MIDTERM 2018

MW01491913

2. (a) UFCF for 2017, after removing effects of excess

↳ EBIT = 300 − 1036 − 1015 − 458 = 491k

= Rev − COGS − SG&A − Dep'n

↳ UFCF = EBIT (1 − Tax Rate) + Dep − Δ Req Cash − Δ AR − Δ Invent + Δ AP − CAPEX

(b) Remove excess cash

Excess Earnings for 2017 using APV version of excess earnings model

unlevered cost of cap = 12%, r_{WACC} = 10%.

(1) Net Income − (1 − T)(interest income) + (1 − T)(interest Expense)

= 294.6k

2) Total cap. invested at beg. of 2017, once excess cash removed

↳ $\text{Equity}_{2016} + \text{Debt}_{2016} - \text{Excess Cash}_{2016} = 1709k$

3) Excess Earnings for 2017 = $UE_{2017} - (TIC_{2016})(r_{UA}) = 294.6 - (1709)(0.12) = \$89.52k$

(c) $V_E = PV(UFCF) + \text{Excess Cash}_{2017} - \text{Debt}_{2017}$ (Most recent year)

3. UFCF = $10b for 4 yrs, + 2%/year after

20% tax rate, r = 11%

(a) Just equity financing

$$V_{UA} = \frac{10}{1.1} + \frac{10}{1.1^2} + \frac{10}{1.1^3} + \frac{10}{(0.11+0.02)1.1^3} = 80.68b$$

(b) Debt + Equity

↳ 60b bond, 5 yr. maturity, 5%/yr cost, Int. Exp. = 3B

$$\hookrightarrow V_{UA} + V_{ITS} = 80.68 + \left[\frac{(0.2)(3)}{1.05} + \cdots \frac{(0.2)(3)}{1.05^5}\right] = 83.28B$$

(c) Liquidate after exactly 10 years for 75b

$$\text{UFCF forgone} = \frac{(10)(0.98^7)}{0.11+0.02} = 66.77B$$

$$\frac{75b - 66.77b}{1.11^{10}} = 2.90b$$

4. Valuing a conglomerate

Discount Rate $= 0.03 + (2)(0.05)$ — r_f, β_i, $E(r_M - r_f)$ Market Risk Premium

Value each division separately

TV business

$$\frac{(2)(1.2)}{1.13} + \frac{(2)(1.2^2)}{(1.13)^2} + \frac{(2)(1.2)^3}{(0.13+0.1)(1.13^2)} \Big)$$

(β)

Cafe Business

$$\frac{(2)(0.9)}{0.08+0.1} = 10B$$

→ $V_{U\ast,\,combined} + V_{ITS,\,acq.} - V_{U\ast,\,pineapple}$

→ $V_{operating\,synergies} = V_{U\ast,\,combined} - [V_{U\ast,\,pineapple} + V_{U\ast,\,tenfeix}]$

Second Edition

Corporate Valuation

Theory, Evidence & Practice

ROBERT W. HOLTHAUSEN
The Wharton School, University of Pennsylvania

MARK E. ZMIJEWSKI
The University of Chicago Booth School of Business

To my sons Mike, Matt, and Jeff, and especially to my wife, Tina, for her support and encouragement throughout the writing of this book.

— RWH

To my patient and understanding wife, Jennifer, my parents, my sister Betty, my children Jason, Kimberly, Kate, and Phillip, and my many wonderful grandchildren.

— MEZ

Editor-in-Chief: George Werthman
Vice President, Brand Management: Marnee Fieldman
Managing Editor: Katie Jones-Aiello
Development Editor: Jocelyn Mousel
Product Developer: Jill Sternard
Digital Marketing Manager: Dana Vinyard
Compositor: T&D Graphics

Photo Credits
Chapter 1: © Getty Images
Chapter 2: © iStock Photo
Chapter 3: © iStock Photo
Chapter 4: © iStock Photo
Chapter 5: © iStock Photo
Chapter 6: © iStock Photo
Chapter 7: © iStock Photo
Chapter 8: © Getty Images
Chapter 9: © iStock Photo
Chapter 10: © Getty Images
Chapter 11: © iStock Photo
Chapter 12: © Getty Images
Chapter 13: © iStock Photo
Chapter 14: © iStock Photo
Chapter 15: © iStock Photo
Chapter 16: © iStock Photo
Chapter 17: © Getty Images

Cambridge Business Publishers, LLC

CORPORATE VALUATION, Second Edition, by Robert W. Holthausen and Mark E. Zmijewski.

STUDENT EDITION ISBN: 978-1-61853-324-1

Printed in the United States of America.
10 9 8 7 6 5 4 3 2

About the Authors

ROBERT W. HOLTHAUSEN is the Nomura Securities Company Professor of Accounting and Finance at The Wharton School of the University of Pennsylvania. He has been on the faculty there since 1989. He is also the Chair of the faculty advisory committee for Wharton Research Data Services (WRDS). Prior to 1989, he was on the accounting and finance faculty at the Graduate School of Business of the University of Chicago for 10 years. Dr. Holthausen earned his doctorate at the University of Rochester, where he also earned his M.B.A. Prior to his academic career, Professor Holthausen worked as a C.P.A. for Price Waterhouse and as a financial analyst with Mobil.

His teaching has been concentrated in the areas of investment management and valuation. Currently, his primary teaching responsibility is for the corporate valuation class he developed for Wharton, which he has taught for almost 30 years. He has teaching experience at the undergraduate, M.B.A., and Ph.D. levels and has won teaching awards from both the undergraduate and M.B.A. programs at Wharton, including the David J. Hauck award for undergraduate teaching, awarded to one tenured faculty member per year. He has taught in many executive education programs at the Wharton School and is the academic director of Wharton's Mergers and Acquisitions Executive Education program.

Professor Holthausen is widely published in both finance and accounting journals. His research has studied the effects of management compensation and governance structures on firm performance, the effects of information on volume and prices, corporate restructuring and valuation, the effects of large block sales on common stock prices, and numerous other topics. His research has appeared in such journals as *The Accounting Review*, *Journal of Accounting Research*, *Journal of Accounting and Economics*, *Journal of Finance*, and *Journal of Financial Economics*. He currently serves as one of the editors of the *Journal of Accounting and Economics*.

Professor Holthausen's consulting and company-specific executive education experiences are varied. In the past, he has consulted with over 20 companies on such diverse activities as serving as a compensation consultant, advising investment companies on the development of fundamental trading rules used to manage equity portfolios, and performing valuation analysis in a variety of situations.

MARK E. ZMIJEWSKI is the Charles T. Horngren Professor of Accounting at The University of Chicago Booth School of Business. He has been a member of Chicago Booth since 1984. Professor Zmijewski earned his doctorate at the State University of New York at Buffalo, where he also earned his B.S. and M.B.A. degrees. Professor Zmijewski's research focuses on the valuation of the firm and its parts, as well as the ways in which various capital market participants use information to value securities. He has published various articles in academic journals such as the *Journal of Accounting Research* and *Journal of Accounting and Economics*, and won the American Accounting Association's Competitive Manuscript Award (1984). He has been an Associate Editor of *The Accounting Review* and on the editorial boards of both the *Journal of Accounting Research* and *The Accounting Review*. In addition to his faculty duties at the University of Chicago, Professor Zmijewski also held the positions of Deputy Dean, Ph.D. Program faculty director, and the Center for Research in Security Prices faculty director. He teaches courses in valuation, mergers and acquisitions, financial analysis, accounting, and entrepreneurship and has won teaching awards for his teaching in both the M.B.A. and Executive M.B.A. programs at Booth.

Professor Zmijewski has consulted with numerous publicly traded and privately owned companies, as well as with entrepreneurs and private equity investors. Professor Zmijewski is a Senior Consultant to Charles River Associates, a consulting firm that provides economic, financial, and management consulting services. He is also a Senior Advisor to, and a member of, the Investment Committee at Patron Capital Partners (Funds IV and V), a private equity investment company with a focus on real estate-related investments. Professor Zmijewski is a founder of Chicago Partners, founded in 1994 and subsequently sold to Navigant Consulting, Inc. Within the time he conducted his consulting through Navigant Economics, he was Navigant Economics' Practice Leader, a member of its management committee, and a member of Navigant Consulting Inc.'s corporate executive committee.

Preface

Welcome to the second edition of *Corporate Valuation: Theory, Evidence & Practice*. We wrote this book to equip our students as well as practitioners—many of whom are our former students—with the current knowledge used to value companies, parts of companies, and the securities issued by companies. Our goal is to provide current conceptual and theoretical valuation frameworks and translate those frameworks into practical approaches for valuing companies. We present the research and descriptive data underpinning these frameworks and use detailed examples to demonstrate how to implement them, often using data from real companies.

> **"*Corporate Valuation: Theory, Evidence & Practice* has been the industry standard on valuation for over two decades, well before it was widely available. The corporate valuation course based on this book is one of the few unstated requirements for graduates of The Wharton School that hope to enter into the field of finance. Having hired dozens of Wharton alumni who have learned valuation from this book, I cannot imagine a more thorough guide or a better reference to learn valuation."**

Ben Frost
Partner, Managing Director
Goldman Sachs Consumer Retail and Mergers Departments

TARGET AUDIENCE

Corporate Valuation: Theory, Evidence & Practice is intended as a college textbook for both graduate and undergraduate courses in valuation. Given the detailed approach, it is also a useful book for practicing professionals. We have been using this material in both valuation-based finance and accounting M.B.A. classes at Chicago Booth and Wharton, as well as in undergraduate finance classes at Wharton, for many years. Although primarily serving as a text in courses that teach valuation, the book can also serve as a background book for case-based courses that include cases on valuation, leveraged buyouts, and mergers and acquisitions. The book can also be used as a "field guide" for those who engage in valuation work. We know that many of our former students refer to our writings in their work involving valuation and security analysis for years after they graduate from our respective institutions.

> **"This is more than a textbook. It's a vital resource for anyone wanting a comprehensive understanding of the financial theory underlying corporate valuation, the mechanics of analyzing financial statements and forecasting cash flows, and a practical framework for assembling this information into a rigorous valuation of the firm. The real world illustrations are superb, and the explanations supporting the methods are clear and comprehensive. Students will find themselves coming back to this book for insights long after the course is completed."**

Wayne Guay
Yageo Professor of Accounting
The Wharton School, University of Pennsylvania

INNOVATIVE, DETAILED, AND PRACTICAL PEDAGOGY

In teaching valuation, we found that students generally lacked the detailed knowledge required to value a company. Although other finance textbooks cover these topics, they do so at a fairly low level of detail and generally do not cover the relevant finance and accounting complexities required to perform valuations. As such, students who use these textbooks typically struggle in the workplace because they either lack the requisite knowledge or fail to understand how to integrate the accounting information with the appropriate finance theory. We integrate the relevant accounting topics with the appropriate finance theory, and demonstrate, using step-by-step examples, how to implement the valuation frameworks we discuss. The book is organized so that instructors can choose not to assign certain chapters or sections of chapters and omit some of these details. In addition, we incorporate relevant empirical evidence and theory from prior studies as well as our own work.

> **"This book contains everything one needs to know to properly value a company. It covers the financial theory of investment analysis, the accounting notions needed to understand, analyze, and forecast financial statements, and many techniques for creating a financial model yielding a rigorous estimate of firm value. It does all that while also providing readers with interesting anecdotes and detailed real-world examples. It is excellent both as the main text for a valuation course, and as the primary reference for practitioners on Wall Street."**
>
> Vincent Glode
> Professor of Finance
> The Wharton School, University of Pennsylvania

Overview of the Structure of the Book

The book consists of six parts. Part I (Chapters 1 through 4) presents an overview of valuation issues and topics, how valuation is used in practice, and the basic tools needed to value a company. These tools include analyzing financial statements, measuring performance, understanding and measuring cash flows, and creating a financial model. Part II (Chapters 5 through 7) discusses the discounted cash flow (DCF) valuation model, including the residual income valuation model. This part of the book demonstrates the equivalence of the alternative forms of the DCF valuation model and when each of the forms is more appropriate to use. Part III (Chapters 8 through 11) discusses how to measure the equity, unlevered, debt, weighted average, and other costs of capital used in the valuation. Part IV (Chapter 12) discusses how to value and measure the cost of capital for warrants, options, and other equity-linked securities. Part V (Chapters 13 and 14) discusses the conceptual framework and practical application of the market multiple valuation method. Finally, Part VI (Chapters 15 through 17) applies and extends these valuation frameworks to specific settings such as highly leveraged transactions, mergers and acquisitions, and cross-border valuations.

Steps in the Valuation Process

In Chapter 1, we provide a top-level overview of the steps in a valuation process used to value a company. These overview steps include analyzing the competitive landscape, analyzing the company and its potential competitive advantage, creating a financial model, measuring the costs of capital, market multiple valuation, and alternative valuation approaches. In the relevant subsequent chapters, we provide detailed steps for each of these overview steps discussed in

Chapter 1. For example, in Chapter 4, we provide a detailed step-by-step process for developing a financial model. These step-by-step process guides are included in many subsequent chapters. We show an example of this step-by-step process from Exhibit 15.8 for leveraged buyout transactions.

EXHIBIT 15.8 Steps in Assessing the Investment Value of Leveraged and Management Buyout Transactions

1. Establish an initial purchase price for the LBO target (for example, based on recent premiums paid in comparable transactions)
2. Develop the target's initial post-LBO capital structure, including the types and terms for the securities to be issued based on market conditions and the buyer's risk preferences
3. Develop a financial model to forecast the post-LBO operations of the target through the expected exit date and incorporate the proposed capital structure into the financial model (see Chapter 4)
4. Forecast all capital structure factors based on the company's capital structure (type of financing, amount of financing, and amount of interest) based on an assumed debt rating, assumed deal terms, and market conditions
5. Assess the target's debt capacity based on the target's expected post-LBO debt rating and ability to service the debt
6. Iterate steps 1 through 5 until the assumed deal terms and the debt capacity (based on the target's post-LBO debt rating and ability to service the debt) align
7. Measure the internal rate of return (IRR) for each equity investor (as well as debt with equity-option features) based on different exit years and exit valuations
8. Set a new price and/or capital structure and iterate steps 1 through 7 until the LBO transaction IRRs meet or exceed the minimum IRR hurdle rate set by the various investors
9. Value the firm and equity using the weighted average cost of capital method to determine the resulting implied exit multiples and IRRs
10. Use the adjusted present value method to value the post-LBO firm and evaluate the investment based on its overall NPV and cost of equity

Real Companies and Detailed Examples Incorporated Throughout

The understanding of valuation and how it plays a role in business decisions is essential to the success of any business and its decision makers. Throughout each chapter, we include real company data and examples to engage students and provide an understanding of how the theory and conceptual frameworks are used in practice. Each chapter contains excerpts and summaries from company financial statements, SEC filings, and new articles illustrating how the topics in the chapter apply to real companies using the Valuation in Practice notes as well as an opening vignette. In addition, each chapter contains one or more detailed examples demonstrating a step-by-step application of the theory and conceptual frameworks discussed in the chapter, which provide an important bridge to help students understand how to apply the concepts. Many of these detailed examples use information from real companies; for example, we use the Xerox Corporation and Affiliated Computer Services, Inc. merger to demonstrate a step-by-step application of the concepts discussed in Chapter 16 on mergers and acquisitions (Exhibit 16.26 is an example of an exhibit detailing a valuation in the context of a real-world acquisition).

EXHIBIT 16.26 Xerox Corporation—Post-merger Valuation

($ in millions, except per share)	
Xerox firm value (after using all excess cash to close the transaction)	$15,905.0
ACS firm value (after using all excess cash to close the transaction)	8,186.8
Value of synergies	1,485.6
Post-merger Xerox firm value (including ACS and synergies)	$25,577.4
Post-merger debt and preferred stock	
Xerox and ACS pro forma combined total debt and liabilities	$11,910.7
Convertible preferred stock	300.0
Post-merger total debt and preferred stock	$12,210.7
Post-merger value of Xerox common equity and options*	$13,366.7
Value of stock options	
ACS stock options assumed in exchange for Xerox equivalent option	$ 298.4
Xerox stock options	56.6
Total value of stock options	$ 355.0
Value of Xerox post-merger common equity	$13,011.7
Post-merger Xerox shares outstanding	
Xerox shares outstanding	877.5
ACS shares outstanding × 4.935	481.9
Total post-merger shares	1,359.4
Value of Xerox post-merger common equity per share	$ 9.572

* This value includes a deduction for Xerox's minority interest but includes any tax benefits from existing options.

The following table lists the real companies discussed in the text by chapter:

Chapter 1	Apple Inc. Altria, Inc. and Kraft Foods Spinoff BMC Software, Inc. Daimler-Benz and Chrysler Merger FMC Corporation	The Gillette Company H. J. Heinz Company Snap, Inc. Xerox Corporation
Chapter 2	Advanced Micro Devices, Inc. Apple Inc. Bloomberg Cisco Systems, Inc. Dell Inc. Delta Airlines, Inc. Dex Media, Inc. Fort Howard Corporation The Fresh Market Inc.	The Gap, Inc. Kroger Co. Main Street Restaurant Group Nike, Inc. Pinnacle Entertainment, Inc. Samsonite Corporation The Sherwin-Williams Company Water Pik Technologies, Inc. Whole Foods Market Inc.
Chapter 3	Alcoa, Inc. Amazon.com Darden Restaurants, Inc. E*Trade Financial Corporation	Facebook Inc. Starbucks Corporation Zillow Group, Inc.
Chapter 4	Alphabet Inc. (Google) Darden Restaurants, Inc. Encana Corporation The Gap, Inc.	Goldcorp Inc. Integra Life Sciences Holdings Corp. Starbucks Corporation Yahoo! Inc.

Chapter 5	Apple Inc. Danaher Corporation Emerging Communications Inc.	Euro Disney S.C.A. Nobel Biocare United Photovoltaics Group Limited
Chapter 6	Equity One, Inc. LinkedIn Corporation Microsoft Corp. The BVA Group LLC Cover-All Technologies Inc. Majesco	Micronas Semiconductor Holding AG Monsanto Company Regency Centers Corporation Syngenta AG TDK Corporation Yahoo! Inc.
Chapter 7	Ball Corporation Crane Co. HSBC Investment Bank plc	Morgan Stanley Dean Witter Rexam PLC Whole Foods Market, Inc.
Chapter 8	America OnLine Berna Biotech SA Colgate Palmolive Company Crucell N.V. Dimensional Fund Advisors Ford Motor Company General Electric Company Honeywell International, Inc. Knight Transportation, Inc. Laureate Education, Inc.	LifeWatch Ltd. McClatchy Newspapers Microsoft Corporation Nichi-Iko Pharmaceutical Co., Ltd. Sagent Pharmaceuticals, Inc. Swift Transportation Company Textron Inc. Time Warner, Inc. Wal-Mart Stores, Inc.
Chapter 9	Advanced Micro Devices Inc. Alcoa Inc. American Axle & Manufacturing	Gap, Inc. Intel Corporation Washington Mutual, Inc.
Chapter 10	Advanced Micro Devices, Inc. Ibbotson Associates Latam Airlines Group, S.A.	Philip Morris International, Inc. TAM S.A.
Chapter 11	Delta Airlines, Inc. Six Flags Entertainment Corporation Sunrun Inc.	United Airlines United Continental Holdings, Inc.
Chapter 12	Alcoa Inc. Alphabet Inc. (Google) The Fresh Market Inc. Intel Corporation	International Business Machines Corp. KapStone Paper and Packaging Corp. Synergy Pharmaceuticals Inc. Yahoo! Inc.
Chapter 13	Altera Corporation Intel Corporation Microsoft Corporation	PepsiCo, Inc. Tesla Motors Inc.
Chapter 14	Calix, Inc. Coca Cola Company Genco Shipping & Trading Limited	Merck & Co., Inc. Microsoft Corporation UAL Corporation (United Airlines)
Chapter 15	FMC Corporation H. J. Heinz Company Kinder Morgan Inc.	Met Life vs. RJR Nabisco RJR Nabisco, Inc.

Chapter 16	Affiliated Computer Services, Inc. (ACS) Autonomy Corporation plc Baker Hughes Incorporated Cingular Wireless and AT&T Wireless Merger Chrysler Corporation Daimler-Benz, AG Halliburton Company Hewlett-Packard Company Jos. A. Bank Clothiers, Inc. LAN Airlines S.A. and TAM S.A. Merger	LATAM Airlines Group S.A. Medivation, Inc. The Men's Wearhouse Inc. PeopleSoft, Inc. Oracle Corporation Pfizer Inc. Sanofi S.A. SIRIUS Satellite Radio Xerox Corporation XM Satellite Radio
Chapter 17	Caraco Pharmaceutical Laboratories Alphabet Inc. (Google) Johnson & Johnson	Merck & Co. Inc. Sun Pharmaceutical Industries Limited Synthes, Inc.

Learning Objectives, Vignettes, and Chapter Organizational Charts

At the beginning of every chapter, we present learning objectives for that chapter, a small vignette of a real-world example that applies to the content of the chapter, and an organizational chart of the chapter. Thus, even before reading the introduction to the chapter, the reader has a sense of the content of the chapter, its importance, and how the chapter will be organized, which makes it easier to learn the material that follows.

Example Learning Objectives

After mastering the material in this chapter, you will be able to:

1. Adjust the value of the firm and its equity for the value created from financing (5.1)
2. Measure firm and equity value using the adjusted present value and weighted average cost of capital valuation models (5.2–5.3)
3. Measure value using the equity free cash flow and dividend valuation models (5.4–5.5)
4. Understand how to measure expected cash flows and risk-adjusted discount rates (5.6)

Example Vignette

EMERGING COMMUNICATIONS INC.

Emerging Communications' valuation using discounted cash flow valuation models—Emerging Communication Inc. (EmCom) owned various subsidiaries whose businesses provided local telephone service, sold and leased telecommunications equipment, and provided cellular telephone service in the U.S. Virgin Islands. EmCom's Chairman and CEO, who already owned a majority of the company's shares, began to acquire EmCom's remaining shares in order to take the company private. The CEO arranged various types of debt financing for the transaction. In order to negotiate a deal price with the CEO, EmCom's board of directors created a special committee drawn from EmCom's Board of Directors. The special committee negotiated a $10.25 price per share. EmCom's Board approved the $10.25 bid and EmCom gave notice to its shareholders of a special meeting to vote on the sale. EmCom's shareholders approved the transaction.[1] According to Delaware law—the state in which the company was incorporated—shareholders not wishing to participate in the transaction can exercise their appraisal rights by petitioning the court to assess the fair value of their stock. Some of EmCom's minority shareholders opted to exercise their appraisal rights under Delaware law. The court concluded that the fair value of EmCom's shares was $38.05 per share ($27.80 per share higher than the deal price) based on a weighted average cost of capital valuation method. According to Bloomberg, Emerging Communications went out of business in 2012 through a Chapter 11 liquidation filing under bankruptcy.

In this chapter, we explore the intricacies of the weighted average cost of capital and adjusted present value discounted cash flow valuation methods and demonstrate ho[illegible]

Example Chapter Organizational Chart

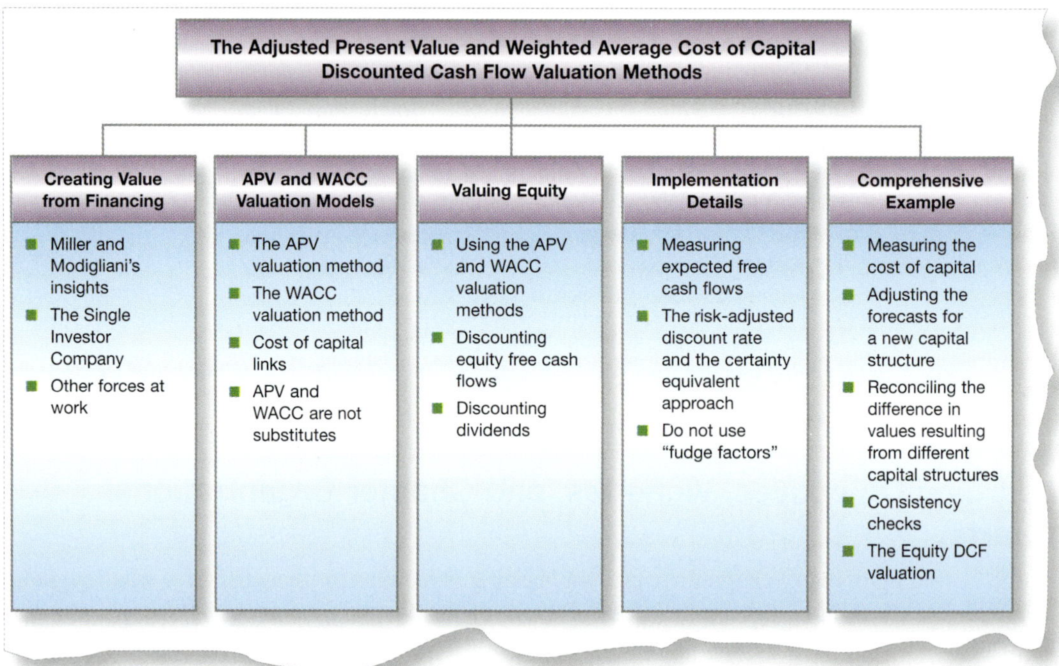

Valuation Keys

Each chapter contains numerous boxed summaries of key concepts and tools called Valuation Keys. The Valuation Keys help focus the reader on the key issue or issues in each section of the chapter.

Valuation Key 13.4

In addition to risk and growth factors, a company's income tax, depreciation, and operating cost structure, as well as its working capital and capital expenditure requirements, are potentially relevant determinants of a company's market multiple, depending on the market multiple and the specific valuation. A determinant that is excluded from the calculation of a market multiple's value driver (denominator) is more likely to be relevant for assessing comparability (for example, income tax cost structure is more likely to be relevant for EBIT, EBITDA, and revenue multiples than unlevered earnings multiples). Of course, all else equal, we prefer multiples that are not sensitive to numerous determinants as it makes the choice of comparable companies easier.

Review Exercises with Solutions Throughout Each Chapter and End-of-Chapter Problems

Applying theory and conceptual frameworks to realistic data is challenging for most students, and it is especially challenging for students with less business experience or previous exposure to finance, management, and other valuation-related business courses. To reinforce concepts presented in each section of the chapter, we include review exercises that allow students to apply the topic discussed in each section. The solutions to the review exercises appear at the end of each chapter. In addition, each chapter contains additional end-of-chapter exercises and problems instructors can assign separately.

Example Review Exercise and Solution

REVIEW EXERCISE 16.1

Valuing Synergies—LATAM Airlines Group

Use the following information (taken from the offering memorandum) to measure the value of the synergies for the LAN and TAM merger discussed in Valuation in Practice 16.5. After the completion of the proposed combination, the breakdown of the expected range of annual pre-tax synergies was estimated to be as follows (realized in full in the fourth year after the merger):

- Increased revenues—$225 million to $260 million from the combination of passenger networks and $120 million to $125 million from the combination of cargo services.
- Cost savings—$15 million to $25 million from the consolidation of frequent flyer programs; $100 million to $135 million from the coordination of airport and procurement activities; $20 million to $25 million from the coordination and improved efficiency of maintenance operations; and $120 million to $130 million from the convergence of information technology systems, the increased efficiency of combined sales and distribution processes, and the increased efficiency in corporate overhead costs.

LAN and TAM expected the one-time merger costs—including banking, consulting, and legal advisory fees—to be between $170 million and $200 million. LAN expected a reduction of approximately $150 million in working capital from not having to inventory as many engines and spare parts, which was expected to be fully realized at the end of 2013.

Use the midpoint of the synergy forecasts in the cal[illegible]ns. Assume that all synergies are actual cash flows, [illegible] tax rate is 30% [illegible]

Review Exercise 16.1: Valuing Synergies—LATAM Airlines Group

Weighted Average Cost of Capital Valuation of Synergies:		10.00%		g=	−10.00%		
Tax rate =		30.0%					
($ in millions)		**Low**	**High**	**Midpoint**			
Passenger revenue		$225	$260	$243			
Cargo revenue		120	125	123			
		$345	$385	$365			
Frequent flyer program consolidation		$ 15	$ 25	$ 20			
Airport/procurement		100	135	118			
Maintenance		20	25	23			
Information technology and other		120	130	125			
		$255	$315	$285			
		$600	$700	$650			
Reduced investment in working capital		$150	$150	$150			
Integration costs and fees		$170	$200	$185			
First year synergies		$171	$200	$185	28.5%		
($ in millions)		**2012**	**2013**	**2014**	**2015**	**2016**	**CV 2016**
Cumulative percentage of synergies achieved			**28.5%**	**50.0%**	**80.0%**	**100.0%**	
Pre-tax revenue synergies			$103.9	$182.5	$292.0	$365.0	$ 328.5
Pre-tax cost synergies			81.1	142.5	228.0	285.0	256.5
Integration costs and fees		−$185.0					
Less: taxes on synergies and costs		55.5	−55.5	−97.5	−156.0	−195.0	−175.5
Reduced investment in working capital savings			150.0				
After-tax costs, fees, synergies and other		−$129.5	$279.5	$227.5	$364.0	$455.0	$ 409.5
Discount factor for continuing value							5.000
Unlevered free cash flow and CV		−$129.5	$279.5	$227.5	$364.0	$455.0	$2,047.5
Discount factor		0.953	0.867	0.788	0.716	0.651	0.651
Present value		−$123.5	$242.3	$179.3	$260.8	$296.3	$1,333.4
Value of synergies	$2,188.5						

Exhibit may contain small rounding errors

FLEXIBLE STRUCTURE

The curricula, instructor preferences, and course lengths vary across schools. Accordingly, to the extent possible, we designed many of the chapters in *Corporate Valuation: Theory, Evidence & Practice* so that they can be taught independently of one another. This design provides flexibility and allows instructors to omit certain chapters in a course. Given the nature of the topics covered in the book, however, some of the chapters are interrelated, and certain concepts in a chapter not included in the curriculum would need to be covered by the instructor separately without assigning the entire chapter. We use this approach at Chicago because we have a quarter rather than a semester course schedule. Also, instructors may wish to supplement the course with cases, which might require omitting certain chapters.

Flexibility for Courses of Varying Lengths

Given differing preferences and needs, we provide the following table of possible course designs. In the semester course, faculty members can cover all 17 chapters in the book (Wharton curriculum). In the quarter course, however, covering the entire book is not practicable. For quarter courses, we outline two alternative approaches—one that focuses more on the details underpinning valuation, omitting the transaction and cross-border valuation chapters, and another that covers the valuation topics in less detail and includes the transaction and cross-border valuation chapters (Chicago curriculum). We also present these two versions of the curriculum for the shorter six-week and five-day courses. The book is also used in Wharton's Executive MBA program in a half-semester format which also includes cases, so the book is flexible in how it can be used.

<table>
<tr><th>Chapter and Topic</th><th>15-Week Semester-Course</th><th>10-Week Valuation Focused</th><th>10-Week Transaction Focused</th><th>6-Week Valuation Focused Mini-Course</th><th>6-Week Transaction Focused Mini-Course</th><th>5-Day Valuation Focused Mini-Course</th><th>5-Day Transaction Focused Mini-Course</th></tr>
<tr><td>Chapter 1
Introduction</td><td>Week 1</td><td rowspan="2">Week 1
Less Detail on Financial Ratios</td><td rowspan="2">Week 1</td><td rowspan="3">Week 1
Overview of Basic Concepts</td><td rowspan="3">Week 1
Overview of Basic Concepts</td><td rowspan="3">Day 1
Overview of Basic Concepts</td><td rowspan="3">Day 1
Overview of Basic Concepts</td></tr>
<tr><td>Chapter 2
Financial Ratios</td><td>Weeks 1 and 2</td></tr>
<tr><td>Chapter 3
Free Cash Flows</td><td>Week 2</td><td>Week 2</td><td rowspan="2">Week 2
Less Detail on Free Cash Flows</td></tr>
<tr><td>Chapter 4
Financial Modeling</td><td>Week 3</td><td>Week 3</td><td>Optional</td><td>Optional</td><td>Optional</td><td>Optional</td></tr>
<tr><td>Chapter 5
Discounted Cash Flow Valuation</td><td>Weeks 4 and 5</td><td>Weeks 3 and 4</td><td>Weeks 3 and 4</td><td>Weeks 2 and 3</td><td>Week 2</td><td>Days 2 and 3</td><td>Day 2</td></tr>
<tr><td>Chapter 6
Continuing (Terminal) Value</td><td>Week 5</td><td>Week 4</td><td>Week 4 or Optional</td><td>Week 3</td><td>Optional</td><td>Day 3</td><td>Optional</td></tr>
<tr><td>Chapter 7
Excess (Residual) Earnings Valuation</td><td>Week 6</td><td>Week 5</td><td>Week 4 or Optional</td><td>Week 4</td><td>Optional</td><td>Day 4</td><td>Optional</td></tr>
<tr><td>Chapter 8
Equity Cost of Capital</td><td>Week 7</td><td>Week 6</td><td>Optional</td><td>Optional</td><td>Optional</td><td>Optional</td><td>Optional</td></tr>
<tr><td>Chapter 9
Non-Equity Costs of Capital</td><td>Week 8</td><td>Week 7</td><td>Optional</td><td>Optional</td><td>Optional</td><td>Optional</td><td>Optional</td></tr>
<tr><td>Chapter 10
Levering and Unlevering</td><td>Week 9</td><td rowspan="2">Week 8</td><td rowspan="2">Week 5</td><td rowspan="2">Week 5</td><td>Optional</td><td>Optional</td><td>Optional</td></tr>
<tr><td>Chapter 11
Weighted Average Cost of Capital</td><td>Week 10</td><td>Optional</td><td>Optional</td><td>Optional</td></tr>
</table>

continued

Chapter and Topic	15-Week Semester-Course	10-Week Valuation Focused	10-Week Transaction Focused	6-Week Valuation Focused Mini-Course	6-Week Transaction Focused Mini-Course	5-Day Valuation Focused Mini-Course	5-Day Transaction Focused Mini-Course
Chapter 12 Option Pricing Model Applications	Week 11	Week 9	Week 6	Optional	Optional	Optional	Optional
Chapter 13 Market Multiple Valuation I; **Chapter 14** Market Multiple Valuation II	Week 12	Week 10	Week 7	Week 6	Week 3	Day 5	Day 3 or Optional
Chapter 15 Leveraged Buyouts	Week 13	Optional	Week 8	Optional	Week 4	Optional	Day 3 or Optional
Chapter 16 Mergers and Acquisitions	Week 14	Optional	Week 9	Optional	Week 5	Optional	Day 4
Chapter 17 Cross-Border Valuation	Week 15	Optional	Week 10	Optional	Week 6	Optional	Day 5

VALUATION FROM A PRACTICAL PERSPECTIVE

Naturally, it is not possible for a textbook or any other book to discuss which of the specific valuation frameworks and applications apply to every valuation context that might arise. Each company and valuation context will have specific and potentially unique facts and circumstances that require the valuation expert to choose the frameworks and implement them in a way that is appropriate for the specific valuation context. The chapters in this book are meant to provide a guide to understanding the alternative frameworks and ways they can be implemented. Valuation experts must use their informed judgments to choose the specific valuation frameworks to use in a valuation and how to best implement them based on the facts and circumstances for the specific valuation.

The second edition of the book contains many useful updates and extensions.

- The Tax Cuts and Jobs Act of 2017 (TCJA): We include discussions of the TCJA throughout the book and how it fundamentally affects valuation. For example, we discuss and provide examples of the effect of the TCJA's interest deductibility limitation on interest tax shields, the new rules regarding net operating loss carryforwards, the implications for the levering and unlevering formulas, multinational valuation, and more. Many of the provisions in the TCJA are common in other countries, so these discussions apply to similar provisions in other countries.
- Changes in accounting rules: We updated the chapters for various changes in accounting rules that affect how we value firms. For example, we discuss and provide examples for the change in accounting for leases in several chapters where pertinent.
- Edited and reorganized certain chapters: We reorganized and edited certain chapters and parts of chapters based on input from teaching assistants and students. For example, we reorganized and edited the comprehensive example in Chapter 5 (discounted cash flow valuation). We expanded, reorganized, and extensively edited Chapter 12 (equity-linked securities) and included more basic examples. Chapters 13 and 14 (market multiples valuation) have been rewritten with new comprehensive examples.
- Additional examples: We added additional examples in various chapters. For example, in Chapter 11, we have a detailed example of how to value a company with net operating loss carryforwards (NOLs) and interest carryforwards.
- Additional companies: Throughout the book we updated and added vignettes and valuation in practice examples to provide more bridges from the concepts in the texts to applications for actual companies.
- Additional problems: We added additional problems in certain chapters.

SUPPLEMENTS

For Instructors

Solutions Manual Created by the authors and contains solutions to each of the problems at the end of the chapters.

PowerPoint Presentations Created and classroom tested by the authors, the PowerPoint slides outline key elements of each chapter and provide additional examples not used in the textbook. Because most of the examples in the PowerPoint presentations are different from those used in the book, instructors are not just repeating what is in the book.

Spreadsheets We provide author-created Excel spreadsheets for the underlying examples in the PowerPoint presentations. This allows instructors to see exactly how the spreadsheets are created and would also allow instructors to create other examples if they so desired.

For Students

Example, Review Exercise, and Problem Data We provide Excel spreadsheets of "hard-coded" data for chapter examples, review exercises, and end-of-chapter problems. We also provide hard-coded solutions to the chapter examples and review exercises. These hard-coded solutions provide students with the template used as well as the data for the problems, and make it easier to solve the problems, as students do not have to input the raw data into an Excel file.

In some cases, the exhibits in the book have small rounding errors because we do not show enough significant digits in order to avoid the clutter of multiple significant digits. When that occurs, the following phrase appears at the bottom of the exhibit: "Exhibit may contain small rounding errors." The Excel spreadsheets provide more significant digits for students who want to refer to them.

Option Pricing Spreadsheet Chapter 12 includes applications of option pricing theory to plain vanilla options, warrants, employee stock options, convertible debt, and financial distress prediction. We provide an Excel file that aids with these applications.

ACKNOWLEDGMENTS

We would especially like to thank Jennifer J. Jones, former faculty member at The University of Chicago Booth School of Business, for the countless hours she has contributed to both editions of the book by helping us review the chapters, examples, solutions, and galleys. Her devotion to detail and to this project has been incredible, and it is fair to say that the book would not be as good as it is, and we might even still be working on it, without her efforts—and for that, we owe her an enormous amount of gratitude.

We would also like to thank our former students at Chicago and Wharton who have used this material in various forms over the years. They have provided valuable feedback and advice that has shaped the content of this book. In addition, we would like to thank Associate Professor Vincent Glode, Professor Wayne Guay, and Professor Michael Roberts at Wharton, for their insights on the book when teaching the corporate valuation class at Wharton. We would also like to thank Keith Bockus, Vice President at Charles River Associates, for his many years of feedback and advice on the content in the book, as well as many staff at Charles River Associates.

This book also benefited from many years of discussions about valuation issues with our colleagues at our respective universities as well as with colleagues at other universities throughout the world.

We would also like to thank The University of Chicago Booth School of Business and The Wharton School for their support during the writing of this book.

We received feedback and suggestions from faculty from around the country during various stages of writing the book. We want to recognize their contribution and thank them for their help.

Ashok Abbott, *West Virginia University*
Jeffrey Allen, *Southern Methodist University*
Peter Brous, *Seattle University*
Tyrone Callahan, *University of Southern California*
Shelly L. Canterbury, *George Mason University*
Ibrahim Elsaify, *Goldey-Beacom College*
Bradford Cornell, *UCLA Anderson*
Steven Ferraro, *Pepperdine University*
Scott Fine, *Case Western Reserve University*
Susan Fleming, *Cornell University*
Cesare Fracassi, *University of Texas*
Amarjit Gill, *New York Institute of Technology*
Benton Gup, *University of Alabama*
Anurag Gupta, *Case Western University*
Alexander Gurvich, *Pace University*
Jeffrey Hart, *University of Iowa*
Michael Ho, *University of Virgina, Darden School*
Narayanan Jayaraman, *Georgia Institute of Technology*
Domingo Castelo Joaquin, *Illinois State University*
Rick Johnston, *Purdue University*
Seth J. Kopchak, *Franklin & Marshall*
Srinivasan Krishnamurthy, *North Carolina State University*
Christian Leuz, *University of Chicago*
Christiano Manfre, *Loyola Marymount University*
Nathan Mauck, *University of Missouri—Kansas City*
William Maxwell, *Southern Methodist University*
Karl Mergenthaler, *Pace University*
Michael Nugent, *University of Cincinnati*
Jamie Pawlukiewicz, *Xavier University*
Peter Pfau, *Pace University*
George Pinteris, *Ohio State University*
Julia Plotts, *University of Southern California*
Annette Poulsen, *University of Georgia*
Andreas Schüler, *Universität der Bundeswehr München*
Richard Shockley, *Indiana University*
Tao Shu, *University of Georgia*
Lenny Soffer, *University of Chicago*
Michel Vetsuypens, *Southern Methodist University*
Joe Wells, *University of Texas—Dallas*
Robert West, *Villanova University*
Jeffrey Zwiebel, *Stanford University*

In addition, we owe particular thanks to George Werthman for believing in this project and for helping us fully develop this book, and we are extremely grateful to Katie Jones-Aiello, Jocelyn Mousel, Jill Sternard, Marnee Fieldman, Debbie McQuade, Terry McQuade, and the entire team at Cambridge Business Publishers for their encouragement, enthusiasm, and guidance.

RWH	*MEZ*
Philadelphia, PA	Chicago, IL

Brief Contents

Contents

CHAPTER 1 Introduction to Valuation 3

CHAPTER 2 Financial Statement Analysis 39

s://www.facebook.com/
og In, Si
facebook

3M

CHAPTER 5 The Adjusted Present Value and Weighted Average Cost of Capital Discounted Cash Flow Valuation Methods 201

CHAPTER 6 Measuring Continuing Value Using the Constant-Growth Perpetuity Model 251

CHAPTER 7 The Excess Earnings (Residual Income) Valuation Method 291

CHAPTER 8 Estimating the Equity Cost of Capital 327

GAP

CHAPTER 10 Levering and Unlevering the Cost of Capital and Beta 435

CHAPTER 11 Measuring the Weighted Average Cost of Capital and Related Valuation Issues 483

CHAPTER 12 The Effects of Stock-Based Compensation and Other Equity-Linked Securities on Discounted Cash Flow Valuations 555

CHAPTER 13 Introduction to Market Multiple Valuation Methods 611

CHAPTER 14 Market Multiple Measurement and Implementation 657

OREO

CHAPTER 16 Mergers and Acquisitions 793

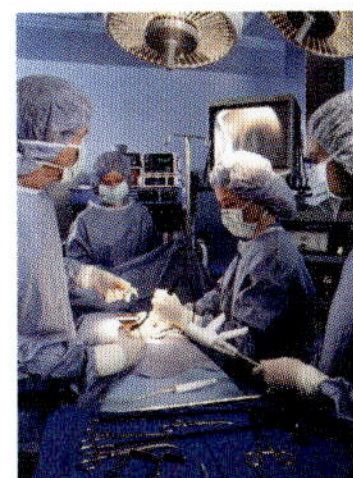

CHAPTER 17 Valuing Businesses Across Borders 855

After mastering the material in this chapter, you will be able to:

1. Explain the different concepts of value (1.1–1.2)
2. Understand the principles underpinning the commonly used valuation methods (1.3)
3. Explain how the different valuation models measure value (1.4–1.6)
4. Describe the ways managers and investors use valuation models (1.7)
5. Outline the steps used in the valuation process (1.8)

CHAPTER

1

Introduction to Valuation

SNAP, INC.

Snap Inc.'s (formerly Snapchat Inc.) primary product is an app called Snapchat. Snapchat, which launched in 2011, is a very popular photo- and video-messaging (free) app.[1] Snap was expected to go public (have an initial public offering) in March 2017. Goodwater Capital analyzed Snap's valuation in February 2017, when Snap was expected to have an offering price in the $14–$16 per share range (fully diluted market capitalization range of $19.9 billion to $22.8 billion).[2] As part of the analysis of Snap's potential value, Goodwater included illustrative forecasts for Snap from 2017 through 2027, which appear in the following table. (For now, ignore the column titled Equation 1.1; we discuss that equation in Section 1.3.)

(in millions of $)*	Equation 1.1	2015A	2016A	2017	2018	2019	2020	2021	2022	2023	2024	2025	2026	2027
Revenue		$ 59	$404	$1,104	$1,942	$2,754	$3,453	$4,321	$5,387	$6,682	$8,237	$10,085	$12,263	$14,811
EBITDA**		−$366	−$491	−$ 616	−$ 340	$ 144	$ 626	$1,035	$1,578	$2,284	$3,185	$ 4,315	$ 5,650	$ 7,280
Earnings before interest and taxes	EBIT	−$382	−$520	−$ 695	−$ 485	−$ 70	$ 347	$ 686	$1,142	$1,744	$2,519	$ 3,499	$ 4,659	$ 6,083
Income taxes	−TAX	−8	−7	−1	−1	−1	1	172	285	436	630	874	1,165	1,521
EBIT − Income tax	EBIT − TAX	−$374	−$513	−$ 694	−$ 484	−$ 69	$ 346	$ 514	$ 857	$1,308	$1,889	$ 2,625	$ 3,494	$ 4,562
Depreciation and amortization	+ NCEXP	15	29	79	145	214	279	349	436	540	666	815	992	1,198
Required cash	−ΔRC	−2	−15	−5	−9	−12	−16	−19	−24	−30	−37	−45	−55	−67
Non-cash operating working capital	−ΔWCO	−15	−152	−50	−87	−124	−155	−194	−243	−301	−371	−454	−552	−666
Required investments	− CAPEX	−19	−66	−110	−194	−275	−345	−432	−539	−668	−824	−1,009	−1,226	−1,481
Unlevered free cash flow	FCF	−$395	−$717	−$ 779	−$ 629	−$ 266	$ 109	$ 217	$ 487	$ 849	$1,323	$ 1,932	$ 2,653	$ 3,546
Annual Percentage Change:														
Revenue			584.7%	173.3%	75.9%	41.8%	25.4%	25.1%	24.7%	24.0%	23.3%	22.4%	21.6%	20.8%
EBITDA**			34.2%	25.5%	−44.8%		334.7%	65.3%	52.5%	44.7%	39.4%	35.5%	30.9%	28.8%
Earnings before interest and taxes			36.1%	33.7%	−30.2%	−85.6%		97.7%	66.5%	52.7%	44.4%	38.9%	33.2%	30.6%
Tax-effected EBIT			37.2%	35.3%	−30.3%	−85.7%		48.6%	66.7%	52.6%	44.4%	39.0%	33.1%	30.6%
Unlevered free cash flow			81.8%	8.7%	−19.3%	−57.7%		98.8%	124.3%	74.3%	55.8%	46.0%	37.4%	33.6%
Margins:														
EBITDA to revenue		−620.3%	−121.5%	−55.8%	−17.5%	5.2%	18.1%	24.0%	29.3%	34.2%	38.7%	42.8%	46.1%	49.2%
EBIT to revenue		−647.5%	−128.7%	−63.0%	−25.0%	−2.5%	10.0%	15.9%	21.2%	26.1%	30.6%	34.7%	38.0%	41.1%
Free cash flow to revenue		−668.6%	−177.5%	−70.6%	−32.4%	−9.7%	3.2%	5.0%	9.0%	12.7%	16.1%	19.2%	21.6%	23.9%

* Forecasts in italic font are authors' estimates.

** EBITDA = Earnings Before Interest, Taxes, Depreciation and Amortization

The chapters in this book provide detailed discussions of the conceptual frameworks and tools needed to value a company such as Snap as well as other privately held and publicly traded companies. The chapters provide conceptual frameworks and the tools to create and analyze forecasts, measure a company's riskiness and costs of capital, and value the company using alternative valuation models such as the discounted cash flow model, the residual income model, the market multiple model, and the leveraged buyout model. The chapters also provide tools to analyze merger and acquisition transactions and how to address the valuation issues that arise when valuing a company across borders. We use the above information for Snap later in this chapter to illustrate how to value a company.

[1] See Snap Inc.'s S-1 Registration Statement filed with the U.S. SEC on February 2, 2017.

[2] Goodwater Capital invests in consumer technology companies. See "Understanding Snapchat—The Next Facebook or Another Twitter?," available on June 25, 2018 at http://www.goodwatercap.com/thesis/understanding-snapchat.

CHAPTER ORGANIZATION

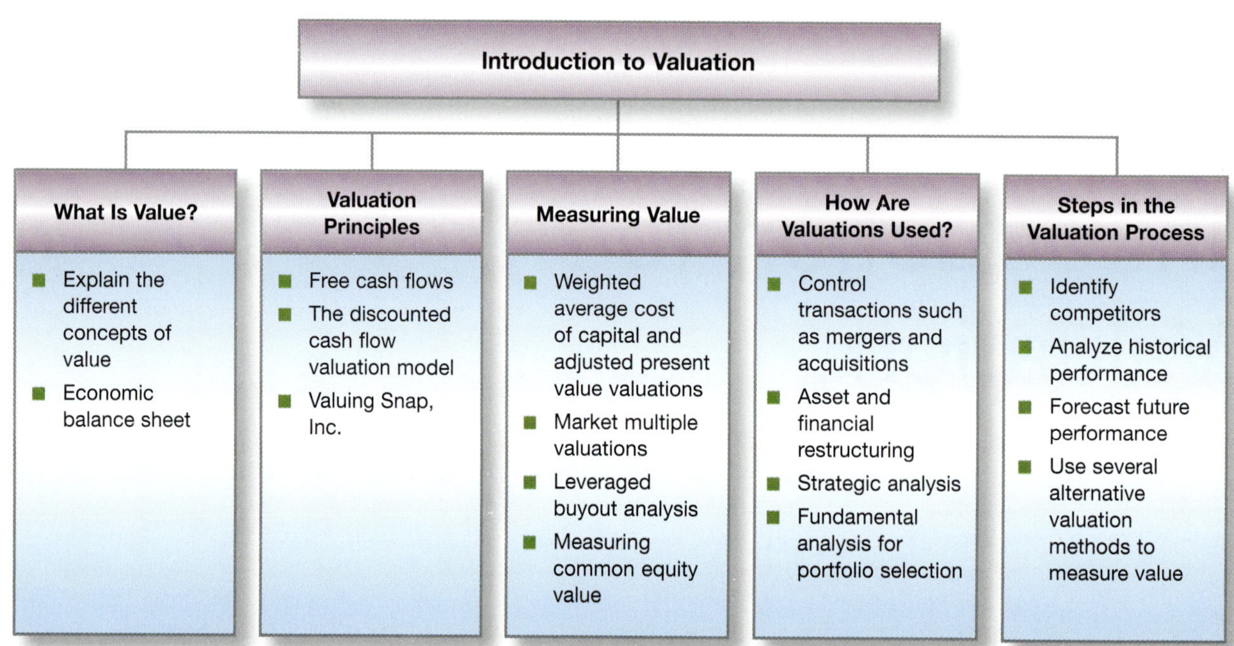

INTRODUCTION

Managers and investors place big bets and take large risks based on the valuation models discussed in this book. They are willing to make those investments and take those risks because they expect to earn sufficient cash in the future from these investments to create value for their companies or superior returns for their investment portfolios. Managers, for example, who acquire other companies, and other investors decide whether or not to make an investment by comparing their assessment of the value—or valuation—of the future cash flows they expect to earn from an investment to the amount they must invest. They select investments for which their valuation of the future cash flows is sufficiently greater than the amount they must invest. The valuation models discussed in this book provide the conceptual frameworks and tools to conduct these analyses.

Since valuation analyses serve as the basis for many decisions managers and investors make every day, all managers and investors benefit from understanding valuation frameworks, how valuation models work, and how to implement those valuation models appropriately. In this book, we present well-accepted methods and valuation models that managers and investors commonly use to measure value. While managers and investors use these valuation models to measure the value of many different types of investments and as the basis of many different decisions, our focus is on measuring the value of a firm and its common equity. We also discuss ways to value certain securities a firm may issue to raise financial capital. Finally, while we do not discuss project valuation directly, many of the valuation methods and tools presented in this book can be used to assess the value of a company's specific investment projects.

In this chapter, you will gain a general understanding of the primary valuation models. Further, you will gain an understanding of the general components of a firm's value. In addition, you will see the various ways that managers and investors use valuation models. For example, the managers of Daimler and Chrysler agreed to merge the two auto manufacturers based in part on the advice of their financial advisors who relied on the models discussed in this book (see Valuation in Practice 1.1). Finally, you will gain an appreciation of the overall valuation process.

1.1 WHAT DO WE MEAN BY "THE VALUE OF A COMPANY"?

LO1 Explain the different concepts of value

Various terms are used to indicate the value of a company, for example, **fair market value**, **market value**, **fair value**, **intrinsic value**, and **fundamental value** to name a few. A widely used description of fair market value of a company is the cash equivalent value at which a willing and unrelated buyer would agree to buy and a willing and unrelated seller would agree to sell the company, when neither party is compelled to act, and when both parties have reasonable knowledge of the relevant available information.[3]

Valuation in Practice 1.1

The Daimler-Benz—Chrysler Merger In November 1998, Daimler-Benz, AG (Daimler) merged with Chrysler Corporation (Chrysler). The merger of Daimler and Chrysler resulted in the formation of a new German company, DaimlerChrysler, AG (DaimlerChrysler). The process started in mid-January 1998, when Mr. Jurgen E. Schrempp, Chairman of Daimler, and Mr. Robert J. Eaton, Chairman and Chief Executive Officer of Chrysler, met and began discussions about a possible merger between the two companies. By late April of that year, they agreed to merge in a **stock-for-stock transaction**. Daimler agreed to an exchange ratio that resulted in a 28%, or more than $7 billion, premium to the Chrysler shareholders.

On the day before they announced the merger, Daimler's market capitalization (or market cap) was over $52.5 billion and Chrysler's market cap was over $26.5 billion, with a combined market cap of over $79 billion. The initial market reaction to the merger announcement was positive. Chrysler's market cap increased by more than $7.5 billion and Daimler's market cap increased by more than $4.5 billion, for a combined increase of more than $12 billion (or 15%).

Mr. Schrempp and Mr. Eaton and their respective boards decided to place their bets, in part, based on the advice of their financial advisors. Credit Suisse First Boston was Chrysler's financial advisor in connection with this merger and the financial advisor for Daimler-Benz was Goldman Sachs. Both financial advisors provided a fairness opinion to their respective clients indicating that the price paid in the merger was fair, and both used the valuation models we discuss in this book as a basis for their conclusions. Of course, we now know that this merger did not work as well as implied by the market's initial reaction to the announcement, as Daimler sold Chrysler in 2007 for more than a $25 billion loss.

Source: See Annex C and Annex D in the DaimlerChrysler AG SEC Form F-4 (Registration Statement). DaimlerChrysler's post-merger financial performance has not yet met pre-merger expectations.

This definition suggests some important characteristics about the valuation context—"arm's length," time-frame constraints, information set, and specific use. For example, a willing and unrelated buyer and seller suggests that the transaction is "arm's length"; that is, it does not include "side payments" or other remuneration (economic or other) beyond the transaction price paid by the buyer to the seller. Neither party being compelled to act suggests a time-frame context—that is, the time frame for the parties to identify and negotiate with each other is such that, whatever it happens to be, it does not affect the price at which a transaction would take place. This component of the definition suggests the transaction is not forced such as might be compelled by a court or a government agency or that might be necessary if the seller is in financial distress or has liquidity issues that it must address quickly. The definition also indicates the importance of the availability of information—that is, the value is based on an information set that is assumed to contain all relevant and available information. Lastly, part of the relevant information is the specific use of the assets being purchased.

In most valuations, the company is valued as an ongoing business (**ongoing value** or **going-concern value**). Certain valuation contexts, however, can value the company presuming that the company will not be operated any longer, **liquidation value (forced and orderly)**, or that the company will be broken up into pieces and the pieces will be operated as separate entities, **breakup value**. Liquidation value is used when the company's assets, either collectively or in parts or individually, are going to be sold or liquidated. Forced liquidation suggests a valuation context in which the time frame to sell the company is sufficiently short such that the company will be sold for less than it would have been sold for given more time, sometimes called a **fire sale** of the asset. Orderly liquidation suggests that the time frame to sell the company does not affect the price at which the company is sold. Breakup value is the value of selling off the different parts of a company—for example, a **conglomerate** selling off all or some of the individual companies it owns.

---

[3] This definition has been adopted by the U.S. Internal Revenue Service to define Fair Market Value, "The fair market value of any interest of a decedent in a business, whether a partnership or a proprietorship, is the net amount which a willing purchaser whether an individual or a corporation, would pay for the interest to a willing seller, neither being under any compulsion to buy or to sell and both having reasonable knowledge of relevant facts." U.S. Internal Revenue Service, 26 CFR 20.2031-3 – Valuation of Interests in Businesses.

Of course, there is not just one universal opinion on the value of a company. Different investors often have differences of opinion regarding the best way to use the company's assets, or they may have different expectations regarding the company's future prospects even if they do agree on the best use of the assets, or they have different assessments of the riskiness of the company's expected cash flows. Naturally, buyers and sellers need not be in exact agreement over the value of a company when they transact. The buyer typically believes the value (to the buyer) is higher than the price paid for it and the seller often believes the value is lower than the price at which it is sold. Naturally, transactions are more likely to occur when the buyer believes a company is worth more (to the buyer) than the seller believes it is worth (to the seller). Nevertheless, valuation models approximate the observed market value of the company so long as the inputs used reflect both a specific valuation context and the information and expectations of the buyers and sellers engaged in market transactions.

1.2 THE ECONOMIC BALANCE SHEET: RESOURCES EQUAL CLAIMS ON RESOURCES

The value of the firm and the value of the securities it issues are related in a very fundamental way. A company is a legal entity, which is essentially a collection of contracts.[4] One of those contracts must be with the owners of the company (shareholders, which could be individuals or another company), because a company cannot own itself. For example, articles of incorporation, corporate bylaws, shareholders agreement (optional), and stock certificates (optional in most states) are the contracts a corporation has with its common equity owners. In almost all cases, the common equity owners of a company have a **residual interest** in the company's assets; that is, the common equity owners get the value that remains after all other contracts are settled. As a result, the value of a company's resources must be equal to the value of the contractual claims on its resources.

Value of Resources = Value of Claims on Resources

Value of the Firm = Value of Non-Equity Claims + Value of Common Equity (Residual Interest)

From this relation, it follows that a change in the value created by a company must be equal to the change in the value of the company's securities (we use the Greek letter delta, Δ, to signify the change in a variable). Said another way, the dollar return on a company's resources must be equal to the dollar return on the claims on its resources.

ΔValue Firm = ΔValue Non-Equity Claims + ΔValue Common Equity

$ Return Firm = $ Return Non-Equity Claims + $ Return Common Equity

We use several forms of these relations to develop various aspects of the valuation models presented throughout this book. It is sometimes useful to depict this relation in more detail using an **economic balance sheet**.

Example Economic Balance Sheet

Exhibit 1.1 is an example of an economic balance sheet. The first point to note about this exhibit is that the value of the company's resources (or the value of the firm) is equal to the value of the claims on its resources (or the value of its securities). This is a useful relation because information available about the securities that a company issues can be used to assess the company's value and cost of capital. The **cost of capital** is the expected rate of return required by investors to invest in a specific investment. Conceptually, it is the opportunity cost of investing in a specific investment that has a certain level of risk. If we invest in an investment, we give up the opportunity to invest in alternative investments; thus, the cost of capital is the market determined return we would expect to earn by investing in alternative investments of equal risk. The cost of capital is particularly relevant in valuation because we use the (after-tax) cost of capital of an investment—also called the **risk-adjusted discount rate**, **required rate of return**, **expected rate of return**, and **hurdle rate**—to discount an investment's expected cash flows in order to measure the value of the investment.

---

[4] See Coase (1937) for an important discussion about why firms exist; Coase, R., "The Nature of the Firm," *Economica* 4 (1937), pp. 386–405.

EXHIBIT 1.1 Economic Balance Sheet for a Hypothetical Company

HYPOTHETICAL COMPANY
Economic Balance Sheet
As of 31 December, Year 5

Resources (Assets)	Market Value
Value of the unlevered (all equity-financed) business operations without excess assets	$ 8,500
Value of the excess assets	500
Value of the unlevered firm	$ 9,000
Value created from financing	1,000
Value of the firm	$10,000

Claims on Resources	Market Value
Value of debt	$ 3,000
Value of preferred stock	2,000
Value of common equity	5,000
Value of securities issued	$10,000

Resources (Assets). The value of a company's resources has two basic components—the **value of the unlevered firm** and the **value created from financing**. The value of the unlevered firm is what the company would be worth if it was entirely financed with common equity but had made all of the same investment decisions. It is essentially the value of the company's operating assets plus the value of any excess assets it might hold. The value created from financing arises when a company is able to raise capital at a cost of capital that is less than the market-determined cost of capital, for example, because of some tax advantage or subsidy. In many tax jurisdictions, payments to **debtholders** in the form of interest are tax deductible at the corporate level whereas payments or flows to **equityholders** are not tax deductible. When a taxing authority allows a company to deduct interest expense to calculate taxable income, the company's debtholders receive the interest payment but the cost to the company is the after-tax amount of interest. As a result, companies have a potential tax advantage of debt relative to other forms of financing, such as equity.

The economic balance sheet does not typically show the value of all the individual components that make up the value of the unlevered firm, but we are able to break it into two components: the value of the company's business operations on an unlevered basis and the value of its excess assets. The value of a company's business operations is the value of the company's ongoing businesses, exclusive of any value created from financing and any value in assets that are not needed for the business. The value of the company's business operations is not the sum of the individual values of the assets that the company needs to operate its businesses when considered separately. Rather, it is the value of those assets when valued together as an ongoing business based on the company's strategy and management's implementation of that strategy. These assets include monetary assets (such as cash and receivables required for the business), physical assets (such as inventory and property, plant, and equipment), intangible assets (such as intellectual property or a superior R&D capability), and the **value of growth opportunities** (also called the **present value of growth opportunities**). Thus, the value of the business operations includes any expected future value creation resulting from anticipated investments. The latter are not assets already-in-place, but they are part of the value of a company.

The value of the company's **excess assets** includes all resources that are not needed to operate the specific business being valued. Excess assets include assets such as **excess cash** and marketable securities (sometimes referred to as cash and cash equivalents); land, buildings, equipment, and patents not needed to run the business; **net pension assets**, and any other asset that is not needed to operate the business based on the company's strategy. Generally, we value excess assets separately and isolate them from our valuation analysis of the company's business.

Claims on Resources. In the bottom section of Exhibit 1.1, Claims on Resources, we show that the value of the firm is equal to the sum of the value of a company's securities. We use a simple capital structure in this exhibit: debt, preferred stock, and common equity. The claims on the company's resources consist of all of the securities issued by the company to raise capital. Keep in mind that companies can

Valuation in Practice 1.2

Apple Inc.'s[5] (Apple) Excess Cash As shown in Exhibit P1.2 (see Problem 1.7), as of the end of fiscal year 2011, Apple had over $116 billion in assets, of which $81 billion (70%) was composed of cash, cash equivalents, and marketable securities ("cash"). Apple had no debt at this time. It was clear that most of the "cash" was an excess asset (excess cash), which is why financial analysts and other market participants began to lobby Apple to begin to distribute its excess cash to its shareholders. In 2012, Apple began a "return of capital" program and began to pay dividends and repurchase its shares. From 2012 through 2016, Apple's return of capital program distributed over $200 billion to its shareholders. In spite of its $200 billion return of capital program, as of the end of its first fiscal quarter in 2017 (quarter ended December 31, 2016), Apple reported total assets of $331 billion, of which $246 billion (74%) was composed of cash, cash equivalents, and marketable securities. Over this period, however, Apple borrowed $77 billion, so its net cash position without debt was $169 billion (67% of its assets with net cash).

In order to value Apple, we would first estimate its actual cash needs for operating the company and its excess cash; in other words, estimate the amount of "cash" Apple needs to implement its current long-term strategy. Estimating required cash is complex for most companies (see Chapters 3 and 4). Part of the analysis to estimate Apple's excess cash requires that we understand why Apple borrowed $77 billion, when it appeared to have so much excess cash on its balance sheet. Is that "cash" really excess cash? It turns out that of the $246 billion in "cash" as of December 31, 2016, over 90% ($230 billion) is from profits of its overseas operations which would be taxed by the U.S. if it was paid (repatriated or upstreamed) to Apple's parent company in the U.S. Apple's CEO stated that the U.S. tax rate would be around 40% (federal and state taxes) on its overseas "cash" if repatriated (based on current U.S. income tax rates) and said it has no plans to do so until U.S. tax rates are reduced.In December of 2017, the passage of the Tax Cuts and Jobs Act of 2017 reduced the U.S. federal tax rate to 21%. In addition, companies are required to pay a tax on earnings that have not been previously repatriated back to the U.S at a 15.5% tax rate on liquid assets (cash and marketable securities) and an 8% tax rate on non-liquid assets as of January 1, 2018. Companies are given 8 years to pay the taxes on these past overseas earnings.

issue different kinds of debt, preferred and common equity, so each of these categories can actually be composed of multiple securities.

All companies have at least one type of claim, called **common equity** (or **equity**). (We use the term *equity* interchangeably with the term *common equity* throughout this book.) The investors who own these securities have a residual interest in the company's resources and almost always control the company. They generally elect the board of directors, which hires and compensates management. Companies can have more than one type of common equity that has different rights, such as different voting rights as well as different dividend rights. Another claim on the resources of the company is the debt that is outstanding. Companies can have different types of debt with varying seniority and differing terms. Debt has seniority over the other claims shown in the economic balance sheet. Most, but not all forms of debt instruments represent a fixed claim on the company's resources.

Companies can also issue another form of security, called **preferred stock**, that typically (but not always) also has a fixed claim on the company's resources. Preferred stock is generally junior to the company's debt instruments, but it is generally senior to the common equity. A company can also issue various classes of preferred stock. In most tax jurisdictions, the dividends paid on preferred stock are not generally tax deductible. In addition, companies can issue debt and preferred stock that are convertible into common equity at the option of the holder. Companies can also have other types of securities, such as contingent claims like **employee stock options** and **stock warrants**, or other debt-like claims, such as **pension liabilities**.

You might be wondering why the value of the company's non-interest-bearing operating liabilities (such as accounts payable or taxes payable) does not show up in the Claims on Resources section of the

---

[5] Apple designs, manufactures, and markets personal computers and related software, services, peripherals, and networking solutions worldwide as well as portable digital music players and related accessories and services, including online sale of third-party audio and video products. See http://investor.apple.com/.

economic balance sheet. **Operating liabilities** result when a company does not have to pay cash for its operating expenses in the same period in which it receives the good or service provided to it. These liabilities are presented on a company's balance sheet as current liabilities (such as accounts payable and other payables), as well as non-current liabilities. From a valuation perspective, we do not consider any of these liabilities as debt but consider them non-interest-bearing operating liabilities. The reason the non-interest-bearing operating liabilities do not appear in the economic balance sheet is that in the normal process of performing a valuation on a going-concern basis, the non-interest-bearing operating liabilities of the company are implicitly netted against the value of the company's assets in the valuation models used to determine the value of the unlevered assets. Since non-interest-bearing operating liabilities are netted out in measuring the resources of the company, none of the claims shown on the economic balance sheet is a non-interest-bearing operating liability. However, since non-interest-bearing operating liabilities have a legal claim on the assets of a company, they do affect the valuation of the company, which we will discuss later in Chapters 3 through 5.

Why is it that in the course of a valuation the **non-interest-bearing liabilities** are implicitly netted out against the value of the company's assets in determining the value of the company's unlevered assets? Because financing costs related to non-interest-bearing operating liabilities are embedded in the company's operating expenses, we do not have an easy way to disentangle the financing cost from the actual operating expense. When a company buys a product or service **on account** from a vendor, the vendor charges the company for the product or service plus an implicit financing charge for not paying at the time the good or service is received. Hence, the financing charge is embedded in the cost of the product or service and cannot be separated from the value of the operations. At this point, we don't discuss how this netting takes place in the various types of valuation methods used, but we will return to this topic when we discuss each type of valuation method in subsequent chapters.

Valuation Key 1.1

The economic balance sheet portrays the value of the resources or assets of the firm considered as a whole, as well as the value of the claims the company has issued. The economic balance sheet shows the value of a company's collective resources and the values of the various claims on its resources (securities issued) at a specific point in time. Naturally, the value of the company's resources or assets is equal to the value of the claims on those resources. This is a fundamental relationship widely used in the valuation frameworks and tools we discuss in the book.

The Economic Balance Sheet Does Not Equal the Accounting Balance Sheet

The economic balance sheet is not like the balance sheets companies publish in their **annual reports** or **quarterly reports**, which are **accounting balance sheets** (unless we indicate otherwise, we use the term **balance sheet** to mean the **accounting balance sheet** prepared by a company for its annual or quarterly report). The economic balance sheet shows the *market* value of a company's collective resources and the market values of the various claims on its resources (securities issued) at a specific point in time. Accountants prepare the accounting balance sheet using specific rules (**Generally Accepted Accounting Principles**, **GAAP**, or **International Financial Accounting Standards**, **IFRS**), which do not, for the most part, purport to measure the market value of a company's resources or claims on its resources. Accountants tend to be conservative in the way they record the assets and liabilities on balance sheets and other **financial statements**; they will, more often than not, recognize losses before they are realized but not recognize gains until they are realized. The result is an accounting system that ignores some important assets that add to the company's value. As a result, the economic balance sheet will generally have a higher value for the company's resources, and therefore a higher value for the claims on its resources, than observed on an accounting balance sheet. Most of this difference in value benefits the company's residual value claimants (common equityholders or shareholders). We observe that the ratio of the market value of equity to the **book value** of equity is, on average, greater than one, which is consistent with these differences. But note that not all companies have market-to-book ratios that are greater than one (see Chapter 13).

REVIEW EXERCISE 1.1

The Market Value Company Economic Balance Sheet

Prepare an economic balance sheet for The Market Value Company as of Year 0 using the following information and the financial statements provided. The company's share price is $12.08 and it has 1,200 shares outstanding. Its debt is trading at a premium, indicating that its market value is equal to 102% of its book value. The company has land valued at $3,000 that is not necessary to operate the business. Based on the amount and type of debt financing, the company creates $3,800 in value from financing.

THE MARKET VALUE COMPANY
Income Statement and Balance Sheet Forecasts

	Year −1	Year 0
Balance Sheet—Assets		
Cash balance	$ 171.4	$ 188.5
Accounts receivable	571.2	628.3
Inventory	286.5	315.2
Total current assets	$1,029.1	$1,132.0
Net property, plant and equipment	7,539.4	8,567.5
Total assets	$8,568.5	$9,699.5
Income Statement		
Revenue	$3,472.0	$3,769.7
Cost of goods sold	−1,473.6	−1,621.0
Gross margin	$1,953.4	$2,148.7
Selling, general and administrative	−479.8	−527.8
Operating income	$1,473.6	$1,621.0
Interest expense	−307.0	−384.0
Income before taxes	$1,166.6	$1,237.0
Income tax expense	−443.3	−470.0
Net income	$ 723.3	$ 766.9

	Year −1	Year 0
Balance Sheet—Liabilities & Equity		
Accounts payable	$ 122.8	$ 135.1
Other current operating liabilities	119.9	131.9
Total current liabilities	$ 242.7	$ 267.0
Debt	4,800.0	5,200.0
Total liabilities	$5,042.7	$5,467.0
Common stock	$1,802.4	$1,802.4
Retained earnings	1,723.3	2,430.0
Total shareholders' equity	$3,525.7	$4,232.4
Total liabilities and equities	$8,568.5	$9,699.5

Exhibit may contain small rounding errors

Solution on pages 34–35.

1.3 VALUATION PRINCIPLES

LO2 Understand the principles underpinning the commonly used valuation methods

An asset has value to an investor because the investor believes the asset will generate cash flows in the future. The value of an asset depends on the magnitude, timing, and risk of the cash flows the investor expects it to generate. Holding everything else constant, the value of an asset increases if the magnitude of its expected cash flows increases, if its expected cash flows arrive sooner, or if its risk (risk-adjusted discount rate) decreases. As we discuss below, the **discounted cash flow (DCF) valuation model** directly results from these valuation principles.

Valuation Key 1.2

The value of an asset depends on the magnitude, timing, and risk of the cash flows (called free cash flows) the investor expects it to generate. The discounted cash flow (DCF) valuation model directly results from these valuation principles.

Introduction to Measuring Free Cash Flows

The DCF model measures the value of an asset as the sum of the expected cash flows the asset generates after adjusting each expected cash flow for its timing and risk. In the context of the valuation of

Valuation Key 1.3

Free cash flows are the cash flows that could be distributed to all of the company's investors after it makes all necessary investments, but without consideration of the taxes saved from any interest expense that arises from debt in its capital structure. They are the free cash flows of the company if it were entirely equity financed.

companies, we refer to those cash flows as the **free cash flows** or the **free cash flows of the unlevered firm**. Free cash flows are the cash flows generated by the company after the collection of its revenues, payment of its expenses, and after making its investments, including investments in working capital. They are the cash flows the company would generate if it was entirely financed with equity. We use the word "free" to describe these cash flows not because they were costless to generate, but because the company is "free" (or able) to distribute these flows to its investors without interfering with the execution of its strategy.

To measure free cash flows, we begin with earnings before interest and taxes, **EBIT**, and deduct income taxes. The income taxes deducted, **TAX**, are the income taxes the company would pay if it had no **interest deductions** (interest expense that is deductible for income tax purposes). The next adjustment is to convert the company's earnings to cash flows. Earnings are not equal to cash flows because earnings include non-cash expenses, non-cash revenues, and other accruals. To convert EBIT to cash flow, we add back any **non-cash expenses or losses (NCEXP)**, for example, depreciation, and subtract any **non-cash revenues or gains (NCREV)**. We also subtract investments, which include any increase in the **required cash balance (Δ RC)**, any increase in **non-cash required operating working capital** (**Δ WCO**, for example, inventory), **capital expenditures (CAPEX)**, and any other required investments for the business. Non-cash required operating working capital does not include any items related to financing costs (such as interest) or income taxes. We show this calculation in Equation 1.1

$$\text{FCF} = \text{EBIT} - \text{TAX} + \text{NCEXP} - \text{NCREV} - \Delta\text{RC} - \Delta\text{WCO} - \text{CAPEX} \tag{1.1}$$

This is the most basic calculation of free cash flows. Naturally, as a company's assets, capital structure, economic transactions, and income tax situations become more complex, the calculation of free cash flows becomes more complex as well. We discuss Snap Inc. (Snap) in the opening vignette. Recall that as part of Goodwater Capital's analysis of Snap's potential value, Goodwater included illustrative forecasts for Snap from 2017 through 2027, which appear in the table in the opening vignette. In the second column of the forecasts, we show each component of the condensed free cash flow formula in Equation 1.1. Snap's free cash flow forecast for 2020 is equal to $109 million.

$$\text{FCF} = \text{EBIT} - \text{TAX} + \text{NCEXP} - \text{NCREV} - \Delta\text{RC} - \Delta\text{WCO} - \text{CAPEX}$$
$$\$109 = \$347 - \$1 + \$279 - \$0 - \$16 - \$155 - \$345$$

Snap's 2020 EBIT forecast is $347 million. Snap is expected to have an income tax expense of only $1 million in 2020 because Snap is expected to use its net operating losses from previous years (net operating loss carryforward, see Chapter 3) to offset its taxable income.[6] Snap's free cash flow in 2020 is $109 million even though its EBIT minus income taxes is more than three times that amount, $346 million. The reason why Snap's free cash flow is less than its earnings is that its required investments in cash ($16 million), working capital ($155 million), and capital expenditures ($345 million) are larger than its non-cash expense, depreciation and amortization ($279 million). We observe this effect in all subsequent years because the forecasts have Snap growing at more than 20% in every year, which requires large investments to support that growth (see Chapters 4 and 6).

[6] The Tax Cuts and Jobs Act of 2017 set limitations on the extent to which net operating losses can reduce taxable income in any one year. Those limitations do not apply to Snap's NOLs because they arose prior to 12/31/17. We discuss this issue in more detail in Chapter 3.

REVIEW EXERCISE 1.2

The Market Value Company Unlevered Free Cash Flow

Use the information in Review Exercise 1.1 to measure the unlevered free cash flow for The Market Value Company for Year 0. The company has $500 in depreciation expense embedded within its cost of goods sold. This is the only depreciation the company records. The company holds no excess cash so the change in cash is its required cash. The tax rate is 38%.

Solution on page 35.

The Discounted Cash Flow Valuation Model

The DCF model adjusts expected free cash flows by using **time value of money principles** to discount each expected free cash flow to the date of the valuation, using a risk-adjusted discount rate that reflects the risk of the asset. The DCF model provides a useful framework to convert the sometimes abstract and qualitative strategic concepts (strategic fit, competitive advantage, market power) into quantitative measures that affect value. This framework involves answering three overarching questions: How does the strategic action affect the magnitude of the free cash flows? How does the strategic action affect the timing of the free cash flows? How does the strategic action affect the underlying risk of the free cash flows?

Since a company does not have a contractually finite life but can exist forever, the DCF model normally discounts a company's free cash flows to infinity. The DCF model to measure the value of the firm, $V_{F,0}$, simplified for an all-equity financed company with a constant (risk-adjusted) cost of capital, r_{UA}, which is termed the **unlevered cost of capital**, is:

$$V_{F,0} = \frac{FCF_1}{(1+r_{UA})^1} + \frac{FCF_2}{(1+r_{UA})^2} + \ldots + \frac{FCF_\infty}{(1+r_{UA})^\infty} = \sum_{t=1}^{\infty} \frac{FCF_t}{(1+r_{UA})^t}$$

The value of the firm is measured at a particular date, which is as of the end of Period 0 in the above formula. Unless we believe the company will liquidate or otherwise go out of business, the assumption that a company has an infinite life complicates our DCF calculations, for it is not possible to forecast and then discount an infinite series of cash flows unless we make a simplifying assumption about the time series of the expected cash flows. The way we typically solve this problem is to develop detailed forecasts for a company's expected cash flows for some finite period of time, say 10 years. Then, we measure the value of the firm at the end of that finite period. We call the value at the end of the finite period of time the company's **continuing value (CV)**; other terms used for this concept are **terminal value**, **residual value**, and **horizon value**. The way we typically implement the infinite forecast horizon is to construct detailed forecasts for the company for C years and measure the continuing value of the firm, $CV_{F,C}$, as of the end of Year C.

The continuing value represents the value of the company as of the end of Year C. Using a continuing value in our DCF model as of the end of Year C, our DCF model becomes

$$V_{F,0} = \sum_{t=1}^{C} \frac{FCF_t}{(1+r_{UA})^t} + \frac{CV_{F,C}}{(1+r_{UA})^C} \tag{1.2}$$

A common way we can measure a company's continuing value is to assume the company's free cash flows grow at a constant rate, g, after the continuing value date and that the discount rate remains constant as well. We call this assumption a **constant growth perpetuity** assumption. As long as the growth rate is constant and less than the constant discount rate, the infinite series present value calculation summarizes to the constant growth perpetuity formula.[7]

$$CV_{F,C} = FCF_{C+1} \times \frac{1}{(r_{UA} - g)} \tag{1.3}$$

[7] This type of constant growth perpetuity valuation model for discounting dividends is called the Gordon growth model; see Myron J., 1962, *The Investment, Financing, and Valuation of the Corporation.* Illinois - Richard D. Irwin.

Substituting the above continuing value into the DCF model we get our widely accepted DCF model with a constant growth perpetuity continuing value:

$$V_{F,0} = \sum_{t=1}^{C} \frac{FCF_t}{(1+r_{UA})^t} + \frac{FCF_{C+1}}{(r_{UA} - g)} \times \frac{1}{(1+r_{UA})^C} \quad \textbf{(1.4)}$$

Illustration of the Discounted Cash Flow Valuation Using Snap Inc.

Recall from the opening vignette that Snap was expected to go public in March 2017, and Goodwater Capital analyzed Snap's valuation in February 2017, when Snap was expected to have an offering price in the \$14–\$16 per share range (fully diluted market capitalization range of \$19.9 billion to \$22.8 billion). As part of the analysis of Snap's potential value, Goodwater included illustrative forecasts for Snap from 2017 through 2027, which appear in the table in the opening vignette and which we use in this illustration of the discounted cash flow valuation.

Anyone interested in owning Snap's stock is naturally interested in Snap's value. Forecasts like those provided by Goodwater are helpful to investors because Snap's value results from the timing, magnitude and riskiness of Snap's free cash flows. Snap presented two years of historical performance data prior to going public. While its revenues grew by over 600% over those two years (from \$59 million to \$404 million), its earnings (for example, earnings before interest, taxes, depreciation and amortization, EBITDA) were negative in both years, and they were more negative in 2016 than they were in 2015 (−\$366 million versus −\$491 million). Because of its investments in working capital and long-term investments, Snap's free cash flows were even more negative than its EBITDA, −\$395 million in 2015 and −\$717 in 2016.

Why did Goodwater Capital expect Snap to have an offering price of \$14–\$16 per share implying a fully diluted market capitalization range of \$19.9 billion to \$22.8 billion? According to the Goodwater Capital forecasts, they expected Snap's performance—for example, EBITDA and free cash flows—to turn positive within a few years and then grow quickly. According to these forecasts, Goodwater Capital expected Snap to have high revenue growth (growing from \$404 million in 2016 to \$14.8 billion in 2027, which is a compound annual growth rate of over 35%). In addition, after a few years of negative EBITDA and negative free cash flows, Goodwater expected Snap's EBITDA to turn positive and then steadily grow to \$7.3 billion by 2027, and its free cash flows to steadily grow to \$3.5 billion, by 2027. Apparently, Goodwater perceived that Snap's positive free cash flows in the later years more than offset its negative free cash flows in the early years resulting in a fully diluted market capitalization with a range of \$19.9 billion to \$22.8 billion.

In order to value Snap using the DCF valuation model in Equation 1.4, we need expected free cash flows for a finite number of years, Snap's cost of capital (or discount rate), and a perpetual growth rate. We already have free cash flow forecasts for eleven years, 2017 through 2027. Around the time of the IPO, analysts used a cost of capital in the 9% to 11% range and a perpetual growth rate in the 2.5% to 3.5% range. For our valuation, we will initially use a 10% discount rate and a 3% perpetual growth rate. Using the DCF valuation model in Equation 1.4, Snap's value is \$21.5 billion.

$$V_{Snap,\,2016} = \frac{-\$779}{1.1} + \frac{-\$629}{1.1^2} + \frac{-\$266}{1.1^3} + \frac{\$109}{1.1^4} + \frac{\$217}{1.1^5} + \frac{\$487}{1.1^6}$$

$$+ \frac{\$849}{1.1^7} + \frac{\$1{,}323}{1.1^8} + \frac{\$1{,}932}{1.1^9} + \frac{\$2{,}653}{1.1^{10}} + \frac{\$3{,}546}{(0.1-0.03)} \times \frac{1}{1.1^{10}} = \$21{,}481 \text{ million}$$

On a fully-diluted basis, Snap has 1,424 million share equivalents outstanding. Based on 1.424 billion shares, the above valuation implies a share price of \$15.09 (\$15.09 = \$21,481/1,424), which is roughly in the middle of the expected range of offer prices of \$14 to \$16. In Exhibit 1.2, we present the above calculations in a typical spreadsheet format.

EXHIBIT 1.2 Discounted Cash Flow Valuation of Snap, Inc.

(in millions of $)	2016	2017	2018	2019	2020	2021	2022	2023	2024	2025	2026	2027
Unlevered free cash flow for continuing value . . .												$ 3,546
Discount factor for continuing value												14.29
Unlevered free cash flow		−$779	−$629	−$266	$109	$217	$487	$849	$1,323	$1,932	$2,653	$50,656
Discount factor.		0.909	0.826	0.751	0.683	0.621	0.564	0.513	0.467	0.424	0.386	0.386
Present value		−$709	−$520	−$200	$ 75	$135	$275	$436	$ 617	$ 819	$1,023	$19,530
Firm value.	$21,481											
Fully diluted shares.	1,424		Discount rate = 10.0%				Long-term growth rate = 3.00%					
Price per share	$ 15.09											

It turned out that the expected $14–$16 initial offering price was too low. Snap's stock went public (initial public offering) in March 2017 at an offering price of $17 per share (fully-diluted market capitalization of $24.2 billion), but even that offering price did not reflect the market's valuation of Snap. Once Snap's stock started trading publicly after the initial public offering, its opening price was $24 per share (fully-diluted market capitalization of $34.3 billion), more than 40% higher than the $17 offering price. One month after Snap's initial public offering, Snap's stock was still trading above the $17 offering price. Its stock price after one month of trading was over $22 per share (fully-diluted market capitalization of $31.3 billion), more than 29% higher than the $17 offering price.

The market apparently ended up with a different assessment of the timing, magnitude and riskiness of Snap's free cash flows than we used in the above $21.5 billion valuation. While the DCF valuation model in Equation 1.4 is fairly straightforward to calculate, the inputs and analyses that underpin the inputs in that valuation model are not. The DCF valuation model (and our basic valuation principles) tell us that in order to justify the market's higher value of Snap, its free cash flows either need to arrive sooner, or be larger, or have less risk.

One way Snap's value could be higher than our $21.5 billion estimate is if Snap can break even on a free cash flow basis sooner than expected in the above forecasts. In the above forecasts, Snap's free cash flows are negative for the next three years (2017 through 2019). If instead, Snap breaks even on a free cash flow basis in 2018 (that is, the 2018 free cash flow is $0 instead of −$629 million), and the dollar change in all future free cash flows remain as reported in the original forecasts, Snap's share price increases from $15.09 to $19.83. Another way Snap's value increases is if Snap has a higher perpetual growth rate. Increasing Snap's perpetual growth rate from 3% to 3.5% increases Snap's share price from $15.09 to $16.14. Combining these two changes increases Snap's share price from $15.09 to $21.07. A third way Snap's value increases is if Snap's cost of capital (discount rate) is lower, say, 9.5%, instead of 10% (lower risk assessment). Decreasing Snap's cost of capital (discount rate) from 10% to 9.5% increases Snap's share price from $15.09 to $16.91. However, combining all three of these changes increases Snap's share price from $15.09 to $23.54, which is in the range of Snap's opening stock price once it began trading publicly. We present this valuation in Exhibit 1.3.

EXHIBIT 1.3 Adjusted Discounted Cash Flow Valuation of Snap, Inc.

(in millions of $)	2016	2017	2018	2019	2020	2021	2022	2023	2024	2025	2026	2027
Unlevered free cash flow for continuing value												$ 4,175
Discount factor for continuing value												16.67
Unlevered free cash flow		−$779	$0	$363	$738	$846	$1,116	$1,478	$1,952	$2,561	$3,282	$69,582
Discount factor.		0.913	0.834	0.762	0.696	0.635	0.580	0.530	0.484	0.442	0.404	0.404
Present value		−$712	$0	$276	$514	$538	$ 648	$ 783	$ 944	$1,131	$1,324	$28,077
Firm value.	$33,524											
Fully diluted shares.	1,424		Discount rate = 9.5%				Long-term growth rate = 3.50%					
Price per share	$ 23.54											
Dollar change in original free cash flow forecasts . . .				$363	$375	$108	$ 270	$ 362	$ 474	$ 608	$ 722	$ 893

Another way our original DCF valuation would increase is if the free cash flow forecast we used to measure Snap's continuing value is too low. A reason why its free cash forecast may be too low is that the company was still growing at more than 20% in that year. High growth requires larger investments than would be required in subsequent years with the same scale of operations after it made the investments necessary to support that scale of operations. Analyzing this potential effect is beyond the scope of our discussion in this chapter (see Chapter 6).[8]

Naturally, while these sensitivity analyses are potentially useful, any meaningful valuation or sensitivity analysis is based on sound conceptual frameworks and analysis, which first requires an understanding of DCF-based valuation models (discussed in Chapters 5 to 7). Developing the inputs used in DCF-based valuation models also requires sound conceptual frameworks and analysis. For example, the eleven years of forecasts are based on a financial model. Analyzing a financial model includes an analysis of the company's historical performance and performance relative to comparable companies, which identifies the key forecast drivers and the magnitude of the key forecast drivers used to develop the forecasts, as well as overall performance measures used to evaluate the forecasts (discussed in Chapters 2 through 4). Similarly, the perpetual growth rate input is based on an analysis of the last year of the free cash flow forecasts, an assessment of macroeconomic forecasts, as well as analyzing comparable companies (Chapter 6). Lastly, assessing the riskiness of a company's assets and its equity requires asset pricing models and analysis based on those models (discussed in Chapters 8 through 12).

REVIEW EXERCISE 1.3

Valuation of Unlevered Free Cash Flows

A company has expected free cash flows of $100.2 million, $114.0 million, and $120.8 million in the next three years. Afterward, the free cash flows will grow in perpetuity by 2% annually. Measure the value of this company as of today using a 12% discount rate.

Solution on page 36.

1.4 MEASURING THE VALUE OF THE FIRM

LO3 Explain how the different valuation models measure value

So far we discussed the general valuation principles and how they relate to the discounted cash flow model, ignoring any value from financing. In this section we discuss two alternative DCF models and other valuation models commonly used to value companies. All of the valuation models discussed in the book can be used in a variety of different contexts and in most industries. When valuing companies, we are most often interested in the value of the common equity and the value of the firm. The models we discuss in this section are commonly used valuation models for valuing the firm. In the following section we discuss how we value common equity.

Two Forms of the Discounted Cash Flow (DCF) Valuation Model

The DCF valuation model is one of the most commonly used valuation methods. In a 1998 survey of large corporations and financial advisors, Bruner et al. (1998) report that 96% of corporations use the DCF valuation method to evaluate investment opportunities and 100% of financial advisors do so.[9] As discussed in the prior section, the value of an investment according to the DCF model is the discounted (or present) value of the expected cash flows of the investment, where the discount rate is the risk-adjusted rate of return, and where the time value of money framework is used to adjust for the timing of the cash flows. The inputs for the DCF model are the magnitude and the timing of the expected cash flows and the risk-adjusted discount rate.

The two DCF methods used to measure the value of the firm are the **adjusted present value method** (**APV**) and the **weighted average cost of capital method** (**WACC**). The latter is sometimes referred to as the **adjusted cost of capital method** for reasons we explain later. Ignoring excess assets, a company derives its value from two broad sources: the value of the company's operations (**unlevered firm value**)

---

[8] In December of 2017, Snap's stock was trading in the $14 to $16 range, consistent with the initial expected offering price. By May of 2018, its stock price was in the $10 to $11 range with a value of approximately $13.5 billion.

[9] See Bruner, R., K. Eades, R. Harris, and R. Higgins, "Best Practices in Estimating the Cost of Capital: Survey and Synthesis," *Financial Practice and Education* (Spring/Summer 1998), pp. 13–28.

and the value that results from the way the company chooses to finance itself (**value from financing**). Both the APV and WACC methods value the company based on the combined value of the company's operations and the value created from financing. While the two methods take somewhat different paths to measure value, both methods yield the same value if consistently implemented. The difference between the two methods is how the methods incorporate the value created from financing in the value of the firm. The APV method incorporates the value from financing directly, via forecasts of cash flows that are attributable to financing choices. The WACC method incorporates the value from financing indirectly, through an adjustment to the discount rate, which is why it is also called the **adjusted cost of capital method**.

You are probably wondering why there are two DCF methods if they yield the same answer. As it turns out, the APV and WACC methods are not substitutes. Given the information available and the valuation assumptions made, only one of the two methods is the more appropriate starting point for a particular valuation analysis. We will come back to this issue in detail when we discuss the DCF methods in Chapter 5. The cash flows used to value the firm (the combined value of the debt, preferred equity, and common equity) are the free cash flows of the unlevered firm (free cash flows) for both DCF valuation methods. The risk-adjusted discounted rate is not the same for the two methods. The risk-adjusted discount rate used to discount the free cash flows reflects the overall riskiness of the company's operations, the unlevered cost of capital, but in the case of the WACC method, we adjust that discount rate to incorporate the potential benefit of a company's capital structure (typically, from the tax deductibility of interest), which is referred to as the weighted average cost of capital.

Instead of performing a going-concern valuation, which is most common, some valuations assume that a company will liquidate as soon as it is practical to do so or after it operates for some period of time. In a liquidation, one assumes that the assets of the company are sold in the most advantageous manner in order to pay off all of its liabilities (including any preferred stock), its other contractual obligations, and any costs associated with closing the business (e.g., employee severance packages, costs of plant closings). To the extent that any cash remains after all of that, the cash is distributed to the equityholders. An orderly liquidation that tries to maximize value usually takes some time to achieve, and the resulting cash flows from the liquidation can be incorporated into a DCF model.

The Discounted Excess Flow Valuation Models

The **discounted excess flow** valuation model has various forms, which are algebraically equivalent to the DCF valuation model. The most basic form is the **excess cash flow** method. In this method, we discount free cash flows in excess of the required free cash flows that are based on the required rate of return and amount of capital invested. The intuition for this model is quite simple. Suppose a company begins by investing $100,000 in land, the required rate of return for the risk of the business is 10%, and this is the only investment the company makes. In this case, the required unlevered cash flow that would result in the value of this company that is equal to the initial investment of $100,000 (called a zero net present value (zero NPV) investment) is $10,000 ($10,000 = $100,000 × 10%) per year in perpetuity. If the company generates an expected annual unlevered cash flow of $10,000 per year and distributes it entirely to its claimholders, it is simply worth the $100,000 investment, creating no additional value above the initial investment. If, however, the company generates an expected annual unlevered cash flow of more than $10,000 a year, the value created is the discounted value of the distribution above $10,000 per year. The value of the company in this case is the $100,000 invested plus the discounted value of the distribution above $10,000 per year. For example, if the company was expected to generate $12,000 per year that it would distribute to its investors, the value of the company would be equal to $120,000, which we could measure as the discounted value of the cash flows (DCF valuation method) or as the initial investment plus the discounted value of the cash flow above the required return [$120,000 = $12,000/0.1 = $100,000 + ($12,000 − $10,000)/0.1].

Another form of this model, called the **excess earnings** or **residual income** valuation model, uses financial accounting information to discount excess accounting earnings. Other forms of the model adjust a company's financial statements in an attempt to refine excess earnings to approximate **excess economic earnings** instead of excess accounting earnings. The accounting-based excess flow models are algebraically equivalent to the DCF model, and therefore the valuation principles we discussed previously are preserved in the excess flow valuation models. Excess flow valuation models are discussed in Chapter 7.

Market Multiple Valuation Models

Market multiple valuation models are used extensively by investment bankers and other valuation experts. Bruner et al. (1998) report that 100% of financial advisors use market multiple methods based on publicly traded comparable companies as well as comparable transactions in their valuation work. A market multiple is a ratio of the value of a firm or its equity scaled by a measure of the firm's performance or scale of operations (value driver). One way to think of a market multiple is the price the market is willing to pay for each dollar of the multiple's denominator (performance measure). The specific forms of market multiples used by managers and investors is extensive. Some of the more common market multiples for valuing the firm are the market value of the firm to **earnings before interest and taxes (EBIT)**; the market value of the firm to **earnings before interest, taxes, depreciation, and amortization (EBITDA)**; the market value of the firm to sales; and the market value of the firm to total assets or invested capital. For the numerator of a market multiple, analysts and investment bankers often subtract "cash" from the market value of the firm, which is called enterprise value. Thus, it is not uncommon to hear investment bankers refer to multiples such as enterprise value to EBITDA, which is the ratio of a company's enterprise value to EBITDA.

To use the **market multiple valuation method** (also called **price multiple**, **comparable company**, or **twin company valuation method**), we first identify a characteristic of the company that we believe is a primary determinant or driver of the company's value. Then, we identify a set of companies that are comparable to the company we are valuing for which we can observe the same value driver as well as each company's value. For each comparable company, we calculate its market multiple by dividing its value by its value driver (for example, divide the market value of the firm by EBIT, called an EBIT multiple). From the multiples of the comparable companies, we choose the appropriate multiple for the company we are valuing. Then, we multiply that multiple by the value driver (in this case EBIT) of the company we are valuing to obtain its estimated value.

The market value estimates in these multiples are typically obtained from prices of publicly traded companies or from prices paid in **control transactions** (such as a merger or tender offer) or possibly from prices of **initial public offerings (IPOs)**. For example, in considering the value of a company being acquired, financial advisors also analyze the market multiple based on transaction prices of comparable companies that have recently been acquired. Or when valuing a company for an initial public offering, the financial advisors also use prices of comparable companies that have recently gone public to measure market multiples. Market multiples based on control transactions or IPO transactions are typically referred to as **comparable transactions multiples** or **comparable deals multiples**. Irrespective of the source of the values of the comparable companies, valuation using multiples relies on the assumption that the prices used in measuring the multiples are appropriate indicators of value for the underlying companies.

The intuition underpinning market multiple valuation models is the notion of the law of one price. That is, if two assets are identical in terms of the magnitude, timing, and riskiness of their cash flows, they should sell for the same price. Further, if two assets are identical in terms of the timing and riskiness of their cash flows, but the cash flows of one asset are exactly two times as large as the cash flows of the other asset in every period, then that asset should sell for twice as much. For example, when using the EBIT multiple, we assume that the value of a company is directly proportional to current earnings before deducting interest or taxes (EBIT). If the value of one firm is $10,000 and its EBIT is $1,000, then the market multiple approach assumes that another firm that is identical in all other relevant respects, except its EBIT is $2,000, will have a value of $20,000. While market multiple valuation is simple to understand, it is quite difficult to implement. The key implementation issues are selecting comparable companies and adjusting the inputs to calculate the multiples so they are aligned with the company being valued. These issues are discussed extensively in Chapters 13 and 14.

Assuming that the values used in calculating the multiples are based on the valuation principles discussed previously and do not misrepresent market values, a market multiple valuation method preserves those valuation principles.

Valuation in Practice 1.3

BMC Software Inc.[10] Leveraged Buyout (Going Private) Transaction Large private equity transactions are often led by one or two private equity investment funds with other funds co-investing smaller amounts. BMC Software Inc. (BMC) is such an example. In May 2013, BMC agreed to be taken private by a group of private equity investors led by Bain Capital Fund X, L.P. and Golden Gate Capital Opportunity Fund, L.P. The total funds required to complete the transaction and pay related fees and expenses were expected to be approximately $8.7 billion. BMC had $1.4 billion of excess cash that could be used to fund part of the deal, resulting in required funding from debt and equity investors of approximately $7.3 billion.

The private equity investors committed up to $1.25 billion in equity and arranged and expected to use debt financing for the remainder. Barclays Bank PLC, Credit Suisse AG Cayman Islands Branch and Royal Bank of Canada (and in some cases, certain of their affiliates), provided commitments for the full amount of the debt financing subject to various terms and conditions. Under the debt commitment letter, the lenders committed to provide up to an aggregate principal amount of $6.23 billion in debt financing, consisting of a $4.2 billion senior secured term loan facility, a $350 million senior secured revolving credit facility, and a $1.68 billion senior unsecured bridge facility. The transaction closed in September 2013. At the time, it was one of the largest and most highly leveraged transactions since 2008.

Leveraged Buyout Valuation Models

Another typical technique used by investment bankers when measuring the value of a company that is put up for sale is to consider whether that company is a candidate for a **leveraged buyout (LBO)** or **private equity** transaction. An LBO is a form of transaction in which a group of private investors acquires the company using extensive debt financing. The ability of a company to support an LBO transaction depends on such characteristics as the magnitude of the expected cash flows, the stability of those cash flows, the extent to which the company already has debt outstanding, and the current condition of the credit markets. A typical LBO analysis makes assumptions about the cash flows a company can generate, the expected post-LBO capital structure, and the required rates of return for various capital providers (bank debt, senior subordinated debt, junior subordinated debt, preferred stockholders, and common stockholders). The analysis then measures the maximum price of the buyout that provides those rates of return to the various capital providers. The maximum price the LBO analysis generates is another indication of value, in this case, conditional on a particular transaction. Conditional on this particular form of transaction, the analysis preserves the valuation principles discussed previously regarding the magnitude, timing, and riskiness of the cash flows. The intricacies of leveraged buyout models are detailed in Chapter 15.

Valuation Key 1.4

The most common methods used to value the firm (the combined value of the debt, preferred equity, common equity, and other potential claims) are the DCF method, the discounted excess flow method (algebraically equivalent to the DCF method), the market multiple valuation method, and LBO analysis.

1.5 MEASURING THE VALUE OF THE FIRM'S EQUITY

The most common way to measure the value of the common equity is to first value the firm using any of the methods previously discussed and then to subtract the value for all of the non-common equity claims, such as debt and preferred stock, warrants and employee stock options, etc. As we discussed previously, operating working capital liabilities such as accounts payable are not included as part of debt because the cost (or value) of these liabilities is implicitly netted out in valuing the company's operations through the way we calculate free cash flows. For example operating liabilities such as accounts payable and taxes payable are not subtracted off because they are already factored into the valuation through the free cash flow forecasts. However, the value of interest-bearing debt, as well as the value of pension liabilities, environmental liabilities, potential settlements from lawsuits, and other liabilities are all subtracted from the value of the firm if they are not factored into the valuation through the free cash flow forecasts.

[10] See the BMC Software Inc. proxy statement filed with the U.S. SEC on May 24, 2013.

In most cases, the value of the non-equity claims—subtracted from the value of the firm to measure the value of the common equity—is an estimate of the market value of those securities. In some situations, however, we do not use market values. Consider a control transaction where a company (the acquirer) is acquiring a firm (the target) and assume the debt of the target has a provision that prohibits control transactions if any of the debt is still outstanding. In that situation, the acquirer would have to retire the debt in order to complete the acquisition. If the debt also required that it could only be retired at a premium to its face value prior to its maturity or some other specific date in the future (a **call premium**), then the value that would be subtracted from the value of the firm would not be the market value of the debt, but rather would be the amount that would have to be paid to call the debt and retire it.

Occasionally, a valuation will be conducted when a liquidation of the business is being contemplated. In a liquidation analysis, we basically appraise the individual assets and perhaps some businesses that can be sold separately. Thus, a liquidation analysis may not involve a DCF valuation but rather just an appraisal of individual assets. Of course, if we can sell a business intact, that would likely call for a DCF valuation of that business. From the value of the individual appraised assets, we subtract the value of the working capital liabilities as well as the amount needed to retire any debt or preferred stock (unless a working capital liability, debt, or preferred stock is transferred to the buyer of any businesses or assets sold). The value of the equity is what remains after subtracting off the appropriate working capital liabilities, debt and preferred stock.

Another way to value common equity is to use a discounted cash flow method that values the common equity directly. This method discounts the equity free cash flows at the equity cost of capital. The free cash flows of the equity are equal to the free cash flows of the unlevered firm adjusted for all cash flows to and from non-equity claims, such as debt and preferred stock issuances or retirements, interest and preferred dividends. As we will see in Chapter 5, using a discounted equity free cash flow model that values the equity directly is difficult to implement precisely. Hence this technique is often reserved for special situations such as valuing financial institutions, which have very high financial leverage.

Certain market multiples value the common equity directly. Instead of valuing the firm or enterprise value using a market multiple such as the EBIT or EBITDA multiple and then subtracting the value of the non-common equity claims, we value the equity directly using a common equity-based multiple. For example, a **P/E multiple** or **price-to-earnings ratio**, defined as price per common share divided by earnings available to common equityholders per share, is one such multiple that values the common equity directly. Another is the **market-to-book ratio**, defined as the market value of the equity to the book value of the equity.

Valuation Key 1.5

The value of a firm's equity can be measured in various ways. The most common method is to value the firm and subtract the value of the non-common equity claims. In certain valuations, for example, valuations of financial institutions, the value of the equity is measured directly by discounting equity free cash flows or using a common equity-based market multiple.

1.6 REAL OPTIONS IN VALUATION

The option pricing framework is another valuation method used in certain situations. Option pricing recognizes that the holder of an asset is not always compelled to act, but instead acts only if it is in the holder's best interest to do so. For example, the holder of a **call option** has the right to buy a specific asset at a specified price, called the **exercise price**, for a certain time period. Thus, if the value of the asset is above the exercise price at the time the call option is about to expire, then the holder of the call will be better off exercising the call and buying the asset at the exercise price. Of course, if the value of the asset is below the exercise price of the call, and if the holder of the call wants to purchase the asset, then the holder will buy the asset in the open market and will not exercise the call. Since it is cheaper to buy the asset in the open market than by exercising the call option, the call will not be exercised.

Early work on the potential applications of option pricing methods recognized that the common equity of a levered firm is similar to a call option on the firm, where the exercise price is equal to the amount owed to the debtholders.[11] In other words, the equityholders have the right to "buy back" the firm

[11] For a discussion of how options are valued and why equity in a firm with debt is like a call option, see Black and Scholes (1973); Black, F., and M. Scholes, "The Pricing of Options and Corporate Liabilities," *Journal of Political Economy* 91 (May–June 1973), pp. 637–654.

from the debtholders by paying off the debtholders, if they choose to do so. If the amount necessary to pay off the debt is greater than or equal to the value of the firm, it is not in the interest of the equityholders to buy the firm back, and they simply do not pay off the debtholders. Obviously, if the value of the company's assets is higher than the amount owed the debtholders, the equityholders are made better off by paying off the debtholders the amount owed.

More recently, managers and investors have recognized that certain investments that companies make have embedded options, so called **real options**. These options include options such as the option to delay investing, the option to expand, the option to abandon, the option to invest, and the option to purchase, among others. DCF valuation models can incorporate certain limited types of optionality correctly; however, companies (for example, startups) or projects with multiple stages of development and multiple decision points to decide whether to continue to invest, or abandon or sell, are not easily valued by DCF models. Market multiple valuation is also difficult because it is typically difficult to identify comparable companies or products with the same optionality and payoffs.

Pharmaceutical companies often use real option valuation to make product decisions because the product (drug) development has such a long investment horizon with multiple decision points during the investment horizon to either continue the investment, change the investment, abandon the investment, or sell it. For example, the product development cycle of a new drug begins with primary scientific research. If successful and the research results in a candidate drug, the research is patented. This is the company's first major decision point to either continue to develop the drug or abandon or sell the research (or patent). The company makes that decision based on the value of the alternatives. If the company decides to continue to develop the drug, the candidate drug is then developed into a specific formula and tested for safety, quality, and stability (pre-clinical testing). After pre-clinical testing, the company has another major decision point to either begin clinical trials, or abandon or sell the intellectual property. Typical testing for human consumption requires multiple (often three) clinical trials and takes several years to complete. The company has a major decision point after the completion of each clinical trial. If the clinical trials are ultimately successful, the company can apply for regulatory approval for one or more specific forms of the drug (for example, oral or injectable) as well as for a specific condition (some drugs ultimately can treat more than one condition). This is another option as the company does not have to seek approval for all forms and conditions at the same time.

Options can be valued in a variety of ways. The specific method that is most appropriate in a given situation is related to the type and quality of information that is available. Financial options, where there is typically a wealth of relevant data, are often valued using models such as the **Black-Scholes Option Pricing Model** and the **Binomial Option Pricing Model**. These models are also used to measure the value of real options in the context of operating decisions. However, in some cases the required data for those models is not readily available and the effect of real options on value is approximated through a DCF model that explicitly considers the options that are embedded in an investment.

Valuation Key 1.6

Certain companies (for example, startups) or projects that have multiple stages of development and multiple decision points that allow management to decide whether to continue to invest, abandon, or sell, have embedded real options. DCF valuation models, and to some extent market multiples, can incorporate certain limited types of optionality correctly. However, companies or projects like this are often best valued using option model valuation tools if the necessary data is available to use those tools.

1.7 HOW MANAGERS AND INVESTORS USE VALUATION MODELS

LO4 Describe the ways managers and investors use valuation models

A valuation analysis, based on the valuation models we discuss in this book, is an important input into the decisions managers and investors make about transactions that involve the sale, purchase, investment, or disinvestment of an entire business or a portion of a business. In addition, these same models are used for non-transactional analyses such as making smaller investment decisions or helping set the strategic direction of a company. Managers of large multinational companies, mid-sized companies, and private corporations all rely on these models to make investment and strategic decisions. Even governments rely on valuation models to make decisions. In this section, we discuss the various ways managers, investors, and others rely on valuation analyses to make important decisions.

Valuation in Practice 1.4

The Kraft/Heinz Merger In February 2013, H. J. Heinz Company agreed to be taken private by Berkshire Hathaway and 3G Capital for $28.75 billion, funded by a combination of common equity, preferred stock (with attached warrants), and debt.[12] The transaction closed in June 2013. Post-LBO Heinz quickly improved its performance, mostly through cost cutting and other increased efficiency initiatives. Less than two years later, in March 2015, Kraft Food Group and Heinz signed a definitive merger agreement to merge to form the Kraft Heinz Company.[13] The terms of the deal were that Kraft shareholders would own 49% of the Kraft Heinz Company and receive a $16.50 cash payment (dividend), which was funded by Heinz shareholders Berkshire Hathaway and 3G Capital. Management expected the merger to be accretive to earnings (i.e., increase earnings) by 2017 from expected synergies of $1.5 billion annually beginning in 2017. This merger resulted in Heinz's equity becoming publicly traded again, allowing for an eventual exit for Berkshire Hathaway and 3G Capital.

The financial advisors in this deal used the discounted cash flow and market multiple valuation methods we discuss in this book.

Control Transactions

Control transaction is a term used to describe any transaction that results in a change of control of a company.[14] A control transaction does not have to involve the sale of the entire company. It could involve the sale of an equity interest (a large block of common stock) so the buyer has sufficient control to make the company's business decisions, or it could involve the sale of only a portion of a company's business. Valuation models are used in these transactions to measure the value of the acquired entity, based on the strategy in place before the transaction (from the perspective of the seller) as well as the value based on the intended strategy after the transaction (from the perspective of the buyer). The parties involved in a potential transaction use these valuations to help negotiate a price.

If a company can use another company's assets more effectively, the company may decide to acquire some or all of the assets of that other company (via an **asset purchase**, **acquisition**, or **merger**). **Mergers and acquisitions (M&As)** is a term that describes transactions in which one company acquires or merges with another company. Acquisitions can entail the purchase of a subset of a company's assets, of all of the company's assets, or of all a company's common stock. After the transaction, the two companies can remain separate legal entities or they can merge into one legal entity. The valuation conducted in an M&A transaction includes the expected standalone cash flows of the target, plus any expected cost or revenue synergies resulting from the transaction. Thus, the relevant cash flow forecasts used in a DCF model would include additional revenues expected to be generated (revenue synergies) and any anticipated reductions in costs (cost synergies) associated with the transaction. The cash flow forecasts may also embed changes in the strategic direction of the enterprise that a new owner might make.

Certain activist investors, such as Carl Icahn, look for companies that are performing poorly relative to their potential and then take a significant stake in the company (see Valuation in Practice 1.6). In many cases, that stake is not a controlling interest. Following that, they often attempt to secure one or more seats on the board of directors in order to try to force management to change the company's operations. Since such investment strategies have inherent uncertainties in being able to get managers to change

---

[12] See the H. J. Heinz Company proxy statement filed with the U.S. SEC on March 27, 2013.

[13] See the Kraft-Heinz Investor Presentation, dated March 25, 2015, and available on June 25, 2018 at http://ir.kraftheinzcompany.com/static-files/44b6766d-efb8-4735-9a4c-9071d8418c79.

[14] See the discussion of the issues and an overview of the early research in this area by Jensen and Ruback (1983); Jensen, M. C., and R. S. Ruback, "The Market for Corporate Control: The Scientific Evidence," *Journal of Financial Economics* 11 (1983), pp. 5–50.

the operations of the company, investors do not take activist positions like this unless they believe the value-creation opportunities are substantial. These value-creation opportunities are evaluated using the valuation methods we discuss in this book.

Sometimes companies attempt an unsolicited acquisition of another company (called a **hostile takeover**). These attempts don't always work out as planned, however. For example, in 2013, the CEO of Jos. A. Bank made an unsolicited bid to acquire another smaller men's retail clothing chain, Men's Wearhouse. The CEO of Men's Wearhouse told investors that the Jos. A. Bank offer was much too low and was an "opportunistic attempt to exploit a temporary dislocation in the Men's Wearhouse stock price." Instead of negotiating to be acquired, Men's Wearhouse first made presentations to its investors explaining why it was undervalued in the market and that the offer from Jos. A. Bank was too low. The battle between the two companies continued and eventually, Men's Wearhouse made an unsolicited bid to acquire Jos. A. Bank and eventually won the battle.[15]

Highly leveraged transactions include leveraged buyouts (LBOs) and **management buyouts (MBOs)**, both of which are **change-of-control** transactions, in which control of the entity shifts. LBOs are transactions in which a group of private investors uses extensive debt financing to purchase an entire company or a part of it, such as a division. The company becomes privately held, because its common stock is no longer publicly traded. MBOs are transactions in which the managers of the company comprise part of the group of private investors, which is not uncommon.[16] Valuation models in support of LBOs and MBOs usually embed the benefits of being private, and the cost savings, tax savings, and working capital reductions associated with running the organization more efficiently. The benefits may also include changes in the strategy of the company.

When companies are bought and sold, it is common for some type of financial advisor, such as an investment bank, to aid in the process. Not only do financial advisors help perform valuations, they play a variety of other roles, such as holding an auction or auction-like process for a company being sold, advising on potential acquirers, helping obtain and evaluate offers, arranging financing, aiding with negotiation tactics, and more.

One of the paramount concerns for a board of directors in any change-of-control transaction, particularly in the U.S, is the potential legal liability associated with not using reasonable business judgment and not basing the decision on relevant available information. The business judgment rule, as it is generally applied in courts, protects the board of directors from legal liability (but not from someone filing a lawsuit) if the directors make a decision with adequate information, on an informed basis, and unmotivated by personal incentives that conflict with the incentives of other shareholders. When making business decisions that involve the sale of an entire business, one role of valuation models for the seller is to assist the board in deciding whether to accept a bid and to protect the board from legal liability by providing the board with adequate information and demonstrating that it is exercising reasonable business judgment.

In almost all change-of-control transactions of publicly traded companies, a consultant, typically an investment bank or other valuation specialist, issues an opinion (**fairness opinion**) that indicates whether the price offered in the transaction is fair, from a financial perspective, to the common equityholders and sometimes to other investors as well. While not formally required by U.S. law, since the groundbreaking Van Gorkom ruling, detailed in Valuation in Practice 1.5, almost all change-of-control transactions involving the sale of a publicly traded company will have a fairness opinion. The valuation expert's judgment on the fairness of the price is based on many of the valuation techniques discussed previously in this chapter.

---

[15] David Gelles, "Once Suitor, Jos. A. Bank Is a Target for Men's Wearhouse," November 26, 2013 8:39 am, available June 25, 2018 at https://dealbook.nytimes.com/2013/11/26/mens-wearhouse-offers-to-buy-jos-a-bank/?_r=0

[16] See Jensen (1986) and Kaplan (1989); Jensen, M. C., "Agency Costs of Free Cash Flow, Corporate Finance, and Takeovers," *American Economic Review* 2 (1986), pp. 323–329; Kaplan, S. N., "The Effects of Management Buyouts on Operating Performance and Value," *Journal of Financial Economics* 24 (1989), pp. 217–254.

Valuation in Practice 1.5

The Van Gorkom Case A fairness opinion is essentially a letter from an independent valuation specialist that tells the board of directors that the price of a proposed transaction is fair. The use of "fairness opinions" has its origins in a Delaware Supreme Court ruling in *Smith v. Van Gorkom* in 1985. Smith was a shareholder of Trans Union, and Van Gorkom was the company's chief executive officer. The lawsuit involved the sale of a company, Trans Union, to a private buyer in 1980. Trans Union's stock was trading below $38 during the year before the sale. Mr. Van Gorkom negotiated a price of $55 with a private buyer, and the buyer gave the company's board of directors three days to accept or decline the offer. Mr. Van Gorkom did not consult the board during the short negotiations process.

Mr. Van Gorkom called for a special board meeting, and after a few hours, the board of directors approved the sale of the company and recommended that shareholders accept the offer. The court ruled that the board of directors of Trans Union did not make its decision to sell the company with sufficient information and that the board of directors was not sufficiently informed about the value of the company. In its ruling, the court also noted the lack of a report by an expert consultant, and the board was held liable for not exercising reasonable business judgment in considering this transaction. Since this ruling, the board of directors in virtually any sale of a public company obtains a fairness opinion.

In rendering a fairness opinion, it is typical to perform a discounted cash flow valuation, a market multiple valuation based on comparable companies, a market multiple valuation based on comparable transactions, and sometimes an analysis of the value that would result from an LBO transaction. An investment banker may also base a fairness opinion, in part, on the process that was used to sell a company and whether there were other bids. In addition, if the company being bought and sold is a public company, it is common to examine the historical trading range of the company's stock price over some recent historical period and to examine the target prices for the company's stock as reported in various analyst reports. The financial advisor generally makes a presentation to the board of directors concerning the valuation, so the board can come to a conclusion as to whether to proceed with the transaction. Between 1994 and 2003, 95% of the deals whose value was at least $10 million had at least one fairness opinion on the target side, and 70% of the same deals had one or more opinions on the acquirer side.[17]

Asset and Financial Restructuring Activities

Companies undertake a variety of asset and financial restructuring activities to increase the value of the firm and maximize shareholder value. **Asset restructuring activities** involve the sale of assets, businesses, or the stock of subsidiaries. **Financial restructuring activities** involve large changes in a company's capital structure. Management sometimes undertakes these activities proactively and sometimes reactively, such as in response to the threat of a takeover. In a **proactive restructuring** activity designed to maximize shareholder value, management uses valuation models to better understand the economic consequences of a restructuring decision. In **reactive restructuring**, a response to a corporate raider or a threat of a **hostile bid**, management uses valuation models to analyze the economic consequences of the offer as well as the economic consequences of alternative defenses and strategies. In these cases, management will try to demonstrate that its actions will increase the per-share value of the company above the amount of the hostile bid.

Asset Restructuring Activities. A company can create value if another company can better use some of its assets, if it can use another company's assets better, or if combining the assets of two companies creates value (synergies). If another company can use a company's assets better (best and highest value use), the company should **divest** (sell off) some of those assets (**asset sale** or **divestiture**).[18] Asset restructuring activities can be of various types. One type of restructuring activity is **corporate**

[17] See Kisgen, D., J. Qian, and W. Song, "Are Fairness Opinions Fair? The Case of Mergers and Acquisitions," *Journal of Financial Economics* (February 2009), pp. 179–207.

[18] Scholarly research shows that, on average, the stock market perceives divestitures as value increasing; see, for example, Klein, L., "The Timing and Substance of Divestiture Announcements: Individual, Simultaneous and Cumulative Effects," *Journal of Finance* (July 1986), pp. 685–696.

downsizing. The goal of corporate downsizing is to reduce the size of, or eliminate, certain businesses or business activities that are not profitable or less profitable than they may potentially be. One way to downsize is by means of **asset sales**, in which a company simply sells some of its assets. For example, a company may sell a manufacturing plant or a patent that it believes a buyer can use more profitably. Another way to downsize is to sell an entire business in a transaction called a **divestiture**. In these transactions, the seller must evaluate the value to potential buyers and attempt to capture as much of the value added by the buyer as possible. The seller must also value the entity being sold as it currently operates it so that it may know whether the bids received will in fact create value for the shareholders relative to continuing to operate the asset or business. In other words, is there a bid for the assets being sold that exceeds the value of those assets if the seller were to continue to operate them? The more potential buyers with whom the seller can negotiate, the more of these benefits the seller can generally capture.

Valuation in Practice 1.6

Xerox Corporation Splits into Two Companies As you will read in Chapter 16, in 2010, Xerox acquired Affiliated Computer Services, Inc. (ACS)—a business processing outsourcing company—for around $6.5 billion (consideration was a combination of cash and Xerox stock). In 2009, ACS reported $6.5 billion in revenues and Xerox reported $15.1 billion in revenues. Xerox revenues peaked in 2011 at $22.6 billion but steadily declined each year through 2015 with revenues of $18 billion. After activist investor Carl Icahn's investment company purchased a block of Xerox stock, he lobbied Xerox to split into two companies. On January 29, 2016, Xerox announced that after a strategic review of the company's portfolio and capital allocation options, the Xerox Corporation Board unanimously approved management's plan to separate Xerox into two independent publicly-traded companies:[19]

> The Document Technology company will continue to be a global leader in document management and document outsourcing with approximately $11 billion in 2015 revenue. . . .
>
> The Business Process Outsourcing (BPO) company will be an industry leader that helps clients improve the flow of work by leveraging its expertise in managing transaction-intensive processes and applying innovations to automate and simplify business processes. With approximately $7 billion in 2015 revenue . . .
>
> **Separation Rationale**
>
> Today's market realities require greater agility and flexibility, the ability to innovate and adapt technology to address clients' fast evolving needs, and a more focused and efficient approach to operations and capital allocation. As a result, it has become increasingly clear that the Document Technology and BPO businesses serve distinct client needs, have different growth drivers, and require customized operating models and capital structures. Thus, the separation of the two businesses will enhance their competitive positions and create significant value creation opportunities, including:
>
> - Enhanced strategic and operational focus. . . .
> - Simplification of organizational structure and resources. . . .
> - Distinct and clear financial profiles. . . .
> - Compelling equity investment cases. As standalone companies, both companies will offer distinct and compelling investment propositions with differentiated financial profiles, growth drivers and business prospects.

Liquidation is an extreme form of asset restructuring in which a company dissolves either a single business or the entire company by selling off all of the assets and paying off any liabilities and any costs of liquidation. If the entire company is liquidated, any remaining cash is distributed to the stockholders. The decision to liquidate is based on a determination that the company is worth more liquidated than operating as a going concern. Again, management has to value the company as a going concern and compare that

[19] See Xerox Corporation for 8-K filing with the U.S. SEC dated January 29, 2017.

value to the liquidation value of the company. The stock market generally reacts positively to news of asset sales, divestitures, and liquidations.[20] The reason for this is that the assets being sold or divested are generally more valuable to a buyer than to the selling company; and in turn, the selling company captures some of that value. In addition, companies that are liquidated are generally quite unprofitable and the shareholders are better off receiving the liquidation proceeds than having the company continue to operate unprofitably, which dissipates any remaining resources.

Other asset restructuring activities involve a company issuing stock in the public markets for one of its subsidiaries. In **spin-offs**, a company distributes shares of a subsidiary (a separate legal entity) to existing shareholders on a pro-rata basis. The subsidiary then becomes a new standalone company that is publicly traded and operates independently of the parent company. A related restructuring activity is an **equity carve-out**. Equity carve-outs involve the **initial public offering** (**IPO**) of the stock of a subsidiary. The parent company takes a subsidiary public and retains some of the ownership, but unlike a spin-off, an equity carve-out allows the parent company to retain control over the subsidiary. The average excess stock return to the parent company when it announces transactions of this sort is generally positive.[21] In many cases, the shares of the subsidiary had not been publicly traded, so there is now an active market for the shares of the subsidiary, which provides the potential for using equity and option grants as an incentive for employees. It also provides some financial flexibility to the company. Many spin-offs occur when the subsidiary's business is not part of the parent's core business.

Valuation in Practice 1.7

Altria, Inc. Spins Off Kraft Foods Altria Group, Inc. (Altria), the parent company of Philip Morris, USA, the largest cigarette maker in the United States, also owned 88.9% of the common stock of Kraft Foods, Inc. (Kraft), itself a public company. On March 30, 2007, after legal wrangling that took several years, Altria successfully spun off its shares of Kraft to its (Altria's) shareholders on a pro-rata basis in a tax-free transaction. When Altria announced the spin-off, it stated the following in its press release:

> The separation of Altria and Kraft will benefit both parties and achieve the following benefits:
>
> - Enhance Kraft's ability to make acquisitions, including by using Kraft stock as acquisition currency, to compete more effectively in the food industry;
> - Allow management of Altria and Kraft to focus more effectively on their respective business and improve Kraft's ability to recruit and retain management and independent directors.
> - Provide greater aggregate debt capacity to both Altria and Kraft; and
> - Permit Altria and Kraft to target their respective shareholder bases more effectively and improve capital allocation within the company.

Source: See Altria Group, Inc. press release dated March 30, 2007, "Altria, Group, Inc. to Spin-off Kraft Foods, Inc.," http://investor.altria.com/phoenix.zhtml?c=80855&p=irol-newsArticle&ID=956368, available on June 25, 2018.

Financial Restructuring Activities. Financial restructuring activities (sometimes referred to as financial engineering) include such actions as issuing debt and repurchasing the company's shares, both of

---

[20] The value of the common stock of selling companies announcing asset sales or divestitures increases approximately 2%, and there is even a greater positive reaction for companies announcing their liquidation. The latter are a peculiar group of companies. For research in this area, see Hite, Owers, and Rogers (1987) and Kose and Ofek (1995); Hite, G. L., J. E. Owers, and R. C. Rogers, "The Market of Interfirm Assets Sales: Partial Sell-Offs and Total Liquidations" *Journal of Financial Economics* 18 (1987), pp. 229–252; Kose, J., and E. Ofek, "Asset Sales and Increase in Focus," *Journal of Financial Economics* 37 (1995), pp. 105–126.

[21] For spin-offs, see the early research by Schipper and Smith, (1983); Schipper, K., and A. Smith, "Effects of Recontracting on Shareholder Wealth: The Case of Voluntary Spin-offs," *Journal of Financial Economics* 12 (1983), pp. 437–467. For research that examines why spin-offs appear to create value for the parent company, see Daley, Mehrota, and Sivakumar (1997); Daley, V., V. Mehrota, and R. Sivakumar, "Corporate Focus and Value Creation: Evidence from Spinoffs, *Journal of Financial Economics* 45 (1997), pp. 257–281. For equity carve-outs, see the early research by Schipper and Smith (1986); Schipper, K., and A. Smith, "Equity Carve-Outs and Seasoned Equity Offerings," *Journal of Financial Economics* 15 (1986), pp. 153–186. For research that investigates the information effects of equity carve-outs, see Slovin, Sushka, and Ferraro (1995); Slovin, M., M. Sushka, and S. Ferraro, "A Comparison of the Information Conveyed by Equity Carveouts, Spinoffs, and Asset Sell-Offs," *Journal of Financial Economics* 37 (1995), pp. 89–104.

which can increase the company's financial leverage. Financial restructuring can also entail the repayment of debt or an exchange offer where equity is issued for debt, reducing the company's financial leverage. Financial restructuring might lead to the issuance of certain securities that have tax advantages; it might be used as a defensive tactic to thwart a hostile takeover; or it might change who has control of a company.

We often observe a company undertaking financial restructuring activities at the same time it is undergoing asset restructuring activities; the circumstances that resulted in the need to restructure the company's assets might also result in a need for the company to adjust its capital structure. An asset restructuring can also create an opportunity for a company to change its capital structure. On the other hand, a company may have to undergo asset restructuring because it changed its financing (capital structure) strategy (see Valuation in Practice 1.8). The role of valuation models in financial restructuring is to measure the effects of the restructuring on the value of the firm and to provide a long-term plan for the company's **financial architecture**. Once these valuations are performed, management is in a much better position to make the appropriate value-creation decision.

One type of financial restructuring is a debt recapitalization. The goal of a **debt recapitalization (debt recap)** is to increase the value of the firm by getting better financial terms, such as lower interest rates; more potential tax benefits associated with a more highly leveraged position; and potential benefits from better management incentives associated with higher debt levels. Why might a large amount of debt improve the efficiency of a company's operations? For some firms, a large debt overhang can be an incentive for managers to operate the firm efficiently because it forces them to generate the cash flows necessary to pay off the debt. A debt recap can also be very effective in creating value in situations where investors believe managers have been using the company's cash flows to invest in negative net present value projects.[22] In this case, the company issues a large amount of debt and pays the proceeds out to shareholders in the form of a special dividend or share repurchase at the time the debt is issued. This forces management to stop investing in negative net present value projects, for it paid out the present value of the expected cash flows to shareholders upfront and is now forced to use the cash flows generated by the business to service the debt. Debt recaps can serve as an effective commitment device to stop wasting resources.

Valuation in Practice 1.8

FMC's Debt Recapitalization FMC Corporation (FMC) is a diversified global chemical company operating in three business segments—agricultural products, specialty chemicals, and industrial chemicals. FMC was one of the first companies to undergo a debt recapitalization. In February 1986, FMC's board of directors approved a financial restructuring of the company. The plan did not treat all shareholders in the same way. Management wanted a larger percentage of the company's stock after the debt recapitalization for both itself and its employee benefit plans. Public shareholders were to receive $70 per share and one new share for each old share.

FMC planned on issuing $1.7 billion in debt to finance the debt recapitalization. The company actually issued more debt and paid more to the shareholders to get them to approve the plan, and it reduced $187 million of excess funding in its pension plans as part of the financing. The cash distribution paid by FMC to its shareholders resulted in FMC having a negative net worth (shareholders' equity) of more than $507 million by the end of 1986.

FMC provides us with an example of a successful debt recapitalization. By the end of 1990, FMC had reduced its debt level substantially and had a positive net worth (book value). FMC outperformed the S&P 500 for almost 10 years following its debt recapitalization.

Source: "FMC Corporation Board Approves Recapitalization Plan," *Wall Street Journal* (February 24, 1986); for the company's announcement of this event and the information we discuss in this paragraph, see Rudin (1987); Rudin, B., "Pension Surplus Lightens FMC Debt Load," *Crain's Chicago Business* (October 26, 1987), p. 38. For a discussion of FMC's post-debt recapitalization performance, see "FMC Corp: It Learns That There Can Be Life After Leverage," *Barron's* vol. 70, no. 18 (April 30, 1990), pp. 41–42.

Another type of financial restructuring is a stock repurchase. **Stock repurchases** are a form of dividend because cash is distributed to the shareholders if they sell their stock back to the company. The stock repurchase does not harm shareholders who do not sell their stock as long as the company does not overpay for the stock it repurchases. If the company has more cash and cash flows than profitable

[22] See Jensen (1986); Jensen, M. C., "Agency Costs of Free Cash Flow, Corporate Finance, and Takeovers," *American Economic Review* 2 (1986), pp. 323–329.

investment opportunities, that cash may be more valuable to the shareholders if the managers distribute it back to shareholders rather than retaining it. An announced stock repurchase plan that buys back the corporation's shares systematically over time can create value for shareholders if the likely alternative is one in which management will reinvest operating cash flows in negative NPV projects. Of course, if the managers have great investment opportunities (positive NPV projects), stockholders would rather have management reinvest the cash instead of paying it out. Managers typically value their companies when contemplating a stock repurchase to see how their valuation compares to the company's market valuation. Managers are more likely to engage in share repurchases when they believe their shares are undervalued. If management feels the company's shares are undervalued, the company may repurchase shares even if the company does not have available cash or cash flow by issuing additional debt. On average, companies that announce leverage-increasing restructuring activities experience positive excess stock returns. Companies that announce leverage-decreasing restructuring activities, on average, experience negative excess stock returns.[23]

Raising Capital

The ability to raise capital is a characteristic of any capitalism-based economy.[24] A company has a variety of different sources from which it can access capital. Capital can be raised from both private and public sources, and capital can be raised in the form of debt, equity, or a security that is a hybrid of the two, such as convertible debt. For example, a company can raise debt capital from private sources (such as a loan from a bank or consortium of banks), or it can raise private equity capital (such as **preferred** or **common stock** from different types of **private equity** investors). Private equity providers include **venture capitalists**, **angel investors**, **LBO sponsors**, and **mezzanine financing funds**. Of course, companies can also issue debt, preferred stock, or equity in the public markets.

The role of valuation models is important when a company raises long-term capital, particularly with equity instruments or instruments that are part debt and part equity. Similar to their role in financial restructuring activities, valuation models measure the effects of raising capital on the value of the firm and, more importantly, serve as a basis for determining the price of the new capital. Valuations help ensure that a firm does not issue new securities below their fair value, which would harm the company's existing claimholders.

Venture capital funds are a source of private equity (both common and preferred) and sometimes debt. The security issued in most venture capital investments is convertible preferred stock with voting rights so the venture capital fund shares in the residual value of the company but also has seniority (priority) over the common shareholders. Companies typically go to venture capital funds for capital when the company is young. For even younger companies, angel investors are more likely to be the very initial sources of funding. Both angel investors and venture capitalists demand very high expected rates of return, so they are an expensive source of capital. However, since angel investors and venture capitalists generally invest in very risky ventures, it is not surprising that these investors demand high expected rates of return. Venture capital funds are typically short lived, so the venture capitalist who raises the fund usually wants to exit investments the fund makes within five years. The two most common ways for the venture capital fund to exit an investment are to sell the company to another investor (typically a company in the same line of business, called a **strategic investor**, or another investment fund, called a **financial investor**) or to have the company issue stock in public markets, called **going public**.

LBO funds are another form of private equity. Many LBO transactions involve public companies or subsidiaries of public companies that are taken private. However, LBO transactions can also involve companies that are already private. As discussed previously, LBO transactions are financed with extensive amounts of debt. The amount of debt in a particular transaction will be a function of the credit market

[23] For research on these topics, see Dan and Mikkelson (1984) and Masulis (1980, 1981); Dan, L. Y., and W. H. Mikkelson, "Convertible Debt Issuance, Capital Structure Change and Financing-Related Information: Some New Evidence," *Journal of Financial Economics* vol. 13, no. 2 (1984), pp. 157–186; Masulis, R. W., "The Effects of Capital Structure Change on Security Prices: A Study of Exchange Offers," *Journal of Financial Economics* vol. 8, no. 2 (1980), pp. 139–177; Masulis, R. W., "The Impact of Capital Structure Change on Firm Value: Some Estimates," *Journal of Finance* vol. 38, no. 1 (1983), pp. 107–126; Vermaelen, T., "Common Stock Repurchases and Market Signaling: An Empirical Study," *Journal of Financial Economics* vol. 9, no. 2 (1981), pp. 138–183.

[24] Rajan and Zingales (2003) discuss this issue thoroughly in Rajan, R., and L. Zingales, *Saving Capitalism from the Capitalists: Unleashing the Power of Financial Markets to Create Wealth and Spread Opportunity*, Crown Publications (2003).

conditions at the time of the transaction, the magnitude and stability of the company's cash flows, and the quality of the company's assets and management team.

An **initial public offering (IPO)** occurs when a company issues stock in publicly traded markets for the first time. If the company is issuing new shares of stock, the offering is called a **primary offering**, and the company receives the proceeds of the transaction. If the company's initial investors are selling some or all of their stock (such as a venture capital fund or management), the offering is called a **secondary offering**, and in this case, the proceeds of the offering go to the selling shareholders. Another type of secondary offering is when a company with publicly traded stock has another stock offering (also called a **seasoned offering**). Regardless of whether this is a primary or secondary offering (or a combination of both), shareholders want to make sure that they are receiving fair value for giving up some of their proportionate ownership in the enterprise. In addition to a source of capital, going public provides a source of liquidity for a company's stock. Highly liquid stock can sometimes act like a form of currency for a company, which can be valuable to its investors as well as to employees who have **employee stock options** or hold other equity claims on the company. Valuation models naturally play a role in setting prices any time a company goes public. The **underwriters** shop the issue to various investors to assess the demand for the shares at various prices. The assessed supply and demand determines the final price at which the company issues its shares. Historically, the issue price undervalues the shares by, on average, close to 19%, as measured by the price one day after the issue. Over the longer term, however, IPO stocks do not perform as well as a control group of stocks. We observe these results for both U.S. and non-U.S. IPOs.[25]

Strategic Analysis and Value-Based Management

Companies use a strategic process to continually revise existing strategies and to develop new strategies, strategic plans, and tactics. They execute their strategic plans and tactics to create value. Valuation models use forecasts from alternative strategic plans and other information to measure the effect of different strategies on the value of the firm. Companies can use valuation models to make many decisions beyond strategic decisions, such as deciding whether to invest in certain projects.

Strategic analysis attempts to identify a company's value-maximizing business strategy. The process involves evaluating the businesses that a firm does or can operate and how it can best organize itself to compete in those respective markets. One element of strategic analysis is to perform a valuation analysis of the feasible alternative strategic initiatives to determine which of the alternative business strategies creates the most shareholder value. Managers then look at the valuation implications of the various strategies as well as the risks inherent in each in order to determine the best path for the company to pursue.

Value-based management is one of many terms that describes how a company can operate all aspects of its business and make all management decisions based on the effect its decisions have on shareholder value. Value-based management systems attempt to provide managers with incentives to maximize shareholder value.[26] The distinguishing feature of a value-based management process is its more formalized and rigorous analysis of the valuation effects of a multitude of decisions and its direct compensation of management based on the value created.[27] A requirement for a value-based management process is a valuation model that is based on the company's specific inputs and outputs. This requirement provides a distinct role for valuation models.

Contracts Between a Company and Its Investors and Employees

A company begins with a contract between the company and its shareholders and perhaps just between the founders at the outset. A company has contracts with every type of investor from whom it raises capital, which could be another company, some other legal entity, or a single individual. Companies also have contracts with their employees. Many of these contracts, especially the contracts of a privately held company, require a valuation of the company to be conducted from time to time.

---

[25] See Ritter and Welch (2002) for a review of the research on IPOs; Ritter, J. R., and I. Welch, "A Review of IPO Activity, Pricing, and Allocations," *Journal of Finance* vol. LVII, no. 4 (August 2002), pp. 1795–1828.

[26] See Martin and Petty (2000) for a detailed discussion of value-based management; Martin, J. D., and J. W. Petty, *Value Based Management: The Corporate Response to the Shareholder Revolution*, Harvard Business School Press (2000).

[27] While we discuss strategy development as a step-by-step linear process, it is actually a dynamic, continually evolving process.

Privately held companies often have a buy/sell agreement. The buy/sell agreement identifies the conditions under which the equity of the company can be bought or sold and at what price; or it delineates the method used to measure this price. Similarly, privately held companies with an employee stock ownership plan (ESOP) or some type of stock option or incentive compensation plan (based on the value of the firm) must conduct a valuation of the company, usually annually, so employees leaving the company can receive the value of their holdings in the ESOP or the value of their stock options. Even publicly traded companies sometimes provide incentives for division managers with compensation schemes based on the value of the separate divisions, which implies that valuations of the separate divisions must be conducted from time to time. Sometimes publicly traded companies create a **special purpose entity (SPE)** in order to isolate certain assets for securitization or self-insurance, to manage risk, or to allocate capital. These SPEs often require a valuation of certain claims or assets of a company.[28]

Regulatory and Legal Uses of Valuation

Governments sometimes sell off government owned businesses in the process of **privatization**. Governments use valuation models to assess the value of the government owned businesses to be sold. Regulatory agencies regularly set allowed rates of return in regulated industries based on a company's cost of capital. Sometimes income tax authorities, such as the Internal Revenue Service (IRS) or state taxing authorities in the U.S., base the amount of taxes owed by a taxpayer on the value of assets. This occurs when someone dies and an estate must pay taxes on the value of the decedent's estate at the time of death. The U.S. IRS also requires a valuation of assets when assets are transferred from one taxpayer to another. The taxpayers can be companies or individuals. Sometimes in an acquisition, a company will be forced to divest of certain assets in order to cure an antitrust issue with an antitrust enforcement agency. In this case, the company will use valuation models to find the cure that maximizes the value of the entity post-transaction.

Courts also rely on valuations when ruling on damages in lawsuits that involve companies. In many of these cases, damages equal the loss in firm value that results from the alleged actions of the defendant. Lawsuits in which damage assessments are likely to rely on a valuation model include those involving patent infringements, theft of trade secrets, business disparagement, breach of contract, appraisal of the value of a merger, and misrepresentation in the purchase of a business or security, among many others.

Identifying Over- and Undervalued Securities

Some investors use valuation models to measure a company's **fundamental value** based on their expectations of the business. They then compare the fundamental value to the price of the company on the stock market in order to identify whether the company is undervalued or overvalued. These investors then take portfolio positions that they hope will yield superior returns. Sometimes these investors are individual investors, investment funds, or other companies. For example, in April 2017, after purchasing a substantial equity interest, Mr. Daniel Lewis, the Managing Partner of Orange Capital, LLC, sent a letter to the CEO of Pinnacle Entertainment outlining the case for Pinnacle to split into two companies to increase share value, which it subsequently did.

Whether an investor can "beat the market"—that is, earn returns on a portfolio that exceed the returns the market would expect for that portfolio given its risk—depends on how good that individual's valuations are relative to the market's valuations and whether the market subsequently learns information that is consistent with the investor's insights.[29] While we do not discuss portfolio management in this book, the valuation methods we discuss can be used in investment management in order to determine what companies to buy, sell, or sell short. At present, billions of dollars are invested in U.S. investment funds alone that base their portfolio decisions on the valuation models we present in this book.

---

[28] See Culp and Niskanen (2003), especially Chapter II-1, for a discussion of SPEs and the use and alleged misuse of SPEs by Enron Corporation; Culp, C., and W. A. Niskanen, editors, *Public Policy Implications of the Enron Failure*, CATO Institute (2003).

[29] See Fama (1994, 1998) for a discussion of the **efficient markets hypothesis**; Fama, G., "Efficient Markets: II," Fiftieth Anniversary Invited Paper, *Journal of Finance* 46 (December 1991), p. 1575–1617; Fama, G., "Market Efficiency, Long-Term Returns, and Behavioral Finance," *Journal of Financial Economics* 49 (September 1998), pp. 283–306.

1.8 AN OVERVIEW OF THE VALUATION PROCESS

LO5 Outline the steps used in the valuation process

Conducting a valuation analysis involves a process that includes completing a series of specific steps. Some of these steps must be completed in a certain order, while others need not be. The process varies somewhat as a function of the type of company as well as the reason for performing the valuation. Here, we describe one approach to organizing the steps in a valuation, which we summarize in this section and in Exhibit 1.4.

EXHIBIT 1.4 An Overview of the Steps in a Typical Company Valuation

1. Identify the company's direct, indirect, and potential competitors as well as any other potential comparable or peer companies (Chapter 2)
2. Analyze historical performance, strategy, and sources of competitive advantage (Chapter 2)
3. Calculate the value of the firm and equity using one of the forms of the discounted cash flow valuation model or excess flow model (Chapters 5–7)
   - Forecast financial statements and free cash flows (Chapters 3 and 4)
   - Measure the business risk of the company and costs of capital (Chapters 8–12)
4. Calculate the value of the firm and its common equity using market multiple valuation methods (Chapter 13–14)
   - Using publicly traded companies
   - Using comparable transactions (if applicable)
5. Consider alternative valuation methods such as a leveraged buyout analysis (Chapter 15)

An early step in any valuation is identifying the company's key competitors as well as any other potential comparable or peer companies (Chapter 2). This step entails identifying the firm's lines of business and then identifying both key competitors and potential competitors for each line of business. Potential competitors include firms that sell similar products in a different geographic area—but could potentially enter the company's geographic area—and companies that might choose to enter a particular line of business. In addition, other firms selling products that the company is thinking of selling are also potential competitors. Finally, firms that sell products that are quite different but have some of the same functionality (e.g., oil and propane gas) may be key competitors as well.

In the second step, we analyze the past performance of the company and its competitors using historical financial information, for example, using the information in the companies' financial statements and relevant market data (Chapter 2). We also identify the strategy of the company and its competitors in an effort to establish the sources of competitive advantage for each company. As part of this analysis we assess whether or not the potential sources of competitive advantage are detectable in the historical data. Once the sources of competitive advantage are identified, we assess the extent to which that competitive advantage is sustainable, and—if it is sustainable—for how long.

In the third step, we measure the value of the firm using one of the forms of the DCF valuation model or excess flow model (Chapter 5 through 7). For both the DCF and excess flow methods, we decide which form of DCF model is the best form to use (for example, the WACC DCF model versus the APV DCF model). We usually measure the continuing value using the cash flow perpetuity model or, in some valuation contexts, we may use a market multiple valuation. Once we analyze the historical performance and sustainability of any identified competitive advantage, we create forecasts of the financial statements and free cash flows and test the reasonableness of those forecasts (Chapters 3 and 4). These forecasts take economic and industry-specific trends into consideration. To the extent the company has important embedded options to consider, the forecasts consider how to embed those option-like features or how to measure the value of these features separately. As part of this valuation, we also measure the company's business risk and costs of capital (Chapters 8 through 12). Estimating the company's cost of capital normally relies on data from the company and from relevant comparable companies. Estimating the company's equity cost of capital normally includes implementing a model of how assets are priced, such as the **Capital Asset Pricing Model (CAPM)**, and how the company's financial structure affects its cost of capital (Chapters 8 and 10). This step includes collecting data on the company being valued and its comparables, choosing an asset pricing model, and implementing the asset pricing model. As part of this process we typically use the companies' costs of non-common equity capital such as the cost of capital for debt, preferred stock, and possibly stock options (Chapters 9 and 12). If using the WACC method, we also measure the weighted average cost of capital (Chapter 11).

Next, in step four, we measure the company's value using a market multiple valuation method (Chapters 13 and 14). This step involves choosing comparable companies appropriate for both the method and the company being valued, choosing the specific multiples to use, adjusting the financial statements of the companies (if the multiples are based on information in the financial statements), measuring the multiples—both numerator and denominator—for each comparable company, choosing the value or range of values for each multiple, and using the multiples to measure the value of the company and its common equity. If there is potential value in the options available to the company, that option value has to be added to the market multiple valuation, or we have to choose comparable companies with the same options in order to embed that value in the measured multiples.

Finally, we consider whether any other valuation methods are appropriate to use. For example, we might consider the value of the firm in an LBO transaction (Chapter 15). In this analysis, we use our projections of cash flows that the company would generate if it did an LBO, determine the most advantageous capital structure possible given credit market conditions and characteristics of the company, and value the company as an LBO transaction based on the required rates of return for its different claimholders. Alternatively, we might consider breaking up or liquidating the company.

The valuation models we discuss in this book are well-accepted and widely-used. However, not all of the valuation models may apply in every circumstance, and the implementation of a valuation model may differ for different companies or at different times for the same company. The choice of the valuation models used and the implementation of the valuation models depend on the valuation context for a specific valuation.

SUMMARY AND KEY CONCEPTS

This chapter has provided an overview of the valuation process and the basic valuation models that are commonly used, including discounted cash flow, discounted excess flow, market multiples, LBO transaction analysis, and the option pricing framework. In addition, we have discussed the economic balance sheet and the sources of value for a company, including the value of its operations, excess assets, and the value from financing.

We discussed a variety of contexts in which valuations are used to analyze and make decisions regarding transactions and to make various types of internal decisions. Further, we have discussed how managers use these valuation methods in their decisions.

This book explores all of the valuation methods discussed in this chapter in detail and gives specific guidance on how to obtain the relevant data necessary in order to implement the models discussed.

ADDITIONAL READING AND REFERENCES

Coase, R., "The Nature of the Firm," *Economica* 4 (1937), pp. 386–405.

Jensen, M. C., "Agency Costs of Free Cash Flow, Corporate Finance, and Takeovers," *American Economic Review* 2 (1986), pp. 323–329.

EXERCISES AND PROBLEMS

P1.1 **Economic Balance Sheet—The Second Market Value Company:** Prepare an economic balance sheet for The Second Market Value Company as of Year 0 using the following information and the financial statements provided in Exhibit P1.1. The company's share price is $8.00 and it has 500 shares outstanding. Its debt is trading at a discount, indicating that its market value is equal to 95% of its book value. The company has land valued at $2,000 that is not necessary to operate the business. Based on the amount and type of debt financing, the company creates $2,200 in value from financing.

EXHIBIT P1.1 The Second Market Value Company Financial Statements

	Year −1	Year 0
Balance Sheet—Assets:		
Cash balance	$ 210.0	$ 230.0
Accounts receivable	690.0	720.0
Inventory	340.0	360.0
Total current assets	$1,240.0	$1,310.0
Net property, plant and equipment	6,030.0	6,220.0
Total assets	$7,270.0	$7,530.0

	Year −1	Year 0
Balance Sheet—Liabilities & Equity:		
Accounts payable	$ 150.0	$ 160.0
Other current operating liabilities	140.0	160.0
Total current liabilities	$ 290.0	$ 320.0
Debt	4,000.0	4,500.0
Total liabilities	$4,290.0	$4,820.0
Common stock	2,160.0	2,160.0
Retained earnings	820.0	550.0
Total shareholders equity	$2,980.0	$2,710.0
Total liabilities and equities	$7,270.0	$7,530.0

	Year −1	Year 0
Income Statement:		
Revenue	$2,340.0	$2,580.0
Cost of goods sold	−510.0	−580.0
Gross margin	$1,830.0	$2,000.0
Selling, general & administrative	−370.0	−460.0
Operating income	$1,460.0	$1,540.0
Interest expense	−530.0	−560.0
Income before taxes	$ 930.0	$ 980.0
Income tax expense	−372.0	−392.0
Net income	$ 558.0	$ 588.0

P1.2 **Unlevered Free Cash Flows—The Second Market Value Company:** Prepare an unlevered free cash flow schedule for The Second Market Value Company as of Year 0 using the information in the previous problem and the financial statements provided in Exhibit P1.1. Note that the company has $500 of depreciation which is part of Cost of Goods Sold and Selling, General and Administrative. The tax rate is 40%. The company holds no excess cash so the change in cash is the change in its required cash.

P1.3 **Basic DCF Valuation #1:** A company has expected free cash flows of $1.45 million, $2.93 million, and $3.2 million in the next three years. Beginning in Year 4, the expected cash flows will grow by 3% in perpetuity. Measure the value of this company as of today using both a 10% and 12% discount rate.

P1.4 **Basic DCF Valuation #2:** A company has expected free cash flows of $1.45 million, $2.93 million, and $3.2 million in the next three years. Beginning in Year 4, the expected cash flows will grow (or decrease) by −5% in perpetuity. Measure the value of this company as of today using both a 10% and 12% discount rate.

P1.5 **Comparison of DCF Valuations:** Compare and discuss the valuations in the previous two problems.

P1.6 **Basic DCF Valuation #3:** A company has expected cash flows of $1.85 million, $2.25 million, and $2.92 million in the next three years. For Years 4 through 10, the free cash flows will grow by 6% annually. Beginning in Year 11, the expected cash flows will grow by 3% in perpetuity. Measure the value of this company as of today using both a 10% and 12% discount rate.

P1.7 **DCF Valuation—Apple Inc.:** Develop a DCF valuation model for Apple Inc. (Apple) using the following information and the financial information in Exhibit P1.2, which includes summary historical financial statements and free cash flows (2010 and 2011) and 11 years of forecasts (2012 through 2022). Use free cash flow forecasts for 11 years (2012 through 2022), a constant growth rate of 2.5% for free cash flows generated in perpetuity after 2022, and a risk-adjusted discount rate of 12.5%. Use the free cash flow forecast for 2022 and constant perpetual growth rate of 2.5% to measure the continuing value of the firm as of the end of 2021. Apple has excess assets it does not need for its operations totaling $70.745 billion. These excess assets include excess cash ($15.127 billion) and long-term securities ($55.618 billion). For simplicity, assume that there is no tax that would be levied on Apple's excess assets if Apple were to distribute them to its shareholders. The free cash flow forecasts exclude any effects from Apple's excess assets.

P1.8 **Economic Balance Sheet—Apple Inc.:** Review Apple Inc.'s (Apple) financial statements in Exhibit P1.2 and its excess assets and valuation from P1.7. Prepare an economic balance sheet for Apple similar to the economic balance sheet in Exhibit 1.1. Discuss potential reasons for the differences between the values on the economic balance sheet and Apple's financial statements.

EXHIBIT P1.2 Apple Inc. Historical and Selected Financial Statement and Free Cash Flow Forecasts

APPLE INC.
Income Statement Forecasts
(for the years ended September 30)

($ in millions)	A2010	A2011	F2012	F2013	F2014	F2015	F2016	F2017	F2018	F2019	F2020	F2021	F2022
Revenue	$65,225	$108,249	$121,239	$132,473	$141,952	$149,796	$156,187	$161,333	$165,438	$169,574	$173,813	$178,159	$182,613
Cost of goods sold	-39,541	-64,431	-72,830	-79,579	-85,273	-89,985	-93,825	-96,916	-99,382	-101,866	-104,413	-107,023	-109,699
Gross margin	$25,684	$ 43,818	$ 48,409	$ 52,894	$ 56,679	$ 59,811	$ 62,363	$ 64,418	$ 66,057	$ 67,708	$ 69,401	$ 71,136	$ 72,914
Research and development	-1,782	-2,429	-3,016	-3,296	-3,532	-3,727	-3,886	-4,014	-4,116	-4,219	-4,324	-4,433	-4,543
Selling, general and administrative	-5,517	-7,599	-9,383	-10,252	-10,986	-11,593	-12,088	-12,486	-12,804	-13,124	-13,452	-13,788	-14,133
Operating income	$18,385	$ 33,790	$ 36,009	$ 39,346	$ 42,161	$ 44,491	$ 46,389	$ 47,918	$ 49,137	$ 50,365	$ 51,624	$ 52,915	$ 54,238
Other income and expense	155	415	0	0	0	0	0	0	0	0	0	0	0
Income before taxes	$18,540	$ 34,205	$ 36,009	$ 39,346	$ 42,161	$ 44,491	$ 46,389	$ 47,918	$ 49,137	$ 50,365	$ 51,624	$ 52,915	$ 54,238
Income tax expense	-4,527	-8,283	-9,002	-9,836	-10,540	-11,123	-11,597	-11,979	-12,284	-12,591	-12,906	-13,229	-13,559
Net income	$14,013	$ 25,922	$ 27,007	$ 29,509	$ 31,621	$ 33,368	$ 34,792	$ 35,938	$ 36,853	$ 37,774	$ 38,718	$ 39,686	$ 40,678

APPLE INC.
Balance Sheet Forecasts
(for the years ended September 30)

($ in millions)	A2010	A2011	F2012	F2013	F2014	F2015	F2016	F2017	F2018	F2019	F2020	F2021	F2022
Cash and marketable securities	$25,620	$ 25,952	$ 12,124	$ 13,247	$ 14,195	$ 14,980	$ 15,619	$ 16,133	$ 16,544	$ 16,957	$ 17,381	$ 17,816	$ 18,261
Accounts receivable	5,510	5,369	8,128	8,881	9,516	10,042	10,470	10,815	11,091	11,368	11,652	11,943	12,242
Inventory	1,051	776	1,406	1,537	1,647	1,738	1,812	1,872	1,919	1,967	2,016	2,067	2,118
Other current assets	9,497	12,891	16,045	17,532	18,787	19,825	20,671	21,352	21,895	22,442	23,003	23,578	24,168
Total current assets	$41,678	$ 44,988	$ 37,703	$ 41,197	$ 44,145	$ 46,584	$ 48,572	$ 50,172	$ 51,449	$ 52,735	$ 54,053	$ 55,405	$ 56,790
Property, plant and equipment	$ 7,234	$ 11,768	$ 17,089	$ 23,167	$ 29,964	$ 37,437	$ 45,541	$ 54,234	$ 63,480	$ 68,762	$ 73,850	$ 78,440	$ 82,579
Accumulated depreciation	-2,466	-3,991	-6,135	-9,114	-12,983	-17,787	-23,557	-30,317	-38,078	-42,315	-46,178	-49,962	-53,274
Property, plant and equipment (net)	$ 4,768	$ 7,777	$ 10,953	$ 14,053	$ 16,981	$ 19,650	$ 21,983	$ 23,918	$ 25,402	$ 26,447	$ 27,672	$ 28,478	$ 29,304
Long-term marketable securities	$25,391	$ 55,618	$ 0	$ 0	$ 0	$ 0	$ 0	$ 0	$ 0	$ 0	$ 0	$ 0	$ 0
Intangible assets	1,083	4,432	4,964	5,424	5,812	6,133	6,395	6,605	6,773	6,943	7,116	7,294	7,477
Other assets	2,263	3,556	4,095	4,474	4,794	5,059	5,275	5,449	5,587	5,727	5,870	6,017	6,167
Total assets	$75,183	$116,371	$ 57,715	$ 65,148	$ 71,732	$ 77,426	$ 82,225	$ 86,144	$ 89,211	$ 91,851	$ 94,712	$ 97,194	$ 99,738
Accounts payable	$12,015	$ 14,632	$ 16,754	$ 18,179	$ 19,473	$ 20,544	$ 21,415	$ 22,117	$ 22,677	$ 23,243	$ 23,825	$ 24,420	$ 25,031
Accrued expenses and other	8,707	13,338	15,561	17,003	18,220	19,227	20,047	20,708	21,235	21,765	22,310	22,867	23,439
Total current liabilities	$20,722	$ 27,970	$ 32,316	$ 35,183	$ 37,693	$ 39,770	$ 41,463	$ 42,825	$ 43,911	$ 45,009	$ 46,134	$ 47,288	$ 48,470
Non-current liabilities	6,670	11,786	12,799	13,985	14,986	15,814	16,489	17,032	17,465	17,902	18,349	18,808	19,278
Total liabilities	$27,392	$ 39,756	$ 45,115	$ 49,168	$ 52,679	$ 55,584	$ 57,951	$ 59,857	$ 61,377	$ 62,911	$ 64,484	$ 66,096	$ 67,748
Common stock (and other)	$10,622	$ 13,774	$ 13,774	$ 13,774	$ 13,774	$ 13,774	$ 13,774	$ 13,774	$ 13,774	$ 13,774	$ 13,774	$ 13,774	$ 13,774
Retained earnings	37,169	62,841	-1,174	2,206	5,279	8,068	10,499	12,513	14,060	15,166	16,454	17,324	18,216
Total shareholders equity	$47,791	$ 76,615	$ 12,600	$ 15,980	$ 19,053	$ 21,842	$ 24,273	$ 26,287	$ 27,834	$ 28,940	$ 30,228	$ 31,098	$ 31,990
Total liabilities and equities	$75,183	$116,371	$ 57,715	$ 65,148	$ 71,732	$ 77,426	$ 82,225	$ 86,144	$ 89,211	$ 91,851	$ 94,712	$ 97,194	$ 99,738

APPLE INC.
Free Cash Flow Forecasts
(for the years ended September 30)

($ in millions)	A2010	A2011	F2012	F2013	F2014	F2015	F2016	F2017	F2018	F2019	F2020	F2021	F2022
Earnings before interest and taxes (EBIT)	$18,540	$ 34,205	$ 36,009	$ 39,346	$ 42,161	$ 44,491	$ 46,389	$ 47,918	$ 49,137	$ 50,365	$ 51,624	$ 52,915	$ 54,238
- Income taxes paid on EBIT	-4,527	-8,283	-9,002	-9,836	-10,540	-11,123	-11,597	-11,979	-12,284	-12,591	-12,906	-13,229	-13,559
Earnings before interest and after taxes	$14,013	$ 25,922	$ 27,007	$ 29,509	$ 31,621	$ 33,368	$ 34,792	$ 35,938	$ 36,853	$ 37,774	$ 38,718	$ 39,686	$ 40,678
+ Depreciation expense	1,027	1,814	2,144	2,978	3,869	4,804	5,771	6,759	7,762	8,771	9,183	9,863	10,110
+/- Working capital and other changes	3,555	9,793	-1,723	1,303	1,191	985	803	646	515	522	535	549	562
- Change in required cash	-4,302	-4,302	-1,299	-1,123	-948	-784	-639	-515	-410	-414	-424	-435	-445
Unlevered cash flow from operations	$14,293	$ 33,227	$ 26,129	$ 32,668	$ 35,734	$ 38,373	$ 40,726	$ 42,829	$ 44,719	$ 46,653	$ 48,013	$ 49,663	$ 50,905
- Capital expenditures (net)	-2,779	-7,955	-5,852	-6,538	-7,185	-7,794	-8,365	-8,904	-9,414	-9,985	-10,582	-10,847	-11,118
Unlevered free cash flow	**$11,514**	**$ 25,272**	**$ 20,277**	**$ 26,129**	**$ 28,548**	**$ 30,579**	**$ 32,361**	**$ 33,925**	**$ 35,305**	**$ 36,668**	**$ 37,431**	**$ 38,816**	**$ 39,787**

Exhibit may contain small rounding errors

P1.9 **Analysis of Free Cash Flows—Frits Seegers Inc.:** Review Exhibit P1.3 for Frits Seegers Inc. and measure the free cash flow for Seegers for Year 0 and six years of forecasts (Year +1 to Year +6) shown. The company does not hold any excess cash, so the change in the cash balance is equal to the change in required cash. The change in Retained Earnings in a year is equal to the company's net income minus the dividends declared by the company in that year. Discuss the major factors that caused the free cash flows to change from year to year.

P1.10 **DCF Valuation—Frits Seegers Inc.:** Value Frits Seegers Inc. as of the end of Year 0 using the information in Exhibit P1.3 and a 13% risk-adjusted discount rate, and a constant growth rate of 3% for free cash flows, generated in perpetuity after Year 6.

EXHIBIT P1.3 Frits Seegers, Inc. Financial Statement—Actual and Forecasts

FRITS SEEGERS INC.
Income Statement and Balance Sheet Forecasts
(for the years ended December 31)

	Actual		Forecast					
	Year -1	Year 0	Year 1	Year 2	Year 3	Year 4	Year 5	Year 6
Income Statement								
Revenue	$1,000.0	$1,100.0	$1,650.0	$2,310.0	$3,003.0	$3,303.3	$3,402.4	$3,504.5
Cost of goods sold	–610.0	–671.0	–1,006.5	–1,409.1	–1,831.8	–2,015.0	–2,075.5	–2,137.7
Gross margin	$ 390.0	$ 429.0	$ 643.5	$ 900.9	$1,171.2	$1,288.3	$1,326.9	$1,366.7
Selling, general & administrative	–120.0	–132.0	–198.0	–277.2	–360.4	–396.4	–408.3	–420.5
Operating income	$ 270.0	$ 297.0	$ 445.5	$ 623.7	$ 810.8	$ 891.9	$ 918.6	$ 946.2
Interest expense	–77.0	–96.0	–112.0	–128.0	–136.0	–144.0	–152.0	–160.0
Income before taxes	$ 193.0	$ 201.0	$ 333.5	$ 495.7	$ 674.8	$ 747.9	$ 766.6	$ 786.2
Income tax expense	–77.2	–80.4	–133.4	–198.3	–269.9	–299.2	–306.7	–314.5
Net income	$ 115.8	$ 120.6	$ 200.1	$ 297.4	$ 404.9	$ 448.7	$ 460.0	$ 471.7
Balance Sheet								
Cash balance	$ 50.0	$ 55.0	$ 82.5	$ 115.5	$ 150.2	$ 165.2	$ 170.1	$ 175.2
Accounts receivable	166.7	183.3	275.0	385.0	500.5	550.6	567.1	584.1
Inventory	118.6	130.5	195.7	274.0	356.2	391.8	403.6	415.7
Total current assets	$ 335.3	$ 368.8	$ 553.2	$ 774.5	$1,006.8	$1,107.5	$1,140.7	$1,175.0
Land	1,550.0	1,825.0	2,155.0	2,501.5	2,651.7	2,701.2	2,752.2	2,804.8
Total assets	$1,885.3	$2,193.8	$2,708.2	$3,276.0	$3,658.5	$3,808.7	$3,893.0	$3,979.8
Accounts payable	$ 50.8	$ 55.9	$ 83.9	$ 117.4	$ 152.7	$ 167.9	$ 173.0	$ 178.1
Other current operating liabilities	35.0	38.5	57.8	80.9	105.1	115.6	119.1	122.7
Total current liabilities	$ 85.8	$ 94.4	$ 141.6	$ 198.3	$ 257.8	$ 283.5	$ 292.0	$ 300.8
Debt	1,200.0	1,400.0	1,600.0	1,700.0	1,800.0	1,900.0	2,000.0	2,100.0
Total liabilities	$1,285.8	$1,494.4	$1,741.6	$1,898.3	$2,057.8	$2,183.5	$2,292.0	$2,400.8
Common stock	$ 383.6	$ 383.6	$ 450.7	$ 564.5	$ 564.5	$ 564.5	$ 564.5	$ 564.5
Retained earnings	215.8	315.7	515.8	813.3	1,036.3	1,060.7	1,036.5	1,014.5
Total shareholders equity	$ 599.4	$ 699.4	$ 966.6	$1,377.7	$1,600.7	$1,625.2	$1,600.9	$1,579.0
Total liabilities and equities	$1,885.3	$2,193.8	$2,708.2	$3,276.0	$3,658.5	$3,808.7	$3,893.0	$3,979.8

Exhibit may contain small rounding errors

SOLUTIONS FOR REVIEW EXERCISES

Solution for Review Exercise 1.1: The Market Value Company Economic Balance Sheet
We have sufficient information to value the claims on the company's resources. The company's share price is $12.08 and it has 1,200 shares outstanding or an equity value of $14,496. Its debt is trading at a premium indicating that its market value is equal to 102% of its book value or $5,304. The resulting value of the firm is $19,800. From that amount we subtract the value of the excess asset, land valued at $3,000, and the value created from debt financing, $3,800, to measure the value of the unlevered operations, $13,000.

THE MARKET VALUE COMPANY Economic Balance Sheet	
Economic Balance Sheet—Resources/Assets	
Value of the unlevered business operations without excess assets	$13,000.0
Value of the excess assets	3,000.0
Value of the unlevered firm	$16,000.0
Value created from financing	3,800.0
Value of the firm	$19,800.0
Economic Balance Sheet—Claims on Resources	
Value of debt	$ 5,304.0
Value of equity	14,496.0
Value of securities issued	$19,800.0

Solution for Review Exercise 1.2: The Market Value Company Unlevered Free Cash Flow

We show the calculation of the unlevered free cash flow below. Notice that the unlevered free cash flow is negative. The negative free cash flow occurred not because the company was unprofitable but because the company invested more cash than it generated. Note that the Capital Expenditures equal the change in the Net Property, Plant and Equipment plus the Depreciation Expense for the Year.

THE MARKET VALUE COMPANY Free Cash Flow Forecasts	
Earnings before interest and taxes (EBIT)	$1,621.0
− Income taxes paid on EBIT	−616.0
Earnings before interest and after taxes	$1,005.0
+ Depreciation	500.0
− Change in accounts receivable	−57.1
− Change in inventory	−28.7
+ Change in accounts payable	12.3
+ Change in current other liabilities	12.0
− Change in required cash balance	−17.1
Unlevered cash flow from operations	$1,426.4
− Capital expenditures	1,528.1
Unlevered free cash flow	−$ 101.7

Income taxes paid on EBIT = 0.38 × \$1,621 = \$616

CAPEX = ΔNet PPE + Depreciation = \$1,028.1 + \$500.0 = \$1,528.1

Solution for Review Exercise 1.3: Valuation of Unlevered Free Cash Flows

We show the calculation of the value of the unlevered free cash flows below.

Cost of capital		12.0%			
Growth rate for free cash flow for continuing value		2.0%			
($ in millions)	**Year 0**	**Year 1**	**Year 2**	**Year 3**	**CV_{Firm} Year 3**
Unlevered free cash flow for continuing value (CV)					$ 123.22
Discount factor for continuing value					10.000
Unlevered free cash flow and CV		$100.20	$114.00	$120.80	$1,232.16
Discount factor		0.893	0.797	0.712	0.712
Present value		$ 89.46	$ 90.88	$ 85.98	$ 877.03
Value of the firm	$1,143.35				
		FCF g =	13.8%	6.0%	2.0%

Exhibit may contain small rounding errors.

$FCF_4 = FCF_3 \times (1 + g) = \$120.80 \times 1.02 = \$123.22$

After mastering the material in this chapter, you will be able to:

1. Know how to access financial information, identify competitors, and use financial statement analysis in valuation (2.1–2.3)
2. Measure the performance of a company using rates of return (2.5–2.7, 2.9, 2.14)
3. Examine a company's asset utilization and working capital management (2.8, 2.10)
4. Analyze a company's fixed assets and financial leverage (2.11–2.13)
5. Assess a company's competitive advantage (2.15)
6. Properly measure financial ratios (2.16)

CHAPTER

Financial Statement Analysis

2

The Kroger Co. and Whole Foods Market Inc. are both large grocery retailers but they have very different business models. Kroger has various store formats that include grocery and multi-department stores, discount, and convenience stores while Whole Foods sells natural foods products without artificial food preservatives, without antibiotics in meat, and without pesticides in vegetables, that are sustainable and consider animal welfare.[1] Financial statement relations, or financial ratios, are ratios of various financial statement items that attempt to measure economic concepts that allow us to identify the effects of these differences on the company's operating performance, operating risk, financial risk, growth, efficiency, and asset utilization. The table on the left presents a subset of the financial ratios we discuss in this chapter for Kroger and Whole Foods.

After mastering the material in this chapter, you will be able to explain such differences as why Whole Foods has a higher rate of return on its assets than Kroger but Kroger has a higher rate of return on its common equity than Whole Foods. You will also be able to use financial ratios to identify comparable companies to assess the operating performance, operating risk, financial risk, growth, efficiency, and asset utilization of the company you are valuing. This analysis will provide useful information for identifying the financial ratios to use to drive forecasts, to assess the reasonableness of the forecasts, to measure a company's costs of capital, and to use in a market multiple valuation.

WHOLE FOODS VERSUS KROGER

	2011	2012	2013	2014	2015
Profitability Ratios:					
Return on Assets					
Kroger.	3.9%	7.5%	6.7%	6.9%	7.3%
Whole Foods . . .	8.4%	9.7%	10.2%	10.3%	9.3%
Unlevered Profit Margin					
Kroger.	1.0%	1.9%	1.8%	1.9%	2.1%
Whole Foods . . .	3.4%	4.0%	4.3%	4.1%	3.5%
Return on Common Equity					
Kroger.	13.0%	36.6%	31.7%	32.0%	33.3%
Whole Foods . . .	12.8%	13.7%	14.3%	15.1%	14.1%
Liquidity Analysis:					
Current Ratio					
Kroger.	0.8	0.7	0.8	0.8	0.8
Whole Foods . . .	1.7	2.2	1.8	1.4	1.2
Quick Ratio					
Kroger.	0.2	0.2	0.2	0.2	0.2
Whole Foods . . .	1.0	1.6	1.2	0.8	0.6
Activity Ratios:					
Asset Turnover					
Kroger.	3.8	4.0	3.6	3.6	3.4
Whole Foods . . .	2.4	2.4	2.4	2.5	2.7
Days to Sell Inventory					
Kroger.	25.4	24.0	24.9	23.9	25.0
Whole Foods . . .	18.9	17.7	17.8	17.5	17.7

	2011	2012	2013	2014	2015
Expense Ratios:					
Cost of Goods Sold to Revenue					
Kroger.	79.1%	79.4%	79.4%	78.8%	77.8%
Whole Foods . . .	62.3%	61.9%	61.6%	61.9%	62.1%
Selling, General and Administrative to Revenue					
Kroger.	16.6%	16.1%	16.1%	16.4%	17.0%
Whole Foods . . .	29.6%	29.2%	29.0%	29.0%	29.0%
Advertising to Revenue					
Kroger.	0.6%	0.6%	0.6%	0.6%	0.6%
Whole Foods . . .	0.4%	0.4%	0.4%	0.4%	0.6%
Debt Factors and Leverage:					
Total Debt to Total Assets					
Kroger.	0.8	0.8	0.8	0.8	0.7
Whole Foods . . .	0.3	0.3	0.3	0.3	0.3
EBITDA* to Interest Expense					
Kroger.	8.9	9.3	10.0	10.6	11.8
Whole Foods . . .	126.8	**	**	**	**
Growth:					
Sales Growth					
Kroger.	10.0%	7.1%	1.7%	10.3%	1.3%
Whole Foods . . .	12.2%	15.7%	10.4%	9.9%	8.4%
EBITDA* Growth					
Kroger.	1.8%	11.2%	3.0%	16.8%	9.5%
Whole Foods . . .	16.5%	26.6%	16.5%	7.2%	5.6%

* EBITDA—Earnings before interest, taxes, depreciation and amortization

** EBITDA to Interest Expense ratio is greater than 1,000

Source: Financial statement inputs from the Compustat® North American Industrial Annual File

[1] See http://www.thekrogerco.com/about-kroger and http://www.wholefoodsmarket.com/company-info, both available on May 27, 2018.

CHAPTER ORGANIZATION

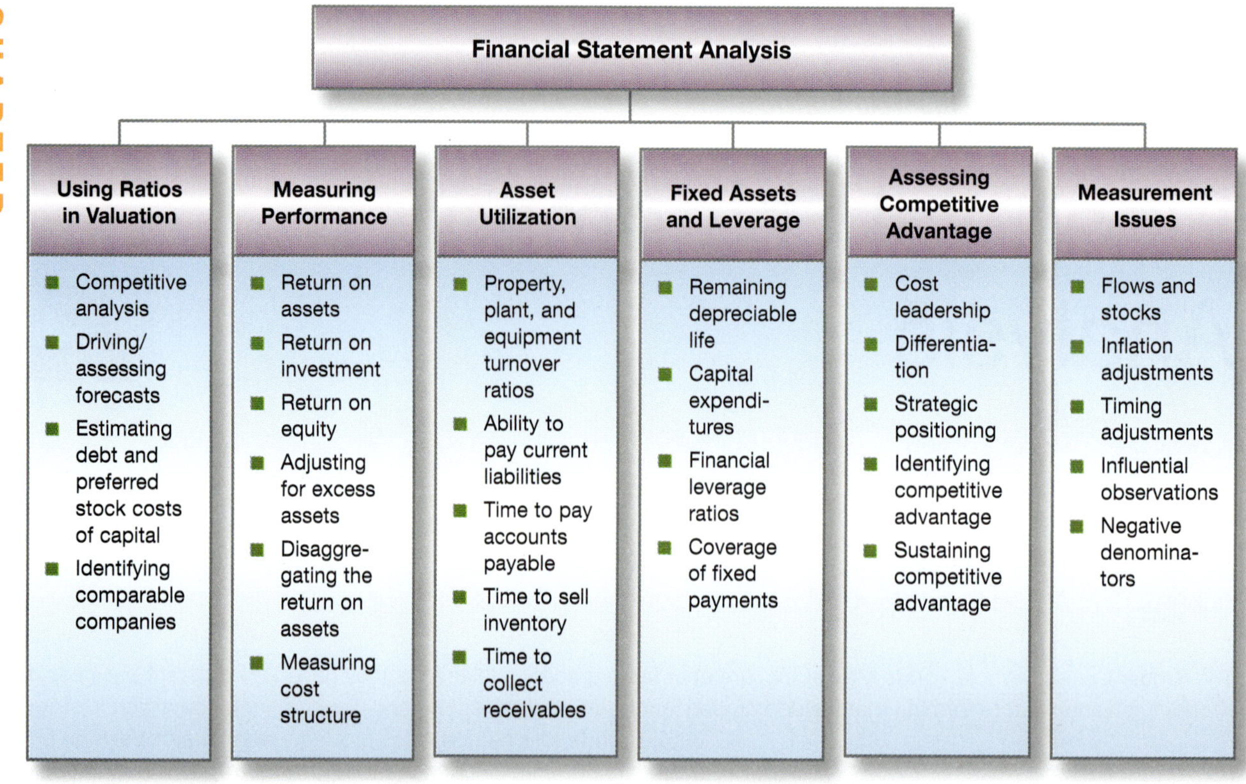

INTRODUCTION

Financial statement relations, or **financial ratios**, are ratios of various financial statement items that attempt to measure certain economic concepts. These economic concepts include such characteristics as a company's operating performance, operating risk, financial risk, growth, efficiency, and asset utilization. We typically use financial ratios to analyze a company relative to other companies, for example, competitors or comparable companies (often called a **cross-sectional analysis**) and relative to itself over time (often called a **time-series analysis**). We use ratios rather than the numbers in the financial statements directly in order to control for the scale or size of the company so that we can make comparisons with other companies or even with the same company over time. For example, instead of comparing operating income as it is reported in the income statement, we compare operating income scaled (divided) by some other financial statement number that reflects the scale of the company, such as the company's sales or assets. Sometimes, we use non-accounting information when calculating financial relations as an alternative way to adjust for scale, such as number of employees, number of stores (or the square feet of retail space), or number of tons of output.

In this chapter, we discuss how to measure and use financial ratios. We begin with a discussion of the ways we use financial ratios when valuing a company. We then discuss the various financial ratios such as accounting-based rates of return, cost structure, asset utilization, working capital management, and financial leverage ratios. It is important to understand that while we use financial ratios as proxies for certain economic concepts, they are, by their nature, accounting-based ratios, not market-based ratios, and therefore are imprecise measures of those economic concepts.

Analyzing the financial statements of a company and its competitors entails the following steps. First, we examine the businesses in which the company operates to identify its potential competitors and potential comparable companies. Second, we adjust the companies' financial statements for differences and potential distortions due to differences, for example, in accounting principles and related estimates, excess assets, the structuring of certain types of transactions (for example, leases), and any other potential distortions. Third, we qualitatively assess whether any of the companies has a potential competitive advantage. We then analyze the companies quantitatively using financial ratios and other performance metrics to assess how the performance amongst the companies has changed over time and the extent to which our assessments of competitive advantage are observable. After conducting the above analyses, we are finally in a position to use the analysis to guide our forecasts, choose comparable companies to measure various costs of capital, and choose comparable companies as the basis to measure market multiples and choose the market multiples to use in our valuation.

2.1 SOURCES OF INFORMATION

Naturally, we need to collect a substantial amount of information in order to analyze a company, its industry, and its comparable companies. We collect information on the industry, the company, its actual and potential competitors, other potential comparable companies, and even its suppliers and customers. In this section, we discuss the sources of such information.

LO1 Know how to access financial information, identify competitors, and use financial statement analysis in valuation

Information About a Company

Many company websites, especially for publicly traded companies, are a rich source of information, usually in the investor relations section of the website. Companies often provide access to the company's annual and quarterly reports, earnings announcements, government-filed reports, press releases, investor conference calls, management presentations made at investor or analyst meetings and information on annual meetings with shareholders (typically transcripts or recordings of important speeches and/or question-and-answer sessions with stockholders). A company's annual and quarterly reports contain, in addition to company financial statements, information about the company's history, operations, operating segments, competition, and more. A company will also issue a press release soon after a significant event occurs. Even privately held companies, which have no public disclosure requirements, often provide substantial financial information on their websites.

Even if a company does not have a website (a rarity, to be sure), publicly traded companies are required to file financials and other reports with the government in almost all countries. For example, in the U.S., publicly traded companies are required to file annual reports (Form 10-K) and quarterly reports (Form 10-Q) with the U.S. Securities and Exchange Commission (SEC). Depending on the type of company (large accelerated filer, accelerated filer, non-accelerated filer), the company must file its 10-K reports within 60, 75, or 90 days of its fiscal year-end and its 10-Q reports within 40 or 45 days of the end of a fiscal quarter. These reports contain extensive information about the company, including (usually limited) information on its industry segments for companies operating in more than one industry segment, and major customers. If a company cannot file its 10-K or 10-Q within the SEC's filing requirements, it must file a Form 12b-25 and explain the reasons why it cannot file on time.[2] Companies must also file a report with the SEC when a significant event occurs for the company (Form 8-K), when it notifies shareholders of a shareholders' meeting (a **proxy statement**), when it proposes to issue certain types of securities (a **registration statement**), and for a variety of other events or circumstances. All of these public filings are available on the SEC's EDGAR website.[3] In addition to filing reports with the SEC, companies often must (or choose to) file reports with other government agencies. For example, the Department of Transportation requires airline and commercial trucking companies to file certain reports. Banks and other financial institutions must file with other various government agencies.

Almost all countries have reporting requirements that companies must meet in order to be listed on an exchange for one or more of its securities to trade publicly. **Foreign private issuers** (foreign companies listed on U.S. securities exchanges) generally file **Form 20-F** as both a registration statement and an annual report. The Form 20-F report is similar in content to the S-1 registration statement and 10-K annual report filed by U.S. companies.

In addition to company-wide financial statements (called **consolidated financial statements**), U.S. generally accepted accounting principles (U.S. GAAP) requires companies to report certain (limited) accounting information—for example, revenues, operating assets, and operating incomes—for each of their operating segments.[4] According to U.S. GAAP, an operating segment is a part of a company for which

---

[2] See Alford, A., J. Jones, and M. E. Zmijewski, "Extensions and Violations of the Statutory SEC Form 10-K Filing Requirements," *Journal of Accounting and Economics* 17 (January 1993), pp. 229–254.

[3] The SEC's EDGAR website contains all public filings of U.S. listed companies. It can be found at http://www.sec.gov.

[4] See Financial Accounting Standards Board, Statement of Financial Accounting Standards No. 131, "Disclosures About Segments of an Enterprise and Related Information," June 1997.

separate financial information is made available and evaluated by management, and that accounts for 10% or more of the company's revenues. The information reported should be the same as the information used internally for decision making. Operating segments are typically of two types: industry segments and geographic segments. U.S. GAAP also requires companies to disclose their major customers, generally defined as customers who purchase 10% or more of the company's good and services. Operating segment information can be useful when valuing a company. However, detailed publicly available information for a company's industry or geographic segment is usually quite limited, and we generally need information not available to the public in order to analyze a segment in detail.

Other sources of information include stock reports and financial analyst reports. Stock reports—such as the *Standard & Poor's Stock Reports* (two-page company summaries)—contain financial and other summary information for publicly traded companies in a quickly accessible and usable form. Analyst reports can provide a wealth of information on the companies analysts follow and often include information about important competitors. Companies often list the analysts who write reports on them on their websites, and analysts following a company are also listed in certain publications (*Nelson's Directory of Investment Research*). We typically classify an analyst as either a sell-side analyst, a buy-side analyst, or an independent research analyst. **Sell-side analysts** work for brokerage companies and make recommendations that brokers use to advise clients on sales and purchases of securities. **Buy-side analysts** work for investment management companies and advise portfolio managers on the stocks they might purchase or sell. **Independent research analysts** work for companies that sell analyst reports to investors. Of course, analysts obtain much of their information from the management and financial statements of companies. Although analysts are likely to be more objective than managers, we know that analysts are, on average, optimistic, although not as optimistic as managers, on average.[5]

The financial press (newspapers, magazines, periodicals, and news websites), financial websites, stock exchanges, and certain services also provide information on companies. Articles in the financial press sometimes serve to collect and summarize information from a variety of sources (the company, its management, financial analysts, reports filed with the government, etc.). Financial websites such as Hoover's Inc., Google Finance, and Yahoo! Finance provide information about companies and their competitors in much the same way some stock reports do. Many stock exchanges provide information on the companies that have securities that trade on that stock exchange. Some companies—for example, Thomson Reuters, Bloomberg, and Morningstar—provide information on a company as well as conduct analyses using that information.

Large archival databases are another source of individual company information. For example, the Center for Research in Security Prices at the University of Chicago maintains a comprehensive database of U.S. stock market data. Standard & Poor's Compustat® is a standardized database containing accounting and some market data. Datastream and other databases provide financial statement and stock price information on companies all over the globe. Such databases allow one to investigate a company and its industry in a variety of ways. Wharton's Research Data Services (WRDS) from the Wharton School at the University of Pennsylvania provides convenient access to many databases with a web-based interface.

Information About an Industry

Extensive information is also available about industries. First, companies often disclose information about the industries in which they operate in their 10-K reports and in annual reports to shareholders. Many financial analysts specialize in certain industries and write industry reports as well as individual company reports. Some companies also issue reports containing information on an industry—for example, *Standard & Poor's Industry Surveys*. Industry financial ratios are also available in some of these publications. Most large industries have an industry or trade association. Such associations often issue industry or trade magazines that contain information on the industry, including various industry statistics. The financial press and financial websites also contain information about industries.

---

[5] Various research studies document the extent to which analysts are optimistic; see, for example, Lin, H., and M. McNichols, "Underwriting Relationships, Analysts' Earnings Forecasts, and Investment Recommendations," *Journal of Accounting and Economics* 25 (1988), pp. 101–127. This article suggests that such optimism sometimes results from a conflict of interest of (at least sell-side) analysts. As it turns out, in the United States, a number of investment banks settled with federal securities regulators on the issue of conflicts of interests faced by their (sell-side) stock analysts. (See https://www.nytimes.com/2003/04/29/business/wall-street-settlement-overview-10-wall-st-firms-reach-settlement-analyst.html, available on May 27, 2018.)

Privately Held (Owned) Companies

While we have extensive information available on publicly traded companies, less information is available about privately held companies in the U.S., unless we have the cooperation of the private company (for example, if we are valuing the company because it is considering an initial public offering). Companies like Dun and Bradstreet, Inc. and Robert Morris Associates collect limited information about privately held companies. Databases that provide some limited valuation data on private companies sold in change-of-control transactions are also available. In some countries outside the U.S., privately held companies are required to file financial statements (e.g., in Germany and the U.K.).

2.2 HOW WE USE FINANCIAL RATIOS IN VALUATION

Scholarly research has shown that financial ratios contain useful information,[6] which provides empirical justification for their widespread use in valuation and other financial analyses. Generally, when we use financial ratios, we typically compare a company to itself over time—a **time-series analysis**—or to other comparable companies—a **cross-sectional analysis**. We often use both types of analyses at the same time—a combined time-series and cross-sectional analysis. While we often use the financial ratios of competitors as "benchmarks" for the company we are analyzing, we often do not have an absolute "benchmark" for what is a "good" or "bad" value.

While we are getting ahead of ourselves a bit, we illustrate this point using the current ratio—the ratio of a company's current assets to its current liabilities. Most companies have more current assets than current liabilities. We typically observe an average current ratio for a broad set of companies in the range of 1.5 to 2. A higher current ratio suggests a more liquid company. But what is a "good" current ratio? Is a good current ratio below the average or above the average? The answer to that question is, "It depends." A low current ratio might suggest potential financial distress; but, if the company has processes in place that allow it to operate more efficiently than other companies and have a low current ratio (for example, very low inventory levels), then a low current ratio might suggest a source of competitive advantage. For example, in the earlier years of mass production of personal computers, Dell had a very low current ratio, and its working capital management techniques were seen as a source of competitive advantage. We face the same benchmarking issue for other types of ratios as well.

Competitive Analysis

Conducting a competitive analysis of a company and its industry provides a general understanding of both the company and its industry, as well as an assessment of the company's position within the industry. We normally conduct a competitive analysis early in the process of valuing a company unless we are able to rely on forecasts provided to us by others, such as management forecasts. Such an analysis can provide insights into the key value drivers of a company's business and help us identify a company's sources of competitive advantage, if any. A competitive analysis often involves analyzing a company's vision, strategy, and strategic objectives.

Measuring the Debt and Preferred Stock Costs of Capital

The debt and preferred stock costs of capital are typically required inputs to measure the unlevered cost of capital. We use these and other costs of capital to unlever the equity cost of capital to measure the unlevered cost of capital, to lever the unlevered cost of capital in order to measure the equity cost of capital, and to measure the weighted average cost of capital. Since a company's debt and preferred stock often are not publicly traded, we often cannot measure its debt and preferred stock costs of capital directly from market

[6] A study that examines accounting-based rates of return directly is Amir, E., I. Kama, and J. Livnat, "Conditional versus Unconditional Persistence of RNOA Components: Implications for Valuation," *Review of Accounting Studies* vol. 16, no. 2 (2011), pp. 302–327. Also see the work of Ou, J., and S. Penman, "Financial Statement Analysis and the Prediction of Stock Returns," *Journal of Accounting and Economics* 11 (1989), pp. 295–330; Holthausen, R., and D. Larcker, "The Prediction of Stock Returns Using Financial Statement Information," *Journal of Accounting and Economics* 15 (1992), pp. 373–412; and Abarbanell, J., and B. Bushee, "Abnormal Stock Returns to a Fundamental Analysis Strategy," *Accounting Review* 73 (1998), pp. 19–45.

data. In such cases, we typically measure the debt and preferred stock costs of capital using market data from comparable companies, and we assess the comparability of companies, in part, using financial ratios.

Creating, Driving, and Assessing the Reasonableness of Financial Forecasts

We use financial ratios to create or "drive" our forecast, and then we use other financial ratios not used to directly create the forecasts to assess the reasonableness of our financial forecasts. As we discuss in Chapter 4, one of the first steps in creating financial forecasts is to identify factors or "**forecast drivers**" to generate the forecasts. Once we forecast the scale of the company, for example, revenues, we typically use financial ratios, such as expense ratios, as forecast drivers for one or more expenses on the income statement. Turnover ratios (the ratio of an item on the income statement to a balance sheet item—for example, revenue to accounts receivable) are another common type of forecast driver. Once we develop our forecasts, we use other financial ratios to help assess the reasonableness of the forecasts. For example, we compare the rates of return (return on assets and return on equity) in our forecasts to the historical rates of return of the company, its industry, and its competitors. We might also use liquidity ratios, asset utilization ratios, and asset composition ratios in a similar manner.

Assessing the Degree of Comparability in Market Multiple Valuation

Financial ratios can be useful in a market multiple valuation when assessing the comparability of the company we are valuing to other companies. We use financial ratios to assess the comparability of profitability, rates of return, cost structures, capital expenditure requirements, growth rates, and business risk. Assessing the comparability of these factors can be important in a market multiple valuation depending on the market multiple used and the valuation context.

Constraints and Benchmarks in Contracts

Investors often use financial ratios as either constraints or benchmarks in contracts. For example, debt contracts—and to some extent preferred stock contracts—often utilize financial ratios as constraints, called **covenants**, to protect investors' rights and provide investors additional rights if the company violates one or more covenants. Investors might require a company to maintain a certain amount of liquidity, limit the amount of debt, or limit dividends by using various financial ratios (see Valuation in Practice 2.4). If a company violates any of these accounting-based covenants, called a **technical default**, the investors typically get additional rights, such as the right to accelerate the maturity of the debt and possibly charge a higher promised return.[7]

Investors use other contract provisions as well to prohibit the company from selling a significant amount of its assets or merging with another company. Investors also use financial ratios as benchmarks (or hurdles). For example, companies might have to meet certain hurdles described in a debt agreement to draw cash from a line-of-credit. Some loans, called performance priced debt, determine the yield spread above U.S. Treasuries or LIBOR the borrower is charged based on accounting performance measures. In addition, companies sometimes use accounting-based measures of performance to compensate managers.

Valuation Key 2.1

We use financial ratios in a variety of ways: to perform a competitive analysis of an industry or of a company within an industry, to assess business risk, to measure the debt and preferred stock costs of capital, to drive and assess the reasonableness of financial forecasts, to assess comparability for a market multiple valuation, and to set constraints or benchmarks in contracts.

---

[7] See Duke, J., and H. Hunt, III., "An Empirical Examination of Debt Covenant Restrictions and Accounting-Related Debt Proxies," *Journal of Accounting and Economics* vol. 1–3 (January 1990), pp. 45–63; and Press, E., and J. Weintrop, "Accounting-Based Constraints in Public and Private Debt Agreements—Their Association with Leverage and Impact on Accounting Choice," *Journal of Accounting and Economics* vol. 1–3 (January 1990), pp. 65–96.

Valuation in Practice 2.1

Example of Restricted Covenants of Advanced Micro Devices, Inc. Advanced Micro Devices has debt agreements restricting it from undertaking certain types of transactions:

> The agreements governing our notes and our Secured Revolving Line of Credit impose restrictions on us that may adversely affect our ability to operate our business. . . .
>
> - incur additional indebtedness;
> - pay dividends and make other restricted payments;
> - make certain investments, including investments in our unrestricted subsidiaries;
> - create or permit certain liens;
> - create or permit restrictions on the ability of certain restricted subsidiaries to pay dividends or make other distributions to us;
> - use the proceeds from sales of assets;
> - enter into certain types of transactions with affiliates;
> - consolidate or merge or sell our assets as an entirety or substantially as an entirety.
>
> . . .
>
> - make asset dispositions other than certain ordinary course dispositions and certain supply chain finance arrangements;
> - make certain loans, make payments with respect to subordinated debt or certain borrowed money prior to its due date; and
> - become party to certain agreements restricting the Loan Parties' ability to enter into any non-arm's-length transaction with an affiliate.

Source: Advanced Micro Devices, Inc. 2015 10-K Report, p. 17.

2.3 IDENTIFYING A COMPANY'S INDUSTRY AND ITS COMPARABLE COMPANIES

To identify a company's comparable companies, we generally begin by identifying a company's existing direct (or "head-to-head") competitors and then identify indirect and potential competitors. For example, to value the Ford Motor Company (Ford), we would first identify what markets Ford serves. Ford competes in the worldwide auto, truck, financing, insurance, and leasing markets. Identifying Ford's competitors in the auto and truck markets is relatively straightforward. Its competitors in the financing, leasing, and insurance business include a much broader group of companies, ranging from other car manufacturers to numerous financial institutions and insurance companies. As discussed earlier, a good starting point for this analysis is Ford's 10-K report.

In its 10-K, Ford provides information on its market share in the U.S. combined car and truck market as well as for its major competitors. For the year ended December 31, 2016, Ford identified its competitors with global presence to include Fiat Chrysler Automobiles, General Motors Company, Honda Motor Company, Hyundai-Kia Automotive Group, PSA Peugeot Citroen, Renault-Nissan B.V., Suzuki Motor Corporation, Toyota Motor Corporation, and Volkswagen AG Group. Ford also provided information on the non-U.S. market, information on the countries that are most important to it at that time, and information on emerging markets that it believes will become more important to it over time.

Ford's indirect competitors are companies that could affect the profitability of the auto industry but that do not directly compete in Ford's markets. Indirect competition may or may not be important for a company. For example, motorcycle manufacturers are indirect competitors for automobile manufacturers, but they do not have a substantive impact on either the profitability of or the demand for automobiles. Reducing the price of motorcycles would likely have a small, if any, impact on the demand for autos.

While indirect competition from motorcycle manufacturers is not likely important for analyzing Ford, potential competition could be important. Potential competitors from China, India, and South Korea could have a significant effect on the worldwide automotive market in the future. Great Wall Automobile Co. of

China started selling sport-utility vehicles in Russia in early 2005 at prices that were approximately 35% lower than other Asian imports. Chery Automobile, another Chinese automaker, is exporting to Europe and other locations. Both companies have plans to enter the U.S. market. All of these new or potential competitors, though small now, will likely influence the worldwide automotive industry over time. This potential competition could be important in valuing Ford, as the increased competition may affect Ford's future profitability.

Once we identify a company's current and potential competitors, we perform a competitive analysis of the industry and determine which companies in the industry, if any, have a competitive advantage. In addition, as we discuss throughout the book, various steps in the valuation process require the identification of comparable companies. The relevant comparable companies used for specific steps in the valuation process are generally a subset of the current and potential competitors of a company, and as we discuss later, can even include companies that are not current or potential competitors of the company being valued.

It is unlikely that a truly comparable company exists for any company (where the companies are comparable on all relevant dimensions, and possibly not on any specific dimension), which is why we often use a portfolio of potentially comparable companies in our analysis. Unfortunately, while the financial relations and underlying accounting data we discuss in this chapter are useful for assessing and identifying comparable companies, their usefulness is limited because of the differences between accounting data and the potentially unobservable economic concepts they represent.

2.4 THE GAP, INC.—AN ILLUSTRATION OF THE CALCULATION AND ANALYSIS OF FINANCIAL RATIOS

In this chapter, we use The Gap, Inc. (GAP) to illustrate the calculation and analysis of financial ratios. GAP is a global retailer operating retail and outlet stores that sell apparel, accessories, and personal care products for men, women, and children. We assume for illustrative purposes that GAP's management believes that the market is substantially undervaluing GAP, as GAP's management believes that it can improve GAP's performance in a variety of ways. In Exhibit 2.1, we present GAP's summary historical financial statements for two years (Year −1 and Year 0) and hypothetical management forecasts of its income statements, balance sheets, and summary free cash flow schedules for six years (Year +1 through Year +6). We do not show GAP's Statement of Cash Flows although we show GAP's operating cash flow at the bottom of the schedule, nor do we show its footnotes and other supplemental disclosures. Rather, we discuss relevant footnotes and other disclosures as needed. Naturally, a complete financial analysis includes a detailed review of all of a company's footnotes and other disclosures in its financial statements but that is beyond the scope of what we cover in this chapter. Sometimes, we make adjustments to the financial statements before computing various ratios and computing market multiples, which we discuss in Chapter 14.

Prior to the end of its Year 0 fiscal year, GAP distributed close to one billion dollars in dividends and share repurchases. This was excess cash that GAP management felt it did not need. GAP had a market capitalization (a measure of firm value) of roughly $11 billion at the end of its Year 0 fiscal year (after the cash distributions to shareholders had been made). The GAP hypothetical forecasts assume that management can improve the company's performance. Management believes it can grow revenues above market expectations, reduce GAP's operating expenses to improve GAP's cost structure, manage GAP's working capital better to reduce its investment in working capital, and reduce GAP's capital expenditure requirements without affecting its planned capital maintenance and expansion forecast. Using a cost of capital of 13.5% and a perpetual growth rate of 2.5% after Year +6, we can use the valuation framework we discussed in Chapter 1 to value GAP using the hypothetical management forecasts. We show this valuation in Exhibit 2.2.

If management can attain these forecasts, this illustration indicates that GAP's market value would be $12.8 billion instead of $11 billion, which is a 16% increase in its value. Naturally, management and GAP's investors would all be pleased with such an improvement in GAP's performance. The issue, of course, is whether such an improvement is feasible. As we discuss in Chapter 4, when discussing forecasting models, we can use financial ratios resulting from the forecasts to help assess the reasonableness of the forecasts.

To analyze GAP's historical performance, we use a set of comparison companies. The comparison companies we use are all companies in the Family Clothing Store industry classification (SIC = 5651), which is the primary industry classification for GAP. The number of companies (other than GAP) in that industry, and for which we can measure the financial ratios, varies between 17 and 19 during any one year. We should note that while all of these companies have the same primary industry classification as GAP, they might not all be equally good competitors. This industry code includes such companies as American Eagle Outfitters,

Inc. and Abercrombie & Fitch, which are direct competitors of GAP. This industry classification, however, also contains such companies as Casual Male Retail Group, Inc., which does not focus on the same type of shopper as GAP but rather focuses on big and tall men, and Nordstrom, Inc., which sells a broader set of merchandise. The companies also vary in business strategy, size, and other characteristics.

EXHIBIT 2.1 The Gap, Inc.—Historical Financial Statement and Free Cash Flows and Hypothetical Management Forecasts

THE GAP, INC.
Financial Statements and Free Cash Flows

Income Statement ($ in millions)	Year −1	Year 0	Year +1	Year +2	Year +3	Year +4	Year +5	Year +6
Revenue	$14,197	$14,664	$15,251	$16,013	$16,814	$17,654	$18,096	$18,548
Cost of goods sold	−7,818	−8,127	−8,349	−8,750	−9,188	−9,647	−9,888	−10,136
Gross margin	$ 6,379	$ 6,537	$ 6,902	$ 7,263	$ 7,626	$ 8,007	$ 8,207	$ 8,413
Depreciation and amortization	−655	−648	−674	−708	−743	−780	−800	−820
Operating expenses	−3,909	−3,921	−4,138	−4,329	−4,546	−4,773	−4,892	−5,015
Operating income	$ 1,815	$ 1,968	$ 2,089	$ 2,226	$ 2,337	$ 2,454	$ 2,515	$ 2,578
Interest expense	−6	−6	0	0	0	0	0	0
Interest income	7	20	22	23	24	25	26	27
Income before taxes	$ 1,816	$ 1,982	$ 2,111	$ 2,249	$ 2,361	$ 2,479	$ 2,542	$ 2,605
Income tax expense	−714	−778	−829	−883	−927	−973	−998	−1,023
Net income	$ 1,102	$ 1,204	$ 1,283	$ 1,366	$ 1,434	$ 1,506	$ 1,544	$ 1,583
Balance Sheet ($ in millions)	**Year −1**	**Year 0**	**Year +1**	**Year +2**	**Year +3**	**Year +4**	**Year +5**	**Year +6**
Cash balance	$ 2,573	$ 1,661	$ 1,727	$ 1,814	$ 1,905	$ 2,000	$ 2,050	$ 2,101
Accounts receivable	0	0	0	0	0	0	0	0
Inventory	1,477	1,620	1,664	1,744	1,831	1,923	1,971	2,020
Other current assets	614	645	671	704	740	777	796	816
Total current assets	$ 4,664	$ 3,926	$ 4,062	$ 4,262	$ 4,476	$ 4,699	$ 4,817	$ 4,937
Property, plant, and equipment	$ 7,427	$ 7,573	$ 7,909	$ 8,341	$ 8,879	$ 9,532	$10,332	$11,151
Accumulated depreciation	−4,799	−5,010	−5,684	−6,392	−7,135	−7,915	−8,714	−9,534
Property, plant, and equipment (net)	$ 2,628	$ 2,563	$ 2,225	$ 1,949	$ 1,744	$ 1,617	$ 1,617	$ 1,617
Other assets	$ 693	$ 576	$ 599	$ 629	$ 660	$ 693	$ 711	$ 729
Total assets	$ 7,985	$ 7,065	$ 6,886	$ 6,841	$ 6,880	$ 7,010	$ 7,145	$ 7,283
Accounts payable	$ 1,027	$ 1,049	$ 1,059	$ 1,110	$ 1,165	$ 1,224	$ 1,254	$ 1,286
Accrued expenses	1,104	1,046	1,088	1,142	1,199	1,259	1,291	1,323
Current portion of long-term debt	0	0	0	0	0	0	0	0
Total current liabilities	$ 2,131	$ 2,095	$ 2,147	$ 2,252	$ 2,365	$ 2,483	$ 2,545	$ 2,609
Long-term debt	0	0	0	0	0	0	0	0
Non-current liabilities	963	890	926	972	1,020	1,071	1,098	1,126
Total liabilities	$ 3,094	$ 2,985	$ 3,072	$ 3,224	$ 3,385	$ 3,554	$ 3,643	$ 3,734
Common stock (and other)	−$ 5,924	−$ 7,687	−$ 7,687	−$ 7,687	−$ 7,687	−$ 7,687	−$ 7,687	−$ 7,687
Retained earnings	10,815	11,767	11,501	11,304	11,182	11,143	11,189	11,236
Total shareholders equity	$ 4,891	$ 4,080	$ 3,814	$ 3,617	$ 3,495	$ 3,456	$ 3,502	$ 3,549
Total liabilities and equities	$ 7,985	$ 7,065	$ 6,886	$ 6,841	$ 6,880	$ 7,010	$ 7,145	$ 7,283
Free Cash Flows ($ in millions)	**Year −1**	**Year 0**	**Year +1**	**Year +2**	**Year +3**	**Year +4**	**Year +5**	**Year +6**
Earnings before interest and taxes (EBIT)	$ 1,822	$ 1,988	$ 2,111	$ 2,249	$ 2,361	$ 2,479	$ 2,542	$ 2,605
− Income taxes paid on EBIT	−716	−780	−829	−883	−927	−973	−998	−1,023
Earnings before interest and after taxes	$ 1,106	$ 1,208	$ 1,283	$ 1,366	$ 1,434	$ 1,506	$ 1,544	$ 1,583
+ Depreciation expense	655	648	674	708	743	780	800	820
+/− Working capital and other changes	165	−313	−6	8	7	8	4	4
− Change in required cash	0	912	−66	−86	−91	−95	−50	−51
Unlevered cash flow from operations	$ 1,926	$ 2,455	$ 1,884	$ 1,995	$ 2,094	$ 2,199	$ 2,298	$ 2,355
− Capital expenditures (net)	−241	−249	−336	−432	−538	−653	−800	−820
Unlevered free cash flow	$ 1,684	$ 2,205	$ 1,549	$ 1,563	$ 1,556	$ 1,545	$ 1,498	$ 1,536
Cash flow from operations	$ 1,922	$ 1,539	$ 1,951	$ 2,082	$ 2,185	$ 2,294	$ 2,348	$ 2,406

Exhibit may contain small rounding errors

EXHIBIT 2.2 The Gap, Inc.'s Discounted Cash Flow Valuation Using Hypothetical Management Forecasts

THE GAP, INC. Discounted Cash Flow Valuation							
Cost of capital	13.5%						
Growth rate for free cash flow for continuing value	2.5%						
Billions of Dollars	**Year 0**	**Year +1**	**Year +2**	**Year +3**	**Year +4**	**Year +5**	**CV_{Firm} Year +5**
Unlevered free cash flow for continuing value (CV)							$ 1,535.5
Discount factor for continuing value							9.091
Unlevered free cash flow and CV		$1,548.9	$1,562.9	$1,555.9	$1,545.4	$1,498.1	$13,959.2
Discount factor		0.8811	0.7763	0.6839	0.6026	0.5309	0.5309
Present value		$1,364.6	$1,213.3	$1,064.1	$ 931.2	$ 795.3	$ 7,411.0
Value of the firm	$12,779.6						

Exhibit may contain small rounding errors

Generally, we would conduct a more detailed analysis of these companies before using them as comparable companies. Identifying a specific set of comparable companies for GAP is beyond what we cover in this chapter. We discuss this issue in more detail later in the book, when we discuss the use of comparable companies in estimating the cost of capital and conducting a price multiples valuation.

2.5 MEASURING A COMPANY'S PERFORMANCE USING ACCOUNTING RATES OF RETURN

LO2 Measure the performance of a company using rates of return

Accounting rates of return attempt to measure the performance of a company. We can measure a company's accounting rates of return in various ways. All of the alternatives are typically a measure of accounting income divided by a measure of the average level of investment used to generate that income. Some rates of return measure the amount of income generated for each dollar of investment; for example, a company with an annual income of $124 million and an investment of $1,240 million has a 10% rate of return on its investment. The 10% rate of return indicates that the company generates $1 of income each year for each $10 of investment. Conceptually, the higher the rate of return, the better the performance, ignoring the many pitfalls of using financial statement information to measure performance. We can compare a company's current rate of return to its historical rates of return in order to assess the change in its accounting-based performance over time, and we can compare it to the rates of return of competitor companies in order to assess its relative accounting-based performance.

Naturally, it is important to ensure that you use a consistent numerator and denominator when measuring a particular rate of return. For example, if the denominator is average assets, then the numerator should be the income generated by those assets; thus, we would measure income before deducting interest expense (on an after-tax basis). If the denominator is average common equity, then the numerator should be income to the common equityholders. Similarly, if we measure income by excluding certain income effects such as the effects of discontinued operations or the effects of excess assets, then we exclude any assets from the denominator that are related to the excluded income.

We discuss three example rate of return measures that attempt to quantify the rate of return related to the company's invested capital: the **return on assets (ROA)**, the **return on investment (ROI)**, and **return on (common) equity (ROE)**. Each of these rates of return attempts to measure the amount of income generated per dollar of invested capital given some specific definition of income and invested capital.

Return on Assets

The numerator in the return on assets (ROA) formula is unlevered income, and the denominator is average total assets for the period over which we are measuring the rate of return. To unlever income, we add back after-tax interest and other effects related to non-equity financing such as preferred dividends if they are already deducted from the measure of income we are using as the starting point in the calculation; we do this to measure the income generated by the assets, which is equivalent to what income would have been had the company been completely financed with equity. The basic formula for computing ROA is

$$\text{ROA} = \frac{\text{Net Income} + (1 - \text{Income Tax Rate for Interest}) \times \text{Interest Expense}}{\text{Average Total Assets}} \tag{2.1}$$

After reviewing GAP's footnote for income taxes (not shown in the chapter), we assume that GAP's **effective income tax rate** (income tax expense divided by income before taxes) of 39.3% (0.393 = $778/$1,982) is reasonable to use as the tax rate for interest. However, as we discuss in Chapters 3 and 4, the effective income tax rate is not always an appropriate assumption to use for the income tax rate for interest. GAP has $6 of interest expense and has no preferred dividends. The return on assets for GAP calculated for Year 0 is

$$\text{ROA}_{\text{GAP, Year 0}} = \frac{\$1{,}204 + (1 - 0.393) \times \$6}{(\$7{,}985 + \$7{,}065)/2} = 0.160$$

In the above formula, we assume that GAP does not have any non-controlling or minority interest positions in the company's subsidiaries (as GAP did not report any minority interest). If GAP had non-controlling interests, we would reverse any impact of **non-controlling** or **minority interest** in the net income of subsidiaries, because the average total assets in the denominator represents the total assets, including any assets attributable to the minority interests. (We discuss non-controlling or minority interests in more detail in Chapters 11 and 14.) We typically measure average total assets—and other financial ratio denominators based on an average—as the beginning-of-year balance plus the end-of-year balance divided by two. This calculation assumes the change in the denominator occurred evenly during the year and that the beginning and ending balances represent the average level of assets during the year. This might not be the case for companies that undertook a major acquisition or divestiture during the year or have a highly seasonal business. In that case, we might compute the average from quarterly reports or perhaps from pro forma financials (based on the assumption that the transaction occurred at the beginning of the year).

Return on Investment

The return on investment (ROI) is similar to the return on assets. The major difference between the two ratios is how we measure the denominator. In addition, the numerator is slightly different as well. The denominator for the return on investment is equal to average invested capital instead of average assets as is used in the return on assets calculation. One way we can measure invested capital is to add the book value of debt, preferred stock and common equity, or—looking at it from the asset side of the balance sheet—we can subtract operating liabilities (accounts payable, wages payable, income taxes payable, deferred income taxes, etc.) from total assets. Some analysts add non-current net deferred tax liabilities to common equity under the assumption that this is not really a liability and that stockholder's equity was reduced when the deferred tax liability was recorded. They would make the same adjustment in calculating return on equity, discussed next. Since the denominator for the return on investment does not include investments by non-controlling or minority shareholders, we do not adjust the numerator for the net income for non-controlling or minority interest as we did in the return on assets calculation.

The reason some analysts prefer return on investment to return on assets is that the implicit financing costs of a company's operating liabilities are embedded in the company's operating expenses. (Recall our discussion of this point in Chapter 1.) The basic formula for the return on investment is

$$\text{ROI} = \frac{\text{Net Income} + (1 - \text{Income Tax Rate for Interest}) \times \text{Interest Expense}}{\text{Average (Book Value of Debt} + \text{Preferred Stock} + \text{Common Equity)}} \tag{2.2}$$

Since GAP has no debt and no preferred stock at the beginning or end of the year, the return on investment for GAP for Year 0 is simply

$$\text{ROI}_{\text{GAP, Year 0}} = \frac{\$1{,}204 + (1 - 0.393) \times \$6}{(\$4{,}891 + \$4{,}080)/2} = 0.269$$

Note that GAP did have a small amount of debt outstanding during the year when it drew down its revolver. If we knew the average debt outstanding over the year, we would include that in the denominator.

Valuation in Practice 2.2

Delta Airlines, Inc.'s Reported Rate of Return on Invested Capital Delta believes that its rate of return on its invested capital (ROIC) is useful to investors. Since the calculation of ROIC (as well as other financial ratios) is not specified within accounting or other standards, Delta uses its own definition.

> We present ROIC as management believes this metric is helpful to investors in assessing our ability to generate returns using its invested capital. ROIC is operating income, adjusted, divided by adjusted average invested capital. We adjust operating income for MTM adjustments and settlements and restructuring and other for the same reasons discussed above for pre-tax income. All adjustments to calculate ROIC are intended to provide a more meaningful comparison of our results to the airline industry and other high quality industrial companies.

Delta provided the following calculation of its ROIC (as well as tables presenting the calculation of the components of its ROIC, not shown here):

(in millions, except % of return)	2015	2014
Operating income	$ 7,802	$ 2,206
Adjusted for:		
Mark-to-market adjustments and settlements	–$ 1,301	$ 2,346
Restructuring and other	35	716
7x annual interest expense included in aircraft rent	172	149
Amortization of retirement actuarial loss	230	112
Operating income, adjusted	$ 6,938	$ 5,529
Adjusted book value of equity	$17,564	$18,518
Average adjusted net debt	6,970	8,215
Adjusted average invested capital	$24,534	$26,733
ROIC	28.3%	20.7%

Source: Delta Airlines, Inc. 2015 10-K Report, p. 48.

Return on (Common) Equity

The return on (common) equity (ROE) measures the amount of income to common equity generated per dollar of equity invested (all measured using financial statement information). The basic formula for the return on equity is

$$ROE = \frac{\text{Net Income} - \text{Preferred Stock Dividends}}{\text{Average Common Equity}} = \frac{\text{Income to Common Equity}}{\text{Average Common Equity}} \quad \textbf{(2.3)}$$

The return on equity for GAP for Year 0 is

$$ROE_{\text{GAP, Year 0}} = \frac{\$1{,}204 - \$0}{(\$4{,}891 + \$4{,}080)/2} = 0.268$$

Since GAP has no debt or preferred stock outstanding at the beginning or end of the year, the ROE and ROI will be very close. The only difference between them, for GAP, is caused by the minimal amount of interest expense from debt outstanding at some point during the year, for we did not know the average debt balance for the denominator in the ROI calculation.

The numerator for the return on (common) equity (ROE) is income available to common equityholders. The denominator is the average (common) equity of the company during the period over which we measure the numerator. Again, we typically measure this average by dividing the sum of the beginning and ending balances of the company's (common) equity by two. Since we do not deduct preferred stock dividends when measuring net income, we deduct it from the numerator to represent the income after all payments to non-common equity securities; in other words, to measure the income available to common equityholders.

Valuation Key 2.2

Rates of return measured using financial statements are popular performance measures. Rates of return measure the amount of income generated per dollar of capital invested, measured in a variety of ways. Alternative types of rates of return measures include return on assets, return on investment, and return on (common) equity.

Adjusting Financial Ratios for Excess Assets

We can use alternative definitions for the numerator in the rate of return calculations; for example, we can exclude certain types of income from the numerator, such as income from excess assets, income from discontinued operations, one-time expenses from reorganizations, and extraordinary items. Regardless of the definition we use, we measure the denominator so it is consistent with the definition of the numerator. For example, if we exclude income from excess assets in the numerator, we also exclude excess assets in the denominator.

Valuation Key 2.3

Eliminating excess assets from rate of return measures is often useful in order to gain a representative measure of the profitability of a company's operations. This is typically the situation when we are using rates of return in a valuation analysis. That said, in some situations eliminating the effect of excess assets is not preferred. For example, we would not eliminate excess assets if we wanted to understand the overall profitability of the company from the investors' perspective.

We use the definition that best fits the context of our analysis—that best fits how we plan to use the financial ratio. No single definition dominates the alternatives in all contexts. For example, if we want to know the overall profitability of a company, we might prefer to include a company's excess assets; however, if we wanted to know the profitability of the company's operations—for example, to compare to comparable companies—we would generally exclude excess assets. The inclusion or exclusion of a company's excess assets can have a substantial effect on its rates of return, and the direction of the effect can be either positive or negative. The direction of the effect depends on the rate of return on the excess assets relative to the rate of return on the company's operations. A way to deal with adjustments such as for excess assets is to first adjust the financial statements for the effect of the excess assets and then compute the ratios with the adjusted financial statements.

Recall from Chapter 1 (Valuation in Practice 1.2), about three-fourths of Apple Inc.'s reported total assets were composed of cash, cash equivalents, and marketable securities. In Valuation in Practice 2.3, we assume all of these assets are excess assets and show the effect of excluding Apple's excess assets on its rates of return.

Valuation in Practice 2.3

Apple Inc.'s Return on Assets and Return on Equity Excluding Excess Assets In its 2016 financial statements, Apple reported that of its $322 billion of assets, it had over $20 billion in cash and cash equivalents, over $46 billion in short-term marketable securities, and over $170 billion in long-term marketable securities. Using Apple's reported income, average total assets, and average common equity, its return on assets is 15% and its return on equity is 37%. These rates of returns, however, do not reflect the rates of return on its operating assets. We assume that all of the cash and short-term marketable securities are required for its operations (which is over $67 billion or over 20% of its assets), and assume its long-term marketable securities are excess assets (non-operating).

continued

continued from previous page

The adjustments to the rate of return on assets calculation include deducting the after-tax income on those investments from the numerator ($2.1 billion) and deducting the average balance of its long-term marketable securities from the denominator ($167.2 billion). The adjustments to the rate of return on equity are to again deduct the after-tax income on those investments from the numerator ($2.1 billion) but, instead of deducting the average balance of its long-term marketable securities from the denominator, we minimize the effect on the denominator by assuming Apple first redeems all of its debt and then deduct only the average balance of its long-term marketable securities net of its debt from the denominator ($99.9 billion). Given that we eliminated Apple's debt, we also add back after-tax interest to the numerator ($0.9 billion). This results in a net adjustment to the numerator of $1.2 billion ($1.2 = $2.1 − $0.9). Measured in this way, Apple's return on assets increases to 32% and its return on equity increases to 186%.

($ in millions)	2016 Reported		ROR	Adjustments	2016 Adjusted		ROR
Return on Assets							
Net income	$ 46,561	=	15.2%	−$ 2,136	$ 44,425	=	32.0%
Average total assets	$306,016			−$167,248	$138,768		
Return on Equity							
Net income	$ 45,687	=	36.9%	−$ 1,262	$ 44,425	=	185.6%
Average common equity	$123,802			−$ 99,870	$ 23,933		

Source: Apple Inc. 2016 10-K Report.

Alternative Ways to Measure Financial Ratio Inputs

Instead of using a measure of accounting income in the numerator, some analysts use some type of cash flow to measure rates of return. For example, we can use unlevered cash flow from operations or free cash flow as the numerator in the return on assets and return on investment equations, and use operating cash flow (adjusted for preferred stock dividends) or equity free cash flow as the numerator in the return on common equity calculation.

Cash flow rate of return measures have become more popular since the standardization of cash flow statements in 1987. Many analysts utilize cash flows from operations for the numerator in equity rate of return measures. One note of caution regarding cash flows from operations is that it does not contain any provision for the replacement of assets, whereas income numbers at least include a depreciation charge. One measure of cash return on assets that captures capital expenditures is free cash flow of the unlevered firm divided by total assets. The limitation of using free cash flow of the unlevered firm in the numerator, however, is that capital expenditures can be "lumpy," that is, large in some years and small in others. Some type of averaging or normalization of capital expenditures can be used to address this issue.

Limitations of Accounting Rates of Return as Measures of Performance

Accounting rates of return have widely recognized limitations as measures of performance.[8] Accounting rates of return focus on the ratio of a measure of earnings in a single year to a measure of investment calculated using financial statement numbers. The percentage change in the value of an investment depends on changes in all expected future cash flows and risk. Thus, accounting earnings, which generally focus on a single period, cannot measure changes in the value of an investment exactly. In addition, historical cost accounting measures of the value of an investment do not reflect market values. Alternative measures that attempt to address some of these limitations involve some sort of longer-term forecast of expected performance and risk.

[8] See, for example, Solomon, E., and J. Lays, "Measurement of Company Profitability: Some Systematic Errors in the Accounting Rate of Return,", in A. Robichek, ed., *Financial Research and Management Decisions*, Wiley (2003), pp. 152–283; and Fisher, F., and J. McGowan, "On the Misuse of Accounting Rates of Return to Infer Monopoly Profits," *American Economic Review* 73 (1983), pp. 82–97.

Even with these limitations, accounting rates of return are widely used measures of performance. We know that accounting earnings and accounting rates of return as measures of performance have an empirically positive correlation with changes in market value as measured by stock returns.[9]

2.6 DISAGGREGATING THE RETURN ON ASSETS

Disaggregating the rates of return into their various components has two important roles in valuation. First, we disaggregate historical rates of return in order to help us better understand why a company is performing well and possibly identify the source and sustainability of a company's potential competitive advantage or, conversely, why a poorly performing firm is performing poorly and possibly at a competitive disadvantage. Second, once we create the financial forecasts, we disaggregate rates of return based on the financial forecasts in order to assess the reasonableness of those forecasts for the components that we do not use to drive the forecasts.

Disaggregating the Return on Assets

The two primary components of a company's return on assets are its unlevered profit margin and its asset utilization. A company's **unlevered profit margin** is equal to unlevered income divided by revenue. A company's **asset utilization** (or **asset turnover**) is equal to the amount of revenue the company generates per dollar of assets. The product of a company's unlevered profit margin and asset utilization ratio is equal to its return on assets (ROA). The basic formulas for unlevered profit margin and asset utilization as well as how to use them to disaggregate the return on assets are as follows:

$$\text{ROA} = \text{Unlevered Profit Margin} \times \text{Asset Utilization}$$

$$\text{ROA} = \frac{\text{Net Income} + (1 - \text{Income Tax Rate}) \times \text{Interest Expense}}{\text{Revenue}} \times \frac{\text{Revenue}}{\text{Average Total Assets}} \tag{2.4}$$

The numerator of the unlevered profit margin formula is identical to the numerator in the return on assets calculation. If there is income attributable to minority interests, the same adjustment must be made to the unlevered profit margin, as discussed with respect to the return on assets calculation. The unlevered profit margin and asset utilization ratios for GAP are

$$\text{ROA}_{\text{GAP, Year 0}} = \frac{\$1{,}204 + (1 - 0.393) \times \$6}{\$14{,}664} \times \frac{\$14{,}664}{(\$7{,}985 + \$7{,}065)/2} = 0.160$$

$$\text{ROA}_{\text{GAP, Year 0}} = 0.082 \times 1.949 = 0.160$$

Valuation Key 2.4

We can disaggregate the return on assets into meaningful components. The components of the return on assets are unlevered profit margin and asset utilization. Decomposing rates of return helps us better understand the source and potential sustainability of a company's return. It will also help us better assess the reasonableness of a set of financial forecasts.

From the formula in Equation 2.4, we observe that even with a low profit margin, a company that has a sufficiently high asset utilization can have the same, or even a higher, return on assets as a company with

[9] For the seminal work on the relation between earnings and stock prices, see Ball, R., and P. Brown, "An Empirical Evaluation of Accounting Income Numbers," *Journal of Accounting Research* (Autumn 1968), pp. 159–178. For research on cash flow and accruals, see Dechow, P., "Accounting Earnings and Cash Flows as Measures of Firm Performance: The Role of Accounting Accruals," *Journal of Accounting and Economics* 18 (1994), pp. 3–42, which shows that current accounting earnings are more informative of a company's valuation than current cash flows, although earnings and cash flows each provide incremental valuation information relative to the other.

a high profit margin. We also observe that two companies can have the same return on assets even though they have very different profit margins. For example, a company with a 10% return on assets that results from having an 8.6% unlevered profit margin and asset utilization ratio of 1.16 (0.1 = 0.086 × 1.16) has the same return on assets as another company that has a profit margin of 27.4% and an asset utilization ratio of only 0.36 (0.1 = 0.274 × 0.36).

Relation Between the Return on Asset Components

In Exhibit 2.3, we show the asset utilization and unlevered profit margin ratios for selected industries with an ROA of approximately 5%.[10]

EXHIBIT 2.3 Return on Assets and Components for Selected Industries

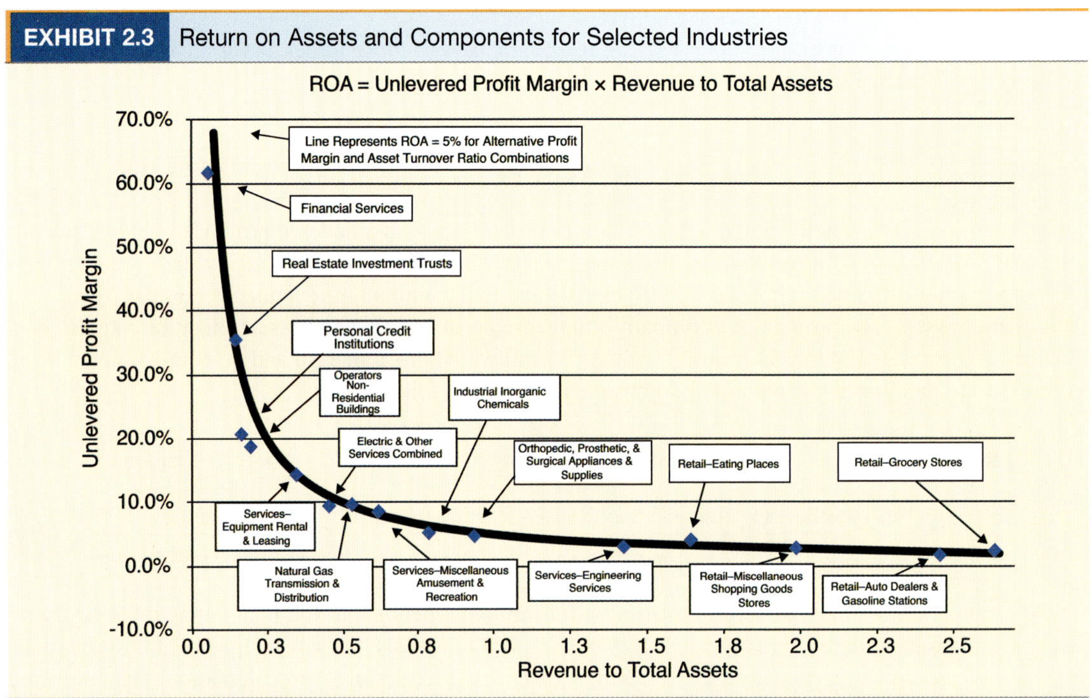

The solid line in the exhibit shows the unlevered profit margin and revenue to total assets combinations that result in a return on assets equal to 5%. For example, a 10% unlevered profit margin and a 0.5 ratio of revenue to total assets results in a 5% return on assets, as does a 2.5% unlevered profit margin and a ratio of revenue to total assets equal to 2.0. The diamonds on the graph show the specific combinations for selected industries. If a diamond is above the solid line, it indicates that the industry's return on assets is somewhat greater than 5%; if it's below the solid line, it indicates that the industry's return on assets is slightly less than 5%. We can quickly observe from this graph that many of the industries have a return on assets that is close to 5 percent, even though they have different—sometimes substantially different—unlevered profit margins. The grocery store industry, for example, is a high-turnover (revenue to total assets of more than 2.5) and low-margin (unlevered profit margin of 2%) business with a return on assets of close to 5%. However, the real estate investment trust business is a low-volume (revenue to total assets of 0.14) and high-margin (unlevered profit margin of 36%) business that also has a return on assets of about 5%.

How Does GAP Perform Relative to Other Companies in Its Industry?

In Exhibit 2.4, we show the ratios for GAP's return on assets, unlevered profit margin, and revenue to total assets for the fiscal years Year −4 through Year 0. We also show various percentiles of the distribution of

[10] This type of analysis was first presented in Selling, T., and C. Stickney, "The Effects of Business Environment and Strategy on a Firm's Rate of Return on Assets," *Financial Analysts Journal* (January–February 1989), pp. 43–52.

those ratios for other companies in the Family Clothing Store industry classification (SIC = 5651), which is the primary industry classification for GAP. The number of companies (other than GAP) in that industry, and for which we could measure the financial ratios, varies between 17 and 20, depending on the year.

EXHIBIT 2.4 Return on Asset and Related Ratios for The Gap, Inc. and the Distribution of Companies in the Family Clothing Store Industry Classification (SIC = 5651)

	Year −4	Year −3	Year −2	Year −1	Year 0
Return on Assets					
The Gap, Inc.	**9.3%**	**10.9%**	**12.6%**	**14.2%**	**16.0%**
10th percentile	2.6%	−1.6%	−15.3%	−2.0%	1.5%
25th percentile	**5.0%**	1.6%	−5.9%	2.9%	5.4%
50th percentile	12.6%	**9.3%**	**7.8%**	5.5%	8.7%
75th percentile	14.8%	15.3%	13.2%	**14.2%**	**15.9%**
90th percentile	15.9%	19.1%	18.9%	18.2%	19.1%
Unlevered Profit Margin					
The Gap, Inc.	**5.1%**	**5.6%**	**6.7%**	**7.8%**	**8.2%**
10th percentile	1.0%	−0.8%	−23.7%	−1.0%	2.7%
25th percentile	2.8%	1.1%	−3.1%	2.2%	3.5%
50th percentile	**5.1%**	**3.9%**	4.2%	3.6%	5.6%
75th percentile	8.4%	9.4%	**6.7%**	**7.8%**	**7.2%**
90th percentile	10.5%	12.4%	11.5%	14.2%	14.2%
Revenue to Total Assets (Utilization or Turnover)					
The Gap, Inc.	**1.84**	**1.92**	**1.89**	**1.83**	**1.95**
10th percentile	1.17	1.14	1.09	1.03	1.20
25th percentile	1.55	1.50	1.48	1.41	1.38
50th percentile	**1.83**	**1.79**	**1.73**	**1.83**	**1.89**
75th percentile	2.37	2.11	2.03	2.07	2.15
90th percentile	3.00	2.73	2.91	2.85	2.81

In Year −4, GAP's return on assets is below the 50th percentile of its industry group and steadily increases during this period and by Year 0, it is above the 75th percentile. We can examine the two primary components of the return on assets to learn more about what caused the change in GAP's return on assets relative to the other companies. It turns out that GAP's unlevered profit margin also steadily increased during this period, from the 50th percentile to above the 75th percentile, while its asset utilization ratio (revenue to total asset) stayed relatively constant, varying between 1.83 and 1.95. Thus, the increase in GAP's unlevered profit margin is the main reason why its return on assets increased relative to that of the other companies.

REVIEW EXERCISE 2.1

The Gap, Inc. Return on Asset Forecasts for Year +1 and Beyond

Use the information in Exhibit 2.1 to calculate GAP's return on assets and its components for one or more of the years in the forecasts (Year +1 through Year +6). Compare GAP's return on assets and its components in the forecasts to GAP's time-series and to SIC 5651 in Exhibit 2.4.

Solution on page 88.

2.7 MEASURING A COMPANY'S COST STRUCTURE USING EXPENSE RATIOS

A company's **cost structure**—that is, the relation between a company's revenues and its costs—can be a source of competitive advantage or competitive disadvantage. Understanding a company's cost structure allows us to more thoroughly understand its accounting-based rates of return because it allows us to understand what drives a company's unlevered profit margin. In addition, we use an analysis of a company's cost structure when we identify comparable companies and usually when we forecast its financial statements and cash flows.

For most expenses, a common way to analyze a company's cost structure is to analyze the **expense ratios** (an expense item divided by operating revenues) for each of its relevant expenses. When comparing the company to itself and to comparable companies, expense ratios often provide useful insights into understanding its profit margin. Common operating expense ratios include the cost of goods sold ratio and the selling, general, and administrative expense ratio.

Certain expense ratios are usually less informative—for example, the income tax expense ratio (income tax expense to revenues) and the expense ratios for such one-time costs as reorganization costs. We typically analyze those types of expenses in other ways. Since generally accepted accounting principles in the U.S. do not generally require companies to use the same accounting principles for financial statement and income tax purposes, analyzing income tax expenses and measuring income tax rates is complex if a company has substantial differences between its tax and book accounting. We analyze a company's income taxes by computing its income tax rates with both income statement information and its income tax footnote disclosures (which we discuss in Chapter 3).

We show the formulas for the **cost of goods sold expense ratio**; **selling, general, and administrative expense ratio**; and **depreciation and amortization expense ratio** below. We can measure other expense ratios in a similar manner.

$$\text{Cost of Goods Sold Expense Ratio} = \frac{\text{Cost of Goods Sold}}{\text{Revenue}} \tag{2.5}$$

$$\text{Selling, General, and Administrative Expense Ratio} = \frac{\text{Selling, General, and Administrative Expense}}{\text{Revenue}} \tag{2.6}$$

$$\text{Depreciation and Amortization Expense Ratio} = \frac{\text{Depreciation and Amortization}}{\text{Revenue}} \tag{2.7}$$

At first glance, one might think managers should minimize a company's expense ratios because it appears that lower expense ratios lead to higher profit margins, higher rates of return, and, therefore, better performance. This conclusion is not always correct for expenses that affect a company's future performance. Generally accepted accounting principles in the U.S. and most other countries tend to **expense an expenditure** for which the future benefits cannot be reasonably measured, even though the expenditure likely has future benefits. Examples of such expenditures include expenditures on marketing and research and development. A company could minimize its expense ratio for marketing (or research and development) to increase its current year profitability. That decision, however, could have negative effects on the company's performance in future years and ultimately destroy value. Thus, minimizing expense ratios is not necessarily consistent with maximizing the value of the firm.

Consistency in the numerator and denominator is important when analyzing financial ratios. For example, excluding non-operating revenues when measuring operating expense ratios requires excluding any related expenses in the numerator. Consistency across companies is also important. Companies sometimes classify costs differently; for example, one company may include depreciation in cost of goods sold and show a line item for depreciation not related to the cost of goods sold, while another company might show all of its depreciation as a separate line item in the income statement. Similarly, companies sometimes use different accounting principles; for example, one company might use the last-in, first-out (LIFO) inventory method, and another company might use the first-in, first-out (FIFO) inventory method. Our goal when measuring financial ratios for comparing them over time or across companies is to adjust the financial statements for all material inconsistencies over time and across companies if the adjustment affects the qualitative results from the analysis.

The Gap, Inc.'s Expense Ratios

In Exhibit 2.5, we show certain expense ratios for GAP for the fiscal years Year −4 through Year 0. We also show various percentiles of the distribution of those ratios for other companies in the Family Clothing Store industry classification (SIC = 5651), which is the primary industry classification for GAP.

EXHIBIT 2.5 Expense Ratios for The Gap, Inc. and the Distribution of Companies in the Family Clothing Store Industry Classification (SIC = 5651)

	Year −4	Year −3	Year −2	Year −1	Year 0
Cost of Goods Sold to Revenue					
The Gap, Inc.	**60.7%**	**59.8%**	**58.0%**	**55.1%**	**55.4%**
10th percentile	52.0%	50.5%	53.9%	**52.6%**	52.7%
25th percentile	57.6%	**56.4%**	**58.0%**	55.8%	**54.8%**
50th percentile	**60.7%**	60.7%	61.8%	61.5%	61.2%
75th percentile	71.7%	73.5%	74.2%	71.6%	71.0%
90th percentile	82.4%	86.6%	97.0%	88.5%	85.3%
Operating Expenses to Revenue					
The Gap, Inc.	**28.1%**	**27.6%**	**26.8%**	**27.5%**	**26.7%**
10th percentile	16.8%	16.7%	16.7%	16.4%	16.9%
25th percentile	23.8%	23.4%	**23.4%**	**23.2%**	23.0%
50th percentile	**25.8%**	**26.7%**	27.4%	28.1%	**26.7%**
75th percentile	34.0%	31.9%	30.7%	32.3%	31.3%
90th percentile	47.0%	47.5%	40.1%	44.3%	38.3%
Depreciation and Amortization to Revenue					
The Gap, Inc.	**3.8%**	**4.0%**	**4.5%**	**4.6%**	**4.4%**
10th percentile	1.9%	2.0%	2.1%	2.1%	2.0%
25th percentile	2.9%	2.9%	3.3%	3.0%	3.3%
50th percentile	**3.2%**	**3.4%**	**3.9%**	**4.1%**	**3.8%**
75th percentile	4.4%	4.7%	4.6%	5.0%	5.3%
90th percentile	4.8%	5.2%	6.4%	8.2%	6.6%
Advertising Expense to Revenue					
The Gap, Inc.	**3.6%**	**3.0%**	**3.0%**	**3.6%**	**3.5%**
10th percentile	0.5%	0.6%	0.5%	0.5%	0.4%
25th percentile	1.2%	1.0%	0.9%	0.8%	1.0%
50th percentile	1.8%	1.7%	1.7%	1.7%	1.9%
75th percentile	**3.5%**	**3.0%**	**2.8%**	**3.0%**	**3.5%**
90th percentile	6.3%	4.5%	4.3%	4.3%	4.6%

Recall that GAP had an increase in its return on assets over the Year −4 to Year 0 period and moved from below the 50th percentile to above the 75th percentile relative to other stores in SIC 5651. This improvement was caused by a steady increase in its unlevered profit margin. Using the expense ratios, we should be able to better understand why this happened. Looking at Exhibit 2.5, it appears that most of this change was caused by a steadily declining ratio of cost of goods sold to revenue (from 60.7% to 55.4%) as GAP moved from the 50th percentile to very near the 25th percentile. GAP's operating expense ratio is roughly around the median for all years, as is its depreciation and amortization expense ratio, and its advertising expense ratio is above the 75th percentile in all years. However, GAP has little systematic movement in the sum of these three expense ratios over time, as the combined ratio for operating expense, depreciation and amortization, and advertising expense to revenue is 35.5% in Year −4 and 34.6% in Year 0. As we discussed earlier, when making such comparisons, we assume that the companies we are analyzing have consistently prepared income statements.

Valuation Key 2.5

A company's cost structure can be a source of its competitive advantage or disadvantage. We use expense ratios—the ratio of an expense line item, such as cost of goods sold, to revenue—to analyze a company's cost structure. We also typically use expense ratios as forecast drivers in financial models.

REVIEW EXERCISE 2.2

The Gap, Inc. Expense Ratio Forecasts for Year +1 and Beyond

Use the information in Exhibit 2.1 to calculate GAP's expense ratios for one or more of the years in the forecasts (Year +1 through Year +6). Compare GAP's expense ratios in the forecasts to GAP's time-series and to SIC 5651 in Exhibit 2.5.

Solution on page 88.

2.8 ANALYZING A COMPANY'S ASSET UTILIZATION USING TURNOVER RATIOS

LO3 Examine a company's asset utilization and working capital management

A company's **asset utilization**—that is, the revenue generated per dollar of investment in a certain type of asset—is another potential source of a company's competitive advantage. Like expense ratios, we often use asset utilization ratios to create or to assess the reasonableness of forecasts. A common way to measure a company's asset utilization is to analyze its **asset utilization** or **turnover ratios**, measured by dividing operating revenues by an operating asset item on its balance sheet. We already discussed the overall measure of asset utilization, which is revenue divided by average total assets. This ratio measures the dollars of revenue generated per dollar of investment in all types of assets. We can disaggregate this overall measure of asset utilization into various components. Turnover ratios provide a sense of whether a company invests more or less in a particular asset, per dollar of revenue, relative to itself over time or relative to its competitors.

Common asset utilization measures include utilization measures for cash, accounts receivable, inventory, other current assets, property, plant, and equipment, and other non-current assets. We typically examine a company's current asset turnover ratios in the context of how the company manages its working capital, which we discuss later in the chapter. Two common asset utilization ratios unrelated to working capital are revenues to average gross (and net) property, plant, and equipment. The formulas for these ratios are as follows:

$$\text{Gross Property, Plant, and Equipment Turnover Ratio} = \frac{\text{Revenue}}{\text{Average Gross Property, Plant, and Equipment}} \quad \textbf{(2.8)}$$

$$\text{Net Property, Plant, and Equipment Turnover Ratio} = \frac{\text{Revenue}}{\text{Average Net Property, Plant, and Equipment}} \quad \textbf{(2.9)}$$

The calculations for the above turnover ratios for GAP are as follows:

$$\text{Gross Property, Plant, and Equipment Turnover Ratio}_{\text{GAP, Year 0}} = \frac{\$14{,}664}{(\$7{,}427 + \$7{,}573)/2} = 1.96$$

$$\text{Net Property, Plant, and Equipment Turnover Ratio}_{\text{GAP, Year 0}} = \frac{\$14{,}664}{(\$2{,}628 + \$2{,}563)/2} = 5.65$$

Again, at first glance, we might conclude that managers should maximize a company's asset utilization because conceptually, higher asset utilization ratios lead to higher rates of return, and therefore, better performance. However, as with expense ratios, this conclusion is only correct if maximizing the asset utilization ratios does not affect the company's future performance in a negative way. For example, cutting inventory levels leads to greater inventory turnover at first, but if customers begin to experience delays in receiving their orders, sales are likely to decline.

The inverse of the overall asset turnover ratio (total assets to revenue) is equal to the sum of the inverse of the turnover ratio for each asset on the balance sheet (for example, cash/revenue, accounts receivable/revenue). We illustrate this calculation using GAP in the next section of the chapter (see Exhibit 2.6). Of the two property, plant, and equipment turnover ratios, the one that feeds into the overall asset turnover ratio is the net property, plant, and equipment turnover ratio.

REVIEW EXERCISE 2.3

The Gap, Inc. Asset Utilization Ratios for Year +1 and Beyond

Use the information in Exhibit 2.1 to calculate GAP's asset utilization ratios for one or more of the years in the forecasts (Year +1 through Year +6). How are GAP's asset utilization ratios in the forecasts changing relative to Year 0?

Solution on page 88.

We do not compare the turnover ratios to those of the companies that are in SIC 5651, for the changes in GAP's return on assets were caused primarily by changes in its unlevered profit margins and not in its asset utilization.

Valuation Key 2.6

Asset utilization can be a source of a company's competitive advantage. We use turnover ratios—the ratio of revenue to an asset line item such as accounts receivable or fixed assets—to analyze a company's asset utilization. We also use these ratios, or working capital management ratios, as forecast drivers in financial models or to assess the reasonableness of the forecasts from a financial model.

2.9 SUMMARY OF DISAGGREGATING THE GAP, INC.'S RATES OF RETURN

In Exhibit 2.6, we present the process of disaggregating a company's rates of return and illustrate this disaggregation using GAP. For now, we concentrate on the return on assets, because the return on equity has additional components we have not yet discussed. The exhibit shows how the return on assets is disaggregated into unlevered profit margin and overall asset utilization (revenue divided by total assets), which can be further analyzed using the corresponding expense ratios and turnover ratios.

EXHIBIT 2.6 Disaggregating the Return on Equity and Return on Assets for The Gap, Inc.

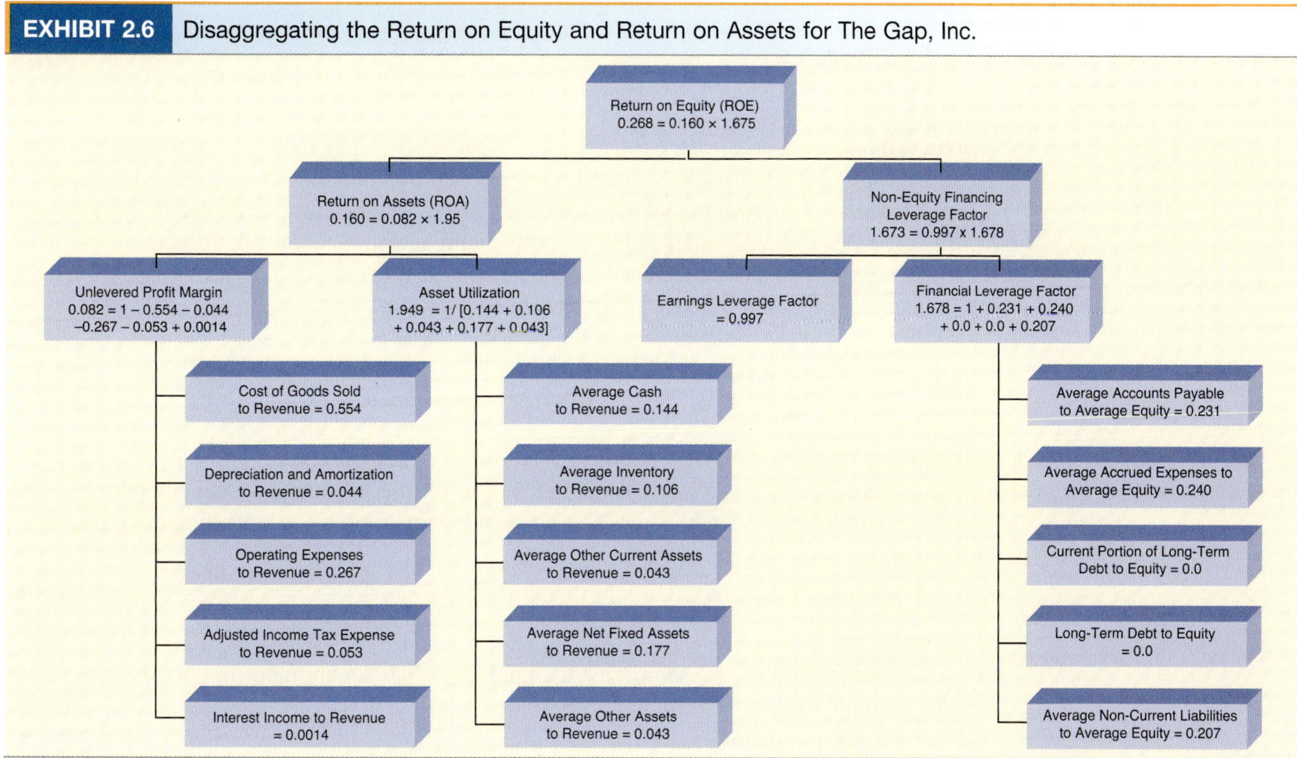

2.10 ANALYZING A COMPANY'S WORKING CAPITAL MANAGEMENT

Working capital is typically defined as current assets minus current liabilities. Most companies have more current assets than current liabilities; therefore, most companies have positive working capital. U.S. generally accepted accounting principles require companies to disclose current assets and current liabilities on their balance sheets. **Current assets** are cash, cash-like assets, and other assets expected to be used or converted into cash within one year or within the company's normal operating cycle, whichever is longer. Examples include cash, accounts receivable, and inventory. **Current liabilities** are liabilities that mature or are discharged within one year. Examples include accounts payable, wages payable, income taxes payable, short-term bank notes, and the current portion of long-term debt. When measuring working capital management financial ratios, we define operating working capital as operating current assets minus operating current liabilities, excluding short-term debt, the current portion of long-term debt, and excess cash. As you recall from Chapter 1 and we discuss in more detail in Chapter 3, when measuring the change in non-cash operating working capital to measure free cash flows, we define non-cash operating working capital as all current and non-current operating assets (excluding cash) less operating liabilities.

Operating working capital is an investment made by the company so that it can operate its business. All else equal, companies prefer to minimize the amount of operating working capital. It is difficult, however, to minimize working capital holding everything else constant. For example, a company could reduce its working capital by requiring all customers to pay in cash; such a policy, however, would also likely have the negative effect of decreasing revenues. A company could also reduce working capital by holding less inventory; however, such a policy would also likely lead to reductions in revenues because it would take longer to deliver products to customers. In addition, a company could reduce its working capital by not paying its accounts payable until after the due dates, but again, this action would likely cost the company additional financing charges, or it might result in an inability to purchase the necessary materials to operate the company. In this section of the chapter, we discuss various ways to analyze working capital.

Ability to Pay Current Liabilities

Analysts often use three ratios to analyze the overall working capital management of a company. These ratios are the current ratio, the quick (or acid test) ratio, and the ratio of cash flow to current liabilities. We calculate the **current ratio** as the ratio of a company's current assets to its current liabilities:

$$\text{Current Ratio} = \frac{\text{Current Assets}}{\text{Current Liabilities}} \tag{2.10a}$$

The current ratio attempts to measure the ability of a company to pay its current liabilities given the relative magnitude of its current assets. Naturally, going-concern companies must continually replenish their current assets such as receivables and inventory, so current assets cannot be depleted. The **quick or acid test ratio** is the ratio of cash, marketable securities, and accounts receivable to current liabilities. This ratio also attempts to measure the ability of a company to pay its current liabilities given the relative magnitude of the company's more liquid current assets.

$$\text{Quick or Acid Test Ratio} = \frac{\text{Cash} + \text{Marketable Securities} + \text{Accounts Receivable}}{\text{Current Liabilities}} \tag{2.10b}$$

The **cash flow to current liabilities ratio** is the ratio of a specific measure of cash flow (cash flow from operations or free cash flows) to current liabilities. This ratio is a measure of the company's ability to pay its current liabilities with its cash flow. The formula for this ratio using operating cash flow is:

$$\text{Operating Cash Flow to Current Liabilities Ratio} = \frac{\text{Operating Cash Flow}}{\text{Current Liabilities}} \tag{2.10c}$$

As with most financial ratios, we can define the numerator and denominator in various ways. Once again, the choice of numerator and denominator depends on the context of the analysis, and consistency between the numerator and denominator is important. Sometimes we exclude short-term debt from current liabilities and excess assets from current assets to focus the analysis on operating assets and liabilities. The calculation of GAP's current, quick, and operating cash flow to current liabilities ratios is shown below. Note, we do not provide the cash flow statement for GAP, but we report its operating cash flow for Year 0 in Exhibit 2.1 of $1,539.

$$\text{Current Ratio}_{\text{GAP, Year 0}} = \frac{\$3{,}926}{\$2{,}095} = 1.87$$

$$\text{Quick or Acid Test Ratio}_{\text{GAP, Year 0}} = \frac{\$1{,}661}{\$2{,}095} = 0.79$$

$$\text{Operating Cash Flow to Current Liabilities Ratio}_{\text{GAP, Year 0}} = \frac{\$1{,}539}{\$2{,}095} = 0.73$$

Excess assets can sometimes have a significant effect on these financial ratios because companies often hold excess assets in various short-term investments (see Valuation in Practice 2.3). A company's current and quick ratios can change significantly if it has significant excess (current) assets and we assume that the company distributed those excess assets to its equityholders or used them to pay off its debt. To illustrate the effect of eliminating an excess asset, we assume 50% of GAP's cash is an excess asset; GAP's current ratio would decrease to 1.5 [1.5 = ($3,926 − 0.5 × $1,661)/$2,095] and its quick ratio would decrease to 0.4 (0.4 = 0.5 × $1,661/$2,095).

Inventories, Accounts Receivable, Accounts Payable, and Trade Cash Cycle Ratios

Inventories, accounts receivable, and accounts payable all involve the production and sales cycle of a company. A company must first purchase materials and services, which it will eventually sell. While a company usually makes these purchases "on credit," the length of the maturity period is typically short. Then, it takes time for the company to produce and sell its inventory, and it takes additional time for the company to collect cash on its credit sales. Thus, companies typically have a **trade cash cycle** or **cash conversion cycle** they must finance—that is, the time from when the company pays its payables until the time it is able to sell its inventory and ultimately collect its receivables.

Before we analyze the cash conversion cycle in more detail, let us first analyze each component of the cash conversion cycle—days of purchases outstanding, days of inventory held, and the accounts receivable collection period. These measures are variations of the turnover ratios we discussed previously. We measure the **days of accounts payable outstanding**, the **days sales held in inventory**, and the **accounts receivable collection period** as

$$\text{Days of Accounts Payable Outstanding} = \frac{\text{Average Accounts Payable}}{\text{Purchases/365}} \tag{2.11}$$

$$\text{Days of Sales Held in Inventory} = \frac{\text{Average Inventory}}{\text{Cost of Goods Sold/365}} \tag{2.12}$$

$$\text{Accounts Receivable Collection Period} = \frac{\text{Average Gross Accounts Receivable}}{\text{Credit Sales/365}} \tag{2.13}$$

Once we measure these ratios, we can measure a company's cash conversion cycle—that is, the time from when it must pay out cash until the time it collects cash. In other words, a company's cash conversion cycle measures the length of time for which the company must finance its purchases. The greater this number, the larger investment the company has to make in receivables and inventory net of payables. The formula for the cash conversion cycle or **trade cash cycle** is:

$$\begin{array}{c}\text{Cash}\\\text{Conversion}\\\text{Cycle}\end{array} = \begin{array}{c}\text{Accounts}\\\text{Receivable}\\\text{Collection}\\\text{Period}\end{array} + \begin{array}{c}\text{Days of}\\\text{Inventory}\\\text{Held}\end{array} - \begin{array}{c}\text{Days of}\\\text{Payables}\\\text{Outstanding}\end{array} \tag{2.14}$$

As with all financial ratios, the above measurement of a company's cash conversion cycle, while commonly used, is a proxy for the underlying economic concept we attempt to measure. For example, it does not include all of the cash a company must pay out to operate its business before it collects cash from receivables, and it does not adjust for the profit margin embedded in accounts receivable. These limitations are in addition to the limitations of using annual averages of the account balances for the financial ratios used in the trade cash cycle formula. That being said, analyzing a cash conversion cycle for a company over time or across companies in cross-section can be informative. In 1988, Dell's cash conversion cycle was almost 60 days, and as it began to work on improving its working capital management, its cash conversion cycle fell steadily. By 1995, its cash conversion cycle was negative for the first time, and by the early 2000s, it was almost −60 days. This occurred through a combination of reducing both the days of inventory held and the accounts receivable collection period while simultaneously leaning on suppliers to extend days payables outstanding. While its competitors instituted the same practices, Dell's trade cash cycle was consistently lower. Dell's cash conversion cycle continued to be negative even through 2016.

Some analysts compute accounts receivable turnover, inventory turnover, and accounts payable turnover ratios instead of the "days" calculations. These turnover ratios are closely related to the above calculations and, in fact, are just the denominator (not divided by 365) over the numerator. Hence, inventory turnover would simply be cost of goods sold divided by average inventory and accounts receivable turnover would simply be credit sales divided by average accounts receivable. You can also simply compute the relevant turnover ratio by dividing 365 by the relevant "days" calculation. These are different from the asset utilization ratios discussed in Section 2.8 because, in that case, every turnover ratio was computed relative to revenues, but here, we try to relate the numerator and the denominator more closely (e.g., inventory and cost of goods sold instead of inventory and revenues).

Analysts also sometimes examine the "quality" of a company's net account receivables by analyzing the ratio of the provision for bad debts to gross accounts receivable (net accounts receivable plus allowance for uncollectible accounts), called the provision for bad debts ratio.

$$\text{Provision for Bad Debts Ratio} = \frac{\text{Allowance for Uncollectible Accounts}}{\text{Gross Accounts Receivable}} \tag{2.15}$$

Below, we show the calculation of GAP's inventory, accounts receivable, and accounts payable ratios. Since GAP does not have any accounts receivable, its accounts receivable collection period is zero and the provision for bad debts ratio is not relevant.

$$\text{Days of Accounts Payable Outstanding}_{\text{GAP, Year 0}} = \frac{(\$1{,}027 + \$1{,}049)/2}{(\$8{,}127 + \$1{,}620 - \$1{,}477)/365} = 45.8$$

$$\text{Days of Sales Held in Inventory}_{\text{GAP, Year 0}} = \frac{(\$1{,}477 + \$1{,}620)/2}{\$8{,}127/365} = 69.5$$

$$\text{Accounts Receivable Collection Period}_{\text{GAP, Year 0}} = 0 \text{ days (no accounts receivable)}$$

$$\text{Trade Cash Cycle}_{\text{GAP, Year 0}} = 0 + 69.5 - 45.8 = 23.7 \text{ days}$$

$$\text{Provision for Bad Debts Ratio}_{\text{GAP, Year 0}} = \text{Not a Meaningful Figure (no accounts receivable)}$$

Even though GAP accepts credit cards, it has no accounts receivable. According to GAP's 10-K report, GAP recognizes revenue and assumes the cash is in transit when a customer purchases merchandise at the register, even if a customer pays with a credit card. Other companies do not follow this same policy for credit card sales. These companies record a receivable because it takes two to three days for a company to receive payment from third-party credit card sales. For example, Nordstrom, Inc., one of GAP's competitors, changed its accounting treatment for this issue and reclassified its two or three days of outstanding credit card balances from cash (which is how GAP treats them) to accounts receivable. Nordstrom also has its own credit cards, which have a longer accounts receivable collection period. Its accounts receivable balances and allowances for uncollectible accounts for Year 0 and Year −1 were \$2,026 and \$2,035, and \$85 and \$76, respectively. Nordstrom's accounts receivable collection period for Year 0, when it had \$9,310 of revenues, was 82.8 days:

$$\text{Accounts Receivable Collection Period} = \frac{[(\$2{,}035 + \$76) + (\$2{,}026 + \$85)]/2}{\$9{,}310/365} = 82.8 \text{ days}$$

Nordstrom has a 4% provision for bad debts for its accounts receivable, which we calculate as

$$\text{Provision for Bad Debts Ratio} = \frac{\$85}{\$2{,}026 + \$85} = 0.04$$

REVIEW EXERCISE 2.4

The Gap, Inc. Working Capital Management Ratio Forecasts for Year +1 and Beyond

Use the information in Exhibit 2.1 to calculate GAP's working capital management ratios for one or more of the years in the forecasts (Year +1 through Year +6). How are GAP's working capital management ratios in the forecasts changing relative to Year 0?

Solution on page 89.

2.11 ANALYZING A COMPANY'S FIXED ASSET STRUCTURE AND CAPITAL EXPENDITURES

LO4 Analyze a company's fixed assets and financial leverage

Naturally, when valuing a company, understanding its capital expenditures (its investments in fixed assets—property, plant, and equipment) is important because, as you recall from Chapter 1, it is an input into measuring free cash flows. We can use both a company's property, plant, and equipment accounts and its depreciation accounts in order to assess the depreciable life of its fixed assets. We can also examine its capital expenditures relative to revenues, depreciation, and earnings. As with most of the financial ratios, these financial ratios can be useful in identifying comparable companies and in preparing and assessing the reasonableness of forecasts.

Depreciable Life (Age)

All else equal, companies with older plant and equipment will have higher capital expenditures in the future. The specific ratios to learn about the age of these assets are:

$$\text{Depreciable Life of Gross Plant} = \frac{\text{Average Gross Property, Plant, and Equipment}}{\text{Depreciation}} \quad \textbf{(2.16)}$$

$$\text{Depreciable Life of Net Plant} = \frac{\text{Average Net Property, Plant, and Equipment}}{\text{Depreciation}} \quad \textbf{(2.17)}$$

The **depreciable life of the net plant** provides an indication of the average remaining life of the net plant, as long as the company uses estimated useful lives that are close to the economic lives. Consider two companies in the same industry that use the same depreciation policies. If one company has a depreciable life of net plant that is smaller than the other, then it is likely that the two companies have assets of different ages. All else equal, this difference has implications for the replacement of those assets. Such analysis can be useful to identify comparable companies or to forecast capital expenditures. Depreciation includes all depreciation—that is, depreciation expense plus additional depreciation taken but capitalized (for example, depreciation included in inventory). Companies sometimes disclose this information in a separate schedule; if not, the cash flow statement can provide information on depreciation in addition to the information provided on the income statement. If possible, we would also exclude non-depreciable assets such as land from the numerator in the above calculations.

We assume that GAP has no amortization of intangible assets. A detailed reading of the footnotes indicates that GAP has a minimal amount of amortization, which we choose to ignore for the purposes of this example. GAP does not disclose the cost of land separately in its 10-K, so we are unable to eliminate it from the calculation as we would like to. The calculations of these ratios for GAP for Year 0 are as follows:

$$\text{Depreciable Life of Gross Plant}_{\text{GAP, Year 0}} = \frac{(\$7{,}427 + 7{,}573)/2}{\$648} = 11.57$$

$$\text{Depreciable Life of Net Plant}_{\text{GAP, Year 0}} = \frac{(\$2{,}628 + \$2{,}563)/2}{\$648} = 4.0$$

However, for GAP (and other retailers), this is just a small proportion of its assets, as many retailers have leased significant amounts of assets and do not record many leased assets on their balance sheets. We will provide more discussion about this issue when we discuss leverage in Section 2.13.

Capital Expenditures

All else equal, companies have larger relative capital expenditures if they are capital intensive, are in need of replacing assets, or are growing. We can analyze a company's capital expenditures relative to its revenues and measures of earnings and cash flows. We can also measure a company's capital expenditures relative to its depreciation. The goal of analyzing these ratios is to help assess, and possibly forecast, a company's capital expenditures. Some example ratios include the following:

$$\text{Capital Expenditures to Revenue} = \frac{\text{Capital Expenditures}}{\text{Revenues}} \quad \textbf{(2.18)}$$

$$\text{Capital Expenditures to EBITDA} = \frac{\text{Capital Expenditures}}{\text{EBITDA}} \quad \textbf{(2.19)}$$

$$\text{Capital Expenditures to Depreciation} = \frac{\text{Capital Expenditures}}{\text{Depreciation}} \quad \textbf{(2.20)}$$

Capital expenditures are often "lumpy"—that is, they are large in some years and small in others, especially for smaller companies. In such situations, we sometimes try to smooth the capital expenditures by using the average over a few years. Again, when we compare companies using these ratios, we either assume that they have similar policies regarding leasing versus buying plant and equipment, or we make the appropriate adjustments in our calculations for the relevant differences.

Below, we show the calculations of these ratios for GAP in Year 0, which had $249 of capital expenditures according to its statement of cash flows.

$$\text{Capital Expenditures to Revenue}_{\text{GAP, Year 0}} = \frac{\$249}{\$14{,}664} = 0.017$$

$$\text{Capital Expenditures to EBITDA}_{\text{GAP, Year 0}} = \frac{\$249}{\$1{,}204 + \$6 + \$778 + \$648} = 0.095$$

$$\text{Capital Expenditures to Depreciation}_{\text{GAP, Year 0}} = \frac{\$249}{\$648} = 0.384$$

Note that our calculation of EBITDA includes interest income in EBITDA; thus, we are assuming it is part of the company's operations. GAP's capital expenditures to revenue ratio is quite small, but remember that GAP leases most of its stores, so the capital expenditure number does not fully reflect its total investment in fixed assets.

2.12 OTHER TYPES OF FINANCIAL STATEMENT RELATIONS—GROWTH, TRENDS, PER SHARE, PER EMPLOYEE, AND PER UNIT OF CAPACITY AND OUTPUT

Analyzing per share measures and growth rates is a standard part of most financial analyses. Historical growth rates—both annual growth rates and compound annual growth rates—are characteristics widely utilized by analysts. Analysts often use historical growth rates as part of the basis for developing forecasts. Analysts sometimes also analyze a company using its financial statement information in combination with its non-financial information. For example, analysts often use a per share measure as an input into the calculation of certain market multiples (for example, the P/E ratio) and to compare a company to itself over time. Analysts also use ratios based on non-financial information in order to analyze a company's historical performance, identify comparable companies, and prepare and assess the reasonableness of forecasts. For example, in the retail industry, analysts often measure such company characteristics as revenue or earnings per square foot of retail space or number of stores.

Employee, Unit of Capacity, and Unit of Output Measures

It is sometimes useful to examine various financial statement items—for example, revenues, assets, cash flows—on a per employee, per unit of capacity, and per unit of output basis. All else equal, we can use such measures as operating income per employee as a proxy for productivity. Similarly, we can use measures based on the unit of capacity as a proxy for capacity utilization.

For GAP, for example, we might measure capacity using the number of square feet of retail space; for paper mills and heavy manufacturing, we might measure capacity using tons of productive capacity; for the airline industry, we might measure capacity using available seat miles. We can use measures based on output to realize the average revenue and cost per unit of output. We might measure revenue per transaction for an online retailer or revenue per check for a restaurant. Naturally, we analyze these measures by comparing the company we are valuing to its comparable companies currently and over time, just as we do for all other financial ratios.

Since many of the financial statement items are affected by inflation but the denominators are not (number of square feet or number of employees, etc.), it may be useful to adjust the numerators in these calculations for inflation in order to restate them in constant dollars (or any other currency) to more readily see real trends. A common inflation index is the Consumer Price Index; another general index that could be more appropriate for manufacturers is the Producer Price Index; however, these indices might not be relevant for all industries. Some industries might face a different price level index than that faced by the general economy (for example, the personal computer manufacturer industry, which has faced decreasing prices at times).

Growth Rates and Trend Analyses

We often measure growth rates for free cash flows and for certain items on the income statement, balance sheet, and cash flow statement. Growth rates are often used to drive revenues in forecasting models. We cannot, however, measure a growth rate if the base year is negative. For example, a company that has earnings last year of \$10, and this year of \$12, has a 20% growth rate (0.2 = \$12/\$10 − 1). The same calculation is not meaningful if that company has earnings last year of −\$10 and this year of \$12; (\$12/−\$10) − 1 is not a meaningful calculation. We discuss this issue—negative denominators—in more detail later.

Sometimes, we also examine the **index trend** of a characteristic of interest, in which we divide all years by the first year to measure the cumulative growth rate. For example, if a company's operating income during a five-year period is \$100, \$110, \$125, \$180, and \$220, its index trend for those five years is 1.0, 1.1, 1.25, 1.8, and 2.2. The index trend in the first year is always equal to 1.0 because we are dividing a number by itself. This feature of the index trend is useful because we can easily compare different characteristics of the company to each other (for example, comparing revenue to operating income), or we can compare one characteristic of the company to that of comparable companies. For example, if the index trend of sales goes from 1 to 1.5 over a five-year period and the index trend of operating income goes from 1 to 2 over the same period, it indicates that the company is likely benefiting from economies of scale as it grows. If the operating income trend index moves in lockstep with sales, then the firm is not experiencing any scale economies.

Growth rates for companies tend to vary somewhat each year, as in the example of operating income immediately above. In the first year the growth rate was 10% (0.1 = \$110/\$100 − 1), and in the second year, the growth rate was 13.64% (0.1364 = \$125/\$110 − 1). Analysts often compute a **compound annual growth rate, CAGR**, which indicates what yearly growth rate would have resulted from the observed growth for the period analyzed. Therefore, in our example above, we would be asking what yearly growth in operating income would have resulted from it growing from \$100 to \$220 in four years. We calculate the compound average growth rate in X, over the period from t to t + n, as

$$CAGR_{t,\,t+n} = \sqrt[n]{\frac{X_{t+n}}{X_t}} - 1 = \left(\frac{X_{t+n}}{X_t}\right)^{\frac{1}{n}} - 1 \tag{2.21}$$

$$CAGR_{t,\,t+4} = \sqrt[4]{\frac{\$220}{\$100}} - 1 = \left(\frac{\$220}{\$100}\right)^{\frac{1}{4}} - 1 = 0.218$$

Therefore, if the company's operating income started at \$100 and grew 21.8% each year for four years, the operating income would have reached \$220.

Per Share Measures

We also measure the per share amount of free cash flows and of various items on an income statement, balance sheet, and cash flow statement. On the income statement, we might analyze revenues, gross margin, operating income, and net income on a per share basis. On the balance sheet, we might analyze the major components of assets as well as their book value on a per share basis. On the cash flow statement, we might analyze cash flow from operations and capital expenditures on a per share basis. Last, we might analyze free cash flow and equity free cash flow on a per share basis. Naturally, rather than analyze all of these per share measures, we choose the per share measures based on the context of the analysis. Normally, these involve parts of the income statement.

To measure a financial statement number on a per share basis, we divide this number by the number of shares outstanding. A company usually reports more than the shares it has outstanding. In addition to the number of shares it has outstanding, it might report the number of shares it is authorized to issue and the number of shares it has issued. The **number of shares outstanding** is equal to the number of shares a company issued net of the number of shares it has repurchased and not reissued, called **treasury shares**.

In the U.S., companies must report two earnings per share measures—basic earnings per share and diluted earnings per share. For **basic earnings per share**, we divide net income to common equity by the weighted average shares outstanding. The **weighted average shares outstanding** is the number of shares outstanding during the year weighted by how long the shares were outstanding during the year. For **diluted earnings per share**, we again divide net income to common equity by the weighted average shares outstanding, but we adjust both the numerator and denominator for the dilutive effects of non-equity securities (such as convertible debt, convertible preferred stock, and stock options) that we assume are converted into common equity. For some companies, the difference between the two earnings per share numbers can be substantial because of their reliance on stock options to compensate employees.

2.13 ANALYZING A COMPANY'S FINANCIAL LEVERAGE AND FINANCIAL RISK

We define financial leverage as the use of non-common equity financing. All else equal, the more non-common equity financing a company uses, the more financial leverage it has. We measure a company's financial leverage and financial risk in three ways using financial statement relations. We use financial leverage ratios to measure the degree to which a company is using financial leverage. We use coverage ratios to measure the ability of a company to service, or cover the payments on, its non-equity securities. When using financial statement values to measure the degree to which a company is using financial leverage, we often use the ratio of a specific measure of non-equity securities (for example, debt) to a specific measure of total investment (for example, total assets or total invested capital). To measure a company's ability to service its non-equity securities, we typically use a ratio of a specific measure of income or cash flow to a specific measure of required payments to non-equity security holders. To measure the ability of the company to repay its debt, we use a ratio of total debt to earnings or cash flow.

As we discuss in many parts of this book, we use market values to measure a company's financial leverage ratio in order to measure its cost of capital or evaluate its capital structure strategy. In this section, we use financial statement numbers to measure financial leverage ratios. We do not recommend using financial leverage ratios based on financial statement numbers to measure a company's cost of capital—for example, to lever and unlever the cost of capital (beta), or to measure the weighted average cost of capital. If that is the case, why are we discussing these ratios that are dependent on financial statement figures? We discuss financial leverage ratios based on financial statement numbers because they are commonly used by analysts and managers, in debt contracts, and by debt rating agencies. Moreover, these leverage ratios are correlated with ratings, yields, and the probability of default. In doing a valuation analysis, we might need to determine if a company is in compliance with its debt covenants, or we might need to estimate its debt rating. As such, we discuss these ratios in this section of the chapter. In Chapter 9, we show how one can use these ratios to estimate a debt rating.

A common way to examine the financial leverage of a company is to examine the ratio of debt and other non-equity financing to total assets (or total invested capital or common equity). For the numerator in our financial leverage ratios, we use such figures as total debt, total debt plus preferred stock, long-term debt, and long-term debt plus preferred stock. When measuring these financial leverage ratios, analysts sometimes net out cash against non-equity claims, assuming that the cash could be used to redeem the non-equity claims. We show three popular financial leverage ratios here. For companies that have other non-equity securities, we could also assign financial leverage ratios to those securities as well.

$$\text{Total Debt to Total Assets} = \frac{\text{Total Debt}}{\text{Total Assets}} \tag{2.22}$$

$$\text{Total Liabilities to Total Assets} = \frac{\text{Total Liabilities}}{\text{Total Assets}} \tag{2.23}$$

$$\text{Total Debt to Common Equity} = \frac{\text{Total Debt}}{\text{Common Equity}} \tag{2.24}$$

From Exhibit 2.1, as of the end of Year 0, GAP has current and non-current liabilities but no debt; however, we can also see that GAP had $6 million in interest expense in Year 0, which means that GAP had a small amount of debt at some point during the year. The debt GAP incurred was associated with drawing on its **line-of-credit**, probably to fund a buildup of inventory during its busy season. For GAP, the calculations of these financial leverage ratios—measured using year-end financial statement data as opposed to market data—are as follows:

$$\text{Total Debt to Total Assets}_{\text{GAP, Year 0}} = \frac{\$0}{\$7{,}065} = 0$$

$$\text{Total Liabilities to Total Assets}_{\text{GAP, Year 0}} = \frac{\$2{,}985}{\$7{,}065} = 0.423$$

$$\text{Total Debt to Common Equity}_{\text{GAP, Year 0}} = \frac{\$0}{\$4{,}080} = 0$$

Measurement Issues—What Is Debt?

Debt is sometimes difficult to define and measure for two reasons. First, not all liabilities on an accounting balance sheet are debt. Accountants define liabilities as:[11] "A liability has three essential characteristics: (a) it embodies a present duty or responsibility to one or more other entities that entails settlement by probable future transfer or use of assets at a specified or determinable date, on occurrence of a specified event, or on demand, (b) the duty or responsibility obligates a particular entity, leaving it little or no discretion to avoid the future sacrifice, and (c) the transaction or other event obligating the entity has already happened."

[11] Financial Accounting Standards Board, *Statement of Financial Accounting Concepts No. 6*, "Elements of Financial Statements," December 1985, p. 36.

While not all liabilities are debt, accountants do not have a specific definition of debt. We use the term **debt** to represent certain types of financing. These include notes, mortgages, bonds (debentures), and other financing instruments that typically have an explicit or implicit interest rate attached to them; thus, from a valuation perspective, we can define debt as an amount contractually owed to another party that has an explicit or implicit interest payment that we can measure. This definition excludes such liabilities as deferred income taxes, unearned revenue, and most other operating liabilities (for example, accounts payable, wages payable, accruals). For other reasons, convertible notes and convertible debt are also not entirely debt, even though accountants may classify them as debt on the financial statements. The convertible feature of convertible debt is a claim on equity, and the value of that convertible feature is not debt.

The second reason it is difficult to define and measure debt is that companies can use debt that does not appear on the balance sheet, called **off-balance-sheet financing**. One example is leases that do not appear on the balance sheet (called operating leases). That said, revised accounting rules will require public companies to recognize the present value of most of these obligations on their balance sheets starting in 2018. We discuss accounting for leases in detail in Chapters 11 and 14. Another example of a contractual obligation not recognized on the balance sheet is a future obligation to make certain payments for fixed or minimum quantities to be delivered in the future. While U.S. GAAP requires companies to disclose the terms of these unconditional requirements (for the next five years) in the footnotes, they do not require that the company record a liability for these payments because the items being purchased have not yet been received.

In addition, companies sometimes create **special purpose vehicles** or **entities (SPVs** or **SPEs)** to transfer risks from the balance sheet to another entity. SPVs and SPEs became highly publicized after the failure of the Enron Corporation. Another term for an entity of this type is a "bankruptcy-remote entity." Regardless of what we call them, the key to such entities is that their operations are limited to the acquisition and financing of specific assets. The SPV or SPE is usually a subsidiary company with an asset and liability structure that isolates it from the parent company. Companies use SPVs and SPEs to isolate financial risk. For example, a company can use an SPV or SPE to finance a large project without putting the entire firm at risk.

Companies can use many other types of financial instruments that may be classified as debt but do not have the characteristics of a debt instrument. These include exchangeable debentures, interest rate swaps, recourse obligations on receivables sold, options, financial guarantees, interest rate caps and floors, futures contracts, forward contracts, and so forth. Many financial instruments have debt-like and equity-like characteristics, and it is important to understand both the economics of these transactions and how the accountant records and discloses them to conduct a detailed financial analysis of a company.

Valuation in Practice 2.4

Example Debt Covenant for Pinnacle Entertainment, Inc. Pinnacle has debt agreements requiring it to have a maximum amount of debt relative to its earnings before interest, taxes, depreciation, and amortization (EBITDA), called a leverage ratio. It is also required to have a minimum amount of EBITDA relative to its interest payments, called an interest coverage ratio. In addition, the interest rate the company is charged depends on its leverage ratio.

> . . . The revolving credit facility bears interest, at our option, at either LIBOR plus a margin ranging from 1.75% to 2.75% or at a base rate plus a margin ranging from 0.75% to 1.75%, in either case based on our Consolidated Total Leverage Ratio, which, in general, is the ratio of Consolidated Total Debt less Excess Cash to Annualized Adjusted EBITDA (as such terms are defined in the Credit Facility).
>
> The Credit Facility has, among other things, financial covenants and other affirmative and negative covenants. As of December 31, 2015, the Credit Facility requires compliance with the following ratios so long as there are outstanding borrowings under our revolving credit facility: (1) maximum Consolidated Total Leverage Ratio of 6.25 to 1.00; (2) minimum Consolidated Interest Coverage Ratio (as defined in the Credit Facility) of 2.00 to 1.00; and (3) maximum Consolidated Senior Secured Debt Ratio of 2.75 to 1.00. In addition, the Credit Facility has covenants that limit the amount of senior unsecured debt we may incur to $3.5 billion, unless our maximum Consolidated Total Leverage Ratio is less than 6.00 to 1.00.

Source: Pinnacle Entertainment, Inc. 2015 10-K Report, pp. 42–43.

Coverage Ratios

Coverage ratios attempt to measure the ability of a company to pay its fixed charges (for example, interest payments). Conceptually, a company with a higher coverage ratio has a greater ability to make interest payments on its debt. To measure coverage ratios, we typically use a ratio of a measure of earnings or cash flow (before the payment of fixed charges) to a measure of fixed charges. A general formula for coverage ratios is

$$\text{Coverage Ratio} = \frac{\text{Earnings Available to Pay Fixed Charges}}{\text{Fixed Charges}}$$

Alternative numerators include earnings before interest and taxes (EBIT), EBIT plus depreciation and amortization (EBITDA), operating cash flow before interest and taxes, and free cash flow before income taxes. Alternative denominators include interest payments and interest payments plus preferred stock dividends (grossed up for income taxes because we use a pre-tax numerator and preferred stock dividends are not tax deductible). Interest includes all interest payments, usually even **capitalized interest**. Typically, companies expense all interest accrued or paid; however, in some cases, when a company borrows money to finance the construction of a long-lived asset, the company will capitalize the interest. In other words, the company will include the interest that accrues during the construction of a building in the value of the asset. Since capitalized interest must be paid like most other interest, we include the capitalized interest in the denominator.

Sometimes companies issue **zero-coupon** or **paid-in-kind** debt, often referred to as **PIK debt**. In this case, the company does not actually pay interest currently. Instead, the principal amount of the loan increases by the amount of the unpaid but accrued interest. Depending on the reason we are calculating the coverage ratio, we might decide not to include the interest from the zero-coupon or paid-in-kind debt. For example, to analyze a company's current ability to pay its fixed charges, we might exclude the interest on the PIK debt, for that portion of the interest is not a current requirement to be paid; the firm does not default for deferring payment since it is not contractually liable for that payment until later. A common adjustment to the financial statements when measuring coverage ratios is to treat non-capitalized (or operating) leases as capital leases, which we discuss in Chapters 11 and 14.

Analysts typically do not include required principal repayments in fixed charges. If the company's ability to refinance its debt is in doubt, you may want to include required principal payments in the denominator. As with all financial ratios, we measure the numerators and denominators consistently. If we include a fixed charge in the denominator, we do not deduct it from the numerator. Basic formulas for some of the common coverage ratios appear below (it is also common to use income from continuing operations instead of net income in the following formulas). We divide the preferred stock dividend by one minus the income tax rate because preferred stock dividends are not tax deductible.

$$\text{EBIT/(INT + PSDiv)} = \frac{\text{Net Income + Interest + Income Taxes}}{\text{Interest + Preferred Stock Dividends/(1 − Income Tax Rate)}} \quad (2.25)$$

$$\text{EBITDA/(INT + PSDiv)} = \frac{\text{Net Income + Interest + Income Taxes + Depreciation + Amortization}}{\text{Interest + Preferred Stock Dividends/(1 − Income Tax Rate)}} \quad (2.26)$$

GAP does not have any preferred stock or debt financing outstanding at the end of fiscal Year 0, but it had a small amount of debt outstanding during the year, resulting in $6 million of interest in Year 0. The coverage ratios for GAP for Year 0 are

$$\text{EBIT/INT}_{\text{GAP, Year 0}} = \frac{\$1{,}204 + \$6 + \$778}{\$6 + \$0/(1 - 0.393)} = 331.3$$

$$\text{EBITDA/INT}_{\text{GAP, Year 0}} = \frac{\$1{,}204 + \$6 + \$778 + \$648}{\$6 + \$0/(1 - 0.393)} = 439.3$$

Our calculations of EBIT and EBITDA for GAP above assume that the interest income is from operations and not from excess assets. If they were from excess assets, an alternative treatment that some analysts use is to reduce the EBIT and EBITDA for the interest income, but then to pay down the debt with the excess assets and calculate a revised interest amount.

Making additional adjustments to our calculations for GAP is beyond the scope of this chapter; however, in a more detailed analysis of GAP, we would consider capitalizing GAP's operating leases as well as those of its competitors. GAP uses a significant amount of operating leases. Most of its stores are leased and GAP also leases most of its offices and distribution facilities. GAP's leases are, for the most part, not capitalized on its balance sheet; rather, GAP recognizes the lease payments as rent expense on its income statement. In GAP's case, capitalizing operating leases will increase financial leverage ratios. In addition, capitalizing those leases would affect its coverage ratios, as would the alternative treatment of including the lease payments as a fixed charge in the denominator if not capitalized.

Debt to Earnings Ratio

The **debt to earnings ratio** (or **net debt to earnings ratio**) attempts to measure the ability of a company to pay back the debt. It is typically measured as debt minus cash and cash-like investments (or **net debt**) to a measure of earnings (EBITDA) or cash flow (free cash flow). This ratio indicates how many years it will take the company to pay back the debt. As with most ratios, this ratio is not meaningful if the denominator is negative. However, it is possible for this ratio to be negative if a company has more cash (and cash like investments) than debt (see Valuation in Practice 2.3).

Valuation Key 2.7

Coverage ratios measure the ability of a company to pay its fixed charges (for example, interest). We measure coverage ratios as the ratio of a measure of income or cash flow to a measure of fixed charges (payments to non-equity security holders).

2.14 DISAGGREGATING THE RETURN ON (COMMON) EQUITY

We can disaggregate the return on equity into three components. The first two components are similar to the components in the return on assets—(levered) profit margin and asset utilization. We measure profit margin using net income to common equity in the numerator, called the **levered profit margin**, for we are disaggregating the return on equity. The third component is a **financial leverage factor** that considers the impact of using non-equity financing—the average of total assets to the average equity. We show the basic formula to disaggregate the return on equity in Equation 2.27.

$$\text{ROE} = \text{Levered Profit Margin} \times \text{Asset Utilization} \times \text{Financial Leverage Factor}$$

$$\text{ROE} = \frac{\text{Net Income} - \text{Preferred Stock Dividends}}{\text{Revenue}} \times \frac{\text{Revenue}}{\text{Average Total Assets}} \times \frac{\text{Average Total Assets}}{\text{Average Equity}} \quad (2.27)$$

The decomposition of the return on equity for GAP using the numbers from Year 0 is

$$\text{ROE}_{\text{GAP, Year 0}} = \frac{\$1{,}204 - \$0}{\$14{,}664} \times \frac{\$14{,}664}{(\$7{,}985 + \$7{,}065)/2} \times \frac{(\$7{,}985 + \$7{,}065)/2}{(\$4{,}891 + \$4{,}080)/2} = 0.268$$

$$\text{ROE}_{\text{GAP, Year 0}} = 0.082 \times 1.95 \times 1.68 = 0.268$$

Return on assets and return on equity are algebraically related to each other. The return on equity is equal to the return on assets multiplied by a non-equity financing leverage factor. The non-equity financing leverage factor has two components. The first component is a **leverage factor for earnings**, and the second is a financial leverage factor that measures the amount of non-equity financing in the balance sheet. We show the relation between the return on assets and return on equity in Equation 2.28.

$$\text{ROE} = \text{ROA} \times \qquad \text{Non-Equity Financing Leverage Factor}$$

$$\text{ROE} = \text{ROA} \times [\ \text{Leverage Factor for Earnings} \times \text{Financial Leverage Factor}\ ]$$

$$\text{ROE} = \text{ROA} \times \left[\frac{\text{Income to Common Equity}}{\text{Net Income} + (1 - \text{Income Tax Rate}) \times \text{Interest Expense}} \times \frac{\text{Average Total Assets}}{\text{Average Equity}} \right] \quad \textbf{(2.28)}$$

The relation between the return on assets and return on equity for GAP is as follows:

$$\text{ROE}_{\text{GAP, Year 0}} = 0.160 \times \left[\frac{\$1{,}204 - \$0}{\$1{,}204 + (1 - 0.393) \times \$6} \times \frac{(\$7{,}985 + \$7{,}065)/2}{(\$4{,}891 + \$4{,}080)/2} \right] = 0.268$$

$$\text{ROE}_{\text{GAP, Year 0}} = 0.160 \times [0.997 \times 1.68] = 0.268$$

$$\text{ROE}_{\text{GAP, Year 0}} = 0.160 \times 1.67 = 0.268$$

In Exhibit 2.6 (which is in Section 2.9), we depict the decomposition of GAP's return on equity, just as we presented the decomposition of the return on assets.

REVIEW EXERCISE 2.5

The Gap, Inc. Return on Equity Forecasts for Year +1 and Beyond

Use the information in Exhibit 2.1 to calculate GAP's return on equity for one or more of the years in the forecasts (Year +1 through Year +6). How is GAP's return on equity in the forecasts changing relative to Year 0?

Solution on page 89.

2.15 ASSESSING COMPETITIVE ADVANTAGE

LO5 Assess a company's competitive advantage

As we discussed in Chapter 1, assessing a company's competitive advantage is part of the valuation process. A company's competitive advantage affects the forecasts we use in our valuation. A competitive advantage is any characteristic that allows a company to compete within its industry so that it performs better than its rivals perform and allows a company to earn a return higher than its cost of capital. Michael Porter identified two primary types of competitive advantage: **cost leadership** and **differentiation**.[12] It is also possible for a company to have a competitive advantage via government or legal avenues by means of patents, licenses to do business, subsidies, and tariffs.

In order to have a competitive advantage, a company has to have the resources and the capabilities or competencies to achieve that competitive advantage. By understanding those capabilities, management and valuation experts are able to understand the nature of a company's competitive advantage and, more importantly, to make predictions about the sustainability of a company's competitive advantage. In the end, we want to forecast a company's free cash flows. Those free cash flows are affected by a company's competitive advantage, the returns associated with that competitive advantage, how long the competitive advantage is sustainable, and the likelihood the company can create new sources of competitive advantage in the future.

A company generally develops a competitive advantage by being a low-cost provider or by differentiating its product or service from those of its competitors. Differentiation can come in the form of specific attributes of the product, servicing of the product, speed of delivery, or perceived and actual quality (brand differentiation). A company can be a low-cost provider by either using its assets more efficiently than its competitors (effectively delivering more sales per dollar of invested assets), for example, by keeping costs of production, marketing, and distribution lower. While some companies are considered low-cost producers, their product offering is often still somewhat differentiated.

[12] See for example, Porter, Michael E., *Competitive Advantage: Creating and Sustaining Superior Performance*, The Free Press (1985).

Cost Leadership as a Competitive Advantage

Companies that are cost leaders have found some way to provide a product or service to a customer at a lower cost. Consider the case of a commodity product (e.g., oil), which does not have any meaningful product differentiation. In a competitive environment, with no differentiation, all producers charge the same price. The only way to achieve superior profitability is to produce and deliver the product to the customer at a lower cost. Companies may be able to achieve lower costs in a variety of ways. Examples include lowering costs by operating with scale-efficient plants, taking advantage of economies of scale (buying power) and scope, using simpler designs that allow for lower costs of production, having technological advantages that lower costs, having a skilled and more efficient workforce, creating low-cost distribution networks, and keeping tight control of overhead, advertising, and research and development (R&D).

Companies that pursue cost leadership strategies must build capabilities and incentives within the organization to achieve that cost advantage. Those capabilities include the design of efficient processes of production or the ability to create technologies for efficient production, tight cost controls on operations, and a reporting system that quickly alerts managers if either the production process or spending gets out of control. In addition, companies pursuing a cost leadership strategy typically create incentives for employees and managers that focus on costs and cost control.

A company pursuing cost leadership as its primary strategy may also attempt to differentiate its products to some degree. So while cost leaders typically have reasonably limited and standardized offerings, they still may engage in differentiation through some mechanism. For example, McDonald's has a limited menu, and the menu is the same every day (except in the case of product introductions). Moreover, its offerings are quite standardized (employees don't ask you how you like your hamburger cooked). That being said, McDonald's still attempts to differentiate itself through branding and innovative product offerings.

Differentiation as a Competitive Advantage

A company pursues a differentiation strategy by offering unique product or service attributes that the customer will value. Thus, pursuing a differentiation strategy entails understanding the product or service attributes that customers value and then supplying those attributes to customers in a unique manner. Differentiation is achieved by emphasizing things such as product quality and design, service quality, branding, and product variety.

A company focused on differentiation typically has capabilities in advertising and branding, product design, engineering skills, R&D, and/or service and distribution networks that focus on maintaining the company's differentiation. An example of a company like this is the BMW Group, which produces BMW automobiles and is considered to be a leader in engineering and design. Another example is Nike, Inc., which advertises, markets, distributes, and sells athletic shoes and apparel and is well known for its focus on branding and promotion.

That said, a company pursuing a differentiation strategy also manages its costs. In the end, customers trade off quality attributes they desire against the cost of those attributes. Automobile manufacturers have improved the design and quality of their cars over time while simultaneously finding manufacturing processes that reduce costs.

Strategic Positioning

Achieving competitive advantage and superior performance does not result by simply choosing a cost advantage objective or a differentiation strategy. Indeed, companies choose a portfolio of combinations of differentiation and cost strategies. Companies with a great degree of differentiation generally have high relative costs and companies with no differentiation generally operate with low costs. However, companies can achieve a competitive advantage with a variety of combinations of differentiation and relative cost strategies.

As a result, a viable strategy in some industries might be to operate with some degree of differentiation, but to give up some relative cost advantage that would have been feasible with no differentiation. Companies will choose to position themselves with the combination of cost effectiveness and differentiation that is both feasible for them and that creates the greatest long-term competitive advantage relative to their peers.

Achieving and Sustaining Competitive Advantage

We discussed some of the capabilities and competencies that a company must create in order to have a competitive advantage. However, sustaining a competitive advantage is not permanent and can erode quickly without ongoing focus and innovation. Once a company has a competitive advantage, other companies will attempt to undermine that competitive advantage. They will attempt to replicate a competitive advantage or eliminate it by creating their own distinct competitive advantage. Companies that were once industry leaders for years have seen their competitive advantages erode and eventually disappear. For example, Eastman Kodak Co.'s (Kodak) core business in film and developing was slowly eroded by film introduced by Fuji Photo Film Co. (Fuji) and by film processing labs that did not rely on Kodak products. Subsequently, Kodak saw new technology, digital cameras, erode its market position even further. A second reason why competitive advantage may be temporary is that shocks external to the industry can alter which companies in an industry have a competitive advantage. For example, an increase in gasoline prices could lead auto manufacturers with more fuel-efficient cars to suddenly have a competitive advantage relative to those who have focused their strategy on large SUVs.

In analyzing the sustainability of competitive advantage, we have to ask: what is the source of the competitive advantage; what are the core competencies that the company has created to sustain that competitive advantage; how easy is it for someone to imitate its success; how likely is it that the nature of the competitive advantage will shift due to either external shocks, changes in regulation, new technologies, competitor innovation, or any other source; and how nimbly can the company react to those shifts in competitive advantage?

Valuation in Practice 2.5

The Fresh Market Inc.'s Competitive Strengths, or Are They? The Fresh Market went public (initial public offering, IPO) in November 2010 at about $32 per share. At the time it went public, The Fresh Market was the industry leader with one of the highest profit margins, rates of return, and growth rates in the grocery store industry. Its stock price almost doubled in 2012 and traded above $62 per share in November of 2012. In its 2012 10-K Report, The Fresh Market described its competitive strengths:

> **Competitive Strengths**
> We attribute our success in large part to the following competitive strengths:
> **Outstanding food quality, store environment and customer service.** We are dedicated to delivering a superior shopping experience that exceeds our customers' expectations . . .
> **Business well positioned for changing industry trends.** We believe that The Fresh Market is well positioned to capitalize on evolving consumer preferences and other trends currently shaping the food retail industry. . . .
> . . .
> **Scalable operations and replicable store model.** We believe that our infrastructure, including our management systems and distribution network, enables us to replicate our profitable store format and differentiated shopping experience. . . .

It turned out that The Fresh Market's competitors eventually were able to replicate and possibly even improve on The Fresh Market's business model and strategy. As a result of increased competition in 2013 and 2014, the company's profit margins and growth rates did not meet the market's expectations and by the end of 2014, The Fresh Market's stock price declined to around $41 per share. The company's performance continued to slip in 2015. In October 2015, the company began conducting a financial review of its strategic alternatives. Around this time, financial analysts were characterizing the company as facing a "competition pinch," consumers were finding high-quality food and organic produce at cheaper prices elsewhere. By the end of 2015, The Fresh Market's stock price declined to around $23.50 per share. In early 2016, the company was acquired by a private equity company at a premium relative to its stock price at that time, which was in the low $20 range but the offer price was well below The Fresh Market's initial offering price of $32 per share.

Source: The Fresh Market 2012 10-K Report and stock prices from the Center for Research in Security Prices, The University of Chicago.

Identifying the Source of Competitive Advantage

Managers often make statements about their companies' competitive advantage, but that does not mean the sources of competitive advantage are real or create value (see Valuation in Practice 2.5). While a company may have certain capabilities, those capabilities may not be unique, or competitors may have compensating capabilities (different capabilities that lead to similar outcomes). If so, the company would not have a competitive advantage. Once you identify a source of competitive advantage and understand the degree of competition in an industry, it is useful to test whether your initial view can be "observed in the data." We can observe a company's competitive advantage in its data in a variety of ways.

One way to identify a company's competitive advantage is by comparing the financial performance of the company to that of its competitors. If we identify a difference in the performance of the company, we then assess whether the difference is due to different accounting technique choices, different classifications of expenses between categories, or something else that would indicate that the differences are not real (the result of accounting differences or short-term effects). If we can conclude that the difference in performance is not the result of accounting differences or short-term effects, we then attempt to identify economic explanations for the difference.

What if we think a company has a competitive advantage but fail to see evidence of the competitive advantage in the data? In that case we must decide if (i) no competitive advantage actually exists, (ii) the competitive advantage, while real, is too small to be detected given the general imprecision and level of aggregation in financial statements, or (iii) management somehow obfuscates the effect of the competitive advantage because it does not want its competitors to see direct evidence of its success.

Assessing the Sustainability of Competitive Advantage

If we document a company's competitive advantage from its historical financial statements, we then assess the sustainability of that competitive advantage. Can a company's competitive advantage last in perpetuity? That is unlikely in a competitive industry, although as we explain in Chapter 6, depending on the discount rate and growth rate, 90% to almost 100% of a company's value is captured within the next 50–100 years of its life. The nature of competition and free markets is that competitors have incentives to eliminate any competitive disadvantage they are experiencing by either imitating another company's competitive advantage or creating a different but equal in value competitive advantage for themselves in a different manner. That said, some companies have been able to sustain competitive advantages for a long time.

We do not have a single way to assess the sustainability of a company's competitive advantage. Rather, we formulate questions to ask, collect as much information as reasonably possible, and then use our judgment to answer them. For example, we might ask: Is it a process or a technology that is patented and difficult to imitate in other ways? If so, how much longer does the patent last, and what is the likelihood that a similar outcome can be achieved through a different process or technology before then? Is the competitive advantage a long-term contract on an important raw material for production that guarantees a supply at a lower price? If so, what is the length of the contract, and could the competition utilize alternative materials with somewhat different manufacturing techniques to lower its costs? Is the competitive advantage a patent on a blockbuster drug? If so, how long will the patent last? Is the competitive advantage the result of a unique process in manufacturing or some support service such as procurement or distribution? If so, how obvious are the necessary capabilities that support that process, and how difficult would it be to replicate the capabilities required for that process?

Valuation Key 2.8

Valuing a company involves assessing a company's sources of competitive advantage and the sustainability of its competitive advantage. This analysis leads directly to an overall picture of the future profitability of the company being valued that will then be embedded in the forecasts.

Fort Howard Corporation

Fort Howard Corporation's (Fort Howard) competitive advantage was its ability to produce a commodity product (tissue paper, toilet paper, etc. for the commercial market) at a lower cost. For years, Fort Howard had a proprietary de-inking technology, which allowed it to use a greater proportion of recycled wastepaper in the production of commercial tissues. At one point, Fort Howard used 100% recycled fiber while major competitors such as Scott Paper, Inc. (Scott Paper) and James River Corporation used 15% and 10% recycled fiber, respectively. At that time, recycled wastepaper was approximately 20% of the cost of non-recycled pulp because most states had passed mandatory recycling laws, and there were relatively few good uses for recycled paper. In fact, Fort Howard created a division that collected recycled paper that gave the company a further cost advantage and allowed it to control the quality of the recycled fiber. Since the end-products were not differentiated in any meaningful way, Fort Howard was able to charge essentially the same prices as its competitors, and consequently enjoyed much higher margins because of its lower cost structure.

How might we have discovered Fort Howard's competitive advantage? Fort Howard continually disclosed in its 10-K that it had a proprietary de-inking technology. For example, it disclosed in one 10-K that, "The de-inking technology employed by the Company allows it to use a broad range of wastepaper grades, which effectively increases both the number of sources and the quantity of wastepaper available for its manufacturing process. The Company believes that its use of wastepaper for substantially all of its fiber requirements gives it a cost advantage over its competitors."[13] Of course, just indicating that it had a proprietary technology did not necessarily imply that the technology was a source of competitive advantage, nor did it quantify it. For example, other companies might have found other ways to achieve the same cost structure as Fort Howard. Analysts also discussed Fort Howard's superior technology and advantageous cost structure. Industry sources indicated the extent to which the tissue manufacturers relied on recycled paper in the manufacturing processes, and those sources corroborated management statements that Fort Howard was the leader in the use of recycled paper.

The Effect of Fort Howard's Competitive Advantage on Its Pricing Strategy. Where would we expect to observe Fort Howard's competitive advantage in its financial statements? Before we address that, first think about whether a cost advantage for Fort Howard would lead management to lower sales prices. Since commercial tissue is a commodity product, the sales price is essentially identical across manufacturers, and determined by industry capacity and demand. Fort Howard's management could have reduced its price in an effort to capture market share or drive out a weakly capitalized competitor. However, since Fort Howard was operating close to its capacity and did not have the resources to expand production facilities aggressively (in fact, it had capital expenditure constraints in its debt contracts), it had no reason to try to increase market share by cutting prices. By dropping prices, it would not capture all the benefits of its competitive advantage since it would have given some of those benefits to its consumers. At the time, Fort Howard had undergone an LBO, was highly levered, had to generate substantial cash flows to service that debt, and was in no position to engage in predatory pricing. Further, it faced competitors that were more strongly capitalized than it was. As such, Fort Howard had no incentive to cut price.

The Effect of Fort Howard's Competitive Advantage on Its Financial Ratios. Now let us think about where we might observe Fort Howard's competitive advantage in its financial statements. We would expect Fort Howard's ratio of cost of goods sold to sales to be lower than that of other companies in the commercial tissue business. Why? We believe we identified a source of competitive advantage that allowed Fort Howard to produce products more cheaply than its competitors were able to. We have no indication that Fort Howard's de-inking technology allowed it to produce more products with less production capacity, but there was some indication that Fort Howard's plants were more expensive, as it suggested in one 10-K: "The Company has invested heavily in its manufacturing operations. . . .the Company's annual capital spending program includes significant investments for the ongoing modernization of each of its mills. For example, as new de-inking technologies and converting equipment are developed, the Company adds such technology and equipment at each mill to maintain low cost structures."[14] If these

[13] See Fort Howard Corporation's 10-K for December 31, 1994, p. 7.

[14] See Fort Howard Corporation's 10-K for December 31, 1994, p. 6.

investments are large relative to those of its competitors, Fort Howard's EBIT margin might be reduced by additional depreciation, and we might expect to see its sales to total assets ratio to be somewhat lower than that of its competitors. Finally, nothing inherent in its strategy should have led to higher or lower selling, general, and administrative expenses (SG&A) relative to its competitors.

In Exhibit 2.7, we show various ratios for Fort Howard Corporation, Fort James Corporation (Fort James, which had been called James River Corporation up until Year 8 when it merged with Fort Howard), and Pope and Talbot, Inc. (Pope and Talbot) up to Year 9. We picked these two competitors because they are largely in the commercial tissue market, and Fort Howard's other competitors in the commercial tissue market also had significant operations in the consumer tissue market, which is not considered a commodity product.

EXHIBIT 2.7 Fort Howard Corporation, Fort James Corporation, and Pope and Talbot, Inc. Preliminary Financial Analysis

	Year 1	Year 2	Year 3	Year 4	Year 5	Year 6	Year 7	Year 8	Year 9
Cost of Goods Sold to Revenue									
Fort James Corporation	72.5%	71.5%	76.6%	75.3%	74.8%	70.2%	66.7%	63.1%	61.3%
Fort Howard Corporation	**52.7%**	**52.5%**	**56.0%**	**58.6%**	**60.5%**	**64.2%**	**53.3%**		
Pope and Talbot, Inc.	84.8%	89.4%	88.6%	83.5%	85.7%	88.8%	86.7%	81.9%	94.9%
EBIT Profit Margin (EBIT to Revenues)									
Fort James Corporation	8.1%	5.3%	1.0%	2.5%	3.1%	7.0%	7.8%	14.6%	15.9%
Fort Howard Corporation	**23.5%**	**23.8%**	**23.5%**	**22.2%**	**23.3%**	**22.2%**	**31.3%**		
Pope and Talbot, Inc.	6.1%	–0.2%	0.9%	7.2%	3.4%	–1.4%	2.1%	4.5%	–7.7%
Sales to Total Assets									
Fort James Corporation	0.94	0.80	0.79	0.76	0.79	0.90	0.82	1.02	0.94
Fort Howard Corporation	**0.30**	**0.32**	**0.33**	**0.45**	**0.77**	**0.97**	**0.97**		
Pope and Talbot, Inc.	1.59	1.43	1.52	1.52	1.33	1.04	1.02	0.84	1.02
Return on Assets (EBIT to Average Total Assets)									
Fort James Corporation	7.6%	4.3%	0.8%	1.9%	2.4%	6.3%	6.4%	14.8%	15.0%
Fort Howard Corporation	**7.1%**	**7.6%**	**7.7%**	**10.1%**	**17.8%**	**21.6%**	**30.3%**		
Pope and Talbot, Inc.	9.6%	–0.3%	1.3%	10.9%	4.4%	–1.5%	2.1%	3.8%	–7.8%

We first review the data through Year 7, the last year for which we have data for Fort Howard. By examining the ratio of cost of goods sold to revenue, we see that Fort Howard has substantially lower cost of goods sold relative to its competitors. It is possible that this is due to some differences in how the three companies classify their costs. An examination of Fort Howard's EBIT to revenue (EBIT profit margin) shows a substantial advantage for Fort Howard. Thus, the advantage in gross margins did not just result from a reclassification of expenses to other line items in the income statement, for the gross margin advantage translates all the way down to EBIT. In addition, this means that higher depreciation charges did not offset the cost advantage of using more recycled fiber. In its last year (Year 7), Fort Howard's EBIT margin is 31.3% relative to 7.8% for Fort James and 2.1% for Pope and Talbot.

An examination of Fort Howard's sales to total assets indicates that its turnover was much lower than that of its competitors until Year 5, likely due to more extensive investments in de-inking equipment and new capacity. However, by Year 6, Fort Howard's turnover ratio is similar to that of both Fort James and Pope and Talbot. Because of its higher EBIT margin, Fort Howard's EBIT return on assets is greater than that of the other two companies in every year except Year 1, when Fort Howard's asset turnover ratio was very low relative to that of the other two companies. By Year 5, Fort Howard's EBIT return on assets is far above the EBIT return on assets of both Fort James and Pope and Talbot. We focus on the EBIT return on assets, instead of the more typical return on assets, in order to remove the effect of some non-recurring charges that were taken by Fort Howard and some of the other companies, such as the write-off of goodwill.

The Sustainability of Fort Howard's Competitive Advantage. Suppose that we were valuing Fort Howard in Year 5, and we were interested in estimating how long Fort Howard's competitive advantage was likely to persist. To do this, we would attempt to understand the nature of its competitive advantage, its current position, and the position of its competitors. Fort Howard had undergone a leveraged buyout and was still highly levered in Year 5. Thus, it wasn't clear how much it could afford to spend on maintaining its competitive edge in the use of recycled paper. Moreover, Fort Howard faced well-capitalized competitors who were likely trying to develop improvements in their own processes for the efficient use of recycled paper.

Of course, an understanding of Fort Howard's technology and that of its competitors would allow us to make more informed judgments on the ability of Fort Howard's competitors to substantially improve their processes and reduce Fort Howard's cost advantage. Interestingly, the company relied on trade secret protection for its proprietary de-inking technology as opposed to seeking patent protection. One advantage of not filing a patent was that competitors were not able to observe how Fort Howard had achieved its superior usage of recycled fiber (and neither can we for purposes of analyzing the sustainability of Fort Howard's competitive advantage). Of course, there is always the danger that the trade secret will slip to the competition.

If the analysis concludes that the current source of competitive advantage is not sustainable, we estimate how long it will take the current advantage to dissipate and whether new sources of competitive advantage can be created by the company. If we believe that Fort Howard will lose its competitive advantage, you will then have to project the level of profitability that it will attain. One approach to the latter issue is to start by examining the level of profitability of other companies in the commercial tissue market. That margin, though much lower than Fort Howard's, is sufficient to keep those companies from exiting the industry, so it is a reasonable prediction of where Fort Howard's margin will wind up once its competitive advantage is eliminated. Interestingly enough, Fort Howard merged with James River in Year 8, and James River's margins improved immediately, suggesting that Fort Howard's competitive advantage was still largely intact at least through Year 9, the last year of data in the exhibit.

Nike, Inc.

Nike, Inc. (Nike) is famous for its athletic shoes and other athletic apparel. It performs market research and designs, markets, and distributes its athletic shoes; but, it outsources the manufacture and assembly of its shoes to companies in other countries. This is not unusual in the footwear industry. For example, Reebok International, Ltd. (Reebok) and Stride Rite Corporation (Stride Rite) have similar operating practices for the manufacture of their products. Lacrosse Footwear, Inc. (Lacrosse) had traditionally manufactured its products in the United States but was in the process of outsourcing the manufacturing overseas.

Nike spends a relatively large amount on endorsements and advertising relative to companies such as Lacrosse, Reebok, and Stride Rite in an attempt to differentiate its apparel and create a source of competitive advantage. If Nike's endorsements and advertising are a source of competitive advantage, where would we expect to see it in the financial statements? First, if it spends more, we should see that its ratio of advertising to revenue exceeds that of its competitors. To the extent that advertising allows it to differentiate its products from those of its competitors who spend relatively little, we should expect to see that Nike's gross margin is higher than that of its competitors. If it is not, then one has to wonder whether Nike gets any advantage from its extensive advertising and endorsements. Of course, we should expect Nike's selling, general, and administrative expenses to be higher since advertising is a component of that cost. Whether Nike's advertising and marketing creates any competitive advantage will depend on whether its bottom line profit margin exceeds that of its competitors after extra advertising and marketing costs are taken into consideration.

The Effect of Nike's Competitive Advantage on Its Financial Ratios. In Exhibit 2.8, we provide various ratios for Nike and its competitors over an eight-year history. Nike's ratio of advertising to revenue always exceeds 10%, whereas Nike's competitors' ratios are generally less than 6%. Thus, Nike does spend substantially more than its competitors on advertising. Does that allow Nike to achieve greater gross margins? An examination of the ratio of cost of goods sold to revenue indicates that Nike's cost of goods sold to revenue is lower than that of its competitors, so Nike's gross margins are greater. Interestingly, Nike's ratio of selling, general, and administrative expenses to revenue is not greater than that of its competitors in spite of the fact that this line item includes advertising. Thus, Nike is doing something to curtail non-advertising SG&A costs, and we would want to try to determine how that had been achieved. Some suggest that because the Nike campus (corporate headquarters) is such a great place to work, employees are willing to work for lower wages because of the environment.

EXHIBIT 2.8 Nike, Inc., Lacrosse Footwear, Inc., Reebok International, Inc., and Stride Rite Corporation Preliminary Financial Analysis

	Year 1	Year 2	Year 3	Year 4	Year 5	Year 6	Year 7	Year 8
Advertising to Revenue								
Lacrosse Footwear, Inc.	1.7%	1.5%	2.2%	2.3%	2.4%	1.7%	2.1%	2.1%
Nike, Inc.	**10.6%**	**11.8%**	**11.1%**	**10.9%**	**10.5%**	**10.4%**	**10.9%**	**11.2%**
Reebok International, Ltd.	5.8%	4.5%	4.4%	3.7%	3.8%	4.8%	4.2%	4.3%
Stride Rite Corporation	5.5%	5.5%	6.4%	6.5%	6.1%	5.7%	4.3%	4.8%
Cost of Goods Sold to Revenue								
Lacrosse Footwear, Inc.	69.5%	69.4%	71.0%	71.5%	71.7%	69.6%	70.4%	67.7%
Nike, Inc.	**58.4%**	**61.6%**	**60.3%**	**58.0%**	**58.9%**	**58.4%**	**56.8%**	**55.1%**
Reebok International, Ltd.	60.6%	61.9%	61.9%	60.2%	60.7%	62.1%	61.6%	60.7%
Stride Rite Corporation	63.7%	61.7%	62.0%	61.5%	61.6%	61.0%	60.7%	59.5%
Selling, General, & Admin Expenses to Revenue								
Lacrosse Footwear, Inc.	19.5%	19.0%	21.7%	25.3%	26.0%	26.8%	27.8%	27.3%
Nike, Inc.	**25.1%**	**27.5%**	**27.6%**	**29.0%**	**28.3%**	**28.5%**	**29.3%**	**30.1%**
Reebok International, Ltd.	30.6%	29.4%	32.4%	33.5%	31.9%	30.5%	30.5%	31.2%
Stride Rite Corporation	32.9%	30.4%	29.9%	29.1%	29.3%	30.4%	29.9%	31.1%
EBIT Profit Margin (EBIT to Revenues)								
Lacrosse Footwear, Inc.	8.3%	9.0%	4.2%	−0.3%	−0.6%	0.2%	−1.0%	3.5%
Nike, Inc.	**14.8%**	**8.8%**	**9.5%**	**10.7%**	**10.5%**	**10.6%**	**11.6%**	**12.6%**
Reebok International, Ltd.	7.6%	7.6%	4.4%	4.8%	5.8%	6.2%	6.9%	7.2%
Stride Rite Corporation	1.2%	6.0%	6.4%	7.7%	6.9%	5.9%	6.5%	7.0%
Return on Assets (EBIT to Average Total Assets)								
Lacrosse Footwear, Inc.	12.1%	13.6%	5.6%	−0.4%	−0.8%	0.3%	−1.4%	5.8%
Nike, Inc.	**29.2%**	**15.7%**	**15.7%**	**17.4%**	**17.1%**	**17.2%**	**18.9%**	**21.2%**
Reebok International, Ltd.	15.4%	15.6%	8.0%	8.4%	10.9%	12.3%	12.7%	13.0%
Stride Rite Corporation	1.5%	8.8%	10.2%	12.9%	10.8%	8.9%	10.1%	11.4%

Not surprisingly, given the above we see that Nike's EBIT profit margins (operating income after depreciation to revenue) are consistently above the competition, indicating that Nike does have some competitive advantage. Finally, Nike's return on assets consistently exceeds the return on assets of the competition by a wide margin. Thus, Nike's competitive advantage is readily observable in its financial statements. Nike's performance has continued at the same pace relative to its competition through its Year 8 fiscal year. While Adidas Group did not file financial statements at the time of the analysis above, it does now, and Nike's return on assets is larger than that of Adidas, which has a relatively similar strategy (Adidas Group now owns Reebok).

2.16 IMPLEMENTATION AND MEASUREMENT ISSUES

LO6 Properly measure financial ratios

The selection of the specific methods used to measure financial ratios depends on why we are analyzing a company. The inputs, and even the specific formula used, can differ in different contexts. Regardless of the specific purpose of our analysis, we typically face certain measurement issues, which is the topic we discuss in this section of the chapter.

Some Basic Measurement Rules

Below, we list some basic measurement rules to follow when developing financial ratio formulas and measuring financial ratios. We refer to "flow" and "stock" variables in our discussion. A **flow variable** represents items on the income statement or cash flow statement. A **stock variable** is a value at a specific time, a balance, such as the items on the balance sheet.

- Flow divided by a flow—divide the most recent flow by the most recent flow. Some financial ratios that fall under this rule are profit margin (but not rate of return on assets or rate of return on equity), coverage of fixed cost (earnings before interest and taxes to interest), and expense ratios (cost of goods sold to sales).

- Stock divided by a stock—use the ending balances (adjusted for seasonality, see below). Relations that fall under this rule are liquidity ratios (current assets to current liabilities) and financial leverage ratios (total debt to equity).
- Flow divided by a stock or a stock divided by a flow—we generally use the most recent flow and the average stock (seasonally adjusted when appropriate). Relations that fall under this rule are rate of return on assets and rate of return on equity. In certain situations, it may be more appropriate to use ending stock balances. For example, we sometimes do this with working capital management ratios (receivables, inventory, and payables).

Seasonality

Some businesses are seasonal in nature; for example, many types of retailers experience most of their sales in the fourth quarter. The cash position of such companies tends to be highest in January and lowest in October, whereas their inventories and short-term debt balances tend to be highest in October and lowest in January. Consequently, many retailers choose a fiscal year-end near the end of January. Thus, using fiscal year-end balances can result in misleading financial ratios depending on the ratio and how it is used. One way to address this issue is to use the average quarterly (or even monthly) balance instead of the ending annual balance. This approach better reflects the average balance of certain balance sheet items over the year. For example, Ford provides monthly revenue data in its annual reports that could be used to make such adjustments.

Quarterly Data

We might be tempted to analyze financial ratios calculated on a quarterly basis—that is, calculate the return on assets, profit margin, turnover ratios, and so forth for each fiscal quarter. This approach does not always work well. Quarter-end balances for both flow and stock variables can be seasonal, which can distort the financial ratios. That is why we typically construct annual data from the last four quarters—usually called **last twelve months (LTM)** or **trailing twelve months (TTM)**. Of course, when making comparisons between companies in the same industry for particular quarters, the use of quarterly data may be appropriate.

Different Fiscal Year-ends

When we compare a company's financial ratios over time, the ratios may be misleading if a company changes its fiscal year-end during our analysis period. Similarly, when comparing a company's financial ratios to the ratios of its comparable companies, the ratio comparisons may be misleading if we are using annual financial statement data and the companies have different fiscal year-ends. Fortunately, we do not observe these issues very frequently. Companies rarely change their fiscal year-ends. In addition, companies in the same industry tend to cluster to a specific fiscal year-end due to industry factors. For example, as we noted earlier, most retail stores in the U.S. use January 31 as their fiscal year-end as opposed to December 31.

Adjusting the Data for Influential Observations (Outliers)

An **outlier** or **influential observation** is an unusual observation that appears to be outside the distribution of other observations. If the observation is truly an outlier, in that it is not part of the distribution of other observations, then using it can be misleading. Sometimes, an outlier is a data error, and sometimes it occurs because the denominator is close to zero; sometimes, however, it is the result of real economic effects.

What do you do with an outlier? First, identify whether it is a data error; if it is, correct it or exclude it if you cannot correct it. Second, identify potential economic rationales for why you should exclude it from your analysis or how you might adjust it to use in your analysis. For example, a company with a stock price of $10 and earnings per share of $0.01 has a price-to-earnings (P/E) ratio of 1,000. We know that a P/E ratio of 1,000 is likely an outlier. We would analyze this issue by assessing the reason for the company's earnings per share of $0.01; for example, ascertain if it is the result of a one-time or non-recurring effect. If it is, then we know that the P/E of 1,000 is merely an artifact of a non-recurring item and not a representative P/E ratio. In this case, we might consider adjusting the P/E ratio by adjusting the earnings for the non-recurring item or by using another definition of earnings that is not affected by the non-recurring item.

Other ways we might address a potential outlier issue include the following. If we are going to use a measure of central tendency or a range of representative values as benchmarks, we might use statistics that are less influenced by outliers (for example, use the median instead of the mean). We can also exclude a certain number or percentage of the observations from each tail of the distribution, called **trimming the distribution**. We can also set a certain number or percentage of the observations in each tail of the distribution at a "reasonable" value, called, **winsorizing the distribution**. Although beyond our discussion, we can also use statistical methods to identify outliers.

Negative Denominators

A negative denominator usually results in a misleading or meaningless financial ratio. For example, a company with negative shareholders' equity of −\$100 and an earnings to common of \$10 will have a negative return on equity of −10% (−0.1 = \$10/−\$100), which is not a meaningful number. Sometimes it is possible to substitute a denominator that does not have a negative value or to invert a ratio to avoid a negative denominator. For example, if we invert a price-to-earnings ratio, the resulting earnings-to-price ratio can never have a negative denominator.

Inflation Adjustments

Naturally, inflation adjustments tend to be less important if inflation is low during the time period analyzed. For a single year, these adjustments are also less important for "flow to flow" ratios because flow variables tend to be similarly affected by inflation. However, even this statement is not correct when one of the flow variables contains depreciation and amortization expenses, because the underlying asset accounts are typically composed of assets purchased in the more distant past. Inflation adjustments are more important for "flow to stock" or "stock to flow" ratios; this is especially important when either the numerator or denominator of a financial ratio is not measured in dollars. For example, examining a time-series of revenues per square foot of retail space or of revenues per employee is more influenced by inflation, because one of the inputs (square feet or number of employees) is not affected by inflation at all.

One of the difficulties in adjusting financial ratios for inflation is the difficulty of identifying the appropriate adjustment factor or inflation index. For example, a computer manufacturer might be experiencing decreasing costs for some raw materials but increasing costs for others. Thus, in many circumstances, an overall inflation index, like the consumer price index, may not be the best way to adjust all of the numbers. As a result, many analysts do not make inflation adjustments in their analyses unless the company is experiencing very high rates of inflation. For example, inflation in Venezuela was over 1,000% in 2017 and the year-on-year inflation rate for April of 2018 was over 13,000%.

The Role of Accounting

The analysis of financial statements obviously relies on financial statement information. As such, expertise in financial statement analysis requires a thorough understanding of the economics of the transactions that parties are engaged in and how the accounting system records those transactions. That is why understanding financial disclosures and generally accepted accounting principles is an important part of any financial analysis.

Generally accepted accounting principles are continually evolving in the United States and throughout the world. Knowledge of changes in generally accepted accounting principles can be important for conducting financial statement analysis. For example, some companies engage in a variety of ways to obtain financing that is not disclosed directly on the balance sheet, called **off-balance-sheet financing**. Standard setting bodies, such as the Financial Accounting Standards Board, respond to these strategies and change accounting principles in an attempt to improve the quality of disclosures. However, the process is never ending, for companies respond to changes in accounting policies with new types of transactions.

Because accounting principles vary from country to country, understanding accounting principles becomes more complicated when using the financial statements of companies in different countries. Apparent differences between two companies from different countries may be driven by differences in accounting principles in the two countries. The good news is that the International Accounting Standards Board

(IASB) is in the process of creating a set of accounting standards called the International Financial Reporting Standards (IFRS). Many countries have adopted IFRS, and many other countries have committed to adopt them in the next few years. At this time, the U.S. has not adopted IFRS and continues to promulgate its own standards through the Financial Accounting Standards Board (FASB). The bad news is that we still observe significant differences in the properties of accounting numbers across countries even when the standards are identical, due to differences in institutions, regulations, monitoring, enforcement, and legal systems. Thus, the properties of accounting numbers across countries are unlikely to ever be the same, even if the standards being used are identical.[15]

"Quality" of the Financial Disclosures

One dimension of the quality of a financial disclosure is its detail and transparency so that the reader can readily understand the economics underpinning it. Another dimension of the quality of a financial disclosure is how well it represents economic reality. As part of a financial analysis, we can assess whether the company tends to choose income-increasing or income-decreasing accounting policies or a mixture of both. Examples of more conservative accounting policy choices include capitalizing rather than expensing leases, expensing rather than capitalizing operating expenses, and consolidating special-purpose entities. We can examine the difference between a company's accounting earnings and its operating cash flows in order to assess a company's accruals. We can even consider the manager's reputation for being either aggressive or conservative, and we consider whether the company structured certain transactions to achieve a "beneficial" accounting treatment.

We might also assess how transparent the company's disclosures are. Do they provide detailed discussions in the management discussion and analysis (MD&A) section of the 10-K? What about in conference calls on the business, the competition, or the company's strategy? Do they appear to obfuscate? Some analysts and researchers run linguistic programs on the MD&A and on the Q&A of conference calls in order to assess how forthcoming management is. Are the segment disclosures useful? Do they provide management forecasts? A company that is more forthcoming in these disclosures is generally consistent with higher overall accounting quality. However, we must keep in mind that management cannot disclose all of its strategy and tactical plans because disclosing it to investors also entails disclosing it to competitors. Thus, management has to make tradeoffs between informing investors and disclosing proprietary information to competitors. One size does not fit all companies.

Accounting Rates of Return Do Not Equal Economic Rates of Return

Throughout the book we attempt to use accounting rates of return to assess economic rates of return; however, evaluating the economic rate of return on existing investments is difficult and often not possible, for we cannot observe a company's actual economic rate of return using accounting data. While we can observe the accounting-based rates of return historically and often in forecasts, which is informative, these rates of return do not equal the economic rate of return on capital. That said, although accounting-based rates of return do not measure a company's actual economic return, empirical evidence indicates that a company's accounting-based rates of return are correlated with its market-based rates of return.

Accounting rates of return do not equal economic rates of return for several reasons. For example, the income and investment base used in calculating accounting rates of return do not represent the economic income and economic investment base underpinning a company's economic rate of return. Accounting book values are largely based on historical costs and not current values, which partially explains the difference between the accounting and economic measurement of the denominator. In addition, expenditures for investments in brand development or company-developed intellectual property, as well as its organizational infrastructure (for example, existing distribution systems and channels), and its human capital, are generally expensed and thus reduce accounting book values. In effect, the accounting system does not treat these expenditures as part of a company's invested capital; however, these investments undoubtedly create value for many companies and the market value of those companies reflects these values. Because of the potential differences between accounting rates of return and the unobservable true economic rate

[15] See Ball, R., A. Robin, and J. Wu, "Incentives Versus Standards: Properties of Accounting Income in Four East Asian Countries," *Journal of Accounting and Economics* (December 2003), pp. 235–270, and Holthausen, R., "Testing the Relative Power of Accounting Standards Versus Incentives and Other Institutional Features to Influence the Outcome of Financial Reporting in an International Setting," *Journal of Accounting and Economics* (December 2003), pp. 271–284.

of return, meaningful comparisons between a company's accounting returns and its cost of capital are often difficult to make. This is why we often use comparable companies to assess the reasonableness of the forecasts, which we discuss in Chapter 4.

Valuation Key 2.9

Understanding a company's accounting choices and policies, as well as the thoroughness of its financial disclosures, is a useful part of the financial analysis of a company.

SUMMARY AND KEY CONCEPTS

We use financial statement relations (financial ratios) in an attempt to measure certain economic concepts, such as a company's performance, operating risk, financial risk, growth, efficiency, and asset utilization. We analyze a company relative to both itself over time (time-series analysis) and other companies (cross-sectional analysis). To measure financial ratios, we divide a number from a company's financial statements by a number that adjusts the numerator for differences in size or scale. For example, we divide operating income by revenues to calculate a company's profit margin.

We use financial ratios in many ways in valuation—to assess the degree of comparability of potential comparable companies, to measure a company's cost of capital, to drive financial forecasts, to evaluate financial forecasts, and to establish constraints or hurdles in contracts. When measuring a company's financial ratios, we address various measurement issues that may arise for a company and for a specific use.

ADDITIONAL READING AND REFERENCES

Ball, R., and P. Brown, "An Empirical Evaluation of Accounting Income Numbers," *Journal of Accounting Research* (Autumn 1968), pp. 159–178.

Beaver, W., P. Kettler, and M. Scholes, "The Association Between Market-Determined and Accounting-Determined Risk Measures," *Accounting Review* (1970), pp. 654–682.

Fisher, F., and J. McGowan, "On the Misuse of Accounting Rates of Return to Infer Monopoly Profits," *American Economic Review* 73 (1983), pp. 82–97.

EXERCISES AND PROBLEMS

P2.1 **Rates of Return Ratios—Cisco Systems, Inc.**: Review the time-series of various rates of return and rates of return components for Cisco Systems, Inc. in Exhibit P2.1. (Cisco manufactures and sells networking and communications products worldwide. It sells its products and services through its direct sales force, distributors, and retail partners.)

a. Discuss the change in the return on assets during this period using its components.

b. Discuss the change in the return on equity during this period using its components.

c. Why are the unlevered and levered profit margins the same in all years, whereas the leverage ratios (as measured by total assets to common equity) are not equal to each other in any year?

EXHIBIT P2.1 Rates of Return and Components for Cisco Systems, Inc.

CISCO Systems, Inc.	Year 1	Year 2	Year 3	Year 4	Year 5	Year 6	Year 7	Year 8	Year 9	Year 10
Return on assets	30.0%	33.9%	23.1%	18.8%	17.7%	11.2%	−3.0%	5.2%	9.6%	13.7%
Return on equity	37.8%	43.5%	29.5%	23.7%	22.3%	14.0%	−3.8%	6.8%	12.6%	18.4%
Unlevered profit margin	21.3%	22.3%	16.3%	16.0%	17.2%	14.1%	−4.5%	10.0%	19.0%	22.5%
Levered profit margin	21.3%	22.3%	16.3%	16.0%	17.2%	14.1%	−4.5%	10.0%	19.0%	22.5%
Revenue to average total assets	1.41	1.52	1.42	1.18	1.03	0.80	0.65	0.52	0.50	0.61
Total assets to common equity	1.26	1.28	1.28	1.26	1.26	1.25	1.27	1.31	1.32	1.35

P2.2 **Rates of Return Ratios—The Sherwin-Williams Company**: Review the time-series of various rates of return and rates of return components for the Sherwin-Williams Company in Exhibit P2.2. (Sherwin-Williams manufactures, distributes, and sells coatings and related products in North America and South America. It operates four segments: paint stores, consumer, automotive finishes, and international coatings.)

a. Discuss the change in the return on assets in the time-series using its components.
b. Discuss the change in the return on equity in the time-series using its components.
c. Why does the return on equity increase much more than the return on assets during this time period?
d. Why is the return on equity less than the return on assets in Year 6?

EXHIBIT P2.2 Rates of Return and Components for the Sherwin-Williams Company

Sherwin-Williams Company	Year 1	Year 2	Year 3	Year 4	Year 5	Year 6	Year 7	Year 8	Year 9	Year 10
Return on assets	9.9%	9.5%	8.8%	7.8%	8.4%	1.4%	8.1%	9.5%	10.0%	10.6%
Return on equity	17.7%	17.5%	17.4%	16.5%	17.8%	1.0%	17.8%	22.0%	23.7%	25.3%
ROE to ROA	1.80	1.84	1.97	2.10	2.11	0.74	2.21	2.31	2.37	2.39
Unlevered profit margin	6.2%	5.9%	6.3%	6.4%	6.8%	1.0%	5.9%	6.5%	6.6%	6.9%
Levered profit margin	6.1%	5.5%	5.3%	5.5%	6.1%	0.3%	5.2%	6.0%	6.1%	6.4%
Revenue to average total assets	1.60	1.61	1.39	1.22	1.23	1.34	1.37	1.47	1.52	1.54
Total assets to common equity	1.81	1.97	2.35	2.45	2.38	2.46	2.49	2.50	2.54	2.56

P2.3 **Working Capital Management Ratios—Dell Inc.**: Review the time-series of various working capital management ratios for Dell Inc. (formerly Dell Computer Corporation) in Exhibit P2.3. (Dell designs, develops, manufactures, and sells computer systems and services around the world.)

a. Discuss the change in Dell's current and quick ratios over the time-series. Is this change "good" or "bad" for Dell? In other words, should Dell try to reverse the trend in its time-series of current and quick ratios?
b. Using Dell's component ratios, discuss the change in Dell's trade cash cycle over the time-series.

EXHIBIT P2.3 Working Capital Management Ratios for Dell Inc.

Dell Inc.	Year 1	Year 2	Year 3	Year 4	Year 5	Year 6	Year 7	Year 8	Year 9	Year 10
Current assets to current liabilities	2.1	1.7	1.5	1.7	1.5	1.5	1.1	1.0	1.0	1.2
Quick ratio	1.5	1.4	1.2	1.5	1.3	1.3	0.8	0.8	0.8	1.0
Days of sales held in inventory	31.4	20.5	9.3	6.6	6.1	5.7	4.9	6.4	7.8	5.4
Accounts receivable collection period	43.6	38.3	35.4	39.7	37.3	31.9	30.2	25.0	27.4	29.9
Accounts payable payment period	38.5	46.8	51.4	52.4	54.1	56.6	67.5	68.9	72.2	74.7
Trade cash cycle	36.5	12.0	–6.8	–6.1	–10.8	–19.0	–32.4	–37.5	–37.0	–39.5

P2.4 **Working Capital Management Ratios—Water Pik Technologies, Inc.**: Review the time-series of various working capital management ratios for Water Pik Technologies, Inc. in Exhibit P2.4. (Water Pik designs, manufactures, and sells personal health care products, swimming pool products, and water heating systems.)

a. Discuss the change in Water Pik's current and quick ratios over the time-series. Is this change "good" or "bad" for Water Pik? In other words, should Water Pik try to reverse the trend in its time-series of current and quick ratios?
b. Using Water Pik's component ratios, discuss the change in Water Pik's trade cash cycle over the time-series.

EXHIBIT P2.4 Working Capital Management Ratios for Water Pik Technologies, Inc.

Water Pik Technologies, Inc.	Year 1	Year 2	Year 3	Year 4	Year 5	Year 6
Current assets to current liabilities	1.8	1.8	2.1	2.3	2.4	2.0
Quick ratio	1.1	1.1	1.4	1.4	1.5	1.1
Days of sales held in inventory	55.8	59.2	67.7	69.3	69.6	91.2
Accounts receivable collection period	74.5	74.0	88.2	98.9	98.4	104.6
Accounts payable payment period	55.4	51.3	49.0	43.9	41.3	52.6
Trade cash cycle	74.9	81.9	106.9	124.3	126.7	143.3

P2.5 **Financial Leverage Ratios—Samsonite Corporation**: Review the time-series of various financial leverage and coverage ratios for Samsonite Corporation in Exhibit P2.5. (Samsonite designs, develops, manufactures, and sells luggage and travel-related consumer products.)

a. Discuss the change in Samsonite's financial leverage and coverage ratios over the time-series.

b. Using its financial leverage and coverage ratios, discuss what you know about its common equity.

c. Which is larger—interest expense or preferred stock dividends—for each year in the time series? (Assume that an income tax rate of zero was used to measure the financial ratios.)

EXHIBIT P2.5 Financial Leverage and Coverage Ratios for Samsonite Corporation

Samsonite Corporation	Year 1	Year 2	Year 3	Year 4	Year 5	Year 6	Year 7	Year 8	Year 9
Total debt to total assets	0.5	0.5	0.3	0.8	0.8	0.8	0.9	0.7	0.7
Preferred stock to total assets	0.0	0.0	0.0	0.3	0.4	0.4	0.5	0.6	0.3
Total debt to common equity	12.7	10.8	0.9	NMF	NMF	NMF	NMF	NMF	NMF
Preferred stock to common equity.	0.0	0.0	0.0	NMF	NMF	NMF	NMF	NMF	NMF
EBIT coverage (interest only)	−0.2	0.7	3.6	0.5	1.1	1.2	0.9	1.5	1.7
EBIT coverage (interest + preferred stock dividends).	−0.2	0.7	3.6	0.4	0.7	0.7	0.5	0.8	1.0

"NMF" = not a meaningful figure

P2.6 **Capital Structure Transactions and Rates of Return Ratios—Jake and Luke Schnall Company:** Use the financial statements in Exhibit P2.6 to calculate the return on assets, return on equity, and their respective top-level components (unlevered profit margin, asset utilization, earnings leverage factor, and financial leverage factor) for the Jake and Luke Schnall Company for Year 10. In addition, for each of the events described below, recalculate the return on assets, return on equity, and their respective components assuming the event occurred at the end of Year 9. Assume that the company distributes an annual dividend to common shareholders equal to net income minus any dividends distributed to preferred stockholders.

a. The company issues additional debt at its current interest rate to fund capital expenditures and raise the working capital necessary to grow the company by 50 percent in Year 10; the new investment will earn an ROA equal to the company's current ROA.

b. Same information as part (a) except the company issues additional preferred stock instead of debt.

c. Same information as part (a) except the company issues additional common stock instead of debt.

d. The company issues additional debt at its current interest rate to repurchase 10 percent of the company's common stock at a price equal to two times its book value.

e. The company refinances all of its existing debt and issues debt in a highly levered transaction. Its new interest rate is 2 percent higher than its previous interest rate. It used the cash proceeds from the debt issuance to repurchase 55 percent of the company's common stock at a price equal to two times its book value.

f. The company issues additional common stock to repurchase all of the existing debt and preferred stock at book value with no taxable gains or losses on the debt.

g. The company sells 20 percent of its business (operating assets and liabilities) at book value with no taxable gain or loss. The sale of the business reduces the company's revenue and all operating expenses by 10 percent. The company uses the cash flow from the sale to redeem debt at book value with no taxable gains or losses on the debt.

h. The company sells 20 percent of its business (operating assets and liabilities) at book value with no taxable gain or loss. The sale of the business reduces the company's revenue and all operating expenses by 10 percent. The company uses the cash flow from the sale to repurchase some of the company's common stock.

EXHIBIT P2.6 Financial Statements for the Jake and Luke Schnall Company

Income Statement ($ in millions)	Rate	Year 10
Operating revenue		$ 5,000
Operating expenses		1,750
Operating income (EBIT)		$ 3,250
Interest expense	7.0%	263
Income before income tax expense (EBT)		$ 2,988
Income tax expense (benefit)	40.0%	1,195
Net income		$ 1,793

Common Equity Balance	Rate	Year 10
Beginning balance		$ 4,875
Net income		1,793
Preferred stock dividends	8.0%	−150
Dividends		−1,643
Ending balance		$ 4,875

Balance Sheet ($ in millions)	Year 9	Year 10
Total current assets	$ 2,500	$ 2,500
Property, plant, and equipment, net	10,000	10,000
Total assets with excess assets	$12,500	$12,500
Total current liabilities	$ 2,000	$ 2,000
Total debt	3,750	3,750
Total liabilities	$ 5,750	$ 5,750
Preferred stock	$ 1,875	$ 1,875
Common stock (equity)	4,875	4,875
Total stockholders' equity	$ 6,750	$ 6,750
Total liabilities and stockholders' equity	$12,500	$12,500

P2.7 **Financial Ratios and Financial Statements—Nate and Evelyn Z's Furniture Company:** Exhibit P2.7 presents certain rates of return, profit margins, and other information on the Nate and Evelyn Z's Furniture Company. Using the information in the exhibit, complete the partial financial statements and calculate the missing financial ratios (shown as "?-#") in Exhibit P2.7. (All financial ratios using balance sheet numbers were calculated using Year 12 ending balances instead of average balances.)

EXHIBIT P2.7 Nate and Evelyn Z's Furniture Company

Income Statement ($ in millions)	Year 12	Financial Ratios	Year 12
Operating revenue	$30,000	Return on assets	17.5%
Operating expenses	?-1	Return on investment	19.4%
Operating income (EBIT)	?-2	Return on equity	?-13
Interest expense	?-3	Unlevered profit margin	14.0%
Income before income tax expense (EBT)	?-4	Total asset utilization (turnover)	?-14
Income tax expense (benefit)	?-5	Levered profit margin (to common)	10.8%
Net income	?-6	Financial leverage factor	2.938

Balance Sheet ($ in millions)	Year 12	Other Information	Year 12
Total assets with excess assets	?-7	Constant income tax rate	30.0%
		Preferred stock dividend rate	9.0%
Total current liabilities	?-8	Change in preferred stock at end of Year 12	$1,000
Total debt	?-9	Preferred stock dividends	$432
Preferred stock	?-10		
Common stock (equity)	?-11		
Total liabilities and stockholders' equity	?-12		

P2.8 **Financial Ratios and Financial Statements—Jeff, Matt and Mike Associates:** You are an analyst and have certain rates of return, profit margins, and other information on the Jeff, Matt, and Mike Associates company. Using the information in Exhibit P2.8, complete the partial financial statements and calculate the missing financial ratios (shown as "?-#") in the exhibit. The company had no purchases or other additions to Intangible Assets. (All financial ratios using balance sheet numbers are calculated using Year 7 ending balances instead of average balances. The company had no sales or retirements of property, plant, and equipment or intangible assets. Essentially all of the company's property, plant, and equipment is depreciable. All changes in financing occur at the end of the fiscal year.)

EXHIBIT P2.8 Financial Statements for Jeff, Matt, and Mike Associates

Income Statement ($ in millions)	Year 7	Other Information	Year 7
Operating revenue	?-1	Income tax rate	30.0%
Cost of goods sold	?-2	Preferred stock dividend rate	9.0%
Selling, general and administrative	?-3	Change in preferred stock	$ 1,000
Depreciation and amortization (All)	?-4	Retained earnings—beginning balance	$ 4,400
Operating income (EBIT)	?-5	Inventory purchases	$12,400
Interest expense	?-6	Capital expenditures (PPEQ)	$15,000
		Beginning of year balance—intangible assets	$ 2,500
Income before income tax expense (EBT)	?-7	Common dividends	$ 3,014
Income tax expense (benefit)	?-8		
Net income	?-9		

Balance Sheet ($ in millions)	Year 7	Financial Ratios (Based on Ending Balances)	Year 7
Cash	?-10	Cost of goods sold expense ratio	28.571%
Accounts receivable	?-11	Selling, general and administrative expense ratio	33.333%
Inventory	?-12	Total liabilities to total assets	0.546
Current assets	?-13	EBITDA to interest	8.000
		EBITDA to fixed charges	4.776
Property, plant and equipment—gross (PPEQ)	?-14	Quick (asset test) ratio	1.531
Accumulated depreciation	?-15	Days of inventory held	133.833
Property, plant and equipment—net	?-16	Accounts receivable collection period	32.776
		Trade cash cycle	103.028
Intangible assets	?-17	Provision for bad debts ratio	4.546%
Total assets with excess assets	?-18	Depreciable life of gross plant	12.500
		Depreciable life of net plant	8.500
		PPEQ investment (CAPEX) to revenues	35.714%
Accounts payable	?-19	PPEQ investment (CAPEX) to depreciation	2.500
Accruals	?-20		
Total current liabilities	$ 3,070	Earnings per share (EPS)—basic	$4.375
Total debt	?-21	Shares outstanding for basic EPS	984.0
Total liabilities	?-22		
Preferred stock	?-23		
Common stock—paid-in-capital	?-24		
Retained earnings	?-25		
Shareholders' equity	?-26		
Total liabilities and stockholders' equity	?-27		

P2.9 **Rates of Return Ratios—Main Street Restaurant Group:** A young analyst was asked to measure the return on assets and return on equity for *the operations* of the Main Street Restaurant Group by using the abbreviated balance sheets and income statements that appear in Exhibit P2.9. (The company operates TGI Friday's and other restaurants.) Based on this information, the analyst calculated the rates of return using the following formulas

$$\text{Return on Assets} = \frac{\text{Net Income} + (1 - \text{Average Tax Rate}) \times \text{Interest Expense}}{\text{Average Total Assets}}$$

$$\text{Return on Equity} = \frac{\text{Net Income}}{\text{Average Common Equity}}$$

a. Comment on the formulas the analyst used to measure the rates of return on the company's operations shown in the exhibit.

b. Using the information in the exhibit, correctly calculate the return on assets and return on equity for the company's operations, for each year for which you have data available.

c. Calculate the components of the correctly calculated return on assets and return on equity for each year for which you have data available.

EXHIBIT P2.9 Abbreviated Balance Sheets and Income Statements for the Main Street Restaurant Group

Main Street Restaurant Group

Balance Sheet (Abbreviated)	Year 1	Year 2	Year 3	Year 4	Year 5	Year 6
Current assets	$ 8.56	$ 13.20	$ 15.82	$ 12.55	$ 9.83	$ 10.04
Plant, property & equip (net)	58.00	63.85	65.23	71.27	68.13	66.45
Other assets	19.96	31.20	31.42	28.58	28.25	26.69
Total assets	$ 86.52	$108.25	$112.47	$112.40	$106.21	$103.18
Total current liabilities	$ 25.22	$ 20.89	$ 23.81	$ 27.58	$ 26.80	$ 29.74
Long term debt	31.51	44.40	47.23	52.00	47.87	42.23
Other liabilities	2.41	2.47	1.22	3.21	2.44	1.92
Total liabilities	$ 59.14	$ 67.76	$ 72.26	$ 82.79	$ 77.11	$ 73.89
Common stock	$ 44.20	$ 53.63	$ 53.66	$ 53.94	$ 54.95	$ 54.95
Retained earnings	–16.82	–13.14	–13.45	–24.33	–25.85	–25.66
Treasury stock	0.00	0.00	0.00	0.00	0.00	0.00
Common equity (total)	$ 27.38	$ 40.49	$ 40.21	$ 29.61	$ 29.10	$ 29.29
Liabilities and shareholders' equity	$ 86.52	$108.25	$112.47	$112.40	$106.21	$103.18
Debt in current liabilities	$ 1.83	$ 2.01	$ 3.01	$ 3.50	$ 3.82	$ 3.85
Average income tax rate	35.0%	35.0%	35.0%	35.0%	35.0%	35.0%
Closing stock price	$ 3.25	$ 3.03	$ 4.94	$ 2.12	$ 2.86	$ 1.60
Common dividends	$ 0.00	$ 0.00	$ 0.00	$ 0.00	$ 0.00	$ 0.00

Main Street Restaurant Group

Income Statement (Abbreviated)	Year 1	Year 2	Year 3	Year 4	Year 5	Year 6
Sales (net)	$141.16	$187.15	$214.26	$229.15	$227.49	$224.75
Cost of goods sold	121.29	161.65	184.86	194.79	200.79	199.75
Gross profit	$ 19.87	$ 25.50	$ 29.40	$ 34.36	$ 26.70	$ 25.00
Selling, general, & admin expenses	9.93	11.15	11.20	12.39	10.08	9.52
Depreciation, depletion, & amortiz	5.65	8.49	9.68	8.36	8.99	8.87
Operating income	$ 4.29	$ 5.86	$ 8.52	$ 13.61	$ 7.63	$ 6.61
Interest expense	2.60	3.62	3.83	3.90	4.52	3.97
Minority interest in income	0.00	0.00	0.00	0.00	0.00	0.00
Non-operating income (expenses)	–0.49	1.69	–3.45	–7.99	–2.08	–1.69
Pretax income	$ 1.20	$ 3.93	$ 1.24	$ 1.72	$ 1.03	$ 0.95
Income taxes	0.42	1.38	0.43	0.60	0.36	0.33
Income before extraordinary items & discontinued oper	$ 0.78	$ 2.55	$ 0.81	$ 1.12	$ 0.67	$ 0.62
Extraordinary items and discontinued operations	–0.17	–0.02	0.00	0.00	0.00	0.00
Net income	$ 0.61	$ 2.53	$ 0.81	$ 1.12	$ 0.67	$ 0.62

SOLUTIONS FOR REVIEW EXERCISES

Solution for Review Exercise 2.1: The Gap, Inc. Return on Assets Year +1 and Beyond

Return on Assets	Year 0	Year +1	Year +2	Year +3	Year +4	Year +5	Year +6
Return on assets	16.0%	18.4%	19.9%	20.9%	21.7%	21.8%	21.9%
Unlevered profit margin	8.2%	8.4%	8.5%	8.5%	8.5%	8.5%	8.5%
Total asset utilization (turnover)	1.95	2.19	2.33	2.45	2.54	2.56	2.57
Return on assets (check)	16.0%	18.4%	19.9%	20.9%	21.7%	21.8%	21.9%

Solution for Review Exercise 2.2: The Gap, Inc. Expense Ratio Forecasts for Year +1 and Beyond

Expense Ratios (to Revenue)	Year 0	Year +1	Year +2	Year +3	Year +4	Year +5	Year +6
Cost of goods sold	55.4%	54.7%	54.6%	54.6%	54.6%	54.6%	54.6%
Gross margin	44.6%	45.3%	45.4%	45.4%	45.4%	45.4%	45.4%
Depreciation and amortization	4.4%	4.4%	4.4%	4.4%	4.4%	4.4%	4.4%
Operating expense	26.7%	27.1%	27.0%	27.0%	27.0%	27.0%	27.0%
Operating income	13.4%	13.7%	13.9%	13.9%	13.9%	13.9%	13.9%
Interest expense	0.0%	0.0%	0.0%	0.0%	0.0%	0.0%	0.0%
Other income (expense), net	0.1%	0.1%	0.1%	0.1%	0.1%	0.1%	0.1%
Income before income tax expense	13.5%	13.8%	14.0%	14.0%	14.0%	14.0%	14.0%
Income tax expense (benefit)	5.3%	5.4%	5.5%	5.5%	5.5%	5.5%	5.5%
Net income	8.2%	8.4%	8.5%	8.5%	8.5%	8.5%	8.5%

Solution for Review Exercise 2.3: The Gap, Inc. Asset Utilization Ratios for Year +1 and Beyond

Asset Utilization (Turnover) Ratios	Year 0	Year +1	Year +2	Year +3	Year +4	Year +5	Year +6
Cash—required (total revenues)	6.93	9.00	9.04	9.04	9.04	8.94	8.94
Accounts receivable, gross (total revenues)							
Inventories (total revenues)	9.47	9.29	9.40	9.40	9.40	9.29	9.29
Other current assets (total revenues)	23.29	23.18	23.29	23.29	23.29	23.02	23.02
Total current assets (total revenues)	3.41	3.82	3.85	3.85	3.85	3.80	3.80
Property, plant, and equipment, net (total revenues)	5.65	6.37	7.67	9.10	10.50	11.19	11.47
Other assets (total revenues)	23.11	25.96	26.08	26.08	26.08	25.77	25.77
Total assets w/o excess assets (total revenues)	2.08	2.21	2.34	2.44	2.52	2.53	2.55
Property, plant, and equipment, gross (total revenues)	1.96	1.97	1.97	1.95	1.92	1.82	1.73
Total assets (total revenues)	2.08	2.21	2.34	2.44	2.52	2.53	2.55

Solution for Review Exercise 2.4: The Gap, Inc. Working Capital Management Ratio Forecasts for Year +1 and Beyond

Working Capital Management Ratios	Year 0	Year +1	Year +2	Year +3	Year +4	Year +5	Year +6
Current ratio (operating liabilities)	1.87	1.89	1.89	1.89	1.89	1.89	1.89
Quick (asset test) ratio	0.79	0.80	0.81	0.81	0.81	0.81	0.81
Cash flow to current liabilities (operating)	0.73	0.91	0.92	0.92	0.92	0.92	0.92
Days of purchases outstanding (payable)	45.81	45.84	44.83	44.77	44.77	45.51	45.51
Days of inventory held	69.55	71.79	71.09	71.03	71.03	71.87	71.87
Accounts receivable collection period							
Trade cash cycle	23.73	25.95	26.26	26.25	26.25	26.36	26.36

Solution for Review Exercise 2.5: The Gap, Inc. Return on Equity Forecasts for Year +1 and Beyond

Return on Equity	Year 0	Year +1	Year +2	Year +3	Year +4	Year +5	Year +6
Return on equity	26.8%	32.5%	36.8%	40.3%	43.3%	44.4%	44.9%
Profit margin (to common)	8.2%	8.4%	8.5%	8.5%	8.5%	8.5%	8.5%
Total asset utilization (turnover)	1.949	2.186	2.333	2.451	2.542	2.557	2.571
Financial leverage factor	1.678	1.767	1.847	1.929	1.998	2.035	2.046
Return on equity (check)	26.8%	32.5%	36.8%	40.3%	43.3%	44.4%	44.9%
Return on assets	16.0%	18.4%	19.9%	20.9%	21.7%	21.8%	21.9%
Leverage factor for earnings	0.997	1.000	1.000	1.000	1.000	1.000	1.000
Financial leverage factor	1.678	1.767	1.847	1.929	1.998	2.035	2.046
Return on equity (check)	26.8%	32.5%	36.8%	40.3%	43.3%	44.4%	44.9%

After mastering the material in this chapter, you will be able to:

1. Measure free cash flows (3.1–3.2)
2. Create a cash flow statement (3.3–3.4)
3. Analyze income tax disclosures (3.5–3.6)
4. Measure the effects of interest deduction limitations and net operating losses on taxes and interest tax shields (3.7)

CHAPTER

3

Measuring Free Cash Flows

Many companies, for example Facebook, use free cash flow measures to manage the company and measure performance:

FACEBOOK, INC.

Free Cash Flow[1]

In addition to other financial measures presented in accordance with U.S. generally accepted accounting principles (GAAP), we monitor free cash flow (FCF) as a non-GAAP measure to manage our business, make planning decisions, evaluate our performance, and allocate resources. . . .

We believe that FCF is one of the key financial indicators of our business performance over the long term and provides useful information regarding how cash provided by operating activities compares to the property and equipment investments required to maintain and grow our business. . . .

We have chosen our definition for FCF because we believe that this methodology can provide useful supplemental information to help investors better understand underlying trends in our business. We use FCF in discussions with our senior management and board of directors. . . .

Facebook provided the following reconciliation of its measure of FCF to what it views as the most comparable GAAP measure, net cash provided by operating activities:

	2012	2013	2014	2015	2016
Net cash provided by operating activities	$2,645	$4,831	$7,326	$10,320	$16,108
Purchases of property and equipment	−1,235	−1,362	−1,831	−2,523	−4,491
Property and equipment acquired under capital leases	−340	−11	0	0	0
Free cash flow	$1,070	$3,458	$5,495	$ 7,797	$11,617

Facebook does not use exactly the same definition of free cash flows that we use to value companies. In this chapter, you will learn additional details about calculating the free cash flows we use in our valuation work, how to create a cash flow statement, and how to analyze income tax disclosures (including those related to net operating losses).

[1] See Facebook, Inc.'s 2016 10-K report, p. 32.

CHAPTER ORGANIZATION

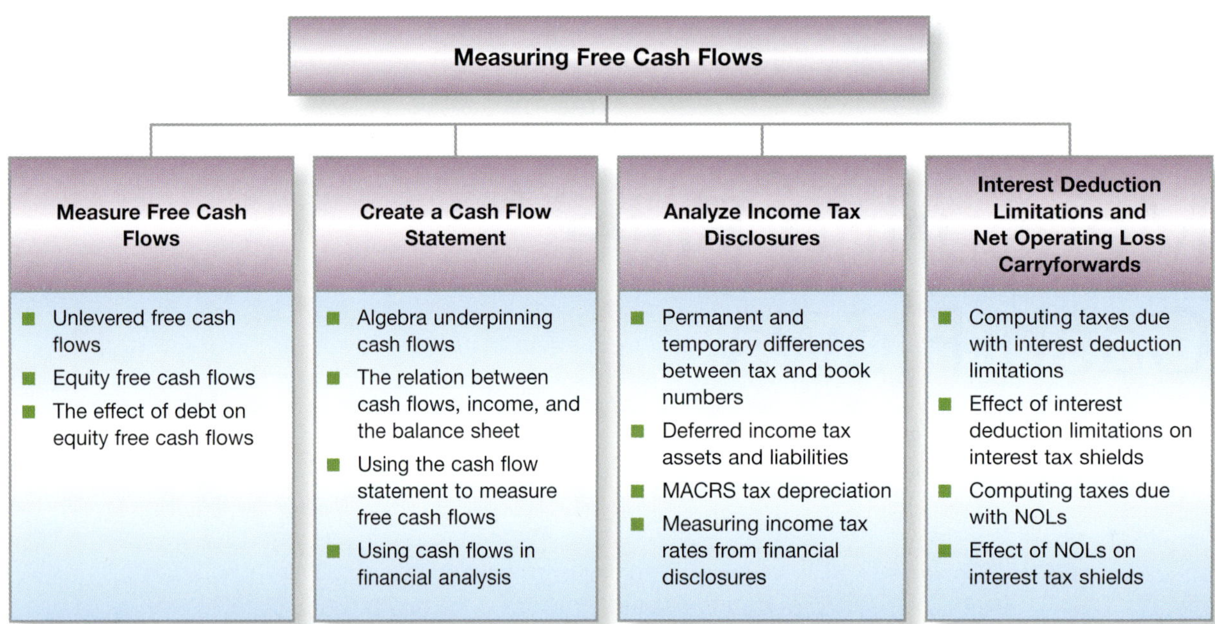

INTRODUCTION

What is a cash flow? The term "cash flow" has many definitions, but most are of little help to an analyst interested in valuation. For example, a net change in a company's cash holdings can be called the net cash flow, but this cash flow would not be very useful for valuing a company. In valuation analysis, an important characteristic of the cash flow concept is the cash flow that is available for distribution to particular security holders (investors). For example, if we were valuing a long-term straight debt instrument that matures in 20 years, the relevant cash flows are the interest and principal payments.

In valuing a company, the relevant cash flows are the (unlevered or asset) free cash flows that we introduced in Chapter 1. Free cash flows are the cash flows available for distribution to all of a company's security holders (debt, preferred stock, common stock), regardless of whether or not the company plans to distribute all of those cash flows to its investors. They are the cash flows measured after a company collects its revenues, pays its expenses, and makes all of the investments necessary to implement its business strategy, including investments in property, plant, and equipment as well as working capital and all other operating assets and liabilities (called net operating working capital). They are the cash flows the company would generate if it was entirely financed with equity, which is why they are called unlevered cash flows. In this chapter, we discuss both the concept of free cash flows and how to measure them. We also discuss another cash flow concept—equity free cash flows. Equity free cash flows are the unlevered free cash flows adjusted for all cash flows to and from non-common equity investors. They represent the cash flows that are available for distribution to the common equityholders, regardless of whether or not the company plans to distribute those cash flows to the equityholders.

After discussing free cash flows, we discuss the cash flow statement, and the similarities and differences with the way we measure free cash flows. We show how operating accrual adjustments used to convert income to operating cash flow in the cash flow statement are essentially the same ones used to measure free cash flows. Thus, it is important to understand the basics of accounting, particularly the cash flow statement, in order to correctly measure free cash flows. We then discuss how to adjust free cash flows for income taxes.

3.1 INTRODUCTION TO MEASURING FREE CASH FLOWS

LO1 Measure free cash flows

The cash flows that we discount are an important input into any discounted cash flow (DCF) valuation. We call these **free cash flows**. If a company only uses common equity financing, then it will have one type of investor and one type of free cash flow, which we call **unlevered free cash flows** or **free cash flows** (**FCF**), for short. If a company uses other types of financing such as debt or preferred stock, we still want to know the free cash flows that are available to all investors. These are the same unlevered free cash flows for the company. When a company uses both non-common equity financing and equity financing, we may want to know the free cash flows that are available to its common equityholders. A company's **equity free cash flows** (**EFCF**) are equal to the company's unlevered free cash flows adjusted for all after-tax cash flows paid to, or received from, non-common equity security holders.

The free cash flows (of the unlevered firm) are not affected by interest expense but interest expense is relevant when measuring the equity free cash flows. Preferred stock dividends do not affect free cash flows, but they do affect equity free cash flows. Since we measure equity free cash flows by adjusting free cash flows for all after-tax flows to or from non-common equity securities, we deduct preferred stock dividends to calculate equity free cash flows (but we do not deduct common dividends). Similarly, changes in financing do not affect free cash flows. However, changes in debt and preferred stock financing affect equity free cash flows, but changes in common equity financing do not. Changes in common equity financing and dividends to common equityholders help reconcile equity free cash flows to the change in cash, but they do not affect free cash flows or equity free cash flows.

Valuation in Practice 3.1

Free Cash Flow Is Not Calculated Based on U.S. Generally Accepted Accounting Principles (GAAP)
Free cash flow is not a measure calculated according to U.S. GAAP; however, the U.S. SEC allows a company to present certain non-GAAP measures in its financial statements as long they meet certain disclosure requirements. The U.S. SEC provided guidance for companies presenting free cash flow measures.

Question: Some companies present a measure of "free cash flow," which is typically calculated as cash flows from operating activities as presented in the statement of cash flows under GAAP, less capital expenditures. Does Item 10(e)(1)(ii) of Regulation S-K prohibit this measure in documents filed with the Commission?

Answer: No. The deduction of capital expenditures from the GAAP financial measure of cash flows from operating activities would not violate the prohibitions in Item 10(e)(1)(ii). However, companies should be aware that this measure does not have a uniform definition and its title does not describe how it is calculated. Accordingly, a clear description of how this measure is calculated, as well as the necessary reconciliation, should accompany the measure where it is used. Companies should also avoid inappropriate or potentially misleading inferences about its usefulness. For example, "free cash flow" should not be used in a manner that inappropriately implies that the measure represents the residual cash flow available for discretionary expenditures, since many companies have mandatory debt service requirements or other non-discretionary expenditures that are not deducted from the measure. Also, free cash flow is a liquidity measure that must not be presented on a per share basis. . . .

Source: See https://www.sec.gov/divisions/corpfin/guidance/nongaapinterp.htm available on May 29, 2018.

Measuring (Unlevered) Free Cash Flows (FCF)

As discussed in Chapter 1, to measure free cash flows, we begin with earnings before interest and taxes, **EBIT**, and deduct income taxes. The income taxes deducted (**TAX**) are the income taxes the company would pay if it had no **interest deductions** (interest expense that is deductible for income tax purposes). The result is the company's **unlevered earnings** (**UE**)—the earnings the company would have if it were all common equity financed. The next adjustment we make is to convert the company's unlevered earnings into unlevered operating cash flows.

Recall from basic accounting that a company's net income is not equal to its cash flow, for earnings contain the effect of non-cash expenses, non-cash revenues, and various other accruals. To convert unlevered earnings to an **unlevered operating cash flow** (**UCFO**), we add back any **non-cash expenses or losses** (**NCEXP**) that affect EBIT (for example, depreciation) and subtract any **non-cash revenues or gains** (**NCREV**) that affect EBIT. We then subtract any increases in **non-cash operating working capital** (**ΔWCO**) (for example, inventory). The non-cash net operating working capital adjustment does not include any items related to financing costs (such as interest) or income taxes, but it does include noncurrent operating assets and noncurrent operating liabilities. While **working capital** is often defined as current assets minus current liabilities, that is not the definition of operating working capital.

Operating working capital is equal to all current assets plus all noncurrent assets not included in the calculation of capital expenditures, minus all liabilities not included in debt financing. We then subtract any increase in the **required cash balance** (**ΔRC**). Here, we have a company's unlevered cash flow from operations (**UCFO**). We then calculate unlevered free cash flow (**FCF**) by subtracting investments—capital expenditures (**CAPEX**) measured net of any long-lived assets sold—from the unlevered cash flow from operations. Note, a company can also have decreases in required cash and non-cash operating working capital as well as negative capital expenditures, all of which would increase cash flows. For example, this is possible for a company that engages in restructuring activities or whose businesses are contracting. We summarized this calculation in Chapter 1 with Equation 1.1:

$$FCF = EBIT - TAX + NCEXP - NCREV - \Delta RC - \Delta WCO - CAPEX \tag{1.1}$$

This is the most basic calculation of free cash flows. Naturally, as a company's assets, capital structure, economic transactions, and income tax situations become more complex, the calculation of free cash flows becomes more complex as well.

Valuation Key 3.1

Free cash flows are the cash flows that could be distributed to all of the company's security holders after making all necessary investments to implement its current operating strategy. They do not, however, take into consideration the taxes saved from any interest expense that arises from the debt in a company's capital structure. These are equivalent to the free cash flows of the company if it were entirely equity financed.

Measuring Equity Free Cash Flows (EFCF)

Equity free cash flows are the free cash flows available for distribution to the common equityholders after all cash flows are paid to, or received from, non-common equity security holders. To measure the equity free cash flows, we begin with a company's unlevered free cash flows. From the unlevered free cash flows, we subtract all of the after-tax cash flows paid to non-common equity security holders, and we add all of the after-tax cash flows received from non-common equity security holders. For a company with debt, preferred stock, and equity financing, this means we subtract after-tax interest, preferred stock dividends, the repayment or retirement of debt, and the repurchase or retirement of preferred stock; likewise, we add the net cash flows resulting from the issuance of debt or preferred stock. Transactions with common equityholders are not considered in the calculation of equity free cash flows. Note, preferred stock dividends and the repurchase or retirement of preferred stock generally do not have any income tax effect. The repayment or retirement of debt, however, can have income tax effects if the debt is repaid or retired at an amount other than book value.

Subtracting after-tax cash interest paid is equivalent to subtracting cash interest paid and then adding back the interest tax shield resulting from the interest expense. We separate after-tax interest into these two components because we will often use the interest tax shields in our valuation of the company. In addition, the interest tax shield is based on tax deductible interest (INT), which may be different from both the interest expense reported in the financial statements and cash interest paid. **Interest tax shields** are the reductions in income taxes that result from interest expense. The interest tax shield is equal to the amount of tax deductible interest multiplied by the **marginal tax rate for interest**, T_{INT}. This income tax rate (T_{INT})—applied to interest expense in order to calculate a company's interest tax shield—is equal to the tax rate that measures the savings in corporate taxes, which results from the interest expense being deducted when calculating a company's taxable income. Note that many countries, including the U.S. since the passage of the Tax Cuts and Jobs Act of 2017, set limitations on the extent to which a company can deduct interest to reduce its taxable income. For example, in the U.S. starting in 2018, deductible interest expense is limited to 30% of what is essentially earnings before interest, taxes, depreciation, and amortization (EBITDA); then in 2022, deductible interest expense will be limited to 30% of essentially earnings before interest and taxes (EBIT). In the U.S., any interest that is not deductible because of this limitation can be carried forward indefinitely and deducted at a later date when the limitation is not binding.

In a straightforward situation, we can easily calculate a company's interest expense. For example, when a company issues debt at its face (or par) value with interest payments that occur at the end of fiscal periods, interest expense is equal to cash interest paid. To simplify calculations, we assume throughout the book that changes in debt occur at the end of the year, and in turn, interest expense is based on the beginning-of-year debt balance. Note, it is not uncommon to base interest expense on the average debt balance in a year. With our simplifying assumption, interest expense is equal to the interest rate (r_{INT}) multiplied by the book value of the debt outstanding at the beginning of the period (D_{t-1}). To calculate cash interest paid (CINT), we adjust interest expense for changes in interest payable and other issues we discuss later (such as **paid-in-kind debt**, which occurs when the interest accrues but is not paid until later).

The interest tax shield (ITS) is equal to the interest expense (which is equal to tax deductible interest), not the cash interest paid, multiplied by the tax rate that measures the tax deduction from interest (marginal tax rate for interest)—T_{INT}.

$$ITS = INT \times T_{INT} = r_{INT} \times D_{t-1} \times T_{INT} \quad \textbf{(3.1a)}$$

To calculate equity free cash flows, we also subtract preferred stock dividends paid (PSDiv). In a straightforward situation, this is equal to the dividend rate of the preferred stock (the preferred stock cost of capital)—r_{PS}—multiplied by the amount of preferred stock outstanding at the beginning of the period (PS_{t-1}).

$$PSDiv = r_{PS} \times PS_{t-1} \quad \textbf{(3.1b)}$$

Typically, we do not make any income tax adjustments for preferred stock dividends, for they are usually not tax deductible. Finally, we add any changes in the company's debt (ΔD) and preferred stock (ΔPS). We show this calculation in Equation 3.2.

$$EFCF = FCF - CINT + ITS - PSDiv + \Delta D + \Delta PS \quad \textbf{(3.2)}$$

Valuation Key 3.2

The equity free cash flows are available for distribution to the common equityholders of the firm after consideration of all required investments and all payments both to and from non-common equity security holders—on an after-tax basis.

How Issuing and Repaying Debt Affects Equity Free Cash Flows

It may be a little confusing at first to understand why issuing and repaying non-common equity securities affect equity free cash flows. When a company issues non-common equity securities (for example, debt or preferred stock), the company has more cash flow that year than it would have had otherwise. The company can then use the cash flow from the non-common equity securities to make new investments, pay dividends, and so forth. The net effect of issuing non-common equity securities is more cash flow available to the company's common equityholders than they would have had otherwise at the time of issuance. On the face of it, this might seem counterintuitive. How can the common equityholders have more cash flow by issuing non-common equity securities? If this were the case, the common equityholders would continue to issue more and more non-common equity securities in order to increase their cash flows, which in turn increases the value of their equity. While it would be nice for money to grow on trees in this way, this is not the effect of issuing non-common equity securities.

If a company issues non-common equity securities today, it pays the security holders an appropriate annual risk-adjusted rate of return, and it also repays the amount of capital raised no later than the maturity date of the security. In the year a company issues non-common equity securities, its equity free cash flow is larger than it would have been otherwise, but for all future years—as the company pays a return to those security holders (interest on debt or dividends on preferred) or repays the capital raised—its equity free cash flows are smaller. Assuming that the company issues non-common equity securities at its risk-adjusted rate of return, and assuming that the company does not get any other benefits from issuing non-common equity securities (such as interest tax shields), the common equityholders are no better off than they would have been had they not issued the non-common equity security.

For example, assume an investor is making a $100 investment in a company today and expects the company to earn and pay the investor $300 at the end of two years. The investor's expected cash flows are

Year 0	Year 1	Year 2
–$100	$0	+$300

If the investor wants to receive a dividend of $50 at the end of Year 1, the investor can have the company borrow $50 for one year at 10% interest and pay the $50 dividend. This creates a new time-series of expected cash flows to the investor. (The cash flow in Year 2 is $245 = $300 − 1.1 × $50.)

Year 0	Year 1	Year 2
–$100	+$50	+$245

The investor was able to shift some of the cash flow from Year 2 to Year 1 by borrowing $50. Naturally, shifting $50 of the expected cash flow from Year 2 to Year 1 did not come without a cost. The investor's expected cash flows in Year 2 decreased by $55 ($55 = 1.1 × $50). Regardless of whether or not it was a good decision, it is clear that borrowing the $50 had a direct positive effect on the expected cash flow in Year 1 and the repayment of the debt and interest had a direct negative effect on the expected cash flow in Year 2. Changing the amount of non-common equity financing has a direct effect on equity free cash flows. Of course, companies can have many reasons why they might decide to issue non-common equity securities. Interest tax shields are one such reason. In addition, if the company has more investment opportunities than available capital, issuing debt may allow it to take advantage of valuable investment opportunities without issuing equity, which is generally more costly to issue than debt.

3.2 THE BOB ADAMS COMPANY EXAMPLE

A few years ago, the Bob Adams Company financed itself with a significant amount of debt. The company is now in a situation in which it plans to make relatively large capital expenditures for the next three years, and some of the debt it had previously issued is maturing. The company's chief financial officer (CFO) prepared a set of forecasts (Exhibit 3.1) that management will use to assess the company's ability to fund the capital expenditures internally and repay the maturing debt.

EXHIBIT 3.1 The Bob Adams Company Balance Sheet and Income Statement Forecasts

THE BOB ADAMS COMPANY
Income Statement and Balance Sheet Forecasts

	Actual Year –1	Actual Year 0	Forecast Year 1	Forecast Year 2	Forecast Year 3
Income Statement					
Revenue	$14,960	$15,708	$16,493	$17,813	$18,882
Operating expenses	–8,976	–9,425	–9,896	–10,688	–11,329
Depreciation expense	–1,500	–1,725	–1,976	–2,305	–2,643
Earnings before interest and taxes	4,484	4,558	4,622	4,820	4,910
Interest expense	0	–1,200	–1,160	–1,150	–1,120
Income before taxes	4,484	3,358	3,462	3,670	3,790
Income tax expense	–1,794	–1,343	–1,385	–1,468	–1,516
Net income	$ 2,690	$ 2,015	$ 2,077	$ 2,202	$ 2,274

continued

EXHIBIT 3.1 The Bob Adams Company Balance Sheet and Income Statement Forecasts *(continued)*

THE BOB ADAMS COMPANY Income Statement and Balance Sheet Forecasts	Actual Year −1	Actual Year 0	Forecast Year 1	Forecast Year 2	Forecast Year 3
Statement of Retained Earnings					
Beginning-of-year balance	$ 4,088	$ 6,196	$ 7,847	$ 9,462	$11,117
Net income	2,690	2,015	2,077	2,202	2,274
Preferred stock dividends	−83	−110	−125	−130	−142
Common equity dividends	−500	−254	−336	−417	−328
End-of-year balance	$ 6,196	$ 7,847	$ 9,462	$11,117	$12,921
Balance Sheet					
Cash	$ 1,496	$ 2,152	$ 2,230	$ 2,362	$ 2,469
Net operating working capital	2,992	3,142	3,299	3,563	3,776
Property, plant, and equipment (net)	15,708	16,493	17,813	18,882	19,815
Total assets	$20,196	$21,787	$23,342	$24,807	$26,061
Debt	$12,000	$11,600	$11,500	$11,200	$10,400
Preferred stock	1,000	1,140	1,180	1,290	1,540
Common stock	1,000	1,200	1,200	1,200	1,200
Retained earnings	6,196	7,847	9,462	11,117	12,921
Total shareholders' equity	$ 7,196	$ 9,047	$10,662	$12,317	$14,121
Total liabilities and equities	$20,196	$21,787	$23,342	$24,807	$26,061

Exhibit may contain small rounding errors

The Bob Adams's Unlevered Free Cash Flows

In this section, we calculate the free cash flows of the Bob Adams Company from the company's income statement and balance sheet. For the Bob Adams Company, which has an income tax rate of 40% on all income statement items, we can use Equation 1.1 and the information in Exhibit 3.1 to measure its free cash flow for Year 0.

We calculate the company's unlevered free cash flows in Exhibit 3.2. To calculate the company's free cash flow for Year 0, we begin with EBIT, $4,558, which we can find on the company's income statement. In this simple example, income taxes on EBIT, TAX, is equal to EBIT multiplied by the income tax rate of 40% (TAX = $1,823 = 0.4 × $4,558) because the income tax rate is 40% on all types of income including interest expense. The only non-cash expense or revenue for this company is depreciation, $1,725 (NCEXP = $1,725, NCREV = $0). The company does not present its non-cash current assets and current liabilities separately on its balance sheet. It only reports the company's net operating working capital exclusive of cash. We can measure the change in the company's net operating working capital by calculating the change on the balance sheet from Year −1 to Year 0 (ΔNWC = $150 = $3,142 − $2,992). Increases in net operating working capital indicate that the company is, on net, investing in net operating working capital (for example, its inventory increases more than its accounts payable does, and the net increase is positive). Increases in net operating working capital indicate an outflow of cash. Assume the company needs an increase in its required cash equal to $75 in Year 0 in order to support the company's growth. Since the company's cash balance increased by $656, the company is holding excess cash of $581 ($581 = $656 − $75) as of the end of Year 0. Assume further that in future years, the forecasted change in the cash balance in the balance sheet represents the change in required cash necessary to operate the business. Using this information, we can calculate the company's unlevered cash flow from operations, $4,235 ($4,235 = $2,735 + $1,725 − $75 − $150).

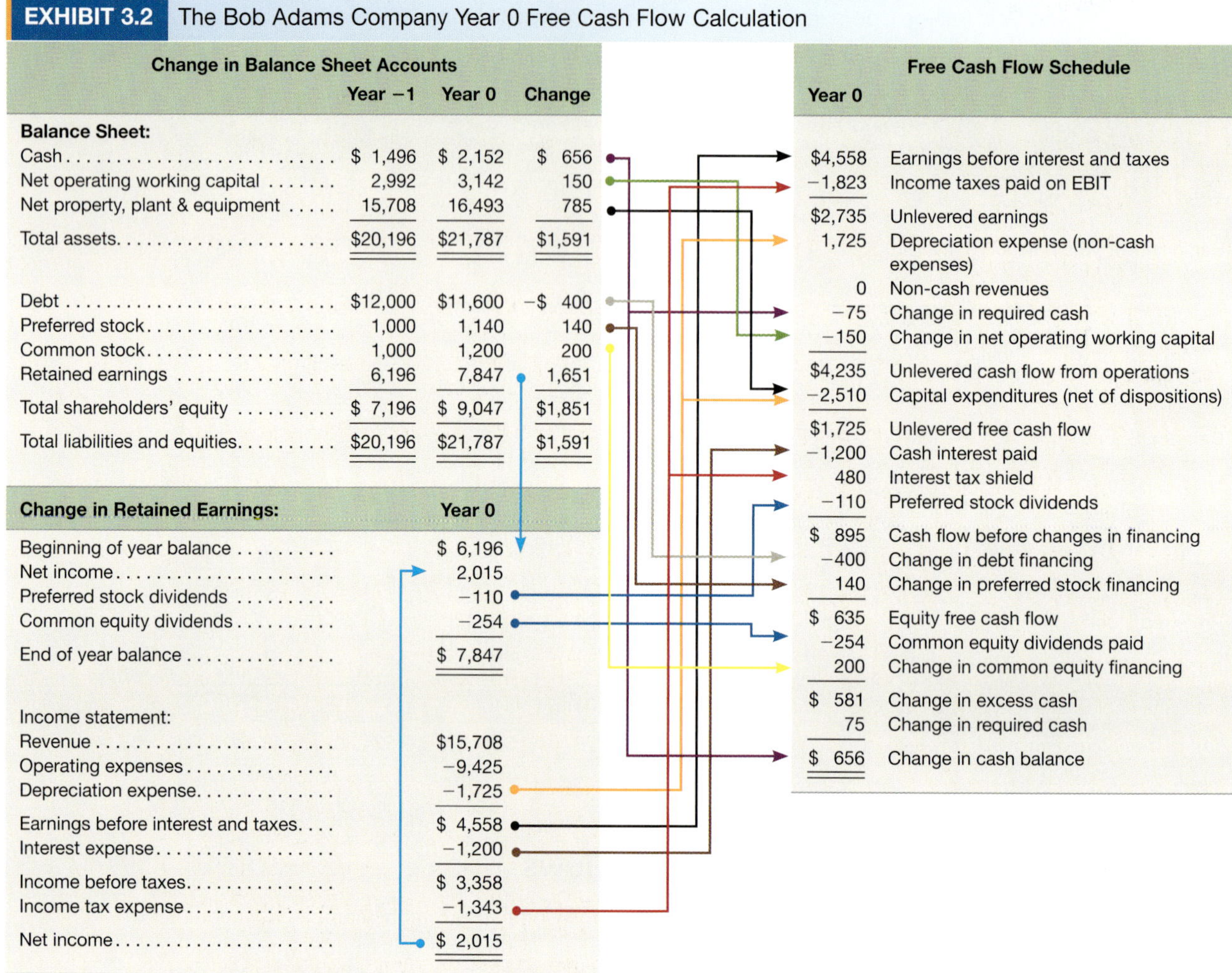

EXHIBIT 3.2 The Bob Adams Company Year 0 Free Cash Flow Calculation

Change in Balance Sheet Accounts

	Year −1	Year 0	Change
Balance Sheet:			
Cash	$ 1,496	$ 2,152	$ 656
Net operating working capital	2,992	3,142	150
Net property, plant & equipment	15,708	16,493	785
Total assets	$20,196	$21,787	$1,591
Debt	$12,000	$11,600	−$ 400
Preferred stock	1,000	1,140	140
Common stock	1,000	1,200	200
Retained earnings	6,196	7,847	1,651
Total shareholders' equity	$ 7,196	$ 9,047	$1,851
Total liabilities and equities	$20,196	$21,787	$1,591

Change in Retained Earnings:	Year 0
Beginning of year balance	$ 6,196
Net income	2,015
Preferred stock dividends	−110
Common equity dividends	−254
End of year balance	$ 7,847
Income statement:	
Revenue	$15,708
Operating expenses	−9,425
Depreciation expense	−1,725
Earnings before interest and taxes	$ 4,558
Interest expense	−1,200
Income before taxes	$ 3,358
Income tax expense	−1,343
Net income	$ 2,015

Free Cash Flow Schedule

Year 0	
$4,558	Earnings before interest and taxes
−1,823	Income taxes paid on EBIT
$2,735	Unlevered earnings
1,725	Depreciation expense (non-cash expenses)
0	Non-cash revenues
−75	Change in required cash
−150	Change in net operating working capital
$4,235	Unlevered cash flow from operations
−2,510	Capital expenditures (net of dispositions)
$1,725	Unlevered free cash flow
−1,200	Cash interest paid
480	Interest tax shield
−110	Preferred stock dividends
$ 895	Cash flow before changes in financing
−400	Change in debt financing
140	Change in preferred stock financing
$ 635	Equity free cash flow
−254	Common equity dividends paid
200	Change in common equity financing
$ 581	Change in excess cash
75	Change in required cash
$ 656	Change in cash balance

We calculate the company's capital expenditures by using information from both the income statement and balance sheet. The balance in the company's net property, plant, and equipment account increases when the company makes capital expenditures and decreases when the company depreciates these assets. Thus, we can calculate capital expenditures in a year as the change in the net property, plant, and equipment account plus depreciation in that year. (The balance in this account also changes if a company sells or retires some of its property, plant, and equipment during the year. However, we assume that the company is not selling or retiring any of its property, plant, and equipment.) Bob Adams Company's capital expenditures are equal to the change in its net property, plant, and equipment account on the balance sheet plus the depreciation on the income statement (CAPEX = \$2,510 = \$16,493 − \$15,708 + \$1,725). From this information, we can complete the calculation of the unlevered free cash flows for the Bob Adams Company in Year 0, \$1,725 (\$1,725 = \$4,235 − \$2,510).

Valuation in Practice 3.2

Amazon.com, Inc.'s Focus on Free Cash Flow As early as 2004, Amazon told its shareholders that its focus is growing free cash flow per share:

> Our Most Important Financial Measure: Free Cash Flow Per Share. Amazon.com's financial focus is on long-term growth in free cash flow per share. Amazon.com's free cash flow is driven primarily by increasing operating profit dollars and efficiently managing both working capital and capital expenditures. . . .

continued

continued from previous page

In its 2016 10-K Report, Amazon reported multiple free cash flow measures:

> We provide multiple measures of free cash flows because we believe these measures provide additional perspective on the impact of acquiring property and equipment with cash and through capital and finance leases.
>
> **Free cash flow** is cash flow from operations reduced by "Purchases of property and equipment, including internal-use software and website development, net," which is included in cash flow from investing activities. . . .
>
> **Free cash flow less lease principal repayments** is free cash flow reduced by "Principal repayments of capital lease obligations," and "Principal repayments of finance lease obligations," which are included in cash flow from financing activities. Free cash flow less lease principal repayments approximates the actual payments of cash for our capital and finance leases. . . .
>
> **Free cash flow less finance lease principal repayments and assets acquired under capital leases** is free cash flow reduced by "Principal repayments of finance lease obligations," which are included in cash flow from financing activities, and property and equipment acquired under capital leases. In this measure, property and equipment acquired under capital leases is reflected as if these assets had been purchased with cash, which is not the case as these assets have been leased. . . .

Source: See Amazon's April 2004 letter to its shareholders, available on May 29, 2018 at http://library.corporate-ir.net/library/97/976/97664/items/162060/2004_shareholderLetter.pdf and Amazon's 2016 10-K Report, pp. 30–31.

Bob Adams's Equity Free Cash Flows

From the above calculation, we learn that, in Year 0, the company generated unlevered cash flow from its operations of $4,235. Of that amount, the company invested $2,510 in capital expenditures. Thus, the company has $1,725 that it can distribute to its investors or if it does not distribute the entire amount, it increases its excess cash. In this section, we calculate the company's equity free cash flows and will learn more about how the company will use the $1,725 of unlevered free cash flow. We continue our calculations for Year 0 in Exhibit 3.2 by calculating the company's equity free cash flows. To calculate a company's equity free cash flows, we begin with its unlevered free cash flow, subtract all of the after-tax cash flows paid to non-common equity security holders (after-tax interest, preferred stock dividends, and the repayment or repurchase of debt and preferred stock, if any), and add all of the after-tax cash flows received from non-common equity security holders (issuance of debt or preferred stock, if any). For the Bob Adams Company, we can use Equation 3.2 and the information in Exhibit 3.1 to measure its equity free cash flow for Year 0, which we show in Exhibit 3.2.

We begin with unlevered free cash flow, $1,725. From that, we subtract cash interest paid, which, for the Bob Adams Company, is simply equal to the debt cost of capital of 10% multiplied by the beginning balance of debt (CINT = $1,200 = 0.1 × $12,000), assuming that the company does not have any change in its interest payable. Next, we add back the interest tax shield on the debt, which is equal to interest expense multiplied by the income tax rate for interest (ITS = $480 = 0.4 × 0.1 × $12,000) because 40% is the tax rate applicable to all income and expenses. We then subtract preferred stock dividends, equal to the preferred stock cost of capital of 11%, multiplied by the beginning balance of preferred stock (PSDIV = $110 = 0.11 × $1,000). We do not tax adjust preferred stock dividends because they are generally not tax deductible. The result of the previous calculation is the available cash flow the company has before changes in its financing, $895 ($895 = $1,725 − $1,200 + $480 − $110). If this cash flow is negative, it indicates the amount of additional financing the company must obtain (or potentially use up some of its available cash); if the cash flow is positive, it indicates the amount of cash available to either pay down debt or preferred stock, pay dividends, repurchase stock, or accumulate excess cash.

We calculate equity free cash flows by adding the change in non-common equity financing—which, in this example, is equal to the repayment of debt of $400 and the issuance of preferred stock of $140. From Exhibit 3.2, we see that the company's equity free cash flow is equal to $635 ($635 = $895 − $400 + $140). The company can use this cash flow to either pay dividends, repurchase stock, or accumulate excess cash. We see in Exhibit 3.2 that the company paid dividends to its common equityholders, $254, and] issued additional equity, $200.

Reconciling Free Cash Flows to Change in Cash Balance

As a preliminary check on our calculations, we should always be able to reconcile a company's equity free cash flow to the change in its cash balance. This reconciliation is useful as a check on our free cash flow and equity free cash flow calculations. As we show in Exhibit 3.2, we begin with equity free cash flow and subtract common dividends and add changes in common equity investments (or common share repurchases) in order to calculate the change in the company's excess cash. For the Bob Adams Company, the change in excess cash in Year 0 is \$581 (\$581 = \$635 − \$254 + \$200). The company increased its excess cash by \$581 because the company generated more equity free cash flow, \$635, than it paid in common equity dividends, \$254, plus it issued additional common equity, \$200. We add the change in required cash to the change in excess cash, which, if we calculated everything correctly, reconciles to the change in the company's cash balance.

Bob Adams Free Cash Flow Forecasts (Year 1 through Year 3)

As we discuss in more detail in Chapter 4, once we begin forecasting the company's free cash flows, we typically no longer assume that the company issues common equity in our explicit forecasts. Further, we typically assume that the company distributes all of its equity free cash flows to its common equityholders; in other words, the company no longer accumulates any excess cash. These are common assumptions we make when valuing a company.

Reviewing the forecasts for Years 1 to 3, we see that the Bob Adams Company's unlevered free cash flows in Exhibit 3.3 declined from \$1,725 in Year 0 to \$1,218 in Year 1 and then grew in Years 2 and 3 but never recovered to the Year 0 free cash flow.

EXHIBIT 3.3 The Bob Adams Company Free Cash Flow Schedule

THE BOB ADAMS COMPANY
Free Cash Flow and Equity Free Cash Flow Forecasts

		Actual Year 0	Forecast Year 1	Forecast Year 2	Forecast Year 3
Earnings before interest and taxes	+ EBIT	\$4,558	\$4,622	\$4,820	\$4,910
Income taxes paid on EBIT	− TAX	−1,823	−1,849	−1,928	−1,964
Unlevered earnings	**= UE**	**2,735**	**2,773**	**2,892**	**2,946**
Depreciation expense (non-cash expenses)	+ NCEXP	1,725	1,976	2,305	2,643
Non-cash revenues	− NCREV	0	0	0	0
Change in required cash	− ΔRC	−75	−79	−132	−107
Change in net operating working capital	− ΔWCO	−150	−157	−264	−214
Unlevered cash flow from operations	**= UCFO**	**4,235**	**4,513**	**4,801**	**5,268**
Capital expenditures (net of dispositions)	− CAPEX	−2,510	−3,295	−3,374	−3,577
Unlevered free cash flow	**= FCF**	**1,725**	**1,218**	**1,427**	**1,691**
Cash interest paid	− CINT	−1,200	−1,160	−1,150	−1,120
Interest tax shield	+ ITS	480	464	460	448
Preferred stock dividends	− PSDIV	−110	−125	−130	−142
Cash flow before changes in financing	**CFBFIN**	**895**	**396**	**607**	**878**
Change in debt financing	+ ΔDFIN	−400	−100	−300	−800
Change in preferred stock financing	+ ΔPSFIN	140	40	110	250
Equity free cash flow	**= EFCF**	**635**	**336**	**417**	**328**
Common equity dividends paid	− CDIV	−254	−336	−417	−328
Change in common equity financing	+ ΔCEFIN	200	0	0	0
Change in excess cash	= ΔXC	581	0	0	0
Change in required cash	+ ΔRC	75	79	132	107
Change in cash balance	**= ΔC**	**\$ 656**	**\$ 79**	**\$ 132**	**\$ 107**

Exhibit may contain small rounding errors

Although the company's unlevered free cash flow did not grow in Year 1, it generated sufficient cash flow in Year 1 and all other years so that its equity free cash flows were positive for every year. We also see in the forecasts that the company does not accumulate any excess cash as the forecasts set common dividends equal to the company's equity free cash flows. This is the standard assumption we make when valuing a company, even if the company does not intend to pay those dividends. We discuss this issue in Chapter 4.

REVIEW EXERCISE 3.1

Frits Seegers, Inc. Free Cash Flow Schedule

Use the information on Frits Seegers to prepare a free cash flow schedule for Year 0 that includes unlevered free cash flows, equity free cash flows, and a reconciliation to the change in the company's cash balance. Assume that the cash shown is required cash for the business and that the only items that affect retained earnings are net income and dividends. Assume that all interest expense is tax deductible in each year and is not subject to the 30% limitation. (Note, for more practice, see Problem 1.9 where more years of data for Frits Seegers, Inc. are presented.)

FRITS SEEGERS INC.
Income Statement and Balance Sheet

	Year −1	Year 0		Year −1	Year 0
Balance Sheet—Assets			**Balance Sheet—Liabilities and Equity**		
Cash balance	$ 50.0	$ 55.0	Accounts payable	$ 50.8	$ 55.9
Accounts receivable	166.7	183.3	Other current operating liabilities	35.0	38.5
Inventory	118.6	130.5	Total current liabilities	85.8	94.4
Total current assets	$ 335.3	$ 368.8	Debt	1,200.0	1,400.0
Land	1,550.0	1,825.0	Total liabilities	$1,285.8	$1,494.4
Total assets	$1,885.3	$2,193.8	Common stock	$ 383.6	$ 383.6
			Retained earnings	215.8	315.7
			Total shareholders' equity	$ 599.4	$ 699.4
			Total liabilities and equities	$1,885.3	$2,193.8

	Year −1	Year 0
Income Statement		
Revenue	$1,000.0	$1,100.0
Cost of goods sold	−610.0	−671.0
Gross margin	$ 390.0	$ 429.0
Selling, general, and administrative	−120.0	−132.0
Operating income	$ 270.0	$ 297.0
Interest expense	−77.0	−96.0
Income before taxes	$ 193.0	$ 201.0
Income tax expense	−77.2	−80.4
Net income	$ 115.8	$ 120.6

Exhibit may contain small rounding errors

Solution on pages 146–147.

3.3 CASH FLOW STATEMENT BASICS

LO2 Create a cash flow statement

The balance sheet and income statement are two widely used and reasonably well-understood financial statements (although many do not recognize their limitations). The statement of cash flows is not as well understood. The cash flow statement prepared by accountants reconciles the change in a company's cash balance with changes in the other items on the balance sheet. Under U.S. accounting principles, the cash flow statement partitions this reconciliation into four parts:

Cash flow from operations
Net cash flows from investing activities
Net cash flows from financing activities
Foreign currency translation adjustment[2]
Change in cash and cash equivalents

In this section, we discuss the algebra underpinning the cash flow statement. We also discuss the relation between the free cash flow schedule and the cash flow statement. What we quickly learn is that the adjustments that we make to unlevered earnings to measure unlevered operating cash flow are mostly the same adjustments that we make to net income to measure cash flow from operations. The information on the cash flow statement is also useful for calculating the investments made by a company and changes in its financing. In this section, we also show how to calculate free cash flows directly from cash flows from operations.

The Algebra Underpinning the Cash Flow Statement

Understanding the algebra that underpins the cash flow statement provides a useful framework for understanding how to prepare a cash flow statement (and free cash flow schedule). The basic accounting identity or equality equates assets (resources) with liabilities and shareholders' equity (claims on the assets). Even though preparing the cash flow statement can be somewhat complex, it is, in reality, merely a restatement of that accounting equality. The cash flow statement reconciles the change in the cash balance on the balance sheet with the changes in all of the other accounts on the balance sheet, and it partitions the changes in a systematic manner (cash flow from operations, cash flow from investing, cash flow from financing, and the foreign currency translation adjustment).

We present a typical balance sheet and statement of retained earnings on the left side of Exhibit 3.4. We present variable names for each of the accounts on the balance sheet, each of the changes in those accounts (column labeled "change"), and each of the components in the retained earnings statement, but we ignore other components of shareholders' equity (such as comprehensive income adjustments) to simplify our discussion.

Using this notation, we can present the equation for the accounting identity (eliminating any time subscripts) as

$$TA = TL + SE$$
$$C + COA + PPEQ + NCOA = COL + INT/P + CLTD + LTD + NCOL + PS + CS + RE$$

The above equality still holds if we restate the equation in terms of the changes in the balance sheet accounts. We use the Greek letter Δ to represent the change in a balance sheet account: $\Delta X = X_t - X_{t-1}$.)

$$\Delta C + \Delta COA + \Delta PPEQ + \Delta NCOA$$
$$= \Delta COL + \Delta INT/P + \Delta CLTD + \Delta LTD + \Delta NCOL + \Delta PS + \Delta CS + \Delta RE$$

If we assume the change in accumulated comprehensive income is zero, then the change in retained earnings increases or decreases each year by the amount of net income net of preferred and common dividends ($\Delta RE = NI - PSDIV - CDIV$). We can substitute this relation into the above equation.

$$\Delta C + \Delta COA + \Delta PPEQ + \Delta NCOA$$
$$= \Delta COL + \Delta INT/P + \Delta CLTD + \Delta LTD + \Delta NCOL + \Delta PS + \Delta CS + NI - PSDIV - CDIV$$

Recall that the cash flow statement reconciles the change in the cash balance with changes in the balances of all of the other balance sheet accounts; thus, we can rearrange the previous equation to approximate a cash flow statement. (The partitioning is actually much more complicated than represented below, so do not take this partitioning as being literally true.)

[2] The foreign currency translation adjustments are beyond the scope of our discussion in this chapter. For the remainder of this chapter, we assume foreign currency translation adjustments are not relevant to either our discussion or our examples.

$$\Delta C =$$
$$+ NI - \Delta COA - \Delta NCOA + \Delta COL + \Delta INT/P + \Delta NCOL \quad [CFO]$$
$$- \Delta PPEQ \quad [CFI]$$
$$+ \Delta CLTD + \Delta LTD + \Delta PS + \Delta CS - PSDIV - CDIV \quad [CFF]$$

In Exhibit 3.4, we show a more detailed and more accurate mapping of the changes in the balance sheet accounts to the cash flow statement. We typically need to use the income statement (which we do not show in Exhibit 3.4) to identify non-cash expenses (depreciation and amortization) and non-cash revenues (gains on dispositions).

EXHIBIT 3.4 Relationships Between Changes in the Balance Sheet Accounts and the Cash Flow Statement

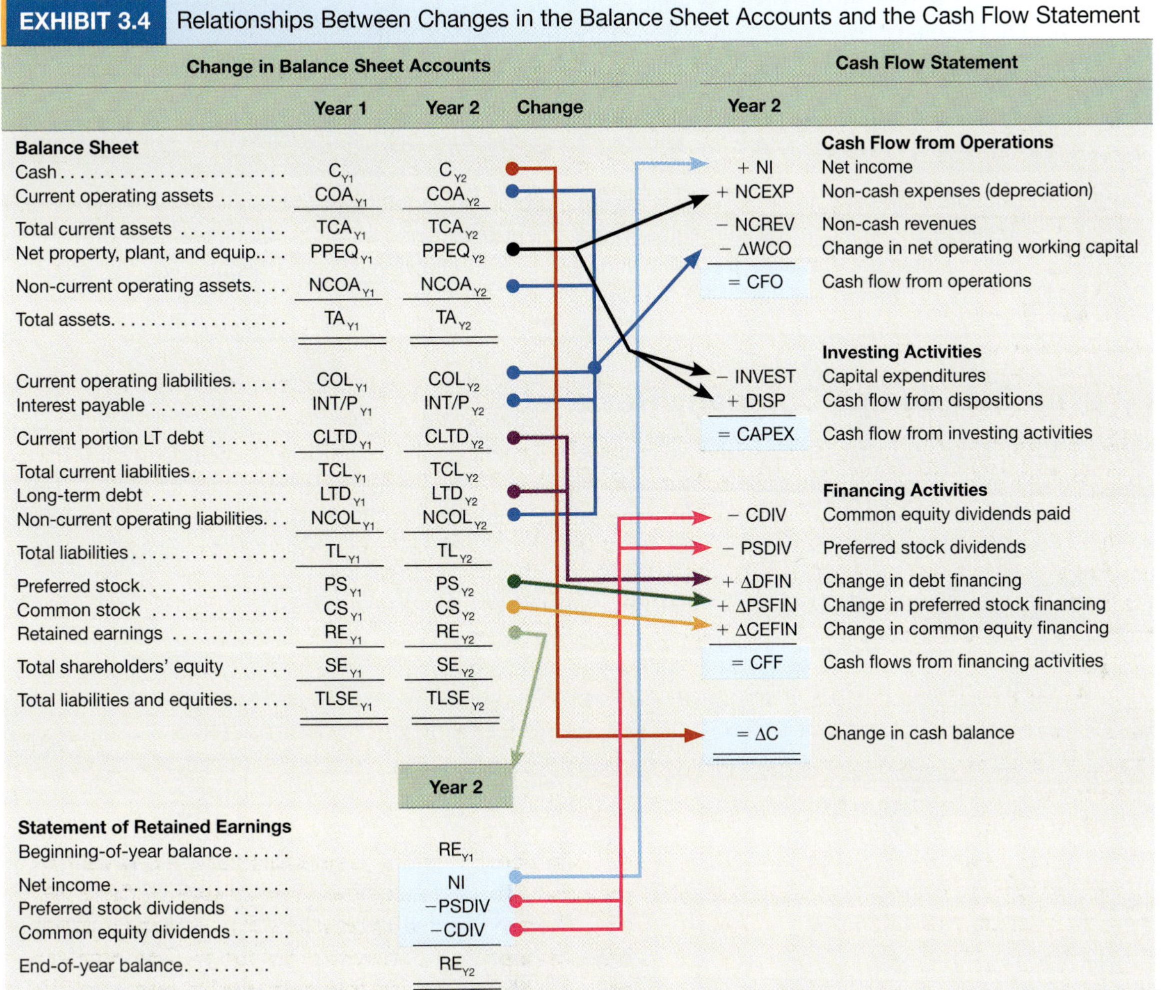

Change in Balance Sheet Accounts

Balance Sheet	Year 1	Year 2	Change
Cash	C_{Y1}	C_{Y2}	
Current operating assets	COA_{Y1}	COA_{Y2}	
Total current assets	TCA_{Y1}	TCA_{Y2}	
Net property, plant, and equip.	$PPEQ_{Y1}$	$PPEQ_{Y2}$	
Non-current operating assets	$NCOA_{Y1}$	$NCOA_{Y2}$	
Total assets	TA_{Y1}	TA_{Y2}	
Current operating liabilities	COL_{Y1}	COL_{Y2}	
Interest payable	INT/P_{Y1}	INT/P_{Y2}	
Current portion LT debt	$CLTD_{Y1}$	$CLTD_{Y2}$	
Total current liabilities	TCL_{Y1}	TCL_{Y2}	
Long-term debt	LTD_{Y1}	LTD_{Y2}	
Non-current operating liabilities	$NCOL_{Y1}$	$NCOL_{Y2}$	
Total liabilities	TL_{Y1}	TL_{Y2}	
Preferred stock	PS_{Y1}	PS_{Y2}	
Common stock	CS_{Y1}	CS_{Y2}	
Retained earnings	RE_{Y1}	RE_{Y2}	
Total shareholders' equity	SE_{Y1}	SE_{Y2}	
Total liabilities and equities	$TLSE_{Y1}$	$TLSE_{Y2}$	

Statement of Retained Earnings	Year 2
Beginning-of-year balance	RE_{Y1}
Net income	NI
Preferred stock dividends	−PSDIV
Common equity dividends	−CDIV
End-of-year balance	RE_{Y2}

Cash Flow Statement

Year 2	
	Cash Flow from Operations
+ NI	Net income
+ NCEXP	Non-cash expenses (depreciation)
− NCREV	Non-cash revenues
− ΔWCO	Change in net operating working capital
= CFO	Cash flow from operations
	Investing Activities
− INVEST	Capital expenditures
+ DISP	Cash flow from dispositions
= CAPEX	Cash flow from investing activities
	Financing Activities
− CDIV	Common equity dividends paid
− PSDIV	Preferred stock dividends
+ ΔDFIN	Change in debt financing
+ ΔPSFIN	Change in preferred stock financing
+ ΔCEFIN	Change in common equity financing
= CFF	Cash flows from financing activities
= ΔC	Change in cash balance

The algebra demonstrates how we can always prepare a cash flow statement given two years of balance sheets, an income statement, and a statement of retained earnings. However, although it is possible to prepare a cash flow statement with only these financial statements, preparing a precise cash flow statement typically requires more detailed information that explains the changes in the balance sheet accounts. This, in turn, allows us to better classify parts of the change in balance sheet accounts into the four categories of cash flows on the cash flow statement. The footnotes in a 10-K are helpful in preparing a more detailed reconciliation. Not having or using that information can result in a misclassification of part or all of a change in a balance sheet account. Such misclassifications may or may not be important, depending on how they affect our free cash flow calculations.

Using the Cash Flow Statement to Measure Free Cash Flows

It is clear from comparing Exhibits 3.2 and 3.4 that the adjustments we make to unlevered earnings to measure unlevered cash flows from operations are very similar to the adjustments we make to net income to measure cash flow from operations. Thus, it is of no surprise that we can calculate free cash flows from cash flow from operations. We begin our calculation with cash flow from operations. The primary difference between cash flow from operations on the cash flow statement and the unlevered cash flow from operations as shown in Exhibit 3.2 is the after-tax cash flow effect of interest deductions and the change in required cash. To measure unlevered cash flow from operations, we add after-tax cash interest paid (cash interest paid minus the interest tax shield) to cash flow from operations and subtract increases in required cash. This is the same unlevered cash flow from operations that we calculated in Exhibits 3.2 and 3.3. When we start with cash flows from operations for our free cash flow calculation, we call it the CFO method. If EBIT is the starting point for the free cash flow calculation, we call it the EBIT method. Once we measure unlevered cash flow from operations using either the EBIT or CFO methods, the remainder of the free cash flow calculation is the same as in Exhibits 3.2 and 3.3. Likewise, the calculation of equity free cash flow and the reconciliation of the equity free cash flow to the change in the cash balance are the same for both the EBIT and CFO methods.

Valuation Key 3.3

The algebra of the accounting system allows us to prepare a statement of cash flows with a comparative balance sheet, income statement, and statement of retained earnings. Once we have prepared a cash flow statement, it makes the calculation of free cash flows relatively straightforward when using either the EBIT method or the CFO method.

The Bob Adams Company Revisited

In Exhibit 3.5, we map changes in the balance sheet accounts to the cash flow statement for Year 0 for the Bob Adams Company. For this company, the only information we need from the income statement is depreciation expense, which we show at the bottom of this exhibit (see Exhibit 3.1 for the income statement).

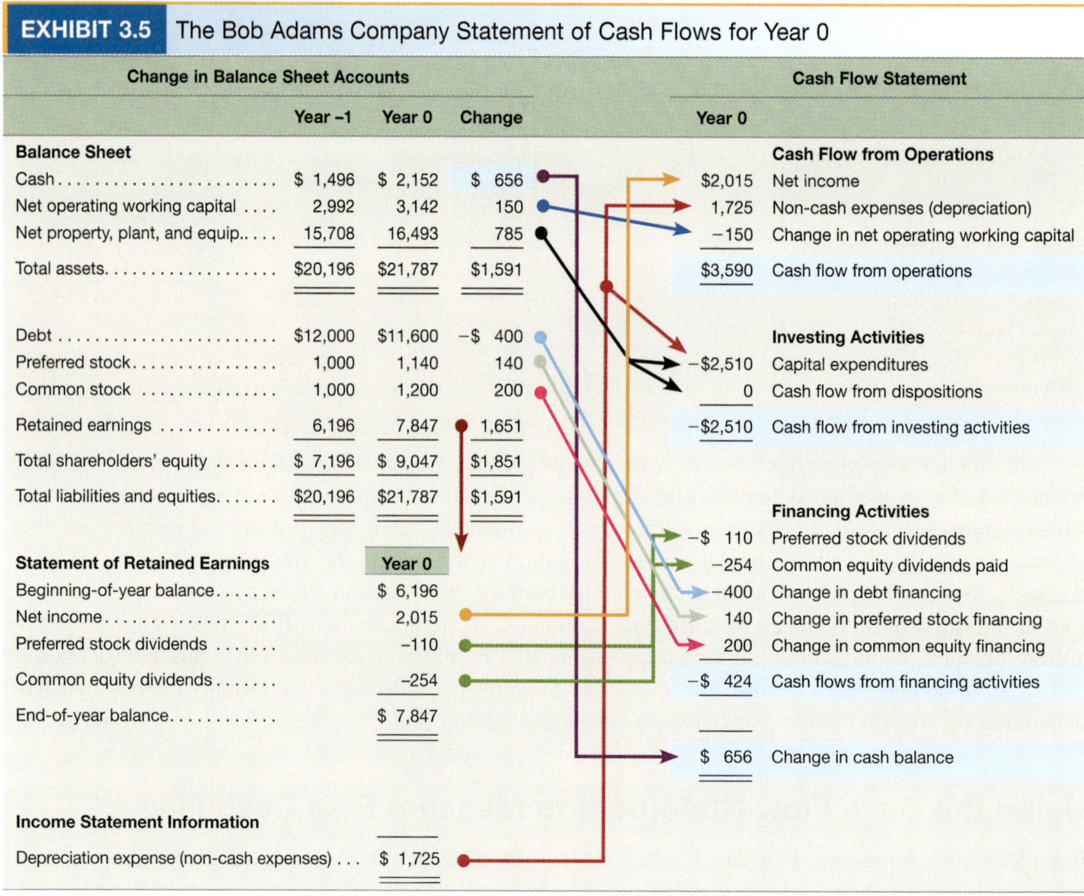

EXHIBIT 3.5 The Bob Adams Company Statement of Cash Flows for Year 0

Change in Balance Sheet Accounts

	Year −1	Year 0	Change
Balance Sheet			
Cash	$ 1,496	$ 2,152	$ 656
Net operating working capital	2,992	3,142	150
Net property, plant, and equip.	15,708	16,493	785
Total assets	$20,196	$21,787	$1,591
Debt	$12,000	$11,600	−$ 400
Preferred stock	1,000	1,140	140
Common stock	1,000	1,200	200
Retained earnings	6,196	7,847	1,651
Total shareholders' equity	$ 7,196	$ 9,047	$1,851
Total liabilities and equities	$20,196	$21,787	$1,591

Statement of Retained Earnings	Year 0
Beginning-of-year balance	$ 6,196
Net income	2,015
Preferred stock dividends	−110
Common equity dividends	−254
End-of-year balance	$ 7,847

Income Statement Information	
Depreciation expense (non-cash expenses)	$ 1,725

Cash Flow Statement

Year 0	
	Cash Flow from Operations
$2,015	Net income
1,725	Non-cash expenses (depreciation)
−150	Change in net operating working capital
$3,590	Cash flow from operations
	Investing Activities
−$2,510	Capital expenditures
0	Cash flow from dispositions
−$2,510	Cash flow from investing activities
	Financing Activities
−$ 110	Preferred stock dividends
−254	Common equity dividends paid
−400	Change in debt financing
140	Change in preferred stock financing
200	Change in common equity financing
−$ 424	Cash flows from financing activities
$ 656	Change in cash balance

Since the Bob Adams Company has a straightforward balance sheet and income statement, and since it did not have any complex transactions, preparing its cash flow statement is relatively straightforward. Capital expenditures is the only number on the cash flow statement that is neither directly from the change column on the balance sheet nor from the income statement or statement of retained earnings. For the cash flow statement, the calculation of capital expenditures is generally the same calculation as the one used for the free cash flow statement. An exception to this occurs when a company has non-cash transactions—for example, purchasing a building by borrowing the money from the seller. We would treat that as a dual transaction on the free cash flow statement—showing both the purchase of the building and the issuance of debt—but nothing would be shown on the cash flow statement according to U.S. GAAP, though U.S. GAAP requires that such non-cash transactions be disclosed separately.

In Exhibit 3.6, we show the cash flow statements for the Bob Adams Company for all years. The cash flow statement for Year 0 is the same cash flow statement that appears in Exhibit 3.5. We prepared the cash flow statements for the remaining years in the same manner. In fact, to do this, we merely copied the formulas in our spreadsheet from the column representing Year 0 to the columns representing Years 1 to 3. Based on the calculations in Exhibit 3.5, we see that each number in the cash flow statement results from a calculation based on two balance sheets, the income statement and/or the statement of retained earnings. Our relatively simple Bob Adams Company example shows how it is possible to create spreadsheet templates in order to calculate a company's cash flow statement and, therefore, its free cash flows from its income statement, balance sheet, and statement of retained earnings. In a financial model, we typically forecast a company's income statements, balance sheets, and supplemental information (for example, more detailed schedules of income taxes and property, plant, and equipment) to calculate the company's cash flow statement and free cash flows.

EXHIBIT 3.6 The Bob Adams Company Statement of Cash Flows Year 0 to Year 3

THE BOB ADAMS COMPANY Cash Flow Statement Forecasts		Actual Year 0	Forecast Year 1	Forecast Year 2	Forecast Year 3
Cash Flow from Operations					
Net income	+NI	$2,015	$2,077	$2,202	$2,274
Depreciation expense (non-cash expenses)	+NCEXP	1,725	1,976	2,305	2,643
Non-cash revenues	−NCREV	0	0	0	0
Change in net operating working capital	−ΔWC	−150	−157	−264	−214
Cash flow from operations	=CFO	$3,590	$3,896	$4,243	$4,703
Investing Activities					
Capital expenditures	−INVEST	−$2,510	−$3,295	−$3,374	−$3,577
Cash flow from dispositions	+DISP	0	0	0	0
Cash flow from investing activities	=CAPEX	−$2,510	−$3,295	−$3,374	−$3,577
Financing Activities					
Common equity dividends paid	−CDIV	−$ 254	−$ 336	−$ 417	−$ 328
Preferred stock dividends	−PSDIV	−110	−125	−130	−142
Change in debt financing	+DFIN	−400	−100	−300	−800
Change in preferred stock financing	+PSFIN	140	40	110	250
Change in common equity financing	+CEFIN	200	0	0	0
Cash flows from financing activities	=CFF	−$ 424	−$ 522	−$ 737	−$1,019
Change in cash balance	=ΔC	$ 656	$ 79	$ 132	$ 107

Exhibit may contain small rounding errors

In Exhibit 3.7, we show the free cash flow calculations for the Bob Adams Company using the cash flow from operations method. We add back after-tax interest to cash flow from operations and subtract the increases in required cash in order to calculate unlevered cash flow from operations, which is the same unlevered cash flow from operations calculated in Exhibit 3.3.

EXHIBIT 3.7 The Bob Adams Company Free Cash Flow Measured Using the Cash Flow Statement

THE BOB ADAMS COMPANY Free Cash Flow Forecasts		Actual Year 0	Forecast Year 1	Forecast Year 2	Forecast Year 3
Cash flow from operations	+CFO	$3,590	$3,896	$4,243	$4,703
Interest paid in cash	+CINT	1,200	1,160	1,150	1,120
Interest tax shield	−ITS	−480	−464	−460	−448
Change in required cash	−ΔRC	−75	−79	−132	−107
Unlevered cash flow from operations	**=UCFO**	**$4,235**	**$4,513**	**$4,801**	**$5,268**
Capital expenditures	−CAPEX	−2,510	−3,295	−3,374	−3,577
Unlevered free cash flow	**=FCF**	**$1,725**	**$1,218**	**$1,427**	**$1,691**

Now that we have the same unlevered cash flow from operations, the remainder of the free cash flow calculation is the same as in Exhibit 3.3. Likewise, the calculation of equity free cash flows and the reconciliation of the equity free cash flows to the change in the cash balance are the same for the cash flow from operations method as they are for the EBIT method, which we presented in Exhibit 3.3. We do not repeat that part of the schedule in the exhibit. While it is useful to understand the cash flow from operations method for its insights into the EBIT method, most practitioners use the EBIT method when they measure free cash flows.

REVIEW EXERCISE 3.2

Frits Seegers, Inc. Cash Flow Statement

Use the information on Frits Seegers in Review Exercise 3.1 to prepare a cash flow statement in order to then calculate the company's unlevered free cash flow using the CFO method. Assume that all interest expense is tax deductible in each year and is not subject to the 30% limitation. (Note, for more practice, see Problem 1.9 where more years of data for Frits Seegers, Inc. are presented.)

Solution on pages 147–148.

3.4 THE RELATIONSHIPS BETWEEN THE FREE CASH FLOW SCHEDULE AND THE CASH FLOW STATEMENT

So far, we discussed how to prepare a free cash flow schedule from a company's income statement, balance sheet, and some supplemental information, and how to prepare a statement of cash flows using the same information. In this section, we discuss the relationships between the various components on the statement of cash flows and the various components on the free cash flow schedule. As we learned from the previous sections, both the statement of cash flows and the free cash flow schedule reconcile the change in the cash balance on the balance sheet with the changes in all of the other accounts on the balance sheet. As it turns out, many of the components on the statement of cash flows are the same as the components on the free cash flow schedule.

The Relationships

The primary difference between the statement of cash flows and the free cash flow schedule is how the changes in the accounts on the balance sheet are organized. The statement of cash flow organizes the changes in the accounts on the balance sheet into cash flow from operations, cash flow from investing activities, and cash flow from financing activities. The free cash flow schedule organizes the changes in the accounts on the balance sheet into unlevered cash flow from operations, unlevered free cash flow, equity free cash flow, and common equity cash flows in order to reconcile equity free cash flow to the change in cash balance. In Exhibit 3.8, we show the relationships between the components on the statement of cash flows and the components on the free cash flow schedule.

EXHIBIT 3.8 The Relations between the Cash Flow Statement and Free Cash Flow Schedule

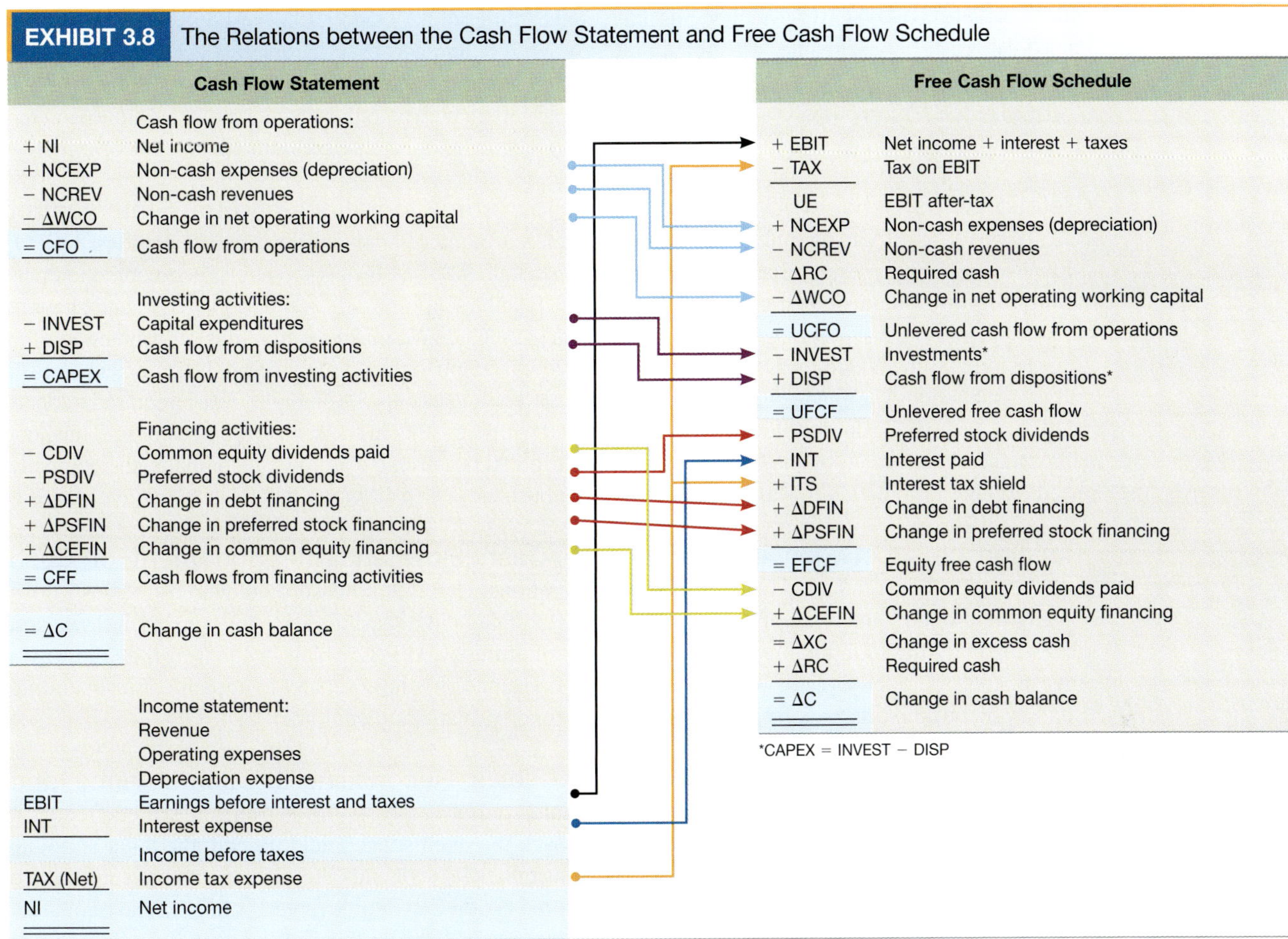

Net Income versus EBIT Starting Points. One of the differences between the statement of cash flows and the free cash flow schedule is the starting point. The starting point for the statement of cash flows is net income, while the starting point for the free cash flow schedule is EBIT. From EBIT we then subtract income taxes on EBIT to obtain unlevered earnings, UE. Since both the statement of cash flows and free cash flow schedule reconcile to the change in the cash balance, the difference in the starting points must be offset with other differences.

As we show at the bottom of the exhibit, net income is equal to EBIT minus interest expense (INT) and minus income taxes, which includes the effect of interest tax shields (TAX (Net)). Interest is deducted on the free cash flow schedule but it is deducted as an adjustment to unlevered free cash flow to measure equity free cash flow. Income taxes are also deducted on the free cash flow schedule. The second line item on the free cash flow schedule deducts income taxes that would be paid on EBIT (that is, ignoring the effect of interest tax shields on income taxes). For a company with positive taxable income, the income tax on EBIT (TAX) is higher than the tax paid on EBIT net of interest (TAX (Net)). The difference in the two income tax numbers is equal to the interest tax shield (ITS). The tax rate on EBIT is equal to the weighted average of the effective income tax rate (on all income) and the marginal tax rate on interest (with weights equal (1 − Interest/EBIT) for the effective tax rate and Interest/EBIT for the marginal tax rate). We add back the interest tax shield on the free cash flow schedule as an adjustment to unlevered free cash flow to measure equity free cash flow. Thus, while the starting points differ, the free cash flow schedule also uses net income to reconcile to the change in the cash balance but partitions net income into multiple components—EBIT, income tax on EBIT (TAX), interest (INT), and the interest tax shield (ITS)—the end result, however, is that the free cash flow schedule also uses net income to reconcile to the change in the cash balance. Another way to say this is that one basic difference between the cash flow from operations and the unlevered cash flow from operations is that interest costs net of the interest tax shields are treated as financing related costs on the free cash flow schedule but part of operations on the cash flow statement.

For example, the net income of the Bob Adams Company in Year 0 is $2,015, which is the starting point for the statement of cash flows in Exhibit 3.5. The starting point in the free cash flow schedule is EBIT minus income taxes on EBIT, which yields unlevered earnings of $2,735 ($2,735 = $4,558 − $1,823). Later in the free cash flow schedule, we subtract interest, $1,200, and add-back the interest tax shield, $480 (or subtract after-tax interest, $720) as part of the calculation of equity free cash flow (NI = EBIT − TAX − INT + ITS; $2,015 = $4,558 − $1,823 − $1,200 + $480). Thus, both the statement of cash flows and the free cash flow schedule essentially use net income to reconcile to the change in the cash balance.

Relationships between Unlevered Cash Flow from Operations and the Statement of Cash Flows. To adjust unlevered earnings to measure unlevered cash flow from operations, UCFO, we make the same types of adjustments made on the statement of cash flows to adjust net income to operating cash flow: add-back non-cash expenses, NCEXP; subtract non-cash revenues, NCREV; and subtract the change in non-cash net operating working capital, ΔWCO.[3] We make an additional adjustment on the free cash flow schedule to measure unlevered cash flow from operations not made on the statement of cash flows—subtracting the change in required cash, ΔRC. Required cash is the amount of cash required to operate the company's business, which typically increases with increases in the scale of the business. Thus, not all of the cash generated by the company can be distributed because, for a growing company, the company needs to invest more cash to support the scale of the business, just as it would invest in more inventory.

Relationships between Unlevered Free Cash Flow and the Statement of Cash Flows. To adjust unlevered cash flow from operations, UCFO, to measure unlevered free cash flow, UFCF, we use the same types of cash flows used in the statement of cash flows to measure cash flow from investing activities: subtracting the net capital expenditures, CAPEX, which is equal to the company's investments in property, plant, and equipment, INVEST, made by the company to implement its operating strategy, net of the proceeds from dispositions of property, plant, and equipment, DISP.[4]

Relationships between Equity Free Cash Flows, Reconciling to Cash Balance, and the Statement of Cash Flows. To calculate equity free cash flows from unlevered free cash flows, we first subtract cash interest paid and add-back the interest tax shield. Recall, the latter is not an adjustment made in the statement of cash flows but rather it reconciles the difference between the two starting points—net income versus EBIT minus income tax on EBIT (unlevered earnings). The remainder of the adjustments to calculate equity free cash flows are the same as three of the types of non-common equity financing cash flows used in the statement of cash flows to measure the cash flow from financing activities: preferred stock dividends, PSDIV; the change in debt financing, ΔDFIN; and the change in preferred stock financing, ΔPSFIN. To reconcile to the change in cash, we first add the common equity cash flows also on the statement of cash flows in the financing section in order to measure the change in excess cash, including common equity dividends, CDIV; and change in common equity financing, ΔCEFIN. Finally, we add back the change in required cash deducted to calculate unlevered free cash flows to reconcile to the change in the cash balance.

Preparing Starbucks Free Cash Flow Schedule Using the Components on Its Statement of Cash Flows

In this section, we use the reported financial statements of Starbucks Corporation (Starbucks) to illustrate the relationships between the various components on the statement of cash flows and the various components on the free cash flow schedule. We use Starbucks because the detail in its financial statements is more representative of a company's financial statements than the Bob Adams Company. We show Starbucks' summarized income statements and balance sheets for Year −1 and Year 0 in Exhibit 3.9. We also show a column of reference numbers. Under "FCF Ref," we list reference numbers that we reference

[3] One difference in the change in non-cash net operating working capital between the statement of cash flows and free cash flow schedule not shown on the exhibit is that any financing related working capital accounts, for example, interest payable, included in the change in non-cash operating working capital on the statement of cash flows would be included as an adjustment to interest to determine cash interest paid in the free cash flow schedule in order to measure equity free cash flow. We illustrate this adjustment later in the Starbucks example in Exhibit 3.10.

[4] One difference in the investing section of the statement of cash flows and adjustments used to measure free cash flow schedule not shown on the exhibit is the purchase and sale of investments included in the statement of cash flows. We would either assume that these investments, for example, investments in marketable securities, are part of the required cash needed to operating the company's business or that they are excess assets and would separate them from the free cash flow calculations. We illustrate this adjustment later in the Starbucks example in Exhibit 3.10.

EXHIBIT 3.9 Starbucks' Income Statements and Balance Sheets

Starbucks Corporation Income Statements ($ in thousands)	Year −1	Year 0	FCF Ref #
Sales	$6,369,300	$7,786,942	
Cost of goods sold	−2,605,212	−3,178,791	
Store and other operating expenses	−2,362,935	−2,947,902	
General and administrative expenses	−357,114	−473,023	
Depreciation and amortization	−340,169	−387,211	
Other operating income	76,648	93,937	
Operating income	$ 780,518	$ 893,952	1
Interest and other income	17,101	23,396	21
Interest expense	−1,272	−11,105	15
Earnings before income taxes	$ 796,347	$ 906,243	
Provision for income taxes	−301,977	−324,770	2
Cumulative effect of accounting change	0	−17,214	
Net earnings	$ 494,370	$ 564,259	

Starbucks Corporation Balance Sheets ($ in thousands)	Year −1	Year 0	FCF Ref #
Cash and cash equivalents	$ 173,809	$ 312,606	12
Short-term investments	133,227	141,038	
Receivables	190,762	224,271	
Inventories	546,299	636,222	
Other current assets	165,237	215,651	
Total current assets	$1,209,334	$1,529,788	
Land, buildings, and equipment, net	1,842,019	2,287,899	
Goodwill and other intangible assets	127,883	199,433	
Long-term investments	261,564	224,904	
Other non-current assets	72,893	186,917	
Total assets	$3,513,693	$4,428,941	
Accounts payable	$ 220,975	$ 340,937	
Short-term debt	277,000	700,000	
Current portion of long-term debt	748	762	
Accrued expenses and other	552,907	661,148	
Interest payable	318	847	
Deferred revenue	175,048	231,926	
Total current liabilities	$1,226,996	$1,935,620	
Long-term debt	2,870	1,958	
Other non-current liabilities	193,565	262,857	
Total liabilities	$1,423,431	$2,200,435	
Common stock and surplus	$ 130,361	$ 40,149	
Retained earnings	1,938,987	2,151,084	
Cumulative comprehensive income (loss)	20,914	37,273	
Total stockholders' equity	$2,090,262	$2,228,506	
Total liabilities and stockholders' equity	$3,513,693	$4,428,941	

on Starbucks' free cash flow schedule to help map the components on the free cash flow schedule to Starbucks financial statements.

The line items on Starbucks' balance sheet are the typical line items we observe for most companies. When we calculate free cash flows, we isolate a company's cash flows from operations from its cash flows from its excess assets. For Starbucks, we assume that all of its cash and cash equivalents are required to operate the company and that all of its investments (short-term investments and long-term investments) are excess assets. These assumptions are, of course, simplistic. First, Starbucks is unlikely to need all of its cash balance ($312 million) to operate the company. In addition, even though some of its long-term investments appear to be investments in government securities and are likely excess assets, at least some of the investments are related to operations and are not excess assets. For example, the company has partial equity interests in various partnerships, especially partnerships outside the United States (Starbucks Coffee Korea Company, Limited, and many others).

With a few exceptions, most of the line items in the income statement are common revenue and expense items that are easily understood. Two of the exceptions, however, are worth noting. The first exception is the line item titled, interest and other income. For simplicity, we assume that this is the income from the company's excess assets. The second exception is the line item titled, cumulative effect of accounting change.

While the details of the accounting change are not relevant to our discussion, recall that accounting changes do not affect cash; they only affect accounting accruals. Thus, this is an expense that Starbucks will add back in its calculation of operating cash flows. The word "cumulative" indicates that the amount adjusts the company's accounting accruals for not only Year 0 but for its entire history. Last, accountants show accounting changes, like this one, net of any income tax effects; thus, the provision for income taxes on the income statement is not related to this accounting change.

On the left side of Exhibit 3.10, we show Starbucks' summarized cash flow statements for Years −1 and 0. Starbucks uses a standard form for its cash flow statement, and most of the items are typical items on the cash flow statement. Comparing Starbucks' cash flow statements to its income statements, we can make several observations. First, we see that Starbucks' cash flow from operations is about twice as large as its net earnings. We can explain much (about 70%) of that difference with the add-back for depreciation and amortization. The remaining difference is largely the result of changes in various net operating working capital accounts. Second, we see that Starbucks' operating cash flow was $923 million in Year −1 and $1.13 billion in Year 0 (an increase of more than 22%), while its earnings grew from $494 million to $564 (an increase of about 14%). The higher growth rate for the company's Year 0 operating cash flow resulted from changes in various accruals.

Measuring Starbucks' Unlevered Free Cash Flow

We show our calculation of Starbucks' free cash flows on the right side of Exhibit 3.10 using the EBIT method. For now, we focus on the column titled "Reported Year 0," which we calculate using both the cash flow statement reported by Starbucks for that period and some additional information from the income statement.

Starbucks' Unlevered Cash Flow from Operations. We begin our EBIT method calculation by identifying (and when necessary, calculating) the company's EBIT from its income statement. We exclude any income statement items that are not related to the company's operations from EBIT. For Starbucks, we exclude the cumulative effect of accounting change because it is unrelated to the company's Year 0 operations; we do the same for interest and other income because we assume it is related to the company's excess assets, which we are not going to treat as ongoing in our forecast. While the interest and other income would be part of the company's free cash flows for this historical period, there is no need to incorporate them in the model that we are going to build to forecast Starbucks. Rather, we exclude their effect from our free cash flow forecasts and value the excess assets separately as of the date of our valuation. The relevant EBIT for our free cash flow calculations is $894 million, which we get from the income statement in Exhibit 3.9 (FCF 1).

If reported EBIT was Starbucks' taxable income, and if there was no change in taxes payable (which does not appear to change in this case based on the information provided), then we would subtract the taxes that the company would pay (cash amount paid) based on its EBIT. Starbucks' **effective income tax rate** or average accounting-based income tax rate is equal to the provision for income taxes in the income statement ($324.8 million) divided by earnings before income taxes ($906.2 million), which is equal to 35.8% (0.358 = $324.8/$906.2). Recall, however, the income tax on EBIT excludes the income tax shelter from interest (interest tax shield), as well as the income taxes paid on income from excess assets because we excluded the income from excess assets from EBIT in the free cash flow schedule. Thus, the effective or average tax rate is not the correct tax rate to use for EBIT unless the tax rate for interest and for income from excess assets is also equal to the effective tax rate.

Based on a review of Starbucks' income tax disclosures (not shown in the chapter), a reasonable rate to use for interest expense, T_{INT}, is 38.4%, which is equal to the sum of Starbucks' federal and net state income tax rates. We assume this is also the applicable income tax rate to use for interest and other income. Income tax on EBIT is equal to the provision for income taxes on the income statement (FCF 2) plus the interest tax shield on interest minus the income tax on the income from excess assets. The interest tax shield is equal to interest expense (FCF 15) multiplied by the tax rate for interest (0.384) and the income tax on income from excess assets is equal to the income from excess assets (FCF 21) multiplied by the corresponding income tax rate, which for Starbucks, we assume is also equal to 38.4%. Based on this calculation, the income tax for EBIT is equal to −$320,050 (−$320,050 = −324,770 −11,105 × 0.384 + 23,396 × 0.384). EBIT minus income taxes (unlevered earnings) is equal to $573,902 ($573,902 = $893,952 − $320,050). Although not shown on the balance sheet or statement of cash flows, Starbucks has deferred tax assets and deferred tax liabilities, which are included on its statement of cash flows in the change in other assets and other liabilities. Later in the chapter, we discuss deferred income taxes and how to use them to measure income tax payments when calculating free cash flows, but for now we ignore them.

EXHIBIT 3.10 Starbucks' Cash Flow Statements and Free Cash Flow Schedule

Starbucks Corporation Cash Flow Statement ($ in thousands)	Reported Year −1	Reported Year 0	FCF Ref #
Net earnings	$ 494,370	$ 564,259	
Depreciation and amortization	367,207	412,625	3
Cumulative effect of accounting change	0	17,214	24
Asset impairment charges	19,464	19,622	4
Adjustments for operating working capital:			
Receivables			5
Inventories	−121,618	−85,527	6
Other current assets			7
Accounts payable	9,717	104,966	8
Accrued expenses and other	30,216	145,427	9
Interest payable	80	529	16
Deferred revenue	53,276	56,547	10
Other, net	70,204	−104,029	11
Net cash provided by operating activities	**$ 922,915**	**$1,131,633**	25
Purchase of investments, net	$ 444,264	$ 21,924	22
Capital expenditures, net	−643,296	−771,230	13
Acquisitions, net of cash acquired	−21,583	−91,734	14
Net cash used by investing activities	**−$ 220,615**	**−$ 841,040**	
Proceeds from issuance of common stock	$ 163,555	$ 276,617	19
Repurchase of common stock	−1,113,647	−854,045	20
Increase (decrease) in short-term debt	277,000	423,000	17
Increase (decrease) in long-term debt	−735	−898	18
Net cash used by financing activities	**−$ 673,827**	**−$ 155,326**	
Effect of exchange rate changes	$ 283	$ 3,530	23
Increase (decrease) in cash	**$ 28,756**	**$ 138,797**	
Cash interest paid	**$ 1,060**	**$ 10,576**	
Cash income taxes	**$ 227,812**	**$ 274,134**	

* FCF 2 + FCF 15 × 0.384 + FCF 21 × 0.384
= −324,770 −11,105 × 0.384 + 23,396 × 0.384 = − $320,050

Starbucks Corporation Free Cash Flows ($ in thousands)	Reported Year 0	FCF Ref #
Earnings before interest and taxes (EBIT)	**$893,952**	1
Income taxes paid on EBIT	−320,050	*
Earnings before interest and after taxes	**$573,902**	Sum
Depreciation and amortization	412,625	3
Asset impairment charges	19,622	4
Receivables		5
Inventories	−85,527	6
Other current assets		7
Accounts payable	104,966	8
Accrued expenses and other	145,427	9
Deferred revenue	56,547	10
Other, net	−104,029	11
Change in required cash balance	−138,797	12
Unlevered cash flow from operations	**$984,736**	Sum
Capital expenditures, net	−771,230	13
Acquisitions, net of cash acquired	−91,734	14
Unlevered free cash flow	**$121,772**	Sum
Interest expense	−11,105	15
Change in interest payable	529	16
Interest tax shield	4,264	−15 × 0.384
Cash flow before changes in financing	**$115,460**	Sum
Increase (decrease) in short-term debt	423,000	17
Increase (decrease) in long-term debt	−898	18
Equity free cash flow	**$537,562**	Sum
Proceeds from issuance of common stock	276,617	19
Repurchase of common stock	−854,045	20
Add back effects of excess assets		
Interest and other income, after-tax	14,412	21 × (1.0 − 0.384)
Purchase of investments	21,924	22
Effect of exchange rate changes	3,530	23
Change in excess cash	**$ 0**	Sum
Change in required cash	138,797	12
Change in cash	**$138,797**	Sum
Marginal tax rate on interest, T_{INT}	38.4%	
Effective tax rate	**35.8%**	

With a few exceptions, we now adjust after-tax EBIT for all of the non-cash revenues, non-cash expenses, and changes in accounting accruals that appear on the cash flow from operations section of Starbucks' cash flow statement in Exhibit 3.10. In addition to all of the company's net operating working capital adjustments (FCF 5 through FCF 11), these adjustments include the adjustments for depreciation and amortization (FCF 3) and asset impairment charges (FCF 4). However, we do not adjust for interest payable (FCF 16), for free cash flows exclude all effects of financing. An alternative way to explain these adjustments is that since we are adjusting EBIT, we do not consider any item in the operating section of the cash flow that is not related to EBIT (since interest is not part of EBIT, we do not consider changes in interest payable).

In addition, in this section of our free cash flow calculation, we also subtract the change in required cash, for it represents an investment in net operating working capital that is similar to the investment in inventory and other operating current assets (FCF 12, $139 million), as we assume the observed change in cash is the change in required cash. We do not adjust after-tax EBIT for the cumulative effect of accounting change (FCF 24) because we excluded this amount when we measured EBIT (FCF 1) so it does not include this amount (whereas net earnings does, which is why this adjustment is in the operating section of the cash flow statement). We added back the asset impairment charges, for they are non-cash expenses, and the company books an expense by writing down the carrying value of some of its assets. The sum of the above items is equal to the company's **unlevered cash flow from operations**—in other words, the cash flow the company generates from its operations before any capital expenditures and before cash flows either to or from its investors. Starbucks' unlevered cash flow from operations is equal to $985 million.

Starbucks' Unlevered Free Cash Flow. To calculate a company's (unlevered) free cash flow, we reduce the company's unlevered cash flow from operations by the amount of capital expenditures necessary for the company to implement its strategic plan. In general, we identify capital expenditure information from the investing section of the company's cash flow statement. Starbucks has three items in the investing section of its cash flow statement presented in Exhibit 3.10. The first item is the purchase of investments (net of sales). Earlier we assumed that these investments shown on the balance sheet are excess assets, and therefore we exclude the purchase or sale of them from our calculation of free cash flows. However, we include the other two items. One of the items—capital expenditures, net (FCF 13, $771 million)—is included in the calculation of free cash flows because it represents investments in the company's operating assets.

The second item—acquisitions, net of cash acquired (FCF 14, $92 million)—represents the net assets acquired by the company through acquisitions, which is also included in the calculation of free cash flows. This item understates the amount paid for acquisitions for two reasons. First, it excludes the cash acquired, but it is likely that this is a relatively small amount. Second, and likely more important, it nets out any debt and other interest-bearing liabilities assumed by the company, and only shows the net amount. Since we are primarily interested in measuring unlevered free cash flows, we want to deduct the total amount of cash investments. Hence, if known, we treat the financing of any investments separately from the investing cash flows rather than showing only the net investment acquired. By netting the debt and other interest-bearing liabilities assumed in the acquisition, we understate the amount invested. We would need additional information to measure the total amount of the investment acquired which we do not have in these exhibits.

A somewhat related issue regarding how accountants prepare cash flow statements (discussed briefly before) is the exclusion of what we refer to as dual purchase / financing transactions. For example, the cash flow statement would exclude the purchase of a manufacturing plant financed by means of a mortgage from the seller. However, to measure free cash flows, we treat the transaction as two transactions: the purchase of the manufacturing plant, which we show as a capital expenditure, and the financing of that purchase with a mortgage. A rather common example of such a dual transaction is the capitalization of leases in which the company records an asset and a liability for the amount of the capitalized lease. In this case, neither the increase in the asset nor the increase in the liability appears on the cash flow statement. Fortunately, accounting standards require companies to disclose such non-cash transactions in supplemental disclosures. Starbucks had no such non-cash transactions in Year 0. Starbucks' (**unlevered**) **free cash flow** is equal to its unlevered cash flow from operations ($985 million) less its capital expenditures and acquisition expenditures ($771 million and $92 million), which equals $122 million ($122 = $985 − $771 − $92).

Measuring Starbucks' Equity Free Cash Flow

To calculate a company's equity free cash flow, we deduct all after-tax cash flows to or from non-common equity investors from the (unlevered) free cash flow. An intermediate calculation between free cash flow and equity free cash flow is the **cash flow before changes in financing** (also often referred to as the **pre-debt repayment cash flow**). To calculate the cash flow before changes in financing, we deduct all after-tax interest and preferred stock dividend cash flows paid to the company's non-common equity investors.

Starbucks does not have any preferred stock, but it does have debt; thus, we calculate Starbucks' cash flow before changes in financing by deducting the after-tax interest paid to debtholders from its free cash flow. Starbucks' interest expense appears on its income statement (FCF 15, $11 million). We adjust interest expense for the change in interest payable (FCF 16, $0.5 million)—which appears on its cash flow statement—to measure the amount of interest it paid in cash. We then add back any interest tax shield from its interest. In this illustration, using a simple calculation to measure its interest tax shield, we multiply the tax rate for interest (calculated earlier as 0.384) by the amount of interest expense (FCF 15 × 0.384, $4 = $11 × 0.384). Starbucks' cash flow before changes in financing is $115 million ($115.5 = $122 − $11 + $0.5 + $4). This cash flow is relevant to Starbucks for executing its capital structure strategy. Since this cash flow is positive ($115.5 million), Starbucks does not need to raise additional capital for this period unless it needs to pay off debt or wants to repurchase common stock or pay dividends.

We calculate Starbucks' equity free cash flow by deducting any change in its non-common equity financing from the cash flow before changes in financing. Starbucks increased its short-term debt by $423 million (FCF 17) and decreased its long-term debt by $1 million (FCF 18). Thus, its equity free cash flow is equal to $537.5 million ($537.5 = $115.5 + $423 − $1).

Reconciling Starbucks' Equity Free Cash Flow to Its Change in Cash Balance

The remainder of the free cash flow schedule in Exhibit 3.10 reconciles Starbucks' equity free cash flow to the change in its cash balance. This reconciliation has three parts. The first part adjusts for the cash flows to and from common equityholders. For Starbucks, these adjustments include an issuance of common stock (FCF 19, \$277 million) and a repurchase of common stock (FCF 20, −\$854 million). You might be wondering why Starbucks issued and repurchased stock in the same year. Most of the issuance of the stock was the exercise of employee stock options or other stock-related compensation. The repurchase of the stock was part of the company's stock repurchase plan. Knowing this, we now understand why Starbucks might have issued the short-term debt; it needed extra cash to be able to repurchase shares for more than \$850 million.

The second part of the reconciliation is for the cash flow resulting from excess assets. Although we do not include it in EBIT, we now include any after-tax interest income—FCF 21 adjusted for taxes, \$14 million = \$23 × (1 − 0.384)—and any increase or decrease in the amount of excess assets (FCF 22, \$22 million), in order to reconcile to the change in cash. The third part takes into consideration the effect of changes in exchange rates. If we add these three parts to equity free cash flow, we arrive at the change in the company's excess cash, which in this case is 0. Next, we add the change in the company's required cash balance (FCF 12) to the change in the company's excess cash to reconcile to the change in the company's total cash balance.

Calculating Starbucks' Free Cash Flow Using the Cash Flow Statement

In Exhibit 3.11, we show the calculation of Starbucks' free cash flow using the cash flow from operations method. Using this method, we begin with a company's cash flow from operations (FCF 25, \$1.131 billion). Next, we adjust it for any effects that we do not consider to be part of the company's operations. For Starbucks, this adjustment includes deducting the income from its excess assets (FCF 21 adjusted for income taxes, which we calculate to be \$14 million in the prior section). Since the change in the company's required cash balance (FCF 12) is deducted when calculating free cash flows (a deduction not made by accountants when measuring cash flow from operations), we also deduct it here. The sum of these amounts is equal to the company's adjusted cash flow from operations.

EXHIBIT 3.11 Starbucks' Free Cash Flow Measured Using the Cash Flow Statement

Starbucks Corporation **Free Cash Flows (\$ in thousands)**	**Reported** **Year 0**	**FCF** **Ref #**
Net cash provided by operating activities	\$1,131,633	25
Remove effects of excess assets on CFO		
Interest and other income, after tax	−14,412	21 × (1.0 − 0.384)
Change in required cash balance	−138,797	12
Adjusted cash flow from operations	**\$ 978,424**	Sum
Interest expense	11,105	15
Change in interest payable	−529	16
Interest tax shield	−4,264	15 × 0.384
Unlevered cash flow from operations	**\$ 984,736**	Sum
Acquisitions, net of cash acquired	−91,734	14
Capital expenditures	−771,230	13
Unlevered free cash flow	**\$ 121,772**	Sum

We add back after-tax cash interest to measure the company's unlevered cash flow from operations. For Starbucks, this adjustment has three parts—adding back interest (FCF 15), subtracting the increase in interest payable (FCF 16), and deducting the interest tax shield (FCF 15 × 0.384). The unlevered cash flow from operations we measure using this method is the same as the unlevered cash flow from operations using the EBIT method. To calculate free cash flow we subtract the amount spent on acquisitions (FCF 14) and capital expenditures (FCF 13). The remaining equity free cash flow and cash reconciliation calculations are the same for both free cash flow calculation methods, so we do not repeat them here.

Using Cash Flows in Financial Analysis and Valuation

Forecasting free cash flows requires an understanding of the company historically as well as in the future. We discussed this issue in Chapter 2 as we sought to analyze the competitiveness of an industry and a company's competitive advantage. One potentially useful financial analysis is to use a company's historical financial statements to calculate its historical free cash flows as we did for Starbucks. Analyzing a company's historical free cash flows can help us think about the company's future free cash flows, which we will forecast from our financial model (discussed in Chapter 4).

Since our purpose for analyzing historical cash flows is to understand the past in order to forecast the future, it is useful to partition the cash flow measures into cash flows related to existing and ongoing operations from cash flows related to "one-time" events or circumstances. For example, even though a company may have experienced effects from foreign currency translation on its balance sheet accounts, we would not generally forecast these effects going forward, as they are non-cash in nature. Hence, we will not likely allow for this complexity in our forecasts.

Unlevered operating cash flows and free cash flows provide a useful complement to earnings as we analyze the performance of a company. Neither earnings measures nor cash flow measures reveal the economic earnings of the company although both types of performance measures can be useful to understand the company's economic earnings. Earnings measures can provide better information on the company's long-run earning power. Cash flow measures can provide information on the resources that can be distributed to claimholders, and they are less easily manipulated than earnings; however, they can match revenues and expenses poorly and not portray future earning power very well. In addition, cash flows are typically more variable than earnings, usually due to "lumpy" capital expenditures and other investments that earnings generally smooth (capital expenditures are not subtracted in calculating earnings but are smoothed using a depreciation charge against earnings over time).

The ratio of unlevered earnings to unlevered cash flow from operations indicates the magnitude of accruals in unlevered earnings. Over the life of the company, its cumulative earnings roughly equal its cumulative cash flow; thus, this ratio is roughly equal to one. However, in any one year, a company's cash flow can be greater than or less than its earnings; in other words, this ratio can be greater than or less than one. A ratio greater than one indicates the company is recording accruals (non-cash items) that increase the company's earnings above its cash flow. It can be useful to understand the reasons why a company's ratio is consistently greater or less than one. One can also examine this ratio over time to discern if earnings and cash flows are both growing at the same rate or different rates. If they are not growing at the same rate, it may be useful to analyze the reasons why this ratio is changing. Cash flows before changes in financing provide a useful measure to understand the flexibility a company has in pursuing its financing strategy. A positive cash flow before changes in financing indicates that the company can either pay down or redeem its non-common equity securities, distribute cash to its owners, or accumulate excess cash. A negative cash flow before changes in financing indicates the need for additional financing or that the company will draw down its cash balance.

Most studies indicate that operating cash flows do not provide a superior ability to predict events—such as bankruptcy—relative to earnings, nor do they explain as much variation in stock returns relative to earnings. However, other studies indicate that earnings and cash flows, when used in conjunction with each other, explain stock price movements more accurately than using either alone.[5]

In valuing a company, it is important to understand where various balance sheet accounts flow into the different sections of the statement of cash flows—operating, investing, and financing. While it is very obvious where some balance sheet accounts flow to the cash flow statement—such as accounts receivable and inventory—it is not equally obvious for some balance sheet accounts—such as other assets or other liabilities. It is important for us to understand this mapping, for if we know exactly how the various balance sheet accounts map into the different partitions of the statement of cash flows, we can more accurately estimate the unlevered free cash flows. We typically are not overly concerned with misclassifying a cash flow or adjustment to the cash flows between operating cash flows and investing cash flows, for

[5] See, for example, Dechow, P., "Accounting Earnings and Cash Flows as Measures of Firm Performance: The Role of Accounting Accruals," *Journal of Accounting and Economics* (July 1994), pp. 3–42.

both are part of the calculation of unlevered free cash flows, which is of primary interest. However, if we misclassify a cash flow or adjustment to the cash flows between the operating and financing sections or between the investing and financing sections, the unlevered free cash flows will be measured incorrectly. Thus, even if we projected the balance sheet and income statement for future years with perfect accuracy, our measured unlevered free cash flows could be forecasted with significant error if we do not know where certain balance sheet accounts map into the statement of cash flows (operating, investing, financing and reconciliation to the change in cash).

We can reconstruct the company's cash flow statement from its income statement, balance sheet, statement of shareholders' equity and supplemental footnote information; we can then use the reconstructed cash flow statements to calculate free cash flows. For most companies, the reconstructed cash flow statements and free cash flow schedules will not be the same as the reported cash flow statement and related free cash flows. This is true for a variety of reasons. However, we can usually learn enough through the reconstruction process to be confident about where the balance sheet accounts map into the statement of cash flows. Once we achieve that, we can be more confident about how the relevant accounts map into the calculation of the free cash flows.

3.5 DIFFERENCES BETWEEN BOOK AND TAX ACCOUNTING AND THE EFFECT ON INCOME TAX RATES

LO3 Analyze income tax disclosures

Measuring income taxes and marginal income tax rates on different types of income and expenses, such as interest, is a necessary step in most valuation analyses. In this section, we provide an overview of income tax issues that can arise when conducting a valuation. The first issue that arises is that the income before tax in a company's financial statements does not represent the taxable income reported to the taxing authority. Thus, the income tax expense (**provision for income taxes**) in the financial statements does not equal the taxes due on the company's tax forms. These differences arise as a result of differences between the accounting rules used to prepare income tax returns and the accounting principles used to prepare financial statements.

Some differences between a company's tax records and its financial statements are **permanent differences**; that is, the revenues and/or expenses on the tax records are permanently different from the revenues and/or expenses in the financial statements. However, a company may also have **temporary differences** between its tax records and its financial statements; that is, the revenues and/or expenses on the tax records are temporarily different from the revenues and/or expenses in the financial statements, but the difference eventually reverses so that the cumulative revenues and expenses are the same in the long run.

Permanent Differences Between Book and Tax Accounting

Permanent differences between income reported on a company's financial statements (**book accounting**) and taxable income reported on the company's tax returns (**tax accounting**) occur because certain revenues or expenses are recognized for financial reporting purposes that differ from the revenues and expenses recognized for income tax purposes. A U.S. example of a permanent difference is the interest on municipal bonds that is not taxable; that is, the investor holding a municipal bond (for example, the bonds of a city or state) does not have to pay federal income taxes on the interest earned on those bonds. The income statement reports income for municipal bond interest but the tax records do not. Other U.S. examples of permanent differences include: compensation expense for certain stock options (expense is not tax deductible), dividends received exclusion (a portion of certain types of dividends received from other corporations is not taxable), the write-down of non-tax deductible goodwill due to impairment (expense is not tax deductible), premiums paid and proceeds received on life insurance policies of key managers (premiums are not tax deductible, and proceeds are not taxable), and fines resulting from the violation of the law (fines are not tax deductible). For a company with only permanent differences, the provision for income taxes (income tax expense) in the financial statements is equal to the income tax that the company must pay to the taxing authority.

The **effective income tax rate** based on the financial statements (provision for income taxes divided by income before taxes) will generally differ from the income tax rate reflected in the company's tax forms. Thus, the effective tax rate in the financial statements does not represent the tax rate for calculating interest tax shields, or the tax rate that the company will pay on additional income, or the income tax rate used for EBIT in the free cash flow schedule.

Assume a company has taxable income equal to \$100,000, but it also has \$10,000 in interest income from non-taxable municipal bonds. Assume further that the company has a 40% tax rate on all types of taxable income. For financial accounting purposes, the company has income before tax equal to \$110,000. For income tax purposes, the company has income equal to \$100,000 and an income tax liability equal to \$40,000 (\$40,000 = 0.4 × \$100,000). Since the municipal bond interest is a permanent difference, the financial accounting records also reflect the \$40,000 income tax liability. The correct calculation and presentation of the company's income taxes is as follows:

	Tax (40%)	Book
Income before interest expense and interest income	\$120,000	\$120,000
Interest expense	−20,000	−20,000
Municipal bond interest		10,000
Taxable income or income before taxes	\$100,000	\$110,000
Income tax payable or expense (provision)	−40,000	−40,000
Net income	\$ 60,000	\$ 70,000
Effective income tax rate	40.0%	36.4%

A permanent difference in net income—between the income tax records and financial statements—causes the effective tax rate implied in the financial statements to differ from the statutory tax rate. The effective tax rate implied in the financial statements is simply calculated as the provision for income taxes (income tax expense) divided by income before tax. In our example, the effective income tax rate is 36.4% (0.364 = \$40,000/\$110,000) rather than 40.0%. This difference is important because the effective tax rate implied in the financial statements does not represent the tax rate used in the calculation of interest tax shields, or the income tax rate that the company pays on its taxable income, or the income tax rate used for EBIT in the free cash flow schedule. U.S. companies are required to reconcile the difference between the U.S. federal statutory rate and the effective income tax rate. The reconciliation is useful because it provides us with information relevant to determining the tax rate the company faces. In this case, the reconciliation would indicate that the company is paying at the 40% tax rate on its taxable income. The reconciliation for the company in our example is as follows:

Reconciliation to the Statutory Rate	
Statutory rate	40.0%
Non-taxable municipal bond interest*	-3.6%
Effective income tax rate	36.4%

*Calculated as 0.4 × \$10,000/\$110,000

The income tax rate for interest, T_{INT}, is an input to measure free cash flows. Given the assumptions in this example, we know the income tax rate for interest is 40%. While in this case it is easy to determine the income tax rate on interest that is not always the case. We illustrate the steps in performing this calculation. First, we measure the interest tax shield, which is equal to the difference between the income taxes paid by the company with and without the interest deduction. In other words, the difference between the income taxes paid if the company did not have debt and its actual income taxes. In the above example, if the company did not have any interest expense, its taxable income would equal its operating income, \$120,000. The income tax on taxable income of \$120,000 is \$48,000 (\$48,000 = 0.4 × \$120,000). As shown in the above table, the income tax on taxable income after deducting interest is \$40,000. The income tax reduction from the interest deduction, that is, the interest tax shield, is \$8,000 (\$8,000 = \$48,000 − \$40,000). Based on the interest tax shield, we measure the income tax rate for interest, T_{INT}, as the interest tax shield divided by the interest deduction, 40% (0.4 = \$8,000/\$20,000). We note that in cases where the company has net operating losses (NOLs) or has interest expense that exceeds the limitation on tax deductible interest, measuring the interest tax shield and the income tax rate for interest is more complicated. We discuss these issues later in the chapter.

In this example, EBIT is equal to the company's income, \$70,000, plus its interest expense, \$20,000, plus its income taxes, \$40,000, or \$130,000 (assuming we include the municipal bond interest in EBIT). The accounting-based income tax on EBIT is equal to actual income tax paid plus the interest tax shield, \$48,000 (\$48,000 = \$40,000 + \$8,000). This income tax is also equal to the income taxes paid because the company only has a permanent difference (no temporary difference), and thus, the accounting-based income tax (income tax expense) is equal to the income tax paid. The accounting-based income tax rate for EBIT is equal to 36.9%, (0.369 = $48,000/$130,000), which is not equal to either the effective tax rate, 36.4%, or the income tax rate for interest, 40%. Although we can calculate the income tax rate on EBIT in this way, we typically do not need this income tax rate because we can calculate the amount of the accounting-based income taxes on EBIT as the actual provision for income taxes (income tax expense) plus the interest tax shield, which does not require knowing this rate. Again, it is important to remember that here we assume that the only difference between book income and tax income is a permanent difference; with temporary differences this calculation is more complex.

REVIEW EXERCISE 3.3

Effect of Permanent Difference on Income Tax Rates

A company has $200,000 of income before interest expense and interest income on both its income statement (book) and tax forms (tax). The company also has $80,000 of interest expense that is also tax deductible and $60,000 of municipal bond interest income that is not taxable. The company has a 40% tax rate on all types of income. Calculate the company's effective tax rate and prepare a reconciliation between its 40% statutory rate and its effective tax rate. Also calculate the company's interest tax shield and the income tax rate for interest. Assume the company's EBIT is $260,000 ($260,000 = $200,000 + $60,000), what is the income tax the company would pay on EBIT? Assume that all interest expense is tax deductible in each year and is not subject to any limitation.

Solution on page 149.

Temporary Differences Between Book and Tax Accounting

A company's income tax expense shown on the income statement usually does not equal the income taxes on its tax forms that are currently payable to various governments. In the past, some countries had close uniformity between book and tax accounting, however in the U.S., and in many other countries now, a company's financial statements are not identical to its income tax records (filed with various tax authorities), and the differences are not just permanent differences.

Temporary differences arise when the revenues and/or expenses on the tax records are temporarily different from the revenues and/or expenses in the financial statements. These temporary differences between the book and tax records eventually reverse themselves so that the cumulative expenses or revenues are the same over the life of the firm. Temporary differences result in the creation of either **deferred income tax asset** or **deferred income tax liability** accounts (or both). Deferred income tax asset or liability accounts arise when the values of the assets and liabilities on a company's financial statements (the **book value** of its assets and liabilities) do not equal the values in its income tax records (the **tax basis** of the assets and liabilities) because of temporary differences. Permanent differences do not create deferred income tax assets or liabilities. If it is more likely than not that the company will not be able to capture the benefit of a deferred tax asset, accounting rules require companies to offset (reduce) the balance of a deferred tax asset using a separate **valuation allowance** account. In other words, if management does not expect to be able to capture the benefits of a deferred tax asset, the company reduces the value of its deferred tax asset for the amount of the asset that it may not be able to capture. A valuation allowance is a contra-asset account and essentially records the reduction in the deferred tax assets in such circumstances.

Deferred tax asset and liability accounts do not represent cash flows. Why do we care about them when valuing a company? We care about deferred income taxes because we typically do not have access to a company's income tax records. Therefore, we use the deferred income tax assets and liabilities in order to measure the company's income tax payable to the tax authorities, which we use to calculate free cash flows. While deferred tax asset and liability accounts are not cash flows in themselves, we use them to calculate income taxes paid by adjusting the provision for income taxes (income tax expense on the income statement).

Conceptually, the balance of a company's net deferred income taxes (that is, the net of the company's deferred tax assets and deferred tax liabilities) is equal to the difference between the book value and tax basis of the company's assets and liabilities, multiplied by the appropriate tax rate. The provision for income taxes reported on the company's income statement is equal to the sum of the income tax on the company's income tax returns and the adjustments for deferred income taxes and other items related to the current period. The deferred tax adjustment to a company's income tax provision is equal to the change in deferred income tax assets and liabilities that relate to the company's operations (for example, excluding any deferred tax assets and liabilities related to excess assets).

More specifically, a deferred tax liability results whenever the book value of an asset is greater than the tax basis of that asset, or when the book value of a liability is less than the tax basis of that liability. This difference occurs when the cumulative expenses deducted for tax purposes are greater than the cumulative expenses deducted for accounting purposes. Conversely, a deferred tax asset results whenever the book value of an asset is less than the tax basis of that asset, or when the book value of a liability is greater than the tax basis of that liability. This difference occurs when the cumulative expenses deducted for tax purposes are less than the cumulative expenses deducted for accounting purposes.

Effects on Valuation Analyses. We use cash income taxes, not income tax expense, in order to measure free cash flows. Understanding the change in deferred income taxes is useful in order to calculate a company's income taxes paid from the company's provision for income taxes (income tax expense) on the income statement. When valuing the equity of a company, we subtract the value of the non-common equity claims from the value of the firm. We do not include deferred tax liabilities as a non-common equity claim just as we do not include the company's operating liabilities in that calculation. In other words, it is incorrect to deduct deferred tax liabilities (or add the value of deferred tax assets) when measuring the value of the common equity, and it is also incorrect to use deferred tax liabilities to measure the capital structure ratios of a company in order to then estimate the company's cost of capital.

Example of a Deferred Tax Liability Resulting from Depreciation

We demonstrate the basic deferred tax issues with a simple example. In Exhibit 3.12, we show a company with $100,000 in income before it deducts depreciation. The company has tax deductible depreciation of $20,000 and reports depreciation on the income statement of $10,000. This is all of the depreciation recorded by the company. The company has a 40.0% income tax rate on taxable income. Since the company has $80,000 in taxable income, it pays $32,000 in income taxes. The company only has $10,000 of depreciation expense for financial reporting purposes for the current year because it uses a slower rate for depreciation for financial reporting purposes, and thus has income before taxes equal to $90,000 in its financial records. Because of the way companies typically recognize depreciation for income tax purposes in the U.S. (on an accelerated basis), this example is the typical situation for most companies.

EXHIBIT 3.12 Income Tax Payable Versus Provision for Income Taxes

	Tax (40%)	Book
Income before depreciation	$100,000	$100,000
Depreciation	–20,000	–10,000
Taxable income or income before taxes	$ 80,000	$ 90,000
Income tax payable (tax) and provision for income taxes (book)	–32,000	??
Income	$ 48,000	??

What is the company's provision for income taxes (income tax expense) for financial reporting purposes? One view is that the provision for income taxes should be equal to the amount payable to the taxing authorities ($32,000), for this is what the company pays. Another view is that reporting a provision for income taxes of $32,000 does not convey complete information because it distorts the implied tax rate the company actually pays. A provision for income taxes equal to $32,000 implies an effective tax rate of 35.6% (0.356 = $32,000/$90,000), which is lower than the statutory tax rate of 40.0% the company actually pays. In the U.S., GAAP requires companies to include in the provision for income taxes any amount that is deferred to future periods.

To calculate the deferred portion of the provision for income taxes, we first measure the **net book value** and the **income tax basis** of the underlying asset. Net book value is equal to the asset's **acquisition cost** (the amount the company originally paid) minus the total amount of depreciation deducted for financial reporting purposes. The tax basis of the asset is equal to the acquisition cost minus the total amount of depreciation deducted for income tax purposes. Assume the company originally paid \$200,000 for the asset three years ago. During the last three years, the company deducted total depreciation of \$90,000 for income tax purposes, which includes \$20,000 of depreciation for this year. Thus, the asset has a tax basis of \$110,000 at the end of the year and \$130,000 at the beginning of the year. Assume the company uses the straight-line depreciation method and expenses \$10,000 in depreciation each year for financial reporting purposes. The net book value of the asset is \$170,000 at the end of the year and \$180,000 at the beginning of the year, which we show in Exhibit 3.13.

We know that the difference between the asset's tax basis and net book value will eventually reverse once the asset is fully depreciated on both the tax and financial accounting records. In the early years, the tax depreciation will be larger than the book depreciation. In the later years, the book depreciation will be larger than the tax depreciation, and eventually the cumulative tax and book depreciation will be equal. Until the difference completely reverses, however, cumulative taxable income will not equal cumulative income reported in the financial statements.

EXHIBIT 3.13 Tax Basis Versus Book Value

	Tax Basis	Book Value	Difference (Book Value - Tax Basis)
Original amount paid (acquisition cost)	\$200,000	\$200,000	\$ 0
Depreciation deducted or expensed as of the beginning of the year	–70,000	–20,000	50,000
Taxable basis or book value as of the beginning of the year	\$130,000	\$180,000	\$50,000
Depreciation deducted or expensed during the current year	–20,000	–10,000	10,000
Taxable basis or book value as of the end of the year	\$110,000	\$170,000	\$60,000

The tax basis of the asset at the end of the year is \$110,000 and its net book value is \$170,000. The difference between the tax basis and book value of \$60,000 is the additional depreciation that has been deducted on the tax records relative to what the company deducted for financial reporting purposes. The income tax effect of this difference is \$24,000 (40.0% × \$60,000), which is the balance required in the deferred tax liability account for this asset as of the end of the current year. The income tax rate for the calculation of deferred income taxes is the rate that the company expects to be paying at the time of the reversal, which may differ from the current income tax rate. In our example, we assume a constant income tax rate for all types of income currently and in future years, so we only use one income tax rate, 40%. The tax basis of the asset at the beginning of the year was \$130,000, and its net book value was \$180,000. The difference between the tax basis and book value of \$50,000 resulted in a deferred tax liability balance of \$20,000 (40.0% × \$50,000) at the beginning of the year.

Recall that the provision for income taxes reported on the company's income statement is equal to the amount of income tax payable (\$32,000 noted earlier) plus the change in its net deferred income taxes (deferred tax assets minus deferred tax liabilities) for the year (\$4,000 = \$24,000 − \$20,000). Thus, the provision for income taxes is equal to \$36,000, of which \$32,000 is currently payable and \$4,000 is deferred (as shown in Exhibit 3.14). Note that recording deferred income taxes in this way results in an effective tax rate implied in the income statement that is equal to the statutory tax rate. The effective income tax rate (implied in the company's income statement) is now 40.0% (0.40 = \$36,000/\$90,000), which is equal to the statutory tax rate. It is not always the case that the effect of a deferred tax adjustment will result in the effective tax rate (provision for income taxes divided by income before taxes) being equal to the statutory tax rate because the provision for income taxes is affected by various types of permanent differences. If the only difference between income taxes paid and the provision for income taxes results from deferred income taxes like those in this example, the deferred income tax adjustment results in an effective tax rate equal to the statutory tax rate.

The \$24,000 in additional deductions recorded on the tax records will reverse in the future because tax depreciation will eventually be lower than book depreciation. By the end of the life over which the asset is depreciated, the cumulative depreciation deducted for tax purposes and for book purposes will be the same. In the future, as the difference reverses, the company will pay higher income taxes than the reported income tax expense in its financial reports; for this reason, accountants classify this timing difference as a liability (something to be paid in the future). Of course, at an aggregate level, the total deferred tax liability on the balance sheet associated with depreciation (or anything else) might not reverse if the company continues to grow. For example, while the deferred tax liability will eventually disappear for an individual asset, the aggregate deferred tax liability associated with depreciation could continue to grow if the company keeps growing.

EXHIBIT 3.14 Income Tax Payable Versus Provision for Income Taxes

	Tax (40%)	Book
Income before depreciation	$100,000	$100,000
Depreciation	–20,000	–10,000
Taxable income or income before taxes	$ 80,000	$ 90,000
Provision for income taxes:		
Current	–$ 32,000	–$ 32,000
Deferred		–4,000
Provision for income taxes—total	–$ 32,000	–$ 36,000
Net income	$ 48,000	$ 54,000
Effective income tax rate	40.0%	40.0%

Valuation Key 3.4

For most companies, an important difference between income for financial reporting and tax purposes is the use of straight-line depreciation for financial reporting purposes and the use of accelerated depreciation for tax purposes. In many valuations, it is useful to model the effect of the accelerated depreciation deductions on free cash flows. Accelerated depreciation deductions in the U.S. are based on the Modified Accelerated Cost Recovery System (MACRS). In addition, there are certain assets that can be entirely expensed in the year purchased, which is essentially an extreme form of accelerated depreciation.

Overview of the Modified Accelerated Cost Recovery System (MACRS)

Naturally, for income tax purposes, tax-paying companies generally prefer to depreciate a capitalized asset as quickly as possible in order to minimize the present value of the income taxes they pay. In the U.S., companies can write off some qualifying assets entirely in the year purchased. Under the Tax Cuts and Jobs Act of 2017, the amount that can be written off for those qualifying assets in one year declines in subsequent years. For other assets (and for the portion of those qualifying assets not written off in the first year), companies use the MACRS depreciation schedules for tax purposes, which we illustrate in Exhibit 3.15. This same approach—depreciate as quickly as possible—is not necessarily the best depreciation method to use for reporting company performance to investors. In the U.S. and in some other countries, generally accepted accounting principles allow companies to use different depreciation methods for income tax and financial reporting purposes. The depreciation method most commonly used in financial reports in the U.S. is the **straight-line depreciation method**. The straight-line depreciation method depreciates the acquisition cost minus salvage value equally over each year of the useful life of the asset.

In the U.S., companies are required to use the MACRS depreciation method for most business and investment property placed in service after 1986. MACRS uses two depreciation systems: the General Depreciation System (GDS) and the Alternative Depreciation System (ADS); however, the ADS system is used in limited situations, and companies use the GDS system for most assets. We use the acronym MACRS when we describe the GDS system. MACRS depreciates a certain percentage of an asset's cost every year. We show these percentages using the "half-year" convention. In other words, regardless of when the asset was purchased, a company depreciates one-half of a full-year of MACRS depreciation in the year acquired. This convention extends the depreciation to one year after the MACRS depreciation period. Companies can adopt other timing conventions as well, and there are elections available to use straight-line depreciation instead of accelerated methods. Since most companies use the straight-line depreciation method for financial reporting purposes and use the MACRS system for income tax purposes, the example in the previous section for depreciation is representative of the situation for most companies in the U.S.

EXHIBIT 3.15 MACRS Depreciation Schedule Using Half-Year Convention

	Depreciation Period (Half-Year Convention)					
Year	**3**	**5**	**7**	**10**	**15**	**20**
SL*	33.333%	20.000%	14.286%	10.000%	6.667%	5.000%
1	33.330%	20.000%	14.290%	10.000%	5.000%	3.750%
2	44.450%	32.000%	24.490%	18.000%	9.500%	7.219%
3	14.810%	19.200%	17.490%	14.400%	8.550%	6.677%
4	7.410%	11.520%	12.490%	11.520%	7.700%	6.177%
5		11.520%	8.930%	9.220%	6.930%	5.713%
6		5.760%	8.920%	7.370%	6.230%	5.285%
7			8.930%	6.550%	5.900%	4.888%
8			4.460%	6.550%	5.910%	4.522%
9				6.560%	5.900%	4.462%
10				6.550%	5.910%	4.461%
11				3.280%	5.900%	4.462%
12					5.910%	4.461%
13					5.900%	4.462%
14					5.910%	4.461%
15					5.900%	4.462%
16					2.950%	4.461%
17						4.462%
18						4.461%
19						4.462%
20						4.461%
21						2.231%
	100%	100%	100%	100%	100%	100%

* SL = straight line depreciation annual percentage

REVIEW EXERCISE 3.4

Deferred Tax Liabilities and Depreciation

Assume a company originally paid $600,000 for an asset three years ago. The asset has a three-year life and zero salvage value at the end of the three years. For the past two years, the company deducted depreciation on this asset for income tax purposes according to the MACRS depreciation schedule using the half-year convention in Exhibit 3.15. It uses straight-line depreciation for financial reporting purposes. In the past, the company had $400,000 of taxable income and book income before deducting depreciation expense, and it expects to have that same income for the foreseeable future. The company has a 40% income tax rate. Calculate the following for Year 3: the amount of tax the company will pay, the depreciation expense and cumulative depreciation expensed for tax and book purposes, the income tax expense shown on the income statement, the net income shown on the income statement, and the balance in its deferred tax asset and liability accounts. Assume the company records a full year of straight-line depreciation in its accounting records in the year it acquires the asset but must use the half-year convention for its tax records.

Solution on pages 149–150.

Example of a Deferred Tax Asset Arising from a Warranty Liability

As we indicated previously, one of the ways a deferred tax asset arises is if the book value of a liability exceeds the tax basis of a liability. One way a deferred tax asset will occur is when a liability is not recognized at all for tax purposes but is recognized for financial reporting purposes. For example, financial reporting rules require companies to estimate warranty liabilities they will incur when they sell a product with a warranty or sell a separate warranty plan such as an extended warranty, whereas the tax rules only allow the deduction when the company pays for warranty work performed. Thus, the company does not have a warranty liability for income tax purposes (tax basis equals zero) but reports an expense or in some cases a reduction in revenue and a corresponding warranty liability for finanical reporting purposes when it has a sale.

Consider the following example. If a company in its first year of operations sold products and booked \$5,000 in estimated warranty expenses, but only incurred actual warranty costs of \$1,000, the difference between book and taxable income is \$4,000. If the company had \$10,000 of income before warranty expenses, its tax records would show \$9,000 of taxable income and \$3,600 of taxes due the taxing authority (assuming a 40% tax rate). For financial reporting purposes, the company would show \$5,000 of income before tax and a provision for income taxes of \$2,000. For financial reporting purposes, at the end of the year, the company would have a \$4,000 warranty liability (\$4,000 = \$5,000 − \$1,000) and would record a deferred tax asset of \$1,600 (\$1,600 = \$4,000 × 40%). The increase in the deferred tax asset from \$0 to \$1,600 indicates that the company's taxes due were \$1,600 higher than the provision for income taxes on its financial reports.

Disclosures of Uncertain Tax Positions

Another type of difference between book and tax accounting is uncertain tax positions. An uncertain tax position is when a company recognizes an expense (or other type of tax benefit) for tax purposes that has a non-zero probability of being rejected by the taxing authority. For example, assume a company recognizes an expense on its income tax forms and initially on its financial statements that has a less than 100% probability of being allowed as a deduction by the taxing authority. If the company concludes that the probability that the expense will be accepted by the taxing authority is less than 50%, the company eliminates the entire tax benefit from the expense by increasing income tax expense and recording an operating liability, called a tax contingency for the unrecognized tax benefit. The company's income tax payable is based on the position it took on its tax return.

If the company concludes that the probability is at least 50% but less than 100% that the expense (or other type of tax benefit) will be accepted by the taxing authority, the company eliminates a portion of the tax benefit from the expense and records a tax contingency for the unrecognized tax benefit liability in the same amount. The company determines the amount recorded as additional tax expense and liability based on its assessment of the potential outcomes and corresponding probabilities based on the technical merits of its position. In either situation, the company's income tax payable is based on the position it took on its tax return with respect to this issue and the increase in the income tax expense and liability recorded for the unrecognized tax benefit is based on the tax benefit it did not recognize in the financial reporting books.[6] The change in the operating liability (tax contingency for unrecognized tax benefit) explains some of the difference between a company's provision for income taxes (income tax expense) and its cash taxes paid.

A required footnote disclosure in the U.S. is a schedule that presents the beginning and ending balance of the contingency for uncertain tax positions and the increases and decreases to that liability. Companies generally disclose increases from positions taken currently or revised assessments of prior positions and decreases due to settlements with tax authorities or a lapse in the statute of limitations (tax years no longer subject to audit). Like many issues in accounting, companies use judgment to decide the amount to record as an additional tax expense and liability for the unrecognized tax benefit; thus, two companies faced with the same tax situation can make different judgments about these issues. Uncertain tax position liabilities are operating liabilities and are used to measure unlevered free cash flows.

3.6 UNDERSTANDING AND ANALYZING INCOME TAX DISCLOSURES

The accounting rules used to prepare financial statements require certain footnote disclosures related to the provision for income taxes on the income statement in addition to disclosures related to deferred income taxes on the balance sheet. These disclosures include the following. For the provision for income taxes, companies must disclose the current and deferred portions of the income tax provision (expense). Companies must also disclose a reconciliation between the **statutory income tax rate** (the income tax rate stated by the government as the income tax rate to be paid on income before adjustments) and the **effective income tax rate** (income tax expense divided by income before taxes). In the footnotes, the company must show a schedule of the company's deferred tax assets (gross and net of any valuation allowance), any valuation allowance, and deferred tax liabilities, and also disclose any net operating loss

[6] FASB Accounting Standards Codification Topic 740, Income Taxes.

carryforwards. On the balance sheet, for fiscal years beginning after December 15, 2016, U.S. accounting rules require companies to classify all deferred taxes as non-current assets or non-current liabilities (prior to that, companies could report a current portion).[7]

Accounting policies require companies to calculate deferred tax assets and liabilities based on the income tax rate that is expected to be in effect at the time that the deferrals reverse. That means companies record changes in the amount of deferred tax assets and deferred tax liabilities when the statutory income tax rate changes, which, on occasion, can be significant. The net change in deferred tax assets and liabilities is an adjustment to income tax expense. Thus, if a company has a greater (smaller) reduction in deferred tax liabilities than in deferred tax assets, the difference will be a reduction (increase) in income tax expense for financial reporting purposes.[8]

The Deferred Income Tax Schedule

U.S. accounting rules require companies to report a **deferred income tax schedule**. The schedule must report the company's deferred tax assets (gross and net of any valuation allowance) and deferred tax liabilities. We present a summarized deferred income tax schedule for 2016, for four companies in Exhibit 3.16: E*Trade Financial Corporation; SeaWorld Entertainment, Inc.; Snap Inc.; and Zillow Group, Inc.

The exhibit presents the various types of deferred income tax assets and liabilities the companies report. All four companies report a deferred tax asset for **net operating loss carryforwards**, which we discuss later in the chapter. Three of the four companies report deferred tax assets for accrued expenses, reserves, and allowances, deferred and stock-based compensation, tax credit carryforwards, and deferred revenue. The first two types of deferred tax assets—deferred tax assets for accrued expenses, reserves, and allowances and deferred and stock-based compensation—represent expenses reported on the income statement at some point in the past (books) but have not yet been deducted for income tax purposes (tax). Tax credit carryforwards represent a reduction to income taxes paid from tax credits (tax) that have not yet been reported on the income statement (books). Deferred revenue represents revenue that has been taxed on the tax forms (tax) but not yet recognized on the income statement (books). All four companies also report a valuation allowance reducing the net deferred tax assets but two of the companies—E*Trade and SeaWorld—have relatively small valuation allowances, while the other two companies—Snap and Zillow—have relatively large valuation allowances. Thus, E*Trade and SeaWorld's managements believe that the companies will likely be able to capture the benefits of almost all of the companies' deferred tax assets, while Snap and Zillow's managements believe that the companies are not as likely to capture the benefits of all of the companies' deferred tax assets. Three of the four companies have fewer deferred tax liabilities than deferred tax assets (before considering valuation allowances). All four companies reported a deferred tax liability for depreciation and amortization, indicating that these companies have deducted more depreciation and amortization for tax purposes (tax) than they expensed on their income statements (books). SeaWorld and Zillow report a deferred tax liability for goodwill and other intangibles indicating that they deducted more amortization of goodwill and other intangibles for tax purposes (tax) than they expensed on their income statements (books).

We can glean valuable information from these disclosures regarding the tax status of the company. For example, the change in the balance of a deferred tax item divided by the appropriate tax rate indicates the difference between the corresponding expense (or revenue) on the financial statement and the deduction (or revenue) on the tax form. Assuming the tax rate is constant for two consecutive years, if a deferred tax liability increases (decreases), this indicates that the related expense on the financial statements is less than (greater than) the tax deduction on the tax forms in the current year, or the related revenue on the financial statements is greater than (less than) the revenue on the tax forms. If

[7] See Financial Accounting Standards Board, Accounting Standards Update 2015-17, *Balance Sheet Classification of Deferred Taxes*.

[8] For example, many companies will record significant changes in the amount of deferred tax assets and deferred tax liabilities because of the Tax Cuts and Jobs Act of 2017, which reduced the U.S. statutory income tax rate from 35% to 21% effective January 1, 2018. Morgan Stanley (MS.N) recorded a $1.4 billion loss in the fourth quarter of 2017 from the revaluation of its deferred income taxes. (see "Morgan Stanley to take $1.25 billion hit in fourth-quarter from tax bill," January 5, 2018, available on May 29, 2018 at https://www.reuters.com/article/us-usa-tax-morgan-stanley/morgan-stanley-to-take-1-25-billion-hit-in-fourth-quarter-from-tax-bill-idUSKBN1EU14L).

a deferred tax asset increases (decreases), this indicates that the related expense on the financial statements is greater than (less than) the tax deduction on the tax forms in the current year, or the related revenue on the financial statements is less than (greater than) the revenue on the tax forms.

EXHIBIT 3.16 Summarized 2016 Deferred Income Tax Schedules for Four Companies

($ in millions; for the 2016 fiscal year)	E*Trade	SeaWorld	Snap	Zillow
Deferred tax assets:				
Net operating losses	$ 676.0	$295.0	$ 33.3	$208.0
Accrued expenses, reserves and allowances, net	335.0		10.9	1.8
Mark to market	160.0			
Deferred and stock-based compensation	43.0		21.1	67.5
Tax credit carryforwards	55.0	6.9	15.9	
Basis differences in investments	14.0			
Deferred revenue		4.7	1.9	5.9
Depreciation and amortization				3.1
Goodwill and other intangible assets			24.1	
Research and development credits				24.3
Self-insurance		9.8		
Acquisition and debt related costs		15.9		
Other	26.0	21.7	1.5	16.2
Total deferred tax assets	$1,309.0	$353.9	$108.6	$326.8
Valuation allowance	−35.0	−0.6	−108.9	−217.4
Total deferred tax assets, net of valuation allowance	$1,274.0	$353.3	−$ 0.3	$109.5
Deferred tax liabilities:				
Depreciation and amortization	−518.0	−326.3	−0.2	−15.9
Goodwill and other intangible assets		−70.4		−193.2
Discount on 2021 Notes not deductible for tax				-34.4
Other		−4.5		
Total deferred tax liabilities	−$ 518.0	−$401.2	−$ 0.2	−$243.4
Net deferred tax assets (liabilities)	$ 756.0	−$ 47.9	−$ 0.5	−$134.0

Sources: 2016 10-K Reports for E*Trade Financial Corporation, SeaWorld Entertainment, Inc., and Zillow Group, Inc.; and Snap Inc.'s Form S-1 Registration Statement dates February 2, 2017.

Valuation in Practice 3.3

Valuation Allowance Account—Zillow versus E*Trade Companies report a valuation allowance against their gross deferred tax assets based on their assessment of whether or not the company will be able to capture the benefits of the deferred tax assets. Zillow concluded that it was not likely to be able to capture the benefits from their deferred tax assets while E*Trade concluded the opposite:

Zillow:

> A valuation allowance against deferred tax assets would be established if, based on the weight of available evidence, it is more likely than not (a likelihood of more than 50%) that some or all of the deferred tax assets are not expected to be realized. . . .
>
> Realization of deferred tax assets is dependent upon the generation of future taxable income, if any, the timing and amount of which are uncertain. We have provided a full valuation allowance against the net deferred tax assets as of December 31, 2016 and 2015 because, based on the weight of available evidence, it is more likely than not (a likelihood of more than 50%) that some or all of the deferred tax assets will not be realized.

continued

continued from previous page

E*Trade:

Management must make judgments to determine income tax expense (benefit), deferred tax assets and liabilities and any valuation allowance to be recorded against deferred tax assets. Changes in our estimates occur periodically due to changes in tax rates, changes in business operations, implementation of tax planning strategies, the expiration of relevant statutes of limitations, resolution with taxing authorities of uncertain tax positions and newly enacted statutory, judicial and regulatory guidance.

The most significant tax related judgment made by management was the determination of whether to provide for a valuation allowance against deferred tax assets. If we were to conclude that a valuation allowance was required, the resulting loss could have a material adverse effect on our financial condition and results of operations. As of December 31, 2016, the Company has no valuation allowance against federal deferred tax assets.

Source: 2016 10-K Reports for Zillow Group, Inc. and E*Trade Financial Corporation

Measuring the Income Tax Rate Used on the Tax Forms

As we discussed earlier, the implied income tax rate used to measure a company's interest tax shields is often not equal to the company's average income tax rate and it is often not equal to the company's statutory income tax rate either. We can develop an estimate of a company's future tax rates (for taxable income in its recent financial statements and for the income tax rate for interest) from the reconciliation of the effective income tax rate and statutory income tax rate. Our goal is to assess the ongoing income tax rates with the information we collect from an analysis of the reconciliation in addition to other relevant information. To estimate the company's income tax rates, we begin with the federal statutory rate and adjust it for other items in the reconciliation that we believe are ongoing and not the result of a permanent difference between book financial statements and tax records. This is only a potential starting point in estimating the appropriate income tax rate for interest tax shields.

In Exhibit 3.17, we present an example of this approach to measuring a company's income tax rate using the tax rate reconciliation of two companies—Darden Restaurants, Inc. (Darden) and Alcoa, Inc. (Alcoa). We can see from the exhibit that Darden's effective tax rate is 31.4% in Year 5 and that it has very few reconciliation items. The first item, state income taxes, reflects the impact of state income taxes (adjusted for the benefit of being able to deduct state income taxes on the federal tax form). This is a common reconciliation item for U.S. companies. Another related, and common, reconciliation item not relevant to Darden but is relevant for Alcoa is the reconciliation item for foreign income taxes. The reconciliation for Alcoa indicates that the taxes it pays on foreign income are below the rates it pays on its U.S. income. Other common reconciliation items are for permanent differences between tax and book income, such as various credits or non-taxable interest and dividend income. Darden reports one of these items—income tax credits—separately. In this case, the credits are due to certain tax rules related to the income of restaurant employees. It does not report any other items specifically but instead reports a combined category labeled "other."

EXHIBIT 3.17 Tax Rate Reconciliation of Darden Restaurants, Inc. and Alcoa, Inc.

	Darden Restaurants, Inc.			Alcoa, Inc.		
	Year 3	Year 4	Year 5	Year 3	Year 4	Year 5
U.S. federal statutory rate	35.0%	35.0%	35.0%	35.0%	35.0%	35.0%
State and local taxes, net of federal benefit	3.0%	3.2%	2.9%			
Taxes on foreign income				-7.5%	-4.3%	-10.1%
Income tax credits	-4.5%	-5.2%	-5.0%			
Permanent differences on restructuring charges				0.5%	3.4%	11.8%
Audit and adjustments to prior years' accruals				-3.3%	-0.1%	-2.8%
Minority interests				0.4%	0.4%	5.0%
Statutory tax rate changes				0.1%	0.2%	3.5%
Other	-0.4%	-1.3%	-1.5%	-0.9%	-0.8%	0.8%
Effective tax rate	33.1%	31.7%	31.4%	24.3%	33.8%	43.2%

We also use this reconciliation to estimate the income tax rate for interest assuming the companies have no NOL carryforwards and no interest expense that is not tax deductible because of the limitation on interest expense that we discuss in the next section (essentially 30% of EBITDA through 2021 and 30% of EBIT thereafter). In this estimate, we only include reconciliation items that would change the interest tax shield. The two most likely items are the U.S. federal statutory rate and the state and local taxes, net of the federal benefit. For Darden, the likely marginal tax rate for computing the interest tax shields in Year 5 is the combined federal and state taxes, 37.9%, as the other items in its reconciliation are unlikely to be affected by changes in its taxable income due to variation in interest expense. Regarding the tax on Darden's overall income, we may or may not use that tax rate in our forecasts, depending on our view of whether or not the income tax credits and the other reconciliation adjustments are ongoing and change with a company's scale. In Darden's case, since the income tax credits of 5% are related to the income of restaurant employees, we would expect them to continue in the future. As such, we would take the magnitude of those credits into consideration in computing Darden's future taxes (multiplying the 5% times Darden's income before tax for financial reporting purposes is a reasonable estimate of the reduction in taxes arising from those credits). Without more information about "other," it is a judgment call as to how to best treat it. Thus, if we ignore other, based on Year 5, Darden's overall income tax rate is 32.9% ($0.329 = 0.35 + 0.029 - 0.05$).

Alcoa has some additional categories. Alcoa has the adjustment for foreign income taxes that we previously mentioned. In addition to audit adjustments, it also has adjustments for restructuring charges, minority interests, and changes in statutory rates. We can use the information in the reconciliation in conjunction with the company's income statement to measure the tax effect of specific line items, such as Alcoa's restructuring charges (discussed in detail in Chapter 14). Alcoa does not indicate that it has any state and local tax effects, which is likely included within its other category. The computation of the taxes and interest tax shields for multinational companies is more complicated than it is for domestic companies. We discuss this issue in the last chapter of the book when we discuss cross-border acquisitions. As with Darden, the tax rates we use in our forecasts depend on our view of whether or not the reconciliation adjustments are ongoing, and for the income tax rate for interest, whether or not the items affect the company's interest tax shields. If we are not anticipating additional restructuring charges, that adjustment would not be included, and the adjustments for the previous year's taxes are also something we would generally not consider to be ongoing.

Note that sometimes companies do not report percentages for each of these items but instead report dollar values. To convert the dollar values into percentages, one takes each item and divides it by income before taxes. See Problem 3.9 involving Google's effective tax rate reconciliation for an example of such a disclosure. We should also note that the reconciliations from the statutory tax rate to the effective tax rate shown in Exhibit 3.17 are from financial statements prior to 2018. The Tax Cuts and Jobs Act of 2017 reduced the federal statutory tax rate for corporations to 21% from the 35% shown in the exhibit.

Valuation Key 3.5

We can develop an estimate of a company's future tax rates (for taxable income in its recent financial statements and the tax rate for interest) from the reconciliation of the effective income tax rate and statutory income tax rate. The relevant characteristics are deciding whether or not an item is ongoing, and for the tax rate for interest, if an item affects the interest tax shield.

3.7 EFFECTS OF INTEREST DEDUCTION LIMITATIONS AND NET OPERATING LOSS CARRYFORWARDS

LO4 Measure the effects of interest deduction limitations and net operating losses on taxes and interest tax shields

In this section, we discuss two common tax rules that affect the magnitude and timing of tax payments due to the government and the magnitude and timing of interest tax shields. The two tax rules are interest deduction limitations or caps on interest, and net operating losses. Both the potential deferred interest deductions created by interest deduction caps (called **interest carryforwards**) and future potential taxable income offsets created by net operating losses (called **net operating loss carryforwards**) can be an important consideration when valuing a company. As we illustrate in this section, interest and net operating loss carryforwards existing before the valuation date can reduce a company's future income tax payments relative to what they would have otherwise been and therefore, all else equal, can increase the value of the firm relative to what the value would have been without the pre-valuation interest and net operating loss carryforwards. On the other hand, interest and net operating loss carryforwards expected after the valuation date defer the benefits of interest tax shields and reduce the value of the interest tax shields.

Interest Deduction Limitations

An **interest deduction cap** (or **interest deduction limitation**) occurs when the tax rules limit the amount of interest a company can deduct for income tax purposes to an amount that is less than the interest expense incurred by the company. The effect of interest deduction caps is that the interest incurred by the company is greater than the interest the company can deduct on its tax forms. Since interest tax shields are based on the company's tax forms, the interest tax shield is no longer equal to the interest recorded by the company (the interest expense shown on a company's income statement) multiplied by the company's marginal income tax rate.

Countries that limit interest deductions often allow a company to use the interest deduction in future years if the company has sufficient income to meet certain profitability conditions.[9] The amount of interest that companies can potentially deduct in the future from previously recorded interest expense that was not tax deductible is called an **interest carryforward**. Companies report the potential future tax benefit from interest carryforwards on their balance sheets as a deferred tax asset. As we explain later in this section (and in Chapter 11), for valuation purposes, we distinguish between interest carryforwards that resulted before the valuation date (**pre-valuation interest carryforwards**) and interest carryforwards that we expect to occur after the valuation date and that are embedded in the forecasts used to value the firm (**post-valuation interest carryforwards**).

In the remainder of this section, we discuss two examples related to the George Conrades Company (Conrades). In all of the Conrades examples, we assume the company's income tax rate on all income is 25%, the tax deduction for interest in any year is limited to 30% of EBIT in that year, interest recorded by the company in excess of the interest deduction cap in a year can be carried forward indefinitely, and the company's EBIT based on its financial statements is the same as its EBIT used to measure its EBIT underpinning its taxable income. In the first interest deduction cap example, we illustrate the effect of interest deduction caps limiting interest deductions to after the valuation date (post-valuation interest carryforwards). In the second example, we illustrate the effects of interest deduction caps on interest deductions created prior to the forecast period or valuation date (pre-valuation interest carryforwards) combined with the effects from post-valuation interest carryforwards.

The George Conrades Company with Post-Valuation Interest Caps. In Exhibit 3.18, we present Conrades' financial statement (income statement) excerpts for two historical years (Years −1 and 0) and five years of forecasts (Years 1 to 5). The exhibit presents the company's EBIT, interest expense, and earnings before income taxes. We also show the interest deduction cap based on 30% of EBIT. Conrades' EBIT in the two past years has been $40,000, resulting in a $12,000 interest deduction cap. Since the company's interest expense in these years is $10,000, the interest deduction cap does not limit the company's ability to deduct all of its interest expense in Years −1 and 0, and therefore, the company does not have any pre-valuation interest carryforward in existence as of the valuation date. In Year 1, however, Conrades' EBIT is expected to decrease to $1,000, which results in an interest deduction cap of $300 ($300 = 0.3 × $1,000), and the company does not expect to be able to deduct all of its interest for income tax purposes, creating a post-valuation interest carryforward. In Year 2, Conrades' EBIT is $60,000 (interest deduction cap of $18,000), which grows each subsequent year by $10,000 (interest deduction cap grows by $3,000 annually) through Year 4, and which allows the company to eventually deduct all of its post-valuation interest carryforwards.

EXHIBIT 3.18 Conrades—Post-Valuation Interest Deduction Cap—Financial Accounting (Income Statement Excerpt) and Interest Deduction Cap

Financial Accounting (Income Statement Excerpt)	Actual		Forecast				
	Year −1	Year 0	Year 1	Year 2	Year 3	Year 4	Year 5
Earnings before interest and taxes	$40,000	$40,000	$ 1,000	$60,000	$70,000	$80,000	$80,000
Interest expense (current)	10,000	10,000	10,000	10,000	10,000	10,000	10,000
Earnings before income taxes	$30,000	$30,000	−$ 9,000	$50,000	$60,000	$70,000	$70,000
Interest deduction cap	$12,000	$12,000	$ 300	$18,000	$21,000	$24,000	$24,000

[9] Caps on the deductibility of interest are relatively common across countries. Under the Tax Cuts and Jobs Act of 2017, interest is limited to 30% of adjusted taxable income, which among other things excludes the effect of net operating losses and any business interest income. In addition, prior to 2022, it also excludes deductions for depreciation and amortization. Interest carryforwards have an infinite life under the 2017 tax code. For purposes of the examples in this chapter, we assume that the interest cap is 30% of EBIT.

In Exhibit 3.19, we calculate the company's taxable income, which includes the calculation of the company's post-valuation interest carryforward. Conrades' taxable income in Years −1 and 0 is the same as its earnings before income taxes on the income statement because all of the company's interest expense is deductible on its tax forms. In Year 1, however, Conrades' interest deduction is limited to \$300 (\$300 = 0.3 × \$1,000), which is \$9,700 lower than its interest expense (\$9,700 = \$10,000 − \$300). The lower interest deduction results in taxable income of \$700 (\$700 = \$1,000 − \$300) while its earnings before income taxes is −\$9,000 for financial reporting purposes. Conrades' income tax in Year 1 is \$175 (\$175 = 0.25 × \$700) even though its earnings before income taxes on its income statement is −\$9,000. As of the end of Year 1, Conrades has a \$9,700 post-valuation interest carryforward, which Conrades can deduct in future years if it has sufficient earnings. Although not shown in the exhibits, Conrades will record a deferred tax asset on its balance sheet for the tax benefit expected from the interest carryforward, and the change in the deferred tax asset in Year 1 will reconcile the provision for income taxes on its income statement (financial reporting) to its income tax due to the government on its tax forms.

EXHIBIT 3.19 Conrades—Post-Valuation Interest Deduction Cap—Levered Company Income Taxes

	Actual		Forecast				
Levered Company (Taxable Income)	**Year −1**	**Year 0**	**Year 1**	**Year 2**	**Year 3**	**Year 4**	**Year 5**
Earnings before interest and taxes	\$40,000	\$40,000	\$1,000	\$60,000	\$70,000	\$80,000	\$80,000
Post-valuation interest carryforward			0	9,700	1,700	0	0
Interest expense (current)	10,000	10,000	300	8,300	10,000	10,000	10,000
Taxable income	\$30,000	\$30,000	\$ 700	\$42,000	\$58,300	\$70,000	\$70,000
Income taxes	7,500	7,500	175	10,500	14,575	17,500	17,500
Earnings	\$22,500	\$22,500	\$ 525	\$31,500	\$43,725	\$52,500	\$52,500
Average tax rate	25%	25%	25%	25%	25%	25%	25%
Post-Valuation Interest Carryforward Balance			**Year 1**	**Year 2**	**Year 3**	**Year 4**	**Year 5**
Beginning interest carryforward			\$ 0	\$ 9,700	\$ 1,700	\$ 0	\$ 0
Change in interest carryforward			9,700	−8,000	−1,700	0	0
Ending interest carryforward			\$9,700	\$ 1,700	\$ 0	\$ 0	\$ 0

Given the \$9,700 interest carryforward as of the end of Year 1, Conrades could deduct up to \$19,700 of interest in Year 2 if it has sufficient earnings (\$19,700 = \$9,700 interest carryforward + \$10,000 current interest). Conrades expects its EBIT to increase to \$60,000 in Year 2, which results in an interest deduction cap of \$18,000, which limits Conrades' Year 2 interest deduction to \$18,000. We first deduct Conrades beginning balance of its interest carryforward, \$9,700, and then current interest of \$8,300 (\$8,300 = \$18,000 − \$9,700). Conrades' interest carryforward decreases to \$1,700 (\$1,700 = \$9,700 balance + \$10,000 current interest − \$18,000 interest expense cap).

Given the \$1,700 interest carryforward, Conrades could deduct up to \$11,700 of interest in Year 3 (\$11,700 = \$1,700 interest carryforward + \$10,000 current interest). Conrades expects its EBIT to increase to \$70,000 in Year 3, which results in an interest deduction cap of \$21,000. In Year 3, Conrades is able to deduct the remaining interest carryforward balance, \$1,700, and all of its current interest, \$10,000. The interest carryforward has a zero balance as of the end of Year 3. Conrades' expected EBIT increases in Years 4 and 5 and its interest remains at \$10,000, so it can deduct all of its current interest and thus, Conrades' taxable income (Exhibit 3.19) is the same as its earnings before income taxes on the income statement (Exhibit 3.18) because it has no interest carryforward and all of the company's current interest is tax deductible.

Interest deduction caps potentially defer the tax deductibility of interest and thus can affect the timing and value of the interest tax shields. The inability to deduct all of its current interest in a year reduces the company's interest tax shield in that year relative to what it would have been had the company deducted all of its current interest for income taxes. On the other hand, deducting all of its current interest plus some amount of interest carryforward in a year increases the company's interest tax shield in that year relative to what it would have been had the company deducted only its current interest for income taxes. Thus, interest deduction caps do not necessarily eliminate interest tax shields if the company later becomes sufficiently profitable, but they can delay them, which reduces their value.

For a company with interest carryforwards that affect the amount of interest deducted for income taxes, it is generally incorrect to measure the interest tax shields by multiplying the interest expense by the company's marginal tax rate because interest recorded by the company in a year does not equal interest deducted for income taxes in that year. We can calculate a company's interest tax shield when it has interest carryforwards as the difference between the company's income tax it would have to pay assuming it is unlevered (without consideration of the interest expense) and the income tax it would pay (after deducting interest expense). We show these calculations for the Conrades example in Exhibit 3.20.

EXHIBIT 3.20 Conrades—Post-Valuation Interest Deduction Cap—Unlevered Company Income Taxes, Interest Tax Shields, and the Implied Marginal Tax Rate for Interest

	Actual		Forecast				
Unlevered Company (Taxable Income)	**Year −1**	**Year 0**	**Year 1**	**Year 2**	**Year 3**	**Year 4**	**Year 5**
Earnings before interest and taxes.	$40,000	$40,000	$ 1,000	$60,000	$70,000	$80,000	$80,000
Income taxes	10,000	10,000	250	15,000	17,500	20,000	20,000
Earnings	$30,000	$30,000	$ 750	$45,000	$52,500	$60,000	$60,000
Average tax rate	25%	25%	25%	25%	25%	25%	25%
Interest Tax Shield			**Year 1**	**Year 2**	**Year 3**	**Year 4**	**Year 5**
Income taxes (unlevered firm)			$ 250	$15,000	$17,500	$20,000	$20,000
Income taxes (with interest deduction)			175	10,500	14,575	17,500	17,500
Correct interest tax shield			$ 75	$ 4,500	$ 2,925	$ 2,500	$ 2,500
Implied Income Tax Rate for Interest Tax Shields			**Year 1**	**Year 2**	**Year 3**	**Year 4**	**Year 5**
Interest tax shield.			$ 75	$ 4,500	$ 2,925	$ 2,500	$ 2,500
Interest expense (current).			$10,000	$10,000	$10,000	$10,000	$10,000
Implied income tax rate for interest tax shields			0.75%	45.00%	29.25%	25.00%	25.00%
Comparison Interest Tax Shield Using Marginal Tax Rate × Interest			**Year 1**	**Year 2**	**Year 3**	**Year 4**	**Year 5**
Interest expense (current).			$10,000	$10,000	$10,000	$10,000	$10,000
Marginal income tax rate			25.0%	25.0%	25.0%	25.0%	25.0%
Interest tax shield using marginal tax rate × interest.			$ 2,500	$ 2,500	$ 2,500	$ 2,500	$ 2,500
Correct interest tax shield			75	4,500	2,925	2,500	2,500
Overstated (understated) interest tax shield			$ 2,425	−$ 2,000	−$ 425	$ 0	$ 0

In the top panel of the exhibit, we calculate Conrades' income taxes as if it had no interest (unlevered firm) in the forecast period. Conrades' EBIT is the same as it was in Exhibit 3.18 but we assume it has no interest and thus, no post-valuation interest carryforward. Income tax in a year is equal to EBIT multiplied by the company's income tax rate of 25%. In the second panel, we calculate Conrades' interest tax shield, which is equal to its income tax assuming the company is unlevered minus its income tax net of its interest deductions (levered firm) from Exhibit 3.19. In the third panel we measure the implied income tax rate for current interest; in other words, the tax rate that could be used to calculate the interest tax shield by multiplying current interest by the implied income tax rate (T_{INT}). As you can see from the exhibit, the implied tax rate is not equal to 25% (the company's average and marginal tax rate) until the company uses all of its current interest and interest carryforwards. In the bottom panel, we compare Conrades' interest tax shield measured using its marginal tax rate of 25%, multiplied by its interest expense to its interest tax shield after including the effects of the interest deduction limitation and post-valuation interest carryforwards.

We begin the interest tax shield calculations in Year 1 because that is the first year of the forecasts. As we discuss in the next example, any interest carryforward from years before the valuation date (pre-valuation interest carryforward) is not included in interest tax shields because any future deductions due to pre-valuation interest carryforwards do not depend on whether the company has debt during the forecasts; hence they are not considered part of the interest tax shields from future financing. Conrades' interest expense in Year 1 is $10,000; thus, multiplying the company's average and marginal tax rate of 25% times interest expense results in a $2,500 interest tax shield ($2,500 = 0.25 × $10,000). This calculation is incorrect, however, because the company was able to deduct only $300 of the $10,000 for income taxes. The interest tax shield in Year 1 is equal to $75 because the company's $175 of income taxes it will pay after deducting interest of $300 (from Exhibit 3.19) is $75 less that what it would pay without deducting any interest ($75 = $250 − $175). Thus, the implied tax rate to correctly measure the company's $75 interest tax shield is 0.75%. The potential future interest deduction (interest carryforward) is $9,700 ($9,700 = $10,000 − $300) and the related potential tax benefit is $2,425 ($2,425 = 0.25 × $9,700), which represents the deferral of the company's interest tax shield.

The interest tax shield in Year 2 is equal to the difference in the income taxes for the levered and unlevered firm, $4,500 ($4,500 = $15,000 − $10,500). The implied tax rate to correctly measure the company's $4,500 interest tax shield (T_{INT}) is 45% (45% = $4,500/$10,000). The company's interest deduction is $2,000 larger than the $2,500 interest tax shield based on the company's $10,000 interest expense multiplied by 25%; thus, in Year 2, the company is able to capture $2,000 of the $2,425 Year 1 deferral of the company's interest tax shield. The interest tax shield in Year 3 is $2,925 ($2,925 = $17,500 − $14,575), and the implied tax rate for interest (T_{INT}) in Year 3 is 29.25% (29.25% = $2,925/$10,000). The company's interest deduction is $425 larger than the $2,500 interest tax shield based on the company's $10,000 interest expense multiplied by 25%, which eliminates its interest carryforward as of the end of Year 3. Since Conrades' interest carryforward at the beginning of Year 4 is $0 and its interest deduction cap does not limit its interest deduction in Year 4, the company's interest tax shield is the company's current interest expense multiplied by 25%, $2,500 ($2,500 = 0.25 × $10,000) in Years 4 and 5.

The George Conrades Company with Pre- and Post-Valuation Interest Caps. In Exhibit 3.21, we present Conrades' financial statement (income statement) excerpts for the previous two years and five years of forecasts. The forecasts in this example are the same as in the previous example but the historical income statements are not. The difference between the two examples is that in this example Years −1 and 0 have only $1,000 of EBIT compared to $40,000 in the previous example. The interest deduction cap for $1,000 EBIT is $300 ($300 = 0.3 × $1,000), which is less than the company's interest expense of $10,000 in both Years −1 and 0. This interest deduction limitation in Years −1 and 0 creates a pre-valuation interest carryforward. As in the previous example, this example also has a post-valuation interest carryforward because the interest deduction cap is less than the company's interest in Year 1.

EXHIBIT 3.21 Conrades—Pre- and Post-Valuation Interest Deduction Cap—Financial Accounting (Income Statement Excerpt) and Interest Deduction Cap

Financial Accounting (Income Statement Excerpt)	Actual		Forecast				
	Year −1	Year 0	Year 1	Year 2	Year 3	Year 4	Year 5
Earnings before interest and taxes....	$ 1,000	$ 1,000	$ 1,000	$60,000	$70,000	$80,000	$80,000
Interest expense (current)...........	10,000	10,000	10,000	10,000	10,000	10,000	10,000
Earnings before income taxes	−$ 9,000	−$ 9,000	−$ 9,000	$50,000	$60,000	$70,000	$70,000
Interest deduction cap	$ 300	$ 300	$ 300	$18,000	$21,000	$24,000	$24,000

In Exhibit 3.22, we calculate the company's taxable income, which includes the calculation of the company's pre-valuation and post-valuation interest carryforwards. We calculate the pre-valuation interest carryforward (the interest carryforward created before the valuation date, which in this example is Years −1 and 0) separately from the post-valuation interest carryforward because the company will capture the tax benefits from the pre-interest carryforward independent of the company's capital structure strategy in the post-valuation period. Thus, reductions in taxable income from the pre-valuation interest are not considered interest tax shields in the post-valuation period because they do not arise from financing decisions in the post-valuation period. The pre-valuation interest carryforwards are a potential tax benefit the company has as of the valuation date and the company does not have to be levered in the post-valuation period to take advantage of them. In Years −1 and 0, Conrades' interest deduction is limited to $300 ($300 = 0.3 × $1,000), which is $9,700 lower than its interest expense ($9,700 = $10,000 − $300). The lower interest deduction results in a taxable income of $700, while its earnings before income taxes for financial reporting purposes is −$9,000. Conrades' income tax is $175 ($175 = 0.25 × $700) in each year even though its earnings before income taxes on its income statement is −$9,000. As of the end of Year 0, Conrades has a $19,400 pre-valuation interest carryforward, which Conrades can deduct in future years if it has sufficient earnings, regardless of whether it is levered in the future.

EXHIBIT 3.22 Conrades—Pre- and Post-Valuation Interest Deduction Cap—Levered Company Income Taxes

	Actual		Forecast				
Levered Company (Taxable Income)	**Year −1**	**Year 0**	**Year 1**	**Year 2**	**Year 3**	**Year 4**	**Year 5**
Earnings before interest and taxes	$1,000	$ 1,000	$ 1,000	$60,000	$70,000	$80,000	$80,000
Pre-valuation interest carryforward	0	300	300	18,000	1,100	0	0
Post-valuation interest carryforward			0	0	19,900	10,100	0
Interest expense (current)	300	0	0	0	0	10,000	10,000
Taxable income	$ 700	$ 700	$ 700	$42,000	$49,000	$59,900	$70,000
Income taxes	175	175	175	10,500	12,250	14,975	17,500
Earnings	$525	$ 525	$ 525	$31,500	$36,750	$44,925	$52,500
Average tax rate	25%	25%	25%	25%	25%	25%	25%
Pre-Valuation Interest Carryforward Balance	**Year −1**	**Year 0**	**Year 1**	**Year 2**	**Year 3**	**Year 4**	**Year 5**
Beginning interest carryforward	$ 0	$ 9,700	$19,400	$19,100	$ 1,100	$ 0	$ 0
Change in interest carryforward	9,700	9,700	−300	−18,000	−1,100	0	0
Ending interest carryforward	$9,700	$19,400	$19,100	$ 1,100	$ 0	$ 0	$ 0
Post-Valuation Interest Carryforward Balance			**Year 1**	**Year 2**	**Year 3**	**Year 4**	**Year 5**
Beginning interest carryforward			$ 0	$10,000	$20,000	$10,100	$ 0
Change in interest carryforward			10,000	10,000	−9,900	−10,100	0
Ending interest carryforward			$10,000	$20,000	$10,100	$ 0	$ 0

In Year 1, Conrades' interest deduction is again limited to $300 ($300 = 0.3 × $1,000), which is again $9,700 lower than its interest expense ($9,700 = $10,000 − $300). We first use the pre-valuation interest carryforward because these tax benefits would be captured by the company independent of its capital structure (assuming it becomes profitable enough) and are essentially considered part of the value of the unlevered firm. In Year 1, we reduce the pre-valuation interest carryforward by $300 to $19,100. None of the Year 1 interest expense is tax deductible in Year 1 because the pre-valuation interest carryforward exceeds the interest deduction cap creating a post-valuation interest carryforward of $10,000.

In Year 2, the company has an interest deduction cap of $18,000 ($18,000 = 0.3 × $60,000). As before, we use the pre-valuation interest carryforward first, reducing its balance to $1,100. Again, none of the Year 2 interest expense is tax deductible in Year 2 because the pre-valuation interest carryforward exceeds the interest deduction cap. Thus, the post-valuation interest carryforward increases by $10,000 resulting in a balance of $20,000. In Year 3, the company has an interest deduction cap of $21,000 ($21,000 = 0.3 × $70,000), which allows the company to deduct the remaining $1,100 pre-valuation interest carryforward and $19,900 of the post-interest carryforward. The resulting balance in the post-valuation interest carryforward is $10,100 ($10,100 = $20,000 balance + $10,000 current interest − $19,900 available deduction). Finally, in Year 4, the company has an interest deduction cap of $24,000 ($24,000 = 0.3 × $80,000), which allows the company to deduct the remaining $10,100 post-valuation interest carryforward and all of its $10,000 of current interest.

As we calculated in Exhibit 3.20, in Exhibit 3.23, we calculate Conrades' income taxes as if it had no interest expense (unlevered firm) in the post-valuation period, its interest tax shield, the implied income tax rate for current interest, and in the bottom panel, we compare Conrades' interest tax shield measured using its marginal tax rate, 25%, multiplied by its interest expense to its interest tax shield after including the effects of the interest deduction limitation. Although we assume the unlevered company has no post-valuation interest, the calculations include the pre-valuation interest carryforward because the company can benefit from the pre-valuation interest carryforward even if it is unlevered in the post-valuation period and is therefore included in the value of the unlevered firm. Because the company's interest deduction depends on the magnitude of a measure of unlevered earnings (EBIT), the unlevered company's deduction of its pre-valuation interest carryforward for the unlevered firm is the same as for the levered firm shown in the previous exhibit.

EXHIBIT 3.23 Conrades—Pre- and Post-Valuation Interest Deduction Cap—Unlevered Company Income Taxes, Interest Tax Shields, and the Implied Marginal Tax Rate for Interest

	Actual		Forecast				
Unlevered Company (Taxable Income)	**Year −1**	**Year 0**	**Year 1**	**Year 2**	**Year 3**	**Year 4**	**Year 5**
Earnings before interest and taxes	$1,000	$ 1,000	$ 1,000	$60,000	$70,000	$80,000	$80,000
Pre-valuation interest carryforward	0	300	300	18,000	1,100	0	0
Interest expense (current)	300	0					
Taxable income	$ 700	$ 700	$ 700	$42,000	$68,900	$80,000	$80,000
Income taxes	175	175	175	10,500	17,225	20,000	20,000
Earnings	$ 525	$ 525	$ 525	$31,500	$51,675	$60,000	$60,000
Average tax rate	25%	25%	25%	25%	25%	25%	25%
Pre-Valuation Interest Carryforward Balance	**Year −1**	**Year 0**	**Year 1**	**Year 2**	**Year 3**	**Year 4**	**Year 5**
Beginning interest carryforward	$ 0	$ 9,700	$19,400	$19,100	$ 1,100	$ 0	$ 0
Change in interest carryforward	9,700	9,700	−300	−18,000	−1,100	0	0
Ending interest carryforward	$9,700	$19,400	$19,100	$ 1,100	$ 0	$ 0	$ 0
Interest Tax Shield			**Year 1**	**Year 2**	**Year 3**	**Year 4**	**Year 5**
Income taxes (unlevered firm)			$ 175	$10,500	$17,225	$20,000	$20,000
Income taxes (with interest deduction)			175	10,500	12,250	14,975	17,500
Correct interest tax shield			$ 0	$ 0	$ 4,975	$ 5,025	$ 2,500
Implied Income Tax Rate for Interest Tax Shields			**Year 1**	**Year 2**	**Year 3**	**Year 4**	**Year 5**
Interest tax shield			$ 0	$ 0	$ 4,975	$ 5,025	$ 2,500
Interest expense (current)			$10,000	$10,000	$10,000	$10,000	$10,000
Implied income tax rate for interest tax shields			0.00%	0.00%	49.75%	50.25%	25.00%
Comparison Interest Tax Shield Using Marginal Tax Rate × Interest			**Year 1**	**Year 2**	**Year 3**	**Year 4**	**Year 5**
Interest expense (current)			$10,000	$10,000	$10,000	$10,000	$10,000
Marginal income tax rate			25.0%	25.0%	25.0%	25.0%	25.0%
Interest tax shield using marginal tax rate × interest			$ 2,500	$ 2,500	$ 2,500	$ 2,500	$ 2,500
Correct interest tax shield			0	0	4,975	5,025	2,500
Overstated (understated) interest tax shield			$ 2,500	$ 2,500	−$ 2,475	−$ 2,525	$ 0

As we show in the exhibit, Conrades' taxable income for the levered and unlevered companies is the same for Years 1 and 2 and therefore, the company has no interest tax shield in either of those years. The result is that the $2,500 interest tax shield that would result from the company's current interest expense in those years is deferred. In Year 3, the company expects to deduct interest of $19,900 from the post-valuation period (see Exhibit 3.22). The resulting interest tax shield in Year 3 is equal to the difference in the income taxes for the levered and unlevered firm, which is $4,975 ($4,975 = $17,225 − $12,250).

The interest tax shield in Year 3 is $2,475 larger than the $2,500 interest tax shield based on the company's $10,000 current interest expense multiplied by a 25% tax rate. The total interest related deduction of $19,900 results in an implied tax rate to correctly measure the company's $4,975 interest tax shield, which is 49.75% (49.75% = $4,975/$10,000). Thus, in Year 3, the company is able to capture $2,475 of the $5,000 deferral of the company's interest tax shield from Years 1 and 2.

In Year 4, the company is able to deduct the remaining post-valuation interest carryforward balance of $10,100 and all of its current interest for a total interest related deduction of $20,100. The interest tax shield in Year 4 is equal to the difference in the income taxes for the levered and unlevered firm, $5,025 ($5,025 = $20,000 − $14,975), and the implied tax rate in Year 3 is 50.25% (50.25% = $5,025/$10,000). Since the interest carryforward at the beginning in Year 5 is $0 and its interest deduction cap does not limit its interest deduction in Year 5, the company's marginal tax rate of 25% multiplied by its current interest expense correctly measures the company's interest tax shield, $2,500 ($2,500 = 0.25 × $10,000).

Valuation Key 3.6

Interest carryforwards can be an important consideration when valuing a company. Interest carryforwards existing before the valuation date (pre-valuation interest carryforwards) can reduce a company's future income tax payments relative to what they would have otherwise been and therefore, all else equal, can increase the value of the firm relative to what the value would have been without the pre-valuation interest carryforwards. On the other hand, interest carryforwards expected after the valuation date (post-valuation interest carryforwards) defer the benefits of interest tax shields during the forecast period and therefore, all else equal, decrease the value of the interest tax shields relative to what the value would have been without the post-valuation interest carryforwards; that is, if the company had been able to fully deduct its current interest expense.

REVIEW EXERCISE 3.5

Measuring the Effect of Interest Deduction Caps

Using the information in the following schedule, calculate the company's taxable income, income taxes due, interest tax shields, and the implied income tax rate for interest. Assume the company's income tax rate on all income is 30%, the tax deduction for interest in any year is equal to 20% of EBIT in that year, and any interest expense above the interest deduction cap in a year can be carried forward indefinitely.

Financial Accounting (Income Statement Excerpt)	Actual		Forecast				
	Year −1	Year 0	Year 1	Year 2	Year 3	Year 4	Year 5
Earnings before interest and taxes. . . .	$ 100	$ 200	$ 500	$40,000	$50,000	$60,000	$70,000
Interest expense (current).	5,000	5,000	5,000	5,000	5,000	5,000	5,000
Earnings before income taxes	−$4,900	−$4,800	−$4,500	$35,000	$45,000	$55,000	$65,000

Solution on pages 150–152.

Net Operating Loss Carryforwards

A **net operating loss** (**NOL**) occurs when a company's revenues are less than its expenses reported on its tax forms; more specifically, for income tax purposes, a company has a net operating loss when its taxable revenue (revenue on the company's income tax forms) is less than its tax-deductible expenses (expenses it deducts on its income tax forms). The amount of future taxable income that companies can shelter with past net operating losses is called a **net operating loss carryforward** (**NOL carryforward**). Companies can have a net operating loss in different income tax jurisdictions in which they operate (different countries or states or provinces) and therefore, can have multiple net operating losses and multiple net operating loss carryforwards applying to different tax jurisdictions. Most countries allow companies to carry forward net operating losses against future taxable income and some countries allow companies to carry back net operating losses against past income. The number of years and the extent to which a company can carry back and carry forward losses are often limited. Countries often also have minimum income tax rules such that a company must pay a minimum amount of tax in some circumstances (that is there can be a limitation on the amount of NOL carryforwards that can be used in any year). A company's ability to use its NOLs may also be limited after it is acquired, and NOLs may be reduced to the extent that a company has debt forgiven in bankruptcy.[10]

Because NOLs can reduce future income tax payments and are sometimes large, they can be an important consideration when valuing a company (see Chapter 11). NOLs can reduce a company's future income tax payments and hence increase free cash flows, which, all else equal, increases the value of the firm. Second, if a company has NOLs that will offset future income, this has the potential effect of also deferring the benefit of the company's interest tax shields, which, all else equal, reduces the value of the interest tax shields. In addition, for NOLs with a limited life, if a company continues to have losses and fails to use its NOL within the allowed carryforward time period, it can lose some of its interest tax shields rather than just deferring them to future years.

Companies record the potential tax benefits from NOL carryforwards as a deferred tax asset, ignoring the time-value-of-money. If management does not expect to be able to use all of the NOLs because the company's expected future taxable income is lower than the amount of the NOLs, the company reduces the value of its NOL deferred tax asset for the amount of the asset that it may not be able to capture via a valuation allowance. While neither a probabilistic (expected value) nor a present value calculation, the valuation allowance can provide information that may be useful in valuing a company's NOL carryforwards (see Exhibit 3.16 and associated discussion), especially for NOLs with a limited life.

The calculations to measure taxable income with the effect of NOL carryforwards are similar to the calculations discussed for interest carryforwards. Unlike interest carryforwards, however, we do not need to keep track of pre-valuation and post-valuation NOL carryforwards separately.[11] You might be saying to yourself that this all sounds very complicated and that surely this is not a very common phenomenon. However, that is not the case, as NOLs are quite common.

Net Operating Loss Carryforwards Are Common. Naturally, start-up companies often have NOL carryforwards, as many companies incur operating losses in the early years of operations. Because these companies do not have previous income to which they can carry back the operating losses, these companies have NOL carryforwards. However, NOL carryforwards are more common across all companies than we might imagine. In Exhibit 3.24, we show the percentage of companies with NOL carryforwards in each year from 2000 through 2016. The sample consists of all companies in the Compustat® North American database with at least $1 million in revenues and market capitalization. The total number of companies in a year ranges from 4,000 to 7,000, depending on the year. This exhibit shows that the proportion of companies with NOL carryforwards has been gradually increasing during this period, with close to 60% of publicly listed companies having some NOLs by 2016. Remember that a company can have different NOLs in different tax jurisdictions; domestic, foreign, states and provinces. To assess the relative magnitude of these NOL carryforwards, we also present the median ratio of NOL carryforward to revenues for companies reporting some amount of NOLs. As you can see, the NOLs as a percent of revenues for the median company initially decreased from around 35% in 2000 to around 20% in 2008 but then increased to between 25% and 30% by the end of 2016. This ratio is quite large for some companies; for example, in 2016, 25% of the companies have NOLs larger than 140% of revenues, 10% of the companies have NOLs larger than 940% of revenues, and 1% of the companies

---

[10] In the U.S., under the Tax Cuts and Jobs Act of 2017, for losses incurred prior to 2018, a company can use an NOL from the current year against the company's taxable income for the previous two years in order to obtain a refund of taxes paid during that period (net operating loss carry back). Further it can offset future income for up to 20 years (net operating loss carryforward). Companies could elect to not carry back pre-2018 losses and just carry them forward, which might be optimal if the company expected to face a higher tax rate in the future than it faced in the past. In addition, for pre-2018 losses, there was no limitation on the amount of taxable income that could be offset from NOLs. For losses incurred after 2017, there is no carryback allowed and the carryforward period is unlimited. Further, post-2017 losses can offset only 80% of taxable income in any year. In the U.S., generally accepted accounting principles require a company to disclose the amount of its NOLs in its income tax disclosures. Countries have many varied income tax rules concerning NOLs.

[11] While there is no reason to keep track of pre-existing NOL carryforwards separately from post-valuation NOL carryforwards, in the U.S., it is important to keep track of the pre-2018 NOL carryforwards separately from the post-2017 NOL carryforwards because of the differences in their lives, whether they can be carried back or not and the extent to which they can offset taxable income (see prior footnote).

EXHIBIT 3.24 Percent of Publicly Listed Companies with NOLs and Median NOLs to Revenues

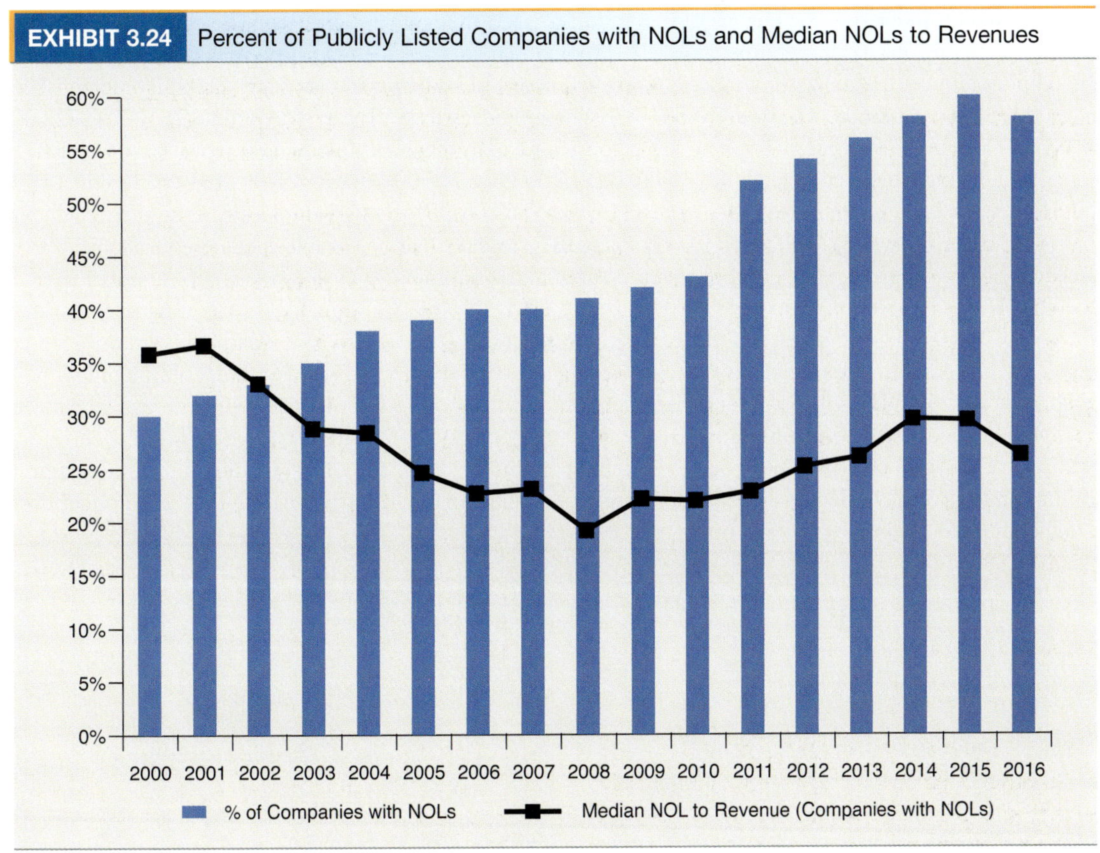

have NOLs larger than 1,000% of revenues. Given the frequency and magnitude of NOL carryforwards, it is important to understand their valuation impact.

The George Conrades Company with Net Operating Loss Carryforwards and No Interest (Unlevered). In this section, we revisit the Conrades example and change EBIT in Years −1 and 0 so that the company has a net operating loss in each year, creating an NOL carryforward. To avoid the complications resulting from interest carryforwards that also result when a company has a net operating loss, we first illustrate the effect of NOL carryforwards assuming Conrades is unlevered (has no interest). In the subsequent example, we embed Conrades' interest as in the previous examples. In both of these examples, we make the same assumptions made in the previous examples and add the assumption that Conrades can offset up to 80% of its taxable income with its NOL carryforwards and that NOLs can only be carried forward.

In Exhibit 3.25, we present Conrades' financial statement (income statement) excerpts for two historical years and five years of forecasts. In this example, however, the company has no interest (is unlevered), and in order to illustrate the effect of NOLs, we assume Conrades' EBIT is −$40,000 in each of the Years −1, 0, and 1.

EXHIBIT 3.25 Conrades (Unlevered)—Net Operating Loss Carryforward—Financial Accounting (Income Statement Excerpt)

Financial Accounting (Income Statement Excerpt)	Actual		Forecast				
	Year −1	Year 0	Year 1	Year 2	Year 3	Year 4	Year 5
Earnings before interest and taxes. . .	−$40,000	−$40,000	−$40,000	$60,000	$70,000	$80,000	$80,000
Interest expense (current).	0	0	0	0	0	0	0
Earnings before income taxes	−$40,000	−$40,000	−$40,000	$60,000	$70,000	$80,000	$80,000

In Exhibit 3.26, we measure the company's taxable income, including the effects of its NOL carryforward. The company pays no income taxes in Year −1 through Year 1 because the company has an operating loss of $40,000 in each year; thus, as of the end of Year 1, the company has an NOL carryforward equal to $120,000. In Year 2, the company has EBIT of $60,000. Conrades can use its NOL to offset 80% (maximum allowed by the assumed tax law) of its $60,000 EBIT to calculate its taxable income equal to $12,000 ($12,000 = $60,000 − 0.8 × $60,000), which reduces its NOL carryforward to $72,000 ($72,000 = $120,000 − $48,000). Similarly, in Year 3, Conrades can use its NOL to offset 80% of its $70,000 EBIT to calculate its taxable income equal to $14,000 ($14,000 = $70,000 − 0.8 × $70,000), which reduces its NOL carryforward to $16,000 ($16,000 = $72,000 − $56,000). In Year 4, Conrades can use the remainder of its NOL carryforward to offset $16,000 of its EBIT to calculate its taxable income equal to $64,000. Because of its losses and net operating loss carryforwards, the company pays no taxes for Years −1 to 1 and then pays taxes of $3,000, $3,500, $16,000, and $20,000, respectively, for Years 2 to 5. Only in Year 5 does the company's average tax rate equal the 25% statutory tax rate (when all the NOL carryforwards are gone).

We eliminated interest in this example to isolate the calculations to measure taxable income when a company has NOL carryforwards. The calculations for a levered company (with interest) are more complicated because a company with EBIT less than or equal to zero will also have an interest carryforward because a company will not be able to deduct any interest if the tax laws include interest deduction limitations as we have demonstrated in the prior Conrades examples. To illustrate these complications, we include interest in the next example.

EXHIBIT 3.26 Conrades (Unlevered)—Net Operating Loss Carryforward—Income Tax Calculations

	Actual		Forecast				
Unlevered Company (Taxable Income)	**Year −1**	**Year 0**	**Year 1**	**Year 2**	**Year 3**	**Year 4**	**Year 5**
Earnings before interest and taxes	−$40,000	−$40,000	−$ 40,000	$ 60,000	$70,000	$80,000	$80,000
Interest expense (current)	0	0	0	0	0	0	0
Taxable income	−$40,000	−$40,000	−$ 40,000	$ 60,000	$70,000	$80,000	$80,000
NOL carryforward used	0	0	0	−48,000	−56,000	−16,000	0
Taxable income after NOL carryforward adjustment	−$40,000	−$40,000	−$ 40,000	$ 12,000	$14,000	$64,000	$80,000
Income taxes	0	0	0	3,000	3,500	16,000	20,000
Earnings	−$40,000	−$40,000	−$ 40,000	$ 9,000	$10,500	$48,000	$60,000
Average tax rate	0%	0%	0%	5%	5%	20%	25%
Net Operating Loss Carryforward Balance	**Year −1**	**Year 0**	**Year 1**	**Year 2**	**Year 3**	**Year 4**	**Year 5**
Beginning NOL carryforward	$ 0	$40,000	$ 80,000	$120,000	$72,000	$16,000	$ 0
Change in NOL carryforward	40,000	40,000	40,000	−48,000	−56,000	−16,000	0
Ending NOL carryforward	$40,000	$80,000	$120,000	$ 72,000	$16,000	$ 0	$ 0

The George Conrades Company with Net Operating Loss Carryforwards and Interest. In Exhibit 3.27, we present Conrades' financial statement (income statement) excerpts for two historical years (Years −1 and 0) and five years of forecasts (Years 1 to 5). In this example we now include the company's interest of $10,000 in each year (Years −1 through 5). This interest is tax deductible but subject to the interest deduction limitation (30% of EBIT) as in the earlier examples.

EXHIBIT 3.27 Conrades—Net Operating Loss Carryforward with Interest Deduction Caps—Financial Accounting (Income Statement Excerpt) and Interest Deduction Cap

	Actual		Forecast				
Financial Accounting (Income Statement Excerpt)	**Year −1**	**Year 0**	**Year 1**	**Year 2**	**Year 3**	**Year 4**	**Year 5**
Earnings before interest and taxes	−$40,000	−$40,000	−$40,000	$60,000	$70,000	$80,000	$80,000
Interest expense (current)	10,000	10,000	10,000	10,000	10,000	10,000	10,000
Earnings before income taxes	−$50,000	−$50,000	−$50,000	$50,000	$60,000	$70,000	$70,000
Interest deduction cap	$ 0	$ 0	$ 0	$18,000	$21,000	$24,000	$24,000

In Exhibit 3.28, we calculate the company's taxable income, which includes the calculation of the company's pre-valuation and post-valuation interest carryforwards. Recall that we track the pre-valuation interest carryforward (the interest carryforward created before the valuation date, which in this example is Years −1 and 0) separately from the post-valuation interest carryforward because the company will capture the tax benefits from the pre-interest carryforward independent of the company's capital structure strategy in the post-valuation period and thus, they are not interest tax shields in the post-valuation period.

EXHIBIT 3.28 Conrades—Net Operating Loss Carryforward with Interest Deduction Caps—Levered Company Income Taxes

	Actual		Forecast				
Levered Company (Taxable Income)	**Year −1**	**Year 0**	**Year 1**	**Year 2**	**Year 3**	**Year 4**	**Year 5**
Earnings before interest and taxes	−$40,000	−$40,000	−$ 40,000	$60,000	$70,000	$80,000	$80,000
Pre-valuation interest carryforward	0	0	0	18,000	2,000	0	0
Post-valuation interest carryforward			0	0	19,000	11,000	0
Interest expense (current)	0	0	0	0	0	10,000	10,000
Taxable income	−$40,000	−$40,000	−$ 40,000	$42,000	$49,000	$59,000	$70,000
NOL carryforward used	0	0	0	−33,600	−39,200	−47,200	0
Taxable income after NOL carryforward adjustment	−$40,000	−$40,000	−$ 40,000	$ 8,400	$ 9,800	$11,800	$70,000
Income taxes	0	0	0	2,100	2,450	2,950	17,500
Earnings	−$40,000	−$40,000	−$ 40,000	$ 6,300	$ 7,350	$ 8,850	$52,500
Average tax rate	0%	0%	0%	5%	5%	5%	25%
Pre-Valuation Interest Carryforward Balance	**Year −1**	**Year 0**	**Year 1**	**Year 2**	**Year 3**	**Year 4**	**Year 5**
Beginning interest carryforward	$ 0	$10,000	$ 20,000	$ 20,000	$ 2,000	$ 0	$ 0
Change in interest carryforward	10,000	10,000	0	−18,000	−2,000	0	0
Ending interest carryforward	$10,000	$20,000	$ 20,000	$ 2,000	$ 0	$ 0	$ 0
Post-Valuation Interest Carryforward Balance			**Year 1**	**Year 2**	**Year 3**	**Year 4**	**Year 5**
Beginning interest carryforward			$ 0	$ 10,000	$20,000	$11,000	$ 0
Change in interest carryforward			10,000	10,000	−9,000	−11,000	0
Ending interest carryforward			$ 10,000	$ 20,000	$11,000	$ 0	$ 0
Net Operating Loss Carryforward Balance	**Year −1**	**Year 0**	**Year 1**	**Year 2**	**Year 3**	**Year 4**	**Year 5**
Beginning NOL carryforward	$ 0	$40,000	$ 80,000	$120,000	$86,400	$47,200	$ 0
Change in NOL carryforward	40,000	40,000	40,000	−33,600	−39,200	−47,200	0
Ending NOL carryforward	$40,000	$80,000	$120,000	$ 86,400	$47,200	$ 0	$ 0

In Year −1, the company cannot deduct any of its interest because EBIT is negative. The company's earnings before income taxes (on the income statement) is −$50,000; however, since the company cannot deduct any interest because EBIT is negative, its taxable income is −$40,000, which creates a $40,000 NOL carryforward. The $10,000 interest in Year −1 creates a pre-valuation interest carryforward of $10,000. In Year 0, the company again has −$40,000 of EBIT and $10,000 of interest, which increases its NOL by $40,000 and increases its pre-valuation interest carryforward by $10,000.

Year 1 is the first year of the post-valuation period during which the company continues to have −$40,000 of EBIT and $10,000 of interest. The operating loss increases Conrades' NOL carryforward by $40,000. None of the current interest is tax deductible in Year 1, which increases its interest carryforward by $10,000; however, since this is the first year of the post-valuation period, we separately keep track of Conrades' post-valuation interest carryforward. At the end of Year 1, the company has a $20,000 pre-valuation interest carryforward, a $10,000 post-valuation interest carryforward, and a $120,000 NOL carryforward.

In Year 2, the company has EBIT of $60,000 (interest deduction cap of $18,000). We first reduce EBIT by $18,000 for interest related deductions (pre-valuation interest carryforward)—which also reduces the pre-valuation interest carryforward—in order to measure the company's $42,000 taxable income before any offset from the NOL carryforward ($42,000 = $60,000 − $18,000). We then reduce its taxable income before any offset from the NOL carryforward ($42,000 = $60,000 − $18,000) by 80%, due to the NOL carryforward, resulting in taxable income of $8,400 ($8,400 = $42,000 − 0.8 × $42,000) and a tax of $2,100. As of the end of Year 2, the company's NOL carryforward balance is $86,400 ($86,400 = $120,000 − $33,600), its pre-valuation interest carryforward balance is $2,000 ($20,000 − $18,000), and its post-valuation interest carryforward balance increases to $20,000 because none of the current year's interest is tax deductible.

In Year 3, the company has EBIT of $70,000 (interest deduction cap of $21,000). We first reduce EBIT by $21,000 for interest related deductions in order to measure the company's taxable income before any offset from the NOL carryforward. The $21,000 of interest related deductions has two components—the remaining $2,000 pre-valuation interest carryforward and $19,000 post-valuation interest carryforward. We then reduce its taxable income before the NOL carryforward offset ($49,000 = $70,000 − $21,000) by 80% due to the NOL carryforward, resulting in taxable income of $9,800 ($9,800 = $49,000 − 0.8 × $49,000) and a tax of $2,450. As of the end of Year 3, the company's NOL carryforward balance is $47,200 ($47,200 = $86,400 − $39,200), its pre-valuation interest carryforward balance is $0, and its post-valuation interest carryforward balance decreases by $9,000 (−$9,000 = $10,000 current interest − $19,000 post-valuation carryforward used) to $11,000.

In Year 4, the company has EBIT of $80,000 (interest deduction cap of $24,000). The company has an $11,000 post-valuation interest carryforward and $10,000 of current interest for a total of $21,000, which is less than the interest deduction cap. Again, we first reduce EBIT by $21,000 for interest related deductions in order to measure the company's taxable income before any offset from the NOL carryforward. The $21,000 of interest related deductions has two components—the remaining $11,000 post-valuation interest carryforward and $10,000 of current interest. We then offset its taxable income before the NOL carryforward offset ($59,000 = $80,000 − $21,000) by the remainder of the NOL carryforward (which coincidentally is exactly equal to 80% of the taxable income before any offset from the NOL carryforward), resulting in taxable income of $11,800 ($11,800 = $59,000 − $47,200) and a tax of $2,950. As of the end of Year 4, the company has used all of its interest carryforwards and NOL carryforwards. In Year 5, the company's interest deduction cap, $24,000, is larger than its interest, $10,000, so the company can deduct all of its interest in Year 5.

As we calculated in earlier similar exhibits, in Exhibit 3.29, we present four panels in which we calculate Conrades' income taxes as if it had no interest expense (unlevered firm) in the post-valuation period, its interest tax shield, the implied income tax rate for current interest, and in the bottom panel, we compare Conrades' interest tax shield measured using its marginal tax rate, 25%, multiplied by its interest expense to its interest tax shield after including the effects of the interest deduction limitation. Although we assume the unlevered company has no post-valuation interest, the calculations include the pre-valuation interest carryforward because the company can benefit from its pre-valuation interest carryforward even if it is unlevered subsequent to the valuation date.

In Years −1 through 1, the company has a $40,000 net operating loss (−$40,000 EBIT) and it has $10,000 of interest in Years −1 and 0. The three years of a net operating loss results in an NOL carryforward of $120,000 as of the end of Year 1. Since the company cannot deduct any interest in Years −1 and 0, and has a net operating loss in Year 1, the unlevered company has a $20,000 pre-valuation interest carryforward as of the end of Year 1.

In Year 2, the unlevered company has EBIT of $60,000 (interest deduction cap of $18,000). We first reduce EBIT by $18,000 for interest related deductions (pre-valuation interest carryforward)—which also reduces the pre-valuation interest carryforward—in order to measure the company's $42,000 taxable income before any offset from the NOL carryforward ($42,000 = $60,000 − $18,000). We then reduce its taxable income before the NOL carryforward offset ($42,000 = $60,000 − $18,000) by 80% for the NOL carryforward, resulting in taxable income of $8,400 ($8,400 = $42,000 − 0.8 × $42,000) and a tax of $2,100. As of the end of Year 2, the company's NOL carryforward balance is $86,400 ($86,400 = $120,000 − $33,600) and its pre-valuation interest carryforward balance is $2,000 ($20,000 − $18,000). The unlevered company does not have any post-valuation interest carryforward.

In both Years 1 and 2, the levered company (see Exhibit 3.28) was not able to deduct any post-valuation period interest, thus, we know that all of its potential interest tax shields in those two years are

EXHIBIT 3.29 Conrades—Net Operating Loss Carryforward with Interest Deduction Caps—Unlevered Company Income Taxes, Interest Tax Shields, and the Implied Marginal Tax Rate for Interest

	Actual		Forecast				
Unlevered Company (Taxable Income)	**Year −1**	**Year 0**	**Year 1**	**Year 2**	**Year 3**	**Year 4**	**Year 5**
Earnings before interest and taxes	−$40,000	−$40,000	−$ 40,000	$ 60,000	$70,000	$80,000	$80,000
Pre-valuation interest carryforward	0	0	0	18,000	2,000	0	0
Interest expense (current)	0	0					
Taxable income	−$40,000	−$40,000	−$ 40,000	$ 42,000	$68,000	$80,000	$80,000
NOL carryforward used	0	0	0	−33,600	−54,400	−32,000	0
Taxable income after NOL carryforward adjustment	−$40,000	−$40,000	−$ 40,000	$ 8,400	$13,600	$48,000	$80,000
Income taxes	0	0	0	2,100	3,400	12,000	20,000
Earnings	−$40,000	−$40,000	−$ 40,000	$ 6,300	$10,200	$36,000	$60,000
Average tax rate	0%	0%	0%	5%	5%	15%	25%
Pre-Valuation Interest Carryforward Balance	**Year −1**	**Year 0**	**Year 1**	**Year 2**	**Year 3**	**Year 4**	**Year 5**
Beginning interest carryforward	$ 0	$10,000	$ 20,000	$ 20,000	$ 2,000	$ 0	$ 0
Change in interest carryforward	10,000	10,000	0	−18,000	−2,000	0	0
Ending interest carryforward	$10,000	$20,000	$ 20,000	$ 2,000	$ 0	$ 0	$ 0
Net Operating Loss Carryforward Balance	**Year −1**	**Year 0**	**Year 1**	**Year 2**	**Year 3**	**Year 4**	**Year 5**
Beginning NOL carryforward	$ 0	$40,000	$ 80,000	$120,000	$86,400	$32,000	$ 0
Change in NOL carryforward	40,000	40,000	40,000	−33,600	−54,400	−32,000	0
Ending NOL carryforward	$40,000	$80,000	$120,000	$ 86,400	$32,000	$ 0	$ 0
Interest Tax Shield			**Year 1**	**Year 2**	**Year 3**	**Year 4**	**Year 5**
Income taxes (unlevered firm)			$ 0	$ 2,100	$ 3,400	$12,000	$20,000
Income taxes (with interest deduction)			0	2,100	2,450	2,950	17,500
Correct interest tax shield			$ 0	$ 0	$ 950	$ 9,050	$ 2,500
Implied Income Tax Rate for Interest Tax Shields			**Year 1**	**Year 2**	**Year 3**	**Year 4**	**Year 5**
Interest tax shield			$ 0	$ 0	$ 950	$ 9,050	$ 2,500
Interest expense (current)			$ 10,000	$ 10,000	$10,000	$10,000	$10,000
Implied income tax rate for interest tax shields			0.00%	0.00%	9.50%	90.50%	25.00%
Comparison Interest Tax Shield Using Marginal Tax Rate × Interest			**Year 1**	**Year 2**	**Year 3**	**Year 4**	**Year 5**
Interest expense (current)			$ 10,000	$ 10,000	$10,000	$10,000	$10,000
Marginal income tax rate			25.0%	25.0%	25.0%	25.0%	25.0%
Interest tax shield using marginal tax rate × interest			$ 2,500	$ 2,500	$ 2,500	$ 2,500	$ 2,500
Correct interest tax shield			0	0	950	9,050	2,500
Overstated (understated) interest tax shield			$ 2,500	$ 2,500	$ 1,550	−$ 6,550	$ 0

deferred ($5,000 = 0.25 × $10,000 × 2). The bottom three panels of the exhibit show these calculations. Since income taxes for the unlevered company equal income taxes for the levered company in both Years 1 and 2, the company has no income tax shield in either year; they are deferred through the post-valuation interest carryforward.

In Year 3, the unlevered company has EBIT of $70,000 (interest deduction cap of $21,000). We first reduce EBIT by $2,000 for the remainder of the company's pre-valuation interest carryforward, in order to measure the company's taxable income before any offset from the NOL carryforward of $68,000 ($68,000 = $70,000 − $2,000). We then reduce its taxable income before the NOL carryforward offset by 80% for the NOL carryforward, resulting in taxable income of $13,600 ($13,600 = $68,000 − 0.8

× $68,000) and a tax of $3,400. As of the end of Year 3, the company's NOL carryforward balance is $32,000 ($32,000 = $86,400 − $54,400) and its pre-valuation interest carryforward balance is now $0. The resulting interest tax shield in Year 3 is equal to the difference in the income taxes for the levered and unlevered firm, which is $950 ($950 = $3,400 − $2,450).

Conrades' interest tax shields in Year 3 were limited to $950 (versus its potential interest tax shields of $7,500 from Years 1 through 3; $7,500 = $10,000 × 3 × 0.25) because it was able to offset 80% of its income using its NOL carryforward even when unlevered. The interest tax shield in Year 3 is $1,550 lower than the $2,500 interest tax shield based on the company's $10,000 interest expense, which increases the amount of deferred interest tax shields from $5,000 to $6,550 ($6,550 = $2,500 + $2,500 + $1,550). The implied tax rate to measure the company's $950 interest tax shield is 9.5%.

In Year 4, as a levered firm (see Exhibit 3.28), Conrades was able to capture not only its potential interest tax shields from the current year but also capture all previously deferred interest tax shields ($9,050 = $10,000 × 4 × 0.25 − $950). The company is able to deduct its remaining post-valuation interest carryforward of $11,000 and all of its current interest for a total interest related deduction of $21,000. The interest tax shield in Year 4 is equal to the difference in the income taxes for the levered and unlevered firm, $9,050 ($9,050 = $12,000 − $2,950), and the implied tax rate for interest in Year 4 is 90.5%. Because the post-valuation interest carryforward at the beginning of Year 5 is $0 and its interest deduction cap does not limit its interest deduction in Year 5, the interest tax shield is just equal to the company's marginal tax rate × interest expense, $2,500 ($2,500 = 0.25 × $10,000).

Valuation Key 3.7

Net operating loss carryforwards (NOLs) can be an important consideration when valuing a company. NOLs can reduce a company's future income tax payments relative to what they would have been otherwise and therefore, all else equal, can increase the value of the firm relative to what the value would have been without the NOLs. On the other hand, NOLs can also defer the benefits of interest tax shields and therefore, all else equal, decrease the value of the interest tax shields relative to what the value would have been without the NOLs. On net, the positive effect on value from the tax savings from NOLs is larger than the decrease in value from the deferred interest tax shields. For levered companies, any year in which a company has a net operating loss, it will also have an increase in its interest carryforward if there are binding limitations on the deductibility of interest. Thus, interest carryforwards are part of the calculation of the effect of NOL carryforwards. We can often glean useful information about NOLs from a company's income-tax-related footnote disclosures in its financial statements.

REVIEW EXERCISE 3.6

Measuring the Effects of Net Operating Loss Carryforwards

Using the information in the following schedule, calculate the company's taxable income, income taxes due, interest tax shields, and the implied income tax rate for interest. Assume the company's income tax rate on all income is 30%, the tax deduction for interest in any year is limited to 20% of EBIT in that year, any interest payment above the interest deduction cap in a year can be carried forward indefinitely, and the company can only use its NOL carryforwards to offset a maximum of 80% of its taxable income before NOL offsets.

Financial Accounting (Income Statement Excerpt)	Actual		Forecast				
	Year −1	Year 0	Year 1	Year 2	Year 3	Year 4	Year 5
Earnings before interest and taxes. . .	−$20,000	−$20,000	−$20,000	$40,000	$50,000	$60,000	$70,000
Interest expense (current).	5,000	5,000	5,000	5,000	5,000	5,000	5,000
Earnings before income taxes	−$25,000	−$25,000	−$25,000	$35,000	$45,000	$55,000	$65,000

Solution on pages 152–153.

SUMMARY AND KEY CONCEPTS

Unlevered free cash flows (or free cash flows) are cash flows available for distribution to all of a company's investors (security holders). In this chapter, we discuss the concept of free cash flows and how to measure them. They are the cash flows we use in discounted cash flow models that measure a company's value. Equity free cash flows are free cash flows adjusted for all cash flows to and from non-common equity investors and represent the amount that could be distributed to the common equity investors. Calculations of free cash flows and equity free cash flows take into consideration the actual taxes the company must pay, and we discussed the information that can be gleaned from the financial statements about the company's taxes.

We also discuss the preparation of a cash flow statement, a free cash flow schedule, and the relationships between the components of the statement of cash flows and the free cash flow schedule. We use most of the calculations and adjustments in the cash flow statement in order to calculate free cash flows and then reconcile free cash flows to the change in the company's cash balance. Constructing a cash flow statement and a free cash flow schedule from a company's balance sheets, income statement, statement of shareholders' equity, and supplemental schedules serves as an introduction to the creation of financial models, which we will discuss in the next chapter. The flow of information and calculations from the income statement and balance sheet into the cash flow statement and a free cash flow schedule, is the same flow and calculations we use in financial modeling.

ADDITIONAL READING AND REFERENCES

Barth, M., D. Cram, and K. Nelson, "Accruals and the Prediction of Future Cash Flows," *The Accounting Review* vol. 76, no. 1 (January 2001), pp. 27–58.

Sloan, R., "Do Stock Prices Fully Reflect Information in Accruals and Cash Flows About Future Earnings?" *The Accounting Review* (July 1996), pp. 289–315.

EXERCISES AND PROBLEMS

P3.1 **Cash Flow Statement and Free Cash Flow Schedule—Tim Schlindwein & Company:** We provide income statements, statements of retained earnings, and balance sheets for Tim Schlindwein & Company (Schlindwein) in Exhibit P3.1. All of the cash flows occur at the end of each year, including capital expenditures and any financing transactions. The company distributes all equity free cash flows to equityholders in the form of dividends; in other words, it does not hold any excess cash. Its income tax rate is 30% on taxable income up to $2,000 and 40% on all additional taxable income. The interest rate the company pays on debt is 8%, and its preferred stock dividend rate is 9% (both based on the company's book value of debt and preferred stock). The company has no sales or retirements of property, plant, or equipment during the period covered by the exhibit. The cash line represents required cash.

a. Calculate Schlindwein & Company's unlevered free cash flow and equity free cash flows for Years 0 through 4.

b. Compare the stability of the company's earnings before interest and taxes, net income, unlevered free cash flows, and equity free cash flows.

EXHIBIT P3.1 Tim Schlindwein & Company Income Statement, Statement of Retained Earnings, and Balance Sheet Forecasts

TIM SCHLINDWEIN & COMPANY
Income Statement, Statement of Retained Earnings, and Balance Sheet Forecasts

	Actual Year −1	Actual Year 0	Forecast Year 1	Forecast Year 2	Forecast Year 3	Forecast Year 4
Income Statement						
Revenue	$ 7,960	$ 8,119	$ 8,931	$ 9,556	$ 9,939	$10,137
Operating expenses	−5,094	−5,196	−5,537	−5,256	−5,466	−5,576
Depreciation expense	−889	−1,005	−1,207	−1,411	−1,610	−1,642
Earnings before interest and taxes	$ 1,977	$ 1,918	$ 2,187	$ 2,889	$ 2,862	$ 2,919
Interest expense	0	−400	−392	−360	−288	−208
Income before taxes	$ 1,977	$ 1,518	$ 1,795	$ 2,529	$ 2,574	$ 2,711
Income tax expense	−593	−455	−538	−812	−830	−885
Net income	$ 1,384	$ 1,062	$ 1,256	$ 1,718	$ 1,745	$ 1,827
Balance Sheet						
Cash	$ 80	$ 81	$ 89	$ 96	$ 99	$ 101
Net operating working capital	318	325	357	382	398	405
Property, plant, and equipment (net)	8,119	8,931	9,556	9,939	10,137	10,340
Total assets	$ 8,517	$ 9,337	$10,003	$10,416	$10,634	$10,847
Debt	$ 5,000	$ 4,900	$ 4,500	$ 3,600	$ 2,600	$ 2,652
Preferred stock	1,000	1,050	1,170	1,430	1,740	1,775
Equity	2,517	3,387	4,333	5,386	6,294	6,420
Total liabilities and equities	$ 8,517	$ 9,337	$10,003	$10,416	$10,634	$10,847
Statement of Retained Earnings						
Beginning-of-year balance	$ 701	$ 1,517	$ 2,387	$ 3,333	$ 4,386	$ 5,294
Net income	1,384	1,062	1,256	1,718	1,745	1,827
Preferred stock dividends	−68	−90	−95	−105	−129	−157
Common equity dividends	−500	−102	−216	−559	−708	−1,544
End-of-year balance	$ 1,517	$ 2,387	$ 3,333	$ 4,386	$ 5,294	$ 5,420

Exhibit may contain small rounding errors

P3.2 **Cash Flow Statement and Free Cash Flow Schedule—Jake and Phil Company:** We provide financial statement forecasts for the Jake and Phil Company in Exhibit P3.2 (comparative balance sheets, an income statement, and statement of retained earnings). During Year 3, the company sold property, plant, and equipment with an acquisition cost of $5,000. Its income tax rate is 40%. The company needs an increase in cash of $1,000 to operate next year. Prepare a Statement of Cash Flows, a Free Cash Flow Schedule using the Earnings Before Interest and Taxes method and a Free Cash Flow Schedule using the Cash Flow from Operations method for Year 3.

EXHIBIT P3.2 Income Statement and Balance Sheet Forecasts for the Jake and Phil Company

Income Statement	Year 2	Year 3
Net revenues	$80,000	$100,000
Gain on sale (other revenues)	0	700
Total revenues	$80,000	$100,700
Cost of goods sold	–$40,000	–$ 50,000
Selling, general and administrative	–20,000	–20,000
Depreciation expense—total	–10,000	–13,000
Total expenses	–$70,000	–$ 83,000
Income before interest and taxes	$10,000	$ 17,700
Interest expense	–1,000	–3,000
Income before taxes	$ 9,000	$ 14,700
Income tax expense	–1,200	–5,880
Net income	$ 7,800	$ 8,820
Beginning retained earnings		7,800
Dividends	0	–4,000
Ending retained earnings	$ 7,800	$ 12,620

Balance Sheet	Year 2	Year 3
Cash and short-term investments	$ 19,500	$ 22,420
Accounts receivable	8,000	18,000
Inventories	2,000	1,500
Total current assets	$ 29,500	$ 41,920
Property, plant and equipment	$100,000	$125,000
Less: accumulated depreciation	–10,000	–22,000
Net property, plant, and equipment	$ 90,000	$103,000
Pre-paid expenses (non-current)	$ 0	$ 3,000
Total assets	$119,500	$147,920
Accounts payable—trade	$ 4,200	$ 8,200
Accrued liabilities (expenses)	6,000	3,500
Interest payable	1,000	1,100
Income taxes payable	500	2,500
Dividends payable	0	1,000
Total current liabilities	$ 11,700	$ 16,300
Long-term debt-A	$ 20,000	$ 20,000
Long-term debt-B	0	15,000
Long-term liabilities	$ 20,000	$ 35,000
Total liabilities	$ 31,700	$ 51,300
Common stock at par	$ 80,000	$ 85,000
Additional paid-in capital	0	0
Foreign currency translation adj	0	0
Retained earnings	7,800	12,620
Treasury stock, at cost	0	–1,000
Total shareholders' equity	$ 87,800	$ 96,620
Total liabilities and equity	$119,500	$147,920

P3.3 **Working Backwards—Cash Flow Statement and Free Cash Flow Schedule—The Missing Data Company:** We provide partially completed calculations for the income statements, balance sheets, retained earnings, and free cash flows for the Missing Data Company in Exhibit P3.3. All of the cash flows occur at the end of each year, including capital expenditures and any financing transactions. The company distributes all equity free cash flows to equityholders in the form of dividends; in other words, it does not hold any excess cash. The interest rate it pays on debt is 7%, and its preferred stock dividend rate is 8% (of the company's book value of preferred stock). All cash flows occur at the end of each year. The tax rate is 25% on the first $4,000 of income and 45% on all income above $4,000. The company has no income taxes payable at the end of any of the three years. Complete the Missing Data Company's income statements, balance sheets, retained earnings, and free cash flow calculations for Years 0 and 1.

EXHIBIT P3.3 Income Statements, Balance Sheets and Free Cash Flow Schedules for the Missing Data Company

Income Statement and Balance Sheet

	Actual Year -1	Actual Year 0	Forecast Year 1
Income Statement			
Revenue	$ 9,568	$9,759	$10,735
Operating expenses	-5,262	-5,368	-5,368
Depreciation expense	-1,091	-1,212	-1,433
Earnings before interest and taxes	$ 3,215	$3,180	$ 3,935
Interest expense	0	?-1	?-1
Income before taxes	$ 3,215	?-2	?-2
Income tax expense	-804	?-3	?-3
Net income	$ 2,411	?-4	?-4
Statement of Retained Earnings			
Beginning-of-year balance	$ 209	$2,060	$ 3,557
Net income	2,411	?-5	?-5
Preferred stock dividends	-60	?-6	?-6
Common equity dividends	-500	?-7	?-7
End-of-year balance	$ 2,060	?-8	?-8
Balance Sheet			
Cash	$ 96	$ 98	$ 107
Net operating working capital	765	781	429
Property, plant, and equipment (net)	12,199	?-9	?-9
Total assets	$13,060	?-10	?-10
Debt	$ 9,000	?-11	?-11
Preferred stock	1,000	?-12	?-12
Equity	3,060	?-13	?-13
Total liabilities and equities	$13,060	?-14	?-14

Free Cash Flow and Equity Free Cash Flow

	Actual Year 0	Forecast Year 1
Earnings before interest and taxes (EBIT)	$3,180	$3,935
− Income taxes paid on EBIT	-795	-984
Earnings before interest and after taxes	$2,385	$2,951
+ Depreciation expense	1,212	1,433
− Change in required cash	?-15	?-15
− Change in net operating working capital	?-16	?-16
− Capital expenditures	-2,432	-2,372
Unlevered free cash flow	?-17	?-17
− Interest paid in cash	?-18	?-18
+ Interest tax shield	158	151
− Preferred stock dividends	?-19	?-19
+ Change in debt financing	-400	-1,300
+ Change in preferred stock financing	140	380
Equity free cash flow	?-20	?-20

Exhibit may contain small rounding errors

P3.4 **Permanent Tax Differences:** A company owns a municipal bond that pays $30,000 interest annually. The company's financial reporting (book) income before income taxes and municipal bond interest is $200,000, which is also equal to the company's taxable income (interest on the municipal bond is not taxable). The company's statutory income tax rate is 30%. Calculate the company's current income tax payable to the taxing authority, its financial reporting or book income before income taxes and provision for income taxes, and its effective income tax rate.

P3.5 **Permanent Tax Differences:** A company's financial reporting (book income) and taxable income (taxable income) before income taxes, municipal bond interest, and warranty expense is $120,000. A company owns a municipal bond that pays $20,000 interest annually, which is not taxable. For this year, the company had an accrued warranty expense equal to $40,000 and a warranty tax deduction equal to $25,000. The company accrues warranty expenses based on expected warranty expenses for current year revenues, resulting in an increase in a warranty accrued liability. The company's warranty liability at the end of the year was equal to $135,000. For income taxes, the company can only deduct warranty expenses when it incurs actual warranty expenditures. The company's statutory income tax rate is 40%. Calculate the company's current income tax payable to the taxing authority, its financial reporting or book income before income taxes and provision for income taxes, and its effective income tax rate.

P3.6 **Effect of Permanent Difference on Income Tax Rates:** A company has $1,200,000 income before interest expense and interest income on both its income statement (book) and tax forms (tax). The company also has $200,000 of interest expense that is tax deductible and $400,000 of municipal bond interest income that is not taxable. The company has a 30% tax rate on all types of income. Calculate the company's effective tax rate and prepare a reconciliation between its 30% statutory rate and its effective tax rate. Also calculate the company's interest tax shield and the income tax rate for interest. Assuming the company's EBIT is $1,600,000 ($1,600,000 = $1,200,000 + $400,000), calculate the income tax the company would pay on EBIT.

P3.7 **Deferred Income Taxes—The Equipment Company:** Assume a company originally paid $400,000 for an asset three years ago. The asset has a ten-year life and zero salvage value at the end of the ten years. During the past three years, the company deducted depreciation on this asset for income tax purposes according to the MACRS depreciation schedule using the half-year convention from Exhibit 3.15. It uses straight-line depreciation for financial reporting purposes. In the past, the company had $100,000 of taxable income and book income before deducting depreciation expense, and it expects to have that same income for the foreseeable future. The company has a 40% income tax rate. Calculate the following for Year 4: the amount of tax the company will pay, the depreciation expense and cumulative depreciation expensed for tax and book purposes, the income tax expense shown on the income statement, the net income shown on the income statement, and the balance in its deferred tax asset and liability accounts.

P3.8 **Deferred Income Taxes—The Warranty Company:** At the end of Year 1, a company records a $5,000 warranty expense and pays $3,000 to fulfill its warranty commitments for that year. The balance for the warranty liability at the beginning of Year 1 was $20,000. At the end of Year 2, the company records an $8,000 warranty expense and pays $9,000 to fulfill its warranty commitments for that year. The company's income tax rate is 40%, and income before warranty expenses is $10,000 for both income tax and financial reporting purposes. For income taxes, the company can only deduct warranty expenses when it incurs actual warranty expenditures. Calculate the following: the amount of tax the company will pay, the income tax expense shown on the income statement, the net income shown on the income statement, and the balance in its deferred tax asset and liability accounts for Year 1 and Year 2.

P3.9 **Statutory Tax Rate Reconciliation—Google Inc.:** Use the information in Exhibit P3.4 for Google Inc. and discuss the components of its statutory income tax rate reconciliation for Years 2 and 3. For each year, calculate Google's effective tax rate and the marginal tax rate for its interest tax shields assuming Google has no NOLs and any interest expense has not been subject to the 30% limitation. Also discuss the tax rates you would use in forecasting Google's after-tax earnings and interest tax shields for income and interest in the United States for Year 4, assuming it will face the same tax regimes in Year 4 as it faced in Year 3. Also using just the Federal statutory tax rate line and the foreign rate differential line, what is your estimate of the tax rate paid on foreign income if 50% of their income is from outside the United States?

EXHIBIT P3.4 Statutory Income Tax Rate Reconciliation for Google

	Google Inc.	
($ in millions)	**Year 2**	**Year 3**
Federal statutory tax rate (35%)	$2,933	$2,049
State taxes, net of federal benefit	302	263
Stock-based compensation expense	63	91
Change in valuation allowance	–41	313
Foreign rate differential	–1,339	–1,020
Federal research credit	–56	–52
Tax exempt interest	–15	–52
Other permanent differences	14	34
Provision for income taxes	$1,861	$1,626

P3.10 **Effect of Interest Deduction Limitations:** Using the information in the following schedule, calculate the company's taxable income, income taxes due, interest tax shields, and the implied income tax rate for interest. Assume the company's income tax rate on all income is 20%, the tax deduction for interest in any year is limited to 30% of EBIT in that year, and any interest payment above the interest deduction cap in a year can be carried forward indefinitely.

	Actual		Forecast				
Financial Accounting (Income Statement Excerpt)	**Year –1**	**Year 0**	**Year 1**	**Year 2**	**Year 3**	**Year 4**	**Year 5**
Earnings before interest and taxes	$1,000	$2,000	$8,000	$40,000	$60,000	$80,000	$90,000
Interest expense (current)	8,000	8,000	8,000	8,000	8,000	8,000	8,000
Earnings before income taxes	–$7,000	–$6,000	$ 0	$32,000	$52,000	$72,000	$82,000

P3.11 Net Operating Losses and Interest Tax Shield (with Carrybacks and No Interest or NOL Limitations): A company has an income tax rate of 30% on all taxable income. It issued $50,000 of 10% debt at its inception; interest is $5,000 per year. The company is a start-up company in the United States. Management has created three scenarios of possible earnings before interest and taxes (EBIT) for the first four years of the company's operations. Management does not expect to change any of its external financing (the company will not issue or repurchase securities). For each scenario, calculate the company's taxable income, income taxes, and interest tax shield for each year. The tax law allows both carrybacks and carryforwards of net operating losses and has no limitations for interest deductions and the usage of NOLs.

		Year 1	Year 2	Year 3	Year 4
a.	Scenario #1, EBIT =	$10,000	$ 0	$10,000	$10,000
b.	Scenario #2, EBIT =	$ 0	$3,000	$10,000	$20,000
c.	Scenario #3, EBIT =	$ 4,000	$4,000	$ 7,000	$10,000

P3.12 Effects of Interest and Net Operating Loss Carryforwards: Using the information in the following schedule, calculate the company's taxable income, income taxes due, interest tax shields, and the implied income tax rate for interest. Assume the company's income tax rate on all income is 20%, the tax deduction for interest in any year is limited to 30% of EBIT in that year, any interest payment above the interest deduction cap in a year can be carried forward indefinitely, and the company can only use its NOL carryforwards to offset a maximum of 80% of its taxable income before NOL offsets.

Financial Accounting (Income Statement Excerpt)	Actual		Forecast				
	Year −1	Year 0	Year 1	Year 2	Year 3	Year 4	Year 5
Earnings before interest and taxes. . .	−$30,000	$5,000	−$50,000	$40,000	$60,000	$80,000	$90,000
Interest expense (current).	8,000	8,000	8,000	8,000	8,000	8,000	8,000
Earnings before income taxes	−$38,000	−$3,000	−$58,000	$32,000	$52,000	$72,000	$82,000

SOLUTIONS FOR REVIEW EXERCISES

Solution for Review Exercise 3.1: Frits Seegers, Inc. Free Cash Flow Schedule

Below, we present the free cash flow schedule for Frits Seegers that includes unlevered free cash flows, equity free cash flows, and a reconciliation to the change in the company's cash balance using the EBIT method. (Note, the problem in the chapter only provided data for you to solve Year 0. The additional years of data are contained in Problem 1.9.)

FRITS SEEGERS INC. Free Cash Flow Forecasts (for the years ended December 31)	Year 0	Year 1	Year 2	Year 3	Year 4	Year 5	Year 6
Earnings before interest and taxes (EBIT)	$297.0	$445.5	$623.7	$810.8	$891.9	$918.6	$946.2
– Income taxes paid on EBIT	–118.8	–178.2	–249.5	–324.3	–356.8	–367.5	–378.5
Earnings before interest and after taxes	$178.2	$267.3	$374.2	$486.5	$535.1	$551.2	$567.7
– Change in accounts receivable	–16.7	–91.7	–110.0	–115.5	–50.1	–16.5	–17.0
– Change in inventory	–11.9	–65.2	–78.3	–82.2	–35.6	–11.8	–12.1
+ Change in accounts payable	5.1	28.0	33.6	35.2	15.3	5.0	5.2
+ Change in current other liabilities	3.5	19.3	23.1	24.3	10.5	3.5	3.6
– Change in required cash balance	–5.0	–27.5	–33.0	–34.7	–15.0	–5.0	–5.1
Unlevered cash flows from operations	$153.3	$130.1	$209.6	$313.6	$460.2	$526.5	$542.3
– Capital expenditures	–275.0	–330.0	–346.5	–150.2	–49.5	–51.0	–52.6
Unlevered free cash flow	–$121.7	–$199.9	–$136.9	$163.5	$410.7	$475.4	$489.7
– Interest paid	–96.0	–112.0	–128.0	–136.0	–144.0	–152.0	–160.0
+ Interest tax shield	38.4	44.8	51.2	54.4	57.6	60.8	64.0
Cash flow before changes in financing	–$179.3	–$267.1	–$213.7	$ 81.9	$324.3	$384.2	$393.7
+ Change in debt financing	200.0	200.0	100.0	100.0	100.0	100.0	100.0
Free cash flow to common equity	$ 20.7	–$ 67.1	–$113.7	$181.9	$424.3	$484.2	$493.7
+ Change in common equity financing	$ 0.0	$ 67.1	$113.7	$ 0.0	$ 0.0	$ 0.0	$ 0.0
– Common equity dividends paid	–20.7	0.0	0.0	–181.9	–424.3	–484.2	–493.7
Change in excess cash	$ 0	$ 0	$ 0	$ 0	$ 0	$ 0	$ 0
+ Change in required cash balance	5.0	27.5	33.0	34.7	15.0	5.0	5.1
Change in cash balance	$ 5.0	$ 27.5	$ 33.0	$ 34.7	$ 15.0	$ 5.0	$ 5.1
Change in cash balance on the balance sheet	$ 5.0	$ 27.5	$ 33.0	$ 34.7	$ 15.0	$ 5.0	$ 5.1

Exhibit may contain small rounding errors

Solution for Review Exercise 3.2: Frits Seegers, Inc. Cash Flow Statement

Below, we present the cash flow statement and use cash flow from operations in order to calculate the company's unlevered free cash flow. (Note, the problem in the chapter only provided data for you to solve Year 0. The additional years of data are contained in Problem 1.9.)

FRITS SEEGERS INC.
Cash Flow Statement Forecasts
(for the years ended December 31)

	Year 0	Year 1	Year 2	Year 3	Year 4	Year 5	Year 6
Cash flows from operations:							
Net income	$120.6	$200.1	$297.4	$404.9	$448.7	$460.0	$471.7
– Change in accounts receivable	–16.7	–91.7	–110.0	–115.5	–50.1	–16.5	–17.0
– Change in inventory	–11.9	–65.2	–78.3	–82.2	–35.6	–11.8	–12.1
+ Change in accounts payable	5.1	28.0	33.6	35.2	15.3	5.0	5.2
+ Change in current other liabilities	3.5	19.3	23.1	24.3	10.5	3.5	3.6
Cash flow from operations	$100.7	$ 90.4	$165.8	$266.7	$388.8	$440.2	$451.4
Investing Activities:							
– Capital expenditures	–$275.0	–$330.0	–$346.5	–$150.2	–$ 49.5	–$ 51.0	–$ 52.6
Financing activities:							
+ Change in debt financing	$200.0	$200.0	$100.0	$100.0	$100.0	$100.0	$100.0
+ Change in common equity financing	0.0	67.1	113.7	0.0	0.0	0.0	0.0
– Common equity dividends paid	–20.7	0.0	0.0	–181.9	–424.3	–484.2	–493.7
Cash flows from financing activities	$179.3	$267.1	$213.7	–$81.9	–$324.3	–$384.2	–$393.7
Change in cash balance	$ 5.0	$ 27.5	$ 33.0	$ 34.7	$ 15.0	$ 5.0	$ 5.1
Change in cash balance on balance sheet	$ 5.0	$ 27.5	$ 33.0	$ 34.7	$ 15.0	$ 5.0	$ 5.1

Exhibit may contain small rounding errors

FRITS SEEGERS INC.
Free Cash Flow Forecasts
(for the years ended December 31)

	Year 0	Year 1	Year 2	Year 3	Year 4	Year 5	Year 6
Cash flow from operations	$100.7	$ 90.4	$165.8	$266.7	$388.8	$440.2	$451.4
Change in required cash balance	–5.0	–27.5	–33.0	–34.7	–15.0	–5.0	–5.1
Adjusted cash flow from operations	$ 95.7	$ 62.9	$132.8	$232.0	$373.8	$435.3	$446.3
Interest expense	96.0	112.0	128.0	136.0	144.0	152.0	160.0
Interest tax shield	–38.4	–44.8	–51.2	–54.4	–57.6	–60.8	–64.0
Unlevered cash flow from operations	$153.3	$130.1	$209.6	$313.6	$460.2	$526.5	$542.3
Capital expenditures	–275.0	–330.0	–346.5	–150.2	–49.5	–51.0	–52.6
Unlevered free cash flow	–$121.7	–$199.9	–$136.9	$163.5	$410.7	$475.4	$489.7

Exhibit may contain small rounding errors

Solution for Review Exercise 3.3: Effect of Permanent Difference on Income Tax Rates

Actual Levered Firm	Tax (40%)	Book
Income before interest expense and interest income	$200,000	$200,000
Interest expense	−80,000	−80,000
Municipal bond interest		60,000
Taxable income or income before taxes	$120,000	$180,000
Income tax payable or expense (provision)	−48,000	−48,000
Net income	$ 72,000	$132,000
Effective income tax rate	40.0%	26.7%
Reconciliation to the statutory rate:		
Statutory rate		40.0%
Non-taxable municipal bond interest[1]		−13.3%
Effective income tax rate		26.7%

[1] Calculated as 0.4 × $60,000/$180,000

Unlevered Firm	Tax (40%)	Book
Income before interest expense and interest income	$200,000	$200,000
Interest expense		
Municipal bond interest		60,000
Taxable income or income before taxes	$200,000	$260,000
Income tax payable or expense (provision)	−80,000	−80,000
Net income	$120,000	$180,000
Effective income tax rate	40.0%	30.8%

Reconciliation to the Statutory Rate:	
Statutory rate	40.0%
Municipal bond interest[1]	−9.2%
Effective income tax rate	30.8%

[1] Calculated as 0.4 × $60,000/$260,000

Interest Tax Shield:	
Income taxes for unlevered firm	$80,000
Actual income taxes paid	48,000
Interest tax shield	$32,000
Interest	80,000
Tax rate for interest, T_{INT}	40.0%

Solution for Review Exercise 3.4: Deferred Tax Liabilities and Depreciation

Below, we show the calculation of tax and book depreciation for this asset.

	MACRS	Tax (40%)	Straight-Line	Book
Amount paid for asset		$600,000		$600,000
Year 1 depreciation	33.33%	$199,980	33.33%	$200,000
Year 2 depreciation	44.45%	$266,700	33.33%	$200,000
Year 3 depreciation	14.81%	$ 88,860	33.33%	$200,000
Year 4 depreciation	7.41%	$ 44,460		$ 0
	100.00%	$600,000	100.00%	$600,000

We measure tax and book accumulated depreciation as of the beginning and end of Year 3. The difference in the tax and book accumulated depreciation is equal to the difference in the tax basis of the asset, which—when multiplied by the income tax rate—measures the deferred tax liability.

Year 3	Tax Basis	Book Value	Difference (Book Value – Tax Basis)	Deferred Income Tax Liability (Asset)
Original amount paid (acquisition cost)	$600,000	$600,000	$ 0	$ —
Depreciation deducted or expensed as of the beginning of the year	–466,680	–400,000	66,680	26,672
Taxable basis or book value as of the beginning of the year	$133,320	$200,000	$ 66,680	$ 26,672
Depreciation deducted or expensed during the current year	–88,860	–200,000	–111,140	–44,456
Taxable basis or book value as of the end of the year	$ 44,460	$ 0	–$ 44,460	–$ 17,784

We can now measure income tax for tax and book purposes. For financial reporting (books), the current income tax is equal to 40% of the taxable income for tax purposes; the deferred tax is equal to the change in the balance of the deferred income tax liability. In Year 3, deferred income taxes reduces tax expense relative to the tax owed because the deferred tax liability decreased this year (and actually became a deferred tax asset). The deferred tax liability became a deferred tax asset at the end of Year 3 because the asset was fully depreciated on the books but it was not fully depreciated on the tax records. In Year 4, $44,460 of depreciation will be deducted on the tax return, but zero depreciation expense will be recorded on the books (income statement).

	Tax (40%)	Book
Net income before depreciation	$400,000	$400,000
Depreciation	–88,860	–200,000
Taxable income or income before taxes	$311,140	$200,000
Provision for income taxes:		
Current	–$124,456	–$124,456
Deferred		44,456
Provision for income taxes—total	–$124,456	–$ 80,000
Net income	$186,684	$120,000
Effective income tax rate	40.0%	40.0%

Solution for Review Exercise 3.5: Measuring the Effect of Interest Deduction Caps

EBIT and Interest Cap

Financial Accounting (Income Statement Excerpt)	Actual		Forecast				
	Year –1	Year 0	Year 1	Year 2	Year 3	Year 4	Year 5
Earnings before interest and taxes	$ 100	$ 200	$ 500	$40,000	$50,000	$60,000	$70,000
Interest expense (current)	5,000	5,000	5,000	5,000	5,000	5,000	5,000
Earnings before income taxes	–$4,900	–$4,800	–$4,500	$35,000	$45,000	$55,000	$65,000
Interest deduction cap	$ 20	$ 40	$ 100	$ 8,000	$10,000	$12,000	$14,000

Calculation of the Company's Taxable Income

	Actual		Forecast				
Levered Company (Taxable Income)	**Year −1**	**Year 0**	**Year 1**	**Year 2**	**Year 3**	**Year 4**	**Year 5**
Earnings before interest and taxes	$ 100	$ 200	$ 500	$40,000	$50,000	$60,000	$70,000
Pre-valuation interest carryforward	0	40	100	8,000	1,840	0	0
Post-valuation interest carryforward			0	0	8,160	6,840	0
Interest expense (current)	20	0	0	0	0	5,000	5,000
Taxable income	$ 80	$ 160	$ 400	$32,000	$40,000	$48,160	$65,000
Income taxes	24	48	120	9,600	12,000	14,448	19,500
Earnings	$ 56	$ 112	$ 280	$22,400	$28,000	$33,712	$45,500
Average tax rate	30%	30%	30%	30%	30%	30%	30%
Pre-Valuation Interest Carryforward Balance	**Year −1**	**Year 0**	**Year 1**	**Year 2**	**Year 3**	**Year 4**	**Year 5**
Beginning interest carryforward	$ 0	$4,980	$9,940	$ 9,840	$ 1,840	$ 0	$ 0
Change in interest carryforward	4,980	4,960	−100	−8,000	−1,840	0	0
Ending interest carryforward	$4,980	$9,940	$9,840	$ 1,840	$ 0	$ 0	$ 0
Post-Valuation Interest Carryforward Balance			**Year 1**	**Year 2**	**Year 3**	**Year 4**	**Year 5**
Beginning interest carryforward			$ 0	$ 5,000	$10,000	$ 6,840	$ 0
Change in interest carryforward			5,000	5,000	−3,160	−6,840	0
Ending interest carryforward			$5,000	$10,000	$ 6,840	$ 0	$ 0

Calculation of the Company's Unlevered Taxable Income, Interest Tax Shield, and Implied Tax Rate for Interest

	Actual		Forecast				
Unlevered Company (Taxable Income)	**Year −1**	**Year 0**	**Year 1**	**Year 2**	**Year 3**	**Year 4**	**Year 5**
Earnings before interest and taxes	$ 100	$ 200	$ 500	$40,000	$50,000	$60,000	$70,000
Pre-valuation interest carryforward	0	40	100	8,000	1,840	0	0
Interest expense (current)	20	0					
Taxable income	$ 80	$ 160	$ 400	$32,000	$48,160	$60,000	$70,000
Income taxes	24	48	120	9,600	14,448	18,000	21,000
Earnings	$ 56	$ 112	$ 280	$22,400	$33,712	$42,000	$49,000
Average tax rate	30%	30%	30%	30%	30%	30%	30%
Pre-Valuation Interest Carryforward Balance	**Year −1**	**Year 0**	**Year 1**	**Year 2**	**Year 3**	**Year 4**	**Year 5**
Beginning interest carryforward	$ 0	$4,980	$9,940	$ 9,840	$ 1,840	$ 0	$ 0
Change in interest carryforward	4,980	4,960	−100	−8,000	−1,840	0	0
Ending interest carryforward	$4,980	$9,940	$9,840	$ 1,840	$ 0	$ 0	$ 0
Interest Tax Shield			**Year 1**	**Year 2**	**Year 3**	**Year 4**	**Year 5**
Income taxes (unlevered firm)			$ 120	$ 9,600	$14,448	$18,000	$21,000
Income taxes (with interest deduction)			120	9,600	12,000	14,448	19,500
Correct interest tax shield			$ 0	$ 0	$ 2,448	$ 3,552	$ 1,500
Implied Income Tax Rate For Interest Tax Shields			**Year 1**	**Year 2**	**Year 3**	**Year 4**	**Year 5**
Interest tax shield			$ 0	$ 0	$ 2,448	$ 3,552	$ 1,500
Interest expense (current)			$5,000	$ 5,000	$ 5,000	$ 5,000	$ 5,000
Implied income tax rate for interest tax shields			0.00%	0.00%	48.96%	71.04%	30.00%

continued

continued from previous page

Comparison Interest Tax Shield Using Marginal Tax Rate × Interest	Year 1	Year 2	Year 3	Year 4	Year 5
Interest expense (current)	$5,000	$ 5,000	$ 5,000	$ 5,000	$ 5,000
Marginal income tax rate	30.0%	30.0%	30.0%	30.0%	30.0%
Interest tax shield using marginal tax rate × interest	$1,500	$ 1,500	$ 1,500	$ 1,500	$ 1,500
Correct interest tax shield	0	0	2,448	3,552	1,500
Overstated (understated) interest tax shield	$1,500	$ 1,500	−$ 948	−$ 2,052	$ 0

Solution for Review Exercise 3.6: Measuring the Effect of Net Operating Loss Carryforwards (with Interest Rate Caps)

EBIT and Interest Cap

Financial Accounting (Income Statement Excerpt)	Actual		Forecast				
	Year −1	Year 0	Year 1	Year 2	Year 3	Year 4	Year 5
Earnings before interest and taxes	−$20,000	−$20,000	−$20,000	$40,000	$50,000	$60,000	$70,000
Interest expense (current)	5,000	5,000	5,000	5,000	5,000	5,000	5,000
Earnings before income taxes	−$25,000	−$25,000	−$25,000	$35,000	$45,000	$55,000	$65,000
Interest deduction cap	$ 0	$ 0	$ 0	$ 8,000	$10,000	$12,000	$14,000

Calculation of the Company's Taxable Income

	Actual		Forecast				
Levered Company (Taxable Income)	Year −1	Year 0	Year 1	Year 2	Year 3	Year 4	Year 5
Earnings before interest and taxes	−$20,000	−$20,000	−$20,000	$40,000	$50,000	$60,000	$70,000
Pre-valuation interest carryforward	0	0	0	8,000	2,000	0	0
Post-valuation interest carryforward			0	0	8,000	7,000	0
Interest expense (current)	0	0	0	0	0	5,000	5,000
Taxable income	−$20,000	−$20,000	−$20,000	$32,000	$40,000	$48,000	$65,000
NOL carryforward used	0	0	0	−25,600	−32,000	−2,400	0
Taxable income after NOL carryforward adjustment	−$20,000	−$20,000	−$20,000	$ 6,400	$ 8,000	$45,600	$65,000
Income taxes	0	0	0	1,920	2,400	13,680	19,500
Earnings	−$20,000	−$20,000	−$20,000	$ 4,480	$ 5,600	$31,920	$45,500
Average tax rate	0%	0%	0%	6%	6%	29%	30%

Pre-Valuation Interest Carryforward Balance	Year −1	Year 0	Year 1	Year 2	Year 3	Year 4	Year 5
Beginning interest carryforward	$ 0	$ 5,000	$10,000	$10,000	$ 2,000	$ 0	$ 0
Change in interest carryforward	5,000	5,000	0	−8,000	−2,000	0	0
Ending interest carryforward	$ 5,000	$10,000	$10,000	$ 2,000	$ 0	$ 0	$ 0

Post-Valuation Interest Carryforward Balance	Year 1	Year 2	Year 3	Year 4	Year 5
Beginning interest carryforward	$ 0	$ 5,000	$10,000	$ 7,000	$ 0
Change in interest carryforward	5,000	5,000	−3,000	−7,000	0
Ending interest carryforward	$5,000	$10,000	$ 7,000	$ 0	$ 0

Net Operating Loss Carryforward Balance	Year −1	Year 0	Year 1	Year 2	Year 3	Year 4	Year 5
Beginning NOL Carryforward	$ 0	$20,000	$40,000	$60,000	$34,400	$ 2,400	$ 0
Change in NOL Carryforward	20,000	20,000	20,000	−25,600	−32,000	−2,400	0
Ending NOL Carryforward	$20,000	$40,000	$60,000	$34,400	$ 2,400	$ 0	$ 0

Calculation of the Company's Unlevered Taxable Income, Interest Tax Shield, and Implied Tax Rate for Interest

	Actual		Forecast				
Unlevered Company (Taxable Income)	**Year −1**	**Year 0**	**Year 1**	**Year 2**	**Year 3**	**Year 4**	**Year 5**
Earnings before interest and taxes	−$20,000	−$20,000	−$20,000	$40,000	$50,000	$60,000	$70,000
Pre-valuation interest carryforward	0	0	0	8,000	2,000	0	0
Interest expense (current)	0	0					
Taxable income	−$20,000	−$20,000	−$20,000	$32,000	$48,000	$60,000	$70,000
NOL carryforward used	0	0	0	−25,600	−34,400	0	0
Taxable income after NOL carryforward adjustment	−$20,000	−$20,000	−$20,000	$ 6,400	$13,600	$60,000	$70,000
Income taxes	0	0	0	1,920	4,080	18,000	21,000
Earnings	−$20,000	−$20,000	−$20,000	$ 4,480	$ 9,520	$42,000	$49,000
Average tax rate	0%	0%	0%	6%	9%	30%	30%

Pre-Valuation Interest Carryforward Balance	**Year −1**	**Year 0**	**Year 1**	**Year 2**	**Year 3**	**Year 4**	**Year 5**
Beginning interest carryforward	$ 0	$ 5,000	$10,000	$10,000	$ 2,000	$ 0	$ 0
Change in interest carryforward	5,000	5,000	0	−8,000	−2,000	0	0
Ending interest carryforward	$ 5,000	$10,000	$10,000	$ 2,000	$ 0	$ 0	$ 0

Net Operating Loss Carryforward Balance	**Year −1**	**Year 0**	**Year 1**	**Year 2**	**Year 3**	**Year 4**	**Year 5**
Beginning NOL Carryforward	$ 0	$20,000	$40,000	$60,000	$34,400	$ 0	$ 0
Change in NOL Carryforward	20,000	20,000	20,000	−25,600	−34,400	0	0
Ending NOL Carryforward	$20,000	$40,000	$60,000	$34,400	$ 0	$ 0	$ 0

Interest Tax Shield	**Year 1**	**Year 2**	**Year 3**	**Year 4**	**Year 5**
Income taxes (unlevered firm)	$ 0	$ 1,920	$ 4,080	$18,000	$21,000
Income taxes (with interest deduction)	0	1,920	2,400	13,680	19,500
Correct interest tax shield	$ 0	$ 0	$ 1,680	$ 4,320	$ 1,500

Implied income tax rate for interest tax shields	**Year 1**	**Year 2**	**Year 3**	**Year 4**	**Year 5**
Interest tax shield	$ 0	$ 0	$ 1,680	$ 4,320	$ 1,500
Interest expense (current)	$5,000	$ 5,000	$ 5,000	$ 5,000	$ 5,000
Implied income tax rate for interest tax shields	0.00%	0.00%	33.60%	86.40%	30.00%

Comparison Interest Tax Shield Using Marginal Tax Rate × Interest	**Year 1**	**Year 2**	**Year 3**	**Year 4**	**Year 5**
Interest expense (current)	$5,000	$ 5,000	$ 5,000	$ 5,000	$ 5,000
Marginal income tax rate	30.0%	30.0%	30.0%	30.0%	30.0%
Interest tax shield using marginal tax rate × interest	$1,500	$ 1,500	$ 1,500	$ 1,500	$ 1,500
Correct interest tax shield	0	0	1,680	4,320	1,500
Overstated (understated) interest tax shield	$1,500	$ 1,500	−$ 180	−$ 2,820	$ 0

After mastering the material in this chapter, you will be able to:

1. Understand the steps in the process of creating a financial model (4.1–4.2)
2. Identify and measure the forecast drivers and create a model to forecast the company's operations (4.3–4.4)
3. Test the model, assess forecast reasonableness, and incorporate the company's capital structure into the model (4.5–4.7)
4. Forecast required cash and measure excess cash (4.8)
5. Forecast income tax rates and payments (4.9)
6. Forecast revenues and capital expenditures at a more detailed level (4.10)

CHAPTER

Creating a Financial Model

4

THE 3M COMPANY

Companies often make public announcements about their future performance, called guidance. These forecasts are usually short term, forecasting no more than the next 12 to 24 months, although some companies provide longer term goals and objectives. For example, in March 2016, the 3M Company publicly disclosed that it ". . . expects 2016 earnings to be in the range of $8.10 to $8.45 per share with organic local-currency sales growth of 1 to 3 percent. 3M also expects free cash flow conversion to be in the range of 95 to 105 percent."[1] The company also provided its five-year objectives:

> At a meeting with investors and analysts at the company's global headquarters today, 3M Chairman, President and Chief Executive Officer Inge G. Thulin will introduce new five-year financial objectives and describe how the company is positioned to deliver consistently strong performance in 2016 and beyond. Thulin will also discuss how 3M's playbook—including its three key levers of portfolio management, investing in innovation, and business transformation—is making 3M even more relevant to customers, more agile and more competitive.
>
> 3M's new five-year financial objectives—covering 2016 through 2020—are:
>
> - 8 to 11 percent growth in earnings per share
> - 2 to 5 percent organic local currency sales growth
> - 20 percent return on invested capital
> - 100 percent free cash flow conversion

In this chapter, we discuss how to build a model of a company's operations and capital structure. Such models forecast a company's financial statements and its free cash flows.

[1] See the 3M Company's 8-K Report filed with the U.S. SEC on March 29, 2016.

CHAPTER ORGANIZATION

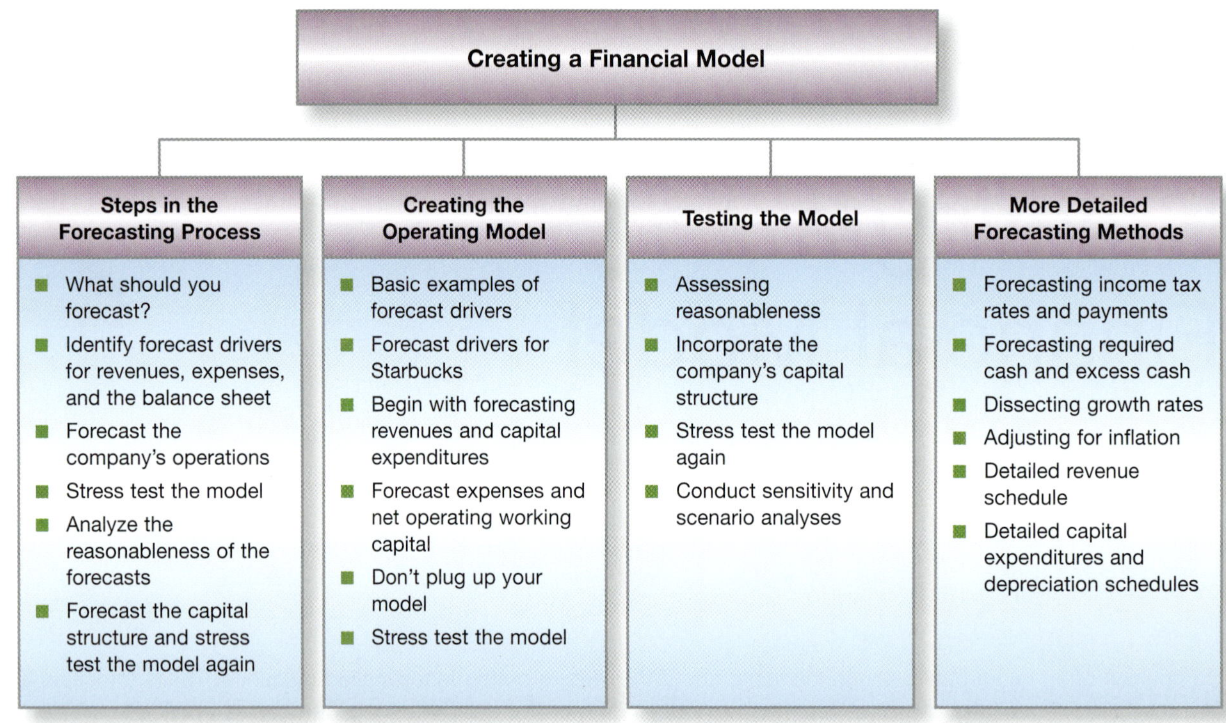

INTRODUCTION

Since a company's value is equal to the present value of its expected free cash flows (adjusted appropriately for any value created from financing), forecasts of its free cash flows and the inputs that we use to measure them—the income statement, balance sheet, and certain financial statement schedules—are important elements in a company's valuation. Forecasts have other uses as well; for example, managers use forecasts for financial planning, bankers and other creditors use forecasts to make credit decisions, and managers, investors, and analysts use forecasts to evaluate various types of investment opportunities. In this chapter, we discuss how to create a financial model with sufficient detail to provide all of the inputs needed to value a company using both the discounted cash flow (DCF) and market multiple valuation methods. We also discuss methods with which to stress test that model and to assess the reasonableness of the forecasts.

A **financial model** is a set of assumptions (or forecast drivers) and relations (or formulas) that produces predictions regarding the future performance of a company. We call these predictions either **forecasts**, **projections**, or **pro forma (financial) statements**. In most valuation contexts, we recommend developing a sufficiently detailed financial model that includes a company's income statement, balance sheet, cash flow statement, free cash flow schedule, and appropriate supporting schedules (for example, debt, fixed assets, and income tax schedules). Sometimes, we create a financial model that is more detailed than what the company reports in its publicly available information (to the extent we have access to such information). For example, we may disaggregate selling, administrative, and general expenses into its components if they are important value drivers for the company, or we may forecast at the divisional level or by geographic region as opposed to the consolidated company level.

Managers of companies, such as 3M (see the opening vignette), sometimes make public forecasts of, or provide investors "guidance" about, their future performance. In the U.S., a company is protected if its actual performance is different from its forecasts if the company follows the "safe harbor" provision of U.S. securities laws. According to the Private Securities Litigation Reform Act of 1995, a company or its management can make "forward-looking statements" (forecasts) and have "safe harbor" protection as long as the statements are not knowingly false (at the time the forecast is made), the company clearly identifies the statements as forward-looking, and the company accompanies the forecasts with meaningful cautionary statements that identify important factors that could cause actual results to differ materially from those in the statement (see Valuation in Practice 4.1 and 4.2).

Valuation in Practice 4.1

Yahoo! Inc.'s Forward Looking Disclosure Like all publicly traded companies in the U.S., Yahoo! identifies any statements about future performance as "forward-looking statements" so that it has the safe harbor protection provided in U.S. securities laws and directs investors to read the "risk factors" described by the company:

> **Forward-Looking Statements**
> In addition to current and historical information, this Annual Report on Form 10-K contains forward-looking statements within the meaning of the Private Securities Litigation Reform Act of 1995. These statements relate to our future operations, prospects, potential products, services, developments, and business strategies. These statements can, in some cases, be identified by the use of terms such as "may," "will," "should," "could," "would," "intend," "expect," "plan," "anticipate," "believe," "estimate," "predict," "project," "potential," or "continue," the negative of such terms, or other comparable terminology. This Annual Report on Form 10-K includes, among others, forward-looking statements regarding our:
>
> - expectations regarding our proposed spin-off of our remaining holdings in Alibaba Group Holding Limited ("Alibaba Group");
> - expectations about revenue, including display, search, and other revenue;
> - expectations about growth in users;
>
> . . .
>
> These statements involve certain known and unknown risks and uncertainties that could cause our actual results to differ materially from those expressed or implied in our forward-looking statements. You are urged to carefully review the disclosures made concerning risks and uncertainties that may affect our business or operating results, which include, among others, those listed in Part 1, Item 1A "Risk Factors" of this Annual Report on Form 10-K. We do not intend, and undertake no obligation, to update or revise any of our forward-looking statements after the date of this Report on Form 10-K to reflect new information, actual results or future events or circumstances.

Source: Yahoo! Inc. 2015 10-K Report.

4.1 AN OVERVIEW OF THE PROCESS OF CREATING A FINANCIAL MODEL

LO1 Understand the steps in the process of creating a financial model

We construct a forecasting model based on a set of assumptions from which we forecast all aspects of a company's performance. We call these assumptions **forecast drivers**, for they are the inputs and relationships that underpin or "drive" the entire financial model. To facilitate changing the forecast drivers to either stress test the model or examine alternative assumptions or scenarios, we place all of the forecast drivers in a separate section of our spreadsheet, typically at the very top or in a separate sheet of the financial model.

Steps in the Process of Creating a Financial Model

We show a summary of the steps used to create a financial model in Exhibit 4.1. Naturally, the specific process used to create a financial model depends on the valuation context. However, the basic process typically involves the steps we show in this exhibit. Before discussing that, it is useful to recall the first two steps of the valuation process that we outlined in Chapter 1. Step 1 was identifying the company's direct, indirect, and potential competitors, and Step 2 was analyzing historical performance, strategy, and sources of competitive advantage. These two steps are useful in the creation of a financial model for a variety of reasons.

We conduct a competitive analysis of the company's industry and assess the company's competitive advantage in order to help us identify and forecast the forecast drivers; to help assess the role that general economic, industry, and comparable company factors could have in developing a financial model; and to assess the reasonableness of the forecasts. For example, a competitive analysis could be useful to develop forecasts for a company's revenue or capacity needs if the company's revenues are linked to its predicted market share, and the size of that market is linked to the general economy through such statistics as the size of the economy or population. Analyzing a company and its industry can also play a role in developing forecasts of the forecast drivers. Recall from Chapter 2 that sometimes we are able to link a company's competitive advantage to certain financial statement relations. For example, we were able to link Nike's competitive advantage that it gets through advertising and promotion to its cost structure and profit margins. In some valuations, we rely on management forecasts, which is common practice when rendering fairness opinions in mergers and acquisitions, and sometimes we are able to use analyst forecasts as part of the basis of our forecasts.

EXHIBIT 4.1 The Steps in the Process of Creating a Financial Model

1	Choose what aspects of the company (financial statements, free cash flows, and supporting schedules) to forecast, the level of aggregation of the forecasts (consolidated, by type of business, by geographic region, etc.), whether to forecast cash flows in real or nominal terms (usually nominal), and the horizon (number of years) to forecast
2	Identify the forecast drivers (assumptions needed) to forecast the scale (revenues, capacity) of the company and forecast those forecast drivers
3	Identify the operating expenses and balance sheet operating items for the model and identify and forecast the forecast drivers (assumptions) to forecast these items
4	Create the basic structure of the financial statements and supporting schedules; ignoring capital structure, forecast each item in the financial model related to the company's operations
5	Stress test the model—make sure the financial statements and schedules articulate, that assets equal liabilities plus equities, and correct calculation errors
6	Analyze the reasonableness of the forecasts of the company's operations; iterate to Step 2 as necessary
7	If needed for the valuation, forecast all capital structure items based on the company's capital structure strategy (type and amount of financing, amount of interest and dividends, etc.)
8	Stress test the model and analyze the reasonableness of the forecasts again; iterate to Step 2 as necessary

In Step 1, we make various decisions about the model's level of detail (line items in the financial statements), the model's level of aggregation (consolidated company, by subsidiary, etc.), and the horizon (number of years) over which we will forecast the explicit year-by-year cash flows. These decisions depend, in part, on the homogeneity of the parts of the company, the availability of information, and the valuation context.

Level of Aggregation

Given sufficient information, we prefer to create separate forecasts for the parts of the company that are not homogeneous, primarily regarding growth rates. For example, suppose a company has two divisions that have different but constant growth rates—5% and 10%. Even though the two divisions have constant but different growth rates, the growth rate of the consolidated company is not constant. The growth rate of the combined divisions increases over time and approaches, but never reaches, the higher of the two divisional growth rates. It is also advantageous to disaggregate forecasts when two divisions have different but constant growth rates and different but constant margins. In this case, the growth rate and the margin will vary every year at the consolidated level, but forecasting at the divisional level will be quite easy. For similar reasons, we often forecast multinational companies at the country level or by geographic regions. Different countries or geographic regions can have different expected inflation rates and different exposure to exchange rate fluctuations and regional economic conditions, all of which can result in different growth rates, profit margins, rates of return, and so forth. As such, we often forecast at the "currency" level for multinational companies if we have sufficient data (see Chapter 17 for a detailed discussion).

Real or Nominal Cash Flow Forecasts

We can create forecasts in either "real" or "nominal" currencies. Unless a company operates in a high-inflation economy, most analysts use nominal currency values and nominal costs of capital in valuation. It is sometimes more difficult to forecast a company's financial statements when the company operates in a highly inflationary economy, for it can be difficult to assess how various inputs or line items in the company's financial statements are affected by inflation. In that situation, it may be easier to create forecasts in real (constant) currency (ignoring inflation) and use real costs of capital (again, ignoring inflation).

Valuation in Practice 4.2

Risk Factors Identified by Alphabet Inc. (Google) Like all publicly traded companies in the U.S., Alphabet Inc. (Google) identifies potential "risk factors" to its business so that it has the safe harbor protection provided in U.S. securities laws for any forward-looking statements it makes in its financial statements. In its 2015 10-K Report, Google identified over eleven pages of "risk factors;" for example:

ITEM 1A. RISK FACTORS

Our operations and financial results are subject to various risks and uncertainties, including those described below, which could adversely affect our business, financial condition, results of operations, cash flows, and the trading price of our common and capital stock.

Risks Related to Our Businesses and Industries

We face intense competition. If we do not continue to innovate and provide products and services that are useful to users, we may not remain competitive, and our revenues and operating results could be adversely affected.

. . .

Our revenue growth rate could decline over time, and we anticipate downward pressure on our operating margin in the future.

Our revenue growth rate could decline over time as a result of a number of factors, including:

- increasing competition,
- changes in property mix, platform mix, and geographical mix
- the challenges in maintaining our growth rate as our revenues increase to higher levels,
- the evolution of the online advertising market, including the increasing variety of online platforms for advertising, and the other markets in which we participate, and
- the rate of user adoption of our products, services, and technologies.

Source: Alphabet Inc. (Google) 2015 10-K Report.

Choice of Horizon for Explicit Year-by-Year Cash Flows

As we discuss in Chapter 1, when we use the DCF valuation method, we typically create detailed forecasts of free cash flows for a finite forecast horizon and then use a cash flow perpetuity model or some other valuation method to measure the value of the firm as of the end of the finite forecast horizon (the continuing value date). Some practitioners use a fixed horizon for their year-by-year forecasts.[2] To the extent it is feasible, we recommend creating detailed forecasts until the company reaches "steady state." We can define steady state in a variety of ways, and the definition depends, in part, on the valuation method we use to measure the continuing value. We will discuss this issue in more detail in Chapter 6 when using a cash flow perpetuity for the continuing value calculation and Chapter 13 when using a market multiple valuation for the continuing value. As we shall see, the choice of horizon relates directly to the point in time in the future at which we will be comfortable performing a continuing value calculation, given the method used for that calculation.

Timing of Cash Flows Within a Year

A company's cash flows—collecting revenues, paying expenses, issuing and repaying debt, and issuing and redeeming other securities—occurs on a continual basis during the year. Even though cash flows are generated continuously throughout the year, it is not reasonable to forecast a company's cash flows without making an assumption that reduces the frequency of the cash flows (monthly, quarterly, yearly, etc.) over a year. The most common assumption for the frequency of cash flows is that they occur annually. If we forecast a company's performance on an annual basis, we assume the cash flows occur at the same time each year.

[2] According to the 2013 Association for Financial Professionals survey, 51% of the respondents use a 5 year horizon for their cash flow forecasts in their DCF models and 26% use 10 years. See, 2013 AFP Estimating and Applying Cost of Capital: Report of Survey Results, October 2013, Association for Financial Professionals.

The most common assumption is to assume that cash flows occur at mid-year (called the **mid-year convention**). If a company's business is seasonal (for example, a retail toy store that sells most of its toys in the fourth quarter), we may assume that cash flows occur sometime after mid-year—maybe at the end of the third quarter. In this book, for both clarity and simplicity, we assume a company's cash flows occur at the end of the year even though the mid-year convention is more commonly used in practice. If we do want to implement the mid-year convention, we can simply take the value we derive from end-of-year discounting and multiply that value by $(1 + r)^{1/2}$, where r is the discount rate used.

The year-end discounting assumption we use in this book affects both the free cash flow calculations and also the way we measure interest expense and interest tax shields. Since we assume that all cash flows occur at the end of the year, we also assume that a company will only issue or repay debt at the end of the year. We calculate a company's interest expense based on the amount of debt issued as of the beginning of the year. Calculating interest expense for the year based on the debt balance at the beginning of the year makes the calculations in the book much clearer with no loss of generality. In practice, it is common to use the company's average debt outstanding in a year in order to calculate interest expense.

4.2 FORECASTING STARBUCKS CORPORATION (STARBUCKS)

Recall that we used Starbucks in the previous chapter to illustrate how to calculate free cash flows. We extend that illustration to this chapter as we use Starbucks to illustrate how to create a financial model. Before we walk through the detailed steps of creating a financial model for Starbucks, we show the outcome of that process. In Exhibits 4.2 through 4.4, we show the company's historical (Years −1 and 0) financial statements, free cash flow schedules and our illustrative forecasts (Years 1 through 5). For brevity, we only

EXHIBIT 4.2 Starbucks Historical Income Statements and Forecasts

STARBUCKS CORPORATION
Income Statement Forecasts
(for the fiscal years ended October)

	Actual		Forecast				
($ in thousands)	**Year −1**	**Year 0**	**Year 1**	**Year 2**	**Year 3**	**Year 4**	**Year 5**
Revenue	$6,369,300	$7,786,942	$9,344,330	$11,680,413	$13,432,475	$14,775,722	$15,514,509
Cost of goods sold	−2,605,212	−3,178,791	−3,831,175	−4,672,165	−5,372,990	−5,910,289	−6,205,803
Gross margin	$3,764,088	$4,608,151	$5,513,155	$ 7,008,248	$ 8,059,485	$ 8,865,433	$ 9,308,705
Store and other operating expenses	−2,362,935	−2,947,902	−3,550,846	−4,380,155	−5,037,178	−5,540,896	−5,817,941
General and administrative expenses	−357,114	−473,023	−560,660	−642,423	−738,786	−812,665	−853,298
Depreciation and amortization	−340,169	−387,211	−425,770	−531,568	−628,526	−724,960	−815,926
Other operating income	76,648	93,937	93,443	116,804	134,325	147,757	155,145
Operating income	$ 780,518	$ 893,952	$ 1,069,323	$ 1,570,907	$ 1,789,319	$ 1,934,670	$ 1,976,686
Interest and other income	17,101	23,396					
Interest expense	−1,272	−11,105	−42,163	−42,163	−42,163	−42,163	−42,163
Income before taxes	$ 796,347	$ 906,243	$1,027,159	$ 1,528,743	$ 1,747,156	$ 1,892,507	$ 1,934,523
Provision for income taxes	−301,977	−324,770	−369,777	−550,348	−628,976	−681,303	−696,428
Cumulative effect of accounting change	0	−17,214					
Net earnings	$ 494,370	$ 564,259	$ 657,382	$ 978,396	$ 1,118,180	$ 1,211,204	$ 1,238,095
Earnings Per Share							
Net earnings	$ 494,370	$ 564,259	$ 657,382	$ 978,396	$ 1,118,180	$ 1,211,204	$ 1,238,095
Common shares outstanding—basic	789,570	766,114	766,114	766,114	766,114	766,114	766,114
Earnings per share—basic	$ 0.63	$ 0.74	$ 0.86	$ 1.28	$ 1.46	$ 1.58	$ 1.62
Retained Earnings (and Other)							
Beginning balance	$1,444,617	$1,938,987	$2,151,084	$ 2,359,849	$ 2,793,551	$ 3,138,676	$ 3,331,740
Net income	494,370	564,259	657,382	978,396	1,118,180	1,211,204	1,238,095
Dividends, stock repurchases, and other	0	−352,162	−448,617	−544,693	−773,056	−1,018,140	−1,036,233
Ending balance	$1,938,987	$2,151,084	$2,359,849	$ 2,793,551	$ 3,138,676	$ 3,331,740	$ 3,533,602

Exhibit may contain small rounding errors

show forecasts through Year 5, but we know that we would likely use a longer forecast horizon for a company in a high growth stage. Starbucks' income statements appear in Exhibit 4.2.

Starbucks' revenues almost double during the five-year forecast period; they increase from $7.8 billion in Year 0 to $15.5 billion in Year 5. Early in this period, its revenues grow by more than 20% annually, but by Year 5, the growth rate decreases to 5%. By Year 5, Starbucks' net income is forecasted to exceed $1.2 billion relative to its net income of $564 million in Year 0. We see that the growth in Starbucks' operating income parallels the growth in its balance sheet. Notice that we eliminated interest and other income from the forecasts because we assume this income statement item results from excess assets that we distribute to shareholders at the beginning of Year 1 (recall from Chapter 3 that we assume Starbucks' short-term and long-term investments are excess assets). We see the effects of this distribution in the balance sheets in Exhibit 4.3 in our elimination of the company's short-term and long-term investments, for we assume these are the excess assets. We discuss identifying excess cash, required cash, and valuation issues related to excess cash later in the chapter.

EXHIBIT 4.3 Starbucks Historical Balance Sheets and Forecasts

STARBUCKS CORPORATION
Balance Sheet Forecasts
(for the fiscal years ended October)

	Actual		Forecast				
($ in thousands)	**Year −1**	**Year 0**	**Year 1**	**Year 2**	**Year 3**	**Year 4**	**Year 5**
Required cash	$ 173,809	$ 312,606	$ 467,217	$ 584,021	$ 671,624	$ 738,786	$ 775,725
Short-term investments	133,227	141,038					
Accounts receivable	190,762	224,271	256,009	320,011	368,013	404,814	425,055
Inventories	546,299	636,222	766,235	934,433	1,074,598	1,182,058	1,241,161
Other current assets	165,237	215,651	280,330	350,412	402,974	443,272	465,435
Total current assets	$1,209,334	$1,529,788	$1,769,791	$2,188,877	$2,517,209	$2,768,930	$2,907,376
Land, buildings, and equipment, net	1,842,019	2,287,899	2,920,103	3,358,119	3,693,931	3,878,627	4,072,558
Goodwill and other intangible assets	127,883	199,433	199,433	199,433	199,433	199,433	199,433
Long-term investments	261,564	224,904	0	0	0	0	0
Other non-current assets	72,893	186,917	186,887	233,608	268,649	295,514	310,290
Total assets	$3,513,693	$4,428,941	$5,076,213	$5,980,037	$6,679,222	$7,142,504	$7,489,658
Accounts payable	$ 220,975	$ 340,937	$ 434,103	$ 530,451	$ 604,181	$ 659,479	$ 686,565
Accrued expenses and other	552,907	661,148	840,990	1,051,237	1,208,923	1,329,815	1,396,306
Interest payable	318	847	7,027	7,027	7,027	7,027	7,027
Deferred revenue	175,048	231,926	280,330	350,412	402,974	443,272	465,435
Short-term and current long-term debt	277,748	700,762	700,762	700,762	700,762	700,762	700,762
Total current liabilities	$1,226,996	$1,935,620	$2,263,212	$2,639,890	$2,923,868	$3,140,355	$3,256,095
Long-term debt	2,870	1,958	1,958	1,958	1,958	1,958	1,958
Other non-current liabilities	193,565	262,857	373,773	467,217	537,299	591,029	620,580
Total liabilities	$1,423,431	$2,200,435	$2,638,943	$3,109,064	$3,463,125	$3,733.342	$3,878,634
Common stock and surplus	$ 130,361	$ 40,149	$ 40,149	$ 40,149	$ 40,149	$ 40,149	$ 40,149
Cumulative comprehensive income (loss)	20,914	37,273	37,273	37,273	37,273	37,273	37,273
Retained earnings	1,938,987	2,151,084	2,359,849	2,793,551	3,138,676	3,331,740	3,533,602
Total shareholders' equity	$2,090,262	$2,228,506	$2,437,271	$2,870,973	$3,216,098	$3,409,162	$3,611,024
Total liabilities and equities	$3,513,693	$4,428,941	$5,076,213	$5,980,037	$6,679,222	$7,142,504	$7,489,658

Exhibit may contain small rounding errors

We show the free cash flow schedule in Exhibit 4.4. Recall from Chapter 3 that in its statement of cash flows, Starbucks combined the change in receivables, change in other current assets, and change in other non-current assets into a single number (other, net). This is why the changes in those accounts show as zeroes in the Years −1 and 0 (the two prior actual years). Since we have line items in the balance sheet for each of those accounts we are forecasting, we model the change in each of these accounts in the free cash flow forecasts. Not surprisingly, given all of the other forecasts, Starbucks has substantial growth in its unlevered free cash flows during this period. Its unlevered free cash flows grow from $122 million in Year 0 to $1.1 billion by Year 5.

EXHIBIT 4.4 Starbucks Historical Free Cash Flow Schedules and Forecasts

STARBUCKS CORPORATION
Free Cash Flow Forecasts
(for the fiscal years ended October)

	Actual		Forecast				
($ in thousands)	**Year −1**	**Year 0**	**Year 1**	**Year 2**	**Year 3**	**Year 4**	**Year 5**
Earnings before interest and taxes (EBIT)	$780,518	$893,952	$1,069,323	$1,570,907	$1,789,319	$1,934,670	$1,976,686
Income taxes paid on EBIT	−295,899	−320,050	−385,968	−566,538	−645,167	−697,493	−712,619
Earnings before interest and after taxes	$484,619	$573,902	$ 683,355	$1,004,368	$1,144,153	$1,237,177	$1,264,067
Depreciation and amortization	367,207	412,625	425,770	531,568	628,526	724,960	815,926
Asset impairment charges	19,464	19,622					
Receivables	0	0	−31,738	−64,002	−48,002	−36,801	−20,241
Inventories	−121,618	−85,527	−130,013	−168,198	−140,165	−107,460	−59,103
Other current assets	0	0	−64,679	−70,082	−52,562	−40,297	−22,164
Accounts payable	9,717	104,966	93,166	96,348	73,731	55,298	27,086
Accrued expenses and other	30,216	145,427	179,842	210,247	157,686	120,892	66,491
Deferred revenue	53,276	56,547	48,404	70,082	52,562	40,297	22,164
Other non-current assets	0	0	30	−46,722	−35,041	−26,865	−14,776
Other non-current liabilities	0	0	110,916	93,443	70,082	53,730	29,551
Other, net	70,204	−104,029					
Change in required cash balance	−28,756	−138,797	−154,611	−116,804	−87,603	−67,162	−36,939
Unlevered cash flow from operations	**$884,329**	**$984,736**	**$1,160,442**	**$1,540,249**	**$1,763,366**	**$1,953,769**	**$2,072,062**
Capital expenditures, net	−664,879	−862,964	−1,057,975	−969,583	−964,338	−909,656	−1,009,857
Unlevered free cash flow	**$219,450**	**$121,772**	**$ 102,468**	**$ 570,665**	**$ 799,028**	**$1,044,112**	**$1,062,205**
Interest expense	−1,272	−11,105	−42,163	−42,163	−42,163	−42,163	−42,163
Interest payable	80	529	6,180	0	0	0	0
Interest tax shield	488	4,264	16,191	16,191	16,191	16,191	16,191
CF before non-equity financing changes	**$218,746**	**$115,460**	**$ 82,675**	**$ 544,693**	**$ 773,056**	**$1,018,140**	**$1,036,233**
Change in debt, net	276,265	422,102	0	0	0	0	0
Equity free cash flow	**$495,011**	**$537,562**	**$ 82,675**	**$ 544,693**	**$ 773,056**	**$1,018,140**	**$1,036,233**
Interest and other income, after-tax	10,534	14,412					
Sale (purchase) of (ST & LT) investments	444,264	21,924	365,942				
Effect of exchange rate changes	283	3,530					
Cash flow before CF to/from common	**$950,092**	**$577,428**	**$ 448,617**	**$ 544,693**	**$ 773,056**	**$1,018,140**	**$1,036,233**
Change in common stock, net	−950,092	−577,428	0	0	0	0	0
Common dividends			−448,617	−544,693	−773,056	−1,018,140	−1,036,233
Change in excess cash	$ 0	$ 0	$ 0	$ 0	$ 0	$ 0	$ 0
Change in required cash balance	28,756	138,797	154,611	116,804	87,603	67,162	36,939
Change in cash balance	**$ 28,756**	**$138,797**	**$ 154,611**	**$ 116,804**	**$ 87,603**	**$ 67,162**	**$ 36,939**

Exhibit may contain small rounding errors

4.3 SELECTING AND FORECASTING THE FORECAST DRIVERS FOR THE COMPANY'S OPERATIONS (STEPS 2 AND 3)

LO2 Identify and measure the forecast drivers and create a model to forecast the company's operations

We now begin our walk through the steps in building the financial model for Starbucks. We assume that we already completed the first step in the process (decide on the level of aggregation, forecast horizon, etc.), and we begin our illustration with Step 2. In Steps 2 and 3 of the forecasting process, we develop a set of forecast drivers for our financial model. In Exhibit 4.5, we show some common forecast drivers used to drive forecasts of various items in the financial statements and supporting schedules for typical companies.

EXHIBIT 4.5 Some Example (Basic) Forecast Drivers

Item in Financial Statement or Supporting Schedule	Typical (Basic) Forecast Driver
Certain Income Statement Items	
Revenue	Growth rates, store openings, square feet, production capacity, and others
Cost of goods sold	Expense ratio, adjusted for fixed cost component
General and administrative	Expense ratio, adjusted for fixed cost component
Selling and marketing	Expense ratio, adjusted for fixed cost component; adjusted for specific costs in marketing plan
Depreciation and amortization	Based on a schedule that incorporates the company's depreciation and amortization methods for financial reporting purposes; might need another schedule for income taxes
Interest expense	Based on a debt schedule
Provision for income taxes	Based on an income tax schedule; might need another schedule for actual income taxes to be paid
Certain Balance Sheet Items—Assets	
Cash	Relationship with revenues; adjusted for potential economies of scale
Accounts receivable	Days to collect trade receivables
Inventory	Days to sell inventory
Property, plant, and equipment (cost)	Formula = Beginning + CAPEX − Dispositions = Ending
Capital expenditures	Based on a schedule that measures capital expenditures needed to maintain the current productive capacity and capital expenditures needed to support expected volume increases
Accumulated depreciation	Formula = Beginning + Depreciation Expense − Dispositions = Ending
Deferred tax assets	Based on a schedule that adjusts for the difference between revenue and expense recognition in the financial statements and income tax forms; might relate to the scale of the company or line items in the financial statements
Certain Balance Sheet Items—Liabilities	
Accounts payable	Days to pay accounts payable
Debt (short-term and long-term)	Based on a debt schedule that is driven by the company's capital structure strategy
Deferred tax liabilities	See deferred tax assets
Common stock (invested capital)	Increases with negative equity free cash flows (at least in the first pass); ultimately affected by the capital structure strategy of the company
Retained earnings	Formula = Beginning + Net Income − Dividends = Ending
Dividends	Positive equity free cash flows (at least in the first pass); ultimately affected by the capital structure strategy of the company

We identify and forecast the forecast drivers using a combination of general economic, industry, and company information. For near-term forecasts, we sometimes rely more on the company's recent history (assuming we have no reason to not rely on its recent history, such as major economic shifts or recent innovations). For longer-term forecasts, we would consider using both the competitive nature of the industry and the sustainability of a company's competitive advantage, if any, in developing how our forecast drivers will evolve over time. Obviously, comparable companies play a role in this assessment as well.

Recall our discussion of Fort Howard in Chapter 2. Fort Howard appeared to have a competitive advantage—its deinking technology—that reduced its cost of goods sold expense ratio. When we forecast Fort Howard's cost of goods sold expense ratio, we might choose a ratio with a value close to its historical value (assuming no change in capacity utilization or industry pricing) for the beginning of the forecast period. As the forecast horizon increases, we might eventually trend the cost of goods sold expense ratio (essentially trending its gross margin) toward the cost of goods sold expense ratios of comparable companies if we want to assume Fort Howard's competitive advantage would erode during this period. Of course, if you assumed that Fort Howard's competitive advantage was sustainable, you would not trend its gross margin to that of its industry counterparts.

In Step 2, we develop a set of forecast drivers for the company's revenues and capacity requirements. We forecast revenue and capacity using forecasting methods that range from something as simple as forecasting an overall growth rate or as complex as aggregating multiple detailed schedules based on prices and quantities of groups of similar products or similar geographic regions. We normally begin forecasting a company's revenue and associated capacity requirements, because many operating expenses, assets, and liabilities are directly or indirectly linked to revenues or capacity. In Step 3, we identify and forecast the forecast drivers we will use for all of the other operating expenses, assets, and liabilities. For example, we might forecast cost of goods sold as a percentage of revenues or inventory as a function of costs of goods sold. We often use the same type of relation used for cost of goods sold—expense ratios—for the other operating expenses (selling and marketing, general and administrative). While it is often reasonable to forecast most operating expenses as completely variable, in certain situations some expense categories can have a fixed component and may even be completely fixed over some range of scale. Thus, as part of identifying and forecasting the forecast drivers, we consider the fixed and variable characteristics of the expense categories we forecast.

Forecast Drivers for the Starbucks Corporation Financial Model

To make the Starbucks illustration as straightforward as possible, we use relatively simple forecast drivers for most of the items we forecast. Remember, our purpose here is to illustrate how to create a financial model; it is not to create the most sophisticated and detailed financial model of Starbucks' operations. The key forecast drivers for Starbucks appear in Exhibit 4.6. We forecast revenues at the company level using a growth rate—$\text{Revenue}_{t+1} = \text{Revenue}_t \times (1 + g_{Rev})$. Revenue forecasts can, and often do, result from a more complex calculation. For example, for a company like Starbucks, we could consider forecasting store openings and closures and we could try to separately model the revenue it gets from selling its products through grocery stores and other outlets. Or, for a company with multiple divisions and products, we could perform a buildup by division or even product (e.g., determining growth at the product or divisional level, which ultimately yields the consolidated company growth rate). We will illustrate a more detailed buildup for forecasting revenue growth later in the chapter. In Exhibit 4.6, we project Starbucks' revenue to grow 20% in Year 1, grow 25% per year for the next year (revenues had grown 22% in Year 0), and then we fade Starbucks revenue growth rate down to 5.0% over the next three years. As stated earlier, at this stage in Starbucks' growth, we might need a longer

EXHIBIT 4.6 Forecast Drivers for the Starbucks Corporation Financial Model

STARBUCKS CORPORATION Forecast Drivers (for the fiscal years ended October)	Actual		Forecast				
	Year −1	Year 0	Year 1	Year 2	Year 3	Year 4	Year 5
Revenue growth rate		22.3%	20.0%	25.0%	15.0%	10.0%	5.0%
Cost of goods sold (% revenue, rev)	40.9%	40.8%	41.0%	40.0%	40.0%	40.0%	40.0%
Store and other operating expenses (% rev)	37.1%	37.9%	38.0%	37.5%	37.5%	37.5%	37.5%
General and administrative (% rev)	5.6%	6.1%	6.0%	5.5%	5.5%	5.5%	5.5%
Other operating income (% rev)	1.2%	1.2%	1.0%	1.0%	1.0%	1.0%	1.0%
Interest and other income			Assume income from excess assets, which we liquidate				
Depreciation (# of years)		9.36	10.00	10.00	10.00	10.00	10.00
Effective income tax rate (for the provision for income taxes)	37.9%	35.8%	36.0%	36.0%	36.0%	36.0%	36.0%
Income tax rate for interest, T_{INT}	38.4%	38.4%	38.4%	38.4%	38.4%	38.4%	38.4%
Required cash balance (% rev)	2.7%	4.0%	5.0%	5.0%	5.0%	5.0%	5.0%
Short-term investments	2.1%	1.8%	Assume to be excess assets, which we liquidate				
Accounts receivable (days to collect)	10.9	10.5	10.0	10.0	10.0	10.0	10.0
Inventory (days to sell)	76.5	73.1	73.0	73.0	73.0	73.0	73.0
Other current assets (% rev)	2.6%	2.8%	3.0%	3.0%	3.0%	3.0%	3.0%
Goodwill and other intangible assets	2.0%	2.6%	No additional goodwill or other intangible assets acquired				
Long-term investments	4.1%	2.9%	Assume to be excess assets, which we liquidate				
Other non-current assets (% rev)	1.1%	2.4%	2.0%	2.0%	2.0%	2.0%	2.0%
Accounts payable (days to pay)		38.1	40.0	40.0	40.0	40.0	40.0
Accrued expenses (% rev)	8.7%	8.5%	9.0%	9.0%	9.0%	9.0%	9.0%
Interest payable (% debt)	0.1%	0.1%	1.0%	1.0%	1.0%	1.0%	1.0%
Deferred revenue (% rev)	2.7%	3.0%	3.0%	3.0%	3.0%	3.0%	3.0%
Other non-current liabilities (% rev)	3.0%	3.4%	4.0%	4.0%	4.0%	4.0%	4.0%
Short-term debt—change from previous year ($)			$0	$0	$0	$0	$0
Long-term debt—change from previous year ($)			$0	$0	$0	$0	$0
Interest rate for debt (beginning balance—assumed)		5.6%	6.0%	6.0%	6.0%	6.0%	6.0%
Cumulative comprehensive income			Assume no change in future years				
Revenues_{t+1} to net property, plant, and equipment	4.2	4.1	4.0	4.0	4.0	4.0	4.0

horizon to forecast Starbucks to steady state, but for purposes of illustrating the creation of a financial model, that level of detail is not needed.

As in Chapter 3, assume Starbucks' short-term and long-term investments are excess assets, and we assume interest and other income represents the income from those excess assets. Although we do not show a DCF valuation for Starbucks based on our forecasts, if we did, we would essentially liquidate the excess assets from the company's balance sheet, distribute their value to the shareholders as of the valuation date (on an after-tax basis), and not include any subsequent income from these assets in our forecasts. In other words, we would not value the excess assets as part of the DCF valuation but instead, use the DCF valuation method to measure the value of the firm without the excess assets and add the value of the excess assets to the DCF valuation to measure the value of the firm.

For simplicity, the financial model we create for Starbucks, forecasts most of the other items on the income statement—cost of goods sold, store and other operating expenses, general and administrative expenses, and other operating income—based on a percentage of revenues. As seen in Exhibit 4.6, comparing Starbucks' actual expense ratios in Year 0 to the forecasted expense ratio projections, we see that the forecasts include some improvements for Year 2, which are then maintained for all future years. Being able to discern whether these are reasonable assumptions is beyond what we are trying to accomplish in this chapter, although we illustrate some ways to assess forecast reasonableness later in the chapter.

Depreciation expense is forecasted using straight-line depreciation over the number of years in the exhibit assuming a zero salvage value. We make the simplifying assumption that the company does not amortize any of its intangible assets, which is consistent with the company's practice. We measure interest expense using the beginning-of-year debt balance. Finally, based on our review of Starbucks' income tax disclosures, a reasonable rate to use for the provision for income taxes on its income statements is 36%, Starbucks' effective tax rate. As you may recall from Chapter 3, however, the marginal income tax rate to use for interest expense, T_{INT}, is 38.4% and not 36%.[3] Although not shown on the balance sheet or statement of cash flows, Starbucks has deferred tax assets and deferred tax liabilities. Starbucks includes the effect of its deferred income taxes on its statement of cash flows in the change in other assets and other liabilities, which we follow when measuring Starbucks' free cash flows.

We also forecast most items on the balance sheet as either a direct or indirect function of revenues. We use "percentage of revenues" to forecast the required cash balance, other current assets, other non-current assets, accrued expenses, deferred revenue, and non-current liabilities. We use "average days to collect receivables" to forecast accounts receivable, "average days to sell inventory" to forecast inventory, and "average days of payables" to forecast accounts payable. Again, these percentages and days assumptions are kept constant at approximately the Year 0 levels.

Recall from Chapter 2 that we often use the average balance of balance sheet items (a stock) to measure financial ratios. For example, we use the average balance of accounts receivable to measure the average number of days it takes a company to collect its accounts receivable. We often use average balances for these ratios because they are the average investments needed to generate the flows (average accounts receivable needed to generate the year's revenues). As discussed earlier, using the average rather than ending balance does not have a significant effect on the financial ratio if the growth in the flow variable during the period is small. This same issue exists in a financial model. For simplicity, we only use ending balances in the Starbucks example, but we could utilize the financial ratios that use average balances discussed in Chapter 2.

We assume the company will not acquire any additional long-term investments or goodwill or other intangible assets. Even though the company may invest in such assets, our assumption is equivalent to assuming that any such assets acquired will create no additional value; in other words, they will be zero net present value investments. This is a simplifying assumption considering Starbucks is partnering and creating joint ventures around the world—activities that are reported as long-term investments on its balance sheet. For land, buildings, and equipment, we assume that the forecasts include expenditures for new locations as well as the refurbishing and replacement of existing locations. For simplicity, we assume that expected inflation is constant and has been factored into our forecast driver for capital expenditures. In our calculations, we also ignore any retirements and dispositions of fixed assets the company may make; this implicitly assumes that retirements and dispositions would have no effect on expected cash flows. We discuss forecasting capital expenditures with a more detailed model later in the chapter.

[3] This model was created before the passage of the Tax Cuts and Jobs Act of 2017. If we were modeling Starbucks after 2017, we would have to consider what the appropriate tax rates would be given the change in the tax code.

Recall that we usually assume that a company does not change its capital structure when we first create a financial model; as such, our initial focus is creating a model for the company's operations. In addition, this means the company will not issue or redeem any short-term or long-term debt. To simplify the calculations further, we assume that interest payable is a function of the amount of debt outstanding. We also assume that the company will not have any change in its cumulative comprehensive income line item within shareholders' equity.

Next, we assume the company will not accumulate any excess cash or other assets. In order to implement this assumption, we forecast the amount of cash the company requires to support the scale of its operations, which naturally increases as the scale of the company's operations increases. We discuss identifying and estimating required cash later in the chapter. The implication of this assumption is that the company uses equity free cash flow (either negative or positive) to balance the company's balance sheet. If Starbucks generates positive equity free cash flows, we assume it will distribute these cash flows to its equityholders (for example, through dividends or a repurchase of equity). If Starbucks has negative equity free cash flow, its existing equityholders will invest the additional cash needed. In other words, if we assume no change in debt financing, then distributions/contributions to/from the company's existing equityholders are equal to its equity free cash flows. Later in the chapter, after we review Starbucks' operating results, we incorporate an illustrative capital structure strategy into the forecasts.

4.4 CREATING A FINANCIAL MODEL FOR THE COMPANY'S OPERATIONS (STEP 4)

We now have all of the forecast drivers and inputs needed in order to create a financial model to forecast the company's operations. The next step is creating the formulas for the financial model in order to forecast each item in the financial model. Since our focus is on the company's operations, we will ignore the company's capital structure strategy in this step of the process.

We can think of Step 4 as having three (sub-) steps. First, we collect all of the forecast drivers (see Exhibit 4.6) in a table at the top of the model or in a separate sheet of the model. Second, we create a basic structure for each of the financial statements and supporting schedules, and we link the financial statements and schedules to each other. Third, we create formulas that use both the relevant forecast drivers and any other forecasts already in the model in order to forecast all of the items in each supporting schedule and financial statement.

These last two substeps can be complex for someone who is creating a financial model for the first time. A financial model typically contains many links throughout the various supporting schedules and financial statements. Recall the lyrics from that old song that describe all of the bones in the body and how they are connected to each other: ". . . the hip bone connected to the back bone, and the back bone connected to the neck bone, and the neck bone connected to the head bone . . . "[4] Financial models essentially work in the same way; each part of a financial model is in some way connected to the other parts. We explain the process of building a financial model as a sequence of events, but it is much more of an iterative process. In general, we do not create an entire financial statement or schedule. Rather, we create part of a financial statement or schedule, which feeds into another financial statement or schedule. Then, we "loop back" to complete the previous financial statement or schedule.[5]

Starbucks' Income Statement Forecasts—Part 1

Given the forecast drivers in Exhibit 4.6, we begin creating the Starbucks financial model by forecasting revenue. Revenue directly drives the cost of goods sold, selling, general and administrative, and most of the other line items in the income statements as all of those items are driven by expense ratios. We summarize the initial calculations for the Year 1 income statement forecast in Exhibit 4.7 (subsequent years' calculations are similar—the formulas need only be copied to future years). In this and the Starbucks' exhibits that follow, we reference each calculation in the exhibit with a number in square brackets

[4] See the lyrics to the song titled, "Dry Bones," composer unknown.

[5] This is somewhat complex the first time you see this, but you have already seen these linkages explained in Chapter 3 in the Bob Adams example. If you have never created a financial model, we urge you to create the Starbucks model on your own to fully understand these linkages. The chapter provides sufficient detail that you should be able to replicate the model exactly.

(e.g., [1]); we do not discuss references to subtotals and totals in the calculations. We begin creating the financial model by forecasting revenues [1]. Using a growth rate for total revenues, we forecast revenues directly in the income statement. If the revenue forecasting model was more complex, we would use one or more separate schedules to forecast revenues, and revenues on the income statement would be linked to these supplemental schedules (see Section 4.10 for an example).

Next, to forecast the expenses that are directly related to revenue, we multiply revenue by the appropriate expense ratio from Exhibit 4.6 in [2], [4], [5], and [6]. We also have sufficient information to forecast interest expense [7], as it is based on the beginning of year debt balance. We do not require a forecast for interest and other income because these are excess assets and assumed to have been liquidated for the purposes of our forecasts used in a DCF valuation. We cannot calculate operating income or income before taxes until we forecast depreciation and amortization. We typically use a separate schedule for land, buildings, and equipment and another schedule for accumulated depreciation. These schedules include forecasts for capital expenditures and depreciation.

EXHIBIT 4.7 Starbucks—Year 1 Income Statement Forecasts

STARBUCKS CORPORATION
Income Statement Forecasts
(for the fiscal years ended October)

($ in thousands)	Year −1	Year 0	Year 1	Calculation	Formulas and Explanation
Revenue	$6,369,300	$7,786,942	$9,344,330	[1] = 7,786,942 × 1.20	= Rev (Last Year) × (1 + g)
Cost of goods sold	−2,605,212	−3,178,791	−3,831,175	[2] = −0.41 × 9,344,330	= Rev × [CGS/Rev]
Gross margin	$3,764,088	$4,608,151	$5,513,155	[3] = [1] + [2]	= Sum
Store and other operating expenses	−2,362,935	−2,947,902	−3,550,846	[4] = −0.38 × 9,344,330	= Rev × [S&OO/Rev]
General and administrative expenses	−357,114	−473,023	−560,660	[5] = −0.06 × 9,344,330	= Rev × [G&A/Rev]
Depreciation and amortization	−340,169	−387,211	−425,770	[12]	= See Exhibit 4.8, [12]
Other operating income	76,648	93,937	93,443	[6] = 0.01 × 9,344,330	= Rev × [OOI/Rev]
Operating income	$ 780,518	$ 893,952	$1,069,323	[15] = [3] + [4] + [5] + [12] + [6]	= Sum
Interest and other income	17,101	23,396		Income from liquidated excess asset	= Forecast not required
Interest expense	−1,272	−11,105	−42,163	[7] = −0.06 × (700,762 + 1,958)	= Interest Rate × Beg bal debt
Income before taxes	$ 796,347	$ 906,243	$1,027,159	[16] = [15] + [7]	= Sum
Provision for income taxes	−301,977	−324,770	−369,777	[17] = −0.36 × [16]	= Tax rate × income before taxes
Cumulative effect of accounting change	0	−17,214		Assumed $0	= Forecast not required
Net earnings	$ 494,370	$ 564,259	$ 657,382	[18] = [16] + [17]	= Sum
Earnings Per Share					
Net earnings	$ 494,370	$ 564,259	$ 657,382	[18]	= [18]
Common shares outstanding—basic	789,570	766,114	766,114	[19] = 766,114	= Assumed constant
Earnings per share—basic	$ 0.63	$ 0.74	$ 0.86	[20] = [18] ÷ [19]	= Quotient
Retained Earnings (and Other)					
Beginning balance	$1,444,617	$1,938,987	$2,151,084	[65] = 2,151,084	= Ending balance (last year)
Net income	494,370	564,259	657,382	[18]	= [18]
Common equity distributions	0	−352,162	−448,617	[62]	= See Exhibit 4.10, [62]
Ending balance	$1,938,987	$2,151,084	$2,359,849	[66] = [65] + [18] + [62]	= Sum

Exhibit may contain small rounding errors

Using Expense Ratios to Forecast Expenses

Naturally, when forecasting expenses we consider other factors besides the ratio of an expense line item to revenue (or revenue growth); for example, we may consider capacity utilization, changes in capacity utilization, and economies of scale. For a given change in revenues and demand, some expenses and balance sheet items may depend entirely on revenue and demand forecasts, some may depend partially on revenue and demand forecasts, and others may not depend on revenue and demand forecasts at all, at least over some range of scale.

A company's operating expense ratios (for example, cost of goods sold as a percentage of its revenues) can change if the company has substantial fixed costs and if its capacity utilization changes during the forecast period. If a company has substantial fixed costs and assuming all else is equal, increasing the company's capacity utilization would decrease the company's ratio of cost of goods sold to revenue. The cost of goods sold to revenue ratio can also change because selling prices per unit change but costs per unit do not. For example, the ratio of cost of goods sold to revenue can change as a function of capacity utilization at the industry level. Prices typically rise when the industry is operating at full capacity, and they fall when there is excess capacity. The ratio of cost of goods sold to revenue can also change when the industry becomes more or less competitive, for such an event can cause changes in gross margins.

However, even so-called fixed costs are not generally fixed over all ranges of output for all periods. A company's rent expense is fixed only until the company's scale increases and it needs to rent additional assets to support its increased scale. Such costs are fixed only until the company begins operating at full capacity with respect to those assets; and then it must rent more assets to expand capacity. Thus, such costs are only fixed over some range of output. Some assets and related costs have an unlimited capacity, such as patents and copyrights; however, these assets typically have a limited life, so the related costs are fixed for unlimited changes in revenues but only for a limited period.

REVIEW EXERCISE 4.1

Financial Model for the Bob Wardrop Company—Part 1

Forecast drivers, financial statements, and certain supporting schedules for the Bob Wardrop Company appear below. In the forecast, assume that the company uses only common equity financing, raises more equity capital when equity free cash flows are negative, and distributes all positive equity free cash flows to common equity-holders in the form of dividends. Forecast the company's income statement for Year 1. Calculate depreciation expense as the beginning balance in gross property, plant, and equipment, divided by the number of years of life.

B. WARDROP COMPANY

Income Statement and Balance Sheet ($ in thousands)	Year 0
Income Statement	
Revenue (Rev)	$1,000
Cost of goods sold (CGS)	−600
Depreciation expense	−167
Earnings before interest and taxes	$ 233
Interest expense	
Income before taxes	$ 233
Income tax expense	−70
Net income	$ 163
Balance Sheet	
Cash	$ 100
Accounts receivable	200
Total current assets	$ 300
Property, plant, and equipment (net)	1,837
Total assets	$2,137
Debt	$ 0
Capital stock	100
Retained earnings	2,037
Liabilities and shareholders' equity	$2,137

Statement of Retained Earnings ($ in thousands)	Year 0
Retained earnings—Beginning of year	$1,873
Net income	163
Common equity dividends	0
Retained earnings—End of year	$2,037

Cash Flow Statement ($ in thousands)	Year 0
Cash flows from operations	
Net income	$ 163
+ Depreciation expense	167
− Change in accounts receivable	−20
Cash flow from operations	$ 310
Investing activities	
− Capital expenditures	−$ 670
Financing activities	
+ Change in debt financing	$ 0
+ Change in common equity financing	0
− Common equity dividends paid	0
Cash flows from financing activities	$ 0
Change in cash balance	−$ 360

Exhibit may contain small rounding errors

continued

continued from previous page

B. WARDROP COMPANY—Forecast Drivers	Actual	Forecast			
	Year 0	Year 1	Year 2	Year 3	Year 4
Operating Drivers					
Revenue growth rate		40.0%	30.0%	20.0%	10.0%
Cost of goods sold (% of revenues)	60.0%	60.0%	60.0%	60.0%	60.0%
Depreciation (# of years, straight-line basis)	10	10	10	10	10
Effective income tax rate (for the provision for income taxes)	30.0%	30.0%	30.0%	30.0%	30.0%
Income tax rate for interest, T_{INT}	40.0%	40.0%	40.0%	40.0%	40.0%
Required cash (% of revenue)	10.0%	10.0%	10.0%	10.0%	10.0%
Accounts receivable (% of revenues)	20.0%	20.0%	20.0%	20.0%	20.0%
Capital expenditures	$670	$700	$610	$360	$200

Plant and Equipment (PPEQ) Schedule ($ in thousands)	Year 0
Beginning PPEQ—gross	$1,667
Capital expenditures	670
Ending PPEQ—gross	$2,337
Beginning accumulated depreciation	$ 333
Depreciation expense	167
Ending accumulated depreciation	$ 500
Net property, plant, and equipment	$1,837

Exhibit may contain small rounding errors

Solution on page 195.

Starbucks' Property, Plant, and Equipment Forecasts

Next, we prepare a separate schedule to forecast the company's depreciation expense and capital expenditures; we also forecast the balance of its accumulated depreciation and of its net land, buildings, and equipment (see Exhibit 4.8). We begin this schedule by forecasting land, buildings, and equipment (gross). We add the beginning balance [8] to capital expenditures for the year [9] in order to calculate its ending balance [10].

We forecast the ending balance of accumulated depreciation [13] by adding the beginning balance [11] to depreciation taken for the year [12]. Depreciation [12] is equal to the beginning balance of land, buildings, and equipment (gross), divided by the average number of years of depreciable life; in this case we use ten years. In order to forecast capital expenditures, we first forecast the total year-end net land, buildings, and equipment needed to generate next year's revenues. The net land, buildings, and equipment balance is equal to revenues next year divided by our forecast driver—the ratio of next year's revenue to this year's ending balance of net land, buildings, and equipment. From this, we subtract the amount of net land, buildings, and equipment the company already owns before adding the depreciation taken this year. The result of this calculation is equal to our forecast of capital expenditures. Recall that we assume Starbucks will not have any retirements or dispositions of its assets.

This is a straightforward and top-level property, plant, and equipment schedule. We illustrate an example of a more detailed forecast of capital expenditures in Section 4.10. Further, we sometimes create depreciation schedules that track each tranche of capital investment (as defined by the year purchased) and then depreciate each tranche separately, and may even have schedules for different types of assets to the extent such information is available. For the beginning balance of plant and equipment, we may or may not have detailed information on these tranches, so we may have to depreciate the existing stock of plant and equipment as one tranche. If we do have enough information, we can depreciate the different tranches of plant and equipment separately. Since we will be forecasting subsequent tranches of capital expenditures, we will always have data on future tranches. In addition, companies often use different methods of depreciation for financial reporting and taxes, and we sometimes create separate depreciation schedules for financial reporting depreciation and tax depreciation. Thus, a financial model's set of depreciation schedules can be quite detailed.

EXHIBIT 4.8 Starbucks—Year 1 Property, Plant and Equipment Related Forecasts

STARBUCKS CORPORATION
Land, Buildings, and Equipment Forecasts
(for the fiscal years ended October)

($ in thousands)	Year −1	Year 0	Year 1	Calculation	Formulas and Explanation
Land, Buildings, and Equipment (GPPEQ)					
Beginning balance (BB)	$2,802,704	$3,467,583	$4,257,703	[8] = 4,257,703	= Ending balance (last year)
Capital expenditures	664,879	862,964	1,057,975	$[9] = [1]_{t+1}/4 - [14]_{t-1} + [12]_t$ $= 11{,}680{,}413/4 - [14]_{t-1} + [12]_t$	$= Rev_{t+1}/[Rev/NetPPEQ]$ $- BBNetPPEQ + Dep$
Retirements and dispositions		−72,844		Assumed to Equal $0	= Forecast not required
Ending balance (EB)	$3,467,583	$4,257,703	$5,315,678	[10] = [8] + [9]	= Sum
Accumulated Depreciation: (AcDep)					
Beginning balance (BB)	$1,258,357	$1,625,564	$1,969,804	[11] = 1,969,804	= Ending balance (last year)
Depreciation expense	367,207	412,625	425,770	$[12] = [10]_{t-1}/10$ years = 4,257,703/10	= Gross PPEQ (last year)/# years
Retirements and dispositions		−68,385		Assumed to Equal $0	= Forecast not required
Ending balance (EB)	$1,625,564	$1,969,804	$2,395,574	[13] = [11] + [12]	= Sum
Net property, plant, and equipment	$1,842,019	$2,287,899	$2,920,103	[14] = [10] − [13]	= Sum

Exhibit may contain small rounding errors

Starbucks' Income Statement Forecasts—Part 2

Now that we have a forecast of depreciation and amortization [12], we can use this forecast in order to complete the income statement forecasts (see Exhibit 4.7). In this illustration, we calculate income taxes [17] by multiplying a constant income tax rate for the provision for income taxes (see the forecast drivers) by income before taxes [16]. As you know from Chapter 3, income tax calculations include the effects of any income taxes payable or receivable and the effects of any deferred income tax assets and liabilities. Earlier in the chapter (and in Chapter 3), we concluded that a reasonable rate to use to calculate Starbucks' provision for income taxes is 36%, Starbucks' effective tax rate, but that its marginal income tax rate to use for interest expense, T_{INT}, is 38.4%, not 36%. Although not shown on the balance sheet or statement of cash flows, Starbucks has deferred tax assets and deferred tax liabilities. Starbucks includes the effect of its deferred income taxes on its statement of cash flows in the change in other assets and other liabilities, which we follow when measuring Starbucks' free cash flows. We now have a forecast of Starbucks' net earnings [18]. We can also calculate the company's earnings per share [20] by dividing net earnings [18] by common shares outstanding, which we assume remain unchanged [19]. While we can begin our forecast for retained earnings, we cannot complete this calculation, for we do not know the company's distributions to equityholders. We will not know that amount until we calculate the company's equity free cash flow. We defer that calculation until then.

Starbucks' Balance Sheet Forecasts—Part 1

Once we have the income statement programmed in the model, we can begin forecasting the balance sheet (see Exhibit 4.9). We begin creating our balance sheet forecasts by forecasting items that are directly or indirectly related to revenues—required cash [21], other current assets [24], other non-current assets [26], accrued expenses and other [29], deferred revenue [30], and other non-current liabilities [31].

Several of our balance sheet forecast drivers are indirectly related to revenues—accounts receivable [22], inventories [23], and accounts payable [28]. We already have forecasts for net, land, buildings, and

EXHIBIT 4.9 Starbucks—Year 1 Balance Sheet Forecasts

STARBUCKS CORPORATION
Balance Sheet Forecasts
(for the fiscal years ended October)

($ in thousands)	Year −1	Year 0	Year 1	Calculation	Formulas and Explanation
Required cash	$ 173,809	$ 312,606	$ 467,217	[21] = 0.05 × 9,344,330	= Rev × [cash/rev]
Short-term investments	133,227	141,038		Liquidated excess asset	= Forecast not required
Accounts receivable	190,762	224,271	256,009	[22] = 9,344,330/365 × 10	= Rev/365 × [days AR]
Inventories	546,299	636,222	766,235	[23] = 3,831,175/365 × 73	= CGS/365 × [days inventory]
Other current assets	165,237	215,651	280,330	[24] = 0.03 × 9,344,330	= Rev × [other current assets/rev]
Total current assets	$1,209,334	$1,529,788	$1,769,791	[25] = [21] + [22] + [23] + [24]	= Sum
Land, buildings, and equipment, net	$1,842,019	$2,287,899	$2,920,103	[14]	= See Exhibit 4.8, [14]
Goodwill and other intangible assets	127,883	199,433	199,433	Assumed constant (GW)	= Forecast not required
Long-term investments	261,564	224,904		Liquidated excess asset	= Forecast not required
Other non-current assets	72,893	186,917	186,887	[26] = 0.02 × 9,344,330	= Rev × [other non-current assets/rev]
Total assets	$3,513,693	$4,428,941	$5,076,213	[27] = [25] + [14] + [26] + GW	= Sum
Accounts payable	$ 220,975	$ 340,937	$ 434,103	[28] = (3,831,175 + (766,235 − 636,222)) /365 × 40	= (CGS + change in inventory)/365 × [days AP]
Accrued expenses and other	552,907	661,148	840,990	[29] = 0.09 × 9,344,330	= Rev × [accrued expenses and other/rev]
Interest payable	318	847	7,027	[34] = 0.01 × (700,762 + 1,958)	= End bal debt × [interest payable/debt bal]
Deferred revenue	175,048	231,926	280,330	[30] = 0.03 × 9,344,330	= Rev × [deferred revenue/rev]
Short-term and current long-term debt	277,748	700,762	700,762	[32] = 700,762 + 0	= Ending balance (last year) + change
Total current liabilities	$1,226,996	$1,935,620	$2,263,212	[35] = [28] + [29] + [34] + [30] + [32]	= Sum
Long-term debt	$ 2,870	$ 1,958	$ 1,958	[33] = 1,958 + 0	= Ending balance (last year) + change
Other non-current liabilities	193,565	262,857	373,773	[31] = 0.04 × 9,344,330	= Rev × [other non-current liabilities/rev]
Total liabilities	$1,423,431	$2,200,435	$2,638,943	[36] = [35] + [33] + [31]	= Sum
Common stock and surplus	$ 130,361	$ 40,149	$ 40,149	[71] = 40,149 + [61]	= Beg bal + change, see Exhibit 4.10, [61]
Cumulative comprehensive income (loss)	20,914	37,273	37,273	Assumed constant (CCI)	= Forecast not required
Retained earnings	1,938,987	2,151,084	2,359,849	[66]	= See Exhibit 4.7, [66]
Total shareholders' equity	$2,090,262	$2,228,506	$2,437,271	[67] = [71] + [66] + CCI	= Sum
Total liabilities and equities	$3,513,693	$4,428,941	$5,076,213	[68] = [36] + [67]	= Sum

Exhibit may contain small rounding errors

equipment [14] from Exhibit 4.8. At this point in creating the financial model, we assume that the amount of debt (short-term [32] and long-term [33]) remains constant. Based on the debt balance, we forecast interest payable [34]. Based on these forecast drivers, inputs, and assumptions, we can forecast all of the asset and liability accounts but not the shareholders' equity accounts.

REVIEW EXERCISE 4.2

Financial Model for the Bob Wardrop Company—Part 2

Use the information in Review Exercise 4.1 to forecast the asset side of the company's balance sheet for Year 1.

Solution on page 196.

The Balance of Shareholders' Equity Is Not a Plug

Total shareholders' equity consists of three accounts—common stock and surplus, cumulative comprehensive income (loss), and retained earnings. (Common stock and surplus is often separated into two accounts—common stock at par value and contributed capital in excess of par value.) We typically assume a company's comprehensive income remains constant in our forecasts because we assume the company will not, on average, have a gain or loss not recorded on the income statement. We know the balance in the capital stock and surplus account is equal to its beginning balance plus the amount received for stock issued minus the amount paid for stock repurchases; however, we do not know the amount of the stock issued or repurchased. We also know that the balance of retained earnings is equal to its beginning balance plus net income for the year minus any distributions to equityholders (such as dividends);

however, we do not yet know the amount of the dividends (or other distributions) the company will pay to its equityholders. As we explain in this section and illustrate in the following section, we measure the company's cash received from stock issuances and the cash distributed through stock repurchases or dividends in the free cash flow schedule.

We know that total shareholders' equity is equal to total assets minus total liabilities. Thus, since we already have a forecast of total assets and total liabilities, we could "plug" for the sum of these two amounts. We do not recommend using such an approach because that procedure can result in a financial model in which the financial statements and free cash flow schedule do not properly articulate (link). In the next section, we describe an approach to calculate these balances that ensures the financial statements and free cash flow schedule properly articulate. This approach uses the checks and balances embedded in financial accounting systems, which can help to reduce errors in the financial model.

In this approach, we treat common equityholders as residual claimants of the company's free cash flows. In other words, if the company generates a positive equity free cash flow, it will distribute that cash—in some manner—to its existing equityholders on a proportionate basis. On the other hand, if the company generates a negative equity free cash flow, we assume that its existing equityholders will make an additional investment in the company to fund the negative free cash flow. We can make this assumption even though we do not actually expect the company to either distribute cash to or secure financing from its current common equityholders. If the company does retain cash not needed for operations, we assume it will invest that cash in zero net present value projects or investments that earn their respective required rates of return. The assumption concerning securing financing from common equityholders is valid as long as we can assume that the company will be able to raise any needed capital at its risk-adjusted cost of capital and with minimal transactions cost.

Starbucks' Free Cash Flow Forecasts

We show the free cash flow schedule in Exhibit 4.10. Creating a free cash flow schedule for forecasts is essentially the same as creating a free cash flow schedule based on historical financial statements, which we discussed and illustrated in Chapter 3. The free cash flow schedule begins with one input from the income statement—EBIT (operating income, [15]). We then deduct the income tax the company would pay on its EBIT [51]. Forecasts for the income tax on EBIT excludes the income tax shelter from interest (interest tax shield, ITS). Thus, the effective or average tax rate is seldom the correct tax rate to use for EBIT. Recall that based on a review of Starbucks' income tax disclosures (not shown in the chapter), a reasonable rate to use for interest expense, T_{INT}, is 38.4%, which is equal to the sum of Starbucks' federal and net state income tax rates. Income tax on EBIT is equal to the provision for income taxes on the income statement [17] (a negative number in the financial statements) minus the interest tax shield [57]. As we discussed in Chapter 3, if there are changes in deferred tax assets and liabilities, we would have to adjust the income tax provision for those as well. The interest tax shield is equal to interest expense [7] multiplied by the tax rate for interest (0.384). We use these two inputs to measure the company's unlevered earnings [52]. Next, we adjust EBIT for accounting accruals. Recall from Chapter 3 that these adjustments are mostly the same adjustments made in a cash flow statement to measure cash flow from operations (see Exhibit 4.11 which follows for Starbucks' cash flow statement)—[37] through [41] and [43] through [45] are the adjustments we make in the Starbucks example. The exception to this rule is that we only pick up adjustments that impact EBIT. If you look at Starbucks' balance sheet, you will see that there is a current liability for interest payable. Since EBIT is before interest, we do not include the change in interest payable in measuring unlevered cash flows since it is before interest. In addition, we include an adjustment for the change in required cash [53], which is just the change in required cash from the balance sheet. We discuss how to forecast required cash in Section 4.8. Lastly, we assume the company will not have any asset impairment charges or accounting changes in the future.

To measure Starbucks' unlevered free cash flow [56], we subtract capital expenditures [9] from its unlevered cash flow from operations [54]. We calculate equity free cash flow by adjusting unlevered free cash flow [56] for after-tax cash interest paid—[7], [42], and [57]—and the change in non-common equity financing [50]. Note that while we ignored the adjustment for change in interest payable in making our adjustments to EBIT (since interest is not part of EBIT), we do include it in calculating cash interest paid from interest expense.

We add the proceeds from the sale of short-term [47] and long-term investments [48] to equity free cash flow [59] in order to measure the cash flow before cash flows to/from common equityholders [60]. If that amount is negative, we assume the company's existing stockholders invest more cash into the

EXHIBIT 4.10 Starbucks—Year 1 Free Cash Flow Schedule Forecasts

STARBUCKS CORPORATION Free Cash Flow Forecasts (for the fiscal years ended October)					
($ in thousands)	**Year −1**	**Year 0**	**Year 1**	**Calculation**	**Formulas and Explanation**
Earnings before interest and taxes (EBIT)	**$780,518**	**$893,952**	**$1,069,323**	**[15]**	**= See Exhibit 4.7, [15]**
Income taxes paid on EBIT	−295,899	−320,050	−385,968	[51] = [17] − [57]	= Provision for income taxes − ITS
Unlevered earnings	**$484,619**	**$573,902**	**$ 683,355**	**[52] = [15] + [51]**	**= Sum**
Depreciation and amortization	367,207	412,625	425,770	[12]	= See Exhbit 4.7, [12]
Asset impairment charges	19,464	19,622		Assumed $0	= Forecast not required
Receivables	0	0	−31,738	[37] = − (256,009 − 224,271)	= − Change in accounts receivable
Inventories	−121,618	−85,527	−130,013	[38] = − (766,235 − 636,222)	= − Change in inventory
Other current assets	0	0	−64,679	[39] = − (280,330 − 215,651)	= − Change in other current assets
Accounts payable	9,717	104,966	93,166	[40] = + (434,103 − 340,937)	= + Change in accounts payable
Accrued expenses and other	30,216	145,427	179,842	[41] = + (840,990 − 661,148)	= + Change in accrued expenses and other
Deferred revenue	53,276	56,547	48,404	[43] = + (280,330 − 231,926)	= + Change in deferred revenue
Other non-current assets	0	0	30	[44] = − (186,887 − 186,917)	= − Change in other non-current assets
Other non-current liabilities	0		110,916	[45] = + (373,773 − 262,857)	= + Change in other non-current liabilities
Other, net	70,204	−104,029		Not used	= Forecast not required
Change in required cash balance	−28,756	−138,797	−154,611	[53] = −(467,217 − 312,606)	= − Change in required cash
Unlevered cash flow from operations	**$884,329**	**$984,736**	**$1,160,442**	**[54] = [52] + [12] + [37] +...+ [41] + [43] + [44] + [45] + [53]**	= Sum
Capital expenditures, net	−664,879	−862,964	−1,057,975	−[9]	= See Exhbit 4.8, [9]
Unlevered free cash flow	**$219,450**	**$121,772**	**$ 102,468**	**[56] = [54] − [9]**	**= Sum**
Interest expense	−1,272	−11,105	−42,163	[7]	= See Exhbit 4.7, [7]
Interest payable	80	529	6,180	[42] = + (7,027 − 847)	= + Change in interest payable
Interest tax shield	488	4,264	16,191	[57] = 0.384 × [7]	= Tax rate × Exhibit 4.7 [7]
CF before non-equity financing changes	**$218,746**	**$115,460**	**$ 82,675**	**[58] = [56] + [7] + [42] + [57]**	**= Sum**
Change in debt, net	276,265	422,102	0	[50] = + (770,762 − 770,762) + (1,958 − 1,958)	= + Change in short-term and long-term debt
Equity free cash flow	**$495,011**	**$537,562**	**$ 82,675**	**[59] = [58] + [50]**	**= Sum**
Interest and other income, after-tax	10,534	14,412	0	Income from liquidated excess asset	= Forecast not required
Sale (purchase) of investments	444,264	21,924	365,942	= [47] + [48] = − (0 − 141,038) − (0 − 224,904)	= − Change in ST and LT investments
Effect of exchange rate changes	283	3,530	0	Assumed $0	= Forecast not required
Cash flow before cash flows to/from common equityholders	**$950,092**	**$577,428**	**$ 448,617**	**[60] = [47] + [48] + [59]**	**= Sum**
Change in common stock, net	−950,092	−577,428	0	[61] = if [60] < 0, − [60], otherwise 0	= − Negative equity free cash flow, 0
Common dividends	0	0	−448,617	[62] = if [60] > 0, − [60], otherwise 0	= − Positive equity free cash flow, 0
Change in excess cash	$ 0	$ 0	$ 0	[63] = [60] + [61] +[62]	= Sum
Change in required cash balance	28,756	138,797	154,611	− [53]	= − [53]
Change in cash balance	**$ 28,756**	**$138,797**	**$ 154,611**	**[64] = [63] − [53]**	**= Sum**

Exhibit may contain small rounding errors

company [61], and if that amount is positive, we assume the company distributes the cash to its investors [62]. You can see the dividends are $448.6 million. In this treatment, we are not treating the sale of the excess asset as a free cash flow. If we did, we would be assuming that these assets are liquidated at the end of Year 1. Recall from our prior discussion that if we did conduct a DCF valuation, we would add the after-tax value of the excess assets to the discounted value of the free cash flows, implicitly assuming that the liquidation and distribution takes place at the valuation date. Thus, we are essentially assuming that the distribution of the proceeds from the sale of the excess assets takes place at the beginning of Year 1.

At the end of the schedule, we reconcile our free cash flow schedule to the change in the cash balance [64] in order to make sure that these calculations articulate with the other financial statements.

Starbucks' Balance Sheet Forecasts—Part 2

Now that we know the amount of capital invested by the company's equityholders—if any—and the distributions to its equityholders, we can complete the retained earnings schedule (Exhibit 4.7, [65], [18], [62], and [66]). We can also use this information to complete the shareholders' equity section of the balance sheet (Exhibit 4.9, [71], [66] and [67]).

Starbucks' Cash Flow Statement Forecasts

Given that we already calculated Starbucks' free cash flow schedule, we can easily create its statement of cash flows. As we did to create the free cash flow schedule, we create a statement of cash flows in the financial model using only information in the income statement, balance sheet, and supporting schedules in the same manner as we discussed in Chapter 3. We have the forecasts necessary to forecast cash flow from operations and investing cash flows from the forecasts in the income statement, balance sheet, and supplemental schedules we have already created. We show the cash flow statement forecasts in Exhibit 4.11. As we assumed in the free cash flow schedule, we assume the company will not have any asset impairment charges or accounting changes.

EXHIBIT 4.11 Starbucks—Year 1 Statement of Cash Flow Forecasts

STARBUCKS CORPORATION Cash Flow Statement Forecasts (for the fiscal years ended October)					
($ in thousands)	**Year −1**	**Year 0**	**Year 1**	**Calculation**	**Formulas and Explanation**
Cash Flows from Operations					
Net earnings	$494,370	$ 564,259	$ 657,382	[18]	= See Exhibit 4.7, [18]
Depreciation and amortization	367,207	412,625	425,770	[12]	= See Exhbit 4.7, [12]
Cumulative effect of accounting change	0	17,214		Assumed $0	= Forecast not required
Asset impairment charges	19,464	19,622		Assumed $0	= Forecast not required
Adjustments for operating working capital:					
Receivables			−31,738	[37] = − (256,009 − 224,271)	= − Change in accounts receivable
Inventories	−121,618	−85,527	−130,013	[38] = − (766,235 − 636,222)	= − Change in inventory
Other current assets			−64,679	[39] = − (280,330 − 215,651)	= − Change in other current assets
Accounts payable	9,717	104,966	93,166	[40] = + (434,103 − 340,937)	= + Change in accounts payable
Accrued expenses and other	30,216	145,427	179,842	[41] = + (840,990 − 661,148)	= + Change in accrued expenses and other
Interest payable	80	529	6,180	[42] = + (7,027 − 847)	= + Change in interest payable
Deferred revenue	53,276	56,547	48,404	[43] = + (280,330 − 231,926)	= + Change in deferred revenue
Other non-current assets			30	[44] = − (186,887 − 186,917)	= − Change in other non-current assets
Other non-current liabilities			110,916	[45] = + (373,773 − 262,857)	= + Change in other non-current liabilities
Other, net	70,204	−104,029		Not used	= Forecast not required
Cash flow from operations	$922,915	$1,131,633	$1,295,261	[46] = [18] + [12] + [37] + ... + [45]	= Sum
Investing Activities					
Purchase of investments, net	$444,264	$ 21,924		Not used	= Forecast not required
Sale (purchase) of short-term investments, net			$ 141,038	[47] = − (0 − 141,038)	= − Change in short-term investments
Sale (purchase) of long-term investments, net			224,904	[48] = − (0 − 224,904)	= − Change in long-term investments
Capital expenditures, net	−643,296	−771,230	−1,057,975	−[9]	= See Exhbit 4.8, [9]
Acquisitions, net of cash acquired	−21,583	−91,734		Assumed $0	= Forecast not required
Net cash used by investing activities	−$220,615	−$ 841,040	−$ 692,033	[49] = [47] + [48] − [9]	= Sum
Financing Activities					
Change in common stock, net	−$950,092	−$ 577,428	$ 0	[61]	= See Exhibit 4.10, [61]
Change in debt, net	276,265	422,102	0	[50] = + (770,762 − 770,762) + (1,958 − 1,958)	= + Change in short-term and long-term debt
Common equity distributions			−448,617	[62]	= See Exhibit 4.10, [62]
Cash flows from financing activities	−$673,827	−$ 155,326	−$ 448,617	[69] = [61] + [50] + [62]	= Sum
Effect of exchange rate changes	$ 283	$ 3,530		Assumed $0	= Forecast not required
Change in cash balance	$ 28,756	$ 138,797	$ 154,611	[70] = [46] + [49] + [69]	= Sum

Exhibit may contain small rounding errors

Cash flow from operations is equal to net earnings [18], plus depreciation and amortization [12], adjusted for changes in all of the operating assets and liabilities as well as interest payable [37] through [45]. Cash flow for investing is equal to the change in short-term [47] and long-term investments [48] minus capital expenditures [9]. We calculate cash flow from financing using information regarding changes in debt financing on the balance sheet, and changes in shareholders' equity from the income statement and free cash flow schedule. We use this information to complete the financing section of the cash flow statement ([50], [61], and [62]) and reconcile to the change in cash [70]. We assume the company does not have any cash flow effect from exchange rate changes.

Valuation Key 4.1

Creating a financial model involves linking a set of forecast drivers (assumptions) and formulas (relations) to a set of financial statements, a free cash flow schedule, and other supporting schedules. One important facet of a good financial model is that the financial statements and various schedules fully articulate with each other; that is, do not "plug" for an item on the balance sheet in order to get your balance sheet to balance (total assets equal total liabilities plus shareholders' equity).

REVIEW EXERCISE 4.3

Financial Model for the Bob Wardrop Company—Part 3

Use the information in Review Exercise 4.1 to forecast the company's cash flow statement, free cash flow schedule, and statement of retained earnings for Year 1; afterward, complete the company's balance sheet (liabilities and shareholders' equity section) that you started in Review Exercise 4.2.

Solution on page 197.

4.5 STRESS TESTING THE MODEL AND ASSESSING THE REASONABLENESS OF THE FORECASTS (STEPS 5 AND 6)

LO3 Test the model, assess forecast reasonableness, and incorporate the company's capital structure into the model

The next step in the forecasting process—Step 5—is to check the model for its calculation accuracy and to stress test the model to make sure the model works properly when we change the forecast drivers. We also repeat this step after Step 7 (capital structure integration) to ensure that we did not introduce new errors when we integrated the capital structure into the financial model. In Step 6, we analyze the reasonableness of the forecasts and revise the forecasts as deemed necessary.

Checking and Stress Testing the Model—Step 5

We check to ensure the financial model works properly in various ways. First, we check that total assets equal the sum of total liabilities and shareholders' equity. We check to make sure that the ending balance in retained earnings is equal to the beginning balance in retained earnings, plus net income, minus dividends and other adjustments (if relevant); that changes in balance sheet accounts are tied to changes in the cash flow statement where appropriate; that the change in the cash balance ties to the free cash flow schedule and statement of cash flows; that depreciation expense (plus any depreciation included in the change in inventory, if any) is deducted from net property, plant, and equipment and net income; and that depreciation is added back to net income in the operating section of the cash flow statement.

We can also use the financial statements to measure the forecast drivers based on the financial statement forecasts to check our formulas. For example, if we use the "days to pay accounts payable" financial ratio as a forecast driver, we can calculate it based on the forecasted financial statements and check that it is the same as the forecast driver. If they are not the same, we have an error in our formulas. At this step, we also verify that even when we change the assumptions in the model, the model continues to work properly. For example, we might change the growth rates and see if the model still works.

Step Back and Ask, "Do the Forecasts Make Sense?"—Step 6, Part 1

We begin this step by reviewing big-picture issues in order to assess whether the forecasts make sense based on our competitive analysis. For example, suppose our forecasts indicate an increase in revenues over the next five years. Are the increases reasonable when compared to the forecasts for the industry (for example, from industry associations or financial analysts)? Can we identify the factors that are driving the sales increase? Is the increase a result of price increases above inflation? If so, why? Does the new pricing make sense given the competition and cost structure of the company and its competitors? If demand for the company's products depends on certain macro conditions (for example, growth in the economy or population), are the forecasts consistent with forecasts of these macro conditions?

Is the increase in revenue a result of increased volume of the same product(s)? If so, is the overall demand in the market expected to increase, or do the forecasts assume the company will take market share away from its competitors? What other factors might affect revenues? For example, could changes in regulations, global competition, or innovations affect demand for the company's products? Questions regarding the source of an increase in revenues may also lead to questions about cost structure and capital investments. For example, is an increase in volume achievable with the projected level of marketing expenses? Is the projected level of production consistent with planned staffing and capital expenditures? Are inventory and other net operating working capital forecasts consistent with the sales increase?

Sometimes we can check the reasonableness of our forecasts by using our forecasting process on earlier years for which data is available—in other words, **back testing** the model. In particular, we might do this for the part of the model that forecasts revenue and capital expenditures if these are based on complex schedules.

Comparing Historical Financial Ratios to the Financial Ratios Based on the Forecasts—Step 6, Part 2

Comparing forecasted financial ratios to a company's historical financial ratios and the financial ratios of comparable companies can be a useful way of analyzing the reasonableness of a set of forecasts. As we indicated previously, examining financial ratios—which were direct forecast drivers—is merely a check on the intended calculations in the model, but it is not an analysis of the reasonableness of the forecasts. However, we can use financial ratios that do not drive the model to help us analyze the reasonableness of the forecasts.

A good starting point for such an analysis is a comparison of the accounting rates of return that we discussed in Chapter 2—the return on assets, return on investment, and potentially the return on equity. We also examine the components of the rate of return ratios (such as the unlevered profit margin and its components and sales to total assets and its components). Other useful financial ratios include various turnover ratios (for example, revenue to fixed assets), asset composition ratios (for example, current assets relative to total assets), liquidity ratios (for example, the current ratio), and various margins (for example, gross margin and operating margin)—assuming we did not use these to drive the forecasts. We would also examine projected growth rates in revenues and their source and other important line items such as free cash flows.

We know that, on average, a company's profitability ratios are likely to move toward those of its comparable companies over a sufficiently long horizon. This is just the nature of a competitive economy. Over the long run, most companies will eventually trend toward the industry average in terms of economic profitability and revenue growth called **mean reversion.** The key issue here, of course, is how to estimate the time period over which this mean reversion will occur. Naturally, we can observe exceptions to this principle. For example, Microsoft Corporation has been able to sustain its competitive advantage longer than many companies have. Dell sustained a competitive advantage for quite some time, but it now appears to have lost that advantage. It is important to keep in mind that while the financial relations and underlying accounting data we discuss throughout this book can be useful for assessing and measuring economic concepts, their usefulness can be limited due to the differences between accounting data and the potentially unobservable economic concepts they represent. Also, comparisons across companies can be limited by differences in the underlying accounting principles used to create the accounting data. Thus, while examining the financial relations in the forecasts is useful for assessing the reasonableness of the forecasts, it is no guarantee of the validity of your forecasts.

Finally, we can compare our forecasts for revenues, earnings, and other performance and operating measures to either financial analyst forecasts or forecasts based upon other forecasting methods (for example, statistical time-series models). At the end of this step, we may revise the model until we conclude that the forecasts are reasonable for our intended purpose.

Starbucks' Historical Financial Ratios and Financial Ratio Forecasts

In Exhibit 4.12, we present some summary financial ratios for Starbucks' forecasts in order to provide a preliminary examination of the reasonableness of the forecasts. In these illustrative forecasts for Starbucks, we observe an initial jump in some of its financial ratios. In Year 2, the return on assets increases from 14.5% to 18.2%, largely due to an increase in its unlevered profit margin and total asset turnover. Reviewing the forecast drivers in Exhibit 4.6, we see reductions in cost of goods sold, store and other operating expenses, and general and administrative expenses (all as a percentage of revenue); these changes explain the increase in the forecasted unlevered profit margin. Revenue to total assets (asset utilization) also increases in Years 2 to 4, but it is not systematically drifting upward over time—often a sign of too little investment, which could merit further analysis. Part of this increase is due to the fact that we paid the short-term and long-term investments (which we assumed were excess assets) out to shareholders. Some additional analysis of the property, plant, and equipment ratios appears in order. Note also that the "days calculations" for receivables, inventory, and payables do not match the forecast drivers for those items in Exhibit 4.6. That occurs because the forecasts use the drivers in Exhibit 4.6 to calculate the ending balance in receivables, inventory, and payables, and the calculations shown in Exhibit 4.12 are based on average balances. We will not analyze the reasonableness of these forecasts further, for we do not show a longer history for Starbucks, nor do we have comparable companies, both of which are things we would likely use in such an analysis. However, it should be apparent that a detailed financial analysis of the forecasts, such as the analysis of The Gap, Inc. we discussed in Chapter 2, could help assess the reasonableness of the forecasts.

EXHIBIT 4.12 Starbucks—Historical Financial Ratios and Forecasts

	Actual	Forecast				
Disaggregating the Rate of Return	**Year 0**	**Year 1**	**Year 2**	**Year 3**	**Year 4**	**Year 5**
Return on assets	14.5%	14.4%	18.2%	18.1%	17.9%	17.3%
Unlevered profit margin	7.4%	7.3%	8.6%	8.5%	8.4%	8.1%
Total asset utilization (turnover)	1.96	1.97	2.11	2.12	2.14	2.12
Return on equity	26.1%	28.2%	36.9%	36.7%	36.6%	35.3%
Profit margin (to common)	7.2%	7.0%	8.4%	8.3%	8.2%	8.0%
Total asset utilization (turnover)	1.96	1.97	2.11	2.12	2.14	2.12
Financial leverage factor	1.84	2.04	2.08	2.08	2.09	2.08
ROE/ROA	1.808	1.960	2.029	2.032	2.042	2.041
Coverage Ratios	**Year 0**	**Year 1**	**Year 2**	**Year 3**	**Year 4**	**Year 5**
EBIT to interest	80.50	25.36	37.26	42.44	45.89	46.88
EBITDA to interest	117.66	35.46	49.87	57.34	63.08	66.23
Working Capital Management Ratios	**Year 0**	**Year 1**	**Year 2**	**Year 3**	**Year 4**	**Year 5**
Current ratio (operating liabilities)	1.2	1.1	1.1	1.1	1.1	1.1
Days of purchases outstanding (payable)	31.4	35.7	36.4	37.6	38.3	39.2
Days of inventory held	67.9	66.8	66.4	68.2	69.7	71.3
Accounts receivable collection period	9.7	9.4	9.0	9.3	9.5	9.8
Trade cash cycle	46.2	40.5	39.1	40.0	40.9	41.8
Property, Plant, and Equipment	**Year 0**	**Year 1**	**Year 2**	**Year 3**	**Year 4**	**Year 5**
Depreciable life of gross plant	9.36	11.24	10.91	10.77	10.63	10.62
Depreciable life of net plant	5.54	6.86	6.32	5.88	5.35	4.99
Capital expenditures to revenues	11.1%	11.3%	8.3%	7.2%	6.2%	6.5%
Capital expenditures to EBIT	96.5%	98.9%	61.7%	53.9%	47.0%	51.1%
Capital expenditures to EBITDA	66.0%	70.8%	46.1%	39.9%	34.2%	36.2%
Capital expenditures to depreciation	209.1%	248.5%	182.4%	153.4%	125.5%	123.8%

Valuation Key 4.2

Assessing the reasonableness of a financial model and its forecasts involves stepping back from the numbers and conducting a competitive analysis, an analysis of competitive advantage, and a financial analysis of the forecasts relative to the company's recent history as well as the recent history and expected performance of its comparable companies.

4.6 INCORPORATING THE COMPANY'S CAPITAL STRUCTURE STRATEGY

It is possible to skip this step if the valuation model does not require specific forecasts for interest and debt balances, for example, the weighted average cost of capital valuation model, a point we discuss in Chapter 5. However, it can be useful to incorporate an estimate of the company's capital structure into the financial model in order to better understand the company's financing needs, to measure the rates of return on equity (sometimes used to set compensation), to forecast coverage ratios and other debt-related ratios, and to assess how close the company will be to any financial-statement-based covenants in its debt contracts.

Fortunately, if we follow all of the first six steps in our forecasting process, the model will already include most of the necessary calculations to incorporate the company's capital structure into the financial model as long as the company has some existing interest-bearing debt on the balance sheet. If we adjust the company's debt balances, interest rates on debt, and other relevant aspects of its capital structure strategy, the model will automatically adjust the forecasts for a change in capital structure.

Once we incorporate the company's capital structure strategy into the model, we again stress test the model and check it for calculation accuracy; naturally, at this juncture, we focus more on the parts of the model affected by the capital structure strategy.

Incorporating an Alternative Capital Strategy in the Financial Model

Starbucks has \$700.8 million in debt that matures in Year 1 (see Exhibit 4.3, short-term and current long-term debt). The financial model does not assume that this debt was paid off in our projected balance sheet (see Exhibit 4.9) because the model initially assumes the current debt levels and interest rates continue. While capital structure decisions do not affect a company's unlevered free cash flows, they do affect its equity free cash flows. For example, for Starbucks in Year 1, had Starbucks paid off its short-term and current long-term debt of \$700.8 million, and it did not issue new debt or preferred stock, its equity free cash flow would decrease from a positive \$82.7 million to a negative \$618.1 million. As we discussed in Chapter 1, and disucss in more detail in Chapter 5, that decline in debt financing would not affect the value of the unlevered firm but it would likely reduce the value of the interest tax shields.

Starbucks had an AAA credit rating as of the end of Year 0. The Starbucks financial model can be used to estimate how much debt it can issue next year (Year 1) and still maintain its AAA debt rating. To illustrate this type of analysis, we use Starbucks' interest coverage ratio (EBIT divided by interest) to predict its debt rating. Naturally, qualifying for a specific debt rating is more complex than maintaining a certain coverage ratio, but using the company's coverage ratio allows us to illustrate how we can incorporate this type of capital structure analysis into a financial model (we discuss the intricacies of debt ratings in more detail in Chapter 9). At the time, the median EBIT coverage ratio of companies with an AAA rating was 21.4 and senior debt with an AAA rating carried an interest rate of 6%.

Assume that at the beginning of Year 1, Starbucks will retire all of its debt (\$702.7 million, see the Year 0 current and long-term debt in Exhibit 4.9) and issue new long-term debt such that its expected interest coverage ratio—based on the projected EBIT for Year 1—is equal to 22.0 (slightly above the median coverage ratio for companies with an AAA debt rating). Starbucks' debt will carry an interest rate of 6%. We calculate the company's debt level in Year 1 with a two-step calculation that we combine into one calculation. First, we calculate the amount of interest Starbucks can have in Year 1, based on the company's EBIT in Year 1 and its target coverage ratio. Next, we calculate the maximum amount of debt the company can issue at the end of Year 1 based on that projected EBIT divided by the target coverage ratio at a 6% interest rate. The combined calculation of the maximum amount of debt is as follows:

$$\text{Maximum Debt}_{\text{Year 1}} = \frac{\dfrac{\text{EBIT}_{\text{Year 1}}}{\text{Target Coverage Ratio}}}{\text{Interest Rate}} = \frac{\dfrac{\$1{,}069{,}323}{22.0}}{0.06} = \$810{,}093$$

The maximum debt issue that allows Starbucks to maintain an interest coverage ratio of 22 (and an AAA rating) is \$810,093 in Year 1. While we do not present an exhibit illustrating the debt issuance, the newly issued debt is \$107.4 million higher than the previous debt balance (\$107.4 = \$810.1 − \$700.8 − \$1.9), resulting in an increase in equity free cash flows and an additional cash distribution to its equityholders of \$107.4 million (assuming no change in interest payable with the increased debt). We note that in all years after Year 1, the company's EBIT continues to increase such that the maximum debt Starbucks could issue and maintain an AAA rating would increase each year. Of course, issuing additional debt has no impact on Starbucks' projected unlevered free cash flows.

This is just one potential capital structure strategy that a firm might pursue. For example, a company might choose to fund its entire cash shortfall before financing by issuing debt, without expecting to maintain a particular bond rating. Another alternative is that a company might pursue a target debt-to-equity capital structure (e.g., fund itself with 20% debt and 80% equity) and manage its capital structure over the long-run with the goal of maintaining that capital structure. Alternatively, given the limitation on the tax deductibility of interest in some countries (e.g., 30% of EBIT), one could calculate the maximum amount of debt the company could issue given the forecasts that would allow for full deductibility of interest.

Valuation Key 4.3

Once we create a financial model that maintains the company's current capital structure strategy (that is, assuming no change in non-common equity financing), we can incorporate the company's capital structure strategy by changing the way we calculate the company's debt balances, interest rates, and balances of all other non-common equity financing items.

Since we only changed the parts of the model that relate to financing, the parts of the company's income statement related solely to its operations (through the Operating Income in Exhibit 4.7) do not change. In addition, the unlevered free cash flows do not change (Exhibit 4.10). If they do change, it is likely that the model has an error in the formulas, for a company's operations are generally assumed independent of its financing decisions. Of course, if raising additional debt causes changes in required cash holdings, for example, then the unlevered free cash flows would change.

It is common, especially in highly levered transactions, for a financial model to include detailed debt schedules that allow for an automatic pay down of debt in order of seniority when the cash available before financing is positive. These schedules sometimes allow for an automatic draw from a line of credit, if the cash available before financing is negative. We illustrate such schedules in Chapter 15 when we discuss highly leveraged transactions called leveraged buy-out transactions.

REVIEW EXERCISE 4.4

Financial Model for the Bob Wardrop Company—Part 4

Use the information in Review Exercise 4.1 (except the information on the company's capital structure). For the company's capital structure, assume the company will issue debt to fund all of the financing needs it cannot fund with internally generated cash flow, and assume that its cost of debt is 10%. The company will pay down all of its debt before it begins to pay any dividends; then, it will distribute all positive equity free cash flows to common equityholders. Using this information, forecast the financial statements and supporting schedules, including a free cash flow schedule, first for Year 1 and then for Year 2. Recall from Review Exercise 4.1 that the company's effective tax rate to measure the provision for income taxes is 30% but its marginal tax rate for interest is 40%.

Solution on page 198.

4.7 SENSITIVITY AND SCENARIO ANALYSES AND SIMULATIONS

Forecasts are predictions of the future, so they are, by nature, uncertain. Given this uncertainty, we often examine our forecasts under alternative scenarios—that is, sets of likely (and even unlikely, though possible) future outcomes. Sensitivity and scenario analyses can be useful tools to help us understand the impact that alternative strategies have on a company's forecasts and valuation. In addition, scenario analysis and simulations can provide a distribution of possible forecasts and valuations based on alternative assumptions we might use in the financial model. Further, a manager or investor might want to know how "bad things can get" before the company violates its debt covenants or is unable to service its debt—as opposed to the company's expected performance (what we use in a DCF valuation).

In a **sensitivity analysis**, we change one or more of a financial model's forecast drivers and examine the impact that these changes have on the forecasts. We can then see how sensitive the value is to variations in specific forecast drivers. In a **scenario analysis**, we develop alternative scenarios in which we change a large number of assumptions in creating each scenario. For example, suppose we are valuing a biotech startup that is working on a single drug that could potentially cure a deadly form of cancer. We might develop a scenario where the drug undergoing testing is approved by the Food and Drug

Administration (FDA), and the efficacy tests indicate that the drug has great benefits with little side effects—turning it into a blockbuster drug with strong demand and excellent pricing. Another scenario is that the drug is approved, but the tests indicate frequent side effects and positive results in a smaller number of patients. Thus, while the drug will be marketable to patients with little hope from any alternative treatments, its sales will not be as impressive. Finally, we could develop a scenario where the FDA does not approve the drug due to serious side effects and poor clinical results at an early stage of testing and further development is abandoned.[6]

A Monte Carlo simulation is more complex than either a sensitivity or scenario analysis. In a **Monte Carlo simulation**, we incorporate a financial model into a simulation software package (for example an Excel add-on). In addition, we input distributional parameters for each forecast driver in the model (for example, assume that the company's ratio of cost of goods sold to revenue is normally distributed with a mean of 55% and a variance of 1.5%) and the correlation among all of the forecast drivers. The simulation software package allows the user to choose from a wide variety of statistical distributions as well as allowing the user to customize the distribution. The simulation then generates distributions of the forecasts by repeatedly sampling across the forecast drivers, based on the distributional assumptions provided. Assuming the financial model calculates the present value of the future cash flows, the simulation will provide a distribution of firm values obtained from the distributional assumptions provided. The mean of the distribution will represent the value of the company at the expected value of the cash flows.

Valuation Key 4.4

Sensitivity analyses, scenario analyses, and simulations can be useful tools to understand the impact that various assumptions have on forecasts and valuations. In addition, these tools can provide a distribution of possible forecasts and valuations based on the distributions of the assumptions in the financial model. One advantage of uncovering which assumptions have the biggest impact on value is that we can then try to refine our information with respect to the most critical drivers of value.

4.8 FORECASTING REQUIRED CASH AND VALUING EXCESS CASH

LO4 Forecast required cash and measure excess cash

As we discussed in all of the earlier chapters, companies require some amount of cash or securities that can be converted into cash to operate their businesses, which we call **required cash**. Some companies require more cash than others, and generally, the amount of cash required to operate the business increases with the scale of the business. Some companies, however, hold more cash (and liquid investments also referred to as cash) than they need to operate the company, called **excess cash**. Recalling the discussion in Chapter 3, excess cash flow results whenever managers do not distribute all of the company's (positive) equity free cash flows to its common equityholders.

Economic research suggests that companies hold excess cash for a variety of reasons.[7] Some multinational companies hold more cash than they need because of repatriation taxes that result from upstreaming cash to the parent company. This depends on the home country's tax system. For example, prior to 2018, U.S. multinational firms paid U.S. taxes on cash they repatriated back to the U.S. parent, whereas those earnings escaped U.S. taxes if the funds were not repatriated back. This is called a worldwide tax system, meaning the home country taxes the earnings of the company from all over the world when it is repatriated back to the parent (more on this in Chapter 17). Of course with the passage of the Tax Cuts and Jobs Act of 2017, companies must now pay taxes on those previously unrepatriated earnings (8% on liquid assets and 15.5% on illiquid assets) and they have eight years in which to do so (8% in each of first five years, 15% in year 6, 20% in year 7 and 25% in year 8, starting in 2018). Thus, U.S. companies can now use those liquid

[6] According to the 2013 Association for Financial Professionals survey, 72% of the respondents use multiple scenarios to evaluate projects and other investment opportunities. See, 2013 AFP Estimating and Applying Cost of Capital: Report of Survey Results, October 2013, Association for Financial Professionals.

[7] See, for example, Bates, T. W., K. M. Kahle, and R. M. Stulz, "Why Do U.S. Firms Hold So Much More Cash than They Used To?," *Journal of Finance* vol. LXIV, no. 5 (October 2009), pp. 1985–2021; Opler, T., et al. "The Determinants and Implications of Corporate Cash," *Journal of Financial Economics* vol. 52 (1999), pp. 3–46; Foleya, C. F., et al., "Why Do Firms Hold so Much Cash? A Tax-Based Explanation," *Journal of Financial Economics* vol. 86, no. 3 (December 2007), pp. 579–607; Simutin, Mikhail, "Excess Cash and Stock Returns," *Financial Management* vol. 39, no. 3 (Autumn 2010), pp. 1197–1222; and Liu, Yixin and David C. Mauer, "Corporate Cash Holdings and CEO Compensation Incentives," *Journal of Financial Economics* vol. 39, no. 3 (Autumn 2010), pp. 83–198.

assets to retire debt, repurchase shares or invest more in their businesses. Another reason for holding excess cash expressed by managers is that they hold excess cash to be able to take advantage of strategic growth opportunities. Companies with risk-taking CEOs may hold excess cash either because their debtholders require the company to have more liquidity or because these CEOs want the flexibility to make more near-term risky investments afforded by holding excess cash. Companies with relatively less easy access to capital markets, or for which raising additional capital is relatively more expensive, may be more likely to hold excess cash. Companies may also hold substantial cash because they feel they are facing a period of economic uncertainty or believe they have riskier cash flows; for example, during the financial crisis around 2008 and 2009, many companies accumulated cash as a cushion against uncertainty.

When we analyze a company, measure its free cash flows, or use one or more valuation methods to value it, we treat cash required to operate the business as a required investment—essentially the economic equivalent of purchasing inventory—and we treat excess cash as an asset not required to operate the business, an **excess asset**, and exclude it from our analysis and valuation of the company's operations. Thus, when we analyze a company, measure its free cash flows, or use one or more valuation methods to value the company, we first partition a company's cash (and liquid investments) balance into the cash the company needs for its operations and to implement its operating strategy (required cash) and the cash the company holds in excess of its required cash (excess cash).

Forecasting the Cash Required to Operate the Business (Required Cash)

Although it is easy to conclude that some companies held substantial excess cash at the end of 2017 (for example, Apple, Alphabet [Google], Microsoft), it is typically not easy to partition a company's cash (and liquid investment) balance into its required and excess components. A common approach is to assume all cash (and liquid investments) are excess cash. One valuation error resulting from this approach is that as the scale of the company increases, we ignore the required investment in cash to support the increase in scale, which overstates unlevered (and equity) free cash flows. The degree of overstatement, of course, depends on the relative amount of cash required to operate the company's business and the expected increase in the scale of the company's business. If the company being valued is a zero (or low) growth company, ignoring any increase in required cash will have little to no effect on the valuation. The second valuation error resulting from this assumption is that it presumes that all cash at the valuation date is available for distribution to the shareholders since it is not required for operations. Both of these errors will overstate the value of the firm; however, these errors are partially or even completely offset through the effect of this assumption on the cost of capital (see Chapters 8 and 11).

One way to identify a company's required cash balance is to examine its cash holdings (scaled, for example, by total assets or revenues) over time and compared to comparable companies. The goal of this analysis is to identify a useful driver (for example, cash holdings to a measure of the scale of the business operations) and the magnitude of the forecast driver to use in a company's financial model. A positive change or drift (intervention) in the time-series of scaled cash holdings relative to comparable companies is consistent with holding excess cash, assuming it is not related to additional required liquidity. Naturally, this approach will not work well if the company and the comparable companies have always held excess cash.

Regardless of the approach used to estimate a company's required cash, once we identify a forecast driver to use in the financial model, we can use sensitivity analysis to assess the effect that changes in required cash have on the value of the firm. Any valuation error resulting from an assumption about changes in required cash will be relatively small for a company that needs relatively little additional cash to operate expected increases in the scale of businesses—for example, companies with low growth rates, companies who arrange lines of credit as part of the company's financing and capital structure strategies and do not need much cash to operate the business.

As we have said previously, we value the excess cash as of the date of the valuation on an after-tax basis separately from the value of the company's operations (the latter would consider any changes in required cash). If a company holds a lot of excess cash it is important to separate it from required cash and value it as of the valuation date.

Valuing Excess Cash

In the previous section, we discuss how to partition a company's cash (and liquid investments) balance into its required cash and excess cash components. After identifying a company's excess cash balance, we must value the company's excess cash. Since companies report cash, cash equivalents, and marketable securities on a fair value basis the starting point of the value of a company's excess cash is, of course, its balance as of the valuation date. However, how the company invests its excess cash (and liquid investments) as well as potential income taxes can affect the valuation of a company's excess cash.

How we treat existing excess cash (and liquid investments) or undistributed future cash flows and the related income (or losses) generated by them depends on the assumption we make about those assets. We typically assume that investments of excess cash earn their respective required rates of return (that is, they do not create or destroy value). In this case, we assume that any excess cash (and liquid investments) in existence as of the valuation date are liquidated and distributed to the common shareholders as of the valuation date based on their after-tax value. For future equity free cash flows that are not needed for the business, we assume they are paid out as dividends even if we do not think the company will make those payouts. This is not a problem as long as we can again assume that the cash not distributed to shareholders will be invested in zero net present value investments and not create (or lose) any value. In other words, this treatment assumes that the company invests its excess cash in investments that just earn their risk-adjusted required rate of return.

If, however, the company subsequently invests its excess cash in investments that are non-zero net present value projects, we value these excess assets separately from the company's business but using the valuation methods discussed throughout the book. If a company invests its excess cash in negative net present value projects, the value of the company will be reduced relative to distributing its excess cash to the shareholders. One complexity that this assumption may create is that the cost of capital to value the investments made using excess cash could be different from the cost of capital to value the company's operations because by definition the investments made with the excess cash are not part of the company's operations. For this reason, we prefer to assume that all non-required cash is distributed to the equityholders.

The after-tax value of any marketable security can of course be less than its fair market value because of appreciation in the amount of the investment which would make it subject to capital gains tax if liquidated. Further, the value of excess cash (and liquid investments) can also have a lower value than the value of the actual individual investments for U.S. multinational companies as of the end of 2017 because they have to pay income tax on those unrepatriated earnings (as discussed above). To give you a sense of the magnitude of the unrepatriated earnings, in 2015, 286 U.S. companies in the Fortune 500 disclosed such investments subject to repatriation tax had a value of $2.1 trillion,[8] which was around 10% of the market capitalization of the entire Fortune 500, approximately $19 trillion at that time. The top ten companies with the largest such investments had $800 billion of such investments (40% of the total subject to repatriation tax), and the top 10% of the companies had $1.4 trillion of such investments (65% of the total). Not all companies face repatriation taxes. Many countries have what is referred to as territorial tax regimes which means they only tax the domestic earnings of their multinational companies (see Chapter 17 for more detail). The U.S. is moving to largely a territorial tax regime starting in 2018, but as mentioned, U.S. multinationals will have to pay a transitional tax on the earnings earned through 2017 that have not been repatriated.

Valuation Key 4.5

Companies require some amount of cash or securities that can be converted into cash to operate their businesses, called required cash. Some companies, however, hold more cash (and liquid investments to which we will refer to all as cash) than they need to operate the company, called excess cash. When we analyze a company, measure its free cash flows, or use one or more valuation methods to value the company, we treat cash required to operate the business as a required investment—essentially the economic equivalent to purchasing inventory—and we treat excess cash as an asset not required to operate the business, and extract it from the analysis and valuation of the company's operations.

[8] See McIntyre, R. S., R. Phillips, and P. Baxandall, Offshore Shell Games 2015, "The Use of Offshore Tax Havens by Fortune 500 Companies," available on May 31, 2018 at https://uspirg.org/sites/pirg/files/reports/USP%20ShellGames%20Oct15%201.3.pdf.

Valuation in Practice 4.3

Integra LifeSciences Holdings Corporation's (Integra) Acquisition Strategy and Its Required Cash Balance At the end of 2000, Integra had a cash (and equivalent) balance of about $15.2 million, and its revenues for that year were $71.6 million. By the end of 2003, Integra's cash balance increased by more than 13 times to $206.7 million, and its revenues grew by about 2.6 times to $185.6 million. Why the large increase in cash relative to revenues? During this period, Integra adopted a strategy of growth by acquisitions. Consequently, it began to build up a large cash balance, enabling the company to take advantage of potential acquisition opportunities as they became available. In its annual filing with the U.S. SEC, Integra stated:

> Our goal is to become a global leader in the development, manufacturing and marketing of medical devices, implants and biomaterials in the neurosurgery, reconstructive surgery and general surgery markets. Key elements of our strategy include ... expanding our product portfolio and market reach through additional acquisitions . . .
>
> We have achieved this growth in our overall business through the development and introduction of new products, the development of our distribution channels and acquisitions.
>
> We regularly evaluate potential acquisition candidates in this market and in other specialty medical technology markets characterized by high margins, fragmented competition and focused target customers.

Thus, for Integra, its cash holdings in excess of its required cash balance for its existing businesses were not an excess asset, for Integra managers thought they needed the additional cash and financial flexibility to implement their acquisition growth strategy, which turned out to be quite successful. Management felt that it would not have been cost effective for Integra to distribute these funds and have to raise capital shortly afterward to fund acquisitions given the transactions costs of raising capital. One way to address the valuation of this cash and acquisition growth strategy is to separate the cash not needed to operate the company from the financial model and then assess the value of Integra's growth strategy through acquisition, given the reduced financing costs it would bear.

Source: See Integra's 2004 10-K Report.

4.9 FORECASTING INCOME TAX RATES AND PAYMENTS

LO5 Forecast income tax rates and payments

The discounted cash flow valuation models use free cash flows that reflect expected income tax payments, not income tax expense (provision for income taxes), and require an estimate of the marginal tax rate for interest, T_{INT} (either to measure the weighted average cost of capital or interest tax shields or both). Thus, a financial model requires adjustments to the accounting income tax expense (provision for income taxes) to measure the effects of expected income tax payments. Also, as part of the calculation of income taxes on EBIT (in the free cash flow schedule), we estimate the company's interest tax shield, which we often base on the marginal tax rate for interest to adjust the cash taxes paid. We forecast a company's income tax rates—an average tax rate to apply to the company's taxable income and a marginal tax rate to measure interest tax shields—based on an analysis of its historical income tax and income tax rate information disclosed in the footnotes to its financial statements.

Forecasting the Average Tax Rate and Adjustments to Forecast Income Taxes Paid

As we discuss in Chapter 3, we forecast the average tax rate, which we will apply to the company's income, by analyzing a company's income tax reconciliation schedule (the schedule that reconciles the statutory federal income tax rate to the company's effective income tax rate; see Section 3.6 and Exhibit 3.17), its breakdown of its provision for income taxes into current, deferred, foreign (and sometimes state and local income taxes), and its deferred tax schedule (see Exhibit 3.16). This analysis includes an assessment of the effect of a company's deferred income taxes on its provision for income taxes, an assessment of which of the company's historical income tax rate adjustments will continue into the future, as well as an analysis of the expected profitability of the company in the financial model.

A common approach to estimating a company's average tax rate is to ignore the difference between book and tax income if the income tax effect of deferred taxes on the company's provision for income taxes is small. Another common approach is to estimate a company's average tax rate by first adjusting its pre-tax income for permanent differences between book and tax income (based on the income tax footnote), and then measure the company's income tax rate based on its current income taxes (ignore the deferred income tax portion of the company's provision for income taxes). Both of these approaches directly estimate the company's income tax payments and not its accounting income tax expense (provision for income taxes). A potential shortcoming of this approach is that the financial model does not provide forecasts of the company's income tax expense and net income, and the difference will be large if the difference between tax and book income is large.

When a company has large differences between its tax and book income, it may be more useful to forecast the company's income tax expense and deferred income tax assets and liabilities and then adjust its income tax expense for the effect of deferred income taxes. This analysis includes an assessment of the effect of a company's deferred income taxes on its provision for income taxes and an assessment of which of the company's historical income tax rate adjustments will continue into the future. The potential shortcoming of this approach is the complexity that it can create in a financial model even if we only model the issues for which book and tax differences are large (for example, book and tax depreciation are often significantly different from each other). This is the more common approach when the company has large differences between book and taxable income.

Forecasting the Marginal Tax Rate for Interest, T_{INT}

As we learned from Chapter 3, a company's average or effective tax rate can differ from its marginal tax rate. The first step in estimating the marginal tax rate for interest is to analyze which of the company's historical income tax rate adjustments in the tax reconciliation schedule apply to interest deductions and will continue into the future. The next step is to analyze the expected profitability of the company forecasts in the financial model. A common assumption is that for a company expected to generate positive taxable income, the statutory federal tax rate (plus the marginal state and local tax rates) may be reasonable to use as the marginal tax rate for interest in a financial model. However, in some circumstances the statutory tax rate may differ markedly from the long-run marginal tax rate for interest.

In Exhibit 4.13, we show the distribution of the estimated marginal federal tax rate before interest deductions (based on the 35% statutory federal tax rate) for a sample of over 12,000 observations for fiscal years ending in 2011 and 2012. The estimated marginal tax rate before interest deductions is based on the published work of Blouin, Core, and Guay (2010)[9] and is available from the Wharton Research Database Services (WRDS).[10] The estimated marginal tax rate before interest deductions is a present value weighted average tax rate for a company considering its past and expected taxable income before interest deductions, so it is not exactly the same tax rate we use in a financial model but should be more similar to the long-term marginal tax rate we might use. Regardless, it provides some useful information about the marginal tax rate to use to forecast interest tax shields in a financial model (note that the study does not embed information about state and local taxes in its assessment of marginal tax rates).

Panel A of the exhibit reports the distribution of the marginal federal tax rate. The median marginal tax rate is 32%, which is close to but less than the then 35% statutory federal rate. About 25% of the companies have a marginal tax rate less than 13% (less than 40% of the 35% statutory federal tax rate) and about 25% of the companies have a marginal tax rate of at least 34% (close to the 35% statutory federal tax rate). Panel B reports the median effective and marginal tax rates for five groups (quintiles) based on pre-tax profit margin (pre-tax income to revenue). This analysis shows that the median marginal tax rates increase as the profitability of the companies increase, with the exception of the highest profit margin group, and that the marginal tax rate is close to the 35% statutory federal tax rate for profitable companies (the top three groups). This analysis also shows that the marginal tax rate is larger than the effective tax rate for all groups. What is clear is that for many firms, utilizing the top 35% statutory tax rate for either the average

[9] Blouin, Jennifer, John Core, and Wayne Guay, "Have the Tax Benefits of Debt Been Overestimated?" *Journal of Financial Economics* vol 98, no. 3 (November 2010), pp. 195–213.

[10] Available on May 31, 2018 for subscribers at https://wrds-web.wharton.upenn.edu/wrds/query_forms/navigation.cfm?navId=95.

or marginal tax rate would overstate the tax rate. Of course, this analysis is based on data from when the U.S. statutory tax rate was 35%, which has now changed to 21% beginning in 2018. The punchline of the study however, has not changed. We do not want to apply the top statutory tax rate as the marginal federal rate for all companies.

EXHIBIT 4.13 Marginal Tax Rate Before Interest Deductions from Blouin, Core, and Guay (2010)

Panel A: Distribution of Marginal Tax Rate Before Interest Deductions

Percentile	Marginal Tax Rate Before Interest Deductions
1st	0.0%
10th	5.5%
25th	13.0%
50th	31.7%
75th	34.3%
90th	35.0%
99th	35.0%
Average	24.7%

Panel B: Median Pre-Tax Profit Margin and Tax Rates by Pre-Tax Profit Margin Quintiles

Pre-Tax Profit Margin Quintile (−2 Lowest, + 2 Highest)	Median Pre-Tax Profit Margin	Median Effective Tax Rate	Median Marginal Tax Rate Before Interest Deductions
−2	−63.5%	0.0%	9.6%
−1	−0.5%	10.0%	29.5%
0	5.9%	32.6%	33.6%
1	13.4%	32.7%	34.0%
2	30.1%	18.0%	32.4%

4.10 MORE DETAILED FORECASTS OF REVENUES AND CAPITAL EXPENDITURES

LO6 Forecast revenues and capital expenditures at a more detailed level

Naturally, forecasting revenues is an important part of most financial models, for as we have seen, revenue forecasts typically drive many of the other forecasts in a financial model. For example, cost of goods sold and selling, general, and administrative expenses are typically driven, at least in part, by revenue forecasts. The same can be said of the company's operating assets (accounts receivable and inventory) and operating liabilities (accounts payable and other accruals).

In a financial model, we sometimes use a simple growth rate, g, to forecast revenues—for example, $\text{revenue}_t = (1 + g) \times \text{revenue}_{t-1}$, in much the same way we did in the Starbucks example. The magnitude of this growth rate, however, is the result of either an implicit or an explicit forecast of macroeconomic factors, industry factors, and company-specific factors that eventually forecast the company's market share (quantity or volume) and prices. In this section, we show how to disaggregate a simple growth rate into its quantity and price components. We also provide an example of a more detailed revenue forecast and discuss capital expenditure forecasts and how they can be related to revenue forecasts. Many models build up a forecast by division, segment, or geographic area.

The Price and Quantity Components of the Revenue Growth Rate

Simply stated, revenue is equal to price multiplied by volume; thus, a revenue growth rate is the result of a growth in volume, a change in price, or both. Disaggregating the revenue growth into its components and other drivers can be helpful in understanding the factors that drive a company's value (value drivers). We can disaggregate the revenue growth rate into its price change ($\Delta p/p = g_p$) and quantity (or volume) change ($\Delta q/q = g_q$) growth rate components.

Assume a company has revenue of $1,000 in Year 0 and $1,476 in Year 1. Its revenue growth rate is 47.6% (0.476 = $1,476/$1,000 − 1). We cannot disaggregate this growth rate unless we know either the number of units sold in each period (q_0 and q_1) or the price at which the units were sold in each period

(p_0 and p_1). Assume that in Year 0, this company sold 1,000 units of output at $1 per unit, and in Year 1, the company sold 1,200 units at $1.23 per unit. The growth rate for the change in price, g_p, is 23% (0.23 = $1.23/$1.00 − 1), and its growth rate for quantity, g_q, is 20% (0.2 = 1,200/1,000 − 1). The company's growth rate for revenues, $g_{rev, total}$, is equal to $(1 + g_p) \times (1 + g_q) - 1$, which in this example is 47.6% (0.476 = 1.23 × 1.2 − 1). Another way to think about the company's growth in revenues is that it is equal to the percentage change in price (price growth rate) of 23% in this example plus its quantity growth rate of 20% adjusted for (multiplied by) 1 plus the percentage change in price.

$$g_{rev, total} = \frac{\Delta p}{p_o} + \left(1 + \frac{\Delta p}{p_o}\right) \times \frac{\Delta q}{q_o} = g_p + (1 + g_p) \times g_q = 0.23 + 1.23 \times 0.20 = 0.23 + 0.246 = 0.476$$

Adjusting Growth Rates for Inflation

We can disaggregate the previous growth formula further to adjust for inflation. To adjust total revenues for the effects of inflation, we first divide revenues by 1 plus the inflation rate, 1 + i, for the period in order to measure the effect of inflation on revenues. Assuming inflation was 2.5% in the previous example, what are the inflation-adjusted (or real) growth rates for revenue and price? We can calculate the real growth rate for revenues by dividing (1 plus) the growth rate for revenues by (1 plus) the inflation rate.

$$g_{rev, real} = \frac{1 + g_{rev, total}}{1 + i} - 1 = \frac{1.476}{1.025} - 1 = 0.44$$

Alternatively, we can calculate the real (inflation-adjusted) change in price and use our original formula to measure real growth in revenues:

$$g_{p, real} = \frac{1 + g_p}{1 + i} - 1 = \frac{1.23}{1.025} - 1 = 0.20$$

$$g_{rev, real} = g_{p, real} + (1 + g_{p, real}) \times g_q = 0.20 + 1.20 \times 0.20 = 0.20 + 0.24 = 0.44$$

Potential Forecast Drivers for Revenues and Capital Expenditures

We use price and volume to forecast revenues in industries that produce a clearly identifiable quantity of products sold with clearly identifiable prices. For example, in the auto industry, we might use the number of cars and the average price per car in order to measure revenue, or we might disaggregate our revenue forecast by brand or by class of car within a brand if the prices and product mixes vary within our forecast period. In other industries, we may use capacity and capacity utilization as measures of volume and use the average price (revenue)—per unit of capacity available or capacity utilized—as a measure of price. For example, for companies in heavy manufacturing industries (such as, steel and paper), the measure used for capacity is the maximum number of tons output (production). In turn, capacity utilization is the actual number of tons of output divided by the maximum number of tons of capacity, and the average revenue per unit of capacity utilized is the average price per ton. The airline industry also uses capacity and capacity utilization to forecast revenues. Capacity is available seat miles and capacity utilization is load factor (percentage of seats occupied); the price is revenue per seat mile (where seat miles is available seat miles × load factor).

For most companies in the retail industry (for example, GAP), we would likely use either number of stores (capacity) in conjunction with average revenue per store (revenue per unit of capacity) or the number of square feet of retail space (capacity) in conjunction with average revenue (price) per square foot of retail space (revenue per unit of capacity). To better understand the driver of growth in a retail chain, we might further disaggregate a measure such as average revenue per square foot of retail space into average number of transactions (number of purchases) per square foot (which we could use to measure capacity and capacity utilization) and average revenue (price) per transaction. We might also inflation adjust the revenue per unit of capacity numbers to understand whether prices are increasing in real terms or whether revenue per transaction or per square foot is rising solely due to inflation. Forecasts in the retail industry are often separated into two components—increases in "same store" or "comparable store" sales (what is the increase in sales expected for stores open for a sufficiently long period of time to attain long-run operating performance) and sales related to new locations. Sometimes, forecasts are adjusted by the number of days available—for example, a store that opens or closes during the year. In addition, some retailers adjust their forecasts for the number of days and weekends between the Thanksgiving and Christmas holidays (which varies across years). They do this to take into account the critically important holiday shopping season that generally occurs between these two holidays. In addition, many retailers use fiscal year-ends that cause the number of weeks per year to vary between 52 and 53. Further, for retailers with a significant online presence, we would have to model their online sales.

Valuation in Practice 4.4

Companies Sometimes Provide Forecasts About Capacity—The Gap, Inc. (GAP) Below is a quote from GAP's 10-K filing with the U.S. SEC. It provides an example of the type of information that we can sometimes glean from a company's financial reports on its value drivers and short-term forecasts.

> . . . Our real estate strategy in fiscal 2005 includes plans to open about 175 new stores, weighted more toward Old Navy. We have announced the launch of a new brand targeted at women over the age of 35 and the expansion of Banana Republic into Japan. . . . We also plan to close about 135 stores in 2005, mainly from Gap brand in North America . . . These growth initiatives and moves will negatively impact operating expenses in fiscal 2005, but will position us to take advantage of future opportunities.
>
> In 2005, we expect earnings per share to grow to $1.41 to $1.45 per share on a fully diluted basis. . . . We expect operating margin to be about 13% and we also expect to generate at least $1 billion in free cash flow.

Note that although GAP plans to increase the number of stores it operates by 40, it plans to build 175 new stores and close 135 stores; thus, we would forecast capital expenditures for 175 new stores and not for 40 net new stores. However, GAP did not continue to open more new stores than it closed. While it varied over the years, in 2009, GAP closed 101 stores and opened only 47, and in 2010 it closed 98 stores and opened only 71. In 2015, the company closed 202 stores and opened about the same number, 197. As we discuss in Chapter 9, in 2016, three of the major credit rating agencies downgraded Gap's credit ratings from BBB− to BB+.

Source: Gap, Inc. 2004, 2010, and 2015 10-K Reports with the U.S. SEC.

Naturally, some industries have similar forecast drivers to other industries. The restaurant industry, for example, has revenue forecast drivers that are similar to those we typically use in the retail industry. As for capacity and capacity utilization, we can use a variety of measures depending on the information available on the company. For example, we might use the number of restaurants, the number of tables served, the number of checks (a restaurant's invoices) issued, or the number of seats. For price, we would use average revenue (price) per unit of capacity; for example, if we used the number of checks as a measure of utilized capacity, we would use the average revenue per check.

Potential Forecast Drivers for Capital Expenditures (and Property, Plant, and Equipment)

We typically, but not always, forecast revenues before we forecast capital expenditures. We base our capital expenditure forecasts on the productive capacity required to support the revenue forecasts. We can classify capital expenditures into various categories; for example, increasing the company's productive capacity; maintaining existing productive capacity—in other words, replacing worn out, expired, or inefficient assets; replacing or enhancing the operating infrastructure of the company (for example, purchasing information technology for ordering materials or scheduling production and distribution); and replacing or expanding the company's administrative offices and equipment (overhead).

When forecasting capital expenditures, we attempt to measure each type of capital expenditure. Using publicly available information, we sometimes forecast all types of capital expenditures together and sometimes we have sufficient information that allows us to analyze the different types of capital expenditures individually.

Valuation in Practice 4.5

Long-Term Company Provided Forecasts (Guidance)—Goldcorp Inc. and Encana Corp. Most companies do not disclose long-term forecasts. A common exception is when a company is being acquired and management discloses long-term (usually five years) forecasts of the company's performance (see Chapters 15 and 16). Another exception is companies with long-term planning cycles. Two examples of such companies are Goldcorp Inc. and Encana Corp.

Goldcorp, a Canadian company, mines and produces gold from a portfolio of mines. Encana, a U.S. company, is a leading North American energy producer focused on producing natural gas, oil and natural gas liquids. Both companies have long planning horizons and, in 2017, provided detailed short-term and less detailed longer-term (five-year) forecasts.

Goldcorp Five-Year Guidance	2017	2018	2019	2020	2021
Gold production (millions oz)	2.5	2.5	2.7	3.0	3.0
All-in sustaining cost ($/oz)	$850	$800	$750	$700	$700
Capital expenditure (in millions $)					
Sustaining	$700	$650	$650	$650	$650
Growth	$600	$400	$150	$250	$100
Sustaining and growth	$1,300	$1,050	$800	$900	$750

Source: Goldcorp January 17, 2017 Guidance available on June 28, 2018 at https://s22.q4cdn.com/653477107/files/doc_downloads/guidance/2017/Goldcorp-Guidance-Jan-2017.pdf.

Encana Five-Year Guidance*	2017	2018	2019	2020	2021
Production (thousand barrels of oil equivalent/day)	340.0	400.0	440.0	550.0	640.0
Capital (in billions $)	$1.1	$1.8	$1.9	$2.4	$2.8
Cash flow (in billions $)	$1.3	$2.0	$2.8	$3.5	$4.2

* Authors' estimate from published chart

Source: Encana Corp May 2017 Guidance available on May 31, 2017 at https://www.encana.com/pdf/investors/presentations-events/corporate-presentation.pdf.

Many companies make productive capacity decisions based on either short- or mid-term revenue forecasts or growth strategies. Short-term decision frameworks like these do not typically work for companies in capital-intensive industries, as it can take these companies years to add productive capacity, and often the incremental change in productive capacity is large (the minimum amount is the amount produced by an efficiently sized plant). Companies operating in these industries must develop long-term industry demand forecasts in order to decide when to add additional productive capacity.

Revenue forecasts often drive capital expenditures as in the above example; a company determines what its revenues (volume and price) are likely to be—perhaps based on forecasts of industry demand and market share—and then adds productive capacity to be able to deliver the forecasted demand. In other cases, capital expenditures are at least a partial driver of forecasted revenues. For example, managers of retail and restaurant chains often consider how many new locations they can open in a given year, and those forecasts of store openings partially drive both capital expenditures and revenues for that period.

Illustration of a More Detailed Revenue Forecast

In this section, we use Darden Restaurants Inc. (Darden) to illustrate how to forecast revenues using a more detailed approach. Darden owns and operates several different chains of casual dining restaurants in the U.S. and Canada under various names. In Darden's case, some of the restaurant chains it operates are mature and growing slowly, while others are new concepts with higher growth potential. Thus, it may be useful to forecast revenues separately for Darden's different restaurant concepts, as they are growing at substantially different rates. In our illustration, we focus on forecasting just one of its restaurant concepts—Olive Garden—using both information provided in Darden's financial statements and our own estimates.

To forecast revenues, given that Darden's Olive Garden restaurants are of similar size, we multiply the number of Olive Garden restaurants by the expected revenue per restaurant. Darden discloses much of this information in its financial statements for the last two years, and we estimate some of the required information to generate the forecasts. We show the revenue forecasts in Exhibit 4.14. In this model, the revenue growth rate is a function of the growth rate in revenue per restaurant—which is a function of price and the volume of food and beverages sold—and the growth rate for the number of restaurants. We first forecast the number of restaurants by forecasting the number of restaurants that will open and the number that will close (see Valuation in Practice 4.4 for an example of such management forecasts). We then multiply the revenue generated per restaurant (for the year we are forecasting) by the number of restaurants open as of the end of the previous year. This calculation makes the simplifying assumption that all restaurants open and close on the last day of the year. Moreover, this assumes that new restaurants do not need to mature over several years before they are operating at normal capacity utilization. To forecast revenues in Year 1, the first year of our forecast, we multiply 561 restaurants (as of the end of Year 0) by average revenue per restaurant of $4.640 million in order to forecast revenues of $2,603 million.

In this illustration, the revenue growth rate for Olive Garden decreases from 8.4% to 6.9% even though the revenue generated per restaurant grows by 5% each year. This decrease results from a decrease in the number of new restaurants opened and an increase in the number of restaurants closed, resulting in a decrease in the growth rate of the number of restaurants open each year (the growth rate in number of restaurants goes from 3.2% down to 1.3%). Since Olive Garden restaurants are roughly the same size, we use average revenue per restaurant in our forecast. If the restaurants varied in size (number of seats), one refinement to consider is forecasting revenues as the number of seats multiplied by revenue generated per seat. An alternative approach for projecting revenues is to forecast the number of invoices or bills multiplied by the average revenue per invoice. Another modeling technique that we sometimes use is modeling the growth in revenue per restaurant as a function of real growth in revenue per restaurant and inflation.

EXHIBIT 4.14 Darden Restaurants Inc.—Olive Garden Revenue Forecasts

	Actual	Forecast				
Olive Garden	**Year 0**	**Year 1**	**Year 2**	**Year 3**	**Year 4**	**Year 5**
Beginning number of restaurants	542	561	579	596	610	621
New restaurants	24	24	24	22	20	18
Closed restaurants	–5	–6	–7	–8	–9	–10
Ending number of restaurants	561	579	596	610	621	629
Growth rate in number of stores		3.2%	2.9%	2.3%	1.8%	1.3%
Sales per restaurant—previous year (× $1,000)		$4,419	$4,640	$4,872	$5,116	$5,372
Growth in revenue per restaurant		5.0%	5.0%	5.0%	5.0%	5.0%
Sales per restaurant—current year (× $1,000)		$4,640	$4,872	$5,116	$5,372	$5,640
Total revenue (× $1,000,000)		$2,603	$2,821	$3,049	$3,277	$3,503
Revenue growth rate			**8.4%**	**8.1%**	**7.5%**	**6.9%**

Illustration of More Detailed Capital Expenditure and Depreciation Forecasts

In this section, we again use Darden to illustrate how to forecast capital expenditures and depreciation using a more detailed approach. We first forecast capital expenditures, which we show in Exhibit 4.15. From the previous exhibit, we have a forecast of the number of restaurants Darden will open each year. We multiply this number by the cost per restaurant for land, buildings, and equipment (which Darden discloses in its 10-K report) in order to measure capital expenditures for new restaurants. For Year 1, we measure capital expenditures for new restaurants by multiplying the 24 new restaurants in Year 1 by the cost of constructing a new restaurant of $3.8 million in order to calculate total capital expenditures for new restaurants of $91.2 million. In subsequent years, we increase capital expenditures for land, building, and equipment per restaurant using a 2.5% inflation rate.

EXHIBIT 4.15 Darden Restaurants Inc. Capital Expenditure Forecasts

	Actual	Forecast				
	Year 0	**Year 1**	**Year 2**	**Year 3**	**Year 4**	**Year 5**
Olive Garden—Capital Expenditures for New Restaurants						
Per restaurant—land (× $1,000)	$ 488	$ 500	$ 513	$ 525	$ 538	$ 552
Per restaurant—buildings (× $1,000)	2,244	2,300	2,358	2,416	2,477	2,539
Per restaurant—equipment (× $1,000)	976	1,000	1,025	1,051	1,077	1,104
Per restaurant—total (× $1,000)	$ 3,707	$ 3,800	$ 3,895	$ 3,992	$ 4,092	$ 4,194
Capital expenditures—land (× $1,000)	$ 11,707	$ 12,000	$ 12,300	$ 11,557	$ 10,769	$ 9,934
Capital expenditures—buildings (× $1,000)	53,854	55,200	56,580	53,162	49,537	45,698
Capital expenditures—equipment (× $1,000)	23,415	24,000	24,600	23,114	21,538	19,869
Capital expenditures—total (× $1,000)	$ 88,976	$ 91,200	$ 93,480	$ 87,832	$ 81,844	$ 75,501
Olive Garden—Capital Expenditures for Existing Restaurants						
Beginning number of restaurants	542	561	579	596	610	621
Closed restaurants	–5	–6	–7	–8	–9	–10
Number of existing restaurants	537	555	572	588	601	611
Per restaurant—buildings (× $1,000)	$ 107	$ 110	$ 113	$ 116	$ 118	$ 121
Per restaurant—equipment (× $1,000)	49	50	51	53	54	55
Per restaurant—total (× $1,000)	$ 156	$ 160	$ 164	$ 168	$ 172	$ 177
Capital expenditures—buildings (× $1,000)	$ 57,629	$ 61,050	$ 64,493	$ 67,954	$ 71,193	$ 74,187
Capital expenditures—equipment (× $1,000)	26,195	27,750	29,315	30,888	32,361	33,721
Capital expenditures—total (× $1,000)	$ 83,824	$ 88,800	$ 93,808	$ 98,843	$103,554	$107,909
Olive Garden—Total Capital Expenditures for Restaurants						
Capital expenditures—land (× $1,000)	$ 11,707	$ 12,000	$ 12,300	$ 11,557	$ 10,769	$ 9,934
Capital expenditures—buildings (× $1,000)	111,483	116,250	121,073	121,116	120,730	119,885
Capital expenditures—equipment (× $1,000)	49,610	51,750	53,915	54,002	53,898	53,590
Capital expenditures—total (× $1,000)	$172,800	$180,000	$187,288	$186,675	$185,397	$183,410
Capital expenditure growth rate		4.2%	4.0%	–0.3%	–0.7%	–1.1%

Exhibit may contain small rounding errors

In addition to capital expenditures for new restaurants, we also measure capital expenditures for existing restaurants. In this illustration, we do this by multiplying the number of existing restaurants (beginning number of restaurants minus the number closed) by an average capital expenditure per existing restaurant. Naturally, Darden does not arrive at its capital expenditures in this way, but if this relation is stable, such an approach is possible to use and is the best estimate based on publicly available information. For Year 1, we measure capital expenditures for existing restaurants by multiplying the 555 existing restaurants (555 = 561 − 6) by the capital expenditures per existing restaurant of $160 thousand in order to calculate a total capital expenditures for existing restaurants figure of $88.8 million. A more detailed analysis might have relied on the age of the restaurants to project the amount spent each year on refurbishing particular restaurant locations.

Capital expenditures for existing restaurants are growing each year based on an increase in capital expenditures per restaurant due to inflation and an increase in the number of existing restaurants; however, capital expenditures for new restaurants decrease during the period because the number of new restaurants decreases during the period.

Note that the revenue growth rate in Exhibit 4.14 is larger than the capital expenditure growth rate in Exhibit 4.15 for all years. Further, the growth rate for capital expenditures decreases and eventually becomes negative in Year 3. Recall that for Darden, revenues are growing because of either an increase in revenues per restaurant (growing at 5% each year), an increase in the number of restaurants, or both. Growth due to an increase in revenues per restaurant is not likely related to capital expenditures based on what we can learn from publicly available information. Rather, it could be the result of increases in price or utilization, which are potentially unrelated to capital expenditures. Thus, having different growth rates for capital expenditures and revenues is feasible in this situation.

In Exhibit 4.16, we present depreciation schedules and a schedule for property, plant, and equipment. We present two depreciation schedules—one for buildings and one for equipment. The acquisition cost of

EXHIBIT 4.16 Darden Restaurants Inc. Depreciation Forecasts and Property, Plant, and Equipment Schedules

($ in thousands)			Forecast				
Buildings	**Depr Years**	**Initial Bal**	**Year 1**	**Year 2**	**Year 3**	**Year 4**	**Year 5**
Existing buildings	12.0	$ 813,474	$ 67,790	$ 67,790	$ 67,790	$ 67,790	$ 67,790
New buildings year 1	20.0	$ 116,250		5,813	5,813	5,813	5,813
New buildings year 2	20.0	121,073			6,054	6,054	6,054
New buildings year 3	20.0	121,116				6,056	6,056
New buildings year 4	20.0	120,730					6,037
Total buildings—depreciation			$ 67,790	$ 73,602	$ 79,656	$ 85,711	$ 91,748

			Forecast				
Equipment	**Depr Years**	**Initial Bal**	**Year 1**	**Year 2**	**Year 3**	**Year 4**	**Year 5**
Existing equipment	4.0	$ 365,460	91,365	91,365	91,365	91,365	
New equipment year 1	8.0	51,750		6,469	6,469	6,469	6,469
New equipment year 2	8.0	53,915			6,739	6,739	6,739
New equipment year 3	8.0	54,002				6,750	6,750
New equipment year 4	8.0	53,898					6,737
Total equipment—depreciation			$ 91,365	$ 97,834	$ 104,573	$ 111,323	$ 26,696
Total depreciation			**$ 159,154**	**$ 171,436**	**$ 184,229**	**$ 197,035**	**$ 118,444**

	Actual	Forecast				
	Year 0	**Year 1**	**Year 2**	**Year 3**	**Year 4**	**Year 5**
Property, Plant, and Equipment—Cost						
Beginning balance	$1,257,554	$1,415,873	$1,578,062	$1,744,051	$1,905,775	$2,062,401
Capital expenditures	172,800	180,000	187,288	186,675	185,397	183,410
Retirements and dispositions	−14,481	−17,811	−21,299	−24,951	−28,771	−32,767
Ending balance	$1,415,873	$1,578,062	$1,744,051	$1,905,775	$2,062,401	$2,213,044
Property, Plant, and Equipment—Accumulated Depreciation						
Beginning balance	$ 548,072	$ 585,879	$ 734,956	$ 894,341	$1,064,453	$1,245,209
Depreciation expense	46,000	159,154	171,436	184,229	197,035	118,444
Retirements and dispositions	−8,193	−10,077	−12,051	−14,117	−16,278	−18,539
Ending balance	$ 585,879	$ 734,956	$ 894,341	$1,064,453	$1,245,209	$1,345,113
Net property, plant, and equipment	$ 829,994	$ 843,106	$ 849,710	$ 841,322	$ 817,192	$ 867,930

Exhibit may contain small rounding errors

the buildings as of the end of Year 0 is $813.5 million, and the buildings have an average life of 12 years; concurrently, newly constructed and renovated buildings have an average life of 20 years. Depreciation for existing buildings is equal to $813.5 million divided by 12 years of remaining life, or $67.8 million. In this illustration, depreciation begins the year after construction and is equal to capital expenditures (for a new building) divided by 20 years. For example, depreciation in Year 2 for buildings constructed in Year 1 (which includes improvement to existing buildings) is equal to capital expenditures in Year 1 of $116.25 million divided by 20 years, which is equal to $5.8 million. We perform the same calculation to measure depreciation for equipment. Notice, however, that for existing equipment as of the end of Year 0 (assumed to have a four-year remaining life), we stop the depreciation after the end of Year 4.

At the bottom of this exhibit, we present the property, plant, and equipment schedule, which includes schedules for gross property, plant, and equipment and accumulated depreciation. These schedules have the same basic format—beginning balance plus increases minus decreases is equal to the ending balance. The increases are either capital expenditures or depreciation. The decreases result from the retirement or disposition of assets—for example, the closing of a restaurant. Retirements and dispositions are based on the number of closed restaurants and an estimate of the original acquisition cost per restaurant, assuming that the average closed restaurant is 10 years old and that construction costs increased by 2.5% per year (the assumed inflation rate). We assume that the buildings of the closed restaurants are half depreciated since they have a twenty-year life and that the equipment is fully depreciated since it has an eight-year life.

SUMMARY AND KEY CONCEPTS

In this chapter, we discussed the process used to create a financial model, which can involve many different types of analyses and decisions, as well as a multitude of calculations. We discussed the flow and structure of financial models and the identification of forecast drivers (assumptions) used in our formulas to forecast each item in the financial statements and supporting schedules. We discussed ways to assess the reasonableness of a financial model and ways by which to embed the company's capital structure strategy into the model. We also extended our discussion to an examination of topics such as excess cash, forecasting tax rates, scenario analysis, sensitivity analysis, and simulations. In addition, we discussed the creation of detailed revenue, capital expenditure, and depreciation schedules.

ADDITIONAL READING AND REFERENCES

Minton, B., and C. Schrand, "The Impact of Cash Flow Volatility on Discretionary Investment and the Costs of Debt and Equity Financing," *Journal of Financial Economics* 54 (1999), pp. 423–460.
Verrecchia, R., "Essays on Disclosure," *Journal of Accounting and Economics* 32 (2001), pp. 97–180.

EXERCISES AND PROBLEMS

P4.1 **Revenue Growth Rate Components Missing Data:** Calculate the number for each of the missing parts to this problem.

	$Quantity_{t-1}$	$Price_{t-1}$	Total $Revenue_{t-1}$	$Quantity_t$	$Price_t$	Total $Revenue_t$	$g_{quantity}$	g_{price}	$g_{Rev, Total}$
a.	10,000	$10.00	?–1	11,000	?–2	?–3	?–4	20.00%	?–5
b.	?–1	?–2	$750,000	60,000	?–3	?–4	20.00%	10.00%	?–5
c.	10,000	?–1	?–2	?–3	$13.80	$151,800	?–4	?–5	26.50%
d.	5,000	?–1	?–2	?–3	$11.00	?–4	5.00%	?–5	15.50%
e.	?–1	?–2	?–3	7,350	?–4	$ 72,000	5.00%	20.00%	?–5

P4.2 **Revenue Growth Rate Components with Inflation Missing Data:** Calculate the number for each of the missing parts to this problem.

	$Quantity_{t-1}$	$Price_{t-1}$	Total $Revenue_{t-1}$	$Quantity_t$	$Price_t$	Total $Revenue_t$	$g_{quantity}$	g_{price}	$g_{Rev, Total}$	Inflation rate	$g_{price, real}$	Revenue from Inflation	$Price_t$ with no Inflation
a.	10,000	?–1	?–2	?–3	$ 1.26	$13,230	?–4	?–5	28.0%	5.0%	?–6	?–7	$ 1.20
b.	5,000	?–1	?–2	?–3	$11.00	?–4	20.0%	?–5	38.6%	5.0%	?–6	?–7	$10.48
c.	?–1	$5.00	?–2	5,500	?–3	?–4	10.0%	23.0%	?–5	2.5%	?–6	$825	?–7
d.	?–1	?–2	$5,000	800	?–3	?–4	20.0%	17.0%	?–5	4.0%	?–6	$270	?–7
e.	?–1	?–2	?–3	1,800	?–4	$ 3,600	5.0%	14.4%	?–5	4.0%	?–6	?–7	$ 1.92

P4.3 **Revenue Growth Rate Components:** Respond to the following questions, assuming each part of the problem is independent of the other parts.

a. Company A has an expected revenue growth rate of 20%, and Company B has an expected revenue growth rate of 10%. Company A has an expected **increase** in its selling prices of 12%, and Company B has an expected **increase** in its selling prices of 10%. Which company has the higher expected increase in volume?

b. Company A has an expected revenue growth rate of 20%, and Company B has an expected revenue growth rate of 10%. Company A has an expected **increase** in its selling prices of 12%, and Company B has an expected **decrease** in its selling prices of –5%. Which company has the higher expected increase in volume?

c. Company A has an expected revenue growth rate of 15%, and Company B has an expected revenue growth rate of 12%. Company A has an expected **increase** in the number of units sold equal to 10%, and Company B has an expected **increase** in the number of units sold equal to 5%. Which company has the higher expected price change?

d. Company A has an expected revenue growth rate of 15%, and Company B has an expected revenue growth rate of 12%. Company A has an expected **decrease** in the number of units sold equal to –10%, and Company B has an expected **decrease** in the number of units sold equal to –5%. Which company has the higher expected price change?

e. Company A has an expected revenue growth rate of –10%, and Company B has an expected revenue growth rate of –5%. Company A has an expected **increase** in the number of units sold equal to 5%, and Company B has an expected **increase** in the number of units sold equal to 10%. Which company has the higher expected price change?

P4.4 **Financial Model (All Equity Financed)—Bob Wardrop Company:** Forecast drivers, financial statements, certain supporting schedules, and other information for the Bob Wardrop Company appear in Review Exercise 4.1. Forecast the financial statements and supporting schedules, including a free cash flow schedule, for Year 2 through Year 4. Note: Year 1 is illustrated in Review Exercises 4.1 to 4.3.

P4.5 **Financial Model (with Debt)—Bob Wardrop Company:** Use the information on the Bob Wardrop Company from the previous problem except for the information on the company's capital structure. For the company's capital structure, assume the company will issue debt to fund all of the financing needs it cannot fund with internally generated cash flow, and assume that its cost of debt is 10%. The company will pay down all of its debt before it begins to pay any dividends; then, it will distribute all positive equity free cash flows to common equityholders. Using the above information, forecast the financial statements and supporting schedules, including a free cash flow schedule for Year 3 and Year 4. Note: Year 1 and Year 2 are illustrated in Review Exercise 4.4.

P4.6 **Financial Model (Debt Held Constant)—Bruce Rigel Company:** The Year 0 financial statements and supporting schedules for the Bruce Rigel Company appear in Exhibit P4.1. Forecast the financial statements and supporting schedules, including a free cash flow schedule, for Year 1 through Year 4. Use the following assumptions and the information in the exhibit as the basis of your forecasts.

a. **Revenue**—The company expects its revenues to grow 25% in Year +1, 30% in Year +2, 20% in Year +3, 10% in Year +4, and 2% thereafter. Expected inflation is 2% per year for the entire forecast horizon. The company expects its selling prices will grow at the expected inflation rate and inflation is already taken into consideration in the projected revenue growth rates.

b. **Cost of Goods Sold**—The company expects its cost of goods sold expense ratio to be 45% in all years.

c. **Depreciation**—The company depreciates its property, plant, and equipment over 20 years. None of the company's property, plant, and equipment will be retired or sold during the five-year forecast period.

d. **Income Taxes**—The company has a 40% effective income tax rate that represents the average income tax rate the company will use to measure its provision for income taxes (income tax expense). The company's marginal tax rate for interest is equal to 45%.

e. **Cash**—The company expects its required cash balance to equal 5% of current year revenues during the entire forecast period. The company does not expect to accumulate any excess cash.

f. **Days to Collect Accounts Receivable**—The company expects to increase its days to collect accounts receivable to 50 days in Year +1 and to 60 days thereafter as a way to extend additional credit to its customers, which is needed to achieve its expected revenue growth (this driver is based on year-end receivables, not average receivables).

g. **Days to Sell Inventory (Inventory Held)**—The company expects to increase its days to sell inventory to 60 days during the forecast period, which is needed to achieve its expected revenue growth (this driver is based on year-end inventory, not average inventory).

h. **Days to Pay Accounts Payable**—The company expects to increase its days to pay its accounts payable to 50 days in all years in the forecast period (this driver is based on year-end payables, not average payables).

i. **Capital Expenditures**—The company must invest $2.5 for each $1 of revenue increase expected in the following year due to volume increases (in other words, revenue increases that result from price increases do not require capital expenditures). Hint: Reread the revenue assumption for this problem.

j. **Capital Structure**—The company will not change its debt financing from its balance in Year 0, and the interest rate on the debt remains at 8% for all years in the forecast period. Current common equityholders will make any necessary investments in the company. Similarly, the company plans to distribute all positive equity free cash flows to its common equityholders in the form of dividends.

EXHIBIT P4.1 The Bruce Rigel Company

Income Statement and Balance Sheet ($ in thousands)	Year 0
Income Statement	
Revenue (Rev)	$20,000
Cost of goods sold (CGS)	−10,200
Depreciation expense	−1,875
Earnings before interest and taxes	$ 7,925
Interest expense	
Income before taxes	$ 7,925
Income tax expense	−3,170
Net income	$ 4,755
Balance Sheet	
Cash	$ 1,800
Accounts receivable	2,192
Inventory	1,397
Total current assets	$ 5,389
Property, plant, and equipment (net)	41,275
Total assets	$46,664
Accounts payable	$ 1,324
Debt	6,000
Total liabilities	$ 7,324
Capital stock	$ 2,000
Retained earnings	37,340
Shareholders' equity	$39,340
Liabilities and shareholders' equity	$46,664

Plant and Equipment (PPEQ) Schedule ($ in thousands)	Year 0
Beginning PPEQ—gross	$37,500
Capital expenditures	11,275
Ending PPEQ—gross	$48,775
Beginning accumulated depreciation	$ 5,625
Depreciation expense	1,875
Ending accumulated depreciation	$ 7,500
Net property, plant and equipment	$41,275

Statement of Retained Earnings ($ in thousands)	Year 0
Retained earnings—beginning of year	$32,952
Net income	4,755
Common equity dividends	−367
Retained earnings—end of year	$37,340

Cash Flow Statement ($ in thousands)	Year 0
Cash flows from operations	
Net income	$ 4,755
+ Depreciation expense	1,875
− Change in accounts receivable	−789
− Change in inventory	−182
+ Change in accounts payable	33
Cash flow from operations	$ 5,692
Investing activities	
− Capital expenditures	−$11,275
Financing activities	
+ Change in debt financing	$ 6,000
+ Change in common equity financing	0
− Common equity dividends paid	−367
Cash flows from financing activities	$ 5,633
Change in cash balance	$ 50

P4.7 **Financial Model (with Varying Debt)—Bruce Rigel Company:** Use all of the information on the B. Rigel Company that appears in the previous problem except for the information on the company's capital structure, including its dividend policy. Instead, use the following information on the company's capital structure strategy and dividend policy. The company knows that its planned capital expenditures over the next few years will require the company to raise additional capital. The company plans to raise all additional capital using debt financing. The company would like to keep its debt level as low as possible; however, the company would like its dividends to grow at least by 10% per year subsequent to the Year 0 dividends, even if the company must borrow additional debt to pay its dividends. The company believes that its interest rate will be 8% if its debt level is less than $10,000 and 9%, if it is between $10,000 and $25,000. Forecast the financial statements and supporting schedules, including a free cash flow schedule, for Year 1 through Year 4.

P4.8 **Financial Model (Capital Structure Based on Maintaining a Debt Rating)—Bruce Rigel Company:** Use all of the information on the B. Rigel Company that appears in Problem 4.6 except for the information on the company's capital structure, including its dividend policy. Instead, use the following information on the company's capital structure strategy and dividend policy. The company knows that its planned capital expenditures over the next few years will require the company to raise additional capital. Although the company would like to maintain an "AAA" credit rating, it is willing to decrease its debt rating for a few years in order to finance its growth. The company will finance all negative free cash flows before changes in financing by refinancing its debt with new debt. The amount of debt and the interest rate for this debt depend on the company's debt rating, which is determined by the interest coverage ratios in the following schedule. Use forecasted EBIT in year t divided by interest expense in year t + 1 (based on the debt outstanding at the end of year t) to determine the rating.

	Credit Rating				
	AAA	AA	A	BBB	BB
Interest rate for credit rating class	8.0%	8.5%	9.0%	9.5%	10.0%
Minimum coverage ratio for credit rating class	22.0	10.0	6.0	4.0	2.0

Once the company begins generating positive free cash flows before changes in financing, the company plans to use them to repay its debt until it regains its AAA credit rating. Once the company regains its AAA credit rating, it plans to maintain that credit rating and distribute all positive equity free cash flows to its equityholders. Forecast the financial statements and supporting schedules, including a free cash flow schedule, for Year 1 through Year 4.

P4.9 **Assessing the Forecasts (Capital Structure Based on Maintaining a Debt Rating—Must complete P4.8 before attempting this problem)—Bruce Rigel Company:** Assess the reasonableness of the forecasts created in P4.8 using the time-series of various financial ratios.

SOLUTIONS FOR REVIEW EXERCISES

Solution for Review Exercise 4.1: Forecasts for Bob Wardrop Company—Part 1

B. WARDROP COMPANY Income Statements ($ in thousands)	Actual Year 0	Forecast Year +1
Income Statement		
Revenue	$1,000	$1,400
Cost of goods sold.	–600	–840
Depreciation expense.	–167	–234
Earnings before interest and taxes.	$ 233	$ 326
Interest expense.		0
Income before taxes.	$ 233	$ 326
Income tax expense.	–70	–98
Net income.	$ 163	$ 228

Solution for Review Exercise 4.2: Forecasts for Bob Wardrop Company—Part 2

B. WARDROP COMPANY
Income Statements and Balance Sheets

($ in thousands)	Actual Year 0	Forecast Year +1
Income Statement		
Revenue	$1,000	$1,400
Cost of goods sold	−600	−840
Depreciation expense	−167	−234
Earnings before interest and taxes	$ 233	$ 326
Interest expense		0
Income before taxes	$ 233	$ 326
Income tax expense	−70	−98
Net Income	$ 163	$ 228
Balance Sheet		
Cash	$ 100	$ 140
Accounts receivable	200	280
Total current assets	$ 300	$ 420
Property, plant, and equipment (net)	1,837	2,303
Total assets	$2,137	$2,723
Debt	$ 0	$ 0
Capital stock	100	458
Retained earnings	2,037	2,265
Liabilities and shareholders' equity	$2,137	$2,723

B. WARDROP COMPANY
Statement of Retained Earnings

($ in thousands)	Actual Year 0	Forecast Year +1
Retained earnings—beginning of year	$1,873	$2,037
Net income	163	228
Common equity dividends	0	0
Retained earnings—end of year	$2,037	$2,265

B. WARDROP COMPANY
Income Tax Schedule

($ in thousands)	Actual Year 0	Forecast Year +1
Earnings before income taxes	$ 233	$ 326
Income tax rate	30.0%	30.0%
Income tax expense	$ 70	$ 98

B. WARDROP COMPANY
Plant and Equipment (PPEQ) Schedule

($ in thousands)	Actual Year 0	Forecast Year +1
Beginning PPEQ—gross	$1,667	$2,337
Capital expenditures	670	700
Ending PPEQ—gross	$2,337	$3,037
Beginning accumulated depreciation	$ 333	$ 500
Depreciation expense	167	234
Ending accumulated depreciation	$ 500	$ 734
Net property, plant and equipment	$1,837	$2,303

Exhibit may contain small rounding error

Note: Review Exercise 4.2 asked you to complete only the asset side of the balance sheet. You cannot complete the liability and shareholder's equity side of the Balance Sheet or the Statement of Retained Earnings before completing Review Exercise 4.3. For convenience, we show both the statement of retained earnings and liability and stockholders' equity side of the balance sheet (partial solution to Review Exercise 4.3) here.

Solution for Review Exercise 4.3: Forecasts for Bob Wardrop Company—Part 3

B. WARDROP COMPANY Cash Flow Statement ($ in thousands)	Actual Year 0	Forecast Year +1
Cash flows from operations		
Net income	$163	$228
+ Depreciation expense	167	234
− Change in accounts receivable	−20	−80
Cash flow from operations	$310	$382
Investing activities		
− Capital expenditures	−$670	−$700
Financing activities		
+ Change in debt financing	$ 0	$ 0
+ Change in common equity financing	0	358
− Common equity dividends paid	0	0
Cash flows from financing activities	$ 0	$358
Change in cash balance	−$360	$ 40

B. WARDROP COMPANY Free Cash Flow and Equity Free Cash Flow ($ in thousands)	Actual Year 0	Forecast Year +1
Earnings before interest and taxes	$233	$326
− Income taxes paid on EBIT	−70	−98
Earnings before interest and after taxes	$163	$228
+ Depreciation expense	167	234
− Change in accounts receivable	−20	−80
Unlevered operating cash flow	$310	$382
− Change in required cash balance	−50	−40
− Capital expenditures	−670	−700
Unlevered free cash flow	−$410	−$358
− Interest paid in cash	0	0
+ Interest tax shield	0	0
Cash flow before changes in financing	−$410	−$358
+ Change in debt financing	0	0
Equity free cash flow	−$410	−$358
+ Change in common equity financing	0	358
− Common dividends	0	0
+ Change in required cash balance	50	40
Change in cash balance	−$360	$ 40

Note: See the solution to Review Exercise 4.2 for the Statement of Retained Earnings and the Liability and Stockholders' Equity side of the Balance Sheet.

Solution for Review Exercise 4.4: Forecasts for Bob Wardrop Company—Part 4

B. WARDROP COMPANY
Income Statement

($ in thousands)	Year 0	Forecast Year +1	Forecast Year +2
Revenue	$1,000	$1,400	$1,820
Cost of goods sold	−600	−840	−1,092
Depreciation expense	−167	−234	−304
Earnings before interest and taxes	$ 233	$ 326	$ 424
Interest expense		0	−36
Income before taxes	$ 233	$ 326	$ 389
Income tax expense	−70	−98	−117
Net income	$ 163	$ 228	$ 272

B. WARDROP COMPANY
Income Tax Schedule

($ in thousands)	Year 0	Forecast Year +1	Forecast Year +2
Earnings before income taxes	$ 233	$ 326	$ 389
Income tax rate	30.0%	30.0%	30.0%
Income tax expense	$ 70	$ 98	$ 117

B. WARDROP COMPANY
Balance Sheet

($ in thousands)	Year 0	Forecast Year +1	Forecast Year +2
Cash	$ 100	$ 140	$ 182
Accounts receivable	200	280	364
Total current assets	$ 300	$ 420	$ 546
Property, plant, and equipment (net)	1,837	2,303	2,609
Total assets	$2,137	$2,723	$3,155
Debt		$ 358	$ 518
Capital stock	$ 100	100	100
Retained earnings	2,037	2,265	2,537
Liabilities and shareholders' equity	$2,137	$2,723	$3,155

B. WARDROP COMPANY
Plant and Equipment (PPEQ) Schedule

($ in thousands)	Year 0	Forecast Year +1	Forecast Year +2
Beginning PPEQ—gross	$1,667	$2,337	$3,037
Capital expenditures	670	700	610
Ending PPEQ—gross	$2,337	$3,037	$3,647
Beginning accumulated depreciation	$ 333	$ 500	$ 734
Depreciation expense	167	234	304
Ending accumulated depreciation	$ 500	$ 734	$1,037
Net property, plant and equipment	$1,837	$2,303	$2,609

B. WARDROP COMPANY
Cash Flow Statement

($ in thousands)	Year 0	Forecast Year +1	Forecast Year +2
Cash flows from operations			
Net income	$163	$228	$272
+ Depreciation expense	167	234	304
− Change in accounts receivable	−20	−80	−84
Cash flow from operations	$310	$382	$492
Investing activities			
− Capital expenditures	−$670	−$700	−$610
Financing activities			
+ Change in debt financing	$ 0	$358	$160
+ Change in common equity financing	0	0	0
− Common equity dividends paid	0	0	0
Cash flows from financing activities	$ 0	$358	$160
Change in cash balance	−$360	$ 40	$ 42

B. WARDROP COMPANY
Free Cash Flow and Equity Free Cash Flow

($ in thousands)	Year 0	Forecast Year +1	Forecast Year +2
Earnings before interest and taxes	$233	$326	$424
− Income taxes paid on EBIT	−70	−98	−131
Earnings before interest and after taxes	$163	$228	$293
+ Depreciation expense	167	234	304
− Change in accounts receivable	−20	−80	−84
Unlevered operating cash flow	$310	$382	$513
− Change in required cash balance	−50	−40	−42
− Capital expenditures	−670	−700	−610
Unlevered free cash flow	−$410	−$358	−$139
− Interest paid in cash	0	0	− 36
+ Interest tax shield	0	0	14
Cash flow before changes in financing	−$410	−$358	−$160
+ Change in debt financing	0	358	160
Equity free cash flow	−$410	$ 0	$ 0
+ Change in common equity financing	0	0	0
− Common dividends	0	0	0
+ Change in required cash balance	50	40	42
Change in cash balance	−$360	$ 40	$ 42

B. WARDROP COMPANY
Statement of Retained Earnings

($ in thousands)	Actual Year 0	Forecast Year +1	Forecast Year +2
Retained earnings—beginning of year	$1,873	$2,037	$2,265
Net income	163	228	272
Common equity dividends	0	0	0
Retained earnings—end of year	$2,037	$2,265	$2,537

Exhibit may contain small rounding error

After mastering the material in this chapter, you will be able to:

1. Adjust the value of the firm and its equity for the value created from financing (5.1)
2. Measure firm and equity value using the adjusted present value and weighted average cost of capital valuation models (5.2–5.3)
3. Measure value using the equity free cash flow and dividend valuation models (5.4–5.5)
4. Understand how to measure expected cash flows and risk-adjusted discount rates (5.6)

The Adjusted Present Value and Weighted Average Cost of Capital Discounted Cash Flow Valuation Methods

CHAPTER 5

EMERGING COMMUNICATIONS INC.

Emerging Communications' valuation using discounted cash flow valuation models—Emerging Communication Inc. (EmCom) owned various subsidiaries whose businesses provided local telephone service, sold and leased telecommunications equipment, and provided cellular telephone service in the U.S. Virgin Islands. EmCom's Chairman and CEO, who already owned a majority of the company's shares, began to acquire EmCom's remaining shares in order to take the company private. The CEO arranged various types of debt financing for the transaction. In order to negotiate a deal price with the CEO, EmCom's board of directors created a special committee drawn from EmCom's Board of Directors. The special committee negotiated a $10.25 price per share. EmCom's Board approved the $10.25 bid and EmCom gave notice to its shareholders of a special meeting to vote on the sale. EmCom's shareholders approved the transaction.[1] According to Delaware law—the state in which the company was incorporated—shareholders not wishing to participate in the transaction can exercise their appraisal rights by petitioning the court to assess the fair value of their stock. Some of EmCom's minority shareholders opted to exercise their appraisal rights under Delaware law. The court concluded that the fair value of EmCom's shares was $38.05 per share ($27.80 per share higher than the deal price) based on a weighted average cost of capital valuation method. According to Bloomberg, Emerging Communications went out of business in 2012 through a Chapter 11 liquidation filing under bankruptcy.

In this chapter, we explore the intricacies of the weighted average cost of capital and adjusted present value discounted cash flow valuation methods and demonstrate how the two methods relate to each other and result in identical valuations if implemented consistently.

[1] See Emerging Communications Inc. Proxy Statement, filed with the Securities and Exchange Commission (SEC) on September 28, 1998.

CHAPTER ORGANIZATION

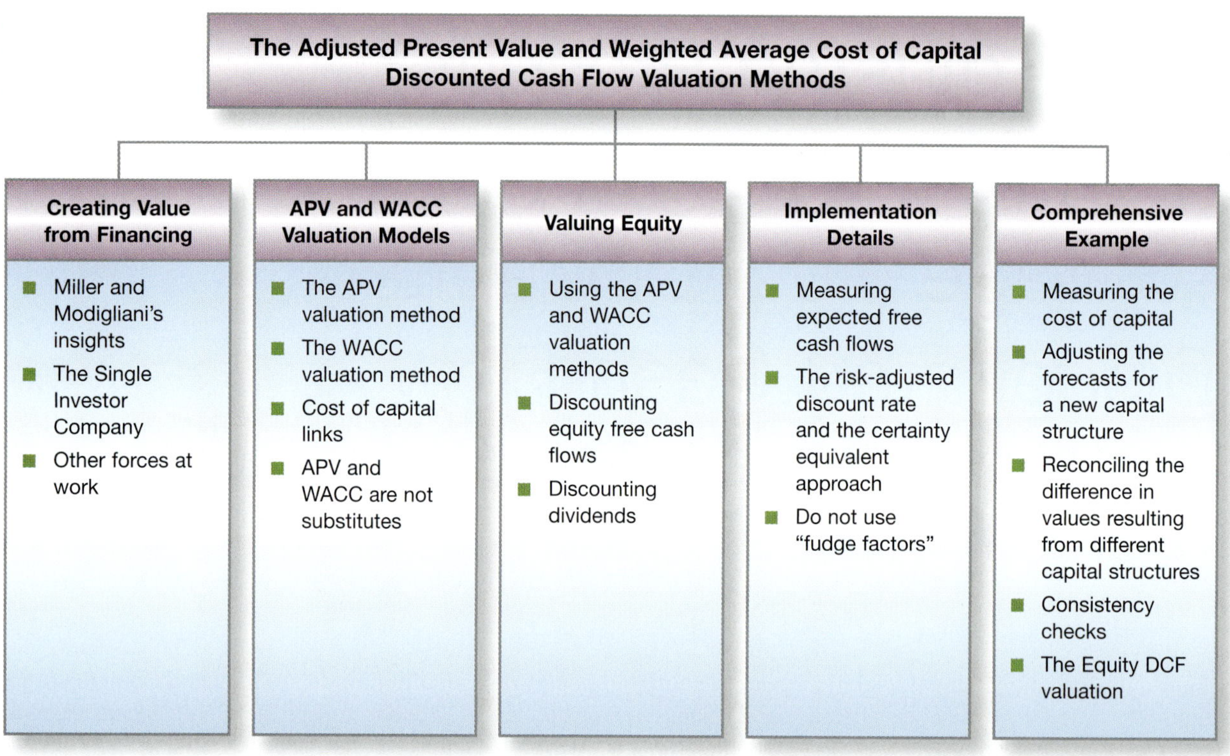

INTRODUCTION

In Chapter 1, we introduced the discounted cash flow (DCF) valuation model. We also discussed that the way a company finances itself may affect the value of the firm, and that the value created from financing is an asset on a company's economic balance sheet. This asset is not a physical asset, but an asset created by the company by financing itself in a particular way that reduced its after-tax cost of capital below the cost of capital required by investors to invest in that security.

We use one of two forms of the DCF valuation model to value the company (measure the value of the firm), which includes any value from financing—the **adjusted present value method (APV)** or the **weighted average cost of capital method (WACC)**. The difference between these two methods is the way in which the methods incorporate the value created from financing. The APV method incorporates the benefit directly by discounting the expected tax benefits from financing. The WACC method incorporates this benefit indirectly through an adjustment to the discount rate; for this reason, the WACC method is also called the **adjusted cost of capital valuation method**. The APV and WACC methods are generally *not* substitutes because the best method to use depends on the context of the valuation, in particular the capital structure strategy of the company.

We begin this chapter with a discussion of how the tax deductibility of interest can create value. We then discuss the APV and WACC valuation methods. We then illustrate how to use these methods and how they relate to each other. We discuss measuring the value of a company's common equity by subtracting the value of the company's non-common equity claims from the value of the firm. We also discuss DCF valuation methods that measure the value of a company's equity directly—the equity discounted cash flow (Equity DCF) method and the dividend discounted cash flow valuation method (Dividend DCF). Finally, in this chapter, we assume the company does not have any excess assets. If the company has excess assets, we would value the company without the excess assets and add the value of the excess assets to the DCF valuation (see Chapter 4).

5.1 CREATING VALUE FROM FINANCING

LO1 Adjust the value of the firm and its equity for the value created from financing

Debt financing can create value for the firm because of the tax deductibility of interest at the corporate level. In the U.S., and in many other tax jurisdictions, interest paid to debtholders is generally tax deductible at the corporate level (potentially subject to some limitations as discussed in Chapter 3), and payments to equityholders (dividends) are not. A company that issues debt and has tax-deductible interest will generally have more cash flows to distribute to its investors (debt and equityholders combined) than a company that does not issue debt. The government essentially subsidizes the cash flow paid to debtholders (interest) because it is tax deductible, unlike the flows (for example, dividends) paid to equityholders. We refer to the incremental cash flows arising from the tax savings from interest as **interest tax shields (ITS)**, and we call the potential value created by the interest tax shields the **value of interest tax shields (V_{ITS})**. The value of interest tax shields is a component of the value created by financing (V_{FIN}), and in most valuations, the value from financing is equal to the value of the interest tax shields net of any countervailing costs.

Insights from Miller and Modigliani and Others

The framework for understanding the effect of a company's capital structure decisions on its value comes from the research of Miller and Modigliani (M&M).[2] M&M established the framework for analyzing how interest tax shields create value and how capital structure decisions affect the relationships among a company's costs of capital. M&M based their initial work in this area on various assumptions. We list some of these assumptions below.

- No one capital market participant (investor or company) sets security prices; everyone is a **price taker**.
- Everyone can transact without incurring any transaction costs (no transaction costs entails no fees for transacting, no costs of processing information, and no direct cost for transferring assets to debtholders in bankruptcy).
- No one can earn **arbitrage profits**.
- Investors and companies borrow and lend at the same rate.
- All capital market participants have the same information and knowledge (no asymmetric information) and investors and companies can write perfect, enforceable contracts that eliminate all agency costs (agency costs between the owner and manager and agency costs between the owners/manager and debtholders).
- Neither investors nor companies pay income taxes.

M&M showed that, if all of their assumptions were correct, capital structure decisions would not affect the value of the firm; in other words, capital structure decisions would be irrelevant as long as the firm did not change its investment decisions because of the change in the capital structure. M&M demonstrated that if this result was not true, investors could buy the mispriced company and personally borrow or lend in order to create an investment that would earn arbitrage profits. They showed that an investor could always buy the equity of an unlevered company by borrowing money to recreate a levered company's financial leverage; thus, both the unlevered company and levered company would have the same value. To explain this concept in a non-academic setting, Professor Miller used a joke attributed to the famous baseball player Yogi Berra: "You better cut the pizza in four pieces because I'm not hungry enough to eat six." Professor Miller would then explain that like Yogi Berra's pizza, no matter how you sliced up the claims on a company's assets (in other words, no matter how many different types of securities a company issued and no matter what capital structure it adopted), its size (value) would not change as long as the company held the investments it made constant.

M&M also showed that a levered firm's equity cost of capital—that is a firm with non-common equity claims such as debt or preferred stock in its capital structure—would be higher (more risky) than that of an unlevered firm. The equity is more risky because the debtholders and preferred holders are paid a fixed amount each period (interest payments or preferred dividends) and their claims have priority (are paid first) over the claims of the common equityholders. M&M showed that the equity cost of capital is equal to the company's unlevered cost of capital, plus a premium for the company's financial leverage

[2] See the following research on this topic: Modigliani, F., and M. H. Miller, "The Cost of Capital, Corporate Finance and the Theory of Investment," *American Economic Review* 48 (1958), pp. 261–297; Modigliani, F., and M. H. Miller, "Corporate Income Taxes and the Cost of Capital: A Correction," *American Economic Review* 53 (June 1963), pp. 433–443; Modigliani, F., and M. H. Miller, "Some Estimates of the Cost of Capital to the Electric Utility Industry, 1954–1957," *American Economic Review* 56 (June 1966), pp. 333–391.

(non-common equity claims). Although M&M based their work on assumptions that are not reflective of the real world, their capital structure irrelevance proposition provides an anchor for our thinking about capital structure decisions and how they could affect the value of the firm.

In their subsequent research, M&M assumed that companies paid income taxes and that interest expense was tax deductible while dividends were not, which roughly mirrored the tax code in the U.S. and many other countries at the time and to this day. They kept all other assumptions the same, including their assumption of no personal income taxes. M&M showed that the tax deductibility of interest reduced the income taxes paid by a company and thus provided more cash flow to the company's investors (debt and equity combined). This, in turn, increased the cash flows the company could pay to its investors (by the amount of the interest tax shields) and decreased the company's overall after-tax cost of capital (weighted average cost of capital). The effect of the interest tax shields was that they decreased a company's corporate taxes and increased the value of the firm because of the additional payouts to the company's investors that were possible.

M&M's research suggests that companies should use as much debt as possible to maximize the value of the firm if there were no limitations on the tax deductibility of interest; however, we know companies do not adopt such a capital structure, even when there are no limitations on the deductibility of interest. Subsequent research identified potential reasons why companies would not maximize their financial leverage, which we call countervailing forces.[3] Some researchers have extended M&M's work by making the original assumptions more robust. For example, M&M assumed that all companies had the same risk and that debt was risk-free, but subsequent research showed that neither is necessary for M&M's results to hold. Other researchers extended M&M's work to companies that refinanced their debt both annually and continuously, and to companies that were not zero-growth perpetuities. Finally, other researchers, including Miller himself, have added additional factors to consider, such as personal income taxes, signaling, agency costs, and financial distress and bankruptcy costs, all of which may mitigate the benefits of financial leverage. First, we illustrate how the tax deductibility of interest can create value, and then we will return to discuss the potential countervailing forces.

The Single Investor Company

To illustrate the value created from financing, we use a simple example of a sole owner deciding whether to finance a company with all equity, with equity and debt when interest is not tax deductible, and with equity and debt when interest is tax deductible. Our company is the Single Investor Company, which has a single investor and manager, regardless of whether equity or equity and debt are issued. We use an example with one investor to avoid any agency costs (costly conflicts between investors or between owners and managers). The Single Investor Company is a startup company that requires $50,000 of financing. All of the company's transactions are in cash, and it does not require other investments in the future other than the initial capital. The company expects to generate earnings before interest and taxes (EBIT) of $10,000 in perpetuity. The company has a 40% income tax rate on all income.

The manager-owner is considering whether to finance the company with $50,000 of equity financing or with $30,000 of equity financing and $20,000 of perpetual debt financing with a 10% interest rate. In either case, the manager-owner is investing $50,000. The manager-owner will select the capital structure that results in a higher firm value. We analyze two income tax cases (regimes). In both cases, the income

[3] For example, Shackelford, D., and T. Shevlin, "Empirical Tax Research in Accounting," *Journal of Accounting and Economics*, 31 (2001), pp. 321–387; and Graham, J. R., "Taxes and Corporate Finance: A Review," Working Paper (July 2001), Fuqua School of Business, Duke University, Durham NC 27708-0120; Hamada, R. S., "Portfolio Analysis, Market Equilibrium, and Corporation Finance," *Journal of Finance* (March 1969), pp. 13–31; Hamada, R. S., "The Effect of the Firm's Capital Structure on the Systematic Risk of Common Stocks," *Journal of Finance* (May 1972), pp. 435–452; Rubinstein, M. E., "A Mean-Variance Synthesis of Corporate Financial Theory," *Journal of Financial and Quantitative Analysis* (March 1973), pp. 167–181; Stiglitz, J. E., "A Re-Examination of the Modigliani-Miller Theorem," *American Economic Review* (December 1969), pp. 187–193; Stiglitz, J. E., "On the Irrelevance of Corporate Financial Policy," *American Economic Review* (December 1974), pp. 851–866; Rubinstein, M. E., "A Mean-Variance Synthesis of Corporate Financial Theory," *Journal of Financial and Quantitative Analysis* (March 1973), pp. 167–181; Conine, T. E., "Corporate Debt and Corporate Taxes: An Extension," *Journal of Finance* (September 1980), pp. 1033–1037; Miles, J. A., and J. R. Ezzell, "The Weighted Average Cost of Capital, Perfect Capital Markets, and Project Life: A Clarification," *Journal of Financial and Quantitative Analysis* vol. 15, no. 3 (1980), pp. 719–730; Miles, J. A., and J. R. Ezzell, "Reformulating Tax Shield Valuation: A Note," *Journal of Finance* vol. 40 (1985), pp. 1485–1492; and Harris, R. S., and J. J. Pringle, "Risk-Adjusted Discount Rates—Extensions from the Average Risk Case," *Journal of Financial Research* vol. 8, no. 3 (1985), pp. 237–244.

tax rate is 40%, but in the first case, interest and dividends are not tax deductible to the company, and in the second case, interest is tax deductible but dividends are not.

In Exhibit 5.1, we examine the effect of using all equity financing and some equity and some debt financing when interest is not tax deductible. The two financing alternatives have identical **revenues**, operating expenses, and **earnings before interest and taxes (EBIT)**. Since interest is not tax deductible, income taxes are also the same, as is the total cash flow generated by the company to distribute to its investor. Here, the only effect of issuing debt is that some of the company's total cash flows are paid to the debtholder (the single investor) in the form of interest. Since the cash flow the company generates for all investors is unchanged, the risk of the cash flows is also unchanged, thus the value of the firm does not change and the equityholder (the single investor) is not better off by issuing debt.

EXHIBIT 5.1 Single Investor Company's Initial Investment, Income Statement, and Cash Flows When Interest Is Not Tax Deductible

SINGLE INVESTOR COMPANY Income Statement Forecast	All Equity	Interest Not Deductible
Initial Investment		
Debt (10% interest rate)	$ 0	$20,000
Equity	50,000	30,000
Total investment	$50,000	$50,000
Income Statement (All Items Are Cash)		
Revenue	$50,000	$50,000
Operating expenses	−40,000	−40,000
Earnings before interest and taxes (EBIT)	$10,000	$10,000
Tax deductible interest	0	0
Earnings before tax	$10,000	$10,000
Income taxes (40%)	−4,000	−4,000
Earnings before non-tax deductible interest	$ 6,000	$ 6,000
Non-tax deductible interest	0	-2,000
Earnings to equityholders	$ 6,000	$ 4,000
Cash flow to debtholders (interest)	0	2,000
Total cash flow to all investors	$ 6,000	$ 6,000
Return on equity	12.0%	13.3%
Return on total investment	12.0%	12.0%

Another lens through which to see this result is comparing the single investor's rate of return with and without debt financing. If the company only uses equity financing, the single investor earns a return on total investment of 12% at the expected EBIT of $10,000. If the company issues debt, the single investor continues to earn a 12% return on total investment at the expected EBIT of $10,000, even though the cost of debt is 10%. The single investor earns 10% on the debt and a higher return on equity, but the return on total investment is still equal to the 12%. Thus, no value is created. Since the total cash flows paid to all investors do not increase after adding debt to the capital structure (when interest is not tax deductible), the single investor will not be better off.

Although issuing debt when interest is not tax deductible does not change either the total cash flows to all investors or the return on total investment, it does make the equity more risky. The risk of the equity increases because the debtholders have first claim on the company's assets and the equityholders have a claim on the residual that remains after satisfying the debtholders' claims. We see this effect on the return on equity. If the equity is made more risky when debt is issued, then the expected return on equity should increase. Although the earnings to equityholders at the expected EBIT of $10,000 are smaller when the company issues debt ($4,000 versus $6,000), the initial equity investment is also smaller ($30,000 versus $50,000) such that the expected return on equity is larger. In the all-equity case, the expected return on equity is 12%, but in the debt and equity financed case, the expected return on equity is 13.33%. As we said before, however, the single investor still holds a portfolio with an expected return of 12% (40% of the portfolio is debt yielding 10%, and 60% of the portfolio is equity returning 13.33%).

We can see that the equity becomes more risky by comparing the return on equity with and without debt to different levels of EBIT. For example, if EBIT turns out to be $5,000 instead of the expected EBIT of $10,000, then the return on equity decreases more in the case with debt and equity financing (ROE for all equity financing decreases from 12% to 6% versus ROE for debt and equity financing decreases from 13.33% to 3.3%). Conversely, if EBIT turns out to be $15,000 instead of the expected EBIT of $10,000, then the return on equity increases more in the case with debt and equity financing (ROE for all equity increases from 12% to 18% versus ROE for debt and equity financing increases from 13.33% to 23.3%).

The higher expected return on equity reflects the fact that the equity is made more risky when we add debt to the capital structure, but it has not made the single investor better off. Why? When interest is not tax deductible, adding debt to the capital structure does not increase the total cash flow to the single investor (debt and equity investors combined), nor does it increase the total return on the single investor's portfolio of debt and equity.

Our conclusions change when a company's interest is tax deductible. In Exhibit 5.2, we show the Single Investor Company's initial investment and income statement for the two financing alternatives (all equity and debt and equity) and for the two income tax regimes (interest is not tax deductible and interest is tax deductible). An income tax regime in which interest is tax deductible has the effect of increasing the earnings to equityholders by $800 ($800 = $4,800 − $4,000) relative to the income tax regime in which interest is not tax deductible. Likewise, the total payoff paid to all investors increases by $800 and the rate of return on the total investment increases from 12% to 13.6%. The $800 increase in total cash flow to all investors goes to the equityholders ($4,800 − $4,000), for both the amount of debt and the interest rate are fixed in both income tax regimes. Thus, equityholders are better off with the debt and equity alternative when interest is tax deductible even after adjusting the valuation for the additional risk of the equity with debt financing.

We can also see the same effect by examining the return on equity. Notice how the return on equity has increased relative to the case in which interest is not deductible. Since the promised payments to debtholders do not change when moving to the case where interest is deductible, the return on equity

EXHIBIT 5.2 Single Investor Company's Initial Investment, Income Statement, and Cash Flows When Interest Is Tax Deductible

SINGLE INVESTOR COMPANY
Income Statement Forecast

	All Equity	Interest Not Deductible	Interest Deductible
Initial Investment			
Debt (10% interest rate)	$ 0	$20,000	$20,000
Equity	50,000	30,000	30,000
Total investment	$50,000	$50,000	$50,000
Income Statement (All Items Are Cash)			
Revenue	$50,000	$50,000	$50,000
Operating expenses	−40,000	−40,000	−40,000
Earnings before interest and taxes (EBIT)	$10,000	$10,000	$10,000
Tax deductible interest	0	0	−2,000
Earnings before tax	$10,000	$10,000	$ 8,000
Income taxes (40%)	−4,000	−4,000	−3,200
Earnings before non-tax deductible interest	$ 6,000	$ 6,000	$ 4,800
Non-tax deductible interest	0	−2,000	0
Earnings to equityholders	$ 6,000	$ 4,000	$ 4,800
Cash flow to debtholders (interest)	0	2,000	2,000
Total cash flow to all investors	$ 6,000	$ 6,000	$ 6,800
Return on equity	12.0%	13.3%	16.0%
Return on total investment	12.0%	12.0%	13.6%

increases to 16% when interest is tax deductible. Indeed, the return on the single investor's portfolio will increase from 12% (12% = \$6,000/\$50,000) to 13.6% (13.6% = \$6,800/\$50,000). The single investor now holds a portfolio composed of 40% debt that yields 10% and 60% equity with a return of 16% ($0.136 = 0.4 \times 0.1 + 0.6 \times 0.16$).

For every \$1 of tax-deductible interest, income tax expense decreases by \$1 multiplied by the company's **income tax rate applicable to interest expense (T_{INT})**. The government, in essence, subsidizes the cash flow paid to debtholders (interest) because the cash flow is tax deductible relative to the flows paid to equityholders. In a straightforward valuation context, this subsidy, called an **interest tax shield (ITS)**, is equal to the income tax rate applicable to the interest deduction, multiplied by the **interest expense deducted (INT)**.

$$ITS = T_{INT} \times INT$$

As we discussed in Chapter 3, a company's average and marginal tax rates can differ from the income tax rate for interest tax shields, T_{INT}, for a variety of reasons that include progressive income tax rates, net operating loss carryforwards, non-deductible interest, and alternative minimum tax calculations (a company might have to pay a minimum amount of income tax based on income items unrelated to interest). In valuing a company, the value of the interest tax shields is, not surprisingly, the discounted value of the expected interest tax shields for the company based on its capital structure strategy. If the Single Investor Company expected to never retire the \$20,000 in debt it had issued nor issue additional debt, the value of the interest tax shields would be \$800 per year in perpetuity discounted at an appropriate risk-adjusted discount rate, a topic we discuss in more detail later in the chapter.

Subsidized Financing. Another way a company can create value from financing is by securing financing with a subsidized (lower than market rate) cost of capital. In general, investors do not knowingly give such subsidies to a for-profit company, but a government might. For example, a government, such as a state or municipal government, might provide subsidized debt financing to provide an incentive for a company to build a plant or office building within its jurisdiction.

Countervailing Forces

For a company with just one investor, the choice appears to be clear. The company should issue as much debt as possible. By issuing debt, the investor converts payments that he or she might receive in the form of dividends to interest and the company can deduct those payments on its tax return reducing the company's income taxes. It is not surprising, then, that governments restrict the owners of small companies from implementing the strategy of having the owners make loans to the company instead of making equity investments. Governments generally do not allow a company to deduct interest expense attributable to loans from its owners, or they will at least restrict the amount that can be deducted. For companies with a large number of diverse owners, these same restrictions do not apply.

The fact that we do not observe companies, even those with a large number of diverse owners, maximizing the amount of debt suggests that countervailing forces must offset some, or perhaps all, of the value created by interest tax shields. These countervailing forces include the transactions cost of enforcing bond covenants, the cost of financial distress, the cost of bankruptcy, agency costs, and the potential for the value of interest tax shields to be offset by personal income taxes paid by the company's investors. Moreover, as we discussed in Chapter 3, if the tax regime imposes limitations on the amount of interest that is deductible for tax purposes (such as in the U.S. starting in 2018), that is another reason why companies might limit the amount of their debt financing.

Agency Costs. When a company has many investors, the interests of the shareholders, debtholders, and managers often come into conflict. We call the costs associated with managing these conflicts **agency costs**. Debt contracts are used to help mitigate the potential agency costs between the debtholders and managers and shareholders and provide the debtholders with rights to protect their principal if the company ever fails to make required **debt service** payments (interest and principal) or violates other provisions of the loan contract. One of these rights is to accelerate the due date of the loan and demand immediate payment. If the amount owed cannot be immediately paid, the debtholders can force the company into bankruptcy. The bankruptcy process can be expensive, and it has both indirect and direct costs associated with it. The more debt a company has, the more incentive the managers and shareholders have to take actions that will benefit themselves yet harm the debtholders. Examples of actions managers and shareholders can take that would hurt the debtholders include investing in riskier projects than anticipated, not investing in projects that create value (because the value created would go to the debtholders), or liquidating assets and distributing the cash to the shareholders.[4] The increase in agency costs associated with more debt in the capital structure mitigates the benefit of the interest tax shields generated by the debt. If we believe that the amount of leverage is sufficiently high that there are some states of the world where the firm would incur financial distress or bankruptcy costs, we would have to take those costs into account in estimating the future expected free cash flows of the firm.

While there are agency cost arguments for why debt in the capital structure may affect the value of the firm negatively, there are also agency cost arguments that suggest debt may increase the value of the firm in some circumstances. In Chapter 1, we said that a large debt overhang could be an incentive for managers to operate the firm efficiently because they are so focused on generating sufficient cash flows to pay off the debt. This is an argument often given in favor of firms undergoing a debt recapitalization or a leveraged buyout.[5]

Personal Income Taxes. Personal income taxes may also have an effect on the value of the interest tax shields. Naturally, investors care about the amount of cash they earn on their investments after all income taxes are paid (both corporate and personal taxes). If the personal income taxes paid on interest from debt investments differ from the personal income taxes paid on earnings from equity investments (dividends and appreciation in value), then this different income tax treatment can affect the value of the company's interest tax shields. This issue is somewhat complicated because the tax laws are complex and not all investors face the same income tax rates. However, under the correct circumstances, personal income taxes can mitigate or eliminate the value of interest tax shields.[6]

Conclusions. As a result, the value created from financing is equal to the value of a company's interest tax shields plus the value of any subsidized financing minus the other expected costs that result from using non-equity financing. The current view is that debt creates some value for a company if the company has a reasonably high probability of generating sufficient taxable income to capture the benefit of its interest tax shields and if the probability of bankruptcy is not too high.[7] In this chapter, we assume that the value from financing is equal to the value of a company's interest tax shields, (V_{ITS}). In other words, $V_{FIN} = V_{ITS}$. In effect, we ignore the other potential benefits and costs of debt financing, such as positive management incentives, the transaction costs of issuing debt, the effect of personal taxes, and the expected costs of financial distress and bankruptcy. We discuss these other effects of debt financing in Chapter 11.

Valuation Key 5.1

If interest is tax deductible, a manager can potentially create value by financing the company with debt. Measuring the value from debt financing is potentially a more complex issue than merely discounting expected interest tax shields at the appropriate risk-adjusted discount rate. We also consider adjustments for the potential effects of personal income taxes, agency costs, and financial distress and bankruptcy, all of which can reduce the value created from debt financing.

---

[4] See Jensen and Meckling (1976) for an important discussion about the agency conflicts between managers, shareholders, and debtholders that result from our inability to write perfect contracts; Jensen M. C., and W. Meckling, "Theory of the Firm: Managerial Behavior, Agency Costs and Capital Structure," *Journal of Financial Economics* 3 (1976), pp. 305–360.

[5] See Jensen (1986); Jensen, M. C., "Agency Costs of Free Cash Flow, Corporate Finance, and Takeovers," *American Economic Review* 2 (1986), pp. 323–329.

[6] See Miller, M. H. "Debt and Taxes," *Journal of Finance* 32 (May 1977), pp. 261–276.

[7] See Rajan and Zingales (1995) and Miller (1989) for reviews of this literature; Rajan, R. G., and L. Zingales, "What Do We Know About Capital Structure? Some Evidence from International Data," *Journal of Finance* 50 (December 1995), pp. 1421–1460; Miller, M. H., "The Modigliani-Miller Propositions After Thirty Years," *Journal of Applied Corporate Finance* vol. 2, no, 1 (Spring 1989), pp. 6–18.

5.2 THE ADJUSTED PRESENT VALUE AND WEIGHTED AVERAGE COST OF CAPITAL VALUATION MODELS

LO2 Measure firm and equity value using the adjusted present value and weighted average cost of capital valuation models

Recall that the value of the firm is equal to the discounted value of the company's free cash flows (FCF). Since, conceptually, a company has an infinite life, we discount the company's cash flows through infinity using an appropriate risk-adjusted discount rate (r). We implement the infinite discounting of a company's cash flows by discounting the company's free cash flows for a finite period, then estimate its continuing (residual or terminal) value (CV) as of the end of the finite period and discount that continuing value back to the valuation date. A common way to measure the company's continuing value is with a free cash flow perpetuity formula. In this section, we implement this generic formula for both the adjusted present value and the weighted average cost of capital valuation methods. Recall from Chapter 4 that the DCF valuation measures the value of the firm without any excess assets. If the firm has excess assets, the value of the excess assets must be added to the DCF valuation.

Adjusted Present Value (APV) Method

Recall that the value of the firm is equal to the sum of the value of the unlevered assets (V_{UA}) and the value from financing. For now, we assume that the value from financing is just due to the value of the interest tax shields (V_{ITS}). In the **adjusted present value (APV) valuation method**, we measure these two components of the value of the firm separately. We measure the value of the unlevered assets, V_{UA}, by discounting the free cash flows at the cost of capital that reflects the risk of these assets, called the **unlevered cost of capital (r_{UA})** or **asset cost of capital**.

Then, to the value of the unlevered firm, we add the value of the company's interest tax shields (V_{ITS}), which is equal to the discounted value of the company's expected interest tax shields (ITS). To the extent the company being valued has meaningful financial distress costs, we would subtract the value of its financial distress costs from the APV valuation. The appropriate risk-adjusted discount rate for the interest tax shields (r_{ITS}) depends on a variety of factors, but for now, we assume that it is appropriate to discount interest tax shields at the unlevered cost of capital ($r_{ITS} = r_{UA}$). We defer a more detailed discussion of this topic until Chapter 10, but note here that it is not uncommon to discount interest tax shields at the cost of debt in some circumstances. Using the assumption that we discount interest tax shields at the unlevered cost of capital, the formula for the APV method using the continuing value of the company's unlevered assets ($CV_{UA,C}$) and the continuing value of the interest tax shields ($CV_{ITS,C}$) as of the end of Year C appears in Equation 5.1.

$$V_F = \sum_{t=1}^{C} \frac{FCF_t}{(1+r_{UA})^t} + \frac{CV_{UA,C}}{(1+r_{UA})^C} + \sum_{t=1}^{C} \frac{ITS_t}{(1+r_{UA})^t} + \frac{CV_{ITS,C}}{(1+r_{UA})^C} \tag{5.1}$$

Using a constant growth perpetuity formula for the continuing values, the equation becomes

$$V_F = \sum_{t=1}^{C} \frac{FCF_t}{(1+r_{UA})^t} + \frac{FCF_{C+1}}{(r_{UA}-g)} \times \frac{1}{(1+r_{UA})^C} + \sum_{t=1}^{C} \frac{ITS_t}{(1+r_{UA})^t} + \frac{ITS_{C+1}}{(r_{UA}-g)} \times \frac{1}{(1+r_{UA})^C} \tag{5.2}$$

Valuation in Practice 5.1

United Photovoltaics Group Limited—Adjusted Present Value (APV) Valuation United Photovoltaics Group Limited is an investor and operator of 25 large solar power plants throughout China. In 2015, the company announced that one of its subsidiaries entered into an equity transfer agreement to sell part of its equity interest and enter into a joint venture agreement with other companies. As part of this transaction, the company, primarily consisting of solar power plant assets, was valued by a financial advisor. The advisor used the adjusted present value and not the weighted average cost of capital valuation method for the reasons we discuss in the chapter—that is, the company's capital structure strategy was to repay the debt over time and had unknown capital structure ratios. The explanation for using the adjusted present value method was:

continued

continued from previous page

Based on the previous borrowing capacity of other solar power plant projects owned by United PV, capital expenditures could be financed up to 70% with a gradual repayment of the outstanding loan by installment and was expected to have no debt from 2028 onwards. As advised by the Management, interest expense would be tax deductible. The estimated cost of borrowing is 6.55% p.a., with reference to the existing long-term best lending rate in China and the loan tenure is expected to be 13 years based on United PV's past borrowing capacity. . . .

Unlike the valuation of a business, where there is usually a long-term stable target debt to equity ratio which enables the use of the weighted average cost of capital ("WACC") to value a going concern business with indefinite life, as the capital structure of a capital intensive project will change due to debt repayment or additional borrowing throughout the operating period, the Adjusted Present Value ("APV") method was used in order to exclude the distortion resulting from the change in capital structure over the operating period. In the valuation, the APV method values projects by discounting projected free cash flows at a rate of return assuming all-equity financing as fundamental value ("Fundamental Value"). The all-equity financing discount rate or required return on assets ("Asset Discount Rate") is adopted. The Fundamental Value plus the present value of the tax shield effect of the interest expense of the financing arrangement to arrive at the fair value of the business enterprise of the Target Company.

Source: Company announcement available on May 27, 2018 at http://www.unitedpvgroup.com/uploads/media/LTN20150227015.pdf.

Valuation Key 5.2

The adjusted present value (APV) valuation method measures the value of the firm by adding the value of the interest tax shields to the value of the unlevered firm. The inputs into the APV valuation method are a company's free cash flows, its interest tax shields, the unlevered cost of capital, and the risk-adjusted discount rate for interest tax shields.

Weighted Average Cost of Capital (WACC) Method

In the **weighted average cost of capital (WACC) valuation method**, instead of measuring the value of the interest tax shields as a separate component of the value of the firm, the WACC valuation method incorporates the value of a company's interest tax shields by adjusting the discount rate we use to discount the company's free cash flows. In other words, the WACC method measures the value of the unlevered firm and the value of the interest tax shields jointly. When we use the WACC method, we discount the same expected unlevered free cash flows as in the APV method, but we discount these cash flows by the weighted average cost of capital rather than the unlevered cost of capital. And like the APV valuation method, to the extent the company being valued has meaningful financial distress costs, we would subtract the value of its financial distress costs from the WACC valuation. If interest tax shields create value, the weighted average cost of capital is lower than the unlevered cost of capital. The formula for the WACC method that uses the continuing value of the company's levered assets ($CV_{F,C}$) appears in Equation 5.3.

$$V_F = \sum_{t=1}^{C} \frac{FCF_t}{(1+r_{WACC})^t} + \frac{CV_{F,C}}{(1+r_{WACC})^C} \tag{5.3}$$

Using a constant growth perpetuity formula for the continuing value, we get

$$V_F = \sum_{t=1}^{C} \frac{FCF_t}{(1+r_{WACC})^t} + \frac{FCF_{C+1}}{(r_{WACC}-g)} \times \frac{1}{(1+r_{WACC})^C} \tag{5.4}$$

The WACC method is sometimes called the adjusted cost of capital method because it "adjusts" the unlevered cost of capital downward to reflect the benefit of the interest tax shields. The difference between the WACC and APV valuation methods is that the APV method adds the discounted value of the interest tax shields to the discounted value of the unlevered free cash flows, whereas the WACC method embeds the value of the interest tax shields into the valuation through a lower discount rate (r_{WACC}). This is not a simple concept to understand immediately, but we will explain it at a big-picture level in this chapter and we will explain it in more depth in Chapter 10.

Valuation in Practice 5.2

Nobel Biocare's Fairness Opinion—Weighted Average Cost of Capital Valuation In September 2014, Danaher Corporation submitted an all-cash public tender offer to the Nobel Biocare shareholders to purchase all publicly held registered shares for a price of CHF 17.10 (Swiss Francs) per share. Nobel Biocare, who develops and markets implant-based dental restoration products, retained Swiss Capital to prepare a fairness opinion assessing the financial appropriateness of the offer from the perspective of the public shareholders of Nobel Biocare. Swiss Capital explained their valuation as follows:

Valuation process . . .

- The discounted cash flow (DCF) method has been used as the primary valuation method to determine the fair value of the Nobel Biocare shares.
- The key assumptions of the underlying business plan have been tested for plausibility in several dialogues with the company management and compared to industry benchmarks . . .
- The DCF method is regarded as one of the most recognized and accurate methods in company valuation
- The DCF method has therefore been applied as the primary valuation method . . .
- The DCF method is based on future free cash flow projections before financing activities. This represents cash flows available to both equity investors and debt providers that are then discounted at the weighted average cost of capital (WACC) . . .
- The long-term free cash flow projections are based on a going-concern assumption (after the end of the planning period). These cash flows are the basis of the terminal value which therefore includes all future cash flows subsequent to the planning periods . . .
- The weighted average cost of capital (WACC) is defined as the cost of capital or required rate of return for equity investors and debt providers. . . .
- Beta [equity cost of capital]: The unlevered beta [unlevered cost of capital] was calculated on the basis of comparable companies and re-levered to the target capital structure for Nobel Biocare. . . .
- As part of the DCF method, sensitivity analyses were also conducted using changes in key value drivers (perpetual growth rate and WACC)

Source: Nobel Biocare fairness opinion available on June 1, 2018 at https://www.nobelbiocare.com/content/dam/Migration%20Assets/Documents/Discover/Company/Investors/Offering/20140926_Nobel%20Biocare%20-%20Fairness%20Opinion_FINAL_FRA.PDF authors added notes within square brackets [ ].

The Weighted Average Cost of Capital

Since we embed the value created by the company's interest tax shields in the weighted average cost of capital, if interest tax shields create value the weighted average cost of capital must be less than the unlevered cost of capital ($r_{WACC} < r_{UA}$). The unlevered cost of capital (r_{UA}) is determined by the risk of the cash flows of the company's operating assets. As stated previously, in this chapter we assume that the riskiness of the interest tax shields is equal to the riskiness of the company's operating assets; in other words, $r_{ITS} = r_{UA}$. From the economic balance sheet in Chapter 1 we know that the value of the firm's assets (unlevered value and value from financing) is equal to the sum of the values of the securities used to finance the firm. From the economic balance sheet it follows that the returns generated on the company's assets are also equal to the returns generated by the securities used to finance the firm (equity, r_E; debt, r_D; preferred, r_{PS}).

$$r_{UA} \times V_{UA} + r_{UA} \times V_{ITS} = r_{UA} \times V_F$$

$$r_{UA} \times V_F = r_D \times V_D + r_{PS} \times V_{PS} + r_E \times V_E$$

The above formula shows that the return on the company's assets (r_{UA}) equals the weighted average returns on the securities used to finance the firm (equity, debt, preferred), weighted by the market value weights in the capital structure. The expected return on the company's operating assets is r_{UA}. We call Equation 5.5 the **unlevering formula** because, as we explain later in this section, we use this formula to unlever a company's equity cost of capital to measure its unlevered cost of capital.

$$r_{UA} = r_E \times \frac{V_E}{V_F} + r_D \times \frac{V_D}{V_F} + r_{PS} \times \frac{V_{PS}}{V_F} \quad (5.5)$$

However, the return on the company's operating assets, r_{UA}, is not the overall after-tax cost of capital for a levered company, because the return paid on debt is tax deductible. The weighted average cost of capital measures the company's after-tax cost of capital. The common way to measure a company's weighted average cost of capital is to measure the after-tax cost of capital of each of the company's securities (sources of financing) and calculate the weighted average of its after-tax costs of capital, using the proportion of the company (proportion of firm value, not book value) financed with each security. Since companies can deduct interest expense when calculating income taxes, the **after-tax debt cost of capital** is equal to the debt cost of capital, multiplied by one minus the corporate tax rate that is applicable to the interest deduction, $(1 - T_{INT}) \times r_D$. Note in the following expression that only the cost of debt is multiplied by 1 minus the company's appropriate tax rate, for payments to the common and preferred equityholders are not tax deductible for the corporation in most tax regimes.

$$r_{WACC} = r_E \times \frac{V_E}{V_F} + (1 - T_{INT}) \times r_D \times \frac{V_D}{V_F} + r_{PS} \times \frac{V_{PS}}{V_F} \quad (5.6)$$

The difference between the weighted average cost of capital and the unlevered cost of capital ($r_{WACC} - r_{UA}$) is equal to the following (subtract Equation 5.5 from Equation 5.6).

$$r_{WACC} - r_{UA} = -T_{INT} \times r_D \times \frac{V_D}{V_F}$$

Thus, we see that the weighted average cost of capital is equal to the unlevered cost of capital, minus the tax savings ($T \times r_D$) from the proportion of the firm financed with debt (V_D/V_F). If the tax rate applicable to interest is zero or the firm uses no debt financing, then of course the weighted average cost of capital is equal to the unlevered cost capital.

$$r_{WACC} = r_{UA} - T_{INT} \times r_D \times \frac{V_D}{V_F} \quad (5.7)$$

Recall that in this chapter we assume that the riskiness of the interest tax shields is equal to the riskiness of the company's operating assets, $r_{ITS} = r_{UA}$. The above formula changes if we assume the discount rate for interest tax shields is not the unlevered cost of capital, which we discuss in Chapters 10 and 11. We also assume that the debt cost of capital, r_D, is equal to the promised yield on the debt, and that the expected interest deduction is equal to the yield on the debt multiplied by the value of the debt. In Chapter 9, we discuss the complications that arise when this is not the case.

Valuation Key 5.3

The weighted average cost of capital (WACC) method discounts the unlevered free cash flows of the firm at the weighted average cost of capital. This method incorporates the value of the interest tax shields in the valuation by using a discount rate that is lower than the unlevered cost of capital (when interest tax shields create value).

The Link between the Unlevered Cost of Capital and the Equity Cost of Capital

We know that the risk of a company's operating assets determines the unlevered cost of capital. We also know that the return on the company's assets is equal to the weighted average return earned by securities used to finance the firm (see Equation 5.5). From the discussion of M&M, we know that the risk of the company's equity, however, depends on the risk of the company's assets—operating risk—and the risk from the company using non-equity financing—financial leverage risk. We can rewrite Equation 5.5 to measure the equity cost of capital by isolating the equity cost of capital on the left-hand-side of Equation 5.5.

$$r_E = r_{UA} + (r_{UA} - r_D) \times \frac{V_D}{V_E} + (r_{UA} - r_{PS}) \times \frac{V_{PS}}{V_E} \quad \textbf{(5.8)}$$

This formula shows that a company's equity cost of capital is equal to its unlevered cost of capital, which reflects the company's operating risk, plus a premium to reflect the risk from financial leverage—one factor due to debt in the capital structure and another due to preferred. We do not show time subscripts in Equation 5.8 because each of the terms in this formula has the same time subscript. In other words, we measure each input at the same point in time. Just as for the weighted average cost of capital, the equity cost of capital and its determinants need not be constant over time. The equity cost of capital changes if we expect the company's business risk or financial risk to change or if we expect economy-wide shifts in required rates of return. We call this formula the **levering formula** because, as we explain later in this section, we use this formula to lever a company's unlevered cost of capital to measure its equity cost of capital.

Again, recall that in this chapter we assume that the riskiness of the interest tax shields is equal to the riskiness of the company's operating assets, $r_{ITS} = r_{UA}$. The above formula changes if we assume the discount rate for interest tax shields is not the unlevered cost of capital, which we discuss in Chapter 10.

Valuation Key 5.4

Since common equityholders are the residual claimants for a company's assets, a company's equity cost of capital is always greater than or equal to its unlevered cost of capital. If a company only issues common equity, then its equity cost of capital is equal to its unlevered cost of capital. If a company issues equity and non-common equity securities, then its equity cost of capital will be equal to its unlevered cost of capital plus a premium related to each non-common equity security it uses to finance the company.

How the Cost of Capital Links Are Used in Practice

The formulas we discuss in this chapter—the **unlevering formula** (Equation 5.5), the **levering formula** (Equation 5.8), and the **weighted average cost of capital formula** (Equation 5.6)—are widely used in practice (see Valuation in Practice 5.2). The cost of capital for the APV valuation model is the unlevered cost of capital. The cost of capital for the WACC valuation model is the weighted average cost of capital.

Using the Cost of Capital Links to Measure the Unlevered Cost of Capital. We use comparable companies to measure a company's unlevered cost of capital if the company's stock is not publicly traded. Even if a company's stock is publicly traded, we often use comparable companies, as well as the company being valued, to measure its unlevered cost of capital for reasons we discuss in Chapter 8.

Once we identify the comparable companies, we use the unlevering formula to measure each company's unlevered cost of capital based on each company's costs of capital for the securities used to finance the firm and its capital structure ratios. For each comparable company, we first measure the costs of capital and the capital structure ratios for all of the securities used to finance the firm. We then use the unlevering formula (Equation 5.5) to measure each company's unlevered cost of capital. Once we measure the unlevered cost of capital for the set of comparable companies (and possibly the company we are valuing if it is publicly traded), we estimate the unlevered cost of capital for the company we are valuing (we describe how we estimate the unlevered cost of capital based on this analysis in more detail in Chapter 10).

As we stated earlier, the formula in this chapter (Equation 5.5) is not the only version of the formula used to measure the unlevered cost of capital. The formula in this chapter assumes that the riskiness of the interest tax shields is equal to the riskiness of the company's operating assets, $r_{ITS} = r_{UA}$. The formula changes if we assume the discount rate for interest tax shields is not the unlevered cost of capital, which we discuss in Chapter 10.

Using the Cost of Capital Links to Measure the Weighted Average Cost of Capital. If a company's stock is not publicly traded, we use comparable companies to help measure its weighted average cost of capital. Even if a company is publicly traded, we often use comparable companies, as well as the company being valued, to measure its weighted average cost of capital for reasons we discuss in Chapter 8. The commonly used formula to measure the weighted average cost of capital (Equation 5.6) requires that we first measure the costs of capital and the capital structure ratios for all of the securities that the company will use in the future.

To measure the weighted average cost of capital, the typical procedure first unlevers the equity costs of capital for comparable companies and the company being valued (if publicly traded) using Equation 5.5. We then estimate an unlevered cost of capital for the company we are valuing based on that analysis (again, we describe how we estimate the unlevered cost of capital in more detail in Chapter 10). We then measure the company's equity cost of capital from the unlevered cost of capital using the levering formula (Equation 5.8). The levering formula requires an estimate of the unlevered cost of capital, the costs of capital and the capital structure ratios for all of the non-common equity securities that the company being valued will use to finance the firm in the future. This may or may not be the capital structure the company used in the past. Once we measure the company's equity cost of capital in this way, we have all of the inputs necessary to measure the company's weighted average cost of capital (using Equation 5.6), again based on the capital structure that the company will use to finance the firm in the future. Although not often used in practice, we can measure the weighted average cost of capital without measuring the equity cost of capital using formulas like Equation 5.7.

The formula in this chapter to measure a company's equity cost of capital from its unlevered cost of capital (Equation 5.8) is not the only version of the formula used to measure the equity cost of capital. The formula in this chapter is derived assuming that the riskiness of the interest tax shields is equal to the riskiness of the company's operating assets, $r_{ITS} = r_{UA}$. The formula changes if we assume the discount rate for interest tax shields is not the unlevered cost of capital, which we discuss in Chapter 10.

The Adjusted Present Value and Weighted Average Cost of Capital Valuation Methods Are Typically Not Substitutes

The APV and WACC valuation methods are not substitutes. Depending on the information available and the valuation assumptions made, only one of the two methods is the better starting point for a particular valuation analysis. For a specific valuation, we will generally not have sufficient information to use both the WACC and APV valuation methods. If we already know all of the information required to use both the APV and WACC valuation methods, we also must know the value of the firm.

We can understand why these methods are not substitutes by comparing the inputs required to implement them. The APV method requires forecasts of the company's free cash flows, interest tax shields, and unlevered cost of capital, and forecasts for interest tax shields require forecasts of the company's debt cost of capital, the tax rate for the interest tax shields, and the amount of debt (dollar magnitude) for each future year. On the other hand, the WACC method requires forecasts of the company's free cash flows and the weighted average cost of capital, and the weighted average cost of capital requires forecasts of the company's equity cost of capital, debt cost of capital, tax rate, cost of preferred stock, and the company's capital structure ratios, which are equal to the proportion of the firm financed with each security (measured in terms of market values). We do not need to know the value of the individual securities for the WACC DCF method; we only need to know the company's target capital structure or capital structure strategy, stated as proportions of the firm financed with each of the securities.

The key difference between the inputs for the two valuation methods is the type of information required about the company's capital structure. The APV method requires forecasts of the magnitude (dollar or other currency amount) of the debt, while the WACC method requires forecasts of the proportion (stated in terms of market values) of the company financed with each type of security. When valuing a company, it is unlikely for us to know both the amount of debt and proportion of debt at the same time, for then, we would implicitly know the value of the firm. For example, if you know that a company has $1,000 in debt and that the company always finances itself with 25% debt, you implicitly know that the value of the firm is $4,000 ($4,000 = $1,000/0.25).

In sum, the primary factor for choosing either the APV or WACC valuation method is the information available, or the assumptions made, about the company's capital structure. A company might not have a formal capital structure strategy or even a plan for financing itself. Regardless, because of the value created from financing, conducting a valuation requires an assumption about how the company will finance itself in the future. If the valuation assumes the company has a target capital structure strategy stated in terms of the proportion of the company financed with certain types of securities, then the WACC valuation method is the best starting point for the valuation. This is the most common assumption that is made in practice. On the other hand, if the valuation assumes the company has a capital structure strategy based on the amount of debt the company will use to finance the firm in each future period, then the APV valuation method is the best starting point. It is also possible to switch from the APV valuation method to the WACC valuation method within the same valuation if we expect the company to switch its capital structure strategy from an expected amount of debt used to finance the firm to a constant proportion of debt used to finance the firm.

Valuation Key 5.5

The adjusted present value and weighted average cost of capital valuation methods are typically not substitutes. The key factor for choosing between the two methods is the information available or the assumptions made about the company's capital structure. Use the WACC method if the company has a target capital structure strategy stated in terms of the proportion of the company financed with non-common equity securities; otherwise, use the APV method when you have forecasts of the dollar magnitude of the debt in future periods.

In practice, managers, analysts, and investors use the WACC valuation method most often and assume that the discount rate is constant. They assume that the company will adopt a target capital structure stated in terms of the proportion of the company financed with non-common equity securities. Such an assumption is not appropriate if a company will have significant changes in its capital structure over time (for example, companies that have just undergone a highly leveraged transaction or a debt recapitalization) or if it intends to pay down its debt according to a specified schedule. In many of these cases, the companies are operating at a capital structure far different from the industry norm and often intend to bring their capital structures back in line with their industry counterparts over time. However, the WACC valuation method has certain limitations even if a company has a target capital structure. We discuss these limitations in Chapter 11. In short, the WACC method is not the best valuation method if a company does not have sufficient taxable income to capture the benefits of its interest tax shields when it pays the interest (for example, startup companies incurring losses in their early years or companies with significant net operating loss carryforwards or companies with interest carryforwards caused by limitations on the deductibility of interest). In Chapter 3, we discussed the complexity of determining the timing and amount of the interest tax shields for companies with net operating loss carryforwards and interest carryforwards. In these situations, the APV valuation method may be easier and the more appropriate method to use.

5.3 THE ANDY ALPER COMPANY

We use the Andy Alper Company (Alper) to illustrate the APV and WACC valuation methods. Mr. Alper started his company at the end of Year 0 by raising \$8,000 in capital—his equity investment of \$3,000, issuing \$1,000 of preferred stock (with a cost of preferred stock of 12%), and borrowing \$4,000 (with a cost of debt of 10%). At the end of Year 0, Mr. Alper purchased two machines, paying \$1,000 for one machine and \$3,000 for the other. He also invested \$3,000 in operating working capital (for example, inventory). Mr. Alper believes he needs to keep the remaining \$1,000 in cash in order to operate the business (required cash). Mr. Alper also believes the company's revenues, free cash flows, and interest tax shields will grow at 5% per year in perpetuity. In addition, all balance sheet items will also grow by 5% in every year. Free cash flow forecasts and summary financial statements appear in Exhibit 5.3. Based on an analysis of publicly traded comparable companies and using the unlevering formula (Equation 5.5), Apler's unlevered cost of capital is 15%. Alper has a 40% corporate tax rate on all types of income and does not have any temporary or permanent differences between its taxable income and accounting income.

Which Valuation Method Do We Use to Value Andy Alper Company?

Deciding on what valuation method to use depends on the information we have available. For Alper, we know its capital structure in terms of the amount of capital issued, and we know the cost of capital for its debt and preferred stock. We also know its unlevered cost of capital and interest tax shields (see Exhibit 5.3). We have not been provided with a capital structure strategy for Alper and have several choices to consider. We discuss four such choices.

One choice is to assume the company will use the capital structure ratios used to initially finance the company, 50% debt (\$4,000/\$8,000), 12.5% preferred stock (\$1,000/\$8,000), and 37.5% common equity (\$3,000/\$8,000), even though these capital structure ratios are not likely based on market values. These capital structure ratios will not be based on market values if Alper's equity investment creates (destroys) value, a positive (negative) net present value project. Regardless, it is the capital structure used to initially finance the company and an option to consider. Since Alper does not have a known (or historical) capital structure, a second option is using a target capital structure that is representative of the comparable companies to Alper. Choosing either of these two options results in a capital structure strategy based on assumed capital structure ratios and we would therefore use the WACC method as the starting point to value Alper.

A third option to consider is that Alper will continue to grow its debt and preferred stock financing at the same growth rate as the company's assets. This option assumes that as the scale of the company increases, its financing will increase proportionately. Lastly, a fourth option is to assume Alper will use the company's free cash flow after paying interest and preferred stock dividends to reduce the amount of debt and preferred stock financing it has. Either of these options allows us to develop forecasts of the dollar amount of the company's debt, and thus, interest expense and interest tax shields. Choosing either of these last two options results in a capital structure strategy based on the dollar amount of outstanding debt (and not capital structure ratios) and we would therefore use the APV method as the starting point to value Alper.

Which is the correct capital structure strategy for Alper? The correct capital structure assumption is the capital structure strategy that Alper intends to use in the future to finance the company. In this section, we examine two of these alternatives. We use the capital structure ratios used to initially finance the company to value Alper using the WACC method, and we use the capital structure strategy that Alper will continue to grow its debt and preferred stock financing at the same growth rate as the company's assets to value Alper using the APV method.

EXHIBIT 5.3 Andy Alper Company's Financial Statement and Free Cash Flow Forecasts

Balance Sheet Forecast	Actual Year 0	Forecast Year +1
Cash	$1,000	$ 1,050
Net operating working capital	3,000	3,150
Net property, plant, and equipment	4,000	4,200
Total assets	$8,000	$ 8,400
Debt (10% interest rate)	$4,000	$ 4,200
Preferred stock (12% dividend rate)	1,000	1,050
Common equity	3,000	3,150
Total liabilities and equities	$8,000	$ 8,400

Free Cash Flow Schedule	Forecast Year +1
Earnings before interest and taxes	$2,067
Income taxes (40% tax rate, T_{INT})	−827
Unlevered earnings after tax	$1,240
Depreciation	2,000
Change in required cash	−50
Change in net working capital	−150
Capital expenditures	−2,200
Unlevered free cash flow (FCF)	$ 840

Income Statement Forecast	Forecast Year +1
Revenue	$10,000
Depreciation expense	−2,000
Operating expenses	−5,933
Earnings before interest and taxes	$ 2,067
Interest expense	−400
Earnings before tax	$ 1,667
Income taxes (40% tax rate)	−667
Earnings after tax	$ 1,000
Preferred stock dividends	−120
Earnings available to equity	$ 880

Alper's Valuation Based on Capital Structure Ratios Used to Initially Finance the Company—The Weighted Average Cost of Capital Valuation Method

In this section, we assume Alper will adopt a capital structure strategy based on the capital structure ratios used to initially finance the firm. These capital structure ratios are not the same as the capital structure ratios based on market values if Alper's equity investment creates or destroys value, but we assume that Alper will adjust its capital structure to those ratios based on market values. Since we know the capital structure ratios, the best starting point to value Alper is the WACC method. The WACC valuation assumes that regardless of the company's current capital structure, the company will refinance its capital structure based on the market value capital structure ratios assumed in the WACC valuation.

Recall Alper's capital structure ratios used to initially finance the company are 50% debt (\$4,000/\$8,000), 12.5% preferred stock (\$1,000/\$8,000), and 37.5% common equity (\$3,000/\$8,000). Alper's debt and preferred stock costs of capital are 10% and 12%, respectively. Alper has a 40% tax rate on all income, so its average and marginal tax rate for interest, T_{INT}, are 40% (we assume that the interest is fully tax deductible because the interest expense is less than 30% of EBIT). The first step in measuring Alper's weighted average cost of capital is to measure its unlevered cost of capital, which we assume was analyzed and equal to 15%. Based on the unlevered cost of capital and the above capital structure information, we can measure Alper's equity cost of capital for this capital structure strategy.

$$r_E = r_{UA} + (r_{UA} - r_D) \times \frac{V_D}{V_E} + (r_{UA} - r_{PS}) \times \frac{V_{PS}}{V_E}$$

$$= 0.15 + (0.15 - 0.1) \times \frac{0.5}{0.375} + (0.15 - 0.12) \times \frac{0.125}{0.375} = 0.2267$$

Once we measure the company's equity cost of capital in this way, we have all of the inputs necessary to measure the company's weighted average cost of capital (Equation 5.6) based on the capital structure that the company will use to finance the firm in the future.

$$r_{WACC} = r_E \times \frac{V_E}{V_F} + (1 - T_{INT}) \times r_D \times \frac{V_D}{V_F} + r_{PS} \times \frac{V_{PS}}{V_F}$$

$$= 0.2267 \times 0.375 + (1 - 0.4) \times 0.1 \times 0.5 + 0.12 \times 0.125 = 0.13$$

We can also measure the weighted average cost of capital without measuring the equity cost of capital (Equation 5.7).

$$r_{WACC} = r_{UA} - T_{INT} \times r_D \times \frac{V_D}{V_F}$$

$$= 0.15 - 0.4 \times 0.1 \times 0.5 = 0.13$$

We now have the inputs necessary to value Alper using the WACC valuation method. Based on this capital structure, the unlevered free cash flow for Year 1 (Exhibit 5.3), and using the WACC valuation method, the value of Alper (firm value) is \$10,500.

$$V_{F,0} = \frac{FCF_1}{r_{WACC} - g} = \frac{\$840}{0.13 - 0.05} = \$10{,}500$$

According to the WACC valuation, Alper created \$2,500 of value from its investment of \$8,000 (\$2,500 = \$10,500 − \$8,000). Later we will use the APV valuation method to better understand the sources of the \$2,500 value created.

The Value of Alper's Equity Based on the Weighted Average Cost of Capital Valuation and the Assumed Recapitalization. As we discuss in more detail later in the chapter, since equityholders are the residual claimants, the value of Alper's equity is equal to the value of the firm minus the value of Alper's debt and preferred stock. Based on this valuation, the value of Alper's equity is \$5,500 (\$5,500 = \$10,500 − \$4,000 − \$1,000) which is above its book value, assuming that the market values of Alper's debt and preferred are equal to their book values. However, based on this valuation, Alper's common equity would be more than 50% of the value of the firm (0.52 = \$5,500/\$10,500) when the assumed capital structure in the WACC valuation assumes that only 37.5% of the company is financed with equity, 50% of the company is financed with debt, and 12.5% with preferred stock. According to the WACC valuation, Alper should have debt and preferred stock outstanding of \$5,250.0 (\$5,250.0 = 0.5 × \$10,500) and \$1,312.5 (\$1,312.5 = 0.125 × \$10,500), respectively. Thus, the WACC valuation assumes that Alper will recapitalize so that post-recapitalization, 50% of the company would be financed with debt, 12.5% with preferred stock, and 37.5% with equity.

We present a summary of the assumed recapitalization in Exhibit 5.4. The WACC valuation assumes Alper has a capital structure with $5,250 of debt and with $1,312.5 of preferred stock. In order to recapitalize to the capital structure, Alper needs to issue additional debt of $1,250 ($1,250 = $5,250 − $4,000) and additional preferred stock of $312.5 ($312.5 = $1,312.5 − $1,000). Since Alper does not need the additional capital for its operations, it will distribute the additional capital to the equityholders, resulting in a post-recapitalization and post-distribution value of the equity equal to $3,937.5 ($3,937.5 = $5,500 − $1,250 − $312.5). Note that the with-distribution value of the equity is $5,500 ($5,500 = $3,937.5 + $1,250.0 + $312.50).

EXHIBIT 5.4 Alper Recapitalization Based on the Weighted Average Cost of Capital Valuation

	Initial	Post Recapitalization	Equity Value
Valuation before recapitalization			
Pre-recapitalization value of equity			$5,500.0
Value of the debt	$4,000.0	$5,250.0	$1,250.0
Value of the preferred	$1,000.0	$1,312.5	312.5
Distribution to equity			$1,562.5
Post-recapitalization value of equity			$3,937.5

Whether or not the company could actually—or would actually—recapitalize its capital structure in this way is relevant to the WACC valuation because if Alper would not recapitalize in this way, we would have to re-value the company based on an alternative assumption about Alper's capital structure that we believe is more indicative of what Alper will actually do.

REVIEW EXERCISE 5.1

The Stuart Essig Perpetuity Company—Part 1

The Stuart Essig Company has an unlevered cost of capital of 12% and an income tax rate of 40%. The company finances itself with 1/3 debt, which has a cost of capital equal to 8%; 1/6 preferred stock, which has a cost of capital of 8.5%; and the remainder with common equity. The company expects its unlevered free cash flows to remain constant in perpetuity. Assume that the company's interest expense is fully tax deductible and that the interest tax shields should be valued at the unlevered cost of capital and that the company holds no excess cash nor any other excess assets. Use this information and the information that follows to value the Stuart Essig Company (firm and equity) as of the end of Year 0 using the WACC valuation method.

Income Statement Forecast	Year 1
Revenue	$180,000
Depreciation expense	−25,000
Operating expenses	−84,000
Earnings before interest and taxes	$ 71,000

Asset Forecast	Year 1
Cash	$ 4,000
Net operating working capital	25,000
Net property, plant, and equipment	120,000
Total assets	$149,000

Unlevered Free Cash Flow Forecast	Year 1
Earnings before interest and taxes	$71,000
Income taxes	−28,400
Unlevered earnings after tax	$42,600
Depreciation expense (non-cash expenses)	25,000
Change in required cash	0
Change in net working capital	0
Capital expenditures	−25,000
Unlevered free cash flows	$42,600

Solution on page 248.

Value of Unlevered Firm and Value of the Interest Tax Shields Embedded in Alper's Weighted Average Cost of Capital Valuation. We know the WACC method embeds the value of a company's interest tax shields in the value of the firm. We can measure the value of the unlevered firm and value of the interest tax shields embedded in a WACC valuation using the APV valuation method. Since we know the post-recapitalization debt in Alper's capital structure, we can measure the interest tax shields assumed in the WACC valuation. We know Alper's unlevered cost of capital, 15%, free cash flow (in Year 1), $840, and long-term growth rate, 5%, but we do not know its expected interest tax shields based on the WACC valuation without some additional analysis.

To measure Alper's expected interest tax shields (in Year 1) based on the WACC valuation, we first measure the expected interest expense, $525, which is equal to the amount of debt as of the end of Year 0 based on the WACC valuation, $5,250 ($5,250 = 0.5 × $10,500), multiplied by the interest rate, 10%. Alper's expected interest tax shields (in Year 1) based on the WACC valuation, $210, is equal to the expected interest expense, $525, multiplied by the marginal tax rate for interest, which in this case is equal to its average tax rate, 40% ($210 = $525 × 0.4).[8] We now have all of the inputs necessary to measure Alper's value using the APV method assuming we discount the interest tax shields at the unlevered cost of capital.

$$V_{F,0} = \frac{FCF_1}{r_{UA} - g} + \frac{ITS_1}{r_{UA} - g}$$

$$= \frac{\$840}{0.15 - 0.05} + \frac{\$210}{0.15 - 0.05}$$

$$= \$8{,}400 + \$2{,}100 = \$10{,}500$$

Given that we used the same assumptions for the APV valuation that we relied on in the WACC valuation, the APV and WACC valuations result in the same firm value. One reason to also value the company using the APV valuation is that it provides additional information not provided in the WACC valuation. From the APV valuation we learn that of the $10,500 in value, the value of the unlevered firm is $8,400 (80%) and the value of the interest tax shields is $2,100 (20%).

Valuation in Practice 5.3

Euro Disney's Valuation Using the Adjusted Present Value Valuation Method In the early 2000s, Euro Disney S.C.A. experienced a downturn in revenues, primarily the result of a prolonged downturn in European travel and tourism combined with challenging general economic and geopolitical conditions in key markets. Euro Disney experienced increased losses as a result of reduced revenues, as well as higher operating costs and marketing expenses in connection with the opening of the Walt Disney Studios Park.

In 2004, Euro Disney and certain companies of the Group negotiated a comprehensive restructuring of its financial obligations with its lenders and The Walt Disney Company. The restructuring provided new cash resources (through issuing equity rights), reduced or deferred certain obligations, and provided Euro Disney with more flexibility to invest in new attractions and in the development of the resort and its surrounding areas. The restructuring required Euro Disney to value its equity. Euro Disney was highly levered at that time and it expected to reduce its debt over time after the restructuring. One of the valuation methods used to value Euro Disney's equity was the adjusted present value (APV) valuation method, which it described as follows:

> ... an alternative method was implemented to confirm results: the Adjusted Present Value Method ("APV"). This method, based on the valuation of the assets adjusted for the impact of the financial structure allows one to ascertain the value of the operational assets of the company without using assumptions pertaining to the financial structure (i.e., flows are discounted at an expected rate of return of assets of 9.3% . . ., a sector beta of 0.92, calculated using a selection of companies operating in the entertainment and hotel industries (including Six Flags, Walt Disney, Club Med, Accor and Whitebread) and a market premium of 5.7%, . . . According to this method, the weight of the terminal value in the value of the assets is 24%. The discounted value of the tax savings linked to the deductibility of financial charges is added to the value of the operational assets (discounted at 5.1%).

Source: Euro Disney S.C.A 2004 Annual Report (with restructuring plan attached)

[8] We note that it is important to calculate the implied or expected interest expense from a WACC valuation in countries where there are limitations on the amount of interest that is deductible. For example, in Alper's case, its expected interest expense ($525) is less than 30% of its EBIT ($2,067), which would satisfy the most stringent limitation of the Tax Cuts and Jobs Act of 2017.

What Were the Sources of the Value Created? Recall Alper initially financed the company with \$8,000 of capital. According to our valuation, the value of Alper is \$10,500. Thus, Alper created \$2,500 (\$2,500 = \$10,500 − \$8,000) of value; said differently, Alper increased the value of the capital invested by over 30% (0.3125 = \$2,500/\$8,000). Since the debt and preferred stock are fixed claims, all of that additional value accrues to Alper's common equityholders, increasing the value of the common equity from \$3,000 to \$5,500 or by over 80% (0.8333 = (\$5,500 − \$3,000)/\$3,000).

The APV valuation provides information to understand how much of the value created results from an increase in the value of the operating (unlevered) company and how much results from debt financing (interest tax shields). Had Alper financed the company with only common equity and preferred stock, its value would have been \$8,400 (value of the unlevered firm). In other words, the value of the operating (unlevered) company increased from the \$8,000 investment to \$8,400 or by \$400 (\$400 = \$8,400 − \$8,000) or by 5% (\$400/\$8,000). The remainder of the value created, \$2,100 (\$2,100 = \$2,500 − \$400) results from the assumption of financing 50% of the company's value with debt. Of the total increase in value, 16% (0.16 = \$400/\$2,500) results from increasing the value of the operating assets and 84% (0.84 = \$2,100/\$2,500) results from the value of the interest tax shields.

Again, whether or not the company could actually—or would actually—recapitalize its capital structure according to the assumed capital structure in the WACC valuation and whether or not countervailing forces would possibly reduce the value of the interest tax shields are additional factors to consider.

Alper's Valuation Based on Growing Its Debt and Preferred Stock Financing at the Free Cash Flow Growth Rate—The Adjusted Present Value Valuation Method

In this section, we assume Alper will adopt a capital structure strategy based on the current amount of debt and preferred stock used to initially finance the firm, and assume the debt and preferred stock financing will grow at the same rate as the company's free cash flows and assets. Since we know the amount of debt in Alper's capital structure, the best starting point to value Alper is the APV method. We know Alper's unlevered cost of capital, 15%, free cash flow (in Year 1), \$840, and long-term growth rate, 5%, but we do not know its expected interest tax shields based on \$4,000 of debt financing without additional calculations.

To measure Alper's expected interest tax shields (in Year 1), we first measure the expected interest expense, \$400.0, which is equal to the amount of debt as of the end of Year 0, \$4,000, multiplied by the interest rate, 10%. Alper's expected interest tax shields (in Year 1), \$160, is equal to the expected interest expense, \$400, multiplied by the marginal tax rate for interest, which in this case is equal to its average tax rate, 40% (\$160 = \$400 × 40%). We now have all of the inputs to measure Alper's value using the APV method.

$$
\begin{aligned}
V_{F,0} &= \frac{FCF_1}{r_{UA} - g} + \frac{ITS_1}{r_{UA} - g} \\
&= \frac{\$840}{0.15 - 0.05} + \frac{\$160}{0.15 - 0.05} \\
&= \$8{,}400 + \$1{,}600 = \$10{,}000
\end{aligned}
$$

The value of the unlevered firm is \$8,400, and the value of the interest tax shields is \$1,600, yielding a total firm value of \$10,000. Recall that the investors initially invested \$8,000. Since the value of the firm is \$10,000, the valuation implies that management will create \$2,000 in value by implementing its business strategy and plan, including the effect of this capital structure strategy. Alper's equity value based on this set of capital structure strategy assumptions is \$5,000 (\$5,000 = \$10,000 − \$4,000 − \$1,000). Given the fixed nature of the debt and preferred stock claims, all else equal, the decrease in the value of the interest tax shields from \$2,100 to \$1,600 (\$500), results in the same decrease in the value of the equity.

Note that the only difference between the WACC valuation and the APV valuations is the value of the interest tax shields. Recall from M&M, the value of the company's operating assets (unlevered firm) is assumed to be independent of its capital structure strategy assuming the investment policy is held fixed. Under the M&M assumptions, different capital structure strategies affect the value of a company's interest tax shields but do not affect the value of the company's operating assets.[9] The capital structure strategy in the WACC valuation assumes that 50% of the firm would be financed with debt, which resulted in initial debt financing of $5,250, while the APV valuation assumes that the company has initial debt financing of $4,000 (or 40% debt financing). All else equal, the capital structure strategy with more debt financing has a larger value because the value of the interest tax shields is larger. One side note, for simplicity, we assume that the cost of debt and the cost of preferred capital stay the same at 10% and 12% respectively, despite the different capital structures, which as we discuss in more detail in Chapter 9, may not be the case.

Costs of Capital Implicit in the Adjusted Present Value Valuation

Now that we know Alper's value based on the APV valuation, we can measure the capital structure ratios implicit in that valuation, which we show in Exhibit 5.5. We can use these capital structure ratios and other information we know to measure Alper's value using the WACC method based on the assumptions in the APV valuation.

EXHIBIT 5.5 Andy Alper Company's Implicit Capital Structure Ratios—APV Valuation

Valuation and Capital Structure Ratios	Year 0	to V_F	to V_E
Value of the firm	$10,000		
Value of the debt	4,000	40.0%	80.0%
Value of the preferred	1,000	10.0%	20.0%
Value of the equity	$ 5,000	50.0%	

Based on the APV valuation, we can calculate Alper's equity cost of capital using Equation 5.8 and its weighted average cost of capital using Equation 5.6.

$$r_E = r_{UA} + (r_{UA} - r_D) \times \frac{V_D}{V_E} + (r_{UA} - r_{PS}) \times \frac{V_{PS}}{V_E}$$

$$= 0.15 + (0.15 - 0.1) \times 0.8 + (0.15 - 0.12) \times 0.2 = 0.196$$

$$r_{WACC} = r_E \times \frac{V_E}{V_F} + (1 - T_{INT}) \times r_D \times \frac{V_D}{V_F} + r_{PS} \times \frac{V_{PS}}{V_F}$$

$$= 0.196 \times 0.5 + (1 - 0.4) \times 0.1 \times 0.4 + 0.12 \times 0.1 = 0.134$$

We now have all of the information we need to value Alper using the WACC method based on a set of assumptions consistent with the APV valuation, and we note that the value is the same.

$$V_{F,0} = \frac{FCF_1}{r_{WACC} - g} = \frac{\$840}{0.134 - 0.05} = \$10{,}000$$

REVIEW EXERCISE 5.2

The Stuart Essig Perpetuity Company—Part 2

Use the information in and solution for Review Exercise 5.1 to value the Stuart Essig Company (firm and equity) using the APV valuation method.

Solution on page 248.

[9] We generally assume, as did M&M, that investment policy is independent of capital structure. If taking on more debt meant, for example, that the company would hold more required cash, that would be a change in the investment policy and we would have to take that into consideration in our cash flow forecasts. By assuming the difference in the value of the firm from the change in the capital structure is due solely to the difference in the value of the interest tax shields, we are also implicitly assuming there is no change in the countervailing forces associated with the change in the capital structure.

5.4 THE DISCOUNTED EQUITY FREE CASH FLOW VALUATION METHOD

LO3 Measure value using the equity free cash flow and dividend valuation models

As we illustrated with the Alper example, we can measure the value of a company's equity using either the APV or the WACC valuation methods by first measuring the value of the firm and then subtracting the value of the non-common equity claims. In this section, we discuss a way to measure the value of the equity directly using the **Equity DCF valuation method**. As we discuss in this section, implementing the Equity DCF valuation method and consistently maintaining the underlying assumptions can be complex.

Valuing Common Equity by First Measuring the Value of the Firm

Common equityholders are the residual claimants of a company; that is, equityholders have a claim on the remaining value of the firm after all other claims against the company's assets are satisfied. Using the economic balance sheet, we can express the value of the firm's common equity as the value of the firm minus the value of each of the non-common equity claims. For a company with debt, V_D, preferred stock, V_{PS}, and any other claims such as warrants and options, V_{OTHER}, this calculation is as follows.

$$V_E = V_F - V_D - V_{PS} - V_{OTHER} \tag{5.9}$$

Valuing the Equity Directly Using the Equity Discounted Cash Flow Method

For reasons we explain in this section, the above approach is the more common approach used to measure a company's equity value in most valuation contexts. However, we can use either the **Equity DCF method** or **Dividend DCF method** to value a company's common equity value directly. In the Equity DCF method we discount the cash flows the company has available to pay its common equityholders (**equity free cash flows**) at the equity cost of capital. Recall from Chapter 3, equity free cash flows are equal to a company's unlevered free cash flows adjusted for all after-tax cash flows paid to or received from all non-common equity claimholders. We can also discount a company's expected common dividend payments at the equity cost of capital. In general, a company's dividends typically do not equal its equity free cash flows. Companies usually adopt a dividend policy that smooths dividends over time so that they are not equal to equity free cash flows period by period. In the long run, however, the sum of a company's common dividends must be equal to the sum of its equity free cash flows (assuming no share repurchases). Thus, as long as the company earns the equity cost of capital on the difference between its dividends and equity free cash flows, these two valuation methods result in the same equity value.

The formula used in the Equity DCF valuation method is similar to the formula used in the WACC method. The differences between the two methods are the calculations of the relevant cash flows and discount rate. In the WACC method, we discount the unlevered free cash flows at the weighted average cost of capital to measure the value of the firm. In the Equity DCF method, we discount the equity free cash flows at the equity cost of capital. The general formula for the Equity DCF method is

$$V_E = \sum_{t=1}^{\infty} \frac{EFCF_t}{(1+r_E)^t}$$

If we construct detailed forecasts for the company for C years and measure the continuing value of the equity ($CV_{E,C}$) as of the end of Year C, the above formula becomes

$$V_E = \sum_{t=1}^{C} \frac{EFCF_t}{(1+r_E)^t} + \frac{CV_{E,C}}{(1+r_E)^C} \tag{5.10}$$

If we use the constant growth perpetuity method to measure the continuing value, the above formula becomes

$$V_E = \sum_{t=1}^{C} \frac{EFCF_t}{(1+r_E)^t} + \frac{EFCF_{C+1}}{(r_E - g)} \times \frac{1}{(1+r_E)^C} \tag{5.11}$$

Valuation Key 5.6

We can measure the value of a company's common equity by valuing the firm using either the APV or WACC valuation methods and subtracting the value of the company's non-common equity claims. An alternative approach is to value the company's common equity directly using the Equity DCF method, which discounts the company's equity free cash flows at the equity cost of capital.

Equity Discounted Cash Flow Model for the Alper Company

We can use Equation 5.11 to measure the value of Alper's equity using the Equity DCF method based on either set of capital structure strategy assumptions used in the previous section. In the previous section, we valued Alper using two alternative capital structure strategies. We already calculated the equity cost of capital for both of these capital structure strategies but we do not know Alper's equity free cash flow for either capital structure strategy. The first capital structure strategy is based on the capital structure ratios used to initially finance the firm (WACC capital structure) and resulted in a recapitalized financing with \$5,250 debt financing and \$1,312.5 preferred stock financing that will grow at the growth rate of the free cash flows and operating assets. The second capital structure is based on the \$4,000 debt and \$1,000 preferred stock financing (APV capital structure) that will grow at the growth rate for the free cash flows and operating assets.

Since we know the amount of Alper's outstanding debt and preferred stock as of the end of Year 0 and we know that Alper grows at 5% in perpetuity, we can easily measure Alper's equity free cash flow for each capital structure strategy. Recall from Chapter 3, the equity free cash flow is equal to unlevered free cash flow minus after-tax interest payments and preferred stock dividends, plus any increase (minus any decrease) in debt or preferred stock financing. Exhibit 5.3 shows Alper's unlevered free cash flow calculation. In Exhibit 5.6, we calculate Alper's equity free cash flow (in Year 1) for both of the alternative capital structure strategies. The equity free cash flow (in Year 1) based on the WACC capital structure is \$695.6 and based on the APV capital structure is \$730. The lower equity free cash flow for the WACC capital structure results from higher interest and preferred stock dividends, which results from higher debt and preferred stock financing.

EXHIBIT 5.6 Alper Equity Free Cash Flows for the Weighted Average and Adjusted Present Value Capital Structure Strategies

Free Cash Flow Schedule	Capital Structure Strategy	
	WACC Capital Structure Strategy	APV Capital Structure Strategy
Unlevered free cash flow (FCF)	\$840.0	\$840.0
Interest paid in cash ($r_D \times V_{D,0}$)	−525.0	−400.0
Interest tax shield ($T_{INT} \times r_D \times V_{D,0}$)	210.0	160.0
Preferred stock dividend ($r_{PS} \times V_{PS,0}$)	−157.5	−120.0
Change in debt ($V_{D,0} \times g$)	262.5	200.0
Change in preferred stock ($V_{PS,0} \times g$)	65.6	50.0
Equity free cash flow (EFCF)	\$695.6	\$730.0
Common dividends	−695.6	−730.0
Change in common equity	0.0	0.0
Change in required cash	50.0	50.0
Change in cash balance	\$ 50.0	\$ 50.0

Based on the WACC capital structure, Alper's equity value (after the recapitalization assumed in the WACC valuation method) using the Equity DCF method is \$3,937.5, the same value we calculated earlier using the WACC valuation method.

$$V_E = \frac{EFCF_1}{(r_E - g)} = \frac{\$695.63}{0.22667 - 0.05} = \$3,937.5$$

Adding the assumed distribution to equityholders from the recapitalization assumed in the WACC valuation method—$1,250 debt and $312.5 preferred stock, $1,562.5 in total—the pre-recapitalization value of Alper's equity is $5,500 again, the same value we calculated earlier using the WACC valuation method.

Based on the APV capital structure, Alper's equity value using the Equity DCF method is $5,000, the same value we calculated earlier using the APV valuation method.

$$V_E = \frac{EFCF_1}{(r_E - g)} = \frac{\$730.0}{0.196 - 0.05} = \$5{,}000$$

While we were easily able to use the Equity DCF valuation method for both the WACC capital structure and APV capital structure, we could do so only because we already knew information about Alper's capital structure that we learned from first measuring Alper's value using the WACC and APV valuation methods, which we discuss in the next section.

Complexities and Limitations of the Equity Discounted Cash Flow Method

The Equity DCF method requires an estimate of the company's equity cost of capital and equity free cash flows. To measure a company's equity cost of capital, we need the company's capital structure ratios in each year. To measure a company's equity free cash flows, however, we need to know the company's after-tax interest expense and any other payments to and from non-common equity security holders in each year. That means that we need to know both a company's capital structure ratios and the amount of each of its non-common equity securities issued, which of course means that we already know the value of the firm. For example, a company financed with 30% debt and which has $3,000 debt outstanding, has a firm value of $10,000 ($10,000 = $3,000/0.3). That is why the WACC and APV valuation methods are the more common starting point in a valuation, even when measuring the value of the common equity.

In the Alper example, we used the WACC valuation that was based on capital structure ratios to determine the dollar amount of debt once we knew the value of the firm. We did this because we had to measure the equity free cash flows before we could implement the Equity DCF method. Further, we used the APV valuation that was based on a known dollar amount of debt to determine the capital structure ratios to determine the equity cost of capital before we could implement the Equity DCF method. Thus, for either capital structure assumption, we had to value the firm first using either the WACC or APV valuation.

From a practical perspective, if the forecasts of the amounts of the non-equity securities are not too different from the amounts that would be needed to maintain the company's target capital structure, the difference in the equity value for a company between the Equity DCF and the APV-based or WACC-based methods will be small. It is cumbersome, of course, to verify that they are not too different.

In some situations, however, using the Equity DCF method as the starting point makes sense. For example, the Equity DCF method is sometimes used for financial institutions, which typically use substantial financial leverage. If a company uses substantial financial leverage in its capital structure, any inaccuracy in the valuation of the firm likely translates into an inaccuracy in the value of the equity. Further, if we first measure the value of the firm using the WACC or APV valuation methods, we also need to know the value of the non-common equity claims to measure the value of the equity. Some companies have substantial non-common equity claims that may be difficult to value—for example, financial institutions. Any valuation inaccuracies of the non-common equity claims translate into an inaccuracy in the value of the equity. Thus, in such situations, any inaccuracy resulting from using the Equity DCF method might be smaller than the inaccuracy resulting from using either the WACC or APV valuation methods and subtracting the value of the non-common equity claims.

Valuation Key 5.7

Although we can measure the value of a company's equity by discounting the company's equity free cash flows at its equity cost of capital, this is not typically the best starting point in a valuation. Usually, the best starting point for a valuation is to use either the APV or the WACC valuation method to value the firm and then subtract the value of the company's non-common equity claims in order to measure the value of its equity.

Assumption About Distributing Equity Free Cash Flows to Equityholders

In the Equity DCF valuation method, we discount equity free cash flows at the equity cost of capital. For positive equity free cash flows, we assume either that the company distributes these cash flows to equityholders or, if the company retains them, that the company invests the equity free cash flows in zero net present value investments. In addition, if the equity free cash flows are invested in zero net present value projects, these investments neither change the value of the firm nor the equity, so we can ignore them. In general, it is easier to assume in the models we create that the equity free cash flows are distributed. The most common form of a cash distribution to equityholders is a dividend; alternatively, the company could repurchase stock at its current market price.[10] For negative equity free cash flows, we implicitly assume that the equityholders are making additional cash investments in the company and that the new shares are sold to equity investors at their fair market value at the time of sale.

REVIEW EXERCISE 5.3

The Stuart Essig Perpetuity Company—Part 3

Use the information in and solutions to Review Exercises 5.1 and 5.2 to measure the company's equity free cash flow in Year 1; afterward, value Stuart Essig Company's equity by discounting the equity free cash flows at the equity cost of capital.

Solution on page 249.

5.5 THE DISCOUNTED DIVIDEND VALUATION MODEL

The **dividend discounted cash flow valuation method** (**Dividend DCF valuation method**) is similar to the Equity DCF valuation method. In fact, if expected dividend distributions equal expected equity free cash flows, the two methods are identical. We know, however, that companies do not usually declare dividends equal to equity free cash flows; rather, companies tend to smooth dividend distributions.[11] Companies have other ways to distribute cash to their shareholders that can have certain advantages, such as share repurchases.

Valuation in Practice 5.4

Apple Inc. Decides to Distribute Cash to Shareholders On March 20, 2012, Apple Inc.'s (Apple) CEO Tim Cook announced that the company would begin to pay dividends and buy back shares. As of December 31, 2011, Apple had close to $100 billion in cash and marketable securities, the largest cash stockpile of any non-financial U.S. corporation at the time. Former CEO Steve Jobs had resisted returning cash to shareholders, arguing that the company needed it for future investments. Apple announced that over the next three years the dividends and share repurchase program would return $45 billion in cash to shareholders. Apple also indicated that approximately $64 billion of its cash holdings was overseas and that Apple would not be repatriating that cash back to the United States to make the cash payouts because of the U.S. taxes that would then have been owed on that income. While Apple's announcement is certainly significant, this is not the largest *one-time* payout by a company at that time. On December 2, 2004, Microsoft Corporation (Microsoft) paid a one-time special dividend of $32 billion—the biggest cash dividend in history.

Sources: Vascellaro, J., "Apple Pads Investor Wallets," *Wall Street Journal* (March 20, 2012), p. A1; and Oster, C., "Microsoft's $32 Billion Payout Sparks a New Interest in Dividends," *Wall Street Journal* (July 22, 2004), p. D2.

---

[10] For a detailed review of the academic literature on how companies pay out cash to shareholders, see Franklin, Allen, and Roni Michaely, "Payout Policy," in George Constantinides, Milton Harris, and Rene Stulz, eds., *Handbook of Economics and Finance* North-Holland Publishing (2003), pp. 337–429.

[11] See Lintner, John, "Distribution of Incomes of Corporations Among Dividends, Retained Earnings, and Taxes," *American Economic Review* vol. 46, no. 2 (1956), pp. 97–113; and Fama, Eugene F., and Harvey Babiak, "Dividend Policy: An Empirical Analysis," *Journal of the American Statistical Association* vol. 63, no. 324 (1968), pp. 1132–1161.

The formula for the Dividend DCF method is the same as the formula for the Equity DCF valuation method, except that we replace equity free cash flows with dividends (DIV). The general formula for the Dividend DCF method is

$$V_E = \frac{DIV_1}{(1+r_E)^1} + \frac{DIV_2}{(1+r_E)^2} + \ldots + \frac{DIV_\infty}{(1+r_E)^\infty} = \sum_{t=1}^{\infty} \frac{DIV_t}{(1+r_E)^t}$$

If we construct detailed forecasts for the company for C years and measure the continuing value of the equity ($CV_{E,C}$) as of the end of Year C, the above formula becomes

$$V_E = \sum_{t=1}^{C} \frac{DIV_t}{(1+r_E)^t} + \frac{CV_{E,C}}{(1+r_E)^C} \quad \textbf{(5.12)}$$

Even though the Dividend DCF and Equity DCF valuation methods are likely to use different expected cash flows to value a particular company's equity (dividends versus equity free cash flows), the two methods yield the same value if the assumptions underlying them are consistently applied. The key assumption that equates the two valuation methods is that whatever the company does with the difference between equity free cash flows and dividends, it does not change the risk of the equity nor change the value of the equity or the firm. If the company's equity free cash flow is greater than its dividend distribution, the company invests in zero net present value projects that neither change the value and risk of the company nor its equity. If the company's equity free cash flow is less than its dividend distribution, the company raises additional equity capital that neither changes the value and risk of the company nor its equity. If this assumption is met, then the discount rate—the equity cost of capital—and the equity valuation are the same for the two methods. The Dividend DCF method has the same limitations as the Equity DCF method.

Valuation Key 5.8

Even though we can measure the value of a company's common equity by discounting its expected dividends at the equity cost of capital, this method—the dividend discounted cash flow method—is not typically the best starting point in a valuation. This method has the same limitations as the Equity DCF valuation method and it is more difficult to implement when dividends do not equal equity free cash flows. It is usually best to use either the APV or the WACC valuation methods to value the firm and then to subtract the value of the company's non-common equity claims in order to measure the value of its equity.

5.6 USEFUL VALUATION CONCEPTS TO KEEP IN MIND

LO4 Understand how to measure expected cash flows and risk-adjusted discount rates

We discuss various conceptual issues and frameworks in this section that should help anchor the implementation of any of the DCF valuation models. We begin with a discussion on the implicit assumption made in DCF valuation models about current and non-current operating liabilities. We then discuss the way inflation should affect the DCF valuation model. Afterward, we discuss the concepts of expected free cash flows and risk-adjusted discount rates. Last, we discuss the misuse of what we call "**fudge factors**," which result when someone arbitrarily adjusts the discount rate for any uncertainty that should only affect the calculation of expected free cash flows and not the risk-adjusted discount rate.

The Value of the Firm Is Net of Its Non-Interest-Bearing Operating Liabilities

In every DCF-based valuation, the value of the firm that we measure is the value of the company's assets (including growth opportunities) net of its non-interest-bearing operating liabilities. In other words, the value of the company's non-interest-bearing operating liabilities is already deducted when we value the firm using any of the DCF valuation methods. The value of the firm includes the value of all interest-bearing debt, preferred stock, common equity, and any options or warrants issued by the firm but it excludes non-interest-bearing operating liabilities.

For example, suppose the value of a firm using a DCF valuation method is \$100 million, and the firm has \$30 million of debt outstanding and \$5 million of accounts payable. The \$100 million firm value represents the value of the company net of its \$5 million in accounts payable. The value of the equity is \$70 million (\$70 = \$100 − \$30). If the company sells its assets, and if the buyer does not assume the company's non-interest-bearing operating liabilities, then the value of the firm is adjusted to reflect the netting of the non-interest-bearing operating liabilities. In other words, if the company sells the assets but retains all of the liabilities, including accounts payable, the value of the company's assets will equal \$105 million (\$105 = \$100 + \$5). If in selling the assets, the purchaser agrees to assume the accounts payable, the purchase price would be \$100 million. If the purchaser assumes both the accounts payable and the debt, the purchase price would be \$70 million.

As we discuss in the previous chapters, the reason we do not treat non-interest-bearing operating liabilities like debt is that we generally do not know their implicit financing charge; hence, we cannot easily treat them like interest-bearing debt. Suppliers of goods and services typically provide a grace period in which invoices can be paid without interest; therefore, any implicit financing charge is embedded in the cost of the good or service. The cost is charged to various operating expenses, which reduces a company's EBIT that, in turn, reduces a company's free cash flows once the cost incurred is paid. As such, non-interest-bearing operating liabilities have already been netted out in valuing the firm.

For now, the important point to understand is that the value of the firm as measured by the DCF methods is net of its non-interest-bearing operating liabilities. Later, in Chapter 11, we discuss the effect of the choice of treating certain contractual obligations as operating versus financing activities.

Using Nominal or Real (Inflation-Adjusted) Cash Flows and Discount Rates

When forecasting cash flows, we can either include the effects of expected inflation (**nominal forecasts**) or exclude them (**real forecasts** or **constant dollar forecasts**). We can also measure discount rates in either nominal or real terms. **Nominal discount rates** (nominal cost of capital estimates) include compensation for expected inflation and **real discount rates** do not. Naturally, we use discount rates that are consistent with the forecasts; we use nominal discount rates with nominal forecasts and real discount rates with real or constant dollar forecasts.

A company's free cash flows can grow as a result of inflation, even if it is not experiencing real growth. Real growth implies that the company is growing at a rate faster than the rate of inflation. Since the effect of inflation is included in the company's nominal cost of capital, we also include the effect of inflation on the company's free cash flows when we use a nominal cost of capital.

Assume our company's expected free cash flows grow at the rate of inflation (i), which is constant in perpetuity. We can value the company using either nominal free cash flow forecasts and nominal discount rates or real (inflation free) cash flow forecasts and real discount rates. We can express the relationship between the nominal ($r_{nominal} = r$) and real (r_{real}) rates of return as

$$r = r_{nominal} = (1 + r_{real}) \times (1 + i) - 1$$

$$r_{real} = \frac{(1 + r)}{(1 + i)} - 1$$

where i is the rate of inflation.

Assume a company's free cash flow for Year 0 is \$100 and its expected outlook for the future is that its cash flows will grow with inflation (i = 2.9%); thus, it will not have any real growth. If the company's nominal cost of capital is 12.5%, we can measure the value of the firm using our perpetuity formula.

$$V_{F,0} = \frac{FCF_0 \times (1 + i)}{r - i}$$

$$V_{F,0} = \frac{\$100 \times (1 + 0.029)}{0.125 - 0.029} = \$1{,}071.88$$

If the company's nominal cost of capital is 12.5%, and if the constant inflation rate is 2.9%, its real cost of capital is equal to 9.33%.

$$r_{real} = \frac{(1+r)}{(1+i)} - 1$$

$$r_{real} = \frac{(1.125)}{(1.029)} - 1 = 0.0933$$

We can then measure the value of the firm using our perpetuity formula and a real discount rate (r_{real}) and real cash flows.

$$V_{F,0} = \frac{FCF_1}{r_{real}}$$

$$V_{F,0} = \frac{\$100}{0.0933} = \$1{,}071.88$$

If we have all of the information we need to precisely convert nominal forecasts and nominal discount rates to real forecasts and real discount rates, then the choice of using either nominal or real forecasts and discount rates is irrelevant, for we end up measuring the same value. The key to deciding which approach to use rests in identifying the approach that results in forecasts that are more accurate. Using a nominal approach is more common for valuation contexts that do not include high rates of expected inflation. In hyperinflationary economies—for example, see Valuation in Practice 5.5—where many contracts and tax regulations are indexed by the rate of inflation, it is common to use real discount rates and real cash flow forecasts.

Valuation in Practice 5.5

Hyperinflationary Venezuela Since the early 2000s until late 2014, Venezuela benefited from high oil prices. The government nationalized many private firms in sectors such as oil and gas, mining and metallurgy, cement, banking and telecommunications. Economic growth and redistribution policies decreased poverty levels and income inequality relative to other countries in the region. However, according to the World Bank:

> Nevertheless, the collapse in international oil prices, along with inadequate macro and microeconomic policies, have significantly affected Venezuela's economic and social performance. The country's reliance on the hydrocarbon sector has sharply increased (oil now accounts for 96 percent of exports). Also, during the economic boom Venezuela did not accumulate savings to mitigate a reversal in terms of trade or to cushion the necessary macroeconomic adjustment. . . .
>
> . . . regulations on private sector participation in the production and distribution of some basic goods, have triggered shortages of basic goods, inflationary pressures, and supply problems in a productive structure that is heavily dependent on imports. . . .
>
> . . . Private consumption has collapsed as runaway inflation eroded incomes. Moreover, investment has plunged, undermined by widespread distortions and uncertainty, causing the capital stock to shrink.

continued

continued from previous page

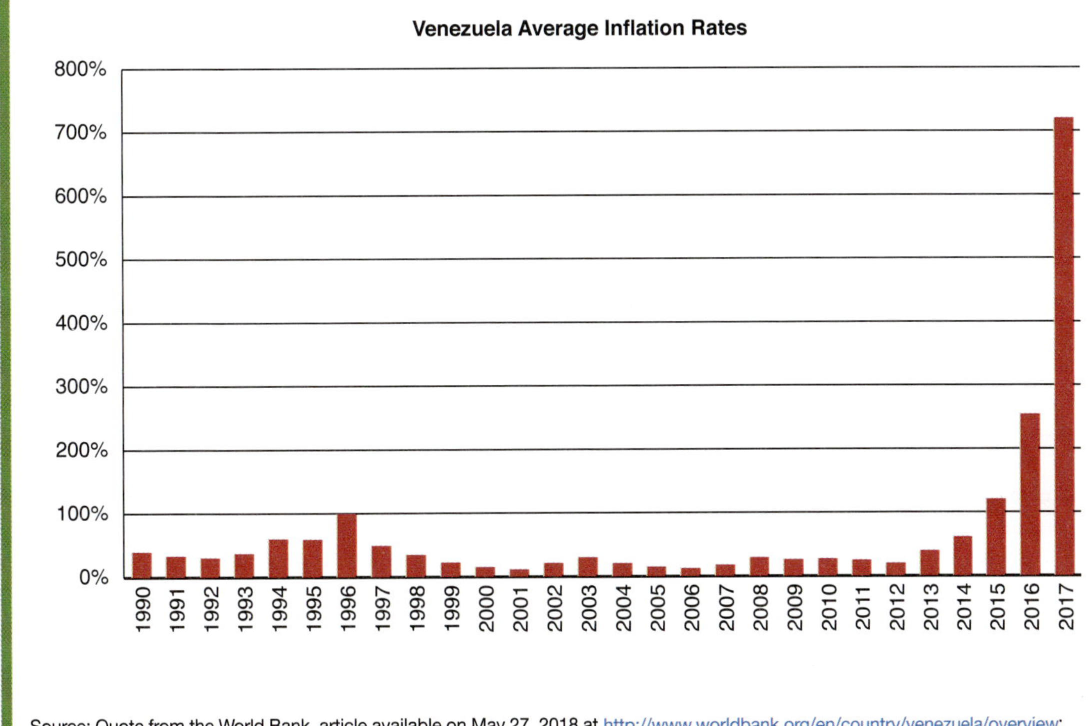

Source: Quote from the World Bank, article available on May 27, 2018 at http://www.worldbank.org/en/country/venezuela/overview; data for chart from International Monetary Fund, World Economic Outlook Database, April 2017

Valuation Key 5.9

We can forecast cash flows and use discount rates that either include inflation (nominal) or exclude inflation (real). The key is to keep forecasts of cash flows and discount rates consistent—nominal and nominal or real and real. The more common approach for low-inflation situations is to use nominal forecasts and discount rates.

The Concept of Expected Free Cash Flows

Since companies typically face various business and financial risks, most assets (such as the stocks or bonds issued by companies) have uncertain future cash flows. In the DCF valuation model, we discount **expected cash flows**. Discounting expected cash flows allows us to perform present value calculations when there are numerous possible outcomes for an investment. We discussed this concept to some extent in previous chapters, but in this section we develop this concept in more detail and draw links to other related issues.

We can readily see the concept of expected value in the context of a game of chance. Assume a casino has a bowl containing 50 red, 40 white, and 10 green balls. You, the player, pay (bet) to play the game and pick one ball from the bowl; you cannot see inside the bowl, and the balls are identical except for color. The relative number of balls of a certain color represents the probability of picking a color; in addition, playing the game multiple times does not affect the **outcome** of any game. You will receive $22 if you pick a red ball, $75 if you pick a white ball, and $690 if you pick a green ball.

How much would you expect to win, on average (before deducting the cost of playing the game), from playing one round of the game? The answer is $110. To calculate the **expected payoff** from playing the game, we multiply the probability of each outcome (0.5, 0.4, and 0.1) by the payoff from that outcome ($22, $75, and $690) and add all of those products together as we show in the following table.

Calculating Expected Values

Color of Ball	Number of Balls in Bowl	Payoff	Probability of Payoff	Expected Payoff
Red	50	$ 22	0.5	$ 11
White	40	$ 75	0.4	30
Green	10	$690	0.1	69
	100		1.0	$110

The payoff will be either $22, $75, or $690, but it will never be $110. How can $110 be the expected value if you will never receive $110, regardless of which ball you pick? To answer, the $110 represents the average payoff you would receive if you made a sufficient number of bets, which is how we expect investors to invest; that is, we expect investors to invest in a diversified portfolio of investments (discussed in Chapter 8).

We calculate expected cash flows in the same way we calculated the expected payoff in the casino game of chance. We multiply the probability of each outcome (sometimes called a **state of nature**, such as the state of the economy) by the cash flow resulting from that outcome. The expected cash flow is the sum of the products (probability × $ outcome) across all possible outcomes. In other words, an expected cash flow is the probability-weighted sum of the cash flows from all of the possible outcomes. In practice, we do not calculate expected cash flows using all possible outcomes because too many outcomes are possible.

Instead, valuation specialists often construct their forecasts based on a single scenario they view as being the most representative as of the date of the forecast. Another common approach is to calculate the forecast as the average of several scenarios. For example, the scenarios could be pessimistic, most likely, and optimistic, with each scenario being weighted by its respective probability. When only one scenario or a few probability-weighted scenarios are used in our valuation models, we implicitly assume that the individual scenario or the expected outcome of a few scenarios represents the expected value of the multiple states of nature. We discussed scenario analysis briefly in Chapter 4.

Sometimes, the cash flows of a project or a firm can be characterized as a chronological sequence of events, where some of these events result in a decision point for a manager or firm. In such cases, we sometimes use decision trees to help guide and structure our analysis. For example, we can use a decision tree to analyze the cash flows of a startup company that is developing a new product. If product development is successful, the company will invest in production facilities; if it is not successful, it will go bankrupt at zero cost and zero liquidation value. A decision tree helps us to better understand the potential cash flow outcomes, better identify the decisions to be made, and better analyze the options available to the company at various points in time. These options are often called "real options." Below we provide a decision tree example.

The company invests $1,000 at the end of Year 0 to develop the product. In one year, the company will either market the product or not, and each outcome has an equal probability of occurring. If the company successfully develops the product, the company will invest $2,000 at the end of Year 1, and it expects the new product to generate a cash flow at the end of Year 2 of either $10,000 if the economy is doing well or $3,000 if the economy is doing poorly. The probability of the economy doing well is 40%, and the probability of the economy doing poorly is 60%. If the company does not develop the project, the company will go bankrupt at zero cost and zero liquidation value at the end of Year 1. For simplicity, we assume that the new product can only be sold in Year 2 and that the company liquidates costlessly at the end of Year 2—even if the product is successful. We can use the following decision tree to help us analyze this investment:

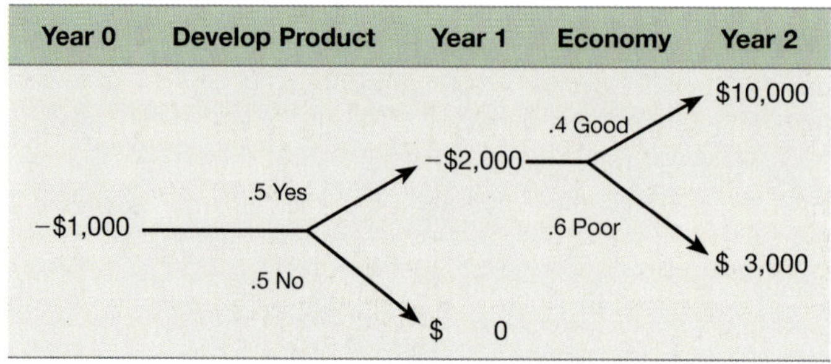

When measuring expected cash flows for each year, we must remember that at the end of Year 0, the company does not yet make the investment decision for the end of Year 1. It will not do so until it observes the outcome of the product development. This is a type of real option. The company can choose to abandon the project at the end of Year 1 if the product development is unsuccessful—an abandonment option.

Let us see what the expected cash flows are for each year. If the company makes the investment at the end of Year 1, the expected cash flow in Year 2 is \$5,800 (\$5,800 = 0.4 × \$10,000 + 0.6 × \$3,000). However, since there is only a 50% chance that it will make the investment in Year 1, the expected cash flow in Year 2 is \$2,900. For Year 1, the expected cash flow is − \$1,000 (−\$1,000 = 0.5 × −\$2,000). For Year 0, the expected cash flow is −\$1,000 as well. If we assume that the appropriate discount rate for valuing the company is 10%, the value of the company will be \$487.60 (\$487.60 = −\$1,000 −\$1,000/1.1 + \$2,900/1.1^2).

An alternative approach that will yield the same value is to calculate the present value of the three possible scenarios and probabilistically weight them. The first scenario is to spend \$1,000 at Year 0 and abandon the company. This scenario has a probability of 0.5 and a net present value of −\$1,000. The second scenario is to spend \$1,000 at Year 0, spend \$2,000 at Year 1, and receive \$3,000 at Year 2. This scenario has a probability of 0.3 (0.3 = 0.5 × 0.6) and has a present value of −\$338.84 (−\$338.84 = −\$1,000 − \$2,000/1.1 + \$3,000/1.1^2). The third scenario is to spend \$1,000 at Year 0, spend \$2,000 at Year 1, and receive \$10,000 at Year 2. This scenario has a probability of 0.2 (0.2 = 0.5 × 0.4) and a present value of \$5,446.28 (\$5,446.28 = −\$1,000 − \$2,000/1.1 + \$10,000/1.1^2). Considering the scenarios together, the value of the company is \$487.60 (\$487.60 = −\$1,000 × 0.5 − \$338.84 × 0.3 + \$5,446.28 × 0.2). Thus, discounting the expected cash flows from each period or calculating the present value of each scenario and probabilistically weighting them yields exactly the same valuation.

To appropriately measure expected cash flows, we use all of the available information to create the most precise, unbiased forecasts possible. Sometimes managers and investors are too optimistic and include all of the good outcomes but leave out one or more of the very bad outcomes—for example, financial failure or some catastrophic event. This error results in forecasts that are too high, creating an upward bias in the forecasts. Alternatively, some managers and investors implicitly consider all of the possible outcomes and then reduce the expected cash flow to be conservative. This approach results in forecasts that are too low, creating a downward bias. The key is to be realistic (remain objective) and neither bias the forecasts by unintentionally ignoring possible outcomes nor intentionally attempting to be conservative.

Valuation Key 5.10

The cash flows we use to value companies are expected cash flows. Expected cash flows represent the probability-weighted cash flows of all of the possible outcomes the company faces (for example, high growth, normal growth, low growth, zero growth, negative growth). The key is to be realistic (remain objective) and not bias the forecasts by unintentionally ignoring possible outcomes or intentionally attempting to be conservative.

The Risk-Adjusted Discount Rate (Cost of Capital)

We use a company's **risk-adjusted discount rate**—also commonly referred to as a **required rate of return**, an **expected rate of return**, **a hurdle rate**, or **the cost of capital**—to discount expected cash flows. A key concept underpinning the measurement of a company's risk-adjusted discount rate is diversification. Investors can reduce or diversify away some of the risk of a single investment by owning a portfolio of investments instead of just a single investment. Investors cannot diversify away all risk, for the outcomes companies face in a country—or even within the world—are not independent, called **systematic risks**.

The reason investors cannot diversify away all of their risk is that while investments do not have identical risks, they do have some of the same risks—for example, the health of the general economy affects many businesses similarly. Risk that investors can diversify away is referred to as **diversifiable risk** or **unsystematic risk**, and the risk that they cannot diversify away is **non-diversifiable risk** or **systematic risk**. The models we typically use to measure a company's risk-adjusted discount rate (see Chapter 8) assume that diversifiable risk does not affect the company's discount rate; that is, investors do not expect to receive compensation for that form of risk because they can easily eliminate it from their portfolios by holding multiple securities. However, risk that is not diversifiable will increase the company's risk-adjusted discount rate.

Consider the following two investments, A and B, and assume these are the only two investments available. Both investments have seven potential states that can occur and each state has a payout (cash flow) for each state. Analyze these two investments and decide which one is more risky and should have the higher discount rate.

State	Probability of State Occuring	Payoff If Outcome Occurs	
		Investment A	Investment B
1	5%	$100	$900
2	10%	$200	$800
3	20%	$400	$600
4	30%	$800	$200
5	20%	$300	$700
6	10%	$600	$400
7	5%	$700	$300
	100%		

Both investments have the same expected payoff of $500. The expected payoff (cash flow) of investment A is $500 ($500 = 0.05 × $100 + 0.1 × $200 + 0.2 × $400 + 0.3 × $800 + 0.2 × $300 + 0.1 × $600 + 0.05 × $700), and has a range of payoffs from $100 to $800. The expected payoff (cash flow) of investment B is also $500 ($500 = 0.05 × $900 + 0.1 × $800 + 0.2 × $600 + 0.3 × $200 + 0.2 × $700 + 0.1 × $400 + 0.05 × $300), and has a range of payoffs from $200 to $900.

Both investments have uncertain outcomes and uncertain payoffs and both have expected cash flows of $500. Which investment is more risky and should have the higher discount rate; in other words, given that they have the same expected payoff (cash flow), that question is equivalent to asking which investment should have the higher price. Investment A has a range of payoffs from $100 to $800 and its most likely outcome is $800 (30% probability, state 4). Investment B has a range from $200 to $900 but its most likely outcome is $200 (30% probability, state 4).

It turns out that both investments have no systematic risk (non-diversifiable risk) even though they have uncertain outcomes. Why? Investors would realize that instead of purchasing investment A or investment B, they can eliminate the uncertainty in the payoff by investing in both A and B. Purchasing investment A and investment B has a $1,000 payoff in every possible state. In state 1, the payoff of investment A is $100 and the payoff of investment B is $900, resulting in a payoff for the portfolio of investments A and B of $1,000. In state 2, the payoffs of investments A and B are $200 and $800, again, resulting in a payoff for the portfolio of investments A and B of $1,000. Continuing this calculation for all of the states, the payoff for the portfolio of investments A and B is $1,000 for every possible state. Investing in both investments eliminates any uncertainty. Since investors would figure this out, both investments would have the same price and the discount rate for both investments is the risk-free rate of return.

Valuation Key 5.11

To calculate the value of a risky investment, we discount *expected* cash flows with *risk-adjusted* discount rates. We take into consideration both diversifiable and non-diversifiable risk in computing expected cash flows, but risk-adjusted discount rates only rise above the risk-free rate when there is non-diversifiable risk.

Don't Use "Fudge Factors"

When we create forecasts for use in a DCF valuation, the forecasts should represent the expected value of the company's future free cash flows. As discussed previously, we measure expected values by probability weighting all potential outcomes that might occur. Naturally, we typically face what appears to be an infinite number of potential outcomes, so probability weighting all of these outcomes is generally not feasible. However, we can select a finite number of potential outcomes in order to approximate the expected value.

Suppose that a company's free cash flow—in perpetuity—will be $133 if the economy is bad, $500 if it is good, and $1,200 if it is booming, and that the probability of a bad, good, and booming economy is 30%, 40%, and 30%, respectively. The expected value of the company's free cash flow is $600 ($600

= 0.3 × $133 + 0.4 × $500 + 0.3 × $1,200). If the company's discount rate is 10%, the value of the company is $6,000 ($6,000 = $600/0.1).

How would we adjust the above valuation—expected free cash flow and discount rate—of the company if we now learn that the success of the company is entirely dependent on the company being awarded a patent next year and that the probability of the company being awarded that patent is 80%? Further, if the patent is awarded to the company, the expected cash flows will be $600 in perpetuity and $0 if the company is not awarded the patent.

Initially, we used the probabilities of outcomes in the general economy to measure the company's expected free cash flows. Do we now include the probability of securing the patent in our expected value calculation? Yes. The outcomes we use to measure the expected values of free cash flows include all potential outcomes, regardless of whether they are related to the general economy (systematic effects) or are company specific (idiosyncratic effects). Thus, in addition to the potential outcomes for the general economy and industry, we—at least implicitly—consider such events as the success of various research and development programs, the approval of drugs, the approval of patents, the weather, the death of a key employee, and so on. Our company has a 20% chance of having $0 free cash flows and an 80% chance of having an expected free cash flow of $600 (in perpetuity). The company's expected free cash flow adjusting for this uncertainty is $480 ($480 = 0.2 × $0 + 0.8 × $600 = 0.8 × $600). An alternative way to calculate this expected value is to incorporate both the probability of the company not obtaining the patent—and the resulting zero free cash flow—and then adjust the probability of each state of the economy for the probability of the company not obtaining the patent; $480 = 0.2 × $0 + (0.8 × 0.3) × $133 + (0.8 × 0.4) × $500 + (0.8 × 0.3) × $1,200.

Should we also adjust the discount rate for this new information? No. Unless the probability of getting the patent is somehow related to the economy and affects the company's non-diversifiable risk, we do not include this uncertainty (company-specific risk) into the discount rate. Thus, adding this uncertainty to the example does not change the discount rate (10%), but it does change the value of the company to $4,800 ($4,800 = $480/0.1) from $6,000 because it reduces the expected cash flow.

Arbitrarily changing the discount rate to adjust for these potential uncertainties—arguing that they are additional "risk factors"—is conceptually flawed. As we discussed earlier, the discount rate should not reflect unsystematic or idiosyncratic risks (risks that can be diversified away). Adjusting the discount rate for these effects will undervalue the company if the expected free cash flows are already adjusted for these uncertainties. If an adjustment is not made when measuring the expected free cash flows, adjusting the discount rate is merely an arbitrary adjustment. For example, if someone were to guess and use an adjustment of 5% for the discount rate, the resulting "adjusted" discount rate would be 15%. The resulting value would then be $4,000 ($4,000 = $600/0.15), which is an error of more than 16%.

Is it possible to make such an adjustment to the discount rate such that the valuation is correct? Algebraically, the answer is yes, but conceptually, the answer is no. If we make this adjustment to the discount rate, we will no longer be using a discount rate that measures value by discounting the company's expected free cash flows, and the free cash flows will no longer be expected free cash flows. In addition, and more important, we would need the correct value of the company before we can calculate the correct adjustment to the discount rate, as there is no theory we can rely on to determine the discount rate adjustment. The only way to accurately adjust the discount rate for this type of risk is to first measure the appropriate value of the company based on the expected cash flows. Then calculate the discount rate—applied to cash flows that differ from the expected value cash flows—that yields the same valuation.

Using our example, we can illustrate how to make such an adjustment. We know the correct value of the firm is $4,800, and the value ignoring the additional uncertainty is $6,000; thus, the correct value is 80% of the value ignoring the additional uncertainty (0.8 = $4,800/$6,000). Using this information, we can adjust the discount rate by this ratio in order to measure the discount rate that we could use to discount the free cash flow that ignores the additional uncertainty. That discount rate is 12.5% (0.125 = 0.1/0.8). Discounting the $600 free cash flow by 12.5%, we get $4,800 ($4,800 = $600/0.125). Note that calculating the adjustment to the discount rate will not be so simple in situations in which the cash flows are not simple perpetuities. That said, it would be simple to solve for that discount rate in a financial model using software such as Excel. Nevertheless, you still need to know the value of the company before you can calculate the discount rate that will yield the correct valuation when applied to cash flows that differ from the expected values.

Adding an adjustment to the discount rate that does not have a conceptual foundation is nothing more than a **fudge factor**. Thus, although adjusting the discount rate for idiosyncratic risks can result in the correct valuation, it is unlikely to do so unless we already know the value of the firm. As you might have guessed, we do not recommend using the "fudge factor" approach.

Valuation Key 5.12

When we create forecasts to use in a DCF valuation, they should represent the expected value of the company's future free cash flows. We measure expected values by probability weighting all of the potential outcomes that might occur. Ignoring the unlikely outcomes and attempting to consider them by adjusting the discount rate in the valuation—arguing that they are additional risk factors for the discount rate—is conceptually flawed and cannot be directly implemented, which is why we call such adjustments "fudge factors."

5.7 COMPREHENSIVE EXAMPLE—DENNIS KELLER, INC.

We use Dennis Keller, Inc. (Keller) to illustrate how to use the various DCF valuation methods discussed in this chapter. Keller is a privately owned company with one owner, Dennis Keller, who is also the company's chief executive officer (CEO). Dennis Keller is considering selling his company to his current chief financial officer (CFO). Based on the company's current strategic plan, Keller prepared forecasts for the company shown in Exhibit 5.7. After Year 3, Keller believes the company's unlevered free cash flows will keep pace with the estimated long-run annual inflation rate of 3%. The company does not hold any excess cash and it faces a tax rate of 40%, $T_C = T_{INT}$, on all income. Keller analyzed several comparable companies and based on the framework in this chapter, unlevered the comparable companies' equity costs of capital to measure their unlevered costs of capital. Based on this analysis, Keller concluded that the best estimate of Keller's unlevered cost of capital is 12%.

Although not the capital structure shown in the forecasts in Exhibit 5.7 (as the debt is held constant at $2 million for Years 1 to 3 in the forecasts), Keller expects to finance the firm (based on market values) with 20% debt (with a cost of capital of 8%) and 80% equity, which we call the *20% debt capital structure*. The CFO plans to use a different capital structure to finance the acquisition. The CFO plans to borrow $20 million at the end of Year 0 and use all of the company's available cash flow to repay the debt in Year 1 through Year 3. As of the end of Year 3, the CFO plans to maintain the capital structure in place at that time and grow the debt at the same rate as the company's free cash flows. We call this capital structure strategy the *$20 million debt capital structure*. The CFO agrees with the forecasts of the unlevered free cash flows prepared by Keller. Since Keller uses a 20% debt capital structure, the best starting point to measure the value of Keller using this capital structure is the WACC valuation method because we know the capital structure ratios but do not know the amount of debt in the capital structure. On the other hand, the CFO plans to use the $20 million debt capital structure (9% cost of capital) for which we know the amount of debt in the capital structure but not the capital structure ratios, so the best starting point for that valuation is the APV valuation method. We know from the chapter that since Keller and the CFO use different capital structures, the value of the firm will differ by the difference in the value of the interest tax shields.

EXHIBIT 5.7 Financial Statement and Unlevered Free Cash Flow Forecasts for Dennis Keller, Inc.

($ in thousands)	Actual		Forecast			
Income Statement:	**Year −1**	**Year 0**	**Year 1**	**Year 2**	**Year 3**	**Year 4**
Revenue	$10,000	$11,000	$12,000	$14,000	$14,420	$14,853
Operating expenses	−2,000	−2,200	−3,600	−4,200	−4,326	−4,456
Depreciation expense	−2,100	−2,600	−3,100	−3,700	−4,077	−4,200
Earnings before interest and taxes	$ 5,900	$ 6,200	$ 5,300	$ 6,100	$ 6,017	$ 6,197
Interest expense	−160	−160	−180	−180	−180	−180
Income before taxes	$ 5,740	$ 6,040	$ 5,120	$ 5,920	$ 5,837	$ 6,017
Income tax expense	−2,296	−2,416	−2,048	−2,368	−2,335	−2,407
Net income	$ 3,444	$ 3,624	$ 3,072	$ 3,552	$ 3,502	$ 3,610

continued

continued from previous page

	Actual		Forecast			
Balance Sheet:	**Year −1**	**Year 0**	**Year 1**	**Year 2**	**Year 3**	**Year 4**
Cash	$ 200	$ 200	$ 200	$ 280	$ 288	$ 297
Net operating working capital	2,000	2,500	1,600	1,820	1,875	1,931
Property, plant & equipment (net)	22,000	24,400	27,300	27,375	28,196	29,042
Total assets	$24,200	$27,100	$29,100	$29,475	$30,359	$31,270
Debt	$ 2,000	$ 2,000	$ 2,000	$ 2,000	$ 2,000	$ 2,060
Common equity	500	10,500	10,500	10,500	10,500	10,500
Retained earnings	21,700	14,600	16,600	16,975	17,859	18,710
Total liabilities and equities	$24,200	$27,100	$29,100	$29,475	$30,359	$31,270
Unlevered Free Cash Flow:						
Earnings before interest and taxes (EBIT)		$ 6,200	$ 5,300	$ 6,100	$ 6,017	$ 6,197
− Income taxes paid on EBIT ($T_C \times$ EBIT)		−2,480	−2,120	−2,440	−2,407	−2,479
Earnings before interest and after taxes		$ 3,720	$ 3,180	$ 3,660	$ 3,610	$ 3,718
+ Depreciation expense		2,600	3,100	3,700	4,077	4,200
− Change in required cash		0	0	−80	−8	−9
− Change in net operating working capital		−500	900	−220	−55	−56
− Capital expenditures		−5,000	−6,000	−3,775	−4,899	−5,046
Unlevered free cash flow		$ 820	$ 1,180	$ 3,285	$ 2,726	$ 2,807

Exhibit may contain small rounding errors

In the remainder of this section, we first use the WACC valuation method to measure the value of Keller based on the 20% debt capital structure. As we did in the Alper example, after we measure the value of the firm using the WACC valuation method, we measure the amount of debt in the 20% capital structure and use that information to also measure the value of the firm using the APV and Equity DCF valuation methods based on the capital structure assumption underlying the WACC valuation. We then use the APV valuation method to measure the value of Keller based on the $20 million debt capital structure. Again, as we did in the Alper example, after we measure the value of the firm using the APV valuation method, we measure the capital structure ratios in the $20 million debt capital structure and use that information to also measure the value of the firm using the WACC and Equity DCF valuation methods based on the capital structure assumption underlying the APV valuation.

Value of Keller Based on the 20% Debt Capital Structure Valuation—The Seller's Perspective

In this section, we measure the value of Keller based on the 20% debt capital structure and use the WACC valuation method. We first measure Keller's equity cost of capital based on Keller's unlevered cost of capital of 12%, an 8% cost of debt and a constant capital structure ratio of 20% debt and 80% equity. We use the capital structure the company expects to use in the future, so its current $2 million of debt outstanding is not relevant because it does not reflect Keller's expected capital structure strategy. Using Equation 5.8 to calculate the company's equity cost of capital based on the 20% debt capital structure, we estimate Keller's equity cost of capital is 13%.

$$r_E = 0.12 + (0.12 - 0.08) \times \frac{0.2}{0.8} = 0.13$$

Based on Keller's 20% capital structure strategy, 8% cost of debt, 40% income tax rate, and 13% equity cost of capital, Keller's weighted average cost of capital (r_{WACC}) is 11.36%.

$$r_{WACC} = 0.13 \times 0.8 + (1 - 0.4) \times 0.08 \times 0.2 = 0.1136$$

Using the free cash flow forecasts in Exhibit 5.7, a 3% growth rate for free cash flows after Year 3, and an 11.36% weighted average cost of capital, Keller's value is $30 million, which we show in Exhibit

5.8. Based on this valuation and \$2 million of outstanding debt, Keller's equity value is \$28 million (\$28 = \$30 − \$2). Note that the 20% debt capital structure assumption in the WACC valuation assumes that Keller will recapitalize the company to 20% debt or \$6 million in total debt (\$6 = \$30 × 0.2) if he does not sell it. If Keller did not recapitalize to its target capital structure, the value of the interest tax shields would not be as high as assumed in the WACC valuation and we would need to adjust the capital structure assumption to correctly value the firm and equity.

EXHIBIT 5.8 CEO's Weighted Average Cost of Capital Valuation of Keller (20% Debt Capital Structure)

(\$ in thousands)	Year 0	Year 1	Year 2	Year 3	CV_{Firm} Year 3
Unlevered free cash flow for continuing value					\$ 2,807
Continuing value capitalization factor $(r_{WACC} - g)^{-1}$					11.962
Unlevered free cash flow and continuing value		\$1,180	\$3,285	\$2,726	\$33,582
Discount factor $(1 + r_{WACC})^{-t}$		0.898	0.806	0.724	0.724
Present value		\$1,060	\$2,649	\$1,974	\$24,317
Value of the firm	**\$30,000**				
Value of outstanding debt	**2,000**				
Value of common equity	**\$28,000**				

Exhibit may contain small rounding errors

Measuring the Value of Keller's Interest Tax Shields and Unlevered Value Embedded in the 20% Debt Capital Structure and Using the APV Valuation Method. Now that we know the value of the firm for the 20% debt capital structure, we can measure the value of the interest tax shields and the value of the unlevered firm using the APV valuation method under the assumption of the 20% debt capital structure underlying the WACC valuation. In order to do this, we forecast the interest tax shields embedded in the WACC valuation, which requires forecasts of the amount of debt in each year that is implicit in the WACC valuation. To generate these forecasts, we first measure the value of the firm at the beginning of each year using the WACC method. The amount of debt for any year is equal to the constant capital structure ratio of 20% debt multiplied by the value of the firm at the beginning of the year.

We can measure the value of the firm in each year by starting at the continuing value date, Year 3, which we already measured in Exhibit 5.8, \$33,582 (\$33,582 = \$2,807.45/(0.1136 − 0.03)).[12] We can also use the WACC method to measure the value of the firm at the end of Years 2, 1 and 0. We measure the value of the firm in Year 2 by discounting both the value of the firm at the end of Year 3 (the continuing value) and the free cash flow in Year 3 for one year by the weighted average cost of capital; more generally, we can use the formula in Equation 5.13.

$$V_{F,t} = \frac{FCF_{t+1}}{1+r_{WACC}} + \frac{V_{F,t+1}}{1+r_{WACC}} \tag{5.13}$$

Using this approach, we measure the value of Keller at the end of Years 2, 1, and 0. We already know the value of the firm as of the valuation date from Exhibit 5.8, \$30,000, but we calculate it again using Equation 5.13 to show that the valuations are identical.

$$V_{F,2} = \frac{\$33{,}581.91 + \$2{,}725.68}{1.1136} = \$32{,}603.80$$

$$V_{F,1} = \frac{\$32{,}603.80 + \$3{,}285.30}{1.1136} = \$32{,}228.00$$

$$V_{F,0} = \frac{\$32{,}228.00 + \$1{,}180.00}{1.1136} = \$30{,}000.00$$

[12] We use more significant digits than shown in the exhibits to avoid rounding errors in the text. See the data file available for this chapter for the precise calculations.

Now that we know the value of the firm in each year, we can use the constant target debt to value ratio, 20%, in order to calculate both the amount of debt and the interest tax shields imbedded in the WACC valuation, which we show in Exhibit 5.9. An advantage of calculating the implied debt and interest expense is to make sure that the interest will be fully deductible if the tax regime imposes limitations on the tax deductibility of interest (like the U.S.). Assuming the limitation was 30% of EBIT, we can see that the interest would be fully deductible.

EXHIBIT 5.9 Interest Tax Shields Implied in the 20% Debt Capital Structure WACC Valuation

($ in thousands)	Year 1	Year 2	Year 3	Year 4
Value of the firm beginning of year.	$30,000	$32,228	$32,604	$33,582
Constant target debt to value ratio	20%	20%	20%	20%
Amount of debt beginning of year	$ 6,000	$ 6,446	$ 6,521	$ 6,716
Interest rate for debt.	8.0%	8.0%	8.0%	8.0%
Interest on debt for Year ($r_D \times V_D$)	$ 480	$ 516	$ 522	$ 537
Tax rate for interest (T_{INT})	40%	40%	40%	40%
ITS implied in WACC valuation (20% debt)	$ 192	$ 206	$ 209	$ 215

We now have sufficient information to value Keller using the APV valuation method based on the assumptions underlying the 20% debt capital structure-based WACC valuation. We present the APV valuation in Exhibit 5.10.

Since we used the same cash flow and discount rate assumptions in the APV valuation as we used in the WACC valuation (the 20% debt capital structure), the valuation of the firm and equity are the same. In the APV valuation, the unlevered free cash flows and interest tax shields are discounted at the unlevered cost of capital. From the APV valuation we learn that the value of Keller's operating assets (unlevered value of the firm) is $27,816 and the value of the interest tax shields embedded in the WACC valuation is $2,184, for a firm value of $30,000.

EXHIBIT 5.10 Adjusted Present Value Valuation of the 20% Debt Capital Structure

($ in thousands)	Year 0	Year 1	Year 2	Year 3	CV Year 3
Value of the Unlevered Firm					
Unlevered free cash flow for continuing value					$ 2,807
Discount factor for continuing value					11.111
Unlevered free cash flow and continuing value		$1,180	$3,285	$2,726	$31,194
Discount factor		0.893	0.797	0.712	0.712
Discounted value		$1,054	$2,619	$1,940	$22,203
Value of the unlevered firm	$27,816				
Value of the Interest Tax Shields					
Interest tax shield for continuing value					$ 215
Discount factor for continuing value					11.111
Interest tax shield and continuing value		$ 192	$ 206	$ 209	$ 2,388
Discount factor		0.893	0.797	0.712	0.712
Present value		$ 171	$ 164	$ 149	$ 1,700
Value of the interest tax shields	$ 2,184				
Value of the firm	**$30,000**	$1,225	$2,783	$2,089	$23,903

Exhibit may contain small rounding errors

Measuring the Value of Keller's Equity Based on the 20% Debt Capital Structure Using the Equity DCF Method. In the 20% debt capital structure WACC valuation of Keller, Keller's equity cost of capital, which we calculated previously as 13%, would not change over time. Although we know the equity cost of capital for the 20% capital structure WACC valuation, we do not know the equity free cash flows based on this capital structure. To measure equity free cash flows for Keller, we subtract after-tax interest and add the change in debt to Keller's unlevered free cash flow (debt is the only non-common equity financing used by Keller).

Exhibit 5.9 calculates Keller's interest and interest tax shields for Years 1 through 4. This exhibit also calculates the amount of debt assumed in the 20% debt capital structure WACC valuation for the end of Years 0 through 3 from which we can calculate the change in debt for Years 1 through 3. Since as of the end of Year 3 Keller is expected to grow at 3%, the change in debt for Year 4 is equal to the debt balance at the beginning of Year 4 (end of Year 3) multiplied by the growth rate ($201 = $6,716 × 0.03). Based on this information and the unlevered free cash flow forecasts, we can measure the equity free cash flows implied by the WACC valuation. We show this calculation in Exhibit 5.11. Note that in this case, the company will be able to pay dividends every year and will require no additional financing.

EXHIBIT 5.11 Equity Free Cash Flows Implied in the 20% Debt Capital Structure-Based Weighted Average Cost of Capital Valuation

	Forecast			
($ in thousands)	**Year 1**	**Year 2**	**Year 3**	**Year 4**
Unlevered free cash flow (FCF)	$1,180	$3,285	$2,726	$2,807
Interest expense paid ($r_D \times V_D$)	−480	−516	−522	−537
Interest tax shield (ITS = $T_{INT} \times r_D \times V_D$)	192	206	209	215
Change in debt	446	75	196	201
Free cash flow to common equity (EFCF)	$1,338	$3,051	$2,608	$2,687

Exhibit may contain small rounding errors

We use Equation 5.11 to measure the value of Keller's equity by discounting the equity free cash flows implied in the 20% debt capital structure and WACC valuation.

$$V_E = \frac{EFCF_1}{(1+r_E)} + \frac{EFCF_2}{(1+r_E)^2} + \frac{EFCF_3}{(r_E - g)} \times \frac{1}{(1+r_E)^2}$$

$$\$24{,}000 = \frac{\$1{,}338}{1.13} + \frac{\$3{,}051}{1.13^2} + \frac{\$2{,}608}{0.13 - 0.03} \times \frac{1}{1.13^2}$$

Note that the equity free cash flows were discounted individually for Years 1 and 2, and the continuing value began in Year 3. We were able to start the continuing value in Year 3 rather than Year 4 because the Year 4 and subsequent free cash flows are assumed to increase annually by the growth rate.[13] The amount calculated using the equity discounted cash flow method of $24 million equals the value of the equity using the WACC valuation method ($24,000 = $30,000 firm value × 0.8 equity/firm value).

Value of Keller Based on the $20 Million Debt Capital Structure—The Buyer's Perspective

The CEO and CFO agreed to a transaction price of $28 million for Keller's equity. The CFO was arranging the following financing in order to purchase Keller. The CFO plans to personally invest $10 million and borrow the remaining amount needed, $20 million, in debt with a 9% interest rate. The $30 million in raised capital will be used to repay the $2 million of existing debt and to purchase the CEO's equity for $28 million, which we summarize in the following sources and uses of funds schedule.

[13] The same equity value will be obtained if you discount Years 1 through 3 individually, and begin the continuing value in Year 4, as shown below:

$$\$24{,}000 = \frac{\$1{,}338}{1.13} + \frac{\$3{,}051}{1.13^2} + \frac{\$2{,}608}{1.13^3} + \frac{\$2{,}687}{0.13 - 0.03} \times \frac{1}{1.13^3}$$

Sources of Funds ($ in thousands)	
New equity invested	$10,000
New debt (9%)	20,000
Total sources of funds	$30,000

Uses of Funds ($ in thousands)	
Value of the equity purchased	$28,000
Existing debt (8%)	2,000
Total uses of funds	$30,000

For the next three years, the CFO plans to use any free cash flow the company generates to pay interest and repay debt. After the end of Year 3, the CFO plans to maintain a constant proportion of debt to equity at whatever that proportion is at the end of Year 3. In other words, the CFO intends to use the debt-to-value ratio, whatever that is, as of the end of the third year, and then maintain the capital structure at that target ratio beyond Year 3 by growing the debt at Keller's long-term growth rate.

The increase in the interest rate for the new debt (from 8% to 9%) reflects the additional risk of having more debt in the capital structure. To make the calculations less complex, we assume that the interest rate on the debt is equal to the debt cost of capital. We also assume that the company's debt cost of capital of 9% will not change, even though the CFO expects the company to reduce the amount of debt it has outstanding to some degree in Years 1 through 3.

Measuring Keller's Value Based on the $20 Million Debt Capital Structure Using the Adjusted Present Value Valuation Method. The CFO is confident that the company can achieve the free cash flow forecasts in Exhibit 5.7. The CFO prepared financial statement and free cash flow forecasts based on the $20 million debt capital structure. The income and balance sheet forecasts appear in Exhibit 5.12. The balance sheet as of the end of Year 0 includes the effects of purchasing the equity for $28 million. As stated previously, the CFO will invest $10 million in equity and issue $20 million of debt. The company will use these funds to pay down the existing debt of $2 million and pay the CEO $28 million for his equity. The net effect of this is an outstanding debt balance of $20 million and a common equity balance of $7.1 million (we will explain the latter after we discuss the free cash flow forecasts).

EXHIBIT 5.12 Income Statement and Balance Sheet Forecasts Based on the $20 Million Debt Capital Structure

($ in thousands)	Actual Year −1	Actual Year 0	Forecast Year 1	Forecast Year 2	Forecast Year 3	Forecast Year 4
Income Statement						
Revenue	$10,000	$11,000	$12,000	$14,000	$14,420	$14,853
Operating expenses	−2,000	−2,200	−3,600	−4,200	−4,326	−4,456
Depreciation expense	−2,100	−2,600	−3,100	−3,700	−4,077	−4,200
Earnings before interest and taxes	$ 5,900	$ 6,200	$ 5,300	$ 6,100	$ 6,017	$ 6,197
Interest expense	−160	−160	−1,800	−1,791	−1,592	−1,433
Income before taxes	$ 5,740	$ 6,040	$ 3,500	$ 4,309	$ 4,424	$ 4,764
Income tax expense	−2,296	−2,416	−1,400	−1,724	−1,770	−1,906
Net income	$ 3,444	$ 3,624	$ 2,100	$ 2,585	$ 2,655	$ 2,859
Balance Sheet						
Cash	$ 200	$ 200	$ 200	$ 280	$ 288	$ 297
Net operating working capital	2,000	2,500	1,600	1,820	1,875	1,931
Property, plant, and equipment (net)	22,000	24,400	27,300	27,375	28,196	29,042
Total assets	$24,200	$27,100	$29,100	$29,475	$30,359	$31,270
Debt	$ 2,000	$20,000	$19,900	$17,689	$15,919	$16,396
Common equity	500	10,500	10,500	10,500	10,500	10,500
Retained earnings	21,700	−3,400	−1,300	1,285	3,940	4,373
Total liabilities and equities	$24,200	$27,100	$29,100	$29,475	$30,359	$31,270

Exhibit may contain small rounding errors

Based on the unlevered free cash flow forecasts in Exhibit 5.7, the CFO also prepared forecasts for the company's expected equity free cash flows and reconciliations to the change in cash, both of which appear in Exhibit 5.13. Since the company does not hold any excess cash, the dividend paid each year is equal to the equity free cash flow. As of the end of Year 0, the company's common equity balance is equal to $10.5 million, which is equal to the $0.5 million balance from Year −1, plus the $10 million invested in Year 0. The retained earnings balance is $21.7 million at the end of Year −1. To that, we add $3.624 million in Net Income for Year 0 and subtract both the $28 million paid to the CEO and the $0.724 million equity free cash flow (equals dividends paid in Year 0, excluding the increase in debt issued), in order to measure the retained earnings balance as of the end of Year 0 of −$3.4 million (−$3,400 = $21,700 + $3,624 − $28,000 − $724).

EXHIBIT 5.13 Equity Free Cash Flow Forecasts Based on the $20 Million Debt Capital Structure

($ in thousands)	Actual Year 0	Forecast Year 1	Forecast Year 2	Forecast Year 3	Forecast Year 4
Equity Free Cash Flow (EFCF)					
Unlevered free cash flow (FCF)	$ 820	$1,180	$3,285	$2,726	$2,807
Interest expense paid ($r_D \times V_{D,t-1}$)	−160	−1,800	−1,791	−1,592	−1,433
Interest tax shield (ITS = $T_{INT} \times r_D \times V_{D,t-1}$)	64	720	716	637	573
Free cash flow minus after-tax interest	$ 724	$ 100	$2,211	$1,770	$1,948
Change in debt	18,000	−100	−2,211	−1,770	478
Equity free cash flow (EFCF)	$18,724	$ 0	$ 0	$ 0	$2,425
Reconciliation to Change in Cash					
Equity free cash flow (EFCF)	$18,724	$ 0	$ 0	$ 0	$2,425
− Common equity dividends paid	−28,724	0	0	0	−2,425
+ Change in common equity financing	10,000	0	0	0	0
Change in excess cash	$ 0	$ 0	$ 0	$ 0	$ 0
Change in required cash	0	0	80	8	9
Change in cash balance	$ 0	$ 0	$ 80	$ 8	$ 9

Exhibit may contain small rounding errors

The CFO knows that based on the $20 million debt capital structure, the APV method—and not the WACC method—is the best valuation method to use to value the company. The CFO used the unlevered cost of capital to discount its interest tax shields for all years. Using the APV method and a 12% cost of capital for the company's unlevered assets, the CFO calculated the value of the firm as of the end of Year 0 to be $34.015 million, which we present in Exhibit 5.14. The CFO assumed that the company would maintain its capital structure ratios in perpetuity after the end of Year 3, and that debt, interest, and interest tax shields would grow at the company's long-term growth rate after that year. The CFO calculated the value of Keller's equity by subtracting the values of each of the non-equity claims from the value of the firm. Since Keller finances itself with debt and equity only, the value of the CFO's equity as of the end of Year 0 is $14.015 million ($14,015 = $34,015 − $20,000).[14]

EXHIBIT 5.14 CFO's Adjusted Present Value Valuation of Keller Based on the $20 Million Debt Capital Structure

($ in thousands)	Year 0	Year 1	Year 2	Year 3	CV Year 3
Value of the Unlevered Firm					
Unlevered free cash flow for continuing value					$ 2,807
Continuing value capitalization factor $(r_{UA} - g)^{-1}$					11.111
Unlevered free cash flow and continuing value		$1,180	$3,285	$2,726	$31,194
Discount factor $(1 + r_{UA})^{-t}$		0.893	0.797	0.712	0.712
Discounted value		$1,054	$2,619	$1,940	$22,203
Value of the unlevered firm	$27,816				

continued

[14] We are assuming that all of the interest expense is tax deductible. We note that if the limitation on deductible interest expense is 30% of EBIT, then not all of the Year 1 interest expense would be deductible, which would impact the APV valuation and the calculation of the equity free cash flows. This would give rise to an interest carryforward, which we discussed in detail in Chapter 3.

continued from previous page

($ in thousands)	Year 0	Year 1	Year 2	Year 3	CV Year 3
Value of the Interest Tax Shields					
Interest tax shield for continuing value					$ 573
Continuing value capitalization factor $(r_{UA} - g)^{-1}$					11.111
Interest tax shield and continuing value of the interest tax shield		$ 720	$ 716	$ 637	$ 6,368
Discount factor $(1 + r_{UA})^{-t}$		0.893	0.797	0.712	0.712
Present value		$ 643	$ 571	$ 453	$ 4,532
Value of the interest tax shields	$ 6,200				
Value of the firm	**$34,015**				
Value of outstanding debt	**20,000**				
Value of common equity	**$14,015**				

Exhibit may contain small rounding errors

Measuring the Value of Keller Based on the $20 Million Debt Capital Structure and Using the Weighted Average Cost of Capital Valuation Method. We can also use the WACC method as a consistency check for an APV valuation. In an APV valuation, we do not know a company's capital structure ratios. We can calculate the company's capital structure ratios based on the $20 million capital structure and the APV valuation by first calculating the value of the firm for each year using the APV method, and then calculating the company's capital structure ratio for each year based on the debt forecasts in Exhibit 5.12. Once we have the capital structure ratios for each year, we can measure the company's equity cost of capital and weighted average cost of capital for each year, and then use the weighted average cost of capital to value the firm. Since the capital structure ratios are changing, both the equity cost of capital and weighted average cost of capital change each year. In Exhibit 5.15, we use the APV method to measure the value of the firm in each year using the data presented in the APV valuation.

EXHIBIT 5.15 Year-by-Year Adjusted Present Value Valuation of the $20 Million Debt Capital Structure

As of the Beginning of the Year ($ in thousands)	Year 1	Year 2	Year 3	CV Year 3
Value of Unlevered Firm				
Unlevered free cash flow for continuing value				$ 2,807
Continuing value capitalization factor $(r_{UA} - g)^{-1}$				11.111
Unlevered free cash flow	$ 1,180	$ 3,285	$ 2,726	
Value of the unlevered firm at year end	29,974	30,285	31,194	
Unlevered value at year end plus unlevered free cash flow	$31,154	$33,571	$33,920	
Discount factor for one year $(1 + r_{UA})^{-1}$	0.893	0.893	0.893	
Beginning of year value of unlevered firm	$27,816	$29,974	$30,285	$31,194
Value of the Interest Tax Shields (ITS)				
Interest tax shield for continuing value				$ 573
Continuing value capitalization factor $(r_{UA} - g)^{-1}$				11.111
Interest tax shields	$ 720	$ 716	$ 637	
Value of the interest tax shields at year end	6,223	6,254	6,368	
End of year ITS plus current year ITS	$ 6,943	$ 6,970	$ 7,004	
Discount factor for one year $(1 + r_{UA})^{-1}$	0.893	0.893	0.893	
Beginning of year value of interest tax shields	$ 6,200	$ 6,223	$ 6,254	$ 6,368
Beginning of year value of the firm	**$34,015**	**$36,197**	**$36,539**	**$37,561**

Exhibit may contain small rounding errors

We perform the same type of calculation in Exhibit 5.15 that we performed for the WACC valuation using Equation 5.13. For example, to calculate the value of the unlevered firm at the beginning of Year 3, we add the continuing value of the unlevered firm, $31,194, to the Year 3 unlevered free cash flow, $2,726, and discount the sum one period at the unlevered cost of capital to arrive at $30,285. We do the same type of calculation with the interest tax shields and find that the value of the firm at the beginning of Year 3 is $36,539. To calculate the value of the unlevered firm at the beginning of Year 2, we take the value of the unlevered firm at the beginning of Year 3 ($30,285), add it to the Year 2 unlevered free cash flow ($3,285), and discount the sum back one period to arrive at $29,974. Doing the same type of calculation with the interest tax shields, we find that the value of the firm at the beginning of Year 2 is $36,197.

Once we know the value of the firm at the beginning of each year, we use the debt forecasts to measure the company's capital structure ratios in each year, which we show in the top panel of Exhibit 5.16.[15] Afterward, we can use our levering formula (Equation 5.8) to measure the equity cost of capital in each year, which we show in the bottom panel of Exhibit 5.16. Note that the equity cost of capital is decreasing each year starting at 16.3% and decreasing to 14.2% by the beginning of Year 4. Assuming market conditions do not change, it will remain at 14.2% thereafter, for the company's capital structure strategy is to adopt a constant capital structure ratio after Year 3 of whatever that capital structure happens to be at that time (from Exhibit 5.16, you can see that the debt-to-value ratio is forecasted to be 42.4%).

Given that the equity cost of capital is decreasing, how should we expect the weighted average cost of capital to change? On the one hand, a decrease in the equity cost of capital would decrease the weighted average cost of capital. However, the decrease in the equity cost of capital is due to a decrease in the use of financial leverage. A decrease in the use of financial leverage places more weight on the equity cost of capital and less weight on the after-tax debt cost of capital in the weighted average cost of capital calculation. The net effect increases the weighted average cost of capital, which we show in Exhibit 5.17, consistent with the work of M&M.

EXHIBIT 5.16 Year-by-Year Capital Structure Ratios Based on the Adjusted Present Value Valuation of the $20 Million Debt Capital Structure

As of the End of the Year ($ in thousands)	Year 0	Year 1	Year 2	Year 3
Value of the firm (V_F)	$34,015	$36,197	$36,539	$37,561
Value of debt (V_D)	20,000	19,900	17,689	15,919
Value of equity (V_E)	$14,015	$16,297	$18,850	$21,643
Value of debt (V_D) to value of the firm (V_F)	58.8%	55.0%	48.4%	42.4%
Value of equity (V_E) to value of the firm (V_F)	41.2%	45.0%	51.6%	57.6%
Value of debt (V_D) to value of equity (V_E)	1.4270	1.2211	0.9384	0.7355

$r_E = r_{UA} + (r_{UA} - r_D) \times \frac{V_D}{V_E}$	Beg of Year 1	Beg of Year 2	Beg of Year 3	Beg of Year 4
Unlevered cost of capital, r_{UA}	12.0%	12.0%	12.0%	12.0%
Cost of debt, r_D	9.0%	9.0%	9.0%	9.0%
Value of debt to value of equity	1.43	1.22	0.94	0.74
Equity cost of capital, r_E	16.3%	15.7%	14.8%	14.2%

Exhibit may contain small rounding errors

EXHIBIT 5.17 Year-by-Year Weighted Average Costs of Capital Based on the Adjusted Present Value of the $20 Million Debt Capital Structure

$r_{WACC} = r_E \times \frac{V_E}{V_F} + (1 - T_{INT}) \times r_D \times \frac{V_D}{V_F}$	Beg of Year 1	Beg of Year 2	Beg of Year 3	Beg of Year 4
Equity cost of capital, r_E	16.3%	15.7%	14.8%	14.2%
Value of equity to value of the firm	41.2%	45.0%	51.6%	57.6%
Cost of the debt r_D	9.0%	9.0%	9.0%	9.0%
Value of debt to value of the firm	58.8%	55.0%	48.4%	42.4%
Income tax rate	40.0%	40.0%	40.0%	40.0%
Weighted average cost of capital, r_{WACC}	9.9%	10.0%	10.3%	10.5%

[15] For simplicity, we assume that the market value and book value of the debt remain equal despite the decline in the use of leverage. We can use the techniques discussed in Chapter 9 to value the debt if necessary.

We now have all of the information we need to use the WACC method in order to measure the value of the firm with a changing capital structure. Note that since the weighted average cost of capital is changing over time, we discount the cash flows using the appropriate present value calculation allowing for varying discount rates.

$$V_F = \frac{FCF_1}{(1+r_{WACC,1})} + \frac{FCF_2}{(1+r_{WACC,1})\times(1+r_{WACC,2})} + \frac{FCF_3 + \dfrac{FCF_4}{(r_{WACC,4}-g)}}{(1+r_{WACC,1})\times(1+r_{WACC,2})\times(1+r_{WACC,3})}$$

$$\$34{,}015 = \frac{\$1{,}180}{1.099} + \frac{\$3{,}285}{1.099\times1.1} + \frac{\$2{,}726 + \dfrac{\$2{,}807}{0.105-0.03}}{1.099\times1.1\times1.103}$$

The continuing value of the firm in this WACC valuation is equal to \$37.561 million [= $FCF_4 \div (r_{WACC,4} - g)$], which is equal to the continuing value from the APV valuation (see Exhibit 5.15; \$37,561 = \$31,194 + \$6,367).

Measuring the Value of Keller's Equity Based on the \$20 Million Debt Capital Structure and Using the Equity DCF Valuation Method. In the APV valuation of the \$20 million debt capital structure, the CFO prepared forecasts of the company's financial statements (Exhibit 5.12) as well as its equity free cash flows (Exhibit 5.13). We already measured Keller's capital structure ratios and its equity cost of capital for each year in Exhibit 5.16. Thus, we have all the information needed to value the company's equity using the Equity DCF method based on the \$20 million debt capital structure. We note that the discounting of the equity free cash flows takes into consideration the changing cost of equity capital in each year.

$$V_E = \frac{EFCF_1}{(1+r_{E,1})} + \frac{EFCF_2}{(1+r_{E,1})\times(1+r_{E,2})} + \frac{EFCF_3 + \dfrac{EFCF_4}{(r_{E,4}-g)}}{(1+r_{E,1})\times(1+r_{E,2})\times(1+r_{E,3})}$$

$$\$14{,}015 = \frac{\$0}{1.163} + \frac{\$0}{1.163\times1.157} + \frac{\$0 + \dfrac{\$2{,}425}{0.142-0.03}}{1.163\times1.157\times1.148}$$

The value of the equity calculated above equals the value of the equity calculated using the APV valuation method (\$14,015 = \$34,015 firm value − \$20,000 debt).

SUMMARY AND KEY CONCEPTS

In this chapter, we discussed how the tax deductibility of interest could increase the value of the firm by the value of the related interest tax shields, and we then learned how the different valuation methods measure this effect. The cash flows created by the tax deductibility of interest, called interest tax shields, are equal to the reduction in income taxes a company pays as a result of the tax deductibility of interest.

In addition, we learned about the relationships between the equity cost of capital and a company's other costs of capital under the assumption that the expected interest tax shields are discounted at the unlevered cost of capital. As we discuss later in the book, those relationships change using other assumptions about valuing a company's interest tax shields, including the discount rate used to value the interest tax shields. We also learned how to compute the weighted average cost of capital.

Further, we illustrated how to implement the APV and WACC discounted cash flow methods. We saw that the method that is the best starting point for our valuation depends on the capital structure strategy of the company and the information we have on its capital structure. In addition, we saw that the Equity DCF method is not a particularly useful starting point in many valuation situations. Although most of the formulas presented in this chapter assumed a company had only three types of financing—debt, preferred stock, and common stock—all of the formulas can easily be adjusted if the company has other sources of financing.

ADDITIONAL READING AND REFERENCES

Myers, S. C., "Interactions of Corporate Financing and Investment Decisions—Implications for Capital Budgeting," *Journal of Finance* 29 (1974), pp. 1–25.

Ruback, R. S., "Downsides and DCF: Valuing Biased Cash Flow Forecasts," *Journal of Applied Corporate Finance* vol. 23, no.2 (2011), pp. 8–17.

EXERCISES AND PROBLEMS

P5.1 **Which Valuation Method to Use:** Assume you were going to value the companies described below. State which valuation method you would use to value the company and discuss why you would use that method.

a. A privately held company has had a stable capital structure strategy using 20% debt financing and 20% preferred stock financing and is expected to use the same capital structure in the future. Value the company as of today.

b. A publicly traded company, which has had no debt for many years, is planning to undergo a debt recapitalization. The plan calls for the company to issue a large amount of debt—about 90% of the value of the firm—and distribute the cash to its equityholders. Over the next ten years, the company plans to repay its debt so that the company will have 20% debt financing at the end of ten years. The company's long-run (after year ten) capital structure strategy is to maintain 20% debt financing. Value the company as of the date of the anticipated debt recapitalization.

c. Company P is acquiring Company S in a cash transaction. Company P has a capital structure strategy of 30% debt financing. Company S is in a different industry than Company P and has a capital structure strategy of 10% debt financing. Company P plans to continue to use its capital structure strategy on a consolidated basis after the transaction. Value Company S for this transaction.

d. A publicly traded company has been changing its capital structure over the past few years as it acquired various companies operating in various industries. The company plans to refinance itself with 20% debt financing. Value the company as of the refinancing.

P5.2 **Basic Valuation Calculations (Interest is Tax Deductible)—The APV Perpetuity Company:** The APV Perpetuity Company does not expect to grow. In other words, it expects its cash flows to remain constant, and it expects to distribute all equity free cash flows to the equityholders in the form of dividends and not hold any excess cash. The company is expected to generate an unlevered free cash flow of $3,000 per year in perpetuity. The company is initially financed with $10,000 equity, $12,000 debt, and $8,000 preferred stock. The company's income tax rate on all income statement items is 40%, and interest is tax deductible. The company does not intend to change the amount of financing it has currently. The company's interest rate, which is equal to its debt cost of capital, is 8%. The company's preferred stock dividend rate (paid on the book value of preferred stock), which is equal to the cost of capital of preferred stock, is 9%. The company's unlevered cost of capital is 10%. The appropriate discount rate for interest tax shields is the unlevered cost of capital for this company.

a. Value the company—the value of the firm and the value of the equity—as of the end of Year 0 using the APV valuation method.

b. Calculate the company's capital structure ratios as of the end of Year 0. Given the company's capital structure strategy, how will these capital structure ratios vary in the future?

c. Calculate the company's weighted average cost of capital as of the end of Year 0.

d. Value the company—the value of the firm—as of the end of Year 0 using the WACC valuation method.

e. Value the equity as of the end of Year 0 using the Equity DCF valuation method.

P5.3 **Basic Valuation Calculations (Interest is Not Tax Deductible)—The APV Perpetuity Company:** In this problem, we value the APV Perpetuity Company from Problem 5.2 in an income tax regime in which interest expense is **not** tax deductible. The underlying information for the APV Perpetuity Company appears in Problem 5.2 with the following exceptions—interest is not tax deductible. If you also completed the previous problem for the APV Perpetuity Company, compare your responses for this problem to your responses for Problem 5.2.

a. Value the company—the value of the firm and the value of the equity—as of the end of Year 0 using the APV valuation method.

b. Calculate the company's capital structure ratios as of the end of Year 0. Given the company's capital structure strategy, how will these capital structure ratios vary in the future?

c. Calculate the company's weighted average cost of capital as of the end of Year 0.

d. Value the company—the value of the firm—as of the end of Year 0 using the WACC valuation method.

e. Value the equity as of the end of Year 0 using the Equity DCF valuation method.

P5.4 Basic Valuation Calculations (Interest is Tax Deductible)—The WACC Perpetuity Company: The WACC Perpetuity Company does not expect to grow. In other words, it expects its cash flows to remain constant, and it expects to distribute all equity free cash flows to the equityholders in the form of dividends; the company does not hold excess cash. The company is expected to generate an unlevered free cash flow of $3,000 per year in perpetuity. The company's income tax rate on all income statement items is 40%, and interest is tax deductible. The company does not have forecasts for the dollar values of its financing but knows it is going to finance itself with 50% debt, 10% preferred stock, and 40% equity. The company does not intend to change the proportions of financing it will have. The company's interest rate, which is equal to its debt cost of capital, is 9%. The company's preferred stock dividend rate (paid on the book value of preferred stock), which is equal to the cost of capital of preferred stock, is 10%. The company's unlevered cost of capital is 11%. The appropriate discount rate for interest tax shields is the unlevered cost of capital for this company.

a. Value the company—the value of the firm and the value of the equity—as of the end of Year 0, using the WACC valuation method and assuming its capital structure strategy was in place at the end of Year 0.
b. Calculate the amount of debt and preferred stock the company would have as of the end of Year 0 based on your WACC valuation.
c. Value the company—the value of the firm—as of the end of Year 0 using the APV valuation method.
d. Calculate the company's equity free cash flow for Year 1, assuming its capital structure strategy was in place at the end of Year 0.
e. Value the equity as of the end of Year 0 using the Equity DCF valuation method, assuming its capital structure strategy was in place at the end of Year 0.

P5.5 Basic Valuation Calculations (Interest is Not Tax Deductible)—The WACC Perpetuity Company: In this problem, we value the WACC Perpetuity Company from Problem 5.4 in an income tax regime in which interest expense is **not** tax deductible. The underlying information on the WACC Perpetuity Company appears in Problem 5.4, with the following exception—interest is not tax deductible. If you also completed the previous problem for the WACC Perpetuity Company, compare your responses for this problem to your responses for Problem 5.4.

a. Value the company—the value of the firm and the value of the equity—as of the end of Year 0, using the WACC valuation method, assuming its capital structure strategy was in place at the end of Year 0.
b. Calculate the amount of debt and preferred stock the company would have as of the end of Year 0 based on your WACC valuation.
c. Value the company—the value of the firm—as of the end of Year 0 using the APV valuation method.
d. Calculate the company's equity free cash flow for Year 1, assuming its capital structure strategy was in place at the end of Year 0.
e. Value the equity as of the end of Year 0 using the Equity DCF valuation method assuming its capital structure strategy was in place at the end of Year 0.

P5.6 Adjusted Present Value Valuation—The Joel Germunder Company: The Joel Germunder Company (Germunder) is a privately held family business that currently uses no debt in its capital structure. The owner-managers have a plan to expand the operations of the company over the next two years. Some of Germunder's younger owner-managers proposed a plan to issue a large amount of debt to not only expand the company's operations but to also pay the owners a one-time, special dividend. The younger owner-managers' plan is to finance the entire transaction by issuing $15 million of 10% debt.

After the company completes its expansion, the plan of the younger owner-managers is to use some of the free cash flows to repay the debt until the end of Year 3, but they will continue to pay some dividends in Years 1 through 3. As of the beginning of Year 4, they expect the company's cash flows to grow at the long-run inflation rate, which they expect to be 2.5%. At the end of Year 3, they believe that the company will have paid down a sufficient amount of debt so that the remaining debt will be used as the basis of a stable target capital structure, and the debt will grow at the overall growth rate of 2.5%. While the leverage of the company will decline some over the first three years, it will not fall enough to change the cost of debt. Moreover, since the debt-to-value ratio will stay the same after Year 3, the cost of debt will remain at 10%. The company does not hold any excess cash, and all equity free cash flows will be paid out as a dividend to shareholders. The company's chief financial officer prepared a set of financial forecasts that reflects this plan. The income statement, balance sheet, and cash flow statement forecasts appear in Exhibit P5.1. The forecasts assume the company will issue the debt at the end of Year 0, which is reflected in the balance sheet for that year. Germunder's income tax rate for all revenues and expenses (including interest) is 40%, and its unlevered cost of capital is 12%.

a. Use the financial statements in Exhibit P5.1 to measure Germunder's unlevered free cash flows in Years 1 through 4.
b. Value Germunder—the entire firm and equity—as of the end of Year 0, using the APV valuation method. Assume that the appropriate discount rate for interest tax shields is the unlevered cost of capital of the company.

c. As of the end of Year 0, what amount and percent of firm value and what percent of equity value does Germunder derive from the value of its interest tax shields?

d. What issues would you suggest the company's management think about before moving forward with this capital structure strategy?

e. As a consistency check on your previous valuation, value Germunder as of the end of Year 0 using all of the above assumptions with the WACC valuation method. Again, assume that the appropriate discount rate for interest tax shields is the unlevered cost of capital for this company.

f. As a consistency check on your previous valuation, value Germunder's equity as of the end of Year 0 using the Equity DCF valuation method. Again, assume that the appropriate discount rate for interest tax shields is the unlevered cost of capital for this company.

EXHIBIT P5.1 Income Statement, Balance Sheet, and Cash Flow Statement Forecasts for the Joel Germunder Company

($ in thousands)	Actual Year −1	Actual Year 0	Forecast Year 1	Forecast Year 2	Forecast Year 3	Forecast Year 4
Income Statement						
Revenue	$ 7,968	$ 8,765	$13,147	$14,462	$14,823	$15,194
Operating expenses	−3,187	−3,506	−5,259	−5,785	−5,929	−6,078
Depreciation expense	−1,000	−1,273	−1,875	−2,226	−2,494	−2,557
Earnings before interest and taxes	$ 3,781	$ 3,986	$ 6,014	$ 6,451	$ 6,400	$ 6,560
Interest expense	0	0	−1,500	−1,440	−1,320	−1,190
Income before taxes	$ 3,781	$ 3,986	$ 4,514	$ 5,011	$ 5,080	$ 5,370
Income tax expense	−1,512	−1,594	−1,805	−2,004	−2,032	−2,148
Net income	$ 2,268	$ 2,392	$ 2,708	$ 3,006	$ 3,048	$ 3,222
Balance Sheet						
Cash	$ 80	$ 88	$ 131	$ 145	$ 148	$ 152
Net operating working capital	1,514	1,665	1,972	2,169	2,224	2,279
Property, plant & equipment (net)	11,686	16,434	18,077	18,529	18,993	19,467
Total assets	$13,280	$18,187	$20,181	$20,843	$21,364	$21,898
Debt	$ 0	$15,000	$14,400	$13,200	$11,900	$12,198
Equity	13,280	3,187	5,781	7,643	9,464	9,701
Total liabilities and equities	$13,280	$18,187	$20,181	$20,843	$21,364	$21,898
Cash Flow Statement						
Cash flows from operations						
Net income		$ 2,392	$ 2,708	$ 3,006	$ 3,048	$ 3,222
+ Depreciation expense		1,273	1,875	2,226	2,494	2,557
− Change in net operating working capital		−151	−307	−197	−54	−56
Cash flow from operations		$ 3,513	$ 4,276	$ 5,036	$ 5,488	$ 5,723
Investing activities						
− Capital expenditures		−$ 6,020	−$ 3,518	−$ 2,678	−$ 2,958	−$ 3,031
Financing activities						
+ Change in debt financing		$15,000	−$ 600	−$ 1,200	−$ 1,300	$ 297
+ Change in common equity financing		0	0	0	0	0
− Common equity dividends paid		−12,485	−114	−1,144	−1,227	−2,985
Cash flows from financing activities		$ 2,515	−$ 714	−$ 2,344	−$ 2,527	−$ 2,688
Change in cash balance		$ 8	$ 44	$ 13	$ 4	$ 4

Exhibit may contain small rounding errors

P5.7 **Weighted Average Cost of Capital Valuation—The Joel Germunder Company:** Before you begin this problem, read the text and review the information in the previous problem for the Joel Germunder Company and use that information but incorporate the changes described below. Some of Germunder's older owner-managers are concerned about the younger owner-managers' plan to issue so much debt to expand the company and pay a large one-time dividend. They agree that the company's cash flows could easily support some debt, but they are concerned about the amount of debt proposed by the younger owner-managers. They hired a consultant who recommended a lower risk capital structure strategy of financing the company with a constant target capital structure of 20% debt (for a debt-to-firm value ratio equal to 20%). The consultant told them that with this target capital structure, their interest rate on debt (and debt cost of capital) would be equal to 8%. Based on this revised capital structure, the older owner-managers would pay out all equity free cash flows as dividends.

a. Use the financial statements in Exhibit P5.1 to measure Germunder's unlevered free cash flows in Years 1 through 4.

b. Value Germunder—the entire firm and its equity—as of the end of Year 0 using the WACC valuation method and the proposed capital structure strategy assuming that interest tax shields are valued at the unlevered cost of capital.

c. Calculate the company's equity free cash flows forecasts based on the older owner-managers' capital structure strategy.

d. Value Germunder's equity as of the end of Year 0 using the Equity DCF valuation method and the proposed capital structure strategy.

e. As a consistency check, value Germunder as of the end of Year 0 using the APV valuation method. Assume that the appropriate discount rate for interest tax shields is the unlevered cost of capital for this company.

f. You must complete the previous problem on the Joel Germunder Company to solve this part of the problem. Analyze the difference between the value of the firm based on the capital structure strategy in the previous problem and the value based on the capital structure strategy in this problem. Reconcile, mathematically, the difference in the value of the firm.

P5.8 Adjusted Present Value Valuation with Debt Recapitalization at the Continuing Value Date—The Joel Germunder Company: The Joel Germunder Company (Germunder) is a privately held, family business that currently uses no debt in its capital structure. The owner-managers have a plan to expand the operations of the company over the next two years. The owner-managers agreed on a plan to issue a large amount of debt to not only expand the company's operations but also pay the owners a one-time, special dividend. Their plan is to finance the entire transaction by issuing $15 million of 10% debt. After the company completes its expansion, their plan is to use some of the free cash flows to repay the debt until the end of Year 3; thus, they will pay some dividends in Years 1 through 3. At the end of Year 3, they plan to refinance the company to a constant target capital structure of 20% debt. As of the beginning of Year 4, they expect the company's cash flows to grow at the long-run inflation rate, which they expect to be 2.5%. The company's chief financial officer prepared a set of financial forecasts that reflects this plan. The income statement, balance sheet, and cash flow statement forecasts appear in Exhibit P5.1. The forecasts assume the company will issue the debt at the end of Year 0, which is reflected in the balance sheet for that year. The forecasts do not, however, reflect the debt recapitalization at the end of Year 3. The debt cost of capital will not change while the company is paying off its debt, but it will decrease to 8% when they recapitalize the company to 20% debt at the end of Year 3. Germunder's income tax rate for all revenues and expenses is 40%, and its unlevered cost of capital is 12%.

a. Use the financial statements in Exhibit P5.1 to measure Germunder's unlevered free cash flows in Years 1 through 4.

b. As of the continuing value date, what amount and percent of its firm value does Germunder derive from the value of its interest tax shields? Assume the appropriate discount rate for interest tax shields is the unlevered cost of capital for this company.

c. As of the continuing value date, what amount and percent of its equity value does Germunder derive from the value of its interest tax shields? Assume the appropriate discount rate for interest tax shields is the unlevered cost of capital for this company.

d. Value Germunder—the entire firm and equity—as of the end of Year 0 using the APV valuation method. Assume that the appropriate discount rate for interest tax shields is the unlevered cost of capital for this company.

e. As of the end of Year 0, what amount and percent of its firm value and equity does Germunder derive from the value of its interest tax shields?

f. What issues would you suggest the company's management think about before moving forward with this capital structure strategy (in other words, what factors related to issuing additional debt are not considered in your APV valuation that might affect the value of the firm and equity)?

g. Value Germunder—the entire firm and equity—as of the end of Year 0 using the WACC valuation method. Again, assume that the appropriate discount rate for interest tax shields is the unlevered cost of capital for this company.

h. Value Germunder's equity as of the end of Year 0 using the Equity DCF valuation method. Again, assume that the appropriate discount rate for interest tax shields is the unlevered cost of capital for this company.

SOLUTIONS FOR REVIEW EXERCISES

Solution for Review Exercise 5.1: The Stuart Essig Perpetuity Company—Part 1

$$r_E = r_{UA} + (r_{UA} - r_D) \times \frac{V_D}{V_E} + (r_{UA} - r_{PS}) \times \frac{V_{PS}}{V_E}$$

$$= 0.12 + (0.12 - 0.08) \times \frac{0.3333}{0.5} + (0.12 - 0.085) \times \frac{0.167}{0.5} = 0.158333$$

$$r_{WACC} = r_E \times \frac{V_E}{V_F} + (1 - T_{INT}) \times r_D \times \frac{V_D}{V_F} + r_{PS} \times \frac{V_{PS}}{V_F}$$

$$= 0.1583 \times 0.5 + (1 - 0.4) \times 0.08 \times 0.333 + 0.085 \times 0.167 = 0.1093$$

$$r_{WACC} = r_{UA} - T_{INT} \times r_D \times \frac{V_D}{V_F}$$

$$= 0.12 - 0.4 \times 0.08 \times 0.333 = 0.1093$$

$$V_{F,O} = \frac{FCF_1}{r_{WACC} - g} = \frac{\$42{,}600}{0.1093333 - 0} = \$389{,}634$$

$$V_{E,O} = V_{F,O} \times \frac{V_E}{V_F}$$

$$= \$389{,}634 \times 0.5 = \$194{,}817$$

Solution for Review Exercise 5.2: The Stuart Essig Perpetuity Company—Part 2

	Value	% Value
Debt	$129,878	33.3%
Preferred stock	64,939	16.7%
Equity	194,817	50.0%
V_F	$389,634	100.0%

Interest Tax Shields	Year 1
Beginning of year debt	$129,878
Cost of debt = interest rate	0.08
Interest expense	$ 10,390
Income tax rate for interest	40%
Interest tax shield	$ 4,156

$$V_{F,O} = \frac{FCF_1}{r_{UA} - g} + \frac{ITS_1}{r_{UA} - g}$$

$$= \frac{\$42{,}600}{0.12 - 0} + \frac{\$4{,}156}{0.12 - 0}$$

$$= \$355{,}000 + \$34{,}634 = \$389{,}634$$

Solution for Review Exercise 5.3: The Stuart Essig Perpetuity Company—Part 3

Equity Free Cash Flows	Year 1
Unlevered free cash flow	$ 42,600
Interest paid in cash	−10,390
Interest tax shield	4,156
Preferred stock dividend	−5,520
Change in debt	0
Change in preferred stock	0
Equity free cash flow (EFCF)	$ 30,846

$$V_E = \frac{EFCF_{C+1}}{(r_E - g)} = \frac{\$30{,}846}{0.158333 - 0} = \$194{,}817$$

After mastering the material in this chapter, you will be able to:

1. Calculate a company's continuing value using the constant-growth perpetuity model (6.1)
2. Measure the growth rate for the constant-growth perpetuity model (6.2)
3. Measure the base-year free cash flow for the constant-growth perpetuity model (6.3)
4. Incorporate real growth and value creation in the constant-growth perpetuity model (6.4)
5. Assess the reasonableness of the inputs in the continuing value calculation (6.5)

Measuring Continuing Value Using the Constant-Growth Perpetuity Model

CHAPTER

6

In 2016, Regency Centers Corporation and Equity One, Inc. agreed to combine through a stock-for-stock merger, in which Equity One merged into Regency and Regency continued as the surviving corporation. In January 2017, the companies issued a joint proxy statement that includes a fairness opinion issued by J. P. Morgan.[1] J.P. Morgan explained its discounted cash flow valuation as follows:

REGENCY CENTERS CORPORATION AND EQUITY ONE, INC. MERGER

> J.P. Morgan conducted a discounted cash flow analysis for the purpose of determining an implied equity value per share for Regency common stock and Equity One common stock. A discounted cash flow analysis is a method of evaluating an asset using estimates of the future unlevered free cash flows generated by the asset and taking into consideration the time value of money with respect to those future cash flows by calculating their "present value." . . . "Terminal value" [continuing value] refers to the capitalized value of all cash flows from an asset for periods beyond the final forecast period.
>
> J.P. Morgan calculated the present value of unlevered free cash flows that each of Regency and Equity One is expected to generate during the period from calendar year 2017 through the end of 2026 . . .
>
> J.P. Morgan also calculated a range of terminal values for each of Regency and Equity One at December 31, 2026 by applying a terminal growth rate ranging from 2.25% to 2.75%, in the case of Regency, and 2.75% to 3.25% in the case of Equity One, to the financial forecasts of each of Regency and Equity One during 2026 to derive terminal period unlevered free cash flows for each of Regency and Equity One. . . .

In this chapter, we explore the intricacies of using the constant-growth cash flow perpetuity model to estimate the continuing value of a company.

[1] See the joint proxy statement issue on January 24, 2017, available at www.SEC.gov.

CHAPTER ORGANIZATION

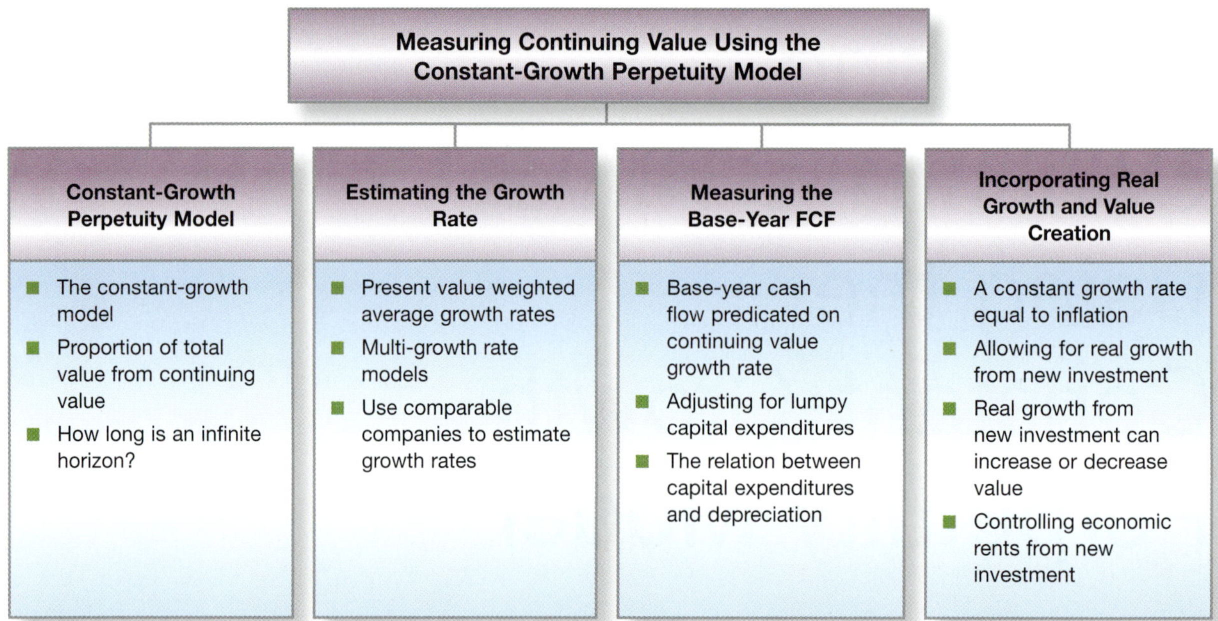

INTRODUCTION

Corporations do not have a predetermined finite life by law, and theoretically, they can continue to operate forever. While companies do not necessarily have an infinite life, when viewing a company as a **going concern**, we assume it will continue to operate for the foreseeable future unless we believe it will liquidate at some future time. Therefore, we typically use a very long forecast horizon for a company's expected free cash flows in a DCF valuation model. Naturally, it is not practicable to forecast (and then discount) an infinite series of cash flows without making some simplifying assumptions.

To address this complication, we typically develop detailed forecasts for a company's expected cash flows for some finite period of time—say, 10 years, and then measure the value of the firm at the end of this finite period, Year 10. We call the value at the end of the finite period the company's **continuing value (CV)**; other terms used for this concept are **terminal value**, **residual value**, and **horizon value**. The continuing value component often ranges from 30% to more than 60%, and sometimes even more than 60%, of the company's total value; thus, continuing value estimates are an important part of valuing companies.

Although we suggest using the free cash flow constant-growth perpetuity method to measure a company's continuing value, the market multiple valuation method is another commonly used valuation method to estimate continuing value. Our suggested approach is to use the constant-growth perpetuity method to measure continuing value and then to calculate the market multiples implied by that continuing value estimate and the underlying forecasts. We compare the implied market multiples based on the constant-growth perpetuity model to the market multiples of a set of comparable companies in order to corroborate our estimate of the continuing value.[2]

It is less common to assume that a company will be liquidated (presumably, because most companies are worth less when liquidated than operating as a going concern) or that the company will be broken up into different parts and sold to various interested parties. This latter type of valuation is called a **breakup value** and presumes that at least some of the parts of the company will continue to operate but under the auspices of multiple owners. A breakup value should be considered if the independent parts of the company can be utilized more effectively when sold to others than when operating as parts of a single conglomerate company.

We introduced the constant-growth perpetuity model in Chapter 1. In this chapter, we discuss the model in more detail and the assumptions we must satisfy in order to use the constant-growth

[2] According to the 2013 Association for Financial Professionals survey, over 50% of the respondents from large or publicly traded companies use the constant-growth perpetuity model to measure continuing value, while only 13% use the market multiple valuation method. See 2013 AFP Estimating and Applying Cost of Capital: Report of Survey Results, October 2013, Association for Financial Professionals.

perpetuity model. We then discuss ways to measure the growth rate and base-year free cash flow for the model. Lastly, we discuss how the model can incorporate real growth (value creation).

Valuation in Practice 6.1

Using Market Multiples to Measure Continuing Value—Microsoft's Acquisition of LinkedIn
In June 2016, Microsoft Corp. (Nasdaq: MSFT) and LinkedIn Corporation (NYSE: LNKD) announced that they entered into a merger agreement under which Microsoft will acquire LinkedIn for $196 per share in an all-cash transaction valued at $26.2 billion. After gaining regulatory approval in the U.S., Europe, and other countries, the transaction closed in December 2016. As part of its fairness opinion, LinkedIn's financial advisor, Qatalyst Partners, used the DCF valuation method to value LinkedIn. In its DCF valuation method, Qatalyst Partners used the market multiple valuation method to measure LinkedIn's continuing (terminal) value:

> . . . calculated by multiplying the estimated Adjusted EBITDA . . . , less any capitalized software and website development costs (excluding capitalized stock-based compensation), which we refer to as the estimated "Modified EBITDA," in calendar year 2020, based on the LinkedIn Projections, by a range of multiples of fully-diluted enterprise value to next-twelve-months estimated Modified EBITDA of 12.0x to 18.0x . . .
>
> . . . Based upon research analyst consensus estimates for calendar year 2017, and using the closing prices as of June 10, 2016, for shares of the selected companies, Qatalyst Partners calculated, among other things, the implied fully diluted enterprise value divided by the estimated consensus Modified EBITDA for calendar year 2017, which we refer to as the "CY17E Modified EBITDA Multiples," for each of the selected consumer internet companies. The median CY17E Modified EBITDA Multiple for the selected consumer internet companies analyzed was 13.4x. . . . Based on an analysis of the CY17E Modified EBITDA Multiples for each of the selected consumer internet companies, Qatalyst Partners selected a representative range of 12.0x to 18.0x . . .

Source: LinkedIn Corporation's Proxy Statement filed with the U.S. SEC on June 13, 2016

6.1 THE CONSTANT-GROWTH PERPETUITY MODEL

LO1 Calculate a company's continuing value using the constant-growth perpetuity model

We often use the constant-growth perpetuity model to estimate continuing value. We first discuss the model and its derivation and we then go on to discuss the assumptions we have to make about the company in order use the constant-growth cash flow perpetuity model to estimate a company's continuing value.

The formula to discount an infinite series of cash flows is as follows:[3]

$$V_0 = \sum_{t=1}^{\infty} \frac{FCF_t}{(1+r)^t}$$

If we assume free cash flows grow at a constant rate, g, after Year 1, we can expand the infinite sum as follows:[4]

$$V_0 = \frac{FCF_1}{(1+r)} \times \left(1 + \frac{(1+g)}{(1+r)} + \frac{(1+g)^2}{(1+r)^2} + \dots + \frac{(1+g)^{\infty-1}}{(1+r)^{\infty-1}}\right) \tag{6.1}$$

We cannot directly calculate the result of this formula, for we cannot directly calculate an infinite series; however, we can nicely summarize the above formula if we make an assumption about the relative magnitudes of the discount rate and growth rate. If the discount rate is equal to the growth rate (r = g), then the last term in the formula is equal to infinity, for an infinite series of 1s is equal to infinity [$\infty = FCF_1/(1 + r) \times (1 + 1 + 1 + \dots)$]. We also arrive at the same answer if the discount rate is less

[3] The discount rate, r, is equal to the unlevered cost of capital for an all-equity company or the weighted average cost of capital for a company with debt.

[4] The free cash flow in period 1 must be greater than zero in order to make the constant-growth assumption.

than the growth rate ($r < g$) because an infinite series of numbers greater than 1 is equal to infinity. If the discount rate is greater than the growth rate ($r > g$), the present value of the constant-growth perpetuity is less than infinity and greater than zero.[5] In this case, we can reduce the above formula to a simple and usable form—the constant-growth perpetuity formula.

$$V_0 = \frac{FCF_1}{(r - g)} \tag{6.2}$$

Using the Free Cash Flow in Year Zero (FCF_0)

Using the above assumptions, we can also adapt the above perpetuity formula to use the free cash flow in Year 0 ($FCF_1 = FCF_0 \times (1 + g_1)$) as follows:

$$V_{F,0} = \frac{FCF_0 \times (1 + g_1)}{r - g} \tag{6.3}$$

The growth rate for Year 1, g_1, does not need to be the same as the growth rate for future years for the formula to correctly calculate the present value. The free cash flow for Year 0 must be greater than 0 in order for the Year 1 free cash flow, $FCF_0 \times (1+g_1)$, to be positive.

Basic Assumptions Underlying the Constant-Growth Perpetuity Model

A valuation must meet certain assumptions in order to use the constant-growth perpetuity model (Equations 6.2 and 6.3): (1) the expected free cash flow in period 1, FCF_1, (assuming a valuation date $t = 0$) is positive; (2) the present value weighted average growth rate is constant; (3) the discount rate is constant; and (4) the growth rate is less than the discount rate. We discuss the implications of these assumptions in this section.

The Positive (t + 1) Free Cash Flow Assumption. In order to use the constant-growth perpetuity model, the expected free cash flow in period 1, FCF_1, (assuming a valuation date $t = 0$) must be positive. Although FCF_1 does not appear in Equation 6.3, the numerator $FCF_0 \times (1 + g_1)$ is the forecast for FCF_1, which must be positive. If the expected free cash flow in period 1 is negative (or zero), applying a constant growth rate results in an infinite series of negative (zero) numbers, which results in a negative (or zero) firm value.

The Constant Growth Rate Assumption. Although not apparent from either Equations 6.2 or 6.3 if the growth rate is greater than or equal to the discount rate, the value of the firm is infinite, which, of course, is not possible. A review of Equation 6.1 shows this result. In Equation 6.1, if the growth rate is equal to the discount rate, Equation 6.1 reduces to $V_0 = FCF_1 / (1 + r) \times [1 + (1 + g) / (1 + r) \times (\infty - 1)]$. Since $(1 + g)/ (1+r) \times (\infty - 1)$ is equal to ∞ and $FCF_1/(1+r)$ is a positive number, any positive number multiplied by infinity is equal to infinity.

The assumption of a constant growth rate, however, does not require the growth rate to be positive. The growth rate can be negative or zero or positive, but it must be less than the discount rate. In addition, although the growth rate used in the model is constant, it can actually equal the present value weighted average of a series of different expected future growth rates for the company. In other words, a company's expected growth rates after the continuing value date do not need to be constant as long as we know the present value weighted average growth rate of all of the company's expected growth rates after the continuing value date. This is a point we discuss in Section 6.2.

The Constant Discount Rate Assumption. As we discuss in Chapters 8 through 11, the determinants of a company's costs of capital (equity, debt, preferred, . . . , weighted average cost of capital) include operating risk, financial risk, and macroeconomic factors such as the risk-free rate of return and the market risk premium. We can think of operating risk as the sensitivity of the company's unlevered cash flows to changes in the economy. The sensitivity of a company's unlevered cash flows to changes in the economy is determined by the sensitivity of its revenue to changes in the economy and the degree of fixed costs in its cost structure (higher fixed costs, more operating risk). In Chapter 5, we discussed a

[5] Recall that we are assuming that the initial cash flow, FCF_1, is positive, that the constant growth rate is a finite number ($-\infty < g < \infty$), and that the discount rate is a finite positive number ($0 < r < \infty$).

company's financial risk and the risk premium resulting from using non-common equity financing (see Equation 5.8). In Chapter 8, we discuss the macroeconomic factors that determine costs of capital such as the risk-free rate of return and the market risk premiums.

Therefore, the constant discount rate assumption assumes that, as of the continuing value date, the company is expected to have constant operating risk, constant financial risk (constant capital structure ratios), and constant expected macroeconomic determinants of the cost of capital. Naturally, it is possible that these factors could be expected to change over time in such a way that the effects on the company's discount rate offset each other, though that is not typical. The typical assumption is these determinants of the company's discount rate are expected to be constant.

The Steady State Company

Although often not practicable, ideally, a valuation includes year-by-year detailed forecasts (**year-by-year forecast horizon**) until the company reaches **steady state**. What is steady state? First, a company in steady state meets the basic assumptions for the constant-growth perpetuity model (expected free cash flow in period 1 is positive, growth rate is constant, discount rate is constant, the growth rate is less than the discount rate). However, a steady state company is also a company that has evolved to the point of generating constant economic returns on its investments. The assumption of a constant economic rate of return results in a constant steady state growth rate for all future periods; that is, $g_{t+1} \approx g_{t+2} \approx g_{t+3}, \ldots, \approx g_{t+\infty}$. In other words, the growth rate is no longer the present value weighted average growth rate of a series of changing growth rates but is a constant growth rate in every future period.

In what situation does a company reach a constant economic rate of return for all future periods? First, the company's existing investments as of the continuing value date have reached steady state; that is, the company's expected economic rate of return on its existing investment and replenishment of that investment is constant. Second, the company's new investment is a constant proportion of its free cash flow generated from its existing assets and earns a constant economic rate of return. Given the perpetual nature of the assumptions, it is likely that the company's steady state economic rate of return approaches its cost of capital; in other words, little, if any, additional value is created from new investments. These assumptions do not change the conclusion that the constant growth rate can be negative or zero or positive.

Estimating the point in time when a company reaches its steady state can be complex, especially for a company in a high-growth stage of its life cycle as of the valuation date. For example, a company like Starbucks will not likely reach its steady state until Starbucks at least saturates the U.S. market with its locations. Further, given we know Starbucks has expanded into other countries, we would also consider when Starbucks would saturate its non-U.S. markets with its locations. We also know Starbucks has been creating new revenue streams. For example, a number of years ago, Starbucks began selling its coffee beans in grocery stores and other retail outlets, which was a new revenue stream beyond revenues generated from its store locations.

When Will a Company Meet the Constant-Growth Perpetuity Model Assumptions?

Asking when a company will meet the constant-growth perpetuity model assumptions is akin to asking how many years of year-by-year detailed forecasts should be used in a valuation. The answer, of course is, it depends. As we just discussed, ideally we forecast year-by-year cash flows until the company reaches steady state, but that is sometimes not practicable. However, it is typically practicable to estimate when a company will meet the basic assumptions underlying the constant-growth perpetuity model even if it has not reached steady state. According to the 2013 Association for Financial Professionals survey, 51% of respondents use a five-year forecast horizon, 26% use a ten-year forecast horizon, 12% use a forecast horizon shorter than five years and 11% use a forecast horizon longer than 10 years.[6]

When a company's year-by-year detailed forecasts do not reach its steady state by the end of the forecast period, and the growth rate in the last year of the detailed forecasts far exceeds the company's steady state growth rate, it naturally is unreasonable to assume a company's free cash flow growth rates are cliff-like and fall precipitously from the high growth rate in the last year of the detailed forecast period to the company's lower steady state growth rate within one year. We can meet the positive free cash flow

[6] See 2013 AFP Estimating and Applying Cost of Capital: Report of Survey Results, October 2013, Association for Financial Professionals.

assumption by extending the year-by-year forecast horizon in the financial model until the expected free cash flow is positive. In most situations, we can also extend the forecast horizon until it is reasonable to assume constant operating risk, and a sustainable (constant) capital structure, and constant expected macroeconomic determinants of the cost of capital. Regarding a sustainable capital structure, most WACC valuations embed a long-term sustainable capital structure strategy as part of the capital structure strategy for the entire valuation, so this assumption is typically not an issue in a WACC valuation. It can be more of an issue in a valuation in which the company has a changing capital structure. For example, in the Keller example in Chapter 5, the CFO's capital structure strategy was to repay as much debt as possible in the first three years and then to maintain the existing capital structure in perpetuity. In such situations, we extend the forecast horizon until we believe the company's capital structure is sustainable (and usually constant in proportionate terms) for the long run. One way to assess the sustainability of a company's capital structure is to examine comparable companies to understand the range of capital structure strategies used by the comparable companies. What is clear is that a company may meet the minimum requirements for using the constant-growth perpetuity model before it reaches steady state.

Extending the forecasts in this way is sometimes called a **three-stage DCF model**, which includes a transition period between the last year of the detailed forecast and the first year the company reaches its constant growth perpetuity or possibly its steady state. Alternatively, the standard DCF model can be adapted so that it is economically equivalent to the 3-stage model by using a blended growth rate in the constant growth perpetuity model. The blended growth rate approach is common and is economically equivalent to the three-stage models as long as the blended growth rate is equal to the present value weighted growth rate in the second and third stages of the three-stage model.

Valuation Key 6.1

When using the constant-growth perpetuity formula, we assume that the growth rate is smaller than the discount rate; otherwise, the resulting value is infinite. In a constant-growth perpetuity model, the continuing value is quite sensitive to the growth rate chosen. We apply the constant-growth cash flow perpetuity model at the point in time the firm is expected to reach steady state.

Value Derived from Continuing Value Is Often More Than 50%

In this section, we illustrate that the proportion of a company's total value derived from its continuing value is often more than 50%. In Exhibit 6.1, we present a chart for a low-growth and a high-growth company and show the proportion of firm value derived from explicit year-by-year forecasts for various horizons. The free cash flows of the low-growth company grow at 5% for the first 5 years and 2% thereafter, while the free cash flows of the high-growth company grow at 30% for the first 5 years and 2% thereafter.

EXHIBIT 6.1 Proportion of Firm Value Derived from Continuing Value at Different Year-by-Year Forecast Horizons

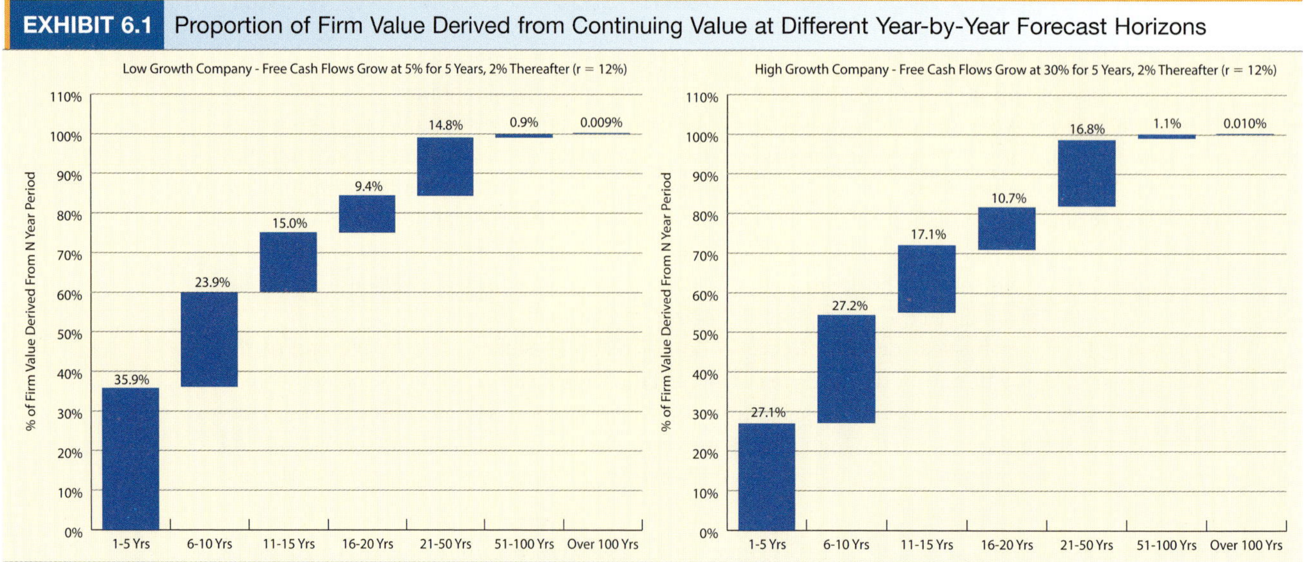

As shown in the exhibit, with a year-by-year forecast horizon of five years, the low-growth company derives 36% of its value from the first five years of its forecast and 64% of its value from its continuing value. Naturally, the value derived from continuing value decreases as the year-by-year forecast horizon increases. For example, if we forecast the low-growth company out 10 years it derives 60% of its value from the first ten years of forecasts (an additional 24% of value from the forecasts for years six to ten) and 40% of its value from the continuing value. The percentage of value derived from the continuing value for the low-growth company with a year-by-year forecast horizon of 15 and 20 years is 25% and 16% respectively. Looking at the high-growth company, the proportion of firm value derived from continuing value increases for the higher growth company because the higher growth rate results in a higher base year free cash flow forecast for the continuing value calculation relative to the free cash flow forecasts for the earlier years. As shown in the exhibit, with a year-by-year forecast horizon of five years, the high-growth company derives 73% of its value from its continuing value. The percentage of value derived from continuing value for the high-growth company with a year-by-year forecast horizon of 10, 15, and 20 years, is 46%, 29%, and 18%, respectively. As shown in the exhibit for both the low- and high-growth companies, 99% of the value of the company is attained within the first 50 years of the year-by-year forecast horizon.

Valuation in Practice 6.2

Year-by-Year Forecast Horizon and Growth Rate—The Battle to Acquire Syngenta Syngenta AG is a publicly traded global Swiss agricultural company (traded on the SIX Swiss Exchange and the New York Stock Exchange), with over 30,000 employees. In February 2015, Monsanto Company made an unsolicited offer to purchase Syngenta with a cash and stock offer. Its offer was rejected by Syngenta's Board of Directors. Monsanto increased its offer but Syngenta's Board again rejected the offer. In February 2016, China National Chemical Corporation (ChemChina) made an all-cash offer for the company for $43 billion, which was accepted by Syngenta's Board.

Syngenta's Board retained N+1 Swiss Capital AG to provide a fairness opinion for the ChemChina offer. Based on the company's business plan, N+1 Swiss Capital used a 15-year forecast horizon and measured the continuing (terminal) value using a 2.5% constant-growth perpetuity model. Even with a 15-year forecast horizon, continuing value was over 50% of the company's value:

> The terminal value is calculated based on an assumed perpetual growth rate of 2.0 to 2.5%, which is in line with consensus equity research analyst forecasts for Syngenta and expected long-term market growth.

Calculation of Value per Syngenta Share	
USDm (unless otherwise stated)	
Present value of free cash flows.	20,949
Present value of terminal value	21,545
Enterprise value	**42,494**
Enterprise value adjustments.	(3,348)
Equity value.	**39,147**
Diluted shares outstanding (m).	92.6
Value per share (USD)	**422.82**
USD/CHF exchange rate	1.0171
Value per share (CHF).	**430.05**

Source: Fairness Opinion on the Public Tender Offer by China National Chemical Corporation to Acquire Syngenta AG dated March 4, 2016; available on May 28, 2018 at https://www.syngenta.com/~/media/Files/S/Syngenta/media-releases/fairness-opinion-english.pdf.

In Exhibit 6.2, we show the percentage of value resulting from cash flows after Year 10 for various combinations of discount rates (varying between 8% and 15%) and constant growth rates (varying between 0% and 5%). This exhibit shows that the percentage of value derived from cash flows after Year

10 has a low of 25% (with a growth rate of 0% and a discount rate of 15%) and a high of 75% (with a growth rate of 5% and a discount rate of 8%). Thus, in many valuations, more than 50% of the total value of the firm is likely derived from the continuing value calculation, even with a year-by-year forecast horizon of 10 years. Naturally, using the more common five-year year-by-year forecast horizon results in an even greater proportion of the total value derived from the continuing value estimate.

EXHIBIT 6.2 Percentage of Firm Value Derived from Continuing Value After Year 10 for Various Combinations of Discount and Growth Rates

	Constant-Growth Rate in Perpetuity					
Discount Rate	**0%**	**1%**	**2%**	**3%**	**4%**	**5%**
8%	46%	51%	56%	62%	69%	75%
9%	42%	47%	51%	57%	63%	69%
10%	39%	43%	47%	52%	57%	63%
11%	35%	39%	43%	47%	52%	57%
12%	32%	36%	39%	43%	48%	52%
13%	29%	33%	36%	40%	44%	48%
14%	27%	30%	33%	36%	40%	44%
15%	25%	27%	30%	33%	37%	40%

Does an Infinite Horizon Really Assume the Company Exists Forever?

It might at first appear that it is the perpetuity assumption that causes continuing values to have such a large effect on a company's total value. Moreover, you might be concerned that it is an inappropriate assumption to assume a company will last forever. However, Exhibit 6.1 shows that cash flows after 100 years contribute less than 0.01% of the total value and that cash flows after 50 years contribute only 1% of the total value. Thus, in most situations, a company derives most of its economic value from the first 50 years of its forecasted cash flows.

Valuation Key 6.2

The cash flows beyond 50 to 100 years typically have a small effect on value when we make an infinite horizon assumption in the continuing value calculation. However, in a typical valuation of a company the continuing value often drives 40% to 60% of a firm's total value and sometimes more.

In Exhibit 6.3, we show the percentage of value derived from the first 50 years of a perpetuity for various combinations of discount rates and growth rates. For discount rates of at least 8% and growth rates of no more than 5%, the first 50 years account for at least 76% of the perpetuity's value. For

EXHIBIT 6.3 Percentage of Constant-Growth Perpetuity Value Derived from the First 50 Years of Cash Flows for Various Combinations of Discount Rates and Growth Rates

	Constant-Growth Rate in Perpetuity					
Discount Rate	**0%**	**1%**	**2%**	**3%**	**4%**	**5%**
8%	98%	96%	94%	91%	85%	76%
9%	99%	98%	96%	94%	90%	85%
10%	99%	99%	98%	96%	94%	90%
11%	99%	99%	99%	98%	96%	94%
12%	100%	99%	99%	98%	98%	96%
13%	100%	100%	99%	99%	98%	97%
14%	100%	100%	100%	99%	99%	98%
15%	100%	100%	100%	100%	99%	99%

growth rates between 2% and 4% and discount rates between 10% and 13%, the first 50 years account for at least 94% of the perpetuity's value. Thus, in economic terms, we are not really assuming an infinite life for a company when we use the cash flow perpetuity model.

Yahoo! and Snap's Continuing Value as a Percentage of Firm Value. As we show in the Appendix, the DCF model we use for Yahoo contains 11 years of detailed forecasts. We use the 11th year to measure Yahoo's continuing value. Its free cash flow in Year 11 is \$5.678 billion. With a 12% discount rate and a 2.5% perpetual growth rate (based on expected inflation) after Year 11, Yahoo's continuing value as of the end of Year 10 is \$59.8 billion.

$$V_{\text{Yahoo, 10}} = \frac{FCF_{11}}{r - g} = \frac{\$5.678}{0.12 - 0.025} = \$59.8$$

The Year 0 present value of Yahoo's Year 10 continuing value is equal to \$19.2 billion [\$19.2 = \$59.8 × $(1.12)^{-10}$]. This value is almost 60% of Yahoo's total Year 0 value of \$32.6 billion, ignoring the value of its excess assets (0.59 = \$19.2/\$32.6), despite the fact that we forecasted 10 years of cash flows before performing the continuing value calculation. Note that we further assumed that Yahoo would not experience any real growth subsequent to Year 10. Given Yahoo's Year 1 expected free cash flow of \$0.985 billion and 12% cost of capital, we know that its free cash flows will have to grow at high rates for many years in order for its Year 0 value to equal \$32.6 billion. In our illustration, we assumed that Yahoo's revenues would grow by more than 20% annually through Year 6, and then we reduced its growth rate to 2.5% or less by Year 9; in spite of this, Yahoo's continuing value is still almost 60% of its total value.

In the Snap Inc. valuation we performed in Chapter 1 (see Exhibit 1.3), the continuing value contributed more of the total value than in the valuation of Yahoo even though we also forecasted explicit year-by-year cash flows for 10 years. In that case, the continuing value was 84% of the total value. Snap's continuing value is such a large part of its total value because its free cash flows for the first two years were negative or zero and then grew at fairly high growth rates for the remainder of the ten-year forecast. Suffice it to say, the continuing value is an important part of the valuation for most companies.

6.2 ESTIMATING THE LONG-TERM GROWTH RATE FOR THE CONSTANT-GROWTH PERPETUITY MODEL

In this section, we discuss estimating the long-term growth rate used in the constant-growth perpetuity model. We first identify some of the factors to consider when estimating the long-term growth rate. We then discuss the concept and calculation of the present value weighted average growth rate. Lastly, we discuss how to use comparable companies to estimate the long-term growth rate.

LO2 Measure the growth rate for the constant-growth perpetuity model

Factors to Consider When Estimating the Long-Term Growth Rate

Factors to consider when estimating the long-term growth rate include macroeconomic factors such as inflation, gross domestic product (GDP) growth, population growth, and the like. Since inflation and GDP growth are generally positive, one might conclude that the long-term expected inflation rate or GDP growth is the lower bound of the long-term constant growth rate. That conclusion is incorrect. The long-term growth rate can be negative or zero because industry and firm specific factors can result in negative or zero growth for a company's free cash flows even in an economy with positive inflation and positive GDP growth. Industry (or product specific) expected price level changes can be negative, zero, or positive. The size of an industry's market can shrink (negative growth) or grow. Firm specific factors such as market share, product innovation, and the like can also result in negative, zero, or positive expected growth. Thus, we take all of these factors into consideration when determining a company's long-term growth rate and the resulting outcome can be positive, zero or negative free cash flow growth rates.

Valuation in Practice 6.3

Long-Term Growth Rate and Inflation—TDK's Tender Offer of Micronas In December 2015, TDK Corporation, a publicly traded company in Japan, launched a public tender offer for the common stock of Micronas Semiconductor Holding AG. Micronas' Board of Directors engaged Ernst & Young Ltd to provide a fairness opinion for the TDK offer.

> To account for Micronas' going concern assumption, an assumption regarding an indefinite growth rate has to be made. In general, the terminal growth rate equals the long-term expected inflation of the corresponding countries the target company is operating in. An indefinite growth rate equal to expected inflation would correspond to an assumption implying that the company's profits will remain constant in real terms. . . . We have calculated for Micronas a revenue weighted long-term inflation rate of 1.8%.

Source: Project Gauss: Fairness Opinion, dated December 21, 2015, available on May 28, 2018 at https://www.micronas.com/sites/default/files/Fairness%20Opinion_e-1.pdf.

The Present Value Weighted Average Growth Rate

Although we eventually assume that a company reaches a point when it meets the assumptions underlying the constant-growth perpetuity model, we might conclude that we have insufficient information to extend the year-by-year forecast horizon until the company reaches its steady state growth rate. Regardless of the reason, valuation models often choose a continuing value date that is before the date when the company is expected to reach its steady state. In order to use the constant-growth perpetuity model before a company reaches its steady state, we can estimate a constant growth rate that represents the present value weighted average growth rate of all of the companies' expected growth rates beyond the point where we stop the year-by-year forecasts.

Even if the year-to-year growth rates in cash flows for a company vary widely over time, we can always express the value of a firm as a function of single growth rate in a constant-growth perpetuity model as long as the first cash flow is positive and the discount rate is constant through time. For example, assume a company's Year 0 free cash flow is \$100, and its expected growth rates are 50% for Year 1, 30% for Year 2, 10% for Year 3, and 3% thereafter. If the company's cost of capital is 12%, the value of the company is \$2,189.36 as of the end of Year 0.

$$V_{F,0}=\frac{\$100\times(1.5)}{(1.12)}+\frac{\$100\times(1.5)\times(1.3)}{(1.12)^2}+\frac{\$100\times(1.5)\times(1.3)\times(1.1)}{(1.12)^3}+\frac{\$100\times(1.5)\times(1.3)\times(1.1)\times(1.03)}{0.12-0.03}\times\frac{1}{(1.12)^3}=\$2{,}189$$

If we know the value of an investment, its discount rate, and its free cash flows in Year 1, we can measure the present value weighted average growth rate for this investment, g_A, by solving Equation 6.2 for the growth rate. The present value weighted average growth rate for this example is 5.15%.

$$g_A=r-\frac{FCF_1}{V_{F,0}} \tag{6.4}$$

$$g_A=r-\frac{FCF_1}{V_{F,0}}=0.12-\frac{\$150}{\$2{,}189}=0.0515$$

In other words, the expected free cash flow growth rates for Year 2 onward of 30%, 10%, and then 3% in perpetuity, are equivalent to assuming a 5.15% growth rate in perpetuity for Year 2 onward (assuming a discount rate of 12%). Although the cost of capital is one of the inputs into this formula, it does not imply that the cost of capital determines the growth rate. On the contrary, the growth rate of the free cash flows and the cost of capital determine the value of the firm and we reverse engineer that relationship to measure the growth rate.

Being able to calculate the present value weighted average growth rate can be useful for presentation purposes, as in many valuations free cash flow forecasts are often shown for five years or even fewer than five years. Equation 6.4 indicates we can measure a company's continuing value regardless of the length of the year-by-year forecast horizon as long as we know the company's present value weighted average growth rate as of the end of the year-by-year forecast horizon. Note we are not advocating that it is appropriate to use a year-by-year forecast horizon of five years and then guess the continuing value growth rate. The point of this discussion is to demonstrate that it is possible to use the constant-growth perpetuity model before a company reaches its steady state (and the company is still experiencing variable cash flow growth rates), which is a common approach in practice.

If we use Year 0 as our base year and use its free cash flow (see Equation 6.3), we can measure the present value weighted average growth rate, g_A—which includes the effect of the growth rate for Year 1 with Equation 6.5.

$$g_A = \frac{1+r}{1+\frac{FCF_0}{V_{F,0}}} - 1 \qquad \textbf{(6.5)}$$

For the above example, the present value weighted average growth rate from Year 1 onward increases from 5.15% to 7.11% because it includes the effect of the growth rate in Year 1 of 50%, which is higher than the present value weighted average growth rate from Year 2 onward.

$$g_A = \frac{1+r}{1+\frac{FCF_0}{V_{F,0}}} - 1 = \frac{1.12}{1+\frac{\$100}{\$2{,}189}} - 1 = 0.0711$$

Yahoo!'s Present Value Weighted Average Growth Rate. In this section, we use the DCF valuation to measure Yahoo's present value perpetual weighted average growth rate as of Year 0 (from Year 1 onward). We know that its Year 0 value is \$32.6 billion after the distribution of excess assets and that its Year 1 free cash flow is \$0.985 billion. With a discount rate of 12%, Yahoo's present value weighted average growth rate for Year 2 onward is equal to 8.98%.

$$g_A = r - \frac{FCF_1}{V_{F,0}} = 0.12 - \frac{\$0.985}{\$32.612} = 0.0898$$

As discussed earlier in this section, we can use a shorter year-by-year forecast horizon and then the present value weighted average growth rate in the constant-growth perpetuity model to measure the same value based on a shorter year-by-year forecast horizon. We demonstrate this approach here with Yahoo.

In Exhibit 6.4, we calculate the year-by-year values of Yahoo for all ten years of the year-by-year forecast horizon. As shown in the exhibit, the value at the end of Year 5 is \$51.4 billion. The present value weighted average growth rate as of the end of Year 6 is 5.3%.

$$g_A = r - \frac{FCF_6}{V_{F,5}} = 0.12 - \frac{\$3{,}443}{\$51{,}380} = 0.0530$$

EXHIBIT 6.4 Yahoo!'s Year-by-Year Valuations and Corresponding Present Value Weighted Average Growth Rates

(in millions of \$)	Year 1	Year 2	Year 3	Year 4	Year 5	Year 6	Year 7	Year 8	Year 9	Year 10	CV Year 10
Cost of capital	12.0%										
Value as of the end of the year	\$35,541	\$39,201	\$43,252	\$47,666	\$51,380	\$54,103	\$55,929	\$56,937	\$58,315	\$59,773	
Unlevered free cash flow	985.0	604.3	653.5	776.6	2,005.5	3,443.1	4,666.1	5,703.3	5,454.4	5,539.9	5,678.4
Value end of year plus unlevered free cash flow	\$36,526	\$39,806	\$43,906	\$48,442	\$53,386	\$57,546	\$60,595	\$62,640	\$63,770	\$65,313	\$ 5,678
Discount factor	0.893	0.893	0.893	0.893	0.893	0.893	0.893	0.893	0.893	0.893	10.53
Value as of the beginning of the year	\$32,612	\$35,541	\$39,201	\$43,252	\$47,666	\$51,380	\$54,103	\$55,929	\$56,937	\$58,315	\$59,773
Present value weighted average growth rate	**9.0%**	**10.3%**	**10.3%**	**10.2%**	**7.8%**	**5.3%**	**3.4%**	**1.8%**	**2.4%**	**2.5%**	**2.5%**

Now that we know the present value weighted average growth rate to apply to Yahoo's Year 6 free cash flow, we can calculate Yahoo's value using only six years of forecasts, which we present in Exhibit 6.5. The resulting value of the firm of \$32.6 billion (without excess cash) is equal to the value calculated using all 11 years of forecasts (see the Appendix and Exhibit A6.3).

EXHIBIT 6.5 Yahoo!'s Valuation Using a Five-Year Forecast Horizon and the Present Value Weighted Average Growth Rate for Year 6 Onward

Cost of capital			12.0%				
Present value weighted average growth rate			5.3%				
($ in millions)	**Year 0**	**Year 1**	**Year 2**	**Year 3**	**Year 4**	**Year 5**	**CV_{Firm}**
Unlevered free cash flow for continuing value							$ 3,443
Discount factor for continuing value							14.922
Unlevered free cash flow and continuing value		$ 985	$ 604	$ 654	$ 777	$2,006	$51,380
Discount factor		0.893	0.797	0.712	0.636	0.567	0.567
Present value		$ 879	$ 482	$ 465	$ 494	$1,138	$29,155
Value of the firm (without excess cash)	**$32,612**						

Exhibit may contain small rounding errors

REVIEW EXERCISE 6.1

Present Value Weighted Average Growth Rate

Assume an investment will generate cash flows at the end of Years 1 through 5 equal to $2,200, $3,240, $3,300, $3,820, and $4,280, respectively. After Year 5, the cash flows will grow at 3% per year in perpetuity. Calculate the present value of these cash flows at the end of Year 0, assuming a discount rate of 12%. Then calculate the present value weighted average growth rate for this investment for Year 2 onward.

Solution on page 287.

A Two-Stage Continuing Value Growth Rate Illustration

In this section, we illustrate the effect of multiple growth rates on the present value weighted average growth rate using a company with two growth rates—a growth rate higher than its steady state growth rate for a finite period and then its steady state growth rate in perpetuity. Assume a company has two free cash flow growth rates, g_1 and g_2, and that its free cash flows will grow at the first growth rate through Year N and then grow at the second growth rate thereafter in perpetuity. Note that the cash flows grow at g_1 for N − 1 years because the first year to which the growth rate applies is the second year. The formula to measure the present value of the free cash flows with two growth rates combines the present value of an N-year annuity with constant growth (g_1) and the present value of a constant-growth perpetuity (g_2).

$$PV_0 = FCF_1\left[\left(\frac{1}{r-g_1} - \frac{1}{r-g_1}\times\frac{(1+g_1)^N}{(1+r)^N}\right) + \left(\frac{1+g_2}{r-g_2}\times\frac{(1+g_1)^{N-1}}{(1+r)^N}\right)\right]$$

For example, assume that a company with a discount rate equal to 13% has an expected free cash flow next year (FCF_1) equal to $1,000, which is expected to grow at 15% for Years 2 through 4 and thereafter grow at 3% in perpetuity. Using the above formula, the present value of this four year annuity and the subsequent perpetuity is $13,243.

$$\$13{,}243 = \$1{,}000\times\left[\left(\frac{1}{0.13-0.15} - \frac{1}{0.13-0.15}\times\frac{(1.15)^4}{(1.13)^4}\right) + \left(\frac{1.03}{0.13-0.03}\times\frac{(1.15)^3}{(1.13)^4}\right)\right]$$

$$\$13{,}243 = \$1{,}000\times[(-50-(-50\times1.0727)+(10.3\times0.933)]$$

$$\$13{,}243 = \$1{,}000\times[13.243]$$

Once we know the value, we can calculate the present value weighted average growth rate using Equation 6.4.

$$g_A = 0.13 - \frac{\$1{,}000}{\$13{,}243} = 0.05449$$

In Exhibit 6.6, we show the present value weighted average growth rate for various combinations of growth rates, two horizons for the first growth rate, and a discount rate of 12%, which demonstrates the effect that multiple growth rates can have on a company's present value weighted average growth rate. The first growth rate can have a large effect on the present value weighted average growth rate. For example, we show that a company with free cash flows growing at 20% for five years and 3% thereafter will have a present value weighted average growth rate of more than 6% with a discount rate of 12%.

EXHIBIT 6.6 Present Value Weighted Average Growth Rate for a Two-Stage Growth Rate Perpetuity

Discount Rate is 12% (r = 12%)	g_2 after Year 5			g_2 after Year 10		
g_1 (through Year N)	0%	3%	5%	0%	3%	5%
10%	3.1%	4.8%	6.0%	5.1%	6.1%	6.9%
15%	4.3%	5.8%	6.9%	6.9%	7.7%	8.3%
20%	5.3%	6.6%	7.6%	8.2%	8.8%	9.3%
25%	6.2%	7.3%	8.2%	9.2%	9.7%	10.1%

The larger the discount rate, the larger the effect of the first growth rate on the present value weighted average growth rate, because the present value of the cash flows coming from the years of the second growth rate is smaller. In addition, the longer the time the first growth rate persists, the larger the weighted average growth rate if g_1 is greater than g_2.

Valuation Key 6.3

It is always possible to express the value of a firm in terms of a single growth rate within a constant-growth free cash flow perpetuity model, as long as the first cash flow is positive and the discount rate is constant through time, even if the year-to-year cash flow growth rates are expected to vary over time.

REVIEW EXERCISE 6.2

Two-Stage Growth Rates

Calculate the present value weighted average growth rate for an investment with a discount rate of 12% and cash flows that grow at g_1 through Year 10 and at g_2 thereafter in perpetuity; use every combination of g_1 (5%, 10%, 15% and 20%) and g_2 (–3%, 0%, 3%).

Solution on page 287.

Using Comparable Companies to Measure Present Value Weighted Average Growth Rates

With sufficient comparability and adequate information, we can sometimes use information for comparable companies to estimate the present value weighted average growth rate if we have sufficient information for a set of comparable companies. If, for a comparable company, we can measure its value and the weighted average cost of capital, and obtain free cash flow estimates for a series of years up to T, we can estimate its present value weighted average growth rate for periods T + 1 onward, by solving for g in the following formula.

$$V_{F,0} = \sum_{t=1}^{T} \frac{FCF_t}{(1+r_{WACC})^t} + \frac{FCF_T \times (1+g)}{(r_{WACC}-g)} \times \frac{1}{(1+r_{WACC})^T}$$

We can solve for g using an iterative process (such as "goal seek" or "solver" functions in spreadsheet software), or we can solve it directly using the following formula.

$$g = r_{WACC} - \frac{FCF_T}{(1+r_{WACC})^{T-1} \times \left[V_{F,0} - \sum_{t=1}^{T-1} \frac{FCF_t}{(1+r_{WACC})^t} \right]}$$

Although the cost of capital is one of the inputs into this formula, it does not imply that the cost of capital determines the growth rate. On the contrary, the growth rate of the free cash flows and the cost of capital determine the value of the firm and we reverse engineer that relationship to measure the growth rate.

We measure the comparable company's firm value from the observed value of its securities in the marketplace and its cost of capital using the methods we discuss in this book. In most valuations, we would have already measured the value of the firm and unlevered cost of capital for the relevant comparable companies, so it is usually easy to calculate the weighted average cost of capital from the inputs used in the measurement of the unlevered cost of capital. For most comparable companies followed by financial analysts, we can use financial analyst forecasts to measure free cash flows for several years. Once we collect this information, we can measure the growth rate using the above formula.

For example, assume we measured the following inputs for a computer technology consulting company: a weighted average cost of capital equal to 9.06%; a firm value equal to \$3,578.8 million; and free cash flow forecasts for the following three years equal to \$259.0 million, \$254.9 million, and \$255.1 million, respectively. Using the above formulas, this company's present value weighted average growth rate for Year 4 and beyond is equal to 2.2%.

$$\$3{,}578.8 = \frac{\$259.0}{(1.0906)^1} + \frac{\$254.9}{(1.0906)^2} + \frac{\$255.1}{(1.0906)^3} + \frac{\$255.1 \times (1+g)}{(0.0906 - g)} \times \frac{1}{(1.0906)^3};\ g = 0.022$$

$$g = r_{WACC} - \frac{FCF_T}{(1+r_{WACC})^{T-1} \times \left[V_{F,0} - \sum_{t=1}^{T-1} \frac{FCF_t}{(1+r_{WACC})^t} \right]}$$

$$g = 0.0906 - \frac{\$255.1}{(1.0906)^2 \times \left(\$3{,}578.8 - \frac{\$259.0}{(1.0906)^1} - \frac{\$254.9}{(1.0906)^2} \right)} = 0.022$$

The perpetual growth rate for this company is in the range of the long-run inflation rate expected at that time. Below, we show the resulting growth rate for this and five other computer technology consulting companies. As we show in Exhibit 6.7, this company (labeled Comparable Company 6) has the highest growth rate among these companies.

EXHIBIT 6.7 Measuring the Implied Growth Rate for Technology Consulting Companies

Technology Consulting Companies ($ in millions)	WACC	Unlevered Free Cash Flow Forecasts Year 1	Year 2	Year 3	Firm Value	Growth Rate
Comparable Company 1	9.83%	$2,442.5	$2,619.2	$2,547.5	$23,310.3	-1.33%
Comparable Company 2	9.45%	$ 336.6	$ 380.1	$ 367.3	$ 3,513.5	-1.16%
Comparable Company 3	9.19%	$ 191.3	$ 171.9	$ 169.2	$ 1,847.4	-0.10%
Comparable Company 4	9.01%	$ 891.6	$ 941.1	$ 924.1	$10,423.6	0.18%
Comparable Company 5	9.83%	$1,443.7	$1,500.4	$1,522.2	$17,507.0	1.39%
Comparable Company 6	9.06%	$ 259.0	$ 254.9	$ 255.1	$ 3,578.8	2.20%
25th percentile						-0.90%
Median						0.04%
75th percentile						1.09%

This analysis shows that the present value weighted average growth rate for Year 4 onward for the selected comparable companies is negative for three of the six comparable companies. The median growth rate is essentially zero, and the 25th and 75th percentiles are −0.9% and 1.1%. These growth rates suggest that, over the long-term, free cash flows will be steady or modestly expanding or declining in this industry. Even a negative long-term free cash flow growth rate, however, does not necessarily mean that the size of this industry will decrease as measured by revenues. The industry may be growing, but increased competition could cause profit margins and, hence, free cash flows to decrease. For example, the microcomputer industry experienced declining margins of this sort for many years.

REVIEW EXERCISE 6.3

Estimating Growth Rates from Comparable Companies

A comparable company has a 10% weighted average cost of capital. Its equity value is currently $12,000, and the value of its debt—the only other financing it uses—is $6,000. It has unlevered free cash flow forecasts for the next three years equal to $1,000, $1,200, and $1,500, respectively. The company is anticipated to maintain a constant proportionate capital structure. Measure the present value weighted average growth rate for the company's continuing value for Year 4 and beyond.

Solution on page 287.

6.3 ESTIMATING THE BASE-YEAR YEAR FREE CASH FLOW

In this section, we discuss some of the factors to consider when estimating the base-year free cash flow for the constant-growth perpetuity model. First, we consider the growth rates of the components of the free cash flow forecasts, which may require extending the year-by-year forecast horizon so that the free cash flow growth rate in the year-by-year forecasts approaches the long-term growth rate. Second, we consider the "lumpy" nature of some types of capital expenditures. Third, we consider a related issue, when depreciable useful life differs from economic useful life. While these issues are not uncommon for individual assets, we typically assume they are less important at the company level. Lastly, we discuss the relation between capital expenditures and depreciation.

LO3 Measure the base-year free cash flow for the constant-growth perpetuity model

Preparing the Base-Year Free Cash Flow Forecast for the Financial Model

Valuations are often based on financial models that grow the scale of the company and free cash flows at a rate that is substantially higher than the long-term growth rate even in the last year of the year-by-year forecast horizon and then, as of the continuing value date, assume the free cash flows grow at a substantially lower long-term growth rate in perpetuity. The degree to which this assumption is correct depends on the required growth in the balance sheet to support the assumed growth in the free cash flows. Consider two extreme example companies.

Company A requires no investments in assets and has no liabilities, and it has all cash revenues and cash expenses, which are proportional to its revenues. For this company, free cash flows equal revenues minus expenses. Since expenses grow at the same rate as revenues, free cash flows grow at the same rate as revenues. For this company, a change in the revenue growth rate results in the same change in the free cash flow growth rate because it has no required growth in the balance sheet to support the assumed growth in the free cash flows.

Company B requires substantial investments in fixed assets (for example, land) and has no liabilities, and it has all cash revenues and no expenses (land is not depreciated). For this company, free cash flows equal revenues minus capital expenditures. While this company's balance sheet (total investment in fixed assets) always grows at the same growth rate as revenues, its capital expenditures (investment in additional fixed assets—that is the change in the balance sheet account) do not if the growth rate in a year is different from the growth rate in the previous year. In a year that the revenue growth rate increases, the growth rate for land (more generally, the growth rate for capital expenditures and the change in working capital) is higher than the revenue growth rate, and free cash flows grow at a rate lower than the revenue growth rate in that year. In a year that the revenue growth rate decreases, the growth rate for land is lower than the revenue growth rate, and free cash flows grow at a rate higher than the revenue growth rate in that period.

In Exhibit 6.8, we provide a simple illustration of the effect of changing revenue growth rates on free cash flow growth rates for a company with required investments in working capital. This company has no capital expenditures and finances itself with 100% equity. Its only expense is an operating expense that is equal to 60% of revenues, and it has a constant income tax rate equal to 30%. The company has only one asset—accounts receivable—that is equal to 40% of revenues. The company's revenues grow by 50% in Year 1 and by 5% thereafter. The exhibit presents one year of actual results and three years of forecasts and the annual growth rates for each line item in the financial model on the right-hand side of the exhibit. The revenue growth rates are 50% for Year 1 and 5% thereafter. Since all of the items in the income statement and all of the assets on the balance sheet are proportional to revenue, the growth rate for every item on the income statement and balance sheet is equal to the revenue growth rate in each year.

EXHIBIT 6.8 Effect of Changing Revenue Growth Rates on Free Cash Flows

Income Statement, Balance Sheet, and Free Cash Flow Forecasts					Growth Rates		
	Actual Year 0	Forecast Year 1	Forecast Year 2	Forecast Year 3	Forecast Year 1	Forecast Year 2	Forecast Year 3
Income Statement							
Revenue	$1,000	$1,500	$1,575	$1,654	50.0%	5.0%	5.0%
Operating expenses	-600	-900	-945	-992	50.0%	5.0%	5.0%
Income before taxes	$ 400	$ 600	$ 630	$ 662	50.0%	5.0%	5.0%
Income tax expense	–120	–180	–189	–198	50.0%	5.0%	5.0%
Net income	$ 280	$ 420	$ 441	$ 463	50.0%	5.0%	5.0%
Balance Sheet							
Total assets = Accounts receivable	$ 400	$ 600	$ 630	$ 662	50.0%	5.0%	5.0%
Shareholders' equity	$ 400	$ 600	$ 630	$ 662	50.0%	5.0%	5.0%
Free Cash Flows							
Earnings before interest and taxes (EBIT)	$ 400	$ 600	$ 630	$ 662	50.0%	5.0%	5.0%
Income taxes paid on EBIT	–120	–180	–189	–198	50.0%	5.0%	5.0%
Earnings before interest and after taxes	$ 280	$ 420	$ 441	$ 463	50.0%	5.0%	5.0%
Change in accounts receivable	–36	–200	–30	–32	450.0%	–85.0%	5.0%
Unlevered free cash flow = Equity FCF	$ 244	$ 220	$ 411	$ 432	–9.7%	86.8%	5.0%

Exhibit may contain small rounding errors

The free cash flow growth rate, however, is not equal to the revenue growth rate in Years 1 and 2 because the free cash flows depend, in part, on changes in the balance sheet. When the revenue growth rate increases from about 10% in Year 0 (not shown in the exhibit but calculable) to 50% in Year 1, the free cash flow growth rate is −9.7% because the growth rate for change in the accounts receivable is 450%. On the other hand, when the revenue growth rate decreases from 50% to 5% in Year 2, the free cash flow growth rate is 86.8% because the growth rate for the change in accounts receivable is −85%. When the revenue growth rate remains at 5% in Year 3, the free cash flow growth rate is equal to the revenue growth rate because the growth rate for the change in accounts receivable is also equal to the revenue growth rate.

If you look carefully at Exhibit 6.8 you can see that once you model the free cash flow for Year 2 which equals $411, you can then safely grow the cash flow forecasts at 5% per year thereafter, because all of the components of the free cash flows are growing at 5 percent subsequent to Year 2. In other words, you will note that the free cash flow for Year 3 of $432 is 5% greater than the free cash flow forecast for Year 2 ($432 = $411 × 1.05).

In the simple example in Exhibit 6.8, the valuation consequences of erroneously growing the free cash flow forecasts for Year 1 at 5% and using that to determine the continuing value instead of using the free cash flow forecasts for Year 2 are extremely large. Assuming a cost of capital of 10%, the correct valuation of the company would be $7,672.7 based on growing the Year 2 forecasts at 5%. Growing the Year 1 forecast at 5% yields a value of $4,400, which is only 57% of the correct value. The correct valuation is

$$V_{F,0} = \frac{\$220}{1.1} + \frac{\$411}{1.1^2} + \frac{\$411 \times (1.05)}{(0.1 - 0.05)} \times \frac{1}{1.1^2} = \$7{,}672.7$$

Whereas the incorrect valuation stemming from applying a 5% growth rate to the Year 1 forecast would be

$$V_{F,0} = \frac{\$220}{1.1} + \frac{\$220 \times (1.05)}{(0.1 - 0.05)} \times \frac{1}{1.1} = \$4{,}400$$

While we used a simple example and the change in accounts receivable to illustrate why the free cash flow growth rate will not always equal the revenue growth rate, any cash flow component based on changes in balances on the balance sheet (all working capital components, capital expenditures, etc.) will have a similar effect. In addition, since we calculate depreciation based on historical capital expenditures, depreciation can also cause a difference between the revenue and free cash flow growth rates. Some cash flow components may take even longer to reach steady state than we show in this simple example. For example, if a financial model assumes that accounts payable is a percentage of total purchases, and total purchases is equal to cost of goods sold plus the change in inventory, then the growth rate for the change in accounts payable will take three years to equal the constant revenue growth rate. Why? It will take two years for the change in inventory to equal the constant revenue growth rate, and the growth rate for the change in accounts payable will take one additional year to equal the constant revenue growth rate.

One way to correctly deal with this issue is to extend the year-by-year forecast horizon until the free cash flow growth rate "settles down" to something that is close to the assumed long-term growth rate used in the continuing value calculation. While it is not necessary to have every component of the free cash flows growing at the same rate in order to accomplish this goal, analyzing every line item provides useful insights into the model. Naturally, analyzing the sensitivity of a valuation to different perpetuity growth rates may require a different base-year free cash flow for each different growth rate so that the investments are consistent with the revenue growth rates.

Valuation Key 6.4

It is often useful to extend the year-by-year forecast horizon to test whether the free cash flow growth rate approaches the growth rate used in the continuing value valuation.

Revenue and Free Cash Flow Growth Rates in the Yahoo! Financial Model. In Exhibit 6.9, we present Yahoo's annual growth rates for both its revenue forecasts and the components of its free cash flow forecasts. We quickly observe that Yahoo's revenue and free cash flow growth rates are never the same until Year 11 even though its revenue growth rate is at the long-term inflation rate of 2.5%

EXHIBIT 6.9 Yahoo! Inc.—Revenue and Free Cash Flow Growth Rates

YAHOO! INC.
Annual Growth Rates for Revenues and Components of Free Cash Flow Forecasts
(for the years ended December 31)

($ in millions)	Year 0	Year 1	Year 2	Year 3	Year 4	Year 5	Year 6	Year 7	Year 8	Year 9	Year 10	Year 11
Revenue	22.2%	25.0%	30.0%	35.0%	40.0%	30.0%	20.0%	12.5%	5.1%	2.5%	2.5%	2.5%
Earnings before interest and taxes (EBIT)	–54.6%	67.2%	30.0%	35.0%	40.0%	30.0%	20.0%	12.5%	5.1%	2.5%	2.5%	2.5%
– Income taxes paid on EBIT	–40.3%	67.8%	30.0%	35.0%	40.0%	30.0%	20.0%	12.5%	5.1%	2.5%	2.5%	2.5%
Earnings before interest and after taxes	–60.4%	66.9%	30.0%	35.0%	40.0%	30.0%	20.0%	12.5%	5.1%	2.5%	2.5%	2.5%
+ Depreciation	34.9%	21.3%	41.1%	37.9%	37.1%	37.9%	35.7%	31.6%	27.0%	17.3%	2.5%	2.5%
+ Amortization	37.4%	0.0%	0.0%	0.0%	0.0%	0.0%	0.0%	0.0%	0.0%	0.0%	0.0%	0.0%
– Change in accounts receivable	–32.0%	–8.6%	94.9%	51.7%	54.3%	5.0%	–13.3%	–24.8%	–54.4%	–48.3%	2.5%	2.5%
– Change in other current assets			211.8%	51.7%	54.3%	5.0%	–13.3%	–24.8%	–54.4%	–48.3%	2.5%	2.5%
– Change in other assets	–72.9%	5369.9%	74.3%	48.5%	44.5%	–25.9%	–50.0%	–72.0%	–217.4%	–321.5%	1.4%	1.4%
+ Change in accounts payable	–3.7%	69.4%	–6.4%	51.7%	54.3%	5.0%	–13.3%	–24.8%	–54.4%	–48.3%	2.5%	2.5%
+ Change in accrued expenses	–17.7%	268.4%	–6.3%	51.7%	54.3%	5.0%	–13.3%	–24.8%	–54.4%	–48.3%	2.5%	2.5%
+ Change in non-current liabilities	–113.5%	–54.9%	52.7%	51.7%	54.3%	5.0%	–13.3%	–24.8%	–54.4%	–48.3%	2.5%	2.5%
– Change in required cash balance		37.5%	50.0%	51.7%	54.3%	5.0%	–13.3%	–24.8%	–54.4%	–48.3%	2.5%	2.5%
Unlevered cash flow from operations	–23.3%	36.2%	–7.8%	25.2%	33.3%	66.2%	42.7%	24.7%	14.9%	–1.7%	2.5%	2.5%
– Capital expenditures (net)	–62.0%	–1.6%	30.0%	35.0%	40.0%	30.0%	20.0%	12.5%	5.1%	2.5%	3.9%	2.5%
Unlevered free cash flow	–214.1%	98.4%	–38.6%	8.1%	18.8%	158.2%	71.7%	35.5%	22.2%	–4.4%	1.6%	2.5%

beginning in Year 9. Yahoo's expense ratios stabilize in Year 2, and its EBIT growth rate is the same as its revenue growth rate afterward because the financial model forecasts each earnings component directly or indirectly as a percentage of revenues.

The growth rates for the adjustments that convert EBIT to free cash flow, however, are not the same as the revenue growth rates until Year 10 for some adjustments and not until Year 11 for others. The working capital adjustments, such as accounts receivable, grow in the way we discussed earlier in this chapter. We have two key points to glean from this analysis. First, when the revenue growth rate increases (decreases), the free cash flow growth rate is often smaller (larger) than the revenue growth rate, indicating that may not be a good point in the forecast horizon to select as the continuing value date. Second, it can take multiple years with a constant long-term revenue growth rate before the free cash flow growth rate will equal the revenue growth rate. The number of years it takes depends on the forecast drivers embedded in the financial model.

Other considerations in the base-year free cash flow are to deal appropriately with capital expenditures, depreciation, and the relationship between them. We discuss that in detail in the next section.

"Lumpy" Capital Expenditures Result in "Lumpy" Free Cash Flows

In this section, we illustrate the effect of "lumpy" capital expenditures on free cash flows. In Exhibit 6.10, we show the financial forecasts and growth rates for the Lumpy CAPEX Company over 24 years, Year 1 to Year 24. The company uses a three-year useful life and straight-line depreciation to amortize its assets for both book and tax purposes, and we assume the three-year useful life is equal to the economic life of the assets. To keep the example simple, we assume the company has no working capital assets or any other assets apart from the depreciable assets; that the company has no working capital liabilities or debt;

EXHIBIT 6.10 The Lumpy CAPEX Company's Financial Forecasts and Growth Rates

	Year 0	Year 1	Year 2	Year 3	Year 4	Year 5	Year 6	...	Year 22	Year 23	Year 24
Income Statement											
Revenue		$150.0	$210.0	$252.0	$252.0	$252.0	$252.0	...	$252.0	$252.0	$252.0
Depreciation expense		–75.0	–105.0	–126.0	–126.0	–126.0	–126.0	...	–126.0	–126.0	–126.0
Income before taxes		$ 75.0	$105.0	$126.0	$126.0	$126.0	$126.0	...	$126.0	$126.0	$126.0
Income tax expense (provision)		–22.5	–31.5	–37.8	–37.8	–37.8	–37.8	...	–37.8	–37.8	–37.8
Net income		$ 52.5	$ 73.5	$ 88.2	$ 88.2	$ 88.2	$ 88.2	...	$88.2	$ 88.2	$ 88.2
Balance Sheet											
Total assets	$225.0	$240.0	$198.0	$297.0	$261.0	$198.0	$297.0	...	$261.0	$198.0	$297.0
Shareholders' equity	$225.0	$240.0	$198.0	$297.0	$261.0	$198.0	$297.0	...	$261.0	$198.0	$297.0
Free Cash Flows											
Earnings before interest and taxes		$ 75.0	$105.0	$126.0	$126.0	$126.0	$126.0	...	$126.0	$126.0	$126.0
Income taxes paid on EBIT		–22.5	–31.5	–37.8	–37.8	–37.8	–37.8	...	–37.8	–37.8	–37.8
Earnings before interest and after taxes		$ 52.5	$ 73.5	$ 88.2	$ 88.2	$ 88.2	$ 88.2	...	$ 88.2	$ 88.2	$ 88.2
Depreciation		75.0	105.0	126.0	126.0	126.0	126.0	...	126.0	126.0	126.0
Unlevered cash flow from operations		$127.5	$178.5	$214.2	$214.2	$214.2	$214.2	...	$214.2	$214.2	$214.2
Capital expenditures	–$225.0	–90.0	–63.0	–225.0	–90.0	–63.0	–225.0	...	–90.0	–63.0	–225.0
Unlevered free cash flow		$ 37.5	$115.5	–$ 10.8	$124.2	$151.2	–$ 10.8	...	$124.2	$151.2	–$ 10.8

	Year 2	Year 3	Year 4	Year 5	Year 6	...	Year 22	Year 23	Year 24
Growth Rates									
Revenue growth rate	40%	20%	0%	0%	0%	...	0%	0%	0%
Earnings before interest and after taxes growth rate	40%	20%	0%	0%	0%	...	0%	0%	0%
Depreciation growth rate	40%	20%	0%	0%	0%	...	0%	0%	0%
Unlevered operating cash flow growth rate	40%	20%	0%	0%	0%	...	0%	0%	0%
Unlevered free cash flow growth rate	**208%**	**–109%**	**NMF**	**22%**	**–107%**	**...**	**NMF**	**22%**	**–107%**
Capital expenditure growth rate	**–30%**	**257%**	**–60%**	**–30%**	**257%**	**...**	**–60%**	**–30%**	**257%**

and that the company will not experience inflation. Again, in order to keep it simple, we also assume the company only has three assets.

Revenues grow at 40% in Year 2, 20% in Year 3, and 0% thereafter. The company's earnings before interest and after taxes, depreciation expense, and unlevered cash flow from operations all grow at the revenue growth rate. The company's free cash flows, however, do not grow at the revenue growth rate; further, the free cash flow growth rate never converges to a zero growth rate even though the revenue growth rate is zero after Year 3. The cause of the varying free cash flow growth rate is the lumpiness of the company's capital expenditures.

We assume that the company invests $1.5 at the end of a year to generate $1 of additional revenues in the following year. At the end of Year 0—the first year of the company's operations—the company has $225 of assets that will generate revenues of $150 in Year 1. Revenues grow by $60 (40%) in Year 2, which requires the company to invest $90 at the end of Year 1, and revenues grow by $42 (20%) in Year 3, which requires the company to invest $63 at the end of Year 2. Although the company's revenues are growing in Year 2, its capital expenditures are decreasing (from $90 to $63, or −30%) because revenues grow less in Year 3 ($42 = $252 − $210) than they do in Year 2 ($60 = $210 − $150).

Since revenues stop growing in Year 4, the company does not need to make any new investments in Year 3 to grow the company's revenues. However, since the company's assets purchased at the end of Year 0 are fully depreciated and have no remaining economic useful life, the company must replace the assets purchased in Year 0. The capital expenditures in Year 3 replace the assets the company purchased in Year 0. Similarly, in Year 4, the company replaces the assets purchased in Year 1, and in Year 5, the company replaces the assets purchased in Year 2. This pattern repeats in perpetuity; thus, the company's capital expenditures and, hence, free cash flow growth rates never converge to the company's "steady state" revenue growth rate (0%). In this case, depreciation is constant from Year 3 onward even though the capital expenditures are lumpy, for the company uses straight-line depreciation. If accelerated depreciation were used instead, the depreciation number would not become constant, which complicates the issue further. We will discuss that complication in the next section.

In Exhibit 6.11, we present valuations of the Lumpy CAPEX Company using different continuing value dates (at which we use a perpetuity valuation method) using a 10% discount rate and a 0% growth rate. The correct value of the firm is equal to $816. The valuation we show under the Year 3 column assumes that the continuing value date is Year 3. In order to measure the value of the firm at the end of Year 0, we discount the free cash flow for Years 1 through 3 and the continuing value at the end of Year 3 (based on the Year 4 free cash flow) discounted to Year 0; specifically:

$$V_{F,0} = \frac{FCF_1}{1+r} + \frac{FCF_2}{(1+r)^2} + \frac{FCF_3}{(1+r)^3} + \frac{FCF_4}{(r-g)} \times \frac{1}{(1+r)^3}$$

$$V_{F,0} = \frac{\$37.5}{1.1} + \frac{\$115.5}{1.1^2} + \frac{-\$10.8}{1.1^3} + \frac{\$124.2}{(0.1-0)} \times \frac{1}{1.1^3} = \$1,055$$

This value is larger than the company's actual value of $816 (29% larger). Since we know that the free cash flows for each year are correct, the reason this valuation exceeds the actual valuation is because the free cash flow used in the continuing value (FCF_4 = $124.2) is too large for the base-year free cash

EXHIBIT 6.11 The Lumpy CAPEX Company Valuation with Varying Continuing Value Dates

	Discounted Cash Flow Valuation Using Actual Free Cash Flows										
Year (t)	**Year 0**	**Year 1**	**Year 2**	**Year 3**	**Year 4**	**Year 5**	**Year 6**	**...**	**Year 22**	**Year 23**	**Year 24**
Free cash flow		$37.5	$115.5	-$ 10.8	$124.2	$151.2	-$ 10.8	...	$124.2	$151.2	-$ 10.8
Continuing value at Year 0				$ 933	$1,033	-$ 67	$ 701	...	$ 186	-$ 12	$ 126
Present value of FCF Year +1 to Year (t)				121	206	300	294	...	706	723	722
Value of the firm at Year 0	$816			$1,055	$1,239	$ 233	$ 995	...	$ 892	$ 711	$ 848
Error in the valuation				29%	52%	−71%	22%	...	9%	−13%	4%
Continuing value (% of total)				88%	83%	−29%	70%	...	21%	−2%	15%
Present value of FCF (% of total)				12%	17%	129%	30%	...	79%	102%	85%
Value of the firm at Year 0				100%	100%	100%	100%	...	100%	100%	100%

Exhibit may contain small rounding errors

flow. If we extend the continuing value date to Year 4, the error is larger (52%) because the base-year free cash flow is even larger than the previous base-year free cash flow (FCF_5 = \$151.2). If we extend the continuing value date to Year 5, the absolute value of the error is even larger (71%), but in this case, the valuation is too low because the base-year free cash flow in the continuing value calculation is negative (FCF_6 = −\$10.8).

In short, we cannot correctly value the firm choosing any of the years as the base-year cash flow for the cash flow perpetuity model. To address this issue, we can either run or model out for, say, 1,000 columns or we can convert the lumpy capital expenditure time-series into an equivalent present value annuity time-series as of the end of Year 3. The repeating capital expenditure time-series is \$90, \$63, and \$225. The present value (using a 10% discount rate) of these capital expenditures is equal to \$302.9 (\$302.9 = \$90/1.1 + \$63/1.1^2 + \$225/1.1^3). We then convert this present value into a three-year annuity with the same present value by substituting capital expenditures of \$121.8 per year (\$121.8 = \$302.9/2.487, where 2.487 is the present value factor of an ordinary annuity for 3 years at 10% interest; the sum of 0.909, 0.828, and 0.751).

We adjust the free cash flows in each period for the difference between the actual capital expenditure and the capital expenditure annuity. We show this calculation in Exhibit 6.12. We also show the different valuations of the Lumpy CAPEX Company for varying continuing value dates. All of the valuations equal \$816—the correct value of the firm.

EXHIBIT 6.12 Using an Annuity to Eliminate the Lumpiness in the Capital Expenditures

Discounted Cash Flow Valuation Using Adjusted Free Cash Flows, Adjusted for Annuity Capital Expenditures											
Year (t)	**Year 0**	**Year 1**	**Year 2**	**Year 3**	**Year 4**	**Year 5**	**Year 6**	**...**	**Year 22**	**Year 23**	**Year 24**
Capital expenditure in FCF					\$ 90.0	\$ 63.0	\$225.0	...	\$ 90.0	\$ 63.0	\$225.0
Annuity for capital expenditures					121.8	121.8	121.8	...	121.8	121.8	121.8
Adjustment to free cash flow					–\$ 31.8	–\$ 58.8	\$103.2	...	–\$ 31.8	–\$ 58.8	\$103.2
Adjusted free cash flow		\$37.5	\$115.5	–\$ 10.8	\$ 92.4	\$ 92.4	\$ 92.4	...	\$ 92.4	\$ 92.4	\$ 92.4
Continuing value at Year 0				\$ 694	\$ 631	\$ 574	\$ 522	...	\$ 113	\$ 103	\$ 94
Present value of FCF Year +1 to Year (t)				121	185	242	294	...	702	712	722
Value of the firm at Year 0	\$ 816			\$ 816	\$ 816	\$ 816	\$ 816	...	\$ 816	\$ 816	\$ 816
Error in the valuation				0%	0%	0%	0%	...	0%	0%	0%
Continuing value (% of total)				85%	77%	70%	64%	...	14%	13%	12%
Present value of FCF (% of total)				15%	23%	30%	36%	...	86%	87%	88%
Value of the firm at Year 0				100%	100%	100%	100%	...	100%	100%	100%

Exhibit may contain small rounding errors

Thus, we correct for the lumpiness in capital expenditures by converting the lumpy series into an annuity with the same present value. First, we must identify the capital expenditure cycle—that is, the period during which capital expenditures are lumpy and the repeating pattern of the lumpiness. The example we used had a three-year cycle, which is likely shorter than most that you will encounter. Our example also assumed a zero growth rate in perpetuity. The issue becomes more complex for a non-zero growth rate; however, converting the lumpy capital expenditure series into either an annuity or an annuity with growth mitigates this problem.

Valuation Key 6.5

We correct for the lumpiness in capital expenditures by converting the lumpy series into an annuity. First, we identify the capital expenditure cycle. Then, we convert the capital expenditures in that cycle to an annuity with the same present value. The alternative is to extend the year-by-year forecast horizon to say, 1,000 years, which, given the current spreadsheet capabilities is also feasible.

REVIEW EXERCISE 6.4

Lumpy Capital Expenditures

A company has $1,200 in annual revenues that are expected to continue in perpetuity with no growth. The company's only expenses are depreciation and income taxes (40% tax rate). The company uses straight-line depreciation with no salvage value and a three-year life for its single fixed asset. The fixed asset has an acquisition cost of $1,200 and must be replaced every three years. The replacement cost of the fixed asset is not expected to change in the future. Below we present the company's income statement and balance sheet for Years 0 and 1. The company was formed on the last day of Year 0 when it invested $1,200 in its fixed asset. The company is all-equity financed, will hold no cash, and has no working capital requirements. The company's cost of capital is 10%. Measure the company's free cash flow for Years 1 through 3. Measure the value of the company at the end of Year 0 using a cash flow perpetuity.

	Actual Year 0	Forecast Year 1
Income Statement		
Revenue		$1,200
Depreciation expense....		−400
Income before taxes....		$ 800
Income tax expense (provision)....		−320
Net income....		$ 480
Balance Sheet		
Total assets = Fixed asset....	$1,200	$ 800
Shareholders' equity....	$1,200	$ 800

Solution on pages 287–289.

Lumpy Income Taxes When Depreciable Life Differs from Economic Life. It is common for an asset's depreciable life for tax purposes to differ from its economic useful life given current tax codes in the U.S. and elsewhere. Indeed, some assets are completely written off in the first year despite having a multi-year economic useful life. While depreciation does not represent a cash flow itself, depreciation affects income tax payments. Even if revenues and all other expenses for tax purposes are identical year-to-year, the company's income tax payments are not the same each year if its depreciable life for tax purposes is not equal to its economic life. This issue can also occur when the company uses accelerated depreciation for tax purposes because depreciation expense will vary every year. While these differences almost always occur at the individual asset level, the key again is whether these differences occur at the aggregate level for the company.

In an example like the Lumpy CAPEX Company where the revenues and EBITDA are constant after Year 3, we could now have two factors driving the difference in the revenue and free cash flow growth rates. The first factor is the lumpy capital expenditures, and the second is varying income taxes due to varying depreciation. We can use an annuity to adjust a company's free cash flows for the non-constant growth rate resulting from the depreciable life of the assets not equaling the economic life of the assets just as we adjusted the capital expenditures in the Lumpy CAPEX example.

Valuation Key 6.6

If the depreciable life of a company's assets is not equal to the economic life of its assets or if the company uses accelerated depreciation for tax purposes, the company's continuing value free cash flows may not have a constant growth rate. We adjust the free cash flows to have a constant growth rate by converting the lumpy income tax and capital expenditure series into an annuity.

Relationship Between Capital Expenditures and Depreciation

Another issue to consider when estimating the base-year for the constant-growth perpetuity model is the relationship between capital expenditures and depreciation. Factors that determine whether capital expenditures are greater than, equal to, or less than depreciation in the base-year free cash flow include price level changes, productivity changes, the depreciable life of the asset, the economic life of the asset, and the company's expected real growth after the continuing value date. For the purposes of this discussion, we assume that the company uses straight-line depreciation and that the depreciable life and economic useful life are the same.

If we assume the company will have no real growth after the continuing value date and the assets it purchases have no change in productivity, then price level changes—either increases or decreases—will affect the relation between capital expenditures and depreciation. If the company is in steady state and prices have remained constant since the initial purchase date of assets, the capital expenditures required to replace those assets (assuming all the assets are identical and 1/Nth of the company's assets are replaced each year where N is the depreciable life of the assets) will equal depreciation. If prices increased over the useful life of the asset, capital expenditures will be greater than depreciation; if prices decreased over the useful life of the asset, capital expenditures will be less than depreciation. Again, this presumes no changes in productivity.

Ignoring the potential offsets from changes in productivity or real growth, in Exhibit 6.13, we compute continuing value capital expenditure to depreciation ratios for varying levels of price level changes (−3% to +3%) and varying years of useful life for the asset (5, 10, 15, ..., 40 years). The exhibit shows how the ratio of capital expenditure to depreciation increases when price levels increase and decreases when price levels decrease. We assume that the firm is in steady state for purposes of these calculations. In particular, if the company uses assets with a five-year life, it replaces one-fifth of these assets every year. If the assets have a 10-year life, we assume the company replaces one-tenth of these assets every year. The effects of the price level changes are magnified as the number of years of useful life increases and as the inflation rate increases. This exhibit indicates that the ratio of capital expenditure to depreciation can easily be more than 1.25 for many assets even with inflation at just 3% (and ignoring all other factors). Of course, the relation between depreciation and capital expenditures at the firm level will depend on the mix of the useful lives of the assets that the firm uses in its operations.

EXHIBIT 6.13 Ratios of Continuing Value Capital Expenditure to Depreciation for Varying Levels of Inflation and Varying Years of Useful Life

	Price Level Changes for Each Year in the Life of the Asset				
Years of Life	**−3.0%**	**−1.5%**	**0.0%**	**1.5%**	**3.0%**
5	91%	96%	100%	105%	109%
10	84%	92%	100%	108%	117%
15	78%	88%	100%	112%	126%
20	72%	85%	100%	116%	134%
25	66%	82%	100%	121%	144%
30	60%	78%	100%	125%	153%
35	55%	75%	100%	129%	163%
40	50%	72%	100%	134%	173%

If the company is experiencing real growth and is investing in capital expenditures to achieve that real growth, the ratio of capital expenditures to depreciation will be even greater than shown in the exhibit. On the other hand, increases in productive capacity can offset the effects of inflation and real growth on the ratio of capital expenditure to depreciation at the continuing value date. In this context, productivity means the ability to purchase the same productive capacity at a lower cost (for example, productivity increases in computing power).

Relation Between CAPEX and Depreciation in the Yahoo! Financial Model. In our continuing value of Yahoo, it is important to consider the relationship between capital expenditures and depreciation and to be certain that we are comfortable with that relationship in the base-year free cash flow. In Exhibit A6.2, Yahoo's Year 11 capital expenditures equal $3.973 billion and its depreciation is

$3.767 billion, resulting in a ratio of capital expenditures to depreciation of 1.055. Remember that the growth rate we assumed for the perpetuity was 2.5%, the expected inflation rate. As such, the continuing value assumes no real growth. The ratio of capital expenditures to depreciation of 1.055 seems consistent with the assumptions in the financial model such as no real growth and the characteristics of Yahoo's assets such as the generally short life of many of Yahoo's capitalized investments, and potential productivity increases in computer-related fields.

Valuation Key 6.7

Inflation (price level changes), real growth, and changes in productivity after the continuing value date affect the ratio of capital expenditures to depreciation used to determine the base-year free cash flow to measure the continuing value. Higher inflation and real growth increase this ratio, whereas increasing productivity decreases this ratio.

6.4 REAL GROWTH AND VALUE CREATION IN THE CONSTANT-GROWTH PERPETUITY MODEL

LO4 Incorporate real growth and value creation in the constant-growth perpetuity model

The long-term growth rate is, of course, an important input into the constant-growth perpetuity model. The long-term growth rate is often assumed to be positive, but it can be either positive or negative depending on the economic context underpinning the valuation. If it is positive and above long-run expected inflation, the growth reflects real growth. One way for a company to grow is by increasing its unlevered operating cash flows without increasing its investment beyond what it has already made; in other words, using excess capacity. While growth like this can occur over a few years, it is less likely to continue in perpetuity or for a long enough period to include in a perpetuity valuation. It is also possible for a company to expect real growth without increasing its scale for other reasons—for example, sales price increases above inflation without corresponding increases in costs—but again this is likely to be short-term in nature. Thus, the more common assumption is that the company will experience real growth by expanding its scale. For example, the growth rate may be linked to growth in an economy or population growth, both of which can result in a growth rate that is higher than inflation (real growth). If we expect a company to exactly keep pace with the real growth of the economies in which it operates, the real growth component of the company's perpetual growth rate is equal to the expected real growth of the economies in which it operates. We might also expect the company to grow with the population to which it sells its goods or services or a sub-group of that population, such as a certain age group.

Valuation in Practice 6.4

Including Real Growth in Continuing Value—The Majesco and Cover-All Technologies Inc. Merger In December 2014, Majesco and Cover-All Technologies Inc. announced that they entered into a merger agreement under which Cover-All would merge into Majesco in a stock-for-stock merger. According to the agreement, each share of common stock of Cover-All would be exchanged for 0.21466 shares of Majesco. The merger closed in June 2015. Cover-All engaged The BVA Group LLC to render a fairness opinion. In its DCF valuation method, BVA used the constant-growth perpetuity model to measure Cover-All's continuing (terminal) value:

> Beyond a discrete five-year cash period, BVA utilized an annuity-in-perpetuity approach to determine the terminal value assuming a long-term growth rate of 3.0 percent. This long-term growth rate was estimated based on the assumption of modest inflation plus a small measure of real growth. The long-term growth rate was below that of expected nominal GDP growth given the limited growth opportunities available to Cover-All on a stand-alone basis without significant investment in upgrading its product suite as well as product marketing and sales effort.

Source: Majesco and Cover-All Technologies Inc.'s joint Proxy Statement filed with the U.S. SEC on March 31, 2015

The growth rate may be linked to long-term product or service market penetration in various markets, including global markets. In this case, real growth cannot occur in perpetuity because all markets will eventually be penetrated, but the growth from expanded market penetration can be sufficiently long enough—say 50 or more years—that including it in the perpetuity valuation is appropriate. Another way to achieve real growth is to find new products and services to offer; think of the new products and services that Apple has introduced since the introduction of the iPod in 2001. It is also possible to link real growth to taking away market share from competing companies, but this is less likely to occur year after year over the long run. Regardless of the cause of the real growth, if we expect real growth from new investment, the expected new investment is included in the calculation of the base-year free cash flow.

Not all positive real growth rates increase the value of the firm. We know that if a company invests in negative net present value projects, its free cash flows might grow, but the value of the firm will decrease. Thus, we must also consider the rate of return the company earns on its investments.

In the remainder of this section, we develop the constant-growth perpetuity model based on two sets of conditions. We first develop the model under the assumption that a company faces inflation but has no real growth opportunities after the continuing value date. Next, we expand the first model that includes inflation to include an assumption for real growth. We illustrate how real growth can create value, have no effect on value, or decrease value, depending on the return earned on the new investment relative to the cost of capital.

A Constant Growth Rate Equal to Inflation (No Real Growth)

Recall from earlier chapters that in DCF models, we either forecast free cash flows in nominal terms and discount the free cash flows at the nominal risk-adjusted discount rate, or we forecast real (inflation-free or constant currency) free cash flows and discount the free cash flows at the real (inflation-free) risk-adjusted discount rate. Performed properly, these two approaches result in the same valuation. If nominal free cash flows, FCF, are growing at inflation, then discounting the nominal free cash flow at the risk-adjusted nominal discount rate, r, using inflation as the constant growth rate, $g = i$, is equivalent to discounting real free cash flows, FCF^{Real}, at the real discount rate, r^{Real}.

$$V_0 = \frac{FCF_1}{r - i} = \frac{FCF_0 \times (1 + i)}{r - i} = \frac{FCF_1^{Real}}{r^{Real}} = \frac{FCF_0^{Real}}{r^{Real}}$$

If nominal free cash flows grow at inflation and have no real growth, then the appropriate growth rate for the constant-growth perpetuity model is inflation, $g = i$. Setting the growth rate equal to inflation in the perpetuity formula does not imply that the company will experience real growth. When discounting at the nominal discount rate, omitting the effect of expected inflation on the growth rate understates value. Of course, the world is not so simple that you can automatically assume that the cash flows will grow with inflation and that the company has no real growth.

The appropriate growth rate can be greater or less than inflation, and it can even be negative. For example, assume we expect computer chip manufacturers to continue to have technological innovations in the design and manufacture of microchips such that product prices are reduced throughout the industry. In this case, the nominal cash flow per unit for these companies can grow at less than inflation; in fact, it can have a negative growth rate per unit, and total nominal cash flows will have a growth rate lower than inflation unless the companies either increase the number of units sold to offset decreasing prices or expand to other products. In other words, the effect of inflation on the growth of nominal cash flows can be offset, in part, by technological advances so that neither revenues nor costs increase as fast as inflation. Competitive pressures can also reduce cash flow growth rates below inflation as well if profit margins are squeezed.

Valuation Key 6.8

Even if the company has zero real growth, the growth rate in the perpetuity model using a nominal discount rate will not be zero if the company's nominal cash flows grow as a result of a decline in the purchasing power of the currency (i.e., inflation).

Real Growth from New Investment Can Decrease the Value of the Firm[7]

Recall that although the conceptually preferred approach to evaluate projects is the **net present value** method, an alternative approach compares the internal rate of return on the investment to the company's required rate of return for that investment. We know a company destroys value if it invests in negative net present value projects, which occurs if a project's internal rate of return is less than its required rate of return. In this section we discuss a framework to assess the value created or destroyed from new investments

We use this framework to illustrate two points related to a company making new investments beyond those necessary to maintain its current scope and scale, which we call new investment. First, ignoring inflation, the nominal free cash flow growth rate is a function of two factors—the proportion of free cash flow (before new investment) invested in new investments and the nominal free cash flow-based rate of return on that new investment, **nominal free cash flow-based rate of return, FCFROI**. Second, the effect of new investment on the value of the firm depends on the free cash flow-based rate of return expected on the new investment relative to the required rate of return on that new investment. Positive real growth destroys value if the free cash flow-based return on the new investment is less than the investment's required rate of return. Growth in free cash flows from new investment only creates value if the return on the new investment is greater than the investment's required rate of return—in other words, if it has a positive net present value.

Assume that new investments have the same risk and, hence, the same required rate of return, r, as the company's existing investments. We use the term "new investment" for investments that result in positive (real) growth in free cash flows beyond those that result from the company's current scale and scope. We include new investments in the model by assuming that the company has new investment opportunities in perpetuity equal to a percentage, I%, of its **free cash flows without new investments, $FCF_{t+1}^{w/o\ NewI}$**. Free cash flow (after making the new investments) is equal to the free cash flow without new investment multiplied by 1 minus the investment percentage, I%; in other words, omitting time subscripts, $FCF = FCF^{w/o\ NewI} \times (1 - I\%)$). The **investment percentage, I%**, sometimes called the **plowback ratio**, represents the percentage of the free cash flow before new investments that is invested in **new investments**; in other words, investments made beyond those required to maintain the company's existing scale or productive capacity. Note that investments do not only represent expenditures a company capitalizes on its balance sheet (for example, working capital and capital expenditures). Investments include any expenditures a company makes that have a life beyond the period in which the expenditure occurs. For example, expenditures for investments in brand development or company-developed intellectual property, as well as a company's organizational infrastructure (such as existing distribution systems and channels), and its human capital, are generally expensed and thus are not included in invested capital even though they likely have a life beyond the period in which the expense is recorded and create value. It is often difficult to measure these investments and determine their economic useful life.

Although the free cash flows without new investment do not include a deduction for new investment, they include the investments needed to maintain the company's scale (productive capacity) as of the continuing value date. Without these investments, the company's free cash flows would decrease over time because of decreasing productive capacity. The **real return on new investment, $FCFROI^{Real}$**, is equal to the cash flow generated by new investment in the following year divided by the amount of the new investment adjusted for inflation, i. The nominal free cash flow-based return on investment is equal to the real return on investment adjusted for inflation.

$$FCFROI = (1 + FCFROI^{Real}) \times (1 + i) - 1$$

$$FCFROI^{Real} = \frac{FCFROI - i}{1 + i}$$

Lastly, we assume a company's free cash flow without new investments, that is, the free cash flow based on maintaining the company's current capacity, grows at the rate of inflation, i.

$$FCF_{t+1}^{w/o\ NewI} = FCF_{t}^{w/o\ NewI} \times (1 + i)$$

$$FCF_{t+2}^{w/o\ NewI} = FCF_{t+1}^{w/o\ NewI} \times (1 + i) = FCF_{t}^{w/o\ NewI} \times (1 + i)^2$$

[7] For additional discussion of this topic, see Bradley, M., and Jarrell, G. A., "Expected Inflation and the Constant-Growth Valuation Model," *Journal of Applied Corporate Finance* 20 (2008), pp. 66–78; and Cornell, B., and R. Gerger, "A Note on Estimating Constant Growth Terminal Value with Inflation," *Business Valuation Review*, Volume 36, Number 4, pp. 117–123.

The growth rate of free cash flows is equal to the ratio of two consecutive free cash flows minus 1. If the company makes new investments for real growth, its free cash flow in Year 1 is equal to its free cash flow without new investment multiplied by 1 minus the investment percentage (I% or the plowback ratio). The free cash flow in Year 2 has two components, both of which are multiplied by 1 minus the plowback ratio (1 − I%) to incorporate new investment in Year 2. The first component is the free cash flow without new investment in Year 2, and the second component is the return on the new investment made in Year 1, adjusted for one year of inflation. Now that we have formulas for the free cash flows for Years 2 and 1, we can measure the growth rate by dividing the free cash flow formula for Year 2 by the free cash flow formula for Year 1.

$$1+g=\frac{FCF_2}{FCF_1}=\frac{(FCF_2^{w/o\ NewI}+FCF_1^{w/o\ NewI}\times I\%\times(1+i)\times FCFROI^{Real})\times(1-I\%)}{FCF_1^{w/o\ NewI}\times(1-I\%)}$$

We can rewrite the free cash flow without investment in Year 2 as the free cash flow without investment in Year 1 adjusted for one year of inflation.

$$1+g=\frac{\left[FCF_1^{w/o\ NewI}\times(1+i)+FCF_1^{w/o\ NewI}\times I\%\times(1+i)\times\frac{FCFROI-i}{1+i}\right]\times(1-I\%)}{FCF_1^{w/o\ NewI}\times(1-I\%)}$$

The resulting growth rate has two components. The first component is equal to the plowback ratio, I%, multiplied by the nominal return on new investment, FCFROI. The second component is equal to the inflation rate multiplied by 1 minus the plowback ratio, which reduces the inflation adjustment for the percentage of the cash flow due to inflation that is invested in new investments.

$$g = I\% \times FCFROI + i \times (1 - I\%) \tag{6.6}$$

If inflation is equal to zero, the second component is equal to zero and FCFROI becomes the real return on investment, $FCFROI^{Real}$. The growth rate (which is now the real growth rate) is equal to the plowback ratio multiplied by the real return on investment ($I\% \times FCFROI^{Real}$). For a given FCFROI, Equation 6.6 can be rearranged to measure the level of new investment required to support an assumed growth rate, $I\% = (g - i)/(FCFROI - i)$.

Substituting Equation 6.6 for the growth rate in the constant-growth perpetuity model shows the way that the rate of inflation, i, the nominal return on new investment, FCFROI, and the plowback ratio, I%, affect continuing value.

$$V_{CV}=\frac{FCF_{CV}^{w/o\ NewI}\times(1+i)\times(1-I\%)}{r-I\%\times FCFROI-i\times(1-I\%)} \tag{6.7}$$

Although the implication of the above formula might not be readily obvious, Equation 6.7 shows that new investment only increases the company's value if its return is greater than its required return. We can restate this formula to make this point a little clearer by partitioning Equation 6.7 into two parts—the value of the firm without new investment and the effect of new investment on the value of the firm without new investment. The second component is greater than 1, that is, the new investment creates value, only if the nominal return on new investment, FCFROI, is greater than the nominal required rate of return r, (so that $FCFROI - i > r - i$).

$$V_{CV}=\frac{FCF_{CV}^{w/o\ NewI}\times(1+i)}{r-i}\times\frac{1-I\%}{1-I\%\times\left(\frac{FCFROI-i}{r-i}\right)}$$

This formula shows that if the company's nominal return on investment is equal to its nominal cost of capital, the last term in our formula is equal to 1, and making new investments—or plowing back free cash flow into the company for real growth—has no effect on the company's value. The company's free cash flows grow, but that growth does not change the value of the firm. If the company's nominal return on its investment is less than its nominal cost of capital, the last term in the above equation is less than 1, and making these new investments decreases the value of the company. On the other hand, if the company's nominal return on its investment is greater than its nominal cost of capital, the last term in our formula is greater than 1, and making these new investments increases the value of the company.

This analysis provides some—albeit limited—insights to guide estimating the long-term growth rate used in the constant-growth perpetuity. As a starting point, assume we developed a base-year free cash flow to represent the company's free cash flow based on the current scale of its operations, its expected performance, and expected long-term inflation—in other words, no real growth free cash flow forecast. The above formulas are typically not applicable to measure this free cash flow because this free cash flow is based on the company continuing its existing business strategy and scale of operations and does not include new investments for real growth, and often does not require the same level of investment as new investments. Thus, we expect the company's long-term growth rate is equal to expected long-term inflation if the company makes no investment for real growth. Then, if we expect the company will make new investment, we would change the growth rate based on Equation 6.6. The major advantage of applying Equation 6.7 is that it explicitly identifies the difference between the rate of return on new investment, FCFROI, and the company's cost of capital, r, embeded in the company's free cash flow forecasts and valuation. Said differently, it allows you to control the size of the economic rents (the difference between the return on investment and the required rate of return on investment) that the company earns on new investment opportunities every year in perpetuity.

For example, assume a company has an expected free cash flow without new investment equal to \$120 in Year 0. It has a required real rate of return of 12% and the inflation rate is 2.5%. The expected free cash flow without new investment in Year 1 is equal to the free cash flow in Year 0, \$120, multiplied by 1 plus the inflation rate, \$123 (\$123 = \$120 × 1.025). Since we include inflation in the free cash flows (nominal free cash flows), we also include inflation in the required real rate of return since we use the nominal required rate of return. The nominal required rate of return is equal to 12% adjusted for inflation, which is 14.8% (0.148 = 1.12 × 1.025 − 1). If the company has no new investments and thus no real growth, the free cash flows grow at the inflation rate, and the value of the firm without any new investments is equal to \$1,000 [\$1,000 = \$123/(0.148 − 0.025)].[8]

Valuation Key 6.9

If we assume that a company's continuing value free cash flows are increasing from real growth due to new investment, and if we can calculate both the percentage of the company's continuing value free cash flow that can be invested and the rate of return on the new investment, we can use these two factors in conjunction with inflation as a guide to measuring the company's growth rate above inflation.

Now, assume the company expects that it can make new investments, in perpetuity, at a rate of 20% of its free cash flow without new investment. If we assume the nominal return on the new investment is equal to 10%, FCFROI = 10%, using Equation 6.6 the growth rate for the free cash flows is equal to 4% [0.04 = 0.2 × 0.1 + 0.025 (1 − 0.2)], which is 1.5% higher than the inflation rate (1.5% is the real growth). However, using Equation 6.7, we see that the new investments decrease the value of the firm to \$911.1 (an 8.9% decrease) even though the company's growth rate increased from 2.5% to 4%.

$$V_0 = \frac{FCF_0^{\text{w/o NewI}} \times (1+i) \times (1-I\%)}{r - I\% \times FCFROI - i \times (1-I\%)} = \$120 \times \frac{(1.025) \times (1-0.2)}{0.148 - 0.2 \times 0.1 - 0.025 \times (1-0.2)} = \frac{\$98.4}{0.108} = \$911.1$$

Why did the value of the company decrease when the growth rate increased? It decreased because the nominal return on the new investment, 10%, is less than the nominal required rate of return of 14.8%. Using Equation 6.7, we show various combinations of the plowback ratio (I%) and the nominal return on new investment in Exhibit 6.14. As is clear from this exhibit, although the company experiences real growth in all of the alternatives where I% is greater than 0, whether or not a company creates or destroys value with that new investment depends on the relative magnitudes of the company's required rate of return, r, and the nominal return on investment, FCFROI.

This analysis, while it provides potential insights about economic rents earned on new investments, is not generally useful to gain insights about the economic rate of return on the reinvestments the firm makes to grow at the rate of inflation. In other words, it does not address how reasonable the forecasts are that yield the base year cash flows without new investment for real growth as of the continuing value

[8] We can use the real free cash flow and real required rate of return to calculate the same value of the firm, \$1,000 (\$1,000 = \$120/0.12).

EXHIBIT 6.14 Value Created or Destroyed (Real Cost of Capital = 12%, Initial Free Cash Flow Without New Investment = \$120, and Inflation = 2.5%)

I%	CFROI	Inflation (i)	FCF_1	g_{FCF}	$[r - g_{FCF}]^{-1}$	V_0	% Change in V_0
0%		2.5%	\$123	2.5%	8.1	\$1,000	
20%	10.0%	2.5%	98	4.0%	9.3	911	–8.9%
20%	14.8%	2.5%	98	5.0%	10.2	1,000	0.0%
20%	18.0%	2.5%	98	5.6%	10.9	1,070	7.0%
40%	10.0%	2.5%	74	5.5%	10.8	794	–20.6%
40%	14.8%	2.5%	74	7.4%	13.6	1,000	0.0%
40%	18.0%	2.5%	74	8.7%	16.4	1,210	21.0%

date. In order to assess the reasonableness of those forecasts, we use tools such as the financial analysis discussed in Chapter 2 to analyze financial statement forecasts as of the continuing value date. We discuss this in more detail in Section 6.5.

Yahoo! with New Investments as of the Continuing Value Date

To illustrate how new investment opportunities affect continuing value, we assume that Yahoo's management believes that in Year 11, and thereafter, it will have additional opportunities to invest a certain percentage of its free cash flow in new investments (a certain percentage of \$5.678 billion in Year 11 and of each subsequent free cash flow before new investments). Should Yahoo make this additional investment each year? The answer, of course, depends on the economic rate of return that Yahoo expects to earn on these new investments.

In Exhibit 6.15, we illustrate the effect resulting from three alternative assumptions regarding Yahoo's new investment opportunities as of the continuing value date. We use the same free cash flow, discount rate, and inflation rate that we used in the continuing value calculation of \$59.8 billion (Appendix Exhibit A6.3), which we show in the first column of this exhibit. In the second column of the exhibit, we assume that Yahoo invests 20% of its free cash flow of \$5.7 billion and that the nominal return on the new investment is 12% as a result of a real rate of return on new investment of 9.27% and inflation of 2.5% (12% nominal, $0.12 = 1.0927 \times 1.025 - 1$). Applying Equation 6.7, we see that this investment strategy is value neutral; even though Yahoo's growth rate increases to 4.4%, which is 1.9% above inflation, its value is unchanged by this investment regardless of the percentage invested in the new investment, for the return on new investment is equal to the required rate of return. In other words, these new investments are zero NPV investments that do not create value.

EXHIBIT 6.15 Yahoo! Inc.—Alternative New Investment Opportunities

	No New Investment	Value Neutral New Investment	Value Creating New Investment	Value Destroying New Investment
Free cash flow (Before investment), Year CV+1 . . .	\$5.678	\$5.678	\$5.678	\$5.678
Nominal required rate of return	12.00%	12.00%	12.00%	12.00%
Inflation.	2.50%	2.50%	2.50%	2.50%
Return on new investment (Real)		9.27%	11.00%	8.00%
Return on new investment (Nominal)		12.000%	13.775%	10.700%
% New investment.		20.00%	20.00%	20.00%
Growth rate.	2.50%	4.40%	4.76%	4.14%
Continuing value.	\$ 59.8	\$ 59.8	\$ 62.7	\$ 57.8
% Change in value.		0.00%	4.90%	-3.31%

In the third column of the exhibit, we increase the real return on the new investment to 11% (13.8% nominal) but maintain all other assumptions. Since the inflation-adjusted return on new investment is larger than Yahoo's cost of capital by 1.8%, this investment increases Yahoo's continuing value to $62.7 billion (a 4.9% increase). The growth rate also increases to 4.8% as a result of the increase in the return on investment. In the last column, we show what would occur if the real return on new investments was only 8%. Although Yahoo's growth rate (4.1%) would be greater than inflation, its continuing value would decrease to $57.8 billion (−3.3%) because the inflation-adjusted return on investment is lower than Yahoo's cost of capital.

These examples illustrate how to evaluate and possibly include new investment opportunities into a continuing value calculation as well as the impact they can have on value—positive, negative, or neutral. As we stated earlier, such value-creating growth only results if the company can identify new investment opportunities in perpetuity (or at least for a substantial number of years) and if the rate of return on these new investments is greater than the company's required rate of return; in other words, the investments must have a positive net present value. The examples also show the potential usefulness of this approach. As we have seen, applying Equation 6.7 gives us the ability to control the spread between the cost of capital and the return on new investment on the investments the company makes for real growth. However, while these formulas provide a framework to understand the relation between new investment, return on new investment, and growth, they are often difficult to implement because of the difficulty identifying and measuring all of the company's investments (expenditures that benefit the company for more than one year).

6.5 ASSESSING THE REASONABLENESS OF THE CONTINUING VALUE ESTIMATE

LO5 Assess the reasonableness of the inputs in the continuing value calculation

One way to analyze the growth rate and base-year free cash flows used in the constant-growth perpetuity model is to compare the company's implicit projected rate of return of its cash flows to its cost of capital (discount rate). If the company were in a steady state by the continuing value date, then we would expect it to earn a constant (economic) rate of return on its invested capital in perpetuity. If the economic rate of return exceeds the cost of capital in the base-year free cash flow, then we are effectively projecting that the company will earn an excess return in perpetuity, for at least 50 years or so. In other words, we are assuming that the company will be able to earn economic rents for a long time and that competition in the industry will not drive the firm's economic rate of return to its cost of capital. As part of this analysis, we would examine the company's competitive advantages and their sustainability as we discuss in Chapter 2.

Evaluating the economic rate of return embedded in a continuing value is difficult and often not possible. We can observe the accounting-based rates of return in our projections, which is informative, but these rates of return do not equal the economic rate of return embedded in the continuing value. Although accounting-based rates of return do not measure a company's actual economic return, empirical evidence indicates that a company's accounting-based rates of return are significantly correlated with its economic rates of return. So how do we evaluate the base year cash flows in the continuing value calculation assuming no real growth? The best approach is to use the forecasts as of the continuing value date that assume no real growth and analyze those financial statements using the various analyses discussed in Chapter 2 in comparison to other similar companies. While this does not provide the economic rate of return embedded in the forecasts, it does provide a way to judge the reasonableness of those forecasts.

Analyzing Yahoo!'s Forecasts

We assume a 2.5% growth rate in Yahoo's continuing value calculation, which is roughly equal to expected long-run inflation as of the valuation date; consequently, we assume that Yahoo will not experience any real growth from new investments after Year 10 in our base-year free cash flow. Using a 2.5% continuing value growth rate assumes, however, that Yahoo's financial performance in Year 11 will continue in perpetuity and grow at the inflation rate. We begin a preliminary investigation of Yahoo's performance at the continuing value date by examining Yahoo's (accounting) rate of returns.

We show Yahoo's return on assets and return on investment in Exhibit 6.16. Recall that we are using a 12% required rate of return for Yahoo. In this exhibit, the accounting rates of return increase during the forecast horizon, reach their highest point in Year 8, and remain at that level through Year 10. By Year 10, Yahoo's return on assets is 21% and its return on investment is 34.2%, both of which are considerably higher than its 12% cost of capital. Do Yahoo's high accounting rates of return indicate that the forecasts for Yahoo result in an economic return that is greater than Yahoo's cost of capital? We know that is not the case because of the way we created this example. We created the Yahoo forecasts so that the Yahoo DCF valuation was equal to Yahoo's actual value observed at the time. By design, the internal rate of return of the DCF valuation is equal to its cost of capital, 12%; therefore, the high accounting rates of return do not indicate that the forecasts assume that Yahoo has an economic return above its cost of capital. However, we were only able measure Yahoo's economic return in the example because we knew Yahoo's actual value, which is not the case in most valuations. If we did not know Yahoo's actual value, we would have no ability to measure Yahoo's internal rate of return (economic return) embedded in the model.

EXHIBIT 6.16 Yahoo! Inc.—Return on Assets, Return on Investment with Profit Margin and Asset Utilization (Turnover) Components

Rate of Return Ratios	Year −1	Year 0	Year 1	Year 2	Year 3	Year 4	Year 5	Year 6	Year 7	Year 8	Year 9	Year 10
Return on assets (ROA)	7.5%	12.9%	14.7%	16.6%	18.6%	19.7%	20.3%	20.8%	20.9%	21.0%	21.0%	21.0%
Unlevered income to revenue. . .	11.7%	15.6%	15.6%	15.6%	15.6%	15.6%	15.6%	15.6%	15.6%	15.6%	15.6%	15.6%
Revenue to total assets	0.640	0.825	0.941	1.063	1.194	1.260	1.302	1.333	1.340	1.345	1.347	1.347
Return on investment (ROI)	8.9%	16.1%	19.4%	22.7%	26.5%	29.1%	31.1%	32.8%	33.7%	34.2%	34.2%	34.2%
Unlevered income to revenue. . .	11.7%	15.6%	15.6%	15.6%	15.6%	15.6%	15.6%	15.6%	15.6%	15.6%	15.6%	15.6%
Revenue to investment.	0.758	1.034	1.241	1.453	1.698	1.862	1.992	2.099	2.158	2.189	2.192	2.192

The investment base used in calculating accounting rates of return (the book value of Yahoo's total assets or capital invested) likely does not represent the investment in a calculation of the economic rate of return. As of Year 0, Yahoo's market value is $32.6 billion after the payout of the excess assets (Appendix Exhibit A6.3) but the book value of its total assets is only $9.2 billion and its invested capital is only $7.6 billion (Appendix Exhibit A6.1). Given the discrepancy between the book value of Yahoo's investment and its market value, it is not a surprise that the accounting rates of return far exceed the economic rate of return. As we discuss at the end of Chapter 2, while the financial relations and underlying accounting data we discuss in Chapter 2 and throughout this book can be useful for assessing and measuring economic concepts, their usefulness is limited because of the differences between accounting data and the (unobservable) economic concepts they represent.

Because of the potential differences between accounting rates of return and the unobservable true economic rate of return for Yahoo on its past investments, meaningful comparisons between Yahoo's accounting returns and its cost of capital are difficult to make. This is why we use comparable companies to assess the reasonableness of the base-year cash flows. In an ideal world, we would attempt to identify companies in the same line of business that are now as mature as the company of interest will be at the continuing value date (Yahoo in this example) and compare our company's financial ratios at the continuing value date to the ratios of those now mature companies.

Valuation Key 6.10

One approach to estimating continuing value is to create a base-year free cash flow that does not include any real growth from new investment, but includes the investment necessary to maintain the company's scale of operations given expected inflation. One way to assess the reasonableness of the base-year cash flow forecasts is to conduct a financial statement analysis relative to a set of comparable companies. We can also then control for any allowable economic rents from new investment intended to achieve real growth.

REVIEW EXERCISE 6.5

Real Growth and Value

Assume a company has expected free cash flows without new investment equal to $1,000 in Year 0. It has a required discount rate of 10%, and the inflation rate is 0%. If the company does not invest any of its free cash flows without new investment in Year 0, its cash flows will not grow. The company believes that it could invest 40% of its free cash flows without new investment in perpetuity. Measure the value of the company and its perpetual growth rate for the free cash flows in four scenarios: no new investment is made, and the company makes the new investment each year and earns an 8%, 10%, or 12% return on its investment annually and in perpetuity.

Solution on page 289.

Using Market Multiples to Assess the Reasonableness of the Continuing Value

Although we will discuss market multiples later in the book, it is helpful to introduce the notion that we can use market multiples to assess the reasonableness of the constant-growth cash flow perpetuity continuing value. In the valuation process we described in Chapter 1, we collect and analyze information on a company's comparable companies. A part of this process entails a calculation of the market multiples for those comparable companies. We often use these market multiples as an alternative way to value the subject company. We can also use multiples, however, to assess the reasonableness of the perpetuity-based continuing value.

When we use the perpetuity-based continuing value formula, we must know the company's expected free cash flow for the year after the continuing value date. We recommend that we measure this free cash flow based on a detailed forecast from our financial model. If we use a financial model, we also have a forecast of the company's income statement and balance sheet for the year of and the year after the continuing value date. Thus, we have sufficient information to calculate market multiples implied by the financial forecasts and the continuing value calculated using the perpetuity formula. For example, the implied earnings before interest and taxes (EBIT) multiple as of the continuing value date is equal to the continuing value divided by the EBIT in the financial model. We then compare the implied multiple to the multiples of appropriately selected comparable companies.

This analysis is useful for examining the perpetuity-based continuing value calculation, but it is not definitive. Two issues arise. The first is the same as it is for all market multiple-based valuations; that is, have we identified the correct set of comparable companies, and are we measuring the multiples correctly? The second issue is concerned with whether a particular multiple measured today is appropriate for the continuing value estimate. Market multiples of competitors measured as of the valuation date may not be appropriate as a benchmark for the continuing value date. For example, if the comparable companies are all at the beginning of a high-growth period as of the valuation date, we know the market multiples of these companies will decline at the end of the high-growth period, and this will likely be near the time of the continuing value date. As such, it may be appropriate to use a different set of comparable companies' multiples as the benchmark at the continuing value date versus the set of comparable companies used to value the company as of the valuation date. If all of the comparable companies are at the same stage of development, none of the existing comparable companies will reflect the likely multiples at the continuing value date and thus there may not be a good set of comparable companies from this industry for assessing the continuing value calculation. The good news is that in many industries, we can find companies at very different stages of their life cycle, so this is often not a problem. If no good comparable companies exist in this industry, then we may need to look at closely related industries. We discuss the use of market multiples as a continuing value calculation in more detail in Chapter 13.

Yahoo!'s Implied Market Multiples

We demonstrate here how to calculate implied market multiples based on both the DCF valuation and the forecasts in the financial model. We illustrate this calculation using one of many alternative market multiples and one of many ways to measure them. The market multiple we will use is the ratio of total market capitalization (firm value) to earnings before interest and taxes (EBIT) in the following year. The implied EBIT multiple for Yahoo's \$59.8 billion continuing value is 6.1, which we calculate as follows (using data from Exhibits A6.2 and A6.3):

$$\frac{V_{\text{Yahoo, 10}}}{\text{EBIT}_{11}} = \frac{\$59.773}{9.871} = 6.1$$

As stated above, the multiples you observe today for a company need not be the appropriate multiples for the continuing value calculation. Yahoo's multiple—calculated based on its value (without excess assets) as of Year 0 divided by our forecasted EBIT for Year 1—is 16.1 (16.1 = \$32,612/\$2,022), far from the implied multiple at the continuing value date. Given all the growth we had to forecast for Yahoo in order to justify its valuation as of Year 0, it is no wonder that the multiple at the time of the valuation far exceeds our implied multiple at the continuing value date when the growth rate is assumed to be just 2.5%.

Valuation Key 6.11

There are a variety of techniques available for assessing the reasonableness of the continuing value used in a valuation. One such technique is to calculate implied market multiples from a continuing value and compare that to market multiples of appropriate comparable companies.

SUMMARY AND KEY CONCEPTS

In this chapter, we discussed how to use the constant-growth perpetuity model to measure a company's continuing value. The continuing value component of the total value of a firm is often 40% to 60% of the value of the firm, but decreases as the number of years in the forecast horizon for detailed forecasts increases. Most of the continuing value results from the first 50 years after the continuing value date; thus, practically speaking, the constant-growth perpetuity model is not really dependent on the firm lasting forever. This chapter reviewed important issues related to the forecast horizon (number of years of explicit year-by-year cash flow forecasts) until we rely on a continuing value calculation, how to create a reasonable base-year free cash flow, how to control for economic rents embedded in the continuing value calculation, and how to estimate the perpetual growth rate used in the constant-growth perpetuity valuation of a company's continuing value.

APPENDIX: Yahoo! Inc.

We use a discounted cash flow valuation of Yahoo! Inc. (Yahoo) at a point in time when it was still a publicly traded company (before being bought by Verizon Communications in 2017) to illustrate the various issues, analyses, and adjustments that we discuss in the chapter. Yahoo had very little debt in its capital structure and $2.3 billion in excess assets (marketable securities). In our illustration, we assume that at the end of Year 0, Yahoo liquidated all of its excess assets, redeemed all of its debt ($0.75 billion), and distributed the remaining proceeds ($1.53 billion). Yahoo had a total market capitalization (firm value) of over $34 billion around this time. We developed a set of forecasts that are consistent with this valuation. In Exhibit A6.1, we show Yahoo's historical and forecasted income statement and balance sheet forecasts.

In Exhibit A6.2, we show the free cash flow forecasts generated from operations for Yahoo. Since we assume that as of the date of our valuation, the company redeems all of its debt, liquidates all of its excess assets, and distributes the net proceeds to its equity holders, we do not include the distribution of the excess assets in the unlevered free cash flows in this exhibit. Note that the other income and expense from the income statement is considered part of the company's operations and is thus included in the EBIT number in the free cash flow forecasts.

We use a 12% unlevered cost of capital (discount rate) and a 2.5% constant free cash flow growth rate for years after Year 11 to value Yahoo. We assume that 2.5% is a reasonable forecast for long-term inflation, so, for now, we are assuming no real growth for Yahoo after Year 11. In Exhibit A6.3, we show Yahoo's DCF valuation. The valuation of Yahoo's operations is $32.6 billion. Yahoo's total value is equal to the sum of the value of its operations and the net excess assets of $2.3 billion, which is roughly equal to its $34.9 billion market capitalization ($34.9 = $32.6 + $2.3) at that time.

EXHIBIT A6.1 Yahoo! Inc.—Historical and Forecasted Income Statements and Balance Sheets

YAHOO! INC.
Income Statement Forecasts
(for the years ended December 31)

($ in millions)	Year −1	Year 0	Year 1	Year 2	Year 3	Year 4	Year 5	Year 6	Year 7	Year 8	Year 9	Year 10	Year 11
Revenue	$ 5,258	$6,426	$ 8,032	$10,442	$14,096	$19,735	$25,655	$30,786	$34,647	$36,406	$37,316	$38,249	$39,205
Cost of goods sold	−2,096	−2,676	−3,213	−4,177	−5,639	−7,894	−10,262	−12,315	−13,859	−14,562	−14,926	−15,300	−15,682
Gross margin	$ 3,161	$3,750	$ 4,819	$ 6,265	$ 8,458	$11,841	$15,393	$18,472	$20,788	$21,844	$22,390	$22,949	$23,523
Product development	−570	−833	−884	−1,149	−1,551	−2,171	−2,822	−3,387	−3,811	−4,005	−4,105	−4,207	−4,313
Selling, general, and administrative	−1,484	−1,976	−2,249	−2,924	−3,947	−5,526	−7,183	−8,620	−9,701	−10,194	−10,449	−10,710	−10,977
Operating income	$ 1,108	$ 941	$ 1,687	$ 2,193	$ 2,960	$ 4,144	$ 5,388	$ 6,465	$ 7,276	$ 7,645	$ 7,836	$ 8,032	$ 8,233
Interest expense			0	0	0	0	0	0	0	0	0	0	0
Other income and expenses	1,556	268	336	436	589	824	1,072	1,286	1,447	1,521	1,559	1,598	1,638
Income before taxes	$ 2,664	$1,209	$ 2,022	$ 2,629	$ 3,549	$ 4,969	$ 6,459	$ 7,751	$ 8,723	$ 9,166	$ 9,395	$ 9,630	$ 9,871
Income tax expense	−768	−458	−768	−999	−1,349	−1,888	−2,455	−2,945	−3,315	−3,483	−3,570	−3,659	−3,751
Net income	$ 1,896	$ 751	$ 1,254	$ 1,630	$ 2,200	$ 3,081	$ 4,005	$ 4,806	$ 5,408	$ 5,683	$ 5,825	$ 5,971	$ 6,120

continued

continued from previous page

YAHOO! INC.
Balance Sheet Forecasts
(for the years ended December 31)

($ in millions)	Year −1	Year 0	Year 1	Year 2	Year 3	Year 4	Year 5	Year 6	Year 7	Year 8	Year 9	Year 10	Year 11
Cash plus marketable securities	$ 2,561	$ 321	$ 402	$ 522	$ 705	$ 987	$ 1,283	$ 1,539	$ 1,732	$ 1,820	$ 1,866	$ 1,912	$ 1,960
Accounts receivable	722	931	1,100	1,430	1,931	2,703	3,514	4,217	4,746	4,987	5,112	5,240	5,371
Other current assets	167	218	241	313	423	592	770	924	1,039	1,092	1,119	1,147	1,176
Total current assets	$ 3,450	$1,470	$ 1,743	$ 2,266	$ 3,059	$ 4,282	$ 5,567	$ 6,680	$ 7,518	$ 7,900	$ 8,097	$ 8,300	$ 8,507
Property, plant, and equipment	$ 1,267	$1,955	$ 2,758	$ 3,802	$ 5,212	$ 7,185	$ 9,751	$12,829	$16,294	$19,118	$22,047	$25,099	$28,228
Accumulated depreciation	−570	−853	−1,220	−1,737	−2,450	−3,428	−4,776	−6,604	−9,011	−11,250	−14,033	−16,885	−19,808
Property, plant, and equipment (net)	$ 698	$1,101	$ 1,538	$ 2,065	$ 2,761	$ 3,757	$ 4,975	$ 6,225	$ 7,284	$ 7,868	$ 8,014	$ 8,214	$ 8,420
Other non-current assets	$ 6,685	$6,662	$ 6,948	$ 7,622	$ 8,740	$10,459	$11,673	$12,161	$12,126	$11,650	$11,941	$12,240	$12,546
Total assets	$10,832	$9,233	$10,229	$11,953	$14,560	$18,499	$22,215	$25,066	$26,928	$27,418	$28,052	$28,754	$29,472
Accounts payable	$ 70	$ 109	$ 161	$ 209	$ 282	$ 395	$ 513	$ 616	$ 693	$ 728	$ 746	$ 765	$ 784
Accrued expenses	1,134	1,365	2,008	2,610	3,524	4,934	6,414	7,697	8,662	9,101	9,329	9,562	9,801
Total current liabilities	$ 1,204	$1,474	$ 2,169	$ 2,819	$ 3,806	$ 5,328	$ 6,927	$ 8,312	$ 9,355	$ 9,830	$10,075	$10,327	$10,585
Long-term debt	750	0	0	0	0	0	0	0	0	0	0	0	0
Non-current liabilities	311	129	161	209	282	395	513	616	693	728	746	765	784
Total liabilities	$ 2,265	$ 1,603	$ 2,329	$ 3,028	$ 4,088	$ 5,723	$ 7,440	$ 8,928	$10,048	$10,558	$10,822	$11,092	$11,370
Common stock (and other)	$ 5,600	$ 5,443	$ 5,443	$ 5,443	$ 5,443	$ 5,443	$ 5,443	$ 5,443	$ 5,443	$ 5,443	$ 5,443	$ 5,443	$ 5,443
Retained earnings	2,966	2,187	2,456	3,482	5,029	7,333	9,332	10,695	11,437	11,417	11,787	12,218	12,660
Total shareholders' equity	$ 8,566	$ 7,630	$ 7,899	$ 8,925	$10,472	$12,776	$14,775	$16,138	$16,880	$16,860	$17,231	$17,661	$18,103
Total liabilities and equities	$10,832	$ 9,233	$10,229	$11,953	$14,560	$18,499	$22,215	$25,066	$26,928	$27,418	$28,052	$28,754	$29,472

Exhibit may contain small rounding errors

EXHIBIT A6.2 Yahoo! Inc.—Historical and Forecasted Free Cash Flow Schedules

YAHOO! INC.
Free Cash Flow Forecasts
(for the years ended December 31)

($ in millions)	Year −1	Year 0	Year 1	Year 2	Year 3	Year 4	Year 5	Year 6	Year 7	Year 8	Year 9	Year 10	Year 11
Earnings before interest and taxes (EBIT)	$2,664	$1,209	$2,022	$2,629	$3,549	$4,969	$6,459	$7,751	$8,723	$9,166	$9,395	$9,630	$9,871
− Income taxes paid on EBIT	−768	−458	−768	−999	−1,349	−1,888	−2,455	−2,945	−3,315	−3,483	−3,570	−3,659	−3,751
Earnings before interest and after taxes	$1,896	$ 751	$1,254	$1,630	$2,200	$3,081	$4,005	$4,806	$5,408	$5,683	$5,825	$5,971	$6,120
+ Depreciation	224	302	367	517	713	977	1,348	1,829	2,406	3,056	3,586	3,675	3,767
+ Amortization	173	238	238	238	238	238	238	238	238	238	238	238	238
− Change in accounts receivable	−272	−185	−169	−330	−501	−772	−811	−703	−529	−241	−125	−128	−131
− Change in other current assets	0	0	−23	−72	−110	−169	−178	−154	−116	−53	−27	−28	−29
− Change in other assets	−35	−10	−523	−912	−1,355	−1,957	−1,451	−725	−203	239	−529	−536	−544
+ Change in accounts payable	32	30	52	48	73	113	118	103	77	35	18	19	19
+ Change in accrued expenses	212	175	643	602	914	1,410	1,480	1,283	965	440	228	233	239
+ Change in non-current liabilities	−518	70	32	48	73	113	118	103	77	35	18	19	19
− Change in required cash balance		−41	−80	−120	−183	−282	−296	−257	−193	−88	−46	−47	−48
Unlevered cash flow from operations	$1,711	$1,331	$1,788	$1,648	$2,063	$2,750	$4,571	$6,522	$8,131	$9,344	$9,186	$9,416	$9,651
− Capital expenditures (net)	−2,146	−816	−803	−1,044	−1,410	−1,973	−2,566	−3,079	−3,465	−3,641	−3,732	−3,876	−3,973
Unlevered free cash flow	**−$ 435**	**$ 515**	**$ 985**	**$ 604**	**$ 654**	**$ 777**	**$2,006**	**$3,443**	**$4,666**	**$5,703**	**$5,454**	**$5,540**	**$5,678**

Exhibit may contain small rounding errors

EXHIBIT A6.3 Yahoo! Inc.—Discounted Cash Flow Valuation

YAHOO! INC.
Discounted Cash Flow Valuation

Cost of capital	12.0%
Growth rate for free cash flow for continuing value	2.5%

($ in millions)	Year 0	Year 1	Year 2	Year 3	Year 4	Year 5	Year 6	Year 7	Year 8	Year 9	Year 10	CV_{Firm} Year 10
Unlevered free cash flow for continuing value												$ 5,678
Discount factor for continuing value												10.526
Unlevered free cash flow and continuing value		$ 985	$ 604	$ 654	$ 777	$2,006	$3,443	$4,666	$5,703	$5,454	$5,540	$59,773
Discount factor		0.893	0.797	0.712	0.636	0.567	0.507	0.452	0.404	0.361	0.322	0.322
Present value		$ 879	$ 482	$ 465	$ 494	$1,138	$1,744	$2,111	$2,303	$1,967	$1,784	$19,245
Value of the firm (without excess cash)	$32,612											
Net excess assets	2,280											
Value of the firm	$34,892											

Exhibit may contain small rounding errors

ADDITIONAL READING AND REFERENCES

Levin, J., and P. Olsson, "Terminal Value Techniques in Equity Valuation–Implications of the Steady State Assumption," SSE/EFI Working Paper Series in Business Administration No. 2000:7 (June 2000).

EXERCISES AND PROBLEMS

P6.1 **Present Value Weighted Average Growth Rate:** Assume an investment will generate cash flows at the end of Years 1 through 5 equal to $200, $240, $300, $420, and $480, respectively; from that point, the investment begins to generate a series of constant-growth perpetual cash flows.

a. Calculate the present value of these cash flows at the end of Year 0, assuming a discount rate of 10% and a 3% constant growth rate for the perpetuity. Calculate the present value weighted average growth rate for this investment.

b. Calculate the present value of these cash flows at the end of Year 0, assuming a discount rate of 10% and a −3% constant growth rate for the perpetuity. Calculate the present value weighted average growth rate for this investment.

P6.2 **Present Value Weighted Average Growth Rate:** Assume an investment will generate cash flows at the end of Years 1 through 5 equal to $2,000, −$3,000, $3,000, $3,900, and $5,000, respectively; from that point, the investment begins to generate a series of constant-growth perpetual cash flows.

a. Calculate the present value of these cash flows at the end of Year 0, assuming a discount rate of 10% and a 3% constant growth rate for the perpetuity. Calculate the present value weighted average growth rate for this investment.

b. Calculate the present value of these cash flows at the end of Year 0, assuming a discount rate of 10% and a −3% constant growth rate for the perpetuity. Calculate the present value weighted average growth rate for this investment.

P6.3 **Present Value Weighted Average Growth Rate:** A company's current, Year 0, free cash flow is $231, and its expected growth rates are 60% for Year 1, 20% for Year 2, 10% for Year 3, 5% for Years 4 and 5, and 3% thereafter. The company's cost of capital is 10%.

a. Measure the present value of the cash flows as of Year 0, and measure the present value weighted average growth rate for the cash flows after Year 0.

b. Measure the present value weighted average growth rate for the cash flows after Year 1.

c. Discuss the change in the present value weighted average growth rate from Year 0 to Year 1.

P6.4 **Multi-Stage Growth Rate:** Calculate the present value weighted average growth rate for an investment with a discount rate of 9% and cash flows that grow through Year 10 at g_1 and at g_2 thereafter in perpetuity, using every combination of g_1 (5%, 10%, and 15%) and g_2 (−3%, 0%, 3%).

P6.5 **Estimating a Perpetual Growth Rate from Comparable Companies:** Straight Shooter Inc.'s CFO is using the DCF valuation model to value his company. The company's CFO collected information about five comparable companies as shown in Exhibit P6.1. Estimate the perpetual growth rate for each of the comparable companies based on this information.

EXHIBIT P6.1 Straight Shooter, Inc.'s Comparable Company Information

		Unlevered Free Cash Flow Forecasts			
($ in millions)	WACC	Year 1	Year 2	Year 3	Firm Value
Comparable Company 1	10.50%	$2,000.0	$2,400.0	$2,600.0	$30,000.0
Comparable Company 2	10.20%	$ 340.0	$ 350.0	$ 360.0	$ 4,200.0
Comparable Company 3	10.10%	$ 200.0	$ 210.0	$ 240.0	$ 2,800.0
Comparable Company 4	9.80%	$1,200.0	$1,400.0	$1,500.0	$20,000.0
Comparable Company 5	9.50%	$ 260.0	$ 250.0	$ 250.0	$ 2,870.0

P6.6 **Lumpy Capital Expenditures:** A company has $1.6 million in annual revenues in Year 1. The company expects revenues to increase by $0.6 million in Years 2 and 3 before remaining constant. Expected inflation is 0% in perpetuity. The company's only expenses are depreciation and income taxes (40% tax rate). The company uses straight-line depreciation with no salvage value and a three-year life for its assets. The fixed asset purchased at the end of Year 0 has an acquisition cost of $3.2 million. All fixed assets purchased must be replaced every three years and depreciation on fixed assets purchased begins the year after they are purchased. The replacement cost of all fixed assets is expected to remain constant in perpetuity. The company will have to invest $1.2 million in fixed assets at the end of Years 1 and 2 to support its revenue growth in Years 2 and 3. The company is all-equity financed, will hold no cash, and has no working capital requirements. The company's cost of capital is 12%. Measure the company's free cash flow for Years 1 through 4. Measure the value of the company as of the end of Year 0.

P6.7 **Growth and Value Creation:** Assume a company has expected free cash flows equal to $12,000 in Year 0, before making any new investments. It has a discount rate of 15%, and the inflation rate is 3%. If the company does not invest any of its free cash flows without new investment in Year 0, its cash flows will grow at the inflation rate. The company believes it could invest 20% of its free cash flows before new investment in perpetuity. Measure the value of the company under four scenarios: no new investment is made; the company makes a new investment each year and earns a 10%, 15%, and 20% nominal return on its investment annually and in perpetuity. What if the company invested 40% of its free cash flows before new investment and earned a 10%, 15%, or 20% nominal return?

P6.8 **Growth Rates and Continuing Value—Ed Kaplan, Inc.:** A young analyst is valuing Ed Kaplan, Inc. as of the end of Year 0. The forecast drivers underpinning the financial statement and free cash flow forecasts for four years appear in Exhibit P6.2, and the resulting income statement, balance sheet, and free cash flow forecasts for three years appear in Exhibits P6.3 and P6.4. The company's unlevered cost of capital is 13% and interest tax shields are valued using the unlevered cost of capital. The company's revenue growth rate is expected to equal 3% in perpetuity beginning in Year 4. The company intends to increase the amount of debt outstanding every year beginning at the end of Year 4 by 3%. To measure the company's continuing value at the end of Year 3, the analyst assumed the Year 3 free cash flow grew at 3% in Year 4 and then continued at that growth rate in perpetuity. The analyst calculated the company's continuing value at the end of Year 3 (CV_3) using the following formula:

$$CV_3 = \frac{FCF_3 \times (1+g)}{r_{UA} - g} + \frac{ITS_3}{r_{UA}}$$

$$CV_3 = \frac{\$852.5(1.03)}{0.13 - 0.03} + \frac{\$320.0}{0.13} = \$8{,}780.75 + \$2{,}461.5 = \$11{,}242.3$$

a. Identify the errors the analyst made in the continuing value calculation.
b. Forecast the company's unlevered free cash flow in Year 4 using the information in the exhibits for this problem.
c. Discuss the difference between the Year 4 growth rates for revenue and the unlevered free cash flow.
d. Calculate the correct value of the firm as of the end of Year 0 and the continuing value of the firm as of the end of Year 3 using the perpetuity valuation.
e. Forecast the company's equity free cash flow in Year 4 using the information in the exhibits for this problem.
f. Calculate the correct value of the equity as of the end of Year 0 and the continuing value of the equity as of the end of Year 3 using the perpetuity valuation.

EXHIBIT P6.2 Ed Kaplan, Inc.—Forecast Drivers

Ed Kaplan, Inc.—Foreast Drivers	Actual	Forecast			
	Year 0	Year 1	Year 2	Year 3	Year 4
Expected inflation	3.0%	3.0%	3.0%	3.0%	3.0%
Revenue growth rate	10.0%	20.0%	20.0%	20.0%	3.0%
Cost of goods sold (% revenue)	20.0%	20.0%	20.0%	20.0%	20.0%
Selling, general and administrative (% revenue)	12.0%	12.0%	12.0%	12.0%	12.0%
Constant income tax rate	40.0%	40.0%	40.0%	40.0%	40.0%
Required cash balance (% revenue)	2.5%	2.5%	2.5%	2.5%	2.5%
Accounts receivable (days to collect)	60.0	60.0	60.0	60.0	60.0
Inventory (days to sell)	70.0	70.0	70.0	70.0	70.0
Accounts payable (days to pay)	30.0	30.0	30.0	30.0	30.0
Other current operating liabilities (% revenue)	3.5%	3.5%	3.5%	3.5%	3.5%
Land based on revenue to land	0.50	0.50	0.50	0.50	0.50
Interest rate on debt	8.0%	8.0%	8.0%	8.0%	8.0%

EXHIBIT P6.3 Ed Kaplan, Inc.—Income Statement and Balance Sheet Forecasts

Ed Kaplan, Inc.—Income Statement and Balance Sheet Forecasts	Actual		Forecast		
	Year −1	Year 0	Year 1	Year 2	Year 3
Income Statement					
Revenue	$10,000.0	$11,000.0	$13,200.0	$15,840.0	$19,008.0
Cost of goods sold	−2,000.0	−2,200.0	−2,640.0	−3,168.0	−3,801.6
Gross margin	$ 8,000.0	$ 8,800.0	$10,560.0	$12,672.0	$15,206.4
Selling, general and administrative	−1,200.0	−1,320.0	−1,584.0	−1,900.8	−2,281.0
Operating income	$ 6,800.0	$ 7,480.0	$ 8,976.0	$10,771.2	$12,925.4
Interest expense	−640.0	−800.0	−800.0	−800.0	−800.0
Income before taxes	$ 6,160.0	$ 6,680.0	$ 8,176.0	$ 9,971.2	$12,125.4
Income tax expense	−2,464.0	−2,672.0	−3,270.4	−3,988.5	−4,850.2
Net income	$ 3,696.0	$ 4,008.0	$ 4,905.6	$ 5,982.7	$ 7,275.3
Balance Sheet					
Cash balance	$ 250.0	$ 275.0	$ 330.0	$ 396.0	$ 475.2
Accounts receivable	1,666.7	1,833.3	2,200.0	2,640.0	3,168.0
Inventory	388.9	427.8	513.3	616.0	739.2
Total current assets	$ 2,305.6	$ 2,536.1	$ 3,043.3	$ 3,652.0	$ 4,382.4
Land	20,000.0	22,000.0	26,400.0	31,680.0	38,016.0
Total assets	$22,305.6	$24,536.1	$29,443.3	$35,332.0	$42,398.4
Accounts payable	$ 166.7	$ 183.3	$ 220.0	$ 264.0	$ 316.8
Other current operating liabilities	350.0	385.0	462.0	554.4	665.3
Total current liabilities	$ 516.7	$ 568.3	$ 682.0	$ 818.4	$ 982.1
Debt	10,000.0	10,000.0	10,000.0	10,000.0	10,000.0
Total liabilities	$10,516.7	$10,568.3	$10,682.0	$10,818.4	$10,982.1
Common stock	$10,419.3	$10,419.3	$10,419.3	$10,419.3	$10,419.3
Retained earnings	1,369.6	3,548.5	8,342.0	14,094.3	20,997.0
Total shareholders equity	$11,788.9	$13,967.8	$18,761.3	$24,513.6	$31,416.3
Total liabilities and equities	$22,305.6	$24,536.1	$29,443.3	$35,332.0	$42,398.4

Exhibit may contain small rounding errors

EXHIBIT P6.4 Ed Kaplan, Inc.—Free Cash Flow Forecasts

Ed Kaplan, Inc.—Free Cash Flow Forecasts	Actual	Forecast		
	Year 0	Year 1	Year 2	Year 3
Earnings before interest and taxes (EBIT)	$7,480.0	$8,976.0	$10,771.2	$12,925.4
− Income taxes paid on EBIT	−2,992.0	−3,590.4	−4,308.5	−5,170.2
Earnings before interest and after taxes	$4,488.0	$5,385.6	$ 6,462.7	$ 7,755.3
− Change in accounts receivable	−166.7	−366.7	−440.0	−528.0
− Change in inventory	−38.9	−85.6	−102.7	−123.2
+ Change in accounts payable	16.7	36.7	44.0	52.8
+ Change in current other liabilities	35.0	77.0	92.4	110.9
− Change in required cash balance	−25.0	−55.0	−66.0	−79.2
Unlevered cash flow from operations	$4,309.1	$4,992.0	$ 5,990.5	$ 7,188.5
− Capital expenditures	−2,000.0	−4,400.0	−5,280.0	−6,336.0
Unlevered free cash flow	$2,309.1	$ 592.0	$ 710.5	$ 852.5
− Interest paid	−800.0	−800.0	−800.0	−800.0
+ Interest tax shield	320.0	320.0	320.0	320.0
Free cash flow before changes in financing	$1,829.1	$ 112.0	$ 230.5	$ 372.5
+ Change in debt financing	0.0	0.0	0.0	0.0
Free cash flow to common equity	$1,829.1	$ 112.0	$ 230.5	$ 372.5

Exhibit may contain small rounding errors

SOLUTIONS FOR REVIEW EXERCISES

Review Exercise 6.1: Present Value Weighted Average Growth Rate

Discounted Cash Flow Valuation							
Cost of capital			12.0%				
Growth rate for free cash flow for continuing value			3.0%				
($ in millions)	Year 0	Year 1	Year 2	Year 3	Year 4	Year 5	CV_{Firm} Year 5
Unlevered free cash flow for continuing value							$ 4,408
Discount factor for continuing value							11.111
Unlevered free cash flow and continuing value		$2,200	$3,240	$3,300	$3,820	$4,280	$48,982
Discount factor		0.893	0.797	0.712	0.636	0.567	0.567
Present value		$1,964	$2,583	$2,349	$2,428	$2,429	$27,794
Value of the firm as of Year 0	$39,546						
Present value weighted average growth rate		6.44%					

$$g = r - \frac{FCF_1}{V_0} = 0.12 - \frac{\$2{,}200}{\$39{,}546} = 0.0644$$

Exhibit may contain small rounding errors

Review Exercise 6.2: Two-Stage Growth Rates

Discount Rate is	12%	g_2 after Year 10	
g_1 (through Year 10)	–3%	0%	3%
5%	2.0%	2.9%	4.0%
10%	4.4%	5.1%	6.1%
15%	6.3%	6.9%	7.7%
20%	7.7%	8.2%	8.8%

Review Exercise 6.3: Estimating Growth Rates from Comparable Companies

$$\$18{,}000 = \frac{\$1{,}000}{(1.1)^1} + \frac{\$1{,}200}{(1.1)^2} + \frac{\$1{,}500}{(1.1)^3} + \frac{\$1{,}500 \times (1+g)}{(0.1-g)} \times \frac{1}{(1.1)^3};\ g = 0.023$$

$$g = r_{WACC} - \frac{FCF_T}{(1+r_{WACC})^{T-1} \times \left[V_{F,0} - \sum_{t=1}^{T-1} \frac{FCF_t}{(1+r_{WACC})^t} \right]}$$

$$g = 0.1 - \frac{\$1{,}500}{(1.1)^2 \times \left(\$18{,}000 - \frac{\$1{,}000}{(1.1)^1} + \frac{\$1{,}200}{(1.1)^2} \right)} = 0.023$$

Review Exercise 6.4: Lumpy Capital Expenditures

Capital expenditures occur in a three-year sequence: \$0, \$0, and \$1,200. Unlevered cash flow from operations is equal to \$880, and thus, unlevered free cash flow occurs in the following three-year sequence: \$880, \$880, −\$320. We can convert the capital expenditure to an annuity of \$363 by dividing the present value of the three-year capital expenditure cash flows by the annuity present value factor formula (we previously showed the annuity present factor formula for an annuity with growth, but the growth rate is zero in this exercise).

$$A = \frac{PV_{CAPEX,0}}{\text{PV of Annuity (3 years, 10\%)}} = \frac{PV_{CAPEX,0}}{\frac{1}{(r-g)} - \frac{1}{(r-g)} \times \frac{(1+g)^3}{(1+r)^3}} = \frac{\frac{\$1{,}200}{1.1^3}}{\frac{1}{(0.1-0)} - \frac{1}{(0.1-0)} \times \frac{1.0^3}{1.1^3}} = \$363$$

We can now adjust the free cash flows by the amount of the annuity, and the cash flows become a constant $517 per year.

Below, we present various schedules providing more detailed calculations. Note that if we value the company using the actual unlevered free cash flow, the company's value will be overstated for years in which it does not have capital expenditures and understated for years it has capital expenditures. The company's value is correct when the cash flows are adjusted for the capital expenditures annuity. The continuing value at Year 3 using the adjusted cash flows is $3,888 with a present value of the actual cash flows for Years 1 through 3 of $1,287. The total of the two present values yields the correct firm value of $5,175.

Income Statement, Balance Sheet, and Free Cash Flow Forecasts

	Year 0	Year 1	Year 2	Year 3	Year 4	Year 5	Year 6
Income Statement							
Revenue		$1,200	$1,200	$1,200	$1,200	$1,200	$1,200
Depreciation expense		–400	–400	–400	–400	–400	–400
Income before taxes		$ 800	$ 800	$ 800	$ 800	$ 800	$ 800
Income tax expense (Provision)		–320	–320	–320	–320	–320	–320
Net income		$ 480	$ 480	$ 480	$ 480	$ 480	$ 480
Balance Sheet							
Total assets = Fixed asset	$1,200	$ 800	$ 400	$1,200	$ 800	$ 400	$1,200
Shareholders' equity	$1,200	$ 800	$ 400	$1,200	$ 800	$ 400	$1,200
Free Cash Flow							
Earnings before interest and taxes		$ 800	$ 800	$ 800	$ 800	$ 800	$ 800
Income taxes paid on EBIT		–320	–320	–320	–320	–320	–320
Earnings before interest and after taxes		$ 480	$ 480	$ 480	$ 480	$ 480	$ 480
Depreciation		400	400	400	400	400	400
Unlevered cash flow from operations		$ 880	$ 880	$ 880	$ 880	$ 880	$ 880
Capital expenditures	–$1,200	0	0	–1,200	0	0	–1,200
Unlevered free cash flow = Equity FCF		$ 880	$ 880	–$ 320	$ 880	$ 880	–$ 320

Property, Plant, and Equipment and Accumulated Depreciation Forecasts

	Year 0	Year 1	Year 2	Year 3	Year 4	Year 5	Year 6
Beginning property, plant, and equipment		$1,200	$1,200	$1,200	$1,200	$1,200	$1,200
Capital expenditures	$1,200	0	0	1,200	0	0	1,200
Retirements				–1,200	0	0	–1,200
Ending property, plant, and equipment	$1,200	$1,200	$1,200	$1,200	$1,200	$1,200	$1,200
Beginning accumulated depreciation		$ 0	$ 400	$ 800	$ 0	$ 400	$ 800
Depreciation expense		400	400	400	400	400	400
Retirements		0	0	–1,200	0	0	–1,200
Ending accumulated depreciation	$ 0	$ 400	$ 800	$ 0	$ 400	$ 800	$ 0
Net property, plant, and equipment	$1,200	$ 800	$ 400	$1,200	$ 800	$ 400	$1,200

Discounted Cash Flow Valuation Using Actual Free Cash Flows							
Year (t)	**Year 0**	**Year 1**	**Year 2**	**Year 3**	**Year 4**	**Year 5**	**Year 6**
Free cash flow		$ 880	$ 880	–$ 320	$ 880	$ 880	–$320
Continuing value at Year 0		$8,000	–$2,645	$6,612	$6,011	–$ 1,987	
Present value of FCF Year +1 to Year t	Correct	800	1,527	1,287	1,888	2,434	
Value of the firm at Year 0	$5,175	$8,800	–$1,117	$7,898	$7,898	$ 447	
Error in the valuation		70%	–122%	53%	53%	–91%	

Discounted Cash Flow Valuation Using Adjusted Free Cash Flows, Adjusted for Annuity Capital Expenditures							
Year (t)	**Year 0**	**Year 1**	**Year 2**	**Year 3**	**Year 4**	**Year 5**	**Year 6**
Actual capital expenditure		$ 0	$ 0	$1,200	$ 0	$ 0	$1,200
Annuity for capital expenditures		363	363	363	363	363	363
Adjustment to free cash flow		–$ 363	–$ 363	$ 837	–$ 363	–$ 363	$ 837
Actual free cash flow		880	880	–320	880	880	–320
Adjusted free cash flow		$ 517	$ 517	$ 517	$ 517	$ 517	$ 517
Continuing value at Year 0		$4,704	$4,277	$3,888	$3,534	$3,213	
Present value of FCF Year +1 to Year t	Correct	470	898	1,287	1,640	1,962	
Value of the firm at Year 0	$5,175	$5,175	$5,175	$5,175	$5,175	$5,175	
Error in the valuation		0%	0%	0%	0%	0%	

Exhibit may contain small rounding errors

Review Exercise 6.5: Real Growth and Value

	No New Investment	Value Neutral New Investment	Value Creating New Investment	Value Destroying New Investment
Free cash flow (Before Investment), Year CV+1	$ 1,000.0	$ 1,000.0	$ 1,000.0	$1,000.0
Nominal required rate of return	10.0%	10.0%	10.0%	10.0%
Inflation	0%	0%	0%	0%
Return on new investment (Real)		10.0%	12.0%	8.00%
Return on new investment (Nominal)		10.0%	12.0%	8.0%
% New investment		40.0%	40.0%	40.0%
Growth rate	0.0%	4.0%	4.8%	3.2%
Continuing value	$10,000.0	$10,000.0	$11,538.5	$8,823.5
% Change in value		0.00%	15.4%	–11.8%

After mastering the material in this chapter, you will be able to:

1. Understand how the excess earnings (residual income) valuation model works (7.1–7.2)
2. Measure firm value using the WACC and APV forms of the excess earnings model (7.3–7.4)
3. Measure equity value using the equity form of the excess earnings model (7.5)
4. Learn about adjustments to earnings and invested capital to evaluate performance and measure "economic earnings" (7.6)

CHAPTER

The Excess Earnings (Residual Income) Valuation Method

Some analysts use the excess earnings (residual income) valuation method as a standard part of their assessment of a company's value; for example, in an analyst report on electronics manufacturing service (EMS) companies, Morgan Stanley Dean Witter states:

MORGAN STANLEY DEAN WITTER

> Residual income valuations depend on the sustainable returns companies generate on current invested capital and the expected returns they will generate on incremental invested capital from the free cash they generate. . . . revenues, costs, and invested capital are linked through ROE, so that the tie into the valuations should be relatively transparent. . . . revenue growth, operating margins, and operating asset turns are key inputs to understanding profitability. As the EMS companies begin to leverage their recent investments, they should start to generate more free cash flow. Thus, valuations also depend on our assumptions regarding how this free cash gets used. As electronic manufacturing service (EMS) companies drive profitability through economies of scale and scope, we see them as natural candidates for a residual income valuation analysis, which focuses on the actual invested capital, plus the related return on that invested capital, specifically operating margins and operating asset turnover (efficiency).[1]

In this chapter, we will learn the ins and outs of residual income valuation models, as these are sometimes used as an alternative to the discounted cash flow model.

[1] Morgan Stanley Dean Witter, "Technology: Electronics Manufacturing Service," Equity Research—Industry, Morgan Stanley Dean Witter, New York (March 28, 2001).

CHAPTER ORGANIZATION

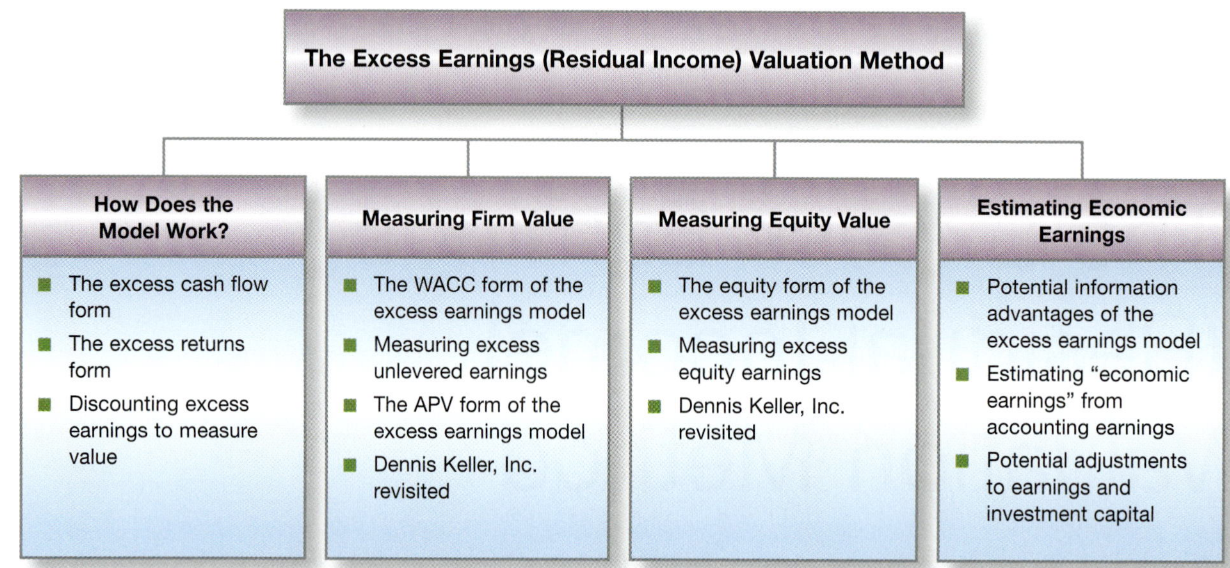

INTRODUCTION

The excess earnings (residual income) valuation method is a specific form of a more general valuation model we call the excess flow model. While it might not be apparent at first glance, all excess flow valuation models—including the excess earnings form—result directly from our fundamental valuation principles and concepts, and they are algebraically equivalent to the discounted cash flow (DCF) valuation models. Like the DCF valuation models, the excess earnings valuation model has an adjusted present value (APV), weighted average cost of capital (WACC), and equity discounted flow (Equity) form. From Chapter 5, we know that, if implemented properly, the APV, WACC, and Equity DCF valuation methods all result in the same valuation. The same statement is true for all forms of the excess earnings model; that is, if implemented properly, all forms of the excess earnings valuation model result in the same valuation, and this valuation is equal to the DCF-based valuation.

If excess earnings models are algebraically equivalent to the DCF model, you might be wondering why someone would bother using an excess earnings model. The reason is that, although the excess earnings valuation model is algebraically equivalent to the DCF valuation model, the inputs are not, and thus, the excess earnings model is another lens through which to analyze a company's value. Because it has different inputs, the excess earnings model can convey additional information that is informative for assessing a company's value beyond that gleaned from a DCF valuation. The excess earnings valuation model separates the value of the firm into two parts—the amount of capital invested as of the valuation date and the value of the firm in excess of its invested capital. The value of the firm in excess of its invested capital is equal to the discounted value of the company's forecasted excess earnings, with excess earnings equal to the difference between the earnings forecast and required earnings (where required earnings are based on capital invested by the company and the risk-adjusted discount rate). The additional information provided by the excess earnings model consists of the excess earnings a company earns every period.

Some companies use commercial forms of the excess earnings valuation models as part of a value-based management system and compensation system. Stern Value Management (formerly, Stern Stewart & Company), for example, uses its economic value added (EVA®) and market value added (MVA®) approaches, which are based on the excess earnings valuation model framework. CSFB HOLT LLC uses its cash flow return on investment approach (CFROI®). McKinsey & Company uses a variety of approaches to help managers create value and become "value managers."

7.1 THE EXCESS CASH FLOW VALUATION FRAMEWORK

LO1 Understand how the excess earnings (residual income) valuation model works

We begin our discussion of the excess earnings valuation model with its most basic form—the **excess free cash flow** form. In this form, the value of the firm is equal to the invested capital as of the valuation date plus the value of the company's discounted excess free cash flows. Excess free cash flow is equal to expected free cash flow minus the risk-adjusted discount rate multiplied by the company's invested capital (required free cash flow). In the following section we extend the excess free cash flow form of the model to the **excess earnings** (**residual earnings** or **residual income**) valuation model. While the formulas might not look like it, keep in mind that each form of the excess earnings model is algebraically equivalent to the DCF valuation model.

Excess Free Cash Flow Form

The value of an investment with an expected return equal to its risk-adjusted required rate of return, r, is equal to the amount invested. For a no-growth perpetuity, if the investment's expected free cash flow is equal to its required return multiplied by the amount of the investment ($FCF = r \times I_0$), then the value of the investment is equal to the amount invested ($V_0 = I_0$). For example, assume Mr. J. Stern purchased an all-equity-financed company with an investment of \$100, I_0. When Mr. Stern purchased the company—now called the J. Stern Company—it had an expected annual free cash flow (FCF) of \$10 in perpetuity and a required rate of return of 10%; thus, its expected return of 10% (0.1 = \$10/\$100) is equal to its required rate of return. If the company distributes its free cash flow at the end of each year to investors, the value of the J. Stern Company will always equal the amount invested, \$100.

Why? Because the company's expected return is equal to its required return and thus, does not create (or destroy) any value. We can also phrase this statement in terms of amounts—since the company's expected free cash flow of \$10 is equal to the company's required cash flow (\$10 = 0.1 × \$100), the value of the company is equal to the value of the investment. We can use the zero-growth DCF perpetuity formula to show this result.

$$V_0 = \frac{FCF_1}{r} = \frac{r \times I_0}{r} = I_0$$

For reasons we explain later, this is an important concept, for it underpins all of the excess flow models. Instead of discounting the total amount of the free cash flow (or earnings) stream, the excess flow models discount the flows in excess of the required free cash flows—called **excess flows** (or **excess earnings**). Since the value of the required free cash flows is equal to the value of the investment, we can calculate the value of the firm by adding the amount of the investment as of the valuation date to the discounted value of the forecasted excess flows. In essence, the excess flow model adds and subtracts the value of the investment from the DCF model valuation, which of course results in the same value as the DCF valuation.

We can illustrate this concept with the J. Stern Company. We know that Mr. Stern could create value if the company's free cash flows were greater than the required free cash flow return of \$10. If Mr. Stern found a way to use the company's assets to generate expected free cash flows of \$12 per year in perpetuity without changing the risk of the company, the value of the company would increase to \$120.

$$V_0 = \frac{FCF_1}{r} = \frac{\$12}{0.1} = \$120$$

In the excess flow model, we calculate the value of the firm as being the investment plus the present value of the discounted excess free cash flows.

$$V_0 = \frac{r \times I_0}{r} + \frac{FCF_1 - r \times I_0}{r} = I_0 + \frac{FCF_1 - r \times I_0}{r}$$

$$V_0 = \frac{0.1 \times \$100}{0.1} + \frac{\$12 - 0.1 \times \$100}{0.1} = \$100 + \frac{\$12 - 0.1 \times \$100}{0.1} = \$120$$

It is important to note that while we added back and subtracted initial investments from the DCF model, we could have added and subtracted any value from the DCF model. For example, we could have multiplied the initial investment by 2. As long as we subtract the required return multiplied by the amount we added (investment multiplied by 2), we are merely adding and subtracting the same amount from the DCF valuation. The reason for using the amount invested instead of another amount (e.g., investment multiplied by 2) is that the excess return has a potential economic meaning and interpretation; that is, the value created or destroyed measured relative to the invested capital (in this case, the excess flow is

\$2 per year with a value created of \$20). For example, although it would have no economic meaning, we could have added \$200 and subtracted r × \$200 in every subsequent period, and we would have still arrived at the same value.

$$V_0 = I_0 + \frac{FCF_1 - r \times I_0}{r} = \$200 + \frac{\$12 - 0.1 \times \$200}{0.1} = \$200 + \frac{\$12 - \$20}{0.1} = \$200 - \$80 = \$120$$

An Excess Returns Presentation of the Excess Flow Model

We can also implement the excess flow model in a returns form, which is merely an alternative way of showing the calculation of an investment's excess flow. In the J. Stern Company example, the \$12 free cash flow is a 12% return on investment (0.12 = \$12/\$100). The company's **excess return**, xr, is equal to its expected return, ER, minus its required return, r. The excess return in this example is 2% (0.02 = 0.12 − 0.1). Using an excess returns approach, the value of a company with a 12% expected return is equal to the initial investment plus the value of the excess return (xr) multiplied by the amount of the investment.

$$V_0 = I_0 + \frac{(ER_1 - r) \times I_0}{r} = I_0 + \frac{xr_1 \times I_0}{r}$$

For the above example, we can value the investment as

$$V_0 = \$100 + \frac{(0.12 - 0.1) \times \$100}{0.1} = \$100 + \frac{0.02 \times \$100}{0.1} = \$120$$

The excess returns presentation is merely an alternative way to calculate the excess flow (or earnings) in each period.

Valuation Key 7.1

The discounted excess flow valuation methods value a firm or investment as the value of the initial investment plus the value of the discounted future returns in excess of the required returns. Properly implemented, all forms of the excess flow valuation methods are equivalent to DCF-based valuations.

REVIEW EXERCISE 7.1

Excess Free Cash Flow Model

A group of investors formed a company at the end of Year 0 by investing \$10.0 million in equity, which was used to purchase assets and provide working capital for the company's operations. The company is financed with only equity and has a 12% cost of capital. The company expects to generate \$1.44 million in annual free cash flows in perpetuity, and the company holds no excess cash. Measure the value of the company using the excess free cash flow model.

Solution on page 320.

7.2 THE EXCESS EARNINGS VALUATION FRAMEWORK

To use the excess earnings valuation method, we discount excess accounting earnings (residual earnings or residual income) instead of excess free cash flows. We measure excess earnings the same way that we measure excess free cash flows, but instead of using free cash flows and cash investment, we use accounting earnings and total invested capital based on the financial statements. The concept of excess or residual earnings is not new. As early as 1890, an economist by the name of Alfred Marshall defined profits in terms of excess earnings and the value of a company in terms of its capitalized excess earnings:

> When a man is engaged in business, his profits for the year are the excess of his receipts from his business during the year over his outlay for his business. The difference between the value of his stock of plant, material, etc. at the end and at the beginning of the year is taken as part of his receipts or as part of his outlay, according as there has been an increase or decrease of value. What remains of his profits after deducting interest on his capital at the current rate (allowing, where necessary, for insurance) is generally called his earnings of undertaking or management. . . .
>
> He would not be, however, willing to continue the business unless he expected his total net gains from it to exceed interest on his capital at the current rate. These gains are called profits. [2]

Valuation in Practice 7.1

HSBC Investment Bank plc Version of the Excess Earnings Valuation Method and Continuing Value To develop excess earnings, HSBC has detailed forecasts for an "explicit forecast period." Then,

> After the explicit forecast period we fade the ROIC down towards the cost of capital and growth down to long-run sustainable levels. The length of the fade period is a judgment based on the sustainability of competitive advantage. . . . The terminal value is a one-off representation of the value of the "continuing period;" i.e., the value of the . . . residual income that the business will generate beyond the end of the "fade" period. By definition the assumption in the continuing period is that the ROIC will be equal to the cost of capital; super-normal returns will have been competed away . . . If using continuing economic residual income in perpetuity to value the continuing period, then, by definition, it should be set at nil.

Thus, HSBC implements the excess flow method by adding the discounted value of the excess earnings, for as long as it believes the ROIC will exceed the company's cost of capital, to current book value. HSBC bases the length of supernormal returns on a judgment of the ability of the company to maintain a competitive advantage. Of course, keep in mind that what is important here is whether the ROIC (based on the book value of the company's investments) exceeds the company's cost of capital. A company's new investments could earn just their cost of capital, but the ROIC, which is based on the historical cost book value of all prior investments, could exceed the company's cost of capital for a very long time.

Source: HSBC Investment Bank plc (HSBC), "Innogy Uncovering Hidden Value," Company Report, HSBC Investment Bank plc, London (September 1, 2000); ROIC is the return on invested capital.

It took quite a few years before Edwards and Bell (1961) explicitly discussed measuring residual earnings using financial statements.[3] Stern Value Management (formerly, Stern Stewart & Company) commercialized the excess earnings valuation method, called economic value added (EVA®).[4] Ohlson (1989, 1995) provided a rigorous development of these models and popularized this valuation method as a research topic and its use in the investment community.[5]

As stated in the introduction, if implemented consistently, the various forms of the excess earnings valuation methods result in the same valuation as the DCF valuation method. At first, this assertion might seem confusing. Everyone who knows how to read a financial statement knows that accounting earnings do not equal free cash flows, so understanding why the discounted excess earnings method results in the same valuation as the DCF models is not straightforward. The equivalence of the excess earnings and DCF valuation models, however, is neither a coincidence nor a mystery; the algebra underlying the two valuation methods is simply equivalent, though that equivalence is not readily transparent at first.

---

[2] Marshall used the term "interest" more broadly than interest on debt. He used it in the same way we use the term "cost of capital." Marshall, A., *Principles of Economics*, first published in 1890, London: Macmillan and Co., Ltd. (1920), retrieved on May 28, 2018 from http://www.econlib.org/library/Marshall/marP8.html, Book II, Chapter IV, paragraph 9.

[3] Edwards, E. and P. Bell , *The Theory and Measurement of Business Income*, Berkeley: University of California Press (1961).

[4] See, for example, Stewart (1991) for a detailed discussion of this approach; Stewart, B.B. III, *The Quest for Value*, Harper Collins Publishers, Inc. (1991).

[5] Ohlson, J. A., "Accounting Earnings, Book Value, and Dividends: The Theory of the Clean Surplus Equation Part I," Columbia University Working Paper, 1989; reprinted in Brief, R. P., and K. V. Peasnell, *Clean Surplus: A Link Between Accounting and Finance*, Garland Publishing, Inc. (1996); and Ohlson, J. A., "Earnings, Book Values and Dividends in Equity Valuation," *Contemporary Accounting Research* vol. 11, no. 2 (1995), pp. 661–688.

How can the excess earnings and DCF valuation models result in the same valuation? The sneak preview answer is simply that the excess earnings valuation model adjusts the calculations for the timing differences between a company's free cash flows and its earnings. A company begins with cash (initial investment) and ends with cash (liquidating dividend). Over the life of the company, the sum of its earnings is equal to the sum of its free cash flows. In order to discount earnings instead of free cash flows, we adjust the calculations for the timing differences between the earnings and cash flows. The mechanics of the discounted excess earnings valuation method implicitly adjust for these timing differences on a present value basis. The result is that the present value of the difference between excess earnings and excess cash flows is equal to zero.

The Excess Free Cash Flow Form

We begin the development of the excess earnings model with a more general form of the excess free cash flow model. For now, assume that r measures an appropriate discount rate based on the riskiness of the cash flows—later in the chapter we will make clear what cost of capital we use in specific forms of the model. The excess free cash flow model for an all-equity company is

$$V_F = I_0 + \sum_{t=1}^{\infty} \frac{FCF_t - r \times I_0}{(1+r)^t}$$

In the next section, we show that the above model is nothing more than adding and subtracting the investment (I_0) from the DCF model.

$$V_F = \sum_{t=1}^{\infty} \frac{FCF_t}{(1+r)^t} + I_0 - \sum_{t=1}^{\infty} \frac{r \times I_0}{(1+r)^t}$$

$$V_F = \sum_{t=1}^{\infty} \frac{FCF_t}{(1+r)^t} + I_0 - \frac{r \times I_0}{r}$$

The Excess (or Residual) Earnings Form

Accountants record revenues and expenses based on generally accepted accounting principles (GAAP) and not based on cash receipts and cash expenses. The difference between cash-basis accounting and GAAP-based accrual accounting is called **accounting accruals**. Examples of accruals include revenues recorded by the company but not yet collected in cash—resulting in an account receivable—or expenses recorded by the company but not paid in cash—resulting in an account payable. Another type of accrual is the result of expensing a previously capitalized investment over its useful life; this is called **depreciation** if the investment is for plant or equipment or **amortization** if the investment is for an intangible asset.

Accounting accruals affect both the income statement and the balance sheet and explain the difference between earnings and cash flows. The balance sheet contains the cumulative amount of the accruals recorded by the company, A. The income statement, on the other hand, contains the change in the company's cumulative accruals, ΔA_t. We can state the difference between accounting earnings and free cash flows as the change in accounting accruals and new cash investments. In other words, free cash flow is equal to accounting earnings, adjusted for the change in accounting accruals and new investment. As long as accruals and investments do not cause a permanent difference between cumulative accounting earnings and cumulative free cash flows, called clean-surplus accounting, over a company's life, the sum of its free cash flows is equal to the sum of its earnings. Eventually, all accruals and investments recorded on the balance sheet reverse. For example, a company collects its receivables, pays its payables, and expenses its previously capitalized cash expenditures. The difference is only a matter of timing.[6]

Recall the basic free cash flow formula from Chapter 3. Unlevered free cash flow is equal to earnings before interest and taxes, EBIT, minus cash income taxes on EBIT, TAX, plus non-cash expenses, NCEXP (an accrual), minus non-cash revenues, NCREV (an accrual), minus the change in required cash, ΔRC, minus the change in non-cash operating working capital, ΔWCO (an accrual), minus capital expenditures, CAPEX.

[6] See Ohlson, J. A., "Earnings, Book Values and Dividends in Equity Valuation," *Contemporary Accounting Research* vol. 11, no. 2 (1995), pp. 661–688.

$$FCF = EBIT - TAX + NCEXP - NCREV - \Delta RC - \Delta WCO - CAPEX$$

We assume the company is all-equity financed, earnings, E, is equal to earnings before interest and taxes less income taxes (E = EBIT − TAX). We also assume that the new cash investment is equal to the change in required cash plus capital expenditures ($\Delta I_t = \Delta RC + CAPEX$), and assume that the remainder of the terms in the above free cash flow formula represent the change in accounting accruals ($\Delta A_t = \Delta WCO + NCREV - NCEXP$). Thus, we can rewrite the free cash flow formula as follows:

$$FCF = E - \Delta A - \Delta I = EBIT - TAX + NCEXP - NCREV - \Delta RC - \Delta WCO - CAPEX$$

The assumptions are not precise, for we assume the change in working capital is only an accrual when, in fact, it contains both accruals (such as the changes in accounts receivable and wages payable) and new investment (such as investments in inventory and prepaid expenses). Using a more precise mapping of the terms in the initial free cash flow formula would have no effect on proving the equivalence of the excess earnings and DCF valuation methods. Lastly, the book value of a company's equity, BVE, is equal to its cumulative investment, I, plus its cumulative accruals, A, or BVE = I + A.

The excess earnings model is equal to

$$V_F = BVE_0 + \sum_{t=1}^{\infty} \frac{E_t - r \times BVE_{t-1}}{(1+r)^t} \tag{7.1}$$

We can rewrite the excess earnings model to show that it is equal to the DCF model. We can restate Equation 7.1 by replacing earnings with the abbreviated free cash flow formula, $E_t = FCF_t + \Delta A_t + \Delta I_t$, and book value with cash investments plus accruals, $BVE_t = A_t + I_t$. Then, we can restate the above equation in terms of the DCF model plus two other components.

$$V_F = (I_0 + A_0) + \sum_{t=1}^{\infty} \frac{[FCF_t + \Delta I_t + \Delta A_t] - r \times (I_{t-1} + A_{t-1})}{(1+r)^t}$$

$$V_F = \sum_{t=1}^{\infty} \frac{FCF_t}{(1+r)^t} + \left[I_0 + \sum_{t=1}^{\infty} \frac{\Delta I_t - r \times I_{t-1}}{(1+r)^t} \right] + \left[A_0 + \sum_{t=1}^{\infty} \frac{\Delta A_t - r \times A_{t-1}}{(1+r)^t} \right]$$

The first term on the right-hand side of above equation is the DCF model. The second term is the investment term, which adds and subtracts the time series of investments. The third term is the accrual term, which adds and subtracts the time series of accruals. Since the first term on the right-hand side of the above equation is equal to the DCF model; the excess earnings model is equal to the DCF model if the second and third terms equal zero.

Since the form of the second and third terms are the same, we only need show that the second term is zero for then it naturally follows that the third term is also equal to zero. In other words, we need to show that

$$0 = I_0 + \sum_{t=1}^{\infty} \frac{\Delta I_t - r \times I_{t-1}}{(1+r)^t}$$

We begin by expanding the infinite series in the above equation. We add back each investment and then subtract it by subtracting the present value of the required returns on that investment. To show this result, we first begin by expanding the above equation:

$$0 = I_0 + \left[\frac{\Delta I_1}{(1+r)^1} - \frac{r \times I_0}{(1+r)^1} \right] + \left[\frac{\Delta I_2}{(1+r)^2} - \frac{r \times I_1}{(1+r)^2} \right] + \left[\frac{\Delta I_3}{(1+r)^3} - \frac{r \times I_2}{(1+r)^3} \right] + \cdots$$

Next we expand each of the changes in the investments and combine like terms.

$$0 = I_0 + \left[\frac{I_1 - I_0}{(1+r)^1} - \frac{r \times I_0}{(1+r)^1} \right] + \left[\frac{I_2 - I_1}{(1+r)^2} - \frac{r \times I_1}{(1+r)^2} \right] + \left[\frac{I_3 - I_2}{(1+r)^3} - \frac{r \times I_2}{(1+r)^3} \right] + \cdots$$

$$0 = I_0 + \left[\frac{I_1}{(1+r)^1} - \frac{(1+r) \times I_0}{(1+r)^1} \right] + \left[\frac{I_2}{(1+r)^2} - \frac{(1+r) \times I_1}{(1+r)^2} \right] + \left[\frac{I_3}{(1+r)^3} - \frac{(1+r) \times I_2}{(1+r)^3} \right] + \cdots$$

We restate the above equation as follows:

$$0 = I_0 + \left[\frac{I_1}{(1+r)^1} - I_0\right] + \left[\frac{I_2}{(1+r)^2} - \frac{I_1}{(1+r)^1}\right] + \left[\frac{I_3}{(1+r)^3} - \frac{I_2}{(1+r)^2}\right] + \dots$$

Each term in the previous equation has an additive inverse such that the value of this equation is zero; in other words, the investment is both added and then subtracted in the excess valuation model.

As we stated in the introduction to this section, we do not need to know very much about accounting in order to understand the simple mechanics that make the excess earnings valuation method equivalent to the DCF valuation method. Accounting rules result in differences between free cash flows and accounting net income in every period (year), and that these differences are recorded in the company's balance sheet. Eventually, over the life of the company, the cumulative difference between free cash flows and earnings (cumulative accruals and investments) net to zero. The mechanics of the model ensure that the present value of the accruals in the excess earnings model is equal to zero.

Extending the J. Stern Company Example to the Excess Earnings Valuation Method

Recall our simple excess cash flow example concerning the J. Stern Company, which is an all-equity-financed company. After Stern purchases the company, the expected free cash flows of the company are equal to \$12 per year, and the company's discount rate is 10%. The company will not grow and will distribute all of its free cash flow to its investors. Thus, the value of the company is \$120. Now, we are going to add some accruals to the J. Stern Company example.

We first extend our example by adding an accrual to the initial balance sheet—that is, the investment (assets and common equity) on the balance sheet will no longer equal the cash investment. We do this by assuming that J. Stern invested \$100, but for whatever reason, the company recorded the investment on both the asset side and equity side of the balance sheet at \$110 ($BVE_0 = \$110$). We can characterize this difference as an accrual of \$10. We also assume that the company's expected earnings is equal to its expected free cash flows for every year—\$12; that is, the company does not have any additional accruals or new investments.

We do not need to know why we recorded this accrual (the difference between the cash invested and the book value of the company). In fact, it could even be an error. The mechanics of the excess flow valuation model are such that such accruals do not affect the valuation of the company; again, it's not magic—only a little algebra at work. Seeing is believing—here is the valuation with the \$10 accrual that increases the book value of equity ($BVE_0 = \$110$).

$$V_F = BVE_0 + \frac{E_1 - r \times BVE_0}{r}$$

$$V_F = \$110 + \frac{\$12 - 0.1 \times \$110}{0.1} = \$120$$

The valuation of the company is still \$120. The accrual not only increased the initial book value of the investment by \$10 (from \$100 to \$110), but it also reduced the excess earnings for every year in the future; because the required return ($r \times BVE$) became larger, the excess earnings became smaller. The present value of the decrease in excess earnings in future years is equal to \$10, which exactly offsets the \$10 accrual, so the valuation is unchanged by adding an accrual to the initial book value. We know that we could have chosen any number for the accrual because the model merely adds back and subtracts that number. That is why having an economic underpinning to the accrual number is important—so that the present value of the excess earnings has some economic meaning.

Now, accruals can also affect earnings such that earnings no longer equal free cash flow every period. The company's expected free cash flows continue to be \$12 per year. Assume the company's expected earnings no longer equal its free cash flows. We expect the company to have a \$10 earnings increasing accrual in Year 1 that reverses in Year 3, and in all other years, its expected earnings are equal to its expected free cash flow. Thus, the company's expected earnings no longer equal its free cash flows in every year (\$12 per year). Earnings increase by \$10 in the year the accrual is recorded (Year 1) and decrease by \$10 in the year the accrual reverses (Year 3). Forecasted earnings equal \$22 in Year 1, \$12 in Year 2, \$2 in Year 3, and \$12 thereafter. Note that the income increasing accrual also increases the book value of equity at the end of Year 1 by \$10 to \$120, and the reversal decreases it by \$10 to \$110 at the end of Year 3.

The mechanics work in the same way as when we added an accrual to the initial book value of the investment. The accrual either increases or decreases earnings relative to cash flows from operations in that year, and it similarly affects the book value of the company's invested capital (investment plus cumulative accruals). Thus, applying the cost of capital to the company's book value exactly offsets the accrual in the earnings when we calculate the present value, even though we had an accrual that created a difference between earnings and cash flow. The calculation is a little more complex because we need to value the excess earnings for Years 1 through 3 separately from the perpetuity, which begins in Year 4.

$$V_E = V_F = BVE_0 + \frac{E_1 - r \times BVE_0}{1+r} + \frac{E_2 - r \times BVE_1}{(1+r)^2} + \frac{E_3 - r \times BVE_2}{(1+r)^3} + \frac{E_4 - r \times BVE_3}{r} \times \frac{1}{(1+r)^3}$$

$$V_E = V_F = \$110 + \frac{\$22 - 0.1 \times \$110}{1.1} + \frac{\$12 - 0.1 \times \$120}{(1.1)^2} + \frac{\$2 - 0.1 \times \$120}{(1.1)^3} + \frac{\$12 - 0.1 \times \$110}{0.1} \times \frac{1}{(1.1)^3}$$

$$V_E = V_F = \$110 + \frac{\$22 - \$11}{1.1} + \frac{\$12 - \$12}{(1.1)^2} + \frac{\$2 - \$12}{(1.1)^3} + \frac{\$12 - \$11}{0.1} \times \frac{1}{(1.1)^3} = \$120$$

REVIEW EXERCISE 7.2

Excess Earnings Model

Use the information from Review Exercise 7.1 and assume that in addition to the initial $10 million investment in the company, the company also recorded a $1 million intangible asset, which has a perpetual life. Also assume that the company's free cash flow is equal to its accounting earnings (for example, depreciation is equal to capital expenditures and that there is no change in working capital). Measure the value of the company using the excess earnings model.

Solution on page 320.

The Articulation of the Income Statement and the Balance Sheet and Comprehensive Income

In order for the sums of accounting earnings and free cash flows to be equivalent over the life of a company, a company's earnings must be comprehensive; that is, net income must reconcile to the change in the book value of equity excluding the effects of the issuance or repurchase of equity or equity distributions (e.g., dividends)—called the **articulation of the income statement and the balance sheet** or the **clean surplus accounting** principle. Another way to say this is that all income must flow through the income statement into shareholders' equity (i.e., no income can bypass the income statement and get booked directly to retained earnings). As shown earlier, the exact accounting rules or principles accountants use to measure accounting earnings are irrelevant to making the model work. Accountants could use any set of accounting principles and the value from the excess earnings valuation method would still be the same as the value from the DCF model as long as the sum of a company's accounting earnings equals the sum of its free cash flows over the life of the company. Naturally, an arbitrary set of accounting rules will not be very informative, but the excess earnings model will still work. We discuss this issue in more detail at the end of the chapter.

If the company's earnings on its income statement are not comprehensive, we need to adjust the earnings in order to make them comprehensive. Thus, forecasts of the financial statements would have to be comprehensive in order to use them in an excess earnings valuation model. It is not necessary to restate the historical financial statements on a comprehensive basis, but the forecasts must be comprehensive. **Comprehensive income** is defined by *Statement of Financial Accounting Concepts No. 6* as "the change in equity of a business enterprise during a period from transactions and other events and circumstances from non-owner sources. It includes all changes in equity during a period except those resulting from investments by owners and distributions to owners."[7]

[7] Financial Accounting Standards Board, *Statement of Financial Accounting Concepts No. 6: Elements of Financial Statements (A Replacement of FASB Concepts Statement No. 3—Incorporating an Amendment of FASB Concepts Statement No. 2)*, December 1985, p. 70.

Valuation in Practice 7.2

Whole Foods Market, Inc.'s (Whole Foods) Use of the EVA® Excess Earnings Model
Whole Foods, a large grocery store chain in the U.S., explained its use of EVA, prior to being acquired by Amazon, as follows:

> We use Economic Value Added ("EVA") to evaluate our business decisions and as a basis for determining incentive compensation. . . . We believe that one of our core strengths is our decentralized culture, where decisions are made at the store level, close to the customer. We believe this is one of our strongest competitive advantages, and that EVA is the best financial framework that team members can use to help make decisions that create sustainable shareholder value.
>
> We use EVA extensively for capital investment decisions, including evaluating new store real estate decisions and store remodeling proposals. We are turning down projects that do not add long-term value to the Company. . . . Our emphasis is on EVA improvement, as we want to challenge our teams to continue to innovate and grow EVA in new ways. We believe that opportunities always exist to increase sales and margins, to lower operating expenses and to make investments that add value in ways that benefit all of our stakeholders. . . .
>
> The Company provides information regarding EVA as additional information about its operating results. EVA is a measure not in accordance with, or an alternative to, generally accepted accounting principles ("GAAP"). The Company's management believes that this additional EVA information is useful to shareholders, management, analysts and potential investors in evaluating the Company's results of operations and financial condition. In addition, management uses these measures for reviewing the financial results of the Company and for budget planning and incentive compensation purposes. . . .
>
> Capital charge is calculated by multiplying weighted average EVA capital by our weighted average cost of capital.

Source: Whole Foods Market, Inc.; was www.wholefoodsmarket.com, Investor Relations—EVA tab (no longer available).

Valuation Key 7.2

As long as the accounting system adheres to clean surplus accounting, the use of accounting earnings instead of cash flows results in the same valuation when using the excess earnings valuation technique. Clean surplus requires that the net income must reconcile to the change in the book value of equity excluding the effects of the issuance or repurchase of equity or equity distributions (e.g., dividends).

Under U.S. GAAP, deviations from clean surplus accounting occur for a variety of reasons, including foreign currency translation adjustments, gains and losses on foreign currency transactions that are economic hedges of a net investment in a foreign entity, a change in the market value of a futures contract that qualifies as a hedge of certain assets reported at fair value, unrealized holding gains and losses on available-for-sale securities, and unrealized holding gains and losses that result from a debt security being transferred from the held-to-maturity category to the available-for-sale category.[8] The items that do not flow through income under U.S. GAAP are generally not the kinds of items we forecast anyway, but if you do forecast them, just remember to run them through net income.

7.3 THE WEIGHTED AVERAGE COST OF CAPITAL FORM OF THE MODEL

LO2 Measure firm value using the WACC and APV forms of the excess earnings model

To value a company using the WACC form of the excess earnings valuation method, we discount the company's unlevered excess earnings and the continuing value of its unlevered excess earnings at the weighted average cost of capital and add its book value of total invested capital as of the valuation

[8] Financial Accounting Standards Board, *Statements of Financial Accounting Standards 130: Reporting Comprehensive Income*, June 1997.

date. Unlevered excess earnings is equal to unlevered earnings minus the required earnings, calculated as total invested capital as of the beginning of the period multiplied by the weighted average cost of capital ($UE_t - r_{WACC} \times TIC_{t-1}$). Conceptually, unlevered earnings are equal to earnings (net income) plus any after-tax interest deducted in calculating earnings.

For a company financed with claims beyond common equity, the book value of a company's **total invested capital (TIC)** is equal to the book value of its debt (D), preferred stock (PS), common equity (BVE), and all other securities used to finance the firm (OTH) but it does not include non-interest-bearing operating liabilities (accounts payable, deferred income taxes, etc.). We can also define total invested capital starting with the other side of the balance sheet—that is, total invested capital is equal to total assets (TA) minus the company's non-interest-bearing operating liabilities (OPL).

$$TIC = D + PS + BVE + OTH = TA - OPL$$

Equation 7.2 is the general formula for the WACC-based unlevered excess earnings valuation method, using a constant growth perpetuity formula to measure the continuing value of excess earnings.

$$V_F = TIC_0 + \sum_{t=1}^{C} \frac{UE_t - r_{WACC} \times TIC_{t-1}}{(1 + r_{WACC})^t} + \frac{UE_{C+1} - r_{WACC} \times TIC_C}{r_{WACC} - g} \times \frac{1}{(1 + r_{WACC})^C} \quad (7.2)$$

An alternative but equivalent way of measuring the continuing value of a company's unlevered excess earnings is to separately measure the continuing value of the firm, $CV_{F,C}$, and subtract the book value of total invested capital as of the continuing value date, TIC_C.

$$V_F = TIC_0 + \sum_{t=1}^{C} \frac{UE_t - r_{WACC} \times TIC_{t-1}}{(1 + r_{WACC})^t} + \frac{CV_{F,C} - TIC_C}{(1 + r_{WACC})^C} \quad (7.3)$$

A useful feature of the continuing value calculation in Equation 7.3 is that we can use a different valuation method for the continuing value—such as an assumed sales price, a value based on a market multiple, or a liquidation value.

Note that in either formula, we can also calculate excess earnings in every year by taking the difference between the return on invested capital, ROIC (unlevered earnings divided by beginning of year total invested capital), and the weighted average cost of capital and then multiply that difference by the beginning-of-year total invested capital. This is the excess returns version of the model.

Dennis Keller, Inc. Revisited—Weighted Average Cost of Capital Form of the Model

In Chapter 5, we used Dennis Keller, Inc. to illustrate the WACC, APV, and Equity DCF valuation models. In this section, we again use the Keller company to illustrate how to implement the various forms of the excess earnings model and to show that this model calculates the same value as the DCF valuation model. In Exhibit 7.1, we reproduce the original income statement and balance sheet forecasts for Keller (Exhibit 5.7 from Chapter 5). Recall that the company's unlevered cost of capital is 12%, its debt cost of capital is 8%, and its capital structure strategy is 20% debt and 80% equity financing. Based on this capital structure and a 40% income tax rate, the company's equity and weighted average costs of capital are 13% and 11.36%, respectively. The growth rate after Year 3 is 3% per year.

To measure the company's unlevered excess earnings, we first measure its unlevered earnings—or earnings before interest and after taxes—which we know is independent of the company's capital structure. We also measure the company's total invested capital for each year in the forecasts (see Exhibit 7.1 for both inputs). While the relative components (debt, preferred, equity) of the company's total invested capital depends on the capital structure, the total amount of its invested capital does not as long as investment policy is fixed; thus, we can use the total invested capital from the original financial projections in Exhibit 7.1 even though the 20% debt capital structure is based on a different mix of debt and equity. Similarly, the $20 million debt capital structure proposed by the CFO changed the amount of debt and equity financing but the total invested capital did not change. To understand this point more fully, remember that we can define total invested capital as total assets less non-interest-bearing operating liabilities. Given the scale of the company's operations remains the same, its total invested capital is the same, regardless of the capital structure strategy, as long as investment policy is held fixed across the different capital structures.

EXHIBIT 7.1 Financial Statement and Unlevered Free Cash Flow Forecasts (Exhibit 5.7)—Dennis Keller, Inc.

($ in thousands)	Actual Year −1	Actual Year 0	Forecast Year 1	Forecast Year 2	Forecast Year 3	Forecast Year 4
Income Statement:						
Revenue	$10,000	$11,000	$12,000	$14,000	$14,420	$14,853
Operating expenses	−2,000	−2,200	−3,600	−4,200	−4,326	−4,456
Depreciation expense	−2,100	−2,600	−3,100	−3,700	−4,077	−4,200
Earnings before interest and taxes	$ 5,900	$ 6,200	$ 5,300	$ 6,100	$ 6,017	$ 6,197
Interest expense	−160	−160	−180	−180	−180	−180
Income before taxes	$ 5,740	$ 6,040	$ 5,120	$ 5,920	$ 5,837	$ 6,017
Income tax expense	−2,296	−2,416	−2,048	−2,368	−2,335	−2,407
Net income	$ 3,444	$ 3,624	$ 3,072	$ 3,552	$ 3,502	$ 3,610
Balance Sheet:						
Cash	$ 200	$ 200	$ 200	$ 280	$ 288	$ 297
Net operating working capital	2,000	2,500	1,600	1,820	1,875	1,931
Property, plant & equipment (net)	22,000	24,400	27,300	27,375	28,196	29,042
Total assets	$24,200	$27,100	$29,100	$29,475	$30,359	$31,270
Debt	$ 2,000	$ 2,000	$ 2,000	$ 2,000	$ 2,000	$ 2,060
Common equity	500	10,500	10,500	10,500	10,500	10,500
Retained earnings	21,700	14,600	16,600	16,975	17,859	18,710
Total liabilities and equities	$24,200	$27,100	$29,100	$29,475	$30,359	$31,270
Unlevered Earnings:						
Earnings before interest and taxes (EBIT)		$ 6,200	$ 5,300	$ 6,100	$ 6,017	$ 6,197
− Income taxes paid on EBIT (T_C × EBIT)		−2,480	−2,120	−2,440	−2,407	−2,479
Earnings before interest and after taxes		$ 3,720	$ 3,180	$ 3,660	$ 3,610	$ 3,718

We show the calculation of Keller's Year 0 total invested capital and its components for the original forecasts, the 20% debt capital structure, and the $20 million debt capital structure in Exhibit 7.2. As of the end of Year 0, Keller has $27,100 in total invested capital regardless of which capital structure the company adopts. The components of Keller's total invested capital, however, depend on the company's capital structure. We can calculate Keller's equity in two ways. We can calculate it as total assets minus operating liabilities minus post-recapitalized debt or as post-recapitalized retained

EXHIBIT 7.2 Total Invested Capital and Its Components for the Original Forecasts, 20% Debt Capital Structure, and $20 Million Debt Capital Structure—Dennis Keller, Inc.

($ in thousands)	Original Forecasts	20% Capital Structure Recapitalization	$20 Million Capital Structure Recapitalization
Total assets net of operating liabilities	$27,100	$27,100	$27,100
Debt in post recapitalization capital structure	2,000	6,000	20,000
Book value of equity	$25,100	$21,100	$ 7,100
Retained earnings pre-recapitalization	$14,600	$14,600	$14,600
Debt refinanced		2,000	2,000
Debt in post recapitalization capital structure		−6,000	−20,000
Retained earnings post- recapitalization	$14,600	$10,600	−$ 3,400
Common stock	10,500	10,500	10,500
Book value of equity	$25,100	$21,100	$ 7,100
Debt in post recapitalization capital structure	2,000	6,000	20,000
Total invested capital	$27,100	$27,100	$27,100

earnings plus common stock plus recapitalized debt. Post-recapitalized retained earnings is equal to retained earnings before the recapitalization minus the change in non-common equity financing, which assumes the company distributed any net increase in non-common equity financing to the shareholders (or that the shareholders proportionately contributed additional capital for any net decrease in non-common equity financing).

We measure the company's required earnings by multiplying the beginning-of-year total invested capital by the weighted average cost of capital. As shown in Exhibit 7.3, in Year 1, the required earnings are $3,079, or 11.36% times $27,100. We measure unlevered excess earnings as the difference between the unlevered earnings forecasts and required earnings. Note that the unlevered earnings is equal to earnings before interest and after taxes from Exhibit 7.1. We calculate this for Year 1 as the EBIT of $5,300 less the tax on EBIT of $2,120 ($2,120 = $5,300 × 0.4) yielding unlevered earnings of $3,180 ($3,180 = $5,300 − $2,120). For Year 1, excess earnings is equal to $101 ($101 = $3,180 − $3,079). We present the calculation of unlevered excess earnings for Years 1 through 4 in Exhibit 7.3. Alternatively, we could measure unlevered excess earnings as the difference in the forecasted rates of return on total invested capital and the weighted average cost of capital multiplied by the beginning balance of total invested capital.

EXHIBIT 7.3 Calculation of Unlevered Excess Earnings Based on the Weighted Average Cost of Capital—Dennis Keller, Inc.

($ in thousands)	Year 1	Year 2	Year 3	Year 4
Unlevered net income	$ 3,180	$ 3,660	$ 3,610	$ 3,718
Beginning of year total invested capital	$27,100	$29,100	$29,475	$30,359
Weighted average cost of capital	11.36%	11.36%	11.36%	11.36%
Required unlevered net income	$ 3,079	$ 3,306	$ 3,348	$ 3,449
Unlevered excess earnings	$ 101	$ 354	$ 262	$ 269

Exhibit may contain small rounding errors

Now that we measured the expected unlevered excess earnings, we can discount the unlevered excess earnings using the weighted average cost of capital. We calculate the company's continuing value using a constant-growth perpetuity formula as follows:

$$CV_{\text{Year 3}} = \frac{\text{Unlevered Excess Earnings}_4}{(r_{\text{WACC}} - g)} = \frac{\$269}{(0.1136 - 0.03)} = \$3{,}223$$

The company's total invested capital at the end of Year 3 is equal to $30,359. If we add the continuing value of the company's excess earnings as of the end of Year 3—$3,223 to the beginning value of the total invested capital at the end of Year 3 ($30,359)—we measure the continuing value of the firm as being $33,582. This is the same continuing value based on the WACC DCF valuation (Exhibit 5.8).

As we will discuss later in the chapter, the $3,223 continuing value of unlevered excess earnings provides information on the expectations for the company. If the company's total invested capital and accounting earnings reasonably represent the company's underlying economic investment and performance, then this continuing value assumes the company will be able to earn a return in excess of its required rate of return (weighted average cost of capital) in perpetuity. This may or may not be a reasonable assumption, for we know from Chapters 2 and 6 that for reasonably competitive markets, a company is likely to only earn its required rate of return in the long run. However, it is important to also remember that excess earnings is based on the book value of total invested capital—not on the market value of the capital—and that excess earnings is based on accounting earnings—not economic earnings. Total invested capital and earnings are accounting numbers based on accounting rules. At best, they measure economic value and performance with error. Thus, it is plausible that rates of return computed based on accounting numbers will be greater than the company's economic cost of capital in perpetuity.

To complete the valuation of Keller, we discount each year's unlevered excess earnings to measure the value of the company's excess earnings as of the end of Year 0, which we calculate to be $2,900. We add that amount to the value of the company's total invested capital at the end of Year 0 of $27,100 in order to measure Keller's firm value of $30,000. We show these calculations in Exhibit 7.4. This value is equal to the WACC DCF valuation we calculated in Chapter 5 (Exhibit 5.8).

EXHIBIT 7.4 Unlevered Excess Earnings Weighted Average Cost of Capital Valuation—Dennis Keller, Inc.

($ in thousands)	Year 0	Year 1	Year 2	Year 3	CV_{Firm} Year 3
Unlevered excess earnings for continuing value					$ 269
Discount factor for continuing value					11.962
Unlevered excess earnings and continuing value		$ 101	$ 354	$ 262	$ 3,223
Discount factor.		0.898	0.806	0.724	0.724
Present value		$ 91	$ 286	$ 189	$ 2,334
Present value of unlevered excess earnings	$ 2,900				
Book value of total invested capital.	27,100				
Value of the firm	$30,000				

Exhibit may contain small rounding errors

REVIEW EXERCISE 7.3

WACC Form of the Excess Earnings Model

Use the income statement, balance sheet, and free cash flow forecasts for State Line Farm, Inc. to value the firm as of the end of Year 0 using the WACC form of the excess earnings model. The company's unlevered cost of capital is 12%, it has a target capital structure of 1/3 debt (which is reflected in the forecasts provided below), it has a cost of debt of 8%, and it has a perpetual growth rate of 2% for excess earnings. Assume interest tax shields are valued using the unlevered cost of capital.

STATE LINE FARM, INC.
Income Statement and Balance Sheet Forecasts

($ in thousands)	Year 0	Year 1	Year 2	Year 3	Year 4
Income Statement					
Revenue		$10,000	$11,000	$11,550	$11,781
Operating expenses.		−6,200	−6,820	−7,161	−7,304
Depreciation expense.		−833	−1,000	−1,146	−1,169
Earnings before interest and taxes.		$ 2,967	$ 3,180	$ 3,243	$ 3,308
Interest expense.		−425	−481	−502	−515
Income before taxes.		$ 2,542	$ 2,699	$ 2,741	$ 2,793
Income tax expense.		−1,017	−1,080	−1,096	−1,117
Net income.		$ 1,525	$ 1,619	$ 1,645	$ 1,676
Balance Sheet					
Cash.	$ 500	$ 500	$ 550	$ 578	$ 589
Inventory.	1,000	2,300	2,530	2,657	2,710
Total current assets	$1,500	$ 2,800	$ 3,080	$ 3,234	$ 3,299
Property, plant, and equipment (net)	8,333	9,167	9,625	9,818	10,014
Total assets.	$9,833	$11,967	$12,705	$13,052	$13,313
Debt	$5,313	$ 6,011	$ 6,279	$ 6,432	$ 6,561
Equity	4,521	5,955	6,426	6,619	6,752
Total equities	$9,833	$11,967	$12,705	$13,052	$13,313

continued

continued from previous page

STATE LINE FARM, INC. **Free Cash Flow and Equity Free Cash Flow Forecasts** **($ in thousands)**	**Year 1**	**Year 2**	**Year 3**	**Year 4**
Earnings before interest and taxes (EBIT)	$2,967	$3,180	$3,243	$3,308
– Income taxes paid on EBIT	–1,187	–1,272	–1,297	–1,323
Earnings before interest and after taxes	$1,780	$1,908	$1,946	$1,985
+ Depreciation expense	833	1,000	1,146	1,169
– Change in inventory	–1,300	–230	–127	–53
– Change in required cash balance	0	–50	–28	–12
– Capital expenditures	–1,667	–1,458	–1,338	–1,365
Unlevered free cash flow	–$ 353	$1,170	$1,599	$1,724
– Interest paid in cash ($r_D \times V_D$)	–425	–481	–502	–515
+ Interest tax shield ($T_{INT} \times r_D \times V_D$)	170	192	201	206
+ Change in debt financing	699	267	153	129
Equity free cash flow	$ 90	$1,148	$1,451	$1,544

Exhibit may contain small rounding errors

Solution on pages 320–321.

7.4 THE ADJUSTED PRESENT VALUE FORM OF THE MODEL

To value a company using the APV form of the excess earnings model, we add the discounted value of the company's unlevered excess earnings and the continuing value of its unlevered excess earnings (all discounted at the company's unlevered cost of capital) to the company's total invested capital as of the valuation date, and then add the value of its interest tax shields, V_{ITS} (exactly as calculated using the APV form of the DCF model). Unlevered excess earnings is equal to unlevered earnings minus the required earnings, where the required earnings is now based on the unlevered cost of capital (rather than the weighted average cost of capital). In other words, required earnings equal total invested capital as of the beginning of the period multiplied by the unlevered cost of capital, or $UE_t - r_{UA} \times TIC_{t-1}$.

Equation 7.4 is the general formula for the APV-based excess earnings valuation method, using a constant growth perpetuity formula to measure the continuing value of the excess earnings.

$$V_F = TIC_0 + \sum_{t=1}^{C} \frac{UE_t - r_{UA} \times TIC_{t-1}}{(1 + r_{UA})^t} + \frac{UE_{C+1} - r_{UA} \times TIC_C}{r_{UA} - g} \times \frac{1}{(1 + r_{UA})^C} + V_{ITS,0} \qquad \textbf{(7.4)}$$

Again, we can use an alternative method to compute the continuing value of the unlevered firm, such as a market multiple or liquidation value. In this case, we measure the continuing value of the unlevered firm, $CV_{UA,C}$, and subtract the book value of its total invested capital as of the continuing value date, TIC_C. Equation 7.5 uses this approach.

$$V_F = TIC_0 + \sum_{t=1}^{C} \frac{UE_t - r_{UA} \times TIC_{t-1}}{(1 + r_{UA})^t} + \frac{CV_{UA,C} - TIC_C}{(1 + r_{UA})^C} + V_{ITS,0} \qquad \textbf{(7.5)}$$

Here again, with either of these two formulas, we can calculate excess earnings every year by taking the difference between return on invested capital and the unlevered cost of capital multiplied by the beginning-of-year total invested capital.

Dennis Keller, Inc. Revisited—Adjusted Present Value Form of the Model

Recall that we used the APV valuation method for the Keller Company in Chapter 5 when we changed the capital structure strategy from 20% debt to an initial amount of debt equal to $20 million and used all available cash flow to reduce the debt over the next three years. Recall Keller's unlevered cost of capital is 12%, and its debt cost of capital is 9% for this capital structure. Since we do not know the company's capital structure ratios for this capital structure strategy, but instead know the expected amount of debt the company will have outstanding at each point in time, we use the APV form of the model to value the company. The additional financial leverage resulted in an increase in the value of the firm from $30,000 to $34,015

(Exhibit 5.14), ignoring financial distress costs and other costs related to the increase in financial leverage. The value of the interest tax shields with this new capital structure strategy is \$6,200.

Valuation in Practice 7.3

Ball Corporation's Acquisition of Rexam PLC In 2016, Ball Corporation acquired Rexam PLC for approximately \$6.1 billion of cash and equity, plus the assumption of approximately \$2.4 billion of net debt. This acquisition made Ball the largest manufacturer of beverage cans in the world. Ball used EVA® to evaluate the purchase:

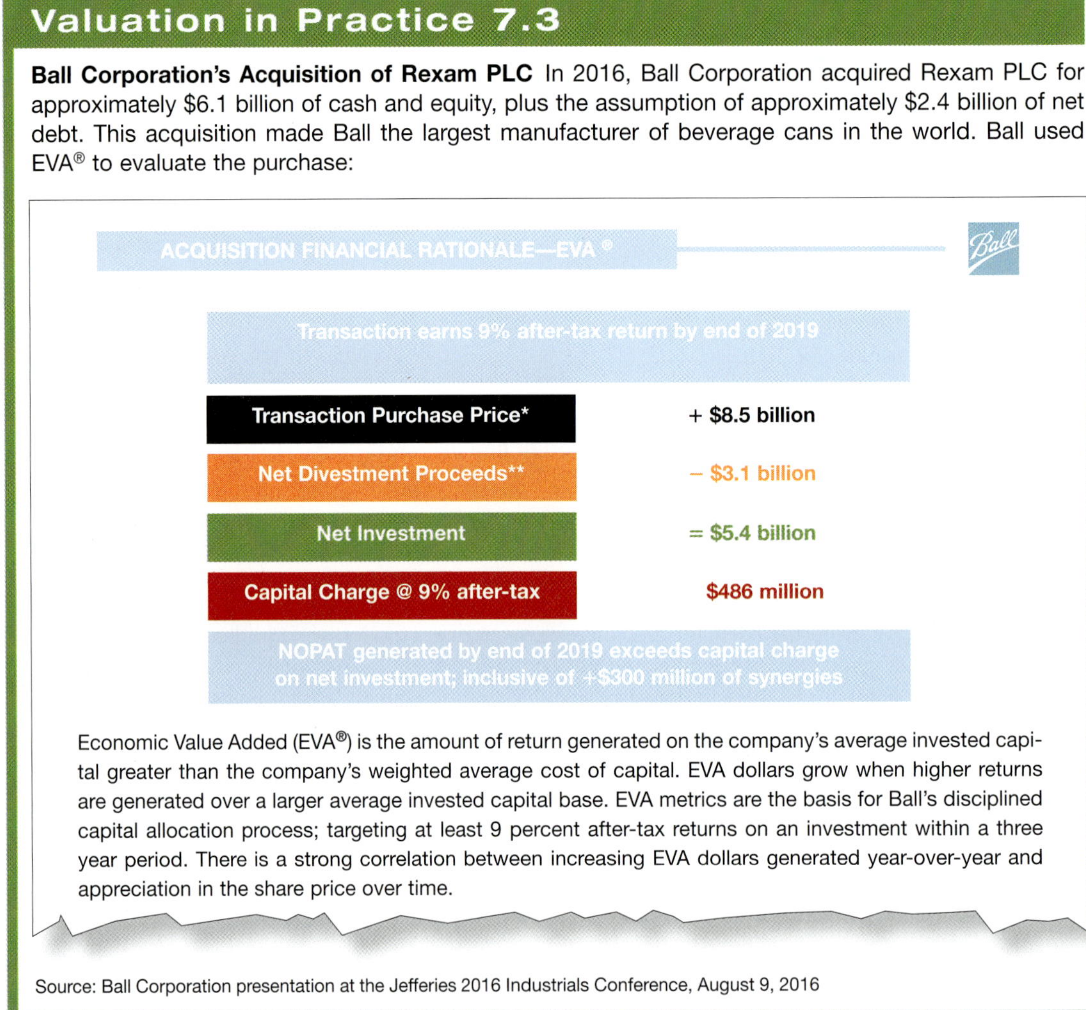

Source: Ball Corporation presentation at the Jefferies 2016 Industrials Conference, August 9, 2016

We measure the company's required earnings and unlevered excess earnings in the top panel of Exhibit 7.5. The only difference between this calculation and the calculation for the WACC form of the excess earnings model (Exhibits 7.3 and 7.4) is the required return. The unlevered earnings and total invested capital in this exhibit are the same as in Exhibit 7.3; thus, the only difference in the calculation of excess unlevered earnings is the cost of capital. We use the unlevered cost of capital for the APV form of the model and weighted average cost of capital for the WACC form of the model. Since the unlevered cost of capital is higher than the weighted average cost of capital, the excess earnings are smaller in the APV form of the model relative to the WACC form of the model.

EXHIBIT 7.5 Excess Earnings Adjusted Present Value Valuation—Dennis Keller, Inc.

(\$ in thousands)	Year 1	Year 2	Year 3	Year 4
Unlevered net income	\$ 3,180	\$ 3,660	\$ 3,610	\$ 3,718
Beginning of year total invested capital	\$27,100	\$29,100	\$29,475	\$30,359
Unlevered cost of capital	12.00%	12.00%	12.00%	12.00%
Required unlevered net income	\$ 3,252	\$ 3,492	\$ 3,537	\$ 3,643
Unlevered excess earnings	–\$ 72	\$ 168	\$ 73	\$ 75

continued

continued from previous page

APV Valuation	Year 0	Year 1	Year 2	Year 3	CV_{Firm} Year 3
Unlevered excess earnings for continuing value					$ 75
Discount factor for continuing value					11.111
Unlevered excess earnings and continuing value . . .		−$ 72	$ 168	$ 73	$ 835
Discount factor (unlevered cost of capital).		0.893	0.797	0.712	0.712
Present value		−$ 64	$ 134	$ 52	$ 594
Present value of unlevered excess earnings	$ 716				
Book value of total invested capital	27,100				
Value of the unlevered firm.	$27,816				
Value of interest tax shields	6,200				
Value of the firm	$34,015				

Exhibit may contain small rounding errors

In the bottom panel of the exhibit, we measure the value of the firm using the APV form of the model by calculating the value of the unlevered firm and adding the value of the interest tax shields. We measure the value of the interest tax shields in the same way we measured them in Chapter 5, but we do not show that calculation in this chapter. We discount each year's unlevered excess earnings at the unlevered cost of capital to measure the value of the company's unlevered excess earnings as of the end of Year 0, which equals $716. We add that amount to the book value of the company's total invested capital at the end of Year 0 to measure the company's unlevered value of $27,816, which is the same valuation we calculated in Chapter 5 (Exhibit 5.14). To measure the value of the firm, we add the value of the interest tax shields—measured in Chapter 5 (Exhibit 5.14)—to the value of the unlevered firm, yielding a firm value of $34,015, which is equal to the APV DCF valuation in Chapter 5 (Exhibit 5.14).

REVIEW EXERCISE 7.4

Adjusted Present Value Form of the Excess Earnings Model

Use the income statement, balance sheet, and free cash flow forecasts, and other information in Review Exercise 7.3 for State Line Farm, Inc., to value the firm as of the end of Year 0 using the APV form of the excess earnings model.

Solution on pages 322–323.

7.5 THE EQUITY DISCOUNTED EXCESS EARNINGS MODEL

LO3 Measure equity value using the equity form of the excess earnings model

If implemented correctly, the equity excess earnings valuation method results in the same equity valuation as the WACC or APV forms of the DCF models. To measure the value of a company's equity using the equity excess earnings valuation method, we discount both the company's excess earnings to the common equityholders and the continuing value of its equity excess earnings—at its equity cost of capital—and add the book value of its common equity, BVE, as of the valuation date. Excess earnings to common equityholders is equal to earnings available to common (earnings after preferred dividends) minus required earnings, calculated as the book value of the common equity as of the beginning of the period multiplied by the equity cost of capital ($E_t - r_E \times BVE_{t-1}$). Equation 7.6 is the general formula for the equity excess earnings valuation method using a constant growth perpetuity formula to measure the continuing value of the excess earnings.

$$V_E = BVE_0 + \sum_{t=1}^{C} \frac{E_t - r_E \times BVE_{t-1}}{(1+r_E)^t} + \frac{E_{C+1} - r_E \times BVE_C}{r_E - g} \times \frac{1}{(1+r_E)^C} \quad \textbf{(7.6)}$$

Again, an alternative way to measure the continuing value of the company's equity excess earnings is to separately measure the company's continuing equity value, CV_E, based on perhaps a market multiple or some other method, and subtract the book value of its equity as of the continuing value date.

$$V_E = BVE_0 + \sum_{t=1}^{C} \frac{E_t - r_E \times BVE_{t-1}}{(1+r_E)^t} + \frac{CV_{E,C} - BVE_C}{(1+r_E)^C} \quad (7.7)$$

In both of the above formulas, we could alternatively compute excess earnings every year by taking the difference between the return on equity (net income available to common divided by beginning-of-period book value of equity) and the equity cost of capital and multiply the difference by the beginning-of-period book value of common equity.

In Chapter 5, we discussed the calculations we need to perform in order to use the Equity DCF valuation method in both the constant target capital structure and changing capital structure valuation contexts. As discussed, the Equity DCF method is difficult to implement directly; either the cost of equity capital is changing each period when the capital structure proportions are not constant, or the implied debt levels—and hence, the interest tax shields and thus, equity free cash flows—are not readily apparent if the capital structure proportions are constant. The same issues arise when implementing the equity excess earnings valuation method.

To implement the equity excess earnings valuation method correctly, we forecast both the income statement and balance sheet in order to measure the company's excess earnings to common equityholders. Earnings to common equityholders and the book value of common equity are directly affected by a company's capital structure. To measure earnings to common equityholders, we deduct after-tax interest and preferred stock dividends from unlevered earnings based on the assumed capital structure strategy. Thus, the earnings forecasts will not be the correct forecasts for use in an equity excess earnings valuation unless they match the assumptions about the capital structure of the firm.

Valuation in Practice 7.4

Morgan Stanley's Residual Income Valuation of Samsung SDI Samsung SDI is a South Korean manufacturer of the rechargeable batteries for the IT industry, automobiles, energy storage systems, and materials used to produce semiconductors, displays, and solar panels. In 2016, Morgan Stanley used the residual income valuation method to value SDI (currency amounts in South Korean Won, ₩):

> **Intrinsic value, based on a residual income (RI) methodology:** Under our RI model, we value Samsung SDI at ₩86,076 for 2016 (₩100,347 previously). In this methodology, we value the stock as a function of its equity plus the present value of net profit generated in excess of the company's cost of equity. We discount the excess returns, or residual income, back to determine their value today. Our residual income valuation model assumes a terminal growth rate of 3%, cost of equity of 11.5% and a beta of 1.0 (all unchanged). . . .

A summary of Morgan Stanley's residual income valuation appears below:

Summary of Morgan Stanley's Residual Income Model (currency amounts in South Korean Won, ₩)

FY Ending Dec. 31	2016E	2017E	2018E	2019E	2020E	2021E	2022E	2023E	2024E	2025E
Forecast Period:										
Total equity (₩ billions)	11,366	11,496	11,691	12,322	12,929	13,595	14,246	14,929	15,661	16,445
Return on average equity	1.9%	1.4%	2.2%	6.3%	7.5%	8.6%	9.1%	9.5%	10.1%	10.5%
Spread [Return on average equity $-r_E$, 11.5%]	−9.6%	−10.1%	−9.3%	−5.2%	−4.0%	−2.9%	−2.4%	−2.0%	−1.4%	−1.0%
Residual income (₩ billions)	−1,084	−1,150	−1,079	−628	−504	−387	−340	−294	−218	−163
PV of forecast period (₩ billions)	−4,454									
Continuing Value:										
Cost of equity	11.50%									
Terminal growth rate	3.0%									
Terminal value multiple	12.12									
Continuing value spread	−12.98%									
PV of continuing value (₩ billions)	−741									
Valuation:										
PV of forecast period (₩ billions)	−4,454									
PV of continuing value (₩ billions)	−741									
Beginning equity capital (₩ billions)	11,253									
Total equity value (₩ billions)	6,058									
No. of common shares (millions)	70.4									
Projected price (EOY)(₩)	86,076									

Source: Morgan Stanley Research, "EV Batteries More Hype than Opportunity," June 2, 2016.

Valuation Key 7.3

Just like the DCF valuation method, there are three different forms of the excess earnings valuation model: the weighted average cost of capital form, the adjusted present value form, and the equity excess earnings form. Properly implemented, all three techniques provide consistent valuations. In addition, all three forms of the excess earnings valuation models have the same advantages and disadvantages as their DCF counterparts.

If we assume a constant proportionate target capital structure in our valuation—the valuation context when we typically use the WACC valuation method—our initial forecasts of the company's debt and book value of equity will likely not reflect the constant target capital structure ratios correctly. Usually, to measure the earnings to common equityholders and the book value of common equity that are consistent with the constant target capital structure ratio assumption, we measure the value of the firm in each year first. If we know the value of the firm in each year, we can use the assumed target capital structure to measure the amounts of non-common equity financing and update the forecasts with these new amounts (see Chapter 5 and the Keller example). This allows us to update our forecasts for earnings to common equityholders and the book value of common equity for the assumed capital structure strategy. If instead, we have forecasts of the amount of debt—the valuation context when we typically use the APV valuation method—the equity cost of capital will vary over time, so we must value the firm every period to compute the varying cost of equity capital (again, see Chapter 5 and the Keller example).

Dennis Keller, Inc. Revisited—Equity Discounted Excess Earnings Form of the Model

We can use the equity discounted excess earnings form of the model for both the Keller 20% debt and \$20 million debt capital structures strategies we examined in the previous two sections of the chapter. However, just as required for the Equity DCF valuations in Chapter 5, we cannot use the equity form of the excess earnings model for either capital structure unless we know the value of the firm in every period. For the 20% debt capital structure, we know the equity cost of capital, 13%, which is constant in all years. We cannot, however, forecast earnings to equity, dividends, or retained earnings, unless we know the value of the firm in each year. Once we know the value of the firm each year, we can forecast the amount of non-common equity securities, interest and preferred dividend payments, other cash flows to or from non-common equity securities, common equity dividends, and retained earnings. For the \$20 million capital structure, we have forecasts of the amount of non-common equity securities, interest and preferred dividend payments, other cash flows to or from non-common equity securities, common equity dividends, and retained earnings. We do not, however, know the equity cost of capital, which changes each year as the capital structure ratios change. Once we know the value of the firm in each year, we can measure the equity cost of capital in each year.

20% Debt Capital Structure Strategy. For the capital structure strategy based on constant capital structure ratios (20% debt and 80% equity), we know the equity cost of capital is 13%. The original forecasts, however, are based on a capital structure with \$2,000 of debt with an 8% interest rate. The \$2,000 debt capital structure—not the 20% debt capital structure—is the basis of the common equity balances (on the balance sheet) and the net income (on the income statements) in the original forecasts in Exhibit 7.1. In order to use the equity discounted excess earnings method we recalculate the forecasts based on the 20% debt capital structure as follows. We calculate the value of the firm in each year using the WACC valuation method, measure the amount of debt the company will have outstanding (20% of the firm value), measure the amount of interest paid in each year (see Exhibit 5.9), and then measure both the common equity balance and the company's net income in each year. We present these calculations in Exhibit 7.6, using information from Chapter 5.

We begin these calculations with a restatement of the common equity balance. The 20% debt capital structure strategy has \$6,000 of debt outstanding at the end of Year 0, because the value of the firm is equal to \$30,000 at the end of Year 0 (\$6,000 = 0.2 × \$30,000). We calculate the amount of debt outstanding each year in the same way. We measure the value of the firm each year using our WACC valuation method, which we discussed in Chapter 5. Since the book value of the assets is unchanged by the capital structure strategy, the initial book value of the common equity (based on \$6,000 of debt) is equal to the book value of the total assets of \$27,100 less the \$6,000 of debt (\$21,100 = \$27,100 − \$6,000). We use this value as the beginning book value of the common equity based on the 20% capital structure, which we calculate two ways in Exhibit 7.2. Net income for this capital structure is equal to the year's unlevered income minus after-tax interest. We know the unlevered income from the original forecasts. Interest is equal to the outstanding debt balance multiplied by the interest rate. The interest tax shield is equal to interest multiplied by the income tax rate. In Year 1, unlevered earnings are \$3,180. Interest expense is equal to 8% of the \$6,000 in debt outstanding as of the beginning of the year (\$480), and the interest tax shield is equal to 40% of the interest (\$192). Thus, net income to common equity in this year is equal to \$2,892 (\$2,892 = \$3,180 − \$480 + \$192). We measure the required equity earnings as the beginning book value of equity multiplied by the equity cost of capital (\$2,743 = \$21,100 × 0.13). We measure excess equity earnings as the difference between the actual equity earnings and the expected common equity earnings (\$149 = \$2,892 − \$2,743).

To calculate the book value of common equity in subsequent years, we add the beginning balance of the book value of the common equity for that year to net income and subtract the common equity dividends. The common equity dividends equal unlevered free cash flow minus interest paid plus the interest tax shield minus the change in debt (Exhibit 5.11). We continue these calculations for each year in our forecasts.

EXHIBIT 7.6 Equity Excess Earnings—20% Debt and 80% Equity Capital Structure Strategy

DENNIS KELLER, INC.
(20% Debt Capital Structure Strategy)
Equity Excess Earnings Valuation

Growth rate for free cash flow for continuing value			3.0%		
Equity cost of capital			13.0%		
(\$ in thousands)	**Year 0**	**Year 1**	**Year 2**	**Year 3**	**Year 4**
Restated Earnings and Common Equity for 20% Debt Capital Structure					
Book value of total assets	\$27,100				
Debt based on 20% debt to value	6,000				
Book value of equity	\$21,100				
Unlevered net income		\$ 3,180	\$ 3,660	\$ 3,610	\$ 3,718
Interest expense*		−480	−515	−522	−537
Interest tax shield*		192	206	209	215
Net income to common equity		\$ 2,892	\$ 3,351	\$ 3,297	\$ 3,396
Net income to common equity		\$ 2,892	\$ 3,351	\$ 3,297	\$ 3,396
Common equity at beginning of year		21,100	22,654	22,954	23,643
Common equity dividends (equity free cash flow, Exhibit 5.11)		−1,338	−3,051	−2,608	−2,687
Total common equity	\$21,100	\$ 22,654	\$ 22,954	\$ 23,643	\$ 24,352
Total common equity at beginning of year		21,100	22,654	22,954	23,643
Common equity cost of capital		13.0%	13.0%	13.0%	13.0%
Required net income to common equity		\$ 2,743	\$ 2,945	\$ 2,984	\$ 3,074
Excess earnings to common equity		\$ 149	\$ 406	\$ 313	\$ 322

* Based on the WACC valuation, see Exhibit 5.9.

In Exhibit 7.7, we discount the excess equity earnings at the 13% equity cost of capital. The discounted value of the excess equity earnings is \$2,900. We add the beginning book value of common equity of \$21,100 to the discounted value of the excess equity earnings in order to measure a value of common equity of \$24,000, which agrees with our post-recapitalization DCF valuation of the equity.

EXHIBIT 7.7 Discounted Equity Excess Earnings—20% Debt Capital Structure Strategy—Dennis Keller, Inc.

($ in thousands)	Year 0	Year 1	Year 2	Year 3	CV_{Equity} Year 3
Excess equity earnings for continuing value					$ 322
Discount factor for continuing value					10.000
Excess equity earnings and continuing value		$ 149	$ 406	$ 313	$ 3,223
Discount factor.		0.885	0.783	0.693	0.693
Present value		$ 132	$ 318	$ 217	$ 2,234
Present value of excess equity earnings	$ 2,900				
Book value of equity.	21,100				
Value of the equity	$24,000				

Exhibit may contain small rounding errors

$20 Million Debt Capital Structure Strategy. For the $20 million debt capital structure strategy, we know the common equity balances and the net incomes in the $20 million debt capital structure-based forecasts are correct (Exhibit 5.12). However, we do not know the equity cost of capital based on this capital structure strategy, because we do not know the debt ratios (stated in terms of market values) for this capital structure strategy. To measure the equity cost of capital, we measure the value of the firm in each year, subtract the value of the outstanding debt to measure the value of the equity in each year, and then measure the company's resulting capital structure ratios in order to measure the company's equity cost of capital in each year. We measured the equity cost of capital in this way in Chapter 5 (Exhibit 5.16).

We present this valuation in Exhibit 7.8. This valuation has the same format as the previous valuation. However, here, we use the book value of the common equity and the net income from the CFO's forecasts of the $20 million debt capital structure strategy (Exhibit 5.12), and we use the changing equity cost of capital that results from the $20 million debt capital structure strategy (Exhibit 5.16). The total common equity is equal to the total invested capital less the value of the debt or the common equity plus retained earnings from Exhibit 5.12. Since the equity cost of capital is changing each year, the discount factor for each year is a cumulative multiplicative factor based upon the annual equity costs of capital for years 1 through N, where N is the period discounted; for example, the Year 3 discount factor of 0.648 $= 1/[(1 + 0.163) \times (1 + 0.157) \times (1 + 0.148)]$. The resulting value of the common equity of $14,015 equals the value of the firm of $34,015 from Exhibit 7.5 less the value of the debt of $20,000.

EXHIBIT 7.8 Discounted Equity Excess Earnings—$20 Million Debt Capital Structure Strategy—Dennis Keller, Inc.

($ in thousands)		Year 1	Year 2	Year 3	Year 4
Net income to common equity.		$2,100	$2,585	$ 2,655	$ 2,859
Total common equity at beginning of year.		$7,100	$9,200	$11,785	$14,440
Common equity cost of capital		16.3%	15.7%	14.8%	14.2%
Required net income to common equity		$1,156	$1,441	$ 1,746	$ 2,051
Excess earnings to common equity.		$ 944	$1,144	$ 909	$ 807
Equity cost of capital		16.3%	15.7%	14.8%	14.2%
	Year 0	**Year 1**	**Year 2**	**Year 3**	**CV_{Equity} Year 3**
Excess equity earnings for continuing value					$ 807
Discount factor for continuing value					8.923
Excess equity earnings and continuing value . . .		$ 944	$ 1,144	$ 909	$ 7,202
Discount factor.		0.860	0.744	0.648	0.648
Present value		$ 812	$ 851	$ 588	$ 4,664
Present value of excess equity earnings	$ 6,915				
Book value of equity	7,100				
Value of the equity	$14,015				

Exhibit may contain small rounding errors

REVIEW EXERCISE 7.5

Equity Discounted Excess Earnings Model

Use the income statement, balance sheet, and free cash flow forecasts, and other information in Review Exercise 7.3 for State Line Farm, Inc., to value the company's equity as of the end of Year 0 using the equity discounted excess earnings model.

Solution on pages 323–324.

7.6 POSSIBLE INFORMATION ADVANTAGES OF THE EXCESS EARNINGS VALUATION METHOD

LO4 Learn about adjustments to earnings and invested capital to evaluate performance and measure "economic earnings"

Since the DCF-based and excess-earnings-based valuations are identical, the only potential advantages the excess earnings valuation method may have over the DCF-based valuation method are that it requires fewer forecast inputs, or that it is easier to implement, or that it provides different information. As we have seen in this chapter, the inputs are essentially the same for the DCF-based and excess-earnings-based models, and both approaches are equally easy (or difficult) to implement; thus, the potential advantages of the excess-earnings-based models, if any, must be informational. This appears to be the major motivation for consultants and managers who use excess-earnings-based models.

Indeed, the commercialized forms of the excess flow models make adjustments to both earnings figures and book values in an attempt to make the excess earnings calculated even more informative with respect to deciding whether a manager creates value for a firm in a given period. The commercialized forms are often implemented for use in compensation systems for managers. The intuition for these models is simple. Given an investment that the firm has made (as measured by the accounting system with some modifications), did the managers generate cash flows or earnings during the current period (again, as measured by the accounting system with some modifications) that exceeded the cash flow or earnings required based on the amount of invested capital and the cost of capital? That is, did they generate excess flows or excess earnings? If they did, the firm's investment has added value. As such, the accounting system is adjusted in order to arrive at a measure of the value delivered in a given period, which is then tied to the compensation system for managers. It is a subject of debate as to how close these measures are to a true measure of the value created in a given period, but that is the intent of these systems. Whether or not they measure value created in a period, these systems do focus on the importance of earning returns on investment in excess of a company's cost of capital. For example, G. Bennett Stewart, III, a founding partner of Stern Stewart & Company (now Stern Value Management), stated,

> EVA® [an excess earnings-based valuation method] is a practical method of estimating the economic profit that is earned, as opposed to the accounting profit. . . . It's really a finance tool for non-finance executives. Finance execs don't need EVA.[9]

Karl-Hermann Baumann, Chairman of the Supervisory Board of Siemens AG, stated,

> We tested discounted cash-flow—it was not much of a success. It is too abstract . . . too far from the current reporting system and our annual financial statements. EVA® removes the confusion, arising from the existence of the several planning measures and creates a common language for everyone—for the simple employee and for the top manager.[10]

Naturally, support for excess earnings valuation models is not unanimous. Armstrong Holdings Inc., the floor-and-ceiling materials company, replaced EVA® with a cash flow measure of performance. E. Follin Smith, CFO, gave the following reason for the switch:

[9] Taub, S., "Which Companies Created the Most Wealth for Shareholders Last Year? Enter MVA—or Market Value Added," *CFO.com* of *CFO Magazine* (July 1, 2003), http://ww2.cfo.com/strategy/2003/07/mvps-of-mva/, retrieved May 28, 2018.

[10] Stern Stewart & Company, "EVA® Implementation at Siemens AG," October 2000, at http://www.eva.com/, p. 6, available November 8, 2003 (no longer available).

> . . .because we want to reward growth and accuracy and meeting budget commitments, which EVA doesn't capture.

Valuation in Practice 7.5

Using EVA® in Compensation Contracts—Crane Co. Crane Co. is a diversified manufacturer of engineered industrial products and operates in the aerospace, engineered materials, merchandising systems, fluid handling, and controls business segments. Crane is a typical example of how companies use EVA® as a basis for compensation:

> The Company's annual incentive compensation program utilizes the principles of economic value added ("EVA"). EVA is defined as the difference between the return on total capital invested in the business (net operating profit after tax, or NOPAT, divided by total capital employed) and the cost of capital, multiplied by total capital employed. . . .
>
> The Committee believes that, compared to such common performance measures as return on capital, return on equity, growth in earnings per share and growth in cash flow, EVA has the highest correlation with the creation of value for shareholders over the long term. . . . Awards are generally uncapped to provide maximum incentive to create value and, because awards may be positive or negative, executives can incur penalties when value is reduced.
>
> . . . Thus, the EVA formula requires the executive to focus on improvement in the Company's balance sheet as well as the income statement. Awards are calculated on the basis of year end results, and award formulas utilize both a percentage of the change in EVA from the prior year, whether positive or negative, and a percentage of the positive EVA, if any, in the current year. EVA awards are calculated for the Company as a whole for the corporate executives.

Source: Crane's DEF 14A (Proxy Statement) filing with the U.S. SEC, dated March 7, 2003.

Adjustments to Earnings and Book Value to Estimate "Economic Earnings"

As we just discussed, various consulting companies have commercialized the excess earnings valuation model. The commercialized versions adjust accounting earnings and invested capital in an attempt to provide more economic content to the measures of excess earnings and the excess return on capital. They adjust both the calculation of the investment and the measure of earnings, affecting the calculation of the required earnings, actual earnings, and therefore the excess earnings.[11]

We sometimes see the term "economic earnings" when reading about these models. The concept of economic earnings to which such writings refer is not the same concept that economists use when using this term. Most economists discuss **economic earnings** in terms of the cash flow distribution plus the change in the value of an investment (or capital gains)—that is, the value you can consume during a period that will make you as well off at the end of the period as you were at the beginning of the period.[12] It is possible to use any valuation method that is consistent with the DCF valuation models to measure economic earnings as economists define it. We would measure economic earnings for a period as the difference in the valuations at two different points in time plus any cash distribution to the investor. When we read about economic earnings in practice, the authors are typically referring to an improved measurement of investments or returns relative to that normally measured by the accounting system. By devising a series of adjustments to the financial statements, consultants attempt to create excess earnings that have more economic content.

[11] See Myers (1996, 1997) for a discussion of how companies are adopting these approaches and choosing among them; Myers, R., "Metric Wars," *CFO: The Magazine for Senior Financial Executives* vol. 12, no. 10 (October 1996), pp. 41–50; Myers, R., "Measure for Measure," *CFO: The Magazine for Senior Financial Executives* vol. 13, no. 11 (November 1997), pp. 41–50.

[12] For seminal work on this topic, see Hicks (1938), who was awarded the Nobel Prize in economics in 1972; Hicks, J. R., *Value and Capital*, Oxford: Clarendon Press (1938), reprinted in Parker, R. H., G. C. Harcourt, and G. Whittington, eds., *Readings in the Concept and Measurement of Income*, 2nd ed., Deddington, Oxon.: Philip Allan, (1986).

Consultants and analysts implementing the commercialized forms of the excess earnings valuation method generally make two types of adjustments to a company's financial statements. The first type of adjustment affects the beginning balance of the balance sheet. These adjustments typically adjust the beginning balance of the balance sheet for the effect of some previous income statement adjustments. For example, they may partially capitalize prior research and development (R&D) expenditures instead of treating them as being expensed when incurred. The second type of adjustment affects the income statement in current and subsequent years and therefore affects the ending balances of the balance sheet in current and subsequent years. For example, they might continue to capitalize future R&D expenditures and then amortize the capitalized value of the R&D over time.

The goal of the adjustments to the income statement and balance sheet is to make the adjusted earnings and book value more closely reflect the determinants of the changes in firm value.[13] While these adjustments may be important in compensation contracts or for measuring performance in a particular year (see Valuation in Practice 7.5), they do not affect the value of the firm or equity we measure based on any of the excess earnings valuation methods. The mechanics of the excess earnings valuation method adjust the calculations to measure the same value, irrespective of the accounting rules used, as long as earnings are comprehensive.

As shown previously in Valuation in Practice 7.3, Ball Corporation uses EVA® to evaluate acquisitions. The Chairman, President and Chief Executive Officer of Ball Corporation, Mr. Hoover also manages the company "down to the plant floor" using EVA®.[14]

> . . . in the early 1990s, we really implemented a program where next year's [EVA®] target for incentive purposes was half the distance between last year's target and last year's actual. So if you are improving that, it means you have to get better every year if you want to make any money. And funny enough, that has a hell of a nice correlation to creating shareholder value. We have seen the market cap of the company go from about $1 billion eight years ago to roughly $5.5 billion today and the enterprise value grow even a little more. . . .
>
> . . . We talk a lot about this idea of behaving as an owner in the company. It is one of our five keys to success and we highlight those behaviors when they occur. We run the EVA incentive plan down to the plant floor. With the beverage can plants in North America, the non-union ones, they are on the same incentive process that I am on. People understand that when you invest money you have to make a return in excess of your cost of capital and if we do that, we create value.

Potential Adjustments for Implementing the Excess Earnings Model

Consultants attempting to implement the excess earnings model for use in, say, a compensation plan must use their best judgment as to how to adjust a company's financial statements. Regardless of the specific adjustments, they typically adjust both the income statement and the balance sheet (beginning and subsequent balances). It is important to adjust the initial balances of the balance sheet, for that is the base used to measure required earnings. In Exhibit 7.9, we summarize some of the types of adjustments a consultant considers making when implementing the excess earnings model.[15]

[13] Whether or not EVA® accomplishes this goal is an empirical issue. For a review of the literature examining this issue, see Biddle, Gary, R. Bowen, and J. Wallace, "Evidence on EVA®," *Journal of Applied Corporate Finance* (Summer 1999), pp. 8–18. The general conclusion is that these adjustments do provide some additional information related to stock price changes.

[14] *The Wall Street Transcript* interview of R. David Hoover, Chairman, President and Chief Executive Officer of Ball Corporation, May 19, 2008.

[15] For a more detailed discussion of these adjustments, see Stewart, G. B. III, "Accounting Is Broken—Here's How to Fix It—A Radical Manifesto," *EVAluation* vol. 5, no. 1 (September 2002), available on June 4, 2018, at http://www.public.asu.edu/~bac524/acctgbroken.pdf; and Young, D., and S. O'Byrne, *EVA and Value-Based Management*, New York: McGraw-Hill (2001), especially Chapter 6.

EXHIBIT 7.9 Possible Income Statement and Balance Sheet Adjustments When Implementing Excess Earnings Valuation Models

	Possible Issue	Possible Adjustments
1.	Management stock options	If company does not expense these options, then expense the value of the options when issued.
2.	Income taxes	Either eliminate or use present value tools to recalculate deferred income taxes. If eliminated, then income tax expense is equal to income taxes paid (other than a short-term income taxes payable).
3.	Research and development	Capitalize expenditures on the balance sheet and amortize when used in future years.
4.	Depreciation (amortization and depletion)	Adjust depreciation to reflect depreciation deducted for income tax purposes or adjust to better reflect economic depreciation (actual loss in value).
5.	Goodwill	If directly written off against equity, reverse write-off and amortize over useful life. If capitalized and amortized, use appropriate amortization period that reflects economic life.
6.	Expense accruals	Either eliminate or adjust expense accrual to reflect actual economic situation—examples include accruals for warranties, allowance for uncollectible accounts, and loan loss reserves.
7.	Pensions	Adjust value of pension assets and pension liabilities to reflect market values; adjust pension expense for cash flow or actual economic cost to company.
8.	Off-balance-sheet financing	Capitalize off-balance-sheet financing instruments—for example, operating leases and special-purpose vehicles, recognizing an expense based on the capitalized value.
9.	Restructuring charges and other write-downs	Capitalize expense on the balance sheet and amortize over the original life of the assets (and liabilities) restructured.
10.	Accounting for mergers	Reverse any excess expense accruals recorded as part of the merger; if an old merger was recorded using the pooling-of-interests (recorded merger using book values) method, restate to purchase (market value at date of transaction) method.
11.	Successful efforts oil & gas accounting	Capitalize exploration-related expenditures on the balance sheet and amortize when used in future years.
12.	Inventory accounting	Restate inventory on the balance sheet to reflect current value; for example, eliminate LIFO reserve by increasing inventory value and adjusting cost of goods sold.

It is important to remember that these adjustments would not change the amount of income taxes paid by the company because the adjustments would not change what the company reports to the taxing authority. Also, since these adjustments are accounting accruals and not cash flows, they do not affect any of the company's cash flows.

SUMMARY AND KEY CONCEPTS

In this chapter we learned how to implement excess earnings valuation models. We discussed the WACC and APV forms of the excess earnings model based on unlevered earnings and the equity excess earnings valuation model based on earnings available to common shareholders. All of these forms of the excess earnings valuation model yield the same valuation as their DCF counterparts if they are consistently implemented. In addition, we have seen that the advantages and disadvantages of each of the forms of the excess earnings valuation methods are the same as those of their DCF counterparts.

ADDITIONAL READING AND REFERENCES

Lundholm, R., and T. O'Keefe, "Reconciling Value Estimates from the Discounted Cash Flow Model and the Residual Income Model," *Contemporary Accounting Research* 18 (Summer 2001), pp. 311–335.

Ohlson, J. A., "Earnings, Book Values and Dividends in Equity Valuation," *Contemporary Accounting Research* vol. 11, no. 2 (1995), pp. 661–688.

EXERCISES AND PROBLEMS

P7.1 **Excess Earnings Valuation—Two-Year Investment Life—The One-Shot Tee-Shirt Company:** At the end of Year 0, an investor creates a company by investing $1,500 in cash for stock, and the company uses all of the cash to buy t-shirts (inventory). At the end of Year 1, the company sells the t-shirts to a vendor for $2,420 but does not collect the revenue in cash until the end of Year 2. At the end of Year 2, the company liquidates itself by paying a liquidating dividend. The company has no operating expenses other than those related to the inventory (cost of goods sold) and does not pay income taxes. We show the company's income statement and balance sheet forecasts in Exhibit P7.1. For all parts of this problem, assume a discount rate of 10%.

EXHIBIT P7.1 Income Statement and Balance Sheet Forecasts for the One-Shot Tee-Shirt Company

ONE-SHOT TEE-SHIRT COMPANY Income Statement and Balance Sheet	Year 0	Year 1	Year 2
Income Statement			
Revenue		$2,420	$ 0
Expenses		-1,500	0
Earnings		$ 920	$ 0
Balance Sheet			
Cash	$ 0	$ 0	$ 0
Receivable	0	2,420	0
Inventory (t-shirts)	1,500	0	0
Total assets	$1,500	$2,420	$ 0
Common stock	$1,500	$1,500	$1,500
Retained earnings		920	-1,500
Total equities	$1,500	$2,420	$ 0

a. Value the company as of the end of Year 0 using the discounted cash flow valuation model.
b. Value the company as of the end of Year 0 using the excess cash flow valuation method.
c. Value the company as of the end of Year 0 using the residual earnings valuation method.

P7.2 **Excess Earnings Valuation with an Intangible Asset—Two-Year Investment Life—The One-Shot Tee-Shirt Company:** At the end of Year 0, an investor creates a company by investing $1,500 in cash for stock, and the company uses all of the cash to buy t-shirts (inventory). The company also issues $200 of stock to another investor who gave the company a customer list (the name of the vendor). The company records a $200 intangible asset at the end of Year 0 for this transaction. At the end of Year 1, the company sells the t-shirts to a vendor for $2,420 but does not collect the revenue in cash until the end of Year 2. At the end of Year 2, the company liquidates itself by paying a liquidating dividend. The company has no operating expenses other than those related to the inventory (cost of goods sold) and does not pay income taxes. We show the company's income statement and balance sheet forecasts in Exhibit P7.2. For all parts of this problem, assume a discount rate of 10%.

EXHIBIT P7.2 Income Statement and Balance Sheet Forecasts for the One-Shot Tee-Shirt Company with an Intangible Asset

ONE-SHOT TEE-SHIRT COMPANY Balance Sheet and Income Statement	Year 0	Year 1	Year 2
Income Statement			
Revenue		$2,420	$ 0
Amortization of intangible		−100	−100
Expenses		−1,500	0
Earnings		$ 820	−$ 100
Balance Sheet			
Cash	$ 0	$ 0	$ 0
Receivable	0	2,420	0
Inventory (t-shirts)	1,500	0	0
Intangible asset	200	100	0
Total assets	$1,700	$2,520	$ 0
Common stock	$1,700	$1,700	$1,700
Retained earnings		820	−1,700
Total equities	$1,700	$2,520	$ 0

a. Value the company as of the end of Year 0 using the discounted cash flow valuation model.
b. Value the company as of the end of Year 0 using the excess cash flow valuation method.
c. Value the company as of the end of Year 0 using the residual earnings valuation method.

P7.3 **Adjusted Present Value Form of the Excess Earnings Valuation Method—Joel Germunder Company (see Problem 5.6):** Use the information and exhibits in Problem 5.6 for the Joel Germunder Company to answer the questions in this problem.

a. Use the adjusted present value form of the excess earnings valuation method to value the Joel Germunder Company (the entire firm and the equity).
b. Use the equity excess earnings form of the excess earnings model to value the common equity of the company.

P7.4 **Weighted Average Cost of Capital Form of the Excess Earnings Valuation Method—Joel Germunder Company (see Problem 5.7):** Use the information and exhibits in Problem 5.7 for the Joel Germunder Company to answer the questions in this problem.

a. Use the weighted average cost of capital form of the excess earnings valuation method to value Germunder and Company (the entire firm and the equity).
b. Use the equity excess earnings form of the excess earnings model to value the common equity of the company.

P7.5 **Weighted Average Cost of Capital Form of the Excess Earnings Valuation Method—B. Stewart Company:** A small group of equity investors plans to start the B. Stewart Company (Stewart). The company needs $10.33 million in initial financing to start the company and another $2.22 million in the second year. The investors arranged for an initial debt financing of $6 million and another $1 million in the following year, all with a 10% cost of debt (interest rate). The equity investors plan to initially invest $4.33 million and $1.22 million in the following year.

The investors hired a consultant to prepare forecasts for the company and to then value it. The forecasts of the company's income statement and balance sheet appear in Exhibit P7.3, and the forecasts of free cash flow appear in Exhibit P7.4. These exhibits show detailed forecasts for the first four years of the company's life. The company's income tax rate is 30% for all taxable income items. The investors believe that beginning in Year 4, the company will grow at the expected long-run inflation rate, which is 3% and that the debt will grow at the same rate from then on as well. Based on an analysis of both comparable companies and other information, the investors concluded that the company's unlevered cost of capital is 12%. Based on the analysis used to measure the company's unlevered cost of capital, the investors concluded that companies similar to Stewart have a target capital structure of one-third debt. The investors asked their valuation consultant to value Stewart using this target capital structure. The valuation consultant explained that the financing in the forecasts might not be consistent with the target capital structure, so they might have to revisit the financing assumptions after the valuation of

Stewart using the WACC based method. Assume that regardless of the capital structure strategy, interest tax shields are valued at the unlevered cost of capital.

EXHIBIT P7.3 Income Statement and Balance Sheet Forecasts for the B. Stewart Company

B. STEWART CORPORATION
Income Statement and Balance Sheet Forecasts

	Actual	Forecast			
($ in thousands)	**Year 0**	**Year 1**	**Year 2**	**Year 3**	**Year 4**
Income Statement					
Revenue		$10,000	$15,000	$17,250	$17,768
Operating expenses		−6,000	−9,000	−10,350	−10,661
Amortization		−500	−500	0	0
Depreciation expense		−833	−1,333	−1,654	−1,704
Earnings before interest and taxes		$ 2,667	$ 4,167	$ 5,246	$ 5,403
Interest expense		−600	−700	−700	−700
Income before taxes		$ 2,067	$ 3,467	$ 4,546	$ 4,703
Income tax expense		−620	−1,040	−1,364	−1,411
Net income		$ 1,447	$ 2,427	$ 3,182	$ 3,292
Balance Sheet					
Cash	$ 1,000	$ 1,000	$ 1,500	$ 1,725	$ 1,777
Inventory	1,000	3,000	4,500	5,175	5,330
Total current assets	$ 2,000	$ 4,000	$ 6,000	$ 6,900	$ 7,107
Intangible asset	1,000	500	0	0	0
Property, plant, and equipment (net)	8,333	12,500	14,375	14,806	15,250
Total assets	$11,333	$17,000	$20,375	$21,706	$22,357
Accounts payable	$ 0	$ 2,000	$ 3,000	$ 3,450	$ 3,554
Debt	6,000	7,000	7,000	7,000	7,000
Equity	5,333	8,000	10,375	11,256	11,804
Total equities	$11,333	$17,000	$20,375	$21,706	$22,357

Exhibit may contain small rounding errors

EXHIBIT P7.4 Free Cash Flow Forecasts for the B. Stewart Company

B. STEWART CORPORATION
Free Cash Flow and Equity Free Cash Flow Forecasts

($ in thousands)	**Year 1**	**Year 2**	**Year 3**	**Year 4**
Earnings before interest and taxes (EBIT)	$2,667	$4,167	$5,246	$5,403
− Income taxes paid on EBIT	−800	−1,250	−1,574	−1,621
Earnings before interest and after taxes	$1,867	$2,917	$3,672	$3,782
+ Depreciation expense	833	1,333	1,654	1,704
+ Amortization expense	500	500	0	0
− Change in inventory	−2,000	−1,500	−675	−155
+ Change in accounts payable	2,000	1,000	450	104
− Change in required cash balance	0	−500	−225	−52
− Capital expenditures	−5,000	−3,208	−2,085	−2,148
Unlevered free cash flow	−$1,800	$ 542	$2,791	$3,235
− Interest paid in cash ($r_D \times V_D$)	−600	−700	−700	−700
+ Interest tax shield ($T_{INT} \times r_D \times V_D$)	180	210	210	210
+ Change in debt financing	1,000	0	0	0
Equity free cash flow	−$1,220	$ 52	$2,301	$2,745

a. Value the company using the weighted average cost of capital form of the discounted cash flow model and the company's target capital structure.

b. Value the company using the weighted average cost of capital form of the excess earnings model and the company's target capital structure.

c. Value the common equity of the company using the equity free cash flow form of the discounted cash flow model and the company's target capital structure.

d. Value the common equity of the company using the equity excess earnings form of the excess earnings model and the company's target capital structure.

7.6 **Adjusted Present Value Form of the Excess Earnings Valuation Method—B. Stewart Company:** Use the information in Problem 7.5 to respond to the questions in this problem.

a. Value the company using the adjusted present value form of the discounted cash flow model and the company's capital structure as forecasted in the exhibits and assume that the debt will grow at the long-run growth rate beginning in Year 4.

b. Value the company using the adjusted present value form of the excess earnings model and the company's capital structure as forecasted in the exhibits.

c. Value the common equity of the company using the equity free cash flow form of the discounted cash flow model and the company's capital structure as forecasted in the exhibits.

d. Value the common equity of the company using the equity excess earnings form of the excess earnings model and the company's capital structure as forecasted in the exhibits.

7.7 **Adjusting the Financial Statements for the Excess Earnings Valuation Method—The Phillip Zee Company:** The Phillip Zee Company financial statements for the first three years of its life which began as of the end of Year 0 are shown in Exhibit P7.5. The company initially recorded an intangible asset for $10,000, and amortized 50% of this intangible asset in each of the first two years of its operation. Assume the company uses equity financing only and does not pay income taxes. The company has a 10% cost of capital. Assume an analyst in devising a compensation plan decides that the intangible asset has an infinite life instead of a two-year life. In other words, the intangible asset does not decrease in value over time.

a. Measure the company's excess earnings in Years 1 through 3 using the company's financial statements.

b. Adjust the company's Year 0 through Year 3 income statements and balance sheets based on the analyst's view of the life of the intangible asset.

c. Discuss the effect that these adjustments have on the company's equity free cash flows.

d. Measure the company's excess earnings in Years 1 through 3 using the company's restated financial statements.

e. Compare the excess earnings calculated in parts *a* and *d*.

EXHIBIT P7.5 Income Statements and Balance Sheets for the Phillip Zee Company

Reported Financial Statements	Year 0	Year 1	Year 2	Year 3
Income Statement				
Revenue		$10,000	$15,000	$17,250
Operating expenses		−6,000	−9,000	−10,350
Amortization		−5,000	−5,000	
Net income		−$ 1,000	$ 1,000	$ 6,900
Balance Sheet				
Net operating working capital	$ 2,000	$ 3,000	$ 4,500	$ 5,175
Intangible asset	10,000	5,000	0	0
Total assets	$12,000	$ 8,000	$ 4,500	$ 5,175
Equity	$12,000	$ 8,000	$ 4,500	$ 5,175
Total equities	$12,000	$ 8,000	$ 4,500	$ 5,175

SOLUTIONS FOR REVIEW EXERCISES

Solution for Review Exercise 7.1: Excess Free Cash Flow Model

In the excess flow model, we calculate the value of the firm as the investment plus the present value of the discounted excess free cash flow.

$$V_0 = I_0 + \frac{FCF_1 - r \times I_0}{r} = \$10 + \frac{\$1.44 - 0.12 \times \$10}{0.12} = \$10 + \frac{\$0.24}{0.12} = \$10 + \$2 = \$12$$

We can also implement the excess flow model in a returns form, which is merely an alternative way to show the calculation of an investment's excess flow. The rate of return is equal to \$1.44 / \$10 or 14.4%.

$$V_0 = I_0 + \frac{(ER_1 - r) \times I_0}{r} = I_0 + \frac{xr_1 \times I_0}{r}$$

$$V_0 = \$10 + \frac{(0.144 - 0.12) \times \$10}{0.12} = \$10 + \frac{0.024 \times \$10}{0.12} = \$12$$

We can use the DCF valuation model to measure the value of the firm as

$$V_0 = \frac{FCF_1}{r} = \frac{\$1.44}{0.12} = \$12$$

Solution for Review Exercise 7.2: Excess Earnings Model

Instead of using the dollar investment and free cash flow, we use the book value of the investment and accounting earnings in the excess earnings model.

$$V_F = BVE_0 + \frac{E_1 - r \times BVE_0}{r}$$

$$V_F = \$11 + \frac{\$1.44 - 0.12 \times \$11}{0.12} = \$11 + \frac{\$0.12}{0.12} = \$11 + \$1 = \$12$$

The firm value of \$12 from the excess earnings model equals the firm value calculated in Review Exercise 7.1 using the excess free cash flow model.

We can also implement the excess earnings model in a returns form—the rate of return is equal to \$1.44 / \$11 or 13.09%.

$$V_0 = BVE_0 + \frac{(ER_1 - r) \times BVE_0}{r} = BVE_0 + \frac{xr_1 \times BVE_0}{r}$$

$$V_0 = \$11 + \frac{(0.1309 - 0.12) \times \$11}{0.12} = \$11 + \frac{0.0109 \times \$11}{0.12} = \$12$$

Solution for Review Exercise 7.3: Weighted Average Cost of Capital Form of the Excess Earnings Model—State Line Farm, Inc.

The equity cost of capital is equal to:

$$r_E = r_{UA} + (r_{UA} - r_D) \times \frac{V_D}{V_E} = 0.12 + (0.12 - 0.08) \times 0.5 = 0.14$$

The weighted average cost of capital is equal to:

$$r_{WACC} = r_E \times \frac{V_E}{V_F} + (1 - T_{INT}) \times r_D \times \frac{V_D}{V_F} = 0.14 \times \frac{2}{3} + 0.08 \times \frac{1}{3} \times (1 - 0.4) = 0.10933$$

The discounted cash flow WACC valuation is equal to:

($ in thousands)	Year 0	Year 1	Year 2	Year 3	CV_{Firm} Year 3
Unlevered free cash flow for continuing value					$ 1,724
Discount factor for continuing value					11.194
Unlevered free cash flow and continuing value		−$ 353	$1,170	$1,599	$19,296
Discount factor		0.901	0.813	0.733	0.733
Present value		−$ 319	$ 950	$1,172	$14,135
Value of the firm	$15,938				

Exhibit may contain small rounding errors

To use the excess earnings model, we first calculate the excess unlevered earnings:

($ in thousands)	Year 1	Year 2	Year 3	Year 4
Earnings before interest and taxes (EBIT)	$2,967	$3,180	$3,243	$3,308
Income tax rate (assuming one tax rate, T_C)	40%	40%	40%	40%
Income taxes	−$1,187	−$1,272	−$1,297	−$1,323
Unlevered earnings, UE	$1,780	$1,908	$1,946	$1,985

($ in thousands)	Year 1	Year 2	Year 3	Year 4
Total invested capital (book value) beginning balance	$ 9,833	$11,967	$12,705	$13,052
Required rate of return, r_{WACC}	10.93%	10.93%	10.93%	10.93%
Required unlevered earnings	$ 1,075	$ 1,308	$ 1,389	$ 1,427
Unlevered earnings, UE	$ 1,780	$ 1,908	$ 1,946	$ 1,985
Required unlevered earnings	1,075	1,308	1,389	1,427
Excess unlevered earnings	$ 705	$ 600	$ 557	$ 558
Return forecast (expectation)	18.1%	15.9%	15.3%	15.2%
Required rate of return	10.9%	10.9%	10.9%	10.9%
Excess return	7.2%	5.0%	4.4%	4.3%

Now we can calculate the value of the firm:

($ in thousands)	Year 0	Year 1	Year 2	Year 3	CV_{Firm} Year 3
Excess unlevered earnings for continuing value					$ 558
Discount factor for continuing value					11.194
Excess unlevered earnings and continuing value		$ 705	$ 600	$ 557	$ 6,245
Discount factor		0.901	0.813	0.733	0.733
Present value		$ 635	$ 487	$ 408	$ 4,574
Value of excess flows	$ 6,105				
Initial total invested capital	9,833				
Value of the firm	$15,938				

Exhibit may contain small rounding errors

The values of the debt and equity are 1/3 of the value of the firm ($5,313) and 2/3 of the value of the firm ($10,625), respectively. Note, this is the same value of the debt on the balance sheet as of the end of Year 0. This is not a coincidence. We created the forecasts for the company based on the target capital structure.

Solution for Review Exercise 7.4: Adjusted Present Value Form of the Excess Earnings Model—State Line Farm, Inc.

The discounted cash flow APV valuation is equal to:

($ in thousands)	Year 0	Year 1	Year 2	Year 3	CV_{Firm} Year 3
Value of the Unlevered Firm					
Unlevered free cash flow for continuing value					$ 1,724
Discount factor for continuing value					10.000
Unlevered free cash flow and continuing value		–$ 353	$1,170	$1,599	$17,238
Discount factor		0.893	0.797	0.712	0.712
Discounted value		–$ 315	$ 932	$1,138	$12,270
Value of the unlevered firm	$14,025				
Value of the Interest Tax Shields					
Interest tax shield for continuing value					$ 206
Discount factor for continuing value					10.000
Interest tax shield and continuing value of the interest tax shield		$ 170	$ 192	$ 201	$ 2,058
Discount factor		0.893	0.797	0.712	0.712
Present value		$ 152	$ 153	$ 143	$ 1,465
Value of the interest tax shields	$ 1,913				
Value of the firm	$15,938				

Exhibit may contain small rounding errors

To use the excess earnings model, we first calculate the excess unlevered earnings, which we calculated in Review Exercise 7.3. The difference in this calculation is that we use the unlevered cost of capital rather than the weighted average cost of capital.

($ in thousands)	Year 1	Year 2	Year 3	Year 4
Total invested capital (book value) beginning balance	$ 9,833	$11,967	$12,705	$13,052
Required rate of return, r_{UA}	12.00%	12.00%	12.00%	12.00%
Required unlevered earnings	$ 1,180	$ 1,436	$ 1,525	$ 1,566
Unlevered earnings (See Review Exercise 7.3)	$ 1,780	$ 1,908	$ 1,946	$ 1,985
Required unlevered earnings	1,180	1,436	1,525	1,566
Excess unlevered earnings	$ 600	$ 472	$ 421	$ 419
Return forecast (expectation)	18.10%	15.94%	15.32%	15.21%
Required rate of return	12.00%	12.00%	12.00%	12.00%
Excess return	6.10%	3.94%	3.32%	3.21%

We then measure the value of the firm using the APV form of the excess earnings model:

($ in thousands)	Year 0	Year 1	Year 2	Year 3	CV_{Firm} Year 3
Value of the Unlevered Firm Using Excess Earnings Valuation					
Unlevered excess earnings for continuing value					$ 419
Discount factor for continuing value					10.000
Excess earnings and continuing value		$ 600	$ 472	$ 421	$ 4,186
Discount factor		0.893	0.797	0.712	0.712
Present value		$ 536	$ 376	$ 300	$ 2,980
Value of unlevered excess earnings	$ 4,192				
Initial total invested capital	$ 9,833				
Value of the unlevered firm	$14,025				
Value of the Interest Tax Shields					
Interest tax shield for continuing value					$ 206
Discount factor for continuing value					10.000
Interest tax shield and continuing value of the interest tax shield		$ 170	$ 192	$ 201	$ 2,058
Discount factor		0.893	0.797	0.712	0.712
Present value		$ 152	$ 153	$ 143	$ 1,465
Value of the interest tax shields	$ 1,913				
Value of the firm	$15,938				

Exhibit may contain small rounding errors

Solution for Review Exercise 7.5: Equity Discounted Excess Earnings Model—State Line Farm, Inc.

The Equity DCF valuation is equal to:

($ in thousands)	Year 0	Year 1	Year 2	Year 3	CV_{Equity} Year 3
Equity free cash flow for continuing value					$ 1,544
Discount factor for continuing value					8.333
Equity free cash flow and continuing value		$ 90	$1,148	$1,451	$12,864
Discount factor		0.877	0.769	0.675	0.675
Present value		$ 79	$ 884	$ 980	$ 8,683
Discounted equity free cash flow V_E	$10,625				

Exhibit may contain small rounding errors

To use the excess earnings model, we first calculate excess equity earnings:

($ in thousands)	Year 1	Year 2	Year 3	Year 4
Common equity (book value, BVE) beginning balance	$ 4,521	$ 5,955	$ 6,426	$ 6,619
Required rate of return, r_E	14.00%	14.00%	14.00%	14.00%
Required earnings	$ 633	$ 834	$ 900	$ 927
Earnings	$ 1,525	$ 1,619	$ 1,645	$ 1,676
Required earnings	633	834	900	927
Excess earnings	$ 892	$ 786	$ 745	$ 749
Return forecast (expectation)	33.73%	27.19%	25.59%	25.32%
Required rate of return	14.00%	14.00%	14.00%	14.00%
Excess return	19.73%	13.19%	11.59%	11.32%

Exhibit may contain small rounding errors

Now, we can measure the value of the equity using the equity form of the excess earnings model:

($ in thousands)	Year 0	Year 1	Year 2	Year 3	CV_{Equity} Year 3
Equity excess earnings for continuing value					$ 749
Discount factor for continuing value					8.333
Excess equity earnings and continuing value		$ 892	$ 786	$ 745	$6,245
Discount factor		0.877	0.769	0.675	0.675
Present value		$ 783	$ 605	$ 503	$4,215
Discounted excess equity flow	$ 6,105				
Initial book value of common equity	4,521				
Common equity value	$10,625				

Exhibit may contain small rounding errors

The resulting value of the common equity of $10,625 equals the value of the equity calculated using the excess earnings model in Review Exercise 7.3 ($10,625 = 2/3 equity × $15,938 firm value).

After mastering the material in this chapter, you will be able to:

1. Understand the underpinnings and implications of the Capital Asset Pricing Model (8.1)
2. Estimate the required inputs for the Capital Asset Pricing Model to estimate the equity cost of capital (8.2–8.7)
3. Adjust the Capital Asset Pricing Model-based equity cost of capital for market capitalization and other potential attributes (8.8–8.9)
4. Estimate the equity cost of capital using the three-factor model or implied cost of capital estimates (8.10–8.11)

CHAPTER

Estimating the Equity Cost of Capital

8

In its fairness opinion, delivered to the Board of Directors of Berna Biotech SA, regarding the fairness, from a financial viewpoint, of Crucell N.V.'s tender offer for Berna Biotech SA's publicly traded shares, PricewaterhouseCoopers explained how it estimated the company's equity cost of capital as follows.[1]

THE BERNA BIOTECH SA FAIRNESS OPINION

The cost of equity is composed of three components: the risk-free interest rate, the equity premium, and a premium for small capitalizations. The equity premium relies on the Capital Asset Pricing Model (CAPM), whereby the company specific risk premium is the product of the "levered" beta and the market risk premium. The "levered" beta is a measure for the specific risk of a company as compared to the market risk and hinges among other things on its capital structure. . . .

- **Risk-free interest rate**

  The risk-free interest rate is derived from the yield of 30-year [government] bonds. This was determined to be 2.55%

- **Market risk premium**

  . . . assumes a market risk premium of 4.77%. This represents the difference between the average return of the Swiss stock market and government bonds, since 1926.

- **. . . Beta**

  The "unlevered" beta leading to the "levered" beta by taking into account the capital structure has been derived from the "unlevered" betas of public companies in the vaccines industry. A value of 1.03 thus corresponds to the average "unlevered" beta from comparable midsize vaccines companies. . . .

- **Premium for small capitalizations**

  The premium for small capitalizations corresponds to the higher risk-return expectations related with an investment in small and mid-caps. It is obtained by the difference between the long-term return of small capitalizations observed and the return estimated by means of the CAPM (Capital Asset Pricing Model). . . . The applied premium of 2.4% has been obtained from an annual study . . .

In this chapter, we discuss how to estimate the cost of equity capital using several commonly used alternative techniques.

[1] PricewaterhouseCoopers' Fairness Opinion delivered to the Board of Directors of Berna Biotech SA, available on May 30, 2018 at www.uebernahme.ch/documentprovider/contentelements/nr/933/lang/3.

CHAPTER ORGANIZATION

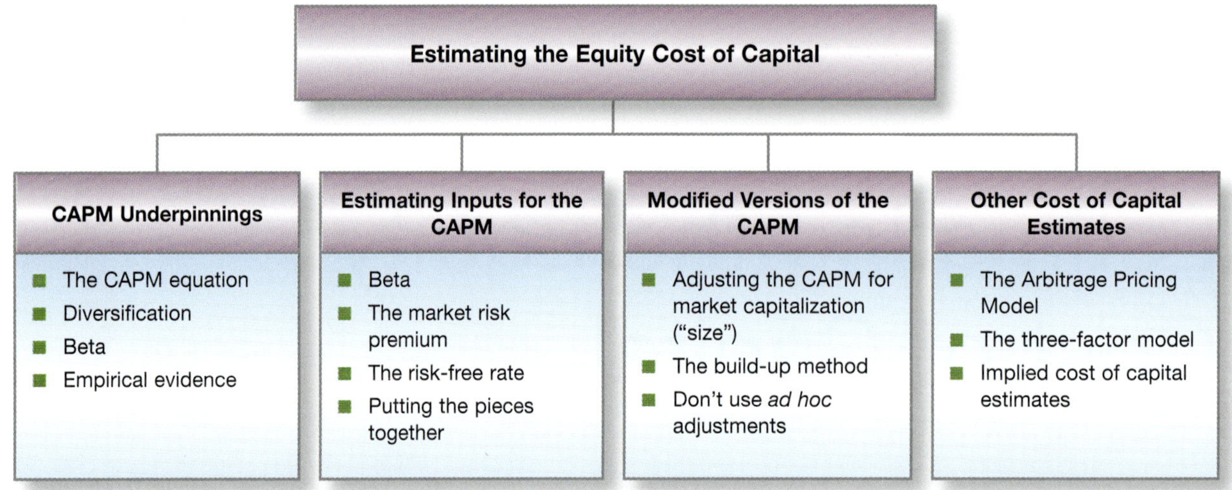

INTRODUCTION

When valuing a company, the end result of the process of estimating the cost of capital is estimating either the unlevered cost of capital (if we are using the adjusted present value valuation method) or the weighted average cost of capital (if we are using the weighted average cost of capital valuation method). When measuring the cost of capital, a valuation usually begins by estimating the equity cost of capital for comparable companies, and if possible, estimating it directly for the company we are valuing.

Most asset pricing models used to estimate the equity cost of capital add one or more company-specific risk premiums to the required return on the risk-free asset. The Capital Asset Pricing Model (CAPM) is the asset pricing model currently used most often to estimate a company's equity cost of capital. In a recent survey, 85% of the companies responded that they used the CAPM to estimate the equity cost of capital, and the other 15% responded that they used a multi-factor model or a dividend discount model or some other method.[2] The CAPM is perhaps the most straightforward asset pricing model. The cost of capital in the CAPM (for equity or any security) is equal to the risk-free rate plus one risk premium. The risk premium is equal to the risk of the security relative to the risk in the market multiplied by the risk premium for holding the market portfolio.

In this chapter we introduce the CAPM and discuss how to implement the CAPM to estimate the cost of equity capital. While the CAPM formula is straightforward, estimating the CAPM is not as straightforward as one might expect. It is more complex to implement because different scholars and different practitioners have varying views on the specific methods they favor in estimating the inputs for the CAPM. We discuss these issues and the trade-offs among alternative methods.

We then examine some alternative methods for estimating the cost of equity capital. The primary alternative to the CAPM used in practice is the CAPM modified for the potential effect of market capitalization. We also discuss alternative empirically-based asset pricing models, and illustrate one of them, the Fama-French three-factor model. Lastly, we also discuss other, less frequently used models, such as the Arbitrage Pricing Model, the Gordon Constant Growth Dividend Model, implied cost of capital models, and the so-called "build-up" method.

8.1 THE CAPITAL ASSET PRICING MODEL

LO1 Understand the underpinnings and implications of the Capital Asset Pricing Model

The **Capital Asset Pricing Model (CAPM)** was developed in the 1960s.[3] It describes how individual securities (assets) are priced in the market under the assumption that investors care about the trade-off they

[2] See 2013 AFP Estimating and Applying Cost of Capital: Report of Survey Results, October 2013, Association for Financial Professionals.

[3] The CAPM is generally attributed to William Sharpe, John Lintner, and Jack Treynor (though Treynor never published his paper). See W. F. Sharpe, "Capital Asset Prices: A Theory of Market Equilibrium Under Conditions of Risk," *Journal of Finance* 19 (1964), pp. 425–442; and J. Lintner, "The Valuation of Risky Assets and the Selection of Risky Investments in Stock Portfolios and Capital Budgets," *Review of Economics and Statistics* 47 (1965), pp. 13–37. The CAPM is often referred to as the Sharpe-Lintner Capital Asset Pricing Model. Lintner, Markowitz, and Sharpe all won the Nobel Prize in Economics for their work on portfolio theory and the Capital Asset Pricing Model.

experience between expected return and risk—specifically, given a specified level of risk, investors prefer more expected return to less expected return. In its standard form, the CAPM describes the relationship between an asset's (or security's) expected return, $E(\tilde{R}_i)$ (which we use as an estimate of the security's cost of capital), and the factors that determine it—the risk-free rate of return, r_F, a measure of the risk of a security, beta or β_i, and a risk premium (or price of risk) per unit of risk, measured against the return on the risk-free asset, called the market risk premium, $[E(\tilde{R}_m) - r_F]$. We show a typical form of the CAPM in Equation 8.1.

$$E(\tilde{R}_i) = r_F + \beta_i\left[E(\tilde{R}_m) - R_F\right] \quad (8.1)$$

Before we discuss the underpinnings of the CAPM, we first begin with a discussion of the benefits of diversification.

The Effects of Diversification

The seminal work of Harry Markowitz addressed the benefits of diversification by deriving the effect of diversification on the expected return and variance of return of a portfolio.[4] This work is important to investors who care about maximizing the expected return on their portfolios (rather than on an individual investment) and assumes that variance (or standard deviation) of returns is the measure of risk used by investors to assess the risk of their portfolios. We can use observed stock returns to measure the historical mean and variance of the stock returns of an individual security. We can also combine stocks into portfolios and use portfolio returns to measure the historical mean and variance of the stock returns of any portfolio.

Markowitz's work demonstrates that increasing the number of randomly picked securities in a portfolio reduces the variance of the portfolio's return without affecting the mean return of the portfolio. We show this effect in Exhibit 8.1. To create Exhibit 8.1, we randomly select portfolios that vary in size from 1 to 125 companies from the New York, American, and NASDAQ stock exchanges that had monthly return data available for ten years. We repeat this random selection 1,000 times for each of the portfolios with different numbers of securities. In this exhibit, we plot the average monthly standard deviation of the return of the 1,000 equally weighted portfolios as a function of the number of securities in the portfolio, and we also report the average mean monthly return for the same portfolios.

EXHIBIT 8.1 Effects of Adding Stocks to a Portfolio on the Standard Deviation and Mean Return of the Portfolio's Stock Returns

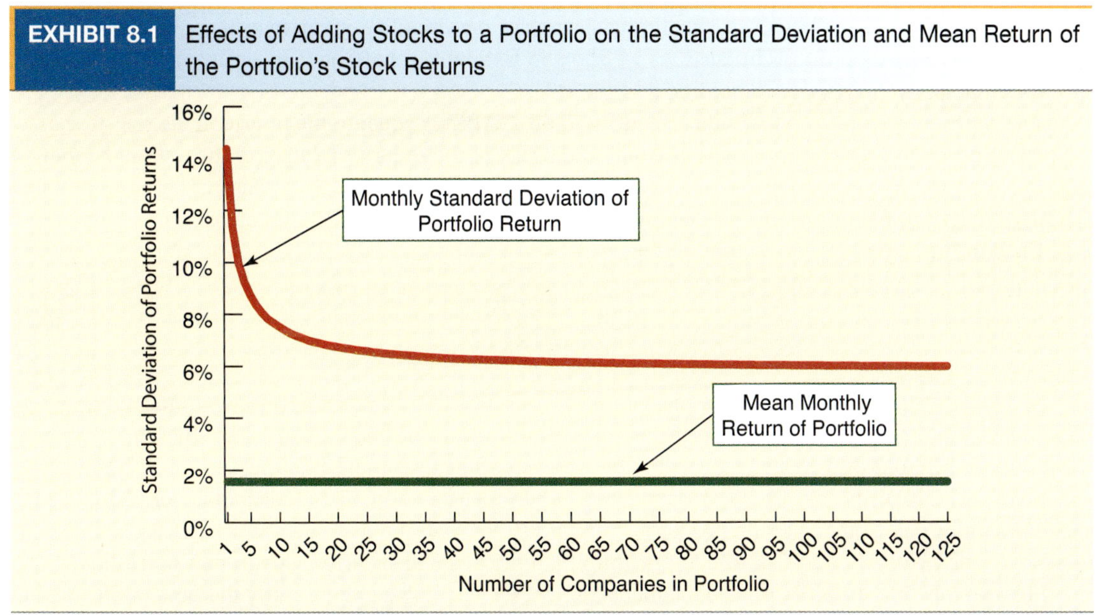

The standard deviation of returns falls rapidly as you add securities to the portfolio. The first security in the 1,000 portfolios has an average standard deviation of 14.4% per month. With three securities the portfolio average standard deviation has fallen to 10%, and at seven securities the portfolio average standard deviation has fallen to 8%. At 15 securities the average standard deviation has fallen under 7%, and at 90 securities the

[4] See H. M. Markowitz, "Portfolio Selection," *Journal of Finance* 7 (1952), pp. 77–91.

average standard deviation is 6%. Thus, by the time 15 firms have entered the portfolio, the portfolio's standard deviation has dropped to one-half of the standard deviation with only one security in the portfolio. The standard deviation decreases even faster by optimally choosing companies as opposed to random selection.[5]

Given this drop in the standard deviation, what do we expect to happen to the expected return to the portfolio as we add securities to it? Given that we randomly picked securities to add to the portfolio, on average, we would expect the portfolios to earn the return on the market. Thus, we anticipate that the return on the portfolio will remain (roughly) constant and (roughly) equal to the return on the market as we add securities to the portfolio. As you can see in the diagram, the mean return of the portfolios is constant.

Valuation Key 8.1

Investors trade off expected return (reward) and standard deviation of returns (risk) in deciding on the portfolio to hold. The benefits of diversification (holding multiple securities in a portfolio instead of a single stock) are that you can reduce the risk of your portfolio without affecting the expected return (reward).

Beta as a Measure of Security Risk

The derivation of the CAPM assumes that investors are concerned about the risk–return trade-off in assessing their portfolios, where risk is determined by the standard deviation of the portfolio's return and return is the expected return of the portfolio. The CAPM, among other things, describes how individual securities are priced (as well as efficient portfolios—that is, portfolios that for a given expected return have minimum risk among all portfolios—and inefficient portfolios—that is, portfolios that for a given expected return do not have the minimum risk among all portfolios). In other words, the question resolved by the CAPM is, given that the relevant measure of risk for an investor's portfolio is the standard deviation of portfolio return, what is the relevant measure of risk for an individual security in an investor's portfolio? As it turns out, the relevant measure of risk for an individual security is not the standard deviation of return of that security; rather, it is the contribution of that security to the standard deviation of the portfolio return, which is measured by beta or β_i in Equation 8.1. In other words, investors are not compensated for the volatility of the individual assets that they hold even though they are concerned about the volatility of their portfolios. The intuitive reason for this result is that investors can eliminate some of the volatility or variance of individual securities by holding diversified portfolios because, as we show in Exhibit 8.1, holding a diversified portfolio reduces the risk of the portfolio relative to holding a single stock.

The expected return of an individual security in the CAPM is equal to the return on the risk-free asset plus a risk premium. The risk premium is equal to the risk of the security relative to the risk in the market multiplied by the risk premium for holding the market portfolio, $[E(\tilde{R}_m) - r_F]$. The risk of an individual security relative to the market (or the security's contribution to the overall market risk), called beta (β), is defined in Equation 8.2.

$$\beta_i = \frac{\text{cov}(\tilde{R}_i, \tilde{R}_m)}{\sigma^2(\tilde{R}_m)} \tag{8.2}$$

A stock's beta measured against a market index indicates the stock's risk relative to the average risk of the stocks in that market index. Whether it adds more or less risk than the average stock to the market index can be inferred by whether the stock's beta measured against that same market index is greater or less than 1. If a security has a beta greater than 1 when measured against a particular portfolio, it adds relatively more risk to the overall riskiness of that portfolio than the average security. If the beta is less than 1, it adds relatively less risk to that portfolio than the average security adds to that portfolio.

For example, if a stock has price movements (as a percentage) that are generally the same as the market portfolio on average, then the stock should have a beta equal to 1. If a stock has a beta of 1, we would expect it to earn a return of 5% above the risk-free return on a day the market earned 5% above the risk-free return. We would expect it to earn 5% below the risk-free return on a day the market earned 5% below the risk-free return. If another stock has a beta of 2, we would expect it to earn a return of 10% above the risk-free return

---

[5] See, for example, M. Statman, "How Many Stocks Make a Diversified Portfolio?" *Journal of Financial and Quantitative Analysis* 22 (September, 1987), pp. 353–364.

on a day the market earned 5% above the risk-free return. Of course, securities will not track the market's return exactly, but a forward looking beta measures how we expect it to move with the market, on average.

In Chapter 5, we discuss risk-adjusted discount rates (cost of capital) in terms of **diversifiable risk** (or **unsystematic risk** or **idiosyncratic risk**) and **non-diversifiable risk (or systematic risk)**. As we discuss in Chapter 5, the models we typically use to measure a company's risk-adjusted discount rate assume that diversifiable risk does not affect the company's discount rate (cost of capital); however, risk that is not diversifiable will increase the company's risk-adjusted discount rate. Systematic risk or non-diversifiable risk in the context of the CAPM, concerns beta or market risk. This is risk that cannot be avoided through diversification. It can only be controlled by choosing a portfolio with a given beta. As an example, an investor could choose to invest in a portfolio with a beta of 2.0 or a beta of 0.5—thus controlling the amount of market risk to bear. Diversifiable risk or idiosyncratic risk is the risk that can potentially be eliminated through diversification. So while idiosyncratic risk is part of the volatility of a security's return, it can be eliminated in a portfolio through diversification. As a consequence, investors are not rewarded for that form of risk, but are rewarded for systematic risk according to the CAPM.

While the CAPM prices any risky asset in theory, the CAPM is mostly used in practice to assess the expected returns (estimate the cost of capital) of common equity securities. We can rewrite the CAPM formula to reflect this use in Equation 8.3.

$$r_{E,i} = r_F + \beta_{E,i} \times MRP \tag{8.3}$$

where $r_{E,i}$ is the expected return on common equity security i, r_F is the rate of return earned on an asset that is completely risk-free, $\beta_{E,i}$ is the equity beta of security i, and MRP is the expected market risk premium (the difference between the expected return on the value-weighted market portfolio of all risky assets less the return earned on the risk-free asset).

The CAPM is a model of expected returns, not the actual returns an investor earned historically or will necessarily earn in any given period in the future. In other words, because this is a model of the returns expected to be earned by risky assets, in any given time period, an investor might earn more or less than the expected return. However, if the model is correct, over the long run and over a large number of assets, the model should describe the mean return an investor will earn.

REVIEW EXERCISE 8.1

Calculating Beta

Information is provided below for three companies. The standard deviation of the market return is 0.05 and the expected market risk premium ($E(R_m) - r_F$) equals 0.06.

Standard deviation of the market return	0.05		
Expected market risk premium	0.06		
	Firm 1	**Firm 2**	**Firm 3**
Standard deviation of firm's return	0.12	0.06	0.10
Covariance of firm's return and market return	0.003	0.0025	0.004

For each company, calculate each firm's beta and the relative risk of the firm's security return to the market return based upon their relative standard deviations. Are beta and the relative standard deviations both measures of the firm's risk?

Solution on page 376.

Valuation Key 8.2

Beta is a measure of how much more or less a particular stock's return moves with the market portfolio. It measures the risk of that stock relative to the market. In the CAPM, the volatility of an individual security's return is not the relevant measure of risk of an individual stock. A security with a high variance of its returns could add relatively little risk to a portfolio if that volatility is diversifiable, which is the risk relevant for determining its expected return and equity cost of capital according to the CAPM.

A Quick Look at Some Betas

Think about some industries and how the stock returns of companies in those industries are likely to move with the overall market return. Would you expect the betas of grocery store chains to have more or less risk than the overall market (have a beta above or below 1)? To answer this question, we would think about how grocery store businesses are affected by upturns and downturns in the economy. Certainly business cycles affect the profitability of grocery stores. In an economic downturn, people probably do not go to the gourmet aisle as often, or eat the finest cuts of meat and fish, and probably buy fewer pre-prepared foods (all of which generally have higher margins), but people still eat. Thus, after thinking about the issue for a few moments, you might not be surprised that grocery stores are generally less risky than the market and have betas that are less than 1. However, beta (risk) differs even within industries, including the grocery store industry. Wal-Mart Stores, Inc. operates mostly discount retail stores, mostly under the Walmart and Sam's Club brand. Revenues from groceries represent about 55% of its total revenues. Whole Foods Market Inc. sells organic and minimally processed foods with minimal artificial food preservatives, antibiotics in meat, and pesticides in vegetables. It is likely that discount grocery stores are less affected by swings in the economy than higher priced grocery stores like Whole Foods. Indeed, at the end of 2015, Wal-Mart's beta was around 0.3 and Whole Foods' beta was around 0.6. Whole Foods has since been acquired by Amazon.com, Inc.

In Exhibit 8.2 we provide estimates of median industry equity betas estimated using 60 months of data ending March 31, 2015. We include all industries with the required data for at least twelve companies available in the Center for Research in Security Prices (CRSP) monthly stock return database.[6] The industry betas range from a low of 0.28 for Electric & Other Services Combined to a high of 2.07 for Television Broadcasting Stations. Recall that equity risk is determined by the riskiness of the business (unlevered beta) and additional risk from financial leverage. Since industries not only differ on business risk but also differ on the degree of financial leverage used to finance the firm (see Chapter 10), the betas in the exhibit do not

EXHIBIT 8.2 Median Equity Betas for U.S. Industries (4-Digit SIC Code) with at Least 12 Observations

SIC Code	Industry Name	Median Beta	Inter-quartile Range	# of Firms
4931	Electric & other services combined	0.28	0.25	20
4911	Electric services	0.40	0.81	45
2086	Bottled & canned soft drinks & carbonated waters	0.42	0.21	13
6035	Savings institution, federally chartered	0.51	0.74	43
6712	Offices of bank holding companies	0.57	0.37	22
5812	Retail-eating places	0.64	0.44	25
6036	Savings institutions, not federally chartered	0.66	0.58	21
4812	Radiotelephone communications	0.72	0.87	12
5810	Retail—eating & drinking places	0.73	0.38	12
6798	Real estate investment trusts	0.74	0.50	156
6221	Commodity contracts brokers & dealers	0.75	0.72	14
1041	Gold ores	0.77	0.86	37
6022	State commercial banks	0.77	0.53	76
6726	Unit investment trusts, face-amount certificate offices, and closed-end management investment offices	0.78	1.10	1,099
6331	Fire, marine & casualty insurance	0.81	0.33	51
4922	Natural gas transmission	0.81	0.56	17
3812	Search, detection, navigation, guidance, aeronautical sys	0.88	0.79	12
3841	Surgical & medical instruments & apparatus	0.91	0.67	39
4813	Telephone communications (no radiotelephone)	0.92	0.59	37
4512	Air transportation, scheduled	0.93	0.54	13
3679	Electronic components, NEC	0.96	0.85	12
6021	National commercial banks	0.98	0.61	69
6211	Security brokers, dealers & flotation companies	0.99	0.51	159
8742	Services—management consulting services	0.99	0.48	16
3663	Radio & tv broadcasting & communications equipment	1.04	0.50	25
3826	Laboratory analytical instruments	1.04	0.23	12
6722	Management investment offices, open-end	1.05	0.37	12
6141	Personal credit institutions	1.06	0.21	12
2834	Pharmaceutical preparations	1.10	0.90	104
7371	Services-computer programming services	1.10	1.12	21
7389	Services-business services, NEC	1.11	0.81	60
3577	Computer peripheral equipment, NEC	1.13	0.94	14
7372	Services-prepackaged software	1.14	0.63	62
7374	Services-computer processing & data preparation	1.16	0.57	16
8731	Services-commercial physical & biological research	1.16	0.89	26
8711	Services-engineering services	1.19	0.62	16
4899	Communications services, NEC	1.20	0.88	17
4841	Cable & other pay television services	1.20	0.70	20
3670	Electronic components & accessories	1.22	0.74	39
3825	Instruments for meas & testing of electricity & elec signals	1.23	0.82	12
3845	Electromedical & electrotherapeutic apparatus	1.24	0.53	18
7373	Services-computer integrated systems design	1.24	0.72	27
7011	Hotels & motels	1.25	0.33	19
6311	Life insurance	1.30	0.57	24
7370	Services-computer programming, data processing, etc.	1.31	0.56	35
4213	Trucking (no local)	1.34	0.54	12
2621	Paper mills	1.36	0.72	12
3570	Computer & office equipment	1.37	0.49	12
7363	Services-help supply services	1.37	0.69	14
6282	Investment advice	1.42	0.56	28
2836	Biological products, (no diagnostic substances)	1.46	0.72	32
6029	Commercial banks, NEC	1.46	0.99	18
3674	Semiconductors & related devices	1.46	0.79	71
1311	Crude petroleum & natural gas	1.47	0.74	95
1389	Oil & gas field services, NEC	1.47	0.21	14
2911	Petroleum refining	1.48	0.94	23
1531	Operative builders	1.52	0.54	15
4412	Deep sea foreign transportation of freight	1.54	0.86	27
3714	Motor vehicle parts & accessories	1.58	0.66	24
3312	Steel works, blast furnaces & rolling mills (coke ovens)	1.59	0.40	17
7359	Services-equipment rental & leasing, NEC	1.62	1.49	12
3661	Telephone & telegraph apparatus	1.63	0.89	13
2821	Plastic materials, synth resins & nonvulcan elastomers	1.64	0.51	13
3711	Motor vehicles & passenger car bodies	1.65	0.63	13
1381	Drilling oil & gas wells	1.77	0.75	16
4833	Television broadcasting stations	2.07	0.95	12
	Median across all companies	1.00		4,887

[6] The Center for Research in Security Prices (CRSP) is at The University of Chicago's Booth School of Business. Since 1960, CRSP has provided research-quality stock return and other market data to researchers and investment practitioners; see www.CRSP.com. Wharton Research Data Services (WRDS) was used in preparing this exhibit. This service and the data available thereon constitute valuable intellectual property and trade secrets of WRDS and/or its third-party suppliers.

only represent differences in business risk. Even so, reviewing the betas down the list of industries should generally make sense. Rate of return regulated utilities have relatively little systematic risk despite their very high leverage. Retail eating places have a risk that is below the average, while industries such as hotels and other lodging places have above average betas. The exhibit also presents the inter-quartile range (75th percentile beta minus the 25th percentile beta) for each industry. The inter-quartile range shows how betas vary even within industry. Such variation is a function of differences in business risks, capital structures, and measurement error. In addition, higher beta industries generally have more variation within the industry.

A Portfolio Beta Is a Weighted Average of the Betas of the Securities in the Portfolio

For a portfolio of N securities, the return of the portfolio is simply the weighted average of the returns to the individual securities in the portfolio. The weights, x_i, are calculated as the market value of security i divided by the total market value of the securities in the portfolio.

$$\tilde{R}_p = \sum_{i=1}^{N} x_i \tilde{R}_i$$

A portfolio beta is the weighted average of the betas of the securities in the portfolio, where the weights are again based on the market values of each security relative to the total market value of the portfolio.

$$\beta_p = \sum_{i=1}^{N} x_i \beta_i \quad (8.4)$$

The implication is that the beta of a portfolio is the weighted average of the betas of the individual securities in the portfolio. If you had two securities in your portfolio and one stock had a beta of 0.4 and the other had a beta of 2.0, and you held equal values of both, your portfolio beta would be 1.2 ($1.2 = 0.4 \times 0.5 + 2.0 \times 0.5$).

The beta of the portfolio with respect to a market portfolio can be written as

$$\beta_p = \frac{\text{cov}(\tilde{R}_p, \tilde{R}_m)}{\sigma^2 (\tilde{R}_m)} \quad (8.5)$$

This expression looks just like the expression for the beta of an individual security except the numerator is now the covariance of the return of the portfolio with the market instead of the covariance of the return of an individual security with the market.

Valuation Key 8.3

The beta of a portfolio is a weighted average of the betas of the individual securities that comprise that portfolio. The weights for each security are determined by the proportion of the portfolio's value stemming from that security.

REVIEW EXERCISE 8.2

Calculating Portfolio Return and Portfolio Beta

In the table below, the market value, beta, and equity security return are listed for four individual equity securities that are contained in a portfolio. Calculate the return to the portfolio and the beta for the portfolio.

	Firm 1	Firm 2	Firm 3	Firm 4
Total equity market value in portfolio (in millions).	$1,000	$3,500	$2,300	$700
Firm beta	0.90	1.07	1.20	1.46
Stock return	5.0%	7.0%	9.0%	10.0%

Solution on page 377.

Further Observations and Empirical Evidence

In addition to describing the risk and return relationship for individual securities, the CAPM has other implications. The first implication is that investors should hold well-diversified portfolios. If they do not, they will bear risk for which they are not compensated. Why? If the portfolio isn't sufficiently well-diversified, then the variance of the portfolio will be driven by idiosyncratic risk. As we discuss earlier in the chapter, investors are not compensated for idiosyncratic risk according to the CAPM. They are only compensated for systematic risk.

The second implication is that corporations should not pursue pure diversification as a strategy. By diversification, we mean investing in different types of businesses when the investment does not create value (a positive net present value investment) through synergies or other types of increases in expected free cash flows. Why? Because investors can diversify themselves. In practice, diversification across industries and countries for investors is usually simple and practically costless because investors have easy access to investing in various index funds that track broad-based indices, such as the S&P 500, as well as many other major indices, including international indices.

The third implication of the CAPM is the main reason we discuss it in this book. The CAPM is a model about the returns that investors demand in expectation for the risk that they are bearing by investing in a security (the common equity of a company for our purposes in this chapter). As such, it provides a method for estimating a company's cost of capital.

Valuation Key 8.4

The Capital Asset Pricing Model is widely used to estimate the cost of equity capital. In addition, the model has important implications for investors and corporations. For investors, the CAPM indicates that it is important to hold well-diversified portfolios. For corporations, the CAPM implies that diversification is not a value-added activity unless it is associated with positive cash flow effects.

Evidence on the Capital Asset Pricing Model

Is the CAPM a reasonable model to use to calculate the cost of capital? That is, does it explain differences in expected returns empirically? Substantial, but certainly not all, scholarly research on this topic suggests that the primary predictions of the CAPM are broadly consistent with the data. However, academicians have identified two shortcomings of the CAPM. First, stock returns appear to be related to measures other than beta (other factors are important), and second, the CAPM-based predicted returns of the high-beta (low-beta) portfolios are too low (high).

While some relatively early evidence investigating the CAPM showed that returns were related to betas and that measures such as the variance of returns were unrelated to returns, subsequent evidence identified departures from the predictions of the CAPM. For example, an early study by Black, Jensen, and Scholes provided evidence that returns were linearly related to beta. A study by Fama and Macbeth[7] indicated that variables such as beta squared and idiosyncratic risk were not priced. However, both of these studies indicated that the relationship between expected return and beta was somewhat "flat" relative to the predictions of the CAPM using data back to the 1930s. Later research also shows that while the relationship between return and beta is positive, it is still flatter than the CAPM predicts. That is, the returns to low-beta stocks are too high and the returns to high-beta stocks are too low relative to the predictions of the CAPM.[8]

One problem, discussed by Richard Roll and others, is that a true test of the CAPM would require us to know the market portfolio, defined as the value-weighted portfolio of all risky assets in the world. Of course, such an index does not exist and is unlikely to ever exist. Since most tests of the CAPM rely only on portfolios of common stock or include a few other types of securities (bonds, preferred stock and real estate but then only with U.S. data), one could argue the CAPM has never been fairly tested, nor likely will it ever be.[9] However, from a practical perspective, what is important to estimating the equity cost of

---

[7] See Black, F., M. Jensen, and M. Scholes, "The Capital Asset Pricing Model: Some Empirical Tests," in M. Jensen, ed., *Studies in the Theory of Capital Markets,* New York: Praeger Publishing (1972), pp. 79–121; and Fama, E., and J. MacBeth, "Risk, Return and Equilibrium: Empirical Tests," *Journal of Political Economy* 81 (1973), pp. 607–636.

[8] See Fama, E., and K. French, *Journal of Economic Perspectives* 18 (Summer 2004), pp. 25–46.

[9] See R. Roll, "A Critique of the Asset Pricing Theory's Tests; Part I: On Past and Potential Testability of the Theory," *Journal of Financial Economics* 4 (March, 1977), pp. 129–176.

capital is that so far, we have not been able to define a proxy for the market return that totally describes expected returns to common equities using the CAPM.

Another problematic issue for the CAPM is that research shows the presence of risk factors other than beta that explain the returns of firms in a systematic way. For example, small firms (in terms of market capitalization of the equity) have, on average, outperformed large firms on a CAPM risk-adjusted basis. In other words, smaller firms over long historical periods had returns that were higher than the CAPM predicted and large firms had returns that were smaller than the CAPM predicted.[10] This is often referred to as the "**size effect**." Interestingly, a large portion (and maybe all) of the size effect occurs in the month of January.[11] Researchers refer to this phenomenon as the "**January effect**." A variety of explanations for the size effect have been considered, such as riskier growth opportunities, time-varying risk premia, liquidity, bid-ask spreads and turn-of-the-year trading; issues in estimating betas; and the effect of taxes, and transactions costs, and more. To date, we have no completely satisfactory explanation for the phenomenon. More recent studies also conclude that a size effect exists. A study from 2013 concluded that when measured over shorter intervals, the size effect is erratic and at times negative; however, over long periods, smaller capitalized stocks persistently outperform larger capitalized stocks based on CAPM excess returns, although the relation is not linear (and is larger for smaller firms).[12] A study in 2017 concluded that after controlling for firm quality (profitability, stability, and growth), the authors document a significant size premium, which is stable through time, not concentrated in microcaps, and more consistent across seasons.[13]

Some interpreted the evidence on the size effect to indicate the existence of a trading rule based on firm size (that is, if you want to beat the market, just buy small stocks). But this interpretation presumes that the risk adjustment in the CAPM is correct. Another interpretation is that the CAPM is not a perfect descriptor of the return-generating process and somehow we are not measuring risk completely with the CAPM beta. In that interpretation, size is a proxy for some element of priced risk that is not captured by beta as we measure it. Academicians generally interpret the evidence on firm size to infer that the CAPM is not a perfect descriptor of the return-generating process.

Despite the uncertainty with regard to interpreting this evidence, the evidence has led some, but not all, valuation experts to estimate a firm's cost of capital using the traditional CAPM with an adjustment based on the firm's approximate market equity capitalization. We discuss the adjustments to the CAPM based on firm size later in the chapter.

In addition to the size effect, other factors appear to be potentially important in explaining the cross-section of expected returns beyond the CAPM; this evidence led to the three-factor and other multi-factor models, which we discuss later in the chapter as well. All of this evidence suggests that the CAPM is not a perfect descriptor of expected returns. That said, the excess market return factor in the CAPM is also a factor in the various multi-factor models, and the CAPM beta is correlated with the betas for the excess market return factor in the multi-factor models. Most likely, until we have an alternative model that clearly dominates the CAPM, it will likely be the most common way for practitioners to estimate the equity cost of capital in a valuation. We next discuss how to implement the CAPM in practice, and later in the chapter we examine some of the alternatives to the CAPM.

Valuation Key 8.5

The evidence on the Capital Asset Pricing Model is mixed. While we observe the basic risk–return relationship predicted by the model, the evidence suggests that it is far from a perfect descriptor of expected returns. Regardless, it continues to be the most widely used model in practice to estimate the equity cost of capital.

---

[10] See Banz, R., "The Relationship Between Return and Market Values of Common Stock," *Journal of Financial Economics* 9 (March, 1981), pp. 3–18.

[11] Keim, Donald B., "Size-Related Anomalies and Stock Return Seasonality: Further Evidence," *Journal of Financial Economics* 9 (June 1983), pp. 13–32.

[12] R. J. Grabowski, and J. P. Harrington, *Risk Premium Report* 2013, Copyright © 2013 Duff & Phelps Corporation, DP132014.

[13] Asness, C., A Frazzini, R. Israel, T. Moskowitz, and L. Pedersen, "Size Matters, if You Control Your Junk," February 2017, Fama-Miller Working Paper; available on May 30, 2018 at SSRN: https://ssrn.com/abstract=2553889.

8.2 AN OVERVIEW ON ESTIMATING THE EQUITY COST OF CAPITAL USING THE CAPITAL ASSET PRICING MODEL

LO2 Estimate the required inputs for the Capital Asset Pricing Model to estimate the equity cost of capital

Estimating the cost of equity capital using the CAPM requires estimates of the three components of the CAPM: the risk-free rate, the company's beta, and the market risk premium. As we stated in the introduction of the chapter, implementing the CAPM can be complex because different scholars and different practitioners have varying views on the specific methods they favor to estimate the inputs for the CAPM. While the CAPM is widely used, the methods used to estimate these components vary significantly in practice.

In the next few sections, we discuss many of the alternative methods used to estimate the three components of the CAPM and discuss some of the trade-offs to consider in making those decisions. Although we have some guiding principles, in the end, like many steps in the valuation process, we use professional judgment as to how to estimate each component of the CAPM. Companies such as investment banks or consulting firms or other companies that conduct valuations, may have certain standard practices to follow to estimate these components. Even then, however, the specific company and valuation context usually requires some refinement to standard practices requiring professional judgment.

Valuation in Practice 8.1

The Equity Costs of Capital in the Knight Transportation, Inc. and Swift Transportation Company Merger In April 2017, Knight Transportation and Swift Transportation Company announced that their boards of directors unanimously approved a merger of Knight and Swift in an all-stock transaction, which will create the industry's largest full truckload company. Under the terms of the agreement, Swift stockholders will own approximately 54 percent and Knight stockholders will own approximately 46 percent of the combined company. According to the companies, Knight is expected to be the accounting acquirer, and the transaction is expected to be accretive to adjusted earnings per share with expected pre-tax synergies of approximately $15 million in the second half of 2017, $100 million in 2018, and $150 million in 2019. The companies' joint financial advisor, Morgan Stanley & Co. LLC, measured the companies' equity costs of capital as follows.

> Morgan Stanley performed a discounted cash flow analysis on each of Swift and Knight, which analysis is designed to provide an implied value of a company on a standalone basis by calculating the present value of the estimated future cash flows and terminal value of that company.
>
> ***Swift Discounted Cash Flow Analysis.***
>
> . . . cost of equity range of 10.9% to 12.9% (which was based on the Capital Asset Pricing Model using a market risk premium of 6.0%, a risk-free rate of 2.4% and a beta of 1.59 for class A shares of Swift that was determined by Morgan Stanley using market data ... as of April 7, 2017, plus a sensitivity adjustment of 1.0% to define the low and high ends of the cost of equity range), . . .
>
> ***Knight Discounted Cash Flow Analysis.***
>
> . . . cost of equity range of 8.1% to 10.1% (which was based on the Capital Asset Pricing Model using a market risk premium of 6.0%, a risk-free rate of 2.4% and a beta of 1.12 for Knight shares that was determined by Morgan Stanley using market data ... as of April 7, 2017, plus a sensitivity adjustment of 1.0% to define the low and high ends of the cost of equity range), . . .

Source: Knight Transportation, Inc. and Swift Transportation Company joint Form S-4 Registration Statement filed with the U.S. SEC on May 23, 2017.

In Exhibit 8.3, we outline the basic steps required to estimate the cost of equity capital using the CAPM. The first step is to decide, which, if any, comparable companies to use to estimate the equity cost of capital, which is generally decided by the suitability of the available comparable companies. We begin with this step because this decision affects subsequent decisions we make and analyses we perform. The second step is to assess the stability of the company's operating assets and capital structure as well as any comparable companies being considered. We perform this analysis because we know beta changes if the company's business risk or financial leverage changes.

EXHIBIT 8.3	Steps in Estimating the Cost of Equity Capital Using the CAPM
1	Decide which comparable companies to use to estimate the equity cost of capital needed in the valuation
2	Assess the stability of the operating assets (asset risk or unlevered company risk) and capital structure (financial leverage risk) of the company we are valuing and comparable companies
3	Estimate the beta of each company's common stock
4	Estimate the market risk premium
5	Estimate the risk-free rate (yield on a risk-free asset at the valuation date)
6	Substitute your estimates in the CAPM equation and calculate the cost of equity

In Steps 3, 4, and 5 of the process, we estimate the three components of the CAPM—beta, the market risk premium, and the risk-free rate of return. Each of these steps has its own process with various steps, which we discuss in subsequent sections of the chapter. The last step is to calculate the CAPM equity cost of capital using the components estimated from the previous three steps.

Before we discuss the many choices that we make when estimating each component, it is useful to understand that the choices we make across the components are not independent of one another. For example, the market index we use to estimate beta is linked to the market index we use to estimate the market risk premium. Also, the risk-free rate we use in the CAPM is linked to the risk-free return we use to measure the market risk premium. We will discuss these interdependencies as we discuss estimating the three components of the CAPM.

8.3 ESTIMATING BETA

Beta, as we already discussed, is a measure of the risk of an asset or security relative to a certain portfolio, which, according to the CAPM, is the market portfolio. When we implement the CAPM, we estimate the beta by measuring the risk of an asset relative to some proxy that we use for the market portfolio. The most common method used to estimate betas is to estimate the parameters of a regression model called the market model. Virtually all estimates of beta begin with an estimate from a market model regression because the statistical formula for the slope parameter of the market model is the same as the formula for beta in the CAPM (Equation 8.2).

We show the primary steps in the process to estimate beta in Exhibit 8.4. The first step is to choose the proxy for the market index. Steps 2 and 3 involve making choices for the time period and return holding period (periodicity) for the stock returns used to estimate the market model. Then, we estimate the model and possibly adjust the beta estimate for such effects as mean reversion. When implementing this process, we use the information from the second step in the cost of equity estimation process in Exhibit 8.3, which is evaluating the stability of the companies' operating risk and financial leverage risk, as it informs us about the time period we should use to estimate beta.

EXHIBIT 8.4	Steps in Estimating Beta of the Company's Common Stock
1	Choose a market index (links to the market risk premium estimation process)
2	Choose an estimation period (length of period and specific dates)
3	Choose the periodicity for the stock return (daily, weekly, or monthly interval)
4	Collect the necessary data and estimate the market model
5	Make adjustments, if any, for mean reversion and other effects

The Equity Cost of Capital Used in Valuation is Forward Looking but Estimated Using Historical Data

When we estimate a company's cost of capital for purposes of valuing it, we require a **forward-looking** estimate of that cost of capital, that is, a cost of capital relevant for discounting future free cash flows. Unfortunately, the regression approach used to measure beta uses historical information, and therefore represents the historical beta. As we discuss next, the estimate of beta can shift from one estimation period to another for the same company. This effect can be due to noise in estimated betas or it can be due to shifts in economic fundamentals, which change the systematic risk of the company or its industry.

Below, we discuss ways that we can adjust betas estimated using historical data so they better represent more forward-looking betas, but it is useful to remember that by necessity we start with something that is historical, not forward looking.

The Market Model

The **market model** represents a direct way to estimate beta using historical information. It can also further strengthen our intuition as to why beta is the measure of risk that is priced in the CAPM. Since we are focused on estimating the cost of equity capital, we focus our discussion on using the market model to estimate equity betas using stock returns; however, it is possible to use the market model for any asset or security if the necessary data are available. We estimate the parameters of the **market model**, one of which is beta, using ordinary least squares regression analysis. Such regressions are typically referred to as **market model regressions**. **Regression analysis** is a statistical method that explains the variation in a **dependent variable** with other variables called **independent variables**. A regression model has one dependent variable and can have one or more independent variables.

The standard market model regression has one independent variable; it is a "simple" regression where the stock return of the company for which we are estimating beta is the dependent variable (left-hand-side variable) and the contemporaneous return on a proxy for the market portfolio is the independent variable (right-hand-side variable). We estimate the regression using a time-series (from $t = 1$ to $t = T$) of the stock returns, R_{it}, and the contemporaneous returns on the market index, R_{mt}.

$$R_{it} = \alpha_i + \beta_i R_{mt} + \varepsilon_{it} \quad t = 1......T \tag{8.6}$$

The market model specifies that the return of a stock is equal to a constant, α_i, plus the asset's beta, β_i, multiplied by the return on the market, plus a shock or noise term. The estimate of β_i is the slope of the fitted regression line, and is an estimate of the beta of the CAPM. The estimated α_i is the intercept of the regression line on the vertical axis.

It is also common to estimate beta by regressing a company's return minus the return on the risk-free asset on the market return minus the return on the risk-free asset called an excess return form of Equation 8.6. Generally, the beta estimates using excess returns are similar to those using Equation 8.6.

$$R_{it} - R_{Ft} = \alpha_i + \beta_i (R_{mt} - R_{Ft}) + \varepsilon_{it} \quad t = 1......T \tag{8.7}$$

Equations 8.6 and 8.7 identify the choices we need to make to estimate beta. While how to measure the company's stock return is clearly defined, the period over which we measure the stock return (**periodicity**) is not; for example, periodicity could be a day, a week, a month, or even part of a day. The number of periods to use to estimate the model is another choice. The market index to use as the proxy for the market portfolio is yet another choice. We discuss the alternatives and guiding principles for making these choices later in the chapter.

Assuming the data meet the assumptions required for ordinary least squares regression (primarily normality, stationarity, and serial independence of the error terms), the estimate of beta, $\hat{\beta}_i$, from a regression is an unbiased estimate of the true beta, β_i; in other words, the expected value of the estimated beta is equal to the true beta. The good news is that market model regressions are generally well specified so that all the properties that a regression should have are generally observed for market model regressions. This is not true universally, however. Of course, even though the expected value of the estimated beta is the true beta, the estimated beta from any particular regression could be above or below the true beta. The standard error of the beta estimate from the regression analysis describes the sampling variability of the beta estimate and thus measures the precision of the estimate (how precisely it is measured).

Return Dichotomization in the Market Model

The market model dichotomizes or disaggregates a company's stock return into two components—the part of the company's stock return explained by movements in the market index and the part of the company's stock return that is not explained by the movements in the market index. We typically describe the latter component as a firm-specific return. The firm-specific component is equal to $\alpha_i + \varepsilon_{it}$ and the market related component is equal to $\beta_i R_{mt}$. Similarly, the market model implies that the stock return variance can also be disaggregated into two parts. The expression for the stock return variance derived in terms of the market model equation is

$$\sigma^2(\tilde{R}_i) = \beta_i^2 \sigma^2(\tilde{R}_m) + \sigma^2(\tilde{\varepsilon}_i)$$

The first component represents the stock return variance related to the variance of the market return, which we call **non-diversifiable risk** or **systematic risk**. The second component is variance not explained by the market, which we call **non-systematic risk**, **unsystematic risk**, or **idiosyncratic risk**. Recall that we used all those terms previously in providing some intuition for the CAPM. If we divide both sides of the above formula by the variance of the stock's returns, we can measure the proportion of a company's stock return explained by the market.

$$\frac{\sigma^2(\tilde{R}_i)}{\sigma^2(\tilde{R}_i)} = 1 = \beta_i^2 \frac{\sigma^2(\tilde{R}_m)}{\sigma^2(\tilde{R}_i)} + \frac{\sigma^2(\tilde{\varepsilon}_i)}{\sigma^2(\tilde{R}_i)}$$

The first term on the right-hand side in the above formula, $\beta_i^2\sigma^2(\tilde{R}_m)/\sigma^2(\tilde{R}_i)$, is the proportion of the variance of the return of the security that can be explained by variation in the market. The r-squared statistic from a market model regression is an estimate of this proportion.

Market Model Estimates for Four Example Companies

In Exhibit 8.5, we show scatter plots of the time-series observations of the monthly with-dividend stock returns of four companies: Colgate Palmolive Co., which is a consumer products company; Ford Motor Co., manufacturer of automobiles and trucks; General Electric Co., which has aircraft engine, power generation, and oil and gas production equipment, financing and various industrial product related businesses; and Textron Inc., which has various aircraft, defense, industrial and financing businesses. We pair the returns for each company with the contemporaneous with-dividend returns on the S&P 500 from April 2012 to March 2017 (60 months of return data in all). We also show the estimated regression lines from estimating a market model regression of the return on each security against the return on the S&P 500.

EXHIBIT 8.5 Scatter Plots and Market Model Regression Lines for Four Companies (using 60 Monthly Returns Ending 3/31/2017)

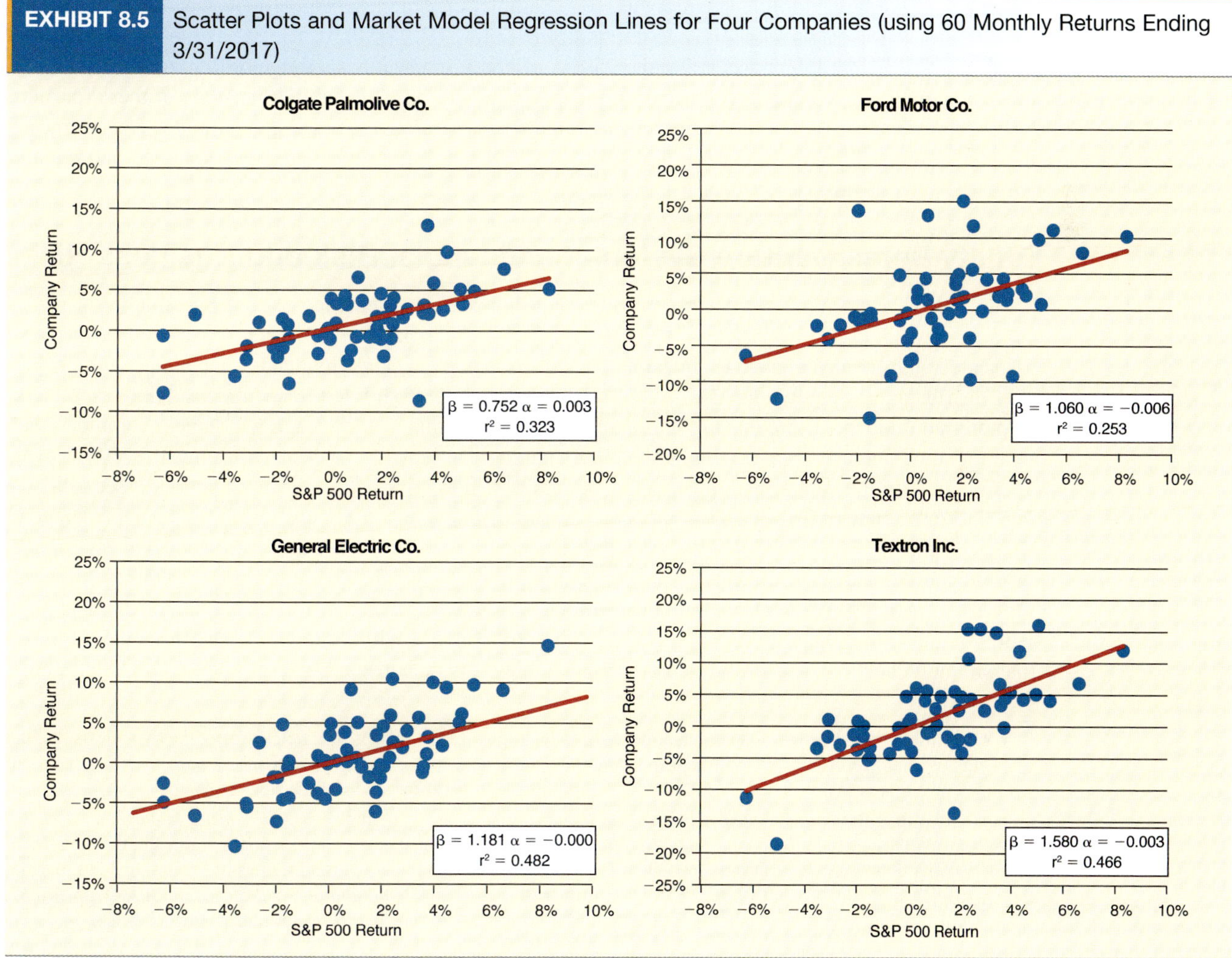

These are fairly typical scatter plots for market model regressions. Since the market does not explain all of the variation of the stock returns of any company, the data points do not all lie on the estimated regression lines. The vertical deviation between each data point and the fitted regression line is the error term, ε_{it}, in the market model equation.

In Exhibit 8.6, we provide certain summary statistics for the market model regressions for these companies. We report the estimated beta, the standard error of the beta estimate, the t-statistic to test if beta is significantly different from zero, the 95% confidence interval for the estimated beta, and the adjusted r-squared of the regression. The betas for the individual companies range from a low of 0.75 for Colgate Palmolive Co. to a high of 1.58 for Textron Inc. All of the betas are statistically significantly different from zero based on the t-statistics,[14] and the adjusted r-squareds of the regressions for the individual companies range from a low of 25% for Ford Motor Company to a high of 48% for General Electric Co.—the latter is reasonably high for a market model regression on an individual company, but GE is a highly diversified company in its own right.

EXHIBIT 8.6 Market Model Regression Statistic for Four Companies (using 60 Monthly Returns Ending 3/31/2017)

	Beta Estimate	Standard Error of Beta	t-statistic	95% Confidence Interval		Adjusted r-squared
				Lower Bound	Upper Bound	
Colgate Palmolive Co.	0.75	0.14	5.26	0.47	1.03	0.32
Ford Motor Co.	1.06	0.24	4.43	0.59	1.53	0.25
General Electric Co.	1.18	0.16	7.35	0.87	1.50	0.48
Textron Inc	1.58	0.22	7.11	1.14	2.02	0.47
Average	1.14	0.19				0.38
Equally weighted portfolio	1.14	0.08	13.84	0.98	1.31	0.77

While all of these beta estimates are statistically different from zero, this exhibit shows that estimates of beta can have large confidence intervals. For example, the smallest standard error is 0.14 for Colgate, which implies it has a 95% confidence interval of 0.47 to 1.03. For Ford, which has the largest standard error among the four companies, 0.24, the 95% confidence interval has a range of 0.59 to 1.53. It should be noted, and we'll see more evidence on standard errors later in Chapter 10, that some of these (particularly Colgate and GE) are reasonably small standard errors relative to the beta estimates (which means they have tighter 95% confidence intervals) than most companies. We discuss the average and equally weighted rows of this exhibit later in the chapter.

Equity Betas Capture Systematic Financial Risk and Business Risk

As we noted earlier in the chapter, a company's equity beta, or systematic risk, has two sources of risk—**financial risk** and **business risk** or **operating risk**.[15] Financial risk is the risk that results from the fixed cost associated with financial leverage (interest payments or preferred stock dividends—payments with priority over distributions to equityholders). **Financial leverage** results from fixed financing costs (interest on debt or preferred dividends). A company with a higher degree of financial leverage will have a common stock with higher systematic risk, or a higher beta, relative to what its beta would be with lower levels of leverage. We refer to the beta of a company's operating or business risk as its unlevered beta or asset beta. We introduced the relation between the equity cost of capital, unlevered cost of capital, and financial leverage in Chapter 5 and those same relations hold with respect to betas, which we discuss in more detail in Chapter 10.

Business risk or operating risk has two components.[16] The first component is operating leverage. **Operating leverage** results from having fixed operating costs. A **fixed cost** is a cost that does not change with volume and a **variable cost** is a cost that directly changes with volume. The world is naturally not that simple. A cost is rarely only fixed or only variable—over a sufficiently large change in volume, most

[14] With 60 observations, any t-statistic greater than 2.0 or less than −2.0 indicates that we can reject the hypothesis that the true beta is equal to zero at the 5% significance level (which means that there is only a 5% chance we are wrong). Consistent with that, note that zero does not fall within the 95% confidence interval for any of these stocks.

[15] See, for example, Brenner, M., and S. Smidt, "Asset Characteristics and Systematic Risk," *Financial Management* (Winter 1978), pp. 33–39, who model the relation between systematic risk and fixed costs, contribution margin, and the covariance of revenues with the market. Also see Mandelker, G., and S. Rhee, "The Impact of the Degrees of Operating and Financial Leverage on Systematic Risk of Common Stock," *Journal of Financial and Quantitative Analysis* (March 1984), pp. 45–57, who empirically document the relation between a company's systematic risk and its operating and financial risk.

[16] See Brenner, M., and S. Smidt, "Asset Characteristics and Systematic Risk," *Financial Management* (Winter 1978), pp. 33–39.

costs vary; and over a sufficiently short time interval, many costs are fixed. Fixed production costs result in a higher degree of operating leverage and, thus, higher business risk.

The second component is **cyclicality**, **revenue cyclicality** or **gross margin cyclicality**. Revenue cyclicality is the sensitivity of a company's revenue (or how sensitive the demand for the company's products and product prices are) to the general economy. Gross margin cyclicality is the sensitivity of a company's gross margin to fluctuations in the economy. The more sensitive a company's revenue or gross margin is to the general economy, the more business risk it has; thus, all else equal, more cyclical companies have more business risk than non-cyclical companies if the cycles of the cyclical companies are positively correlated with the economy.

For example, we know that the automobile and construction industries are more cyclical than the food processing and mining industries; thus, the automobile and construction industries have higher business risk. Examples of factors that might drive the revenue cyclicality component of a company's business risk are its sensitivity to general economic growth, inflation, the cost of borrowing in the economy, input prices, and the ability to adjust prices.

If a company does not use any financial leverage, then its equity beta is a measure of its operating or business risk and is equal to its unlevered beta. If a company uses financial leverage, its equity beta is determined by both its business risk and financial risk.

We illustrate the relation between equity betas and financial leverage using a publicly traded company, McClatchy Newspapers.[17] McClatchy's stock was trading in the $40 range in early 2000 and increased to the $70 range by mid-2004. McClatchy's performance began to decline in 2005 and its stock price decreased by over 90% by 2009. As the company's stock price declined by over 90%, its financial leverage increased. In Exhibit 8.7, we show McClatchy's estimated beta from January 2000 through December 2015 as well as the company's total debt to total capital ratio for this same period. We estimated beta using 60 monthly returns.[18] These are rolling 60 month betas, meaning that for every month, we add the most recent observation and drop the oldest observation used in the previous month's estimation. The chart illustrates the relation between a company's equity beta and its financial leverage—all else equal, the higher a company's financial leverage, the higher its equity beta.

EXHIBIT 8.7 Relation between Financial Leverage and Equity Betas—McClatchy Newspapers

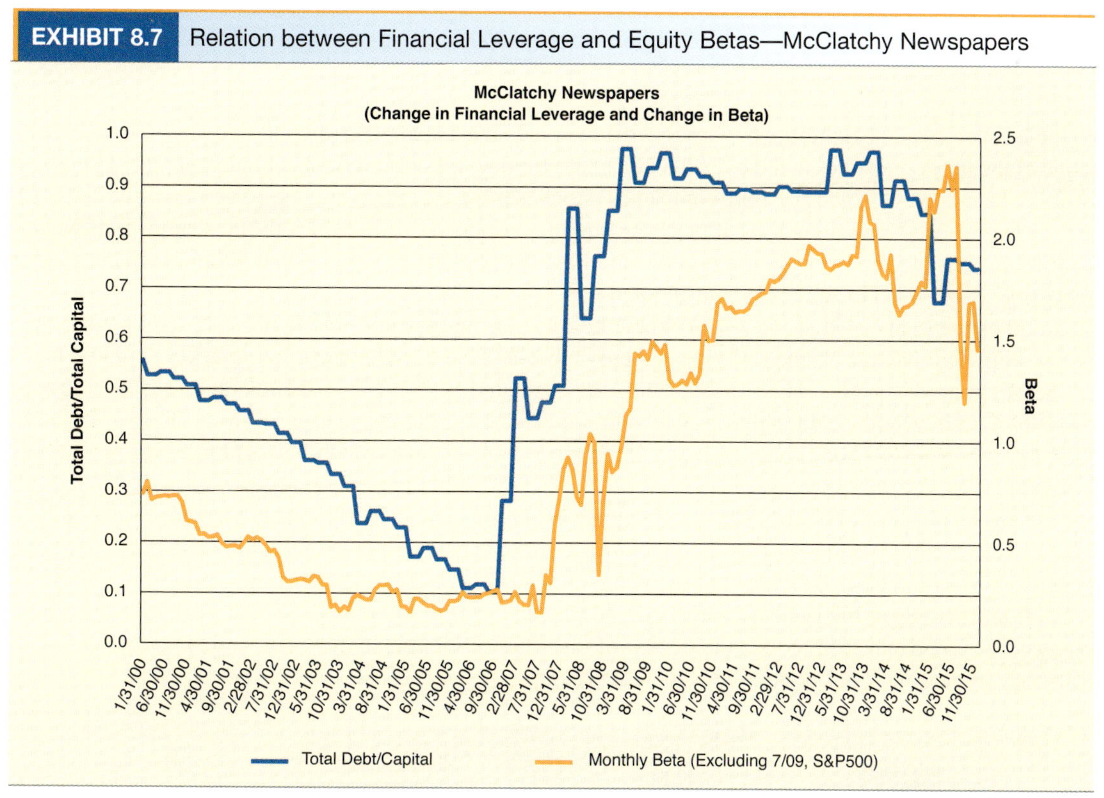

[17] McClatchy Newspapers started in California in 1857 and now operates in 29 U.S. markets publishing newspapers. Its operations include daily newspapers, Websites and mobile applications, mobile news and advertising, video products, publications, direct marketing, direct mail services and community newspapers.

[18] For reasons we explain later in the chapter (see Exhibit 8.10), we exclude July 2009 when we estimate beta.

The Market Model Applied to Portfolios

Just as the CAPM is applicable to both individual securities and portfolios of securities, the market model is also applicable to both. The market model regression in terms of portfolio p is shown in Equation 8.8.

$$\tilde{R}_{pt} = \alpha_p + \beta_p \tilde{R}_{mt} + \tilde{\varepsilon}_{pt} \quad t = 1......T \tag{8.8}$$

And the variance of the portfolio's return based on the market model is

$$\sigma^2(\tilde{R}_p) = \beta_p^2 \sigma^2(\tilde{R}_m) + \sigma^2(\tilde{\varepsilon}_p)$$

What happens to $\sigma^2(\tilde{\varepsilon}_p)$ as the number of securities in the portfolio increases, that is, approaches the securities in the market portfolio used to estimate the market model? In the limit, $\sigma^2(\tilde{\varepsilon}_p)$ approaches zero, implying that all of the variation in a portfolio's return can be explained by variation in the market in conjunction with the beta of the portfolio. Consequently, the r-squared of a market model regression approaches 1.0 (100%) as the portfolio becomes more diversified and more similar to the market used to estimate the market model. Thus, for a well diversified portfolio, all of the risk is based on the portfolio beta in conjunction with overall market risk. Since portfolio betas are just the weighted average of the betas of the securities in the portfolio, you should now have some intuition for why beta is the measure of risk that is priced in the CAPM even though investors measure portfolio risk by its variance.

REVIEW EXERCISE 8.3

Systematic Risk and Unsystematic Risk

Assume a portfolio has monthly stock returns with a standard deviation of 0.155, and the standard deviation of the market portfolio of monthly returns is 0.06. The portfolio has an estimated beta of 1.3. Calculate the proportion of the portfolio's stock return variance that represents systematic risk and the proportion that represents unsystematic risk. Is the portfolio well diversified?

Solution on page 377.

In the last two rows of Exhibit 8.6, we show the average beta, standard error, and r-squared of the regressions of the four companies and the results of a market model regression for an equally weighted portfolio of the four companies (add the four companies' stock returns together for each period and divide by 4). In Exhibit 8.8 we show the scatter plot of the equally weighted portfolio. From the scatter plot, we see that the returns are closer to the regression line than they are in any of the individual company scatter plots in Exhibit 8.5. The portfolio beta is equal to 1.14, which is equal to the average of the betas of the four companies. This is what we would expect because we know from Equation 8.4 that a portfolio beta is the weighted average of the individual security betas. Also as we expect, the market explains more of the variance of the four security portfolio (the r-squared is 77%) than the average (38%) and more than any individual stock. In addition, the standard error of the four-stock portfolio beta is lower, 0.08, than the average, 0.19, and lower than any individual stock, indicating the 95% confidence interval has a smaller range.

These results are not surprising. As we increase the number of securities in a portfolio, we reduce the amount of idiosyncratic risk in the portfolio, and that generally decreases the standard error of the beta estimate of the portfolio. That is why using comparable companies can increase the precision of our beta estimate (reduces the standard error). While we can never eliminate all of the uncertainty, the use of comparable companies can reduce the degree of uncertainty. Of course, the comparable companies must truly be comparable if this technique is to actually improve our estimates of the cost of capital.

Valuation Key 8.6

A market model regression is the standard method for developing initial beta estimates. Understanding the market model provides useful intuition as to why the CAPM suggests that beta is the relevant measure of the risk of a security.

EXHIBIT 8.8 Scatter Plot of an Equally Weighted Portfolio of the Four Companies in Exhibit 8.6

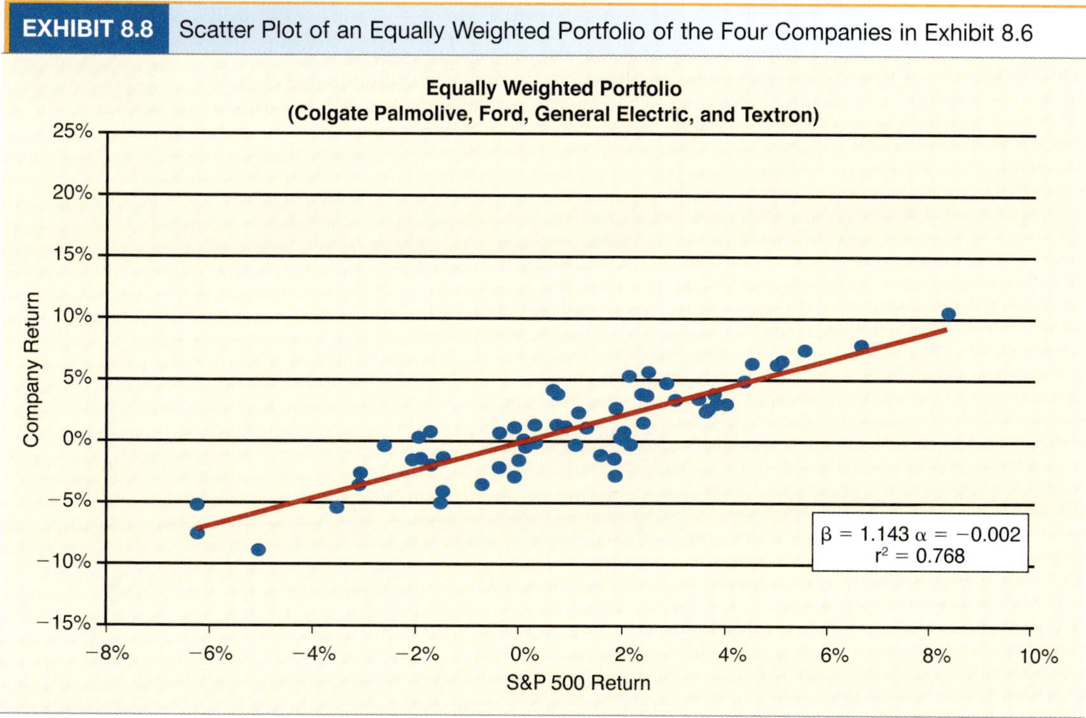

Beta Estimation: Choosing the Proxy for the Market Portfolio (Market Index)

The market portfolio in the theoretical derivation of the CAPM is the value-weighted index of all risky assets. While that is the theoretical construct, in practice, we implement the model differently as estimates of the returns to such a market portfolio are not available. Thus, one factor to consider in the choice of an index is what securities to include in the index. Since we use the CAPM to price equity securities, we typically use a broad-based stock market index and do not include other types of assets such as bonds, real estate, private equity investments, and so forth. The primary reason for not including these other assets is the abundance of stock return data and the relative paucity of return data for other types of assets.

One factor to consider when choosing a market index to estimate beta is what market index you will choose to estimate the market risk premium. The two choices are linked to each other in that the same index should be used to estimate both beta and the market risk premium. For example, assume we can use either a broad market index of stocks to estimate the beta for a company and market risk premium or an index of these same stocks and a broad index of corporate bonds. We know that the risk (volatility) of a broad-based stock index is higher than the risk (volatility) of that same broad-based stock index combined with a bond index because bonds have less risk than stocks. We also know that the expected return on a stock-only index will be greater than the expected return on the combined stock and bond index. As such, the market risk premium estimated using the stock-only index would be larger than the market risk premium estimated using the combined stock and bond index. We would also expect a company's estimated stock beta to be higher using the stock and bond combined index than when using the stock-only index because beta is a measure of relative risk, that is, an asset's risk judged relative to a particular portfolio or index. If we use one index to estimate a company's beta and use a different index to estimate the market risk premium, the estimates will be inconsistent. While using a stock index versus using a combined stock and bond index is a somewhat extreme example, the same issues arise when mixing other indices. For example, we would not want to estimate a company's beta against the Wilshire 5000 and then estimate the market risk premium from the S&P 500.

Two additional factors to consider are whether to include dividends in the calculation of the returns to a stock index and whether to use a value-weighted or equal-weighted average index. Since the stock returns investors earn include the effect of dividends, we recommend using a market index that also includes the effect of dividends to estimate beta. Some indices, such as the S&P 500 as it is normally calculated, do not include the dividend component in the calculation of the return on the index. We recommend including dividends. Whenever we use the returns to the S&P 500 in this book, we have calculated the returns with dividends. The last factor we discuss regarding the construction of the index is the weighting of the firms in the market index, usually either an equal or a value weighting. The CAPM assumes that the market portfolio is a value-weighted index of all risky assets, but practitioners use both equal-weighted and value-weighted indices, though value-weighted indices such as the S&P 500 are more commonly used.[19]

Domestic or World Index. An issue that we discuss later in the book (see Chapter 17) is whether to use a domestic index or a world index. As we explain in more detail later, the choice depends on the appropriate reference portfolio for the investors buying or owning the company being valued. If we are valuing a U.S. company with almost all U.S. investors, who primarily hold U.S. securities, we would choose a domestic index like the S&P 500. However, if we believed that investors in that U.S. company held a diversified world portfolio regardless of where they resided, we would use a world index. The former view of the world assumes that capital markets are segmented while the latter view assumes that capital markets are integrated and that capital flows freely around the world. We discuss this issue in greater detail in Chapter 17, and for now we just assume that markets are segmented, meaning that if we are interested in valuing a U.S. company, we would use a U.S. stock market index. Analogously, if we were valuing a Japanese firm, we would use a Japanese stock market index.

Beta Estimation: Choosing the Time Period for the Estimation and Time Interval (Periodicity) for Measuring Returns

Earlier we discussed the potential issues with beta estimates because we estimate betas using a company's historical (observed) stock returns regressed on a market index of observed returns. We also discussed how betas can shift because of changes in a company's capital structure or because of changes in the underlying business risk of the company, or because of fundamental changes in the overall market. Fortunately, we can measure returns over virtually any time interval (**periodicity**)—hourly, daily, weekly, monthly, quarterly, annually, or longer. We can use the choice of the number of observations, chronological time period, and time interval used to estimate beta to address any potential spurious bias or changes in a company's underlying risk factors. For the purposes of a valuation, the goal of these choices is to estimate the company's forward looking beta for the long-term. Generally, all else equal, we prefer to use more observations, a longer chronological time period, and a longer return period to estimate beta.

Choosing the Number of Observations and Time Period. A basic principle in statistics is that, all else equal, the precision of regression parameters, and thus, the precision of a beta estimate, increases with more observations; hence, all else equal, we prefer to use more observations to estimate beta. It turns out, however, that all else is not always equal and we face tradeoffs between increasing the number of observations and stability of the company's beta (changes in the underlying risk factors). The more observations used, the more likely there has been a shift in the company's beta. Using monthly data, it is quite common to use 60 monthly observations, if the data are available and if there is no obvious indication that the beta has shifted. Some scholarly research indicates that 60 months of data is a reasonable time period over which to measure beta.[20] But we can sometimes get reasonable estimates of beta with as few as 30 observations, depending on the company and the circumstances. If we do not have a sufficient stable history of monthly returns, we would use a shorter return interval (for example, weekly or daily data). However, most of the research focuses on estimating beta for the short-term (often one month), and not for the very long term used in a DCF valuation. Fama and French (1997) show that for short-term forecasts of one month, the past 60 months of returns works best; however, for longer-term forecasts, they document that, when estimating betas for industries (not individual companies), estimation periods of up to 26 years work best for longer forecast horizons of a year or longer.[21] This evidence suggests that industry betas are mean reverting (a topic we discuss next) and using the longer time period

[19] On March 21, 2005, the weighting in the S&P 500 was changed to be based on the market value of the public float (shares held by the public) as opposed to the total number of shares outstanding. Wal-Mart and Microsoft have the biggest number of shares not in the public float and will accordingly now have less of an impact on the S&P 500. Had the S&P 500 index been calculated using the new rule from September 2003 to March 16, 2005, the difference in the return would have been 0.13%. See M. Krantz, *USA Today*, March 21, 2005 at http://www.usatoday.com/money/markets/us/2005-03-21-sp-usat_x.htm.

[20] See Alexander, G., and N. Chervany, "On the Estimation and Stability of Beta," *Journal of Financial and Quantitative Analysis* 15 (1980), pp. 123–137. They show that four- and six-year estimation periods are superior to alternative estimation periods varying between one and nine years.

[21] See Fama, E., and K. French, "Industry Costs of Equity," *Journal of Financial Economics* 43 (1997), pp. 153–193.

dampens the effect of any wanderings the industry beta may take from its underlying mean. This approach has not been studied at the company level as of yet.

Time Interval (Periodicity) for Measuring Returns. The shorter the periodicity (time interval) we choose to measure a return, the more likely that we will encounter statistical issues when we estimate the market model. One statistical issue is that over shorter return intervals, such as daily returns, the returns are more likely to be auto-correlated (last period's return is related to the next period's return). This is much less of an issue for monthly returns. Another issue is that the shorter the return interval, the greater the likelihood that the period over which the return on the stock is measured will not match the period over which the return on the market is measured because stocks might not trade precisely at the end of each interval. When this occurs we say that the returns are non-synchronous. In order to estimate the beta properly, the period over which the stock returns and index returns are measured must be matched. The more infrequently a stock trades, the more likely we encounter non-synchronous returns. We observe this effect for daily return intervals for many stocks. For stocks trading infrequently, this effect can even occur in monthly return intervals to some extent, and it is more likely to occur in emerging markets where trading is less frequent.

One method we can use to correct for non-synchronous trading is to include both lead and lagged market returns in the market model regression.[22] In other words, we estimate the following regression:

$$R_{it} = \alpha_i + \beta_{i,lag}R_{mt-1} + \beta_i R_{mt} + \beta_{i,lead}R_{mt+1} + \varepsilon_{it} \quad t = 1......T \tag{8.9}$$

The advantage of this technique is that if the returns are non-synchronous, the lead and lag terms help correct for the non-synchronicity. To calculate the estimated beta from this version of the market model, we simply add the three beta terms together, $\beta_{i,lag} + \beta_i + \beta_{i,lead}$.

Using Daily or Weekly Data to Adjust for Changes in Operations and Capital Structure. We indicated that monthly returns may have advantages relative to daily or weekly data if we believe infrequent trading potentially exists. However, a company's risk characteristics are more likely to shift the longer the time period used for estimating beta. The underlying business risk can shift because of major acquisitions, divestitures, shifts in the company's primary business, or simply because of structural shifts in the economy that cause the underlying business to have a different systematic risk in relation to the overall market. To address this issue, we might use either weekly or daily returns so we can estimate the beta over a shorter time period. Alternatively, we may be able to measure beta prior to the structural shift and then adjust the beta for the structural shift.

Valuation in Practice 8.2

Estimating Laureate Education, Inc.'s Beta After a Major Divestiture Laureate Education, Inc. ("the Company" or "Laureate") is focused exclusively on providing a superior higher education experience through a leading global network of accredited campus-based and online universities and other higher education institutions ("higher education institutions" or "schools").

Sylvan Learning Systems, Inc. sold the principal operations that comprised its K–12 educational services segments. As a result, the Company changed its name from Sylvan Learning Systems, Inc. to Laureate Education, Inc. The selling price of the K–12 segment was $283.4 million dollars, which was roughly 35% of Sylvan Learning Systems' total firm value prior to the sale. In addition to the significant divestiture, Laureate reduced its market value debt to equity ratio from approximately 25% to 6%.

Suppose you were interested in valuing Laureate 21 months after the sale. How would you estimate its beta given its new business mix? The significant divestiture and change in leverage make it difficult to use monthly data because we have only 21 monthly returns since the changes took place. If we estimate Laureate's beta using the 21 monthly returns, we obtain a beta estimate of 0.31 with a standard error of 0.70 for a 95% confidence interval of −1.15 to 1.77, not a particularly useful result. Using 18 months of daily returns prior to the transaction, the company's beta estimate is 0.51. Using 18 months of daily returns after the transaction, Laureate's beta is 1.02. Thus, despite the decline in

continued

[22] See M. Scholes, and J. Williams, "Estimating Betas from Nonsynchronous Data," *Journal of Financial Economics* 5 (1977), pp. 309–327; Dimson, E., "Risk Measurement When Shares Are Subject to Infrequent Trading," *Journal of Financial Economics* 7 (1979), pp. 197–226.

continued from previous page

leverage, Laureate's equity beta approximately doubled with the shift in operations. The estimated post-transaction beta of 1.02 has a standard error of 0.09 for a 95% confidence interval from 0.84 to 1.20. This example illustrates the potential benefit of using a shorter time period for estimation in conjunction with higher-frequency data for estimating beta when there has been a shift in a company's operations.

Source: See Laureate Education, Inc.'s December 31, 2004 10-K Report, p. 3.

When using daily data, a common rule of thumb is to use one to two years of data (a typical year has approximately 250 trading days). When using weekly data, it is a fairly common practice to use two years of data (104 observations). The advantage of daily and weekly data relative to monthly data is that we use a more recent history of returns to estimate beta, but we have to make sure the beta estimation does not have statistical issues such as asynchronous returns.

Valuation Key 8.7

Before attempting to estimate a company's equity beta, first assess the stability of the company's business risk and risk from financial leverage. Changes in operations or capital structure can cause instability in beta estimates measured in periods that span such changes. Using a shorter return interval (weekly or daily) may provide a sufficient number of observations to estimate beta after such shifts occur.

Mean Reversion in Estimated Betas and Adjusted Betas

Research indicates that estimated betas have a tendency to revert toward the mean of the market beta, which is one. This effect is often referred to as **mean reversion** in estimated betas. The betas we estimate from a market model equal the true beta plus noise (measurement error). In other words, we cannot observe a company's true beta. On average, estimated betas that are greater than one have positive noise terms (or positive measurement error), and estimated betas that are less than one have negative noise terms (negative measurement error). Thus, on average, but not for every company, beta estimates that are greater than one tend to be upward biased and estimated betas that are less than one tend to be downward biased, even though, on average, beta is an unbiased estimate of the true beta. Naturally, companies with higher than average financial leverage and higher than average operating risk will have equity betas greater than the average beta.

Marshall Blume conducted a study of this phenomenon in 1971.[23] He divided his observations into six different time periods and examined how betas moved between one time period and the next time period. For each adjacent two time periods, he estimated a regression using the second period's beta for each security i as the dependent variable and the first period's beta for each security i as the independent variable (which we refer to as $\beta_{i,2}$ and $\beta_{i,1}$). On average across all of his regressions of adjacent time periods, he found that: $\beta_{i,2} = 0.371 + 0.635\ \beta_{i,1}$.

That finding is of course consistent with the mean reversion phenomena. This formula implies that the best prediction of the beta you will observe in the second period if the first period's beta is 2.0 is equal to 1.641 ($1.641 = 0.371 + 0.635 \times 2.0$). If the first period's estimated beta is 0.4, the best prediction of that beta in period 2 is 0.625 ($0.625 = 0.371 + 0.635 \times 0.4$). Thus, the best prediction of next period's beta is that it is closer to one. Recall from Exhibit 8.2 in which we present median industry betas, some industries tend to have higher betas than others. To the extent industry betas are stable, we would not expect companies in a high (low) beta industry, for example, a highly leveraged industry, to revert toward the average beta across all companies, but instead could well revert toward their industry's mean beta. We discuss this issue in Chapter 10.

Blume's findings could result from a statistical issue (the measurement error we have been discussing) or it could simply be that over time, firms choose projects that naturally move them closer to 1. Subsequent work shows that we still observe substantial mean reversion whether we run the regression as discussed earlier or when we perform the regression in reverse ($\beta_{i,2}$ becomes the independent variable and $\beta_{i,1}$ becomes the dependent variable). The result also stands for portfolios or for individual securities.[24]

---

[23] See Blume, M. E., "On the Assessment of Risk," *Journal of Finance* 26 (1971), pp. 1–10.

[24] See Elgers, P. T., J. R. Haltiner, and W. H. Hawthorne, "Beta Regression Tendencies: Statistical and Real Causes," *Journal of Finance* 34 (March, 1979), pp. 261–263.

The same pattern exists if we use every other day to estimate betas or even and odd months. Thus, this result appears to be a statistical issue, not an economic one; fortunately, we have procedures to adjust for this effect if necessary.

Some practitioners and suppliers of commercial estimates adjust beta and provide so-called **adjusted betas**. For many, the technique they use follows from the work of Blume. Bloomberg, for example, provides both historical and adjusted betas. Bloomberg's adjusted beta is Bloomberg Adjusted Beta = 0.33 + 0.67 × Historical Beta. Using comparable companies to estimate a company's beta can mitigate this issue as long as the degree to which the comparable companies are too high or too low is not correlated across the comparable companies.

Valuation Key 8.8

Beta estimates appear to regress toward the mean beta of 1.0 because of statistical reasons. Thus, if the regression estimate of beta is above 1.0, we might adjust it downward; if it is below 1.0, we might adjust it upward. There is also evidence of reversion toward the mean industry beta. Various adjustment processes are available to adjust for these effects.

Using Commercially Available Betas

An alternative to estimating beta directly is to use commercially available CAPM-based beta estimates or even commercially available cost of capital estimates. If the choice is to use a commercially available estimate, we first identify the assumptions and choices underlying the estimation and then follow the process outlined in this chapter to decide, which, if any, of the beta estimates are appropriate for the valuation.

Many commercial services use monthly data; however, Bloomberg, for example, uses weekly data as a default (although the user can specify the use of monthly data). The advantage of using returns measured over a shorter interval is that we can generally estimate betas over a shorter and more recent time period, because given the same period of time (say, number of years) we get more observations when each return is computed over a shorter interval. For example, the services that use monthly data generally use 60 monthly observations or five years of data, whereas Bloomberg uses 104 weeks of weekly observations or two years of data. Depending on the company and its characteristics, using more recent data might provide a better forward-looking estimate.

In Exhibit 8.9, we present six commercially available beta estimates for the four companies for which we estimated beta (see Exhibit 8.6). All of the betas are estimated using the S&P500 Index as the proxy

EXHIBIT 8.9 Commercially Available Betas for the Four Companies in Exhibit 8.6

Published as of July 7, 2017	Colgate Palmolive Co.	Ford Motor Co.	General Electric Co.	Textron Inc.
Bloomberg				
Equity Beta	0.78	1.28	1.03	1.18
Adjusted Equity Beta	0.85	1.19	1.02	1.12
Capital IQ 5 Year Beta	0.81	1.15	1.22	1.56
Google Finance	0.82	1.04	1.25	1.55
Thomson One	0.87	1.15	1.03	1.32
Yahoo Finance	0.74	1.35	1.10	1.52
Zacks	0.82	1.03	1.25	1.55
Average	0.81	1.17	1.13	1.40
Exhibit 8.6 (as of March 31, 2017)	0.75	1.06	1.18	1.58

Bloomberg	Estimated using two years of weekly returns and the S&P 500 index; adjusted beta = 0.333 + 0.667 × beta
Capital IQ 5	Estimated using five years of monthly returns and the S&P 500 index.
Google Finance	Not officially published; appears to be estimated using five years of monthly returns and the S&P 500 index.
Thomson One	Estimated using 1,300 (approximately five years) of daily returns and the S&P 500 index.
Yahoo Finance	Estimated using three years of monthly returns and the S&P 500 index.
Zacks	Not officially published; appears to be estimated using five years of monthly returns and the S&P 500 index.

for the market index. Four of the betas are estimated using monthly data, one using weekly data, and one using daily data. One of the betas is estimated using two years of data, another uses three years of data, while the others use five years of data. The betas of Textron vary the most—the difference between the maximum and minimum beta divided by the mean is more than 30%. The betas of Colgate Palmolive vary the least—the difference between the maximum and minimum beta divided by the mean is about 15%. It is typically not possible to analyze why commercial beta estimates differ from each other because of a lack of sufficiently detailed data.

Potential Spurious Effects of Company Specific Information on Beta

We estimate beta using a company's historical (observed) stock returns regressed on a market index of observed returns. These are observed stock returns, not expected stock returns. As a result, a company can experience a positive or negative stock return for reasons unrelated to the market that we use to estimate beta. If it happens that the company experiences a large positive stock return in a period, say month, that is unrelated to the market, and at the same time the market has a positive (negative) stock return, that large monthly return can result in an upward (downward) impact on beta. On the other hand, if it happens that the company experiences a large negative stock return in a period, say month, that is unrelated to the market, and at the same time the market has a positive (negative) stock return, that monthly return can result in a downward (upward) impact on beta. The extent of this impact depends not only on the relative returns in that month but also in the other months used to estimate beta.

We illustrate this effect using what turned out to be an extreme example, McClatchy Newspapers. McClatchy Newspapers stock was trading in the $40 range in early 2000 and increased to the $70 range by mid-2004. McClatchy's performance began to decline rapidly in 2005 and its stock price decreased by over 90% by 2009. In July 2009, McClatchy announced unexpected positive performance, which was preceded and also followed by unexpected positive performance of some of its competitors. This and other positive news about the company resulted in a 358% stock return for McClatchy in July 2009. In that month the S&P 500 had a 7.4% return. It turns out that these contemporaneous positive price movements had a large effect on McClatchy's beta, even when estimated over 60 months.

In Exhibit 8.10, we show McClatchy's estimated beta (rolling 60 month beta) including and excluding July 2009. McClatchy's beta increased from 1.4 as of June 2009 to 3.6 as of July 2009. McClatchy's

EXHIBIT 8.10 Example of the Spurious Effect of Company Specific Information on Beta—McClatchy Newspapers

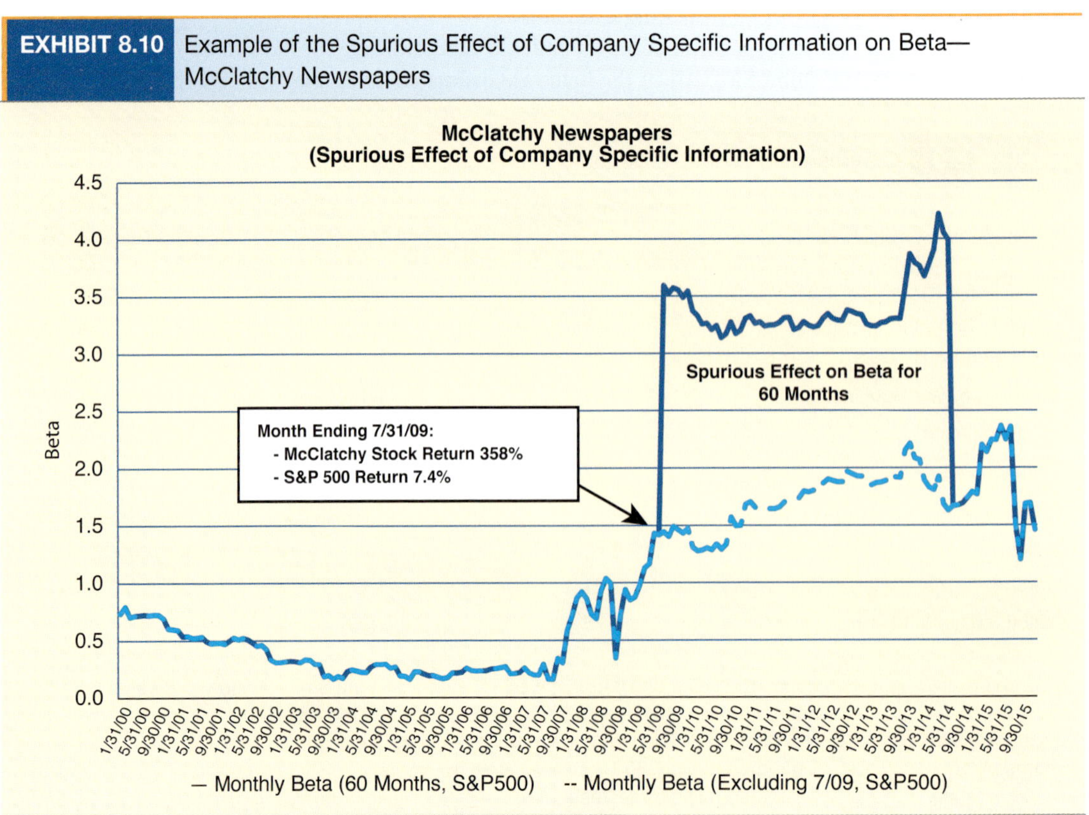

estimated beta remained at this high level for five years (June 2014), when July 2009 was no longer included when estimating beta. The chart also shows the effect of excluding that one month. While McClatchy is an extreme example—a 358% return in a month is unusual—it clearly shows how stock price movements unrelated to the market movements, can impact beta estimates. We can compare betas estimated using alternative estimation periods (for example, one year, two years, five years) and alternative periodicity (for example, daily, weekly, monthly returns) to help identify potential influential observations. Using comparable companies' betas can mitigate this issue as long as such spurious effects are not correlated across the comparable companies (a point we discuss in more detail in Chapter 10).

8.4 ADJUSTING ESTIMATED BETAS FOR CHANGES IN RISK (NON-STATIONARY BETAS)

In this section, we illustrate ways we can use the basic principle that a portfolio beta is equal to the weighted average of the betas of each investment. We apply this concept to a company's unlevered (or asset) beta—that is, a company's unlevered beta is equal to the weighted average of the unlevered betas of each part of the company's business—to illustrate how to adjust betas for changes in a company's operations or to exclude excess assets. Recall that a company's betas will change if either financial or operating risk changes.

Adjustments to Beta for Changes in Operations

If we have sufficient information, we can make direct adjustments for changes in certain types of operations (beta of the operations or unlevered beta) and for changes in capital structure. We discuss how to adjust betas for changes in capital structure in Chapter 10. Here we discuss how to adjust betas for changes in operations.

Recall from Equation 8.4 that the beta of a portfolio is simply the weighted average of the betas of the securities in the portfolio, where the weights are relative market values. This same principle is also applicable to the composition of a company's unlevered beta or asset beta. An unlevered beta is the weighted average of the betas of the firm's assets (or projects). As it turns out, this is a useful result and sometimes can help us adjust betas for changes in operations.

To see how we might use this relation, assume that we were interested in estimating what America OnLine (AOL) and Time Warner, Inc.'s (Time Warner) beta would be after they merged in January 2001. In other words, assume it is early in the year 2000, but the merger will not close until early 2001. We could forecast what AOL/Time Warner's beta would be after the merger as follows. First, we would estimate Time Warner's beta and AOL's beta separately. Then, we would calculate the weighted average beta based on the relative weights. In this case, the companies merged in a stock-for-stock transaction, so the companies' economic balance sheets were essentially merged together, and thus, the post-merger capital structure is a weighted average of the pre-merger capital structures. In order to make this assumption, we also assume that value will neither be created nor destroyed by the merger. Had this not been the case, we would have used unlevered betas of the two companies and then relevered the unlevered beta for the anticipated post-merger capital structure.

In the case of AOL and Time Warner, the equity beta of the combined company should equal the market value weighted average of the equity betas, assuming there are no subsequent changes in capital structure. If the total amount of debt stays the same after the merger but the value of the firm increases from synergies, then the amount of financial leverage will decrease. Also, in some transactions, capital structures might be expected to change and appropriate adjustments would have to be made for that. For purposes of this analysis, we assume the leverage of the company is expected to stay the same.

At the time of the merger announcement, AOL's equity was 42% of the total equity value of AOL and Time Warner, and Time Warner was 58% of the total. AOL's pre-merger beta was approximately 2.7 and Time Warner's pre-merger beta was 1.2. Weighting the pre-merger betas by the market values at the time of announcement yields an estimate of the combined firm's beta of 1.83 ($1.83 = 0.42 \times 2.7 + 0.58 \times 1.2$). Hence, we would anticipate a combined beta of approximately 1.8. It turns out that the post-merger beta was in the 2.1 range, higher than we anticipated.

Our analysis did not predict the post-merger beta correctly because two changes occurred that our calculation did not anticipate. First, AOL/Time Warner issued more debt subsequent to the transaction and thus the amount of debt of the combined firm was greater than our calculation anticipated. Second, by the time of the close of the merger, the market values of both companies had decreased by approximately one-third and the post-merger company was more highly levered than expected. The value of the combined company continued to fall subsequent to the close, thus making the company even more highly levered in the months and years after the closing. As such, it is not a surprise that the beta of AOL/Time Warner turned out to be greater than our prediction of 1.8 since that calculation presumed there would be no increase in leverage, which proved to be incorrect.

In the case of AOL and Time Warner, we made our prediction by working with the equity betas directly. Had we known that the capital structures were going to change, we could have first calculated unlevered betas, weighted the unlevered betas based on the market values of AOL and Time Warner, and then adjusted the unlevered betas for the new capital structure of the merged entity. We discuss levering and unlevering betas in Chapter 10, but it is analogous to levering and unlevering cost of capital estimates as discussed in Chapter 5.

Direct Adjustments to Unlevered Betas for Excess Assets and Divestitures

The basic principle that a company's unlevered (asset) beta is equal to the weighted average unlevered betas of its projects is useful to make adjustments for excess assets or for divestitures. For example, one estimate of Microsoft's equity beta is 1.07. Since Microsoft did not have any significant debt during the estimation period used, its unlevered beta was also around 1.07. During this time period, Microsoft had about 20% of its market value in various types of cash instruments and marketable securities, which we will assume were all excess assets and have a beta of 0.15. Using this principle, we can estimate Microsoft's unlevered beta for its operations. Its unlevered beta for its operations would be $\beta_{\text{unlevered operations}}$ in the following formula.

$$\beta_{\text{unlevered company}} = 0.2 \times \beta_{\text{marketable securities}} + (1 - 0.2) \times \beta_{\text{unlevered operations}}$$

$$1.07 = 0.2 \times 0.15 + (1 - 0.2) \times \beta_{\text{unlevered operations}}$$

Solving the above formula for $\beta_{\text{unlevered operations}}$, we estimate the unlevered beta of Microsoft's operations to be approximately 1.30.

We could perform a similar calculation for a company that was going to divest itself of a division or spin it off, if we wanted to estimate the beta of the remaining assets. Similarly, if we have sufficient information, we can use this same principle to estimate the unlevered beta of one of the business segments of a company. The above cannot be used on equity betas for levered companies because financial leverage also affects equity betas. To use this approach, we first unlever the company's equity beta (see Chapter 10).

Valuation Key 8.9

The beta of a portfolio is equal to the weighted average beta of the securities that make up that portfolio. Similarly, the beta of a company's assets—the company's unlevered beta—is equal to the weighted average beta of the assets (or projects) in which the company invests. We can use this relationship to make adjustments to beta for changes in the company's assets and to exclude the effect of a company's excess assets on its beta.

Shifting Betas in the Future

It is possible that we might anticipate beta shifting in the future because of expected changes in the underlying economics of a company. For example, suppose you are valuing a firm that produces jets for the government and has a five-year backlog for those planes, sold on a "cost plus" basis. Business beyond five years depends on the company obtaining additional contracts. It is possible that the risk of the first five years of cash flows is different from the risk of the cash flows beyond five years. The government may purchase more planes when the economy is good and tax revenues are high than when the economy is poor and tax receipts are down. In that case, the relevant beta for the first five years of cash flows for this company could be smaller than the beta of the cash flows starting in Year 6.

REVIEW EXERCISE 8.4

Adjusting Estimated Betas

Part 1—Assume Company A that operates in the transportation equipment industry and has an estimated equity beta of 1.7 is planning to merge with Company B that operates in the trucking and warehousing industry and has an estimated equity beta of 1.0. At the time of the announcement of the merger, Company B's equity was twice the market value of Company A's equity. Estimate the combined firm's equity beta after the merger, assuming that debt in the merged entity will be equal to the pre-merger debt of Company A and Company B combined and the merger is not expected to create or destroy value.

Part 2—Company C has an estimated beta of 1.5 and does not have any debt or other non-common equity financing. The company has 30% of its total market value invested in marketable securities that have an estimated beta of 0.4 and are assumed to be excess assets. Estimate the unlevered beta for Company C's operations.

Solution on page 377.

REVIEW EXERCISE 8.5

Bloomberg Adjusted Betas

Calculate the Bloomberg adjusted beta for each of the comparable companies and the portfolio of comparable companies that appear in the table below. Assume all companies are unlevered.

	Beta Estimate	Standard Error of Beta	t-statistic
Comparable Company #1	0.900	0.50	1.80
Comparable Company #2	1.100	0.40	2.75
Comparable Company #3	1.350	0.60	2.25
Comparable Company #4	1.500	0.45	3.33
Comparable company average beta	1.213		
Company being valued	1.100	0.56	1.96

Solution on page 378.

8.5 ESTIMATING THE MARKET RISK PREMIUM

The market risk premium represents the expected return, above the return on the risk-free asset, demanded by the market to induce investors to invest in the market portfolio. More practically, it is the difference between the expected return on a proxy for the overall market less the return offered on a risk-free investment. At the current time, there is considerable debate about the most accurate way to estimate the market risk premium. While there is some debate about the most appropriate proxy for the market portfolio and the proxy for the risk-free rate, the majority of the debate on implementing the CAPM is about how to estimate the expected market risk premium once the proxies are chosen for the market and the risk-free rate. For years, the most common approach was to calculate the historical average market risk premium over some long prior historical period. While this method is still used most often, other methods have been developed and are being used. Many of these methods use historical data, but some do not.

In Exhibit 8.11, we summarize the steps in estimating the market risk premium, and discuss them in this section of the chapter.

EXHIBIT 8.11 Steps in Estimating the Market Risk Premium

1	Decide which statistic to use to measure the market risk premium (average, geometric mean, or some other procedure)
2	Choose a market index (links to the beta estimation process) and a proxy for the risk-free asset (links to estimating the risk-free yield)
3	Choose an estimation period (how long of a period and specific beginning and ending dates)
4	Make adjustments, if any, for survivorship bias or other effects

The 1926 to 2016 U.S. Return Experience

Before we discuss the market risk premium, we first examine some historical security returns. Our goal is to glean some general information about the magnitude of the returns of different kinds of assets to help you understand some of the debate about estimating the market risk premium. Exhibit 8.12 presents the annual returns on various classes of assets measured over the 1926–2016 period.

EXHIBIT 8.12 Total Annual U.S. Returns 1926–2016

Return Series	Geometric Mean	Arithmetic Mean	Standard Deviation
S&P 500	10.0%	12.0%	19.9%
Small stocks	12.1%	16.6%	31.9%
Long-term corp bonds	6.0%	6.3%	8.4%
Long-term gov't bonds	5.5%	6.0%	9.9%
Intermediate-term gov't bonds	5.1%	5.3%	5.6%
U.S. Treasury Bills	3.4%	3.4%	3.1%
Inflation	2.9%	3.0%	4.1%

Source: See *Stocks, Bonds, Bills and Inflation* by Duff and Phelps, John Wiley and Sons, Inc., 2017. Reprinted with permission.

Each line in the exhibit represents the return for a different class of assets traded in the U.S. between 1926 and 2016. The S&P 500 is the with-dividend returns earned on the Standard and Poor's 500, which tend to be large capitalization stocks. Small stocks represent the returns to a portfolio of small stocks, but the construction of that series has changed somewhat over time.[25] The long-term corporate bonds are the returns earned on the Citigroup Long-Term High-Grade Corporate Bond Index (formerly Salomon Brothers High-Grade Corporate Bond Index). The long-term government bonds are 20 year bonds (bonds issued by the U.S. Treasury with a maturity of 20 years, or as close to that as possible). The bonds are held for a year, sold, and the proceeds are reinvested in a new 20-year bond (assuming no taxes). The intermediate government bond, which is also issued by the U.S. Treasury, is similar to the long-term government bond except that the bonds are bought when they have a maturity of five years, are held for a year, and the proceeds are reinvested in a new five-year bond (again, assuming no taxes). The U.S. Treasury Bill series is obtained by buying a U.S Treasury Bill with one month to go until it matures, holding it for a month, and then reinvesting in another Treasury bill with a one-month maturity (again with no taxes).[26] Inflation is measured by the Consumer Price Index (CPI).

Exhibit 8.12 presents the arithmetic mean annual return, the geometric mean annual return, and the standard deviation of the annual returns for each type of asset. The arithmetic mean return, $\bar{R}_A$, is the simple average annual return and is calculated as

$$\bar{R}_A = \frac{1}{T}\sum_{t=1}^{T} R_t \quad \textbf{(8.10)}$$

Thus, it measures the simple average yearly return over the period 1926–2016.

The geometric mean return, R_G, is estimated as

$$R_G = \left[\prod_{t=1}^{T}(1+R_t)\right]^{1/T} - 1 \quad \textbf{(8.11)}$$

[25] From 1926 until 1981, the series was the value-weighted index of the lowest quintile of the New York Stock Exchange. Between 1982 and March, 2001, the series represents the performance of Dimensional Fund Advisors (DFA) Small Company Fund, which is a value-weighted portfolio of the lowest quintile of the NYSE plus any stocks on the AMEX or NASDAQ with market capitalization less than or equal to the highest-valued company in the lowest quintile of the NYSE (though stocks with a market cap of less than $10 million are not purchased). Starting in April 2001, the series represents the performance of DFA's Micro Cap Fund, which is a portfolio composed of the stocks with the smallest 5% of market capitalization across the NYSE, AMEX, and NASDAQ. DFA manages passive small company stock funds that take the passive side of transactions for their benchmark portfolios. Thus, the performance of their funds includes the transactions costs they receive for always taking the passive side of a transaction. See *Stocks, Bonds, Bills and Inflation,* by Duff and Phelps, John Wiley and Sons, Inc., Chapter 3. Reprinted with permission.

[26] U.S. Treasury Bills are a debt obligation of the U.S. Treasury that have maturities of one year or less (typically issued with maturities of 91 days, 182 days, or 52 weeks).

The geometric mean return, say, for the S&P 500, indicates the annually compounded return over the 1926–2016 time period if someone would have invested $1 in the S&P 500 on January 1, 1926, and held that position until December 31, 2016 (and reinvested all cash distributions without taxes). One dollar invested in the S&P 500 in the beginning of 1926 would have grown to $6,035.12 by the end of 2016, which is equivalent to an annual return every year of 10.0%, the geometric mean. The geometric mean return is always less than the arithmetic mean return as long as the time-series experiences both up and down movements. We focus our discussion on the arithmetic mean return for now.

From the information in Exhibit 8.12, we can estimate the real risk-free rate of return earned over this period as the difference between the average annual return on one-month U.S. Treasury Bills and the average annual increase in the CPI, which is 0.4% (0.4% = 3.4% − 3.0%). We would not use longer-term U.S. debt securities for this calculation because the return on these securities includes a maturity premium.

We can measure the average maturity premium as the difference in the average annual returns of long-term government bonds and short-term Treasury bills. Measured this way, on average, investors earned 2.6% (2.6% = 6.0% − 3.4%) more per year by holding U.S. securities that matured in 20 years as opposed to a one-month maturity. Since investors holding a 20-year bond bear the risk of unanticipated inflation and shifts in required real risk-free returns, it is not surprising that they demand a premium for holding long-term bonds relative to short-term bills. The maturity premium measured between intermediate-term government bonds and Treasury bills is 1.9% (1.9% = 5.3% − 3.4%).

In addition to the maturity premium, the returns on long-term corporate bonds also include a default premium. The default premium compensates investors for the possible default on the bonds. One measure of the default premium is the difference between the average annual return on high-grade long-term corporate bonds and long-term government bonds. The average difference is 0.3% (0.3% = 6.3% − 6.0%) per year. Of course, default premiums relative to non-investment-grade (more risky) bonds would be larger, and we discuss this further in Chapter 9.

Two proxies for the market risk premium are the difference in the average annual returns between the S&P 500 and U.S. Treasury Bills and the difference in the average annual returns between the S&P 500 and U.S. long-term government bonds. From Exhibit 8.12, we can calculate both of these proxies for this period. The average market risk premium measured using the S&P 500 and U.S. Treasury Bills has been 8.6% (8.6% = 12.0% − 3.4%). Using the S&P 500 and U.S. long-term government bonds, the average market risk premium has been 6.0% (6.0% = 12.0% − 6.0%). We can also calculate a market risk premium relative to intermediate-term government bonds, which would result in a market risk premium estimate of 6.7% (6.7% = 12.0% − 5.3%).

The mean difference in average annual returns between small stocks and the S&P 500 has been 4.6% (4.6% = 16.6% − 12.0%) during this period. The returns of small stocks are much more volatile than the returns of large stocks as well. The standard deviation of annual returns is 19.9% for large stocks and 31.9% for small stocks.

Choice of the Proxy for the Market Portfolio (Market Index)

Recall from our earlier discussion that, generally, we estimate beta using the same market index that we use to measure the market risk premium. Thus, the issues regarding the choice of index for measuring the market risk premium are essentially the same as the issues we discuss regarding beta estimation. The key issues are what securities to include in the index, what weighting method to use, and whether to include dividends. Recall from our discussion about estimating beta that we generally include dividends to calculate the index returns and generally use a value-weighted index. We also generally use an index composed of stocks rather than stocks and other assets. That is why some academics and practitioners often refer to the market risk premium as the equity risk premium. We use the term market risk premium but keep in mind that we use a portfolio of common stocks as a proxy for the market portfolio.

Choice of Proxy for the Risk-Free Return to Measure the Market Risk Premium

The CAPM uses an expected (forward-looking) risk-free rate—that is, the yield on the risk-free asset as of the date of our valuation—the expected return of a riskless security at the date of our valuation. However, we also use historical risk-free rates of return to estimate the market risk premium if we estimate the market risk premium using historical returns. As you might expect, our choice of the risk-free asset we use to measure the yield (which we discuss in the next section of the chapter) affects the risk-free rate we use to estimate the market risk premium.

Valuation in Practice 8.3

LifeWatch Ltd.'s Equity Cost of Capital LifeWatch Ltd. is a public company traded on the SIX Swiss Exchange; whose main commercial unit, which accounted for all of its patient services and all of its third-party revenues, was LifeWatch Services Inc., a Delaware-incorporated company. In January 2017, Aevis Victoria SA, announced a public tender offer for all publicly held registered shares of LifeWatch. In February 2017, LifeWatch announced that it will solicit additional offers and in March 2017, the company's board of directors' special committee unanimously recommended to LifeWatch's shareholders to reject the Aevis offer. In April 2017, BioTelemetry Inc. offered to purchase each share of the company's stock for 0.1457 shares of BioTelemetry common stock plus CHF 10.00 in cash or, at the choice of each LifeWatch shareholder, 0.2185 shares of BioTelemetry Common Stock plus CHF 8.00 in cash. The company's board of director's special committee unanimously recommended to LifeWatch's shareholders to accept the BioTelemetry offer. In April 2017, LifeWatch's financial advisor, Raiffeisen Switzerland Cooperative, measured the company's equity cost of capital as follows.

Risk-free interest rate

To determine the risk-free interest rate, long-term interest yields of public issuers are used. As LifeWatch is mainly active in the US, the risk-free rate is based on the current yield of 30-year US government bonds on 24 March 2017, which amounted to 3.0%, approximately.

Equity risk premium

. . . Market participants demand risk premiums as compensation for taking on entrepreneurial risk. Since investors take on a special risk when investing in a company, a risk premium on top of the risk-free rate must be added to the risk-free rate. . . .

The company-specific risk premium is derived by multiplying the beta factor of the company by the market risk premium. The beta factor is a measure of the company-specific risk in relation to market risk. The market risk premium is the difference in the returns on equity and risk-free investments. . . ., the United States Long-Horizon Equity Risk Premia (1926-2015) amounted to 6.9%.

To derive the beta factor for LifeWatch, we used the beta factors of comparable companies. . . . To ensure that the beta factors are effectively comparable, they were adjusted by the company-specific leverage (debt-adjusted or unlevered beta). . . . By taking a certain degree of typical leverage . . . into account, a relevered beta of 0.96 results, resulting in costs of equity of 9.6% for the US Core Business and GE Cooperation activities.

Source: Fairness Opinion Regarding the Public Exchange and Cash Offer by Cardiac Monitoring Holding Company, LLC, Malvern, Pennsylvania, USA, (Domicile: Wilmington, Delaware, USA), for all publicly held registered shares of Life Watch Ltd., Zug ("Life Watch") April 21, 2017, available on June 26, 2018 at www.takeover.ch/documentprovider/contentelements/nr/3053/lang/3.

In the U.S., the most common choices for the historical risk-free rate returns to measure the market risk premium are U.S. government bonds (intermediate-term or long-term) and U.S. Treasury Bills. Advocates of using U.S. Treasury Bills often make the argument that while long-term U.S. government bonds might be free of default risk, they are not free of risk due to variation in expected inflation and variation in real required risk-free returns. The risk of unexpected inflation or shifts in real rates that an investor must bear increases with the maturity of a bond that has a fixed coupon rate. Suppose an investor buys a 10-year government bond at face value, when expected inflation is 2% per year. After purchasing the bond, an economic shock occurs, increasing expected inflation to 5%. If that occurs, the price of the bond will fall to reflect the increase in the required nominal rate of return that investors demand because of the increase in expected inflation. The price falls because the coupon is fixed and the only way that a new investor in the bond can earn the new higher required nominal return is to purchase the bond below face value. Thus, the purchaser of a long-term government bond is not really buying a completely risk-free security; it may be free of default risk, but it is not free of all risk as its price will fluctuate over time.

On the other hand, short maturity U.S. Treasury Bills are not as affected by these risks and are thus better proxies for the risk-free return over a short period. A strategy of rolling over an investment in one-month Treasury bills yields a return series that is very close to risk-free, assuming the risk of the U.S. government defaulting within a month is remote. Moreover, while changes in expected inflation or shifts in real required rates of return can occur within a month, the amount of risk that an investor would bear due to either factor is quite small given a one-month maturity. At the end of the month, the investor purchases a new one-month Treasury bill, which should reflect current expectations of inflation and investors' required rates of return on a risk-free asset.

Despite the fact that government bonds are riskier than Treasury bills, using long-term or intermediate-term government bonds to measure the market risk premium has many advocates. Fortunately, this choice does not have a large impact on the CAPM cost of capital, because we make an offsetting adjustment when estimating the risk-free yield. In fact, as we discuss later, for a security whose beta is exactly equal to 1, the choice between using one-month Treasury bills and long-term government bonds to measure the market risk premium will have no impact on the cost of capital estimated.

If we choose to use government bonds to estimate the market risk premium, we face the choice of using either the long-term or intermediate-term government bond. This choice of long-term versus intermediate-term bonds is based on the bond that we want to use to measure the risk-free yield as of the date of the valuation. If we are valuing a long-term investment, such as a company, we would generally measure the market risk premium using a long-term bond. If we are valuing a project that generated cash flows for, say, five years, we would measure the market risk premium using intermediate-term government bonds.

When calculating the returns on government bonds, we often use the total return on the government bond. However, some practitioners advocate using the income return on government bonds instead of the total return. If you buy a 20-year bond at face value and hold it for a year and then sell it, the return on the bond has two components. One component is the income return (the interest rate on the bond multiplied by the face value) and the other return component is the capital gain or loss on the bond. The value of the bond changes due to shifts in real rates of return or expectations of inflation, thus resulting in a capital gain or loss component. If you measure the market risk premium by subtracting the income return on long-term government bonds from the S&P 500, the market risk premium measured over the 1926 to 2016 period is 6.9%, almost a full percentage point higher than the market risk premium estimated using the total return on the long-term government bond.[27]

If we choose to use a long-term government bond to estimate the market risk premium and the yield, how long a bond should we use? Many advocate using a 20- or 30-year bond, because it more closely captures the duration of the cash flows when valuing a company. However, as a matter of practice, the U.S. government does not always issue bonds with a long maturity. For example, the U.S. government did not issue 30-year bonds before 1977. The U.S. Treasury stopped issuing them in 2001. Beginning in February, 2006, the U.S. government began issuing 30-year bonds again. In addition, for a time, the U.S. government did not issue bonds with more than a 10-year maturity. Remember that no matter what term to maturity you choose, we match the maturity of the bond for purposes of estimating both the yield and the market risk premium.

Another alternative some advocate using is the return on a very high-grade long-term corporate bond instead of the return on a government bond. The justification for this alternative is that the income from U.S. government bonds is tax-free at the state level (although it is taxed at the federal level). The argument is that the returns on government bonds are affected by their preferential tax status, suggesting they are priced to return a lower, pre-state-tax rate of return. U.S. corporate bonds are taxable at both the federal and state level, and hence they do not have that tax advantage. However, even high-grade corporate bonds, such as an AAA-rated bond, have some default risk, which would be embedded in the bond returns.

The Historical Approach to Estimating the Market Risk Premium

One way to estimate the market risk premium is to calculate annual returns on the chosen market portfolio and risk-free asset for some historical time period and then calculate the "mean" difference between the return on the market portfolio and the return on the risk-free asset. This is similar to what we have been discussing given the data in Exhibit 8.12. To use this approach, we choose the time period over which to measure the "average" and how to measure the "mean" (arithmetic mean versus geometric mean).

[27] See *Stocks, Bonds, Bills and Inflation* by Duff and Phelps, John Wiley and Sons, Inc., 2017, Exhibit 10.9, pp. 10–21.

In using this approach, the arithmetic mean return is generally used because it is the conceptually correct estimate if annual returns are independent through time (knowing last period's return does not help you predict next period's return). Since evidence indicates that annual returns are generally independent over time, the arithmetic mean is typically adopted in lieu of the geometric mean estimate.

A common technique is to use all of the data available since 1926 because 1926 is the oldest readily available year for which we have data that we believe is quite accurate. This approach assumes that the expected market risk premium has not changed over 90 years, and therefore using more data provides a more precise estimate. Using a long time period ensures that the estimation period encompasses all types of economic and political conditions, such as war, peace, expansions, contractions, rampant inflation, oil price shocks, assassinations, natural disasters, and so forth.

An alternative to using all the data back to 1926 is to estimate the market risk premium over shorter time periods, say, the last 20 or 30 years. One effect of using a shorter time period is that the estimated market risk premium varies more from one year to the next because the addition of one new observation and the dropping of the oldest observation has a larger effect when using 20 years of observations than it does using, say, 80 years of observations. Of course, just because the market risk premium estimated this way varies over time, it does not mean that the estimates are incorrect or inappropriate.

From Exhibit 8.12, we can use the historical arithmetic average based on data from 1926–2016, utilizing the return on the S&P 500 and the return on one of the government bond or Treasury bill series. Using the total return on long-term government bonds, the expected market risk premium is 6.0% (6.0% = 12.0% − 6.0%), using the intermediate-term government bonds, the expected market risk premium is 6.7% (6.7% = 12.0% − 5.3%), and using U.S. Treasury Bill returns, the expected market risk premium is 8.6% (8.6% = 12.0% − 3.4%). While the difference between the expected market risk premium using the long-term government bonds and the U.S. Treasury Bill returns is 2.6% (2.6% = 8.6% − 6.0%), for reasons we explain in the following section on estimating the risk-free yield, its net effect on the CAPM expected return is substantially less than that.

Instead of using the S&P 500 index, it is also possible to use other indices. For example, using the return for the top 20% of the companies traded in the U.S. in the CRSP database, the average return on the market from 1926 through 2016 is 11.8% (versus 12.0% for the S&P 500 in Exhibit 8.12), which, all else equal, decreases the market risk premium by 0.2% However, using the return for a broader index, for example, all of the companies traded in the U.S. in the CRSP database, the average return on the market from 1926 through 2016 is 11.3% (versus 12.0% for the S&P 500 in Exhibit 8.12), which, all else equal, decreases the market risk premium by 0.7%.[28]

It is also common to use the income return on the risk-free asset rather than the total return to measure the market risk premium. The income return from 1926 through 2016 for the long-term government bond is 5.1% (versus 6.0% for the total return reported in Exhibit 8.12).[29] The market risk premium increases by 0.9% using the income return on the risk-free asset (long-term government bond) rather than the total return, 6.9% (6.9% = 12.0% − 5.1%).

Another common approach for estimating the market risk premium, based on the work of Ibbotson and Chen (2003), is the supply-side approach, which also uses income returns on the risk-free asset rather than total return.[30] The supply-side model adjusts the market return by extracting the part of the return that resulted from the change in market's forecast for the growth in earnings (based on changes in the price to earnings ratio). The resulting market risk premium is roughly 1% lower or 6% (again, using the income return on the risk-free asset rather than the total return), though the difference depends on the measurement period.[31]

Although calculating the market risk premium starting in 1926 is the most common time period used, the time period is a choice. In Exhibit 8.13 we present the market risk premium calculated through the end of 2016 but starting at different points in time based on the S&P 500 index less the income return on long-term government bonds. The chart shows that the choice of the time period used to estimate the market risk premium has an effect on the estimate of the market risk premium. Using only the most recent five

[28] See *Stocks, Bonds, Bills and Inflation* by Duff and Phelps, John Wiley and Sons, Inc., 2017, Exhibit 10.9, pp. 10–21.

[29] See *Stocks, Bonds, Bills and Inflation* by Duff and Phelps, John Wiley and Sons, Inc., 2017, Exhibit 10.9, pp. 10–21.

[30] Ibbotson, R. and P. Chen, "Long-run Stock Returns: Participating in the Real Economy," *Financial Analysts Journal*, vol. 59, no. 1 (2003), pp. 88–98; and Ibbotson, Roger G., "The Equity Risk Premium," Research Foundation Publications, Dec 2011, pp. 18–26. Data for the supply-side market risk premium is, as of March 2018, available from Duff and Phelps, https://costofcapital.duffandphelps.com, last accessed on March 27, 2018.

[31] See *Stocks, Bonds, Bills and Inflation* by Duff and Phelps, John Wiley and Sons, Inc., 2017, Exhibit 10.9, pp. 10–27–10–30.

years, the market risk premium is over 12% but using the most recent 10 years, the market risk premium decreases to 5.3%. The market risk premium is in the range of 4.9% to 6.1% measured using the most recent 20 to 60 years; however, the range of the market risk premium increases to 6.6% to 6.9% when measured over the most recent 70 to 91 years.

EXHIBIT 8.13 Market Risk Premium as of 2016 Using Different Starting Points

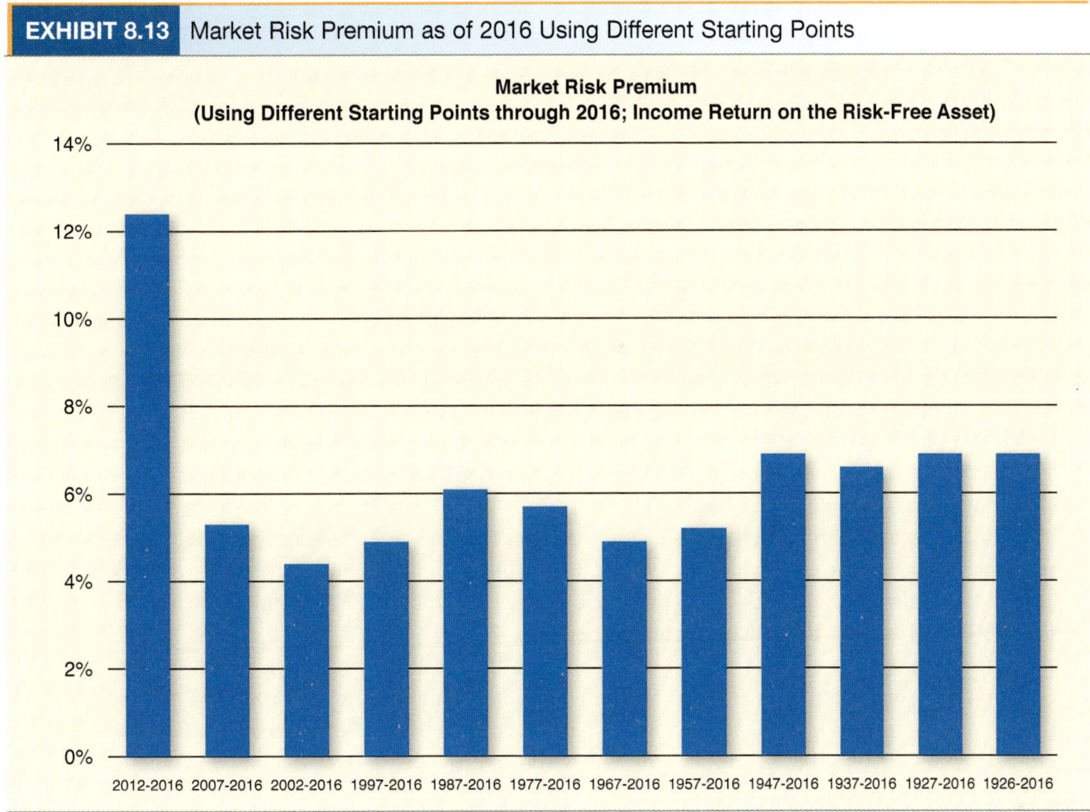

Not everyone who uses the historical approach uses estimates back to 1926. Some practitioners estimate the market risk premium using the S&P 500 index in excess of the long-term government bond since 1950, which results in a market risk premium of approximately 5.0%. Advocates for using data since 1950 argue that markets are less risky now and that risk premiums should be smaller now than they were in the first half of the twentieth century.[32] Others use data starting in 1926 but do not use data from 1942 through 1951 because the U.S. Federal Reserve and the U.S. Treasury were attempting to control interest rates in the U.S. because of World War II.[33]

Another issue associated with using realized returns to compute the market risk premium is that the estimated risk premium could be upward biased because of "survivorship bias" in our proxy for the market portfolio. An example of survivorship bias is to use historical returns of the companies that were listed continuously for the past 20 years. That sample would obviously exclude companies that were listed for some time during the period but failed and were delisted, which would likely upward bias our historical returns.

Some have applied similar logic to estimating the market risk premium using only U.S. data (even though that data does include companies which have failed and delisted). They argue that the U.S. stock market has been wildly successful. Thus, because the U.S. market survived and prospered, using historical data on only the U.S. market overstates the premium an investor should expect, as there have been stock markets that literally disappeared. Of course in 1926, no one knew for certain that the U.S. stock market would survive and prosper. For example, the U.S. stock market earned a real return of 4.3% during the twentieth century versus a median real return of 0.8% for other countries. Academic evidence suggests

[32] See Petit, J., I. Gulic, and A. Park, "The Equity Risk Measurement Handbook," *Stern Stewart Research EVAluation* (March, 2001).

[33] Pratt, S. and R. Grabowski, *Cost of Capital: Applications and Examples*, 5th edition, Wiley, pp. 119–121.

that an adjustment for such survivorship bias is probably between 30 and 70 basis points—that is, take the historical market risk premium and subtract 0.3% to 0.7%.[34]

Another assumption made when using the historical approach is the assumption that the risk premium has remained constant over a relatively long time period. Some argue that the market risk premium varies over time and, in particular, that it has declined since the depression in the first half of the twentieth century. One way to accommodate that belief is to use a shorter time period that does not extend all the way back to 1926 or to adjust the returns observed in the earlier years, which is the topic we discuss next.

Time Variation in Estimating the Market Risk Premium

Recent research suggests that the expected market risk premium decreased during the second half of the twentieth century. Mayfield (2004) provides evidence of a structural shift in the underlying volatility process occurring after the depression in the 1930s and concludes that average historical estimates of the market risk premium using data back to 1926 overstate the expected premium. Mayfield argues that as investors recognized that expected volatility decreased, stock prices rose because of the declining market risk premium. Since that rise in stock prices is embedded in historical returns but was due to a decline in risk, the effect of the decline in risk should be excluded when estimating the expected market risk premium. Using data through 2000, Mayfield claims that the average market risk premium (measured relative to Treasury bills) since 1940 is 5.6% in contrast to the historical premium relative to Treasury bills of 8.2% starting at 1926 and ending in 2000 (when Mayfield's data ends), indicating that the historical estimates are approximately 2.6% too high.[35]

Pastor and Stambaugh as well as Fama and French come to somewhat similar conclusions using different approaches. Pastor and Stambaugh use a longer history of data and a different methodology than Mayfield. Using data back to 1834, they provide evidence that the market risk premium (again, measured relative to U.S. Treasury Bills) has fluctuated between 4% and 6%. As of the end of 1999, Pastor and Stambaugh estimated the market risk premium at 4.8%, suggesting the historical risk premium relative to Treasury bills (measured back to 1926 and ending at that same time) was about 3.7% too high.[36] Fama and French, similar to Mayfield, argue that the high average return observed using data back to 1926 is due to a decline in the market risk premium, which in turn produced a large capital gain. Using data from 1872 to 2000, they estimate that the historical average excess return overstates the market risk premium substantially, by between 2.65% and 3.6% (depending on the model used).[37]

While these three articles do not come to the same conclusion regarding the exact point estimate of the market risk premium, nor do they provide evidence about which of the alternatives is the best measure of the market risk premium, they all suggest that estimates of the market risk premium using the historical approach are too high, when using data back to 1926. Using Mayfield's estimates, an estimate of the market risk premium relative to Treasury bills is 5.6% and from that we can infer that the market risk premium relative to long-term government bonds would be about 4.2%.[38] Those numbers lie within the range produced by Fama and French. None of these studies have been updated for more recent data.

Estimates of the Market Risk Premium from Market Participants

Graham and Harvey have surveyed CFOs every quarter from June of 2000 asking them their current estimate of the market risk premium (judged relative to the 10-year U.S. Treasury Bond). Over the 17 years of their survey, the risk premium estimates have varied widely. At the end of the first quarter of 2017 survey, the mean risk premium estimate for the S&P 500 relative to the 10-year U.S. government

[34] See Jorion, P., and W. Goetzmann, "Global Stock Markets in the Twentieth Century," *Journal of Finance* 54 (June, 1999), pp. 953–974.

[35] See Mayfield, E. Scott, "Estimating the Market Risk Premium," *Journal of Financial Economics* 73 (2004), pp. 465–496.

[36] See Pastor, L., and R. Stambaugh, "The Equity Premium and Structural Breaks," *Journal of Finance* 56 (August, 2001), pp. 1207–1239. The change in prices since 1999 would likely change Pastor and Stambaugh's estimate of the market risk premium since 1999, but they have not updated their study at this time.

[37] See Fama, E., and K. French, "The Equity Premium," *Journal of Finance* 57 (April, 2002), pp. 637–659.

[38] Mayfield does not discuss the market risk premium relative to long-term government bonds. To estimate the 4.2%, we calculated the difference in returns between long-term government bonds and U.S. Treasury Bills between 1940 and 2000 (Mayfield's estimation period). That difference is 1.4%.

bond across all CFOs who responded to the survey was 4.2%, with a range across industry groups of 3.1% to 8.4%.[39]

Another 2017 survey of finance and economics professors, analysts and managers of companies asked respondents for their estimates of the risk-free rate and market risk premium to estimate the equity cost of capital.[40] The average and median market risk premium for the U.S. were both 5.7% across 1,617 respondents; the standard deviation was 1.5% with a minimum of 1.2% and a maximum of 12%. The average and median risk-free rate for the U.S. were both 2.5% across 1,617 respondents; the standard deviation was 1.0% with a minimum of 0.0% and a maximum of 6.9%.

Estimates of the Market Risk Premium from Implied Cost of Capital Estimates

Another approach for estimating the market risk premium is to measure implied cost of capital estimates using forecasts of earnings or cash flows in conjunction with currently observed stock prices. The way this approach is implemented is to use analysts' forecasts or forecasts derived from a model to estimate short-term and intermediate-term growth rates for a company's free cash flows or excess earnings. For a long-term growth rate, this approach typically uses either long-term industry growth rates or forecasted growth rates for the economy. Once we know a company's price, its current free cash flows or excess earnings, and short- and long-term growth rates of free cash flows or excess earnings, we can solve for the internal rate of return that equates discounted expected free cash flows or excess earnings to the company's current stock price. This yields an implied cost of capital for a company.

To use this approach to estimate the market risk premium for an index of stocks such as the S&P 500, we would average the individual companies' implied cost of capital estimates based on market capitalizations for all stocks in the S&P 500 to solve for the value-weighted average expected return on the S&P 500. To then estimate the market risk premium, say relative to long-term government bonds, we would subtract the current yield on the long-term government bond, and the resulting difference is an estimate of the market risk premium. Bloomberg uses a procedure like this to estimate market risk premiums for different countries. Several academic papers have also utilized this approach. The estimates from these models depend in part on the price levels seen in the market. In the late 1990s and early 2000, when values were quite high relative to current earnings, these models often gave estimates of the market risk premium under 3%.[41] We discuss implied cost of capital estimates more thoroughly in a subsequent section of the chapter, as they are a standalone alternative to using the CAPM that can be applied to individual companies to estimate the equity cost of capital.

Uncertainty in Estimates of the Market Risk Premium

One of the difficulties in estimating the CAPM revolves around our uncertainty about the expected market risk premium. While there is uncertainty about estimated betas, the economic importance of the uncertainty about the estimated market risk premium dominates any uncertainty about estimation errors in beta (assuming, for now, that the CAPM is a perfect model). Fama and French conclude that the uncertainty about the market risk premium alone translates into a standard error of industry cost of capital estimates in their study of approximately 3.01% per year, while including uncertainty about an industry's true beta increases the standard error by only 0.14% to 3.15%.[42]

Where Does All of the Evidence Leave Us?

Recent evidence suggests that the expected market risk premium is overstated using the historical approach back to 1926. However, this empirical work is not definitive. Mehra and Prescott discuss these issues as well as alternative rationales for why we may have observed such large historical market risk premiums. Those explanations include factors such as changes in taxes and regulation, compensation for the chance of

---

[39] The results of the CFO surveys can be found at http://www.cfosurvey.org/.

[40] Fernandez, P., V. Pershin, and I. Acín, "Discount Rate (Risk-Free Rate and Market Risk Premium) used for 41 countries in 2017: a survey," April 17, 2017; available on May 30, 2018 at SSRN: https://ssrn.com/abstract=2954142.

[41] J. Claus and J. Thomas, "Equity Premia as Low as Three Percent? Evidence from Analysts' Earnings Forecasts for Domestic and International Stock Markets," *Journal of Finance* 56 (2001), pp. 1629–1666; and Gebhardt, W., C. Lee, and B. Swaminathan, "Toward an Implied Cost of Capital," *Journal of Accounting Research* 39 (2001), pp. 135–176.

[42] See Fama, E., and K. French, "Industry Costs of Equity," *Journal of Financial Economics* 43 (1997), pp. 153–193.

a cataclysmic event, and more. None of their explanations, however, can completely explain the magnitude of the observed market risk premiums to date. Without an explanation, Mehra and Prescott conclude: "In the absence of this [a plausible explanation for the high market risk premium], and based on what we currently know, we can make the following claim: over the long horizon the equity premium is likely to be similar to what it has been in the past. . . ."[43] Thus, there is far from a unanimous view on this important issue.

Valuation Key 8.10

Estimating the market risk premium is an important part of implementing the Capital Asset Pricing Model. At the current time, there is not a broad consensus concerning the best way to estimate the market risk premium, and estimates of the market risk premium vary widely. More recent evidence suggests that using the long-term average historical market risk premium may overstate the expected market risk premium; however, the "jury is still out" on this issue.

8.6 ESTIMATING THE RISK-FREE RATE OF RETURN TO USE IN THE CAPM

We can estimate the risk-free rate in the CAPM using the yield on a risk-free security, measured as of the valuation date. The good news is that for most U.S. government securities, we can observe this yield. In Exhibit 8.14, we summarize the steps in estimating the forward-looking risk-free rate of return, and discuss them in this section of the chapter. The first two choices are choosing the proxy for the risk-free asset and the maturity of that proxy. Then, depending on those choices, we adjust the proxy for any risk-premium embedded in it, if required.

EXHIBIT 8.14 Steps in Estimating the Risk-Free Rate of Return (Yield on a Risk-Free Asset at the Valuation Date)

1	Choose a proxy for the risk-free asset (U.S. government bond or corporate AAA bond)
2	Choose a maturity for the risk-free asset proxy based on the length of the cash flow forecasts being utilized
3	Make adjustments, if any, for risk premium embedded in the risk-free asset proxy
4	Use one rate to discount all periods or different rates for each period

As we discussed generally, the choice of the proxy (U.S. government bonds versus AAA corporate bonds) and the choice of maturity (short-term, intermediate-term, and long-term maturity) are linked to our choices for the market risk premium. The driver of both choices is based on the duration of the cash flows that we are valuing, which governs the maturity that we use for estimating the risk-free yield.

If we are discounting nominal free cash flow forecasts, we include investors' expectations for inflation in the discount rate, and this is captured in the risk-free rate we use. We can use different risk-free rates for each period by choosing a risk-free estimate of the expected return for each future period using the yield curve or we might just simply measure the time-weighted average rate of return that investors demand over the relevant horizon. The latter approach is the more common approach. Of course, if the **term structure of interest rates** as of the valuation date is such that the **yield curve**[44] is very steep (rates changing with maturity), we might choose to estimate the cost of capital period by period.

The most common practice is to match, as closely as practicable given the asset that is being valued, the maturity (or duration) of the proxy for the risk-free asset to the duration of the cash flows being discounted. For example, if we are discounting cash flows for five years, we would use the yield on an intermediate-term bond. When we value a firm, we generally assume the firm has an infinite life and has a long duration. As such, when measuring the risk-free rate for valuing a firm, we generally use the yield on a long-term bond.

Recall from the previous section that we observe a maturity premium between different maturities of government bonds. We adjust the risk-free rate for this maturity premium if we use a different proxy for

[43] See Mehra, R., and E. Prescott, "The Equity Premium in Retrospect," in G. Constantinides, M. Harris, and R. Stulz, eds., *Handbook of the Economics of Finance*, Elsevier B.V. (2003), pp. 887–936.

[44] The term structure of interest rates is the relationship between interest rates and maturity of debt securities with the same default risk. The yield curve is a graph of the term structure of interest rates. The yield curve is generally rising with maturity.

the risk-free asset to measure the market risk premium and the yield on the risk-free asset in the CAPM. As such, if we estimate the market risk premium using one-month U.S. Treasury Bills, we adjust the yield on the risk-free asset if it is not a one-month U.S. Treasury Bill yield (which it typically is not when valuing a firm because we typically match the yield to the duration of the cash flows we are valuing). In such situations, we subtract an estimate of the maturity premium from the yield on the risk-free asset used in the CAPM. For example, assume we used the historical approach and measured the market risk premium as the difference between the returns on the S&P 500 and the return on U.S. Treasury Bills between 1926 and 2016. Further assume that we also used the yield on a long-term government bond as of the valuation date for the risk-free yield in the CAPM. In that case, we would use a market risk premium of 8.6% and a yield on the risk-free asset equal to the yield on the long-term government bond less the historical maturity premium of 2.6%. If we were using the yield on an intermediate-term government bond for the yield on the risk-free asset, we would subtract the historical maturity premium for intermediate-term bonds of 1.9% from the yield on the intermediate-term bond.

Valuation Key 8.11

When valuing a company, the risk-free rate of return in the CAPM is normally measured as the yield on a long-term government bond as of the date of the valuation. We would adjust that yield for the expected maturity premium if the market risk premium is measured against a short maturity security, such as U.S. Treasury Bills. The maturity premium adjustment to the risk-free yield is not required when the market risk premium is measured against long-term government bonds.

8.7 PUTTING THE PIECES TOGETHER

Using the CAPM to estimate the expected return of a security requires estimates of three inputs—the yield on the risk-free asset, beta, and the market risk premium. As we discuss in this chapter, we can estimate each of these inputs in various ways, and we generally use data from different time periods to estimate the different inputs for the CAPM. We use the observed yield on a proxy for the risk-free asset as of the valuation date. We usually estimate beta using historical data (two to five years are common, but we may use other periods depending on the valuation context). We might use a very long time-series of data to estimate the historical market risk premium or we might use more current data from implied cost of capital estimates.

Informed Judgment and Guiding Principles (Links)

Estimating the cost of capital using the CAPM requires a certain amount of informed judgment. Fortunately, we have some guiding principles we can use when making choices because certain inputs are linked to each other in certain ways. The first link is between the proxy we use for the market index to estimate beta and the proxy we use to measure the market risk premium; generally, we use the same proxy in the estimation of both inputs. The second link is between the proxy for the return on the risk-free asset we use to estimate the market risk premium and the proxy we use for the yield on the risk-free asset as of the valuation date. Generally, this link is based in part on the duration of the cash flows we are valuing. The type of security (government bond versus corporate bond) and the maturity of the security (long-term, intermediate-term, or short-term maturity) should be consistent or adjusted to maintain consistency, such as the maturity premium adjustment discussed previously.

CAPM Example Using Our Four Companies

Assume that we estimated the following inputs for the CAPM to determine the cost of equity capital for our four companies: Colgate Palmolive Co., Ford Motor Co., General Electric Co., and Textron Inc. We illustrate the effect of choosing alternative sets of assumptions to implement the CAPM for these four companies.

- Proxy for the yield on the risk-free asset is the yield on the long-term government bond on our valuation date, 3.0%.
- Two estimates of beta for each company in Exhibit 8.6 based on the S&P 500
  - Betas in Exhibit 8.6 (based on the S&P 500)

- Betas in Exhibit 8.6 (based on the S&P 500) using the Bloomberg adjustment, Bloomberg Adjusted Beta = 0.33 + 0.67 × Historical Beta.

- Three estimates of the market risk premium
  - 8.6%, based on 1926 through 2016 returns on the S&P 500 and U.S. Treasury Bills
  - 6.0%, based on 1926 through 2016 returns on the S&P 500 and the long-term government bonds
  - 4.2%, based on Mayfield's research, which is based on the difference between the returns on the S&P 500 and long-term government bonds.
- A maturity premium equal to 2.6% for U.S. long-term government bonds relative to U.S. Treasury Bills, based on the 1926–2016 returns.

The above assumptions result in six different CAPM-based equity cost of capital estimates (two alternative betas and three alternative market risk premiums) for each company. We show the calculation of each of the six estimates as well as the average, the minimum, and maximum estimates for each of our four companies in Exhibit 8.15. We use Textron to discuss the exhibit because it has the beta farthest from 1.0 and thus, has the largest variation in the equity cost of capital across the six alternatives. Textron's beta is 1.580 in Exhibit 8.6. Applying the CAPM to the first set of assumptions (no Bloomberg adjustment and a market risk premium equal to 6.0%), Textron's estimated equity cost of capital is 12.5% (0.125 = 0.03 + 1.580 × 0.06). If we adjust Textron's beta using the Bloomberg adjustment process, its adjusted beta is equal to 1.388 (1.388 = 0.33 + 0.67 × 1.580), and its estimated equity cost of capital (holding the other inputs con-

EXHIBIT 8.15 Alternative CAPM-Based Equity Cost of Capital Estimates for Our Four Companies

			Beta		Market Risk Premium			
Company	Equity Cost of Capital Estimate	Yield on Risk-Free Asset	Exhibit 8.6	Bloomberg Adjusted	Historical Based on U.S. Treasury Bill	Historical Based on U.S. Long-Term Gov Bond	Mayfield	Maturity Risk Premium
Colgate Palmolive Co.	7.5%	3.0%	0.752			6.0%		
	6.9%	3.0%	0.752		8.6%			2.6%
	6.2%	3.0%	0.752				4.2%	
	8.0%	3.0%		0.834		6.0%		
	7.6%	3.0%		0.834	8.6%			2.6%
	6.5%	3.0%		0.834			4.2%	
Average/Low/High	7.1%	6.2%	8.0%					
General Electric Co	10.1%	3.0%	1.181			6.0%		
	10.6%	3.0%	1.181		8.6%			2.6%
	8.0%	3.0%	1.181				4.2%	
	9.7%	3.0%		1.121		6.0%		
	10.0%	3.0%		1.121	8.6%			2.6%
	7.7%	3.0%		1.121			4.2%	
Average/Low/High	9.3%	7.7%	10.6%					
Ford Motor Co	9.4%	3.0%	1.060			6.0%		
	9.5%	3.0%	1.060		8.6%			2.6%
	7.5%	3.0%	1.060				4.2%	
	9.2%	3.0%		1.040		6.0%		
	9.3%	3.0%		1.040	8.6%			2.6%
	7.4%	3.0%		1.040			4.2%	
Average/Low/High	8.7%	7.4%	9.5%					
Textron Inc	12.5%	3.0%	1.580			6.0%		
	14.0%	3.0%	1.580		8.6%			2.6%
	9.6%	3.0%	1.580				4.2%	
	11.3%	3.0%		1.388		6.0%		
	12.3%	3.0%		1.388	8.6%			2.6%
	8.8%	3.0%		1.388			4.2%	
Average/Low/High	11.4%	8.8%	14.0%					

stant) is equal to 11.3% (0.113 = 0.03 + 1.388 × 0.06). For Textron, which had a beta more than 50% above the average beta, the Bloomberg adjustment procedure reduced the cost of equity capital estimate by 1.2%.

Using the returns on the S&P 500 and U.S. Treasury Bills to estimate the market risk premium of 8.6%, our estimate of the risk-free yield would be 0.4% (3.0% current yield on the long-term government bond less the historical maturity premium on long-term government bonds of 2.6%). Our estimate of Textron's cost of equity capital using a beta of 1.58 is 14.0% (0.14 = 0.03 − 0.026 + 1.580 × 0.086). Note that had Textron's beta been exactly equal to one, the choice of the proxy for the risk-free return in estimating the market risk premium (long-term government bond or treasury bills) would not have made any difference. However, in this case, since Textron's beta is greater than 1, using U.S. Treasury Bills to estimate the market risk premium results in a higher cost of capital than when using long-term U.S. government bonds (14.0% versus 12.5%). For example, Ford has the beta closest to 1.0, 1.060, and the difference between using U.S. Treasury Bills and long-term government bond returns to estimate the market risk premium is only 0.1% (9.4% versus 9.5%).

If we use the 4.2% market risk premium estimate inferred from Mayfield (the difference between the return on the S&P 500 and long-term government bonds), our estimate for Textron's equity cost of capital using an unadjusted beta is equal to 9.6% (0.096 = 0.03 + 1.580 × 0.042). In this case the difference in the estimate of the cost of capital relative to the historical approach using long-term government bonds is 2.8% [0.0284 = 0.1248 – 0.0964 = 1.580 × (0.06 – 0.042)]. The lowest equity cost of capital is using the Mayfield market risk premium and the Bloomberg adjusted beta which equals 8.8% (0.088 = 0.03 + 1.388 × 0.042). The range of CAPM-based equity cost of capital estimates for Textron across the alternative estimates is 8.8% to 14%, with an average of 11.4%. The range of 5.2% (0.052 = 0.140 − 0.088) is 45% of the average equity cost of capital estimate (0.45 = 0.052/0.114). This is the largest variation because Textron's beta is 50% higher than the average beta. However, the equity cost of capital also varies (range/average) for the other three companies and is at least 24% (Ford has a range from 7.4% to 9.5% and an average of 8.7%).[45] Still you can see that variation in the way the CAPM is implemented can lead to substantial variation in the estimated cost of equity capital.

REVIEW EXERCISE 8.6

Alternative CAPM-Based Equity Cost of Capital Estimates for Four Comparable Companies in Review Exercise 8.5

Calculate the cost of equity capital for the four comparable companies in Review Exercise 8.5 using the alternative assumptions used to measure the equity cost of capital in Exhibit 8.15; in other words, create a table similar to Exhibit 8.15 for the four comparable companies in Review Exercise 8.5.

Solution on page 378.

How Finance Professionals Put the Pieces Together[46]

As we stated in the introduction, the CAPM is the most widely used model for estimating a company's equity cost of capital. Finance professionals tend to use a commercial source for beta estimates, and Bloomberg is the dominant source (65% of the respondents use Bloomberg). Recall Bloomberg allows the user to make certain choices to estimate beta. Most financial professionals use five years of monthly data to estimate beta. The second most common way to estimate beta is using weekly data over one to three years. About 50% of the financial professionals use adjusted betas. Finance professionals split about evenly on using comparable companies or not.

For the market risk premium, most financial professionals use a range of 4% to 6%, updated at least annually, with less than 20% using a market risk premium under 4% and roughly 20% using a market risk premium of 6% or more. For the risk-free rate, about 50% use a maturity of at least 10 years, 14% use a maturity of 5 years, and about 30% use a U.S. Treasury Bill rate on bills with a maturity of one year or less. Most companies use either the current yield or a forecasted yield. About one-third apply either a floor of 4% or a cap of 8% or both on the risk-free rate.

---

[45] It is common for practitioners to use a range of up to ±2% when valuing a company.

[46] 2013 AFP Estimating and Applying Cost of Capital: Report of Survey Results, October 2013, Association for Financial Professionals.

As we state in various parts of this chapter (and the book), the inputs for the CAPM are based on various choices. The chapter provides some guiding principles for these choices, but, in the end, the choices depend on the facts and circumstances of the valuation and the informed views of the valuation expert.

8.8 ADJUSTING THE CAPITAL ASSET PRICING MODEL FOR MARKET CAPITALIZATION

LO3 Adjust the Capital Asset Pricing Model-based equity cost of capital for market capitalization and other potential attributes

Earlier in the chapter, we discussed the empirical evidence that the CAPM overstates the returns to large firms and understates the returns to small firms. One reason this evidence is of interest is that it represents another method for estimating a firm's equity cost of capital. In order to more fully understand this approach, let's examine the data in Exhibit 8.16.

The deciles are constructed by ranking New York Stock Exchange firms based on their market capitalization (market value of the common equity) as of the last trading day in March, June, September, and December of every year, ranking them from largest to smallest, and then identifying the largest one-tenth of the firms as decile 1, the next largest one-tenth as decile 2, and so on, until the smallest one-tenth of the firms are identified as decile 10. The quarterly decile cutoffs are based only on NYSE companies in existence at the end of every quarter, and then all companies on the NYSE, AMEX, and NASDAQ exchanges are assigned to the appropriate size decile based on the NYSE deciles. The return in excess of the long-term government bond is calculated as the value-weighted return for each decile portfolio every year less the income return from investing in a 20-year U.S. government bond for the year. The return in excess of the CAPM is calculated as the value-weighted return for each decile portfolio less the return predicted by the CAPM given the portfolio's beta. The last column provides information on the market value of the common stock of the largest firm in each decile as of 2016. Because the size effect is nonlinear and largest in the smallest decile, it is also common to partition the smallest size decile (10th decile) into two or more sub-groups. Others have used smaller groupings of firms, for example, 25 size-based portfolios instead of 10.[47] Although the exhibit measures the size premium as of 2016 starting in 1926, it is not clear that the best forward-looking size premium should be measured in that way. All of the issues for selecting the time period to measure the market risk premium apply to measuring the size premium.

EXHIBIT 8.16 Size Premium Relative to the Risk-Free Return and the CAPM from January 1926 Through 2016 for 10 Deciles of Firm Size

Decile	Beta	Arithmetic Mean	Return in Excess of Risk-Free Rate (actual)	Return in Excess of Risk-Free Rate (predicted by CAPM)	Size Premium Relative to the CAPM	Common Stock Market Value (Largest Firm in Decile—Millions)
1—largest......	0.92	11.05%	6.04%	6.38%	−0.35%	$609,163.5
2.............	1.04	12.82%	7.81%	7.19%	0.61%	24,233.7
3.............	1.11	13.57%	8.55%	7.66%	0.89%	10,711.2
4.............	1.13	13.80%	8.78%	7.80%	0.98%	5,676.7
5.............	1.17	14.62%	9.60%	8.09%	1.51%	3,512.9
6.............	1.17	14.81%	9.79%	8.14%	1.66%	2,390.9
7.............	1.25	15.41%	10.39%	8.67%	1.72%	1,570.0
8.............	1.30	16.14%	11.12%	9.04%	2.08%	1,030.4
9.............	1.34	16.97%	11.96%	9.28%	2.68%	567.8
10—smallest.....	1.39	20.27%	15.25%	9.66%	5.59%	262.9

Source: See *Stocks, Bonds, Bills and Inflation*, by Duff and Phelps, John Wiley and Sons, Inc., 2017, Chapter 7. Reprinted with permission.

Add the Decile Risk Premium to the Risk-Free Rate. Given the relation between size and returns, one approach for using the results in the exhibit to determine a firm's cost of equity capital is to add the historical return in excess of the long-term government bond for the size decile of which the firm is currently a member to the long-term government bond yield. That is

[47] R. J. Grabowski, and J. P. Harrington, *Risk Premium Report 2013*, Copyright © 2013 Duff & Phelps Corporation, DP132014.

$$r_E = r_F + \text{Return in Excess of LT Govt Bond for Size Decile} \tag{8.12}$$

This technique presumes that beta plays no role whatsoever in setting expected returns and that only size matters. This is not the most common usage of this data, but we illustrate its implementation because some practitioners do use this technique.

Implementing this technique requires approximate knowledge of the size (market capitalization) of the firm. As such, if the firm were not publicly traded, one would probably have to use a price multiple technique to approximate the market value in the absence of any other indication or use an iterative DCF approach (choose a decile, measure the value, compare the value from the DCF to the decile, and so forth). In addition, if the firm grows through time sufficiently to change deciles, this technique suggests that the required rate of return would decline through time. Of course implementing that would be difficult and is not typically done.

As an example, the arithmetic mean return on firms in the eighth decile has been 16.1%. More importantly, the eighth decile risk premium relative to long-term U.S. government bonds has been 11.1%. If long-term government bonds were yielding 3.0%, this would suggest that the equity cost of capital for firms in the eighth decile of firm size is 14.1% (0.141 = 0.03 + 0.111).

Adjusting the CAPM for the Historical Size Mispricing. The more commonly used technique for estimating the cost of equity capital using the results in the exhibit is to estimate the cost of capital from the CAPM and adjust the CAPM cost of capital for the historical deviation from CAPM pricing for a firm of that approximate market capitalization, which we show in Equation 8.13.

$$r_E = r_F + \beta_E \times \text{MRP} + \text{Adjustment for CAPM Size Mispricing} \tag{8.13}$$

As in the previous approach, this approach requires approximate knowledge of market capitalization of the firm. For example, suppose a company has a market capitalization of approximately $700 million and a beta of 1.2. A firm with a market value of $700 million is in decile 8 in Exhibit 8.16. If long-term government bonds were yielding 3.0%, this would suggest an equity cost of capital (estimating the market risk premium relative to long-term government bonds as 6.0%) of 12.28% (0.1228 = 0.03 + 1.2 × 0.06 + 0.0208). The 2.08% that is added in this calculation is the adjustment for CAPM size mispricing for the eighth decile per Exhibit 8.16.

The same issue exists here as for the previous method if the firm is expected to grow or decline through time. That is, as the value moves up or down, the size decile might differ, resulting in a different cost of capital. Again, such adjustments would be difficult to make and are not generally used in practice.

Valuation in Practice 8.4

Sagent Pharmaceuticals' Equity Cost of Capital In July 2016, Nichi-Iko Pharmaceutical Co., Ltd., a Japanese corporation, made a tender offer to purchase the shares of Sagent Pharmaceuticals, Inc., a U.S. corporation. The boards of directors of the companies supported the tender offer and signed a merger agreement prior to the announcement. By the end of August 2016, over 85% of Sagent common stock had been validly tendered and all conditions to the tender offer were satisfied, which enabled Nichi-Iko to complete the acquisition of the other shares. Sagent's financial advisor, Perella Weinberg, measured Sagent's equity cost of capital as follows.

> Perella Weinberg calculated the 5-year monthly historical Bloomberg adjusted beta for each of the selected peer companies. Perella Weinberg then unlevered each beta using each such company's normalized capital structure and marginal tax rate. The median levered beta for these peer companies was 1.10, while the median unlevered beta for these companies was 0.84. Perella Weinberg then used this median unlevered beta of 0.84 as a "medium" case, while applying "low" and "high" beta sensitivities of 0.74 and 0.94, respectively. Perella Weinberg then re-levered these unlevered betas, using Sagent's normalized debt / capital ratio of 25% and their marginal tax rate of 40% (based on information provided by Sagent management), to derive a range of levered betas of 0.89 to 1.13. Cost of equity was calculated using the levered betas, a market risk premium of 7% (based on Duff & Phelps' long-term historical equity risk premium), the 10-year US Treasury yield of 1.37%, and an applicable size premium of 2.7% (based on Duff & Phelps' size premium data). As a result, Sagent's cost of equity was calculated to range from 10.28% to 11.96%.

Source: Sagent Pharmaceuticals' Schedule 14D-9 (Amendment No. 3) filed with the U.S. SEC on August 18, 2016.

An alternative technique is to use fewer groupings than the 10 deciles shown in Exhibit 8.16. In this technique, adjustments are constructed for three different portfolios, a mid-cap (stocks in deciles 3 to 5), low-cap (stocks in deciles 6 to 8), and micro-cap (stocks in deciles 9 and 10) portfolio, with no adjustment made to the CAPM for stocks that are in decile portfolios 1 and 2 (see Exhibit 8.17). Note that the companies in the first two deciles, for which no adjustment is made, represent approximately 75% of the market capitalization of the NYSE, AMEX, and NASDAQ markets.

EXHIBIT 8.17 Size Premium Relative to the Risk-Free Return and the CAPM from January 1926 Through 2016 for Three Portfolios of Firm Size

Group	Beta	Arithmetic Mean	Return in Excess of Risk-Free Rate (actual)	Return in Excess of Risk-Free Rate (predicted by CAPM)	Size Premium Relative to the CAPM	Common Stock Market Value (Largest Firm in Portfolio—Millions)
Mid-cap (Deciles 3–5).	1.12	13.82%	8.80%	7.79%	1.02%	$10,711.2
Low-cap (Deciles 6–8)	1.22	15.26%	10.24%	8.49%	1.75%	2,390.9
Micro-cap (Deciles 9–10) . . .	1.35	18.04%	13.02%	9.35%	3.67%	567.8

Source: See *Stocks, Bonds, Bills and Inflation*, by Duff and Phelps, John Wiley and Sons, Inc., 2017, Chapter 7. Reprinted with permission.

If we were to apply this data to our example of a company with an approximate market capitalization of $700 million and a beta of 1.2 (continuing to assume that the risk-free rate is 3% and the market risk premium is 6.0%), we would estimate the equity cost of capital to be 11.95% ($0.1195 = 0.03 + 1.2 \times 0.06 + 0.0175$).

Valuation Key 8.12

Evidence on the historically observed size premium is used by some practitioners to adjust the CAPM by the amount the CAPM has historically misestimated the returns earned by portfolios of securities with varying market capitalizations. The size adjustment is negligible for the firms that are as large as the firms in the top two deciles of the NYSE.

8.9 THE BUILD-UP METHOD

The build-up method is another technique used to estimate the cost of capital. Unfortunately, many implementations of the build-up method in practice are *ad hoc* because practitioners identify components and use premiums for the components that are purely subjective and not based on scientific evidence.

Typical Formulation of the Build-Up Method

A common formulation for the build-up method starts with the risk-free rate, adds a general equity risk premium, and adds (or subtracts) an industry risk premium depending on whether the industry is considered to be more or less risky than the average industry in the market. It then may add a premium for size and finally may add a company-specific risk factor. So the build-up method might look like the following.

$$r_E = r_F + \text{MRP} + \text{ISRP} + \text{Adjustment for CAPM Size Mispricing} + \text{CSRP} \quad (8.14)$$

where ISRP is an industry-specific risk premium and CSRP is a company-specific risk premium.

The addition of the industry-specific risk premium can be sensible if it is constructed and estimated properly. However, not every practitioner who adds an industry-specific risk premium bases the estimate of the industry-specific premium on any economic evidence. Instead, these adjustments are often based on subjective assessments and thus have little foundation. We have already discussed the adjustment to the CAPM for market capitalization and the evidence for and against making that adjustment. As such, we have little to add here, except for one point. When adding an industry-specific risk premium, the industry risk premium should not also incorporate a size adjustment. The same issue arises when adding a company-specific risk premium.

The potential subjectivity in the build-up method increases greatly when practitioners add company-specific risk premiums because the rationalizations for company-specific premiums are often tenuous and not supported by economic evidence. As such, they are essentially just subjective judgments.The reasons often given for these company-specific factors are based on a wide variety of items, such as leverage; dependence on a key executive, key supplier, or important customer; risk of competition; and more. The reasons for a company-specific risk premium are only limited by one's imagination. Many of the reasons we listed for a company-specific risk premium largely reflect idiosyncratic risks. As we discuss in Chapter 5, idiosyncratic risks should be accounted for in the expected cash flows, not in the cost of capital, as diversifiable risk should not affect the cost of capital according to the theory underlying all asset pricing models in modern finance.

There are many complexities and alternatives with respect to estimating the cost of capital. Obviously, valuation experts must make a variety of informed judgments when estimating the cost of capital. Many use the CAPM, but they will implement it differently. Others may use an alternative model such as the Fama-French model, which we discuss next. Despite the differences in these models, there is some scientific basis for many of the alternative models and many of the alternative ways in which the models are implemented in practice. One thing we would strongly urge is that you not use *ad hoc* models. In our opinion, the build-up method can lead to completely *ad hoc* and unsupportable estimates of the cost of capital if constructed or estimated improperly.

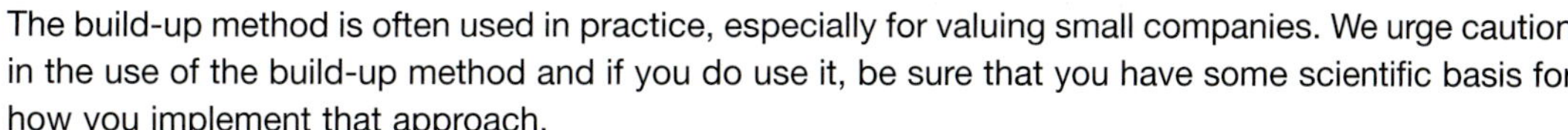

The build-up method is often used in practice, especially for valuing small companies. We urge caution in the use of the build-up method and if you do use it, be sure that you have some scientific basis for how you implement that approach.

8.10 MULTI-FACTOR MODELS

LO4 Estimate the equity cost of capital using the three-factor model or implied cost of capital estimates

Arbitrage Pricing Theory (APT) is a theoretical equilibrium pricing model that is a competitor to the CAPM.[48] The APT starts with the premise that multiple macroeconomic factors affect the actual returns that assets will experience. Further, it assumes that different assets will respond differently to these macroeconomic factors. For example, the returns earned by some businesses may be more sensitive to shifts in expected inflation rates than others. Or perhaps some businesses are more sensitive to the cost of energy than others. In addition, the model assumes, like the CAPM, that idiosyncratic shocks also affect an asset's return. As in the CAPM, the APT assumes that all of the idiosyncratic risk can be diversified away by holding a well-diversified portfolio. Further, because the idiosyncratic risk can be eliminated, it will not be priced. Sound familiar? But unlike the CAPM, because multiple macroeconomic forces affect the pricing of assets and affect companies differently, more than one risk factor will appear in the pricing equation, whereas the CAPM has only one risk factor, market risk.

Besides the evidence on the size effect documented by Banz and Keim, researchers have identified other variables that appear to be potentially important in explaining the cross-section of expected returns beyond beta from the CAPM. For example, Basu documented that returns for stocks with high ratios of earnings to price exceeded the return predicted by the CAPM, and Statman documented that stocks with high book-to-market ratios (the book value of the common stock divided by the market value of the common stock) had higher returns than predicted by the CAPM.[49]

Fama and French updated the evidence from these and other earlier studies that had documented the empirical shortcomings of the CAPM and from that, developed what is known as the Fama and French three-factor model. In particular, they documented significant explanatory power for predicting expected returns from size, earnings-to-price ratios, book-to-market ratios, and debt-to-equity ratios even in the

[48] See Ross, S., "The Arbitrage Theory of Capital Asset Pricing," *Journal of Economic Theory* 13 (1976), pp. 341–360.

[49] See Basu, S., "Investment Performance of Common Stocks in Relation to Their Price-Earnings Ratios: A Test of the Efficient Market Hypothesis," *Journal of Finance* 12 (1977), pp. 129–156; and Statman, D., "Book Values and Stock Returns," *The Chicago MBA: A Journal of Selected Papers* 4 (1980), pp. 25–45.

presence of beta.[50] As such, Fama and French proposed a three-factor model that includes market risk, size, and book-to-market factors.[51] This model is not based on any underlying theory for why size and book-to-market might represent risks that are not diversifiable and might be priced. Instead, the model is motivated from the previously described empirical work that shows that size and the market-to-book ratio help explain the cross-section of expected returns even in the presence of the CAPM beta. You can think of the three-factor model as an alternative attempt to specify the APT. However, it does not rely on standard macroeconomic factors (like inflation risk) as is more typical of implementations of the APT.

Fama and French and other researchers have continued this line of research and have developed other empirically-based multi-factor asset pricing models. For example, Carhart (1997) proposed a four-factor model,[52] and Pastor and Stambaugh (2003) added a liquidity factor to the Fama and French three-factor model.[53] Hou, Zue, and Zhang (2015) developed a q-factor model,[54] and Fama and French more recently developed a five-factor model.[55] While all of these models have been shown to "beat" the CAPM, at least in the short-term, at the current time, the CAPM (and CAPM with a size adjustment) continues to be the most widely used model for estimating a company's cost of capital in practice. Of the various multi-factor models, the Fama and French three-factor model is the most well-known, and we use that model to illustrate how to estimate a multi-factor model.

The Fama and French Three-Factor Model and Its Estimation

Fama and French start with the CAPM (risk-free rate plus sensitivity [beta] multiplied by the market risk premium) and add two other factors: the sensitivity of a stock's return to the difference in returns between diversified portfolios of small and large market capitalization companies multiplied by the small minus big firm risk premium, and the stock's sensitivity to the difference in returns between diversified portfolios of high and low book-to-market stocks multiplied by the expected risk premium on high minus low book-to-market portfolios.

The equation of the three-factor model is as follows:

$$r_E = r_F + \beta_{MRP}\,[MRP] + \beta_{SMB}[SMB] + \beta_{HML}\,[HML] \tag{8.15}$$

where r_E is the return on equity, r_F is the risk free rate, β_{MRP} is the sensitivity of a stock's return to the market risk premium (MRP), β_{SMB} is the sensitivity of a stock's return to the small minus big risk premium (SMB), and β_{HML} is the sensitivity of a stock's return to the high minus low book-to-market risk premium (HML).

The three factors can be viewed as empirically documented risk factors, each with a risk premium—MRP, SMB, and HML. SMB measures the difference in returns between small and big companies. Certain firms may prosper more when the environment for small firms is better than that for large firms and vice-versa. This would be reflected in different sensitivities to the SMB factor. In addition, if HML is negative, it means that high-book-to-market firms have performed worse than low-book-to-market firms. Firms with high sensitivity to the HML factor are likely to perform poorly and distressed firms may perform particularly poorly when the HML factor is negative. Again, this would be reflected in the company's sensitivity to the HML factor. We illustrate this calculation in Exhibit 8.18 for the same four stocks in Exhibit 8.6.

To estimate the three-factor model we estimate the sensitivity of a stock's return to each of the three risk factors, which requires a time series of the returns on a company's stock and the return on each of the risk premiums on a periodic basis, such as monthly return data. Fortunately, Ken French maintains

---

[50] See Fama, E., and K. French, "The Cross-Section of Expected Stock Returns," *Journal of Finance* 47 (1992), pp. 427–463; and Fama, E., and K. French, "Multifactor Explanations of Asset Pricing Anomalies," *Journal of Finance* 51 (1996), pp. 55–84.

[51] See Fama, E., and K. French, "Common Risk Factors in the Returns on Stocks and Bonds," *Journal of Financial Economics* 33 (1993), pp. 3–56; and Fama, E., and K. French, "Multifactor Explanations of Asset Pricing Anomalies," *Journal of Finance* 51 (1996), pp. 55–84.

[52] Carhart, Mark M., "On Persistence in Mutual Fund Performance," *Journal of Finance* 52 (1997), pp. 57–82.

[53] Pastor, Lubos, and Robert F. Stambaugh, "Liquidity Risk and Expected Stock Returns," *Journal of Political Economy* 111 (2003), pp. 642–685.

[54] Hou, Kewei, Chen Xue, and Lu Zhang, "Digesting Anomalies: An Investment Approach," *Review of Financial Studies* 28 (2015), pp. 650–705.

[55] Fama, Eugene F., and Kenneth R. French, "A Five-Factor Asset Pricing Model," *Journal of Financial Economics* 116 (2015), pp. 1–22.

the returns to the three factors (and the five factors for the Fama and French five-factor model) on his website.[56] We estimate the model by regressing a company's stock returns on the returns associated with the three factors to determine a stock's sensitivity to each of the factors. We then use estimates of the historical risk premiums in conjunction with the sensitivities to estimate the risk premium for a stock. In the exhibit, we compare the three-factor risk premium to the risk premium calculated using the CAPM using the beta from Exhibit 8.6. Note that to estimate the cost of equity capital for either model, we add an estimate of the risk-free rate to the risk premium estimates shown in Exhibit 8.18.

At the top of Exhibit 8.18, we show the risk premiums for each of the risk factors for the Fama and French three-factor model. These are the average annual risk premiums from 1927 through 2016 using all of the companies available in the CRSP database, which is a broad index, rather than the S&P 500. The market risk premium (MRP) in the model is based on U.S. Treasury Bills. We estimate the parameters using 60 months of data ending in March 2017. The beta for the CAPM is similar to the parameter for the market risk premium in the three-factor model—Colgate has the lowest beta, followed by Ford, General Electric, and Textron. However, the other factors in the three-factor model affect the overall risk premium, which is the important difference in the models.

While the risk premiums vary across the models, Colgate has the lowest risk premium, Textron has the highest risk premium, and General Electric and Ford are in the middle for both models. General Electric has the most similar risk premiums from the two models (10.0% versus 9.9%), and Colgate has the most dissimilar risk premiums from the two models (2.2% versus 6.3%). The CAPM beta and the market risk premium beta for the three-factor model are very similar across the two models, hence the market risk premiums are similar across the two models. However, in the case of Colgate, it has a large negative parameter for the size and book-to-market factors, which reduces Colgate's risk premium in the three-factor model which explains why Colgate's risk premiums are so different under the two models. The risk premiums are similar for an equally weighted portfolio of the four companies (9.7% versus 9.6%).

EXHIBIT 8.18 Firm-Specific Risk Premiums from the Three-Factor and CAPM Models for Our Four Companies

	Three-Factor Model				CAPM	
	MRP	SMB	HML		MRP	
Risk Premiums	0.0836	0.0329	0.0512		0.0836	
	Three-Factor Model Sensitivities					
	β_{MRP}	β_{SMB}	β_{HML}	Three-Factor Risk Premium	CAPM β	CAPM Risk Premium
Colgate Palmolive Co.	0.777	−0.622	−0.442	2.2%	0.752	6.3%
General Electric Co.	1.168	−0.395	0.297	10.0%	1.181	9.9%
Ford Motor Co.	1.077	−0.120	0.508	11.2%	1.060	8.9%
Textron Inc.	1.466	0.522	0.287	15.4%	1.580	13.2%
Equally weighted portfolio	1.122	−0.153	0.163	9.7%	1.143	9.6%

In Exhibit 8.19, we present the median risk premiums for the three-factor and CAPM models for the 20 industries with the lowest beta and 20 industries with the highest beta in Exhibit 8.2. The correlation between the two risk premiums is 96%, and it is statistically significant. Although the average parameter for the market risk premium for the three-factor model is lower than beta in the CAPM (1.04 versus 1.12), on average, the risk premium from the three-factor model is 1.1% higher than the CAPM risk premium (10.4% versus 9.3%). The risk premium from the three-factor model is higher even though the coefficient for the market risk premium is lower because the parameters for the size and book-to-market factors are both, on average, positive. The largest difference in the risk premiums is 3.9% (SIC = 3812, Search, Detection, Navigation, Guidance, Aeronautical Sys, 11.2% versus 7.3%).

[56] See http://mba.tuck.dartmouth.edu/pages/faculty/ken.french/data_library.html.

EXHIBIT 8.19 Industry Risk Premiums from the Fama-French Three-Factor and CAPM Models (Estimated using 60 months of data)

		Three-Factor Model Sensitivities			Three-Factor Risk Premium	CAPM β	CAPM Risk Premium
		β_{MRP}	β_{SMB}	β_{HML}			
	Risk premiums	0.0830	0.0325	0.0491			0.0830
Panel A: 20 Industries with the Lowest CAPM Betas as of March 31, 2015							
4931	Electric & other services combined	0.29	−0.23	0.05	1.9%	0.28	2.3%
4911	Electric services	0.38	−0.09	0.03	3.0%	0.40	3.3%
2086	Bottled & canned soft drinks & carbonated waters	0.56	−0.08	0.42	6.5%	0.42	3.5%
6035	Savings institution, federally chartered	0.44	0.24	0.07	4.8%	0.51	4.3%
6712	Offices of bank holding companies	0.52	0.26	0.01	5.3%	0.57	4.7%
5812	Retail-eating places	0.60	0.25	−0.01	5.7%	0.64	5.3%
6036	Savings institutions, not federally chartered	0.57	0.31	0.12	6.3%	0.66	5.4%
4812	Radiotelephone communications	0.81	−0.51	−0.04	4.9%	0.72	6.0%
5810	Retail-eating & drinking places	0.66	0.60	0.06	7.7%	0.73	6.1%
6798	Real estate investment trusts	0.71	0.10	0.13	6.8%	0.74	6.2%
6221	Commodity contracts brokers & dealers	0.65	0.04	0.00	5.5%	0.75	6.2%
1041	Gold ores	0.65	0.40	−0.12	6.1%	0.77	6.4%
6022	State commercial banks	0.69	0.53	0.10	7.9%	0.77	6.4%
6726	Unit investment trusts, face-amount certificate offices, and closed-end management investment offices	0.78	−0.10	0.05	6.4%	0.78	6.5%
6331	Fire, marine & casualty insurance	0.74	0.25	0.18	7.9%	0.81	6.7%
4922	Natural gas transmission	0.93	−0.61	0.10	6.2%	0.81	6.7%
3812	Search, detection, navigation, guidance, aeronautical sys	0.93	0.53	0.35	11.2%	0.88	7.3%
3841	Surgical & medical instruments & apparatus	0.73	0.73	0.06	8.7%	0.91	7.5%
4813	Telephone communications (no radiotelephone)	0.97	−0.30	0.08	7.4%	0.92	7.7%
4512	Air transportation, scheduled	0.86	0.32	−0.01	8.1%	0.93	7.7%
Panel B: 20 Industries with the Highest CAPM Betas as of March 31, 2015							
2621	Paper mills	1.13	1.07	0.35	14.6%	1.36	11.3%
3570	Computer & office equipment	1.08	0.99	0.51	14.7%	1.37	11.3%
7363	Services-help supply services	1.31	0.73	0.41	15.2%	1.37	11.4%
6282	Investment advice	1.34	0.32	0.06	12.5%	1.42	11.8%
2836	Biological products, (no diagnostic substances)	1.31	0.84	0.16	14.4%	1.46	12.1%
6029	Commercial banks, NEC	1.40	−0.24	0.06	11.1%	1.46	12.1%
3674	Semiconductors & related devices	1.29	0.65	0.22	13.9%	1.46	12.2%
1311	Crude petroleum & natural gas	1.32	0.07	0.27	12.6%	1.47	12.2%
1389	Oil & gas field services, NEC	1.40	0.22	0.17	13.2%	1.47	12.2%
2911	Petroleum refining	1.45	−0.13	0.04	11.8%	1.48	12.3%
1531	Operative builders	1.31	0.85	0.12	14.2%	1.52	12.6%
4412	Deep sea foreign transportation of freight	1.46	0.47	0.12	14.2%	1.54	12.8%
3714	Motor vehicle parts & accessories	1.46	0.81	0.08	15.1%	1.58	13.1%
3312	Steel works, blast furnaces & rolling mills (coke ovens)	1.47	0.20	−0.07	12.5%	1.59	13.2%
7359	Services-equipment rental & leasing, NEC	1.49	0.69	0.11	15.2%	1.62	13.5%
3661	Telephone & telegraph apparatus	1.47	0.84	0.07	15.3%	1.63	13.6%
2821	Plastic materials, synth resins & nonvulcan elastomers	1.54	0.58	0.17	15.5%	1.64	13.6%
3711	Motor vehicles & passenger car bodies	1.53	0.78	0.07	15.6%	1.65	13.7%
1381	Drilling oil & gas wells	1.66	0.35	0.18	15.8%	1.77	14.7%
4833	Television broadcasting stations	1.84	0.59	0.61	20.2%	2.07	17.2%
	Average	1.04	0.33	0.13	10.4%	1.12	9.3%

Almost all of the estimation issues that arise for the CAPM are relevant for the three-factor model, only now we are estimating the risk premiums associated with three risk factors instead of one and the sensitivity of a company's stock to three factors instead of one. For example, what is the best way to estimate the risk premiums for the three different factors? Should we use the historical approach? If so, should we use the arithmetic or geometric mean? What time period should we use? Should we use some approach other than the mean historical approach? How many observations should we use to estimate factor sensitivities? Should we use monthly, weekly, or daily return data? The list goes on. Naturally, these issues also apply to the other multi-factor models as well.

The imprecision in our estimates of the cost of capital that are obtained from the three-factor model is similar to what we discussed earlier in the chapter regarding the CAPM. Fama and French again conclude that the imprecision in the factor risk premiums is the major cause of error even if the three-factor model is the correct model. Again, they find that the standard errors of the overall risk premium introduced by uncertainty about the risk premiums associated with the three factors, assuming one knew the sensitivities with certainty and that the three-factor model was correct, amount to 3.17% per year.

Valuation Key 8.14

The multi-factor models are an alternative method for estimating a company's cost of capital. The three-factor model is widely used in academic studies and is seeing some use in practice, but the CAPM (and CAPM with a size adjustment) continue to dominate in practice. Use of the three-factor model requires estimating the sensitivity of a stock's return to the three different factors and estimating the risk premiums for each of the factors.

REVIEW EXERCISE 8.7

Three-Factor Risk Premiums for Four Comparable Companies in Review Exercise 8.5

Use the information in Review Exercise 8.5, assumptions in Exhibit 8.18, and the information that appears below to calculate the three-factor and CAPM risk premiums for the four comparable companies; in other words, create a table similar to Exhibit 8.18 for the four comparable companies in Review Exercise 8.5.

	Three-Factor Model Sensitivities		
	β_{MRP}	β_{SMB}	β_{HML}
Comparable Company #1	0.900	0.300	0.250
Comparable Company #2	0.800	0.100	0.900
Comparable Company #3	1.500	−0.200	0.500
Comparable Company #4	1.100	0.600	0.200

Solution on page 379.

8.11 IMPLIED COST OF CAPITAL ESTIMATES

Earlier in the chapter, we briefly discuss estimating the market risk premium by first estimating the expected rate of return on a stock from the current price and forecasts of earnings or free cash flows and then aggregating those individual estimates of expected returns across all firms in a market to determine an estimate of the expected return on the market.[57] Essentially, given a set of forecasts of cash flows or excess earnings derived from forecasts of analysts or from a model, we solve for the discount rate that equates that stream of projected cash flows or excess earnings with the currently observed price. The discount rate or internal rate of return is an implied cost of capital for the firm—implied by current prices and forecasts. These implied cost of capital estimates can be used as a measure of a company's equity cost of capital. We discuss this technique in further detail here and start with a simple model to develop the intuition.

The Constant Dividend Growth Model

If we assume that a company's dividends and share repurchases will grow by a constant proportion each year and if we assume that the cost of equity capital is constant through time, then the price per share of the company is equal to

$$P_0 = \frac{DIV_1}{(r_E - g)} \quad \textbf{(8.16)}$$

where

P_0 = the price per share of the company's stock today.
DIV_1 = the expected dividend and share repurchases per share for the next year.
r_E = the cost of equity capital.
g = the expected annual growth rate in dividends and share repurchases.

[57] Easton, Peter, "Estimating the Cost of Capital Implied by Market Prices and Accounting Data," *Foundations and Trends in Accounting* vol. 2, no. 4 (2007), pp. 241–364.

This is nothing more than a constant growth perpetuity model applied to dividends and share repurchases. Rearranging this formula suggests that the cost of equity capital is equal to

$$r_E = g + \left(\frac{DIV_1}{P_0}\right)$$

where $\frac{DIV_1}{P_0}$ is often referred to as the firm's dividend yield (including share repurchases).

This formulation is obviously a simplification in that it assumes that the company's dividends and amounts spent on share repurchases will grow by the same proportionate amount each year. As such, this model only has any chance of producing reasonable estimates of the cost of equity capital for companies that are very stable, mature, growing slowly, and paying dividends or repurchasing shares. We do not generally recommend the use of the constant dividend growth model as a means of estimating the cost of equity capital.

Implied Cost of Capital Estimates from Forecasts of Excess Earnings or Cash Flows

A variation of the constant growth model is to develop short-term, intermediate-term, and long-term free cash flow or excess earnings forecasts in an effort to solve for the expected return (internal rate of return), which when used to discount the projected cash flow or excess earnings forecasts yields the currently observed stock price. In this case, the models are not typically applied to assumptions about dividend growth, but are instead applied to either free cash flows or excess earnings. However, the intuition is similar to the constant dividend growth model. We solve for the rate of return that equates the cash flow forecasts or forecasts of excess earnings with the publicly observed price. Unlike the constant growth dividend model, these models do not have a closed-form solution to estimate the cost of equity capital when allowing for varying growth rates. Thus, the solution is an iterative one, just like measuring the internal rate of return.

Many of the variations in this method relate to how many years to forecast explicit year-by-year free cash flows or excess earnings, how to determine the intermediate and long-term growth rates (for example, use long-term industry outlooks or expected inflation), and how and when to transition between the intermediate- and long-term growth rates.[58]

All of these models can be applied using either analyst forecasts or forecasts that come from a forecasting model. A disadvantage of using analyst forecasts is the biases of analysts and the staleness of analyst forecasts. Another disadvantage is that analysts tend not to follow small market capitalization companies, so the sample of companies for which we can measure implied cost of capital estimates from analysts' forecasts is limited. Academic research suggests that controlling for some of the known biases of analysts and controlling for the fact that some analyst forecasts are "stale" at any given point in time, implied cost of capital measures have desirable properties. However, without controls for the known biases and staleness, the estimates do not exhibit these desirable properties.[59]

Recent research suggests that estimating the implied equity cost of capital from earnings forecasts derived from a simple cross-sectional model has superior properties to using analysts' forecasts—the implied cost of capital estimates are a better proxy for expected returns using the forecasts from the cross-sectional model.[60] As such, there is promise for this technique and we expect research to continue to attempt to exploit this technique to estimate the cost of capital. These models have several potential advantages. First, all of the inputs and analysis is forward looking. Second, we do not have to make any presumption about which asset pricing model is best, nor do we need to estimate parameters such as the market risk premium. However, we do have to assume that observed prices in the market are rational, that we can collect or estimate reliable forecasts of free cash flows or excess earnings, and that the models correctly estimate the intermediate and long-term growth rates.

[58] See Appendix A of Hou, K., M. van Dijk, and Y. Zhang, "The Implied Cost of Capital: A New Approach," *Journal of Accounting and Economics* 53 (2012), pp. 504–526, for a discussion of some of the alternative ways of estimating implied costs of capital.

[59] See Guay, W., S. P. Kothari, and S. Shu, "Properties of Implied Cost of Capital Estimates Using Analysts' Forecasts," *Australian Journal of Management* 36 (2011), pp. 125–149.

[60] See Hou, K., M. van Dijk, and Y. Zhang, "The Implied Cost of Capital: A New Approach," *Journal of Accounting and Economics* 53 (2012), pp. 504–526.

SUMMARY AND KEY CONCEPTS

In this chapter, we discuss the Capital Asset Pricing Model and how to implement it in practice. The CAPM is the most commonly used model to estimate the cost of equity capital in practice, but that does not mean that the CAPM is necessarily more accurate than the other models. We have discussed the issues associated with estimating the CAPM inputs—a company's beta, the risk-free rate, and market risk premium. The CAPM is a model; it is not a perfect statement of exactly how the world works. In addition, even if the CAPM was the perfect model, estimates of the CAPM inputs would result in noisy estimates of the cost of capital from the CAPM. We discuss the variety of ways that practitioners and academics implement the CAPM, and that some of the differences in estimation lead to substantial differences in the estimated equity cost of capital. Suffice it to say that two individuals working independently might not agree on a company's cost of capital even if both individuals were using the CAPM.

We also discuss alternatives to the CAPM for estimating the equity cost of capital. Such alternatives include the size adjustment to the CAPM, the build-up method, arbitrage pricing theory, the multi-factor models, and implied cost of capital models. The CAPM and all the alternative models have a large number of estimation issues associated with them, and all of this introduces uncertainty into our estimates of the cost of capital.

One caveat to our discussion of estimating the cost of equity capital is worth noting before concluding this chapter. The methods discussed in this chapter for estimating the cost of capital are not directly relevant for valuing private companies as private companies, since these methods all presume that investors hold well-diversified portfolios and that the assets are readily marketable. As such, we often make adjustments to the valuation of private companies when using these methods for estimating the cost of equity. We discuss these adjustments later in the book. Of course, we sometimes value a private company as if it were a public company, such as for an initial public offering, in which case the kinds of adjustments we discuss later are unnecessary.

ADDITIONAL READING AND REFERENCES

Fama, E., and K. French, "The Capital Asset Pricing Model: Theory and Evidence," *Journal of Economic Perspectives* 18 (Summer, 2004), pp. 25–46.

Fama, E., and K. French, "Multifactor Explanations of Asset Pricing Anomalies," *Journal of Finance* 51 (1996), pp. 55–84.

EXERCISES AND PROBLEMS

P8.1 **Calculating Beta:** Information is provided below for three companies. The standard deviation of the market return is 0.055 and the expected market risk premium $[(E(R_m) - r_F]$ equals 0.065. For each company, calculate the firm beta, and the relative risk of the firm's security return to the market return based upon their relative standard deviations. Are beta and the relative standard deviations both measures of the firm's risk?

	Firm 1	Firm 2	Firm 3
Standard deviation of firm's return	0.108	0.066	0.101
Covariance of firm's return and market return	0.0027	0.0032	0.0042

P8.2 **Calculating Portfolio Return and Portfolio Beta:** In the table below, the total equity market value, beta, and equity security return is listed for four individual equity securities. Assume you create a portfolio with these four securities. Calculate the return to the portfolio and the beta for the portfolio.

	Firm 1	Firm 2	Firm 3	Firm 4
Total firm equity market value (in millions)	$ 990	$3,675	$2,714	$ 581
Firm beta	0.78	1.06	0.96	1.47
Firm security return	5.8%	6.5%	7.7%	8.3%

P8.3 **Systematic Risk and Unsystematic Risk:** Assume a portfolio has monthly stock returns with a standard deviation of 0.12, and the standard deviation of the market portfolio of monthly returns is 0.05. The portfolio has an estimated beta of 1.2. Calculate the proportion of the portfolio's stock return variance that represents systematic risk and the proportion that represents unsystematic risk. Is the portfolio well diversified?

P8.4 **Adjusting Beta for an Anticipated Merger:** Assume Company A that operates in the retail industry and has an estimated beta of 1.6 is planning to merge with Company B that produces food related products and has an estimated beta of 0.8. At the time of the announcement of the merger, Company A was three times the size of Company B. Estimate the combined firm's beta after the merger assuming that the merger is not expected to create or destroy value and that the pre-merger debt of the two companies will remain outstanding after the merger occurs.

P8.5 **Adjusting Beta for Non-Operating Assets:** Company C has an estimated beta of 1.3 and uses no debt or other non-common equity financing. The company has 20% of its total market value invested in marketable securities that have an estimated beta of 0.1 and are assumed to be excess assets. Estimate the unlevered beta for Company C's operations.

P8.6 **Bloomberg Adjusted Betas:** Calculate the Bloomberg adjusted beta for each of the comparable companies and the portfolio of comparable companies that appear in the table for this problem. All of the companies are unlevered.

	Beta Estimate	Standard Error of Beta	t-statistic
Comparable Company #1	0.970	0.500	1.94
Comparable Company #2	1.310	0.550	2.38
Comparable Company #3	1.420	0.710	2.00
Comparable Company #4	1.580	0.700	2.26
Comparable company average beta	1.320		
Company being valued	1.110	0.600	1.85

P8.7 **Alternative CAPM-Based Equity Cost of Capital Estimates for Four Comparable Companies in Problem 8.6:** Calculate the cost of equity capital for the four comparable companies in Problem 8.6 using the alternative assumptions used to measure the equity cost of capital in Exhibit 8.15; in other words, create a table similar to Exhibit 8.15 for the four comparable companies in the previous problem.

P8.8 **Three-Factor Risk Premiums for Four Comparable Companies in Problem 8.6:** Use the information in Problem 8.6, assumptions in Exhibit 8.18, and the information that appears below to calculate the three-factor and CAPM Risk Premiums for the four comparable companies; in other words, create a table similar to Exhibit 8.18 for the four comparable companies in Problem 8.6.

	Three-Factor Model Sensitivities		
	β_{MRP}	β_{SMB}	β_{HML}
Comparable Company #1	0.820	0.340	0.930
Comparable Company #2	1.250	0.090	0.890
Comparable Company #3	1.320	−0.200	1.260
Comparable Company #4	1.650	0.670	0.320

P8.9 **Estimating Beta Using Monthly Stock Return Data:** Exhibit P8.1 presents monthly stock returns and the market capitalization of the equity for four companies, as well as the monthly returns for the S&P 500 and the three factors of the three-factor model.

a. Estimate the CAPM betas for each of the four stocks using regression analysis and 60 months of stock return data and an equally weighted portfolio of the four stocks.

b. Discuss the various statistics from the regression analysis including the statistical significance and 95% confidence interval of each beta.

c. Identify any of the companies that have a beta which is reliably (at the 95% confidence interval) different from the market beta.

d. Calculate the Bloomberg adjusted beta for each company.

EXHIBIT P8.1 Stock Returns for the Honeywell International, Inc. (HON), Boeing Company (BA), McDonalds Corporation (MCD), Oracle Systems Corporation (ORCL), S&P 500, and the Three Fama-French Factors

S&P 500 = S&P 500 value-weighted return with dividends
FF $R_m - R_f$ = Fama–French Market Factor
FF – SMB = Fama–French SMB Factor
FF – HML = Fama-French HML Factor
Ticker Ret = Stock Return for Ticker

DATE	HON RET	BA RET	MCD RET	ORCL RET	S&P 500	FF $R_m - R_f$	FF – SMB	FF – HML
Month 1	1.0%	0.8%	0.0%	0.1%	1.5%	1.4%	–0.4%	–0.4%
Month 2	2.1%	–2.2%	–1.5%	–4.3%	–1.9%	–1.9%	1.1%	0.7%
Month 3	–0.7%	1.9%	3.1%	10.3%	1.1%	0.7%	–0.1%	–0.6%
Month 4	17.6%	4.6%	7.2%	3.7%	4.4%	3.5%	–2.1%	–0.7%
Month 5	7.3%	8.6%	4.7%	3.1%	3.4%	3.2%	0.1%	0.0%
Month 6	–2.8%	–4.4%	0.4%	1.7%	–1.7%	–2.0%	0.8%	–1.5%
Month 7	2.2%	7.6%	–5.7%	–3.0%	–3.1%	–3.8%	–2.6%	–4.4%
Month 8	–1.9%	–6.2%	2.9%	6.1%	1.5%	0.8%	–0.2%	–1.6%
Month 9	5.9%	8.6%	10.6%	6.8%	3.7%	3.2%	–2.2%	–3.3%
Month 10	1.6%	–6.1%	9.7%	2.4%	1.7%	1.7%	0.4%	–4.7%
Month 11	–5.9%	–5.8%	0.4%	–9.0%	–4.1%	–4.9%	–2.5%	–1.8%
Month 12	8.7%	–5.5%	0.8%	11.9%	–0.6%	–0.8%	0.6%	–3.1%
Month 13	–4.1%	–4.9%	–9.0%	–9.0%	–6.1%	–6.3%	–1.3%	8.2%
Month 14	–2.1%	0.0%	1.7%	–8.5%	–3.1%	–3.2%	0.1%	–4.3%
Month 15	–1.9%	–10.2%	3.1%	4.0%	–0.3%	–0.9%	0.8%	–1.1%
Month 16	5.3%	14.1%	6.8%	6.6%	4.9%	4.6%	–2.5%	–0.4%
Month 17	0.8%	–2.0%	–0.4%	9.5%	1.3%	1.9%	3.2%	–4.3%
Month 18	–15.7%	–20.6%	–4.6%	–8.1%	–8.3%	–8.4%	–0.1%	–8.8%
Month 19	1.1%	–7.0%	6.4%	2.5%	–0.7%	–0.7%	2.5%	6.2%
Month 20	–0.8%	7.9%	4.3%	1.9%	1.5%	1.5%	3.3%	2.3%
Month 21	–17.2%	–12.5%	–0.5%	–7.4%	–8.5%	–9.6%	0.2%	3.3%
Month 22	–26.7%	–8.6%	–6.1%	–9.9%	–16.7%	–17.2%	–2.9%	–7.5%
Month 23	–7.6%	–18.0%	2.3%	–12.0%	–7.4%	–7.8%	–4.3%	–5.7%
Month 24	17.8%	0.1%	5.9%	10.2%	1.2%	1.8%	2.9%	–0.1%
Month 25	–0.1%	–0.8%	–6.7%	–5.1%	–8.3%	–7.9%	0.9%	–5.4%
Month 26	–17.4%	–24.9%	–9.1%	–7.7%	–10.4%	–9.9%	–0.8%	–8.3%
Month 27	3.8%	13.2%	4.4%	16.3%	8.8%	8.8%	0.9%	5.1%
Month 28	12.0%	12.6%	–2.3%	7.3%	9.4%	10.2%	10.6%	19.7%
Month 29	7.2%	13.0%	10.7%	1.3%	5.5%	5.3%	–1.5%	7.3%
Month 30	–5.3%	–5.2%	–1.7%	9.3%	0.2%	0.4%	2.0%	–4.8%
Month 31	10.5%	1.0%	–4.2%	3.6%	7.4%	7.8%	2.4%	3.4%
Month 32	6.9%	16.9%	3.1%	–1.1%	3.5%	3.2%	–1.1%	7.3%
Month 33	1.1%	9.0%	1.5%	–4.8%	3.7%	4.2%	2.9%	0.6%
Month 34	–3.4%	–11.7%	2.7%	1.5%	–1.8%	–2.5%	–4.1%	–1.7%
Month 35	8.0%	10.6%	8.8%	4.6%	6.0%	5.6%	–3.1%	–0.1%
Month 36	1.9%	3.3%	–1.3%	11.1%	1.9%	2.8%	5.7%	–0.2%
Month 37	–1.4%	12.0%	0.0%	–5.8%	–3.6%	–3.5%	0.4%	3.5%
Month 38	4.7%	4.9%	3.1%	6.9%	3.0%	3.4%	1.2%	0.6%
Month 39	12.7%	15.0%	4.5%	4.3%	6.1%	6.3%	1.8%	1.6%
Month 40	4.9%	–0.2%	5.8%	0.8%	1.6%	2.1%	4.4%	2.6%
Month 41	–9.3%	–10.9%	–4.5%	–12.7%	–8.0%	–7.9%	0.3%	–1.8%
Month 42	–8.7%	–2.2%	–1.5%	–4.9%	–5.4%	–5.7%	–1.9%	–1.7%
Month 43	9.8%	8.6%	5.9%	10.4%	7.2%	7.3%	–0.5%	1.0%
Month 44	–8.2%	–9.7%	5.6%	–7.6%	–4.5%	–4.8%	–2.8%	–1.7%
Month 45	12.5%	8.8%	2.0%	22.9%	9.0%	9.6%	3.6%	–2.7%
Month 46	7.2%	6.2%	4.4%	9.6%	3.9%	4.0%	0.4%	–1.5%
Month 47	6.2%	–9.2%	1.5%	–7.9%	0.0%	0.6%	3.5%	–0.5%
Month 48	6.9%	2.3%	–2.0%	15.7%	6.7%	6.8%	0.8%	4.7%
Month 49	5.4%	6.5%	–4.0%	2.5%	2.3%	2.1%	–2.1%	0.6%
Month 50	4.0%	4.2%	3.6%	2.7%	3.2%	3.5%	1.6%	0.0%

continued

continued from prior page

EXHIBIT P8.1 Stock Returns for the Honeywell International, Inc. (HON), Boeing Company (BA), McDonalds Corporation (MCD), Oracle Systems Corporation (ORCL), S&P 500, and the Three Fama-French Factors

S&P 500 = S&P 500 value-weighted return with dividends
FF $R_m - R_f$ = Fama–French Market Factor
FF – SMB = Fama–French SMB Factor
FF – HML = Fama-French HML Factor
Ticker Ret = Stock Return for Ticker

DATE	HON RET	BA RET	MCD RET	ORCL RET	S&P 500	FF $R_m - R_f$	FF – SMB	FF – HML
Month 51	3.1%	2.7%	0.5%	1.6%	0.1%	0.6%	2.1%	–1.6%
Month 52	2.5%	7.9%	2.9%	7.8%	2.9%	3.0%	–0.8%	–1.7%
Month 53	–2.2%	–1.7%	4.9%	–4.8%	–1.1%	–1.3%	–0.6%	–0.7%
Month 54	0.1%	–5.3%	3.4%	–3.8%	–1.6%	–1.7%	–0.6%	–1.0%
Month 55	–10.9%	–4.7%	2.6%	–6.9%	–2.0%	–2.3%	–1.2%	–1.2%
Month 56	–9.3%	–4.4%	5.2%	–8.2%	–5.5%	–6.0%	–2.8%	–2.3%
Month 57	–8.2%	–9.5%	–2.9%	2.4%	–7.0%	–7.5%	–2.9%	–2.0%
Month 58	19.3%	8.7%	5.7%	14.3%	10.9%	11.3%	3.6%	3.2%
Month 59	4.1%	5.1%	3.6%	–4.3%	–0.3%	–0.3%	0.2%	–1.8%
Month 60	0.4%	6.8%	5.0%	–18.2%	0.9%	0.9%	–0.8%	0.9%

P8.10 **Alternative CAPM-Based Equity Cost of Capital Estimates for the Four Companies in Problem 8.9:** Calculate the cost of equity capital for the four comparable companies in Problem 8.9 using the alternative assumptions used to measure the equity cost of capital in Exhibit 8.15; in other words, create a table similar to Exhibit 8.15 for the four companies in the previous problem. However, do not use the Mayfield estimate of the market risk premium in this example (for each company you will have four different cost of capital estimates—two betas [adjusted and unadjusted] and two market risk premium estimates).

P8.11 **Estimating Three-Factor Risk Factor Betas and Risk Premiums for the Four Companies in Problem 8.9:** Use the information in Problem 8.9 to estimate the three-factor risk factor betas for the four companies in Problem 8.9. Use the assumptions in Exhibit 8.18 and the other information for this problem and calculate the three-factor risk premiums and the CAPM risk premiums for the four companies. Compare these risk premiums to the risk premiums from the CAPM and Bloomberg adjusted betas estimated in Problem 8.10.

SOLUTIONS FOR REVIEW EXERCISES

Review Exercise 8.1: Calculating Beta

Standard deviation of the market return	0.05		
Expected market risk premium	0.06		
	Firm 1	**Firm 2**	**Firm 3**
Standard deviation of firm's return	0.12	0.06	0.10
Covariance of firm's return and market return	0.003	0.0025	0.004
Firm beta	1.20	1.00	1.60
Firm standard deviation/market std. dev.	2.40	1.20	2.00

The betas are calculated by dividing the covariance of the individual security return and the market return by the variance (standard deviation squared) of the market return. The relative risk of the individual security to the market as measured by standard deviations is calculated by dividing the individual security standard deviation by the market return standard deviation. Beta is a measure of how much more or less an individual stock's return moves with the market portfolio (a measure of risk) whereas the volatility of an individual security's return does not measure risk. Firm 3 has the highest beta or risk measure of 1.6, but Firm 1 has the highest relative standard deviation as compared to the market of 2.4. The relative standard deviation measure indicates the relative volatility of the individual firm's return and the market, but does not measure risk. Firm 2 happens to have the lowest beta of 1.0 and lowest relative standard deviation measure of 1.2.

Review Exercise 8.2: Calculating Portfolio Return and Portfolio Beta

	Firm 1	Firm 2	Firm 3	Firm 4
Total equity market value in portfolio (in millions)	$1,000	$3,500	$2,300	$ 700
Firm beta	0.90	1.07	1.20	1.46
Stock return	5.0%	7.0%	9.0%	10.0%
Firm market value/total market value	13.3%	46.7%	30.7%	9.3%
Return to the portfolio	7.6%			
Portfolio beta	1.124			

To compute the weights, we simply determine the proportion of each firm's market value to the total value of the portfolio. We then use the weighted average returns and weighted average betas to compute the portfolio return of 7.6% and the portfolio beta of 1.12.

Review Exercise 8.3: Systematic Risk and Unsystematic Risk

Portfolio standard deviation of returns	0.155
Market portfolio standard deviation of returns	0.060
Portfolio estimated beta	1.300
Systematic risk	25.3%
Unsystematic risk	74.7%

We can use the following formula to measure the proportion of systematic risk

$$\frac{\sigma^2(\tilde{R}_i)}{\sigma^2(\tilde{R}_i)} = 1 = \beta_i^2 \frac{\sigma^2(\tilde{R}_m)}{\sigma^2(\tilde{R}_i)} + \frac{\sigma^2(\tilde{\varepsilon}_i)}{\sigma^2(\tilde{R}_i)}$$

(Keep in mind that standard deviations were given in the problem so those amounts must be squared to arrive at variances that are used in the formula.) The proportion of the variance of the security return that is systematic is calculated to be 25%. The unsystematic proportion is therefore 75% (= 1 − 0.25). The portfolio is not well diversified.

Review Exercise 8.4: Adjusting Estimated Betas

Part 1	Company A	Company B
Beta	1.70	1.00
Percentage of the merged company	33.3%	66.7%
Estimated beta after the merger	1.233	

The estimated beta for the combined company is 1.23. This is just a value-weighted average of the pre-merger betas. Note this calculation presumes that the merger neither creates nor destroys value and that the pre-merger debt of the companies remains with the merged entity.

Part 2	
Beta (levered = unlevered) for the company	1.500
% of market value in excess assets	30.0%
Beta for marketable securities	0.400
Beta for unlevered operations (excludes excess assets)	1.971

The estimated beta for unlevered operations is 1.97. To calculate it, we solve for the beta of the operations knowing the unlevered beta of the company is 1.5 and that the excess assets have a beta of 0.4 and represent 30% of the market value of the firm.

Review Exercise 8.5: Bloomberg Adjusted Betas

	Beta Estimate	Standard Error of Beta	Bloomberg Adjusted Beta
Comparable Company #1	0.90	0.50	0.933
Comparable Company #2	1.10	0.40	1.067
Comparable Company #3	1.35	0.60	1.235
Comparable Company #4	1.50	0.45	1.335
Company being valued	1.10	0.56	1.067
Comparable company average beta	1.213		1.142
Average beta of comps and company being valued	1.190		

The Bloomberg adjusted beta is 0.33 + 0.67 × unadjusted beta.

The comparable company average beta and average beta of the comparable companies and the company being valued are just equally weighted averages.

Review Exercise 8.6: Alternative CAPM-Based Equity Cost of Capital Estimates for Four Comparable Companies in Review Exercise 8.5

			Beta		Market Risk Premium			
Company	Equity Cost of Capital Estimate	Yield on Risk-Free Asset	Review Exercise 8.5	Bloomberg Adjusted	Historical Based on U.S. Treasury Bill	Historical Based on U.S. Long-Term Gov Bond	Mayfield	Maturity Risk Premium
Comparable Company #1 . . .	8.4%	3.0%	0.900			6.0%		
	8.1%	3.0%	0.900		8.6%			2.6%
	6.8%	3.0%	0.900				4.2%	
	8.6%	3.0%		0.933		6.0%		
	8.4%	3.0%		0.933	8.6%			2.6%
	6.9%	3.0%		0.933			4.2%	
Average	7.9%							
Comparable Company #2 . . .	9.6%	3.0%	1.100			6.0%		
	9.9%	3.0%	1.100		8.6%			2.6%
	7.6%	3.0%	1.100				4.2%	
	9.4%	3.0%		1.067		6.0%		
	9.6%	3.0%		1.067	8.6%			2.6%
	7.5%	3.0%		1.067			4.2%	
Average	8.9%							
Comparable Company #3 . . .	11.1%	3.0%	1.350			6.0%		
	12.0%	3.0%	1.350		8.6%			2.6%
	8.7%	3.0%	1.350				4.2%	
	10.4%	3.0%		1.235		6.0%		
	11.0%	3.0%		1.235	8.6%			2.6%
	8.2%	3.0%		1.235			4.2%	
Average	10.2%							
Comparable Company #4 . . .	12.0%	3.0%	1.500			6.0%		
	13.3%	3.0%	1.500		8.6%			2.6%
	9.3%	3.0%	1.500				4.2%	
	11.0%	3.0%		1.335		6.0%		
	11.9%	3.0%		1.335	8.6%			2.6%
	8.6%	3.0%		1.335			4.2%	
Average	11.0%							

The betas of the companies come from Review Exercise 8.5. The market risk premium measured from the S&P 500 less one-month U.S. Treasury Bills is 8.6%, the market risk premium measured from the S&P 500 less U.S. Long-Term Government Bonds is 6.0%, the market risk premium per Mayfield is 4.2% and the maturity premium is 2.6%.

Review Exercise 8.7: Three-Factor Risk Premiums for Four Comparable Companies in Review Exercise 8.5

	Three-Factor Model				CAPM MRP	
	MRP	SMB	HML			
Risk premiums	0.0836	0.0329	0.0512		0.0836	
	Three-Factor Model Sensitivities			Three-Factor Risk Premium	CAPM β	CAPM Risk Premium
	β_{MRP}	β_{SMB}	β_{HML}			
Comparable Company #1	0.900	0.300	0.250	9.8%	0.900	7.5%
Comparable Company #2	0.800	0.100	0.900	11.6%	1.100	9.2%
Comparable Company #3	1.500	−0.200	0.500	14.4%	1.350	11.3%
Comparable Company #4	1.100	0.600	0.200	12.2%	1.500	12.5%
Comparable company portfolio beta	1.300	−0.300	0.500	12.4%	1.213	10.1%

After mastering the material in this chapter, you will be able to:

1. Understand how companies finance their operations (9.1)
2. Use credit ratings, recovery rates, and default rates to analyze the yield to maturity, the cost of debt, and expected default loss (9.2)
3. Measure the debt and preferred stock costs of capital (9.3)
4. Use credit rating models to estimate a company's credit rating (9.4)
5. Use financial distress (bankruptcy) models to estimate a company's default probability (9.5)

Measuring the Cost of Capital for Debt and Preferred Securities

CHAPTER

GAP, INC.

In May, 2016, Gap, Inc.[1] (Banana Republic, Old Navy, Athleta, and Intermix clothing brands) lost its investment grade (BBB−) credit rating, when three of the major credit rating agencies downgraded Gap, Inc.'s credit ratings from BBB− to BB+. Falling below an investment grade credit rating will prevent some investors, who only invest in investment grade debt (BBB− and higher), from investing in Gap's debt.

The downgrades were issued after Gap reported continued declines in its revenues for the first quarter of 2016. Expected continued sales and earnings declines, volatile gross margins, and the need for a transformative expense reduction program, are some of the reasons given for the downgrade.

In this chapter, we examine the ways in which companies finance their operations with debt and preferred financing, how to estimate the cost of that financing, and the role of credit ratings.

[1] See, Business Wire, "Fitch Downgrades The Gap, Inc.'s IDR to 'BB+'; Outlook Stable." May 11, 2016 09:25 AM Eastern Daylight Time. Gap Inc. is a leading global apparel retail company offering apparel, accessories, and personal care products. Gap operates stores in the U. S., Canada, the U. K., France, Ireland, Japan, Italy, China, Hong Kong, Taiwan, and Mexico and franchisees throughout Asia, Australia, Europe, Latin America, the Middle East, and Africa. (Gap, Inc.'s 2015 SEC 10-K Report.)

CHAPTER ORGANIZATION

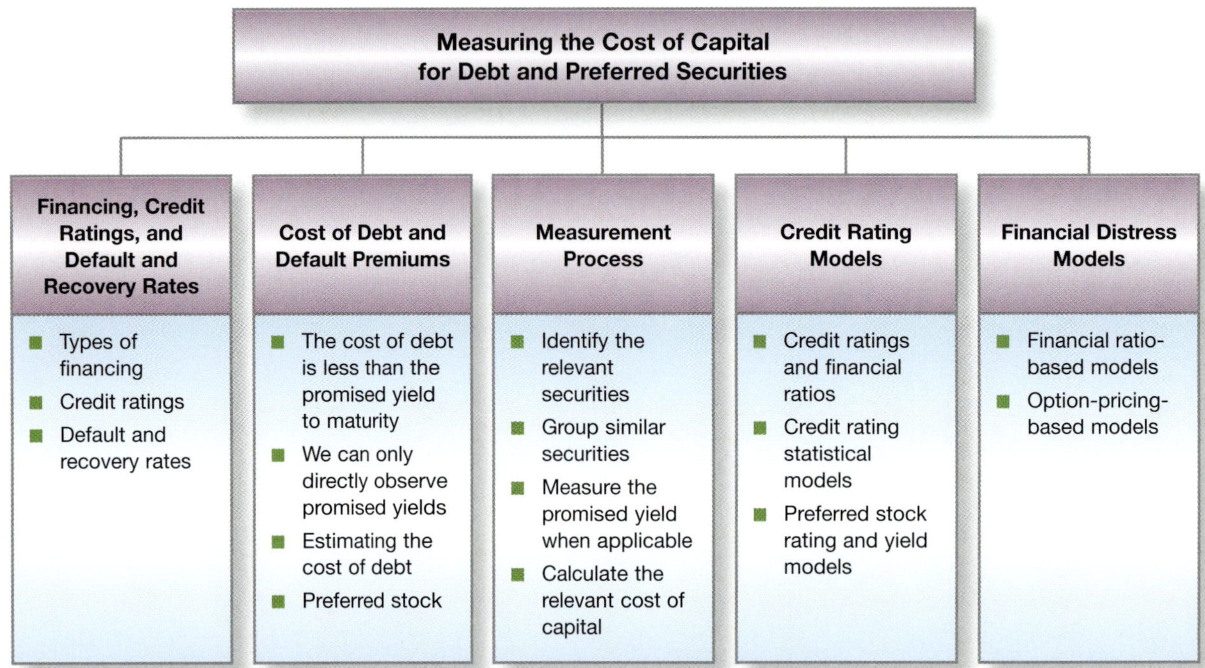

INTRODUCTION

In the previous chapter, we discussed how to measure the equity cost of capital. After common equity, the most widely used source of financing is debt financing; however, companies also use other sources of financing such as preferred stock and securities that are convertible into another security (for example, debt or preferred that are convertible into equity as well as warrants and employee stock options). These other financing sources are relevant to a valuation analysis because the levering, unlevering, and weighted average cost of capital formulas include a component for each type of financing used by the company in its capital structure. The focus of this chapter is measuring the cost of capital for debt and preferred securities without conversion privileges. In Chapter 12, we discuss measuring the cost of capital for equity-linked securities such as convertible debt, convertible preferred, warrants, and employee stock options.

We can measure the cost of capital for debt and preferred stock in various ways. Recall the Capital Asset Pricing Model (CAPM) and the other asset pricing models used to measure the equity cost of capital. We can use models similar to these models along with other asset pricing models and other techniques to measure the cost of capital for debt and preferred stock. We sometimes use comparable companies to measure various costs of capital. To do the latter, we identify comparable companies whose debt and preferred stock have similar risk characteristics as the debt and preferred stock of the company which we are valuing and use the observed costs of capital for the comparable companies. We can use statistical models (credit rating and bankruptcy prediction models) to assess the risk of a company's debt and preferred securities in order to help select the comparable companies.

An important caveat to our discussion in this and the previous chapter is that the models and methods available to measure costs of capital are evolving, and none of them fully explains the variation we observe in returns. Factors such as liquidity, regulation, and other factors, including some that are likely yet to be discovered, affect security prices and thus affect the cost of capital. On the state of our understanding of discount rates, Cochrane concludes "Discount rates vary a lot more than we thought. Most of the puzzles and anomalies that we face amount to discount-rate variation we do not understand. Our theoretical controversies are about how discount rates are formed. We need to recognize and incorporate discount-rate variation in applied procedures. We are really only beginning these tasks."[2]

[2] Cochrane, John, "Presidential Address: Discount Rates," *The Journal of Finance* vol. LXVI, no. 4 (August 2011), pp. 1047–1108.

9.1 TYPES OF NON-COMMON-EQUITY SECURITIES

In this section of the chapter, we provide a summary of alternative sources of financing. We present a list of the alternative sources of financing in Exhibit 9.1. This list is not meant to be exhaustive, but rather, it presents the most prevalent sources of financing companies use.

LO1 Understand how companies finance their operations

EXHIBIT 9.1 Alternative Sources of Financing

Debt	Equity
Short-Term Debt	**Preferred or Preference Stock**
Bank debt (secured or unsecured) Revolving line of credit Commercial paper	Fixed or variable dividend rate (usually fixed) Callable Convertible (into common stock) Publicly traded or privately placed Cumulative dividends (if not paid) Required redemption (redemption price) Liquidation price
Long-Term Debt	**Common Stock**
Mortgage (secured) Notes (secured or unsecured) Capital lease (secured) Debentures or bonds Senior or subordinated (junior) Sinking fund or no sinking fund Callable Putable Convertible (into preferred stock or common stock) or with warrants Publicly traded or privately placed Fixed or floating interest rate (with/without a collar or cap, inflation adjusted, income based, equity linked) Covenants (performance hurdles or restricting actions) Zero-coupon and pay-in-kind debt (see debentures for characteristics)	Class A (voting) Class B Voting (more rights or fewer rights than Class A) or non-voting Higher priority or same priority (as Class A) Fixed or variable or no dividend rate **Equity Derivatives** Convertible components of debt and preferred stock Employee stock options Warrants Rights offering
Quasi Long-Term Debt	
Operating leases	
Swaps	
Interest rate and other swaps	

The exhibit shows that companies have many available alternative sources of financing. Naturally, one of the company's goals is to finance itself at the lowest possible cost in order to maximize the value of the firm and the value of its common equity. Recall that a company's unlevered free cash flows represent the cash flow available for distribution to all of the company's investors—in other words, to the investors of every source of financing used by a company (excluding non-interest-bearing operating liabilities)—before consideration of any benefits from interest tax shields. Based on the contracts for the different forms of financing, investors in different securities have different claims, and the varying claims have different rights and priorities on the company's unlevered free cash flows. These, as well as other, differences result in different costs of capital for different sources of financing. Claims that are more senior or have higher priority over other claims generally have a lower cost of capital.

How Do Companies Finance Their Balance Sheets?

In Exhibit 9.2, we show the distribution of the different types of financing that companies use to finance their operations based on the book values reported in their financial statements.[3] In this chart, we present the

[3] The sample consists of 4,023 companies with complete information for their 2015 fiscal years available in the Compustat® North American Industrial Annual File and not classified as financial institutions or insurance companies

distribution in terms of the average proportion of a company's balance sheet that is financed with various types of debt, operating liabilities, and equities (excluding leases, employee stock options, warrants, and rights). This chart presents financing percentages based on book values, not market values. Recall that in estimating the weighted average cost of capital, we use weights based on market values, not book values, and we do not include operating liabilities when measuring the capital structure. We discuss market value-based capital structure proportions in Chapter 11 when we discuss the weighted average cost of capital.

EXHIBIT 9.2 How Companies "Finance" Their Balance Sheets

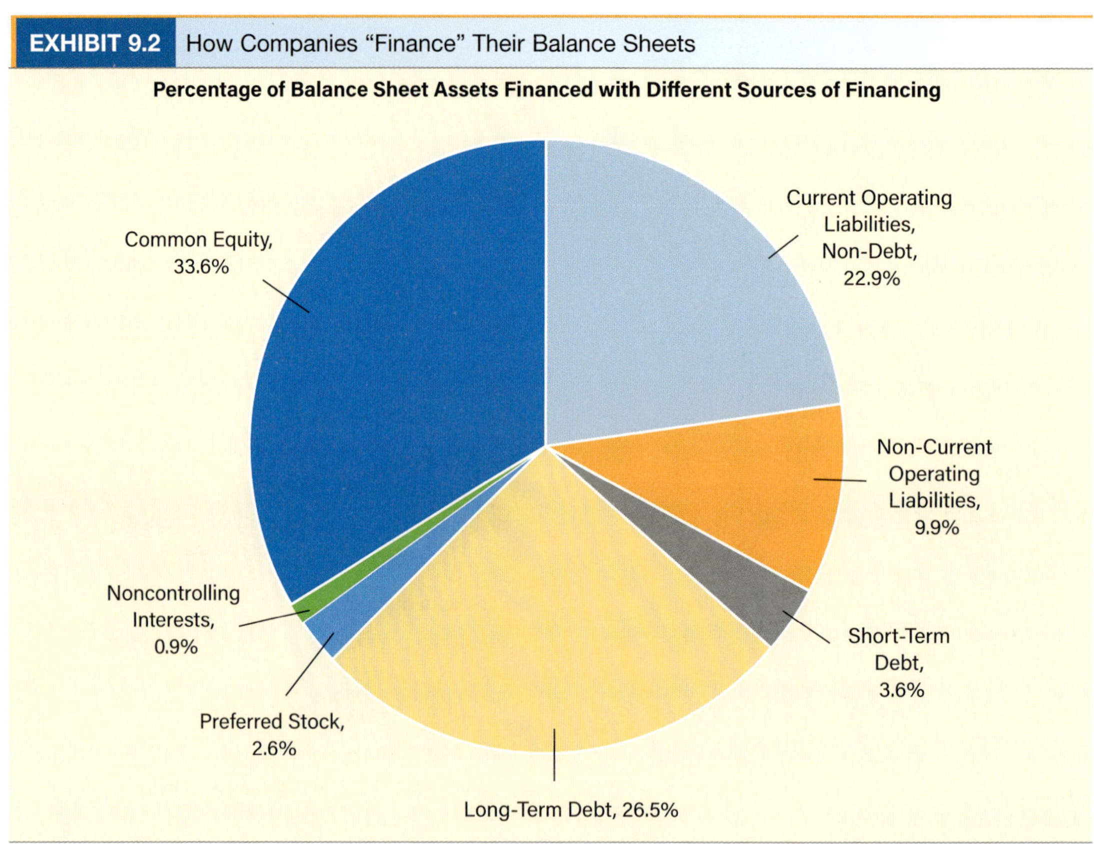

On average, common stock financing (on a book value basis) accounts for 33.6% of the companies' total assets, and long-term debt accounts for 26.5% of the total. Short-term debt accounts for 3.6% of the total, and preferred stock accounts for 2.6% of the total. Current non-interest-bearing operating liabilities and other long-term non-interest-bearing operating liabilities account for 22.9% and 9.9% of the total, respectively. Thus, on average, non-interest-bearing operating liabilities finance 32.8% of the companies' assets.

Valuation Key 9.1

Companies use many different types of non-common-equity securities to finance their operations. Different non-common-equity claims have different maturity dates, different rights, and different priorities of claims on a company's unlevered free cash flows. These differences result in different costs of capital for different sources of financing.

Preferred stock is a different form of non-common-equity financing than debt. Like common equity, it pays dividends rather than interest, but it typically does not have a maturity date. In general, it legally has equity status—thus, it cannot force a company into bankruptcy—and has priority on claims before common equity but after debt. Its dividends are either cumulative or non-cumulative. If dividends are cumulative, missed dividends become dividends in arrears that must be paid before the company makes distributions to common shareholders. Preferred stock can be convertible (typically into common stock), be callable by the company, be redeemable (at the option of the company or be required after certain events), have a floating dividend rate, and even participate in a company's profits. From the exhibit we know that, on average, preferred stock accounts for a small portion of the total financing of companies.

Further, we know that many companies do not issue preferred stock. In this sample, 80% of the companies use debt financing, but only 10% of the companies use preferred stock financing. Preferred stock financing is more likely to be used in certain industries such as the oil and gas extraction, textile mill products, and lumber and wood products (except furniture) industries.

Valuation in Practice 9.1

Washington Mutual, Inc. Issuance of 7.75% Series R Non-Cumulative Perpetual Convertible Preferred Stock Washington Mutual, Inc.* announced that it was going to increase its public offering to 3,000,000 shares of 7.75% Series R Non-Cumulative Perpetual Convertible Preferred Stock, priced at $1,000 per share, resulting in a $3.0 billion issuance before transactions costs. In its amended prospectus, dated December 12, 2007, Washington Mutual described this security as follows:

> Washington Mutual, Inc. is offering 3,000,000 shares of our 7.75% Series R Non-Cumulative Perpetual Convertible Preferred Stock, referred to as the Series R Preferred Stock.
>
> Dividends on the Series R Preferred Stock will be payable quarterly in arrears, when, as and if declared by our board of directors, at a rate of 7.75% per year on the liquidation preference of $1,000 per share. . . . Dividends on the Series R Preferred Stock will be non-cumulative. If for any reason our board of directors does not declare full cash dividends on the Series R Preferred Stock for a dividend period, we will have no obligation to pay any dividends for that period, . . . However, . . ., we may not declare or pay dividends on or redeem or purchase our common stock or other junior securities during the next succeeding dividend period.
>
> Each share of the Series R Preferred Stock may be converted at any time, at the option of the holder, into 47.0535 shares of our common stock (which reflects an approximate initial conversion price of $21.25 per share of common stock) plus cash in lieu of fractional shares, subject to anti-dilution adjustments. . . .
>
> On or after December 18, 2012, if the closing price of our common stock exceeds 130% of the conversion price for 20 trading days during any consecutive 30 trading day period . . ., we may at our option cause some or all of the Series R Preferred Stock to be automatically converted into common stock at the then prevailing conversion rate.
>
> Investing in the shares of Series R Preferred Stock involves risks. See "Risk Factors" beginning on page S-11.

* Washington Mutual, Inc. was a financial services company that served consumers and small to medium-sized businesses. Its assets were eventually sold to JPMorgan Chase.

Current and Non-Current Operating Liabilities Not Included in Non-Common-Equity Financing

Although we show all of the typical liabilities and equities we see on balance sheets in Exhibit 9.2 (including non-interest-bearing operating liabilities), our focus in this chapter is measuring the cost of capital for debt and preferred stock. Recall that when valuing a company, we implicitly "net" non-interest-bearing current and non-current operating liabilities against the value of the company's operations and excess assets; in other words, the value of the firm is measured net of its non-interest-bearing operating liabilities.

We "net" non-interest-bearing liabilities against the value of the company because financing costs related to non-interest-bearing-operating liabilities are embedded in the company's operating expenses, and we do not have an easy way of disentangling them. For example, when a company buys a product or service on account from a vendor, the vendor charges the company for the product or service plus an implicit financing charge for not paying at the time the good or service is received. Hence, the financing charge is embedded in the cost of the product or service and cannot be easily partitioned from the value of the operations.

Thus, we do not include all of a company's liabilities as part of its capital structure. We use the term *debt* to represent certain types of financing such as notes, mortgages, and bonds (debentures). From a valuation perspective, we define debt to be an amount contractually owed to another party that has an explicit or implicit interest payment *that we can measure*. This definition excludes current and non-current operating liabilities (for example, accounts payable, wages payable, accruals, etc.) as well as liabilities such as deferred income taxes and deferred revenue.

The Cost of Capital for Warrants, Employee Stock Options, and Other Equity-Linked Securities

In this chapter we focus our discussion on measuring the cost of capital of straight debt and preferred stock; however, the levering, unlevering, and weighted average cost of capital formulas require us to know the cost of capital and the capital structure ratio for each of the securities a company uses to finance itself. These securities include equity-linked securities such as warrants, employee stock options, convertible debt, and other similar securities. We introduce these securities in this chapter and discuss them in greater detail in Chapter 12. These securities have characteristics that are similar, but are not identical, to the stock option contracts for which the Black-Scholes Option Pricing Model was developed.[4]

One important feature of these securities is that they are dilutive; if the holder of such a security exercises the option in the security, the company issues additional shares of stock, which dilutes the ownership interest of the pre-existing shares. In general, equity-linked securities issued by companies have a longer term to maturity than options traded on option exchanges. Various researchers have extended the Black-Scholes Option Pricing Model to measure the value and cost of capital of warrants, employee stock options, convertible debt, and other similar equity-linked securities, which we discuss in Chapter 12. Convertible debt is a security that has a coupon interest rate and maturity date (among other provisions) just like a straight-debt security. However, it also has an option for the holder to convert the bond into common stock (or sometimes even into preferred stock).

9.2 CREDIT RATINGS, RECOVERY RATES, DEFAULT RATES, AND YIELD TO MATURITY VERSUS THE COST OF DEBT

LO2 Use credit ratings, recovery rates, and default rates to analyze the yield to maturity, the cost of debt and expected default loss

Unlike common equity, debt and preferred stock have contractually promised payments. Thus, measuring the cost of capital requires an assessment of both the promised payments and the company's ability to make those payments. The likelihood of default and the expected recovery in case of default are a function of various factors such as the riskiness of the firm's unlevered cash flows, the company's financial leverage, the magnitude and timing of the payments that the firm is required to make to all of its non-common-equity investors, the extent to which the debt is secured by the firm's assets, and the value of its non-secured assets. Different securities issued by the same company can have different costs of capital due to differences in the terms of the contracts, which include maturity, seniority, and security or collateral features. In addition, restrictions or **debt covenants** in the contracts also affect the cost of debt. For example, a corporation may agree to limit the total amount of indebtedness that it can have, or it may agree to restrict the sale of its assets, common stock repurchases, or dividends. In addition, it may agree to meet certain financial measures (for example, a minimum coverage ratio) while the debt is outstanding. If the company does not meet these conditions, it is in technical default even though it hasn't missed any required payments. Technical default provides the creditors with additional rights and typically forces the company to renegotiate the terms of the agreement with the creditors or receive a waiver for the technical default. Such restrictions or covenants tend to reduce the cost of debt because they protect the lender.

Fortunately, credit rating agencies provide assessments of the ability of a company to meet the obligations of its debt and preferred stock. A credit rating agency assesses the creditworthiness of a debtor as an entity or with respect to specific securities. These ratings and the market data associated with them provide useful information for measuring the costs of debt and preferred stock.

Credit Rating Agencies and Credit Ratings

Credit ratings (also called debt or bond ratings, depending on the entity or security rated) on the debt securities of companies, municipalities, and governments are issued by various credit rating agencies. These rating agencies include, among others, Moody's Investors Service, Inc. (Moody's); Standard & Poor's (S&P); Fitch, Inc. (Fitch); and Dominion Bond Rating Services, Limited (DBRS)—a Canadian company. In the

[4] Black, F., and M. Scholes, "The Pricing of Options and Corporate Liabilities," *Journal of Political Economy* vol. 81, no. 3 (May/June 1973), pp. 637–654.

United States, all of these credit rating agencies, as well as others, are designated by the U.S. SEC as **Nationally Recognized Statistical Rating Organizations** (NRSROs) and they operate in many markets around the world (as of December 2015, the U.S. SEC approved ten NRSROs).[5] In addition to these global credit rating agencies, many rating agencies have their focus in a single country or region. For example, Asia, China, Japan, Malaysia, Indonesia, Korea, Thailand, and the Philippines all have local credit rating agencies, as do some countries in Latin America such as Columbia, Chile, Ecuador, Panama, and Peru.

Credit ratings indicate the likelihood of timely repayment of principal and interest by the borrower, as well as expected recovery rates in the event of default. Higher probabilities of repayment and higher recovery rates are associated with higher ratings. As such, ratings measure default risk and also incorporate recovery rates in the event of default. However, they do not measure overall market interest rate risk—that is, the risk that the value of the bond may change due to fluctuations in market-wide interest rates.

For example, S&P rates bonds AAA, AA, A, BBB, BB, B, CCC, CC, C, and D. The D rating is reserved for bonds that have defaulted. Ratings between AA and CCC are assigned gradients of + or − to show their relative standing within the major rating classifications. For example, an A-rated bond can be rated A+, A, or A−. Bonds rated BBB− or above are generally considered **investment-grade bonds**, and those rated below BBB− are **non-investment grade**, and may be referred to as speculative or **junk bonds**. Some institutions and funds are prohibited from holding bonds that are not investment grade.

Moody's has a similar ranking system: Aaa, Aa, A, Baa, Ba, B, Caa, Ca, and C with gradations of 1, 2, and 3 within the rating categories of Aa to B. Thus, an Aa-rated bond can be rated Aa1, Aa2, or Aa3. Much like S&P, Dominion Bond Rating Services uses rating categories of AAA to D and denotes three gradations between AA and C. Fitch's also has rating categories that are similar to those of S&P.[6]

In Exhibit 9.3, we show the distribution of credit ratings for a sample of publicly traded companies for which S&P had a current credit rating in 2008 (Panel A) and in 2015 (Panel B) available in S&P's CapitalIQ database.

Exhibit 9.3 shows that fewer companies have credit ratings in the highest (AAA and AA) and lowest (CCC, CC, C, and D) categories. The proportion of ratings in each class, especially those in the middle of the distribution, changes over time, depending on the state of the economy. If the economy is weaker, as it was in 2008 (Panel A), we observe more companies in the B categories; conversely, if the economy is strong, as it was in 2015 (Panel B), we observe a shift in the ratings as more ratings exist in the BBB categories. In 2015, 53% of the companies had investment grade (BBB−) or better credit ratings, while in 2008, only 38% of the companies had investment grade or better credit ratings.

Valuation Key 9.2

Debt and preferred stock ratings measure the likelihood of default and incorporate information on expected recovery in the event of default. Rating agencies use factors such as the riskiness of the firm's cash flows, the firm's leverage ratio, the payments that the firm is required to make to all of its lenders, and the extent to which the debt is secured by assets in order to develop these ratings.

Recovery and Default Rates

As stated earlier, credit ratings reflect both the **default rates** (likelihood of default) and the anticipated **recovery rates** in the event of default; the lower the rating, the more likely the company will default on its promised payments and, generally, the lower the recovery will be. The term "dividend omission" is generally used instead of "default" when discussing preferred stock because not paying or omitting a preferred stock dividend is generally not a violation of its associated contract.

Empirically, we observe that the higher the rating, the higher the recovery rate. Therefore, the percentage of the promised payments on a security that is recovered when a company defaults is negatively

[5] See U.S. SEC Staff, *Annual Report on Nationally Recognized Statistical Rating Organizations*, December 2015, available on May 31, 2018 at https://www.sec.gov/ocr/reportspubs/annual-reports/2015-annual-report-on-nrsros.pdf.

[6] For more information on the credit agencies and their ratings methodologies as well as some statistics on ratios for various credit ratings, see http://www.standardandpoors.com/ratings/ and http://www.moodys.com.

EXHIBIT 9.3 Distribution of Company Current Credit Ratings in Standard and Poor's

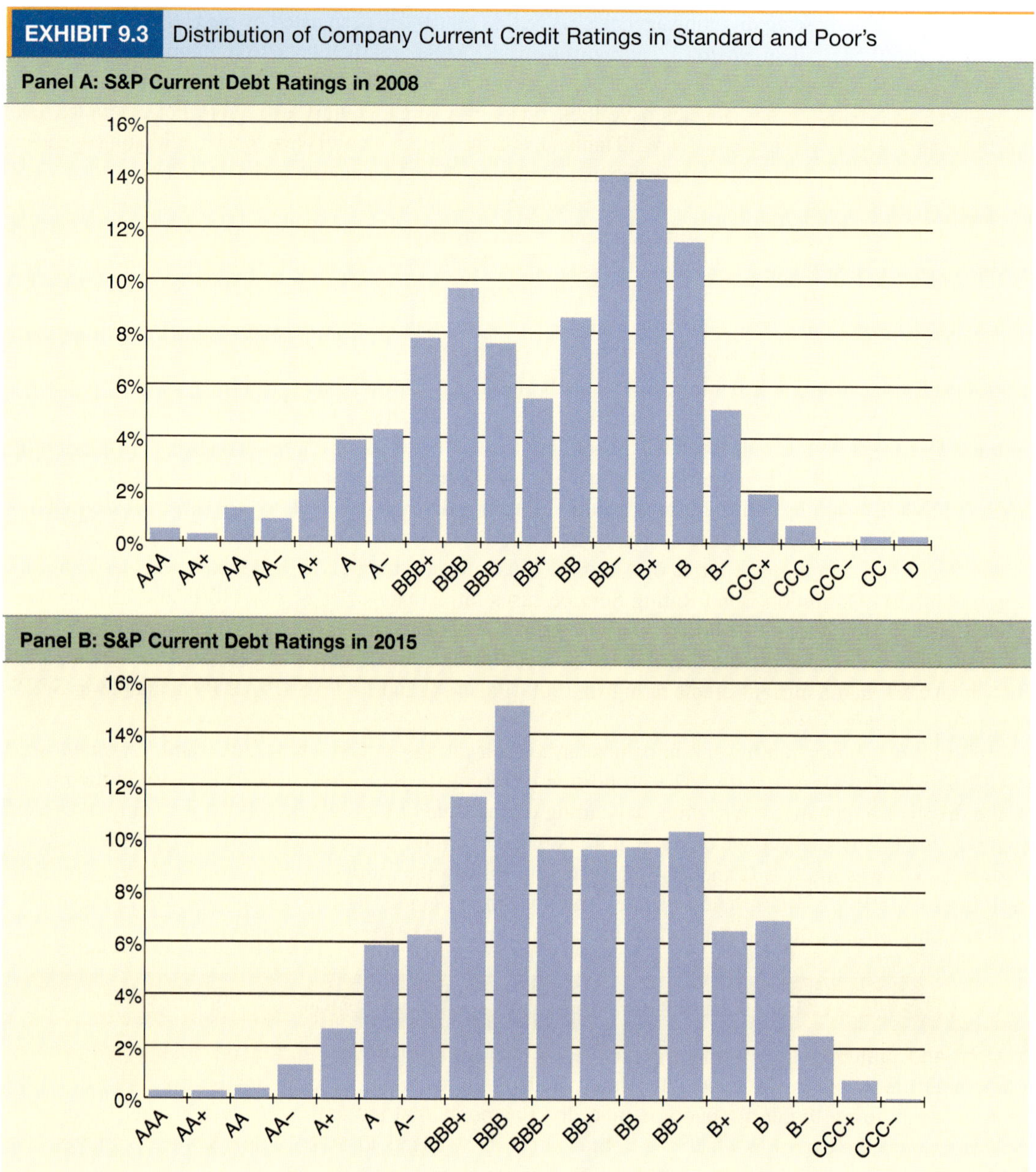

correlated with default rates.[7] In Exhibit 9.4, we present recovery rates for debt, measured based on seniority and type of security.

The first column of recovery rates presents recovery rates based on market prices 30 days after the default event; in other words, it is the percentage of the amount owed (including accrued interest and outstanding principal) that would be received if the investor sold the security in the market 30 days after the default. The second column of recovery rates is based on the ultimate outcome; in other words, it is the percentage of the amount owed (including accrued interest and outstanding principal) that an investor ultimately received from holding the security until it was redeemed or liquidated. These two columns do not represent "apples-to-apples" comparisons because the ultimate recovery rates in the second column typically require the investor to wait longer than 30 days to receive the recovered amount. Since the recovery rates are not adjusted for the time value of money, they cannot be directly compared to one another. As we would expect, this exhibit shows that secured debt and more senior debt have higher recovery rates.

[7] See the discussion on page 10 in *Corporate Default and Recovery Rates*, 1920–2007, Moody's Investors Service, February 2008, reprinted with permission. To the best of our knowledge, this is the last publication in which Moody's reported the detailed information for preferred stocks.

EXHIBIT 9.4 Average Recovery Rates for Certain Types of Debt Securities (1983-2015) from Moody's Investors Service*

Type of Security	Based on Trading Prices after Default	Ultimate Recovery
Bank Loans		
Senior secured	66.6%	
Senior unsecured	47.1%	
All		80.4%
Bonds		
Senior secured	53.4%	63.3%
Senior unsecured	37.6%	48.8%
Senior subordinated	31.1%	
Subordinated	31.9%	
Junior subordinated	24.2%	
All subordinated		28.2%

* See Exhibits 7 and 8 in *Moody's Corporate Default and Recovery Rates*, 1920–2015, Moody's Investors Service, February 2016, reprinted with permission.

Average recovery rates vary over time. In Exhibit 9.5 we present a chart of the average annual recovery rates for a subset of the debt securities shown in the previous exhibit. The relative ranks of the recovery rates of the four debt securities are generally the same. Senior Secured Loans generally have the highest recovery rate, the Senior Secured Bonds have the second highest recovery rate, the Senior Unsecured Bonds have the third highest recovery rate, and the Senior Subordinated Bonds have the lowest recovery rate. All of the recovery rates vary over time but generally have the same relative ranking over time. This exhibit indicates that in times of a recession (economic boom), recovery rates may be lower (higher) than average recovery rates.

EXHIBIT 9.5 Average Recovery Rates for Certain Types of Debt Securities (1996–2015) from Moody's Investors Service*

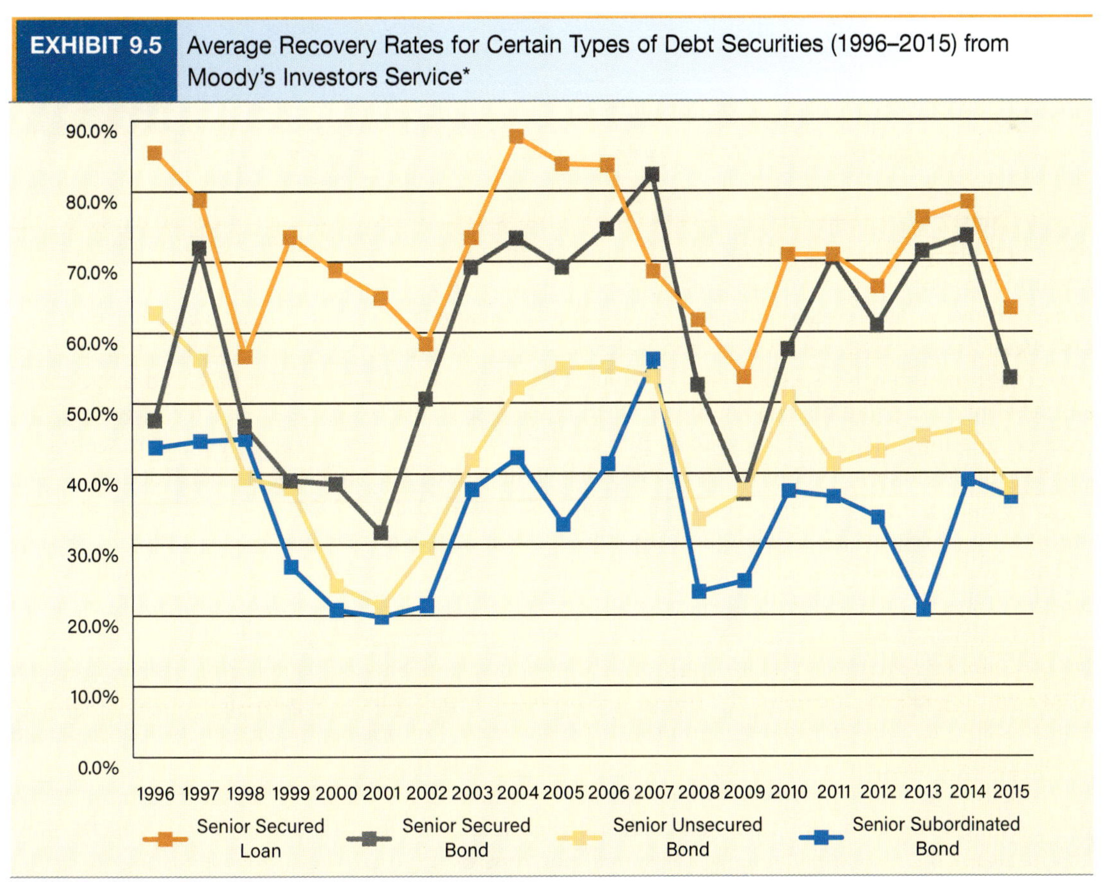

*See Exhibit 20 in *Moody's Corporate Default and Recovery Rates*, 1920–2015, Moody's Investors Service, February 2016, reprinted with permission.

In Exhibit 9.6, we present average recovery rates—based on market prices 30 days after the default event—for senior unsecured bonds partitioned by the bond's credit rating as measured by Moody's. This exhibit presents average recovery rates by rating class within a given number of years until default. The Year 1 column in this exhibit is the recovery rate after the bond was rated in the rating class for that row if it defaulted within the first year; the Year 2 column is the recovery rate after the bond was rated in the rating class for that row if it defaulted in the first or second year; and so forth. We do not report the statistics for Aaa bonds because at most five Aaa bonds defaulted in the first five years after they had been rated Aaa; and three of those bonds were Icelandic bank bonds, which had an average recovery of 3.33%, and thus, the recovery rates are not generally representative of Aaa bonds. This exhibit shows that, on average, for a given column (number of years after the bond was rated), higher ratings generally have slightly higher recovery rates. For example, recovery rates on investment-grade debt are greater than the recovery rates on speculative-grade debt in all five years.

EXHIBIT 9.6 Average Recovery Rates by Credit Ratings of Senior Unsecured Bonds by Year Prior to Default (1983–2015) from Moody's Investors Service*

Senior Unsecured Bond Rating	Year 1	Year 2	Year 3	Year 4	Year 5	Average
Aaa	(Too Few Observations to Report)**					
Aa	37.2%	39.0%	38.1%	44.0%	43.2%	40.3%
A	30.4%	42.6%	45.0%	44.5%	44.2%	41.3%
Baa	42.9%	44.4%	44.7%	44.6%	44.4%	44.2%
Ba	44.5%	43.5%	42.6%	42.3%	42.4%	43.1%
B	37.6%	36.6%	36.9%	37.3%	37.9%	37.3%
Caa–C	38.0%	38.4%	38.4%	38.9%	39.0%	38.5%
Investment grade	40.0%	43.5%	44.4%	44.6%	44.4%	43.4%
Speculative grade	38.3%	38.1%	38.2%	38.6%	39.0%	38.4%
All ratings	38.3%	38.5%	38.7%	39.2%	39.5%	38.8%

* See Exhibit 21 in *Moody's Corporate Default and Recovery Rates*, 1920–2015, Moody's Investors Service, February 2016, reprinted with permission.

** We did not report the rates for Aaa bonds because only five bonds defaulted and three of those bonds were Icelandic bank bonds, which had an average recovery of 3.33%, and thus, the recovery rates are not generally representative of Aaa bonds.

In Exhibit 9.7, we show recovery rates for preferred stock—based on market prices 30 days after the default event—as measured by Moody's. The rows in the exhibit represent different "default" events or impairments and subsequent or contemporaneous events relative to the default event. In addition, we also present recovery rates based on whether the dividends are cumulative or not. The two columns of recovery rates represent the recovery rates for preferred stock issued directly by the company (Corporate or Non-Trust) and through a special-purpose vehicle (Trust). The exhibit shows that preferred stock recovery rates are higher with dividend omissions than in the case of distress exchanges, which have a higher recovery rate than Chapter 11 bankruptcy filings. A distressed exchange occurs when a debt security is exchanged for another security (or securities) that diminishes the company's financial obligation and helps the company avoid default. Corporate or non-trust preferred shares have a higher recovery rate than preferred stock issued by a special-purpose entity, and cumulative preferred stock has a higher recovery rate than non-cumulative preferred stock. Not surprisingly, the recovery rates on debt are generally higher than the recovery rates on preferred stock.

In Exhibit 9.8, we provide data on the cumulative weighted average default rate of bonds that default N years into the future (N-year horizon) from Moody's Investors Service. Moody's recognizes a default if the company misses or delays payment of interest or principal, if the company files for bankruptcy or experiences other legal impediments to making timely interest or principal payments, or if a distressed exchange occurs.

Moody's measures cumulative weighted average default rates which we report in Exhibit 9.8 by first forming a cohort of similarly rated bonds for each year, 1983 to 2015. Moody's tracks each cohort and measures the annual default rate for annual horizons of up to 20 years, after adjusting for rating

EXHIBIT 9.7 Average Recovery Rates for Various Types of Preferred Stock (1983–2007) from Moody's Investors Service*

	Corporate (Non-Trust)	Trust
All issuances	23%	12%
Dividend omission	35%	18%
Distress exchange	22%	
Chapter 11	16%	11%
Missed payment	19%	9%
Other	2%	6%
Preferred Impairment Contemporaneous with Bond Default		
Cumulative dividends	20%	
Non-cumulative	13%	
Dividend Omission with Subsequent Bond Default		
Cumulative dividends	34%	
Non-cumulative	26%	
Dividend Omission with no Subsequent Bond Default		
Cumulative dividends	42%	
Non-cumulative	33%	
All Issuances		
Cumulative dividends		18%
Non-cumulative		7%

*See Exhibits 8, 45, and 46 in Emery, K., S. Ou, J. Tennant, F. Kim, and R. Cantor, *Corporate Default and Recovery Rates*, 1920–2007, Moody's Investors Service, February 2008, reprinted with permission.

withdrawals.[8] Moody's uses the weighted average annual default rates to calculate the cumulative default rates in Exhibit 9.8 for an N-year horizon by multiplying the series of one minus each default rate for each year from year-one to year-N and then subtracts the resulting number from 1. For example, the cumulative weighted average eight-year default rate is equal to 1 − (1 − first-year weighted average default rate) × (1 − second-year weighted average default rate) × ... × (1 − eighth-year weighted average default rate). We can use the cumulative weighted average default rates in Exhibit 9.8 to estimate the weighted average default rate for a specific year by dividing one-minus the cumulative weighted average default rate for that horizon by one-minus cumulative weighted average default rate for the previous horizon and then subtract the resulting number from 1; for example, the weighted average default rate estimate for the eighth year for B3 rated debt is equal to 4.7% [$0.047 = 1 - (1 - 0.394)/(1 - 0.364)$].

Although not shown, the annual default rates decline over time for lower credit ratings. In other words, if a company does not default in the first year after the rating, it is less likely to default in the second year; and if a company does not default for two years, it is even less likely to default in the third year, and so forth. For example, for Ca-C rated debt, the annual default rates for years 1 through 5 are 27.7%, 12.2%, 10.1%, 8.9%, and 5.4%, respectively.

In Exhibit 9.8, we present the cumulative weighted average default rates from Moody's Investors Service for the period 1983–2015. The default and recovery rates in this exhibit are averages over more than 30 years. Annual average default rates vary over time. In Exhibit 9.9 we present a chart of the annual default rates for a subset of the credit ratings shown in the previous exhibit. All of the default rates vary over time and the lower the credit rating, the higher the variation.

[8] The number of bonds in the cohort decreases in the subsequent horizons if Moody's no longer rates the bond, however, the bond remains in its cohort even if Moody's changes its rating. A debt rating can be withdrawn by Moody's for various reasons such as the debt matures or Moody's no longer has adequate information to rate the debt security. For the details of these calculations see, J. Tung and A. Metz, Glossary of Moody's Ratings Performance Metrics – Special Comment, Moody's Investors Service, September 30, 2011, pp. 2–4.

EXHIBIT 9.8 Average Cumulative Issuer-Weighted Global Default Rates (1983–2015) from Moody's Investors Service*

Rating	Cumulative Percent of Companies in Rating Class that Defaulted N Years in the Future									
	1	2	3	4	5	6	7	8	9	10
Aaa	0.0%	0.0%	0.0%	0.0%	0.1%	0.1%	0.1%	0.1%	0.1%	0.1%
Aa1	0.0%	0.0%	0.0%	0.1%	0.1%	0.2%	0.2%	0.2%	0.2%	0.2%
Aa2	0.0%	0.0%	0.1%	0.2%	0.4%	0.5%	0.5%	0.7%	0.8%	0.9%
Aa3	0.0%	0.1%	0.2%	0.3%	0.4%	0.5%	0.7%	0.8%	0.8%	0.9%
A1	0.1%	0.2%	0.5%	0.7%	0.9%	1.1%	1.4%	1.6%	1.7%	1.9%
A2	0.1%	0.2%	0.3%	0.6%	0.8%	1.2%	1.5%	1.9%	2.3%	2.8%
A3	0.1%	0.2%	0.4%	0.6%	0.9%	1.2%	1.5%	1.8%	2.2%	2.5%
Baa1	0.1%	0.4%	0.7%	1.0%	1.2%	1.5%	1.8%	2.0%	2.2%	2.4%
Baa2	0.2%	0.5%	0.8%	1.2%	1.6%	2.0%	2.4%	2.9%	3.3%	3.8%
Baa3	0.3%	0.7%	1.1%	1.7%	2.3%	2.9%	3.5%	4.1%	4.8%	5.4%
Ba1	0.5%	1.5%	2.8%	4.1%	5.5%	6.8%	7.9%	8.7%	9.5%	10.5%
Ba2	0.8%	1.9%	3.4%	4.9%	6.3%	7.3%	8.3%	9.5%	10.8%	12.1%
Ba3	1.5%	4.1%	7.4%	10.8%	13.7%	16.4%	19.0%	21.4%	23.5%	25.5%
B1	2.2%	5.9%	9.9%	13.7%	17.5%	20.9%	24.4%	27.5%	30.2%	32.2%
B2	3.3%	8.3%	13.3%	18.0%	21.8%	25.2%	28.2%	30.6%	32.9%	35.0%
B3	5.4%	11.7%	17.9%	23.2%	28.2%	32.6%	36.4%	39.4%	41.7%	43.2%
Caa1	5.1%	11.9%	18.2%	23.4%	27.9%	31.6%	34.2%	35.8%	37.6%	40.0%
Caa2	11.5%	20.6%	28.0%	34.3%	39.4%	43.6%	47.2%	51.0%	53.9%	56.5%
Caa3	20.5%	32.5%	40.9%	46.5%	51.2%	53.4%	55.9%	58.9%	59.6%	59.6%
Ca–C	27.7%	36.5%	42.9%	48.0%	50.8%	51.6%	52.0%	52.9%	53.4%	53.4%
Investment-grade	0.1%	0.3%	0.5%	0.7%	1.0%	1.3%	1.5%	1.8%	2.1%	2.3%
Speculative-grade	4.2%	8.6%	12.8%	16.5%	19.7%	22.4%	24.9%	26.9%	28.8%	30.3%
All-rated	1.6%	3.3%	4.8%	6.0%	7.1%	8.1%	8.9%	9.5%	10.2%	10.7%

*See Exhibit 32 in *Moody's Corporate Default and Recovery Rates*, 1920–2015, Moody's Investors Service, February 2016, reprinted with permission.

EXHIBIT 9.9 Annual Issuer-Weighted Global Average Default Rates (1996–2015) from Moody's Investors Service*

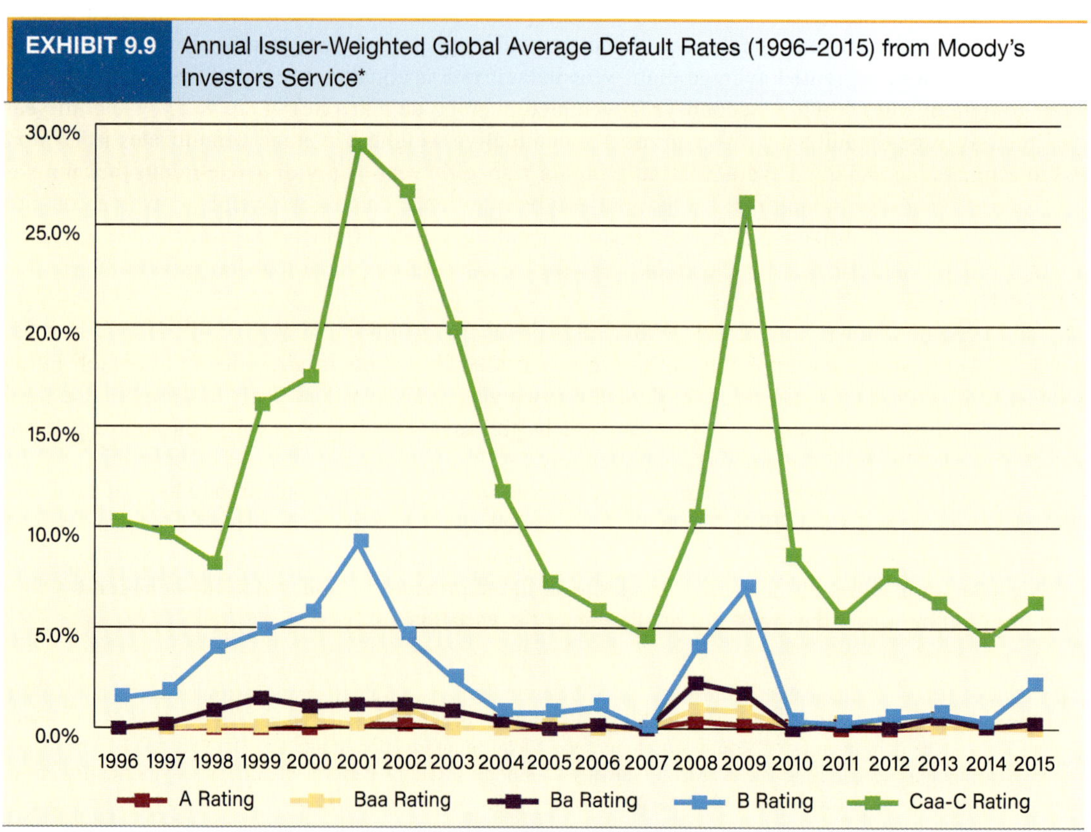

* See Exhibit 30 in *Moody's Corporate Default and Recovery Rates*, 1920–2015, Moody's Investors Service, February 2016, reprinted with permission.

Rating	11	12	13	14	15	16	17	18	19	20
Aaa	0.1%	0.1%	0.1%	0.1%	0.1%	0.1%	0.1%	0.1%	0.1%	0.1%
Aa1	0.2%	0.2%	0.2%	0.3%	0.4%	0.5%	0.5%	0.5%	0.5%	0.5%
Aa2	1.1%	1.3%	1.4%	1.5%	1.5%	1.7%	2.0%	2.2%	2.5%	2.7%
Aa3	1.0%	1.2%	1.4%	1.5%	1.6%	1.6%	1.7%	1.9%	2.2%	2.6%
A1	2.1%	2.3%	2.6%	2.9%	3.2%	3.5%	3.8%	4.1%	4.3%	4.4%
A2	3.2%	3.5%	3.9%	4.3%	4.8%	5.3%	6.0%	6.6%	7.1%	7.6%
A3	2.8%	3.1%	3.5%	3.9%	4.5%	5.0%	5.4%	6.0%	6.6%	7.2%
Baa1	2.8%	3.3%	3.9%	4.3%	5.0%	5.7%	6.5%	7.1%	7.3%	7.5%
Baa2	4.4%	5.1%	5.8%	6.4%	6.9%	7.4%	7.9%	8.5%	9.3%	9.9%
Baa3	6.0%	6.6%	7.3%	8.1%	8.7%	9.7%	10.9%	12.0%	13.1%	13.9%
Ba1	11.5%	12.5%	13.3%	14.0%	15.1%	16.2%	17.0%	18.1%	19.9%	21.5%
Ba2	13.3%	14.5%	15.3%	16.2%	17.5%	18.3%	19.2%	19.9%	20.9%	21.1%
Ba3	27.2%	28.7%	30.7%	32.9%	34.7%	36.6%	38.1%	39.4%	40.3%	41.0%
B1	33.8%	35.2%	37.0%	38.9%	40.3%	41.4%	42.6%	44.1%	45.6%	47.2%
B2	36.5%	37.9%	39.0%	39.9%	41.2%	42.3%	43.0%	43.6%	43.9%	44.8%
B3	44.4%	45.4%	46.1%	46.8%	47.0%	47.3%	48.6%	48.9%	48.9%	48.9%
Caa1	41.4%	42.3%	43.3%	43.7%	43.7%	43.7%	43.7%			
Caa2	58.3%	58.8%	58.8%	58.8%	59.6%	61.3%	61.7%	61.7%	61.7%	61.7%
Caa3	59.6%	59.6%	59.6%	59.6%	59.6%	59.6%	59.6%			
Ca–C	54.1%	55.2%	55.9%	55.9%	55.9%	55.9%	55.9%	55.9%	55.9%	55.9%
Investment-grade	2.6%	3.0%	3.3%	3.6%	4.0%	4.4%	4.8%	5.2%	5.6%	6.0%
Speculative-grade	31.6%	32.8%	34.0%	35.1%	36.2%	37.3%	38.2%	39.1%	40.1%	41.0%
All-rated	11.2%	11.7%	12.1%	12.6%	13.1%	13.6%	14.0%	14.5%	15.0%	15.3%

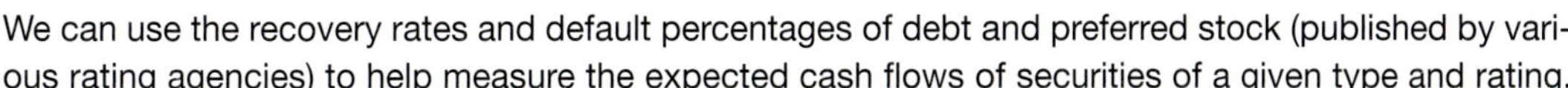

Valuation Key 9.3

We can use the recovery rates and default percentages of debt and preferred stock (published by various rating agencies) to help measure the expected cash flows of securities of a given type and rating.

The Promised Yield to Maturity versus the Cost of Debt

Usually, at this point in a chapter, we would discuss the process to implement the concepts in the chapter. Before we do that, however, we first discuss a topic that is not well understood and affects the process we use. A potentially important issue to consider when estimating the cost of capital for debt and preferred securities is the difference between the promised yield and the cost of capital. The **debt cost of capital** we use in our valuation formulas is equal to the required or expected rate of return based on the riskiness of the expected cash flows. The **promised yield** is equal to the rate of return the investor would realize if the debt is fully paid and the company does not default, but those are not the expected cash flows unless the default risk is non-existent.

A debt contract specifies the magnitude and timing of the agreed-upon cash payments, which we call promised payments. However, recall that the expected cash flows for a given period equal the sum of the cash flows in each possible state (or outcome that might occur) for that period, each multiplied by its respective probability of occurring. Naturally, when investors make investments in debt securities, they assess the likelihood of the debtor defaulting on the agreed-upon cash payments, and they then forecast the amount they expect to recover in default. We measure expected cash flows by adjusting the promised payments for both the probability of default and the amount expected to be recovered in each possible state. Thus, the promised yield to maturity, which is based on the magnitude and timing of the promised cash flows, is larger than the debt cost of capital that is based on the expected cash flows. (Although we will discuss preferred stock later in the chapter, this issue also pertains to it; that is, the cost of capital for preferred stock is less than the promised dividend yield on preferred stock unless the default risk is zero.)

We use a simple example to illustrate these calculations. Assume a one-period debt agreement has two possible outcomes—default and no default and which has the following terms. One year after the execution of the contract, the company will pay the investor 9% annual interest—called the **coupon rate**—on the **face (or par) value** of the loan plus the $1,000 face (or par) value. The promised payments for this debt agreement, all to be made at the end of one year, are $90 of interest plus $1,000 of principal, or $1,090 ($1,090 = $1,000 × 0.09 + $1,000). These promised payments are the maximum payments the company would ever pay under the contract. If the investor's expected cash flows are equal to the maximum promised payments (in other words, there is no chance of default), then the 9% rate of interest (which is also the promised yield, assuming the bond is valued at $1,000) is the cost of capital for this security. However, if the expected cash flows are less than the promised cash flows, then the cost of capital must be less than the promised yield. In this example, we assume the price of the bond is equal to $973.09.

Yield to maturity. We can often observe prices and promised yields to maturity for publicly traded and sometimes even for privately held debt securities (for privately held debt this occurs at the date of issue or when traded in a secondary loan market). For all debt securities, we can also observe the timing and magnitude of the promised payments. We are not, however, able to directly observe the debt cost of capital. With the readily observable data, investors and the financial press calculate the promised yield to maturity or, more simply, the **yield to maturity (YTM)**. In the example, we observe a promised interest payment of $90, a promised principal payment of $1,000, and a price of $973.09. The investment's internal rate of return when based on the price of the bond and the promised cash flows is equal to 12%. This is the promised yield to maturity; it is not the debt cost of capital if the probability of default is non-zero and the expected recovery is less than 100%.

$$\$973.09 = \frac{\$1{,}000 \times 0.09 + \$1{,}000}{1 + \text{YTM}}$$

$$\text{YTM} = \frac{\$1{,}090}{\$973.09} - 1 = 0.12014$$

We cannot typically calculate the yield to maturity using this simple formula but must use the more general form of the internal rate of return formula:

$$0 = \frac{\text{PrInt}_1}{(1+\text{YTM}_0)} + \frac{\text{PrInt}_2}{(1+\text{YTM}_0)^2} + \frac{\text{PrInt}_3}{(1+\text{YTM}_0)^3} + \cdots + \frac{\text{PrInt}_T + \text{PrPrinc}_T}{(1+\text{YTM}_0)^T} - \text{Price}_0 \quad (9.1)$$

where PrInt_t and PrPrinc_t are, respectively, promised payments in period t for interest and principal, respectively and YTM_0 is the yield to maturity based on the price at time 0.

Cost of Debt r_D. Now assume investors assess a 4% probability of the company defaulting on the promised payments, and if the company defaults, the investor will be paid $0 interest and 60% of the principal ($600 = $1,000 × 0.6). We can measure the expected cash flows as follows. The expected interest payment is equal to $86.40 ($86.40 = $1,000 × 0.09 × 0.96), which is $3.60 (or 4%) less than the $90 promised interest payment. The expected principal payment is equal to $984.00 [$984.00 = $1,000 × 0.96 + $1,000 × 0.6 × (1 − 0.96)], which is $16.00 (or 1.6%) less than the $1,000 promised principal payment. The total expected cash flow (expected interest and principal) is $1,070.40.

Valuation Key 9.4

Expected cash flows from debt or preferred stock are equal to the probability weighted cash flows under different states of the world. These consist of the cash flows the investor expects to receive if the company defaults times the probability of default, plus the promised cash flows the investor will receive if the company does not default times the probability of no default.

	Promised	No-Default State	Default State	Expected	
Debt (coupon) interest rate	9.0%				
Face value	$1,000.00				
Probability		96.0%	4.0%		
Recovery rate—interest		100.0%	0.0%		
Recovery rate—principal		100.0%	60.0%		
Cash Payments:					
Interest	$ 90.00	$ 86.40	$ 0.00	$ 86.40	96.0%
Principal	1,000.00	$960.00	$24.00	984.00	98.4%
Total	$1,090.00			$1,070.40	98.2%

Exhibit may contain small rounding errors

The issue we face when valuing a company is that we neither directly observe the debt cost of capital nor do we observe the expected cash flows. However, we often observe or can measure the price of the debt issue. If we know the price, promised payments, probability of default, and expected recovery rates, the debt cost of capital, r_D, is equivalent to calculating an internal rate of return based on the expected payments and the price of the debt. Note that the debt cost of capital is less than the promised yield to maturity when the default probability is non-zero.

$$\$973.09 = \frac{\$86.40 + \$984.00}{1 + r_D}$$

$$r_D = \frac{\$86.40 + \$984.00}{\$973.09} - 1 = 0.1$$

Valuation Key 9.5

The debt cost of capital we use in valuation formulas—like the weighted average cost of capital and levering and unlevering formulas—is equal to the required or expected rate of return, which is based on the timing, magnitude, and riskiness of the expected cash flows. We can calculate the debt cost of capital using an internal rate of return formula if we know the price and expected cash flows. Expected cash flows are based on the promised payments, the probability of default, and the expected recovery rates in the event of default. Simply calculating the internal rate of return from the promised payments and the current price will not yield the debt cost of capital unless the default probability is zero.

Typically, we cannot use the simple formula above to measure the debt cost of capital, because most debt agreements have a longer term to maturity and other complicating characteristics; we can, however, use the more general form of the internal rate of return formula:

$$0 = \frac{E_0(CF_1)}{(1+r_D)} + \frac{E_0(CF_2)}{(1+r_D)^2} + \frac{E_0(CF_3)}{(1+r_D)^3} + \cdots + \frac{E_0(CF_T)}{(1+r_D)^T} - \text{Price}_0 \quad \textbf{(9.2)}$$

where $E_0(CF_t)$ is the expected cash flow for period t as of time 0, and Price_0 is the price of the bond at time 0. As we discuss in more detail in the next section, measuring the expected cash flows from the investment requires that we know the promised cash flows, which we can observe from the contract, but it also requires that we know the expected default and recovery rates. Note that the default and recovery rates from Exhibits 9.4, 9.6, 9.7, and 9.8 are averages over many years, and while these statistics may be good approximations for a normal state of the economy, they may not be good approximations for either a boom or bust economy. For example, in times of a recession, default probabilities may be higher and recovery rates may be lower than those portrayed in the exhibits (see Exhibits 9.5 and 9.9 for evidence of this variation).

Expected Default Loss. Since we measured the promised yield using promised payments rather than expected payments, the yield to maturity is higher than the debt cost of capital. We call the difference between the yield to maturity and the debt cost of capital the **expected default loss**, E(DL).

$$E(DL) = YTM - r_D \qquad (9.3)$$

$$0.02014 = 0.12014 - 0.10$$

The expected default loss is the amount of the promised yield to maturity that an investor does not expect to receive, for the investor knows that the expected cash flows are less than the promised cash flows. We can use one or more alternative methods to measure expected default losses and the cost of debt, depending on the data available. Once we measure both the promised yield and the expected default loss, we can measure the debt cost of capital with the following formula:

$$r_D = YTM - E(DL) \qquad (9.4)$$

$$0.10 = 0.12014 - 0.02014$$

Valuation Key 9.6

We measure the promised yield to maturity or yield to maturity (YTM) using promised interest and principal payments rather than expected interest and principal payments; thus, the promised yield to maturity is larger than the debt cost of capital. The difference between the promised yield to maturity and the debt cost of capital is called the expected default loss.

REVIEW EXERCISE 9.1

Debt Cost of Capital

Assume the company has a $1,000 debt agreement that will pay the investor at the end of one year the coupon interest rate of 12% plus the $1,000 face value of the debt. Assume the investor believes the company has a 3% probability of defaulting on the promised payments. If the company defaults, the investor will be paid no interest and 50% of the face value of the debt at the end of year 1.

a. Calculate the expected cash flows for the debt.

b. Assume the investor requires an expected annual rate of return of 14% for a debt security with this level of risk. Calculate the amount the investor would be willing to pay for this debt security.

c. Ignore part b, and instead assume the debt security is sold for $1,019.81. Calculate the debt cost of capital implied by this price. Why is the issue price greater than the face value of the debt?

d. Calculate the yield to maturity assuming the value of the debt is $1,019.81.

e. Calculate the expected default loss assuming the value of the debt is $1,019.81.

Solution on pages 428–429.

9.3 MEASURING THE DEBT AND PREFERRED STOCK COSTS OF CAPITAL

LO3 Measure the debt and preferred stock costs of capital

In this section, we discuss the process of measuring the cost of debt and preferred capital. To do that we collect information on the debt and preferred forms of financing the company will use. As part of the data collection process, we also collect information on the equity-linked derivative securities that the company will use such as convertible forms of debt and preferred, as well as options and warrants. We do not discuss estimation of the costs of capital for equity-linked derivative securities until Chapter 12, so for now we focus on estimating non-convertible debt and preferred stock costs of capital. Once we have information on the debt and preferred forms of financing, we estimate their yields as well as their costs of capital. Some of the methods we discuss to estimate the debt and preferred costs of capital assume that you have an assessment of the debt or preferred stock rating. In some cases, the debt and preferred stock is rated and thus obtaining that assessment is easy. In other cases, we must estimate the rating. In this section, we presume we know or have an estimate of the rating of the debt and preferred stock. In the next section, we discuss ways to estimate those ratings when they are not readily available.

An Overview of the Process for Measuring the Debt and Preferred Stock Costs of Capital

The process of measuring the cost of capital depends on both the type of security, the specific contractual terms of that security, and the measurement approach we use. In this section, we describe the process to measure the debt and preferred stock costs of capital. We show these steps in Exhibit 9.10. The first step in the process is to identify all the sources of debt, preferred stock, and other types of non-common-equity financing. These are the securities we expect the company to use to finance itself in the future, which may or may not be the same mix of securities it uses currently. As part of that process, we collect information on the equity-linked derivative securities, though we do not discuss estimating their cost of capital until Chapter 12.

A useful starting point for this process is to prepare a financing schedule that lists all of the debt securities a company uses currently and then adjust that list for the securities the company plans to use in the future. The debt financing schedule includes such information on each security as its description, book value, face value, coupon rate of interest, maturity, current promised yield to maturity, rating, market value, proportion of capital structure, and any other key features. The long-term debt and other footnotes in a company's 10-K are a good starting point for collecting information about a company's existing debt. The 10-K is also a valuable source of information about other forms of non-equity financing—such as preferred stock, warrants, and options.

EXHIBIT 9.10 Overview Summary of Steps to Measure the Non-Common-Equity Costs of Capital

1	For each company being valued and comparable companies, identify each source of non-common-equity financing used or expected to be used to finance the company (debt, preferred stock, warrants, convertible securities, etc.)
2	For convertible securities, partition the value of the convertible feature (if material)
3	Group similar securities that have similar contractual terms (for example, maturity, secured/unsecured, priority of claims, callability)
4	Collect or estimate the company's and specific securities' ratings, the yield to maturity (for debt) and dividend yield (for preferred stock)
5	For highly rated securities, for example, for AAA, AA, and A rated debt, use the yield to maturity as the cost of debt. For less highly rated debt and preferred securities, measure the cost of debt or preferred using one or more of the methods we discuss in this chapter
6	Measure the cost of capital for other non-common-equity securities that are equity-linked derivative securities such as options, warrants and debt and preferred with convertible features (discussed in Chapter 12)

Since securities with convertible features—such as convertible debt and convertible preferred stock—have features of multiple types of securities, in Step 2, we partition such securities into their non-equity and equity-linked components. For example, we partition a convertible debt issue into a non-convertible debt security and an equity-linked option security. In the third step, we group securities of the same type that have similar features. We use maturity, security, seniority, callability, and other features to group debt securities.

In the fourth step, we collect or measure the company's and specific securities' ratings, the yield to maturity (for debt) and dividend yield (for preferred stock). For highly rated securities, for example, for AAA, AA, and A rated debt, the fifth step is using the yield to maturity as the cost of debt. For less highly rated debt and preferred securities, the fifth step is measuring the cost of debt or preferred using one or more of the methods we discuss in this section of the chapter. Naturally, we might use one method for one group of securities and another method (or even multiple methods) for another group of securities. The last step in the process is to measure the costs of capital for equity-linked derivative securities (which we discuss in detail in Chapter 12).

Measuring the Yield to Maturity

We often want to estimate the promised yield to maturity on debt or the yield on preferred stock to estimate their costs of capital by adjusting the promised yield of either debt or preferred stock for the expected default loss. Using this approach, we measure both the promised yield and the expected default loss, and then we measure the cost of capital as the difference between the two. Later in this section, we discuss a variety of ways to measure the expected default loss. As we shall see, there are also methods we can use to measure the cost of debt or preferred without estimating the expected default loss. But first, we will outline ways to estimate the promised yields.

Publicly Traded Debt and Preferred Stock Securities. If the company has publicly traded debt or preferred stock, we can observe the promised yield directly or the price of the security from which we can then calculate the promised yield. In addition, publicly traded debt and preferred stock are often rated by credit rating agencies, so we can often observe the rating for the security as well. If a rating is not available, then we can estimate it by using a rating model or any of the other methods we discuss later in the chapter.

Debt and Preferred Stock That Are Not Publicly Traded. We can observe the promised yield and value of a security at the time the company issues the security and after issuance if the debt trades in the secondary loan market even if the company's securities are not publicly traded. Naturally, how useful the issuance price is depends on how recent it is, whether the company had or anticipates material changes in its financial leverage or operating risk, and whether the economy-wide interest rates have changed since the debt was issued. We can adjust for such changes using the various methods we discuss in this chapter, but the historical yields will not be particularly useful if the underlying factors that determine the cost of debt have changed. If only the risk-free interest rates changed and general economy-wide default premiums did not change, we can adjust the date of issuance information for the change in the risk-free rate as long as the company's risk did not change, that is, its financial leverage and operating risk did not change.

If the company did not issue all its securities recently, then we can measure the promised yields using another approach. One approach is the grouping approach that we discussed earlier in which we group similar securities. If one of the securities in a group is publicly traded or was issued recently, we would use the same cost of capital for the other securities in that group.

If none of the approaches just described is feasible, an alternative approach is to estimate the rating for the security using the methods described later in the chapter and to then measure the promised yields from the current promised yields for bonds of that rating, maturity, and so forth.

Expected Changes in Capital Structure or Operating Risk. We use the expected capital structure—not the current capital structure—when we value a company. Thus, we base the costs of capital on the company's expected capital structure and expected operating risk. When we expect a company's capital structure or operating risk to change, we estimate the company's rating and yield to maturity based on the expected capital structure and operating risk. In this situation, we use forecasts of the company's financial statements in addition to other information based on the new capital structure and potential change in operations in order to estimate its rating.

We can analyze the effect of such changes in two ways. We can establish how much debt (and preferred stock) the company must issue to fund its activities and forecast the financial statements based on that capital structure and estimate the rating. Alternatively, we can begin by specifying a minimally accepted rating, and based on this rating and the company's projected operating results, we can estimate how much debt and preferred stock the company can issue and still maintain that rating. In either approach, we use pro-forma financial statement forecasts to measure the relevant financial ratios and other information to estimate the credit rating. We illustrated this procedure in Chapter 4 when we added debt to the financial model we created for Starbucks.

When constructing the forecasts, we integrate the new capital structure into all of the components of the financial statements—balance sheet, income statement, statement of free cash flows, and other schedules—in order to understand all of the effects of the new capital structure. The income statement effects include a change in interest expense and the resulting change in income taxes; the balance sheet effects include a change in both long-term debt and, most likely, short-term debt. Total assets may or may not be affected by the new capital structure depending on whether the change in capital structure is tied to a change in investing activities. If the company is issuing new debt and/or preferred and all of the proceeds are being used to repurchase shares or pay a one-time dividend, then the assets of the company will not change.

If we expect a major change in operations, we would do the same thing that we would do for a change in capital structure; that is, we create pro-forma financial statements that reflect the changes in operations and then assess the likely rating based on our pro-forma forecasts. For example, if a company makes a major acquisition or is engaged in a major divestiture, we can create pro-forma financial statement forecasts to see the impact of these changes on the company's various financial ratios in comparison to the historical financials. We discuss how to use pro-forma financial statements to estimate credit ratings in Section 9.4.

Valuation Key 9.7

One way to measure the debt or preferred stock cost of capital is to measure the promised yield and adjust it for the expected default loss. We can often measure promised yields for publicly traded securities or debt traded in the secondary loan market directly. For securities that are not publicly traded, we can estimate a rating and use published yields for that rating to measure the promised yield for a company and then adjust it for the expected default loss. Knowing or estimating the rating allows us to also implement the CAPM-based approach for estimating the cost of debt.

Measuring the Cost of Debt Using the Internal Rate of Return Approach

The internal rate of return approach for measuring the cost of debt is based on the formula in Equation 9.2. The inputs into this formula are the expected cash flow at each date the debt contract requires the company to make a promised payment and the current price of the debt. If the debt is callable, the likelihood the debt will be called has to be taken into consideration in determining the expected cash flows. The debt cost of capital is equal to the rate of return (discount rate) that equates the current price to the present value of the expected cash flows. Measuring the expected cash flows for the debt requires that we know the promised cash flows, which we can observe from the contract, but it also requires that we estimate the default and recovery rates at each date the debt contract requires the company to make a promised payment. Measuring the expected cash flow for the previous one-period example is straightforward, but it is more complex for multi-period securities. This complexity arises from the fact that the company may default on the debt in any period.

Valuation in Practice 9.2

American Axle Manufacturing Holdings, Inc.'s Yield to Maturity and Minimum Expected Default Loss In 2008, the credit rating of American Axle & Manufacturing Holdings, Inc. (AXL)[9] declined to CCC+ with a negative outlook. A CCC+ credit rating indicates that the company has a high probability of defaulting on its obligations (see Exhibit 9.8). AXL had unsecured senior debt securities, "5.25% Notes," which matured in roughly five years. The 2008 outstanding principal was $250 million, and its fair value as disclosed in the company's 10-K report was $68.8 million. The difference between the principal and fair value represents a discount of 72.5%, and a yield to maturity of about 42% (see the calculation in the chapter). At this time, AXL's equity beta was around 2.0. Assuming a risk-free rate of 3% and a market risk premium at the high end of 7.5%, AXL's CAPM-based equity cost of capital was 18% ($0.18 = 0.03 + 2.0 \times 0.075$). Since a company's cost of debt must be less than its equity cost of capital, the expected default loss on AXL's debt was at least 24% ($0.24 = 0.42 - 0.18$).

At every promised payment date, we measure the expected cash flow based on both the company not defaulting in that period and on the company defaulting in that period. If the company does not default, the cash flow payments are equal to the interest payment in each period until the debt matures, and at maturity the cash flow is equal to the interest payment plus the principal payment. The expected cash flow is equal to the probability of not defaulting in any period through that date multiplied by the cash flow for that period. If the company defaults, the cash flow is equal to the amount of principal and interest expected to be recovered. The expected cash flow is equal to the probability that the company does not default in previous periods but defaults in the current period multiplied by the cash flow expected to be recovered for that period.

American Axle Manufacturing Holdings, Inc. (AXL). Recall from Valuation in Practice 9.2 that, in 2008, AXL's credit rating declined to CCC+, and the value of its $250 million 5.25% notes declined to $68.8 million resulting in a 42% yield to maturity for that debt security. We can measure the promised yield to maturity for this note using Equation 9.1. The annual promised interest payments were

[9] American Axle Manufacturing Holdings, Inc. was the principal supplier of driveline components to General Motors Corporation (GM) for its rear-wheel drive light trucks and SUVs manufactured in North America. See the company's 2008 Form 10-K filing for the relevant information.

\$13.125 million (13.125 = 0.0525 × 250), and the promised principal payment (to be paid in roughly five years) was \$250 million. Given this, the yield to maturity for this note was

$$0=\frac{\$13.125}{(1+\mathrm{YTM}_0)}+\frac{\$13.125}{(1+\mathrm{YTM}_0)^2}+\frac{\$13.125}{(1+\mathrm{YTM}_0)^3}+\frac{\$13.125}{(1+\mathrm{YTM}_0)^4}+\frac{\$13.125+\$250}{(1+\mathrm{YTM}_0)^5}-\$68.8$$

$$\mathrm{YTM}_0=42.2\%$$

Clearly, investors in AXL's debt were uncertain that they would receive these promised payments. Therefore, AXL's debt cost of debt capital for this note was not 42.2%, for the yield to maturity did not consider the expected cash flows given expected recovery rates and the likelihood of default. We use Equation 9.2 to measure the cost of debt for this note. The inputs into that formula are the price of the note, the probability of default, and recovery rate for each year. To illustrate this calculation, we assume a constant recovery rate of 25% for each year for the interest and principal. This recovery rate is lower than the recovery rate shown in Exhibit 9.6 because 2008 was the year in which the financial crisis and recession began (see Exhibit 9.5). We assume that the conditional probabilities of default (that is, conditional on not defaulting until that point in time) equal 56%, 48%, 40%, 32%, and 24% for 2009 through 2013, respectively. Given the promised payments, the probabilities of default, and the recovery rates at each point in time, we can calculate the expected cash flows (versus promised cash flows) for each year. Once we calculate the expected cash flows, we can calculate the cost of debt using Equation 9.2.

In this illustration, each year has two possible outcomes—default and no default. If the company defaults, the company pays the investor the expected recovery rate multiplied by the sum of the principal and interest for that year; if the company does not default, the company pays the investor the promised interest payment, but if it is the final year, the company pays the promised principal in addition to the interest payment. To calculate the expected cash flow in a year, we multiply each outcome by its respective probability in that year.

$$E_0(CF_t) = prob_{\text{no default},\,t} \times (PrInt_t + PrPrinc_t) + prob_{\text{default},\,t} \times recov_t \times (PrInt_t + PrPrinc_t) \quad \textbf{(9.5)}$$

Here, $prob_{default,t}$ and $prob_{no\ default,t}$ are the probabilities that the company will and will not default in period t, respectively; $recov_t$ is the expected recovery rate (percentage collected) in period t for interest and principal if the company defaults in period t; finally, $PrInt_t$, and $PrPrinc_t$ are as we defined earlier.

For example, in 2009, the company had a default probability of 56%, and the recovery rate was equal to 25%; thus, the expected cash flow was equal to

$$\$42.61 = 0.56 \times 0.25 \times (\$13.125 + \$250) + (1 - 0.56) \times \$13.125$$

Note that the expected cash flow of \$42.61 million is larger than the promised payment of \$13.1 million. To explain, the promised payment is the promised interest payment. However, the expected cash flow considers the expected cash flows in both the no-default (promised interest payment only) and default (recovered interest and principal payments) states—the latter of which can have a cash flow that is larger than the promised interest payment if the probability of default is as large as it is for AXL and the recovery rate is sufficiently high. Of course, after the amount is recovered subsequent to default, there are no further payments.

We continue to use this same approach for 2010 through 2013, but also adjust the expected cash flows in these years for the probability that the company will not default prior to that point in time. The company has a probability of not defaulting in 2009 of 44% (0.44 = 1 − 0.56). In 2010, the company has a 48% probability of defaulting. Hence, the probability of the company not defaulting in 2009 and defaulting in 2010 is 21.1% [0.211 = 0.48 × (1 − 0.56)]. The probability of the company not defaulting in both 2009 and 2010 is 22.9% [0.229 = (1 − 0.56) × (1 − 0.48)]. Thus, for 2010, the expected cash flow is equal to

$$\$16.90 = 0.211 \times 0.25 \times (\$13.125 + \$250.0) + 0.229 \times \$13.125$$

$$\$16.90 = \$13.89 + \$3.01$$

We show a calculation of the expected cash flows for all years in Exhibit 9.11.

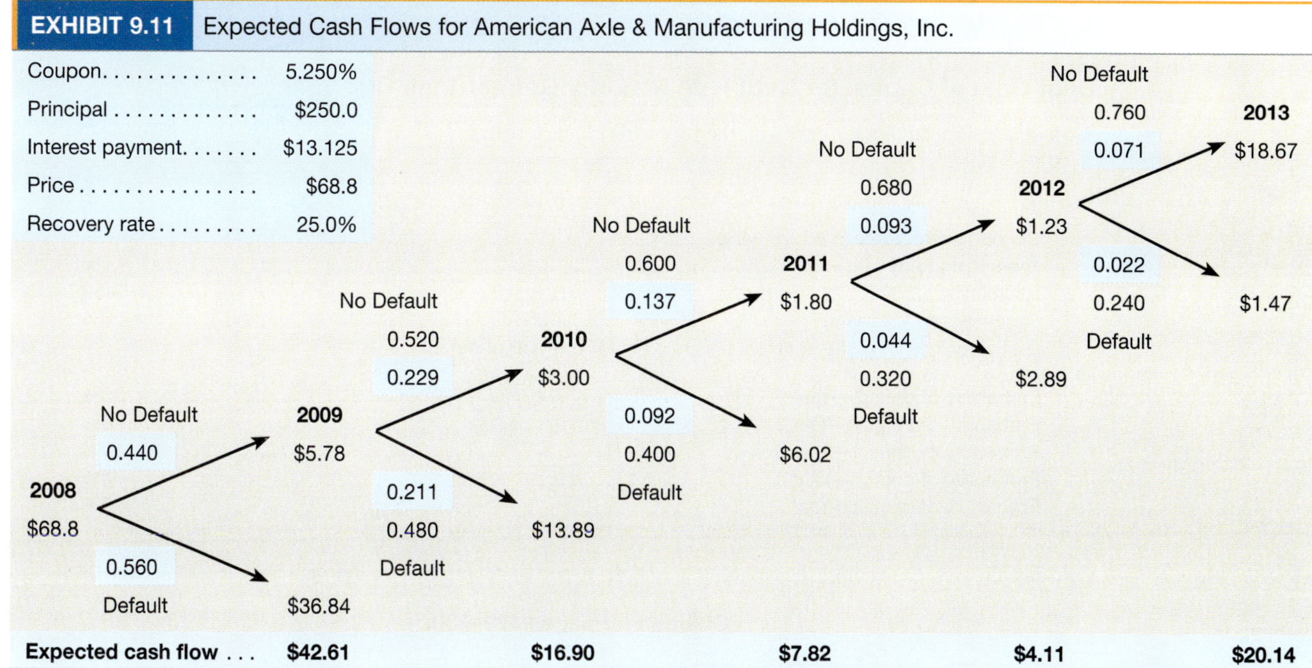

Exhibit may contain small rounding errors

Given the expected cash flows, we can use Equation 9.2 to calculate AXL's cost of debt.

$$0 = \frac{\$42.61}{(1+r_D)^1} + \frac{\$16.90}{(1+r_D)^2} + \frac{\$7.82}{(1+r_D)^3} + \frac{\$4.11}{(1+r_D)^4} + \frac{\$20.14}{(1+r_D)^5} - \$68.8$$

$$r_D = 13.8\%$$

The expected default loss is 28.4% (0.284 = 0.422 − 0.138), which is 72.4% of the spread between AXL's yield to maturity (42.2%) and the U.S. government bond rate at the time of 3% [0.724 = 0.284 ÷ (0.422 − 0.03)]. We can measure expected recovery rates and year-by-year default probabilities with the information published by credit rating agencies adjusted potentially for any company-specific and economy-specific information. We note, however, while the recovery and default rates in these exhibits may be useful to use in a normal state of the economy for the average company, they may not be as useful for either a boom or recession economy or if the company is different from the average company. For example, in times of a recession, default probabilities may be higher and recovery rates may be lower than those portrayed in the exhibits (see Exhibits 9.5 and 9.9). We can use models to estimate the default probability (sometimes called financial distress or financial failure or bankruptcy probabilities) and we discuss two such models later in the chapter. A summary of the yield to maturity and cost of debt calculations for American Axle is as follows.

	Yield to Maturity		Cost of Debt
2008	−$ 68.80		−$68.80
2009	$ 13.125		$42.61
2010	$ 13.125		$16.90
2011	$ 13.125		$ 7.82
2012	$ 13.125		$ 4.11
2013	$263.125		$20.14
Internal rate of return	42.2%		13.8%
Risk-free YTM, $r_{F,YTM}$	3.0%	Default loss	28.4%
Spread = YTM − $r_{F,YTM}$	39.2%	% of spread	72.4%

REVIEW EXERCISE 9.2

Debt Cost of Capital for Debt with Maturity Greater than One Year

Assume the company issues debt with the following characteristics:

Face value of debt	$600
Coupon interest rate (paid annually)	8%
Years to maturity	5
Issue price	$460
Recovery rate (all years)	50%
(Recovery rate is for the principal plus interest for the year of default)	
Probability of default—Year 1	30%
Probability of default—Year 2	20%
Probability of default—Year 3	15%
Probability of default—Year 4	5%
Probability of default—Year 5	5%

Calculate the yield to maturity, the cost of debt, and the expected default loss for this debt issue as of the issue date.

Solution on pages 429–430.

Measuring the Preferred Stock Cost of Capital Using the Adjusted Promised Yield Approach

We use essentially the same conceptual framework to measure the cost of capital for preferred stock as we use to measure the debt cost of capital. The primary differences between debt and preferred stock securities are that debt typically has required interest payments and a defined term to maturity, whereas preferred stock often has no mandatory dividend payments and no maturity. Dividend payments must be paid before common shareholders receive distributions if the dividends are cumulative, but not paying preferred dividends only results in an arrearage (dividends in arrears), not a default. For non-cumulative preferred, not paying preferred dividends generally just means that you cannot pay common dividends for some time period (see Valuation in Practice 9.1). Not paying interest results in a default on the debt issue, consequently resulting in a renegotiation of the debt or the company filing for bankruptcy. Thus, for preferred stock, we may have to use the perpetuity formulas instead of Equations 9.1 and 9.2.

Valuation Key 9.8

The conceptual framework we use to measure the cost of capital for preferred stock is essentially the same as the one we use to measure the debt cost of capital.

Measuring the Cost of Debt Using the Expected Default Loss Approach

Although expected default losses are not widely available, in this section we illustrate how to measure the cost of debt using expected default losses, based on the **yield spread**. A yield spread is equal to the difference between the yield on a corporate debt security and the yield on a U.S. government bond (risk-free bond) of the same maturity. The yield spread represents the sum of the systematic risk premium for that debt security and the expected default loss. We can use the percentage of the yield spread that is equal to the expected default loss (EDL%) to measure the systematic risk premium (SRP) for that debt security [SRP = (1 − EDL%) × yield spread]. We can measure the cost of debt by adding the yield on the risk-free bond to the systematic risk premium.

To begin, we review bond yield spreads in order to learn about their properties. In Exhibit 9.12, we show the average annual bond yield spreads over U.S. Treasury Bonds for various bond ratings from January 1997 through June 2016. This chart shows that bond yield spreads change over time and that higher-rated bonds have smaller spreads than lower-rated bonds. The yield spreads for the various bond ratings generally change in the same direction. The chart also shows the unusually large increase in spreads during the financial crisis beginning in September 2008.

EXHIBIT 9.12 Average Promised Yield Spread over U.S. Treasury Bonds, January 1997 through June 2016*

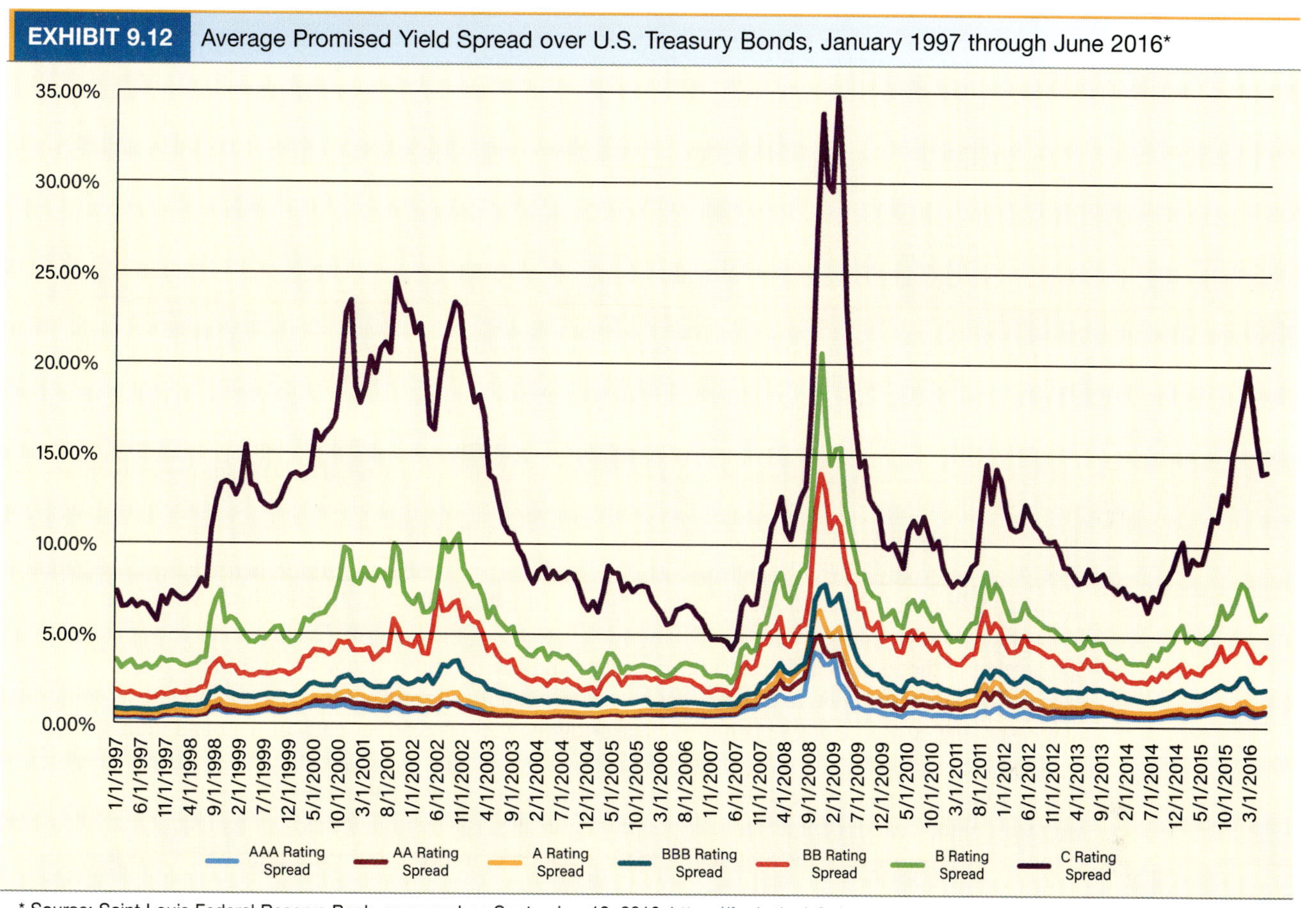

* Source: Saint Louis Federal Reserve Bank, accessed on September 12, 2016, https://fred.stlouisfed.org.

In a study conducted by Elton et al. (2001),[10] the authors analyzed the difference between the yield to maturity on corporate bonds and U.S. government bonds of the same maturity using three factors—expected default losses, state income taxes, and systematic risk factors. The authors used a sample of over 90,000 monthly bond prices from the Lehman Brothers Fixed Income Database with the sample period ending in 1998. Unfortunately, this empirical evidence on expected default losses does not provide information on bonds rated below BBB (but we know expected default losses increase in the lower rating categories) and the study has not been updated; however, this is the best empirical evidence we have at this point in time on expected default losses by rating category.

The authors calculated the proportion of the yield spread attributable to the expected default loss for AA, A, and BBB rated bonds for a maturity between 2 and 10 years. The calculation of the expected default losses was based on both default probabilities and recovery rates—similar to the calculations we presented earlier in the chapter for American Axle. For each combination of credit rating and maturity, the authors calculated the expected default loss and the yield spread. In Exhibit 9.13, we show the percentage of the yield spread that is attributable to the expected default loss for every rating/maturity combination the authors estimate. The exhibit shows that the expected default loss as a percentage of the yield spread increases as the

[10] Elton, Edwin J., M. Gruber, D. Agrawal, and C. Mann, "Explaining the Rate Spread on Corporate Bonds," *The Journal of Finance* vol. LVI, no. 1 (February 2001), pp. 247–277.

credit rating decreases and as the maturity increases. Since spreads increase with longer maturities and with more poorly rated debt, expected default losses increase with longer maturities and lower ratings.

EXHIBIT 9.13 Expected Default Losses as a Percentage of the Spread of Industrial Bonds over U.S. Government Bonds (Elton et al. [2001])

Maturity	AA	A	BBB
2	1.0%	8.5%	12.4%
3	1.9%	9.3%	15.0%
4	2.6%	10.3%	17.9%
5	3.4%	11.4%	20.9%
6	4.4%	12.6%	23.9%
7	5.1%	13.9%	26.7%
8	5.9%	15.1%	29.5%
9	7.0%	16.4%	32.1%
10	8.0%	17.8%	34.7%

The empirical evidence on expected default losses from this study indicates that they are not large for highly rated debt; thus, the promised yield and the cost of debt will be quite close. The expected default loss for AA bonds will be very small when these percentages (8% or less) are multiplied by the AA yield spreads (AA yield spreads average around 1%—see Exhibit 9.12). Thus the expected default losses for AA bonds are generally 8 basis points or less. For A-rated debt (BBB-rated debt) maturing in 10 years, the expected default loss is 18% (35%) of the spread. The expected default losses for A bonds and BBB bonds based on average spreads of 1.4% and 2.1% would be 25 and 73 basis points respectively. Thus, the difference between promised yields and the cost of debt is generally not large for highly rated debt. Of course, during the financial crisis, the yield spreads increased (see Exhibit 9.12) indicating the expected default losses likely increased. As the rating declines further and as the maturity lengthens, the percentage of the spread that is the expected default loss increases and the promised yield becomes an even more biased estimate of the cost of debt. In Exhibit 9.14, we present an illustration of how to use expected default losses to measure the cost of debt. We begin by measuring the yield spread for each of the bond ratings. We then multiply the yield spread by the expected default loss percentage to measure the expected default loss. The risk premium is equal to the difference between the yield spread and the expected default loss. Finally, we measure the cost of debt as the risk premium plus the risk-free rate (yield). Alternatively, you can just compute the cost of debt by subtracting the expected default loss from the promised yield to maturity.

EXHIBIT 9.14 Illustration of Measuring the Cost of Debt Using Expected Default Loss Percentages for Bonds with a 10-Year Maturity

	Research Reported Percentages		
June 2015	AA	A	BBB
Yield to maturity (YTM)	2.14%	2.53%	3.44%
Risk-free rate (yield)	1.49%	1.49%	1.49%
Yield spread	0.65%	1.04%	1.95%
Expected default loss %	7.96%	17.83%	34.66%
Expected default loss	0.05%	0.19%	0.68%
Cost of debt, r_D	2.09%	2.34%	2.76%
r_D as % of YTM	97.6%	92.5%	80.2%

American Axle & Manufacturing Holdings, Inc. (AXL) Revisited. Recall that the expected default loss we computed previously for AXL was 72.4% of the spread between AXL's yield to maturity and the U.S. government bond rate. This percentage exceeds the largest expected default loss percentage in Exhibit 9.13 for a five-year maturity, which is 20.9% for the BBB debt. The percentages in this exhibit, however, are calculated for debt rated BBB or higher; thus, these percentages are unlikely to be useful for the AXL example given its CCC+ rating. Since we know that the ratio of the expected default loss to the spread increases as the credit rating decreases, we would expect that AXL's expected default loss as a proportion of its spread (in relation to U.S. government bonds) would be much larger than those reported in this exhibit. Unfortunately, at this writing, this study has not been updated for more recent time periods, nor has anyone computed similar statistics for lower rated debt. This limits the usefulness of this approach especially given the relatively modest expected default losses for investment grade bonds. However, we do not have any empirical evidence to calibrate it precisely. We will now turn to other ways to estimate the cost of debt.

Using the Capital Asset Pricing Model to Measure the Cost of Debt

An alternative way to measure the debt and preferred stock costs of capital is to use an asset pricing model like the CAPM, the three-factor model, or an empirical variation of these models—such as the model in Fama and French (1993).[11] The specific process used to implement one of these asset pricing models varies depending on the specific model. We know that even highly rated debt is somewhat risky and includes both default and liquidity risk, because its promised yield is larger than the yield on a risk-free security, but the risk premium for highly rated debt is quite small.

In Exhibit 9.15, we show the beta (measured against the S&P 500 index) for various bond rating categories based on the Bank of America Merrill Lynch US Corporate Master Index[12] and measured over the previous 60 months for each date shown. The first observation from this exhibit is that betas consistently increase as the bond ratings decrease. The second observation is that bond rating betas change over time.

Recall that a beta of 1.0 indicates a risk that is equal to the average risk in the overall market (and recall that the market index used in this exhibit is the S&P 500 index, not an index of bonds). In Exhibit 9.16, we report the estimated betas using the prior 60 months as of June, 2016. The betas of the AAA, AA, and A ratings are all generally small and near zero, especially when considered in conjunction with a market risk premium of 6 percent; however, the betas for the non-investment grade ratings are much higher. The betas that predate the financial crisis in 2008 are all lower than the betas of the same rating during and for some time after the financial crisis. Prior to the financial crisis in 2008, the betas of investment grade bonds were all around 0. During the financial crisis, the betas of investment grade bonds increased to between 0.05 (AAA rated debt) and 0.25 (A and BBB rated debt). Since the financial crisis, the betas of investment grade bonds decreased—the betas of AAA, AA, and A rated bonds are again around 0 and the betas of BBB rated bonds are around 0.1. Prior to the financial crisis in 2008, non-investment grade bonds had higher betas, which increased even more during the financial crisis. Since the financial crisis, the betas of non-investment grade bonds decreased to a range of 0.35 (BB rated debt) to 0.7 (C rated debt).

An adaptation of the CAPM to estimate the cost of debt assumes that debt with a rating of AA or higher has a zero expected default loss; in other words, the promised yield to maturity for such debt is equal to its cost of capital. This assumption is consistent with the betas for AA rated debt in Exhibit 9.15, which are close to zero. To use this method, we first measure the difference between the betas of A, BBB, BB, B, and C rated debt and the beta of the AA rated debt, called the incremental beta. We multiply the incremental beta by the market risk premium to measure the risk premium above debt with an AA rating. We add the yield to maturity for AA rated debt at the time we are estimating the cost of debt to the estimated risk premium for a rating class to measure the cost of debt. The justification underpinning this approach is that the CAPM measures systematic risk and therefore the measured cost of capital does not include the effect of unsystematic risk (which should not be included in the cost of debt). Of course, an alternative to this approach is to use the CAPM directly (Chapter 8) in conjunction with the risk-free yield and market risk premium once you know the beta of a bond or bond rating. However, recall from Chapter 8, yields on government bonds are affected by their preferential tax status, suggesting they are priced to return a lower, pre-state-tax rate of return. That said, the difference between using this approach or using the CAPM directly is generally small.

---

[11] For example, for debt securities, see Fama, E., and French, K., "Common Risk Factors in the Returns on Stocks and Bonds," *Journal of Financial Economics* 33 (1993), pp. 3–56.

[12] See Bank of America Merrill Lynch US Corporate Master Index tracking the performance of US dollar denominated investment grade rated corporate debt publicly issued in the US domestic market. Each rating subset includes all securities with a given investment grade rating. Available from the St. Louis Federal Reserve Bank, accessed on September 12, 2016, https://fred.stlouisfed.org.

EXHIBIT 9.15 Bond Betas by Bond Rating (60 Month Rolling Betas)

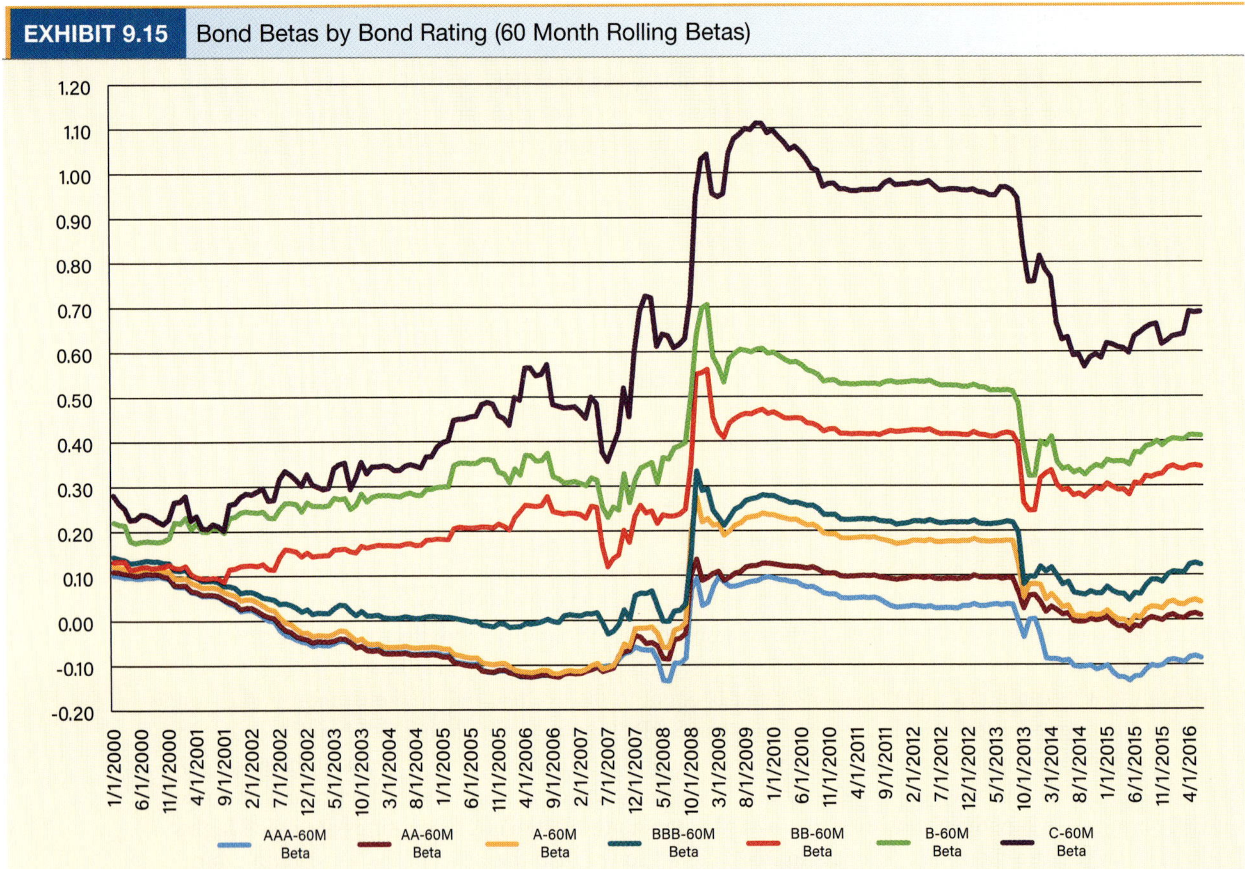

* Source: Bank of America Merrill Lynch US Corporate Master Index available from the Saint Louis Federal Reserve Bank, accessed on September 12, 2016, https://fred.stlouisfed.org.

In Exhibit 9.16, we illustrate how to use incremental CAPM betas to measure the cost of debt. The first three rows of this exhibit show the estimated beta and its respective t-statistic and p-value (testing for whether the estimated beta is statistically different from zero) for the various bond ratings. (We estimated the bond betas using 60 months of bond returns ending in June 2016.) First, the only investment grade bond with a statistically significant beta is the BBB rated bond. Thus, the betas of the AAA, AA, and A rated bonds are not significantly greater than 0. The betas for the other bond betas are positive and statistically significant and range from 0.12 (BBB rating) to 0.69 (C rating).

EXHIBIT 9.16 Illustration of Measuring the Cost of Debt Using Incremental Debt Betas (June, 2016)

	AAA	AA	A	BBB	BB	B	C
Bond beta	−0.088	0.008	0.037	0.120	0.342	0.410	0.685
T-statistic	−1.931	0.202	0.867	2.514	8.141	8.827	7.933
Probability	5.8%	84.1%	38.9%	1.5%	0.0%	0.0%	0.0%
Incremental beta relative to beta for AA rating			0.029	0.112	0.334	0.402	0.677
Assumed market risk premium			6.0%	6.0%	6.0%	6.0%	6.0%
Incremental cost of capital			0.18%	0.67%	2.00%	2.41%	4.06%
Yield to maturity for AA rated debt			2.14%	2.14%	2.14%	2.14%	2.14%
Cost of debt, r_D			2.32%	2.81%	4.14%	4.55%	6.20%
Yield to maturity			2.53%	3.44%	5.15%	7.43%	15.10%
Cost of debt, r_D			2.32%	2.81%	4.14%	4.55%	6.20%
Expected default loss			0.21%	0.63%	1.01%	2.88%	8.90%

Exhibit may contain small rounding errors

In the next row we measure the incremental betas of each of the bond ratings below the AA rating relative to the beta for the AA rating. Then, we multiply the incremental beta by the appropriate market risk premium (see Chapter 8) to measure the risk premium for that bond rating relative to the AA rated debt. Here we use a market risk premium of 6 percent. Remember, since the betas are measured against the S&P 500 index, we must use an estimate of the market risk premium for the S&P 500, even though we are pricing bonds. To measure the cost of debt, we add the yield to maturity for the AA bonds (assumed equal to the cost of debt of the AA rated bonds) to the risk premium. In the last three rows we measure the expected default loss based on this approach. As in the previous section, the expected default losses increase with decreases in the bond rating and are roughly consistent with the expected default loss magnitudes reported in Exhibit 9.14.

Valuation Key 9.9

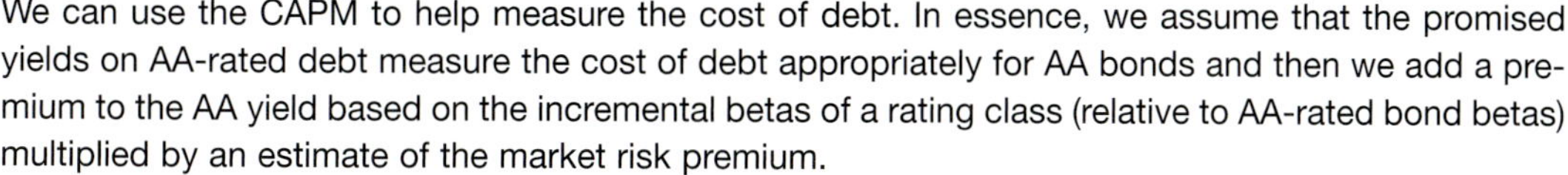

We can use the CAPM to help measure the cost of debt. In essence, we assume that the promised yields on AA-rated debt measure the cost of debt appropriately for AA bonds and then we add a premium to the AA yield based on the incremental betas of a rating class (relative to AA-rated bond betas) multiplied by an estimate of the market risk premium.

American Axle & Manufacturing Holdings, Inc. (AXL) Revisited. We can use this adaptation of the CAPM for AXL. At the end of 2008, the yield to maturity of AA rated debt was around 7.2%, which we assume to be equal to its cost of debt for AA bonds. From Exhibit 9.15, we can estimate the incremental beta for C rated bonds was around 1.0 in 2008. Assuming a market risk premium of 6%, the risk premium for C rated bonds at this time was 6% ($0.06 = 1 \times 0.06$). Based on this analysis, the cost of debt for C rated bonds at this time was 13.2% ($0.132 = 0.06 + 0.072$), which is similar to the cost of debt based on the internal rate of return approach.[13]

REVIEW EXERCISE 9.3

Debt Cost of Capital Estimated Using the CAPM

The LLJ Company had debt on its books as of June, 2016, with a credit rating of B. The yield to maturity of AA-rated debt at that time was 2.14%, which we assume is equal to its cost of debt. Use the data in Exhibit 9.16 to estimate the debt cost of capital for the LLJ Company *at the end of June, 2016*. For purposes of this review exercise, assume the market risk premium is 6.5% at the end of June, 2016.

Solution on page 430.

Using Credit Default Swaps to Measure Default Risk and Recovery Rates

A **credit default swap** (**CDS**) is a contract in which the issuer provides the purchaser of the credit default swap protection against the risk of default on one or more debt obligations issued by a country or company, called a **reference entity**; thus, a CDS is essentially an insurance policy that protects the purchaser against the loss of principal resulting from the default by the issuer. If certain pre-specified default events occur, the premium payments stop and the issuer of the CDS pays the buyer the par value for the bond and the CDS issuer receives the bond. If no default event occurs during the term of the contract, the purchaser of the protection continues to pay the premium for the term of the contract. The insurance premium paid by the purchaser is a periodic premium over the life of the contract, which is often called the CDS spread, and is quoted in basis points per annum of the contract's notional (or par) value. These contracts were first issued in the late 1990s for sovereign debt but expanded to corporate bonds, mortgage-backed securities, and local government debt.

The CDS spread is, in part, a measure of the premium required by investors to bear a firm's default risk. Default risk has two components, the probability of default and the expected recovery rate. To the extent CDS spreads measure the default risk premium, we can potentially use them to help measure a company's debt cost of capital. In Exhibit 9.17, we present average CDS spreads for different credit ratings, maturities, and durations. These results show that CDS spreads increase with lower credit ratings, longer maturities, and longer durations.

---

[13] The AXL example occurred at the end of 2008 during the global financial crisis, so we used the incremental beta as of the end of 2008 to measure AXL's cost of debt at the time.

EXHIBIT 9.17 Credit Default Spreads for Different Bond Ratings, Maturities, and Durations for January 2001 to December 2008*

Credit Rating	CDS Spread	Std Dev of Spread	Maturity	CDS Spread	Std Dev of Spread	Duration	CDS Spread	Std Dev of Spread
AAA	0.16	0.17	Short	0.31	0.79	Short	0.35	0.82
AA	0.32	0.51	2	0.51	0.84	2	0.55	0.86
A	0.45	0.74	3	0.62	0.79	3	0.79	0.92
BBB	0.86	0.94	4	0.79	0.83	4	0.81	0.81
			Long	0.83	0.79	Long	0.75	0.52

* This exhibit is taken from Li, Haitao, Weina Zhang, and Gi Hyun Kim, "The CDS-Bond Basis and the Cross Section of Corporate Bond Returns," *NUS RMI Quarterly Newsletter*, Issue 7, May 2011 Working Paper, December 2011, Stephen M. Ross School of Business, University of Michigan, Ann Arbor, MI 48109.

Callen, Livnat, and Segal (2007) document that CDS spreads are related to credit ratings but they vary substantially within a given rating.[14] Hull, Predescu, and White (2004) examine the relationship between bond yields and CDS spreads, and whether changes in CDS spreads anticipate credit rating announcements.[15] The authors document that the CDS spreads anticipate negative credit events such as a downgrade, negative watch, or negative outlook, but they do not find evidence that they anticipate positive rating events.

More specific to our adjustment of a company's promised yield, Das and Hanouna (2009) developed a model to estimate a forward-looking probability of default and expected recovery rate using a company's stock price and its volatility in conjunction with the company's CDS spread.[16] The authors developed a methodology to estimate the present value of premiums paid on the CDS for a given maturity given no default and the losses if the reference entity defaults based on an estimated recovery rate and the probability of default. Their results indicate that recovery rates are inversely related to expected default rates, as we observed in Exhibits 9.5, 9.6, 9.8, and 9.9. Such models are an alternative to using historical default and recovery rates to estimate expected cash flows and are potentially useful since they are forward looking and presumably would measure appropriate default and recovery rates irrespective of the state of the economy. Once we know the expected cash flows and the price of a bond, we can measure the cost of debt.

Valuation in Practice 9.3

Alcoa Inc.'s Downgrade to a BBB− Credit Rating In February 2009, the credit rating of Alcoa Inc.[17] was downgraded. In its 10-K filing, the company discussed the downgrade as follows:

> Alcoa's cost of borrowing and ability to access the capital markets are affected not only by market conditions but also by the short- and long-term debt ratings assigned to Alcoa's debt by the major credit rating agencies. . . .
>
> In February 2009, Standard & Poor's Ratings Services (S&P) and Fitch Ratings (Fitch) each lowered Alcoa's long-term debt rating to BBB−; . . . and both indicated that the current outlook is negative. Also in February 2009, Moody's Investors Service lowered Alcoa's long-term debt rating to Baa3 . . .
>
> Although the company has available to it committed revolving credit facilities to provide liquidity, these recent downgrades in Alcoa's credit ratings, as well as any additional downgrades, will increase Alcoa's cost of borrowing and could have a further adverse effect on its access to the capital markets, . . . An inability to access the capital markets could have a material adverse effect on Alcoa's financial condition, results of operations or cash flow.

[14] Callen, J. L., J. Livnat, and D. Segal, "The Impact of Earnings on the Pricing of Credit Default Swaps," *The Accounting Review* vol. 84, no. 5 (2009), pp. 1363–1394.

[15] Hull, J. C., M. Predescu, and A. White, "The Relationship Between Credit Default Swap Spreads, Bond Yields, and Credit Rating Announcements," *Journal of Banking & Finance* vol. 28, no. 11 (November 2004), pp. 2789–2811.

[16] Das, Sanjiv, and Paul Hanouna, "Implied Recovery," *Journal of Economic Dynamics and Control* vol. 33, no. 11 (2009), pp. 1837–1857.

[17] Alcoa Inc. produces primary aluminum, fabricated aluminum, and alumina. See the company's 2008 10-K filing at page 21 and other pages for a discussion of its credit rating downgrade.

CDS spreads are driven in part by both idiosyncratic and systematic expected default losses. Since CDS spreads include the systematic component of expected default losses, the adjustment to the yield to maturity is not as simple as subtracting the observed CDS spread for the bond. Moreover, CDS spreads are not driven solely by default losses. For example, there is some counterparty risk (the risk that the seller of the protection cannot cover the buyer's losses), and that is priced in the CDS spread as well. Thus, we cannot merely adjust the yield to maturity by the entire CDS spread to estimate the cost of debt, as we have to isolate the component of the CDS spread that is not related to counterparty risk or systematic risk. Given the factors reflected in the CDS spread, we know that the adjustment for the expected default loss should be no larger than the CDS spread if credit default swaps are priced accurately and if the length of the contract matches the maturity of the debt.

Measuring the Cost of Debt—Summary

We discussed multiple ways to estimate the cost of debt when the default risk is non-zero and the recovery rate is less than 100%. The first approach was to estimate expected cash flows using information about default probabilities and recovery rates. Then, given the price of the bond and the expected cash flows, we estimate the internal rate of return of the bond, which provides an estimate of the cost of the debt. The second approach discussed was to use the historical evidence on the percentage of the yield spread between like-maturity U.S. government bonds and corporate debt that is attributable to the expected default loss for bonds of a particular rating and maturity. Once we estimate the expected default loss, we subtract it from the corporate debt's promised yield to estimate the cost of debt. The third approach was to estimate betas of debt of various rating categories, compute the incremental beta for that rating category relative to AA bonds, and then use the yield on the AA bonds and add it to the incremental beta multiplied by an estimate of the relevant market risk premium. We also discussed potentially using information from CDS spreads to calculate expected cash flows from a debt instrument to calculate the cost of debt in conjunction with the price of the bond or to adjust the yield to maturity for expected default losses. Unfortunately, neither of these techniques using CDS spreads is particularly straightforward.

While, all else equal, default losses increase as the credit rating decreases, it is common for practitioners to use the yield to maturity as the cost of debt for all investment grade (BBB− or better) rated debt. For bonds below investment grade, some practitioners use the BBB yield and others add a small premium to the BBB yield which they hold constant regardless of the below investment grade rating. Yet other practitioners use the yield to maturity as the cost of debt for below investment grade debt and suggest that a justification for this approach is that including the expected default loss in the cost of debt is a way to adjust a valuation for financial distress costs (see Chapter 5). While we occasionally see this approach in practice, it has no theoretical or empirical justification and we do not suggest using that approach. As we discuss in Chapter 11, to the extent necessary and practical to do so, we adjust the cash flow forecasts for the effects of financial distress.

9.4 CREDIT RATING MODELS

LO4 Use credit rating models to estimate a company's credit rating

Using a company's credit rating in combination with its current promised yields to maturity provides useful information for measuring the company's debt cost of capital. Not all companies have a current credit rating or have promised yields to maturity that are observable. In such cases, we can use estimation methods to measure the company's likely credit rating. For example, we know from our discussion of financial ratios in Chapter 2 that those ratios provide information about a company's financial performance, financial condition, and risk. We also know that credit rating agencies use financial ratios, various other metrics, and qualitative information to assign credit ratings. In this section, we illustrate how we use financial ratios and a statistical model to assess a company's credit rating. These estimated credit ratings can, in turn, be used to estimate the cost of debt.

Credit rating models combine various financial ratios and other factors into a metric to classify a company into a credit rating category. The ultimate goal of a credit rating model is to develop a model that mimics the assessments of the rating agencies. Since such models only attempt to reproduce the ratings of rating agencies, the model can only be as good as the work of the rating agencies. Before we illustrate how to develop and use such a model, we examine the relation between credit ratings and certain financial ratios, and we illustrate how to estimate a credit rating with a set of financial ratios.

Valuation in Practice 9.4

Advanced Micro Devices, Inc. Downgrade to a CCC+ (Caa1) Credit Rating[18] In its 2015 SEC 10-K report, Advanced Micro Devices discussed its recent credit rating downgrade:

> We regularly assess markets for external financing opportunities, including debt and equity financing. Additional debt or equity financing may not be available when needed or, if available, may not be available on satisfactory terms. The health of the credit markets may adversely impact our ability to obtain financing when needed. Any downgrades from credit rating agencies such as Moody's or Standard & Poor's may adversely impact our ability to obtain external financing or the terms of such financing. In July 2015, Moody's lowered our corporate credit rating to Caa1 from B3 and our senior unsecured debt rating to Caa2 from Caa1. Furthermore, in October 2015, Standard & Poor's lowered our corporate credit rating to CCC+ from B− and our senior unsecured debt rating to CCC from B−.
>
> Credit agency downgrades or concerns regarding our credit worthiness may impact relationships with our suppliers, who may limit our credit lines. Our inability to obtain needed financing or to generate sufficient cash from operations may require us to abandon projects or curtail planned investments in research and development or other strategic initiatives. If we curtail planned investments in research and development or abandon projects, our products may fail to remain competitive and our business would be materially adversely affected.

Estimating Credit Ratings Using Financial Ratios

In Exhibit 9.18, we present the median financial ratios in 2015 for different credit ratings published by S&P and the financial ratios available in CapitalIQ (we do not examine the gradients for ratings between AA and CCC due to limited sample sizes). The financial ratios generally vary monotonically across the rating classes. Financial ratios that measure profitability or coverage generally decrease as the ratings decrease, and financial leverage ratios generally increase as the ratings decrease. We note that the rating agencies make many adjustments to the financial statements, for example, capitalizing operating leases, before assigning a rating. The financial ratios that we use in the exhibit are taken directly from the company's financial statements.

EXHIBIT 9.18 Median Financial Ratios by Credit Rating

2015 Medians	AAA	AA	A	BBB	BB	B	CCC
Return on assets	8.8%	7.5%	8.2%	7.1%	4.9%	3.4%	−3.2%
Return on capital	12.8%	11.1%	13.1%	9.8%	6.6%	4.5%	−4.4%
EBITDA to average total assets	16.4%	15.1%	15.5%	14.0%	11.2%	9.3%	1.7%
EBITDA margin	33.1%	25.9%	17.9%	17.7%	14.1%	11.8%	0.9%
EBIT margin	27.3%	20.8%	14.5%	13.6%	9.2%	5.7%	−1.2%
Debt to capital	0.294	0.372	0.401	0.423	0.553	0.659	0.757
EBITDA to interest	35.0	32.2	20.3	12.9	6.2	3.3	1.4
EBIT to interest	28.9	27.0	16.5	9.8	4.5	1.7	0.9
Number of bonds	2	13	52	154	161	85	6

One way to estimate a company's credit rating is to compare the median financial ratios of specific ratings published by rating agencies to the ratios of a particular company. In Exhibit 9.19, we show the financial ratios for 2015 for Advanced Micro Devices (AMD, see Valuation in Practice 9.4). We conduct the analysis for 2013–2015 to illustrate how the financial ratios and ratings changed over time for Advanced Micro Devices.

[18] Advanced Micro Devices, Inc. a global semiconductor company that produces and sells microprocessors, motherboard chipsets, embedded processors, and graphics processors for servers, workstations, and personal computers. See the company's 2015 10-K filing at page 281 and other pages for a discussion of its credit rating downgrade.

EXHIBIT 9.19 Financial Ratios for Advanced Micro Devices Compared to Credit Rating-Based Financial Ratios, 2015

	Advanced Micro Devices					
	2013		2014		2015	
Financial Ratio/Metric	**Ratio**	**Rating**	**Ratio**	**Rating**	**Ratio**	**Rating**
Return on assets	0.4%	B–CCC	−5.4%	< CCC	−14.2%	< CCC
Return on capital	0.9%	B–CCC	−12.4%	< CCC	−30.6%	< CCC
EBITDA to average total assets. . .	9.6%	BB–B	9.3%	B	−6.0%	< CCC
EBITDA margin.	7.9%	B−CCC	6.4%	B - CCC	−4.6%	< CCC
EBIT margin	3.4%	B−CCC	2.7%	B - CCC	−8.8%	< CCC
Debt to capital	0.79	< CCC	0.92	< CCC	1.22	< CCC
EBITDA to interest	2.36	B–CCC	1.99	B−CCC	−1.16	< CCC
EBIT to interest.	1.02	B–CCC	0.84	< CCC	−2.20	< CCC
Actual rating		B−		B−		CCC+

We compare each of the ratios for AMD to the distribution of the respective ratio across credit ratings in Exhibit 9.19, and we show what rating corresponds to the ratios of the company. The exhibit shows that the 2013 ratios are mostly between the B and CCC credit rating ratios except for the EBITDA to Average Total Assets ratio, which is between the BB and B credit rating ratios, and the debt to capital ratio which is below CCC. This is generally consistent with the company's B− credit rating at that time. The company's financial ratios deteriorated in 2014. As a result, many, but not all, of its ratios indicate a CCC credit rating or below for the company, though it still retained its B− rating from S&P. The 2015 ratios show further deterioration in the company's financial condition; its rates of returns are lower, interest coverage ratios are lower, and its leverage ratio is higher. As a result, the company's 2015 ratios are all below the median ratios for a CCC rating, and, as noted in Valuation in Practice 9.4, the company's credit ratings declined from B− to CCC+ that year.

Sometimes, classifying a company's credit rating in this way can be difficult because different ratios often indicate a different rating, and we have no way to systematically combine the ratios into one rating. In the next section, we illustrate how to use a statistical model to address this issue.

REVIEW EXERCISE 9.4

Using Financial Ratios to Estimate a Credit Rating

Estimate the Snap Company's credit rating at the end of Year 0 using the company's financial statements given below, and the distribution of key financial ratios for different credit ratings given in Exhibit 9.18.

SNAP COMPANY Balance Sheets and Income Statement ($ in thousands)	Year −1	Year 0
Income Statement		
Revenue		$26,243
Operating expenses		−9,447
Depreciation expense.		−1,939
Earnings before interest and taxes.		$14,857
Interest expense.		−1,028
Income before taxes.		$13,829
Income tax expense		−5,532
Net income		$ 8,297

SNAP COMPANY Unlevered Free Cash Flow Statement ($ in thousands)	Year 0
Unlevered operating cash flow	$9,796
− Change in required cash balance	−119
− Capital expenditures	−926
Unlevered free cash flow.	$8,751

continued

continued from previous page

Balance Sheet		
Total current assets	$ 4,974	$ 6,460
Property, plant, and equipment (net)	31,275	30,262
Total assets	$36,249	$36,722
Account payable	$ 1,037	$ 1,347
Debt	12,845	13,487
Total liabilities	$13,882	$14,834
Capital stock	$12,000	$12,000
Retained earnings	10,367	9,888
Shareholders' equity	$22,367	$21,888
Liabilities and shareholders' equity	$36,249	$36,722

Solution on pages 430–431.

The HZ Credit Rating Model

Credit rating models have been studied for more than 50 years. For example, Horrigan (1966), Pinches, and Mingo (1973), and Kaplan and Urwitz (1979) are early examples that document such models can correctly classify credit ratings.[19] All of these and many subsequent models use a company's financial ratios and other metrics to predict (or classify) its credit rating. More recent models have attempted to use artificial intelligence and neural net estimation methods to better predict the ratings assigned by credit rating agencies. Various commercial versions of bond rating models exist. Some of these models use financial ratios and other metrics and some of the models are based on option-theoretic approaches and some use prices from credit default swaps.

In this section, we develop a financial-ratio-based credit rating model to illustrate how such a model is developed and used. We use a sample of 1,148 companies for which S&P had a current senior unsecured credit rating for the company and for which we could compute the necessary financial ratios. We show the distribution of company credit ratings for the sample and how we aggregate these into a smaller number of broader rating categories in Exhibit 9.20.

Because of the small number of observations in certain categories, we aggregated the 21 different credit ratings into six broader rating groups in order to have a reasonable number of observations in each group.[20] We use five independent (or explanatory) variables used in other credit rating models. The five variables are a performance measure (EBIT to the Average of Total Debt plus Shareholders' Equity), the inverse of interest coverage (Interest to EBITDA), the inverse of debt coverage (Average Total Debt to Cash Flow from Operations minus Capital Expenditures), financial leverage (Total Debt to Total Debt plus Shareholders' Equity), and capital expenditures coverage (Capital Expenditures to EBITDA). We present the parameter estimates and summary statistics for the model in Exhibit 9.21.

[19] Horrigan, J. O. "The Determination of Long-Term Credit Standing with Financial Ratios," *Empirical Research in Accounting: Selected Studies, Supplement to V.4. Journal of Accounting Research* (1966); Kaplan, R. S., and G. Urwitz, "Statistical Models of Bond Ratings: A Methodological Inquiry," *Journal of Business* 52 (1979), pp. 231–261; and Pinches, G. E., and K. A. Mingo, "A Multivariate Analysis of Industrial Bond Ratings," *Journal of Finance* 28 (1973), pp. 1–18.

[20] The 21 credit ratings are D, CC, CCC−, CCC, CCC+, B−, B, B+, BB−, BB, BB+, BBB−, BBB, BBB+, A−, A, A+, AA−, AA, AA+, and AAA.

EXHIBIT 9.20 Distribution of Company Credit Ratings for the HZ Credit Rating Model Sample

	Original Sample			Aggregated HZ Sample	
S & P Rating	**Number**	**%**		**Number**	**%**
AAA	6	0.5%			
AA+	3	0.3%			
AA	15	1.3%			
AA–	10	0.9%	AA– to AAA	34	3.0%
A+	23	2.0%			
A	45	3.9%			
A–	49	4.3%	A– to A+	117	10.2%
BBB+	90	7.8%			
BBB	111	9.7%			
BBB–	87	7.6%	BBB– to BBB+	288	25.1%
BB+	63	5.5%			
BB	99	8.6%			
BB–	161	14.0%	BB– to BB+	323	28.1%
B+	159	13.9%			
B	132	11.5%			
B–	58	5.1%	B– to B+	349	30.4%
CCC+	22	1.9%			
CCC	8	0.7%			
CCC–	1	0.1%			
CC	3	0.3%			
D	3	0.3%	CCC+ & Below	37	3.2%
Total	1,148	100.0%		1,148	100.0%

EXHIBIT 9.21 The HZ Credit Rating Model

Variable (Logit Model Estimation)	Coefficients*	Standard Error	Chi-Square Statistic	Probability
Intercept for CCC+ & below	–5.632	0.301	350.616	0.000
Intercept for B– to B+	–1.669	0.237	280.591	0.000
Intercept for BB– to BB+	–0.072	0.251	489.255	0.000
Intercept for BBB– to BBB+	1.663	0.270	727.915	0.000
Intercept for A– to A+	3.447	0.317	820.815	0.000
EBIT to average total debt + Shareholders' equity	–5.387	0.540	99.546	0.000
Interest to EBITDA	2.441	0.300	66.262	0.000
Average total debt to CFO – Capital expenditures	–0.002	0.001	1.505	0.220
Total debt to total debt + Shareholders' equity	2.092	0.202	107.058	0.000
Capital expenditures to EBITDA	–0.182	0.091	3.982	0.046

CFO = Cash flow from operations

EBITDA = Earnings before interest, taxes, depreciation, and amortization

*The reported intercept coefficients represent the coefficients for a rating class. The difference between the intercept coefficients for a rating class and those of the lowest rating class provides the incremental intercept coefficient for that rating class, which is the relevant coefficient for the standard error, chi-square, and probability statistics.

The overall model is statistically significant, and all but one of the coefficients for the independent variables are statistically significant (the column labeled probability indicates the statistical significance of each variable). The one explanatory variable that is not statistically significant in this sample (but is used in other credit rating models) is Total Debt to Cash Flow from Operations minus Capital Expenditures, which has a coefficient that is essentially zero.

A positive coefficient in this model indicates that, holding everything else constant, the larger the value of the variable, the lower the debt rating; a negative coefficient indicates that, holding everything else constant, the larger the value of the variable, the higher the debt rating. As such, the positive coefficient for the inverse of the coverage ratio (Interest to EBITDA) indicates that as interest rises relative to EBITDA, the company is likely to have a lower rating. Further, the negative coefficient for company performance (EBIT to average Total Debt + Shareholders' Equity) indicates that a higher-performing company is more likely to have a higher credit rating, as expected. Similarly, if a company has a lot of investment opportunities and is plowing a larger proportion of its EBITDA into capital expenditures, it is likely to have a higher credit rating. The positive coefficient on the leverage ratio (Total Debt to Total Debt + Shareholders' Equity) indicates that as leverage goes up, the company is likely to have a lower rating. The remaining variable (Total Debt to CFO − Capital Expenditures) is insignificant given its near-zero coefficient.

Note that the results of the logistic model include five intercepts—one intercept for each category with the exception of the AA− to AAA category. These intercepts are important when we use the model to classify a company's credit rating, but for now the key observation is that all of the intercept coefficients are reliably different from zero, indicating that the estimated model can distinguish companies' credit ratings across groups. The statistical test for the intercept is actually a test of whether or not the difference between adjacent intercepts is statistically significant. We present the predictive (classification) ability of our model in Exhibit 9.22.

EXHIBIT 9.22 Classifications from the HZ Credit Rating Model on the 1,148 Sample Observations

	Sample Classifications						
Actual	**CCC+ & Below**	**B− to B+**	**BB− to BB+**	**BBB− to BBB+**	**A− to A+**	**AA− to AAA**	**Total % Correct**
CCC+ & below	19%	78%		3%			
B− to B+	2%	63%	26%	8%	0%	1%	
BB− to BB+	0%	28%	41%	28%	3%	1%	
BBB− to BBB+		11%	36%	51%	2%		
A− to A+		5%	15%	73%	6%	2%	
AA− to AAA		9%	6%	74%	12%		
Total % correct							45%

Exhibit may contain small rounding errors

The model predicts about 45% of the credit ratings correctly and the vast majority of the predictions (over 90%) are within one rating class of the actual rating. The model correctly classifies 19% of the CCC+ & below group, 63% of the B− to B+ group, 41% of the BB− to BB+ group, 51% of the BBB− to BBB+ group, only 6% of the A− to A+ group, and 0% of the AA− to AAA group.

In Exhibit 9.23, we show the calculation of the credit rating score for Advanced Micro Devices for 2013–2015. As discussed earlier, its credit rating in 2013 and 2014 was B−; in the following year, its financial condition deteriorated so far that its credit rating was downgraded to CCC+. The credit rating model calculates a probability for each of the credit rating groups. The credit rating group with the highest probability is the predicted credit rating for the company. We measure the probability by first calculating the credit rating score for each of the credit ratings using its associated intercept. We calculate a credit rating score by adding the intercept for that rating to the product of each of the model's financial ratios for the company and the respective coefficient for each financial ratio. The resulting credit rating score is a number that can theoretically vary between +/− infinity. Given the logistic regression estimation method we use, we convert the credit rating score, which we label HZ, into a probability using the following formula, where $\exp^{-HZ}$ is the exponential function of –HZ.

$$\text{Cumulative Probability} = \frac{1}{1+\exp^{-HZ}}$$

This probability is the cumulative probability that the credit rating is lower than or equal to the credit rating for that group. The probability for a credit rating group is equal to the difference between its cumulative probability and the cumulative probability of the adjacent lower credit rating group. Doing this, we calculate probabilities for five of the six credit ratings. The probability for the remaining credit rating is equal to 1 minus the sum of the other five probabilities.

EXHIBIT 9.23 The HZ Credit Rating Model Applied to Advanced Micro Devices in 2013–2015*

		Advanced Micro Devices					
2013 Financial Data—Actual Rating B−:	**Coefficients**	**CCC+ & Below**	**B− to B+**	**BB− to BB+**	**BBB− to BBB+**	**A− to A+**	**AA− to AAA**
Intercept for CCC+ & below	−5.632	−5.632					
Intercept for B− to B+	−1.669		−1.669				
Intercept for BB− to BB+	−0.072			−0.072			
Intercept for BBB− to BBB+	1.663				1.663		
Intercept for A− to A+	3.447					3.447	
EBIT to average total debt + Shareholders' equity	−5.387	0.070	0.070	0.070	0.070	0.070	
Interest to EBITDA	2.441	0.424	0.424	0.424	0.424	0.424	
Average total debt to CFO − Capital expenditures	−0.002	−8.871	−8.871	−8.871	−8.871	−8.871	
Total debt to total debt + Shareholders' equity	2.092	0.791	0.791	0.791	0.791	0.791	
Capital expenditures to EBITDA	−0.182	0.201	0.201	0.201	0.201	0.201	
HZ credit rating score		−3.338	0.625	2.222	3.957	5.741	
Cumulative probability		0.0343	0.6514	0.9022	0.9812	0.9968	1.0000
Probability of credit rating		**3.43%**	**61.71%**	**25.08%**	**7.90%**	**1.56%**	**0.32%**
2014 Financial Data—Actual Rating B−:							
Intercept for CCC+ & below	−5.632	−5.632					
Intercept for B− to B+	−1.669		−1.669				
Intercept for BB− to BB+	−0.072			−0.072			
Intercept for BBB− to BBB+	1.663				1.663		
Intercept for A− to A+	3.447					3.447	
EBIT to average total debt + Shareholders' equity	−5.387	0.062	0.062	0.062	0.062	0.062	
Interest to EBITDA	2.441	0.503	0.503	0.503	0.503	0.503	
Average total debt to CFO − Capital expenditures	−0.002	−11.461	−11.461	−11.461	−11.461	−11.461	
Total debt to total debt + Shareholders' equity	2.092	0.922	0.922	0.922	0.922	0.922	
Capital expenditures to EBITDA	−0.182	0.270	0.270	0.270	0.270	0.270	
HZ credit rating score		−2.841	1.123	2.719	4.455	6.238	
Cumulative probability		0.0552	0.7545	0.9382	0.9885	0.9981	1.0000
Probability of credit rating		**5.52%**	**69.93%**	**18.37%**	**5.03%**	**0.95%**	**0.19%**
2015 Financial Data—Actual Rating CCC+:							
Intercept for CCC+ & below	−5.632	−5.632					
Intercept for B− to B+	−1.669		−1.669				
Intercept for BB− to BB+	−0.072			−0.072			
Intercept for BBB− to BBB+	1.663				1.663		
Intercept for A− to A+	3.447					3.447	
EBIT to average total debt + Shareholders' equity	−5.387	−0.190	−0.190	−0.190	−0.190	−0.190	
Interest to EBITDA	2.441	1.000	1.000	1.000	1.000	1.000	
Average total debt to CFO − Capital expenditures	−0.002	−7.025	−7.025	−7.025	−7.025	−7.025	
Total debt to total debt + Shareholders' equity	2.092	1.223	1.223	1.223	1.223	1.223	
Capital expenditures to EBITDA	−0.182	−0.519	−0.519	−0.519	−0.519	−0.519	
HZ credit rating score		0.498	4.461	6.058	7.793	9.577	
Cumulative probability		0.6219	0.9886	0.9977	0.9996	0.9999	1.0000
Probability of credit rating		**62.19%**	**36.67%**	**0.91%**	**0.19%**	**0.03%**	**0.01%**

Exhibit may contain small rounding errors

* Note: The financial ratios are listed in the table, and the HZ credit rating score is the sum of each ratio multiplied by the applicable coefficient and the appropriate intercept.

We calculate the probabilities for Advance Micro Devices in 2013, as follows. The CCC+ group has a credit rating score of −3.338, and the corresponding probability is 0.0343. For the B− to B+ group with a credit rating score of 0.625, the corresponding cumulative probability is 0.6514 which we interpret as the company having a 65.14% probability that its credit rating is no higher than B− to B+. The probability for the B− to B+ group is the difference between the two cumulative probabilities, or 61.71% (0. 6171 = 0.6514 − 0.0343). The cumulative probability for the BB− to BB+ group is 0.9022, and its probability is 25.08% (0.2508 = 0.9022 − 0.6514). The probability of the last group, AA− to AAA, is equal to 1 minus the cumulative probability of the previous rating class, A; this difference is equal to 0.32% (0.0032 = 1 − 0.9968).

For the 2013 ratios, the credit rating with the highest probability is the B− to B+ group, which is Advanced Micro Devices' actual credit rating at that time. The next most likely rating is the BB− to BB+ rating—with a probability of 25.08%. As we had discussed earlier, the financial condition of the company deteriorated in the following two years (as evidenced in the 2014 and 2015 panels in the exhibit). For 2015, the effect of this deterioration in financial condition on the credit rating model was an increase in the probability of the lowest rating group from 3.43% in 2013 and 5.52% in 2014 to 62.19% in 2015, resulting in the CCC rating group having the highest probability. As noted in Valuation in Practice 9.4, Advanced Micro Devices' credit rating was downgraded in 2015 from B− to CCC+.

Note that given the sample used, senior unsecured debt ratings, one would have to adjust the rating for debt issues that are secured or collateralized or for debt issues that are junior or junior subordinated. It is not unusual for a company with many different kinds of debt instruments outstanding to have different ratings on its debt as a function of security, seniority, and maturity.

All such classification or prediction models of this kind must make an assumption about the relative cost of misclassifying a company. In our illustration, we assumed that the misclassification cost was constant for each credit rating group, and we chose the credit rating group with the highest probability. If we assume the misclassification costs are not equal, we would adjust the model for the relative misclassification costs.

REVIEW EXERCISE 9.5

Using the HZ Credit Rating Model to Estimate a Credit Rating

Apply the HZ Credit Rating Model to the Snap Company given in Review Exercise 9.4. What is the probability that Snap's credit rating falls within each of the six credit rating categories used in the HZ model in Year 0?

Solution on page 431.

Valuation Key 9.10

We can use credit rating models to estimate the credit rating of a company that does not have a current credit rating or for one that is planning to change its capital structure or operations. We then use the estimated credit rating as an input in the process of measuring the promised yield and debt cost of capital.

Preferred Stock Rating Models

We observe fewer companies with preferred stock, and information such as that in Exhibit 9.18 is not as readily available; the same is true of preferred stock rating models like the credit rating model we just illustrated. One approach we can use to estimate a preferred stock rating is to adjust the company's credit rating. Since preferred stock generally has a lower priority of claims relative to debt, deferral of dividend payments, and other characteristics specific to preferred stock, we lower the credit rating to estimate the company's preferred stock rating.

A reduction of one rating (one notch, not an entire rating) is typically the minimum reduction for preferred stock. Factors considered include the deferral of dividends (which are optional as opposed to those required by either covenants of other securities or regulators), cumulative versus non-cumulative dividends, subordination, payment risk, specific default and distress risk, and potential government support. For example, in 2005, MetLife Inc. issued $2.1 billion of non-cumulative perpetual preferred.

This security was rated BBB, which was three notches below the company's A credit rating. One reason provided for this reduction was that the preferred security had both optional and mandatory dividend deferrals.[21]

Yield Prediction Models

The alternative to using a credit rating model is to use a yield prediction model. In a yield prediction model, we create a model that explains cross-sectional variation in yield spreads with a procedure similar to that of a bond rating model. In other words, we use variables such as leverage, size, profitability, interest coverage, and specific bond terms to estimate yields. The potential advantage of a yield prediction model is that it is a more direct approach if the ultimate goal is to predict a promised yield to maturity.

9.5 BANKRUPTCY PREDICTION AND FINANCIAL DISTRESS MODELS

LO5 Use financial distress (bankruptcy) models to estimate a company's default probability

Recall from earlier in the chapter that assessing a company's probability of bankruptcy or financial distress may be useful for assessing a company's risk of default. We discuss two types of financial distress, financial failure, or bankruptcy prediction models. One type is based on financial ratios and the second type is based on option pricing models. The financial ratio-based models combine various financial ratios and other factors into a financial distress metric that can be used to predict the likelihood of companies entering bankruptcy or a state of financial distress within a specified period. The financial ratios are typically measures of company performance and financial leverage. The option-pricing-based models predict the probability that the value of a company's assets in the future will fall below the amount of debt the company has outstanding using option pricing models. We illustrate both of these types of models in this section.

The HZ Financial-Ratio-Based Bankruptcy Prediction Model

Financial-ratio-based bankruptcy prediction models have as long a history as debt rating models. Edward Altman conducted one of the first studies of this sort in 1968.[22] He developed his model using a sample of 33 bankrupt and 33 non-bankrupt manufacturing companies. He used the following five financial ratios in his model: working capital/total assets; retained earnings/total assets; earnings before interest and taxes/total assets; market value of equity/book value of total debt; and sales/total assets. Altman's model correctly classified 94% of the bankrupt companies and 97% of the non-bankrupt companies, one year prior to a company filing for bankruptcy. Altman tested his model on another (hold-out) sample of 25 bankrupt and 66 non-bankrupt companies and was able to correctly classify 94% of the bankrupt companies and 79% of the non-bankrupt companies in this sample, again one year prior to a company filing for bankruptcy.

Depending on where in the business cycle the economy is, 0.1% to 4% of publicly traded companies file for bankruptcy in a typical year. Between 1986 and 2008, approximately an average of 1.2% of U.S. publicly traded companies filed for bankruptcy each year, with a high of 4.0% and a low of 0.27% in any one year. Thus, Altman's hold-out sample of 25 (27.5%) bankrupt companies and 66 non-bankrupt companies (72.5%) is not representative of the actual population and overstates the ability of the model to make correct predictions.[23] Regardless, Altman's study began a long series of research projects developing financial distress models, and numerous authors (including Altman) have refined Altman's original approach. These refinements include extending the model to other industries and privately held companies, using a sample that is more representative of the population of companies (to

---

[21] For additional information on this issue, see "Criteria: Assigning Ratings to Hybrid Capital Issues," *Standard & Poor's Viewpoint*, Standard & Poor's, May 8, 2006.

[22] See Altman, E. I "Financial Ratios, Discriminant Analysis and Prediction of Corporate Bankruptcy," *Journal of Finance* (September 1968), pp. 589–610.

[23] See Zmijewski, M. E. "Methodological Issues Related to the Estimation of Financial Distress Prediction Models," *Journal of Accounting Research* 22 (Supplement 1984), pp. 59–82.

avoid problems that may arise if some underlying characteristic of the sampled companies differs from that of the population), addressing the problems that arise if the proportion of companies in the sample (bankrupt v. non-bankrupt) is not representative of the population, carefully collecting the historical data to represent a predictive context, and making various adjustments to the financial ratios and other metrics in the model.

In this section we illustrate the use of a financial ratio-based bankruptcy prediction model, which we call the HZ Bankruptcy Prediction Model. We use a sample of 2,719 companies composed of 354 (13%) bankrupt companies and 2,365 (87%) non-bankrupt companies, somewhat over-sampling the bankrupt group. We use five financial ratios in the model, which we show in Exhibit 9.24. The dependent variable is equal to one for bankrupt companies and zero for non-bankrupt companies; thus, a positive (negative) coefficient for a financial ratio indicates that the larger the financial ratio, the higher (lower) the probability of bankruptcy. We use a logistic regression model as we did for the debt rating model, but we now have a dependent variable with only two outcomes (bankrupt/not bankrupt) versus the six debt rating categories in the debt rating model. The financial statements for the bankrupt companies are the annual financial statements made available up to 12 months prior to when the company files for bankruptcy. Thus, the model is predicting the probability of bankruptcy within 12 months of the financial statement date.

EXHIBIT 9.24 The HZ Bankruptcy Prediction Model

Bankrupt sample	354	13.0%
Non-bankrupt sample	2,365	87.0%
Total sample	2,719	100.0%

Variable	Coefficients	Standard Error	Chi-Square Statistic	Probability
Intercept	–3.099	0.302	105.350	0.000
Net income to average total assets	–0.756	0.227	11.080	0.001
Current assets to current liabilities	–0.176	0.063	7.733	0.005
UCFO to average total liabilities	–1.192	0.388	9.425	0.002
EBITDA to interest (10 if no debt)	–0.029	0.007	17.343	0.000
Total liabilities to total assets	2.326	0.330	49.746	0.000
Pseudo R-squared	26.7%			

UCFO = Unlevered cash flow from operations
EBITDA = Earnings before interest, taxes, depreciation and amortization

The overall model is statistically significant, and the coefficient for each of the independent (or explanatory) variables is statistically significant as well (see the probability column). All of the coefficients in this model are negative except for one. The coefficients are consistent with our discussion of how to interpret financial ratios in Chapter 2. The performance measure (net income to average total assets), liquidity measure (current assets to current liabilities), debt coverage (unlevered cash flow from operations to average total liabilities), and interest coverage (EBITDA to interest) all have negative coefficients. The negative coefficient indicates that a company with a higher financial ratio (higher performance, liquidity, cash flow to debt, and coverage) has a lower probability of bankruptcy. The positive coefficient for the ratio of total liabilities to total assets (financial leverage) is also consistent with our previous discussion—companies with higher financial leverage have a higher probability of bankruptcy.

Altman's model had a high correct prediction rate for the sample used in that study; however, the sample in that study greatly overrepresented the bankruptcy group and the methodology did not control for that oversampling. Increasing the relative size of the non-bankruptcy group will result in lower overall prediction rates. While our sample is more representative, we also have a sample that somewhat overrepresents bankrupt companies (13% versus the lower than 2% in the population). We present the predictive (classification) ability of our model in Exhibit 9.25. We show that the model predicts about 80% of both the bankrupt and non-bankrupt companies over the next 12 months.[24]

EXHIBIT 9.25 Classifications from the HZ Bankruptcy Prediction Model on the 2,719 Sample Observations

	Sample Classifications		
Actual	**Non-Bankrupt**	**Bankrupt**	**Overall**
Non-bankrupt	80%	20%	
Bankrupt	17%	83%	
Overall			81%

Using a cutoff value of −0.99 for the financial distress metric maximizes the number of correct predictions for this sample.

In Exhibit 9.26, we provide the classifications from the model for various cutoffs based on the model's bankruptcy score. We partition the companies into five groups based on the financial distress metric—lowest probability of bankruptcy to highest probability of bankruptcy. The percentage of bankrupt companies increases in each group from 0% bankrupt for the group with the lowest probability of bankruptcy to 1%, to 4%, to 17%, and finally to 43% for the group with the highest probability of bankruptcy.

EXHIBIT 9.26 Probability of Bankruptcy Groupings Using the HZ Bankruptcy Prediction Model on the 2,719 Sample Observations

	Sample Classifications		
Probability	**% Non-Bankrupt**	**% Bankrupt**	**Cutoff Value**
Lowest	100%	0%	−3.63
Lowest +	99%	1%	−2.24
Medium	96%	4%	−1.46
Medium +	83%	17%	−1.05
Highest	57%	43%	> −1.05

Similar to the debt rating model, in Exhibit 9.27, we show the calculation of the bankruptcy prediction score for Advanced Micro Devices for 2013–2015. We measure the bankruptcy prediction score for a company by adding the intercept to the product of each of the model's financial ratios for the company and its respective coefficient. We convert the bankruptcy prediction rating score, which we again label HZ, into a probability using the formula below, where $\exp^{-HZ}$ is the exponential function of −HZ.

$$\text{Probability of Bankruptcy} = \frac{1}{1+\exp^{-HZ}}$$

According to the model, as of 2013, Advanced Micro Devices had a 20% probability of filing for bankruptcy within the next 12 months. In the following year, its financial condition deteriorated, and its probability of filing for bankruptcy within a year increased to 23.7%. As we observed when applying the credit rating model to Advanced Micro Devices, the company deteriorated even further in 2015; and its credit rating declined from B− to CCC+ and its probability of filing for bankruptcy within one year increased to 38.1%.

These probabilities for Advanced Micro Devices are higher than the default rates we presented in Exhibit 9.8. The cumulative default rates for the B− (B3) rating do not increase to 23% until four years

[24] When making these predictions, we assume that our goal is to maximize the number of correct predictions; in other words, we assume that the cost of incorrectly predicting each group is equal. It may be more likely that the cost of incorrectly predicting a bankrupt company is more than the cost of incorrectly predicting a non-bankrupt company. For example, consider the extreme example of a financial institution not making a one-year loan to a company because it thought the company was going to go bankrupt. Assume that the financial institution does not have another customer to lend this money to and that it loses the interest on the loan (and only the interest) relative to investing the money in government securities. Also, assume that if the financial institution makes the loan and that the company does go bankrupt, the financial institution will lose both the interest and principal of the loan. We can quickly see that the relative cost of incorrectly predicting no bankruptcy when a company goes bankrupt—principal plus interest—is substantially larger (probably by more than 20 times) than the cost of not making a loan when the company does not go bankrupt but we predicted it would—the spread between the interest rate on the loan and the government rate of return.

after the company was rated; and cumulative default rates for the CCC+ (Caa1) rating do not increase to even 36% until eight years after the company was rated. Potential explanations for these differences include the following two reasons. First, it is possible that Advanced Micro Devices was a below average company within its rating categories which is consistent with the analysis summarized in Exhibit 9.19 that compared the ratios of Advanced Micro Devices to the median ratios for different debt ratings. Consistent with that, in 2016 there was a lot of speculation regarding the potential for AMD to go bankrupt. Second, estimating the model on a sample in which bankrupt firms are over sampled can result in overstated bankruptcy probabilities.

EXHIBIT 9.27 The HZ Bankruptcy Prediction Model Applied to Advanced Micro Devices, 2013–2015

		Advanced Micro Devices—Data		
Variable	**Coefficients**	**2013**	**2014**	**2015**
Intercept	−3.099			
Net income to average total assets	−0.756	−0.02	−0.11	−0.21
Current assets to current liabilities	−0.176	1.78	1.90	1.65
UCFO to average total liabilities	−1.192	−0.04	−0.03	−0.06
EBITDA to interest	−0.029	2.36	1.99	−1.16
Total liabilities to total assets	2.326	0.87	0.95	1.13
HZ (bankruptcy prediction) score		−1.387	−1.168	−0.486
Probability of bankruptcy		20.0%	23.7%	38.1%

Valuation Key 9.11

Bankruptcy or financial distress prediction models can be used to assess the probability that a company will be in a state of financial distress within a certain period of time. We can use these models to help assess a company's debt cost of capital.

REVIEW EXERCISE 9.6

Using the HZ Bankruptcy Prediction Model to Estimate the Probability of Bankruptcy

Using the financial information for the Snap Company given in Review Exercise 9.4, and the HZ Bankruptcy Prediction Model, calculate the probability that Snap will file for bankruptcy in the next 12 months.

Solution on page 432.

Option Pricing-Based Financial Distress Models

Another type of financial distress prediction model is an option pricing-based model. We review the basics of option pricing in the appendix. The financial distress prediction model is based on the Merton model and its variations.[25] These models consider such company factors as financial leverage, market value, and the volatility of a company's equity. Using this and other information, the model estimates the volatility of the underlying assets and predicts the probability of financial distress.

For a particular horizon (number of years in the future), this model measures the probability that the value of the company's assets will be less than the amount of the company's debt (the definition of financial distress or financial failure in the model). The debt maturity input, T, is unable to fully map the theoretical construct of the original model, as there is no option contract being settled up at this date. Even though we use this input to represent the horizon, it has a broader and more complex interpretation than a horizon or simple term to maturity. Note that this is not the same as going bankrupt, for a company

[25] Merton, R.C., "On the Pricing of Corporate Debt: The Risk Structure of Interest Rates," *Journal of Finance* vol. 29, no. 2 (May 1974), pp. 449–470.

can have the value of its assets fall below the principal value of its debt and not file for bankruptcy. The model below is based on the model in Hillegeist et al. (2004).[26] In this model, the value of the equity is measured using Equation 9.6.

$$V_E = V_A \times e^{-d_A \times T_D} \times N(d_1) - X_D \times e^{-r_F \times T_D} \times N(d_2) + (1 - e^{-d_A \times T_D}) \times V_A \quad \textbf{(9.6)}$$

where all terms are defined as:

V_A = value of the company's assets
V_E = value of the company's common equity
r_F = risk-free rate of return
d_A = continuously compounded dividend rate (rate based on V_A)
T_D = maturity of the company's debt
X_D = amount due on the company's debt

$$d_1 = \frac{\ln(V_A / X_D) + \left[r_F - d_A + (\sigma_A^2/2)\right] \times T_D}{\sigma_A \times \sqrt{T_D}}$$

$d_2 = d_1 - \sigma_A \times \sqrt{T_D}$
r_A = the expected return on the company's assets (often the unlevered cost of capital)
σ_A = the volatility or standard deviation of the company's expected return on its assets
$N(x)$ = the standard cumulative normal[27]

We can measure the probability that the value of the assets will be less than the value of the debt claims for a certain horizon, T (for example, one year, three years, five years, etc.), and we define this to be the probability of financial distress in the model, $Prob_{\text{Financial Distress}}$.[28]

$$Prob_{\text{Financial Distress}} = N\left(-\frac{\ln(V_A / X_D) + \left[r_A - d_A (\sigma_A^2/2)\right] \times T_D}{\sigma_A \times \sqrt{T_D}}\right) \quad \textbf{(9.7)}$$

The probability of financial distress is a function of the expected growth in the value of the assets, r_A (the expected return on the assets, which is normally set to be equal to the unlevered cost of capital), the horizon, the volatility of the value of the company's assets, and the difference between the value of the assets and the amount due on the company's debt. Holding all else constant, the larger the difference between the value of the assets and amount due on the company's debt or the larger the expected growth in the value of the assets, the smaller the probability of financial distress; the longer the horizon or the larger the volatility of the value of the company's assets, the higher the probability of financial distress.

In the case of publicly traded companies, we can typically measure the following inputs for the model—the value of the equity, V_E; the standard deviation of the annual return on equity, σ_E; the amount due on the company's debt, X_D; the horizon, T_D; the risk-free rate of return, r_F; the expected dividends paid by the company, and the expected rate of return on the company's assets (often set equal to the unlevered cost of capital), r_A. We assume we cannot observe the value of the company's assets because we cannot measure the value of the company's non-equity claims; we also assume that we cannot measure the volatility of the assets. If we cannot measure the value of the assets, we also cannot observe the dividend rate based on the value of the company's assets, d_A; however, once we estimate the value of the company's assets as we describe below, we can calculate the continuously compounded dividend rate on the company's assets as the expected dividend divided by the value of the company's assets, continuously compounded.

---

[26] Hillegeist, S. A., E. K. Keating, D. P. Cram, and K. G. Lundstedt, "Assessing the Probability of Bankruptcy," *Review of Accounting Studies* 9 (2004), pp. 5–34.

[27] N(x) is the probability that a normally distributed random variable will be less than x standard deviations above the mean. If x is, say, 2, then the probability will be close to 1.0 (.9972 to be exact).

[28] The model assumes that T is the maturity of a company's debt, which is assumed to be zero-coupon debt with the same maturity date. We illustrate the model for a shorter horizon—one or three years—to illustrate how to use this model even though this assumption varies from the theoretical model—see Hillegeist et al. (2004) for a discussion of this point. Other research studies develop more complex models that address this issue. See, for example, Black, F., and J. Cox, "Valuing Corporate Securities: Some Effects of Bond Indenture Provisions," *Journal of Finance* vol. 31, no. 2 (1976), pp. 351–367; and Geske, R., "The Valuation of Corporate Liabilities as Compound Options," *Journal of Financial and Quantitative Analysis* vol. 12, no. 4 (1977), pp. 541–552.

If we cannot observe the value of the company's assets, V_A, and the volatility of the assets, σ_A, we can measure these two inputs by simultaneously solving the equity valuation formula (Equation 9.6) and the optimal hedge formula, which we show in Equation 9.8:

$$\sigma_E = \frac{\sigma_A \times N(d_1) \times V_A \times e^{-d_A \times T_D}}{V_E} \quad \textbf{(9.8)}$$

To simultaneously solve these two equations, we choose values for the volatility of the company's assets, σ_A, and the value of the assets, V_A. For each iteration, we calculate the dividend rate as the expected dividends divided by the value of the assets, continuously compounded in that iteration. We then use these values in conjunction with the other inputs to calculate the results of Equation 9.8. Since we observe the value of the equity (which we can also calculate using Equation 9.6) and volatility of the equity (which we can also calculate using Equation 9.8), we can choose a value of the assets and volatility of the assets that solves Equation 9.8. Thus, we compare the observed values to the calculated values and use an iterative process until the observed and calculated values are equal.

If we can observe either the value of the company's assets or the volatility of the assets, we can solve for the other term directly using one of the two formulas. If we know the value of the assets but not the volatility of the assets, we can use Equation 9.8 to calculate the volatility of the assets before measuring the probability of financial distress. If we know the volatility of the assets but not the value of the assets, we can use Equation 9.6 to calculate the value of the assets before measuring the probability of financial distress. We can sometimes measure the volatility of the assets from a publicly traded, unlevered, comparable company.

In Exhibit 9.28, we show the results of estimating the option-theoretic financial distress prediction model for Advance Micro Devices in 2013–2015, using three different horizons (one year, three, and five years) and two different expected returns on assets (we chose 5% and 0% in this example). We measure the other inputs as follows: we measure the value of the equity, V_E, as the number of shares outstanding multiplied by the price on the "as of date"; we collected the standard deviation of the annual return on equity, σ_E, from the company's 10-K report; and we measure the dividend rate, d_A, as the dividend divided by the market value of the assets (value of the firm), continuously compounded, which is 0.0% for this company. We use the book value of the company's debt reported in the company's financial statements for the amount due on the company's debt, X_D, and we use the one-year risk-free rate of return, r_F.

EXHIBIT 9.28 The Option Pricing Model-Based Financial Distress Model Applied to Advanced Micro Devices, 2013–2015

	Advanced Micro Devices		
Inputs:	**2013**	**2014**	**2015**
Outstanding debt	$2,058.0	$2,212.0	$2,262.0
Value of the common equity	$2,627.0	$2,256.0	$1,938.0
Standard deviation of equity	56.00%	58.00%	60.00%
Dividend yield (based on value of assets)	0.00%	0.00%	0.00%
Risk-free rate	2.00%	2.00%	2.00%
Assuming a 5% Annual Return:			
1-year probability of financial distress	0.5%	0.9%	1.5%
3-year probability of financial distress	9.9%	12.8%	15.6%
5-year probability of financial distress	16.5%	26.1%	30.2%
Assuming a 0% Annual Return:			
1-year probability of financial distress	0.8%	1.5%	2.2%
3-year probability of financial distress	15.1%	19.2%	22.9%
5-year probability of financial distress	25.9%	37.0%	41.8%

This exhibit shows that the probability of financial distress increases as the horizon increases and the rate of return on the assets decreases. Given the company's financial deterioration between 2013 and 2015, we also observe an increase in the probability of financial distress over this period. In 2013, the one-year horizon probability of financial distress was between 0.5% and 0.8%, depending on the assumed return on assets. This is less than the probability we measured using the HZ financial statement-based model. Assuming a 5% return on assets, the one-year horizon probability increases to 0.9% in 2014 and 1.5% in 2015, consistent with the company's deterioration but again, lower than the probabilities we estimated using the financial ratio-based models and lower than the one-year default rates for B− (B3) debt or CCC+ (Caa1) debt in Exhibit 9.8, both of which have one-year default rates of over 5%.

We know that using a longer horizon results in a higher probability of financial distress. To illustrate this effect, we also use a three- and a five-year horizon. In 2013, assuming a 5% return, the company's probability of financial distress increases from under 1% based on the one-year horizon to 9.9% based on the three-year horizon and to 16.5% based on the five-year horizon. We observe similar increases assuming a 0% return on assets. Further, the three- and five-year horizon probabilities are more consistent with the financial ratio-based probabilities of bankruptcy for the company and the three- and five-year default rates for B3 and Caa1 debt in Exhibit 9.8.

Which Approach Works Better (Ratio-Based or Option Pricing-Based Financial Distress Models)?

The study by Hillegeist et al. (2004) compared two approaches. It compared the option pricing-based model we discussed earlier to updated versions of two financial ratio models—the model in Altman (1968)[29] and the model in Ohlson (1980).[30] The study reported that the option pricing-based approach worked better than the financial ratio-based approach; however, both approaches work in that they both predict bankruptcy. Arora, Bohn, and Zhu (2005)[31] provide evidence that an option-theoretic-based model known as the K-V model[32]—which is now a proprietary model owned by Moody's and is now known as the KMV model—as well as option-theoretic-based models similar to those developed by Hull and White (2000)[33] outperform the Merton model.

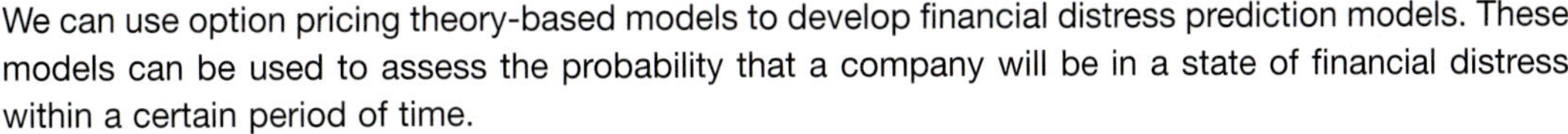

Valuation Key 9.12

We can use option pricing theory-based models to develop financial distress prediction models. These models can be used to assess the probability that a company will be in a state of financial distress within a certain period of time.

SUMMARY AND KEY CONCEPTS

The levering, unlevering, and weighted average cost of capital formulas we use to measure the cost of capital in a valuation analysis include a component for each type of financing used by a company in its capital structure. In this chapter, we discussed how to measure the costs of capital for a company's straight debt and preferred claims. The most frequently issued non-common-equity security is debt financing; however, even debt financing varies considerably based on the terms and provisions of its contract.

For a straight or pure debt contract, we measure the value of the debt by discounting the promised payments (interest and principal) at the promised yield to maturity. We can observe the promised payments from the terms of the contract, and we can observe the promised yield to maturity directly if the debt is traded. If the debt is not traded, we can measure the promised yield by using the company's credit rating, which we can either observe or directly measure from the company's underlying financial and market data. The promised yield is not, however, the company's cost of capital for the debt. The promised yield is equal to the cost of

[29] Altman, E., "Financial Ratios, Discriminant Analysis and the Prediction of Corporate Bankruptcy," *Journal of Finance* 23 (1968), pp. 589–609.

[30] Ohlson, J., "Financial Ratios and the Probabilistic Prediction of Bankruptcy," *Journal of Accounting Research* 19 (1980), pp. 109–131.

[31] Arora, N., J. Bohn, and F. Zhu, "Reduced Form vs. Structural Models of Credit Risk: A Case Study of Three Models," *Journal of Investment Management* vol. 3, no. 4 (2005), pp. 43–67.

[32] See Vasicek, O., *Credit Valuation*, 1984, Moody's KMV, for background on this model.

[33] See Hull, J., and A. White, "Valuing Credit Default Swaps: No Counterparty Default Risk," *Journal of Derivatives* 8 (2000), pp. 29–40.

debt plus the expected default loss. We discussed multiple ways to estimate a company's cost of debt. We can use similar methods for preferred stock.

Companies also issue equity-linked securities such as warrants, employee stock options, and debt and preferred stock that are convertible into common equity. We can use models based on option pricing theory to measure the value and cost of capital for these securities. We delay discussion of those topics to Chapter 12.

ADDITIONAL READING AND REFERENCES

Kaplan, R. S., and G. Urwitz, "Statistical Models of Bond Ratings: A Methodological Inquiry," *Journal of Business* 52 (1979), pp. 231–261.

Merton, R. C., "On the Pricing of Corporate Debt: The Risk Structure of Interest Rates," *Journal of Finance* vol. 29, no. 2 (May 1974), pp. 449–470.

Zmijewski, M. E. "Methodological Issues Related to the Estimation of Financial Distress Prediction Models," *Journal of Accounting Research* 22 (Supplement 1984), pp. 59–82.

APPENDIX: AN OVERVIEW OF THE BLACK-SCHOLES AND MERTON OPTION PRICING MODELS

Like all securities, an option is a contract. What differentiates options from many other securities is that an option provides the holder of the option contract the right (but not an obligation) to buy or sell the underlying security at a set price. The option is a **derivative security**, so called because its value depends in part on the value of another asset. There are two basic options—call and put options. A **call option** is an option to purchase an underlying security at a certain price for a specified period. The option may be exercisable on the date the option expires (**expiration date**)—a **European option**—or it may be exercisable any time before the expiration date—an **American option**. Examples of call options on common stock issued by companies and relevant to measuring firm value include employee stock options, warrants, convertible debt, and convertible preferred stock. A **put option** is an option to sell the underlying security at a certain price for a specified period, but companies generally do not issue put options on their common stock.

Option pricing theory is valuable in many different types of settings. In addition to company-issued options, investors issue options on a company's stock to other investors. These options not only include "plain vanilla" put and call options but also include "exotic" options. Exotic options include Asian options, which have payoffs that depend on the average prices of the underlying assets over a specified period, and rainbow options, which have payoffs that depend on multiple securities or events. Investors write option contracts on stocks, credit contracts, foreign currency, commodities, and even the weather. These options can be used by investors and corporations to hedge certain risks.

Another type of option is an option that is embedded within an investment opportunity. Any investment contains an embedded option if it can be changed during its life as an investor learns more about it; for example, if an investment can be deferred, contracted, expanded, or abandoned before completion. These options are called **real options**. They can be used in such various settings as research and development valuations, patent valuations, and natural resource investments. Discounted cash flow approaches cannot always capture all of the value derived from the embedded options. In such circumstances, an option pricing framework is more appropriate if the necessary information is available to utilize this approach.

The seminal works of Black and Scholes (1973) and Merton (1973) and other related works by these authors and others underpin many of the option pricing models used today.[34] We assume the reader already has some understanding of both option pricing theory and these models, so what follows is only a summary review of the Black-Scholes and Merton option pricing models. Just as with many models used in valuation, these option pricing models make certain assumptions about markets, information, and the characteristics of the options. Since these assumptions are unlikely to hold exactly in a specific circumstance, they are simply estimates of the value of the options. Nevertheless, these models are widely used in practice. The focus of the discussion in this appendix is on the valuation of basic call options.

Key Factors that Determine the Value of an Option

Black and Scholes developed their option pricing model under the assumption that the option could not be exercised until the expiration date (**European option**). They assumed that markets are frictionless—that is, markets have no transactions costs or taxes—and that investors have the same instantaneous and costless access to information. They also assumed that investors have no restrictions on their ability to engage in short sales, that assets trade continuously, that the risk-free rate is known and stationary, and that the company does not pay dividends (Merton eliminated this last restriction). They also assume that it is not the company issuing the option; hence, there will be no dilution of the existing shareholders associated with the exercise of the option.

[34] Black, F., and M. Scholes, "The Pricing of Options and Corporate Liabilities," *Journal of Political Economy* vol. 81, no. 3, (May/June 1973), pp. 637–654; and Merton, R. C., "Theory of Rational Option Pricing," *Bell Journal of Economics and Management Science* vol. 4, no. 1 (Spring 1973), pp. 141–183.

Based on these assumptions, we know two key factors relevant to option pricing, because they are part of the option's contract: the **strike** or **exercise price** (X_{Option}), at which the option can be exercised, and the length of the contract—or the amount of time to the expiration date (T_{Option}). We discuss these factors from the perspective of an investor who purchases a call option on a stock. All else equal, the investor prefers to have a lower exercise price because the investor will have to pay less for the stock. Similarly, all else equal, the investor prefers to have a longer time to expiration because the longer the time to expiration, the longer the stock price has to grow above the exercise price. In addition, since the difference between the stock price and the strike price determines the payoff at the expiration of the option, all else equal, the investor prefers a higher stock price (P_E). Thus, so far, we have identified three factors that clearly determine the value of an option—stock price, exercise price, and time to expiration.

The Black-Scholes option pricing model includes two additional factors that affect the option's value. The first factor is the variance of the stock price. Since the call is worth more the greater the spread between the stock price and the exercise price, the investor prefers a higher probability that the stock price will be higher than the exercise price. All else equal, the larger the variance of the stock price, the higher the probability that the stock price will be larger than the exercise price. Thus, all else equal, a call is worth more when written on a stock with a higher variance. The last factor in the Black-Scholes Option Pricing Model is the risk-free rate of return. The time value of money is relevant to option pricing because the investor pays the exercise price at the exercise date. Thus, the value of the option today takes the present value of the exercise price into consideration. Black and Scholes show that an investor can hedge an investment so that any adjustment for the time value of money will be at the risk-free rate of return. All else equal, the higher the risk-free rate of return, the lower the present value of the exercise price and thus the higher the value of the option. To summarize, all else equal, the value of an option increases with increases in the stock price, the variance of the stock price, the time to expiration of the option, and the risk-free rate; it decreases with increases in the strike price.

Merton adds one additional factor: dividends. As we know, when a company pays a dividend, it reduces the company's assets and, thus, its equity value (ignoring any informational value of the dividend). All else equal, the stock price of a company that pays dividends will have a lower value by the amount of the dividends paid. The Black-Scholes model assumes dividends are not paid, but Merton includes dividend distributions. The higher the dividend yield, the lower the value of the option.

Valuation in Practice A9.1

Intel Corporation's Valuation of Its Equity Incentive Plan As described in its 10-K report, Intel Corporation (Intel) uses the Black-Scholes Option Pricing Model to measure the fair value of stock options and stock purchase rights granted:

> . . . use the Black-Scholes option-pricing model for estimating the fair value of options granted under the company's equity incentive plans and rights to acquire stock granted under the company's stock purchase plan. The weighted average estimated values of employee stock option grants and rights granted under the stock purchase plan, as well as the weighted average assumptions that were used in calculating such values . . . , were based on estimates at the date of grant as follows:

	Stock Options			Stock Purchase Plan		
	2004	2005	2006	2004	2005	2006
Estimated value per option.	$10.79	$6.02	$5.21	$6.38	$0	$6.02
Expected life (in years)	4.2	4.7	4.9	0.5	0.5	0.5
Risk-free interest rate.	3.0%	3.9%	4.9%	1.4%	3.2%	5.0%
Volatility	50.0%	26.0%	27.0%	30.0%	23.0%	29.0%
Dividend yield.	0.6%	1.4%	2.0%	0.6%	1.3%	2.1%

Source: See Intel's 2006 10-K report filed with the U.S. SEC and available on the company's website, www.intel.com.

The Black-Scholes and Merton Option Pricing Models

We know that the value of a call option at the exercise date is equal to the price of the stock minus the exercise price. For example, if an investor exercises a call option at the expiration date when the stock price is $12 and the exercise price is $10, the investor will earn $2; thus, the value of this option immediately before it expires is very close to $2. Naturally, valuing an option one year before the exercise date is more complex, for we do not know the value of the stock at the exercise date; however, we know the current stock price, the variability of the stock price, the length of the option contract, and the strike price. We can use these factors to estimate the expected payoff from the call option. The Black-Scholes Option Pricing Model, which is the continuous version of the discrete time binomial model for pricing options, does just that. The form of this model is

$$P_C = P_E \times N(d_1) - X_C \times e^{-r_F \times T_C} \times N(d_2) \quad \text{(A9.1)}$$

where:

P_C = price of a European call option
P_E = common stock price per share
T_C = time to expiration of the call option (in years)
X_C = exercise or strike price of the call option

$$d_1 = \frac{\ln\left(\frac{P_E}{X_C}\right) + (r_F + \sigma_E^2/2) \times T_C}{\sigma_E \times \sqrt{T_C}}$$

$$d_2 = d_1 - \sigma_E \times \sqrt{T_C}$$

r_F = risk-free rate of return
$N(x)$ = the standard cumulative normal[35]
σ_E = the standard deviation of the company's continuously compounded annual returns

This formula might not be intuitive, but we can think of it as measuring the difference between the present value of the expected stock price at expiration minus the present value of the strike price.

Valuation Key A9.1

The Black-Scholes Option Pricing Model prices a European call option (option only exercisable at the expiration date) based on five factors. All else equal, the value of an option increases with increases in the stock price, variance of the stock price, time to expiration, and risk-free rate; it decreases with increases in the strike price.

As long as the option's underlying security does not pay dividends, Merton shows that the Black-Scholes option pricing formula can be used to value an American option even though it can be exercised before the expiration date. The intuition underpinning this conclusion is that the value of the option is always greater than the value of exercising the option and owning the stock; thus, the option will not be exercised early, and the value of the American option will be the same as the value of the European option. Merton also derives an adjustment for a European call option for a stock that pays dividends.

It is clear that, all else equal, if a company pays dividends, the value of the option decreases because the value of the stock at the exercise date will be lower. Merton adjusts the option pricing model for dividends by assuming the company pays a constant dividend yield (dividend divided by stock price, continuously compounded). He adjusts the pricing formula by essentially reducing the value of the first component in the option pricing formula by discounting the stock price by the dividend yield as follows:

$$P_C = P_E \times e^{-d_E \times T_C} \times N(d_1) - X_C \times e^{-r_F \times T_C} \times N(d_2) \quad \text{(A9.2)}$$

All terms are as defined earlier with an adjustment to d_1 as follows:

$$d_1 = \frac{\ln\left(\frac{P_E}{X_C}\right) + (r_F - d_E + \sigma_E^2/2) \times T_C}{\sigma_E \times \sqrt{T_C}}$$

$$d_2 = d_1 - \sigma_E \times \sqrt{T_C}$$

d_E = annual continuously compounded dividend yield

Merton's formula for valuing a European call option is not applicable to an American call option for a dividend-paying stock. If an option holder can exercise an option before the expiration date, it may be more valuable to do so before the dividend reduces the stock price. In order to value the option, we must examine the value of the option before each expected dividend payment while considering such factors as the expected drop in stock price after the dividend and the time to expiration remaining after the dividend. The **binomial option method** can be used to value these options.

[35] N(x) is the probability that a normally distributed random variable will be less than x standard deviations above the mean. If x is, say, 2, then the probability will be close to 1.0 (.9972 to be exact).

Valuation Key A9.2

Merton shows that the Black-Scholes option pricing formula can be used to value an American option as long as the underlying security does not pay dividends. He also develops an option pricing model for a European call option for a stock that pays dividends.

We do not walk through a detailed example using the Black-Scholes and Merton option pricing models, as we presume the reader already has familiarity with these models. However, Review Exercise A9.1 utilizes these models to value a European call option for those in need of a refresher.

REVIEW EXERCISE A9.1

Valuation of a Basic European Call Option

A European call option provides the holder of the option the right to purchase a share of a company's stock for $12 per share three years from today. The stock is currently trading at $10, does not pay dividends, and has a standard deviation on its annual return of 30%. The risk-free rate of return is 5%. What is the value of this option today? How will the value of the option change if the company changes its dividend policy and begins to pay a regular dividend (continuously compounded) equal to 5% of its stock price?

Solution on pages 432–433.

EXERCISES AND PROBLEMS

P9.1 **Debt Cost of Capital and Promised Yield:** Assume the company has a debt agreement with the following characteristics:

Face value of the debt	$1,000
Debt coupon interest rate (paid annually)	10%
Debt term (# years)	1
Probability of default	20%
Recovery rate—Interest paid upon default	0%
Recovery rate—Principal paid upon default	40%

a. Calculate the expected cash flows for the debt.

b. Assume the investors require an expected annual rate of return of 13% for a debt security with this level of risk. Calculate the amount the investors would be willing to pay for this debt security.

c. Ignore part b, and instead assume the debt security is sold for $880.73. Calculate the debt cost of capital implied in this price.

P9.2 **Yield to Maturity and Expected Default Loss:** Using the information in P9.1, calculate the yield to maturity and expected default loss for parts b and c.

P9.3 **Debt Cost of Capital for Debt with Maturity Greater than One Year:** Assume the company issues debt with the following characteristics:

Face value of debt (in millions)	$100
Coupon interest rate (paid annually)	12%
Years to maturity	5
Issue price	$75
Recovery rate (all years)	40%
(Recovery rate is for the principal plus interest for the year of default)	
Probability of default—Year 1	30%
Probability of default—Year 2	25%
Probability of default—Year 3	20%
Probability of default—Year 4	15%
Probability of default—Year 5	10%

Calculate the yield to maturity, the cost of debt, and the expected default loss for this debt issue.

P9.4 **Debt Cost of Capital Estimated Using the CAPM—PMJ Company:** The PMJ Company had debt on their books at the end of 2015 with a credit rating of B. The yield to maturity of AA rated debt at that time was approximately 3.5%, which we assume is equal to its cost of debt. Use the data in Exhibit 9.16 other than the YTM of the AA rated debt to estimate the debt cost of capital for the PMJ Company at the end of 2015. Assume the market risk premium is 6%.

P9.5 **Using Financial Ratios to Estimate a Credit Rating—Viking Company:** Estimate the Viking Company's credit rating at the end of Year 0 using the company's financial statements given below, and the distribution of key financial ratios for different credit ratings given in Exhibit 9.18.

Viking Company Balance Sheets and Income Statement ($ in thousands)	Year –1	Year 0
Income Statement		
Revenue		$12,290
Operating expenses		–4,793
Depreciation expense		–1,920
Earnings before interest and taxes		$ 5,577
Interest expense		–1,148
Income before taxes		$ 4,429
Income tax expense		–1,329
Net income		$ 3,100
Balance Sheet		
Total current assets	$ 1,904	$ 2,044
Property, plant & equipment (net)	30,894	29,553
Total assets	$32,798	$31,596
Account payable	$ 626	$ 672
Debt	16,399	16,563
Total liabilities	$17,025	$17,235
Capital stock	$ 8,000	$ 8,000
Retained earnings	7,773	6,361
Shareholders' equity	$15,773	$14,361
Liabilities and shareholders' equity	$32,798	$31,596

Viking Company Unlevered Free Cash Flow Statement ($ in thousands)	Year 0
Unlevered operating cash flow	$5,735
– Change in required cash balance	–5
– Capital expenditures	–578
Unlevered free cash flow	$5,152

Exhibit may contain small rounding errors

P9.6 **Using the HZ Credit Rating Model to Estimate a Credit Rating—Viking Company:** Apply the HZ Credit Rating Model to the Viking Company given in P9.5. What is the probability that Viking's credit rating falls within each of the six credit rating categories used in the HZ model in Year 0?

P9.7 **Using the HZ Bankruptcy Prediction Model to Estimate the Probability of Bankruptcy—Viking Company:** Using the financial information for the Viking Company given in P9.5, and the HZ Bankruptcy Prediction Model, calculate the probability that Viking will file for bankruptcy in the next twelve months.

SOLUTIONS FOR REVIEW EXERCISES

Review Exercise 9.1: Debt Cost of Capital

Assume the company has a one-period $1,000 debt agreement that will pay the investor at the end of one year the coupon interest rate of 12% plus the $1,000 face value of the debt. Assume the investors believe the company has a 3% probability of defaulting on the promised payments. If the company defaults, the investors will be paid no interest and 50% of the face value of the debt at the end of Year 1.

	Promised	No Default State	Default State	Expected	
Debt (coupon) interest rate	12.0%				
Face value	$1,000.00				
Probability		97.0%	3.0%		
Recovery rate—interest		100.0%	0.0%		
Recovery rate—principal		100.0%	50.0%		
Interest	$ 120.00	$116.40	$ 0.00	$ 116.40	97.0%
Principal	$1,000.00	$970.00	$15.00	$ 985.00	98.5%
Total	$1,120.00			$1,101.40	98.3%
Debt cost of capital	14.0%			0.877	
Present value				$ 966.14	96.6%
Part C—Implied debt cost of capital					
Assumed debt issue price	$1,019.81				
Total expected cash flows	$1,101.40				
Implied debt cost of capital	8%				

Exhibit may contain small rounding errors

a. The expected cash flows for the debt equal $116.40 for interest plus $985 for the principal or a total of $1,101.40.

b. The investors would be willing to invest $966.14 in this security (= $1,101.40 expected cash flows × 0.8772 present value factor for one year at 14% or = $1,101.4/1.14).

c. The implied debt cost of capital is 8% (0.08 = $1,101.40 expected cash flows/$1,019.81 issue price of the debt − 1). The issue price is higher than the face value of the debt (issued at a premium) because the expected cash flows result in a return that exceeds the debt cost of capital when valued using the face value of the bond, even after taking into account the default risk. Thus, in order to earn just the debt cost of capital, the bond has to be selling at a premium to its face value.

d. The yield to maturity is 9.82%.

$$\text{YTM} = 0.0982 = \frac{[(1{,}000 \times 0.12) + 1{,}000]}{1{,}019.81} - 1$$

e. $\text{E(DL)} = \text{YTM} - r_D = 9.82\% - 8\% = 1.82\%$

Review Exercise 9.2: Debt Cost of Capital for Debt with Maturity Greater than One Year

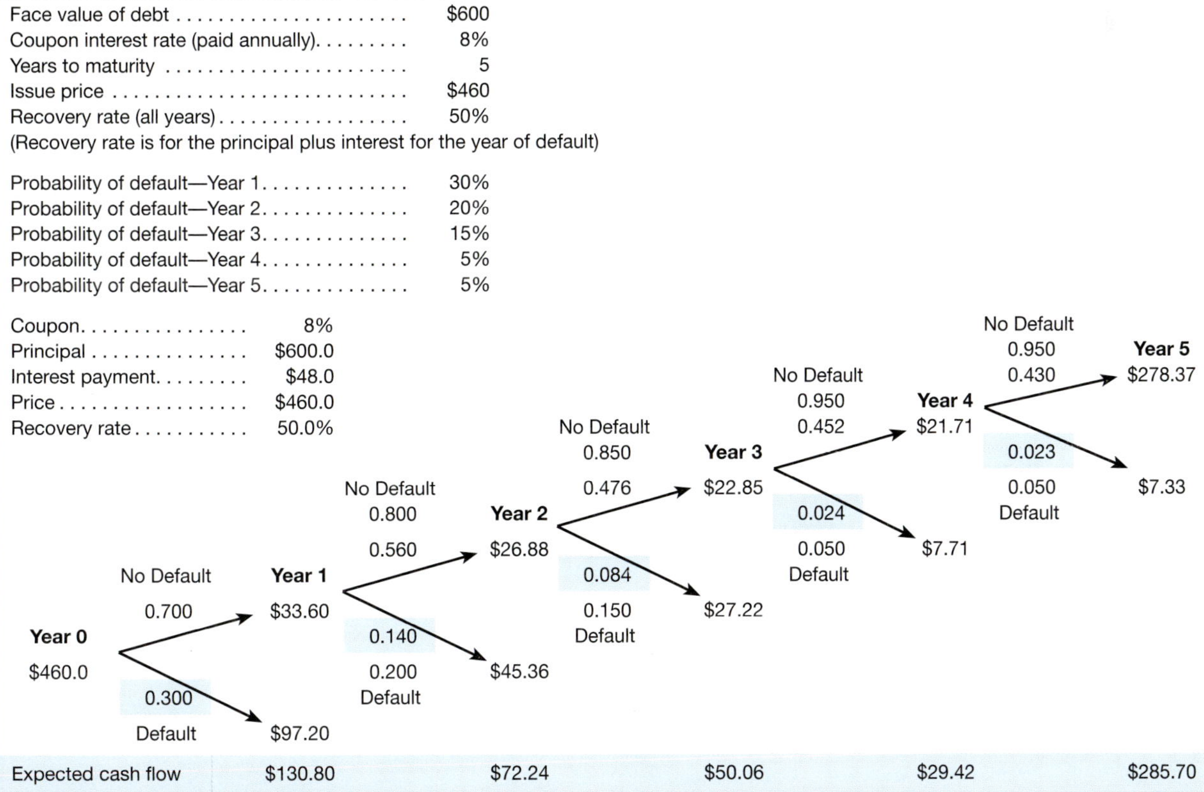

Face value of debt	$600
Coupon interest rate (paid annually)	8%
Years to maturity	5
Issue price	$460
Recovery rate (all years)	50%

(Recovery rate is for the principal plus interest for the year of default)

Probability of default—Year 1	30%
Probability of default—Year 2	20%
Probability of default—Year 3	15%
Probability of default—Year 4	5%
Probability of default—Year 5	5%

Coupon	8%
Principal	$600.0
Interest payment	$48.0
Price	$460.0
Recovery rate	50.0%

Expected cash flow	$130.80	$72.24	$50.06	$29.42	$285.70

Exhibit may contain small rounding errors

Using Equation 9.1 with the promised cash flows, the YTM is

$$0=\frac{\$48}{(1+YTM_0)^1}+\frac{\$48}{(1+YTM_0)^2}+\frac{\$48}{(1+YTM_0)^3}+\frac{\$48}{(1+YTM_0)^4}+\frac{\$48+\$600}{(1+YTM_0)^5}-\$460$$

YTM = 15%

Using Equation 9.2 with the expected cash flows, the cost of debt is

$$0=\frac{\$130.80}{(1+r_D)^1}+\frac{\$72.24}{(1+r_D)^2}+\frac{\$50.06}{(1+r_D)^3}+\frac{\$29.42}{(1+r_D)^4}+\frac{\$285.70}{(1+r_D)^5}-\$460$$

$r_D = 6.5\%$

The expected default loss is 8.5% (0.085 = 0.15 − 0.065).

Review Exercise 9.3: Debt Cost of Capital Estimated Using the CAPM

Debt cost of capital for AA rated debt	2.14%
Market risk premium	6.5%
Incremental beta for B rating	0.402
Risk premium	2.61%
Estimated debt cost of capital for B rating	4.75%

The estimated debt cost of capital is 4.75% (0.0475 = 0.0214 + (0.402 × 0.065)).

Review Exercise 9.4: Using Financial Ratios to Estimate a Credit Rating

Financial Ratios	Ratio	Rating
Return on Assets	24.4%	AAA
Return on Capital	25.3%	AAA
EBITDA to Average Total Assets	46.0%	AAA
EBITDA Margin	64.0%	AAA
EBIT Margin	56.6%	AAA
Debt to Capital	0.38	AA–A
EBITDA to Interest	16.34	A–BBB
EBIT to Interest	14.46	A–BBB

Table may contain small rounding errors

$$\text{Return on Assets}=\frac{[8{,}297+(1-0.4)\times 1{,}028]}{[(36{,}249+36{,}722)/2]}=0.244$$

$$\text{Return on Capital}=\frac{[8{,}297+(1-0.4)\times 1{,}028]}{[((12{,}845+22{,}367)+(13{,}487+21{,}888))/2]}=0.253$$

$$\frac{\text{EBITDA}}{\text{Average Total Assets}}=\frac{(14{,}857+1{,}939)}{[(36{,}249+36{,}722)/2]}=0.460$$

$$\text{EBITDA Margin}=\frac{(14{,}857+1{,}939)}{26{,}243}=0.640$$

$$\text{EBIT Margin}=\frac{14{,}857}{26{,}243}=0.566$$

$$\text{Debt to Capital} = \frac{13{,}487}{(13{,}487 + 21{,}888)} = 0.38$$

$$\text{EBITDA to Interest} = \frac{(14{,}857 + 1{,}939)}{1{,}028} = 16.34$$

$$\text{EBIT to Interest} = \frac{14{,}857}{1{,}028} = 14.46$$

The financial ratios for the Snap Company correspond with credit ratings ranging from AAA to BBB which illustrates the fact that using financial ratio distributions to estimate a credit rating can be difficult. Two of the ratios are between the median financial ratios for credit ratings between A and BBB and another ratio is between the medians for AA and A rated bonds and five of the ratios are consistent with an AAA rating. Given just the information in the financial ratios, we would anticipate that Snap Company would have an A or AA rating.

Review Exercise 9.5: Using the HZ Credit Rating Model to Estimate a Credit Rating

Variable (Logit Model Estimation)	Coefficients	CCC+ & Below	B− to B+	BB− to BB+	BBB− to BBB+	A− to A+	AA− to AAA
Intercept for CCC+ & below	−5.632	−5.632					
Intercept for B− to B+	−1.669		−1.669				
Intercept for BB− to BB+	−0.072			−0.072			
Intercept for BBB− to BBB+	1.663				1.663		
Intercept for A− to A+	3.447					3.447	
EBIT to average total debt + Shareholders' equity	−5.387	0.421	0.421	0.421	0.421	0.421	
Interest to EBITDA	2.441	0.061	0.061	0.061	0.061	0.061	
Average total debt to CFO − Capital expenditures	−0.002	1.595	1.595	1.595	1.595	1.595	
Total debt to total debt + Shareholders' equity	2.092	0.381	0.381	0.381	0.381	0.381	
Capital expenditures to EBITDA	−0.182	0.055	0.055	0.055	0.055	0.055	
HZ credit rating score		−6.965	−3.002	−1.405	0.330	2.114	
Cumulative probability		0.001	0.047	0.197	0.582	0.892	1.000
Probability of credit rating		**0.1%**	**4.6%**	**15.0%**	**38.5%**	**31.0%**	**10.8%**

$$\text{EBIT to Average Debt} + \text{Shareholders' Equity} = \frac{14{,}857}{[((12{,}845{+}22{,}367) + (13{,}487 + 21{,}888))/2]} = 0.421$$

$$\text{Interest to EBITDA} = \frac{1{,}028}{(14{,}857 + 1{,}939)} = 0.061$$

$$\text{Average Total Debt to CFO} - \text{CAPEX} = \frac{[(12{,}845 + 13{,}487)/2]}{(9{,}796 - 1{,}028 \times (1 - 0.4) - 926)} = 1.595$$

Note: CFO = UCFO − Interest Expense × (1 − Tax Rate)

$$\text{Total Debt to Total Debt} + \text{Shareholders' Equity} = \frac{13{,}487}{(13{,}487 + 21{,}888)} = 0.381$$

$$\text{CAPEX to EBITDA} = \frac{926}{(14{,}857 + 1{,}939)} = 0.055$$

The credit rating with the highest probability is the BBB− to BBB+ group with a probability of 38.5%, but the probability for the A− to A+ group is quite close at 31%. This result indicates that the range of most likely credit ratings is quite wide—from A+ to BBB−.

Review Exercise 9.6: Using the HZ Bankruptcy Prediction Model to Estimate the Probability of Bankruptcy

Variable	Coefficients	Year 0
Intercept	−3.099	
Net income to average total assets	−0.756	0.23
Current assets to current liabilities	−0.176	4.80
UCFO to average total liabilities	−1.192	0.68
EBITDA to interest	−0.029	16.34
Total liabilities to total assets	2.326	0.40
HZ bankruptcy prediction score		−4.465
Probability of bankruptcy in 12 months		1.1%

$$\text{Net Income to Average Total Assets} = \frac{8{,}297}{((36{,}249 + 36{,}722)/2)} = 0.23$$

$$\text{Current Assets to Current Liabilities} = \frac{6{,}460}{1{,}347} = 4.80$$

$$\text{UCFO to Average Total Liabilities} = \frac{9{,}796}{((13{,}882 + 14{,}834)/2)} = 0.68$$

$$\text{EBITDA to Interest} = \frac{(14{,}857 + 1{,}939)}{1{,}028} = 16.34$$

$$\text{Total Liabilities to Total Assets} = \frac{14{,}834}{36{,}722} = 0.40$$

The HZ Financial Distress Model predicts only a 1.1% probability that Snap will file for bankruptcy in the next twelve months.

Review Exercise A9.1: Valuation of a Basic European Call Option

With no dividends:

Assumptions for Option Valuation		
Stock price	$ 10.00	P_E
Exercise price	$ 12.00	X_C
Annualized standard deviation	30.00%	σ_E
Dividend yield, continuously compounded	0.00%	d_E
Maturity in years	3	T_C
Risk-free rate	5.0%	r_F
Key Calculations		
d_1	0.198	
$N(d_1)$	0.578	
d_2	−0.322	
$N(d_2)$	0.374	
Price of the call option	$1.923	P_C

With annual continuously compounded dividend yield = 5%

Assumptions for Option Valuation		
Stock price	$ 10.00	P_E
Exercise price	$ 12.00	X_C
Annualized standard deviation	30.00%	σ_E
Dividend yield, continuously compounded	5.00%	d_E
Maturity in years	3	T_C
Risk-free rate	5.0%	r_F
Key Calculations		
d_1	−0.091	
$N(d_1)$	0.464	
d_2	−0.611	
$N(d_2)$	0.271	
Price of the call option	$1.195	P_C
Change in value	−37.8%	

After mastering the material in this chapter, you will be able to:

1. Implement the process of levering and unlevering and its use in valuation (10.1)
2. Choose the appropriate discount rate for a company's interest tax shields (10.2)
3. Lever a company's unlevered cost of capital and unlevered beta (10.3–10.4)
4. Unlever a company's equity cost of capital and equity beta (10.5)
5. Use comparable companies to estimate betas (10.6)
6. Avoid common errors in the levering and unlevering process (10.7)

Levering and Unlevering the Cost of Capital and Beta

CHAPTER

10

LAN Airlines S.A. (LAN), a Chilean Company, and TAM S.A. (TAM), a Brazilian company, along with their respective controlling shareholders entered into an exchange offer agreement (prospectus dated May 10, 2012) to combine LAN and TAM to form the airline with the largest fleet of aircraft of any airline in Latin America. The combined companies were named as LATAM Airlines Group, S.A. after the combination was completed. BTG Pactual, which served as the financial advisor for TAM, is an internationally recognized investment banking firm with experience in providing strategic advisory services for transactions in Latin America. BTG Pactual conducted a discounted cash flow analysis. BTG's estimates of the cost of capital for TAM, "were determined based on (i) an unlevered beta of TAM, (ii) a target capital structure of 50% debt to total capital, (iii) country risk in Chile and (iv) the long-horizon expected equity premium." Banco Bradesco BBI S.A. (Bradesco) was elected by TAM's minority shareholders to file an independent appraisal report. In its appraisal report, Bradesco describes in detail how the equity betas for LAN and TAM were computed and the exact method used to unlever those betas and then relever them for the relevant target capital structure.[1]

LATAM AIRLINES GROUP, S.A.

In this chapter, we discuss the levering and unlevering process used to measure a company's equity cost of capital based on its comparable companies and its expected capital structure. In particular, we explore alternative relationships between the equity cost of capital, the unlevered cost of capital, and the company's other costs of capital that are determined by the company's capital structure strategy and the inherent risk of its interest tax shields.

[1] See the Offer to Exchange Each Common Share, Preferred Share and American Depositary Share of TAM S.A. for 0.90 of a Common Share of LAN Airlines, S.A., dated May 10, 2012.

CHAPTER ORGANIZATION

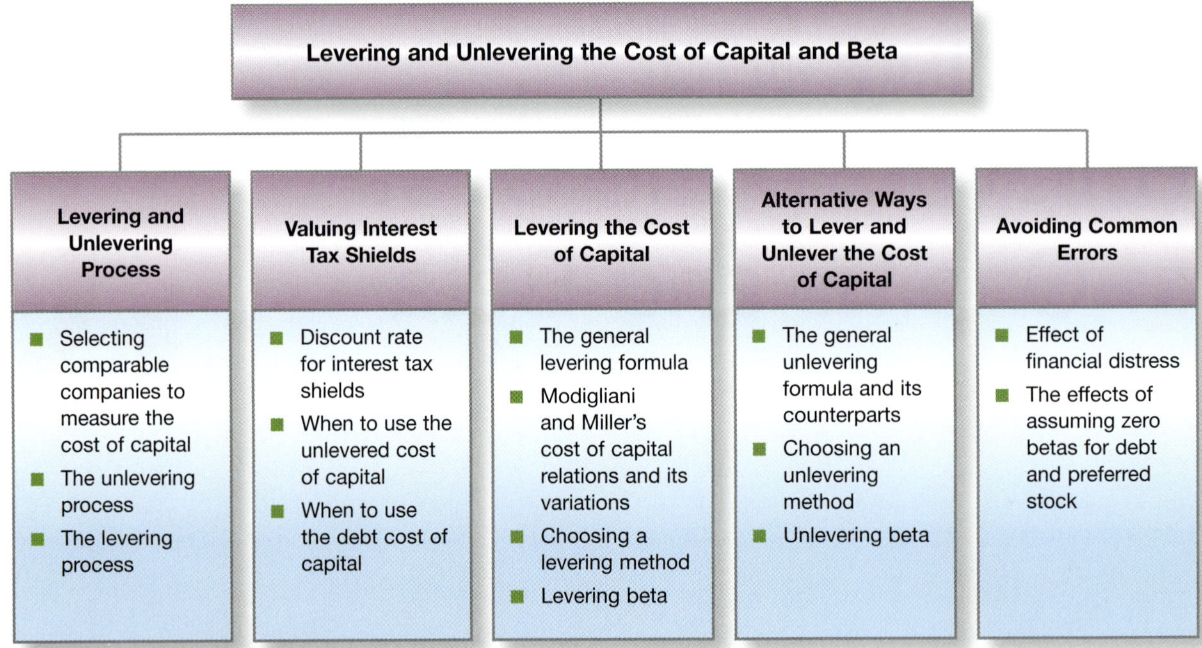

INTRODUCTION

In Chapter 5, we discussed the rudiments of the levering and unlevering process and introduced one specific form of the relationship between a company's equity cost of capital, its unlevered cost of capital, and the company's other costs of capital. In this chapter, we explore the levering and unlevering process in more detail. As it turns out, the levering and unlevering formulas have multiple forms that depend on the risk (as well as the magnitude and timing) of the company's interest tax shields, which in turn depends on the company's capital structure strategy. In other words, alternative assumptions about how to value the interest tax shields affect the relationship among the various costs of capital. In this chapter, we provide a framework for assessing the riskiness of the company's interest tax shields based on the company's capital structure strategy, which in turn leads to a specific form of the relationship between the various costs of capital for the levering and unlevering process.

More specifically, we can measure a company's unlevered cost of capital from its equity and other costs of capital, given its capital structure strategy. We call this the **unlevering process** because we remove the effects of financial leverage from the equity cost of capital in order to measure the unlevered cost of capital. We can also use these relationships to measure a company's equity cost of capital from its unlevered and non-equity costs of capital given its capital structure strategy. We call this the **levering process** because we adjust the company's unlevered cost of capital for the company's capital structure strategy. Most valuations use either the unlevering or levering process, or both processes.

In this chapter, we also show how to use these same relationships to lever and unlever the beta (or systematic risk) from the Capital Asset Pricing Model (CAPM). We demonstrate that if we use the CAPM to measure the cost of capital, using the levering and unlevering relationships that are stated in terms of CAPM betas and then applying the CAPM results in the same costs of capital that we would have calculated had we used the levering and unlevering relationships based on the costs of capital directly.

As part of our discussion, we explain how the weighted average cost of capital discounted cash flow (DCF) method embeds the value of a company's interest tax shields into the valuation based on varying assumptions about their risk, magnitude, and timing. We also show that an important reason why the weighted average cost of capital valuation method measures the value of the interest tax shields correctly under different assumptions is the choice of the levering formula that indicates how to value the interest tax shields.

10.1 AN OVERVIEW OF THE UNLEVERING AND LEVERING PROCESS

LO1 Implement the process of levering and unlevering and its use in valuation

We typically use either the weighted average cost of capital (WACC) or the adjusted present value (APV) valuation method to measure a company's value when using a discounted cash flow (DCF) valuation method. The weighted average cost of capital is the discount rate for the WACC valuation method. It requires measuring a company's after-tax costs of capital for its equity and each of its non-equity securities. To use the APV valuation method, we use two discount rates—the unlevered cost of capital and the cost of capital for the company's interest tax shields, which may or may not be equal to the unlevered cost of capital.

We often use comparable companies to measure the unlevered and equity costs of capital for the company we are valuing for two reasons. First, if the company we are valuing does not have publicly traded equity, we cannot estimate the company's equity cost of capital directly with an asset pricing model (such as the CAPM). Second, even if we can use an asset pricing model directly for the company we are valuing, we often use comparable companies to measure the unlevered or equity cost of capital for the company we are valuing in order to reduce the measurement error in our estimates, a topic we previously discussed in Chapter 8.

Identifying and Selecting Comparable Companies

How do we choose comparable companies for estimating the cost of capital? To begin, first think about what we are trying to achieve. We know that the unlevered cost of capital measures the risk of the unlevered assets of a firm. Therefore, we select comparable companies whose underlying business risk is the same as that of the company we are valuing. The business risk of a company is determined by its revenue or gross margin cyclicality and its operating leverage, which we discussed in Chapter 8. When choosing comparable companies for measuring the cost of capital, we implicitly assume that the comparable companies have the same revenue or gross margin cyclicality and operating leverage as the company we are valuing. In other words, the revenues and gross margins of those companies should all react similarly to changes in overall economic conditions and they should have similar cost structures. We know that the equity cost of capital is affected by both a company's business risk and its financial risk. However, the unlevering process removes the effect of capital structure risk (the financial risk) from the equity cost of capital, allowing us to use comparable companies that have different financial risk to measure the unlevered cost of capital as long as they have similar business risk.

To choose comparable companies that we believe have the same underlying business risk, we typically begin by identifying companies that are broadly in the same line of business as the company we are valuing. In addition, we assess the similarity of the companies' production processes and cost structures—in particular, the extent to which they have similar proportions of variable and fixed costs (operating leverage)—and potentially the similarity of growth opportunities.[2] The degree of operating leverage could be different if two firms use very different production processes or have different business models. For example, a restaurant chain that leases all of its locations is likely to have a higher fixed cost structure than a restaurant chain that uses a franchise model for its business where the company neither leases nor owns any of its restaurant locations.

Once we have selected the comparable companies, we begin the unlevering process by measuring the equity cost of capital for each comparable company and for the company we are valuing, if possible. We then unlever the equity cost of capital of each company to measure each company's unlevered cost of capital using one or more of the formulas we present in this chapter. Based on our analysis of the unlevered costs of capital for these companies, we select a value or range of values for the unlevered cost of capital for the company we are valuing based on the unlevered costs of capital of the comparable companies and the alternative unlevering formulas used. We discuss different ways to weight, or choose from the distribution of, the unlevered cost of capital estimates later in the chapter. If we are using the adjusted present value method to value the company, we use our estimate of the unlevered cost of capital.

If we are using the weighted average cost of capital method to value the company, we lever the unlevered cost of capital for the expected capital structure, often called the **target capital structure**, of the company we are valuing in order to measure the company's equity cost of capital. That estimate, in conjunction with the company's other costs of capital, allows us to measure the company's weighted average cost of capital. As we discuss later, when we select a formula to lever the unlevered cost of capital, we are also measuring the weighted average cost of capital based on a particular assumption about the valuation of the interest tax shields.

Unlevering and levering the CAPM beta is an alternative to unlevering and levering the cost of capital. Unlevering and levering betas is the more popular alternative in practice than unlevering and levering

---

[2] All else equal, companies with more growth opportunities have higher risk. See, Bernardo, A., Chowdhry, B., Goyal, A., 2007, "Growth Options, Beta, and the Cost of Capital," *Financial Management* 36, pp. 5–17; and Da, Zhi, R. Guo, and R. Jagannathan, 2012, "CAPM for Estimating the Cost of Equity Capital: Interpreting the Empirical Evidence," *Journal of Financial Economics*, 103, pp. 204–220.

the costs of capital directly, which is undoubtedly attributable to the popularity of the CAPM in practice. As we show later in the chapter, unlevering and levering beta is equivalent to unlevering and levering the cost of capital as long as the costs of capital are appropriately measured by the CAPM.

As an alternative to unlevering the equity cost of capital, we use essentially this same process to unlever the equity betas of the comparable companies and the company we are valuing. For example, we can unlever the equity betas of each company to estimate each company's unlevered beta and then use the CAPM to measure the unlevered cost of capital (see Chapter 8). If we need to measure the company's equity cost of capital, we lever the unlevered beta to obtain the equity beta of the firm we are valuing based on its target capital structure and then use the CAPM to measure the equity cost of capital. Unlevering the equity cost of capital that is based on the CAPM or unlevering the equity beta and then applying the CAPM, results in the same unlevered cost of capital estimate. The same is true for levering the unlevered cost of capital or levering an unlevered beta to estimate the equity cost of capital—as long as the CAPM is used in both processes.

The Steps in the Unlevering Process

We unlever a company's cost of capital using estimates of its equity cost of capital, the costs of capital of each of its non-equity securities, and its capital structure strategy. Instead of unlevering the equity cost of capital directly, we can also unlever the equity beta. We call this process the unlevering process, and summarize the processes for unlevering the equity cost of capital and equity beta in Exhibit 10.1.

EXHIBIT 10.1 The Steps in the Unlevering Process

	Unlevering the Equity Cost of Capital Directly	Unlevering the Capital Asset Pricing Model Beta, β
For each comparable company (and the company being valued, when relevant):		
1	Measure the company's equity cost of capital, r_E, using an asset pricing model	Measure the company's equity beta, β_E, using the Capital Asset Pricing Model
2	Measure the cost of capital for each of its non-equity securities (e.g., r_D, r_{PS})	Measure the beta for each of its non-equity securities (e.g., β_D, β_{PS})
3	Measure the capital structure ratios or the value of each security (e.g., V_E/V_F, V_D/V_F, V_{PS}/V_F or V_E, V_D, V_{PS})	Same
4	Measure the income tax rate for interest tax shields, T_{INT}, discount rate, r_{ITS}, and any other information needed to measure the value of the company's interest tax shields, V_{ITS}	Same
5	Choose the appropriate unlevering formula for that company	Same
6	Measure the company's unlevered cost of capital, r_{UA}	Measure the company's unlevered beta, β_{UA}
Based on the distribution of the estimates of the unlevered costs of capital or betas:		
7	Measure the unlevered cost of capital (or range of the unlevered costs of capital) that best reflects the operating risk of the company being valued, r_{UA}	Measure the unlevered beta (or range of unlevered betas) that best reflects the operating risk of the company being valued, β_{UA}
8	Not relevant	Measure the company's unlevered cost of capital using the Capital Asset Pricing Model, if needed for the valuation

The Steps in the Levering Process

Once we measure the unlevered cost of capital for the company we are valuing based on the comparable companies and company of interest, we measure the equity cost of capital for the company we are valuing based on the estimate of the unlevered cost of capital, the costs of capital of the company's non-equity securities, and the capital structure strategy that is relevant for the valuation. Alternatively, instead of calculating the equity cost of capital directly from the unlevered cost of capital, we can first calculate the equity beta from the unlevered beta and then calculate the equity cost of capital using the CAPM. Either way, we call this the levering process, and summarize the processes for levering the unlevered cost of capital and unlevered beta in Exhibit 10.2. We then use the equity cost of capital and the other information used in this process to measure a company's weighted average cost of capital.

EXHIBIT 10.2 The Steps in the Levering Process

	Levering the Unlevered Cost of Capital, r_{UA}	Levering the Unlevered Capital Asset Pricing Model Beta, β_{UA}
For the company being valued:		
1	Measure the company's unlevered cost of capital or range of unlevered costs of capital, r_{UA} (see Exhibit 10.1)	Measure the company's unlevered beta, β_{UA}, or range of unlevered betas (see Exhibit 10.1)
2	Measure the expected capital structure ratios or the value of each of the company's non-equity securities (e.g., V_E/V_F, V_D/V_F, V_{PS}/V_F or V_E, V_D, V_{PS})	Same
3	Measure the cost of capital for each of the company's non-equity securities based on the company's expected future capital structure (e.g., r_D, r_{PS})	Measure the beta for each of the company's non-equity securities (e.g., β_D, β_{PS})
4	Measure the income tax rate, T_{INT}, discount rate, r_{ITS}, and any other information needed to measure the value of the company's interest tax shields, V_{ITS}	Same
5	Choose the appropriate levering formula	Same
6	Measure the company's equity cost of capital, r_E	Measure the company's equity beta, β_E
7	Not relevant	Measure the company's equity cost of capital, r_E, using the Capital Asset Pricing Model

Valuation Key 10.1

The unlevering and levering processes are used in most DCF valuations. If we are valuing a company using the APV method, we use the unlevering process to measure the unlevered cost of capital for the company being valued (if it is publicly traded) as well as for the relevant publicly traded comparable companies. If we are valuing a company using the WACC method, we typically begin by using the unlevering process to measure the company's unlevered cost of capital if we have comparable companies to work with or if the company is considering a change in capital structure; and then, we use the levering process to measure the company's equity cost of capital and ultimately its weighted average cost of capital.

Measuring the Inputs

The inputs necessary to lever and unlever either the cost of capital or CAPM beta are similar. Both require estimates of a company's capital structure ratios and potentially its income tax rates. Naturally, levering and unlevering the cost of capital requires estimates of the companies' costs of capital, while levering and unlevering betas requires estimates of the companies' betas. How we measure the inputs when we lever a company's unlevered cost of capital or unlevered beta for the company we are valuing, however, differs on one fundamental dimension from how we measure the inputs when we unlever a company's cost of capital or beta for the comparable companies and the company being valued.

We typically use comparable companies (and the firm being valued if publicly traded) to measure the unlevered cost of capital either by unlevering the companies' equity cost of capital or its equity beta. Even if we unlever the equity cost of capital, we often use the CAPM and, thus, beta, to measure the equity cost of capital. Since we typically measure beta using historical data (see Chapter 8), which reflects the company's weighted average capital structure over the estimation period, the capital structure ratios we use to unlever beta are the company's weighted average capital structure ratios over the estimation period. Naturally, if a company's capital structure is approximately constant, then the company's current capital structure ratios should be sufficiently similar to its weighted average capital structure ratios. A company's income tax rate for interest tax shields (if needed) is measured over the estimation period as well, although income tax rates tend to be more constant over time than capital structure ratios.

Once we have an estimate of what we believe is a company's forward looking unlevered cost of capital or unlevered beta, we lever the unlevered cost of capital or unlevered beta for the company we are valuing using the company's forward looking or expected capital structure and tax rates and not its historical or current capital structure ratios and income tax rates. Doing so results in a forward looking estimate of the company's equity cost of capital or equity beta.

10.2 SELECTING THE DISCOUNT RATE AND MEASURING THE VALUE OF INTEREST TAX SHIELDS

LO2 Choose the appropriate discount rate for a company's interest tax shields

We first assess the risk of a company's interest tax shields in order to measure the discount rate with which we—either explicitly, using the APV valuation method, or implicitly, using the WACC valuation method—value a company's interest tax shields. Companies adopt various types of capital structure strategies. Some companies adopt a target capital structure stated in terms of a target debt to total value ratio that is defined in terms of market values. For example, a past survey of chief financial officers (CFOs) indicated that about 10% of the CFOs surveyed had a strict target debt ratio, 34% had "a somewhat tight target range," 37% had a "flexible target range," and the remaining 19% had "no target."[3] Some companies—for example, companies that undergo a debt recapitalization—may have a strategy of paying down their outstanding debt for a certain number of years until the debt level reaches a certain long-run target capital structure ratio. Regardless of which capital structure strategy a company adopts, the capital structure strategy (how a company intends to manage its capital structure) affects the risk, as well as the magnitude and timing, of the interest tax shields and therefore, their value.

The Conditions When the Cost of Debt Is a Reasonable Discount Rate for Interest Tax Shields

If the risk of a company's interest tax shields, or some of the company's interest tax shields, is solely determined by the company's ability to generate sufficient taxable income to capture the benefits of its interest tax shields (assuming that interest is fully tax deductible even if it reduces the company's taxable income to zero), then the risk of the underlying debt is a reasonable measure of the risk of the interest tax shields. Why? Because the debt's required rate of return—as set by lenders in an arm's-length transaction—indicates the company's ability to generate sufficient cash flows to meet its required payments. Further, this risk should be similar to the risk that the company can generate sufficient taxable income to be able to use the interest tax shields (to utilize those tax deductions). In such cases, we use the debt cost of capital as the discount rate for the interest tax shields. We discuss how limitations on the deduction of interest, such as those in the Tax Cuts and Jobs Act of 2017 (discussed in Chapter 3), may alter our thinking on the riskiness of the interest tax shields later in this section.

In this chapter, we assume that the cost of debt, r_D, can be used to calculate a company's expected interest expense deduction for income tax purposes. This may not be the case for all firms. The cost of debt at the date of issuance may not equal the current cost of debt, for the company's cost of debt can change over time because of shifts in the real risk-free rate of return or expected inflation as market conditions change. We discuss the implications of this difference later in the chapter, but for now, we assume that the current cost of debt multiplied by the value of the debt equals a company's expected interest expense deduction for income tax purposes.

Given these assumptions, the value of the interest tax shields at time 0, when the discount rate for all interest tax shields is equal to the cost of debt, $V_{ITS@r_D,0}$, is equal to

$$V_{ITS@r_D,0} = \sum_{t=1}^{\infty} \frac{ITS_t}{(1+r_{D,t})^t} = \sum_{t=1}^{\infty} \frac{r_{D,t} \times V_{D,t} \times T_{INT,t}}{(1+r_{D,t})^t}$$

Under what circumstances is a company's cost of debt a reasonable discount rate for its interest tax shields? One such circumstance is when the amount of the outstanding debt that the firm will keep in the future is independent of the value of the firm, the amount of debt is modest relative to the value of the firm, and tax laws do not impose limitations on the deductibility of interest. If we know the amount of debt a company has outstanding and that it will not change if the value of the firm changes, the only risk is related to the company's ability to generate sufficient taxable income to take advantage of its interest tax shields; as such, the cost of debt is a reasonable discount rate to use for the company's interest tax shields resulting from the company's current outstanding debt. In so doing, we assume that the risk of

[3] See Graham, J. R., and C. R. Harvey, "The Theory and Practice of Corporate Finance: Evidence From the Field," *Journal of Financial Economics* 60 (2001), pp. 187–243.

refinancing the debt when it matures is not related to the riskiness of the business as the amount of debt is well below the company's debt capacity.

An extreme example of this situation is a company with zero expected growth in perpetuity, a fixed amount of perpetual debt outstanding, and facing a constant tax rate in perpetuity.[4] In this case, it is reasonable to discount the interest tax shields at the cost of debt. The value of the interest tax shields is equal to

$$V_{ITS@r_D} = \frac{ITS}{r_D} = \frac{r_D \times V_D \times T_{INT}}{r_D} = T_{INT} \times V_D \qquad \textbf{(10.1)}$$

Valuation in Practice 10.1

Companies Can Increase Financial Leverage by Repurchasing Equity: Philip Morris International, Inc. (PM) The Board of Directors of Philip Morris International Inc. (NYSE/Euronext Paris: PM) announced a new three-year share repurchase program of $18 billion on June 13, 2012. It was anticipated that the new program would be initiated August 1, 2012, following completion of the existing three-year program of $12 billion that began in May 2010 and that would conclude ahead of schedule. As previously announced, Philip Morris had a share repurchase target for 2012 of $6.0 billion.

Because of the recent share repurchases, the book value of shareholders' equity as of March 31, 2012, was only $112 million, so that share repurchases could drive the book value of shareholders' equity negative. The scheduled repurchases will also increase the company's debt-to-equity ratio (as measured in market values).

Source: For more information, visit Philip Morris' website at www.pmi.com/investors.

The Conditions When the Unlevered Cost of Capital Is a Reasonable Discount Rate for the Interest Tax Shields[5]

On the other hand, if the risk of a company's interest tax shields is linked directly to the riskiness of the company's assets, then the unlevered cost of capital is a reasonable discount rate for the company's interest tax shields. For example, if the company has a constant target capital structure (in terms of the proportion of debt to equity), then the amount of its debt—and in turn, the amount of its interest tax shields—depends on the value of the firm in each future period. Since the amount of the interest tax shields is directly linked to the value of the firm, the risk of a company's interest tax shields is approximately the risk of the company's underlying assets—the unlevered cost of capital. The presumption here is that a firm will adjust its capital structure in order to maintain a constant proportionate capital structure—if the value of the firm decreases, the firm reduces its debt; if the value of the firm increases, the firm increases its debt.

An extreme example of this situation is when a company has a strategy of a constant debt-to-value capital structure and issues debt with a very short maturity such that it must continually refinance its debt. As the company's value changes, the company correspondingly changes the amount of its outstanding debt. The risk of the interest tax shields depends on not only the ability of the company to capture the benefits of its interest tax shields but also on the amount of debt the company will have outstanding. The amount of debt the company will have outstanding depends directly on the value of the firm.[6] Given these assumptions, the value of the interest tax shields at time 0, when the discount rate for all interest tax shields is the unlevered cost of capital, $V_{ITS@r_{UA},0}$, is equal to

$$V_{ITS@r_{UA},0} = \sum_{t=1}^{\infty} \frac{ITS_t}{(1+r_{UA,t})^t} = \sum_{t=1}^{\infty} \frac{r_D \times V_{D,t} \times T_{INT,t}}{(1+r_{UA,t})^t}$$

---

[4] These are some of the assumptions made by Modigliani, F., and M. H. Miller, "Corporate Income Taxes and the Cost of Capital: A Correction," *American Economic Review* 53 (June 1963), pp. 433–443, which we introduced in Chapter 5 and discuss in more detail in the next section.

[5] For a discussion of this approach see, Ruback, R. S., "A Simple Approach to Valuing Risky Cash Flows," *Financial Management* vol. 31, no. 2 (Summer, 2002), pp. 85–103.

[6] See Harris, R. S., Pringle, J. J. "Risk-adjusted Discount Rates—Extensions from the Average Risk Case," *Journal of Financial Research* vol. 8, no. 3 (1985), pp. 237–244, which examines the continuous financing assumption thoroughly; for an additional explanation and a discrete time version of the Harris and Pringle model, see Taggart Jr., R. A., "Consistent Valuation and Cost of Capital Expressions with Corporate and Personal Taxes," *Financial Management* vol. 20 (1991), pp. 8–20.

Discount Rate for Interest Tax Shields with Annual Refinancing

Some firms follow a strict target capital structure strategy, but, of course, even these companies do not refinance continually. Even if a company pursues a target capital structure policy in terms of some fixed target debt-to-equity ratio, such capital structures are "sticky" because of adjustment costs. In other words, the transactions costs of adjusting the capital structure are not zero. Whether a company issues debt, issues equity, calls debt, or repurchases shares, it will incur transactions costs. As such, managers do not instantaneously adjust their debt levels for every fluctuation in the value of a company's equity. In this section we illustrate how to measure the value of the interest tax shields when the company adjusts its capital structure annually.

If a company only adjusts to its target capital structure annually, we know the exact amount of debt the company will have for the first year subsequent to the valuation date because it will not make adjustments to the level of its debt during that year. If the company sets the amount of debt outstanding as of the valuation date based on the value of the firm and the target debt-to-equity ratio, the riskiness of the interest tax shields for the first year is the company's ability to generate sufficient taxable income to take advantage of its interest tax shields. For subsequent years, however, the amount of debt (and therefore the magnitude of the interest tax shields) depends on the value of the firm at each successive year. At the end of each year, we assume the firm will refinance itself to maintain a constant target capital structure, so the amount of debt the company will issue (or retire) depends on the value of the firm at the end of each subsequent year (each annual refinancing date).[7]

As of Year 0, we know the interest tax shield that is available in Year 1, but as of Year 0, future interest tax shields depend on the value of the firm at each subsequent year-end. Thus, it is reasonable to use the cost of debt to discount the interest tax shield in Year 1 and to use the unlevered cost of capital to discount the value of all remaining interest tax shields as of the end of Year 1, back to Year 0. So the value of all the interest tax shields at Year 0, $V_{ITS,0}$, is

$$V_{ITS,0} = V_{ITS@r_D,0} + V_{ITS@r_{UA},0} = \frac{r_D \times V_{D,0} \times T_{INT}}{1+r_D} + \frac{V_{ITS,1}}{1+r_{UA}} \tag{10.2}$$

Interest Deduction Limitations or Caps

Recall from Chapter 3, some countries limit the amount of interest a company can deduct for income tax purposes.[8] Naturally, interest deduction caps can affect the expected amount and riskiness (discount rate) of interest tax shields, depending on the interest deduction limitation rules. For example, if the interest deduction caps, such as in the U.S. and the U.K., are a function of the company's performance (for example, a percentage of EBITDA), then the interest deduction cap affects how we measure the expected amount of a company's interest deduction and it affects the riskiness (discount rate) of the interest tax shields.

It is obvious that a limitation on the deduction of interest that is a function of the company's performance has the potential to increase the riskiness of the tax shield relative to no interest deduction cap. All else equal, imposing a limitation on the tax deductibility of interest based on a function of the company's performance would make it more likely to value a company's interest tax shields at the unlevered cost of capital rather than at the cost of debt, even for a zero-growth company with a fixed amount of perpetual, fixed interest rate, debt. For example, consider valuing such a zero-growth, perpetual debt, company for which its interest expense is near the interest deduction cap. Although the company is not expected to grow, its performance is still uncertain and thus, its performance will fluctuate such that the company may not be able to deduct all of its interest. Thus, even in the perpetual debt case, interest deduction caps can make interest tax shields riskier than the underlying debt resulting in a discount rate for interest tax shields that is greater than the cost of debt.

[7] Miles and Ezzell extended Modigliani and Miller's original work for a company that refinances itself annually to maintain a constant capital structure. See: Miles, J. A., and J. R. Ezzell, "The Weighted Average Cost of Capital, Perfect Capital Markets, and Project Life: A Clarification," *Journal of Financial and Quantitative Analysis* vol. 15, no. 3 (1980), pp. 719–730; and Miles, J. A., and J. R. Ezzell, J.R. (1985), "Reformulating Tax Shield Valuation: A Note," *Journal of Finance* vol. 40 (1985), pp. 1485–1492.

[8] Under the U.S. Tax Cuts and Jobs Act of 2017, the deduction for interest expense is limited to 30% of adjusted taxable income, which is essentially a company's EBITDA (excluding any business interest income) through tax years beginning before January 1, 2022 and essentially a company's EBIT (excluding any business interest income) thereafter.

Guidelines for Choosing Discount Rates for Interest Tax Shields

None of the discussed capital structure strategies is reflective of the actual capital structure strategies of real companies. These examples, however, provide a useful framework to guide the selection of a discount rate for interest tax shields that is bounded between the cost of debt and unlevered cost of capital ($r_D \le r_{ITS} \le r_{UA}$). While this range of discount rates for interest tax shields is reasonable for most companies, under certain conditions, even the cost of debt is too high for discounting the interest tax shields of some companies—or at least some of the interest tax shields of certain companies.[9] One intuitive rule of thumb we can glean from our framework is that if a company has existing debt and if management does not intend to adjust the debt (for example, early repayment) as a function of the company's performance, and if the amount of interest expense is not near any limitation on the tax deductibility of interest, a reasonable cost of capital for the existing debt's interest tax shields prior to maturity is the debt cost of capital ($r_{ITS} = r_D$ for debt outstanding), which approximates the risk that the company's taxable income will be sufficiently high that it will be able to use the interest tax shields. In addition, consider the survey on capital structure strategies discussed previously in which 10% of the companies indicated they had a very strict target debt ratio and 34% said they had a strict target range. For these companies, it is probably reasonable to value their interest tax shields at the unlevered cost of capital. However, even for such companies, they might have a minimum amount of debt they would maintain in their capital structure, and thus, a portion of the company's interest tax shields would be discounted at the cost of debt. Limitations on the tax deductibility of interest such as 30% of EBIT or EBITDA make it more likely that we would discount interest tax shields at the unlevered cost of capital, especially if the interest expense is near the limitation.

Our framework is not as clear for debt a company expects to issue to either replace existing debt once it matures or to finance growth if the firm does not have a target debt ratio. If a company is already using a substantial amount of financial leverage and does not have much additional debt capacity, the amount of new or replacement debt the company can issue is likely dependent on the future value of the firm. In this situation a reasonable cost of capital for interest tax shields from new or replacement debt is the unlevered cost of capital. On the other hand, if the company is not using much financial leverage, has substantial additional debt capacity, and if the value of the firm is relatively stable, the debt a company issues in the future will be less dependent on the value of the firm. Such a company might have a policy of having some amount of debt—that may even be modestly increasing—that is largely independent of its value for some finite period of time. In this case, we could use the cost of debt to value the tax shields.

This framework also provides the following additional intuition—in the long run, it is unlikely that the amount of debt a company will issue, above some minimal amount of total debt, will be independent of the company's value. Eventually, the risk of the interest tax shields from debt, above some minimal amount of debt, approaches the risk of the unlevered cost of capital of the company. As such, the discount rate for the interest tax shields is often the unlevered cost of capital in continuing value calculations. Thus, it is possible, and even likely, that the best way to discount interest tax shields is to discount certain interest tax shields—such as the interest tax shields for existing debt or a modest amount of debt—at the cost of debt and the remaining interest tax shields at the unlevered cost of capital. This valuation of interest tax shields is a combination of the previous two formulas for discounting certain interest tax shields at the cost of debt and discounting certain interest tax shields at the unlevered cost of capital.

$$V_{ITS,0} = \sum_{t=1}^{\infty} \frac{ITS_{t,@r_{UA}}}{(1 + r_{UA,t})^t} + \sum_{t=1}^{\infty} \frac{ITS_{t,@r_D}}{(1 + r_{D,t})^t} \quad \textbf{(10.3)}$$

$$V_{ITS,0} = V_{ITS@r_{UA,0}} + V_{ITS@r_{D,0}} \quad \textbf{(10.3')}$$

We note that when we use the weighted average cost of capital DCF method and apply a constant weighted average cost of capital, we are assuming that the company is pursuing a constant debt-to-value capital structure strategy. In other words, the valuation assumes that if the value of the company increases (or decreases), the company adjusts the amount of debt outstanding to have a constant proportionate capital structure. Using the alternative unlevering methods we discuss in this chapter can be useful to identify a range of unlevered costs of capital (or range of equity costs of capital) to use in a valuation.

---

[9] For example, if a company has a policy of not increasing (or even decreasing) its debt when it is performing well, it might be the case that the discount rate for interest tax shields is lower than the cost of debt. See: Grinblatt, M., and S. Titman, *Financial Markets and Corporate Strategy*, 2nd ed., McGraw-Hill Companies, Inc. (2002).

Valuation Key 10.2

The selection of a discount rate for interest tax shields is a complex issue. For outstanding debt (and even for low future levels of debt), when the amount of debt is independent of the value of the firm, the cost of debt is a reasonable discount rate for the interest tax shields $r_{ITS} = r_D$. When the amount of outstanding debt is closely tied to the value of a firm, such as an assumption of a constant proportionate capital structure, the unlevered cost of capital is a reasonable discount rate for interest tax shields $r_{ITS} = r_{UA}$. Naturally, these are the two polar cases and the discount rate for interest tax shields for some companies can be a mix of the cost of debt and the unlevered cost of capital.

10.3 LEVERING THE UNLEVERED COST OF CAPITAL

LO3 Lever a company's unlevered cost of capital and unlevered beta

In this section, we develop an intuitive framework for estimating a company's levered (or equity) cost of capital based on its unlevered, debt, and other costs of capital, as well as its capital structure ratios. For the purposes of this chapter, we assume that the value from financing is equal to the value of a company's interest tax shields, V_{ITS} ($V_{FIN} = V_{ITS}$), and any potential effects of financial distress, bankruptcy costs, agency costs, and personal income taxes have no significant impact on the value from debt financing. In other words, we assume that the present value of a company's expected interest tax shields—discounted at the appropriate discount rate—captures the entire effect of financial leverage on the value of the firm.[10]

The Economic Balance Sheet

The starting point for the informal derivation of the various formulas to lever a company's cost of capital is the economic balance sheet, which we introduced in Chapter 1. On the economic balance sheet, the market value of a company's resources (its assets) is equal to the market value of the claims on those assets (securities such as debt, preferred and common equity). The value of a company's assets is composed of the value of its unlevered assets, V_{UA}, and the value of its interest tax shields, V_{ITS} (remember, we are assuming that interest tax shields are the only valuation impact of financing). The values of the claims on these assets that we discuss in this chapter are the value of its debt, V_D, the value of its preferred stock, V_{PS}, and the value of its equity, V_E (we discuss the effect of a company using other, equity-linked, securities in Chapter 12). For such a company, the economic balance sheet is equal to the following:

$$V_{UA} + V_{ITS} = V_D + V_{PS} + V_E$$

Since the value of a company's assets is equal to the value of its securities, it is reasonable to assume that the dollar returns on its assets and securities—measured as the beginning value of an asset or security multiplied by its respective cost of capital or return—also follows this relationship. That is, the dollar return on a company's resources is equal to the dollar return of the company's securities. The company has a value and cost of capital for each of its assets and securities. The cost of capital for the unlevered assets is $r_{UA.}$ For now, we use a cost of capital for the interest tax shields, r_{ITS}, and we do not make any assumptions regarding its relationships to other costs of capital. The economic balance sheet equation expressed in terms of dollar returns is equal to:

$$r_{UA} \times V_{UA} + r_{ITS} \times V_{ITS} = r_D \times V_D + r_{PS} \times V_{PS} + r_E \times V_E$$

Using the above formula as our starting point, we develop a general relationship between a company's equity cost of capital and its other costs of capital (the unlevered cost of capital and the costs of capital for its non-common equity securities). Note if a company finances itself with non-common equity securities other than debt and preferred stock, for example, warrants or stock options, the above formula would include a component for each of those non-common equity securities as well, which would carry through the rest of the formulas in this chapter.

[10] See Grinblatt and Liu for a formal framework for a broad class of dynamic debt policies that depend on the asset's free cash flows, value, and past performance, and derive the tax-adjusted cost of capital for free cash flows and analyze the conditions under which the weighted average cost of capital is an appropriate discount rate. Grinblatt, Mark and Jun Liu, "Debt Policy, Corporate Taxes, and Discount Rates," *Journal of Economic Theory*, 2008, vol. 141, issue 1, pp. 225-254.

The General Levering Formula

If we rearrange the terms in the above formula so that the equity cost of capital is on the left side, we can derive a formula to measure the equity cost of capital.[11]

$$r_E = r_{UA} + (r_{UA} - r_D) \times \frac{V_D}{V_E} + (r_{UA} - r_{PS}) \times \frac{V_{PS}}{V_E} - (r_{UA} - r_{ITS}) \times \frac{V_{ITS}}{V_E} \quad \textbf{(10.4)}$$

The key insight to glean from this levering formula is that a company's equity cost of capital is always greater than its unlevered cost of capital when the company uses debt or preferred financing, since both the cost of debt and cost of preferred are less than the unlevered cost of capital. If a company only issues common equity, its equity cost of capital is equal to its unlevered cost of capital, for all of the other components are equal to zero. Two components of the formula add premiums to the unlevered cost of capital for the debt and preferred financing issued by the company, the implication being that a company's equity cost of capital becomes riskier than the unlevered cost of capital as the company issues more debt and preferred stock. These two components reflect the fact that the equity becomes riskier as the firm promises to pay greater fixed amounts to the debtholders and preferred equityholders who have seniority over the common equityholders. The last term in the formula, however, decreases the equity cost of capital when the discount rate for interest tax shields is less than the unlevered cost of capital—in other words, when the company creates an asset through financing (the value of the interest tax shields)—that is potentially less risky than the company's business risk (the risk of the company's unlevered assets). The last term potentially mitigates the increase in the cost of equity from having debt in the capital structure.

We do not show time subscripts in the previous formula because we measure each input at the same point in time. As in the weighted average cost of capital formula, the equity cost of capital and the inputs to the right of the equality sign need not be constant over time. These costs of capital will change if the company's business risk or financial risk changes or if economy-wide shifts in required rates of return (for example, an increase or decrease in the risk-free rate of return) occur.

Valuation Key 10.3

Common equityholders are the residual claimants of a company's assets, and hence, a company's common equity cost of capital is always greater than its unlevered cost of capital when the company issues debt or preferred. If a company issues debt and preferred securities, then its equity cost of capital is equal to its unlevered cost of capital plus a premium related to the amount of debt and preferred it uses, with a potential downward adjustment related to the risk of its interest tax shields.

[11] We derive this formula by isolating the equity cost of capital on the left-hand side of the formula.

$$r_E = r_{UA} \times \frac{V_{UA}}{V_E} + r_{ITS} \times \frac{V_{ITS}}{V_E} - r_D \times \frac{V_D}{V_E} - r_{PS} \times \frac{V_{PS}}{V_E}$$

Then, from the economic balance sheet, we know that the sum of the value of a company's securities minus the value of its interest tax shields is equal to the value of the unlevered firm, ($V_{UA} = V_E + V_D + V_{PS} - V_{ITS}$). We substitute this relationship in the above formula and rearrange terms to get

$$r_E = r_{UA} \times \left(\frac{V_E + V_D + V_{PS} - V_{ITS}}{V_E}\right) - r_D \times \frac{V_D}{V_E} - r_{PS} \times \frac{V_{PS}}{V_E} + r_{ITS} \times \frac{V_{ITS}}{V_E}$$

$$r_E = r_{UA} \times \left(\frac{V_E}{V_E} + \frac{V_D}{V_E} + \frac{V_{PS}}{V_E}\right) - r_{UA} \times \frac{V_{ITS}}{V_E} - r_D \times \frac{V_D}{V_E} - r_{PS} \times \frac{V_{PS}}{V_E} + r_{ITS} \times \frac{V_{ITS}}{V_E}$$

$$r_E = r_{UA} \times \left(1 + \frac{V_D}{V_E} + \frac{V_{PS}}{V_E}\right) - r_D \times \frac{V_D}{V_E} - r_{PS} \times \frac{V_{PS}}{V_E} - (r_{UA} - r_{ITS}) \times \frac{V_{ITS}}{V_E}$$

$$r_E = r_{UA} + (r_{UA} - r_D) \times \frac{V_D}{V_E} + (r_{UA} - r_{PS}) \times \frac{V_{PS}}{V_E} - (r_{UA} - r_{ITS}) \times \frac{V_{ITS}}{V_E}$$

Levering Formulas for Specific Simplifying Assumptions for the Value of Interest Tax Shields

We now use the above general formula and apply it to a series of special cases where we can write the present value of the interest tax shields, V_{ITS}, using expressions that rely on, say, the debt and unlevered costs of capital and the amount of debt.

Value All Interest Tax Shields at the Unlevered Cost of Capital or When Interest Is Not Tax Deductible (V_{ITS} = 0). If interest is not tax deductible, then the value of a company's interest tax shields, V_{ITS}, is, by definition, zero.[12] If the value of a company's interest tax shields is equal to zero, the last term in the levering formula (Equation 10.4) is equal to zero. Moreover, if the discount rate for all of a company's interest tax shields is equal to the unlevered cost of capital ($r_{ITS} = r_{UA}$), then the risk of the company's assets (operating assets and interest tax shields) is the same, and, again, the last term in Equation 10.4 is equal to zero.[13]

Thus, if either the discount rate for all of a company's interest tax shields is equal to the unlevered cost of capital, or if interest is not tax deductible (in other words, the value of a company's interest tax shields is equal to zero), then the levering formula becomes

$$r_E = r_{UA} + (r_{UA} - r_D) \times \frac{V_D}{V_E} + (r_{UA} - r_{PS}) \times \frac{V_{PS}}{V_E} \qquad \textbf{(10.5)}$$

Equation 10.5 should look familiar. This is the equation we discussed in Chapter 5 when we assumed that interest tax shields were valued at the unlevered cost of capital.

Value Certain Interest Tax Shields at the Cost of Debt and the Remaining Interest Tax Shields at the Unlevered Cost of Capital. As we discussed in the previous section, it is possible, and even likely, that the best way to discount interest tax shields is to discount certain interest tax shields—such as the interest tax shields for existing debt or a modest amount of debt—at the cost of debt and the remaining interest tax shields at the unlevered cost of capital. We replace the adjustment for the effect of interest tax shields in Equation 10.4 with two adjustments—an adjustment for interest tax shields discounted at the cost of debt and an adjustment for interest tax shields discounted at the unlevered cost of capital (see Equations 10.3 and 10.3'). As shown in Equation 10.6, only interest tax shields discounted at the cost of debt have a direct effect on the equity cost of capital

$$r_E = r_{UA} + (r_{UA} - r_D) \times \frac{V_D}{V_E} + (r_{UA} - r_{PS}) \times \frac{V_{PS}}{V_E} - (r_{UA} - r_D) \times \frac{V_{ITS@r_D}}{V_E} - (r_{UA} - r_{UA}) \times \frac{V_{ITS@r_{UA}}}{V_E}$$

$$r_E = r_{UA} + (r_{UA} - r_D) \times \frac{V_D}{V_E} + (r_{UA} - r_{PS}) \times \frac{V_{PS}}{V_E} - (r_{UA} - r_D) \times \frac{V_{ITS@r_D}}{V_E}$$

$$r_E = r_{UA} + (r_{UA} - r_D) \times \frac{V_D - V_{ITS@r_D}}{V_E} + (r_{UA} - r_{PS}) \times \frac{V_{PS}}{V_E} \qquad \textbf{(10.6)}$$

We should note that interest tax shields discounted at the unlevered cost of capital have an indirect effect on the equity cost of capital through their impact on the value of the equity and hence the leverage ratio.

The intuition underpinning this formula is that with no tax shields or with tax shields valued at the unlevered cost of capital, the risk of all of the company's assets equals the unlevered cost of capital. However, if some of the interest tax shields are valued at the debt cost of capital, the equityholders have a claim to a portfolio of assets with less risk, on average, than a portfolio of assets with risk only equal to

---

[12] See: Modigliani, F., and M. H. Miller, "The Cost of Capital, Corporate Finance and the Theory of Investment," *American Economic Review* 48 (1958), pp. 261–297. Stiglitz and Rubinstein show that M-M's work holds even if companies have risky debt; see See Stiglitz, J. E., "A Re-Examination of the Modigliani-Miller Theorem," *American Economic Review* (December 1969), pp. 187–193; Stiglitz, J. E., "On the Irrelevance of Corporate Financial Policy," *American Economic Review* (December 1974), pp. 851–866; Rubinstein, M. E., "A Mean-Variance Synthesis of Corporate Financial Theory," *Journal of Financial and Quantitative Analysis* (March 1973), pp. 167–181; and Conine, T. E., "Corporate Debt and Corporate Taxes: An Extension," *Journal of Finance* (September 1980), pp. 1033–1037.

[13] This is a special case of the model in Miles and Ezzell; see: Miles, J. A., and J. R. Ezzell, "The Weighted Average Cost of Capital, Perfect Capital Markets, and Project Life: A Clarification," *Journal of Financial and Quantitative Analysis* vol. 15, no. 3 (1980), pp. 719–730; and Miles, J. A., and J. R. Ezzell, J.R. (1985), "Reformulating Tax Shield Valuation: A Note," *Journal of Finance* vol. 40 (1985), pp. 1485–1492.

the unlevered cost of capital. This reduction in the average risk of the company's assets (operating assets and interest tax shields) partially mitigates the increase in the equity cost of capital resulting from the company's financial leverage relative to what it would have been if interest was not tax deductible or if all tax shields were valued at the unlevered cost of capital.

Valuation Key 10.4

If the appropriate discount rate for some of a company's interest tax shields is the debt cost of capital, the increase in the cost of equity capital from using financial leverage is partially mitigated because the company has an asset—the value of its interest tax shields—that is not as risky as the company's unlevered assets. This effect also lowers the weighted average cost of capital.

Equation 10.6 requires an estimate of the present value of the company's interest tax shields that are discounted at the cost of debt, $V_{ITS@r_D}$. We can calculate this present value based on forecasts of the outstanding debt for which the discount rate for the corresponding interest tax shields is the cost of debt. We can also make simplifying assumptions about the valuation of the interest tax shields discounted at the cost of debt and substitute those expressions for $V_{ITS@r_D}$ in Equation 10.6 to obtain simpler forms of the levering formula to use. We illustrate such an approach next.

A Fixed Amount of Perpetual Debt. Previously, we discussed the risk and valuation of interest tax shields for a zero-growth company with a fixed amount of perpetual debt and a discount rate for interest tax shields equal to the cost of debt (see Equation 10.1).[14] For a company with a fixed amount of perpetual debt, we can restate the levering formula for interest tax shields discounted at the cost of debt (Equation 10.6) by substituting the present value of the tax shield discounted at the cost of debt ($V_{ITS@r_D}$) in this case with the expression $[(T_{INT} \times V_D \times r_D)/r_D = T_{INT} \times V_D]$ for the value of interest tax shields discounted at the cost of debt. Under certain conditions, this formula is the same for a growing company that has a fixed amount of perpetual debt and uses a constant debt-to-value ratio to manage its debt. The fixed amount of debt has to be sufficiently small so that the probability of the total debt outstanding falling below the fixed amount of debt is insignificant, and the discount rate for the interest tax shields from any new debt resulting from the company's growth is the unlevered cost of capital. The resulting levering formula is

$$r_E = r_{UA} + (r_{UA} - r_D) \times (1 - T_{INT}) \times \frac{V_D}{V_E} + (r_{UA} - r_{PS}) \times \frac{V_{PS}}{V_E} \quad \textbf{(10.7)}$$

Annual Refinancing to Rebalance to a Target Capital Structure. Previously, we also discussed the risk and valuation of interest tax shields for a company that refinances its debt annually (see Equation 10.2). For this type of company, we discount the interest tax shield for the first year after the valuation date at the cost of debt, and discount the remaining interest tax shields at the unlevered cost of capital as of the valuation date.[15] We can restate our levering formula with the present value of the interest tax shields discounted at the cost of debt (Equation 10.6) by substituting an expression for the present value of the interest tax shields discounted at the cost of debt, which in this case is just $(r_D \times V_D \times T_{INT})/(1 + r_D)$.

$$r_E = r_{UA} + (r_{UA} - r_D) \times \left(1 - \frac{r_D \times T_{INT}}{1 + r_D}\right) \times \frac{V_D}{V_E} + (r_{UA} - r_{PS}) \times \frac{V_{PS}}{V_E} \quad \textbf{(10.8)}$$

This levering formula yields a similar result to the levering formula assuming the discount rate for all interest tax shields is the unlevered cost of capital (Equation 10.5). Using reasonable values for r_D and T_{INT} results in a value of the term in large brackets that is close to 1; for example, if the cost of debt is 10%, and if the tax rate is 40%, the term in the large brackets is equal to 0.96. When the expression in the large brackets is close to 1 it is almost equivalent to assuming that all of the tax shields are discounted

[14] See Modigliani, F., and M. H. Miller, "Corporate Income Taxes and the Cost of Capital: A Correction," *American Economic Review* 53 (June 1963), pp. 433–443; and Modigliani, F., and M. H. Miller, "Some Estimates of the Cost of Capital to the Electric Utility Industry, 1954–1957," *American Economic Review* 56 (June 1966), pp. 333–391.

[15] See Miles, J. A., and J. R. Ezzell, "The Weighted Average Cost of Capital, Perfect Capital Markets, and Project Life: A Clarification," *Journal of Financial and Quantitative Analysis* vol. 15, no. 3 (1980), pp. 719–730; and Miles, J. A., and J. R. Ezzell, J.R. (1985), "Reformulating Tax Shield Valuation: A Note," *Journal of Finance* vol. 40 (1985), pp. 1485–1492.

at the unlevered cost of capital, which makes sense because only the first year's interest tax shield has a current discount rate equal to the cost of debt when we use the annual refinancing assumption.

Valuation Key 10.5

If we assume a company continually refinances its debt to a proportionate target capital structure, we value all of a company's interest tax shields at the company's unlevered cost of capital. This is an extreme assumption about capital structure strategy (one that no firm practices), but there is relatively little difference in the value of the tax shields (and hence the value of the firm) between this assumption and the assumption that management adjusts the firm's capital structure on an annual basis to its target capital structure. This is a reasonable presumption for many firms.

The Booth Company—Levering the Unlevered Cost of Capital

The Booth Company (Booth) is a privately held company and has adopted a capital structure strategy of financing itself with 60% debt, 10% preferred stock, and 30% equity. We assume that Booth's cost of debt is 8% and its cost of preferred stock financing is 9%. We further assume that Booth expects to maintain this capital structure in the future. The company has a 40% income tax rate on all income. Management expects Booth to generate free cash flows of $800 in perpetuity and plans to distribute all equity free cash flows each year (it will retain no excess cash). Since Booth is not growing, the dollar magnitude of debt and preferred stock it will have in its capital structure will stay constant. Booth's unlevered cost of capital is 10%. In this section, we illustrate the use of each of the above levering formulas to measure the equity cost of capital and then the resulting weighted average cost of capital and valuation. Note that we are just illustrating the use of the various formulas. In a real valuation setting, we choose the formula that best fits the capital structure strategy of the firm that we are levering.

Value the Interest Tax Shields at the Unlevered Cost of Capital. Assuming the discount rate for interest tax shields is the company's unlevered cost of capital, then Booth's equity cost of capital (using Equation 10.5) and weighted average cost of capital are, respectively,

$$r_E = 0.1 + (0.1 - 0.08) \times \frac{0.6}{0.3} + (0.1 - 0.09) \times \frac{0.1}{0.3} = 0.1433$$

$$r_{WACC} = 0.1433 \times 0.3 + 0.08 \times (1 - 0.4) \times 0.6 + 0.09 \times 0.1 = 0.0808$$

Notice that the equity cost of capital is higher than the unlevered cost of capital because of the leverage and the weighted average cost of capital is less than the unlevered cost of capital because of the tax deductibility of interest. If we assume the company generates cash flows of $800 in perpetuity, the value of Booth using the WACC valuation method is

$$V_F = \frac{FCF_1}{r_{WACC}} = \frac{\$800}{0.0808} = \$9{,}901$$

We can replicate this valuation using the adjusted present value (APV) method by discounting the tax shields at the unlevered cost of capital. At a value of $9,901 and a 60% debt-to-value capital structure ratio, the company would have $5,940.6 of debt ($5,940.6 = $9,901 × 0.6) with an interest tax shield of $190.1 ($190.1 = $9,901 × 0.6 × 0.08 × 0.4). The resulting APV valuation is

$$V_F = \frac{FCF_1}{r_{UA}} + \frac{ITS_1}{r_{UA}} = \frac{\$800}{0.10} + \frac{\$190.1}{0.10} = \$9{,}901$$

From this example, we can see clearly that in this case the WACC DCF method valued the tax shields at the unlevered cost of capital. Note that we ignored the amount of preferred financing in utilizing the APV method, as it does not create any additional interest tax shields. Although we assumed that Booth's growth rate is zero, for this levering formula, the only effect of assuming a non-zero growth rate is to change the value of the firm. The equity cost of capital and weighted average cost of capital are unchanged, and the WACC and APV-based valuations would be equal to each other though different than the value in the zero growth case.

Assume Interest Is Not Tax Deductible. Assuming that interest is not tax deductible, the equity cost of capital is unchanged, or 14.33%, because the levering formula is the same (Equation 10.5). However, the weighted average cost of capital is not the same. It is equal to the unlevered cost of capital, 10%, because the tax rate used in the weighted average cost of capital formula would be zero (interest is not tax deductible).

$$r_{WACC} = 0.1433 \times 0.3 + 0.08 \times (1 - 0) \times 0.6 + 0.09 \times 0.1 = 0.10$$

The value of the company is lower, $8,000, because the value of the interest tax shields is zero. The difference of $1,901 ($1,901 = $9,901 − $8,000) is due solely to the value of the interest tax shields.

$$V_F = \frac{FCF_1}{r_{WACC}} = \frac{\$800}{0.10} = \$8{,}000$$

It should be obvious that an APV valuation of the company would be exactly the same ($800/0.10). Thus, here the WACC valuation method assigned no value to the interest tax shields because the tax rate in the weighted average cost of capital formula was set to zero.

A Fixed Amount of Perpetual Debt. Alternatively, assuming the discount rate for interest tax shields is the company's cost of debt and that the debt is perpetual, then Booth's equity cost of capital (using either Equations 10.6 or 10.7) and weighted average cost of capital are, respectively,

$$r_E = 0.1 + (0.1 - 0.08) \times (1 - 0.4) \times \frac{0.6}{0.3} + (0.1 - 0.09) \times \frac{0.1}{0.3} = 0.1273$$

$$r_{WACC} = 0.1273 \times 0.3 + 0.08 \times (1 - 0.4) \times 0.6 + 0.09 \times 0.1 = 0.076$$

Notice that Booth's equity cost of capital is lower than it was when its interest tax shields were discounted at the unlevered cost of capital. This is because the tax shields are valued at the cost of debt, thus mitigating the impact of debt on the cost of equity capital. Booth's weighted average cost of capital is lower than it was before because the equity cost of capital is lower. Again, assuming the company generates cash flows of $800 in perpetuity, the value of Booth using the WACC valuation method is

$$V_F = \frac{FCF_1}{r_{WACC}} = \frac{\$800}{0.076} = \$10{,}526$$

The lower weighted average cost of capital naturally results in a higher valuation. In this case, the valuation when we assume that the interest tax shields are valued at the cost of debt is $625 (6.3%) higher than it was when we valued the interest tax shields at the unlevered cost of capital ($625 = $10,526 − $9,901). As we observe by comparing the APV valuations, this entire difference results from the assumption that the risk of the interest tax shields is now lower as the discount rate for the interest tax shields is now the cost of debt rather than the unlevered cost of capital.

We can replicate this valuation using the adjusted present value method by discounting the tax shields at the debt cost of capital. At a value of $10,526, the company would have debt of $6,315.6 ($6,315.6 = $10,526 × 0.6) with an interest tax shield of $202.1 ($202.1 = $10,526 × 0.6 × 0.08 × 0.4). The APV valuation is

$$V_F = \frac{FCF_1}{r_{UA}} + \frac{ITS_1}{r_D} = \frac{\$800}{0.10} + \frac{\$202.1}{0.08} = \$10{,}526$$

Note that the value of the unlevered firm—that is the company's operations assuming no debt financing—is the same, $8,000 ($8,000 = $800/0.1), regardless of the discount rate used to value the interest tax shields. The discount rate used to value the unlevered firm is always the company's unlevered cost of capital. The only change in these valuations is the discount rate used to value the interest tax shields.

Finally, contrary to the previous case, this case with both a perpetual and a fixed amount of debt requires a zero growth rate assumption for the free cash flows of the firm because a non-zero growth rate results in changing capital structure ratios, which is inconsistent with assuming a constant proportionate capital structure in the WACC valuation method. We discuss this issue at the end of the chapter.

Annual Refinancing to Rebalance to a Target Capital Structure. If instead of making the simplifying assumption that the discount rate for all of Booth's interest tax shields is its unlevered cost of capital, we assume Booth refinances its capital structure annually back to its target capital structure, then Booth's equity cost of capital (using Equation 10.8), weighted average cost of capital, and valuation are, respectively,

$$r_E = 0.1 + (0.1 - 0.08) \times \left(1 - \frac{0.08 \times 0.4}{1.08}\right) \times \frac{0.6}{0.3} + (0.1 - 0.09) \times \frac{0.1}{0.3} = 0.1421$$

$$r_{WACC} = 0.1421 \times 0.3 + 0.08 \times (1 - 0.4) \times 0.6 + 0.09 \times 0.1 = 0.080444$$

$$V_F = \frac{FCF_1}{r_{WACC}} = \frac{\$800}{0.080444} = \$9{,}945$$

Thus, the impact of assuming that the Booth Company adjusts to its target capital structure with an annual lag is similar to that of assuming that the company refinances itself continually—a weighted average cost of capital of 0.0804 compared to 0.0808 and valuation of $9,945 compared to $9,901.

As it turns out, to show that the WACC and APV methods are equivalent takes a bit more discussion about the annual refinancing assumption. To use the APV valuation method, we use forecasts of the company's interest tax shields. With a value of $9,945, Booth will have $5,967 of debt ($5,967 = $9,945 × 0.6) with annual interest tax shields of $191 ($191 = $5,967 × 0.08 × 0.4). Calculating the present value of the interest tax shields involves some subtleties we have not yet discussed. Recall that as of the valuation date, the end of Year 0, we know the amount of debt outstanding. As a result, we know the amount of the interest tax shield available for Year 1. The only uncertainty of the interest tax shield for Year 1 is the company's ability to use the interest tax shield in that year. Therefore, as we discussed earlier, a reasonable discount rate to use for the Year 1 interest tax shield is the cost of debt.

For the interest tax shield in Year 2, the situation is more complex. As of the end of Year 1, we know the amount of debt outstanding and the interest tax shield available for Year 2. This is a situation similar to the situation we have for the Year 1 interest tax shield, so we use the cost of debt to discount the Year 2 interest tax shield from Year 2 to Year 1. The risk of the Year 2 interest tax shield as of the end of Year 0, however, is greater than the risk as of the end of Year 1. At the end of Year 0, the amount of debt the company will have at Year 1 depends on the value of the firm at the end of Year 1, as does the interest tax shield we expect to have for Year 2. To account for this additional risk, we use the unlevered cost of capital to discount the Year 2 interest tax shield from Year 1 to Year 0.

Therefore, we discount the Year 2 interest tax shield from Year 2 to Year 1 at the cost of debt, and from Year 1 to Year 0 at the unlevered cost of capital. Combining these calculations results in the following formula for discounting the Year 2 interest tax shield

$$\frac{ITS_2}{(1 + r_{UA}) \times (1 + r_D)}$$

Extending this logic forward to Year N, we discount the Year N interest tax shields from Year N to Year N − 1 at the cost of debt, and from Year N − 1 to Year 0 at the unlevered cost of capital.

$$\frac{ITS_N}{(1 + r_{UA})^{N-1} \times (1 + r_D)}$$

In other words, we discount each interest tax shield at the debt cost of capital for its last year and at the unlevered cost of capital for all remaining years.[16]

[16] Another way to think about this issue is as follows. We can measure the present value of the interest tax shields at Year 0 by discounting the interest tax shield for Year 1 at the cost of debt and discounting the value of all remaining interest tax shields as of the end of Year 1 at the unlevered cost of capital.

$$V_{ITS,0} = \frac{ITS_1}{1 + r_D} + \frac{V_{ITS,1}}{1 + r_{UA}}$$

We can perform the same calculation to measure the value of the interest tax shields as of the end of Year 1.

$$V_{ITS,1} = \frac{ITS_2}{1 + r_D} + \frac{V_{ITS,2}}{1 + r_{UA}}$$

If we substitute the above valuation of the interest tax shields as of the end of Year 1 into the valuation of the interest tax shields as of the end of Year 0, we get

$$V_{ITS,0} = \frac{ITS_1}{1 + r_D} + \frac{ITS_2}{(1 + r_D) \times (1 + r_{UA})} + \frac{V_{ITS,2}}{1 + r_{UA}}$$

If we extend this process forward, we can see that we are discounting each interest tax shield for one year at the cost of debt and for all remaining years at the unlevered cost of capital.

We often use perpetuity formulas to measure the continuing value of a company's interest tax shields. Since we do not discount all interest tax shields at the same discount rate, our standard perpetuity valuation formula does not work. We adjust that formula so that we discount each interest tax shield at the cost of debt for one year and at the unlevered cost of capital for the remaining years.

$$V_{ITS} = \frac{ITS_1}{r_{UA} - g} \times \frac{(1 + r_{UA})}{(1 + r_D)}$$

We now have all of the information required to value Booth using the APV method:

$$V_F = \frac{FCF_1}{r_{UA}} + \frac{r_D \times T_{INT} \times V_D}{r_{UA}} \times \frac{(1 + r_{UA})}{(1 + r_D)}$$

$$V_F = \frac{\$800}{0.1} + \frac{0.08 \times 0.4 \times \$5{,}967}{0.1} \times \frac{(1.1)}{(1.08)} = \$8{,}000 + \$1{,}945 = \$9{,}945$$

Thus, both the APV and WACC methods provide consistent estimates. Moreover, the WACC method embedded the value of the interest tax shields using the assumption that each yearly tax shield is discounted at the cost of debt for the last year and at the unlevered cost of capital for each prior year (in the case of the first year's tax shield, there is only the last year).

Summary. This example illustrates that, like the APV valuation method, the WACC valuation method is capable of valuing the interest tax shields under a variety of assumptions; for example, when the value of the tax shields is zero, when they are valued using the unlevered cost of capital or the debt cost of capital, or when they are valued under more complicated assumptions like the annual refinancing case—a combination of the debt and unlevered costs of capital. This example also illustrates that the levering formula is one of the factors that allows the WACC valuation method to embed the value of a company's interest tax shields into the weighted average cost of capital discount rate, including the riskiness of the tax shields.

The Booth example is a simple no-growth perpetuity. Although we do not demonstrate this point, we can always reconcile the valuations from the WACC and APV valuation methods, even for firms with varying growth rates as long as we use the same assumptions about the capital structure and the valuation of the interest tax shields in the WACC and APV valuations. One final note bears repeating. This example uses a simplified no-growth company to illustrate the use of the various levering formulas. In an actual valuation, we choose one or a combination of formulas that best fit the capital structure strategy and valuation context of the firm for which we are levering its unlevered cost of capital.

REVIEW EXERCISE 10.1

The Palm Company—Levering the Unlevered Cost of Capital

The Palm Company (Palm) is a privately held company and has adopted a capital structure strategy of financing itself with 30% debt, 20% preferred stock, and 50% equity. We assume that Palm's cost of debt is 7% and preferred stock cost of financing is 8%, that neither the debt nor preferred have a maturity, and that Palm expects to maintain this capital structure in the future. The company has a 45% income tax rate on all income. Management expects Palm to generate a free cash flow of $100 each year in perpetuity, and Palm plans to distribute all equity free cash flows each year (in other words, it will not have any excess cash). Since Palm is not growing, the dollar magnitude of debt and preferred stock it will have in its capital structure will stay constant. Palm's unlevered cost of capital is 12%. Measure Palm's equity cost of capital and weighted average cost of capital based on the following alternative assumptions for the discount rate for interest tax shields:

a. discount the interest tax shields at the unlevered cost of capital,

b. discount the interest tax shields at the cost of debt (assume this is a zero-growth company with a fixed amount of perpetual debt), and

c. discount the interest tax shields assuming annual refinancing (using the debt cost of capital for one year and unlevered cost of capital for subsequent years).

Solution on pages 477–478.

Choosing a Levering Method

The fifth step in the levering process (see Exhibit 10.2) is choosing the appropriate levering formula. The choice of the levering formula depends on the company we are valuing and the specific valuation context. As discussed earlier, the primary factor in this decision is the risk of the interest tax shields. The most reasonable method for levering the cost of capital depends on how closely both the company and the valuation context in which we are valuing the company meet the underlying assumptions for a particular levering method or formula. In particular, factors such as the company's capital structure strategy—which includes the degree of financial leverage, the riskiness of that financial leverage, and the maturity of that financial leverage—as well as the company's expected growth rate, have a role in choosing a levering method. In Exhibit 10.3, we summarize the formulas we discuss in this section.

EXHIBIT 10.3 Formulas to Lever the Unlevered Cost of Capital

Equity Cost of Capital

Discount rate for interest tax shields is the unlevered cost of capital or interest is not tax deductible:

$$r_E = r_{UA} + (r_{UA} - r_D) \times \frac{V_D}{V_E} + (r_{UA} - r_{PS}) \times \frac{V_{PS}}{V_E} \qquad (10.5)$$

Discount rate for certain interest tax shields is the cost of debt:

$$r_E = r_{UA} + (r_{UA} - r_D) \times \frac{V_D - V_{ITS@r_D}}{V_E} + (r_{UA} - r_{PS}) \times \frac{V_{PS}}{V_E} \qquad (10.6)$$

Discount rate is the cost of debt for a zero-growth company with a fixed amount of perpetual debt:

$$r_E = r_{UA} + (r_{UA} - r_D) \times (1 - T_{INT}) \times \frac{V_D}{V_E} + (r_{UA} - r_{PS}) \times \frac{V_{PS}}{V_E} \qquad (10.7)$$

Discount rate based on the annual refinancing assumptions:

$$r_E = r_{UA} + (r_{UA} - r_D) \times \left(1 - \frac{r_D \times T_{INT}}{1 + r_D}\right) \times \frac{V_D}{V_E} + (r_{UA} - r_{PS}) \times \frac{V_{PS}}{V_E} \qquad (10.8)$$

While no company likely meets any of the following alternative assumptions exactly, the following (relatively extreme) examples help guide the choice of a levering formula. If we believe a company pursues a strict constant target capital structure policy that is stated in terms of the proportion of debt to firm value, it is likely reasonable to use either the continuous refinancing assumption (all interest tax shields valued at the unlevered cost of capital) or the annual refinancing assumption since both yield similar valuations. If a company has a substantial amount of debt with a short maturity and has little additional debt capacity, it is again likely reasonable to use either the continuous refinancing assumption or the annual refinancing assumption. On the other hand, if the company does not use much debt, has substantial additional debt capacity, has a long maturity that the company will rollover when the debt matures, has a very low or zero-growth rate, and does not plan to issue additional debt, it is likely reasonable to use the formulas developed for situations in which a zero-growth company has a fixed amount of perpetual debt. If the company plans to pay down debt according to a schedule that does not depend on the value of the firm, we may just want to use the formula where we measure the present value of the interest tax shields discounted at the cost of debt. Using the formulas in Equation 10.5—$r_{ITS} = r_{UA}$ for all interest tax shields—and Equation 10.7, assuming a fixed amount of perpetual debt with $r_{ITS} = r_D$—is one way to estimate a range for the weighted average cost of capital.

Using the formula developed for the situation in which a zero-growth company has a fixed amount of perpetual debt—the Modigliani and Miller-based model—is the most common way to lever the unlevered cost of capital in practice, which is then used to estimate the weighted average cost of capital. Using this formula is not always reasonable and we discuss the limitations of using this approach in Section 10.7. However, one point to keep in mind is this: if the comparable companies and the company we are valuing have similar capital structure strategies, the process of unlevering the common equity cost of capital or beta for the comparable companies and relevering the resulting unlevered cost of capital or beta, will yield similar estimates regardless of which of the formulas we use.

Valuation Key 10.6

The primary factor to consider when choosing a levering formula is the risk of the company's interest tax shields. Factors such as the company's capital structure strategy—which includes the degree of financial leverage, the riskiness of that financial leverage, and the maturity of that financial leverage—as well as the company's expected growth rate, have a role in choosing a levering method.

10.4 LEVERING THE UNLEVERED (ASSET) BETA FROM THE CAPITAL ASSET PRICING MODEL

In this section we discuss an alternative, but equivalent, levering process based on the CAPM. As we discussed in Section 10.1, to use this approach, we first measure the CAPM common equity betas of the comparable companies and potentially the company we are valuing (if it is publicly traded) and then unlever the common equity betas to measure the unlevered beta for the company we are valuing. Once we measure the unlevered beta for the company we are valuing, we use the CAPM to measure the unlevered cost of capital if we are using the APV valuation method, or we lever the unlevered beta to measure the equity beta of the company we are valuing. Once we measure the equity beta we can use the CAPM to measure the equity cost of capital and then the weighted average cost of capital.

Miller and Modigliani[17](M&M) developed their theory of capital structure and levering and unlevering assuming, among other things, that all companies have the same risk, issue only debt and equity, and have debt that is risk-free. Other researchers—for example, Hamada, Stiglitz, and Rubinstein—extended this work. Hamada and Rubinstein show that M&M's work holds even if all companies do not have the same risk.[18] Stiglitz and Rubinstein show that M&M's work holds even if companies have risky debt.[19]

As we discussed in Section 10.1, unlevering and levering CAPM betas is the more popular alternative in practice than unlevering and levering the costs of capital directly. However, the choice of unlevering and levering betas or unlevering and levering costs of capital does not affect the outcome of a valuation as long as we use consistent assumptions and data, because the two approaches result in the same cost of capital for the company we are valuing. That said, practitioners often use shortcuts in the beta approach that induce errors in the levering and unlevering process and that result in violations of basic corporate finance theory. We discuss these shortcuts and their potential errors in Section 10.7. We summarize the steps in the levering process for beta, which are similar to the steps in the cost of capital levering process, in Exhibit 10.2.

Using the Capital Asset Pricing Model to Measure Beta from an Observed Cost of Capital

Recall from Chapter 8 that we can write the CAPM as

$$E(\tilde{R}_i) = R_F + \beta_i[E(\tilde{R}_m) - R_F]$$

---

[17] See the following research on this topic: Modigliani, F., and M. H. Miller, "The Cost of Capital, Corporate Finance and the Theory of Investment," *American Economic Review* 48 (1958), pp. 261–297; Modigliani, F., and M. H. Miller, "Corporate Income Taxes and the Cost of Capital: A Correction," *American Economic Review* 53 (June 1963), pp. 433–443; and Modigliani, F., and M. H. Miller, "Some Estimates of the Cost of Capital to the Electric Utility Industry, 1954–1957," *American Economic Review* 56 (June 1966), pp. 333–391.

[18] See Hamada, R. S., "Portfolio Analysis, Market Equilibrium, and Corporation Finance," *Journal of Finance* (March 1969), pp. 13–31; Hamada, R. S., "The Effect of the Firm's Capital Structure on the Systematic Risk of Common Stocks," *Journal of Finance* (May 1972), pp. 435–452; and Rubinstein, M. E., "A Mean-Variance Synthesis of Corporate Financial Theory," *Journal of Financial and Quantitative Analysis* (March 1973), pp. 167–181.

[19] See Stiglitz, J. E., "A Re-Examination of the Modigliani-Miller Theorem," *American Economic Review* (December 1969), pp. 187–193; Stiglitz, J. E., "On the Irrelevance of Corporate Financial Policy," *American Economic Review* (December 1974), pp. 851–866; Rubinstein, M. E., "A Mean-Variance Synthesis of Corporate Financial Theory," *Journal of Financial and Quantitative Analysis* (March 1973), pp. 167–181; and Conine, T. E., "Corporate Debt and Corporate Taxes: An Extension," *Journal of Finance* (September 1980), pp. 1033–1037.

Sometimes, we know the cost of capital (or discount rate) for an asset or security but do not know its CAPM beta, nor can we easily measure it. This situation occurs when we observe the cost of debt or preferred stock but cannot easily measure the debt or preferred beta. In these cases, we can use the following formula to measure the implied CAPM beta from any cost of capital estimate based on the risk-free rate and the market risk premium that we are using for the CAPM to estimate the cost of equity.

$$\beta_i = \frac{E(\tilde{R}_i) - R_F}{\left[E(\tilde{R}_m) - R_F\right]} \tag{10.9}$$

For example, assume we know that a company's debt cost of capital is 8%. In addition, assume that in order to estimate the equity cost of capital we are assuming that the risk-free rate of return is 4% and that the market risk premium is 6%. From this information, the company's implied debt beta is 0.67, which, as we know from Chapter 9, is the beta of debt with a credit rating of around C (see Exhibit 9.16).

$$\beta_D = \frac{E(\tilde{R}_i) - R_F}{\left[E(\tilde{R}_m) - R_F\right]} = \frac{0.08 - 0.04}{0.06} = 0.67$$

Naturally, it might be useful to estimate a company's debt beta using a market model regression, although it is often difficult to estimate betas on specific publicly traded debt securities because they trade infrequently. All that the calculation of implied betas is doing is providing the levering and unlevering formulas stated in terms of betas with the relative cost of capital for equity, debt and preferred. It is important to use the risk-free rate and the market risk premium in this calculation that we use in estimating the equity cost of capital or unlevered cost of capital. If they are not consistent, then the results from levering and unlevering the cost of capital and levering and unlevering betas will not be the same.

Integrating the Capital Asset Pricing Model into the Levering Formula

Since the CAPM return is equal to the risk-free rate plus a premium for risk (measured as beta multiplied by the market risk premium), we can substitute the CAPM formula for each cost of capital term in the general levering formula (Equation 10.4) and eliminate the redundant terms by subtracting the risk-free rate from both sides of the equation and dividing both sides of the equation by the market risk premium. After substituting the CAPM formula in the general levering formula, we obtain

$$\beta_E = \beta_{UA} + (\beta_{UA} - \beta_D) \times \frac{V_D}{V_E} + (\beta_{UA} - \beta_{PS}) \times \frac{V_{PS}}{V_E} - (\beta_{UA} - \beta_{ITS}) \times \frac{V_{ITS}}{V_E}$$

Once we derive the above general formula for levering betas, we can derive all of the formulas for levering beta for the special cases (Equations 10.5–10.8) we discussed in the previous section. We show a summary of the levering formulas in terms of betas in Exhibit 10.4. Note that the formulas look very similar to those in Exhibit 10.3, but for the fact that betas substitute for the various cost of capital terms (but for one instance in the annual refinancing formula).

The Booth Company Revisited—Levering the Unlevered Beta

Continuing with our Booth Company example, we measure Booth's equity beta using its unlevered beta, debt beta, and preferred stock beta. We know the cost of capital for each of Booth's non-equity securities (debt with an 8% cost of capital and preferred stock with a 9% cost of capital) and the company's income tax rate for all income (40%). Booth's unlevered cost of capital is 10%. We assume that the risk-free rate is 4% and that the market risk premium (MRP) is 6%. Given this information, we can measure Booth's debt, preferred stock, and unlevered betas. Using Equation 10.9 to measure the implied betas, Booth's debt beta is 0.667 [0.667 = (0.08 − 0.04)/0.06], its preferred stock beta is 0.833 [0.833 = (0.09 − 0.04)/0.06], and its unlevered beta is 1.0 [1.0 = (0.1 − 0.04)/0.06]. In the remainder of this section, we measure the equity beta and resulting CAPM equity cost of capital based on the alternative assumptions (see Equations 10.10–10.13 in Exhibit 10.4).

EXHIBIT 10.4 Formulas to Lever the CAPM Unlevered Beta

Equity Beta	
Discount rate for interest tax shields is the unlevered cost of capital or interest is not tax deductible:	
$\beta_E = \beta_{UA} + (\beta_{UA} - \beta_D) \times \frac{V_D}{V_E} + (\beta_{UA} - \beta_{PS}) \times \frac{V_{PS}}{V_E}$	(10.10)
Discount rate for certain interest tax shields is the cost of debt:	
$\beta_E = \beta_{UA} + (\beta_{UA} - \beta_D) \times \frac{V_D - V_{ITS@r_D}}{V_E} + (\beta_{UA} - \beta_{PS}) \times \frac{V_{PS}}{V_E}$	(10.11)
Discount rate is the cost of debt for a zero-growth company with a fixed amount of perpetual debt:	
$\beta_E = \beta_{UA} + (\beta_{UA} - \beta_D) \times (1 - T_{INT}) \times \frac{V_D}{V_E} + (\beta_{UA} - \beta_{PS}) \times \frac{V_{PS}}{V_E}$	(10.12)
Discount rate based on the annual refinancing assumptions:	
$\beta_E = \beta_{UA} + (\beta_{UA} - \beta_D) \times \left(1 - \frac{r_D \times T_{INT}}{1 + r_D}\right) \times \frac{V_D}{V_E} + (\beta_{UA} - \beta_{PS}) \times \frac{V_{PS}}{V_E}$	(10.13)

Value the Interest Tax Shields at the Unlevered Cost of Capital. If we assume the discount rate for the interest tax shields is equal to the company's unlevered cost of capital, then, using Equation 10.10, Booth's equity beta is equal to 1.72. An equity beta of 1.72 results in an equity cost of capital equal to 14.33%, which is exactly what we calculated previously in levering the unlevered cost of capital assuming that interest tax shields are discounted at the unlevered cost of capital (or interest is not tax deductible).

$$\beta_E = 1 + (1 - 0.667) \times \frac{0.6}{0.3} + (1 - 0.833) \times \frac{0.1}{0.3} = 1.72$$

$$r_E = 0.04 + 0.06 \times 1.72 = 0.1433$$

A Fixed Amount of Perpetual Debt. Alternatively, if we assume the discount rate for interest tax shields is equal to the company's cost of debt for a company with a fixed amount of perpetual debt, then, using either Equation 10.11 or 10.12, Booth's equity beta is equal to 1.456. An equity beta of 1.456 results in an equity cost of capital equal to 12.73%, again exactly equal to what we obtained when we levered the unlevered cost of capital under the assumption of a fixed amount of perpetual debt.

$$\beta_E = 1 + (1 - 0.667) \times (1 - 0.4) \times \frac{0.6}{0.3} + (1 - 0.833) \times \frac{0.1}{0.3} = 1.456$$

$$r_E = 0.04 + 0.06 \times 1.456 = 0.1273$$

Annual Refinancing to Rebalance to a Target Capital Structure. Lastly, if we assume Booth only refinances its capital structure annually (rather than refinancing continuously), then, using Equation 10.13, Booth's equity beta is equal to 1.702. An equity beta of 1.702 results in an equity cost of capital equal to 14.21%, again exactly what we obtained previously under the annual refinancing assumption.

$$\beta_E = 1 + (1 - 0.667) \times \left(1 - \frac{0.08 \times 0.4}{1.08}\right) \times \frac{0.6}{0.3} + (1 - 0.833) \times \frac{0.1}{0.3} = 1.702$$

$$r_E = 0.04 + 0.06 \times 1.702 = 0.1421$$

REVIEW EXERCISE 10.2

The Palm Company—Levering Beta

Use both the information in Review Exercise 10.1 and the following information to measure Palm's equity beta. First, measure Palm's unlevered beta, debt beta, and preferred stock beta assuming that the market risk premium is 6% and that the risk-free rate is 4%. Then, measure Palm's equity beta and equity cost of capital based on the following alternative assumptions for the discount rate for interest tax shields:

a. discount the interest tax shields at the unlevered cost of capital,

b. discount the interest tax shields at the cost of debt (remember that this is a zero-growth company with a fixed amount of perpetual debt), and

c. discount the interest tax shields assuming annual refinancing (using the debt cost of capital for one year and unlevered cost of capital for subsequent years).

Solution on page 478.

10.5 UNLEVERING THE EQUITY COST OF CAPITAL AND EQUITY BETA

LO4 Unlever a company's equity cost of capital and equity beta

In the previous section we assume we know the company's unlevered cost of capital. In this section we discuss how to estimate the unlevered cost of capital based on the equity and other costs of capital, capital structure ratios, and the tax rate of the comparable companies and perhaps the company being valued. To measure the unlevered cost of capital, we unlever a company's equity cost of capital by using a formula that eliminates the premiums resulting from the use of non-equity securities embedded in the equity cost of capital. As we illustrated with the levering formulas, we can also unlever CAPM equity betas to measure the unlevered cost of capital. We unlever the equity beta to determine the unlevered beta that we then use in conjunction with the CAPM to determine the unlevered cost of capital or that we would then lever back up for the capital structure of the company we are valuing to determine the company's equity beta. The specific process and formula we use to measure a company's unlevered cost of capital or unlevered beta depends on the particular company we are unlevering and the valuation context.

Unlevering the Equity Cost of Capital

Fortunately, the conceptual framework for developing the unlevering formulas is identical to the conceptual framework we used to develop the levering formulas. Again, we begin with the economic balance sheet formula expressed in terms of dollar returns—that is, the dollar return on the company's assets is equal to the dollar return on the company securities—and solve for the unlevered cost of capital. In other words, instead of solving for the equity cost of capital in each of the formulas, we solve for the unlevered cost of capital. Thus, each levering formula has an unlevering formula counterpart, which we show in Exhibit 10.5. In this exhibit, we show two forms of the unlevering formulas. Depending on the inputs available, one or both of these forms may be calculable.[20]

The Bakwin Company—Unlevering the Equity Cost of Capital

Assume we collected the following information for the Bakwin Company, a comparable company for which we want to measure the unlevered cost of capital:

[20] The reduced forms of the unlevering formulas are derived by multiplying the initial formulas by V_{UA}/V_E and then dividing by V_{UA}/V_E. In Equation 10.14, since $V_{ITS} = 0$ this leads to $V_{UA} = V_F = V_D + V_E + V_{PS}$. In the other two reduced forms of the unlevering formulas, V_{ITS} is not equal to zero, which results in more complex formulas, but the same process was used to derive them.

Income tax rate for interest (T_{INT})	40.0%
Value of debt	$10,000
Value of preferred stock	$ 4,000
Value of equity	$ 6,000
Debt cost of capital	6.0%
Preferred stock cost of capital	7.0%
Equity cost of capital	18.667%

We use the alternative unlevering formulas in Exhibit 10.5 to measure the unlevered cost of capital for the comparable company using different assumptions about the discount rate for interest tax shields. As we demonstrate in the remainder of this section, the unlevered cost of capital varies between 10% and 11%, depending on which set of assumptions we make.

EXHIBIT 10.5 The Unlevering Formula Counterparts to the Levering Formulas for the Cost of Capital

Using the Value of the Securities as Inputs | **Using the Capital Structure Ratios as Inputs**

Discount rate for interest tax shields is the unlevered cost of capital or interest is not tax deductible:

$$r_{UA} = r_E \times \frac{V_E}{V_F} + r_D \times \frac{V_D}{V_F} + r_{PS} \times \frac{V_{PS}}{V_F} \quad (10.14)$$

$$r_{UA} = \frac{r_E + r_D \times \frac{V_D}{V_E} + r_{PS} \times \frac{V_{PS}}{V_E}}{1 + \frac{V_D}{V_E} + \frac{V_{PS}}{V_E}} \quad (10.14')$$

Discount rate for certain interest tax shields is the cost of debt:

$$r_{UA} = r_E \times \frac{V_E}{V_F - V_{ITS@r_D}} + r_D \times \frac{V_D - V_{ITS@r_D}}{V_F - V_{ITS@r_D}} + r_{PS} \times \frac{V_{PS}}{V_F - V_{ITS@r_D}} \quad (10.15)$$

Not Available

Discount rate is the cost of debt for a zero-growth company with a fixed amount of perpetual debt:

$$r_{UA} = r_E \times \frac{V_E}{V_F - T_{INT} \times V_D} + r_D \times (1 - T_{INT}) \times \frac{V_D}{V_F - T_{INT} \times V_D} + r_{PS} \times \frac{V_{PS}}{V_F - T_{INT} \times V_D} \quad (10.16)$$

$$r_{UA} = \frac{r_E + r_D \times (1 - T_{INT}) \times \frac{V_D}{V_E} + r_{PS} \times \frac{V_{PS}}{V_E}}{1 + (1 - T_{INT}) \times \frac{V_D}{V_E} + \frac{V_{PS}}{V_E}} \quad (10.16')$$

Discount rate based on the annual refinancing assumptions:

$$r_{UA} = r_E \times \frac{V_E}{Z} + r_D \times \left(1 - \frac{r_D \times T_{INT}}{1 + r_D}\right) \times \frac{V_D}{Z} + r_{PS} \times \frac{V_{PS}}{Z}$$

$$Z = V_F - \frac{r_D \times T_{INT}}{1 + r_D} \times V_D \quad (10.17)$$

$$r_{UA} = \frac{r_E + r_D \times \left(1 - \frac{r_D \times T_{INT}}{1 + r_D}\right) \times \frac{V_D}{V_E} + r_{PS} \times \frac{V_{PS}}{V_E}}{1 + \left(1 - \frac{r_D \times T_{INT}}{1 + r_D}\right) \times \frac{V_D}{V_E} + \frac{V_{PS}}{V_E}} \quad (10.17')$$

Value the Interest Tax Shields at the Unlevered Cost of Capital. If we assume the discount rate for interest tax shields is equal to the company's unlevered cost of capital or that interest is not tax deductible, then the comparable company's unlevered cost of capital is equal to 10%, using either Equation 10.14, or the equivalent alternative version of this formula, Equation 10.14'. The calculation of the comparable company's unlevered cost of capital assuming the discount rate for all interest tax shields is the unlevered cost of capital and using Equation 10.14 is as follows

$$r_{UA} = 0.18667 \times \frac{\$6{,}000}{\$20{,}000} + 0.06 \times \frac{\$10{,}000}{\$20{,}000} + 0.07 \times \frac{\$4{,}000}{\$20{,}000} = 0.10$$

The calculation of the comparable company's unlevered cost of capital assuming the discount rate for all interest tax shields is the unlevered cost of capital and using Equation 10.14' is as follows

$$r_{UA} = \frac{0.18667 + 0.06 \times \frac{\$10{,}000}{\$6{,}000} + 0.07 \times \frac{\$4{,}000}{\$6{,}000}}{1 + \frac{\$10{,}000}{\$6{,}000} + \frac{\$4{,}000}{\$6{,}000}} = 0.10$$

A Fixed Amount of Perpetual Debt. Alternatively, if we assume the discount rate for interest tax shields is equal to the company's cost of debt (zero growth with a fixed amount of perpetual debt), then the comparable company's unlevered cost of capital is equal to 11% using Equation 10.16, or the equivalent alternative version of this formula, Equation 10.16'. The calculation of the comparable company's unlevered cost of capital assuming the discount rate for all interest tax shields is the debt cost of capital and using Equation 10.16 is as follows

$$r_{UA} = 0.18667 \times \frac{\$6{,}000}{\$20{,}000 - 0.4 \times \$10{,}000} + 0.06 \times (1 - 0.4) \times \frac{\$10{,}000}{\$20{,}000 - 0.4 \times \$10{,}000} + 0.07 \times \frac{\$4{,}000}{\$20{,}000 - 0.4 \times \$10{,}000} = 0.11$$

The calculation of the comparable company's unlevered cost of capital assuming the discount rate for all interest tax shields is the debt cost of capital and using Equation 10.16' is as follows

$$r_{UA} = \frac{0.18667 + 0.06 \times (1 - 0.4) \times \frac{\$10{,}000}{\$6{,}000} + 0.07 \times \frac{\$4{,}000}{\$6{,}000}}{1 + (1 - 0.4) \times \frac{\$10{,}000}{\$6{,}000} + \frac{\$4{,}000}{\$6{,}000}} = 0.11$$

Annual Refinancing to Rebalance to a Target Capital Structure. Lastly, if we assume the comparable company refinances its capital structure annually, then the comparable company's unlevered cost of capital is 10.05% using Equation 10.17, or the equivalent alternative version of this formula, Equation 10.17'. The calculation of the comparable company's unlevered cost of capital assuming the discount rate for all interest tax shields is the unlevered cost of capital other than for the first year which is discounted at the debt cost of capital and using Equation 10.17 is as follows

$$r_{UA} = 0.18667 \times \frac{\$6{,}000}{\$20{,}000 - \frac{0.06 \times 0.4}{1.06} \times \$10{,}000} + 0.06 \times \left(1 - \frac{0.06 \times 0.4}{1.06}\right) \times \frac{\$10{,}000}{\$20{,}000 - \frac{0.06 \times 0.4}{1.06} \times \$10{,}000} + 0.07 \times \frac{\$4{,}000}{\$20{,}000 - \frac{0.06 \times 0.4}{1.06} \times \$10{,}000} = 0.1005$$

The calculation of the comparable company's unlevered cost of capital assuming the discount rate for all interest tax shields is the unlevered cost of capital other than for the first year which is discounted at the debt cost of capital and using Equation 10.17' is as follows

$$r_{UA} = \frac{0.18667 + 0.06 \times \left(1 - \frac{0.06 \times 0.4}{1.06}\right) \times \frac{\$10{,}000}{\$6{,}000} + 0.07 \times \frac{\$4{,}000}{\$6{,}000}}{1 + \left(1 - \frac{0.06 \times 0.4}{1.06}\right) \times \frac{\$10{,}000}{\$6{,}000} + \frac{\$4{,}000}{\$6{,}000}} = 0.1005$$

REVIEW EXERCISE 10.3

The Date Company—Unlevering the Equity Cost of Capital

Use the information in the table below to measure Date Company's unlevered cost of capital based on the following alternative assumptions for the discount rate for interest tax shields:

a. discount the interest tax shields at the unlevered cost of capital,
b. discount the interest tax shields at the cost of debt (assume this is a zero-growth company with a fixed amount of perpetual debt), and
c. discount the interest tax shields assuming annual refinancing (using the debt cost of capital for one year and unlevered cost of capital for subsequent years).

Income tax rate for interest (T_{INT})	45.0%
Value of debt	$5,000
Value of preferred stock	$3,000
Value of equity	$2,000
Debt cost of capital	8.0%
Preferred stock cost of capital	9.0%
Equity cost of capital	26.5%

Solution on pages 478–479.

Unlevering the CAPM Equity Beta

Like we did for the unlevering formulas utilizing the various costs of capital in Exhibit 10.5, we can derive unlevering formulas utilizing the betas of the different securities. We summarize these formulas in Exhibit 10.6. Just as we observed for the levering formulas, the beta version of the unlevering formulas replaces various costs of capital from the formulas in Exhibit 10.5 with their respective betas and we present two forms of most of the formulas.

EXHIBIT 10.6 The Unlevering Formula Counterparts to the Levering Formulas for the Capital Asset Pricing Model Beta

Using the Value of the Securities as Inputs		Using the Capital Structure Ratios as Inputs	
Discount rate for interest tax shields is the unlevered cost of capital or interest is not tax deductible:			
$\beta_{UA} = \beta_E \times \frac{V_E}{V_F} + \beta_D \times \frac{V_D}{V_F} + \beta_{PS} \times \frac{V_{PS}}{V_F}$	(10.18)	$\beta_{UA} = \frac{\beta_E + \beta_D \times \frac{V_D}{V_E} + \beta_{PS} \times \frac{V_{PS}}{V_E}}{1 + \frac{V_D}{V_E} + \frac{V_{PS}}{V_E}}$	(10.18')
Discount rate for certain interest tax shields is the cost of debt:			
$\beta_{UA} = \beta_E \times \frac{V_E}{V_F - V_{ITS@r_D}} + \beta_D \times \frac{V_D - V_{ITS@r_D}}{V_F - V_{ITS@r_D}} + \beta_{PS} \times \frac{V_{PS}}{V_F - V_{ITS@r_D}}$	(10.19)	Not Available	
Discount rate is the cost of debt for a zero-growth company with a fixed amount of perpetual debt:			
$\beta_{UA} = \beta_E \times \frac{V_E}{V_F - T_{INT} \times V_D} + \beta_D \times (1 - T_{INT}) \times \frac{V_D}{V_F - T_{INT} \times V_D} + \beta_{PS} \times \frac{V_{PS}}{V_F - T_{INT} \times V_D}$	(10.20)	$\beta_{UA} = \frac{\beta_E + \beta_D \times (1 - T_{INT}) \times \frac{V_D}{V_E} + \beta_{PS} \times \frac{V_{PS}}{V_E}}{1 + (1 - T_{INT}) \times \frac{V_D}{V_E} + \frac{V_{PS}}{V_E}}$	(10.20')
Discount rate is based on the annual refinancing assumptions:			
$\beta_{UA} = \beta_E \times \frac{V_E}{Z} + \beta_D \times \left(1 - \frac{r_D \times T_{INT}}{1 + r_D}\right) \times \frac{V_D}{Z} + \beta_{PS} \times \frac{V_{PS}}{Z}$; $Z = V_F - \frac{r_D \times T_{INT}}{1 + r_D} \times V_D$	(10.21)	$\beta_{UA} = \frac{\beta_E + \beta_D \times \left(1 - \frac{r_D \times T_{INT}}{1 + r_D}\right) \times \frac{V_D}{V_E} + \beta_{PS} \times \frac{V_{PS}}{V_E}}{1 + \left(1 - \frac{r_D \times T_{INT}}{1 + r_D}\right) \times \frac{V_D}{V_E} + \frac{V_{PS}}{V_E}}$	(10.21')

The Bakwin Company Revisited—Unlevering the CAPM Equity Beta

Continuing with our Bakwin Company example, we measure Bakwin's unlevered beta using its CAPM equity beta, debt beta, and preferred stock beta. We know the cost of capital for each of Bakwin's securities (debt with a 6% cost of capital, preferred stock with a 7% cost of capital, and an 18.667% equity cost of capital) and the company's income tax rate for all income (40%). We assume that the risk-free rate is 4% and that the market risk premium (MRP) is 6%. Given this information, we can measure Bakwin's debt, preferred stock, and equity betas. Using Equation 10.9 to measure the implied betas, Bakwin's debt beta is 0.333 [0.333 = (0.06 − 0.04)/0.06], its preferred stock beta is 0.5 [0.5 = (0.07 − 0.04)/0.06], and its equity beta is 2.445 [2.445 = (0.18667 − 0.04)/0.06]. In the remainder of this section, we measure Bakwin's unlevered beta and resulting CAPM unlevered cost of capital based on the alternative assumptions (see Equations 10.18–10.21 in Exhibit 10.6).

Value the Interest Tax Shields at the Unlevered Cost of Capital. If we assume the discount rate for interest tax shields is equal to the company's unlevered cost of capital or that interest is not tax deductible, then the comparable company's unlevered beta is equal to 1.0, using either Equation 10.18, or the equivalent alternative version of this formula, Equation 10.18'. The calculation of the comparable company's unlevered beta assuming the discount rate for all interest tax shields is the unlevered cost of capital and using Equation 10.18 is as follows

$$\beta_{UA} = 2.445 \times \frac{\$6{,}000}{\$20{,}000} + 0.333 \times \frac{\$10{,}000}{\$20{,}000} + 0.5 \times \frac{\$4{,}000}{\$20{,}000} = 1.0$$

The calculation of the comparable company's unlevered beta assuming the discount rate for all interest tax shields is the unlevered cost of capital and using Equation 10.18' is as follows

$$\beta_{UA} = \frac{2.445 + 0.333 \times \frac{\$10{,}000}{\$6{,}000} + 0.5 \times \frac{\$4{,}000}{\$6{,}000}}{1 + \frac{\$10{,}000}{\$6{,}000} + \frac{\$4{,}000}{\$6{,}000}} = 1.0$$

If we plug our unlevered beta estimate into the CAPM equation with a 4% risk-free rate and 6% market risk premium, we find the unlevered cost of capital is equal to 10% (0.10 = 0.04 + 1.0 × 0.06) which is the same result we obtained when we unlevered the equity cost of capital previously and assumed that interest tax shields were discounted at the unlevered cost of capital or interest was not tax deductible.

A Fixed Amount of Perpetual Debt. Alternatively, if we assume the discount rate for interest tax shields is equal to the company's cost of debt (zero-growth with a fixed amount of perpetual debt), then the comparable company's unlevered beta is equal to 1.167, using either Equation 10.20, or the equivalent alternative version of this formula, Equation 10.20'. The calculation of the comparable company's unlevered beta assuming the discount rate for all interest tax shields is the debt cost of capital and using Equation 10.20 is as follows

$$\beta_{UA} = 2.445 \times \frac{\$6{,}000}{\$20{,}000 - 0.4 \times \$10{,}000} + 0.333 \times (1 - 0.4) \times \frac{\$10{,}000}{\$20{,}000 - 0.4 \times \$10{,}000}$$
$$+ 0.5 \times \frac{\$4{,}000}{\$20{,}000 - 0.4 \times \$10{,}000} = 1.167$$

The calculation of the comparable company's unlevered beta assuming the discount rate for all interest tax shields is the debt cost of capital and using Equation 10.20' is as follows

$$\beta_{UA} = \frac{2.445 + 0.333 \times (1 - 0.4) \times \frac{\$10{,}000}{\$6{,}000} + 0.5 \times \frac{\$4{,}000}{\$6{,}000}}{1 + (1 - 0.4) \times \frac{\$10{,}000}{\$6{,}000} + \frac{\$4{,}000}{\$6{,}000}} = 1.167$$

If we plug our unlevered beta estimate into the CAPM equation with a 4% risk-free rate and 6% market risk premium, we find the unlevered cost of capital is equal to 11% (0.11 = 0.04 + 1.167 × 0.06) which is the same result we obtained when we unlevered the equity cost of capital previously under the assumption of a fixed amount of perpetual debt.

Annual Refinancing to Rebalance to a Target Capital Structure. If we assume the comparable company refinances its capital structure annually, then the comparable company's unlevered beta is 1.008, using either Equation 10.21, or the equivalent alternative version of this formula, Equation 10.21'. The calculation of the comparable company's unlevered beta assuming the discount rate for all interest tax shields is the unlevered cost of capital other than for the first year which is discounted at the debt cost of capital and using Equation 10.21 is as follows

$$\beta_{UA} = 2.445 \times \frac{\$6{,}000}{\$20{,}000 - \frac{0.06 \times 0.4}{1.06} \times \$10{,}000} + 0.333 \times \left(1 - \frac{0.06 \times 0.4}{1.06}\right) \times \frac{\$10{,}000}{\$20{,}000 - \frac{0.06 \times 0.4}{1.06} \times \$10{,}000}$$
$$+ 0.5 \times \frac{\$4{,}000}{\$20{,}000 - \frac{0.06 \times 0.4}{1.06} \times \$10{,}000} = 1.008$$

The calculation of the comparable company's unlevered beta assuming the discount rate for all interest tax shields is the unlevered cost of capital other than for the first year which is discounted at the debt cost of capital and using Equation 10.21' is as follows

$$\beta_{UA} = \frac{2.445 + 0.333 \times \left(1 - \frac{0.06 \times 0.4}{1.06}\right) \times \frac{\$10{,}000}{\$6{,}000} + 0.5 \times \frac{\$4{,}000}{\$6{,}000}}{1 + \left(1 - \frac{0.06 \times 0.4}{1.06}\right) \times \frac{\$10{,}000}{\$6{,}000} + \frac{\$4{,}000}{\$6{,}000}} = 1.008$$

If we plug our unlevered beta estimate into the CAPM equation with a 4% risk-free rate and 6% market risk premium, we find the unlevered cost of capital is equal to 10.05% (0.1005 = 0.04 + 1.008 × 0.06) which is the same result we obtained when we unlevered the equity cost of capital previously when using the annual refinancing assumption.

When the Cost of Debt Is the Discount Rate for Some but Not All Interest Tax Shields

The unlevering formulas in Equations 10.15 (to unlever the equity cost of capital) and 10.19 (to unlever the equity beta), are useful when the cost of debt is the discount rate for some, but not all of a company's interest tax shields. The most likely situation in which these formulas will be used is when a company has existing debt and plans to refinance that debt based on a debt-to-value ratio when the debt matures. Given that lenders naturally have a limit on how much debt the company can borrow relative to the value of the underlying assets, this situation is common for companies with high leverage-based capital structures. This assumes that the company will not retire the existing debt early to maintain a target debt-to-value capital structure if the value of the firm falls below the amount necessary to maintain the target debt-to-value ratio.

In such situations, it may be reasonable to use the cost of debt for the discount rate for the interest tax shields from the existing debt and the unlevered cost of capital for the discount rate for the interest tax shields from the refinanced debt based on the debt-to-value ratio. For example, assume the debt outstanding for the Bakwin Company matures in ten years and the Bakwin Company intends to refinance that debt when it matures based on a specific debt-to-value ratio. The specific debt-to-value ratio is irrelevant to our calculations because the only debt that directly affects the calculation of the unlevered cost of capital or unlevered beta is the debt for which the cost of debt is the discount rate for the resulting interest tax shields.

The Bakwin Company has $10,000 of debt outstanding, which has a 6% interest rate. Since Bakwin has a 40% income tax rate on all income, its interest tax shield based on this debt is $240 ($240 = $10,000 × 0.6 × 0.4). The present value of ten years of interest tax shields of $240 is $1,766

$$\$1{,}766 = \$240 \times \left(\frac{1}{0.06} - \frac{1}{0.06} \times \frac{1}{1.06^{10}}\right)$$

Once we measure the present value of the interest tax shields discounted at the cost of debt, we can measure the unlevered cost of capital using Equation 10.15 as follows

$$r_{UA} = 0.18667 \times \frac{\$6{,}000}{\$20{,}000 - \$1{,}766} + 0.06 \times \frac{\$10{,}000 - \$1{,}766}{\$20{,}000 - \$1{,}766} + 0.07 \times \frac{\$4{,}000}{\$20{,}000 - \$1{,}766} = 0.1039$$

Finally, we can measure the unlevered beta using Equation 10.19 as follows

$$\beta_{UA} = 2.445 \times \frac{\$6{,}000}{\$20{,}000 - \$1{,}766} + 0.333 \times \frac{\$10{,}000 - \$1{,}766}{\$20{,}000 - \$1{,}766} + 0.5 \times \frac{\$4{,}000}{\$20{,}000 - \$1{,}766} = 1.065$$

If we plug our unlevered beta estimate into the CAPM equation with a 4% risk-free rate and 6% market risk premium, we find the unlevered cost of capital is equal to 10.39% (0.1039 = 0.04 + 1.065 × 0.06) which is the same result we obtained when we unlevered the equity cost of capital.

Again, this assumes that Bakwin would not retire the existing debt early if the value of the firm fell below the amount necessary to be consistent with its debt-to-value target capital structure. For example, let us assume that their target debt-to-value ratio is 40%. Therefore, we are assuming that if the value of the firm fell below $25,000 (which would support $10,000 of debt at a 40% debt-to-value ratio), Bakwin would not retire any of the existing debt.

REVIEW EXERCISE 10.4

The Date Company—Unlevering Equity Beta

Use both the information in Review Exercise 10.3 and the following information to measure Date's unlevered beta. First, measure Date's equity beta, debt beta, and preferred stock beta, assuming the market risk premium is 6% and the risk-free rate is 4%. Then, measure Date's unlevered beta and unlevered cost of capital based on the following alternative assumptions for the discount rate for interest tax shields:

a. discount the interest tax shields at the unlevered cost of capital,

b. discount the interest tax shields at the cost of debt (assume the company will have zero growth with fixed amount of perpetual debt), and

c. discount the interest tax shields assuming annual refinancing (using the debt cost of capital for one year and unlevered cost of capital for subsequent years).

Solution on page 479.

Choosing an Unlevering Method

As in the levering process, the most reasonable unlevering method to use in a valuation depends on how closely a company meets the underlying assumptions for a particular unlevering method. If a company either maintains a target capital structure in terms of proportions of debt and equity or has a substantial amount of debt with a short maturity, and with little additional debt capacity, then it is likely reasonable to use the formulas that discount all interest tax shields at the unlevered cost of capital or that rely on the annual refinancing assumptions. If a company does not use much debt, has substantial additional debt capacity, is not nearing any limitation on the tax deductibility of interest, and the company has a forecast of its debt schedule, the general formula for discounting tax shields at the cost of debt might be the most relevant. If a company has relatively little debt with a long maturity, has a low growth rate, and does not plan to issue additional debt, then the relevant formulas developed for a zero-growth company with a fixed amount of perpetual debt might be reasonable to use.

Given the alternative capital structures used by companies, the same unlevering formula is unlikely the best formula to use for every comparable company and no single formula will be exactly correct. Rather, we examine each comparable company individually to assess which set of assumptions underlying the alternative unlevering formulas best fits the capital structure strategy of each company.

Valuation Key 10.7

The conceptual framework for developing unlevering formulas is identical to the conceptual framework used to develop the levering formulas. Each formula is based on a specific set of underlying assumptions based on a company's capital structure strategy and the resulting discount rate applicable for that strategy. When unlevering a company, we use the unlevering formula that best fits the capital structure strategy of the particular company being unlevered.

10.6 USING COMPARABLE COMPANIES TO ESTIMATE BETAS

LO5 Use comparable companies to estimate betas

One of the reasons we use comparable companies to estimate a company's beta, even when the company is publicly traded, is to increase the precision of our estimates. In order to shed further light on why we do this, we estimated the standard errors of the portfolio betas for the portfolios we described in Exhibit 8.1 (recall we constructed portfolios with the number of firms in the portfolio ranging from 1 to 125 and we constructed 1,000 portfolios of each size of portfolio). When we estimate the portfolio betas, the average standard error across the 1,000 replications for the portfolio of just one firm was 0.26 (think about what that implies about a 95% confidence interval—the point estimate plus or minus 0.52). Increasing the portfolio to just five firms decreases the average standard error of the portfolio beta to 0.13—a decrease of 50%. With a portfolio of 10 firms, the average standard error of the portfolio beta was 0.10. Thus, if we have a set of truly comparable companies, we can gain precision in the estimate of the cost of capital by using a set of comparable companies.

Using Individual Betas (Instead of Portfolio Betas) to Improve Precision

When we use comparable companies, we generally do not estimate a portfolio beta of the comparable companies. Rather, we estimate each company's beta separately. We could estimate a portfolio beta for the comparable companies if we could assume that the capital structure of the company we are valuing is close to the average capital structure embedded in the portfolio of comparable companies. Since that assumption is often not met, generally, after estimating each company's beta, we use the unlevering process on each of the comparable companies (using the most appropriate unlevering formula for each company) to measure each comparable company's unlevered beta. Once we measure the unlevered betas of the comparable companies, we use the distribution of the unlevered betas to measure the unlevered beta of the company we are valuing. Even though we do not estimate portfolio betas directly in this method, we achieve a similar reduction in the standard error as indicated by the standard error of the portfolio beta by using the unlevered betas of the comparable companies in this way.

Of course, when we use comparable companies, we are assuming that the business risk (unlevered cost of capital) is the same. One of the trade-offs we make in choosing comparable companies is that generally, the standard error of the portfolio beta declines by increasing the number of comparable companies, but as we add comparable companies, the degree of comparability (e.g., the similarity of the business risk) likely decreases.

What information does the standard error of the beta provide about the precision of the beta? It is possible for a company's beta to shift over time due to changes in its operations, changes in its capital structure, or changes in market conditions. The standard error provides information about the imprecision of the beta estimate based on the historical data, which could be the result of such shifts or the inability of the market to explain the company's stock return. The standard error does not provide definitive information that a shift occurred. We analyze the companies whose betas we plan to estimate in order to ensure that shifts in operations or capital structure have not occurred—or if they have occurred, we make appropriate adjustments for those changes when possible. If shifts in operations or capital structure have occurred and appropriate adjustments are not possible, we will likely eliminate that firm as a comparable company.

Measuring a Company's Unlevered Beta from Its Comparable Companies' Unlevered Betas

After we unlever all of the comparable company betas, we can use alternative ways to assess the unlevered beta to use for the company we are valuing. We have a distribution of unlevered betas and can use the mean, median, a range of betas, a point on the distribution (if we believe the company's unlevered beta is higher or lower than the median or average beta), or we can calculate a weighted average. For example, we might use market values to weight betas or we might decide to assign more weight to companies that are similar in size. We could also use some other characteristic that we believe is correlated with the degree of comparability depending on our assessment of the best weighting method.

If we believe the comparable companies are equally comparable, we can also use the precision of the unlevered beta estimates to weight the betas, using the standard errors of the unlevered betas for weights, called a **precision weighted beta**:

$$\beta_{\text{Precision Weighted}} = \frac{\sum_{i=1}^{N} \beta_i \left(\frac{1}{\sigma_{SE,\,\beta_i}} \right)}{\sum_{i=1}^{N} \left(\frac{1}{\sigma_{SE,\,\beta_i}} \right)} \tag{10.22}$$

where $\sigma_{SE,\,\beta_i}$ is the standard error of company i's unlevered beta. For example, assume we had two companies that had the following unlevered betas and standard errors of the unlevered betas.

Firm	β_i	σ_{SE,β_i}	$\frac{1}{\sigma_{SE,\beta_i}}$
A	1.0	0.4	2.5
B	2.0	0.1	10.0

An equally weighted average of those two betas would give us an estimated beta of 1.5. But a precision weighted average of those two betas would yield a beta of 1.8 [1.8 = (1.0 × 2.5 + 2.0 × 10.0)/(2.5 + 10.0)]. As can be seen from this formula, the beta that is estimated more precisely is given more weight in the calculation.

The above calculation requires estimates of the unlevered betas as well as the standard errors of the unlevered betas. However, when we estimate the market model, we observe the equity betas and the standard errors of the equity betas (assuming the company has leverage), and not unlevered betas or the standard errors of the unlevered betas. Under a reasonable set of assumptions, it can be shown that the standard error of the unlevered beta for a company is the standard error of the equity beta multiplied by the equity-to-value ratio (V_E/V_F). Note that if the company has no leverage (i.e., $V_E = V_F$), the standard error of the unlevered beta and equity beta are the same. To the extent the company has leverage, the standard error of the unlevered beta will be smaller than the standard error of the equity beta.

Vasicek developed another technique for estimating the unlevered beta from a set of companies, which is an alternative to the precision weighted beta, called the **Vasicek adjusted beta**.[21] This method adjusts a company's beta toward the mean of any specified portfolio's beta (a market beta or comparable company group beta or industry beta). The adjustment is a function of the precision of the beta estimate of the individual company relative to the precision of the betas from the comparison portfolio.

$$\text{Vasicek Adjusted } \beta_i = \frac{\sigma^2_{\beta_p}}{\sigma^2_{SE,\beta_i} + \sigma^2_{\beta_p}} \times \beta_i + \frac{\sigma^2_{SE,\beta_i}}{\sigma^2_{SE,\beta_i} + \sigma^2_{\beta_p}} \times \beta_p \quad \textbf{(10.23)}$$

where:

β_i = the beta for security i
β_p = the mean beta of some peer group, the market, or the industry
σ^2_{SE,β_i} = the square of the standard error of the historical beta estimate for security i
$\sigma^2_{\beta_p}$ = the variance of the betas in the peer group, market, or industry.

Using this adjustment method, the adjusted beta is a weighted average of the beta of the company being valued and the mean beta of a benchmark portfolio. For example, suppose we estimated the betas of 10 comparable companies and they were very close to one another with little variation but the precision of the beta of the company of interest, its standard error, was large. In this case, the Vasicek method would weight the mean beta of the comparable companies more heavily than the beta of the firm of interest.

Valuation Key 10.8

Choosing comparable companies can increase the precision of our beta estimates. We are generally forced to make a trade-off between more precise beta estimates using more comparable companies and the degree of comparability. We typically do not estimate a portfolio equity beta for the comparable companies because of capital structure differences. We estimate individual company equity betas, unlever the equity betas, and use the distribution of unlevered betas to measure the unlevered beta of the company we are valuing using one or more of the available techniques for weighting the individual unlevered betas.

[21] See Vasicek, O. A., "A Note on Using Cross-Sectional Information in Bayesian Estimation of Security Betas," *Journal of Finance* 28 (1973), pp. 1233–1239.

Valuation in Practice 10.2

Ibbotson Associates Estimates Beta in Multiple Ways Ibbotson Associates produced several alternative estimates of beta. One of its estimates uses the Vasicek method to adjust beta estimates back to a peer industry group. Ibbotson Associates uses monthly data and generally uses 60 months of observations.

For the CAPM model, we provide several equity beta statistics including traditional levered and unlevered ordinary least squares (OLS) estimates, levered and unlevered Sum Beta (including lag) estimates, peer group betas and levered and unlevered adjusted betas. Each of these statistics is intended to provide the user with additional information regarding the actual equity beta of each individual company . . .

To estimate the beta of a company, monthly total returns of the company's stock, in excess of the risk-free asset, are regressed against the monthly total returns of the stock market in excess of the return on the risk-free asset. In all of the CAPM beta regressions, the total returns of the S&P 500 are used as the proxy for the market returns. The series used as a proxy for the risk-free asset is the yield on the 30 day T-bill. Total returns for both individual stocks and the market proxy are determined by calculating price appreciation and dividend reinvestment. A sixty-month time frame is used for the regression. If fewer than sixty months of data are available for a company, the beta is then calculated using the months of data that are available with a minimum of thirty-six months as acceptable.

Based on the theory that over time a company's beta tends towards its industry's average beta, we present an adjusted beta for each company. The adjusted beta is a weighted average of the company's regression beta and its peer group beta. . . . The amount of shrinkage is calculated using a formula first suggested by Vasicek. With Vasicek's formula, the greater the statistical confidence of the regression beta, the more the adjustment will be toward the regression beta; the less the statistical confidence of the regression beta, the more the adjustment will be toward the industry beta.

Source: *Ibbotson Beta Book First 2010 Edition*, Morningstar, Inc. (2010)

REVIEW EXERCISE 10.5

Bloomberg, Precision, and Vasicek Adjusted Betas

Calculate the Bloomberg adjusted beta (see Chapter 8) for each of the comparable companies and the portfolio of comparable companies that appear in the table below. Also calculate the precision weighted beta and the Vasicek adjusted beta for the company being valued using the four comparable companies and the company being valued. Assume all company betas are unlevered.

	Beta Estimate	Standard Error of Beta	t-statistic
Comparable Company #1	0.900	0.50	1.80
Comparable Company #2	1.100	0.40	2.75
Comparable Company #3	1.350	0.60	2.25
Comparable Company #4	1.500	0.45	3.33
Comparable company average beta	1.213		
Company being valued	1.100	0.56	1.96

Solution on page 480.

10.7 LIMITATIONS OF THE LEVERING AND UNLEVERING FORMULAS

In this section we discuss some of the limitations of the levering and unlevering formulas. One issue results from assuming the value of the debt financing is equal to the value of the interest tax shields. In other words, these formulas do not consider any of the countervailing effects from debt financing, such as financial

LO6 Avoid common errors in the levering and unlevering process

distress costs. Another limitation results from assuming that the current cost of debt multiplied by the value of the debt is equal to the expected interest tax shields. We then discuss the limitations using the levering and unlevering methods that assume a company has a fixed amount of perpetual debt and the assumption that non-common equity betas are zero. We explore these limitations and their effects in this section.

Considering Financial Distress Costs When Choosing Comparable Companies

Now that we understand the levering and unlevering process, we raise an issue regarding the choice of comparable companies. In deriving the levering and unlevering formulas, we assumed that there are no countervailing forces associated with issuing debt—in other words, issuing debt creates interest tax shields, but does not increase **bankruptcy costs**, **financial distress costs**, or **agency costs**. For example, if a highly levered capital structure results in non-negligible expected costs of financial distress and those costs affect the cost of capital estimates, then the levering and unlevering formulas will result in incorrect estimates of either the cost of capital or beta. In other words, if the company we are valuing has modest amounts of leverage, but we are using a highly levered comparable company with significant expected financial distress costs embedded in the cost of capital, the unlevered cost of capital for the highly levered comparable will include the effects of financial distress. This effect occurs because the levering and unlevering formulas only make adjustments for the value and riskiness of the interest tax shields—they do not make adjustments for the effects of financial distress costs on the cost of capital.

We suggest using comparable companies that do not have totally different expected financial distress costs. So, if the company we are valuing has negligible expected financial distress costs, we probably do not want to use comparable companies with significant expected financial distress costs embedded in their costs of capital. Similarly, if the company we are valuing has high expected financial distress costs which impact the company's cost of capital, and we use comparable companies with minimal expected financial distress costs, we likely would underestimate the cost of capital for the company being valued.

Valuation in Practice 10.3

Companies Can Reduce Financial Leverage by Issuing Equity: Advanced Micro Devices, Inc. (AMD) Recall from Valuation in Practice 9.4 that in 2015, Moody's and Standard & Poor's lowered AMD's corporate credit rating. In an attempt to reduce its financial leverage, in 2016, AMD issued $700 million of common stock and $600 million of convertible debt. AMD's stated intention was to "use the net proceeds of this [common stock] offering, together with the net proceeds of the anticipated Convertible Notes Offering . . ., to repay up to $226 million of our borrowings under the Amended and Restated Loan and Security Agreement ... and to purchase up to $1,020 million aggregate total consideration of our Senior Notes . . ."

Source: Advanced Micro Devices, Inc. Prospectus for the common stock offering (SEC Form 424(b)(5)) dated September 6, 2016.

Does the Cost of Debt Multiplied by the Value of the Debt Measure Expected Interest Tax Shields?

We often assume that the current cost of debt multiplied by the value of the debt measures expected interest tax shields. That is likely correct for any newly issued debt, but is not necessarily correct for debt that was issued previously. It is also not likely correct if the company has net operating loss carryforwards or interest carryforwards arising from limitations on the deductibility of interest (see Chapters 3 and 11). Assume the company's default probability has not changed but that its cost of debt has changed since the existing debt was issued, for example, because the inflation rate has changed or the real risk-free rate of return demanded by investors has changed. In some situations, this change can cause problems for the levering and unlevering formulas because the current cost of debt multiplied by the current value of the debt will not measure the expected interest tax shields.

We briefly discuss the levering formulas to provide some intuition on this issue. First, the formula for valuing all of the interest tax shields at the unlevered cost of capital—the continuous refinancing assumption (or assuming interest is not tax deductible), Equation 10.5, is not affected by this issue because nowhere in that formula do we assume that the expected interest tax shields are equal to the cost of debt times the value of the debt. The same is true of Equation 10.6, where we calculate the present value of the tax shields discounted at the cost of debt, $V_{ITS@r_D}$, as long as we correctly measure the expected interest tax shields based on the original cost of debt and book value of the debt and discount them at the current cost of debt.

So far so good, but the same is not true for the perpetual debt, zero-growth assumption contained in the levering formula shown in Equation 10.7. That formula assumes that the current cost of debt multiplied by the value of the debt is the expected interest tax shield. That will not be the case if the cost of debt and value of the debt has changed since the debt was issued. The expected interest tax shield will be the effective rate of interest at the time of issuance multiplied by the book value of debt and not the current cost of debt multiplied by the value of the debt. The good news is that the effects are somewhat countervailing, so the error is not likely to be too large. Suppose inflation increased and the cost of debt is now higher than it was when the debt was issued. The countervailing effect is that the value of the debt will decrease. While the current cost of debt multiplied by the current value of the debt is not likely to yield the exact expected interest tax shield, and therefore the tax rate multiplied by the value of the debt will not yield the present value of the interest tax shields, the error is likely to be reasonably small. The error in the annual refinancing formula (Equation 10.8) is likely to be insignificant, as the only expected interest tax shield measured with error by assuming the current cost of debt multiplied by the current value of the debt is the first period's interest tax shield.

In summary, we do not believe this issue is likely to lead to a significant error in valuation in the levering and unlevering process in most situations.

Limitations of Modigliani and Miller's Levering and Unlevering Formulas

Earlier in the chapter, we discussed the levering and unlevering formulas for a zero-growth company with a fixed amount of perpetual debt and a discount rate for interest tax shields that is equal to the cost of debt (see Equations 10.1, 10.7, 10.12, 10.16 and 10.20).[22] These formulas do not generally apply to a growing company or to a company that is expected to change the dollar amount of debt it has outstanding. Although this levering formula is widely used to lever and unlever the cost of capital, it is not always the best and sometimes it is not a reasonable way to lever or unlever a company's cost of capital or beta. Naturally, the extent of the error caused by using this formula in a valuation context in which it does not apply depends on the specific valuation context. For example, if the comparable companies and the company we are valuing have similar capital structure strategies, the process of unlevering the common equity cost of capital or beta for the comparable companies and relevering the resulting unlevered or beta cost of capital using the same formula for each, will result in an appropriate outcome regardless of which of the formulas we use. But again, that assumes that all the companies have similar capital structure strategies.

We illustrate the potential error based on different valuation contexts in the following example. Assume a company with an unlevered cost of capital of 10% expects to follow a capital structure strategy with 70% debt and 10% preferred stock. The debt has an 8% cost of capital and the preferred stock has a 9% cost of capital. The company has an income tax rate equal to 40%, and a $1,000 expected free cash flow in Year 1 that has a present value weighted perpetual growth rate of 5%. If we assume that the discount rate for interest tax shields is the cost of debt and that the present value of the interest tax shields is equal to the tax rate multiplied by the value of the debt ($T_{INT} \times V_D$)—which means that the debt is not expected to grow—the company's equity cost of capital and weighted average cost of capital are

$$r_E = 0.10 + (0.10 - 0.08) \times (1 - 0.4) \times \frac{0.7}{0.2} + (0.10 - 0.09) \times \frac{0.1}{0.2} = 0.147$$

$$r_{WACC} = 0.147 \times 0.2 + 0.08 \times (1 - 0.4) \times 0.7 + 0.09 \times 0.1 = 0.072$$

Based on the WACC valuation method the value of the company is equal to $45,454.5.

$$V_{F,0} = \frac{FCF_1}{r_{WACC} - g} = \frac{\$1{,}000}{0.072 - 0.05} = \$45{,}454.5$$

[22] See: Modigliani, F. and M. H. Miller, "Corporate Income Taxes and the Cost of Capital: A Correction," *American Economic Review* 53 (June 1963), pp. 433–443; Modigliani, F. and M. H. Miller, "Some Estimates of the Cost of Capital to the Electric Utility Industry, 1954–1957," *American Economic Review* 56 (June 1966), pp. 333–391.

However, the assumptions in this valuation are internally inconsistent. The company's free cash flows are growing at 5%; thus, the company's value will grow at 5%. The levering formula assumes that the company will not issue additional debt, but the weighted average cost of capital formula assumes that the company will follow a constant capital structure strategy of 70% debt, which assumes debt will grow with the value of the firm. These assumptions are inconsistent with each other. If the correct valuation context is no increase in debt, then the valuation from the WACC method shown above is vastly overstated. We can measure the correct valuation for this valuation context using the APV valuation method.

The assumption underpinning the levering formula is that the company will not issue or retire debt. Even though the WACC valuation is overstated, we assume for illustrative purposes the company will issue \$31,818.2 in debt outstanding in perpetuity (\$31,818.2 = 70% × \$45,454.5). In other words, we assume that the company believed the valuation was correct and issued \$31,818.2 of debt. The interest tax shield from this debt is \$1,018.2 (\$1,018.2 = \$31,818.2 × 0.08 × 0.4). If we assume the amount of debt is fixed and that the interest tax shields are valued at the cost of debt, the APV valuation of the company is \$32,727.3, which is far less than the WACC valuation.

$$V_{F,0} = \frac{FCF_1}{r_{UA} - g} + \frac{r_D \times T_{INT} \times V_D}{r_D}$$

$$V_F = \frac{\$1{,}000}{0.1 - 0.05} + \frac{0.08 \times 0.4 \times \$31{,}818.2}{0.08} = \$20{,}000 + \$12{,}727.3 = \$32{,}727.3$$

The difference between the WACC and APV valuations is \$12,727.2 (\$12,727.2 = \$45,454.5 − \$32,727.3) or about 39%. The WACC valuation assumes that the company's weighted average cost of capital of 7.2% is constant in perpetuity based on a 70% debt-to-value ratio. However, given a 5% perpetual growth rate in the free cash flows, the value of the firm will grow over time at the same rate but the levering formula assumes that the debt will not grow. With a growing firm and a fixed amount of debt, the debt-to-value ratio decreases over time and thus, the weighted average cost of capital increases over time. Thus, assuming a constant 7.2% weighted average cost of capital understates the weighted average cost of capital in this valuation context and the resulting valuation is overstated relative to having a fixed amount of debt.

Now let us assume that the company continues to believe that the value of the firm is \$45,454.5 and the company's capital structure strategy is to issue \$31,818.2 in debt and grow the debt with the value of the firm. Our objective is to measure the error in the company's valuation based on this capital structure strategy; it is not to assume a different capital structure policy. So again, the valuation context matters. In order to do that, we can use the APV valuation method to value the firm. The APV valuation method requires an assumption about the discount rate for the company's interest tax shields based on this capital structure strategy. As discussed earlier in the chapter, we have three choices—use the cost of debt, use the unlevered cost of capital, or use the cost of debt for certain interest tax shields and the unlevered cost of capital for the remaining interest tax shields.

Given that the company plans to issue additional debt as the company grows, it is unlikely that the cost of debt is a reasonable discount rate to use for all interest tax shields given it is so highly levered. Thus, we do not consider the cost of debt as the discount rate for all interest tax shields as a reasonable assumption for this capital structure strategy. The company's capital structure strategy may be closest to the continuous refinancing assumption discussed earlier in the chapter, which would indicate that the company should discount interest tax shields at the unlevered cost of capital. While we might argue that the company should have levered the company's unlevered cost of capital using Equation 10.5 (continuous refinancing assumption), which would have resulted in a lower valuation, that is irrelevant for purposes of this discussion because that is not what we are assuming the company did, as we assume it issued \$31,818.2 of debt.

Assuming the correct discount rate for all interest tax shields is the unlevered cost of capital we can measure the valuation error in the company's original valuation based on its capital structure strategy of issuing \$31,818.2 in debt and growing the debt with the value of the firm.

$$V_{F,0} = \frac{FCF_1}{r_{UA} - g} + \frac{r_D \times T_{INT} \times V_D}{r_{UA} - g}$$

$$V_F = \frac{\$1{,}000}{0.1 - 0.05} + \frac{0.08 \times 0.4 \times \$31{,}818.2}{0.1 - 0.05} = \$20{,}000 + \$20{,}363.6 = \$40{,}363.6$$

Assuming the company's capital structure strategy is to issue \$31,818.2 in debt and grow the debt with the value of the firm, and the discount rate for all interest tax shields is the unlevered cost of capital, the correct value of the firm is \$40,363.6 indicating that the original WACC-based valuation overstates value of the firm by \$5,090.9 (\$5,090.9 = \$45,454.5 − \$40,363.6) or by about 13%.

Instead of assuming the discount rate for all interest tax shields is the cost of debt or the unlevered cost of capital, we examine the assumption that the discount rate for interest tax shields from the company's existing debt is the cost of the debt and the discount rate from additional debt resulting from the company's growth is the unlevered cost of capital. This valuation context may be reasonable, for example, for a company with existing debt with a very long-term maturity or for a company with a relatively small amount of existing debt and substantial additional debt capacity.

$$V_F = \frac{FCF_1}{r_{UA} - g} + ITS_1 \times \left(\frac{1}{r_D} + \frac{1}{r_{UA} - g} - \frac{1}{r_{UA}} \right)$$

$$= \frac{\$1,000}{0.10 - 0.05} \times \$1,018.2 \times \left(\frac{1}{0.08} + \frac{1}{0.10 - 0.05} - \frac{1}{0.1} \right)$$

$$= \$20,000 + \$22,909.1 = \$42,909.1$$

Assuming the company's capital structure strategy is to issue \$31,818.2 in debt and grow the debt with the value of the firm, and the discount rate for interest tax shields from the company's existing debt is the cost of the debt and the discount rate for interest tax shields from additional debt is the unlevered cost of capital, the correct value of the firm is \$42,909.1 indicating that the original WACC-based valuation overstates value of the firm by \$2,545.5 (\$2,545.5 = \$45,454.5 − \$42,909.1) or by about 6%.[23]

So in summary, using the M&M perpetual debt formula and the WACC valuation method resulted in a valuation of \$45,454.5. Based on that valuation, if we assume the company issued \$31,818.2 of debt, we see widely varying estimates of firm value depending on what we assume is the firm's capital structure strategy and the right way to value the tax shields. If we assume the debt does not grow and interest tax shields are discounted at the cost of debt, the value of the firm would only be \$32,727.3. If we assume the debt will grow, but the right way to value all the tax shields is at the unlevered cost of capital, then the value of the firm would be \$40,363.6. Finally, if we assume that we discount the tax shields on the \$31,818.2 of debt at the cost of debt and all the tax shields from the growing debt at the unlevered cost of capital, then the resulting valuation is \$42,909.1.

Of course, we would argue that the best way to value the company and to figure out how much debt to have issued would have been based on the continuous refinancing levering formula which values all the tax shields at the unlevered cost of capital. If we had done this, the value of the firm would have only been \$36,231.9 and the firm would have only issued \$25,362.3 of debt (\$25,362.3 = \$36,231.9 × 0.7).

$$r_E = 0.10 + (0.10 - 0.08) \times \frac{0.7}{0.2} + (0.10 - 0.09) \times \frac{0.1}{0.2} = 0.175$$

$$r_{WACC} = 0.175 \times 0.2 + 0.08 \times (1 - 0.4) \times 0.7 + 0.09 \times 0.1 = 0.0776$$

$$V_{F,0} = \frac{FCF_1}{r_{WACC} - g} = \frac{\$1,000}{0.0776 - 0.05} = \$36,231.9$$

The difference in the valuation would be \$9,222.6 (\$9,222.6 = \$45,454.5 − \$36,231.9) indicating that our valuation based on the perpetual debt levering formula overstated the value of the firm (and the amount of debt it would issue) by about 25%.

It should be clear from these examples that the M&M perpetual debt levering formula will always overstate the valuation of a growing company with constant capital structure ratios. Thus, we note that we do not recommend using this levering formula for companies for which this levering method results in a significant valuation error. Such companies are companies with a high debt-to-value ratio, or which

[23] Another alternative valuation context similar to this one is one in which some minimal amount of debt grows with the value of the firm for which the discount rate for interest tax shields is the cost of debt and the remainder of the company's debt, also growing with the value of the firm, has interest tax shields discounted at the unlevered cost of capital. See Grinblatt and Liu for a formal framework based on this type of valuation context; Grinblatt, Mark and Jun Liu, "Debt Policy, Corporate Taxes, and Discount Rates," *Journal of Economic Theory*, 2008, vol. 141, issue 1, pp. 225–254.

do not have additional debt capacity, or have a high present value weighted average perpetual growth rate or intend to follow a reasonably strict debt-to-value target capital structure. We illustrated the overstated valuation by levering the unlevered cost of capital. The identical error occurs if we lever the unlevered beta instead of the unlevered cost of capital.

Although we do not illustrate the valuation errors resulting from using the corresponding unlevering formulas (see Equations 10.16 and 10.20), the same issues exist, although the resulting error is in the opposite direction. Assuming a company issues a fixed amount of perpetual debt for which the discount rate for interest tax shields is the cost of debt, when the expectation is that the company will grow or when the correct discount rate for interest tax shields is the unlevered cost of capital, results in an unlevered cost of capital that is overstated. All else equal, an overstated unlevered cost of capital results in an understated valuation. Naturally, we have partially offsetting errors if we use Equations 10.16 or 10.20 to unlever a comparable company's cost of capital (or beta) and then use Equations 10.7 and 10.12 to lever the cost of capital (or beta) of the company we are valuing. The degree of the offset depends on the similarity of the company's capital structure strategies, growth rates, and income tax rates for interest.

Valuation Key 10.9

The assumptions that a company has a fixed amount of perpetual debt and that the discount rate for the company's interest tax shields is the company's debt cost of capital serve as the basis for the most widely used levering and unlevering formulas (often called the Modigliani and Miller or M&M levering and unlevering formulas). However, the levering and unlevering formulas based on these assumptions are inconsistent for many companies and result in valuation errors when applied to a growing company. The degree of the error depends on the difference between the company's correct valuation context and the assumed valuation context—no growth perpetual debt—underpinning these formulas.

Assuming Zero Debt and Preferred Stock Betas

As we discuss in this chapter, Modigliani and Miller developed levering and unlevering formulas for the cost of capital assuming a zero-growth company issuing a fixed amount of riskless debt ($r_D = r_F$) and no other non-common equity securities. Hamada extended that work to beta by assuming the CAPM determined the cost of capital.[24] Hamada continued to assume that the company issued riskless debt and no other non-common equity securities. Since riskless debt has a zero beta, Hamada developed the levering and unlevering formulas assuming the beta of debt is zero. These formulas are the most commonly used formulas for levering and unlevering beta, which assume the betas of all non-common equity securities are zero.

However, from Chapter 9 we know that most companies issue risky debt. Thus, even though a company's debt and preferred stock securities are less risky than its equity, we also know that these non-equity securities are not risk-free. In this section, we discuss the effect of assuming that these non-equity securities are risk-free. Assuming that debt and preferred betas are equal to zero $\beta_D = \beta_{PS} = 0$, which is equivalent to assuming that the debt and preferred are risk-free, we develop levering and unlevering formulas under that assumption and illustrate the valuation errors that result. We show that the zero debt beta assumption might be reasonable to use for companies that have very highly rated debt (debt with low default risk) because the cost of such debt is close to the risk-free rate. However, it is not a reasonable assumption to use for many companies. Despite that, this assumption is commonly used in the practice community.

Levering Formulas with Zero Betas for Debt and Preferred Securities. Assuming zero betas for debt and preferred, we show the simplified levering and unlevering formulas in Exhibit 10.7. The effect of making this assumption on the levering formulas is that the equity beta resulting from the levering process is higher than it would be otherwise. To illustrate this point, we use the levering formula assuming the discount rate for all interest tax shields is the unlevered cost of capital.

[24] Hamada, R. S., "Portfolio Analysis, Market Equilibrium, and Corporation Finance," *Journal of Finance* (March 1969), pp. 13–31; Hamada, R. S., "The Effect of the Firm's Capital Structure on the Systematic Risk of Common Stocks," *Journal of Finance* (May 1972), pp. 435–452.

$$\beta_E = \beta_{UA} + (\beta_{UA} - \beta_D) \times \frac{V_D}{V_E} + (\beta_{UA} - \beta_{PS}) \times \frac{V_{PS}}{V_E}$$

Assuming both the debt and preferred stock betas equal zero, this formula becomes

$$\beta_E = \beta_{UA} + \beta_{UA} \times \frac{V_D}{V_E} + \beta_{UA} \times \frac{V_{PS}}{V_E}$$

$$\beta_E = \beta_{UA} \times \left(1 + \frac{V_D}{V_E} + \frac{V_{PS}}{V_E}\right)$$

Since a company's true debt and preferred stock betas are lower than its unlevered beta but not equal to zero, assuming a zero beta for debt or preferred stock increases the equity beta above its true value given a properly measured unlevered beta. Since the capital structure ratios do not change as a result of this assumption, the higher equity cost of capital results in a higher weighted average cost of capital. In addition, the WACC and APV valuation methods will no longer result in the same valuation, confirming the inconsistency.

In Exhibit 10.8, we show an example of levering a company's unlevered beta assuming zero debt and preferred betas when, in fact, those betas are not equal to zero. The company's unlevered beta is 1.0. The risk-free rate of return is 5%, the market risk premium is 6%, and the income tax rate is 40%. We assume that the discount rate for all interest tax shields is the unlevered cost of capital. The company has an expected free cash flow for the next period equal to $1,000, which the company expects to grow at 3% in perpetuity.

EXHIBIT 10.7 The Levering and Unlevering Formulas for the Capital Asset Pricing Model Beta Assuming Debt and Preferred Securities Have a Zero Beta

Levering Formula		Unlevering Formula	
Discount rate for interest tax shields is the unlevered cost of capital or interest is not tax deductible:			
$\beta_E = \beta_{UA} \times \left(1 + \frac{V_D}{V_E} + \frac{V_{PS}}{V_E}\right)$	(10.24)	$\beta_{UA} = \frac{\beta_E}{1 + \frac{V_D}{V_E} + \frac{V_{PS}}{V_E}}$	(10.28)
Discount rate for certain interest tax shields is the cost of debt:			
$\beta_E = \beta_{UA} \times \left(1 + \frac{V_D - V_{ITS@r_D}}{V_E} + \frac{V_{PS}}{V_E}\right)$	(10.25)	$\beta_{UA} = \frac{\beta_E}{1 + \frac{V_D - V_{ITS@r_D}}{V_E} + \frac{V_{PS}}{V_E}}$	(10.29)
Discount rate is the cost of debt for a zero-growth company with a fixed amount of perpetual debt:			
$\beta_E = \beta_{UA} \times \left[1 + (1 - T_{INT}) \times \frac{V_D}{V_E} + \frac{V_{PS}}{V_E}\right]$	(10.26)	$\beta_{UA} = \frac{\beta_E}{1 + (1 - T_{INT}) \times \frac{V_D}{V_E} + \frac{V_{PS}}{V_E}}$	(10.30)
Discount rate based on the annual refinancing assumptions:			
$\beta_E = \beta_{UA} \times \left[1 + \left(1 - \frac{r_D \times T_{INT}}{1 + r_D}\right) \times \frac{V_D}{V_E} + \frac{V_{PS}}{V_E}\right]$	(10.27)	$\beta_{UA} = \frac{\beta_E}{1 + \left(1 - \frac{r_D \times T_{INT}}{1 + r_D}\right) \times \frac{V_D}{V_E} + \frac{V_{PS}}{V_E}}$	(10.31)

EXHIBIT 10.8 Example of Levering Formulas for the Capital Asset Pricing Model Beta Assuming Debt and Preferred Securities Have a Zero Beta

Company We Are Valuing:			
Free cash flow	$1,000.00		
Growth rate (constant in perpetuity)	3.0%		
Cost of debt	8.0%	Cost of preferred stock	9.0%
Debt beta	0.500	Preferred stock beta	0.667
Debt to firm value	50.0%	Preferred to firm value	20.0%
Using Betas for All Securities:		**Assuming Zero Non-Equity Betas:**	
$\beta_E = \beta_{UA} + (\beta_{UA} - \beta_D) \times V_D/V_E + (\beta_{UA} - \beta_{PS}) \times V_{PS}/V_E$	2.056	$\beta_E = \beta_{UA} \times (1 + V_D/V_E + V_{PS}/V_E)$	3.333
Equity cost of capital	17.33%	Equity cost of capital	25.00%
Weighted average cost of capital	9.400%	Weighted average cost of capital	11.700%
Value of the Firm—WACC Method	**$ 15,625**	**Value of the Firm—WACC Method**	**$11,494**
		Valuation error	-26.4%

The company we are valuing is a highly leveraged company. It uses 50% debt financing (with a cost of debt of 8%) and 20% preferred stock financing (with a cost of preferred of 9%). We first calculate the implied betas of the debt and preferred using the cost of debt and cost of preferred stock, the assumptions about the risk-free rate and market risk premium, and Equation 10.9. Then, using the unlevered beta of 1.0, a debt beta of 0.5, and a preferred stock beta of 0.667, we measure an equity beta of 2.056 [$2.056 = 1 + (1 - 0.5) \times 0.5/0.3 + (1 - 0.667) \times 0.2/0.3$], again assuming the discount rate for all interest tax shields is the unlevered cost of capital. The equity cost of capital for the company is 17.33% ($0.1733 = 0.05 + 2.056 \times 0.06$). The company's weighted average cost of capital is 9.4% [$0.094 = 0.1733 \times 0.3 + 0.08 \times (1 - 0.4) \times 0.5 + 0.09 \times 0.2$].[25] The correct value of the company is equal to $15,625 [$\$15,625 = \$1,000/(0.094 - 0.03)$]. We present this valuation at the bottom of the left-hand side of the exhibit.

If we assume the company's non-equity betas equal zero, the equity beta is 3.333 [$3.333 = 1 \times (1 + 0.5/0.3 + 0.2/0.3)$] instead of 2.056 from when we used the implied debt and preferred betas. The equity cost of capital for the company is 25% ($0.25 = 0.05 + 3.333 \times 0.06$) instead of 17.33%, and the company's weighted average cost of capital is 11.7% [$0.117 = 0.25 \times 0.3 + 0.08 \times (1 - 0.4) \times 0.5 + 0.09 \times 0.2$] instead of 9.4%. The higher weighted average cost of capital results in a value of $11,494 [$\$11,494 = \$1,000/(0.117 - 0.03)$] instead of $15,625, which is a valuation error of −26%.

The problems with this approach are twofold. First, the levered equity beta is too high and the resulting valuation is too low. Second, the assumption of zero betas causes violations of basic corporate finance theory. We can see this easily from the above example. With an unlevered beta of 1.0, a risk-free rate of 5%, and a market risk premium of 6%, the unlevered cost of capital is 11% ($0.11 = 0.05 + 1 \times 0.06$). The value of the unlevered firm with $1,000 of free cash flow growing at 3% is $12,500 [$\$12,500 = \$1,000/(0.11 - 0.03)$]. However, note that the value of the company with debt and preferred financing assuming zero debt and preferred betas is $11,494 (see Exhibit 10.8), which is less than the value of the unlevered firm, $12,500. Thus, the measured value of the firm is lower with debt and the associated value of the interest tax shields than without debt—a clear violation of one of the very basic tenets of corporate finance. Since the value of the unlevered firm is $12,500, it should also be clear that the APV valuation method will not reconcile to the valuation of $11,494 but will be greater than $12,500 as long as the interest tax shields create value. Further, assuming a zero beta for preferred stock when it is not zero will result in the amount of preferred stock leverage affecting the value of the firm, which it should not. Similarly, assuming a zero beta for debt when it is not zero will result in debt leverage affecting the value of the firm even if income tax rates are zero (or if interest is not tax deductible).

Unlevering Formulas with Zero Betas for Debt and Preferred Securities. As we demonstrated in the previous section, levering betas under the assumption that the betas for a company's debt and

[25] Again, we do not adjust the company's weighted average cost of capital or valuation for countervailing forces that could reduce the embedded value of the company's interest tax shields.

preferred securities are equal to zero results in an equity beta that is higher than it would be if the levering were done properly. In Exhibit 10.9, we show an example of unlevering a comparable company's equity cost of capital assuming a zero beta for its debt and preferred securities. The comparable company has an equity beta equal to 2.11, uses 60% debt financing and 10% preferred stock financing, and has a cost of debt of 8% and a cost of preferred stock of 9%. The risk-free rate of return is 5% and the market risk premium is 6%.

EXHIBIT 10.9 Example of Unlevering Formulas for the Capital Asset Pricing Model Beta Assuming Debt and Preferred Securities Have a Zero Beta

Comparable Company Capital Structure and Market Data:			
Observed equity beta	2.11		
CAPM equity cost of capital	17.7%		
Equity to firm value	30.0%		
Cost of debt	8.0%	Cost of preferred stock	9.0%
Debt beta	0.500	Preferred stock beta	0.667
Debt to firm value	60.0%	Preferred to firm value	10.0%
Company We Are Valuing (Only Equity Financing):			
Free cash flow	$1,000.00		
Growth rate (constant in perpetuity)	3.0%		
Unlevered Beta Using Betas for All Securities:		**Unlevered Beta Assuming Zero Non-Equity Betas:**	
$\beta_{UA} = \beta_E \times V_E/V_F + \beta_D \times V_D/V_F + \beta_{PS} \times V_{PS}/V_F$	1.000	$\beta_{UA} = \beta_E/(1 + V_D/V_E + V_{PS}/V_E)$	0.633
Unlevered cost of capital	11.00%	Unlevered cost of capital	8.80%
Value of Unlevered Firm	**$ 12,500**	**Value of Unlevered Firm**	**$17,242**
		Valuation error	38%

Using the equity beta of 2.11 and the betas of the company's implied debt and preferred securities based on Equation 10.9 (a debt beta of 0.5 and a preferred stock beta of 0.667), we measure the comparable company's unlevered beta to be equal to 1, again assuming the discount rate for all interest tax shields is the unlevered cost of capital.[26] The unlevered cost of capital for the company is 11% (0.11 = 0.05 + 1.0 × 0.06). The value of the company we are valuing, which has free cash flows of $1,000 and a growth rate of 3% for the cash flows and no debt in its capital structure, is equal to $12,500 [$12,500 = $1,000/(0.11 − 0.03)]. If we assume the betas of the comparable company's non-equity securities are equal to zero, the resulting unlevered beta is 0.633.[27] The resulting unlevered cost of capital for the company is 8.8% (0.088 = 0.05 + 0.633 × 0.06), and the estimated value of the company is now equal to $17,242 [$17,242 = $1,000/(0.088 − 0.03)]—a valuation error of about 38%. Thus, when we unlever the equity beta while assuming that the debt and preferred betas are zero, the resulting unlevered cost of capital is too low.

Valuation Key 10.10

Practitioners often assume that the betas of a company's debt and preferred securities are equal to zero. We do not recommend making this assumption for companies with risky debt or preferred stock (for example, companies with low credit ratings) because it implicitly assumes that the cost of debt and preferred are equal to the risk-free rate, which is not true for almost all companies. For companies with risky debt and preferred stock, this assumption can lead to significant errors in the estimation of the cost of capital and, as we have shown, can lead to violations of the most basic principles of corporate finance.

[26] We calculate the unlevered beta as follows:

$$\beta_{UA} = \frac{2.11 + 0.5 \times \frac{0.6}{0.3} + 0.667 \times \frac{0.1}{0.3}}{1 + \frac{0.6}{0.3} + \frac{0.1}{0.3}} = 1.0$$

[27] We calculate the unlevered beta as follows:

$$\beta_{UA} = \frac{2.11}{1 + \frac{0.6}{0.3} + \frac{0.1}{0.3}} = 0.633$$

SUMMARY AND KEY CONCEPTS

We discussed two processes used to measure a company's cost of capital based on its capital structure strategy. The first process, called levering the cost of capital, is based on the relationship between the equity cost of capital and the other costs of capital, conditional on the company's capital structure strategy. The second process, called unlevering the cost of capital, is based on the relationship between the unlevered cost of capital and the other costs of capital, also conditional on the company's capital structure strategy. In general, we use the unlevering process to measure the unlevered cost of capital for the comparable companies and the company being valued if it is publicly traded. If we are using the APV valuation method, we need not use the levering process as we already have measured the unlevered cost of capital. But if we are using the WACC valuation method, we relever the unlevered cost of capital based on the capital structure of the company being valued to measure its equity cost of capital, which we then use to measure the weighted average cost of capital.

The issues related to the effects of a company's capital structure decisions on its value are numerous and complex, which also affects which levering and unlevering method we use. We do not have a single method for levering a company's cost of capital, and as such, we do not have a single method for measuring a company's weighted average cost of capital from both its unlevered cost of capital and the cost of capital of each of its non-equity securities. We also do not have a single unlevering method. We must, therefore, analyze a company's capital structure strategy to choose which approach is the most reasonable one to lever and unlever the cost of capital. Instead of unlevering and levering the cost of capital, we can use a similar approach to lever and unlever betas if we are using the CAPM to measure the equity and unlevered costs of capital. Just as for our levering and unlevering formulas for the cost of capital, we do not have a single method for levering and unlevering a company's betas.

The framework in this chapter shows how the weighted average cost of capital embeds the value of the interest tax shields using alternative assumptions about the riskiness of the interest tax shields, and how the WACC valuation method adjusts for the riskiness of the interest tax shields through the choice of the levering formula.

Finally, we discuss some of the common mistakes that practitioners make in levering and unlevering the costs of capital and betas. First, we showed that the use of the Miller and Modigliani perpetual debt formula applied to a growing firm is problematic. Second, we showed that the use of levering and unlevering formulas with the common assumption that debt and preferred betas are equal to zero can result in valuation errors and violate some of the standard principles of corporate finance.

ADDITIONAL READING AND REFERENCES

Hamada, R. S., "Portfolio Analysis, Market Equilibrium, and Corporation Finance," *Journal of Finance* (March 1969), pp. 13–31.

Hamada, R. S., "The Effect of the Firm's Capital Structure on the Systematic Risk of Common Stocks," *Journal of Finance* (May 1972), pp. 435–452.

Miles, J. A., and J. R. Ezzell, "Reformulating Tax Shield Valuation: A Note," *Journal of Finance* vol. 40 (1985), pp. 1485–1492.

EXERCISES AND PROBLEMS

P10.1 **Levering the Unlevered Cost of Capital:** A company's management is considering alternative ways of financing the company. Going forward, the company plans to adopt a target capital structure with some combination of short-term and long-term debt as well as preferred stock and common equity. Below, we show the three options management is considering.

		Option 1	Option 2	Option 3
Debt to firm value		10.0%	10.0%	70.0%
Preferred stock to firm value		40.0%	10.0%	10.0%
Unlevered cost of capital		10.0%	10.0%	10.0%
Debt cost of capital		6.0%	6.0%	7.0%
Preferred stock cost of capital		9.0%	8.0%	8.0%
Equity cost of capital		???	???	???
Income tax rate for all income		40.0%	40.0%	40.0%
Unlevered free cash flow		$1,000	$1,000	$1,000
Perpetual growth rate		3.0%	3.0%	3.0%
Risk-free rate	4.0%			
Market risk premium	6.0%			

a. For each option, calculate the equity cost of capital and weighted average cost of capital under the assumption that interest is tax deductible and that (i) the discount rate for interest tax shields is the unlevered cost of capital, (ii) the discount rate for interest tax shields is the debt cost of capital (zero-growth with fixed amount of perpetual debt), and (iii) the company refinances itself annually to a target capital structure (use the debt cost of capital for the first year and the unlevered cost of capital for subsequent years).

b. For each option and each alternative assumption about valuing the tax shields:
   i. Value the firm and the equity using the WACC valuation method.
   ii. Value the firm using the APV valuation method.
   iii. Value the equity using the Equity Free Cash Flow valuation method.
   iv. Explain any discrepancies between the valuations.

P10.2 **Levering Unlevered Beta:** Use the information from P10.1. Answer P10.1 (Part A only) but calculate the equity beta and then use the CAPM to calculate the equity cost of capital.

P10.3 **Levering the Unlevered Cost of Capital:** A company is going to finance itself with the capital structure shown below. The company will generate a perpetual series of cash flows that will not grow. Management plans to measure the value of the firm and the value of each of its securities based on the information below and some additional assumptions outlined in each part of the problem. For each part of the problem, measure the value of the firm using the WACC valuation method and measure the value of each of the securities the company uses to finance itself. Then use the APV method to value the firm. Finally, measure the company's equity free cash flow and use the Equity Free Cash Flow valuation method to value the company's equity.

Debt to firm value	40.0%
Preferred stock to firm value	20.0%
Unlevered cost of capital	12.0%
Debt cost of capital	9.0%
Preferred stock cost of capital	10.0%
Equity cost of capital	???
Income tax rate for interest (T_{INT})	40.0%
Unlevered free cash flow	$1,000
Growth rate	0.0%

a. Assume the company is going to issue short-term debt and continually refinance itself such that the discount rate for the company's interest tax shields is equal to the unlevered cost of capital.

b. Assume that the company is going to issue long-term debt and preferred stock such that the discount rate for the company's interest tax shields is equal to the debt cost of capital.

c. Assume that the company annually refinances itself to maintain a constant proportionate capital structure.

d. Compare the equity cost of capital, weighted average cost of capital, value of the firm, value of each of the company's securities, and equity free cash flow for parts (a), (b) and (c) of the problem. Explain how and why they differ.

P10.4 **Unlevering the Equity Cost of Capital—Low Leverage & High Leverage Companies:** Below, we show the information for two potential comparable companies. Calculate the unlevered cost of capital based on the following assumptions. Neither company expects its free cash flows to grow.

	Low Leverage Company	High Leverage Company
Income tax rate for interest (T_{INT})	35.0%	45.0%
Value of debt	$ 4,000	$45,000
Value of preferred stock	$ 1,000	$ 0
Value of equity	$15,000	$ 5,000
Maturity of debt (years)	Perpetual	Perpetual
Debt cost of capital	5.0%	8.0%
Preferred stock cost of capital	6.0%	
Equity cost of capital	11.8%	28.0%

a. Assume that interest is tax deductible and that the discount rate for all interest tax shields is the unlevered cost of capital.

b. Assume that interest is tax deductible and that the discount rate for all interest tax shields is the cost of debt.

c. Assume that interest is tax deductible but that the company refinances its debt at the end of each year (annual refinancing).

P10.5 **Unlevering the Equity Beta—Low Leverage & High Leverage Companies:** Use the information from P10.4 and assume that the risk-free rate is 4% and that the market risk premium is 6%. Respond to each part of P10.4 but calculate the unlevered beta instead of the unlevered cost of capital.

P10.6 **Unlevering the Equity Cost of Capital:** For each comparable company below, choose an unlevering method and measure the company's unlevered cost of capital. Explain why you chose the unlevering method you chose. Summary information appears below.

	Company A	Company B	Company C
Income tax rate for interest (T_{INT})	30.0%	40.0%	30.0%
Value of debt	$ 3,000	$28,000	$45,000
Value of preferred stock	$ 1,000	$ 4,000	
Value of equity	$16,000	$ 8,000	$ 5,000
Maturity of debt (years)	1	50	5
Debt cost of capital	5.0%	8.0%	8.0%
Preferred stock cost of capital	8.0%	8.5%	
Equity cost of capital	11.8%	16.2%	28.0%

Company A is a company that has had a stable capital structure strategy; it generally adjusts its financing to its target capital structure on a regular basis. Company B is a company that had issued a very long-term bond to finance an expansion. This is the only debt the company ever issued. The company has a very low growth rate, it funds its investments internally, and has no plans to issue additional debt. Company C has had very little debt historically. About five years ago, the company went through a debt recapitalization. The company issued debt and repurchased some of its shares, and it announced a new capital structure strategy which was to repay all of the debt by the end of its ten-year maturity. Over the last five years, the company has repaid its debt as per its capital structure strategy. The company's current debt has a five-year maturity, and the company plans to repay 20% of this balance at the end of each of the next five years. The company plans to operate with no debt after it repays its current debt. The company's equity cost of capital reflects its current capital structure strategy and debt outstanding.

P10.7 **Assuming Zero Non-Equity Betas:** For each part of the problem, measure the equity beta, equity cost of capital, and weighted average cost of capital under the assumptions that interest is tax deductible and that (i) the discount rate for interest tax shields is the unlevered cost of capital, (ii) the discount rate for interest tax shields is the debt cost of capital, and (iii) the company refinances itself annually to a target capital structure (use the debt cost of capital for the first year and the unlevered cost of capital for subsequent years).

a. Assume non-equity betas are equal to the betas implied by the cost of capital stated for each security.

b. Assume non-equity betas are equal to zero and use the debt and preferred stock costs of capital stated in the problem to measure the weighted average cost of capital. What violations of standard corporate finance theory do you observe?

Risk-free cost of capital	4.0%		
Market risk premium	6.0%		
	Company 1	**Company 2**	**Company 3**
Debt to firm value	10.0%	20.0%	60.0%
Preferred stock to firm value	40.0%	20.0%	20.0%
Unlevered CAPM beta	1.000	1.000	1.000
Debt cost of capital	6.0%	6.0%	7.0%
Preferred stock cost of capital	7.0%	6.5%	7.5%
Equity cost of capital	???	???	???
Income tax rate for interest (T_{INT})	40.0%	40.0%	40.0%

P10.8 **Incorrect Valuation Assumptions:** A privately held company finances itself with long-term debt and preferred stock using the capital structure shown below. The company's current free cash flow is $100, and it expects to generate a series of cash flows that will grow at 3% per year in perpetuity. The company plans to maintain its current capital structure strategy of 50% debt and 20% preferred stock in perpetuity, refinancing the company on an ongoing basis.

Initial debt to firm value	50.0%
Initial preferred stock to firm value	20.0%
Unlevered cost of capital	12.0%
Debt cost of capital	8.0%
Preferred stock cost of capital	9.0%
Equity cost of capital	???
Tax rate on all income	40.0%

The company's chief financial officer (CFO) measured the company's equity cost of capital using the following formula.

$$r_E = r_{UA} + (r_{UA} - r_D) \times (1 - T_{INT}) \times \frac{V_D}{V_E} + (r_{UA} - r_{PS}) \times \frac{V_{PS}}{V_E}$$

The CFO valued the company and its equity using the WACC valuation method. The CFO wants to check the WACC valuation by using the APV valuation method but is unsure how to use this valuation method to check the WACC valuation. The CFO calculated a $15,152 firm value using the WACC valuation method.

a. Reproduce the CFO's equity cost of capital, weighted average cost of capital, and WACC valuation and compare it to an APV valuation. Are the valuations consistent?

b. Use the WACC valuation method to value the firm and the equity correctly by discounting the tax shields at the unlevered cost of capital. Use the APV valuation method to value the firm, and use the Equity Free Cash Flow valuation method to value the company's equity. Are the valuations consistent?

P10.9 **Bloomberg, Precision, and Vasicek Adjusted Betas:** Calculate the Bloomberg adjusted beta (see Chapter 8) for each of the comparable companies and the portfolio of comparable companies that appear in the table for this problem. All of the companies are unlevered. Also calculate the precision weighted beta for the four comparable companies and the company being valued based on the unadjusted betas as well as the equally weighted beta of the five companies. In addition, compute the Vasicek adjusted beta for the company being valued based on the unadjusted betas. Compare the comparable company average beta (based on the unadjusted betas), comparable company precision weighted beta, and Vasicek adjusted beta.

	Beta Estimate	Standard Error of Beta	t-statistic
Comparable Company #1	0.970	0.500	1.94
Comparable Company #2	1.310	0.550	2.38
Comparable Company #3	1.420	0.710	2.00
Comparable Company #4	1.580	0.700	2.26
Comparable company average beta	1.320		
Company being valued	1.110	0.600	1.85

SOLUTIONS FOR REVIEW EXERCISES

Review Exercise 10.1: The Palm Company—Levering the Unlevered Cost of Capital

a. If we assume the discount rate for interest tax shields is equal to the company's unlevered cost of capital, then Palm's equity cost of capital (using Equation 10.5) and weighted average cost of capital are, respectively,

$$r_E = 0.12 + (0.12 - 0.07) \times \frac{0.3}{0.5} + (0.12 - 0.08) \times \frac{0.2}{0.5} = 0.1660$$

$$r_{WACC} = 0.1660 \times 0.5 + 0.07 \times (1 - 0.45) \times 0.3 + 0.08 \times 0.2 = 0.1105$$

b. Alternatively, if we assume the discount rate for interest tax shields is equal to the company's cost of debt, then Palm's equity cost of capital (using Equation 10.7) and weighted average cost of capital are, respectively,

$$r_E = 0.12 + (0.12 - 0.07) \times (1 - 0.45) \times \frac{0.3}{0.5} + (0.12 - 0.08) \times \frac{0.2}{0.5} = 0.1525$$

$$r_{WACC} = 0.1525 \times 0.5 + 0.07 \times (1 - 0.45) \times 0.3 + 0.08 \times 0.2 = 0.1038$$

Notice that Palm's equity cost of capital is now less than it was before. The reason for this is that the tax shields in the formula are valued at the cost of debt, thus mitigating the impact of debt on the cost of equity capital.

c. Lastly, if we assume Palm refinances its capital structure annually (rather than issuing perpetual debt and preferred stock), then Palm's equity cost of capital (using Equation 10.8) and weighted average cost of capital are, respectively,

$$r_E = 0.12 + (0.12 - 0.07) \times \left(1 - \frac{0.07 \times 0.45}{1.07}\right) \times \frac{0.3}{0.5} + (0.12 - 0.08) \times \frac{0.2}{0.5} = 0.1651$$

$$r_{WACC} = 0.1651 \times 0.5 + 0.07 \times (1 - 0.45) \times 0.3 + 0.08 \times 0.2 = 0.1101$$

Thus, the impact of assuming that the Palm Company adjusts to its target capital structure with an annual lag is similar to that of assuming continual refinancing (i.e., a discount rate for interest tax shields equal to the unlevered cost of capital).

Review Exercise 10.2: The Palm Company—Levering Beta

Palm's debt beta is 0.5 [0.5 = (0.07 − 0.04)/0.06], its preferred stock beta is 0.667 [0.667 = (0.08 − 0.04)/0.06], and its unlevered beta is 1.333 [1.333 = (0.12 − 0.04)/0.06].

a. If we assume the discount rate for interest tax shields is equal to the company's unlevered cost of capital, then Palm's equity beta is equal to 2.10, which results in an equity cost of capital of 16.66%.

$$\beta_E = 1.333 + (1.333 - 0.5) \times \frac{0.3}{0.5} + (1.333 - 0.667) \times \frac{0.2}{0.5} = 2.10$$

$$r_E = 0.04 + 0.06 \times 2.10 = 0.166$$

b. Alternatively, if we assume the discount rate for interest tax shields is equal to the company's cost of debt, then Palm's equity beta is equal to 1.875, which results in an equity cost of capital of 15.25%.

$$\beta_E = 1.333 + (1.333 - 0.5) \times (1 - 0.45) \times \frac{0.3}{0.5} + (1.333 - 0.667) \times \frac{0.2}{0.5} + 1.875$$

$$r_E = 0.04 + 0.06 \times 1.875 = 0.1525$$

c. Lastly, if we assume Palm refinances its capital structure annually (rather than issuing perpetual debt and preferred stock), its equity beta is 2.085.

$$\beta_E = 1.333 + (1.333 - 0.5) \times \left(1 - \frac{0.07 \times 0.45}{1.07}\right) \times \frac{0.3}{0.5} + (1.333 - 0.667) \times \frac{0.2}{0.5} = 2.085$$

$$r_E = 0.04 + 0.06 \times 2.085 = 0.1651$$

Review Exercise 10.3: The Date Company—Unlevering the Equity Cost of Capital

Below we use the unlevering formulas to measure the unlevered cost of capital for the Date Company based on several alternative assumptions for the discount rate for interest tax shields.

a. If we assume the discount rate for interest tax shields is equal to the company's unlevered cost of capital, then the comparable company's unlevered cost of capital is equal to 12%.

$$r_{UA} = 0.265 \times \frac{\$2{,}000}{\$10{,}000} + 0.08 \times \frac{\$5{,}000}{\$10{,}000} + 0.09 \times \frac{\$3{,}000}{\$10{,}000} = 0.12$$

$$r_{UA} = \frac{0.265 + 0.08 \times \dfrac{\$5{,}000}{\$2{,}000} + 0.09 \times \dfrac{\$3{,}000}{\$2{,}000}}{1 + \dfrac{\$5{,}000}{\$2{,}000} + \dfrac{\$3{,}000}{\$2{,}000}} = 0.12$$

b. Alternatively, if we assume the discount rate for interest tax shields is the company's cost of debt (zero-growth with fixed amount of perpetual debt), then the comparable company's unlevered cost of capital is equal to 13.2%.

$$r_{UA} = 0.265 \times \frac{\$2{,}000}{\$10{,}000 - 0.45 \times \$5{,}000} + 0.08 \times (1 - 0.45) \times \frac{\$5{,}000}{\$10{,}000 - 0.45 \times \$5{,}000} + 0.09 \times \frac{\$3{,}000}{\$10{,}000 - 0.45 \times \$5{,}000} = 0.132$$

$$r_{UA} = \frac{0.265 + 0.08 \times (1 - 0.45) \times \dfrac{\$5{,}000}{\$2{,}000} + 0.09 \times \dfrac{\$3{,}000}{\$2{,}000}}{1 + (1 - 0.45) \times \dfrac{\$5{,}000}{\$2{,}000} + \dfrac{\$3{,}000}{\$2{,}000}} = 0.132$$

c. Lastly, if we assume Date refinances its capital structure annually, then the comparable company's unlevered cost of capital is equal to just over 12.1%.

$$r_{UA} = 0.265 \times \frac{\$2{,}000}{\$10{,}000 - \frac{0.08 \times 0.45}{1.08} \times \$5{,}000} + 0.08 \times \left(1 - \frac{0.08 \times 0.45}{1.08}\right) \times \frac{\$5{,}000}{\$10{,}000 - \frac{0.08 \times 0.45}{1.08} \times \$5{,}000} + 0.09 \times \frac{\$3{,}000}{\$10{,}000 - \frac{0.08 \times 0.45}{1.08} \times \$5{,}000} = 0.121$$

$$r_{UA} = \frac{0.265 + 0.08 \times \left(1 - \frac{0.08 \times 0.45}{1.08}\right) \times \frac{\$5{,}000}{\$2{,}000} + 0.09 \times \frac{\$3{,}000}{\$2{,}000}}{1 + \left(1 - \frac{0.08 \times 0.45}{1.08}\right) \times \frac{\$5{,}000}{\$2{,}000} + \frac{\$3{,}000}{\$2{,}000}} = 0.121$$

Review Exercise 10.4: The Date Company—Unlevering Equity Beta

Below we use the unlevering formulas to measure the unlevered beta for the Date Company based on alternative assumptions for the discount rate for interest tax shields.

a. If we assume the discount rate for interest tax shields is the company's unlevered cost of capital, then the comparable company's unlevered cost of capital is equal to 12% (0.12 = 0.04 + 1.333 × 0.06).

$$\beta_E = \frac{0.265 - 0.04}{0.06} = 3.75$$

$$\beta_D = \frac{0.08 - 0.04}{0.06} = 0.667$$

$$\beta_{PS} = \frac{0.09 - 0.04}{0.06} = 0.833$$

$$\beta_{UA} = 3.750 \times \frac{\$2{,}000}{\$10{,}000} + 0.667 \times \frac{\$5{,}000}{\$10{,}000} + 0.833 \times \frac{\$3{,}000}{\$10{,}000} = 1.333$$

$$\beta_{UA} = \frac{3.750 + 0.667 \times \frac{\$5{,}000}{\$2{,}000} + 0.833 \times \frac{\$3{,}000}{\$2{,}000}}{1 + \frac{\$5{,}000}{\$2{,}000} + \frac{\$3{,}000}{\$2{,}000}} = 1.333$$

b. Alternatively, if we assume the discount rate for interest tax shields is the company's cost of debt (zero-growth with fixed amount of perpetual debt), then the comparable company's unlevered cost of capital is equal to 13.2% (0.132 = 0.04 + 1.527 × 0.06).

$$\beta_{UA} = 3.750 \times \frac{\$2{,}000}{\$10{,}000 - 0.45 \times \$5{,}000} + 0.667 \times (1 - 0.45) \times \frac{\$5{,}000}{\$10{,}000 - 0.45 \times \$5{,}000} + 0.833 \times \frac{\$3{,}000}{\$10{,}000 - 0.45 \times \$5{,}000} = 1.527$$

$$\beta_{UA} = \frac{3.750 + 0.667 \times (1 - 0.45) \times \frac{\$5{,}000}{\$2{,}000} + 0.833 \times \frac{\$3{,}000}{\$2{,}000}}{1 + (1 - 0.45) \times \frac{\$5{,}000}{\$2{,}000} + \frac{\$3{,}000}{\$2{,}000}} = 1.527$$

c. Lastly, if we assume Date uses annual refinancing of its capital structure, then the comparable company's unlevered cost of capital is equal to 12.1% (0.121 = 0.04 + 1.345 × 0.06).

$$\beta_{UA} = 3.750 \times \frac{\$2{,}000}{\$10{,}000 - \frac{0.08 \times 0.45}{1.08} \times \$5{,}000} + 0.667 \times \left(1 - \frac{0.08 \times 0.45}{1.08}\right) \times \frac{\$5{,}000}{\$10{,}000 - \frac{0.08 \times 0.45}{1.08} \times \$5{,}000} + 0.833 \times \frac{\$3{,}000}{\$10{,}000 - \frac{0.08 \times 0.45}{1.08} \times \$5{,}000} = 1.345$$

$$\beta_{UA} = \frac{3.750 + 0.667 \times \left(1 - \frac{0.08 \times 0.45}{1.08}\right) \times \frac{\$5{,}000}{\$2{,}000} + 0.833 \times \frac{\$3{,}000}{\$2{,}000}}{1 + \left(1 - \frac{0.08 \times 0.45}{1.08}\right) \times \frac{\$5{,}000}{\$2{,}000} + \frac{\$3{,}000}{\$2{,}000}} = 1.345$$

Review Exercise 10.5: Bloomberg, Precision, and Vasicek Adjusted Betas

Precision Weighted Beta	Beta Estimate	Standard Error of Beta	1/ Standard Error	Bloomberg Adjusted Beta
Comparable Company #1	0.90	0.50	2.00	0.933
Comparable Company #2	1.10	0.40	2.50	1.067
Comparable Company #3	1.35	0.60	1.67	1.235
Comparable Company #4	1.50	0.45	2.22	1.335
Company being valued	1.10	0.56	1.79	1.067
Comparable company average beta	1.213			1.142
Average beta of comps and company being valued	1.190			
Precision weighted beta	1.189			
Sum of 1/standard error	10.175			
Vasicek adjusted beta—company being valued	1.196			
Vasicek inputs:				
Variance of the comparable company betas	0.0530			
Standard error squared—company being valued	0.3136			
Weight for company being valued	0.1445			
Weight for comparable company portfolio beta	0.8555			

The Bloomberg adjusted beta is 0.33 + 0.67 × unadjusted beta.

The comparable company average beta and average beta of the comparable companies and the company being valued are just equally weighted averages.

The precision weighted beta is calculated using Equation 10.22 and the Vasicek adjusted beta is based on Equation 10.23. In this case the average beta, precision-weighted beta and Vasicek adjusted beta are all quite close to one another with a range of 1.19 to 1.21.

2012

2. Valuation

Advertising – UFCF = 600, 900, 1350, 5% g forever, r_{UA} = 13%, $\frac{V_D}{V_F}$ = 50% (annually + refinancing), r_D = 6%

Gaming – UFCF = 88, 110, 138, r_{UA} = 8%, $\frac{V_E}{V_F}$ = 100%. | T_C = 40%, No excess assets, V_F = ?

V_{adv}: $r_E = r_{UA} + (r_{UA} - r_D)\left(1 - \frac{(r_D)(T_C)}{1+r_D}\right)\left(\frac{V_D}{V_E}\right) = 0.13 + (0.13 - 0.06)\left(1 - \frac{0.06(0.4)}{1.06}\right)\left(\frac{1}{1}\right) = 19.842\%$

$r_{WACC} = r_E\left(\frac{V_E}{V_F}\right) + (1 - T_{INT})(r_D)\left(\frac{V_D}{V_F}\right) = 0.198\left(\frac{1}{2}\right) + (0.6)(0.06)\left(\frac{1}{2}\right) = 11.72\%$

$V_{adv.} = \frac{600}{1.1172} + \frac{900}{1.1172^2} + \frac{\frac{1350}{1.1172^3}}{1 - \frac{1.05}{1.1172}} = 17353.56$

$V_{gaming} = \Delta\ r_E = r_{UA} = r_{WACC} = 8\%$.

$r_{WACC} = r_E\left(\frac{V_E}{V_F}\right) = r_E$ $V_{adv} = \frac{88}{1.08} + \frac{110}{1.08^2} + \frac{\frac{138}{1.08^3}}{1 - \frac{1.05}{1.08}} = 4119.547$

$V_F = V_{adv} + V_{gaming} = 21473.112$

3. Multiples

(a) $EV/EBIT$ = ? → $EV = 275$, $EBIT = 15$ → $\frac{EV}{EBIT} = 18.\bar{3}$

(b) Req. cash = 10, EBIT = 5 but exp. EBIT = 7, V_F = ?

$V_F = (18.\bar{3})(7) + 10$ (7: EBIT; 10: Req. Cash)

4. UFCF = 100 forever, $r_{UA} = 15\%$, $T_C = 40\%$

(a) $r_D = 7\%$, Continuous Refinancing, $\frac{V_D}{V_F} = 60\%$, $V_E = ?$

$r_E = 27\%$, $r_{WACC} = 13.32\%$, $V_F = 750.751$, $V_E = 300.300$

(b) Perpetual Debt, $r_D = 7\%$, $\frac{V_D}{V_F} = 60\%$, $V_E = ?$

WACC $r_E = 22.2\%$, $r_{WACC} = 11.4\%$, $V_F = 877.193$, $V_E = 350.877$

OR APV $V_F = PV(UFCF) + PV(ITS)$

$$V_F = \frac{100}{0.15 \to r_{UA}} + \frac{(0.4)(0.7)(0.6V_F)}{0.07}$$

$V_F = 877.19$, $V_E = 350.87$

(c) r_E is diff. b/c discount rate applied to ITS's is higher in (a). ITS are safer, but w/ same exp. value, in second scenario, which is why firm is worth more in second scenario

1. (a) r_{UA} comps vs. P-E comps – r_{UA} comps (match only op. risk and distress situation), P-E comps (match of future growth, cap. structure, cap. re-investment policies}, etc. + adjust for acct. techniques used to measure earnings, transitory shocks

(b) EFCF issue – EFCF needs V_D, r_E needs $\frac{V_D}{V_F}$ so need V_F, V_D, V_E before valuing firm to properly use EFCF method

(c) Diversified Portfolio for Historic Equity β – Not portfolio resembling firm/specialized portfolio – want Russell 3000

(d) Change in DIV. impacting Equity Value

Current $\to g = (1 - \text{Payout Ratio})(ROE)$ Future

$g = (1-0.15)(0.10) = 0.085 \to \frac{DIV}{r_E - g}$ $g = (1-0.5)(0.10) = 0.05 \to \frac{DIV}{r_E - g}$

$\frac{DIV}{0.12-0.085} = 28.57\,DIV$ vs $\frac{3.5DIV}{0.12-0.05}$ ($\frac{0.5}{0.15}$) $= 47.142\,DIV \to \frac{47.12}{28.57} = 65\%$ increase

(e) Leases

(i) Decision to capitalize airplane leases obfuscates valuation based on $\frac{EV}{EBITDA}$

↳ OPEX impacted by elimination of operating lease expense from EBITDA. This OPEX replaced by interest exp. and dep'n exp. (both not part of EBITDA). Assets (or debt) also included as part of EV. Over, multiple should change w/ choice of acct. treatment for leases

(ii) Sol'n to problem

↳ Treat all leases the same way for all companies

(f) Insider Info – Jail if person aware trade based on insider info, Jail if Dept. of Justice criminally prosecutes

(g) ↑IRR – Problem w/ investing in highly leveraged LBOs b/c they produce highest IRR

↳ ↑Leverage → ↑Risk → ↑Cost of capital – can't know if value is created just by looking at IRR

(h) WACC r_{ITS} – r_{ITS} used to compute r_E in WACC so riskiness of interest tax shields accounted for

(i) LBO Firm Change – firms that go through LBO change a lot, ↑leverage, ↑Value for shareholders, & Diff. cost of capital, Diff. multiples, use multiples of post-LBO firms instead

(j) Same WACC for acquisition – only appropriate if both firms have same op. risk (r_{UA})

(k) Uncertainty → Discount Rate – Discount rate shouldn't change b/c uncertainty is idiosyncratic

(l) Value through LBO Process – Tax benefit of leverage, reduction in agency problems, improvement in op. performance, transfers from bondholders (those w/ no protections/covenants

After mastering the material in this chapter, you will be able to:

1. Measure the weighted average cost of capital (11.1)
2. Measure a company's target capital structure and income tax rate for interest tax shields (11.2)
3. Standardize the treatment of liabilities as debt versus operating liabilities (11.3–11.4)
4. Value a company with interest and net operating loss carryforwards (11.5)
5. Adjust the value created by debt financing for potential countervailing forces (11.6)

Measuring the Weighted Average Cost of Capital and Related Valuation Issues

CHAPTER 11

On January 8, 2015, Sunrun, Inc. announced the close of $195 million of senior credit facilities to support the growth of Sunrun's residential solar business. According to the company's press release:

SUNRUN, INC.

> Sunrun will use the funds to help more Americans install high quality solar systems on their homes and reduce their electricity costs. This is Sunrun's first syndicated financing and signifies a new source of capital for the company.
>
> "This financing significantly reduces Sunrun's cost of capital, which will help us lower costs for homeowners and also positions the company well for continued growth," said Jason Cavaliere, VP of Project Finance at Sunrun. "The strength of our project portfolio and operating history, among other factors, allowed us to achieve a lower interest rate and longer tenor [time to expiration] than any publicly announced residential solar backleverage facility."[1]

In this chapter, we will discuss many of the intricacies associated with measuring the weighted average cost of capital. We will also explore the other effects of debt financing on the value of the firm.

[1] Source: Sunrun, Inc. is the largest dedicated residential solar company in the U.S., and designs, installs, finances, insures, monitors and maintains the solar panels for homeowners. The company's website is www.sunrun.com.

CHAPTER ORGANIZATION

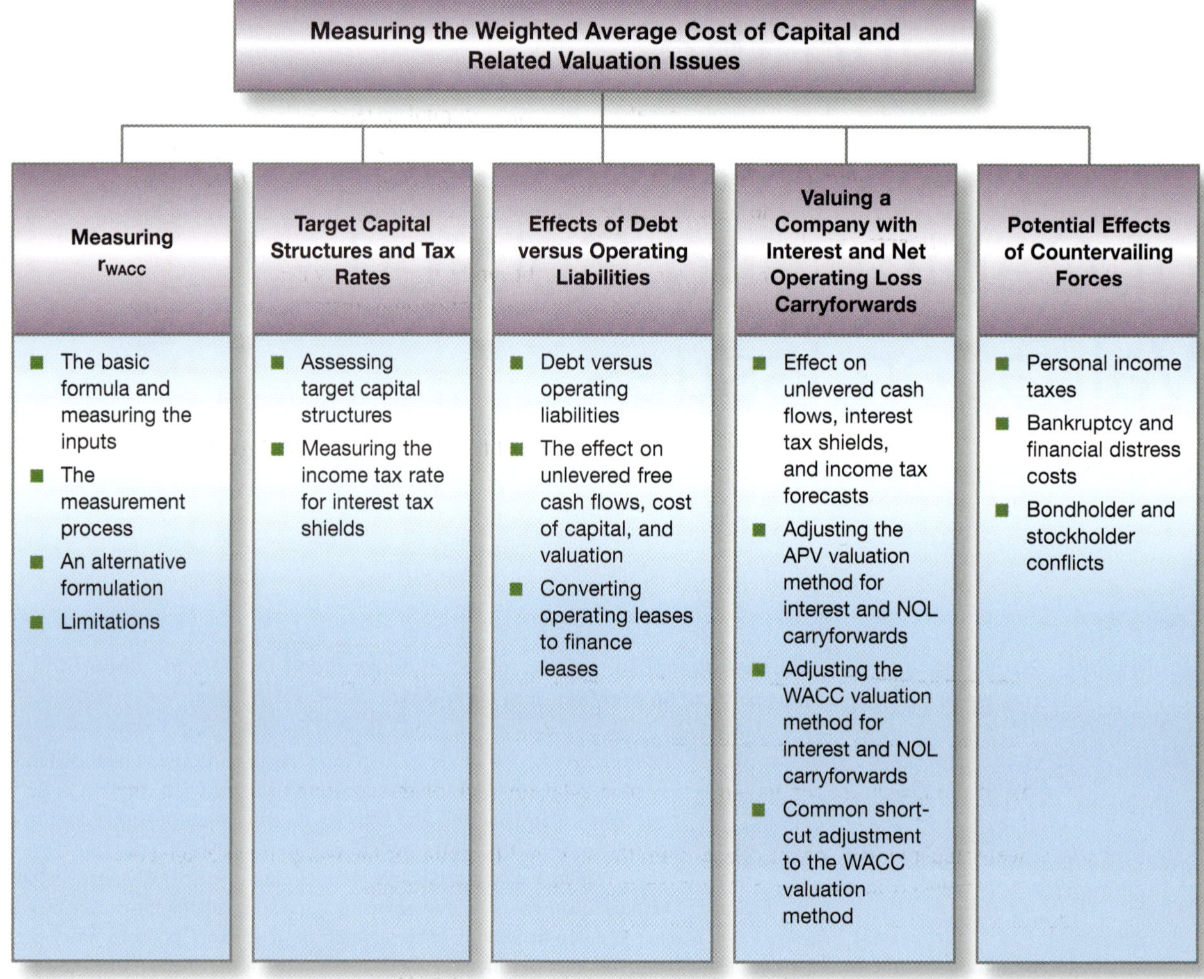

INTRODUCTION

In this chapter, we discuss the process of, and the more complex issues related to, measuring the weighted average cost of capital and the resulting valuation issues. Recall from previous chapters that the WACC valuation method embeds the value of the interest tax shields into the valuation by using a discount rate—the weighted average cost of capital—that is lower than the unlevered cost of capital used to measure the value of the unlevered firm in the APV valuation method. Using a lower discount rate results in a higher discounted value of the unlevered cash flows, and this increase in value is equal to the value of the interest tax shields.

In this chapter, we present a more detailed discussion of measuring a company's weighted average cost of capital, r_{WACC}, than our discussion in Chapter 5. Specifically, we discuss the weighted average cost of capital inputs in more detail. In addition, we discuss the measurement of a company's capital structure and capital structure ratios, the adjustment for excess assets, minority interest positions, unconsolidated affiliates, leases, and pensions (and similar benefits). We then discuss two common valuation issues that arise when using the WACC valuation method. The first is how to adjust the WACC valuation method when a company has interest and net operating loss carryforwards and the company does not benefit from interest expense when it is paid (recall the initial discussion of this issue in Chapter 3). The second is the effect of classifying a liability as an operating liability instead of debt (or the converse). We also discuss topics related to measuring the benefits from debt financing. A review of the academic literature suggests that the benefits of debt associated with interest tax shields may be reduced by the effect of such items as personal taxes, agency costs, and the magnitude and likelihood of incurring **financial distress costs**. As such, the value of debt financing cannot be measured solely by valuing the interest tax shields. We also discuss circumstances in which the weighted average cost of capital method cannot measure the value of the interest tax shields correctly, whereas the adjusted present value method results in the correct value.

11.1 THE WEIGHTED AVERAGE COST OF CAPITAL—OVERVIEW

LO1 Measure the weighted average cost of capital

The **weighted average cost of capital**, r_{WACC}, is the after-tax cost of capital investors require to finance the company's expected or **target capital structure**. We summarize the process of measuring the weighted average cost of capital in Exhibit 11.1. We calculate a company's weighted average cost of capital by averaging its equity cost of capital and the cost of capital for each of its non-common equity securities (debt, preferred stock, warrants, employee stock options, etc.), on an after-tax basis. Since companies usually do not have capital structures with equal amounts of debt, preferred stock, warrants, and equity, we cannot use a simple average to calculate the weighted average cost of capital. Instead, we weight each cost of capital by the proportion of the firm—measured using market values—that is financed with each respective security.

EXHIBIT 11.1 An Overview of the Process to Measure the Weighted Average Cost of Capital

1	Estimate the equity cost of capital, r_E
2	Estimate the cost of capital for each non-common equity security (e.g., r_D, r_{PS})
3	Determine the proportions of a company's securities in its target capital structure (based on market values) (e.g., V_E/V_F, V_D/V_F, V_{PS}/V_F as well as warrants, options, etc.), making appropriate adjustments for excess assets, unconsolidated affiliates, minority interest, leases, etc.
4	Estimate the tax rate for interest (T_{INT}) and any other information needed to value the interest tax shields
5	Calculate the weighted average cost of capital, r_{WACC}, using the standard weighted average cost of capital formula

If we have all of the necessary inputs—the cost of capital for each of the company's securities, the income tax rate for interest tax shields, and the proportion of the firm financed with each security—we can measure the weighted average cost of capital with the standard formula for the weighted average cost of capital that we introduced in Chapter 5, to which we added a warrant component, and to which we would add additional components for each additional type of security used to finance the firm.

$$r_{WACC} = r_E \times \frac{V_E}{V_F} + r_D \times (1 - T_{INT}) \times \frac{V_D}{V_F} + r_{PS} \times \frac{V_{PS}}{V_F} + r_W \times \frac{V_W}{V_F} \tag{11.1}$$

where: r_{WACC} = the weighted average cost of capital
r_E = cost of equity capital
r_D = cost of debt capital
r_{PS} = cost of preferred stock capital
r_W = cost of capital for warrants and/or rights offerings
V_D/V_F = capital structure ratio for debt
V_{PS}/V_F = capital structure ratio for preferred stock
V_W/V_F = capital structure ratio for warrants and/or rights offerings
V_E/V_F = capital structure ratio for equity
T_{INT} = the appropriate tax rate to measure the tax deduction for interest

Recall that we typically use the WACC method when we expect the company to manage its capital structure using constant proportions of debt, equity, preferred stock, and other securities issued by the firm. We measure all of the inputs for the weighted average cost of capital using market costs of capital (see Chapters 8–10 and 12) and target capital structure ratios based on relative market values. For example, some companies have a stated capital structure strategy based on target capital structure ratios. As such, we do not need to know the values of the numerators and denominators because we know the forward looking capital structure ratios. On the other hand, if we are measuring the weighted average cost of capital for a publicly traded company, and know the values of all of its securities, then we can measure the company's capital structure ratios directly and analyze its historical capital structure ratios. We can use the analysis of the company's historical capital structure ratios to either confirm a stated capital structure strategy or forecast the company's forward looking capital structure ratios. Note that the standard weighted average cost of capital formula (Equation 11.1) only makes a tax adjustment to the cost of debt and not the other securities. None of the other terms for equity, preferred, and warrants are tax-adjusted because those generally do not lead to tax deductions at the corporate level. If they did, we would adjust Equation 11.1 accordingly. By now it should be clear that the weights to measure the weighted average cost of capital represent expected capital structure ratios, and the costs of capital reflect the expected cost of capital based on the company's forward looking or target capital structure, capital structure strategy, and business risk.

We do not show time subscripts in the weighted average cost of capital formula, for all of the terms in the formula share the same time subscript (in other words, we measure each input at the same point in time). A company's weighted average cost of capital is not necessarily constant over all future years. The weighted average cost of capital changes over time if we expect its inputs to change over time—for example, if we expect changes in a company's capital structure ratios, costs of capital, or income tax rate for measuring the interest tax shields. The inputs also change if we predict a company's business risk or financial risk will change. For example, if the company expects to sell one or more of its businesses, its business risk will change if the businesses expected to be sold have a different business risk than the remaining businesses. In addition, shifts in required costs of capital can occur because of shifts in expected inflation, changes in required real risk-free rates of return, and variation in market risk premiums.

If we use a weighted average cost of capital that is constant over time, we assume that the firm will keep the proportions of debt, preferred stock, equity, and any other claims constant over time and that the operating risk and financial risk of the firm will remain constant. We also assume that the real risk-free rate of return, expected inflation, and market risk premium are constant. Under these assumptions, if the value of the equity increases or decreases, we assume the company will adjust its capital structure to maintain the assumed constant capital structure strategy. In Chapter 10, we discussed why companies may not continuously make these adjustments due to transactions costs. However, using a constant weighted average cost of capital presumes the company will manage its capital structure to maintain some perceived target.

Of course, if a company anticipates changing its capital structure, then the company's current costs of capital will not be useful for calculating its weighted average cost of capital under the new capital structure. For example, a change in the proportion of debt used by a company will cause changes in the other costs of capital as well. Thus, conducting analyses of alternative capital structures requires changing all of the costs of capital. For example, a common error is to not vary the costs of capital with different leverage ratios. We have already provided all of the necessary tools to estimate the effect of a change in a company's capital structure on its various debt, preferred, and equity costs of capital in Chapters 9 and 10.

Valuation Key 11.1

The weighted average cost of capital is used to value the firm and to value projects that are of average risk. It is based on the after-tax cost of capital of each of the claims that the firm issues, weighted according to target capital structure weights as measured by market values.

How the Weighted Average Cost of Capital Embeds the Value of Interest Tax Shields

It is useful to think about the weighted average cost of capital from a different perspective to understand exactly how it adjusts the unlevered cost of capital to embed the value of the interest tax shields in the WACC DCF method. We can illustrate this effect using the general levering formula we derived in Chapter 10 (Equation 10.4), which measures the equity cost of capital as a function of the unlevered cost of capital and the debt and preferred stock costs of capital. If we substitute the general levering formula for the equity cost of capital into the weighted average cost of capital formula (Equation 11.1), we see that the weighted average cost of capital is determined by a company's unlevered cost of capital, debt cost of capital, cost of capital for interest tax shields, tax rate for computing the interest tax shields, and the proportion of debt to firm value and potentially the proportion of the value of the interest tax shields to firm value.

$$r_{WACC} = r_{UA} - r_D \times T_{INT} \times \frac{V_D}{V_F} - (r_{UA} - r_{ITS}) \times \frac{V_{ITS}}{V_F} \tag{11.2}$$

The second term in the above weighted average cost of capital formula reduces the unlevered cost of capital for the tax deductibility of interest; in addition, if the company's interest tax shields have less risk than its operating assets (for example, if they are valued at the cost of debt), the third term reduces the weighted average cost of capital even further for this risk reduction. If the discount rate for interest tax shields is equal to the unlevered cost of capital, the third term is equal to zero. Further, if interest is not tax deductible, $T_{INT} = 0$, the last two terms of the formula equal zero, and the weighted average cost of capital is just equal to the unlevered cost of capital.

This formula does not contain terms for the equity cost of capital or preferred stock cost of capital. This is neither a coincidence nor a mystery. In Equation 11.2, we substituted the levering formula for the equity cost of capital term in Equation 11.1, and the equity cost of capital and the preferred stock cost of capital terms drop out of the formula. Recall that issuing preferred stock does not affect the weighted average cost of capital, for preferred stock dividends are not tax deductible and, thus, have no tax advantage over the equity cost of capital. Of course, if preferred stock dividends were tax deductible, then the formulas in Chapter 10 and the standard weighted average cost of capital formula (Equation 11.1) would be adjusted for this tax benefit.

We can derive an expression for the weighted average cost of capital for each of the special levering cases we discussed in Chapter 10. We summarize these formulas in Exhibit 11.2. On the left-hand-side of the exhibit we show the levering formulas from Chapter 10 and on the right-hand-side we show the corresponding weighted average cost of capital formula resulting from substituting the levering formula for the equity cost of capital in Equation 11.1. As it turns out, there are situations, especially with warrants and options, where these expressions are useful and make our calculations simpler. We will highlight their potential usefulness with warrants and options in Chapter 12.

EXHIBIT 11.2 Weighted Average Cost of Capital Formulas Based on the Unlevered Cost of Capital

Equity Cost of Capital		Corresponding Weighted Average Cost of Capital Formulas	
Discount rate for interest tax shields is the unlevered cost of capital or interest is not tax deductible:			
$r_E = r_{UA} + (r_{UA} - r_D) \times \frac{V_D}{V_E} + (r_{UA} - r_{PS}) \times \frac{V_{PS}}{V_E}$	(10.5)	$r_{WACC} = r_{UA} - r_D \times T_{INT} \times \frac{V_D}{V_F}$	(11.3)
Discount rate for certain interest tax shields is the cost of debt:			
$r_E = r_{UA} + (r_{UA} - r_D) \times \frac{V_D - V_{ITS@r_D}}{V_E} + (r_{UA} - r_{PS}) \times \frac{V_{PS}}{V_E}$	(10.6)	$r_{WACC} = r_{UA} - r_D \times T_{INT} \times \frac{V_D}{V_F} - (r_{UA} - r_D) \times \frac{V_{ITS@r_D}}{V_F}$	(11.4)
Discount rate is the cost of debt for a zero-growth company with a fixed amount of perpetual debt:			
$r_E = r_{UA} + (r_{UA} - r_D) \times (1 - T_{INT}) \times \frac{V_D}{V_E} + (r_{UA} - r_{PS}) \times \frac{V_{PS}}{V_E}$	(10.7)	$r_{WACC} = r_{UA} \times \left(1 - T_{INT} \times \frac{V_D}{V_F}\right)$	(11.5)
Discount rate based on the annual refinancing assumptions:			
$r_E = r_{UA} + (r_{UA} - r_D) \times \left(1 - \frac{r_D \times T_{INT}}{1 + r_D}\right) \times \frac{V_D}{V_E} + (r_{UA} - r_{PS}) \times \frac{V_{PS}}{V_E}$	(10.8)	$r_{WACC} = r_{UA} - (1 + r_{UA}) \times \frac{r_D \times T_{INT}}{(1 + r_D)} \times \frac{V_D}{V_F}$	(11.6)

Target Long-Term Capital Structure and the Free Cash Flow Perpetuity Method

Recall that the free cash flow perpetuity formula assumes that the company has a constant discount rate and a constant growth rate. If we are using the weighted average cost of capital as the discount rate in the free cash flow perpetuity model, then we need a constant discount rate that, in turn, requires a constant weighted average cost of capital. Of course, it is possible for a company's capital structure to change and for the weighted average cost of capital to remain the same if, for some reason, the costs of capital or income tax rate for interest changes in a way that offsets the effect of the change in the company's capital structure. Even though this is possible, this set of circumstances is unlikely to occur; thus, from a practical perspective, this requires the company to use a target capital structure that it will adhere to over time. The assumption of a constant target capital structure at the continuing value date is likely reasonable to make for most companies—especially when they have reached the steady state required for using the perpetuity method. In the absence of countervailing evidence such as a stated forward looking capital structure strategy or one based on a relatively stable historical capital structure, we can use a typical industry capital structure, although as we illustrate in the next section, while we observe differences in the capital structure across industries, we also observe substantial variation of companies' capital structures within most industries.

REVIEW EXERCISE 11.1

Measuring the Weighted Average Cost of Capital

Calculate the weighted average cost of capital using Equations 11.1 and 11.2. Assume that the company's securities are publicly traded, that its debt is currently trading at 100% of book value, and that its preferred stock is currently trading at 95% of its book value. The company's stock price is currently $12 per share, and the company has 1,000 shares of stock outstanding, which is net of 100 treasury shares. The risk-free rate is 5%, and the market risk premium is 6%. The company issued the debt and preferred stock at par value. The company has an equity beta equal to 2.5. The company's debt has a yield to maturity equal to 8%, which includes a 1% expected default loss, and the cost of capital for the preferred stock is equal to 8.5%. The income tax rate on all income is 30%. The company plans to continually refinance itself to have a constant capital structure strategy based on its current capital structure ratios.

	Year 1	Year 2
Income Statement		
Revenue		$20,000
Operating expenses		−8,000
Depreciation expense		−5,200
Earnings before interest and taxes		$ 6,800
Interest expense		−800
Income before taxes		$ 6,000
Income tax expense		−1,800
Net income		$ 4,200
Balance Sheet		
Total current assets	$ 4,000	$ 6,000
Property, plant, and equipment (net)	32,000	34,000
Total assets	$36,000	$40,000
Account payable	$ 1,000	$ 1,200
Debt	10,000	12,000
Total liabilities	$11,000	$13,200
Preferred stock	$ 8,000	$ 8,000
Capital stock	2,000	2,000
Retained earnings	15,000	16,800
Shareholders' equity	$25,000	$26,800
Liabilities and shareholders' equity	$36,000	$40,000

Solution on pages 540–541.

Limitations of the Weighted Average Cost of Capital Valuation Method

In this section, we discuss certain limitations of the WACC valuation method; in other words, situations when the WACC valuation method is not capable of valuing the firm correctly. One way to address these valuation issues is to use the APV valuation method.

Interest and Net Operating Loss Carryforwards. In Chapter 3, we discuss **interest** and **net operating loss carryforwards** (NOLs) and how to identify when a company with interest and NOL carryforwards will capture the tax benefit of its interest deduction. Among other things, we learned that interest and NOL carryforwards can cause timing differences between when the company receives its interest tax shield benefits and when it pays (or accrues) the interest. The standard implementation of the WACC valuation method will incorrectly value the firm because of the difference between the assumed timing of the interest tax shield benefits using the WACC valuation method and the expected timing of the interest tax shield benefits resulting from the effect of any interest and NOL carryforwards. A straightforward way to value a company in such situations is to forecast the period-by-period timing and magnitude of the interest tax shields and use the APV valuation method to value the firm. One constraint using the APV valuation method is the requirement of forecasts of the company's capital structure. We cannot forecast the timing and magnitude of the interest tax shields unless we have forecasts of the company's capital structure. Later in the chapter we show one way the WACC valuation method can be adjusted to correctly value the firm that has interest and NOL carryforwards, which is not the standard implementation of the WACC valuation method.

Capitalized Interest. Most taxing authorities require companies to capitalize interest in certain situations, for example, while a company is paying interest to fund a construction project or manufacture inventory that takes a long time to build, such as a yacht. In such situations, the **capitalized interest** is attached to the value of an asset—for example, a building or work-in-process inventory. When interest is capitalized to the carrying value of a building during its construction phase, the capitalized interest is not tax deductible until it is amortized through the subsequent depreciation expense on that building. For work-in-process inventory, the capitalized interest will be added to the carrying value of the inventory, and eventually, it will be expensed through cost of goods sold. For example, if it takes five years to build a yacht that is later sold, the interest incurred is capitalized for five years and then is expensed as part of cost of goods sold.

It should be apparent that the capitalization of interest causes a timing difference between when the interest is paid or accrued and when the tax benefit from the interest is received. Note that the interest will never be shown as interest expense on the financial statements, but this is irrelevant. What is relevant is the timing difference between when the benefit of the interest is received relative to when it is paid or accrued. The WACC valuation method cannot correctly measure the value of the firm with such a timing difference between when the interest is paid and when the interest is actually deductible; however, this timing difference is not an issue for the APV valuation method as long as we keep track of when the interest will actually be deductible. Of course, if the amount of the capitalized interest is small, it is unlikely that it will lead to a meaningful valuation error, which is the case for most companies. On another note, we need only be concerned about interest that is capitalized in the forecasts. Any previously capitalized interest will simply be embedded in depreciation expense or cost of goods sold, which does not cause a problem for the WACC method. Any capitalized interest prior to the valuation date is no different than any other asset that the firm owns as of the valuation date, and it is not dependent on debt financing subsequent to the date of the valuation.

Paid-in-Kind Interest. **Paid-in-kind interest** or **PIK interest** is interest that is accrued and not paid until a future period—which could be in a few years or not until the debt matures. The interest that is accrued, but not paid, increases the principal amount of the loan. For financial reporting purposes, the interest accrued on the **paid-in-kind debt** (or **zero coupon debt**) is reported as interest expense even though it is not paid. In many situations, paid-in-kind interest is tax deductible in the period in which it is expensed for financial reporting purposes. In these situations and assuming the company follows its target capital structure, the weighted average cost of capital correctly values the interest tax shields because we include the PIK debt as part of the capital structure when we compute the weighted average cost of debt and capital structure ratios.

In certain circumstances, however, paid-in-kind interest is not tax deductible when it is expensed for financial reporting purposes or potentially not at all. The U.S. income tax code has a provision called the **AHYDO** (**applicable high-yield discount obligation**) rules. This provision potentially postpones the tax benefits of paid-in-kind interest until the interest is paid in cash (often at maturity, but possibly sooner) or can even convert the interest into dividends, meaning the interest will never be deductible.

If the rules apply, and the interest tax shield is postponed until it is paid in cash, the weighted average cost of capital method will not value the interest tax shields correctly. If we include the paid-in-kind debt in the capital structure as debt, and if the cost of that debt is used in calculating the weighted average cost of debt, the weighted average cost of capital will presume the interest is deductible in that period. Again, the adjusted present value method does not have this limitation but we need a forecast of the tax deductible interest in each future period. Further, any PIK interest that will be treated as a dividend will not generate any interest tax shield and can just be ignored in an APV and WACC valuation.

Cost of Debt Is Not the Same as the Effective Interest Rate. As we discussed in Chapter 10, some (but not all) of the levering and unlevering formulas assume that the cost of debt multiplied by the value of the debt is equal to the expected interest tax shield and errors can result when that assumption is not correct. The weighted average cost of capital method also makes that same assumption. If the cost of debt at the time of debt issuance differs from the cost of debt at the valuation date due to significant changes in expected default losses or shifts in inflation or shifts in required real returns on a risk-free asset, the WACC DCF method as normally applied will not value the interest tax shields correctly. We do not discuss this issue in detail here, as we discussed it to some extent in Chapter 10, but one can readily understand that when we measure the weighted average cost of capital using the cost and value of debt at the valuation date we may not properly reflect the value of the tax shields in these circumstances.

Generally, this error should be small since the change in the cost of debt is offset by a change in the market value of the debt if the cost of debt shifts. For example, if a company issues debt at face value and then inflation increases and investors demand a higher rate of return on the debt, the cost of debt will go up, but the value of the debt will fall. Conversely, if the cost of debt has fallen since the debt was issued, the market value of the debt will rise. As such, while the new cost of debt times the value of the debt may not exactly equal the expected interest tax shields, the error is likely to be small. If we think this issue could lead to significant errors in our valuation, the easiest approach is to use the APV valuation method and compute the period-by-period interest tax shields based on the true expected interest tax shields, not the current cost of debt multiplied by the value of debt. We would continue using the APV method until such time as all the affected debt is retired. At that point, one can switch to the WACC valuation method if it is desirable to do so.

Valuation Key 11.2

In situations such as when a company has interest and net operating loss carryforwards, capitalized interest, paid-in-kind debt subject to AHYDO rules, and when the current cost of debt multiplied by the value of the debt does not equal the expected interest tax shields, the WACC valuation method as normally applied cannot incorporate the present value of the interest tax shields correctly. In all of these cases, if the effect is likely to be material, we can value the interest tax shields correctly by using the APV valuation method.

11.2 MEASURING TARGET CAPITAL STRUCTURES AND THE INCOME TAX RATE FOR INTEREST TAX SHIELDS

LO2 Measure a company's target capital structure and income tax rate for interest tax shields

Previous chapters (as well as Chapter 12) discuss how to measure the cost of capital inputs for the weighted average cost of capital. In this chapter we discuss two other inputs—capital structure ratios and the income tax rate for interest tax shields.

Assessing a company's capital structure strategy is the preliminary step in measuring a company's capital structure ratios. Naturally, if a company has a specified target capital structure ratio it plans to use in the future, we use that capital structure strategy in the valuation. However, if the company does not have a forward looking capital structure or if the company is going to be sold to an unknown buyer, then assessing the company's capital structure is typically necessary, which raises the issue of identifying the likely or best capital structure strategy for the company to follow.

Do companies have an optimal capital structure, and if so, how can we determine the optimal capital structure for a company? This question has been the subject of academic and practitioner research for more than 50 years and provides useful principles to guide our thinking about capital structure strategies; however, the specific choice of an optimal capital structure remains largely unresolved. Different capital structure theories make different assumptions about the costs and benefits of issuing various securities, and as such, the different theories result in different optimal capital structures. We know that a company's optimal capital structure is contingent on many forces, some of which we discuss later in this chapter.[2] Moreover, the personal preferences of managers can impact the capital structure decision as well.

---

[2] For reviews of this literature see Graham, John R. and Mark T. Leary, "A Review of Empirical Capital Structure Research and Directions for the Future," *Annual Review of Financial Economics* vol. 3 (December 2011), pp. 309–345; and Parsons, Christopher and Sheridan Titman, "Empirical Capital Structure: A Review," *Foundations and Trends in Finance* vol. 3, no. 1 (2008), pp. 1–93.

In this section we also discuss some of the complexities that arise when measuring the income tax rate for interest tax shields. As we discussed in previous chapters, in any given period, a company's interest tax shield is equal to the reduction in income taxes that results from the company's interest expense deduction for that period. Conceptually, it is the difference between the income tax a company would pay if it had no interest expense deduction and the actual income tax the company pays. Even though the concept is straightforward, we are unable to observe a company's interest tax shield directly; it does not appear in the company's financial statements or its income tax filings.

We know that the weighted average cost of capital is an appropriate discount rate for valuing the firm, which is why it is of interest to us as valuation specialists. The weighted average cost of capital is also the appropriate discount rate for valuing "scale expansions" (increasing the size of the firm by scaling up all of its elements proportionately) or for valuing projects that have the "average" risk of existing operating assets, assuming the firm's capital structure strategy remains constant. However, the weighted average cost of capital is not an appropriate discount rate for all of the firm's projects. For example, it is not appropriate for projects that are either more or less risky than the average risk of the firm's existing operating assets or for projects that will result in changes in the company's capital structure. For many projects, it is more appropriate to use a project-specific cost of capital or hurdle rate that will differ from the weighted average cost of capital.

VALUATION IN PRACTICE 11.1

How Do Companies Measure Cost of Capital Inputs? A survey of large U.S. companies, investment banks, and leading textbooks documents that

> The estimation approaches are broadly similar across the three samples in several dimensions.
>
> - Discounted Cash Flow (DCF) is the dominant investment-evaluation technique.
> - WACC is the dominant discount rate used in DCF analyses.
> - Weights are based on *market* not book value mixes of debt and equity.
> - The after-tax cost of debt is predominantly based on *marginal* pretax costs, and *marginal* or *statutory* tax rates.

Source: Bruner, R. F., K. M. Eades, R. S. Harris, and R. C. Higgins, "Best Practices in Estimating the Cost of Capital: Survey and Synthesis," *Financial Practice and Education* (Spring/Summer 1998), pp. 13–28; the specific quote is on page 15.

Measuring Target Capital Structure Ratios

The framework underpinning the WACC valuation method as well as the levering and unlevering formulas discussed in Chapter 10 is based on market value capital structure ratios; thus, we use market values to measure capital structure ratios. If the company (or the buyer of the company) has a stated forward looking capital structure strategy, we base the company's target capital structure ratios on that strategy. If the company does not have an explicit capital structure strategy, we analyze the company's historical capital structure ratios to assess the company's implicit capital structure strategy. Thus, in assessing the target capital structure, we typically examine how the company managed its capital structure in the recent past. This review provides useful information on whether the general assumption of a constant proportionate capital structure underlying the use of the WACC method is reasonable. In the absence of a stated company strategy or plan, using a recently observed capital structure as the target is often a viable option, especially if the capital structure proportions have been reasonably constant over the last few years.

If current capital structure weights do not reflect the company's stated capital structure strategy, we assume that the company will adjust its financing to its target capital structure reasonably quickly. If this is not the expectation, then using the target capital structure in the weighted average cost of capital method may not be appropriate. Rather, we might need to use an alternative capital structure until such time as we expect the company to refinance itself to its target capital structure. If the company expects to change capital structures over time—for example, if a company with high financial leverage plans to pay down its debt over a number of years in order to eventually achieve a long-run target capital structure—then the weighted average cost of capital will also vary over time. In this situation, the APV valuation method is likely the more appropriate method to use until the company reaches a constant target capital structure. At the point in time when the company reaches its target capital structure, we can switch from an APV valuation to a WACC valuation.

Operating Liabilities Are Not Part of a Company's Capital Structure. Capital structure ratios exclude **operating liabilities** that are included in **operating working capital** (such as accounts payable, wages payable, as well as non-current operating liabilities). Most operating liabilities are current liabilities, but some are not (such as non-current deferred income tax liabilities). Any interest-bearing debt, such as bank debt, is part of the capital structure—as are common stock, preferred stock, warrants, rights offerings, and employee stock options.

Other contractual obligations—such as operating leases, finance leases, pensions, and post-retirement benefits—may or may not be part of the capital structure, depending on how we choose to treat them. We discuss the issue of including them or treating them as operating liabilities in more detail later in the chapter, but essentially, these liabilities can be treated as either an operating activity—affecting the company's operating risk—or a financing activity—affecting the company's financial risk. How we classify a liability as either debt or an operating liability is particularly relevant when using comparable companies either to measure the costs of capital or market multiples. We discuss the effect of alternative classifications on the costs of capital later in this chapter and discuss the effect on market multiples in Chapter 14.

Industry Capital Structures. Companies in the same industry often have similar capital structures, although we also observe a substantial amount of variation within industries as well. Companies sometimes use target capital structures that are observable in their industry as a guide to deciding on their own target capital structure. As we discussed earlier, industry capital structure ratios may be useful when valuing a company. For example, suppose we are advising a company on the value of a division it is considering selling. Rather than using the capital structure used by the selling company—which may reflect many different types of businesses—we would use a capital structure based on the industry capital structure for the business of the division, as potential buyers would likely believe it to be a reasonable capital structure strategy for the asset. This is also a common assumption to make when we cannot easily measure the value of a company's capital structure ratios, for example, with a private company, and the company does not have a capital structure strategy. Naturally, this is only one alternative to consider when choosing a capital structure for valuing an entity. For example, if we decided that the cash flows of the entity were capable of supporting a leveraged buyout transaction, we might perform another valuation based on that capital structure and valuation method (see Chapter 15).

In Exhibit 11.3, we present data on average capital structure ratios for industries with at least 30 companies in 2015 based on two-digit SIC codes. These are the equally weighted average capital structures for these industries. For purposes of creating this exhibit, we measure debt and preferred stock using book values (given the relative paucity of data on the market values of debt and preferred) and we measure the common equity using market values; all are measured as of the 2015 fiscal year-end of each company.[3] Market capitalization represents the sum of the book values of debt and preferred plus the market value of the equity.

In the exhibit, we sort the industries by common equity to total market capitalization. For the entire sample, companies, on average, use 63.7% equity financing, 35.6% debt financing, and 0.8% preferred stock financing. The standard deviation of the percentage of equity financing is 25.7%, indicating substantial variation across industries. As we can quickly see from this exhibit, the amount of debt financing used varies significantly across industries; the Business Services industry group finances itself, on average, with 12.4% debt, whereas other industries such as Amusement and Recreation Services; Water Transportation; Electric, Gas, and Sanitary Services; and Health Services use 40% or more debt. One note of caution when examining this table: we have not included off-balance-sheet financing in the capital structure ratios. For example, we have not capitalized operating leases, and some of these industries use substantial amounts of operating leases (retail stores, restaurants, and others). In addition, we have not included other types of claims such as employee stock options or warrants.

While the exhibit reports the average capital structure ratios across industries, it does not give a very good sense of the variation in capital structure ratios within industries. For example, the Fabricated Metal Products, Except Machinery and Transportation Equipment group, on average, has 76% equity financing and 24% debt financing. Not shown in the exhibit is the fact that this industry has a range of equity

[3] This sample is the same sample of companies used in Chapter 9—2015 data for all U.S. publicly traded companies with a market capitalization greater than $1 million with available data in the CapitalIQ database. The total sample has 5,259 companies for 2015 and the number of companies in an industry in the exhibit varies from 30 (the minimum number we required) to 649. The total number of companies within the industries shown in the exhibit is 4,570 (87% of the total in the CapitalIQ database for 2015).

EXHIBIT 11.3 Average Capital Structure Ratios for Selected Industries

		Weighted Average by Broad Industry Group				
Industry SIC Code	Industry Description	Short-Term Debt to Market Cap	Long-Term Debt to Market Cap	Total Debt to Market Cap	Preferred Stock to Market Cap	Common Equity to Total Market Cap
	All companies in the sample	5.3%	30.3%	35.6%	0.8%	63.7%
56	Apparel and accessory stores	0.0%	8.5%	8.6%	0.0%	91.4%
73	Business services	0.4%	12.0%	12.4%	0.0%	87.6%
36	Electronic and other electrical equipment and components, except computer equipment	0.8%	12.6%	13.5%	0.2%	86.3%
87	Engineering, accounting, research, management, and related services	0.0%	14.0%	14.1%	0.0%	85.9%
59	Miscellaneous retail	0.2%	14.2%	14.4%	0.0%	85.6%
29	Petroleum refining and related industries	2.8%	13.2%	16.0%	0.0%	84.0%
38	Measuring, analyzing, and controlling instruments; photographic, medical and optical goods; watches and clocks	0.8%	15.3%	16.0%	0.0%	83.9%
28	Chemicals and allied products	1.0%	14.9%	15.9%	0.3%	83.8%
58	Eating and drinking places	0.2%	17.6%	17.7%	1.6%	80.6%
20	Food and kindred products	2.7%	18.0%	20.7%	0.8%	78.5%
26	Paper and allied products	1.0%	20.7%	21.7%	0.0%	78.3%
50	Wholesale trade-durable goods	1.3%	21.3%	22.6%	0.2%	77.2%
34	Fabricated metal products, except machinery and transportation equipment	0.2%	23.7%	23.9%	0.0%	76.1%
63	Insurance carriers	1.4%	24.5%	25.9%	0.4%	73.7%
35	Industrial and commercial machinery and computer equipment	2.0%	24.2%	26.2%	0.1%	73.7%
99	Nonclassifiable establishments	1.1%	30.8%	31.8%	0.5%	67.7%
51	Wholesale trade-non-durable goods	0.9%	34.8%	35.7%	0.2%	64.1%
48	Communications	0.1%	37.3%	37.4%	0.0%	62.6%
37	Transportation equipment	3.7%	34.7%	38.4%	0.0%	61.5%
10	Metal mining	0.2%	39.1%	39.2%	0.5%	60.3%
13	Oil and gas extraction	0.5%	38.8%	39.3%	0.6%	60.2%
33	Primary metal industries	0.4%	40.4%	40.8%	0.1%	59.1%
79	Amusement and recreation services	0.0%	43.3%	43.3%	0.0%	56.6%
44	Water transportation	0.1%	43.5%	43.6%	0.4%	56.0%
49	Electric, gas, and sanitary services	2.1%	43.6%	45.7%	0.3%	53.9%
67	Holding and other investment offices	10.7%	35.1%	45.8%	0.8%	53.4%
80	Health services	0.1%	47.1%	47.2%	0.1%	52.7%
65	Real estate	2.6%	51.7%	54.2%	0.2%	45.6%
60	Depository institutions	18.6%	37.3%	55.9%	2.3%	41.8%
62	Security and commodity brokers, dealers, exchanges, and services	24.3%	39.8%	64.1%	1.4%	34.5%
61	Non-depository credit institutions	10.7%	76.4%	87.2%	3.2%	9.7%
	Across industry averages					
	10th percentile	0.1%	13.2%	14.1%	0.0%	45.6%
	25th percentile	0.2%	16.4%	16.9%	0.0%	56.3%
	50th percentile—median	0.9%	30.8%	31.8%	0.2%	67.7%
	75th percentile	2.4%	39.4%	43.5%	0.5%	82.2%
	90th percentile	10.7%	43.6%	54.2%	1.4%	85.9%

financing from 23% to 100%. Also not shown in the exhibit, is that every industry has at least one company with more than 95% equity financing and most industries have at least one company that is highly levered and likely in financial distress. Thus, it is important to note that there is variation in the capital structure ratios within industry groups.

Potential Adjustments for Excess Cash and Other Excess Assets. Recall that we typically value a company's **excess assets** separately from its operating assets; the most typical example of this is a company holding more cash than it needs to operate its businesses (excess cash). In previous chapters, we discussed how to adjust the free cash flows and the costs of capital for excess cash. To measure the weighted average cost of capital, we use both the adjusted costs of capital and the relevant capital structure ratios for the assets we are valuing—that is, the capital structure ratios for the assets we are valuing (excluding excess assets) for the company's target capital structure. Of course, after measuring the value of the firm without the excess assets, we add the value of the excess assets to the value of the firm without excess assets in order to measure the total firm value.

In certain circumstances, we might decide to not exclude the excess assets from our DCF valuation (for example, we believe the company will retain the excess assets). In these circumstances, we would not adjust the free cash flows or costs of capital for the elimination of the excess cash, but rather, we would include the income flows from the excess cash in the free cash flows, and we would choose the target capital structure for the company with the retention of excess cash taken into consideration—companies may elect to hold more debt in their capital structure if they retain excess cash as opposed to if they had no excess cash.

Potential Adjustments for Noncontrolling (Minority) Interests. If a parent company owns between 50% and 100% of a subsidiary, the parent usually consolidates it. Consolidation means that the parent company reports 100% of the subsidiary's assets, liabilities, revenues, and expenses on its own financial statements. If the parent company owns less than 100% of the subsidiary, the parent company shows an allocation—a deduction for the parent company—of the subsidiary's income or loss and common equity attributable to the minority shareholders—called **noncontrolling interest** or **minority interest**—on its financial statements for the proportion of the subsidiary not owned by the parent company.

Fortunately, relatively few companies have significant minority interest. For example, for the sample of companies used in Exhibit 11.3, for the 2015 fiscal year, only 28% reported noncontrolling interest on the balance sheet. Of those reporting non-zero noncontrolling interests, more than 50% reported a book value of minority interests to total assets of less than 0.6%. The 25th and 75th percentiles of this ratio for these companies is 0.1% and 2.4%, respectively. These results show that, for the majority of companies, the effect of minority interest is likely to be quite small. That said, however, when it is significant, we should consider the impact of minority interests when we value a company.

Suppose that we are valuing a company with significant minority interests and that we believe we should adjust for that minority interest in our valuation. Conceptually, this adjustment is fairly straightforward. One way to make the adjustment is to value the company, including the value of the minority interest, and then deduct the value of the minority interest, essentially treating it as a non-common equity claim on the company's assets. However, it is sometimes very difficult to collect the information we need to make this adjustment.

To be more specific, if we can assume that the weighted average cost of capital for the less than 100% owned subsidiaries is the same as the parent company's weighted average cost of capital, we can then measure the weighted average cost of capital as follows. Since the consolidated company reports 100% of the subsidiaries' non-equity financing, we can add the market value of the minority interest claims to the value of the parent company's common equity. We measure the capital structure ratios using 100% of the debt, preferred stock, and equity (including minority interest); the latter is equal to 100% of the total parent company equity plus the value of the minority interest. If the subsidiary is publicly traded, this is a straightforward calculation, but if it is not, we have to use other valuation methods to value the minority interests depending on the information that is available. To measure the value of the firm, we discount the unlevered free cash flows (including cash flows that might be attributable to the minority interests) using the weighted average cost of capital, which measures the value of the firm plus the value of the minority interests. We then subtract the value of the minority interests to arrive at the value of the firm.

An alternative way to make this adjustment is to extract the effect of the part of the subsidiary that the parent company does not own from both the unlevered free cash flows and the components of the weighted average cost of capital. Naturally, depending on the level of information that is available, this exercise can be tedious or next to impossible.

Potential Adjustments for Unconsolidated Affiliates. Generally, the term **unconsolidated affiliate** refers to a partially owned company, which can be an equity investment in an unrelated company or an investment in a joint venture, that is not consolidated by the parent company; the ownership percentage

VALUATION IN PRACTICE 11.2

Six Flags Entertainment Corporation While noncontrolling interests is not typically a large component of the company's financial statements, they can be large for some companies. An example is Six Flags, which is the largest regional theme park operator in the U.S., with 16 regional theme and water parks; Six Flags also has one theme park in Mexico City and one in Montreal.

Six Flags does not own 100% of all of its theme parks. The company consolidates these partnerships

> as subsidiaries in our consolidated financial statements as we have determined that we have the power to direct the activities of those entities that most significantly impact the entities' economic performance and we have the obligation to absorb losses and receive benefits from the entities that can be potentially significant to these entities. The equity interests owned by non-affiliated parties in the Partnership Parks are reflected in the accompanying consolidated balance sheets as redeemable noncontrolling interests. . . . The portion of earnings or loss attributable to non-affiliated parties . . . is reflected as net income attributable to noncontrolling interests in the accompanying consolidated statements of operations.

In 2015, 20% of Six Flags net income and 18% of its total assets were allocated to noncontrolling interests in these partnerships:

Six Flags Entertainment Corporation

Abbreviated Income Statement	2014	2015
Total revenue	$1,175,793	$1,263,938
Operating and other gains and expenses	−1,061,759	−1,071,083
Net income	$ 114,034	$ 192,855
Net income attributable to noncontrolling interests	−38,012	−38,165
Net income attributable to Six Flags Entertainment Corp	$ 76,022	$ 154,690

Abbreviated Liabilities and Stockholders' Equity	2014	Percentage of Total Assets	2015	Percentage of Total Assets
Current liabilities	$ 231,671	10%	$ 272,058	11%
Long-term debt	1,373,605	57%	1,498,022	62%
Other noncurrent liabilities	150,180	6%	198,423	8%
Total liabilities	$1,755,456	73%	$1,968,503	81%
Noncontrolling interests	437,545	18%	435,721	18%
Stockholders' equity	223,895	9%	24,216	1%
Liabilities and stockholders' equity	$2,416,896	100%	$2,428,440	100%

Source: Six Flags Corporation 2015 10-K filing available on the company's website https://www.sixflags.com.

is usually at least 20% but less than 50%. Investments of this sort are not consolidated but reported on the parent company's financial statements on one line presenting the net effect of the investment in the appropriate financial statement. The income statement shows one line that represents the income effect of unconsolidated affiliates (the firm's proportionate share of the income or loss of its unconsolidated affiliates). The cash flow statement has a similar line item, but it converts the income effect into a cash effect. The balance sheet also shows the investment on one line, presenting the book value of the parent company's equity in the unconsolidated affiliate (the original investment plus the cumulative proportionate share of income since the original investment less any dividends received, adjusted for purchase premiums and discounts).

Using the same sample of companies used previously, 19.3% of the companies report a value for earnings from unconsolidated affiliates. Of these companies, 68% reported positive earnings from unconsolidated affiliates and 32% reported negative earnings from unconsolidated affiliates. Of those companies reporting positive earnings from unconsolidated affiliates, the median earnings effect to shareholders' equity was 0.7% (25th and 75th percentiles of 0.2% and 2.2%, respectively). Of those companies reporting negative earnings from unconsolidated affiliates, the median earnings effect to shareholders' equity was −0.3% (25th and 75th percentiles of −1.7% and −0.1%, respectively).

To the extent information permits and if the amount of unconsolidated affiliates is considered material, we can treat unconsolidated affiliates in essentially the same way we treat excess assets. We measure the costs of capital as we discussed in previous chapters. In order to calculate the target weights for the weighted average cost of capital, we subtract the value of the company's ownership in the unconsolidated affiliate from the value of the equity, and hence the value of the firm. If the risk of the unconsolidated affiliate is different from the company's risk (without the unconsolidated affiliate), we would consider adjusting the company's equity beta using the techniques we discussed in Chapter 8 to adjust out the effect of excess assets—assuming we can measure the equity cost of capital of the unconsolidated affiliate. In order to make any of these adjustments, we must, of course, measure the value of the company's ownership in the unconsolidated affiliate either from market data if available, market multiples, or some other technique.

Once we measure the weighted average cost of capital and the unlevered free cash flows without the effect of the unconsolidated affiliates, we discount these free cash flows by the weighted average cost of capital. Doing so provides an estimate of the value of the firm without the value of the unconsolidated affiliate. To measure the total value of the firm, we add the value of the unconsolidated affiliates.

Potential Adjustments for Off-Balance-Sheet Entities. Companies use certain types of off-balance-sheet entities such as **special-purpose entities** (sometimes called **special-purpose vehicles**) and other types of joint ventures and partnerships for a variety of reasons. Companies can use special-purpose entities and limited partnerships for business ventures with other companies for tax or management incentives. For example, sometimes, companies set up limited partnerships to finance research and development activities.[4] A company typically uses special-purpose entities to either remove or separate assets or liabilities from its balance sheet in what is usually an attempt to mitigate some type of risk. The risk can be embedded in the transferred assets—thus removing that risk from the company—or embedded in the company—thus removing that risk from the transferred assets.

For these entities, one key issue to consider is whether the creditors of the off-balance-sheet entity have claims against the company that set up the entity. An off-balance-sheet entity with creditors that do not have claims against the company is said to be **bankruptcy remote**. If the creditors of the off-balance-sheet entity do not have claims against the company, then we exclude the debt of the off-balance-sheet entity when we measure the weighted average cost of capital of the company. If the off-balance-sheet creditors have a claim against the company, then the financing of the entity (or at least the firm's proportionate share of the financing) is generally considered as part of the company's capital structure. Further, even if the company is not contractually obligated to support the entity, the company may voluntarily choose to support the entity's claims. Management may voluntarily support these claims to avoid a loss in investor confidence in the company, which could affect the company's ability to raise capital in the future.[5] This is called implicit recourse or moral recourse, and if this is the expectation, then the supported debt should be included in the company's capital structure. Last, income tax rules vary by the type of entity and by circumstances of the entity, which need to be considered when we include the financing of these entities in the company's capital structure.

One other issue is that if the off-balance-sheet entity is likely to produce cash flows that the company will receive, we must obviously include those cash flows in our valuation.

Valuation Key 11.3

The weighted average cost of capital is based on target market value weights. Include only the relevant claims in the cost of capital calculation and make adjustments as needed for excess assets, noncontrolling (or minority) interests, unconsolidated affiliates and off-balance-sheet entities.

Measuring the Income Tax Rate for Interest Tax Shields

Since we cannot observe a company's interest tax shield directly, we typically estimate the income tax rate for interest tax shields by multiplying the company's interest expense deduction by an income tax

[4] See, Beatty, A., P. Berger, and J. Magliolo, "Motives for Forming Research and Development Financing Organizations," *Journal of Accounting and Economics* 19 (1995), pp. 411–442.

[5] For a discussion of special-purpose entities, see Gorton, G., and N. Souleles, "Special Purpose Vehicles and Securitization," in: *The Risks of Financial Institutions*, Eds. Carey, M., and Stulz, R., University of Chicago Press for the National Bureau of Economic Research, Inc. (2006), pp. 549–602.

rate we believe measures the company's interest tax shield, T_{INT}. This is an implicit income tax rate—not an income tax rate set by the government. This income tax rate depends on both the cumulative effect of complex tax laws and regulations and a company's particular income tax situation at a specific point in time. Ignoring issues that arise due to personal income taxes for a moment (more on this later), the same issues arise for the income tax rate used in the weighted average cost of capital calculation.

If we have the necessary information, we can measure the implied income tax rate for a company's interest tax shield, T_{INT}, by dividing a company's interest tax shield by its interest expense deduction. While we do not generally have the information for that calculation, it is a useful frame of reference to help understand the concept we are trying to measure. The implied income tax rate that we use to measure a company's after-tax cost of debt depends on a variety of factors. Tax rules can create complexities in measuring the appropriate tax rate to use for estimating a company's interest tax shields, for example, complexities created by limitations on the deductibility of interest and net operating losses. The tax rate for interest tax shields may not even be the marginal tax rate on the company's taxable income. It can even be a tax rate that exceeds the company's marginal tax rate if the tax code has graduated corporate tax rates and if the interest expense keeps the company out of the next highest tax bracket. Alternatively, various factors can reduce the income tax rate for interest tax shields below the statutory income tax rate. In this section, we discuss some of these factors.[6]

Before we begin, we note that many of these issues are relevant for assessing the taxes that the organization will pay on its total taxable income. While we discuss some of these isssues in Chapter 3, the topics we discuss here also can relate to the measurement of the relevant free cash flows.

In this section we discuss progressivity in corporate income tax rates, income tax credits, and state and local taxes.[7] In addition to these factors, we incorporate the probability of the company actually capturing the benefit of its interest tax shields when we forecast the company's interest tax shields. While foreign taxes are important and potentially confusing for valuing multinational companies, we postpone our discussion of that topic until the last chapter of the book, where we discuss valuing cross-border acquisitions and multinational valuation. Lastly, we discuss the empirical evidence on this issue.

Progressive Corporate Income Tax Rates. Some countries, such as France, India, the Netherlands, Portugal and Taiwan have **progressive corporate income tax rates**. In fact, until 2018, U.S. statutory tax rates were progressive corporate income tax rates at low levels of income; for example, the statutory income tax rate was 15% for taxable income up to \$50,000 and 25% for taxable income greater than \$50,000 and less than \$75,000. A company with \$60,000 of income would face a total tax bill of \$10,000 ($\$10{,}000 = 0.15 \times 50{,}000 + 0.25 \times 10{,}000$). Between \$75,000 and \$100,000 of taxable income, the tax rate was 34%, and between \$100,000 and \$335,000, the tax rate was 39%. The increased tax rate between \$100,000 and \$335,000 essentially meant that if a company had \$335,000 in income, it was effectively paying 34% on all its income [$0.34 = (\$50{,}000 \times 0.15 + \$25{,}000 \times 0.25 + \$25{,}000 \times 0.34 + \$235{,}000 \times 0.39)/\$335{,}000$]. Of course, the effect of this graduated rate means that, within certain ranges of income, a company might actually have a tax rate for its interest tax shields, T_{INT}, of 39%. For example if a company had \$100,000 of taxable income and its deductions included \$50,000 of interest expense, the interest tax shield would be \$19,500 ($\$19{,}500 = 0.39 \times 50{,}000$).[8] It should be obvious that the progressivity of a tax law is relevant for measuring the unlevered free cash flows as well. Of course, as of 2018, the U.S. Corporate Income tax rate is a flat 21%.

Tax Credits. Income tax credits reduce the amount of income taxes a company must pay on a dollar-for-dollar basis; that is, for every dollar of income tax credit, the taxpayer reduces income taxes due by a dollar.

---

[6] For an extensive review of the academic literature on this topic, see Shackelford, D., and T. Shevlin, "Empirical Tax Research in Accounting," *Journal of Accounting and Economics* 31 (2001), pp. 321–387; and Graham, J. R., "Taxes and Corporate Finance: A Review," *Review of Financial Studies* 16 (2003), pp. 1074–1128.

[7] For a more detailed discussion of these factors, see, Graham, J. R., and M. Lemmon, "Measuring Corporate Tax Rates and Tax Incentives: A New Approach," *Journal of Applied Corporate Finance* 11 (1998), pp. 54–65.

[8] The progressiveness of U.S. tax rates continued. For taxable income between \$335,000 and \$10 million, the tax rate was 34%; between \$10 million and \$15 million of taxable income, the tax rate was 35%; and between \$15 million and \$18.333 million of taxable income, the tax rate was 38% (which effectively means that the company pays a 35% tax rate on all taxable income if taxable income is at least \$18.333 million). Again, in this range, T_{INT} would be 38%. Afterward, the statutory income tax rate is a constant 35%. The statutory tax rate is the income tax rate set by the government on taxable income. In most of our discussion, we assume that governments have one statutory tax rate (which is quite common) in order to reduce the complexity of the calculations.

Examples of income tax credits allowed by U.S. tax law include research and development tax credits, foreign tax credits and various tax credits for investing in renewable energy (such as wind and solar power). Research and development tax credits provide incentives for companies to engage in these activities by providing a 20% tax credit for research and development expenditures above a certain base. Previously, U.S. tax laws also provided for investment tax credits. At one time, investment tax credits provided incentives for companies to purchase qualified assets by providing as high as a 10% tax credit on the amount spent on qualifying purchases (various types of fixed assets). Naturally, a company might not have sufficient income taxes to use its tax credits in the year it earns them. In most cases, tax credits can be carried forward against taxes in future years. As we discussed in Chapter 3, tax credits reduce a company's effective tax rate, and these credits always affect the reconciliation between the federal statutory tax rate and the company's effective tax rate, which is what companies must report in their tax footnote. Tax credits do not generally affect the income tax rate used to value the interest tax shields unless they reduce the taxes that the company has to pay to zero (before the consideration of interest expense) or make the interest expense not fully deductible after they are considered. As we discussed in Chapter 3, the tax credits a company has and that are part of the reconciliation between the statutory and effective rate are important to consider in calculating the unlevered free cash flows.

State and Local Income Taxes. In most states and in some municipalities in the U.S., companies pay state and local government income taxes. State and local income taxes have the effect of increasing a company's income taxes. This effect is less than a dollar for each dollar of tax paid to state and local governments, because in general, these income taxes are deductible when calculating federal income taxes. For example, a 10% state income tax rate that is deductible for federal income taxes, assuming the relevant federal income tax rate is 35%, is effectively a 6.5% income tax rate [$0.065 = 0.1 \times (1 - 0.35)$] above the federal statutory tax rate. As discussed in Chapter 3, the reconciliation between the statutory and effective tax rates always shows the effects of state and local taxes net of the federal tax benefit.

Interest expense is generally tax deductible on state tax returns, so the tax rate used to calculate the after-tax cost of debt includes federal, state, and local taxes. In the absence of more detailed knowledge, an estimate of the tax rate for the interest tax shields is the federal statutory tax rate plus the effect of state and local income taxes, net of the federal tax benefit that is reported in the reconciliation of the federal statutory tax rate to the effective tax rate (ignoring foreign taxes for now). One caveat, the state and local tax rates that are observable in the reconciliation represent average state and local tax rates—not marginal tax rates.

Valuation Key 11.4

The calculation of the appropriate tax rate with which to assess the benefit of interest tax shields, T_{INT}, is a potentially complex calculation. Because of progressive tax structures, state and local taxes, limitations on interest deductions, and tax credits, it is often appropriate to use a tax rate that differs from the federal statutory tax rate when estimating the weighted average cost of capital. These same items impact how we compute the taxes due when measuring the unlevered free cash flows.

Evidence on the Use of the Federal Statutory Tax Rate to Estimate the Tax Rate for Interest Tax Shields, T_{INT}. A common way to measure the tax rate for interest tax shields and the weighted average cost of capital, T_{INT}, is to use the federal statutory tax rate (now 21% in the U.S.) plus the after-tax effect of state and local taxes (which we call the combined statutory rate). It turns out that if it is possible that the company may experience losses in future years (at least with some positive probability), the expected tax rate will be less than the combined statutory rate. Shevlin (1987, 1990) and Graham (1996a, 1996b) conducted the early research on estimating a company's marginal income tax rate.[9] A more recent article by Blouin, Core, and Guay (2010) provides more evidence on this issue and extends the earlier research of Shevlin and Graham.[10] These (and other) researchers provide extensive empirical

[9] See Shevlin, T., "Taxes and Off-Balance Sheet Financing: Research and Development Limited Partnerships," *The Accounting Review* 62 (1987), pp. 480–509; Shevlin, T., "Estimating Corporate Marginal Tax Rates with Asymmetric Tax Treatment of Gains and Losses," *The Journal of the American Taxation Association* 12 (1990), pp. 51–67; Graham, J. R., "Debt and the Marginal Tax Rate," *Journal of Financial Economics* 41 (1996a), pp. 41–73; and Graham, J. R., "Proxies for the Corporate Marginal Tax Rate," *Journal of Financial Economics* 42 (1996b), pp. 187–221.

[10] See Blouin, J., J. Core, and W. Guay, "Are Firms Under-Leveraged? Evidence from Improved Estimates of Marginal Tax Rates," *Journal of Financial Economics* (November 2010), pp. 195–213. Also see, Menichini, Amilcar A. (2016) "On the Value and Determinants of the Interest Tax Shields," *Review of Quantitative Finance and Accounting*, Forthcoming.

evidence that marginal federal income tax rates are often less than the company's federal statutory income tax rate (these researchers did not investigate state and local taxes in performing their calculations).

Blouin, Core, and Guay (2010) find that about one-fourth of the publicly traded firms have an average tax rate that is considerably lower than the statutory rate. Smaller-size companies, companies reporting current losses, and companies with net operating losses are more likely to have marginal tax rates not equal to the statutory tax rate than large, profitable companies without net operating losses. Thus, at least for some firms, using the federal statutory tax rate for all years to calculate the interest tax shields can misstate the value of the interest tax shields as well as the after-tax cash flows. This research suggests that a large number of companies will not pay taxes at the statutory tax rate, and hence the value of the interest tax shields need not necessarily be evaluated based on the statutory tax rates.[11] This of course would impact the tax rate used in computing the after-tax cost of debt in the weighted average cost of capital formula. This result has implications for the income taxes paid on other income as well. The recent change in the U.S. tax law would somewhat reduce the proportion of publicly traded firms not facing the 21% statutory tax rate, but the overall message of this study remains.

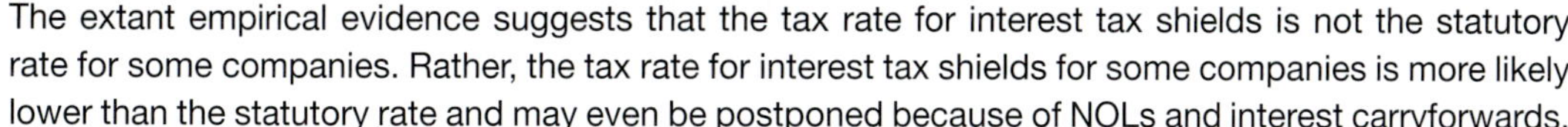

Valuation Key 11.5

The extant empirical evidence suggests that the tax rate for interest tax shields is not the statutory rate for some companies. Rather, the tax rate for interest tax shields for some companies is more likely lower than the statutory rate and may even be postponed because of NOLs and interest carryforwards.

11.3 THE EFFECTS OF TREATING LIABILITIES AS DEBT VERSUS OPERATING LIABILITIES

LO3 Standardize the treatment of liabilities as debt versus operating liabilities

In Chapter 3, we discussed the effects of treating liabilities as debt versus operating liabilities on free cash flows. In Chapter 5, we discussed the effects of treating liabilities as debt versus operating liabilities on the value of the firm. In this section, we quickly review those discussions and also discuss the effect of treating liabilities as debt versus treating them as operating liabilities on the unlevered and weighted average costs of capital. We show that the unlevered cost of capital, and the resulting weighted average cost of capital are lower for a company treating a liability, for example, operating leases, as debt relative to treating the liability as an operating liability. The conclusion is that consistency in the treatment of liabilities as debt versus operating liabilities becomes relevant when using comparable companies to measure the unlevered cost of capital.

The Debt versus Operating Liability Issue

We know from the definition of unlevered free cash flows in Chapter 3, that treating a liability as debt results in recording payments related to that liability as interest expense or a reduction in principal, neither, of which, affect the calculation of unlevered free cash flows. On the other hand, treating that same liability as an operating liability results in recording any payments related to that liability as an operating expense, which directly reduces unlevered free cash flows. The equity free cash flows are independent of the treatment of the liability because the cash payments related to the liability are deducted either as interest or principal payments (when treated as debt) or as operating expenses (when treated as an operating liability). Both treatments result in the same equity free cash flows. Since the equity free cash flows are identical, the treatment as debt or as an operating liability also does not affect the equity cost of capital and therefore, does not affect the value of the equity. All else equal, the value of the equity is independent of the treatment of a liability as debt or as an operating expense.

Although the value of the equity is the same, we know from Chapter 5 that the value of the firm is equal to the sum of the values of the securities used to finance the firm (see Equation 5.9). The securities used to finance the firm include securities such as common stock, preferred stock, debt and other related interest bearing contractual agreements, employee stock options, and any other equity-linked securities. They do not include operating liabilities such as accounts payable, accrued expenses, and non-current operating liabilities. Other contractual obligations—such as operating or capitalized leases (see the Appendix), pensions,

[11] See Section 4.9 and Exhibit 4.13 for a more detailed discussion of this study.

and post-retirement health benefits—may or may not be part of the capital structure, depending on how we choose to treat them. Given that the value of the firm is equal to the sum of the values of the securities used to finance the firm, firm value when treating a liability as debt must be higher than firm value when treating it as an operating liability, and the difference must be equal to the present value of the cash payments of the liability treated as debt.

As we show in the following lease example, the value is higher for two reasons. First, as we discuss earlier in this section, the unlevered free cash flows are higher when treating the liability as debt. Second, the unlevered cost of capital and the resulting weighted average cost of capital are lower when treating the liability as debt. The riskiness of the unlevered free cash flows is higher when treating a liability as an ongoing operating liability because of the operating leverage created by that expense; however, treating that same liability as debt shifts the operating leverage to financial leverage, which lowers the operating risk, and the corresponding cost of capital, of the unlevered free cash flows.[12] The combination of the two effects increases the value of the firm by the present value of the payments on the liability. We illustrate these points in a lease example.

The Perpetual Leasing Company

The Perpetual Leasing Company leases all of its assets using three-year leases. The company's income tax rate is 40% on all income, has an equity cost of capital of 15%, a cost of capital for its leases of 10%, and expected free cash flows continuing at their current level in perpetuity. We assume the company has adopted the new U.S. lease accounting rules.[13] (We discuss these accounting rules and contrast them with the current lease accounting rules in the Appendix.) Based on these accounting rules, the company will capitalize its leases on its balance sheet (unless the lease duration is less than 12 months). On the effective date of the lease, the company records a lease asset and lease liability equal to the present value of the lease payments, discounted at 10% (we assume the company incurs no costs at the time the lease is executed). After initially recording the lease assets and liability, if the lease is treated as an operating lease, the company records the lease payment as an operating expense. If the lease is treated as a finance lease, the company treats the lease liability as debt and records the lease payment as interest expense and a repayment of the principal of the lease liability (debt). The company also amortizes the leased asset when the lease is treated as a finance lease.

The company is in a zero-growth steady state. The value of the lease liability (or debt) on the balance sheet is always equal to the present value of all future lease payments discounted at the company's cost of debt. The company has three identical leases for the same amount and every year one of the leases expires and a new lease with the same terms is signed. Thus, at the end of every year, there is a new lease (with three years remaining), a lease with two years remaining and a lease with one year remaining. The table below shows the lease amortization for one such lease. Remembering that every year the three leases will have different end dates, adding up the balance in the liability across the three years means that in any year, there will be $22,000 worth of lease liability. Further, if the lease is treated as a financing lease, the interest every year will be $2,200 (adding up the interest across the three years).

Annual Payment	$ 4,287.3			
Implicit Interest Rate	10.0%	3.0	Life of Lease	
Present Value of Lease Payments	$10,661.8			
	Beginning Lease Liability	**Implicit Interest**	**Lease Payment**	**Ending Lease Liability**
Year 1	$10,661.8	$1,066.2	$ 4,287.3	$7,440.7
Year 2	$ 7,440.7	$ 744.1	$ 4,287.3	$3,897.5
Year 3	$ 3,897.5	$ 389.8	$ 4,287.3	$ 0.0
Total	$22,000.0	$2,200.0	$12,861.8	

[12] Research shows the market participants recognize the risks regardless of the treatment of a liability as debt or as an operating liability; see, for example, Bratten, Brian, Preeti Choudhary, and Katherine Schipper, "Evidence that Market Participants Assess Recognized and Disclosed Items Similarly when Reliability is Not an Issue," *The Accounting Review* vol. 88, no. 4 (2013) pp. 1179–1210.

[13] Financial Accounting Standards Board, (FASB) Accounting Standards Update No. 2016-02, *Leases*, which supersedes FASB Accounting Standards Codification (ASC) Topic 840, *Leases*, and creates ASC 842, *Leases*.

In Exhibit 11.4, we show the company's income statements, balance sheets, and free cash flow schedule for the current year and next year. Since the company is in a zero-growth steady state, its balance sheets, income statements, and free cash flows are the same for the two years. The company's equity free cash flows are the same for both the operating and finance lease treatments, $1,200, but the unlevered free cash flows are not. The unlevered free cash flow treating the lease liability as an operating liability is the same as its equity free cash flow, $1,200 because the company has no other non-common equity securities. Treating the lease as a finance lease, the lease asset is treated like a capital expenditure ($10,661.8) at the inception of each lease which is subsequently amortized using the straight-line method over the life of the lease. The unlevered free cash flow treating the lease liability as debt, $2,520, is larger by the amount of the after-tax interest ($1,320 = $2,520 − $1,200 = $2,200 − $880). Note, we do not observe any reductions in the lease liability on the free cash flow schedule because the company is in a zero-growth steady state and any lease that expires is replaced with a new identical lease.

EXHIBIT 11.4 Perpetual Leasing Company—Operating Liability versus Debt Treatment

	Operating Lease		Finance Lease	
Income Statements and Balance Sheets	**Actual Year 0**	**Forecast Year 1**	**Actual Year 0**	**Forecast Year 1**
Revenue	$14,861.8	$14,861.8	$14,861.8	$14,861.8
Lease expense	−12,861.8	−12,861.8	0.0	0.0
Finance lease asset amortization	0.0	0.0	−10,661.8	−10,661.8
Earnings before interest and taxes	$ 2,000.0	$ 2,000.0	$ 4,200.0	$ 4,200.0
Interest expense	0.0	0.0	−2,200.0	−2,200.0
Income before taxes	$ 2,000.0	$ 2,000.0	$ 2,000.0	$ 2,000.0
Income tax expense	−800.0	−800.0	−800.0	−800.0
Net income	$ 1,200.0	$ 1,200.0	$ 1,200.0	$ 1,200.0
Cash	$ 1,862.8	$ 1,862.8	$ 1,862.8	$ 1,862.8
Lease asset	22,000.0	22,000.0	22,000.0	22,000.0
Deferred tax asset	0.0	0.0	0.0	0.0
Total assets	$23,862.8	$23,862.8	$23,862.8	$23,862.8
Lease liability	$22,000.0	$22,000.0	$ 0.0	$ 0.0
Lease debt	0.0	0.0	22,000.0	22,000.0
Equity	1,862.8	1,862.8	1,862.8	1,862.8
Total liabilities and equities	$23,862.8	$23,862.8	$23,862.8	$23,862.8

	Operating Lease		Finance Lease	
Free Cash Flow Schedule	**Actual Year 0**	**Forecast Year 1**	**Actual Year 0**	**Forecast Year 1**
Earnings before interest and taxes	$2,000.0	$2,000.0	$ 4,200.0	$ 4,200.0
− Income taxes on EBIT	−800.0	−800.0	−1,680.0	−1,680.0
Earnings before interest and after taxes	$1,200.0	$1,200.0	$ 2,520.0	$ 2,520.0
+ Lease asset amortization	0	0	10,661.8	10,661.8
+ Change in operating lease liability	0	0	0	0
+ Deferred tax adjustment	0	0	0	0
Unlevered cash flow from operations	$1,200.0	$1,200.0	$13,181.8	$13,181.8
− Capital lease increases (CAPEX)	0	0	−10,661.8	−10,661.8
Unlevered free cash flow	$1,200.0	$1,200.0	$ 2,520.0	$ 2,520.0
Implicit interest on finance leases	0	0	−2,200.0	−2,200.0
Interest tax shield	0	0	880.0	880.0
Free cash flow minus after-tax interest	$1,200.0	$1,200.0	$ 1,200.0	$ 1,200.0
Change in finance lease liability	0	0	0	0
Equity free cash flow	$1,200.0	$1,200.0	$ 1,200.0	$ 1,200.0

The Value of the Perpetual Leasing Company Treating the Lease as an Operating Liability. The valuation of the company treating the lease as an operating lease is straightforward because the company has no other non-common equity financing; in other words, the company's equity cost of capital is equal to the unlevered cost of capital, which is equal to the weighted average cost of capital, 15% (given). The value of the firm and its equity is equal to

$$V_F = V_E = \frac{\$1,200}{0.15} = \$8,000$$

The Value of the Perpetual Leasing Company Treating the Lease as Debt. The valuation of the company treating the lease as debt is also straightforward because the company has no other non-common equity financing and we know the value of the lease debt from the balance sheet. The value of the firm is equal to the value of the equity, $8,000, plus the value of the lease debt, $22,000, or $30,000. The company's debt to value ratio is equal to 0.7333 [0.7333 = $22,000/($8,000 + $22,000)]. As you will see shortly, we could also have derived the capital structure ratios using the adjusted present value valuation method. Although in this simple example, we measure the value of the firm directly once we know the value of the equity, as the goal of this example is to illustrate the effect that the operating lease versus debt treatment has on the company's cost of capital. Given that the company is continually rolling over the leases (debt), we assume the appropriate discount rate for all interest tax shields is the unlevered cost of capital, r_{UA}. Based on this assumption, the company's unlevered and weighted average costs of capital are equal to

$$r_{UA} = r_E \times \frac{V_E}{V_F} + r_D \times \frac{V_D}{V_F}$$

$$r_{UA} = 0.15 \times (1 - 0.7333) + 0.1 \times 0.7333 = 0.11333$$

$$r_{WACC} = r_E \times \frac{V_E}{V_F} + (1 - T_{INT}) \times r_D \times \frac{V_D}{V_F}$$

$$r_{WACC} = 0.15 \times (1 - 0.7333) + (1 - 0.4) \times 0.1 \times 0.7333 = 0.084$$

For the reasons we discussed earlier, the unlevered cost of capital decreases from 15% to 11.333% and the weighted average cost of capital decreases from 15% to 8.4%. It is important to recognize that the unlevered cost of capital varies with the treatment of the leases, a point we will emphasize with respect to comparable companies. According to our framework, the increase in the free cash flow and the decrease in the costs of capital should increase the value of the firm by the amount of the lease debt, $22,000, using either the APV or WACC valuation methods. We have all of the inputs necessary to value the company treating the lease as debt using both the APV and WACC valuation methods. The value of the firm using the WACC valuation method, $V_{F,WACC}$, is equal to the value of the firm using the APV valuation method, $V_{F,APV}$, $30,000.

$$V_{F,WACC} = \frac{FCF_1}{r_{WACC}} = \frac{\$2{,}520}{0.084} = \$30{,}000$$

$$V_{F,APV} = \frac{FCF_1}{r_{UA}} + \frac{ITS_1}{r_{UA}} = \frac{\$2{,}520}{0.11333} + \frac{\$880}{0.11333} = \$22{,}235.3 + \$7{,}764.7 = \$30{,}000$$

The increase in the value of the firm is, as expected, equal to the value of the lease debt, $22,000.

This example illustrates the potential effect of using comparable companies that have inconsistent treatments of liabilities, a point we will discuss in more detail at the end of this section. Before that, we briefly discuss examples other than leases for which this issue can arise.

Other Examples of the Debt versus Operating Liability Issue

This same valuation issue potentially arises in other situations. Even if accounting rules require companies to use a specific accounting method in a given circumstance, companies still have some discretion. For example, conditional on the characteristics of a lease contract, accounting rules typically determine whether or not a lease must be treated as an operating lease or a finance lease. However, companies often have discretion over the characteristics of the lease contract, and hence they have discretion over whether or not a lease must be treated as a finance lease. In addition, cross-country differences in accounting rules may create situations in which the treatments are different.

Consider pensions under U.S. GAAP. Under U.S. GAAP, pension expense is treated as an operating expense even though it includes an implicit interest component. The interest component of pension expense is not reported as interest expense in the financial statements. As such, without adjusting the financial statements and free cash flows, the pension liability will be treated as an operating liability—not debt—in order to be consistent with the income statement treatment. However, consider a case where two companies are identical in all respects (including their pension obligations), but one company has a pension liability, and the other company fully funds its pension plan obligation by issuing debt. In essence, the latter company converts its operating liability into a financing liability. If we unlever the equity costs of capital for these two companies, the unlevered cost of capital will not be the same because for the company showing the pension liability, we treat the pension liability as an operating liability, not debt.

If we adjust the reported numbers to treat the pension liability as a financing activity and unlever accordingly, the two companies will have the same unlevered cost of capital. In general, we cannot observe if a company makes this type of trade-off, so if this is an important issue, we would consider converting the operating liability into debt to ensure consistent treatment between the comparable companies and the company we are valuing. As was the case with leases, this adjustment treats the pension liability as debt, reverses the interest expense component of the pension expense, and treats it as interest expense. In addition, for the company we are valuing, we adjust the unlevered free cash flows by treating the interest expense component of the pension expense as interest expense—not as an operating expense. A similar issue might arise with post-retirement benefits because many companies do not even partially fund their post-retirement benefits (and unlike the case for pensions, even partial funding is not required by law), and some companies at least partially fund these liabilities.

Conclusions

While the treatment of a liability as either debt or an operating liability does not affect the value of the company's equity, it affects the value of the firm, the unlevered free cash flows, and the unlevered and weighted average cost of capital. In particular, first, the treatment of a liability as debt or as an operating liability has no effect on the equity cost of capital or the value of the equity because the equity free cash flows are the same. Second, the unlevered free cash flows are generally higher when the liability is treated as debt because cash flows related to debt increase interest expense and reduce (repay) the debt, which do not affect unlevered free cash flows, while cash flows related to an operating liability increase operating expenses, which directly reduce unlevered free cash flows. Third, the unlevered and weighted average costs of capital are lower when the liability is treated as debt because the operating leverage from the operating liability, which increases the unlevered cost of capital, is then treated as financial leverage, which does not affect the unlevered cost of capital. The end result is that the value of the firm when a liability is treated as debt is larger than the value of the firm when the liability is treated as an operating liability and the difference is equal to the value of the liability.

One tempting conclusion to draw from this discussion is that given the value of the equity is the same for both treatments, it makes no difference whether we treat a liability as debt or an operating liability, for the value of the equity is the same. All we have to remember is that if we treat the liability as debt, we subtract the capitalized value of the lease obligations from the value of the firm in order to calculate the value of the equity. This approach is reasonable as long as we can measure the equity cost of capital for the company we are valuing without using comparable companies and if the company's forward-looking capital structure strategy is its existing capital structure. Our example shows that when we observe the equity cost of capital directly, both the adjusted present value and weighted average cost of capital valuation methods result in the same valuation for the value of the equity regardless of the treatment of a liability as debt or as an operating liability. Suppose, however, that we use comparable companies and measure each company's unlevered cost of capital. Now, consistency in the treatment of a company's specific liability (for example, operating leases) as debt or as an operating liability is potentially relevant because the unlevered cost of capital depends on the treatment.

For example, if the comparable companies use operating leases in the same proportions as each other and as the company we are valuing, we can ignore this issue. Any finance leases are part of the financing structure of the company, and operating lease payments are part of the unlevered free cash flows. The fact that the companies have a mix of operating and finance leases causes no complication as long as the relative use of each type of leasing is the same across all companies. How do we know if the relative use of leases is the same? In order to make this assessment, we can examine the lease liability for the operating leases under the new U.S. GAAP standard as the company will have already determined the capitalized value of the lease liability for the operating leases (see the Appendix if this is confusing to you) and determine if the ratio of the total value of the operating leases capitalized to total firm value (including the capitalized value of the operating leases) is approximately the same across firms. However, if the comparable companies do not use operating leases in the same proportion as that of the company we are valuing, the only way to lever and unlever the cost of capital is to treat the leases of all companies as either all finance leases or all operating leases.

Valuation Key 11.6

While the treatment of a liability as either debt or an operating liability does not affect the value of the company's equity, it affects the value of the firm, unlevered free cash flows, and the unlevered and weighted average cost of capital. Consistency in the treatment of a company's specific liability (for example, leases) as an operating lease or a finance lease becomes potentially relevant when using comparable companies to measure the unlevered and weighted average costs of capital.

REVIEW EXERCISE 11.2

Operating Versus Finance Leases and Valuation

In Year 0, a company entered into a perpetual lease on property. The property has a value of $5,000 at the end of Year 0, the implicit cost of debt is 9% (which is not expected to change over time), and the annual lease payment is $450 each year in perpetuity. The company expects to have revenues of $800 in Year 1 that will then grow at 2% in perpetuity and to have no other expenses apart from expenses related to the lease. In order to grow at 2% per year, the company expects to increase its leased property by 2% each year starting at the end of Year 1 (new leases will also be perpetual leases). The company's tax rate on all income is 30%. All revenues and expenses are paid in cash. The company has no assets or liabilities other than those related to the lease. Assume today is the end of Year 0. The company has an 18% equity cost of capital, and the discount rate for interest tax shields (including those from finance leases) is equal to the unlevered cost of capital. Value the company as of the end of Year 0, assuming the company treats the lease as operating; value the company again, assuming the company treats the lease as a finance lease. Prepare the company's income statement and free cash flow schedule for Year 1 for each lease treatment. Use the weighted average cost of capital, equity DCF, and APV valuation methods to value the company.

Solution on pages 541–542.

11.4 CONVERTING OPERATING LEASES TO FINANCE (OR CAPITAL) LEASES

In this section we illustrate how to treat operating leases as finance leases for the comparable companies and for the company we are valuing, that is, how to convert a company's financial statements and free cash flows so that all leases are treated as finance leases. We use United Airlines' 2014 financial statements for these illustrations (United Continental Holdings, Inc., see Valuation in Practice 11.3). United's 2014

VALUATION IN PRACTICE 11.3

United Airlines (United Continental Holdings, Inc.)—2014 Lease Footnote United Airlines leases various types of equipment and property—primarily aircraft and airport facilities. United outlined its capital and operating leases in its 2014 10-K report as follows.

United leases aircraft, airport passenger terminal space, aircraft hangars and related maintenance facilities, cargo terminals, other airport facilities, other commercial real estate, office and computer equipment and vehicles.

At December 31, 2014, United's scheduled future minimum lease payments under operating leases having initial or remaining noncancelable lease terms of more than one year, aircraft leases, including aircraft rent under CPAs and capital leases (substantially all of which are for aircraft) were as follows (in millions):

2014 10-K	Year	Capital Leases	Operating Leases
	2015	$ 168	$ 2,729
	2016	154	2,370
	2017	115	2,236
	2018	104	1,750
	2019	38	1,448
	After 2019......	495	9,829
Total		$1,074	$20,362
Interest		393	
Present value		$ 681	

* Note—the authors combined all operating leases

continued

continued from previous page

Aircraft operating leases have initial terms of six to twenty-eight years, with expiration dates ranging from 2015 through 2024. Under the terms of most leases, United has the right to purchase the aircraft at the end of the lease term, in some cases at fair market value, and in others, at fair market value or a percentage of cost. United has facility operating leases that extend to 2041.

United is the lessee of real property under long-term operating leases at a number of airports where we are also the guarantor of approximately $1.5 billion of underlying debt and interest thereon as of December 31, 2014. . . .

Source: The company operates globally as a scheduled passenger airline through its principal subsidiary, United Airlines, Inc.; United's 2014 10-K, Footnote 13, "Leases and Capacity Purchase Agreements."

financial statements were issued before the release of the new accounting rules in 2016 (see the appendix to this chapter). The process used to convert operating leases based on the 2014 accounting rules is very similar to the process to convert operating leases based on the accounting rules released in 2016 that become effective for fiscal years starting on or after December 15, 2018. In the previous section, we discuss when converting operating leases to finance leases is relevant in a DCF-based valuation. In Chapter 14, we discuss when converting operating leases to finance leases is relevant in a market multiple valuation.

United as a Comparable Company. First, assume United is a comparable company in a valuation. Using United's 2014 footnote disclosure for leases, we identify its operating lease obligations for 2015 through 2019. The footnote disclosure also provides a lump sum for all lease obligations due in years after 2019. In Exhibit 11.5, we show United's 2013 and 2014 operating lease disclosures and measure the present value of the operating lease payments for both years.[14]

For the 2014 disclosure, we assume that the lease payments after 2019 will remain constant at $1,448 million annually until the year in which we use up the residual amount remaining of the total $9,829 million due after 2019, which is $1,141 million in 2026. We assume that United's implicit interest rate for these leases is 9% and that the leases have an average life of 7 years. We make similar assumptions for the 2013 operating lease disclosure.

We can see from the exhibit that the present values of the lease obligations for 2013 and 2014 are, respectively, $12,331.7 and $13,033.3 million. If United was a comparable company, we would treat the capitalized values of the operating lease obligations as debt if we were going to unlever United's equity cost of capital and use the cost of debt of 9% for the lease component of United's debt.

As an estimate of the cost of debt for the operating leases, we use the discount rate already used by the company for its capitalized (finance) leases on its balance sheet, if known. If that rate is not available, we generally use the interest rate on a senior secured loan of a similar maturity (or something slightly less than that rate) because in bankruptcy, a lessor is typically more protected than a secured lender, as the lessor can take the asset back in bankruptcy, which is not necessarily true for a secured lender.[15] We note that once the new accounting standard is in place, companies will compute the capitalized value of the lease liability for the operating leases, so that this information will be given and we will not have to calculate the present value of the operating lease payments. We should also note that while we have assumed we want to treat all leases as finance (capitalized) leases in this example, one can also decide to treat all leases as operating leases. Which will be easier to do will depend on how the comparable companies and the company of interest treat their leases.

United as the Company Being Valued. Now suppose that United was the company that we were valuing. In order to treat United's operating leases as capital or finance leases (debt), we would also have to remeasure United's unlevered free cash flows assuming that all leases are capitalized (treated as finance leases). One way to do this is to recast the financial statements and recompute the unlevered free cash flows. We demonstrate this approach for 2014.

[14] The source of the information for the 2013 numbers is United's 2013 10-K, Footnote 13, "Leases and Capacity Purchase Agreements," which we do not show in the chapter.

[15] See Eisfeldt, A., and A. Rampini, "Leasing, Ability to Repossess and Debt Capacity," *Review of Financial Studies* 22 (2009), pp. 1621–1657.

We use the present value of the leases as of the end of 2013 to measure both the amount of implicit interest on the capitalized operating leases and the amount of lease amortization in 2014. The interest on the lease obligation is equal to 9% multiplied by the December 31, 2013, present value of the leases ($1,109.9 = 0.09 × $12,331.7). Given a 7-year average life, the 2014 lease amortization is $1,761.7 million (see Exhibit 11.5).

EXHIBIT 11.5 United Airlines—Present Value of Lease Payments as of December 31, 2013, and December 31, 2014

Operating Lease Payments as of December 31, 2013 ($ in millions)				Operating Lease Payments as of December 31, 2014 ($ in millions)			
Year	**Payment**	**PV Factor**	**Present Value**	**Year**	**Payment**	**PV Factor**	**Present Value**
2014	$2,793	0.917	$2,562.4				
2015	2,368	0.842	1,993.1	2015	$2,729	0.917	$2,503.7
2016	2,014	0.772	1,555.2	2016	2,370	0.842	1,994.8
2017	1,884	0.708	1,334.7	2017	2,236	0.772	1,726.6
2018	1,496	0.650	972.3	2018	1,750	0.708	1,239.7
2019	1,496	0.596	892.0	2019	1,448	0.650	941.1
2020	1,496	0.547	818.4	2020	1,448	0.596	863.4
2021	1,496	0.502	750.8	2021	1,448	0.547	792.1
2022	1,496	0.460	688.8	2022	1,448	0.502	726.7
2023	1,496	0.422	631.9	2023	1,448	0.460	666.7
2024	341	0.388	132.1	2024	1,448	0.422	611.7
				2025	1,448	0.388	561.1
				2026	1,141	0.356	405.7
Present value as of 12/31/2013			$12,331.7	Present value as of 12/31/2014			$13,033.3
				2014 lease payment net of interest			1,683.1
Implicit interest rate			9.0%				$14,716.4
Implicit interest expense for 2014			$1,109.9	Less: Present value as of 12/31/2013			12,331.7
				Present value of new leases in 2014			$2,384.7
Assumed remaining average life			7				
Lease asset amortization for 2014			$1,761.7	Rent in 2014 if operating leases			$2,793.0

We use the change in the present value of the leases—adjusted for lease payments net of implicit interest on the lease—in order to measure the present value of the new leases in 2014, which represent a capital investment that year. In other words, the value of the new leases entered into in 2014 of $2,384.7 million is equal to the present value of the leases as of December 31, 2014 of $13,033.3 million, plus the principal of the capitalized leases that was paid in 2014 of $1,683.1 million (equal to the 2014 lease payment net of interest, $1,683.1 = $2,793.0 − $1,109.9), minus the present value of the leases in 2013 of $12,331.7 million. The new leases reduce the unlevered free cash flows, as they are treated as a capital expenditure.

REVIEW EXERCISE 11.3

Capitalizing Operating Leases—Part 1

Use the information in the following financial disclosures to measure the present value of the outstanding operating lease obligations as of the end of Year 0 and Year 1, assuming annual lease payments and an 8% discount rate. Also measure the present value of the additions to the lease obligations (new leases), the implicit interest on the capitalized lease obligations, and the lease asset amortization (assuming a 10-year life) for Year 1.

continued

continued from previous page

Year 0 Financial Disclosure		
Year	**Capital Leases**	**Operating Leases**
Year 1	$ 800	$1,200
Year 2	760	1,000
Year 3	710	900
Year 4	630	700
Year 5	250	600
After Year 5	2,000	5,400
Total	$5,150	$9,800
Total interest	1,583	
Present value	$3,567	

Year 1 Financial Disclosure		
Year	**Capital Leases**	**Operating Leases**
Year 2	$ 850	$1,100
Year 3	810	990
Year 4	760	770
Year 5	670	660
Year 6	270	630
After Year 6	2,160	5,670
Total	$5,520	$9,820
Total interest	1,703	
Present value	$3,817	

Solution on page 543.

In Exhibit 11.6, we show United's 2014 summary income statement and balance sheet. In the first column of the exhibit, we show the company's reported numbers. In the next five columns, we show the adjustments to capitalize its operating leases. We assume the company capitalized its leases as of the end of 2013 by recording the capitalized lease assets and capitalized lease obligation equal to the present value of the 2013 lease payments, $12,331.7 million. This is the first adjustment shown, under the column labeled Beginning of Year Balance.

EXHIBIT 11.6 United Airlines—2014 Summary Income Statement and Balance Sheet with and Without Capitalizing Its Operating Leases

United Airlines Summarized Financial Statements ($ in millions)	2014 Reported	Beginning of Year Balance	Adjust Rent Expense	Amortization of Finance Lease Asset	Income Taxes	Acquisition of Additional Leases	2014 Adjusted
Income Statement							
Revenues	$38,901.0						$38,901.0
Rent expense	−2,725.0		$2,793.0				68.0
Depreciation and amortization	−1,679.0						−1,679.0
Amortization of operating leases				−$1,761.7			−1,761.7
All other operating expenses	−32,124.0						−32,124.0
Operating income	$ 2,373.0		$2,793.0	−$1,761.7	$ 0.0	$ 0.0	$ 3,404.3
Interest expense	−735.0						−735.0
Miscellaneous, net	−510.0						−510.0
Lease interest			−1,109.9				−1,109.9
Income before taxes	$ 1,128.0		$1,683.1	−$1,761.7	$ 0.0	$ 0.0	$ 1,049.5
Income taxes	4.0				28.3		32.3
Net income	$ 1,132.0		$1,683.1	−$1,761.7	$28.3	$ 0.0	$ 1,081.7
Balance Sheet							
Current assets	$ 8,181.0						$ 8,181.0
Net property, plant, and equipment	19,467.0						19,467.0
Other assets	10,460.0						10,460.0
Deferred tax asset, net					$28.3		28.3
Capitalized operating leases		$12,331.7		−$1,761.7		$2,384.7	12,954.7
Total assets	$38,108.0	$12,331.7	$ 0.0	−$1,761.7	$28.3	$2,384.7	$51,091.0
Current operating liabilities	$12,513.0						$12,513.0
Other liabilities	12,269.0						12,269.0
Deferred tax liability, net					$ 0.0		0.0
Debt	10,691.0						10,691.0
Capitalized operating leases		$12,331.7	−$1,683.1			$2,384.7	13,033.3
Total liabilities	$35,473.0	$12,331.7	−$1,683.1	$ 0.0	$ 0.0	$2,384.7	$48,506.3
Shareholders' equity	2,635.0		1,683.1	−1,761.7	28.3		2,584.7
Total liabilities and shareholders' equity	$38,108.0	$12,331.7	$ 0.0	−$1,761.7	$28.3	$2,384.7	$51,091.0

Exhibit may contain small rounding errors

To convert the 2014 income statement, we first add back rent expense and then deduct interest expense and also reduce the lease liability on the balance sheet (see Exhibit 11.5 for these calculations). The net adjustment of $1,683.1 reduces the capitalized operating lease (debt) on the balance sheet as this represents the payment of principal. Then, we amortize the capitalized lease asset (based on the ending 2013 balance and assuming an average 7-year remaining life), and we record the provision for income taxes, which includes adjusting for deferred income taxes (using a 36% marginal income tax rate). Even though the company has a zero income tax expense (it used its NOL carryforwards to shelter its income), we assume that the marginal tax rate for the change in the company's expenses is 36% in order to illustrate the effect of taxes in our example. That is, we tax effect (at 36%) any difference in income between United's reported and revised income based on the capitalization of its operating leases.

The income tax adjustment of $28.3 is the change in net income before tax of −$78.6 (−$78.6 = $1,683.1 − $1,761.7) multiplied by 36%. Since the cash flows are unaffected by converting the operating leases, this tax adjustment results in an increase in the company's net deferred tax asset. Assuming no deferred tax effect in 2013, the net deferred tax effect in 2014 is equal to the difference between the 2014 balance of the lease liability of $13,033.3 and the lease asset of $12,954.7, multiplied by 36% ($28.3 = ($13,033.3 − $12,954.7) × 0.36). Finally, we record the additional leases for 2014 of $2,384.7 (see Exhibit 11.5 for this calculation). Keep in mind that all changes in net income affect shareholders' equity due to the change in retained earnings.

We present a summary free cash flow schedule for 2014 in Exhibit 11.7. This exhibit has the same columns as the previous exhibit. The first adjustment we make to the income statement and balance sheet—recording the beginning balance—is not relevant for measuring free cash flows because it does not represent a cash flow in 2014. The other adjustments in the previous exhibit carry over to the free cash flow statement. The income tax adjustment for free cash flows includes an adjustment for the change in EBIT equal to a tax increase of $371.3 ($371.3 = $1,031.3 × 0.36 where $1,031.3 = $2,898.3 − $1,867.0), and a decrease in income taxes due to the increase in the interest tax shield of $399.5 ($399.5 = $1,109.9 × 0.36) and the deferred tax adjustment of $28.3 discussed earlier. As stated previously, capitalizing the company's operating leases has no effect on equity free cash flows even though it affects net income. However, notice that the unlevered cash flow from operations increases from $3,260.0 to $5,653.5. This increase is largely offset by the increase in the company's capital expenditures so that the company's free cash flows increase from $1,461.0 to $1,469.7.

EXHIBIT 11.7 United Airlines—2014 Summary Free Cash Flow Schedule

Summarized Free Cash Flow Schedule ($ in millions)	2014 Reported	Adjust Rent Expense	Amortization of Finance Lease Asset	Income Taxes	Acquisition of Additional Leases	2014 Adjusted
Earnings before interest and taxes (EBIT)	$1,867.0	$2,793.0	−$1,761.7			$2,898.3
− Income taxes paid on EBIT	4.0			−$371.3		−367.3
Earnings before interest and after taxes	$1,871.0	$2,793.0	−$1,761.7	−$371.3	$ 0	$2,531.1
+ Depreciation and amortization	1,679.0					1,679.0
+ Amortization of operating leases			1,761.7			1,761.7
− Change in net working capital	−268.0					−268.0
+ Change in non-current liabilities and other	−22.0			−28.3		−50.3
− Change in required cash balance	0.0					0.0
Unlevered cash flow from operations	$3,260.0	$2,793.0	$ 0	−$399.5	$ 0	$5,653.5
− Capital expenditures (net)	−1,799.0					−1,799.0
− Increase in finance lease assets					−2,384.7	−2,384.7
Unlevered free cash flow	$1,461.0	$2,793.0	$ 0	−$399.5	−$2,384.7	$1,469.7
− Interest paid	−735.0	−1,109.9				−1,844.9
+ Interest tax shield				399.5		399.5
+ Change in non-common equity	−1,071.0					−1,071.0
+ Change in finance lease obligations		−1,683.1			2,384.7	701.6
Free cash flow to common equity	−$ 345.0	$ 0	$ 0	$ 0	$ 0	−$ 345.0
+ Change in common and other	−204.0					−204.0
− Common dividends and repurchases	−212.0					−212.0
Change in excess cash	−$ 761.0	$ 0	$ 0	$ 0	$ 0	−$ 761.0
+ Change in required cash balance	0.0					0.0
Change in cash balance without investments	−$ 761.0	$ 0	$ 0	$ 0	$ 0	−$ 761.0
Change in investments	−457.0					−457.0
Change in cash balance on the balance sheet	−$1,218.0					−$1,218.0

Exhibit may contain small rounding errors

These adjustments affect unlevered free cash flows because rent expense is an operating expense and decreases unlevered free cash flow, whereas interest and the repayment of the capitalized lease obligation are financing related and do not affect unlevered free cash flows. We also adjust the unlevered free cash flows for the increase in the capitalized lease assets, which we treat as a capital expenditure. We might also decide it is easier to treat all leases as operating leases. While we do not illustrate that, it is straightforward to do so if you understand how to convert all leases to finance (capitalized) leases.

We discuss the new U.S. lease accounting rules in the appendix. The primary change in the accounting rules is capitalizing both operating and finance leases. Once these accounting rules become effective, operating leases will be capitalized on the balance sheet. However, accounting rules continue to require companies to record the expense from operating leases as an operating expense instead of interest expense. Thus, the income statement and free cash flow adjustments we illustrate in this section generally extend to the new lease accounting rules as well.

Valuation Key 11.7

We must assure consistency in the treatment of leases between the company being valued and the comparable companies used to estimate the company's unlevered cost of capital, which sometimes requires treating a company's operating leases as capital (or finance) leases. One can also decide to treat all leases as operating leases.

REVIEW EXERCISE 11.4

Capitalizing Operating Leases—Part 2

Use the information presented in Review Exercise 11.3 and the following financial information to restate the company's Year 1 income statement, balance sheet, and free cash flow schedule so that all operating leases are capitalized (treated as finance leases) as of the end of Year 0 onward. The company's income tax rate is 40% on all income.

Summarized Financial Statements	Year 1 Reported
Income Statement	
Revenues	$22,000.0
Rent expense	−2,000.0
Depreciation and amortization	−3,000.0
Amortization of operating leases	0.0
All other operating expenses	−10,000.0
Operating income	$ 7,000.0
Interest expense	−1,000.0
Lease interest	0.0
Income before taxes	$ 6,000.0
Income taxes	−2,400.0
Net income	$ 3,600.0
Balance Sheet	
Current assets	$ 8,000.0
Net property, plant, and equipment	20,000.0
Other assets	5,000.0
Deferred tax asset	0.0
Capitalized operating leases	0.0
Total assets	$33,000.0
Current operating liabilities	$ 7,000.0
Other liabilities	10,000.0
Deferred tax liability	0.0
Debt	13,000.0
Capitalized operating leases	0.0
Total liabilities	$30,000.0
Shareholders' equity	3,000.0
Total liabilities and shareholders' equity	$33,000.0

Summarized Free Cash Flow Schedule	Year 1 Reported
Earnings before interest and taxes (EBIT)	$7,000.0
− Income taxes paid on EBIT	−2,800.0
Earnings before interest and after taxes	$4,200.0
+ Depreciation and amortization	3,000.0
+ Amortization of operating leases	0.0
− Change in net working capital	500.0
+ Change in non-current liabilities and other	100.0
− Change in required cash balance	−50.0
Unlevered cash flow from operations	$7,750.0
− Capital expenditures (net)	−3,000.0
− Increase in capital lease assets	0.0
Unlevered free cash flow	$4,750.0
− Interest paid	−1,000.0
+ Interest tax shield	400.0
+ Change in non-common equity	0.0
+ Change in capital lease obligations	0.0
Free cash flow to common equity	$4,150.0

Solution on pages 543–544.

11.5 VALUING A COMPANY WITH INTEREST AND NET OPERATING LOSS CARRYFORWARDS

LO4 Value a company with interest and net operating loss carryforwards

In Chapter 3 (Section 3.7), we discuss two common tax rules that affect the magnitude and timing of income tax payments and interest tax shields—**interest deduction limitations** or **interest deduction caps** and **net operating losses**. Both the potential deferred interest deductions created by interest deduction caps (**interest carryforwards**) and future potential taxable income offsets created by net operating losses (**net operating loss carryforwards**) can be an important consideration when valuing a company. In this section, we discuss how to value a company with interest and NOL carryforwards.

We illustrate how NOL carryforwards can reduce a company's future income tax payments relative to what they would have otherwise been and therefore, all else equal, can increase the value of the firm relative to what the value would have been without the NOL carryforwards. We also illustrate how NOL carryforwards defer the benefits of interest tax shields and therefore, all else equal, decrease the value of the interest tax shields relative to what the value would have been without the NOL carryforwards. On net, the positive effect on value from the tax savings is larger than the decrease in value from the deferred interest tax shields. For levered companies, any year in which a company has a net operating loss, it will also have an increase in its interest carryforward, thus, interest carryforwards are part of the calculation of the effect of NOL carryforwards. We separate interest carryforwards into two groups: those arising before the valuation date (**pre-valuation interest carryforward**) and those arising after the valuation date (**post-valuation interest carryforward**).

VALUATION IN PRACTICE 11.4

Delta Airlines, Inc.'s Net Operating Losses After experiencing several years of financial losses, filing and emerging from bankruptcy, and merging with Northwest Airlines, as of December 31, 2013, Delta had over $15 billion of U.S. federal pre-tax NOLs with a potential tax benefit of over $5 billion. Because of its previous losses and low expected profitability, prior to December 2013, Delta recorded a valuation allowance for the entire amount of the tax benefit of its NOLs. In 2013, however, based on its increased profitability and a positive outlook, Delta reversed almost the entire valuation allowance, concluding that it was more likely than not to capture the benefits of the NOLs:

> We periodically assess whether it is more likely than not that we will generate sufficient taxable income to realize our deferred income tax assets. We establish valuation allowances if it is not likely we will realize our deferred income tax assets. In making this determination, we consider all available positive and negative evidence and make certain assumptions. We consider, among other things, projected future taxable income, scheduled reversals of deferred tax liabilities, the overall business environment, our historical financial results and tax planning strategies. We recorded a full valuation allowance in 2004 due to our cumulative loss position at that time, compounded by the negative industry-wide business trends and outlook.
>
> At December 31, 2013, we released substantially all of the valuation allowance against our net deferred tax assets, resulting in an $8.3 billion benefit in our provision for income taxes. During 2014 and 2015, we continued our trend of sustained profitability. After considering all available positive and negative evidence, we released additional valuation allowances related to net operating losses and capital loss carryovers in each of those years. . . .

In 2014 and 2015, Delta did not pay any U.S. federal income taxes, a tax benefit of over $2 billion. As of December 31, 2015, Delta had approximately $9.5 billion of U.S. federal pre-tax NOLs with a potential tax benefit of over $3 billion. Delta stated that its NOLs would not begin to expire until 2024 and that it would not pay any cash federal income taxes before 2018, indicating that it would be able to capture the $3.5 billion of tax benefit by no later than December 31, 2018.

Source: Delta Airlines operates as a global scheduled passenger airline. See the company's 2013 and 2015 10-K filing for the information used in this valuation in practice.

The George Conrades Company. Throughout this section we use the George Conrades Company to discuss how to value a company with interest and NOL carryforwards. This is the same company we used in Chapter 3 (Section 3.7) to illustrate the effects of interest and NOL carryforwards on the magnitude and timing of a company's income tax payments and the magnitude and timing of its interest tax shields. As in the previous Conrades example in Chapter 3, we assume the company's income tax rate on all income is 25%, the tax deduction for interest in any year is limited to 30% of EBIT in that year, interest recorded by the company in excess of the interest deduction cap in a year can be carried forward indefinitely, the company's EBIT based on its financial statements is the same as its EBIT used to measure EBIT underpinning its taxable income, and Conrades can offset up to 80% of its taxable income in any one year with its NOL carryforwards. In addition, we also assume Conrades has a 15% unlevered cost of capital, an 8% interest rate (which is equal to the cost of debt), a discount rate for interest tax shields equal to the unlevered cost of capital ($r_{ITS} = r_{UA}$), and a long-term growth rate (Year 6 onward) equal to 2%. Given the 8% interest rate (cost of debt) and $10,000 of interest expense every year, we assume that Conrades has $125,000 of debt outstanding each year.

Effect on Unlevered Cash Flows, Interest Tax Shields, and Income Tax Forecasts

Since we already discussed the effect of interest and NOL carryforwards on unlevered cash flows, interest tax shields, and income tax forecasts in Chapter 3 (Section 3.7), we do not repeat that discussion here. (See Exhibits 3.27 through 3.29 and the related discussion.) Exhibit 11.8 is a reproduction of Exhibit 3.27, in which we present Conrades' financial statement (income statement) excerpts for two historical years (Years −1 and 0) and five years of forecasts (Years 1 to 5). The exhibit presents the company's EBIT, interest expense (assumed to equal interest payment), and earnings before income taxes. We also show the interest deduction cap based on 30% of EBIT.

EXHIBIT 11.8 Conrades Financial Accounting Income Statement Excerpt and Interest Deduction Cap (see Exhibit 3.27)

Financial Accounting (Income Statement Excerpt)	Actual		Forecast				
	Year −1	Year 0	Year 1	Year 2	Year 3	Year 4	Year 5
Earnings before interest and taxes....	−$40,000	−$40,000	−$40,000	$60,000	$70,000	$80,000	$80,000
Interest expense (current)...........	10,000	10,000	10,000	10,000	10,000	10,000	10,000
Earnings before income taxes	−$50,000	−$50,000	−$50,000	$50,000	$60,000	$70,000	$70,000
Interest deduction cap	$ 0	$ 0	$ 0	$18,000	$21,000	$24,000	$24,000

Conrades: The Levered Cash Flows Including Interest and NOL Carryforwards. Conrades had a net operating loss (negative EBIT) in the two past years (Years −1 and 0) of −$40,000, which continues in Year 1 (first year of forecasts). Conrades is expected to turn around its operations by Year 2 and generate EBIT equal to $60,000, which increases to $70,000 in Year 3, and to $80,000 in each of Years 4 and 5. Conrades' negative EBIT in Years −1 and 0 results in a $0 interest deduction cap. Since the company's interest for these years is $10,000, the interest deduction cap limits the company's ability to deduct any of its interest in Years −1 and 0, which creates a pre-valuation interest carryforward of $20,000 as of the end of Year 0. In Year 1, the first year of the forecasts, Conrades' negative EBIT again results in a $0 interest deduction cap, which creates a post-valuation interest carryforward of $10,000. The three years of a −$40,000 EBIT result in an NOL carryforward of $120,000 as of the end of Year 1. We present these calculations and the calculations for Years 2 through 5 in Exhibit 11.9, which is a reproduction of Exhibit 3.28.

EXHIBIT 11.9 Conrades—Levered Company Income Taxes Including Interest and Net Operating Loss Carryforwards—(see Exhibit 3.28)

	Actual		Forecast				
Levered Company (Taxable Income)	**Year −1**	**Year 0**	**Year 1**	**Year 2**	**Year 3**	**Year 4**	**Year 5**
Earnings before interest and taxes	−$40,000	−$40,000	−$40,000	$60,000	$70,000	$80,000	$80,000
Pre-valuation interest carryforward	0	0	0	18,000	2,000	0	0
Post-valuation interest carryforward			0	0	19,000	11,000	0
Interest expense (current)	0	0	0	0	0	10,000	10,000
Taxable income	−$40,000	−$40,000	−$40,000	$42,000	$49,000	$59,000	$70,000
NOL carryforward used	0	0	0	−33,600	−39,200	−47,200	0
Taxable income after NOL carryforward adjustment	−$40,000	−$40,000	−$40,000	$ 8,400	$ 9,800	$11,800	$70,000
Income taxes	0	0	0	2,100	2,450	2,950	17,500
Earnings	−$40,000	−$40,000	−$40,000	$ 6,300	$ 7,350	$ 8,850	$52,500
Average tax rate	0.00%	0.00%	0.00%	5.00%	5.00%	5.00%	25.00%
Pre-Valuation Interest Carryforward Balance	**Year −1**	**Year 0**	**Year 1**	**Year 2**	**Year 3**	**Year 4**	**Year 5**
Beginning interest carryforward	$ 0	$10,000	$20,000	$20,000	$ 2,000	$ 0	$ 0
Change in interest carryforward	10,000	10,000	0	−18,000	−2,000	0	0
Ending interest carryforward	$10,000	$20,000	$20,000	$ 2,000	$ 0	$ 0	$ 0
Post-Valuation Interest Carryforward Balance			**Year 1**	**Year 2**	**Year 3**	**Year 4**	**Year 5**
Beginning interest carryforward			$ 0	$10,000	$20,000	$11,000	$ 0
Change in interest carryforward			10,000	10,000	−9,000	−11,000	0
Ending interest carryforward			$10,000	$20,000	$11,000	$ 0	$ 0
NOL Carryforward Balance	**Year −1**	**Year 0**	**Year 1**	**Year 2**	**Year 3**	**Year 4**	**Year 5**
Beginning NOL carryforward	$ 0	$40,000	$ 80,000	$120,000	$86,400	$47,200	$ 0
Change in NOL carryforward	40,000	40,000	40,000	−33,600	−39,200	−47,200	0
Ending NOL carryforward	$40,000	$80,000	$120,000	$ 86,400	$47,200	$ 0	$ 0

Conrades pays no income taxes in Years −1 through +1. Even though Conrades has EBIT equal to $60,000 in Year 2, Conrades does not pay income taxes based on the $60,000 EBIT because it can offset $18,000 of that income with its pre-valuation interest carryforward and 80% or $33,600 [$33,600 = 0.8 × ($60,000 − $18,000)] of its remaining taxable income using its NOL carryforward. Since Conrades' pre-valuation interest carryforward exceeds its interest deduction cap, it cannot deduct any of its current interest, which increases the balance of its post-valuation interest carryforward to $20,000. In Year 3, Conrades has an interest deduction cap of $21,000, and it uses its remaining pre-valuation interest carryforward of $2,000 and $19,000 of its post-valuation interest carryforward to meet that cap, but none of its current interest. In Year 4, Conrades' interest deduction cap exceeds its combined post-valuation interest carryforward and current interest, so it can deduct all of its interest and its remaining interest carryforward balance.

Conrades: Unlevered Cash Flows Including Pre-Valuation Interest and NOL Carryforwards. Recall from Chapter 3, we can measure a company's interest tax shields for the forecasts by subtracting the income taxes it pays including the effects of interest from the income taxes it would pay if it had no interest deductions. In Exhibit 11.10, we calculate Conrades' income taxes, its pre-valuation interest carryforwards, its NOL carryforwards, its interest tax shields, and unlevered free cash flows assuming Conrades has no interest during the forecast periods. Note, however, we include the interest carryforwards from the pre-valuation period because that is an asset that company has as of the valuation date, even though we assume it has no interest in the post-valuation period. Exhibit 11.10 is a partial reproduction of Exhibit 3.29 and also includes a calculation of Conrades' unlevered free cash flows. We assume that Conrades makes no investment in working capital and that its CAPEX is equal to its depreciation. Thus, its unlevered free cash flows are equal to its EBIT less income taxes on EBIT.

EXHIBIT 11.10 Conrades—Unlevered Income Taxes and Free Cash Flows Including Pre-Valuation Interest and Net Operating Loss Carryforwards (see Exhibit 3.29)

	Actual		Forecast				
Unlevered Company (Taxable Income)	**Year −1**	**Year 0**	**Year 1**	**Year 2**	**Year 3**	**Year 4**	**Year 5**
Earnings before interest and taxes	−$40,000	−$40,000	−$ 40,000	$60,000	$70,000	$80,000	$80,000
Pre-valuation interest carryforward	0	0	0	18,000	2,000	0	0
Interest expense (current)	0	0					
Taxable income	−$40,000	−$40,000	−$ 40,000	$42,000	$68,000	$80,000	$80,000
NOL carryforward used	0	0	0	−33,600	−54,400	−32,000	0
Taxable income after NOL carryforward adjustment	−$40,000	−$40,000	−$ 40,000	$ 8,400	$13,600	$48,000	$80,000
Income taxes	0	0	0	2,100	3,400	12,000	20,000
Earnings	−$40,000	−$40,000	−$ 40,000	$ 6,300	$10,200	$36,000	$60,000
Average tax rate	0.00%	0.00%	0.00%	5.00%	5.00%	15.00%	25.00%
Pre-Valuation Interest Carryforward Balance	**Year −1**	**Year 0**	**Year 1**	**Year 2**	**Year 3**	**Year 4**	**Year 5**
Beginning interest carryforward	$ 0	$10,000	$ 20,000	$20,000	$ 2,000	$ 0	$ 0
Change in interest carryforward	10,000	10,000	0	−18,000	−2,000	0	0
Ending interest carryforward	$10,000	$20,000	$ 20,000	$ 2,000	$ 0	$ 0	$ 0
NOL Carryforward Balance	**Year −1**	**Year 0**	**Year 1**	**Year 2**	**Year 3**	**Year 4**	**Year 5**
Beginning NOL carryforward	$ 0	$40,000	$ 80,000	$120,000	$86,400	$32,000	$ 0
Change in NOL carryforward	40,000	40,000	40,000	−33,600	−54,400	−32,000	0
Ending NOL carryforward	$40,000	$80,000	$120,000	$ 86,400	$32,000	$ 0	$ 0
Interest Tax Shield			**Year 1**	**Year 2**	**Year 3**	**Year 4**	**Year 5**
Income taxes (unlevered firm)			$ 0	$ 2,100	$ 3,400	$12,000	$20,000
Income taxes (with interest deduction)			0	2,100	2,450	2,950	17,500
Correct interest tax shield			$ 0	$ 0	$ 950	$ 9,050	$ 2,500
Unlevered Free Cash Flow			**Year 1**	**Year 2**	**Year 3**	**Year 4**	**Year 5**
EBIT			−$ 40,000	$60,000	$70,000	$80,000	$80,000
Income taxes			0	2,100	3,400	12,000	20,000
Unlevered free cash flow			−$ 40,000	$57,900	$66,600	$68,000	$60,000

The underlying calculations for the unlevered firm in Exhibit 11.10 are the same as the calculations in the previous exhibit with two exceptions—$0 interest after the valuation date and, thus, $0 post-valuation interest carryforwards in the forecasts—so naturally the income taxes differ (are higher). The important parts of this exhibit are the bottom two panels—the calculation of Conrades' interest tax shields and unlevered free cash flows. Conrades has $0 interest tax shields in Years 1 and 2 because it was not able to deduct any current interest in those years. Conrades interest tax shields in Year 3 are limited to $950 (versus its potential interest tax shields of $7,500 from Years 1 through 3; $7,500 = $10,000 × 3 × 0.25) because it was able to offset 80% of its income using its NOL carryforward. In Year 4, however, Conrades was able to capture not only its potential interest tax shields from the current year but also capture all previously deferred interest tax shields ($9,050 = $10,000 × 4 × 0.25 − $950).

In the bottom panel, we calculate the company's unlevered free cash flows, which is equal to EBIT minus income taxes assuming the company has no interest in the forecasts, which we calculate in the top panel of the exhibit. These are the unlevered free cash flows that include the effects of pre-valuation interest and NOL carryforwards. The unlevered free cash flows in this panel and the interest tax shields in the previous panel are the cash flows we use to value the firm including the effects of the interest (pre- and post-valuation) and NOL carryforwards.

Conrades: Unlevered Cash Flows Excluding Interest and NOL Carryforwards. We can calculate the effect of the company's interest and NOL carryforwards on its cash flows (unlevered free cash flows and interest tax shields) by subtracting the unlevered free cash flows and interest tax shields including the effects of interest and NOL carryforwards from the unlevered free cash flows and interest tax shields excluding the effects of interest and NOL carryforwards.

In order to perform that calculation, we must first calculate Conrades' unlevered free cash flows and interest tax shields for Years 1 to 5, excluding all interest and NOL carryforwards, which we present in Exhibit 11.11. As part of these calculations, we assume the company has no interest deduction cap and it has a negative income tax if it has negative taxable income. In other words, income tax in a year is equal to EBIT multiplied by the income tax rate, even if EBIT is negative. Doing this essentially assumes that the company gets a cash payment from the government. Also, since EBIT is equal to the company's unlevered pre-tax cash flow given the assumptions stated previously, EBIT minus income tax on EBIT is equal to the company's unlevered free cash flow. For example, in Year 1, EBIT is −\$40,000 and income tax on EBIT is −\$10,000 (−\$10,000 = −\$40,000 × 0.25), resulting in an unlevered free cash flow in Year 1 of −\$30,000. In Year 2, the company's unlevered free cash flow is \$45,000 (\$45,000 = \$60,000 − \$60,000 × 0.25). Given these assumptions, the company's interest tax shield in a year is equal to its marginal tax rate for interest multiplied by its interest expense in that year. In other words, we are assuming the company gets the benefit of the interest tax shield in the year it incurs the interest expense, regardless of its profitability. Given all of this, we are assuming away NOL and interest carryforwards and realizing the tax benefits of the interest deduction in the years of losses and the year in which interest is incurred.

EXHIBIT 11.11 Conrades—Unlevered Free Cash Flows and Interest Tax Shields Excluding All Interest and Net Operating Loss Carryforwards

	Year 1	Year 2	Year 3	Year 4	Year 5
EBIT	−\$40,000	\$60,000	\$70,000	\$80,000	\$80,000
Income taxes	−10,000	15,000	17,500	20,000	20,000
Unlevered free cash flow	−\$30,000	\$45,000	\$52,500	\$60,000	\$60,000
Interest expense	\$10,000	\$ 10,000	\$10,000	\$ 10,000	\$ 10,000
Income tax rate	25%	25%	25%	25%	25%
Interest tax shield	\$ 2,500	\$ 2,500	\$ 2,500	\$ 2,500	\$ 2,500

In the top panel of Exhibit 11.12, we calculate the effect of the company's interest and NOL carryforwards on its cash flows (unlevered free cash flows and interest tax shields) by subtracting the unlevered free cash flows and interest tax shields including the effects of interest and NOL carryforwards (Exhibit 11.10) from the unlevered free cash flows and interest tax shields excluding the effects of interest and NOL carryforwards (Exhibit 11.11). The sum of the differences in the unlevered free cash flows is \$25,000 (\$25,000 = −\$10,000 + \$12,900 + \$14,100 + \$8,000 + \$0) and the sum of the differences in the interest tax shields is \$0 (\$0 = −\$2,500 − \$2,500 − \$1,550 + \$6,550), resulting in a sum of the total differences of \$25,000.

The sum of the differences in the unlevered free cash flows is \$25,000 because the company had pre-valuation interest and pre-valuation NOL carryforwards equal to \$100,000 (\$100,000 = \$20,000 + \$80,000, Exhibit 11.9), which were completely utilized. The (undiscounted) tax benefits of these pre-existing carryforwards is \$25,000 (\$25,000 = \$100,000 × 0.25). The sum of the differences in interest tax shields is equal to \$0 because the company was able to capture all of the interest tax shields from its interest in the forecasts by Year 4.

EXHIBIT 11.12 Conrades—Unlevered Free Cash Flows and Interest Tax Shields Including and Excluding Interest and NOL Carryforwards Compared

	Year 1	Year 2	Year 3	Year 4	Year 5
Difference in Free Cash Flows and Interest Tax Shields (Compare Exhibit 11.10 and 11.11)					
Free cash flows including interest and NOL carryforwards	−$40,000	$57,900	$66,600	$68,000	$60,000
Free cash flows excluding interest and NOL carryforwards	−30,000	45,000	52,500	60,000	60,000
Difference	−$10,000	$12,900	$14,100	$ 8,000	$ 0
Interest tax shields including interest and NOL carryforwards	$ 0	$ 0	$ 950	$ 9,050	$ 2,500
Interest cash flows excluding interest and NOL carryforwards	2,500	2,500	2,500	2,500	2,500
Difference	−$ 2,500	−$ 2,500	−$ 1,550	$ 6,550	$ 0
Difference in free cash flows and interest tax shields	−$12,500	$10,400	$12,550	$14,550	$ 0
NOL Carryforward and Interest Carryforward (Created) and Used (See Exhibit 11.9)					
Change in NOL balance (NOLs used)	−$40,000	$33,600	$39,200	$47,200	$ 0
Change in pre-valuation interest carryforward	0	18,000	2,000	0	0
Change in post-valuation interest carryforward	−10,000	−10,000	9,000	11,000	0
Total	−$50,000	$41,600	$50,200	$58,200	$ 0
Tax rate	25%	25%	25%	25%	25%
Tax benefit	−$12,500	$10,400	$12,550	$14,550	$ 0

REVIEW EXERCISE 11.5

Valuing a Company with Interest and NOL Carryforwards—Part 1

Use the information in the following schedule, which contains two years of historical performance and five years of forecasts, to value the firm as of the end of Year 0 using the following assumptions. Assume the company's income tax rate on all income is 35%, the tax deduction for interest in any year is capped at 45% of EBIT in that year, any interest payment above the interest deduction cap in a year can be carried forward indefinitely, the company can only use its NOL carryforwards to offset a maximum of 80% of its taxable income before NOL offsets, and the company's EBIT based on its financial statements is equal to its EBIT for income taxes. Also assume the company's unlevered cost of capital is 12%, its interest rate (and debt cost of capital) is 9%, its discount rate for its interest tax shields is equal to its unlevered cost of capital, and its long-term growth rate (Year 6 onward) is 3%. Assume the company makes no investment in working capital and that CAPEX is equal to depreciation.

a. Calculate the company's income taxes and interest and NOL carryforwards for the levered company (including interest in the forecasts). (Similar to Exhibit 11.9.)

b. Calculate the company's income taxes and interest and NOL carryforwards for the unlevered company (excluding interest in the forecasts but including interest in Years −1 and 0). (Similar to Exhibit 11.10.)

c. Calculate the company's income taxes and interest tax shields assuming the company can deduct all of its interest for income taxes and the company receives a tax refund if its EBIT is negative. (Similar to Exhibit 11.11.)

d. Calculate the effect of the company's interest and NOL carryforwards on the company's cash flows (unlevered free cash flows and interest tax shields) by subtracting the unlevered free cash flows and interest tax shields including the effects of interest and NOL carryforwards from the unlevered free cash flows and interest tax shields excluding the effects of interest and NOL carryforwards. Compare these differences to the sum of the interest and NOL carryforwards. (Similar to Exhibit 11.12.)

continued

continued from previous page

Financial Accounting (Income Statement Excerpt)	Actual Year −1	Actual Year 0	Forecast Year 1	Forecast Year 2	Forecast Year 3	Forecast Year 4	Forecast Year 5
Earnings before interest and taxes. . .	−$10,000	−$10,000	−$10,000	$28,000	$32,000	$36,000	$32,000
Interest expense (current).	4,000	6,000	8,000	8,000	8,000	8,000	8,000
Earnings before income taxes	−$14,000	−$16,000	−$18,000	$20,000	$24,000	$28,000	$24,000
Interest deduction cap.	$ 0	$ 0	$ 0	$12,600	$14,400	$16,200	$14,400

Solution on pages 544–546.

Adjusting the APV Valuation Model for Interest and NOL Carryforwards

We know that the APV valuation method correctly measures the value of the firm with interest and NOL carryforwards as long as we correctly measure unlevered free cash flows and interest tax shields so that they include the effect of interest and NOL carryforwards.

Conrades Adjusted Present Value-Based Valuation Including the Effect of Interest and NOL Carryforwards in Its Cash Flows. We know Conrades' unlevered cost of capital is 15% and its long-term growth rate (Year 6 onward) is 2%. We also know Conrades' unlevered free cash flows and interest tax shields including the effect of its interest and NOL carryforwards (Exhibit 11.10). This is all of the information we need to measure the value of the firm using the adjusted present value valuation model, which we show in Exhibit 11.13. Given its interest and NOL carryforwards, Conrades' unlevered value is equal to $355,554 and the value of its interest tax shields is equal to $16,794, resulting in a firm value of $372,348.

EXHIBIT 11.13 Conrades—Adjusted Present Value Valuation Including the Effect of the Company's Interest and Net Operating Loss Carryforwards in the Company's Unlevered Free Cash Flows and Interest Tax Shields

Adjusted Present Value Valuation	Year 0	Year 1	Year 2	Year 3	Year 4	CV Year 4
Unlevered free cash flows for continuing value						$ 60,000
Continuing value discount factor						7.692
Unlevered free cash flows and continuing value		−$40,000	$57,900	$66,600	$68,000	$461,538
Discount factor.		0.870	0.756	0.658	0.572	0.572
Present value of unlevered free cash flows	$355,554	−$34,783	$43,781	$43,791	$38,879	$263,886
Interest tax shield for continuing value.						$ 2,500
Continuing value discount factor						7.692
Interest tax shield and continuing value.		$ 0	$ 0	$ 950	$ 9,050	$ 19,231
Discount factor, $r_{ITS} = r_{UA}$		0.870	0.756	0.658	0.572	0.572
Present value of interest tax shields.	$ 16,794	$ 0	$ 0	$ 625	$ 5,174	$ 10,995
Value of the firm	$372,348					

The previous valuation embeds the cash flow effects of Conrades' interest and NOL carryforwards in its unlevered free cash flows and interest tax shields. Earlier in this section we explained how the difference in a company's cash flows resulting from its interest and NOL carryforwards in a year is equal to the interest and NOL carryforwards created or used in that year multiplied by the company's tax rate (Exhibit 11.12). Thus, an alternative way to measure the value of the firm is to first measure the value of the firm using the APV valuation method excluding the effect of the company's interest and NOL carryforwards (see Exhibit 11.11 for Conrades) and separately value the pre- and post-valuation interest and NOL carryforwards (see Exhibit. 11.12 for Conrades). We show this valuation in Exhibit 11.14.

EXHIBIT 11.14 Conrades—Adjusted Present Value Valuation Separately Valuing the Effect of the Company's Interest and Net Operating Loss Carryforwards

Adjusted Present Value Valuation	Year 0	Year 1	Year 2	Year 3	Year 4	CV Year 4
Unlevered free cash flows for continuing value						$ 60,000
Continuing value discount factor						7.692
Unlevered free cash flows and continuing value (Exhibit 11.11)		−$30,000	$45,000	$52,500	$60,000	$461,538
Discount factor		0.870	0.756	0.658	0.572	0.572
Value of unlevered free cash flows	$340,650	−$26,087	$34,026	$34,520	$34,305	$263,886
Interest tax shield for continuing value						$ 2,500
Continuing value discount factor						7.692
Interest tax shield and continuing value (Exhibit 11.11)		$ 2,500	$ 2,500	$ 2,500	$ 2,500	$ 19,231
Discount factor, $r_{ITS} = r_{UA}$		0.870	0.756	0.658	0.572	0.572
Value of interest tax shields	$ 18,133	$ 2,174	$ 1,890	$ 1,644	$ 1,429	$ 10,995
Value of the firm	$358,783					
Effect of NOL Carryforwards						
Change in NOL balance (NOLs used) (Exhibit 11.12)		−$40,000	$33,600	$39,200	$47,200	$ 0
Tax rate		25%	25%	25%	25%	25%
Tax benefit		−$10,000	$ 8,400	$ 9,800	$11,800	$ 0
Discount factor, $r_{NOL} = r_{UA}$		0.870	0.756	0.658	0.572	
Value of NOL carryforwards	$ 10,846	−$ 8,696	$ 6,352	$ 6,444	$ 6,747	
Effect of Pre-Valuation Interest Carryforwards						
Change in pre-valuation interest carryforwards (Exhibit 11.12)		$ 0	$18,000	$ 2,000	$ 0	$ 0
Tax rate		25%	25%	25%	25%	25%
Tax benefit		$ 0	$ 4,500	$ 500	$ 0	$ 0
Discount factor, $r_{Pre\text{-}iCF} = r_{UA}$		0.870	0.756	0.658	0.572	
Value of pre-valuation interest carryforwards	$ 3,731	$ 0	$ 3,403	$ 329	$ 0	
Effect of Post-Valuation Interest Carryforwards						
Change in post-valuation interest carryforwards (Exhibit 11.12)		−$10,000	−$10,000	$ 9,000	$11,000	$ 0
Tax rate		25%	25%	25%	25%	25%
Tax benefit		−$ 2,500	−$ 2,500	$ 2,250	$ 2,750	$ 0
Discount factor, $r_{Post\text{-}iCF} = r_{UA}$		0.870	0.756	0.658	0.572	
Value of post-valuation interest carryforwards	−$ 1,013	−$ 2,174	−$ 1,890	$ 1,479	$ 1,572	
Value of all carryforwards	$ 13,565					
Value of the firm	$372,348					

Naturally, the two APV valuations result in the same firm value, $372,348, as long as we assume the discount rate is the unlevered cost of capital for all cash flows (unlevered free cash flows and interest tax shields), which means that we implicitly assume that the discount rates for its pre-valuation and post-valuation interest carryforwards ($r_{Pre\text{-}iCF}$ and $r_{Post\text{-}iCF}$) and NOL carryforwards (r_{NOL}) are also equal to the unlevered cost of capital. We can, however, relax this assumption and use different discount rates for the pre-valuation, post-valuation, and NOL carryforwards. The highest discount rate applicable to these carryforwards is the unlevered cost of capital, but it is possible that one or more of these carryforwards are less risky than the company's unlevered assets. The riskiness of these carryforwards naturally depends on the approach we use to value them and the specific facts and valuation context for a particular valuation.[16]

[16] Although we do not show these calculations in the text, given the APV valuation in Exhibit 11.14, we can also use the WACC valuation method to measure the same value of the firm including the effects of the company's interest and NOL carryforwards by using the forecasted debt amounts and the varying yearly r_{WACC} (determined using the year-by-year capital structure ratios implied in the forecasted debt amounts). The process is the same as the process discussed in Chapter 5.

REVIEW EXERCISE 11.6

Valuing a Company with Interest and NOL Carryforwards—Part 2

Using the information and assumptions in Review Exercise 11.5, measure the value of the firm by separately valuing the firm without interest and NOL carryforwards and then add the value of the pre-valuation and post-valuation interest carryforwards and NOL carryforwards. Assume the company's capital structure strategy is based on the forecasts and the long-term growth rate. (Use the APV valuation method, similar to Exhibit 11.14.)

Solution on page 547.

Adjusting the Weighted Average Cost of Capital Valuation Model for Interest and NOL Carryforwards

We discuss the effects of interest and NOL carryforwards on free cash flows and interest tax shields in Chapter 3 and also earlier in this section. The effect of these carryforwards on interest tax shields is such that the assumed timing relation between a company's recognition of its interest expense and its tax deductibility that underpins the WACC valuation model does not hold. In this section, we explain how we can adjust the WACC valuation method to correctly measure the value of a company with interest and NOL carryforwards. In order to adjust the WACC valuation model, we assume that the company knows its capital structure ratios excluding the effect on value from the company's interest and NOL carryforwards. In other words, the capital structure ratios are not based on the value of those carryforwards.

The process is as follows. We first value the company excluding the effect of any interest or NOL carryforwards using the WACC valuation method. We then calculate the pre-valuation, post-valuation, and NOL carryforwards based on the capital structure assumed in the WACC valuations. Doing this entails calculating the implied interest from the capital structure implied by the WACC valuation (see Chapter 5 for a refresher on this calculation). Finally, we separately value the company's pre-valuation, post-valuation, and NOL carryforwards to which we add the WACC valuation that excluded the valuation effect of the company's interest and NOL carryforwards.

For Conrades, we already have the unlevered free cash flows without NOLs from the previous section and we know the company's cost of debt, the unlevered cost of capital, and the income tax rate. The only additional information we need to measure the company's weighted average cost of capital is its capital structure ratios. For Conrades, we assume a capital structure strategy of 28% debt and 72% common equity based on the value of the firm excluding the effect on firm value from the company's interest and NOL carryforwards. Conrades' equity cost of capital is 17.72% [$0.1772 = 0.15 + (0.15 - 0.08) \times 0.28/0.72$], assuming the discount rate for interest tax shields is equal to the unlevered cost of capital. The resulting weighted average cost of capital for Conrades is 14.44% [$0.1444 = 0.1772 \times 0.72 + 0.08 \times (1 - 0.25) \times 0.28$].

Based on the unlevered free cash flows in Exhibit 11.11, the value of the firm as shown in Exhibit 11.15 is equal to $359,359. This valuation is $576 larger than the APV-based value of the firm using the same unlevered free cash flows, $358,783, shown in Exhibit 11.14 but neither of these valuations has considered the valuation effects of the interest and NOL carryforwards. We know that since the unlevered firm values are the same in both valuations (same unlevered free cash flows), then the difference must be that the value of the interest tax shields embedded in the WACC valuation is $576 larger than the value of the interest tax shields embedded in the APV valuation, which we show later in this section.

EXHIBIT 11.15 Conrades—Weighted Average Cost of Capital Valuation Excluding the Effect of the Company's Interest and Net Operating Loss Carryforwards

WACC Valuation Excluding Interest and NOL Carryforwards	Year 0	Year 1	Year 2	Year 3	Year 4	CV Year 4
Unlevered free cash flow for continuing value						$ 60,000
Discount factor for continuing value						8.039
Unlevered free cash flow and continuing value		−$30,000	$45,000	$52,500	$60,000	$482,315
Discount factor, r_{WACC}		0.874	0.764	0.667	0.583	0.583
Firm value ignoring interest carryforwards and NOLs	$359,359	−$26,215	$34,360	$35,029	$34,982	$281,203

In Exhibit 11.16, we present the year-by-year WACC valuations excluding the valuation effect of Conrades' interest and NOL carryforwards. Now that we know the value of the firm in each year, we can measure the amount of debt assumed in the WACC valuation (28% debt to value ratio) and the corresponding interest, which we also present in this exhibit.

In Exhibit 11.17, we calculate Conrades' income taxes, its pre-valuation and post-valuation interest carryforwards, its NOL carryforwards, its interest tax shields, and unlevered free cash flows for each year during the forecast period. This exhibit includes the same calculations as we perform in Exhibit 11.9 but they are based on the capital structure assumed in the WACC valuation instead of the capital structure in the forecasts. This exhibit provides the amount of pre-valuation, post-valuation, and NOL carryforwards created or used in each year during the forecast period based on the WACC valuation. Comparing the interest assumed in the WACC valuation in this exhibit to that in the forecasts (Exhibit 11.8) shows that the interest assumed in the WACC valuation is smaller than that in the forecasts in Years 1 and 2 but larger for Years 3 onward.

EXHIBIT 11.16 Conrades—Year-by-Year Weighted Average Cost of Capital Valuation Excluding the Effect of the Company's Interest and Net Operating Loss Carryforwards

	Year 1	Year 2	Year 3	Year 4	CV Year 4
Unlevered free cash flow for continuing value					$ 60,000
Discount factor for continuing value					8.039
Unlevered free cash flow	−$ 30,000	$ 45,000	$ 52,500	$ 60,000	
Value of the unlevered firm at year end	$441,250	$459,967	$473,886	$482,315	
Unlevered value at year end plus unlevered free cash flow	$411,250	$504,967	$526,386	$542,315	
Discount factor for one year	0.874	0.874	0.874	0.874	
Beginning of year V_F (ignoring interest and NOL carryforwards)	$359,359	$441,250	$459,967	$473,886	$482,315
As of the End of Year	**Year 0**	**Year 1**	**Year 2**	**Year 3**	**Year 4**
Value of the firm (V_F)	$359,359	$441,250	$459,967	$473,886	$482,315
Debt to value	28%	28%	28%	28%	28%
Value of debt	$100,620	$123,550	$128,791	$132,688	$135,048
Interest rate (cost of debt)	8%	8%	8%	8%	8%
Interest (in following year)	$ 8,050	$ 9,884	$ 10,303	$ 10,615	$ 10,804
Tax rate	25%	25%	25%	25%	25%
Interest × tax rate (potential interest tax shield)	$ 2,012	$ 2,471	$ 2,576	$ 2,654	$ 2,701
Interest deduction cap (in the following year)	$ 0	$ 18,000	$ 21,000	$ 24,000	$ 24,000

EXHIBIT 11.17 Conrades—Levered Company Income Taxes Including Interest and Net Operating Loss Carryforwards Based on the Weighted Average Cost of Capital Valuation Assumed Debt

Financial Accounting (Income Statement Excerpt)	Actual Year −1	Actual Year 0	Forecast Year 1	Forecast Year 2	Forecast Year 3	Forecast Year 4	Forecast Year 5
Earnings before interest and taxes	−$40,000	−$40,000	−$ 40,000	$ 60,000	$70,000	$80,000	$80,000
Interest expense (current)	10,000	10,000	8,050	9,884	10,303	10,615	10,804
Earnings before income taxes	−$50,000	−$50,000	−$ 48,050	$ 50,116	$59,697	$69,385	$69,196
Interest deduction cap	$ 0	$ 0	$ 0	$ 18,000	$21,000	$24,000	$24,000
Levered Company (Taxable Income)	**Actual Year −1**	**Actual Year 0**	**Forecast Year 1**	**Forecast Year 2**	**Forecast Year 3**	**Forecast Year 4**	**Forecast Year 5**
Earnings before interest and taxes	−$40,000	−$40,000	−$ 40,000	$ 60,000	$70,000	$80,000	$80,000
Pre-valuation interest carryforward	0	0	0	18,000	2,000	0	0
Post-valuation interest carryforward			0	0	17,934	9,237	0
Interest expense (current)	0	0	0	0	1,066	10,615	10,804
Taxable income	−$40,000	−$40,000	−$ 40,000	$ 42,000	$49,000	$60,148	$69,196
NOL carryforward used	0	0	0	−33,600	−39,200	−47,200	0
Taxable income after NOL carryforward adjustment	−$40,000	−$40,000	−$ 40,000	$ 8,400	$ 9,800	$12,948	$69,196
Income taxes	0	0	0	2,100	2,450	3,237	17,299
Earnings	−$40,000	−$40,000	−$ 40,000	$ 6,300	$ 7,350	$ 9,711	$51,897
Average tax rate	0.00%	0.00%	0.00%	5.00%	5.00%	5.38%	25.00%
Pre-Valuation Interest Carryforward Balance	**Year −1**	**Year 0**	**Year 1**	**Year 2**	**Year 3**	**Year 4**	**Year 5**
Beginning interest carryforward	$ 0	$10,000	$ 20,000	$ 20,000	$ 2,000	$ 0	$ 0
Change in interest carryforward	10,000	10,000	0	−18,000	−2,000	0	0
Ending interest carryforward	$10,000	$20,000	$ 20,000	$ 2,000	$ 0	$ 0	$ 0
Post-Valuation Interest Carryforward Balance			**Year 1**	**Year 2**	**Year 3**	**Year 4**	**Year 5**
Beginning interest carryforward			$ 0	$ 8,050	$17,934	$ 9,237	$ 0
Change in interest carryforward			8,050	9,884	−8,697	−9,237	0
Ending interest carryforward			$ 8,050	$ 17,934	$ 9,237	$ 0	$ 0
NOL Carryforward Balance	**Year −1**	**Year 0**	**Year 1**	**Year 2**	**Year 3**	**Year 4**	**Year 5**
Beginning NOL carryforward	$ 0	$40,000	$ 80,000	$120,000	$86,400	$47,200	$ 0
Change in NOL carryforward	40,000	40,000	40,000	−33,600	−39,200	−47,200	0
Ending NOL carryforward	$40,000	$80,000	$120,000	$ 86,400	$47,200	$ 0	$ 0

In Exhibit 11.18, we separately value the company's pre-valuation, post-valuation, and NOL carryforwards using the unlevered cost of capital to which we add the WACC valuation excluding the valuation effect of the company's interest and NOL carryforwards. The value of the pre-valuation, post-valuation, and NOL carryforwards is $13,709, which when added to the previous valuation results in a firm value of $373,068.[17]

[17] The WACC valuation method used here assumes different debt amounts (debt equals 28% of firm value) than the APV valuation method (forecasted debt) which leads to different firm values. While we do not show the calculation in the text, we can use the APV valuation method to replicate the WACC valuation. To do so, discount the unlevered free cash flows embedding the NOL carryforward into those estimates at the unlevered cost of capital and value the interest tax shields from Exhibit 11.16 at the unlevered cost of capital.

EXHIBIT 11.18 Conrades—Weighted Average Cost of Capital Valuation Separately Including the Effect of the Company's Interest and Net Operating Loss Carryforwards

WACC Valuation—using debt based on WACC capital structure to measure interest and NOL carryforwards	Year 0	Year 1	Year 2	Year 3	Year 4	CV Year 4
Unlevered free cash flow for continuing value						$ 60,000
Discount factor for continuing value						8.039
Unlevered free cash flow and continuing value		−$30,000	$45,000	$52,500	$60,000	$482,315
Discount factor, r_{WACC}		0.874	0.764	0.667	0.583	0.583
Firm value ignoring interest carryforwards and NOLs	$359,359	−$26,215	$34,360	$35,029	$34,982	$281,203
Effect of NOL Carryforwards						
Change in NOL balance (NOLs used)		−$40,000	$33,600	$39,200	$47,200	$ 0
Tax rate		25%	25%	25%	25%	25%
Tax benefit		−$10,000	$ 8,400	$ 9,800	$11,800	$ 0
Discount factor, $r_{NOL} = r_{UA}$		0.870	0.756	0.658	0.572	
Value of NOL carryforwards	$ 10,846	−$ 8,696	$ 6,352	$ 6,444	$ 6,747	
Effect of Pre-Valuation Interest Carryforwards						
Change in pre-valuation interest carryforwards		$ 0	$18,000	$ 2,000	$ 0	$ 0
Tax rate		25%	25%	25%	25%	25%
Tax benefit		$ 0	$ 4,500	$ 500	$ 0	$ 0
Discount factor, $r_{Pre\text{-}iCF} = r_{UA}$		0.870	0.756	0.658	0.572	
Value of pre-valuation interest carryforwards	$ 3,731	$ 0	$ 3,403	$ 329	$ 0	
Effect of Post-Valuation Interest Carryforwards						
Change in post-valuation interest carryforwards		−$ 8,050	−$ 9,884	$ 8,697	$ 9,237	$ 0
Tax rate		25%	25%	25%	25%	25%
Tax benefit		−$ 2,012	−$ 2,471	$ 2,174	$ 2,309	$ 0
Discount factor, $r_{Post\text{-}iCF} = r_{UA}$		0.870	0.756	0.658	0.572	
Value of post-valuation interest carryforwards	−$ 868	−$ 1,750	−$ 1,868	$ 1,430	$ 1,320	
Value of all interest carryforwards	$ 13,709					
Value of the firm	$373,068					

In this valuation, we discount the pre-valuation, post-valuation, and NOL carryforward related cash flows at the unlevered cost of capital in order to compare them to the corresponding APV valuation in Exhibit 11.14. Recall from the earlier discussion, the discount rate for the interest and NOL carryforwards will depend on the approach and valuation context of the specific valuation. The WACC valuation is $720 larger than the APV valuation ($720 = $373,068 − $372,348). Recall, the WACC valuation excluding the valuation effects of the interest and NOL carryforwards is $576 larger than the corresponding APV valuation and this difference is augmented by the difference in the valuation of the interest and NOL carryforwards in the WACC versus APV valuations of $144 ($13,709 versus $13,565).

REVIEW EXERCISE 11.7

Valuing a Company with Interest and NOL Carryforwards—Part 3

Using the information and assumptions in Review Exercise 11.5, measure the value of the firm including and excluding interest and NOL carryforwards and assuming the company's capital structure strategy is to finance 1/3 of the firm with debt and 2/3 with common equity excluding interest and NOL carryforwards. (Similar to Exhibits 11.15 through 11.18.)

Solution on page 547–550.

A Common "Short-Cut" Adjustment to the WACC Valuation Method

A common "short-cut" method used to adjust the WACC valuation method for interest and NOL carryforwards is to first value the company excluding the effect of any interest or NOL carryforwards using the WACC valuation method as we did in the previous section. Instead of calculating the pre-valuation, post-valuation, and NOL carryforwards based on the capital structure assumed in the WACC valuations, this method uses the interest forecasts as the basis of those calculations, and then separately values the company's pre-valuation and post-valuation interest carryforwards, and NOL carryforwards. Those carryforwards can be discounted at the rate that best approximates their riskiness, though the most common assumption is to discount them at the weighted average cost of capital. We present this approach in Exhibit 11.19. In this case the valuation from the short-cut method and the correct valuation are very close because the interest expense assumptions are very similar. How close the two valuations will be to each other hinges on how close the interest expense assumptions are. Note that the value of the interest and NOL carryforwards here is $13,875, which is slightly larger than the value obtained in Exhibit 11.14 ($13,565). The difference is due to the fact that the discount rate used in Exhibit 11.14 is the unlevered cost of capital while the discount rate used here is the weighted average cost of capital.

EXHIBIT 11.19 Conrades—"Short-Cut" Weighted Average Cost of Capital Valuation Separately Including the Effect of the Company's Interest and Net Operating Loss Carryforwards Based on the Company's Debt Forecasts

"Short-Cut" WACC Valuation—using debt forecasts (not WACC debt) to measure interest and NOL carryforwards	Year 0	Year 1	Year 2	Year 3	Year 4	CV Year 4
Unlevered free cash flow for continuing value						$60,000
Discount factor for continuing value						8.039
Unlevered free cash flow and continuing value		−$30,000	$45,000	$52,500	$60,000	$482,315
Discount factor, r_{WACC}		0.874	0.764	0.667	0.583	0.583
Firm value ignoring interest carryforwards and NOLs	$359,359	−$26,215	$34,360	$35,029	$34,982	$281,203
Effect of NOL Carryforwards						
Change in NOL balance (NOLs used)		−$40,000	$33,600	$39,200	$47,200	$ 0
Tax rate		25%	25%	25%	25%	25%
Tax benefit		−$10,000	$ 8,400	$ 9,800	$11,800	$ 0
Discount factor, $r_{NOL} = r_{WACC}$		0.874	0.764	0.667	0.583	
Value of NOL carryforwards	$ 11,094	−$ 8,738	$ 6,414	$ 6,539	$ 6,880	
Effect of Pre-Valuation Interest Carryforwards						
Change in pre-valuation interest carryforwards		$ 0	$18,000	$ 2,000	$ 0	$ 0
Tax rate		25%	25%	25%	25%	25%
Tax benefit		$ 0	$ 4,500	$ 500	$ 0	$ 0
Discount factor, $r_{Pre\text{-}iCF} = r_{WACC}$		0.874	0.764	0.667	0.583	
Value of pre-valuation interest carryforwards	$ 3,770	$ 0	$ 3,436	$ 334	$ 0	
Effect of Post-Valuation Interest Carryforwards						
Change in post-valuation interest carryforwards		−$10,000	−$10,000	$ 9,000	$11,000	$ 0
Tax rate		25%	25%	25%	25%	25%
Tax benefit		−$ 2,500	−$ 2,500	$ 2,250	$ 2,750	$ 0
Discount factor, $r_{Post\text{-}iCF} = r_{WACC}$		0.874	0.764	0.667	0.583	
Value of post-valuation interest carryforwards	−$ 989	−$ 2,185	−$ 1,909	$ 1,501	$ 1,603	
Value of all carryforwards	$ 13,875					
Value of the firm	$373,234					
Valuation Error						
Correct WACC valuation	$373,068					
Short-cut method	373,234					
Difference	−$ 166	0.0%				

Valuation Key 11.8

The adjusted present value valuation method measures the value of a company with interest and NOL carryforwards as long as the unlevered free cash flows and interest tax shields incorporate the effect of the NOL and interest carryforwards. The weighted average cost of capital valuation method does not correctly measure the value of a company with NOL and interest carryforwards; however, adjustments can be made to the standard implementation of that valuation method to correctly value a company with NOL carryforwards. The shortcut method, often used by practitioners, can, but need not, approximate the correct value.

REVIEW EXERCISE 11.8

Valuing a Company with Interest and NOL Carryforwards—Part 4

Using the information and assumptions in Review Exercise 11.5, use the "short-cut" method to measure the value of the firm by separately valuing the firm without interest and NOL carryforwards and then add to that the value of the pre-valuation and post-valuation interest carryforwards and NOL carryforwards using the weighted average cost of capital as the discount rate. Assume the company's capital structure strategy is to finance 1/3 of the firm with debt and 2/3 with common equity excluding interest and NOL carryforwards. (See Exhibit 11.19.)

Solution on page 550–551.

11.6 OTHER FACTORS THAT AFFECT THE VALUE CREATED FROM DEBT FINANCING

LO5 Adjust the value created by debt financing for potential countervailing forces

The extant research and the valuations of practitioners conclude that financial leverage increases the value of the firm based on the effects embedded in the weighted average cost of capital or by the discounted value of the interest tax shields in the APV valuation method. However, the effects of capital structure decisions on the value of a firm and its costs of capital are complex and far from resolved.[18] These factors include:

- **Personal Income Taxes:** So far, we have assumed that personal income taxes do not affect our calculations. This assumption holds if investors do not pay income taxes on their investment income or if investors are taxed equally on all forms of income (interest, dividends, and capital gains). Since personal income taxes paid on investment income affects investor wealth, personal income taxes are relevant to the returns that investors will demand on different assets if the returns on different assets have different implicit or explicit tax rates. Personal income taxes can also affect the extent that debt in the capital structure increases the value of the firm (the value of interest tax shields). In particular, personal income taxes may reduce the benefits of debt depending on how various forms of investment income are taxed.
- **Financial Distress Costs:** **Financial distress costs** take into account how the cash flows and costs of capital of a company are affected by suppliers, customers, and capital providers. These costs can be substantial for a company with a high probability of experiencing financial distress and can include **bankruptcy costs**. The costs of bankruptcy equal the difference in the value of a company's assets before it goes bankrupt and after it emerges from bankruptcy or liquidates. The costs of bankruptcy include the legal, accounting, consulting, and other fees involved in the bankruptcy process, as well as the indirect costs of bankruptcy from operating inefficiently while in bankruptcy.

[18] See Rajan and Zingales (1995), Miller (1989), and Myers (2001) for reviews of this issue and literature; Rajan, R. G., and L. Zingales, "What Do We Know About Capital Structure? Some Evidence from International Data," *Journal of Finance* 50 (December 1995), pp. 1421–1460; Miller, M. H., "The Modigliani-Miller Propositions After Thirty Years," *Journal of Applied Corporate Finance* vol. 2, no. 1 (Spring 1989), pp. 6–18; and Myers, S. C., "Capital Structure," *Journal of Economic Perspectives* vol. 15, no. 2 (Spring 2001), pp. 81–102.

- **Agency Costs from Debt:** Conflicts of interest between debtholders and owners and managers can create costs from issuing debt, a type of **agency cost**, because those conflicts of interest need to be monitored and mitigated. For example, debtholders might be concerned that the firm will issue debt and use the proceeds from the debt to make a distribution to shareholders instead of investing the proceeds in the company. Or the company could decide to issue additional debt that will make the existing debt less valuable. Debtholders recognize that equityholders can take actions that can reduce the value of their debt claims. Debtholders either require a higher return to compensate them for the expected losses from such actions or the company writes a contract (a debt agreement or bond indenture) that contains certain terms, called **debt covenants**, that limit or preclude it from taking certain actions (such as selling off assets, making distributions to equityholders or issuing additional debt). Such debt covenants reduce the company's yield to maturity and cost of debt. The agency costs associated with issuing debt increase with the amount of leverage, and can reduce the net benefits of debt.[19]
- **Agency Costs from Manager–Owner Conflicts:** In Chapter 5, we discussed the benefits of interest tax shields for a company with one investor/manager. Once we have different owners and managers, conflicts of interest can arise between them, another type of agency cost. Issuing debt is one way to potentially reduce these conflicts. One way for managers to ensure that large free cash flows are paid out to shareholders instead of being invested in unprofitable projects is to issue a large amount of debt and pay a one-time dividend or announce a share repurchase program; this way, the large free cash flows are required to service the debt. A large amount of debt also provides managers with the incentive to make decisions so that the company continues to generate free cash flows and increase firm value.[20]
- **Information (Pecking Order), Product Market, and Industry Influences:**[21] If managers have more information than investors (asymmetric information in favor of managers), investors may interpret the managers' decisions to issue more debt or equity as a signal of the future expected performance of the company; however, the net effect on the value of the firm is unclear. For example, issuing debt can imply that the managers believe the stock is undervalued, and issuing equity can indicate that managers believe that the stock is overvalued. On the other hand, if managers have more information than investors, all securities issued to external markets for additional financing may be undervalued. Because of these issues, to the extent that it is practicable, managers tend to first use internally generated funds before issuing securities externally. Debt is the next source of funds, for the asymmetric information is likely to have a smaller effect on the pricing of debt than on the pricing of equity.

In the remainder of this chapter we discuss some of these factors in more detail. We first discuss the effect of personal income taxes on the tax rate for interest tax shields. We then discuss financial distress costs, which includes a discussion of some types of agency costs.

The Potential Effects of Personal Income Taxes on the Costs of Capital and the Value from Debt Financing

In 1977, Miller extended his previous work with Modigliani by considering the effect of personal income taxes on the Modigliani and Miller framework.[22] In this section, we discuss the implications of Miller's research and subsequent research on the potential effects of personal income taxes on the value of interest tax shields and the levering and unlevering formulas.[23] This issue continues to be largely unresolved, in large part, because the necessary data are not available to test and estimate the potential effects of personal income taxes. However, understanding the theory and its implications provides a framework for thinking about the value of the interest tax shields and provides a cautionary note on valuing them.

---

[19] See Jensen, M. C., and W. H. Meckling, "Theory of the Firm: Managerial Behavior, Agency Costs and Capital Structure," *Journal of Financial Economics* (1976), pp. 305–360.

[20] See Jensen, M. C., "Agency Costs of Free Cash Flow, Corporate Finance and Takeovers," *American Economic Review* 76 (1986), pp. 323–329.

[21] See Myers, S. C., and N. S. Majluf, "Corporate Financing and Investment Decisions When Firms Have Information That Investors Do Not Have," *Journal of Financial Economics* vol. 13, no. 2 (1984), pp. 187–221.

[22] Miller, M. H., Debt and Taxes, *Journal of Finance* 32 (1977), pp. 261–275.

[23] See DeAngelo and Masulis (1980) and Kim (1989) for discussions of this point: DeAngelo, H. and R. W. Masulis, "Optimal Capital Structure Under Corporate and Personal Taxation," *Journal of Financial Economics* 8, (1980), pp. 3–29; Kim, E. H., "Optimal Capital Structure in Miller's Equilibrium," in S. Bhattacharya and G. Constantinides, editors, *Financial Markets and Incomplete Information*, Rowman and Littlefield, (Totowa, NJ, 1989), pp. 36–48.

The Fundamental Issue. Naturally, investors make investment decisions after considering all of the income taxes payable on investment returns, including personal income taxes, yet the valuation of interest tax shields and levering and unlevering formulas we discussed up until this point ignore personal income taxes. Miller assumes that investors will adjust rates of returns on different investments (for example, equity, debt, preferred stock) so that investments with the same risk will have the same expected return after adjusting for all income taxes, including personal income taxes. If two investments have the same risk, but incomes from the investments have different personal income tax rates, then investors will demand a gross-up (or increase) of the expected return on the investment with the higher personal tax rate so that after personal income taxes, the two investments have the same after-tax expected return.

Miller shows that personal income taxes become relevant for assessing the value of interest tax shields when the returns on different types of investments have different personal income tax rates. For example, since interest is tax deductible at the corporate level, companies do not pay taxes on tax deductible interest. The only tax on interest is the personal income tax the investor pays on interest income. For every one dollar of pre-corporate tax cash interest distribution from the borrowing company, the after-tax amount debtholders retain is (1 − personal tax rate on interest income). On the other hand, income to equityholders in the form of dividends is first taxed at the corporate level at the corporate tax rate when the company generates income and is then taxed again at the personal tax rate when the company distributes the income to the equityholders. For a one dollar pre-corporate tax distribution from the company to the equityholders, the after-tax amount equityholders retain is (1 − corporate tax rate) × (1 − personal tax rate on equity returns).

Assume for illustrative purposes that the debt and equity are equally risky (or are both riskless). If the combined corporate and personal tax effect on interest income from debt (1 − personal tax rate on interest income) is equal to the combined corporate and personal tax effect on income from equity, (1 − corporate tax rate) × (1 − personal tax rate on equity returns), then capital structure is irrelevant, for debt has no tax advantage over equity. If, however, the combined corporate and personal tax effect on interest income from debt is less than the combined corporate and personal tax effect on income from equity, then debt is tax advantaged and interest tax shields create value. In this case, for every dollar of pre-corporate tax cash distribution, debtholders retain more than equityholders after corporate and personal taxes. The effective tax rate advantage (disadvantage) of debt is equal to

1 − [(1 − corporate tax rate) × (1 − personal tax rate on equity returns)/(1 − personal tax rate on interest income)]

We ignored personal income taxes previously by assuming the special case that all personal income is taxed at the same rate. In this case, the value of the interest tax shields is equivalent to the value of interest tax shields assuming personal income taxes are zero. Based on this assumption, the result is that the effective tax rate advantage of debt is equal to the corporate tax rate. For example, assume the personal income tax rate on all income is 40% and the corporate tax rate on all income is 21%. The effective tax rate advantage of debt is 21% (0.21 = 1 − [(1 − 0.21) × (1 − 0.4)/(1 − 0.4)]. If, however, personal tax rates on interest income are higher than personal tax rates on equity returns (tax rates for dividends and capital gains), then it is possible that debt could be tax advantaged but by less than the corporate tax rate, or debt could be tax neutral (zero value of interest tax shields, a theory proposed by Miller), or debt could even be tax disadvantaged. Continuing the previous example, assume the corporate tax rate on all income is 21% but the personal tax rates on interest income and equity returns differ from one another—assume the personal tax rate on interest income is 37% and the personal tax rate for dividends and capital gains is 20% (these are approximately the top U.S. 2018 federal income tax rates before the 3.8% additional tax on certain income from long-term capital gains, dividends, and other types of investments). Assuming these tax rates, the effective tax rate advantage of debt decreases to −0.3% (−0.003 = 1 − [(1 − 0.21) × (1 − 0.2)/(1 − 0.37)], which means debt is tax disadvantaged. Essentially, the tax advantage of debt is wiped out.

Because investors do not pay tax on capital gains until the investor realizes the capital gain by selling the investment, equity investors are likely able to defer paying capital gains taxes, potentially indefinitely. For example, if the investor does not sell the investment but it becomes part of the investor's estate, a tax may never be paid on the appreciation of the security. Continuing the previous example, assume the tax rate for dividends and capital gains is 20% but investors defer one-third of the tax on equity indefinitely, reducing the effective personal income tax rate on equity to 13.3% [0.1333 = 0.2 × (1 − 0.333)]. Assuming these tax rates, debt becomes disadvantaged relative to equity as the effective tax rate to debt becomes −8.7% (−0.087 = 1 − [(1 − 0.21) × (1 − 0.1333)/(1 − 0.37)].

However, before concluding that debt has little to no tax advantage, we must think about both the marginal or representative investor who sets security prices and the personal income tax rates of different investors. Not-for-profit organizations, such as university endowments, generally do not pay any income taxes. Income taxes on pension fund earnings are generally paid by the beneficiary only after retiring and withdrawing funds from the pension fund at the personal tax rate on the entire distribution from the pension fund (assuming the individual did not make any after-tax contributions to the pension). Taxes on the pension fund distribution are independent of how the pension fund earned its return (interest or dividends or capital gains). As such, the pension fund faces a zero personal income tax rate because it pays no taxes, and its holders pay tax on the distribution regardless of whether the pension earns dividends, capital gains, or interest income. Again, continuing the previous example, now assume the relevant personal income tax rate for interest is 13.3% rather than 37% and the personal tax rate on equity continues to be 13.3%. Assuming these tax rates, the effective tax rate advantage for debt is back to 21% $(0.21 = 1 - [(1 - 0.21) \times (1 - 0.1333)/(1 - 0.1333)]$. Thus, it is clear, that we need to know the relevant personal tax rates for income on debt and equity for the marginal investors in order to estimate the potential effect of personal income taxes. As we discuss in the next section, we have limited information about these tax rates.

What We Know about the Tax Rates of the Marginal or Representative Investor. Even though we know statutory tax rates and tax rules and laws, this information is insufficient to estimate the potential effect of personal taxes on the value of interest tax shields for two reasons. First, the relevant tax rate is the personal tax rate faced by the marginal or representative investor who is investing in debt or equity and setting the market price, which is not observable. Second, we must understand how different investors expect to postpone the realization of capital gains.

We have relatively little information about the effective personal income tax rates of the marginal investors needed to resolve this issue. Graham analyzed research on the exchange of traditional (dividend paying) preferred stock for monthly income preferred stock.[24,25] Based on the results of this study, Graham estimated a personal income tax rate on interest income of roughly 13%. While this conclusion is far from definitive, it is one estimate of the personal tax rate on interest income. A tax rate of 13% for the marginal investor for debt suggests that the tax advantage of debt is still substantive, even if the personal tax rate on equity is zero, which is unlikely.

Several research studies show that changes in the tax code, which have made debt less tax advantageous (assuming personal taxes matter), have affected the amount of debt that companies use. In particular, both the reduction in the capital gains tax rate and the dividends tax rate to 15%, which reduced the personal tax rate on equity, were associated with a shift from debt financing to equity financing that is consistent with personal taxes affecting the value of the interest tax shields. In addition, researchers who estimate forward looking (implied) equity costs of capital have shown that the same two tax law changes reduced the equity cost of capital, which is again consistent with personal taxes affecting the pricing of securities.[26]

The lack of available data and research about the personal tax rates for these marginal investors leads us to agree with Graham, who summarizes the situation nicely: "The truth is that we know very little about the identity or tax-status of the marginal investor(s) between any two sets of securities, and deducing this information is difficult."[27]

Miller's Capital Structure Irrelevance Theory. To understand Miller's capital structure irrelevance theory, assume, for the ease of illustration, the tax on all equity-related income (dividends and capital gains) is zero, debtholders have personal tax rates between 0% and 40% for debt related income, and the corporate tax rate is 35% on all income for all companies; and that companies are risk-free so that both debt and equity have no risk.

Miller argues that since not-for-profit organizations and pensions do not pay personal income taxes, companies will issue debt to these organizations first because this debt will not be tax disadvantaged relative to equity for these investors. Therefore, debt has a tax advantage for corporations because tax-exempt

---

[24] Graham, J. R., "Taxes and Corporate Finance: A Review," *The Review of Financial Studies* 16, (2003), p. 1096.

[25] See Engel, E. M. Erickson, and E. Maydew, "Debt-Equity Hybrid Securities," *Journal of Accounting Research* 37, (1999), pp. 249-274.

[26] Dhaliwal, D.S., L. Krull and O. Li, "The Effect of 2003 Tax Act on Cost of Equity Capital," *Journal of Accounting & Economics*. (2007) and Dhaliwal, D.S., M. Erickson and L. Krull, "The Effect of Personal Taxes on a Firm's Decision to Issue Debt vs. Equity," *Journal of the American Taxation Association*, (2007).

[27] Graham, J. R., "Taxes and Corporate Finance: A Review," *The Review of Financial Studies* 16, (2003), p. 1086.

investors will not demand a premium above the equity return to hold the debt (remember that the personal tax rate on equity is assumed to be zero and that debt and equity have the same risk). Once the tax exempt investors purchase as much debt as they are willing to purchase (so that they are now fully invested), companies will issue debt to investors with very low tax rates for debt related income. The company must pay these investors a higher rate of return than what it paid to the tax-exempt investors in order to entice them to hold debt instead of equity. However, when companies pay a premium to entice the investors taxed at a low personal tax rate to hold debt, they must pay the same premium to the tax-exempt investors.

Miller argues that in aggregate, companies will continue to entice more individuals to hold debt as long as the corporate tax savings from the interest deduction is greater than the premium the company must pay a taxed investor in order to entice them to hold debt over equity. Once the after (corporate and personal) tax returns on debt and equity are equal, the company is indifferent about enticing this group of investors to hold debt, for the premium it must pay is exactly equal to the interest tax shield it will get. Miller argues that once the economy is in equilibrium, capital structure for the individual company is a matter of irrelevance. Hence, interest tax shields have no value to the equityholders because the before tax interest rate has already been grossed up to compensate individuals for the personal tax they will bear which exactly offsets the benefit of the interest tax shield to the corporation. The issue of whether or not companies issue debt to the point where the next debt investor is taxed at the level of the corporate tax rate is unresolved at this time. If the tax-exempt or low tax bracket investors hold all of the debt and have the ability to invest more, then debt is tax advantaged.

Conclusions about the Potential Effects of Personal Income Taxes on Levering and Unlevering Formulas and the Value Created from Debt Financing. At first, we might think that we only need to substitute an adjusted tax rate for interest tax shields into our levering and unlevering formulas to adjust these formulas for personal income taxes. Unfortunately, such a substitution is incomplete. Taggart shows that in order to adjust the levering and unlevering formulas for the cost of debt, we not only need to make an adjustment for the income tax rate, but we also need to adjust the cost of debt for the difference between personal income tax rates on equity and debt.[28] In other research, Dobbs and Miller discuss the nonlinear nature of the adjustment that has to be made in order to adjust the levering and unlevering formulas for personal income taxes.[29] Cooper and Nyborg develop levering and unlevering formulas for the continuous refinancing and annual refinancing cases with personal taxes and risky debt.[30] In addition, Vandell and Stevens show that even the form of the Capital Asset Pricing Model likely changes with personal taxes.[31]

All of these frameworks, however, require knowledge about the personal tax rates of the marginal investor on the income from debt and from equity investments. Based on the state of the academic literature today, adjusting the levering and unlevering formulas for personal income taxes is not practicable because of the inherent difficulty in measuring the personal income tax rates of the marginal debt and equity investors that is required when unlevering the equity cost of capital to measure the unlevered cost of capital, or relevering the unlevered cost of capital to measure the equity cost of capital. The WACC valuation method requires an estimate of the cost of equity with personal taxes and likely requires unlevering the cost of capital of comparable companies. The APV valuation method requires an estimate of the income tax rate for interest tax shields and also likely requires unlevering the cost of capital of comparable companies. As is clear from the above discussion, we do not have the required information about the personal tax rates for the marginal investors to implement either of these valuation methods.

In conclusion, the effect of personal income taxes on the value of interest tax shields—and consequently, on the value of the firm—is largely unresolved. Until researchers are able to analyze this issue more fully and develop a method to estimate the relevant personal tax rates, estimating the potential effects of personal taxes is not practicable. That said, though a practical implementation is not available at this time, it is helpful to understand that the value of interest tax shields may be reduced by the effect

---

[28] Taggart Jr., R. A., 1991, "Consistent Valuation and Cost of Capital Expressions with Corporate and Personal Taxes," *Financial Management* 20, pp. 8–20.

[29] Dobbs, I. M., and A. D. Miller, 2002, "Capital Budgeting, Valuation and Personal Taxes," *Accounting and Business Research* 32, pp. 227–243.

[30] Cooper, I. and K. Nyborg, "Tax-adjusted Discount Rates with Investor Taxes and Risky Debt," *Financial Management* (Summer 2008), pp. 365–379.

[31] For a review of this issue, see, R. F. Vandell and J. L. Stevens, "Personal Taxes and Equity Security Pricing," *Financial Management*, vol. 11, no. 1 (Spring, 1982), pp. 31–40.

of personal income taxes. Understanding the theory and implications provides a framework for thinking about how to value interest tax shields and provides a cautionary note for valuing interest tax shields.

Valuation Key 11.9

Given a tax code that is similar to that in the United States, the effect of personal taxes potentially mitigates the benefit of the interest tax shields. Our inability to observe or empirically estimate the personal tax rates for the marginal investor on the income from debt and equity investments that is implicit in the pricing of these securities reduces our ability to consider the potential effect of personal taxes on the value of the firm.

The Effects of Financial Distress Costs on the Value Created from Debt Financing

In this section, we provide a more detailed discussion of the effects of financial distress costs on the value created from debt financing: specifically, we discuss both the magnitude of, and likelihood that a firm will experience, financial distress costs from debt financing. We first describe financial distress costs, then discuss the empirical evidence on the magnitude of financial distress costs, and finally discuss its implications for valuation.

The Types of Financial Distress Costs. **Financial distress costs** are the expected value of the costs that arise due to the possibility that a company will be unable to meet its principal and interest payments. Conceptually, we separate **economic distress costs**—that is, the expected costs of a company failing, even if it has no debt—from financial distress costs, but the two are intertwined. Even unlevered firms experience economic distress costs if the company's business model has a high probability of failing, for example by starting to experience losses. Financial distress costs are the costs a levered company incurs in addition to the costs of economic distress experienced by an unlevered firm. Examples of financial distress costs include the following:

- Loss of customers, employees, and suppliers when they become concerned that the firm may go out of business due to the debt in the company's capital structure.
- Being denied access to the capital markets because of the existing debt in the company's capital structure.
- Costs of conflicts of interest between stockholders and debtholders, which increase with financial leverage.
- Indirect costs of bankruptcy (i.e., the costs of inefficient operations while in bankruptcy proceedings).
- Direct costs of bankruptcy (i.e., the legal, accounting, and court costs associated with bankruptcy proceedings to determine how the assets are to be split among the claimants).

Financial distress costs are the additional expected costs from having debt in the capital structure. A levered company that incurs a negative economic shock may find itself renegotiating its lending terms with creditors in an effort to stave off bankruptcy. If these renegotiations fail, the company can be forced to file for bankruptcy. Creditors may decide that they are better off liquidating the firm than allowing the firm to continue as a going concern or the company may decide that it needs protection from creditors' actions that is provided in bankruptcy.

Issuing debt can cause conflicts between debtholders and equityholders because the equityholders can take actions that impose costs on the debtholders. The agency costs associated with issuing debt increase as the amount of financial leverage increases, for the debtholders have more to lose as leverage increases (note that the financial leverage can increase from increasing debt but also from a decline in the value of the equity). As these agency costs increase, debtholders will charge the company a higher cost of debt in an effort to price protect themselves from the actions they expect the company to take that are not in the debtholders' best interests. As a consequence, contracts with debtholders typically restrict the kinds of actions that managers might take to reduce their cost of debt, through the use of **debt covenants**.

For example, a company may enter into a debt contract that restricts the amount of dividends and share repurchases it can make, restricts how much additional debt it can issue, restricts the amount of assets that it can sell, and requires commitments to maintain certain minimum interest coverage ratios, a minimum net worth, or certain maximum leverage ratios. If a company does not meet these restrictions, it is in default on its debt agreements—called a **technical default**. Not meeting these restrictions allows the lenders to renegotiate the terms of the contract and even demand accelerated repayment of the loan. These restrictions can, in turn, impose costs on the company and reduce the value of the firm, for the company may be precluded from taking the appropriate actions to maximize firm value. The company, of course, trades off the cost of these restrictions against the borrowing costs it saves by restricting its actions. In some cases, the company must agree to such restrictions in order to obtain additional financing or renew its current financing.

In bankruptcy, the conflicts between debtholders and equityholders may be large. The debtholders will generally want to preserve capital and recover as much of their capital as possible. The equityholders, realizing that they are likely to get little or nothing, would be more inclined to take a very risky bet (make risky investments) with the company's remaining assets to see if that would yield some return to them—essentially, they have nothing to lose in this situation.

Companies bear two types of bankruptcy costs when undergoing a bankruptcy process—direct bankruptcy costs and indirect bankruptcy costs. Direct bankruptcy costs arise because the bankruptcy process itself is expensive. A company going through bankruptcy incurs the costs of lawyers, accountants, and investment bankers, as well as incurs transactions costs of securing additional financing if needed. Indirect costs of bankruptcy arise because the firm may not operate as efficiently while in bankruptcy. In some bankruptcies, management is replaced, and in others, existing management may have to get court approval to engage in certain types of activities; all of which makes managing the business less efficient. At the very least, the bankruptcy process distracts management's focus. Various research studies examining bankruptcy costs suggest that bankruptcy costs can be up to 5% of the value of the firm.[32]

Bankruptcy costs likely vary by the type of company. An example of a company with low bankruptcy costs is a company with a single investment in real estate with a well-written mortgage contract. Ownership of an investment of this sort can transfer from the pre-bankruptcy owners to the debtholders with relatively low transactions costs. Thus, in this case, the difference between the value of the company's assets immediately before and after the bankruptcy is likely to be relatively small. At the other extreme, a company with mostly intangible assets (a service company or research and development intensive company) may not even survive bankruptcy unless the creditors believe the company's chances for success are substantial and consider it worthwhile to raise additional capital; thus, bankruptcy costs for these firms are relatively high.[33]

Empirical Research on the Magnitude of Value of Financial Distress Costs. Andrade and Kaplan estimated the costs of financial distress for a sample of companies that underwent highly leveraged transactions and subsequently experienced financial distress.[34] Of 136 highly leveraged firms, 39 experienced some type of financial distress. Their estimates of financial distress costs varied depending on the specific tests and subsample examined. Some of the estimates were zero and some ranged between 10% and 20% of total firm value, conditional on the firm experiencing financial distress. They concluded from their analysis that the expected financial distress costs for firms that are healthy and not highly levered are relatively low because the probability of financial distress is quite low for these firms. They also attempted to control for economic distress by examining a subsample of companies that had

---

[32] See, for example, Warner, J., "Bankruptcy, Absolute Priority, and the Pricing of Risky Debt Claims," *Journal of Financial Economics* (May 1977a), pp. 239–276; Warner, J., "Bankruptcy Costs: Some Evidence," *Journal of Financial Economics* (May 1977b), pp. 337–347; White, M. J., "Bankruptcy Costs and the New Bankruptcy Code," *Journal of Finance* (May 1983), pp. 477–488; and Weiss, L., "Bankruptcy Resolution: Direct Costs and Violation of Priority of Claims," *Journal of Financial Economics* vol. 27, no. 2 (1990), pp. 285–314.

[33] For a discussion of the potential effects of salvage value on capital structure decisions, see Scott, J. H. Jr., "A Theory of Optimal Capital Structure," *Bell Journal of Economics* (Spring 1976), pp. 33–54.

[34] Andrade, G., and S. Kaplan, "How Costly Is Financial (Not Economic) Distress? Evidence from Highly Leveraged Transactions that Became Distressed," *The Journal of Finance* vol. 53, no. 5 (October 1998), pp. 1443–1493.

no economic shock to their business—that is, no economic distress. These companies experienced no evidence of significant financial distress costs.

Elkamhi, Ericsson, and Parsons address the effects of economic shocks on financial distress costs in more detail. They show that if estimates of expected financial distress costs are first adjusted for the effects of future economic shocks, they are substantially lower than estimated in previous research. They conclude that expected financial distress costs average less than 1% of current firm value and thus, are generally far too small to offset the expected tax benefits of debt. Finally, they concluded that expected financial distress costs are higher when the risk premium in debt markets is high and when a firm has high systematic risk.[35]

Other researchers analyzed the financial distress issue from another perspective. Instead of estimating the value of the expected financial distress costs, they estimated default costs. The value of financial distress costs is based on expected default costs and the timing and the probability of default. We discuss the last two topics in Chapter 9. Davydenko, Strebulaev, and Zhao examined a large sample of firms with observed prices of debt and equity that defaulted on their debt, and they conclude that the cost of default for an average defaulting firm is 22% of the market value of assets.[36] The costs are substantially higher for investment-grade firms (29%) than for highly levered bond issuers (20%). In another study, Glover concludes that previous research understates the average firm's expected cost of default due to a sample selection bias.[37] Since credit markets price default costs, firms with higher costs of default choose lower amounts of leverage, reducing the probability of default. Glover estimates the expected cost of financial distress and concludes that the average firm expects to lose as much as 45% of firm value in default, but that the sample of firms that actually default experiences default losses of 25% of firm value—firms with lower expected financial distress costs are more likely to take on more leverage and default.

Adjusting Free Cash Flows for Financial Distress. When we discussed the various DCF valuation methods in Chapter 5, we discussed the concept of expected value and how to use this concept to measure expected free cash flows. Recall that expected free cash flows are equal to the sum of the probabilities of the potential outcomes multiplied by their respective free cash flows. Both economic distress and financial distress are possible outcomes, and those scenarios, if they have a non-trivial likelihood of occurring, should naturally be embedded in the expected free cash flows. If a valuation's expected free cash flow forecasts implicitly or explicitly incorporate the possible outcomes of economic distress and financial distress, we effectively will have incorporated financial distress costs into the valuation, assuming we have measured the cost of capital correctly. The financial distress prediction models in Chapter 9 can provide an assessment of the probability of financial distress.

One way to adjust the free cash flows is to create scenarios that consider what will happen to the company if it experiences varying degrees of financial distress. This approach focuses on specific financial distress costs. What will be the loss of customers given the type of business we are valuing? Are we selling a durable good with a need for maintenance and parts, or are we selling a non-durable good with no service component? How will suppliers tighten their credit policies? Will the company lose key employees? What will creditors do if we violate our debt covenants, or worse, miss a payment? If the company files for bankruptcy, what kinds of costs will the company face? Once we develop the cash flows for the financial distress scenarios, as well as the non-financial distress scenarios, we measure expected free cash flows by multiplying the probability of each scenario by its respective expected free cash flows.

An alternative approach for considering financial distress costs is to use an estimate of the costs of financial distress from the empirical work we cited previously based on the type of firm, its current financial situation, and the general economic conditions. The disadvantage of this approach is that it may not fully take into account the likely variation in financial distress costs across firms that we just discussed.

---

[35] Elkamhi, R., J. Ericsson, and C. Parsons, "The Cost and Timing of Financial Distress." *Journal of Financial Economics* 105, no. 1 (July 2012), pp. 62–81.

[36] Davydenko, S. A., I. A. Strebulaev, and X. Zhao, "A Market-Based Study of the Cost of Default," *Review of Financial Studies* vol. 25, issue 10 (2012), pp. 2959–2999.

[37] Glover, B., "The Expected Cost of Default," *Journal of Financial Economics* vol. 119, issue 2 (February 2016), pp. 284–299.

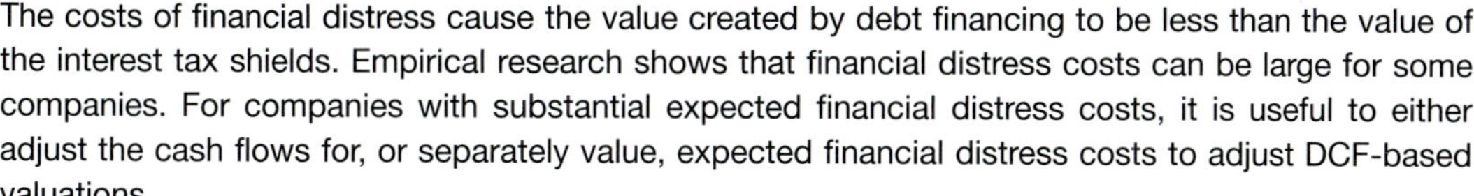

Valuation Key 11.10

The costs of financial distress cause the value created by debt financing to be less than the value of the interest tax shields. Empirical research shows that financial distress costs can be large for some companies. For companies with substantial expected financial distress costs, it is useful to either adjust the cash flows for, or separately value, expected financial distress costs to adjust DCF-based valuations.

SUMMARY AND KEY CONCEPTS

In this chapter, we discussed how to measure the weighted average cost of capital and issues related to specific valuation contexts—the existence of noncontrolling or minority interests, unconsolidated affiliates, and excess assets. We also discussed the effect of the accounting treatment of liabilities classified as debt versus an operating liability using lease accounting as an example. In essence, we learned that it does not matter whether we treat a liability as an operating liability or debt, but what is relevant is using the same assumption for all of the comparable companies and the company we are valuing.

We also discussed certain situations in which the weighted average cost of capital cannot measure the value of the interest tax shields correctly, at least as normally implemented. In most of these situations, the timing of when the interest deduction occurs differs from when the weighted average cost of capital assumes it to occur. The issues discussed include interest carryforwards, net operating losses, capitalized interest, paid-in-kind interest when AHYDO rules apply, and certain cases where the cost of debt has changed since the debt was issued. We also showed how the weighted average cost of capital valuation method can be adjusted to value a firm with interest and net operating loss carryforwards correctly.

We discussed complications associated with calculating the value of the interest tax shields. We learned that the value of the firm is equal to the value of the unlevered firm plus the value of the interest tax shields adjusted for any impact from personal income taxes minus the present value of the expected costs of financial distress and agency costs. Ignoring the effect of personal income taxes on interest tax shields and the countervailing forces of financial distress costs and agency costs can lead to upward-biased estimates of the value of debt financing and the value of the firm.

ADDITIONAL READING AND REFERENCES

Miller, M. H., "Debt and Taxes," *Journal of Finance* 32 (1977), pp. 261–275.

Myers, S. C., and N. S. Majluf, "Corporate Financing and Investment Decisions When Firms Have Information That Investors Do Not Have," *Journal of Financial Economics* vol. 13, no. 2 (1984), pp. 187–221.

Taggart Jr., R. A., "Consistent Valuation and Cost of Capital Expressions with Corporate and Personal Taxes," *Financial Management* 20 (1991), pp. 8–20.

APPENDIX: Financial Statement and Free Cash Flow Effects of Leases

In this appendix, we summarize the U.S. lease accounting rules. The Financial Accounting Standards Board changed the accounting rules for lease accounting in 2016, which is effective for fiscal years beginning on or after December 15, 2018 (companies can voluntarily adopt the standard before that date).[38] The International Accounting Standards Board also changed its lease accounting rules,[39] which we discuss at the end of this section. In the U.S., the primary change in the accounting rule pertains to operating leases, which are not currently capitalized on the balance sheet. We discuss the new U.S. accounting rules in the remainder of this appendix and identify the primary difference between those accounting rules and the current accounting rules.[40] We also illustrate how the treatment of leases impacts the financial statements and free cash flows as a function of whether we treat the leases as finance leases or operating leases.

[38] Financial Accounting Standards Board, (FASB) Accounting Standards Update No. 2016-02, *Leases*, which supersedes FASB Accounting Standards Codification (ASC) Topic 840, *Leases*, and creates ASC 842, *Leases*.

[39] International Accounting Standards Board (IASB), International Financial Reporting Standard (IFRS) No. 16, which becomes effective for fiscal years beginning on or after January 1, 2019—companies can voluntarily adopt the standard before that date.

[40] We do not discuss various adjustments to the leases for impairment, lease modifications, and other issues that do not generally arise in a valuation.

Lease Accounting. A lease is a contract that grants the right to control the use of certain property, plant, and equipment for a specified period of time for certain consideration. The lease contract has two parties—the **lessee** and the **lessor**. The lessee leases the property from the lessor. The accounting rules we discuss in this section pertain to the lessee because that is the most common issue that arises when valuing a company. A lease with a term of no more than twelve months is considered a short-term lease. The accounting for short-term leases is straightforward. The company recognizes rent or lease expense as the company uses the property. All other leases are capitalized on the balance sheet as of the effective date of the lease, but not all leases that are capitalized on the balance sheet are treated in the same way.

Capitalizing a lease on a balance sheet records two components—an asset, called a **right-of-use asset**, and a liability, called a **lease liability**. Companies must classify each lease as either an **operating lease** or a **finance lease**. A finance lease is a lease that meets certain criteria that essentially transfers the risks and rewards of ownership of the property to the lessee. They include criteria related to the degree to which the term of the lease is equal to the property's economic useful life, certain types of purchase options, the degree to which the present value of the lease payments (including any residual value guarantee) is equal to the property's fair value, or the lessee-specific specialized nature of the property. If the lease does not meet the criteria for a finance lease, then it is an operating lease.

Whether a lease is classified as an operating lease or a finance lease, on the effective date of the lease, the company records a lease liability equal to the present value of the lease payments. The discount rate is equal to the implicit rate charged by the lessor or if not knowable, the company's incremental cost of capital for similar secured debt. The company also records a right-of-use asset equal to the present value of the lease payments, plus any initial payments made to the lessor, minus any incentives or value received from the lessor, plus any initial direct costs incurred by the company related to executing the lease. Under these rules, as of the effective date of the lease, the value of the lease asset is always greater than or equal to the value of the liability. Companies record the same initial value of the lease asset and lease liability independent of its classification (operating versus finance lease). The company's cash flow statement treats recording the initial asset and liability values of the lease as a non-cash transaction because no cash changes hands, except for any initial costs incurred or direct costs paid to execute the lease. While the accounting rules at the inception of a lease are essentially the same regardless of the lease's classification, with leases treated as a finance lease, to calculate the free cash flows, we treat the recording of the initial asset and liability values as a dual transaction—the purchase of an asset reducing unlevered free cash flows (CAPEX) and an increase in liabilities (debt) increasing equity free cash flows. That is not how we treat operating leases in the calculation of free cash flows, which we describe next.

After the effective date, the accounting rules for operating and finance leases differ. For an operating lease, the company records an operating expense, called lease expense, equal to the sum (not the present value) of the lease payments plus or minus any other adjustments used in the initial valuation of the lease asset divided by the term of the lease. If there are no adjustments and the lease payment is the same every period, the lease expense is just the periodic lease payment. This is the only expense recognized for the lease, which is classified as an operating expense (it does not have an interest component). The value of the lease asset on the balance sheet decreases by the lease expense minus the implicit interest on the lease for that period (lease discount rate × beginning balance of the lease liability) and any amortization of initial payments or direct costs incurred at inception.[41] The value of the lease liability decreases by the lease payment in that period minus the implicit interest on the lease for that period (effective interest rate method). The lease payment reduces net income and consequently reduces cash flows from operations since cash flows from operations are measured beginning with net income. If we are treating the lease as an operating lease, we use the same treatment in the free cash flow schedule as the cash flow statement (see Section 11.4). In other words, it is just treated as an operating expense which reduces the free cash flows.

The accounting for finance leases is mostly unchanged. The company records an operating expense for the straight-line amortization of the lease asset and interest expense for the implicit interest on the lease. The value of the lease asset decreases by the amount amortized and the value of the lease liability decreases by the lease payment in that period minus the implicit interest on the lease for that period (effective interest rate method). On the cash flow statement, the company adds back the amortization of the lease asset to net income in order to measure cash flow from operations and reports the decrease in the lease liability in the financing section to measure cash flow from financing. The interest expense is included with all of the other interest expense of the company which reduces net income and hence operating cash flows. The treatment in the free cash flow statement mirrors any other treatment of cash interest paid, a change in debt and depreciation on an asset.

The difference in the lease accounting (current and new) rules and lease related income tax regulations results in the recognition of deferred income taxes from the difference in the value of the lease assets and liabilities. Recall from Chapter 3 that a deferred income tax asset results whenever the book value of a liability for financial reporting purposes exceeds the value of that liability on the tax records (tax basis); and that a deferred tax liability results whenever the book value of an asset for financial reporting purposes exceeds the tax basis of that asset. The amount of the deferred tax asset or liability is equal to the difference in the book and tax basis of the asset or liability multiplied by the income tax rate.

---

[41] Generally, a difference between the lease expense and the lease payment (or from the change in the lease asset and lease liability) results from the amortization of any initial payments made to the lessor or any initial direct costs incurred by the company related to executing the lease or if the lease payments change over time. Otherwise, the lease expense and the lease payment and the change in the lease asset and the change in the lease liability are equal. Any amortization of initial payments and direct costs would appear as an addback in the operating section of the cash flows statement.

The U.S. tax regulations generally allow a deduction for leases when a payment is made and do not recognize the capitalization of lease payments as an asset or liability (tax basis equal to zero). Since the value of the lease asset and lease liability on the income tax records is zero, the value of the corresponding deferred income tax asset and deferred income tax liability is equal to the value of the lease asset or liability multiplied by the income tax rate, and the net deferred income tax asset or liability is equal to the difference in the book values of the lease asset and lease liability multiplied by the income tax rate. From the above discussion, we know this difference is zero or small for operating leases and somewhat larger for finance leases.

Lastly, the new U.S. lease accounting rules differ from the new international accounting rules in various ways, though they are generally similar with one important exception. The new international accounting rules essentially treat all leases as if they are finance leases, in other words, as if the lease liability is the equivalent of debt.

The Mark Hoplamazian Company. The Mark Hoplamazian Company is a start-up company that operates a chain of hotels. The company's focus is operating hotels, not investing in the real estate and thus, the company plans to lease all of its hotels. The CEO and Chairman of the company, Mark Hoplamazian, is considering leasing a large chain of hotels beginning in 2018. Assume the lease contracts could be written so that the lease terms meet the criteria for either operating lease accounting or finance lease accounting. Mark would like to know how the different accounting rules affect the company's income statements, balance sheets, and free cash flows. To illustrate the financial statement and free cash flow effects resulting from the differences in the accounting rules for operating leases versus financing leases, we use a shortened, three-year term, of the proposed lease.

The lease contract begins on the last day of Year 0 and ends on the last day of Year 3. The lease has three annual payments equal to $4,000, and it has a 10% implicit interest rate. We assume the company incurred no other costs in executing the lease. The present value of the three lease payments is $9,947.4, which is capitalized as the lease asset, called a **right-of-use asset**, and lease liability as can be seen in Exhibit A11.1.[42] We present the liability amortization table in Exhibit A11.1. The exhibit presents the annual interest and reduction in the liability over its three-year term. For each period, interest expense is equal to the beginning balance of the lease obligation multiplied by the implicit interest rate. The difference between the lease payment and interest is equal to the reduction in the lease obligation. For example, in Year 1, interest is equal to $994.7 ($994.7 = $9,947.4 × 0.1) and the reduction in the lease obligation is $3,005.3 ($3,005.3 = $4,000.0 − $994.7).

EXHIBIT A11.1 Hoplamazian Company—Three-Year Operating versus Finance Lease Example

$ in thousands	Beginning Lease Obligation	Implicit Interest	Lease Payment	Ending Lease Obligation	Change in Liability
Year 1	$9,947.4	$ 994.7	$ 4,000.0	$6,942.1	$3,005.3
Year 2	6,942.1	694.2	4,000.0	3,636.4	3,305.7
Year 3	$3,636.4	363.6	4,000.0	0.0	3,636.4
Total		$2,052.6	$12,000.0		$9,947.4

Exhibit may contain small rounding errors

In Exhibit A11.2, we present Hoplamazian's income statements and balance sheets for both the operating lease and finance lease treatments of the three-year life of the lease. At the end of Year 0, the company has assets equal to $1,000 in required cash, which remains constant over time, and the present value of the lease payments, called a **right-of-use asset**, of $9,947.4. At the end of Year 0 the company also has a lease liability equal to the value of the right-of-use asset value and equity of $1,000. This is true regardless of whether the lease is treated as an operating lease or a finance lease. Assume the company has a policy of distributing all equity free cash flows to its equityholders, and its income tax rate is 40% on all income. We present the operating lease treatment in the first set of columns in the exhibit. The company has revenues of $10,000.0 in each year and has no expenses other than the lease expense. Thus, each year, its pre-tax income is equal to $6,000.0, its income tax is equal to $2,400.0, and its net income is equal to $3,600.0. The company writes down the carrying value of the right-of-use asset based on the effective interest method, which tracks the decrease in the lease liability in each year. Since, in this example, the book value of the right-of-use asset is equal to the book value of the lease liability, the operating lease treatment does not result in any net deferred income taxes (the deferred tax assets and liabilities are the same in each year) as can be seen in Exhibit A11.3. Recall from the discussion of the accounting rules, however, if the lease had unequal lease payments, the lease expense is equal to the average lease payment (straight-line amortization of the sum of the lease payments over the life of the term of the lease).

[42] The value of the lease payments is equal to the present value of a three-period annuity discounted at 10%.

$$\$9{,}947.4 = \$4{,}000 \times \left(\frac{1}{0.1} - \frac{1}{0.1} \times 1.1^{-3}\right)$$

EXHIBIT A11.2 Hoplamazian Company—Operating versus Finance Lease Income Statements and Balance Sheets

	Operating Lease				Finance Lease					
($ in thousands)	Actual Year 0	Forecast Year 1	Forecast Year 2	Forecast Year 3	Actual Year 0	Forecast Year 1	Forecast Year 2	Forecast Year 3	Total Operating Lease	Total Finance Lease
Income Statement										
Revenue		$10,000.0	$10,000.0	$10,000.0		$10,000.0	$10,000.0	$10,000.0	$30,000.0	$30,000.0
Lease expense		–4,000.0	–4,000.0	–4,000.0					–12,000.0	0.0
Finance lease asset amortization						–3,315.8	–3,315.8	–3,315.8	0.0	–9,947.4
Earnings before interest and taxes		$ 6,000.0	$ 6,000.0	$ 6,000.0		$ 6,684.2	$ 6,684.2	$ 6,684.2	$18,000.0	$20,052.6
Interest expense						–994.7	–694.2	–363.6	0.0	–2,052.6
Income before taxes		$ 6,000.0	$ 6,000.0	$ 6,000.0		$ 5,689.5	$ 5,990.0	$ 6,320.6	$18,000.0	$18,000.0
Income tax expense		–2,400.0	–2,400.0	–2,400.0		–2,275.8	–2,396.0	–2,528.2	–7,200.0	–7,200.0
Net income		$ 3,600.0	$ 3,600.0	$ 3,600.0		$ 3,413.7	$ 3,594.0	$ 3,792.3	$10,800.0	$10,800.0
Cash	$ 1,000.0	$ 1,000.0	$ 1,000.0	$ 1,000.0	$ 1,000.0	$ 1,000.0	$ 1,000.0	$ 1,000.0		
Right-of-use asset	9,947.4	6,942.1	3,636.4	0.0	9,947.4	6,631.6	3,315.8	0.0		
Deferred tax asset						124.2	128.2	0.0		
Total assets	$10,947.4	$ 7,942.1	$ 4,636.4	$ 1,000.0	$10,947.4	$ 7,755.8	$ 4,444.0	$ 1,000.0		
Deferred tax liability						$ 0.0	$ 0.0	$ 0.0		
Lease liability	$ 9,947.4	$ 6,942.1	$ 3,636.4	$ 0.0	$ 9,947.4	6,942.1	3,636.4	0.0		
Equity	1,000.0	1,000.0	1,000.0	1,000.0	1,000.0	813.7	807.7	1,000.0		
Total liabilities and equities	$10,947.4	$ 7,942.1	$ 4,636.4	$ 1,000.0	$10,947.4	$ 7,755.8	$ 4,444.0	$ 1,000.0		
Sum of lease amortization and interest expense						$ 4,310.5	$ 4,010.0	$ 3,679.4		$12,000.0

The finance lease treatment is more complex than the operating lease treatment. First, over the life of the lease, the lease payments of $12,000.0 are expensed by amortizing the right-of-use asset of $9,947.4 plus expensing interest on the outstanding lease obligation, equal to $2,052.6 over the life of the lease (see Exhibit A11.2). Because finance lease accounting amortizes the right-of-use asset generally using the straight line method and recognizes interest using the effective interest method, the sum of the lease amortization and interest expense is never equal to $4,000 in any year. As shown in Exhibit A11.2, the sum of the lease amortization and interest expense is greater than the lease payment in the early years of the lease and less than the lease payment in the later years of the lease.

Second, because the decrease in the right-of-use asset and decrease in the lease liability do not track each other as they do for the operating lease, the company generally records a net deferred tax asset for the lease, which eventually decreases to zero over the term of the lease. Since the value of the lease obligation on the income tax records is zero, the value of the deferred income tax asset is equal to the value of the finance lease obligation multiplied by the income tax rate; for example, at the end of Year 2, the deferred tax asset is equal to $1,454.5 ($1,454.5 = 0.40 × $3,636.4; see Exhibit A11.3). Also since the value of the lease asset on the income tax records is zero, the value of the deferred income tax liability is equal to the value of the lease asset multiplied by the income tax rate; for example, the end of Year 2 deferred tax liability is equal to $1,326.3 ($1,326.3 = 0.40 × $3,315.8; see Exhibit A11.3). Income tax expense for financial reporting purposes is equal to income taxes payable, $2,400.0 each year, minus the change in the deferred tax asset plus the change in the deferred tax liability; for example, the Year 2 income tax expense is equal to $2,396.0 [$2,396.0 = $2,400 – ($1,454.5 – $2,776.9) + ($1,326.3 – $2,652.6)]. For financial reporting purposes, in Year 1 the deferred tax asset of $2,776.9 ($1,454.5 in Year 2) and the deferred tax liability of $2,652.6 ($1,326.3 in Year 2) are offset and reported as a net deferred tax asset of $124.2 ($128.2 in Year 2).

EXHIBIT A11.3 Hoplamazian Company—Operating versus Finance Lease Deferred Income Taxes

	Operating Lease				Finance Lease			
$ in thousands	Actual Year 0	Forecast Year 1	Forecast Year 2	Forecast Year 3	Actual Year 0	Forecast Year 1	Forecast Year 2	Forecast Year 3
Deferred tax asset (DTA)	$3,979.0	$2,776.9	$1,454.5	$0.0	$3,979.0	$2,776.9	$1,454.5	$0.0
Deferred tax liability (DTL)	3,979.0	2,776.9	1,454.5	0.0	3,979.0	2,652.6	1,326.3	0.0
Net deferred tax asset (liability)	$ 0.0	$ 0.0	$ 0.0	$0.0	$ 0.0	$ 124.2	$ 128.2	$0.0

Since our focus is on valuation, a key issue to consider is how the different classification of expenses for operating versus finance leases affects a company's free cash flows. We know that the accounting method does not affect the company's lease payments or its income tax payments, and thus, does not affect its equity free cash flows. However, the unlevered free cash flows are not equal for the two methods. The finance lease method assumes the company essentially purchased the right-of-use asset and financed that purchase with debt. Thus, both the magnitude and timing of the unlevered free cash flows change. We show this effect in Exhibit A11.4.

From this exhibit, we observe the following. First, treating a lease as either an operating lease or finance lease, does not affect the equity free cash flows. Second, if we use the finance lease treatment, the unlevered free cash flows over the life of the lease will be higher than the unlevered free cash flows based on the operating lease treatment. The lease payments ($12,000) are all treated as operating expenses in the operating lease method, and they reduce unlevered free cash flows; however, the finance lease method treats the implicit interest embedded in the lease payments as a cost of financing and not a reduction in the unlevered free cash flows. Thus, over the life of the lease the sum of the unlevered free cash flows from the finance lease method is larger than the unlevered free cash flows from the operating lease method by the amount of the after-tax implicit interest embedded in the lease payments. Over the life of Hoplamazian's lease, the sum of the unlevered free cash flows under the finance lease method includes deductions equal to the present value of the lease payments, $9,947.4 for the amortization of the lease asset. The $2,052.6 of implicit interest expense, however, does not impact the unlevered free cash flows. The after-tax effect of this difference on the unlevered free cash flows is $1,231.6 [$1,231.6 = $12,031.6 − $10,800 = (1 − 0.4) × $2,052.6]. Note that total tax payments under the finance lease equal $7,200 ($7,200 = $8,021 − $821) which is the same as under the operating lease although the affect on unlevered free cash flows differs across the two types of leases. As we explain in Section 11.4, as a result of the larger free cash flows (and lower cost of capital), treating a liability as debt versus an operating liability has the effect of increasing the value of the firm by the amount of the debt.

EXHIBIT A11.4 Hoplamazian Company—Operating versus Finance Lease Free Cash Flow Schedule

	Operating Lease				Finance Lease					
($ in thousands)	**Actual Year 0**	**Forecast Year 1**	**Forecast Year 2**	**Forecast Year 3**	**Actual Year 0**	**Forecast Year 1**	**Forecast Year 2**	**Forecast Year 3**	**Total Operating Lease**	**Total Finance Lease**
Earnings before interest and taxes	$0.0	$6,000.0	$6,000.0	$6,000.0	$ 0.0	$6,684.2	$6,684.2	$6,684.2	$18,000.0	$20,052.6
− Income taxes on EBIT	0	−2,400.0	−2,400.0	−2,400.0	0	−2,673.7	−2,673.7	−2,673.7	−7,200.0	−8,021.0
Earnings before interest and after taxes	$0.0	$3,600.0	$3,600.0	$3,600.0	$ 0.0	$4,010.5	$4,010.5	$4,010.5	$10,800.0	$12,031.6
− Change in required cash		0.0	0.0	0.0		0.0	0.0	0.0	0.0	0.0
+ Right-of-use lease asset amortization						3,315.8	3,315.8	3,315.8	0.0	9,947.4
+ Deferred tax adjustment						−124.2	−4.0	128.2	0.0	−0.0
Unlevered cash flow from operations	$0.0	$3,600.0	$3,600.0	$3,600.0	$ 0.0	$7,202.1	$7,322.3	$7,454.5	$10,800.0	$21,979.0
− Capital lease increases (CAPEX)					−9,947.4					−9,947.4
Unlevered free cash flow	$0.0	$3,600.0	$3,600.0	$3,600.0	−$9,947.4	$7,202.1	$7,322.3	$7,454.5	$10,800.0	$12,031.6
Implicit interest on finance leases					0	−994.7	−694.2	−363.6	0.0	−2,052.6
Interest tax shield					0	397.9	277.7	145.5	0.0	821.0
Free cash flow minus after-tax interest	$0.0	$3,600.0	$3,600.0	$3,600.0	−$9,947.4	$6,605.3	$6,905.8	$7,236.4	$10,800.0	$10,800.0
Change in finance lease liability					9,947.4	−3,005.3	−3,305.8	−3,636.4	0.0	0.0
Equity free cash flow	$0.0	$3,600.0	$3,600.0	$3,600.0	$ 0.0	$3,600.0	$3,600.0	$3,600.0	$10,800.0	$10,800.0

REVIEW EXERCISE A11.1

A Simple Lease Example

A lease contract begins on the last day of Year 0 and ends on the last day of Year 3. The lease has three annual payments equal to $5,000. The appropriate discount rate for the lease is 8%. Prepare a lease amortization table, an income statement, balance sheet, and free cash flow schedule for the term of the lease, using both the operating and finance lease acccounting methods. Assume the company has $8,000 in revenue each year and that the income tax rate is 30% on all income. The company has a policy of distributing all equity free cash flows to its equityholders each period. The company has no assets other than $400 in required cash that remains constant over time.

Solution on pages 551–553.

EXERCISES AND PROBLEMS

P11.1 **Measuring the Weighted Average Cost of Capital:** Calculate the weighted average cost of capital using both Equations 11.1 and 11.2. Assume the company's securities are publicly traded, that its debt is currently trading at 100% of par value, and that its preferred stock is currently trading at 110% of its par value. The company's stock price is currently $8 per share, and the company has 5,000 shares of stock outstanding, which is net of 1,000 treasury shares. The risk-free rate is 4%, and the market risk premium is 6%. The company issued the debt and preferred stock at par value. The company has an equity beta equal to 1.5. The company has an effective interest rate equal to 7.5%, which includes an 0.5% default premium, and the cost of capital for the preferred stock is equal to 7.5%. The income tax rate on all income is 40%. The company plans to have a constant capital structure strategy based on its current capital structure ratios. The company's income statement and balance sheets are given below.

	Year 1	Year 2
Income Statement		
Revenue		$12,000
Operating expenses		−6,000
Depreciation expense		−5,200
Earnings before interest and taxes		$ 800
Interest expense		−450
Income before taxes		$ 350
Income tax expense		−105
Net income		$ 245
Balance Sheet		
Total current assets	$ 2,000	$ 3,000
Property, plant, and equipment (net)	12,000	12,000
Total assets	$14,000	$15,000
Accounts payable	$ 1,000	$ 1,000
Debt	6,000	6,000
Total liabilities	$ 7,000	$ 7,000
Preferred stock	$ 4,400	$ 4,600
Capital stock	5,000	5,000
Retained earnings	−2,400	−1,600
Shareholders' equity	$ 7,000	$ 8,000
Liabilities and shareholders' equity	$14,000	$15,000

P11.2 **Operating Versus Finance Leases and Valuation:** In Year 0, a company entered into a perpetual lease on certain property. The property has a value of $25,000, the cost of debt is 12%, and its annual lease payment is $3,000. The company expects all of the cash flows to grow at 3% in perpetuity and it expects to increase the amount of leased property at the same rate beginning at the end of Year 1 (all new leases are perpetual leases). The company has revenues of $5,000 in Year 1 and has no other expenses other than those related to the lease. The company's tax rate on all income is 45%. All revenues and expenses are paid in cash. The company has no assets or liabilities other than those related to the lease. Assume today is the end of Year 0. The company has a 22% equity cost of capital, and the discount rate for interest tax shields is equal to the unlevered cost of capital. Value the company as of the end of Year 0 assuming the company treats the lease as an operating lease, and value the company again assuming the company treats the lease as a capital or finance lease, treating the present value of the lease payments as debt. As part of the valuation, prepare the company's income statement and free cash flow schedule for Year 1 under each lease treatment. Use the weighted average cost of capital, equity DCF, and APV valuation methods to value the company.

P11.3 **Capitalizing Operating Leases—Part 1:** Use the information presented in the following financial disclosures to measure the present value of the outstanding operating lease obligations as of the end of Years 0 and 1, assuming annual payments and a 7% discount rate. Also measure the present value of the additions to the lease obligations (new leases), the implicit interest on the capitalized lease obligations, and the lease asset amortization (assuming a 10-year life) for Year 1.

Year 0 Financial Disclosure		
Year	**Finance Leases**	**Operating Leases**
Year 1	$ 1,200	$ 3,600
Year 2	1,160	3,480
Year 3	1,110	3,330
Year 4	1,030	3,090
Year 5	1,000	3,000
After Year 5	8,000	27,000
Total	$13,500	$43,500
Total interest	5,979	
Present value	$ 7,521	

Year 1 Financial Disclosure		
Year	**Finance Leases**	**Operating Leases**
Year 2	$ 1,400	$ 4,000
Year 3	1,400	3,900
Year 4	1,300	3,700
Year 5	1,200	3,400
Year 6	1,200	3,300
After Year 6	9,600	29,700
Total	$16,100	$48,000
Total interest	7,154	
Present value	$ 8,946	

P11.4 **Capitalizing Operating Leases—Part 2:** Use the information presented in Problem 11.3 and the following financial information to restate the company's Year 1 income statement, balance sheet, and free cash flow schedule so that all operating leases are capitalized as of the end of Year 0 onward. The company's income tax rate is 35% on all income. The Year 1 operating lease payment of $3,600 reported in the footnote is included in the total rent expense reported of $10,000.

Summarized Financial Statements	Year 1 Reported
Income Statement	
Revenues	$40,000.0
Rent expense	−10,000.0
Depreciation and amortization	−6,000.0
Amortization of operating leases	0.0
All other operating expenses	−5,000.0
Operating income	$19,000.0
Interest expense, net	−2,000.0
Lease interest	0.0
Income before taxes	$17,000.0
Income taxes	−5,950.0
Net income	$11,050.0
Balance Sheet	
Current assets	$20,000.0
Net property, plant, and equipment	60,000.0
Other assets	10,000.0
Deferred tax asset	0.0
Capitalized operating leases	0.0
Total assets	$90,000.0
Current operating liabilities	$10,000.0
Other liabilities	20,000.0
Deferred tax liability	0.0
Debt	20,000.0
Capitalized operating leases	0.0
Total liabilities	$50,000.0
Shareholders' equity	40,000.0
Total liabilities and shareholders' equity	$90,000.0

Summarized Free Cash Flow Schedule	Year 1 Reported
Earnings before interest and taxes (EBIT)	$19,000.0
− Income taxes paid on EBIT	−6,650.0
Earnings before interest and after taxes	$12,350.0
+ Depreciation and amortization	6,000.0
+ Amortization of operating leases	0.0
− Change in net working capital	4,000.0
+ Change in non-current liabilities and other	1,000.0
− Change in required cash balance	−400.0
Unlevered cash flow from operations	$22,950.0
− Capital expenditures (net)	−10,000.0
− Increase in capital lease assets	0.0
Unlevered free cash flow	$12,950.0
− Interest paid	−2,000.0
+ Interest tax shield	700.0
+ Change in non-common equity	0.0
+ Change in capital lease obligations	0.0
Free cash flow to common equity	$11,650.0

P11.5 **Capitalizing Operating Leases Again—Part 1:** Use the information presented in the following financial disclosures to measure the present value of the outstanding operating lease obligations as of the end of Years 0 and 1, assuming annual payments and a 6% discount rate. Also measure the present value of the additions to the lease obligations (new leases), the implicit interest on the capitalized lease obligations, and the lease asset amortization (assuming a 10-year life) for Year 1.

Year 0 Financial Disclosure		
Year	**Finance Leases**	**Operating Leases**
Year 1	$ 400	$ 1,200
Year 2	380	1,140
Year 3	360	1,080
Year 4	300	900
Year 5	250	750
After Year 5	2,000	6,750
Total	$3,690	$11,820
Total interest	1,088	
Present value	$2,602	

Year 1 Financial Disclosure		
Year	**Finance Leases**	**Operating Leases**
Year 2	$ 450	$ 1,400
Year 3	400	1,300
Year 4	400	1,200
Year 5	300	1,000
Year 6	300	800
After Year 6	2,400	7,200
Total	$4,250	$12,900
Total interest	1,280	
Present value	$2,970	

P11.6 **Capitalizing Operating Leases Again—Part 2:** Use the information presented in Problem 11.5 and the following financial information to restate the company's Year 1 income statement, balance sheet, and free cash flow schedule so that all operating leases are capitalized as of the end of Year 0 onward. The company's income tax rate is 45% on all income. The Year 1 operating lease payment of $1,200 from the footnote is included in the total rent expense reported of $5,000.

Summarized Financial Statements	Year 1 Reported
Income Statement	
Revenues	$10,000.0
Rent expense	−5,000.0
Depreciation and amortization	−2,000.0
Amortization of operating leases	0.0
All other operating expenses	−1,000.0
Operating income	$ 2,000.0
Interest expense, net	−500.0
Lease interest	0.0
Income before taxes	$ 1,500.0
Income taxes	−675.0
Net income	$ 825.0
Balance Sheet	
Current assets	$ 8,000.0
Net property, plant, and equipment	12,000.0
Other assets	2,000.0
Deferred tax asset	0.0
Capitalized operating leases	0.0
Total assets	$22,000.0
Current operating liabilities	$ 6,000.0
Other liabilities	2,000.0
Deferred tax liability	0.0
Debt	10,000.0
Capitalized operating leases	0.0
Total liabilities	$18,000.0
Shareholders' equity	4,000.0
Total liabilities and shareholders' equity	$22,000.0

Summarized Free Cash Flow Schedule	Year 1 Reported
Earnings before interest and taxes (EBIT)	$ 2,000.0
− Income taxes paid on EBIT	−900.0
Earnings before interest and after taxes	$ 1,100.0
+ Depreciation and amortization	2,000.0
+ Amortization of operating leases	0.0
− Change in net working capital	4,000.0
+ Change in non-current liabilities and other	1,000.0
− Change in required cash balance	−400.0
Unlevered cash flow from operations	$ 7,700.0
− Capital expenditures (net)	−10,000.0
− Increase in capital lease assets	0.0
Unlevered free cash flow	−$ 2,300.0
− Interest paid	−500.0
+ Interest tax shield	225.0
+ Change in non-common equity	0.0
+ Change in capital lease obligations	0.0
Free cash flow to common equity	−$ 2,575.0

P11.7 **Valuing a Company with Interest and Net Operating Loss Carryforwards:** Use the information in the following schedule, which contains two years of historical performance and five years of forecasts, to value the firm as of the end of Year 0 using the following assumptions. Assume the company's income tax rate on all income is 40%, the tax deduction for interest in any year is limited to 55% of EBIT in that year, any interest payment above the interest deduction cap in a year can be carried forward indefinitely, the company can only use its NOL carryforwards to offset a maximum of 80% of its taxable income before NOL offsets, and the company's EBIT based on its financial statements is equal to its EBIT for income taxes. Also assume the company's unlevered cost of capital is 10%, its interest rate (and debt cost of capital) is 8%, its discount rate for its interest tax shields is equal to its unlevered cost of capital, and its long-term growth rate (Year 6 onward) is 2.5%. Also assume that the company makes no investments in working capital and that CAPEX is equal to depreciation.

a. Calculate the company's income taxes and interest and NOL carryforwards for the levered company (including interest in the forecasts). (Similar to Exhibit 11.9.)

b. Calculate the company's income taxes and interest and NOL carryforwards for the unlevered company (excluding interest in the forecasts but including interest in Years 1 and 0). (Similar to Exhibit 11.10.)

c. Calculate the company's income taxes and interest tax shields assuming the company can deduct all of its interest for income taxes and the company receives a tax refund if its EBIT is negative. (Similar to Exhibit 11.11.)

d. Calculate the effect of the company's interest and NOL carryforwards on the company's cash flows (unlevered free cash flows and interest tax shields) by subtracting the unlevered free cash flows and interest tax shields including the effects of interest and NOL carryforwards from the unlevered free cash flows and interest tax shields excluding the effects of interest and NOL carryforwards. Compare these differences to the sum of the interest and NOL carryforwards. (Similar to Exhibit 11.12.)

e. Measure the value of the firm by separately valuing the firm without interest and NOL carryforwards and then adding the value of the pre-valuation and post-valuation interest carryforwards and NOL carryforwards and assuming the company's capital structure strategy is based on the forecasts and the long-term growth rate. (Use the APV valuation method, similar to Exhibit 11.14.)

f. Measure the value of the firm including and excluding interest and NOL carryforwards and assuming the company's capital structure strategy is to finance 45% of the firm with debt and 55% with common equity excluding interest and NOL carryforwards. (Similar to Exhibits 11.15 through 11.18.)

g. Use the "short-cut" method to measure the value of the firm by separately valuing the firm without interest and NOL carryforwards and then adding the value of the pre-valuation and post-valuation interest carryforwards and NOL carryforwards using the weighted average cost of capital as the discount rate. Assume the company's capital structure strategy is to finance 45% of the firm with debt and 55% with common equity excluding interest and NOL carryforwards. (Similar to Exhibit 11.19.)

Financial Accounting (Income Statement Excerpt)	Actual Year −1	Actual Year 0	Forecast Year 1	Forecast Year 2	Forecast Year 3	Forecast Year 4	Forecast Year 5
Earnings before interest and taxes. . .	−$15,000	−$15,000	−$15,000	$38,000	$42,000	$46,000	$32,000
Interest expense (current).	8,000	10,000	12,000	12,000	12,000	12,000	12,000
Earnings before income taxes	−$23,000	−$25,000	−$27,000	$26,000	$30,000	$34,000	$20,000
Interest Deduction Cap	$ 0	$ 0	$ 0	$20,900	$23,100	$25,300	$17,600

P11.8 **Valuing a Company with Interest and Net Operating Loss Carryforwards:** Use the information in the following schedule, which contains two years of historical performance and five years of forecasts, to value the firm as of the end of Year 0 using the following assumptions. Assume the company's income tax rate on all income is 30%, the tax deduction for interest in any year is limited to 33.333% of EBIT in that year, any interest payment above the interest deduction cap in a year can be carried forward indefinitely, the company can only use its NOL carryforwards to offset a maximum of 75% of its taxable income before NOL offsets, and the company's EBIT based on its financial statements is equal to its EBIT for income taxes. Also assume the company's unlevered cost of capital is 11%, its interest rate (and debt cost of capital) is 9%, its discount rate for its interest tax shields is equal to its unlevered cost of capital, and its long-term growth rate (Year 6 onward) is 2%. Also assume that the company makes no investments in working capital and that CAPEX is equal to depreciation.

a. Calculate the company's income taxes and interest and NOL carryforwards for the levered company (including interest in the forecasts). (Similar to Exhibit 11.9.)

b. Calculate the company's income taxes and interest and NOL carryforwards for the unlevered company (excluding interest in the forecasts but including interest in Years 1 and 0). (Similar to Exhibit 11.10.)

c. Calculate the company's income taxes and interest tax shields assuming the company can deduct all of its interest for income taxes and the company receives a tax refund if its EBIT is negative. (Similar to Exhibit 11.11.)

d. Calculate the effect of the company's interest and NOL carryforwards on the company's cash flows (unlevered free cash flows and interest tax shields) by subtracting the unlevered free cash flows and interest tax shields including the effects of interest and NOL carryforwards from the unlevered free cash flows and interest tax shields excluding the effects of interest and NOL carryforwards. Compare these differences to the sum of the interest and NOL carryforwards. (Similar to Exhibit 11.12.)

e. Measure the value of the firm by separately valuing the firm without interest and NOL carryforwards and then adding the value of the pre-valuation and post-valuation interest carryforwards and NOL carryforwards and assuming the company's capital structure strategy is based on the forecasts and the long-term growth rate. (Use the APV valuation method, see Exhibit 11.14.)

f. Measure the value of the firm including and excluding interest and NOL carryforwards and assuming the company's capital structure strategy is to finance 25% of the firm with debt and 75% with common equity excluding interest and NOL carryforwards. (Similar to Exhibits 11.15 through 11.18.)

g. Use the "short-cut" method to measure the value of the firm by separately valuing the firm without interest and NOL carryforwards and then adding the value of the pre-valuation and post-valuation interest carryforwards and NOL carryforwards using the weighted average cost of capital as the discount rate. Assume the company's capital structure strategy is to finance 25% of the firm with debt and 75% with common equity excluding interest and NOL carryforwards. (Similar to Exhibit 11.19.)

Financial Accounting (Income Statement Excerpt)	Actual Year −1	Actual Year 0	Forecast Year 1	Forecast Year 2	Forecast Year 3	Forecast Year 4	Forecast Year 5
Earnings before interest and taxes. . .	−$ 8,000	−$ 8,000	−$ 8,000	$38,000	$42,000	$46,000	$32,000
Interest expense (current).	4,000	6,000	8,000	8,000	8,000	8,000	8,000
Earnings before income taxes	−$12,000	−$14,000	−$16,000	$30,000	$34,000	$38,000	$24,000
Interest Deduction Cap	$ 0	$ 0	$ 0	$12,667	$14,000	$15,333	$10,667

P11.9 Appendix Problem—A Simple Lease Example—Part 1: A lease contract begins on the last day of Year 0 and ends on the last day of Year 3. The lease has three annual payments equal to $25,000. The appropriate discount rate for the lease is 9%. Prepare a lease amortization table similar to the one in Exhibit A11.1 treating the lease as a finance lease.

P11.10 Appendix Problem—A Simple Lease Example—Part 2: Use the information in Problem P11.9 and the following information to prepare an income statement, balance sheet, and free cash flow schedule for the three years of the lease assuming the lease is an operating lease, and again assuming the lease is a finance lease. Assume the company has $30,000 in revenue each year and that the income tax rate is 45% on all income. The company has a policy of distributing all equity free cash flows to equityholders each period. The company has no assets other than $1,500 in required cash that remains constant over time.

SOLUTIONS FOR REVIEW EXERCISES

Review Exercise 11.1: Measuring the Weighted Average Cost of Capital

Market Value of Debt	
Price	100%
Market value of debt	$12,000
Market Value of Preferred	
Price	95%
Market value of preferred	$ 7,600
Market Value of Equity	
Price	$ 12.00
Shares	1,000
Market value of equity	$12,000
Market value of firm	$31,600

continued

continued from previous page

Market Value of Equity	
Debt-to-firm value	38.0%
Preferred-to-firm value	24.1%
Equity-to-firm value	38.0%
	100.0%
Risk-free rate	5.00%
Market risk premium	6.00%
Equity beta	2.5
Equity cost of capital	20.00%
Yield on debt	8.00%
Less: Expected default loss	1.00%
Cost of debt	7.00%
Cost of preferred	8.50%
Income tax rate	30.00%
Weighted average cost of capital #1	11.50%
$r_{WACC} = 0.20 \times 0.38 + 0.07 \times (1 - 0.3) \times 0.38 + 0.085 \times 0.241 = 0.115$	
Unlevered cost of capital	12.30%
Weighted average cost of capital #2	11.50%
$r_{WACC} = 0.123 - 0.07 \times 0.3 \times 0.38 = 0.115$	

Note: $r_{ITS} = r_{UA}$ when a company continually refinances itself to maintain a constant capital structure strategy (see Chapter 10).

Review Exercise 11.2: Operating versus Finance Leases and Valuation

Income Statement and Free Cash Flow Schedule for Year 1		**Operating Lease Method**	**Finance Lease Method**
Income Statement			
Revenues		$800	$800
Rent expense		–450	
Interest expense			–450
Pretax income		$350	$350
Income taxes	30.0%	–105	–105
Net income		$245	$245
Free Cash Flow Schedule			
Earnings before interest and taxes		$350	$800
– Income taxes paid on EBIT	30.0%	–105	–240
Earnings before interest and after taxes		$245	$560
– Increase in capital lease assets	2.0%		–100
Unlevered free cash flow		$245	$460
– Interest paid		n/a	–450
+ Interest tax shield	30.0%	n/a	135
+ Change in non-common equity		0	0
+ Change in capital lease obligations		n/a	100
Free cash flow to common equity		$245	$245

continued

continued from previous page

Values as of Year 0		Operating Lease Method	Finance Lease Method
Value of the property = Lease obligation		$5,000	$5,000
Value of the equity	18.0%	$1,531	$1,531
Debt-to-firm value		—	76.6%
Unlevered cost of capital		18.0%	11.1%

$$r_{UA} = r_E \times \frac{V_E}{V_F} + r_D \times \frac{V_D}{V_F}$$

$$r_{UA} = 0.18 \times \frac{\$1{,}531}{\$1{,}531 + \$5{,}000} + 0.09 \times \frac{\$5{,}000}{\$1{,}531 + \$5{,}000} = 0.111 \text{ for finance lease}$$

	Operating Lease Method	Finance Lease Method
Weighted average cost of capital	18.0%	9.043%
Value of the firm using WACC method	$1,531	$6,531
Value of debt	0	5,000
Value of equity	$1,531	$1,531
Value of the Firm Using APV Method		
Value of the unlevered firm	$1,531	$5,049
Value of the interest tax shields		1,482
Value of the firm	$1,531	$6,531
Value of debt	0	5,000
Value of equity	$1,531	$1,531

WACC for finance lease = $r_{UA} - r_D \times T_{INT} \times V_D/V_F$ = 0.1111 − 0.09 × 0.30 × $5,000/$6,531 = 0.09043

Value of the firm using WACC:

Operating lease: $245/(0.18 − 0.02) = $1,531

Finance lease: $460/(0.09043 − 0.02) = $6,531

Value of the firm using APV:

Operating lease: $245/(0.18 − 0.02) = $1,531

Finance lease: $460/(0.1111 − 0.02) + $135/(0.1111 − 0.02) = $5,049 + $1,482 = $6,531

Equity DCF both lease methods = $245/(0.18 − 0.02) = $1,531

Review Exercise 11.3: Capitalizing Operating Leases—Part 1

Operating Lease Payments as of end of Year 0

Year	Payment	PV Factor	Present Value
Year 1	$1,200	0.926	$1,111.1
Year 2	1,000	0.857	857.3
Year 3	900	0.794	714.4
Year 4	700	0.735	514.5
Year 5	600	0.681	408.3
Year 6	600	0.630	378.1
Year 7	600	0.583	350.1
Year 8	600	0.540	324.2
Year 9	600	0.500	300.1
Year 10	600	0.463	277.9
Year 11	600	0.429	257.3
Year 12	600	0.397	238.3
Year 13	600	0.368	220.6
Year 14	600	0.340	204.3
Year 15			0.0
Present value as of end of Year 0			$6,156.7
Implicit interest rate			8.0%
Implicit interest expense for Year 1			$ 492.5
Assumed remaining average life			10
Lease asset amortization for Year 1			$ 615.7

Operating Lease Payments as of end of Year 1

Year	Payment	PV Factor	Present Value
Year 2	$1,100	0.926	$1,018.5
Year 3	990	0.857	848.8
Year 4	770	0.794	611.3
Year 5	660	0.735	485.1
Year 6	630	0.681	428.8
Year 7	630	0.630	397.0
Year 8	630	0.583	367.6
Year 9	630	0.540	340.4
Year 10	630	0.500	315.2
Year 11	630	0.463	291.8
Year 12	630	0.429	270.2
Year 13	630	0.397	250.2
Year 14	630	0.368	231.6
Year 15	630	0.340	214.5
Present value as of end of Year 1			$6,070.9
Year 1 interest			−492.5
Year 1 lease payment			1,200.0
			$6,778.3
Present value as of end of Year 0			6,156.7
Present value of new leases in Year 1			$ 621.7
Rent in Year 1			$1,200.0

Exhibit may contain small rounding errors

Review Exercise 11.4: Capitalizing Operating Leases—Part 2

Summarized Financial Statements	Year 1 Reported	Beginning of Year Balance	Adjust Rent Expense	Amortization of Finance Lease Asset	Income Taxes	Acquistion of Additional Leases	Year 1 Adjusted
Income Statement							
Revenues	$22,000.0						$22,000.0
Rent expense	−2,000.0		$1,200.0				−800.0
Depreciation and amortization	−3,000.0						−3,000.0
Amortization of operating leases				−$615.7			−615.7
All other operating expenses	−10,000.0						−10,000.0
Operating income	$ 7,000.0	$ 0.0	$1,200.0	−$615.7	$ 0.0	$ 0.0	$ 7,584.3
Interest expense	−1,000.0						−1,000.0
Lease interest			−492.5				−492.5
Income before taxes	$ 6,000.0	$ 0.0	$ 707.5	−$615.7	$ 0.0	$ 0.0	$ 6,091.8
Income taxes	−2,400.0				−36.7		−2,436.7
Net income	$ 3,600.0	$ 0.0	$ 707.5	−$615.7	−$36.7	$ 0.0	$ 3,655.1

continued

continued from previous page

Summarized Financial Statements	Year 1 Reported	Beginning of Year Balance	Adjust Rent Expense	Amortization of Finance Lease Asset	Income Taxes	Acquistion of Additional Leases	Year 1 Adjusted
Balance Sheet							
Current assets	$ 8,000.0						$ 8,000.0
Net property, plant, and equipment	20,000.0						20,000.0
Other assets	5,000.0						5,000.0
Deferred tax asset					$ 0.0		0.0
Capitalized operating leases asset		$6,156.7		–$615.7		$621.7	6,162.7
Total assets	$33,000.0	$6,156.7	$ 0.0	–$615.7	$ 0.0	$621.7	$39,162.7
Current operating liabilities	$ 7,000.0						$ 7,000.0
Other liabilities	10,000.0						10,000.0
Deferred tax liability					$ 36.7		36.7
Debt	13,000.0						13,000.0
Capitalized operating leases liability		$6,156.7	–$707.5			$621.7	6,070.9
Total liabilities	$30,000.0	$6,156.7	–$707.5	$ 0.0	$ 36.7	$621.7	$36,107.6
Shareholders' equity	3,000.0		707.5	–615.7	–36.7		3,055.1
Total liabilities and shareholders' equity	$33,000.0	$6,156.7	$ 0.0	–$615.7	$ 0.0	$621.7	$39,162.7

Summarized Free Cash Flow Schedule	Year 1 Reported	Adjust Rent Expense	Amortization of Finance Lease Asset	Income Taxes	Acquistion of Additional Leases	Year 1 Adjusted
Earnings before interest and taxes (EBIT)	$7,000.0	$1,200.0	–$615.7			$7,584.3
– Income taxes paid on EBIT	–2,800.0			–$233.7		–3,033.7
Earnings before interest and after taxes	$4,200.0	$1,200.0	–$615.7	–$233.7	$ 0.0	$4,550.6
+ Depreciation and amortization	3,000.0					3,000.0
+ Amortization of operating leases			615.7			615.7
– Change in net working capital	500.0					500.0
+ Change in non-current liabilities & other	100.0			36.7		136.7
– Change in required cash balance	–50.0					–50.0
Unlevered cash flow from operations	$7,750.0	$1,200.0	$ 0.0	–$197.0	$ 0.0	$8,753.0
– Capital expenditures (net)	–3,000.0					–3,000.0
– Increase in capital lease assets					–621.7	–621.7
Unlevered free cash flow	$4,750.0	$1,200.0	$ 0.0	–$197.0	–$621.7	$5,131.3
– Interest paid	–1,000.0	–492.5				–1,492.5
+ Interest tax shield	400.0			197.0		597.0
+ Change in non-common equity		0.0				0.0
+ Change in capital lease obligations		–707.5			621.7	–85.8
Free cash flow to common equity	$4,150.0	$ 0.0	$ 0.0	$ 0.0	$ 0.0	$4,150.0

Exhibit may contain small rounding errors

Review Exercise 11.5—Valuing a Company with Interest and NOL Carryforwards—Part 1

a. Calculate the company's income taxes and interest and NOL carryforwards for the levered company (including interest in the forecasts). (Similar to Exhibit 11.9.)

Levered Company (Taxable Income)	Actual Year −1	Actual Year 0	Forecast Year 1	Forecast Year 2	Forecast Year 3	Forecast Year 4	Forecast Year 5
Earnings before interest and taxes	−$10,000	−$10,000	−$10,000	$28,000	$32,000	$36,000	$32,000
Pre-valuation interest carryforward	0	0	0	10,000	0	0	0
Post-valuation interest carryforward			0	2,600	13,400	7,000	0
Interest expense (current)	0	0	0	0	1,000	8,000	8,000
Taxable income	−$10,000	−$10,000	−$10,000	$15,400	$17,600	$21,000	$24,000
NOL carryforward used	0	0	0	−12,320	−14,080	−3,600	0
Taxable income after NOL carryforward adjustment	−$10,000	−$10,000	−$10,000	$ 3,080	$ 3,520	$17,400	$24,000
Income taxes	0	0	0	1,078	1,232	6,090	8,400
Earnings	−$10,000	−$10,000	−$10,000	$ 2,002	$ 2,288	$11,310	$15,600
Average tax rate	0.00%	0.00%	0.00%	7.00%	7.00%	29.00%	35.00%
Pre-Valuation Interest Carryforward Balance	**Year −1**	**Year 0**	**Year 1**	**Year 2**	**Year 3**	**Year 4**	**Year 5**
Beginning interest carryforward	$ 0	$ 4,000	$10,000	$10,000	$ 0	$ 0	$ 0
Change in interest carryforward	4,000	6,000	0	−10,000	0	0	0
Ending interest carryforward	$ 4,000	$10,000	$10,000	$ 0	$ 0	$ 0	$ 0
Post-Valuation Interest Carryforward Balance			**Year 1**	**Year 2**	**Year 3**	**Year 4**	**Year 5**
Beginning interest carryforward			$ 0	$ 8,000	$13,400	$ 7,000	$ 0
Change in interest carryforward			8,000	5,400	−6,400	−7,000	0
Ending interest carryforward			$ 8,000	$13,400	$ 7,000	$ 0	$ 0
NOL Carryforward Balance	**Year −1**	**Year 0**	**Year 1**	**Year 2**	**Year 3**	**Year 4**	**Year 5**
Beginning NOL carryforward	$ 0	$10,000	$20,000	$30,000	$17,680	$ 3,600	$ 0
Change in NOL carryforward	10,000	10,000	10,000	−12,320	−14,080	−3,600	0
Ending NOL carryforward	$10,000	$20,000	$30,000	$17,680	$ 3,600	$ 0	$ 0

b. Calculate the company's income taxes and interest and NOL carryforwards for the unlevered company (excluding interest in the forecasts but including interest in Years −1 and 0). (Similar to Exhibit 11.10.)

Unlevered Company (Taxable Income)	Actual Year −1	Actual Year 0	Forecast Year 1	Forecast Year 2	Forecast Year 3	Forecast Year 4	Forecast Year 5
Earnings before interest and taxes	−$10,000	−$10,000	−$10,000	$28,000	$32,000	$36,000	$32,000
Pre-valuation interest carryforward	0	0	0	10,000	0	0	0
Interest expense (current)	0	0					
Taxable income	−$10,000	−$10,000	−$10,000	$18,000	$32,000	$36,000	$32,000
NOL carryforward used	0	0	0	−14,400	−15,600	0	0
Taxable income after NOL carryforward adjustment	−$10,000	−$10,000	−$10,000	$ 3,600	$16,400	$36,000	$32,000
Income taxes	0	0	0	1,260	5,740	12,600	11,200
Earnings	−$10,000	−$10,000	−$10,000	$ 2,340	$10,660	$23,400	$20,800
Average tax rate	0.00%	0.00%	0.00%	7.00%	17.94%	35.00%	35.00%
Pre-Valuation Interest Carryforward Balance	**Year −1**	**Year 0**	**Year 1**	**Year 2**	**Year 3**	**Year 4**	**Year 5**
Beginning interest carryforward	$ 0	$ 4,000	$10,000	$10,000	$ 0	$ 0	$ 0
Change in interest carryforward	4,000	6,000	0	−10,000	0	0	0
Ending interest carryforward	$ 4,000	$10,000	$10,000	$ 0	$ 0	$ 0	$ 0

continued

continued from previous page

NOL Carryforward Balance	Year −1	Year 0	Year 1	Year 2	Year 3	Year 4	Year 5
Beginning NOL carryforward	$ 0	$10,000	$20,000	$30,000	$15,600	$ 0	$ 0
Change in NOL carryforward	10,000	10,000	10,000	−14,400	−15,600	0	0
Ending NOL carryforward	$10,000	$20,000	$30,000	$15,600	$ 0	$ 0	$ 0

Interest Tax Shield	Year 1	Year 2	Year 3	Year 4	Year 5
Income taxes (unlevered firm)	$ 0	$ 1,260	$ 5,740	$12,600	$11,200
Income taxes (with interest deduction)	0	1,078	1,232	6,090	8,400
Correct interest tax shield	$ 0	$ 182	$ 4,508	$ 6,510	$ 2,800

Unlevered Free Cash Flow	Year 1	Year 2	Year 3	Year 4	Year 5
EBIT	−$10,000	$28,000	$32,000	$36,000	$32,000
Income taxes	0	1,260	5,740	12,600	11,200
Unlevered free cash flow	−$10,000	$26,740	$26,260	$23,400	$20,800

c. Calculate the company's income taxes and interest tax shields assuming the company can deduct all of its interest for income taxes and the company receives a tax refund if its EBIT is negative. (Similar to Exhibit 11.11.)

	Year 1	Year 2	Year 3	Year 4	Year 5
EBIT	−$10,000	$28,000	$32,000	$36,000	$32,000
Income taxes	−3,500	9,800	11,200	12,600	11,200
Unlevered free cash flow	−$ 6,500	$18,200	$20,800	$23,400	$20,800
Interest expense	$ 8,000	$ 8,000	$ 8,000	$ 8,000	$ 8,000
Income tax rate	35%	35%	35%	35%	35%
Interest tax shield	$ 2,800	$ 2,800	$ 2,800	$ 2,800	$ 2,800

d. Calculate the effect of the company's interest and NOL carryforwards on the company's cash flows (unlevered free cash flows and interest tax shields) by subtracting the unlevered free cash flows and interest tax shields including the effects of interest and NOL carryforwards from the unlevered free cash flows and interest tax shields excluding the effects of interest and NOL carryforwards. Compare these differences to the sum of the interest and NOL carryforwards. (Similar to Exhibit 11.12.)

	Year 1	Year 2	Year 3	Year 4	Year 4
Difference in Free Cash Flows and Interest Tax Shields (Compare Exhibit 11.10 and 11.11)					
Free cash flows including interest and NOL carryforwards	−$10,000	$26,740	$26,260	$23,400	$20,800
Free cash flows excluding interest and NOL carryforwards	−6,500	18,200	20,800	23,400	20,800
Difference	−$3,500	$ 8,540	$ 5,460	$ 0	$ 0
Interest tax shields including interest and NOL carryforwards	$ 0	$ 182	$ 4,508	$ 6,510	$ 2,800
Interest cash flows excluding interest and NOL carryforwards	2,800	2,800	2,800	2,800	2,800
Difference	−$ 2,800	−$ 2,618	$ 1,708	$ 3,710	$ 0
Difference in free cash flows and interest tax shields	−$ 6,300	$ 5,922	$ 7,168	$ 3,710	$ 0
NOL Carryforward and Interest Carryforward (Created) and Used (See Exhibit 11.9)					
Change in NOL balance (NOLs used)	−$10,000	$12,320	$14,080	$ 3,600	$ 0
Change in pre-valuation interest carryforward	0	10,000	0	0	0
Change in post-valuation interest carryforward	−8,000	−5,400	6,400	7,000	0
Total	−$18,000	$16,920	$20,480	$10,600	$ 0
Tax rate	35%	35%	35%	35%	35%
Tax benefit	−$ 6,300	$ 5,922	$ 7,168	$ 3,710	$ 0

Review Exercise 11.6—Valuing a Company with Interest and NOL Carryforwards—Part 2

Using the information and assumptions in Review Exercise 11.5, measure the value of the firm by separately valuing the firm without interest and NOL carryforwards and then add the value of the pre-valuation and post-valuation interest carryforwards and NOL carryforwards. Assume the company's capital structure strategy is based on the forecasts and the long-term growth rate. (Use the APV valuation method, similar to Exhibit 11.14.)

Adjusted Present Value Valuation	Year 0	Year 1	Year 2	Year 3	Year 4	CV Year 4
Unlevered free cash flows for continuing value						$ 20,800
Continuing value discount factor						11.111
Unlevered free cash flows and continuing value		−$ 6,500	$18,200	$20,800	$23,400	$231,111
Discount factor		0.893	0.797	0.712	0.636	0.636
Value of unlevered free cash flows	$185,257	−$ 5,804	$14,509	$14,805	$14,871	$146,875
Interest tax shield for continuing value						$ 2,800
Continuing value discount factor						11.111
Interest tax shield and continuing value		$ 2,800	$ 2,800	$ 2,800	$ 2,800	$ 31,111
Discount factor, $r_{ITS} = r_{UA}$		0.893	0.797	0.712	0.636	0.636
Value of interest tax shields	$ 28,276	$ 2,500	$ 2,232	$ 1,993	$ 1,779	$ 19,772
Value of the firm	$213,533					
Effect of NOL Carryforwards						
Change in NOL balance (NOLs used)		−$10,000	$12,320	$14,080	$ 3,600	$ 0
Tax rate		35%	35%	35%	35%	35%
Tax benefit		−$ 3,500	$ 4,312	$ 4,928	$ 1,260	$ 0
Discount factor, $r_{NOL} = r_{UA}$		0.893	0.797	0.712	0.636	
Value of NOL carryforwards	$ 4,621	−$ 3,125	$ 3,438	$ 3,508	$ 801	
Effect of Pre-Valuation Interest Carryforwards						
Change in pre-valuation interest carryforwards		$ 0	$10,000	$ 0	$ 0	$ 0
Tax rate		35%	35%	35%	35%	35%
Tax benefit		$ 0	$ 3,500	$ 0	$ 0	$ 0
Discount factor, $r_{Pre\text{-}iCF} = r_{UA}$		0.893	0.797	0.712	0.636	
Value of pre-valuation interest carryforwards	$ 2,790	$ 0	$ 2,790	$ 0	$ 0	
Effect of Post-Valuation Interest Carryforwards						
Change in post-valuation interest carryforwards		−$ 8,000	−$ 5,400	$ 6,400	$ 7,000	$ 0
Tax rate		35%	35%	35%	35%	35%
Tax benefit		−$ 2,800	−$ 1,890	$ 2,240	$ 2,450	$ 0
Discount factor, $r_{Post\text{-}iCF} = r_{UA}$		0.893	0.797	0.712	0.636	
Value of post-valuation interest carryforwards	−$ 855	−$ 2,500	−$ 1,507	$ 1,594	$ 1,557	
Value of all carryforwards	$ 6,556					
Value of the firm	$220,089					

Review Exercise 11.7—Valuing a Company with Interest and NOL Carryforwards—Part 3

Using the information and assumptions in Review Exercise 11.5, measure the value of the firm including and excluding interest and NOL carryforwards and assuming the company's capital structure strategy is to finance 1/3 of the firm with debt and 2/3 with common equity excluding interest and NOL carryforwards. (Similar to Exhibits 11.15 through 11.18.)

WACC valuation excluding interest and NOL carryforwards:

WACC Valuation Excluding Interest and NOL Carryforwards	Year 0	Year 1	Year 2	Year 3	Year 4	CV Year 4
Unlevered free cash flow for continuing value						$ 20,800
Discount factor for continuing value						12.579
Unlevered free cash flow and continuing value		−$ 6,500	$18,200	$20,800	$23,400	$261,635
Discount factor, r_{wacc}		0.901	0.812	0.732	0.660	0.660
Firm value ignoring interest carryforwards and NOLs	$212,256	−$ 5,858	$14,785	$15,229	$15,442	$172,658

Year-by-year WACC valuations excluding interest and NOL carryforwards:

	Year 1	Year 2	Year 3	Year 4	CV Year 4
Unlevered free cash flow for continuing value					$ 20,800
Discount factor for continuing value					12.579
Unlevered free cash flow	−$ 6,500	$ 18,200	$ 20,800	$ 23,400	
Value of the unlevered firm at year end	241,998	250,297	256,904	261,635	
Unlevered value at year end plus unlevered free cash flow	$235,498	$268,497	$277,704	$285,035	
Discount factor for one year	0.901	0.901	0.901	0.901	
Beginning of year V_F (ignoring interest and NOL carryforwards)	$212,256	$241,998	$250,297	$256,904	$261,635
As of the End of Year	**Year 0**	**Year 1**	**Year 2**	**Year 3**	**Year 4**
Value of the firm (V_F)	$212,256	$241,998	$250,297	$256,904	$261,635
Debt to value	33.33%	33.33%	33.33%	33.33%	33.33%
Value of debt	$ 70,752	$ 80,666	$ 83,432	$ 85,635	$ 87,212
Interest rate (cost of debt)	9.00%	9.00%	9.00%	9.00%	9.00%
Interest (in following year)	$ 6,368	$ 7,260	$ 7,509	$ 7,707	$ 7,849
Tax rate	35%	35%	35%	35%	35%
Interest × tax rate (potential interest tax shield)	$ 2,229	$ 2,541	$ 2,628	$ 2,697	$ 2,747
Interest deduction cap (in the following year)	$ 0	$ 12,600	$ 14,400	$ 16,200	$ 14,400

Income taxes and interest and NOL carryforwards based on the WACC valuation assumed capital structure:

Levered Company (Taxable Income)	**Actual Year −1**	**Actual Year 0**	**Forecast Year 1**	**Forecast Year 2**	**Forecast Year 3**	**Forecast Year 4**	**Forecast Year 5**
Earnings before interest and taxes	−$10,000	−$10,000	−$10,000	$28,000	$32,000	$36,000	$32,000
Pre-valuation interest carryforward	0	0	0	10,000	0	0	0
Post-valuation interest carryforward			0	2,600	11,028	4,137	0
Interest expense (current)	0	0	0	0	3,372	7,707	7,849
Taxable income	−$10,000	−$10,000	−$10,000	$15,400	$17,600	$24,156	$24,151
NOL carryforward used	0	0	0	−12,320	−14,080	−3,600	0
Taxable income after NOL carryforward adjustment	−$10,000	−$10,000	−$10,000	$ 3,080	$ 3,520	$20,556	$24,151
Income taxes	0	0	0	1,078	1,232	7,195	8,453
Earnings	−$10,000	−$10,000	−$10,000	$ 2,002	$ 2,288	$13,362	$15,698
Average tax rate	0%	0%	0%	7%	7%	30%	35%
Pre-Valuation Interest Carryforward Balance	**Year −1**	**Year 0**	**Year 1**	**Year 2**	**Year 3**	**Year 4**	**Year 5**
Beginning interest carryforward	$ 0	$ 4,000	$10,000	$10,000	$ 0	$ 0	$ 0
Change in interest carryforward	4,000	6,000	0	−10,000	0	0	0
Ending interest carryforward	$ 4,000	$10,000	$10,000	$ 0	$ 0	$ 0	$ 0
Post-Valuation Interest Carryforward Balance			**Year 1**	**Year 2**	**Year 3**	**Year 4**	**Year 5**
Beginning interest carryforward			$ 0	$ 6,368	$11,028	$ 4,137	$ 0
Change in interest carryforward			6,368	4,660	−6,891	−4,137	0
Ending interest carryforward			$ 6,368	$11,028	$ 4,137	$ 0	$ 0
NOL Carryforward Balance	**Year −1**	**Year 0**	**Year 1**	**Year 2**	**Year 3**	**Year 4**	**Year 5**
Beginning NOL carryforward	$ 0	$10,000	$20,000	$30,000	$17,680	$ 3,600	$ 0
Change in NOL carryforward	10,000	10,000	10,000	−12,320	−14,080	−3,600	0
Ending NOL carryforward	$10,000	$20,000	$30,000	$17,680	$ 3,600	$ 0	$ 0

WACC valuation including interest and NOL carryforwards:

WACC Valuation—using debt based on WACC capital structure to measure interest and NOL carryforwards	Year 0	Year 1	Year 2	Year 3	Year 4	CV Year 4
Unlevered free cash flow for continuing value						$ 20,800
Discount factor for continuing value						12.579
Unlevered free cash flow and continuing value		−$ 6,500	$18,200	$20,800	$23,400	$261,635
Discount factor, r_{wacc}		0.901	0.812	0.732	0.660	0.660
Firm value ignoring interest carryforwards and NOLs	$212,256	−$ 5,858	$14,785	$15,229	$15,442	$172,658
Effect of NOL Carryforwards						
Change in NOL balance (NOLs used)		−$10,000	$12,320	$14,080	$ 3,600	$ 0
Tax rate		35%	35%	35%	35%	35%
Tax benefit		−$ 3,500	$ 4,312	$ 4,928	$ 1,260	$ 0
Discount factor, $r_{NOL} = r_{UA}$		0.893	0.797	0.712	0.636	
Value of NOL carryforwards	$ 4,621	−$ 3,125	$ 3,438	$ 3,508	$ 801	
Effect of Pre-Valuation Interest Carryforwards						
Change in pre-valuation interest carryforwards		$ 0	$10,000	$ 0	$ 0	$ 0
Tax rate		35%	35%	35%	35%	35%
Tax benefit		$ 0	$ 3,500	$ 0	$ 0	$ 0
Discount factor, $r_{Pre\text{-}iCF} = r_{UA}$		0.893	0.797	0.712	0.636	
Value of pre-valuation interest carryforwards	$ 2,790	$ 0	$ 2,790	$ 0	$ 0	
Effect of Post-Valuation Interest Carryforwards						
Change in post-valuation interest carryforwards		−$ 6,368	−$ 4,660	$ 6,891	$ 4,137	$ 0
Tax rate		35%	35%	35%	35%	35%
Tax benefit		−$ 2,229	−$ 1,631	$ 2,412	$ 1,448	$ 0
Discount factor, $r_{Post\text{-}iCF} = r_{UA}$		0.893	0.797	0.712	0.636	
Value of post-valuation interest carryforwards	−$ 653	−$ 1,990	−$ 1,300	$ 1,717	$ 920	
Value of all interest carryforwards	$ 6,758					
Value of the firm	$219,014					

Review Exercise 11.8—Valuing a Company with Interest and NOL Carryforwards—Part 4

Using the information and assumptions in Review Exercise 11.5, use the "short-cut" method to measure the value of the firm by separately valuing the firm without interest and NOL carryforwards and adding the value of the pre-valuation and post-valuation interest carryforwards and NOL carryforwards using the weighted average cost of capital as the discount rate. Assume the company's capital structure strategy is to finance 1/3 of the firm with debt and 2/3 with common equity excluding interest and NOL carryforwards. (Similar to Exhibit 11.19.)

"Short-Cut" WACC Valuation—Using Debt Forecasts (Not WACC debt) to Measure Interest and NOL Carryforwards	Year 0	Year 1	Year 2	Year 3	Year 4	CV Year 4
Unlevered free cash flow for continuing value						$ 20,800
Discount factor for continuing value						12.579
Unlevered free cash flow and continuing value		−$ 6,500	$18,200	$20,800	$23,400	$261,635
Discount factor, r_{WACC}		0.901	0.812	0.732	0.660	0.660
Firm value ignoring interest carryforwards and NOLs	$212,256	−$ 5,858	$14,785	$15,229	$15,442	$172,658
Effect of NOL Carryforwards						
Change in NOL balance (NOLs used)		−$10,000	$12,320	$14,080	$ 3,600	$ 0
Tax rate		35%	35%	35%	35%	35%
Tax benefit		−$ 3,500	$ 4,312	$ 4,928	$ 1,260	$ 0
Discount factor, $r_{NOL} = r_{WACC}$		0.901	0.812	0.732	0.660	
Value of NOL carryforwards	$ 4,788	−$ 3,155	$ 3,503	$ 3,608	$ 831	
Effect of Pre-Valuation Interest Carryforwards						
Change in pre-valuation interest carryforwards		$ 0	$10,000	$ 0	$ 0	$ 0
Tax rate		35%	35%	35%	35%	35%
Tax benefit		$ 0	$ 3,500	$ 0	$ 0	$ 0
Discount factor, $r_{Pre\text{-}iCF} = r_{WACC}$		0.901	0.812	0.732	0.660	
Value of pre-valuation interest carryforwards	$ 2,843	$ 0	$ 2,843	$ 0	$ 0	
Effect of Post-Valuation Interest Carryforwards						
Change in post-valuation interest carryforwards		−$ 8,000	−$ 5,400	$ 6,400	$ 7,000	$ 0
Tax rate		35%	35%	35%	35%	35%
Tax benefit		−$ 2,800	−$ 1,890	$ 2,240	$ 2,450	$ 0
Discount factor, $r_{Post\text{-}iCF} = r_{WACC}$		0.901	0.812	0.732	0.660	
Value of post-valuation interest carryforwards	−$ 802	−$ 2,524	−$ 1,535	$ 1,640	$ 1,617	
Value of all carryforwards	$ 6,829					
Value of the firm	$219,085					
Valuation Error						
Correct WACC valuation	$219,014					
Short-cut method	219,085					
Difference	−$ 71	0.0%				

Review Exercise A11.1: A Simple Lease Example—Part 2

Lease amortization table:

	Beginning Lease Liability	Implicit Interest	Lease Payment	Ending Lease Liability	Change in Liability
Year 1	$12,885.5	$1,030.8	$ 5,000.0	$8,916.3	$ 3,969.2
Year 2	$ 8,916.3	$ 713.3	$ 5,000.0	$4,629.6	$ 4,286.7
Year 3	$ 4,629.6	$ 370.4	$ 5,000.0	$ 0.0	$ 4,629.6
Total		$2,114.5	$15,000.0		$12,885.5

Income statements and balance sheets:

Simple Lease Example	Operating Lease Actual Year 0	Operating Lease Forecast Year 1	Operating Lease Forecast Year 2	Operating Lease Forecast Year 3	Finance Lease Actual Year 0	Finance Lease Forecast Year 1	Finance Lease Forecast Year 2	Finance Lease Forecast Year 3	Total Operating Lease	Total Finance Lease
Income Statement										
Revenue		$8,000.0	$8,000.0	$8,000.0		$8,000.0	$8,000.0	$8,000.0	$24,000.0	$24,000.0
Lease expense		−5,000.0	−5,000.0	−5,000.0					−15,000.0	0.0
Finance lease asset amortization						−4,295.2	−4,295.2	−4,295.2	0.0	−12,885.5
Earnings before interest and taxes		$3,000.0	$3,000.0	$3,000.0		$ 3,704.8	$3,704.8	$3,704.8	$ 9,000.0	$11,114.5
Interest expense						−1,030.8	−713.3	−370.4	0.0	−2,114.5
Income before taxes		$3,000.0	$3,000.0	$3,000.0		$2,674.0	$2,991.5	$3,334.5	$ 9,000.0	$ 9,000.0
Income tax expense		−900.0	−900.0	−900.0		−802.2	−897.5	−1,000.3	−2,700.0	−2,700.0
Net income		$2,100.0	$2,100.0	$2,100.0		$1,871.8	$2,094.1	$2,334.1	$ 6,300.0	$ 6,300.0
Balance Sheet										
Cash	$ 400.0	$ 400.0	$ 400.0	$ 400.0	$ 400.0	$ 400.0	$ 400.0	$ 400.0		
Right-of-use asset	12,885.5	8,916.3	4,629.6	0.0	12,885.5	8,590.3	4,295.2	0.0		
Deferred tax asset						97.8	100.3	0.0		
Total assets	$13,285.5	$9,316.3	$5,029.6	$ 400.0	$13,285.5	$9,088.1	$4,795.5	$400.0		
Deferred tax liability						$ 0.0	$ 0.0	$ 0.0		
Lease liability	$12,885.5	$8,916.3	$4,629.6	$ 0.0	$12,885.5	8,916.3	4,629.6	0.0		
Equity	400.0	400.0	400.0	400.0	400.0	171.8	165.9	400.0		
Total liabilities and equities	$13,285.5	$9,316.3	$5,029.6	$ 400.0	$13,285.5	$9,088.1	$4,795.5	$ 400.0		
Sum of lease amortization plus interest expense						$5,326.0	$5,008.5	$4,665.5		$15,000.0

Exhibit may contain small rounding errors.

Deferred income tax schedule:

Simple Lease Example	Operating Lease Actual Year 0	Operating Lease Forecast Year 1	Operating Lease Forecast Year 2	Operating Lease Forecast Year 3	Finance Lease Actual Year 0	Finance Lease Forecast Year 1	Finance Lease Forecast Year 2	Finance Lease Forecast Year 3
Deferred tax asset (DTA)	$3,865.6	$2,674.9	$1,388.9	$0.0	$3,865.6	$2,674.9	$1,388.9	$0.0
Deferred tax liability (DTL)	3,865.6	2,674.9	1,388.9	0.0	3,865.6	2,577.1	1,288.5	0.0
Net deferred tax asset (liability)	$ 0.0	$ 0.0	$ 0.0	$0.0	$ 0.0	$ 97.8	$ 100.3	$0.0

Free cash flow schedule:

Simple Lease Example	Operating Lease Actual Year 0	Operating Lease Forecast Year 1	Operating Lease Forecast Year 2	Operating Lease Forecast Year 3	Finance Lease Actual Year 0	Finance Lease Forecast Year 1	Finance Lease Forecast Year 2	Finance Lease Forecast Year 3	Total Operating Lease	Total Finance Lease
Earnings before interest and taxes	$0.0	$3,000.0	$3,000.0	$3,000.0	$ 0.0	$3,704.8	$3,704.8	$3,704.8	$9,000.0	$11,114.5
− Income taxes on EBIT	0	−900.0	−900.0	−900.0	0	−1,111.5	−1,111.5	−1,111.5	−2,700.0	−3,334.4
Earnings before interest and after taxes	$0.0	$2,100.0	$2,100.0	$2,100.0	$ 0.0	$2,593.4	$2,593.4	$2,593.4	$6,300.0	$7,780.2
− Change in required cash		0	0	0		0	0	0	0	0
+ Right-of-use lease asset amortization						4,295.2	4,295.2	4,295.2	0	12,885.5
+ Change in operating lease liability									0	0
+ Deferred tax adjustment						−97.8	−2.5	100.3	0	0
Unlevered cash flow from operations	$0.0	$2,100.0	$2,100.0	$2,100.0	$ 0.0	$6,790.7	$6,886.0	$6,988.9	$6,300.0	$20,665.6
− Capital lease increases (CAPEX)					−12,885.5				0	−12,885.5
Unlevered free cash flow	$0.0	$2,100.0	$2,100.0	$2,100.0	−$12,885.5	$6,790.7	$6,886.0	$6,988.9	$6,300.0	$7,780.2
Implicit interest on finance leases	0	0	0	0	0	−1,030.8	−713.3	−370.4	0	−2,114.5
Interest tax shield	0	0	0	0	0	309.3	214.0	111.1	0	634.4
Free cash flow minus after-tax interest	$0.0	$2,100.0	$2,100.0	$2,100.0	−$12,885.5	$6,069.2	$6,386.7	$6,729.6	$6,300.0	$6,300.0
Change in finance lease liability					12,885.5	−3,969.2	−4,286.7	−4,629.6	0	0
Equity free cash flow	$0.0	$2,100.0	$2,100.0	$2,100.0	$ 0.0	$2,100.0	$2,100.0	$2,100.0	$6,300.0	$6,300.0

2014 - Cost of Capital - $\beta_E = 1.5$, $\beta_D = 0.5$, $\frac{V_D}{V_F} = \frac{1}{3}$ (annual refinancing), $T_C = 40\%$, $r_F = 5\%$, $E(r_m) - r_F = 4\%$, $E(r_m) = 7\%$, UFCF = 100 for perpetuity

2\. (a) $r_{UA} = ? \rightarrow r_{UA} = 7.68\%$

(b) $r_{UA} = 10\%$, $r_E = ?$, $\frac{V_D}{V_F} = 0.5$, $r_D = 7\%$ (continuous refinancing) $\rightarrow r_E = 13\%$

(c) $V_E = ? \rightarrow V_F = 1162.711$, $V_E = V_F(0.5) = 581.395$, $r_{WACC} = 8.6\%$

(d) $PV(ITS) = ? \rightarrow PV(ITS) = V_{levered} - V_{unlevered} = \frac{FCF}{r_{WACC}} - \frac{FCF}{r_{UA}} = \frac{100}{0.086} - \frac{100}{0.1} = 162.791k$

or $PV(ITS) = \frac{(T_C)(r_D)(V_D)}{(1+r_{UA})^t} = \frac{(0.4)(0.07)(581.395)}{0.1 \rightarrow \text{perpetuity}} = 162.791k$

4\. Cap. Structure - UFCF = 250 for 3 yrs, $T_C = 40\%$, $r_{UA} = 13\%$

(a) $\frac{V_D}{V_F} = 25\%$, $r_D = 7\%$, $V_F = ? \rightarrow r_E = 15\%$, $r_{WACC} = 12.3\%$, $V_F = \frac{250}{1.123} + \frac{250}{1.123^2} + \frac{250}{1.123^3} = 597.4$

(b) $V_{ITS} = ?$ $V_{D,t} = (V_{F,t}) / \left(\frac{V_D}{V_F}\right)$

for each year $V_{D,0} = (V_{F,0})\left(\frac{V_D}{V_F}\right) = (597.4)(0.25) = 149.344 \rightarrow ITS_0 = (T_C)(r_D)(V_D) = (0.4)(0.07)(149.344)$

$V_{D,1} = \left(\frac{250}{1.123} + \frac{250}{1.123^2}\right)(0.25) = 105.2 \rightarrow ITS_1 = (0.4)(0.07)(105.2) = 2.946$

$V_{D,2} = \left(\frac{250}{1.123}\right)(0.25) = 55.654 \rightarrow ITS_2 = (0.4)(0.07)(55.654) = 1.558$

After mastering the material in this chapter, you will be able to:

1. Adjust a discounted cash flow valuation for the expected issuance of stock-based compensation (12.1)
2. Adjust a discounted cash flow valuation for a company's previously issued and outstanding stock-based compensation and other equity-linked securities (12.2)
3. Value warrants and employee stock options, and other option-based equity-linked securities to allocate total equity to common equity and options (12.3)
4. Measure the cost of capital of warrants and employee stock options and unlever the cost of capital of companies with warrants and employee stock options (12.4)
5. Analyze the debt and option components of convertible debt and measure its cost of capital (12.5)

The Effects of Stock-Based Compensation and Other Equity-Linked Securities on Discounted Cash Flow Valuations

CHAPTER 12

Synergy Pharmaceuticals Inc.[1]—uses various employee stock options and restricted stock units to recruit, retain, and incent employees. It also issued warrants when it issued stock and issued convertible debt. The company describes these securities in its 10-K report:

SYNERGY PHARMACEUTICALS INC.

Share-Based Compensation

We rely heavily on incentive compensation in the form of stock options to recruit, retain and motivate directors, executive officers, employees and consultants. Incentive compensation in the form of stock options and restricted stock units is designed to provide long-term incentives, develop and maintain an ownership stake and conserve cash during our development stage. . . .

Share-based compensation is recognized as an expense in the financial statements based on the grant date fair value. Upon adoption of ASC Topic 718 "Compensation—Stock Compensation," we selected the Black-Scholes option pricing model as the most appropriate model for determining the estimated fair value for stock-based awards. . . . (2014 10-K, p. 38)

Warrants

We have issued common stock warrants in connection with the execution of certain equity financings. . . . The fair value of warrants deemed to be derivative instruments is determined using the Black-Scholes or Binomial option-pricing models using varying assumptions regarding volatility of our common share price, remaining life of the warrant, and risk-free interest rates at each period end. . . . (2014 10-K, p. 39)

Convertible Debt—7.50% Convertible Senior Notes due 2019

The notes are unsecured, senior obligations and bear interest at a rate of 7.50% per year, payable semiannually . . . The notes are convertible, at any time, into shares of our common stock at an initial conversion rate of 321.5434 shares per $1,000 principal amount of notes, which is equivalent to an initial conversion price of $3.11 per share. The net proceeds from this offering were approximately $187.3 million, after deducting estimated expenses and the initial purchasers' discount. (2014 10-K, p. 35)

[1] Synergy Pharmaceuticals Inc. is a biopharmaceutical company focused primarily on the development of drugs to treat gastrointestinal, or GI, disorders and diseases; see Synergy Pharmaceuticals Inc.'s 2014 10-K report, pp. 38–39.

CHAPTER ORGANIZATION

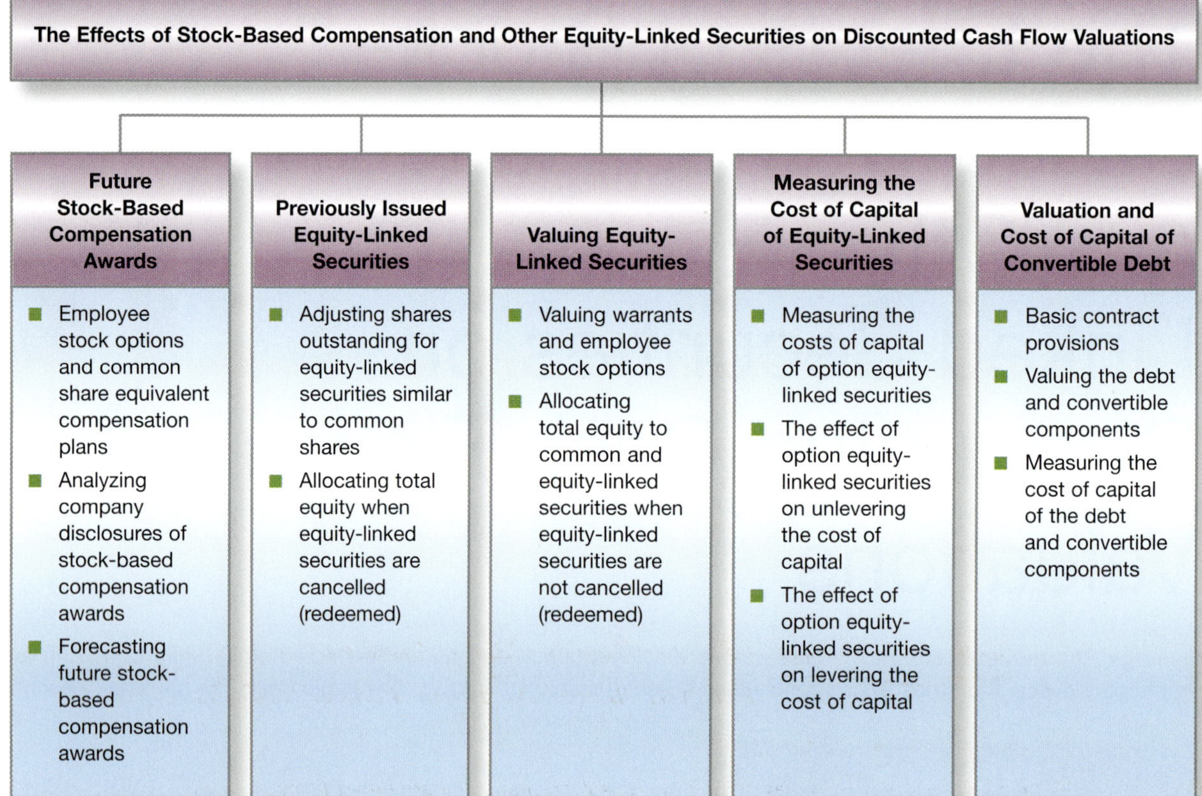

INTRODUCTION

Companies use stock-based compensation (a form of equity-linked securities) of various types as part of the total compensation paid to certain employees. The goals of such compensation plans are typically to attract and retain employees as well as to better align the incentives of employees to those of the company's shareholders. While stock-based compensation is a non-cash transaction on the date it is awarded to the employee, it is, of course, dilutive to the company's equity value. Thus, we adjust a DCF valuation for the dilution of the company's common equity in two ways. First, we adjust the forecasted free cash flows in a DCF valuation for the dilution of the company's common equity that results from the expected issuance of future stock-based compensation (after the valuation date). Second, we adjust a DCF valuation for the dilution of the company's common equity that results from stock-based compensation previously awarded and outstanding as of the valuation date.

We use the term **equity-linked security** to represent both the contracts underpinning stock-based compensation plans such as employee stock options and restricted stock units as well as other types of equity-linked securities such as warrants and convertible securities used as part of a company's capital structure strategy (see the opening vignette about Synergy Pharmaceuticals, Inc.). The goals of issuing such securities, which we discuss later in the chapter, vary across the different securities. Like employee stock options, we also adjust a DCF valuation for the dilution of the company's common equity that results from these other types of equity-linked securities previously issued and outstanding as of the valuation date. However, we do not make the same adjustment to the forecasted free cash flows for these securities that we make for the future issuance of employee stock options or restricted stock because the company issues these securities as part of its capital structure strategy and not as payment for compensation or some other operating expense.

Adjusting a DCF valuation for the dilution of the company's common equity that results from stock-based compensation and other equity-linked securities previously awarded and outstanding as of the valuation date requires an allocation of the value of the company's total equity to its common equity and each of its equity-linked securities. This allocation is straightforward if we measure the value of the company's equity using a DCF valuation and the company's equity-linked securities will be cancelled (redeemed) at the implied stock price, which is often the situation in an acquisition. However, this allocation requires a valuation model to value the equity-linked securities if we measure the value of the company's equity using a DCF valuation and the company's equity-linked securities will not be cancelled (redeemed).

Lastly, measuring the cost of capital for a company's equity-linked securities can also be relevant in a DCF valuation when using comparable companies or the company of interest to measure the unlevered cost of capital, if they have a significant proportion of their capital structure composed of equity-linked securities. For such companies, the equity cost of capital already reflects the effects of the equity-linked securities. This issue arises for companies that use a substantial amount of employee stock options, warrants, or convertible debt and convertible preferred stock as part of their capital structure strategy. It turns out that ignoring the cost of capital for the equity-linked securities for such a company understates its unlevered cost of company. This issue also arises when measuring a company's weighted average cost of capital when using a company's observed equity cost of capital.

We discuss each of these issues in this chapter—adjusting a DCF valuation for the company's equity-linked securities previously issued and outstanding as of the valuation date, adjusting a DCF valuation for the dilution of the company's common equity that results from the expected issuance of future stock-based compensation (after the valuation date), and valuing and measuring the costs of capital for equity-linked securities.

12.1 ADJUSTING DISCOUNTED CASH FLOW VALUATIONS FOR THE EXPECTED ISSUANCE OF FUTURE STOCK-BASED COMPENSATION

LO1 Adjust a discounted cash flow valuation for the expected issuance of stock-based compensation

Companies often compensate employees using compensation plans that are either directly or indirectly related to the performance of the companies' common stock, called **stock-based compensation** or **share-based compensation** or **equity-based compensation** plans. The goals of such compensation plans are typically to attract and retain employees as well as better align the incentives of employees with the company's shareholders (see Valuation in Practice 12.1). In some stock-based plans, the company uses stock market performance or other measures believed to be related to stock market performance in order to pay cash bonuses to the employees. The cash bonus may be deferred and may require certain service or other performance requirements before it is paid. Regardless of the specific type of stock-based compensation, a company incurs an economic cost when it grants stock-based compensation to its employees even if no cash flows occur at the grant date or even anytime in the future. In this section, we consider how to include the economic cost of future grants of stock-based compensation into a DCF valuation. We first begin with an overview of the common types of stock-based compensation.

VALUATION IN PRACTICE 12.1

Intel Corp. Intel explains why it uses stock-based compensation in its 2014 10-K report:

> **We must attract, retain, and motivate key employees.**
> To be competitive, we must attract, retain, and motivate executives and other key employees. Hiring and retaining qualified executives, scientists, engineers, technical staff, and sales representatives are critical to our business, and competition for experienced employees can be intense. To help attract, retain, and motivate qualified employees, we use share-based and other performance-based incentive awards such as restricted stock units and cash bonuses. If our share-based or other compensation programs cease to be viewed as competitive and valuable benefits, our ability to attract, retain, and motivate employees could be weakened, which could harm our results of operations.

Source: Intel Corp. 2014 10-K report, p. 23; Intel manufactures and sells semiconductor chips and related products globally.

In stock-based compensation plans that are settled by issuing stock, the company does not pay the employee in cash; in fact, it may have a cash inflow as a result of paying an employee with this type of compensation (for example, when employees purchase stock by exercising stock options). Regardless of whether the company settles the stock-based compensation with stock or cash, the common shareholders have borne an economic cost as of the date the stock-based compensation is awarded. Even if companies settle the stock-based compensation with stock, companies sometimes repurchase shares in anticipation of issuing shares to employees, which results in a cash outflow for the company.

When we value a company, we adjust our valuation for all forms of compensation paid to employees. If the company incurs an economic cost for compensating an employee, we adjust our valuation, financial model, and free cash flows for that economic cost even if it does not involve a direct cash outflow. As we discussed in Chapter 4, we adjust our valuation for cash compensation by including forecasts for all of its forms (annual salaries, bonuses, and hourly wages) in the free cash flow forecasts via the income statement and balance sheet forecasts. For equity-based compensation, we make equivalent adjustments, but they are not as straightforward as cash compensation adjustments. To begin, we discuss equity-based compensation in general and then discuss the types of adjustments we make for future grants of equity-based compensation.

Overview of Stock-Based Compensation

One type of equity-based compensation is **employee stock options**, where the company issues stock options to its employees—giving them rights to purchase a specified number of shares at a specific price (**exercise** or **strike price**) during a certain period. Another similar type of stock-based compensation is **stock appreciation rights (SAR)**, which grants the employee the right to receive the value of the appreciation of a share of stock from the grant date to the expiration date. The company can typically settle the amount owed the employee in cash, common stock, or even some other type of security. These awards typically vest over three to five years and the employee has the right to exercise the option or receive the appreciation in the stock over a longer time period than the vesting period, often seven to ten years from the date of grant.

The accounting for equity-based compensation consists of valuing the stock-based compensation and recording it as an expense over the vesting period, adjusting for any expected forfeitures or cancellations. A company usually values stock options or stock appreciation rights using the Black-Scholes or Merton option pricing model (which were discussed in Chapter 9). The company records an expense over the vesting period equal to the value of the compensation at the date of grant. Companies can use either a straight-line or an accelerated form of amortization to expense the grant date value over the vesting period.

A company may also issue other types of equity-linked securities that are similar to common shares (**common share equivalents**). For example, companies award stock-based compensation such as **restricted stock**, **restricted stock units**, and **performance awards** (see Valuation in Practice 12.2). These types of stock-based compensation typically vest over a period of years or if certain performance hurdles are met. With restricted stock units and similar types of awards, the company does not actually issue any stock until they vest. Even after they vest, the company may not issue the underlying restricted stock, but may issue another type of security or pay the employee the cash equivalent value, depending on the contractual terms of the stock-based compensation plan. These types of stock-based compensation are not transferable before vesting; however, even the restricted stock has limited transferability because it is not registered with the U.S. SEC until the restrictions are lifted. For publicly traded companies, unregistered stock cannot be sold on the stock exchange until it is registered or unless it meets certain conditions.[2]

A company typically values these types of stock-based compensation by multiplying the number of shares by their value at the date of grant, which is often the underlying share price. The company expenses this value over the vesting period or at the end of the vesting period if vesting depends on meeting certain performance criteria. Once the company issues restricted stock and it vests, the restricted shares are included in the company's outstanding shares. Depending on the specifics of

[2] See Rule 144 under the Securities Act of 1933, which allows for the limited sale of such securities under the exemption set forth in Section 4(1) of the Securities Act.

the compensation plan, the restricted shares may or may not have dividend and voting rights while restricted.

In the U.S., the tax effects of stock options and stock appreciation rights are similar. At the date of exercise, exercising the option or stock appreciation right results in taxable income to the employee. The taxable income is based on the difference between the market value of the stock on the exercise date and the exercise price for an option and on the appreciation in the stock's value from the grant date for a stock appreciation right. The exercise also results in a tax deduction for the corporation in the same amount. To be somewhat more precise, here we refer to non-qualified stock options that are issued with a strike or exercise price that is no lower than the company's current stock price (out-of-the-money). Companies can also issue qualified stock options (also called incentive stock options) that are treated differently, and corporations can issue non-qualified options that are in-the-money.

VALUATION IN PRACTICE 12.2

Yahoo Inc. Yahoo uses various forms of stock-based compensation as discussed in its 2014 10-K report:

> **Stock Plans.** The Stock Plan provides for the issuance of stock-based awards to employees, including executive officers, and consultants. The Stock Plan permits the granting of incentive stock options, non-statutory stock options, restricted stock, restricted stock units, stock appreciation rights, and dividend equivalents. . . .
>
> The Stock Plan permits the granting of restricted stock and restricted stock units (collectively referred to as "restricted stock awards"). The restricted stock award vesting criteria are generally the passing of time, meeting certain performance-based objectives, or a combination of both, and continued employment through the vesting period (which varies but generally does not exceed four years). Restricted stock award grants are generally measured at fair value on the date of grant based on the number of shares granted and the quoted price of the Company's common stock. Such value is recognized as an expense over the corresponding service period. . . .
>
> Options granted under the Directors' Plan before May 25, 2006 generally become exercisable, based on continued service as a director, . . . Such options generally expire seven to 10 years after the grant date. . . . Restricted stock units granted under the Directors' Plan generally vest in equal quarterly installments over a one-year period following the date of grant . . . Non-employee directors are also permitted to elect an award of restricted stock units or a stock option under the Directors' Plan in lieu of a cash payment of their quarterly Board retainer and any cash fees for serving on committees of the Board. Such stock options or restricted stock unit awards granted in lieu of cash fees are fully vested on the grant date.
>
> From time to time, the Company also assumes stock-based awards in connection with corporate mergers and acquisitions, which awards become payable in shares of the Company's common stock.

Source: Yahoo Inc. 2014 10-K report, pp. 135–136; Yahoo is a multinational technology company that offers a Web portal, search engines, email, market information, mapping, and various other online products and services.

Most corporations issue non-qualified stock options that are out-of-the-money or at-the-money (strike price is greater than or equal to the stock price when issued). With a qualified stock option, the corporation receives no tax deduction, and when the stock is sold, the employee only pays capital gains taxes on the difference between the market value of the stock and the exercise price. If an option is issued in-the-money, it is automatically non-qualified. In this case, the employee pays income tax on the difference between the market value and the exercise price whenever the option vests (not at exercise) and the company receives a tax deduction.

For restricted stock or restricted stock units, the employee pays a tax based on the fair market value of the stock whenever the restricted stock or restricted stock unit (or their equivalent) vests, and the company receives a deduction for the same amount at the same time.[3]

[3] An employee can make a section 83(b) election, which will cause the employee's entire grant to be taxed at the date of grant based on the grant date value. If those restricted stock units never vest, the employee does not get a refund of the tax. If the 83(b) election is made, the company gets the entire tax deduction at the date of grant (not at the date of vesting). There are also certain deferrals of tax on restricted stock in some cases for private companies. We ignore both of these alternative treatments in subsequent discussions on the taxation of restricted stock.

Analysis of Financial Statement Disclosures of Stock-Based Compensation

As we discussed in the previous section, in the U.S., companies record an expense over the vesting period of stock-based compensation, which is equal to the value of the compensation at the date of grant. Companies provide various disclosures related to stock-based compensation. The income statement includes the amount of the expense for stock-based compensation on the relevant line items (cost of goods sold, SG&A, R&D, etc.) as well as a reduction in the provision for income taxes (and an increase in a deferred tax asset in the balance sheet related to that expense). The statement of cash flows includes an add back of non-cash compensation expense in the operating section, and potentially an adjustment for the excess tax benefits from stock-based awards and proceeds from the exercise of stock options in the financing section. The statement of shareholders' equity also includes any cash settlements for vested or exercised stock-based compensation. A company's footnotes accompanying its financial statements provide more detailed information about a company's stock-based compensation activities in a year. For example, for each plan: a company must describe the general terms of the plan and disclose the number of stock-based compensation awards outstanding at the beginning and end of the fiscal year; the weighted average exercise price (if any), and contractual life of the awards granted, cancelled, forfeited, expired and vested/exercised; and the value of the awards granted in the current year. In this section we use Google, Inc.[4] to illustrate the disclosures companies provide about the effect of share-based compensation on their income and cash flow statements.

Google Inc.'s Income Statement. In Exhibit 12.1, we present Google's summarized income statement. We show Google's reported numbers in the first column of that exhibit, which include the share-based compensation expenses. In the second column, we show a common-sized income statement based on the reported numbers. In the third column, we show the share-based expenses and tax effects that Google reports in its footnote disclosures, and in the fourth column, we show what percentage of the reported number for a given line on the income statement comes from share-based compensation expense. Google includes stock-based expenses in four expense categories—cost of sales (2%), research and development (22%), sales and marketing (9%), and general and administrative (12%). Overall, Google's stock-based expenses decreased its pre-tax income from operations by 24% relative to what it would have reported had it not had to expense its share-based compensation. Without its equity-based compensation expense, Google's net income to revenue would have been 26% instead of 21% that they reported.

EXHIBIT 12.1 Google Inc.'s 2014 Summary Income Statement and the Effects of Stock-Based Compensation

Year Ended December 31, 2014 (in millions)	Reported Including Stock-Based Compensation	% of Revenue	Stock-Based Compensation*	% of Line Item	Reported Excluding Stock-Based Compensation	% of Revenue
Revenues	$66,001				$66,001	
Cost of revenues	−$25,691	−39%	$ 535	2%	−$25,156	−38%
Research and development	−9,832	−15%	2,200	22%	−7,632	−12%
Sales and marketing	−8,131	−12%	715	9%	−7,416	−11%
General and administrative	−5,851	−9%	725	12%	−5,126	−8%
Total costs and expenses	−$49,505	−75%	$4,175	8%	−$45,330	−69%
Income from operations	$16,496	25%	$4,175	25%	$20,671	31%
Interest and other income, net	763	1%	0	0%	763	1%
Pre-tax income from continuing operations	$17,259	26%	$4,175	24%	$21,434	32%
Provision for income taxes	−3,331	−5%	−867	26%	−4,198	−6%
Net income from continuing operations	$13,928	21%	$3,308	24%	$17,236	26%

*Excludes $104 million of stock-based compensation related to discontinued operations; total stock based compensation is equal to $4,279 ($4,279 = $104 + $4,175).

[4] The exhibits from Google were summarized from Google's 2014 10-K report.

Google Inc.'s Cash Flow Statement. In Exhibit 12.2, we present Google's summarized cash flow statement. Google's cash flow statement includes four line items related to its stock-based compensation plans. Two of these line items appear in the calculation of cash flow from operations. The first line item is an add-back for "stock-based compensation expense." Companies record an expense for stock-based compensation over the vesting period based on the value of the stock-based compensation as of the grant date. Google recorded over $4 billion for stock-based compensation in 2014 (see Exhibit 12.1). Stock-based compensation expense is a non-cash expense and as such, is added back to net income to calculate cash flow from operations.

The next line item is the "excess tax benefits from stock-based awards." Recall that although a company does not actually get the tax deduction for employee stock options until the employee exercises the option and pays tax on the gain, the company records a deferred tax asset when it records stock-based compensation expense based on the value of the stock-based compensation on the grant date. The excess tax benefits from stock-based awards occur when the actual tax benefit received on the exercise date is larger than the benefit recorded through the deferred income tax asset. The excess tax benefits from stock-based awards reduce the company's income tax expense and taxes to be paid in the current year. Accounting rules, however, require companies to classify this benefit as a cash flow from financing activities because it related to a previously issued security (issued on the grant date). Thus, excess tax benefits from stock-based awards are subtracted from cash flows from operations and reclassified as financing in the financing section of the cash flow statement.

EXHIBIT 12.2 Google Inc.'s 2014 Summary Cash Flow Statement and the Effects of Stock-Based Compensation

Year Ended December 31, 2014 (in millions)	Reported
Operating activities	
Net income	$14,444
Adjustments:	
Depreciation expense and loss on disposals	3,523
Amortization and impairment	1,456
Stock-based compensation expense	4,279
Excess tax benefits from stock-based awards	−648
Deferred income taxes	−104
Gains and other	−938
Changes in assets and liabilities:	
Accounts receivable, prepayments, and other assets	−1,182
Income taxes, net	283
Accounts payable, accrued expenses, other liabilities	1,193
Deferred and accrued revenue share	70
Net cash provided by operating activities	$22,376
Investing activities	
Purchases of property and equipment	−$10,959
Acquisitions, net of cash acquired, and purchases of intangibles and other assets	−4,888
Proceeds from divestiture of businesses	386
Net investments in securities and other	−5,594
Net cash used in investing activities	−$21,055
Financing activities	
Net payments related to stock-based award activities	−$ 2,069
Excess tax benefits from stock-based award activities	648
Net change in debt	−18
Net cash provided by (used in) financing activities	−$ 1,439
Effect of exchange rate changes	−$ 433
Net increase (decrease) in cash and cash equivalents	−$ 551
Cash and cash equivalents at beginning of period	18,898
Cash and cash equivalents at end of period	$18,347

The other two line items appear in the financing section of Google's cash flow statement. The first line item, "net payments related to stock-based compensation," represents the cash paid by Google to settle some of its share-based compensation that vested that year. Companies can often settle stock-based compensation when exercised with cash or other securities, and this line item represents the stock-based compensation Google settled in cash. Google also received cash proceeds from the exercise of stock options which must have gone into the calculation of "net payments related to stock-based compensation." Sometimes you will see a line item for proceeds from the exercise of stock options or proceeds from the issuance of equity in the financing section that reflects proceeds from the exercise of stock options. The last line item is the reclassified excess tax benefits from stock-based awards from operating to financing.

Naturally, the valuation issue is measuring a company's free cash flows and whether or not the issue is sufficiently important to consider. Google's income statement indicates a relatively large stock-based compensation expense in 2014. While its 2014 expense was larger than previous years, Google disclosed that it estimates stock-based compensation expense will be around $4.3 billion in 2015 and $5.5 billion in 2016 related to stock awards outstanding as of December 31, 2014, which does not include future awards. Thus, stock-based compensation appears to be a relevant factor for assessing Google's valuation, which requires an adjustment for the economic cost resulting from the stock-based compensation.

Google Inc.'s Free Cash Flows. In Exhibit 12.3, we present Google's free cash flow schedule. For purposes of this analysis, we treat the gains (losses), interest and other income, net, and net investments in securities and other, as related to Google's excess assets and do not include their effects in the free cash flow calculation.

The first column of the free cash flow schedule measures Google's free cash flows using the treatment of the equity-based grant expense in its cash flow statement—that is, adding back stock-based compensation expense or $4,279 because it is a non-cash expense. These adjustments—stock-based compensation expense and the excess tax benefit from stock-based compensation—are the adjustments on Google's cash flow statement. The deferred income tax effect of the stock-based compensation is not disclosed separately in Google's income or cash flow statements but it is available in Google's accompanying footnote disclosures, and amounts to $889.

In the second column of the free cash flow schedule, we adjust free cash flows by removing the related adjustments in Google's cash flow statement for stock-based compensation, and the deferred tax effects related to its stock-based compensation. Thus, we treat the share-based compensation and its tax effect as having cash flow consequences (a cash outflow) in the calculation of Google's free cash flows. We do not reverse the adjustment for the excess tax benefit from share-based compensation as this adjustment is from previously granted options that are being exercised, not from new option grants; however, forecasts for this item should be zero for future option grants.

Since stock-based compensation expense and the related deferred income tax effect are not cash flows, we reclassify these adjustments as the equivalent of issuing a form of common equity. In other words, we treat stock-based compensation as two events—a cash expense equal to the after-tax stock-based compensation expense and the issuance of a form of equity, essentially, assuming the employee was paid cash compensation and purchased options from the company. These adjustments reconcile the equity free cash flows to the change in the company's cash balance. Our treatment of the stock-based compensation reduces Google's unlevered free cash flow and equity free cash flow by over $3 billion (over 57%). If Google's numbers for this year are representative of the proportionate annual effect of its stock-based compensation on its free cash flows, a valuation of Google would be substantially lower than it would have been had we ignored these effects.

Valuation Key 12.1

Companies often compensate employees using compensation plans that are either directly or indirectly related to the performance of the companies' common stock, called stock-based compensation, in an attempt to attract and retain employees as well as better align the incentives of employees with the shareholders. A company incurs an economic cost when it grants stock-based compensation to its employees even if no cash flows occur.

EXHIBIT 12.3 Google Inc.'s 2014 Summary Free Cash Flow Statement and the Effects of Stock-Based Compensation

Free Cash Flow Schedule ($ in millions)	Based on Reported	Reported Numbers Adjusted	Difference	
Earnings before interest and taxes (EBIT)	$16,496	$16,496	$ —	
Income taxes paid on EBIT	−3,184	−3,184	0	
Earnings before interest and after taxes	$13,312	$13,312	$ 0	
Depreciation and amortization	4,979	4,979	0	
Excess tax benefit from share-based compensation	−648	−648	0	
Share-based compensation	4,279	0	4,279	
Deferred income taxes	−104	785	−889	
Other, net	−938	−938	0	
Adjustments for operating working capital, net	364	364	0	
Change in required cash balance (assumed)	100	100	0	
Unlevered cash flow from operations	$21,344	$17,954	$3,390	−15.9%
Additions to property, plant and equipment	−15,847	−15,847	0	
Proceeds from divestitures, net and other	386	386	0	
Unlevered free cash flow	$ 5,883	$2,493	$3,390	−57.6%
Interest expense	0	0	0	
Interest tax shield	0	0	0	
Cash flow before non-common equity financing changes	$ 5,883	$ 2,493	$3,390	
Change in debt, net	−18	−18	0	
Equity free cash flow	$ 5,865	$ 2,475	$3,390	−57.8%
Interest and other income, net	1,132	1,132	0	
Net investments in securities and other	−5,594	−5,594	0	
Effect of exchange rate changes	−433	−433	0	
Cash flow before cash flows to/from common	$ 970	−$ 2,420	$3,390	
Change in common stock, net			0	
Excess tax benefit from share-based compensation	648	648	0	
Net payments related to stock-based award activities	−2,069	−2,069	0	
Share-based compensation		4,279	−4,279	
Deferred income taxes (share-based compensation)		−889	889	
Common dividends			0	
Change in excess cash	−$ 451	−$ 451	$ 0	
Change in required cash balance	−100	−100	0	
Change in cash balance	−$ 551	−$ 551	$ 0	

Forecasting the Issuance and Free Cash Flow Effects of Future Stock-Based Compensation

It is clear that regardless of the specific type of stock-based compensation, a company incurs an economic cost when it grants stock-based compensation even if no cash flows occur at the grant date. Stock-based compensation has two—either direct or indirect—effects on the company's free cash flows. The first effect, an indirect effect on cash flows, is the economic cost of the equity-based compensation resulting from the expected dilution of the existing equity. The second effect, a direct effect on cash flows, is the income tax benefits the company receives from the stock-based compensation.

The effect of the expected dilution of the existing equity is an indirect effect on the company's cash flows because it does not directly reduce free cash flows. The actual dilution of the equity results from increasing the number of common shares outstanding, which does not occur on the grant date. The implicit effect on cash flow is the cost to the company to repurchase shares of stock so that it can reissue those shares to settle the equity-based compensation contract at the exercise date, net of any proceeds received from the exercise of stock options. Those cash flow effects require a forecast of the company's stock price at both the grant date and exercise date. For share equivalent stock-based compensation, the actual dilution occurs on the date it vests. For option stock-based compensation, the actual dilution occurs on the date the employee exercises the option. In a DCF valuation, however, the relevant dilution for a valuation is the expected dilution and not the actual dilution that occurs.

Once we forecast the economic cost from the dilution, forecasting the tax benefit is less difficult. Companies receive the tax benefit when either the stock-based compensation vests or is exercised, which we implicitly or possibly explicitly forecast when we forecast the economic cost of the dilution. However, just as we discussed the effect of net operating loss carryforwards on interest tax shields, they can have a similar effect on the tax benefit from stock-based compensation. Research shows that some companies cannot use the tax deduction from the exercise of the options.[5]

In this section, we illustrate some of the potential ways to forecast the economic effects of future stock-based compensation. The most appropriate method to use, of course, depends on the specific facts and circumstances, and the valuation context for a specific valuation.

Expected Dilution from Share Equivalent Stock-Based Compensation. For share equivalent stock-based compensation, the actual dilution occurs on the date it vests but the DCF valuation model requires a forecast of the expected, not the actual, dilution. The dilution is equal to the number of shares issued (or that must be issued) on the vesting date. Assume we are valuing a firm as of the end of Year 0 using the DCF valuation model. As part of the valuation, we are forecasting the expected dilution that will occur from restricted stock units that are expected to be granted at the end of Year 1. Further, assume these restricted stock units vest at the end of Year 2, at which time the company will issue the common shares.

In order to forecast the expected dilution, we first forecast the expected number of units that will vest. Not all of the restricted stock units granted will vest because some employees will leave the company before the vesting date or not meet other vesting criteria. Next, we forecast the company's expected stock price as of the vesting date, Year 2. The expected stock price as of the vesting date measures the expected cost of the dilution of the equity and thus, the resulting indirect effect on the company's free cash flows, for each restricted stock unit as of the end of Year 2. The company's potential tax benefit from this grant is based on the value of the restricted stock unit as of the vesting date, Year 2.

Since the value of the company's stock as of the end of Year 1 is equal to the present value of the company's stock as of the end of Year 2, we can measure the expected cost of the dilution and tax benefit using the value of the restricted stock units on the grant date. The present value of the economic cost of the expected dilution from share equivalent stock-based compensation is equal to the value of the restricted stock units on the grant date. The value of the restricted stock units on the grant date is equal to the expected number of restricted stock units that will vest multiplied by the company's expected share price on that date. The expected tax benefit is equal to the value of the restricted stock units on the grant date that will vest multiplied by the appropriate tax rate.

Given that the expense is recorded over the vesting period, the accounting for share equivalent stock-based compensation and their valuation impact do not have a one-to-one correspondence. In other words, the present value of the expense recorded will be less than the value of the grant. If a firm is in steady-state with respect to the amount of share equivalent stock-based compensation it is awarding, this is not an issue, but it will be an issue if share equivalent stock-based compensation is increasing or decreasing over time.

Expected Dilution from Option Stock-Based Compensation. For option stock-based compensation, the actual dilution occurs on the date the employee exercises the option. Of course, no dilution occurs if the employee does not exercise the option. The actual dilution is equal to the number of shares issued minus the shares that can be repurchased from the cash paid for those shares based on the strike price. For example, if an employee exercises 150 options with a strike price of \$10, when the company's stock price is \$15, then the dilution is 50 shares or \$750 [$50 = 150 - (150 \times \$10)/\$15$; $\$750 = 150 \times (\$15 - \$10)$]. However, the DCF valuation model requires a forecast of the expected, not the actual, dilution.

Like share equivalent stock-based compensation, in order to forecast the expected dilution, we first forecast the expected number of options that will vest. Next, we forecast the company's expected stock price as of the grant date, Year 1, which is the likely strike price for the options awarded. We also forecast the company's stock price as of the exercise date. The employee can typically exercise the option during

[5] Sullivan estimated that the tax deductions for options exceeded net income for eight of the forty largest U.S. companies in 2000, including, Microsoft, AOL, Cisco Systems, Amgen, Dell Computer, Sun Microsystems, Qualcomm, and Lucent; see, Sullivan, M, "Stock Options Take \$50 Billion Bite Out of Corporate Taxes," *Tax Notes*, (March 2002), pp. 1396–1401.

a specified period of time. In our discussion here, we assume the employee will exercise the options on the last day during that period. The difference between the expected stock price and the expected strike price on the exercise date, called **intrinsic value**, measures the expected cost of dilution of the equity and thus, the indirect effect on the company's free cash flows, for each option as of the exercise date. The company's potential tax benefit from each of these options is equal to the expected intrinsic value on the exercise date (that is, the difference between the expected stock price and the expected strike price on the exercise date) multiplied by the appropriate tax rate.

The value of the option on the grant date, which is, approximately, the present value of the expected intrinsic value on the exercise date, can be measured directly using various option pricing models. Thus, the expected dilution from option stock-based compensation, and the related effect on the company's free cash flows, is equal to the value of the options on the grant date. The value of the options on the grant date is equal to the expected number of options that will be exercised multiplied by the value of the options on the grant date. The expected tax benefit is equal to the value of the options on the grant date multiplied by the appropriate tax rate.

As with share equivalent stock-based compensation, given that the expense is recorded over the vesting period of the options or stock appreciation rights, accounting for stock options and stock appreciation rights do not have a one-to-one correspondence to the effect they have on value. In other words, the present value of the expense recorded will be less than the value of the grant. If a firm is in steady-state with respect to the amount of option related compensation it is awarding, this is not an issue, but it will be an issue if option related compensation is increasing or decreasing over time.

Forecasting the Effect of Expected Dilution from Stock-Based Compensation on Free Cash Flows. The above discussion indicates that in order to forecast the expected effect of dilution from stock-based compensation on free cash flows, we require a valuation of the company's stock price in every year in the forecast period and for the continuing value. This is not an easy task to complete because the expected stock price at a point in time will reflect the dilution from all expected stock-based compensation that will be issued in the future. An alternative approach is to assume the company awards stock-based compensation based on some dimension of the scale or the performance of the company. For example, we might assume that a company will base the value of its stock-based compensation on its cash-compensation (labor costs), or its free cash flows (excluding stock-based compensation), or even revenues. Accounting rules require companies to disclose information that can be used to help identify such relations.

One approach for forecasting the effect of the stock-based compensation on a company's free cash flows is to analyze the company's historical expense ratios, which include its stock-based compensation expense (**expense ratio method**). Since companies include stock-based compensation expense in the income statement, forecasting all of a company's line items in its income statements in a financial model embeds the cash flow effects of equity-based compensation grants as long as they are not eliminated when measuring the company's free cash flows. For example, for Google (see Exhibit 12.1), its research and development expense is 15% of revenues including stock-based compensation expense. Of that 15%, 3% is related to stock-based compensation expense. The choice of the expense ratio depends on the information available and which of the alternative scaling factors is best to forecast the stock-based compensation expense. As noted previously however, the accounting for stock-based compensation requires the expense to be amortized over the vesting period, and is not fully recognized at the date of grant.[6]

An alternative approach is to use the company's footnote disclosures to identify the value of the stock-based compensation granted in a year (**grant date value method**) to analyze the company's grant-date value ratios. To use this approach, we first eliminate the stock-based compensation expense in the income statement. We then scale the value of the stock-based compensation granted in a year, adjusted for expected forfeitures, by the best scaling factor for forecasting the value of the stock-based compensation granted in the year and use that ratio to forecast a separate line item for the value of the stock-based compensation granted in a year. The value of the stock-based compensation granted in a year is what was awarded, not what is expected to vest. We would adjust the value awarded by the percentage of awards not expected to vest.

[6] Unlike U.S. accounting rules, international financial accounting rules require companies to expense the cost of employee stock options based on the intrinsic value of the options and not the value of the options at the grant date, which makes this approach more difficult to implement. See International Financial Accounting Standards for stock-based compensation (IFRS 2, *Share-based Payment*).

Google's footnote disclosures for the year-ended December 31, 2014 indicate that it granted 15.520 million shares (restricted stock units) at a weighted-average grant-date fair value of $573.71 in 2014, indicating that Google granted $8.9 billion of restricted stock units in 2014. Google also reports that they expect 21.958 million shares to vest of the 24.619 unvested shares at December 31, 2014 for an expected vesting rate of 0.891 (0.891 = 21.958/24.619). Multiplying the 89.1% by $8.9 billion suggests that the expected value of the grants this year that will ultimately vest is $7.9 billion. For forecasting purposes, we would choose an appropriate scalar for the $7.9 billion such as a specific expense (labor) or possibly revenue. Of course, since the number and the value of the awards a company grants in a given year may fluctuate, an analysis of several years may be helpful in forecasting the awards. Note that in 2014 for Google, this approach results in a much higher estimate of the effect of share-based compensation than the $4.3 billion expensed in that year (Exhibit 12.3), suggesting that analyzing multiple years of data may be useful. For example, the lower amount could be due to Google steadily increasing the amount of equity-linked compensation over the last few years.

A third approach uses the ex post or actual value of the stock-based compensation that vested or that was exercised in a year (**exercise date value method**) to analyze the company's exercise-date value ratios. To use this approach, we again first eliminate the stock-based compensation expense in the income statement. We then scale the actual value of the stock-based compensation that vested or that was exercised in a year by the best scaling factor for forecasting the actual value of the stock-based compensation that vested or that was exercised in a year and use that ratio to forecast a separate line item for the value of the stock-based compensation granted in a year. Google disclosed in its December 31, 2014 footnote disclosures that 10.743 million shares vested in 2014. Using a weighted average value per unit in 2014 of $573.71 results in a $6.2 billion valuation of the awards that vested. This estimate is between the previous two estimates discussed, again suggesting that analyzing multiple years of data may be useful.

Naturally, each of these, and other, potential forecasting methods has tradeoffs and the choice is based on the expected future stock-based compensation awards, the valuation context, and the available information.

Assumptions Underpinning the Alternative Forecasting Methods for the Effect of the Expected Cost of Dilution from Stock-Based Compensation on Free Cash Flows. Naturally, certain assumptions underpin each of these forecasting methods. All of the methods assume that we have sufficient information and can identify reasonable forecast drivers for stock-based compensation. Our forecast models will likely evolve as we have more time-series information on the relation between grant-date value for equity-based compensation grants and other forecast drivers.[7]

The first two methods—expense ratio and grant date value approaches—assume the company correctly valued the stock-based compensation as of the grant date. Any valuation error in the stock-based compensation can cause a valuation error in the DCF valuation. Companies typically use the valuation models discussed in the accounting standards to value stock options and stock appreciation rights. These models include the Black-Scholes and Merton option pricing models and lattice models such as the binomial model. These valuation models are widely accepted models for valuing certain types of options. The models depend on certain factors (estimates of the volatility of the company's stock return, dividend yield, and risk-free rate), so we must assume that the company uses reasonable assumptions in the model. [8]

The expense ratio method assumes that the amortization of the previously granted options over their vesting period reasonably measures the value of the stock-based compensation on the grant date. If a company's stock grants are related to its scale and the firm is growing (shrinking), then stock-based compensation expense underestimates (overestimates) the value of the equity-based compensation to some degree. The effect also depends on whether the company uses an accelerated form of amortizing the grants to expense or uses a straight-line method. The second approach—grant date value approach—does not suffer from this issue but it faces other issues. If a company's stock-based compensation awards are lumpy—for example, launches a new plan every few years—then the adjustment to the free cash flows based on the grant date value method will not measure the expected effect if based on only one year. As mentioned earlier, we would likely want to look at several years of data.

---

[7] See, for example, Bettis, J., J. Bizjak, and M. Lemmon, "Exercise Behavior, Valuation and the Incentive Effect of Employee Stock Options," *Journal of Financial Economics* vol. 76 (2005), pp. 445–470.

[8] While not yet a well-developed market, some investment banks are offering products to companies that allow the company to "sell" the liability to fulfill the equity-based compensation contracts to the bank. The product allows companies to hedge the potential cost of having to repurchase stock at higher prices and address the uncertain shareholder dilution caused by equity-based compensation. If this market develops, we may be able to use third-party valuations to value a company's equity-based compensation.

The exercise date value method—the actual value approach—is based on the actual effect previously granted stock-based compensation had on free cash flows and not the expected effect it will have on free cash flows. Naturally, if the valuation models work well and we analyze a sufficiently long historical time period, we would expect the actual effect to equal the expected effect. However, if the past performance of the company's stock was unusually good (bad), the actual approach would over (under) estimate the expected effect. In sum, all of the approaches are subject to limitations and a historical analysis can shed light on the ability of each approach to reasonably forecast the effect of stock-based compensation on a company's free cash flows. The best method to use can vary across companies.

The J. J. Jones Company. The J. J. Jones Company uses restricted stock as part of the compensation paid to its employees. We begin by reviewing the following information for the J.J. Jones Company and use the expense-based, grant value-based, and the exercise date value methods to measure the company's potential forecast drivers for its stock-based compensation (restricted stock units) for Year 1. We assume the restricted stock units vest annually over three years and the appropriate way to scale stock-based compensation is (a) revenue and (b) cash labor costs.

We first calculate the amount that would be expensed in Year −1 which is equal to the units granted in Years −4, −3 and −2 multiplied by the value at the grant date in each year divided by 3 and then multiplied by the percentage expected to vest (85%). The percentage expected to vest (85%) is equal to the units expected to vest divided by each year's ending balance of the unvested units, which is 85% in every year. The amount that would be expensed in Year −1 based on the grants in Years −4, −3 and −2 is equal to $1,367 [$1,367 = (($14.19 × 105.8 + $15.04 × 106.8 + $15.94 × 107.8) × 0.85)/3]. The grant date value expected to vest in Year −1, is equal to the units granted in Year −1 (108.8) multiplied by the value at the grant date ($16.89) and by the percentage expected to vest (85%). As such, the grant date value expected to vest is $1,562 ($1,562 = $16.89 × 108.8 × 0.85). This is the expected cost of the restricted stock granted in Year −1. The value from the second calculation (grant value-based) will generally be higher than the value from the first calculation (expense-based) for a company that is growing and issuing more equity-based compensation each year. Finally, to use the exercise date value method, we calculate the restricted stock vested in Year −1 at the vesting date value, which is equal to the units vested in Year −1 (90.8) multiplied by the value at the vesting date ($16.89), which is equal to $1,534. This is the ex post cost of the value that was vested.

Restricted Stock Units	Year −4	Year −3	Year −2	Year −1	Year 0
Unvested units beginning balance	208.3	210.3	212.3	214.3	216.3
Units granted	105.8	106.8	107.8	108.8	109.8
Units vested	−88.3	−89.1	−89.9	−90.8	−91.6
Units forfeited	−15.6	−15.7	−15.9	−16.0	−16.2
Unvested units ending balance	210.3	212.3	214.3	216.3	218.3
Units expected to vest	178.7	180.4	182.1	183.8	185.6
Weighted average date value per unit					
Units granted—value at grant date	$ 14.19	$ 15.04	$ 15.94	$ 16.89	$ 17.91
Units vested—value at grant date	$ 11.91	$ 12.62	$ 13.38	$ 14.19	$ 15.04
Units vested—value at vesting date	$ 14.19	$ 15.04	$ 15.94	$ 16.89	$ 17.91
Current stock price	$ 14.19	$ 15.04	$ 15.94	$ 16.89	$ 17.91
Revenue	$15,869	$17,138	$18,509	$19,990	$21,589
Total labor costs (cash + stock-based)	$ 8,620	$ 9,223	$ 9,868	$10,559	$11,298

The final step in all three methods is to scale the above values to measure the ratio used to forecast stock based compensation. The J. J. Jones Company has two potential ways to scale the above values—revenues and labor costs. When we divide by revenue, the three different computations vary between 6.8% and 7.8%. As expected, the compensation expense to revenue yields the lowest percentage because the company is growing. When we divide by cash labor costs of $9,192, the forecast drivers range between 14.9% and 17%, again with the compensation expense to cash labor costs yielding the lowest expense ratio. Note that to calculate the cash labor costs we must take the total labor costs for Year −1 ($10,559) and subtract the compensation expense we calculated of $1,367. We summarize these calculations in the following table.

Restricted Stock Units Forecast Drivers	Year −1
RSU stock-based compensation expense	$ 1,367
Granted—Grant date value expected to vest	$ 1,562
Vested—Exercise date value	$ 1,534
Total cash labor costs	$ 9,192
Total revenue	$19,990
Units expected to vest	85.0%
Expense/Revenue	6.8%
Granted—Grant date value expected to vest/Revenue	7.8%
Vested—Exercise date value/Revenue	7.7%
Expense/Cash labor costs	14.9%
Granted—Grant date value expected to vest/Cash labor costs	17.0%
Vested—Exercise date value/Cash labor costs	16.7%

Which of the three methods and two scalars are the most appropriate to use to forecast the company's stock-based compensation? That depends on the factors the company used and its plans to use stock-based compensation in the future. Without specific information from the company, we use the historical information to make that assessment. In addition to measuring the economic cost of the restricted stock or RSU grants, we must also take into consideration their tax benefits as discussed previously.

Valuation Key 12.2

Stock-based compensation has two effects on the company's free cash flows—an indirect effect from the expected dilution of the existing equity and a direct effect from expected income tax benefits. We typically forecast both of these effects by either including stock-based compensation in the company's operating expenses or by including a separate operating expense for stock-based compensation. We describe three approaches for measuring stock-based compensation—an expense approach, a grant date approach, and an ex post exercise date approach.

REVIEW EXERCISE 12.1

Forecasting Future Stock-Based Compensation

Review the above information for the J. J. Jones Company.

a. Use the expense-based, grant value-based, and exercise date value methods to measure the company's potential forecast drivers for its stock-based compensation (restricted stock units) for Year 0, assuming the restricted stock units vest annually over three years and the appropriate way to scale stock-based compensation is (a) revenue and (b) cash labor costs.

b. Use the forecast drivers from the previous part of the problem to forecast the stock-based compensation effect on free cash flows in Year 1, assuming the forecast for revenues in Year 1 is $24,000 and the forecast for cash labor cost in Year 1 is $11,000.

Solution on page 604.

LO2 Adjust a discounted cash flow valuation for a company's previously issued and outstanding stock-based compensation and other equity-linked securities

12.2 ADJUSTING A DISCOUNTED CASH FLOW VALUATION FOR PREVIOUSLY ISSUED AND OUTSTANDING EQUITY-LINKED SECURITIES

The goal of many valuations is to not only measure the value of the firm, but also measure the value of the common stock and the corresponding stock price. We typically measure the value of the common equity by subtracting the value of the debt, preferred stock, and other non-common equity claims from the value of the firm. And we typically measure the per share price by dividing the value of the equity by the number of outstanding shares. However, when a firm previously issued and still has outstanding equity-linked securities, measuring the value of a company's common equity and the corresponding share price requires more steps, which can become somewhat complicated.

When a company previously issued and still has outstanding equity-linked securities as of the valuation date, a DCF valuation typically measures the value of a company's total equity claims (common stock, employee stock options, warrants, and convertible securities) and not just the value of the common stock. After measuring the value of the total equity, we allocate the total equity to the common equity and the equity-linked securities by adjusting the shares outstanding for equity-linked securities that are similar to common shares (for example, restricted stock) and by subtracting the value of equity-linked securities from total equity value (for example, employee stock options and warrants).

The Effect of Option-Based Equity-Linked Securities Is Already Included in the Weighted Average Cost of Capital Used in a Discounted Cash Flow Valuation

In a weighted average cost of capital DCF valuation, we typically know (assume) the proportion of the company that will be financed with debt, preferred stock, and other non-common equity claims, and the remainder of the capital structure will be equity. For example, the target capital structure might be 25% debt, 10% preferred stock, and the remaining 65% equity. We typically do not know (assume) the proportion of the equity that is common equity versus employee stock options versus other equity-linked securities. Thus, when we apply the appropriate levering formula to measure the company's equity cost of capital, we are actually measuring the company's **total equity cost of capital, r_{TE}**, which is the weighted average of the costs of capital of the common equity and all of the option-based equity-linked securities. We use warrants throughout this section as an example of the effect of option-based securities on the weighted average cost of capital.

$$r_{TE} = r_E \times \frac{V_E}{V_{TE}} + r_W \times \frac{V_W}{V_{TE}} \quad \textbf{(12.1)}$$

$$r_{TE} = r_E \times \frac{P_E \times S_E}{P_E \times S_E + P_W \times S_W} + r_W \times \frac{P_W \times S_W}{P_E \times S_E + P_W \times S_W} \quad \textbf{(12.1')}$$

If we wanted to measure r_E instead of r_{TE}, we can add a component for warrants to the levering formula in Equation 10.5 (which assumes the discount rate for interest tax shields is the unlevered cost of capital), or any of our other levering formulas. In other words, if we assume the value of a company's total equity claims is equal to the value of the common equity and the value of the company's outstanding warrants, V_W, which has a corresponding warrant cost of capital, r_W, the formula in Equation 10.5 is as follows.

$$r_E = r_{UA} + (r_{UA} - r_D) \times \frac{V_D}{V_E} + (r_{UA} - r_{PS}) \times \frac{V_{PS}}{V_E} + (r_{UA} - r_W) \times \frac{V_W}{V_E} \quad \textbf{(10.5 adjusted for warrants)}$$

If we exclude the component for warrants, the levering formula measures the total equity cost of capital, which is equal to the weighted average common equity and warrant costs of capital.[9]

[9] Using the same framework used in Chapter 10, the levering formula measures the combined or total equity cost of capital, r_{TE}, if we exclude the component for warrants:

$$r_{UA} \times V_{UA} + r_{ITS} \times V_{ITS} = r_D \times V_D + r_{PS} \times V_{PS} + r_W \times V_W + r_E \times V_E$$

$$r_E \times \frac{V_E}{V_E + V_W} + r_W \times \frac{V_W}{V_E + V_W} = r_{UA} \times \frac{V_{UA}}{V_E + V_W} + r_{ITS} \times \frac{V_{ITS}}{V_E + V_W} - r_D \times \frac{V_D}{V_E + V_W} - r_{PS} \times \frac{V_{PS}}{V_E + V_W}$$

$$r_{TE} = r_{UA} + (r_{UA} - r_D) \times \frac{V_D}{V_{TE}} + (r_{UA} - r_{PS}) \times \frac{V_{PS}}{V_{TE}} - (r_{UA} - r_{ITS}) \times \frac{V_{ITS}}{V_{TE}}$$

$$\text{For } r_{ITS} = r_{UA} \Rightarrow r_{TE} = r_{UA} + (r_{UA} - r_D) \times \frac{V_D}{V_{TE}} + (r_{UA} - r_{PS}) \times \frac{V_{PS}}{V_{TE}}$$

$$r_{TE} = r_{UA} + (r_{UA} - r_D) \times \frac{V_D}{V_{TE}} + (r_{UA} - r_{PS}) \times \frac{V_{PS}}{V_{TE}} \quad \textbf{(12.2)}$$

Most relevant to our valuation is that using the total equity cost of capital in the weighted average cost of capital formula results in the same (and appropriate) cost of capital using separate components for both the common equity and warrant costs of capital. The weighted average cost of capital formula including separate components for common equity and warrants is as follows.

$$r_{WACC} = r_E \times \frac{V_E}{V_F} + r_W \times \frac{V_W}{V_F} + r_D \times (1 - T_{INT}) \times \frac{V_D}{V_F} + r_{PS} \times \frac{V_{PS}}{V_F} \quad \textbf{(11.1)}$$

Substituting the total equity cost of capital for the common equity components results in the identical weighted average cost of capital.[10] Thus, we can measure the appropriate weighted average cost of capital as long as we know the total equity cost of capital and the other components for non-common equity securities.

$$r_{WACC} = r_{TE} \times \frac{V_{TE}}{V_F} + r_D \times (1 - T_{INT}) \times \frac{V_D}{V_F} + r_{PS} \times \frac{V_{PS}}{V_F} \quad \textbf{(12.3)}$$

It is important to note that this entire discussion assumes that we have measured the unlevered cost of capital correctly. As we discuss later in the chapter, if we are going to use the firm that has issued warrants (or options) to measure its own unlevered cost of capital, then we will need to measure the value and cost of capital of the warrants (options) in order to unlever the equity cost of capital correctly. Or if we are using comparable companies with warrants and options, we will need to measure the value and cost of capital of the warrants and options to unlever the comparable companies' equity costs of capital correctly.

Valuation Key 12.3

In a weighted average cost of capital DCF valuation, we typically know (assume) the proportion of the company that will be financed with debt, preferred stock, and the remainder of the capital structure will be equity. Thus, when measuring the equity cost of capital based on a known unlevered cost of capital, that equity cost of capital is the weighted average of all equity-linked claims, in other words, the cost of capital for total equity, r_{TE}.

Adjusting the Shares Outstanding for Outstanding Share Equivalent Equity-Linked Securities

We adjust (increase) the company's outstanding shares for equity-linked securities, generally, resulting from stock-based compensation, that have sufficiently similar characteristics to common stock (**share equivalents**). These securities generally result from stock-based compensation awards such as restricted stock, restricted stock units, and performance awards. The resulting number of shares (**equivalent outstanding shares**) adjusts the number of shares outstanding for the dilution of the common equity resulting from these types of equity-linked securities.

The first step in making the adjustment to the company's shares outstanding is to identify which of the stock-based compensation plans should be used to adjust the company's shares outstanding (equivalent outstanding shares) and which of the plans should be valued directly (option-based equity-linked securities). The second step is to measure any benefits from the income tax deductions related to the outstanding

[10] To see that Equation 12.3 is equivalent to Equation 11.1, the standard formula for measuring the weighted average cost of capital, substitute Equation 12.1 into Equation 12.3 and combine terms to derive the standard weighted average cost of capital formula, Equation 11.1 that includes warrants.

$$r_{TE} = r_E \times \frac{V_E}{V_{TE}} + r_W \times \frac{V_W}{V_{TE}}$$

$$r_{WACC} = r_E \times \frac{V_E}{V_F} + r_D \times (1 - T_{INT}) \times \frac{V_D}{V_F} + r_{PS} \times \frac{V_{PS}}{V_F} + r_W \times \frac{V_W}{V_F}$$

share equivalent equity-linked securities. The next step is to adjust the number of shares outstanding for the share equivalents resulting from the equity-linked shares outstanding, after considering the benefits from any related income tax deductions.

One way to adjust our valuation for restricted stock, restricted stock units and share-based performance awards is to add the value of the expected tax benefit to the value of the company's total equity and add the total number of common shares expected to result from the equity-linked securities to the company's outstanding shares. We first measure the value of the total equity by subtracting the value of the non-common equity claims (for example, debt and preferred stock) from the value of the firm. The value of total equity is equal to the value of the common stock plus the value of any common equity-linked securities.

$$V_{TE} = V_F - V_D - V_{PS}$$

To illustrate the adjustment for expected tax benefits not included in the DCF valuation, we assume that the value of the restricted stock is equal to the current stock price and that the present value of the future stock price is approximately equal to today's stock price. Remember that when restricted stock vests in the future, it confers a tax benefit for the firm based on the number of shares that vest multiplied by stock price at the time of vesting multiplied by the company's marginal tax rate. Therefore, the present value of the tax benefits from the existing grants of restricted stock equals the current stock price multiplied by the number of shares that we expect will vest in the future multiplied by the future marginal tax rate for the restricted stock tax benefit, T_{RS}. We add the present value of the tax benefit from the restricted stock, $P_E \times S_{RS} \times T_{RS}$, to the value of the total equity, V_{TE}, the sum of which is equal to the share price of the common equity, P_E, multiplied by the sum of the number of shares of common equity outstanding as of the valuation date, S_E, and the number of shares of restricted stock, S_{RS}.

$$V_{TE} + P_E \times S_{RS} \times T_{RS} = P_E \times S_E + P_E \times S_{RS}$$
$$V_{TE} = P_E \times S_E + P_E \times S_{RS} \times (1 - T_{RS})$$

We can restate the above formula to solve for the stock price.

$$P_E = \frac{V_{TE}}{S_E + S_{RS} \times (1 - T_{RS})}$$

Valuation Key 12.4

We adjust common shares outstanding for stock-based compensation that is the equivalent of common shares. Once we identify which of the stock-based compensation plans should be used to adjust the company's shares outstanding (equivalent outstanding shares), we measure any related benefits from the income tax deductions. We then adjust the number of shares outstanding for the share equivalents resulting from the equity-linked shares outstanding.

The Sally Company's Restricted Stock Units. Assume the DCF valuation of the Sally Company's total equity, V_{TE}, is \$100 million. The Sally Company has 8 million shares outstanding and 2 million unvested restricted stock units, which have a tax benefit equal to the value of the restricted stock multiplied by the future marginal tax rate for restricted stock units, 40%. The per share value of Sally is equal to \$10.87 per share.

$$P_E = \frac{V_{TE}}{S_E + S_{RS} \times (1 - T_{RS})} = \frac{\$100}{8 + 2 \times (1 - 0.4)} = \$10.87$$

The value of the tax benefit of the restricted shares, $P_E \times S_{RS} \times T_{RS}$, is \$8.70 million (\$8.70 = \$10.87 × 2 × 0.4). The value of the total equity including the value of the tax benefit of the restricted shares is \$108.7. Dividing the value of the total equity including the value of the tax benefit of the restricted shares by the total number of shares results in the \$10.87 share price (\$10.87 = \$108.7/(8 + 2)).

VALUATION IN PRACTICE 12.3

The Fresh Market, Inc. We use The Fresh Market Inc.[11] to illustrate the types of stock-based compensation companies use to compensate employees and members of the board of directors. Below we provide excerpts from the company's 10-K report outlining its five different stock-based compensation plans—stock options, restricted stock units, restricted stock awards, performance share awards, and performance share units.

9. Share-based Compensation

The Company grants share-based awards under the 2010 Omnibus Incentive Compensation Plan. . . .

Stock Options—2010 Omnibus Incentive Compensation Plan

Options are granted at an option price equal to the closing price of the Company's common stock on the grant date and vest in 25% annual increments on each of the first four anniversaries of the grant date. Options expire ten years from the grant date. The Company uses the Black-Scholes option pricing model to estimate the fair value of stock options at the grant date. . . .

Restricted Stock Units—2010 Omnibus Incentive Compensation Plan

The RSUs vest in 25% annual increments on each of the first four anniversaries of the grant date and the fair value is equal to the closing price of the Company's common stock on the grant date. . . .

Restricted Stock Awards for Non-Employee Directors—2010 Omnibus Incentive Compensation Plan

The Company grants RSAs to its non-employee directors. RSAs vest at the earlier of one year from the date of grant or the next annual meeting of stockholders. The fair value of the RSAs is equal to the closing price of the Company's common stock on the grant date. . . .

Performance Share Awards—2010 Omnibus Incentive Compensation Plan

The Performance Share Award Agreement, approved by the Board of Directors in March 2012, provides for the issuance of performance shares ("Performance Shares") . . .

Performance Share Units—2010 Omnibus Incentive Compensation Plan

. . . The PSUs are subject to performance conditions and time-based cliff vesting on the last day of the performance period, as defined below, and settle in shares of the Company's common stock upon vesting. The fair value of the PSUs is equal to the closing price of the Company's common stock on the grant date.

All of The Fresh Market's stock-based compensation except the stock options would be used to adjust The Fresh Market's shares outstanding to measure its equivalent outstanding shares. For the stock options, we measure the value of the stock options separately and subtract that value from the value of the total equity.

Allocating the Value of the Combined or Total Equity to Common Stock and Outstanding Warrants When the Securities Will Be Cancelled (Redeemed)

Allocating the value of the combined or total equity to common stock and outstanding option equity-linked securities—such as employee stock options and warrants—requires that we subtract the value of the option equity-linked securities from the value of the total equity. However, the value of the option equity-linked securities depends on the stock price. In this section we assume the company's option equity-linked securities will be cancelled (redeemed) at the company's stock price. Such situations often occur when a company is being acquired, especially for cash. In figuring out what price to bid for the shares, it is important to take into consideration the value of the warrants and options since your bid for the common shares affects the amount

[11] The Fresh Market Inc. is a specialty grocery retailer focused on offering high-quality and high-margin food products, with an emphasis on fresh, premium perishables; it opened its first store in 1982 and had revenues of $1.7 billion in the fiscal year ended January 25, 2015; see The Fresh Market Inc.'s 2015 10-K report, pp. 76–80.

necessary to redeem the warrants and options. Later in the chapter we discuss the allocation process when the company's equity-linked securities will not be cancelled (redeemed), which requires a valuation model to separately value the equity-linked securities. We begin our discussion using warrants because warrants do not have any potential tax effects and in the following section we discuss employee stock options.

The value of an option-like security prior to its expiration date is generally greater than its **intrinsic value**. Intrinsic value is equal to the difference between the price of the underlying security (stock price for warrants and employee stock options) and the price at which the underlying security can be purchased, called the **exercise** or **strike price**. Intrinsic value is positive when the price of the underlying security is greater than the exercise price (**in-the-money**). Intrinsic value is zero if the price of the underlying security is less than or equal to the exercise price (**out-of-the-money**). However, as long as the option-like security has not expired, the option has value even if its intrinsic value is zero, and that value can be measured using an option pricing model, which we discuss later in the chapter. In this part of the chapter we assume the company's option equity-linked securities will be cancelled (redeemed) based on the company's stock price, in other words, they are exercised, and therefore, the value of any option equity-linked securities is equal to their intrinsic value.

We first measure the value of the total equity by subtracting the value of the non-common equity claims (for example, debt and preferred stock) from the value of the firm. Thus, the value of total equity is equal to the value of the common stock plus the value of any common equity-linked securities.

$$V_{TE} = V_F - V_D - V_{PS}$$

The value of the total equity is equal to the share price of the common equity, P_E, multiplied by the number of shares of common equity outstanding as of the valuation date, S_E, plus the value of a warrant, P_W, multiplied by the number or warrants outstanding, S_W.

$$V_{TE} = P_E \times S_E + P_W \times S_W \qquad \textbf{(12.4)}$$

Because the warrants will be exercised as of the valuation date, the value of each warrant is equal to its intrinsic value. We know that the maximum value of the stock price without the warrants is V_{TE}/S_E, which is the stock price ignoring the effects of the warrants. If the strike price is greater than the maximum stock price, the intrinsic value of the warrant will be zero; if the strike price is less than the maximum stock price, the intrinsic value will be equal to difference between the stock price and the warrant strike price, $P_W = P_E - X_W$. If the company has one option equity-linked security with one strike price that is less than the maximum stock price, we can directly measure the company's stock price from the formula in Equation 12.4.

$$P_E = \frac{V_{TE} + X_W \times S_W}{S_E + S_W} \qquad \textbf{(12.5)}$$

The value of a warrant, P_W, is equal to the stock price minus its exercise price.

$$P_W = \frac{V_{TE} + X_W \times S_W}{S_E + S_W} - X_W = P_E - X_W \qquad \textbf{(12.6)}$$

We can adopt the above formulas to a company that has more than one type of option equity-linked security, or one type of option equity-linked security with multiple strike prices, by adding additional terms to the numerator and denominator for each of the additional securities with options that are in-the-money while simultaneously considering any restricted stock. However, we can no longer directly measure the stock price using the above formula but we must iterate to determine if each of the option-based equity-linked securities with a specific exercise price is dilutive (has a strike price less than the calculated stock price) while simultaneously considering any restricted stock.

Knuth Company—Allocating Total Equity to Common Equity and Warrants. Assume that the value of the Knuth Company's total common equity is $105 million and its outstanding shares is 10 million. Assume further that the Knuth Company also has 5 million warrants outstanding, which have an $8 exercise price ($X_W$ = $8) and will be cancelled (redeemed) at the valuation date based on the company's stock price.

The Knuth Company's maximum stock price of $10.5 (total common equity value divided by equivalent shares outstanding) is greater than the strike price of the warrants, $8; thus the option is in-the-money. Using the formulas in Equations 12.5 and 12.6, the company's stock price is $9.667 and its warrant price is $1.667.

$$P_E = \frac{V_{TE} + X_W \times S_W}{S_E + S_W} \Rightarrow \$9.667 = \frac{\$105 + \$8 \times 5}{10 + 5}$$

$$P_W = P_E - X_W \Rightarrow \$9.667 - \$8 = \$1.667$$

We can check our work by recalculating the value of the total equity as the sum of the value of the common equity plus the value of the warrants (Equation 12.4), which should equal $105 million.

$$V_{TE} = P_E \times S_E + P_W \times S_W \Rightarrow \$105 = \$9.667 \times 10 + \$1.667 \times 5$$

REVIEW EXERCISE 12.2

Allocating Total Equity to Common Equity and Warrants That Are Cancelled on the Valuation Date

Review the following information for the Triple J Company. Measure the company's stock price and warrant price based on the reported valuation and assuming the warrants will be cancelled on the valuation date. Triple J has 48,000.0 warrants outstanding that have a $31.20 exercise price, and which expire in 4.0 years.

Value of the firm	$10,000,000	Unlevered cost of capital	12.0%
Value of the debt	$ 3,000,000	Unlevered free cash flow next year	$880,000
Common shares authorized	630,000	Equity free cash flow next year	$528,000
Common shares issued	250,000	Weighted average cost of capital	10.800%
Common treasury shares	50,000	Risk-free rate	2.0%
Income tax rate on all income	40.0%	Annualized standard deviation (Volatility)	30.00%

Solution on page 604.

Allocating the Value of the Combined or Total Equity to Common Stock and Outstanding Employee Stock Options When the Securities Will Be Cancelled (Redeemed)

The only difference between allocating total equity when we have warrants versus when we have employee stock options is that employee stock options have potential tax benefits for the company while warrants typically do not. Like warrants, we first measure the value of the total equity by subtracting the value of the non-equity claims (for example, debt and preferred stock) from the value of the firm. The value of total equity is equal to the value of the common stock plus the value of any equity-linked securities. However, as we discussed with restricted stock, employee stock options may also provide the company with an additional tax deduction, which is not typically included in a DCF valuation and that tax benefit depends on the difference between the stock price at the time of exercise and the exercise price for the previously issued options. Thus, similar to share equivalent equity-linked securities (restricted stock units), we increase the value of the total equity by the benefit of the tax deduction from the employee stock options.

When measuring the value of a company using publicly traded or estimated prices for the equity, and other securities used to finance the firm, we would automatically include the market's assessment of the value of this tax benefit in the value of the firm as it would be reflected in the value of the equity. This is often how we measure firm value for comparable companies when we are analyzing the cost of capital or market multiples. However, when we value a company using a discounted cash flow method, we typically do not include the value of the tax benefits for employee stock options previously issued and outstanding as of the valuation date even though we forecast the effect of future option grants. This is the same issue we encountered with the tax benefit from restricted stock. When we do not include the tax benefit from employee stock options in our initial DCF valuation, we must measure and include this tax benefit separately.

One way to measure the present value of the option tax shelter for existing options is to multiply the future marginal tax rate for the option-related expense deduction, T_{SO}, by the value of the options. This calculation assumes that the tax rate multiplied by the value of the options is a reasonable measure of the present value of the tax benefit from the options, which is generally a reasonable assumption to make, particularly when the options are redeemed in a merger.

Like warrants, we first measure the value of the total equity by subtracting the value of the non-equity claims (for example, debt and preferred stock) from the value of the firm. The value of total equity is equal to the value of the common stock plus the value of any common equity-linked securities. We add the value of the tax benefit from the employee stock options, $P_{ESO} \times S_{ESO} \times T_{ESO}$, to the value of the total equity, V_{TE}, which is equal to the share price of the common equity, P_E, multiplied by the number of shares of common equity outstanding as of the valuation date, S_E, plus the value of an employee stock option, P_{ESO}, multiplied by the number of employee stock options outstanding, S_{ESO}.

$$V_{TE} + P_{ESO} \times S_{ESO} \times T_{ESO} = P_E \times S_E + P_{ESO} \times S_{ESO} \tag{12.7}$$

$$V_{TE} = P_E \times S_E + P_{ESO} \times S_{ESO} \times (1 - T_{ESO}) \tag{12.7'}$$

Because the employee stock options will be exercised at the valuation date, the value of an employee stock option is equal to its intrinsic value. If the strike price of the employee stock options is greater than the maximum stock price (the stock price ignoring the options), the intrinsic value of the option will be zero; if the strike price is less than the maximum stock price, the intrinsic value of the employee stock options will be equal to the difference between the stock price and the stock option strike price, $P_{ESO} = P_E - X_{ESO}$. If the company has one class of option equity-linked securities with one strike price that is less than the maximum stock price, we can directly measure the company's stock price restating the formula in Equation 12.7'.

$$P_E = \frac{V_{TE} + X_{ESO} \times S_{ESO} \times (1 - T_{ESO})}{S_E + S_{ESO} \times (1 - T_{ESO})} \tag{12.8}$$

The value of an employee stock option, P_{ESO}, is equal to the stock price minus its exercise price.

$$P_{ESO} = \frac{V_{TE} + X_{ESO} \times S_{ESO} \times (1 - T_{ESO})}{S_E + S_{ESO} \times (1 - T_{ESO})} - X_{ESO} = P_E - X_{ESO} \tag{12.9}$$

Again, we can adopt the above formulas to a company that has more than one type of option equity-linked security, or one type of option equity-linked security with multiple strike prices, by adding additional terms to the numerator and denominator for each of the additional securities with options that are in-the-money while simultaneously considering any restricted stock. However, we can no longer directly measure the stock price using the above formula but we must iterate to determine if each options-based equity-linked security with a specific exercise price is dilutive (has a strike price less than the calculated stock price) while simultaneously considering any restricted stock.

Knuth Company—Allocating Total Equity to Common Equity and Employee Stock Options. We use all of the information for the Knuth Company that we used for the warrant example but we will now assume the warrants are actually employee stock options and the company's income tax rate related to the employee stock options is 40%. Knuth Company's total common equity value is $105 million (without the tax benefit of the employee stock options), the outstanding shares is 10 million, the company has 5 million employee stock options outstanding, which have an $8 exercise price ($X_{ESO}$ = $8), which will be cancelled (redeemed) at the valuation date based on the company's stock price.

The Knuth Company's maximum stock price of $10.5, calculated earlier in this section, is greater than the strike price of the employee stock options, $8. Since the tax benefit from the employee stock options increases the total value of the equity, both the stock price and price of the employee stock option increase. Using the formulas in Equations 12.8 and 12.9, the company's stock price is $9.923 and its ESO price is $1.923.

$$P_E = \frac{V_{TE} + X_{ESO} \times S_{ESO} \times (1 - T_{ESO})}{S_E + S_{ESO} \times (1 - T_{ESO})} \Rightarrow \frac{\$105 + \$8 \times \$5 \times (1 - 0.4)}{10 + 5 \times (1 - 0.4)} = \$9.923$$

$$P_{ESO} = P_E - X_{ESO} \Rightarrow \$9.923 - \$8 = \$1.923$$

The tax benefit from the employee stock options is equal to $P_{ESO} \times S_{ESO} \times T_{ESO}$ or $3.846 million ($3.846 = $1.923 × 5 × 0.4). We can check our work using the stock price and employee stock option price and either the formula in Equation 12.7 or 12.7'.

$$V_{TE} + P_{ESO} \times S_{ESO} \times T_{ESO} = P_E \times S_E + P_{ESO} \times S_{ESO}$$

$$\$105 + \$1.923 \times 5 \times 0.4 = \$9.923 \times 10 + \$1.923 \times 5 = \$108.846$$

$$V_{TE} = P_E \times S_E + P_{ESO} \times S_{ESO} \times (1 - T_{ESO}) \Rightarrow \$105 = \$9.923 \times 10 + \$1.923 \times 5 \times (1 - 0.4)$$

Note here that both the price per share and the value of each employee stock option is higher in this example than when we assumed the securities were warrants. This is due to the fact that the employee stock options provide a tax benefit which increases the value of the firm relative to the case where the equity-linked securities are warrants.

Valuation Key 12.5

A DCF valuation typically requires an allocation of the value of the combined or total equity to common stock and outstanding option equity-linked securities—such as employee stock options and warrants existing as of the valuation date. If the option-like securities will be cancelled on the valuation date, the value of the options is equal to their intrinsic value and the allocation can be calculated directly. If they will not be cancelled on the valuation date, then they are valued based on an option pricing model and the allocation is based on an iterative process (numerical methods). Employee stock options may have certain tax benefits that are not included in the DCF valuation and would be added to the DCF valuation when allocating the total equity.

REVIEW EXERCISE 12.3

Allocating Total Equity to Common Equity and Employee Stock Options That Are Cancelled on the Valuation Date

Review the following information for the Triple J Company. Measure the company's stock price and the value of an employee stock option based on the reported valuation and assuming the employee stock options will be cancelled on the valuation date. (Note—this review exercise is a continuation of Review Exercise 12.2, although all of the relevant information is repeated here.)

	Employee Stock Options		
	Options	Weighted Avg Exercise Price	Weighted Avg Remaining Term
Beginning Balance	60,000.0	$24.00	
Granted	40,000.0	$30.00	
Exercised	−34,000.0	$28.80	
Forfeited/Expired	−6,000.0	$30.00	
Ending balance	60,000.0	$31.80	3.5
Expected to exercise	48,000.0	$31.20	4.0

continued

continued from previous page

Value of the firm	$10,000,000.0	Unlevered cost of capital	12.0%
Value of the debt	$ 3,000,000.0	Unlevered free cash flow next year	$880,000.0
Common shares authorized	630,000.0	Equity free cash flow next year	$528,000.0
Common shares issued	250,000.0	Weighted average cost of capital	10.800%
Common treasury shares	50,000.0	Risk-free rate	2.0%
Income tax rate on all income	40.0%	Annualized standard deviation (volatility)	30.00%

Solution on page 605.

12.3 VALUING WARRANTS, EMPLOYEE STOCK OPTIONS, AND OTHER OPTION-BASED EQUITY-LINKED SECURITIES

LO3 Value warrants and employee stock options, and other option-based equity-linked securities to allocate total equity to common equity and options

In the previous section, we assumed the company's option-based equity-linked securities were cancelled on the valuation date. In that situation, the value of the option is equal to its intrinsic value. However, if the options are not cancelled on the valuation date, we value options using an option pricing model, like the Black-Scholes-Merton option pricing model discussed in Chapter 9. Seminal works of Black and Scholes (1973) and Merton (1973) and other related works by these and other authors underpin many of the option pricing models used today.[12] In this section, we illustrate how to use a variation of the Black-Scholes and Merton option pricing models to value the options and allocate the DCF-based valuation of the company's total equity to the common equity and the options.

The Black-Scholes and Merton Option Pricing Models

We know that the value of a call option at the exercise date is equal to its intrinsic value, the price of the stock minus the exercise price. However, prior to the expiration date, the value of the option is larger than its intrinsic value. The difference between the value of the option and its intrinsic value is sometimes called the **time value of the option**. For a non-paying dividend firm, the time value is positive as long as the stock price has a non-zero probability of exceeding the exercise price at the expiration date. Naturally, valuing an option before the exercise date is more complex, for we do not know the value of the stock at the exercise date; however, we know the current stock price, the variability of the stock price, the length of the option contract, the strike price, and any expected dividend payments. We can use these factors to estimate the expected payoff from the call option. The Black-Scholes and Merton option pricing models, which are the continuous versions of the discrete time binomial model for pricing options, does just that. The form of this model is

$$P_C = P_E \times e^{-d_E \times T_C} \times N(d_1) - X_C \times e^{-r_F \times T_C} \times N(d_2) \tag{12.10}$$

where:

P_C = price of a European call option
P_E = common stock price per share
T_C = time to expiration of the call option (in years)
X_C = exercise or strike price of the call option

$$d_1 = \frac{\ln\left(\frac{P_E}{X_C}\right) + (r_F - d_E + \sigma_E^2/2) \times T_C}{\sigma_E \times \sqrt{T_C}}$$

$d_2 = d_1 - \sigma_E \times \sqrt{T_C}$
d_E = annual continuously compounded dividend yield
r_F = risk-free rate of return
$N(x)$ = the standard cumulative normal
σ_E = the standard deviation of the company's continuously compounded annaul returns

[12] Black, F., and M. Scholes, "The Pricing of Options and Corporate Liabilities," *Journal of Political Economy* vol. 81, no. 3, (May/June 1973), pp. 637–654; and Merton, R. C., "Theory of Rational Option Pricing," *Bell Journal of Economics and Management Science* vol. 4, no. 1 (Spring 1973), pp. 141–183.

Recall that this formula for valuing a European call option, an option that cannot be exercised until the expiration date, is not applicable to an American call option, an option that can be exercised until the expiration date, for a dividend-paying stock. If an option holder can exercise an option before the expiration date, it may be more valuable to do so before the dividend reduces the stock price. While the Black-Scholes and Merton option pricing models are widely used to value option-like securities that are not issued by companies, when a company issues the option, the model must be adjusted for dilution resulting from the issuance of the options.

Valuation in Practice 12.4

Intel Corporation's Valuation of Its Equity Incentive Plan As described in its 10-K report, Intel Corporation (Intel) uses the Black-Scholes Option Pricing Model to measure the fair value of stock options and stock purchase rights granted:

> . . . use the Black-Scholes option-pricing model for estimating the fair value of options granted under the company's equity incentive plans and rights to acquire stock granted under our stock purchase plan. We based the weighted average estimated value of employee stock option grants and rights granted under the stock purchase plan, as well as the weighted average assumptions used in calculating the fair value on estimates at the date of grant for each period as follows:

	Stock Options			Stock Purchase Plan		
	2014	2013	2012	2014	2013	2012
Estimated value per option.	$3.61	$3.11	$4.22	$5.87	$4.52	$5.47
Expected life (in years)	5.1	5.2	5.3	0.5	0.5	0.5
Risk-free interest rate	1.7%	0.8%	1.0%	0.1%	0.1%	0.1%
Dividend yield	3.6%	3.9%	3.3%	3.2%	4.0%	3.3%
Volatility	23.0%	25.0%	25.0%	22.0%	22.0%	24.0%

> We base the expected volatility on implied volatility because we have determined that implied volatility is more reflective of market conditions and a better indicator of expected volatility than historical volatility. We use historical option exercise data as the basis for determining expected life, as we believe that historical data provides a reasonable basis upon which to estimate the expected life input for valuing options using the Black-Scholes model.

Source: See Intel's 2014 10-K report, p. 98

Measuring the Price (Value) of Warrants and Employee Stock Options

Warrants and employee stock options are similar to call options. For example, a warrant is a security issued by a company that gives the holder the right (but not the obligation) to purchase a certain number of shares of the company's stock at a fixed price on or before a specified date. One difference between a company issuing a warrant and investors issuing option contracts to each other is the dilution in the company's equity that occurs from issuing warrants that does not occur when investors issue options to each other.

Daves and Ehrhardt (2007) developed a pricing model and a cost of capital model for warrants and employee stock options.[13] In this analysis, we assume warrants are the only equity-linked security outstanding and that they are exercisable on their expiration date. If the company has other equity-linked securities outstanding, we would include all such securities in this analysis. As we might expect, the formula for the value of a warrant is similar to the Black-Scholes and Merton option pricing formulas but it is adjusted for the dilution effect of the warrants.

[13] Daves, P. R., and Ehrhardt, M., "Convertible Securities, Employee Stock Options and the Cost of Equity," *The Financial Review* vol. 42, no. 2 (May 2007), pp. 267–288, available at SSRN: http://ssrn.com/abstract=990906 or DOI: 10.1111/j.1540-6288.2007.00171.x.

$$P_W = \frac{S_E \times CR}{S_E + S_W \times CR} \times \left[\left(P_E \times e^{-d_E \times T_W} + P_W \times \frac{S_W}{S_E} \right) \times N(d_1) - X_W \times e^{-r_F \times T_W} \times N(d_2) \right] \quad \textbf{(12.11)}$$

All terms are as defined earlier, and

P_W = price per warrant
S_E = number of common shares outstanding
S_W = number of warrants outstanding
CR = conversion ratio or the number of common shares exchanged for each warrant
d_E = continuously compounded dividend yield
T_W = time to expiration of the warrant in years
X_W = the exercise or strike price of the warrant

$$d_1 = \frac{\ln\left(\dfrac{P_E \times e^{-d_E \times T_W} + P_W \times \dfrac{S_W}{S_E}}{X_W} \right) + (r_F + \sigma_Q^2/2) \times T_W}{\sigma_Q \times \sqrt{T_W}}$$

$$d_2 = d_1 - \sigma_Q \times \sqrt{T_W}$$

σ_Q = the standard deviation of the expected annual return on the total value of the common stock and warrants, V_Q

We can measure the standard deviation, σ_Q, of the expected annual return on the total value of the common stock and warrants using Equation 12.12:

$$\sigma_Q = \sigma_E \times P_E \times \frac{S_E + S_W \times \omega_E}{S_E \times P_E + S_W \times P_W} \quad \textbf{(12.12)}$$

We can calculate the last term in the numerator of Equation 12.12 (which is equal to the partial derivative of the warrant price with respect to the stock price) using Equation 12.13:

$$\omega_E = \frac{S_E \times CR \times e^{-d_E \times T_W} \times N(d_1)}{S_E + S_W \times CR \times [1 - N(d_1)]} \quad \textbf{(12.13)}$$

First, the price of the warrant is on both sides of Equation 12.11. In addition, as is apparent from Equation 12.11, the warrant pricing model is circular because $N(d_1)$ in Equation 12.11 depends on σ_Q (Equation 12.12), which depends on ω_E (Equation 12.13), which also depends on $N(d_1)$. Because the calculation of the warrant price is circular, we solve for the warrant price numerically using an iterative process. Spreadsheet software typically provides a way to solve circular equations such as Equations 12.11–12.13 numerically. First, enable the iterative function in the spreadsheet, which allows the calculation of indirect circular references. Then, use an iterative function in the spreadsheet (for example, goal seek or solver) to calculate the warrant price.

The iterative process begins by choosing (informed guess) a warrant price. Based on the chosen price, calculate the warrant price using Equations 12.11–12.13 numerically. For example, if the calculated warrant price is lower (higher) than the chosen price, choose a lower (higher) warrant price and recalculate Equations 12.11–12.13. Continue this iterative process until the absolute value of the difference between the chosen warrant price and the calculated warrant price is sufficiently close to zero.

A company's **dividend yield** is equal to a company's annualized periodic dividend payout divided by its stock price, D%. If the company distributes dividends annually, it is equal to the company's annual dividend divided by its stock price. If the company distributes dividends semi-annually or quarterly, dividend yield is typically measured as the company's most recent periodic dividend divided by its stock price multiplied by the number of dividend distributions per year. Dividend yield does not include any special dividends the company may distribute from time to time. The **continuously compounded annual dividend yield** measures a company's dividend yield had the company continuously distributed dividends instead of distributing dividends periodically. For example, assume a company distributes a dividend of 10% of its stock price annually (D% = 10%). The continuously compounded dividend—roughly the average continuous return during the year—is equal to the natural log of one plus the annual dividend yield, 9.531% (0.09531 = ln(1.1)). The continuously compounded dividend represents the continuously compounded return earned during the year resulting in an annual return of 10% ($0.10 = e^{0.09531} - 1$).

In a DCF valuation, however, we may not have an observable dividend yield but, instead, assume the company will not retain any excess cash; in other words, the company will distribute all of the company's equity free cash flows to its common shareholders. Based on this assumption, the **DCF-based annual dividend yield**, D%, is equal to the equity free cash flow, $EFCF_1$, divided by the value of the common equity, $V_{E,0} = P_{E,0} \times S_{E,0}$; in other words, the DCF-based annual dividend yield is equal to $D\% = EFCF_1/(P_{E,0} \times S_{E,0})$. When we calculate the dividend yield in this way, the iterative solution takes into consideration that the dividend yield changes with variation in the price per share. The continuously compounded annual dividend yield, d_E, is equal to the natural log of 1 + D%.

$$d_{E,1} = \ln\left(1 + \frac{EFCF_1}{P_{E,0} \times S_{E,0}}\right) \tag{12.14}$$

Of course, we may have a different estimate of the expected annual dividend yield for a company that we believe is more reliable and wish to rely on, so we can use that dividend yield instead, in which case that input is fixed in the model.

Valuation Key 12.6

Outstanding warrants—and other option-based equity-linked securities—dilute a company's common equity, and thus, the Black-Scholes and Merton option pricing models are not always the best valuation models for such securities. Warrant pricing models adjust the valuation for the dilution from the warrants and require the use of an iterative process (numerical methods).

Valuing Synergy Pharmaceuticals Inc.'s Warrants When the Stock Price is Observable. Recall from the opening vignette that Synergy Pharmaceuticals Inc. (SPharma) has convertible debt, warrants, and employee stock options. We are going to value SPharma's warrants ignoring SPharma's convertible debt and employee stock options (assume they do not exist). SPharma's common stock and its warrants are publicly traded. In early July 2015, 17 months before the warrants were going to expire, SPharma's stock price was \$9.76 and its warrants were trading at \$5.15 per share (high and low prices on that day were \$5.24 and \$4.98, respectively).

According to SPharma's 10-K, the company has approximately 96.6 million common shares and 5.6 million warrants outstanding. Each warrant has the right to purchase one share of SPharma's common stock for \$5 and the warrants expire on December 1, 2016. In its footnote regarding how it valued the options, SPharma's 10-K indicates that it does not currently nor does it intend to pay dividends in the foreseeable future. The 10-K also reports a volatility (standard deviation of its annual stock return) between 52% and 60%—we use the midpoint of that range, 56%, in our valuation of the warrants. We use a risk-free rate of 2%. To illustrate this calculation, we will use \$4.76 as the initial warrant price, which is equal to its intrinsic value (\$4.76 = \$9.76 − \$5.00).

Below, we show the inputs into Equations 12.11–12.13. Notice some of the inputs depend on the solution to another equation and must be solved numerically using a spreadsheet.

$$P_W = \frac{96.6 \times 1}{96.6 + 5.6 \times 1} \times \left[\left(\$9.76 \times e^{-0 \times 17/12} + \$4.76 \times \frac{5.6}{96.6}\right) \times N(d_1) - 5.00 \times e^{-0.02 \times 17/12} \times N(d_2)\right]$$

Equation 12.11 has two inputs, d_1 and d_2, which are separate formulas.

$$d_1 = \frac{\ln\left(\frac{\$9.76 \times e^{-0 \times 17/12} + \$4.76 \times \frac{5.6}{96.6}}{\$5.00}\right) + (0.02 + \sigma_Q^2/2) \times 17/12}{\sigma_Q \times \sqrt{17/12}}$$

$$d_2 = d_1 - \sigma_Q \times \sqrt{17/12}$$

The formulas for d_1 and d_2 have one input, σ_Q, which is the formula in Equation 12.12.

$$\sigma_Q = 0.56 \times 9.76 \times \frac{96.6 + 5.6 \times \omega_E}{96.6 \times 9.76 + 5.6 \times \$4.76}$$

The formula for σ_Q has one input, ω_E, which is the formula in Equation 12.13.

$$\omega_E = \frac{96.6 \times 1 \times e^{-0 \times 17/12} \times N(d_1)}{96.6 + 5.6 \times 1 \times (1 - N(d_1))}$$

We solved the above system of equations numerically using spreadsheet software and calculated a warrant price equal to \$5.213. Since the calculated warrant price, \$5.213, is larger than the chosen price, \$4.76, we increase the chosen price and resolve the system of equations again. By iterating the chosen warrant price in this way, a chosen warrant price of \$5.234 resulted in a calculated warrant price of the same amount. The other calculated results from the model for d_1, d_2, σ_Q, and ω_E are 1.4095, 0.7287, 0.5720, and 0.9164, respectively. Note that the calculated warrant price of \$5.234 is between the high (\$5.24) and low (\$4.98) on the day SPharma's stock price was \$9.76, the assumed date of the valuation.

Applying the Warrant Pricing Model to Employee Stock Options. Employee stock options have different characteristics than warrants, which are inconsistent with the assumptions underlying the warrants and other option pricing models. For example, option pricing theory assumes that the options are traded and that the holder can hedge the risk of options by short-selling stock or by performing some other similar action. However, employee stock options typically have provisions that do not allow trading and include forfeiture, the employee cannot typically hedge the risk, and employees may have inside information on the company.[14] Another assumption in the option pricing models (for a non-dividend paying company) is that investors will not exercise the option until the expiration date. Research shows, however, that employees, on average, exercise early and diversify when the value sacrificed by exercising early is relatively low and their degree of risk aversion is relatively high.[15] Ignoring the early exercise of the options would overstate the value of the option and the corresponding tax benefits, which is why companies use the expected exercise date and not the term of the option when valuing the option at the grant date.[16]

In this chapter, we use a warrant pricing model to value employee stock options. However, U.S. accounting rules allow companies to use the Black-Scholes option pricing model to value options, which ignores the dilutive effect of employee stock options. Naturally, this is not an issue if the employee stock options are relatively small. Research shows, however, that the warrant pricing model, with an adjustment for the tax benefit from the options, is a more accurate valuation method.[17] The issue in a DCF valuation is the economic cost to the company and not the value of the options to the employee. Using the warrant pricing model to value employee stock options assumes the cost to the company of granting the option to the employee is similar to the value the company would have received by issuing a warrant to an outside investor, which is likely a reasonable approach.

Allocating the Value of the Combined or Total Equity to Option-Based Equity-Linked Securities When the Securities Will Not Be Cancelled (Not Redeemed)

As we discussed in the previous section, in a DCF valuation, we typically measure the value of a company's total equity claims by subtracting non-equity claims (debt and preferred stock) from the value of the firm and then allocate the value of the total equity to the company's common equity, warrants, and employee stock options. Recall that the warrant and employee stock option prices depend on the stock

[14] For a discussion of this issue, see Hall, B., and K. Murphy, "Stock Options For Undiversified Executives," *Journal of Accounting and Economics* vol. 33, no. 11 (February 2002), pp. 3–42.

[15] Huddart, Steven, "Employee Stock Options," *Journal of Accounting & Economics*, 18 (1994), pp. 207–231.

[16] Huddart, Steven, and Lang, M., 1996. "Employee Stock Option Exercises, An Empirical Analysis," *Journal of Accounting & Economics*, 21 (1996), pp. 5–43.

[17] See Feng Li and M. H. Franco Wong, "Employee Stock Options, Equity Valuation, and the Valuation of Option Grants Using a Warrant-Pricing Model," *Journal of Accounting Research* vol. 45, no. 1, (2005), pp. 97–131.

price and the stock price also depends on the warrant and employee stock option prices. This circularity does not prevent us from directly calculating the stock price. In the previous section, assuming the warrants and employee stock options are in-the-money, and will be cancelled on the valuation date, we derived a formula to directly calculate the stock price.

However, if the warrants and employee stock options will not be cancelled on the valuation date, we can no longer derive a formula to directly calculate the stock price. In this situation, we use the formula in Equation 12.4 and the pricing model for warrants, and the formula in Equation 12.7' and the pricing model for employee stock options. For example, assume the company has only common equity and warrants outstanding. To allocate the company's total equity, we first choose a stock price. For example, choose a stock price equal to the total equity divided by the shares outstanding. This stock price is too high, of course, because it is the stock price if the company did not also have warrants. Based on the chosen stock price, we calculate the warrant price using Equations 12.11–12.13. Once we calculate the warrant price for the chosen stock price, we use the stock price and warrant price to calculate the value of the total equity based on those prices (Equation 12.4; $V_{TE} = P_E \times S_E + P_W \times S_W$). If the value of the total equity based on the calculated prices is greater than the value of the total equity from the DCF valuation (adjusted for equivalent shares), then the chosen stock price is too high. We then choose a lower stock price and continue the iterative process until the value of the total equity based on the calculated prices is equal to the value of the total equity from the DCF valuation.

Valuation Key 12.7

A DCF valuation typically requires an allocation of the value of the combined or total equity to common stock and outstanding option equity-linked securities—such as employee stock options and warrants existing as of the valuation date. If the option-like securities are not cancelled on the valuation date, they are valued based on an option pricing model that accounts for the dilution of the common equity and the allocation is based on an iterative process (numerical methods).

Knuth Company—Allocating Total Equity to Common Equity and Warrants Revisited. Recall from earlier in this section that the value of Knuth Company's total common equity is \$105 million and the outstanding shares is 10 million. The Knuth Company also has 5 million warrants outstanding, which have an \$8 exercise price (X_W = \$8). In this example, we assume the warrants will not be cancelled (redeemed) at the valuation date. The Knuth Company's maximum stock price is \$10.5, but this assumes the warrants are worthless.

We need additional information to value the warrants using the warrant pricing model—the expiration date is 2 years, the risk-free rate is 5%, the total equity cost of capital is 12.26%, and the common stock's annual volatility is 45%. From a DCF model, the Knuth Company's equity free cash flow is \$7.622 million. If we use an initial stock price of \$10.5, its annual dividend yield is equal to 7.26% [0.0726 = \$7.622/(\$10.5 × 10)] and its continuously compounded annual dividend yield is equal to 7.01% [0.0701 = ln(1 + 0.0726)]. To measure the value of the common equity and warrant, we choose a stock price and for each stock price chosen, we use the pricing model to solve for the warrant price. We iterate on different stock prices until we satisfy Equation 12.4, $V_{TE} = P_E \times S_E + P_W \times S_W$.

For the Knuth Company, we begin by assuming the stock price is \$10.5 even though we know that price is too high as it does not allocate any of the value of the total equity value to the value of the 5 million warrants. Using a \$10.5 stock price in the pricing model, results in a \$3.071 warrant price. However, the total value of the equity based on those two prices, \$120.4 million, is greater than the DCF valuation of the total equity of \$105 million.

$$V_{TE} = P_E \times S_E + P_W \times S_W \Rightarrow \$120.4 = \$10.5 \times 10 + \$3.071 \times 5$$

We iterate by choosing a lower stock price, calculating the value of the warrant, and evaluating the total value of the equity based on those two prices and the DCF valuation of the total equity. It turns out that a stock price of \$9.367, resulting in a warrant price of \$2.267, are the prices that result in a value of the total equity that is equal to the value of the total equity from the DCF valuation.

$$V_{TE} = P_E \times S_E + P_W \times S_W \Rightarrow \$105 = \$9.367 \times 10 + \$2.267 \times 5$$

Note that each time we use a different stock price in our iteration, we also have a different continuously compounded annual dividend yield. The annual dividend yield for the \$9.367 stock price is equal to 8.14% [0.0814 = \$7.622/(\$9.367 × 10)] and its continuously compounded annual dividend yield is equal to 7.82% [0.0782 = ln (1 + 0.0814)]. The other outputs from the warrant pricing model for d_1, d_2, σ_Q, and ω_E are 0.6850, −0.0455, 0.5165, and 0.5735, respectively.

When we assumed the warrants were going to be cancelled on the valuation date, the prices of the stock and the warrants were \$9.667 and \$1.667. Assuming the warrants are not going to be cancelled will increase the value of a warrant above its intrinsic value as long as the expected stock return implicit in the valuation model is more than the dividend yield.[18] Assuming the warrants will not be cancelled, the value of the warrants increased from \$1.667 to \$2.267 (an increase of 36.0%) and the stock price decreased from \$9.667 to \$9.367 (a decrease of 3.1%).

REVIEW EXERCISE 12.4

Allocating Total Equity to Common Equity and Warrants (Not Cancelled on the Valuation Date)

Review the information in Review Exercise 12.2 for the Triple J Company. Measure the company's stock price and warrant price based on the reported valuation and assuming the warrants will not be cancelled on the valuation date; in other words, use the warrant valuation model to allocate the total equity of Triple J.

Solution on pages 605–606.

Knuth Company—Allocating Total Equity to Common Equity and Employee Stock Options Revisited. We use all of the information for the Knuth Company that we used for the previous employee stock option example but assume the options will not be cancelled on the expiration date. Knuth Company's total common equity value is \$105 million, the outstanding shares is 10 million, the company has 5 million employee stock options outstanding, which have an \$8 exercise price (X_{ESO} = \$8). The employee stock options have an expiration date of 2 years, the risk-free rate is 5%, the total equity cost of capital is 12.26%, and the common stock's annual volatility is 45%, and the Knuth Company's equity free cash flow to measure the continuously compounded dividend yield is \$7.622 million. These are the same assumptions we used for valuing Knuth's warrants.

Since the tax benefit from the employee stock options increases the total value of the equity, both the stock price and price of the employee stock option will be higher than in the case where we assumed the options were warrants. Using a 40% tax rate, the formula in Equation 12.7' and the above iterative process, the company's stock price is \$9.743 and its warrant price is \$2.525. The annual dividend yield for the \$9.743 stock price is equal to 7.82% [0.0782 = \$7.622/(\$9.743 × 10)] and its continuously compounded annual dividend yield is equal to 7.53% [0.0753 = ln(1 + 0.0782)]. The other outputs from the warrant pricing model for d_1, d_2, σ_Q, and ω_E are 0.7577, 0.0253, 0.5179, and 0.5999, respectively.

The tax benefit from the employee stock options is equal to $P_{ESO} \times S_{ESO} \times T_{ESO}$ or \$5.05 million (\$5.05 = \$2.525 × 5 × 0.4). The total value of the equity is equal to \$110.05, which is the DCF valuation of \$105 million plus the tax benefit of \$5.05 million from employee stock options. We can check our work using the stock price and employee stock option price and either Equation 12.7 or 12.7'.

$$V_{TE} + P_{ESO} \times S_{ESO} \times T_{ESO} = P_E \times S_E + P_{ESO} \times S_{ESO}$$

$$\$105 + \$2.525 \times 5 \times 0.4 = \$9.743 \times 10 + \$2.525 \times 5 = \$110.05$$

$$V_{TE} = P_E \times S_E + P_{ESO} \times S_{ESO} \times (1 - T_{ESO}) \Rightarrow \$105 = \$9.743 \times 10 + \$2.525 \times 5 \times (1 - 0.4)$$

[18] The effect of dividends on the value of a warrant or other equity-linked option securities such as employee stock options is more complex if the warrants are exercisable any time before the expiration date (American option setting) and the valuation model in this section must be adapted for such a circumstance.

When we assumed the employee stock options were going to be cancelled on the valuation date, the prices of the stock and the warrants were $9.923 and $1.923. Assuming the employee stock options were not going to be cancelled will increase the value of an employee stock option above its intrinsic value as long as the expected stock return implicit in the valuation model is more than the dividend yield.[19] Assuming the employee stock options will not be cancelled, the value of the employee stock options increased from $1.923 to $2.525 (31.3%) and the stock price decreased from $9.923 to $9.743 (1.8%).

REVIEW EXERCISE 12.5

Allocating Total Equity to Common Equity and Employee Stock Options (Not Cancelled on the Valuation Date)

Review the information in Review Exercise 12.3 for the Triple J Company. Measure the company's stock price and the value of an employee stock option based on the reported valuation and assuming the employee stock options will not be cancelled on the valuation date; in other words, use the employee stock option valuation model to allocate the total equity of Triple J.

Solution on pages 606–607.

12.4 MEASURING THE COST OF CAPITAL FOR OPTION-BASED EQUITY-LINKED SECURITIES

LO4 Measure the cost of capital of warrants and employee stock options and unlever the cost of capital of companies with warrants and employee stock options

The cost of capital for warrants and employee stock options is, in essence, a levered common equity cost of capital because we invest less in a warrant than in a share of stock. The leverage effect of option-based equity-linked securities relative to the underlying stock is not always immediately apparent. We often think of the common shareholders as the residual claimants, and that they hold the security with the highest amount of risk; however, warrants have more risk than the underlying equity. As we discussed earlier in the chapter, a company's total equity cost of capital is not affected by the allocation of the total equity to common equity and equity-linked securities. The total cost of equity is equal to the weighted average of the equity and warrant (employee stock option) costs of capital. Given that the warrant cost of capital is essentially a levered common equity cost of capital, and thus, higher than the common equity cost of capital, the company's common equity cost of capital decreases after it issues warrants because its total equity cost of capital is constant and is equal to the weighted average of the common equity cost of capital and the warrant (employee stock option) cost of capital.

In Exhibit 12.4, we illustrate this effect on the beta (and hence on the equity cost of capital) from issuing warrants. We assume the company in the exhibit is initially financed with only common equity and has an equity beta equal to 2.0. The blue diamonds in the exhibit show a random set of market returns and corresponding stock returns for a company with a beta of 2.0, and a small normally distributed random error. The line through these diamonds represents the estimate of the market model and the slope of the line is equal to the company's beta, which is equal to 2.0.

The red dots in the exhibit represent the equity returns of the company after it issues warrants. To hold the company's investments (assets) constant, we assume the company repurchases common equity with the proceeds from issuing the warrants. To more clearly show the effect of issuing warrants, we assume the stock price, $12, is above the exercise price, and the company issues warrants equal to the number of common shares outstanding. Since the warrants share in the upside and downside, the equityholders end up giving up some of the upside and downside. Thus, for a given change in the value of the assets, the warrants dampen the equity returns (the equity returns are closer to zero). In this case, the equity beta for the company with the warrants is 1.12—a reduction of 44%. Thus, issuing warrants—or other equity-linked securities—reduces the company's equity beta and reduces its equity cost of capital.

We formally show the effect of issuing warrants on the equity cost of capital in Equation 12.15. The term r_{TE} is the value-weighted average cost of capital for all the equity-linked securites a company uses to finance the firm, which is equal to the common equity cost of capital if the company only has

[19] The effect of dividends on the value of a warrant is more complex if the warrants are exercisable any time before the expiration date (American option setting) and the valuation model in this section must be adapted for such a circumstance.

common equity securites. Equation 12.15 shows that once a company issues warrants, r_E, is a function of its total equity cost of capital, r_{TE}, and the risk-free rate, r_F. The weights on r_{TE}, and r_F are between zero and one and they sum to one; thus, the common equity cost of capital is lower than the total equity cost of capital.

$$r_E = r_{TE} \times \frac{S_E \times P_E + S_W \times P_W}{S_E \times P_E + S_W \times P_E \times \omega_E} + r_F \times \frac{S_W \times P_E \times \omega_E - S_W \times P_W}{S_E \times P_E + S_W \times P_E \times \omega_E} \quad \textbf{(12.15)}$$

We show the relation between the warrant cost of capital and the equity cost of capital in Equation 12.16. The cost of capital for the warrants, r_W, is equal to the risk-free rate plus the stock's equity risk premium adjusted for the leverage from the warrant. The leverage adjustment is a function of two factors: the ratio of the stock price to the warrant price (which adjusts the return for the relative investments) and the last term in the equation (which is equal to the partial derivative of the warrant price with respect to the stock price and is defined in Equation 12.13). The leverage effect, which is the product of the last two terms, is always greater than or equal to 1.

$$r_W = r_F + (r_E - r_F) \times \frac{P_E}{P_W} \times \omega_E \quad \textbf{(12.16)}$$

If we use the iterative process we describe to measure the warrant price, we have all of the inputs necessary to measure the warrant cost of capital using Equation 12.16. If we know the price of the warrant—for example, because it is publicly traded—we can measure the partial derivative, ω_E, directly using Equations 12.12 and 12.13.

EXHIBIT 12.4 Effect of Issuing Warrants on Equity Returns and Equity Beta

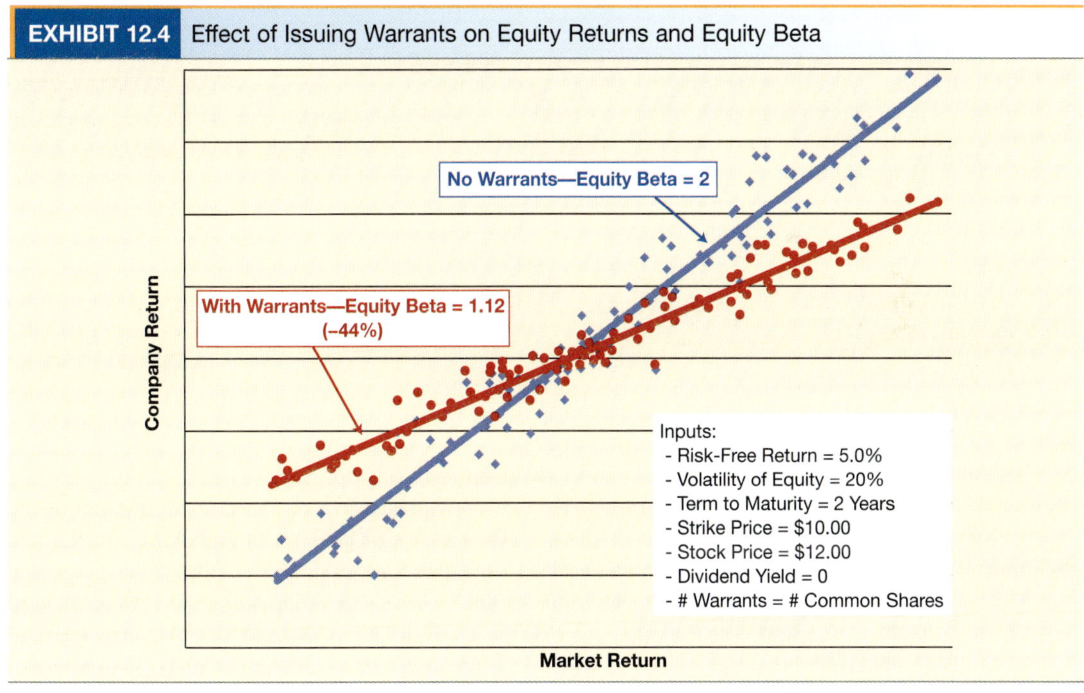

If we assume the CAPM is the asset pricing model for the common equity cost of capital, $r_E = r_F + \beta_E \times MRP$, then Equation 12.16 can be rewritten in terms of the CAPM, see Equation 12.17. Assuming the CAPM is the asset pricing model for the common equity cost of capital, the risk premium for the warrant cost of capital is equal to the risk premium for the common equity multiplied by the leverage factor for the warrant, $(P_E/P_W) \times \omega_E$.[20]

[20] Although under certain circumstances accounting rules require companies to record certain types of warrants, stock-based compensation, and other convertible securities as debt (see Accounting Standards Codification 480-10-25), research shows that employee stock options, and by inference, other equity-linked securities, have the characteristics of equity and are riskier than common equity. See, Barth, Mary, Leslie Hodder, and Stephen Stubben, "Financial Reporting for Employee Stock Options: Liabilities or Equity?," *Review of Accounting Studies*. vol. 18, issue 3 (September 2013), pp. 642–682.

$$r_W = r_F + \beta_E \times MRP \times \frac{P_E}{P_W} \times \omega_E \quad (12.17)$$

Note that the warrant cost of capital depends on the company's stock price and thus, the warrant cost of capital changes if the company's stock price changes.

Valuation Key 12.8

We can use option pricing models to measure the cost of capital for option-based equity-linked securities such as warrants and other types of option-based equity-linked securities.

Determinants (Inputs) of the Valuation and Cost of Capital of Option-Based Equity-Linked Securities

From what we just discussed, it is clear that the warrant cost of capital is a function of various determinants such as the exercise price, the stock price, the volatility of the equity, the time to the expiration of the warrants, the dividend yield, the equity cost of capital, and the risk-free rate of return. In Exhibit 12.5, we summarize these relations. We know from option pricing theory that, holding everything else constant, the value of the option increases with increases in the stock price, the volatility of the equity, the risk-free rate, and the time to expiration; we also know it decreases with increases in the exercise price, and the dividend yield. The same is true for warrants, of course, as shown in the exhibit.

EXHIBIT 12.5 Effect of Various Factors on the Value and Cost of Capital of Warrants

	Warrant	
Factor Increasing	**Value**	**Cost of Capital**
Stock price	+	−
Volatility of common stock	+	−
Risk-free rate	+	−
Time to expiration	+	−
Exercise (strike) price	−	+
Dividend yield	−	+
Equity cost of capital − r_F	0	+

Holding everything else constant, the value of an option does not depend on the equity cost of capital, but we can clearly see from Equation 12.16 that the warrant cost of capital is a function of the equity risk premium (equity cost of capital minus the risk-free rate or beta multiplied by the market risk premium, Equation 12.17). As we can see from the exhibit, the warrant cost of capital is an increasing function of the equity cost of capital, but the value of the warrants is independent of (does not vary with) the equity cost of capital. For the other factors, the warrant cost of capital moves in the opposite direction of the value of the warrants; in other words, holding everything else constant, the warrant cost of capital decreases with increases in the stock price, the volatility of the equity, the risk-free rate, and the time to expiration; it increases with increases in the exercise price, and the dividend yield.

Synergy Pharmaceuticals Inc.'s Warrant Cost of Capital. Recall that we calculated the value of SPharma's warrants as well as d_1, d_2, σ_Q, and ω_E. Using this information and SPharma's common equity cost of capital, we can measure its warrant cost of capital. We estimated SPharma's common equity beta regressing SPharma's daily stock returns from June 3, 2015 through September 30, 2015 on the market index (see Chapter 8 for a discussion of how to estimate beta). The chart in Exhibit 12.6 presents scatterplots of SPharma's stock returns (blue diamonds) against the market return and SPharma's warrant returns (red dots) against the market return. The lines represent the predicted returns from a market model regression of SPharma's stock return (blue line) and warrant return (red line) on the market return.

SPharma's common equity beta is 2.193 (t-statistic, 5.0). Assuming a 2% risk-free rate and a 6% market risk premium, SPharma's common equity cost of capital is 15.16% (0.1516 = 0.02 + 2.193 × 0.06), which has a risk premium of 13.16% (0.1316 = 2.193 × 0.06). Based on this information and the estimates from the warrant pricing model, we can estimate SPharma's warrant cost of capital, 24.49%, using either Equation 12.16 or 12.17.

$$r_W = r_F + (r_E - r_F) \times \frac{P_E}{P_W} \times \omega_E = 0.02 + (0.1516 - 0.02) \times \frac{9.76}{5.234} \times 0.9164 = 0.2449$$

$$r_W = r_F + \beta_E \times MRP \times \frac{P_E}{P_W} \times \omega_E = 0.02 + 2.193 \times 0.06 \times \frac{9.76}{5.234} \times 0.9164 = 0.2449$$

The warrant leverage factor (LF_W) is 1.71.

$$LF_W = \frac{P_E}{P_W} \times \omega_E = \frac{9.76}{5.234} \times 0.9164 = 1.71$$

We also estimated SPharma's warrant beta by regressing SPharma's daily warrant returns from June 3, 2015 through September 30, 2015 on the market returns. SPharma's warrant beta is 3.318 (t-statistic, 4.7) and the 95% confidence interval is from 1.899 to 4.738. The warrant beta implied from the warrant pricing model's cost of capital is 3.75 [3.75 = (r_W − r_F) /MRP = (0.245 − 0.02)/0.06], which is the same beta we measure if we multiply the common equity beta, 2.193, by the warrant cost of capital risk premium leverage factor, 1.71 (3.75 = 2.193 × 1.71). The warrant beta implied by the warrant pricing model is within the 95% confidence interval from the market model regression used to estimate the warrant beta and is reasonably close to the point estimate.

EXHIBIT 12.6 Synergy Pharmaceuticals Inc.'s Common Equity and Warrant Returns and Betas

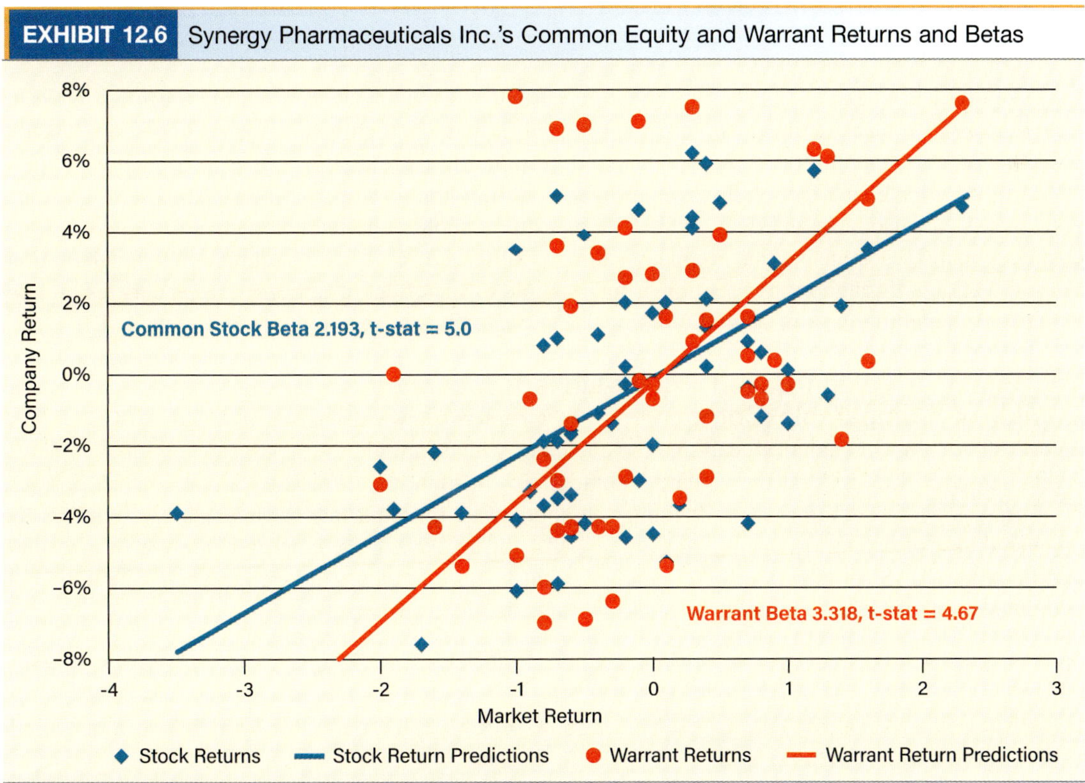

What is SPharma's cost of capital for its total equity, r_{TE}? We know that the total equity cost of capital is equal to the weighted average of the common equity, r_E, and warrant, r_W, costs of capital, with the weights equal to the proportion of the value each claim has to the value of the total equity, V_{TE}, see Equation 12.1. Since most, 97%, of the value of the total equity is common equity, the cost of capital for the total equity will be close to, but higher than, the common equity cost of capital, r_{TE} = 0.1544, r_E = 0.1516.

$$r_{TE} = r_E \times \frac{P_E \times S_E}{P_E \times S_E + P_W \times S_W} + r_W \times \frac{P_W \times S_W}{P_E \times S_E + P_W \times S_W}$$

$$r_{TE} = 0.1516 \times \frac{\$9.76 \times 96.6}{\$9.76 \times 96.6 + \$5.234 \times 5.6} + 0.2449 \times \frac{\$5.234 \times 5.6}{\$9.76 \times 96.6 + \$5.234 \times 5.6} = 0.1544$$

Valuation in Practice 12.5

KapStone Paper and Packaging Corporation's Warrants On August 19, 2005, the KapStone Paper and Packaging Corporation (KapStone) issued 20,000,000 units ("Units") for $6.00 per Unit as part of its initial public offering. Each Unit consisted of one share of the company's common stock and two warrants. According to the company, each warrant entitled the holder to purchase one share of common stock at an exercise price of $5.00 from the company, and the warrant expired on August 15, 2009. After issuance, the warrants detached from the common stock and traded separately. The warrants were also redeemable by the company at a price of $0.01 per warrant upon 30 days' notice after the warrants became exercisable, and their stock price is at least $8.50 per share for any 20 trading days within a 30-day trading period. The company included this provision to be able to force conversion.

Source: See KapStone Paper and Packaging Corporation (KapStone) 2008 10-K report.

The Effect of Option-Based Equity-Linked Securities When Measuring the Unlevered Cost of Capital of a Publicly Traded Company

Since option-based equity-linked securities are part of a company's capital structure, they have an effect on how we measure the costs of capital for publicly traded companies for which we observe the value of the common equity. If they represent a sufficiently large component of a company's capital structure, they have an effect on how we unlever a publicly traded company's cost of capital. Warrants and options can also have an effect on how we measure a publicly traded company's weighted average cost of capital if we are using that company's directly observed cost of equity capital in that calculation. We use warrants throughout this section as an example of the effect of option-based securities on how we unlever the equity cost of capital of comparable companies or the company being valued.

The Effect of Option-Based Equity-Linked Securities on Unlevering the Cost of Capital of Comparable Companies. In Chapter 10, we discussed alternative formulas for unlevering the cost of capital. Recall that the choice of which formula to use depends on the company's capital structure strategy and the valuation context. To illustrate the effect of warrants on the unlevering formulas, we use the formulas assuming the appropriate discount rate for interest tax shields is the unlevered cost of capital ($r_{ITS} = r_{UA}$), Equation 10.14 for unlevering the common equity cost of capital and Equation 10.18 for unlevering the common equity beta. We adjust these formulas by including an additional component for option-based securities, specifically, warrants.

$$r_{UA} = r_E \times \frac{V_E}{V_F} + r_D \times \frac{V_D}{V_F} + r_{PS} \times \frac{V_{PS}}{V_F} + r_W \times \frac{V_W}{V_F} \quad \text{(10.14 adjusted for warrants)}$$

$$\beta_{UA} = \beta_E \times \frac{V_E}{V_F} + \beta_D \times \frac{V_D}{V_F} + \beta_{PS} \times \frac{V_{PS}}{V_F} + \beta_W \times \frac{V_W}{V_F} \quad \text{(10.18 adjusted for warrants)}$$

The other unlevering formulas in Chapter 10 are adjusted in the same way, that is, by including an additional component for warrants or employee stock options. A company that has outstanding option-based securities has a common equity beta and equity cost of capital that reflects the reduction in risk caused by the outstanding option-based securities; therefore, ignoring the effect of the option-based securities results in an unlevered cost of capital or beta that is too low. Naturally, if the weight of the option-based securities is a small component of a company's capital structure, including them will not have a large effect on the unlevered cost of capital. However, as we show later in this section, if the weight for option-based securities is relatively large, including them can have a relatively large effect on the unlevered cost of capital.

Measuring the Weighted Average Cost of Capital of a Publicly Traded Company Based on Its Common Equity Cost of Capital. A similar issue arises when measuring the weighted average cost of capital of a publicly traded company based on its common equity cost of capital, for example, by estimating its beta and applying the CAPM. Since the company's common equity beta reflects the reduction in risk caused by the outstanding option-based securities, excluding them in a weighted average cost of capital results in a weighted average cost of capital that is too low. Recall that we briefly discussed this issue in Chapter 11 and already included a component for warrants in the weighted average cost of capital formula in Equation 11.1.

$$r_{WACC} = r_E \times \frac{V_E}{V_F} + r_D \times (1 - T_{INT}) \times \frac{V_D}{V_F} + r_{PS} \times \frac{V_{PS}}{V_F} + r_W \times \frac{V_W}{V_F} \quad \textbf{(11.1)}$$

One of the common assumptions made when using the weighted average cost of capital valuation method is that the weighted average cost of capital is constant, which implies that the capital structure strategy is constant. In order to have a constant capital structure, a company with warrants in its capital structure will continue to have warrants as part of its capital structure, which means the company will reissue warrants if they expire and adjust the amount of common equity as the warrants are exercised.

KapStone Paper and Packaging Corporation. KapStone issued units of stock and warrants in its initial public offering in 2005 (Valuation in Practice 12.5). The warrants detached from the stock and traded separately. In this section, we measure KapStone's unlevered cost of capital and its weighted average cost of capital as of June 30, 2008, with and without including the effect of its warrants in order to demonstrate the potential impact of option-linked equity securities on cost of capital estimates. We use KapStone in this illustration because it had a substantial number of warrants, 40 million, relative to its number of common shares outstanding, 28.4 million, and thus, the dilutive effect of the warrants could be relatively large.

At the end of June 2008, KapStone's stock price was \$6.67 and its warrant price was \$1.91. KapStone does not pay common dividends and the annual volatility of its equity is 24.4%. KapStone's equity beta was 0.83333 and its common equity cost of capital was 8.0% (the risk-free rate is 3% and the market risk premium is 6%, 0.08 = 0.03 + 0.83333 × 0.06). The risk premium for the common equity is 5% (0.05 = 0.08 − 0.03). We used the warrant pricing model to measure ω_E in order to measure KapStone's warrant cost of capital using either Equations 12.16 or 12.17.

$$r_W = r_F + (r_E - r_F) \times \frac{P_E}{P_W} \times \omega_E \Rightarrow 0.03 + (0.08 - 0.03) \times \frac{6.67}{1.91} \times 0.9134 = 0.1898$$

$$r_W = r_F + \beta_E \times MRP \times \frac{P_E}{P_W} \times \omega_E \Rightarrow 0.03 + 0.8333 \times 0.06 \times \frac{6.67}{1.91} \times 0.9134 = 0.1898$$

KapStone's common equity cost of capital at this time was 8.0% and its warrant cost of capital was 18.98%. Given the market value of KapStone's equity (189.4 million = \$6.67 × 28.4 million) and warrants (76.4 million = \$1.91 × 40 million), its weighted average cost of capital for its total equity, r_{TE}, is equal to 11.16%.

$$r_{TE} = r_E \times \frac{V_E}{V_E + V_W} + r_W \times \frac{V_W}{V_E + V_W}$$

$$0.1116 = 0.08 \times \frac{189.4}{189.4 + 76.4} + 0.1898 \times \frac{76.4}{189.4 + 76.4}$$

The total equity cost of capital has an implied beta. β_{TE}, equal to 1.36 (1.36 = (0.1116 − 0.03)/0.06). In other words, all else equal, if KapStone had not issued these warrants but issued only common equity, its common equity beta would be equal to 1.36 (versus 0.8333). It turns out that KapStone did not issue additional warrants when these warrants expired and did not intend to do so in the future. As expected, the chart in Exhibit 12.7 shows KapStone's common equity beta and an equally weighted industry common equity beta from July 2008 through September 2009.[21] As seen from this chart, KapStone's common equity beta increased from well below the industry beta to around the industry beta as the expiration date of the warrants approached (August, 2009).

EXHIBIT 12.7 KapStone Paper and Packaging Corporation's Equity Beta Before and After the Expiration of Its Warrants

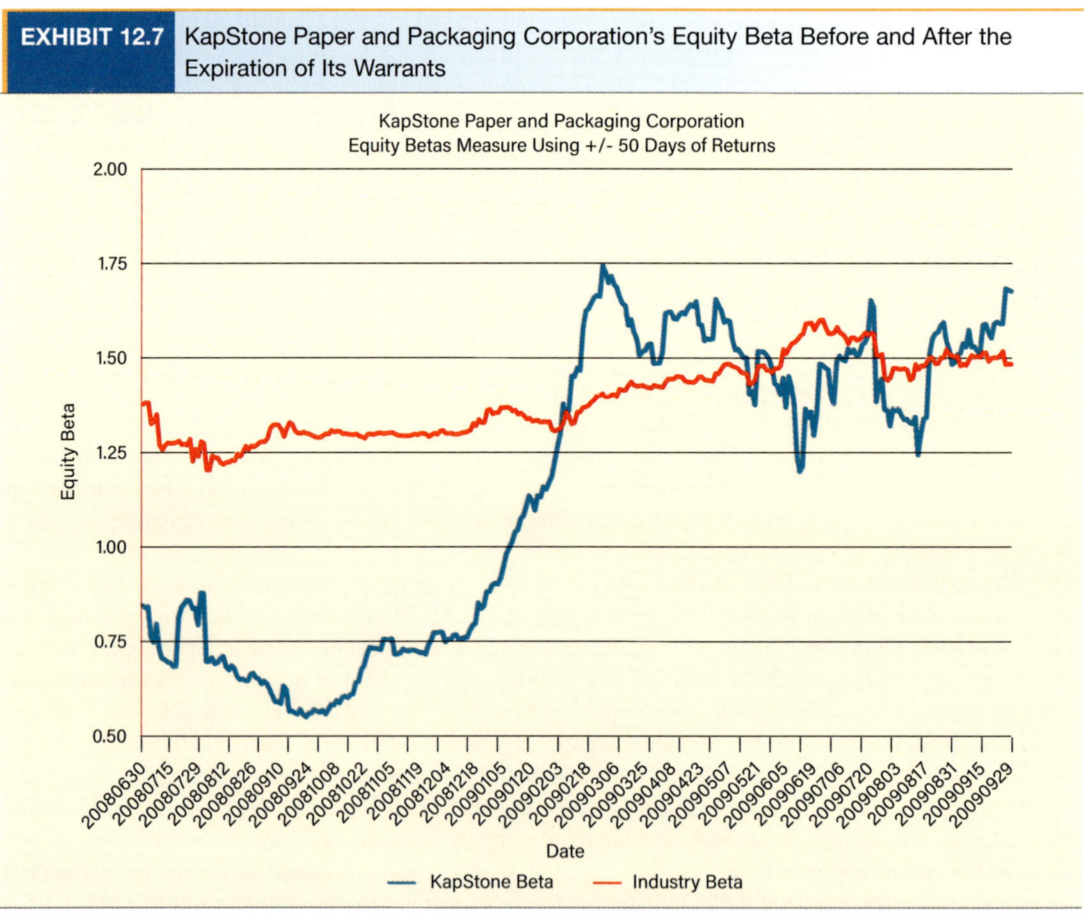

In Exhibit 12.8, we calculate KapStone's unlevered cost of capital excluding and including its warrants in its capital structure; in other words, when we exclude the warrants we assume the only financing the company uses is common equity and $240 million of debt. When we exclude the warrants, the company's capital structure is 55.9% debt and 44.1% equity. With a cost of debt of 6.5% and an equity cost of capital of 8%, its unlevered cost of capital is 7.16%. Ignoring the warrants, of course, is wrong, as the equity cost of capital is diminished because of the warrants. When we correctly include the warrants, the company's capital structure is 47.4% debt, 37.4% equity, and 15.1% warrants. KapStone's correct unlevered cost of capital is 8.95%. For KapStone, excluding the warrants from its capital structure understated its unlevered cost of capital by 1.79%. Excluding warrants from KapStone's capital structure results in a similar error when measuring its weighted average cost of capital. KapStone's weighted average cost of capital excluding the warrants is 5.71%, while its correct weighted average cost of capital including the warrants is 7.71%.

We chose KapStone because its warrants had a large effect on its unlevered and weighted average cost of capital. Most companies are not as affected by their equity-linked securities. However, KapStone illustrates that for companies for which warrants or employee stock options or other option-based equity-linked securities is a sufficiently large component of the company's capital structure, the impact can be relevant for measuring the unlevered cost of capital or weighted average cost of capital. Finally, we note that the equity and warrant cost of capital change over time as the warrants approach the expiration date. The only way for the company to have a constant equity cost of capital is to assume

[21] Beta is measured by regressing 50 daily stock returns before and after a date on the market index. We eliminated five of KapStone's 317 daily returns because they were outliers resulting from KapStone's low stock price during some of this period.

EXHIBIT 12.8 KapStone Paper and Packaging Corporation's Costs of Capital Excluding and Including the Effects of Warrants

Excluding the Effect of Warrants	Price	Units	Value	Weight	r_i	r_{UA}	r_{WACC}
Value of the debt			$240.0	55.9%	6.50%	3.63%	2.18%
Value of common equity	$6.670	28.40	189.4	44.1%	8.00%	3.53%	3.53%
Value of the firm			$429.4	100.0%		7.16%	5.71%

Including the Effect of Warrants	Price	Units	Value	Weight	r_i	r_{UA}	r_{WACC}
Value of the debt			$240.0	47.4%	6.50%	3.08%	1.85%
Value of common equity	$6.670	28.40	189.4	37.4%	8.00%	3.00%	3.00%
Value of warrants	$1.910	40.00	76.4	15.1%	18.98%	2.87%	2.87%
Value of the firm			$505.8	100.0%		8.95%	7.71%

the company will maintain its capital structure, which will include the characteristics of the warrants. However, the weighted average cost of capital and the total equity cost of capital will stay the same as the equity and warrant cost of capital change over time as long as the company keeps the proportion of debt and other non-common equity related securities (e.g., preferred stock) constant.

REVIEW EXERCISE 12.6

Measuring the Unlevered Cost of Capital for a Comparable Company with Outstanding Warrants

A company has 20,000 shares of common stock and 5,000 warrants outstanding. Each warrant has the right to purchase one share of the company's stock in five years at $12 per share, which is the current stock price. The value of a warrant is $8.775. The standard deviation of the stock's annual return is 24%. The company has a continuously compounded dividend yield of 5%. The company has $200,000 of outstanding debt with a 9% cost of capital. The company's equity cost of capital is 14%, its equity beta is 1.6667, the marginal tax rate for interest tax shields is 40%, the risk-free rate is 4%, and the market risk premium is 6%. Ignore the warrants and calculate the company's unlevered cost of capital and weighted average cost of capital, assuming that the company's current capital structure (without the warrants) represents its long-run capital structure and that the discount rate for interest tax shields is the unlevered cost of capital. Using these same assumptions, calculate the company's unlevered cost of capital and weighted average cost of capital that includes the effect of the warrants.

Solution on page 607.

12.5 CONVERTIBLE DEBT

LO5 Analyze the debt and option components of convertible debt and measure its cost of capital

Convertible debt is a security that has a coupon interest rate and maturity date (among other provisions) like straight-debt as well as an option to convert the bond into common stock (or possibly preferred stock). While convertible debt is a small percentage of the total debt outstanding, it is not an uncommon way to finance a company. Over the ten years ending in 2015, 20% of U.S. publicly traded companies that had some debt outstanding, had convertible debt outstanding. For companies with convertible debt, convertible debt is, on average, 16% of the total debt outstanding. Why do companies issue convertible debt? Research shows that it is useful for some companies to issue convertible debt as a less expensive way to issue equity ("back door" way to issue equity).[22] Research also shows that companies issuing convertible debt outperform the industry prior to issuing the debt and underperform afterward.[23]

[22] See, for example, Stein, Jeremy, "Convertible Bonds as a Back Door to Equity Financing," *Journal of Financial Economics* 32, (1992), pp. 3–21.

[23] Lewis, C. M., Rogalski R. J., and Seward, J. K. "The Long-Run Performance of Firms That Issue Convertible Debt: An Empirical Analysis of Operating Characteristics and Analyst Forecasts," *Journal of Corporate Finance*7 (2001), pp. 447–474.

A survey of companies found that 58% of the managers who considered issuing convertible debt considered convertible debt a way of issuing equity.[24] Interestingly, that survey also found 42% considered convertible debt cheaper financing than straight debt. That perception is incorrect. Convertible debt might, at first, seem like cheap debt because of its lower coupon rate, but it is not. The cost of capital for the convertible debt is equal to the weighted average of the cost of capital for the straight-debt component and the cost of capital for the conversion feature, which is higher than the cost of debt for straight debt. As we illustrate later in this section, while the yield-to-maturity on convertible debt considers only the coupon payments and the return of the principal upon maturity, it does not consider the expected cost of dilution associated with issuing equity if the debt is converted to equity.

Convertible Debt Contract Provisions

Convertible debt (and convertible preferred stock) can have many different provisions (or conditions) in its contracts. Like straight debt, convertible debt has a coupon rate, coupon timing, a principal amount (or par value), and a maturity date. Furthermore, it can be issued at a premium (issued at a price above the par value) or at a discount (issued at a price below par value). Unlike straight debt, convertible debt has a conversion provision that gives an investor the right to convert the debt into a certain number of shares of common stock. The conversion ratio is the number of shares of stock into which a debt or preferred stock security can be converted. This ratio is typically adjusted for stock splits and stock dividends, so the underlying economics do not change with these events. However, the conversion ratio can change over time as specified in the contract—based on, for example, the passage of time or on some characteristic of the company (such as stock price). Recall option pricing models assume that the investor will not exercise an option early for a non-dividend paying firm. For convertible securities, the option pricing models assume the investor will not exercise the option before the date the debt is callable, or if not callable, before it matures; thus, the **conversion price** is equal to par value (or the call price if it is callable) divided by the conversion rate. Depending on market conditions and the circumstances of the company issuing the convertible security, the conversion price is usually set 10% to 30% higher than the stock price on the issue date.

A call provision is very common in convertible debt securities. A call provision gives the company the right to call or repurchase its debt. In addition, it is common to have an initial period during which the company cannot call the debt—the hard non-call period. The call provision also includes a call price that is often greater than the principal (or par) value and it can also change over time. Another type of call provision is one in which the call activates only after the company's stock price increases to a value specified in the contract, or if the company meets some other performance condition. On the investor side, a less common provision is the put provision, which gives the investor the right to sell back—or put—the debt to the company after a certain point in time at a certain price. The put provision has various characteristics that are similar to what we described for the call provision.

Valuation Key 12.9

Convertible debt securities (and convertible preferred stock) have many different provisions (or conditions) in their contracts. Like straight debt, convertible debt has a coupon rate, coupon timing, a principal amount (or par value), and a maturity date, various types of debt covenants, and it can be issued at a premium or discount. Unlike straight debt, convertible debt has a conversion provision that gives the investor the right to convert the debt into a certain number of shares of stock. A call provision is very common in convertible debt securities, and it gives the company the right to repurchase its debt at a specified price beginning sometime before the maturity date.

One measure of the **intrinsic value** of the convertible debt any time the conversion option is in-the-money is the price of the stock multiplied by the number of common shares that will be received if the debt is converted, called the **if-converted value**. The value of the convertible debt is normally higher than that if the conversion option is in-the-money, as the option provides additional value over

[24] See Graham, J. R. and C. R. Harvey, "The Theory and Practice of Corporate Finance: Evidence from the Field," *Journal of Financial Economics* 60 (May 2001), pp. 187–243.

simply converting. Another common measure of intrinsic value is the ratio of the stock price to the conversion price—sometimes called the **parity ratio**. If the parity ratio is greater than 1, the conversion feature is "in-the-money"; if it is less than 1, the conversion feature is "out-of-the-money." Because the option to convert the bond into stock has value, we expect a convertible bond to always trade above the value of the straight debt component (what the debt would be worth without the conversion feature) or its value if it is converted—whichever is higher. In Exhibit 12.9, we show this relationship for an illustrative convertible note assuming there is no probability of default.

EXHIBIT 12.9 Valuation of Convertible Debt Compared to Its If-Converted Value at Different Stock Prices

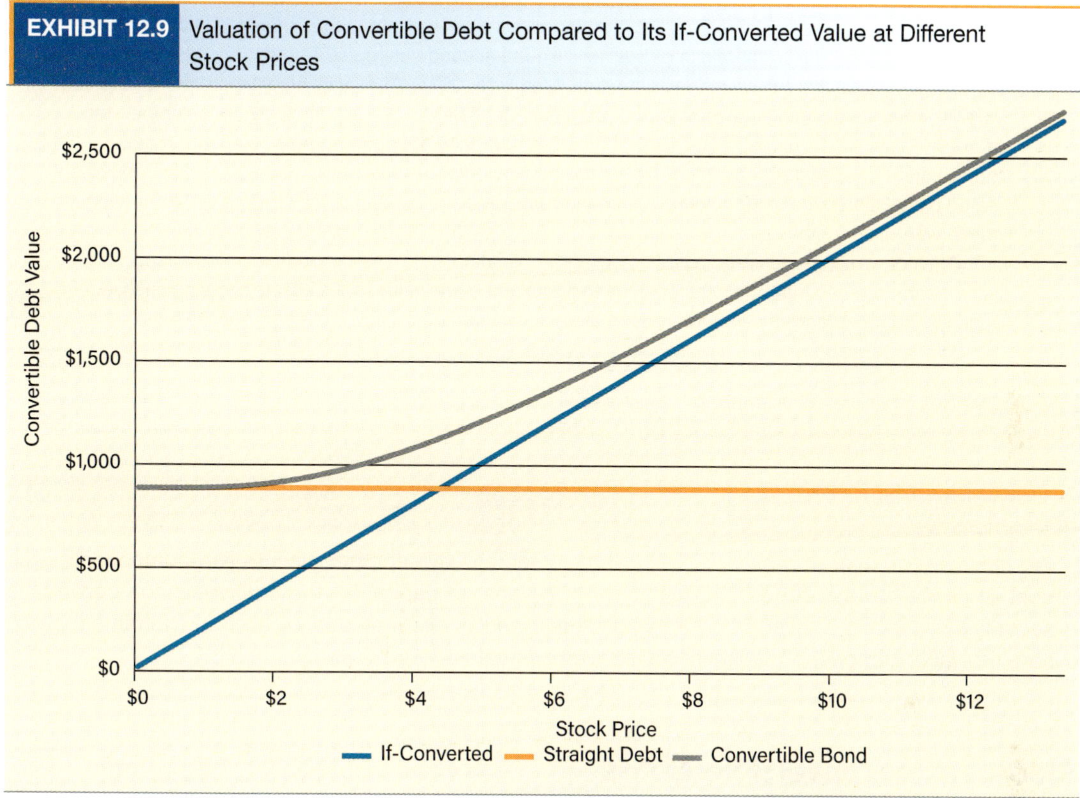

The Valuation and Cost of Capital of Convertible Debt

We measure the value and cost of capital for a convertible security by separating it into two components—the value and cost of capital for the security if it were not convertible and the value and cost of capital for the convertible feature. For a convertible debt issue, we know from the terms of the contract what the contractual or promised payments for the interest and the principal are. Using the methods discussed in Chapter 9, we can measure the promised yield and cost of debt for straight debt with the same risk. We can often analyze other debt instruments issued by the same company to measure the promised yield on a straight debt issue with similar risk; this yield is then assigned to the underlying straight debt component of the convertible security. We can then measure the value of the straight-debt component using the promised payments of the convertible security in conjunction with the promised yield for straight-debt with the same default risk and maturity as the convertible debt.

The second component is the convertible feature, and we need to measure both the value and the cost of capital for this component. If we know the value of the convertible security because, for example, it is publicly traded or was recently issued, we can measure the value of the convertible feature directly. The value of the convertible feature is equal to the difference between the value of the convertible security and the value of the first component (the value of the underlying security if it were not convertible). If we do not know the value of the convertible security, we must use a warrant pricing model to value the convertible feature. Fortunately, we can usually use the same formulas and methods used for warrants to measure the value and cost of capital of the convertible feature.

Valuation in Practice 12.6

Alcoa Inc.'s Issuance of Convertible Notes (and Common Equity) In spite of a downgrade in its credit rating, Alcoa Inc. (see Valuation in Practice 9.3) was able to issue both common equity and convertible notes shortly afterward. In its 10-Q report, the company stated:

> On March 24, 2009, Alcoa issued $575 [million] of 5.25% convertible notes due 2014 (the "convertible notes"). . . . Interest on the convertible notes is payable semi-annually . . .
>
> Alcoa does not have the right to redeem the convertible notes prior to the stated maturity date. Holders of the convertible notes have the option to convert their notes into shares of Alcoa's common stock at any time prior to the close of business on the second scheduled trading day (March 13, 2014) immediately preceding the stated maturity date (March 15, 2014). The initial conversion rate for the convertible notes is 155.4908 shares of Alcoa's common stock per $1,000 (in whole dollars) principal amount of notes (89,407,210 shares), equivalent to a conversion price of approximately $6.43 per share, . . . On the issuance date of the convertible notes, the market price of Alcoa's common stock was above the stated conversion price of $6.43 creating a beneficial conversion option to the holders, as the convertible notes were "in-the-money." . . .
>
> The convertible notes are general unsecured obligations. . . . The convertible notes effectively rank junior to any secured indebtedness of Alcoa to the extent of the value of the assets securing such indebtedness, and are effectively subordinated to all debt and other liabilities of Alcoa's subsidiaries.

Source: Available on June 14, 2018 at http://www.annualreports.com/HostedData/AnnualReportArchive/a/NYSE_AA_2009.pdf.

Valuation Key 12.10

We measure the cost of capital for a convertible security by separating it into two components—the cost of capital for the convertible feature and the cost of capital for the equivalent non-convertible security if it were not convertible. We can use the formulas and methods we used for warrants to measure the value and cost of capital of the convertible feature.

Alcoa Inc.'s Convertible Notes

We use Alcoa's convertible notes as described in Valuation in Practice 12.6 to illustrate how to measure the value and cost of capital of convertible debt. The total par value of the $1,000 notes is $575 million. The debt was issued for $641 million, which results in a 2.795% effective rate (or yield-to-maturity), based on a coupon rate of 5.25%, paid semi-annually, and maturing in five years from the date of issue. The conversion rate is 155.4908 common shares per $1,000 note, resulting in a conversion price of $6.4312 per share of common stock ($6.4312 = $1,000/155.4908). On the day the debt was issued, the company's stock price was $6.70 per share, so the conversion feature was in-the-money. In total, the notes are convertible into 89.4 million shares of common stock (89,407,210 = [$575.0 million/$1,000] × 155.4908).

Valuing the Components of Alcoa's Convertible Debt as of the Issuance Date. To value the conversion feature at issuance, we first separate the $641 million initial value of the notes into its straight debt and convertible feature components. To simplify the calculations, we ignore the fact that the term of the notes is a few days less than five years as well as certain features of the notes that make them more complex to value, such as the fact that the notes can be converted prior to the expiration date of the conversion feature. In Exhibit 12.10, we show three valuations for the straight-debt component. In the first valuation, we value the debt using the coupon rate of interest. The promised interest payments, which occur every six months, equal $15.094 million ($15.094 = $575.0 × 2.625%). On the maturity date, the promised payment is equal to the interest payment plus the repayment of the principal of $575 million. In the second component, we value the debt at its effective rate of interest (yield-to-maturity). In the third valuation, we value the notes using the promised yield of Alcoa's unsecured straight debt with the same maturity, which we assume to be 9% at the time.

EXHIBIT 12.10 Alcoa Inc. Convertible Debt Valuation as of the Issuance Date

($ in millions except per share amounts)	Coupon Rate	Effective Rate (YTM)	Straight-Debt Rate
Annual interest rate	5.250%	2.795%	9.000%
Semi-annual interest rate	2.625%	1.388%	4.500%
September 15, 2009	$ 15.094	$ 15.094	$ 15.094
March 15, 2010	$ 15.094	$ 15.094	$ 15.094
September 15, 2010	$ 15.094	$ 15.094	$ 15.094
March 15, 2011	$ 15.094	$ 15.094	$ 15.094
September 15, 2011	$ 15.094	$ 15.094	$ 15.094
March 15, 2012	$ 15.094	$ 15.094	$ 15.094
September 15, 2012	$ 15.094	$ 15.094	$ 15.094
March 15, 2013	$ 15.094	$ 15.094	$ 15.094
September 15, 2013	$ 15.094	$ 15.094	$ 15.094
March 15, 2014	$590.094	$590.094	$590.094
Value of straight debt notes	$575.000	$641.000	$489.691
Market price of the notes			$641.000
Value of the conversion provision			$151.309
Number of shares			89,407,210
Value of conversion feature per share			$ 1.692

($ in millions except per share amounts)	Shares	Price	Value
Value of notes (ignoring accrued interest)			$ 489.7
Value of conversion feature	89,407,210	$ 1.692	151.3
Value of convertible note			$ 641.0
Value if converted	89,407,210	$ 6.700	599.0
Value of note in excess of converted value			$ 42.0

If we discount the same promised payments by the 9% discount rate, we find that the value of the straight debt component is equal to $489.7 million. Since the notes were issued for $641 million, the implied value of the conversion feature is $151.3 million ($151.3 = $641.0 − $489.7). The notes are convertible into 89,407,210 shares; thus, the per-share value of the conversion feature is $1.692 ($1.692 = $151.3/89.407) as of the issuance date. At the bottom of the exhibit, we compare the value of the notes to the value of the notes if converted. As expected, the $641.0 million value (straight debt of $489.7 million and conversion feature of $151.3 million) is larger than the value of the notes if converted by $42.0 million ($42.0 = $641 − 89.407 × $6.7).

The Cost of Capital for Alcoa's Convertible Debt at the Issuance Date. Recall for Alcoa's convertible debt its yield-to-maturity is 2.795%, while it is 9.0% for its straight debt. Thus, convertible debt might seem like "cheap debt" but it is not. The cost of capital for the convertible debt is equal to the weighted average of the cost of capital for the straight debt and the cost of capital for the conversion feature. This weighted average must be higher than the cost of capital for the straight debt because the cost of capital for the conversion feature is larger than that cost of capital for the straight debt.

We can glean some intuition as to why this is the case if we measure the internal rate of return (yield-to-maturity) assuming that the principal is repaid when the debt matures (see the middle column of numbers in Exhibit 12.10) versus that the principal is converted into equity. Alcoa's current stock price is $6.70, its equity cost of capital is equal to 12%, its dividend yield is 3%, and the conversion feature of the debt has a five-year term. For a quick calculation, assume that the company's stock price will increase by 9% (12% − 3%) each year or to $10.3088 on the date the debt matures ($10.31 = $6.70 × 1.09^5). Since the stock price will be greater than the exercise price of $6.4312, the debt will convert at a value of $921.679 million ($921.679 = 89.407 × $10.3088). In the following table, we calculate the internal rate of return (yield-to-maturity) assuming that the principal is repaid when the debt matures versus that the principal is converted into equity.

This table shows that the cost of capital for the convertible debt, 11.44%, is greater than the cost of capital for straight debt. This back-of-the-envelope example illustrates why convertible debt is not cheap debt.

Dates of payments	IRR of Interest and Principal	IRR of Interest and Conversion
Initial loan	−$641.000	−$641.000
September 15, 2009	$ 15.094	$ 15.094
March 15, 2010	$ 15.094	$ 15.094
September 15, 2010	$ 15.094	$ 15.094
March 15, 2011	$ 15.094	$ 15.094
September 15, 2011	$ 15.094	$ 15.094
March 15, 2012	$ 15.094	$ 15.094
September 15, 2012	$ 15.094	$ 15.094
March 15, 2013	$ 15.094	$ 15.094
September 15, 2013	$ 15.094	$ 15.094
March 15, 2014	$ 590.094	$1,055.693
Internal rate of return (semi-annual)	1.39%	5.56%
Internal rate of return (annual)	2.79%	11.44%

Using the above and some additional information about Alcoa in conjunction with the warrant pricing model, we first measure the cost of capital for the conversion feature of its convertible debt. In the following table we summarize Alcoa's inputs for the warrant pricing model.

Risk-free rate of return	2.1%
Equity cost of capital	12.000%
Annual volatility of equity	34.0%
Dividend yield continuously compounded	3.000%
Expiration of warrants (in years)	5.0
Face value per note	$1,000.00
Conversion ratio per $1,000 note	155.4908
Exercise price of conversion feature	$ 6.4312
Current stock price	$ 6.700
Common shares outstanding	974,372,426
Marginal tax rate for interest	40.0%

In the following table we summarize the output from the warrant pricing model. The cost of capital for the conversion feature is 23.8%,[25] which is, as expected, higher than Alcoa's equity cost of capital of 12%.

Stock price/Warrant price	$6.700	$1.690
Volatility, σ_E/Risk-free rate	34.00%	2.10%
d_1 and d_2	0.4192	−0.3616
σ_Q	0.3492	
ω_E	0.5531	
Equity and warrant costs of capital	12.00%	23.80%
Combined total equity cost of capital	12.27%	

[25] The cost of debt for the conversion feature is equal to the following (Equation 12.16).

$$r_w = r_F + (r_E - r_F) \times \frac{P_E}{P_W} \times \omega_E = 0.021 + (0.12 - 0.021) \times \frac{6.70}{1.690} \times 0.5531 = 0.238$$

From equation 12.1', the total equity cost of capital is as follows:

$$r_{TE} = 0.12 \times \frac{\$6.70 \times 974.372426}{\$6.70 \times 974.372426 + \$1.69 \times 89.407210} + 0.2380 \times \frac{\$1.69 \times 89.407210}{\$6.70 \times 974.372426 + \$1.69 \times 89.407210} = 0.12267$$

The cost of capital for the convertible debt is equal to the weighted average of the cost of capital for the straight debt and the cost of capital for the conversion feature, 12.49%.

At Issue Date	Value	Weight	r_i	r_{CD}
Value of the straight debt	$489.7	76.4%	9.00%	6.88%
Value of the convertible feature	151.3	23.6%	23.80%	5.62%
Value of the convertible debt	$641.0	100.0%		12.49%

Alcoa One Year Later. It turned out that Alcoa's stock price more than doubled over the next year. Since Alcoa's convertible debt was not publicly traded, which is common, we use the warrant pricing model to measure the value of the components of Alcoa's convertible debt and their cost of capital. In the following table we present Alcoa's inputs and outputs for the warrant pricing model one year later.

Risk-free rate of return	2.1%
Total equity cost of capital	12.267%
Annual volatility of equity	60.0%
Dividend yield continuously compounded	1.200%
Expiration of warrants (in years)	4.0
Face value per note	$1,000.00
Conversion ratio per $1,000 note	155.4908
Exercise price of conversion feature	$ 6.4312
Current stock price	$ 14.000
Common shares outstanding	974,372,426

Notice that in addition to Alcoa's stock price increasing from $6.70 per share to $14.00, several other inputs changed. Its annual volatility increased from 34% to 60%, its dividend yield decreased from 3% to 1.2%, and the time to expiration decreased by one year. Also notice that several of the inputs did not change. The risk-free rate remained at 2.1% and all of the terms of the convertible note remained the same. One difference that we illustrate later in this section but preface here is the increase in Alcoa's equity cost of capital. At the issuance date we measured Alcoa's total equity cost of capital as 12.27%. In the absence of changes in the risk free rate or the business risk of Alcoa, we assume that its total equity cost of capital did not change since the date when it issued the convertible debt. Given that the value of the conversion feature increased over this period, its cost of capital likely decreased, resulting in an increase in the equity cost of capital.

In the following table we summarize the inputs and output from the warrant pricing model. Since the stock price increased, the value of the conversion feature increased. The value of the conversion feature also increased from the decrease in the dividend yield and increase in volatility. On the other hand, the conversion feature expires in four years rather than five, which has the opposite effect. Overall, the value of the conversion feature increases from $1.69 to $8.838. The increase in the value of the conversion feature results in a decrease in the cost of capital of the conversion feature, which results in an increase in the equity cost of capital.

Warrant Pricing Model Inputs and Output	2010		2009	
Stock price/Warrant price	$14.000	$8.838	$6.700	$1.690
Volatility, σ_E/Risk-free rate	60.00%	2.10%	34.00%	2.10%
d_1 and d_2	1.3252	0.1016	0.4192	−0.3616
σ_Q	0.6118		0.3492	
ω_E	0.8576		0.5531	
Equity and warrant costs of capital	12.07%	15.65%	12.00%	23.80%
Combined total equity cost of capital	12.27%		12.27%	
Warrant cost of capital leverage factor		1.3586		2.1923

Warrant cost of capital leverage factor = $(P_E/P_W) \times \omega_E$

In Exhibit 12.11, we value the straight-debt component of the convertible debt, which increases from $489.7 million to $503.9 million. Since the straight-debt is valued at a discount (relative to its par value), the value of the debt will increase as it matures. Thus, the value of the debt increased because we assumed the cost of capital for the straight-debt component did not change and the time to maturity decreased by one year.

EXHIBIT 12.11 Valuation of Alcoa Inc. Convertible Debt One Year Later

($ in millions except per share amounts)	Straight-Debt Rate
Annual interest rate	9.000%
Semi-annual interest rate	4.500%
September 15, 2010	$ 15.094
March 15, 2011	$ 15.094
September 15, 2011	$ 15.094
March 15, 2012	$ 15.094
September 15, 2012	$ 15.094
March 15, 2013	$ 15.094
September 15, 2013	$ 15.094
March 15, 2014	$590.094
Value of straight debt notes	**$503.888**

The value of the conversion feature increases from $1.69 to $8.838, which results in a decrease in the cost of capital for the conversion feature from 23.80% to 15.65%. Even though the cost of capital for the conversion feature decreased, the cost of capital for the convertible debt increased from 12.5% to 13.1%. It increased to 13.1% because the value of the conversion feature increased from $151.3 million to $790.2 million and thus, accounts for a larger proportion of the value of the convertible debt.

One Year Later	Value	Weight	r_i	r_{CD}
Value of the straight debt	$503.9	38.9%	9.00%	3.50%
Value of the convertible feature	790.2	61.1%	15.65%	9.55%
Value of the convertible debt	$1,294.1	100.0%		13.06%

REVIEW EXERCISE 12.7

Convertible Debt

A company issued $2 million of $1,000 face-value convertible bonds with an 8% annual coupon payment. The bonds mature in six years. Each bond is convertible into 100 shares of the company's stock at the end of the six years. The company's straight debt has a yield to maturity and a cost of capital equal to 10%. The bonds are currently trading at $1,100. The company has 1 million shares of stock outstanding, and its stock is trading at $8.45 per share. Its equity cost of capital is 15%, the annual volatility of equity is 40%, the continuously compounded dividend yield is 5%, the income tax rate for interest tax shields is 40%, and the risk-free rate is 4%. This is the only financing the company uses to finance the company. Using the warrant pricing model, calculate the value of the conversion feature of these bonds based on a per convertible share value basis, the cost of capital for this conversion feature, and the cost of capital for the convertible debt. In addition, calculate the value of the conversion feature of these bonds based on a per convertible share value basis by comparing the value of the bond if it were straight debt to the market value of the bond.

Solution on pages 608–609.

SUMMARY AND KEY CONCEPTS

In this chapter, we focused on various aspects of valuing a company for which option pricing models are useful. Our focus is on option-like securities that are typically written by a company on its common stock. These options include employee stock options, warrants, and convertible bonds and preferred stock. We discuss how to value them and measure their cost of capital.

We discussed in detail the different forms of equity-based compensation that are paid to employees by companies—including stock options, stock appreciation rights, restricted stock, and restricted stock units. We discussed the accounting and tax treatments of this form of compensation and we discussed how to measure the economic value that the firm gives to employees when it provides equity-based compensation. Finally, we discussed in detail how to adjust a company's valuation for existing equity-based compensation as of the valuation date, as well as how to deal with grants of equity-based compensation that will occur after the valuation date.

We showed how to use an option pricing model to estimate both the value and the cost of capital for warrants and the convertible feature of convertible debt or preferred. We also showed the potential importance of taking into consideration the value and cost of capital for option-like securities in unlevering the equity cost of capital or in computing the weighted average cost of capital discount rate.

ADDITIONAL READING AND REFERENCES

Black, F., and M. Scholes, "The Pricing of Options and Corporate Liabilities," *Journal of Political Economy* vol. 81, no. 3 (May/June 1973), pp. 637–654.

Merton, R. C., "On the Pricing of Corporate Debt: The Risk Structure of Interest Rates," *Journal of Finance* vol. 29, no. 2 (May 1974), pp. 449–470.

EXERCISES AND PROBLEMS

P12.1 **Forecasting Future Stock-Based Compensation #1—Triple J Company:** Review the following information and Exhibit P12.1 for the Triple J Company.

EXHIBIT P12.1 Triple J Company's Employee Stock Option and Other Information

Employee Stock Options	Year −4	Year −3	Year −2	Year −1	Year 0
Outstanding options beginning balance	292.5	297.3	302.1	307.0	312.0
Options granted	105.9	107.7	109.4	111.2	113.0
Options exercised	−85.8	−87.2	−88.6	−90.0	−91.5
Options forfeited	−15.4	−15.6	−15.9	−16.2	−16.4
Outstanding options ending balance	297.3	302.1	307.0	312.0	317.1
Percent forfeited each year before vesting	5.0%	5.0%	5.0%	5.0%	5.0%
Weighted average date value per unit					
Options granted—value at grant date	$ 9.52	$ 10.53	$ 11.64	$ 12.88	$ 14.24
Options exercised—value at grant date	$ 7.04	$ 7.78	$ 8.61	$ 9.52	$ 10.53
Options exercised—value at vesting date	$ 9.55	$ 10.56	$ 11.68	$ 12.92	$ 14.29
Current stock price	$36.61	$ 40.49	$ 44.78	$ 49.53	$ 54.77
Revenue	$9,869	$11,053	$12,380	$13,865	$15,529
Total labor costs	$4,714	$ 5,299	$ 5,956	$ 6,695	$ 7,525

a. Use the expense ratio-based, grant date value-based, and exercise date value-based forecasting methods to measure the company's potential forecast drivers for its stock-based compensation (employee stock options) for Year 1, assuming the employee stock options vest annually over three years and will be exercised in three years. Also, assume the appropriate way to scale stock-based compensation is (a) revenue and (b) cash labor costs.

b. Forecast the stock-based compensation effect on free cash flows in Year 0 based on the revenues and cash labor costs in Year 0 (see Exhibit P12.1).

P12.2 **Forecasting Future Stock-Based Compensation #2—Triple J Company:** Review the information in Problem P12.1 for the Triple J Company.

a. Use the expense ratio-based, grant date value-based, and exercise date value-based forecasting methods to measure the company's potential forecast drivers for its stock-based compensation (employee stock options) for Year 0, assuming the employee stock options vest annually over three years and will be exercised in three years. Also, assume the appropriate way to scale stock-based compensation is (a) revenue and (b) cash labor costs.

b. Forecast the stock-based compensation effect on free cash flows in Year 1 assuming the forecast for revenues in Year 1 is $17,000 and the forecast for cash labor cost in Year 1 is $7,000.

P12.3 Allocating Total Equity to Common Equity and Warrants That Will be Cancelled on the Valuation Date #1—Addison Inc.: Review the information in Exhibit P12.2 for the Addison Inc. Calculate the company's stock price and warrant price based on the reported valuation and assuming the warrants will be cancelled on the valuation date. Addison Inc. has 330,000.0 warrants outstanding that have a $20 exercise price, and which expire in 4.0 years.

EXHIBIT P12.2 Addison Inc.'s Stock Based Compensation Related Other Information

Value of the firm	$8,000,000.0	Unlevered cost of capital	12.0%
Value of the debt	$2,000,000.0	Unlevered free cash flow next year	$480,000.0
Common shares authorized	550,000.0	Equity free cash flow next year	$240,000.0
Common shares issued	220,000.0	Weighted average cost of capital	11.000%
Common treasury shares	20,000.0	Risk-free rate	3.0%
Income tax rate on all income	40.0%	Annualized standard deviation (volatility)	45.00%
Exercise price	$ 20.0	Expiration (in years)	4.0

P12.4 Allocating Total Equity to Common Equity and Employee Stock Options That Will be Cancelled on the Valuation Date #2—Evelyn Associates: Review the information in Exhibit P12.3 for the Evelyn Associates. Calculate the company's stock price and the value of an employee stock option based on the reported valuation and assuming the employee stock options will be cancelled on the valuation date.

EXHIBIT P12.3 Evelyn Associates' Stock Based Compensation Related Other Information

	Employee Stock Options		
	Options	Weighted Avg Exercise Price	Weighted Avg Remaining Term
Beginning balance	300,000.0	$20.00	
Granted	200,000.0	$30.00	
Vested/exercised	−167,000.0	$21.80	
Forfeited/expired	−28,000.0	$22.80	
Ending balance	305,000.0	$25.10	3.5
Expected to vest/exercise	244,000.0	$24.00	4.0

Value of the firm	$12,000,000.0	Unlevered cost of capital	12.0%
Value of the debt	$4,000,000.0	Unlevered free cash flow next year	$720,000.0
Common shares authorized	630,000.0	Equity free cash flow next year	$400,000.0
Common shares issued	250,000.0	Weighted average cost of capital	10.667%
Common treasury shares	50,000.0	Risk-free rate	3.0%
Income tax rate on all income	40.0%	Annualized standard deviation (Volatility)	45.00%

P12.5 Allocating Total Equity to Common Equity and Warrants That Will Not be Cancelled on the Valuation Date #1—Addison Inc.: Review the information in P12.3 for Addison Inc. Measure the company's stock price and warrant price based on the reported valuation and assuming the warrants will not be cancelled on the valuation date; in other words, use the warrant valuation model to allocate the total equity. The debt cost of capital is 10%.

P12.6 Allocating Total Equity to Common Equity and Employee Stock Options That Will Not be Cancelled on the Valuation Date #2—Evelyn Associates: Review the information in Exhibit P12.3 for Evelyn Associates. Measure the company's stock price and the value of an employee stock option based on the reported valuation and assuming the warrants will not be cancelled on the valuation date; in other words, use the warrant valuation model to allocate the total equity. The debt cost of capital is 10%.

P12.7 Measuring the Warrant Cost of Capital: On January 1, 2017, 3 years before a company's warrants were going to expire, the company's stock price was $10.00. According to the company's 10-K report, the company has approximately 100 million common shares and 20 million warrants outstanding. Each warrant has the right to purchase one share of common stock for $8.00. The company's 10-K indicates that it pays dividends annually at a constant dividend yield. The company's current dividend is $0.50 per share. The 10-K also reports a volatility of 45%. The company's equity cost of capital is 12% (r_E) and the risk-free rate is 3% (r_F). Calculate: (a) the intrinsic value of the warrant; (b) the value of the warrant based on the warrant pricing model (time value of the warrant); (c) the warrant cost of capital (r_W); and (d) the total equity cost of capital (r_{TE}). The market risk premium is 6%.

P12.8 **Allocating Total Equity to Common Equity and Warrants That Are Not Cancelled on the Valuation Date #3:** A Company has an unlevered cost of capital of 10%, which is also the discount rate for interest tax shields; the company also has an income tax rate of 30%. The company finances itself with 40% debt, which has a cost of capital equal to 7%; finances itself with 10% preferred stock, which has a cost of capital of 7.5%; and the remainder with common equity. The company expects its unlevered free cash flows to remain constant in perpetuity. The company holds no excess cash or excess assets. Use the information that follows to calculate the company's stock price, assuming it has 2,000 shares of common stock outstanding at the end of Year 0—the valuation date. Afterward, calculate the company's stock price, assuming the company issued 1,000 warrants with an exercise or strike price equal to $5 and immediately paid out the proceeds to shareholders as of the end of Year 0. The warrants and the common equity together account for 50% of the capital structure. The company expects to follow a consistent dividend policy and pay all available cash flows to its shareholders in the form of dividends. The warrants can be exercised at the end of two years, their expiration date. At the date of issuance, the risk-free rate was 4%, and the company's annualized standard deviation of its stock return is 40%.

Income Statement Forecast	Year 1
Revenue	$120,000
Depreciation expense	−20,000
Operating expenses	−96,859
Earnings before interest and taxes	$ 3,141

Asset Forecast	Year 1
Cash	$ 4,000
Net operating working capital	25,000
Net property, plant and equipment	120,000
Total assets	$149,000

Unlevered Free Cash Flow Forecast	Year 1
Earnings before interest and taxes	$ 3,141
Income taxes	−942
Unlevered earnings after tax	$ 2,198
Depreciation expense (non-cash expenses)	20,000
Change in required cash	0
Change in net working capital	0
Capital expenditures	−20,000
Unlevered free cash flows	$ 2,198

Exhibit may contain small rounding errors

P12.9 **Allocating Total Equity to Common Equity and Warrants That Are Not Cancelled on the Valuation Date #4:** A Company has an unlevered cost of capital of 12%, which is also the discount rate for interest tax shields; and the company has an income tax rate of 45%. The company finances itself with 40% debt, which has a cost of capital equal to 7%; finances itself with 10% preferred stock, which has a cost of capital of 8%; and the remainder with common equity. The company expects its unlevered free cash flows to grow at 6% in perpetuity. The company holds no excess cash or excess assets. Use the information that follows to calculate the company's stock price, assuming it has 20,000 shares of common stock outstanding at the end of Year 0—the valuation date. Next, calculate the company's stock price, assuming the company issued 5,000 warrants with an exercise or strike price equal to $3 and immediately paid the proceeds out to shareholders as of the end of Year 0. The warrants and the common equity together account for 50% of the capital structure. The company expects to follow a consistent dividend policy and pay all available cash flows to its shareholders in the form of dividends. The warrants can be exercised at the end of two years, their expiration date. At the date of issuance, the risk-free rate was 4%, and the company's annualized standard deviation of its stock returns is 40%.

Balance Sheet Forecast	Year 0	Year 1
Cash	$ 12,000	$ 12,720
Net operating working capital	36,000	38,160
Net property, plant, and equipment	60,000	63,600
Total assets	$108,000	$114,480
Debt	$ 80,000	$ 84,800
Preferred stock	20,000	21,200
Common equity	8,000	8,480
Total liabilities and equities	$108,000	$114,480

Income Statement Forecast	Year 1
Revenue	$120,000
Depreciation expense	−24,000
Operating expenses	−66,982
Earnings before interest and taxes	$ 29,018
Interest expense	−5,600
Earnings before tax	$ 23,418
Income taxes	−10,538
Earnings after tax	$ 12,880
Preferred stock dividends	−1,600
Earnings available to common equity	$ 11,280

Free Cash Flow Schedule	Year 1
Earnings before interest and taxes	$29,018
Income taxes	−13,058
Unlevered earnings after tax	$15,960
Depreciation	24,000
Change in required cash	−720
Change in net working capital	−2,160
Capital expenditures	−27,600
Unlevered free cash flow (FCF)	$9,480
Interest paid in cash ($r_D \times D$)	−5,600
Interest tax shield ($T_{INT} \times r_D \times D$)	2,520
Preferred stock dividend ($r_{PSDIV} \times PS$)	−1,600
Change in debt	4,800
Change in preferred stock	1,200
Equity free cash flow (EFCF)	$10,800
Common dividends	−10,800
Change in common equity	0
Change in required cash	720
Change in cash balance	$ 720

P12.10 Allocating Total Equity to Common Equity and Warrants That Are Not Cancelled on the Valuation Date #5—Stuart Essig Company: The Stuart Essig Company has an unlevered cost of capital of 10% and an income tax rate of 40% on all types of income and expenses. The company finances itself with 50% debt, which has a cost of capital equal to 9%; with 20% preferred stock, which has a cost of capital of 9.5%; and the remainder with common equity. The company expects its unlevered free cash flows to remain constant in perpetuity. The company holds no excess cash or excess assets and expects to pay $3,600 in common dividends in Year 1. Interest tax shields are valued using the unlevered cost of capital. Based on the forecasts and capital structure strategy, the value of the company (firm) is equal to $100,000.

Use the following information to measure the company's stock price, assuming it has 10,000 shares of common stock outstanding at the end of Year 0—the valuation date. Next, calculate the company's stock price and warrant price, assuming the company issued 5,000 warrants as of the end of Year 0 and immediately distributed the proceeds to its shareholders. The company expects to follow a consistent dividend policy and to distribute all available cash flows to its shareholders in the form of dividends. Each warrant can purchase one share of stock for $1 and can be exercised at the end of five years, the expiration date. At the date of issuance, the risk-free rate was 5%, and the company's annualized standard deviation of its stock return was 45%. Lastly, instead of warrants, assume the company issued 5,000 employee stock options with the same terms as the above warrants, assume the employee stock options have the tax benefits described in the chapter, and assume the company reduced the employee's annual cash compensation by the value of the employee stock options upon issuing the employee stock options.

Income Statement Forecast	Year 1
Revenue	$180,000.0
Depreciation expense	−25,000.0
Operating expenses	−141,333.3
Earnings before interest and taxes	$ 13,666.7

Balance Sheet Forecast—Assets	Year 1
Cash	$ 4,000.0
Net operating working capital	25,000.0
Net property, plant, and equipment	120,000.0
Total assets	$149,000.0

Unlevered Free Cash Flow Forecast	Year 1
Earnings before interest and taxes	$13,666.7
Income taxes	−5,466.7
Unlevered earnings after tax	$ 8,200.0
Depreciation expense (non-cash expenses)	25,000.0
Change in required cash	0.0
Change in net working capital	0.0
Capital expenditures	−25,000.0
Unlevered free cash flows	$ 8,200.0

P12.11 Unlevering the Cost of Capital for a Company with Warrants #1: A company has 100,000 shares of common stock and 10,000 warrants outstanding. Each warrant has the right to purchase three shares of the company's stock at the end of five years at $9 per share. The value of a warrant is $3.50 per warrant, and the company's stock price is $8 per share. The standard deviation of the stock's annual return is 30%. The company has a continuously compounded dividend yield of 6%. The company has $100,000 of outstanding debt that has an 8% cost of capital. The company's common equity cost of capital is 15%, and the risk-free rate is 5%. The company's income tax rate is 40% on all income.

a. Ignore the warrants and calculate the company's unlevered cost of capital and weighted average cost of capital, assuming that the company's current capital structure (without the warrants) represents its long-run capital structure, and that the discount rate for interest tax shields is the unlevered cost of capital.

b. Using these same assumptions, calculate the company's unlevered cost of capital and weighted average cost of capital, but now include the effect of the warrants.

P12.12 Unlevering the Cost of Capital for a Company with Warrants #2: A company has 10,000 shares of common stock and 5,000 warrants outstanding. Each warrant has the right to purchase two shares of the company's stock at the end of ten years at $5 per share, which is the company's current stock price. The standard deviation of the stock's annual return is 40%. The company has a continuously compounded dividend yield of 2%. The company has $40,000 of outstanding debt that has an 8% cost of capital. The company's common equity cost of capital is 10%, and the risk-free rate is 4%. The company's income tax rate is 30% on all income.

a. Ignore the warrants and calculate the company's unlevered cost of capital and weighted average cost of capital, assuming that the company's current capital structure (without the warrants) represents its long-run capital structure, and that the discount rate for interest tax shields is the unlevered cost of capital.

b. Using these same assumptions, calculate the company's unlevered cost of capital and weighted average cost of capital, but now include the effect of the warrants.

P12.13 Convertible Bonds with an Observable Price: A company issues $1 million of $1,000 face value convertible bonds with a 6% annual coupon payment. The bonds mature in 5 years. Each bond is convertible into 200 shares of the company's stock at the end of the 5 years. If the company had straight debt outstanding, it would have a yield to maturity and a cost of capital of 9%. The bonds were issued today at $1,200. The company has 1 million shares of stock outstanding, and its stock is trading at $4.50 per share. Its common equity cost of capital is 15%, the standard deviation of its annual stock return is 60%, its continuously compounded dividend yield is 4.75%, and the risk-free rate is 3.25%. This is the only financing the company uses to finance the company. Calculate the value of the conversion feature of these bonds on a per convertible share value and calculate the cost of capital for this conversion feature and for the convertible bond. The income tax rate is 40%.

P12.14 Convertible Bonds with an Unobservable Price: A few years ago, a company issued $1 million of $1,000 face value convertible bonds with a 6% annual coupon payment. Each bond is convertible into 100 shares of the company's stock at the end of 5 years from today. The company has 500,000 shares of stock outstanding and its stock is trading at $11 per share. Its common equity cost of capital is 12%, the standard deviation of its annual stock return is 44%, it has a continuously compounded dividend yield of 3.90%, and the risk-free rate is 3.0%. If the company had straight debt outstanding, it would have a yield to maturity and cost of debt of 10%. This is the only financing the company uses to finance itself. Calculate the value of the conversion feature of these bonds on a per convertible share value and calculate the cost of capital for this conversion feature and for the convertible bond. The value of a bond is $1,200 and the income tax rate is 40%.

SOLUTIONS FOR REVIEW EXERCISES

Review Exercise 12.1: Forecasting Future Stock-Based Compensation

Restricted Stock Units Forecast Drivers	Year −1	Year 0	Forecast Year 1
RSU stock-based compensation expense	$ 1,367	$ 1,463	
Granted—grant date value expected to vest	1,563	1,672	
Vested—exercise date value	1,534	1,641	
Total cash labor costs	9,192	9,836	$11,000
Total revenue	$19,990	$21,589	24,000
Units expected to vest	85.0%	85.0%	
Expense/revenue	6.8%	6.8%	1,626
Granted—grant date value/revenue × expected to vest %	7.8%	7.7%	1,859
Vested—exercise date value/revenue	7.7%	7.6%	1,824
Expense/cash labor costs	14.9%	14.9%	1,636
Granted—grant date value/cash labor costs × expected to vest %	17.0%	17.0%	1,870
Vested—exercise date value/cash labor costs	16.7%	16.7%	$ 1,835
Company's expected cost of stock-based awards as a percentage of total cash labor costs	17.0%	17.0%	

Review Exercise 12.2: Allocating Total Equity to Common Equity and Warrants That Are Cancelled on the Valuation Date

Solution—Warrants:

Common shares issued	250,000.0
Common treasury shares	−50,000.0
Shares outstanding	200,000.0
Value of the firm	$10,000,000.0
Value of the debt	−3,000,000.0
Value of the total equity	$ 7,000,000.0

Warrants	48,000.0
Weighted average exercise price	$ 31.20
Total exercise price	$1,497,600.0
Value of total equity	7,000,000.0
Total equity + exercise	$8,497,600.0
Share equivalents outstanding	200,000.0
Warrants	48,000.0
Total	248,000.0
Stock price	$ 34.26
Weighted average exercise price	31.20
Warrant price	$ 3.06

Review Exercise 12.3: Allocating Total Equity to Common Equity and Employee Stock Options That Are Cancelled on the Valuation Date

Solution—Employee Stock Options:

Common shares issued	250,000.0
Common treasury shares	−50,000.0
Shares outstanding	200,000.0
Value of the firm	$10,000,000.0
Value of the debt	−3,000,000.0
Value of the total equity	$ 7,000,000.0
Stock price	$ 34.52
Shares outstanding	200,000.0
Value of common equity	$ 6,904,335.7
Option price	$ 3.32
Options expected to exercise	48,000.0
Value of options	$ 159,440.6
Total value of equity	$ 7,063,776.2

Options expected to exercise	48,000.0
1 − Income tax rate	60.0%
Weighted average exercise price	$ 31.20
Total exercise price	$ 898,560.0
Value of total equity	7,000,000.0
Total equity + exercise	$7,898,560.0
Share equivalents outstanding	200,000.0
Options expected to exercise	48,000.0
1 − Income tax rate	60.0%
Total	228,800.0
Stock price	$ 34.52
Weighted average exercise price	31.20
Option price	$ 3.32
Option price	$ 3.32
Options expected to exercise	48,000.0
Income tax rate	40.0%
Tax benefit of options	$ 63.776.2
Adjusted total equity value	7,000,000.0
Total value of equity	$7,063,776.2

*Includes rounding errors.

Review Exercise 12.4: Allocating Total Equity to Common Equity and Warrants (Not Cancelled on the Valuation Date)

	Assumptions	Input	Calculate
Risk-free rate, r_F	2.00%		
Number of common shares outstanding, S_E	200,000.00		
Number of ESO/warrants outstanding, S_W	48,000.00		
Conversion ratio, CR	1		
Continuously compounded annual dividend yield, d_E	7.50%		
Stock price, P_E	$ 33.911		
Time to maturity of the ESO/warrants in years, T_W	4		
Strike or exercise price, X_W	$ 31.200		
Standard deviation of annual equity returns, σ_E	30.00%		
Value of ESO/warrants, P_W		$4.537	
Compare calculated value of ESO/warrants, P_W			$4.537
Calculations:			
ω_E			0.3806
σ_Q			0.3172
d_1			0.1689
d_2			−0.4656

Capital Structure Including Warrants	Price	Units	Value	Weight
Observed value of the debt			$ 3,000,000.0	30.0%
Observed value of the preferred			0.0	0.0%
Value of equity	$33.911	200,000.00	6,782,211.3	67.8%
Value of ESO/warrants	$ 4.537	48,000.00	217,788.7	2.2%
Value of the firm			$10,000,000.0	100.0%

			without Warrants/ESOs	
Capital Structure Excluding Warrants	**Implied Price**	**Units**	**Value**	**Weight**
Observed value of the debt			$ 3,000,000.0	30.0%
Observed value of the preferred			0.0	0.0%
Measured value of combined equity	$35.00	200,000.00	7,000,000.0	70.0%
Value of the firm			$10,000,000.0	100.0%

Review Exercise 12.5: Allocating Total Equity to Common Equity and Employee Stock Options (Not Cancelled on the Valuation Date)

	Assumptions	Input	Calculate
Risk-free rate, r_F	2.00%		
Number of common shares outstanding, S_E	200,000.00		
Number of ESO/warrants outstanding, S_W	48,000.00		
Conversion ratio, CR	1		
Continuously compounded annual dividend yield, d_E	7.41%		
Stock price, P_E	$ 34.317		
Time to maturity of the ESO/warrants in years, T_W	4		
Strike or exercise price, X_W	$ 31.200		
Standard deviation of annual equity returns, σ_E	30.00%		
Value of ESO/warrants, P_W		$4.744	
Compare calculated value of ESO/warrants, P_W			$4.744
Calculations:			
	ω_E		0.3898
	σ_Q		0.3175
	d_1		0.1954
	d_2		−0.4397

Capital Structure Including ESOs	Price	Units	Value	Weight
Observed value of the debt			$ 3,000,000.0	29.7%
Observed value of the preferred			0.0	0.0%
Value of equity	$34.317	200,000.00	6,863,362.5	68.0%
Value of ESO/warrants	$ 4.744	48,000.00	227,729.1	2.3%
Value of the firm			$10,091,091.6	100.0%

Tax Effect of ESOs:	$ 91,091.6

			without Warrants/ESOs	
Capital Structure Excluding ESOs	**Implied Price**	**Units**	**Value**	**Weight**
Observed value of the debt			$ 3,000,000.0	30.0%
Observed value of the preferred			0.0	0.0%
Measured value of combined equity	$35.00	200,000.00	7,000,000.0	70.0%
Value of the firm			$10,000,000.0	100.0%

Review Exercise 12.6: Valuation and Cost of Capital for Warrants

	Shares/ Warrants	Price	Valuation ($ in thousands)	Capital Structure Weight	Cost of Capital	Unlevered Cost of Capital	Weighted Average Cost of Capital
Excluding (Ignoring) Warrants:							
Common	20,000	$12.000	$240.00	54.5%	14.0%	7.6%	7.6%
Debt			200.00	45.5%	9.0%	4.1%	2.5%
			$440.00	100.0%		11.7%	10.1%

Other Information:

Income tax rate	40.0%
Risk-free rate of return	4.0%
Annual volatility of equity	24.0%
Exercise price of warrants	$12.00
Expiration of warrants (in years)	5.00
Dividend yield, continuously compounded	5.0%
Conversion ratio	1.0

$$r_W = r_F + (r_E - r_F) \times P_E/P_W \times \omega_E$$
$$0.336 = 0.04 + (0.14 - 0.04) \times \$12/\$1.755 \times 0.43298$$

$$r_W = r_F + \beta_E \times MRP \times P_E/P_W \times \omega_E$$
$$0.336 = 0.04 + 1.6667 \times 0.06 \times \$12/\$1.755 \times 0.43298$$

	Shares/ Warrants	Price	Valuation ($ in thousands)	Capital Structure Weight	Cost of Capital	Unlevered Cost of Capital	Weighted Average Cost of Capital
Including Warrants:							
Common	20,000	$12.000	$240.00	53.5%	14.0%	7.5%	7.5%
Warrants	5,000	$ 1.755	8.78	2.0%	33.6%	0.7%	0.7%
Debt			200.00	44.6%	9.0%	4.0%	2.4%
			$448.78	100.0%		12.2%	10.6%

ω_E	0.43298
σ_Q	25.66%
d_1	0.2797
d_2	−0.2941

Exhibit may contain small rounding errors

Review Exercise 12.7: Warrant Valuation and Cost of Capital

The inputs into the warrant valuation model and the resulting values are:

	Assumptions	Iterate Numerically	Formulas
Risk-free rate, r_F	4.00%		
Number of common shares outstanding, S_E	1,000,000		
Number of warrants outstanding, S_W	200,000		
Conversion ratio, CR	1		
Continuously compounded annual dividend yield, d_E	5.00%		
Stock price, P_E	$ 8.450		
Time to maturity of the warrants in years, T_W	6		
Strike or exercise price, X_W	$10.000		
Standard deviation of annual equity returns, σ_E	40.00%		
Warrant price, P_W		$1.874	
Compare calculated value of P_W			$1.874
Calculations:			
		d_1	0.3433
		d_2	−0.6771
		σ_Q	0.4166
		ω_E	0.4379

Summary output:		
Stock price/Warrant price	$8.450	$1.874
Volatility, σ_E/Risk-free rate	40.00%	4.00%
d_1 and d_2	0.3433	−0.6771
σ_Q	0.4166	
ω_E	0.4379	
Equity and warrant costs of capital	15.000%	25.72%
Combined total equity cost of capital		15.46%
Warrant cost of capital leverage factor		1.9749

From equation 12.1', the total equity cost of capital is as follows:

$$r_{TE} = 0.15 \times \frac{\$8.45 \times 1{,}000{,}000}{\$8.45 \times 1{,}000{,}000 + \$1.874 \times 200{,}000} + 0.2572 \times \frac{\$1.874 \times 200{,}000}{\$8.45 \times 1{,}000{,}000 + \$1.874 \times 200{,}000} = 0.1546$$

$$\text{Warrant cost of capital leverage factor} = (P_E/P_W) \times \omega_E = \frac{\$8.45}{\$1.874} \times 0.4379 = 1.9749$$

"Straight debt" value of the bond compared to its market value

The inputs:

Inputs:			
Total face value	$2,000,000.0	Risk-free rate of return	4.0%
Face value per note	$ 1,000.00	Equity cost of capital	15.000%
Value of a bond	$ 1,100.00	Annual volatility of equity	40.0%
Number of bonds	2,000.00	Continuously compounded dividend yield	5.000%
Conversion ratio per bond	100	Expiration of warrants (in years)	6.0
Annual coupon rate	8.000%	Exercise price of conversion feature	$10.0000
Straight debt yield-to-maturity	10.000%	Current stock price	$ 8.450
Maturity (Years) from date of issue	6	Common shares outstanding	1,000,000

Discounted cash flow valuation of the promised payments at the straight debt rate, comparison to current value, and value of convertible feature:

	Coupon Rate	Current Yield-to-Maturity Rate	Straight-Debt Rate
Annual Interest Rate	8.000%	5.968%	10.000%
Year 1	160,000	160,000	160,000
Year 2	160,000	160,000	160,000
Year 3	160,000	160,000	160,000
Year 4	160,000	160,000	160,000
Year 5	160,000	160,000	160,000
Year 6	2,160,000	2,160,000	2,160,000
Value of straight debt notes	$2,000,000	$2,200,000	$1,825,790
Market price of the notes			$2,200,000
Value of the conversion provision			$ 374,210
Number of shares	100	2,000	200,000
Value of conversion feature per share			$ 1.871

	Shares	Price	Value
Value of notes (ignoring accrued interest)			$1,825,789.6
Value of conversion feature	200,000	$1.871	374,210.4
Value of convertible note			$2,200,000.0
Value if converted	200,000	$8.450	1,690,000.0
Value of note in excess of converted value			$ 510,000.0

After mastering the material in this chapter, you will be able to:

1. Use market multiples to value a company and its equity (13.1–13.2)
2. Identify the characteristics that drive market multiples (13.3–13.4)
3. Choose comparable companies to use in a market multiple valuation (13.5)
4. Adjust for transitory changes when measuring market multiples (13.6)
5. Analyze and measure continuing values using market multiples (13.7)

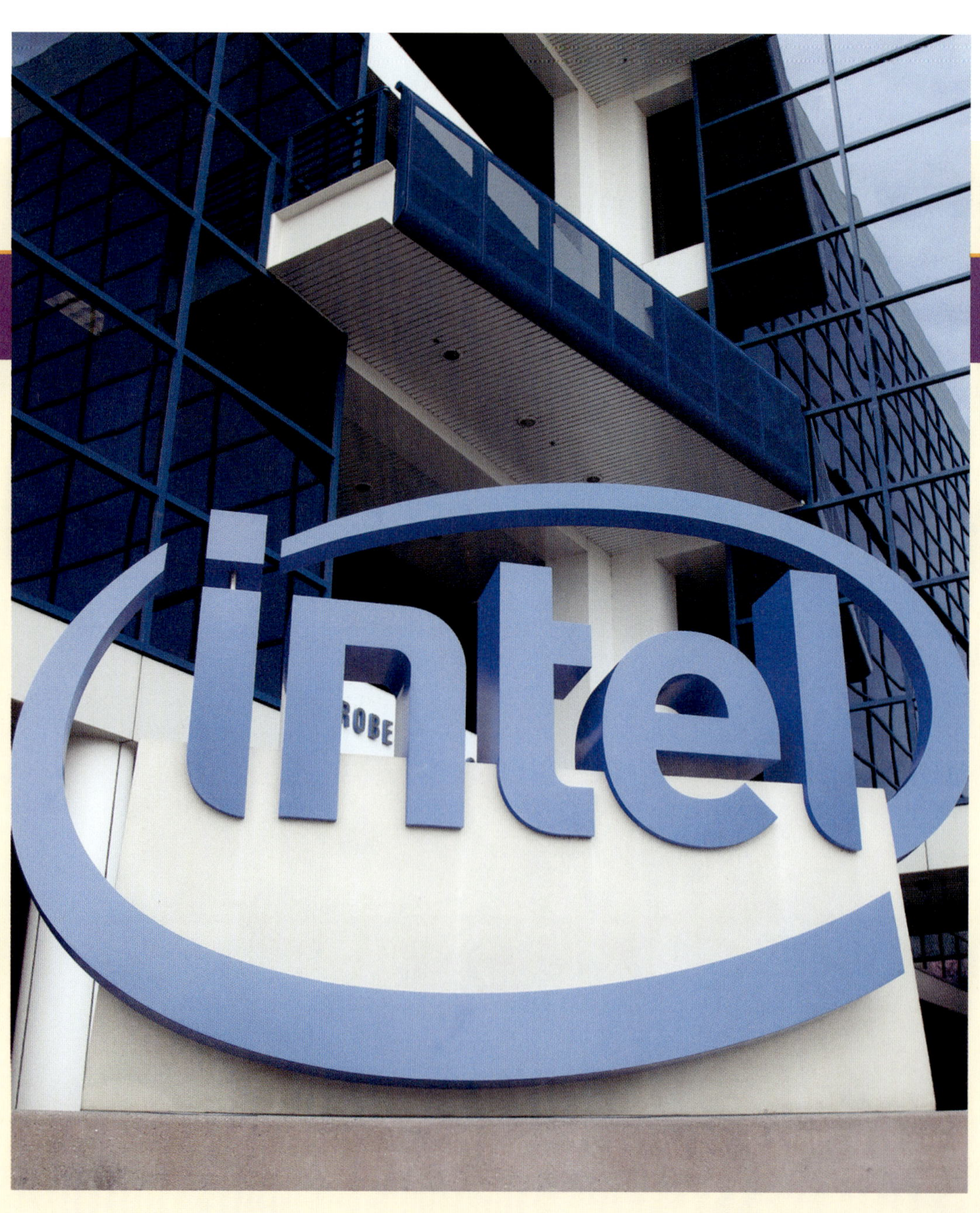

CHAPTER 13

Introduction to Market Multiple Valuation Methods

INTEL AND ALTERA CORPORATIONS

On May 31, 2015, Intel Corporation (Intel) and Altera Corporation (Altera) signed a merger agreement for Intel to purchase all of the common stock of Altera for $54 per share ($16.7 billion in total).[1] Altera's board hired Goldman Sachs & Co (Goldman) to assess the fairness of this transaction to its shareholders. In assessing the fairness of the transaction, Goldman used discounted cash flow, market multiple (public companies and transactions), and other valuation assessments to form its fairness opinion.

Goldman selected ten comparable companies for its market multiple valuation, stating, "Although none of the selected companies is directly comparable to Altera, the companies included were chosen because they are publicly traded companies with operations that for purposes of analysis may be considered similar to certain operations of Altera."[2] In its market multiple valuation, Goldman used EBITDA, revenue, and price-to-earnings multiples based on estimates from the Institutional Brokers' Estimate System and Bloomberg.

Goldman also used income-based transaction multiples from 15 transactions stating, "While none of the companies that participated in the selected transactions are directly comparable to Altera, the companies that participated in the selected transactions are companies with operations that, for the purposes of analysis, may be considered similar to certain of Altera's results, market size and product profile."[3]

In this chapter, you will learn the basics of market multiple valuation including the process used, the fundamental determinants that affect variation in market multiples across firms and over time, and how to choose comparable companies.

[1] See Altera Corporation's proxy statement dated August 24, 2015 (Altera August 24, 2015 Proxy) for the details regarding this merger.

[2] Altera August 24, 2015 Proxy, p. 46.

[3] Altera August 24, 2015 Proxy, p. 48.

CHAPTER ORGANIZATION

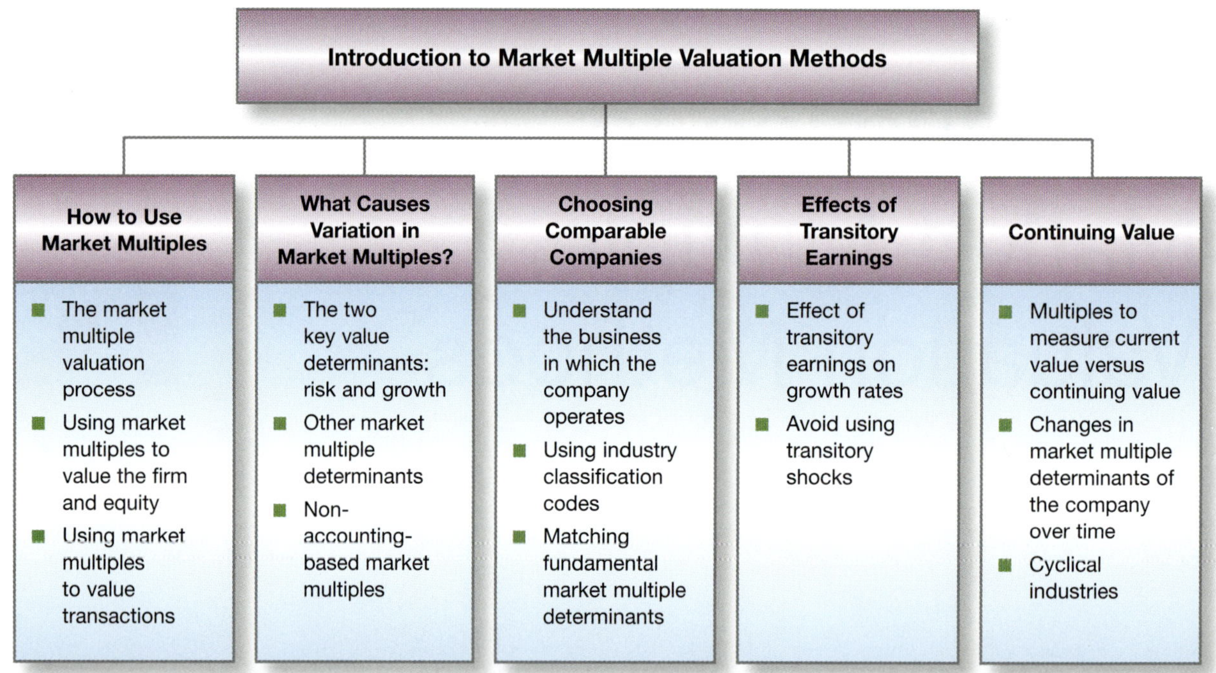

INTRODUCTION

In a **market multiple valuation**, we first identify comparable companies. We then measure the observed relation, or market multiple, between each comparable company's market value and the value driver of the multiple, typically an accounting-based measure, such as earnings or EBIT. This relation or market multiple represents the market value per unit of the value driver, and it is a measure of the amount the market is willing to "pay" for a current unit of the value driver of the multiple. We value the company of interest using its value driver for the chosen multiple and the comparable companies' market multiples; for example, if the relation between the comparable companies' equity market values and current earnings is 15, and if the company we are valuing has current earnings of $1,000, we would multiply the earnings of the company we are valuing by the earnings market multiple of the comparable companies to measure the market value of the equity for the company of $15,000 ($15,000 = 15 × $1,000).

Don't be fooled by the seeming simplicity of the market multiple valuation method. If performed correctly, it is actually complex and time consuming due to various comparability and measurement issues. So while the first two lines in this introduction seem simple—"identify comparable companies" and "measure the observed relation or market multiple"—those two steps are difficult to do well.

We do not view market multiple valuation as an alternative but rather as a complement to a discounted cash flow (DCF) valuation. We can use market multiple valuation as of the valuation date or as of the continuing (or terminal) value date for a DCF valuation. Some investment bankers use market multiple valuation to directly measure a company's continuing value in a DCF valuation. We recommend a somewhat different approach, which is to use market multiples as a tool to analyze the continuing value by examining various multiples implied by a constant-growth perpetuity model (see Chapter 6). At one time, market multiple valuation was the predominant valuation method used by the investment banking community. Now, when valuing companies, investment bankers most often use a market multiple valuation in conjunction with a DCF valuation.[4]

Alternative names for the market multiple valuation method include **comparable company valuation**, **multiple valuation**, **price multiple valuation**, **guideline company valuation**, **relative valuation analysis**, **direct comparison approach**, and **twin company approach**. As you can quickly see from

[4] See, DeAngelo, L., "Equity Valuation and Corporate Control," *Accounting Review* 65 (1990), pp. 93–112 for a discussion of the use of market multiples in rendering fairness opinions; and Kaplan, S., and R. Ruback, "The Valuation of Cash Flow Forecasts: An Empirical Analysis," *The Journal of Finance* vol. L, no. 4 (September, 1995), pp. 1093–1095 for evidence on the usefulness of using market multiples and DCF valuations.

the various names used to describe the market multiple valuation methods, comparable companies—or "**comps**"—are an important part of this valuation method. The key issues in valuing companies using market multiples are choosing appropriate comparable companies that would be priced similarly to the company being valued and making adjustments to the financial statements so that distortions to the valuation do not arise from accounting differences or certain events that render the financial statement numbers less useful for a market multiple valuation.

We use market multiple valuation to measure both a company's firm value and common equity value. We also use market multiple valuation to measure the value of an anticipated transaction (acquisition, leveraged buyout, IPO) by using similar transactions involving comparable companies. Alternative names for a market multiple analysis based on transactions are **precedent transaction analysis**, **comparable transaction analysis**, and **comparable acquisitions analysis**.

The goals of this and the next chapter are to discuss the conceptual underpinning and process of market multiple valuation. In this chapter, we focus on the conceptual framework of the market multiple valuation method and its relation to the DCF valuation method, and we highlight the implicit assumptions made when using the various market multiples. For now, we ignore many of the measurement and implementation issues faced in market multiple valuations, but we will discuss these issues in detail in the next chapter.

13.1 THE MARKET MULTIPLE VALUATION PROCESS

LO1 Use market multiples to value a company and its equity

The basic approach in the market multiple valuation process is to first identify the relevant set of comparable companies for a particular valuation. We then measure the firm value and/or equity value of each comparable company. We divide (or scale) each comparable company's market value by an appropriate value driver (for example, EBITDA) to measure the multiple for each comparable company. After measuring all of the multiples for comparable firms, we determine the appropriate value (or range of values) of the multiple to use for the company being valued. We then multiply the multiple from the comparable companies by the value driver (say, EBITDA) for the company of interest. The result is a measure of the value of the firm or equity, depending on the multiple chosen. Of course, we sometimes use more than one multiple when we perform this work. Further, we sometimes measure the relevant value driver by using either very recent historical data or forecasts. We summarize the steps in the market multiple valuation process in Exhibit 13.1.

EXHIBIT 13.1 An Overview of the Valuation Process Using Market Multiples

1	Identify potential comparable companies (key competitors and other companies with potentially similar market multiple determinants)
2	Collect historical and forward-looking (forecasts) financial and market information for potential comparable companies
3	Identify the characteristics of the company being valued that determine variation in market multiples
4	Assess the comparability of the financial statements and adjust the financial statements to align the financial statements of the comparable companies and the company being valued
5	Assess the comparability of the potential comparable companies based on the characteristics that drive variation in the chosen market multiples and choose the comparable companies
6	Select the appropriate market multiples to use for the company being valued, given the specific valuation context
7	Measure the market value of the equity and firm, as well as the value drivers of the market multiples selected, for the comparable companies at each relevant date
8	Measure the selected multiples for each comparable company
9	Assess the relevant range and measure of central tendency (mean, median) of the multiples to use
10	Measure the relevant value driver for the company being valued and value the company using the market multiples. Assess the reasonable range and consistency of valuations across the different multiples

Some steps in the market multiple valuation process overlap with steps in our overall valuation process. For example, the first two steps in the market multiple valuation process are to identify potential comparable companies and to collect and analyze historical information and forecasts for these companies. These steps are similar to the first two steps in the overall valuation process. The third step in a market multiple valuation, identifying the market multiple determinants of the company being valued that drive variation in market multiples, is similar to what we do when we forecast a company's financial statements and free cash flows. Thus, in most cases, we will have already worked through the first three steps of the market multiple valuation process if we already completed a discounted cash flow valuation of the company.

13.2 COMMONLY USED MARKET MULTIPLES

As you might expect, most of the common value drivers of market multiples used by analysts, investment bankers, and valuation specialists are accounting-based. Some are based on the income statement and statement of cash flows—such as earnings; earnings before interest and taxes (EBIT); earnings before interest, taxes, depreciation, and amortization (EBITDA); revenue; sales; operating cash flows; and free cash flow (FCF). Others are based on the balance sheet—such as total invested capital, total assets, tangible assets, stockholders' equity, and net tangible equity. A multiple's value driver can also be non-accounting-based, such as a measure of productive capacity, number of employees, square feet of retail space, or population in an area served.

Firm Value versus Enterprise Value

Many valuation specialists use multiples based on **enterprise value** instead of the value of the firm. The market value of the firm is equal to the market value of the firm's common equity, options granted, preferred stock, long-term debt, short-term debt, and any other securities issued, such as warrants. Enterprise value is similar to the value of the firm, but instead of using total debt, we use debt minus cash and marketable securities, which is equal to net debt. When we measure a multiple based on enterprise value, we also eliminate any income effect due to the cash and marketable securities used to arrive at net debt. If cash exceeds debt, the net debt will be negative.

By subtracting total cash and marketable securities from debt in order to measure net debt for computing enterprise value, we essentially assume that all cash is available to pay off debt, and hence the company does not require cash to run its business. This is unlikely to cause any problems as long as the comparable companies and the company we are valuing have comparable cash requirements that are proportional to value. Using enterprise value circumvents the issue of estimating required cash. In this book, we sometimes show multiples based on the value of the firm and at other times we use enterprise value.

To use the enterprise value approach, we multiply the market multiple based on the enterprise value and chosen value driver of the comparable companies by the relevant value driver of the market multiple for the company we are valuing. This calculation measures the enterprise value of the company. To measure the value of the firm, we add the value of the company's cash and marketable securities to its enterprise value.

Market Multiples Used to Value the Firm and Equity

We summarize some of the commonly used multiples in Exhibit 13.2. In the first panel of the exhibit, we list market multiples used to measure firm value or enterprise value, and in the second panel, we list market multiples used to value the equity.

Even though free cash flow is a logical value driver to use for a market multiple, it is not very popular, the reasons for which we discuss later in the chapter. We introduce it first because it links directly to the DCF valuation model and it is useful for identifying some of the key assumptions underlying the use of market multiples. The first of the earnings-based multiples is the unlevered earnings multiple—measured as earnings (net income) plus after-tax interest. We use unlevered earnings rather than earnings (net income) to measure the value of the firm. Since we are measuring the value of the firm, we do not deduct interest expense, for it is a flow available to the debtholders—similarly, we would not deduct preferred dividends, as it is a flow available to preferred holders. Unlevered earnings is similar to unlevered free cash flows but it does not include any adjustments for non-cash items (such as depreciation) and investments in fixed assets or working capital.

EXHIBIT 13.2 Some Commonly Used Market Multiples

	Market Multiple Name	Value Driver
Market Multiples to Value the Firm or Enterprise (Numerator Is Market Value of Firm or Enterprise Value)		
1	Free cash flow multiple	Unlevered free cash flow
2	Unlevered earnings multiple	Earnings after taxes plus after-tax interest
3	EBIT multiple	Earnings before interest and taxes
4	EBITDA multiple	Earnings before interest, taxes, depreciation, and amortization
5	Revenue (sales) multiple	Revenue or sales
6	Total invested capital (similar alternatives are tangible assets, total assets) multiple	Total invested capital
7	Non-accounting value driver (productive capacity, number of employees, square feet of retail space, population in area served)	Relevant non-accounting value driver
Market Multiples to Measure Equity Value (Numerator Is Market Value of Equity or Price per Share)		
1	Equity free cash flow multiple	Equity free cash flow
2	Price-to-earnings multiple	Earnings available to common shareholders (or earnings per share)
3	Market-to-book (similar alternative is tangible net equity) multiple	Book value of equity
4	Non-accounting value driver (productive capacity, number of employees, square feet of retail space, population in area served)	Relevant non-accounting value driver for equity

Two of the more popular earnings-based multiples used to value the firm are the EBIT and EBITDA multiples. Again, both EBIT and EBITDA are measures of earnings before interest, so they represent flows that relate to total firm value as opposed to the equity value. EBIT and EBITDA are of course even further removed from unlevered free cash flows than unlevered earnings. Revenue multiples are also used, though less popular, and by their nature cannot adjust for differences in the cost structure of the company and the comparable companies, and thus, are more difficult to use because of the difficulty of identifying comparable companies. Next in the panel are market multiples based on some measure of the investments made by the company—total assets, total invested capital, tangible assets, and so on. These multiples are also used less often. In order to use market multiples based on total invested capital, we assume the comparable companies and the company we are valuing have the same value relative to the amount of invested capital. Financial institutions are sometimes valued based on total capital.

The last type of multiple in this panel is based on non-accounting measures. We would use a non-accounting value driver to measure a multiple if it is the best predictor of a company's future performance (free cash flows). For example, assume that all of the companies in a certain industry have essentially the same investments, accruals, cost structure, and relation between revenues and some non-accounting measure, Z—say, the number of square feet of retail floor space. If the non-accounting measure, Z, is a better indicator of the company's future free cash flows than current or forecasted accounting-based measures, using a market multiple based on this non-accounting measure may be a more reasonable multiple to use to value the company. Naturally, this is a rather strong set of assumptions, but financial analysts, investment bankers, and investors sometimes use non-accounting-based multiples that are specific to particular industries. We explore the logic underlying these multiples in more detail later in the chapter.

As long as we know or can estimate the value of each of the company's non-equity securities, we can use any of the market multiples in the first panel of Exhibit 13.2 to value a company's equity. The value of the company's equity is equal to the value of the firm less the value of the company's non-equity securities. For the multiples in the second panel, we measure each market multiple by dividing the value of the company's equity by a specific value driver. The value drivers of these multiples are, for the most part, analogous to the value drivers of multiples based on the value of the firm; however, in general, we only measure the value driver based on the claims of the equityholders. Thus, we use equity free cash flow, earnings (more specifically, net income available to common shareholders), and the book value of equity as the value drivers.

While we use value drivers that reflect the equityholders' claims for most of the equity value multiples, that is not true for either the multiple of equity value to sales or market multiples based on equity values to non-accounting measures. The value drivers of these multiples measure the activity (for example, sales) that results from all of the company's investments—not from just its equity.

REVIEW EXERCISE 13.1

Basic Calculation of Market Multiples

Below, we present summary financial statements and a free cash flow schedule for an example company. Use this information to measure the free cash flow and financial statement-based market multiples from Exhibit 13.2. Measure the market multiple using the end of Year 0 firm or equity value and the Year 0 value driver. The value of the company's equity at the end of Year 0 is $1,656.3, and the value of the firm is $2,070.3.

High-Growth Company
Financial Statements and Free Cash Flows

($ in millions)	Year −1	Year 0	Year 1	Year 2	Year 3	Year 4	Year 5	Year 6
Income Statement								
Revenue	**$ 980.4**	**$1,000.0**	**$1,080.0**	**$1,231.2**	**$1,255.8**	**$1,280.9**	**$1,306.6**	**$1,332.7**
Operating expenses	−686.3	−700.0	−756.0	−861.8	−879.1	−896.7	−914.6	−932.9
Depreciation expense	−62.8	−64.1	−69.2	−78.9	−80.5	−82.1	−83.8	−85.4
Interest expense	−29.2	−32.5	−33.1	−36.7	−37.8	−38.6	−39.3	−40.1
Income before taxes	$ 202.0	$ 203.4	$ 221.6	$ 253.7	$ 258.4	$ 263.6	$ 268.9	$ 274.3
Income tax expense	−80.8	−81.4	−88.7	−101.5	−103.4	−105.4	−107.6	−109.7
Net income	**$ 121.2**	**$ 122.1**	**$ 133.0**	**$ 152.2**	**$ 155.1**	**$ 158.2**	**$ 161.3**	**$ 164.6**
Balance Sheet								
Net working capital	$ 196.1	$ 200.0	$ 216.0	$ 246.2	$ 251.2	$ 256.2	$ 261.3	$ 266.5
Property, plant, and equipment (net)	967.8	1,006.3	1,130.9	1,083.5	1,035.2	986.0	935.7	884.5
Total assets	$1,163.9	$1,206.3	$1,346.9	$1,329.8	$1,286.4	$1,242.2	$1,197.0	$1,151.0
Debt	$ 405.9	$ 414.1	$ 458.7	$ 472.5	$ 481.9	$ 491.6	$ 501.4	$ 511.4
Equity	758.0	792.2	888.2	857.3	804.5	750.6	695.6	639.6
Total liabilities and equities	$1,163.9	$1,206.3	$1,346.9	$1,329.8	$1,286.4	$1,242.2	$1,197.0	$1,151.0
Free Cash Flows								
Earnings before interest and taxes (EBIT)		$ 235.9	$ 254.8	$ 290.4	$ 296.2	$ 302.2	$ 308.2	$ 314.4
− Income taxes paid on EBIT		−94.4	−101.9	−116.2	−118.5	−120.9	−123.3	−125.8
Earnings before interest and after taxes		$ 141.5	$ 152.9	$ 174.3	$ 177.7	$ 181.3	$ 184.9	$ 188.6
+ Depreciation expense		64.1	69.2	78.9	80.5	82.1	83.8	85.4
− Change in net working capital		−3.9	−16.0	−30.2	−4.9	−5.0	−5.1	−5.2
− Capital expenditures		−102.6	−193.8	−31.6	−32.2	−32.8	−33.5	−34.2
Unlevered free cash flow		**$ 99.2**	**$ 12.2**	**$ 191.4**	**$ 221.1**	**$ 225.5**	**$ 230.1**	**$ 234.7**
− Interest paid		−32.5	−33.1	−36.7	−37.8	−38.6	−39.3	−40.1
+ Interest tax shield		13.0	13.3	14.7	15.1	15.4	15.7	16.0
+ Change in debt financing		8.1	44.6	13.8	9.4	9.6	9.8	10.0
Free cash flow to common equity		**$ 87.8**	**$ 37.0**	**$ 183.2**	**$ 207.9**	**$ 212.1**	**$ 216.3**	**$ 220.6**

Exhibit may contain small rounding errors

Solution on page 652.

Market Multiples Vary Over Time

In order to gain some understanding of the magnitude of some typical market multiples and how they vary over time, in Exhibit 13.3 we present a chart of the EBITDA and price-to-earnings multiples described in Exhibit 13.2. We report the median market multiple for a sample of company-years from 2000 through 2015. This sample is based on all companies in the CapitalIQ[5] database of U.S. companies that have a market capitalization of at least $1 million for which CapitalIQ reports either the EBITDA or price-to-earnings multiple. Throughout the chapter, we refer to this dataset as the "CapitalIQ Market Multiple" dataset.

This exhibit shows the variation over time in market multiples. For example, over this time period, the median P/E has a range of roughly 12 (2008, the year of the financial crisis) to 20 (2005). Excluding 2008, the median P/E has a range of roughly 15 to 20. The median EBITDA multiple has a range of 6 (2008, the year of the financial crisis) to 11 (2013). Excluding 2008, the median EBITDA multiple has a range of roughly 8 to 11.

EXHIBIT 13.3 Time-Series of Median Market Multiples in the U.S.

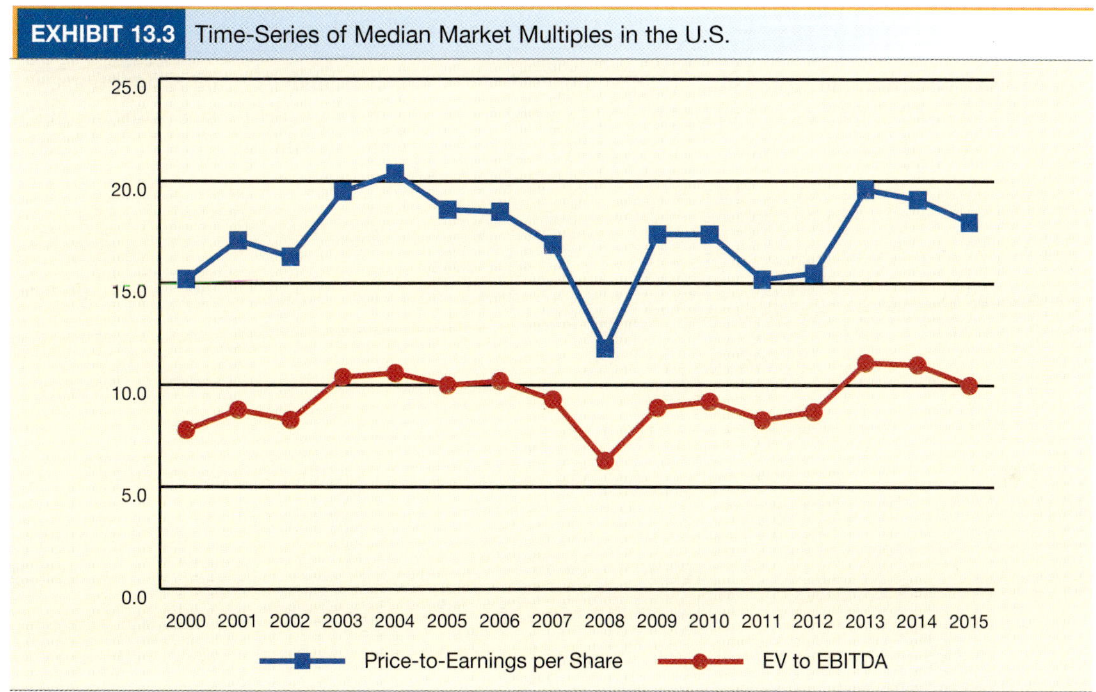

Valuation Key 13.1

One key factor in choosing a market multiple with which to value a company is how closely the value driver of the multiple maps to economic value. Some market multiples are based on earnings numbers or cash flows—such as earnings; earnings before interest and taxes (EBIT); earnings before interest, taxes, depreciation, and amortization (EBITDA); revenue or sales; and free cash flow. Others are based on balance sheet items—such as total invested capital, total assets, tangible assets, stockholders' equity, and net tangible equity. The value driver in a multiple can sometimes be non-accounting-based—such as productive capacity, number of employees, square feet of retail space, and population in an area served.

[5] S&P Capital IQ, a part of S&P Global, Inc., is a "leading provider of multiasset class, unrivaled data, delivered in real time through innovative platforms with insightful analysis." See, http://www.spcapitaliq.com/about-us/about-us.html.

13.3 RISK AND GROWTH VALUE DETERMINANTS OF MARKET MULTIPLES

LO2 Identify the characteristics that drive market multiples

To understand the framework underpinning the market multiple valuation method, we begin by reviewing the discounted cash flow (DCF) valuation model. We show how the market multiple valuation model is linked to the DCF valuation. Indeed, we see that they can be equivalent. Initially, we focus on multiples based on free cash flows, but later in the chapter, we extend our discussion to market multiples commonly used by analysts, investment bankers, and valuation specialists.

The Relation Between the Discounted Cash Flow Model and Free Cash Flow Multiples

From the DCF valuation model, we can measure the value of an *all-equity-financed firm* as

$$V_{F,0} = \frac{FCF_1}{1+r} + \frac{FCF_2}{(1+r)^2} + \frac{FCF_3}{(1+r)^3} + \cdots + \frac{FCF_\infty}{(1+r)^\infty}$$

As we know from our discussion of continuing value in Chapter 6, under certain assumptions, we can restate the DCF valuation as a constant-growth perpetuity—where $g_{1,\infty}$ is the present value weighted average growth rate for the company's free cash flows from Year 1 in perpetuity.

$$V_{F,0} = \frac{FCF_1}{r - g_{1,\infty}}$$

We can use this formula to rewrite our market multiple valuation formula for the free cash flow multiple, MM[FCF], as

$$MM[FCF] = \frac{V_{F,0}}{FCF_1} = \frac{1}{r - g_{1,\infty}} \quad \textbf{(13.1)}$$

If we use the free cash flow from Year 0 (instead of Year 1), then this formula must include the growth rate from Year 0 to Year 1.

$$MM[FCF] = \frac{V_{F,0}}{FCF_0} = \frac{(1+g_{0,1})}{r - g_{1,\infty}} \quad \textbf{(13.2)}$$

Note that we are assuming an all-equity-financed firm, so the unlevered cost of capital is the same as the weighted average and equity costs of capital ($r_{UA} = r_{WACC} = r_E = r$). These formulas can be used to measure market multiples for a firm with debt, but the appropriate cost of capital would be the weighted average cost of capital in that case. The formulas can also be used to calculate equity market multiples, and in that case, you would use the value of the equity and the equity free cash flows and the appropriate discount rate would be the equity cost of capital.

As these formulas illustrate, the free cash flow multiple is equivalent to the capitalization factor in the constant growth perpetuity model. It is similar to a "price" that the market would pay for a dollar of free cash flow, conditional on the riskiness of the cash flows and expectations of the future growth of these cash flows. As is true with the perpetuity model, the base year free cash flow must be positive in order to use the market multiple valuation method. The clear implication from this formula is that we must match comparable companies on both risk and growth in order to use a free cash flow multiple. Because the value of a company is equal to the risk-adjusted present value of the company's expected cash flows, the determinants in this formula (growth and risk) underpin all market multiples—not just free cash flow multiples. No matter what market multiple we use, we must assess the comparability of potential comparable companies based on risk and free cash flow growth. As we will soon show, comparability for all multiples requires that characteristics beyond risk and growth must also be comparable, but the free cash flow multiple will be less sensitive to many of these other characteristics.

Valuation Key 13.2

All market multiples have at least two common determinants—risk and growth. A company's risk factors and growth factors are relevant determinants of a company's market multiples for assessing comparability when evaluating potential comparable companies.

REVIEW EXERCISE 13.2

Risk and Growth Drivers of Market Multiples

Use the information in Review Exercise 13.1 and the company's costs of capital and growth rates to calculate the company's multiple of firm value to unlevered free cash flow and its multiple of equity value to equity free cash flow at Year 0 using the Year 0 value drivers. The company's equity cost of capital is 13%, and its weighted average cost of capital is 11.36%. In order to solve this exercise, you will have to refer back to Equations 6.4 and 6.5 to solve for the present value weighted average growth rate.

Solution on pages 652–653.

Valuation in Practice 13.1

Financial Analysts and Investors Know the Effect of Growth on Market Multiples: The "PEG" Ratio Many financial analysts and investors use the price-to-earnings (P/E) multiple as a basis for screening stocks (identifying potentially over- and undervalued stocks). One way they use the P/E multiple is in the calculation of the PEG (price-to-earnings-to-growth) ratio. The PEG ratio is equal to the P/E multiple divided by a measure of the company's growth rate (measured as a percentage). For example, if a company has a stock price of $15 per share and an earnings per share of $1.2, its P/E multiple is 12.5 (12.5 = $15/$1.2). We know that a company's growth rate affects all of its market multiples—the higher the growth rate, the higher the market multiple. The PEG ratio attempts to adjust for this growth rate effect.

If our example company has a growth rate of 10%, then its PEG ratio is 1.25 (1.25 = 12.5/10); if it has a growth rate of 25%, then its PEG ratio is .5 (.5 = 12.5/25). What does this calculation tell us? The financial analysts and investors who use PEG ratios suggest that a PEG ratio substantially greater than 1 might indicate an overvalued stock and that a PEG ratio substantially less than 1 might indicate an undervalued stock. No systematic studies document this alleged gold mine empirically, but research shows that this heuristic metric is widely used by financial analysts.

Source: For a detailed discussion and derivation of the PEG ratio and the adjustments one might make to it, see, Easton, P., "PE ratios, PEG ratios, and Estimating the Implied Expected Rate of Return on Equity Capital," *The Accounting Review* vol. 79, no. 1 (January 2004).

Why Free Cash Flow Multiples Are Not Very Popular

Since free cash flow is directly linked to value, we might expect free cash flow multiples to be the most common type of multiple used. They are not; in fact, free cash flow multiples are less popular than many of the other multiples shown in Exhibit 13.2. They are not as popular as other multiples for two related reasons: free cash flows are negative more often than earnings measures (such as EBITDA), and free cash flow multiples have more extreme observations (outliers) or transitory shocks than other multiples. The investments in capital expenditures, acquisitions, and working capital that companies make tend to vary from year to year, resulting in free cash flows that are more variable and more often negative than earnings-based measures. Thus, the choice of the appropriate measure of free cash flows for the value driver is generally difficult.

One approach that one might take to implement a free cash flow multiple is to consider what a "normal level" of investment might be for the firm given its projected growth (thus removing the lumpiness of the investment series). This approach can produce a more reasonable base from which the growth rates are computed. In addition, normalizing the investment may make the free cash flows positive, thus allowing the use of that multiple. We are most likely to use one of the free cash flow multiples if the company we are valuing and our selected comparable companies have low and reasonably stable growth. In any event, free cash flow multiples are not popular in spite of their potential superior ability to control for variation in the determinants that affect multiples of the company being valued.

Valuation Key 13.3

In spite of their inherent conceptual superiority, free cash flow multiples are not very popular because of the frequency of negative value drivers and the "lumpiness" of a company's investments (changes in net working capital and capital expenditures). This "lumpiness" causes free cash flows to vary more from year to year than earnings-based measures, which makes it difficult to judge the correct base to use for calculating the free cash flow multiple. One way to address this issue is to "normalize" investments.

REVIEW EXERCISE 13.3

Free Cash Flow Market Multiples

Use the information in Review Exercise 13.1 to measure the free cash flow and financial statement-based market multiples in Exhibit 13.2 for Year 1. Measure the market multiple using the end of Year 1 firm or equity value and the Year 1 value driver. Assume that the value of the company's equity at the end of Year 1 is $1,834.6 and that the value of the firm is $2,293.3. Compare the Year 0 multiples calculated in Review Exercise 13.1 to the Year 1 multiples.

Solution on page 653.

13.4 ADDITIONAL FACTORS TO CONSIDER WHEN ASSESSING COMPARABILITY

We know from the previous analysis that free cash flow multiples have two determinants—risk and free cash flow growth—and that these determinants affect all market multiples. The implication of this result is that we should match companies based on these two underlying factors in order to identify comparable companies, regardless of which multiple we use. In this section we investigate the potential value of considering additional factors—such as cost structure, working capital management, capital expenditure requirements, capital structure, and other components of value—when we identify comparable companies.

We use a very simple financial model of PepsiCo, Inc., and a simple simulation, to illustrate how factors other than risk and growth can determine market multiples and thus, comparability. Naturally, the results of such a simulation are based on the underlying financial model, which varies depending on the available information and valuation context.

When Is a Factor Relevant for Assessing Comparability?

If a factor, for example, the free cash flow growth rate, affects both a multiple's market value (numerator) and value driver (denominator) by the same percentage, it will have no effect on that market multiple. For example, assume a comparable company's income tax rate differs from the income tax rate of the company we are valuing—say, 40% for the comparable company versus 20% for the company we are valuing. If the two companies are exactly the same save for their income tax rates, then the comparable company will have lower free cash flows and a lower value relative to the company we are valuing.

In a simple perpetuity situation, assume the free cash flows and the value of the comparable company are 25% lower than that of the company we are valuing [$-0.25 = (1 - 0.4)/(1 - 0.2) - 1$]. Its free cash flow market multiple, however, is the same because the numerator and value driver are both 25% lower. This is not, however, the case for EBIT. The companies have the same EBIT, but the value of the comparable company (numerator) is 25% lower. In this simple example, this difference results in an EBIT multiple for the comparable company that is 25% lower than the correct multiple for the company being valued. Naturally, the effects of income tax rates and other factors are more complex than the assumptions used in this example, so we cannot make such a straightforward adjustment for actual companies. However, the example clearly demonstrates that comparability of the future tax rates faced by both the comparable companies and the company being valued becomes more relevant when using EBIT, EBITDA, and revenue multiples than when using unlevered earnings and free cash flow multiples.

In general, market multiple determinants other than growth and risk are not as relevant for assessing comparability when using the free cash flow multiple as they are for other multiples; and they are likely to be more relevant for the revenue and total asset (and other balance-sheet-based) multiples. When we calculate free cash flows, we generally adjust the free cash flow for the market multiple determinants other than risk and growth. Both the free cash flow and therefore the value of the firm are similarly affected, and thus the free cash flow multiple is not as affected as other multiples for a difference in these other market multiple determinants. This is not the case for other multiples, and hence other multiples are generally disadvantaged relative to the free cash flow multiples. Unfortunately, as discussed earlier, the free cash flow multiple has various other disadvantages that generally make it less useful than earnings-based multiples.

What additional market multiple determinants should we consider? In Chapter 4 we discuss financial models and the determinants (assumptions) in those models that determine the free cash flow forecasts and valuation. Each assumption is a potential determinant to consider. A determinant (assumption) in the financial model is relevant for assessing comparability if a change in the determinant has a different proportionate effect on the company's market value (numerator) relative to the proportionate effect it has on the value driver (denominator) used as the basis for the multiple. If a determinant affects both the market value and value driver by the same proportion, that determinant is irrelevant for assessing comparability because the ratio of the numerator to the denominator (the multiple) is unchanged. Any determinant (assumption) in a financial model that affects (determines) a multiple is relevant for assessing comparability.

PepsiCo, Inc. (Pepsi) Simulation

We know that many of the forecast drivers underpinning a company's financial model can be a determinant of the company's market multiples (multiples) and thus, relevant for assessing comparability in a market multiples-based valuation. As you recall from Chapter 4, a financial model is the equivalent of a set of algebraic equations that are a function of the forecast drivers used in the financial model. We can examine the determinants of different multiples by using the set of algebraic equations to specify the relationship between the forecast drivers and each multiple. In this section we develop a simple financial model for PepsiCo, Inc. (Pepsi)[6] and use the set of algebraic equations in the Pepsi financial model to both derive and simulate the effect that various risk factors and forecast drivers can have on a company's multiples, which indicates the factors that are relevant to assess comparability. The goal of this simulation is not to create the ultimate financial model and DCF valuation for Pepsi, but is to use a simple financial model and DCF valuation to identify the determinants of the commonly used multiples. These relations provide guidance on how to assess comparability when selecting comparable companies for a multiple valuation.

Overview of the Financial Model, Discounted Cash Flow Valuation and Simulation. At the end of its 2014 fiscal year (December 27, 2014), Pepsi was trading with an equity market capitalization of roughly $138.6 billion, after eliminating $4.7 billion in assumed excess cash and short-term marketable securities. We assume that Pepsi will maintain its capital structure at 24% debt (3.5% cost of debt) and

[6] PepsiCo, Inc. is a leading global food and beverage company with brands that include Frito-Lay, Gatorade, Pepsi-Cola, Quaker and Tropicana. Pepsi uses authorized bottlers, contract manufacturers and other third parties to make, market, distribute and sell a wide variety of beverages, foods and snacks, serving customers and consumers in more than 200 countries and territories. (See PepsiCo, Inc.'s 2014 SEC 10-K Report or Annual Report to Shareholders.)

has an 8% weighted average cost of capital (r_{WACC} = 8%). Based on these assumptions, Pepsi's debt is $43.8 billion and its total market capitalization is $182.4 billion.[7] We assume Pepsi does not hold any excess cash in the future.

Revenues drive Pepsi's financial model. We use Pepsi's present value weighted average growth rate (4%) to forecast Pepsi's revenues from 2015 onward. We drive Pepsi's cost structure (other than income tax expense and interest) using its 2014 relation between its cost structure and revenues (cost of goods sold is 46.5% of revenues; selling, general and administrative expenses are 35% of revenues; and depreciation is 4% of revenues). We use the simplifying assumption that Pepsi's average income tax rate (25% globally) is equal to its marginal income tax rate for interest. We use these and other forecast drivers to forecast Pepsi's income statement through 2025. We present these forecast drivers and Pepsi's income statement forecasts for selected years in Exhibit 13.4 (we show two years of actuals and three years of the forecasts—2015, 2020 and 2025).

EXHIBIT 13.4 PepsiCo Inc.—Income Statement Forecast Drivers and Historical and Forecasted Income Statements

($ in millions)	A-12/2013	A-12/2014	F-12/2015	F-12/2020	F-12/2025
Income statement forecast drivers					
Growth rate			4.0%	4.0%	4.0%
Cost of goods sold	47.0%	46.3%	46.5%	46.5%	46.5%
Selling, general and administrative	34.2%	35.2%	35.0%	35.0%	35.0%
Depreciation	4.2%	4.1%	4.0%	4.0%	4.0%
Income tax rate	23.7%	25.1%	25.0%	25.0%	25.0%
Income statement					
Revenue	$66,415	$66,683	$69,339	$84,290	$102,466
Cost of goods sold	−31,243	−30,884	−32,242	−39,195	−47,647
Gross margin	35,172	35,799	37,096	45,095	54,819
Selling, general and administrative	−22,694	−23,501	−24,269	−29,502	−35,863
Depreciation and amortization	−2,773	−2,717	−2,774	−3,372	−4,099
Other operating income	0	0	0	0	0
Operating income	9,705	9,581	10,054	12,222	14,858
Interest and other income	97	85	0	0	0
Interest expense	−911	−909	−1,532	−1,863	−2,264
Income before taxes	8,891	8,757	8,522	10,359	12,593
Income tax expense	−2,104	−2,199	−2,130	−2,590	−3,148
Non-controlling interests	−47	−45	0	0	0
Net earnings	$ 6,740	$ 6,513	$ 6,391	$ 7,770	$ 9,445

Exhibit may contain small rounding errors

We also drive most of the line items on Pepsi's balance sheet based on Pepsi's 2014 relation between a balance sheet item and revenues. For example, accounts receivable is 10% of revenues, inventory is 5% of revenues, accounts payable is 19% of revenues, and so forth. Capital expenditures has two components—replacing depreciated assets (4% of revenues) plus adding capacity for growth (5% of the change in revenues).[8] We assume certain balance sheet items do not grow. For example, we assume goodwill and other intangible assets remains constant (no amortization and no acquisitions). Balance sheet debt is equal to the debt implied by the weighted average cost of capital valuation in each year (recall this calculation from Chapter 5). We present these forecast drivers and Pepsi's balance sheet forecasts for the same selected years in Exhibit 13.5.

The above forecasts and forecast drivers provide all of the information we need to measure Pepsi's free cash flows. Recall from Chapters 1 and 3 (Equation 1.1) that free cash flow is equal to unlevered earnings (EBIT − Income Tax) plus non-cash expenses or losses (NCEXP) minus non-cash revenues or gains (NCREV) minus the change in non-cash operating working capital (ΔWCO) minus the change

[7] For purposes of this example, we treated certain other liabilities in the financial statements as debt.

[8] In this example, we assume that replacement capital expenditures are equal to depreciation. See Chapter 6 for a detailed discussion of the relation between capital expenditures and depreciation.

EXHIBIT 13.5 PepsiCo Inc.—Balance Sheet Forecast Drivers and Historical and Forecasted Balance Sheets

($ in millions)	A-12/2013	A-12/2014	F-12/2015	F-12/2020	F-12/2025
Balance sheet forecast drivers (% of revenue)					
Required cash balance			6.0%	6.0%	6.0%
Accounts receivable	10.5%	10.0%	10.0%	10.0%	10.0%
Inventory	5.1%	4.7%	5.0%	5.0%	5.0%
Other current assets	3.3%	3.2%	3.5%	3.5%	3.5%
Other non-current assets	6.1%	5.3%	5.5%	5.5%	5.5%
Accounts payable	18.9%	19.5%	19.0%	19.0%	19.0%
Non-current liabilities	9.0%	8.0%	8.0%	8.0%	8.0%
Capital expenditures—growth (% × Δ Rev)	4.0%	3.9%	5.0%	5.0%	5.0%
Capital expenditures—Maintenance (% × Rev)	4.2%	4.1%	4.0%	4.0%	4.0%
Balance sheet[1]					
Cash	$ 9,375	$ 4,001	$ 4,160	$ 5,057	$ 6,148
Short-term investments	303	0	0	0	0
Accounts receivable	6,954	6,668	6,934	8,429	10,247
Inventories	3,409	3,334	3,467	4,215	5,123
Other current assets	2,162	2,334	2,427	2,950	3,586
Total current assets	22,203	16,337	16,988	20,651	25,104
Land, buildings, and equipment, net	18,575	17,244	17,377	18,124	19,033
Goodwill and other intangible assets	32,652	29,053	29,053	29,053	29,053
Other non-current assets	4,048	3,668	3,814	4,636	5,636
Total assets	$77,478	$66,302	$67,231	$72,464	$ 78,826
Accounts payable	$12,533	$12,670	$13,174	$16,015	$ 19,469
Short-term and current long-term debt	5,306	5,076	5,076	5,076	5,076
Total current liabilities	17,839	17,746	18,250	21,091	24,545
Long-term debt	29,264	38,702	40,445	50,261	61,992
Other long-term obligations	5,986	5,335	5,547	6,743	8,197
Total liabilities	53,089	61,782	64,243	78,096	94,734
Common stock and surplus	4,120	4,140	4,140	4,140	4,140
Other shareholders' equity	−26,151	−35,684	−35,684	−35,684	−35,684
Retained earnings	46,420	36,064	34,533	25,913	15,636
Total shareholders' equity	24,389	4,520	2,989	−5,631	−15,908
Total liabilities and equities	$77,478	$66,302	$67,231	$72,464	$ 78,826

Exhibit may contain small rounding errors

[1] The 2014 balance sheet is restated to eliminate assumed excess cash and short-term investments.

in the required cash balance (ΔRC) minus capital expenditures (CAPEX). We use this basic formula to measure Pepsi's free cash flows in Exhibit 13.6.

$$FCF = EBIT - TAX + NCEXP - NCREV - \Delta RC - \Delta WCO - CAPEX \quad (1.1)$$

Pepsi's free cash flows decreased from 2014 to 2015 primarily because of a relative decrease in the change in its non-cash operating working capital and an increase in its capital expenditures. Since Pepsi's financial model uses its present value weighted average growth rate to forecast its revenues, and since we drive all of the inputs into free cash flows as a percentage of revenue, beginning in 2016, Pepsi's free cash flows grow at its present value weighted average growth rate of 4% (3.983% to be exact). Based on these free cash flow forecasts, an 8% weighted average cost of capital, and a continuing value growth rate equal to Pepsi's present value weighted average growth rate (4%), we measure the value of Pepsi (firm value) and its equity in Exhibit 13.7 of $182.4 billion and $138.6 billion, respectively.

EXHIBIT 13.6 PepsiCo Inc.—Historical and Forecasted Free Cash Flow Schedules

($ in millions)	A-12/2013	A-12/2014	F-12/2015	F-12/2020	F-12/2025
Earnings before interest and taxes (EBIT)	$9,705	$9,581	$10,054	$12,222	$14,858
Income taxes paid on EBIT	−2,297	−2,406	−2,514	−3,056	−3,714
Earnings before interest and after taxes	7,408	7,175	7,541	9,167	11,143
Depreciation and amortization	2,773	2,717	2,774	3,372	4,099
Other adjustments	228	91	0	0	0
Change in receivables	−88	−343	−266	−323	−392
Change in inventories	4	−111	−133	−161	−196
Change in other current assets	−51	80	−93	−113	−137
Change in accounts payable	1,007	1,162	505	613	746
Change in other non-current assets	0	0	−146	−178	−216
Change in other non-current liabilities	−600	−682	212	258	314
Change in required cash balance	0	0	−159	−194	−235
Unlevered cash flow from operations	10,681	10,089	10,234	12,441	15,124
Capital expenditures, net	−2,665	−2,629	−2,906	−3,533	−4,295
Unlevered free cash flow	8,016	7,460	7,328	8,908	10,829
Interest expense	−911	−909	−1,532	−1,863	−2,264
Interest tax shield	216	228	383	466	566
Cash flow before change in debt	7,321	6,779	6,179	7,511	9,131
Change in debt, net	1,094	703	1,743	2,119	2,374
Equity free cash flow	$ 8,415	$ 7,482	$ 7,922	$ 9,631	$11,505

Exhibit may contain small rounding errors

EXHIBIT 13.7 PepsiCo Inc.—Weighted Average Cost of Capital Valuation

Weighted average cost of capital 8.00% Continuing value growth rate 3.98%

($ in millions)	A-12/ 2014	F-12/ 2015	F-12/ 2016	F-12/ 2017	F-12/ 2018	F-12/ 2019	F-12/ 2020	F-12/ 2021	F-12/ 2022	F-12/ 2023	F-12/ 2024	CV/ 2024
Unlevered free cash flow for continuing value (CV)												$ 10,829
Discount factor for continuing value												24.891
Unlevered free cash flow and CV		$7,328	$7,620	$7,923	$8,239	$8,567	$8,908	$9,263	$9,632	$10,016	$10,414	$269,556
Discount factor		0.926	0.857	0.794	0.735	0.681	0.630	0.583	0.540	0.500	0.463	0.463
Present value		$6,785	$6,533	$6,290	$6,056	$5,831	$5,614	$5,405	$5,204	$ 5,010	$ 4,824	$124,856
Value of the firm	$182,408											
Value of existing debt	43,778											
Equity value	$138,630											

In Exhibit 13.8, we present the calculation of the accounting-based multiples in Exhibit 13.2 using Pepsi's December 2014 firm value, equity value and the 2015 forecasts of the relevant denominators. More specifically, the multiples equal the company's firm value or equity value as of December 2014 divided by the 2015 forecast for the cash flow and income statement-based denominators and the 2014 balance for the balance sheet-based denominators. As reported in the top panel of Exhibit 13.8, Pepsi's firm value-based multiples include a free cash flow multiple of 24.9 and an unlevered earnings multiple of 24.2. Naturally, since EBIT is larger than unlevered earnings, the EBIT multiple of 18.1 is smaller than the unlevered earnings multiple. Similarly, the EBITDA multiple of 14.2 is smaller than both the EBIT and unlevered free cash flow multiples for the same reason. Pepsi's revenue multiple is 2.6, and its total invested capital (TIC) multiple is 3.8.

EXHIBIT 13.8 PepsiCo Inc.—Market Multiples as of December 2014

	Numerator	Denominator	Multiple
Total firm value-based multiples:			
Unlevered free cash flow multiple	$182,408	$ 7,328	24.9
Unlevered earnings multiple		7,541	24.2
EBIT multiple		10,054	18.1
EBITDA multiple		12,828	14.2
Revenue (sales) multiple		69,339	2.6
Total invested capital multiple		$48,297	3.8
Equity value-based multiples:			
Equity free cash flow multiple	$138,630	$ 7,922	17.5
P/E or earnings multiple		6,391	21.7
Market-to-book multiple		$ 4,520	30.7

In the bottom panel of Exhibit 13.8, we report the company's equity-value based multiples. The equity free cash flow multiple is 17.5 and the net income (or P/E) multiple is 21.7. The market-to-book multiple of 30.7 is large because the book value of Pepsi's equity is much smaller than its market value, most likely because the value of Pepsi's brands and other intangible assets are not included on Pepsi's financial statements.

In the remainder of this section, we use the Pepsi financial model and valuation to illustrate how variation in risk factors and the forecast drivers (growth, cost structure, and required investments) causes variation in multiples. We also illustrate how variation in risk factors and the forecast drivers affects the various multiples differently. We illustrate these effects in two ways. First, we use the algebraic relations embedded in the Pepsi financial model to measure the relation between a multiple and its determinants (Pepsi's risk factors and its various forecast drivers). Second, we show the same relations using the Pepsi financial model and valuation to simulate the same effects. We change Pepsi's risk factors and forecast drivers to measure the effect of the change on Pepsi's valuation, its financial statement and free cash flow forecasts, and its multiples.

Before we present the results of the simulation, it is useful to aggregate some of Pepsi's forecast drivers in order to reduce the complexity of Pepsi's multiple relations. We aggregate the cost of goods sold and selling, general and administrative forecast drivers into one forecast driver called operating expenses (OE%), which is 81.5%. We also aggregate all of Pepsi's operating working capital forecast drivers including required cash into one forecast driver called net operating working capital (NOWC%), which is 3%. We summarize Pepsi's risk factors and forecast drivers in Exhibit 13.9.

EXHIBIT 13.9 PepsiCo Inc.—Forecast Driver and Risk Factor Summary

	Description of Forecast Driver/Risk Factor	Variable	Value	Value	How It Is Used
1	Revenue growth rate	g	3.983%		$R_1 = R_0 \times (1 + g)$
2	Income tax rate	TAX%	25.000%		$E_1 = EBIT_1 \times (1 - TAX\%)$
3	Operating expenses	OE%	81.500%		$OE_1 = R_1 \times OE\%$
	Cost of goods sold			46.50%	
	Selling, general & admin			35.00%	
4	Depreciation expense	DEPR%	4.000%		$DEPR_1 = R_1 \times DEPR\%$
5	Δ Net operating working capital	NOWC%	3.000%		$\Delta NOWC_1 = g \times R_0 \times NOWC\%$
	Required cash balance			6.00%	
	Accounts receivable			10.00%	
	Inventory			5.00%	
	Other current assets			3.50%	
	Other non-current assets			5.50%	
	Accounts payable			−19.00%	
	Other non-current liabilities			−8.00%	
6	Capital expenditures—growth	CAPEX%	5.000%		$CAPEX_1 = g \times R_0 \times CAPEX\%$
7	Capital expenditures—depreciation	DEPR%	4.000%		$DEPR_1 = R_1 \times DEPR\%$
8	Weighted average cost of capital	r_{WACC}	8.000%		Discount Rate (Risk)
9	Financial leverage	D/V	24.000%		Discount Rate (Risk)

We use the risk factors and forecast drivers in Exhibit 13.9 as the basis of our Pepsi simulation. In Exhibit 13.10, we summarize the results of the Pepsi simulation for the firm value-based multiples. This exhibit is organized in the following way. We present a set of rows for each of the risk factors and forecast drivers. Each set of rows illustrates the effect of a change in a risk factor or one of the forecast drivers on the different multiples shown in the columns. For a set of rows, the first row presents the original values from the Pepsi financial model and valuation (see Exhibit 13.8); the second row presents the revised value for the risk factor or forecast driver and the resulting multiples; the third row presents the percentage change in firm value and the percentage change in the denominators of each of the multiples; and the last row presents the percentage change in the multiple.

EXHIBIT 13.10 PepsiCo Inc.—Illustration of the Effects of Changes in Risk and Forecast Drivers on Firm Value-Based Market Multiples

	Financial Model Assumption	% Change in Firm Value	Free Cash Flow Multiple	Unlevered Earnings Multiple	EBIT Multiple	EBITDA Multiple	Revenue Multiple	Total Invested Capital Multiple
Risk (discount rate).	8.00%		24.9	24.2	18.1	14.2	2.6	3.8
New assumption and multiples	9.00%		19.9	19.4	14.5	11.4	2.1	3.0
% Change in underlying variable		−19.9%	0.0%	0.0%	0.0%	0.0%	0.0%	0.0%
% Change in multiples			−19.9%	−19.9%	−19.9%	−19.9%	−19.9%	−19.9%
Financial leverage.	24.00%		24.9	24.2	18.1	14.2	2.6	3.8
New assumption and multiples	0.00%		23.6	23.0	17.2	13.5	2.5	3.6
% Change in underlying variable		−5.0%	0.0%	0.0%	0.0%	0.0%	0.0%	0.0%
% Change in multiples			−5.0%	−5.0%	−5.0%	−5.0%	−5.0%	−5.0%
Growth rate.	3.98%		24.9	24.2	18.1	14.2	2.6	3.8
New assumption and multiples	3.48%		22.1	21.6	16.2	12.7	2.3	3.4
% Change in underlying variable		−11.2%	−0.1%	−0.5%	−0.5%	−0.5%	−0.5%	0.0%
% Change in multiples			−11.1%	−10.8%	−10.8%	−10.8%	−10.8%	−11.2%
Capital expenditures growth to revenue . .	5.00%		24.9	24.2	18.1	14.2	2.6	3.8
New assumption and multiples	15.00%		24.9	23.3	17.5	13.7	2.5	2.1
% Change in underlying variable		−3.6%	−3.6%	0.0%	0.0%	0.0%	0.0%	71.4%
% Change in multiples			0.0%	−3.6%	−3.6%	−3.6%	−3.6%	−43.8%
Operating working capital	3.00%		24.9	24.2	18.1	14.2	2.6	3.8
New assumption and multiples	0.00%		24.9	24.5	18.3	14.4	2.7	4.0
% Change in underlying variable		1.1%	1.1%	0.0%	0.0%	0.0%	0.0%	−4.1%
% Change in multiples			0.0%	1.1%	1.1%	1.1%	1.1%	5.5%
Income tax rate	25.00%		24.9	24.2	18.1	14.2	2.6	3.8
New assumption and multiples	30.00%		24.9	24.1	16.6	13.0	2.4	3.5
% Change in underlying variable		−8.6%	−8.6%	−8.3%	0.0%	0.0%	0.0%	0.0%
% Change in multiples			0.0%	−0.3%	−8.6%	−8.6%	−8.6%	−8.6%
Depreciation expense %	4.00%		24.9	24.5	18.3	14.4	2.7	4.0
New assumption and multiples	5.00%		24.9	24.2	18.2	15.2	2.8	4.0
% Change in underlying variable		−9.5%	−9.5%	−9.2%	−9.2%	0.0%	0.0%	0.0%
% Change in multiples			0.0%	−0.3%	−0.3%	−9.5%	−9.5%	−9.5%
Operating expense %	81.50%		24.9	24.2	18.1	14.2	2.6	3.8
New assumption and multiples	82.50%		24.9	24.1	18.1	14.0	2.4	3.5
% Change in underlying variable		−7.2%	−7.2%	−7.0%	−7.0%	−5.5%	0.0%	0.0%
% Change in multiples			0.0%	−0.2%	−0.2%	−1.8%	−7.2%	−7.2%

The percentage change in the multiple is equal to one minus the percentage change in the numerator value divided by one plus the percentage change in the denominator minus 1. The more sensitive the multiple is to a change in a value driver or risk factor, the more important that value driver or risk factor is for assessing comparability.

Free Cash Flow Market Multiple—Risk and Growth Determinants. Recall the formula for the free cash flow multiple.

$$V_{F,0} = FCF_1 \times \frac{1}{r_{WACC} - g}$$

$$MM[FCF] = \frac{V_{F,0}}{FCF_1} = \frac{1}{r_{WACC} - g}$$

According to this formula, as long as the company's free cash flows can be represented by a constant growth rate perpetuity, the free cash flow multiple has two determinants—risk and growth.[9] We have two risk factors for Pepsi—r_{WACC} and financial leverage and one growth factor, g. Thus, according to this formula, none of the other forecast drivers should have an effect on the free cash flow multiple because the percentage change in the value of the firm caused by a change in a forecast driver is equal to the percentage change in free cash flow. We can see these effects illustrated in Exhibit 13.10.

The first two factors in Exhibit 13.10, r_{WACC} and leverage, are risk factors. Increasing r_{WACC} or decreasing leverage, decreases the value of the firm but has no effect on free cash flow; thus, the percentage change in the free cash flow multiple is equal to the percentage change in the value of the firm. Growth, however, does have an effect on all future free cash flows. Decreasing the growth rate decreases free cash flow but not as much as the decrease in firm value, which is affected by the decrease in all future free cash flows not only the decrease in the 2015 free cash flow; thus, the percentage change in the free cash flow multiple is only somewhat less than the percentage change in the value of the firm. However, for all of the remaining forecast drivers, the percentage change in the forecast driver is equal to the percentage change in the value of the firm, so the free cash flow multiple is unchanged. And of course, what we want is a multiple that is not sensitive to very many determinants. This analysis shows that as long as the company's free cash flows can be represented by a constant growth rate perpetuity, the free cash flow multiple has only two determinants—risk and growth. All of the firm value-based multiples are a decreasing function of risk and an increasing function of growth, but as we shall see, the other firm value-based multiples have determinants beyond risk and growth.

Unlevered Earnings Market Multiple—Includes a Plowback Ratio Determinant. The unlevered earnings multiple has all of the same determinants as the free cash flow multiple (risk and growth) and it has an additional determinant, the plowback ratio (required investment in net operating working capital and capital expenditures to support growth). In order to analyze the unlevered earnings (and other earnings-based multiples), we must restate the free cash flow formula in Equation 13.1 as a function of unlevered earnings. We can restate the basic formula to measure Pepsi's free cash flow for Year 1 using its forecast drivers: unlevered earnings is equal to $EBIT_1 \times (1 - TAX\%)$; depreciation is equal to the depreciation percentage multiplied by revenues in Year 1 ($DEPR\% \times R_1$); the change in net operating working capital is equal to the net operating working capital percentage multiplied by the growth in Revenues ($NOWC\% \times g \times R_0$); and capital expenditures is equal to the sum of two components—maintaining its net fixed assets (the same as depreciation, $DEPR\% \times R_1$) and increasing its investment in fixed assets to support growth ($CAPEX\% \times g \times R_0$).

$$\begin{aligned} FCF_1 = {} & EBIT_1 \times (1 - TAX\%) + DEPR\% \times R_1 - NOWC\% \times g \times R_0 \\ & - DEPR\% \times R_1 - CAPEX\% \times g \times R_0 \end{aligned}$$

We can simplify this equation because we add back depreciation as a non-cash expense but we also subtract it as a component of capital expenditures and we can combine some of the terms. This

[9] Based on Pepsi's firm value and free cash flow (Exhibit 13.8), its free cash flow multiple is 24.9, which, given Pepsi's financial model we can also calculate as follows.

$$MM[FCF_1] = \frac{V_{F,0}}{FCF_1} = \frac{1}{r_{WACC} - g}$$

$$MM[FCF] = \frac{\$182{,}408}{\$7{,}328} = \frac{1}{0.08 - 0.03983} = 24.9$$

simplification results in the following formula for free cash flows that is a function of unlevered earnings (UE_1)

$$FCF_1 = UE_1 - (NOWC\% + CAPEX\%) \times g \times R_0$$

We can substitute the above formula in our derivation of the free cash flow multiple as follows.

$$V_{F,0} = [UE_1 - (NOWC\% + CAPEX\%) \times g \times R_0] \times \frac{1}{r_{WACC} - g}$$

$$MM[UE] = \frac{V_{F,0}}{UE_1} = \left(1 - \frac{(NOWC\% + CAPEX\%) \times g \times R_0}{UE_1}\right) \Big/ (r_{WACC} - g)$$

While this formula may seem complex, the intuition underpinning it is not. The unlevered earnings multiple also has the risk and growth determinants but it has an additional component, (NOWC% + CAPEX%) × g × R_0/UE_1. This component represents the proportion of unlevered earnings that must be invested in net operating working capital and capital expenditures to support growth, which is commonly called the plowback ratio, PB_{UE}. We can restate the plowback ratio in terms of the forecast drivers by restating unlevered earnings in Year 1 as equal to revenues in Year 0 multiplied by 1 plus the growth rate, multiplied by 1 minus the expense ratios, and multiplied by 1 minus the income tax rate.

$$PB_{UE} = \frac{(NOWC\% + CAPEX\%) \times g \times R_0}{R_0 \times (1+g) \times (1 - OE\% - DEPR\%) \times (1 - TAX\%)}$$

$$PB_{UE} = \frac{(NOWC\% + CAPEX\%) \times g}{(1+g) \times (1 - OE\% - DEPR\%) \times (1 - TAX\%)}$$

Thus, the unlevered earnings multiple is decreasing in risk and increasing in the growth rate, just as the free cash flow multiple, but it is also decreasing in the plowback ratio (the proportion of unlevered earnings that must be invested in net operating working capital and capital expenditures to support growth).[10]

$$MM[UE] = \frac{V_{F,0}}{UE_1} = (1 - PB_{UE}) / (r_{WACC} - g) \quad \textbf{(13.3)}$$

We illustrate these relations using the Pepsi simulation summarized in Exhibit 13.10. The net operating working capital and capital expenditure investments required to support growth have an effect on the unlevered earnings multiple because both of these forecast drivers affect firm value but have no effect on unlevered earnings. The larger the proportion of earnings that must be reinvested in the firm to support growth, the lower the unlevered earnings multiple. The EBIT, EBITDA, revenue, and total invested capital multiples also have these same determinants. All of these multiples are a decreasing function of net operating working capital and capital expenditure requirements. The other forecast drivers (operating expenses, depreciation expense, and tax rate) also have an effect on the unlevered earnings multiple (see the formula for PB_{UE}, but these effects are small because both the firm value and unlevered earnings are similarly affected by a change in these forecast drivers).

[10] Based on Pepsi's firm value and unlevered earnings (Exhibit 13.8), its unlevered earnings multiple is 24.2, which, given Pepsi's financial model we can also calculate as follows.

$$MM[UE] = \frac{V_{F,0}}{UE_1} = \left(1 - \frac{(NOWC\% + CAPEX\%) \times g}{(1+g) \times (1 - OE\% - DEPR\%) \times (1 - TAX\%)}\right) \Big/ r_{WACC} - g$$

$$MM[UE] = \frac{\$182,408}{\$7,541} = \left(1 - \frac{(0.03 + 0.05) \times 0.03983}{(1.03983) \times (1 - 0.815 - 0.04) \times (1 - 0.25)}\right) \Big/ (0.08 - 0.03983) = 24.2$$

Earnings before Interest and Taxes (EBIT) Market Multiple—Includes an Income Tax Cost Structure Determinant. The EBIT multiple has all of the same determinants as the unlevered earnings multiple (risk, growth, and plowback ratio) and it has an additional determinant, income tax cost structure. We already restated the basic formula used to measure free cash flows (Equation 1.1) to measure Pepsi's free cash flow for Year 1 based on EBIT, which we can then use to identify the determinants of the EBIT multiple.

$$V_{F,0} = [EBIT_1 \times (1 - TAX\%) - (NOWC\% + CAPEX\%) \times g \times R_0] \times \frac{1}{r_{WACC} - g}$$

$$MM[EBIT] = \frac{V_{F,0}}{EBIT_1} = 1 - TAX\% - \left(\frac{(NOWC\% + CAPEX\%) \times g \times R_0}{EBIT_1} \right) \Big/ (r_{WACC} - g)$$

$$PB_{EBIT} = \frac{(NOWC\% + CAPEX\%) \times g}{(1+g) \times (1 - OE\% - DEPR\%)}$$

$$MM[EBIT] = \frac{V_{F,0}}{EBIT_1} = (1 - TAX\% - PB_{EBIT}) / (r_{WACC} - g) \quad \textbf{(13.4)}$$

Like the unlevered earnings multiple, the EBIT multiple also includes a plowback component, but measured as the proportion of EBIT instead of unlevered earnings, PB_{EBIT}. The additional factor that drives EBIT multiples is the company's income tax cost structure. The higher a company's income tax rate, the lower its value but EBIT is unaffected.[11] The other forecast drivers (operating expenses and depreciation expense) also have an effect on the EBIT multiple but these effects are small because both the firm value and EBIT are similarly affected by a change in these forecast drivers. We illustrate this additional effect in the Pepsi simulation summarized in Exhibit 13.10. In addition to the factors that affect the unlevered earnings multiple (risk, growth, net operating working capital, and capital expenditure investments), a company's income tax cost structure is also a major determinant of EBIT multiples but not so for unlevered earnings multiples. The higher a company's income tax cost structure, the lower its EBIT multiple. This same effect exists for the EBITDA, revenue, and total invested capital multiples. All of these multiples are a decreasing function of the company's income tax cost structure.

Earnings before Interest, Taxes, Depreciation and Amortization (EBITDA) Market Multiple—Includes a Depreciation Cost Structure Determinant. The EBITDA multiple has all of the same determinants as the EBIT multiple (risk, growth, plowback ratio, and income tax cost structure) and it has an additional determinant, depreciation cost structure. We can restate the basic formula used to measure free cash flows (Equation 1.1) to measure Pepsi's free cash flow for Year 1 based on EBITDA and derive the EBITDA multiple similar to how we derived the EBIT multiple formula ($EBIT_1 = EBITDA_1 - DEPR\% \times R_1$).

[11] Based on Pepsi's firm value and EBIT (Exhibit 13.8), its EBIT multiple is 18.1, which, given Pepsi's financial model we can also calculate as follows.

$$MM[EBIT] = \frac{V_{F,0}}{EBIT_1} = 1 - TAX\% - \left(\frac{(NOWC\% + CAPEX\%) \times g}{(1+g) \times (1 - OE\% - DEPR\%)} \right) \Big/ (r_{WACC} - g)$$

$$MM[EBIT] = \frac{\$182,408}{\$10,054} = 1 - 0.25 - \left(\frac{(0.03 + 0.05) \times 0.03983}{(1.03983) \times (1 - 0.815 - 0.04)} \right) \Big/ (0.08 - 0.03983) = 18.1$$

$$V_{F,0} = [(EBITDA_1 - DEPR\% \times R_1) \times (1 - TAX\%) - (NOWC\% + CAPEX\%) \times g \times R_0] \times \frac{1}{r_{WACC} - g}$$

$$MM[EBITDA] = \frac{V_{F,0}}{EBITDA_1} = \left(1 - TAX\% - \frac{DEPR\% \times R_1 \times (1 - TAX\%)}{EBITDA_1} - \frac{(NOWC\% + CAPEX\%) \times g \times R_0}{EBITDA_1}\right) \Big/ r_{WACC} - g$$

$$PB_{EBITDA} = \frac{(NOWC\% + CAPEX\%) \times g}{(1+g) \times (1 - OE\%)}$$

$$MM[EBITDA] = \frac{V_{F,0}}{EBITDA_1} = \left(1 - TAX\% - \frac{DEPR\% \times (1 - TAX\%)}{(1 - OE\%)} - PB_{EBITDA}\right) \Big/ (r_{WACC} - g) \qquad \textbf{(13.5)}$$

Like the EBIT multiple, the EBITDA multiple also includes a plowback component, but measured as the proportion of EBITDA, PB_{EBITDA}. The additional factor that drives EBITDA multiples is the depreciation cost structure, based on the Pepsi financial model and our assumption that maintenance CAPEX is related to depreciation. A higher depreciation cost structure indicates higher required maintenance investment; thus, the higher a company's depreciation cost structure, the lower its value but EBITDA is unaffected.[12] The other forecast driver (operating expenses) also has an effect on the EBITDA multiple but these effects are small because both firm value and EBITDA are similarly affected by a change in this forecast driver. We illustrate this additional effect in the Pepsi simulation summarized in Exhibit 13.10. In addition to the factors that affect the EBIT multiple (risk, growth, net operating working capital, capital expenditure investments, and income tax cost structure), a company's depreciation cost structure is a determinant of EBITDA multiples. The higher a company's depreciation cost structure, the lower its EBITDA multiple. This same effect exists for the revenue and total invested capital multiples. Both of these multiples are a decreasing function of the company's depreciation cost structure.

Revenue Market Multiple—Add All Other Components of a Company's Cost Structure. The revenue multiple has all of the same determinants as the EBITDA multiple (risk, growth, plowback ratio, income tax cost structure, depreciation cost structure) and it has additional determinants – all of the company's operating cost structure factors (for example, cost of goods sold, research and development, and selling, general and administrative). For Pepsi, we combined its operating cost structure into one forecast driver, OE%. We can restate the basic formula used to measure free cash flows (Equation 1.1) to measure Pepsi's free cash flow for Year 1 based on revenue and derive its revenue multiple similar to how we derived the EBIT multiple formula [$EBIT_1 = R_1 \times (1 - OE\% - DEPR\%)$].

$$V_{F,0} = [R_1 \times (1 - OE\% - DEPR\%) \times (1 - TAX\%) - (NOWC\% + CAPEX\%) \times g \times R_0] \times \frac{1}{r_{WACC} - g}$$

$$MM[Revenue] = \frac{V_{F,0}}{R_1} = \left(1 - TAX\% - (OE\% + DEPR\%) \times (1 - TAX\%) - \frac{(NOWC\% + CAPEX\%) \times g \times R_0}{R_1}\right) \Big/ (r_{WACC} - g)$$

$$PB_{Revenue} = \frac{(NOWC\% + CAPEX\%) \times g}{(1+g)}$$

$$MM[Revenue] = \frac{V_{F,0}}{R_1} = [1 - TAX\% - (OE\% + DEPR\%) \times (1 - TAX\%) - PB_{Revenue}] / (r_{WACC} - g) \qquad \textbf{(13.6)}$$

[12] Based on Pepsi's firm value and EBITDA (Exhibit 13.8), its EBITDA multiple is 14.2, which, given Pepsi's financial model we can also calculate as follows.

$$MM[EBITDA] = \frac{V_{F,0}}{EBITDA_1} = \left(1 - TAX\% - \frac{DEPR\% \times (1 - TAX\%)}{(1 - OE\%)} - \frac{(NOWC\% + CAPEX\%) \times g}{(1+g) \times (1 - OE\%)}\right) \Big/ (r_{WACC} - g)$$

$$MM[EBITDA] = \frac{\$182{,}408}{\$12{,}828} = \left(1 - 0.25 - \frac{0.04 \times (1 - 0.25)}{(1 - 0.815)} - \frac{(0.03 + 0.05) \times 0.03983}{(1.03983) \times (1 - 0.815)}\right) \Big/ (0.08 - 0.03983) = 14.2$$

The revenue multiple also includes a plowback ratio measured as a proportion of revenue ($PB_{Revenue}$), the income tax cost structure, and the depreciation cost structure.[13] The additional factors that drive revenue multiples are all of the components that drive the company's cost structure. Based on the Pepsi financial model, a higher operating cost structure (or the lower its profit margin) results in a lower value but it has no effect on revenue. We illustrate this additional effect in the Pepsi simulation summarized in Exhibit 13.10. In addition to the factors that affect the EBITDA multiple (risk, growth, net operating working capital, capital expenditure investments, income tax cost structure, and depreciation cost structure), all of the components of a company's cost structure are determinants of revenue multiples. Thus, the revenue multiple will typically be a more difficult multiple for which to identify comparable companies, and, thus, it is often the case that revenue multiples are not as useful in a market multiples valuation. These same effects exist for the total invested capital multiple, which we discuss next.

Total Invested Capital Market Multiple—More Sensitive to Investment Requirements to Support Growth. The total invested capital multiple has all of the determinants that the revenue multiple has but it is more sensitive to required investments to support growth. We do not need to restate the basic formula used to measure free cash flows (Equation 1.1) to measure the total invested capital multiple. The total invested capital multiple is equal to the unlevered earnings multiple multiplied by the rate of return earned on the beginning balance of the company's total invested capital.[14]

$$MM[TIC] = \frac{V_{F,0}}{TIC_0} = \frac{V_{F,0}}{UE_1} \times \frac{UE_1}{TIC_0} = MM[UE] \times \frac{UE_1}{TIC_0} \quad (13.7)$$

Since the determinants of unlevered earnings include a company's entire cost structure [$UE_1 = R_1 \times (1 - OE\% - DEPR\%) \times (1 - TAX\%)$], the total invested capital multiple has the same determinants as the revenue multiple (risk, growth, and all of the other forecast drivers) but it is more sensitive than the revenue multiple to investment requirements. We know that the unlevered earnings multiple is a decreasing function of the plowback ratio; however, total invested capital is an increasing function of the plowback ratio, which reduces the return on total invested capital. For a given amount of growth, an increase in the amount of required investment decreases the value of the firm but increases total invested capital. We illustrate this additional effect in the Pepsi simulation summarized in Exhibit 13.10. The simulation shows that all of the factors that affect the revenue multiple (risk, growth, net operating working capital, capital expenditure investments, income tax cost structure, depreciation cost structure, and all of the components of a company's cost structure) also affect the total invested capital multiple but the total invested capital multiple is more sensitive than the revenue multiple to investment requirements (capital expenditures and working capital investments).

[13] Based on Pepsi's firm value and revenue (Exhibit 13.8), its revenue multiple is 2.6, which, given Pepsi's financial model we can also calculate as follows.

$$MM[Revenue] = \frac{V_{F,0}}{R_1} = \left(1 - TAX\% - (OE\% + DEPR\%) \times (1 - TAX\%) - \frac{(NOWC\% + CAPEX\%) \times g}{(1+g)}\right) / (r_{WACC} - g)$$

$$MM[Revenue] = \frac{\$182{,}408}{\$69{,}339} = \left(1 - 0.25 - (0.815 + 0.04) \times (1 - 0.25) - \frac{(0.03 + 0.05) \times 0.03983}{(1.03983)}\right) \Big/ (0.08 - 0.03983) = 2.6$$

[14] Based on Pepsi's firm value and total invested capital (Exhibit 13.8), its total invested capital multiple is 3.8, which, given Pepsi's financial model we can also calculate as follows.

$$MM[TIC] = \frac{V_{F,0}}{TIC_0} = MM[UE] \times \frac{UE_1}{TIC_0}$$

$$MM[TIC] = \frac{\$182{,}408}{\$48{,}297} = 24.2 \times \frac{\$7{,}541}{\$48{,}297} = 3.8$$

Valuation Key 13.4

In addition to risk and growth factors, a company's income tax, depreciation, and operating cost structure, as well as its working capital and capital expenditure requirements, are potentially relevant determinants of a company's market multiple, depending on the market multiple and the specific valuation. A determinant that is excluded from the calculation of a market multiple's value driver (denominator) is more likely to be relevant for assessing comparability (for example, income tax cost structure is more likely to be relevant for EBIT, EBITDA, and revenue multiples than unlevered earnings multiples). Of course, all else equal, we prefer multiples that are not sensitive to numerous determinants as it makes the choice of comparable companies easier.

Before we move on to our discussion of equity based multiples it is important to note one additional thing. The specific algebraic formulas we have provided for the market multiples in this chapter are based on the assumptions of the simplistic financial model we used to value Pepsi. Alternative model assumptions could lead to different formulas for each of the market multiples, thus we are not suggesting that these formulas can be used to determine the appropriate multiple for any company simply by plugging in estimates of the variables in the equations.

REVIEW EXERCISE 13.4

Using Market Multiple Determinants to Measure Multiples

Use the abbreviated income statements and balance sheets for this all-equity financed company to measure its market multiples (free cash flow, unlevered earnings, EBIT, EBITDA, revenue, and total invested capital) using two approaches—(i) the value of the firm divided by the market multiple value driver in Year 1 for the free cash flow, unlevered earnings, EBIT, EBITDA and revenue, and Year 0 for total invested capital and (ii) the formulas derived in the Pepsi simulation. The company has the same forecast drivers in its financial model as Pepsi although the magnitudes of the forecast drivers are different. The company's operating expenses, depreciation, and net operating working capital are a constant percent of revenues; its capital expenditures are equal to depreciation plus a constant percentage of the growth in revenues; and its revenues and free cash flows grow at a constant rate into perpetuity. The company's firm value is \$10,000 and its cost of capital is 14%. (*Hint:* First, measure the company's free cash flows; next, measure the company's growth rate and each of the other forecast drivers; then measure the company's market multiples using the two approaches.)

Forecast Driver		Year 0	Year 1
	Revenue	\$6,983.2	\$ 7,262.6
60.0%	Operating expenses	−4,189.9	−4,357.5
	EBITDA	2,793.3	2,905.0
10.0%	Depreciation	−698.3	−726.3
	EBIT	2,095.0	2,178.8
	Interest	0.0	0.0
	EBT	2,095.0	2,178.8
40.0%	Taxes	−838.0	−871.5
	Earnings	\$1,257.0	\$1,307.3
10.0%	Net operating assets	\$ 698.3	\$ 726.3
	Net fixed assets	1,500.0	1,779.3
	Total assets less operating liabilities	\$2,198.3	\$2,505.6

Exhibit may contain small rounding errors

Solution on pages 653–654.

Equity Value-Based Market Multiples. While financial leverage affects the value of the firm, it does not affect any of the denominators for the firm value-based multiples; thus, changes in financial leverage affect only the numerators in the firm value-based market multiples and not the denominators.

That is not the case for the equity value-based multiples. Financial leverage affects both the value of the equity and the denominators of all of the equity value-based multiples except the revenue multiple. As a result, the formulas for the equity value-based multiples are more complex than the formulas for the firm value-based multiples and we do not derive them here. However, in Exhibit 13.11, we present the results of the Pepsi simulation for the equity free cash flow, earnings (P/E), and market-to-book multiples. The format of that exhibit is the same as Exhibit 13.10.

The determinants of the equity value-based multiples are directionally similar to their respective counterparts for the firm value-based multiples, although the relative effect is sometimes greater for the equity value-based multiples. For example, the determinants of the equity free cash flow multiple are similar to the determinants of the unlevered free cash flow multiple, although the equity free cash flow multiple is affected to some extent by changes in the cost structure forecast drivers where the unlevered free cash flow multiple is not. The determinants of the earnings (P/E) multiple are also similar to the determinants of the unlevered earnings multiple except the effect of the same change for each of the determinants is larger for the earnings (P/E) multiple. While the determinants of the market-to-book

EXHIBIT 13.11 Pepsi, Inc. Illustration of the Effects of Changes in Risk and Forecast Drivers on Equity Value-Based Multiples

	Financial Model Assumption	% Change in Equity Value	Equity Free Cash Flow Multiple	P/E or Earnings Multiple	Market-to-Book Multiple	Revenue (Sales) Multiple
Risk (discount rate)	9.70%		17.5	21.7	30.7	2.0
New assumption and multiples	10.91%		13.1	15.4	7.7	1.5
% Change in underlying variable		−26.2%	−1.5%	3.6%	193.1%	0.0%
% Change in multiples			−25.1%	−28.8%	−74.8%	−26.2%
Financial leverage	24.00%		17.5	21.7	30.7	2.0
New assumption and multiples	0.00%		17.7	17.2	2.7	1.9
% Change in underlying variable		−6.6%	−7.5%	18.0%	968.6%	0.0%
% Change in multiples			1.0%	−20.8%	−91.3%	−6.6%
Growth rate	3.98%		17.5	21.7	30.7	2.0
New assumption and multiples	3.48%		15.5	18.2	12.6	1.7
% Change in underlying variable		−14.7%	−3.4%	1.4%	108.3%	−0.5%
% Change in multiples			−11.7%	−15.9%	−59.1%	−14.3%
Capital expenditures %	5.00%		17.5	21.7	30.7	2.0
New assumption and multiples	15.00%		17.3	20.5	3.3	1.9
% Change in underlying variable		−4.8%	−3.6%	0.7%	798.2%	0.0%
% Change in multiples			−1.2%	−5.4%	−89.4%	−4.8%
Operating working capital %	3.00%		17.5	21.7	30.7	2.0
New assumption and multiples	0.00%		17.6	22.0	68.8	2.0
% Change in underlying variable		1.4%	1.1%	−0.2%	−54.8%	0.0%
% Change in multiples			0.3%	1.6%	124.4%	1.4%
Income tax rate	25.00%		17.5	21.7	30.7	2.0
New assumption and multiples	30.00%		16.8	20.7	14.9	1.8
% Change in underlying variable		−11.3%	−7.5%	−6.9%	83.1%	0.0%
% Change in multiples			−4.1%	−4.7%	−51.5%	−11.3%
Depreciation Expense %	4.00%		17.5	21.7	30.7	2.0
New assumption and multiples	5.00%		16.9	20.9	14.0	1.8
% Change in underlying variable		−12.4%	−9.5%	−9.1%	91.7%	0.0%
% Change in multiples			−3.3%	−3.6%	−54.3%	−12.4%
Operating expense %	81.50%		17.5	21.7	30.7	2.0
New assumption and multiples	82.50%		17.1	21.1	16.4	1.8
% Change in underlying variable		−9.5%	−7.2%	−6.9%	83.1%	0.0%
% Change in multiples			−2.4%	−2.7%	−46.6%	−9.5%

multiple are the same as the total invested capital multiple, the effect is again larger for the market-to-book multiple because total invested capital is not affected by the amount of debt the company issues but the amount of equity issued is affected. Lastly, the equity value-based revenue multiple has the same determinants and effects as the firm value-based revenue multiple but again the effect of a given change in one of the determinants is larger for the equity value-based revenue multiple.

Valuation Key 13.5

Equity value-based multiples have determinants similar to their corresponding firm value-based multiples, but the effect of a change in a determinant is often larger for equity value-based multiples. As with firm valued-based multiples, multiples which are not as sensitive to changes in as many determinants facilitate the choice of comparable companies.

Does Firm Size Matter When Assessing Comparability?

Controlling for the size of the comparable companies is common. However, we are not aware of any theoretical models that include size as a determinant of market multiples. The empirical research is mixed on whether or not controlling for size is helpful for choosing comparable companies after controlling for industry and other market multiple determinants.[15] On the other hand, some evidence indicates that firm size is correlated with certain value-relevant factors of a company; for example, we know that size appears to be correlated with stock returns even after controlling for expected returns measured using the CAPM (see Chapter 8).

In Exhibit 13.12, we show the median EBITDA multiples for five different enterprise value-based size groups (based on the CapitalIQ Market Multiple Sample for 2015). This exhibit shows that the median EBITDA multiple decreases as the firms become smaller. While this exhibit provides some limited evidence that market multiples may be related to enterprise value in some way, this exhibit ignores all of the determinants that affect EBITDA multiples. It may be the case that after controlling for the EBITDA multiple determinants discussed previously, enterprise value is no longer correlated with firm size and not relevant for assessing comparability. Given the uncertainty as to which of the market multiple determinants are important in a specific valuation, and the difficulty to forecast such determinants for all of the comparable companies, controlling for firm size is likely to be useful if estimates of the other determinants are not available.

EXHIBIT 13.12 Median EBITDA Multiples by Enterprise Value Size Groups (U.S. Companies, 2015)

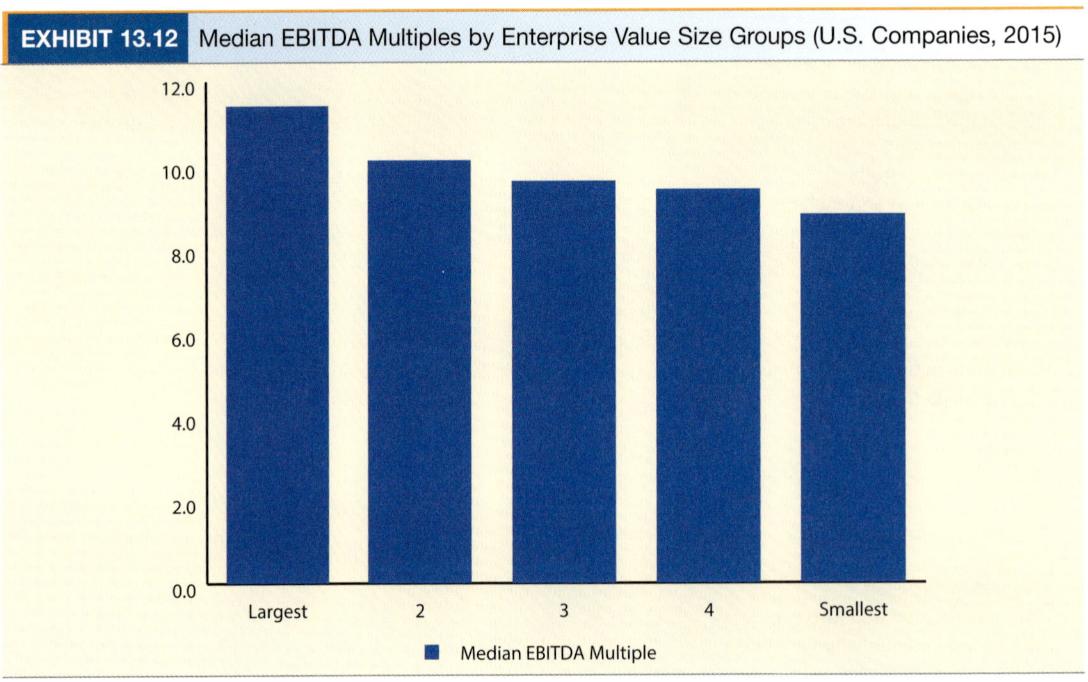

[15] See for example, Alford, A., "The Effect of the Set of Comparable Companies on the Accuracy of the Price Earnings Valuation Method," *Journal of Accounting Research* 30 (1992), pp. 94–108; and Beatty, R., S. Riffe, and R. Thompson, "The Method of Comparables and Tax Court Valuations of Private Firms: An Empirical Investigation," *Accounting Horizons* (September, 1999), pp. 177–199.

REVIEW EXERCISE 13.5

Change in Market Multiples from a Change in Market Multiple Determinants

Use the information in Review Exercise 13.1 to examine the change in market multiples resulting from a change in the determinants of free cash flows in that financial model (assumptions) described below. For each of the changes in the determinants, measure the changes in the multiples of firm value to free cash flow, unlevered earnings, EBIT, EBITDA, and revenue. Measure the market multiple using the end of Year 0 firm value and Year 0 value driver.

- The initial valuation of the company used a 2% perpetual growth rate. If the perpetual growth rate increases to 4%, the company's value increases by 4.7%.
- The initial valuation of the company used a 12% unlevered cost of capital. If the unlevered cost of capital decreases to 10%, the company's value increases by 29.6%.
- The company has a 70% operating expense ratio (% of revenue) in Year 0 and the forecasts. If the operating expense ratio decreases to 60% in Year 0 and the forecasts, the company's value increases by 37%. Assume this change has no effect on working capital.

Solution on page 654.

Assumptions Underlying Non-Accounting-Based Market Multiples

As we discussed earlier, analysts sometimes use non-accounting-based market multiples. Using non-accounting-based market multiples might not seem useful, but consider the following example. A friend tells you that she is going to buy a wireless telephone company and the price she is going to pay is $200 multiplied by the number of people living in the geographic region served by the company. You are shocked that she is going to buy a company based on a valuation model that ignores cash flows and risk, and you quickly challenge the reasonableness of her decision. Your friend tells you that she agreed to pay this price because $200 is well below the average multiple of market capitalization to population (sometimes called the **price-per-pop**) of all wireless telephone companies operating in regions with demographics that are similar to the company she is buying.

You begin to analyze her statement. You know that the market values of comparable companies reflect the market's expectations about future cash flows and risk, which provides a link to value. However, dividing firm value by population seems to ignore the important drivers of value. Your friend then tells you that she knows that all wireless telephone companies make similar capital investments and have similar cost structures that are a function of the number of customers served. She also tells you that both the average revenue per customer and the percentage of the people in the population who are wireless customers are similar for all comparable companies.

You quickly realize that all companies of this type have essentially the same relations between the population and all of the factors that determine cash flows in a financial model. As such, knowing the population is key to forecasting future cash flows. You conclude that your friend's analysis did not ignore cash flows and risk and that her valuation analysis might not be as crazy as you had first thought. You now conclude that this method might provide an accurate assessment of value, depending on the similarity of the comparable companies. Thus, properly done, market multiple valuations based on non-accounting-based value drivers can implicitly incorporate fundamental valuation principles.

As it turns out, companies in the wireless communications industry sometimes must purchase licenses from the government in order to have the right to service a population in a specific area. The government typically limits the number of licenses for each area. Since the population in an area for which a company has a license is a good measure of the company's potential customers in that area, the population in a service area is sometimes used as a value driver. Naturally, this is not the only market multiple determinant investors examine. The number of subscribers, the penetration rate (number of subscribers divided by population), and the churn rate (average length of time a customer stays with the company) are all value relevant characteristics for companies in this industry.[16] The important determinants of variation in non-accounting-based market multiples include all of the same drivers for accounting-based multiples,

[16] See Amir, E., and B. Lev, "Value-Relevance of Nonfinancial Information: The Wireless Communications Industry," *Journal of Accounting and Economics* 2 (1996), pp. 3–30, for a discussion and empirical examination of the market multiple determinants for this industry. Financial analysts sometimes use the ratio of market value to population to analyze wireless telecommunications companies. Another ratio they use is market value to number of subscribers.

which we discussed earlier; in addition, they also share the assumption that the relation between the non-accounting-based value driver and free cash flow is the same.

13.5 THE PROCESS FOR IDENTIFYING COMPARABLE COMPANIES

LO3 Choose comparable companies to use in a market multiple valuation

Identifying comparable companies is an important step in many different facets of any valuation analysis. However, identifying comparable companies is usually the most important as well as the most difficult step in a market multiple based valuation. While selecting comparable companies might not appear to be too difficult, we often quickly conclude that not many, if any, companies are truly comparable to the company we are valuing for purposes of a market multiple valuation. As we learned earlier in the chapter, risk factors and growth rates are determinants of all market multiples and therefore are relevant for assessing comparability and identifying comparable companies. Further, we know from the Pepsi simulation, that variation in other forecast drivers can also cause variation in market multiples, and the degree to which a forecast driver causes variation in a multiple differs for different multiples. The implication of this result is that the factors relevant for assessing comparability are different for different multiples. The process for identifying comparable companies naturally begins with understanding the company's business and identifying its competitors but this is only the first part of the process. Assessing comparability based on the determinants that cause variation in the multiples used to value the firm is also critically important.

Understand the Businesses in Which the Company Operates

The first step in identifying potential comparable companies is to understand the businesses in which the company operates. Analyzing a company's financial statements and filings with the government (such as its 10-K and proxy statements filed with the U.S. Securities and Exchange Commission) is usually the best starting point to collect this information. The company always discusses its lines of business in these documents.

After understanding the businesses in which the company operates, we identify its competitors. Fortunately, we have a variety of sources with which to identify a company's competitors. The company typically identifies its primary competitors in its financial statements and other public filings. In addition, analyzing the industries (business segments) in which the company operates is another way we can identify the company's competitors. Keep in mind that because many companies operate in more than one industry, it is often useful to identify all of the industries in which the company has significant operations.

Industry association publications and financial analyst reports also typically provide information about key competitors, even for private companies. Certain financial websites also contain information on competitors of companies. We can also examine companies that have the same industry code. While industry codes provide an indication of industry, companies with the same industry code may not be direct competitors, while some companies with different industry codes are direct competitors. In addition, the primary industry code only indicates a portion of a company's business for companies operating in more than one industry.

One popular classification system used to identify a company's industry is the Standard Industrial Classification (SIC) system maintained by the U.S. Department of Labor. The SIC system was developed in the 1930s, and it has been revised multiple times based on the economy's changing industrial composition. Current definitions come from the 1987 Standard Industrial Classification (SIC) Manual.[17] We can analyze SIC codes at the one-, two-, three-, or four-digit level. The one- and two-digit levels, however, are not very useful for many applications, including market multiples. It is usually best to start at the three- or four-digit level if you are relying on SIC codes. However, if you only had a handful of observations at the three-digit and four-digit levels, you could choose to analyze companies at the two-digit level. Given the "noise" in these industry classifications, it is typically useful to use other sources of information to identify direct competitors.

The Pepsi simulation illustrates that industries—as well as firms within industries—that have different values for the market multiple determinant will have different multiples. In Exhibit 13.13, we show

[17] You can find SIC industry definitions and a searchable manual at the U.S. Department of Labor's website available on June 15, 2018 at https://www.osha.gov/pls/imis/sic_manual.html.

the median Enterprise Value to EBITDA and Price-to-earnings multiples for 14 industries as of December 2015 at the four-digit level of aggregation. We again use the CapitalIQ Market Multiple sample for 2015 to create this exhibit.[18] This exhibit shows how market multiples vary across industries at a point in time, suggesting that matching companies based on industry can be a useful step when identifying comparable companies. However, as we discuss in the next section, identifying direct competitors is only the first step for identifying comparable companies, and identifying direct competitors may not be useful for identifying comparable companies if the other companies in the industry are not comparable based on the relevant market multiple determinants.

EXHIBIT 13.13 Median Enterprise Value/EBITDA and P/E Multiples for Selected Industries (U.S. Companies, 2015)

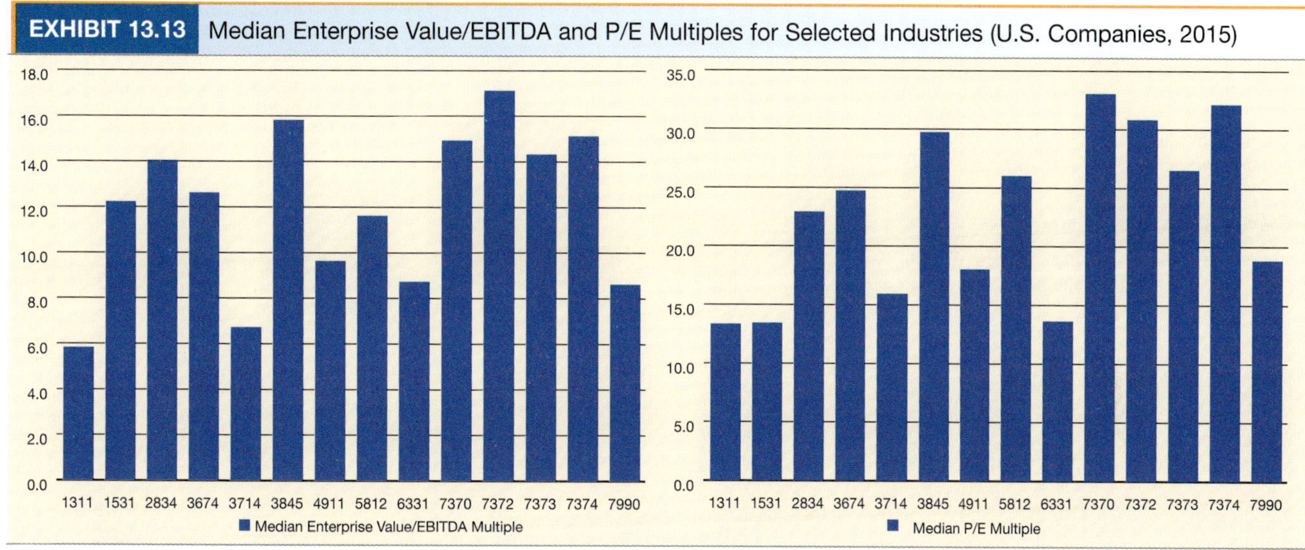

Identifying Competitors and Companies in the Same Industry Is Only the Starting Point

While identifying a company's direct competitors is usually a useful starting point to identify comparable companies, it is usually insufficient for choosing the final set of comparables for a market multiple valuation. Choosing close competitors usually controls for business risk, for close competitors usually, but not always, have similar business risks. However, simply selecting close competitors is generally not sufficient to ensure the companies are comparable, because even direct competitors are not always comparable based on the relevant market multiple determinants. This variation exists because of many of the factors we have been discussing. In Exhibit 13.14, we show as of December 2015 the distributions of the enterprise value to EBITDA and P/E multiples using the same dataset for the 14 industries used in Exhibit 13.13. The distributions in this exhibit show a substantial amount of variation within industries.

[18] The descriptions for the industries in this exhibit are:
1311 Crude Petroleum & Natural Gas
1531 Operative Builders
2834 Pharmaceutical Preparations
3674 Semiconductors & Related Devices
3714 Motor Vehicle Parts & Accessories
3845 Electromedical & Electrotherapeutic Apparatus
4911 Electric Services
5812 Retail-Eating Places
6331 Fire, Marine & Casualty Insurance
7370 Services-Computer Programming, Data Processing, Etc.
7372 Services-Prepackaged Software
7373 Services-Computer Integrated Systems Design
7374 Services-Computer Processing & Data Preparation
7990 Services-Miscellaneous Amusement & Recreation

EXHIBIT 13.14 Distributions of Market Multiples for Selected Industries (U.S. Companies, 2015)

SIC Code =	1311	1531	2834	3674	3714	3845	4911	5812	6331	7370	7372	7373	7374	7990
Enterprise value to earnings before interest, taxes, depreciation, and amortization:														
Number of firms	114	21	46	62	26	24	29	53	45	111	61	26	29	23
Mean.	7.9	17.5	24.4	18.0	7.4	25.6	9.6	12.5	13.1	25.5	32.3	20.1	16.9	9.7
5th percentile	2.5	10.2	2.2	4.7	3.7	8.4	5.3	6.2	4.1	5.6	7.2	6.5	9.3	3.5
10th percentile	3.1	10.5	5.5	4.8	4.5	10.6	6.5	7.1	5.4	7.1	8.3	7.3	9.6	4.9
25th percentile	3.7	11.2	9.6	7.4	5.3	11.8	8.3	9.0	6.6	11.3	10.4	10.3	11.7	6.4
50th percentile	5.8	12.2	14.0	12.6	6.7	15.8	9.6	11.6	8.7	14.9	17.1	14.3	15.1	8.6
75th percentile	9.1	20.0	25.2	19.1	9.4	23.5	10.7	14.1	10.6	25.1	34.7	18.3	17.0	10.5
90th percentile	12.7	28.0	64.3	32.1	10.9	26.9	12.6	19.5	12.8	53.9	75.8	48.2	21.1	13.1
95th percentile	21.6	33.1	91.9	58.9	11.7	58.4	13.9	28.6	18.0	90.5	102.8	55.9	24.6	14.4
75th to 25th ratio	2.4	1.8	2.6	2.6	1.8	2.0	1.3	1.6	1.6	2.2	3.3	1.8	1.4	1.6
90th to 10th ratio	4.1	2.7	11.7	6.6	2.4	2.5	1.9	2.8	2.4	7.6	9.1	6.6	2.2	2.7
Share price to fully diluted earnings per share before extraordinary items:														
Number of Firms. . . .	37	19	44	41	23	20	24	43	45	72	45	21	22	18
Mean.	30.3	12.5	43.4	37.0	16.2	32.4	27.0	29.9	15.2	57.1	42.2	46.2	35.8	34.8
5th percentile	1.8	1.4	1.3	12.2	6.0	10.3	12.4	11.9	6.2	9.6	3.6	16.9	13.4	2.3
10th percentile	2.6	5.0	7.4	14.8	6.6	10.7	12.9	15.1	7.9	11.2	9.9	17.4	18.5	5.3
25th percentile	4.2	11.2	13.8	18.5	11.9	18.6	15.9	20.9	10.3	23.1	18.3	22.0	23.3	9.7
50th percentile	13.3	13.4	22.9	24.7	15.9	29.7	18.0	26.0	13.6	33.0	30.8	26.5	32.1	18.8
75th percentile	25.3	15.2	53.9	35.7	20.3	40.8	21.5	33.3	17.1	65.6	58.6	40.7	45.8	39.5
90th percentile	56.9	17.5	109.3	75.8	26.3	52.7	42.5	39.8	20.6	128.1	83.7	87.6	58.9	70.5
95th percentile	162.1	20.3	138.7	88.7	28.5	64.5	92.2	67.2	23.9	187.3	91.2	148.8	61.4	111.3
75th to 25th ratio . . .	6.0	1.4	3.9	1.9	1.7	2.2	1.4	1.6	1.7	2.8	3.2	1.9	2.0	4.1
90th to 10th ratio . . .	21.9	3.5	14.9	5.1	4.0	4.9	3.3	2.6	2.6	11.4	8.5	5.0	3.2	13.3

Thus, while a company's product lines, customer types, market segments, types of operation, and so forth are all potentially relevant aspects to consider when identifying comparable companies, they are only relevant to the extent they match companies on the relevant market multiple determinants. Choosing comparable companies is tantamount to trying to figure out where in the distribution of market multiples for an industry the company being valued is located. For example, if we are interested in valuing a company in the pharmaceutical preparations industry (SIC 2834) based on its EBITDA multiple, we must decide where in the distribution the company lies. The 10th to 90th percentiles for this industry range from 5.5 to 64.3. Based on a company's characteristics, we must decide whether it is more comparable to the median firm in the industry, or whether it is more likely to be closer to the 10th or 90th percentile of the distribution, or somewhere else.

The conceptual framework discussed in this chapter provides a guide for what market multiple determinants we should examine when identifying comparable companies, even if they are competitors that operate in the same industry. Remember that the goal is to identify (comparable) companies that sell for the same multiple of earnings (or whatever multiple we decide to use) as the company being valued. Thus, we need to control for all of the relevant market multiple determinants that we identified in our conceptual framework that affect a particular multiple by appropriately selecting comparable companies.

In other words, we identify competitors, we analyze both the company being valued and the competitors with respect to characteristics that cause the variation in market multiples. One trade-off will become apparent when attempting this analysis. A valuation expert must achieve a balance between having a sufficient number of comparables for measuring the market multiples and the comparability of these comparables. The larger the set of comparable companies, the more likely that "noise" in the market multiples is eliminated. However, in order for that "noise" to be eliminated, the companies must be truly comparable.

Since the choice of comparables necessitates analyzing such issues as growth and profitability, analysts' reports and historical financial statements of individual companies, in addition to analysts' reports on the industry, can be useful. Financial statements allow one to analyze the recent history of growth and profitability. In addition, analyzing the financial statements helps us understand the comparability of the financial statements across firms as well as the extent to which unusual or non-recurring items have affected the reported performance of the company (more on this latter topic in the next section).

Valuation in Practice 13.2

New Entrant with New Technology in the Auto Industry Tesla designs, develops, manufactures, and sells fully electric vehicles and advanced electric vehicle powertrain components and was the first company to commercially produce a U.S. federally-compliant electric vehicle, the Tesla Roadster. Tesla was incorporated in 2003 and went public on the NASDAQ in 2010. As we show in the following chart, Tesla's Enterprise value/EBITDA multiple is over 600 while the more traditional automakers have EBITDA multiples around 10 or less as of December 31, 2014, suggesting that Tesla's technology is a driver for long-term growth. Tesla's EBITDA multiple was not the result of non-recurring events that negatively impacted Tesla's EBITDA. Tesla's revenue multiple (not shown in the chart) is around 9, which is 10 to 20 times higher than the revenue multiple of the more traditional automakers.

Enterprise Value/EBITDA Multiples for Selected Automobile Manufacturers

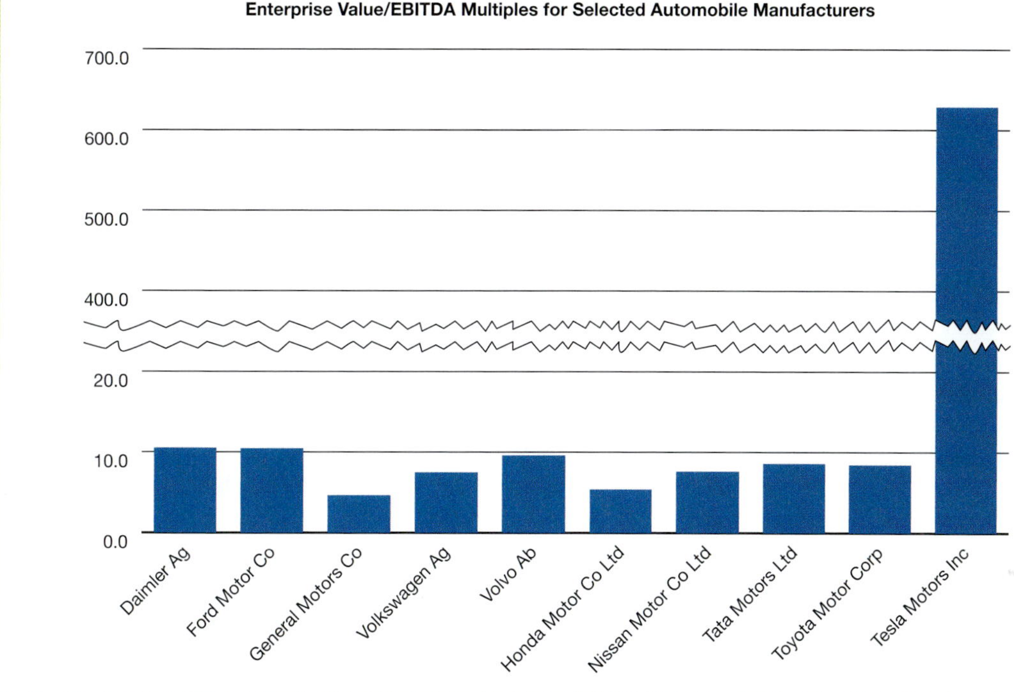

Analysts' reports provide some insight into market expectations for near- and long-term growth prospects as well as forecasts of future profitability. However, empirical evidence indicates that on average, analysts have a slight optimistic bias. In addition, for companies that are performing very well (very poorly), they also tend to believe that the superior (inferior) performance will last longer than it actually will. In addition, empirical studies show that controlling for the historic growth rate is not very useful relative to controlling for expectations of future growth when trying to understand variation in price multiples.[19] Moreover, controlling for the known biases of analysts is useful.

Valuation Key 13.6

Identifying comparable companies is an important part of any market multiple analysis. We typically begin by identifying a company's competitors and other companies in the same industry. We then analyze future risk, growth, profitability, investment requirements, and other relevant determinants of the market multiple we are using in order to select the most comparable set of companies for the company being valued.

[19] Alford (1990) shows that controlling for historic growth rates is not important after controlling for industry. However, Zarowin (1990) shows that controlling for expected growth is important, for it dominates over other factors. See Alford, A., "The Effect of the Set of Comparable Companies on the Accuracy of the Price-Earnings Valuation Method," *Journal of Accounting Research* 30 (1992), pp. 94–108; and Zarowin, P., "What Determines Earnings-Price Ratios: Revisited," *Journal of Accounting, Auditing, and Finance* 5 (1990), pp. 439–457.

13.6 TRANSITORY SHOCKS AND MARKET MULTIPLES

LO4 Adjust for transitory changes when measuring market multiples

A company can experience temporary changes in its earnings and free cash flows, called transitory shocks. We know that the expected growth rate is important in selecting comparable companies. In this section, we explore the issue of transitory shocks and its effect on earnings and free cash flow growth rates, and hence its effect on market multiples and selecting comparable companies.

Consider what happens to a potential comparable company that has a negative transitory shock to its earnings or free cash flow in the year in which we measure its market multiples. If the market believes that the transitory shock will only affect the firm for a single year, the value of the company is unlikely to decline substantially if at all, for the market expects the company to quickly recover. In this situation, the company's market multiples will rise temporarily, because earnings and free cash flow decrease temporarily, whereas value does not. In the following year, the transitory shock disappears, and the company's earnings and free cash flows will grow at an abnormally high rate because of the elimination of the transitory shock. Naturally, the opposite will occur for a firm that has a positive transitory shock to its earnings or free cash flow. This firm's market multiples will be low in the year that the positive transitory shock occurs, for its market value will not increase in proportion to the transitory shock. In the following year, when the positive transitory shock dissipates, earnings and free cash flow growth will be either low or perhaps even negative.

In Exhibit 13.15, we present actual free cash flows for Year −1 and Year 0 and free cash flow forecasts for Year 1 through Year 4 for two companies—the Risen Company (Risen) and Habibi Corporation (Habibi). Risen and Habibi have the same cost of capital and are 100% equity financed. As we show in the exhibit, we have sufficient information to value both of these companies using a DCF valuation method. Risen is one-half of the size of Habibi (see the relative Year 0 firm values). We plan to use Habibi as a comparable company for Risen. Given that the companies have the same risk (same unlevered cost of capital), we begin by assessing the growth rates of the two companies. Since we measured the value of both of these companies (which is not the typical valuation context), we can measure the present value weighted average growth rate subsequent to Year 1 ($r_{UA} - FCF_1/V_{F,0}$ from Equation 6.4), which is equal to 2.3% for both companies (Risen 0.023 = 0.12 − \$47.5/\$491.9; Habibi 0.023 = 0.12 − \$95.0/983.8). If we use the Year 1 free cash flow to measure the free cash flow multiple for each company, we see that the free cash flow multiples are the same for both companies, 10.4 (Risen 10.4 = \$491.9/\$47.5; Habibi 10.4 = \$983.8/\$95). Thus, Habibi would be a perfect comparable company for Risen.

EXHIBIT 13.15 The Effect of Transitory Shocks on Market Multiples

Risen Company (\$ in millions)	**Year −1**	**Year 0**	**Year 1**	**Year 2**	**Year 3**	**Year 4 Onward**
Free cash flow	\$40.0	\$ 44.0	\$ 47.5	\$ 49.9	\$51.4	\$ 52.4
Growth rate		10.0%	8.0%	5.0%	3.0%	2.0%
Cost of capital		12.0%				
Value as of end of Year 0		\$491.9				

Habibi Corporation (\$ in millions)	**Year −1**	**Year 0**	**Year 1**	**Year 2**	**Year 3**	**Year 4 Onward**
Free cash flow	\$80.0	\$ 20.0	\$ 95.0	\$ 99.8	\$102.8	\$104.8
Growth rate		-75.0%	375.2%	5.0%	3.0%	2.0%
Cost of capital		12.0%				
Value as of end of Year 0		\$983.8				

However, if we were to use the Year 0 free cash flow to measure the free cash flow multiple, we see that the multiples are not the same—11.2 for Risen (11.2 = \$491.9/\$44.0) and 49.2 for Habibi (49.2 = \$983.8/\$20.0). They are different because the negative transitory shock in Habibi's free cash flow in Year 0 caused the present value weighted average growth rates of the two companies to differ, using the Year 0 free cash flow as the base year. We measure the present value weighted average growth rate, using Year 0 as the base year, as follows (from Equation 6.5):

$$g_A = \frac{1+r}{1+\dfrac{FCF_0}{V_{F,0}}} - 1$$

Valuation in Practice 13.3

Effect of Transitory Shocks on Microsoft's Market Multiples Microsoft Corp.'s earnings decreased from $22 billion in 2014 to $12 billion 2015 mostly as a result of a $10 billion impairment and restructuring charge for its phone hardware business. Over that same period, Microsoft's enterprise value increased from $279 billion to $288 billion.

(In millions, adjusted for excess assets) Year Ended June 30	2014	2015
Revenue	$ 86,833	$ 93,580
Cost of goods sold	−27,078	−33,038
Research and development	−11,381	−12,046
Sales and marketing	−15,811	−15,713
General and administrative	−4,677	−4,611
Impairment, integration, and restructuring	−127	−10,011
Income before income taxes (EBIT)	27,759	18,161
Provision for income taxes	−5,733	−6,196
Unlevered earnings	$ 22,026	$ 11,965
Enterprise value	$278,502	$288,173

As a result, Microsoft's EBIT multiple increased by over 50% and its unlevered earnings multiple increased by over 90%. As we show in the following chart, however, treating the impairment and restructuring charge as a transitory shock and eliminating it in the calculation of the multiples shows that Microsoft's EBIT and unlevered earnings multiples were similar to its historical multiples.[20]

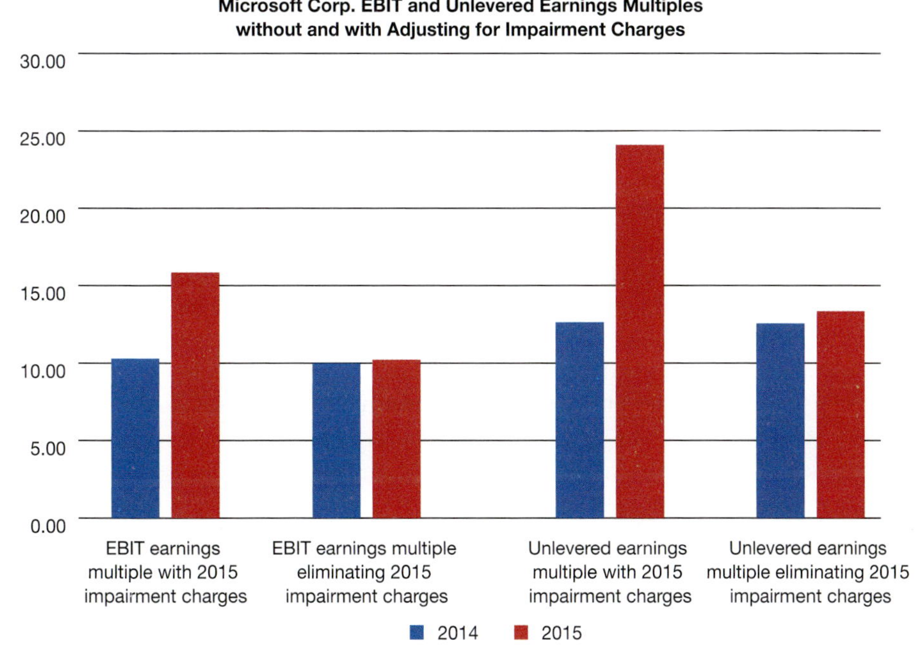

Risen's present value weighted average growth rate, using Year 0 as the base year, is 2.8% [0.028 = (1 + 0.12)/(1 + 44/491.9) − 1], and the growth rate for Habibi is 9.8% [0.098 = (1 + 0.12)/(1 + 20/983.8) − 1]. The difference in the present value weighted average growth rates results in a large difference between the market multiples of the two companies (49.2 vs. 11.2). When we use Year 0 as the base year, it is no longer sufficient for us to have comparable growth rates beginning in Year 1.

[20] Based on the footnotes to Microsoft's financial statements, the marginal tax rate for the impairment and restructuring charges was approximately 4% for computing unlevered earnings, which results because certain foreign subsidiary impairment and restructuring charges were not tax deductible in the U.S.

This difference in the market multiples illustrates the potential effect of using a value driver (denominator) that contains a transitory component. In this case, it should be clear that Habibi is not a good comparable for Risen when measuring the multiple based on the Year 0 free cash flow. In Chapter 14, we discuss techniques to make adjustments for non-recurring items.

Valuation Key 13.7

When selecting comparable companies, we must ensure that the companies have the same short-run and long-run growth rates. Even if two companies have the same long-run growth rate, the market multiples of the companies can be substantially different if the short-run growth rates are different. We sometimes observe this effect when one of the companies has a nonrecurring (one-time) or transitory shock to its current performance.

13.7 ANALYZING AND MEASURING CONTINUING VALUE MULTIPLES

LO5 Analyze and measure continuing values using market multiples

Recall from the introduction to this chapter, we recommend using multiples as a tool to analyze the continuing value measured using a discounted cash flow perpetuity, while others use multiples to measure continuing value directly. Regardless of the approach used, market multiple valuation techniques are useful when measuring continuing value in a DCF valuation. The market multiples used to analyze or measure a company's continuing or terminal value are not always the same as those used when valuing a company (or its equity) as of the valuation date. Since the continuing value date is some number of years after the valuation date, the main question or challenge here is to forecast how the market multiples will evolve by the continuing value date. Thus, in order to use market multiples to analyze or measure continuing value, the ***future*** growth and performance prospects (including capital expenditure and working capital requirements) at the continuing value date of the company being valued must be the same as the ***current*** growth and performance prospects of the comparable companies that will be used to measure the continuing value market multiples from current data. As such, the best comparable companies for a market multiple valuation of a company on the valuation date can differ from the best comparable companies to assess the multiple at the company's continuing value date. For example, if the expected growth rate, expected profitability, or other market multiple determinants are different at the continuing value date than at the valuation date, the comparable companies for the current valuation and the continuing value calculation would be different. In this section we discuss three effects that can cause continuing value multiples to differ from the multiples at the value date—changing growth rates, cyclical industries, and variation in market multiples over time.

Changing Growth Rates

We illustrate the effect of changing growth rates by demonstrating the change in market multiples of a company with high initial revenue growth of 25% in Year 1, which declines to 20% and 8% in the next two years, and then to 2% thereafter. In Exhibit 13.16, we present summary financial statement and free cash flow forecasts for such a company along with a valuation of that company. The firm value to EBIT multiple declines from 10.9 to 8.0 during the forecast period, a decline of over 25%, as a result of the decreasing growth rate. The multiples of firm value to unlevered earnings and EBITDA decline by over 25% as well, while the firm value to free cash flow multiple declines even more, from 58.8 to 10.5. The decrease in the multiples directly corresponds to the decline in the present value weighted average growth rate that occurs during the forecast period.

While this example illustrates the effect that decreasing growth rates can have on how we select comparable companies to estimate the continuing value, assessing comparability when using market multiples to measure the continuing value requires using comparable companies that currently have market multiple determinants that are similar to the expected market multiple determinants of the company of interest at the continuing value date. The expected market multiple determinants could be quite different at the continuing value date than the company's current market multiple determinants, for example, if the company is currently growing rapidly and is very profitable due to some competitive advantage that will not be sustainable at the continuing value date.

EXHIBIT 13.16 Year-by-Year Valuation and Market Multiples

High-Growth Company
Financial Statements and Free Cash Flows

($ in millions)	Year −1	Year 0	Year 1	Year 2	Year 3	Year 4	Year 5	Year 6
Income Statement								
Revenue	**$490.2**	**$500.0**	**$625.0**	**$750.0**	**$810.0**	**$826.2**	**$842.7**	**$859.6**
Operating expenses	–343.1	–350.0	–437.5	–525.0	–567.0	–578.3	–589.9	–601.7
Depreciation expense	–16.3	–16.7	–20.8	–25.0	–27.0	–27.5	–28.1	–28.7
Interest expense	–11.5	–12.8	–13.1	–14.3	–15.1	–15.5	–15.8	–16.1
Income before taxes	$119.2	$120.5	$153.6	$185.7	$200.9	$204.8	$208.9	$213.1
Income tax expense	–35.8	–36.2	–46.1	–55.7	–60.3	–61.4	–62.7	–63.9
Net income	**$ 83.4**	**$ 84.4**	**$107.5**	**$130.0**	**$140.6**	**$143.4**	**$146.2**	**$149.2**
Balance Sheet								
Net working capital	$ 98.0	$100.0	$125.0	$150.0	$162.0	$165.2	$168.5	$171.9
Property, plant, and equipment (net)	251.6	318.3	380.8	395.8	379.6	363.1	346.2	329.0
Total assets	$349.7	$418.3	$505.8	$545.8	$541.6	$528.3	$514.8	$500.9
Debt	$142.3	$145.2	$159.3	$168.0	$172.2	$175.6	$179.1	$182.7
Equity	207.3	273.1	346.5	377.8	369.4	352.7	335.7	318.3
Total liabilities and equities	$349.7	$418.3	$505.8	$545.8	$541.6	$528.3	$514.8	$500.9
Free Cash Flows								
Earnings before interest and taxes (EBIT)		$133.3	$166.7	$200.0	$216.0	$220.3	$224.7	$229.2
− Income taxes paid on EBIT		–40.0	–50.0	–60.0	–64.8	–66.1	–67.4	–68.8
Earnings before interest and after taxes		$ 93.3	$116.7	$140.0	$151.2	$154.2	$157.3	$160.5
+ Depreciation expense		16.7	20.8	25.0	27.0	27.5	28.1	28.7
− Change in net working capital		–2.0	–25.0	–25.0	–12.0	–3.2	–3.3	–3.4
− Capital expenditures		–83.3	–83.3	–40.0	–10.8	–11.0	–11.2	–11.5
Unlevered free cash flow		$ 24.7	$ 29.2	$100.0	$155.4	$167.5	$170.9	$174.3

($ in millions)	Year 1	Year 2	Year 3	Year 4	Year 5	CV_{Firm} Year 5
Unlevered free cash flow for continuing value (CV)						$ 174.3
Discount factor for continuing value						10.277
End of year value of firm	$1,593.0	$1,679.9	$1,721.6	$1,756.0	$1,791.0	
Unlevered free cash flow	29.2	100.0	155.4	167.5	170.9	
	$1,622.2	$1,779.9	$1,877.0	$1,923.5	$1,962.0	
Discount factor	0.895	0.895	0.895	0.895	0.895	
Beginning of year value of firm	$1,451.9	$1,593.0	$1,679.9	$1,721.6	$1,756.0	$1,791.1

	Year 0	Year 1	Year 2	Year 3	Year 4	Year 5
Annual growth rates						
Revenue	2.0%	25.0%	20.0%	8.0%	2.0%	2.0%
Free cash flow		18.1%	242.9%	55.4%	7.8%	2.0%
Firm value market multiples						
Free cash flow multiple	58.8	54.6	16.8	11.1	10.5	10.5
Unlevered earnings multiple	15.6	13.7	12.0	11.4	11.4	11.4
EBIT multiple	10.9	9.6	8.4	8.0	8.0	8.0
EBITDA multiple	9.7	8.5	7.5	7.1	7.1	7.1

Exhibit may contain small rounding errors

Even though we illustrated this concept using a declining revenue growth rate, the same type of effect occurs as a result of declining profitability or any other change in a market multiple determinant that affects a market multiple used to assess value that occurs between the valuation date and the continuing value date.

Cyclical Industries

A related issue arises for companies in cyclical industries. As we show in Exhibit 13.17, the market multiples of companies in cyclical industries vary over time depending on where the industry is in its cycle. Based on historical measures of the value driver, multiples tend to be the highest when the industry is coming out of the trough of the cycle, and the lowest soon after it passes the peak of the cycle. For example, if we use current information to value a company when the industry is at the trough of its cycle, the market multiples we measure reflect the market multiples at the trough of the cycle, which could be appropriate for that valuation. However, for the continuing value calculation, we want to make sure that our valuation reflects the typical valuation of these companies. Thus, for our continuing value calculation, we probably want to estimate market multiples that are reflective of the midpoint of the cycle in conjunction with forecasts of the financial statements of the company being valued that are based on the midpoint of the cycle.

EXHIBIT 13.17 Free Cash Flows, Firm Value, and Market Multiples for Cyclical Industries

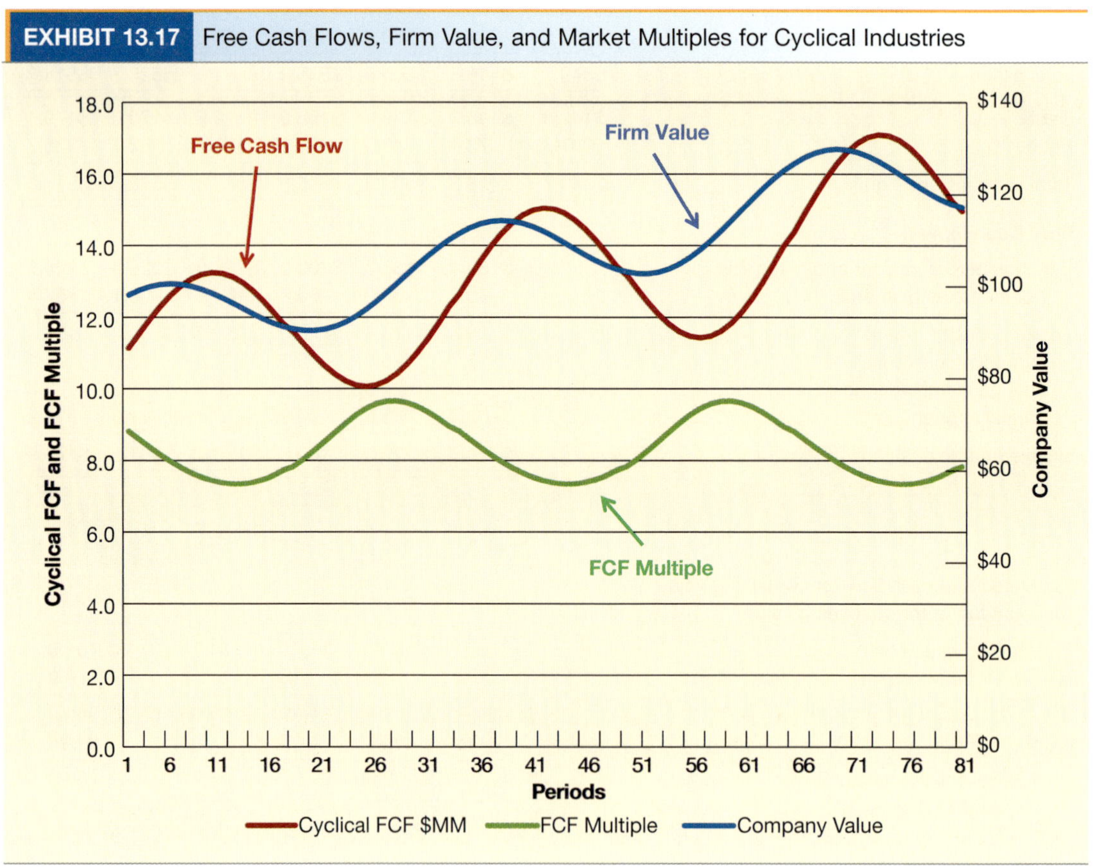

Effect of Market Multiples Varying Over Time

As we demonstrated in Exhibit 13.3, market multiples vary over time because of general economic conditions. Just as with cyclical industries, we expect market multiples to be higher as a slow- or negative-growth economy begins to recover and move into a period of high expected growth; again, this is based on historical measures of the value driver. Suppose current market valuations are quite high; by this we mean that the price-to-earnings ratios in the economy are on the high end of their historic distribution. If the price-to-earnings multiple is high relative to its long-run historical average, and if we are using market multiples to measure a company's continuing value, say, 10 years from now, we will have to decide whether or not the high current market valuations are permanent or whether multiples are likely to regress back toward their long-run average (perhaps because of diminished expectations of growth or because of increases in required rates of return for the economy). Thus, we have a variety of reasons why current market multiples may not reflect expected market multiples at the continuing value date.

Valuation Key 13.8

Current market multiples of comparable companies may not be appropriate to use in all situations, even if the comparable companies are indeed currently comparable. You might have to adjust the current market multiples when using them to measure continuing value because the company's prospects can be different at the continuing value date from what they are currently.

REVIEW EXERCISE 13.6

Evolution of Market Multiples

Use the information in Review Exercise 13.1 as well as the information below to measure the multiples of firm value to unlevered free cash flow and EBITDA, as well as the equity value to equity free cash flow and P/E multiples for Years 0 through 5, using the value as of the end of Year t divided by the value driver in Year t. Also calculate the company's unlevered free cash flow and equity free cash flow multiples using the company's costs of capital and growth rates. The company's equity cost of capital is 13%, and its weighted average cost of capital is 11.36%. The company's valuation as of the end of Years 0 through 5 appears below.

($ in millions)	Year 1	Year 2	Year 3	Year 4	Year 5	CV_{Firm} Year 5
Unlevered free cash flow for continuing value (CV)						$ 234.7
Discount factor for continuing value						10.684
End of year value of firm.	$2,293.3	$2,362.4	$2,409.7	$2,457.9	$2,507.0	
Unlevered free cash flow	12.2	191.4	221.1	225.5	230.1	
	$2,305.5	$2,553.8	$2,630.8	$2,683.4	$2,737.1	
Discount factor.	0.898	0.898	0.898	0.898	0.898	
Beginning of year value of firm.	$2,070.3	$2,293.3	$2,362.4	$2,409.7	$2,457.9	$2,507.0
Beginning of year value of debt	414.1	458.7	472.5	481.9	491.6	501.4
Beginning of year value of equity.	$1,656.3	$1,834.6	$1,889.9	$1,927.7	$1,966.3	$2,005.6

Exhibit may contain small rounding errors

Solution on page 655.

SUMMARY AND KEY CONCEPTS

The market multiple valuation model is a widely used valuation method. We sometimes use it in conjunction with DCF valuation methods as another way to value a company and its equity. This chapter provides a conceptual underpinning for the use of the market multiple technique, and it provides information regarding how to think about comparability as a function of company characteristics and different market multiples. DCF valuation methods rely heavily on the reasonableness of the assumptions underpinning the free cash flow forecasts of the company being valued and the discount rate used to discount the free cash flows. The market multiple valuation method, on the other hand, relies heavily on the choice of comparable companies and the observed valuations of those companies.

ADDITIONAL READING AND REFERENCES

Alford, A., "The Effect of the Set of Comparable Companies on the Accuracy of the Price-Earnings Valuation Method," *Journal of Accounting Research* 30 (1992), pp. 94–108.

Bhojraj, S., and C. Lee, "Who Is My Peer? A Valuation-Based Approach to the Selection of Comparable Companies," *Journal of Accounting Research* vol. 40, no. 2 (May, 2002), pp. 407–439.

EXERCISES AND PROBLEMS

P13.1 **Basic Market Multiple Calculations—Growing Company:** We present summary financial statements and a free cash flow schedule for the Growing Company in Exhibit P13.1 and present a valuation of the company and its equity in Exhibit P13.2. Use this information to measure the free cash flow and financial statement-based market multiples in Exhibit 13.2 for Year 0 through Year 5, using the value of the firm or equity as of the end of Year t divided by the relevant value drivers in Year t. Also calculate the company's unlevered free cash flow and equity free cash flow multiples, using the company's costs of capital and growth rates for each year.

EXHIBIT P13.1 The Growing Company Financial Forecasts

Growing Company Financial Statements and Free Cash Flows ($ in millions)	Year −1	Year 0	Year 1	Year 2	Year 3	Year 4	Year 5	Year 6
Income Statement								
Revenue	**$776.7**	**$800.0**	**$840.0**	**$1,050.0**	**$1,155.0**	**$1,189.7**	**$1,225.3**	**$1,262.1**
Operating expenses	−543.7	−560.0	−588.0	−735.0	−808.5	−832.8	−857.7	−883.5
Depreciation expense	−64.7	−66.7	−70.0	−87.5	−96.3	−99.1	−102.1	−105.2
Interest expense	−17.1	−19.0	−19.5	−21.9	−23.4	−24.2	−24.9	−25.7
Income before taxes	$151.2	$154.4	$162.5	$ 205.6	$ 226.8	$ 233.6	$ 240.6	$ 247.8
Income tax expense	−52.9	−54.0	−56.9	−72.0	−79.4	−81.7	−84.2	−86.7
Net Income	**$ 98.3**	**$100.3**	**$105.6**	**$ 133.6**	**$ 147.4**	**$ 151.8**	**$ 156.4**	**$ 161.1**
Balance Sheet								
Net working capital	$ 77.7	$ 80.0	$ 84.0	$ 105.0	$ 115.5	$ 119.0	$ 122.5	$ 126.2
Property, plant, and equipment (net)	472.5	439.2	544.2	544.2	476.8	407.4	335.9	262.3
Total assets	$550.2	$519.2	$628.2	$ 649.2	$ 592.3	$ 526.4	$ 458.4	$ 388.5
Debt	$189.7	$195.4	$219.2	$ 234.3	$ 241.9	$ 249.2	$ 256.7	$ 264.4
Equity	360.4	323.7	408.9	414.9	350.3	277.2	201.8	124.1
Total liabilities and equities	$550.2	$519.2	$628.2	$ 649.2	$ 592.3	$ 526.4	$ 458.4	$ 388.5
Free Cash Flows								
Earnings before interest and taxes (EBIT)		$173.3	$182.0	$ 227.5	$ 250.3	$ 257.8	$ 265.5	$ 273.5
− Income taxes paid on EBIT		−60.7	−63.7	−79.6	−87.6	−90.2	−92.9	−95.7
Earnings before interest and after taxes		$112.7	$118.3	$ 147.9	$ 162.7	$ 167.5	$ 172.6	$ 177.7
+ Depreciation expense		66.7	70.0	87.5	96.3	99.1	102.1	105.2
− Change in net working capital		−2.3	−4.0	−21.0	−10.5	−3.5	−3.6	−3.7
− Capital expenditures		−33.3	−175.0	−87.5	−28.9	−29.7	−30.6	−31.6
Unlevered free cash flow		**$143.7**	**$ 9.3**	**$ 126.9**	**$ 219.5**	**$ 233.5**	**$ 240.5**	**$ 247.7**
− Interest paid		−19.0	−19.5	−21.9	−23.4	−24.2	−24.9	−25.7
+ Interest tax shield		6.6	6.8	7.7	8.2	8.5	8.7	9.0
+ Change in debt financing		5.7	23.8	15.0	7.7	7.3	7.5	7.7
Free cash flow to common equity		**$137.0**	**$ 20.4**	**$ 127.7**	**$ 212.0**	**$ 225.0**	**$ 231.8**	**$ 238.7**

Exhibit may contain small rounding errors

EXHIBIT P13.2 The Growing Company Valuation

Discounted Cash Flow Valuation	
Growth rate for continuing value	3.000%
Unlevered cost of capital	13.000%
Debt to value	10.000%
Equity cost of capital	13.333%
Weighted average cost of capital	12.650%

($ in millions)	Year 1	Year 2	Year 3	Year 4	Year 5	CV_{Firm} Year 5
Unlevered free cash flow for continuing value (CV)						$ 247.7
Discount factor for continuing value						10.363
End of year value of firm	$2,192.2	$2,342.6	$2,419.4	$2,492.0	$2,566.8	
Unlevered free cash flow	9.3	126.9	219.5	233.5	240.5	
	$2,201.5	$2,469.5	$2,639.0	$2,725.5	$2,807.2	
Discount factor	0.888	0.888	0.888	0.888	0.888	
Beginning of year value of firm	$1,954.3	$2,192.2	$2,342.6	$2,419.4	$2,492.0	$2,566.8
Beginning of year value of debt	195.4	219.2	234.3	241.9	249.2	256.7
Beginning of year value of equity	$1,758.8	$1,973.0	$2,108.4	$2,177.5	$2,242.8	$2,310.1

Exhibit may contain small rounding errors

P13.2 Measuring the Change in Market Multiples Resulting from a Change in Market Multiple Determinants—The Growing Company: Use the information in Problem 13.1 to examine the change in the firm value market multiples computed in Problem 13.1 resulting from a change in the market multiple determinants described below. For each of the changes in the market multiple determinants, measure the changes in the multiples of firm value to free cash flow, unlevered earnings, EBIT, EBITDA, and revenue. Measure the market multiple using the end of Year 0 firm value and Year 0 value driver (denominator).

a. The initial valuation of the company used a 3% perpetual growth rate. If the perpetual growth rate decreases to 2%, the company's value decreases by −4.1%.

b. The initial valuation of the company used a 13% unlevered cost of capital. If the unlevered cost of capital decreases to 12%, the company's value increases by 12.9%.

c. The initial valuation of the company used a 70% operating expense ratio (% of revenue). If the operating expense ratio decreases to 65%, the company's value increases by 18.3%.

d. The initial valuation of the company used a 1.2 ratio of revenue to gross property, plant and equipment. If the ratio of revenue to gross property, plant and equipment increases to 1.5, the company's value increases by 1.4%.

e. The initial valuation of the company used a 10% net operating working capital ratio (% of revenue). If the net working capital ratio increases to 15%, the company's value decreases by −1.3%.

f. The initial valuation of the company used a 35% income tax rate. If the income tax rate increases to 40%, the company's value decreases by −5.6%.

P13.3 The Trouble with Market Multiple Based Contracts—P.R. Value Inc.: You are a consultant and have been hired by the board of directors of P. R. Value, Inc.—a privately held firm—to evaluate the reasonableness of the proposed implementation of an employment contract for an employee, which describes a method for valuing the company's common stock. The employee owns 6,500 shares of the company's stock and decides that now is the best time to leave the company. The company uses the valuation method described in the employment agreement in order to determine the price at which it buys back shares of employees who retire, die, or leave for other reasons. The salient parts of the contract are as follows: the price-earnings ratio for each of the comparable companies (C&B, FH, M&M, and A&A) shall be measured by dividing the average trading price for a corporation's stock during the month of December preceding the date of death or retirement by such corporation's reported audited earnings per share for the fiscal year preceding the date of death or retirement; average the four price-earnings ratios and multiply by the earnings per share of P. R. Value to determine the buyout price per share. The relevant information for the four comparable companies follows:

Using Reported Earnngs	C&B	FH	M&M	A&A
Average selling price	$42.86	$47.30	$47.74	$43.54
Earnings per share	$2.220	$2.020	$2.490	$0.050

The A&A Company had a loss associated with a change in accounting principles of $2.05 per share in the most recent year. The earnings per share for P. R. Value, Inc. is $1.25.

P13.4 **Free Cash Flow Multiple and Growth Rates 1:** You are valuing a company as of the end of Year 0. The company is privately owned and 100% equity financed. The company's free cash flow for the current year, Year 0, is $40 million, and management expects a free cash flow of $46.8 million next year (Year 1). Management expects the company's free cash flows to grow at a present value weighted average growth rate of 4%, using Year 0 as the base year. The company has one comparable company, which also uses only equity financing. The value of the comparable company is $1,283.3 million. Its free cash flow for the current year, Year 0, is $60 million, and management expects its free cash flow to be $115.5 million in the following year, Year 1. Management believes that the two companies have the same cost of capital of 12%.

a. What is the free cash flow multiple of the comparable company based on its Year 0 and Year 1 free cash flows? Why are they different?

b. Value the privately owned company using the free cash flow market multiples of the comparable company based on both the Year 0 and Year 1 free cash flows. Why are the valuations different, and which one is more likely to be the better valuation?

c. Measure the value of the privately owned company using the discounted cash flow valuation method, and compare it to the free cash flow multiple valuations.

P13.5 **Free Cash Flow Multiple and Growth Rates 2:** You are valuing a company as of the end of Year 0. The company is privately owned and 100% equity financed. The company's free cash flow for the current year, Year 0, is $10 million, and management expects a free cash flow of $11.5 million next year (Year 1). Management expects the company's free cash flows to grow at a present value weighted average growth rate of 3%, using Year 0 as the base year. The company has one comparable company which also uses only equity financing. The value of the comparable company is $2.308 billion. Its free cash flow for the current year, Year 0, is $200 million, and management expects its free cash flow to be $300 million in the following year, Year 1. Management believes that the two companies have the same cost of capital of 15%.

a. What is the free cash flow multiple of the comparable company based on its Year 0 and Year 1 free cash flows? Why are they different?

b. Value the privately owned company using the comparable company's free cash flow market multiple based on both the Year 0 and Year 1 free cash flows. Why are the valuations different, and which one is more likely to be the better valuation?

c. Measure the value of the privately owned company using the discounted cash flow valuation method, and compare it to the free cash flow multiple valuations.

P13.6 **Using Market Multiple Determinants to Measure Multiples:** Use the abbreviated income statements and balance sheets for the all-equity financed company in Exhibit P13.3 to measure its market multiples (free cash flow, unlevered earnings, EBIT, EBITDA, revenue, and total invested capital) using two approaches—(i) the value of the firm divided by the market multiple value driver in Year 1 for the free cash flow, unlevered earnings, EBIT, EBITDA and revenue, and Year 0 for total invested capital and (ii) the formulas derived in the Pepsi simulation. The company has the same forecast drivers in its financial model as Pepsi, although the magnitudes of the forecast drivers are different. The company's operating expenses, depreciation, and net operating working capital are a constant percent of revenues; its capital expenditures are equal to depreciation plus a constant percentage of the growth in revenues; and its revenues and free cash flows grow at a constant rate into perpetuity. The company's firm value is $2,000 and its cost of capital is 12%. (*Hint:* First, measure the company's free cash flows; next, measure the company's growth rate and each of the other forecast drivers; then measure the company's market multiples using the two approaches.)

EXHIBIT P13.3 Using Market Multiple Determinants to Measure Market Multiples

	Year 0	Year +1
Revenue	$ 970.9	$1,000.0
Operating expenses	−436.2	−449.2
EBITDA	534.7	550.8
Depreciation	−194.2	−200.0
EBIT	340.5	350.8
Interest	0.0	0.0
EBT	340.5	350.8
Taxes	−102.2	−105.2
Earnings	238.4	245.5
Net operating assets	242.7	250.0
Net fixed assets	1,941.7	2,000.0
Total assets less operating liabilities	$2,184.5	$2,250.0

Exhibit may contain small rounding errors

P13.7 **Valuation Error from Imperfect Comparable Companies—No Perfectly Comparable Company:** The No Perfectly Comparable Company's (NPC) revenues as well as its income statement and free cash flow components grow at a constant growth rate, see Exhibit P13.4 for abbreviated income statements and balance sheets. The DCF valuation of the company is $10,000 and its cost of capital is 14%.

An analyst valued the NPC using a comparable company. The comparable company was comparable on all relevant market multiple determinants except that it has an income tax rate equal to 75% of the NPC's income tax rate and an operating expense ratio equal to 90% of the NPC's Operating Expense ratio. Measure the percentage error in NPC's valuation resulting from using each of the following market multiples of the comparable company to value NPC—free cash flow, unlevered earnings, EBIT, EBITDA, revenue, and total invested capital.

EXHIBIT P13.4 No Perfectly Comparable Company (NPC)

	Year 0	Year +1
Revenue	$7,843.1	$8,000.0
Operating expenses	−4,705.9	−4,800.0
EBITDA	3,137.3	3,200.0
Depreciation	−784.3	−800.0
EBIT	2,352.9	2,400.0
Interest	0.0	0.0
EBT	2,352.9	2,400.0
Taxes	−941.2	−960.0
Earnings	1,411.8	1,440.0
Net operating assets	1,568.6	1,600.0
Net fixed assets	10,431.4	10,640.0
Total assets less operating liabilities	$12,000.0	$12,240.0

Exhibit may contain small rounding errors

P13.8 **Assessing Comparability of an Unlevered Company—ValCo:** Your company has been hired to value ValCo as of the end of Year 0. ValCo is a privately owned, 100% equity-financed company. A research analyst working at the company identified four potential publicly traded comparable companies: COMP A, COMP B, COMP C, and COMP D. The research analyst is confident that the free cash flows of ValCo and its comparable companies have the same risk (that is, all companies have an unlevered cost of capital equal to 12%) and the same growth rate (4%), but they do not have identical cost structures and investment requirements. The financial statements and free cash flows for ValCo and the four potential comparable companies appear in Exhibits P13.5 and P13.6. The research analyst calculates various firm value and equity value market multiples for each of the comparable companies, which also appear in these exhibits.

a. Discuss why the comparable companies have the same free cash flow market multiple even though they do not have the same cost structures or investment requirements.

b. For each comparable company, discuss why each of the accounting-based market multiples might not be the best market multiple for ValCo, and discuss whether the comparable company's market multiple is too high or too low.

EXHIBIT P13.5 Selected Data for ValCo and Potential Comparable Companies

	ValCo	COMP A	COMP B	COMP C	COMP D
Income Statement (Year 1)					
Revenue (sales)	$188.8	$1,067.2	$307.8	$271.4	$338.6
– Operating expenses (costs)	−85.0	−480.2	−110.8	−122.1	−152.4
– Depreciation	−37.8	−213.4	−61.6	−43.4	−84.7
Earnings before interest and taxes	$ 66.1	$ 373.5	$135.4	$105.9	$101.6
– Interest	0.0	0.0	0.0	0.0	0.0
Earnings before income taxes	$ 66.1	$ 373.5	$135.4	$105.9	$101.6
– Income tax expense	−26.4	−119.5	−54.2	−42.3	−40.6
Earnings	$ 39.7	$ 254.0	$ 81.3	$ 63.5	$ 61.0
Balance Sheet (Year 1)					
Total invested capital (net)	$261.9	$1,479.8	$426.8	$376.4	$587.0
Debt	$ 0.0	$ 0.0	$ 0.0	$ 0.0	$ 0.0
Equity	261.9	1,479.8	426.8	376.4	587.0
Debt and equity	$261.9	$1,479.8	$426.8	$376.4	$587.0
Balance Sheet (Year 0)					
Total invested capital (net)	$251.8	$1,422.9	$410.4	$361.9	$564.4
Debt	$ 0.0	$ 0.0	$ 0.0	$ 0.0	$ 0.0
Equity	251.8	1,422.9	410.4	361.9	564.4
Debt and equity	$251.8	$1,422.9	$410.4	$361.9	$564.4
Free Cash Flow (Year 1)					
Earnings before interest and taxes	$ 66.1	$ 373.5	$135.4	$105.9	$101.6
– Income tax expense	−26.4	−119.5	−54.2	−42.3	−40.6
Unlevered earnings	$ 39.7	$ 254.0	$ 81.3	$ 63.5	$ 61.0
Depreciation	37.8	213.4	61.6	43.4	84.7
Investment	−47.8	−270.4	−78.0	−57.9	−107.2
Unlevered free cash flow	$ 29.6	$ 197.1	$ 64.8	$ 49.0	$ 38.4
After-tax interest	0.0	0.0	0.0	0.0	0.0
New debt	0.0	0.0	0.0	0.0	0.0
Equity free cash flow	$ 29.6	$ 197.1	$ 64.8	$ 49.0	$ 38.4

Exhibit may contain small rounding errors

EXHIBIT P13.6 Selected Valuations and Multiples for ValCo's Potential Comparable Companies

Market Multiples Based on the Value of the Firm	COMP A	COMP B	COMP C	COMP D
Value of the firm	$2,463.4	$810.6	$612.9	$479.7
Free cash flow multiple	12.5	12.5	12.5	12.5
Unlevered earnings multiple	9.7	10.0	9.7	7.9
EBIT multiple	6.6	6.0	5.8	4.7
EBITDA multiple	4.2	4.1	4.1	2.6
Revenue (sales) multiple	2.3	2.6	2.3	1.4
Total invested capital multiple	1.7	2.0	1.7	0.9
Market Multiples to Measure the Value of the Equity (Numerator is Market Value of the Equity):				
Value of equity	$2,463.4	$810.6	$612.9	$479.7
Equity free cash flow multiple	12.5	12.5	12.5	12.5
Price-to-earnings multiple	9.7	10.0	9.7	7.9
Revenue (sales) multiple	2.3	2.6	2.3	1.4
Market-to-book	1.7	2.0	1.7	0.9

P13.9 **Assessing Comparability—Levered Co.:** Your company has a consulting engagement to value Levered Co. as of the end of Year 0. Levered Co. is a privately owned company. A research analyst working at the company identified four potential comparable companies: COMP A, COMP B, COMP C, and COMP D, all of which are publicly traded. The research analyst is confident that the free cash flows of Levered Co. and its comparable companies have the same risk (an unlevered cost of capital equal to 10%) and same growth rate (2%) but that they do not have identical cost structures or investment requirements. The financial statements and free cash flows for Levered Co. and the four potential comparable companies appear in Exhibit P13.7. The values and relevant multiples appear in Exhibit P13.8. Your research analyst calculated various firm value and equity value market multiples for each of the comparable companies, which also appear in these exhibits.

a. For each comparable company, discuss why the free cash flow multiples are or are not the same.
b. For each comparable company, discuss why each of the accounting-based market multiples might not be the best market multiple to value the Levered Co., and discuss whether the comparable company's market multiple is too high or too low.

EXHIBIT P13.7 Selected Data for Levered Co. and Potential Comparable Companies

	Levered Co.	COMP A	COMP B	COMP C	COMP D
Income Statement (Year 1)					
Revenue (sales)	$246.5	$1,375.5	$530.4	$379.1	$374.5
– Operating expenses (costs)	−147.9	−825.3	−190.9	−227.5	−224.7
– Depreciation	−56.0	−312.6	−147.3	−51.7	−124.8
Earnings before interest and taxes	$ 42.6	$ 237.6	$192.1	$ 99.9	$ 25.0
– Interest	−6.8	−44.5	−33.2	−17.0	−2.0
Earnings before income taxes	$ 35.7	$ 193.1	$159.0	$ 82.9	$ 22.9
– Income tax expense	−10.7	−34.8	−47.7	−24.9	−6.9
Earnings	$ 25.0	$ 158.4	$111.3	$ 58.0	$ 16.1
Balance Sheet (Year 1)					
Total invested capital (net)	$228.6	$1,275.5	$601.1	$351.5	$509.3
Debt	$ 87.3	$ 566.8	$422.8	$217.3	$ 25.8
Equity	141.3	708.7	178.3	134.2	483.5
Debt and equity	$228.6	$1,275.5	$601.1	$351.5	$509.3
Balance Sheet (Year 0)					
Total invested capital (net)	$224.1	$1,250.5	$589.3	$344.7	$499.3
Debt	$ 85.5	$ 555.7	$414.5	$213.1	$ 25.3
Equity	138.5	694.8	174.8	131.6	474.0
Debt and equity	$224.1	$1,250.5	$589.3	$344.7	$499.3
Free Cash Flow (Year 1)					
Earnings before interest and taxes	$ 42.6	$ 237.6	$192.1	$ 99.9	$ 25.0
– Income tax expense	−12.8	−42.8	−57.6	−30.0	−7.5
Unlevered earnings	$ 29.8	$ 194.8	$134.5	$ 70.0	$ 17.5
Depreciation	56.0	312.6	147.3	51.7	124.8
Investment	−60.5	−337.6	−159.1	−58.6	−134.8
Unlevered free cash flow	$ 25.3	$ 169.8	$122.7	$ 63.1	$ 7.5
After-tax interest	−4.8	−36.5	−23.2	−11.9	−1.4
New debt	1.7	11.1	8.3	4.3	0.5
Equity free cash flow	$ 22.2	$ 144.5	$107.8	$ 55.4	$ 6.6

Exhibit may contain small rounding errors

EXHIBIT P13.8 Selected Valuations and Multiples for Levered Co.'s Potential Comparable Companies

	COMP A	COMP B	COMP C	COMP D
Market Multiples Based on the Value of the Firm				
Value of the firm	$2,222.7	$1,658.0	$852.3	$101.2
Free cash flow multiple	13.1	13.5	13.5	13.5
Unlevered earnings multiple	11.4	12.3	12.2	5.8
EBIT multiple	9.4	8.6	8.5	4.1
EBITDA multiple	4.0	4.9	5.6	0.7
Revenue (sales) multiple	1.6	3.1	2.2	0.3
Total invested capital multiple	1.8	2.8	2.5	0.2
Market Multiples to Measure the Value of the Equity (Numerator is Market Value of the Equity)				
Value of equity	$1,667.0	$1,243.5	$639.2	$ 75.9
Equity free cash flow multiple	11.5	11.5	11.5	11.5
Price-to-earnings multiple	10.5	11.2	11.0	4.7
Revenue (sales) multiple	1.2	2.3	1.7	0.2
Market-to-book	2.4	7.1	4.9	0.2

SOLUTIONS FOR REVIEW EXERCISES

Solution for Review Exercise 13.1: Basic Calculation of Market Multiples

Year 0 Market Multiples	Value	Value Driver	Multiple
Firm Value Market Multiples			
Free cash flow multiple	$2,070.3	$ 99.2	20.88
Unlevered earnings multiple	$2,070.3	$ 141.5	14.63
EBIT multiple	$2,070.3	$ 235.9	8.78
EBITDA multiple	$2,070.3	$ 300.0	6.90
Revenue (sales) multiple—firm value	$2,070.3	$1,000.0	2.07
Total assets multiple	$2,070.3	$1,206.3	1.72
Equity Value Market Multiples			
Equity free cash flow multiple	$1,656.3	$ 87.8	18.87
P/E or earnings multiple	$1,656.3	$ 122.1	13.57
Revenue (sales) multiple—equity value	$1,656.3	$1,000.0	1.66
Market-to-book multiple	$1,656.3	$ 792.2	2.09

Solution for Review Exercise 13.2: Risk and Growth Drivers of Market Multiples

Year 0 Market Multiples	Value	Denominator	Multiple
Firm value to free cash flow multiple	$2,070.3	$99.2	20.88
Present value weighted average growth rate unlevered FCF	10.77%	$= r_{WACC} - FCF_1/V_{F,0}$	
Growth rate $Year_0$ / $Year_1$	−87.65%		
Weighted average cost of capital	11.36%		
$(1+g_{0,1})/(r_{WACC} - g_{1,\infty})$	20.88		
Equity value to equity free cash flow multiple	$1,656.3	$87.8	18.87
Present value weighted average growth rate equity FCF	10.77%	$= r_E - EFCF_1/V_{E,0}$	
Growth rate $Year_0$ / $Year_1$	−57.90%		
Equity cost of capital	13.00%		
$(1 + g_{0,1})/(r_E - g_{1,\infty})$	18.87		

Note—The present value weighted average growth rate is calculated using Equation 6.4:

$$g_A = r - \frac{FCF_1}{V_{F,0}}$$

Solution for Review Exercise 13.3: Free Cash Flow Market Multiples

Firm Value Market Multiples	Year 0	Year 1
Free cash flow multiple	20.88	187.27
Unlevered earnings multiple	14.63	15.00
EBIT multiple	8.78	9.00
EBITDA multiple	6.90	7.08
Revenue (sales) multiple—firm value	2.07	2.12
Total assets multiple	1.72	1.70
Equity Value Market Multiples		
Equity free cash flow multiple	18.87	49.64
P/E or earnings multiple	13.57	13.80
Revenue (sales) multiple—equity value	1.66	1.70
Market-to-book multiple	2.09	2.07

The only market multiples that vary a great deal from Year 0 to Year 1 are those multiples that are based on free cash flows as the free cash flows vary much more than earnings or assets.

Solution for Review Exercise 13.4: Using Market Multiple Determinants to Measure Multiples

Forecast Driver		Year 0	Year +1
	Revenue	$6,983.2	$7,262.6
60.0%	Operating expenses	−4,189.9	−4,357.5
	EBITDA	2,793.3	2,905.0
10.0%	Depreciation	−698.3	−726.3
	EBIT	2,095.0	2,178.8
	Interest	0.0	0.0
	EBT	2,095.0	2,178.8
40.0%	Taxes	−838.0	−871.5
	Earnings	1,257.0	1,307.3
10.0%	Net operating assets	698.3	726.3
	Net fixed assets	1,500.0	1,779.3
	Total assets less operating liabilities	$2,198.3	$2,505.6
	EBIT		2,178.8
	TAX		−871.5
	Depreciation		726.3
	Net operating assets		−27.9
100.0%	CAPEX		−1,005.6
	Free cash flow		1,000.0
Earnings to Beg Total invested capital			59.5%
14.0%	Discount rate		Firm Value
4.0%	Growth (= 7,262.6/6,983.2 − 1 = 0.04)		$10,000.0

Exhibit may contain small rounding errors

CAPEX = change in net fixed assets plus depreciation = (1,779.3 − 1,500.0) + 726.3 = 1,005.6

CAPEX growth % = change in net fixed assets / change in revenue = (1,779.3 − 1,500.0) / (7,262.6 − 6,983.2) = 100%

continued

continued from previous page

Multiples	FV-Based	Formula
Free cash flow	10.000	10.000
Unlevered earnings	7.650	7.650
EBIT	4.590	4.590
EBITDA	3.442	3.442
Revenue	1.377	1.377
Total invested capital	4.549	4.549

Free cash flow = 1/(0.14 − 0.04) = 10.0

Unlevered earnings = (1 − ((0.1 + 1.0) × 0.04) / ((1 + 0.04) × (1 − 0.6 − 0.1) × (1 − 0.4))) / (0.14 − 0.04) = 7.65

EBIT =(1 − 0.4 − ((0.1 + 1.0) × 0.04) /((1 + 0.04) × (1 − 0.6 − 0.1)))/(0.14 − 0.04) = 4.59

EBITDA = (1 − 0.4 − (0.1 × (1 − 0.4))/(1 − 0.6) − ((0.1 + 1.0) × 0.04)/((1 + 0.04) × (1 − 0.6)))/(0.14 − 0.04) = 3.442

Revenue = (1 − 0.4 − (0.6 + 0.1) × (1 − 0.4) − ((0.1 + 1.0) × 0.04)/(1 + 0.04))/(0.14 − 0.04) = 1.377

Total invested capital = MM [UE] × UE / beginning TIC = 7.65 × 1,307.3/2,198.3 = 4.549

Solution for Review Exercise 13.5: Change in Market Multiples from a Change in Market Multiple Determinants

Financial Model Assumption and Market Multiple Determinant	Determinant	% Change in Value of Firm	Free Cash Flow Multiple	Unlevered Earnings Multiple	EBIT Multiple	EBITDA Multiple	Revenue Multiple
Continuing value growth rate	2.0%		20.88	14.63	8.78	6.90	2.07
New assumption and multiples	4.0%		21.86	15.32	9.19	7.23	2.17
% Change in multiples			4.7%	4.7%	4.7%	4.7%	4.7%
% Change in underlying variable		4.7%	0.0%	0.0%	0.0%	0.0%	0.0%
Unlevered cost of capital	12.0%		20.88	14.63	8.78	6.90	2.07
New assumption and multiples	10.0%		27.06	18.96	11.38	8.94	2.68
% Change in multiples			29.6%	29.6%	29.6%	29.6%	29.6%
% Change in underlying variable		29.6%	0.0%	0.0%	0.0%	0.0%	0.0%
Operating expenses (% rev)	70.0%		20.88	14.63	8.78	6.90	2.07
New assumption and multiples	60.0%		17.83	14.08	8.45	7.09	2.84
% Change in multiples			−14.6%	−3.8%	−3.8%	2.8%	37.0%
% Change in underlying variable		37.0%	60.5%	42.4%	42.4%	33.3%	0.0%
New value driver			$159.2	$201.5	$335.9	$400.0	$1,000.0

Solution for Review Exercise 13.6: Evolution of Market Multiples

	Year 0	Year 1	Year 2	Year 3	Year 4	Year 5
Firm value market multiples						
Free cash flow multiple	20.88	187.27	12.34	10.90	10.90	10.90
EBITDA multiple	6.90	7.08	6.40	6.40	6.40	6.40
Equity market multiples						
Equity free cash flow multiple	18.87	49.64	10.32	9.27	9.27	9.27
P/E or earnings multiple	13.57	13.80	12.41	12.43	12.43	12.43
Present value weighted average growth rate unlevered FCF	10.77%	3.01%	2.00%	2.00%	2.00%	2.00%
Growth rate Year t+1/Year t FCF	−87.65%	1462.74%	15.54%	2.00%	2.00%	2.00%
$(1 + g_{t,t+1})/(r_{WACC} - g_{t+1,\infty})$	20.88	187.27	12.34	10.90	10.90	10.90
Present value weighted average growth rate equity FCF	10.77%	3.01%	2.00%	2.00%	2.00%	2.00%
Growth rate Year t+1/Year t equity FCF	−57.90%	395.64%	13.49%	2.00%	2.00%	2.00%
$(1 + g_{t,t+1})/(r_E - g_{t+1,\infty})$	18.87	49.64	10.32	9.27	9.27	9.27

After mastering the material in this chapter, you will be able to:

1. Measure market multiples using first principles (14.1)
2. Conduct an initial review of financial statements (14.2)
3. Measure market multiple numerators (14.3)
4. Measure market multiple denominators (14.4)
5. Make adjustments to market multiple numerators and denominators (14.5–14.9)
6. Choose an appropriate market multiple and range (14.10)

CHAPTER

14

Market Multiple Measurement and Implementation

MERCK & CO., INC. (MERCK)

Merck & Co., Inc. (Merck) is a global health care company that creates and sells prescription medicines, vaccines, biologic therapies, and animal health products.[1] The common equity related claims of Merck were valued at approximately $167 billion as of the end of 2014. The value of its debt was a little less than the value of its cash and marketable securities. Its **enterprise value** was a little less than the value of its equity, $160.3 billion. For 2014, Merck's EBITDA was $24.4 billion, resulting in an EBITDA multiple of 6.6 using reported numbers adjusted for cash and investments (6.6 = 160.3/24.4).

Financial analysts, however, reported a higher EBITDA multiple for Merck (range of 9.0 to 11.2). Why? Because they made various adjustments to Merck's EBITDA (denominator) in order to better represent Merck's long run performance; in addition, some of the adjustments to the denominator required adjustments to the numerator. Potential adjustments to EBITDA include Merck's non-recurring expenses, net operating loss carryforwards, acquisitions, divestitures, noncontrolling interests, and income from unconsolidated affiliate companies. In the following chart we present Merck's EBITDA multiple before making any adjustments other than eliminating cash and investments (dark blue bar) and show how these adjustments either increase or decrease Merck's EBITDA multiple.[2] In this chapter we explain how to both identify and make these adjustments.

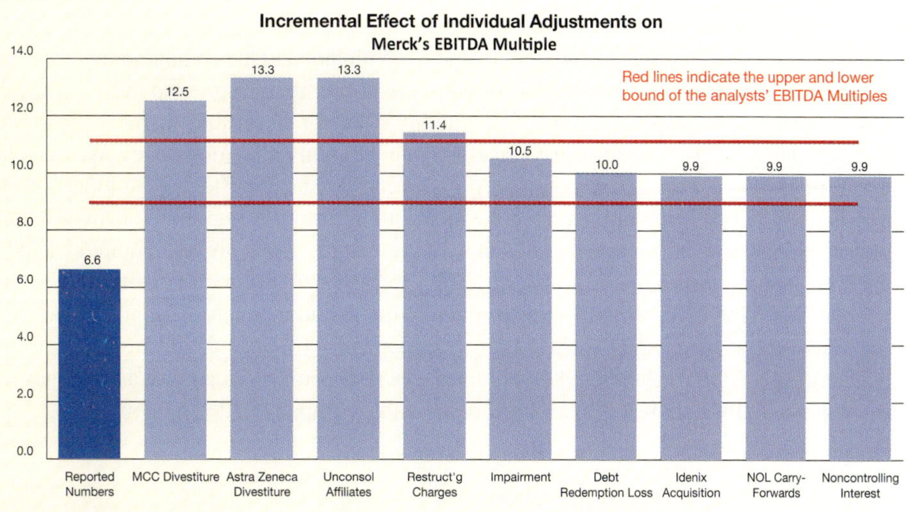

[1] See Merck's 2014 10-K filing with the U.S. Securities and Exchange Commission for the 2014 fiscal year.

[2] The chart reflects the cumulative effect of the adjustments as you move to the right. The resulting effect of a particular adjustment depends on the order in which the adjustments are made.

CHAPTER ORGANIZATION

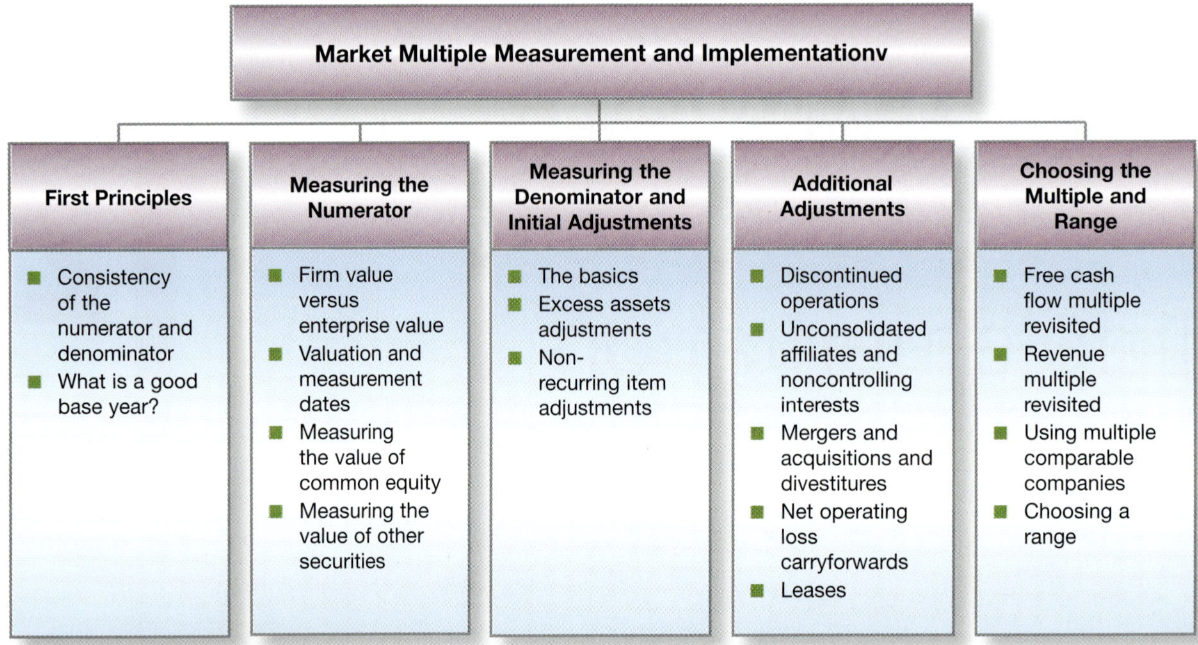

INTRODUCTION

In Chapter 13, we discussed the market multiple valuation process and the conceptual framework underpinning it. We also described the commonly used market multiples and discussed some cross-sectional (across firms and industries) and time-series characteristics of the distributions of these multiples. We discussed the relevance of various factors for assessing the comparability (risk, growth, cost structure, working capital management, capital expenditure requirements, and capital structure) of comparable companies and how the importance of such factors for assessing comparability differs across multiples.

In this chapter, we focus our discussion on how to measure market multiples using financial statement data. Measuring market multiple inputs based on financial statement data is more complex than merely observing the numerator and denominator of a multiple and performing simple division. The numerator is usually less complex to measure, but even this calculation can become complicated, and both the numerator and denominator can require various adjustments to their basic calculations.

The goals of these adjustments are twofold. First, we make adjustments to increase the consistency between the claims on the company's value as represented in the numerator and denominator. Second, we make adjustments to increase the comparability of the company we are valuing to its comparable companies. For example, making adjustments to exclude the effects of a company's excess (idle or non-operating) assets increases the consistency of the numerator and denominator and the comparability across companies. Similarly, adjustments that remove the effects of one-time or non-recurring items from a company's financial statements also increase consistency and comparability. Many of these adjustments relate to accounting treatments and accounting rules, both of which can affect comparability and consistency. We classify these adjustments into four types—excess assets, non-recurring effects, transaction effects (resulting from merger and acquisition and divestiture transactions), and effects resulting from differences or changes in accounting principles underpinning the financial statements. Some of these adjustments are not required when using forecasts—for example, non-recurring items; however, using forecasts can still require certain adjustments—for example, unconsolidated affiliates—and forecasts often do not include the information to make those adjustments.

Throughout the chapter we use Merck & Company (Merck) to illustrate the various calculations and adjustments used to measure market multiples (see the opening vignette for an overview of Merck) under the assumption that we are using Merck as a comparable company in a valuation.

14.1 FIRST PRINCIPLES FOR MEASURING MARKET MULTIPLES

LO1 Measure market multiples using first principles

In this section, we discuss three basic principles that guide how we measure market multiple inputs. The first principle is consistency in measuring a multiple's numerator and denominator. We measure a multiple's numerator based on the values of a certain set of securities—typically, either all of the securities (firm or enterprise value) or the common equity claims. We should therefore measure the denominator based on the same claims or securities that are represented in the numerator. Like many basic principles, this principle seems obvious; however, the subtleties in the way we measure earnings can make this principle difficult to follow.

The second principle is to measure a numerator that represents the value of the company's long-term operating performance. Thus, we exclude the value of excess assets and the anticipated value from the expected sale of part of the business. The third principle follows from the second principle: use a denominator that represents the long-term operating performance of the company. In other words, choose a denominator that represents a good base year for measuring the company's long-term performance. The denominators we use to measure market multiples are typically operating-based, and they may require adjustments in order to reflect the company's long-run performance.

Principle 1: Consistency of Claims Represented in the Numerator and Denominator

Even though it is simple in concept, consistency between the claims in the numerator and denominator is not always straightforward to discern. For example, a multiple that is measured by dividing the value of the firm by earnings before interest, taxes, depreciation, and amortization (the EBITDA multiple) has a reasonably consistent numerator and denominator because the numerator measures the claims related to all of the company's investors, and the denominator measures the flows that are potentially payable to all of the claimholders. However, the EBITDA multiple does not take into account the portion of EBITDA that is payable to the tax authorities and it does not consider required investments, both of which are reflected in the numerator. As we discussed in Chapter 13, these determinants then have to be controlled for through the use of comparable companies; that is, the company being valued and the comparable companies need to have similar tax cost structures and require similar investments.

A multiple that really does not have a consistent numerator and denominator is the multiple measured by dividing the common equity value by revenue. This inconsistency arises because the numerator represents equity claims only and the denominator represents flows related to investors (debtholders, preferred stockholders, and common equityholders), as well as all suppliers, employees, and tax authorities. Two otherwise identical companies with different capital structures will have different multiples of equity value to revenue merely because they have different capital structures. It may be possible to use a market multiple that is defined as the market value of the firm to revenue, but doing so requires that all firms have the same cost structure, investment requirements, tax structure, risk and growth prospects. Finding comparable companies for such a multiple can be a daunting task. However, the degree of complexity in assessing comparability increases even more when we utilize a multiple of equity value to revenue, because it further mixes the claimholders represented in the numerator and denominator. Even though consistency between the numerator and the denominator is useful, assessing comparability can be a complex problem, as we saw in Chapter 13.

A multiple's numerator and denominator can also have more subtle inconsistencies. Measuring the earnings multiple as the market value of a company's equity to net income might seem to have a consistent numerator and denominator because the claimholders in both the numerator and denominator are the same—the common shareholders. However, if the company has preferred stock and pays preferred stock dividends, then the denominator does not represent the flow to common shareholders unless we use income available to common instead of net income. In addition, the numerator and denominator might not be consistent if a company has outstanding stock options, stock appreciation rights, or other securities (such as convertible debt) that can dilute the ownership interests of the common shareholders. In such cases, we must either adjust the numerator, the denominator, or both so that the value of the claims in the numerator and the flow in the denominator represent the same claimholders, which we discuss later in the chapter.

Principles 2 and 3: Use a Numerator and Denominator that Represent the Value of the Company's Long-Run Operating Performance

The market value of a firm or its equity represents the value of the company's long-term performance, plus the value of any business being sold, plus the value of any excess assets. Unless the comparable companies and the company we are valuing have similar businesses being sold and similar excess assets, we typically adjust the numerator in a market multiple to exclude such effects. Such adjustments to the numerator often lead to changes in the denominator. Including the effects of these items in the numerator and denominator can cause differences between the comparable companies and the company we are valuing, so we generally make the appropriate adjustments for these items. Naturally, we cannot calculate a meaningful multiple if a company has a negative denominator. The ratio of firm or equity value to a negative denominator is nonsensical. This issue is similar to using a negative free cash flow in a constant growth perpetuity formula; that is, it does not fit the assumptions underlying the formula. Given that the numerator represents the value of the company's long-term performance, our denominator should represent a good base year for the company's long-term performance. This issue is somewhat similar to the base year issue for continuing values that are measured using a free cash flow perpetuity (recall this discussion in Chapter 6). We should therefore adjust the denominator for any effect that is not representative of the company's long-term performance. For example, the effect of any gain, loss, or cash proceeds from the sale of either a business or a non-recurring item would have to be adjusted to remove the effect from the denominator.

Timing Issues

For market multiple denominators based on a stock (balance sheet value)—such as the book value of shareholders' equity or the book value of total invested capital—we usually rely on the last fiscal period (year or quarter or possibly month) that is closest to the valuation date. Since the denominator is a balance sheet value, quarterly financial statements may provide the information closest to the valuation date.

For market multiple denominators based on a flow (income or cash flow statement)—such as revenues, earnings, EBIT, and EBITDA—we have more choices as to the period for which we measure the denominator. The typical alternatives include the last fiscal year, the **last twelve months (LTM)** or **trailing twelve months (TTM)**, six-months historical and six-months forecast, the next-fiscal-year forecast, or the forecast for the fiscal year two or more years out. Note that the timing convention used to measure the multiples has to match the measured denominator for the company being valued. For example, if we use EBIT measured over the TTM to calculate the multiples for the comparable companies, we use the TTM of EBIT for the firm being valued.

Last Fiscal Year. Measuring the variables from the last fiscal year entails identifying the relevant numbers from the most recent annual financial statement or 10-K filing. This is relatively straightforward. The potential problem with using the last fiscal year is that the information may be stale. For example, if we are valuing a company with a December 31 year-end when it is late October, the last-fiscal-year results will be based on the performance of the company starting 22 months ago and ending 10 months ago. Another potential disadvantage of this alternative is that we might be measuring the denominator over different time periods for the comparable companies with different fiscal year-ends. Using different time periods results in different multiples if either the companies' situations or the conditions of the general economy or industry change substantially during the different measurement periods.[3]

Last Twelve Months (LTM) or Trailing Twelve Months (TTM). Most companies only issue quarterly (and not monthly) financial statements, so using the LTM generally means using the financial statements for the last four quarters available before the valuation date. If the valuation date falls after the date that annual financial statements are available and before the date that the year's first quarterly financial statements are available, then the LTM is equivalent to the last fiscal year.

To calculate the LTM that does not coincide with the fiscal year-end, we use a combination of quarterly and annual financial statements. For example, assume we are measuring the LTM of earnings as of April 30, 2018, for a company that has a fiscal year-end of December 31, and that the quarterly financial statements for the quarter ending on March 31, 2018, are available by April 30. To measure the LTM of earnings we have available as of April 30, 2018, we begin with the December 31, 2017, annual earnings. We subtract the earnings for the March 31, 2017, quarter from the annual earnings (to measure the earnings for the last three quarters of that year) and add the earnings for the March 31, 2018, quarter. To calculate the LTM of earnings as of June 30, 2018, we subtract the earnings for the six months ending June 30, 2017, from the

[3] One advantage of using annual versus quarterly financial statements is that they are audited, whereas quarterly financial statements are only reviewed by the auditor.

annual earnings recorded on December 31, 2017, (to measure the earnings for the last two quarters of that fiscal year), and add the earnings for the six months ending June 30, 2018. The advantage of this approach is that the denominator is measured for a time period that is closer to the valuation date; in other words, the information is less stale.

Forecasts. We can use a forecast of the denominator instead of the most recent historical result (assuming forecasts are available). Using forecasts instead of the most recently observed value can have two potential advantages. First, forecasts might represent a better base with which to capture long-run growth rates, for they are less likely to contain transitory or one-time effects. Second, market prices are based on expectations of the future, so it is consistent to use forecasted denominators. Using analyst forecasts has advantages but it also has disadvantages. One potential problem with using financial analyst forecasts is that analysts do not always provide forecasts for the denominator we are using. While most analysts forecast earnings per share, not all analysts make public their forecasts of free cash flows, revenues, EBIT, or EBITDA. Another potential problem is that analysts may not provide sufficient information to make some of the adjustments we describe in this chapter.

As a result, we often have no clear choice as to whether we want to use the most recent actual value or a forecast. Limited empirical research suggests that, on average, using forecasts is better than using historical information, but we cannot generalize these results for all situations; this is especially true since the empirical evidence is not based on multiples that include all of the adjustments we discuss in this chapter, which are more likely to improve multiples based on historical financial results than those based on forecasts.[4] This is undoubtedly why we observe analysts and others using a combination of multiples based on both historical results and forecasts.

Alternative forecast measures include using a six-month forecast (in conjunction with the most recent six months of actual results), a forecast of the next fiscal year, and a forecast for two or more fiscal years out. The next-fiscal-year forecast is only a complete one-year forecast at the beginning of a company's fiscal year. As a company's fiscal year progresses, the next-fiscal-year forecast becomes a combination of actual results reported for the year to date and the forecast for the remainder of the fiscal year (as analysts update their forecasts periodically during the year, often after quarterly results are released).

Sources for forecasts include individual financial analyst reports or the consensus of many financial analysts' forecasts from companies such as I/B/E/S (Institutional Brokers Estimate Service), First Call, and Zach's Investment Research. I/B/E/S and First Call are owned by Thomson Reuters Corporation.

Valuation Key 14.1

For market multiples based on a stock (balance sheet) variable in the denominator, we usually rely on the fiscal period (year or quarter or even month) that is closest to the valuation date. For market multiples based on a flow (income or cash flow statement) variable—variables such as free cash flows, revenues, earnings, EBIT, and EBITDA—we typically choose from alternatives that include the last fiscal year, the last twelve months (or trailing twelve months), a combination of six months of historical results and six months of forecast results, the next-fiscal-year forecast, or the forecast for the fiscal year two or more years out.

Partial Fiscal Periods. Companies can report a partial fiscal period (part of a year or quarter) for several reasons. One reason is a change in the company's fiscal year-end. Companies do not change their fiscal year-end very often, but if a company changes its fiscal year-end, it will report a partial period (year or quarter) for one of its financial statements. We do not have an exact way to adjust for a partial period financial statement. We can extrapolate the missing part of the period from the following period, but this approach is not exact, especially for seasonal businesses.

Companies that come out of bankruptcy (or a reorganization) typically report a partial fiscal period for the part of the fiscal year or quarter prior to the date they emerge from bankruptcy as well as for the

---

[4] See Liu, J., D. Nissim, and J. Thomas, "Equity Valuation Using Multiples," *Journal of Accounting Research* 40 (2002), pp. 135–172, who examine this and other issues for a large sample of companies; and, Kim, M., and J. Ritter, "Valuing IPOs," *Journal of Financial Economics* 53 (1999), pp. 409–437, who examine this and other issues for a sample of initial public offerings (IPOs).

period after they emerge from bankruptcy. Again, the partial year limits our ability to calculate the market multiple denominators using historical data. A slightly different and less important issue occurs when a company uses a specified point in a year—for example, the last Saturday of August—rather than a fixed date. Fiscal years determined on this basis will not have the same number of days each year.

Valuation in Practice 14.1

Genco Shipping & Trading Limited (Genco) Emergence from Bankruptcy. On April 21, 2014, Genco filed a prepackaged bankruptcy plan. Genco continued to operate its businesses as "debtors-in-possession" and emerged from bankruptcy on July 9, 2014. As a result of emerging from bankruptcy, Genco reported the results of 2014 in two separate periods—prior to July 9, 2014 and after July 9, 2014. The challenge in measuring multiples of a company that has such an event is measuring its long-run expected performance.

> Upon the Company's emergence from the Chapter 11 Cases on July 9, 2014, the Company adopted fresh-start reporting in accordance with provisions of the Financial Accounting Standards Board ("FASB") Accounting Standards Codification ("ASC") 852, "Reorganizations" ("ASC 852"). Upon adoption of fresh-start reporting, the Company's assets and liabilities were recorded at their value as of the fresh-start reporting date. . . . As a result of the adoption of fresh-start reporting, the Company's consolidated balance sheets and consolidated statements of operations subsequent to July 9, 2014 will not be comparable in many respects to our consolidated balance sheets and consolidated statements of operations prior to July 9, 2014. (2014 10 K, p. F 11)

Source: Genco Shipping & Trading Limited 2014 10-K Report

14.2 INITIAL FINANCIAL STATEMENT REVIEW

LO2 Conduct an initial review of financial statements

A common starting point for measuring a company's market multiples is to review its most recent annual (and sometimes its most recent quarterly) financial statements. We review quarterly financial statements if the quarterly financial statements are more recent than the annual financial statements relative to the valuation date. We review annual financial statements even if they are not the most recent financial statements because they typically contain more detailed information than quarterly financial statements. The goal of reviewing a company's financial statements is twofold. First, we identify all the securities we must use to measure the company's market multiple numerators, and second, we identify potential adjustments to the company's market multiple denominators, which can result in adjustments to the numerators as well. In this section, we limit our review to the financial statements and certain selected financial statement schedules, but ignore other information that may be useful such as analysts' reports, management forecasts, etc. In subsequent sections we review Merck's other schedules and footnotes.

Identifying the securities to include in the market multiple numerators is essentially equivalent to the process we use to identify securities to include when measuring the weighted average cost of capital (see Chapter 11). We include all securities used to finance the firm and exclude all (current and non-current) operating liabilities. Identifying potential adjustments to market multiple denominators requires a somewhat different and often more complex analysis than discussed in earlier chapters. In the remainder of the chapter we use Merck (see the opening vignette to the chapter) to illustrate the process of measuring a company's market multiples. Before we do that, we first discuss the categories of potential adjustments.

Categories of Potential Adjustments to Market Multiple Denominators

The goal of adjusting the denominator is to measure a denominator that better represents the long-run performance of the company. We present a list of the more common categories of such adjustments in Exhibit 14.1, and discuss specific examples of each of these categories in more detail later in the chapter using Merck's data as of December 31, 2014.

EXHIBIT 14.1 Summary of Typical Adjustments to Market Multiple Denominators

Type of Adjustment	Adjustment to Income Statement	Adjustment to Balance Sheet	Adjustment to Enterprise Value
Excess assets	Eliminate effect	Eliminate balance	Subtract value
Non-recurring revenues/gains and expenses/losses	Eliminate effect	Typically none	Typically none
Mergers and acquisitions	Add pre-merger income	Typically none	Typically none
Divestitures	Eliminate pre-sale income	Typically none	Typically none
Discontinued operations	Eliminate effect	Eliminate balance	Subtract value
Unconsolidated affiliates	Eliminate effect	Eliminate balance	Subtract value
Noncontrolling interests	Combine into income	Combine into equity	Add value
Non-capitalized leases	Convert to capitalized	Convert to capitalized	Add value

The first category of potential adjustments is **excess assets**, which is any asset that is not required for the company's ongoing operations, for example, land investments not needed for operations or **net operating loss carryforwards (NOLs)** among others. We adjust the income statement by eliminating all income effects from the excess assets, and we adjust the balance sheet by eliminating the amount shown on the balance sheet for the excess assets, which typically has a corresponding effect on retained earnings. Since we adjust the denominator in this way, we similarly subtract the value of the excess assets when measuring enterprise value. This is analogous to the treatment of cash and marketable securities that we always make when calculating multiples. We subtract all cash and marketable securities in determining enterprise value and we adjust the denominators for any income earned by those assets.

The second category of potential adjustments is **non-recurring items** (for example, one-time gains or losses from the disposition of assets or redemption of liabilities, restructuring charges and impairment charges). We adjust the income statement by eliminating all income effects resulting from the non-recurring item, and we adjust the balance sheet by reversing any effects of recording the non-recurring item on the balance sheet. Although we are adjusting the denominator for the non-recurring item, we typically do not need to adjust the numerator because the effect of the (previously disclosed) non-recurring item is usually already reflected in the enterprise value and equity value.

The third category of potential adjustments is **mergers and acquisitions**. When a company (acquirer) acquires another company (target), it begins recording the income and cash flows from the target as of the acquisition closing date. Unless the target was acquired at the end of a year, the income statement and statement of cash flows of the acquirer includes only a partial year of income and cash flows from the target, which is unlikely to represent the long-term performance of the post transaction company. In order to measure the long-term performance of the combined company, we adjust the combined company's income statement (statement of cash flows) by including the income (cash flows) of the target for the part of the current fiscal year occurring before the closing date. Again, we typically do not adjust the numerator because the effect of the (previously disclosed) merger or acquisition is already reflected in the enterprise value and equity value.

The fourth category of potential adjustments is **divestitures**. The adjustment for divestitures is basically the opposite of the adjustment for mergers and acquisitions. Since as of the closing date, enterprise value and the balance sheet no longer include the value of the operations that were divested, we adjust the company's income statement and statement of cash flows to exclude the income and cash flows that were recorded for the divested operations for the part of the current fiscal year occurring before the closing date. If the divestiture resulted in cash holdings, we would of course adjust for the cash resulting from the divestiture in calculating enterprise value.

The fifth category of potential adjustments is **discontinued operations**. A discontinued operation is a part of the company's operations for which it has a plan to divest or has divested and meets certain criteria to qualify as a discontinued operation. The effect of discontinued operations is often presented as a one-line item on the income statement and it is also isolated on the balance sheet. Discontinued operations can show up as a few lines on the statement of cash flows (one in each section typically). We adjust the income statement (statement of cash flows) by eliminating all income (cash flow) effects from discontinued operations, and we adjust the balance sheet by eliminating the amount shown on the balance sheet. Since we adjust the denominator in this way, we similarly subtract the value of any discontinued operations from enterprise value and equity value. We should note that many businesses that a company might choose to divest itself of will not qualify for treatment as a discontinued operation.

The sixth category is **unconsolidated affiliates**. An unconsolidated affiliate is a company (affiliate) in which the company has an investment in the affiliate's equity but the company does not consolidate the affiliate into the company's financial statements. Instead, the company's investment is recorded as a one-line item on the company's income statement and balance sheet. If large and we have sufficient information, we exclude the unconsolidated affiliate when measuring denominators by eliminating all income or cash flow effects from the unconsolidated affiliate. We adjust the balance sheet by eliminating the book value of that investment on the balance sheet. In order to exclude the unconsolidated affiliate from the numerators, we subtract the value of the unconsolidated affiliate from enterprise value and equity value. If an unconsolidated affiliate is not publicly traded, we may have to estimate its value using a price multiple or some other valuation technique.

The seventh category is **noncontrolling interests (minority interests)**. When a parent company partially owns a consolidated subsidiary, the parent records all of the subsidiary's revenues and expenses on the consolidated income statement and records all of the subsidiary's assets and liabilities on the consolidated company's balance sheet. Similarly for the cash flow statement. However, the income (loss) attributable to the portion of the consolidated subsidiary not owned by the parent is subtracted (added) on the consolidated income statement. Further, on the balance sheet, the noncontrolling interests are shown as part of total equity. We adjust the income statement so that all of the subsidiary's income is included in the company's consolidated income (as if the company owned 100 percent of the subsidiary), and we adjust the balance sheet to include the noncontrolling interests as part of shareholders' equity. Since we adjust the denominator in this way, we add the value of the noncontrolling interests to enterprise value and equity value. Again, if not publicly traded, we would have to estimate the value of the noncontrolling interest.

The last category is **leases**. As we discussed in Chapter 11, recent changes in the accounting rules will require companies to capitalize essentially all lease obligations with a contractual term longer than twelve months.[5] The new accounting rules continue to classify leases as either financing or operating and for operating leases the lease expense will continue to be treated solely as an operating expense. In order to adjust the income statement to convert operating leases to financing leases under the current or new accounting rules, we eliminate any effects of the operating leases on the income statement (operating lease expense) and add the effects of treating the operating lease as a financing lease (amortize the lease asset as a non-cash operating expense and record interest on the lease liability). Based on the current rules, we adjust the balance sheet for operating leases by adding the value of the leased asset and lease liability as well as some other potential adjustments. Since we adjust the denominator in this way, we add the value of the capitalized leases to enterprise value. Under the new accounting rules an operating liability will appear on the balance sheet for operating leases with a term of more than 12 months, but we treat the operating lease liability as debt when measuring the numerators and denominators.

Initial Review of Merck & Co., Inc.'s Financial Statements

In this section, we provide an illustration of how to conduct an initial review of a company's financial statements and selected financial statement schedules in order to identify potential securities to use to measure the company's market multiple numerators and potential adjustments to make to the company's market multiple denominators under the assumption that we will use Merck as a comparable company.

What We Initially Learn from Merck's Income Statement and Schedule of Other Income. We begin our illustration by analyzing Merck's income statement presented in Exhibit 14.2. Merck's income statement does not provide much help to identify the securities to use to measure its market multiple numerators; however, it does identify a number of potential adjustments to make to its denominators.

Merck's income statement includes four line items that identify potential adjustments to the denominators for the year ending December 31, 2014—restructuring charges ($1.0 billion), a potential non-recurring expense, equity income from affiliates (unconsolidated affiliates, $257 million), and noncontrolling interests ($14 million, net of tax). In 2014, Merck reported other (income) and expenses on a net basis equal to $11.4 billion of income, which is about two-thirds of its income before taxes (0.66 = $11.4/$17.3). In its footnotes, Merck provided a schedule with more detail about the $11.4 billion of other income presented on a net basis in its income statement. We present that schedule in Exhibit 14.3. Finally, the fact that the weighted average diluted shares is greater than the weighted average basic shares suggests that some form of equity based compensation, convertible securities or warrants are part of the capital structure.

[5] FASB ASC Topic 842, Leases, issued February 25, 2016. Topic 842 replaces ASC Topic 840, Leases. The new accounting rules become effective no later than fiscal years beginning after December 15, 2018.

EXHIBIT 14.2 Merck & Co., Inc.—Abbreviated Consolidated Statement of Income

Consolidated Statement of Income (USD $) In Millions, unless otherwise specified	Dec. 31, 2012	Dec. 31, 2013	Dec. 31, 2014
Sales	$47,267	$44,033	$42,237
Materials and production	$16,446	$16,954	$16,768
Marketing and administrative	12,776	11,911	11,606
Research and development	8,168	7,503	7,180
Restructuring costs	664	1,709	1,013
Equity income from affiliates (net of tax)	−642	−404	−257
Other (income) expense, net	1,116	815	−11,356
Total costs, expenses and other	38,528	38,488	24,954
Income before taxes	8,739	5,545	17,283
Taxes on income	2,440	1,028	5,349
Income (loss) from continuing operations	6,299	4,517	11,934
Discontinued operations	0	0	0
Net income	6,299	4,517	11,934
Less: Net income for noncontrolling interests (net of tax)	131	113	14
Net income attributable to Merck & Co., Inc.	$ 6,168	$ 4,404	$11,920

In Millions, except per share amounts	Dec. 31, 2012	Dec. 31, 2013	Dec. 31, 2014
Basic earnings per common share	$2.03	$1.49	$4.12
Weighted average shares for basic EPS	3,038.424	2,955.705	2,893.204
Earnings per common share assuming dilution	$2.00	$1.47	$4.07
Weighted average shares for diluted EPS	3,084.000	2,995.918	2,928.747

EXHIBIT 14.3 Merck & Co., Inc.—Abbreviated Schedule of Other Income and Expense, Net

In Millions, unless otherwise specified	Dec. 31, 2012	Dec. 31, 2013	Dec. 31, 2014
Interest income	−$ 232	−$264	−$ 266
Interest expense	714	801	732
Exchange losses	185	290	180
Gain on disposal of consumer care			−11,209
Loss on extinguishment of debt			628
Other, net	449	−12	−1,421
Other (income) expense	$1,116	$ 815	−$11,356

Exhibit 14.3 provides additional information to identify a number of potential adjustments to make to Merck's denominators. Merck indicates it had a gain on the sale of its Consumer Care group of $11.2 billion. The company also reported a $628 million loss on the extinguishment of debt, which is a potential non-recurring expense.[6]

What We Initially Learn from Merck's Balance Sheet. We present Merck's balance sheet in Exhibit 14.4. The balance sheet is typically more useful for identifying securities to include in the numerators than for identifying potential adjustments to the denominators. Merck's balance sheet indicates that it has at least two types of securities used to finance the firm, debt (short- and long-term) and common equity. Merck's balance sheet also has three line items to potentially measure "cash"—cash and cash equivalents, short-term investments, and (non-current) investments. It is likely we would include

[6] This schedule also indicates that Merck has cash and other securities generating over $266 million in interest income and debt that has interest expense of over $732 million, as well as a goodwill impairment, which is part of other, net. We discuss "cash" and debt in more detail when we discuss the balance sheet. Exchange losses related to foreign currency effects occurred in every year and are likely to recur in the future as either gains or losses, though we may not forecast them.

both cash and cash equivalents and short-term investments to measure "cash"; however, we would likely need additional information, which we would find in the footnotes to the financial statements, to decide whether or not to include (non-current) investments in "cash."

EXHIBIT 14.4 Merck & Co., Inc.—Abbreviated Consolidated Balance Sheet

In Millions, unless otherwise specified	Dec. 31, 2013	Dec. 31, 2014
Cash and cash equivalents	$ 15,621	$ 7,441
Short-term investments	1,865	8,278
Accounts receivable	7,184	6,626
Inventories	6,226	5,571
Deferred income taxes and other current assets	4,789	5,257
Total current assets	35,685	33,173
Investments	9,770	13,515
Property, plant and equipment, gross	33,094	31,140
Less: accumulated depreciation	18,121	18,004
Property, plant and equipment, net, total	14,973	13,136
Goodwill	12,301	12,992
Other intangibles, net	23,801	20,386
Other assets	9,115	5,133
Total assets	$105,645	$98,335
Loans payable and current portion of long-term debt	$ 4,521	$ 2,704
Trade accounts payable	2,274	2,625
Accrued and other current liabilities	9,501	10,523
Income taxes payable	251	1,606
Dividends payable	1,321	1,308
Total current liabilities	17,868	18,766
Long-term debt	20,539	18,699
Deferred income taxes	6,776	4,266
Other non-current liabilities	8,136	7,813
Merck & Co., Inc. stockholders equity		
Common stock	1,788	1,788
Other paid-in capital	40,508	40,423
Retained earnings	39,257	46,021
Accumulated other comprehensive loss	−2,197	−4,323
Stockholders' equity before deduction for treasury stock	79,356	83,909
Less treasury stock, at cost	29,591	35,262
Total Merck & Co., Inc. stockholders' equity	49,765	48,647
Noncontrolling interests	2,561	144
Total equity	52,326	48,791
Total liabilities and equity	$105,645	$98,335

What We Initially Learn from Merck's Cash Flow Statement. We present Merck's cash flow statement in Exhibit 14.5. Merck's cash flow statement both confirms and supplements the information gleaned from Merck's income statement and balance sheet. The operating section of the cash flow statement confirms the need for the potential adjustment for the gain on the divestiture of the Consumer Care group, the loss on the extinguishment of debt, and income from unconsolidated affiliates. It also shows an adjustment for intangible asset impairment of $1.2 billion, which differs from the restructuring charges shown on the income statement, and is not shown as a separate line item on the income statement. The operating section of the cash flow statement reports the existence of share-based compensation, and the financing section reports the existence of stock options, which is another security used to finance the company. In the investing section, Merck reports that the proceeds from the Consumer Care group divestiture was $14 billion, and it also reports that it acquired a company (Acquisition of Idenix Pharmaceuticals, Inc. net of cash, $3.7 billion). It also shows the sale and purchase of securities, which approximates the changes in these accounts on the balance sheet.

EXHIBIT 14.5 Merck & Co., Inc.—Abbreviated Consolidated Statement of Cash Flows

In Millions, unless otherwise specified	Dec. 31, 2012	Dec. 31, 2013	Dec. 31, 2014
Net income	$ 6,299	$ 4,517	$11,934
Depreciation and amortization	6,978	6,988	6,691
Intangible asset impairment charges	200	765	1,222
Gain on divestiture of Merck Consumer Care	0	0	−11,209
Loss on extinguishment of debt	0	0	628
Equity income from affiliates	−642	−404	−257
Dividends and distributions from equity method affiliates	291	237	185
Deferred income taxes	669	−330	−2,600
Share-based compensation	335	276	278
Change in current asset and current liabilities	−1,158	−826	1,637
Non-current liabilities	−1,747	−132	190
Other non-current	−1,203	563	−839
Net cash provided by operating activities	10,022	11,654	7,860
Capital expenditures	−1,954	−1,548	−1,317
Purchases of securities and other investments	−12,841	−17,991	−24,944
Proceeds from sales of securities and other investments	7,783	16,298	15,114
Divestiture of Consumer Care business, net of cash divested	0	0	13,951
Acquisition of Idenix Pharmaceuticals, Inc., net of cash	0	0	−3,700
Cash inflows from net investment hedges	39	350	195
Other	168	−257	327
Net cash used in investing activities	−6,805	−3,148	−374
Net change in short-term borrowings	624	−159	−460
Payments on debt	−22	−1,775	−6,617
Proceeds from issuance of debt	2,562	6,467	3,146
Purchases of treasury stock	−2,591	−6,516	−7,703
Dividends paid to stockholders	−5,116	−5,157	−5,170
Other dividends paid	−120	−120	−77
Proceeds from exercise of stock options	1,310	1,210	1,560
Other	86	60	208
Net cash used in financing activities	−3,267	−5,990	−15,113
Effect of exchange rate changes	−30	−346	−553
Net (decrease) increase in cash and cash equivalents	−80	2,170	−8,180
Cash and cash equivalents at beginning of year	13,531	13,451	15,621
Cash and cash equivalents at end of year	$13,451	$15,621	$ 7,441

What We Initially Learn from Merck's Income Tax Reconciliation Schedule. We present an extract from Merck's income tax footnote in addition to its income tax reconciliation schedule. We present Merck's income tax reconciliation between its effective tax rate (30.9% in 2014, .309 = $5,349/$17,283) and the 35% U.S. statutory rate in Exhibit 14.6 (recall that starting in 2018, the statutory rate dropped to 21%). This schedule confirms and supplements the information gleaned from Merck's financial statements. In addition, we can use this schedule to measure the tax effect of specific adjustments. This schedule includes line items for the divestiture of the Consumer Care group, restructuring, and intangible asset impairment charges.

Taxes on Income

The effective income tax rates of 30.9% in 2014, 18.5% in 2013 and 27.9% in 2012 reflect the impacts of acquisition and divestiture-related costs and restructuring costs, partially offset by the beneficial impact of foreign earnings. The effective income tax rate for 2014 reflects the impact of the gain on the divestiture of MCC being taxed at combined U.S. federal and state tax rates. . . . The effective income tax rate for 2014 also includes the unfavorable impact of an additional year of expense for the non-tax deductible health care reform fee that the Company recorded in accordance with final regulations issued in the third quarter by the IRS.

EXHIBIT 14.6 Merck & Co., Inc.—Taxes on Income–Reconciliation between Effective Tax Rate and U.S. Statutory Rate

In Millions, unless otherwise specified	Dec. 31, 2012	Dec. 31, 2013	Dec. 31, 2014	Dec. 31, 2014
Total income before taxes (adjusted for net of tax items)	$8,740	$5,546	$17,283	
U.S. statutory rate applied to income before taxes	3,059	1,941	6,049	35.0%
Differential arising from:				
Foreign earnings.	−1,955	−1,316	−1,486	−8.6%
Tax settlements	−113	−497	−89	−0.5%
Amortization of purchase accounting adjustments	905	934	865	5.0%
Divestiture of Merck Consumer Care.		0	440	2.5%
Restructuring	62	224	289	1.7%
U.S. health care reform legislation.	60	65	134	0.8%
Intangible asset impairment charges	40	56	148	0.9%
State taxes	31	44	7	0.0%
Other.	362	−342	−1,008	−5.8%
Taxes on income (effective tax rate).	$2,451	$1,109	$ 5,349	30.9%

If the tax reconciliation footnote does not provide information about an adjustment for a particular item we are adjusting, we use the company's marginal tax rate to measure the income tax effect of the adjustment because we have no other information. We multiply the pre-tax adjustment by the company's marginal tax rate to measure the tax effect. However, if the tax reconciliation footnote does provide information about an adjustment for a particular item we are adjusting, we do not use the marginal tax rate to make the tax adjustment but instead, we use the statutory income tax rate multiplied by the income effect of the adjustment and add or subtract the income tax effect noted in the tax reconciliation footnote. We use the statutory income tax rate instead of the company's marginal tax rate to measure the income tax effect when we have information in the tax reconciliation footnote because the line items in the tax reconciliation footnote measure the effect of that item on the company's taxes relative to the statutory rate. Recall the starting point (and sometimes the ending point) to measure a company's marginal tax rate is typically the statutory rate plus the marginal effect of the state and other income tax rates such as local income taxes (see the discussion about measuring marginal tax rates in Chapter 3, Section 3.6).

Merck's tax reconciliation footnote does not show the effect of state and other income tax rates, so we assume that Merck's marginal tax rate is equal to the federal statutory rate, 35%. Had Merck's tax reconciliation footnote included a marginal effect of the state and other income tax rates, we would have assumed that Merck's marginal tax rate was equal to the statutory rate plus the marginal effect of the state and other income tax rates. Thus, for Merck, we always use 35% to adjust for the income tax effect regardless of whether the adjustment has a corresponding line item in the tax reconciliation footnote because we assume Merck's marginal rate is equal to the federal statutory rate. We use the tax reconciliation schedule to measure the tax effect related to specific events and transactions. If the schedule includes a line item for an adjustment we are making to measure the company's market multiples, we can use the information by adding or subtracting the amount shown on the schedule to the tax implied by the statutory rate for that item. For example, Merck reports the gain on the divestiture of the Consumer Care group as $11.209 billion. If that gain were taxable at the U.S. statutory rate, the tax would be $3.923 ($3.923 billion = 0.35 × $11.209 billion). The tax reconciliation schedule, however, indicates that Merck's total tax on that gain was $440 million higher than the tax based on the 35% U.S. statutory rate. Thus, according to this schedule, Merck paid income taxes of $4.363 ($4.363 = $3.923 + 0.440) billion (a tax rate of 38.9% = $4.363/$11.209) on this gain. Potential causes of the higher income tax rate are state taxes as well as the use of accelerated depreciation for the Consumer Care group such that the income tax basis of that investment was lower than the amount recorded in the accounting records resulting in a larger gain for tax purposes. We discuss the other relevant line items when we make the actual adjustments to the denominators.

Summary of What We Initially Learn from Reviewing Merck's Financial Statements and Selected Schedules. The initial review of Merck's financial statements and two schedules identified at least three securities used to value the firm—equity, debt, stock options (and possibly other share-based compensation). This analysis also identified potential adjustments to the denominators—

excess assets ("cash"), non-recurring expenses (restructuring charges, asset impairment charges), a merger and acquisition (Idenix Pharmaceuticals, Inc.), divestitures (Consumer Care Group), unconsolidated affiliates, and noncontrolling interests. The only types of potential adjustments shown in Exhibit 14.1 and not identified for Merck are discontinued operations and non-capitalized leases.

It is useful to keep in mind that this initial review of the financial statements is only the starting point of our analysis and does not necessarily identify all of the securities used to finance the firm nor all of the potential adjustments to make to the denominators. The next step is to conduct a more detailed analysis of all of the financial statement footnotes and supplemental schedules, which we will conduct later in the chapter.

14.3 MEASURING MARKET MULTIPLE "NUMERATORS"

LO3 Measure market multiple numerators

Measuring the numerator is usually less complex than addressing the other issues involved in using the market multiple valuation method. Although it is usually easier to measure, it still requires making several calculations addressing various measurement issues. The first issue is specifying the concept of value we are measuring. The second issue is timing; for a given valuation date, we must decide as of what date (or dates) to measure the market value of the comparable companies. The third issue, or series of issues, is measuring the components of the value of the firm. A fourth issue is knowing what adjustments to make to the numerator in order to maintain consistency between the numerator and denominator.

Value of the Firm's Operations and Enterprise Value as Alternative Numerators

Recall that the value of the firm is equal to the sum of the value of each of a company's securities (common equity, preferred equity, debt, options, and so forth), including off-balance-sheet financing but excluding operating liabilities. We typically exclude excess or non-operating assets from our analysis and adjust a market multiple valuation separately for these assets. Thus, we adjust firm value by deducting the value of excess assets and any value that results from expected short-term, non-recurring events. For example, if a company announces that it is going to sell off one of its businesses, we would exclude the value of that business that is embedded in the value of the firm. The resulting calculation is the value of the firm's ongoing operations plus any value from financing. We make corresponding adjustments to the denominator to exclude any effect resulting from the business being sold.

However, since many companies hold excess cash, and since excess cash is not reported separately by the company, it is common to exclude all cash and other short-term and long-term investments not required for the company's operations (marketable securities) from the company's value when calculating multiples, called enterprise value, and which is the more common numerator of many market multiples rather than firm value. For a company with no excess assets, the difference between the value of the firm and its enterprise value is required cash. Using enterprise value implicitly assumes that the company has no required cash or, alternatively, that all of the companies used in the analysis have the same relative cash requirements (that is, relative to enterprise value). Since enterprise value is the more common concept used, we focus the remainder of our examples on measuring enterprise value. Net debt is equal to the value of the firm's debt less the company's cash and marketable securities. Thus, an equivalent way to measure enterprise value is to add the value of the equity to the value of the net debt and the value of any other securities used to finance the firm.

We can measure equity-based multiples in more than one way. One way to measure the numerator for equity-based multiples is to use the total value of the company's equity, which includes the value of the company's common stock, restricted stock, warrants, employee stock options and other common equity-linked securities. Using this approach, we measure the value of the numerator and denominator using the total value of the equity and total earnings to equityholders. An alternative approach is to use the price per share and earnings per share of the equity. In the latter approach, we face the issue of knowing how to measure per share earnings. For example, companies report basic earnings per share and fully diluted earnings per share. Ideally, we subtract the value of excess cash from the value of the equity when we measure equity-based multiples, but again, since excess cash is not reported, it is often easier to subtract all of the cash and marketable securities from the value of the equity. Some valuation experts do not subtract the value of the cash and marketable securities from the value of the equity when measuring equity-based multiples, especially when the numerator is the company stock price, for example, when measuring a price-to-earnings ratio.

Relation Between the Valuation Date and the Measurement Date for Value (Numerator)

Given a valuation date, we must decide the date for measuring the value of the comparable companies' securities. One option is to use the most recent value of the firm (or equity) for the comparable companies or measure the average value over the last month, quarter, or year. In general, unless we have a clear reason to do otherwise, we measure the value of the firm (or equity) for the comparable companies as of the date the company is being valued (valuation date) or as reasonably close to that date as possible. With very thinly traded stocks that are subject to large bid-ask spreads, it may be useful to use an average over several days or use the average of the bid and the ask prices.

In general, we do not recommend using an average value that is computed over a long time period. For example, if we were using market multiples to value firms in the technology sector after the large decline in the value of technology stocks in April 2000, it would have been hard to argue that the pre-April 2000 market multiples were the relevant multiples to use to assess the current value in, say, June of 2000. Similarly, arguing that we should use values from July of 2008 to measure the value of a security after October of 2008 when the economy was in the throes of the financial crisis would have been equally problematic; the S&P 500 index fell from 1,284.91 on July 1, 2008, to 848.92 on October 27, 2008, a decline of 33%.

While we do not generally recommend using an average value when using market multiples to estimate value as of the valuation date, we have a somewhat different view when market multiples are used to measure the continuing value (terminal value, residual value). It may be the case that an average of market multiples over a historical period is appropriate for measuring continuing value. For example, if we have a company in a cyclical industry, rather than choose a multiple at the peak or trough of the cycle, it is more sensible to calculate the average multiple over the cycle in order to measure continuing value. Thus, as discussed in Chapter 13, the multiple we choose to measure a company's continuing value can be quite different from the multiple we use to measure the same company's current value.

Measuring the Value of the Common Equity Shares

Measuring the value of the common equity shares for a publicly traded comparable company is typically one of the easier calculations for measuring multiples. To measure the value of the equity, we typically multiply the number of **shares outstanding** by the market price per share. It is incorrect to use the number of **shares issued** instead of the number of shares outstanding, because the number of shares issued includes shares that the company originally issued but later bought back to be held as **treasury stock** or **treasury shares**. Companies often hold treasury shares for employee or shareholder stock purchase plans and employee equity-based compensation, such as employee stock options. A company typically reports the number of shares issued, the number of treasury shares, and the number of shares outstanding in its financial statements. Sometimes companies issue more than one type (class) of common equity. In such cases, we calculate the value of each class of equity and add these values together to measure the value of the equity.

Since most companies issue their financial statements quarterly (at least in the United States), we do not know the exact number of shares outstanding between the quarterly financial statements. In both a company's 10-K and 10-Q filings with the U.S. SEC, we can obtain the number of shares outstanding on two dates—a date close to the date on which the company filed its report with the U.S. SEC and the date of the fiscal period end. By researching a company's website for public announcements, we can also identify large issuances and repurchases of stock and adjust the shares outstanding accordingly when necessary.

Measuring the Value of Debt and Preferred Stock

We measure the value of the debt and preferred stock based on the market value of these claims. If these claims are publicly traded, we can observe their market prices. If the securities are not publicly traded, we review the company's financial statements for useful information to value the securities. Fortunately, companies must provide an assessment of the "fair" value of their financial instruments in their 10-Ks, which includes most types of debt but does not include preferred stock. Thus, when confronted with this issue, the starting point is analyzing the company's 10-K and 10-Q filings. Recall the discussion for valuing debt and preferred stock in Chapter 9.

Once we value a subset of the debt and preferred stock securities, we often use these values as the basis for valuing other securities, making adjustments for differences in the contracts, time to maturity, and so forth. For example, if a firm has some publicly traded debt with observable prices and yields, we can use this information to help value the non-publicly traded claims.

We can also use a company's book values to value securities that were issued recently, making adjustments for changes in the economic conditions underlying the securities' value. Thus, we can use the book value of these securities as a proxy for the market value of these claims if market conditions and the company's financial situation did not change substantially since the date the claims were issued. On the other hand, if market conditions or the company's financial situation have changed substantially since the date the securities were issued, we cannot rely solely on book values.

Measuring the Value of Stock Options and Other Equity-Linked Securities

Companies can have a variety of equity-linked securities that may or may not be publicly traded. The most common examples of such securities are employee stock options, restricted stock awards, and stock appreciation rights. Companies can also attach an option feature to other securities, such as convertible preferred stock or convertible debt. Such option features may be linked to the security for its entire term to maturity or may detach (become separate securities) after the company issues it. For example, a company may issue a bond with an attached warrant (option), and depending on the contract, the warrant may or may not be detachable after the investor purchases the security. Finally, companies also issue equity-based securities to raise capital (warrants). We discussed the valuation of convertible securities and warrants in Chapter 12.

As discussed in Chapter 12, we can measure the value of stock options and other equity-based securities using an option pricing model. It is common for companies to use option pricing models such as a Black-Scholes Option Pricing type of model in order to value employee stock options and related securities.

Some valuation experts exclude the value of stock options and other equity-linked securities when measuring multiples. For example, they calculate enterprise value by summing the value of the common equity, preferred equity, and debt, ignoring the value of stock options and other equity-linked securities. The underlying assumption in such valuations is that the relative value of the stock options and other equity-based securities is the same for the comparable companies as the company we are valuing. Whether that is a reasonable assumption to make depends on the particular company being valued and the comparable companies.

Measuring the Value of Other Securities and Off-Balance-Sheet Financing

Companies occasionally issue securities other than equity, debt, preferred stock, and common equity-linked securities. The key is to identify the existence of these securities—typically through an examination of the company's financial statements and filings with the government—and measure their value. In addition, sometimes companies issue claims that are not reported on their financial statements; we call these claims **off-balance-sheet claims**. A review of the company's financial statement footnotes often provides useful information on these claims.

Adjustments to the Numerator as a Result of Adjustments to the Denominator

We measure the denominators of market multiples in a manner that best reflects the long-run performance of the comparable companies and the firm being valued. As a result, we often make adjustments to the denominators so that they better reflect the company's long-run performance. Any time we adjust the denominator to exclude a portion of earnings or cash flows for the effect of an asset or liability, we will often have to adjust the numerator for that same effect. For example, if we exclude the effects of an excess asset from the denominator, we also subtract the value of the excess asset from the numerator.

Valuation Key 14.2

We measure the enterprise value for each comparable company by summing the values of each comparable company's securities used to finance the company and subtracting the value of the company's cash and marketable securities. We identify a company's issued securities by examining its financial statements and other filings with the government and by researching the company in both the financial press and analyst reports. We measure the value of a company's securities in a variety of ways; sometimes we can use quoted prices, sometimes we can use the company's fair value disclosure, sometimes we must conduct our own valuation, and in some circumstances, we may be able to use book values for debt and preferred stock.

Measuring Merck's Enterprise Value and Equity Value as of December 31, 2014

In this section we illustrate how to measure market multiple numerators by measuring Merck's enterprise value and equity value as of December 31, 2014. Merck finances itself with common equity, share-based compensation, employee stock options, and various forms of debt.

Value of Merck's Common Equity. We begin this calculation by measuring the value of Merck's common equity shares and equity-linked securities that are similar to common shares. We are able to collect the following information about Merck's outstanding shares from its 2014 10-K report.

In Millions, unless otherwise specified	Dec. 31, 2012	Dec. 31, 2013	Dec. 31, 2014
Basic earnings per common share.	\$2.03	\$1.49	\$4.12
Weighted average shares for basic EPS	3,038.424	2,955.705	2,893.204
Earnings per common share assuming dilution.	\$2.00	\$1.47	\$4.07
Weighted average shares for diluted EPS	3,084.000	2,995.918	2,928.747
Common stock, shares authorized		6,500.000	6,500.000
Common stock, shares issued.		3,577.104	3,577.104
Treasury stock, shares		649.577	738.963
Common shares outstanding at 10-K filing date Jan 31, 2015.			2,838.193

Since our valuation date is December 31, 2014, we measure Merck's stock price and its number of outstanding common shares as of that date. Merck's closing common share price on December 31, 2014 was \$56.79, which we can easily collect from a variety of public sources. Merck provides various share numbers. The number of shares used to calculate earnings per share is not the correct number to use because these are weighted average shares for the year and not the year-end number of shares. The correct number of shares to use is the number of shares issued minus the number of shares repurchased and held in treasury (**treasury stock**). The correct number of common shares to use for Merck is 2,838.14 million (2,838.1402 = 3,577.1035 – 738.9633). Note that Merck also discloses the number of shares outstanding as of the 10-K filing date (January 31, 2015). We would use that number of shares—possibly adjusted for other information—if we had a valuation date on or after January 31, 2015 but before the disclosure of its 10-Q for the first quarter of 2015.

Recall that we also include other types of equity-linked securities that are similar to common shares to measure a company's total number of adjusted shares outstanding when measuring the value of its equity. Merck's footnote on **share-based compensation** discusses two types of such shares.[7]

[7] As we discussed in Chapter 12, certain share-based compensation securities may have beneficial income tax effects. Since we are using market values to measure enterprise value or the value of the equity, those tax benefits should be reflected in the market values used.

Share-Based Compensation Plans

The Company has share-based compensation plans under which the Company grants restricted stock units ("RSUs") and performance share units ("PSUs") to certain management level employees. In addition, employees and non-employee directors may be granted options to purchase shares of Company common stock at the fair market value at the time of grant. These plans were approved by the Company's shareholders. . . .

. . . RSUs are stock awards that are granted to employees and entitle the holder to shares of common stock as the awards vest. The fair value of the stock option and RSU awards is determined and fixed on the grant date based on the Company's stock price. PSUs are stock awards where the ultimate number of shares issued will be contingent on the Company's performance against a pre-set objective or set of objectives. The fair value of each PSU is determined on the date of grant based on the Company's stock price. Over the PSU performance period, the number of shares of stock that are expected to be issued will be adjusted based on the probability of achievement of a performance target and final compensation expense will be recognized based on the ultimate number of shares issued. RSU and PSU distributions will be in shares of Company stock after the end of the vesting or performance period, generally three years, subject to the terms applicable to such awards.

A summary of nonvested Restricted Stock Units (RSU) and Performance Stock Units (PSU) activity—shares in thousands is as follows:

	RSUs Number of Shares	Weighted Average Grant Date Fair Value	PSUs Number of Shares	Weighted Average Grant Date Fair Value
Nonvested January 1, 2014	91,340	$40.07	16,730	$35.98
Granted	47,760	$58.13	12,240	$62.94
Vested.	−68,660	$36.36	−7,230	$33.97
Forfeited	−14,100	$46.22	−2,920	$45.49
Nonvested December 31, 2014 . . .	56,340	$46.66	18,820	$52.81

To measure Merck's total number of adjusted shares outstanding, we add the 56.34 million restricted stock units and the 18.82 million performance share units to its 2,838.1402 million shares outstanding. The resulting total number of adjusted shares outstanding is 2,913.3002 million. Note, if we expect additional forfeitures before the restricted stock units and performance share units vest, we would adjust those numbers downward for expected future forfeitures. The value of Merck's common equity, which we use to measure its enterprise value and equity value, is equal to the following.

($ in millions)	Units	Unit Price	Enterprise Value	Equity Value
Value of common stock	2,913.300	$56.79	$165,446	$165,446

Value of Merck's Employee Stock Options. Merck also awards **employee stock options** as part of the compensation to certain employees. Merck's footnote on share-based compensation discusses its employee stock options.

Share-Based Compensation Plans

Employee stock options are granted to purchase shares of Company stock at the fair market value at the time of grant. These awards generally vest one-third each year over a three-year period, with a contractual term of 7–10 years. . . .

The Company uses the Black-Scholes option pricing model for determining the fair value of option grants. In applying this model, the Company uses both historical data and current market data to estimate the fair value of its options. The Black-Scholes model requires several assumptions including expected dividend yield, risk-free interest rate, volatility, and term of the options. The expected dividend yield is based on historical patterns of dividend payments. The risk-free rate is based on the rate at

continued

continued from previous page

grant date of zero-coupon U.S. Treasury Notes with a term equal to the expected term of the option. Expected volatility is estimated using a blend of historical and implied volatility. The historical component is based on historical monthly price changes. The implied volatility is obtained from market data on the Company's traded options. The expected life represents the amount of time that options granted are expected to be outstanding, based on historical and forecasted exercise behavior. . . .

Summarized information relative to stock option plan activity—options in thousands is as follows:

	Number of Options	Weighted Average Exercise Price	Weighted Average Remaining Contractual Term—Years
Outstanding January 1, 2014	115,805	$38.75	
Granted	4,872	$58.14	
Exercised	−39,293	$39.71	
Forfeited	−5,249	$45.28	
Outstanding December 31, 2014	76,135	$39.05	3.85
Expected to vest December 31, 2014	74,000	$38.00	3.60
Exercisable December 31, 2014	65,324	$37.56	3.21

We can use the warrant option valuation model in Chapter 12 to value Merck's employee stock options. An alternative way to measure the value of these options is to use the intrinsic value (the value they would have if exercised on the valuation date). We know from Chapter 12 that intrinsic value is lower than actual value because it does not include the value of the optionality. For Merck, the intrinsic value of the expected number of options that will vest is $1.39 billion ($1.39 billion = 74.0 million × ($56.79 − $38.00)). We calculated the total adjusted shares outstanding in the previous calculation, and we can collect the number of employee stock options expected to vest, the average term to maturity, and other required inputs from Merck's footnote. Using these inputs and the valuation model in Chapter 12, the value of the employee stock options is $21.616 per option (footnote inputs and calculations not shown). The total value of these options using the warrant option valuation model is $1.6 billion compared to a $1.4 billion intrinsic value. We can add the value of Merck's employee stock options to the value of Merck's common equity to measure the total value of Merck's equity claims.

($ in millions)	Units	Unit Price	Enterprise Value	Equity Value
Value of common stock	2,913.300	$56.79	$165,446	$165,446
Employee stock options	74.000	$21.616	1,600	1,600
Total equity			$167,046	$167,046

Value of Merck's Debt. In order to measure the value of the firm or enterprise value, we add the value of non-equity securities to the value of the equity. The only substantial non-equity securities Merck used for financing is debt. Merck issued a variety of debt securities, which we show in the following schedule taken from Merck's 10-K report.

Long-term debt (excluding current portion) in Millions	2013	2014
2.80% notes due 2023	$ 1,749	$ 1,749
5.00% notes due 2019	1,293	1,291
4.15% notes due 2043	1,246	1,246
1.125% euro-denominated notes due 2021		1,218
1.875% euro-denominated notes due 2026		1,210
3.875% notes due 2021	1,148	1,150
2.40% notes due 2022	1,000	1,000

continued

continued from previous page

Long-term debt (excluding current portion) in Millions	2013	2014
Floating-rate borrowing due 2018	1,000	1,000
1.10% notes due 2018	998	999
0.70% notes due 2016	997	998
1.30% notes due 2018	975	984
2.25% notes due 2016	866	858
6.50% notes due 2033	1,306	812
2.50% euro-denominated notes due 2034		603
6.55% notes due 2037	1,143	597
Floating-rate borrowing due 2016	500	500
3.60% notes due 2042	492	493
5.85% notes due 2039	749	418
5.75% notes due 2036	498	371
5.95% debentures due 2028	498	356
6.40% debentures due 2028	499	326
6.30% debentures due 2026	249	152
6.00% notes due 2017	1,095	
4.00% notes due 2015	1,029	
4.75% notes due 2015	1,023	
Other	186	368
Total	$20,539	$18,699

The above schedule presents only the long-term portion of Merck's debt. From Merck's balance sheet we can collect the book value of the current portion of Merck's long-term debt as well as any short-term debt (see loans payable and current portion of long-term debt), which is $2.704 billion. The total value of Merck's debt is $21.403 billion ($21.403 = $18.699 + $2.704). This is the book value of Merck's debt and not the market value of Merck's debt. We discussed the various ways to value debt in Chapter 9, which we can use to value Merck's debt. Merck discloses its valuation of its debt in the "fair value measurements" footnote of its 10-K report, which is equal to $22.5 billion.

Fair Value Measurements

Fair value is defined as the exchange price that would be received for an asset or paid to transfer a liability (an exit price) in the principal or most advantageous market for the asset or liability in an orderly transaction between market participants on the measurement date. The Company uses a fair value hierarchy which maximizes the use of observable inputs and minimizes the use of unobservable inputs when measuring fair value. There are three levels of inputs used to measure fair value with Level 1 having the highest priority and Level 3 having the lowest:

- Level 1—Quoted prices (unadjusted) in active markets for identical assets or liabilities.
- Level 2—Observable inputs other than Level 1 prices, such as quoted prices for similar assets or liabilities, or other inputs that are observable or can be corroborated by observable market data for substantially the full term of the assets or liabilities.
- Level 3—Unobservable inputs that are supported by little or no market activity.

Level 3 assets or liabilities are those whose values are determined using pricing models, discounted cash flow methodologies, or similar techniques with significant unobservable inputs, as well as assets or liabilities for which the determination of fair value requires significant judgment or estimation. . . .

Some of the Company's financial instruments, such as cash and cash equivalents, receivables and payables, are reflected in the balance sheet at carrying value, which approximates fair value due to their short-term nature. . . .

The estimated fair value of loans payable and long-term debt (including current portion) at December 31, 2014, was $22.5 billion compared with a carrying value of $21.4 billion and at December 31, 2013, was $25.5 billion compared with a carrying value of $25.1 billion. Fair value was estimated using recent observable market prices and would be considered Level 2 in the fair value hierarchy.

Based on the above calculations, Merck's firm value is equal to $189.5 billion.

($ in millions)	Units	Unit Price	Enterprise Value	Equity Value
Value of common stock	2,913.300	$56.79	$165,446	$165,446
Employee stock options	74.000	$21.616	1,600	1,600
Total equity			$167,046	$167,046
Total debt			22,500	
Value (with cash and investments)			$189,546	$167,046

Merck's Enterprise Value. As we discuss in the beginning of this section, enterprise value is equal to firm value minus "cash," essentially treating all cash as an excess asset. Cash includes the first line on the balance sheet, often titled cash and cash equivalents, and it typically also includes short- and long-term marketable securities. Merck's balance sheet shows cash and cash equivalents of $7.441 billion, short-term investments of $8.278 billion, and (long-term) investments of $13.515 billion, totaling $29.234 billion. Merck's footnote for investments discusses the market values of these amounts.

> At December 31, 2014, the total of worldwide cash and investments was $29.2 billion, including $15.7 billion of cash, cash equivalents and short-term investments, and $13.5 billion of long-term investments. Generally 80%–90% of these cash and investments are held by foreign subsidiaries and would be subject to significant tax payments if such cash and investments were repatriated in the form of dividends. The Company records U.S. deferred tax liabilities for certain unremitted earnings, but when amounts earned overseas are expected to be indefinitely reinvested outside of the United States, no accrual for U.S. taxes is provided. The amount of cash and investments held by U.S. and foreign subsidiaries fluctuates due to a variety of factors including the timing and receipt of payments in the normal course of business. . . .

This footnote indicates that 80% to 90% of Merck's cash and investments have a potential income tax liability. Economic research indicates that such tax liabilities reduce the value of cash and investments that are held by foreign subsidiaries.[8] We do not address this issue in our illustration and use the value of cash and investments reported by Merck, but one could reduce the value of cash holdings for the potential tax liability on cash expected to be repatriated.[9] Subtracting off all cash and short-term and long-term investments, we find that Merck's enterprise value is $160.3 billion. Recall from our earlier discussion that we can calculate equity-based multiples in different ways. For example, price-to-earnings multiples generally do not include employee stock options or a reduction for excess cash. If "cash" is mostly excess cash, however, then deducting cash to measure the total value of the equity can be useful.

($ in millions)	Units	Unit Price	Enterprise Value	Equity Value
Value of common stock	2,913.300	$56.79	$165,446	$165,446
Employee stock options	74.000	$21.616	1,600	1,600
Total equity			$167,046	$167,046
Total debt			22,500	
Value (with cash and investments)			$189,546	$167,046
Cash			−7,441	−7,441
Short-term investments			−8,278	−8,278
Long-term investments			−13,515	−13,515
Value (without cash and investments)			$160,312	$137,812

[8] See, for example, Bryant-Kutcher, L., L. Eiler and D. Guenther, "Taxes and Financial Assets: Valuing Permanently Reinvested Foreign Earnings," *National Tax Journal*, Vol. 61, No. 4, Part 1 (December, 2008), pp. 699–720; and Campbell, J., D. Dhaliwal, L. Krull, and C. Schwab, "U.S. Multinational Corporations' Foreign Cash Holdings: An Empirical Estimate and Its Valuation Consequences," Working Paper (March 2014).

[9] As we discussed in Chapter 1, the Tax Cuts and Jobs Act of 2017 reduced the U.S. federal tax rate to 21%. In addition, companies are required to pay a tax on earnings that have not been previously repatriated back to the U.S at a 15.5% tax rate on liquid assets (cash and marketable securities) and an 8% tax rate on non-liquid assets. Companies are given 8 years to pay the taxes on these past overseas earnings. Thus, if we were doing this analysis for Merck as of December 31, 2017, we could estimate the present value of that U.S. tax liability.

REVIEW EXERCISE 14.1

Measuring Market Multiple Numerators

Below we present an income statement and balance sheet for the Multiple Company. The company's debt and preferred stock are recorded on the balance sheet at par value. The debt and preferred stock are currently trading at 102% and 98% of their respective par values. The company's debt has a 7% interest rate and the dividend yield for its preferred stock is 8%. The company has 10,000 shares of outstanding stock trading at $10 per share. The company also has 2,000 employee stock options outstanding, which the company valued at $2 per option. The company's income tax rate on all income is 40%. Calculate the company's enterprise value and equity value as discussed in the previous sections of this chapter. (Note: Only make adjustments for factors discussed in previous sections of this chapter.) Without making any adjustments to the income statement, also calculate the company's unlevered earnings, EBIT, EBITDA, revenue, and P/E multiples. *Hint:* Measure the unlevered earnings as net income plus after-tax interest expense and measure EBIT as net income plus interest expense plus income tax expense. EBITDA is just EBIT plus depreciation and amortization.

	Year 2
Revenue	$30,000
Operating expenses	−21,000
Depreciation expense	−8,000
Operating earnings	$ 1,000
Earnings from unconsolidated affiliates	2,000
Investment income (on cash)	600
Interest expense	−840
Income before taxes	$ 2,760
Income tax expense	−1,104
Minority interest (net of tax)	−400
Net income	$ 1,256

	Year 1	Year 2
Cash	$12,000	$12,000
Other current assets	5,000	5,000
Equity in unconsolidated affiliates	11,000	11,000
Property, plant, and equipment (net)	36,000	38,000
Total assets	$64,000	$66,000
Account payable	$ 3,000	$ 4,000
Debt	12,000	12,000
Total liabilities	$15,000	$16,000
Minority interest	$ 5,000	$ 6,000
Preferred stock	$ 5,000	$ 5,000
Capital stock	3,000	3,000
Retained earnings	36,000	36,000
Shareholders' equity	$44,000	$44,000
Liabilities and shareholders' equity	$64,000	$66,000

Solution on page 729.

14.4 BASICS OF MEASURING MARKET MULTIPLE "DENOMINATORS"

Measuring the denominator is often more complex than measuring the numerator, although some adjustments to the denominator can require additional adjustments to the numerator, which can also be complex. Here, we discuss the basic measurement of various denominators, and adjustments for the effects of removing cash when measuring enterprise value.

LO4 Measure market multiple denominators

Measuring the Denominators—Basic Calculations

In this section, we discuss how to measure denominators for various market multiples. The specific calculation depends on the specific circumstances of the company, but the basic underlying calculations are the same.

Unlevered Earnings-Based and Unlevered Cash Flow-Based Denominators. We can use various earnings-based multiples to measure enterprise value, such as unlevered earnings, EBIT, and EBITDA. As we discussed in Chapter 13, in some situations we can also use unlevered free cash flow-based multiples to measure enterprise value. To measure unlevered earnings, we begin with net income and add back after-tax interest expense. To measure EBIT, we begin with net income and add back interest expense and income taxes.[10] To measure EBITDA, we begin with EBIT and add back depreciation and amortization (from the cash flow statement). When we measure the denominator for an enterprise value multiple, we adjust the unlevered earnings for the after-tax income on all cash and marketable securities. For the EBIT and EBITDA multiples, we exclude all interest income on the cash and marketable securities, but we do not adjust for the tax effect on interest income, as these earnings measures are pre-tax measures.

We can also use a revenues multiple to measure enterprise value. We usually use net revenues from the income statement for the denominator, which does not require any adjustments for interest income from cash and marketable securities as revenues do not include interest income.

Earnings-Based and Equity Free Cash Flow-Based Denominators. We can use earnings-based and equity free cash flow-based multiples to measure equity value. The most commonly used multiple is based on earnings per share to common shareholders, often referred to as the P/E ratio.

Per Share Calculations. Companies report two sets of earnings per share figures with the income statement—basic and fully diluted earnings per share. The weighted average shares outstanding used to measure basic earnings per share assumes no dilution for outstanding equity-linked securities such as employee stock options, convertible debt, and convertible preferred stock. It is based on the actual weighted average number of shares outstanding during the year. The weighted average shares outstanding used to measure fully diluted earnings per share includes—based on accounting rules—the effects of the dilution of earnings as a result of outstanding securities that are convertible into common stock. Fully diluted per share multiples are no smaller than basic per share multiples, because fully diluted earnings per share is no larger than basic earnings per share. For most companies, however, the difference between the fully diluted and basic number of shares is not large.

The total-equity-based multiples may not have the same values as per-share-based multiples, for they are often based on different numbers of shares. The total equity-based multiples are usually based on the share price and shares outstanding and the value of the company's other equity-linked securities at the valuation date and earnings or cash flows, whereas per share multiples are based on the share price at the valuation date divided by the per share earnings, which are based on a weighted average number of shares outstanding. There is no definitive relation between the total-equity-based multiples and the share-based multiples. Rather, it depends on whether the company increases or decreases the number of shares outstanding over the year, and it depends on other adjustments that are made.

Naturally, since these alternative multiples typically result in different valuations, a question arises as to which alternative is best. In truth, all three alternatives provide a different perspective on value, and which alternative is best depends on the situation. Total equity value multiples use the actual number of shares outstanding at the valuation date even though they are not per share multiples. Of course, this is the correct value for the numerator, but it may not be the correct value for the denominator; for example, assume that a company with a December fiscal year-end issued a large number of shares on December 31 to acquire another company on that date. The equity value reflects the acquisition, but the earnings do not. In this case, using a weighted average number of shares outstanding might be more appropriate (unless we adjust the earnings for the acquisition, which we argue is the more appropriate adjustment to make).

Balance Sheet Based Denominators. We can use various balance sheet based denominators to measure enterprise value and common equity value. To measure enterprise value, we use total invested capital as the value driver. Total invested capital is equal to the sum of the book values of debt, preferred stock, and common equity. For common equity values, we measure the book value of equity, sometimes measured on a per share basis. For denominators used in enterprise value and common equity value multiples, we generally subtract total cash and marketable securities from the total invested capital and book value of the equity; however, for per share-based equity multiples we do not.

[10] In some circumstances, it is possible to use operating income as the starting point to measure EBIT, which can exclude certain expenses, gains, and losses that we might eventually exclude through our adjustments. However, it is also possible we might not exclude some of these expenses, gains, and losses.

Changes in Accounting, Correction of Errors, and Restated Financial Statements[11]

A company may change accounting principles voluntarily or because of changes in generally accepted accounting principles (GAAP). A company may also change accounting estimates (for example, the usable life of its assets). Mandatory changes in GAAP typically provide a transition process for companies to change to the new accounting method. Voluntary changes in accounting principles require a retrospective adjustment of the financial statements in the year of the change, while a change in accounting estimate does not.

In a retrospective adjustment, the company adjusts its financial statements for the different accounting principles in prior accounting periods as if that principle had always been used. To make a retrospective adjustment, the company records the cumulative effect of the change in the book value of the assets and liabilities as of the beginning of the first period presented in the financial statements. The company then makes an offsetting adjustment to retained earnings (or to other appropriate components of equity).

If a company identifies an unintentional error made in its financial statements for previous years, the company follows essentially the same process as the one to address a change in accounting principles. If the error or misstatement was intentional, then the company will restate its previous financial statements. Regardless of whether a company provides restated financial statements or corrects errors in its financial statements, we should examine the effect of the restatement or correction on our assessment of the recurring earnings of the company.

Merck & Co., Inc., Measuring the Denominators—Basic Calculations. We illustrate the above basic calculations and adjustments for excess assets using Merck. For enterprise-based multiples, we measure Merck's pre-adjusted unlevered earnings, EBIT, EBITDA, and revenue based on the information in Merck's summarized income statement in Exhibit 14.2. For the common equity-based multiples, we measure Merck's earnings and earnings per share numbers using the numbers reported on Merck's income statement.[12]

We begin by calculating Merck's pre-adjusted unlevered earnings, EBIT, and EBITDA. Merck's unlevered earnings is equal to Net Income Attributable to Merck & Co., Inc. plus Merck's after-tax interest expense. Net income is reported on Merck's income statement, Exhibit 14.2, as $11.920 billion. After-tax interest is equal to interest expense multiplied by one minus Merck's tax rate. The tax rate used to measure after-tax interest is the marginal tax rate for interest, T_{INT}, which is the same tax rate we use to measure interest tax shields and the weighted average cost of capital. Based on the information in the tax reconciliation schedule in Exhibit 14.6, and assuming all of Merck's debt is U.S. debt, Merck's marginal tax rate for interest is 35% (35% federal plus any state income tax rate, which we assume is zero for our illustration given Merck does not report any state tax effect in its reconciliation). Although Merck's interest expense is not shown on its income statement, it is reported on Merck's supplemental schedule for other income, Exhibit 14.3 ($732 million). Based on this information, the calculations of Merck's after-tax interest and pre-adjusted unlevered income are, respectively, as follows.

$$\text{After-tax Interest} = \$476 = (1 - 35\%) \times \$732$$
$$\text{Unlevered Earnings} = \$12{,}396 = \$11{,}920 + \$476$$

For EBIT and EBITDA, we also begin with Net Income Attributable to Merck & Co., Inc. instead of operating income and make specific adjustments to account for the difference between the two starting points later in the chapter. EBIT is equal to Net Income Attributable to Merck & Co., Inc. plus interest expense and income tax expense. Merck's income tax expense is also reported on Merck's income statement, Exhibit 14.2 ($5.349 billion). Depreciation does not appear on Merck's income statement but

[11] An accounting change is a change in an accounting principle or an accounting estimate, or an accounting entity; see *Statement of Financial Accounting Standards No. 154*, "Accounting Changes and Error Corrections: a Replacement of APB Opinion No. 20 and FASB Statement No. 3," May 2005.

[12] Because free cash flow multiples are not commonly used, we do not include them in the Merck illustration.

it does appear on its cash flow statement, Exhibit 14.5 ($6.691 billion). Based on this information, the calculations of Merck's pre-adjusted EBIT and EBITDA are as follows.[13]

$$\text{EBIT} = \$18{,}001 = \$11{,}920 + \$732 + \$5{,}349$$

$$\text{EBITDA} = \$24{,}692 = \$18{,}001 + \$6{,}691$$

It is important to note exactly how we calculated unlevered earnings, EBIT and EBITDA. We did so by starting with net income attributable to Merck and then adjusting it. Keeping this in mind will help you understand the adjustments we make later.

Merck's balance sheet, Exhibit 14.4, provides information regarding its shareholders' equity and total invested capital. Shareholders' equity is available directly from Merck's balance sheet on the line Total Merck & Co., Inc. stockholders' equity ($48.647 billion). Total invested capital is equal to the sum of Merck's debt and shareholders' equity. As seen on Merck's balance sheet, Merck has both short- and long-term debt ($2.704 billion and $18.699 billion, respectively). Based on this information, the calculation of Merck's pre-adjusted total invested capital is as follows.

$$\text{Total Invested Capital} = \$70{,}050 = \$2{,}704 + \$18{,}699 + \$48{,}647$$

Adjusting Market Multiple Inputs for Excess Assets

A company may own an asset that is neither necessary for the company's current operations nor for the execution of its strategy. We call such an asset an excess asset. Since comparable companies typically do not have the same excess assets, and since excess assets are not part of current operations or strategy, we remove the effects of excess assets from a market multiple's numerator and denominator. A common excess asset is excess cash and marketable securities, but companies can have a variety of other excess assets as well. For example, a company may decide that it no longer needs certain assets or parts of the company for its current operations and strategy. Such assets might even involve an entire division.

The value of a company's excess assets is embedded in its value (both the value of the firm and the value of its equity). The company's income statement and cash flow statement may or may not reflect the effect of its excess assets depending on whether those excess assets affect cash flows and income. Even if a company's financial statements reflect the effect of its excess assets, the relation between the value of these excess assets and their effect on the company's financial statements—in other words, the market multiple for the excess assets—is likely to be different from the market multiple for the company's operations (see Valuation in Practice 14.2). If we do not eliminate the effect of the excess assets on the comparable companies' numerators and denominators, we are either assuming that the effect is the same for all comparable companies and the company we are valuing or that the market multiple for the excess assets is the same as the market multiple for the companies' operations. Neither assumption is likely to be correct.

For example, assume a company owns unused land that it does not need for its business. Assume that the land has no effect on the company's income statement and that the company records the land on its balance sheet at its historic cost. Since the value of the company includes the market value of its excess assets, any earnings-based market multiple will be higher than an earnings-based market multiple of the same company without that excess asset. Balance sheet based multiples will be affected as well. Thus, unless the market multiple for the excess asset is the same as the market multiple for the company's operations, including excess assets in measuring a company's market multiples results in market multiples that do not properly reflect the market multiples for its operations.

In general, we adjust for most types of excess assets in the same way. For comparable companies, we eliminate the effect of a company's excess assets on the enterprise value of the firm (or equity) as well as the effect of excess assets on any denominator that we might be using. The adjustment to the numerator should adjust the value on an after-tax basis (as if the company were selling the excess assets). The denominator adjustment may or may not be on an after-tax basis depending on whether the denominator is a before tax or after tax number. We then measure the comparable companies' market multiples using the adjusted numerators and denominators. When it comes to cash, because it is difficult to disentangle

[13] Some analysts also add-back stock-based compensation to measure EBITDA because it is a non-cash expense. Recall from Chapter 12, however, we suggest treating stock-based compensation as a dual transaction—cash assumed to be paid as compensation and employee stock options (or other stock-based compensation securities) issued to the employee for cash.

excess cash from required cash, we usually remove all of the cash when calculating enterprise value and common equity value and remove any interest income attributable to cash from the denominator.

Valuation in Practice 14.2

Microsoft's Market Multiples With and Without Its Excess "Cash" As of June 30, 2015, Microsoft Corporation (Microsoft) reported that it had approximately \$96.5 billion in cash and short-term investments (cash). Microsoft's firm value at this time was approximately \$403.7 billion. Thus, about 24% of Microsoft's value was the value of its cash, most of which was not needed for its operations (0.24 = \$96.5/\$403.7). Its EBITDA for the last 12 months was \$25.2 billion (including interest income from the cash) and its interest income was \$1.5 billion. If we measure Microsoft's EBITDA multiple based on firm value (including cash and interest income of \$1.5 billion), it is 16.0 (16.0 = \$403.7/\$25.2); however, if we measure Microsoft's EBITDA multiple based on enterprise value (excluding cash and interest income of \$1.5 billion), it is 13.0 (13.0 = \$307.2/\$23.7), which is about 20% lower. Thus, in order to use Microsoft as a comparable company, we would eliminate the effect of its large cash holdings on its numerators and denominators of the multiples we calculate. If we do not adjust Microsoft's multiple for its large cash holdings, the resulting multiple will be too high for a comparable company without similar cash holdings.

To value a company with excess assets, we remove all of the effects of excess assets on the numerator and denominator for all of the comparable companies, and we remove the effect of excess assets on the measured denominator of the company we are valuing. We then apply these multiples to the measured denominator of the company we are valuing in order to value the company without its excess assets. To measure the enterprise value of the company, we add the value of the company's excess assets (other than cash and marketable securities) to the value obtained from the multiple calculations. To value the firm, we add the value of all of the cash and marketable securities to the enterprise value.

Valuation Key 14.3

Adjusting market multiple inputs for excess assets requires that we remove the value of the excess assets from the numerators. For flow-based multiples, we must also remove the effect of the excess assets on the flow, appropriately adjusting for taxes where necessary. For balance sheet based multiples, we must remove the reported value of the excess assets from the balance sheet.

Adjusting Merck's Income Statement for the Cash and Cash-Like Assets Subtracted from Firm Value to Measure Enterprise and Total Equity Values. Merck's enterprise value is equal to its firm value minus its cash and cash equivalents, short-term investments, and non-current investments. Since enterprise value excludes the value of these assets, the denominators must also exclude the effects of these assets on the denominators. In order to adjust the earnings-based denominators, we subtract the effect of these assets on income. The only item on Merck's income statement, Exhibit 14.2, which likely relates to these assets is other income. The schedule for other income, Exhibit 14.3, has two items that could relate to income from these assets. The first is interest income (\$266 million) and the second is other, net (\$1.421 billion). It seems clear that interest income is related to these assets, however, since we do not have any additional information about the composition of other, net, we assume this amount is unrelated to these assets.

Based on these assumptions, the only adjustment to make to the earnings-based denominators is to exclude the effects of interest income. In order to exclude the effects of interest income on earnings and unlevered earnings, subtract after-tax interest income, which requires the marginal tax rate for interest income. The footnote for investments indicated that 80%–90% of the cash and investments are held by foreign subsidiaries and would be subject to significant tax payments if repatriated back to the United States. Thus, the U.S. federal rate is unlikely the appropriate marginal tax rate for interest income. The information in the tax reconciliation schedule in Exhibit 14.6 shows that lower average foreign tax rates reduced the 35% federal statutory rate by 8.6%. This information does not provide information about

Merck's marginal (or even average) foreign tax rate but it is the only information available and for this illustration we assume that the tax rate for interest income is 26.4% (0.264 = 0.35 − 0.086) as Merck did not plan to repatriate this income back to the U.S.[14]

The adjustment for the denominators depends on the specific denominator. For earnings and unlevered earnings, we subtract the after-tax effect of the cash on income, $196 million ($196 = (1 − 0.264) × $266). EBIT and EBITDA require a similar adjustment but using pre-tax interest income, $266 million. Shareholders' equity and total invested capital require a different type of adjustment. One way to exclude the effects of these assets is to eliminate these assets on the balance sheet and reduce shareholders' equity. This approach assumes these assets either never existed or they were liquidated at their respective book values and the cash distributed to shareholders. It essentially treats these assets as if they were excess assets. In the following schedule, we summarize all of the effects on the numerators and denominators we use in this chapter as a result of the adjustments made for the cash subtracted to measure enterprise and total equity values.

"Cash"	Total adjustment	Cash and cash equivalents	Short-term investments	Investments	Interest income	Tax effect	Retained Earnings
Enterprise value	−$29,234	−$7,441	−$8,278	−$13,515			
Unlevered earnings	−196				−$266	$70	
EBIT	−266				−266		
EBITDA	−266				−266		
Revenue	$0						
Total invested capital	−29,234						−$29,234
Total equity value	−29,234	−$7,441	−$8,278	−$13,515			
Earnings	−196				−$266	$70	
Book value of equity	−$29,234						−$29,234

Merck's Market Multiples Based on Reported Numbers. We now have sufficient information to measure Merck's market multiples based on its reported numbers adjusted for the cash subtracted to measure enterprise value. We calculate five enterprise value-based multiples—unlevered earnings, EBIT, EBITDA, revenue, and total invested capital. The first four multiples are earnings-based and the last multiple is based on the balance sheet. We also calculate two total equity-based multiples. We show the calculation of the denominator other than revenue (which does not require any adjustment for subtracting cash and investments from enterprise and total equity values) in the following schedule.

Without Adjusting Reported Numbers	Earnings	Unlevered Earnings	EBIT	EBITDA
Merck's reported earnings	$11,920	$11,920	$11,920	$11,920
Interest income	−266	−266	−266	−266
Tax adjustment interest income	70	70		
Interest expense		732	732	732
Tax adjustment interest expense (@ 35% U.S. statutory rate)		−256		
Provision for taxes			5,349	5,349
Depreciation and amortization				6,691
Earnings measure	$11,724	$12,200	$17,735	$24,426

	Total Invested Capital	Shareholders' Equity
Merck's shareholders' equity	$48,647	$48,647
Short- and long-term debt	21,403	
	$70,050	$48,647
Cash and investments	−29,234	−29,234
	$40,816	$19,413

[14] Remember that this example uses data prior to the passage of the 2017 Tax Cuts and Jobs Act.

In Exhibit 14.7, we calculate Merck's market multiples based on the information in the previous schedule, which does not adjust Merck's reported financial statements numbers other than removing cash from enterprise and equity values and the effect of cash on Merck's income statement and balance sheet. For example, based on the above enterprise value and EBITDA, we measure an EBITDA multiple equal to 6.6 (6.6 = 160,312/24,426). As we show in the opening vignette, financial analysts reported a higher EBITDA multiple for Merck (9.0 to 11.2) because they made additional adjustments to Merck's EBITDA denominator, which also required adjustments to its numerator. In the remainder of this chapter we illustrate some of these adjustments. We walk through the numerator and denominator effects for each of these adjustments one at a time. Once we have demonstrated all of the adjustments, we show their impact on Merck's market multiples.

EXHIBIT 14.7 Merck & Co., Inc.—Market Multiples Based on Reported Numbers Adjusted for Cash Subtracted to Measure Enterprise Value and Other Denominator Effects

	2014 Reported Adjusted for Cash & Investments	
	Inputs	**Multiple**
Market multiples based on enterprise value	**$160,312**	
Unlevered earnings (NI + After-tax interest)	12,200	13.1
Earnings before interest and taxes (EBIT)	17,735	9.0
EBITDA	24,426	6.6
Revenue	42,237	3.8
Total invested capital	$ 40,816	3.9
Market multiples based on equity value	**$137,812**	
Earnings	11,724	11.8
Book value shareholders' equity	$ 19,413	7.1

Adjusting for Merck's Net Operating Loss Carryforwards. Another example of an excess asset is net operating loss carryforwards (NOLs). We discussed NOLs in Chapters 3 and 11 in the context of their effect on measuring interest tax shields and free cash flows and their effect on the value of the firm. NOLs are specific to a tax jurisdiction (a country or even state/province within a country). In addition, NOLs may be specific to a part of a company, for example, certain subsidiaries, rather than the consolidated company. As a result, a company may have substantial NOL carryforwards but still pay income taxes because the NOLs cannot shelter income from all parts of the company and from all tax jurisdictions. NOLs can affect the way we measure market multiples due to their potential effect on comparability and their impact on long-run performance. Using pre-tax multiples (EBIT, EBITDA, and revenue) does not eliminate the effect of NOLs.

We typically treat NOL carryforwards as an excess asset to increase comparability and measure long-run performance. In order to calculate the market multiples for a company with NOLs, we remove all of the effects of the NOLs on the numerator and denominator. In order to adjust the denominator, we restate the company's income taxes to what they would be if the company did not have NOLs. To adjust the numerator, we subtract the value of the NOLs from enterprise value and common equity value. As we discuss in Chapters 3 and 11, the discount rate for the expected cash flows from the NOL carryforwards is related to the company's asset or unlevered cost of capital, for the underlying risk of these cash flows depends in part on the cash flows generated by the company's assets.

Companies record the potential tax benefits from NOL carryforwards as a deferred tax asset, ignoring the time-value-of-money. If management does not expect to be able to use all of the NOLs because the company's expected taxable income is lower than the amount of the NOLs, the company reduces the value of its NOL deferred tax asset for the amount of the asset that it may not be able to capture. The company records this reduction to the deferred tax asset by creating a **valuation allowance**. A valuation allowance is a contra-asset account and essentially records the reduction in the deferred tax assets in such circumstances. While neither a probabilistic (expected value) nor a present value calculation, the valuation allowance can provide information that may be useful in valuing a company's NOL carryforwards (see Valuation in Practice 14.3).

Merck's NOL carryforward footnote states that it has NOL carryforwards in both U.S. and various foreign jurisdictions. Merck has $203 million of NOL carryforwards in foreign jurisdictions but it offset the deferred tax asset for these NOLs (and other foreign tax issues) with a valuation allowance of $265 million. The valuation allowance suggests that Merck has not and does not expect to benefit from the $203 million of NOLs in foreign jurisdictions. Based on this assumption, no adjustment is necessary to either the market multiple numerators or denominators for the foreign NOLs. This is not the case for Merck's $175 million of U.S. NOL carryforwards that it expects to fully utilize. We decrease the numerator by the value of Merck's U.S. NOLs and decrease any after-tax denominator by eliminating the NOL tax benefit included in income.

Net Operating Loss Carryforwards

The Company has net operating loss ("NOL") carryforwards in several jurisdictions. As of December 31, 2014, $203 million of deferred taxes on NOL carryforwards relate to foreign jurisdictions, none of which are individually significant. Valuation allowances of $265 million have been established on these foreign NOL carryforwards and other foreign deferred tax assets. In addition, the Company has approximately $175 million of deferred tax assets relating to various U.S. tax credit carryforwards and NOL carryforwards, all of which are expected to be fully utilized prior to expiry.

In our illustration, we assume that Merck benefited from a $100 million tax reduction from the U.S. NOLs in the current year, and that Merck expects to utilize approximately $100 million of the remaining $175 million amount in 2015 and the remainder in 2016. Using Merck's unlevered cost of capital of 8.5% to discount its expected tax benefits from the NOLs results in a $156 million[15] valuation of the NOLs as of our valuation date. To adjust the numerators, we subtract this amount from both enterprise value and equity value. For earnings and unlevered earnings, we subtract the $100 million tax benefit this year; however, we make no adjustment to the EBIT, EBITDA, and revenue denominators because these denominators are not affected by income taxes. For shareholders' equity and total invested capital, we eliminate the $175 million deferred tax associated with the NOLs[16]—which has a current, $100 million, and non-current portion $75 million—against retained earnings. In the following schedule we summarize all of the effects on the numerators and denominators from the adjustments made for NOLs.

Net Operating Loss Carryforwards	Total Adjustment	Value of NOLs	Tax Effect	Retained Earnings
Enterprise value	−$156	−$156		
Unlevered earnings	−100		−$100	
EBIT	0			
EBITDA	0			
Revenue	0			
Total invested capital	−175			−$175
Total equity value	−156	−$156		
Earnings	−100		−$100	
Book value of equity	−$175			−$175

Valuation Key 14.4

We can treat NOL carryforwards as an excess asset to increase the comparability of our comparable companies and the company we are valuing. We would restate a comparable company's income taxes to what they would be if the company did not have NOL carryforwards, and we would subtract the value of the NOL carryforwards when calculating the enterprise value and common equity value.

[15] $156 = $100.0/1.085 + $75/1.085^2.

[16] Recall from Chapter 3, that at the time (2014), deferred income taxes were shown on the balance sheet as either a net deferred tax current asset or liability and a net deferred non-current asset or liability. Merck has a net deferred tax current asset and a net deferred tax non-current liability. The adjustment reduces Merck's net deferred tax current asset by $100 million and increases its net deferred tax non-current liability by $75 million.

Valuation in Practice 14.3

At the end of 2014, Calix, Inc. had a common equity value of roughly $380 million. At that time it had NOLs in various tax jurisdictions that had a potential tax benefit of around $670 million. If the company were to realize the tax benefits from these NOLs in the near-term, then a large part of its equity value would be composed of the value of the NOLs. According to the company, however, the value of its NOLs is small because the company expects to receive these benefits in the distant future or not at all.

> Since inception, we have incurred operating losses and accordingly have federal and state net operating loss carry-forwards of $549.1 million and $119.1 million, respectively, as of December 31, 2014. The U.S. federal net operating loss carryforwards will expire at various dates beginning in 2019 and through 2033, if not utilized. The state net operating loss carryforwards will expire at various dates beginning in 2015 and through 2033, if not utilized. . . . These two items account for the bulk of our net deferred tax asset of $212.9 million as of December 31, 2014. Excluding our foreign operations, we have recorded a full valuation allowance against the net deferred assets at each balance sheet date presented. We believe that based on the available evidence and history of operating losses, it is more likely than not that we will not be able to utilize all of our deferred assets before expiration. . . .

Source: Calix, Inc. is a leading global provider of broadband communications access systems and software for fiber- and copper-based network architectures. Calix, Inc. 2014 10-K filing.

14.5 ADJUSTING MARKET MULTIPLE INPUTS FOR NON-RECURRING ITEMS

LO5 Make adjustments to market multiple numerators and denominators

We discussed transitory shocks and non-recurring items in Chapter 13 at a conceptual level. If a company has a large, for example, negative non-recurring item, then the multiple is likely to be large relative to the correctly measured multiple that captures a company's long-term future performance. The opposite occurs for a positive non-recurring item.

By definition, a one-time past expense that results in a one-time negative (or positive) effect on earnings or free cash flows has no effect on a company's future performance. Non-recurring items are similar, but not as exact as the one-time effect we just described. In general, we remove the effects of all non-recurring items on a market multiple's denominator, appropriately adjusting for income taxes where necessary. Non-recurring items typically require an adjustment to the denominator but not to the numerator because we normally measure the multiple subsequent to the disclosure of the non-recurring item. As such, any impact on value will already be reflected in the values used to measure the numerators.

In order to identify non-recurring items, we begin by reviewing the company's income statement, footnotes, the management discussion and analysis (MD&A), conference call presentations, company press releases, and analysts' reports. One challenge with trying to identify non-recurring items is that companies are not required to identify something that is non-recurring.

Once we identify a potential non-recurring item, we then decide whether or not, or how much of the item, is non-recurring. For example, we might think that a restructuring charge is non-recurring, but this may or may not be the case. We make the non-recurring assessment by analyzing the company's historical performance; does it usually have some type of restructuring charge? We may conclude that only part or none of the restructuring charge is non-recurring. Another example of a potential non-recurring item is the write-down of an asset or impairment charge. We might not always think of asset impairments as being non-recurring. For example, retail store chains and restaurants often write down the values of underperforming locations. Continuing impairments may suggest deterioration in the business plan of the retailer and that future impairments may be expected.

Valuation Key 14.5

In general, adjusting market multiple inputs for non-recurring items does not require an adjustment to market multiple numerators. For flow-based denominators, we remove the effect of the non-recurring item on the flow and appropriately adjust for taxes where necessary. For balance sheet based multiples (such as total invested capital or the book value of shareholders' equity), no adjustment is normally made.

To value a company using market multiples, we remove the effects of the non-recurring items on the denominators of the comparable companies and the company we are valuing. We then apply the market multiples of the comparable companies to the adjusted measure of the denominator of the company we are valuing. Usually, no further adjustments are necessary. Generally, no adjustment is made to the denominators for balance sheet based multiples. However, another approach is to adjust shareholders' equity or total invested capital for the effect of the non-recurring item. Whether to include these adjustments or not depends on the particular circumstances. In this chapter, we will make these adjustments to illustrate them but note that we often do not make these adjustments to the balance sheet based denominators.

Restructuring Charges

Although **restructuring charges** do not have a specific definition, they are generally charges (expenses on the income statement) that result from certain types of events or transactions that consolidate or relocate operations, or abandon or dispose of assets. Examples of such events or transactions include a change in the company's strategic plan, response to declines in demand, or response to increasing costs. Certain types of restructuring charges, for example, employee termination costs, are expensed and recorded as liabilities and charged to operations when the company commits to a restructuring plan, while other types of restructuring charges may not be recognized until actually incurred. Restructuring charges are generally not tax deductible until actually incurred and deferred income tax assets are recorded until they become tax deductible. Restructuring charges are a common type of non-recurring charge, although in some circumstances they may be considered to be partially recurring if they are expected to repeat in the future. For example, for a company performing poorly, they may go through a sequence of restructuring activities in which case the initial restructuring charge may be followed by others.

Valuation in Practice 14.4

Coca-Cola Enterprises Inc.'s Write-Down of Its Franchise License Intangible Assets—A Non-Recurring Item In 2006, Coca-Cola Enterprises Inc. wrote down its franchise license intangible assets, which it described as follows:

We do not amortize our goodwill and franchise license intangible assets. Instead, we test these assets for impairment annually (as of the last fiscal day of October), or more frequently if events or changes in circumstances indicate they may be impaired. . . .

We performed our 2006 annual impairment tests of goodwill and franchise license intangible assets as of October 27, 2006. . . . The results of the impairment test of our North American franchise license intangible assets indicated that their estimated fair value was less than their carrying amount. As such, we recorded a $2.9 billion ($1.8 billion net of tax, or $3.80 per common share) non-cash impairment charge to reduce the carrying amount of these assets to their estimated fair value. . . .

($ in millions)	2004	2005	2006
Revenues	$18,190	$18,743	$19,804
Cost of sales	−10,771	−11,185	−11,986
Selling and administrative expenses	−5,983	−6,127	−6,391
Franchise impairment charge			−2,922
Operating (loss) income	$ 1,436	$ 1,431	−$ 1,495
Interest and other, net	−618	−641	−623
Income (loss) before income taxes	$ 818	$ 790	−$ 2,118
Income tax expense (benefit)	−222	−276	975
Net income (loss)	$ 596	$ 514	−$ 1,143

continued

continued from previous page

This write-down is a potential non-recurring item. The factors the company attributes to this write-down are a reduction in the expected growth rate, increased costs, pricing pressures, and increased interest rates. We would consider these factors to decide the amount of this write-down that we would classify as non-recurring; for example, will the slowing growth rate and shrinking margins stabilize or continue to worsen?

Source: Coca-Cola Enterprises, Inc. 2006 Form 10-K, Consolidated Statement of Operations and Footnote 1—Significant Accounting Policies—Goodwill and Franchise License Intangible Assets.

Adjusting for Merck's Restructuring Charges. Merck's income statement (Exhibit 14.2) reports restructuring charges of $1.013 billion; however, Merck had other restructuring charges recorded within other line items on Merck's income statement. An excerpt from Merck's restructuring charge footnote summarizes these charges.

Restructuring Charges

In 2013, the Company announced a global restructuring program (the "2013 Restructuring Program") as part of a global initiative to sharpen its commercial and research and development focus. As part of the program, the Company expects to reduce its total workforce by approximately 8,500 positions. . . . The Company will also reduce its global real estate footprint and continue to improve the efficiency of its manufacturing and supply network. The Company recorded total pretax costs of $1.2 billion in both 2014 and 2013 related to this restructuring program. Since inception of the 2013 Restructuring Program through December 31, 2014, Merck has recorded total pretax accumulated costs of approximately $2.5 billion . . .

In 2010, subsequent to the Merck and Schering-Plough Corporation ("Schering-Plough") merger (the "Merger"), the Company commenced actions under a global restructuring program (the "Merger Restructuring Program") designed to streamline the cost structure of the combined company. Further actions under this program were initiated in 2011. The actions under this program primarily reflect the elimination of positions in sales, administrative and headquarters organizations, as well as from the sale or closure of certain manufacturing and research and development sites and the consolidation of office facilities. The Company recorded total pretax costs of $730 million in 2014, $1.1 billion in 2013 and $951 million in 2012 related to this restructuring program. Since inception of the Merger Restructuring Program through December 31, 2014, Merck has recorded total pretax accumulated costs of approximately $7.9 billion and eliminated approximately 28,410 positions comprised of employee separations, as well as the elimination of contractors and vacant positions. . . .

Year Ended December 31, 2014	Separation Costs	Accelerated Depreciation	Other	Total
2013 restructuring program				
Materials and production		$204	$ 23	$ 227
Marketing and administrative		142	3	145
Research and development		273	9	282
Restructuring costs	$566		28	594
	566	619	63	1,248
Merger restructuring program				
Materials and production		225	30	255
Marketing and administrative		56		55
Research and development			−1	1
Restructuring costs	108		311	419
	108	281	341	730
	$674	$900	$404	$1,978

Merck's footnote reports that it had $1.978 billion in restructuring charges in 2014. Merck also discloses the income statement line items against which Merck recorded those charges. Merck's footnote also indicates that Merck had restructuring charges in previous years and is likely to have some restructuring charges at least in the near future; thus, one is faced with deciding what part, if any, of Merck's restructuring charges should be treated as non-recurring. For the purpose of our illustration, we assume that all of Merck's restructuring charges are non-recurring.

The restructuring charges reduced Merck's pre-tax income by $1.978 billion. We measure the income tax effect of those charges using Merck's tax reconciliation schedule (Exhibit 14.6). Based on the tax reconciliation schedule, we know that the income tax effect of the restructuring charges is equal to the 35% statutory income tax rate less the $289 million (1.7%) increase shown in the reconciliation from the statutory rate to the effective rate. The $289 million increase in the taxes shown on the tax reconciliation schedule indicates that not all of the restructuring charges will be tax deductible at the statutory rate. The resulting income tax effect of the restructuring charges is equal to $403 million (0.35 × $1,978 − $289), a marginal tax rate of around 20% (0.20 = $403/$1,978).

Since the value of the restructuring charges is already reflected in Merck's value, we do not adjust the numerators but we do adjust the denominators. For earnings and unlevered earnings, we add back the after-tax effect of the restructuring charge, $1.575 billion ($1.575 = $1.978 − $0.403), while we add back the entire $1.978 billion to adjust EBIT and EBITDA. Revenue requires no adjustment because the restructuring charges did not affect revenue (it was recorded in various expenses). Based on other information in its 10-K report, we assume that none of the 2014 costs have been paid in cash as of the end of 2014. For shareholders' equity and total invested capital, we eliminate the entire after-tax effect of the restructuring charges against retained earnings because none of the restructuring charges are paid in cash.[17] Had Merck paid some of the restructuring charges in cash, then we would only eliminate the non-cash part of the restructuring charge. In the following schedule we summarize all of the effects on the numerators and denominators from the adjustments made for restructuring charges.

Restructuring Charges	Total Adjustment	Materials and Production	Marketing and Administration	Research and Development	Restructuring Charge	Tax Effect
Enterprise value	$ 0					
Unlevered earnings	1,575	$482	$200	$283	$1,013	−$403
EBIT	1,978	482	200	283	1,013	
EBITDA	1,978	482	200	283	1,013	
Revenue	0					
Total invested capital	1,575	482	200	283	1,013	−403
Total equity value	0					
Earnings	1,575	482	200	283	1,013	−403
Book value of equity	$1,575	$482	$200	$283	$1,013	−$403

REVIEW EXERCISE 14.2

Measuring Market Multiple Denominators

Use the information from Review Exercise 14.1 and the following information to adjust the company's financial statements similar to the adjustments just discussed for the effects related to its cash balance and for its non-recurring items. In Year 2, the company incurred a non-recurring operating expense of $4,000, which is included in operating expenses. Also, using the adjusted financial statements, calculate the company's multiples of enterprise value to unlevered earnings, EBIT, EBITDA, and revenue multiples, as well as its P/E multiple. *Hint*: Calculate unlevered earnings, EBIT, and EBITDA as in Review Exercise 14.1 using the adjusted financial statements.

Solution on page 730.

Impairment Charges

Impairment charges result from writing down the balance sheet or book value of a long-lived asset because the book value of the asset is greater than its recoverable amount. U.S. GAAP requires companies

[17] As we indicated previously, we do not often make adjustments to shareholders' equity and total invested capital for restructuring charges, but said we would illustrate those adjustments. In this case, the adjustments to shareholders' equity and total invested capital would be the $1.575 billion after tax effect of the restructuring charge, which would increase retained earnings.

to determine if an impairment charge is necessary by comparing the undiscounted value of the expected cash flows from the asset to the asset's book value. When the book value of the asset is greater than the undiscounted value, the impairment charge is equal to the difference between the fair value of the asset (that can be measured by the discounted value of the cash flows) and the asset's book value. A company must disclose the amount of the impairment charge, the method used to measure the value of the asset, a description of the asset that is impaired and the events and circumstances resulting in the impairment. Impairment charges must be reported as part of the company's continuing operations. Like restructuring charges, impairment charges are a common type of non-recurring charge, although they may also be considered recurring if they are expected to repeat in the future.

Adjusting for Merck's Impairment Charges. Recall the operating section of Merck's cash flow statement (Exhibit 14.5) shows an adjustment (an add back) for intangible asset impairment of $1.222 billion, which differs from the restructuring charges shown on the income statement. We extracted part of Merck's footnote that discusses the impairment charge.

Goodwill and Other Intangibles

In 2014, the additions to goodwill in the Pharmaceutical segment primarily resulted from the acquisition of Idenix and the reductions resulted both from the sale of MCC . . . Also, during the third quarter of 2014, the Company recorded an impairment charge on the goodwill related to the Supera joint venture.

The Company performed its most recent annual impairment test as of October 1, 2014 and concluded that goodwill was not impaired. During 2014 and 2013, the Company recorded impairment charges related to marketed products of $1.072 billion and $486 million, respectively, within Material and production costs. . . . During 2014, sales of these products were adversely affected by loss of market share or patient treatment delays in markets anticipating the availability of new therapeutic options. . . .

During 2014, the Company recorded $49 million of IPR&D impairment charges within Research and development expenses primarily as a result of changes in cash flow assumptions for certain compounds . . .

Merck's footnote reports that it recorded impairment charges of $1.072 billion in material and production costs, $0.049 billion in research and development costs, and the remainder in goodwill. As with its restructuring charge, Merck indicates that it had impairment charges in 2014, so again, one is faced with deciding what part, if any, of Merck's impairment charges should be treated as non-recurring. For the purposes of our illustration, we assume that all of Merck's impairment charges are non-recurring.

The impairment charges reduced Merck's pre-tax income by $1.222 billion. We measure the income tax effect of the charges using Merck's tax reconciliation schedule (Exhibit 14.6). Based on the tax reconciliation schedule, we know that the income tax effect of the impairment charges is equal to the 35% statutory income tax rate less the $148 million (0.9%) increase in the taxes shown on the tax reconciliation schedule. The $148 million increase in the taxes shown on the tax reconciliation schedule indicates that not all of the impairment charges will be tax deductible at the statutory tax rate. The resulting income tax effect of the impairment charges is equal to $280 million (0.35 × $1,222 − $148), a marginal tax rate of around 23% (0.23 = $280/$1,222).

Like restructuring charges, since the value of the impairment charges is already reflected in Merck's value, we do not need to adjust the numerators. For earnings and unlevered earnings, we add back the after-tax effect of the impairment charges, $942 million ($942 = $1,222 − $280), while we add back the entire $1.222 billion to adjust EBIT and EBITDA. Revenue requires no adjustment because the impairment charges did not affect revenue. Impairment charges are non-cash charges, and we assume the income tax effect is a deferred income tax. Like restructuring charges, it is a judgment call as to whether to remove the effect of the impairment charge on shareholders' equity and total invested capital, but we often do not make those adjustments. However, as in the case of restructuring charges, we illustrate what those adjustments would be. For shareholders' equity and total invested capital, we eliminate the entire after-tax effect of the impairment charges against retained earnings. In the following schedule we summarize all of the effects on the numerators and denominators from the adjustments made for impairment charges.

Impairment Charges	Total Adjustment	Materials and Production	Research and Development	Other (Income) and Expense	Tax Effect	Retained Earnings
Enterprise value	$ 0					
Unlevered earnings	942	$1,072	$49	$101	−$280	
EBIT	1,222	1,072	49	101		
EBITDA	1,222	1,072	49	101		
Revenue	0					
Total invested capital	942					$942
Total equity value	0					
Earnings	942	$1,072	$49	$101	−$280	
Book value of equity	$ 942					$942

Gains and Losses from Debt Redemptions and Repurchases

Gains and losses from debt redemption and repurchases occur when a company redeems or repurchases its debt before it matures. The difference between the book value of the debt and the amount paid to redeem or repurchase the debt is the gain or loss. Other types of gains and losses on the redemption of securities often have adjustments similar to gains and losses from debt redemptions.

Adjusting for Merck's Loss on Debt Redemption. Based on Merck's other income schedule (Exhibit 14.3), we know that it either repurchased or redeemed a debt security with a book value that was less than the amount for which it was redeemed. As a result, Merck recorded a loss on the extinguishment of debt for $628 million. The loss reduced Merck's pre-tax income by $628 million. We have no additional information on Merck's tax reconciliation schedule so we assume that this loss is tax deductible at Merck's marginal tax rate of 35%. Since the loss is already reflected in Merck's value, we do not adjust the numerators. For earnings and unlevered earnings, we add back the after-tax effect of the loss on debt redemption, $408 million ($408 = $628 × [1 − 0.35]), while we add back the entire $628 million to adjust EBIT and EBITDA. Revenue requires no adjustment because the loss did not affect revenue. We make no adjustment for shareholders' equity or total invested capital because we assume this is a cash transaction. In the following schedule we summarize all of the effects on the numerators and denominators from the adjustments made for the loss on debt redemption.

Loss on Debt Redemption	Total Adjustment	Other Income	Tax Effect
Enterprise value	$ 0		
Unlevered earnings	408	$628	−$220
EBIT	628	628	
EBITDA	628	628	
Revenue	0		
Total invested capital	0		
Total equity value	0		
Earnings	408	$628	−$220
Book value of equity	$ 0		

14.6 ADJUSTING MARKET MULTIPLE INPUTS FOR PARTIALLY OWNED COMPANIES

Partially owned companies include both consolidated subsidiaries for which the parent company does not own 100% of the equity—called noncontrolling interests or sometimes minority interests—as well as unconsolidated equity investments of the parent—called unconsolidated affiliates. The adjustments we make for these two types of partially owned companies are different and, to some extent, the opposite of one another. The adjustments for noncontrolling interests involve including the portion of the equity not owned by the parent in the numerators and denominators. The adjustments for unconsolidated affiliates, on the other hand, involve excluding the investment and the income from the numerators and denominators.

Noncontrolling Interest (Minority Interest)

Many companies invest in, and control, other companies by purchasing and holding a majority of their stock. If a company (which we will call the P Company) owns more than 50% of another company (which we will call the S Company), P Company generally consolidates S Company's financial statements because S is a **subsidiary** of the P Company. **Noncontrolling interest** on a company's consolidated financial statements represents the ownership interest in the subsidiary's stock that is not owned by the parent company; thus, we generally observe minority interest or noncontrolling interest line items on a company's financial statements any time the company owns at least 50% but less than 100% of the stock of a subsidiary. Owners of the S Company's shares other than the P Company are called **minority shareholders**.

In the consolidation process, the parent company (P Company) that owns less than 100%—say, z%—of its subsidiary (S Company) adds 100% of S Company's assets to its assets, 100% of S Company's liabilities to its liabilities, and z% of S Company's stockholders' equity to its equity. The consolidation process, however, is incomplete at this point, for P Company's consolidated assets (which include 100% of S Company's assets) are greater than its consolidated liabilities and shareholders' equity (which include 100% of S Company's liabilities but only z% of its shareholders' equity). This difference is equal to (1 − z)% of S Company's shareholders' equity. The company records this amount as a noncontrolling interest and presents it on its balance sheet as a separate line item as part of consolidated shareholders' equity.[18]

When less than 100% of a subsidiary is acquired, the parent company records the subsidiary's assets and liabilities at fair value as of the purchase date, and it records goodwill if the fair value of the assets minus the fair value of the liabilities is less than the purchase price paid. The parent company records the noncontrolling interest in that subsidiary without any adjustments for the difference between book value and fair value or for the goodwill implied in the transaction. Thus, the noncontrolling interest on P Company's consolidated balance sheet represents the claims of the minority shareholders on the book value of S Company's shareholders' equity.

In the consolidation process for the income statement, P Company adds 100% of S Company's revenues to its own revenues and 100% of S Company's expenses to its own expenses. The resulting earnings, therefore, include 100% of the earnings of S Company even though the P Company only owns—and thus only has claims on—z% of S Company's earnings. To adjust the consolidated earnings for S Company's earnings, on which P Company has no claims, P Company records a reduction (or allocation) of the profit or loss of (1 – z)% of S Company's after tax net income or loss for the noncontrolling interest in the earnings of S Company. P Company's consolidated net income is equal to its own net income from its businesses plus z% of S Company's after tax income. Thus, the noncontrolling interest on P Company's consolidated income statement represents the claims of the minority shareholders on the net income of S Company.

Since companies typically do not present the financial statements of their subsidiaries, we generally do not have sufficient information to remove (1 − z)% of S Company's operations from every line item of P Company's consolidated financial statements. Thus, to adjust a company's market multiple denominators, we normally remove the minority interest from the income statement, balance sheet, and cash flow statement. By this, we mean that we measure the income statement and cash flow statement as if the parent owns 100% of the subsidiary, and on the balance sheet, the noncontrolling interest will be treated as part of shareholders' equity. This is usually a straightforward task. When we do this, however, we implicitly assume that both the subsidiary and the parent should have similar market multiples. In some circumstances, it may be better to remove the subsidiary's impact from every line item on the balance sheet, income statement, and cash flow statement (as if the subsidiary was not owned by the parent) in order to measure the parent's value without the subsidiary. We would make this adjustment if we conclude that the multiples of the subsidiary and of the parent are different and if the parent's multiple is the appropriate multiple to use for valuing another company. Unfortunately, we seldom have sufficient information from public filings to make this kind of adjustment.

The parent company's market value does not include the market value of the minority interest claims. Thus, to adjust a company's market multiple numerators, we add the market value of the minority interest shareholders' stock in the subsidiary to the numerator because the value driver includes 100% of the subsidiary's revenue, expenses, assets, and liabilities. This adjustment is straightforward if the subsidiary's stock is publicly traded (so that its market value is equal to the subsidiary's price per share multiplied by the shares outstanding that are not owned by the parent company). If the subsidiary is not publicly traded, valuing the minority interest can be complex because we often have limited information for the subsidiary. We can use

[18] See FASB ACS Topic 810, Consolidation; formerly, Statement of Financial Accounting Standard No. 160, "Noncontrolling Interests in Consolidated Financial Statements," December, 2007.

both the available information on the subsidiary and the valuation methods in this book, such as an equity-based market multiple, to value the subsidiary's common equity.

Let's assume that the subsidiary is in the same line of business as the parent company and that as a consequence, it should have a similar multiple. In this case, in order to value the company using multiples, we adjust for the effects of the minority interests in the numerator and denominator of all of the comparable companies that have minority interests (effectively measuring the multiples as if every subsidiary is 100% owned by the parent) and similarly adjust the relevant denominator measures of the company we are valuing. In other words, we add the value of the minority interest position to the numerator, and we include the relevant income or cash flow or equity investment that is attributable to the minority shareholders in the denominator. We then apply these multiples to the relevant measure of the denominator of the company we are valuing, including the value of the minority interest income or cash flow the company does not own. Then to measure the enterprise value of the company we are valuing that does not own 100% of all its subsidiaries, we subtract the value of the minority interest claims.

Adjusting for Merck's Noncontrolling Interests (Minority Interests). Information about a company's noncontrolling interests appears in its income statement and balance sheet (see Exhibits 14.2 and 14.4). The line item in the income statement represents the allocation of income of certain Merck consolidated subsidiaries for which Merck owns less than 100%. The line item in the equity portion of Merck's balance sheet represents the equity of those subsidiaries not owned by Merck. Merck provides some additional information about these noncontrolling interests in its footnotes.

> **Noncontrolling Interests**
> Net income attributable to noncontrolling interests was $14 million in 2014, $113 million in 2013 and $131 million in 2012. . . .

Recall from the previous discussion, the value of the noncontrolling interests is not reflected in Merck's enterprise value but 100% of the revenues, expenses, assets and liabilities are. Thus, we add the value of the noncontrolling interests to Merck's enterprise value and equity. These interests are relatively small for Merck so Merck does not provide detailed information for them. In this illustration, we use a P/E multiple of 20 to value the noncontrolling interests, which is in the range of multiples for companies similar to Merck. The resulting valuation is net income of $14 million multiplied by 20, or $280 million.

As we did for other income statement line items presented on an after-tax basis, for all of the earnings multiples (earnings, unlevered earnings, EBIT and EBITDA), we add back the (after-tax) noncontrolling interest of $14 million.[19] Revenue requires no adjustment because the deduction did not affect revenue. We reclassify the noncontrolling interest on the balance sheet to equity, which increases total invested capital and shareholders' equity by that amount, $144 million. In the following schedule we summarize all of the effects on the numerators and denominators from the adjustments made for noncontrolling interests.

Noncontrolling Interests	Total Adjustment	Value of NC Interests	Noncontrolling Interests	Common Equity
Enterprise value	$280	$280		
Unlevered earnings	14		$14	
EBIT	14		14	
EBITDA	14		14	
Revenue	0			
Total invested capital	144			$144
Total equity value	280	$280		
Earnings	14		$14	
Book value of equity	$144			$144

Unconsolidated Affiliates

If the P Company owns an investment in another company (which we will call the Z Company), and does not consolidate Z Company's financial statements with its own financial statements, Z Company is an

[19] As before, remember, we calculated EBIT as net income − interest income + interest expense + provision for taxes and EBITDA as EBIT + depreciation and amortization. Had we instead calculated EBIT and EBITDA starting from Income before taxes, the adjustment for noncontrolling interests would be different.

unconsolidated affiliate. Typically, companies consolidate investments in other companies if they own more than 50% of a company; thus, the difference between a consolidated subsidiary and an unconsolidated affiliate is typically the amount of ownership interest.

On a company's financial statements, line items related to unconsolidated subsidiaries or unconsolidated affiliates indicate that the company has equity investments in other companies (affiliates) that it does not consolidate. The most likely—but not the only—reason the company chooses not to consolidate an equity investment is that it has a 50% or less ownership interest in that company.[20] The effect of unconsolidated affiliates on the company's income statement represents an allocation of the affiliate's income based on the company's equity ownership; that is, it is the affiliate's net income multiplied by the company's percentage ownership of that affiliate. Companies normally use this treatment when they own between 20% and 50% of a company.

Since the company's income statement does not reflect the revenues or expenses of the affiliate (the only effect on the income statement is the one line item that represents the company's allocation of the affiliate's net income or loss, normally presented net of tax), we cannot measure the unlevered earnings, EBIT, or EBITDA of the affiliate without supplemental information about the unconsolidated affiliate. Therefore, we treat unconsolidated affiliates in a way that is similar to how we treat excess assets.

The value of a company's unconsolidated affiliates is embedded in its value (in both the enterprise value and the value of its equity). We remove the value of the unconsolidated affiliates from the enterprise value and the common equity value. We also remove the effects of the unconsolidated affiliates on the company's income statement and cash flows—as well as such balance sheet denominators as total invested capital or shareholder's equity.

To value a company using multiples with unconsolidated affiliates, we remove all of the effects of the unconsolidated affiliates from the numerator and the denominator for all of the comparable companies and from the relevant measures of the denominators of the company we are valuing. We then apply these multiples to the denominator measures of the company we are valuing in order to value the company without its unconsolidated affiliates. To measure the enterprise value of the firm, we add the value of the company's unconsolidated affiliates.[21]

Valuation Key 14.6

Adjusting market multiple inputs for unconsolidated affiliates requires the removal of the value of the unconsolidated affiliates from the numerators. For flow-based multiples, we remove the after-tax effect of the unconsolidated affiliates on the flow. For balance sheet based multiples, we remove the book value of the unconsolidated affiliates from the balance sheet.

Adjusting for Merck's Unconsolidated Affiliates. Merck has various investments in unconsolidated affiliates (which include joint ventures). In mid-2014, Merck's equity investment in one of its relatively large joint ventures, AstraZeneca, was sold. We discuss this transaction later in the chapter when we discuss divestitures. In this section, we focus on Merck's remaining unconsolidated affiliates, which were not sold in 2014. Below is an extract of Merck's unconsolidated affiliates footnote that summarizes the effect of these investments.

Equity Income from Affiliates

On June 30, 2014, AstraZeneca Group Plc ("AstraZeneca") exercised its option to purchase Merck's interest in Merck's joint venture with AstraZeneca. As a result of AstraZeneca's exercise of its option, the Company no longer records equity income from AstraZeneca . . . Equity income from affiliates, which reflects the performance of the Company's joint ventures and other equity method affiliates, declined 36% in 2014 to $257 million compared with 2013. The decline was driven primarily by the termination of the Company's relationship with AstraZeneca.

[20] Under certain limited conditions, a company does not have to consolidate an equity investment of greater than 50% ownership—such as lack of control of the company because of regulation or government control.

[21] If we ever need to measure the income tax effects from unconsolidated affiliates, it is useful to know that when one corporation receives dividends from another it does not control, 50% of those dividends are not taxable (the so-called dividends received exclusion). If a company faces a marginal tax rate of 25%, then the effective tax on income from an unconsolidated affiliate would be 12.5% ($0.125 = 0.5 \times 0.25$).

Joint Ventures and Other Equity Method Affiliates—Equity Income from Affiliates (Details) (USD $)			
In Millions	Dec. 31, 2012	Dec. 31, 2013	Dec. 31, 2014
Equity income from affiliates—Other	$ 21	$ 52	$ 65
Equity income from affiliates—AstraZeneca LP	621	352	192
Equity income from affiliates	$642	$404	$257

Joint Ventures and Other Equity Method Affiliates (Excluding AstraZeneca)			
In Millions	Dec. 31, 2012	Dec. 31, 2013	Dec. 31, 2014
Sales (total)	$1,295	$1,326	$1,370
Materials and production costs	573	581	577
Other expense, net	705	691	641
Income before taxes (total)	$ 17	$ 54	$ 152

Looking at the table we see that the equity income from affiliates excluding AstraZeneca is $65 million. We essentially treat unconsolidated affiliates as an excess asset and subtract their value from the numerator. We again use a P/E multiple of 20 in this illustration as we did for the noncontrolling interests. The resulting valuation is based on the $65 million of net income multiplied by 20 or $1.3 billion.

As we did for other income statement line items presented on an after-tax basis, for all of the earnings multiples (earnings, unlevered earnings, EBIT and EBITDA), we subtract the after-tax effect of the income of $65 million. Revenue requires no adjustment because the equity income net of tax did not affect revenue. We write off the book value of the unconsolidated affiliates against shareholders' equity and total invested capital to eliminate it from Merck's balance sheet. Merck discloses the book value of this unconsolidated affiliate as $382 in Other Assets. In the following schedule we summarize all of the effects on the numerators and denominators from the adjustments made for the unconsolidated affiliates.[22]

Unconsolidated Affiliates	Total Adjustment	Value of Unconsolidated Affiliates	Equity Income from Affiliates	Retained Earnings
Enterprise value	−$1,300	−$1,300		
Unlevered earnings	−65		−$65	
EBIT	−65		−65	
EBITDA	−65		−65	
Revenue	0			
Total invested capital	−382			−$382
Total equity value	−1,300	−$1,300		
Earnings	−65		−$65	
Book value of equity	−$ 382			−$382

14.7 ADJUSTING MARKET MULTIPLE INPUTS FOR CORPORATE TRANSACTIONS

Corporate transactions are transactions in which a company buys (acquires) another company or when the company sells (divests) one of the companies it owns. The effect of a corporate transaction is reflected in the market value of the company by the date the acquisition or divestiture transaction closes, and possibly earlier if the company announces the transaction earlier and the probability that it will close is very high. Accounting records, however, reflect the revenues and expenses of the company acquired or divested for the part of the fiscal year that the company was owned. As a result, market multiple denominators do not reflect the company's long-term performance in a year a corporate transaction occurred.

To align the denominators with the long-run performance of the company for a merger or acquisition, we include the acquired company's revenues and expenses for that part of the year prior to the date the transaction closed. Conversely, to align the denominators with the long-run performance of the company for a divestiture, we exclude the divested company's revenues and expenses for that part of the year prior to the date the transaction closed. We discuss both of these adjustments in more detail in this section of the chapter.

[22] You will note in the table above that there is income from unconsolidated affiliates from AstraZeneca which we have not adjusted for here. That is because AstraZeneca was sold and we deal with all aspects of that later in the next section of the chapter.

Mergers and Acquisitions

Mergers and acquisitions are similar to each other. They represent a company's purchase of another company's assets or equity. A divestiture, on the other hand, is the opposite of a merger or acquisition. Divestitures represent the sale of a company's business (division or subsidiary). The common feature of these transactions in relation to measuring market multiples is that they can result in market multiple inputs in the denominators that are inconsistent with the market values used in the numerators. When we measure a company's market value after one of these transactions, it will represent the value of the post-transaction company. The financial statements, however, generally represent a mix of the pre- and post-transaction company in the year of the acquisition.

When a company acquires a controlling interest in another company, it usually records the assets and liabilities of the acquired company on its financial accounting records at the appraised value of the company's assets and liabilities. If the company pays more for the acquired company than the appraised value of its assets minus the value of its liabilities, the company will record goodwill on its books in the amount of the difference.

As of the purchase date, the company's market value represents the post-acquisition market value of the company. Similarly, the company's balance sheet represents the post-acquisition balance sheet. Its income statement and cash flow statements, however, only include the flows (revenues, expenses, cash flows, and so forth) of the acquired company after the transaction closes. Thus, if a company purchases another company, say, nine months into the acquirer's fiscal year, then the acquirer's annual income statement and cash flow statement in the year of the acquisition only includes the last three months of the acquired company's flows. Income statement or cash flow-based market multiples will have inconsistent denominators that are not only inconsistent with the numerators but are also not representative of the performance of the post-transaction company.

Fortunately, we can often collect information to at least partially adjust a company's financial statements. The acquiring company sometimes presents pro forma information in its financial statements. The pro forma information presents the company's income statements (and possibly other financial statements) as if the two companies were combined as of the beginning of the fiscal year. Most companies do not provide pro forma cash flow statements; thus, we will need to create cash flow statements from pro forma income statements and balance sheets if we are using a cash flow-based multiple.

We can use pro forma information to adjust the denominator so that it is more consistent with the numerator (post-transaction company), but the pro forma results do not include expected synergies or transaction-related financing effects. The management's discussion of the transaction is sometimes useful for understanding the expected synergies that may be embedded in the company's market value. Transaction-related financing is usually disclosed as well. If the acquired company was publicly traded, it may be possible to use its pre-acquisition financial statements to create pro forma financial statements.

Adjusting for Merck's Mergers and Acquisitions. Merck had various merger and acquisition transactions during its 2014 fiscal year. We will illustrate how to adjust for merger and acquisition transactions using Merck's 2014 acquisition of Idenix Pharmaceuticals, Inc. Since Merck acquired Idenix on August 5, 2014, Merck's income statement and statement of cash flows reflect Idenix's operations for approximately five months. Merck's value, however, reflects the entire effect of the Idenix acquisition. We extracted part of Merck's acquisition and divestiture footnote that summarizes the effect of this transaction.

> **Acquisitions, Divestitures, Research Collaborations and License Agreements**
> . . . In August 2014, Merck completed the acquisition of Idenix Pharmaceuticals, Inc. ("Idenix") for approximately $3.9 billion in cash ($3.7 billion net of cash acquired). . . . The transaction was accounted for as an acquisition of a business; accordingly, the assets acquired and liabilities assumed were recorded at their respective fair values as of the acquisition date. The determination of fair value requires management to make significant estimates and assumptions. Merck recognized an intangible asset for IPR&D of $3.2 billion related to MK-3682 (formerly IDX21437), net deferred tax liabilities of $856 million and other net assets and liabilities of approximately $20 million. . . . The excess of the consideration transferred over the fair value of net assets acquired of $1.4 billion was recorded as goodwill that was allocated to the Pharmaceutical segment and is not deductible for tax purposes. . . . This transaction closed on August 5, 2014; accordingly, the results of operations of the acquired business have been included in the Company's results of operations beginning after that date.

In 2014, prior to the closing of the acquisition, Idenix had revenue of $1.428 billion, pre-tax operating profit of $224.6 million. Since the value of the acquisition is already reflected in Merck's value, we do not adjust the numerators. For earnings and unlevered earnings, we add the after-tax effect (using Merck's 35% tax bracket) of the pre-acquisition earnings, $146 million ($146 = $224.6 × [1 – 0.35]). We add the entire pre-acquisition, pre-tax operating profit of $225 million to adjust EBIT and EBITDA. Unlike the types of adjustments discussed previously, we also adjust revenue and add Idenix's pre-acquisition revenues of $1.428 billion to Merck's revenues. Since Merck's balance sheet at year-end reflects the acquisition of Idenix, we make no adjustments to shareholders' equity or total invested capital. In the following schedule we summarize all of the effects on the numerators and denominators from the adjustments made for this acquisition.[23]

Idenix acquisition	Total Adjustment	Revenue	Materials and Production	Marketing and Administration	Research and Development	Tax Effect
Enterprise value	$ 0					
Unlevered earnings	146	$1,428	−$568	−$393	−$243	−$79
EBIT	225	1,428	−568	−393	−243	
EBITDA	225	1,428	−568	−393	−243	
Revenue	1,428	1,428				
Total invested capital	0					
Total equity value	0					
Earnings	146	$1,428	−$568	−$393	−$243	−$79
Book value of equity	$ 0					

Valuation in Practice 14.5

Medtronic acquisition of Covidien plc. On January 26, 2015, Medtronic completed the acquisition of Covidien plc, a public limited company organized under the laws of Ireland (Covidien) in a cash and stock transaction valued at approximately $50 billion. . . .

Actual and Pro Forma Impact

The Company's consolidated financial statements for the fiscal year ended April 24, 2015 include Covidien's results of operations from the Acquisition Date through April 24, 2015. Net sales and operating loss attributable to Covidien during this period and included in Medtronic's consolidated financial statements for the fiscal year ended April 24, 2015 total $2.683 billion and $423 million, respectively. The $423 million operating loss includes $623 million of amortization from the step-up in fair value of inventory acquired, $379 million of intangible asset amortization, $218 million of acquisition related charges, and $142 million of restructuring charges, net, all of which relate to the Covidien acquisition.

Here is a comparison of the company's reported results and the pro forma results as if the company was acquired on the first day of the fiscal year; in other words, including the roughly nine months of operations prior to the transaction closing date.

	As Reported	Pro Forma	% Change
Net Sales	$20.261 billion	$28.369 billion	40%
Net Income	$ 2.675 billion	$ 3.944 billion	47%

Source: Medtronic is the global leader in medical technology. Medtronic was founded in 1949 and today serves hospitals, physicians, clinicians, and patients in approximately 160 countries worldwide. Medtronic 10-K filing for the fiscal year ending April 2015.

[23] Note that in the Idenix acquisition table, we have allocated the amounts to Material and Production, Marketing and Administration and Research and Development based on the proportion that each cost is to total costs for Merck as a whole.

Divestitures

A divestiture is the sale of a part of a company; in other words, a company sells one or more (but not all) of its businesses. Earlier in this section, we discussed discontinued operations. If a company decides to sell one of its businesses and issues financial statements before the sale is completed, it will identify the assets, liabilities, and income from this business as a discontinued operation as long as the sale represents a strategic shift that has a major effect on the company's operations. In these situations, divestitures do not cause an inconsistency between the numerator and the denominator in the pre-divesture period because the company has already isolated the divestiture as a discontinued operation; this is true as long as the company isolated the discontinued operation for the entire year and as long as we use the information related to the discontinued operations to make the adjustments that we described earlier.

Of course, as indicated before, the numerator needs to be adjusted downward for the value of the discontinued operations. Once the company completes the disposition of the discontinued operation, we do not need to adjust the numerator for the multiples, for the cash proceeds have already been received. If the company is holding cash from the disposition, the cash will be removed when we calculate the enterprise value.

Companies may divest a business without isolating it as a discontinued operation. In this situation, the company's income statement will include the operations of the divested company for the part of the year during which it owned the divested company. We generally review the footnote and other disclosures included with the financial statements in order to identify information so that we can remove the operations of the divested company for that partial year.

Valuation Key 14.7

Divestitures and mergers and acquisitions can result in a combination of pre- and post-transaction income statements and cash flow statements. We adjust these financial statements in order to make them consistent with the post-transaction company.

Adjusting for Merck's Divestitures. Merck also had various divestiture transactions during its 2014 fiscal year. We illustrate how to adjust for divestitures using two of Merck's large divestitures – one which involved the sale of a 100% owned business (Merck Consumer Care or MCC) and one which involved the sale of an interest in a joint venture recorded as an unconsolidated affiliate (AstraZeneca). We begin with the sale of MCC and show an extracted part of Merck's acquisition and divestiture footnote that summarizes the effect of this transaction.

Acquisitions, Divestitures, Research Collaborations and License Agreements

On October 1, 2014, the Company completed the sale of its Merck Consumer Care ("MCC") business to Bayer AG ("Bayer") for $14.2 billion ($14.0 billion net of cash divested), less customary closing adjustments as well as certain contingent amounts . . . Under the terms of the agreement, Bayer acquired Merck's existing over-the-counter business, including the global trademark and prescription rights for Claritin and Afrin. The Company recognized a pretax gain from the sale of MCC of $11.2 billion in 2014.

Merck Consumer Care (MCC) ($ in millions)	Dec. 31, 2012	Dec. 31, 2013	Dec. 31, 2014
Revenue	$1,952	$1,894	$1,547
Pre-tax operating profit (authors estimate)	$ 514	$ 498	$ 407

A divestiture involves two types of adjustments. The first adjustment eliminates the gain or loss on the transaction. The second adjustment eliminates pre-divestiture revenues and expenses. Merck's footnote discloses that it had an $11.2 billion gain from the MCC transaction. Elsewhere in its financial statements, Merck discloses that MCC had $1.5 billion of pre-divestiture revenue and $407 million of pre-divestiture pre-tax operating profit.

The gain increased Merck's pre-tax income by $11.2 billion. We measure the income tax effect of that gain using Merck's tax reconciliation schedule (Exhibit 14.6). Based on the tax reconciliation schedule, we know that the income tax effect of the gain is equal to the 35% statutory income tax rate plus the $440 million (2.5%) increase in taxes shown on the tax reconciliation schedule. The $440 million increase in the taxes shown on the tax reconciliation schedule indicates that the book value of the net assets sold is more than its tax basis, possibly because of accelerated depreciation.

Since the value of the divestiture is already reflected in Merck's value, we do not adjust the numerators. In order to adjust the non-recurring gain—the first adjustment—we deduct the after-tax effect of the gain, $6.8 billion from earnings and unlevered earnings ($6.846 = $11.209 − $4.363; tax effect of $4.363 = $11.209 × 0.35 + $0.440). Further, we deduct the $11.2 billion pre-tax gain to adjust EBIT and EBITDA. Revenue requires no adjustment for the gain. For the second adjustment, we adjust Merck's income statement by eliminating MCC's pre-divestiture revenues and expenses. For earnings and unlevered earnings, we deduct the pre-divestiture after-tax income generated by MCC. We adjust the pre-tax income of $407 million for income taxes using Merck's marginal 35% income tax rate, which results in a pre-divestiture after-tax income of $265 million ($265 = $407 × [1 − 0.35]). We adjust EBIT and EBITDA by the pre-divestiture, pre-tax operating profit of $407 million. Like the adjustment for mergers and acquisitions, revenue also requires an adjustment but instead of adding revenue, we subtract pre-divestiture revenues of $1.547 billion. Since Merck already recorded the divestiture on its balance sheet (eliminated all of MCC's assets and liabilities), we make no adjustments to shareholders' equity or total invested capital.

The overall adjustment to Merck's earnings and unlevered earnings is $7.1 billion ($7.110 = $6.846 + $0.265),[24] while the overall adjustment to EBIT and EBITDA is $11.6 billion ($11.616 = $11.209 + $0.407). In the following schedule we summarize all of the effects on the numerators and denominators from the adjustments made for this divestiture.[25]

MCC Divestiture	Total Adjustment	Revenue	Materials and Production	Marketing and Administration	Research and Development	Other Income	Tax Effect
Enterprise value	$ 0						
Unlevered earnings	−7,110	−$1,547	$538	$372	$230	−$11,209	$4,506
EBIT	−11,616	−1,547	538	372	230	−11,209	
EBITDA	−11,616	−1,547	538	372	230	−11,209	
Revenue	−1,547	−1,547					
Total invested capital	0						
Total equity value	0						
Earnings	−7,110	−$1,547	$538	$372	$230	−$11,209	$4,506
Book value of equity	$ 0						

Next we discuss the sale of Merck's interest in AstraZeneca, which was recorded as an unconsolidated affiliate.[26] We show an extract from Merck's acquisition and divestiture footnote that summarizes the effect of this transaction.

AstraZeneca LP

In 1982, Merck entered into an agreement with Astra AB ("Astra") to develop and market Astra products under a royalty-bearing license. In 1993, a joint venture business carried on by Astra Merck Inc. ("AMI") was established, in which Merck and Astra each owned a 50% share. . . .

In 1998, Merck and Astra completed the restructuring of the ownership and operations of the joint venture whereby Merck would receive revenue from the sale of KBI (formerly AMI) products to AstraZeneca ("AstraZeneca") and also partnership returns for the distribution of these products by AstraZeneca.

Merck earned revenue based on sales of KBI products and such revenue [*assume this is a royalty with no expenses*] was $463 million, $920 million and $915 million in 2014, 2013 and 2012, respectively, . . . In addition, Merck earned certain Partnership returns which were recorded in Equity income from affiliates. These partnership returns aggregated $192 million, $352 million and $621 million in 2014, 2013 and 2012, respectively.

continued

[24] Includes a rounding error of $0.001

[25] Note that the tax adjustment of $4,506 is the sum of the tax adjustment of $4,363 and $143 ($143 = 407 × 0.35). Also note, that as before, we have allocated the amounts to Material and Production, Marketing and Administration and Research and Development based on the proportion that each cost is to total costs for Merck as a whole.

[26] The actual ownership structure and accounting for AstraZeneca was more complex than we describe but we simplified it for this illustration.

continued from previous page

> On June 30, 2014, AstraZeneca exercised its option to purchase Merck's interest in KBI for $419 million in cash. The Company recognized $91 million as a gain in 2014 within Other (income) expense, net based on this transaction. As a result of AstraZeneca exercising its option, as of July 1, 2014, the Company no longer records equity income from AstraZeneca (partnership returns) and sales of KBI have terminated.

The adjustments for the AstraZeneca divestiture involve three types of adjustments. The first is to eliminate the gain or loss on the transaction and the second is to eliminate the AstraZeneca related pre-divestiture equity income from affiliates. Merck's footnote reports that it had a $91 million gain from this transaction and equity income from this affiliate of $192 million. The third is to eliminate the $463 million of (assumed royalty) revenue from Merck's revenue. Since we have no additional information regarding income taxes, we assume the applicable income tax rate is 35% for these adjustments, except for the $192 equity income from affiliates because that is reported net of tax.

Like MCC, since the value of the divestiture is already reflected in Merck's value, we do not adjust the numerators. In order to adjust for the non-recurring gain, the first adjustment, we deduct the after-tax effect of the gain, $59 million ($59 = $91 × [1 − 0.35]), from earnings and unlevered earnings, while we deduct the entire $91 million to adjust EBIT and EBITDA. Revenue requires no adjustment for the gain. Next, for the second adjustment, we eliminate the pre-divestiture equity income from affiliates. As we did for other income statement line items presented on an after-tax basis, for all of the earnings multiples (earnings, unlevered earnings, EBIT and EBITDA), we deduct the pre-divestiture after-tax income, $192 million (recall equity income from affiliates is reported on an after-tax basis). Revenue does not require an adjustment. Finally, for the third adjustment, we adjust earnings and unlevered earnings by the after-tax effect of the royalty income (which we assume had no related expenses) of $301 million ($301 = $463 × [1 − 0.35]), and we adjust EBIT, EBITDA, and Revenue by $463 million. Since Merck already recorded the divestiture on its balance sheet, we make no adjustments to shareholders' equity or total invested capital. The overall adjustment to Merck's earnings and unlevered earnings is $552 million ($552 = $59 + $192 + $301),[27] while the overall adjustment to EBIT and EBITDA is $746 million ($746 = $91 + $192 + $463). In the following schedule, we summarize all of the effects on the numerators and denominators from the adjustments made for this divestiture.[28]

AstraZeneca Divestiture	Total Adjustment	Revenue = Income (Royalties)	Equity Income from Affiliates	Other (Income) Expense	Tax Effect
Enterprise value	$ 0				
Unlevered earnings	−552	−$463	−$192	−$91	$194
EBIT	−746	−463	−192	−91	
EBITDA	−746	−463	−192	−91	
Revenue	−463	−463			
Total invested capital	0				
Total equity value	0				
Earnings	−552	−$463	−$192	−$91	$194
Book value of equity	$ 0				

14.8 COMPARISON OF MERCK'S MARKET MULTIPLES BASED ON REPORTED AND ADJUSTED INPUTS

In this section, we summarize all of the adjustments made to Merck's market multiple numerators and denominators and examine the incremental effect of each of the adjustments. We begin with a review of the adjustments to Merck's enterprise value and equity value, followed by a review of the adjustments to Merck's income statement and balance sheets. We then compare Merck's multiples using its reported numbers to its multiples using its adjusted numbers and examine the incremental effect of each of the adjustments conditional on the prior adjustments.

[27] Includes a rounding error of $0.001.

[28] The total tax adjustment of $194 is the sum of 0.35 × 91 + 0.35 × 463.

Merck's Adjusted Enterprise Value and Equity Value

As we show in Exhibit 14.8, before making adjustments to Merck's denominators, we calculated the firm value equal to $189.5 billion and total equity value equal to $167.0 billion. We then subtracted Merck's cash and investments from its firm value to measure Merck's enterprise value of $160.3 billion and subtracted its cash and investments from its total equity value to measure a $137.8 billion value of Merck's equity excluding cash and investments.

EXHIBIT 14.8 Merck & Co., Inc.—Summary of Adjustments to Enterprise and Equity Values

($ in millions)	Units	Unit Price	Enterprise Value	Equity Value
Value of common stock	2,913.300	$56.79	$165,446	$165,446
Employee stock options	74.000	$21.616	1,600	1,600
Total equity			$167,046	$167,046
Total debt			22,500	
Value (with cash and investments)			$189,546	$167,046
Cash			−7,441	−7,441
Short-term investments			−8,278	−8,278
Long-term investments			−13,515	−13,515
Value (without cash and investments)			$160,312	$137,812
Net operating loss carryforwards			−156	−156
Restructuring charges			0	0
Impairments			0	0
Mergers and acquisitions			0	0
Divestiture MCC			0	0
Divestiture AstraZeneca			0	0
Noncontrolling/minority interest			280	280
Unconsolidated affiliates—remaining			−1,300	−1,300
Loss on debt redemption			0	0
Adjusted value			$159,136	$136,636

In addition, we made three adjustments to Merck's enterprise and total equity values based on the nine adjustments made to the denominators. We eliminated the value of Merck's NOLs ($156 million) and the value of its unconsolidated affiliates ($1.3 billion). We also added the value of Merck's noncontrolling interests ($280 million). The other adjustments made to the denominators did not affect Merck's enterprise or total equity value because the effect of the transaction or event for which we made these adjustments was already reflected in Merck's value. The resulting adjusted enterprise value and total equity value are, respectively, $159.1 billion and $136.6 billion.

Merck's Adjusted Income Statement and Balance Sheet

We present Merck's income statement adjustments in Exhibit 14.9 and the balance sheet adjustments in Exhibit 14.10. For both exhibits, the first column presents the summarized reported financial statement. The second column presents the adjustments for the cash and investments subtracted from firm value to measure enterprise value. The next nine columns present the adjustments for the various transactions and events we discussed previously in the chapter. The last column presents Merck's adjusted income statement and balance sheet. We use this adjusted income statement and balance sheet to then measure the adjusted denominators.

In the table below, we use the adjusted numbers (right hand most column) from Exhibits 14.9 and 14.10 to calculate Merck's earnings, unlevered earnings, EBIT, EBITDA, total invested capital and book value of equity market multiples. These are just the standard calculations one would make to compute these multiples, but they are based on the 10 adjustments made to Merck's financial statements.

EXHIBIT 14.9 Merck & Co., Inc.—Summary of the Income Statement Adjustments

Abbreviated Income Statement (in 000,000s)	2014 Reported	Cash and Investments	NOLs	Restructuring Charges	Impairment	Loss on Debt Redemption	Noncontrolling/ Minority Interest	Unconsol Affiliates	Mergers & Acquisition Idenix	Divestiture MCC	Divestiture AstraZeneca	2014 Adjusted
Sales	$42,237								$1,428	−$ 1,547	−$463	$41,655
Materials and production	$16,768			−$ 482	−$1,072				568	−538		15,244
Marketing and administrative	11,606			−200					393	−372		11,427
Research and development	7,180			−283	−49				243	−230		6,861
Restructuring costs	1,013			−1,013								0
Equity (income) loss from affiliates (net of tax)	−257							$65			192	0
Other (income) expense, net	−11,822				−101	−$628				11,209	91	−1,251
Total costs, expenses and other	24,488	$ 0	$ 0	−1,978	−1,222	−628	$ 0	65	1,203	10,069	283	32,280
Operating income	17,749	0	0	1,978	1,222	628	0	−65	225	−11,616	−746	9,375
Interest income	266	−266										0
Interest expense	−732											−732
Income before income taxes	17,283	−266	0	1,978	1,222	628	0	−65	225	−11,616	−746	8,643
Provision for income taxes	−5,349	70	−100	−403	−280	−220			−79	4,506	194	−1,661
Income (loss) from continuing operations	11,934	−196	−100	1,575	942	408	0	−65	146	−7,110	−552	6,982
Income (loss) from discontinued operations, net	0											0
Net income	11,934	−196	−100	1,575	942	408		−65	146	−7,110	−552	6,982
Less: net income to noncontrolling interests	14						−14					0
												0
Earnings available to Merck's common equity	$11,920	−$196	−$100	$1,575	$ 942	$408	$14	−$65	$ 146	−$ 7,110	−$552	$ 6,982
Tax rate	35.0%	26.4%	35.0%	35.0%	35.0%	35.0%	35.0%	35.0%	35.0%	35.0%	35.0%	35.0%
Tax adjustment from tax reconciliation			−$100	$ 289	$ 148					$ 440		
Marginal tax rate for adjustment	30.9%	26.4%		20.4%	22.9%	35.0%	0.0%	0.0%	35.0%	38.8%	26.0%	19.2%
Tax effect for items shown net of tax							$ 8	−$35			−$103	−$ 131

EXHIBIT 14.10 Merck & Co., Inc.—Summary of the Balance Sheet Adjustments

Abbreviated Balance Sheet (in 000,000s)	2014 Reported	Cash and Investments	NOLs	Restructuring Charges	Impairment	Loss on Debt Redemption	Noncontrolling/ Minority Interest	Unconsol Affiliates	Mergers & Acquisition Idenix	Divestiture MCC	Divestiture AstraZeneca	2014 Adjusted
Assets:												
Cash and cash equivalents	$ 7,441	−$ 7,441										$ 0
Short-term investments	8,278	−8,278										0
Accounts receivable	6,626											6,626
Inventories	5,571											5,571
Deferred income taxes and other current assets	5,257		−$100									5,157
Total current assets	33,173	−15,719	−100	$ 0	$ 0	$0	$ 0	$ 0	$0	$0	$0	17,354
Investments	13,515	−13,515										0
Property, plant and equipment, net	13,136			900								14,036
Goodwill	12,992											12,992
Other intangibles, net	20,386				1,222							21,608
Other assets	5,133							−382				4,751
Total assets	$98,335	−$29,234	−$100	$ 900	$1,222	$0	$ 0	−$382	$0	$0	$0	$70,741
Liabilities and shareholders equity:												
Loans payable and current portion of long-term debt	$ 2,704											$ 2,704
Trade accounts payable	2,625											2,625
Accrued and other current liabilities	10,523											10,523
Income taxes payable	1,606											1,606
Dividends payable	1,308											1,308
Total current liabilities	18,766	$ 0	$ 0	$ 0	$ 0	$0	$ 0	$ 0	$0	$0	$0	18,766
Long-term debt	18,699											18,699
Deferred income taxes (DTL − DTA)	4,266		75	403	280							5,024
Other non-current liabilities	7,813			−1,078								6,735
Total liabilities	49,544	0	75	−675	280	0	0	0	0	0	0	49,224
Common stock	1,788											1,788
Other paid-in capital	40,423						144					40,567
Retained earnings	46,021	−29,234	−175	1,575	942			−382				18,747
Accumulated other comprehensive loss	−4,323											−4,323
Stockholders' equity before treasury stock	83,909	−29,234	−175	1,575	942	0	144	−382	0	0	0	56,779
Less treasury stock, at cost	35,262											35,262
Total Merck & Co., Inc. stockholders' equity	48,647	−29,234	−175	1,575	942	0	144	−382	0	0	0	21,517
Noncontrolling interests	144						−144					0
Total equity	48,791	−29,234	−175	1,575	942	0	0	−382	0	0	0	21,517
Total liabilities and shareholders equity	$98,335	−$29,234	−$100	$ 900	$1,222	$0	$ 0	−$382	$0	$0	$0	$70,741

Using Adjusted Numbers (Exhibit 14.9)	Earnings	Unlevered Earnings	EBIT	EBITDA
Merck's earnings	$6,982	$6,982	$6,982	$ 6,982
Interest expense		732	732	732
Tax adjustment interest expense		−256		
Provision for taxes			1,661	1,661
Depreciation and amortization				6,691
Earnings measure	$6,982	$7,458	$9,375	$16,066

Using Adjusted Numbers (Exhibit 14.10)	Total Invested Capital	Shareholders' Equity
Merck's shareholders' equity	$21,517	$21,517
Short- and long-term debt	21,403	
	$42,920	$21,517

Comparison of Merck's Market Multiples Based on Reported and Adjusted Inputs

In Exhibit 14.11, we present the inputs for Merck's market multiples based on its reported numbers adjusted only for cash and investments, and on its adjusted numbers as well as Merck's multiples. The amounts used in the "Reported Adjusted for Cash & Investments" column differ from the earlier basic calculations as the inputs in the table have been adjusted for cash and investments. Merck's adjusted enterprise value is $159.1 billion, or a decrease of 0.7% from its unadjusted enterprise value of $160.3 billion. Merck's adjusted total equity value is $136.6 billion, or a decrease of 0.9% from its unadjusted equity value of $137.8 billion. While the absolute magnitude of these adjustments to value may appear large, the percentage changes are not large and thus, will have less than a 1% effect on the difference between the multiples measured on a reported and adjusted basis.

EXHIBIT 14.11 Merck & Co., Inc.—Summary of Unadjusted and Adjusted Market Multiples

	2014 Reported Adjusted for Cash & Investments		2014 Reported Adjusted for All Adjustments		% Change in Input	% Change in Multiple
	Inputs	Multiple	Inputs	Multiple		
Market multiples based on enterprise value	$160,312		$159,136		−0.7%	
Unlevered earnings (NI + After-tax interest)	12,200	13.1	7,458	21.3	−38.9%	62.4%
Earnings before interest and taxes (EBIT)	17,735	9.0	9,375	17.0	−47.1%	87.8%
EBITDA	24,426	6.6	16,066	9.9	−34.2%	50.9%
Revenue	42,237	3.8	41,655	3.8	−1.4%	0.7%
Total invested capital	$ 40,816	3.9	$ 42,920	3.7	5.2%	−5.6%
Market multiples based on equity value	$137,812		$136,636		−0.9%	
Earnings	11,724	11.8	6,982	19.6	−40.4%	66.5%
Book value shareholders' equity	$ 19,413	7.1	$ 21,517	6.4	10.8%	−10.5%

The effect of the adjustments on Merck's earnings-based denominators, however is much larger. Unlevered earnings declined by 39%, EBIT by 47% and EBITDA by 34%. Further, earnings declined by 40%. Revenue and the two balance sheet denominators had much smaller changes—revenues decreased by 1.4%, total invested capital increased by 5.2%, and shareholders' equity increased by 10.8%.

The last column shows the percentage change in multiple resulting from the changes in the inputs. Naturally, given the small changes in the numerators, it is the change in the denominators that drives most of the change in the multiples. EBIT, which had the largest decrease from the adjustments, has the largest increase in the multiple, 88%. The unlevered earnings, EBITDA and earnings multiples had increases of 62%, 51% and 67% respectively. The revenue and balance sheet based multiples have smaller changes in the 1% to 10% range.

Note that as we discussed in the opening vignette of the chapter, Merck's EBITDA multiple is equal to 6.6 based on the unadjusted numbers. Based on the adjustments we made in the chapter, we now estimate it to be 9.9. In that opening vignette, we also indicated that analysts' estimates of Merck's EBITDA multiple had a range from 9.0 to 11.2. Thus, the adjustments we have made here put us very close to the midpoint of the estimates of the analysts.

What is probably obvious is that the percentage change in a multiple is a function of the percentage change in the numerator and denominator of that multiple; specifically, the percentage change in a multiple is equal to one plus the percentage change in the numerator divided by one plus the percentage change in the denominator, minus one.

$$\%\text{ change in multiple} = \frac{1 + \%\text{ change in the numerator}}{1 + \%\text{ change in the denominator}} - 1$$

For example, Merck's adjusted unlevered earnings decreased by 38.9% and its enterprise value decreased by 0.7%, resulting in a 62% increase ($0.62 = [1 - 0.007]/[1 - 0.389]$) in the unlevered earnings multiple.

In Exhibit 14.12, we present the incremental effect of the individual adjustments on the unlevered earnings and EBIT multiples. Keep in mind that the incremental effect we measure for an individual adjustment depends on the order it was added to the analysis. We begin with the two large positive effects—the MCC and AstraZeneca divestitures. The adjustment for the MCC divestiture did not affect the numerators but the effect on EBIT was large, a decrease of 66%. The result was an increase in the EBIT multiple from 9.0 based on the reported numbers to 26.2, or a 190% increase. The AstraZeneca divestiture also increased the earnings-based multiples because it had no effect on Merck's value but decreased EBIT by an additional 12%. The EBIT multiple increased from 26.2 to 29.8, or 14%. The only other adjustment that had a positive effect on the multiples was the adjustment for unconsolidated affiliates increasing the EBIT multiple to 30.0.

The largest negative effect on the multiples was from the restructuring charges. The adjustment for the restructuring charges did not affect the numerators but the effect on EBIT was large, an increase of 37% given the adjustments discussed already. The EBIT multiple decreased from 30.0 to 21.8, or −27%. The next largest negative effect on the EBIT multiples was from the impairment charges. The adjustment for the impairment charges also did not affect the numerators but the effect on EBIT was an additional increase of 17%, which decreased the EBIT multiple from 21.8 to 18.7, or about −14%. The effect on the EBIT multiples from the adjustments for the loss on the debt redemption, the Idenix acquisition, NOLs and noncontrolling interests are, respectively, −7%, −2%, −0.1% and 0.0%. The final adjusted EBIT multiple is 17.0.

EXHIBIT 14.12 Merck & Co., Inc.—Effect of Individual Adjustments on the Unlevered Earnings and EBIT Multiples

		[1]	[2]	[3]	[4]	[5]	[6]	[7]	[8]	[9]
Abbreviated Balance Sheet (in $ Millions)	**Reported Numbers**	**MCC Divestiture**	**AstraZeneca Divestiture**	**Unconsol Affiliates**	**Restructuring Charges**	**Impairment**	**Debt Redemption Loss**	**Idenix Acquisition**	**NOL Carry Forwards**	**Noncontrolling Interest**
Enterprise value	$160,312	$160,312	$160,312	$159,012	$159,012	$159,012	$159,012	$159,012	$158,856	$159,136
% change in enterprise value		0.0%	0.0%	−0.8%	0.0%	0.0%	0.0%	0.0%	−0.1%	0.2%
Unlevered earnings	$ 12,200	$ 5,090	$ 4,538	$ 4,473	$ 6,047	$ 6,990	$ 7,398	$ 7,544	$ 7,444	$ 7,458
% change in unlevered earnings		−58.3%	−10.8%	−1.4%	35.2%	15.6%	5.8%	2.0%	−1.3%	0.2%
Unlevered earnings multiple	13.1	31.5	35.3	35.6	26.3	22.8	21.5	21.1	21.3	21.3
% change in unlevered earnings multiple		139.7%	12.2%	0.6%	−26.0%	−13.5%	−5.5%	−1.9%	1.2%	0.0%
EBIT	$ 17,735	$ 6,119	$ 5,373	$ 5,308	$ 7,286	$ 8,508	$ 9,136	$ 9,361	$ 9,361	$ 9,375
% change in EBIT		−65.5%	−12.2%	−1.2%	37.3%	16.8%	7.4%	2.5%	0.0%	0.1%
EBIT multiple	9.0	26.2	29.8	30.0	21.8	18.7	17.4	17.0	17.0	17.0
% change in EBIT multiple		189.8%	13.9%	0.4%	−27.1%	−14.4%	−6.9%	−2.4%	−0.1%	0.0%

REVIEW EXERCISE 14.3

Adjusting Market Multiple Numerators and Denominators

Use the information from Review Exercise 14.1, Review Exercise 14.2, and the following information to adjust the company's financial statements for effects related to its Unconsolidated Affiliates and Minority Interest similar to the adjustments in Exhibit 14.8 to Exhibit 14.11. Also calculate the company's unlevered earnings, EBIT, EBITDA, revenue, and P/E multiples using the adjusted financial statements. Assume earnings from the unconsolidated affiliates are taxed at a 40% tax rate. The market value of the Multiple Company's interest in the unconsolidated affiliates is $28,000. The market value of the minority interest in the Multiple Company's subsidiary is $5,600. HINT: Calculate unlevered earnings, EBIT, and EBITDA as in Review Exercise 14.1 using the adjusted financial statements.

Solution on pages 731–732.

14.9 ADJUSTING MARKET MULTIPLE INPUTS FOR LEASES AND DISCONTINUED OPERATIONS

In this section we discuss two other common adjustments that we did not have to make with Merck. One adjustment is for leases and the other is for discontinued operations. As we discussed in Chapter 11, recent changes in the accounting rules will require companies to capitalize essentially all lease obligations with a contractual term longer than twelve months.[29] The new accounting rules continue to classify leases as either financing or operating but require companies to capitalize the present value of the lease payments regardless of how a lease is classified. When a company treats a lease as financing (under the current or new rules) it capitalizes the present value of the lease payments for the leased asset and it records an asset (leased asset) and liability (lease liability) equal to the present value of these payments. Every period, the company amortizes (expenses) the leased asset and recognizes interest expense for the lease liability. Over the life of the lease, the sum of the expenses for a financing lease (depreciation and interest) will equal the sum of the lease payments. In the early years of a lease, however, a financing lease has higher expenses than an operating lease, which reverses in later years even though the cash flows (lease payments) are identical for both.

Under current rules, operating leases do not appear as assets or liabilities, but we simply record lease expense for the lease payments every period. Under the new rules, we will continue to record those lease payments as an expense, but we will record both a right-of-use (ROU) asset and a lease liability equal to the present value of the remaining lease payments at any point in time. As the lease continues, both the carrying value of the asset and liability will be reduced by the same amount every period as the present value of the lease payments declines.

The most common adjustment for leases when computing market multiples is to adjust operating leases as if they were financing leases. In order to adjust the income statement to convert operating leases to financing leases under the current or new accounting rules, we eliminate the effects of the operating leases on the income statement (operating lease expense) and add the effects of treating the operating lease as a financing lease (amortize the lease asset as a non-cash operating expense and record interest expense on the lease liability).

In order to adjust the balance sheet and enterprise value, based on the current rules, which do not capitalize operating leases, we adjust the balance sheet by adding the value of the leased asset and lease liability. We also make adjustments to deferred income taxes resulting from the difference in expenses and retained earnings. Since we adjust the denominator in this way, we add the value of the capitalized leases to enterprise value, treating the capitalized leases as debt. Based on the new accounting rules, we would also add the value of the leases to the enterprise value.

Adjusting for United Airlines Leases

Since Merck does not have very many non-capitalized leases, we use United Airlines (United Continental Holdings, Inc.) to illustrate the effect that capitalizing leases can have on a company's market multiples.[30] Recall that we used United in our discussion of leases in Chapter 11. We summarize some of that discussion here and then discuss the effect of capitalizing leases on market multiples, which is a potentially important issue for assessing comparability.

Using a 9% discount rate, we calculate the present value of United's operating lease obligations as of the end of 2013 and 2014, which are equal to approximately $12,331.7 million and $13,033.3 million, respectively. We do this by discounting the reported future lease payments as we illustrated for United in Chapter 11 (see Exhibit 11.5 for the details of these calculations).[31] In Exhibit 14.13, we show United's 2014 summary income statement and balance sheet. In the first column of the exhibit, we show

[29] FASB ASC Topic 842, *Leases*, issued February 25, 2016. Topic 842 replaces ASC Topic 840, *Leases*. The new accounting rules become effective no later than fiscal years beginning after December 15, 2018.

[30] United Continental Holdings, Inc. (United Airlines) transports people and cargo through its mainline operations, which use jet aircraft with at least 118 seats, and its regional operations. In October 2010, United Airlines, Continental Airlines, Inc., and various subsidiary companies merged to form this company. See United Continental Holdings 2014 10-K filing.

[31] Note that under the new rules, companies will compute the present value of leases that have a lease term of more than 12 months. Thus, we will not have to compute that amount as it will be given. We would still need to make all the adjustments to the multiples described here, but the present value of the lease payments will be provided.

the company's reported numbers. In the second column, we summarize the necessary adjustments to the company's income statement and balance sheet to capitalize its operating leases. (See Chapter 11 for a discussion of these adjustments.) We add back the amount of rent expense included in the reported income statement, and we subtract interest expense and amortization on the capitalized operating lease before adjusting the taxes. We assume that the operating leases have a remaining life of 7 years. United had essentially a zero effective income tax rate but we assume its marginal tax rate is 36%.

EXHIBIT 14.13 United Airlines—2014 Summary Income Statement and Balance Sheet with and without Capitalizing Operating Leases

United Airlines Summarized Financial Statements ($ in millions)	2014 Reported	Adjustments to Capitalize Operating Leases	2014 Adjusted	Percentage Effect of Adjustment
Revenues	$38,901.0		$38,901.0	0%
Rent expense	−2,725.0	$ 2,793.0	68.0	
Depreciation and amortization	−1,679.0		−1,679.0	
Amortization of operating leases		−1,761.7	−1,761.7	
All other operating expenses	−32,124.0		−32,124.0	
Operating income	2,373.0	1,031.3	3,404.3	43%
Interest expense, net	−735.0		−735.0	
Miscellaneous, net	−510.0		−510.0	
Lease interest		−1,109.9	−1,109.9	
Income before taxes	1,128.0	−78.5	1,049.5	−7%
Income taxes	4.0	28.3	32.3	
Net income	$ 1,132.0	−$ 50.3	$1,081.7	−4%
Current assets	$ 8,181.0		$8,181.0	
Net property, plant, equipment	19,467.0		19,467.0	
Other assets	10,460.0	$ 28.3	10,488.3	
Capitalized operating lease asset		12,954.7	12,954.7	
Total assets	$38,108.0	$12,983.0	$51,091.0	34%
Current operating liabilities	$12,513.0		$12,513.0	
Other liabilities	12,269.0		12,269.0	
Debt	10,691.0		10,691.0	
Capitalized operating lease liability	0.0	$13,033.3	13,033.3	
Total liabilities	35,473.0	13,033.3	48,506.3	37%
Shareholders' equity	2,635.0	−50.3	2,584.7	
Total liabilities and shareholders' equity	$38,108.0	$12,983.0	$51,091.0	34%
Marginal tax rate	36.0%			

In the top panel of Exhibit 14.14, we show United's equity value and enterprise value with and without the value of the capitalized leases. In the bottom panel of that exhibit, we show the effect of capitalizing United's operating leases on six multiples— earnings, unlevered earnings, EBIT, EBITDA, revenue, and total invested capital. In the first set of rows of the exhibit, we calculate the denominator of each multiple with and without capitalizing the company's operating leases. In the following rows, we calculate United's multiples with and without capitalizing its operating leases. At the very bottom of the exhibit, we show the percentage change in the numerator, denominator, and multiple from capitalizing the leases. The company's common equity (earnings) multiple increases by 5% as a result of capitalizing its operating leases. The unlevered earnings, EBIT, and EBITDA multiples decrease by 0%, 9%, and 21%, respectively. Since revenue is unaffected, the revenue multiple increased by the percentage increase in enterprise value, 41%. The total invested capital multiple decreased by 28% because the denominator increased by 97% while enterprise value increased by only 41%.

United has relatively more operating leases than most other companies, but in general, this example illustrates the potentially large and varying effect that capitalizing operating leases can have on a company's market multiples and, hence, how it can affect comparability. The key is that when substantial differences exist in terms of the extent of leasing and the type of leases (operating or financing), we should treat the leases of the comparable companies and the company being valued in a similar way in order to increase comparability.

EXHIBIT 14.14 United Airlines—2014 Market Multiples with and without Capitalizing Operating Leases

Valuation ($ in millions)	Enterprise Value	Equity Value
Shares outstanding	379.500	379.500
Price/share	$ 66.89	$ 66.89
Market value of equity	$25,384.8	$25,384.8
Options and other securities		
Debt	10,691.0	
Cash	−4,348.0	−4,348.0
Value without capitalizing leases	$31,727.8	$21,036.8
Capitalized operating leases	13,033.3	
Value with capitalizing leases	$44,761.0	$21,036.8
% Increase in enterprise value	41.1%	

($ in millions)	Common Equity Multiple	Unlevered Earnings Multiple	EBIT Multiple	EBITDA Multiple	Revenue Multiple	Total Invested Capital
Denominator						
Earnings	$ 1,132.0	$ 1,132.0	$ 1,132.0	$ 1,132.0		
Interest		735.0	735.0	735.0		
Tax adjustment		−264.6	−4.0	−4.0		
Depreciation and amortization				1,679.0		
Earnings without capitalizing operating leases	$ 1,132.0	$ 1,602.4	$ 1,863.0	$ 3,542.0		
Rent expense	2,793.0	2,793.0	2,793.0	2,793.0		
Interest on leases	−1,109.9					
Amortization of leases	−1,761.7	−1,761.7	−1,761.7			
Tax adjustment	28.3	−371.3				
Earnings with capitalizing leases	$ 1,081.7	$ 2,262.5	$2,894.3	$ 6,335.0		
Multiple without capitalizing leases						
Value without capitalizing operating leases	$21,036.8	$31,727.8	$31,727.8	$31,727.8	$31,727.8	$31,727.8
Denominator without capitalizing operating leases	1,132.0	1,602.4	1,863.0	3,542.0	38,901.0	13,326.0
Multiple without capitalized operating leases	18.58	19.80	17.03	8.96	0.82	2.38
Multiple with capitalizing leases						
Value with capitalizing operating leases	$21,036.8	$44,761.0	$44,761.0	$44,761.0	$44,761.0	$44,761.0
Denominator with capitalizing operating leases	1,081.7	2,262.5	2,894.3	6,335.0	38,901.0	26,309.0
Multiple with capitalized operating leases	19.45	19.78	15.47	7.07	1.15	1.70
Percentage change						
Percentage change in numerator	0.0%	41.1%	41.1%	41.1%	41.1%	41.1%
Percentage change in denominator	−4.4%	41.2%	55.4%	78.9%	0.0%	97.4%
Percentage change in multiple	4.6%	−0.1%	−9.2%	−21.1%	41.1%	−28.5%

Discontinued Operations

A **discontinued operation** is defined as one or more components of an entity that is held for sale or has been disposed of previously. Once a company adopts a plan to sell one of its businesses, accounting principles require the company to isolate the assets held for sale (and related liabilities) as discontinued operations for all years presented in the company's financial statements if disposal of the component(s) represents a strategic shift that has a major effect on the company's operations.[32] If the disposal of the

[32] For the U.S. GAAP for discontinued operations, see, Discontinued Operations, ASC 205-20 (also see ASU 2014-08, Reporting Discontinued Operations and Disclosure of Disposals of Components of an Entity). Note, if the company does not intend to sell the business but plans to abandon, distribute or exchange the assets for similar productive assets, then the company does not record the discontinued operation until the company disposes of the assets.

component(s) does not represent a strategic shift that has a major effect on the company's operations, the company reports the gain or loss from the divestiture within the operating income section of the income statement in the year the divesture occurs. We discussed divestitures previously in this chapter.

The company must present discontinued operations separately from continuing operations. For example, for discontinued operations, the company must disclose—in the income statements or footnotes—the pretax profit or loss of each discontinued operation, major line items constituting pretax profit or loss, and either total operating and total investing cash flows or depreciation, amortization, capital expenditures, and significant non-cash operating and investing items. These more detailed disclosures typically appear in the footnotes and only a one-line after-tax gain or loss on the continuing operation is shown on the income statement. Further, on the company's balance sheet, the assets and liabilities of the discontinued operations are segregated from the assets and liabilities of the continuing operations. The company must also restate the assets of the discontinued operations to their fair value. These disclosures must be provided for all periods presented in the financial statements.

We treat discontinued operations as an excess asset in order to improve both consistency between the numerator and denominator, to better reflect the company's long-run performance and to enhance comparability with other companies. The market value of the company will reflect both the present value of the expected after-tax net proceeds from the sale of the discontinued operations and the anticipated cash flows from the discontinued operations up to the date of sale. It is unlikely that the earnings of the discontinued operations reflect this value. Thus, discontinued operations are likely to have a different multiple from that of the company's continuing operations. Moreover, discontinued operations are often in a different line of business or geographic region, making them less comparable to either the company's other operations or the operations of the comparable companies. Thus, since we want to measure the long-term performance of the company, we eliminate the effect of the discontinued operations from both the numerator and the denominator.

Adjusting the Value of a Company with Discontinued Operations. If we have a comparable company with discontinued operations, we remove the value of the discontinued operations from the numerator of any multiple we calculate (enterprise value or equity value) on a present value and after-tax basis, and we also make sure to exclude the discontinued operations in any denominators we measure. As such, we will have a multiple that is solely based on the comparable company's continuing operations. Ideally, we will also adjust the numerator for the present value of the cash flows expected to be received between the valuation date and the date the discontinued operations are sold (exclusive of the sale proceeds). Sometimes, we know the expected income or loss, but we may not know the expected cash flows or the timing of these cash flows; though that information is sometimes reported in the footnotes.

We multiply the adjusted denominators of the company to be valued (removing any discontinued operations from its denominators if it has any) by the multiples of the comparable companies (as measured based solely on these companies' continuing operations) in order to measure the value of the continuing operations of the company being valued. If the company being valued has discontinued operations, we then add the present value of the expected sale proceeds of the company's discontinued operations on an after-tax basis, which should be disclosed in the company's 10-K; this amount is not, however, disclosed on a present value basis and may need to be adjusted for the time value of money. We also need to add in the present value of any after-tax cash flows up to the date of the sale.

REVIEW EXERCISE 14.4

Market Multiples and Operating Leases

For the LeaseIT Corporation, use the following information to measure the P/E, unlevered earnings, EBIT, EBITDA, and revenue multiples, with and without capitalizing its operating leases. Assume a marginal tax rate of 40% applies to all income.

Present value of operating leases—beginning balance	$ 1,996.3
Present value of operating leases—ending balance	$ 2,100.0
Annual lease payment	$ 500.0
Amortization period in years	5
Lease discount rate	8.0%
Market value of equity	$ 5,000.0
Market value of firm	$ 9,500.0

continued

continued from previous page

LeaseIT Corporation Summarized Income Statement	Reported	LeaseIT Corporation Summarized Balance Sheet	Reported
Revenues	$7,000.0	Cash	$ 400.0
Rent expense	−500.0	Other current assets	2,000.0
Depreciation and amortization	−2,000.0	Net property, plant, and equipment	8,000.0
Amortization of operating leases	—	Other assets	2,000.0
All other operating expenses	−3,000.0	Capitalized operating leases	—
Operating income	$1,500.0	Total assets	$12,400.0
Interest expense, net	−400.0		
Lease interest	—	Current operating liabilities	$ 1,000.0
Income before taxes	$1,100.0	Other liabilities	1,500.0
Income taxes	−440.0	Debt	4,500.0
		Capitalized operating leases	—
Net income	$ 660.0	Total liabilities	$ 7,000.0
		Shareholders' equity	5,400.0
		Total liabilities and shareholders' equity	$12,400.0

Solution on pages 732–733.

14.10 SELECTING AMONG ALTERNATIVE MARKET MULTIPLES AND ESTABLISHING A RANGE

LO6 Choose an appropriate market multiple and range

Naturally, the perfect comparable company rarely, if ever, exists when using market multiple valuation methods. Thus, we naturally face trade-offs when choosing among the potential comparable companies and alternative market multiples. From Chapter 13, we know that the importance and dimensions of comparability increase as we move up the line items on the income statement, for example, from unlevered earnings to EBIT to EBITDA to revenues. However, as we move up the income statement, the probability of negative denominators decreases. Similarly, the importance and dimensions of comparability are larger for balance sheet based multiples than they are for most income statement based multiples. Free cash flow multiples, on the other hand, have the fewest relevant dimensions of comparability (primarily growth, risk, and capital structure). However, they also are the most difficult multiples for which to find a good base year because free cash flows tend to be highly variable. In addition, they often have negative denominators. Further, with respect to the income statement, net income is more likely to be negative than EBIT, which is more likely to be negative than EBITDA and finally revenue should never be negative.

These trade-offs can then push us to move up the line items on the income statement (EBIT, EBITDA, and revenue). In the end, the decision as to which multiple to use in a valuation depends on the particular valuation context, the comparable companies, and the company being valued.

Even after we complete the arduous process of measuring the multiples and identifying the best comparable companies, our work is still not complete. We use the multiples from the comparable companies to identify a range of values for each multiple and/or a measure of central tendency to be used to value the company. If we were to identify comparable companies that are exactly comparable on all relevant dimensions to the company we are valuing and make all of the necessary adjustments, all of the market multiples should work equally and perfectly well. In that case, we would not have to choose a subset of market multiples, we would not need a range or measure of central tendency, and we would not have to accept comparable companies that are not truly comparable. By now, it should come as no surprise that such a perfect situation does not arise. Thus, we almost always make trade-offs by selecting comparable companies that are not truly comparable, and that, in turn, affects the range of market multiple values we observe from our analysis.

Negative Denominators Can Eliminate a Multiple from Consideration

Naturally, we cannot use a denominator to measure a market multiple if it has a negative value. When we have a negative denominator, we either make an adjustment to it (for example, add back a non-recurring item) so that it is positive, use a forecast of it two or three years into the future when it is expected to be positive, or use a different multiple. For example, we might be able to salvage an unlevered earnings multiple by adjusting it for unusual or non-recurring items. If the denominator remains negative, then we are forced to move up the lines in the income statement and not use that particular multiple. Of course, if all of a company's earnings-based numbers are negative, we can use revenue multiples, for revenues are never negative. We know, however, that revenue multiples are more sensitive to differences in comparability—particularly differences in cost structures—than earnings-based multiples.

Revenue Multiples Can Be Appropriate When We Conclude the Cost Structure Will Change

Generally, revenue multiples are difficult to use because they assume the cost structures of the comparable companies and the company we are valuing are identical; however, they can be useful when we believe a company's cost structure will change to that of a comparable company's cost structure. For example, if we believe that we can purchase a company and change its cost structure to that of the comparable companies, revenue multiples will be able to provide valuations consistent with this belief. Naturally, changing cost structures in this way is not always easy, but if we want to make such an assumption, revenue multiples may be appropriate to use. Consider companies such as Laboratory Corporation of America (LabCorp) or Quest Diagnostics that do medical testing. Both of these companies have acquired many smaller labs over the years and they know that most of their cost structure—with their scale economies—will be in place in the acquired labs within a matter of days. In this case, they may actually be able to use a revenue multiple to value these acquisitions. Of course, they have to worry (and they do) about whether any of the revenue of the labs will be lost because of the acquisition.

Valuation Key 14.8

Choosing the most appropriate multiples is usually done after we make adjustments and assess comparability. If we have comparable companies that are perfectly comparable on all dimensions and make all of the necessary adjustments, all of the multiples will result in the same valuation. Realistically, however, that is not the situation we typically encounter, and we must choose multiples based on the particular valuation context for a company at the time we are valuing it (which includes the characteristics of the available comparable companies).

Using Multiple Comparable Companies to Offset Differences

We always make trade-offs when we select comparable companies. One comparable company might be more comparable on certain dimensions than another comparable company, and that comparable company might be more comparable on other dimensions. We might also use two companies that are not exactly comparable to the company we are valuing but have differences that are expected to be offsetting. For example, we might use two companies that are comparable on many dimensions—one with slightly lower growth prospects than the company being valued and the other with slightly better growth prospects. If we include both companies, on average, our portfolio of companies could be comparable and will capture the growth prospects of the company we are valuing.

All else equal, we prefer to use more comparable companies, but all else is rarely equal. Typically, we must make trade-offs between the number of comparable companies we include in our analysis versus the comparability of the comparable companies—including a greater number of comparable companies generally reduces the comparability of the firms we are using, however, using more comparable companies may allow us to offset differences as well.

Does the Variation in Multiples Across Companies Line Up According to Expectations?

A potentially useful analysis to conduct before we compute the multiples for the comparable companies is to think about which companies' multiples are likely to be the highest, which will be in the middle of the range, and which will be at the low end. We make this assessment based on our understanding of the risk, growth, profitability, investment requirements, and so forth, of the comparable companies. If the multiples line up according to our expectations, it indicates that we have a good understanding of the characteristics of the comparables and that we have managed to make the necessary adjustments to the financial statements such that these characteristics are visible in the multiples. If we are successful, we probably have a good idea of where in the range of the multiples the company we are valuing belongs. Of course, if we are unsuccessful in this regard, it may mean that the companies are not very comparable or that we have not made the necessary adjustments we need to make.

Establishing a Reasonable Range of Values and Measuring Central Tendency

If we have a reasonable number of comparable companies, we can choose a reasonable range of values and calculate a measure of central tendency for each market multiple used in our valuation. This task is easier if we have a large number of comparable companies, which again is often not the case. With respect to establishing a range of market values, we begin by assessing the reasonableness of the distribution of values. For example, is the range reasonably narrow or is it large? If the variation is large, we might revisit our adjustment process or conclude that one or more of the companies we chose are not truly comparable to the company being valued. Alternatively, we might include additional comparable companies in order to attempt to reduce the differences across the portfolio of comparable companies.

Possible measures of central tendency include the equally weighted mean (called the mean or average), the value weighted mean, and the median. If we have some extreme outliers in our distribution of market multiples or if the distribution is not symmetric, the mean may be a poor measure of central tendency. An alternative approach is to truncate or trim the distribution of market multiples before calculating the mean; for example, we might truncate the distribution at the 5th and 95th percentiles and set all market multiples above (below) the 95th (5th) percentile equal to the 95th (5th) percentile. The median (50th percentile) is not influenced by outliers if the distribution is relatively symmetric.

Selecting the Range of Values (or Value) to Use in Our Valuation

Once we have narrowed the range of values to a reasonable degree and have a measure of central tendency, we select the final range of values (or value) to use in our valuation. This is an easy task if our comparable companies have a high degree of comparability to the company we are valuing. In this situation, the measure of central tendency is a reasonable value to use in our valuation. If the comparable companies are not equally comparable, we would have to consider eliminating some of the less comparable of the companies or choosing another point in the distribution other than the central tendency (for example, the 25th or 75th percentile), by which we implicitly (or explicitly) weight the comparable companies by their degree of comparability—the more comparable, the more weight. Finally, if the multiples line up across the comparable companies as anticipated, we may be able to simply use a subset of the comparable companies in order to choose a range or measure of central tendency.

Valuation Key 14.9

We almost always need to make trade-offs when we select our portfolio of comparable companies, market multiples, and range of values to use in our valuation. We usually have little choice but to use our informed, personal judgment when making these decisions. Our goal is to select a portfolio of comparable companies, specific market multiples, and range of values that are appropriate for the company we are valuing.

REVIEW EXERCISE 14.5

Valuing a Company Using Market Multiples

Below, we present an income statement and balance sheet for the ValueIT Company. The company's debt and preferred stock balance sheet values are approximately equal to their market values. ValueIT Company has a 30% income tax rate on all income. The company has land in its Net Property, Plant, and Equipment that is not used in its operations, and the land has no effect on the company's revenues or expenses. The current market value of the land is $6,000. Use the market multiples from Review Exercise 14.3 to measure ValueIT's enterprise value and equity value as of the end of Year 1.

continued

continued from previous page

Income Statement	Year 1
Revenues	$5,000.0
Operating expenses	−2,500.0
Depreciation expense	−1,300.0
Operating income	$1,200.0
Interest expense	−480.0
Interest income (cash and equivalents)	200.0
Income before income taxes and other Items	$ 920.0
Provision for income taxes	−276.0
Net income	$ 644.0
Dividends on preferred stock	−350.0
Earnings available to common shareholders	$ 294.0

Balance Sheet	Year 1
Assets	
Cash and equivalents	$ 1,000.0
Net (non-cash) working capital	2,000.0
Total current assets	$ 3,000.0
Property, plant, and equipment, net	30,000.0
Total assets	$33,000.0
Liabilities and Shareholders' Equity	
Non-current operating liabilities	$ 8,000.0
Long-term debt	8,000.0
Total liabilities	$16,000.0
Perpetual preferred stock	$ 5,000.0
Common stock	12,000.0
Total shareholders' equity	$17,000.0
Total liabilities and shareholders' equity	$33,000.0

Solution on page 734.

SUMMARY AND KEY CONCEPTS

The market multiple valuation method is widely used. We use market multiple valuation methods to value the company and its equity as of both the valuation date and the continuing value date. The market multiple valuation method relies heavily on the comparability of the comparable companies. In the previous chapter, we discussed the determinants of different market multiples and assessing comparability based on those determinants. In this chapter, we discuss comparability based on adjusting a company's historical financial statements, which can also apply to financial statement forecasts. As illustrated in this chapter, adjusting historical financial statements can be a difficult task and often relies on estimates of unknown information. Depending on the adjustments that must be made, using financial statement forecasts instead of historical financial statements may be a better way to measure market multiples (e.g., eliminating a non-recurring item).

We make adjustments to increase the consistency of the numerator and denominator of the market multiples we might use as well as to increase the comparability across companies. Adjusting the numerators and denominators of the market multiples is time-consuming and detailed work. However, if we do not make appropriate adjustments to the multiples, the usefulness of the estimated market multiples is usually sacrificed and the market multiple valuations are likely to contain errors. We demonstrated the adjustment process in detail using Merck & Co. Inc. and United Airlines, Inc. for typical adjustments that are made. As is probably obvious, many kinds of adjustments are potentially important, and making such adjustments requires a detailed reading of the company's financial statements.

If we are able to identify a company that is comparable on all dimensions to the company we are valuing and if we make all of the necessary adjustments to the multiples and the company being valued, all of the common market multiples will work equally well. The perfect comparable company, however, does not exist, so we are always trading off the number of comparable companies we use with how comparable the companies are to the company being valued, and we are always considering which of the market multiples are best suited for the situation we face.

ADDITIONAL READING AND REFERENCES

Liu, J., D. Nissim, and J. Thomas, "Equity Valuation Using Multiples," *Journal of Accounting Research* 40 (2002), pp. 135–172.

Ramanlal, P., S. Mann, and W. Moore, "Convertible Preferred Stock Valuation: Tests of Alternative Models," *Review of Quantitative Finance and Accounting* 10 (1998), pp. 303–319.

EXERCISES AND PROBLEMS

P14.1 **Measuring Market Multiple Numerators—Multiple Company:** Below, we present an income statement and balance sheet for the Multiple Company. The company's debt and preferred stock are recorded on the balance sheet at par value. The debt and preferred stock are currently trading at 95% and 105% of their respective par values. The company's debt has an 8% interest rate and the dividend yield for its preferred stock is 9%. The company has 50,000 shares of outstanding stock trading at $8 per share. The company also has 10,000 employee stock options outstanding that the company valued at $3 per option. The company's income tax rate on all income is 30%. Calculate the company's enterprise value and equity value in order to measure the company's market multiples as discussed in the previous sections of this chapter. Calculate the company's enterprise value to unlevered earnings, EBIT, EBITDA, revenue, and P/E multiples without making any adjustments to the income statement. *Hint*: Measure the unlevered earnings as net income plus after-tax interest expense and measure EBIT as net income plus interest expense plus income tax expense.

	Year 2
Revenue	$200,000
Operating expenses	−120,000
Depreciation expense	−50,000
Operating earnings	$ 30,000
Earnings from unconsolidated affiliates	14,000
Investment income (on cash)	5,000
Interest expense	−6,400
Income before taxes	$ 42,600
Income tax expense	−12,780
Minority Interest (net of tax)	−17,000
Net income	$ 12,820

	Year 1	Year 2
Cash	$ 80,000	$ 80,000
Other current assets	30,000	32,000
Equity in unconsolidated affiliates	70,000	72,000
Property, plant, and equipment (net)	240,000	250,000
Total assets	$420,000	$434,000
Accounts payable	$ 20,000	$ 24,000
Debt	80,000	80,000
Total liabilities	$100,000	$104,000
Minority interest	$ 84,000	$ 87,000
Preferred stock	$ 32,000	$ 32,000
Capital stock	20,000	20,000
Retained earnings	184,000	191,000
Shareholders' equity	$236,000	$243,000
Liabilities and shareholders' equity	$420,000	$434,000

P14.2 **Measuring Market Multiple Denominators—Multiple Company:** Use the information from Problem 14.1 as well as the following information to adjust the company's financial statements for effects related to its cash balance and its non-recurring items. In Year 2, the company incurred a non-recurring operating expense of $24,000, which is included in operating expenses. Also calculate the company's enterprise value to unlevered earnings, EBIT, EBITDA, revenue, and P/E multiples using the adjusted financial statements. *Hint*: Measure the unlevered earnings as net income plus after-tax interest expense and measure EBIT as net income plus interest expense plus income tax expense using the adjusted financial statements.

P14.3 **Adjusting Market Multiple Numerators and Denominators—Multiple Company:** Use the information from Problem 14.1 and Problem 14.2 as well as the following information to adjust the company's financial statements for effects related to its unconsolidated affiliates and minority interest. Also calculate the company's enterprise value to unlevered earnings, EBIT, EBITDA, revenue, and P/E multiples using the adjusted financial statements. Earnings from the unconsolidated affiliates are taxed at a rate of 30%. The market value of the Multiple Company's interest in the unconsolidated affiliates is $196,000. The market value of the minority interest in Multiple Company's subsidiary is $238,000. *Hint*: Measure the unlevered earnings as net income plus after-tax interest expense and measure EBIT as net income plus interest expense plus income tax expense using the adjusted financial statements.

P14.4 **Valuing a Company Using Market Multiples—Multiple Value Company:** Below, we present an income statement and balance sheet for the Multiple Value Company. The company's debt and preferred stock balance sheet values are approximately equal to their market values. The Company has a 40% income tax rate on all income. The company has land included in its Property, Plant, and Equipment, Net that it does not use in its operations, and the land has no effect on the company's revenues or expenses. The current market value of the land is $15,000. Use the market multiples from Problem 14.3 to measure the company's enterprise value and equity value as of the end of Year 1.

Income Statement	Year 1
Revenues	$50,000.0
Operating expenses	–25,000.0
Depreciation expense	–15,000.0
Operating income	$10,000.0
Interest expense	–2,160.0
Interest income (cash and equivalents)	200.0
Income before income taxes and other items	$ 8,040.0
Provision for income taxes	–3,216.0
Net income	$ 4,824.0
Dividends on preferred stock	–680.0
Earnings available to common shareholders	$ 4,144.0

Balance Sheet	Year 1
Assets	
Cash and equivalents	$ 5,000.0
Net (non-cash) working capital	10,000.0
Total current assets	$15,000.0
Property, plant, and equipment, net	75,000.0
Total assets	$90,000.0
Liabilities and Shareholders' Equity	
Non-current operating liabilities	$ 8,000.0
Long-term debt	27,000.0
Total liabilities	$35,000.0
Perpetual preferred stock	8,000.0
Common stock	47,000.0
Total shareholders' equity	$55,000.0
Total liabilities and shareholders' equity	$90,000.0

P14.5 **Market Multiple and Operating Leases—Leasing Company:** For the Leasing Company, use the following information to measure the P/E, and enterprise value to unlevered earnings, EBIT, EBITDA, and revenue multiples with and without capitalizing its operating leases.

Present value of operating leases—beginning balance	$ 70,235.8
Present value of operating leases—ending balance	$ 74,000.0
Annual lease payment	$ 10,000.0
Amortization period in years	10
Lease discount rate	7.0%
Market value of equity	$266,760.0
Market value of firm	$320,760.0

Leasing Company Summarized Income Statement	Reported
Revenues	$150,000.0
Rent expense	–10,000.0
Depreciation and amortization	–8,000.0
Amortization of operating leases	—
All other operating expenses	–97,500.0
Operating income	$ 34,500.0
Interest expense, net	–4,860.0
Lease interest	—
Income before taxes	$ 29,640.0
Income taxes	–11,856.0
Net income	$ 17,784.0

Leasing Company Summarized Balance Sheet	Reported
Cash	$ 15,000.0
Other current assets	37,500.0
Net property, plant, and equipment	120,000.0
Other assets	7,500.0
Capitalized operating leases	—
Total assets	$180,000.0
Current operating liabilities	$ 26,000.0
Other liabilities	15,000.0
Debt	54,000.0
Capitalized operating leases	—
Total liabilities	$ 95,000.0
Shareholders' equity	85,000.0
Total liabilities and shareholders' equity	$180,000.0

P14.6 **Market Multiple Valuation—Tina H's Dog Toys, Inc.:** Tina H's Dog Toys, Inc. is a privately held company. You have been hired to value the company's firm value and equity using market multiple valuation methods. An analyst already identified potential comparable companies for your analysis—Mike's Dog Wonderland, Inc., Matt's Pet Supply Company, and Jeff's Dog Heaven, Inc. The analyst also prepared a summary of some accounting and market information, as well as some forecast data for your analysis as shown in Exhibit P14.1. Some of the companies own various marketable securities that they do not need to operate their businesses. These companies record such investments at cost and show dividend income from these investments as a separate line item on the income statement. Operating income is equal to operating revenues minus all operating expenses but excludes interest expense, income taxes, and any extraordinary items (which the company shows as a separate line item in the income statement net of income taxes). Net income is measured after deducting all

EXHIBIT P14.1 Summary Information for Tina H's Dog Toys, Inc. and Comparable Companies

	Mike's Dog Wonderland			Matt's Pet Supply Co.			Jeff's Dog Heaven, Inc.			Tina H's Dog Toys, Inc.		
($ in thousands, except per share amounts)	Actual Year 0	Forecast Year 1	Forecast Year 5	Actual Year 0	Forecast Year 1	Forecast Year 5	Actual Year 0	Forecast Year 1	Forecast Year 5	Actual Year 0	Forecast Year 1	Forecast Year 5
Primary Income Statement Items												
Revenue (sales)	$614.5	$643.7	$880.2	$101.6	$112.7	$280.2	$179.6	$180.4	$299.4	$126.5	$127.1	$176.6
Operating income	$130.5	$126.5	$161.7	$ 32.0	$ 36.2	$ 89.2	$ 31.9	$ 34.9	$ 54.7	$ 31.0	$ 33.1	$ 44.2
Net income	$ 33.3	$ 33.7	$ 92.4	$ 22.0	$ 24.1	$ 54.3	$ 18.0	$ 19.8	$ 32.0	$ 18.3	$ 19.5	$ 26.2
Other Items in the Income Statement												
Depreciation expense	$ 41.5	$ 47.3	$ 60.1	$ 10.7	$ 11.7	$ 28.4	$ 9.4	$ 10.3	$ 14.7	$ 6.9	$ 7.6	$ 9.1
Interest expense	$ 14.7	$ 16.2	$ 19.6	$ 6.0	$ 6.8	$ 9.5	$ 4.2	$ 4.4	$ 5.6	$ 4.3	$ 4.5	$ 5.3
Dividends from investments	$ 0	$ 0	$ 0	$ 10.8	$ 10.8	$ 10.8	$ 0	$ 0	$ 0	$ 1.4	$ 1.4	$ 1.4
Extraordinary item (net of income taxes)	−$ 42.0	−$ 38.0	$ 0	$ 0	$ 0	$ 0	$ 0	$ 0	$ 0	$ 0	$ 0	$ 0
Preferred stock dividends	$ 6.5	$ 7.3	$ 8.9	$ 2.3	$ 2.6	$ 3.7	$ 2.8	$ 3.1	$ 3.9	$ 2.1	$ 2.4	$ 2.8
Primary Balance Sheet Items												
Cash balance	$ 2.5	$ 3.3	$ 5.1	$ 1.3	$ 1.6	$ 2.9	$ 0.6	$ 0.7	$ 0.8	$ 0.5	$ 0.6	$ 0.7
Marketable securities	$ 0	$ 0	$ 0	$ 94.5	$ 94.5	$ 94.5	$ 0	$ 0	$ 0	$ 19.2	$ 19.2	$ 19.2
Total assets	$321.9	$354.0	$442.3	$151.4	$173.0	$241.0	$ 82.0	$ 94.3	$128.5	$ 76.9	$ 82.1	$ 94.9
Common equity	$ 49.4	$ 65.6	$102.1	$ 25.2	$ 32.5	$ 58.8	−$ 6.9	−$ 1.7	$ 12.5	−$ 3.5	−$ 2.6	−$ 2.5
Free Cash Flows (Before Extraordinary Items and Dividends from Investments)												
Unlevered free cash flow	$ 55.6	$ 50.0	$ 92.2	$ 13.1	$ 0.1	$ 49.3	$ 16.9	$ 10.4	$ 31.8	$ 17.4	$ 16.3	$ 26.5
Equity free cash flow	$ 61.1	$ 48.2	$ 80.5	$ 20.4	$ 7.7	$ 45.2	$ 16.4	$ 11.5	$ 27.6	$ 16.3	$ 15.3	$ 23.1
Market Values												
Marketable securities	$ 0			$131.2			$ 0			$ 32.5		
Debt	$190.7			$ 92.5			$ 53.3			$ 53.6		
Preferred stock	$ 81.7			$ 33.6			$ 35.5			$ 26.8		
Common equity:												
Shares authorized	183.35			315.36			214.52			23.12		
Shares issued	121.01			208.14			141.58			18.50		
Shares outstanding	108.91			187.32			127.42			17.02		
Price at end of Year 0	$5.838			$1.572			$1.627					
Average price per share in December of Year 0	$6.422			$1.729			$1.790					

expenses, includes other income (dividends from investments) and includes the effect of extraordinary items. All of the companies have the same income tax rate, 35%, and all income is taxed at the same rate.

a. Calculate each comparable company's unlevered earnings, EBIT, EBITDA, revenue, and P/E multiples using the adjusted financial statements.

b. Value Tina H's Dog Toys, Inc. and its equity using market multiple valuation methods and using each comparable company.

P14.7 **Market Multiple Valuation—F. Hill Enterprises:** F. Hill Enterprises (Hill) is a privately held company that records and distributes musical recordings in a variety of formats. It is a reasonably large company for a privately held company and has several direct competitors that are publicly traded. You have been engaged to value Hill (its firm value and its equity value) using market multiple valuation methods. An analyst has already prepared a summary of some accounting and market information, as well as some forecast data for your analysis shown in Exhibit P14.2 (on the next page). In addition, the analyst identified three publicly traded potential comparable companies for Hill, all of which are its direct competitors—T. McGraw Corporation (McGraw), W. Nelson Company (Nelson), and T. Keith, Inc. (Keith). Further, the analyst reviewed the financial leverage of Hill and its three competitors and concluded that their capital structures were similar. Finally, the analyst found that the companies all had the same income tax rate, 40%, and that this rate applies to all forms of income.

a. Calculate each comparable company's unlevered earnings, EBIT, EBITDA, revenue, and P/E multiples using the adjusted financial statements.

b. Value Hill and its equity using market multiple valuation methods and using each comparable company.

P14.8 **Comprehensive Market Multiple Calculation—L. Messaglia Company:** In Exhibit P14.3, we present an income statement and balance sheet for the L. Messaglia Company. The company's debt and preferred stock are recorded on the balance sheet at par value and were issued a few years ago. The preferred stock is currently trading at its par value. The company's convertible bonds have a 6% interest rate. The company's straight debt has a 9% cost of capital and interest rate. The convertible bonds mature in 5 years. The equity cost of capital is 12%. The company's outstanding stock is trading at $12 per share. The company's income tax rate is 35% on all income. The company's income from unconsolidated affiliates is from dividends received; 70% of the intercompany dividends are excluded from income taxes. The value of the company's investments in its unconsolidated affiliates is $171,600, and the value of the minority interests is equal to $84,000. The current risk-free rate is 4%, and the company's stock has a 40% annual volatility. Depreciation and amortization expense was $48,305 in Year 1. The value of the company's discontinued operations is $18,000.

a. Making all of the appropriate adjustments, calculate the company's enterprise value and equity value as of the end of Year 1 for the purpose of measuring the company's market multiples.

b. Making all of the appropriate adjustments, calculate the company's enterprise value to unlevered earnings, EBIT, EBITDA, revenue, and P/E multiples.

EXHIBIT P14.3 Summary Information for the L. Messaglia Company

Income Statement	Year 0	Year 1
Revenues	$100,000	$120,000
Operating expenses	−50,000	−57,600
Restructuring and impairment costs		−9,600
Operating income	$ 50,000	$ 52,800
Equity in pretax earnings of unconsolidated affiliates	10,000	13,200
Income on cash and equivalents	600	840
Interest expense	−10,200	−10,680
Income before income taxes and other items	$ 50,400	$ 56,160
Provision for income taxes	−15,120	−16,848
Minority interest (net of tax)	−5,000	−6,000
Income (loss) from continuing operations	$ 30,280	$ 33,312
Income (loss) from discontinued operations (net of tax)	0	−7,200
Net income	$ 30,280	$ 26,112
Dividends on preferred stock	−5,310	−5,310
Earnings available to common shareholders	$ 24,970	$ 20,802
Common dividends	$ 9,882	$ 10,402

Balance Sheet	Year 0	Year 1
Assets		
Cash and equivalents	$ 15,000	$ 16,800
Current operating assets	18,000	20,400
Discontinued operations current assets		4,800
Total current assets	$ 33,000	$ 42,000
Property, plant and equipment, net	300,000	348,000
Other non-current assets	15,000	15,600
Investments in unconsolidated affiliates	20,000	21,600
Total assets	$368,000	$427,200
Liabilities and Shareholders' Equity		
Current operating liabilities	$ 9,000	$ 13,200
Short-term debt	40,000	56,000
Discontinued operations liabilities		14,400
Total current liabilities	$ 49,000	$ 83,600
Convertible bonds[1]	150,000	150,000
Other long-term liabilities	9,000	13,200
Total liabilities	$208,000	$246,800
Minority interest	$ 50,000	$ 60,000
Series A 9% perpetual preferred stock	$ 59,000	$ 59,000
Common stock[2]	10,000	10,000
Retained earnings	41,000	51,400
Total shareholders' equity	$110,000	$120,400
Total liabilities and shareholders; equity	$368,000	$427,200

[1] 6% Convertible Bond, each bond issued and outstanding at $1,000 par value. Each bond is convertible into 100 shares of common stock.

[2] Common Stock, 60,000 shares authorized, 40,000 shares issued and outstanding as of the end of Year 1.

EXHIBIT P14.2 Summary Information for F. Hill and Comparable Companies

	T. McGraw Corporation			W. Nelson Company			T. Keith, Inc.			F. Hill Company		
($ in thousands, except per share amounts)	Actual Year 0	Forecast Year 1	Forecast Year 5	Actual Year 0	Forecast Year 1	Forecast Year 5	Actual Year 0	Forecast Year 1	Forecast Year 5	Actual Year 0	Forecast Year 1	Forecast Year 5
Primary Income Statement Items												
Revenue (sales)	$235.8	$259.3	$642.4	$630.3	$664.4	$819.9	$366.5	$400.2	$825.4	$260.5	$286.5	$684.7
Operating income	$ 54.0	$ 61.0	$149.7	$ 89.1	$ 94.7	$114.8	$ 89.4	$ 99.7	$210.0	$ 66.3	$ 75.5	$170.5
Net income	−$ 13.2	−$ 5.5	$ 82.0	$ 56.3	$ 59.5	$ 70.3	$ 47.7	$ 53.5	$116.4	$ 37.1	$ 42.2	$ 95.4
Other Items in the Income Statement												
Depreciation expense	$ 45.0	$ 49.2	$120.1	$131.5	$144.4	$164.0	$ 73.3	$ 80.0	$152.4	$ 52.2	$ 56.3	$137.7
Interest expense	$ 6.1	$ 6.8	$ 13.1	$ 7.1	$ 7.4	$ 9.4	$ 10.0	$ 10.5	$ 16.1	$ 7.5	$ 8.2	$ 14.4
Dividends from investments	$ 0	$ 0	$ 0	$ 11.8	$ 11.8	$ 11.8	$ 0	$ 0	$ 0	$ 3.0	$ 3.0	$ 3.0
Extraordinary item (net of income taxes)	−$ 42.0	−$ 38.0	$ 0	$ 0	$ 0	$ 0	$ 0	$ 0	$ 0	$ 0	$ 0	$ 0
Preferred stock dividends	$ 2.8	$ 3.1	$ 6.0	$ 2.6	$ 2.9	$ 3.7	$ 6.7	$ 7.5	$ 11.5	$ 3.9	$ 4.4	$ 7.7
Primary Balance Sheet Items												
Cash balance	$ 5.3	$ 8.3	$ 17.7	$ 29.2	$ 30.3	$ 34.6	$ 3.1	$ 5.3	$ 13.2	$ 7.6	$ 10.8	$ 19.4
Marketable securities	$ 0	$ 0	$ 0	$144.2	$144.2	$144.2	$ 0	$ 0	$ 0	$ 69.4	$ 69.4	$ 69.4
Total assets	$240.1	$331.4	$618.4	$721.9	$753.1	$871.4	$307.9	$384.8	$654.0	$323.0	$424.4	$696.8
Common equity	$105.6	$165.2	$353.8	$583.2	$606.4	$692.8	$ 61.8	$105.4	$264.8	$151.2	$216.2	$388.7
Free Cash Flows (Before Extraordinay Items and Dividends from Investments)												
Unlevered free cash flow	$ 6.7	−$ 54.7	$ 71.8	$ 23.8	$ 25.6	$ 54.6	$ 39.0	−$ 17.2	$106.9	$ 18.2	−$ 56.1	$ 84.0
Equity free cash flow	$ 18.8	−$ 30.2	$ 65.7	$ 24.1	$ 26.3	$ 48.8	$ 45.3	$ 2.5	$ 97.2	$ 30.4	−$ 29.0	$ 76.7
Market Values												
Marketable securities	$ 0			$144.2			$ 0			$ 69.4		
Debt	$ 94.1			$101.7			$147.6			$114.5		
Preferred stock	$ 40.3			$ 37.0			$ 98.4			$ 57.2		
Common equity:												
Shares authorized	153.35			315.36			214.52			23.12		
Shares issued	101.21			208.14			141.58			18.50		
Shares outstanding	91.09			187.32			127.42			17.02		
Price at end of Year 0	$3.445			$1.727			$4.505					
Average price per share in December of Year 0	$3.790			$1.900			$4.955					

P14.9 **Comprehensive Market Multiple Calculations—IT Happens Inc.:** Review the financial statements, schedules, and footnote extracts for IT Happens Inc. (Exhibits P14.4 to P14.8), and respond to the following questions using a valuation date of December 31, 2015. Assume the following:

- All cash is distributed to the company's shareholders when measuring enterprise value.
- Unlevered income (unlevered earnings) is equal to Net Income attributable to company + After-Tax Interest Expense.
- EBIT is equal to Net Income attributable to company + Interest Expense + Income Taxes.
- EBITDA is equal to EBIT + Depreciation and Amortization.
- Total Invested Capital is equal to Debt + Total Company Shareholders' Equity.
- Assume intrinsic value is an appropriate estimate of the fair market value of employee stock options.
- The company's costs of capital are as follows.

(Hint—recall from the chapter, if the tax reconciliation footnote does not provide information about an adjustment for a particular item we are adjusting, we use the company's marginal tax rate to measure the income tax effect of the adjustment because we have no other information. We multiply the pre-tax adjustment by the company's marginal tax rate to measure the tax effect. However, if the tax reconciliation footnote does provide information about an adjustment for a particular item we are adjusting, we do not use the marginal tax rate to make the tax adjustment but instead, we use the statutory income tax multiplied by the income effect of the adjustment and add or subtract the income tax effect noted in the tax reconciliation footnote. In the example in the chapter, Merck's tax reconciliation footnote does not show an effect of state and other income tax rates, so we assumed that Merck's marginal tax rate was equal to the federal statutory rate, 35%. Thus, for Merck, we always start by using 35% to adjust for the income tax effect regardless of whether the adjustment has a corresponding line item in the tax reconciliation footnote because we assume Merck's marginal rate is equal to the statutory rate. If there is a line item adjustment in the tax reconciliation footnote, the 35% tax was then adjusted for the amount of the line item in the tax reconciliation.)

IT Happens Inc.—Costs of Capital	Dec. 31, 2015
Debt	8.00%
Equity	12.00%
Employee Stock Options	19.00%
Unlevered	10.00%
Weighted Average Cost of Capital	9.00%

a. **Initial Financial Statement Review:** Review the information in Exhibits P14.4 through P14.8 to identify potential securities to use to measure the company's enterprise and equity value, and to identify potential adjustments to the company's market multiple value drivers (unlevered earnings, EBIT, EBITDA, revenue, total invested capital, earnings, and book value of equity). List the securities as well as the potential adjustments you might make based on this initial review.

b. **Measuring Enterprise Value:** Measure IT Happens Inc.'s enterprise value without making any additional adjustments resulting from the adjustments one might make to the financial statements to measure the value drivers (denominators). The company's stock-based compensation footnote appears below.

Stock-Based Compensation

The Company has share-based compensation plans under which the Company grants restricted stock units ("RSUs"), performance share units ("PSUs") and employee stock options ("ESOs") to certain employees and directors. These plans were approved by the Company's shareholders. Employee stock options are granted to purchase shares of Company stock at the fair market value at the time of grant. These awards generally vest one-third each year over a three-year period, with a contractual term of 7-10 years. RSUs are stock awards that are granted to employees and entitle the holder to shares of common stock as the awards vest. The fair value of the stock option and RSU awards is determined and fixed on the grant date based on the Company's stock price. PSUs are stock awards where the ultimate number of shares issued will be contingent on the Company's performance against a pre-set objective or set of objectives. The fair value of each PSU is determined on the date of grant based on the Company's stock price. For RSUs and PSUs, dividends declared during the vesting period are payable to the employees only upon vesting.

The Company uses the Black-Scholes option pricing model for determining the fair value of option grants. In applying this model, the Company uses both historical data and current market data to estimate the fair value of its options. The Black-Scholes model requires several assumptions including expected dividend yield, risk-free interest rate, volatility, and term of the options. The expected dividend yield is based on historical patterns of dividend payments. The risk-free rate is based on the rate at grant date of zero-coupon U.S. Treasury Notes with a term equal to the expected term of the option. Expected volatility is estimated using a blend

continued

continued from previous page

of historical and implied volatility. Specific information about RSUs, PSUs, and ESOs appears below.

Years Ended December 31 Options issued during year:	2013	2014	2015
Expected dividend yield (continuously compounded)	1.5%	1.5%	1.5%
Risk-free interest rate	2.0%	2.0%	2.0%
Expected volatility	35.0%	35.0%	35.0%
Expected life -years	10.0	10.0	10.0

Summarized information relative to stock option plan activity—options in thousands is as follows:

# in thousands (except per share amounts)	Number of Options	Weighted Average Exercise Price	Weighted Average Remaining Contractual Term-Years	Aggregate Intrinsic Value
Outstanding January 1, 2015	118	$21.00		
Granted	47	35.00		
Exercised	−38	35.00		
Forfeited	−30	32.00		
Outstanding December 31, 2015	97	25.00	6.00	$1,260
Expected to vest December 31, 2015	92	21.00	5.00	1,560
Exercisable December 31, 2015	49	$20.00	4.00	$ 880

A summary of nonvested Restricted Stock Units and Performance Stock Units activity—shares in thousands is as follows:

Shares in thousands	RSUs Number of Shares	Weighted Average Grant Date Fair Value	PSUs Number of Shares	Weighted Average Grant Date Fair Value
Nonvested January 1, 2015	98	$25.00	79	$23.00
Granted	25	35.00	16	35.00
Vested	−13	35.00	−8	35.00
Forfeited	−7	33.00	−4	28.00
Nonvested December 31, 2015	103	$27.00	83	$27.00

c. **Market Multiples Based on Reported Financial Statements:** Measure IT Happens Inc.'s unlevered earnings, EBIT, EBITDA, revenue, total invested capital market multiples using a December 31, 2015 valuation date and the company's reported financial statements (that is, without making any additional adjustments resulting from the adjustments one might make to the financial statements to measure the value drivers).

d. **Excess Assets:** Measure the change in unlevered earnings, EBIT, EBITDA, revenue, total invested capital, and enterprise value that would result from adjusting the company's financial statements for **Excess Land Assets** in order to appropriately calculate a market multiple using that item. The company's Property, Plant and Equipment footnote appears below.

Property, Plant, and Equipment

The Company's balance sheet details the company's property, plant and equipment ("PPEQ"). The Company's PPEQ decreased because it transferred certain assets related to discontinued operations during the most recent fiscal year. The assets transferred to discontinued operations did not have any associated accumulated depreciation. The Company has land that it does not use for its business operations but is included in PPEQ. The land has a carrying value and appraised value shown below. The company leases this land to a farmer, who pays all expenses—for example, real estate taxes—related to the land. The annual pre-tax rental payment is shown below. The company plans to sell this land sometime in the near future.

continued

continued from previous page

In Millions	Carrying Value	Appraised Value	Annual Pre-Tax Rent
	$500	$500	$50

e. **Net Operating Loss Carryforwards:** Measure the change in unlevered earnings, EBIT, EBITDA, revenue, total invested capital, and enterprise value that would result from adjusting the company's financial statements for **Net Operating Loss Carryforwards** in order to appropriately calculate a market multiple using that item. The company's Net Operating Loss Carryforwards footnote appears in Exhibit P14.8.

f. **Restructuring Charges:** Measure the change in unlevered earnings, EBIT, EBITDA, revenue, total invested capital, and enterprise value that would result from adjusting the company's financial statements for Restructuring Charges in order to appropriately calculate a market multiple using that item. The company's Restructuring Charges footnote appears below.

Restructuring Charges

In the most recent fiscal year, the Company announced a restructuring program as part of an initiative to increase its focus. As part of the program, the Company expects to reduce its total workforce, which will result in various related costs. None of these costs have been paid as of the end of the current fiscal year and were recorded in long-term liabilities. The specific pre-tax costs recorded in the current fiscal year appear below.

In Millions	
Restructuring Charges in current fiscal year	$500

g. **Impairment Charges:** Measure the change in unlevered earnings, EBIT, EBITDA, revenue, total invested capital, and enterprise value that would result from adjusting the company's financial statements for **Impairment Charges** in order to appropriately calculate a market multiple using that item. The company's Impairment Charges footnote appears below.

Goodwill and Other Intangibles

The Company performed its most recent annual impairment test and concluded that goodwill was impaired as follows:

In Millions	
Impairment of Goodwill	$400

h. **Acquisitions:** Measure the change in unlevered earnings, EBIT, EBITDA, revenue, total invested capital, and enterprise value that would result from adjusting the company's financial statements for **Acquisitions** in order to appropriately calculate a market multiple using that item. The company's Acquisitions footnote appears below.

Acquisition:

In the most recent fiscal year, the Company acquired a 100% interest in a new subsidiary. The Company recorded assets and liabilities related to this acquisition show below. Also shown below are the subsidiary's summary income statements for the periods pre and post acquisition. The Company began recording the subsidiary's revenue and expenses after the acquisition.

continued

continued from previous page

Consolidated Statement of Income (USD $) In Millions, unless otherwise specified	**Post Acquisition**	**Pre Acquisition**
Sales	$2,400	$2,040
Operating Expenses	−1,300	−1,110
Depreciation	−200	−170
Income Before Taxes	$900	$760
Taxes on Income	−360	−304
Net Income Attributable to Company	$ 540	$ 456

Consolidated Balance Sheet (USD $) In Millions, unless otherwise specified	**Post Acquisition**
Accounts receivable	$ 200
Inventories	400
Total current assets	600
Property, Plant and Equipment, Gross	2,000
Less: accumulated depreciation	−600
Property, Plant and Equipment, Net, Total	1,400
Goodwill and Other Intangibles	1,000
Total Assets	$3,000
Trade accounts payable	$ 200
Accrued and other current liabilities	400
Total current liabilities	600
Other Non-current Liabilities	1,000
Total Liabilities	1,600
Common stock	$100
Other paid-in capital	800
Retained earnings	500
Total equity	1,400
Total Liabilities and Equity	$3,000
Purchase Price	$1,400

i. **Dispositions (Divestitures):** Measure the change in unlevered earnings, EBIT, EBITDA, revenue, total invested capital, and enterprise value that would result from adjusting the company's financial statements for **Dispositions (Divestitures)** in order to appropriately calculate a market multiple using that item. The company's Dispositions (Divestitures) footnote appears below.

Disposition:
In the most recent fiscal year, the company sold one of its subsidiaries. Summary financial statements for that subsidiary as of the date of the sale are shown below.

Consolidated Statement of Income (USD $) In Millions, unless otherwise specified	**Pre-Disposition**
Sales	$600
Operating Expenses	−400
Depreciation	−100
Income Before Taxes	100
Taxes on Income	−40
Net Income Attributable to Company	$ 60

continued

continued from previous page

Consolidated Balance Sheet (USD $) In Millions, unless otherwise specified	**Pre-Disposition**
Accounts receivable	$ 100
Inventories	200
Total current assets	300
Property, Plant and Equipment, Gross	500
Less: accumulated depreciation	−100
Property, Plant and Equipment, Net, Total	400
Goodwill and Other Intangibles	400
Total Assets	$1,100
Trade accounts payable	$ 100
Accrued and other current liabilities	200
Total current liabilities	300
Other Non-current Liabilities	300
Total Liabilities	600
Common stock	50
Other paid-in capital	250
Retained earnings	200
Total company stockholders' equity	500
Total Liabilities and Equity	$1,100
Cash Received or Paid	$ 300
Gain (Loss)	−$ 200

j. **Discontinued Operations:** Measure the change in unlevered earnings, EBIT, EBITDA, revenue, total invested capital, and enterprise value that would result from adjusting the company's financial statements for **Discontinued Operations** in order to appropriately calculate a market multiple using that item. The company's Discontinued Operations footnote appears below.

Discontinued Operations

Consistent with its strategy of having more efficient and effective operations, the Company decided to discontinue certain operating units. The Company recorded an operating loss (net of income taxes) in the current fiscal year and transferred all of the net assets to Other Assets. The company expects to sell these operations within the next few years for approximately the value measured by the Company's CFO and shown below, which represents the current value of those operations.

In Millions	**Company's Ownership**	**Carrying Value**	**CFO's Valuation**
	100%	$500	$500

k. **Noncontrolling Interests:** Measure the change in unlevered earnings, EBIT, EBITDA, revenue, total invested capital, and enterprise value that would result from adjusting the company's financial statements for **Noncontrolling Interests** in order to appropriately calculate a market multiple using that item. The company's Noncontrolling Interests footnote appears below.

Noncontrolling Interest

The company owns less than 100% of one of its consolidated subsidiaries. The company's CFO conducted a valuation of this subsidiary and concluded the value of 100% of the subsidiary's common equity is as shown below.

In Millions	Company's Ownership	CFO's Valuation	Annual Net Income
	70%	$8,100	$540

l. **Equity Method Affiliates:** Measure the change in unlevered earnings, EBIT, EBITDA, revenue, total invested capital, and enterprise value that would result from adjusting the company's financial statements for **Equity Method Affiliates** in order to appropriately calculate a market multiple using that item. The company's Equity Method Affiliates footnote appears below.

Equity Method Affiliates

Equity income from affiliates, which reflects the performance of the Company's equity method affiliates is shown below. The CFO concluded that the value of these companies is a multiple of EBIT as shown below.

In Millions, unless otherwise specified	2013	2014	2015
Company's percentage ownership in the affiliate	30.0%	30.0%	30.0%
Equity income from affiliates	$50	$75	$150
Summary information for the affiliate companies:			
Sales	$4,000	$6,500	$12,500
Operating income (EBIT)	$ 500	$ 800	$1,500
Income tax rate on all income	40.0%	40.0%	40.0%
EBIT Multiple	7.80	8.20	8.00

m. **Debt Redemption:** Measure the change in unlevered earnings, EBIT, EBITDA, revenue, total invested capital, and enterprise value that would result from adjusting the company's financial statements for **Debt Redemption** in order to appropriately calculate a market multiple using that item.

n. **Market Multiples Based on Reported Financial Statements:** Measure IT Happens Inc.'s unlevered earnings, EBIT, EBITDA, revenue, and total invested capital market multiples using a December 31, 2015 valuation date and the company's adjusted financial statements (that is, making any additional adjustments resulting from the adjustments one might make to the financial statements to measure the value drivers).

EXHIBIT P14.4 IT Happens Inc.—Consolidated Statements of Income and Market Data

	IT Happens Inc.		
Consolidated Statement of Income (USD $) In Millions, unless otherwise specified	**Dec. 31, 2013**	**Dec. 31, 2014**	**Dec. 31, 2015**
Sales	$ 5,000	$ 8,000	$10,000
Operating expenses	−3,500	−5,600	−7,000
Depreciation	−800	−900	−900
Amortization	−100	−200	−300
Restructuring and impairment costs			−900
Equity income from affiliates (net of tax)	50	75	150
Other income (expense), net	0	0	−100
Operating income	650	1,375	950
Interest and other investment income	140	150	170
Interest expense	−170	−190	−210
Income before taxes	620	1,335	910
Taxes on income	−176	−434	−303
Income (loss) from continuing operations	444	901	607
Discontinued operations (net of tax)			−200
Net income	444	901	407
Less: net income attributable to noncontrolling interests	50	75	162
Net income attributable to company	$ 394	$ 826	$ 245
Basic earnings per common share	$ 1.19	$ 2.23	$ 0.64
Weighted average shares for basic eps	330.0	370.0	380.0
Common stock, shares authorized (millions)	1,000.0	1,000.0	1,000.0
Common stock, shares issued (millions)	400.0	424.0	454.0
Treasury stock, shares (millions)	40.0	52.0	61.0
Stock price at fiscal year-end	$ 17.00	$ 32.00	$ 38.00
Shares outstanding and stock price as of the 10-K filing date 1/31/2016		400.0	$ 40.00

EXHIBIT P14.5 IT Happens Inc.—Consolidated Balance Sheets

Consolidated Balance Sheet (USD $) In Millions, unless otherwise specified	IT Happens Inc. Dec. 31, 2014	Dec. 31, 2015
Cash and cash equivalents	$ 4,000	$ 3,167
Short-term investments	400	500
Accounts receivable	550	1,000
Inventories	520	900
Net deferred income tax assets	420	660
Total current assets	5,890	6,227
Investments	1,200	1,400
Equity affiliates	500	650
Property, plant and equipment, gross	8,000	10,500
Less: accumulated depreciation	−1,000	−2,400
Property, plant and equipment, net, total	7,000	8,100
Goodwill and other intangibles	1,200	1,100
Other assets	100	700
Total assets	$15,890	$18,177
Trade accounts payable	$ 200	$ 400
Accrued and other current liabilities	750	1,000
Income taxes payable	100	180
Total current liabilities	1,050	1,580
Long-term debt	2,100	1,300
Net deferred income tax liabilities	700	900
Other non-current liabilities	800	2,300
Total liabilities	4,650	6,080
Common stock	2,000	2,100
Other paid-in capital	7,340	8,028
Retained earnings	3,900	4,107
Stockholders' equity before deduction for treasury stock	13,240	14,235
Less treasury stock, at cost	−3,000	−3,300
Total company stockholders' equity	10,240	10,935
Noncontrolling interests	1,000	1,162
Total equity	11,240	12,097
Total liabilities and equity	$15,890	$18,177

EXHIBIT P14.6 IT Happens Inc.—Consolidated Statements of Cash Flows

Consolidated Statement of Cash Flows (USD $ in Millions)	IT Happens Inc.	
	Dec. 31, 2014	Dec. 31, 2015
Net income	$ 901	$ 407
Depreciation	900	900
Amortization	200	300
Restructuring		500
Impairment costs		400
(Gain) loss on disposition		200
(Gain) loss on debt redemption		−100
Equity income from affiliates	−75	−150
Deferred income taxes	−32	−40
Accounts receivable	−280	−350
Inventories	−143	−180
Trade accounts payable	80	100
Accrued current liabilities	40	50
Income taxes payable	64	80
Other non-current assets		−100
Other non-current liabilities	240	300
Net cash provided by operating activities	1,895	2,317
Capital expenditures	−1,200	−1,500
Net purchases of securities and other investments	−200	−300
Goodwill and other intangibles		0
Divestiture		300
Acquisition		−1,400
Net cash used in investing activities	−1,400	−2,900
Redemption of debt	0	−1,700
Issuance of debt	1,100	1,000
Purchases of treasury stock	−200	−300
Dividends paid to stockholders	−180	−200
Proceeds from issuance of common stock	400	950
Net cash used in financing activities	1,120	−250
Net (decrease) increase in cash and cash equivalents	1,615	−833
Cash and cash equivalents at beginning of year	2,385	4,000
Cash and cash equivalents at end of year	$ 4,000	$ 3,167

EXHIBIT P14.7 IT Happens Inc.—Investments, Fair Value Measurements, and Other Income Footnotes

Investments

At December 31, 2015, the value of the company's cash and cash equivalents, short-term investments, and investments is equal to their carrying value. The non-cash investments consists primarily of U.S. Government Bonds of various maturities.

Fair Value Measurements

Fair value is defined as the exchange price that would be received for an asset or paid to transfer a liability (an exit price) in the principal or most advantageous market for the asset or liability in an orderly transaction between market participants on the measurement date. The Company uses a fair value hierarchy which maximizes the use of observable inputs and minimizes the use of unobservable inputs when measuring fair value. There are three levels of inputs used to measure fair value with Level 1 having the highest priority and Level 3 having the lowest: Level 1—Quoted prices (unadjusted) in active markets for identical assets or liabilities. Level 2—Observable inputs other than Level 1 prices, such as quoted prices for similar assets or liabilities, or other inputs that are observable or can be corroborated by observable market data for substantially the full term of the assets or liabilities. Level 3—Unobservable inputs that are supported by little or no market activity. Level 3 assets or liabilities are those whose values are determined using pricing models, discounted cash flow methodologies, or similar techniques with significant unobservable inputs, as well as assets or liabilities for which the determination of fair value requires significant judgment or estimation.

Some of the Company's financial instruments, such as cash and cash equivalents, receivables and payables, are reflected in the balance sheet at carrying value, which approximates fair value due to their short-term nature. The estimated fair value of long-term debt as a percentage of carrying value is shown below.

Fair value as a % of carrying value	110%

Other Income:

The details of the company's other income is shown below. In the most recent fiscal year, the company sold one of its subsidiaries. See the summary financial statements for the subsidiary that was sold presented in a later footnote. The company also redeemed debt. The pre-tax income effects for each of these transactions are shown below.

Other Income (Expense), Net (Details) (USD $) In Millions, unless otherwise specified	**2013**	**2014**	**2015**
Gain (loss) on disposition			−$200
Gain (loss) on debt redemption	—	—	100
Other income (expense), net	$0	$0	−$100

EXHIBIT P14.8 IT Happens Inc.—Income Tax Footnotes

Income Taxes

The company's effective tax rate differs from the US Statutory rate due to various differences between tax reporting and financial reporting as well as from the payment of income taxes to various states in the US. A reconciliation of this difference appears below. Also presented below are the balances of the company's deferred tax assets and liabilities.

The Company has net operating loss ("NOL") carryforwards. The potential tax benefit from these NOLs has been recorded as a deferred tax asset, all of which are expected to be fully utilized prior to expiration. In each future year, the Company expects to be able to use the same amount of the NOL tax benefit as it did in the current fiscal year until the Company utilizes all of its current NOLs.

Taxes on Income—Reconciliation Between Effective Tax Rate and US Statutory Rate

In Millions, unless otherwise specified	Dec. 31, 2013	Dec. 31, 2014	Dec. 31, 2015
U.S. statutory rate applied to income before taxes %	35.0%	35.0%	35.0%
Differential arising from:			
Net operating loss carryforwards	−10.0%	−9.0%	−8.8%
Disposition			−4.4%
Restructuring			−2.2%
Intangible asset impairment charges			3.3%
Debt redemption			1.1%
State taxes	5.0%	5.0%	5.0%
Other	3.3%	2.3%	4.3%
Total, Tax Rate	33.33%	33.33%	33.33%
U.S. statutory rate applied to income before taxes $	$217	$467	$319
Differential arising from:			
Net operating loss carryforwards	−62	−120	−80
Disposition	0	0	−40
Restructuring	0	0	−20
Intangible asset impairment charges	0	0	30
Debt redemption	0	0	10
State taxes	31	67	46
Other	−10	20	39
Taxes on income	$176	$434	$303

Taxes on Income—Deferred Income Taxes (Details) (USD $) In Millions, unless otherwise specified	Dec. 31, 2015 Assets	Dec. 31, 2015 Liabilities
Intangibles		$ 300
Inventory		300
Accelerated depreciation		700
Equity investments	$ 200	
Operating liabilities	480	
Compensation related, assets	100	
Net operating loss carryforwards	800	
Other	130	170
Subtotal, assets	1,710	
Valuation allowance (all related to operating liabilities)	−480	
Deferred tax assets and liabilities	$1,230	1,470
Net		−$ 240

SOLUTIONS FOR REVIEW EXERCISES

Solution for Review Exercise 14.1: Measuring Market Multiple Numerators

Market Value of Debt	
Price	102
Market value of debt	$ 12,240
Market Value of Preferred	
Price	98
Market value of preferred	$ 4,900
Market Value of Options	
Price	$ 2.00
Shares	2,000
Market value of options	$ 4,000
Market Value of Common Equity	
Price	$ 10.00
Shares	10,000
Market value of common equity	$100,000

Market Value	Enterprise Value	Equity Value
Debt	$ 12,240	
Preferred stock	4,900	
Options	4,000	$ 4,000
Common equity	100,000	100,000
Subtotal	$121,140	$104,000
Cash and equivalents	−12,000	−12,000
Total	$109,140	$ 92,000

Market Multiples	Numerator	Denominator	Multiple
Net income		$ 1,256	
Interest expense		840	
Interest tax shield		−336	
Unlevered earnings	$109,140	$ 1,760	62.0
EBIT	$109,140	$ 3,200	34.1
Depreciation		8,000	
EBITDA	$109,140	$11,200	9.7
Revenue	$109,140	$30,000	3.6
Net income		$ 1,256	
Preferred stock dividends		−400	
Net income to common	$ 92,000	$ 856	107.5

EBIT of \$3,200 = Net Income \$1,256 + Interest Expense \$840 + Income Taxes \$1,104

Solution for Review Exercise 14.2: Measuring Market Multiple Denominators

	Year 1	Year 2	Cash and Equivalents	Non-recurring Expenses	Year 2 Adjusted
Revenue		$30,000			$30,000
Operating expenses		−21,000		$4,000	−17,000
Depreciation expense		−8,000			−8,000
Operating earnings		$ 1,000	$ 0	$4,000	$ 5,000
Pre-tax earnings from unconsolidated affiliates		2,000			2,000
Interest income (on cash and equivalents)		600	−600		0
Interest expense		−840			−840
Income before taxes		$ 2,760	−$ 600	$4,000	$ 6,160
Income tax expense		−1,104	240	−1,600	−2,464
Minority interest (net of tax)		−400			−400
Net income		$ 1,256	−$ 360	$2,400	$ 3,296
Cash and equivalents	$12,000	$12,000	−$12,000		$ 0
Other current assets	5,000	5,000			5,000
Investments in unconsolidated affiliates	11,000	11,000			11,000
Property, plant, and equipment (net)	36,000	38,000			38,000
Total assets	$64,000	$66,000	−$12,000	$ 0	$54,000
Accounts payable	$ 3,000	$ 4,000			$ 4,000
Debt	12,000	12,000			12,000
Total liabilities	$15,000	$16,000	$ 0	$ 0	$16,000
Minority interest	$ 5,000	$ 6,000			$ 6,000
Preferred stock	$ 5,000	$ 5,000			$ 5,000
Capital stock	3,000	3,000			3,000
Retained earnings	36,000	36,000	−$12,000		24,000
Shareholders' equity	$44,000	$44,000	−$12,000	$ 0	$32,000
Liabilities and shareholders' equity	$64,000	$66,000	−$12,000	$ 0	$54,000

Market Multiples	Numerator	Denominator	Multiple
Net income		$ 3,296	
Interest expense		840	
Interest tax shield		−336	
Unlevered earnings	$109,140	$ 3,800	28.7
EBIT	$109,140	$ 6,600	16.5
Depreciation		8,000	
EBITDA	$109,140	$14,600	7.5
Revenue	$109,140	$30,000	3.6
Net income		$ 3,296	
Preferred stock dividends		−400	
Net income to common	$ 92,000	$ 2,896	31.8

EBIT OF $6,600 = Net Income $3,296 + Interest Expense $840 + Income Taxes $2,464

Solution for Review Exercise 14.3: Adjusting Market Multiple Numerators and Denominators

	Year 1	Year 2	Cash and Equivalents	Non-recurring Expenses	Unconsolidated Affiliates	Minority Interest	Year 2 Adjusted
Revenue		$30,000					$30,000
Operating expenses		−21,000		$4,000			−17,000
Depreciation expense		−8,000					−8,000
Operating earnings		$ 1,000	$ 0	$4,000	$ 0	$ 0	$ 5,000
Pre-tax earnings from unconsolidated affiliates		2,000			−2,000		0
Interest income (cash and equivalents)		600	−600				0
Interest expense		−840					−840
Income before taxes		$ 2,760	−$ 600	$4,000	−$ 2,000	$ 0	$ 4,160
Income tax expense		−1,104	240	−1,600	800		−1,664
Minority interest (net of tax)		−400				400	0
Net income		$ 1,256	−$ 360	$2,400	−$ 1,200	$ 400	$ 2,496
Cash and equivalents	$12,000	$12,000	−$12,000				$ 0
Other current assets	5,000	5,000					5,000
Investments in unconsolidated affiliates	11,000	11,000			−$11,000		0
Property, plant, and equipment (net)	36,000	38,000					38,000
Total assets	$64,000	$66,000	−$12,000	$ 0	−$11,000	$ 0	$43,000
Account payable	$ 3,000	$ 4,000					$ 4,000
Debt	12,000	12,000					12,000
Total liabilities	$15,000	$16,000	$ 0	$ 0	$ 0	$ 0	$16,000
Minority interest	$ 5,000	$ 6,000				−$6,000	$ 0
Preferred stock	$ 5,000	$ 5,000					$ 5,000
Capital stock	3,000	3,000					3,000
Retained earnings	36,000	36,000	−$12,000		−$11,000	$6,000	19,000
Shareholders' equity	$44,000	$44,000	−$12,000	$ 0	−$11,000	$6,000	$27,000
Liabilities and shareholders' equity	$64,000	$66,000	−$12,000	$ 0	−$11,000	$ 0	$43,000

Market Value	Enterprise Value	Equity Value
Debt	$ 12,240	
Preferred stock	4,900	
Options	4,000	$ 4,000
Common equity	100,000	100,000
Subtotal	$121,140	$104,000
Cash and equivalents	−12,000	−12,000
Previous total	$109,140	$ 92,000
Unconsolidated affiliates	−28,000	−28,000
Minority interest	5,600	5,600
Total	$ 86,740	$ 69,600

Market Multiples	Numerator	Denominator	Multiple
Net income		$ 2,496	
Interest expense		840	
Interest tax shield		−336	
Unlevered earnings	$86,740	$ 3,000	28.9
EBIT	$86,740	$ 5,000	17.3
Depreciation		8,000	
EBITDA	$86,740	$13,000	6.7
Revenue	$86,740	$30,000	2.9
Net income		$ 2,496	
Preferred stock dividends		−400	
Net income to common	$69,600	$ 2,096	33.2

EBIT of $5,000 = Net Income $2,496 + Interest Expense $840 + Income Taxes $1,664

Solution for Review Exercise 14.4: Market Multiples and Operating Leases

	Reported	Adjustments	Adjusted
Revenues	$ 7,000.0		$ 7,000.0
Rent expense	−500.0	$ 500.0	0.0
Depreciation and amortization	−2,000.0		−2,000.0
Amortization of operating leases		−399.3	−399.3
All other operating expenses	−3,000.0		−3,000.0
Operating income	$ 1,500.0	$ 100.7	$ 1,600.7
Interest expense, net	−400.0		−400.0
Lease interest		−159.7	−159.7
Income before taxes	$ 1,100.0	−$ 59.0	$ 1,041.0
Income taxes	−440.0	23.6	−416.4
Net income	$ 660.0	−$ 35.4	$ 624.6
Cash	$ 400.0		$ 400.0
Other current assets	2,000.0	$ 23.6	2,023.6
Net property, plant, and equipment	8,000.0		8,000.0
Other assets	2,000.0		2,000.0
Capitalized operating leased asset		2,041.0	2,041.0
Total assets	$12,400.0	$2,064.6	$14,464.6
Current operating liabilities	$ 1,000.0		$ 1,000.0
Other liabilities	1,500.0	$ 0.0	1,500.0
Debt	4,500.0		4,500.0
Capitalized operating lease obligations		2,100.0	2,100.0
Total liabilities	$ 7,000.0	$2,100.0	$ 9,100.0
Shareholders' equity	5,400.0	−35.4	5,364.6
Total liabilities and shareholders' equity	$12,400.0	$2,064.6	$14,464.6

	Capitalized Lease Balance
Lease liability—beginning balance	$1,996.3
Interest expense	159.7
Lease payment	-500.0
Subtotal	$1,656.0
Lease liability—ending balance	2,100.0
Present value of new leases	$ 444.0
Lease asset—beginning balance	$1,996.3
Amortization	-399.3
Present value of new leases	444.0
Lease asset—ending balance	$2,041.0

Valuation	Equity Value	Enterprise Value
Market value of equity	$5,000.0	$ 5,000.0
Debt		4,500.0
Market value of equity and firm	$5,000.0	$ 9,500.0
Cash	-400.0	-400.0
Market value without capitalizing leases	$4,600.0	$ 9,100.0
Capitalized operating leases		2,100.0
Market value with capitalizing leases	$4,600.0	$11,200.0

	P/E	Unlevered Earnings Multiple	EBIT Multiple	EBITDA Multiple	Revenue Multiple
Denominator					
Earnings	$ 660.0	$ 660.0	$ 660.0	$ 660.0	
Interest		400.0	400.0	400.0	
Tax adjustment		−160.0	440.0	440.0	
Depreciation and amortization				2,000.0	
Earnings without capitalizing operating leases	$ 660.0	$ 900.0	$ 1,500.0	$ 3,500.0	
Rent expense	500.0	500.0	500.0	500.0	
Interest on leases	−159.7				
Amortization of leases	−399.3	−399.3	−399.3		
Tax adjustment	23.6	−40.3			
Earnings with capitalizing leases	$ 624.6	$ 960.4	$ 1,600.7	$ 4,000.0	
Multiple Without Capitalizing Leases					
Value without capitalizing operating leases	$4,600.0	$ 9,100.0	$ 9,100.0	$ 9,100.0	$ 9,100.0
Denominator without capitalizing operating leases	660.0	900.0	1,500.0	3,500.0	7,000.0
Multiple without capitalized operating leases	6.97	10.11	6.07	2.60	1.30
Multiple With Capitalizing Leases					
Value with capitalizing operating leases	$4,600.0	$11,200.0	$11,200.0	$11,200.0	$11,200.0
Denominator with capitalizing operating leases	624.6	960.4	1,600.7	4,000.0	7,000.0
Multiple with capitalized operating leases	7.36	11.66	7.00	2.80	1.60
Percentage change	5.7%	15.3%	15.3%	7.7%	23.1%

Solution for Review Exercise 14.5: Valuing a Company Using Market Multiples

Year 1	Unlevered Earnings	EBIT	EBITDA	Net Income to Common
Net income	$644.0	$ 644.0	$ 644.0	$644.0
Preferred stock dividends				−350.0
Interest expense	480.0	480.0	480.0	
Interest tax shield	−144.0			
Income taxes		276.0	276.0	
Depreciation and amortization			1,300.0	
Total (before adjustment for excess cash)	$980.0	$1,400.0	$2,700.0	$294.0
Interest income (cash and equivalents)	−200.0	−200.0	−200.0	−200.0
Income taxes	60.0			60.0
Total (after all adjustments)	$840.0	$1,200.0	$2,500.0	$154.0

Year 1	Unlevered Earnings	EBIT	EBITDA	Revenue	Net Income to Common
ValueIT Company's value drivers	$ 840.0	$ 1,200.0	$ 2,500.0	$ 5,000.0	$ 154.0
Market multiple (Review Exercise 14.3)	28.91	17.35	6.67	2.89	33.21
	$24,287.2	$20,817.6	$16,680.8	$14,456.7	$ 5,113.7
Long-term debt					8,000.0
Perpetual preferred stock					5,000.0
Enterprise value	$24,287.2	$20,817.6	$16,680.8	$14,456.7	$18,113.7
Cash and equivalents	1,000.0	1,000.0	1,000.0	1,000.0	1,000.0
Excess asset (land)	6,000.0	6,000.0	6,000.0	6,000.0	6,000.0
Value of firm with excess assets	$31,287.2	$27,817.6	$23,680.8	$21,456.7	$25,113.7
Long-term debt	−8,000.0	−8,000.0	−8,000.0	−8,000.0	−8,000.0
Perpetual preferred stock	−5,000.0	−5,000.0	−5,000.0	−5,000.0	−5,000.0
Common equity value with excess assets	$18,287.2	$14,817.6	$10,680.8	$ 8,456.7	$12,113.7
% Difference from Unlevered Earnings Valuation					
Value of firm with excess assets	0.0%	−11.1%	−24.3%	−31.4%	−19.7%
Equity value with excess assets	0.0%	−19.0%	−41.6%	−53.8%	−33.8%

After mastering the material in this chapter, you will be able to:

1. Understand LBO activity, deal characteristics, and the role of financial sponsors (15.1)
2. Decide when to consider an LBO transaction (15.2)
3. Understand the steps for analyzing and valuing an LBO transaction (15.3)
4. Use an LBO model to analyze and value an LBO transaction (15.4)
5. Use DCF models to further analyze LBO transactions (15.5)

CHAPTER

Leveraged Buyout Transactions

15

The **RJR Nabisco, Inc.** leveraged buyout is one of the more famous (and early) leveraged buyouts. The book, *Barbarians at the Gate: The Fall of RJR Nabisco*, which became a television movie describes the events and corporate battles around this transaction. RJR Nabisco was a manufacturer of cigarettes and food products (such as Oreo Cookies and Ritz Crackers). It was created by the merger of RJ Reynolds Tobacco Company and Nabisco Brands in the mid-1980s. By the late 1980s, RJR's stock price was "languishing," and in 1989, Kohlberg Kravis & Roberts (KKR), a private equity firm, purchased RJR Nabisco in a highly leveraged buyout transaction for close to $25 billion, which at the time was the largest leveraged buyout transaction on record.[1]

RJR NABISCO

Analysts thought that RJR was a good LBO candidate because it had stable cash flows, steady growth in both up and down business cycles (its unlevered beta was 0.7), low capital expenditure requirements, low financial leverage, and a high likelihood of being able to improve its operating cost structure. KKR funded the equity investment of $1.5 billion, and it issued various forms of debt securities and preferred stock with equity "kickers" for the remainder of the financing. The issuance of the additional debt increased RJR's debt-to-value ratio from roughly 5% to approximately 95%, and the increased debt increased its equity beta from roughly 1 to over 9.5.

In this chapter, we delve into the world of leveraged buyouts to understand the motivations for undertaking an LBO, how they are structured, and how to analyze an LBO transaction.

[1] KKR did not start the bidding for this company. The company's chief executive officer offered $74 per share in an attempt to take the company private. This initial bid was characterized as a "low-ball bid" and KKR responded with a $90 bid. As a result of a bidding war that was primarily between the chief executive officer and KKR, KKR bought the company for more than $100 per share. The premium paid to RJR's stockholders was over $9 billion. For a more detailed discussion, see Michel, A., and I. Shaked, "RJR Nabisco: A Case Study of a Complex Leveraged Buyout," *Financial Analysts Journal* (September–October 1991), pp. 15–27.

CHAPTER ORGANIZATION

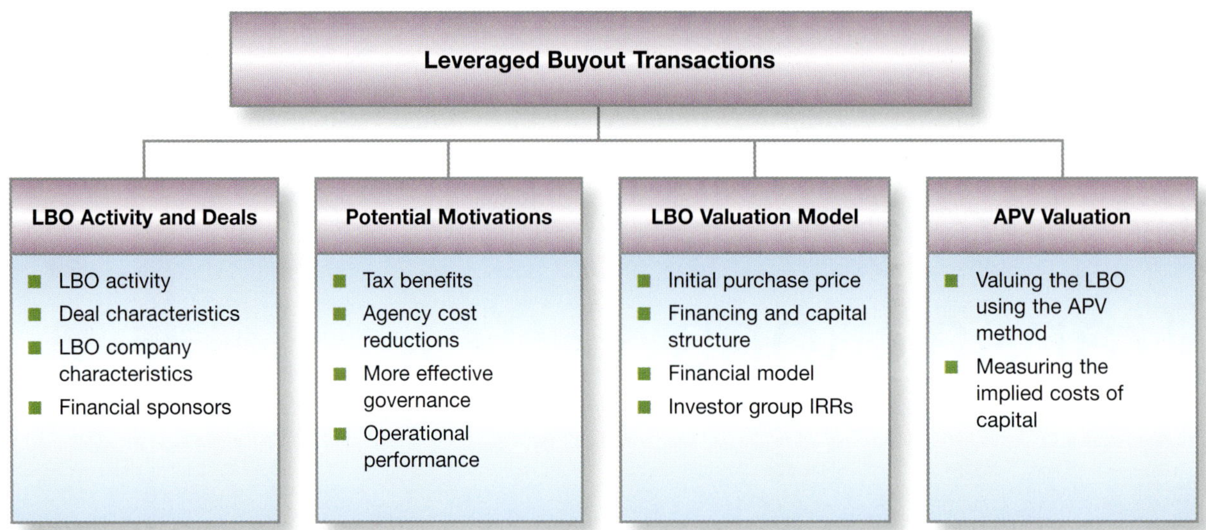

INTRODUCTION

This chapter focuses on certain types of acquisition transactions financed with a large proportion of debt financing—**leveraged buyout** (**LBO**) and **management buyout** (**MBO**) transactions. The target company in the transaction is either a publicly traded or privately held company but the acquirer (buyer) is typically a privately held entity. The post-LBO company uses all of the company's assets as collateral for the additional debt. Next, the company issues unsecured debt. The unsecured debt issued in these transactions is typically high-yield debt (below investment grade)—also called **junk bonds**. While the post-transaction company's equity securities are privately held, its debt and preferred stock may be publicly traded. In a **going private** transaction, publicly held companies become privately held after the transaction, and they often use this type of financial structure. Investors also use this type of financial structure to acquire companies that are already privately owned.

Valuation in Practice 15.1

H. J. Heinz Company Leveraged Buyout by Berkshire Hathaway Inc. and 3G Capital Partners Ltd.[2]—The Transaction In February 2013, Heinz announced that it entered into a definitive merger agreement related to a leveraged buyout transaction with a subsidiary owned by Berkshire Hathaway Inc. and an investment fund affiliated with 3G Capital Partners Ltd. The consideration paid to shareholders and the holders of restricted stock units was $72.50 in cash for each share (or unit). Further, the holders of employee stock options were paid the difference between $72.50 and the exercise price of their options. Heinz was delisted from the New York Stock Exchange after the transaction closed. The uses and sources of capital (in billions of $) for the transaction are as follows.

Uses of Funds		Sources of Funds*	
$24.3	Purchase of equity securities	$ 4.1	3G Capital equity
4.2	Repayment of debt	4.1	Berkshire Hathaway equity
0.3	Fees	8.0	Berkshire Hathaway preferred
$28.8	Total uses of funds	9.5	Senior secured debt
		3.0	Second lien note
		$28.8	Total sources of funds

* Does not include $2.0 billion revolving credit agreement which will not be drawn to close the transaction

[2] H. J. Heinz Company and its subsidiaries manufacture and market an extensive line of food products throughout the world. Its principal products include ketchup, condiments and sauces, frozen food, soups, beans and pasta meals, infant nutrition and other food products. See the Heinz proxy statement filed with the U.S. SEC on March 27, 2013 for more details about this transaction.

MBOs are leveraged transactions in which the current management continues to manage the post-transaction company and the term is generally reserved for situations where the management team is the party that initiates the transaction. Aside from conflicts of interest that occur when current managers participate in the purchase of the company, the valuation issues for LBOs and MBOs are generally the same. Note that current management often continues to manage the post-transaction company, even if the transaction was initiated by a **financial sponsor** or a **private equity firm**. Thus, even though the focus of our discussion is mostly on LBOs, the analyses, financial models, and valuation methods we discuss for LBOs also apply to MBOs.

In this chapter, we first provide descriptive information about these types of transactions and also discuss how leveraged buyout transactions are structured and what types of firms are normally candidates for a leveraged buyout. We discuss how leveraged buyouts increase the incentives of both management and monitors—such as the board of directors—and can potentially create wealth for the investors. We also discuss the extant empirical evidence on the performance of leveraged buyout transactions and the role of financial sponsors in these transactions. Finally, we discuss how to analyze these transactions. As it turns out, the option for a company to go private in a leveraged buyout transaction is often an alternative strategy for a company attempting to create more value for shareholders. This is why an LBO analysis is sometimes used as another valuation method by an investment bank that is serving as a financial advisor to a target of an acquisition.

15.1 LEVERAGED BUYOUT ACTIVITY, DEAL CHARACTERISTICS, AND THE ROLE OF THE FINANCIAL SPONSOR

LO1 Understand LBO activity, deal characteristics, and the role of financial sponsors

As we document in the exhibits that follow, the extent of LBO activity varies over time and across global regions. (We do not distinguish MBO transactions from LBO transactions.) In this section, we present descriptive characteristics of LBO transactions. We use the Thomson Financial database to collect the sample of transactions we examine.[3] We select transactions that were completed or were still pending between 2000 and 2015, that had a value (enterprise value) of at least $10 million, and we included both publicly traded and privately held acquirers and targets. We provide descriptive information on the enterprise value of these transactions both globally and for 12 countries/regions: Africa, Asia, Australia and other Oceania Countries, China, China—Hong Kong, European Union, Europe, Middle East, North America without the U.S., South and Central America and the Caribbean, United Kingdom (U.K.), and the United States (U.S.).[4] Based on these criteria, we examine 3,989 completed public and private LBO transactions. In this section, we also describe the characteristics of leveraged buyouts in terms of both the deal structure of the transaction and the types of companies for which leveraged buyout transactions most commonly occur. While the focus of this chapter is on leveraged buyouts, we also discuss leveraged recapitalizations in this section. Lastly, we discuss the role of financial sponsors—who they are and what they do.

Time-Series of Leveraged Buyout Transactions

In Exhibit 15.1, we present the time-series of both the size (enterprise value) of global LBO transactions and the percentage of global merger and acquisition transactions that were LBO transactions from 2001 through 2015. Prior to 2006, LBO transactions, while initially growing, stabilized at around $100 billion annually and were a relatively small part of all merger and acquisition transactions, between 1.5% and 5.2%. LBO transactions increased substantially in the following two years and peaked in 2007 at over $500 billion. During this period, LBO transactions as a percentage of merger and acquisitions transactions increased as well and peaked at more than 11%. Some have argued that low interest rates and low stock prices (relative to rising corporate profits) created ideal conditions for the LBO market in 2006 and 2007.[5]

---

[3] Thomson Reuters database of global mergers and acquisitions activity, which includes LBO activity. The database covers over 1,000,000 transactions, including more than 300,000 US-target and more than 700,000 non-US-target transactions, whether complete or uncompleted. Thomson's data were formerly collected by Securities Data Corporation and accessed through a program called SDC Platinum.

[4] Classifications are based on United Nations classifications (http://unstats.un.org/unsd/methods/m49/m49regin.htm). Europe includes countries such as Iceland, Norway, Russia, Serbia, Switzerland, Turkey, Ukraine and Yugoslavia.

[5] See, for example, http://money.cnn.com/2007/08/06/markets/privateequitybubble.fortune/index.htm (cited as of June 18, 2018).

LBO transactions plummeted with the financial crisis and recession in 2008, decreasing to $217 billion (6.5% of all merger and acquisition transactions). They decreased again to under $80 billion in 2009 as the recession continued and as the credit markets remained in flux, but increased as the global economy began to recover slowly from the recession and has stabilized in the $150 to $200 billion range annually (6% to 8% of all merger and acquisition transactions).

EXHIBIT 15.1 Time-Series of Global Leveraged Buyout Transactions

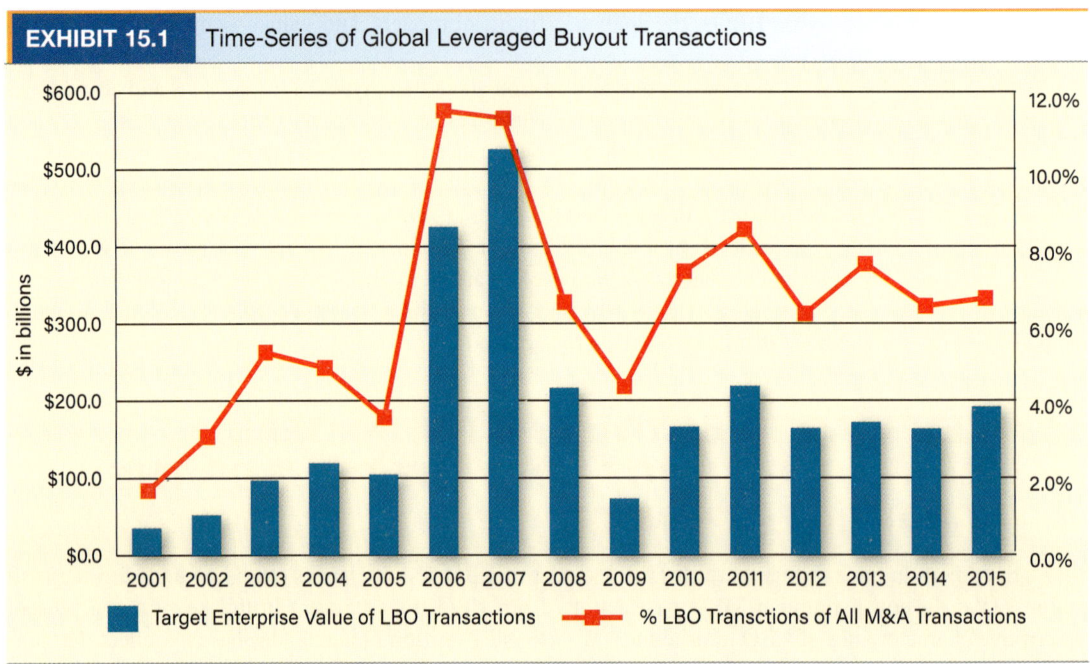

In Exhibit 15.2, we present regional market shares of the value of global LBO transactions based on the country of the target. We measure the market share metric as the value of the LBO transactions in that country or region in 2011 through 2015, divided by the total market value of all global LBO transactions during that period. The U.S. and European Union have the largest market shares, 30% and 21%, respectively. The next largest market shares are Asia and the U.K.

EXHIBIT 15.2 Target Enterprise Value-Based "Market Share" of 2011–2015 Global Leveraged Buyout Transactions

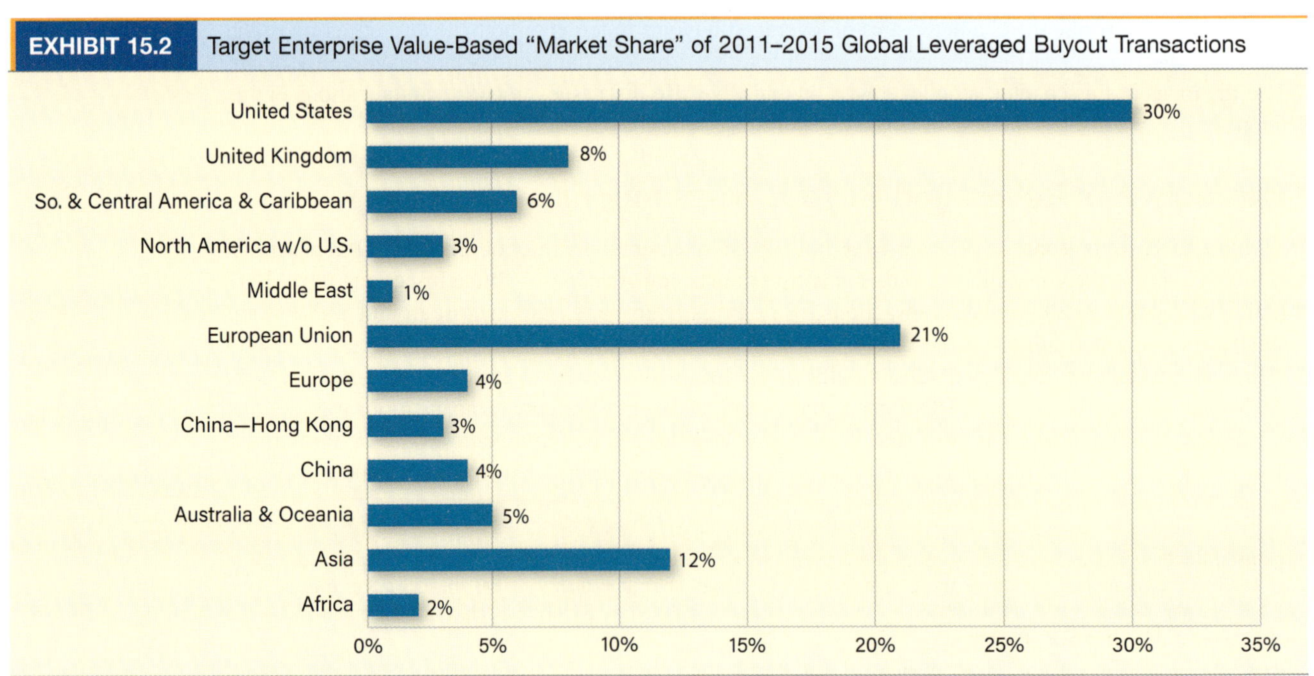

Home Country Preference

In Exhibit 15.3, we present the percentage of LBO transactions for which the target and acquirer are from the same country (based on enterprise value of the target). This percentage is a measure of the acquirers' home country preference. One minus this percentage represents the percentage of cross-border LBO transactions.

EXHIBIT 15.3 Home Country Preference—Target Enterprise Value-Based 2011–2015 Percentage of Global Leveraged Buyout Transactions with Acquirer and Target from Same Country

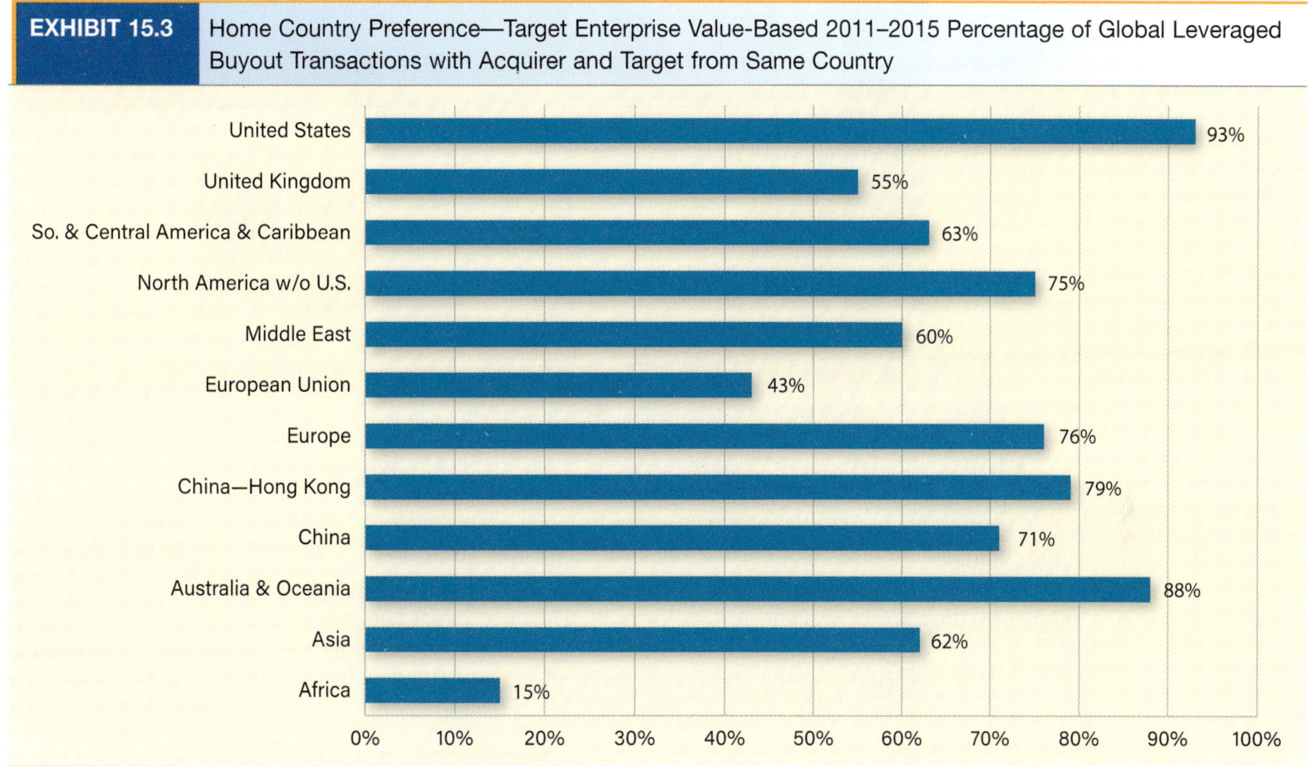

The country with the highest home country preference is the U.S., where over 90% of the enterprise value of LBO transactions by U.S. acquirers involve a U.S. target. The rest of North America, Europe (excluding the E.U.), China, China–Hong Kong, and Australia all have more than a 70% home country preference. African acquirers have the lowest home country preference, 15%, and thus also the most cross-border transactions, 85%.

Private versus Public Targets and Acquirers

In Exhibit 15.4, we present the percentage of global LBO transactions (based on enterprise value) of privately held and publicly traded targets as well as privately held and publicly traded acquirers from 2011 to 2015. The first set of bars reports the types of targets, and the second set of bars reports the types of acquirers.

For the targets, the exhibit shows that about 70% of the total enterprise value are publicly traded, 20% are subsidiaries of a publicly traded company, and under 10% are privately held. In the 1970 to 2007 sample of LBOs in Kaplan and Strömberg (2009), 27% of the total enterprise value of LBO transactions was comprised of public-to-private transactions. In addition, 23% consisted of independent private companies, 30% consisted of divisions of other companies, 20% consisted of secondary LBOs (a private equity firm buying a company from another private equity firm), and 1% was purchased out of distress.[6] For the acquirers, most LBO funds are not publicly traded although they may be part of a publicly traded management company. Thus, only 6% of the acquirers are publicly traded and over 90% are privately held or part of publicly traded companies.

[6] See Kaplan S., and P. Strömberg, "Leveraged Buyouts and Private Equity," *Journal of Economic Perspectives* vol. 23, no. 1 (2009), pp. 1–27.

EXHIBIT 15.4 Target Enterprise Value-Based 2011–2015 Percentage of Global Leveraged Buyout Transactions by Types of Targets and Acquirers in Global Leveraged Buyout Transactions

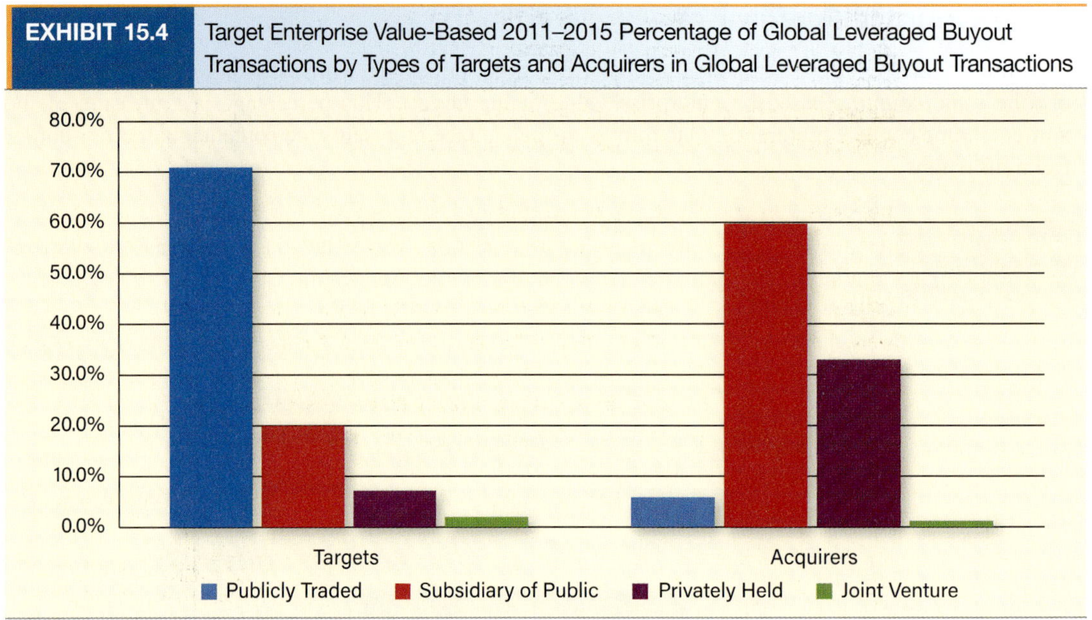

Premiums Paid and Transaction Market Multiples

In this section, we present the premiums paid to target shareholders in LBO transactions and the transaction multiples implied by the LBO transactions by year from 2001 to 2015. Thomson One measures transaction premiums in terms of changes in the publicly traded common equity market prices of target companies; thus, we only report results for publicly traded target companies. In Exhibit 15.5, we report the time-series of one-week transaction premiums.[7] In this exhibit we present the median premium and 25th and 75th percentiles of the premiums across all global LBO transactions in a year. The transaction premiums vary over time. The medians range between 14% (2014) and 34% (2008). The median over all years (not reported on the chart) is 22%. The 25th and 75th percentiles illustrate the fairly large range of premiums paid in any one year. The difference between the 75th and 25th percentiles (called the interquartile range) is generally around 30% with the smallest range equal to 23% (2005) and the largest range equal to 46% (2008).

EXHIBIT 15.5 Time-Series of One-Week Stock Price Premiums Paid in Global Leveraged Buyout Transactions

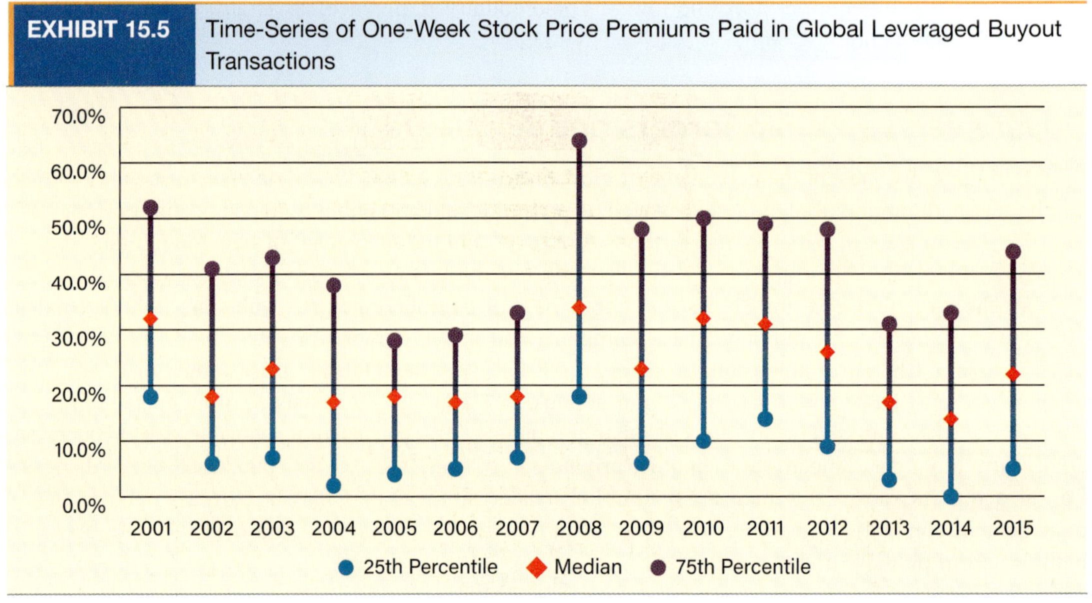

[7] Thomson One divides the closing price of the target company—immediately after the merger announcement—by the target's closing price one week earlier.

In Exhibit 15.6, we present the time-series of LBO EBITDA transaction multiples from 2001 to 2015. In this exhibit we present the median multiple and 25th and 75th percentiles of the EBITDA multiples across all global LBO transactions in a year. Like the premiums in the previous exhibit, the transaction multiples also vary over time. The medians range between 7.6 (2009) and 12.2 (2007). The median over all years (not reported on the chart) is 11.4. The 25th and 75th percentiles again illustrate the fairly large range of EBITDA transaction multiples in any one year.

EXHIBIT 15.6 Time-Series of EBITDA Transaction Multiples Paid in Global Leveraged Buyout Transactions

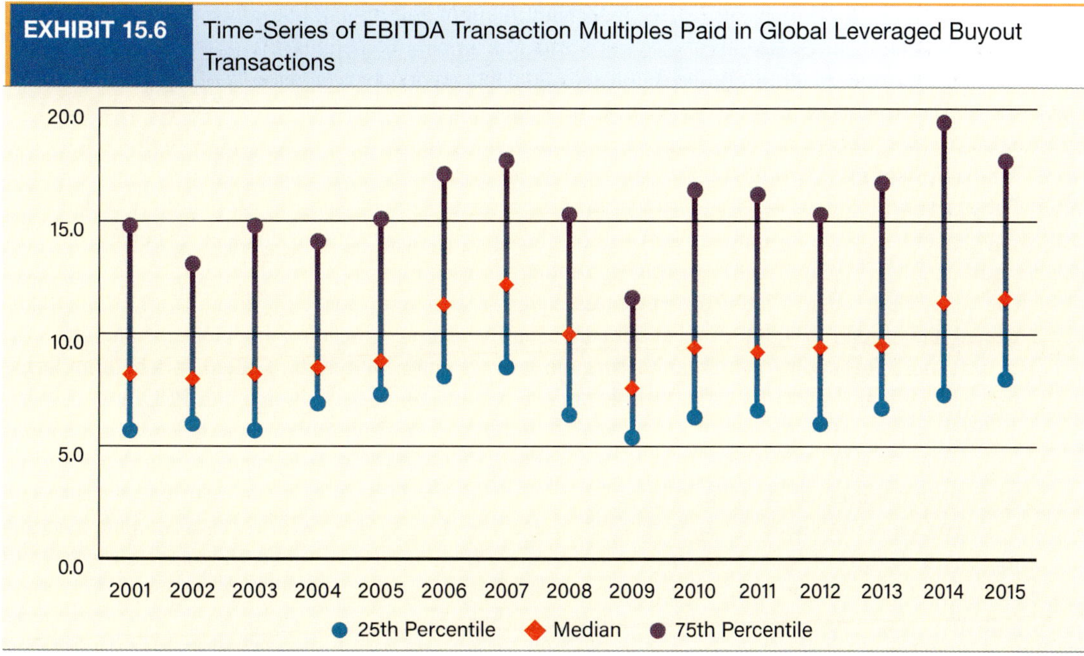

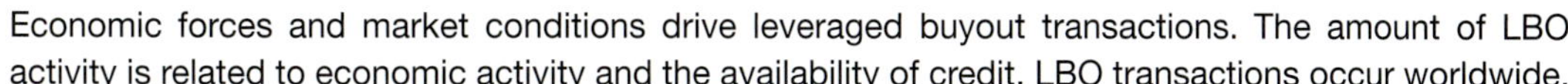

Economic forces and market conditions drive leveraged buyout transactions. The amount of LBO activity is related to economic activity and the availability of credit. LBO transactions occur worldwide.

Leveraged Buyout Deal Characteristics

Although leveraged buyouts do not have a specific definition, they have certain distinguishing deal characteristics that include the following. First, the transaction is financed with a large proportion of debt. Second, the ownership in the firm becomes concentrated. Third, the ownership stake of management increases substantially. Fourth, the board of directors usually becomes smaller, and a large proportion of the equity ownership is represented by those who sit on the board. In this section, we focus on just the capital structure characteristics, and we will discuss the other characteristics afterward.

Debt Financing. A large proportion of the capital structure in LBO transactions is debt. The amount of debt financing depends on credit market conditions, the characteristics of the company (for example, the stability of the cash flows), the quality of the management team, and the quality of the financial sponsor. Guo, Hotchkiss, and Song (2011) report that for their 1990 to 2006 sample, the ratio of debt to total capital for the average firm increased from 23.7% prior to the LBO to 69.9% at the close of the transaction. For the average firm in their sample, 39% of the capital was bank debt, 10% was private debt, 16% was publicly traded debt, and 4% was pay-in-kind debt.[8] Pay-in-kind or PIK debt contracts do not pay interest in the first few years after an LBO, but the accrued interest increases the principal amount due as time passes.

[8] Guo, S., E. Hotchkiss, and W. Song, "Do Buyouts (Still) Create Value?" *Journal of Finance* vol. 66, no. 2 (April 2011), pp. 479–517.

Companies issue various forms of debt in an LBO. The proportions of the specific types of debt vary over time due to changing conditions in the credit markets. Bank debt or senior loan funds are loans secured with the company's assets. These claims have the highest priority in the capital structure. It is common for this source to represent 40% to 60% of the capital structure and for it to be issued in tranches. The first tranche—usually issued by banks—is likely to have a six- to seven-year maturity with an amortization of the principal amount over time such that its average maturity is as short as four years. This tranche typically represents about one-third of the senior secured financing. The next tranche (or two) may be securitized and is often sold to institutional investors. These loans are often not amortizing, but rather, they have so called **bullet payments** on maturity (meaning the entire principal amount is then due). This tranche (or tranches) often accounts for about two-thirds of the senior secured debt and may have a maturity of eight or nine years. All of these senior secured loans are typically floating-rate notes that are pegged to LIBOR.[9]

The next source of debt funding is unsecured senior and senior subordinated debt, including high-yield debt. The maturity of these instruments is longer than that of bank debt and is usually in the range of 8 to 12 years. These securities represent 15% to 30% of the total capital structure. Offerings for publicly traded high-yield debt typically have a minimum of $200 million; thus, publicly traded high-yield debt is not available for smaller transactions. If the transaction is not large enough to use public high-yield debt, a private placement of such debt may be used if available. In some cases, a warrant is attached to the debt to enhance the debtholder's expected rate of return. These forms of debt are usually **cash pay** (meaning the interest is paid in cash).

The next source of funding is mezzanine financing, which can be in the form of either debt or preferred stock. Mezzanine financing is often convertible into equity and can be a combination of PIK for some time followed by a cash pay. It is important to be aware that the rules regarding high-yield discount obligations adopted by various taxing authorities (including the U.S.) may delay or nullify the interest deduction on zero-coupon or paid-in-kind debt.[10] Suffice it to say that the debt and preferred equity portion of the capital structure can be very complicated, with numerous different securities issued with varying contractual terms.

Although a discussion of the alternative corporate structures used in these transactions is beyond the scope of this chapter, sponsors often form a **holding company** to purchase the company's stock. The holding company owns the operating company and has no other assets other than the stock of the operating company. Equity investors in the transaction own all of the shares in the holding company. Sometimes, sponsors use the holding company to issue subordinated debt if it is not issued by the LBO company. Since the loan covenants on the debt issued by the operating company generally prohibit dividend payments to the holding company, the holding company has no cash to make interest and principal payments. In this case, the notes will have to be zero-coupon notes in which the periodic interest that is earned simply increases the outstanding principal amount due. In order to pay off the holding company notes, the holding company has to at least partially exit the investment so that the holding company has a cash infusion from the sale of its stock in the operating company.

Common Equity. The remainder of the capital structure is common equity. Obviously, since the amount of debt a company can issue fluctuates with changes in credit market conditions, and since leveraged buyout transactions typically utilize as much debt in the deal as possible, the amount of common equity varies over time as well. For example, in 1987, common equity represented, on average, less than 10% of the capital structure of the LBOs, which increased steadily until 2001, when the average equity increased to 41%. In 2006 and 2007, the average common equity decreased to around 33%. In 2009, after the credit crisis unfolded, the average increased to around 51% of the capital structure and then decreased to around 40% when the credit markets recovered to some extent in 2010, where it has roughly remained through at least the first quarter of 2012.[11] Between 2015 and 2017, the average equity contribution was approximately 45% to 50% of the capital structure.

The common equity includes both new common equity and **rollover equity**, equity from the pre-LBO company (typically owned by the management team) that is then rolled over into the new entity. Rollover equity is usually a relatively small percentage of the total capital structure. The new common equity comes

[9] For a review of the typical leverage structure in LBOs, see Axelson, U., T. Jenkinson, P. Strömberg, & M. Weisbach, "Borrow Cheap, Buy High? The Determinants of Leverage and Pricing in Buyouts," 2012, CEPR Discussion Paper, 8914, LSE, London, UK.

[10] As we discussed in Chapters 3 and 11, some taxing authorities (including in the U.S. since the 2017 Tax Cuts and Jobs Act) impose limitations on the amount of interest from any form of debt that can be deducted. Given the amount of debt used in some LBO transactions, these limitations could prove binding.

[11] See Eckbo, B. and Karin S. Thorburn, "Corporate Restructuring," *Foundation Trends in Finance* vol. 7, no. 3 (2012), pp. 159–288.

from various types of investors. First, a **private equity fund** managed by the financial sponsor typically invests a relatively large amount of the total equity. The management team also often invests in the company beyond its rollover equity. Lastly, the financial sponsor sometimes seeks other investments from other investors (for example, see Valuation in Practice 15.1, the financial advisor, 3G Capital, raised additional investments from Berkshire Hathaway). The financial sponsor's fund may purchase different types of equity or equity-linked securities than management (such as convertible preferred) that ensure that the fund earns some minimum return on its investment before management participates in part or full.

Valuation in Practice 15.2

Kinder Morgan Inc. Management Buyout[12] In 2007, in one of the largest management-led buyouts in history, top management took Kinder Morgan Inc. private in a $13.5 billion deal. Morgan Chief Executive Richard Kinder and other executives paid over a 20% premium for the company. Mr. Kinder owned around 18% of the company's shares at the time of the acquisition. Mr. Kinder and others contributed around $2.9 billion of their existing shares to the newly private company, with another $4.5 billion coming from private-equity investors Goldman Sachs Capital Partners, American International Group Inc., the Carlyle Group, and others. Mr. Kinder formed Kinder Morgan in the 1990s with roughly $40 million in assets he bought from Enron Corp. According to the company, the transaction was financed with the following sources of capital.

> Financing of the Merger. The merger agreement does not contain any condition relating to the receipt of financing by Parent and Acquisition Co. Parent estimates that the total amount of funds necessary to consummate the transaction, including debt to be incurred or to remain outstanding in connection with the merger, is approximately $22.4 billion. This amount is expected to be provided through a combination of:
>
> - up to $5.0 billion in new equity financing from the Sponsor Investors, based on the rollover commitments received to date from the Rollover Investors, approximately $2.9 billion in rollover equity financing from Richard D. Kinder and the other Rollover Investors,
> - approximately $7.3 billion in new debt financing, and
> - approximately $7.2 billion of existing indebtedness of Kinder Morgan expected to remain outstanding in connection with the merger.

Guo, Hotchkiss, and Song (2011) report that, in their sample, management is a part of the equity contribution in over 60% of the deals and that the average (median) management equity to total equity is 12.8% (6.5%). Management also receives additional equity incentives for performance above agreed upon hurdles. Kaplan and Strömberg (2009) report that in 43 U.S. leveraged buyouts that took place from 1996 to 2004, the CEO owned 5.4% of the equity via stock and options, and the management team, as a whole, owned 16%. Similar structures have been reported for leveraged buyouts in the U.K. as well.

Valuation Key 15.2

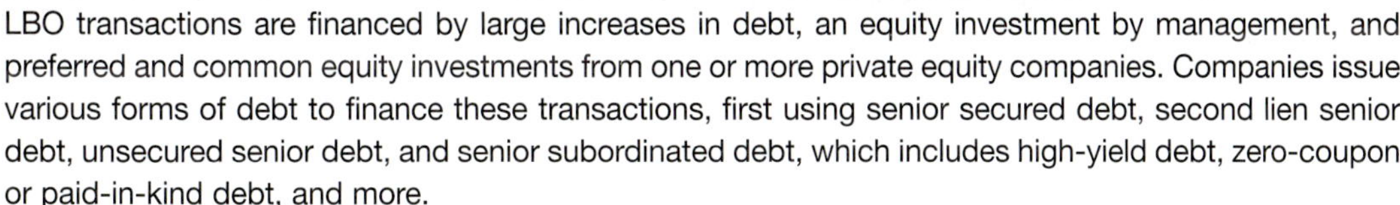

LBO transactions are financed by large increases in debt, an equity investment by management, and preferred and common equity investments from one or more private equity companies. Companies issue various forms of debt to finance these transactions, first using senior secured debt, second lien senior debt, unsecured senior debt, and senior subordinated debt, which includes high-yield debt, zero-coupon or paid-in-kind debt, and more.

As suggested earlier, two or more different private equity firms will sometimes both contribute to buy a company. This often happens when the size of the deal is too large for one private equity firm to write the equity check necessary for the transaction (see Valuation in Practice 15.2). Guo, Hotchkiss, and Song (2011) report that more than one private equity firm is involved in 27.7% of their sample from 1990 to 2006.

[12] Kinder Morgan is one of the largest energy infrastructure companies in North America using its pipelines to transport natural gas, gasoline, crude oil, carbon dioxide, and other gases, and owns terminals that store and handle petroleum products, chemicals and other products. See the Kinder Morgan proxy statement filed with the U.S. SEC on November 15, 2006 for more details about this transaction.

Deal Characteristics: Leveraged Buyouts Versus Leveraged Recapitalizations. LBOs and **leveraged recapitalizations** (**leveraged recaps**) have one important characteristic in common: they result in a large increase in the amount of financial leverage used in a company's capital structure. While the focus of this chapter is on LBOs, it is useful to discuss leveraged recapitalizations in order to identify the key characteristics on which they differ. In a leveraged recap, the company borrows against the assets and cash flows of the company and then distributes that cash to its shareholders by either paying a large one-time dividend to the shareholders or through stock buybacks. In a leveraged recap, the managers sometimes do not participate in the share repurchases and they sometimes get shares in lieu of cash when there is a one-time dividend (see Valuation in Practice 15.3). In some cases, the company also issues new shares in exchange for existing shares.

Both leverage recaps and LBOs result in a substantial increase in leverage for the company. However, in an LBO, new equity investors purchase the company from the pre-LBO equity investors, whereas leveraged recaps do not result in new equity investors unless there is a specific equity sale component associated with the transaction. If the leveraged recap is conducted by a public company, the company will continue to be publicly traded after the transaction, whereas a publicly traded company will become private after an LBO transaction.

Leveraged recapitalizations can be used for a variety of purposes. If a company wants to buy out a particular investor, investor group, or family member, the company can raise debt and buy back the shares of that individual or group. If the founders of a private company want to cash out some of their shares in order to better diversify their wealth, the founders can raise debt and have the corporation buy back some of their shares or pay them (and other shareholders, if any) a one-time dividend. A leveraged transaction can also be used to return capital to all shareholders. Finally, a leveraged recapitalization can be used as a defense against a **hostile takeover**. In some transactions, management significantly increases its proportionate share of the equity and offers shareholders a large cash dividend in order to thwart a hostile takeover (see Valuation in Practice 15.3).

Valuation in Practice 15.3

FMC Corporation Leveraged Recapitalization FMC is a diversified chemical company with leading positions in agricultural, consumer, and industrial markets. In late 1985, FMC management sensed a possible hostile takeover as it became clear that an investor was accumulating shares of the company. At the time, FMC shares were trading for approximately $70 per share. On February 20, 1986, FMC offered its shareholders a cash distribution as well as an exchange of shares. The offer identified three distinct investor groups and treated each one differently. For each existing share, public shareholders were offered $70 per share plus one new share. The employee thrift plan was offered $25 per share and four new shares, and the management team was offered no cash and five and two-thirds shares. If the post-debt recap price of the new shares was $15 per share, all three offers were each worth $85. Given the deal structure, if the stock price fell below (rose above) $15, management stood to lose (gain) the most from this transaction, and thus it had a strong incentive to improve the company's performance.

At the time of the FMC announcement, the price of the existing shares jumped to $85, implying a post-deal value of $15 for each new share. It turned out that Mr. Ivan Boesky had been accumulating the shares, and the market apparently sensed that the bidding for FMC was not complete. Consequently, the price climbed to $100. Eventually, in order to thwart Boesky, FMC gave the public shareholders $80 per share plus a new share. As a result of the transaction, insiders at FMC increased their ownership from 14% to 41%, making it virtually impossible for Boesky to take over the firm. However, do not feel too bad for Mr. Boesky, the value of the old shares rose by $30 per share (or 40% relative to the value of FMC's shares prior to the recap announcement). Finally, FMC's cash flows increased considerably in the years following the leveraged recap.

Characteristics of Potential Leveraged Buyout Candidates

What kinds of companies are good candidates for an LBO transaction? One major concern in an LBO transaction is the ability of the company to service its debt in order to avoid default or bankruptcy. What kinds of characteristics might mitigate this issue? One characteristic is stable cash flows. We generally do not see LBO transactions taking place in highly cyclical industries or with companies that have highly volatile cash flows. In addition, most LBO companies have substantial unused debt capacity prior to the transaction and may have excess cash that can be used to pay off the debt immediately after the company is purchased (or the pre-LBO company distributes the excess cash to its shareholders before the transaction closes, which reduces the transaction price). If the company has a non-core business or excess assets, the post-LBO company typically has a plan to sell these assets to help service or pay down the debt. Guo, Hotchkiss, and Song (2011) report that over one-third of the firms in their sample sold at least $10 million of assets in the first three years following the LBO transaction.

In most LBOs, the existing management team continues to manage the company—at least at the beginning. A company with a strong management team that is risk tolerant and will respond positively to high-powered incentives, increases the likelihood of a successful transaction. We know that many incumbent CEOs depart relatively quickly after a transaction closes. Acharya, Hahn, and Kehoe (2012) found that one-third of the CEOs in their sample were replaced in the first 100 days after the transaction.[13] Another characteristic is low capital expenditure requirements; in other words, modern, up-to-date plant and equipment that will not need replacement soon.

Lastly, the potential for expense reductions or other efficiencies—such as lower operating costs and improved working capital management—is also a characteristic of a good LBO candidate. One basic LBO strategy is to buy a business that will have a higher value if it is managed more efficiently; in other words, buy the company at a purchase price that largely reflects its current inefficient operations, and then create financial incentives for management to improve the company's performance and cash flows.

These characteristics are potentially useful for identifying LBO candidates. However, over time, we have seen LBO transactions in more and more industries, not all of which have these features. For example, in the mid- to late 1980s, LBOs were predominately observed in the manufacturing and retail industries. In the 1990s, LBO transactions spread to such industries as information technology, media, telecommunications, financial services, and health care. During this period, manufacturing and retail firms became a less important part of overall LBO activity (Kaplan and Strömberg, 2009). In the 2000s, more LBO transactions occurred in companies in the services and infrastructure businesses. Despite the spread of LBO transactions into other industries, manufacturing businesses still represent a relatively large percentage of LBO transactions. For example, in the sample of LBOs from 1990 to 2006 in Guo, Hotchkiss, and Song (2011), 36% of the sample companies operated in manufacturing businesses, whereas only 28% operated in service industries.

Over time, we have seen more LBO transactions undertaken in which the strategy underlying an LBO was to grow the business rather than to reduce costs and achieve certain efficiencies. In some cases, these more "entrepreneurial" LBO transactions involve acquisitions by the post-LBO company or by the same private equity fund and then two or more portfolio companies are combined to create a stronger company.

Valuation Key 15.3

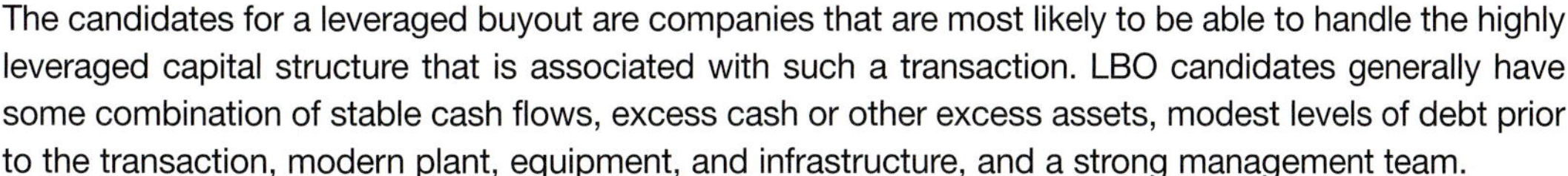

The candidates for a leveraged buyout are companies that are most likely to be able to handle the highly leveraged capital structure that is associated with such a transaction. LBO candidates generally have some combination of stable cash flows, excess cash or other excess assets, modest levels of debt prior to the transaction, modern plant, equipment, and infrastructure, and a strong management team.

Financial Sponsors—Who They Are and What They Do

The terms financial sponsor, private equity firm, and leveraged buyout firm are often used interchangeably. There are many financial sponsors. Some of the largest are Blackstone Group, Kohlberg, Kravis, Roberts & Co. (KKR), Texas Pacific Group (TPG), Apollo Global Management, Goldman Sachs Capital Partners and Carlyle Group. Financial sponsors establish private equity funds, raise capital from investors, and then invest those funds in private equity transactions, many, of which, are LBOs. While a fund is invested in a company, the financial sponsor is actively engaged with the management of the company and requires representation on the board of directors. Some private equity firms do not specialize or even invest in leveraged transactions, but our discussion here is limited to those that do.

[13] Acharya, V., M. Hahn, and C. Kehoe, "Corporate Governance and Value Creation: Evidence from Private Equity," *Review of Financial Studies*, 2012, vol. 26 (2012), pp. 368–402.

Private Equity Firms and Private Equity Funds. Private equity firms are generally partnerships or limited liability corporations, and they are generally private. However, between 2007 and 2012 all of the management companies (not the funds) of the financial sponsors named in the prior paragraph, except Apollo Global Management, went public. Private equity firms raise funds for equity investments by establishing private equity funds, which are basically commitments at some specified amount from various investors (such as endowments, pension funds, other institutions, and high net worth individuals) to provide capital when needed for investments. The private equity firm is a general partner in each of the funds launched, and the investors in the private equity fund are limited partners.

Usually, each fund has a fixed life of 10 years. The fund typically invests most of the capital within the first four to five years and then liquidates the investments during the remaining term of the fund. The term of the fund can typically be extended for a limited period to provide sufficient time for an orderly liquidation of investments. Thus, given the nature of the fund's term, the expectation is that the fund will invest in and exit from these companies within 10 years. Covenants usually constrain certain actions that a private equity firm can take with respect to the investments of the fund—such as restrictions on the percentage that a fund can invest in one company or in one industry and restrictions on the amount of leverage that the fund can use in aggregate across all portfolio companies.

The limited partners who invest in a fund make a commitment to invest a certain amount of capital in the fund. The commitment period usually lasts for about five to six years, which is the expected investment period. The private equity firm does not receive funds from the limited partners until it has an investment to make in a particular company. When the private equity firm (the general partner) is ready to close a transaction, it sends the limited partners a **capital call**, and the limited partners are obligated to transfer capital to the fund within an agreed-upon time frame that is set forth in the contract between the limited partners and general partner; this period is typically 10 days.

Successful private equity firms raise new funds every three to five years, and as such, they are constantly both trying to make new investments and to exit from previous investments. How successful a private equity fund will be in raising subsequent funds depends, in part, on how their previous funds have performed. Private equity firms with successful track records can raise capital more easily than those without any record of accomplishment or those with a weak or mediocre track record.

A private equity firm receives compensation in a variety of ways. First, a private equity firm charges an annual management fee of about 2% of the capital committed for at least the first five years during the investment period. The purpose of this fee is to pay for the cost of operating the fund. Many funds decrease the fee, for example, by 25 basis points per year, over the following five years, as it is less expensive to operate the fund after it is fully invested. Over the 10-year life of a fund, the total fee with that structure would be 16.25% of the capital committed with the remaining 83.75% being invested in portfolio companies. In addition to management fees, a private equity firm also charges various deal and monitoring fees to the portfolio companies. For example, the private equity firm often charges a fee for buying and selling the portfolio company—similar to an advisory fee that is charged by an investment bank. It is not uncommon for some of these deal and monitoring fees to be shared with the limited partners in the fund.

The last form of compensation that a private equity firm receives is a percentage of the profits of the fund—often referred to as **carried interest**. For example, a private equity firm often receives 20% of the profits of the fund. Profits are defined differently by different funds; sometimes, the profits are based on the committed capital, and sometimes the profits are based on only the capital invested in portfolio companies. If profits are based on committed capital, cash received from the sale of portfolio companies is distributed to the investors in accordance with the proportion of the capital that they had contributed to the fund. Once all of the committed capital has been returned, the private equity firm receives 20% of every dollar distributed. Sometimes the carried interest depends on meeting certain performance hurdles beyond returning capital. Some of the carried interest can be paid as the fund liquidates investments and a final settling up occurs when the fund is completely liquidated.

Metrick and Yasuda (2010) simulate the fees and carried interest earned by using actual contracts and information on how actual funds perform. They show that the mean total revenue to private equity firms is $17.80 per $100 invested, $11.64 of which is fixed per the contract and $6.16 of which is variable and is a function of how the fund performs.[14]

[14] Both the fee structures and carried interest calculations vary across funds and can be much more complex than the relatively simple structures described here. For a thorough analysis of many of the alternative structures that are used, see Metrick, A., and A. Yasuda, "The Economics of Private Equity Funds," *Review of Financial Studies* vol. 23, no. 6 (2010), pp. 2303–2341.

What Do Private Equity Firms Do Besides Raise Funds and Buy/Sell Companies?

Private equity firms buy companies and help the companies raise other forms of capital—such as debt and preferred stock. As such, they are not only deciding which companies to buy but also arranging the financing for the companies as well, often charging a fee for doing so. As discussed earlier, the debt structures of these deals are complex, and they are tailored to particular companies within the limits of what the credit markets are willing to consider lending at the time.

Exits most often take the form of a sale to a strategic buyer, a sale to an LBO-backed firm, an IPO, a sale to another financial sponsor, a sale to management, or bankruptcy. Thus, the private equity firm is also involved in selling the companies in which it is invested in order to liquidate the fund. If it cannot exit its transactions, it will not be able to distribute funds to its investors, and hence it will have difficulty in raising subsequent funds. Kaplan and Strömberg (2009, Table 2) report statistics regarding the type of exit and exit timing for their sample of LBOs from 1970 to 2007, which we provide in Exhibit 15.7.

EXHIBIT 15.7 Data on Type of Exit and Time to Exit for LBO Transactions*

Type of Exit	% of Deals
Bankruptcy	6%
IPO	14%
Sold to strategic buyer	38%
Sold to financial sponsor	24%
Sold to financial sponsor-backed firm	5%
Sold to management	1%
Other/Unknown	11%
Deals Exited Within	**% of Deals**
24 months (2 years)	12%
60 months (5 years)	42%
72 months (6 years)	51%
84 months (7 years)	58%

* Table 2 of Kaplan, S., and P. Strömberg, "Leveraged Buyouts and Private Equity" *Journal of Economic Perspectives* vol. 23, no. 1 (2009), pp. 121–146.

These data do not reveal more recent time trends. Kaplan and Strömberg (2009) document that IPOs are now a much less common form of exit than they were from the 1970s to mid-1990s, and selling the company to another financial sponsor or to a company that has already undergone an LBO is more common now than it was in the 1970s and 1980s. It is also interesting to note that despite the generally high leverage in these companies, only 6% of the known outcomes ended in bankruptcy, suggesting that such firms usually have the necessary characteristics to service the high leverage from the LBO transaction. Including the 11% of transactions for which the exit is unknown, the overall failure rate increases to 17%. Harford and Kolasinski (2011) examine 788 large U.S. LBO transactions that occurred between 1993 and 2001, tracking exit status through 2009. They find 10% of the portfolio companies exit through an IPO, 36% through a sale to a strategic buyer, 30% through a sale to a financial buyer, and 15% become financially distressed.[15] Time to exit is, of course, also important to a private equity firm as it tries to close out its funds in 10 to 12 years. Kaplan and Strömberg (2009) also provide data on exits. Across their entire sample, the median time to exit is six years. However, some transactions take longer to exit.

Another role of private equity firms is monitoring and advising. Private equity firms typically have multiple seats on the board of directors of portfolio companies and typically control the board. Guo, Hotchkiss and Song (2011) report that on average, private equity firms hold 50% of the director seats. Further, private equity firms actively participate in the governance of their portfolio companies. Acharya, Hahn, and Kehoe (2012) document that LBO companies usually have 12 formal director meetings every year and that representatives of the private equity firm hold numerous informal meetings with the LBO management team. In addition, they find that one-third of the CEOs are replaced in the first 100 days after the date of the transaction.[16] Also, private equity firms (or at least the larger ones) often hire former operating executives

[15] Harford, J., and A. Kolasinski, "Do Private Equity Returns Result from Wealth Transfers and Short-Termism? Evidence from a Comprehensive Sample of Large Buyouts," *Management Science* vol. 60, no. 4 (2014), pp. 888-902.

[16] Acharya, V., M. Hahn and C. Kehoe, "Corporate Governance and Value Creation: Evidence from Private Equity," *Review of Financial Studies* vol. 26 (2012), pp. 368–402.

from various industries to help advise the management teams of their portfolio companies. Indeed, many private equity firms are organized around an industry focus. These former operating executives play a significant role as they advise the private equity firm's portfolio companies and advise the private equity firm on whether to buy a particular company.

Valuation in Practice 15.4

H. J. Heinz Company Leveraged Buyout—The Initial Exit[17] In February 2013, Heinz announced that it entered into a definitive merger agreement related to a leveraged buyout transaction with a subsidiary owned by Berkshire Hathaway Inc. and an investment fund affiliated with 3G Capital Partners Ltd. (see Valuation in Practice 15.1). The transaction closed in June 2013. The post-LBO company was able to reduce the company's costs quickly and in about two years merged with the Kraft Foods Group, Inc., whose stock was publicly traded on NASDAQ.

In March 2015, Heinz and Kraft jointly announced that they had entered into a definitive merger agreement to create The Kraft Heinz Company, forming the third largest food and beverage company in North America and fifth largest food and beverage company in the world and summarized the transaction as follows:

> Under the terms of the agreement, which has been unanimously approved by both Heinz and Kraft's Boards of Directors, Kraft shareholders will own a 49% stake in the combined company, and current Heinz shareholders will own 51% on a fully diluted basis. Kraft shareholders will receive stock in the combined company and a special cash dividend of $16.50 per share. The aggregate special dividend payment of approximately $10 billion is being fully funded by an equity contribution by Berkshire Hathaway and 3G Capital. . . .
>
> Warren Buffett, Chairman and CEO of Berkshire Hathaway said, "I am delighted to play a part in bringing these two winning companies and their iconic brands together. This is my kind of transaction, uniting two world-class organizations and delivering shareholder value. I'm excited by the opportunities for what this new combined organization will achieve."

This transaction provided Berkshire Hathaway Inc. and 3G Capital Partners Ltd. a path to exit over time.

Valuation Key 15.4

Certain private equity firms raise capital for the funds they manage for investors so they can invest in companies through leveraged buyouts. They arrange the debt financing to purchase these companies, sit on the board of directors, monitor and provide advice to their portfolio companies, and design the equity incentives of the management team. Eventually, they attempt to exit their investments through the sale of the companies to strategic buyers, to other financial buyers, or via initial public offerings.

How Do Private Equity Funds Perform? Data on the performance of private equity funds is limited, for they are not required to publish disclosures regarding their investment performance. Three studies that have examined fund performance are Kaplan and Schoar (2005), Phalippou and Gottschalg (2009), and Harris, Jenkinson, and Kaplan (2014).[18] Kaplan and Schoar (2005) study private equity funds from 1980 to 2001. They conclude that, net of fees, a limited partner (investor) in the average private equity fund earned less than the Standard and Poor's 500 Index. Their estimates indicate that investors earned between

[17] At that time, Kraft Foods Group, Inc., was one of the largest consumer packaged food and beverage companies in North America and manufactured and marketed food and beverage products, including cheese, meats, refreshment beverages, coffee, packaged dinners, refrigerated meals, snack nuts, dressings, and other grocery products, primarily in the United States and Canada, under various brands. See the joint merger announcement dated March 25, 2015, last accessed on June 18, 2018 at http://news.heinz.com/press-release/finance/hj-heinz-company-and-kraft-foods-group-sign-definitive-merger-agreement-form-k and Kraft's proxy statement filed with the U.S. SEC on June 2, 2015.

[18] See Kaplan, S., and A. Schoar, "Private Equity Performance: Returns, Persistence and Capital Flows," *Journal of Finance* vol. 40, no. 4 (2005), pp. 1791–1823, Phalippou, L., and O. Gottschalg, "The Performance of Private Equity Funds," *Review of Financial Studies* vol. 22, no. 4 (2009), pp. 1747–1776; and Harris, R., T. Jenkinson, and S. Kaplan, "Private Equity Performance: What Do We Know?" *The Journal of Finance* vol. 69, no. 5 (2014), pp. 1851–1882.

3% and 7% less than an equivalent investment in the S&P 500 over the life of the fund (note that this is not the annual return difference but the total return difference over the fund's life). Phalippou and Gottschalg (2009) perform a slightly different analysis and risk adjust the returns for their sample of funds from 1980 to 2003. They find that the average fund performance, net of fees, is 3% per year below that of the S&P 500 and that adjusting for risk increases the underperformance to 6% per year. Both studies find strong evidence of persistence in fund performance—in other words, if a private equity firm's current fund performs well; it is likely that the next fund will perform well too.

A more recent study by Harris, Jenkinson, and Kaplan (2014) discusses potential biases in the reported results of the two studies just discussed that could lead to downward-biased estimates of fund performance. They use data provided by over 200 institutional investors that are limited partners in private equity funds (investors such as pension funds, endowments, etc.) that track the investors' cash investments and cash returns from each fund in which they invest. The data cover over 1,400 funds from 1984 to 2008 and represent approximately 60% of the capital committed to private equity funds over this time period. The authors show that, on average, the funds in this sample earn returns in excess of the S&P 500 on a risk-adjusted basis of more than 3% annually and over 20% over the life of the fund. The median risk-adjusted return of the funds is approximately 12% over the life of the fund. Of course, this sample is subject to a selection bias in that institutional investors presumably invest in the funds of the general partners in which they have the most confidence, and thus the results may be an upward-biased estimate of the average performance of all private equity funds. Nevertheless, the data suggest the limited partners earn a positive return on a risk-adjusted basis.

15.2 POTENTIAL MOTIVATIONS, ECONOMIC FORCES, AND ECONOMIC RESEARCH

LO2 Decide when to consider an LBO transaction

In this section, we describe the potential motivations underlying an LBO transaction that might lead to value creation for LBO investors. Potential motivations associated with an LBO include:

- the tax advantage arising from increased interest tax shields,
- a reduction in agency costs associated with the issuance of debt,
- a reduction in agency costs due to management incentives,
- more effective monitoring by the board of directors,
- information asymmetry advantages for insiders (relative to public investors), and
- wealth transfers from employees and pre-buyout debtholders to equityholders.

Potential Tax Benefits from Increased Interest Tax Shields

One potential reason for an increase in the value of a company is the potential tax advantages from increasing the financial leverage of the firm. The amount of value the interest tax shields create depends on:

- the appropriate discount rate for the interest tax shields (cost of debt or unlevered cost of capital),
- the firm's marginal tax rate for interest tax shields,
- the effect of personal taxes on the value of interest tax shields, and
- the amount of debt outstanding in each year before the exit transaction and the long-term post-exit capital structure, as well as the extent to which the interest is fully deductible for tax purposes.

Estimates of the proportion of the total price paid that is attributable to interest tax shields in an LBO transaction depend on assumptions made in the calculation. For example, Kaplan (1989) finds that the value of the interest tax shields can vary from 14% to 130% of the premium paid to pre-buyout shareholders, depending on the assumptions made.[19]

In acquisitions with a corporate buyer, treating the acquisition as taxable to the target can provide tax benefits to the acquirer and not impose a tax burden on the target if the target has a high basis in the

[19] See S. Kaplan, "Management Buyouts: Evidence on Taxes as a Source of Value," *Journal of Finance* vol. 44, no. 3 (1989), pp. 611–632.

assets or has net operating loss carryforwards. In these two situations, the target pays little to no tax and the assets are stepped up in value for income tax purposes, providing future tax write-offs for the buyer. However, since the purchaser in an LBO is often a limited partnership (a private equity fund) and not a corporation, no step-up in basis is allowed.

Potential Agency Cost Reductions from Increased Debt—Jensen's Free Cash Flow Theory

The incentive effects associated with debt present another potential benefit associated with an LBO. Jensen (1986) argues that increasing leverage creates pressure on managers to not waste resources because they must meet interest and principal payments in order to avoid default, removal, or bankruptcy.[20] Jensen describes this as the "free cash flow" problem—incumbent managers in companies with weak corporate governance, large cash flows, and poor investment opportunities are more likely to waste those cash flows in negative net present value projects in order to empire build. Jensen argues that in situations such as this, if the managers of these companies were to substantially increase leverage and pay the proceeds of the debt issuance to shareholders (as a one-time dividend or share repurchase), the managers essentially commit to not wasting future cash flows. This commitment arises because they have already given the future cash flows to the shareholders in the form of a one-time dividend or share repurchase and must now rely on using future operating cash flows to service the debt. As a result, they will not have the cash to invest in negative net present value projects until the debt has been paid down—at least in part.

Managers who have worked at companies that have undergone a leveraged buyout usually discuss the tremendous pressure they felt to generate cash flows in order to meet all of the required interest and principal payments. The pressure from the leverage, in conjunction with the equity incentives and the investment risk that managers bear from their personal investment in the company, provides a strong incentive to produce cash flows and not waste resources.

Potential Agency Cost Reductions from Management Ownership

Many studies examine the effects of managerial ownership on reducing the agency costs between managers and equityholders. Jensen and Meckling (1976) discuss both the agency costs associated with the separation of ownership and control and how managerial incentives to maximize firm value are diminished as the manager owns a smaller proportionate share of the company. Indeed, the interests of a CEO without any equity incentives may be more aligned with debtholders' interests than equityholders' interests. Managers of publicly traded companies generally own stock, options, and other forms of equity compensation in order to provide them with incentives that more closely align their interests with those of the shareholders. Scholarly research shows how stock, options, and other forms of equity compensation provide incentives for the managerial team (see Core, Guay, and Larcker [2003] and Armstrong, Guay, and Weber [2010] for reviews of this literature).[21]

As discussed earlier, the management team often rolls over equity into the new company in addition to making a cash investment. Given their equity incentives and personal investment, the managers' wealth is at risk, yet the managers also stand to gain a tremendous amount if the transaction succeeds. Even though it is true that equity incentives are much more commonly used in public corporations now than in the 1980s (when LBOs gained popularity), the ownership percentages in LBO transactions—and the resulting upside and downside for management—is greater than that in most public corporations.

More Effective Monitoring by the Board of Directors

Researchers have also examined the role of the board of directors in monitoring and advising management. Jensen (1993) argues that many boards of directors are ineffective because board culture discourages conflict, the CEO determines the agenda and information provided to the board, managers and

[20] See M. Jensen, "Agency Costs of Free Cash Flow, Corporate Finance and Takeovers," *American Economic Review* vol. 76, no. 2 (1986), pp. 323–329.

[21] Core, J., W. Guay, and D. Larcker, "Executive Equity Compensation and Incentives: A Survey," *Federal Reserve Economic Policy Review* (2003), pp. 27–50, and Armstrong, C., W. Guay, and J. Weber, "The Role of Information and Financial Reporting in Corporate Governance and Debt Contracting," *Journal of Accounting and Economics* 50 (2010), pp. 179–234.

non-managers on the board have little equity ownership, boards are too large, and the CEO and board chair positions are frequently held by the same person. Crystal (1991) argues that boards of directors are ineffective in setting appropriate levels of compensation because outside directors are essentially hired and can be removed by the CEO. Core, Holthausen, and Larcker (1999) show that ineffective boards tend to pay the CEO too much relative to expected compensation (given economic determinants of pay) and that these companies perform poorly.[22]

When firms undergo an LBO, the board structure changes significantly—at least relative to the board structure of the companies when they were public. First, post-LBO boards are generally small (usually about five to seven members), and they are controlled by the private equity firm. As discussed previously, Guo, Hotchkiss, and Song (2014) report that on average, private equity firms hold 50% of the director seats, represent a significant percentage of the ownership of a corporation and have a vested interest in having a positive outcome, whereas in a typical public corporation, the board holdings and associated incentives are more modest. Also, as discussed previously, private equity firms actively participate in the governance of their portfolio companies and have many formal and informal meetings per year. Thus, the active involvement of the board of directors after an LBO is quite extensive and can lead to better performance.

Information Asymmetry Advantage of Insiders

Critics of LBO transactions argue that inherent conflicts of interest exist when managers participate in the transaction because they have inside information that other shareholders do not have regarding the likely future performance of the business. These critics contend that managers share this information with financial sponsors, giving the sponsors an unfair advantage in choosing LBO companies. Kaplan (1989) examined forecasts released to the public by the management team in various SEC filings leading up to LBO transactions and found that the subsequent performance of the LBOs was slightly worse on average and certainly no better than what was forecasted.[23] In addition, the market for corporate control is competitive and many proposed LBOs end up being taken over by other bidders, including strategic buyers. Further, in many of these transactions, there are significant equity holdings by non-participating insiders who sell their equity stakes in the transaction. If the deal price is unfair, these individuals are irrationally selling their shares. Thus, there is no compelling evidence that any value created for the LBO investors is due to information asymmetry between the insiders and other shareholders.

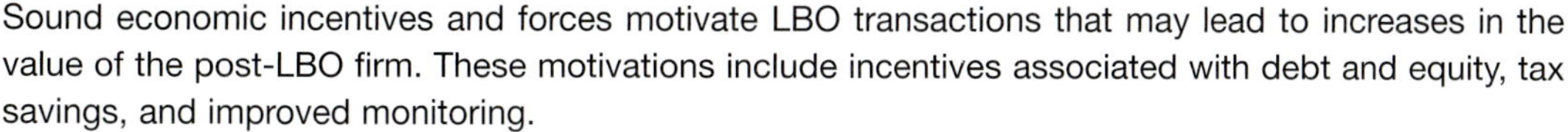

Valuation Key 15.5

Sound economic incentives and forces motivate LBO transactions that may lead to increases in the value of the post-LBO firm. These motivations include incentives associated with debt and equity, tax savings, and improved monitoring.

Wealth Transfer from Employees and Pre-Buyout Bondholders

Some critics of LBO transactions argue that part of the wealth increase experienced by those participating in the transaction is due to wealth transfers from employees and pre-buyout lenders. Kaplan and Strömberg (2009) reviewed the evidence on layoffs from a variety of studies. All of these studies concluded that, on average, growth in employment in companies undergoing LBOs was more modest than that in other companies in the same industry, but the studies did not find evidence that LBO firms were, on average, reducing their work forces. The evidence reviewed by Kaplan and Strömberg (2009) suggested that the same general results held outside the United States. In particular, they note that studies on employment in LBOs in the U.K. indicated that employment growth is similar to that of non-buyout firms in the same industry but that wages increased more slowly, and that a study of French LBOs indicated that job and wage growth was greater for LBO firms than it was for a sample of similar non-buyout firms.

---

[22] See Jensen, M., "The Modern Industrial Revolution, Exit, and the Failure of Internal Control Systems," *Journal of Finance* 48 (1993), pp. 831–880; and Core, J., R. Holthausen, and D. Larcker, "Corporate Governance, Chief Executive Officer Compensation and Firm Performance," *Journal of Financial Economics* vol. 51, no. 3 (1999), pp. 371–406.

[23] Kaplan, S., "The Effects of Management Buyouts on Operating Performance and Value," *Journal of Financial Economics* vol. 24, no. 2 (1989), pp. 217–254.

Valuation in Practice 15.5

Met Life vs. RJR Nabisco After the RJR Nabisco (RJR) LBO, Metropolitan Life sued RJR. Metropolitan Life claimed that it had held $225 million in RJR bonds that had fallen in value by $40 million because of the RJR leveraged buyout transaction—a decline of almost 20% of the value of the bonds. The bonds that Metropolitan Life owned in RJR had no restrictions on the right of RJR to engage in a change of control nor any restrictions on the amount of debt that RJR could issue. Metropolitan Life sued RJR, arguing that RJR had not acted in good faith. The court dismissed most of the suit, concluding that Metropolitan Life was a sophisticated lender with an intimate familiarity with the kinds of restrictive covenants often found in bond indentures that could have protected its investment against a transaction such as this. Further, it knew that these bonds did not contain these provisions and chose to hold the bonds anyway.

Metropolitan Life appealed the court rulings, but on January 25, 1991, before the appeals finished, RJR announced that it had settled the claim with Metropolitan Life—though the exact terms were not disclosed.

Little empirical evidence exists on the extent to which pre-LBO debtholders experience losses from LBO transactions. We do, however, know that lenders who have bond covenants that either prohibit a change in control without approval or put limitations on the extent that debt can be raised (these are common bond covenants) do not experience losses from these transactions. The reason for this is that in order to close the transaction, the bonds have to be retired. That said, in some LBO transactions bondholders experience losses (see Valuation In Practice 15.5). Despite the fact that in some cases pre-LBO bondholders lose value, this issue is generally not considered a significant source of value creation for buyers in LBO transactions, especially since more and more bond contracts (agreements) include change of control covenants that protect bondholders from such losses.

Who Can Pay More for a Company—A Financial Buyer (LBO) or Strategic Buyer?

We outlined the potential benefits from LBO transactions. Naturally, financial buyers compete with strategic buyers, which raises the issue of who can pay more for a company? Who can pay more depends on the characteristics of the target company and economic conditions.

Using data on auctions of companies, Gorbenko and Malenko (2014) estimate valuations (maximum willingness to pay) of strategic and financial bidders from their bids.[24] They find that while a typical target is valued more highly by strategic bidders, 22.4% of targets are valued more highly by financial bidders for companies that are mature and poorly-performing. They find that valuations of financial bidders are correlated with aggregate economic and credit market conditions. They conclude that different targets appeal to different types of bidders, rather than that strategic bidders always value targets more highly because of synergies. It is also true that the probability of a financial sponsor outbidding a strategic investor increases when credit market conditions are good (meaning relatively cheap and plentiful credit), since financial sponsors typically use much more leverage than strategic investors. As you can see from Exhibit 15.1, LBO transactions were a much higher proportion of overall M&A activity just prior to the financial crisis when credit was relatively cheap and plentiful.

The Effects of LBOs on Operating Performance and Firm Values

In the previous section, we discussed the motivation, economic forces, and valuation-creation strategies underpinning LBOs. In this section, we review the extant empirical literature that examines the effects of LBOs on operating performance and value. As noted previously, LBO transactions became popular in the late 1970s, and several empirical studies have examined the effect of early LBOs on operating performance. We first summarize the evidence from two of these studies—Smith (1990) and Kaplan (1989).[25] Afterward, we review studies that examined the post-LBO operating performance of more recent transactions.

[24] Gorbenko, Alexander S. and Andrey Malenko, "Strategic and Financial Bidders in Takeover Auctions," *Journal of Finance* vol. 69, no. 6 (December 2014), pp. 2513–2555.

[25] See Smith, A., "Corporate Ownership Structure and Performance," *Journal of Financial Economics* vol. 27, no. 1 (1990), pp. 143–164; and Kaplan, S., "The Effects of Management Buyouts on Operating Performance and Value," *Journal of Financial Economics* vol. 24, no. 2 (1989), pp. 217–254.

The Effect of LBOs on Operating Performance—The Early Years (1970s–mid-1980s). Examining transactions from 1977 to 1986, Smith (1990) documents a median increase in operating cash flows to assets of 4.3% (adjusted for industry performance) from the year before to the year after the transactions and a median increase of 5.9% from the year before to two years after the transactions; the average pre-transaction operating cash flows to assets was 23.9%. Thus, these increases were 18% and 25% of the pre-transaction operating cash flows to assets. Using EBITDA to assets, Kaplan (1989) shows percentage increases of 17% and 36% (that are analogous to Smith's 18% and 25%).

Part of the increase in operating cash flows documented by Smith is due to improvements in working capital. In particular, by reducing the number of days in inventory and receivables and by lengthening the number of days in payables, a firm can experience an increase in operating cash flows. Smith documents such a decrease in working capital. In particular, the median working capital operating cycle or trade cycle (days in inventory, plus days in accounts receivable, less days in accounts payable) decreased by over 11 days from the year before to the year after the transaction, and it decreased by over 13 days from the year before to two years after the transaction; the pre-transaction level was 73.8 days. Thus, these effects represent a decline in the working capital operating cycle of 15% to 18%.

An issue that naturally arises is whether the improvements in the cash flows were a result of layoffs or from reducing expenditures that reduce the long-run performance of the firm—expenditures for advertising, maintenance, and research and development (R&D). Kaplan finds no reduction in the absolute level of employment, but as discussed previously, the LBO firms were adding employees at a slower rate than their industry counterparts. In particular, he finds that the median increase in employees was 1% across all LBO sample firms, and for the firms that had no divestitures, the growth rate in employees was 5%. Adjusting these results for changes in industry employment, the median percentage change was a negative 12% for all LBO sample companies and negative 6% for those companies having no divestitures. Smith examines the expenditures on advertising, maintenance, and R&D as a percentage of sales and finds no evidence of decreases, suggesting that the companies are not cutting back on these activities.

Smith documents a significant decline in capital expenditures to sales from the year before to the year after the transaction, but she does not find a significant decline from the year before to two years after the transaction. Based on the median level of capital expenditures to sales of 3.4% prior to the transaction, Smith shows that the median industry-adjusted reduction to this ratio is 0.3% for the year after the transaction—a median percentage change of negative 9.2%, which is statistically significant. From the year before to two years after the transaction, the median industry-adjusted percentage change was only negative 3.1% and insignificant. Whether the reduction in capital expenditures is value increasing or decreasing is not known. It could be that the firms were cash constrained and, at least for some time, were unable to make the investments that should have been made. Alternatively, it could have been that the pre-LBO companies were overinvesting beyond what was optimal and that the incentives associated with the LBO solved the overinvestment problem.

For a subset of 25 LBO transactions in which the exit values from the LBO were estimable, Kaplan (1989) estimates the total return to all buyout investors from the date of the going-private transaction (based on the total transaction price and not just on the value of the equity) to the date of exit. The average time to exit was 2.7 years, and the median nominal total return from the going-private date to exit date was 111.3%. The total market-adjusted return (which adjusts for both the market movement and beta of the companies) was 28%. In 22 of the 25 transactions, the market-adjusted returns were positive. He also reports a nominal total return to the equityholders of 786% over the 2.7 years. This evidence suggests that value is created from these transactions, but this evidence includes the effect of an obvious selection bias in terms of the companies for which one can find an exit value. That said, there are reasons to believe that these numbers might also underestimate the value created. For example, in the study, the debt is valued at book value at exit, and there is reason to believe that the value of the debt was greater than the book value at exit since in many cases, the leverage had been reduced. Thus, the remaining debt should have been less risky than when it was issued, and it should have had a market value that exceeded book value.

Of course, even if there is value created at the company level, this may not imply that there are excess returns for the limited partner investors in private equity funds given the fees charged by the private equity firms, a topic we discussed previously.

The Effect of LBOs on Operating Performance—More Recent Transactions. Much of the recent research examined the post-LBO performance of LBOs in the U.K., France, and Sweden. Kaplan and Strömberg (2009) summarize that evidence and conclude that the evidence is consistent with previous research on earlier transactions in the U.S. In particular, the evidence suggests that LBO transactions enhance performance.

Two recent papers, however, document less improvement in performance subsequent to an LBO using U.S. data—Guo, Hotchkiss, and Song (2011) and Cohn, Mills, and Towery (2014).[26] Guo, Hotchkiss, and Song examine LBOs completed between 1990 and 2006. They report percentage changes in industry-adjusted EBITDA to assets of 7.1% for Year −1 to Year +1 and 2.6% for Year −1 to Year +2, but those changes are not statistically significant. The most analogous numbers in Kaplan (1989) are 16.6% and 36.1%. However, in a different analysis using the same sample and examining firms from Year −1 to the last year before exit (including exit through bankruptcy), they report a change of 10.9%, which is statistically significant. This result is not as large as the result reported by Kaplan, but it indicates performance improvements. They also report that firms that had a loss in the year prior to their respective LBO transactions experienced a very significant positive improvement.

The paper by Cohn, Mills, and Towery (2014) uses U.S. tax return data. Previously, other U.S. studies relied on public information. As such, there was a potential selection bias in the sample of firms in those studies, as the firms needed to have publicly traded debt and preferred stock as part of the LBO transaction or they had to exit from the transaction in such a way that revealed their financial information publicly (e.g., an IPO). No such selection bias exists in the Cohn, Mills, and Towery study. Their sample consists of LBOs that closed between 1995 and 2007. They show a median industry-adjusted change in income before interest and federal taxes, divided by assets from Year −1 to Year +2, of 2.3%. The median ratio in the year prior to the transaction was 4.7% for their sample firms. A change of 2.3% is not large in absolute terms, but the percentage improvement in operating performance is substantive (almost 50%). It is not clear, however, why the base is so small for this sample of firms. Kaplan (1989) used a somewhat similar measure (though his measure was before depreciation and was based on financial reporting income and not taxable income), and his median measure for the year before the transaction for his sample was 13.1%. In addition, Cohn, Mills, and Towery show that firms with a loss in the year prior to the LBO transaction had a significantly positive change in performance, similar to what was found by Guo, Hotchkiss, and Song.

Interestingly, in spite of the weaker operating performance improvement that is documented by Guo, Hotchkiss, and Song, they analyze the returns to post-buyout capital on their sample and find similar results regarding value creation as in Kaplan. In particular, they find a median return to total post-buyout capital of 95.8% and median market- and risk-adjusted returns of 40.9%; recall that Kaplan's numbers were 111% and 28%. If performance improvement is as small as found in the Guo, Hotchkiss, and Song sample, the value creation must be due to either an increase in the growth prospects of the portfolio companies or market timing by the private equity firms.

Valuation Key 15.6

The preponderance of evidence on the performance of LBOs suggests that, on average, the firms that undergo these transactions improve both their operating performance and working capital management. The evidence also suggests that, on average, the number of employees retained by LBO firms does not decline (though they do not hire as quickly as their industry counterparts). LBO firms do, however, reduce capital expenditures—at least for a short time—relative to their industry counterparts, but do not reduce expenditures for maintenance, advertising, or R&D.

15.3 STEPS IN ASSESSING THE INVESTMENT VALUE OF LEVERAGED BUYOUT TRANSACTIONS

LO3 Understand the steps for analyzing and valuing an LBO transaction

LBO and MBO transactions are complicated business transactions with numerous factors that drive value. As a consequence, assessing the investment value of these transactions can be complex. We begin this section with a discussion of the steps involved in assessing the potential investment value of leveraged

[26] See Guo, S., E. Hotchkiss, and W. Song, "Do Buyouts (Still) Create Value?" *Journal of Finance* vol. 66, no. 2 (April 2011), pp. 479–517; and Cohn, J., L. Mills, and E. Towery, "The Evolution of Capital Structure, Operating Performance, and Organizational Form after Leveraged Buyouts: Evidence from U.S. Corporate Tax Returns," *Journal of Financial Economics* vol. 111, no. 2 (2014), 469–494.

buyout transactions. The methods and valuation tools used in the process to assess investment value are not new; however, the process combines these methods and valuation tools in a way that is specific to the special characteristics of these highly leveraged transactions.

In Exhibit 15.8, we present an outline of the steps used in assessing the investment value of a proposed LBO transaction. These steps include two iterative processes, neither of which involves a discounted cash flow valuation. Given the changing capital structure (repaying debt with free cash flows) and unknown capital structure ratios, the weighted average cost of capital valuation method is not a useful valuation method. While the adjusted present value valuation method is applicable for this valuation context, it is not commonly used. Instead, the common practice is to compare an investor's internal rate of return (IRR) to the investor's required rate of return or hurdle rate for such transactions.

EXHIBIT 15.8 Steps in Assessing the Investment Value of Leveraged and Management Buyout Transactions

1. Establish an initial purchase price for the LBO target (for example, based on recent premiums paid in comparable transactions)
2. Develop the target's initial post-LBO capital structure, including the types and terms for the securities to be issued based on market conditions and the buyer's risk preferences
3. Develop a financial model to forecast the post-LBO operations of the target through the expected exit date and incorporate the proposed capital structure into the financial model (see Chapter 4)
4. Forecast all capital structure factors based on the company's capital structure (type of financing, amount of financing, and amount of interest) based on an assumed debt rating, assumed deal terms, and market conditions
5. Assess the target's debt capacity based on the target's expected post-LBO debt rating and ability to service the debt
6. Iterate steps 1 through 5 until the assumed deal terms and the debt capacity (based on the target's post-LBO debt rating and ability to service the debt) align
7. Measure the internal rate of return (IRR) for each equity investor (as well as debt with equity-option features) based on different exit years and exit valuations
8. Set a new price and/or capital structure and iterate steps 1 through 7 until the LBO transaction IRRs meet or exceed the minimum IRR hurdle rate set by the various investors
9. Value the firm and equity using the weighted average cost of capital method to determine the resulting implied exit multiples and IRRs
10. Use the adjusted present value method to value the post-LBO firm and evaluate the investment based on its overall NPV and cost of equity

The first iterative process calculates the price, capital structure, and terms for the securities issued so that they are consistent with both the market conditions and the buyer's risk preferences. The second iterative process determines whether the offer price and capital structure from the first iterative process meets the investors' rate-of-return hurdles (in other words, whether the expected rates of return are acceptable to the LBO investors). The second iterative process embeds the first iterative process as the capital structure and purchase price affect these calculations.

The first iterative process (Steps 1 through 6) begins with setting an initial offer price for the LBO target—based on, for example, premiums paid in comparable transactions. Once we set an initial price (Step 1), we then model an initial post-LBO capital structure that includes the amount and types of securities and the financial terms of those securities (Step 2). Concurrently, we develop a financial model (Chapter 4) for the target's post-LBO operations and incorporate the proposed capital structure using interest rates and other financial terms based on assumed debt ratings (Steps 3 and 4). Based on the financial model and market conditions (interest rates and other financial terms for various types of debt securities), we assess the debt rating (Chapter 9) and the ability of the company to service the debt (Step 5).

In Step 6, we iterate Steps 1 through 5 until the debt rating in Step 5 is equal to the debt rating assumed for the interest rates and, based on the financial model, the company can service the debt based on the assumed contractual terms. For example, if the debt rating in Step 5 is lower than the debt rating implicit in the interest rate used in the financial model, we either reduce the amount of debt and related terms in the capital structure, which increases the debt rating or we raise the interest rate. If the debt rating in Step 5 is higher than the debt rating implicit in the interest rate used in the financial model, we either increase the amount of debt in the capital structure or reduce the interest rate on the debt. Moreover, if the financial model indicates that the company cannot meet the required principal and interest payments, we reduce the amount of debt in the model or lengthen the maturity; on the other hand, if the financial model indicates the company can service additional debt, we may choose to increase the amount of debt in the capital structure. After we complete this process, we will have an offer price, a capital structure, and a set of related financial terms that are consistent with market rates and conditions.

While we now have an offer price, a capital structure, and a set of related financial terms that are consistent with market rates and conditions, we do not know whether the proposed LBO transaction is an acceptable investment. Using the net present value method is the preferred way to assess whether or not an investment increases value, but most investors make that assessment in an LBO analysis by comparing the expected IRRs for different investors to the hurdle rates required by those investors. Different types of investors—for example, management, financial sponsors, mezzanine debtholders—have different expected IRRs and different hurdle rates.

Thus, the next step in the process (Step 7) is to measure the internal rates of return (IRRs) of the proposed LBO transaction to various investors based on the investment parameters resulting from the first iterative process and from an estimate of the price at which the company will be sold at exit. In practice, investors most often use market multiples instead of a DCF valuation method to value the company at alternative exit dates in an LBO model. The second iterative process (Step 8) adjusts the offer price and capital structure (and possibly even the operating forecasts) until the IRRs of the proposed investment meet investor hurdle rates. However, any changes to the offer price, capital structure, or operating forecasts require rerunning the first iterative process to ensure that the new investment parameters are based on a feasible capital structure.

An alternative way to measure the exit value at different dates is to use a discounted cash flow analysis (Step 9). For example, use the weighted average cost of capital valuation to estimate exit values based on a standard industry capital structure at the time of exit, indicating what the value of the company will likely be for either a sale to a strategic buyer or a sale in an IPO transaction.

Finally, in Step 10, we use the adjusted present value method to value the firm and measure the company's capital structure ratios, implied equity cost of capital and beta. We compare the implied equity cost of capital to the minimum investor hurdle rates we used for the equity investors in the LBO analysis. We note that, in practice, most investors stop analyzing the LBO at Step 8.

These processes provide investors with a way to assess the highest price the investor would bid for a company in an LBO transaction as well as evaluate alternative prices in a negotiation.

Valuation Key 15.7

An assessment of the investment value of a proposed leveraged buyout transaction includes two iterative processes to ensure the assumptions underlying the proposed transaction are both consistent with market conditions and able to meet investors' required hurdle rates. We use various valuation methods and tools in this analysis, including financial modeling, tools to assess debt ratings and the ability to service debt, and tools to assess the internal rate of return to various investors.

15.4 THE JOHN EDWARDSON & COMPANY LEVERAGED BUYOUT TRANSACTION

LO4 Use an LBO model to analyze and value an LBO transaction

In this section, we use a detailed example to illustrate how to assess the investment value of LBOs and MBOs. To do so, we follow the 10 steps outlined in the previous section. Due to space constraints, we do not show the entire iterative process, but rather, we show only the final proposed model. The company of interest is John Edwardson & Company (Edwardson), which is a publicly traded company in the retail computer industry that sells a variety of products related to computers and computer networks. A financial sponsor is assessing the investment value of a leveraged buyout of Edwardson.

Initial Price and Capital Structure (Steps 1–2)

In this section we illustrate the first two steps in the LBO valuation process. First, we illustrate how to measure the initial price paid for the equity. Second, we illustrate how to prepare a sources and uses of funds schedule and how to measure the fully diluted equity percentages.

Initial Price. In Exhibit 15.9, we present a summary of the offer price for Edwardson's equity and options. The company's current stock price is $40 per share and the company has 200 million shares outstanding, which will also equal the post-transaction shares outstanding. The company has a current price-to-earnings (P/E) ratio of 13.1, and its firm value to EBIT, EBITDA, and revenue multiples equal 8.3, 5.7, and 1.8, respectively. The assumed deal premium is 20%. The resulting offer price is $48 per share, with transaction multiples of 15.7 for the price-to-earnings ratio and 9.7, 6.7, and 2.1 for the firm value to EBIT, EBITDA, and revenue multiples, respectively. Given the deal premium of 20%, the deal stock price, $48, is 20% higher than the current stock price of $40. The 20% increase in the deal stock price increases the P/E ratio by that same percentage. The firm value multiples increase by less than 20% because the 20% premium applies to the stock price but not the non-equity financing. As a result, firm value increases by less than 20% and the firm-value based market multiples increase by the increase in firm value.

EXHIBIT 15.9 John Edwardson & Company LBO—Offer Price for the Equity and Options

			Market Multiples			
			P/E	**EBIT**	**EBITDA**	**Revenue**
Current stock price	$40.00		13.054	8.313	5.715	1.829
Deal premium	20.0%					
Deal stock price	$ 48.00		15.665	9.696	6.666	2.133
Number of fully diluted shares outstanding	213.06	million				
Purchase price of equity	$10,227.00	million				

Pre-LBO Outstanding Options as of End of Year 0 (Liquidation of Options)

Year Issued	**Exercise Price**	**Number of Options = Shares Issued (m)**	**Buyback Shares (m)**	**Net Increase in Shares (m)**
Issued Year −6	$30.00	4.00	2.50	1.50
Issued Year −5	$31.00	4.50	2.91	1.59
Issued Year −4	$31.50	5.00	3.28	1.72
Issued Year −3	$33.00	6.00	4.13	1.88
Issued Year −2	$34.00	7.00	4.96	2.04
Issued Year −1	$35.50	8.00	5.92	2.08
Issued Year 0	$36.00	9.00	6.75	2.25
		43.50	30.44	13.06

Exhibit may contain small rounding errors

As shown in the exhibit, the total offer price for the company's equity and options is $10.2 billion, which is equal to the offer price per share, multiplied by the number of shares outstanding, plus the cost of cashing out existing stock options and any other equity-based derivative equity securities. Edwardson has no convertible debt or convertible preferred, but it does have 43.5 million options outstanding with various exercise prices. In the bottom panel of Exhibit 15.9, we calculate the cost of cashing out the stock options by using the treasury stock method, which is a common way to measure the effect of options on an offer.

To use the treasury stock method, we subtract the number of shares that can be bought back at the offer price (with proceeds received from the exercise of the options) from the number of shares issued in order to measure the net increase in shares. The number of shares that can be repurchased is equal to the total proceeds received divided by the offer price. The total proceeds equal the number of options multiplied by the exercise or strike price. For example, for options issued in Year −6, the company will issue 4 million shares. The number of shares the company can repurchase is equal to the 4 million shares, multiplied by the $30 exercise price (yielding total proceeds of $120 million), divided by the $48 offer price; this equals 2.5 million shares. Thus, the net effect of these options is an additional 1.5 million shares.[27] The net increase in shares from the buyout of all of the options is 13.1 million shares, and the total offer price is $10.2 billion ($10,227 million = $48 × 213.06 million equivalent shares).

[27] An alternative to increasing the number of shares using the treasury stock method is to measure the cost of buying out the options and adding that amount to the cost of repurchasing the shares outstanding. The cost of buying out the options is equal to the difference between the exercise price and the offer price, multiplied by the number of options. This calculation, of course, results in the same total offer price.

Sources and Uses of Funds and Equity Ownership. In Exhibit 15.10, we present a schedule detailing how the proposed transaction will be financed (a sources and uses schedule) along with the post-LBO capital and ownership structures. The first two columns of numbers present the sources and uses in dollars and percentages. The uses portion of the schedule delineates each of the costs of closing the transaction, which includes payments to the current equityholders and payments to redeem all other securities (such as debt and preferred stock). This schedule also details all financing fees paid and the fees paid to the sponsor, to lawyers, to accountants, to financial advisors, and to other consultants. An analysis of Edwardson's balance sheet concludes that Edwardson has $117.7 million in excess cash and that all of Edwardson's $1 billion of debt and all of its $725.0 million of preferred stock would have to be redeemed in order to proceed with the transaction.

EXHIBIT 15.10 John Edwardson & Company LBO—Sources and Uses, Capital Structure, and Deal Terms

Sources and Uses of Cash—LBO Financing ($ in millions)	Amount	%	Coupon = YTM	Maturity (Years)	Post-LBO Capital Structure	Common Shares Issued	Common Shares Issued (% Owned)	Warrants and Options Issued (% of Total Shares)	Fully Diluted Equity Allocation
Sources									
Excess cash	$117.67	1.0%							
Debt assumed	0.00	0.0%							0.00%
Revolver	100.00	0.8%	4.50%	5	0.82%				0.00%
Senior secured note (bank debt)	3,620.00	29.2%	6.00%	7	29.51%				0.00%
Subordinated note (unsecured debt)	1,810.00	14.6%	10.00%	9	14.75%				0.00%
Mezzanine debt	3,020.00	24.4%	12.00%	10	24.62%			4.00%	4.00%
Preferred stock—assumed	0.00	0.0%							0.00%
Preferred stock—new	0.00	0.0%							0.00%
Common equity									0.00%
Sponsor investment	3,380.00	27.3%			27.55%	181.86	90.93%		85.23%
Management rollover	200.00	1.6%			1.63%	10.76	5.38%	1.35%	6.39%
Management new investment	137.11	1.1%			1.12%	7.38	3.69%	0.92%	4.38%
Total sources	$12,384.78	100.0%			100.00%	200.00	100.00%	6.27%	100.00%
Uses									
Common equity									
Non-management shares purchased	$10,027.00	81.0%							
Management rollover	200.00	1.6%							
Preferred stock—redeemed	725.00	5.9%							
Debt redeemed	1,000.00	8.1%	Fee Rate	Total					
Financing fees—debt	253.50	2.0%	3.00%		Debt without revolver—amortize				
Financing fees—revolver	0.00	0.0%	0.50%	$300.0	Expense annually as incurred				
Sponsor fees	119.52	1.0%	1.00%		Based on deal value (deal cost) before fees				
Other fees and expenses	59.76	0.5%	0.50%		Based on deal value (deal cost) before fees				
Total uses	$12,384.78	100.0%							

Exhibit may contain small rounding errors

The total investment (uses) for the proposed transaction is $12.4 billion, which includes the amount paid to equityholders and option holders, $725 million to redeem outstanding preferred stock, $1 billion to redeem existing debt (see Exhibit 15.11 for the company's pre- and post-LBO balance sheet), and $433 million in various fees. We assume existing debt and preferred stock must be redeemed and are redeemable at par value, which equals their respective book values. The sponsor intends to finance this transaction (the sources) by first using Edwardson's $117.7 million in excess cash, issuing various debt securities equaling $8.6 billion, and investing $3.7 billion of equity (including the management's contribution to equity from rollover equity and new investment).

The $8.6 billion in debt is composed of $3.6 billion of 7-year, 6.0% senior secured bank debt; $1.8 billion of 9-year, 10% subordinated unsecured debt; and $3.0 billion of 10-year, and 12% mezzanine debt. In addition, the company is arranging a $300 million revolving line of credit that has a five-year term, a 4.5% interest rate on the amount drawn, and a 0.5% annual fee on the total line of credit. The sponsor plans to use \$100.0 million from this revolver in order to finance the transaction and use the remainder as needed for company operations after the transaction closes. The sponsor will invest \$3.4 billion in common stock. Current management will roll over its \$200 million in common stock and will invest an additional \$137 million in common stock. The financing of the deal is roughly 30% secured bank debt (including the revolver), 15% unsecured subordinated debt, and 24% mezzanine debt for almost 70% debt in total, with the remaining required funds coming from excess cash and 30% common equity. We assume for purposes of modeling, that the terms of the debt contracts require the company to use all of its available cash flow to reduce its debt, beginning with the secured debt before retiring any unsecured debt; however, it may pay down the revolver at any time.

The mezzanine debt includes an "equity kicker" equal to 4% of the common equity ownership on a fully diluted basis. Management will also be given additional performance-based equity equal to 2.27% of the common equity ownership on a fully diluted basis. These equity-linked securities dilute the common equity that exists as of the closing date. We show the fully diluted ownership percentages in the last column of Exhibit 15.10. For example, management will own, in total, 9.07% of the post-LBO shares. Those shares are diluted by the warrants and options equating to 6.27% of the post-LBO fully diluted shares (see total warrants and options issued shown in the second-to-last column in Exhibit 15.10), but management has options equating to 2.27% of the post-LBO fully diluted shares; thus, management's new shares on a fully diluted basis are equal to 10.77% (10.77% = 9.07% × (1 − 6.27%) + 2.27%). We use the fully diluted ownership structure to allocate the exit proceeds available to the combined equity claims (the exit value of the firm minus the debt outstanding on the exit date).

REVIEW EXERCISE 15.1

Sources and Uses, Capital Structure, and Deal Terms

A group of managers plans to offer to purchase the company they manage with the help of a financial sponsor. The company's current stock price is \$16 per share, and the company has 100 million shares outstanding; the company has a current price-to-earnings ratio equal to 14.91 and a firm-value-to-EBITDA multiple equal to 7.05. Management owns 3 million shares of the outstanding stock. After considering the company's expected performance and alternative strategies to the LBO transaction (including alternative acquisition offers), the deal premium is set at 25%. The company has no convertible debt or convertible preferred stock, but it has 20 million stock options outstanding—all with an exercise price equal to \$11.20.

In addition to redeeming the existing stock and options, management and its financial sponsor will also redeem all outstanding debt (par value of \$600 million) and preferred stock (par value of \$100 million) at its par value (which is equal to its book value). Initial fees will equal \$101.94 million (3% on the debt financing, 1% to the sponsor and 0.5% for other fees), but these fees do not include fees for the revolver loan. The sponsor intends to finance this transaction by using \$34.61 million in excess cash held by the company, issuing various debt securities equal to \$1.96 billion, investing \$730 million of its own equity, and having management invest \$153.33 million in equity from rollover equity and new investment. The composition of the \$1.96 billion in debt is \$880 million of 7-year, 5.0% senior secured bank debt; \$410 million of 9-year, 9% subordinated unsecured debt; and \$670 million of 10-year, 11% mezzanine debt (which has an "equity kicker" equal to 5% of the fully diluted post-LBO shares). In addition, the company will arrange a \$300 million revolving line of credit with a 5-year term, a 4.5% interest rate on the amount drawn, and a 0.5% annual fee on the total amount of the line of credit. The sponsor plans to use \$100.0 million of the revolver in order to finance the transaction. Management has an "equity kicker" equal to 4.1% of the fully diluted post-LBO shares. The company will have 200 million post-transaction shares outstanding.

Calculate the purchase price of the equity and prepare a sources and uses schedule similar to the one in Exhibit 15.10.

Solution on page 786.

Financial Model, Capital Structure, and Debt Rating (Steps 3–5)

In Steps 3 through 5, we develop a post-LBO financial model that incorporates the proposed capital structure, and we assess the target's debt capacity based on the target's post-LBO debt rating and ability to service the debt. We then iterate the post-LBO financial model and capital structure until the operating performance supports the proposed capital structure.

Pro Forma Closing Balance Sheet. In Exhibit 15.11, we present the pro forma closing balance sheet for the proposed transaction, which is the starting balance sheet for the financial model. The pro forma closing balance sheet begins with the pre-LBO balance sheet, which we assume is for the end of Year 0.

EXHIBIT 15.11 John Edwardson & Company LBO—Pro Forma Closing Balance Sheet

($ in millions)	Year −1	Year 0	Redeem Existing Securities	Fees	Issue LBO Securities—Use Excess Cash	Year 0 Post-LBO Closing
Cash balance	$ 326.4	$ 285.8			−$ 117.7	$ 168.1
Accounts receivable	680.0	700.4				700.4
Inventory	401.4	393.8				393.8
Total current assets	$1,407.8	$1,379.9				$1,262.3
Property, plant, and equipment	$4,640.0	$5,365.1				$5,365.1
Accumulated depreciation	−1,344.0	−1,904.3				−1,904.3
Property, plant, and equipment (net)	$3,296.0	$3,460.8				$3,460.8
Capitalized fees	$ 0	$ 0		$432.8		$ 432.8
Total assets	$4,703.8	$4,840.7				$5,155.9
Accounts payable	$ 291.9	$ 286.4				$ 286.4
Other current operating liabilities	108.8	112.1				112.1
Total current liabilities	$ 400.7	$ 398.4				$ 398.4
Total debt	1,000.0	1,000.0	−$1,000.0		8,550.0	8,550.0
Total liabilities	$1,400.7	$1,398.4				$8,948.4
Preferred stock	$ 725.0	$ 725.0	−725.0			$ 0
Common stock	1,000.0	1,000.0	−1,000.0		3,717.1	3,717.1
Retained earnings	1,578.1	1,717.3	−9,227.0			−7,509.7
Total shareholders' equity	$3,303.1	$3,442.3				−$3,792.6
Total liabilities and equities	$4,703.8	$4,840.7				$5,155.9

Exhibit may contain small rounding errors

First, we redeem all debt, preferred, and other non-common equity securities that are not assumed in the transaction. We also eliminate the old equity, issue the new equity, and capitalize any fees. We redeem the equity by eliminating the book value of the common stock, $1,000 million, and then reducing retained earnings for the remainder of the amount paid for the equity, $9,227 million ($9,227 = $10,227 − $1,000). To simplify the example and discussion, we capitalize all of the fees related to the transaction (non-financing fees), $179.3 million ($179.3 = $119.52 + $59.76) as well as the fees to issue the debt, $253.5 million, or $432.8 million in total. We expense the $179.3 million of fees related to the transaction in Year 1 and assume they are tax deductible when expensed. This treatment is not completely consistent with accounting standards and tax regulations in the U.S. Companies record certain transaction related fees as part of the cost of the investment. These transaction related fees are generally not tax deductible as an expense but they increase the taxable basis of the investment and thus, reduce the gain or increase the loss when the investment is liquidated. We also capitalize the debt issuance costs as an asset and amortize it on a straight-line basis over the life of the corresponding debt agreement, which is also not consistent with the accounting rules and tax regulations in the U.S. In the U.S., debt issuance costs are netted against the amount of debt issued; in other words, the debt on the balance sheet is equal to the amount borrowed net of the debt issuance costs. They are generally amortized for accounting and tax purposes based on the effective interest method (like an original issue discount on debt). However, to simplify the example and discussion, we capitalize all of the fees related to the transaction and debt issuance. We expense the fees related to the transaction in Year 1 and use the straight-line method to amortize the debt issuance costs.

In this illustration, we use "recap accounting," which essentially treats the payment to shareholders as a return of capital up to their original investment and treats the rest of the payment to the equityholders as a reduction in retained earnings. With this method of accounting, there is no goodwill created, and there is no step-up in the book value of the assets for financial reporting purposes. We use this method because it requires fewer assumptions to create the model without compromising the reader's understanding of how LBOs are analyzed. If the company uses acquisition accounting (purchase accounting), which is typical in LBO transactions, the company will appraise all of its assets and liabilities, write-up (or down) the assets and liabilities to their appraised value, and record any goodwill (the excess of the purchase price above the appraised value of the net assets). Goodwill can be negative if the purchase price is less than the appraised value; however, accounting rules require various adjustments before a company can record negative goodwill.

Post-LBO Financial Model. In Exhibit 15.12, we present the forecast assumptions used in the financial model. These drivers show the improvements that the sponsors and management expect to make in the operating performance of the company. We have modeled this as a classic LBO, which contemplates increases in margins through decreases in costs of goods sold and selling, general, and administrative expenses. In addition, we assume that improvements in working capital management will occur through a decrease in days of receivables, a decrease in days of inventory, and an increase in days of payables. We do not assume a reduction in capital expenditures in the early years of the transaction, but we do assume an initial increase in revenue growth.

EXHIBIT 15.12 John Edwardson & Company LBO—Financial Model Drivers (Assumptions, calculated using year-end and not average balances)

	Year 0	Year 1	Year 2	Year 3	Year 4	Year 5	Year 6	Year 7	Year 8	Year 9	Year 10	Year 11
Expected inflation (Year 11 is a long-run expectation)	3.00%	3.00%	3.00%	3.00%	3.00%	3.00%	3.00%	3.00%	3.00%	3.00%	3.00%	3.00%
Treasury Bonds—20-year	5.00%	5.00%	5.00%	5.00%	5.00%	5.00%	5.00%	5.00%	5.00%	5.00%	5.00%	5.00%
LIBOR—3-month	4.00%	4.00%	4.00%	4.00%	4.00%	4.00%	4.00%	4.00%	4.00%	4.00%	4.00%	4.00%
Revenue growth rate	3.00%	5.00%	8.00%	8.00%	10.00%	5.00%	3.00%	3.00%	3.00%	3.00%	3.00%	3.00%
Cost of goods sold (% revenue)	46.00%	46.00%	45.00%	44.00%	44.00%	44.00%	44.00%	44.00%	44.00%	44.00%	44.00%	44.00%
Selling, general, and administrative (% revenue)	22.00%	22.00%	21.00%	20.00%	20.00%	20.00%	20.00%	20.00%	20.00%	20.00%	20.00%	20.00%
Constant income tax rate	40.00%	40.00%	40.00%	40.00%	40.00%	40.00%	40.00%	40.00%	40.00%	40.00%	40.00%	40.00%
Required cash balance (% revenue)	3.00%	3.00%	2.00%	2.00%	2.00%	2.00%	2.00%	2.00%	2.00%	2.00%	2.00%	2.00%
Accounts receivable (days to collect)	45.6	45.6	43.1	40.6	40.6	40.6	40.6	40.6	40.6	40.6	40.6	40.6
Inventory (days to sell)	55.8	54.8	52.7	50.7	50.7	50.7	50.7	50.7	50.7	50.7	50.7	50.7
Accounts payable (days to pay)	40.7	45.4	45.5	45.5	45.1	45.3	45.4	45.4	45.4	45.4	45.4	45.4
Other current operating liabilities (% revenue)	2.0%	2.0%	2.5%	3.0%	3.0%	3.0%	3.0%	3.0%	3.0%	3.0%	3.0%	3.0%
Capital expenditures—based on revenue to net property, plant, and equipment	1.70	1.70	1.75	1.80	1.80	1.80	1.80	1.80	1.80	1.80	1.80	1.80

In Exhibits 15.13 through 15.15, we present the post-LBO income statement, balance sheet, and free cash flow forecasts from the financial model; all of these forecasts are based on the company's operating strategy, the changes the sponsor and management expect to make to improve the company's operations, and the proposed capital structure. The income statement forecasts in Exhibit 15.13 reflect the expected revenue growth and any efficiency expected to be gained in the cost structure. The decrease in interest expense reflects the pay-down of debt as cash becomes available to retire some of the debt.[28]

[28] We treat all interest expense as being tax deductible in the year expensed. As we have discussed previously, in some countries, there are limitations on the amount of interest that can be deducted for tax purposes (see Chapters 3 and 11). For example, the limitations imposed by the 2017 Tax Cuts and Jobs Act would be binding given the forecasts for Edwardson. See Chapter 3 for more details about these limitations and how we carryforward interest expense to future years.

EXHIBIT 15.13 John Edwardson & Company LBO—Income Statement Forecasts

($ in millions)	Year −1	Year 0	Year 1	Year 2	Year 3	Year 4	Year 5	Year 6	Year 7	Year 8	Year 9	Year 10	Year 11
Revenue	$5,440.0	$5,603.2	$5,883.4	$6,354.0	$6,862.4	$7,548.6	$7,926.0	$8,163.8	$8,408.7	$8,661.0	$8,920.8	$9,188.4	$9,464.1
Cost of goods sold	−2,627.5	−2,577.5	−2,706.3	−2,859.3	−3,019.4	−3,321.4	−3,487.4	−3,592.1	−3,699.8	−3,810.8	−3,925.2	−4,042.9	−4,164.2
Gross margin	$2,812.5	$3,025.7	$3,177.0	$3,494.7	$3,842.9	$4,227.2	$4,438.6	$4,571.7	$4,708.9	$4,850.1	$4,995.6	$5,145.5	$5,299.9
Selling, general, and administrative	−1,256.6	−1,232.7	−1,294.3	−1,334.3	−1,372.5	−1,509.7	−1,585.2	−1,632.8	−1,681.7	−1,732.2	−1,784.2	−1,837.7	−1,892.8
Other expenses			−179.3										
Depreciation expense	−544.0	−560.3	−588.3	−635.4	−686.2	−754.9	−792.6	−816.4	−840.9	−866.1	−892.1	−918.8	−946.4
Operating income	$1,011.8	$1,232.7	$1,115.1	$1,525.0	$1,784.2	$1,962.6	$2,060.8	$2,122.6	$2,186.3	$2,251.9	$2,319.4	$2,389.0	$2,460.7
Interest expense	−48.0	−60.0	−797.2	−791.2	−768.7	−744.3	−715.6	−674.2	−629.9	−566.5	−486.4	−386.5	−257.0
Income before taxes	$ 963.8	$1,172.7	$ 317.9	$ 733.8	$1,015.6	$1,218.3	$1,345.2	$1,448.4	$1,556.3	$1,685.3	$1,833.0	$2,002.5	$2,203.6
Income tax expense	−385.5	−469.1	−127.1	−293.5	−406.2	−487.3	−538.1	−579.4	−622.5	−674.1	−733.2	−801.0	−881.5
Net income	$ 578.3	$ 703.6	$ 190.7	$ 440.3	$ 609.3	$ 731.0	$ 807.1	$ 869.0	$ 933.8	$1,011.2	$1,099.8	$1,201.5	$1,322.2
Earnings Per Share													
Net income	$ 578.3	$ 703.6	$ 190.7	$ 440.3	$ 609.3	$ 731.0	$ 807.1	$ 869.0	$ 933.8	$1,011.2	$1,099.8	$1,201.5	$1,322.2
Preferred stock dividends	−40.6	−50.8											
Net income to common equity	$ 537.7	$ 652.9	$ 190.7	$ 440.3	$ 609.3	$ 731.0	$ 807.1	$ 869.0	$ 933.8	$1,011.2	$1,099.8	$1,201.5	$1,322.2
Common shares outstanding (m)	200.0	200.0	200.0	200.0	200.0	200.0	200.0	200.0	200.0	200.0	200.0	200.0	200.0
Basic earnings per share	$ 2.689	$ 3.264	$ 0.954	$ 2.201	$ 3.047	$ 3.655	$ 4.035	$ 4.345	$ 4.669	$ 5.056	$ 5.499	$ 6.007	$ 6.611
Effect of Dilutive Securities													
Management stock options (net shares, m)	11.1	13.1											
Common shares outstanding (m)	200.0	200.0											
Adjusted shares outstanding	211.1	213.1											
Diluted earnings per share	$ 2.547	$ 3.064											
Retained Earnings													
Beginning balance	$1,043.4	$1,578.1	−$7,509.7	−$7,319.0	−$6,878.7	−$6,269.4	−$5,538.4	−$4,731.3	−$3,862.3	−$2,928.5	−$1,917.3	−$ 817.5	$ 384.0
Net income	578.3	703.6	190.7	440.3	609.3	731.0	807.1	869.0	933.8	1,011.2	1,099.8	1,201.5	1,322.2
Preferred stock dividends	−40.6	−50.8											
Common equity dividends	−3.0	−513.7	0.0	0.0	0.0	0.0	0.0	0.0	0.0	0.0	0.0	0.0	0.0
Ending balance	$1,578.1	$1,717.3	−$7,319.0	−$6,878.7	−$6,269.4	−$5,538.4	−$4,731.3	−$3,862.3	−$2,928.5	−$1,917.3	−$ 817.5	$ 384.0	$1,706.2

Exhibit may contain small rounding errors

The balance sheet forecasts in Exhibit 15.14 also reflect the pay-down of the debt. We note that the capitalized fees are declining as they are expensed over time. We expense non-financing fees in the first year, and amortize the financing fees on a straight-line basis over the life of the respective loans with which they are associated.[29] Notice that debt is shown as one line on the balance sheet and, in order to simplify the balance sheet and discussion, we do not separate short-term from long-term debt. In Exhibit 15.16, we show a detailed debt schedule that separates each debt security.

In Exhibit 15.15, we present the free cash flow forecasts. The company's cash flows (before capital expenditures) are positive in every year, and the company generates sufficient cash flow to fund all of its anticipated capital expenditures. Given that LBO transactions typically maximize the amount of debt in the capital structure, it is common for a post-LBO company to finance most or all of its capital expenditures from internally generated funds. Debt covenants often require this internal funding or sometimes limit capital expenditures to a specified dollar amount even if they are funded internally.

The company also generates sufficient free cash flows to pay all of its after-tax interest costs as is shown in the "cash flow after interest and preferred stock dividends" line also called "pre-debt repayment cash flow" in some models. Based on the financial model, the company is able to pay off the revolver in the first year.

The Debt Schedule. Naturally, various schedules underpin the summary financial statement and free cash flow forecasts in our example. We show one set of these schedules in Exhibit 15.16, which

[29] Note, as stated previously, under U.S. GAAP and U.S. tax regulations, financing fees are essentially treated as original issue discounts and are amortized using the effective interest rate method.

EXHIBIT 15.14 John Edwardson & Company LBO—Balance Sheet Forecasts

($ in millions)	Year −1	Year 0 Post-LBO Opening	Year 1	Year 2	Year 3	Year 4	Year 5	Year 6	Year 7	Year 8	Year 9	Year 10	Year 11
Cash balance	$ 326.4	$ 168.1	$ 176.5	$ 127.1	$ 137.2	$ 151.0	$ 158.5	$ 163.3	$ 168.2	$ 173.2	$ 178.4	$ 183.8	$ 189.3
Accounts receivable	680.0	700.4	735.4	750.1	762.5	838.7	880.7	907.1	934.3	962.3	991.2	1,020.9	1,051.6
Inventory	401.4	393.8	406.0	413.0	419.4	461.3	484.4	498.9	513.9	529.3	545.2	561.5	578.4
Total current assets	$1,407.8	$1,262.3	$1,317.9	$1,290.2	$1,319.1	$1,451.0	$1,523.6	$ 1,569.3	$ 1,616.3	$ 1,664.8	$ 1,714.8	$ 1,766.2	$ 1,819.2
Property, plant, and equipment	$4,640.0	$5,365.1	$6,230.3	$7,049.4	$8,008.0	$8,972.5	$9,897.2	$10,849.6	$11,830.7	$12,841.1	$13,881.9	$13,843.3	$13,803.6
Accumulated depreciation	−1,344.0	−1,904.3	−2,492.7	−3,128.1	−3,814.3	−4,569.2	−5,361.8	−6,178.1	−7,019.0	−7,885.1	−8,777.2	−8,585.5	−8,388.0
Property, plant, and equipment (net)	$3,296.0	$3,460.8	$3,737.7	$3,921.3	$4,193.7	$4,403.3	$4,535.4	$ 4,671.5	$ 4,811.7	$ 4,956.0	$ 5,104.7	$ 5,257.8	$ 5,415.6
Capitalized fees	$ 0.0	$ 432.8	$ 222.9	$ 192.3	$ 161.7	$ 131.1	$ 100.5	$ 69.9	$ 39.2	$ 24.2	$ 9.1	$ 0.0	$ 0.0
Total assets	$4,703.8	$5,155.9	$5,278.4	$5,403.8	$5,674.4	$5,985.4	$6,159.5	$ 6,310.6	$ 6,467.2	$ 6,645.0	$ 6,828.5	$ 7,024.0	$ 7,234.8
Accounts payable	$ 291.9	$ 286.4	$ 338.3	$ 357.4	$ 377.4	$ 415.2	$ 435.9	$ 449.0	$ 462.5	$ 476.4	$ 490.6	$ 505.4	$ 520.5
Other current operating liabilities	108.8	112.1	117.7	158.9	205.9	226.5	237.8	244.9	252.3	259.8	267.6	275.7	283.9
Total current liabilities	$ 400.7	$ 398.4	$ 456.0	$ 516.3	$ 583.3	$ 641.6	$ 673.7	$ 693.9	$ 714.7	$ 736.2	$ 758.3	$ 781.0	$ 804.4
Total debt	1,000.0	8,550.0	8,424.4	8,049.2	7,643.4	7,165.1	6,499.9	5,761.9	4,963.8	4,109.0	3,170.6	2,141.9	1,007.0
Total liabilities	$1,400.7	$8,948.4	$8,880.3	$8,565.5	$8,226.7	$7,806.7	$7,173.6	$ 6,455.8	$ 5,678.6	$ 4,845.1	$ 3,928.9	$ 2,922.9	$ 1,811.4
Preferred stock	$ 725.0	$ 0.0	$ 0.0	$ 0.0	$ 0.0	$ 0.0	$ 0.0	$ 0.0	$ 0.0	$ 0.0	$ 0.0	$ 0.0	$ 0.0
Common stock	1,000.0	3,717.1	3,717.1	3,717.1	3,717.1	3,717.1	3,717.1	3,717.1	3,717.1	3,717.1	3,717.1	3,717.1	3,717.1
Retained earnings	1,578.1	−7,509.7	−7,319.0	−6,878.7	−6,269.4	−5,538.4	−4,731.3	−3,862.3	−2,928.5	−1,917.3	−817.5	384.0	1,706.2
Total shareholders' equity	$3,303.1	−$3,792.6	−$3,601.9	−$3,161.6	−$2,552.3	−$1,821.3	−$1,014.2	−$ 145.2	$ 788.6	$ 1,799.8	$ 2,899.7	$ 4,101.1	$ 5,423.3
Total liabilities and equities	$4,703.8	$5,155.9	$5,278.4	$5,403.8	$5,674.4	$5,985.4	$6,159.5	$ 6,310.6	$ 6,467.2	$ 6,645.0	$ 6,828.5	$ 7,024.0	$ 7,234.8

Exhibit may contain small rounding errors

EXHIBIT 15.15 John Edwardson & Company LBO—Free Cash Flow Forecasts

($ in millions)	Year 1	Year 2	Year 3	Year 4	Year 5	Year 6	Year 7	Year 8	Year 9	Year 10	Year 11
Earnings before interest and taxes (EBIT)	$1,115.1	$1,525.0	$1,784.2	$1,962.6	$2,060.8	$2,122.6	$2,186.3	$2,251.9	$2,319.4	$2,389.0	$2,460.7
− Income taxes paid on EBIT	−446.0	−610.0	−713.7	−785.1	−824.3	−849.0	−874.5	−900.7	−927.8	−955.6	−984.3
Earnings before interest and after taxes	$ 669.0	$ 915.0	$1,070.5	$1,177.6	$1,236.5	$1,273.6	$1,311.8	$1,351.1	$1,391.6	$1,433.4	$1,476.4
+ Depreciation expense	588.3	635.4	686.2	754.9	792.6	816.4	840.9	866.1	892.1	918.8	946.4
− Change in accounts receivable	−35.0	−14.7	−12.4	−76.2	−41.9	−26.4	−27.2	−28.0	−28.9	−29.7	−30.6
− Change in inventory	−12.2	−7.1	−6.4	−41.9	−23.1	−14.5	−15.0	−15.4	−15.9	−16.4	−16.8
+ Change in accounts payable	51.9	19.1	20.0	37.7	20.8	13.1	13.5	13.9	14.3	14.7	15.2
+ Change in other liabilities	5.6	41.2	47.0	20.6	11.3	7.1	7.3	7.6	7.8	8.0	8.3
+ LBO fees—expensed	179.3	0.0	0.0	0.0	0.0	0.0	0.0	0.0	0.0	0.0	0.0
− Change in required cash balance	−8.4	49.4	−10.2	−13.7	−7.5	−4.8	−4.9	−5.0	−5.2	−5.4	−5.5
Cash flow before capital expenditures	$1,438.6	$1,638.3	$1,794.9	$1,858.9	$1,988.6	$2,064.4	$2,126.4	$2,190.2	$2,255.9	$2,323.5	$2,393.2
− Capital expenditures	−865.2	−819.1	−958.6	−964.5	−924.7	−952.4	−981.0	−1,010.4	−1,040.8	−1,072.0	−1,104.1
Unlevered free cash flow	$ 573.4	$ 819.3	$ 836.4	$ 894.3	$1,063.9	$1,112.0	$1,145.4	$1,179.7	$1,215.1	$1,251.6	$1,289.1
− Interest paid	−766.6	−760.6	−738.1	−713.7	−685.0	−643.6	−599.3	−551.4	−471.3	−377.5	−257.0
+ Interest tax shield	318.9	316.5	307.5	297.7	286.2	269.7	252.0	226.6	194.6	154.6	102.8
− Preferred stock dividends	0.0	0.0	0.0	0.0	0.0	0.0	0.0	0.0	0.0	0.0	0.0
Cash flow after interest and preferred stock dividends	$ 125.6	$ 375.2	$ 405.8	$ 478.3	$ 665.1	$ 738.1	$ 798.0	$ 854.9	$ 938.4	$1,028.7	$1,134.9
+ Change in debt financing	−125.6	−375.2	−405.8	−478.3	−665.1	−738.1	−798.0	−854.9	−938.4	−1,028.7	−1,134.9
+ Change in preferred stock financing	0.0	0.0	0.0	0.0	0.0	0.0	0.0	0.0	0.0	0.0	0.0
Free cash flow to common equity	$ 0.0	$ 0.0	$ 0.0	$ 0.0	$ 0.0	$ 0.0	$ 0.0	$ 0.0	$ 0.0	$ 0.0	$ 0.0
+ Change in common equity financing	0.0	0.0	0.0	0.0	0.0	0.0	0.0	0.0	0.0	0.0	0.0
− Common equity dividends paid	0.0	0.0	0.0	0.0	0.0	0.0	0.0	0.0	0.0	0.0	0.0
Change in excess cash	$ 0.0	$ 0.0	$ 0.0	$ 0.0	$ 0.0	$ 0.0	$ 0.0	$ 0.0	$ 0.0	$ 0.0	$ 0.0
+ Change in required cash balance	8.4	−49.4	10.2	13.7	7.5	4.8	4.9	5.0	5.2	5.4	5.5
Change in cash balance	$ 8.4	−$ 49.4	$ 10.2	$ 13.7	$ 7.5	$ 4.8	$ 4.9	$ 5.0	$ 5.2	$ 5.4	$ 5.5

Exhibit may contain small rounding errors

presents the schedules related to debt—the debt balance, interest expense, and capitalized loan cost amortization schedules. The first two schedules present the debt balance and the repayments (or in the case of the revolver, the repayments and draws) of the debt. These schedules show that the company did not need to draw additional funds from the revolver after the transaction was closed, and, in fact, the revolver was paid down completely by the end of Year 1. Recall that senior secured debt is often issued in tranches with at least one of the tranches requiring amortization of the principal amount. Here, we did not model multiple tranches of senior debt, but if we had modeled one or two tranches with required principal payments starting in the first year, we would have potentially had to borrow more from the revolver in the first few years in order to make those payments.

EXHIBIT 15.16 John Edwardson & Company LBO—Debt Schedule Forecasts

($ in millions)	Total	Year 0	Year 1	Year 2	Year 3	Year 4	Year 5	Year 6	Year 7	Year 8	Year 9	Year 10	Year 11
Balance at Year End													
Revolver (total commitment in 1st column) . . .	$ 300.0	$ 100.0	$ 0.0	$ 0.0	$ 0.0	$ 0.0	$ 0.0	$ 0.0	$ 0.0	$ 0.0	$ 0.0	$ 0.0	$ 0.0
Debt assumed		0.0	0.0	0.0	0.0	0.0	0.0	0.0	0.0	0.0	0.0	0.0	0.0
Senior secured note (bank debt)		3,620.0	3,594.4	3,219.2	2,813.4	2,335.1	1,669.9	931.9	133.8	0.0	0.0	0.0	0.0
Subordinated note (unsecured debt)		1,810.0	1,810.0	1,810.0	1,810.0	1,810.0	1,810.0	1,810.0	1,810.0	1,089.0	150.6	0.0	0.0
Mezzanine debt		3,020.0	3,020.0	3,020.0	3,020.0	3,020.0	3,020.0	3,020.0	3,020.0	3,020.0	3,020.0	2,141.9	1,007.0
All debt issued at par		$8,550.0	$8,424.4	$8,049.2	$7,643.4	$7,165.1	$6,499.9	$5,761.9	$4,963.8	$4,109.0	$3,170.6	$2,141.9	$1,007.0
Repayment at Year End													
Total cash available for repayment.	−$7,543.0		$ 125.6	$ 375.2	$ 405.8	$ 478.3	$ 665.1	$ 738.1	$ 798.0	$ 854.9	$ 938.4	$1,028.7	$1,134.9
Revolver	$ 100.0		−$ 100.0	$ 0.0	$ 0.0	$ 0.0	$ 0.0	$ 0.0	$ 0.0	$ 0.0	$ 0.0	$ 0.0	$ 0.0
Debt assumed	0.0		0.0	0.0	0.0	0.0	0.0	0.0	0.0	0.0	0.0	0.0	0.0
Senior secured note (bank debt)	3,620.0		−25.6	−375.2	−405.8	−478.3	−665.1	−738.1	−798.0	−133.8	0.0	0.0	0.0
Subordinated note (unsecured debt)	1,810.0		0.0	0.0	0.0	0.0	0.0	0.0	0.0	−721.0	−938.4	−150.6	0.0
Mezzanine debt	2,013.0		0.0	0.0	0.0	0.0	0.0	0.0	0.0	0.0	0.0	−878.1	−1,134.9
Total debt repaid.	$ 7,543.0		−$ 125.6	−$ 375.2	−$ 405.8	−$ 478.3	−$ 665.1	−$ 738.1	−$ 798.0	−$ 854.9	−$ 938.4	−$1,028.7	−$1,134.9

Interest Expense	Coupon = YTM	Revolver Fee	Year 1	Year 2	Year 3	Year 4	Year 5	Year 6	Year 7	Year 8	Year 9	Year 10	Year 11
Revolver	4.500%	0.5%	$ 6.0	$ 1.5	$ 1.5	$ 1.5	$ 1.5	$ 0.0	$ 0.0	$ 0.0	$ 0.0	$ 0.0	$ 0.0
Debt assumed	0.000%		0.0	0.0	0.0	0.0	0.0	0.0	0.0	0.0	0.0	0.0	0.0
Senior secured note (bank debt)	6.000%		217.2	215.7	193.2	168.8	140.1	100.2	55.9	8.0	0.0	0.0	0.0
Subordinated note (unsecured debt)	10.000%		181.0	181.0	181.0	181.0	181.0	181.0	181.0	181.0	108.9	15.1	0.0
Mezzanine debt	12.000%		362.4	362.4	362.4	362.4	362.4	362.4	362.4	362.4	362.4	362.4	257.0
Amortization of fees			30.6	30.6	30.6	30.6	30.6	30.6	30.6	15.1	15.1	9.1	0.0
Amortization of discount/premium on debt . . .			0.0	0.0	0.0	0.0	0.0	0.0	0.0	0.0	0.0	0.0	0.0
Assume interest expense = interest deductible			$797.2	$791.2	$768.7	$744.3	$715.6	$674.2	$629.9	$566.5	$486.4	$386.5	$257.0
Weighted average interest rate.			8.97%	9.03%	9.17%	9.34%	9.56%	9.90%	10.40%	11.11%	11.47%	11.91%	12.00%

Amortization of Fees	Fee %	Total Fees	Year 1	Year 2	Year 3	Year 4	Year 5	Year 6	Year 7	Year 8	Year 9	Year 10	Year 11
Debt assumed													
Senior secured note (bank debt)	3.000%	$108.6	$15.5	$15.5	$15.5	$15.5	$15.5	$15.5	$15.5				
Subordinated note (unsecured debt)	3.000%	54.3	6.0	6.0	6.0	6.0	6.0	6.0	6.0	$ 6.0	$ 6.0		
Mezzanine debt	3.000%	90.6	9.1	9.1	9.1	9.1	9.1	9.1	9.1	9.1	9.1	$9.1	
Amortization of fees		$253.5	$30.6	$30.6	$30.6	$30.6	$30.6	$30.6	$30.6	$15.1	$15.1	$9.1	$0.0

Exhibit may contain small rounding errors

As can be seen from the debt schedule, the company does not quite have sufficient cash flows to pay down its senior secured debt by the time the debt matures in seven years. The company could pay off the secured debt by the end of Year 8. The company also does not have sufficient cash flows to pay down its subordinated note (unsecured) by the time the debt matures in nine years. The forecasts show that the company is able to pay down its unsecured debt by the end of Year 10. Finally, the mezzanine debt will not be paid down by its maturity (Year 10). Thus, the company may need to refinance the debt in Year 7 or use its revolver to meet the maturity dates of the senior secured debt and subordinated note. This could be an impediment to securing the debt to finance this transaction and it would be up to the various lenders as to whether the capital structure needs to be altered in some way, such as allowing slightly longer maturities or potentially issuing less debt and requiring more equity.

Of course, the company's need to refinance the debt or draw on the revolver will not arise if it exits from the transaction by the end of Year 7 (recall the median exit time is six years). Regardless, the company's forecasts support its ability to refinance its debt. It is unlikely that lenders who are comfortable with these forecasts will view this as a major problem, especially if they think an exit is likely to occur within seven years. That said, note how three years after the transaction, Edwardson still has almost 90% of the original deal debt outstanding. Kaplan (1990) shows that for the sample of leveraged buyouts completed between 1980 and 1986, 85% of the debt was still outstanding one full year after the transactions, 75% was still outstanding at the end of two years, and 71% was still outstanding at the end of three years. Thus, Edwardson's pay-down is somewhat behind the average documented in Kaplan's study. One potential avenue for the company to accelerate the pay-down of the debt is to reduce the company's capital expenditures in the early years—that, of course, will necessitate greater capital expenditures in later years and may reduce revenues in the early years.

We measure interest expense in the middle section of Exhibit 15.16. Interest expense is equal to the coupon rate (recall that all debt is assumed to be issued at par), multiplied by the outstanding balance at the end of the previous year, plus the amortization of any fees (which appears in the last panel in the exhibit). As we do throughout the book, we do not calculate interest expense based on the weighted average debt outstanding during the year, but rather we base it on the year-end balance from the previous year. To the extent that principal payments are made during the year, our calculation overstates the amount of interest expense. The weighted average interest rate is equal to the interest expense for a given year (excluding fee amortization), divided by the outstanding balance at the end of the previous year. For the purposes of this model (which has to convince lenders that the company has the capacity to support this capital structure), we use the yield-to-maturity (equal to the coupon rate for these debt issues) and make no adjustment for the expected default loss we discussed in Chapter 9 because we assume the company will have a successful exit, which requires that it makes all of its interest payments. We will come back to this topic in a later section when we discuss the APV valuation of the company.

Assessing the Debt Rating Implied in the Financial Model. The next step is assessing the debt rating of the company and comparing it to the assumed debt rating. In Exhibit 15.17, we show the financial leverage and performance measures that are often used to assess a company's debt rating; these are also used in the HZ credit rating model discussed in Chapter 9. We use this model to assess the unsecured debt ratings of the company for each year even though the debt rating at the time of the transaction is generally the most relevant (unless the debt rating is expected to decline over time). In this case, the company's initial debt rating is a B rating. Its debt rating increases to BB by the end of Year 5, to BBB by the end of Year 8, and to A by the end of Year 11. The increase in the debt rating strengthens the argument that the company could likely refinance itself if necessary. As an alternative to the HZ credit rating model, we can also use the information on financial ratios and debt ratings in order to determine the likely rating (Chapter 9).

Note that the iterative process requires us to assess whether the unsecured debt rating from the financial model is consistent with the assumption we made about the yield on the unsecured debt issued. A rating of B has a median yield to maturity of 11% at the time of the transaction (see the yield to maturity column). In Exhibit 15.10, we assume that subordinated debt and mezzanine debt have yield to maturities of 10% and 12%, respectively; thus, our assumptions about the capital structure and of the debt yield seem reasonable given the financial model. If the financial model indicated that the debt rating in Year 1 was CCC+ and below, we would either change the capital structure or change the assumption about the yields until everything was internally consistent.

Investor Internal Rate of Return (Steps 7–8)

As we discussed earlier, financial sponsors typically use an IRR approach to evaluate proposed LBO transactions. At the time that this chapter was written, private equity sponsors were requiring a 20% to 30% expected rate of return on such investments (depending on both the risk of the business and the capital structure), and mezzanine investors were requiring around a 15% rate of return. Sponsors measure the IRR at alternative exit dates in order to assess the most profitable time to exit the company and to assess how sensitive the success of the deal is to the timing of the exit. These calculations are, of course, dependent on the exit value, which private equity firms often estimate using market multiples. Financial

EXHIBIT 15.17 John Edwardson & Company LBO—Debt Rating Forecasts

	For Unsecured Debt												
	Yield to Maturity	**Cost of Debt**	**Year 1**	**Year 2**	**Year 3**	**Year 4**	**Year 5**	**Year 6**	**Year 7**	**Year 8**	**Year 9**	**Year 10**	**Year 11**
EBIT to average total debt + shareholders' equity . . .			0.233	0.314	0.358	0.376	0.381	0.382	0.385	0.386	0.387	0.388	0.388
Interest to EBITDA			0.468	0.366	0.311	0.274	0.251	0.229	0.208	0.182	0.151	0.117	0.075
Total debt to CFO – capital expenditures			62.843	24.710	18.376	14.561	9.663	7.757	6.182	4.778	3.360	2.071	0.883
Total debt to total debt + shareholders' equity			1.747	1.647	1.501	1.341	1.185	1.026	0.863	0.695	0.522	0.343	0.157
Capital expenditures to EBITDA			0.508	0.379	0.388	0.355	0.324	0.324	0.324	0.324	0.324	0.324	0.324
Probability of Debt Rating													
CCC+ & Below.	N/A	N/A	9.3%	4.3%	2.3%	1.4%	0.9%	0.6%	0.4%	0.3%	0.2%	0.1%	0.1%
B– to B+	11.0%	8.7%	75.1%	66.2%	52.9%	41.0%	32.2%	24.5%	17.9%	12.5%	8.5%	5.5%	3.5%
BB– to BB+.	9.0%	7.6%	12.0%	21.7%	30.7%	36.0%	37.9%	37.2%	34.2%	29.2%	23.2%	17.1%	11.8%
BBB– to BBB+	8.0%	6.9%	3.0%	6.3%	11.3%	17.0%	22.3%	28.0%	33.7%	38.4%	40.7%	39.8%	35.3%
A– to A+	7.0%	6.6%	0.5%	1.2%	2.3%	3.8%	5.5%	7.9%	11.1%	15.6%	21.4%	28.3%	35.3%
AA– to AAA	6.0%	6.0%	0.1%	0.3%	0.5%	0.8%	1.2%	1.8%	2.6%	3.9%	6.0%	9.1%	14.1%
Debt Rating			**B**	**B**	**B**	**B**	**BB**	**BB**	**BB**	**BBB**	**BBB**	**BBB**	**A**

sponsors generally do not use a DCF approach; instead, they tend to rely on a market multiple valuation to assess the value at exit. We know from Chapters 13 and 14 that market multiples depend on a company's long-term growth rate and are not constant over time if the company's long-term growth rate changes over time. We discuss this issue in more detail later in this section.

A common assumption made about the exit multiple is that it is equal to the original deal multiple. Whether that is a reasonable approach, of course, depends on the valuation context of the company at the time of exit relative to its condition at the time of the LBO. If the company has reduced capital expenditures, R&D, and maintenance during the LBO, the company is likely to experience a contraction in its multiples by the time of the exit. On the other hand, if the company is more efficient or its growth prospects have improved, it is possible for the company's multiple to have increased.

In Exhibit 15.18, we present the exit value for Edwardson for every year during the forecast period using an EBITDA multiple equal to 6.67, which is the LBO transaction "deal multiple." For each year of the forecast period, the exit value of the firm is equal to the EBITDA multiple multiplied by the EBITDA forecast. The value of the equity (including the value of the warrants and options) in any given year is equal to the value of the firm minus the value of the outstanding debt at the end of that year. The value of the equity ranges from \$2.9 billion in Year 1 to \$19.9 billion in Year 10. The value of the equity increases in each year for several reasons. First, based on the forecasts, EBITDA increases in each year; second, the EBITDA multiple is constant; and third, the company reduces its debt in each year.

Since the company does not distribute cash flows to the equityholders before the exit year, the IRR calculation for equityholders has two cash flows—the initial investment and the exit year cash flow. In the investment year, the sponsor invests \$3.4 billion and collects fees equal to \$120 million. We net the fees against the investment in order to measure the Year 0 investment (financial sponsors do not always net their fees against their investment). The exit year distribution is equal to the value of the equity, multiplied by the fully diluted equity ownership (which was shown in Exhibit 15.10). The internal rate of return for the sponsor, who owns 85.2% of the fully diluted equity, ranges from –23.4% in Year 1 to 32.1% in Year 3. After Year 3, the IRR decreases each year until it reaches 17.9% in Year 10. Equity investors only receive a (cash flow) return on their investment on the exit date; thus, the investors' IRR increases in a year only if the percentage change in the investors' net cash flow at the exit in that year is greater than the IRR in the previous year. For example, the IRR in Year 2 is 28.9% and the percentage change in the net cash flow (and the exit value of the equity) in Year 3 is 38.9%; thus, the IRR in Year 3 increases. However, starting in Year 4, the percentage change in the net cash flow (and the exit value of the equity) is less than the IRR in the previous year so the IRR decreases in every year beginning in Year 4. Clearly, a relatively early exit from this transaction will be important to the sponsor given the forecasts. We should note that these IRRs do not represent the returns that the fund inves-

EXHIBIT 15.18 John Edwardson & Company LBO—Exit Value Forecasts and Sponsor Internal Rates of Return

($ in millions)	EBITDA Multiple		Year 1	Year 2	Year 3	Year 4	Year 5	Year 6	Year 7	Year 8	Year 9	Year 10
EBITDA			$ 1,703.4	$ 2,160.4	$ 2,470.4	$ 2,717.5	$ 2,853.4	$ 2,939.0	$ 3,027.1	$ 3,117.9	$ 3,211.5	$ 3,307.8
Debt outstanding			$ 8,424.4	$ 8,049.2	$ 7,643.4	$ 7,165.1	$ 6,499.9	$ 5,761.9	$ 4,963.8	$ 4,109.0	$ 3,170.6	$ 2,141.9
Exit value—firm (using deal multiple)	6.666		$11,354.5	$14,400.7	$16,467.6	$18,114.3	$19,020.1	$19,590.7	$20,178.4	$20,783.7	$21,407.2	$22,049.5
Exit value—debt			8,424.4	8,049.2	7,643.4	7,165.1	6,499.9	5,761.9	4,963.8	4,109.0	3,170.6	2,141.9
Exit value—equity			$ 2,930.2	$ 6,351.5	$ 8,824.2	$10,949.3	$12,520.1	$13,828.8	$15,214.5	$16,674.8	$18,236.7	$19,907.6
% change in equity value				116.8%	38.9%	24.1%	14.3%	10.5%	10.0%	9.6%	9.4%	9.2%
Sponsor (% fully diluted participation in exit)		85.2%										
Investment		−$3,380.0										
Fees		$ 119.5										
Dividends	None											
Other payments	None											
Participation in exit			$ 2,497.5	$ 5,413.5	$ 7,521.0	$ 9,332.3	$10,671.1	$11,786.5	$12,967.6	$14,212.2	$15,543.4	$16,967.6
Net cash flow		−$3,260.5	$ 2,497.5	$ 5,413.5	$ 7,521.0	$ 9,332.3	$10,671.1	$11,786.5	$12,967.6	$14,212.2	$15,543.4	$16,967.6
% change in net cash flow				116.8%	38.9%	24.1%	14.3%	10.5%	10.0%	9.6%	9.4%	9.2%
IRR	**Exit Yr**											
−23.4%	Year 1	−$3,260.5	$ 2,497.5									
28.9%	Year 2	−3,260.5	0.0	$ 5,413.5								
32.1%	Year 3	−3,260.5	0.0	0.0	$ 7,521.0							
30.1%	Year 4	−3,260.5	0.0	0.0	0.0	$ 9,332.3						
26.8%	Year 5	−3,260.5	0.0	0.0	0.0	0.0	$10,671.1					
23.9%	Year 6	−3,260.5	0.0	0.0	0.0	0.0	0.0	$11,786.5				
21.8%	Year 7	−3,260.5	0.0	0.0	0.0	0.0	0.0	0.0	$12,967.6			
20.2%	Year 8	−3,260.5	0.0	0.0	0.0	0.0	0.0	0.0	0.0	$14,212.2		
18.9%	Year 9	−3,260.5	0.0	0.0	0.0	0.0	0.0	0.0	0.0	0.0	$15,543.4	
17.9%	Year 10	−3,260.5	0.0	0.0	0.0	0.0	0.0	0.0	0.0	0.0	0.0	$16,967.6

Exhibit may contain small rounding errors

tors earn (even if every investment in the fund achieved a return identical to this one), as these calculations do not consider the fees the fund investors have to pay the sponsors. While we do not show it here, one could separately model the IRR to the limited partners (investors) of the fund separate from the financial sponsors, by adjusting the limited partners' returns for both the carried interest and the typical contribution that is not invested directly in the portfolio companies (the fees paid to the fund's sponsors).

The other two groups of investors with equity claims are the managers and mezzanine investors. We present the expected IRRs for these investors in Exhibit 15.19. The IRR for the managers, who own 10.8% of the fully diluted equity, ranges from −6.4% in Year 1 to 42.4% in Year 2. After Year 2, the IRR decreases each year until it is equal to 20.3% in Year 10. The IRRs for the sponsor and management differ for two reasons. First, the sponsor receives upfront fees, which in this case, increases the IRR of the sponsor relative to the managers because the managers paid the same price as the sponsors for their shares but did not receive any fees. Second, and the more dominant effect is that the managers receive additional equity for their performance, which increases the IRR of the managers relative to the sponsors. Equity incentives to management often increase over time as the management team meets certain performance criteria. As such, the amount of dilution from the equity incentives can change with changes to the assumption about the exit year. We do not, however, model that complication in this example.

Lastly, the mezzanine investors have both a debt and equity claim. Assuming the company makes all promised interest and principal payments on a timely basis, the lower bound of their IRR is the interest rate of 12%. The cash flows in the IRR calculation include the investments, the interest paid, the principal paid, and the mezzanine investors' share of the equity exit value. The mezzanine investors own 4% of the fully diluted equity. The internal rate of return for the mezzanine investors starts at 15.9% in Years 1 and 2. After Year 2, the IRR decreases each year until it is equal to 13.4% in Year 10.

EXHIBIT 15.19 John Edwardson & Company LBO—Management and Mezzanine Investor Internal Rates of Return

($ in millions)			Year 1	Year 2	Year 3	Year 4	Year 5	Year 6	Year 7	Year 8	Year 9	Year 10
Management % diluted participation in exit and exit equity value		10.8%	$2,930.2	$6,351.5	$8,824.2	$10,949.3	$12,520.1	$13,828.8	$15,214.5	$16,674.8	$18,236.7	$19,907.6
Investment		−$337.1										
Fees												
Dividends												
Other payments												
Participation in exit			$ 315.5	$ 683.9	$ 950.2	$ 1,179.0	$ 1,348.2	$ 1,489.1	$ 1,638.3	$ 1,795.6	$ 1,963.7	$ 2,143.7
Net cash flow		−$337.1	$ 315.5	$ 683.9	$ 950.2	$ 1,179.0	$ 1,348.2	$ 1,489.1	$ 1,638.3	$ 1,795.6	$ 1,963.7	$ 2,143.7
% change in net cash flow				116.8%	38.9%	24.1%	14.3%	10.5%	10.0%	9.6%	9.4%	9.2%
IRR	**Exit Yr**											
−6.4%	Year 1	−$337.1	$ 315.5									
42.4%	Year 2	−337.1	0.0	$ 683.9								
41.3%	Year 3	−337.1	0.0	0.0	$ 950.2							
36.8%	Year 4	−337.1	0.0	0.0	0.0	$ 1,179.0						
31.9%	Year 5	−337.1	0.0	0.0	0.0	0.0	$ 1,348.2					
28.1%	Year 6	−337.1	0.0	0.0	0.0	0.0	0.0	$ 1,489.1				
25.3%	Year 7	−337.1	0.0	0.0	0.0	0.0	0.0	0.0	$ 1,638.3			
23.3%	Year 8	−337.1	0.0	0.0	0.0	0.0	0.0	0.0	0.0	$ 1,795.6		
21.6%	Year 9	−337.1	0.0	0.0	0.0	0.0	0.0	0.0	0.0	0.0	$ 1,963.7	
20.3%	Year 10	−337.1	0.0	0.0	0.0	0.0	0.0	0.0	0.0	0.0	0.0	$ 2,143.7

($ in millions)			Year 1	Year 2	Year 3	Year 4	Year 5	Year 6	Year 7	Year 8	Year 9	Year 10
Mezzanine debt % diluted participation in exit and exit equity value		4.0%	$2,930.2	$6,351.5	$8,824.2	$10,949.3	$12,520.1	$13,828.8	$15,214.5	$16,674.8	$18,236.7	$19,907.6
Investment		−$3,020.0										
Fees												
Interest paid			$ 362.4	$ 362.4	$ 362.4	$ 362.4	$ 362.4	$ 362.4	$ 362.4	$ 362.4	$ 362.4	$ 362.4
Repayment of principal			3,020.0	3,020.0	3,020.0	3,020.0	3,020.0	3,020.0	3,020.0	3,020.0	3,020.0	3,020.0
Participation in exit			117.2	254.1	353.0	438.0	500.8	553.2	608.6	667.0	729.5	796.3
Net cash flow		−$3,020.0	$3,499.6	$3,636.5	$3,735.4	$ 3,820.4	$ 3,883.2	$ 3,935.6	$ 3,991.0	$ 4,049.4	$ 4,111.9	$ 4,178.7
% change in net cash flow				3.9%	2.7%	2.3%	1.6%	1.3%	1.4%	1.5%	1.5%	1.6%
IRR	**Exit Yr**											
15.9%	Year 1	−$3,020.0	$3,499.6									
15.9%	Year 2	−3,020.0	362.4	$3,636.5								
15.4%	Year 3	−3,020.0	362.4	362.4	$3,735.4							
14.9%	Year 4	−3,020.0	362.4	362.4	$362.4	$3,820.4						
14.5%	Year 5	−3,020.0	362.4	362.4	362.4	362.4	$ 3,883.2					
14.1%	Year 6	−3,020.0	362.4	362.4	362.4	362.4	362.4	$ 3,935.6				
13.9%	Year 7	−3,020.0	362.4	362.4	362.4	362.4	362.4	362.4	$ 3,991.0			
13.7%	Year 8	−3,020.0	362.4	362.4	362.4	362.4	362.4	362.4	362.4	$ 4,049.4		
13.5%	Year 9	−3,020.0	362.4	362.4	362.4	362.4	362.4	362.4	362.4	362.4	$ 4,111.9	
13.4%	Year 10	−3,020.0	362.4	362.4	362.4	362.4	362.4	362.4	362.4	362.4	362.4	$ 4,178.7

It is apparent from this example that the highest IRR does not occur in the same year for all investors due to different investment amounts and claims on the cash flows. The sponsor achieves the highest IRR in Year 3, while the managers achieve the highest IRR in Year 2. The mezzanine providers achieve the highest IRR with an exit date of no later than Year 2.

15.5 USING DISCOUNTED CASH FLOW VALUATION MODELS TO EVALUATE LBO TRANSACTIONS (STEPS 9 AND 10)

LO5 Use DCF models to further analyze LBO transactions

The typical LBO analysis uses IRR analyses to evaluate LBO investments. While the conceptual frameworks and underpinnings of IRRs and discounted cash flow valuation models are similar, they are not the same in all respects. Corporate finance textbooks explain why making decisions based on **net present value (NPV)**, which is equal to the difference between the value of an investment and the amount invested, is in many circumstances a better approach to use. In earlier chapters, we explained the benefits of using discounted cash flow models to measure continuing values as an alternative to using market multiples.

In this section, we illustrate how to use discounted cash flow valuation models to assess the investment value of LBO transactions. First, we illustrate how to use the weighted average cost of capital valuation method to measure exit values. This approach is another lens through which to measure exit values and thus, to evaluate an LBO transaction. Second, we illustrate how to use the adjusted present value valuation method to measure the value of the LBO investment and the equity cost of capital, equity beta, and weighted average cost of capital implied in the LBO investment.

Using the Weighted Average Cost of Capital Valuation Method to Measure Exit Values—Step 9 (Another View of Steps 7–8)

We can also measure the exit value using the weighted average cost of capital method instead of an exit multiple. In this case, we assess the likely exit value based on the assumption that the company is sold to a strategic buyer or sold via an IPO. As a consequence of this assumption, we assume the company adopts a more typical capital structure at the time of exit—for example, a typical industry capital structure as opposed to a highly levered capital structure. As we discussed earlier, this is not a method that is generally used but it is another lens by which to evaluate the potential exit value.

REVIEW EXERCISE 15.2

Measuring the Internal Rate of Return

Use the information in Review Exercise 15.1 and the following information to measure the internal rates of return (on a fully diluted equity ownership basis) to the financial sponsor, management, and mezzanine debtholders; assume an exit value based on the EBITDA deal multiple. EBITDA was $346.08 in Year 0. Management has prepared the following forecasts to be used to assess the value of the LBO transaction.

($ in millions)	Year −1	Year 0 Post-LBO Opening	Year 1	Year 2	Year 3	Year 4	Year 5	Year 6	Year 7	Year 8	Year 9	Year 10	Year 11
Cash balance	$ 89.6	$ 57.7	$ 48.0	$ 37.4	$ 26.0	$ 27.0	$ 28.1	$ 29.2	$ 30.1	$ 31.0	$ 31.9	$ 32.9	$ 33.8
Accounts receivable	186.7	192.3	186.6	180.2	173.0	179.9	187.1	194.6	200.5	206.5	212.7	219.0	225.6
Inventory	125.4	123.1	121.6	114.8	107.8	107.1	111.3	115.8	119.3	128.7	138.6	149.0	153.4
Total current assets	$ 401.7	$ 373.0	$ 356.2	$ 332.5	$ 306.8	$ 314.0	$ 326.6	$ 339.6	$ 349.8	$ 366.1	$ 383.2	$ 400.9	$ 412.9
Property, plant, and equipment	$1,124.8	$1,261.6	$1,344.4	$1,435.9	$1,491.4	$1,564.9	$1,719.3	$1,872.6	$2,116.5	$2,458.9	$2,634.3	$2,604.3	$2,573.4
Accumulated depreciation	−300.8	−404.6	−512.6	−624.9	−741.7	−863.1	−989.5	−1,120.8	−1,256.1	−1,395.5	−1,539.1	−1,476.2	−1,411.4
Property, plant, and equipment (net)	$ 824.0	$ 857.0	$ 831.8	$ 811.0	$ 749.7	$ 701.8	$ 729.8	$ 751.7	$ 860.3	$1,063.3	$1,095.2	$1,128.1	$1,161.9
Capitalized fees	$ 0	$ 101.9	$ 51.7	$ 44.5	$ 37.4	$ 30.2	$ 23.1	$ 15.9	$ 8.8	$ 5.4	$ 2.0	$ 0.0	$ 0.0
Total assets	$1,225.7	$1,331.9	$1,239.7	$1,188.0	$1,093.9	$1,046.0	$1,079.5	$1,107.3	$1,218.9	$1,434.9	$1,480.4	$1,529.0	$1,574.8
Accounts payable	$ 62.7	$ 61.5	$ 72.0	$ 79.7	$ 87.2	$ 86.6	$ 90.1	$ 93.7	$ 96.5	$ 104.1	$ 112.1	$ 120.5	$ 124.1
Other current operating liabilities	56.0	57.7	96.0	137.3	142.7	148.5	154.4	160.6	165.4	170.3	175.5	180.7	186.1
Total current liabilities	$ 118.7	$ 119.2	$ 168.0	$ 217.0	$ 230.0	$ 235.0	$ 244.4	$ 254.2	$ 261.9	$ 274.4	$ 287.5	$ 301.2	$ 310.2
Total debt	600.0	2,060.0	1,894.4	1,702.5	1,459.9	1,222.6	1,044.6	842.3	706.5	688.7	529.1	393.1	242.7
Total liabilities	$ 718.7	$2,179.2	$2,062.3	$1,919.5	$1,689.9	$1,457.6	$1,289.0	$1,096.6	$ 968.3	$ 963.1	$ 816.6	$ 694.3	$ 552.9
Preferred stock	$ 100.0	$ 0.0	$ 0.0	$ 0.0	$ 0.0	$ 0.0	$ 0.0	$ 0.0	$ 0.0	$ 0.0	$ 0.0	$ 0.0	$ 0.0
Common stock	200.0	883.3	883.3	883.3	883.3	883.3	883.3	883.3	883.3	883.3	883.3	883.3	883.3
Retained earnings	207.0	−1,730.6	−1,706.0	−1,614.8	−1,479.3	−1,295.0	−1,092.9	−872.6	−632.8	−411.5	−219.5	−48.7	138.6
Total shareholders' equity	$ 507.0	−$ 847.3	−$ 822.7	−$ 731.5	−$ 595.9	−$ 411.7	−$ 209.6	$ 10.7	$ 250.6	$ 471.8	$ 663.8	$ 834.7	$1,021.9
Total liabilities and equities	$1,225.7	$1,331.9	$1,239.7	$1,188.0	$1,093.9	$1,046.0	$1,079.5	$1,107.3	$1,218.9	$1,434.9	$1,480.4	$1,529.0	$1,574.8

continued

continued from previous page

($ in millions)	Year 1	Year 2	Year 3	Year 4	Year 5	Year 6	Year 7	Year 8	Year 9	Year 10	Year 11
Earnings before interest and taxes (EBIT)	$208.8	$311.9	$376.3	$445.4	$463.2	$481.7	$496.1	$449.1	$398.8	$345.0	$355.4
− Income taxes paid on EBIT . . .	−83.5	−124.8	−150.5	−178.1	−185.3	−192.7	−198.5	−179.6	−159.5	−138.0	−142.1
Earnings before interest and after taxes	$125.3	$187.2	$225.8	$267.2	$277.9	$289.0	$297.7	$269.5	$239.3	$207.0	$213.2
+ Depreciation expense.	108.0	112.3	116.8	121.5	126.3	131.4	135.3	139.4	143.6	147.9	152.3
− Change in accounts receivable	5.6	6.4	7.2	−6.9	−7.2	−7.5	−5.8	−6.0	−6.2	−6.4	−6.6
− Change in inventory	1.5	6.8	6.9	0.8	−4.3	−4.5	−3.5	−9.4	−9.9	−10.4	−4.5
+ Change in accounts payable . .	10.5	7.7	7.5	−0.6	3.5	3.6	2.8	7.6	8.0	8.4	3.6
+ Change in other liabilities.	38.3	41.3	5.5	5.7	5.9	6.2	4.8	5.0	5.1	5.3	5.4
+ LBO fees − expensed.	43.1	0.0	0.0	0.0	0.0	0.0	0.0	0.0	0.0	0.0	0.0
− Change in required cash balance.	9.7	10.6	11.5	−1.0	−1.1	−1.1	−0.9	−0.9	−0.9	−1.0	−1.0
Cash flow before capital expenditures	$342.0	$372.2	$381.2	$386.6	$401.1	$417.1	$430.4	$405.1	$378.9	$350.8	$362.5
Capital expenditures	−82.8	−91.5	−55.5	−73.5	−154.4	−153.3	−243.9	−342.4	−175.5	−180.7	−186.1
Unlevered free cash flow	$259.1	$280.7	$325.7	$313.1	$246.7	$263.8	$186.5	$ 62.7	$203.4	$170.1	$176.4

Exhibit may contain small rounding errors

Solution on pages 787–788.

In Exhibit 15.20, we use the weighted average cost of capital method to measure the exit values and implied multiples based on those exit values. We use a weighted average cost of capital of 10.34%, which is based on an unlevered cost of capital of 11%, a constant debt-to-value ratio of 25% at exit (regardless of when exit occurs), a cost of debt capital of 6.6%, and a marginal tax rate of 40%. The 25% debt-to-value capital structure is based on an assessment of the typical capital structure in Edwardson's industry. Because we assume a constant debt-to-value capital structure, we assume the unlevered cost of capital is the discount rate for tax shields after exit. As such, we use the levering formula that values all interest tax shields at the unlevered cost of capital (Equation 10.5). In addition, we assume a 3% continuing value growth rate beyond Year 10.[30]

EXHIBIT 15.20 John Edwardson & Company LBO—Weighted Average Cost of Capital Valuation of Exit Values

Weighted Average Cost of Capital Valuation

r_E	r_D	V_D/V_F	T_{INT}	r_{WACC}	Continuing Value Growth Rate
12.467%	6.600%	25.000%	40.000%	10.340%	3.000%

($ in millions)	Year 0	Year 1	Year 2	Year 3	Year 4	Year 5	Year 6	Year 7	Year 8	Year 9	Year 10
Weighted average cost of capital valuation of the firm . . .	$12,331.7	$13,033.5	$13,561.9	$14,127.8	$14,694.3	$15,149.8	$15,604.3	$16,072.4	$16,554.6	$17,051.2	$17,562.7
Value of debt	8,550.0	8,424.4	8,049.2	7,643.4	7,165.1	6,499.9	5,761.9	4,963.8	4,109.0	3,170.6	2,141.9
Weighted average cost of capital valuation of the equity. . .	$ 3,781.7	$ 4,609.1	$ 5,512.7	$ 6,484.4	$ 7,529.2	$ 8,649.8	$ 9,842.4	$11,108.5	$12,445.6	$13,880.6	$15,420.9
EBITDA.	$1,793.0	$1,703.4	$2,160.4	$2,470.4	$2,717.5	$2,853.4	$2,939.0	$3,027.1	$3,117.9	$3,211.5	$3,307.8
Implied firm value to EBITDA	6.878	7.651	6.278	5.719	5.407	5.309	5.309	5.309	5.309	5.309	5.309
Exit Value Multiple and Values Used											
Deal multiple—firm value to EBITDA		6.666	6.666	6.666	6.666	6.666	6.666	6.666	6.666	6.666	6.666
% Difference with weighted average cost of capital valuation.		−12.9%	6.2%	16.6%	23.3%	25.5%	25.5%	25.5%	25.5%	25.5%	25.5%
Exit value—equity (using deal multiple)		$2,930.2	$6,351.5	$8,824.2	$10,949.3	$12,520.1	$13,828.8	$15,214.5	$16,674.8	$18,236.7	$19,907.6
% Difference with weighted average cost of capital valuation.		−36.4%	15.2%	36.1%	45.4%	44.7%	40.5%	37.0%	34.0%	31.4%	29.1%

Exhibit may contain small rounding errors

[30] Note that by using the weighted average cost of capital based on the cost of debt at the assumed time of exit, we are valuing the interest tax shields after exit based on expected interest tax shields, not interest tax shields based on promised yields.

We use the EBITDA in the financial forecasts and the year-by-year weighted average cost of capital-based exit values from Exhibit 15.20 to measure the implied market multiples for each year. This exhibit shows that the market multiples decline from Year 1 to Year 5. For example, the EBITDA multiple is 7.7 in Year 1 and decreases to 5.3 by Year 5, where it then remains constant through Year 10. This decline results from a decline in the long-term growth rate over the first few years but by Year 5, both the value of the firm and EBITDA grow at the 3% long-term growth rate. The implied EBITDA multiple based on the weighted average cost of capital-based exit value is lower than the deal multiple for every year except for Years 0 and 1.

In Exhibit 15.21, we use the weighted average cost of capital-based exit values to measure the sponsor IRRs. If we compare the IRRs in Exhibit 15.21 to those in Exhibit 15.18, we see that the IRRs based on the weighted average cost of capital-based exit values are, for the most part, less than those in Exhibit 15.18 (the exception being for Year 1). They are less because in all years but Year 1, the value of the firm from the weighted average cost of capital valuation is below the market multiple valuation based on the EBITDA deal multiple.

EXHIBIT 15.21 John Edwardson & Company LBO—Sponsor Internal Rates of Return Based on the Weighted Average Cost of Capital Valuation of Exit Values

($ in millions)		**Year 1**	**Year 2**	**Year 3**	**Year 4**	**Year 5**	**Year 6**	**Year 7**	**Year 8**	**Year 9**	**Year 10**
Exit value—firm (weighted average cost of capital valuation)		$13,033.5	$13,561.9	$14,127.8	$14,694.3	$15,149.8	$15,604.3	$16,072.4	$16,554.6	$17,051.2	$17,562.7
Exit value—equity		$ 4,609.1	$ 5,512.7	$ 6,484.4	$ 7,529.2	$ 8,649.8	$ 9,842.4	$11,108.5	$12,445.6	$13,880.6	$15,420.9
Sponsor (% fully diluted participation in exit)	85.2%										
Investment	−$3,380.0										
Fees	$ 119.5										
Dividends	None										
Other payments	None										
Participation in exit		$ 3,928.4	$ 4,698.6	$ 5,526.8	$ 6,417.3	$ 7,372.4	$ 8,388.9	$ 9,468.0	$10,607.6	$11,830.7	$13,143.5
Net cash flow	−$3,260.5	$ 3,928.4	$ 4,698.6	$ 5,526.8	$ 6,417.3	$ 7,372.4	$ 8,388.9	$ 9,468.0	$10,607.6	$11,830.7	$13,143.5

IRR	**Exit Yr**											
20.5%	Year 1	−$3,260.5	$ 3,928.4									
20.0%	Year 2	−3,260.5	0.0	$ 4,698.6								
19.2%	Year 3	−3,260.5	0.0	0.0	$ 5,526.8							
18.4%	Year 4	−3,260.5	0.0	0.0	0.0	$ 6,417.3						
17.7%	Year 5	−3,260.5	0.0	0.0	0.0	0.0	$ 7,372.4					
17.1%	Year 6	−3,260.5	0.0	0.0	0.0	0.0	0.0	$ 8,388.9				
16.5%	Year 7	−3,260.5	0.0	0.0	0.0	0.0	0.0	0.0	$ 9,468.0			
15.9%	Year 8	−3,260.5	0.0	0.0	0.0	0.0	0.0	0.0	0.0	$10,607.6		
15.4%	Year 9	−3,260.5	0.0	0.0	0.0	0.0	0.0	0.0	0.0	0.0	$11,830.7	
15.0%	Year 10	−3,260.5	0.0	0.0	0.0	0.0	0.0	0.0	0.0	0.0	0.0	$13,143.5

REVIEW EXERCISE 15.3

WACC-Based Exit Value

Use the information in Review Exercises 15.1 and 15.2 to measure the weighted average cost of capital-based exit values and implied EBITDA multiples; compare the implied EBITDA multiples in each year to the deal EBITDA multiple (see Exhibit 15.20). To measure the weighted average cost of capital, assume that as of the exit date, the company will use a capital structure equal to 25% debt and 75% common equity, resulting in a 5.9% cost of debt and 10.033% cost of equity. As of Year 11, the company expects its free cash flows to grow at 3% in perpetuity. Recalculate the internal rate of return to the financial sponsor using the weighted average cost of capital-based exit values (see Exhbit 15.21).

Solution on page 788.

As we discussed in Chapters 13 and 14, multiples are a function of growth and profitability, as well as other factors. The use of a constant deal multiple across different years in order to assess the exit value presumes no changes in future growth opportunities and profitability over time, which is almost never the case except for mature, constant-growth companies. When estimating IRRs for alternative exit dates, assessing the expected growth and operating performance of the company at each exit date is relevant regardless of which valuation method—market multiple or discounted cash flow—we use. Based on the financial model we used for this company, which has decreasing growth over time, it is unlikely that the appropriate exit multiple would be greater than the deal multiple beyond the first year or two.[31]

Valuation Key 15.8

When estimating IRRs for alternative exit dates, assessing the expected growth and operating performance of the company at each exit date is relevant regardless of which valuation method—market multiple or discounted cash flow—we use. Using more than one valuation method provides alternative lenses by which to evaluate the exit values and IRRs.

Adjusted Present Value Method Valuation, Net Present Value of the Investment, Implied Equity Costs of Capital, and Equity Betas (Step 10)

In this section use use the adjusted present value valuation method to accomplish two goals. The first is to measure the value of the LBO investment and the resulting **net present value (NPV)** of the LBO investment (value of the LBO investment on the transaction closing date minus the amount invested). The second is to measure the equity cost of capital, equity beta, and weighted average cost of capital implied in the LBO investment. We can compare the equity cost of capital against the IRRs in the LBO model in order to assess whether the hurdle rate for the IRR is sufficiently high given the riskiness of the equity investment.

The Adjusted Present Value Valuation of an LBO Investment

The inputs to measure the value of the firm using the adjusted present value method are the unlevered free cash flows, the unlevered cost of capital, the expected (not promised) interest tax shields, the discount rate for the interest tax shields, the continuing capital structure strategy, and the growth rate for the continuing value. Edwardson's unlevered cost of capital is 11%. The market risk premium is 6%, and the risk-free rate is 5%, implying an unlevered beta of 1.0. Continuing our approach used at the end of the previous section, we measure the continuing value of the firm by re-capitalizing the firm to a long-term target capital structure using the weighted average cost of capital valuation method. This approach requires a long-term growth rate and target capital structure. The long-term growth rate after Year 10 is equal to the inflation rate of 3%. In this initial analysis, we assume exit is at the end of Year 10, hence, beyond Year 10, the company plans to maintain a 25% debt-to-value ratio with a cost of debt of 6.6%; thus, the interest tax shields will grow at the long-term growth rate after Year 10.

Recall our discussion of the discount rate for interest tax shields in Chapter 10. In general, we use either the company's cost of debt or its unlevered cost of capital. We use the cost of debt to value interest tax shields that are already contracted as of the valuation date and are managed independently of the value of the firm. Further, we use the unlevered cost of capital to value interest tax shields that are not yet contracted and thus dependent on the value of the firm. Edwardson has debt contracts in place for the interest tax shields through Year 10. Afterward, the company will refinance its debt to a target capital structure based on the value of the firm. Based on this assumption, we might conclude that we should use the debt cost of capital to discount the interest tax shields through Year 10 and the unlevered cost of capital to discount the interest tax shields from the continuing value calculation. That said, as a starting point, we first assume that the discount rate for all interest tax shields is the unlevered cost of capital for ease of calculation. Later, we discuss the additional value resulting from the assumption that the discount rate for interest tax shields is the cost of debt for interest tax shields through the refinancing date (up to the exit date), through Year 10.

---

[31] Note that deal multiples can also increase if the company improves or if the sponsor exits when market valuations are generally higher. Evidence in Acharya, Hahn, and Kehoe (2012) indicates that for their sample of Western European LBOs from 1995 to 2005, the average EBITDA multiple increases by two relative to the increase in the industry EBITDA multiple (from the entry to the exit of the LBO). See Acharya, V., M. Hahn, and C. Kehoe, "Corporate Governance and Value Creation: Evidence from Private Equity," *Review of Financial Studies* vol. 26 (2012), pp. 368–402.

As shown in Exhibit 15.22, the value of the firm is $13.0 billion—the value of the unlevered firm is $11.26 billion and the value of the interest tax shields is $1.79 billion.[32] Since the investors invested $12.3 billion (net of cash), the net present value of the LBO investment is $780 million, which is also equal to the net present value to the equity investors (the value of the equity is $4.5 billion relative to the equity investment of $3.72 billion). Had we assumed the discount rate for interest tax shields was equal to the cost of debt through Year 10, the value of the interest tax shields would have increased by $157 million (calculation not shown). That would increase the net present value of the investment by about 20% and the value of the equity by about 4%.

EXHIBIT 15.22 John Edwardson & Company LBO—Adjusted Present Value Valuation

($ in millions)	Year 0	Year 1	Year 2	Year 3	Year 4	Year 5	Year 6	Year 7	Year 8	Year 9	Year 10	CV Year 10
Value of the Unlevered Firm												
Unlevered free cash flow for continuing value....												$ 1,289.1
Discount factor for continuing value												12.500
Unlevered free cash flow and continuing value ...		$573.4	$819.3	$836.4	$894.3	$1,063.9	$1,112.0	$1,145.4	$1,179.7	$1,215.1	$1,251.6	$16,113.8
Discount factor..........................		0.9009	0.8116	0.7312	0.6587	0.5935	0.5346	0.4817	0.4339	0.3909	0.3522	0.3522
Discounted value		$516.5	$664.9	$611.5	$589.1	$ 631.4	$ 594.5	$ 551.7	$ 511.9	$ 475.0	$ 440.8	$ 5,675.0
Value of the unlevered firm..................	$11,262.4											
Value of the Interest Tax Shields												
Interest tax shield for continuing value.........												$ 115.9
Discount factor for continuing value												12.500
Interest tax shield and continuing value of ITS ...		$269.6	$267.2	$258.2	$248.4	$ 215.7	$ 199.2	$ 181.4	$ 142.6	$ 119.4	$ 91.1	$ 1,448.9
Discount factor, r_{UA}		0.9009	0.8116	0.7312	0.6587	0.5935	0.5346	0.4817	0.4339	0.3909	0.3522	0.3522
Present value		$242.9	$216.9	$188.8	$163.7	$ 128.0	$ 106.5	$ 87.4	$ 61.9	$ 46.7	$ 32.1	$ 510.3
Value of the interest tax shields	$ 1,785.0											
Value of the firm V_F w/o excess assets.........	$13,047.4											

Net Present Value of Investment	Firm Value		Equity Value	
Value..................................	$13,047.4		$4,497.4	
Purchase price paid (sources – excess cash)	12,267.1		3,717.1	
Net present value of investment..............	$ 780.3	6.0%	$ 780.3	17.4%

This valuation assumes that investors will not exit from the transaction until Year 10, at an exit value based on a recapitalization of the debt to the company's target capital structure. In Exhibit 15.23 we show the effect of assuming earlier exit dates based on recapitalizing the debt to the target capital structure at the exit date. Based on this analysis, the maximum net present value results from exiting in Year 9. An exit at Year 9 does not, however, maximize the investors' IRRs as shown previously.

EXHIBIT 15.23 John Edwardson & Company LBO—Net Present Value of LBO Investment at Alternative Exit Dates

($ in millions)	Year 1	Year 2	Year 3	Year 4	Year 5	Year 6	Year 7	Year 8	Year 9	Year 10
Firm value, Year 0.......	$12,501.3	$12,648.3	$12,771.7	$12,873.9	$12,944.4	$12,997.4	$13,035.2	$13,051.0	$13,055.0	$13,047.4
Purchase price paid.....	12,267.1	12,267.1	12,267.1	12,267.1	12,267.1	12,267.1	12,267.1	12,267.1	12,267.1	12,267.1
Net present value.......	$ 234.2	$ 381.2	$ 504.6	$ 606.8	$ 677.3	$ 730.3	$ 768.1	$ 783.9	$ 787.9	$ 780.3
% Of purchase price	1.9%	3.1%	4.1%	4.9%	5.5%	6.0%	6.3%	6.4%	6.4%	6.4%
Equity value, Year 0	$ 3,951.3	$ 4,098.3	$ 4,221.7	$ 4,323.9	$ 4,394.4	$ 4,447.4	$ 4,485.2	$ 4,501.0	$ 4,505.0	$ 4,497.4
Purchase price paid.....	3,717.1	3,717.1	3,717.1	3,717.1	3,717.1	3,717.1	3,717.1	3,717.1	3,717.1	3,717.1
Net present value.......	$ 234.2	$ 381.2	$ 504.6	$ 606.8	$ 677.3	$ 730.3	$ 768.1	$ 783.9	$ 787.9	$ 780.3
% Of purchase price	6.3%	10.3%	13.6%	16.3%	18.2%	19.6%	20.7%	21.1%	21.2%	21.0%

[32] Note, as mentioned previously in this chapter, we are assuming that there is no limitation on the deductibility of interest for tax purposes. Also note that these are expected interest tax shields as they are based on the cost of debt (Exhibit 15.24 shows the calculation of these interest tax shields).

EXHIBIT 15.24 John Edwardson & Company LBO—Capital Structure and Expected Interest

($ in millions)	Total	Year 0	Year 1	Year 2	Year 3	Year 4	Year 5	Year 6	Year 7	Year 8	Year 9	Year 10	Year 11
Debt rating			B	B	B	B	BB	BB	BB	BBB	BBB	BBB	A
Debt cost of capital for unsecured debt.			8.70%	8.70%	8.70%	8.70%	7.60%	7.60%	7.60%	6.90%	6.90%	6.90%	6.60%
Balance at Year End												Debt Recapitalization	
Revolver (total commitment in 1st column) . . .	$300.0	$ 100.0	$ 0.0	$ 0.0	$ 0.0	$ 0.0	$ 0.0	$ 0.0	$ 0.0	$ 0.0	$ 0.0		
Debt assumed		0.0	0.0	0.0	0.0	0.0	0.0	0.0	0.0	0.0	0.0		
Senior secured note (bank debt)		3,620.0	3,594.4	3,219.2	2,813.4	2,335.1	1,669.9	931.9	133.8	0.0	0.0		
Subordinated note (unsecured debt)		1,810.0	1,810.0	1,810.0	1,810.0	1,810.0	1,810.0	1,810.0	1,810.0	1,089.0	150.6		
Mezzanine debt		3,020.0	3,020.0	3,020.0	3,020.0	3,020.0	3,020.0	3,020.0	3,020.0	3,020.0	3,020.0		
All debt issued at par		$8,550.0	$8,424.4	$8,049.2	$7,643.4	$7,165.1	$6,499.9	$5,761.9	$4,963.8	$4,109.0	$3,170.6	$4,390.7	$4,522.4

Expected Interest and Tax Deduction	Cost of Debt	Fee	Year 1	Year 2	Year 3	Year 4	Year 5	Year 6	Year 7	Year 8	Year 9	Year 10	Year 11
Revolver	4.500%	0.5%	$ 6.0	$ 1.5	$ 1.5	$ 1.5	$ 1.5	$ 0.0	$ 0.0	$ 0.0	$ 0.0	$ 0.0	
Debt assumed			0.0	0.0	0.0	0.0	0.0	0.0	0.0	0.0	0.0	0.0	
Senior secured note (bank debt)	6.000%		217.2	215.7	193.2	168.8	140.1	100.2	55.9	8.0	0.0	0.0	
Subordinated note (unsecured debt)	Rating-based rate		157.5	157.5	157.5	157.5	137.6	137.6	137.6	124.9	75.1	10.4	
Mezzanine debt	Rating-based rate		262.7	262.7	262.7	262.7	229.5	229.5	229.5	208.4	208.4	208.4	
Expected cash interest expense			$643.4	$637.4	$614.9	$590.5	$508.7	$467.3	$423.0	$341.3	$283.5	$218.8	$289.8
Amortization of fees			30.6	30.6	30.6	30.6	30.6	30.6	30.6	15.1	15.1	9.1	0.0
Amortization of discount/premium on debt . . .													
Expected interest tax deduction			$674.0	$668.0	$645.5	$621.1	$539.3	$497.9	$453.6	$356.4	$298.6	$227.8	$289.8
Weighted average cost of debt			7.88%	7.93%	8.02%	8.13%	7.53%	7.66%	7.87%	7.18%	7.27%	7.19%	6.60%
Interest tax shield			$269.6	$267.2	$258.2	$248.4	$215.7	$199.2	$181.4	$142.6	$119.4	$ 91.1	$115.9
Tax rate for interest tax shields based on cash interest, T_{INT}			40.0%	40.0%	40.0%	40.0%	40.0%	40.0%	40.0%	40.0%	40.0%	40.0%	40.0%

The expected interest tax shields in Exhibit 15.22 do not equal the promised interest payments (coupon rate × debt outstanding), rather they equal the expected interest payments (cost of debt × debt outstanding). In Exhibit 15.24, we present information on the company's debt rating, cost of debt, debt balance (including the debt recapitalization at the end of Year 10), interest (tax-deductible interest expense and cash interest paid), weighted average cost of debt, and interest tax shields. The cost of debt for the unsecured debt adjusts the yield-to-maturity (in this case the coupon rate) for the expected default loss as discussed in Chapter 9 (we assume no expected default losses for the secured debt). We measure the expected interest payments using the cost of debt based on the debt rating from the HZ credit rating model—and not the promised yield—and then add the amortization of the loan fees to determine the expected interest expense. The interest tax shield is equal to the expected interest expense multiplied by the 40% tax rate (assuming no limitation on the deductibility of interest for tax purposes). We also calculate the weighted average cost of debt for each period based on the cost of debt for each instrument. We assume that the debt is **performance priced debt**, meaning the coupon is adjusted annually in response to any changes in the rating. While this assumption may not be applicable to many LBOs as much of the debt is unlikely to be performance priced, we make this simplifying assumption to simplify the calculations and discussion. This adjustment is also appropriate if the company were to refinance itself in the future.

We can use the APV approach from Exhibit 15.22 to measure the value of the firm for every year in the forecast period, and we show this valuation in Exhibit 15.25. We use these valuations to subsequently measure the implied capital structure ratios, cost of equity, and equity beta in the next section.

EXHIBIT 15.25 John Edwardson & Company LBO—Year-by-Year Adjusted Present Value Valuations Assuming Exit at the End of Year 10

Beginning of Year Value ($ in millions)	Year 1	Year 2	Year 3	Year 4	Year 5	Year 6	Year 7	Year 8	Year 9	Year 10	CV Year 10
Value of the Unlevered Firm											
Unlevered free cash flow for continuing value											$ 1,289.1
Discount factor for continuing value											12.500
Unlevered free cash flow	$ 573.4	$ 819.3	$ 836.4	$ 894.3	$ 1,063.9	$ 1,112.0	$ 1,145.4	$ 1,179.7	$ 1,215.1	$ 1,251.6	
End of year value of unlevered firm	11,927.9	12,420.7	12,950.7	13,480.9	13,899.9	14,316.9	14,746.4	15,188.8	15,644.5	16,113.8	
Unlevered firm value + unlevered free cash flow	$12,501.3	$13,240.0	$13,787.0	$14,375.2	$14,963.8	$15,428.9	$15,891.8	$16,368.5	$16,859.6	$17,365.4	
Discount factor for one year, r_{UA}	0.901	0.901	0.901	0.901	0.901	0.901	0.901	0.901	0.901	0.901	
Value of the unlevered firm at beginning of year	$11,262.4	$11,927.9	$12,420.7	$12,950.7	$13,480.9	$13,899.9	$14,316.9	$14,746.4	$15,188.8	$15,644.5	$16,113.8
Value of the Interest Tax Shields Discounted at the Unlevered Cost of Capital											
Interest tax shield for continuing value											$ 115.9
Discount factor for continuing value											12.500
Interest tax shield (ITS)	$ 269.6	$ 267.2	$ 258.2	$ 248.4	$ 215.7	$ 199.2	$ 181.4	$ 142.6	$ 119.4	$ 91.1	
Value of the ITSs at end of year	1,711.8	1,632.9	1,554.3	1,476.8	1,423.5	1,381.0	1,351.5	1,357.6	1,387.4	1,448.9	
Value of the ITSs at end of year plus ITS	$ 1,981.4	$ 1,900.1	$ 1,812.5	$ 1,725.3	$ 1,639.3	$ 1,580.1	$ 1,532.9	$ 1,500.1	$ 1,506.9	$ 1,540.1	
Discount factor for one year, r_{UA}	0.901	0.901	0.901	0.901	0.901	0.901	0.901	0.901	0.901	0.901	
Value of the ITSs at beginning of year	$ 1,785.0	$ 1,711.8	$ 1,632.9	$ 1,554.3	$ 1,476.8	$ 1,423.5	$ 1,381.0	$ 1,351.5	$ 1,357.6	$ 1,387.4	$ 1,448.9
Value of the firm at beginning of year	$13,047.4	$13,639.7	$14,053.6	$14,504.9	$14,957.7	$15,323.5	$15,697.9	$16,097.9	$16,546.4	$17,031.9	$17,562.7

REVIEW EXERCISE 15.4

Adjusted Present Value Valuation of the LBO Transaction

Use the information in Review Exercises 15.1 through 15.3 and the following information to measure the value of the firm as of Year 0 of the LBO transaction using the APV valuation method. Assume the company's unlevered cost of capital is equal to 9% and as of the end of Year 10, the company will recapitalize its capital structure to 25% debt and 75% common equity as described in Review Exercise 15.3. In addition, assume that all of its cash flows will grow at 3% in perpetuity as of the end of Year 11 and that the appropriate discount rate for all interest tax shields is equal to the unlevered cost of capital. Forecasts for the company's expected debt levels and interest deductions appear below.

($ in millions)	Total	Year 0	Year 1	Year 2	Year 3	Year 4	Year 5	Year 6	Year 7	Year 8	Year 9	Year 10	Year 11
Debt rating			B	B	B	BB	BBB	BBB	BBB	BBB	BBB	BBB	BBB
Debt cost of capital for unsecured debt			7.70%	7.70%	7.70%	6.60%	5.90%	5.90%	5.90%	5.90%	5.90%	5.90%	5.90%
Balance at Year End												Debt Recapitalization	
Revolver (total commitment in 1st column)	$300.0	$ 100.0	$ 0.0	$ 0.0	$ 0.0	$ 0.0	$ 0.0	$ 0.0	$ 0.0	$ 0.0	$ 0.0		
Debt assumed		0.0	0.0	0.0	0.0	0.0	0.0	0.0	0.0	0.0	0.0		
Senior secured note (bank debt)		880.0	814.4	622.5	379.9	142.6	0.0	0.0	0.0	0.0	0.0		
Subordinated note (unsecured debt)		410.0	410.0	410.0	410.0	410.0	374.6	172.3	36.5	18.7	0.0		
Mezzanine debt		670.0	670.0	670.0	670.0	670.0	670.0	670.0	670.0	670.0	529.1		
All debt issued at par		$2,060.0	$1,894.4	$1,702.5	$1,459.9	$1,222.6	$1,044.6	$842.3	$706.5	$688.7	$529.1	$815.1	$839.5

Expected Interest Deduction (Based on r_D)	Cost of Debt	Fee	Year 1	Year 2	Year 3	Year 4	Year 5	Year 6	Year 7	Year 8	Year 9	Year 10	Year 11
Revolver	4.500%	0.5%	$ 6.0	$ 1.5	$ 1.5	$ 1.5	$ 1.5	$ 0.0	$ 0.0	$ 0.0	$ 0.0	$ 0.0	
Debt assumed			0.0	0.0	0.0	0.0	0.0	0.0	0.0	0.0	0.0	0.0	
Senior secured note (bank debt)	5.000%		44.0	40.7	31.1	19.0	7.1	0.0	0.0	0.0	0.0	0.0	
Subordinated note (unsecured debt)	Rating-based rate		31.6	31.6	31.6	27.1	24.2	22.1	10.2	2.2	1.1	0.0	
Mezzanine debt	Rating-based rate		51.6	51.6	51.6	44.2	39.5	39.5	39.5	39.5	39.5	31.2	
Expected cash interest expense			$133.2	$125.4	$115.8	$91.8	$72.3	$61.6	$49.7	$41.7	$40.6	$31.2	$48.1
Amortization of fees			7.1	7.1	7.1	7.1	7.1	7.1	7.1	3.4	3.4	2.0	0.0
Expected interest tax deduction			$140.3	$132.5	$122.9	$98.9	$79.5	$68.8	$56.8	$45.1	$44.0	$33.2	$48.1

Exhibit may contain small rounding errors

Solution on pages 789–790.

Implied Equity Costs of Capital, Equity Betas, and Weighted Average Costs of Capital

In Exhibit 15.26, we measure the equity cost of capital and equity beta for each year. We see that the equity cost of capital is 16.9% as of the beginning of Year 1 and generally declines over time to 11.9% as of the beginning of Year 10. Similarly, the equity beta is 1.99 as of the beginning of Year 1 declining to 1.15 as of the beginning of Year 10. We also show the geometric average equity cost of capital from the transaction date through Year 10, which is 13.8%. The Year 11 equity cost of capital and beta increase because of the recapitalization at the end of Year 10 as the recapitalization increases the company's leverage. The levering formula to measure the cost of equity is based on valuing the interest tax shields at the unlevered cost of capital (Equation 10.5).

EXHIBIT 15.26 John Edwardson & Company LBO—Implied Equity Cost of Capital, Equity Beta, and the Weighted Average Cost of Capital

As of the Beginning of Year ($ in millions)	Year 1	Year 2	Year 3	Year 4	Year 5	Year 6	Year 7	Year 8	Year 9	Year 10	Year 11
Value of the firm (V_F)	$13,047	$13,640	$14,054	$14,505	$14,958	$15,323	$15,698	$16,098	$16,546	$17,032	$17,563
Value of debt (V_D)	8,550	8,424	8,049	7,643	7,165	6,500	5,762	4,964	4,109	3,171	4,391
Value of equity (V_E)	$ 4,497	$ 5,215	$ 6,004	$ 6,862	$ 7,793	$ 8,824	$ 9,936	$11,134	$12,437	$13,861	$13,172
Unlevered cost of capital, r_{UA}	11.00%	11.00%	11.00%	11.00%	11.00%	11.00%	11.00%	11.00%	11.00%	11.00%	11.00%
Debt cost of capital, r_D	7.88%	7.93%	8.02%	8.13%	7.53%	7.66%	7.87%	7.18%	7.27%	7.19%	6.60%
Debt to common equity ratio	1.901	1.615	1.341	1.114	0.919	0.737	0.580	0.446	0.330	0.229	0.333
Equity cost of capital, r_E	16.93%	15.96%	15.00%	14.20%	14.19%	13.46%	12.81%	12.70%	12.23%	11.87%	12.47%
Equity to firm value	0.345	0.382	0.427	0.473	0.521	0.576	0.633	0.692	0.752	0.814	0.750
Debt cost of capital, r_D	7.88%	7.93%	8.02%	8.13%	7.53%	7.66%	7.87%	7.18%	7.27%	7.19%	6.60%
Debt to firm value	0.655	0.618	0.573	0.527	0.479	0.424	0.367	0.308	0.248	0.186	0.250
Income tax rate, T_{INT}	40.00%	40.00%	40.00%	40.00%	40.00%	40.00%	40.00%	40.00%	40.00%	40.00%	40.00%
Weighted average cost of capital, r_{WACC}	8.93%	9.04%	9.16%	9.29%	9.56%	9.70%	9.84%	10.11%	10.28%	10.46%	10.34%
Geometric average equity cost of capital, r_E	13.8%		Geometric Average Weighted Average Cost of Capital, r_{WACC}							9.7%	
Equity beta	1.99	1.83	1.67	1.53	1.53	1.41	1.30	1.28	1.21	1.15	1.24

This information is useful because it indicates that the equity cost of capital does not exceed 17%. As such, IRRs above 17% result in positive net present value investments from the management's and sponsor's perspectives. Of course, financial sponsors understand that their investors expect their investments in the private equity fund to yield satisfactory returns net of the fees paid, so the IRRs estimated for the limited partners naturally consider these fees. Since the cost of equity declines every year as the capital structure is becoming less levered, the minimum IRR need not be equal to the maximum equity cost of capital in order for this investment to earn a positive risk-adjusted return for the financial sponsor and management.

Valuation Key 15.9

Most analyses of potential LBOs compare the projected equity IRRs to hurdle rates for the overall fund. An alternative approach is to use the adjusted present value valuation method to measure the net present value of the investment and the implied equity costs of capital and betas.

We also measure the weighted average cost of capital for each year based on the equity cost of capital. Although the equity cost of capital is decreasing as the financial leverage decreases, the weighted average cost of capital increases as the company is becoming less levered. In Exhibit 15.27 we use the varying weighted average costs of capital in Exhibit 15.26 and discount the free cash flows of the unlevered firm, to show that we can replicate the APV valuation shown in Exhibit 15.22 (just as we demonstrated back in Chapter 5 with the Keller example).

EXHIBIT 15.27 John Edwardson & Company LBO—Weighted Average Cost of Capital Valuation

($ in millions)	Year 0	Year 1	Year 2	Year 3	Year 4	Year 5	Year 6	Year 7	Year 8	Year 9	Year 10	Year 10
Unlevered free cash flow for continuing value												$1,289.1
Discount factor for continuing value												13.624
Unlevered free cash flow and continuing value		$573.4	$819.3	$836.4	$894.3	$1,063.9	$1,112.0	$1,145.4	$1,179.7	$1,215.1	$1,251.6	$17,562.7
Discount factor—annual r_{WACC}*		0.918	0.842	0.771	0.706	0.644	0.587	0.535	0.485	0.440	0.398	0.398
Present value		$526.3	$689.7	$645.0	$631.1	$ 685.3	$ 652.9	$ 612.2	$ 572.7	$ 534.9	$ 498.7	$ 6,998.6
Value of the firm w/o excess assets.	$13,047.4											

*The discount factors use the annual r_{WACC} from Exhibit 15.26. For example, the discount factor for Year 2 = 1/[(1 + 0.0893) × (1 + 0.0904)] = 0.842.

REVIEW EXERCISE 15.5

Post-LBO Equity and Weighted Average Costs of Capital

Use the information in Review Exercises 15.1 through 15.4 to i) calculate the value of the firm at the beginning of each year from Years 1 to 11 using the APV DCF method; ii) measure the year-by-year post-LBO equity and weighted average costs of capital; and iii) value the firm as of Year 0 using the WACC DCF method.

Solution on pages 790–791.

SUMMARY AND KEY CONCEPTS

In this chapter, we discuss leveraged buyouts and management buyouts. These transactions rely extensively on debt financing. We discuss the incidence of leveraged buyouts, the characteristics of their deal structures, and the characteristics of companies that generally undergo leveraged buyouts. In addition, we discuss potential motivations for leveraged buyouts, and the role of private equity firms in these transactions.

We discuss and illustrate an LBO financial model and the IRR approach commonly used to evaluate LBO transactions. The tools that we use to do so draw on all of the elements that we have already discussed in the book, but they are combined in such a way that the focus is on the particular characteristics of LBO transactions. One key outcome of an LBO analysis is to confirm that the capital structure assumed in the financial model is feasible. In particular, this requires that the interest rate assumed in the model is consistent with both current market yields for debt and the credit risk of the debt in the transaction; it also requires that the company demonstrate that it can meet the required principal and interest payments. The second key output of an LBO analysis is the internal rates of return potentially earned by various investors as a function of different assumed exit dates.

As we discuss, this analysis is an iterative process in which we begin with an assumed offer price; then, based on this price, we make an assumption about the capital structure and the yields on different debt instruments used to finance the transaction. Based on the financial model for the post-LBO company, we assess whether the assumed capital structure is consistent with both current market conditions and whether the company can service the debt. If the capital structure "works," we measure the IRR to various investors at alternative exit dates to assess whether the minimum hurdle rates demanded by various investors are met.

We also discuss two alternative lenses by which to evaluate an LBO transaction. The first is using the weighted average cost of capital valuation method to measure exit values, instead of the commonly used market multiple approach. The second is using the adjusted present value valuation method to measure the net present value of the investment and the implied equity costs of capital and betas.

ADDITIONAL READING AND REFERENCES

Core, J., R. Holthausen, and D. Larcker, "Corporate Governance, Chief Executive Officer Compensation and Firm Performance," *Journal of Financial Economics* vol. 53, no. 3 (1999), pp. 371–406.

Kaplan, S. N., and P. Strömberg, "Leveraged Buyouts and Private Equity," *Journal of Economic Perspectives* 23 (2009), pp. 121–146.

Smith, A., "Corporate Ownership Structure and Performance," *Journal of Financial Economics* vol. 27, no. 1 (1990), pp. 143–164.

EXERCISES AND PROBLEMS

P15.1 **Sources and Uses, Capital Structure, and Deal Terms—T. Burrus Company:** A group of managers is making an offer to purchase the company they manage—the T. Burrus Company. The company's current stock price is $12 per share, and the company has 250 million shares outstanding; the company has a current price-to-earnings ratio equal to 14.37 and a firm-value-to-EBITDA multiple equal to 5.25. Management owns 12.5 million shares of the outstanding stock. After considering the company's expected performance and alternative strategies to the LBO transaction (including alternative acquisition offers), the deal premium is set at 20%. The company has no convertible debt or convertible preferred stock, but it does have 50 million stock options outstanding, all with an exercise price equal to $7.20.

In addition to redeeming the existing stock and options, management and its financial sponsor will redeem all outstanding debt (par value of $300 million) and preferred stock (par value of $100 million) at their par values (all of which are equal to their book values). Initial fees will equal $161.1 million (3% for the debt financing, 1% to the sponsor, and 0.5% for other fees). These fees do not include fees for a revolver loan. The sponsor intends to finance this transaction by using $141 million in excess cash held by the company, issuing various debt securities equaling $3.19 billion, investing $750 million of its own equity, and having management invest $240.1 million in equity from rollover equity and new investment. The composition of the $3.19 billion in debt is $1.39 billion of 7-year, 7.0% senior secured bank debt; $880 million of 9-year, 11% subordinated unsecured debt; and $920 million of 10-year, 13% mezzanine debt, which has an "equity kicker" equal to 4% of the fully diluted post-LBO shares. In addition, the company is arranging a $400 million revolving line of credit that has a five-year term, a 4% interest rate on the amount drawn, and a 0.5% annual fee on the total amount of the line of credit. Management has an "equity kicker" equal to 4.3% of the fully diluted post-LBO shares. The sponsor plans to use $200.0 million from the revolver to finance the transaction. The company will have 500 million post-transaction shares outstanding.

Calculate the purchase price of the equity and prepare a sources and uses schedule similar to the one in Exhibit 15.10.

P15.2 **Measuring the Internal Rate of Return—T. Burrus Company:** Use the information in Problem 15.1 and the following information to measure the internal rates of return to the financial sponsor, management, and mezzanine debtholders; assume an exit value based on the deal EBITDA multiple. T. Burrus Company's management prepared the forecasts shown in Exhibit P15.1 to assess the value of the LBO transaction.

P15.3 **WACC-Based Exit Value—T. Burrus Company:** Use the information in Problems 15.1 and 15.2 and Exhibits P15.1 and P15.2 to measure the WACC-based exit values and implied EBITDA multiples; compare the implied EBITDA multiples in each year to the deal EBITDA multiple (see Exhibit 15.20). To measure the weighted average cost of capital, assume that as of the exit date, the company will use a capital structure of 20% debt and 80% common equity, which will result in a 7.5% cost of debt and a 11.875% cost of equity. As of Year 11, the company expects its free cash flows to grow at 2% in perpetuity. Recalculate the internal rate of return to the financial sponsor using the WACC-based exit values.

P15.4 **Adjusted Present Value Valuation of the LBO Transaction—T. Burrus Company:** Use the information in Problems 15.1 through 15.3, Exhibits P15.1 and P15.2 and the following information to measure the year-by-year APV valuation of the LBO transaction. Assume the company's unlevered cost of capital is equal to 11%; as of the end of Year 10, the company will recapitalize its capital structure to the one described in Problem 15.3. In addition, assume that all of its cash flows will grow at 2% in perpetuity as of the end of Year 11 and that the appropriate discount rate for interest tax shields is equal to the unlevered cost of capital. See the debt and interest schedules in Exhibit P15.2.

P15.5 **Post-LBO Equity and Weighted Average Costs of Capital—T. Burrus Company:** Use the information in Problems 15.1 through 15.4 and Exhibits P15.1 and P15.2 to measure the year-by-year post-LBO equity and weighted average costs of capital. Use these costs of capital to measure the value of the firm (using the WACC valuation method) and the value of the equity (using the equity DCF valuation method).

P15.6 **Sources and Uses, Capital Structure, and Deal Terms—H. Stauffer Company:** A group of managers is making an offer to purchase the company they manage—the H. Stauffer Company. The company's current stock price is $8 per share, and the company has 130 million shares outstanding; the company has a current price-to-earnings ratio equal to 7.52 and a firm value to EBITDA multiple equal to 4.98. Management owns 2.6 million shares of the outstanding stock. After considering the company's expected performance and alternative strategies to the LBO transaction (including alternative acquisition offers), the deal premium is set at 20%. The company has no convertible debt or convertible preferred stock, but it does have 26 million stock options outstanding, all with an exercise price equal to $4.8.

In addition to redeeming the existing stock and options, management and its financial sponsor will redeem all outstanding debt (par value of $400 million), and preferred stock (par value of $200 million) at their par values (which are equal to their book values), which are given in Exhibit P15.3. Initial fees will equal $71.59 million (3% for the debt financing, 1% to the sponsor, and 0.5% for other fees). These fees do not include fees for a revolver loan. The sponsor intends to finance this transaction by using $12.36 million in excess cash held by the company, issuing various debt securities equaling $1.4 billion, investing $440 million of its own equity, and having management invest $92.03 million in equity from rollover equity and new investment. The composition of the $1.4 billion in debt is $400 million of seven-year, 7.0% senior secured bank debt; $400 million of nine-year, 11% subordinated unsecured debt; and $600 million of ten-year, 13% mezzanine debt, which has an "equity kicker" equal to 4% of the fully diluted post-LBO shares. In addition, the company is arranging a $200 million revolving line of credit that has a five-year term, a 4.5% interest rate on the amount drawn, and a 0.5% annual fee on the total amount of the line of credit. Management has an "equity kicker" equal to 3.2% of the post-LBO shares. The sponsor plans to use $100.0 million from the revolver to finance the transaction. The company will have 260 million post-transaction shares outstanding.

Calculate the purchase price of the equity and prepare a sources and uses schedule similar to one in Exhibit 15.10.

EXHIBIT P15.1 Forecasts for the T. Burrus Company

Income Statement Forecasts ($ in millions)	**Year −1**	**Year 0**	**Year 1**	**Year 2**	**Year 3**	**Year 4**	**Year 5**	**Year 6**	**Year 7**	**Year 8**	**Year 9**	**Year 10**	**Year 11**
Revenue	$2,304.0	$2,350.1	$2,397.1	$2,636.8	$2,900.5	$3,190.5	$3,445.8	$3,583.6	$3,655.3	$3,728.4	$3,802.9	$3,879.0	$3,956.6
Cost of goods sold	−822.5	−799.0	−815.0	−896.5	−957.2	−957.2	−1,033.7	−1,075.1	−1,096.6	−1,118.5	−1,293.0	−1,318.9	−1,345.2
Gross margin	$1,481.5	$1,551.1	$1,582.1	$1,740.3	$1,943.3	$2,233.4	$2,412.0	$2,508.5	$2,558.7	$2,609.9	$2,509.9	$2,560.1	$2,611.3
Selling, general, and administrative	−870.9	−846.0	−862.9	−922.9	−986.2	−893.3	−964.8	−1,003.4	−1,023.5	−1,043.9	−1,331.0	−1,357.6	−1,384.8
Other expenses			−65.4										
Depreciation expense	−253.4	−258.5	−263.7	−290.0	−319.1	−351.0	−379.0	−394.2	−402.1	−410.1	−418.3	−426.7	−435.2
Operating income	$ 357.1	$ 446.5	$ 390.0	$ 527.4	$ 638.1	$ 989.1	$1,068.2	$1,110.9	$1,133.1	$1,155.8	$ 760.6	$ 775.8	$ 791.3
Interest expense	−19.0	−24.0	−335.4	−334.1	−327.2	−309.5	−280.9	−251.5	−214.2	−152.8	−139.4	−96.2	−47.8
Income before taxes	$ 338.1	$ 422.5	$ 54.7	$ 193.3	$ 311.0	$ 679.5	$ 787.3	$ 859.4	$ 919.0	$1,003.0	$ 621.2	$ 679.6	$ 743.5
Income tax expense	−148.8	−185.9	−24.1	−85.1	−136.8	−299.0	−346.4	−378.2	−404.3	−441.3	−273.3	−299.0	−327.1
Net income	$ 189.3	$ 236.6	$ 30.6	$ 108.3	$ 174.1	$ 380.5	$ 440.9	$ 481.3	$ 514.6	$ 561.7	$ 347.8	$ 380.6	$ 416.4
Earnings Per Share													
Net income	$ 189.3	$ 236.6	$ 30.6	$ 108.3	$ 174.1	$ 380.5	$ 440.9	$ 481.3	$ 514.6	$ 561.7	$ 347.8	$ 380.6	$ 416.4
Preferred stock dividends	−5.6	−7.0											
Net income to common equity	$ 183.7	$ 229.6	$ 30.6	$ 108.3	$ 174.1	$ 380.5	$ 440.9	$ 481.3	$ 514.6	$ 561.7	$ 347.8	$ 380.6	$ 416.4
Common shares outstanding (m)	250.0	250.0	500.0	500.0	500.0	500.0	500.0	500.0	500.0	500.0	500.0	500.0	500.0
Basic earnings per share	$ 0.735	$ 0.918	$ 0.061	$ 0.217	$ 0.348	$ 0.761	$ 0.882	$ 0.963	$ 1.029	$ 1.123	$ 0.696	$ 0.761	$ 0.833
Effect of Dilutive Securities													
Management stock options (net shares, m)	21.3	25.0											
Common shares outstanding (m)	250.0	250.0											
Adjusted shares outstanding	271.3	275.0											
Diluted earnings per share	$ 0.677	$ 0.835											
Retained Earnings													
Beginning balance	$ 331.8	$ 512.5	−$3,121.0	−$3,090.4	−$2,982.1	−$2,808.0	−$2,427.4	−$1,986.6	−$1,505.3	−$ 990.7	−$ 429.0	−$ 81.2	$ 299.4
Net income	189.3	236.6	30.6	108.3	174.1	380.5	440.9	481.3	514.6	561.7	347.8	380.6	416.4
Preferred stock dividends	−5.6	−7.0											
Common equity dividends	−3.0	−203.1	0.0	0.0	0.0	0.0	0.0	0.0	0.0	0.0	0.0	0.0	−15.6
Ending balance	$ 512.5	$ 539.0	−$3,090.4	−$2,982.1	−$2,808.0	−$2,427.4	−$1,986.6	−$1,505.3	−$ 990.7	−$ 429.0	−$ 81.2	$ 299.4	$ 700.2

Exhibit may contain small rounding errors

continued

continued from previous page

EXHIBIT P15.1 Forecasts for the T. Burrus Company (cont.)

Balance Sheet Forecasts ($ in millions)	Year −1	Year 0	Year 1	Year 2	Year 3	Year 4	Year 5	Year 6	Year 7	Year 8	Year 9	Year 10	Year 11
Cash balance	$ 368.6	$ 235.0	$ 239.7	$ 210.9	$ 174.0	$ 191.4	$ 206.7	$ 215.0	$ 219.3	$ 223.7	$ 228.2	$ 232.7	$ 237.4
Accounts receivable	352.0	359.0	366.2	402.8	443.1	487.4	526.4	547.5	558.4	569.6	581.0	592.6	604.5
Inventory	45.7	44.4	45.3	49.8	53.2	53.2	57.4	59.7	60.9	62.1	71.8	73.3	74.7
Total current assets	$ 766.3	$ 638.4	$ 651.2	$ 663.6	$ 670.3	$ 732.0	$ 790.6	$ 822.2	$ 838.7	$ 855.5	$ 881.0	$ 898.6	$ 916.6
Property, plant, and equipment	$1,066.2	$1,337.8	$1,668.1	$1,916.3	$2,182.8	$2,470.0	$2,872.0	$3,278.1	$3,692.4	$4,537.5	$4,976.9	$5,027.0	$5,078.1
Accumulated depreciation	−413.4	−671.9	−935.6	−1,225.7	−1,544.7	−1,895.7	−2,274.7	−2,668.9	−3,071.0	−3,481.1	−3,899.4	−3,928.0	−3,957.1
Property, plant, and equipment (net)	$ 652.8	$ 665.9	$ 732.4	$ 690.6	$ 638.1	$ 574.3	$ 597.3	$ 609.2	$ 621.4	$1,056.4	$1,077.5	$1,099.0	$1,121.0
Capitalized fees	$ 0.00	$ 161.1	$ 84.0	$ 72.4	$ 60.7	$ 49.1	$ 37.4	$ 25.8	$ 14.1	$ 8.5	$ 2.8	$ 0.0	$ 0.0
Total assets	$1,419.1	$1,465.4	$1,467.7	$1,426.6	$1,369.2	$1,355.4	$1,425.3	$1,457.2	$1,474.2	$1,920.3	$1,961.3	$1,997.7	$2,037.6
Accounts payable	$ 91.4	$ 88.8	$ 90.6	$ 99.6	$ 106.4	$ 106.4	$ 114.9	$ 119.5	$ 121.8	$ 124.3	$ 143.7	$ 146.5	$ 149.5
Other current operating liabilities	115.2	117.5	119.9	131.8	145.0	159.5	172.3	179.2	182.8	186.4	190.1	193.9	197.8
Total current liabilities	$ 206.6	$ 206.3	$ 210.4	$ 231.5	$ 251.4	$ 265.9	$ 287.1	$ 298.6	$ 304.6	$ 310.7	$ 333.8	$ 340.5	$ 347.3
Total debt	300.0	3,390.0	3,357.5	3,187.1	2,935.7	2,526.9	2,134.7	1,673.8	1,170.2	1,048.5	718.5	367.7	0.0
Total liabilities	$ 506.6	$3,596.3	$3,568.0	$3,418.6	$3,187.1	$2,792.8	$2,421.8	$1,972.4	$1,474.8	$1,359.2	$1,052.3	$ 708.2	$ 347.3
Preferred stock	$ 100.0	$ 0.0											
Common stock	300.0	990.1	990.1	990.1	990.1	990.1	990.1	990.1	990.1	990.1	990.1	990.1	990.1
Retained earnings	512.5	−3,121.0	−3,090.4	−2,982.1	−2,808.0	−2,427.4	−1,986.6	−1,505.3	−990.7	−429.0	−81.2	299.4	700.2
Total shareholders' equity	$ 912.5	−$2,130.9	−$2,100.3	−$1,992.0	−$1,817.9	−$1,437.3	−$ 996.5	−$ 515.2	−$ 0.6	$ 561.1	$ 908.9	$1,289.5	$1,690.3
Total liabilities and equities	$1,419.1	$1,465.4	$1,467.7	$1,426.6	$1,369.2	$1,355.4	$1,425.3	$1,457.2	$1,474.2	$1,920.3	$1,961.3	$1,997.7	$2,037.6

Free Cash Flow Forecasts ($ in millions)	Year 0	Year 1	Year 2	Year 3	Year 4	Year 5	Year 6	Year 7	Year 8	Year 9	Year 10	Year 11
Earnings before interest and taxes (EBIT)	$446.5	$390.0	$527.4	$638.1	$989.1	$1,068.2	$1,110.9	$1,133.1	$1,155.8	$760.6	$775.8	$791.3
− Income taxes paid on EBIT	−196.5	−171.6	−232.0	−280.8	−435.2	−470.0	−488.8	−498.6	−508.5	−334.7	−341.4	−348.2
Earnings before interest and after taxes	$250.0	$218.4	$295.3	$357.3	$553.9	$ 598.2	$ 622.1	$ 634.6	$ 647.2	$425.9	$434.4	$443.1
+ Depreciation expense	258.5	263.7	290.0	319.1	351.0	379.0	394.2	402.1	410.1	418.3	426.7	435.2
− Change in accounts receivable	-7.0	−7.2	−36.6	−40.3	−44.3	−39.0	−21.1	−10.9	−11.2	−11.4	−11.6	−11.9
− Change in inventory	1.3	−0.9	−4.5	−3.4	0.0	−4.3	−2.3	−1.2	−1.2	−9.7	−1.4	−1.5
+ Change in accounts payable	-2.6	1.8	9.1	6.7	0.0	8.5	4.6	2.4	2.4	19.4	2.9	2.9
+ Change in other liabilities	2.3	2.4	12.0	13.2	14.5	12.8	6.9	3.6	3.7	3.7	3.8	3.9
+ LBO fees—expensed		65.4	0.0	0.0	0.0	0.0	0.0	0.0	0.0	0.0	0.0	0.0
− Change in required cash balance	−7.4	−4.7	28.8	36.9	−17.4	−15.3	−8.3	−4.3	−4.4	−4.5	−4.6	−4.7
Cash flow before capital expenditures	$495.1	$538.9	$594.0	$689.6	$857.6	$ 939.9	$ 996.2	$1,026.2	$1,046.7	$841.8	$850.2	$867.2
− Capital expenditures	−271.6	−330.3	−248.2	−266.6	−287.1	−402.0	−406.1	−414.3	−845.1	−439.4	−448.2	−457.2
Unlevered free cash flow	$223.6	$208.6	$345.8	$423.0	$570.5	$ 537.9	$ 590.0	$ 611.9	$ 201.6	$402.4	$402.0	$410.0

Exhibit may contain small rounding errors

EXHIBIT P15.2 T. Burrus Company—Debt and Interest Schedules

($ in millions)	Total	Year 0	Year 1	Year 2	Year 3	Year 4	Year 5	Year 6	Year 7	Year 8	Year 9	Year 10	Year 11
Debt rating			B	B	B	BB	BBB	A	A	A	BBB	A	A
Debt cost of capital for unsecured debt			10.00%	10.00%	10.00%	9.00%	8.00%	7.50%	7.50%	7.50%	8.00%	7.50%	7.50%
Balance at Year End:												Debt Recapitalization	
Revolver (total commitment in 1st column)	$400.0	$ 200.0	$ 167.5	$ 0.0	$ 0.0	$ 0.0	$ 0.0	$ 0.0	$ 0.0	$ 0.0	$ 0.0		
Debt assumed		0.0	0.0	0.0	0.0	0.0	0.0	0.0	0.0	0.0	0.0		
Senior secured note (bank debt)		1,390.0	1,390.0	1,387.1	1,135.7	726.9	334.7	0.0	0.0	0.0	0.0		
Subordinated note (unsecured debt)		880.0	880.0	880.0	880.0	880.0	880.0	753.8	250.2	128.5	0.0		
Mezzanine debt		920.0	920.0	920.0	920.0	920.0	920.0	920.0	920.0	920.0	718.5		
All debt issued at par		$3,390.0	$3,357.5	$3,187.1	$2,935.7	$2,526.9	$2,134.7	$1,673.8	$1,170.2	$1,048.5	$718.5	$983.2	$1,002.9

Expected Interest Deduction (Based on r_D)	Cost of Debt	Fee	Year 1	Year 2	Year 3	Year 4	Year 5	Year 6	Year 7	Year 8	Year 9	Year 10	Year 11
Revolver	4.000%	0.5%	$ 10.0	$ 8.7	$ 2.0	$ 2.0	$ 2.0	$ 0.0	$ 0.0	$ 0.0	$ 0.0	$ 0.0	
Debt assumed			0.0	0.0	0.0	0.0	0.0	0.0	0.0	0.0	0.0	0.0	
Senior secured note (bank debt)	7.000%		97.3	97.3	97.1	79.5	50.9	23.4	0.0	0.0	0.0	0.0	
Subordinated note (unsecured debt)	Rating-based rate		88.0	88.0	88.0	79.2	70.4	66.0	56.5	18.8	10.3	0.0	
Mezzanine debt	Rating-based rate		92.0	92.0	92.0	82.8	73.6	69.0	69.0	69.0	73.6	53.9	
Expected cash interest expense			$287.3	$286.0	$279.1	$243.5	$196.9	$158.4	$125.5	$87.8	$83.9	$53.9	$73.7
Amortization of fees			11.7	11.7	11.7	11.7	11.7	11.7	11.7	5.7	5.7	2.8	0.0
Amortization of discount/premium on debt	None												
Expected interest tax deduction			$299.0	$297.7	$290.8	$255.1	$208.5	$170.1	$137.2	$93.5	$89.6	$56.6	$73.7
Weighted average cost of debt			8.5%	8.5%	8.8%	8.3%	7.8%	7.4%	7.5%	7.5%	8.0%	7.5%	7.5%
Interest tax shield			$131.5	$131.0	$127.9	$112.3	$91.8	$74.8	$60.4	$41.1	$39.4	$24.9	$32.4

Exhibit may contain small rounding errors

P15.7 Post-LBO Balance Sheet—H. Stauffer Company: Use the information in Problem 15.6 and Exhibit P15.3 to prepare a pro forma closing balance sheet for the H. Stauffer Company as of the end of Year 0.

EXHIBIT P15.3 Historical Financial Statements and Free Cash Flow Schedule for the H. Stauffer Company

(in millions)	Year −1	Year 0
Income Statement		
Revenue	$1,000.0	$1,030.0
Cost of goods sold	−378.0	−370.8
Gross margin	$ 622.0	$ 659.2
Selling, general, and administrative expense	−315.0	−309.0
Depreciation expense	−40.0	−41.2
Operating income	$ 267.0	$ 309.0
Interest expense	−26.0	−32.0
Income before taxes	$ 241.0	$ 277.0
Income tax expense	−96.4	−110.8
Net income	$ 144.6	$ 166.2
Balance Sheet		
Cash balance	$ 32.0	$ 33.0
Accounts receivable	208.3	214.6
Inventory	52.5	51.5
Total current assets	$ 292.8	$ 299.0
Property, plant, and equipment	$2,060.0	$2,121.8
Accumulated depreciation	−440.0	−481.2
Property, plant, and equipment (net)	$1,620.0	$1,640.6
Capitalized fees	$ 0.0	$ 0.0
Total assets	$1,912.8	$1,939.6
Accounts payable	$ 42.0	$ 41.2
Total debt	400.0	400.0
Total liabilities	$ 442.0	$ 441.2
Preferred stock	$ 200.0	$ 200.0
Common stock	600.0	600.0
Retained earnings	670.8	698.4
Total shareholders' equity	$1,470.8	$1,498.4
Total liabilities and equities	$1,912.8	$1,939.6

(in millions)	Year 0
Free Cash Flows	
Earnings before interest and taxes (EBIT)	$309.0
− Income taxes paid on EBIT	−123.6
Earnings before interest and after taxes	$185.4
+ Depreciation expense	41.2
− Change in accounts receivable	−6.3
− Change in inventory	1.0
+ Change in accounts payable	−0.8
+ LBO fees—expensed	0.0
− Change in required cash balance	−1.0
Cash flow before capital expenditures	$219.6
− Capital expenditures	−61.8
Unlevered free cash flow	**$157.8**
− Interest paid	−32.0
+ Interest tax shield	12.8
− Preferred stock dividends	−14.0
Cash flow after interest and preferred stock dividends	124.6
+ Change in debt financing	0.0
+ Change in preferred stock financing	0.0
Free cash flow to common equity	**$124.6**
+ Change in common equity financing	0.0
− Common equity dividends paid	−124.6
Change in excess cash	$ 0.0
+ Change in required cash balance	1.0
Change in cash balance	$ 1.0

(in millions)	Year −1	Year 0
Retained Earnings		
Beginning balance	$540.4	$670.8
Net income	144.6	166.2
Preferred stock dividends	−11.2	−14.0
Common equity dividends	−3.0	−124.6
Ending balance	$670.8	$698.4

Exhibit may contain small rounding errors

P15.8 Financial Statement and Free Cash Flow Forecasts—H. Stauffer Company: Use the information in Problems 15.6 and 15.7 to create a financial model for the H. Stauffer Company. The company must use all available cash flows (after investments) to pay down debt. Assume all cash flows occur at the end of each year; thus, the company's capital expenditures in a given year are the capital expenditures necessary to support the revenues in the following year. Use the following forecast drivers for Years 1–11.

Expected inflation (Year 11 is a long-run expectation)	3.00%
Treasury Bonds—20-year	5.00%
LIBOR—3-month	3.50%
Revenue growth rate	3.00%
Cost of goods sold (% revenue)	36.00%
Selling, general and administrative (% revenue)	30.00%
Constant income tax rate on all income	40.00%
Required cash balance (% revenue)	2.00%
Accounts receivable (days to collect)	75.0
Inventory (days to sell)	50.0
Accounts payable (days to pay)	40.0
CAPEX—based on gross PPEQ to rev.	2.00
Depreciation (% of beginning gross PPEQ)	2.00%

Use the EBITDA coverage ratio to estimate the company's credit rating based on the following schedule.

		For Unsecured Debt	
EBITDA for Debt Rating:	**EBITDA Coverage Ratio Hurdle**	**Yield to Maturity**	**Cost of Debt**
CCC+ & Below	0.5	N/A	N/A
B− to B+	1.0	12.0%	10.0%
BB− to BB+	4.0	10.5%	9.0%
BBB− to BBB+	7.0	9.0%	8.0%
A− to A+	12.0	8.0%	7.5%
AA− to AAA	18.0	7.0%	7.0%

a. Use the above assumptions to create a financial model that produces an income statement, balance sheet, and free cash flow schedule for Years 1 through 11 assuming the LBO is consummated. These are the forecasts that management prepared before the LBO transaction. (We refer to these forecasts as the Pre-LBO Forecasts.)

b. Management believes that it can improve the company's performance after the LBO transaction; specifically, management believes that it can reduce both the cost of goods sold and the selling, general, and administrative expenses by 1% of revenue in Years 2 through 4 and that it can maintain this performance in Years 5 onward. Management also believes that it can grow revenues by 5% in Years 2 through 4 (3% in all other years). Using these revised assumptions (LBO Forecasts), create a second financial model that produces an income statement, balance sheet, and free cash flow schedule for Years 1 through 11. These are the forecasts management prepared conditional on completing the LBO transaction. (We refer to these forecasts as the Post-LBO Forecasts.)

c. Discuss the change in the company's expected performance.

P15.9 Measuring the Internal Rate of Return—H. Stauffer Company: Use the information in Problems 15.6 through 15.8 to measure the internal rates of return to the financial sponsor, management, and mezzanine debtholders, assuming an exit value based on the deal EBITDA multiple. Measure the internal rate of return based on the Pre-LBO Forecasts and the Post-LBO Forecasts.

P15.10 Adjusted Present Value Valuation of the LBO Transaction—H. Stauffer Company: Use the information in Problems 15.6 through 15.8 and the following information for this question. Assume the company's unlevered cost of capital is equal to 12%; as of the end of Year 10, the company will recapitalize its capital structure to 20% debt and 80% common equity. In addition, assume that all of its cash flows will grow at 3% in perpetuity as of the end of Year 11 and that the appropriate discount rate for interest tax shields is the unlevered cost of capital.

a. Measure the year-by-year APV valuation of the LBO transaction using the Pre-LBO Forecasts.

b. Measure the year-by-year APV valuation of the LBO transaction using the Post-LBO Forecasts.

P15.11 Post-LBO Equity and Weighted Average Costs of Capital—H. Stauffer Company: Use the information in Problems 15.6 through 15.10 to measure the year-by-year post-LBO equity and weighted average costs of capital based on the Post-LBO forecasts. Use these costs of capital to measure the value of the firm (using the WACC valuation method) and the value of the equity (using the equity DCF valuation method).

SOLUTIONS FOR REVIEW EXERCISES

Solution for Review Exercise 15.1: Sources and Uses, Capital Structure, and Deal Terms

		Market Multiples				
		P/E	EBIT	EBITDA	Revenue	
Current stock price	$ 16.00	14.91	10.08	7.05	2.12	
Deal premium	25.0%					
Deal stock price	$ 20.00	18.64	11.87	8.31	2.49	
Number of fully diluted shares outstanding	108.8	million				
Purchase price of equity	$2,176.0	million				

Pre-LBO Outstanding Options as of End of Year 0 (Liquidation of Options)				
Year Issued	Exercise Price	Number of Options = Shares Issued (m)	Buyback Shares (m)	Net Increase in Shares (m)
Various	$11.20	20.0	11.2	8.8

Sources and Uses of Cash—LBO Financing ($ in millions)	Amount	%	Coupon = YTM	Maturity (Years)	Post-LBO Capital Structure	Common Shares Issued	Common Shares Issued (% Owned)	Warrants & Options Issued (% of Total Shares)	Fully Diluted Equity Allocation
Sources									
Excess cash	$34.61	1.2%							
Debt assumed	0.00	0.0%							0.00%
Revolver	100.00	3.4%	4.50%	5	3.40%				0.00%
Senior secured note (bank debt)	880.00	29.6%	5.00%	7	29.90%				0.00%
Subordinated note (unsecured debt)	410.00	13.8%	9.00%	9	13.93%				0.00%
Mezzanine debt	670.00	22.5%	11.00%	10	22.76%			5.00%	5.00%
Preferred stock—assumed	0.00	0.0%							0.00%
Preferred stock—new	0.00	0.0%							0.00%
Common equity									
Sponsor investment	730.00	24.5%			24.80%	165.28	82.64%		75.12%
Management rollover	60.00	2.0%			2.04%	13.58	6.79%	1.60%	7.77%
Management new investment	93.33	3.1%			3.17%	21.13	10.57%	2.50%	12.10%
Total sources	$2,977.94	100.0%			100.00%	200.00	100.00%	9.10%	100.00%

Uses			Fee Rate	Total	
Common equity					
Non-management shares purchased	$2,116.00	71.1%			
Management rollover	60.00	2.0%			
Preferred stock—assumed	0.00	0.0%			
Preferred stock— redeemed	100.00	3.4%			
Debt assumed	0.00	0.0%			
Debt redeemed	600.00	20.1%			
Financing fees—debt	58.80	2.0%	3.00%		Debt without Revolver - Amortize
Financing fees—revolver	0.00	0.0%	0.50%	$300.0	Expense Annually as Incurred
Sponsor fees	28.76	1.0%	1.00%		Based on deal value (deal cost) before fees
Other fees and expenses	14.38	0.5%	0.50%		Based on deal value (deal cost) before fees
Total uses	$2,977.94	100.0%			

Exhibit may contain small rounding errors

Solution for Review Exercise 15.2: Measuring the Internal Rate of Return

($ in millions)	EBITDA Multiple		Year 1	Year 2	Year 3	Year 4	Year 5	Year 6	Year 7	Year 8	Year 9	Year 10
EBITDA			$ 316.8	$ 424.2	$ 493.1	$ 566.8	$ 589.5	$ 613.1	$ 631.5	$ 588.5	$ 542.3	$ 492.9
Debt outstanding			$1,894.4	$1,702.5	$1,459.9	$1,222.6	$1,044.6	$ 842.3	$ 706.5	$ 688.7	$ 529.1	$ 393.1
Exit value—firm (using deal multiple)	8.310		$2,632.5	$3,525.4	$4,097.8	$4,710.3	$4,898.7	$5,094.7	$5,247.5	$4,890.2	$4,506.7	$4,095.8
Exit value—debt			1,894.4	1,702.5	1,459.9	1,222.6	1,044.6	842.3	706.5	688.7	529.1	393.1
Exit value—equity			$ 738.2	$1,822.9	$2,637.9	$3,487.7	$3,854.1	$4,252.3	$4,541.0	$4,201.5	$3,977.6	$3,702.7
Sponsor (% fully diluted participation in exit)		75.1%										
Investment		−$730.0										
Fees		$ 28.8										
Dividends	None											
Other payments	None											
Participation in exit			$ 554.5	$1,369.4	$1,981.6	$2,620.0	$2,895.3	$3,194.4	$3,411.3	$3,156.2	$2,988.0	$2,781.5
Net cash flow		−$701.2	$ 554.5	$1,369.4	$1,981.6	$2,620.0	$2,895.3	$3,194.4	$3,411.3	$3,156.2	$2,988.0	$2,781.5

IRR	Exit Yr											
−20.9%	Year 1	−$701.2	$ 554.5									
39.7%	Year 2	−701.2	0.0	$1,369.4								
41.4%	Year 3	−701.2	0.0	0.0	$1,981.6							
39.0%	Year 4	−701.2	0.0	0.0	0.0	$2,620.0						
32.8%	Year 5	−701.2	0.0	0.0	0.0	0.0	$2,895.3					
28.8%	Year 6	−701.2	0.0	0.0	0.0	0.0	0.0	$3,194.4				
25.4%	Year 7	−701.2	0.0	0.0	0.0	0.0	0.0	0.0	$3,411.3			
20.7%	Year 8	−701.2	0.0	0.0	0.0	0.0	0.0	0.0	0.0	$3,156.2		
17.5%	Year 9	−701.2	0.0	0.0	0.0	0.0	0.0	0.0	0.0	0.0	$2,988.0	
14.8%	Year 10	−701.2	0.0	0.0	0.0	0.0	0.0	0.0	0.0	0.0	0.0	$2,781.5

Exhibit may contain small rounding errors

($ in millions)			Year 1	Year 2	Year 3	Year 4	Year 5	Year 6	Year 7	Year 8	Year 9	Year 10
Management (% fully diluted participation in exit)		19.9%										
Investment		−$153.3										
Fees	None											
Dividends	None											
Other payments	None											
Participation in exit			$146.7	$362.4	$524.4	$693.3	$766.2	$845.3	$902.7	$835.2	$790.7	$736.0
Net cash flow		−$153.3	$146.7	$362.4	$524.4	$693.3	$766.2	$845.3	$902.7	$835.2	$790.7	$736.0

IRR	Exit Yr											
−4.3%	Year 1	−$153.3	$146.7									
53.7%	Year 2	−153.3	0.0	$362.4								
50.7%	Year 3	−153.3	0.0	0.0	$524.4							
45.8%	Year 4	−153.3	0.0	0.0	0.0	$693.3						
38.0%	Year 5	−153.3	0.0	0.0	0.0	0.0	$766.2					
32.9%	Year 6	−153.3	0.0	0.0	0.0	0.0	0.0	$845.3				
28.8%	Year 7	−153.3	0.0	0.0	0.0	0.0	0.0	0.0	$902.7			
23.6%	Year 8	−153.3	0.0	0.0	0.0	0.0	0.0	0.0	0.0	$835.2		
20.0%	Year 9	−153.3	0.0	0.0	0.0	0.0	0.0	0.0	0.0	0.0	$790.7	
17.0%	Year 10	−153.3	0.0	0.0	0.0	0.0	0.0	0.0	0.0	0.0	0.0	$736.0

($ in millions)		Year 1	Year 2	Year 3	Year 4	Year 5	Year 6	Year 7	Year 8	Year 9	Year 10
Mezzanine debt (% fully diluted participation in exit)	5.0%										
Investment	−$670.0										
Fees	None										
Interest paid		$ 73.7	$ 73.7	$ 73.7	$ 73.7	$ 73.7	$ 73.7	$ 73.7	$ 73.7	$ 73.7	$ 58.2
Repayment of principal		670.0	670.0	670.0	670.0	670.0	670.0	670.0	670.0	670.0	529.1
Participation in exit		36.9	91.1	131.9	174.4	192.7	212.6	227.1	210.1	198.9	185.1
Net cash flow	−$670.0	$780.6	$834.8	$875.6	$918.1	$936.4	$956.3	$970.8	$953.8	$942.6	$772.4

IRR	Exit Yr											
16.5%	Year 1	−$670.0	$780.6									
17.3%	Year 2	−670.0	73.7	$834.8								
16.6%	Year 3	−670.0	73.7	73.7	$875.6							
16.1%	Year 4	−670.0	73.7	73.7	$73.7	$918.1						
15.2%	Year 5	−670.0	73.7	73.7	73.7	73.7	$936.4					
14.7%	Year 6	−670.0	73.7	73.7	73.7	73.7	73.7	$956.3				
14.1%	Year 7	−670.0	73.7	73.7	73.7	73.7	73.7	73.7	$970.8			
13.4%	Year 8	−670.0	73.7	73.7	73.7	73.7	73.7	73.7	73.7	$953.8		
12.9%	Year 9	−670.0	73.7	73.7	73.7	73.7	73.7	73.7	73.7	73.7	$942.6	
12.6%	Year 10	−670.0	73.7	73.7	73.7	73.7	73.7	73.7	73.7	73.7	214.6	$772.4

Solution for Review Exercise 15.3: WACC-Based Exit Value

Weighted average cost of capital valuation

r_E	r_D	V_D/V_F	T_{INT}	r_{WACC}	Continuing Value Growth Rate
10.033%	5.900%	25.000%	40.000%	8.410%	3.000%

($ in millions)	Year 0	Year 1	Year 2	Year 3	Year 4	Year 5	Year 6	Year 7	Year 8	Year 9	Year 10
Weighted average cost of capital valuation of the firm	$3,054.4	$3,052.2	$3,028.2	$2,957.2	$2,892.8	$2,889.4	$2,868.5	$2,923.2	$3,106.4	$3,164.2	$3,260.2
Value of debt	2,060.0	1,894.4	1,702.5	1,459.9	1,222.6	1,044.6	842.3	706.5	688.7	529.1	393.1
Weighted average cost of capital valuation of the equity	$ 994.4	$1,157.8	$1,325.7	$1,497.3	$1,670.2	$1,844.8	$2,026.2	$2,216.8	$2,417.8	$2,635.1	$2,867.1
EBITDA	$ 346.1	$ 316.8	$ 424.2	$ 493.1	$ 566.8	$ 589.5	$ 613.1	$ 631.5	$ 588.5	$ 542.3	$ 492.9
Implied firm value to EBITDA	8.826	9.635	7.138	5.997	5.104	4.902	4.679	4.629	5.279	5.835	6.615
Exit Value Multiple and Values Used											
Deal multiple—firm value to EBITDA		8.310	8.310	8.310	8.310	8.310	8.310	8.310	8.310	8.310	8.310
% difference with weighted average cost of capital valuation		−13.7%	16.4%	38.6%	62.8%	69.5%	77.6%	79.5%	57.4%	42.4%	25.6%
Exit value—equity		$ 738.2	$1,822.9	$2,637.9	$3,487.7	$3,854.1	$4,252.3	$4,541.0	$4,201.5	$3,977.6	$3,702.7
% difference with weighted average cost of capital valuation		−36.2%	37.5%	76.2%	108.8%	108.9%	109.9%	104.9%	73.8%	50.9%	29.1%

($ in millions)		Year 1	Year 2	Year 3	Year 4	Year 5	Year 6	Year 7	Year 8	Year 9	Year 10
Exit value—firm (weighted average cost of capital valuation)		$3,052.2	$3,028.2	$2,957.2	$2,892.8	$2,889.4	$2,868.5	$2,923.2	$3,106.4	$3,164.2	$3,260.2
Exit value—equity		$1,157.8	$1,325.7	$1,497.3	$1,670.2	$1,844.8	$2,026.2	$2,216.8	$2,417.8	$2,635.1	$2,867.1
Sponsor (% fully diluted participation in exit)	75.1%										
Investment	−$730.0										
Fees	$28.8										
Dividends	None										
Other payments	None										
Participation in exit		$ 869.8	$ 995.9	$1,124.8	$1,254.7	$1,385.8	$1,522.1	$1,665.3	$1,816.3	$1,979.6	$2,153.8
Net cash flow	−$701.2	$ 869.8	$ 995.9	$1,124.8	$1,254.7	$1,385.8	$1,522.1	$1,665.3	$1,816.3	$1,979.6	$2,153.8

IRR	Exit Yr											
24.0%	Year 1	−$701.2	$ 869.8									
19.2%	Year 2	−701.2	0.0	$ 995.9								
17.1%	Year 3	−701.2	0.0	0.0	$1,124.8							
15.7%	Year 4	701.2	0.0	0.0	0.0	$1,254.7						
14.6%	Year 5	−701.2	0.0	0.0	0.0	0.0	$1,385.8					
13.8%	Year 6	−701.2	0.0	0.0	0.0	0.0	0.0	$1,522.1				
13.2%	Year 7	−701.2	0.0	0.0	0.0	0.0	0.0	0.0	$1,665.3			
12.6%	Year 8	−701.2	0.0	0.0	0.0	0.0	0.0	0.0	0.0	$1,816.3		
12.2%	Year 9	−701.2	0.0	0.0	0.0	0.0	0.0	0.0	0.0	0.0	$1,979.6	
11.9%	Year 10	−701.2	0.0	0.0	0.0	0.0	0.0	0.0	0.0	0.0	0.0	$2,153.8

Exhibt may contain small rounding errors

Solution for Review Exercise 15.4: Adjusted Present Value Valuation of the LBO Transaction

($ in millions)	Total	Year 0	Year 1	Year 2	Year 3	Year 4	Year 5	Year 6	Year 7	Year 8	Year 9	Year 10	Year 11
Debt rating			B	B	B	BB	BBB	BBB	BBB	BBB	BBB	BBB	BBB
Debt cost of capital for unsecured debt.			7.70%	7.70%	7.70%	6.60%	5.90%	5.90%	5.90%	5.90%	5.90%	5.90%	5.90%
Balance at Year End												Debt Recapitalization	
Revolver (total commitment in 1st column)	$300.0	$ 100.0	$ 0.0	$ 0.0	$ 0.0	$ 0.0	$ 0.0	$ 0.0	$ 0.0	$ 0.0	$ 0.0		
Debt assumed		0.0	0.0	0.0	0.0	0.0	0.0	0.0	0.0	0.0	0.0		
Senior secured note (bank debt)		880.0	814.4	622.5	379.9	142.6	0.0	0.0	0.0	0.0	0.0		
Subordinated note (unsecured debt)		410.0	410.0	410.0	410.0	410.0	374.6	172.3	36.5	18.7	0.0		
Mezzanine debt		670.0	670.0	670.0	670.0	670.0	670.0	670.0	670.0	670.0	529.1		
All debt issued at par		$2,060.0	$1,894.4	$1,702.5	$1,459.9	$1,222.6	$1,044.6	$842.3	$706.5	$688.7	$529.1	$815.1	$839.5

Expected Interest Deduction (Based on r_D)	Cost of Debt	Fee	Year 1	Year 2	Year 3	Year 4	Year 5	Year 6	Year 7	Year 8	Year 9	Year 10	Year 11
Revolver	4.500%	0.5%	$ 6.0	$ 1.5	$ 1.5	$ 1.5	$ 1.5	$ 0.0	$ 0.0	$ 0.0	$ 0.0	$ 0.0	
Debt assumed			0.0	0.0	0.0	0.0	0.0	0.0	0.0	0.0	0.0	0.0	
Senior secured note (bank debt)	5.000%		44.0	40.7	31.1	19.0	7.1	0.0	0.0	0.0	0.0	0.0	
Subordinated note (unsecured debt)	Rating-based rate		31.6	31.6	31.6	27.1	24.2	22.1	10.2	2.2	1.1	0.0	
Mezzanine debt	Rating-based rate		51.6	51.6	51.6	44.2	39.5	39.5	39.5	39.5	39.5	31.2	
Expected cash interest expense			$133.2	$125.4	$115.8	$91.8	$72.3	$61.6	$49.7	$41.7	$40.6	$31.2	$48.1
Amortization of fees			7.1	7.1	7.1	7.1	7.1	7.1	7.1	3.4	3.4	2.0	0.0
Expected interest tax deduction			$140.3	$132.5	$122.9	$98.9	$79.5	$68.8	$56.8	$45.1	$44.0	$33.2	$48.1
Weighted average cost of debt			6.81%	7.00%	7.22%	6.78%	6.50%	6.58%	6.75%	6.38%	6.39%	6.28%	5.90%
Interest tax shield			$56.1	$53.0	$49.2	$39.6	$31.8	$27.5	$22.7	$18.0	$17.6	$13.3	$19.2

Exhibit may contain small rounding errors

Below the calculation of the debt recapitalization at the end of Year 10 is presented:

Continuing Value Using WACC Method ($ in millions)	CV Year 10
Unlevered free cash flow for continuing value (Year 11)	$ 176.4
Discount factor for continuing value	18.48
Continuing value of the firm	$3,260.2
Debt to value ratio for continuing value	25.0%
Amount of debt as of continuing value date	$ 815.1
Debt cost of capital and interest rate for continuing value	5.9%
Interest in Year 11	$ 48.1
Income tax rate for interest	40.0%
Interest tax shield in Year 11	$ 19.2
Amount of debt as of continuing value date	$ 815.1
Debt in the forecasts at the continuing value date	529.1
Debt issued (redeemed) at the continuing value date	$ 286.0
Continuing value of the firm	$3,260.2
Preferred stock to firm value	0%
Value of preferred stock as of continuing value date	$ 0.0
Amount of preferred stock as of continuing value date	$ 0.0
Preferred stock in the forecasts at the continuing value date	0.0
Preferred stock issued (redeemed) at the continuing value date	$ 0.0
Continuing value of the firm	$3,260.2
Common equity to firm value	75%
Value of common equity as of continuing value date	$2,445.2

Exhibit may contain small rounding errors

All Interest Tax Shields discounted at r_{UA}:

Adjusted Present Value Valuation ($ in millions)	**Year 0**	**Year 1**	**Year 2**	**Year 3**	**Year 4**	**Year 5**	**Year 6**	**Year 7**	**Year 8**	**Year 9**	**Year 10**	**CV Year 10**
Value of the Unlevered Firm												
Unlevered free cash flow for continuing value												$ 176.4
Discount factor for continuing value												16.667
Unlevered free cash flow and continuing value . . .		$259.1	$280.7	$325.7	$313.1	$246.7	$263.8	$186.5	$62.7	$203.4	$170.1	$2,939.6
Discount factor.		0.917	0.842	0.772	0.708	0.650	0.596	0.547	0.502	0.460	0.422	0.422
Discounted value		$237.7	$236.3	$251.5	$221.8	$160.3	$157.3	$102.0	$31.4	$ 93.7	$ 71.8	$1,241.7
Value of the unlevered firm.	$2,805.7											
Value of the Interest Tax Shields												
Interest tax shield for continuing value.												$ 19.2
Discount factor for continuing value												16.667
Interest tax shield and continuing value of ITS . . .		$ 56.1	$ 53.0	$ 49.2	$ 39.6	$ 31.8	$ 27.5	$ 22.7	$18.0	$ 17.6	$ 13.3	$ 320.6
Discount factor (r_{UA})		0.917	0.842	0.772	0.708	0.650	0.596	0.547	0.502	0.460	0.422	0.422
Present value		$ 51.5	$ 44.6	$ 38.0	$ 28.0	$ 20.7	$ 16.4	$ 12.4	$ 9.0	$ 8.1	$ 5.6	$ 135.4
Value of the interest tax shields	$ 369.8											
Value of the firm V_F w/o excess assets	$3,175.5											

Net Present Value of Investment	Firm Value	Equity Value
Value.	$3,175.5	$1,115.5
Purchase price paid (sources – excess cash)	2,943.3	883.3
Net present value of investment.	$ 232.2	$ 232.2

Exhibit may contain small rounding errors

Solution for Review Exercise 15.5: Post-LBO Equity and Weighted Average Costs of Capital

Beginning of Year Value ($ in millions)	**Year 1**	**Year 2**	**Year 3**	**Year 4**	**Year 5**	**Year 6**	**Year 7**	**Year 8**	**Year 9**	**Year 10**	**CV Year 10**
Value of the Unlevered Firm											
Unlevered free cash flow for continuing value											$ 176.4
Discount factor for continuing value											16.667
Unlevered free cash flow	$ 259.1	$ 280.7	$ 325.7	$ 313.1	$ 246.7	$ 263.8	$ 186.5	$ 62.7	$ 203.4	$ 170.1	
End of year value of unlevered firm	2,799.1	2,770.3	2,693.9	2,623.3	2,612.7	2,584.0	2,630.0	2,804.1	2,853.0	2,939.6	
Unlevered firm value + unlevered free cash flow	$3,058.2	$3,051.0	$3,019.6	$2,936.4	$2,859.4	$2,847.8	$2,816.6	$2,866.7	$3,056.4	$3,109.7	
Discount factor for one year, r_{UA}.	0.917	0.917	0.917	0.917	0.917	0.917	0.917	0.917	0.917	0.917	
Value of the unlevered firm at beginning of year	$2,805.7	$2,799.1	$2,770.3	$2,693.9	$2,623.3	$2,612.7	$2,584.0	$2,630.0	$2,804.1	$2,853.0	$2,939.6
Value of the Interest Tax Shields Discounted at the Unlevered Cost of Capital											
Interest tax shield for continuing value.											$ 19.2
Discount factor for continuing value											16.667
Interest tax shield (ITS).	$ 56.1	$ 53.0	$ 49.2	$ 39.6	$ 31.8	$ 27.5	$ 22.7	$ 18.0	$ 17.6	$ 13.3	
Value of the ITSs at end of year	347.0	325.2	305.3	293.2	287.8	286.2	289.2	297.2	306.3	320.6	
Value of the ITSs at end of year plus ITS	$ 403.1	$ 378.2	$ 354.4	$ 332.7	$ 319.6	$ 313.7	$ 311.9	$ 315.2	$ 323.9	$ 333.9	
Discount factor for one year, r_{UA}.	0.917	0.917	0.917	0.917	0.917	0.917	0.917	0.917	0.917	0.917	
Value of the ITSs at beginning of year	$ 369.8	$ 347.0	$ 325.2	$ 305.3	$ 293.2	$ 287.8	$ 286.2	$ 289.2	$ 297.2	$ 306.3	$ 320.6
Value of the firm at beginning of year.	$3,175.5	$3,146.0	$3,095.5	$2,999.2	$2,916.4	$2,900.5	$2,870.1	$2,919.2	$3,101.2	$3,159.3	$3,260.2

continued

continued from previous page

Beginning of Year Value ($ in millions)	Year 1	Year 2	Year 3	Year 4	Year 5	Year 6	Year 7	Year 8	Year 9	Year 10	Year 11
Value of the firm (V_F)	$3,175.5	$3,146.0	$3,095.5	$2,999.2	$2,916.4	$2,900.5	$2,870.1	$2,919.2	$3,101.2	$3,159.3	$3,260.2
Value of debt (V_D)	2,060.0	1,894.4	1,702.5	1,459.9	1,222.6	1,044.6	842.3	706.5	688.7	529.1	815.1
Value of equity (V_E)	$1,115.5	$1,251.7	$1,393.0	$1,539.3	$1,693.9	$1,855.9	$2,027.8	$2,212.7	$2,412.6	$2,630.2	$2,445.2

Equity Cost of Capital	Year 1	Year 2	Year 3	Year 4	Year 5	Year 6	Year 7	Year 8	Year 9	Year 10	Year 11
Unlevered cost of capital, r_{UA}	9.00%	9.00%	9.00%	9.00%	9.00%	9.00%	9.00%	9.00%	9.00%	9.00%	9.00%
Debt cost of capital, r_D	6.81%	7.00%	7.22%	6.78%	6.50%	6.58%	6.75%	6.38%	6.39%	6.28%	5.90%
Debt to common equity ratio	1.847	1.513	1.222	0.948	0.722	0.563	0.415	0.319	0.285	0.201	0.333
Equity cost of capital, r_E	13.04%	12.03%	11.17%	11.11%	10.80%	10.36%	9.94%	9.84%	9.74%	9.55%	10.03%
Equity beta	1.507	1.339	1.196	1.185	1.134	1.060	0.989	0.973	0.957	0.925	1.006
Geometric average equity cost of capital to exit year	13.04%										

Weighted Average Cost of Capital, r_{WACC}	Year 1	Year 2	Year 3	Year 4	Year 5	Year 6	Year 7	Year 8	Year 9	Year 10	Year 11
Equity cost of capital, r_E	13.04%	12.03%	11.17%	11.11%	10.80%	10.36%	9.94%	9.84%	9.74%	9.55%	10.03%
Equity to firm value	35.13%	39.79%	45.00%	51.32%	58.08%	63.99%	70.65%	75.80%	77.79%	83.25%	75.00%
Debt cost of capital, r_D	6.81%	7.00%	7.22%	6.78%	6.50%	6.58%	6.75%	6.38%	6.39%	6.28%	5.90%
Debt to firm value	64.87%	60.21%	55.00%	48.68%	41.92%	36.01%	29.35%	24.20%	22.21%	16.75%	25.00%
Income tax rate, T_{INT}	40.00%	40.00%	40.00%	40.00%	40.00%	40.00%	40.00%	40.00%	40.00%	40.00%	40.00%
Weighted average cost of capital, r_{WACC}	7.23%	7.31%	7.41%	7.68%	7.91%	8.05%	8.21%	8.38%	8.43%	8.58%	8.41%
Geometric average weighted average cost of capital, r_{WACC}	7.96%										

($in millions)	Year 0	Year 1	Year 2	Year 3	Year 4	Year 5	Year 6	Year 7	Year 8	Year 9	Year 10	Year 10
Unlevered free cash flow for continuing value												$176.40
Discount factor for continuing value												18.484
Unlevered free cash flow and continuing value		$259.1	$280.7	$325.7	$313.1	$246.7	$263.8	$186.5	$62.7	$203.4	$170.1	$3,260.2
Discount factor—annual r_{WACC}*		0.933	0.869	0.809	0.751	0.696	0.644	0.595	0.549	0.507	0.467	0.467
Present value		$241.6	$243.9	$263.5	$235.2	$171.7	$170.0	$111.1	$34.4	$103.1	$ 79.4	$1,521.5
Value of the firm	$3,175.5											

* The discount factors use the annual r_{WACC} from the table immediately above. For example, the discount factor for Year 2 = 1/[(1 + 0.0723) × (1 + 0.0731)] = 0.869.

After mastering the material in this chapter, you will be able to:

1. Understand the motivations for mergers and acquisitions and whether or not, on average, they create value (16.1–16.3)
2. Identify and value synergies (16.4)
3. Value and analyze an M&A deal (16.5–16.6, 16.9)
4. Measure a negotiation range (16.7–16.8)

CHAPTER

Mergers and Acquisitions

16

PFIZER, INC.—MEDIVATION, INC.'S "WHITE KNIGHT"

On April 28, 2016, Sanofi S.A. sent an unsolicited offer letter to Medivation's CEO in which Sanofi offered to purchase Medivation's stock for $52.50 cash per share or $9.4 billion in total.[1] On April 29, 2016, Medivation announced that its Board of Directors unanimously rejected Sanofi's offer because it undervalued the company. Naturally, other potential acquirers became interested in acquiring Medivation and Medivation's management became interested in them. The market appeared to be expecting other bids because the company's stock was trading at close to $60 at this time.

Sanofi continued its hostile takeover attempt and on May 25, 2016 it filed a contested solicitation sent to Medivation's shareholders (U.S. SEC PREC14A), "We are seeking your support for the removal of the Company Board . . . , because we believe that the Company Board is not acting, and will not act, in your best interests. Specifically, despite the fact that the $52.50 per share price offered by Sanofi represents a premium of over 50% over the two-month volume weighted average price prior to there being takeover rumors, the Company Board has refused even to engage with us regarding our Proposed Offer. . . . " On June 13, 2016, Medivation sent its shareholders a letter stating, ". . . Sanofi's consent solicitation is an essential element of its plan to seize control of Medivation by means of an opportunistically-timed proposal that substantially undervalues Medivation, its leading oncology franchise and its wholly owned, innovative late-stage pipeline. . . . In considering Sanofi's proposals, the Board believes it is important to keep in mind that neither Sanofi nor its nominees currently have a duty to act in the best interests of Medivation and its stockholders."

On July 13, 2016, Medivation announced that it entered into confidentiality agreements with a number of parties that have expressed interest in exploring a potential transaction and that it entered into a confidentiality agreement with Sanofi and that Sanofi agreed to terminate its consent solicitation. Finally, on August 22, 2016, Pfizer and Medivation jointly announced that they entered into a definitive merger agreement under which Pfizer would acquire Medivation through a tender offer for Medivation's shares for $81.50 a share in cash or approximately $14 billion in total. On September 28, 2016, Pfizer announced the successful completion of its acquisition of Medivation.

In this chapter, we discuss mergers and acquisitions—why they take place, the evidence on value creation, and how to analyze and value an M&A deal.

[1] Sanofi S.A. is a French pharmaceutical company and one of the largest global prescription sales companies. Medivation, Inc. is a U.S. biopharmaceutical company focused on the development and commercialization of medically innovative therapies to treat serious diseases for which there are limited treatment options, which, at this time, had one commercial product for the treatment of certain types of prostate cancer. Pfizer Inc. is a U.S. global pharmaceutical company and one of the largest pharmaceutical companies in the world. See Medivation's various U.S. SEC filings from May 2016 through September 2016 available at www.sec.gov.

CHAPTER ORGANIZATION

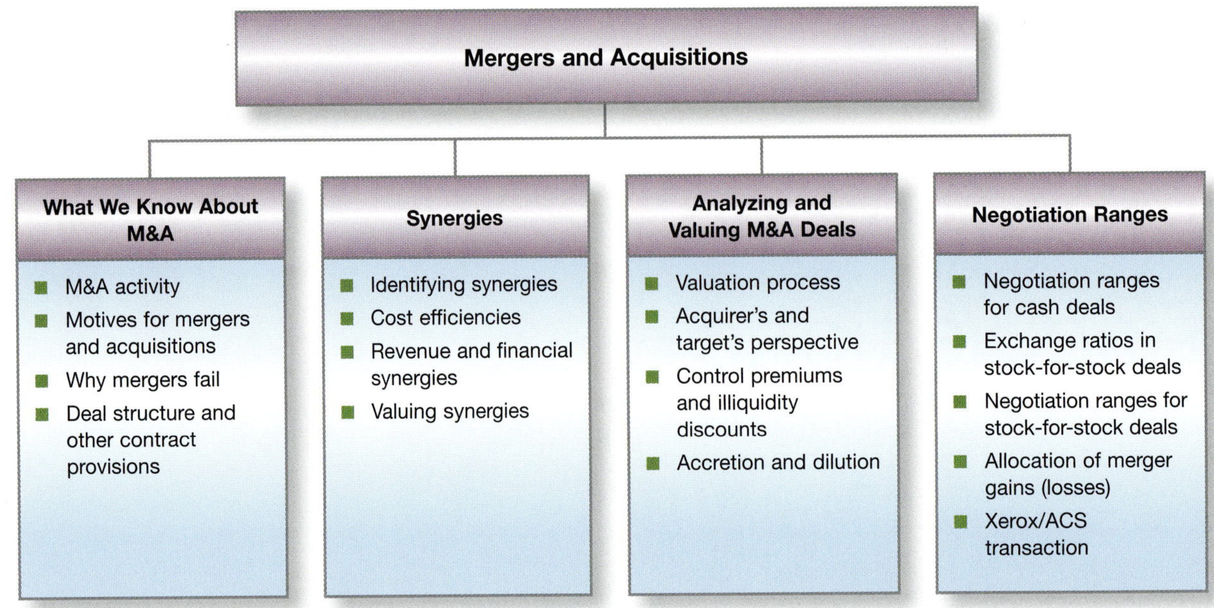

INTRODUCTION

We use the term "merger and acquisition" (M&A) to describe a transaction in which a buyer (the **acquiring company** or **acquirer**) purchases another company (the **target company**). The acquirer can accomplish this purchase by either purchasing the target's assets directly or purchasing the target's stock from its shareholders.

An **asset acquisition** typically involves the sale of a target's assets to the acquiring company. The acquirer may purchase the assets of the entire company, the assets of a subsidiary or division of the company, or only specific assets of the company. The acquirer may also assume some, or sometimes all, of the liabilities and other obligations associated with the assets acquired.

A **stock acquisition** involves the sale of stock from the shareholders of the target company to the acquiring company. In a stock acquisition, the acquirer may purchase less than 100% of the target's stock. If the acquirer purchases more than 50% of the voting interest in a company, the acquirer will own a **controlling interest**. With more than 50% of the target company's voting power, the owner of the controlling interest typically has the power to make all decisions for the company, and thus has control over the company's activities.

In this chapter, we discuss how M&A transactions can create value, the evidence on whether or not M&A transactions create value and for whom, what factors determine an M&A transaction's success or failure, various aspects of deal structure, and how to analyze an M&A transaction. Our analysis of M&A transactions includes how to value them, how to assess whether or not a transaction is **accretive** (increases) or **dilutive** (decreases) to earnings per share and a company's market multiples, how the gains are shared in a merger, and analyzing **exchange ratios** (the number of shares of the acquirer given for every target share in a stock-for-stock transaction). We then illustrate the valuation issues related to M&A transactions with a specific example—the acquisition of Affiliated Computer Services, Inc. by Xerox Corporation.

16.1 WHAT DO WE KNOW ABOUT MERGER AND ACQUISITION TRANSACTIONS?

LO1 Understand the motivations for mergers and acquisitions and whether or not, on average, they create value

In this section we show that the number and value of M&A transactions vary over time and across global regions. Regardless of the country, M&A transactions are more common during certain time periods than others. Various scholars document the existence of such merger waves.[2] These studies show that merger

[2] See, for example, Shleifer, A., and R. Vishny, "Stock Market Driven Acquisitions," *Journal of Financial Economics* 70 (2003), pp. 295–311; Rhodes-Kropf, M., and S. Viswanathan, "Market Valuation and Merger Waves," *The Journal of Finance* vol. 24, no. 6 (December 2004), pp. 2685–2718; and Harford, J., "What Drives Merger Waves?" *Journal of Financial Economics* 77 (2005), pp. 529–560.

waves depend on various industry and macroeconomic circumstances. The United States, the United Kingdom and countries that comprise the European Union have historically been the dominant countries for both the number and value of M&A transactions; however, more recently, M&A transactions have become more common in other countries. In addition, because of globalization, **cross-border M&A** transactions (where the acquirer and target are headquartered in different countries) have increased in importance as well. We discuss cross-border valuation in Chapter 17.

Using the merger database from Thomson One,[3] we select transactions that were completed between 2001 and 2015 with a value (enterprise value) of at least $10 million. We provide descriptive information on the number and enterprise value of transactions for 12 countries and geographic regions. These countries/regions include Africa, Asia, Australia and other Oceania Countries, China, China—Hong Kong, Europe, Middle East, North America without the U.S., South and Central America and the Caribbean, United Kingdom (U.K.), and the United States (U.S.). Based on these criteria, we initially examine 44,839 completed public and private M&A transactions that resulted in either 100% ownership of the target or a majority ownership of the target.

Time-Series of Merger and Acquisition Transactions

In Exhibit 16.1, we present descriptive information on the time-series of the total enterprise value and number of M&A transactions across the 12 regions.

EXHIBIT 16.1 Times-Series of Global Merger and Acquisition Transactions

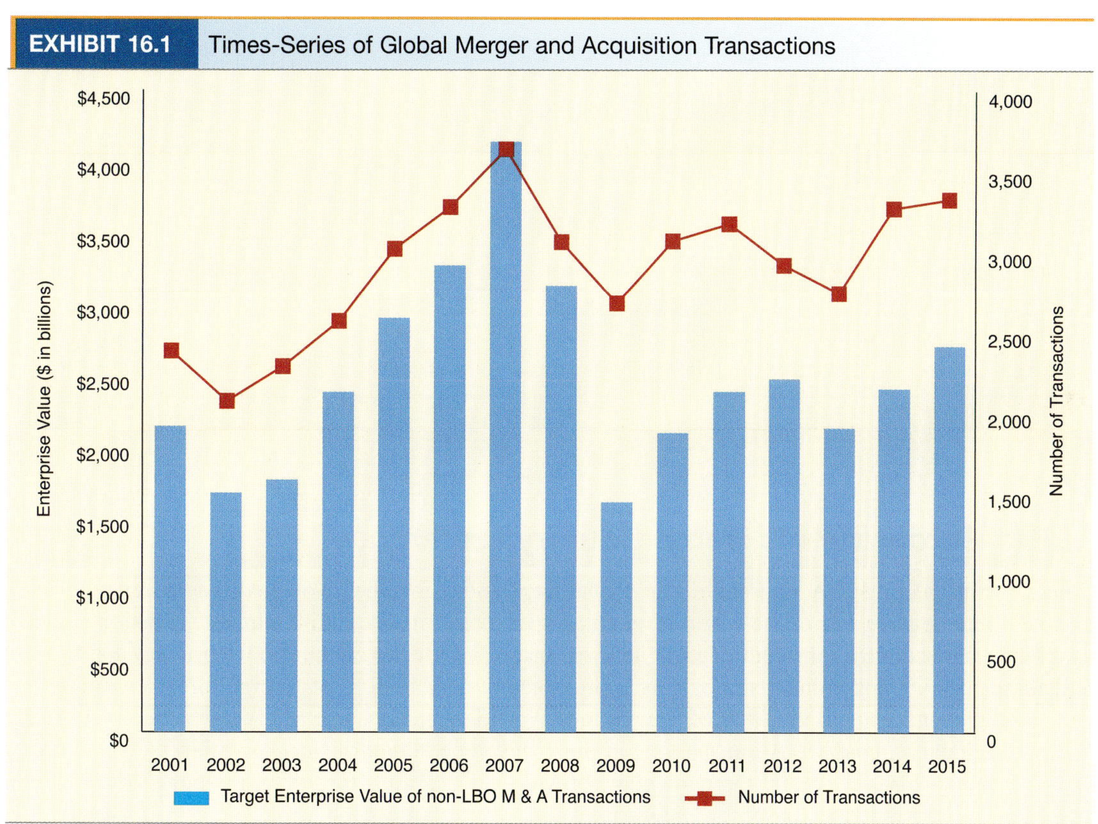

The peak years in terms of the value of global transactions were 2006 and 2007 (2006 with a value over $3 trillion and 2007 with a value over $4 trillion) followed closely by 2008. The time period from 2004 through 2008 was an era of economic growth, tremendous liquidity and low interest rates, both of which drove M&A activity for that period. Finally, the decrease in the number and value of M&A transactions in 2009 demonstrates the effect of the economic and financial crisis that unfolded in the fall of 2008. Because of such events like the ones just described, neither the number of transactions nor the size of the transactions indicates a clear upward or downward trend, which is consistent with the existence of merger waves that are dependent on various industry and macroeconomic circumstances.

[3] We report results from Thomson One, which we discuss in Chapter 15.

For example, deregulation may release backlogged acquisition demand, technological innovation may require asset reallocations, liquidity in the capital markets may make capital more accessible, and higher-than-average market valuations (and possible overvaluations) may drive companies to use stock to purchase other companies.

In Exhibit 16.2, we present a measure of regional market share of the total value of global M&A transactions over 2011–2015. We measure this market share metric as the value of the transactions in that country or region in a given year, divided by the total market value of the transactions in that year. Over this time period, the U.S. has the largest market share at 36%, followed by the E.U. at 21%.

EXHIBIT 16.2 Target Enterprise Value-Based "Market Share" of 2011–2015 Global Merger and Acquisition Transactions

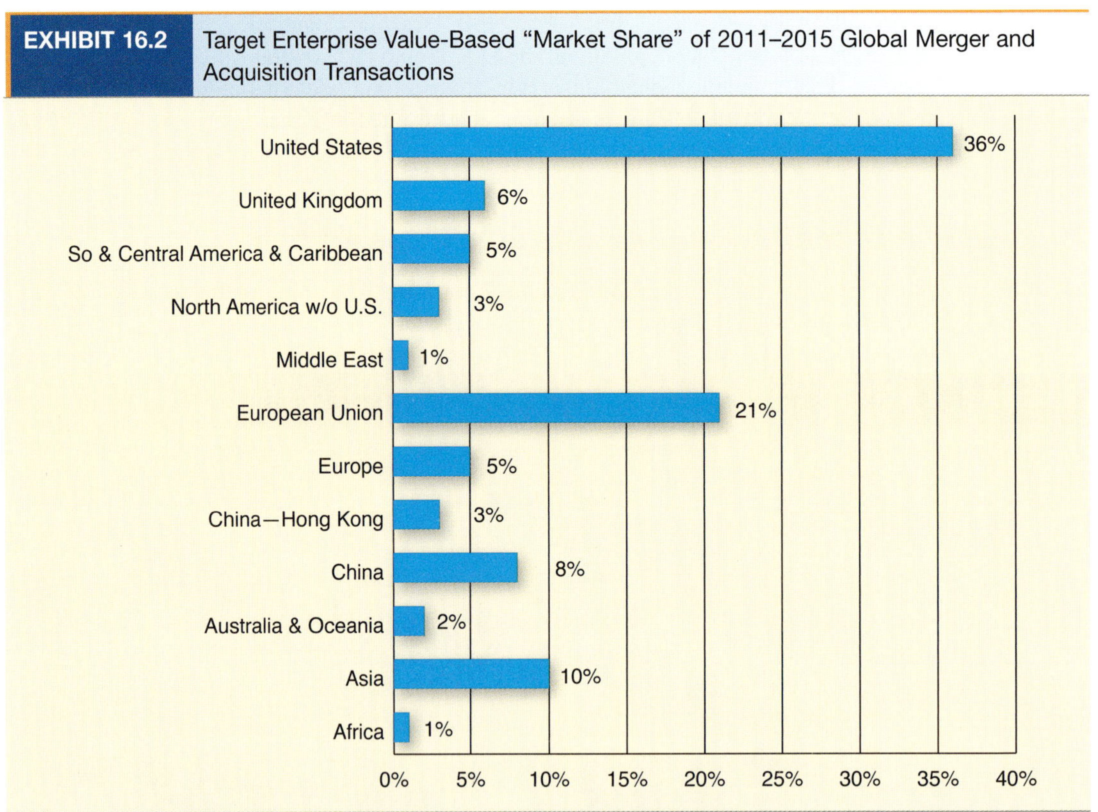

Cross-Border versus Home Country Preference

One motivation for M&A transactions is global expansion (in other words, the acquirer moves its business into new regions of the world through acquisitions). An alternative global expansion strategy is to enter new countries through **organic growth** or **greenfield investments**. It turns out that acquiring companies is the dominant strategy, as approximately 80% to 90% of foreign direct investment in developing countries is in the form of acquisitions. While companies use M&A transactions to extend their global reach, most M&A transactions in more developed countries occur within the same country. In Exhibit 16.3, we present the percentage of M&A transactions for which the target and acquirer are from the same region (based on enterprise value of the target). This percentage is a measure of the acquirers' home country preference, while one minus this percentage represents the percentage of cross-border transactions.

The countries with the highest home country preference are the U.S. and China, with 85% of the M&A transactions having a target and acquirer from the same region, followed closely by Asia. South and Central America (including the Caribbean) and the E.U., all have more than a 65% home country preference. Africa has the lowest home country preference, 26%, and thus the most cross-border transactions.

EXHIBIT 16.3 Home Country Preference—Target Enterprise Value-Based 2011–2015 Percentage of Global Merger and Acquisition Transactions with Acquirer and Target from Same Region

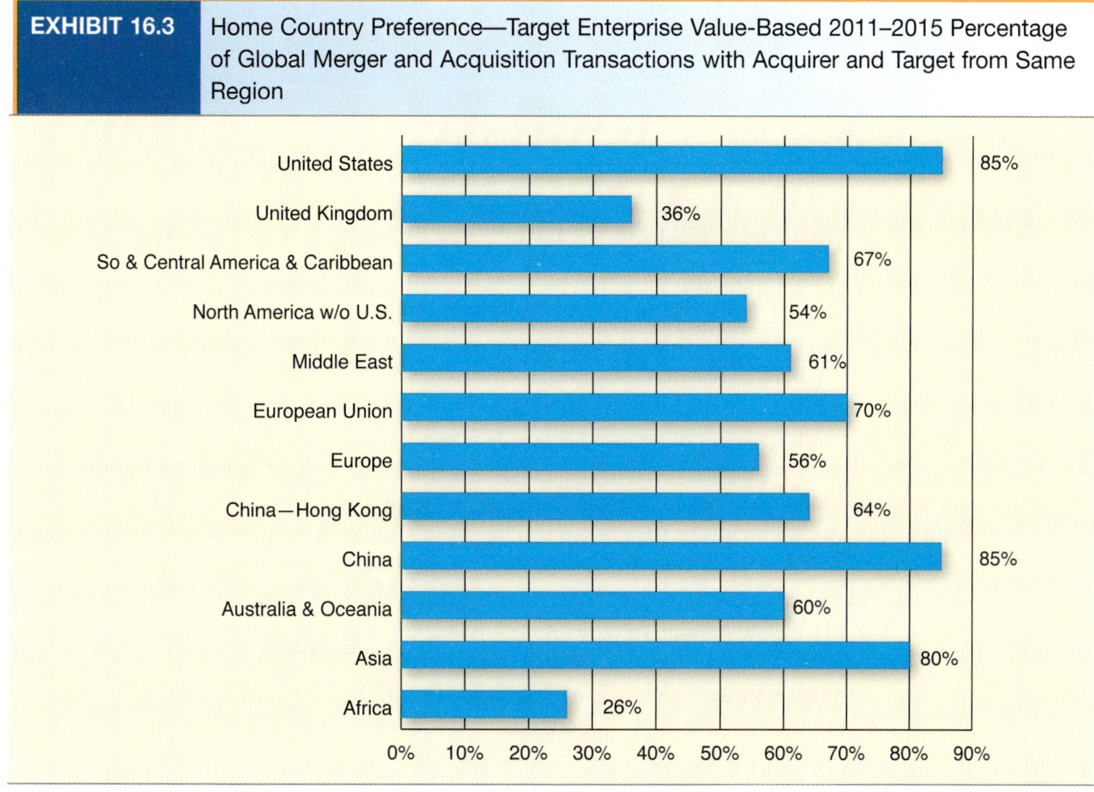

Private versus Public Targets and Acquirers

As discussed at the beginning of this section, the M&A transactions in the sample include both privately held and publicly traded targets and acquirers. In Exhibit 16.4, we present the percentages of the value of the transactions for both privately held and publicly traded targets as well as privately held and publicly traded acquirers.

EXHIBIT 16.4 Target Enterprise Value-Based 2011–2015 Percentage of Global Merger and Acquisition Transactions by Types of Targets and Acquirers in Global Merger and Acquisition Transactions

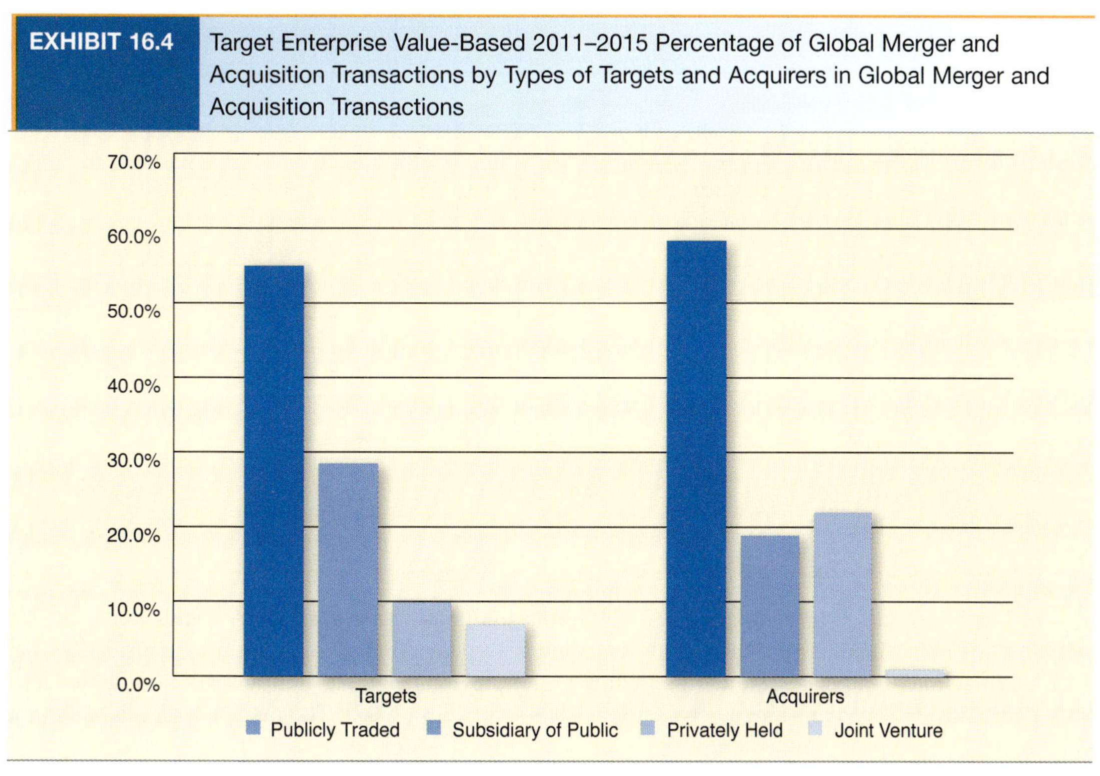

The first set of four bars reports the percentage of privately held and publicly traded targets purchased based on the value of the transactions. For the targets, the exhibit shows that about 55% of the targets are publicly traded, 28% are subsidiaries of a publicly traded company, and under 10% are privately held. The second set of four bars focuses on the acquirers. For the acquirers, 77% are publicly traded or subsidiaries of publicly traded companies and 22% are privately held companies.

Merger Premiums and Market Multiples

In this section, we present the merger premiums paid to target shareholders and the transaction multiples implied by M&A transactions by geographic region. Thomson One measures merger premiums based on changes in the publicly traded market prices of target companies; thus, we report merger premiums for the publicly traded target companies. Although transaction multiples based on enterprise value are available for both privately held and publicly traded targets, these multiples may not be the same for reasons that we discuss later in the chapter. As such, we only report transaction multiples for publicly traded target companies. Thus, the dataset we use in Exhibits 16.5 and 16.6 has about 10,000 observations.

In Exhibit 16.5, we report the average five-day merger premiums, which measure the premium relative to the closing price five days before the announcement of the transaction. In this exhibit we present the median premium and 25th and 75th percentiles of the premiums across all global M&A transactions in a year. The transaction premiums vary over time. The medians range between 16% (2004) and 27% (2001, 2008, 2011, and 2012). The median over all years (not reported on the chart) is 22%, which is the same premium we report in Chapter 15 for global LBO transactions. The 25th and 75th percentiles illustrate the fairly large range of premiums paid in any one year. The difference between the 75th and 25th percentiles (called the interquartile range) is generally around 35% with the smallest interquartile range equal to 27% (2006) and the largest interquartile range equal to 47% (2009).

EXHIBIT 16.5 Time-Series of One-Week Premiums Paid in Global Merger and Acquisition Transactions

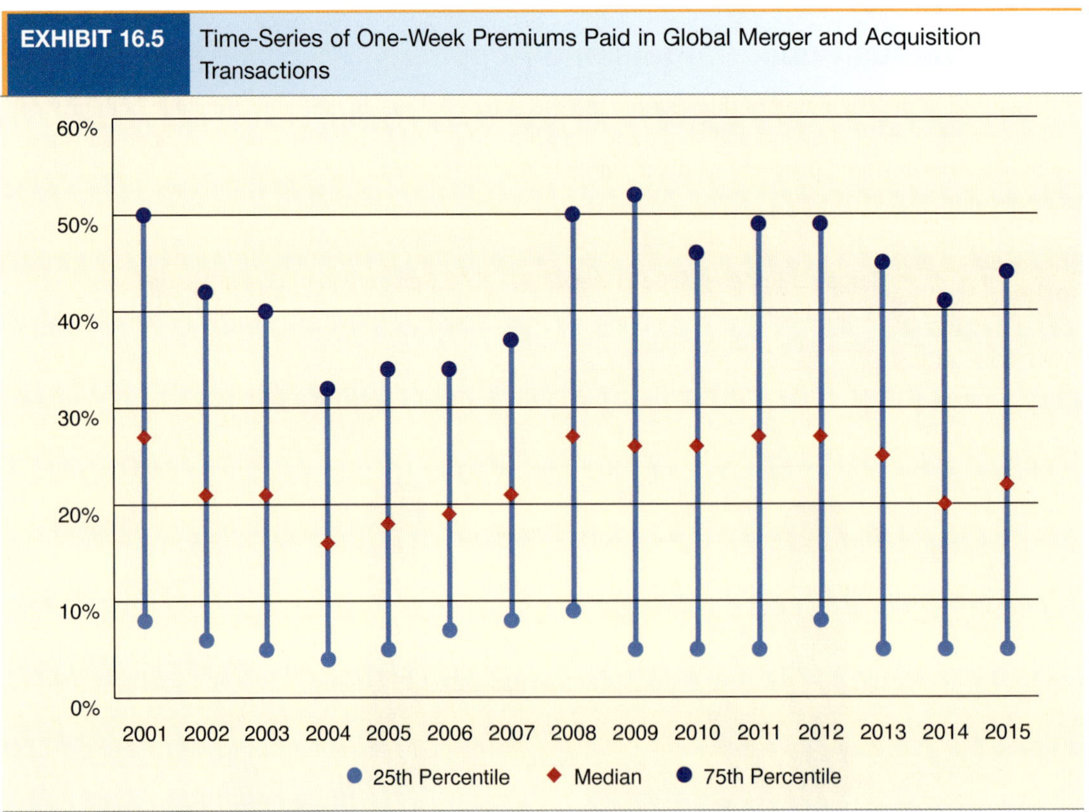

In Exhibit 16.6, we present EBITDA transaction multiples for global M&A transactions. In this exhibit we present the median multiple and 25th and 75th percentiles of the multiples across all global M&A transactions in a year. Like the premiums in the previous exhibit, the transaction multiples also vary over time. The medians range between 9.6 (2009) and 13.3 (2007). The median over all years (not reported on the chart) is 11.4. The 25th and 75th percentiles again illustrate the fairly large range of EBITDA transaction multiples in any one year.

EXHIBIT 16.6 Time-Series of EBITDA Transaction Multiples in Global Merger and Acquisition Transactions

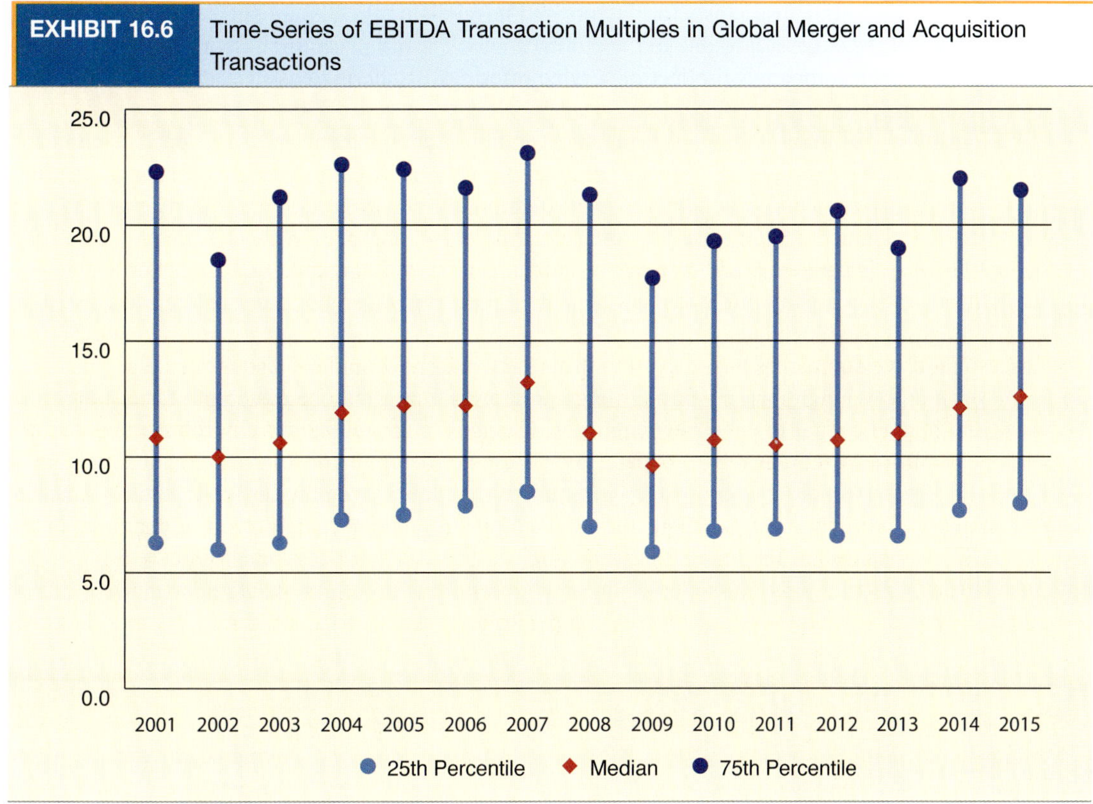

16.2 WHAT MOTIVATES MERGERS AND ACQUISITIONS, AND DO THEY CREATE VALUE?

Naturally, the overarching motivation for acquisitions is to create value for shareholders. However, managers of acquiring companies may also be motivated to acquire companies for personal reasons, which may or may not create value for the shareholders. In this section, we summarize the scholarly research on how acquisitions perform, for example, whether or not they lead to economic efficiency, and whether or not they create value for the shareholders of both the acquiring and target companies. We also discuss the reasons why mergers often fail to create value.

What Motivates Merger and Acquisition Transactions?

Naturally, managers should first develop a complete strategic plan in which they identify the opportunities with which to grow the company and establish, enhance, and protect their competitive advantages in order to create value for the company's shareholders. Moreover, a strategic plan informs the acquisition process by identifying the goals that are best attained organically and the goals that are best attained through acquisitions. An acquisition can help a company establish a competitive advantage, raise barriers to imitation, raise barriers to entry, raise barriers to substitution, enhance or protect power over the supply chain, provide access to foreign markets, and so on.

More specifically, acquirers attempt to create value through acquisitions by taking advantage of various economic forces or regulatory frictions by increasing scale and scope, efficiently entering new markets (especially new global markets), combining complementary resources, capturing superior or new technology and expertise, reacting to changes in regulation, reducing capacity in the industry, removing inefficient management, and capturing tax benefits that otherwise would have been lost. Also, if management believes a company's stock is overvalued, managers may be motivated to use the company's stock as currency to purchase other companies.

A company can create value from increasing its scale or its scope. Scale efficiencies may arise from spreading fixed costs over a larger scale of activities (for example, sharing fixed cost infrastructure investments or research and development activities) and from increased purchasing power. For example, a large company that performs diagnostic tests for doctors and hospitals might acquire smaller labs, and reduce the cost structure of the smaller labs due to the purchasing power of the acquirer. Scope efficiencies may arise from increasing a company's product or service offerings by sharing costs related to these product or service offerings.

An acquisition can create value if companies combine complementary assets or if a company acquires assets needed to improve its products, reduce its costs, or increase its revenues, such as combining a company with very good products but weak distribution channels with a company that has very good distribution channels. Alternatively, a manager might use an acquisition to acquire technology, intellectual property (patents or trade secrets), or human capital with valuable expertise. For example, a larger pharmaceutical company might acquire a smaller biotech company in order to acquire new drugs in the early stages of development.

Forces that drive companies to try to grow faster and enter new markets also motivate acquisitions. Companies can enter foreign markets through organic growth, but it may be easier and faster to acquire the assets and human capital to enter new countries. Changes in the regulatory environment sometimes provide opportunities for companies to expand. For example, deregulation can make acquisitions possible, or even necessary in order to compete, where they were not feasible previously. Regulatory changes can also affect the profitability of an acquisition, which may motivate acquisitions. For example, in the 1990s and 2000s, changes in the regulations affecting the financial services industry made acquisitions both feasible and potentially profitable; however, more recently, changes in regulation have made it more difficult and more costly for financial services companies to expand across borders.

Valuation in Practice 16.1

Managers Forecast Synergies to Value the Benefits from a Merger—Daimler-Benz and Chrysler Merger Naturally, when two companies merge, the managers of both companies measure the value of the merger based on the potential synergies resulting from combining the two companies. In May 1998, Daimler-Benz, AG (Daimler) and Chrysler Corporation (Chrysler) announced the merger of the two companies. The shareholders approved the merger and the companies merged in November 1998. The companies disclosed certain forecasts and the value drivers resulting from the merger. For example, Daimler's management stated,

> . . . the reasons for the business combination including, among other things, general consolidation in the automotive industry and the strong potential for synergies between the constituent companies, the company profile of Chrysler, the transaction structure, organizational issues relating to the structure and composition of the DaimlerChrysler Management Board and Supervisory Board and the prospects for enhancing the value of the combined entity in the future. . . .
>
> The opportunities for significant synergies afforded by a combination of Chrysler and Daimler-Benz—based not on plant closings or lay-offs, but on such factors as shared technologies, distribution, purchasing and know-how. Management expects benefits of $1.4 billion in the first year of merged operations, and annual benefits of $3 billion within three to five years.

The stock market also thought that this merger had significant and positive potential synergies. When the companies announced the merger, Daimler's stock price rose from $102.0625 to $111.375 (from the day before the announcement to the day after), and its market capitalization rose from $52.8 billion to $57.6 billion ($4.8 billion). Chrysler's stock price rose from $41.4375 to $53.8125, and its market capitalization rose from $26.8 billion to $34.8 billion ($8.0 billion). The combined increase in market capitalization was close to $13 billion. It turned out, however, that the synergies did not materialize, and after paying over $36 billion for Chrysler, Daimler eventually sold it for less than $1 billion.

Source: See the DaimlerChrysler AG SEC Form F-4 (Registration Statement) at www.sec.gov.

Holding everything else constant, changes in industry capacity will change product prices. When an industry has too much capacity, reducing capacity is necessary to increase margins to allow the remaining companies to earn the required rate of return in order to survive. Companies are also motivated to reduce industry capacity by eliminating competition in order to earn economic rents. Antitrust regulatory bodies around the world, however, are responsible for preventing the latter type of acquisitions if they violate antitrust laws.

A poorly managed company can become an acquisition target if its inefficiency has a sufficient impact on value. The management of an acquiring company may purchase a poorly managed target company in order to make changes to the target's strategy, operations, and management that will increase its value. For example, many of the acquisitions of oil companies in the 1980s were motivated by potential value creation resulting from changing the companies' operating strategies—in particular, their exploration strategies.

Sometimes, a company states that it acquired another company in order to diversify the company's products and services even though the acquisition has no cost or revenue synergies. Historically, some companies have made acquisitions that were pure diversification plays. However, scholarly research does not provide any definitive evidence that pure diversification strategies create substantial value in well-developed economies. In fact, some studies suggest that pure diversification destroys value because management may lose focus, and the allocation of capital within the organization might not be based on the investments that can create the most value for the company; however, other studies suggest that diversification is a more neutral activity with minimal benefits. On the other hand, it appears that diversification in countries with less-developed capital markets can help create a company's internal capital market and avoid the high costs of obtaining external financing in such markets.[4]

Valuation Key 16.1

Economic forces drive mergers and acquisitions. The reasons for mergers in industries vary over time with the life cycle of the industry and other economic factors. Whatever the motivation for an acquisition, it should be tied to the company's strategy and serve to either establish, enhance, and/or protect the company's competitive advantage.

Do Merger and Acquisition Transactions Create Value, and If They Do, for Whom?

A large number of studies from both academics and consulting firms have addressed this issue in various ways. A number of studies assess value creation by examining the short-run stock market performances of the acquirer and target around the time the acquisition is announced and between the time of announcement and the close of the transaction. Other studies examine long-run stock market performance or long-run operating performance (normally one to three years after the acquisition). Using stock market performance to draw conclusions about gains in economic efficiency and value creation assumes that market participants understand the valuation implications of acquisitions—either at the time of announcement or subsequent to the acquisition—as they observe post-merger performance and price the stocks accordingly. Since these studies do not examine individual acquisitions but instead examine a large sample of acquisitions, it might be possible that the market does not understand the ramifications of one particular acquisition, but it is much harder to argue that it does not understand (at least on average) the implications across a large sample of acquisitions.

This evidence suggests that mergers and acquisitions are generally good for economic efficiency; in other words, the combined returns to the acquirer and the target (weighted by their respective market values), are, on average, positive after controlling for overall stock market performance. However, the evidence indicates that, on average, the preponderance of the gains (if not all of the gains) go to the target shareholders and not the acquirer's shareholders. Risk-adjusted stock returns to target shareholders are

[4] See Berger, P., and E. Ofek, "Diversification's Effect on Firm Value," *Journal of Financial Economics* 37 (1995), pp. 39–65, which suggests that diversified firms sell at a 13% to 15% discount relative to the sum of the standalone components. Also, see Villalonga, B., "Diversification Discount or Premium? New Evidence from the Business Information Tracking Series," *Journal of Finance* 59 (2004), pp. 475–502, which suggests that there is no diversification discount. Also, see Khanna, T., and K. Palepu, "Is Group Affiliation Profitable in Emerging Markets? An Analysis of Diversified Indian Business Groups," *Journal of Finance* 55 (2000), pp. 867–891, on the benefits of conglomerate groups in emerging markets.

significant and positive whereas most studies show zero or modest negative returns to acquirers, indicating that, on average, the target companies capture all of the wealth creation and maybe even more. What is clear from the literature is that many acquisitions are expected to be and appear to turn out to be either zero net present value projects or negative net present value projects for the acquirer. Analyzing the three years subsequent to the merger, Mitchell and Stafford (2000) show that, on average, acquirers lose 5% and that these returns are significantly negative.[5] However, the variation around the average return is large, thus, some transactions create substantial value whereas others destroy substantial value.

Some studies attempt to discern the factors that are associated with better or worse performance for the acquirer. The evidence strongly indicates that mergers financed with stock, as opposed to no stock, are more likely to experience negative returns. Mitchell and Stafford (2000) show that acquisitions financed with stock lost, on average, 9% over the three years following an acquisition, whereas those financed with no stock lost only 1.4%. A potential explanation for this result is that managers are more likely to use stock to finance an acquisition if they believe that their stock is overvalued, leading them to buy some hard assets before the market discovers that the stock is overvalued. As such, using stock may be a signal to the market that it has overvalued the acquiring company. An alternative reason companies use stock to acquire other companies is insufficient cash and debt capacity for the acquisition; to help secure a particular tax treatment and deal structure; and to share the risk of the transaction with the target. A recent paper by Savor and Qu (2009) suggests that most of the negative stock performance associated with acquisitions financed with stock is due to the overvaluation of the stock and not due to managers using their paper currency too loosely or paying too much relative to acquisitions financed with cash. Indeed, they show that companies that failed to close their stock-for-stock transactions for exogenous reasons (such as an antitrust issue) fared worse than companies that completed their stock-for-stock transactions.[6]

Valuation Key 16.2

The evidence on whether mergers and acquisitions create value is reasonably clear from both academic and practitioner studies. Almost all of the studies conclude that, on average, mergers and acquisitions increase economic efficiency. However, most of the gains go to target shareholders. Some studies find, on average, significant negative returns to the acquirers, and some find insignificant returns to acquirers; the variance around the mean is large indicating that some mergers create substantial value while others destroy substantial value.

Why do some acquirers overpay? We consider an overpayment to have occurred for a merger transaction when the value of the acquirer's stock decreases as a result of the merger. In such cases, regardless of the strategic benefits of an acquisition and the economic efficiencies, the acquirer pays more than what is economically justified based on the expected benefits of the merger. Reasons why an acquirer might pay too much include conflicts of interests, psychological factors, and errors in judgment.

A competitive auction process often leads to an increase in the premium paid relative to a situation in which the process has only one bidder. Auctions have become more common over time due to changes in case and securities laws. An acquirer may overpay if the acquirer is overly optimistic in its forecast of the synergies or future performance of the combined companies. In an auction, the winning bidder may be too optimistic about the merger even if, on average, all of the bidders have rational expectations—the so-called winner's curse. In order to avoid overbidding in an auction, bidders must conduct a thorough analysis of the benefits of the acquisition and establish a firm walk-away price that they will not violate without new and substantive positive information.

The nature of the acquisition process can sometimes create incentives and environments that lead to overbidding. For example, an acquirer's financial advisors may have a conflict of interest because they are often compensated based on "success fees;" in other words, they only receive their fees if the transaction closes. The managers of the acquiring company might have incentives—either financial or psychological—to overbid. For example, managerial compensation may be linked to either the size or

[5] There are hundreds of studies that have examined the stock price and accounting performance associated with mergers and acquisitions. Two studies that examine a sample over many years are M. Mitchell and E. Stafford, "Managerial Decisions and Long-Term Stock Price Performance," *Journal of Business* 73 (2000), pp. 287–329 and G. Andrade, M. Mitchell and E. Stafford, "New Evidence and Perspectives on Mergers," *Journal of Economic Perspectives* 15 (2001), pp. 103–120.

[6] See Savor, P., and Q. Lu, "Do Stock Mergers Create Value for Acquirers?" *Journal of Finance* 64 (2009), pp. 1061–1097.

growth of the overall company without an appropriate adjustment for its risk-adjusted performance. From a psychological perspective, managers of the acquiring company may become too personally invested in acquiring the target. Managers often invest many hours of their own time in addition to a sizeable amount of the company's resources; as such, they do not want to "lose" the deal—a **sunk cost** phenomenon. If a target is slipping away, a manager may resort to changing the valuation at the last minute in order to justify a higher bid.

Factors Affecting the Ability of Mergers to Create Value

Mergers and acquisitions are complicated business transactions with numerous elements that have to be managed successfully in order to create value. Even if a merger makes sense economically, it is difficult for an acquisition to be free of unforeseen events and negative surprises. The goal, of course, is to avoid having such unforeseen events and surprises derail the success of an acquisition. What are some of the reasons why an acquisition fails to create value for the acquirer? At the most basic level, of course, the acquirer just paid too much, and that is most likely to occur because of errors in process, expectations, and execution.

Acquisition Strategy. One factor that contributes to the success or failure of a merger is the underlying acquisition strategy. The acquisition may not fit within the company's strategy (e.g., buying a company for non-strategic reasons), or the company's acquisition strategy may be flawed. Another strategy-related success or failure is anticipating (or failing to anticipate) the strategic responses of its competitors. For example, suppose that a company operates in a competitive industry and that the company completes an acquisition that reduces its costs; in turn, the company assumes this will increase its operating margins. If the company is able to achieve these higher margins, the company's competitors will, to the extent possible, take actions to achieve similar cost savings. If the competitors manage to do so, product prices are likely to fall and reduce margins to their previous competitive level. Thus, though the company may benefit from an improvement in operating margins for some limited amount of time, the improvement will not be permanent. If the company fails to anticipate this response, the merger may fail to create value, for the acquirer may have forecasted more persistent benefits than actually materialized and, hence, overpaid for the target.

Due Diligence. In a friendly (as opposed to a hostile) merger, **due diligence** is a process that usually begins after the target and acquirer sign a non-binding letter of intent. The due diligence process allows the acquirer to perform a more detailed examination and analysis of the target's accounting, financial, and legal records. The ultimate goal of a due diligence process is primarily an assessment of the value of the acquisition—a test of the investment thesis. In addition to analyzing the accounting and legal records and documents and various financial aspects of the transaction, the due diligence process investigates such non-financial aspects as the quality of the executives and work force, the culture of the target, and how well or poorly the cultures of the acquirer and target fit together. The due diligence process also affords the acquirer the opportunity to begin developing an integration plan. All of these are important aspects of the due diligence process.

A 2004 Bain and Company survey of 250 senior managers with M&A responsibilities showed that only 30% of the managers surveyed were satisfied with their due diligence.[7] In particular, the Bain survey reported that about two-thirds of the managers ignored the integration challenges that were apparent in the due diligence and, as such, overestimated the synergies. The survey also noted that about one-half of the managers indicated that their due diligence process failed to uncover and highlight such key issues as the target being "dressed up for sale," the stuffing of a sales channel, the treatment of expenses as non-recurring or extraordinary, and cutbacks on maintenance, capital expenditures, and research and development. More than 45% of the managers indicated that due diligence failed to uncover conflicting strategies of the target and acquirer, and more than one-third indicated that neither the valuation nor the bid was updated for the findings of the due diligence process.

---

[7] Cullinan, G., J. Le Roux, R. Weddigen, Bain and Company Brief Newsletter, April 28, 2004, http://www.bain.com/publications/articles/when-to-walk-away-from-a-deal-newsletter.aspx (accessed June 23, 2018).

Valuation in Practice 16.2

The Due Diligence Failure in Hewlett-Packard Company's Acquisition of the Autonomy Corporation plc On August 18, 2011, Hewlett-Packard Company (HP) entered into an offer agreement with Autonomy to acquire all of the company's stock for £25.50 ($42.11) per share in cash.[8] The total value of the offer was about $10.2 billion. Autonomy's stock was trading at $23.53 the day before the announcement (market capitalization of $5.7 billion). As shown in the following chart, investors did not agree with HP's acquisition strategy. On the day of the announcement, Autonomy's market capitalization increased by over $4 billion but HP's market capitalization declined by over $10 billion, basically the entire value HP bid for Autonomy. The acquisition closed in November 2011.

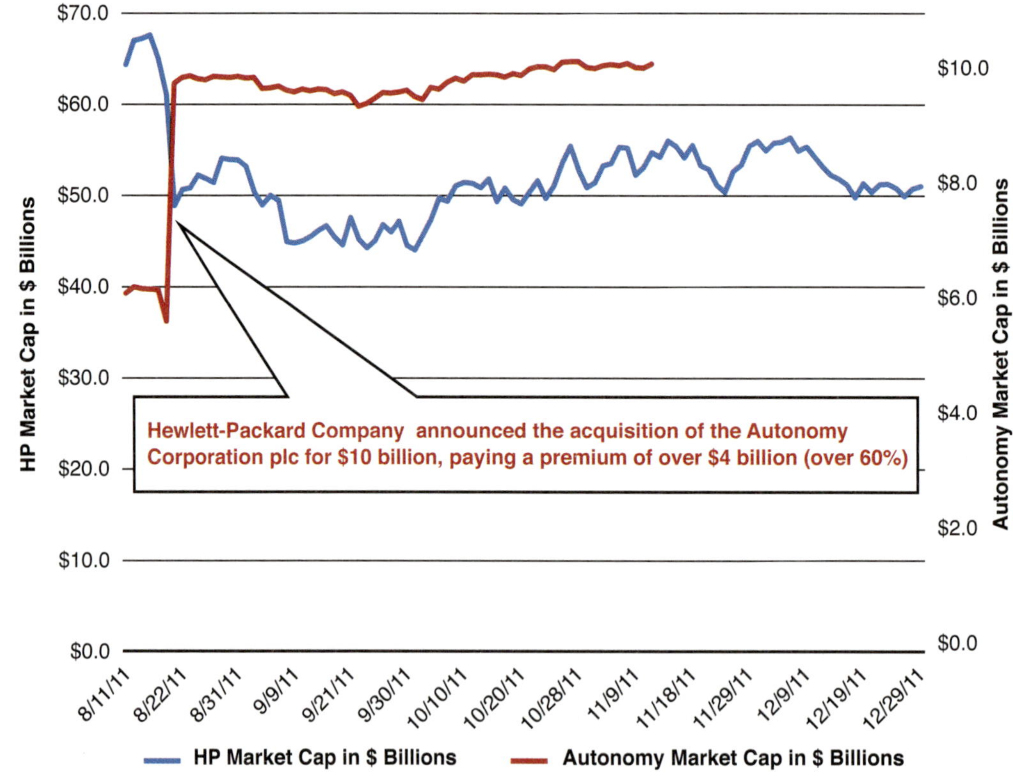

The market's reaction to HP's acquisition strategy was prescient because on November 20, 2012, about one year after the close of the Autonomy acquisition, HP announced:

> Following the completion of its annual review of its goodwill and purchased intangible assets for impairment, on November 20, 2012, HP announced that it recorded a non-cash charge for the impairment of goodwill and intangible assets within its Software segment of approximately $8.8 billion in the fourth quarter of its 2012 fiscal year. The majority of this impairment charge relates to accounting improprieties and disclosure failures at Autonomy Corporation plc ("Autonomy") that occurred prior to HP's acquisition of Autonomy, misrepresentations made to HP in connection with its acquisition of Autonomy, and the impact of those improprieties, failures and misrepresentations on the expected future financial performance of the Autonomy business over the long-term. . . .

Integration Planning and Execution. A successful acquisition requires that management successfully execute a well-thought-out **integration plan**. Naturally, the integration of the operations of

[8] At that time, Hewlett-Packard Company was a provider of products, technologies, software, solutions and services to individual consumers, businesses, and government. Autonomy Corporation plc, a U.K. company, was a provider of infrastructure software for the enterprise that helps organizations to derive value from their information as well as mitigate related risks. See HP's 2011 10-K Report and it's 8-K Report filings around these dates for the relevant information (available on www.sec.gov).

two companies is important for a merger to be successful unless the companies continue to operate on a standalone basis after the acquisition. Integration includes combining operations, eliminating redundant or unnecessary operations or personnel, and integrating cultures and compensation plans. A timetable with clear milestones is important to an integration plan—what does the acquirer need to accomplish in the first 30 days, 60 days, 90 days, and so forth? The integration plan includes detailed, well-developed plans to achieve revenue and cost synergies as well as plans to incur the one-time and ongoing costs of integrating the target, as well as having specific managers developing and executing the integration plan. Communication strategies for customers, employees, and investors are a part of the integration process. Both employees and customers are at risk when two companies announce an acquisition. An integration plan also considers the cultural issues associated with the transaction.

For example, the Daimler-Chrysler merger failed in spite of a strong positive stock market reaction to the merger announcement (see Valuation in Practice 16.1). Cultural differences between the two companies appear to have played an important role in the failure, as they prevented operations and management from being successfully integrated. The two companies also held very different views on compensation. As a result of these differences and the increasing control of Daimler over the merged company, performance and employee satisfaction at Chrysler decreased substantially, resulting in the departures of many of Chrysler's key executives and engineers.[9]

An integration plan is multifaceted, complex, and continually evolving, which is why successful integration plans are often developed, revised, and implemented by a special integration team composed of members from each company. The integration team works with the managers throughout the company to execute the plan and reacts to integration issues as they arise. The integration team revises the plan and takes proactive actions to address the issues that arise in order to maximize the likelihood of achieving the goal of the merger.

A recent survey by Deloitte[10] reports that about 70% of the companies surveyed had an integration plan ready to execute when the merger closed, which was important to the success of the merger. The keys factors identified for a successful integration plan were a dedicated integration team composed of managers from both companies and across functions (accounting, finance, marketing, sales, strategy, and so forth), executive level support and review, and transparent and consistent communications. Reasons why an integration was not successful were transition challenges that were not anticipated, a slower than anticipated process, unexpected delays in the process, and ineffective management.

The Acquisition Process. A well-run acquisition process contributes to the success of a merger and includes well-run due diligence and integration planning and execution discussed previously. The strategic rationale for the acquisition should inform all elements of the acquisition process—such as the valuation, negotiation strategy, deal structure, due diligence, and integration planning. In a well-run process, the due diligence process updates the valuation, integration plan, and negotiations taking place. A well-run acquisition process actively considers whether or when to walk away from a deal. This can happen in the negotiation stage, in the due diligence process, or in response to a competing bid that exceeds the walk-away price. A well-run acquisition process extends beyond the closing of the merger and even beyond the integration process. For example, it includes longer term post-acquisition budgets based on the assumptions in the valuation model that justified the merger price, with operational personnel signing off on these budgets. It includes tracking the success or failure of the merger in order to ensure that the acquisition is meeting its financial and strategic goals. If these goals are not being met, proactive steps are taken to put the acquisition back on track. After every acquisition, the M&A team identifies and reviews the lessons learned from the acquisition so that mistakes are not repeated in subsequent transactions, and the lessons learned are used to develop an "M&A playbook."

Cross-Border Acquisitions

Cross-border acquisitions are even more complex to execute successfully, and the risk of failure is higher. In a cross-border acquisition, cultural issues can be even more difficult to manage than a domestic

---

[9] Weber, R. A., and C. F. Camerer, "Cultural Conflict and Merger Failure: An Experimental Approach," *Management Science* vol. 49, no. 4 (April 2003), pp. 400–415.

[10] McGee, T., T. Thomas, and R. Thomson, *Deloitte Integration Report 2015—Putting the Pieces Together*, Deloitte Development Company LLC.

acquisition. Moreover, cross-border acquisitions have the added complexity of accommodating two different legal and regulatory environments and two different tax jurisdictions.[11]

Mitigating Risks

A company has a limited number of ways to mitigate risks in an acquisition transaction. For example, it is possible to buy insurance for certain risks (such as environmental liabilities and the expropriation of assets by a foreign government), but these insurance products are limited in scope and can be expensive. In addition, an acquirer can transfer some of the risk to the target by having contingent payments such as an **earn-out provision**. **Escrow accounts** are also used to mitigate risks in a transaction. Earn-outs and escrow accounts are generally used with targets that are private companies, and we discuss them later in the chapter. Acquiring a company with at least some stock consideration also mitigates some of the risk because if the deal winds up destroying value, the target shareholders will bear some of the resulting loss; of course, if the transaction does well, they stand to gain more, but this is how risk sharing works.

Valuation Key 16.3

Acquisitions fail to meet their strategic and financial goals for many reasons. However, a well-run acquisition process can mitigate the risk of failure. In addition, in certain circumstances, the acquirer may be able to shift some of the risk onto the target.

16.3 DEAL STRUCTURE, INCOME TAXES, AND OTHER CONTRACT PROVISIONS

Deal structure and other contract provisions have implications for the value and risk of a transaction. Deal structure and income taxes are complex topics that we only introduce in this chapter. Deal structure can influence a number of important factors—the form of payment; the tax effects of the transaction; how, if at all, risk is shared between the acquirer and target; whether the acquirer is responsible for the target's liabilities; whether contracts and items (such as leases) are still in effect after the target is acquired; whether the shareholders of both the target and acquirer have to vote on the merger; and whether minority shareholders will exist after the transaction.

It is often important for a company's existing contracts to remain in effect after the transaction. For example, if the target has leases or long-term contracts with suppliers and customers that are both advantageous and would be difficult to renegotiate on the same terms, then keeping those contracts in effect after the transaction may be important. Of course, some contracts may have change-of-control provisions that require the contract to be renegotiated whenever a change of control occurs. The issue of whether a vote is required by the shareholders (of either the acquirer or the target) speaks to the potential risk of completing a transaction, for approval has to be sought. Whether or not minority shareholders survive the transaction is important, as minority shareholders can be costly and disruptive to management.

A common goal in designing the deal structure is to maximize the size of the "economic pie," which often requires adjusting the purchase price or other elements of the merger agreement for the effects of the deal structure on each party. For example, the offer price that an acquirer will be willing to pay and that a target will be willing to accept is influenced by whether the transaction is tax free to the target and its shareholders. Associated with the tax effect on the target and its shareholders is whether the acquirer can take a step-up in the tax basis of the assets. A tax-free transaction is tax free at the time of the transaction. If a target shareholder receives shares of the acquirer's stock in a tax-free transaction, the target shareholder does not pay taxes on the gain resulting from the transaction at that time but will pay taxes on any gain upon the ultimate sale of the acquirer's shares. Obviously, the deal structure and the form of

[11] See KPMG, "Unlocking the Keys to Shareholder Value," *Mergers and Acquisitions Global Research Report* (1999).

the transaction affect both the buyer's valuation of the target and the target's valuation of the offer—for both tax and other reasons.

Valuation in Practice 16.3

Be Careful What You Wish For—Jos. A. Bank Clothiers, Inc.'s Attempt to Acquire The Men's Wearhouse On September 18, 2013, three months after the executive chairman and former CEO of Men's Wearhouse, Inc. was fired by the board of directors, Jos. A. Bank Clothiers, Inc. submitted an indication of interest to acquire the outstanding shares of Men's Wearhouse at $48 per share in cash, a 42.4% premium over the previous day's closing price.[12] On October 9, 2013, Men's Wearhouse issued a press release rejecting the Jos. A. Bank proposal concluding that the Jos. A. Bank proposal significantly undervalued the Company and failed to reflect its growth strategy and upside potential. Men's Wearhouse also announced that it had adopted a shareholder rights plan and that the company's board had amended and restated the company's bylaws, all in an attempt to make it more difficult for the company to be acquired without board approval.

On November 7, 2013, an equity investor holding over 9% of the company's shares sent a letter to the board of Men's Wearhouse expressing disappointment in the response to the Jos. A. Bank indication of interest and that the board's fiduciary duties required it to evaluate the company's strategic alternatives, including soliciting competing proposals to acquire the company, analyzing a leveraged recapitalization of the company, and entering into a dialogue with Jos. A. Bank regarding a possible combination. On November 26, 2013, Men's Wearhouse announced that it submitted a proposal to Jos. A. Bank to acquire all of the outstanding shares of Jos. A. Bank common stock for $55.00 per share in cash, representing an implied enterprise value of approximately $1.2 billion. Jos. A. Bank rejected that offer and instead attempted to acquire outdoor-wear maker Eddie Bauer as a takeover defense.

Finally, on March 11, 2014 the boards of Men's Wearhouse and Jos. A. Bank Clothiers announced that they had entered into a definitive agreement under which Men's Wearhouse would acquire all of the outstanding shares of common stock of Jos. A. Bank for $65.00 per share in cash, or total consideration of $1.8 billion. The merger was completed on June 14, 2014.

Types of Transactions

Cash Purchase of Assets. In a cash purchase of assets, the buyer pays cash for the assets of the target. In this form of transaction, the liabilities of the target are not transferred to the buyer unless it is agreed upon in the purchase agreement or if the liabilities are not separable from the assets. For example, under U.S. law, if a company buys a chemical plant, it cannot escape the environmental liabilities associated with the plant, even if it did nothing to contribute to the environmental issue. The target company pays a tax on the sale of the assets if it sells them at a gain, and target shareholders generally pay a tax if and when the proceeds are distributed to them. For the buyer, the taxable basis of the assets is equal to the payment made, and this has to be allocated across the assets and potentially to goodwill—the latter if the purchase price exceeds the value allocated to the inventory, other tangible assets, and intangible assets. In these transactions, the tax basis of the assets is normally stepped up for the buyer, which is beneficial to the acquirer if a large portion of the purchase price can be allocated to inventory and depreciable assets. The contracts of the target are typically not transferred to the buyer in an asset purchase. Therefore, leases and contracts with suppliers and customers will not survive.

Purchase of Stock Using Cash and Debt. Another type of transaction is the purchase of the target's stock using cash or debt payments. The most common way to acquire a company's stock is to use cash—48.1% of the M&A transactions in the sample discussed in Section 16.1 are 100% cash transactions. In this form of transaction, the acquirer buys the target's stock directly from the target's shareholders. In the U.S., M&A transactions occur in one of two ways—a **merger** or a **tender offer**. In a merger, the acquirer and the target's boards agree to merge at a specific price and then the target's shareholders

[12] Tailored Brands, Inc., the parent company of Men's Wearhouse, Inc., is a retailer of men's clothing through a network of stores in the U.S. and Canada as well as e-commerce websites. Jos. A. Bank Clothiers, Inc. was also a retailer of men's clothing. See the companies' various U.S. SEC filings from September 2013 through June 2014 available at www.sec.gov.

must vote to approve the merger. In a tender offer, the acquirer makes an offer to the target's shareholders to purchase the target's shares, which often has a condition that a minimum percentage of the target's shares must be tendered (sold).[13] Each target shareholder pays a tax based on the difference between the consideration received and the shareholders' taxable basis in the stock. The target pays no tax.[14] The acquirer effectively assumes all of the target's liabilities, and all existing contracts (leased assets and agreements with suppliers and customers) stay in force unless they have change-in-control termination clauses. No shareholder vote is needed, but of course, the target shareholders have to tender their shares, and those who do not tender will become minority shareholders.

Purchase of Stock Using Stock and Potentially Other Consideration. While the most common way to acquire a company's stock is to use cash, the next most likely method is to use the acquirer's stock plus some amount of cash—32.6% of the M&A transactions in the sample discussed in Section 16.1 are a mix of stock and cash. For these transactions, the mix of stock and cash is, on average, 53% and 47%, respectively. Lastly, about 20% of the M&A transactions in this sample are 100% stock. Many, but not all, of these transactions can be tax free to the target and to the target shareholders. If the transaction is tax free, there is no step-up in the tax basis of the assets for the acquirer. In order to qualify as tax free, there are certain requirements that must be met. For example, in the simplest form of a pure stock-for-stock merger, the acquirer can only exchange voting common stock or voting preferred stock and must control at least 80% of the votes after the transaction. If cash or other consideration is given in a stock-for-stock transaction, there are generally restrictions on the amount of non-voting stock consideration that can be given before the entire transaction is considered taxable. If the transaction meets these restrictions and qualifies for tax-free treatment, some tax is levied to the extent of the cash and other consideration, but the entire transaction will not be taxable.

Purchase of Assets Using Stock and Potentially Other Consideration. In a stock-for-assets merger, the acquirer exchanges shares of its voting stock for the assets of the company. These types of transactions are not common. To qualify as a tax-free transaction, no more than 20% of the consideration may be in a form that is not voting common stock, and the acquirer must acquire at least 70% of the fair market value of the gross assets and 90% of the fair market value of the net assets. If the acquirer assumes any liabilities, they count toward meeting the 20% rule if anything other than voting common stock is used as consideration. Such transactions do not have a step-up in basis of the assets for the acquirer.

Other Common Contract Provisions

In addition to deal structure, other contract provisions affect the underlying economics of a transaction and how the parties allocate the risks.

Earn-outs are payments made after the close of a transaction (usually over several years). The amount of the payment, if any, is contingent upon the performance of the target over a specified time period. This is one way to bridge a difference in views on the value of the target. The size of the earn-out is usually related to the degree of this difference. For example, if the founder of a target is more optimistic about the future of the business than the acquirer, an earn-out can be structured such that the acquirer will pay more if certain performance goals are met after the transaction closes. Earn-outs are most common when the target is a private company, but we occasionally observe them for public targets. Earn-outs may also be useful to retain a founder or the target company's management. Earn-outs are usually based on such financial measures as earnings, revenues, and EBITDA, but sometimes, they are based on non-financial measures—for example, successful clinical trials or FDA approval for a new drug. Earn-outs can be used in both taxable and tax-free transactions.

Earn-outs, while useful, may have negative effects on behavior or outcomes. For example, assume a target is deeply integrated into the acquirer's business and, for the most part, does not operate independently. If the target fails to achieve the performance goals set in the earn-out, the parties will likely disagree over why

[13] For a discussion of mergers versus tender offers see, Offenberg, D., and C. A. Pirinsky, "How Do Acquirers Choose between Mergers and Tender Offers?" *Journal of Financial Economics* vol. 116, no. 2 (2015), pp. 331–342.

[14] The target pays no tax unless the parties agree to a special income tax treatment called a 338 election. The acquirer can treat the transaction as a purchase of stock, or it can treat it as an asset purchase (a section 338 election). In the latter case, the target pays income taxes as if it were an asset purchase and the acquirer can step up the basis in the assets. This is particularly useful if the target has net operating losses that can offset the gain it will recognize from the asset sale. The unused net operating losses of the target can also be used by the acquirer.

the failure occurred—specifically, those who are to receive the earn-out may believe that the acquirer interfered with the target's ability to perform. Earn-outs may also provide incentives for the target's management to act in unintended ways if they are the potential recipients of the earn-out. For example, in order to achieve the maximum earn-out, the target management might reduce expenditures such as advertising, research and development, and maintenance, or not make investments that do not pay off until after the earn-out expires. These actions can increase earnings in the short run but not be in the best long-run interests of the company.

It is also common for the parties to agree that some proportion of the consideration will be held in **escrow**. If the buyer identifies some problem after the acquisition, then the escrow can be used to make the buyer whole. An example of this type of issue is observing that working capital is less than what the target predicted would be in place at the date of close.

In a stock-for-stock transaction, the parties agree to an **exchange ratio**, which is the number of shares of the acquirer's stock that will be exchanged for each share of the target's stock. Once the exchange ratio is fixed, the target's shareholders bear the risk of the acquirer's shares potentially declining in value. For example, the market may react negatively to the announcement of the transaction (see Valuation in Practice 16.2), causing the acquirer's share price to decline. In order to mitigate this risk, **floors** are sometimes included in the deal terms, meaning that the deal will not take place if the acquirer's share price falls below a certain amount or that the **exchange ratio** will have to be adjusted. On the other hand, if the acquirer's share price rises substantially, the acquirer may want to be protected against paying more than a desired maximum amount. In this case, a **cap** is sometimes included in the deal terms that specifies a maximum price above which the deal will not take place or the exchange ratio will be adjusted. Including a floor and a cap in the deal terms creates what is known as a **collar**. If the deal simply has a fixed exchange ratio with no collar, then the consideration that will ultimately be received is linearly related to the acquirer's share price. If the deal is for a fixed value, the ultimate number of shares that will be issued is uncertain, which will move inversely with the acquirer's share price. Naturally, merging parties can use different variations of floors, caps, and collars to protect each party from certain types of risks.

A **material adverse change clause (MAC)** allows the acquirer to rescind the deal if the target's business experiences certain types of contractually specified negative effects. When an acquirer invokes this clause, the target often disagrees with the acquirer's conclusion that a MAC occurred and either negotiates a settlement with the acquirer or initiates a legal proceeding to force the acquirer to purchase the company. A well-known MAC lawsuit involved Enron in the month prior to its filing for bankruptcy. Enron was supposed to be acquired by Dynegy, but a few days after the merger was announced, Enron announced a major restatement of its financial statements. A few weeks later, Dynegy indicated that it would not proceed with the acquisition and relied on the MAC clause to do so. Enron sued, but the case was eventually dropped.

In many acquisitions, the parties agree to **termination fees** (or **breakup fees**) in case one of the parties fails to close the transaction (unless certain conditions are met that allow one side to terminate the deal). Termination fees are meant to compensate the other party for its costs as well as to invoke a penalty in order to make sure that both parties close. Bates and Lemmon (2003) study termination fees and find that, on average, the fee is approximately 3% of the deal value. They also find that if the contract contains a termination fee, a higher incidence of deal completion is observed. In their sample (which ended in the late 1990s), termination fees paid to the acquirer by the target were much more prevalent than termination fees paid by the acquirer to the target.[15] Interestingly, in a few more recent transactions, the deal terms allowed the target to require the acquirer to pay a large termination fee if the acquisition was blocked by antitrust authorities, effectively imposing all of the antitrust risk on the acquirer (see Valuation in Practice 16.4).

A **no shop clause** or a **no solicitation** or **exclusivity provision** prevents a target from pursuing offers from other potentially interested parties for a specified amount of time—usually 45 to 60 days. The rationale for a "no shop" clause is that once a letter of intent is signed, the acquirer will expend considerable time and resources for due diligence, arranging financing and other activities, and a no shop clause provides the buyer some protection. A **go shop** clause gives the target an opportunity to continue shopping for another buyer. A "go shop" clause allows the target company to actively pursue higher bidders and better offers; however, the target's board of directors can always consider unsolicited offers to meet its fiduciary duty to shareholders. This is particularly important if the company has neither been shopped extensively nor been through an auction process. From the acquirer's perspective, this reduces the likelihood that the target will be sued by its shareholders, which can be costly and lead to delays in closing the transaction. Of course, it also increases the probability of the target identifying a higher competing bid.

---

[15] Bates, T., and M. Lemmon, "Breaking Up Is Hard to Do? An Analysis of Termination Fee Provisions and Merger Outcomes," *Journal of Financial Economics* 69 (2003), pp. 469–504.

Valuation in Practice 16.4

The $3.5 Billion Termination Fee Paid in the Halliburton Company and Baker Hughes Incorporated Proposed Merger One example of a very large termination fee is the Halliburton-Baker Hughes merger, a merger of two of the world's top oil-services companies.[16] In November 2014, Halliburton Company and Baker Hughes Incorporated entered into a plan of merger in a stock plus cash merger. Each share of Baker Hughes common stock would receive 1.12 shares of Halliburton common stock plus $19.00 in cash. The deal was valued at $35 billion. Baker Hughes's board was not initially interested in the merger because of concerns that the merger would not be approved by the regulatory agencies. Halliburton, who believed it could achieve over $2 billion in cost savings annually, agreed to a $3.5 billion termination fee if the merger could not close because it was legally prohibited from doing so or if it could not meet the divestiture conditions required by the regulators by a specified date. Baker Hughes agreed to pay a $1.5 billion termination fee if the company board rescinded its recommendation to its stockholders to approve the merger, if the company entered into a definitive agreement with another company offering a better price, or if the company's stockholders did not approve the merger.

It turned out that U.S. regulators sued to stop the merger and the proposed merger was eventually terminated in 2016 and Halliburton paid Baker Hughes a $3.5 billion termination fee.

A **lock-up right** gives an acquirer the right to buy shares at a specified price if another party acquires the company. The price is often set at the current market value (or lower) at the time the lock-up right is executed. Targets often give lock-up rights to friendly buyers in an attempt to thwart a takeover by an unfriendly suitor. Asset lock-up rights give an acquirer the ability to buy certain assets or divisions if another buyer acquires the company. These rights are also used to thwart takeover attempts by unfriendly suitors.

Valuation Key 16.4

The specific form of a transaction can affect the value of the target to the bidder and the value that the target shareholders will receive. Taxes are a major consideration in the design of the deal structure. The bidder's valuation of the target and the target's valuation of the offer must consider the tax consequences of the deal. In addition, the deal structure affects both the liabilities that the acquirer is assuming and the status of the target's existing contracts. Contract provisions also affect who bears certain risks in a transaction.

16.4 SYNERGIES

LO2 Identify and value synergies

Synergies result from combining the operations of the two companies resulting in free cash flows that are higher than when the companies operate as separate, **standalone**, companies. If achieved, synergies increase the value of the post-merger company above the sum of the values of the standalone companies. In general, there are two types of synergies—increases in revenues and reductions in costs, or cost efficiencies. Revenue and cost synergies result from some of the economic forces that motivate M&A transactions. Synergies can also reduce required investments. It is also possible to have financial synergies, but these are not as common and are usually small in magnitude.

Valuation Key 16.5

A synergy is a change in the performance of the post-merger company as a result of combining the assets (both tangible and intangible) of the two companies. Synergies are typically increases in performance that result from increases in revenues and/or decreases in costs.

It is relatively easy to generate ideas about the potential synergistic effects of an acquisition. However, forecasting synergies with a reasonable degree of accuracy and then capturing them after

[16] Halliburton Company is one of the world's largest providers of products and services to the energy industry with over 50,000 employees and operating in approximately 70 countries. Baker Hughes Incorporated is a global supplier of oilfield services, products, technology and systems in the oil and natural gas industry and provides industrial products and services in the chemical products and other industries. See the companies' various U.S. SEC filings from November 2014 through June 2016 available at www.sec.gov.

the merger is not easy. Many cost efficiencies are more easily quantified than revenue synergies, but both can be difficult to forecast and difficult to achieve. Naturally, not all of the value creation that is expected to occur in a merger results from combining the assets of the two companies—for example, replacing bad management could create value without any synergies, but it is a result of the merger. It is also possible for non-synergistic value creation to occur by acquiring a company, breaking it up into different pieces, and selling the pieces, never integrating it into any of the acquirer's operations. In this case, the acquisition has no synergistic value—only value from breaking the company up into more sensible component businesses.

Cost Efficiency Synergies

Cost efficiency synergies (or cost efficiencies) are cost reductions that result from combining the operations of two companies. A company can gain cost efficiencies if it can use its fixed costs to support a larger scale of operations. A company can also gain cost efficiencies if it can lower its variable costs, which typically results from economies of scale or scope. Naturally, if two companies are combined, the surviving company only needs one chief executive officer, one chief financial officer, one treasury function, one legal department, and so forth. Moreover, it only needs one board of directors and one corporate headquarters; thus, combining two companies eliminates these costs even though the company might need additional layers of management as a result of the increase in the company's scale, or the legal department might need more attorneys than the acquiring firm currently has to service the expanded corporation. The costs of being a public company include the costs of following regulatory rules and regulations, holding annual meetings, maintaining investor relations, and so forth, which decrease as a result of two public companies combining.

When companies combine, they have a variety of ways to share their existing infrastructures and other fixed costs in order to reduce their post-merger cost structure. Companies can share research and development functions to reduce headcount and share patents in order to increase patent utilization. They may also share production facilities in order to gain better capacity utilization, share distribution channels and sales forces in order to reduce headcount and increase productivity, and share infrastructures (such as software platforms, delivery systems, back office services, and marketing costs) in order to reduce headcount and other costs.

Another type of cost reduction results from more efficient procurement. To the extent that companies negotiated different prices for different goods and services (office supplies, computer equipment, travel, manufacturing components, etc.), costs can be reduced by adopting the least expensive pricing for both companies. In addition, an increase in scale may provide the company with more market power over its suppliers, leading to further cost reductions.

Companies may also be able to lower combined income taxes by using, for example, foreign income tax credits or net operating loss carryforwards that are not being utilized. A recent survey by Deloitte reports most companies believe they achieved the synergies expected from the transaction and were able to achieve those synergies within two years of the transaction closing. The survey also reported that income tax effects were an important part of the synergies in about 50% of the transactions.[17]

Revenue Synergies

Companies can share distribution channels and brands in order to better promote the products of the other company. It is possible that the target or the acquirer has better marketing or a better sales force than the other, in which case they can increase revenues after the companies are combined. Acquirers often characterize international acquisitions as a way of gaining quicker access to international markets. Sharing brands or customer lists in order to grow revenues into a new customer base—especially globally—is another common type of revenue synergy. These revenue synergies are called **cross-selling** in which the acquirer sells its products to the customers of the target, and the target sells its products to the customers of the acquirer. Other revenue synergies result from better product innovation, for example, from combined research and development efforts.

---

[17] McGee, Tom, Trevear Thomas, and Russell Thomson, *Deloitte Integration Report 2015—Putting the Pieces Together*, Deloitte Development Company LLC.

Valuation Key 16.6

Cost efficiency synergies include savings from eliminating redundant costs such as the C-suite (CEO, CFO, etc.), a board of directors, and public company costs. They also occur from cost sharing, additional market power with suppliers, and technology sharing. Revenue synergies can result from brand sharing, as well as sharing distribution channels and customer lists, and other cross-selling approaches. Revenue synergies are generally harder to forecast and achieve than cost synergies.

Financial Synergies

We know a company can create value by issuing debt if it can capture the benefits of the resulting interest tax shields. If the target company is, for some reason, underutilizing debt in its capital structure, the acquirer can increase value by financing an acquisition with debt and moving the target to its optimal capital structure. We know that part of the value creation associated with leveraged buyouts is related to the highly levered capital structures (see Chapter 15). Such an increase in value is not a synergy per se, for this increase in value can be achieved independently of the acquisition, but it can still create value that results from a merger.

Valuation in Practice 16.5

Synergies in the LATAM Airlines Group Merger

In 2012, LAN Airlines S.A. (LAN), a Chilean company; TAM S.A. (TAM), a Brazilian company; and their respective controlling shareholders entered into an exchange offer agreement and an implementation agreement in order to combine LAN and TAM to form LATAM Airlines Group S.A. According to both companies, the businesses of LAN and TAM were highly complementary from both a geographic and business line perspective.

The companies expected to achieve substantial synergies and cost reductions by coordinating flights at their hubs. By harmonizing the flight schedules of LAN's and TAM's complementary passenger networks, LATAM was expected to be able to offer better services to its customers in the form of more connections, more travel alternatives, new destinations, extended lounge access, and more extensive frequent flyer programs. LAN expected all of this to result in increased passenger revenues and better benefits to customers. The companies also expected the merger to create substantial opportunities for LATAM's international cargo business by optimizing the cargo network, creating efficiencies and cost savings in the cargo business through coordinated freight planning, sharing best practices, and deploying new routes with the combination of passenger and cargo revenue. LAN estimated that the combined synergies arising from the proposed combination could increase LATAM's annual operating income (before depreciation and taxes) over time by \$600 million to \$700 million. Of the total expected annual pre-tax synergies, between \$170 million and \$200 million is achievable within the first year after the transaction's completion. Approximately 40% of the total potential synergies were expected to be generated from increased revenues from the passenger business, 20% to be generated from increased revenues from the cargo business, and the remaining 40% of the potential synergies to be generated from cost savings.

Source: Offer to Exchange Each Common Share, Preferred Share and American Depositary Share of TAM S.A. for 0.90 of a Common Share of LAN AIRLINES S.A. Represented by American Depositary Shares or Brazilian Depositary Shares dated May 10, 2012—see pp. 142–145.

A financial synergy results if the merger reduces the combined weighted average cost of capital. All else equal, we know that a company's cost of capital will decrease if it can reduce its operating leverage. If the combination allows the ratio of fixed to variable costs to decline due to economies of scale, operating leverage should fall. If the overall operating leverage declines, the company's risk decreases, assuming everything else remains constant. Another way to reduce the cost of capital is to reduce financial distress costs. If a target company is facing high financial distress costs, combining the target company with a complementary acquiring company can reduce the target company's financial distress costs and, in turn, reduce its cost of capital.

Synergy Uncertainty

Some synergies are more quantifiable than others are, and most synergies have at least some degree of uncertainty associated with their magnitude and timing. Some of the factors that affect this uncertainty are the innate achievability of the synergy, the cost of achieving the synergy, and the ability of the companies to create a feasible plan to capture the synergy. For example, eliminating the C-suite of the target company is quantifiable and definite, but the cost of closing plants or the effect of increased market power with suppliers may be difficult to estimate precisely. In addition, even though a reduction in headcount (from combining research and development departments) is both quantifiable and relatively certain, quantifying the revenue synergies from new products is much more difficult and uncertain, and forecasting how much business the customers of both companies will do with each other is also difficult and uncertain.

Even though some cost efficiencies are quantifiable and relatively certain, the time needed to achieve all the synergies and how long the synergies will last are both uncertain. Moreover, to the extent that they are achievable, revenue synergies may take longer to achieve than many types of cost savings. It may also be useful to consider how long each synergy will result in a competitive advantage as their effect may dissipate over time. For example, if an industry is consolidating and capturing scale economies, an acquirer is likely to see margin improvements if it is on the leading edge of that consolidation. However, after the industry has consolidated, and once the scale economies have been captured by its competitors, it is possible that prices will decrease, reducing margins until they return to the level that just sustains the industry. Thus, the increase in profit margins associated with the cost synergies may not be sustainable. On the other hand, if the merging companies are lagging behind the consolidation within the industry, prices may already reflect the industry consolidation and the effect of the synergies may be ongoing.

Valuing Expected Synergies from Amberjack Inc.'s Example Acquisition of Tarpon Inc.

In this section we illustrate the valuation of synergies by valuing the expected synergies from Amberjack Inc.'s acquisition of Tarpon Inc. Amberjack offered Tarpon's shareholders 1.25 shares of Amberjack stock for each share of Tarpon stock in a stock-for-stock acquisition. Amberjack is a steady-state company with free cash flows growing at the inflation rate. Pre-merger data for Amberjack and Tarpon are presented in Exhibit 16.7. More specifically, it shows Tarpon's pre-merger production capacity (tons), revenue, EBIT and unlevered free cash flows; as well as Amberjack's EBIT. Amberjack expects to create value from this transaction by decreasing Tarpon's costs and increasing Tarpon's capacity (and revenues) more quickly than they would have increased otherwise.

EXHIBIT 16.7 Selected Pre-Merger Data for Amberjack Inc. and Tarpon Inc.

Selected Pre-Merger Data	A2017	F2018	F2019	F2020	F2021	F2022	F2023	F2024	F2025	F2026	F2027	F2028
Tarpon's pre-merger capacity	200	204	208	212	216	221	225	230	234	239	244	250
Tarpon's pre-merger revenue	$4,000.0	$4,182.0	$4,372.3	$4,571.2	$4,779.2	$4,996.7	$5,224.0	$5,461.7	$5,710.2	$5,970.0	$6,241.7	$6,560.4
Tarpon's pre-merger EBIT	$ 300.0	$ 313.7	$ 327.9	$ 342.8	$ 358.4	$ 374.7	$ 391.8	$ 409.6	$ 428.3	$ 447.8	$ 468.1	$ 492.0
Tarpon's pre-merger unlevered free cash flow	$ 320.0	$ 334.6	$ 349.8	$ 365.7	$ 382.3	$ 399.7	$ 417.9	$ 436.9	$ 456.8	$ 477.6	$ 499.3	$ 590.4
Amberjack EBIT	$ 566.5	$ 583.4	$ 603.9	$ 625.0	$ 639.1	$ 653.4	$ 668.1	$ 683.2	$ 698.5	$ 714.3	$ 730.3	$ 746.8

Measuring Expected Cost Efficiencies, Revenues Synergies, and Integration Costs.

In Exhibit 16.8, we present synergy drivers and the resulting synergy free cash flow effects (2018 through 2028) for this acquisition. As shown in the exhibit, Amberjack expects to decrease Tarpon's costs in three ways. First, Amberjack expects to decrease Tarpon's overhead costs by $50 million in 2018 by eliminating certain executive positions and the board of directors, and public company related costs. Tarpon previously expected these costs to have increased at expected inflation. Second, Amberjack expects to reduce Tarpon's cost of goods sold by 2% by using some of its excess capacity and producing Tarpon's products at Amberjack's lower production cost structure, which yields a savings in 2018 of $50.18 million, and which grows every year. Third, Amberjack expects to reduce Tarpon's general, selling, and administrative expenses by 5% by using its logistics platform and distribution network resulting in a first year savings of $36.59 million, which also grows every year. The exhibit presents the free cash flow effect for each of these synergies.

EXHIBIT 16.8 Selected Forecast and Synergy Drivers for Amberjack Inc.'s Acquisition of Tarpon Inc.

Selected Forecasts and Synergy Drivers	A2017	F2018	F2019	F2020	F2021	F2022	F2023	F2024	F2025	F2026	F2027	F2028
Synergy drivers:												
Expected inflation	2.5%	2.5%	2.5%	2.5%	2.5%	2.5%	2.5%	2.5%	2.5%	2.5%	2.5%	2.5%
Production—reduction in cost of goods sold	%CGS	2.0%	2.0%	2.0%	2.0%	2.0%	2.0%	2.0%	2.0%	2.0%	2.0%	2.0%
Logistics and distribution—decreased cost	%SG&A	5.0%	5.0%	5.0%	5.0%	5.0%	5.0%	5.0%	5.0%	5.0%	5.0%	5.0%
Labor harmonization—increased cost	%SG&A	−4.0%	−4.0%	−4.0%	−4.0%	−4.0%	−4.0%	−4.0%	−4.0%	−4.0%	−4.0%	−4.0%
Synergy free cash flow effects (in millions):												
Reduce overhead (including public company costs)		$ 50.00	$ 51.25	$ 52.53	$ 53.84	$ 55.19	$ 56.57	$ 57.98	$ 59.43	$ 60.92	$ 62.44	$ 64.00
Production—reduction in cost of goods sold		$ 50.18	$ 55.22	$ 60.48	$ 67.29	$ 68.97	$ 70.69	$ 72.46	$ 74.27	$ 76.13	$ 78.03	$ 79.98
Logistics and distribution cost reduction		$ 36.59	$ 40.27	$ 44.10	$ 49.06	$ 50.29	$ 51.55	$ 52.84	$ 54.16	$ 55.51	$ 56.90	$ 58.32
Labor harmonization—increased cost		−$ 29.27	−$ 32.21	−$ 35.28	−$ 39.25	−$ 40.23	−$ 41.24	−$ 42.27	−$ 43.33	−$ 44.41	−$ 45.52	−$ 46.66
Faster expansion—change in free cash flows			−$ 87.36	−$ 120.00	$ 122.33	$ 117.55	$ 112.29	$ 106.53	$ 100.24	$ 93.38	$ 85.92	$ 9.45
Other forecasts (in millions except capacity data):												
Tarpon's post-merger capacity	200	204	219	234	254	254	254	254	254	254	254	254
Change in EBIT from change in capacity	$ 0.0	$ 0.0	$ 17.2	$ 35.1	$ 62.1	$ 56.3	$ 50.0	$ 43.3	$ 35.9	$ 28.1	$ 19.6	$ 7.9
Tarpon's post-merger revenue	$4,000.0	$4,182.0	$4,601.7	$5,039.8	$5,607.4	$5,747.6	$5,891.2	$6,038.5	$6,189.5	$6,344.2	$6,502.8	$6,665.4

Amberjack expects Tarpon to incur higher labor costs as a result of the merger because the salaries of some of Tarpon's employees will be increased to the higher Amberjack salaries. The salary increase is equal to 4% of general, selling, and administrative expenses of the post-merger general, selling, and administrative expenses or an additional cost of $29.27 million in 2018, which will also grow every year as shown in the exhibit. Because Amberjack has more human and financial capital than Tarpon, it also expects to create value by expanding Tarpon's capacity (and revenues) more quickly than Tarpon would have. Amberjack believes that Tarpon has the capacity to sell 254 million tons of its product. It currently has 200 million tons of capacity. The exhibit presents the post-merger forecasts for the number of tons of capacity and the free cash flow effects of the faster expansion. Lastly, Amberjack expects the merger integration to take two years and to incur tax deductible merger integration costs of $200 million in 2018 and $150 million in 2019.

In Exhibit 16.9, we present four charts that present the pre- and post-merger forecast for capacity, revenues, EBIT, and unlevered free cash flow resulting solely from the capacity expansion. The difference between the two lines on each of the charts represents the difference in the pre- and post-merger for each of these four measures of scale and performance based on the capacity increase. The charts show that the increase in capacity has a corresponding increase in revenues and EBIT. However, the effect on unlevered free cash flows is not the same. The faster growth requires more capital expenditures, which in turn reduces the post-merger unlevered free cash flows during the higher growth period, 2019 and 2020. Afterwards, the capacity expansion causes the post-merger unlevered free cash flows to be higher than the pre-merger unlevered free cash flows until 2028, when the capacity, revenues, earnings, and unlevered free cash flows are the same.

Valuing the Synergies, Net of Integration and Other Costs. In Exhibit 16.10, we value the synergies Amberjack expects from the acquisition of Tarpon based on the cash flow effects of the synergies shown in Exhibit 16.8. The selected forecasts and synergy drivers in Exhibit 16.8 provide much of the information required to value the expected synergies. Other information required includes the cost of capital for each of the synergies, which we assume is 10%, the income tax rate for each of the synergies, which we assume is 40%, and the long-term growth rate for each of the synergies, which we assume is expected inflation. The past capital structure strategy for both companies and the post-merger capital structure is 25% debt and 75% common equity, resulting in a weighted average cost of capital for the pre- and post-merger companies of 10%. We separate the value of the net synergies into three components—cost efficiencies (overhead, production, and logistics and distribution cost reductions) net of integration costs, the cost of harmonizing the labor across the two companies, and the revenue synergies.

The present value of the cost efficiencies (overhead, production, and logistics and distribution cost reductions), net of integration costs is $1,057.7 million (Panel A). The present value of the cost of harmonizing the labor across the two companies is $283.8 million (Panel B), resulting in a present value of the net cost efficiencies of $773.9 million. The present value of the revenue synergies is equal to $280.3 million (Panel C), which almost offsets the negative synergy from harmonizing the labor across the two companies and results in the value of all of the net synergies and integration costs of $1,054.2 million (Panel D).

EXHIBIT 16.9 Effects of Tarpon Inc.'s Faster Expansion Resulting from the Acquisition

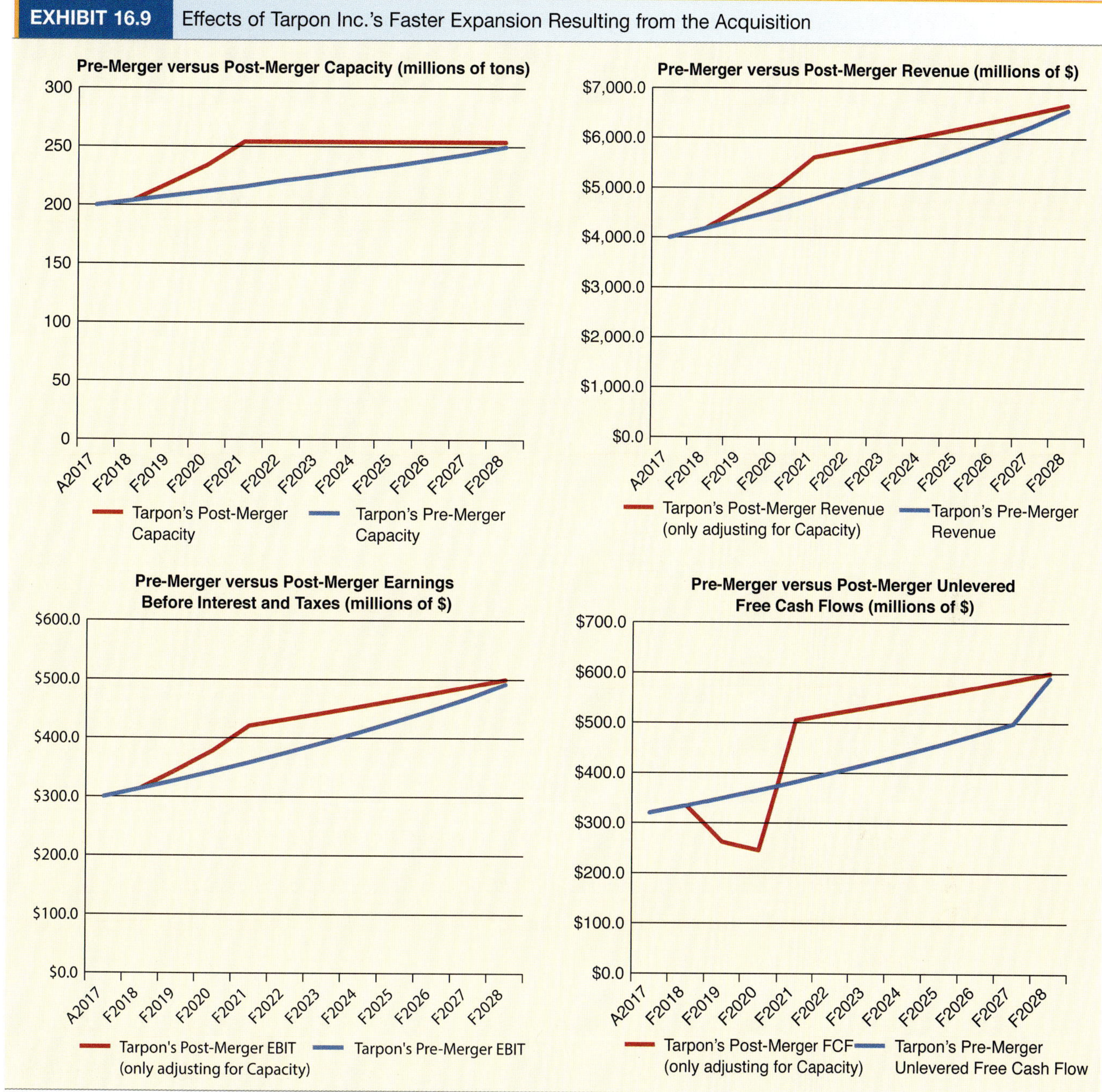

In this valuation, we assume that the cost synergies continue in perpetuity. Earlier in this section we discussed the potential issues associated with making this assumption. In Exhibit 16.11, we present the cumulative present value of the net cost efficiencies (line with blue diamonds), the revenue synergies (line with red dots), and the total of the net synergies (dark blue bars). The chart shows that the cumulative present value of the net cost efficiencies is not positive until 2021and that the cumulative present value of the faster expansion synergies is not positive until 2023. The result is that the cumulative present value of all of the net synergies is not positive until 2022. After 2023, the cumulative present value of the synergies increases as the cumulative present value of both the net cost efficiencies and revenue synergies increase.

EXHIBIT 16.10 Valuation of Expected Net Synergies from the Amberjack Inc. / Tarpon Inc. Acquisition

In millions, except Per Share data	A2017	F2018	F2019	F2020	F2021	F2022	F2023	F2024	F2025	F2026	F2027	F2028
Panel A—Valuation of Overhead, Production Logistic and Distribution Cost Efficiencies (Synergies) Net of Integration Costs:												
Continuing value growth rate												2.50%
Reduce overhead (including public company costs)		$ 50.0	$ 51.2	$ 52.5	$ 53.8	$ 55.2	$ 56.6	$ 58.0	$ 59.4	$ 60.9	$ 62.4	$ 64.0
Production—reduction in cost of goods sold		50.2	55.2	60.5	67.3	69.0	70.7	72.5	74.3	76.1	78.0	80.0
Logistics and distribution cost reduction		36.6	40.3	44.1	49.1	50.3	51.5	52.8	54.2	55.5	56.9	58.3
Merger integration costs		−200.0	−150.0									
Pre-tax cost efficiencies		−$ 63.2	−$ 3.3	$157.1	$170.2	$174.5	$178.8	$183.3	$187.9	$192.6	$197.4	$ 202.3
Income tax	40.0%	25.3	1.3	−62.8	−68.1	−69.8	−71.5	−73.3	−75.1	−77.0	−79.0	−80.9
Change in unlevered free cash flows (FCFs)		−$ 37.9	−$ 2.0	$ 94.3	$102.1	$104.7	$107.3	$110.0	$112.7	$115.5	$118.4	$ 121.4
Perpetuity factor												13.333
Change in free cash flows and continuing value		−$ 37.9	−$ 2.0	$ 94.3	$102.1	$104.7	$107.3	$110.0	$112.7	$115.5	$118.4	$1,618.5
Discount factor		0.909	0.826	0.751	0.683	0.621	0.564	0.513	0.467	0.424	0.386	0.386
Present value	$1,057.7	−$ 34.5	−$ 1.6	$ 70.8	$ 69.7	$ 65.0	$ 60.6	$ 56.4	$ 52.6	$ 49.0	$ 45.7	$ 624.0
Panel B—Valuation of Long-Term Labor Harmonization Costs:												
Continuing value growth rate												2.50%
Labor harmonization—increased cost		−$ 29.3	−$ 32.2	−$ 35.3	−$ 39.3	−$ 40.2	−$ 41.2	−$ 42.3	−$ 43.3	−$ 44.4	−$ 45.5	−$ 46.7
Income tax	40.0%	11.7	12.9	14.1	15.7	16.1	16.5	16.9	17.3	17.8	18.2	18.7
Labor harmonization—after tax		−$ 17.6	−$ 19.3	−$ 21.2	−$ 23.6	−$ 24.1	−$ 24.7	−$ 25.4	−$ 26.0	−$ 26.6	−$ 27.3	−$ 28.0
Perpetuity factor												13.333
Change in free cash flows and continuing value		−$ 17.6	−$ 19.3	−$ 21.2	−$ 23.6	−$ 24.1	−$ 24.7	−$ 25.4	−$ 26.0	−$ 26.6	−$ 27.3	−$ 373.3
Discount factor		0.909	0.826	0.751	0.683	0.621	0.564	0.513	0.467	0.424	0.386	0.386
Present value	−$ 283.8	−$ 16.0	−$ 16.0	−$ 15.9	−$ 16.1	−$ 15.0	−$ 14.0	−$ 13.0	−$ 12.1	−$ 11.3	−$ 10.5	−$ 143.9
Panel C—Valuation of Faster Expansion of Capacity and Increased Growth:												
Continuing value growth rate												2.50%
Faster expansion—change in free cash flows		$ 0.0	−$ 87.4	−$120.0	$122.3	$117.5	$112.3	$106.5	$100.2	$ 93.4	$ 85.9	$ 9.4
Perpetuity factor												13.333
Change in FCFs and continuing value		$ 0.0	−$ 87.4	−$120.0	$122.3	$117.5	$112.3	$106.5	$100.2	$ 93.4	$ 85.9	$ 126.0
Discount factor		0.909	0.826	0.751	0.683	0.621	0.564	0.513	0.467	0.424	0.386	0.386
Present value	$ 280.3	$ 0.0	−$ 72.2	−$ 90.2	$ 83.6	$ 73.0	$ 63.4	$ 54.7	$ 46.8	$ 39.6	$ 33.1	$ 48.6
Panel D—Valuation of All Synergies:												
Present value of all synergies	$1,054.2	−$ 50.5	−$ 89.8	−$ 35.2	$137.2	$123.0	$110.0	$ 98.1	$ 87.2	$ 77.3	$ 68.3	$ 528.7

EXHIBIT 16.11 Cumulative Valuation of Expected Synergies from the Amberjack Inc./Tarpon Inc. Acquisition

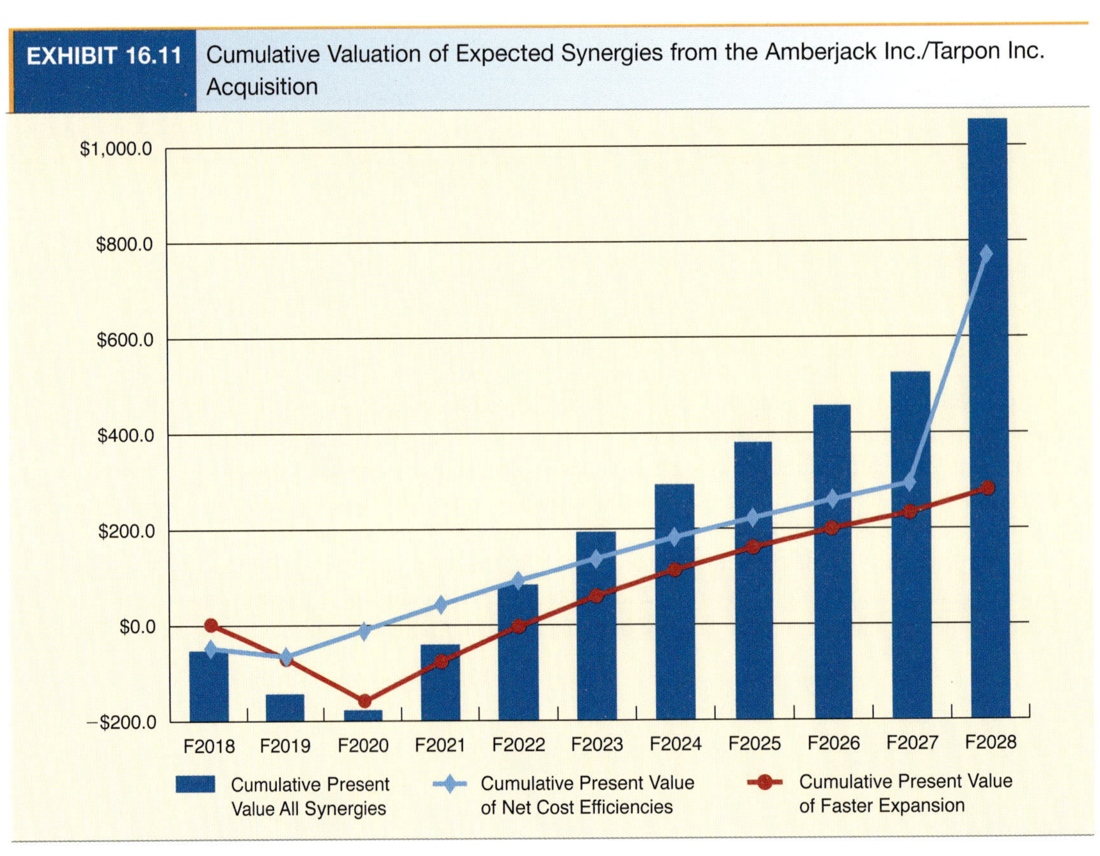

The chart illustrates the effect of assuming a constant growth perpetuity for the cost efficiencies and harmonization of the labor costs. The constant growth perpetuity for the net cost efficiencies increases the present value of all of the synergies by roughly 100%, from $525.6 million (F2027) to $1,054.2 million (F2028, which includes the continuing value estimate of the net synergies). Thus, assuming competition forces Amberjack to decrease prices in 2027 such that the price decrease eliminates the net benefit of all the synergies afterward, the value of the synergies is only $525.6 million. Given the uncertainty of the timing and magnitude of at least certain synergies, we should consider various scenarios or potential outcomes that might occur. For example, eliminating the benefit of all the synergies after 2022 results in a value of all of the synergies of only $84.7 million.

REVIEW EXERCISE 16.1

Valuing Synergies—LATAM Airlines Group

Use the following information (taken from the offering memorandum) to measure the value of the synergies for the LAN and TAM merger discussed in Valuation in Practice 16.5. After the completion of the proposed combination, the breakdown of the expected range of annual pre-tax synergies was estimated to be as follows (realized in full in the fourth year after the merger):

- Increased revenues—$225 million to $260 million from the combination of passenger networks and $120 million to $125 million from the combination of cargo services.
- Cost savings—$15 million to $25 million from the consolidation of frequent flyer programs; $100 million to $135 million from the coordination of airport and procurement activities; $20 million to $25 million from the coordination and improved efficiency of maintenance operations; and $120 million to $130 million from the convergence of information technology systems, the increased efficiency of combined sales and distribution processes, and the increased efficiency in corporate overhead costs.

LAN and TAM expected the one-time merger costs—including banking, consulting, and legal advisory fees—to be between $170 million and $200 million. LAN expected a reduction of approximately $150 million in working capital from not having to inventory as many engines and spare parts, which was expected to be fully realized at the end of 2013.

Use the midpoint of the synergy forecasts in the calculations. Assume that all synergies are actual cash flows, that LATAM's average income tax rate is 30%, and that fees are deductible in 2012. Further assume that 28.5% of the annual synergies will be achieved by the end of the first year after the merger (2013), that 50% of the annual synergies will be achieved by the end of the second year after the merger (2014), that 80% will be achieved by the end of the third year (2015), and 100% will be achieved by the end of the fourth year. Further, assume that the synergies will begin to erode at a rate of 10% per year, beginning in the fifth year after the merger. The weighted average cost of capital for valuing the synergies is 10%. Calculate the value of the synergies as of mid-year 2012, which we assume is the merger close date. Thus, the end-of-year 2012 cash flows are only a half-year away and so on for subsequent years. Examine the sensitivity of the value of the synergies to variation in the weighted average cost of capital between 9% and 11% and to variation in the continuing value growth rates between −20% and 0%.

Solution on pages 849–850.

16.5 OVERVIEW OF HOW TO VALUE MERGER AND ACQUISITION TRANSACTIONS

LO3 Value and analyze an M&A deal

The value of a post-merger company after completing an M&A transaction is equal to the sum of the values of the standalone companies plus the value of the synergies and other efficiencies created, minus the present value of the costs associated with the transaction and integration adjusted for tax and other considerations. In general, we value M&A transactions with all the same valuation methods and processes discussed in previous chapters, but now, we also need to measure the value of the synergies, efficiencies, and costs associated with the transaction and integration. We also consider the tax effects of the transaction and other relevant elements of the deal structure. The typical valuation methods used include the discounted cash flow method and the market multiples method. Market multiple valuations are based on comparable transactions or on publicly traded comparable companies adjusted for a merger premium. Discounted cash flow valuation models have more ability to value specific synergies and the other effects on cash flows than market multiple valuation methods. We briefly discuss the methods used to value an acquisition (from the acquirer's perspective) before discussing the types of techniques used by investment bankers in rendering fairness opinions; we then discuss the valuation issue from the target's perspective. We also discuss control premiums (minority discounts) and liquidity premiums (illiquidity discounts).

The Acquirer's Perspective on Valuation

The first step is to value the target on a standalone basis as it is currently being operated. If the company is publicly traded, this valuation can be compared to the company's market value. Understanding the market's valuation is useful as the market price already builds in expectations of future growth and profitability prospects expected by the market. The standalone value is the bid that would leave the target shareholders no better or worse off assuming that they did not have to pay any income taxes as a result of the transaction.

In order to answer the question of how much value the transaction can create, we first must understand how the acquirer intends to utilize the target. We measure the increase in value by valuing the incremental cash flows from operating the target more efficiently than it was operated previously, plus the incremental cash flows from the synergies, minus the incremental cash flows for integration and transaction costs. The acquisition might also have an effect on how the acquirer manages itself, which would also be considered in the valuation of the acquisition. As indicated previously, we measure all incremental cash flows on an after-tax basis and include all relevant incremental income taxes related to the transaction.

Market multiple valuations are based on either precedent transactions or publicly traded companies (adjusted for merger premiums). These analyses, however, are more useful for understanding what price might be acceptable to the target and not for estimating the value of the combined companies to the acquirer. Thus, a market multiple valuation may help inform the negotiation process and provide input into the likelihood of a target accepting an offer at a certain price, but these analyses do not provide a clear indication of how the target company will create value for the acquirer—that perspective normally comes from a discounted cash flow (DCF) valuation. Recent premiums or valuations based on precedent transactions can provide some, albeit limited, guidance from which a range of reasonable values for the synergies from the current deal might be gauged.

From the acquirer's perspective, the negotiating range for the transaction is between two values. The minimum value is equal to the standalone value of the target as it is currently operating (assuming the transaction is tax free to the target and its shareholders). The maximum value is equal to the target's standalone value plus the value of the net synergies. If the acquirer's bid is equal to the maximum value, the expected net present value of the acquisition (or the value created) for the acquirer will be zero. In other words, the investment will simply earn its cost of capital. As such, in order to create value, the acquirer must submit a bid that is less than the maximum value as defined earlier. At the other end of the range, the target is unlikely to accept a bid equal or even close to its standalone value, especially if the transaction is taxable to the target shareholders.

The Target's Perspective on Valuation

While the parties might not agree on the value of the acquisition, the target and acquirer use standard valuations methods—the discounted cash flow method, market multiples of publicly traded companies (adjusted for merger premiums), a premium analysis, the market multiples from precedent transactions, and a leveraged buyout analysis. Naturally, the target company's management, board of directors, and shareholders want to know that the offer is reasonable; indeed, it is the fiduciary responsibility of the board and officers, and they will look extensively at other transactions involving similar companies and even at other transaction types (such as a leveraged buyout) in order to make this determination. Thus, targets often rely more heavily on market-based valuations (to the extent that they are reasonably comparable), for these valuations rely more heavily on the market prices of other transactions.

Publicly traded target companies (and often larger private companies with minority shareholders) hire financial advisors to render a fairness opinion for any offer that the target expects to accept. As discussed in Chapter 1, the practice of securing a fairness opinion has been common since the Van Gorkom case (see Valuation in Practice 1.5). The board of directors also uses other information to assess the fairness of any offer. For example, if the company is extensively shopped to potential buyers, yet no other bids emerge, the board of directors will have a better idea of the likelihood that higher bids can be obtained.

In a stock-for-stock transaction, we must value the acquirer with the target on a post-transaction basis. Since the target shareholders are receiving stock in the acquirer, we need to value the acquirer post-transaction to understand the offer being made to the target shareholders. Without performing this valuation, we do not have any basis for even understanding if the target shareholders are being offered a premium.

In the merger of ACS and Xerox (see Section 16.9), the fairness opinions rendered by the advisors for both companies utilized various valuation methods and conducted other analyses. The analyses included analyses of the stock trading history of both companies, deal premiums, precedent transaction premiums, and valuations based on precedent transaction multiples, public company trading multiples, analysts' forecasts of future projected prices, discounted cash flow, and a leveraged buyout analysis.

Valuation Key 16.7

Acquirers rely most heavily on a discounted cash flow analysis to measure the value of the target and the related net synergies to the acquirer. However, the acquirer also knows that the target and its financial advisors rely on a variety of valuation methods and merger premium analyses to assess the fairness of a deal. Hence, the other valuation methods we discuss throughout the book inform the acquirer of the likely offer a target might expect to receive and be willing to accept.

Control Premiums (Minority Discounts)

Minority discounts (the inverse of **control premiums**) may occur when a company has diffusely held ownership. Agency cost theory suggests that because of the inherent conflict between a company's management and its owners, the shares of such a company can trade at a lower price than if the manager owned 100% of the company.[18] A control premium—as it relates to mergers and acquisitions—is the increase in value that results from reducing or eliminating the agency costs that result from the inherent conflict between managers and owners. The factors underlying a control premium include the power to elect directors, appoint management, set compensation, control the company's strategy, and make investment decisions. If an acquirer purchases more than 50% of the voting interest in a target company, the acquirer will own a controlling interest. When an acquirer has a controlling interest, it will gain control over decision making in that company. With more than 50% of the voting power in the target company, the owner of the controlling interest has the power to make all decisions for the company and, thus, has control over the target company's activities.

Control alone, however, does not imply the elimination or even a reduction of agency costs. For example, if a publicly traded target that has diffuse ownership is acquired by a publicly traded acquirer that has diffuse ownership, the agency costs may either stay the same, increase, or decrease, depending on the relative effectiveness of the governance structures of the target and acquirer. If the target has a governance structure that controls agency costs more efficiently than the acquirer's governance structure, a purchase of the target by that acquirer may not lead to a reduction in agency costs. In other words, the control value results from the ability to replace poorly performing management that is not maximizing the value of the firm.

A minority discount is the inverse of a control premium. For example, assume that the value of a company's stock is $10 per share when the company is optimally managed (no agency costs) and $8 per share when the company's shares are diffusely held and the company is managed suboptimally. The control premium in this example is 25% ($0.25 = \$10/\$8 - 1$), and the minority discount is 20% ($0.2 = 1 - \$8/\$10$). Thus, the control premium (CP) and the minority discount (MD) are related in the following way: $MD = CP/(CP + 1)$. In our example, the minority discount is $0.2 = 0.25/1.25$.

Should M&A valuations include a control premium, or, in other words, should M&A valuations exclude a minority discount? If so, how do we measure them? It is not at all apparent if an acquirer purchases a control position in a target company, whether the acquirer should include a control premium in its valuation. As stated earlier, whether or not an increase in value from control results from the transaction depends on the relative effectiveness of the target and acquirer to control agency costs.

---

[18] See, for example, Jensen, M., and W. Meckling, "Theory of the Firm: Managerial Behavior, Agency Costs, and Ownership Structure," *Journal of Financial Economics* 3 (1976), pp. 305–360. Conflicts between groups of shareholders can also exist, and another type of control premium can occur when a shareholder has a majority ownership position and control of the shares. This type of control premium is based on the assumption that control provides the ability of the controlling shareholder to engage in self-dealing, which occurs when a controlling shareholder benefits at the expense of minority shareholders.

If we value a target company using a discounted cash flow valuation based on free cash flow forecasts that include the effect of any change in agency costs after the acquisition, we do not adjust for a minority discount or control premium because the discounted cash flow valuation already incorporates the extent to which agency costs will persist or are eliminated after the acquisition.

Now consider a valuation of a target that is based on market multiples measured using publicly traded and diffusely owned comparable companies. Assume for a moment that the extent of any agency costs or ineffective governance structure affects the value of a firm but not any of the denominators used in the multiple valuation. Some might argue that the valuation implicitly includes a minority discount (excludes a control premium), but that depends on the effectiveness of the governance structure of the comparables used in the multiples valuation. The value of the target will exceed the multiple valuation if the governance structure of the target post-transaction is more effective than the governance structure of the comparables used in the market multiple valuation and if the agency costs only affect the numerator. However, it is important to recognize that if both the numerator and the denominator of a market multiple are impacted by a minority discount in identical proportions (for example, both value and earnings are 10% lower), it is possible that the market multiples will not be affected by minority discounts or ineffective governance at all. Cornell (2013) develops an economic model and concludes that in order to estimate the value of a company exclusive of the added value associated with synergies that may be realized in an M&A transaction, no upward adjustment of a comparable company market multiple valuation is required to account for control.[19]

Some argue that in order to assess the control premium, the valuations of publicly traded comparable companies should be increased by the typical premiums paid in mergers. It is important to note that observed merger premiums do not equal control premiums; in fact, for the reasons discussed earlier, it is possible for a bid to not include any control premium even when the merger premium is large. It is incorrect to conclude that merger premiums merely reflect control premiums. Rather, merger premiums often reflect the fact that some of the synergy gains are allocated to the target shareholders in a transaction. Indeed, if you recall our review of the studies on whether M&A activity creates value for acquirers and targets, empirical evidence suggests that, on average, all economic gains from mergers (and maybe more than 100% of the gains) are given to the target shareholders. In addition, some of the premiums can also be compensation to the target shareholders for the taxes they will have to pay in a transaction.

The takeaway from this discussion is that we want to be careful when we "tack on" control premiums in valuations in an M&A setting and if we do, we use company specific information to measure the control premium. Moreover, it is misguided to think that merger premiums are synonymous with control premiums, for merger premiums also reflect the synergies that are allocated to the target shareholders in the deal price.

Valuation Key 16.8

A control premium—as it relates to mergers and acquisitions—is the increase in value of a company's equity that results from the elimination or reduction of agency costs inherent in the conflict between managers and owners. The factors underlying a control premium include the power to elect directors, appoint management, set compensation, control the company's strategy, and make investment decisions. A minority discount is the inverse of a control premium. Control premiums do not equal the premium paid in a merger as some of that premium represents the value of the synergies allocated to the target shareholders.

Liquidity Premiums (Illiquidity Discount)

Liquidity premiums, **illiquidity discounts**, or **discounts for non-marketability** are concepts related to how much time it takes to sell an asset and the cost of selling it. All else equal, investors prefer to hold assets that can be sold quickly at a price that reflects their underlying value when sold without undue time pressure.[20] We cannot observe liquidity premiums (or illiquidity discounts) directly; thus, researchers attempt to estimate illiquidity discounts based on empirical analysis.

Researchers estimate illiquidity discounts using various indirect approaches. One approach is to compare the prices of restricted stocks (stocks that cannot be sold for some time period—say, three years)

[19] Cornell, Bradford, "Guideline Public Company Valuation and Control Premiums: An Economic Analysis," *Journal of Business Valuation and Economic Loss Analysis* vol. 8, no. 1 (2013), pp. 53–70.

[20] This concept of liquidity is discussed in Keynes, J., *A Treatise on Money*, Vol. 2, London (1930).

to the prices of freely traded stocks for companies that have both types of stocks.[21] Another approach examines private stock issuances in private companies just prior to the company going public through an initial public offering (IPO) in order to estimate the difference between the prices paid in the private equity transaction and the IPO. Another approach compares transaction multiples for privately held company M&A transactions to publicly held company M&A transactions.[22] Unfortunately, the results from these studies do not converge to provide a straightforward way of adjusting value for illiquidity discounts, as the discounts measured in these studies vary.

Together, the results of these studies show that illiquidity discounts vary over time and across estimation methods. In general, these studies do not examine illiquidity discounts by industry, so we do not have many insights into whether these discounts vary across industries. However, the studies consistently document the existence of illiquidity discounts, which can have implications for how we value an entity. Longstaff (2001) uses an option valuation approach to measure the illiquidity discount, and he begins by examining an investor's inter-temporal portfolio choice when the investor's trading is restricted;[23] he shows that a 35% illiquidity discount is plausible. The research documents differences between public company and private company transaction multiples, suggesting the potential existence of illiquidity discounts for privately held companies. On the other hand, these differences may be due to systematic differences between public and private companies.

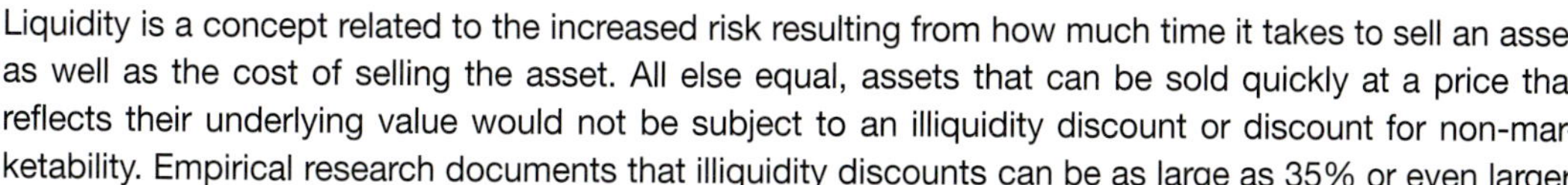

Valuation Key 16.9

Liquidity is a concept related to the increased risk resulting from how much time it takes to sell an asset as well as the cost of selling the asset. All else equal, assets that can be sold quickly at a price that reflects their underlying value would not be subject to an illiquidity discount or discount for non-marketability. Empirical research documents that illiquidity discounts can be as large as 35% or even larger.

De Franco et al. (2011)[24] estimate cross-sectional regressions, controlling for growth, size, and profit margin in the estimation of private company discounts, and they show discounts between 20% and 40%. Interestingly, they show that having a Big 4 auditor mitigates this discount (or, in other words, the discount is even worse for private companies with non-Big 4 auditors). Of course, this does not mean that every company should hire a Big 4 auditor if it wants to be sold, for there are costs associated with hiring a Big 4 auditor in terms of additional audit fees, additional costs of personnel, additional internal control costs, and so forth.

In general, the discounted cash flow and market multiple valuation methods do not include an illiquidity discount. Generally, the discounted cash flow approach does not include illiquidity discounts because it uses a cost of capital measured from publicly traded stocks. We have no asset pricing model for private and illiquid companies. As such, in order to apply an illiquidity discount, one has to calculate the "as-if" public company equity value and then apply a discount to the equity value. Market multiples for public companies would also generally not include an illiquidity discount. Transaction multiples from private companies may include synergies and control premiums, and may or may not include illiquidity discounts. However, if the synergies and potential control premiums are the same in public company and

[21] For restricted stock studies, see Wruck, K. H., "Equity Ownership Concentration and Firm Value: Evidence from Private Equity Financings," *Journal of Financial Economics* vol. 23, no. 1 (1989), pp. 3–28; Silber, William L., "Discounts on Restricted Stock: The Impact of Illiquidity on Stock Prices," *Financial Analysts Journal* (July–August 1991), pp. 60–64; Hertzel, Michael, and Richard L. Smith, "Market Discounts and Shareholder Gains for Placing Equity Privately," *Journal of Finance* (1993), pp. 459–485; Pratt, Shannon P., *Business Valuation Discounts and Premiums*, 2nd ed., New York, NY: John Wiley and Sons (1999); Bajaj, Mukesh, David J. Denis, Stephen P. Ferris, and Atulya Sarin, "Firm Value and Marketability Discounts," *Journal of Corporate Law* (2001); and Barclay, M. J., C. G. Holderness, and D. P. Sheehan, "Private Placements and Managerial Entrenchment," *Journal of Corporate Finance* 13 (2007), pp. 461–484.

[22] For private company sales transactions see, Koeplin, J., A. Sarin, and A. Shapiro, "The Private Company Discount," *Journal of Applied Corporate Finance* vol. 12, no. 4 (2007), pp. 94–101; Officer, M. S., "The Price of Corporate Liquidity: Acquisition Discounts for Unlisted Targets," *Journal of Financial Economics* vol. 83, no. 3 (2007), pp. 571–98; Paglia, J. K., and M. Harjoto, "The Discount for Lack of Marketability in Privately Owned Companies: A Multiples Approach," *Journal of Business Valuation and Economic Loss Analysis* vol. 5, no. 1 (2010), Article 5; and De Franco, G., I. Gavious, J. Y. Jin, and G. D. Richardson, "Do Private Company Targets that Hire Big 4 Auditors Receive Higher Proceeds?" *Contemporary Accounting Research* 28 (2011), pp. 215–262.

[23] Longstaff, Francis A., "Optimal Portfolio Choice and the Valuation of Illiquid Assets," *Review of Financial Studies* 14 (2001), pp. 407–431.

[24] De Franco, G., I. Gavious, J. Y. Jin, and G. D. Richardson, "Do Private Company Targets that Hire Big 4 Auditors Receive Higher Proceeds?" *Contemporary Accounting Research* XX (2011), pp. 1–48.

private company transaction multiples, and if other determinants are controlled for as well (growth, profitability, etc.), the difference between the multiples may give an estimate of the private company discount, especially when the buyer is a private company as well.

The resolution of this issue is unclear. We should consider several factors when we are deciding whether to include an illiquidity discount. For example, if we are valuing a private company because it is about to issue publicly traded stock in an IPO, we would not include an illiquidity or private company discount, as it is going public. In the case in which a private company is being purchased by a public company, the public company might argue that there should be a discount for non-marketability, but the private company will likely argue that once it is acquired, it will no longer be private. Obviously, the resolution of this debate depends on the relative negotiating power of the two parties, which will likely be influenced by the number of potential acquirers interested in acquiring the private company. To include an illiquidity discount, we estimate its magnitude by relying on some of the extant empirical evidence.

16.6 IS THE MERGER AND ACQUISITION TRANSACTION ACCRETIVE OR DILUTIVE?

In addition to valuing the company using the methods we discussed earlier, managers also analyze the effect of a potential transaction on the post-merger company's earnings and other performance measures. These managers may be concerned about the effects of the transaction on the company's debt covenants, compensation agreements, and other contracts, or they may be concerned with the difficulty of explaining to analysts and investors why a merger is value increasing when the common measures of performance—such as earnings per share—are not accretive (increasing). The focus of this section is on measuring the accretive or dilutive (decreasing) effect of a transaction on earnings per share. We can, of course, examine whether a transaction is accretive to value or to something other than earnings per share, but earnings per share is often used for analyzing accretion and dilution. Managers of public companies are interested in knowing what the likely effect is on earnings per share so that they can provide investors with information on the likely earnings impact, which can be negative in the short run even if the transaction creates value.

Accretive and Dilutive Effects on Earnings and Other Performance Measures

To analyze a transaction's accretive or dilutive effects on an acquirer, we create a financial model and measure various performance metrics for the post-merger company. The financial model can be as simple as measuring the effect of the transaction on earnings or as complex as creating a complete and detailed financial model for the entire post-merger company.

To measure the accretion or dilution of earnings before interest and taxes and earnings per share, we begin with the financial statements of the standalone companies. We measure any financing costs that affect earnings and the related income tax effects in order to measure the after-tax financing costs. Some of these costs might be short term (bridge financing), but some may be long term (long-term debt issued to finance the transaction). In addition, the financing might involve the use of excess cash, the after-tax proceeds from the sale of excess assets (the assets that do not fit the post-merger strategy of the company), or newly issued shares. We also adjust the financials for revenue and cost synergies, other efficiencies, integration costs, and other costs of the transaction. We then measure the post-merger earnings on an after-tax basis and adjust the number of shares outstanding of the acquirer if the acquirer issues stock as part of the transaction to measure the post-transaction earnings per share. We then compare the relevant metric (earnings or earnings per share) of the acquirer with and without the transaction.

Accretion and Dilution of Amberjack Inc.'s Earnings per Share. In this section, we measure the accretion or dilution of Amberjack's earnings per share resulting from its acquisition of Tarpon. As discussed previously, Amberjack offered Tarpon's shareholders 1.25 shares of Amberjack stock for each share of Tarpon stock in a stock-for-stock acquisition. Recall Amberjack is a steady-state company with free cash flows growing around inflation. Also remember in Exhibit 16.8, we presented selected forecasts for both companies and synergy drivers prepared by Amberjack for this acquisition and in

Exhibit 16.10 we calculated the effects of these synergies on the company's cash flows and post-merger value. Also, recall that the cost of capital for each of the synergies, which is equal to both companies' weighted average cost of capital, is 10% for all synergies; the income tax rate for each of the synergies is 40%; the long-term growth rate for each of the synergies, which we assume is equal to expected inflation, is 2.5%; and the past capital structure strategy for both companies and the post-merger capital structure is to finance the company with 25% debt and 75% common equity.

In Exhibit 16.12, we measure the 2020 post-merger earnings by combining the companies' standalone income statements and adjusting the combined income statements for the synergies. We illustrate this calculation for 2020 because this is the first year without integration costs. The first two columns of the exhibit present the standalone income statements for each company, and the third column is equal to the combination of the standalone companies. The combined company is the post-merger company without any synergies. Operating income is equal to the sum of the operating incomes of the two companies. Earnings per share is equal to the sum of the incomes available to common shareholders divided by the post-merger shares. Since the post-merger shares (650) is equal to the acquirer's shares (400) plus the target's shares multiplied by the exchange ratio (200 × 1.25), instead of the sum of the pre-merger shares, earnings per share is not equal to the weighted average of the two standalone earnings per share. In this acquisition, the post-merger earnings per share without synergies is equal to $0.594 ($0.594 = $385.9/650). The resulting earnings per share is smaller than the earnings per share of either company ($0.594 versus $0.630 and $0.668) because the 1.25 exchange ratio increased the number of post-merger shares. Thus, the merger is dilutive to Amberjack's earnings per share without the synergies, meaning that Amberjack's earnings per share would go down post-transaction without synergies.

EXHIBIT 16.12 Accretion (Dilution) of Amberjack Inc.'s 2020 Earnings per Share

In millions, except per share data	Amberjack	Tarpon	Combined	Faster Expansion	Overhead	Production	Logistics & Dist	Labor Costs	Synergy Total	Post Merger	%
Sales	$10,000.0	$4,571.2	$14,571.2								
Cost of goods sold and occupancy costs	6,000.0	2,742.7	8,742.7			−$60.5					
Gross profit	$ 4,000.0	$1,828.5	$ 5,828.5								
Selling, general and administrative expenses	1,875.0	800.0	2,675.0		−$52.5		−$44.1	$35.3			
Depreciation and amortization	1,250.0	571.4	1,821.4								
Other expenses	250.0	114.3	364.3								
Operating income	$ 625.0	$ 342.8	$ 967.8	$35.1	$52.5	$60.5	$44.1	−$35.3	$157.0	$1,124.8	16.2%
Interest expense	204.7	120.1	324.7							324.7	
Income before income taxes	$ 420.3	$ 222.8	$ 643.1						$157.0	$ 800.1	24.4%
Provision for income taxes	168.1	89.1	257.2						62.8	320.0	
Net income	$ 252.2	$ 133.7	$ 385.9						$ 94.2	$ 480.0	24.4%
Preferred stock dividends											
Income available to common shareholders	$ 252.2	$ 133.7	$ 385.9						$ 94.2	$ 480.0	24.4%
Earnings per share	$ 0.630	$ 0.668	$ 0.594						$0.145	$ 0.739	24.4%
Weighted average shares outstanding	400.0	200.0	650.0	1.250		Exchange Ratio			650.0	650.0	

Exhibit may contain small rounding error

The next five columns in the exhibit present the effect of the synergies on earnings. Exhibit 16.8 provides the effect of the faster expansion on EBIT, which is not equal to the effect on unlevered free cash flows as well as the effects of the other synergies and costs from the merger. The resulting increase in operating income from the net synergies is $157.0 million, which is an increase of 16.2% relative to the combined company. After deducting income taxes, the increase in net income from the net synergies is $94.2 million and the per share increase is $0.145, which is an increase of 24.4% relative to the combined income. The percentage increase in net income is higher than the percentage increase in operating income because interest expense does not increase from the synergies because this is a stock-for-stock acquisition. Had the consideration paid in the acquisition included a cash payment and the acquirer issued debt to finance that payment, then any additional financing cost (such as interest) would be deducted from the synergies.[25] Finally, the resulting earnings per share increases from $0.594 for

[25] We note that because the value of Amberjack has gone up by more than the standalone value of Tarpon because of the value of the synergies (see Exhibit 16.10), the company may issue additional debt at some point if it wishes to maintain the assumed debt-to-value ratio of 25%. This increase in debt is usually not considered in accretion and dilution analysis, though we could do so. Had additional debt been issued to fund the transaction, that additional debt is normally considered.

the combined company to \$0.739 for the post-merger company with synergies (\$0.739 = \$480.0/650 = \$0.594 + \$0.145); thus, the transaction will be accretive to Amberjack's earnings per share in 2020 (\$0.630 versus \$0.739). Often, the acquirer is most concerned about whether the transaction is accretive relative to its standalone EPS at the time of the transaction. In this case, Amberjack's EPS increases from \$0.575 to \$0.739, an increase of 28.5%. Thus, the 2020 EPS is accretive relative to Amberjack's 2017 standalone EPS.

In Exhibit 16.13, we present a chart of the post-merger earnings per share forecasts and Amberjack's standalone earnings per share. The red line with dots presents Amberjack's standalone actual earnings per share for 2017 and a forecast of its standalone earnings per share for 2018 through 2028. Amberjack's earnings per share on a standalone basis increases from \$0.575 in 2017 to \$0.749 in 2028, which is an average growth rate about equal to expected inflation during this period of 2.5%. The post-merger earnings per share begins in 2018 at \$0.473 and increases to \$0.739 in 2020 (see Exhibit 16.12). The lower earnings per share in 2018 and 2019 results from the merger integration costs incurred in the first two years after the merger, thus the merger is dilutive to earnings per share in the first two years. The post-merger earnings per share increases to \$0.922 by 2028. Thus, the merger is accretive to Amberjack's earnings per share beginning in 2020. The increase from Amberjack's 2017 earnings per share of \$0.575 to the post-merger 2028 earnings per share of \$0.922 has an average growth rate of 4.4%.

EXHIBIT 16.13 Accretion (Dilution) of Amberjack Inc.'s Earnings per Share, 2018–2028

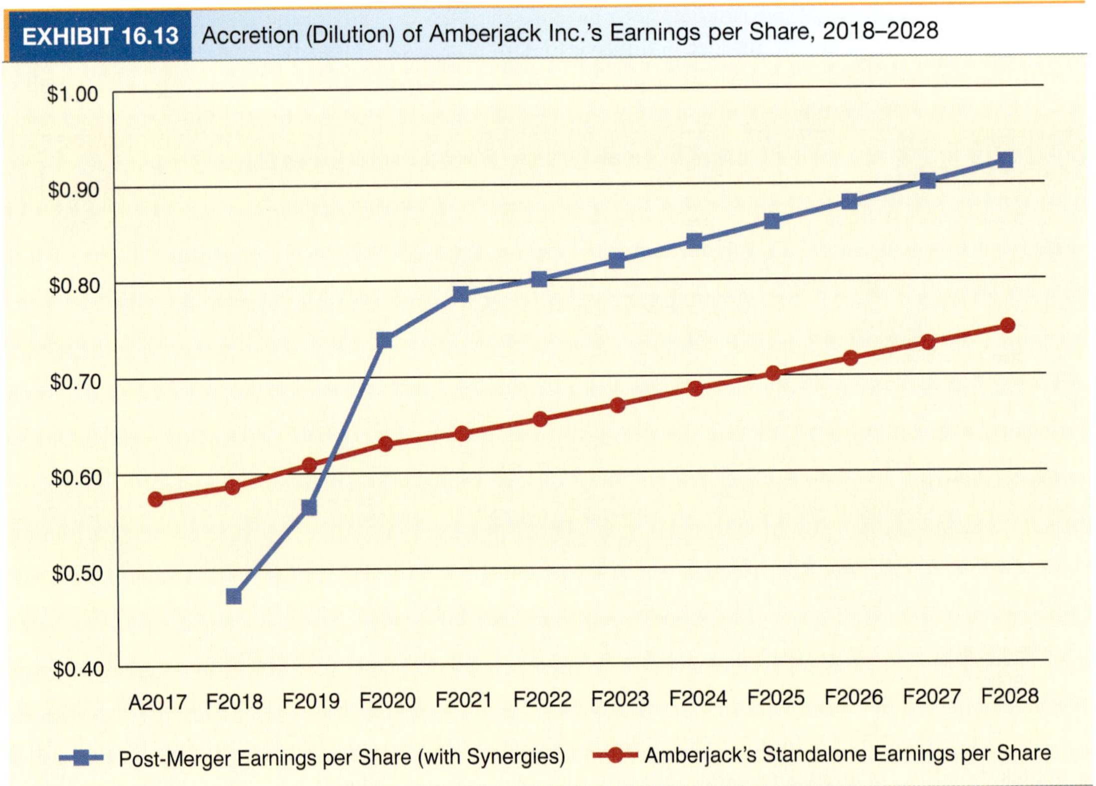

Valuation Key 16.10

In addition to assessing the effect of an M&A transaction on value, acquiring managers often assess the accretive or dilutive effects of the transaction on performance measures such as earnings per share. To measure the accretive or dilutive effects of a transaction, we create a financial model of the post-merger company and examine the effect of the merger on various performance measures. The post-merger company includes both standalone companies and the effects of the transaction on these companies (synergies, transactions costs, integration costs, etc.).

REVIEW EXERCISE 16.2

Measuring Earnings Accretion

A company (the acquirer) purchased another company (the target) for a 20% premium over the target's stock price of $25 per share; the acquirer's stock price at that time was $23 per share. The acquirer financed the transaction with $4,000 of excess cash and $2,000 of debt, the latter of which had a 6% cost of capital and interest rate. The interest tax shields from the incremental debt were valued at $400. As a result of the merger, the companies expected to be able to annually increase revenues by $30 and decrease expenses by $270 for some period; in total, these synergies were valued at $1,500. The company planned to amortize any purchase premium at an average rate of 4.5% per year, which is tax deductible, and the resulting tax shelter from this amortization was valued at $150. The reported interest income was all due to the excess cash being used in the transaction. Assume an income tax rate of 40%. Prepare a post-merger income statement and balance sheet (similar to Exhibit 16.12) and analyze the impact on earnings and earnings per share.

	Standalone Acquirer	Standalone Target
Income Statement		
Revenues	$4,000.0	$2,750.0
Operating expenses	−2,280.0	−1,790.0
Interest income	60.0	20.0
Interest expense	−180.0	−60.0
Income taxes	−640.0	−368.0
Earnings	$ 960.0	$ 552.0
Shares outstanding	400.0	200.0
Earnings per share	$ 2.400	$2.760

	Standalone Acquirer	Standalone Target
Balance Sheet		
Excess cash	$ 3,000.0	$1,000.0
Operating assets	8,000.0	5,000.0
Total assets	$11,000.0	$6,000.0
Debt	$ 3,000.0	$1,000.0
Equity	8,000.0	5,000.0
Liabilities and equity	$11,000.0	$6,000.0

Solution on page 850.

Accretive and Dilutive Effects on Market Multiples

Managers may also be concerned with the effect of an M&A transaction on the acquirer's market multiples. Without synergies and with a price for the target equal to its standalone value, the post-merger market multiples of the acquirer are equal to the weighted average of the multiples of the target and the acquirer. The calculation of the post-merger market multiples becomes more complex for a transaction with synergies and when the price paid is greater than the target's standalone value. M&A transactions can affect earnings, value, capital structure, and the number of shares outstanding—all of which can affect the post-merger company's market multiples. Even if a merger has synergies, an increase in earnings per share does not necessarily mean that the merger created value for the acquirer, if an acquirer overpays for the target company (pays more than the value of the standalone target plus the synergies less costs).

Accretion and Dilution of Amberjack Inc.'s Market Multiples. In this section, we measure the accretion or dilution of Amberjack's market multiples resulting from its acquisition of Tarpon. In Exhibit 16.14, we measure the 2020 post-merger EBIT and P/E market multiples by combining the companies' standalone market values, adjusting the combined market values for the value of the synergies, and then dividing the post-merger value by the post-merger earnings measured in Exhibit 16.12. The first two columns of Exhibit 16.14 present the standalone enterprise values of each company, and the third column is equal to the combination of the standalone enterprise values. As we did for Exhibit 16.12, we hold the debt constant and equal to the sum of the combined debt from the combined companies.

EXHIBIT 16.14 Accretion (Dilution) of Amberjack Inc.'s 2020 Market Multiples

					Post-Merger	
In millions	**Amberjack F2020**	**Tarpon F2020**	**Combined 2020**	**Synergies 2020**	**2020**	**% Change**
Panel A—Earnings Before Interest and Taxes Multiple:						
Equity vaue	$ 7,944.2	$4,755.4	$12,699.6	$1,636.7	$14,336.3	
Value of debt	2,648.1	1,585.1	4,233.2		4,233.2	
Firm value.	$10,592.3	$6,340.5	$16,932.8	$1,636.7	$18,569.5	
Cash	−529.6	−317.0	−846.6		−846.6	
Enterprise value	$10,062.7	$6,023.5	$16,086.1	$1,636.7	$17,722.9	10.2%
EBIT	$ 625.0	$ 342.8	$ 967.8	$ 157.0	$ 1,124.8	16.2%
EBIT multiple	16.1	17.6	16.6	10.4	15.8	−5.2%
Panel B—Price-to-earnings Multiple:						
Exchange ratio			1.250			
Shares outstanding	400.00	200.00	650.00	650.00	650.00	
Stock price	$ 19.861	$ 23.777	$ 19.538	$ 2.518	$ 22.056	12.9%
Earnings per share (EPS)	$ 0.630	$ 0.668	$ 0.594	$ 0.145	$ 0.739	24.4%
P/E—Price to EPS	31.5	35.6	32.9	17.4	29.9	−9.3%

Exhibit may contain small rounding error

In Panel A of the exhibit, we calculate the EBIT multiple by dividing enterprise value by the corresponding EBIT in Exhibit 16.14. Amberjack's standalone EBIT multiple is 16.1 and Tarpon's EBIT multiple is 17.6. The combined company's EBIT multiple without including the synergies is equal to the weighted average of the two standalone multiples, 16.6. The post-merger EBIT multiple, which includes the value of the synergies, is 15.8, or 5.2% lower than the combined multiple. We can understand why the post-merger multiple is lower by measuring the multiple for the synergies. The 2020 value of the synergies is $1,636.7 million (sum of the present values of all synergies that are expected after 2020, see Exhibit 16.10 for the expected synergies by year) and the increase in operating income (EBIT) is $157 million. The resulting multiple for the synergies is 10.4. The weighted average of the combined company EBIT multiple of 16.6 and the synergies multiple of 10.4 results in a post-merger EBIT multiple of 15.8, a decrease of 5.2%. As you may recall from Chapters 13 and 14, another way to glean an understanding of the decrease in the post-merger EBIT multiple is to compare the percentage increase in enterprise value resulting from the synergies, 10.2%, to the increase in EBIT, 16.2%. Since EBIT is increasing more than enterprise value, the EBIT multiple decreases by 5.2% $[-0.052 = (1 + 0.102)/(1 + 0.162) - 1]$. Often the acquirer is interested in how the multiple will change from its pre-acquisition standalone value. In this case, Amberjack's EBIT multiple will decrease from 16.1 in 2017 to 15.8 in 2020, a decrease of 1.9%.

We perform the same set of calculations for the price-to-earnings multiple in Panel B of the exhibit. The one difference between the calculation of the EBIT and P/E multiples is that the exchange ratio affects the P/E multiple but not the EBIT multiple since the P/E multiple is based on share price and earnings per share. To measure the P/E multiple for each of the columns in the exhibit, we first measure the per share value and earnings per share. We measured the earnings per share in Exhibit 16.12. We measure the value per share by dividing the equity value in Panel A by the number of shares in Panel B. Amberjack's standalone P/E multiple is 31.5 and Tarpon's standalone P/E multiple is 35.6. The combined company's P/E multiple is 32.9 before considering synergies. The value of the synergies is $2.518 per share and the earnings per share effect of the synergies is $0.145 per share. The resulting multiple for the synergies is 17.4. The weighted average of the combined company P/E multiple of 32.9 and the synergies multiple of 17.4 results in a post-merger P/E multiple of 29.9, a decrease of 9.3% $[-0.093 = (1 + 0.129)/(1 + 0.244) - 1]$. As stated above, the acquirer is often interested in how the multiple will change from its pre-acquisition standalone value. In this case, Amberjack's P/E multiple will decrease from 31.3 in 2017 to 29.9, a decrease of 4.5%.

In Exhibit 16.15, we present a chart of the EBIT and P/E multiple forecasts for both the post-merger company and Amberjack as a standalone company. The red line with diamonds presents Amberjack's standalone actual P/E multiple for 2017 and a forecast of its standalone P/E multiples for

2018 through 2028, and the red line with dots presents Amberjack's standalone actual EBIT multiple for 2017 and a forecast of its standalone EBIT multiples for 2018 through 2028. The two blue lines present the P/E (squares) and EBIT (triangles) multiples for the post-merger company. Both the P/E and EBIT multiples are higher for the post-merger company than Amberjack as a standalone company in 2018 and 2019, which is driven by the lower EBIT and earnings resulting from the integration costs in those years. Then, from 2020 onward, both the P/E and EBIT multiples are lower for the post-merger company than Amberjack as a standalone company. The P/E and EBIT multiples for Amberjack are constant over time because the company is growing at the inflation rate, while the P/E and EBIT multiples of the post-merger companies decline over time because of a decreasing growth rate.

EXHIBIT 16.15 Accretion (Dilution) of Amberjack Inc.'s Market Multiples, 2018–2028

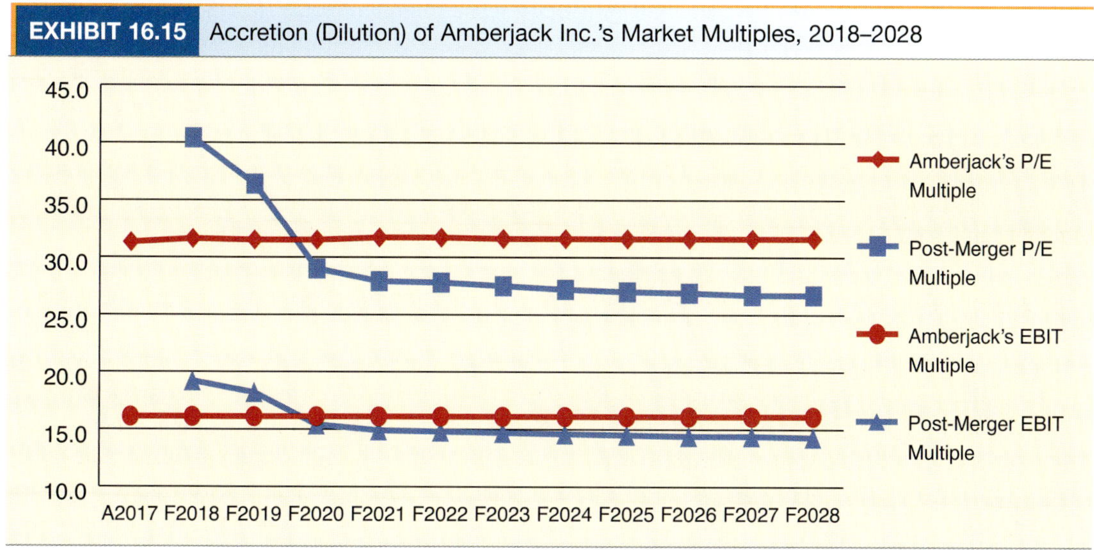

REVIEW EXERCISE 16.3

Effect of Accretion on Market Multiples

Use the information in Review Exercise 16.2 to measure the post-merger firm value, equity value, stock price, and P/E multiple. Compare these values to the acquirer's standalone values.

Solution on page 850.

16.7 CASH-BASED TRANSACTIONS—NEGOTIATION RANGES AND ALLOCATION OF GAINS

LO4 Measure a negotiation range

Naturally, the price paid in an M&A transaction is negotiated based on the value of the equity of the standalone target and the value created by the acquisition, net of all transaction and integration costs. We assume the acquirer and target will not agree to a price that will decrease their pre-merger standalone equity values. In other words, the maximum price that the acquirer will pay is the price at which its equity value is unchanged and the minimum price that the target will accept is the minimum price at which the target's shareholders are not made worse off. Given the post-merger equity value of the company, these constraints set the price range within which the acquirer and target negotiate. For the purpose of our discussion, we ignore deal-related income taxes and other transaction costs the target or its shareholders might have to bear. For example, if the transaction is taxable to the target's shareholders, it is unlikely that they will agree to a transaction that takes place at the target's current standalone value because on an after-tax basis, the target shareholders will be worse off after the transaction. In this section, terms such as standalone value of the acquirer or target, price, post-merger value, and so forth, refer to equity values and not firm values.

Cash Deal

We begin our discussion of negotiation ranges with an example of a cash deal with the following equity values. The standalone values of the target and acquirer are \$1,000 and \$2,000, respectively. Assume that the expected value creation from this acquisition is \$300; however, since the outcome of the merger is uncertain, we assume that the potential outcomes—the value created or destroyed—ranges from a gain of \$1,200 to a loss of \$600. Thus, the value of the post-merger company ranges from \$2,400 to \$4,200 (\$2,400 = \$1,000 + \$2,000 − \$600; \$4,200 = \$1,000 + \$2,000 + \$1,200) with an expected value of \$3,300 (\$3,300 = \$1,000 + \$2,000 + \$300).

The Minimum Price the Target Will Accept. The minimum price that the target shareholders will accept is equal to its standalone equity value, V_T = \$1,000. This minimum value stays constant, independent of the range of potential post-merger outcomes, and the target will never accept a price that is lower than its standalone value. The maximum price that the acquirer will pay is the amount it can pay without reducing its standalone value of \$2,000. This maximum is equal to the post-merger value of the company, minus the standalone value of the acquirer ($V_P - V_A$). The maximum value is a function of the values of the potential outcomes. We show the minimum and maximum prices for a range of possible outcomes in Exhibit 16.16.

The Maximum Price the Acquirer Will Pay. The maximum price is \$1,300 when the value of the synergies is equal to its expected value of \$300 (\$1,300 = \$3,300 − \$2,000). The premium paid to the target is equal to the acquisition price, minus the target's standalone value, $V_{T,\ Premium} = V_{T,\ Paid} - V_T$. The premium paid to the target at this price is \$300 (\$300 = \$1,300 − \$1,000), which is equal to the expected value of the synergies. However, the maximum price—and hence the maximum premium—increases as the value of the expected synergies increases. When the value of the synergies is equal to zero, the maximum and minimum price lines intersect; this is the value neutral point—the point at which the maximum and minimum prices are equal to each other. When the value of the synergies is negative, the maximum value the acquirer will be willing to pay is below the minimum value the target will accept.

EXHIBIT 16.16 Negotiation Strategy Minimum and Maximum Price for a Cash Deal

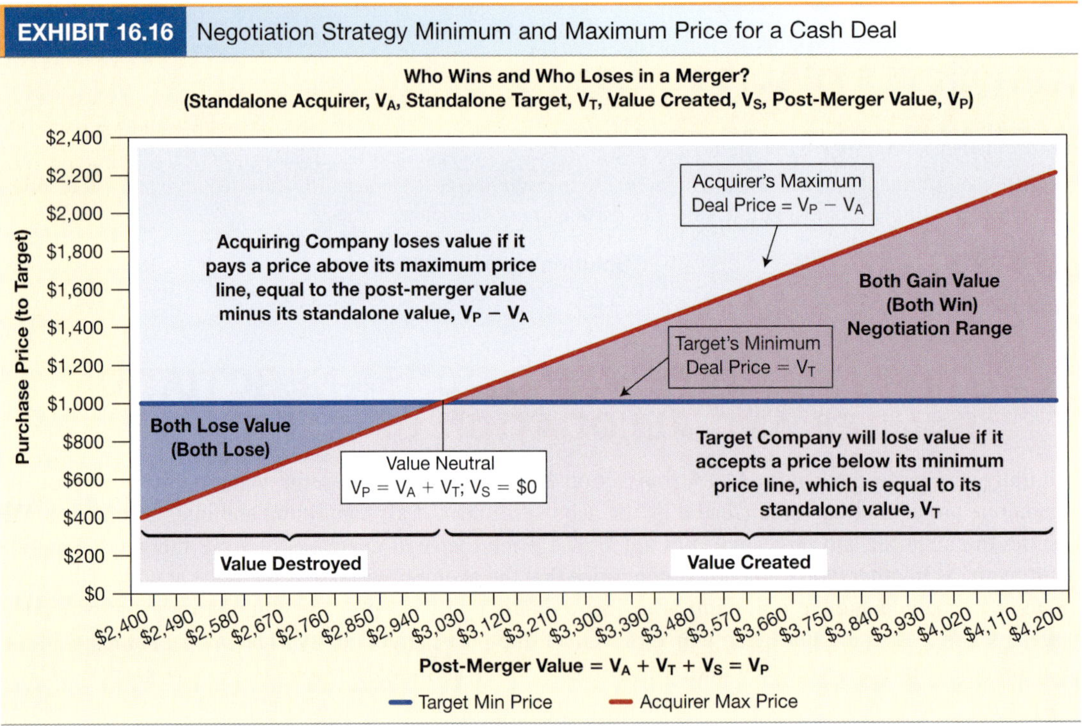

The Negotiation Range. The parties negotiate between the maximum and minimum prices shown in the exhibit. The acquirer increases its value (in expectation) as long as it negotiates a price below its maximum price, and the target increases its value as long as it negotiates a price above its minimum price.

In short, both parties will increase their values as long as they negotiate a price between the minimum and maximum prices; however, this can occur only if the transaction is expected to create value (to the right of the neutral value point in the exhibit). To the left of the neutral value point, one party must lose value in order for the other party to gain value, and it is possible for both parties to lose value.

Deal Risk and the Allocation of Gains and Losses. In cash deals, the acquirer bears all of the deal risk (the uncertainty of the actual outcome of the merger). The upside of bearing all of the deal risk is larger than expected returns if the actual outcome is better than expected; of course, the downside of bearing all of the deal risk is lower than expected returns if the actual outcome is worse than expected. We illustrate this effect with our example. Assume that the negotiated cash price for the target is $1,200—a $200 premium. In the first column of Exhibit 16.17, we present the allocation of the gain from the merger based on the expected value of the synergies of $300. The target captures 67% (0.667 = $200/$300) of the expected gain (20% of its standalone value; 0.2 = $200/$1,000), and the acquirer captures 33% (0.333 = $100/$300) of the expected gain (5% of its standalone value; 0.05 = $100/$2,000).

Since this is a cash deal, the target's gain is 20% of its standalone value regardless of the actual outcome of the merger. In a cash deal, the target does not share in any additional merger gain if the merger turns out to be more valuable than originally expected, nor does it share in any loss if the merger turns out to be less valuable than originally expected. In the next two sets of columns of the exhibit, we illustrate the merger gains and losses when actual outcomes differ from the expected outcome.

The first actual outcome is a merger gain of $800, which is $500 higher than originally expected. Here, the target only captures $200 (25%) of the actual gain (which is, again, 20% of its standalone value), and the acquirer captures $600 (75%) of the actual gain (which is 30% of its standalone value versus the expected 5%). The second actual outcome is a merger loss of −$400, which is $700 lower than originally expected. The target's merger premium remains unchanged at $200, but now, the acquirer suffers the $400 actual merger loss in addition to the $200 premium paid to the target; thus, the acquirer suffers a 30% loss relative to its standalone value (−0.30 = −$600/$2,000) instead of the 5% expected gain.

EXHIBIT 16.17 Allocation of Merger Gain (Loss) for the Cash Deal Example

	Actual Outcome Equals Expected Outcome			Actual Outcome Is Greater Than Expected Outcome			Actual Outcome Is Less Than Expected Outcome		
Cash Deal–Equity Values	**Outcome**	**% Split**	**% Gain**	**Outcome**	**% Split**	**% Gain**	**Outcome**	**% Split**	**% Gain**
Standalone value of acquirer	$2,000			$2,000			$2,000		
Standalone value of target	1,000			1,000			1,000		
Combined standalone value	$3,000			$3,000			$3,000		
Value created (merger gain (loss))	300			800			−400		
Post-merger value	$3,300			$3,800			$2,600		
Overall gain or (loss) on acquisition	$ 300		10.0%	$ 800		26.7%	−$ 400		−13.3%
Post-merger value to target (cash received)	$1,200	36.4%		$1,200	31.6%		$1,200	46.2%	
Standalone value of target	−1,000			−1,000			−1,000		
Gain (loss) to target—merger premium	$ 200	66.7%	20.0%	$ 200	25.0%	20.0%	$ 200	nmf	20.0%
Post-merger value to acquirer	$2,100	63.6%		$2,600	68.4%		$1,400	53.8%	
Standalone value of acquirer	−2,000			−2,000			−2,000		
Gain or (loss) to acquirer	$ 100	33.3%	5.0%	$ 600	75.0%	30.0%	−$ 600	nmf	−30.0%

The point within the negotiation range at which the parties negotiate a final deal price depends on a variety of factors, such as relative bargaining power, market conditions, income taxes, and such agency problems as owner–manager conflicts of interest. For example, all else equal, the target has more negotiating power if it has the ability to create synergies with more than one acquirer. Of course, not all acquirers have the same ability to create synergies with a target. For example, if the acquisition process is competitive, the acquirer with the highest ability to create synergies will most likely win the auction if it pays an acquisition price that is equal to the maximum price of the acquirer with the second highest ability to create synergies (assuming that none of the acquirers is overly optimistic in their forecasts).

Valuation Key 16.11

The target's minimum price is equal to its standalone value, and the acquirer's maximum price is equal to the post-merger value of the company minus the acquirer's standalone value. When the transaction is expected to create value, the negotiation range is the difference between the maximum price the acquirer is willing to pay and the minimum price the target is willing to accept. The parties negotiate within this range, and the final deal price depends on a variety of factors such as relative bargaining power, market conditions, income taxes, and such agency problems as owner-manager conflicts of interest.

REVIEW EXERCISE 16.4

Negotiation and Allocation of Synergies—Cash Deals

The standalone equity values of the target and acquirer are $4,000 and $10,000, respectively. The acquirer has 1,000 shares outstanding, and the target has 2,000 shares outstanding. Assume the expected value creation from this acquisition is $3,000, but since the outcome of the merger is uncertain, assume a set of potential outcomes that ranges from a merger gain of $5,000 to a merger loss of $2,500. Assuming that the acquirer pays $6,000 in cash for the target's equity, calculate the gain or loss to the acquirer and target when the actual outcome of the merger is the expected, highest, and lowest outcome.

Solution on page 851.

16.8 STOCK-BASED TRANSACTIONS—NEGOTIATION RANGES AND ALLOCATION OF GAINS

Not all acquisitions are cash deals. As we discussed earlier in the chapter, acquirers often issue other securities instead of or in addition to cash. In some acquisitions, the acquirer exchanges its stock for the target's stock, called a **stock-for-stock merger**. In a stock-for-stock merger, the target's shareholders exchange their ownership interests for ownership interests in the post-merger company. The number of shares of the acquirer that can be exchanged for one of the target's shares is called the **exchange ratio**. For example, if the acquirer exchanges 1.5 shares of its stock for every share of the target's stock, the exchange ratio is 1.5.

Although the concept of an exchange ratio is straightforward, negotiating it based on the economics underlying the acquisition and deciding on how the gains are to be split between the acquirer and the target can be complex. All else equal, a higher exchange ratio allocates more post-merger shares to the target, which, in turn, allocates a higher proportion of the post-merger value to the target; in other words, a higher exchange ratio results in a higher acquisition price paid to the target shareholders. Analogous to the cash deal, the acquirer will have a maximum exchange ratio that it will offer, and the target will have a minimum exchange ratio that it will accept. However, no one knows with certainty what the price of the acquirer's shares will be after the merger closes. Thus, the parties face uncertainty about the ultimate value of the shares that will be exchanged in the transaction. This is why floors and caps (discussed earlier) are often used in stock-for-stock acquisitions, though floors and caps can only protect the parties through to the close of the transaction.

Minimum and Maximum Exchange Ratios

We begin our discussion with the case of no change in value or zero synergies. When no value is created (no synergies), the maximum and minimum prices will intersect, and thus the minimum and maximum exchange ratios are equal. Once we introduce value creation into the merger, the minimum and maximum prices and the minimum and maximum exchange ratios are no longer the same.

Valuation in Practice 16.6

Exchange Ratio in the LATAM Airlines Group Merger Below are the factors that LAN Airlines S.A. and TAM S.A. (see Valuation in Practice 16.5) considered in determining the exchange ratio:

> To define a range of exchange ratios and implied premiums acceptable to both parties, the parties reviewed the exchange ratios and implied premiums in comparable transactions during the last five years. The comparable transactions were selected after taking into account many different criteria, of which the most important were the industry in which the companies operated, the size of the transaction, board and key management representation, whether the companies continued to operate under their own names or a new or combined name, future headquarters locations, the ultimate relative share ownership of the two groups of shareholders, the form of consideration (e.g., cash, stock or a combination thereof) and whether the synergies were shared proportionally to the new ownership or otherwise. In addition to the criteria described above, the companies were valued using several different quantitative methodologies, including an analysis of the historical relative share trading prices, an analysis of historical and projected multiples of enterprise value to earnings before interest, taxes, depreciation, amortization and rentals based on public information, discounted cash flows based on free cash flow public projections, a contribution analysis and a comparison of research analysts' target prices. Finally, the parties took into account the net present value of estimated synergies and how they should be allocated.

Source: Offer to Exchange Each Common Share, Preferred Share and American Depositary Share of TAM S.A. for 0.90 of a Common Share of LAN AIRLINES S.A. Represented by American Depositary Shares or Brazilian Depositary Shares dated May 10, 2012—see p. 140.

Exchange Ratio with Zero Synergies (No Value Created or Destroyed). Since the acquirer is issuing shares to the target company, the number of shares held by the acquiring shareholders remains fixed. Shares are issued only to the target shareholders. The only way that the allocation of the post-merger company to the acquirer's shareholders will equal the acquirer's standalone value is when the acquirer's post-merger price per share, P_P, equals its pre-merger price per share, P_A ($P_P = P_A$). The value of the acquirer before the merger or standalone value, V_A, is equal to the number of acquirer shares, S_A, multiplied by the pre-merger price per share of the acquirer, P_A ($V_A = P_A \times S_A$). This value must equal the value of the shares of the acquirer's shareholders after the merger—the number of acquirer shares, S_A, multiplied by the post-merger price of the acquirer, P_P, ($P_P \times S_A$).

The minimum exchange ratio that the target is willing to accept is the exchange ratio that results in a post-merger value for the target's shareholders equal to the target's pre-merger or standalone value ($V_T = P_T \times S_T$). The post-merger value for the target's shareholders is equal to the number of shares held by the target's shareholders, multiplied by the exchange ratio and the post-merger price, which is also equal to the acquirer's pre-merger price ($P_P \times S_T \times ER = P_A \times S_T \times ER$). The exchange ratio that results in a post-merger value (for the target's shareholders) equal to the target's standalone value is the ratio of the target's price to the acquirer's price, P_T/P_A:

$$P_T \times S_T = P_A \times S_T \times ER_{MIN=MAX,Synergies=0}$$

$$ER_{MIN=MAX,Synergies=0} = \frac{P_T \times S_T}{P_A \times S_T} = \frac{P_T}{P_A} \tag{16.1}$$

Recall that in the previous (cash deal) example, the standalone values of the target and acquirer are \$1,000 and \$2,000, respectively and the expected value creation is \$300. In addition, now assume that the acquirer has 200 shares outstanding at a price of \$10 per share and that the target has 50 shares outstanding at a price of \$20 per share. If instead of \$300, the merger is expected to be value neutral (no value created), then the minimum exchange ratio the target would accept is equal to the maximum exchange ratio the acquirer would pay and is equal to the ratio of the two stock prices, 2.0 (2.0 = \$20/\$10).

This exchange ratio results in a post-merger value for the shareholders of the target and acquirer that is equal to the standalone values. Multiplying the 2.0 exchange ratio by 50 (the number of target shares) results in 100 shares in the post merger company for the target shareholders. The acquirer has 300 post-merger shares, 200 (66.7%) of which are held by the acquirer's pre-merger shareholders and 100 (33.3%) of which are held by the target's shareholders. If we multiply the post-merger value of \$3,000 (\$3,000 = \$2,000 + \$1,000; recall we assume no value is created) by these ownership percentages, the value of the post-merger shares of the acquirer's pre-merger shareholders is equal to the acquirer's standalone value, \$2,000, and the value of the post-merger shares of the target's shareholders is equal to the target's standalone value, \$1,000.

Minimum Exchange Ratio When Synergies Create Value. The minimum exchange ratio that the target will accept is the exchange ratio that allocates 100% of the value created (or destroyed) to the acquirer. The post-merger price, P_P, is no longer equal to the acquirer's price because the post-merger price includes the value created from the synergies. The post-merger value of the company, V_P, is equal to the post-merger price, P_P, multiplied by the number of post-merger shares, which is equal to the acquirer's shares plus the shares issued to the target's shareholders [$V_P = P_P \times (S_A + S_T \times ER)$]. The minimum exchange ratio that the target is willing to accept is the exchange ratio that results in a post-merger value for the target's shareholders ($P_P \times S_T \times ER$) that is equal to its standalone value ($V_T = P_T \times S_T$). We measure the minimum exchange ratio as follows:

$$P_T \times S_T = P_P \times S_T \times ER_{MIN}$$

$$ER_{MIN} = \frac{P_T \times S_A}{V_P - V_T} = \frac{P_T}{P_A + V_S / S_A} \tag{16.2}$$

Recall that when the value of the synergies, V_S, is equal to zero, the minimum exchange ratio is equal to the maximum exchange ratio, which is equal to the ratio of the target's stock price to the acquirer's stock price. When the value of the synergies is not equal to zero, Equation 16.2 shows that the minimum exchange ratio is equal to the ratio of the target's stock price to the acquirer's stock price, adjusted for the per share effect of the value of the synergies. Thus, when the value of the synergies is positive, the minimum exchange ratio decreases relative to the minimum exchange ratio when the value of the synergies is equal to zero. We show this effect in the example. We now assume the value of the synergies is equal to the expected value of \$300 and that the post-merger value of the company is \$3,300 (\$3,300 = \$2,000 + \$1,000 + \$300). Using this information, the minimum exchange ratio is equal to 1.739. The exchange ratio is lower than in the previous case of zero value created because the post-merger value of the firm is larger.

$$ER_{MIN} = \frac{P_T \times S_A}{V_P - V_T} = \frac{P_T}{P_A + V_S / S_A} = \frac{\$20 \times 200}{\$3{,}300 - \$1{,}000} = \frac{\$20}{\$10 + \$300/200} = 1.739$$

We check our calculation of the exchange ratio in Exhibit 16.18. Multiplying the minimum exchange ratio by 50 (the number of target shares) results in 86.96 shares, which is the amount of stock issued by the acquirer in exchange for the target's stock. The acquirer has 287 post-merger shares, 200 (69.7%) of which are held by the acquirer's original shareholders and 87 (30.3%) of which are held by the target's shareholders. Multiplying the post-merger value by these ownership percentages shows that the value of the post-merger shares of the acquirer's pre-merger shareholders is \$2,300, which is equal to the acquirer's standalone value, plus 100% of the expected synergies. The value allocated to the target's shareholders is \$1,000, which is equal to the target's standalone value. Thus, 1.739 is the minimum exchange ratio the target would accept because a lower exchange ratio would result in a post-merger value for the target's shareholders that is less than the target's standalone value. The resulting stock price is \$11.50, \$1.50 larger per share than the acquirer's pre-merger stock price, reflecting the allocation of all of the synergies to the acquirer's pre-merger shareholders (\$1.50 = \$300/200).

EXHIBIT 16.18 Minimum Exchange Ratio—All Value Created (Destroyed) to Acquirer—Target's Value Is Equal to Its Standalone Value

ER_{MIN}	1.739			
Shares issued to target = $ER_{MIN} \times S_T$	86.96	1.739	50	
Post-Merger—Check	**Shares**	**%**	**Value**	**Price (P_P)**
Acquirer shares (not changed)	200.00	69.7%	\$2,300	\$11.50
Target shares	86.96	30.3%	1,000	\$11.50
Total shares	286.96	100.0%	\$3,300	\$11.50

Maximum Exchange Ratio When Synergies Create Value. The maximum exchange ratio is the exchange ratio that allocates 100% of the merger's gain to the target. Since the acquirer's shareholders are not issued additional shares and we are not allocating any value of the synergies to them, the value of their pre-merger shares must be left unchanged and the post-merger price must be equal to the acquirer's pre-merger price ($P_P = P_A$). Thus, the maximum exchange ratio is the exchange ratio at which the post-merger price is equal to the acquirer's pre-merger price ($P_A = P_P$). The post-merger price of the company, $P_P = P_A$, is equal to the post-merger value of the company, V_P, divided by the post-merger number of shares ($S_A + S_T \times ER$). We can measure this maximum exchange ratio as

$$P_A = \frac{V_P}{S_A + S_T \times ER_{MAX}}$$

$$ER_{MAX} = \frac{V_P - V_A}{P_A \times S_T} = \frac{P_T + V_S/S_T}{P_A} \qquad \textbf{(16.3)}$$

When the value of the synergies is not equal to zero, Equation 16.3 shows that the maximum exchange ratio is equal to the ratio of the target's stock price, adjusted for the per share effect of the value of the synergies, to the acquirer's stock price. Thus, when the value of the synergies is positive, the maximum exchange ratio increases relative to the minimum exchange ratio when the value of the synergies is equal to zero. We show this effect using the prior example. Now, the maximum exchange ratio is equal to 2.6, and the resulting post-merger price, P_P, is equal to P_A ($10).

$$ER_{MAX} = \frac{V_P - V_A}{P_A \times S_T} = \frac{P_T + V_S/S_T}{P_A} = \frac{\$3{,}300 - \$2{,}000}{\$10 \times 50} = \frac{\$20 + \$300/50}{\$10} = 2.6$$

EXHIBIT 16.19 Maximum Exchange Ratio—All Value Created (Destroyed) to Target—Acquirer's Value Is Equal to Its Standalone Value

ER_{MAX}	2.600			
Shares issued to target = $ER_{MAX} \times S_T$	130.00	2.600	50	
Post-Merger—Check	**Shares**	**%**	**Value**	**Price (P_P)**
Acquirer shares (not changed)	200	60.6%	$2,000	$10.00
Target shares	130	39.4%	1,300	$10.00
Total shares	330	100.0%	$3,300	$10.00

We check our calculation of the exchange ratio in Exhibit 16.19. Multiplying the maximum exchange ratio by 50 (the number of target shares) results in 130 shares of the acquirer's stock being issued to the target's shareholders in exchange for the target's stock. The number of post-merger shares is 330, 200 (60.6%) of which are held by the acquirer's original shareholders and 130 (39.4%) of which are held by the target's shareholders. Multiplying the post-merger value by these ownership percentages shows that the value of the post-merger shares of the acquirer's pre-merger shareholders is $2,000, which is equal to the acquirer's standalone value. The value allocated to the target's shareholders is $1,300, which is equal to the target's standalone value, plus 100% of the expected synergies. Thus, 2.6 is the maximum exchange ratio the acquirer would accept because a higher exchange ratio would result in a post-merger value for the acquirer's shareholders that is less than the acquirer's standalone value. The post-merger stock price remains at the acquirer's pre-merger stock price of $10, reflecting the allocation of all of the synergies to the target's shareholders.

Valuation Key 16.12

In some acquisitions, the acquirer's stock is exchanged for the target's stock, called a stock-for-stock merger. The number of shares of the acquirer's stock that is exchanged per share for the target's stock is called the exchange ratio. The exchange ratio affects the acquisition price paid for the target. A higher exchange ratio allocates more post-merger shares to the target, which, in turn, allocates a higher proportion of the post-merger value to the target and thus, a higher price paid for the target.

Exchange Ratio-Based Negotiation Range. We measure the negotiation range by calculating the minimum and maximum exchange ratios at various points within the range of post-merger values. We present a chart of the minimum and maximum exchange ratios for this example in Exhibit 16.20. The maximum exchange ratio increases as the expected value of the post-merger company increases, for all of the synergies are allocated to the target in the calculation of the maximum exchange ratio. The minimum exchange ratio decreases as the value of the post-merger company increases, and this change is non-linear. It decreases, because as the post-merger value of the company increases, the number of shares that are issued to the target's shareholders to maintain the target's standalone value decreases.

EXHIBIT 16.20 Negotiation Strategy Minimum and Maximum Exchange Ratio for a Stock-for-Stock Acquisition

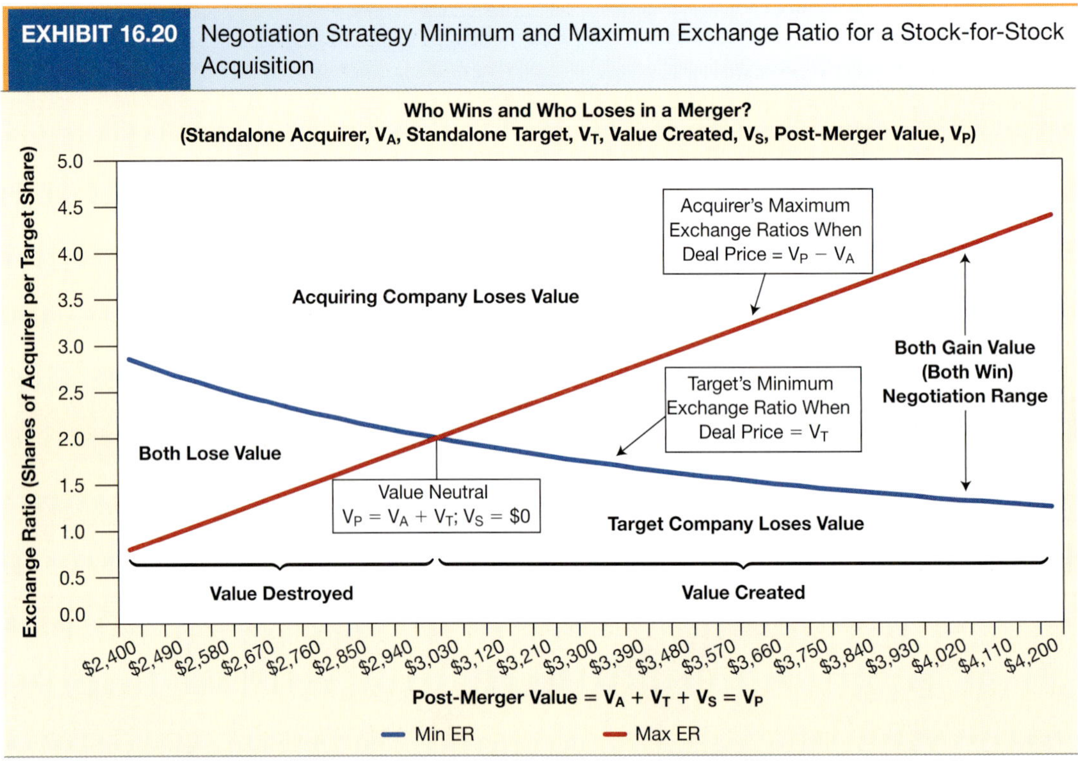

The Exchange Ratio for Proportional Allocation of the Post-Merger Value

We can also calculate the exchange ratio for a specific proportional allocation of the post-merger company to the acquirer's shareholders, C_A, and the target's shareholders, $C_T = 1 - C_A$. Since no additional shares are issued to the acquirer's shareholders, the proportion of the post-merger company allocated to the acquirer's shareholders is equal to

$$C_A = \frac{S_A}{S_A + S_T \times ER_{C_A}} \tag{16.4}$$

Using the above relation, we can solve for the exchange ratio as follows:

$$ER_{C_A} = \frac{S_A}{S_T} \times \frac{C_T}{C_A} \tag{16.5}$$

Equation 16.5 adjusts the ratio of the parties' pre-merger shares outstanding (S_A/S_T) by the ratio of the post-merger proportional ownership, C_T/C_A. Assume in the above example that the parties agreed to allocate the post-merger value with $C_A = 65\%$ to the acquirer's pre-merger shareholders and $C_T = 35\%$ to the target's shareholders. Based on this allocation, $C_T/C_A = 0.5385$ ($0.5385 = 0.35/0.65$). The ratio of the pre-merger shares of the target to the acquirer is 0.25 ($0.25 = 50/200$). The exchange ratio to adjust the number of the target's post-merger shares to the agreed upon proportion is 2.154 ($2.154 = 200/50 \times 0.35/0.65$). The resulting number of post merger shares is equal to 307.69 ($307.69 = 200 + 50 \times$

2.154), and the proportion of the post-merger value owned by the target's shareholders is 35% (0.35 = 107.69/307.69). The post-merger value allocated to the target's shareholders is $1,155 (35% of $3,300), a premium of $155 over the target's standalone value.

Allocating Synergies Based on the Proportion of Pre-Merger Standalone Values

Assume the companies agree to base the allocation of synergies and post-merger value on the companies' relative pre-merger standalone values. In other words, the parties agree to allocate $C_A = V_A/(V_A + V_T)$ to the acquirer's shareholders and $C_T = V_T/(V_A + V_T)$ to the target's shareholders. We can substitute these proportions into the above formula for C_A in order to allocate synergies in terms of the companies' relative pre-merger standalone values:

$$ER_{C_A=\frac{V_A}{V_A+V_T}} = \frac{S_A}{S_T} \times \frac{V_T}{V_A+V_T} \Big/ \frac{V_A}{V_A+V_T}$$

$$ER_{C_A=\frac{V_A}{V_A+V_T}} = \frac{P_T}{P_A} \quad \textbf{(16.6)}$$

Note that this is the same formula as the zero synergies formula; thus, as long as the parties agree to allocate synergies and post-merger value on their relative pre-merger standalone values, the appropriate exchange ratio is equal to the ratio of the target's pre-merger price to the acquirer's pre-merger price, P_T/P_A.

Allocation of Merger Gains and Losses in a Stock-for-Stock Merger

Recall that in the cash deal example (see Exhibit 16.17), the merger gain to the target was fixed by the deal price, and all of the potential variation in the merger gain accrued to the acquirer. In a stock-for-stock merger, the two parties share in any changes in the actual value created or destroyed by the merger. Recall that the standalone values of the target and acquirer are $1,000 and $2,000, respectively, and while the expected value created from this acquisition is $300, the potential outcomes—value created or destroyed—range from a merger gain of $1,200 to a merger loss of −$600. We show the allocation of the gain and loss for the expected outcome and two outcomes that differ from the expected outcome in Exhibit 16.21.

EXHIBIT 16.21 Allocation of Merger Gain (Loss) for Stock-for-Stock Deal Example

	Actual Outcome Equals Expected Outcome			Actual Outcome Is Greater than Expected Outcome			Actual Outcome Is Less than Expected Outcome		
Stock Deal–Equity Values	**Outcome**	**% Split**	**% Gain**	**Outcome**	**% Split**	**% Gain**	**Outcome**	**% Split**	**% Gain**
Standalone value of acquirer	$2,000			$2,000			$2,000		
Standalone value of target	1,000			1,000			1,000		
Combined standalone value	$3,000			$3,000			$3,000		
Value created (merger gain (loss))	300			800			−400		
Post-merger value	$3,300			$3,800			$2,600		
Overall gain or (loss) on acquisition	$ 300		10.0%	$ 800		26.7%	−$ 400		−13.3%
Post-merger value to target (stock received)	$1,200	36.4%		$1,382	36.4%		$ 945	36.4%	
Standalone value of target	−1,000			−1,000			−1,000		
Gain (loss) to target—merger premium	$ 200	66.7%	20.0%	$ 382	47.7%	38.2%	−$ 55	13.6%	−5.5%
Post-merger value to acquirer	$2,100	63.6%		$2,418	63.6%		$1,655	63.6%	
Standalone value of acquirer	−2,000			−2,000			−2,000		
Gain or (loss) to acquirer	$ 100	33.3%	5.0%	$ 418	52.3%	20.9%	−$ 345	86.4%	−17.3%

As in the cash deal shown in Exhibit 16.17, we assume the parties negotiate the deal based on the expected value of the synergies and that they agree to allocate $200 of the synergies to the target. We continue to use that allocation of the expected synergies but in a stock-for-stock merger. Now, the target's shareholders end up owning 36.4% of the post-merger company, which is equal to the proportion of the value that they were assigned in the cash deal (0.364 = $1,200/$3,300). Using Equation 16.5, the exchange ratio resulting in this allocation of post-merger value is equal to 2.285 (2.285 = 200/50 × 0.3636/0.6364). The resulting number of post merger shares is equal to 314.25 (314.25 = 200 + 50 × 2.285) which gives 36.4% of the shares (0.3636 = 114.25/314.25) to the target's shareholders. In a stock-for-stock merger, the target's shareholders share in any changes in the post-merger value that result from differences between the expected and actual outcome of the merger.

For example, assume the actual outcome for the stock-for-stock merger results in a merger gain of $800, which is $500 higher than originally expected. In this outcome, the post-merger value of the shares issued to the target increases from $1,200 to $1,382 (or by 36.4% of the $500 increase in the value of the synergies). The value of the shares held by the acquirer's original shareholders increases from $2,100 to $2,418 (or by 63.6% of the $500 increase in the value of the synergies). When this same outcome occurred in the cash deal, the target shareholders received none of the increase in value (see Exhibit 16.17); thus, the target's share of the post-merger value decreased below 36.4% in the cash deal. Now assume the actual outcome is a merger loss of −$400, which is $700 lower than originally expected. In this outcome, the post-merger value of the newly issued shares to the target's shareholders decreases from $1,200 to $945 (or by 36.4% of the $700 decrease in the value of the synergies). The value of the shares held by the acquirer's original shareholders decreases from $2,100 to $1,655 (or by 63.6% of the $700 decrease in the value of the synergies). When this outcome occurred in the cash deal, the target shareholders did not share the effects of the decrease in value. As a result, in the cash deal, the target shareholders end up with 46.2% of the value, while the acquiring shareholders only end up with 53.8% of the value (see Exhibit 16.17) when there is a merger loss of −$400.

REVIEW EXERCISE 16.5

Allocation of Synergies—Stock-for-Stock Deals

Use the information in Review Exercise 16.4 to respond to the following questions regarding stock-for-stock transactions.

a. Measure the exchange ratio and resulting stock price that allocates $6,000 of the post-merger value (based on the expected outcome) to the target.

b. Measure the exchange ratio and resulting stock price that allocates the value of the synergies based on the relative standalone values of the two companies.

c. Based on a post-merger value equal to the expected outcome for the merger, calculate the target's minimum exchange ratio, the acquirer's maximum exchange ratio, and the resulting stock prices.

d. Assuming the acquirer allocates $6,000 of the post-merger value based on the expected outcome to the target in a stock-for-stock transaction, calculate the gain or loss to the acquirer and target when the actual outcome of the merger is the expected, highest, and lowest outcome.

Solution on pages 852–853.

16.9 THE XEROX CORPORATION AND AFFILIATED COMPUTER SERVICES, INC. MERGER

Stock-for-stock swaps involve more complex valuation issues than a cash M&A transaction because the post-merger stock price of the acquirer is an important component, and sometimes the only component, of the consideration paid to the target shareholders. In these transactions, the target shareholders assess the value of the acquirer, the target, and the value created by the transaction in order to measure the negotiation range for the exchange ratio and the post-merger stock price of the acquirer. In this section, we use Xerox's acquisition of ACS to illustrate these valuation issues. The companies announced the merger on September 27, 2009, and the merger closed on February 5, 2010. The terms of the acquisition involved a cash payment to the ACS shareholders as well as an exchange of ACS stock for shares of Xerox stock.

Xerox's public disclosures identified a variety of potential cost and revenue synergies from the merger and provided five-year forecasts for both companies created by the respective management teams.

Although the common stock of both companies was publicly traded as of the date of the merger, the publicly traded stock prices may not have reflected the fundamental standalone values of the companies because the management forecasts were not disclosed to the market before the merger announcement. As such, the financial advisors for both companies conducted a valuation of the standalone values of both companies as well as the expected value created by the transaction.

The Deal

ACS and Xerox each had two financial advisors. ACS's financial advisors were Citigroup Global Markets Inc. (Citi) and Evercore Group L.L.C. (Evercore). Xerox's financial advisors were Blackstone Advisory Services L.P. (Blackstone) and J.P. Morgan Securities Inc. (JPM). Between May 2009 and June 2009, the financial advisors of ACS and Xerox discussed a potential transaction between the two companies as well as alternative structures for the deal. Over a two-month negotiation process, the Xerox board of directors held special meetings in which management discussed various aspects of the acquisition. The topics discussed included the strategic rationale for the combination, ACS's fit within Xerox's business process outsourcing strategy, the expected cost and revenue synergies, the strengths of ACS's business process outsourcing business, the challenges associated with the transaction, how ACS was to be managed, and potential integration issues.

At the same time, the financial advisors of ACS conducted an analysis of the effects of potential strategic transaction announcements on the stock price of ACS and the potential effects of the ACS announcement on Xerox's stock price.[26] The ACS board established $62 per ACS share as the lowest price it would accept, and although it instructed its financial advisors to include a floor to protect the value of its shares from falling in case Xerox's stock price fell following the transaction announcement, Xerox did not agree to the floor.[27] On September 27, 2009, the companies finalized and announced the merger. In its public filing, ACS described the merger as follows:

> On September 27, 2009, Xerox Corporation ("Xerox"), Boulder Acquisition Corp. ("Merger Sub"), a wholly-owned subsidiary of Xerox, and Affiliated Computer Services, Inc. ("ACS") entered into an Agreement and Plan of Merger (the "Merger Agreement"), providing for the acquisition of ACS by Xerox. Subject to the terms and conditions of the Merger Agreement, which has been approved by the boards of directors of all parties (and recommended by a special committee of independent directors of ACS), ACS will be merged with and into Merger Sub (the "Merger").
>
> As a result of the merger, each outstanding share of ACS's *Class A* common stock, other than shares owned by Xerox, Merger Sub, or ACS (which will be cancelled) and other than those shares with respect to which appraisal rights are properly exercised and not withdrawn (collectively, "Excluded Shares"), will be converted into the right to receive a combination of (i) 4.935 shares of common stock of Xerox ("Common Stock") and (ii) $18.60 in cash, without interest.
>
> As a result of the merger, each outstanding share of *Class B* common stock of ACS, other than Excluded Shares, will be converted into the right to receive (i) 4.935 shares of Common Stock, (ii) $18.60 in cash, without interest and (iii) a fraction of a share of a new series of convertible preferred stock to be issued by Xerox and designated as Series A Convertible Perpetual Preferred Stock ("Convertible Preferred Stock") . . .
>
> Source: Affiliated Computer Services, Inc., Form 8-K, dated September 29, 2009.

ACS had 91.04 million Class A shares and 6.6 million Class B shares outstanding for a total of 97.64 million shares outstanding; thus, the cash consideration for the merger was $1.8 billion ($1,816 million = $18.60 × 97.64 million).

---

[26] Xerox's Amendment No. 4 to Form S-4, dated December 23, 2009, contains fairly detailed descriptions of the analyses the financial advisors conducted in order to assess the "fairness, from a financial point of view, to the holders of the Class A common stock of Affiliated Computer Services, Inc. ("ACS") of the Class A Merger Consideration."

[27] Xerox never agreed to the floor, and thus an analysis of what Xerox's stock price would be post-merger became important to ACS's evaluation of the Xerox offer. Affiliated Computer Services, Inc. Form 8-K, dated September 29, 2009, p. 1.

Post-Merger Value of Xerox

To estimate the post-merger enterprise value of Xerox, we measure the value of Xerox as a standalone company and combine this value with both the standalone value of ACS and the value of the Xerox/ACS synergies, net of all transaction and integration costs. With this analysis, we include the effects of financing on the values of the standalone companies; for example, Xerox used ACS's excess cash, refinanced some debt, repaid some debt, issued new debt, and issued new shares of stock in order to finance the transaction. We also consider the effects of financing on the value of the combined companies.

To measure the post-merger stock price of Xerox, we subtract post-merger debt, convertible preferred, and any other non-common equity claims—such as stock options—from the value of the post-merger firm in order to measure the value of the post-merger common equity. After we calculate the post-merger common equity shares outstanding, we calculate the post-merger stock price by dividing the post-merger value of common equity by the post-merger shares outstanding. Using the post-merger stock price and the cash component of the deal, we measure the gain to ACS shareholders relative to ACS's publicly traded stock price.

Valuation in Practice 16.7

Affiliated Computer Services, Inc. Super Voting Common Stock and Effective Voting Control
Affiliated Computer Services, Inc. (ACS) was founded by Mr. Darwin Deason in 1988. Mr. Deason served as ACS's chief executive officer until 1999 and as its Chairman of the Board of Directors until ACS merged with Xerox Corporation in 2010. ACS had two types of common stock outstanding—Class A and Class B. The Class A common was publicly traded on the New York Stock Exchange, and each share had one vote. The Class B common was privately held (mostly by Mr. Deason) and each share had 10 votes.

According to ACS's 2009 SEC 10-K report,

> As of August 20, 2009, 91,042,152 shares of Class A common stock and 6,599,372 shares of Class B common stock were outstanding. . . .
>
> In addition, as of August 20, 2009, Darwin Deason beneficially owns 6,599,372 shares of Class B common stock and 2,140,884 shares of the Class A common stock and controls approximately 43.6% of our total voting power (based on shares of both classes of common stock outstanding). As a result, Mr. Deason has the requisite voting power to significantly affect many of our significant decisions, including the power to block corporate actions such as an amendment to most provisions of our certificate of incorporation.

Source: See Affiliated Computer Services, Inc. 2009 SEC 10-K filing, p. 19.

Standalone Values of ACS and Xerox. The financial advisors used the various valuation methods we discuss in this book to measure the standalone values of ACS and Xerox. We assume that both companies have excess cash before the transaction and that Xerox uses all of the excess cash of both companies to finance the transaction. Based on the management forecasts, costs of capital, expected long-term growth rates, market multiples, and other market information, the standalone firm value of ACS without excess cash is estimated at $8.2 billion, and the standalone firm value of Xerox without excess cash is $15.9 billion. Based on the $8.2 valuation, ACS's equity was equal to $6.1 billion. The market capitalization of its equity at this time was $4.9 billion (which includes a $300 million premium for ACS's Class B common stock). Thus, ACS's common stock was undervalued by roughly $1.2 billion. Reasons for this undervaluation include management's more optimistic forecasts that were unknown to the market at this time as well as the founder's controlling interest in the company (see Valuation in Practice 16.7).

Valuation of Xerox/ACS Synergies. Xerox discussed various types of synergies, fees, restructuring charges, and integration costs in its Form S-4 filed with the SEC.[28] Xerox expected the transaction to create $250 million in tax credits, which we assume Xerox will use in the first year of the merger.

[28] Xerox Corporation Amendment No. 4 to Form S-4, dated December 23, 2009, p. C-2, which is an excerpt from Citi's fairness opinion letter.

Xerox discussed both cost and revenue synergies (for example, cross-selling products and services), but it only provided forecasts for cost synergies. In addition, financial analysts were less confident that Xerox would attain the potential revenue synergies. For these reasons, we do not include any potential revenue synergies in our valuation.

We assume that ACS's weighted average cost of capital of 9.08% is appropriate for valuing the synergies. To make this assumption, we assume that the synergies were of similar risk to ACS's free cash flows and that the post-merger capital structure was similar to the pre-merger ACS capital structure. The forecasted synergies for the first five years are shown in Exhibit 16.22 along with the related consuting fees, restructuring charges, and integration costs. We assume a percentage growth rate of −5% for the synergies beginning in the year ending June 2013. For the year ending June 2010, the cash flows are discounted for one-half year as the merger closed in February 2010, and that timing is maintained across the subsequent years. As shown in the exhibit, the value of the synergies, net of transaction and integration costs, is $1.486 billion.

EXHIBIT 16.22 Valuation of Xerox Corporation/Affiliated Computer Services, Inc. Synergies

Weighted average cost of capital valuation of synergies		9.08%		g =	−5.00%		
Tax rate =		36.0%					

($ in millions)		June-10	June-11	June-12	June-13	June-14	CV June-14
Pre-tax cost synergies		$ 95.0	$300.0	$300.0	$285.0	$270.8	$ 257.2
Investment banker fees		−50.0	−183.0				
Restructuring charges and integration costs		−45.0	−30.0				
Less: taxes		0.0	−31.3	−108.0	−102.6	−97.5	−92.6
After-tax cost synergies		$ 0.0	$ 55.7	$192.0	$182.4	$173.3	$ 164.6
Income tax credits		$250.0					
Unlevered free cash flow for continuing value (CV)							$ 164.6
Discount factor for continuing value							7.104
Unlevered free cash flow and CV		$250.0	$ 55.7	$192.0	$182.4	$173.3	$1,169.4
Discount factor		0.957	0.878	0.805	0.738	0.676	0.676
Present value		$239.4	$ 48.9	$154.5	$134.6	$117.2	$ 791.0
Value of synergies	$1,485.6						

Post-Merger Financing. Xerox planned to finance the transaction with excess cash and additional debt of $2.7 billion and to issue shares to ACS shareholders. Xerox planned to redeem some existing ACS debt ($1.8 billion) and provide cash compensation to ACS shareholders ($1.8 billion). In Exhibit 16.23, based on Xerox's financing plan, we present sources and uses of cash for the transaction. The financing and related fees totaled $222 million (these are separate from the consulting and other fees related to implementing the post-merger integration plan in Exhibit 16.22). The net effect of the transaction was to eliminate the excess cash holdings of Xerox and ACS by $1.1 billion. We assume that Xerox was using all of ACS's excess cash as well as all of its own excess cash to finance the transaction.

The book value of Xerox's debt as of June 30, 2009 (including its liability to a subsidiary trust issuing preferred stock) was $8.3 billion, and the market value of these securities was $8.7 billion. The market value of ACS's pre-merger debt was $2.3 billion, but Xerox planned to redeem $1.8 billion of this debt; thus, the post-merger debt attributable to ACS was $0.5 billion. In addition to the existing debt, Xerox planned to issue $2.7 billion in additional debt in order to redeem the ACS debt and pay the $1.8 billion cash consideration to the ACS shareholders. Exhibit 16.24 presents the expected market value of the post-merger debt, which included Xerox's pre-merger debt, the new debt issued in the transaction, and the remaining amount of ACS outstanding debt. After the merger, Xerox was expected to have $11.9 billion in debt and trust preferred stock outstanding. In addition, Xerox planned to issue $300 million in convertible preferred stock to the ACS Class B shareholders as extra compensation for the Class B shares.

EXHIBIT 16.23 ACS/Xerox Merger Sources and Uses of Cash and Post-Merger Cash Balance

Sources and Uses of Cash ($ in millions)			
Sources			
Expected new senior unsecured notes	$1,950.0		
Revolving credit facility	750.0		
Total sources of cash	$2,700.0		
Uses			
Repayment of ACS's debt	$1,771.0		
Cash consideration to ACS common stock at $18.60 per share	1,816.1		
Fees and various transactions costs	222.0		
Total uses	$3,809.1		
Net effect on cash	−$1,109.1		
Cash and Cash Equivalents (expected at the closing date)	**Balance**	**Required**	**Excess**
Xerox	$1,159.0	$558.9	$ 600.1
ACS	559.0	50.0	509.0
Net effect on cash	−1,109.1		
Pro forma combined cash balance (no excess cash)	$ 608.9	$608.9	$1,109.1

EXHIBIT 16.24 Xerox Corporation—Post-Merger Debt

($ in millions)	
Market value of Xerox existing debt (including trust preferred)	$ 8,686.4
Market value of additional new borrowings	2,700.0
Market value of remaining ACS debt	524.3
Total market value of post-merger combined debt	$11,910.7

REVIEW EXERCISE 16.6

Merger Sources and Uses Schedule

An acquirer makes an offer to purchase a target company. The target company's current stock price is $10 per share, and the target company has 100 million shares outstanding. Given the expected synergies from the acquisition, the deal premium is negotiated to be 25%. The target has no convertible debt or convertible preferred stock, but it does have 50 million stock options outstanding with an exercise price equal to $9. The acquirer will assume the debt and preferred stock of the target, buy out the option holders, and finance the acquisition with $200 million of its own excess cash, $100 million of the target's excess cash, and the remainder with debt. Initial fees will equal $47.3 million (3% on the debt financing and 1% for other fees). These fees do not include fees for a revolver loan. The debt issued to finance the transaction includes $400 million of seven-year, 6.0% senior secured bank debt and $700 million of nine-year, 8% subordinated unsecured debt; the remainder is financed with a revolving line of credit. The revolving line of credit of $200 million has a five-year term, a 4% interest rate on the amount drawn, and a 0.5% annual fee on the total amount of the line of credit. Calculate the purchase price of the equity and prepare a sources and uses schedule similar to the one in Exhibit 16.23.

Solution on page 853.

Post-Merger Xerox Common Shares and Stock Options Outstanding. To measure the post-merger per share value of Xerox, we first measure the number of post-merger common shares outstanding and the number of options outstanding, which we show in Exhibit 16.25. To calculate the number of Xerox shares issued to ACS shareholders, we multiply the number of Class A and Class B shares by the 4.935 exchange ratio. We perform a similar calculation for the number of Xerox options issued to the ACS employees for their existing options using the option exchange ratio of 7.085, as the ACS options were not cashed out at the time of the transaction, but instead were converted into Xerox options.

EXHIBIT 16.25 Xerox Corporation—Post-Merger Common Shares Outstanding

Shares and Options Outstanding	
Xerox—Number of Shares and Options Outstanding (millions)	
Common shares	869.08
Restricted stock units and performance shares	6.45
Convertible securities	1.99
Total Xerox shares outstanding	877.52
Total number of Xerox options	28.4
ACS—Number of Shares and Options Outstanding	
Class A	91.04
Class B	6.60
Total ACS shares outstanding	97.64
× ACS/Xerox exchange ratio	4.935
Total number of ACS converted shares	481.86
ACS options	14.4
Option exchange ratio	7.085
Total number of ACS converted options	102.1

Post-Merger Xerox Value. We now have all of the inputs necessary to measure the post-merger value of Xerox and the implied post-merger stock price. As we show in Exhibit 16.26, to calculate the post-merger value of Xerox of $25.6 billion, we add the standalone values of ACS and Xerox to the value of the synergies net of integration costs and fees. This calculation assumes that Xerox management will be able to manage ACS at the same level of efficiency that ACS management expected, that the transaction will not interfere with the ability of the Xerox management team to manage Xerox, that the projected synergies will be achieved, and that the value-weighted capital structure of the two companies represents the post-merger capital structure. We use the value of ACS and the value of Xerox without its excess cash, as we assume Xerox will use all excess cash of both companies to fund the transaction.[29]

From the value of the firm of $25.6 billion, we subtract the value of Xerox's post-merger debt (Exhibit 16.24) and the value of the convertible preferred stock to measure the value of the common equity and options of $13.4 billion. The value of the equity securities includes the value of the Xerox stock options (including the ACS converted options), which we subtract in order to measure the post-merger value of Xerox's common equity. To do this, we use the iterative approach we discussed in Chapter 12 to simultaneously solve for the value per option and the equity value per share.

Recall that since the value of the outstanding stock options is a function of the per share value of the underlying equity, we calculate the value of the options when we calculate the per share value of the common equity. We solve this equality using an iterative process, changing the value of the stock price until the sum of the value of the equity and the value of the outstanding equity-based compensation contracts equals the value of the equity and the options. In this case, the calculations are slightly more

[29] For simplicity, we assume that the fees and transaction costs of $222.0 million (shown in Exhibit 16.23) were not tax deductible. However, most of these fees were probably tax deductible, and fees related to arranging the debt financing would typically be amortized to interest expense over the life of the loans (see Chapter 15 for the typical treatment of these financing fees).

complicated, for the terms of the preexisting Xerox options differ from the terms of the ACS options that were converted into Xerox options, but the approach is the same. In this example, we assume the above valuation includes the value of any tax shelter from the options. If the initial valuation excluded the value of the tax shelter (as would likely be the case in a DCF valuation), we measure the value of the tax shelter from the options and increase our initial valuation for the value of the tax shelter as we discussed in Chapter 12. On the other hand, if the valuations were based on publicly traded prices of the company's claims, then it is likely that the value includes the tax shelter from the options.

We show the calculation of the stock price in Exhibit 16.26. Using the initial valuations, the value of the post-merger firm is $25.6 billion. From this value, we subtract the value of the post-merger debt and preferred stock of $12.2 billion in order to measure the initial value of the common equity and options, which is $13.4 billion. We assume this value includes the value of the tax shelter from options and use our iterative approach and find the value of the options is $355.0 million. The resulting common equity value is $13.012 billion, and after dividing this by the post-merger number of shares, the value per share is $9.572.

EXHIBIT 16.26 Xerox Corporation—Post-merger Valuation

($ in millions, except per share)	
Xerox firm value (after using all excess cash to close the transaction)	$15,905.0
ACS firm value (after using all excess cash to close the transaction)	8,186.8
Value of synergies	1,485.6
Post-merger Xerox firm value (including ACS and synergies)	$25,577.4
Post-merger debt and preferred stock	
Xerox and ACS pro forma combined total debt and liabilities	$11,910.7
Convertible preferred stock	300.0
Post-merger total debt and preferred stock	$12,210.7
Post-merger value of Xerox common equity and options*	$13,366.7
Value of stock options	
ACS stock options assumed in exchange for Xerox equivalent option	$ 298.4
Xerox stock options	56.6
Total value of stock options	$ 355.0
Value of Xerox post-merger common equity	$13,011.7
Post-merger Xerox shares outstanding	
Xerox shares outstanding	877.5
ACS shares outstanding × 4.935	481.9
Total post-merger shares	1,359.4
Value of Xerox post-merger common equity per share	$ 9.572

* This value includes a deduction for Xerox's minority interest but includes any tax benefits from existing options.

Allocation of the Gain to ACS and Xerox Shareholders

In Exhibit 16.27, we calculate the allocation of the gain from the merger to Xerox and ACS shareholders. Consider the valuation effects of the merger on ACS. The value of the Xerox post-merger shares to the ACS shareholders is equal to the $9.57 per share value multiplied by the number of Xerox shares that the ACS shareholders received, 481.86 million. The Class A and Class B shareholders also received a cash payment of $1.8 billion, and the Class B shareholders received $300 of Xerox preferred shares.[30] As we show in the exhibit, the percentage increase in value for the Class A and Class B shareholders of ACS is 36.9% and is 8.2% for the Xerox shareholders. The allocation of the merger gain—relative to pre-merger market capitalization, which includes the undervaluation of ACS—is 74.1% to ACS shareholders and 25.9% to Xerox shareholders. Note that although part of the consideration for this merger was paid with Xerox stock, the cash payment to the ACS shareholders ($1.8 billion) was about equal to the gain from the merger ($1.8 billion).

EXHIBIT 16.27 Xerox Corporation—Allocation of the Gain from the Merger

($ in millions, except per share)	ACS Total	Xerox Total	Total
Shares issued to ACS shareholders/Xerox outstanding shares	481.86	877.52	1,359.38
Value of Xerox post-merger common equity per share	$ 9.572	$ 9.572	$ 9.572
Value of Xerox post-merger shares	$4,612.3	$8,399.4	$13,011.7
Plus: cash payment for ACS shares	1,816.1		1,816.1
Value of the merger consideration without Class B preferred shares	$6,428.4	$8,399.4	$14,827.8
Value of Class B preferred shares	300.0		300.0
Value of the merger consideration with Class B preferred shares	$6,728.4	$8,399.4	$15,127.8
Pre-merger market capitalization	$4,613.6	$7,765.2	$12,378.8
Value of Class B preferred shares	300.0		300.0
Pre-merger market capitalization of the merger consideration	$4,913.6	$7,765.2	$12,678.8
Increase over pre-merger market capitalization	$1,814.8	$ 634.2	$ 2,449.0
Percentage increase in pre-merger value	36.9%	8.2%	19.3%
Allocation of total increase	74.1%	25.9%	

Negotiation Range for the Xerox Corporation and Affiliated Computer Services Inc.

As we learned from the previous section, the exchange ratio negotiation range is a function of the standalone per share prices and shares outstanding of the two merging parties and the value of the synergies. In this section, we compute the minimum and maximum exchange ratios for the Xerox/ACS transaction and compare them to the actual exchange ratio of 4.935. Measuring the Xerox/ACS exchange ratio range is more complex than we discussed in the previous section for two reasons. First, some of the consideration paid to ACS's shareholders was non-common stock. Second, Xerox will finance some of the non-common stock consideration and transaction fees with debt and the Xerox and ACS stock options were not cancelled as part of the transaction. Recall that the formulas to measure the negotiation range require, for each company, standalone company common equity prices and the value of the synergies on a per share basis based upon the shares of each company. In the following table, we measure the standalone stock prices of the two merging parties.

[30] Recall from Valuation in Practice 16.7 that ACS had two classes of common stock. In this analysis, we assume that all of the Class B shares are converted into Class A shares and that all of the shares are treated (valued) equally. Naturally, since the Class B shares had super voting rights (10 votes per share), and since these shares were essentially owned by one individual (providing that individual with effective voting control and the ability to prevent an acquisition from occurring), the Class B shares would be valued at a higher price than the Class A shares. We assume the premium for the Class B shares is $300 million in total, and the premium is achieved by issuing the Class B shareholder convertible preferred stock in addition to what the Class A shareholders received. Again, as stated earlier, we do not perform an explicit valuation of the convertible preferred in this chapter. See Lease, R., J. McConnell, and W. Mikkelson, "The Market Value of Control in Publicly Traded Corporations," *Journal of Financial Economics* 11 (1983), pp. 439–473, who show that the average premium for stocks with superior voting rights is 5.44%.

	Standalone Values	
	Xerox	ACS
Firm value without excess cash		$8,186.9
Excess cash		509.0
Firm value with excess cash		8,695.9
Market value of existing debt and existing stock options (calculated separately and not shown)		−2,577.3
Value of common equity before distributions		$6,118.6
Cash distribution to ACS shareholders		−1,816.1
Xerox preferred stock issued to Class B common		−300.0
Common equity	$7,765.2	$4,002.5
Pre-merger shares	877.5	97.6
Share Price	$ 8.849	$ 40.992

Exhibit may contain small rounding errors

Recall from Exhibit 16.27, Xerox's standalone equity value was $7.765 billion and it had 877.52 million shares outstanding, resulting in a $8.849 value per share. The calculation of the standalone value of the common equity of ACS is more complex and equal to the value of the firm without excess cash ($8.19 billion, Exhibit 16.26), plus excess cash ($0.51 billion, Exhibit 16.23) minus the value of the standalone debt and existing stock options ($2.58 billion, calculation not shown). Based on this calculation, ACS's standalone equity value is equal to $6.12 billion. Because ACS's shareholders will receive $1.82 billion in a cash distribution and $0.3 billion in Xerox convertible preferred stock (both shown in Exhibit 16.27), we reduce ACS's standalone common equity value by the value of these distributions. ACS's resulting standalone equity value after these distributions is $4.0 billion or $40.992 per share.

Before we measure the value of the synergies per share, we first adjust the value of the synergies for transaction costs and an allocation of the value of the synergies to existing stock options ($241.6 million, calculation not shown). These adjustments decrease the value of the synergies of $1.49 billion (Exhibit 16.26) to $1.24 billion.

We calculate the per share net value of the synergies to common equity in the following table.

	Xerox	ACS
Net synergies to common equity	$1,243.9	$1,243.9
Pre-merger shares	877.5	97.6
Value of net synergies per pre-merger share	$ 1.418	$ 12.740

We now have all of the required information to measure the minimum and maximum exchange ratios for the Xerox/ACS merger. Using the formula in Equation 16.2, the minimum exchange ratio ACS's shareholders would accept is 3.993.

$$ER_{MIN} = \frac{P_T}{P_A + V_S/S_A} = \frac{\$40.992}{\$8.849 + \$1.418} = 3.993$$

And using the formula in Equation 16.3, the maximum exchange ratio Xerox's shareholders would accept is 6.072

$$ER_{MAX} = \frac{P_T + V_S/S_T}{P_A} = \frac{\$40.992 + \$12.740}{\$8.849} = 6.072$$

The actual exchange ratio of 4.935 is close to the 5.032 midpoint of the minimum and maximum exchange ratios [5.032 = (3.993 + 6.072)/2] indicating that the parties had close to a 50:50 split of the net value of the synergies to common equity.

We know the minimum and maximum exchange ratios vary based on the value of the post-merger equity (the sum of the standalone values and the net value of the synergies to common equity). In Exhibit 16.28, we show a chart of the minimum and maximum exchange ratios for the Xerox/ACS merger after considering non-stock consideration. The point in the chart at which the red horizontal line indicating the agreed upon exchange ratio of 4.935 intersects with Xerox's maximum exchange ratio line (dark blue line) is the minimum post-merger market capitalization of the firm that does not destroy value for Xerox. We can estimate from the chart that as long as the post-merger value of the equity is at least $12.0 billion, Xerox shareholders will not be worse off than they were without the merger. For ACS, the point in the chart at which the red horizontal line indicating the agreed upon exchange ratio of 4.935 intersects with ACS's minimum exchange ratio line (light blue line) is the minimum post-merger market capitalization so that the merger does not destroy value for ACS. We can also estimate from the chart that as long as the post-merger value is at least $11.3 billion, the value of the post-merger Xerox shares paid to ACS shareholders will not be less than ACS's adjusted stand-alone value of $4.0 billion. However, the $1.82 billion cash distribution paid to ACS shareholders provided them with considerable protection from such a downside.

EXHIBIT 16.28 Exchange Ratio Negotiation Range for the Xerox/ACS Merger After Considering Non-Stock Consideration

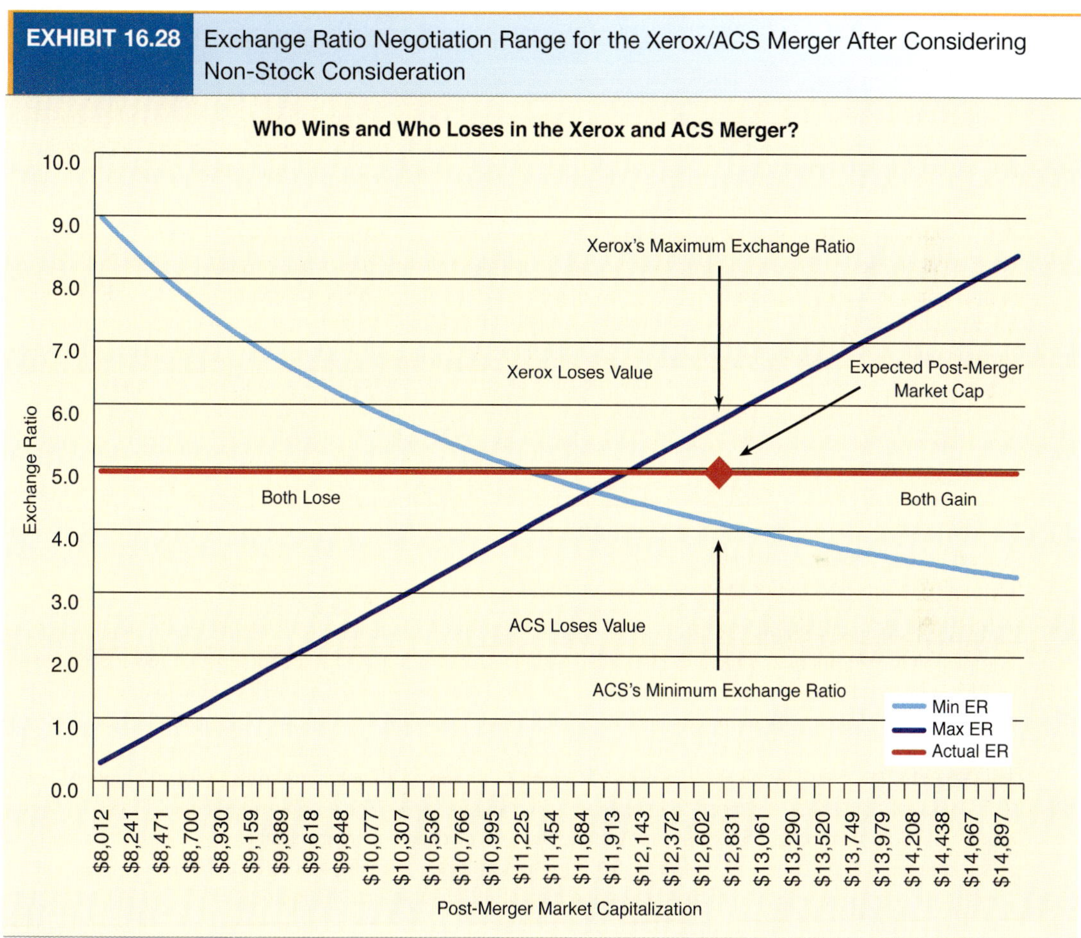

SUMMARY AND KEY CONCEPTS

In this chapter, we discussed the valuation issues related to mergers and acquisitions. Mergers and acquisitions are an important component of corporate strategy, and worldwide M&A activity is significant. In this chapter, we provided some descriptive statistics on the amount of global M&A activity, the typical premiums paid, what motivates M&A transactions, whether and for whom acquisitions create value, and why mergers may fail to create value for acquirers. We also discussed fundamental deal structure, contract provisions, and the income tax ramifications associated with various deal structures. We then discussed how to analyze and value M&A transactions, including the valuation of synergies and analyzing accretion and dilution, exchange ratios, and the allocation of expected gains from a merger between the target and acquirer.

We illustrated that cash transactions are more straightforward to evaluate, for the consideration given to the target shareholders is easy to evaluate. When payment to the target shareholders is in the form of debt, convertible securities, or the common stock of the acquirer, the acquisitions are more difficult to evaluate, for one has to assess the value of these securities that are paid as consideration. This is particularly true when the stock of the acquirer is paid as consideration, for one has to estimate the post-merger value of the acquirer's stock. We discussed the negotiation range for an acquisition as well as a variety of issues related to exchange ratios (the ratio of acquirer shares given per share of the target).

ADDITIONAL READING AND REFERENCES

Andrade, G., M. Mitchell, and E. Stafford, "New Evidence and Perspectives on Mergers," *Journal of Economic Perspectives* 15 (2001), pp. 103–120.

Savor, P., and Q. Lu, "Do Stock Mergers Create Value for Acquirers?" *Journal of Finance* 64 (2009), pp. 1061–1097.

EXERCISES AND PROBLEMS

P16.1 **Valuing Synergies—Oracle Acquisition of PeopleSoft**: Oracle Corporation acquires another business software applications vendor, PeopleSoft, Inc., for approximately $10.3 billion. Oracle expects to achieve various synergies, and its strategy is to continue to support existing versions of PeopleSoft software solutions, create Oracle software to replace all of PeopleSoft's software, and then migrate PeopleSoft customers to Oracle software. Assume that as a result of the merger, the company expects annual selling and administrative costs to decrease by $750 million, annual research and development costs to decrease by $300 million, and annual general and administrative costs to decrease by $200 million. Also, assume that Oracle will be able to migrate about 80% of PeopleSoft's customers (roughly 10,000) and $3 billion in revenue but that it will lose the remaining 20%. Assume that the company will incur $400 million in fees, expenses, and integration- and synergy-related costs in the first year after the merger and none thereafter. Assume that the appropriate discount rate for discounting synergies is 12%; that the post-merger income tax rate is 40% on all income; that revenues are expected to grow with inflation, which is expected to be 3% annually; and that variable costs are, on average, 55% of revenues.

Measure the value of the synergies, assuming that the cost synergies begin in the first year after the merger, remain constant for the following two years despite inflation, and then decline at a rate of 10% in perpetuity beginning in the fourth year after the merger. Also assume that the migration of the customers will take place immediately after the merger and impact the Year 1 cash flows.

P16.2 **Valuing Synergies—SiriusXM Radio Inc.:** Sirius Satellite Radio and XM Satellite Radio announced the completion of their merger, which will be called SiriusXM Radio Inc. XM shareholders will receive 4.6 shares of Sirius common stock for each share of XM stock. The company states that it will be able to offer consumers new packages in audio entertainment and that it will offer subscribers the option of expanding their subscriptions to include the "Best of Both" services. SiriusXM Radio states that it expects to begin realizing synergies immediately. The company expects to achieve synergies of approximately $400 million in 2009, net of costs. The company states that it expects synergies to grow beyond 2009. The combined revenues of the two companies equal approximately $2.2 billion. Assume the expected post-merger variable cost is 65% of revenues. Also, assume that the company will incur $200 million in fees, expenses, and integration and synergy related costs in the first year after the merger and none thereafter. Assume that the appropriate discount rate for discounting synergies is 13%; that the post-merger income tax rate is 40% on all income; that annual inflation is expected to be 3%; and that the breakdown of the expected 2009 pre-tax synergies, all of which are cash flows, is estimated as follows:

- $300 million revenue increase from an increase in the number of channels that is expected to grow with inflation.
- $105 million from a reduction in costs for the design and production of radios for automobiles provided to auto manufacturers
- $60 million from a reduction in costs for the design and production of non-auto radios
- $50 million from the reduction in costs for the production of overlapping entertainment channels
- $20 million from a reduction in marketing costs
- $20 million from the reduction in corporate overhead costs
- $40 million from a reduction in information and other technology costs from eliminating overlapping technologies

Measure the value of the synergies, assuming the cost synergies grow 50% in 2010 and then decline at a rate of 20% in perpetuity; assume revenue synergies continue in perpetuity.

P16.3 **Measuring Earnings Accretion/Dilution—Cash Deal:** A company (acquirer) purchases another company (target) for a 25% premium over the target's current stock price, which is $5 per share. The acquirer's stock price is $10 per share. The acquirer finances the transaction with all of its available excess cash, and it finances the remainder with debt, which has an 8% cost of capital and interest rate. The value of the interest tax shields from the incremental debt is $640. As a result of the merger, the companies expect to be able to increase annual revenues by $50 and decrease annual expenses by $200, which, in total, the companies value at $1,500. The company will amortize any purchase premium at an average rate of 5% per year, and the company values the tax shelter from the amortization at $400. Prepare a post-merger income statement and balance sheet.

	Standalone Acquirer	Standalone Target
Income Statement		
Revenues	$4,000.0	$2,750.0
Operating expenses	−2,213.3	−1,826.7
Interest income	40.0	20.0
Interest expense	−320.0	−240.0
Income taxes	−602.7	−281.3
Earnings	$ 904.0	$ 422.0
Shares outstanding	1,000.0	800.0
Earnings per share	$ 0.904	$ 0.528

	Standalone Acquirer	Standalone Target
Balance Sheet		
Excess cash	$ 2,000.0	$1,000.0
Operating assets	8,000.0	5,000.0
Total assets	$10,000.0	$6,000.0
Debt	$ 4,000.0	$3,000.0
Equity	6,000.0	3,000.0
Liabilities and equity	$10,000.0	$6,000.0

P16.4 **Measuring Value and Market Multiple Accretion/Dilution—Cash Deal:** Use the information in Problem 16.3 to measure the post-merger firm value, equity value, stock price, and P/E multiple. Compare these values to the acquirer's standalone values.

P16.5 **Measuring Earnings Accretion/Dilution—Stock-for-Stock Deal:** A company (acquirer) purchases another company (target) for a 42.5% premium over the target's then current stock price, which was $10 per share. The acquirer's stock price at that time was $11 per share. The acquirer finances the transaction by issuing common stock to the shareholders of the target company in exchange for all of the target's common stock. The exchange ratio is 1.25. As a result of the merger, the companies expect to be able to increase annual revenues by $200, and decrease annual expenses by $400, which in total, the companies value at $3,200. The company will amortize any purchase premium at an average rate of 5% per year, and the company values the tax shelter from the amortization at $1,000. Prepare a post-merger income statement and balance sheet.

	Standalone Acquirer	Standalone Target
Income Statement		
Revenues	$14,000.0	$3,600.0
Operating expenses	−9,066.7	−2,160.0
Interest income	0.0	0.0
Interest expense	−600.0	−240.0
Income taxes	−1,733.3	−480.0
Earnings	$ 2,600.0	$ 720.0
Shares outstanding	2,000.0	800.0
Earnings per share	$ 1.300	$ 0.900

	Standalone Acquirer	Standalone Target
Balance Sheet		
Excess cash	$ 0.0	$ 0.0
Operating assets	20,000.0	6,000.0
Total assets	$20,000.0	$6,000.0
Debt	$10,000.0	$4,000.0
Equity	10,000.0	2,000.0
Liabilities and equity	$20,000.0	$6,000.0

P16.6 **Measuring Value and Market Multiple Accretion/Dilution—Stock-for-Stock Deal:** Use the information in Problem 16.5 to measure the post-merger firm value, equity value, stock price, and P/E multiple. Compare these values to the acquirer's standalone values.

P16.7 **Negotiation and Allocation of Merger Gains—Cash Deal:** The standalone equity values of the acquirer and target are \$5,000 and \$3,000, respectively. The acquirer has 500 shares outstanding, and the target has 1,500 shares outstanding. Assume that the expected value created from this acquisition is \$1,000, but since the outcome of the merger is uncertain, assume a set of potential outcomes (value created or destroyed) that range from a merger gain of \$2,000 to a merger loss of \$1,000. Assuming the acquirer pays \$3,500 for the target's shares, calculate the gain or loss to the acquirer and target when the actual outcome of the merger is the expected, highest, and lowest outcome (see Exhibit 16.17).

P16.8 **Negotiation and Allocation of Merger Gains—Stock-for-Stock Deal:** Use the information in Problem 16.7 to respond to the following questions.

a. Measure the exchange ratio and resulting stock price that allocates \$5,500 of the post-merger value (based on the expected outcome) to the acquirer.

b. Measure the exchange ratio and resulting stock price that allocates the value of the synergies based on the relative standalone values of the two companies.

c. Based on a post-merger value equal to the expected outcome for the merger, calculate the target's minimum exchange ratio, the acquirer's maximum exchange ratio and the resulting stock prices.

d. Assuming the exchange ratio is 0.2121, calculate the gain or loss to the acquirer and target when the actual outcome of the merger is the expected, highest, and lowest outcome (see Exhibit 16.21).

P16.9 **Sources and Uses:** An acquirer makes an offer to purchase a target company. The target company's current stock price is \$3 per share, and it has 300 million shares outstanding. Given the expected synergies from the acquisition, the deal premium is negotiated at 20%. The target has no convertible debt or convertible preferred stock, but it does have 100 million stock options outstanding, all with an exercise price equal to \$3. The acquirer has to redeem the debt and preferred stock of the target for \$100 million and \$200 million, respectively and buy out the option holders. The acquirer plans to finance the acquisition with \$100 million of its own excess cash and \$20 million of the target's excess cash; it plans to finance the remainder with debt. Initial fees will equal \$47.4 million (3% on the debt financing and 1% for other fees). These fees do not include fees for a revolver loan. Debt issued to finance the transaction includes \$400 million of seven-year, 7.0% senior secured bank debt and \$800 million of nine-year, 9% subordinated unsecured debt; the remainder is financed with a revolving line of credit. The revolving line of credit of \$300 million has a five-year term, a 4% interest rate on the amount drawn, and a 0.5% annual fee on the total amount. Calculate the purchase price of the equity and prepare a sources and uses schedule similar to the sources and uses schedule in Exhibit 16.23.

P16.10 **Negotiation Range and Allocation of Synergies—LATAM Airline Group:** See Valuation in Practice 16.5, Valuation in Practice 16.6, and Review Exercise 16.1 for background information for this problem. The stock price of the acquiring company, LAN, prior to the merger announcement was approximately \$18 per share, and LAN had 339.36 million shares outstanding. TAM, the target company, had a stock price of \$14.60 and 156.21 million shares outstanding. Assume that the value of the synergies (merger gain) was expected to be \$3 billion but range from a loss of \$2 billion to a gain of \$5 billion. The companies agreed to an exchange ratio of 0.9.

a. Calculate the exchange ratio that would allocate 70% of the post-merger value to LAN shareholders.

b. Calculate the minimum exchange ratio that TAM shareholders would be willing to accept.

c. Calculate the maximum exchange ratio that LAN shareholders would be willing to accept.

d. Calculate the exchange ratio that would allocate the merger gain based on the relative standalone equity values of the two companies.

e. Based on the actual exchange ratio of 0.9, calculate the post-merger value and the allocation of the merger gain for the shareholders of each company when the actual outcome of the merger is the expected, highest and lowest outcome.

P16.11 **Negotiation Range and Allocation of Synergies—XM Sirius Radio Merger:** See Problem 16.2 for background information for this problem. The stock price of the acquiring company, Sirius, prior to the merger announcement was approximately \$3.7 per share, and Sirius had 1,460 million shares outstanding. XM, the target company, had a stock price around \$14 and 314 million shares outstanding. Assume the value of the synergies (merger gain) was expected to be \$1 billion but ranged from a loss of \$2 billion to a gain of \$3 billion. The companies agreed to an exchange ratio of 4.6.

a. Calculate the exchange ratio that would allocate 70% of the post-merger value to Sirius shareholders.

b. Calculate the minimum exchange ratio that XM shareholders would be willing to accept.

c. Calculate the maximum exchange ratio that Sirius shareholders would be willing to accept.

d. Calculate the exchange ratio that would allocate the merger gain based on the relative standalone equity values of the two companies.

e. Based on the actual exchange ratio of 4.6, calculate the post-merger value and the allocation of the merger gain for the shareholders of each company when the actual outcome of the merger is the expected, highest and lowest outcome.

SOLUTIONS FOR REVIEW EXERCISES

Review Exercise 16.1: Valuing Synergies—LATAM Airlines Group

Weighted Average Cost of Capital Valuation of Synergies:	10.00%		g=	−10.00%	
Tax rate =	30.0%				

($ in millions)	**Low**	**High**	**Midpoint**
Passenger revenue	$225	$260	$243
Cargo revenue	120	125	123
	$345	$385	$365
Frequent flyer program consolidation	$ 15	$ 25	$ 20
Airport/procurement	100	135	118
Maintenance	20	25	23
Information technology and other	120	130	125
	$255	$315	$285
	$600	$700	$650
Reduced investment in working capital	$150	$150	$150
Integration costs and fees	$170	$200	$185
First year synergies	$171	$200	$185

28.5%

($ in millions)		**2012**	**2013**	**2014**	**2015**	**2016**	**CV 2016**
Cumulative percentage of synergies achieved			**28.5%**	**50.0%**	**80.0%**	**100.0%**	
Pre-tax revenue synergies			$103.9	$182.5	$292.0	$365.0	$ 328.5
Pre-tax cost synergies			81.1	142.5	228.0	285.0	256.5
Integration costs and fees		−$185.0					
Less: taxes on synergies and costs		55.5	−55.5	−97.5	−156.0	−195.0	−175.5
Reduced investment in working capital savings			150.0				
After-tax costs, fees, synergies and other		−$129.5	$279.5	$227.5	$364.0	$455.0	$ 409.5
Discount factor for continuing value							5.000
Unlevered free cash flow and CV		−$129.5	$279.5	$227.5	$364.0	$455.0	$2,047.5
Discount factor		0.953	0.867	0.788	0.716	0.651	0.651
Present value		−$123.5	$242.3	$179.3	$260.8	$296.3	$1,333.4
Value of synergies	$2,188.5						

Exhibit may contain small rounding errors

		Continuing Value Growth Rate				
		−20.00%	**−15.00%**	**−10.00%**	**−5.00%**	**0.00%**
	9.00%	$1,734.6	$1,976.4	$2,345.4	$2,978.0	$4,313.4
	9.50%	$1,689.1	$1,918.2	$2,264.8	$2,850.4	$4,052.5
r_{WACC}	10.00%	$1,645.3	$1,862.6	$2,188.5	$2,731.7	$3,818.2
	10.50%	$1,603.1	$1,809.4	$2,116.2	$2,621.0	$3,606.6
	11.00%	$1,562.6	$1,758.5	$2,047.7	$2,517.6	$3,414.7

25th percentile	$1,809.4
50th percentile	$2,188.5
75th percentile	$2,850.4
Mean	$2,457.1

Note: The investment synergy does not increase income taxes because it does not affect income but only the amount of investment.

Review Exercise 16.2: Measuring Earnings Accretion

	Standalone Acquirer	Standalone Target	Financing	Expenses and Asset Changes	Synergies	Post-Merger Company
Income Statement						
Revenues	$ 4,000.0	$2,750.0			$ 30.0	$ 6,780.0
Operating expenses	−2,280.0	−1,790.0		−$ 45.0	270.0	−3,845.0
Interest income	60.0	20.0		−80.0		0.0
Interest expense	−180.0	−60.0	−$ 120.0			−360.0
Income taxes	−640.0	−368.0	48.0	50.0	−120.0	−1,030.0
Earnings	$ 960.0	$ 552.0	−$ 72.0	−$ 75.0	$180.0	$ 1,545.0
Shares outstanding	400.0	200.0	400.0	400.0	400.0	400.0
Earnings per share	$ 2.400	$ 2.760	−$ 0.180	−$ 0.188	$0.450	$ 3.863
Balance Sheet						
Excess cash	$ 3,000.0	$1,000.0	$2,000.0	−$6,000.0		$ 0
Operating assets	8,000.0	5,000.0		1,000.0		14,000.0
Total assets	$11,000.0	$6,000.0	$2,000.0	−$5,000.0	$ 0	$14,000.0
Debt	$ 3,000.0	$1,000.0	$2,000.0			$ 6,000.0
Equity	8,000.0	5,000.0		−$5,000.0		8,000.0
Liabilities and equity	$11,000.0	$6,000.0	$2,000.0	−$5,000.0	$ 0	$14,000.0
Rates of Return (excluding excess assets & using ending balances)						
Return on assets	12.9%	11.5%				12.6%
Return on equity	18.5%	13.5%				19.3%

Review Exercise 16.3: Effect of Accretion on Market Multiples

	Standalone Acquirer	Standalone Target	Financing	Excess Cash	Value of Synergies	Post-Merger Company Including Synergies
Firm value	$12,200.0	$6,000.0	$ 400.0	−$3,850.0	$1,500.0	$16,250.0
Debt	3,000.0	1,000.0	2,000.0	0.0	0.0	6,000.0
Equity value	$ 9,200.0	$5,000.0	−$1,600.0	−$3,850.0	$1,500.0	$10,250.0
Shares outstanding	400.0	200.0			400.0	400.0
Price per share	$ 23.00	$ 25.00			$ 3.75	$ 25.63
Earnings per share	$ 2.400	$ 2.760			$ 0.450	$ 3.863
Price-to-earnings ratio	9.6	9.1			8.3	6.6

Review Exercise 16.4: Negotiation and Allocation of Synergies—Cash Deals

	Value	Shares	Price		Symbol
Standalone Equity Values					
Standalone value of acquirer	$10,000	1000	$10.00		V_A
Standalone value of target	$ 4,000	2000	$ 2.00		V_T
Combined standalone value	$14,000				$V_A + V_T$
Potential Outcomes of Value Created or Destroyed (Synergies)					
Expected value of value created	$ 3,000				$E(V_S)$
Lower bound of value created (destroyed)	−$ 2,500				V_S
Upper bound of value created (destroyed)	$ 5,000				V_S
Potential Outcomes of the Post-Merger Equity Value					
Expected value of post-merger company	$17,000				$E(V_P)$
Lower bound of post-merger company	$11,500				V_P
Upper bound of post-merger company	$19,000				V_P
Negotiated Deal					
Expected value created (merger gain (loss))	$ 3,000				$E(V_S)$
Expected value of post-merger equity	$17,000				$E(V_P)$
Premium paid to target	$ 2,000	66.7%	% of Synergies Allocated		$V_{T,\ premium}$
Standalone value of target	4,000				V_T
Amount paid for target	$ 6,000	50.0%	% Premium Paid for Target		$V_{T,\ paid}$

	Expected Outcome Used in Deal Negotiation			Actual Outcome with More Value Created			Actual Outcome with Value Destroyed		
Cash Deal–Equity Values	**Outcome**	**% Split**	**% Gain**	**Outcome**	**% Split**	**% Gain**	**Outcome**	**% Split**	**% Gain**
Standalone value of acquirer	$10,000			$10,000			$10,000		
Standalone value of target	4,000			4,000			4,000		
Combined standalone value	$14,000			$14,000			$14,000		
Value created (merger gain (loss))	3,000			5,000			−2,500		
Post-merger value	$17,000			$19,000			$11,500		
Overall gain or (loss) on acquisition	$ 3,000		21.4%	$ 5,000		35.7%	−$ 2,500		−17.9%
Post-merger value to target (cash received)	$ 6,000	35.3%		$ 6,000	31.6%		$ 6,000	52.2%	
Standalone value of target	−4,000			−4,000			−4,000		
Gain (loss) to target—merger premium	$ 2,000	66.7%	50.0%	$ 2,000	40.0%	50.0%	$ 2,000	nmf	50.0%
Post-merger value to acquirer	$11,000	64.7%		$13,000	68.4%		$ 5,500	47.8%	
Standalone value of acquirer	−10,000			−10,000			−10,000		
Gain or (loss) to acquirer	$ 1,000	33.3%	10.0%	$ 3,000	60.0%	30.0%	−$ 4,500	nmf	−45.0%

Review Exercise 16.5: Allocation of Synergies—Stock-for-Stock Deals ($ in millions)

Exchange Ratio Based on a Percentage Allocation of Value				
	S_A/S_T	S_A	S_T	
S_A/S_T	0.50	1,000	2,000	
		C_A	S_T	
$C_A \times S_T$	1,294	64.7%		
ER_{CA}	0.273			
Shares issued to target = $ER_{CA} \times S_T$	545.45		2,000	
Post-Merger—Check	**Shares**	**%**	**Value**	**Price**
Acquirer shares (not changed)	1,000	64.7%	$11,000	$11.00
Target shares	545	35.3%	$ 6,000	$11.00
Total shares	1,545	100.0%	$17,000	$11.00

Exchange Ratio to Allocate Synergies and Total Value by Relative Standalone Values				
	ER	P_T	P_A	S_T
ER	0.200	$2.00	$ 10.00	
Shares issued to target = ER × S_T	400.00			2000
Post-Merger—Check	**Shares**	**%**	**Value**	**Price**
Acquirer shares (not changed)	1,000	71.4%	$12,143	$12.14
Target shares	400	28.6%	$ 4,857	$12.14
Total shares	1,400	100.0%	$17,000	$12.14

Minimum Exchange Ratio—All Value Created (Destroyed) to Acquirer—Target's Value Is Equal to Its Standalone Value				
	$P_T \times S_A$	P_T	S_A	
$P_T \times S_A$	$2,000	$2	1,000	
		V_P	V_T	S_T
$V_P - V_T$	$13,000	$17,000	$4,000	
ER_{MIN}	0.154			
Shares issued to target = $ER_{MIN} \times S_T$	307.69			2,000
Post-Merger—Check	**Shares**	**%**	**Value**	**Price**
Acquirer shares (not changed)	1,000	76.5%	$13,000	$13.00
Target shares	308	23.5%	$ 4,000	$13.00
Total shares	1,308	100.0%	$17,000	$13.00

Maximum Exchange Ratio—All Value Created (Destroyed) to Target—Acquirer's Value Is Equal to Its Standalone Value				
	$V_P - V_A$	V_P	V_A	
$V_P - V_A$	$7,000	$17,000	$10,000	
		P_A	S_T	
$P_A \times S_T$	$20,000	$10	2,000	
ER_{MAX}	0.350			
Shares issued to target = $ER_{MAX} \times S_T$	700.00			
Post-Merger—Check	**Shares**	**%**	**Value**	**Price**
Acquirer shares (not changed)	1,000	58.8%	$10,000	$10.00
Target shares	700	41.2%	$ 7,000	$10.00
Total shares	1,700	100.0%	$17,000	$10.00

Stock Deal–Equity Values	Expected Outcome Used in Deal Negotiation			Actual Outcome with More Value Created			Actual Outcome with Value Destroyed		
	Outcome	% Split	% Gain	Outcome	% Split	% Gain	Outcome	% Split	% Gain
Standalone value of acquirer	$10,000			$10,000			$10,000		
Standalone value of target	4,000			4,000			4,000		
Combined standalone value	$14,000			$14,000			$14,000		
Value created (merger gain (loss))	3,000			5,000			−2,500		
Post-merger value	$17,000			$19,000			$11,500		
Overall gain or (loss) on acquisition	$ 3,000		21.4%	$ 5,000		35.7%	−$ 2,500		−17.9%
Post-merger value to target (stock received)	$ 6,000	35.3%		$ 6,706	35.3%		$ 4,059	35.3%	
Standalone value of target	−4,000			−4,000			−4,000		
Gain (loss) to target—merger premium	$ 2,000	66.7%	50.0%	$ 2,706	54.1%	67.6%	$ 59	nmf	1.5%
Post-merger value to acquirer	$11,000	64.7%		$12,294	64.7%		$ 7,441	64.7%	
Standalone value of acquirer	−10,000			−10,000			−10,000		
Gain or (loss) to acquirer	$ 1,000	33.3%	10.0%	$ 2,294	45.9%	22.9%	−$ 2,559	nmf	−25.6%

Review Exercise 16.6: Merger Sources and Uses Schedule

Current stock price	$ 10.00			
Deal premium	25.0%			
Deal stock price	$ 12.50			
Number of fully diluted shares outstanding	114.0		100.00	14.00
Purchase price of equity	$1,425.0			

Pre-Merger Outstanding Options as of End of Year 0 (Liquidation of Options)				
Year Issued	Exercise Price	Number of Options = Shares Issued (m)	Buyback Shares (m)	Net Increase in Shares (m)
Various	$9.00	50.0	36.0	14.0

Sources and Uses of Cash—Merger Financing ($ in millions)	Amount	%	Coupon = YTM	Maturity (Years)
Sources				
Excess cash—acquirer	$ 200.0	13.6%		
Excess cash—target	100.0	6.8%		
Revolver	72.3	4.9%	4.00%	5
Senior secured note (bank debt)	400.0	27.2%	6.00%	7
Subordinated note (unsecured debt)	700.0	47.5%	8.00%	9
Preferred stock—new	0.0	0.0%		
Common equity	0.0	0.0%		
Total sources	$1,472.3	100.0%		
Uses				
Common equity	$1,425.0	96.8%		
Preferred stock—redeemed	0.0	0.0%		
Debt redeemed	0.0	0.0%		
Initial fees:			Fee rate	Total
Financing fees—debt	33.0	2.2%	3.0%	
Financing fees—revolver			0.5%	$200
Other fees and expenses	14.3	1.0%	1.0%	
Total uses	$1,472.3	100.0%		

Note: The treasury stock method (see Chapter 15) was used to calculate the number of shares issued for the target's outstanding options.

After mastering the material in this chapter, you will be able to:

1. Explain how cross-border valuations differ from within-country (domestic) valuations (17.1)
2. Use exchange rate theories to forecast exchange rates (17.2–17.3)
3. Measure income taxes for a cross-border valuation (17.4)
4. Measure discount rates and adjust free cash flows for country-specific risks (17.5–17.6)
5. Explain the limitations of using cross-border market multiples and measure exchange rate exposure (17.7–17.8)

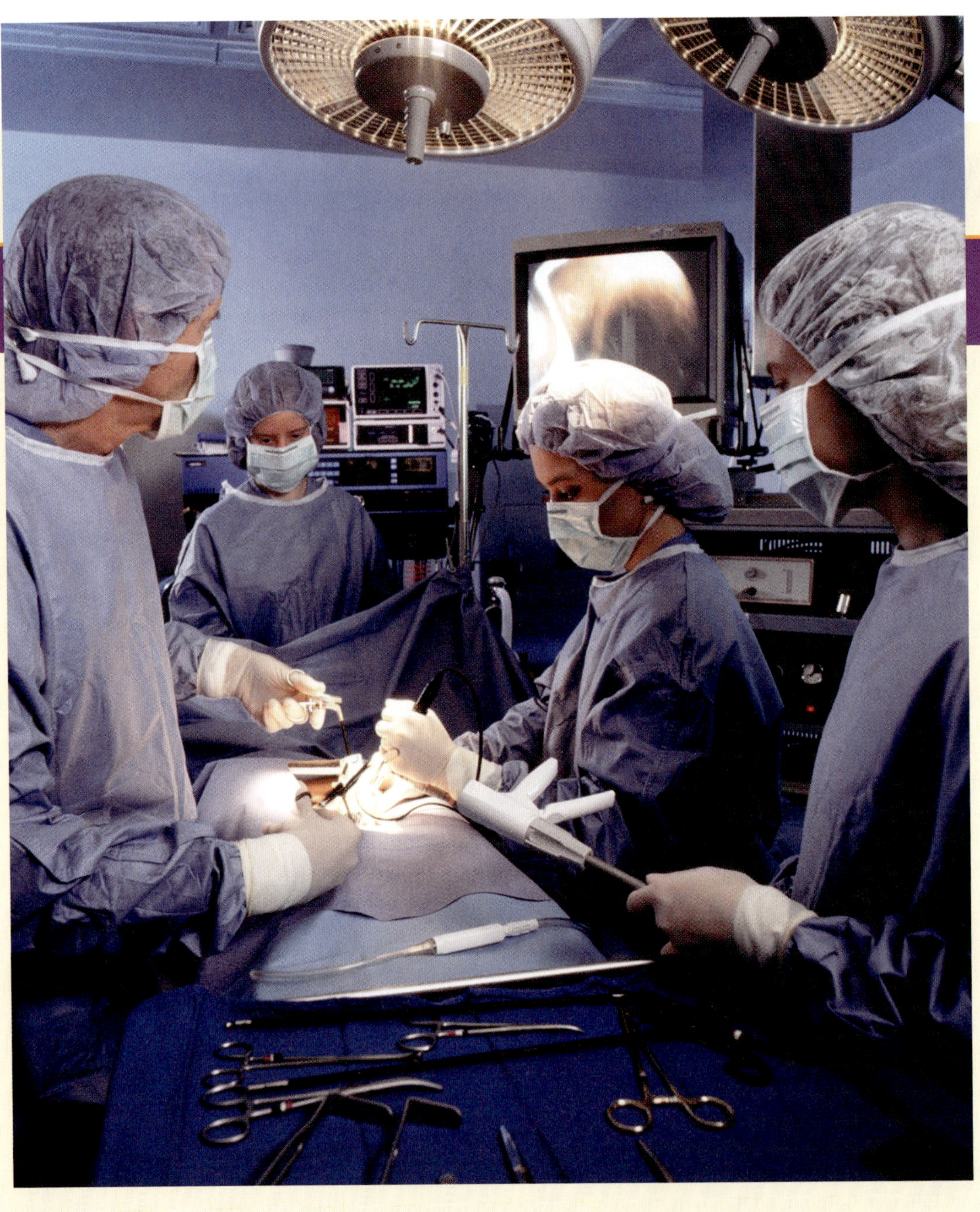

CHAPTER

17

Valuing Businesses Across Borders

SYNTHES, INC.

A common reason for cross-border acquisitions is to gain access to new markets, technology, or products. On April 27, 2011, Johnson & Johnson (J&J), a U.S. company, announced a definitive merger agreement with Synthes, Inc. (Synthes), a Swiss Company. J&J announced that it would acquire Synthes for $21.3 billion in a cash and stock purchase of Synthes' shares (a 27% premium relative to the closing stock price 30 days prior to the announcement). The companies stated the following reasons for the merger:[1]

> Together, the companies will offer surgeons and patients a unique breadth and depth of technology and service worldwide to meet their orthopedic needs. . . . Synthes is widely respected for its innovative high-quality products, world-class R&D capabilities, its commitment to education, the highest standards of service, and extensive global footprint. The combination presents a significant opportunity to jointly bring our products, services and educational offerings to the next level. . . . Together, we will be a more attractive and exciting company for our employees, and a more resourceful partner for our customers. . . .

In this chapter, we explore and highlight the key differences between the valuation of a company operating in a single country and the valuation of a cross-border acquisition target or a multinational company.

[1] See Johnson and Johnson's Form 8-K, filed with the U.S. Securities and Exchange Commission (SEC) on August 7, 2011.

CHAPTER ORGANIZATION

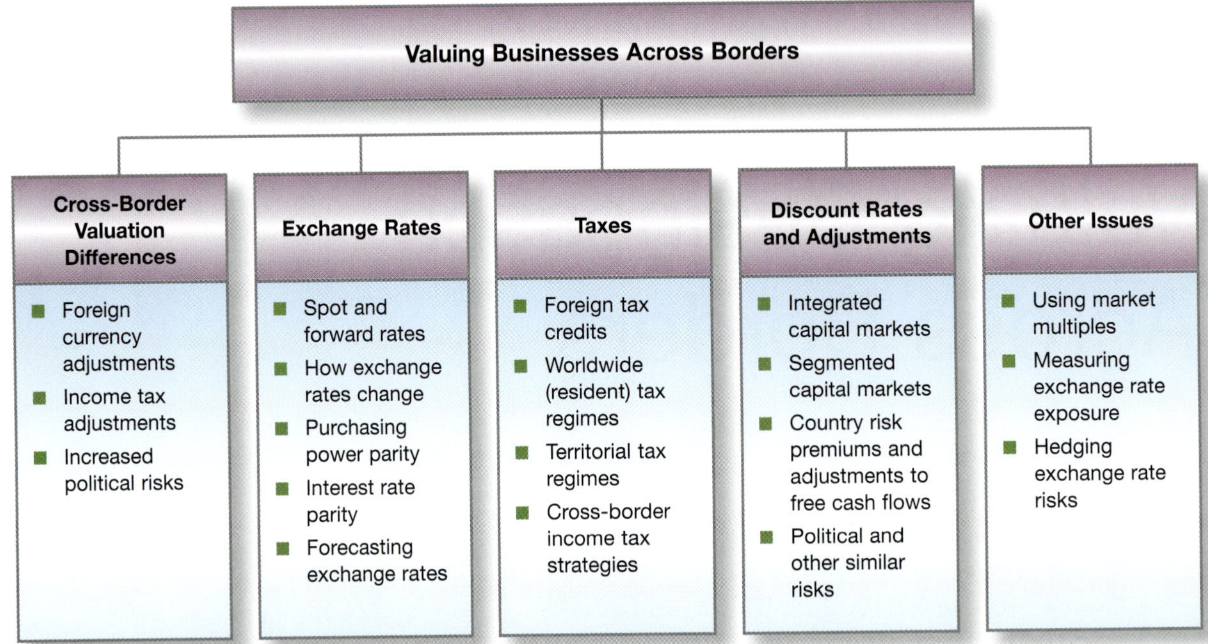

INTRODUCTION

Not that long ago, companies generated most of their revenues and incurred most of their expenses in the country in which they were located (their home or domestic markets). One reason cited for the focus of business activities in domestic markets is that business activities conducted outside of domestic markets are potentially more uncertain. This uncertainty results from different political, legal, and regulatory environments as well as from operating in a different environment and culture, making it more difficult for a company to generate revenues and manage its operations efficiently. These uncertainties exist for all cross-border expansions, but they are generally greater when companies expand into countries with less developed economies and legal systems.

In spite of these uncertainties, cross-border mergers and acquisitions have become more popular as business has become more global. Companies gain access to new markets, technology, and products by expanding globally. They can also gain access to more resources and to cheaper inputs in the production process (such as labor). In addition, innovations in technology have reduced and are continuing to reduce the barriers to conducting business across borders. The Internet, for example, has made it easier, quicker, and less costly to communicate and transfer information over long distances; it is also said to be "shrinking the globe," reducing some of the environmental and cultural differences as well as some of the uncertainties of doing business in other parts of the world.

Up until now, we assumed that companies operated in the same country in which they were located and that the country in which they operated had well-established capital markets. The valuation models and frameworks discussed throughout the previous chapters also apply to cross-border valuations; however, the implementation of these models and frameworks is typically more complex in a cross-border valuation. In this chapter, we now assume that a company—located and operating in one country—is investing in another company (or project) that is located and operating in another country (or countries)—in short, a cross-border valuation.

We discuss how to adjust the valuation models and tools discussed in the previous chapters to value cross-border business activities. The adjustments we make address foreign currency exchange rate issues, income and other types of taxes resulting from a cross-border investment, and cost-of-capital estimation issues. In addition, we discuss issues that specifically arise for cross-border valuations of companies in emerging markets. Finally, since cross-border business activities create potential exposure to unexpected changes in foreign currency exchange rates (the price at which one can convert one type of currency into another type of currency), we discuss exchange rate exposure and how it is hedged. Although the context of this chapter is the valuation of a cross-border acquisition, everything discussed is germane to valuing multinational companies or projects in a foreign country.

17.1 HOW CROSS-BORDER VALUATIONS ARE DIFFERENT

LO1 Explain how cross-border valuations differ from within-country (domestic) valuations

This chapter focuses on a valuation context in which a company located and operating in one country is investing in a company located and operating in another country. We refer to the first company as the **investing company** and the second company as the **foreign** or **cross-border company**. We refer to the currency for the investing company as the **investor currency** or **home currency** and to the currency for the foreign company as the **foreign currency**. Even if a company's cross-border business activities take place in a country with well-established capital markets and legal systems, valuing cross-border activities requires certain adjustments to the implementation of the valuation models and frameworks. We typically make additional adjustments if the foreign company is operating in a developing economy.

Potential Adjustments to Free Cash Flow Forecasts

Various types of issues can arise in cross-border valuations that may require an adjustment to the free cash flows used in a DCF valuation model. These issues include:

- **Exchange Rate Forecasts:** Our goal in a cross-border valuation is to value the cross-border company based on the investor's currency, which requires exchange rate forecasts.
- **Taxes:** An investor (company) in a company located in another country may incur additional (or fewer) taxes simply because the investor is a foreigner, for example, if the target repatriates earnings (pays dividends) to a foreign acquirer. These taxes can include income taxes and withholding taxes on dividends, as well as other types of explicit or implicit taxes, including import and export taxes or tariffs, quotas, and employment taxes.
- **Nominal or Real Forecasts and Discount Rates:** Some countries experience periods of hyperinflation. To the extent that a cross-border company operates in a hyperinflationary economy, we consider whether to value the company in nominal or real terms (nominal free cash flow forecasts with a nominal discount rate or real free cash flow forecasts with a real discount rate).
- **Timing of Cash Flows:** Regulatory limitations on the repatriation of earnings and cash flows can affect the timing of when cash is available for distribution to the investors of a foreign company. Although not directly a timing issue, liquidity issues (the ability to sell the asset if needed or expected) are issues we might also consider.
- **Increased Political and Other Foreign Country Related Risks:** In addition to the potential outcomes normally considered when developing free cash flow forecasts, increased uncertainty from political or other foreign country risks might require additional adjustments when measuring expected free cash flows.

Potential Adjustments to the Risk-Adjusted Discount Rate

Similarly, various types of issues can arise in cross-border valuations that may require an adjustment to the risk-adjusted discount rate used in the DCF valuation model. These issues include:

- **Asset Pricing Model Risk Factors and Risk Premiums:** We may adjust how we estimate risk factors such as the Capital Asset Pricing Model (CAPM) beta and whether or not to include other risk factors such as a risk factor for currency risk.
- **Political and Other Foreign Country Related Risks (Country Credit Rating):** In the previous section, we discussed potential adjustments to the expected free cash flows due to country-specific risks. If these risk factors are systematic risk factors, they also affect the cost of capital. We adjust the discount rate for country-related risks if the risks are systematic in nature and not embedded in the risk factors in our asset pricing model (for example, beta in the CAPM). An example of a potential systematic risk might be a country's fiscal policies, which can result in a country-specific systematic risk factor if they affect interest rates, inflation, or other macroeconomic factors that affect the value of the firm.
- **Capital Structure and Tax Deductibility of Interest:** Tax regulations may affect the amount and type of debt a company can issue for which interest is tax deductible. We adjust a valuation for any constraints on capital structure and the tax deductibility of interest. Differences in bankruptcy laws may also affect financial distress costs.

Valuation Key 17.1

While the discounted cash flow valuation model and framework continue to apply in cross-border valuations, specific characteristics of these valuations require adjustments to the implementation of the DCF valuation model. We adjust our free cash flow forecasts and risk-adjusted discount rates relative to the more standard procedures previously discussed.

Investor Currency (Centralized) and Foreign Currency (Decentralized) Discounted Cash Flow Valuation Approaches

We implement the DCF valuation model to value cross-border companies using one of two approaches to convert the valuation of the cross-border company into the investor's local currency, called the investor currency (centralized) approach and the foreign currency (decentralized) approach. The primary difference between the two approaches is the timing of when we convert the foreign currency to the investor's currency. In the centralized approach, we convert the foreign currency to the investor's currency in the forecasting model, and we convert each year's forecasted foreign currency free cash flows to investor currency free cash flows using exchange rate forecasts. In the decentralized approach, we convert the foreign currency to the investor's currency after valuing the company in its own currency by converting the value of the company stated in the foreign currency to the value of the company stated in the investor's currency using the spot exchange rate as of the valuation date. In Exhibit 17.1, we present an outline of the steps underpinning the two approaches.

EXHIBIT 17.1 Comparison of the Investor Currency (Centralized) and Local Currency (Decentralized) DCF Approaches

Investor Currency or Centralized Approach (Discount Investor Currency Cash Flows)	Foreign Currency or Decentralized Approach (Discount Foreign Currency Cash Flows)
1 Choose a reinvestment/repatriation (upstream cash flows) policy	1 Same as the investor currency or centralized approach
2 Assess special tax effects resulting from ownership by a foreign company	2 Same as the investor currency or centralized approach
3 Assess specific country risks affecting expected free cash flows	3 Same as the investor currency or centralized approach
4 Develop a financial model incorporating Steps 1 through 3 and forecast free cash flows in the company's local currency	4 Same as the investor currency or centralized approach
5 Develop forecasts for the exchange rates for all periods in the forecast horizon of the financial model and convert the local currency free cash flows to the investor's currency	
6 Measure the cost of capital based on the investor's currency, adjusting for any country-specific systematic risks	5 Measure the cost of capital based on the foreign currency, including any country-specific systematic risks
7 Discount the free cash flows from Step 5 using the discount rate from Step 6	6 Discount the free cash flows from Step 4 using the discount rate from Step 5
	7 Convert the value of the firm measured in the foreign currency to the value of the firm measured in the investor's currency at the exchange rate as of the valuation date

The first four steps of the DCF valuation are the same in both approaches. The first step focuses on the income tax effects of repatriating cash flows from a foreign company to an investor company. We begin by choosing a reinvestment or repatriation policy to understand the effects of repatriating cash flows—typically income tax effects. If a company chooses a repatriation policy that prevents or delays the distribution of free cash flows to the investor company, we consider the effect it may have on the valuation of the free cash flows (though cash is often invested in marketable securities that earn their cost of capital). The second step focuses on other potential income tax effects resulting from cross-border ownership.

In Step 3, we assess specific country risks that might affect the free cash flow forecasts. We use this step more frequently for foreign companies located and operating in developing economies. It includes such risks as the expropriation of assets or income by the government, unclear or inconsistently interpreted regulations, the difficulty of enforcing contracts, bureaucracy, and corruption; generally, these risks are more likely and more severe in developing countries than in developed countries. The fourth step develops the financial model discussed in Chapter 4, but now we include the adjustments from the first three steps.

Since the two approaches differ in terms of their remaining steps, we discuss them separately and begin with the investor currency (centralized) approach. In Step 5 of the centralized approach, we convert the foreign currency-denominated free cash flows in the financial model to the investor currency. In order to perform this conversion, we first develop exchange rate forecasts for all periods in the financial model. We use these exchange rate forecasts to convert the foreign currency-denominated free cash flow forecasts for each year into investor currency-denominated free cash flow forecasts. In Step 6, we measure the various costs of capital needed to measure the risk-adjusted discount rate for the foreign investment in terms of the investor's currency, including the effect of any country-specific systematic risks. Since we convert free cash flow forecasts to the investor's currency, we measure the costs of capital and risk-adjusted discount rate for the foreign investment in terms of the investor's currency. Lastly, in Step 7, we discount the investor currency-denominated free cash flow forecasts at the investor currency risk-adjusted discounted rate to value the firm.

For the foreign currency (decentralized) approach, we do not convert the free cash flows to the investor currency. Instead, in Step 5, we measure the various costs of capital needed to measure the risk-adjusted discount rate, again including the effect of any country-specific systematic risks. Since the free cash flow forecasts are denominated in the foreign currency, we measure the costs of capital and risk-adjusted discount rate for the foreign investment in terms of the foreign currency. In Step 6, we discount the foreign currency-denominated free cash flow forecasts at the foreign currency risk-adjusted discount rate for the foreign investment in terms of the foreign currency. Lastly, in Step 7, we convert the foreign currency-denominated firm value to the investor currency with the current (or spot) exchange rate as of the valuation date. Of the two approaches, the investor currency (centralized) approach is more commonly used to value cross-border acquisitions and in valuing multinational companies. We will explain this in more detail later.

Regardless of which approach we use, we always use a consistent basis for measuring the free cash flows and discount rate. In the investor approach, we discount investor currency free cash flows at the investor currency discount rate; in the foreign currency approach, we discount the foreign currency free cash flows at the foreign currency discount rate.

Valuation Key 17.2

We can use one of two approaches—the investor currency (centralized) approach or the foreign currency (decentralized) approach—to adjust the DCF valuation model to value cross-border acquisitions or multinational companies. The primary difference between the two approaches is the timing of the conversion from the foreign currency to the investor currency. In the investor currency (centralized) approach, which is the more common approach, we perform this conversion for each free cash flow in the financial model, while in the foreign currency (decentralized) approach, we perform this conversion after we value the company in its own currency.

Example Illustrating the Centralized and Decentralized Approaches

A company in the U.S., Booth Investor Group, is purchasing a company in Russia, the Ananiev Group. Booth is attempting to value the Ananiev Group in U.S. dollars (USD). After repatriation, taxes, and country-related risks are considered, the free cash flow forecasts of Ananiev for the next three years, stated in Russian rubles (RUB), are 10,000 RUB, 12,340 RUB, and 12,760 RUB; also, the continuing value of the company as of the end of Year 3 is 190,000 RUB. The current exchange rate is 27.8 RUB/USD, and exchange rate forecasts for the next three years for the price of $1 in Russian Rubles (RUB/USD) are 28.91, 30.28, and 31.78. The appropriate risk-adjusted discount rate for this company's cash flows, stated in USD, is 10% and is constant in each year. To simplify the example, we assume both Booth and Ananiev are only financed with common equity.

In Panel A of Exhibit 17.2, we present the DCF valuation of the company using the investor currency (centralized) approach. We first convert the free cash flow and continuing value forecasts from rubles to dollars, using the exchange rate forecasts. Next, we discount the expected free cash flow and continuing value (stated in USD) by the constant cost of capital of 10% in order to measure their present values. The value of the firm is equal to $5,444.1.

EXHIBIT 17.2 Example Illustrating the Equality of the Two DCF Approaches

Panel A—Investor Currency/Centralized Approach	Year 0	Year 1	Year 2	Year 3	$CV_{Firm, Yr 3}$
Free cash flow and continuing value (in RUB × 1,000)		10,000	12,340	12,760	190,000
Exchange rate forecast (RUB/USD)		28.913	30.279	31.784	31.784
Free cash flow and continuing value (USD × 1,000)		$ 346	$ 408	$ 401	$ 5,978
Risk-adjusted discount factor for investor currency	10.0%	0.909	0.826	0.751	0.751
Present value (in USD × 1,000)		$ 314.4	$ 336.8	$ 301.6	$4,491.3
Value of the firm (in USD ×1,000)	$ 5,444.1				

Panel B—Foreign Currency/Decentralized Approach	Year 0	Year 1	Year 2	Year 3	$CV_{Firm, Yr 3}$
Free cash flow and continuing value (in RUB × 1,000)		10,000	12,340	12,760	190,000
Risk-adjusted discount rate in r_{RUB}.		14.42%	15.20%	15.47%	15.47%
Discount factor for foreign currency.		0.874	0.759	0.657	0.657
Present value (in RUB × 1,000)		8,739.7	9,362.0	8,383.5	124,837.6
Value of the firm (in RUB × 1,000)	151,322.9				
Current or spot exchange rate (RUB/USD)	27.80				
Value of the firm (in USD × 1,000)	$ 5,444.1				

Exhibit may contain small rounding errors

In Panel B of the exhibit, we present the DCF valuation of the company using the foreign currency (decentralized) approach. This approach requires an appropriate risk-adjusted discount rate for the free cash flow and continuing value forecasts stated in rubles. For now, assume the appropriate risk-adjusted discount rates based on the foreign currency for the next three years are 14.42%, 15.20%, and 15.47%. We will explain how to calculate these discount rates from the 10% investor discount rate and the forecasted exchange rates in the next section of the chapter. We use these discount rates to measure the present value of the free cash flow and continuing value forecasts stated in rubles. Recall that since the discount rate changes in each period, the discount factor is the product of the individual one-period discount factors; for example, the discount factor for Year 2 is $(1.1442)^{-1} \times (1.1520)^{-1}$, and the discount factor for Year 3 is the discount factor for Year 2 multiplied by $(1.1547)^{-1}$. The value of the firm, stated in rubles, is 151,322.9 RUB. We convert this value to USD using the current exchange rate of 27.8 in order to arrive at a value of $5,444.1, which is identical to the value calculated using the investor currency or centralized approach.

As is clear from this example, forecasting exchange rates is an important aspect of the investor currency (centralized) approach, for this approach uses these exchange rate forecasts directly; however, we also implicitly use exchange rate forecasts to implement the foreign currency (decentralized) approach. As we might suspect from our example, in order for the two approaches to yield the same valuation, the exchange rate forecasts must be linked to the appropriate risk-adjusted discount rates for the free cash flow and continuing value forecasts stated in rubles. We discuss this link later in the chapter when we discuss exchange rate theories and exchange rate forecasts. Again, for reasons we discuss later, the investor currency (centralized) approach—convert cash flows and discount them at the investor currency cost of capital—is the more common approach.

Valuation Key 17.3

While the investor currency (centralized) approach uses exchange rate forecasts directly, the foreign currency (decentralized) approach also uses exchange rate forecasts to convert the discount rate from one currency to the discount rate for another currency.

REVIEW EXERCISE 17.1

Investor Currency (Centralized) and Foreign Currency (Decentralized) Discounted Cash Flow Valuation Approaches

A company in France is purchasing a company in the U.S. The French company is attempting to value the U.S. company in euros. After repatriation, taxes, and country-related risks are taken into consideration, the free cash flow forecasts of the U.S. company for the next three years, stated in USD, are $1.2 million, $1.4 million, and $1.7 million, respectively; also, the continuing value of the company as of the end of Year 3 is $180 million. The current and forward exchange rates appear in Exhibit P17.1 in the problem section of the chapter. The appropriate risk-adjusted discount rate for this company's cash flows, stated in euros, is 12% and is constant in each year. The appropriate discount rates for discounting USD for the next three years are 10.978%, 11.207%, and 11.361%, respectively. Both of the companies are only financed with common equity. Measure the value of the U.S. company in euros using both the investor currency and foreign currency discounted cash flow methods.

Solution on page 910.

Other Potential Economic Forces Affecting Cross-Border Valuations[2]

Depending on the relation between the foreign company's expected free cash flows and unexpected changes in exchange rates or the exchange rate forecasts we use in the valuation, we could have additional adjustments in a cross-border valuation.

The first potential adjustment results from a relation between the foreign company's free cash flows and unexpected changes in exchange rates—more specifically, the covariance between the foreign company's free cash flows and the exchange rate. This covariance could be non-zero if unexpected changes in the exchange rate cause either the foreign company's revenues (quantity or price) or its cost structure to change. If this covariance is not equal to zero, it can affect value. Generally, however, we assume that the foreign company's free cash flows, denominated in the foreign currency, are not related to the exchange rate; that is, we typically assume that unexpected changes in the exchange rate do not cause a change in the foreign currency-denominated free cash flows or that the covariance between them is sufficiently small to allow us to ignore it in the valuation.

The second potential adjustment results from using forecasted exchange rates that differ from market-based exchange rates. If we used forecasted exchange rates that differ from market-based exchange rates, we can partition the cross-border valuation into two parts: the value based on market-based exchange rates and the change in value that results from using exchange rate forecasts that differ from the market-based exchange rates.

17.2 EXCHANGE RATE BASICS

LO2 Use exchange rate theories to forecast exchange rates

Regardless of which form of the DCF valuation model we implement, we use exchange rate forecasts to either convert cash flows from the foreign currency to the investor's currency or to measure the appropriate risk-adjusted discount rate in the foreign currency. Understanding the determinants of exchange rates is also important because they can affect the demand for a company's products or its cost structure. In addition, given the global nature of capital markets, unexpected exchange rate changes can affect the impact of financing decisions. In this section, we discuss the basic concepts of exchange rates, forward contracts, and how to think about changes in exchange rates.

Spot and Forward Exchange Rates

We can think of an **exchange rate** as the price of one currency for one unit of another currency. Terms used to discuss current and future exchange rates are the spot rate and future expected spot rate or forward

[2] For a detailed discussion of the issues in this section, see O'Brien, Thomas J., "Foreign Exchange and Cross-Border Valuation," *Journal of Corporate Finance* (Spring/Summer 2004), pp. 147–154; O'Brien, Thomas J., "The Global CAPM and a Firm's Cost of Capital in Different Currencies," *Journal of Corporate Finance* (Fall 1999), pp. 73–79; and Butler, Kirt, Tom O'Brien, and Gwinyai Utete, "A Fresh Look at Cross-Border Valuation and FX Hedging Decisions," *Journal of Applied Finance* 23 (2), 2013.

rate. Terms used to describe changes in exchange rates include exchange rate appreciation (or increases in value) and exchange rate depreciation (or decreases in value). The **spot rate** is the current exchange rate for immediate delivery of a currency (actually, most of the time, delivery typically takes about two days for the transaction to clear).

With a few exceptions, exchange rates involving U.S. dollars are traded and quoted as the number of units of a non-U.S. currency per one U.S. dollar (USD or \$), denoted, $S_{non\text{-}USD/\$}$. Examples of exceptions include the U.K.'s British Pound Sterling (GBP or £) and the euro (EUR or €), which are traded based on the number of USD per GBP ($S_{\$/£}$) or euro ($S_{\$/€}$). However, we can always invert the exchange rate to measure the price of a non-U.S. currency in USD, denoted $S_{\$/non\text{-}USD} = 1/S_{non\text{-}USD/\$}$. For example, assume a company in the U.S. (which uses the U.S. dollar for its currency) is buying products in the U.K. and must pay for the products with £. In order to complete this transaction, the U.S. company must exchange \$ for £, in other words, purchase £. If \$100 purchases £61.36, then the exchange rate is 1.63 \$/£, stated as $S_{\$/£} = 1.63$ (1.63 = \$100/£61.36) or $S_{£/\$} = 0.6136$, which is equal to the inverse of the $S_{\$/£}$ exchange rate (0.6136 = £61.36/\$100).

Valuation in Practice 17.1

Caraco Pharmaceutical Laboratories, Ltd. (a U.S. Company) Acquired by Sun Pharmaceutical Industries Limited (an Indian Company) It is common for a company to first enter a foreign market through an agreement with a local company in that foreign market. If successful, these relationships sometimes evolve into the acquisition of the company in the foreign market, which is the case of Caraco and Sun Pharma. On February 22, 2011, Caraco Pharmaceutical Laboratories, Ltd. (Caraco), a U.S. company, announced that it had entered into a "going private" merger agreement with Sun Pharmaceutical Industries Limited ("Sun Pharma"), an Indian company.

The relationship between the companies began in March 1996, when Caraco and Sun Pharma announced an agreement to produce and market Sun Pharma's generic anti-convulsant drug in the United States. Their relationship expanded intermittently from 1996 to 1998, and from 1998 to 2002, Sun Pharma made loans to Caraco totaling approximately \$12 million. In a later agreement, Sun Pharma agreed to provide Caraco with 25 mutually agreed-upon generic drugs over a five-year period. During 2004, Sun Pharma acquired 3,452,291 additional shares of Caraco common stock for \$9.00 per share, and it paid \$11,744,964 for options in order to purchase an additional 1,679,066 shares of common stock with exercise prices ranging from \$0.68 to \$3.50. From 2007 onward, Caraco entered into marketing agreements with Sun Pharma for Caraco to purchase selected product formulations offered by Sun Pharma.

Source: See Caraco Pharmaceutical Laboratories, Ltd. Form 8-K (Current Report) and PRER14A (Preliminary Proxy Statement), filed with the U.S. SEC on February 22, 2011, and May 6, 2011, respectively.

A **forward contract** (or forward transaction) is a contract to exchange a specified amount of one currency for a specified amount of another currency at some specified future point in time based on a specified exchange rate, called the **forward rate**. The forward currency market is very large and liquid for currencies of countries with developed economies. Currencies of countries with developed economies generally have forward contracts that mature between the short term (one day) and long term (up to several years), while currencies of countries with early-development-stage economies generally have forward contracts with only shorter-term maturities. In Exhibit 17.3, we present the spot and forward exchange rates for several country-pair exchange rates.

Each exchange rate has a bid rate and an ask rate. The **ask rate** is the home currency price at which the market maker is willing to sell the foreign currency or the price asked by the market maker of the customer interested in buying the foreign currency. The **bid rate** is the home currency price at which the market maker is willing to buy the foreign currency or the price offered by the market maker to the customer interested in selling the foreign currency. It is typical to measure the **actual exchange rate** as the midpoint between the bid and ask rates. The spread between the bid and ask rates (as a percentage of the midpoint) indicates the liquidity in that particular foreign currency market. Exhibit 17.3 also presents this percentage spread between the ask and bid exchange rates (labeled Ask/Bid). As one might expect, the percentage spread increases as the term of the forward contract increases. In addition, the percentage spread is smaller for exchange rates between established economies.

EXHIBIT 17.3 Selected Direct and Indirect Spot and Forward Exchange Rates for Different Country-Pairs*

		Forward Rates				
	Spot Rate	**1 Year**	**2 Year**	**3 Year**	**4 Year**	**5 Year**
Indian Rupee / U.S. Dollar (USD)						
Bid	44.22	45.99	47.67	49.40	50.60	51.70
Ask	44.22	46.14	48.10	50.10	51.90	53.20
Midpoint	44.22	46.07	47.89	49.75	51.25	52.45
Ask/Bid	0.0%	0.3%	0.9%	1.4%	2.6%	2.9%
U.S. Dollar (USD) / Indian Rupee						
Bid	0.0226	0.0217	0.0208	0.0199	0.0193	0.0188
Ask	0.0227	0.0217	0.0210	0.0202	0.0197	0.0193
Midpoint	0.02	0.02	0.02	0.02	0.02	0.02
Ask/Bid	0.1%	0.0%	1.0%	1.5%	2.1%	2.7%
Indian Rupee / U.K. Pound (GBP)						
Bid	72.04	74.63	77.00	79.47	81.26	83.14
Ask	72.06	74.91	77.76	80.73	83.53	85.91
Midpoint	72.05	74.77	77.38	80.10	82.40	84.53
Ask/Bid	0.0%	0.4%	1.0%	1.6%	2.8%	3.3%
Japanese Yen / Indian Rupee						
Bid	1.75	1.66	1.58	1.49	1.40	1.33
Ask	1.75	1.67	1.60	1.51	1.44	1.37
Midpoint	1.75	1.67	1.59	1.50	1.42	1.35
Ask/Bid	0.0%	0.4%	1.0%	1.5%	2.8%	3.3%
Indonesian Rupiah / U.S. Dollar (USD)						
Bid	8.46	8.70	9.64	10.27	10.89	11.49
Ask	8.47	8.73	9.75	10.44	11.12	11.79
Midpoint	8.46	8.71	9.70	10.36	11.00	11.64
Ask/Bid	0.1%	0.2%	1.1%	1.6%	2.1%	2.6%
U.S. Dollar (USD) / U.K. Pound (GBP)						
Bid	1.63	1.62	1.62	1.61	1.61	1.61
Ask	1.63	1.62	1.62	1.61	1.61	1.61
Midpoint	1.63	1.62	1.62	1.61	1.61	1.61
Ask/Bid	0.0%	0.1%	0.1%	0.2%	0.2%	0.4%
U.S. Dollar (USD) / Japanese Yen						
Bid	0.0130	0.0130	0.0131	0.0134	0.0137	0.0141
Ask	0.0130	0.0130	0.0132	0.0134	0.0137	0.0142
Midpoint	0.01	0.01	0.01	0.01	0.01	0.01
Ask/Bid	0.0%	0.1%	0.1%	0.1%	0.3%	0.4%
Russian Ruble / U.S. Dollar (USD)						
Bid	27.78	28.90	30.20	31.69	33.17	34.46
Ask	27.81	28.93	30.35	31.88	33.52	34.80
Midpoint	27.80	28.91	30.28	31.78	33.35	34.63
Ask/Bid	0.1%	0.1%	0.5%	0.6%	1.1%	1.0%

* Source—Bloomberg.

Currency Appreciation and Depreciation, Premiums and Discounts, and Real Exchange Rates

Naturally, spot rates change over time as a function of the relative underlying macroeconomic conditions of two countries. **Currency appreciation** and **currency depreciation** indicate whether a currency is becoming stronger (appreciating) relative to another currency or weaker (depreciating) relative to another currency. We measure the appreciation and depreciation of one currency based on the change in its value relative to the other currency. An increase in the value of one currency indicates that the currency **appreciated** or became **stronger** relative to the other currency. A decrease in the value of the currency indicates that the currency **depreciated** or became **weaker** relative to the other currency. For example, a spot rate ($S_{\$/£}$) of 1.6 means that the value of the £ stated in USD is 1.6. An increase in the spot rate ($S_{\$/£}$) from 1.6 to 1.8 means that the value or price of a £ in USD increased; thus, the value of the £ **appreciated** or became **stronger** relative to the USD by 12.5% (0.125 = 1.8/1.6 − 1). On the other hand, if the spot rate decreases from 1.6 to 1.3, that means that the value of the £ decreased relative to the USD; thus, the value of the £ decreased and **depreciated**, or became **weaker**, relative to the USD by 18.8% (−0.188 = 1.3/1.6 − 1).

An appreciation of one currency implies the depreciation of the other currency. The above example, in which the spot rate ($S_{\$/£}$) increased from 1.6 to 1.8, also implies that it now takes $1.8 to purchase £1.0 when it previously took $1.6 to purchase £1.0, indicating that the USD depreciated. We measure the depreciation of the USD based on the value of the USD in £ ($S_{£/\$}$), decreasing from 0.625 (0.625 = 1/1.6) to 0.556 (0.556 = 1/1.8) or by 11.0% (−0.110 = 0.556/0.625 − 1). If the spot rate ($S_{\$/£}$) decreases from 1.6 to 1.3, it means that it takes $1.3 to purchase £1.0 when it previously took $1.6 to purchase £1.0, indicating that the USD appreciated relative to the £. Again, we measure the appreciation of the USD based on the value of the USD in £ ($S_{£/\$}$), increasing from 0.625 (0.625 = 1/1.6) to 0.769 (0.769 = 1/1.3) or by 23.1% (0.231 = 0.769/0.625 − 1). The percentage appreciation of one currency is not equal to the percentage depreciation of the other currency. One point to remember, the change in one exchange rate (one country-pair) does not indicate the overall strength or weakness of a currency. Instead of using the change in one exchange rate, we typically use a weighted average of the changes in a group of exchange rates, weighted by relative trade flows for each pair of countries.

Investors trade **forward contracts** at a premium or at a discount relative to the spot rate, called the forward rate premium (or forward rate discount). The **forward rate premium** is the percentage difference between the forward and spot exchange rates—that is, the ratio of the forward rate to the spot rate minus 1. We typically present the forward rate premium on an annualized basis by multiplying the percentage by 360 over the length of the contract in days. A contract with a forward rate premium has a forward rate that is larger than the spot rate, and it indicates that, in the future and relative to the spot rate, the foreign currency is trading at a premium relative to the home currency. For example, the spot Indian rupee/USD exchange rate is 44.22 (Exhibit 17.3) and the forward rate for a five-year forward contract is 52.45; thus, the USD is selling at a forward rate premium relative to the Indian rupee of 18.6% (0.186 = 52.45/44.22 − 1) over the five-year period, or 3.7% annually. As we explain in the next section, because inflation rates and interest rates in India are higher than in the United States, the USD sells at a premium in subsequent years to prevent arbitrage opportunities. Conversely, a contract with a **forward rate discount** has a spot rate that is larger than the forward rate. For example, the Japanese Yen/Indian rupee spot rate is 1.75 (Exhibit 17.3) and the forward rate for the five-year forward contract is 1.35; thus, the Japanese Yen is selling at a forward rate discount relative to the Indian rupee of 22.9% (−0.229 = 1.35/1.75 − 1) over the five-year period, or a discount of 4.6% per year. Again, as we explain in the next section, the reason that the Japanese Yen is trading at a forward rate discount is that both inflation and interest rates in Japan are lower than in India.

The **real exchange rate** is the spot exchange rate divided by the relative price levels of the two countries; in other words, it is a nominal exchange rate (previously discussed) adjusted for the relative expected inflations between the two countries. Changes in real exchange rates provide information about changes in the relative competitiveness of the countries. Two important issues in using real exchange rates are the selection of the base year and the use of the correct price indices. Price indices used in real exchange rates can include the consumer price index, wholesale price index, producers' price index, and gross domestic product deflator. Another approach adjusts nominal exchange rates for the relative prices of tradable and non-tradable goods. Regardless of the approach and index used, a decline in the real exchange rate—say, over the last five years—indicates a real depreciation of one currency relative to another currency.

17.3 EXCHANGE RATE THEORIES AND FORECASTING METHODS

Naturally, in order to develop exchange rate forecasts, we must first understand why and how exchange rates change over time. Fortunately, we have some well-established exchange rate theories to help us. These theories explain how the relative underlying macroeconomic conditions of two countries determine the exchange rates between the two countries. All of the exchange rate theories rely on a "no arbitrage condition." Generally, **arbitrage** occurs when an investor can earn a positive risk-free return with no investment by exploiting a difference in prices of the same asset in different markets—for example, by buying in the market in which the asset has a lower price and simultaneously selling that asset in the market with the higher price. A **no arbitrage condition** exists when market forces set prices so that no arbitrage opportunity exists. In the remainder of this section, we explain how to use exchange rate theories to forecast exchange rates.

Purchasing Power Parity and Relative Purchasing Power Parity

In its most basic form, purchasing power parity assumes the **law of one price**—namely, all products and services each have one global price. Assuming all products and services each have one price, **purchasing power parity** asserts that the ratio of prices in different currencies determines exchange rates. Although the underpinning of the theory utilizes average prices across a large group of products and services, we illustrate it using one asset (gold) in order to highlight the intuition underlying this theory. Assume gold is equally valuable to everyone in the world; in other words, if the world had one currency, one agreed-upon unit of gold would have the same price throughout the world. If gold is selling in the U.S. for $1,000 per unit and it is selling in the U.K. for £625 per unit, as long as gold can be easily bought and sold across borders, the purchasing power parity theory predicts that the USD/GBP exchange rate will be $S_{\$/£} = 1.6$ (1.6 = $1,000/£625). Although purchasing power parity is one of the oldest and longest lasting exchange rate theories, it turns out that it does not explain movements in exchange rates in the short run, but it appears to work well over the longer-run.[3] Reasons why this theory does not explain exchange rate movements include various transactions costs (such as shipping costs) and market frictions (such as government regulations or interventions).

Relative purchasing power parity relaxes the assumption of the law of one price underpinning purchasing power parity, and, instead of assuming that relative prices determine exchange rates, it assumes that changes in the relative prices (relative inflation rates) in two countries determine the change in exchange rates. **Relative purchasing power parity** asserts that changes in exchange rates result from changes in the relative prices of the goods in two countries. Relative purchasing power parity asserts that the ratio of the expected future spot rate to the current spot rate is equal to the ratio of (1 plus) the expected inflation rates, i, of the two countries over that same period. While relative purchasing power is somewhat better than purchasing power parity at explaining exchange rate changes, it has less explanatory power over the short-run and more over the longer-run.[4] In order to use this theory to forecast an exchange rate (expected exchange rate, S^E) N periods into the future, we multiply the current spot rate by the ratio of the expected relative inflation rates over the period.

$$S^E_{HC/FC,\,t+N} = S_{HC/FC,\,t} \times \frac{(1+i_{HC})^N}{(1+i_{FC})^N} \tag{17.1}$$

For example, assume that the current (time t) spot exchange rate is $S_{HC/FC} = 2.0$ and that the expected annual inflation is 5% for the home country and 10% for the foreign country. Based on this information, the relative purchasing power parity theory predicts the exchange rate using the above equation for one, two, and five years are as follows:

$$S^E_{HC/FC,\,t+1} = 2.0 \times \frac{(1.05)}{(1.1)} = 1.91;\ S^E_{HC/FC,\,t+2} = 2.0 \times \frac{(1.05)^2}{(1.1)^2} = 1.82;\ S^E_{HC/FC,\,t+5} = 2.0 \times \frac{(1.05)^5}{(1.1)^5} = 1.58$$

The exchange rate declines and the home currency appreciates because of lower inflation in the home country.

Covered and Uncovered Interest Rate Parity (and the International Fisher Effect)

Financial assets are subject to fewer market frictions or interventions and lower transactions costs than non-financial assets; in other words, financial assets are more easily and efficiently tradable relative to many non-financial assets. In addition, investors can purchase forward contracts for many currencies and horizons. Assuming no arbitrage and free movement of capital such that an investor can freely invest across borders (no market frictions or transactions costs), we can relate forward contract exchange rates to current spot rates using relative interest rates across countries.

For example, assume an investor can either invest in the home country and earn the home country's interest rate, r_{HC}, or invest abroad and buy a forward contract to convert the foreign deposit with foreign interest back to the home currency. If the investor invests abroad, the investor will earn the foreign

[3] Lothian, James R., and Mark P. Taylor, "Real Exchange Rate Behavior: The Recent Float from the Perspective of the Past Two Centuries," *Journal of Political Economy* vol. 104, no. 3 (1996), pp. 488–509.

[4] See Lothian and Taylor (1996), cited previously.

country's interest rate, r_{FC}, for that certain period, adjusted for the forward rate premium. We call this condition **covered interest rate parity**, because an investor is covered by the forward contract, and the investor is not taking any risk in the transaction (assuming no deposit risk and the forward contract settles up as written). If the cost of investing locally and of investing in a foreign country are identical, then investors will move capital strategically to invest in the country that provides the highest return in terms of the home country currency. The ability to move capital globally in order to earn the highest return creates a potential arbitrage opportunity for investors. Since many investors have the ability to execute such an investment strategy, capital will move globally until it eliminates any arbitrage opportunities. Thus, given the liquidity and low transaction costs in many financial markets, market forces prevent such arbitrage opportunities from occurring systematically. Empirically, we observe that covered interest rate parity generally holds for shorter horizons after accounting for transactions costs, income tax effects, and the bid-ask spread. For longer horizons, we not only have higher transactions costs (including larger bid-ask spreads), but we also have an increase in the probability of government intervention—for example, restricting foreign deposits and the ability to move funds out of the country. The empirical evidence on longer horizons is more limited.[5]

Uncovered interest rate parity establishes the relation we would expect between current and future spot rates if such investors did not use forward contracts to establish a known return but instead made an uncovered investment in another country's financial assets (an investment not covered by a forward contract).[6] If the forward rate were an unbiased estimate of the expected future spot rate, the expected returns on a covered and uncovered investment would be the same. However, the covered investment's return is known, while the uncovered investment's return is uncertain. If forward rates are unbiased predictors of expected future spot rates, we can use uncovered interest rate parity for forecasting expected future spot rates in which the expected future spot rate is a function of the current spot rate and the relative interest rates in the two countries over the period.

$$S^E_{HC/FC,\,t+N} = S_{HC/FC,\,t} \times \frac{(1+r_{HC})^N}{(1+r_{FC})^N} \tag{17.2}$$

If interest rates are not constant over time, Equation 17.2 becomes

$$S^E_{HC/FC,\,t+N} = S_{HC/FC,\,t} \times \frac{1+r_{HC,\,t+1}}{1+r_{FC,\,t+1}} \times \frac{1+r_{HC,\,t+2}}{1+r_{FC,\,t+2}} \times \frac{1+r_{HC,\,t+3}}{1+r_{FC,\,t+3}} \times \cdots \times \frac{1+r_{HC,\,t+N}}{1+r_{FC,\,t+N}} \tag{17.3}$$

Continuing our previous example, where expected inflation in the home (foreign) country is 5% (10%), assume the current spot exchange rate today (time t) is $S_{HC/FC} = 2.0$, the annual interest rate in the home country is 7.1% for the next five years and the annual interest rate in the foreign country is 14.4% for the next five years. These assumptions assume that the real interest rate is 2% in the home country (0.02 = 1.071/1.05 − 1) and 4% in the foreign country (0.04 = 1.144/1.10 − 1). Based on this information, uncovered interest rate parity provides a way to forecast the exchange rate.

$$S^E_{HC/FC,\,t+1} = 2.0 \times \frac{(1.071)}{(1.144)} = 1.87;\; S^E_{HC/FC,\,t+2} = 2.0 \times \frac{(1.071)^2}{(1.144)^2} = 1.75;\; S^E_{HC/FC,\,t+5} = 2.0 \times \frac{(1.071)^5}{(1.144)^5} = 1.44$$

The empirical evidence on uncovered interest rate parity is also mixed. To the extent it works, it generally works better for longer-horizon forecasts.

The expected exchange rates based on relative purchasing power parity are all larger than the expected exchange rates we calculated based on uncovered interest rate parity. Why? To answer, the relative difference in the inflation rates, (1.05)/(1.1), is not as large as the relative difference in interest rates, 1.071/1.144. What might cause this difference? To answer this question, we explore the link between the two theories using the Fisher Effect.

The Fisher Effect specifies the relation between the nominal interest rate and the real interest rate and inflation, $1 + r_{HC} = (1 + r_{Real\ HC}) \times (1 + i_{HC})$. The International Fisher Effect examines the ratio of

[5] See, for example, Popper, H., "Long-Term Covered Interest Parity—Evidence from Currency Swaps," *Journal of International Money and Finance* vol. 12, no. 4 (1993), pp. 439–48.

[6] For a review of uncovered interest rate parity and some more recent empirical work, see, Chinn, Menzie D., "The (Partial) Rehabilitation of Interest Rate Parity: Longer Horizons, Alternative Expectations and Emerging Markets," *Journal of International Money and Finance* vol. 25, no. 1 (February 2006), pp. 7–21.

interest rates of two countries and asserts that the real rate of interest is constant across countries, assuming no arbitrage. If the real interest rate is constant and the same across countries, then the ratio of (1 plus) the interest rates of two countries (a key factor in uncovered interest rate parity) is equal to the ratio of (1 plus) the inflation rates of two countries. If this condition holds, then the relative purchasing power forecasts and the uncovered interest rate parity forecasts are equal to each other:

$$\frac{(1+r_{HC})}{(1+r_{FC})}=\frac{(1+r_{Real,\,HC})\times(1+i_{HC})}{(1+r_{Real,\,FC})\times(1+i_{FC})}=\frac{(1+i_{HC})}{(1+i_{FC})}$$

In our previous example, we assumed a 2% real interest rate for the home country and a 4% real interest rate for the foreign country; thus, the change in the exchange rates resulted from both differences in the inflation rates and differences in the real interest rates between the two countries. If we had used a 2% real interest rate for both countries, the home country interest rate would have continued to be 7.1%, but the foreign country interest rate would have decreased to 12.2% (0.122 = 1.02 × 1.10). Using these interest rates for the two countries results in the same exchange rate forecasts as we had calculated using relative purchasing power parity:

$$S^E_{HC/FC,\,t+1}=2.0\times\frac{(1.071)}{(1.122)}=1.91;\ S^E_{HC/FC,\,t+2}=2.0\times\frac{(1.071)^2}{(1.122)^2}=1.82;\ S^E_{HC/FC,\,t+5}=2.0\times\frac{(1.071)^5}{(1.122)^5}=1.58$$

Are Forward Rates Unbiased and Efficient Forecasts of Future Spot Rates? (The Forward Premium Puzzle)

If forward rates were unbiased and efficient forecasts of future spot rates, we could use forward rates to forecast exchange rates. However, an unbiased forecast does not have to be the most accurate forecast. For a forecast to be unbiased, it only has to have a forecast error with an expected value of zero; thus, an unbiased forecast does not have to be the best forecast. Even if forward rates were unbiased forecasts of future spot rates, we would still need to test alternative forecasting models and compare the accuracy of these models for their relative forecast accuracy across different horizons. Relative forecast accuracy is one measure for describing an efficient forecast. An efficient forecast is one that incorporates all available information as of the forecast date; thus, if a forward rate is efficient, it is relatively more accurate than alternative forecasts.

Are forward rates unbiased and efficient forecasts of future spot rates? Overall, empirical evidence provides mixed evidence on the issue of what results in the best forecast. It turns out that the forward rate premium (or discount) fails to accurately predict the direction of the change in the spot rate, especially for shorter-term maturities. The issue is mitigated over longer horizons.[7] One explanation for the forward rate premium puzzle is the risk premium required by investors.[8] For longer maturities, some of the empirical evidence suggests that forward rates are sufficiently unbiased,[9] but some traders suggest that they may not be efficient.[10] More recent research concludes that interest rate differentials are not sufficient to explain changes in spot rates and that the current deviation in purchasing power parity is also an important determinant of changes in exchange rates.[11]

---

[7] See, Chinn, M. D., and Meredith, G., "Monetary Policy and Long Horizon Uncovered Interest Parity," *IMF Staff Papers* vol. 51, no. 3 (2004), pp. 409–430.

[8] See Verdelhan, A., "A Habit-Based Explanation of the Exchange Rate Risk Premium," *The Journal of Finance* vol. LXV, no. 1 (February 2010), pp. 123–146.

[9] See, Chinn, M., and Frankel, J., "Patterns in Exchange Rate Forecasts for 25 Currencies," *Journal of Money, Credit and Banking* vol. 26, no. 24 (1994), pp. 759–770; and Chinn, M., and Frankel, J., "Survey Data on Exchange Rate Expectations: More Currencies, More Horizons, More Tests," in Dickinson, D., and W. Allen, eds., *Monetary Policy, Capital Flows and Financial Market Developments in the Era of Financial Globalization: Essays in Honour of Max Fry,* London and New York: Routledge (2002).

[10] For an example of a discussion of how traders might exploit inefficiencies in forward rates, see, Baz, Jamil, Frances Breedon, Vasant Naik, and Joel Press, "Optimal Portfolios of Foreign Currencies—Trading on the Forward Bias," *Journal of Portfolio Management* (Fall 2001), pp. 1–10.

[11] Boudoukh, Jacob, Matthew Richardson, and Robert F. Whitelaw, "New Evidence on the Forward Premium Puzzle," *Journal of Financial and Quantitative Analysis* vol. 51, no. 3 (2016), pp. 875–897.

Understanding the Discount Rates Used in the Investor Currency (Centralized) and Foreign Currency (Decentralized) DCF Approaches

Recall the example illustrating the equivalence of the two approaches for adjusting the DCF valuation model (Exhibit 17.2). In that example, the appropriate risk-adjusted discount rate for the investor currency (USD) stated free cash flows was 10% and constant for all three years. The appropriate discount rates for the foreign currency (ruble) free cash flows for the next three years were 14.4%, 15.2%, and 15.5%. We can use the exchange rate theories to explain the relation between the discount rates and exchange rates.

We know from the exchange rate theories that exchange rate forecasts are linked to current spot rates by either relative interest rates or relative inflation rates. If real interest rates are constant across two countries, relative inflation rates are equivalent to relative interest rates. Thus, instead of using the relative interest rates or inflation rates to adjust the discount rate from a home or local currency-based discount rate to a foreign currency-based discount rate, we use relative exchange rate forecasts; specifically, we use the ratio of the exchange rate forecast for year t to the exchange rate forecast for year t − 1. This ratio measures the implicit interest rate embedded in these forecasts.

In our example, we use forward exchange rates for expected exchange rates. In Exhibit 17.4, we adjust the investor currency discount rate for the annual percentage change in the forward rate. For Year 1, the ratio of the forward rate to the spot rate is 1.04. To measure the discount rate for the project in rubles, we multiply this ratio by 1 plus the investor discount rate for the project (1.1) to arrive at a discount rate of 14.42% (0.1442 = 1.04 × 1.10 − 1). For Year 2, we measure the ratio of the forward rate in Year 2 to the forward rate in Year 1, which is 1.047 and yields a discount rate of 15.20% for the project in rubles (0.152 = 1.047 × 1.10 − 1). Note that if the discount rate for the investor's currency remains constant in future years and the exchange rate between the investor's currency and the foreign currency is expected to continue to change, the discount rate in the foreign currency will continue to change as well.

EXHIBIT 17.4 Calculation of the Discount Rates Used in the Example Illustrating the Equality of the Two DCF Valuation Approaches (See Exhibit 17.2)

Investor to Foreign Discount Rate	Year 1	Year 2	Year 3
Exchange rate forecast = Forward rate (RUB/USD) in period t.	28.913	30.279	31.784
Exchange rate forecast = Forward rate (RUB/USD) in period t − 1	27.796	28.913	30.279
Ratio ≈ $(1 + r_{RUB})/(1 + r_{USD}) \approx (1 + i_{RUB})/(1 + i_{USD})$	1.040	1.047	1.050
One + risk-adjusted discount rate for USD, r_{USD}	1.100	1.100	1.100
Risk-adjusted discount rate for project in foreign currency, r_{RUB}	14.42%	15.20%	15.47%

Exhibit may contain small rounding errors

This link between exchange rates and discount rates assumes that markets are fully integrated. If they are not fully integrated, then the link can be eroded or possibly broken. If markets are not fully integrated, the investor currency or centralized approach—which converts cash flows stated in terms of the investor's home currency and discounts them at the investor's home currency cost of capital—is the more appropriate approach to use to measure value.

REVIEW EXERCISE 17.2

Discount Rates for the Investor Currency (Centralized) and Foreign Currency (Decentralized) Approaches

Measure the discount rates for discounting U.S. dollars (USD) provided in Review Exercise 17.1.

Solution on page 910.

Practical Applications of Exchange Rate Theories and Other Potential Methods of Forecasting Exchange Rates

We discussed three ways to forecast future spot rates based on the relative purchasing power parity theory, the uncovered interest rate parity theory based on relative interest rates, and forward rates, assuming they are unbiased and efficient forecasts of future spot rates. In addition, researchers and investors have developed more complex forecasting models that include additional predictor variables. Variables in such models can include other macroeconomic information on the countries' potential actions, events, or policies, which can affect exchange rates, yet are not embedded in relative inflation and interest rates. We call this type of model fundamentals-based because they rely on fundamental predictor variables hypothesized to be linked causally to exchange rates. Another type of model is based on technical analysis, which is the study of trends in the exchange rates and sometimes includes information on trading volume.

It is common to use forward rates when available and traded in liquid markets, especially for the first few years in a forecast horizon. After the first few years, forecasts from either the relative purchasing power parity or uncovered interest rate parity forecasting methods (or both) are also common. Relative purchasing power parity, however, implies that real exchange rates do not change; thus, it may not be a good method if we believe the current real exchange rate is not sustainable over the long run.

Although we will not discuss the issue in detail here, both parity models assume that market conditions and forces set exchange rates; however, we know that some countries have exchange rate policies that can interfere with market-determined exchange rates. We call market-determined exchange rates **floating exchange rates**, and we refer to a mostly government-determined rate as a **fixed exchange rate**. Some exchange rates are pegged to another, more stable exchange rate, which we call **pegged exchange rates**. Why do governments have exchange rate policies? One reason is to reduce variability in exchange rates, which can discourage foreign investment. Fixed exchange rate policies are still subject to market forces; thus, governments have to counteract these market forces by buying or selling their own and other currencies and setting interest rates. Do government exchange rate policies affect what exchange rate forecasts we use? Since market forces are still at work, stable exchange rate policies will probably not cause us to deviate from the steps we outlined in this chapter. However, unexpected changes in government policies can cause issues when using these models.

We also know that government intervention can affect interest rates, especially in the short run, such that neither relative purchasing power parity nor uncovered interest rate parity forecasts are accurate predictors of expected spot rates, especially in the short run. In Exhibit 17.5, we present interest rates (yield to maturities, or YTMs) for government bonds and expected inflation rates for the countries for which we showed spot and future exchange rates in Exhibit 17.3. Recall that a global financial crisis and severe recession occurred around 2008, and since then many governments have been attempting to keep interest rates low in order to stimulate the economy.

Valuation Key 17.4

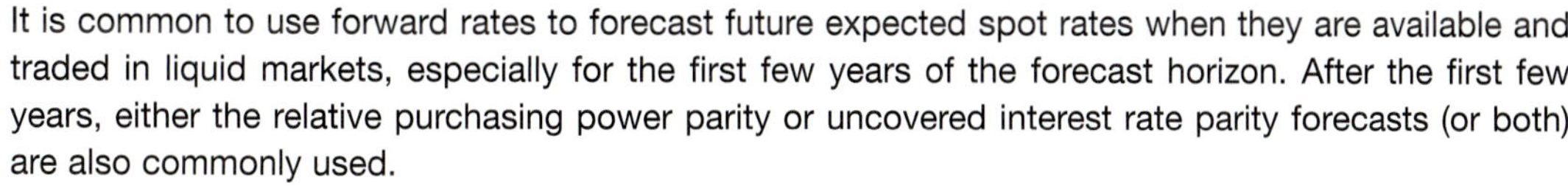

It is common to use forward rates to forecast future expected spot rates when they are available and traded in liquid markets, especially for the first few years of the forecast horizon. After the first few years, either the relative purchasing power parity or uncovered interest rate parity forecasts (or both) are also commonly used.

From this exhibit, we see that interest rates are lower than expected inflation rates for the first two years for all countries and for the first five years for some countries, resulting in negative real interest rates as measured using the Fisher Effect. From this exhibit, we can also see that real interest rates vary across countries. The U.S. and the U.K. generally have similar real rates, especially for longer horizons, and Indonesia generally has real rates that are higher than both the U.S. and U.K. rates. It is an open issue as to whether the differences in these real rates are, in fact, real differences or the result of market frictions such as government regulations or interventions. The negative real rates are consistent with the effect of government intervention in response to the economic crisis that started in 2008.

In Exhibit 17.6, we use both relative purchasing power parity and uncovered interest rate parity to forecast the exchange rates in Exhibit 17.3. We compare our forecasts using the relative interest and

EXHIBIT 17.5 Interest Rates (Government Bond Yields) and Expected Inflation Rates for Different Countries*

	1 Year	2 Year	3 Year	4 Year	5 Year	10 Year	30 Year
United States							
Interest rate	0.20%	0.37%	0.54%	1.32%	2.05%	2.75%	4.08%
Inflation rate	1.50%	1.90%	1.90%	2.00%	2.00%	2.10%	2.10%
Implied real rate	−1.28%	−1.50%	−1.33%	−0.66%	0.05%	0.63%	1.94%
United Kingdom (Great Britain)							
Interest rate	0.48%	0.61%	0.78%	1.18%	1.54%	2.80%	4.00%
Inflation rate	1.58%	2.00%	2.00%	2.00%	2.00%	2.00%	2.00%
Implied real rate	−1.08%	−1.36%	−1.20%	−0.80%	−0.46%	0.79%	1.96%
India							
Interest rate	6.96%	7.53%	8.11%	8.38%	8.46%	8.56%	8.72%
Inflation rate	8.00%	8.00%	7.50%	7.50%	7.50%	7.50%	7.50%
Implied real rate	−0.97%	−0.43%	0.57%	0.82%	0.89%	0.98%	1.13%
Japan							
Interest rate	0.12%	0.16%	0.20%	0.28%	0.37%	1.04%	2.23%
Inflation rate	0.30%	0.30%	0.50%	0.50%	0.50%	0.50%	0.50%
Implied real rate	−0.18%	−0.14%	−0.30%	−0.22%	−0.13%	0.54%	1.72%
Russia							
Interest rate	5.10%	5.67%	6.24%	6.81%	7.08%	7.63%	7.92%
Inflation rate	7.65%	7.65%	7.15%	7.15%	7.15%	7.15%	7.15%
Implied real rate	−2.37%	−1.84%	−0.85%	−0.32%	−0.07%	0.45%	0.72%
Indonesia							
Interest rate	4.36%	4.82%	5.82%	6.18%	6.44%	6.93%	8.50%
Inflation rate	6.32%	6.32%	5.36%	5.36%	5.36%	5.36%	5.36%
Implied real rate	−1.84%	−1.41%	0.44%	0.78%	1.03%	1.49%	2.98%
Implied real rate standard deviation	0.76%	0.67%	0.82%	0.71%	0.60%	0.38%	0.78%

* Interest rates are government bond yield-to-maturity rates quoted in Bloomberg. If a maturity was not available, but longer and shorter maturities were both available, we interpolated the rate. Expected U.S. inflation rates are from the *President's Economic Report*; other inflation rates are from Bloomberg or are the authors' estimates. Data is as of August 1, 2011.

inflation rates from the previous exhibit to the midpoint of the bid and ask rates in Exhibit 17.3. As we can see from this exhibit, relative to the spot rate, all of the forecasts move in the same direction as the forward rates over the five-year horizon (see the column titled "Year 5 to Spot Rate"). We can also see that some of the differences between the forecasts and forward rates (not shown in the exhibit) are relatively small (such as the case for USD/GBP, which is less than 1%) whereas some are larger (as for the Rupee/Pound). We show the average difference across the five years for the RPPP and UIRP forecasts. The average differences for the first five exchange rates are much larger than those for the last three exchange rates. Overall, the average (absolute value) forward rate difference is 4.7% for the relative purchasing power parity forecasts and 5.7% for the uncovered interest rate parity forecasts. However, the magnitude of the (absolute value) differences is not random.

Factors that may explain these differences include the following. First, for differences between the uncovered interest rate parity forecasts and the forward rates, the interest rates might not represent the rates used by the market makers issuing the forward contracts. Second, for differences between the relative purchasing power parity forecasts and the forward rates, the real rates of interest may differ, violating the assumption of constant real interest rates. Finally, frictions in the capital markets—such as flow of capital controls or restrictions in India—may mean that other factors determine forward rates in addition to relative interest rates or relative inflation rates. For example, in this exhibit, the smallest (absolute value) differences occur for countries with well-developed economies—the USD/GBP forecasts from both approaches have average differences of no more than 1%. The forecasts for countries with less developed economies tend to have larger differences. In addition, the differences increase with the horizon. The average (absolute value) difference in Year 1 is less than 2% for both forecast methods before increasing in subsequent years.

EXHIBIT 17.6 Exchange Rate Forecasts Based on Relative Purchasing Power Parity and Uncovered Interest Rate Parity Compared to Forward Exchange Rates

		Forward Rates						
	Spot Rate	1 Year	2 Year	3 Year	4 Year	5 Year	Year 5 to Spot Rate	Average Forward Rate Difference
Indian Rupee / U.S. Dollar (USD)								
Midpoint	**44.22**	**46.07**	**47.89**	**49.75**	**51.25**	**52.45**	**18.6%**	
RPPP	44.22	47.05	49.86	52.60	55.44	58.43	32.1%	6.3%
UIRP	44.22	47.20	50.57	54.38	58.17	61.82	39.8%	9.7%
U.S. Dollar (USD) / Indian Rupee								
Midpoint	**0.023**	**0.022**	**0.021**	**0.020**	**0.020**	**0.019**	**–15.8%**	
RPPP	0.023	0.021	0.020	0.019	0.018	0.017	–24.3%	–5.7%
UIRP	0.023	0.021	0.020	0.018	0.017	0.016	–28.5%	–8.5%
Indian Rupee / U.K. Pound (GBP)								
Midpoint	**72.05**	**74.77**	**77.38**	**80.10**	**82.40**	**84.53**	**17.3%**	
RPPP	72.05	76.61	81.11	85.49	90.09	94.95	31.8%	7.1%
UIRP	72.05	76.69	81.97	87.94	94.20	100.62	39.6%	10.3%
Japanese Yen / Indian Rupee								
Midpoint	**1.75**	**1.67**	**1.59**	**1.50**	**1.42**	**1.35**	**–22.9%**	
RPPP	1.75	1.62	1.51	1.41	1.32	1.23	–29.5%	–6.1%
UIRP	1.75	1.63	1.52	1.41	1.31	1.21	–30.8%	–6.2%
Indonesian Rupiah / U.S. Dollar (USD)								
Midpoint	**8.46**	**8.71**	**9.70**	**10.36**	**11.00**	**11.64**	**37.6%**	
RPPP	8.46	8.86	9.25	9.56	9.88	10.20	20.6%	–6.6%
UIRP	8.46	8.81	9.21	9.69	10.15	10.59	25.1%	–5.4%
U.S. Dollar (USD) / U.K. Pound (GBP)								
Midpoint	**1.63**	**1.62**	**1.62**	**1.61**	**1.61**	**1.61**	**–1.1%**	
RPPP	1.63	1.63	1.63	1.63	1.63	1.63	–0.3%	0.8%
UIRP	1.63	1.62	1.62	1.62	1.62	1.63	–0.1%	0.5%
U.S. Dollar (USD) / Japanese Yen								
Midpoint	**0.0130**	**0.0130**	**0.0131**	**0.0134**	**0.0137**	**0.0142**	**9.3%**	
RPPP	0.0130	0.0131	0.0133	0.0135	0.0137	0.0139	7.4%	0.2%
UIRP	0.0130	0.0130	0.0130	0.0130	0.0132	0.0134	3.4%	–2.7%
Russian Ruble / U.S. Dollar (USD)								
Midpoint	**27.80**	**28.91**	**30.28**	**31.78**	**33.35**	**34.63**	**24.6%**	
RPPP	27.80	29.48	31.14	32.75	34.40	36.14	30.0%	3.1%
UIRP	27.80	29.16	30.70	32.44	34.19	35.88	29.1%	2.1%

REVIEW EXERCISE 17.3

Exchange Rate Forecasts

Use the information in Exhibit 17.5 and Exhibit P17.2 to forecast the U.S. dollar/Polish zloty exchange rate for the next five years using relative purchasing power parity and uncovered interest rate parity.

Solution on page 910.

17.4 OVERVIEW OF POTENTIAL INCOME AND OTHER TAX ISSUES IN A CROSS-BORDER SETTING

LO3 Measure income taxes for a cross-border valuation

Foreign source income is becoming a larger part of total income for many companies; for example, since 1990, the foreign income of the S&P 500 grew from 32% to 50% of total pre-tax income.[12] In

[12] For a more detailed review of many of these issues—especially from a U.S. perspective—and a summary of the scholarly research, see, Blouin, Jennifer, "Taxation of Multinational Corporations," *Foundations and Trends® in Accounting* vol. 6, no. 1 (2012), pp. 1–64, http://dx.doi.org/10.1561/1400000017 accessed June 24, 2018.

a cross-border valuation, income and other tax issues can have unforeseen effects and are often more complex than for within-country valuations. In a cross-border valuation, we consider the tax laws and regulations of the various taxing authorities of both the investor's home country and the foreign company's country; we also consider tax and other treaties between the two countries and possibly even treaties between these countries and other countries. Types of direct and indirect taxes include income taxes at the national level (and other levels in the country), value-added taxes (a form of sales tax on the supply chain, abbreviated as VAT), various types of withholding taxes (such as withholding on payments for dividends, interest, royalties, payments to contractors, and rent), import duties, fringe benefits, and other payroll-related taxes.

The first type of tax issue we may face in a cross-border valuation is that, independent of any tax issues caused by cross-border ownership, the foreign company's country may have income taxes or other taxes that the investor's country does not have. An investor must include the effect of all of these taxes in any cross-border valuation. For example, the United States does not have a national sales tax (VAT), but other countries have a VAT paid on each stage of the production process. A U.S. company investing in a foreign company subject to a VAT has to be aware of the VAT and include its effect in a cross-border valuation. Because these types of taxes are paid by the foreign company independent of cross-border ownership, these types of taxes are typically included in the foreign company's financial statements and easily identified.

Second, countries sometimes offer tax incentives to attract foreign investment, especially in developing countries, which we would include in a cross-border valuation by measuring the value of these subsidies separately, as we would for other types of subsidies. To add further complexity, each country can have additional taxes or regulations for companies with cross-border ownership; thus, the third type of tax issue in a cross-border valuation is that income or other taxes (or an equivalent) may be paid by the investor because of cross-border ownership.

The type of tax regime for the home country is also relevant in a cross-border valuation. There are two basic types of tax regimes in the world, although no country follows either one of these tax regimes completely. The first type of income tax regime is the **resident tax regime** or **worldwide tax regime**, which taxes the total worldwide income of its residents and businesses. Worldwide tax regime countries address double taxation issues with a foreign tax credit or a deduction for foreign income taxes paid. Countries with a worldwide tax regime sometimes allow a company to defer paying income taxes on the earnings of a foreign subsidiary until the subsidiary repatriates these earnings to the parent company, making this tax regime more similar to the territorial or source tax regime. The second type of income tax regime is the **territorial tax regime** or **source tax regime**. Generally, countries have been moving more towards territorial tax regimes and away from worldwide tax regimes; for example, in 2009, Japan and the U.K. moved to tax regimes that are closer to a territorial tax regime. In addition, over 75% of the member countries of the Organization for Economic Coordination and Development (OECD) have tax regimes that are more like a territorial tax regime. However, no country has a purely worldwide or purely territorial tax regime due to various deferrals, tax credits, tax deductions, and other regulations.

Prior to the 2017 Tax Cuts and Jobs Act (TCJA), the U.S. had a worldwide tax system, but allowed credits against U.S. income taxes for taxes paid to foreign countries, similar to the foreign tax credits we describe in the chapter. In addition, if the earnings of foreign subsidiaries were not repatriated back to the U.S. parent, then the earnings were not taxed in the U.S. until they were repatriated, if ever. With the passage of the 2017 TCJA, the taxation of the foreign income of a U.S. parent changed considerably, and in many ways became more like a territorial tax system. Under the TCJA, the U.S. imposed a 15.5% tax rate on unrepatriated earnings of foreign subsidiaries of U.S. companies invested in liquid investments (like cash and marketable securities) and 8% on non-liquid investments (like property, plant, and equipment), and the calculation of the amount of unrepatriated earnings goes back to 1986. The tax on these unrepatriated earnings is payable over eight years (8% of the tax is paid in each of the first 5 years, 15% in year 6, 20% in year 7, and 25% in year 8). According to some sources, Apple has approximately $250 million in cash that has not been repatriated back to the U.S. on which they will now have to pay taxes (see Valuation in Practice 1.2). This is a transitional provision and does not apply to income earned after 2017.

Even though the income of foreign subsidiaries of a U.S. parent is not generally taxed starting in 2018 with the adoption of a territorial-like tax system under the TCJA, the TCJA has a provision for the taxation of "global intangible low-taxed income" (GILTI). Under this provision, the income of a foreign subsidiary that exceeds 10% of its qualified tangible assets is taxable to the U.S. parent, whether repatriated or not. From 2018 to 2025, 50% of this income is excluded from the tax, resulting in a 10.5% effective tax rate on this income given the 21% statutory tax rate under TCJA, and starting in 2026, 37.5% of this income is excluded from tax resulting in an effective tax rate of 13.125%. The purpose of the GILTI provisions is to tax companies who transferred intangible assets and used various transfer pricing and tax treaty strategies in an attempt to reduce their tax bills (see Valuation in Practice 17.3).

The provisions of the 2017 TCJA are quite complicated and we have only scratched the surface in this discussion. Other provisions include a Base Erosion and Anti-Abuse Tax (BEAT) provision, which taxes certain payments made by U.S. corporations to foreign related parties like a subsidiary. This tax only applies to U.S. Corporations with over $500 million of gross receipts. For example, if a U.S. corporation paid interest, royalties, and service fees to a foreign related party, the U.S. Corporation may have to pay additional tax on those deductions that reduced its U.S. taxable income. Another provision is the Foreign Derived Intangible Income (FDII) provision, which provides incentives for U.S. corporations to retain their intellectual property in the U.S. Thus, while the GILTI and BEAT provisions are potentially unfavorable to U.S. corporations with foreign operations because they could increase their U.S. taxes, the FDII provisions are potentially favorable to U.S. corporations with foreign operations. Suffice it to say that the provisions of the TCJA are complicated and corporations will likely respond by shifting assets and adjusting transfer pricing strategies to reduce their tax burden. Further, it is likely that other countries may change their tax codes in response to the TCJA.

Valuation Key 17.5

In a cross-border valuation, we consider the tax laws and regulations of both the investor's home country and the foreign company's country, as well as treaties between the two countries and possibly even between these countries and other countries. Independent of any cross-border issues, the foreign company's country can have income taxes or other taxes that the investor's country does not have. To add further complexity, each country can have additional taxes or regulations for a company with cross-border ownership.

In Exhibit 17.7, we present the corporate income tax rates for the OECD and BRIC (Brazil, Russia, India, China) countries for 2017.[13] The 2017 corporate tax rates vary from 12.5% (Ireland) to 39.1% (U.S.). The average (median) tax rates are 25.1% (25.0%). From 2005 through 2017, corporate tax rates decreased on average by 3.2% (median decrease is 3.4%), with 63.2% of the countries reducing their corporate income tax rates over this period. Beginning in 2018, the U.S. corporate tax rate decreases from 39.1% to 21.0%, which is below the median income tax rate and only 1% above the 25th percentile; however, we do not know how other countries will react to the U.S. corporate tax rate decrease.

[13] Source: Bazel, P., J. Mintz, and A. Thompson, *2017 Tax Competitiveness Report: The Calm Before the Storm*, University of Calgary, School of Public Policy, SPP Research Paper, Volume 11:7, February 2018.

EXHIBIT 17.7 Corporate Income Tax Rates for OECD and BRIC Countries

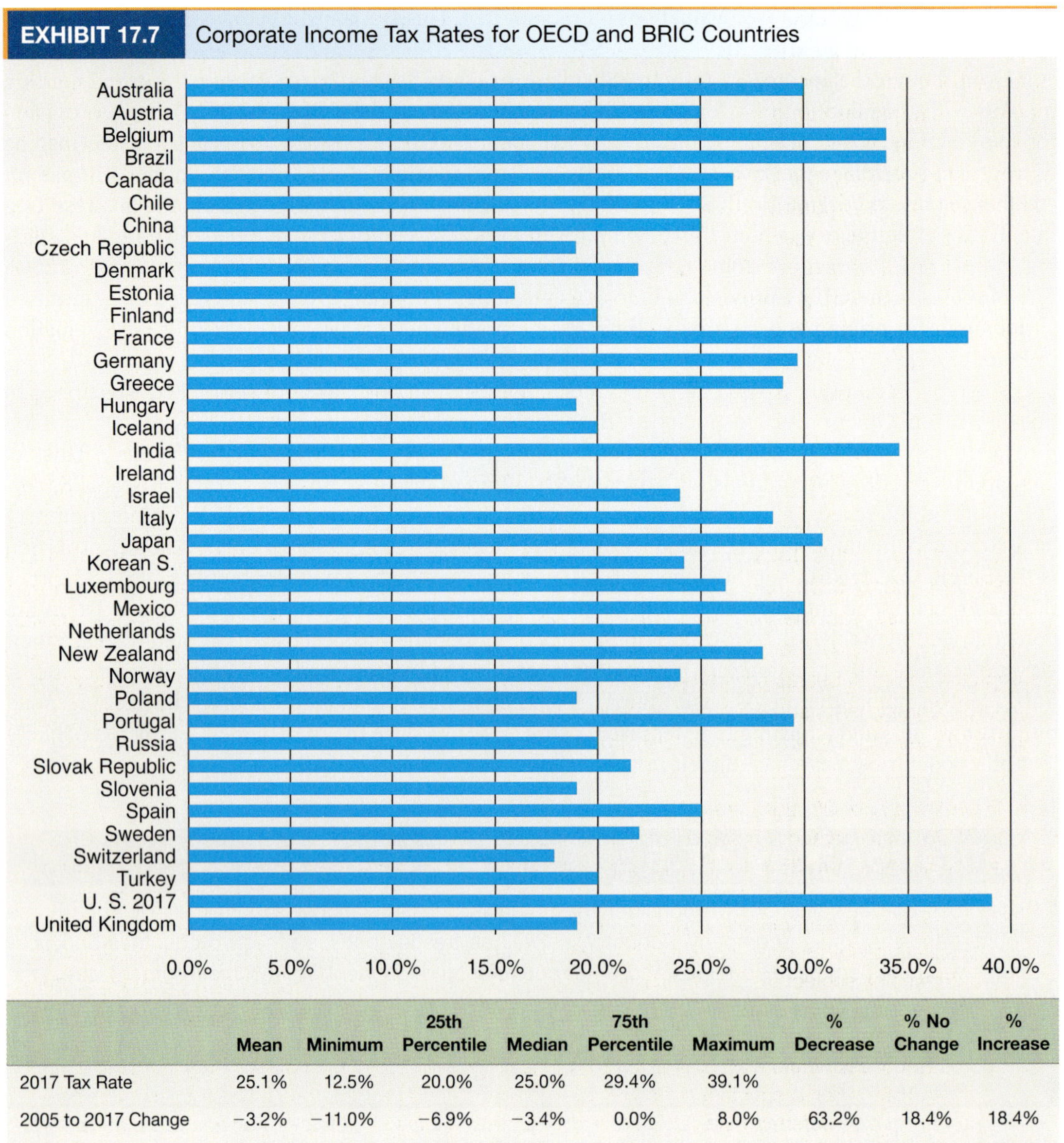

	Mean	Minimum	25th Percentile	Median	75th Percentile	Maximum	% Decrease	% No Change	% Increase
2017 Tax Rate	25.1%	12.5%	20.0%	25.0%	29.4%	39.1%			
2005 to 2017 Change	−3.2%	−11.0%	−6.9%	−3.4%	0.0%	8.0%	63.2%	18.4%	18.4%

In addition to taxing income of foreign companies, many countries impose a withholding tax on dividends paid to a foreign parent. The withholding tax rates vary from 0% in some countries to as high as 35%. If the earnings are reinvested locally, then there is no withholding tax levied.

Foreign Tax Credits and Deferral of Foreign Income for Worldwide (Resident) Tax Regimes

A foreign tax credit can eliminate or at least reduce double taxation on foreign income. Ignoring country-specific rules, generally, countries following a worldwide tax regime provide taxpayers with foreign tax credits that limit the tax payment to the higher of the investor country's tax rate or the foreign country's tax rate in a worldwide tax regime. If the foreign tax rate is less than the domestic tax rate, an investor company will have an incremental tax liability (due to the home country) on foreign earnings equal to foreign earnings multiplied by the difference in the tax rates. In such situations, the investor company has an **excess limit position**. On the other hand, if the foreign tax rate is higher than the domestic tax rate, an investor company will have no tax liability to the home country on that income. In this situation, the investor has an **excess credit position**. When allowable by the home country taxing authorities, companies prefer to offset an excess limit position from one country with an excess credit position from another country in order to minimize total income tax payments.

Naturally, the specific regulations and limitations on the use of foreign tax credits vary across countries. In this section, we will provide a high-level overview of the general types of regulations that govern foreign tax credits. Some regulations limit foreign tax credits based on the source of income. In some countries, companies can pool—under certain conditions and limitations—foreign income across countries to offset an excess limit position with an excess credit position in order to minimize total income tax payments. Pooled income allows companies to offset excess credits from high-tax countries with excess limits from low-tax countries. Companies can accomplish this offsetting in a variety of ways—for example, by simultaneously receiving dividend remittances from affiliates in high-tax and low-tax countries.

The deferral of taxes on foreign income is a common component of a worldwide tax regime. It is a way for a country with a worldwide tax regime to have an effective tax rate more similar to that of a territorial tax regime. As we discuss in the previous section, a common way for countries to defer taxes on foreign income is by not recognizing the foreign income as taxable income until the income is distributed to the investor company. Again, countries have various regulations that govern the deferral of taxes on foreign income.

Valuation in Practice 17.2

Merck & Co., Inc.'s Taxation of Unrepatriated Foreign Earnings Under the 2017 Tax Cuts and Jobs Act Merck & Co., Inc. (Merck) is a global health care company that develops and sells prescription medicines, vaccines, biologic therapies, and animal health products.[14] Merck generates substantial earnings outside the U.S. As we discussed previously, the 2017 Tax Cuts and Jobs Act in the U.S. imposes a 15.5% tax rate on unrepatriated earnings of foreign subsidiaries of U.S. companies invested in liquid investments and 8% on non-liquid investments. The tax on these unrepatriated earnings must be paid over eight years. Merck states the following with respect to the new U.S. tax regulations:

> On December 22, 2017, new U.S. tax legislation known as the Tax Cuts and Jobs Act of 2017 (TCJA) was enacted. Among other provisions, the TCJA reduced the U.S. federal corporate statutory tax rate from 35% to 21% effective January 1, 2018, requires companies to pay a one-time transition tax on undistributed earnings of certain foreign subsidiaries, and creates new taxes on certain foreign sourced earnings. The Company reflected the impact of the TCJA in its 2017 financial statements as described below. However, application of certain provisions of the TCJA was and remains subject to further interpretation and in these instances the Company made a reasonable estimate of the effects of the TCJA. No changes to these amounts were recognized in the first quarter of 2018 and they remain provisional.
>
> The one-time transition tax is based on the Company's post-1986 undistributed earnings and profits (E&P). For a substantial portion of these undistributed E&P, the Company had not previously provided deferred taxes as these earnings were deemed by Merck to be retained indefinitely by subsidiary companies for reinvestment. The Company recorded a provisional amount for its one-time transition tax liability of $5.3 billion. Merck has not yet finalized its calculation of the total post-1986 undistributed E&P for these foreign subsidiaries. The transition tax is based in part on the amount of undistributed E&P held in cash and other specified assets; therefore, this amount may change when the Company finalizes its calculation of post-1986 undistributed foreign E&P and finalizes the amounts held in cash or other specified assets.

Worldwide (Resident) and Territorial (Source) Tax Regime Example—The Holdem Company (with Two Foreign Subsidiaries, Lo-Tx Inc. and Hi-Tx Company)

We illustrate the differences between the worldwide and territorial tax regimes, including the effects of foreign tax credits and the deferral of income, with the Holdem Company (Holdem). Holdem is a holding company with no revenues or expenses other than the revenues and expenses of its foreign subsidiaries. It is located in a country (home country) that defers the recognition of foreign-sourced income as taxable

[14] See Merck's March 31, 2018 10-Q filing with the U.S. Securities and Exchange Commission for the first quarter of 2018.

income until the company declares it as a dividend. When the foreign subsidiary declares a dividend, the dividend declared and any related direct and indirect tax paid on that dividend (for example, a withholding tax on dividends) becomes taxable income to the parent company (in other words, the dividends on a pre-tax basis). The home country allows a foreign tax credit for all taxes paid on income to the foreign government including any withholding taxes from the foreign income of Lo-Tx and Hi-Tx. Holdem has an income tax rate of 40% on all taxable income before adjustments for foreign tax credits.

Holdem has two foreign subsidiaries. One of the subsidiaries, Lo-Tx Inc. (Lo-Tx), is located in a foreign country that has an income tax rate of 10% on all income and a dividend withholding tax of 10%. The other subsidiary, Hi-Tx Company (Hi-Tx), has an income tax rate of 45% on all income and no dividend withholding tax. Lo-Tx and Hi-Tx each have foreign taxable income of $1,000. In the first three columns of Exhibit 17.8, we present the tax calculations for the two subsidiaries and the holding company, assuming each company declares 100% of its after-tax earnings in dividends to Holdem.

EXHIBIT 17.8 Example of Worldwide and Territorial Tax Regimes

	100% Dividend Payout			Strategic Dividend Payout		
	Lo-Tx Inc.	Hi-Tx Co.	Holdem Co. (Pooled)	Lo-Tx Inc.	Hi-Tx Co.	Holdem Co. (Pooled)
Foreign Income Tax						
Foreign taxable income	$1,000.0	$1,000.0	$2,000.0	$1,000.0	$1,000.0	$2,000.0
Foreign income tax rate	10.0%	45.0%		10.0%	45.0%	
Foreign income tax liability	$ 100.0	$ 450.0	$ 550.0	$ 100.0	$ 450.0	$ 550.0
After-tax foreign income	$ 900.0	$ 550.0	$1,450.0	$ 900.0	$ 550.0	$1,450.0
Territorial effective tax rate w/o WH tax	10.0%	45.0%	27.5%	10.0%	45.0%	27.5%
Foreign Dividend Withholding (WH) Tax						
Dividend payout ratio	100.0%	100.0%		0.0%	80.0%	
Dividend declared	$ 900.0	$ 550.0	$1,450.0	$ 0.0	$ 440.0	$ 440.0
Withholding tax rate	10.0%	0.0%		10.0%	0.0%	
Withholding tax	$ 90.0	$ 0.0	$ 90.0	$ 0.0	$ 0.0	$ 0.0
Dividend distributed	$ 810.0	$ 550.0	$1,360.0	$ 0.0	$440.0	$440.0
Total foreign tax liability	$ 190.0	$ 450.0	$ 640.0	$ 100.0	$ 450.0	$ 550.0
Territorial effective tax rate after WH tax	19.0%	45.0%	32.0%	10.0%	45.0%	27.5%
Investor Country Income Tax						
Foreign income tax liability	$ 100.0	$ 450.0	$ 550.0	$ 100.0	$ 450.0	$ 550.0
Dividend payout ratio	100.0%	100.0%		0.0%	80.0%	
Allocated foreign income tax liability	$ 100.0	$ 450.0	$ 550.0	$ 0.0	$ 360.0	$ 360.0
Dividend declared	900.0	550.0	1,450.0	0.0	440.0	440.0
Investor country taxable income	$1,000.0	$1,000.0	$2,000.0	$ 0.0	$ 800.0	$ 800.0
Investor country tax rate	40.0%	40.0%	40.0%	40.0%	40.0%	40.0%
Investor country tax before credits	$ 400.0	$ 400.0	$ 800.0	$ 0.0	$ 320.0	$ 320.0
Foreign tax credit for foreign income tax	–100.0	–450.0	–550.0	0.0	–360.0	–360.0
Foreign tax credit for foreign WH tax	–90.0	0.0	–90.0	0.0	0.0	0.0
Additional U.S. income tax	$ 210.0	$ -	$ 160.0	$ -	$ -	$ -
Worldwide Tax (After Foreign Tax Credits)						
Total worldwide tax	$ 400.0	$ 450.0	$ 800.0	$ 100.0	$ 450.0	$ 550.0
Total worldwide tax rate	40.0%	45.0%	40.0%	10.0%	45.0%	27.5%

Holdem's Income Taxes Assuming a Territorial Tax Regime. In the top panel of Exhibit 17.8, we calculate the foreign income tax liability for each subsidiary. Lo-Tx has a taxable income of

$1,000 and a 10% tax rate, and thus it has a $100 foreign income tax liability. Hi-Tx also has a taxable income of $1,000, but it has a 45% tax rate, and thus it has a $450 foreign income tax liability. Holdem's weighted average income tax rate is equal to 27.5%, excluding the withholding taxes on dividends. The above foreign income tax calculations, however, do not include withholding taxes on dividends paid to the parent. If no dividends were paid, the total tax bill of Holdem would be $550. Recall, however, that we assume that both companies distribute all of their earnings in dividends, and that the foreign country in which Lo-Tx is located has a 10% withholding tax on dividends, while the foreign country in which Hi-Tx is located does not have withholding tax on dividends.

In the next panel of the exhibit, we present the withholding tax on the dividends declared. Both companies declare 100% of their after-tax income as a dividend—$900 for Lo-Tx and $550 for Hi-Tx. Lo-Tx pays a 10% ($90) withholding tax on its dividends. Hi-Tx pays no withholding tax. Thus, Lo-Tx distributes an $810 dividend, and Hi-Tax distributes a $550 dividend. The total foreign tax liability for the two companies is equal to $190 (19%) for Lo-Tx and $450 (45%) for Hi-Tx. These are the companies' income tax liabilities under a territorial tax regime, including withholding taxes on dividends when all after-tax earnings are distributed as dividends. Given these conditions, Holdem's weighted average income tax rate is equal to 32.0% (instead of 27.5%). The formula for the foreign tax rate, $T_{F\text{-}Total}$, for each country—including the foreign income tax, $T_{F\text{-}In}$, and withholding tax, $T_{F\text{-}WH}$—with full repatriation of income is as follows.

$$T_{F\text{-}Total} = T_{F\text{-}In} + (1 - T_{F\text{-}In}) \times T_{F\text{-}WH} \tag{17.4}$$

$$T_{F\text{-}Total,\ Lo\text{-}Tx} = 0.1 + (1 - 0.1) \times 0.1 = 0.19$$

$$T_{F\text{-}Total,\ Hi\text{-}Tx} = 0.45 + (1 - 0.45) \times 0.0 = 0.45$$

Holdem's Income Taxes Assuming a Worldwide Tax Regime. So far, we described the taxes that Holdem would pay if it were taxed in a territorial tax regime, as it would have no tax due to its home country. Now we calculate Holdem's taxes if Holdem was taxed by its home country with a worldwide tax regime. After calculating total taxes for each of the foreign companies, we calculate the investor's home country's income tax based on the country's 40% tax rate and adjust that amount for the foreign taxes paid. Recall the foreign tax liability is equal to the taxable income in the foreign country multiplied by the foreign country's income tax rate. The pre-withholding tax-based dividend payout ratio is equal to the sum of dividends declared plus the withholding tax on dividends divided by the taxable income in the foreign country. Foreign taxable income in the home country is equal to the pre-withholding tax dividend declared plus a proportionate share of the foreign income tax liability equal to the percentage of after-tax earnings declared as a dividend, the dividend payout ratio. Since both companies declared 100% of their after-tax earnings as dividends, we add 100% of their foreign income tax liability to the dividend declared in order to measure the investor country taxable income, which is equal to the taxable income in the foreign country, $1,000. When the dividend payout ratio is less (or more) than 100%, then the foreign country taxable income in the home country is less than (more than) the taxable income in the foreign country. We illustrate this situation in the right-hand set of columns in Exhibit 17.8 labeled Strategic Dividend Payout, which we discuss in the next section.

The investor country income tax is 40% of each company's taxable income, which is $400 for each company. To measure the tax liability for the investor's home country, we deduct the foreign tax liability (income and withholding taxes) allocated to the taxable income for the investor country, which is equal to 100% because both companies have a dividend payout ratio equal to 100%. For Lo-Tx, the foreign tax credits equal $190 ($100 income tax and $90 withholding tax), and the additional investor country income tax liability is equal to $210 ($210 = $400 − $100 − $90), which we call an excess limit. For Hi-Tx, the foreign tax credits equal $450, and it has no additional investor country income tax liability. In fact, Holdem has unused tax credits or excess credits of $50 ($50 = $450 − $400) from Hi-Tx.

The total worldwide tax regime tax liability, as a percentage of total income, is equal to 40% for Lo-Tx and 45% for Hi-Tx. The effective tax rate for each company is equal to the larger of the investor country tax rate (T_{HC} or 40%) and the foreign country tax rate (19% for Lo-Tx and 45% for Hi-Tx). In other words, for each foreign company, the effective tax rate, with full repatriation of dividends, is the

$$\text{Maximum}\ [T_{HC},\ T_{F\text{-}In} + (1 - T_{F\text{-}In}) \times T_{F\text{-}WH}] \tag{17.5}$$

If the home country's tax regulations do not allow Holdem to offset Hi-Tx's $50 excess credit against Lo-Tx's $210 excess limit, the total tax paid by Holdem is $850 ($850 = $400 + $450), and the weighted average of the two worldwide tax rates is equal to 42.5% [0.425 = ($400 + $450)/($1,000 + $1,000)]. However, if the investor country's tax regulations allow Holdem to apply the foreign tax credits on a pooled basis, then Holdem can use its excess credit to offset $50 of the $210 excess limit and reduce its tax liability to the investor country to $160 for Lo-Tx, and Holdem's total tax liability is equal to $800 ($800 = $450 + $100 + $90 + $160), which is equal to a weighted average tax rate of 40% [(0.4 = $800/($1,000 + $1,000)].

REVIEW EXERCISE 17.4

Worldwide (Resident) and Territorial (Source) Tax Regimes

A foreign subsidiary of a U.K. company has the equivalent of £10,000 in taxable income for both the foreign taxing authority and the U.K. taxing authority. The foreign income tax rate is 30% on all income with a 5% withholding tax on dividends; assume the U.K. income tax rate is 45% on all income paid out in dividends. The parent company intends to pay out all of the foreign subsidiary's after-tax income in dividends to the parent company. Calculate the income taxes payable based on both a territorial tax regime and a worldwide tax regime.

Solution on page 911.

Strategic Dividend Payout Scenario. In the last three columns of Exhibit 17.8, labeled Strategic Dividend Payout, we present the same set of calculations for Hi-Tx, Lo-Tx, and Holdem, but we change the dividend payout ratios. All of the data are the same as in the previous set of columns, but Lo-Tx does not distribute any dividends, and Hi-Tx has an 80% dividend payout ratio. The top section of the calculations—foreign income tax—is the same as before because the foreign country's taxable income and tax rates do not change. However, now the withholding tax on dividends is equal to zero for both companies, for Lo-Tx does not distribute any dividends, and the country in which Hi-Tx operates does not have a withholding tax. Thus, the foreign overall tax rate (equivalent to the territorial tax regime tax rate) is equal to 10% instead of 19% for Lo-Tx and remains unchanged for Hi-Tx. Lo-Tx not paying dividends reduces the overall weighted average tax rate from 32% to 27.5%.

The investor's home country income taxes also change if it is a worldwide tax regime. Since Lo-Tx does not distribute dividends, Holdem has no home country taxable income for Lo-Tx. Since Hi-Tx has a dividend payout ratio of 80%, resulting in a dividend of $440 ($440 = $550 × 80%), Holdem's taxable income for Hi-Tx is $800 instead of $1,000 [$800 = (0.8 × $450) + $440]. Thus, Holdem's home country income tax liability before foreign tax credits is zero for Lo-Tx (because Holdem has no taxable income to report from Lo-Tx) and $320 for Hi-Tx (because Hi-Tx has $800 of taxable income). Since Hi-Tx's dividend payout ratio is 80%, the allowable foreign tax credits are 80% of its foreign tax liability ($360 = $450 × 0.8). Hi-Tx continues to have a foreign tax in excess of its potential investor country tax liability, and thus has no additional tax liability to the investor's home country. The resulting worldwide income tax rates are 10% for Lo-Tx, 45% for Hi-Tx, and 27.5% for Holdem. Because Holdem defers recognition of Lo-Tx's taxable income by not distributing Lo-Tx's after-tax income as dividends, it is able to reduce its worldwide weighted average income tax rate to the same rate that would have resulted had it been taxed under a territorial tax regime. In this scenario, Holdem has an excess foreign tax credit of $40, which it may be able to carry forward to use in a future period. However, while the income tax is lower for Lo-Tx this year, the income tax is not eliminated but deferred until Lo-Tx upstreams the earnings to Holdem, assuming Holdem does not have other more tax efficient ways to use the earnings of Lo-Tx instead of paying dividends to Holdem, which we discuss in the next section.

An Overview of Strategies to Minimize Tax Liabilities and Manage Cash

As is evident in the previous example, different tax rates, foreign tax credit regulations, and withholding taxes all have an effect on a company's total tax liability as well as on its ability to manage its cash. On the one hand, companies typically prefer to transfer cash to the part of the company that has the best use for it, but on the other hand, companies also want to minimize the present value of their tax payments. Continuing with the previous example, since Lo-Tx pays a withholding tax on any dividends distributed, it would, all else equal, prefer not to pay a dividend in order to avoid paying this withholding tax. Similarly, since Lo-Tax has a lower income tax rate than Holdem, and since Holdem pays taxes based on a worldwide tax regime, Holdem would prefer to defer—either temporarily or permanently—recognition of Lo-Tx's income on its tax return. Both of these frictions provide Holdem with incentives to find alternatives for the free cash flow generated by Lo-Tx. The issue that arises, of course, is how to use these retained funds in order to provide the maximum value to shareholders.

Valuation in Practice 17.3

Google Inc. Income Tax Strategies Google Inc. (Google) uses transfer pricing and tax treaty strategies to reduce its income tax liability and defer income recognition in the United States with an approach called the "Double Irish" and the "Dutch Sandwich":

> Reports from Dutch regulatory filings say that Alphabet Inc.'s Google saved $3.6 billion in taxes in 2015 alone by moving $15.5 billion offshore. The reports about the $3.6 billion savings—in just one year—aren't flattering. Yet the move is legal and is decades old. In Google's case, the layering of tax-advantaged companies has been in place since 2004. And Google isn't the only one in Silicon Valley's elite that use it. Facebook flipped more than $700 million to the Cayman Islands as part of a "Double Irish" tax reduction strategy.

As many U.S. companies have done, Google transferred certain intellectual property and certain business activities to a subsidiary in Ireland, which has a lower tax rate (12.5%) than that of the U.S. It prearranged transfer prices for these activities with the U.S. government. In addition to this shift in income, it reduced its taxes in Ireland by paying royalties through a company in the Netherlands to another Irish company taxed in Bermuda, which has no income taxes. Because of certain tax agreements between Ireland and the Netherlands, Google can transfer these payments without incurring tax liabilities. Google then paid the subsidiary in Bermuda without being taxed, which is allowed by the Netherlands. While Google paid U.S. income taxes on all of its earnings that it repatriated, it deferred its taxable income in the United States by not paying the company located in the United States dividends from these foreign operations.

Source: See Wood, Robert, "How Google Saved $3.6 Billion Taxes from Paper 'Dutch Sandwich'" Forbes, December 22, 2016, available on June 25, 2018 at https://www.forbes.com/sites/robertwood/2016/12/22/how-google-saved-3-6-billion-taxes-from-paper-dutch-sandwich/#3cefdd631c19.

A potential way used to upstream cash flow but avoid paying dividends is for the parent company to fund part of the investment in the foreign company with a loan (instead of only equity) from the parent company. Naturally, foreign taxing authorities are aware of this tactic and limit interest rates and total interest deductions, as well as the relative amount of debt financing from the parent. Another potential strategy to avoid a dividend payment is for Holdem to use Lo-Tx's free cash flows for other positive net present value investments, assuming such investments fit with Holdem's strategy. Scholarly research indicates that firms facing higher repatriation tax burdens hold higher levels of cash, which they hold abroad in affiliates that trigger high tax costs when repatriating earnings.[15] Alternatively, Holdem could invest the free cash flows in passive, low-risk, or risk-free investments and borrow against those investments, again assuming such a strategy fits with Holdem's overall financial strategy.[16] Potential political risks—for example, risk of expropriation of assets—are also a consideration when making these decisions. Another way to avoid withholding taxes is to pay a series of dividends based on tax treaties among a group of countries that have a zero withholding tax rate (see Valuation in Practice 17.3).

Hi-Tx has a higher income tax rate than Holdem. Foreign tax credits may allow Holdem to offset its excess credits from Hi-Tx against the excess limits of Lo-Tx, but if it cannot do this, Holdem could opt to shift income from Hi-Tx to Holdem. In one potential strategy for shifting income, which can also be used in certain circumstances to avoid repatriation (withholding) taxes, Holdem can charge Hi-Tx management

---

[15] Foley, C. Fritz, J. C. Hartzell, S. Titman, and G. Twite, "Why Do Firms Hold So Much Cash? A Tax-Based Explanation," working paper, University of Texas at Austin, 2007.

[16] See Altshuler, R., and H. Grubert, "Repatriation Taxes, Repatriation Strategies, and Multinational Financial Policy," *Journal of Public Economics* 87 (2003), pp. 73–107.

fees, rents, royalties, and allocation of various corporate overhead expenses. These payments can shift income from Hi-Tx to Holdem if they meet the various tax regulations, thus reducing the overall tax rate so it moves toward Holdem's domestic tax rate.[17]

Valuation Key 17.6

Companies use various strategies to minimize the present value of income taxes related to foreign subsidiaries. These strategies include deferring income by not repatriating earnings, shifting income from one company to another through royalties and fees, and borrowing against the passive investments resulting from the free cash flows of a foreign subsidiary.

Another way companies potentially shift income from high-tax jurisdictions to lower-tax jurisdictions is through transfer pricing. A company may design a product in one country, produce its components in other countries, assemble the product in another country, and distribute and sell the product in yet another country. At each stage in the supply and value chain, the parent company must set a transfer price for the relevant goods used and services performed. This situation may provide a company an opportunity to shift income across taxing jurisdictions. Companies need to consider tariffs as well when they set transfer prices as they want to minimize their income taxes and fees or taxes such as tariffs.

Naturally, tax authorities are aware of these incentives and have various regulations and methods to prevent companies from using inappropriate transfer pricing. Using a market or an arm's length price (the price at which two unrelated parties will trade) is the preferred method for setting a transfer price (called the comparable uncontrolled pricing method), but many times, such prices do not exist. Other common methods include the resale pricing method and the cost plus pricing method (detailed discussions of which are beyond the scope of this book). Transferring intangible assets to low- or zero-tax jurisdictions is another common strategy used by companies. Such shifting is more valuable for companies subject to a territorial tax regime, for any tax reduction is permanent. For a company subject to a worldwide tax regime, the value results from the present value of the tax deferral. Similarly, a company can use its financial strategy to shift tax deductible interest to higher tax rate jurisdictions, but again, taxing authorities have various ways to prevent inappropriate uses of this strategy. For example, we discussed the GILTI and BEAT provisions of the 2017 Tax Cuts and Jobs Act that are attempts to overcome some of these potential strategies.

The Bottom Line on Taxes in a Cross-Border Valuation

It is apparent that cross-border income tax issues can be complex. We have only scratched the surface in this chapter. Moreover, to compute the taxes that a company pays on the income of a foreign subsidiary requires knowledge of:

- the implicit taxes (such as VAT taxes), as well as any tariffs,
- the company's complete tax picture (the home country's tax regime, the foreign country's tax regime, the tax treaty between the countries, whether it has unused FTCs from other subsidiaries, etc.),
- how the company plans to operate the subsidiaries (whether it will transfer goods and services between subsidiaries and at what prices),
- whether it will use corporate structures to defer taxes, and
- what its repatriation policy is going to be with respect to foreign income

Without this information, a more straightforward approach may be informative. As a first pass, compute the taxes for a worst-case scenario—when 100% of the earnings are repatriated as a dividend back to the parent company. If the parent company is taxed based on a territorial tax regime, then the maximum tax rate that it will face on income will be $T_{F\text{-}Total} = T_{F\text{-}In} + (1 - T_{F\text{-}In}) \times T_{F\text{-}WH}$. If, on the other hand, the parent company is taxed based on a worldwide tax regime, then the maximum tax rate that it will face on that income will be the maximum of T_{HC}, and $T_{F\text{-}In} + (1 - T_{F\text{-}In}) \times T_{F\text{-}WH}$.

[17] See Grubert, H., "Taxes and the Division of Foreign Operating Income Among Royalties, Interest, Dividends and Retained Earnings," *Journal of Public Economics* 68 (1998), pp. 269–290.

An alternative (and possible upside case) is that no dividends are ever repatriated. If the parent company is taxed based on a territorial tax regime, then the maximum tax rate that it will face on income will be the foreign income tax rate—$T_{F\text{-}Total} = T_{F\text{-}In}$. If, on the other hand, the parent company is taxed based on a worldwide tax regime, ignoring the potential deferral of non-repatriated earnings under some worldwide tax regimes, then the maximum tax rate that it will face on income will be the maximum of the home country tax rate or the foreign country income tax rate—Maximum $[T_{HC}, T_{F\text{-}In}]$. Of course, in a worldwide tax regime with deferral of tax on non-repatriated earnings the maximum tax rate would be $T_{F\text{-}In}$.

17.5 MEASURING THE EQUITY COST OF CAPITAL

LO4 Measure discount rates and adjust free cash flows for country-specific risks

Various complications arise in cross-border valuations when estimating the equity cost of capital. Even though we discuss this issue in the context of cross-border valuations, much of this discussion will be relevant for domestic valuations as well. Many of the complications in estimating the cost of equity capital in a cross-border valuation stem from the question of whether the world has one global integrated capital market or has multiple capital markets that are segmented by country or region. If markets were completely integrated, then all investors would agree on one risk premium for a given investment in a given currency; in other words, for a given currency, every investment would have the same amount of risk (for example beta) and the same market risk premium. It would not matter whether the investor was in the U.S., U.K., India, or China—the risk premium for an investment would be the same. However, if the world's capital markets are segmented rather than integrated, then investors would not necessarily agree on the risk premium associated with a given investment. An investor in the U.S. might view an investment made in a company in Germany as having a different cost of capital than how a German investor might view that same investment because the risk premium, either the amount of risk or market risk premium or both, for a U.S. investor might be different from that for a German investor.

In this section, we explore how to estimate the cost of equity capital given these two different views of the world's capital markets.[18] One complicating factor is that the world is probably neither completely integrated nor completely segmented, so our two approaches likely provide a reasonable range of discount rates for the discount rate based on partially integrated markets. Another complicating feature is whether risk premiums are affected by foreign currency exchange rate risk and political risk and, if so, how to best estimate these effects. In addition, estimating discount rates is more difficult, especially in emerging economies due to a lack of data. We discuss emerging markets later in the chapter, but for now, we discuss approaches to estimating the cost of capital for assets that are traded in markets that are reasonably liquid.

Integrated Capital Markets

If capital markets are integrated, we would expect equity investors across the world to demand the same risk premium for a given investment measured in a given currency. One implication of this assertion is that all investors use the same measure of risk, such as the systematic risk or beta of an investment from the CAPM. In addition, besides using the same measure of risk, investors must also use the same benchmark portfolio for measuring risk. Within the framework of the CAPM, these implications assume that investors diversify their portfolios across a broad array of securities from around the globe—investing beyond their local markets—and that the benchmark portfolio approximates a world market portfolio that spans at least all equity securities—and possibly all assets—from around the globe on a value-weighted basis. In order to achieve full integration, we would also expect real risk-free rates to be the same across markets and prices of currencies to be in equilibrium (such that the various parity conditions discussed previously hold).

The International CAPM (ICAPM) assumes that capital markets are integrated.

$$r_{E,i}^{HC} = r_F^{HC} + \beta_{E,i}^{W} \times [E(R_{WorldMkt}^{HC} - R_F^{HC})] + \sum_{k=1}^{n} \gamma_{i,k} \times E\left[R_F^{FC_k} + \%\Delta S\left(\frac{HC}{FC_k}\right) - R_F^{HC}\right] \quad (17.6)$$

where:

[18] For an excellent discussion of these issues, see, Bodnar, G., B. Dumas, and R. Marston, "Cross-Border Valuation: The International Cost of Equity Capital," NBER Working Paper #w10115, November 2003.

$r^{HC}_{E,i}$ = expected rate of return (measured in the home currency) on an equity security "i" outside the home country

r^{HC}_{F} = home currency risk-free rate

$\beta^{W}_{E,i}$ = beta of security i measured with respect to the world market risk premium

$E(R^{HC}_{WorldMkt} - R^{HC}_{F})$ = world market risk premium measured against the return on the home country risk-free rate

$\gamma_{i,k}$ = the sensitivity of security i to returns on foreign currency k in excess of the home country risk-free asset

$R^{FC_k}_{F} + \%\Delta S\left(\frac{HC}{FC_k}\right) - R^{HC}_{F}$ = the relevant risk premium for the investment in foreign currency k

We do not discuss the last term in the ICAPM in detail because, generally, the effects of the systematic risk of currencies on an equity security are not economically meaningful, and we typically estimate the ICAPM without estimating the effects of the risks of foreign currencies.

In order to estimate the ICAPM for, say, a U.S. company estimating the equity cost of capital for a U.K. firm it might acquire, we use historical £-denominated returns of the equity for the U.K. firm for, say, the last 60 months and convert those returns into U.S. dollar-based returns using historical exchange rates. We also measure the world market returns in U.S. dollars for the last 60 months. We estimate the market model using the U.K. firm's returns (denominated in dollars) on the dollar-denominated world market index returns in order to estimate $\beta^{W}_{E,i}$. We multiply our estimated beta by our estimate of the dollar-denominated world market risk premium, which is measured in relation to the appropriate U.S. risk-free security; to this, we then add the current yield of the appropriate U.S. risk-free security in order to measure the dollar-denominated required rate of return for the U.K. firm's equity. Assuming that the cost of equity is the appropriate discount rate for the cash flows we are discounting, we use this discount rate to discount the future cash flows of the U.K. company that we converted into U.S. dollars with the relevant future expected exchange rates (the investor currency or centralized approach discussed earlier).

Are equity markets completely integrated? No, but they have been becoming more integrated over time, and we know that cross-border investment flows also continue to grow over time. For example, in Chapters 15 and 16, we document substantial cross-border leveraged buyout (LBO) and merger and acquisition (M&A) activity. In addition, many mutual funds allow investors to purchase securities of foreign companies with relatively low transaction costs. Moreover, the diversification benefits for investors increase when the investors hold foreign investments, which provides incentives for investors to invest abroad. Finally, the correlations between stock market indices across countries have increased over time, which is another indication that economic ups and downs tend to be shared globally.

The World Market Index and Market Risk Premium. Using the international CAPM to measure a company's equity cost of capital requires an appropriate world market index to estimate both the company's beta and the market risk premium. If capital markets are fully integrated, even for U.S. valuations, we would replace the CAPM and related input estimates in Chapter 8 with the international CAPM and the related input estimates for the international CAPM.

Recall from Chapter 8 that the theoretical market portfolio is the investment opportunity set available to current and potential investors consisting of a globally diversified market value-weighted portfolio. In Chapter 8, we used a domestic index to calculate the cost of capital—in particular, we used the S&P 500, which would be consistent with a segmented markets view for a U.S. investor. In estimating a cost of capital using an integrated capital markets perspective, common world market portfolios used for estimating the cost of equity capital are those available from MSCI Inc.[19] MSCI began calculating global indices of publicly traded equities in late 1969. Initially, MSCI distributed the MSCI World Index, available from 1970. The MSCI World Index is a portfolio of publicly traded equities traded in 23 countries such as the U.S., Canada, the U.K. and many European countries, Israel, Australia, Hong Kong, Japan, New Zealand, and Singapore.

In the late 1980s, MSCI began distributing the MSCI Emerging Markets Index and the combination of World and Emerging Markets Indices, the MSCI ACWI Index, available from 1988. The MSCI Emerging Markets Index includes the publicly traded equities in 24 countries in the Americas, Europe, Middle East,

---

[19] MSCI distributes global equity indices and other content, applications, and services to support the needs of global institutional investors throughout their investment processes.

Africa, and Asia. In late 2007, MSCI began distributing the MSCI Frontier Markets Index and the combination of the World, Emerging Markets, and Frontier Indices, the MSCI ACWI & Frontier Markets Index, available from December 2007. The MSCI Frontier Markets Index includes the publicly traded equities in 22 countries in the Americas, Europe, Middle East, Africa, and Asia. Since these are market-weighted indices and the relative market value of the Emerging and Frontier markets is small, the three indices (MSCI, MSCI ACWI and the MSCI ACWI & Frontier Markets indices) are highly correlated (above 0.99). Thus, the MSCI World Index is often the index chosen because it is available for the longest time-series.

These series are each available in three forms—a gross total return index (including full reinvestment of all return of capital distributions or dividends), a net total return index (net of country-specific withholding taxes), and price-based returns (ignoring return of capital distributions). Since return of capital distributions are typically a relatively small part of a return index, these alternative indices are also highly correlated (for example, for the World index the correlations are higher than 0.99).

In Exhibit 17.9, we present the average annual returns and standard deviation of returns of the various world indices produced by MSCI as well as the S&P 500.[20] In the first three columns of the exhibit, we present annual stock return data from 1970 to 2015 for the S&P 500, the MSCI World Index and the MSCI World Index excluding the U.S. As can be seen, the average returns of the three indices are quite similar, ranging from 11.0% to 11.8%, suggesting that market risk premiums based on these three indices would be similar using the historical approach discussed in Chapter 8. The annual standard deviation of returns of the MSCI World Index is similar to the S&P 500 (14.8% vs. 15.3%) while the MSCI World Ex-U.S. Index has a larger standard deviation at 17.1%.

In the last three columns of the exhibit, we report the mean annual returns and standard deviation of returns for S&P 500, the MSCI ACWI World Index (the combination of the World and Emerging Markets indices), and the MSCI ACWI World Index excluding the U.S. for the 1991–2015 period (the period during which the MSCI ACWI World Index is available). Over this shorter period, which includes the global financial crisis, the MSCI ACWI World Index and the MSCI ACWI Ex-U.S. World Index earned average returns of 9.3% and 8.1%, respectively, which were not as high as the S&P 500, 11.6%. The annual standard deviations of the MSCI ACWI World Index and the MSCI ACWI Ex-U.S. World Index are 15% and 16.7%, respectively, which are larger than that of the S&P 500, 14.3%.

EXHIBIT 17.9 Annual MSCI Global Index Returns Compared to the S&P 500 Index Returns

	1970–2015			1991–2015		
	S&P 500 Index	MSCI World Index	MSCI World Ex-U.S. Index Non-U.S. Developed Markets	S&P 500 Index	MSCI ACWI World Index	MSCI ACWI EX-U.S. Index Non-U.S. Developed and Emerging Markets
Average	11.8%	11.0%	11.6%	11.6%	9.3%	8.1%
Standard deviation	15.3%	14.8%	17.1%	14.3%	15.0%	16.7%

In Exhibit 17.10, we present the correlation of two of the MSCI indices, MSCI World Ex-U.S. Index (non-U.S. developed markets) and the MSCI ACWI Ex-U.S. index (non-U.S. developed and emerging markets) with the S&P 500. We measure the correlation using 60 months of overlapping or rolling data. The chart shows that from the mid-1970s through the mid-1990s, the correlation was never higher than 0.62 and had an overall negative trend, decreasing to under 0.4 by 1996. However, in the late 1990s, the correlation quickly increased and reached 0.8 by 2000. Since 2000, the correlation generally varies between 0.8 and 0.9. Thus, the returns on these world indices, which exclude the U.S., are highly correlated with returns on the S&P 500. Note that this does not mean that individual country indices are highly correlated.

Segmented Markets

Even though there are economic forces that are integrating the world's capital markets, other economic forces and frictions have kept complete integration somewhat at bay. For example, many countries impose restrictions on foreign investment in such industries as natural resource industries. As we discuss

[20] We use the indices including dividends and before any withholding taxes in this exhibit.

EXHIBIT 17.10 Correlations of the MSCI Global Indices and the S&P 500*

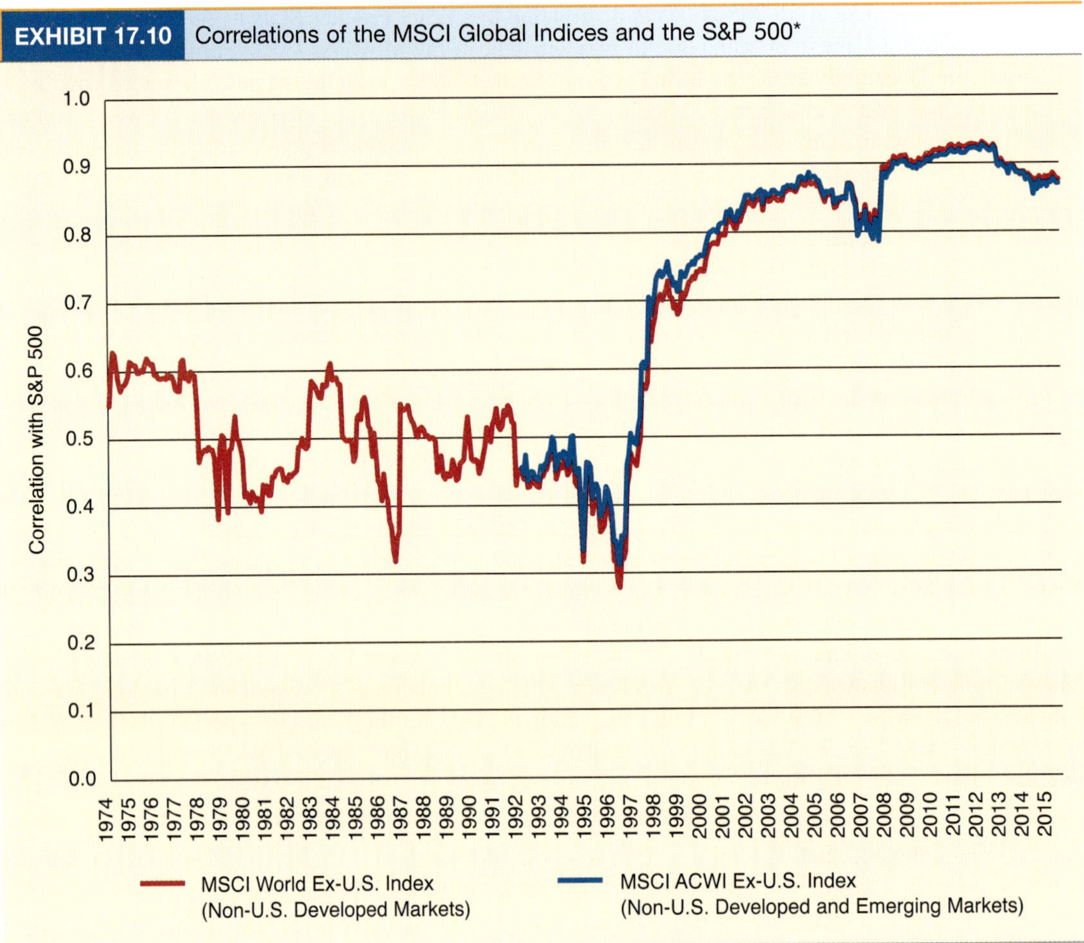

* Correlations as of a given date are based on the past 60 monthly observations.

earlier, some countries have tax policies that affect domestic investors and foreign investors differently. These tax policies usually work to limit foreign investment by taxing income on foreign investment at a higher rate (for example, the withholding tax on dividends paid to a foreign investor). In addition, the inability of foreign investors to garner the same amount of information as domestic investors can also limit foreign investment.

Another limitation on integration is the home bias of investors—that is, the proclivity to invest more in one's own country than in the global market even though global investment is optimal from a diversification perspective. Investors may have valid economic reasons (such as tax and information issues) not to hold a world portfolio in the proportions that each country's market represents, and, as such, these investors are biased toward investing in their domestic economy. For example, in 2012, the U.S. stock market represented 53% of the value of the MSCI ACWI Index (the combination of World and Emerging Markets Indices), but U.S. investors held about 77% of their portfolio in U.S. stocks. The home bias is even more apparent in other countries. One study examined 37 countries in 2003, when U.S. equity markets were 45% of the worldwide equity market. In 18 of the 37 countries, the holdings of U.S. equity securities (as a percentage of total equity securities held) were 1% or less; 13 countries held less than 10%; the rest held less than 20% (except the Netherlands, which held 29%).[21] The home bias is just as prevalent when calculating a country's total foreign holdings of equity to total equity held relative to the proportion of the world's equity market capitalization that comes from outside that country. Thus, the observed home bias does not just apply to U.S. investors or U.S. stocks.

If markets are fully segmented, the implication is that shareholders use their local market to benchmark the risk of an investment. In other words, a U.S. investor would judge the risk of any investment against a

[21] See Yago, G., J. Barth, T. Li, S. Malaiyandi, and T. Phumiswasana, "Home Bias in Global Capital Markets: What Is the Potential Demand for U.S. Asset-Backed Securities?" *Milken Institute Capital Studies*, 2006, available at http://www.milkeninstitute.org/publications/view/281, accessed June 24, 2018.

portfolio of U.S. stocks while a U.K. investor would assess the risk of an asset against a portfolio of U.K. stocks. To understand the implication of fully segmented markets for estimating the cost of capital, consider a U.S. company potentially acquiring a company in India. If markets are segmented, the U.S. company would estimate the risk of the Indian company within a CAPM framework by using, say, the Indian company's last 60 monthly returns after converting them into U.S. dollars from Indian rupees with historical exchange rates. The U.S. company would then estimate beta for the investment using returns on a U.S. stock market index such as the S&P 500. The estimate of the cost of equity capital is equal to the appropriate U.S. risk-free rate, plus the estimated beta, multiplied by the market risk premium for the S&P 500 that is estimated relative to the U.S. risk-free rate. The expected free cash flows equal the rupee-denominated expected free cash flows—converted to USD at the relevant expected future exchange rates between dollars and rupees.

On the other hand, if an Indian company were potentially acquiring the same company, it would estimate the beta of the Indian company based on that company's returns (denominated in Indian rupees) and the returns of a broad-based Indian stock market index such as the SENSEX. The estimate of the cost of equity capital is equal to the appropriate Indian risk-free rate, plus the beta estimated against the SENSEX multiplied by an estimate of the market risk premium for the SENSEX, estimated relative to the appropriate Indian risk-free rate. The expected free cash flows to be discounted equal the expected free cash flows in Indian rupees.

The U.S. investor could estimate either a lower or higher cost of capital for the potential Indian investment than the Indian investor depending on the difference in the beta estimates, the risk-free rates, and the market risk premiums in the U.S. and India. It is likely that the beta estimate for the U.S. investor would be lower than for the Indian investor. Of course, the expected free cash flows for the two investors might also be different due to different taxes, different regulations, political risks, differences in perceived synergies, and the other reasons we discuss in this chapter.

Implications for Domestic Investments

It is useful to note that the issue of how to estimate the cost of capital is not just an issue specific to cross-border valuation. In Chapter 8, the discussion focused on U.S. data, which assumed the segmented markets view of the world was appropriate and that the investor was from the U.S. and the company being valued was a U.S. company. If markets were completely integrated, a U.S. firm investing in a project in the U.S. or buying a U.S. target would use the global market portfolio as the benchmark portfolio for estimating both beta and the market risk premium.

Valuation Key 17.7

Finance theory provides a relatively clear guide on how to estimate the cost of capital if markets are either completely segmented by country or fully integrated globally. If they are integrated, we use a world market index as a benchmark for risk, while if they are segmented, we use a stock market index from the investor's home country as a benchmark for risk.

What if Markets Are Neither Fully Integrated nor Completely Segmented?

While finance theory provides a relatively clear guide on how to estimate the cost of capital if the world's capital markets are either fully integrated globally or completely segmented by country, finance theory does not provide a strong guide for when capital markets are in neither state but are somewhere in between. Some researchers have proposed a hybrid model, which includes two risk factors—one for risk measured against a country benchmark and one for risk measured against a world market benchmark. To estimate the effect of the two factors, one could estimate a multiple regression of a firm's returns against the country index and the world index. Bodnar, Dumas, and Marston (2003)[22] estimated this hybrid model for a variety of countries and companies and found that the betas estimated with respect to the country benchmark were generally large and significant and that the betas estimated with respect to the world index were often small and insignificant. The authors were careful to note that although estimating these models is an interesting empirical analysis

---

[22] Bodnar, Gordon, Bernard Dumas, and Richard Marston, "Cross-Border Valuation: The International Cost of Equity Capital," 2003, fourth draft, working paper, Johns Hopkins University.

to see whether the country or world dominates in explanatory power, this hybrid form of the CAPM has no theoretical foundation. As such, and similar to the market capitalization-based size adjustment to the CAPM, these models may be estimable, but we cannot provide a rigorous theoretical justification for computing a firm's cost of capital using them.

As with the hybrid model, other solutions to the world's capital markets being neither integrated nor segmented have been proposed, and like the hybrid model, these alternatives have no theoretical foundation. For example, one proposed solution is for a valuation expert to estimate the risk premium with a beta estimated with respect to the country index (with no world index in the regression) to estimate the country beta, and then multiply it by the country risk premium to estimate the risk premium. The valuation expert will then measure the risk premium with the beta estimated with respect to the world index (with no country index in the regression), and then multiply it by the world portfolio risk premium. Finally, the valuation expert will then assign weights to the two risk premiums such that the weights sum to 1; the assigned weights are based on the judgment of the valuation expert.

So, given the state of the research on this topic, what do we recommend for estimating the cost of capital? In our view, it makes sense to calculate the cost of capital using both the integrated and segmented market approaches. In some cases, these estimates will be reasonably close, in other cases, they will not, but it provides a range of values. As we show earlier in the chapter, fortunately for U.S. investors, since 2000, the correlation between global capital markets and U.S. capital markets is in the 80% to 90% range. This likely mitigates the difference in discount rates assuming integrated versus segmented markets for U.S. investors.

Arwana Citramulia TBK PT Beta and Equity Cost of Capital Estimates

Arwana is an Indonesian company that manufactures and distributes ceramic tiles almost entirely within Indonesia. The company was founded in 1993 and is headquartered in West Jakarta, Indonesia and is publicly traded on the Jakarta Stock Exchange (an emerging market according to MSCI). Arwana has a market capitalization of around $300 million, which, as we know from Chapter 8, is a relatively small market capitalization based on U.S. equities. In this section, we illustrate how to measure Arwana's beta and equity cost of capital from both a U.S. and Indonesian investor's perspective.

Arwana's Beta from a U.S. Investor's Perspective. From a U.S. investor's perspective, we first convert Arwana's stock returns from the local currency (Indonesia rupee, IDR) to returns based on the investor currency (U.S. dollar, USD). We can do this in two ways. We can convert Arwana's stock prices and dividend payments using concurrent IDR/USD spot rates and calculate stock returns based on USD prices and dividends. Alternatively, we can convert the IDR returns directly by adjusting each return for the percentage change in the IDR/USD spot over the return period. In the following table, we illustrate how to calculate the IDR-denominated and USD-denominated stock returns for Arwana. As we show in the table, Arwana's IDR-denominated stock return on May 19, 2016 was 7.563% and the one-day percentage change in the IDR/USD exchange rate on that day was 1.167%. Thus, Arwana's USD-denominated stock return on that day is equal to 6.322% (0.06322 = 1.07563/1.01167 − 1).

	5/18/16	5/19/16	Return
Arwana stock price (IDR)	595.0	640.0	7.563%
Arwana ex-date dividend (IDR)		0.0	
Arwana stock price + dividend (IDR)	595.0	640.0	7.563%
IDR/USD spot rate	13,455.0	13,612.0	1.167%
Arwana stock price + dividend (USD)	$ 0.0442	$ 0.0470	6.322%

Once we measure Arwana's USD-denominated stock returns, we measure its beta assuming integrated markets and segmented markets. We use the return on the USD-denominated MSCI World Index (Developed Markets, including U.S. equities) as the world market index to measure Arwana's USD beta assuming integrated markets. We use the return on the S&P 500 Index to measure Arwana's USD beta assuming segmented markets. We measure Arwana's betas using monthly returns from January 2011 through June 2016. Arwana's beta assuming integrated markets is 0.95 while its beta assuming segmented markets is 0.97. Both betas are statistically significant, although the adjusted r-squared is only 7% assuming integrated markets and 6% assuming segmented markets. Consistent with our previous discussion regarding the relatively high correlation of MSCI World and the S&P 500 indices, the difference in Arwana's betas assuming integrated versus segmented market is only 0.02 (0.95 versus 0.97) for a U.S. investor.

Arwana Citramulia TBK PT	Beta Estimate	Standard Error of Beta	t-statistic	95% Confidence Interval Lower Bound	95% Confidence Interval Upper Bound	Adjusted r-squared
Investor/Foreign currency (USD):						
MSCI World Index—Integrated markets . . .	0.95	0.36	2.59	0.22	1.67	0.07
S&P 500 Index—Segmented markets	0.97	0.40	2.43	0.18	1.77	0.06
Local/Home currency (Indonesian Rupee):						
Jakarta Stock Exchange	1.28	0.30	4.21	0.67	1.88	0.18

Arwana's Beta from an Indonesian Investor's Perspective. From an Indonesian investor's perspective assuming segmented markets, we measure Arwana's IDR beta using its IDR-denominated stock returns and the IDR-denominated returns of the Jakarta Stock Exchange Index. Recall that Indonesia is an emerging market. The correlation between the USD-denominated returns of the Jakarta Stock Exchange Index and the returns on the USD-denominated MSCI World Index and the S&P 500 is only around 0.45. As we show in the preceding table, Arwana's beta is 1.28 measured against the Jakarta Stock Exchange Index and it is statistically significant. The adjusted r-squared is 0.18. While the 95% confidence intervals of the three estimates of beta overlap and are not likely statistically different from each other, based on the three point estimates, the IDR beta is more than 30% higher than the USD beta, indicating that Arwana has more systematic risk from an Indonesian investor's perspective. Does a higher beta result in a higher equity cost of capital for the Indonesian investor? Not necessarily because the effect of a higher beta can be offset by either a lower Indonesian risk-free rate or a lower Indonesian market risk premium.

We could also calculate the beta from an Indonesian investor's perspective assuming integrated markets. To do this, we would regress the IDR-denominated returns of Arwana on the IDR-denominated MSCI World Index returns. We do not tabulate these results, but as you would expect, that beta is much lower measured against the World Index than the beta measured against the Jakarta Stock Exchange, 0.67.

Arwana's Equity Cost of Capital. We can use our estimates of beta to measure Arwana's CAPM equity cost of capital from both a U.S. and Indonesian investor's perspective. To measure Arwana's CAPM equity cost of capital from a U.S. investor's perspective assuming integrated markets, we collect the USD-denominated U.S. long-term risk-free rate, 3%, and estimate the market risk premium, 5.76%, based on the USD-denominated MSCI World Index, which we used to estimate the integrated markets-based beta. Based on these inputs we can calculate Arwana's USD equity cost of capital assuming integrated markets, 8.5%, which we show in the table below (integrated markets, $0.0845 = 0.03 + 0.95 \times 0.0576$).

Arwana Citramulia TBK PT	Beta Estimate	Market Risk Premium	Company Risk Premium	Risk-Free Rate	CAPM Equity Cost of Capital
Investor/Foreign currency (USD):					
MSCI World Index—Integrated markets	0.95	5.76%	5.45%	3.00%	8.45%
S&P 500 Index—Segmented markets	0.97	6.00%	5.83%	3.00%	8.83%
Local/Home currency (Indonesian Rupee):					
Jakarta Stock Exchange	1.28	8.00%	10.23%	5.02%	15.25%

To measure Arwana's CAPM equity cost of capital from a U.S. investor's perspective assuming segmented markets, we collect the USD-denominated U.S. long-term risk-free rate, 3%, and estimate the market risk premium, 6%, based on the S&P 500 Index, which we used to estimate the segmented markets-based beta. Based on these inputs we can calculate Arwana's USD equity cost of capital assuming segmented markets, 8.8%, which we show in the table (segmented markets, $0.0883 = 0.3 + 0.97 \times 0.06$).

To measure Arwana's CAPM equity cost of capital from an Indonesian investor's perspective assuming segmented markets, we estimate the Indonesian long-term risk-free rate and the Indonesian market risk premium. It turns out that not only does Arwana have a higher beta for an Indonesian investor, Indonesia has a higher risk-free rate and market risk premium. The Indonesian long-term government bond rate was 7.54% at this time. Given that Indonesia is an emerging market, the return on the Indonesian long-term government bond is not likely a risk-free return. One way to estimate the risk premium embedded in the Indonesian long-term government bond return is to compare it to the U.S. long-term government bond return similar to how we estimate the market risk premium (see Chapter 8). Another way to estimate this risk premium is to compare long-term inflation rates and assuming real risk-free interest rates are the same in the U.S. (2%) and Indonesia, adjust the U.S. risk-free rate for the difference in inflation rates between the U.S. and Indonesia (4%). Adjusting the U.S. risk-free rate for the difference in inflation rates results in an IDR-denominated risk-free rate of 5.02% [(0.0502 = (1.03 ÷ 1.02) × 1.04 – 1)], indicating a risk premium of 2.52% embedded in the Indonesian long-term government bond return (0.0252 = 0.0754 − 0.0502).

We estimate Indonesia's market risk premium at 8%.[23] Based on these inputs Arwana's IDR-denominated CAPM equity cost of capital for an Indonesian investor assuming segmented markets is 15.25% (0.1525 = 0.0502 + 1.28 × 0.08). Does the higher equity cost of capital for an Indonesian investor result in a lower valuation than for say a U.S. investor? Again, not necessarily for a variety of reasons. First, remember that the USD-denominated equity cost of capital assumes we will discount USD-denominated free cash flows. Thus, we would have to take the IDR-denominated forecasted free cash flows of Arwana and convert them into USD-denominated free cash flows using estimates of future exchange rates between the U.S. dollar and Indonesian rupee. Because inflation is higher in Indonesia than in the U.S., this process will systematically impact the USD-denominated free cash flows. In addition, because a foreign investor in Indonesia pays a withholding tax of 20% and may have additional political or other country-specific risks (for example, expropriation risk), those factors could reduce the expected free cash flows for a foreign investor. Thus, we would need to carry out a complete valuation to determine whether the value to an Indonesian investor is less than the value to say a U.S. investor.

Lack of a Publicly Traded Comparable Company in the Relevant Market

Sometimes, especially with less developed economies, we are unable to find a firm in the same country that is comparable to the firm we are valuing; hence, we cannot estimate the betas for comparable companies in a particular country with respect to either the country index or the world index. This is even more critical if the firm we are valuing is privately held. A potential solution to this problem is to assume that the unlevered beta of a particular business, with respect to that business' country, is the same across countries.[24]

Assume that markets are segmented and that we are valuing a telephone company from Indonesia that is a private company. Further, assume that there are no publicly traded telephone companies in Indonesia. We could estimate the betas of telephone companies from different countries (measured with respect to each telephone company's home country index). In other words, we assume that the beta of a telephone company with respect to a country index is the same across countries. This would provide an estimate for an Indonesian telephone company's beta against the Indonesian stock market. If instead we assume the world's capital markets are integrated, we would estimate the beta of the Indonesian telephone company with respect to the world market by using the estimate of the beta of the Indonesian telephone company (derived from telephone companies in other countries) multiplied by the beta of the Indonesian stock market with respect to the world market. In either of these approaches, it is probably best to use countries at approximately the same level of economic development and that have similar laws and regulations for the type of business being valued.

Bodnar, Dumas, and Marston (2003) discussed the logic of this approach and tested it on various stocks from four different countries. What they found was that this approach worked reasonably well in the French, U.S., and Belgium markets, which are considered to be developed markets by MSCI, but worked less well

---

[23] This is the market risk premium in the survey reported in Fernandez, P., A. Ortiz, and I. Fernandez Acín, "Market Risk Premium Used in 71 Countries in 2016: a Survey with 6,932 Answers," available at SSRN: https://papers.ssrn.com/sol3/papers.cfm?abstract_id=2776636, accessed June 24, 2018.

[24] See Lessard, D. R., "Incorporating Country Risk in the Valuation of Offshore Projects," *Journal of Applied Corporate Finance* (1996), pp. 52–63.

in the less developed Polish market, considered to be an emerging market by MSCI. While this issue has not been studied more extensively, the latter finding suggests that this approach is not as useful for companies operating in less developed economies, which is when we would most likely need to use it.

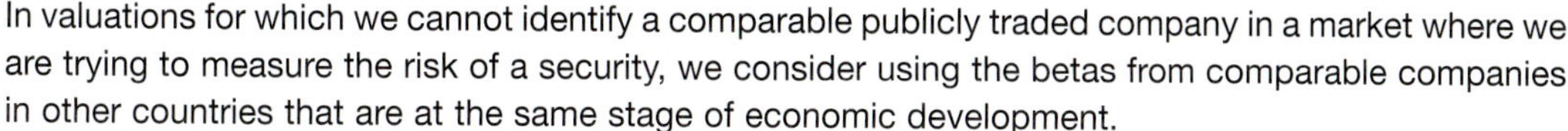

Valuation Key 17.8

In valuations for which we cannot identify a comparable publicly traded company in a market where we are trying to measure the risk of a security, we consider using the betas from comparable companies in other countries that are at the same stage of economic development.

17.6 CROSS-BORDER VALUATION IN LESS DEVELOPED OR TROUBLED ECONOMIES OR EMERGING MARKETS

In this section, we discuss additional adjustments to consider when conducting a cross-border valuation of a foreign company that is located—or has its primary business activities—in a less developed economy or an emerging market. Such cross-border valuations require special consideration, for the expected free cash flows of such companies can be affected by additional risk factors. As we discussed earlier in this chapter, these additional risk factors can be either unsystematic or systematic in nature. If they are unsystematic, we adjust the expected free cash flows for the unsystematic risks, but we do not adjust the discount rate. If the risks are systematic, we adjust the expected free cash flows if the additional systematic risks affect the probabilities, magnitudes, or timing of the free cash flows. We also adjust the discount rate if these country-specific systematic risks are not already embedded in the discount rate through the asset pricing model (for example, the CAPM) used to estimate the company's systematic risk (for example, beta).

Adjusting Expected Free Cash Flows for Country-Specific Risks

Country-specific risks can be related to various economic, political, or other types of risk. Economic-related risks include the riskiness of the country's economy, the degree of financial leverage used by the country, and the risks associated with the country's currency (exchange rate risk). Political risks are risks that affect a company's expected free cash flows that result from political decisions. They can affect a company's operations, as is the case for risks related to promulgation, interpretation, enforcement of regulations and laws, and targeted special direct or indirect taxes to a foreign owner. They can also affect ownership and the ability to transfer assets to another entity—examples include expropriation, confiscation, reduced ability to sell assets, and reduced ability to transfer funds or assets outside the country. Lastly, they can disrupt business—consider government instability, revolution, wars, strikes, or riots. To adjust our valuation for these risks, we either explicitly or implicitly

- identify the effect on free cash flows associated with each risk,
- assess the probabilities of the various outcomes,
- estimate which periods might be affected by the outcomes (for example, the potential effect of increased tax rates resulting from a political election held in three years if a certain political party is elected), and
- adjust the valuation based on the risks.

We can adjust the valuation for these additional risks in one of two ways. First, we can measure the expected effect of the risk on each unadjusted future free cash flow and deduct that amount from the unadjusted free cash flows before discounting them. Alternatively, we can measure the effect of the additional risk on the unadjusted value of the firm and deduct that amount from the unadjusted value of the firm. As we discussed in Chapter 5, although it might be tempting, increasing the discount rate to account for these risks is not appropriate, as we have no basis for making this adjustment.

Valuation in Practice 17.4

Venezuela's Potential Expropriation of Oil Fields Venezuela encouraged global oil companies to invest in its oil fields with favorable terms, including a minority stake in the state oil company, Petroleos de Venezuela S.A. (PDVSA). Global oil companies such as Exxon Mobil and Chevron invested more than $16 billion in the country. In 1998, after Hugo Chavez was elected president, the country began a series of changes to the country's laws and taxes in what some interpret to be an expropriation of the oil reserves developed by these companies. In 2004, Venezuela raised royalty rates from 1% to 16.6% and reinterpreted tax rates, increasing the back taxes of foreign investors by $4 billion. In 2005, Venezuela announced that the existing agreements would have to be changed such that PDVSA would own a minimum of 51%, and it increased its royalty to 30%. Finally, in 2006, Venezuela mandated that PDVSA take operational control of the fields, and it set a deadline of May 1, 2007, for PDVSA to take operational control and a deadline of June 26, 2007, for companies to sign new agreements.

Source: See Witten, Emily A., "Arbitration of Venezuelan Oil Contracts: A Losing Strategy?" *Texas Journal of Oil, Gas, and Energy Law* vol. 4, no. 1 (2009), pp. 56–88.

Usually, we cannot observe the probabilities of these country-specific risks, but it is sometimes possible to get assessments of country-specific risks from consulting services and publications; these include Euromoney Country Risk, AM Best, Economist Intelligence Unit, and International Country Risk Guide.[25] Risks assessed by these groups include such risks as the expropriation of assets, the failure to gain regulatory approval of a project, and the uncertain enforcement of laws and contracts in the legal system. These consulting companies provide assessments on such economy characteristics as credit risks, economic policies, political stability (leadership, military in politics, religion in politics, etc.), favorable or unfavorable conditions for foreign investors, government corruption, political tensions, quality of governmental systems and processes, likelihood of war (both internally and externally), expropriation or confiscation, and foreign trade collection experience.

Valuation Key 17.9

Cross-border valuations require special consideration if the expected free cash flows of the company can be affected by additional risk factors that are not already included in the free cash flow forecasts or the discount rate. These additional risk factors can be either unsystematic or systematic in nature. If they are unsystematic, we adjust the expected free cash flows, but we do not adjust the discount rate; if they are systematic, we adjust the expected free cash flows if they affect the probabilities, magnitudes, or timing of the free cash flows and adjust the discount rate if these risks are not embedded in the systematic risk measured using an asset pricing model like the CAPM.

RiskTel's Valuation

Let us consider an example in which we value a telephone company, RiskTel Company, which operates the only mobile and landline telephone service on a remote country-island in the Pacific Ocean, which has a developing economy. This country-island, Riskie Key, is a fast growing resort island. RiskTel's management developed a financial model with two sets of forecasts based on an assumption about Riskie Key's economic growth—a high-growth and a low-growth scenario. If Riskie Key experiences low growth, RiskTel will have an annual growth of 5% in its free cash flows for the next three years; if Riskie Key experiences high growth, RiskTel will have an annual growth of 20% in its free cash flows for the first three years. Experts expect Riskie Key's growth scenario—either high growth or low growth—to resolve

[25] For example, regarding the International Country Risk Guide: "International Country Risk Guide is one of the world's best commercial sources of country risk analysis and ratings. Updated monthly, ICRG monitors 140 countries. Each 200+ page issue provides financial, political, and economic risk information and forecasts. ICRG's statistical tables assign values to the 22 indicators underlying ICRG's business-oriented model for quantifying risk, examining such country-specific elements as currency risk, political leadership, the military and religion in politics, and corruption." Available on June 26, 2018, at https://epub.prsgroup.com/products/international-country-risk-guide-icrg.

itself in Year 1 and the high- or low-growth rates to continue for Years 2 and 3. After Year 3, management expects the company's free cash flows to grow at the inflation rate of 2%, regardless of the growth scenario that occurs in the earlier years. Experts assess a 60% chance of the high-growth scenario occurring and a 40% chance of the low-growth scenario occurring. The Year 0 free cash flow is equal to $100, the discount rate is equal to 12%, and we are valuing RiskTel as of the end of Year 0.

RiskTel's Initial Valuation. We measure and value both the expected free cash flows for the high- and low-growth scenarios and the overall expected free cash flows. We present this analysis in Panel A of Exhibit 17.11. The free cash flows for the high-growth scenario are equal to the $100 Year 0 (the base year) free cash flow, multiplied by the appropriate growth rate factor (1.2 in Year 1, 1.2^2 in Year 2, and 1.2^3 in Year 3). Similarly, we measure the free cash flows for the low-growth scenario using a growth rate of 5%.

RiskTel's continuing value for both scenarios is equal to the Year 3 free cash flow, multiplied by the long-term growth rate factor (1.02), and divided by the discount rate (12%) minus the long-term growth rate (2%). The column titled "Scenario Present Value" measures the present value of the discounted free cash flows and the continuing value as of the end of Year 0. The value of the high-growth scenario is $1,599, and the value of the low-growth scenario is $1,104. To measure the value of RiskTel, we weight each of the scenario values by their respective probability; after taking a sum of these weighted values, we arrive at a firm value of $1,401. Alternatively, we can measure the value of RiskTel by first measuring the expected free cash flows and then discounting them. In this case, we measure the expected free cash flows by probability weighting the high- and low-growth cash flows in each year, which we show in the line labeled "Expected cash flow valuation." Both approaches result in the same valuation of $1,401.

EXHIBIT 17.11 RiskTel Company Free Cash Flows and Valuation Excluding and Including the Effect of the Extremist Political Party Expropriating Assets

Panel A: Scenario and Expected Cash Flow Valuation Excluding the Effect of the Political Risks

	Scenario Prob	Probability-Weighted Value	% of Value	Scenario Present Value	Year 1	Year 2	Year 3	$CV_{Year\ 3}$
High growth . . .	60%	$ 959.69	68.5%	$1,599.49	$120.00	$144.00	$172.80	$1,762.56
Low growth. . . .	40%	$ 441.80	31.5%	$1,104.49	$105.00	$110.25	$115.76	$1,180.78
	100%	$1,401.49						
Expected Cash Flow Valuation.				$1,401.49	$114.00	$130.50	$149.99	$1,529.85

Panel B: Scenario and Expected Cash Flow Valuation Including the Effect of the Political Risks

	Scenario Prob	Probability-Weighted Value	% of Value	Scenario Present Value	Year 1	Year 2	Year 3	$CV_{Year\ 3}$
High growth . . .	60%	$ 860.09	68.4%	$1,433.49	$118.80	$141.13	$167.67	$1,539.19
Low growth. . . .	40%	$ 397.14	31.6%	$ 992.85	$103.95	$108.06	$112.32	$1,031.14
	100%	$1,257.23						
Expected cash flow valuation.				$1,257.23	$112.86	$127.90	$145.53	$1,335.97

Example 1: RiskTel's Valuation Including the Political Risks. We continue our RiskTel example and include political risks (which we assume to be non-systematic). We assume the island-country has an annual election for control of the government. If the extremist party takes control of the government in any given year, it will expropriate all of RiskTel's assets; this election outcome only has a 1% chance of occurring in any given year. However, if this election outcome does occur, RiskTel's subsequent future cash flows will equal zero, and the government will not pay any value for the expropriated assets. How should we incorporate this risk scenario into our valuation of RiskTel? If the likelihood of a government takeover by an extremist party is independent of the economy, which may or may not be the case, this risk is unsystematic. We only have two sets (high- and low-growth scenarios) of expected free cash flows to adjust for the probability that the cash flows will equal zero if the extremist party takes control. We discussed how to perform these types of adjustments in Chapter 5, but we review them again here. If, however, this risk is systematic, we not only adjust expected free cash flows but also adjust the discount rate for a systematic

risk component, assuming it is not already taken into account in the risk factors that have been included in our discount rate (for example, in beta from the CAPM).

The cash flows in Panel A of Exhibit 17.11 do not consider this political risk. Assuming that this risk is not systematic, we adjust the expected free cash flows but not the discount rate. We first examine the effect of the 1% chance of this political outcome occurring in any given year. If the political outcome occurred, it would reduce all future expected free cash flows to zero. In such a situation—that is, the possibility that all future cash flows will be reduced to zero—the adjustment we make to our calculations is straightforward. Consider the expected free cash flow in Year 1 in the high-growth case. Instead of an expected free cash flow of $120, we have a 99% chance of an expected free cash flow of $120 and a 1% chance of an expected free cash flow of $0, which results in an expected cash flow of $118.8 ($118.8 = 0.99 × $120 + 0.01 × $0). We present the results of these calculations in Panel B of Exhibit 17.11.

We measure the high-growth expected free cash flows in subsequent years by multiplying the previous year's free cash flow by the growth rate factor (1.2) and then multiplying that sum by 1 minus the probability of the negative political outcome occurring (0.99 = 1.0 − 0.01). For example, the expected free cash flow in Year 2, $141.13, is equal to the expected free cash flow in Year 1, $118.8, multiplied by 1.2 and then by 0.99 ($141.13 = $118.8 × 1.2 × 0.99 = $100 × 1.2^2 × 0.99^2). Similarly, to include the effect of this political risk in the continuing value, we adjust the denominator for the probability of the bad outcome (zero cash flows), in essence treating it like a negative growth rate.[26] The perpetuity formula is equal to the Year 3 expected free cash flow multiplied by the growth rate factor (1.02), multiplied by 0.99, and divided by the discount rate (0.12) minus the long-term growth rate (0.02) plus the probability of the political outcome occurring (0.01). We show the valuation for the high-growth scenario here.

$$\$1{,}433.49 = \frac{\$100 \times 1.2 \times 0.99}{1.12} + \frac{\$100 \times 1.2^2 \times 0.99^2}{(1.12)^2} + \frac{\$100 \times 1.2^3 \times 0.99^3}{(1.12)^3} + \frac{\$100 \times 1.2^3 \times 1.02 \times 0.99^4}{(0.12 - 0.02 + 0.01)} \times \frac{1}{(1.12)^3}$$

The only difference between the calculations for the high- and low-growth scenarios is the growth rate factor for the first three years (1.2 for the high-growth scenario versus 1.05 for the low-growth scenario). In this exhibit, we also show the value of the low-growth scenario, which equals $993. To measure the value of RiskTel including the effect of this political risk, we probability weight each of the scenario values, resulting in a value of $1,257—which is about a 10% reduction in value by including the political risk. As before, we can also measure the value of RiskTel by first measuring and then discounting the expected free cash flows. We measure the expected free cash flows by probability weighting the high- and low-growth cash flows for each year, which we show in the line labeled "Expected cash flow valuation." Both approaches result in the same valuation of $1,257.

REVIEW EXERCISE 17.5

Country-Specific Risks—1

A company operates in a country that will have a national election at the end of each year. If the S party wins the election, the S party will expropriate the assets of the company, and the company will be paid $0 for its assets. The probability of the S party winning the election is 2% in any given year. The Year 0 free cash flow for the company is $1,000. For the first three years, the company expects its cash flow to grow at 30% each year if the economy is doing well and −5% each year if the economy is doing poorly. The probability of the economy doing well is 25% in each year. For all outcomes, the economy and the company's free cash flows are expected to grow at 3% in perpetuity after Year 3. The appropriate discount rate is 15%. Measure the value of the firm under both economic scenarios (the economy doing well and the economy doing poorly), ignoring the probability of the company's assets being expropriated; then measure the value of the firm under both economic scenarios including the effects of the potential expropriation.

Solution on page 911.

26 We note that this simple adjustment to the growth rate works for this example because the bad outcome results in zero cash flows for all future periods. The adjustment is more complex if that is not the case. For a discussion of these issues, see Ruback, R. S., "Downsides and DCF: Valuing Biased Cash Flow Forecasts," *Journal of Applied Corporate Finance* vol. 23, no. 2 (2011), pp. 8–17.

Example 2: RiskTel's Valuation Including the Risk of Default on Sovereign Debt. Now, we will use a more complex country-specific risk scenario—instead of the political risk from the election of an extreme party, we discuss how to adjust a valuation for the Riskie Key government defaulting on its debt. We assume the government issued substantial debt in order to build the infrastructure necessary to support its resorts and tourist traffic. As a result, the country's credit rating is low, for it is a small emerging economy with substantial debt. The ability of Riskie Key to service its debt depends on which of the two growth scenarios the country experiences. If Riskie Key experiences the high-growth scenario, which will continue through Year 3, it will not default on its debt. If it experiences the low-growth scenario in Year 1, which will continue through Year 3, it has a 30% probability of defaulting on its debt in both Years 2 and 3. If Riskie Key defaults on its debt, the resort developers will cease to invest in the island. In that case, even RiskTel's low-growth forecasts will be optimistic in comparison to the scenario in which Riskie Key defaults on its debt, which results in a negative growth rate of 35% in the year of default through Year 3, after which growth will increase to 2% per year. To simplify the example, we assume that if Riskie Key does not default by Year 3, it will not default subsequently, and it will grow at 2% per year.

It is clear that we need to adjust the cash flow forecasts for the effects of the government potentially defaulting on its debt. Do we also adjust the discount rate? We would only adjust the discount rate if this additional risk factor was systematic in nature and not already embedded in the other risk factors used to measure RiskTel's discount rate; for example, it may be embedded in the CAPM beta. In this example, we assume this risk does not require us to adjust the discount rate.

The adjustments we make to the expected free cash flows to account for the potential default on the sovereign debt are more complex than the adjustments we made in the previous example because the bad outcome does not result in zero future cash flows but a negative growth rate for future cash flows. These calculations quickly become quite tedious, even for this simple example. We present the calculation of RiskTel's expected free cash flows in Panel A of Exhibit 17.12. The expected free cash flow in Year 1 is equal to the sum of the probability-weighted high- and low-growth outcomes. The probability-weighted outcome is equal to the Year 0 cash flow multiplied by the growth rate factor multiplied by the probability of the outcome. It is \$42 for the low-growth scenario (\$42 = \$100 × 1.05 × 0.40) and \$72 for the high-growth scenario (\$72 = \$100 × 1.2 × 0.60). The expected cash flow is the sum of the two probability-weighted outcomes (\$114 = \$42 + \$72). This is the same Year 1 expected cash flow we calculated in Panel A of Exhibit 17.11, since there is no chance of default in Year 1.

Since both the high- and low-growth scenarios are determined in Year 1 for all three years, and since no default occurs in the high-growth state, the probability-weighted expected cash flow for Year 2 in the high-growth scenario is equal to the Year 1 expected cash flow multiplied by the growth factor (\$86.40 = \$72 × 1.2). However, the low-growth scenario has two potential outcomes in Year 2—default and no default. If the government does not default, the expected cash flow is equal to the Year 1 cash flow multiplied by the low-growth factor, 1.05, which we probability adjust to measure the probability-weighted expected cash flow (\$30.87 = \$42.00 × 1.05 × 0.70). If the government defaults, the expected cash flow is equal to the Year 1 cash flow multiplied by the default growth factor (0.65 = 1 + −0.35), which we again probability adjust to measure the probability-weighted expected cash flow (\$8.19 = \$42.00 × 0.65 × 0.30). The expected cash flow of \$125.46 for Year 2 is the sum of the three probability-weighted outcomes (\$125.46 = \$86.40 + \$30.87 + \$8.19).

In Year 3, we have four different scenarios: high growth, low growth with default in Year 2, low growth with default in Year 3, and low growth with no default. For the high-growth scenario, the Year 3 probability-weighted expected free cash flow is equal to \$103.68 (\$103.68 = \$86.40 × 1.2). For the low-growth scenario with default in Year 2, the probability-weighted expected free cash flow is equal to \$5.32 [\$5.32 = \$8.19 × (1 − 0.35)]. We have two potential outcomes for the low-growth scenario without default in Year 2: default in Year 3 and no default in Year 3. If the government does not default in Year 3, the expected cash flow is equal to the Year 2 cash flow multiplied by the low-growth factor (1.05), which we probability adjust to measure the probability-weighted expected cash flow (\$22.69 = \$30.87 × 1.05 × 0.70). If the government defaults in Year 3, the expected cash flow is equal to the Year 2 cash flow multiplied by the default growth factor (0.65 = 1 + −0.35), which we again probability adjust to measure the probability-weighted expected cash flow (\$6.02 = \$30.87 × 0.65 × 0.30). The expected cash flow in Year 3 of \$137.71 is the sum of the four probability-weighted outcomes (\$137.71 = \$103.68 + \$5.32 + \$6.02 + \$22.69).

Recall that to simplify this example, we assume that after Year 3, RiskTel's free cash flows will grow at 2%, regardless of what occurred in the earlier years. Thus, the continuing value in Year 3 of \$1,404.67 is equal to the Year 3 expected cash flow of $137.71, multiplied by the growth factor of 1.02 and divided by the discount rate of 12% minus the growth rate of 2%. We can discount both the expected free cash flows and continuing value to measure RiskTel's value of $1,300, which we show in Panel B of the exhibit. RiskTel's value decreases by 7% from this risk (compare $1,401 shown in Panel A of Exhibit 17.11 to $1,300 in Panel B of Exhibit 17.12).

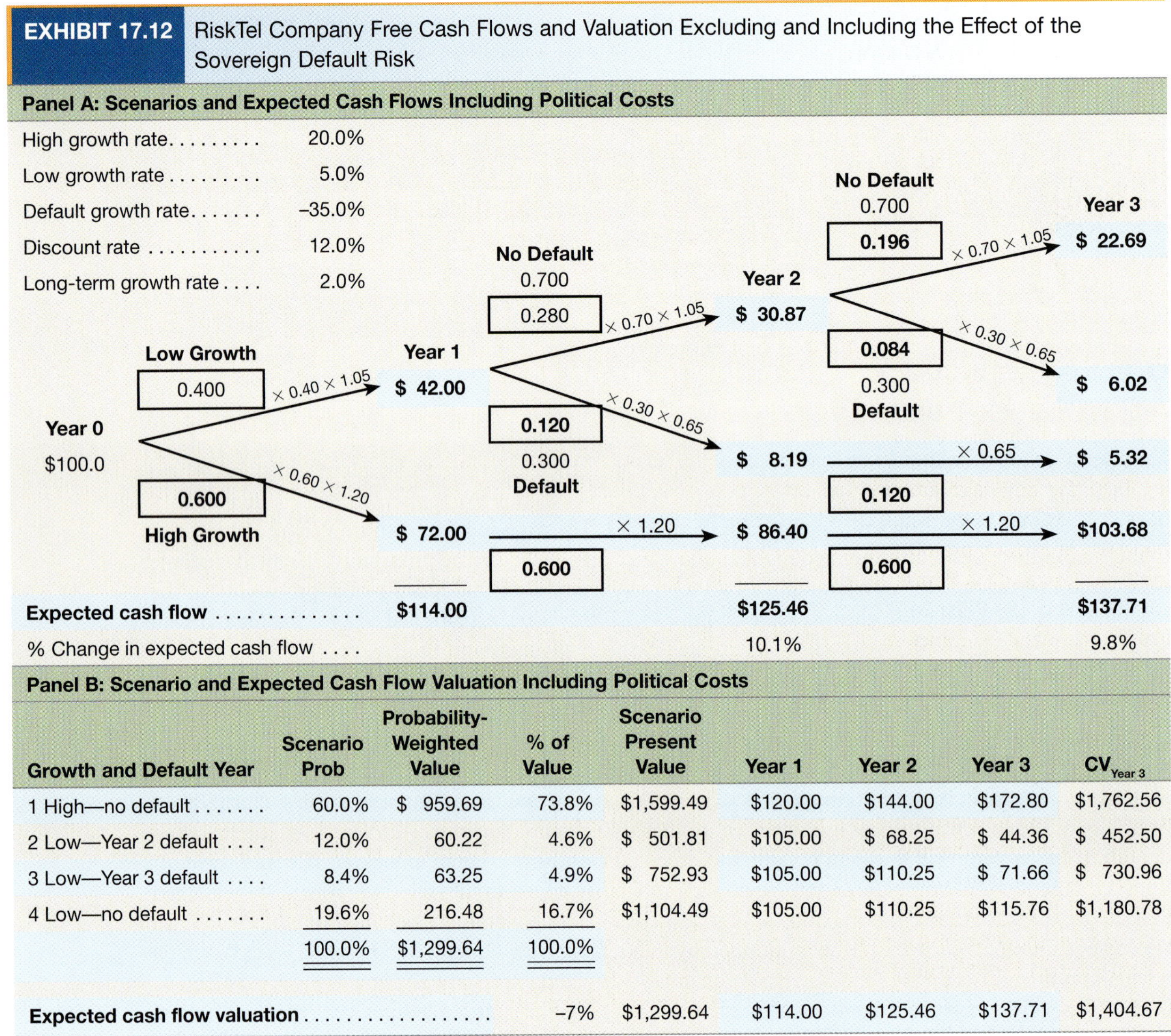

EXHIBIT 17.12 RiskTel Company Free Cash Flows and Valuation Excluding and Including the Effect of the Sovereign Default Risk

Panel B: Scenario and Expected Cash Flow Valuation Including Political Costs

Growth and Default Year	Scenario Prob	Probability-Weighted Value	% of Value	Scenario Present Value	Year 1	Year 2	Year 3	$CV_{Year\ 3}$
1 High—no default.......	60.0%	$ 959.69	73.8%	$1,599.49	$120.00	$144.00	$172.80	$1,762.56
2 Low—Year 2 default....	12.0%	60.22	4.6%	$ 501.81	$105.00	$ 68.25	$ 44.36	$ 452.50
3 Low—Year 3 default....	8.4%	63.25	4.9%	$ 752.93	$105.00	$110.25	$ 71.66	$ 730.96
4 Low—no default.......	19.6%	216.48	16.7%	$1,104.49	$105.00	$110.25	$115.76	$1,180.78
	100.0%	$1,299.64	100.0%					
Expected cash flow valuation..................			–7%	$1,299.64	$114.00	$125.46	$137.71	$1,404.67

An alternative way we can measure this value is by probability weighting the values of the four scenarios—high growth, low growth with default in Year 2, low growth defaulting in Year 3, and low growth with no default. We calculate the free cash flows for the high-growth scenario by multiplying the Year 0 free cash flow ($100) by the appropriate growth factor for each of the three years—1.2, 1.2^2, 1.2^3, respectively. The value of this cash flow stream is $1,599, which has a 60% chance of occurring (see the column titled "Scenario Present Value").

The other three scenarios each begin with the $105 low-growth expected free cash flow in Year 1 ($105 = $100 × 1.05). For the scenario of low growth with no default, we use the same calculation used for the high-growth scenario, but we use the low-growth factor of 1.05. The value of this scenario is $1,104, which has a 19.6% chance of occurring (0.196 = 0.4 × 0.7 × 0.7). We calculate the free cash flows for the low-growth scenario with default in Year 2 using the default growth rate in Years 2 and 3. We calculate the free cash flows for the low-growth scenario with default in Year 3 by using the default growth rate in Year 3. We present the probability-weighted valuations for these two scenarios in Panel B of the exhibit. Of course, the probability of all four scenarios sums to 1. The sum of all of the probability-weighted scenario valuations is again equal to $1,300.

REVIEW EXERCISE 17.6

Country-Specific Risks—2

A company operates in a country that may default on its debt if it experiences low economic growth. If the country experiences high growth in Year 1, it will continue to do so through Year 3, and it will not default on its debt; in this scenario, the company's free cash flows will grow at 15% for Years 1 through 3 and 3% thereafter. The probability of the country having high growth in Year 1 is 20%. If the country experiences low growth in Year 1, it will continue to do so through Year 3, and it will have a 40% probability of defaulting on its debt in both Years 2 and 3. If the country experiences low growth in a given year but does not default on its debt, the company's free cash flows will grow at 4%. If the country defaults on its debt, the company will have a negative growth rate of 20% in the year of the default through Year 3 and a positive growth rate of 3% thereafter. If the country does not default by Year 3, it will not default subsequently, and the country and company's free cash flows will have a positive growth rate of 3% per year. The company's discount rate is 13%, and its Year 0 free cash flow is $1,000. Measure the value of the firm, ignoring the default on country's debt and including the default on the country's debt.

Solution on page 912.

Using Insurance and Insurance Premiums as an Alternative to Adjusting for Political Risks

Various government-related organizations and private insurers offer insurance with various terms regarding both the coverage amount and time horizon in order to mitigate or limit some types of political risks. For example, the Multilateral Investment Guarantee Agency (MIGA) is a member of the World Bank Group, which promotes foreign direct investment in developing countries. It provides political risk insurance guarantees to private sector investors and lenders in order to protect investments against noncommercial risks.[27] The Political Risk Insurance Center (PRI-Center) provides free access to political risk management and insurance resources. It was established in 2006 as part of the MIGA mandate to promote direct foreign investment in developing countries. The U.S. has the Overseas Private Investment Corporation.[28] It is a U.S. government organization that provides investors who invest in foreign countries with financing, guarantees, political risk insurance, and support for private equity investment funds.

To the extent that insurance eliminates certain risks—that is, shifts the entire risk from the investor to the insurer—the only adjustment necessary to adjust for these risks is to include the cost of the insurance in our expected free cash flows. It is difficult to insure against all of the risk over a long horizon when considering an investment in a foreign country, but it is often possible to insure against some of the risk for various limited horizons. For example, it is common for such insurance to be limited to certain types of political risks, limited to the amount of invested capital or the book value of the assets; it is also common to limit the term of such insurance to no more than 20 years. It is also sometimes possible to insure a limited part of the earnings stream.[29]

As we discussed earlier, adjusting expected free cash flows for such risks requires that we measure the expected effect of the risk on free cash flows and deduct that amount from the free cash flows. One way we measure the effect of risk on the free cash flows is to estimate the probability that a bad outcome will occur and to multiply it by the effect that the bad outcome will have on the cash flow. An insurance premium provides an estimate of that calculation plus a return (or profit) to the insurer. We can reduce either the premium or the embedded profit in order to use the insurance premiums to adjust the cash flows to the expected cash flows in the discounted cash flow model. Of course, if an acquirer is buying a company and buying the insurance, we would include the entire insurance premium when calculating the value of the insured target to the acquirer.

---

[27] See, available on June 24, 2018, https://www.miga.org/who-we-are.

[28] See, available on June 24, 2018, https://www.opic.gov/who-we-are/overview.

[29] See, Gordon, Kathryn, "Investment Guarantees and Political Risk Insurance: Institutions, Incentives and Development," Organization for Economic Cooperation and Development (OECD) Investment Policy Perspectives 2008, © OECD 2008.

Estimating the Equity Cost of Capital in Emerging Markets

Estimating the equity cost of capital for a company with business operations in a developing economy can be difficult for reasons beyond those we already discussed in Chapter 8 and earlier in this chapter. First, additional difficulties can arise when estimating the CAPM beta or the parameters of other asset pricing models. Second, developing economies may have systematic risks that are not captured by the CAPM or other asset pricing models. These additional country-specific risk factors may not affect all companies located in that country equally, however; and they could also affect companies not located in that country but doing substantial business in that country. Unfortunately, scholarly research has not provided theoretically-based asset pricing models to estimate the cost of capital of companies operating in developing economies and academics and practitioners have not reached a consensus on an empirically-based estimation model. With those caveats in mind, we provide an overview of the issues.

Assume that a U.S. company is implementing both the integrated and segmented methods to estimate the cost of capital of a company in an emerging market and that it is using the CAPM. Implementing these approaches can be more difficult for a company in an emerging market. First, in many emerging economies, the stock market is not liquid, and trading may be infrequent. How severe this problem will be depends on how infrequently the stocks trade. Regardless of whether we estimate betas against a world index, a U.S. index, or even the local country index, this issue is problematic. Thus, irrespective of whether one adopts a segmented or integrated view of the world, some adjustment for infrequent trading such as estimating betas with lead and lagged market returns—as discussed in Chapter 8—may be relevant.

Another issue in taking the segmented view is that the composition of the market (the relative values of the industry segments) can be different in emerging economies than it is in developed countries. For example, Nokia is listed on the Helsinki stock exchange in Finland and in 2000 represented 70% of the market value of the Helsinki stock exchange which fell to 13% by 2013. As such, the weight of the telecommunications industry in the Finnish stock market varied dramatically over time and at least in some periods is very different than it is in such markets as the U.S. or world market. Hence, if Nokia was contemplating the purchase of another company listed on the Helsinki exchange, it could arrive at a beta for that company (estimated against the local index) that is very different from one that is estimated against a world index. In situations like this, we have to consider whether the segmented markets approach is reasonable for estimating the cost of capital and if we thought that it was, we might have to adjust the market index.

Third, when regressing the returns of a company in a developing country on either a U.S. stock market index (like the S&P 500), a world index, or the index of another developed country, we will likely estimate betas that are very close to zero or are statistically insignificant.[30] The implication of this is that the cost of capital for the company should be very low and near or at the U.S. risk-free rate. Although, in theory, this is possible if the risk of the investment is completely diversifiable, for most practitioners and managers, this assumption seems untenable—even if cash flows are adjusted for political risks, default risk, and so forth. In light of these issues, practitioners and academics have struggled to identify ways to empirically estimate a cost of capital for companies in emerging markets with a more intuitive outcome—that is, a higher cost of capital. A variety of mostly ad hoc alternatives have been developed, and we highlight a few of them next.

Sovereign Spread Model. In this approach, a country risk premium is typically added to the equity cost of capital, which is first estimated using the CAPM (assuming either segregated or integrated markets). The most common method for estimating the country risk premium is to add a sovereign spread to the discount rate, such as the difference between the yield on a long-maturity bond issued by the country (denominated in U.S. dollars) and the yield on a similar maturity U.S. government bond. If the country has not issued bonds payable in U.S. dollars, one would adjust the yield on the country's bonds for exchange rate effects such as the difference in expected inflation between the two countries.

This approach has several potential drawbacks. First, it assumes that the country risk premium is the same for all projects and companies, for this technique makes the same adjustment to the CAPM

[30] Even the betas of an emerging economy stock market index (and not just of a particular company) with respect to the S&P 500 or a world index may have a beta that is close to zero and insignificant. An index of all emerging economies considered jointly has a correlation of about 0.9 with both the S&P 500 and the world index, but this is not true for most emerging markets when considered in isolation.

regardless of the sector of the economy. In other words, if some sectors of the economy are impacted more by country risk factors than other sectors, this adjustment would be inappropriate. Another drawback is that this adjustment presumes that the sovereign spread represents a systematic risk, but some country risk may be diversifiable with respect to an investor in another country. If the risk, or part of the risk, is non-systematic or diversifiable, then adding this spread to determine the cost of capital is not appropriate. Finally, we have no empirical evidence to support the assumption that a country's credit risk represents purely systematic risk. In short, even though this is an approach used in practice, it is grounded in neither theory nor empirical evidence.[31]

Relative Volatilities Assumption. Another approach is to substitute the ratio of the volatility of the foreign stock market relative to the volatility of the U.S. stock market (assuming segmented markets)—or the volatility of the foreign stock market relative to the volatility of the world stock market (assuming integrated markets)—for beta. Volatility is most often measured as the standard deviation of stock returns. Most emerging economies have greater volatility than either the U.S. or world markets, and hence the estimated betas—based on the relative volatilities—tend to be larger than 1 if this technique is used—and certainly higher than zero.[32] Some go a step further and even include the sovereign spread as an additional factor to this approach.[33] The drawbacks to this technique are similar to those of adding the sovereign credit spread to the CAPM estimate. Even if the sovereign credit spread is not added, the model assumes that relative volatilities measure systematic risk, and all companies within a country would have the same cost of capital since the relative volatilities are based on aggregate market data.

Valuation Key 17.10

There are various difficulties in estimating the cost of capital for an investment in emerging economies. The major problem is that betas of such investments—judged relative to a world index, a U.S. index, or the index of another developed country—are likely to be close to zero. Therefore, typical CAPM approaches may imply a zero risk premium. Practitioners and academics have put forth a variety of alternatives, but these are not based on any compelling theoretical underpinnings.

Summary. Rather than discuss all of the different asset pricing model variants that have been tried, we provide our overall conclusion.[34] The integrated and segmented views of estimating the cost of capital under the CAPM have justifiable theoretical underpinnings, but the implementation of these techniques is likely to lead to the conclusion that the risk premium for investments in at least some emerging economies is low. This outcome is potentially justifiable if the risks within emerging economies are largely idiosyncratic with respect to an investor in a developed country. If this is the case, and if we include adjustments for such risks when measuring expected free cash flows, then the CAPM approach (as discussed earlier in the chapter) is a reasonable approach. As discussed earlier, the betas of stock market indices from emerging economies (not just of individual companies)—with respect to the world index, the S&P 500, and other developed country indices—are relatively low, which is consistent with this view. Of course, it is important that the idiosyncratic risks be carefully analyzed and included in the cash flow forecasts as we demonstrated in this section of the chapter. Even though it seems intuitively unrealistic for the risk premium of investments in emerging economies to be relatively low, the alternative models that attempt to increase risk premium estimates are neither firmly grounded in theory nor have strong empirical evidence that endorses their usage. Certainly, this area needs additional inquiry and study.

---

[31] See Kruschwitz, L., A. Löffler, and G. Mandl, "Damodaran's Country Risk Premium: A Serious Critique," *Business Valuation Review* vol. 31, no. 2–3 (Summer/Fall 2012), pp. 75–84.

[32] There is evidence that returns in emerging economies seem to be more highly correlated with volatility than with betas. See Harvey, C., "Drivers of Expected Returns in International Markets," *Emerging Market Quarterly* 4 (2000), pp. 32–49.

[33] See Godfrey, S., and R. Espinosa, "A Practical Approach to Calculating Costs of Equity for Investments in Emerging Markets," *Journal of Applied Corporate Finance* 9 (Fall 1996), pp. 80–89. The authors recognize that the sovereign spread and the relative volatilities may be capturing a similar risk, and therefore they multiply the estimated beta by 0.6 based on the relative volatilities. There is no strong justification for this adjustment.

[34] For a review of a variety of other alternative methods that have been proposed, see Sabal, J., "The Discount Rate in Emerging Markets: A Guide," *Journal of Applied Corporate Finance* 16 (2004), pp. 155–166.

17.7 CHALLENGES USING MARKET AND TRANSACTIONS MULTIPLES ACROSS BORDERS

LO5 Explain the limitations of using cross-border market multiples and measure exchange rate exposure

In this section, we discuss the additional challenges and limitations we face when attempting to use market multiples or transaction multiples in cross-border valuations. To conduct a cross-border valuation with market or transaction multiples, we use the framework and process outlined in Chapters 13 and 14. Although the framework does not change for a cross-border valuation, how we implement the models does. It may or may not be reasonable to use multiples measured from comparable companies in one country in order to value a company in another country, especially if one of the potential comparable companies has substantial business operations in a developing economy. It may or may not even be reasonable to use multiples measured from comparable companies from the target's country in order to value a company being acquired by an investor in another country. For example, the comparable domestic companies from the target's country may face a different tax structure than a foreign investor buying the target. As we might expect from our discussions in Chapters 13 and 14, the degree of appropriateness depends on the facts and circumstances of the particular valuation conducted.

Cross-Border Market Multiples

In Exhibit 17.13, we report the median earnings before interest, taxes, and depreciation (EBITDA) multiples for nine broad industry groups across 16 countries. Similar to the sample used in Chapter 13, the sample used for this exhibit is based on all companies in the CapitalIQ[35] database of global companies that have a market capitalization of at least $1 million and for which CapitalIQ reports an EBITDA multiple, all measured as of December 31, 2015. The initial sample consists of 25,399 companies across 116 countries. In the exhibit, we only include countries having at least 400 companies with complete information and report an industry multiple for a country if the country has at least eleven companies in that industry.

In Panel A, we report the median EBITDA multiple for all of the companies within each of the 16 countries. The number of observations varies from 414 (Singapore) to 2,892 (Japan). The number of companies across the 16 countries is 19,102 (75% of all 25,399 companies across the 116 countries in the total sample). The median EBITDA multiple ranges from 7.1 (Japan) to 35.8 (China); and the 10th and 90th percentiles across the medians of the 16 countries are 8.3 and 11.9, respectively. These results clearly show differences in market multiples across countries, which suggests potential challenges using market multiples across borders.

Naturally, understanding the causes of cross-country variation in market multiples is important in deciding whether to use cross-country multiples in a particular valuation. For example, we know that market multiples differ across industries; thus, some of the cross-country variation can be due to industry differences across countries. Using appropriate comparable companies would mitigate this issue. We also know that since many of the denominators of the market multiples are numbers from financial statements, cross-country differences in accounting principles can also cause cross-country differences in market multiples. It may be possible to adjust the accounting information for these differences. Further, even for companies in the same industry, the expected growth and profitability of industry counterparts for two different countries can be very different. In addition, to the extent that capital markets are not integrated, the valuations for ostensibly the same company in different countries could be different and a difference in the valuations across countries would cause cross-country differences in the market multiples.

To examine industry differences across the 16 countries, in Panel B of Exhibit 17.13, we present the median EBITDA multiple for the nine industry groups by country. In order to be included in the exhibit, a country had to have at least eleven companies in that industry. Three countries tend to have either the highest or lowest EBITDA multiples. China has the highest median EBITDA multiple in all nine industry groups and Japan tends to have the lowest median EBITDA multiple across nine industry groups (lowest in 5 industries). The rank of most of the other countries tends to vary across the nine industry groups. In the last two columns on the right side of the exhibit, we present the 10th and 90th percentiles of the median EBITDA multiples for the 16 countries. Depending on the industry, the 90th percentile of the median EBITDA multiples across the 16 countries is 48% to 111% larger than the 10th percentile. These results clearly show differences in median market multiples across countries even within broad industry groups, which again suggests potential challenges using market multiples across borders.

[35] S&P Capital IQ, a part of S&P Global, is a "leading provider of multiasset class, unrivaled data, delivered in real time through innovative platforms with insightful analysis." See, http://www.spcapitaliq.com/about-us/about-us.html, accessed June 24, 2018.

EXHIBIT 17.13 Median Earnings Before Interest, Taxes, and Depreciation (EBITDA) Multiples for Selected Countries and Industry Groups[36]

	Australia	Canada	China	France	Germany	Hong Kong	India	Japan	Malaysia	Poland	Singapore	South Korea	Taiwan	Thailand	United Kingdom	United States	10th Percentile	90th Percentie
Panel A: EBITDA Multiple for All Companies with Available Data in a Country with at least 400 Companies																		
Multiple	9.7	8.7	35.8	9.1	10.5	10.5	11.3	7.1	9.5	7.9	9.3	10.1	9.6	12.5	10.7	10.0	8.3	11.9
# of Obs	536	703	2,771	427	430	745	2,364	2,892	731	536	414	1,259	1,361	492	753	2,688	414	2,892
Panel B: EBITDA Multiple for Companies within an Industry with at Least 11 Companies																		
Industry																		
20	11.2	12.9	29.7	12.9	9.6	11.9	12.2	9.6	13.7	6.7	8.9	11.2	12.3	12.2	13.2	13.6	9.2	13.6
28	12.9	11.1	36.7	10.6	8.1	10.3	11.9	6.9	9.9	9.6		12.8	13.0	8.9	14.8	11.5	8.4	14.1
35		6.6	55.3	9.5	9.2	8.7	13.8	5.9	9.6	6.6	5.7	11.2	8.8	8.1	10.1	10.0	6.2	12.8
36		9.5	48.4	9.7	11.1	8.5	13.7	5.9	8.0	7.8	9.3	7.7	7.9	11.6	10.9	10.9	7.8	12.8
37		8.3	38.9	12.1	8.4		10.7	4.7	7.9		10.4	7.0	10.5			8.4	7.0	12.1
49	9.2	12.5	17.0	6.7	10.3	12.2	12.3	7.8	8.3	3.7		7.1	11.2	12.0	12.2	10.1	6.8	12.4
50		9.3	55.8			14.9	16.8	7.1	11.4	7.6	13.9	13.2	12.6	13.6	9.9	8.5	7.8	16.4
65	11.0	16.9	22.4	18.3	20.6	12.0	12.3	10.9	9.1	16.9	15.5		16.0	15.7	11.5	17.1	10.9	19.7
73	15.8	11.1	78.4	10.1	14.8	15.7	12.6	7.9	14.1	7.6	12.1	13.4	12.3	13.5	12.9	13.6	9.0	15.7

Using Within-Country Market Multiples in a Cross-Border Valuation

Of course, using market multiples measured from companies within the same country helps us to avoid some of these issues. However, other potential issues can arise if the investor is not in the same country, and we are conducting a cross-border valuation. For example, within-country market multiples do not consider valuation differences that result from segmented capital markets. In addition, they may not consider the income tax differences, other tax differences, and increased political or other foreign country risks that occur in specific cross-border valuations (but are not reflected to the same degree in the market values of the local companies).

Valuation Key 17.11

We can use the market multiple valuation model in cross-border valuations, but we often have to adjust how we measure market multiples. We may also have to adjust the market-multiple-based valuation for such factors as income tax differences, other tax differences, and foreign country risks that occur in a specific cross-border valuation (but are not reflected to the same extent in the market values of the local companies). Similar issues occur for transaction-based multiples.

[36] SIC (Industry Code): Industry Description
20: Food And Kindred Products
28: Chemicals And Allied Products
35: Industrial And Commercial Machinery And Computer Equipment
36: Electronic And Other Electrical Equipment And Components, Except Computer Equipment
37: Transportation Equipment
49: Electric, Gas, And Sanitary Services
50: Wholesale Trade-durable Goods
65: Real Estate
73: Business Services

Using Transaction Multiples in a Cross-Border Valuation

We face the same overarching issues using transaction multiples that we face using market multiples in a cross-border context. The one exception, of course, is when we can identify comparable cross-border transactions (where the acquirers and targets are from the same two countries we face in our valuation). If we are able to identify comparable cross-border transactions, we may then be able to use transaction multiples in the ways discussed in Chapter 16 for mergers and acquisitions.

17.8 EXCHANGE RATE EXPOSURE AND HEDGING BASICS

Exchange rate exposure exists when the value of an asset or liability to an investor changes because of unexpected changes in an exchange rate. Naturally, cross-border ownership usually results in exchange rate exposure, for unexpected changes in the exchange rates can affect the investor's valuation of the firm. Hence, the potential hedging of exchange rate exposure is an issue that naturally arises in the context of cross-border ownership. **Exchange rate exposure** is a measure of the sensitivity of an asset's value—or in the case of a cross-border valuation, a firm's value—to unexpected or real changes in exchange rates. As it turns out, and we explain later, purely domestic companies can also face exchange rate exposure.

We classify economic exchange rate exposure into three types: operating exposure, transaction exposure, and financing exposure. Operating exposure results from a company's operations, while the other two types of exposure are related to specific transactions and financing instruments that a company uses that are stated in terms of a foreign currency. Another type of exchange rate exposure is translation exposure. Translation exposure is not an economic exposure, but it represents the effect of exchange rate changes on a company's financial statements, which may or may not be associated with some form of economic exposure. Exchange rate exposure creates uncertainty that, depending on the economic context, managers may or may not want to hedge. In this section, we discuss exchange rate exposure and its hedging.

Operating Exchange Rate Exposure

Operating exchange rate exposure is the risk associated with changes in the value of one or more of a company's operating cash flow streams because of unexpected changes in exchange rates. It is clear from our cross-border DCF valuation model that cross-border ownership creates exchange rate exposure, as the value of the firm (to the owner) is a function of the exchange rate. Unexpected changes in exchange rates can affect the demand for a company's products, the revenue a company generates from these products, and the cost of producing these products. These effects subsequently affect the company's decisions concerning such issues as pricing, investment, marketing, and production—all of which can affect expected free cash flows. We can use the cross-border DCF valuation model to measure both the company's exchange rate exposure and the total value that is exposed to exchange rate risk for particular currencies. Alternatively, if we do not have a sufficiently detailed financial model, companies can use more top-level models to measure exchange rate exposure. These models use a percentage of the revenues and profit margins from each of a company's foreign operations to measure exposure.[37] Other models estimate the exchange rate risk using a regression model of prices or returns explained by changes in various exchange rates and other fundamental variables.[38]

Cross-border ownership results in operating exchange rate exposure because the company operates in a different currency than the investor's currency. However, operating exchange rate exposure is, of course, a much broader issue and occurs in economic contexts other than cross-border ownership. Consider a company that produces its products domestically but sells its products in foreign countries. This company has exchange rate exposure because unexpected changes in the exchange rates between the home and foreign countries in which it sells its products will affect the prices at which the company can sell its products, the quantity of the products sold, and the profits the company earns on its foreign sales.

---

[37] See Bodnar, G., Dumas, B., and Marston, R., "Pass-Through and Exposure," *Journal of Finance* 57 (2002), pp. 199–231; and Bartram, S., G. Brown, and B. Minton, "Resolving the Exposure Puzzle: The Many Facets of Exchange Rate Exposure," *Journal of Financial Economics* 95 (2010), pp. 148–173.

[38] See, for example, Pantzalis, Christos, Betty J. Simkins, and Paul A. Laux, "Operational Hedges and the Foreign Exchange Exposure of U.S. Multinational Corporations," *Journal of International Business Studies* vol. 32, no. 4 (2001), pp. 793–812.

Consider another company that produces and sells all of its products within the country in which it is located but purchases inputs for the production of its products from foreign vendors with transactions that are denominated in other currencies. This company has exchange rate exposure because changes in exchange rates between the home and foreign countries from which it purchases its inputs will affect the prices at which the company can sell its products, the quantity of the products sold, and the profits the company earns on its domestic sales. Even a company that purchases all of its inputs and sells all of its products domestically can face exchange rate exposure if it competes with foreign companies. Such a company faces exchange rate exposure because unexpected appreciation or depreciation of the foreign companies' currency can affect the prices at which the foreign companies compete in the company's domestic market.

For a company acquiring a company in another country where both companies operate in their own country, then the entire cash flow stream of the target has exchange rate exposure to the acquiring company. On the other hand, for a company that produces and sells its products completely within its domestic country but purchases inputs for its products in other countries in transactions denominated in foreign currencies, it faces exchange rate exposure from the cost of the inputs it purchases in foreign countries with transactions denominated in foreign currencies. Similarly, a company that produces its products completely within its domestic country but sells its products in other countries in transactions denominated in foreign currencies, faces exchange rate exposure from its revenue stream due to transactions denominated in foreign currencies. If these three companies are identical in all respects but for the cash flow stream that is affected by exchange rate exposure, which company has the largest exchange rate exposure? The answer depends on the relative sizes of the cash flow streams. The larger the cash flow stream that is denominated in foreign currency, the larger the exchange rate exposure.

We can use the DCF valuation model to measure exposure if the model includes the effect of exchange rates on the free cash flows. We illustrate this approach in Exhibit 17.14 for a company located in the U.K. (U.K. Sub) and owned by a company in the U.S. (U.S. Parent). We first assume U.K. Sub purchases its products from U.S. Parent in transactions denominated in USD. The Year 1 expected cash revenue for U.K. Sub is £1,200. The total cost of its products is $1,600 and it has no other expenses. U.K. Sub has no capital expenditure requirements and is only financed with common equity. For simplicity, we also assume that no taxes are levied on the income of U.K. Sub. Assume that the USD discount rate for the free cash flows is 10%, that U.K. Sub has a zero expected future growth rate, and that the current and expected future exchange rate is 2 $/£. As we show in the second column, U.K. Sub has revenue of $2,400 ($2,400 = 2 $/£ × £1,200), expenses equaling $1,600, and a resulting expected free cash flow of $800 ($800 = $2,400 − $1,600). With a 10% discount rate and zero growth rate, its value in USD is $8,000 ($8,000 = $800/0.10).

EXHIBIT 17.14 Exchange Rate Exposure—Only Revenues in £

		Exchange Rates $/£		
	Year 1	**2.000**	**2.100**	**1.900**
Revenue (cash in £)	£1,200.0	$ 2,400.0	$ 2,520.0	$ 2,280.0
Expenses (cash in USD)	−$1,600.0	−1,600.0	−1,600.0	−1,600.0
Unlevered free cash flow		$ 800.0	$ 920.0	$ 680.0
Discount rate (in USD, no growth)		10.0%	10.0%	10.0%
Value of U.K. Sub in USD		$ 8,000.0	$ 9,200.0	$ 6,800.0
Percentage change in value			15.0%	−15.0%
Change in value			$ 1,200.0	−$ 1,200.0
Percentage change in exchange rate			5.0%	−5.0%
Total amount of exposure in USD			$24,000.0	$24,000.0
Present value of revenue stream		$24,000.0		

If the expected future exchange rate was to unexpectedly increase by 5% to 2.1 $/£ (while U.K. Sub's expected revenues and the USD discount rate remain unchanged), the USD value of the U.K. company increases to $9,200 (or by $1,200 or 15%). The value increases because the value of the £ increased unexpectedly, or appreciated, relative to the USD; thus, the £-denominated free cash flows are more valuable and are thus higher when converted to USD-denominated free cash flows. Instead of increasing, if the expected future exchange rate was to unexpectedly decrease by 5% to 1.9 $/£, the USD value of U.K. Sub decreases to $6,800 or, again, by $1,200 or 15% because the £-denominated free cash flows are less valuable and are thus lower when converted to USD-denominated free cash flows ($2,280 versus $2,400).

We measure exchange rate exposure as the sensitivity of the value of the U.S. company's investment in the U.K. company to unexpected changes in the $/£ exchange rate. In our example, we observe that a 5% unexpected change in the exchange rate results in a 15% change in the value of U.K. Sub; thus, the sensitivity of the value of U.S. Parent's investment in U.K. Sub to the $/£ exchange rate is 3 (3 = 0.15 change in value/0.05 change in exchange rate). In other words, based on our DCF valuations, an x% change in the exchange rate results in a 3x% change in the value of the firm. What is the amount or value exposed to the exchange rate risk? The total amount of exposure in USD is equal to the present value of U.K. Sub's revenue stream, $24,000 ($24,000 = $2,400/0.10). Another way to measure the total amount of exposure in USD is to divide the change in value by the percentage unexpected change in the exchange rate ($24,000 = $1,200/0.05).

In Exhibit 17.15, we present an alternative scenario in which U.K. Sub produces its products in the U.K. with £-denominated inputs and sells all of its products domestically; thus, U.K. Sub's entire free cash flow stream (revenues net of expenses) is exposed to $/£ exchange rate risk instead of just the revenue stream. Again, we can use the DCF valuation model to measure the exposure to unexpected changes in the $/£ exchange rate. U.K. Sub's Year 1 expected cash revenues and cash expenses are, respectively, £1,200 and £800; thus, the company's free cash flow is £400. Using the $/£ exchange rate of 2.0, the converted USD free cash flow is equal to $800. Assuming that the USD discount rate for the free cash flows is again 10% and that the company has a zero growth rate, the value of the firm in USD is $8,000 ($8,000 = $800/0.10). Although this is the same value as previously, the two companies have different $/£ exchange rate exposures because they have different cash flow streams exposed to the $/£ exchange rate risk.

EXHIBIT 17.15 Exchange Rate Exposure—All Cash Flows in £

		Exchange Rates $/£		
	Year 1	**2.000**	**2.100**	**1.900**
Revenue (cash in £)	£1,200.0	$2,400.0	$2,520.0	$2,280.0
Expenses (cash in £)	−£ 800.0	−1,600.0	−1,680.0	−1,520.0
Unlevered free cash flow	£ 400.0	$ 800.0	$ 840.0	$ 760.0
Discount rate (in USD, no growth)		10.0%	10.0%	10.0%
Value of U.K. Sub in USD		$8,000.0	$8,400.0	$7,600.0
Percentage change in value			5.0%	−5.0%
Change in value			$ 400.0	−$ 400.0
Percentage change in exchange rate			5.0%	−5.0%
Total amount of exposure in USD			$8,000.0	$8,000.0

If the expected future exchange rate unexpectedly increases by 5% to 2.1 $/£, the USD value of U.K. Sub increases to $8,400 (or by $400 or 5%) because the USD free cash flows increase by $40 in perpetuity. If the expected future exchange rate unexpectedly decreases by 5% to 1.9 $/£, the USD value of U.K. Sub decreases to $7,600 (or by $400 or 5%) because the company's free cash flows decrease by $40 in perpetuity. A 5% unexpected change in the exchange rate results in a 5% change in the value of the firm; thus, the sensitivity of the value of the U.S. company's investment in U.K. Sub to changes in the $/£ exchange rate is 1 (1 = 0.05 change in value/0.05 change in exchange rate). The first company has an exchange rate exposure of 3× because its entire revenue stream is exposed to the $/£ exchange rate risk, but the second company offsets some of the revenue exchange rate exposure by also incurring its expenses in the same currency (£).

What is the amount or value exposed to the exchange rate risk now? We can again measure the exposure by multiplying the value of the investment by the sensitivity of the value of the investment to changes in the exchange rate. In the first example in Exhibit 17.14, the value of the investment is $8,000 and the sensitivity is 3, so the exposure is $24,000 ($24,000 = $8,000 × 3). In the second example in Exhibit 17.15, the value of the investment is also $8,000, but the sensitivity is 1, so the exposure is $8,000

($8,000 = $8,000 × 1). This calculation is equivalent to the calculation shown in the exhibit that divides the change in value by the percentage change in the exchange rate. In the first scenario, the change in the value of the investment is $1,200 and the percentage change in the exchange rate is 5%, so the exposure is $24,000 ($24,000 = $1,200/0.05). In the second scenario, the change in the value of the investment is $400 and the percentage change in the exchange rate is 5%, so the exposure is $8,000 ($8,000 = $400/0.05).

In the first example, in which U.K. Sub's revenues are exposed to $/£ exchange rate fluctuations, the total exchange rate exposure is equal to the present value of the revenue stream of $24,000. The implication of this exposure is that U.S. Parent will have to enter into a hedging strategy that has a present value of $24,000. In the second example, the company incurs its expenses in the U.K, which reduces the amount of its exposure to the present value of the free cash flows of $8,000. The hedge would be the opposite stream of £-denominated cash flows as those in U.K. Sub—in this case, U.S. Parent would need £-denominated expenses or a £-denominated liability to offset the net positive £-denominated cash flows in U.K. Sub. Naturally, measuring exchange rate exposure is more difficult when measuring more complex relationships—for example, direct and indirect effects of changes in the exchange rates on a company and its competitors.

Valuation Key 17.12

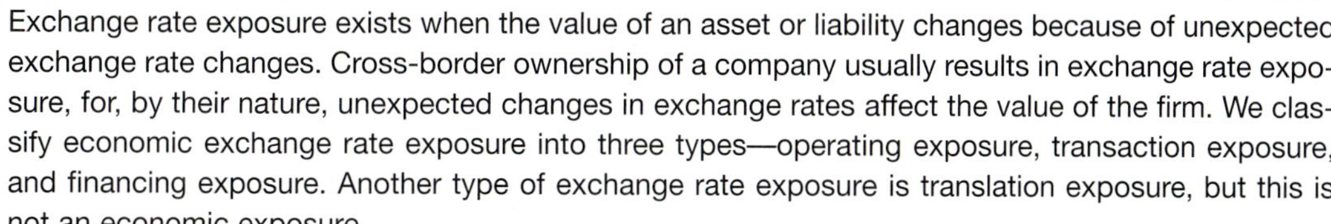

Exchange rate exposure exists when the value of an asset or liability changes because of unexpected exchange rate changes. Cross-border ownership of a company usually results in exchange rate exposure, for, by their nature, unexpected changes in exchange rates affect the value of the firm. We classify economic exchange rate exposure into three types—operating exposure, transaction exposure, and financing exposure. Another type of exchange rate exposure is translation exposure, but this is not an economic exposure.

REVIEW EXERCISE 17.7

Measuring Exchange Rate Exposure

A company is located in France (French Sub) and owned by a company in the U.K. (U.K. Parent). French Sub purchases its products from U.K. Parent in transactions denominated in £. The Year 1 expected cash revenue for France Sub is €1.85 million. The total cost of its products is £0.99 million, and it has no other expenses. French Sub has no capital expenditure requirements and is financed with only common equity. For simplicity, we also assume that no taxes will be levied on the income of French Sub. Assume that the £ discount rate for the free cash flows is 12%, that French Sub has a zero expected growth rate in perpetuity, and that the current and expected future exchange rate is 0.9 £/€. Measure the value of French Sub in £. Measure the value of the firm assuming the £/€ exchange rate unexpectedly changes to 0.990; do this again assuming that the exchange rate unexpectedly changes to 0.810. Measure U.K. Parent's exposure to the euro, and measure the change in the U.K. company's exposure to the euro if its French Sub were to purchase its products with transactions denominated in euros at a total cost of €1.10 million.

Solution on page 913.

Transaction and Financial Exchange Rate Exposure

Transaction exposure and financing exposure are conceptually the same economic construct as operating exposure, but they apply to a subset of the cash flow streams of the company and are usually finite in their term. Transaction exchange rate exposure applies to net foreign currency-denominated transactions that have fixed monetary values in a foreign currency and are fixed (or agreed upon) at a time prior to the date the transaction settles (is paid). Examples include fixed price sales, purchase contracts, receivables, and payables stated in terms of a foreign currency. Financial exchange rate exposure applies to the net foreign currency-denominated financing instruments issued by the company. The common example of such exposure is a company issuing a debt instrument with payments that are denominated in a foreign currency. The common reason a company issues such a debt instrument is to hedge against either transaction or operating exchange rate exposure. Companies operating in countries with less stable exchange rates sometimes issue debt securities denominated in the currency of a country that has more stable exchange rates.

Translation Exposure

Companies that consolidate their foreign subsidiaries' financial statements must translate the foreign currency-denominated financial statements into the parent company's currency. Accounting regulatory bodies throughout the world have rules that companies must follow when they translate the financial statements of their foreign subsidiaries to their own currency. These rules have the company translate the foreign currency-denominated income statement and balance sheet, which often creates a translation gain or loss that is shown in either the income statement or the retained earnings section of the balance sheet. Thus, in addition to economic exchange rate exposure, companies also have translation exchange rate exposure. These translation gains and losses, however, do not generally represent a change in the value of the firm. Thus, translation exposure may relate more to the uncertainty of a company's accounting-based earnings and balance sheet due to the effects of foreign currency translation.

Should Managers Hedge?

A **hedge** is the creation of a position in an asset or liability or expected future cash flow that has the opposite risk of the risk the investor or company is attempting to eliminate. If the asset or liability is completely hedged, the value of the company will no longer be affected by that risk. For example, assume that a U.S. company enters into a contract to purchase inventory with a payment of £100 due in three months and that the company wants to hedge its exposure to unexpected $/£ exchange rate fluctuations. If the company does not hedge its contracted £100 payment due in three months, it is subject to exchange rate risk or fluctuations in the value of a USD relative to a £. The company has a £100 liability position that has $/£ exchange rate exposure. The company can hedge this exposure if it creates an asset position with the same $/£ exchange rate exposure. For example, the company can convert USD today and invest them in a £-denominated money market account such that at the end of three months the value of the money market account will be £100.

The goal of hedging is not to change the expected value of the asset or liability; rather, the goal of hedging is to eliminate or at least reduce the uncertainty about an expected value created by exchange rate risk. As we saw from the two examples in Exhibits 17.14 and 17.15, both companies have the same firm value of $8,000; however, the second company, which hedged part of its exchange rate exposure from revenues with expenses denominated in the same currency, had less exposure to unexpected $/£ fluctuations as a result of this hedge. This is a common hedging method used in such circumstances. For example, Toyota, one of the world's largest producers of automobiles, produces most of the cars sold in the U.S. within the U.S.[39]

Valuation Key 17.13

A hedge is the creation of a position in an asset or liability that has the opposite risk of the risk the investor or company is attempting to eliminate in order for the investor or company to be unaffected by that risk. The goal of hedging is not to change the expected value of the asset or liability, but rather, it is to eliminate or at least reduce the uncertainty about the expected value that an investor or company faces.

Before we discuss hedging methods in more detail, we first consider whether a company should hedge against exchange rate exposure. Recall that hedging does not change the value of the hedged asset or liability in its own right. At best, it is a zero net present value activity; thus, it may not be in the company's interest—or the shareholders' interest—to hedge its exchange rate exposures unless it can create value through some other means or its shareholders do not want to bear a risk that they are unable to effectively hedge themselves. The primary argument against hedging is that shareholders can hedge such risk themselves in their own investment portfolios. An investor can hold a portfolio that naturally diversifies this risk. As such, any hedging the company does is unnecessary.

In some situations, it may be possible for hedging to have a positive effect on the value of the firm.[40] For example, if hedging reduces the probability of financial distress, it can reduce expected financial distress costs, other agency costs, or the cost of capital. Hedging might also allow the company to have better

[39] See, Fantz, Ashley, "What Makes a Car American?" CNN, December 12, 2008, http://www.cnn.com/2008/US/12/12/american.cars/, accessed June 24, 2018.

[40] See Smithson, C., and B. J. Simkins, "Does Risk Management Add Value? A Survey of the Evidence," *Journal of Applied Corporate Finance* 17 (2005), pp. 8–17, for a review of the literature on this issue.

strategic planning and to better execute its strategic plan. Further, if additional volatility due to exchange rate fluctuations creates noise in the public information about a company that its management cannot credibly disentangle for investors, then hedging may provide better information to investors. To overcome this, some managers provide non-GAAP earnings and revenues to indicate what earnings would have been without currency movements and provide guidance (forecasts) assuming no shifts in exchange rates. Finally, if management has a comparative information advantage that allows it to hedge more effectively than shareholders are able, and if shareholders want to hedge that risk, then hedging can potentially create value.[41]

Valuation Key 17.14

Since hedging does not increase value in its own right, it may not be in the shareholders' interest for a company to hedge. The primary argument against hedging is that shareholders can hedge such risk themselves via investment strategy. Hedging can have a positive effect on the value of the firm if hedging reduces the probability of financial distress, thereby reducing expected financial distress costs, other agency costs, or the cost of capital. Hedging might also allow the company to have better strategic planning, better execute its strategic plan, and increase informational transparency for its investors.

What Methods Can a Company Use to Hedge Its Exchange Rate Exposure?

It is easier for a company to hedge against transaction and financing exposure as opposed to operating exposure. To perfectly hedge exposure, we must identify a matching asset or liability that has an expected cash flow stream with the opposite exposure and that perfectly matches—in timing (and thus term) and in magnitude—the cash flow stream we are hedging. In other words, we match both the value and the duration of the asset or liability position we are hedging. Since the timing (duration) and magnitude of transactions and financing instruments are typically contractually set, it is easier to identify an appropriate hedging instrument for these risks. However, a company does not want to hedge all of its contracts that are denominated in foreign currency, for it will likely incur more hedging costs than necessary. A company should examine its net exchange rate exposure across all of its transactions and hedge only the net exposure.

Financial hedges are the most direct way to hedge transaction or financing exchange rate exposure. Examples of such hedging instruments include forward exchange rate contracts, exchange rate futures contracts, and **currency swaps** (two companies agree to swap a specified amount of currency at a specified rate). To hedge liability positions, we can convert the appropriate amount of home currency into foreign currency and invest the foreign currency in money market investments. Conversely, for asset positions, we can borrow the appropriate amount of foreign currency, convert it into home currency, and invest it domestically. A characteristic that financial hedges tend to share is that the amount and duration of the foreign currency hedged is set contractually. That is why they can be useful methods for hedging transaction or financial exposure, but they are not as useful for hedging operational exchange rate exposure.

The more efficient way for a company to hedge its operating exposure is by using an operating hedge or real hedge from another part of its operations. In the example shown in Exhibit 17.14, U.S. Parent is exposed to \$/£ risk because U.K. Sub's revenues are in £. Thus, the entire revenue stream is exposed to unexpected changes in the \$/£ exchange rate. In the example shown in Exhibit 17.15, the company used a partial operating hedge by incurring the costs of U.K. Sub in £. An alternative way U.S. Parent could have hedged this exposure was to purchase inputs for its U.S. production from suppliers in the U.K. Assuming U.S. Parent could purchase £1,200 in inputs annually that is equal to the £1,200 of revenue from the U.K. subsidiary and that changes in the cash flow from purchases were perfectly correlated with the changes in U.K. Sub's revenues, U.S. Parent would have a perfect hedge. Any change in the USD value of U.K. Sub resulting from an unexpected change in the exchange rate would be completely offset by a change in the present value of the cost of future inputs purchased in the U.K. Naturally, such hedges have to make financial sense in their own right; for example, U.S. Parent would not begin purchasing inputs in the U.K. if the cost was higher than purchasing them in the U.S.; but, if the costs were the same, U.S. Parent could

[41] See DeMarzo, P. M., and D. Duffie, "Corporate Financial Hedging with Proprietary Information," *Journal of Economic Theory* 53 (1991), pp. 261–286; and DeMarzo, P. M., and D. Duffie, "Corporate Incentives for Hedging and Hedge Accounting," *Review of Financial Studies* 8 (1995), pp. 743–771.

use its purchases in the U.K. as a real hedge. More broadly, companies can use outsourcing, procurement of various inputs, the location of their production facilities, and sales and marketing management strategies to manage exchange rate risks.

SUMMARY AND KEY CONCEPTS

In this chapter, we discussed how to adjust our valuation methods for a cross-border acquisition. The major changes to our normal valuation methodology include forecasting exchange rates to measure the expected cash flows; estimating the cost of capital for a cross-border acquisition using alternative views of the capital markets (particularly the segmented and integrated views); incorporating the complexities of two (and potentially more) tax regimes in our valuation; and adjusting for political and country risk. While this chapter has primarily discussed these issues in the context of a cross-border acquisition, everything discussed is also relevant for the valuation of a multinational firm or a project in a foreign country. In addition, we discussed the topic of exposure to foreign currency exchange rate risk and how firms might hedge that risk.

Suffice it to say that valuing cross-border acquisitions and multinational companies is more time consuming and more complex than valuing a company whose activities are all within the confines of a single country.

ADDITIONAL READING AND REFERENCES

Brunera, R. F., R. M. Conroya, J. Estradab, M. Kritzmanc, and W. Lia, "Introduction to Valuation in Emerging Markets," *Emerging Markets Review* 3 (2002), pp. 310–324.

Stulz, René M., "Globalization of Capital Markets and the Cost of Capital: The Case of Nestlé," *Journal of Applied Corporate Finance* (Fall 1995), pp. 30–38.

EXERCISES AND PROBLEMS

P17.1 **Investor Currency (Centralized) and Foreign Currency (Decentralized) DCF Approaches—Spain/Russia:** A company in Spain is acquiring a company in Russia, and the Spanish company is attempting to value the Russian company in euros. After repatriation, taxes, and country-related risks are taken into consideration, the free cash flow forecasts of the Russian company for the next three years, stated in rubles, are 322.2 RUB million, 365.4 RUB million, and 430.7 RUB million, respectively; also, the continuing value of the company as of the end of Year 3 is 4,290.2 RUB million. The appropriate risk-adjusted discount rate for this company's cash flows, stated in euros, is 11% and is constant in each year. Both companies are only financed with common equity. Use the information in Exhibit P17.1 to measure the value of the Russian company in euros under both the investor currency and foreign currency discounted cash flow methods.

EXHIBIT P17.1 Selected Euro Exchange Rates

		Forward Rates				
	Spot Rate	1 Year	2 Year	3 Year	4 Year	5 Year
U.S. Dollar (USD)/Euro						
Exchange rate	1.425	1.412	1.402	1.394	1.390	1.393
U.K. Pound (GBP)/Euro						
Exchange rate	0.874	0.870	0.867	0.866	0.864	0.864
Russian Ruble/Euro						
Exchange rate	39.613	40.841	42.462	44.297	46.348	48.231

P17.2 **Investor Currency (Centralized) and Foreign Currency (Decentralized) DCF Approaches—U.K./France:** A company in the U.K. is acquiring a company in France, and the U.K. company is attempting to value the French company in GBP. After repatriation, taxes, and country-related risks are taken into consideration, the free cash flow forecasts of the French company for the next three years, stated in Euros, are €22.2 million, €25.4 million, and €30.7 million, respectively; also, the continuing value of the company as of the end of Year 3 is €290.5 million. The appropriate risk-adjusted discount rate for this company's cash flows, stated in GBP, is 14% and is constant in each year. Both companies are only financed with common equity. Use the information in Exhibit P17.1 to measure the value of the French company in GBP under both the investor currency and foreign currency discounted cash flow methods.

P17.3 **Exchange Rates:** Use the information in Exhibit P17.1 to calculate the following exchange rates: U.S. Dollar (USD) / U.K. Pound (GBP), Russian Ruble / U.S. Dollar (USD), and Russian Ruble / U.K. Pound (GBP).

P17.4 **Exchange Rate Forecasts—U.K. Pound (GBP) / Polish Zloty:** Use the information in Exhibits 17.5 and P17.2 to forecast the U.K. Pound (GBP) / Polish Zloty exchange rate for the next five years using relative purchasing power parity and uncovered interest rate parity, and compare these forecasts to the forward rates.

EXHIBIT P17.2 Poland Exchange Rates, Inflation Rates, and Interest Rates

		Forward Rates				
	Spot Rate	1 Year	2 Year	3 Year	4 Year	5 Year
U.S. Dollar (USD)/Polish Zloty						
Exchange rate	0.357	0.345	0.336	0.320	0.306	0.300
U.K. Pound (GBP)/Polish Zloty						
Exchange rate	0.219	0.213	0.208	0.199	0.190	0.186
Russian Ruble/Polish Zloty						
Exchange rate	9.911	9.985	10.167	10.160	10.201	10.373
Poland						
Interest rate.		4.10%	4.50%	5.40%	6.00%	6.20%
Inflation rate		5.50%	5.00%	4.80%	4.80%	4.80%
Implied real rate		−1.33%	−0.48%	0.57%	1.15%	1.34%

P17.5 **Exchange Rate Forecasts—Russian Ruble / Polish Zloty:** Use the information in Exhibits 17.5 and P17.2 to forecast the Russian Ruble / Polish Zloty exchange rate for the next five years using relative purchasing power parity and uncovered interest rate parity, and compare these forecasts to the forward rates.

P17.6 **Worldwide (Resident) and Territorial (Source) Tax Regimes:** A foreign subsidiary of a French company has the equivalent of €100,000 in taxable income. The foreign income tax rate is 25% on all income with a 10% withholding tax on dividends; the French income tax rate is 50%.

a. Calculate the income taxes payable based on both a territorial tax regime and a worldwide tax regime, assuming the parent company pays out all of the foreign subsidiary's after-tax income in dividends to the parent company.

b. Calculate the income taxes payable based on both a territorial tax regime and a worldwide tax regime, assuming the parent company pays out none of the foreign subsidiary's after-tax income in dividends.

P17.7 **Country-Specific Risks—1:** A company operates in a country that has undergone a revolution and now has a new military controlled government. It is unclear whether the new government will expropriate the assets of the company. If the new government expropriates the assets of the company, the company will be paid $0 for its assets. The probability of expropriation is equal to 60% in Year 1; if no expropriation takes place in Year 1, the probability of expropriation in Year 2 is 30%; and if no expropriation takes place in Year 1 or Year 2, the probability of expropriation in Year 3 is 10%; and 0% thereafter if expropriation does not occur in the first three years. The Year 0 free cash flow for the company is $10,000. The company expects its cash flow to grow at −10% in Years 1 through 3 if the economy is doing well and −20% in each of those years if the economy is doing poorly. The probability of the economy doing well is 20% for Years 1 through 3. After Year 3, the economy and the company's free cash flows are expected to grow at 3% in perpetuity for all outcomes. The company's discount rate is equal to 18%.

a. Measure the value of the firm for both economic scenarios (economy doing well and economy doing poorly), ignoring the potential expropriation of the company's assets; then measure the value of the firm under both economic scenarios while including the effects of the potential expropriation.

b. Measure the value of the firm for both economic scenarios while including the effects of the potential expropriation of the company's assets and assuming the probability of expropriation is 1% per year instead of 0% in Year 4 onward.

P17.8 **Country-Specific Risks—2:** A company operates in a country that is in political turmoil, and there is a possibility that it will experience a revolution in which the military will depose the current president. If the country experiences high growth in Year 1, which will continue through Year 3, the country's president will remain in power, and the company's free cash flows will grow at 25% in Years 1 through 3 and 5% thereafter. The probability of the country having high growth in Year 1 is 10%. If the country experiences low growth in Year 1, which will continue through Year 3, the country has an 80% probability of having a revolution in either Year 2 or Year 3. If the country experiences low growth in a given year but the president remains in power, the company's free cash flows will grow at 1% through Year 3 and 5% thereafter. If the president is deposed, the company will have a negative growth rate of 35% in the year the president is deposed through Year 3, and it will have a growth rate of 5% thereafter. If the president is not deposed by Year 3, the president will not be deposed subsequently, and the country's and company's free cash flows will grow at 5% per year. The company's discount rate is 18%, and its Year 0 free cash flow is $800. Measure the value of the firm, but ignore the possibility of the president being deposed; do this again, but this time, factor in the possibility of the president being deposed.

P17.9 **Exchange Rate Exposure:** A company is located in the U.S. (U.S. Sub) and owned by a company in the U.K. (U.K. Parent). U.S. Sub purchases its products from U.K. Parent in transactions denominated in £. The Year 1 expected cash revenue for U.S. Sub is $22.5 million. The total cost of its products is £9.1 million, and it has no other expenses. U.S. Sub has no capital expenditure requirements and is financed with only common equity. For simplicity, assume that no taxes will be levied on the income of U.S. Sub. Assume that the £ discount rate for the £-denominated free cash flows is 14%, that U.S. Sub has a zero expected growth rate in perpetuity, and that the current and expected future exchange rate is 0.5 £/$. Measure the value of U.S. Sub in £.

a. Measure the value of the firm assuming the £/$ exchange rate unexpectedly changed to 0.6.
b. Measure the value of the firm assuming the £/$ exchange rate unexpectedly changed to 0.4.
c. Measure U.K. Parent's exposure to the USD.
d. Measure the change in U.K. Parent's exposure to the USD if its U.S. Sub purchased its products with transactions denominated in $ at a total cost of $18.2 million rather than from U.K. Parent.

17.10 **Cross-Border Valuation and Exchange Rate Exposure—Comprehensive Problem:** The BW Company (BW) is considering acquiring an Asian wholesale distribution company, Buy From Asia Ltd. (BFA). BFA operates in a country called Zed (a new developing country, so do not be concerned if you have not heard of it). All of BFA's costs are denominated in Zed's local currency (the Zed, $\hat{Z}$). All of BFA's sales transactions are also denominated in $\hat{Z}$s.

BW purchases 80% of its goods from BFA with purchase transactions denominated in $\hat{Z}$. All of BW's other cash flows are in U.S. dollars (USD, $). The goal of this acquisition is to increase BW's revenues and reduce its cost of goods sold by having better control over its purchasing through quicker access to new products and higher quality products at lower prices.

BW's management prepared a set of forecasts for two years for BFA in its local currency ($\hat{Z}$) and for BW in USD (see Exhibit P17.3). BW's management expects BFA to grow at the local long-term inflation rate after Year 2. The income tax rate in Zed's country is 15% on all income. If BW upstreams BFA's "profits" (more precisely, equity free cash flows) in the form of dividends, it will have to pay a 10% dividend withholding tax. The unlevered free cash flows shown in the financial forecasts assume that BW does not upstream any of BFA's "profits." Assume that for this country/acquisition, BW would not pay any U.S.-based income tax regardless of whether or not BFA upstreams dividends to BW. BW's management measured BFA's U.S.-based unlevered cost of capital for acquiring BFA, $r_{USD/\hat{Z}}$, equal to 12%.

a. Use the free cash flow forecasts assuming BW will not upstream any dividends, and use the forward exchange rates to measure the USD value of BFA using the **decentralized or foreign currency** discounted cash flow valuation approach.
b. Use the free cash flow forecasts assuming BW will not upstream any dividends, and use the forward exchange rates to measure the USD value of BFA using the **centralized or investor currency** discounted cash flow valuation approach.
c. Adjust BFA's Year 2 free cash flow forecasts assuming that BW will upstream all of BFA's equity free cash flows to BW in the form of dividends.
d. Use the free cash flow forecasts from the previous question (assuming the company upstreamed its dividends) and the forward exchange rates to measure the effect on the USD value of BFA resulting from BW upstreaming BFA's "profits" (equity free cash flows in the form of dividends). Use either the investor currency (centralized approach) or the foreign currency (decentralized approach) to respond to the question.
e. Measure BW's exposure to $\hat{Z}$ prior to the acquisition of BFA.
f. Measure BW's exposure to $\hat{Z}$ after BW's acquisition of BFA.

EXHIBIT P17.3 BW Company and Buy From Asia Ltd (BFA) Financial and Selected Market Data

	BW Company (All Numbers are in $1,000s)				Buy From Asia Ltd (BFA) (All Numbers are in Ẑ 1,000s)			
Millions	**Year −1**	**Year 0**	**Year 1**	**Year 2**	**Year −1**	**Year 0**	**Year 1**	**Year 2**
Revenue	$10,000	$12,000	$15,000	$15,300	37,500.0	46,530.0	59,625.0	$ 61,414
Cost of goods sold	−6,000	−7,200	−9,000	−9,180	−15,000.0	−18,612.0	−23,850.0	−24,565.5
Selling, general & administrative	−1,200	−1,440	−1,680	−1,796	−7,500.0	−9,306.0	−11,925.0	−12,282.8
Income before taxes	$ 2,800	$ 3,360	$ 4,320	$ 4,324	15,000.0	18,612.0	23,850.0	24,565.5
Income tax expense	−700	−840	−1,080	−1,081	−2,250.0	−2,791.8	−3,577.5	−3,684.8
Net income	**$ 2,100**	**$ 2,520**	**$ 3,240**	**$ 3,243**	**12,750.0**	**15,820.2**	**20,272.5**	**20,880.7**
Cash balance	$ 500	$ 600	$ 750	$ 765	1,875.0	2,326.5	2,981.3	3,070.7
Inventory	600	720	900	918	1,500.0	1,861.2	2,385.0	2,456.6
Other current assets	1,000	1,440	1,800	1,836	3,750.0	5,583.6	7,155.0	7,369.7
Total current assets	$ 2,100	$ 2,760	$ 3,450	$ 3,519	7,125.0	9,771.3	12,521.3	12,896.9
Non-current assets	10,000	12,000	15,000	15,300	37,500.0	46,530.0	59,625.0	61,413.8
Total assets	**$12,100**	**$14,760**	**$18,450**	**$18,819**	**44,625.0**	**56,301.3**	**72,146.3**	**74,310.6**
Accounts payable	$ 600	$ 864	$ 1,080	$ 1,102	1,500.0	2,233.4	2,862.0	2,947.9
Common stock	5,000	5,000	5,234	5,234	5,000.0	5,000.0	5,000.0	5,000.0
Retained earnings	6,500	8,896	12,136	12,483	38,125.0	49,067.9	64,284.3	66,362.8
Total liabilities and equities	**$12,100**	**$14,760**	**$18,450**	**$18,819**	**44,625.0**	**56,301.3**	**72,146.3**	**74,310.6**

	BW Company (All Numbers are in $1,000s)			Buy From Asia Ltd (BFA) (All Numbers are in Ẑ 1,000s)		
	Year 0	**Year 1**	**Year 2**	**Year 0**	**Year 1**	**Year 2**
Earnings before interest and taxes (EBIT)	$3,360	$4,320	$4,324	18,612.0	23,850.0	24,565.5
− income taxes paid on EBIT	−840	−1,080	−1,081	−2,791.8	−3,577.5	−3,684.8
Earnings before interest and after taxes	$2,520	$3,240	$3,243	15,820.2	20,272.5	20,880.7
− Change in inventory	−120	−180	−18	−361.2	−523.8	−71.6
− Change in other current assets	−440	−360	−36	−1,833.6	−1,571.4	−214.7
+ Change accounts payable	264	216	22	733.4	628.6	85.9
− Change in required cash balance	−100	−150	−15	−451.5	−654.8	−89.4
Unlevered cash flow from operations	$2,124	$2,766	$3,195	13,907.3	18,151.1	20,590.9
− Capital expenditures	−2,000	−3,000	−300	−9,030.0	−13,095.0	−1,788.8
Unlevered free cash flow	**$ 124**	**−$ 234**	**$2,895**	**4,877.3**	**5,056.1**	**18,802.1**

	Year 1	**Year 2**	**Future Yrs**
United States			
Interest rate	3.00%	3.00%	3.00%
Inflation rate	2.00%	2.00%	2.00%
Implied real rate	0.98%	0.98%	0.98%
Zed - Ẑ			
Interest rate	7.00%	5.98%	4.96%
Inflation rate	5.00%	4.00%	3.00%
Implied real rate	1.90%	1.90%	1.90%

		Forward Rates		
	Spot Rate	**1 Year**	**2 Year**	**3 Year**
Zed - Ẑ/ U.S. dollar (USD)				
Spot and forward rates	5.000	5.170	5.300	5.370
U.S. dollar (USD) /Zed - Ẑ				
Spot and forward rates	0.200	0.193	0.189	0.186

SOLUTIONS FOR REVIEW EXERCISES

Review Exercise 17.1: Investor Currency (Centralized) and Foreign Currency (Decentralized) Discounted Cash Flow Valuation Approaches

Investor Currency/Centralized Approach	Year 0	Year 1	Year 2	Year 3	$CV_{Firm, Yr 3}$
Free cash flow and continuing value (in USD × 1,000)		$1,200.0	$1,400.0	$1,700.0	$180,000.0
Exchange rate forecast (USD/Euro)		1.412	1.402	1.394	1.394
Free cash flow and continuing value (Euro)		€ 849.9	€ 998.6	€1,219.5	€129,124.8
Risk-adjusted discount factor for Euro	12.0%	0.893	0.797	0.712	0.712
Present value		€ 758.80	€ 796.06	€ 868.02	€91,908.50
Value of the firm (in Euro × 1,000)	€94,331.38				

Foreign Currency/Decentralized Approach	Year 0	Year 1	Year 2	Year 3	$CV_{Firm, Yr 3}$
Free cash flow and continuing value (in USD × 1,000)		$ 1,200.0	$ 1,400.0	$ 1,700.0	$180,000.0
Risk-adjusted discount rate for USD $r_\$$		10.978%	11.207%	11.361%	11.361%
Discount factor for foreign currency (USD)		0.901	0.810	0.728	0.728
Present value in foreign currency		$ 1,081.3	$ 1,134.4	$ 1,236.9	$130,969.6
Value of the firm	$134,422.2				
Current or spot exchange rate (USD/Euro)	1.425				
Value of the firm	€ 94,331.4				

Review Exercise 17.2: Discount Rates for the Investor Currency (Centralized) and Foreign Currency (Decentralized) Approaches

Investor to Foreign Discount Rate	Year 1	Year 2	Year 3
Exchange rate forecast = Forward rate (USD/Euro) in period t	1.412	1.402	1.394
Exchange rate forecast = Forward rate (USD/Euro) in period t-1	1.425	1.412	1.402
Ratio $\approx (1 + r_\$)/(1 + r_€) \approx (1 + i_\$)/(1 + i_€)$	0.991	0.993	0.994
One + Risk-adjusted discount rate for Euros, $r_€$	1.120	1.120	1.120
Risk-adjusted discount rate in foreign currency, $r_\$$	10.978%	11.207%	11.361%

Exhibit may contain small rounding errors

Review Exercise 17.3: Exchange Rate Forecasts

	Spot Rate	Forward Rates and Forecasts				
		1 Year	2 Year	3 Year	4 Year	5 Year
U.S. Dollar (USD)/Polish Zloty						
Actual	0.357	0.345	0.336	0.320	0.306	0.300
RPPP		0.343	0.333	0.324	0.315	0.307
		−0.4%	−0.8%	1.3%	3.1%	2.3%
UIRP		0.344	0.330	0.315	0.301	0.289
		−0.4%	−1.8%	−1.6%	−1.7%	−3.6%

Review Exercise 17.4: Worldwide (Resident) and Territorial (Source) Tax Regimes

Foreign Income Tax	
Foreign taxable income	£10,000.0
Foreign income tax rate	30.0%
Foreign income tax liability	£ 3,000.0
After-tax foreign income	£ 7,000.0
Territorial effective tax rate w/o WH tax	30.0%

Foreign Dividend Withholding (WH) Tax	
Dividend payout ratio	100.0%
Dividend declared	£ 7,000.0
Withholding tax rate	5.0%
Withholding tax	£ 350.0
Dividend distributed	£ 6,650.0
Total foreign tax liability	£ 3,350.0
Territorial effective tax rate after WH tax	33.5%

Investor Country Income Tax	
Foreign income tax liability	£ 3,000.0
Dividend payout ratio	100.0%
Allocated foreign income tax liability	£ 3,000.0
Dividend declared	7,000.0
Investor country taxable income	£10,000.0
Investor country tax rate	45.0%
Investor country tax before credits	£ 4,500.0
Foreign tax credit for foreign income tax	−3,000.0
Foreign tax credit for foreign WH tax	−350.0
Additional U.K. income tax	£ 1,150.0

Worldwide Tax (After Foreign Tax Credits)	
Total worldwide tax	£ 4,500.0
Total worldwide tax rate	45.0%

Review Exercise 17.5: Country-Specific Risks—1

Scenario and Expected Cash Flow Valuation Excluding Effect of the Political Risk

Economy Doing	Scenario Prob	Probability-Weighted Value	% of Value	Scenario Present Value	Year 1	Year 2	Year 3	$CV_{Year\ 3}$
Well	0.250	$4,063.01	43.9%	$16,252.05	$1,300.00	$1,690.00	$2,197.00	$18,857.58
Poorly	0.750	$5,183.25	56.1%	$ 6,911.00	$ 950.00	$ 902.50	$ 857.38	$ 7,359.14
	1.000	$9,246.26						
Expected cash flow valuation				$ 9,246.26	$1,037.50	$1,099.38	$1,192.28	$10,233.75

Scenario and Expected Cash Flow Valuation Including Effect of the Political Risk

Economy Doing	Scenario Prob	Probability-Weighted Value	% of Value	Scenario Present Value	Year 1	Year 2	Year 3	$CV_{Year\ 3}$
Well	0.250	$3,374.38	43.6%	$13,497.51	$1,274.00	$1,623.08	$2,067.80	$14,908.83
Poorly	0.750	$4,365.80	56.4%	$ 5,821.07	$ 931.00	$ 866.76	$ 806.95	$ 5,818.14
	1.000	$7,740.18						
Expected cash flow valuation			−16%	$ 7,740.18	$1,016.75	$1,055.84	$1,122.17	$ 8,090.81

Review Exercise 17.6: Country-Specific Risks—2

Scenario and Expected Cash Flow Valuation Excluding Country Default

	Scenario Prob	Probability-Weighted Value	% of Value	Scenario Present Value	Year 1	Year 2	Year 3	$CV_{Year\ 3}$
High growth	20.0%	$ 2,792.82	24.8%	$13,964.09	$1,150.00	$1,322.50	$1,520.88	$10,856.64
Low growth	80.0%	$ 8,461.39	75.2%	$10,576.74	$1,040.00	$1,081.60	$1,124.86	$ 8,029.75
	100.0%	$11,254.21	100.0%					
Expected cash flow valuation				$11,254.21	$1,062.00	$1,129.78	$1,204.07	$ 8,595.13

Scenarios and Expected Cash Flows Including Country Default

High growth rate	15.0%
Low growth rate	4.0%
Default growth rate	–20.0%
Discount rate	13.0%
Long-term growth rate	3.0%

Year 0: $1,000.00
- Low Growth 0.800 → Year 1: $ 832.00
  - No Default 0.600 (0.480) → Year 2: $ 519.17
    - No Default 0.600 (0.288) → Year 3: $ 323.96
    - Default 0.400 (0.192) → $ 166.13
  - Default 0.400 (0.320) → $ 266.24 → 0.320 → $ 212.99
- High Growth 0.200 → $ 230.00 → 0.200 → $ 264.50 → 0.200 → $ 304.18

	Year 1	Year 2	Year 3
Expected cash flow	**$1,062.00**	**$1,049.91**	**$1,007.26**
		–1.1%	–4.1%

Scenario and Expected Cash Flow Valuation Including Country Default

Growth and Default Year	Scenario Prob	Probability-Weighted Value	% of Value	Scenario Present Value	Year 1	Year 2	Year 3	$CV_{Year\ 3}$
1 High—no default	20.0%	$2,792.82	28.9%	$13,964.09	$1,150.00	$1,322.50	$1,520.88	$15,665.01
2 Low—Year 2 default	32.0%	2,171.06	22.5%	$ 6,784.56	$1,040.00	$ 832.00	$ 665.60	$ 6,855.68
3 Low—Year 3 default	19.2%	1,640.41	17.0%	$ 8,543.82	$1,040.00	$1,081.60	$ 865.28	$ 8,912.38
4 Low—no default	28.8%	3,046.10	31.6%	$10,576.74	$1,040.00	$1,081.60	$1,124.86	$11,586.10
	100.0%	$9,650.39	100.0%					
Expected cash flow valuation				$ 9,650.39	$1,062.00	$1,049.91	$1,007.26	$10,374.79

Review Exercise 17.7: Measuring Exchange Rate Exposure

		Exchange Rates £/€		
Only Revenues in € × millions	**Year 1**	**0.900**	**0.990**	**0.810**
Revenue (cash in €)	€1.850	£ 1.665	£ 1.832	£ 1.499
Expenses (cash in £)	−£0.990	−£ 0.990	−£ 0.990	−£ 0.990
Unlevered free cash flow		£ 0.675	£ 0.842	£ 0.509
Discount rate (in £, no growth)		12.0%	12.0%	12.0%
Value of French sub. in £		£ 5.625	£ 7.013	£ 4.238
Percentage change in value			24.7%	−24.7%
Change in value			£ 1.388	−£ 1.388
Percentage change in exchange rate			10.0%	−10.0%
Total exposure			£13.875	£13.875
Present value of revenue stream		£13.875		

		Exchange Rates £/€		
All Cash Flows in € × millions	**Year 1**	**0.900**	**0.990**	**0.810**
Revenue (cash in €)	€1.850	£1.665	£ 1.832	£ 1.499
Expenses (cash in €)	−€1.100	−£0.990	−£ 1.089	−£ 0.891
Unlevered free cash flow	€0.750	£0.675	£ 0.743	£ 0.608
Discount rate (in £, no growth)		12.0%	12.0%	12.0%
Value of the French sub. in £		£5.625	£ 6.188	£ 5.063
Percentage change in value			10.0%	−10.0%
Change in value			£ 0.563	−£ 0.562
Percentage change in exchange rate			10.0%	−10.0%
Total exposure			£ 5.625	£ 5.625

Index

A

B

Note: The letter e indicates an exhibit on that page.

Note: The letter e indicates an exhibit on that page.

D

Note: The letter e indicates an exhibit on that page.

Note: The letter e indicates an exhibit on that page.

Note: The letter e indicates an exhibit on that page.

Note: The letter e indicates an exhibit on that page.

Note: The letter e indicates an exhibit on that page.

Note: The letter e indicates an exhibit on that page.

N

O

P

Q

R

Note: The letter e indicates an exhibit on that page.

Note: The letter e indicates an exhibit on that page.

V

W

X

Y

Note: The letter e indicates an exhibit on that page.

Z

Note: The letter e indicates an exhibit on that page.